OBITUARIES FROM THE TIMES 1961-1970

including an Index to all Obituaries and Tributes appearing in The Times during the years 1961-1970

Compiler: **Frank C. Roberts** (Home News Editor, *The Times* 1965-1968)

NEWSPAPER ARCHIVE DEVELOPMENTS LIMITED
Reading, RG3 2DF England

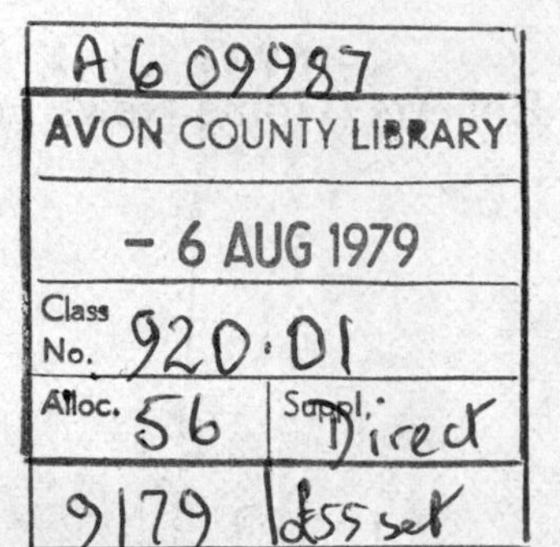

Newspaper Archive Developments Limited,
16 Westcote Road,
Reading RG3 2DF, England.

ISBN 0 903713 98 5

The idea for this book was put forward by
Godfrey Smith, Associate Editor, *The Sunday Times*

Print and typography Consultant Hardy Boer

Text setting in Monophoto by
Thomson Press (India) Ltd,
New Delhi, India
and printed in Great Britain by
Lowe & Brydone (Printers) Ltd,
Thetford, Norfolk

PREFACE

The obituaries in *The Times* have been a classic source for scholars and researchers for many years. They provide a substantial account of the lives of distinguished British men and women and of many people from outside Britain as well. They are widely used in libraries where the bound volumes of *The Times* or microfilms are available. It has now been decided that it would be a good idea to publish them as a reference book which also, we believe, makes a fascinating book of contemporary history.

This volume, which will be followed by further volumes, contains the obituaries from *The Times* between 1961 and 1970. It is in two parts. The second contains an index of all entries appearing in the obituary columns of *The Times* between January 1, 1961 and December 31, 1970. The first part reprints in full an alphabetically-arranged selection of about 1,500 obituary notices of the period. The selection has been made with regard to the public importance of the subject of the obituary, the intrinsic interest of what was written about him, and the need to reflect the wide range of nationalities and walks of life which *The Times* obituary columns encompass. The obituaries are reprinted as they appeared on the day of publication, subject to minor changes of style (to clarify date of death, for instance) and to correct any errors which have been noticed in the original. The date on which each obituary appeared is given in italics beneath it.

What is published here is in no sense a revision of what was published at the time. The length of each entry and the judgments it contains stand as they stood then, however inclined one might be ten or fifteen years later to modify some of those judgments. The book is therefore both a biographical record and a record of the opinions expressed by *The Times* contemporaneously.

Because we have selected the 1,500 most interesting obituaries over a ten year period—that is, on average, one obituary to every two days in the period—we have altered the balance between the British and the overseas obituaries. Normally *The Times* reckons to cover only the more important overseas lives, while including a wide range of obituaries of people who have had distinguished careers in a purely British but not in an international context. Of the 1,500 entries in this book, 61 per cent are British and 39 per cent are overseas and, as a result, the book does contain almost all the major international figures who died in the period. Nearly 150 of the obituaries come from the United States, over 60 each from France and Germany and over 30 from the Soviet Union.

There are some 120 obituaries of heads of state, rulers and leading statesmen and a further 280 of politicians and administrators. There are over 160 in each of the categories of literature, the theatre, cinema and broadcasting, and industry. Journalism and law have about 50 each.

Of the reprinted obituaries that are reprinted in full, the longest, naturally, is that of Sir Winston Churchill, which is 13,500 words long.

It was a period in which the great statesmen of the war died and the obituaries include as well as Sir Winston Churchill, President Eisenhower, de Gaulle, Adenauer and Attlee. They also include the obituary of Pope John XXIII and that of Bertrand Russell. There are, tragically enough, obituaries of a number of people who were murdered by judicial process or assassinated, including of course President Kennedy.

All of these obituaries are *The Times* obituaries. We receive and publish many appreciations contributed from outside. We have not republished these appreciations, interesting though many of them are.

It will be noticed that there are a number of obituaries which have not been republished, of figures who might be expected to appear, where we considered that the original obituary notice, written with knowledge available at the time, might be generally misleading.

Obituaries are a very important part of the coverage of *The Times* as a journal of record and they go back, though not with their present regularity, to the very early days of *The Times,* when we published obituary notices of some of those who suffered in the French Revolution. We attach great importance to ensuring the quality of these obituaries and believe that this volume is not unworthy as a representation of them.

June 1975.

WILLIAM REES-MOGG
Editor of *The Times*

COMPILER'S NOTE

The decade that brought the deaths in alternate years of John F. Kennedy (1963), Winston Churchill (1965), Konrad Adenauer (1967) and Dwight Eisenhower (1969) virtually ended together with the life of Charles de Gaulle in November 1970. Churchill's career in the arc lights, described in pages 139–148 of this volume, had lasted for over 70 years, from the era of the charge at Omdurman to the aftermath of nuclear bombing. By comparison, Kennedy (see page 434 onwards) was for one decade in the eyes of the world; Adenauer (p. 6) for scarcely two decades; and de Gaulle (197) for about three decades, making together less than Churchill's span of seven.

Not only in France was the close of a decade the end, or very nearly the end, of an epoch. Nasser (576) had just died in Egypt; Salazar (699) in Portugal; Sukarno (766) in Indonesia; and, an echo from 50 years back, Kerensky (440) had recently died still in exile.

In Britain the year 1970, with which this volume closes, saw the end of the life stories of Slim (737) and Dowding (224), Bertrand Russell (691) and E. M. Forster (275), Barbirolli (48) and, among those who died with careers cut short, Iain Macleod (512)—Hugh Gaitskell (290) had been lost seven years earlier—with yet another hope of the new generation, Lillian Board (82).

In many obituaries are unfolded the achievements and failures of civil servants, scientists, law-givers and lawyers, fighting men and women, rulers, adventurers, explorers and spies, philosophers and writers, artists and musicians, and dons who laid their stamp on youth. The book is not about death; it is about the life of our times.

"By my troth I care not; a man can die but once; we owe God a death . . . and, let it go which way it will, he that dies this year is quit for the next." Ernest Hemingway's obituary records that he used this quotation from the recruit in King Henry IV Part II "as a touchstone of conduct". In this volume appear many recruits to life who bore themselves according to that touchstone and thereby achieved the more.

F. C. R.

A

Deryck Abel, who died on February 13, 1965, had been editor of the *Contemporary Review* since July, 1960. He was 46.

Deryck Robert Endsleigh Abel was born in September, 1918 at Salisbury, and educated at the Tottenham Secondary School and the London School of Economics. During the war he served in the 69th Searchlight Regiment R.A., until he was seriously wounded and lost a leg.

Abel had two consuming interests in life: his work as journalist, editor, and writer, and the advancement of the Liberal Party. Until 1960 he was able largely to combine these interests. He belonged at first to the diminishing free trade wing of the party. He was directing secretary of the Free Trade Union, 1954–57, and editor of the *Free Trader*, 1951–58. He wrote *A History of British Tariffs*, 1923–42. Within the Liberal Party hierarchy he made steady progress, becoming chairman of the National Party Executive, 1957–59, and vice-president of the party in 1960. He contested St. Albans in 1950, Torquay in 1951, and Worthing in 1959. Abel came to recognize that the future of the party did not lie in a doctrinaire approach to free trade but in the far broader base of radical and social reform combined with private enterprise.

During these years he was a prolific freelance writer, with a particular concern for economic affairs and personal liberty. It was thus appropriate for him to write the biography of Sir Ernest Benn in 1960. *Ernest Benn, Counsel for Liberty*, was certainly his most important book, being a thorough, understanding, and workmanlike study of the great libertarian. This book was followed in 1961 by a penetrating historical survey of the Channel tunnel projects in *Channel Undergound*.

It is, however, as editor of the *Contemporary Review* that Abel will be most widely remembered: this became his overriding interest and indeed passion. It was a difficult task to succeed Dr. G. P. Gooch who had edited and directed the *Review* for 49 years and had built up a world-wide circulation and established for it the highest standing, especially in the fields of public and foreign affairs and of historical study.

Abel did maintain this reputation of the *Review*, and at the same time he added a new degree of freshness and vigour. He widened the scope of contributions, especially on travel and literary subjects. He attracted new contributors from both sides of the Atlantic and encouraged younger writers. During his editorship the *Review* was brought more up to date with a new cover and modern layout. He frequently contributed to the *Review*. As in most of his literary work, his style if not inspiring was solid, penetrating, and dedicated. He wrote with erudition, a high regard for details, and always with complete integrity.

Abel was twice married, his first marriage having been dissolved in 1962. He is survived by his widow and a son and daughter by his first marriage.

February 15, 1965.

Admiral Jean-Marie Charles Abrial, the French naval commander at Dunkirk during the evacuation of the British expeditionary force in 1940, died at Dourgne in the Tarn in December, 1962. He was 83.

Traditional rivalries with the British service die hard in the French Navy, and, as commander-in-chief, Nord, Abrial's relations with the British command were not easy during the Dunkirk operations. These feelings unhappily festered into open hatred, which probably caused him to throw in his lot with the Vichy Government. He made vehement denunciations in public of "British treachery" at Dunkirk, and after the liberation he was tried and convicted by the French High Court of Justice on charges of having had intelligence with the enemy. He was sentenced to 10 years' imprisonment and national degradation, but was released in 1947 and has lived in retirement since then at his home in the Tarn.

BEACHHEAD DEFENDED

His command as "Admiral Nord" with headquarters at Dunkirk extended during the German envelopment to land forces defending the beachhead, and the embarkation of so many allied troops is attributed in large measure to his courage and energy. He left his forward command post on superior orders only when all hope was lost of saving more men.

He was taken prisoner but quickly released, and at the end of 1940 was appointed by Vichy as Governor-General of Algeria, where the Mers-el-Kebir episode would have done nothing to placate his animosity against the British. He was relieved in Algeria by General Weygand, and after the allied landings in North Africa in 1942 served as State Secretary for the Navy in the Vichy Government, a post in which he shared responsibility for the scuttling of the French fleet at Toulon. He left the service of Vichy, a disillusioned and embittered man, more than a year before the war ended.

Abrial passed out of the French Naval Academy in 1896 and was a lieutenant-commander at the beginning of the First World War.

CRUISER COMMAND

He commanded the cruiser Tourville in 1927, and in 1936 was appointed chief of staff of the First Squadron. A year later he became a member of the Supreme Naval Council and was commanding French naval forces in the north on the outbreak of war in 1939.

December 21, 1962.

Joe Randolph Ackerley, author and for many years literary editor of the *Listener*, died suddenly at his Putney home on June 4, 1967, at the age of 70. He was born on November 4, 1896, the son of Roger Ackerley, a director of the firm of banana importers. Elders and Fyffes, and went to school at Rossall. From 1914 to 1918 he served in the First World War, finishing up as captain. In 1917 he was taken prisoner and spent eight months in Germany. Subsequently he was interned in Switzerland for a year. From this latter experience derived both his only play. *The Prisoners of War* (1925) and an anthology, *Escapers All* (1932). The three years after his release he spent reading law at Cambridge. There followed a period during which he worked for an Indian maharaja as companion, private secretary and tutor to his son—brilliantly described in his minor classic *Hindoo Holiday* (1932)—before he began on his 24 fruitful and influential years as literary editor of the *Listener*.

As an editor Joe Ackerley was incomparable. Out of friendship and admiration for him writers as distinguished as E. M. Forster, Edwin Muir and Christopher Isherwood were prepared to contribute anonymous reviews; he had an astonishing knack for discerning talent in the unknown young; and though he would rarely countenance an illogical or ill-formulated sentence, he would never attempt to delete or modify an opinion with which he disagreed. But the price of this dedication to a job which he loved was that, apart from his marvellous letters, he wrote nothing himself for almost two decades. In 1956 there at last appeared *My Dog Tulip*, a book about his much loved Alsatian Queenie, which shocked many doglovers used to regarding dogs merely as extensions of themselves, by the astonishing and sometimes alarming accuracy of its observation.

In 1960 Ackerley published his only novel *We Think the World of You*, winner of the W. H. Smith Award and certainly his finest work. Obviously based, like all Ackerley's writing, on personal experience—he would often declare that he was incapable of inventing, just as he was incapable of lying—it is a book deceptively short and cool and light. At once excruciatingly funny and excruciatingly sad, it brings the unobtrusive artistry of a master to its telling of the strange story of the transference of the narrator's love to a dog from its master.

The key both to Ackerley's writing and to his character was his obsession with the exact truth. He had no use for assumptions or attitudes taken over, unexamined, from others, however distinguished. Every idea, every incident, every person must be appraised by the light of his own acutely perceptive intelligence. Incapable of producing the minor insincerities that are the small change of daily life, he could on occasion be a formidable companion but his candour, though sometimes ruthless, was so totally free of malice that it rarely left a wound.

After his sister, what he cared about most in life were his friends, and to them he was prodigal in his sympathy, his attention, and his kindness. His books are full of love for the spontaneous, the warmhearted and the humble, and of dislike for the calculating, the pompous, and the priggish. In that they reflected his own luminous nature. A man of immense courtesy and charm, and of rare and fastidious taste, he will not be forgotten as either friend or writer. On the last page of his last diary he had inscribed from the *Antigone* of Sophocles the line: "We have only a little time to please the living, but all eternity to love the dead." In his life time, now seemingly so short, he gave pleasure to innumerable people, both famous and unknown.

June 6, 1967.

Dr. W. G. S. Adams, C.H., Warden of All Souls College, Oxford, from 1933 to 1945, died on January 30, 1966, in co. Donegal. He was 91.

William George Stewart Adams, born on November 8, 1874, was the son of John Adams, rector of St. John's Grammar School, Hamilton, Lanarkshire. John Adams was an educational pioneer, a friend of Livingstone, who left his sons with him on one of his visits from Africa. Bonar Law was one of his pupils.

Adams went from Glasgow University to Balliol College with a Snell exhibition, and from graduation onwards he led the life of a student and lecturer on social questions in Manchester, Chicago and Oxford, where he was first Reader (1910–12) and then Gladstone Professor of Political Theory and Institutions (1912–33). In 1910 he was elected to a Fellowship of All Souls. From 1912 to 1924 he was a member of the Hebdomadal Council. In this early period A. L. Smith and Canon Barnett impressed Adams deeply. In the spring of 1904 he had met Sir Horace Plunkett, before becoming for five years an officer of the Department of Agriculture and Technical Instruction in Ireland. Plunkett helped to make a farmer of Adams and until he died in 1932 was a major influence in a life much of which was devoted to the improvement of the nation's agriculture by means of innumerable commissions and committees. Adams put his spare time into running a farm of his own and for many years he served as chairman of the Federation of Young Farmers' Clubs.

IN CHINA

University administration in Britain, in America and in China was one of his abiding interests. In 1931–32 he was a member of a delegation with Sir Reginald Johnston and Professor Roxby, which visited China on behalf of the Universities China Committee and produced a report. In 1942 Adams became chairman of the committee. He had a good deal to do with launching the degree course in philosophy, politics, and economics at Oxford. As the holder of the cardinal chair in politics Adams fought hard and successfully for the "equipollence" of politics with the other live subjects. Apart from himself, there was no other person in Oxford exclusively charged to teach for it, but gradually colleges detailed their modern history tutors to teach in the politics of the new school, and later they began to appoint Fellows in politics alone. The present large and flourishing Sub-Faculty of Politics at Oxford is a witness to Adams's faith in his subject at times when it was somewhat despised and when weaker men might have allowed it to fall into a subordinate position.

PRESERVING AMENITIES

At All Souls he and his wife were much given to hospitality and there were memorable weekends when fellows and friends were given an opportunity of meeting distinguished guests. Adams was one of the first to work for the preservation of Oxford amenities and he put a lot of energy into begging money for this cause in the twenties. Adams himself was not given to writing and he published little either as Gladstone Professor or as Stevenson Lecturer in Citizenship. The Stevenson Lectures, delivered in Glasgow, were never printed.

When in December, 1916, Lloyd George became Prime Minister. Adams joined the group of personal secretaries, with Philip Kerr (Lord Lothian) as one of his colleagues. Adams was at first charged with labour questions but the appointment of Plunkett as chairman of the Irish Convention (July, 1917) meant that Adams took over Irish questions and acted as liaison between Plunkett and the Prime Minister. He edited the War Cabinet reports for 1917 and 1918.

STRONG FAITH

Adams returned to Oxford in 1919 and became a member of the Royal Commission on Oxford and Cambridge Universities. The rest of his public life was mainly divided between the Development Commission (1923–49) and the National Council of Social Service of which he was chairman (1920–49). As in all his activities Adams brought to bear on the work of the commission his own personal experience, his own strong faith, a spirit of eagerness and adventure and a belief in the value of those new endeavours for the well-being of the countryside whose leaders had won his admiration and respect. He showed, perhaps, his strongest concern, for here his fundamental beliefs were involved, in the fostering of co-operation, both for the benefit of farmers and of fishermen.

CO-OPERATIVE CONTACTS

Throughout his service as a commissioner Adams took every opportunity to maintain his personal contacts with the Agricultural Co-operative movement in England, Scotland, Wales and Ireland. He had high regard for Miss Grace Hadow as one of the forces in the enrichment of rural life. He watched in Oxfordshire the beginnings of the Rural Community Council movement and was its president for many years, and during the 30 years of his chairmanship of the National Council of Social Service he was its inspirer and the supporter of all who sought to advance a vigorous and variegated country life. He actively encouraged the provision of village halls, the revitalizing of the ancient crafts of the countryside, the introduction of new industries, and the furtherance of Women's Institutes. He gave much encouragement to the West Highland Survey, which aimed at finding both the meaning of Highland distress and the way to a new prosperity.

STRONG CHARACTER

To all these manifold public services Adams contributed a character of great strength, loyalty and sincerity, wise and persuasive counsel, a vision of a better life and an incurable optimism in the possibility of its attainment. His colleagues felt for him a deep affection.

He married in 1908 Muriel, daughter of William Lane, of Killiney, co. Dublin. They had one son. Adams was made a Companion of Honour in 1936. He was a D.C.L. (Oxford) and an hon. LL.D. of Glasgow and Manchester.

February 1, 1966.

Dr. Konrad Adenauer, who died on April 19, 1967, was Chancellor of western Germany from 1949 to 1963.

Taking office at 73, he managed to translate the limited and stubborn virtues of an old-fashioned town councillor into statesmanship, even greatness. He can justly be called the father of his truncated country, having nurtured its growth from a squalid and demoralized ruin into the shiny, prosperous and well-armed cornerstone of Europe that we know today. He can take an honourable place beside Signor de Gasperi and M. Schuman as one of the architects of the postwar Christian Democratic order in Europe. His place in history is assured, and his contribution already acknowledged with respect and admiration.

Yet he has not left a living myth behind him. In the last years of his chancellorship some of his virtues became vices. His clarity of purpose became inflexibility, his firm leadership autocracy. He outstayed his time and saw the obedient machine of Bonn politics grow awkward, rebellious and bitter. After he resigned the Chancellorship under pressure he remained active as chairman of the Christian Democratic Party, a disgruntled and worried old man plotting against his successor, Dr. Erhard, whom he had always disliked. It was an unhappy spectacle but had the one merit of preventing him becoming a burdensome object of worship to later generations.

In the early days of the Federal Republic it had been Dr. Adenauer's great virtue that he possessed absolute confidence in himself and the unshakable conviction that west Germany must be welded firmly into Europe and the Atlantic community. For the German people perhaps his greatest contribution was that he restored their self-respect, brought them friends, and gave them a role to play in the world. A towering figure at the height of his powers, he possessed the air of inevitability that marks a man who seems destined for a particular moment in history.

LOCAL GOVERNMENT LADDER

But when the moment passed he stayed on. Changes in the communist world, the death of Mr. Dulles, President Kennedy's search for accommodation with Russia, the split between Paris and Washington—all this required an adaptation of which Dr. Adenauer proved incapable in his old age. The development of west German democracy also made new demands. It became restive under his iron hand. Methods that were appropriate in the chaotic uncertainty of the early days became restrictive and humiliating.

The final verdict of history may well be that while Dr. Adenauer nurtured German democracy in its infancy he delayed its maturity. But he had very little faith in the stability of judgment of his own people. This is one of the essential keys to his domestic and foreign policies. It helps to explain both his virtues and his faults, his extraordinary contribution and the way in which he helped to undermine it.

Konrad Adenauer was born at Cologne on January 5, 1876. His father, Konrad Adenauer, was a clerk (*Kanzleirat*) at the Cologne law Courts, a fairly humble official, who in the war of

1866 had achieved the distinction, then uncommon in the Prussian army, of promotion from the ranks to a commission for bravery in the field. The family's means were small, but the young Konrad formed his own ambition to enter the legal profession, and on leaving the Cologne Gymnasium succeeded in spending three years at the universities of Munich, Freiburg, and Bonn. The practice of law led him to politics and to a rapid ascent of the ladder of local government, partly through the chance that he was employed between 1904 and 1906 as deputy to Justizrat Kausen, a counsel at the Cologne court of appeal. Kausen was at the same time chairman of the city branch of the Centre Party.

Cologne was growing in size and wealth. The Liberals were in course of being displaced after a long ascendancy in the government of Cologne by an alliance of Catholic Centre and Conservatives. Adenauer, a strong Catholic, conservative in outlook, entered municipal politics at the most favourable moment and quickly showed himself a gifted and energetic administrator. As a leading young member of the Centre Party he was appointed eleventh *Beigeordneter*, or town deputy, in charge of taxation, in 1906 at the age of 30. Six years later the support of his party and the high opinion which the conservative Chief Burgomaster, Wallraf, had formed of his youngest deputy secured him the appointment of first *Beigeordneter*.

COLOGNE'S EXPANSION

Adenauer, whose appointment as first deputy was criticized on account of his youth, his inexperience, his reputation as a party man, and his clericalism, was elected Burgomaster without dissent—there were 52 favourable votes and two blank papers in 1917 when Wallraf went to a high Government post in Berlin. The Prussian Crown conferred the rank of Chief Burgomaster and summoned him to sit in the Prussian Upper House.

At about this time Adenauer was badly hurt in a motor accident, breaking the cheekbones and the ridge of the nose, and losing the use of some facial muscles. This gave his face its sometimes forbidding immobility in later life and left him with an intermittent tendency to insomnia which never left him.

Adenauer's government of Cologne from 1917 to 1933 saw many national disasters—defeat in war, British occupation, the Ruhr occupation and the Rhineland troubles, the depression, and the rise of Nazism, but in his city it was marked by striking municipal expansion.

As early as 1919 he realized a plan prepared before the war to revive the University of Cologne, which had been extinct since the end of the eighteenth century. The university later made him an honorary doctor of all its faculties in turn. He established the Rhineland Museum, spent large sums on the splendid new fair buildings across the river, extended the civic boundaries, built new suburbs and garden cities, laid out the first fast motor road in Germany, remodelled the Rhine harbour, and developed new sites for industry. He was a bold and confident borrower. The Government in Berlin grumbled. But his personal position was unshakable.

He was chairman of the Prussian State Council (the Republican successor to the *Herrenhaus*) and his voice in the national politics of the Centre Party was influential. On two occasions, in 1921 and 1926, when his party had the opportunity of nominating the Reich Chancellor, Adenauer came almost within reach of the Chancellorship, but in the end it eluded him until after the Second World War. He was reelected for a second 12-year term, but when the Nazis came to power he was summarily removed: a group of party men had called at the Rathaus early in March, 1933, demanding that he hoist the swastika flag on the Rathaus tower, and he refused. A party press campaign accused him of corruption and revived old charges of Rhineland separatism from the years which had followed the First World War. A commission of inquiry spent some time in searching for evidence against him on either count, but none was found. In the end he was allowed to live through the Nazi regime quietly, unmolested except for short periods of arrest in 1934 and 1944.

UNEXPLAINED DECISION

The American Military Government reinstated Adenauer in the office of Chief Burgomaster in June, 1945. In the following October—Cologne and its Government district having been transferred to British Military Government—Adenauer was summarily dismissed. The reason was given that he had shown "insufficient energy", in particular in preparing emergency dwellings for the winter. The decision has never yet been fully explained. The task of government did, indeed, at that time, verge on the impossible. Repeated heavy bombing had reduced great areas of Cologne to a shapeless heap of rubble; yet some hundreds of thousand of people were living in odd corners in the ruins, and disbanded soldiers and evacuated people were still flowing back from distant parts of the dismembered Retch. The extent of the destruction of Cologne had caused the centre of government of the North Rhine Province to be placed not there but at Düsseldorf. Government on a larger scale than the municipality was only beginning to reappear.

Adenauer may well have been insufficiently compliant. The word "obstructive" was used of him at the time. Indeed, it would have been unlike him if he had not accepted his reinstatement as merely right and proper, and set about to reconstruct his somewhat personal system of rule as it had worked in the past. By disposition he was imperious. He had known the office of Chief Burgomaster of Cologne when it had been clothed in power and dignity. Most puzzling, however, was the apparent omission of British Military Government to reflect that the decision to dismiss Adenauer might be of any political consequence. As it happened his second wife was ill in Cologne, and the standard military regulation for the treatment of dismissed officials did not permit a deposed mayor to enter the town to see her. He felt these blows bitterly.

Adenauer set himself to build a successor to the Centre Party which should be capable of winning power nationally. The Centre had been Catholic and moderate conservative and Adenauer began with his old friends in their Middle Rhine stronghold; but the design required that the new party should be wider. Like the new model Catholic parties in France and Italy, the Christian Democratic Union cast a wider social net than its predecessor, taking in an active trade union wing. Adenauer and his friends went on to seek the alliance of the evangelical churchmen; this alone, in a country more than half Protestant, gave them the chance of outnumbering the Social Democrats. Bitter experience under the Nazis had shaken the traditional passivity of the Lutheran Church in politics. The time was ripe for a broad "Christian" political alliance, and Adenauer was the chief of its lay architects on the Catholic side.

Party political life, extinguished since 1933, revived with the communal and Kreis elections in the three western zones in 1946, followed by the formation of the *Länder* with their different constitutional structure. The Christian Democrats gradually assembled enough electoral strength to give their leader the most influential single voice in the construction of the Federal Republic.

Adenauer, their chairman from 1946, remained always the administrator in politics, He had not the dramatic qualities of Schumacher, his Social Democrat opponent in the formative postwar years, but his leadership was solid and untiring and on essential matters judicious. Some external factors helped him by hindering the Social Democrats. Soviet policy cut off Germany east of the Elbe and ensured that the new German state when it came to be formed would be a west German state governed from the Catholic Rhine. The dismantling of industry in its concentrations on the Ruhr and lower Rhine damaged British influence and, by association, the Social Democrats. Adenauer himself attributed dismantling mainly to British fears of German industrial competition, and said so tirelessly. The reputation of disliking the British was still with him when he became the first Federal Chancellor in 1949.

The genesis of the German Federal Republic can be traced to the American offer of economic fusion between the zones in July, 1946, which led to the Anglo-American bizone with its administrative agencies dispersed in Minden, Frankfurt, and other towns and thence to the Economic Council at Frankfurt. This functional union was essentially unworkable without united political institutions; the pressure for such institutions grew and the arguments against them melted away as western relations with the Russians deteriorated and the four-Power experiment became manifestly hopeless.

Thus the decision to summon the Parliamentary Council to draw up a provisional constitution followed within a few weeks of the failure of the London Conference of Foreign Ministers in December, 1947. France decided early in 1948 that no alternative remained but to join her zone to the two bigger western zones. The informal dissolution of the Control Council was followed by tripartite currency reform in the west, and, almost simultaneously, by the blockade of Berlin in June, 1948. The Parliamentary Council, made up of delegates from the Diets of the *Länder*, met at Bonn in the following September and elected Adenauer as its chairman. In May, 1949, the Basic Law was adopted and the Occupation Statute promulgated.

ELECTED CHANCELLOR

In the electoral campaign for the first Federal Parliament many party attitudes and many speeches, including some of Adenauer's, aroused fears abroad of a revival of nationalist politics in Germany. He was elected Chancellor on September 15, 1949, by 202 votes in a House of 402, and formed a coalition Government of the Christian Democratic and Christian Social Unions, together with the Free Democrats and the German Party. The coalition proved stable enough to last throughout the four years of the first Bundestag.

By the end of 1949 the demand—from Allied and German quarters—for a German contribution to western defence was not far off, but the dismantling of industry was still going on, along lines fixed by the desire to make physically impossible a revival of German military strength. Six weeks after he took office he proposed a solution to the dismantling question: dismantling for reparations should stop, but the Federal Republic should bind itself to cooperate in the control of its heavy industrial output through the Ruhr Authority and in the disarmament control through the Military Security Board. He urged closer economic relations with France and the Benelux countries, and the ending of the state of war, together with the relaxation of restrictions on shipbuilding and the granting of the right to the Federal Republic to establish consulates abroad. The Petersberg Agreement, his first success as Chancellor in dealing with the Allies, conceded some of what he asked; the rest came by stages. By the autumn of 1950 the Korean War had transformed Germany's diplomatic position, causing the western Powers under American leadership to seek her aid as an ally. With this change it became possible for Adenauer to press for political independence for the Federal Republic in place of the qualified internal autonomy which it enjoyed when he took office. In March, 1951, the Federal Republic was permitted to reestablish its Foreign Office. Adenauer became Foreign Minister as well as Chancellor.

The journey to independence was still long and not wholly free from errors of judgment and bursts of impatience on Adenauer's part. Like other politicians, he wished to show results. When the German Contract and the Treaty of Paris were signed in May, 1952, purporting to end the occupation and to accept the Federal Republic into a military union with five other Continental states of western Europe, he claimed a success which proved to be hypothetical.

At this time his political opponents often accused him of indifference to the unification of all Germany. Probably east Germany, and Berlin itself, meant less to him emotionally than to most Germans. This did not make him indifferent to the presence of a communist regime on the Elbe. But it was his way to take problems one by one, and to concern himself first with the possible. He was content to seek as a first necessity a prosperous, consolidated, and internationally respectable German State in close association with western Europe. From 1952 until the summer of 1954 he had to fight unremittingly to defend what then turned out to be his dream; against the advocates of national interest; against the passionate Social Democrat critics of the "Little Europe" which they held to be clerical, reactionary, and the negation of the German interest; and against disillusionment.

NATIONAL SOVEREIGNTY

He himself, a man rarely given to illusions, resisted disillusionment beyond the point at which the Government of M. Mendes-France had made it plain that the European Defence Community no longer had any hope of French acceptance. When the French National Assembly killed the project at the end of August, 1954, Adenauer's disappointment was profound, bitter, and in some ways misdirected against M. Mendes France personally. He recovered his judgment, devoted himself with Sir Anthony Eden to the salvaging of a new European defence system from the wreckage, and quickly changed his view of M. Mendes-France as the new project of alliance took shape.

The new and politically less fanciful system was expressed in the treaties signed at Paris in October 1954. To secure the French signature to them he was obliged to concede more to French requirements in the Saar than probably any other German statesman of his day would have done.

Adenauer did not limit his struggle to reestablish an internationally respectable German State to negotiations with the allied High Commissioners and their governments. In 1953 Parliament approved restitution and indemnification to the extent of DM.3,500m. for Jews and others who had suffered under the Nazi regime because of their race.

On May 5, 1955, only 10 years after the surrender, the Federal Republic attained national sovereignty as a free and equal partner with the west; an event which could be regarded as the crowning achievement of Adenauer's career.

In the autumn of 1955 he was invited to Moscow but the visit was not a success. Adenauer seemed to believe he could manage the Russians as he had managed others. He was proved wrong; the Soviet Government was not prepared to discuss reunification, and to arrange the return of less than 10,000 prisoners (it was believed that at least 80,000 were still in the Soviet Union) Adenauer agreed to an exchange of ambassadors.

Worse was to follow. The division of Germany was deepened further a week later when the Soviet Government recognized east Germany as a sovereign state. The east German regime assumed control of all west German traffic between Berlin and the Federal Republic.

Adenauer's protests went unanswered, but his reaction was characteristic. He declared in the Bundestag that recognition of east Germany by any country in diplomatic relations with the Federal Republic would be regarded as an unfriendly act. This contrasted oddly with the exchange of ambassadors with the Soviet Union, but it was not the first or last time when it seemed that only his allies were obliged to follow his policy. The profitable trade between the two Germanies flourished and in 1958 he sold 1m. tons of coal to east Germany to alleviate distress in the Ruhr coalfields. One of his Ministers, Herr Schaffer, was also allowed to discuss reunification with an east German representative on two occasions.

He had relinquished the Foreign Ministry to Herr von Brentano in May, 1955, but remained firmly in control of foreign policy. This was strongly influenced by his Moscow visit, though it was not at first apparent. The visit had convinced him that the Soviet Government was not interested in German reunification except on its own terms, but he continued to insist upon free All-German elections and the right to remain within NATO. Conscription was made law, and the decision was taken to equip the army with weapons capable of carrying nuclear warheads. Rockets and missiles were ordered from the United States, and discussions were opened with France and Italy to manufacture missiles. By the end of 1958 the Bundeswehr was well on its way to becoming the largest national force under NATO command.

PRESIDENTIAL CANDIDATE

Adenauer was then almost 83. Throughout the lengthy preparations for the 1960 summit conference Adenauer remained inflexibly opposed to negotiations, especially over Berlin, and he saw the failure in Paris as proof of his political infallibility. Certainly it seemed to do him no harm at home. With the Social Democratic opposition in disarray, he contemptuously refused an offer of bipartisanship in foreign policy and at the age of 84 confidently prepared to fight his fourth federal election.

If the attainment of national sovereignty was the crowning achievement of Adenauer's career, he was at his most confident in 1960. His party had been returned in the 1957 elections with an overwhelming majority, but this singular event in German political history had not persuaded the party that Adenauer was its only possible leader. His inflexible foreign policy and authoritarian methods were resented by many, and there was a widespread feeling that the party had proved itself and was entitled to a larger say in the running of the country's affairs. Elation was undisguised when, in 1959, he declared his willingness to be candidate for the presidency. Certainly he believed that with a Chancellor of his own choosing he could concentrate on foreign affairs and control the country's destiny from the presidential palace.

This was not to the liking of the party. It seized upon the constitutional safeguards against presidential rule, and was determined that Professor Erhard, the popular Economics Minister, should become Chancellor. Adenauer found the majority of the parliamentary party arrayed against him until he withdrew his candidacy for the presidential office. Opposition withered when it became clear that he intended to remain as Chancellor.

He had cause for satisfaction. The European Economic Community, which he regarded as an instrument of political unity, was pronounced as a success, and relations with France, after a period of doubt following upon the return of

General de Gaulle, were firmly established.

After the ratification of the Rome treaties Adenauer became increasingly impatient with British policies towards western Europe. The Anglo-American alliance was resented, and he did not bother to control his public temper. Disparaging remarks about Britain that seemed calculated to lower western confidence in the firmness of the British people were widely attributed to him.

MEETING WITH MACMILLAN

An exchange of visits with Mr. Macmillan brought little improvement; indeed, Adenauer could not forgive the Prime Minister's visit to Moscow that led to the abortive summit meeting. While declaring that an economic division of western Europe must be avoided, he viewed it with remarkable equanimity.

On January 5, 1961, Adenauer celebrated his eighty-fifth birthday, and Germany celebrated with him. The occasion was a remarkable demonstration of the affection in which the veteran leader was held and also, incidentally, of his stamina, for although Adenauer had only just recovered from a severe cold he stood for hour after hour to receive congratulations.

Although during the election campaign Adenauer's energy and assurance never deserted him, he once or twice fumbled the ball. His suggestion that "Russia was aiding the socialists", and his references to Herr Brandt's changes of name and nationality, were widely regarded as in poor taste. More serious was his inaction in the days immediately following the east Germans' building of a wall through the heart of Berlin on August 13. This cost him votes, and when the results of the elections on September 17 were known, it was seen that for the first time the Chancellor had lost his overall majority in the Bundestag. The seats of the Christian Democrats and their allies fell from 270 to 241. In the end, although the Free Democrats had said that they would never serve under Adenauer as Chancellor, he was duly reelected and the Free Democrats fell into line. Those of his own supporters who had been prepared to throw him over were brought to heel.

A new crisis in the relations between Bonn and Washington came to a head in April with the disclosure in Bonn of details about the so called American "package deal" submitted to Russia, and was interpreted by the United States Government as an attempt to sabotage the talks. It took a lot of explaining away in the months that followed, culminating in a visit to Bonn by Mr. Dean Rusk, the United States Secretary of State, in June.

Meanwhile, the Chancellor had journeyed to Paris for the first act of what was probably to prove the most historic event of his long career and of postwar German development. The pomp and ceremony displayed in his honour, the warmth of General de Gaulle's welcome, the solemn *te Deum* at Rheims cathedral, and the symbolic Franco-German military parade at Mourmelon Camp deeply moved him. They had their counterpart in the hero's welcome given to General de Gaulle when he returned the visit in the autumn, and spoke in German before huge and enthusiastic crowds. For the Chancellor, it marked the apotheosis of a policy which had begun with Robert Schuman and the Coal and Steel Community a decade before. The reconciliation between the two countries was emotionally welcomed by Germans of all parties and persuasions; but the increasingly egocentric policies of de Gaulle, his barely disguised opposition to Britain's entry into the EEC, and suspicion of American aims in Europe, aroused growing misgiving. In October the Bundestag adopted by a large majority a resolution approving the necessity of Britain's membership; and Dr. Schroder enhanced his reputation as candidate for the Chancellorship by an impressive speech on Britain's behalf.

His reluctance to be pinned down to any date for his retirement was enhanced by the determination of a majority of his party to choose to succeed him Professor Erhard, for whose political ability he had scant regard—and demonstrated it.

UNEASY COALITION

The uneasy coalition with the Free Democrats, whose views on domestic policy, and especially on relations with eastern Europe, produced frequent stresses and strains, was tried to breaking point in the autumn in the scandal over the *Spiegel* affair, involving alleged revelations of a military secret by an extremely aggressive weekly, which had some months earlier acquired notoriety by its exposure of scandals bound up with Herr Strauss, the Defence Minister. His personal intervention in the affair, the circumstances of the arrest of several members of the magazine's staff, without the knowledge of F.D.P. Ministers in the Cabinet, led to their mass resignation in December. They refused to reenter the Government unless Herr Strauss withdrew. Dr. Adenauer made desperate efforts to remain in power, even making overtures to the Socialists, whom he had always branded as unreliable. Finally a Government reshuffle was achieved; but at the price of the Chancellor's much firmer commitment—this time exacted by his own party—that he retire in the autumn of 1963. The *Spiegel* affair, the discovery that a prominent Nazi prosecutor had been appointed to one of the highest judicial offices in the state, and a series of other scandals, all strengthened in the eyes of public opinion the impression of decline and of the end of an era.

FRANCO-GERMAN TREATY

It was an ironic twist of fate that the signing of the Franco-German Treaty in Paris in January, 1963, which put the final seal on the new relationship between the two former hereditary enemies, should be an occasion not for satisfaction and rejoicing but for confusion and misunderstanding at home and abroad. General de Gaulle's brutal veto of Britain's entry at Brussels 10 days later produced another estrangement from the United States, apprehension of the military clauses of the treaty, and the suspicion in Britain that Dr. Adenauer had not used all his influence to dissuade the French President from his designs. These suspicions were echoed in Germany herself, and increased the Chancellor's political isolation.

Then to the surprise and initial disbelief of the country the C.D.U. leaders suddenly decided to put an end to the "eternal manoeuvrings" over Adenauer's successor. Suddenly in a series of top level meetings in April that year, they summoned up all their courage, electing before the old Chancellor's eyes the man he had resisted for years, Dr. Erhard, the successful Economics Minister. This step was intended to give the Chancellor no alternative but to keep the promise extracted from him two years before and finally step down that autumn. The decisive considerations were electoral: there was unanimous opposition from the *Länder* party executives to his staying and there was urgent need for the new man to have time to work himself in with the electorate before the 1965 general election. Adenauer, always a realist, accepted and promised to support his successor but had the assurance from the party managers that he would retain the office of party chairman.

The decision taken, almost the whole of that summer passed in Germany in the consciousness that an historic era was ending. It was crowned by the visits, and the public tributes to the great statesman, within a few days of each other by President Kennedy and President de Gaulle. If they were the last political triumphs of *der Alte* they also served to emphasize how far he had brought his country since 1949, with Germany now courted by two of her former leading enemies. But with France there were already differences lurking before Adenauer had gone, including German resistance on Common Market agricultural prices and French opposition to the M.L.F., which the Chancellor wanted.

After 14 years as Chancellor he made his departure with dignity. It was a departure, it is true, with a characteristically Adenauer flavour, warnings of the dangers of Germany's exposed position from Russia, promises to help his party fight social democracy and all its works, and telling everyone that he was in no mood to accept the praise that flooded in as a funeral oration. He took a last demonstration of the German people's gratitude at a vast rally in his native Cologne, where he proclaimed his consciousness that he had "done his duty to the last".

OFFICE RELINQUISHED

At an historic sitting of the Bundestag on October 15 he formally gave up office only a few weeks away from his eighty-eighth birthday, returning to the deputies' benches he left in 1949. The politicians' farewell speeches showed full awareness of the greatness of the country's debt to him, but they were all strangely without human warmth, in spite of the moment.

For months the changeover appeared to have gone more smoothly than anyone had dared to expect. Once or twice the former Chancellor made public speeches which attracted attention—he put the blame on Britain for holding up the Common Market's political progress—but in the summer of 1964 he became politically active again, intervening as the Erhard Government ran into pressure from France. Adenauer saw the reconciliation with France as the crowning achievement of his life's work and probably felt he must act if the most precious part of his political legacy was so soon threatened. The unsuccessful visit by President de Gaulle to Bonn for talks with Dr. Erhard in July caused the former Chancellor to line up with Herr Strauss, the former Defence Minister, and they both sought to urge the Government to make a beginning to a European political union with France *"à deux"*, as the phrase went, if all the Six were not willing as well. The Government, however, resisted these pleadings and Adenauer significantly failed to get the C.D.U. behind him.

Returning from his summer holidays, when he had finally began writing his memoirs, Adenauer provoked a storm in early November by sharply criticizing the Government in a mass circulation newspaper interview, and urging reaching agreement with President de Gaulle at almost any price. This was at the time the French President was threatening to leave both the E.E.C. and NATO, and signing a new trade treaty with Moscow. The former Chancellor, who believed deeply in his special relationship with the French leader, sounded a warning that France might one day ally herself again with Russia against Germany, a fear he often expressed openly during these last years. The dispute was patched up in the C.D.U. but the decline, by now, in Adenauer's effective power over the other party leaders, once his lieutenants, was made manifest in the hints to him that if such attacks on Dr. Erhard continued he would lose the party chairmanship. In the face of still continuing Opposition electoral gains the party was deeply concerned about Adenauer's effect on their chances in 1965.

SUBSTANTIAL VICTORY

It need not have worried. Dr. Erhard won a substantial victory, and Dr. Adenauer could hardly conceal his disappointment. He felt strongly that Dr. Erhard and Dr. Schröder, the Foreign Minister, were between them wrecking his life's work—the reconciliation with France, and he continued to criticize them at every opportunity. But the seeds of Dr. Erhard's fall had already been sown. Before the 1965 election he and his party had been so nervous that they had showered the electorate with various expensive presents that went against all their promises of financial stringency and did much to bring about the budgetary crisis of October, 1966. It was from this crisis that the present coalition Government emerged, with Dr. Kiesinger at its head.

Dr. Adenauer was now a happier man, for the new Government was pledged to restore relations with France, and Dr. Kiesinger soon paid a successful visit to Paris. But Dr. Adenauer was still haunted by his old fears that his allies would do a deal with Russia at the expense of Germany. He never fully accepted the new priorities according to which relaxation in Europe was to be pursued for its own sake, and without formal progress towards German reunification. The draft non-proliferation treaty seemed to confirm all his fears, and he reacted violently, calling it a new version of the Morgenthau plan that was to have made Germany a pastoral nation after the Second World War. Thus he ended his life in a rather incongruous alliance with the very nationalistic elements that he had tried to contain by welding west Germany into a European community.

He was twice married and had seven children. His first wife, Emma Weyer, died in 1916, leaving two sons and a daughter. His second wife, Auguste Zinsser, died in 1948. There were two sons and two daughters of the second marriage.

April 20, 1967.

Halide Edib Adivar, on of the most gifted and influential Turkish writers of her generation, and a woman of action who fought alongside Mustafa Kemal Ataturk in the Turkish war of independence of 1921–22, died in Istanbul in January, 1964, at the age of 79. Halide Edib was born and brought up in the darkest period of Abdul Hamid's dictatorship and in the days when about the only thing a Turkish woman was expected to do in public was to wear a veil. But from her early days she was deeply involved in all the most active and revolutionary intellectual movements of her time.

Born in 1884, she graduated from the old American girls' college at Uskudar (Scutari), in Istanbul, in 1901. She was the first Turkish girl ever to pass through this college. Here she laid the foundation of an Anglo-Saxon education, for she was a pioneer in this sense, too, that whereas almost all Turkish cultural contacts with the west up to that time had come from France or Germany, Halide Edib was one of the first Turks to feel and transmit to her own people an English and American culture. For the whole of her adult life she had a perfect command of English, and many of her finest books were written directly in the English language.

Before and after the Young Turk Revolution of 1908 which finally broke the despotic rule of Abdul Hamid, Halide Edib was a leading member of the circle of revolutionary-minded intellectuals which included such figures as the philosopher Riza Tevfik, the writer Huseyin Camid and the novelist Yakub Kadri. With Ziya Gokalp and Hamdullah Suphi she founded the Turk Ocaklari (nation-wide Turkish nationalist organization) and was for a time captured by the then fashionable Pan Turanianism or Pan Turkism which later became moderated among its exponents to an ardent Turkish patriotism. This period, the last days of the Ottoman Empire, was a ferment of ideas in which Halide Edib and others conceived a reformed and modernized Turkey which Kemal Ataturk, at the time unknown, was later to carry out.

Halide Edib first won fame with her novel *Handan*, written in 1912, a love story of a young woman of good culture who is dominated by the personality of a socialist intellectual. In the same year she wrote *Yeni Turan* (the new Turan), a novel into which she put some of her strongest feelings of Turkish nationalism.

AT THE FRONT

In 1917 Halide, now divorced from her first husband, the well known mathematician Salih Zeki, married Dr. Adnan Adivar, later to become one of the leading Turkish political figures. Together in 1919 they escaped from allied-occupied Istanbul to join Ataturk's forces in Anatolia. During the great battle of the River Sakarya, where Turkish nationalists turned the tide against Greek invaders. Halide Edib, then in another part of Turkey, cabled to Ataturk in Ankara asking for a job at the front. She went there and was given the rank of a corporal and later was promoted sergeant-major.

When the war of independence ended and Ataturk established his complete personal mastery over Turkey both Halide and her husband rejected Ataturk's dictatorship, but later supported President Inönü, with whom her relations were always good. She retired completely from public life—though she continued writing up to the end—but after the death of her husband she lived in seclusion in Istanbul.

Halide Edib wrote about a dozen novels which were translated into western and other languages but some of her finest work was in her memoirs of the war of independence, written in English, such as *Turkey Faces West* and *The Turkish Ordeal,* which are valuable not only for historical data but for her descriptions of such men as Kemal Ataturk, whom she presents in a light which is a good deal more interesting, and probably more realistic, than the hero worshipping conformism of the present day. But her antagonism to Ataturk and her disapproval of some of his most drastic reforms, especially the abolition of the Muslim caliphate, make her writings unfashionable for the present generation in Turkey. One of her best known books written in English was *The Clown's Daughter* which she herself translated into Turkish.

Besides being a strong, original writer and a personality of the first magnitude Halide Edib was a brilliant speaker and her rousing addresses in Istanbul and Izmir at the beginning of the war of independence whipped large crowds to action. She was a woman in whom passion and intellect were remarkably blended. Her books are well worth reading today. In her younger days she was a keen horsewoman, a fine shot, and was always very active.

She is survived by two sons of her first marriage.

January 15, 1964.

General Charles Ailleret, the chief of staff of the French armed forces, died on March 9, 1968, in an air crash on the island of Réunion, in the Indian Ocean, while on an official tour of inspection. He was 60.

The French Government had just decided to prolong his appointment for another year beyond retiring age, in order to enable him to work out the bases of the new French nuclear strategy.

General Ailleret, the most senior soldier of France since 1962, was a rare combination of the intellectual and the military man of action. One of the very few senior officers to hold the Doctorate of Law, he was at the same time a licensed parachute instructor, a judo black belt, and retained throughout his life a love of challenge and of violent sports. He had scant respect for armchair strategy. He played a key part, first in the build up of the French nuclear forces;

and more latterly, was in complete harmony with the military conceptions of General de Gaulle in the elaboration of the theory of protection of French territory from all points of the compass known in this country as "azimuthal defence".

STAFF CONSTRAINED

The direct and detailed interest that General de Gaulle has taken in defence matters since he came to power in 1958 has tended to limit the scope for any of his staff to assert his personality and his views. This was true of General Ailleret, as of his predecessors. But he was no mere executant, and brought to the practical elaboration of the Gaullist strategy a sharp mind and a firm stand. His physical appearance underlined his strength of character: small of stature, tough and close knit, with weatherbeaten features, he disdained protocol and would often be seen stalking training grounds in combat dress, his sleeves rolled up for action.

ARTILLERY SUBALTERN

Charles Ailleret was born on March 26, 1907, at Gassicourt, near Paris. He attended the Lycée Louis-le-Grand, entered the École Polytechnique in 1926 and graduated as a second lieutenant in the artillery two years later. He was to remain in that arm until the outbreak of war.

Following the collapse of France, he commanded the Northern area of the underground army until his arrest and deportation to Buchenwald concentration camp in 1944. On repatriation in March the following year, he was appointed military attaché to Moscow, for two years. Promoted to colonel in 1946, he commanded an infantry demi-brigade, and later served on the staff of S.H.A.P.E.

In 1952, he received command of the special weapons branch, which included the French nuclear weapon, and supervised the first two nuclear tests at Reggane in the Sahara in 1960. Brigadier-general in 1956, a major-general in 1959, he commanded the Constantine area and cabled Paris at the time of the 1961 generals' putsch: "I'm exercising my command normally."

Supreme commander of French forces in Algeria, he was appointed chief of staff of the armed forces in 1962.

SENSATIONAL ARTICLE

An ardent defender of the principle of an "independent" French defence, based on the "dis-integration" of the French forces from Nato and their conversion to a strategic nuclear force, he published, in October, 1967, in the *Revue de la Défense Nationale*, a sensational article on "azimuthal defence" developing the principles set out by General de Gaulle in 1959, on the need for France to be prepared in an age of I.C.B.M.s to ward off attacks from any quarter, and not merely from the east.

He died before being able to settle the controversy between the Air Force and the Navy as to which should assume the responsibility for doing so. His wife and daughter also perished in the same aircraft, and he is survived by a son.

March 11, 1968.

Richard Ainley, who died in London on May 18, 1967, was an actor whose career as a young man had been followed with great interest and whose virtual retirement from the theatre as the result of a very serious war wound had caused general regret.

His birth on December 23, 1910, took place near the end of the year in which his father, Henry Ainley, had played a succession of leading parts in Shakespeare for Beerbohm Tree at His Majesty's. Richard was educated abroad and made his debut in Martin Harvey's company on tour in 1928, using the name Richard Riddle, and not assuming his father's name until some years later, when he felt that audiences had accepted him on his own merits.

Meanwhile he had served an apprenticeship of three seasons under Harcourt Williams at the Old Vic and one season at Barry Jackson's Malvern Festival, playing, in the Waterloo Road, the Lion to Sir John Gielgud's Emperor in *Androcles and the Lion*, Orsino to Dame Edith Evans's Viola, and Laertes in the Hamlet of both Robert Harris and Robert Speaight.

As the King's young secretary—"he played it to perfection" was the opinion of the leading man—Richard Ainley supported Gielgud in *Richard of Bordeaux*, and after a brief appearance as Edward II in Hugh Ross Williamson's play about Edward and Piers Gaveston, he returned to the New Theatre as Rosencrantz—Anthony Quayle was the Guildenstern—to Gielgud's Hamlet in 1934.

Under Robert Atkins he played the name part in the morality play, *Everyman*, at the Q, he was seen as the doctor in *Uncle Vanya*, and in 1938 he joined the company at the Queens for the last play in Gielgud's season, appearing as Bassanio to the Portia of Dame Peggy Ashcroft.

GRAVELY WOUNDED

During the last season before the outbreak of the Second World War his roles included Ludwig II of Bavaria in a play about Elizabeth of Austria, and the announcer of Johnson's impending death in J.B. Priestley's short-lived but well remembered *Johnson over Jordan*.

During the war Ainley, having made his American debut in Frederick Lonsdale's *Foreigners* in 1939, served in the United States Mechanized Cavalry and was gravely wounded in Germany when his armoured vehicle struck a mine. Notwithstanding, he was again seen in 1947 as Everyman, and in 1949 as Faust in a production in Regent's Park commemorating Goethe's bicentenary, but he was now greatly handicapped by lameness. Thereafter his contributions to the art of the drama took the form of broadcasting, of adjudication at the Dominion Drama Festival in Canada in 1958, and of a tour of duty as principal of the British Old Vic Theatre School from 1961 to 1963.

From his father he inherited looks, voice and charm; everything but the spark of greatness which Harry Ainley on his good days showed, but which Richard did not. His tenderness for his father and for his father's flawed greatness was as unmistakable as their physical resemblance. In later years, when the talk would turn on the theatre in Richard Ainley's company, it would be Harry this and Harry that and Harry all the time; and there would be no regret in it, but only admiration.

He was married three times, first to Ethel Glendinning, who had acted with him at the Old Vic, secondly to Miss Betzi Beaton, thirdly to Dr. Rowena Woolf.

May 23, 1967.

Professor Ian Aird, CH.M., F.R.C.S., who died suddenly in London on September 17, 1962, at the age of 57, had been professor of surgery in the University of London and director of the surgical unit at the Postgraduate Medical School at Hammersmith since 1946.

His name came prominently before the public in 1953 when he undertook the separation of the infant Siamese twins, Boko and Tomo, who had been brought to London by air from Kano, West Africa. The operation was successfully performed and although one of the twins subsequently died, the other survived.

In May, 1962, he led the team operating on the Nigerian Siamese twins, Joan and Jennifer Amadu, at Hammersmith Hospital. Jennifer died during the five-hour operation, but Joan survived.

Ian Aird was born on July 4, 1905, the son of William Aird and Jean Elizabeth Binnie, and was educated at George Watson's College and at the University of Edinburgh. He qualified as M.B., Ch.B. Edinburgh in 1928 and was awarded the Thomson scholarship, the Wightman Prize and the Annandale Gold Medal. He visited Paris, Vienna, and the United States for the purpose of postgraduate study, and obtained the F.R.C.S. Edinburgh in 1930 and the Ch.M., with high commendation, in 1935. His appointment as surgeon to the Royal Hospital for Sick Children and assistant surgeon to the Royal Infirmary, Edinburgh, followed, and he rapidly acquired a reputation as a coach. In 1946 he was invited to succeed to the chair of surgery in the London Postgraduate Medical School, following Professor G. Grey Turner. He was admitted F.R.C.S. England (*ad eundem*) in 1947, and he was an examiner in surgery for the Royal College of Surgeons of England and Edinburgh and for the Universities of London, Birmingham and Malaya. He was the author of *A Companion in Surgical Studies* (1949), probably one of the best surgical textbooks to be published in recent years, and of numerous articles. During the 1939–45 war he served as a lieutenant-colonel, R.A.M.C., and was twice mentioned in dispatches.

He married in 1936 Margaret, daughter of William Goodman Cowes, of Buenos Aires. There were a son and a daughter of this marriage.

September 18, 1962.

Anna Akhmatova, Russia's greatest woman poet, died on March 5, 1966, in a nursing home near Moscow at the age of 76.

Her concern with individual experience, whether in love or when confronted with the impersonal machinery of the state, was incompatible with the Socialist realism demanded by

Zhadanov in Stalinist days; her work was seen as harmful to Soviet youth and in 1946 she was expelled from the Union of Soviet Writers. However the tide turned after Stalin's death and the Soviet press on the day after she died described her as "a great Russian and Soviet poet".

In June, 1965, she came to Britain as a guest of the British Council and, during her visit, Oxford University conferred on her an honorary D.Litt.

Anna Andreyevna Akhmatova, *née* Gorenko (she adopted her mother's maiden name Akhmatova as a pseudonym) was born near Odessa on June 23, 1889. She spent her childhood in Tsarskoe Selo, and most of her adult life in St. Petersburg—Leningrad, a city with which her personal experience and her poetry were deeply and at times poignantly associated. From 1910 to 1918 she was married to the poet Gumilev, with whom she took a leading part in launching the Acmeist movement which marked a reaction from Symbolism and a return to the classical tradition in Russian poetry. In 1921 he was shot for counter-revolutionary activity. She achieved fame with her first two volumes of verse, *Evening* (1912) and *Beads* (1914). These were followed by further collections. *The White Flock* (1917) and *Anno Domini* (1922).

PROLONGED SILENCE

The growing distaste which her poetry of intimate human emotions aroused in Soviet officialdom forced her thereafter into periods of prolonged silence. But, though her next volume of verse did not appear until 1940, she was able during those years to publish several distinguished studies of Pushkin's work. In September, 1941, she was evacuated from Leningrad (then under German blockade) to Tashkent whence, after a grave illness, she returned to her home city in June, 1944. A further ordeal overtook her two years later: a violent attack made on her by Zhdanov, motivated by the continued popularity of her poetry, particularly among the young, led to her temporary expulsion from the Union of Soviet Writers. In the more relaxed literary atmosphere that followed Stalin's death she was able to publish new poems which in addition to her earlier qualities of terseness and precision, revealed her vivid sense of the past, often compounded of tragedy or tinged with sadness, and her abiding love of her native land. Yet this nostalgia for the past and the religious inspiration of much of her poetry prevented full official recognition: and the poetic masterpieces of her later years, *Poem Without A Hero* and *Requicm*, were published abroad.

After the death in 1960 of Pasternak (whom she knew well and valued highly) Anna Akhmatova remained the greatest surviving representative of a remarkable generation of Russian poets who were active in the first quarter of this century. Of these Innokenty Annensky exercised perhaps the most immediate influence on her lyric poetry, at once intimate and restrained. In her literary tastes she was discriminating and inclined to fastidiousness. Pushkin, Dostoevsky and Kafka were perhaps the writers she admired most. She disliked Turgenev and, though she generously encouraged fresh talent, had little use for some of the younger Soviet poets who are popular today.

In her latter years she was held in honour and reverence by all true writers and lovers of literature in Russia: a reverence enhanced by the dignity with which she bore her personal trials, and not unmixed with awe, induced by her queenly bearing and her sometimes sharp tongue. She suffered neither fools nor knaves gladly. And at the close of a life during which he was constantly harassed by officialdom, she preserved to the last her literary integrity, her high moral standards, and her Christian faith.

In the end, too, Madame Akhmatova's enforced isolation was mitigated by the honour she received abroad. She travelled to Italy to receive the Taormina Prize; and in June of 1965 she went—for the first time—to England, to receive an honorary doctorate at Oxford. This was an experience as moving to her as it was to her friends and her admirers, some of whom had come from far to pay tribute to the greatest living Russian poet.

March 7, 1966.

Chief Samuel Ladoke Akintola, Premier of the Western Region of Nigeria, who was killed on January 15, 1966, during the revolution in Nigeria, at the age of 55, was a controversial figure in Nigerian politics.

Popularly known as "S.L.A.", Chief Akintola began his career as a teacher at Baptist Academy, Lagos, where he taught from 1930 to 1942. While he was still teaching, he became interested in freelance journalism and edited a religious journal, the *Nigerian Baptist*, from 1939 to 1943. In 1942 he resigned his teaching appointment in sympathy with three dismissed members of the Baptist Teachers Union (of which he was secretary) for their part in an agitation by the union. The same year he joined the Nigerian Railway as a clerk but a few months later he left to join the *Daily Service*—one of Nigeria's former leading dailies.

Chief Akintola was editor of the newspaper until 1946 when he went to the United Kingdom on a British Council scholarship to study local government. This gave him an opportunity to study law at Lincoln's Inn and he was called to the Bar in 1949.

On his return to Nigeria in 1950, he resumed active politics and led the agitation for the separation of Oshun Division from the jurisdiction of Ibadan Divisional Council. When Chief Obafemi Awolowo founded the Action Group in 1951, Chief Akintola rallied his people around the new party and later became Deputy Leader.

So great was his influence in shaping the Action Group's policies and national affairs that he was regarded as the automatic successor when Chief Awolowo relinquished the premiership of the Western Region late in 1959 to contest the federal elections of that year.

In May, 1962, the rift between him and his leader took a violent turn in the Western House of Assembly and the police had to use tear gas to disperse the members. The Federal government stepped in and declared a state of emergency that lasted six months. Chief Akintola resigned from the Action Group and formed a new party—the United People Party. An inquiry set up during the emergency to probe the affairs of six of the region's statutory corporations cleared Chief Akintola's name of all blame and after the lifting of the emergency he was returned to power in January, 1963, at the head of a coalition government formed by his new party.

In the election in the Western Region in October, 1965—the first since the constitutional crisis of 1962—Akintola's party, now named the Nigerian National Democratic Party which enjoyed help and support from the Northern People's Congress, retained power. There were however few illusions about the fairness of the election, and well documented reports gave a picture of corruption, intimidation and skulduggery.

Akintola was for many years a member of the Federal Parliament and was one of the first set of Central Ministers appointed in 1952. After the 1954 general elections he was Leader of Opposition in the Centre until invited to join a national government in 1957.

January 17, 1966.

Field Marshal Lord Alanbrooke, who died on June 17, 1963 at his Hampshire home at the age of 79, held high command in the field for only a brief period in 1940, but has been universally recognized as one of the greatest—intellectually and in military knowledge probably the greatest—soldiers of his generation. As Chief of the Imperial General Staff during the greater part of the Second World War he exercised behind the scenes a profound influence upon its course. He possessed a gift for lucid explanation and exposition which was an invaluable asset at international conferences and also enabled him to succeed in the task, in which so many soldiers have failed, of talking convincingly to the politician. He was as much at home in Whitehall as with his fellow soldiers and the leaders of the other fighting services.

Alan Francis Brooke, Field Marshal Viscount Alanbrooke, K.G., G.C.B., O.M., G.C.V.O., D.S.O., was the sixth son of Sir Victor Brooke, third baronet, of Brookeborough, co. Fermanagh, and of Alice Sophia, daughter of Sir Alan Bellingham, third baronet. He was born in the south of France at Bagnères de Bigorre, where his parents were then living, on July 23, 1883. Sir Victor Brooke was a warm friend of James Roosevelt, father of Franklin Delano, and this friendship was always borne in mind by the future President of the United States. Alan Brooke's early education was obtained at a French lycée, with the result that he grew up virtually bilingual. He afterwards passed through the Royal Military Academy Woolwich, and was gazetted second lieutenant in the Royal Artillery in December, 1902. His early service was spent in Ireland. In 1906 he went to India and was posted to N. Battery, R.H.A., and when war with Germany broke out in 1914 he was commanding the R.H.A. Ammunition Column at Secunderabad.

In September of that year he landed at Marseilles with the Secunderabad Cavalry

Brigade in the Indian Cavalry Corps. A few weeks later, during the Battle of la Basée, he was promoted captain, and in January, 1915, became Staff Captain—subsequently Adjutant—R.H.A., 2nd Indian Cavalry Division. In November he went to the 18th Division as Brigade Major R.A., and in this capacity he served through the Battle of the Somme, having been promoted major in April, 1916. He became Staff Officer R.A. at the headquarters of the Canadian Corps in February, 1917, and later in the year G.S.O.2 R.A., remaining with the Canadians through all their battles until nearly the end of the war. In September, 1918, however, he was transferred to the First Army as G.S.O.1 R.A. He was awarded the D.S.O. in 1917 and a bar to this decoration in 1918. In January, 1919, he was made a brevet lieutenant-colonel.

Brooke had emerged from the war with the reputation of a most capable and promising staff officer, and he was selected to attend the first post-war course at the Staff College. In 1920, after graduation, he became G.S.O.2 of the Northumbrian Division, Territorial Army. In 1923 he returned to the Staff College as an instructor, remained there for four years, and then studied for a year at the Imperial Defence College. After a year on regimental duty he was appointed Commandant of the School of Artillery at Larkhill, his promotion to colonel being antedated to 1923. From 1932 to 1934 he was Army Instructor at the Imperial Defence College. He then received command of the 8th Infantry Brigade at Plymouth. In June, 1935, he was promoted to major-general, and later that year became Inspector of Artillery. He vacated this post in 1935 on appointment to that of Director of Military Training at the War Office.

In 1937 Brooke became commander of an experimental formation known as the "Mobile Division", but passed on in the following year to become Commander of the Anti-Aircraft Corps, an appointment which was enlarged to that of G.O.C.-in-C. Anti-Aircraft Command in 1939. Once again he was scarcely given time to settle down, becoming G.O.C.-in-C., Southern Command in 1939, in succession to General Wavell. The Southern was the most important of the home commands at the time, and it was understood that the appointment carried with it the command of an army corps in any expeditionary force which might be sent abroad in the event of war with Germany. And in 1939, on the out-break of war, he went out to France in command of the II Corps. He had been promoted to the rank of lieutenant-general the previous year.

In the retreat to Dunkirk and the operations covering the evacuation from that port in 1940 Brooke displayed consummate ability. Almost immediately after his return to England he was selected to go back to France and to take command of British troops still in the country, that is, south of the Somme. There was still some slight hope of French resistance continuing, in which case the British Government intended to send the maximum assistance. That hope was rapidly dispelled by the situation which Brooke discovered after landing at Cherbourg on June 12. The French armies were in dissolution. He strongly advocated a second evacuation, but remained in France until the French Government asked the Germans for an armistice.

A DAUNTING RESPONSIBILITY

Back in England Brooke returned for a period of a few weeks to the Southern Command, but was then appointed Commander-in-Chief Home Forces. This was a position of serious and indeed daunting responsibility. Almost all the equipment of the expeditionary forces had been lost and the troops in the United Kingdom had to be provided with obsolete weapons, while in many cases weapons were altogether lacking. All the Commander-in-Chief's great energy, ability, and experience were devoted to the task of reequipment, training, and preparation of defence against invasion. The air victory in the Battle of Britain removed the danger for 1940, though there still seemed to be a possibility of its recurrence. Brooke was in that year promoted to the rank of general and awarded the K.C.B., his C.B. dating from 1937.

At the end of 1941 he was appointed to succeed his old friend and fellow-Ulsterman, General Sir John Dill, as Chief of the Imperial General Staff. He took over that office at a black moment, when the Japanese were in the full flood of victory and Singapore already appeared doomed to fall. In some quarters regret was expressed that he should have given up his command, since he was considered to be of all British soldiers of his generation the most likely to shine in the field. But as the war developed it is certain that his services could not have been more valuable in any capacity than they were at the War Office from now to the end of hostilities and during the period of the immediate aftermath. He established the best possible relations with the Americans and exercised a strong influence upon the future course of allied strategy, especially before the military expansion of the United States had reached its greatest height and the American commanders had acquired experience.

After that the Americans were naturally less inclined to accept advice as a matter of course from any foreigner, however experienced and able, but they still paid great respect to his views, knowing that these always had a firm basis. It has been suggested that he was inclined to overrate the progress made by the gun in the unending duel with the tank and to consider that the opportunities of the latter would henceforth prove to be much more limited against a first-class enemy than in the invasion of north-west Europe. If so, he was not alone in this mistake. It is certain, however, that both on the Chiefs of Staffs Committee and in his relations with commanders-in-chief or allied supreme commanders in the field his personality, strategic insight, and knowledge were elements of strength.

He worked very long hours without showing undue fatigue. He also travelled immense distances and as the war progressed was more and more often absent from London, knowing that the affairs of Whitehall and the War Office itself could safely be left for considerable periods in the hands of the Vice-Chief, Lieutenant-General Nye. He liked to obtain his information and "briefing" from the same small group of men, so that though he was the dominant personality in the War Office, he was hardly known by sight to the majority of its inmates and there were people on the same floor who never caught sight of him for months on end; but those who served him had no reason to complain of any lack of gratitude or regard.

The immense burden that fell on Brooke's shoulders, and the skill and determination with which he shouldered it, are convincingly described in Sir Arthur Bryant's *The Turn of the Tide,* which is based on Brooke's war diaries.

DISTURBING BOOK

This book created a considerable stir when it was published in 1957, chiefly because it portrayed the irritations as well as the glories that fell to those who worked under Sir Winston Churchill in the direction of the war—although Lord Alanbrooke made it clear in his foreword to the book that any irritations or impatience at the defects that arose out of Sir Winston's very greatness were insignificant when set against the magnitude of his achievement.

The book shows how Brooke gradually developed his own technique for dealing with the Prime Minister by steady argument from facts to prevent Britain's strategy from outrunning her resources. In his diary Brooke records his disappointment in August, 1943, when the Prime Minister handed over to the Americans, during the Quebec conference, the appointment of Supreme Commander for the invasion of Europe. Brooke had earlier voluntarily given up the chance of taking over the North African Command before El Alamein because he thought he could serve a more useful purpose by remaining with the Prime Minister, and he had been promised the Supreme Commander's appointment by Churchill. It was, he records, "a crushing blow" and it was delivered without sympathy or regrets. But Brooke survived it to record his final judgment on Churchill: "He is quite the most difficult man to work with that I have ever struck, but I would not have missed the chance of working with him for anything on earth."

CRITICAL COMMENTS

Two years later a sequel was published, *Triumph in the West*, once again written by Sir Arthur Bryant and based on Alanbrooke's diaries. As well as chronicling, as its title indicates, the victories of the allied forces, it provoked renewed controversy by critical comments on American strategic thinking and particularly on General Eisenhower's technical military capacities as a commander.

Brooke was advanced to G.C.B. in 1942, in which year he also became A.D.C. General to the King. He was created a field marshal on January 1, 1944. In 1945 he was created Baron Alanbrooke, of Brookeborough, County Fermanagh, in the peerage of the United Kingdom and later advanced to a viscounty. He was awarded the Order of Merit and made K.G. in 1946. He also received a number of the highest foreign decorations, and received honorary degrees from many British universities. He was appointed Colonel Commandant R.A.

(1939–1957), R.H.A. (1940–1957), Glider Pilot Regiment (1942–1951) and H.A.C. (1946–1954). He left the War Office in the summer of 1946 after the most memorable tenure of the appointment of C.I.G.S. in the history of that office.

After retirement from the Army he continued to lead an active life, assuming many directorships in the City and holding a number of public offices. He was Master Gunner, St. James's Park from 1946 to 1956; Constable of the Tower of London from 1950 to 1955; and H.M. Lieutenant for the County of London from 1950 to 1957. At the Coronation in 1953 he was Commander of the Parade and Lord High Constable of England in the Abbey ceremonies. In 1949 he became Chancellor of Queen's University, Belfast. Alanbrooke was also a former president of the Zoological Society of London, holding office from 1951 to 1954. He was made G.C.V.O. in 1953.

Coming from a family devoted to sport, Lord Alanbrooke was a keen shot and fisherman. Later in life he took to bird-watching, an interest which he pursued in his scanty leisure all through the war and in which he found welcome refreshment of mind. He was a remarkably good and amusing conversationalist, and when he relaxed no respecter of persons or indeed of reputations.

He married first, in 1914, Jane Mary, elder daughter of Colonel John Richardson, Rossfad, Ballinamallard, County Fermanagh. She was killed in a motor accident in 1925. In 1929 he married Benita, widow of Sir Thomas Lees, second baronet, eldest daughter of Sir Harold Pelly, fourth baronet. There were one son and one daughter of each marriage. His elder son, the Hon. Thomas Brooke, now succeeds to the peerage.

June 18, 1963.

The former King Zog of Albania died in hospital in Paris on April 9, 1961. He was 65.

Ahmed Zog was born in the castle of Burgayet on October 8, 1895, the son of Djemal Pasha, head of one of the foremost Albanian clans. After his father's death he was sent to school in Constantinople and there acquired a good knowledge of Turkish.

With the heavy hand of the Turk never far away fighting was in his blood and in 1913, when only 18, Aubrey Herbert referred to him as "a reader of Shakespeare and a fine fighting man". In the First World War he served in the Austrian armed forces and if he cared little enough for his masters he learnt much about military life which he was able to turn to good account in 1921 when he found himself C.-in-C. of the Albanian Forces. That same year he was made Minister of the Interior—he had actually held the post briefly once before—in the sixth Albanian postwar Cabinet. A year later he was Prime Minister. A limited amount of administrative reform was carried through under the guidance of foreign advisers but the country lacked the foreign financial help that was needed to develop its modest resources.

He had a difficult course to steer for it would be far from the truth to say that he led a united people. By 1924 his position had become untenable, an attempt was made on his life—there were to be others—and he retired with his colleagues to his native mountains on the Serbo-Albanian border. It was a case of *reculer pour mieux sauter*, for later in 1924 he returned to expel his successor.

In January, 1925, a national assembly voted for the proclamation of a republic and on February 1 Zog was elected President; nominally President but actually dictator of his country.

In a country such as Albania a president of the type of a Fallières or a Hainisch would have been useless; nor was Ahmed Zog, with his personality and his antecedents, likely to be of this type. Rather was he a ruler after the fashion of Yuan-Shih-Kai and Pilsudski—strong, efficient and where necessary ruthless. His enemies accused him of cruelty; stern he certainly was in his repression of the revolt of the northern Catholic tribes of the Dukagjini in November, 1926, and in his execution of the Catholic priest who had inspired that revolt, in defiance of the time-honoured immunity from execution which rebellious Albanian clergy had previously enjoyed. Even some of his friends deprecated the compulsory "benevolence" of half a napoleon per family levied on the people of Scutari for the construction of his country house on the shores of that lake, while others criticized equally the compulsory display of his portrait in every shop in Albania.

NATIONALIST IDEALS

Yet all these things were done by him not from vanity or from a love of being autocratic but of set purpose. Ahmed Zog was, when he became President, one of the few real patriots in his country and he knew it: was one of the few Albanians who placed the ideal of Albanian nationality above that of tribal, regional or sectarian particularism. He was determined to create, if such a thing were possible, a united if not a uniform Albania, and he knew that the only hope of success lay in the strong personal rule of one man.

Zog slowly consolidated his position, Italy had obtained a substantial commercial interest in Albania, but while well aware of his need for foreign support Zog was concerned lest that support should become crucial and jeopardize the independence of his country. Events, however, forced his hand; an insurrection in 1926 led to the signing of the pact of Tirana under which Italy and Albania recognized that any disturbance directed against the established situation of Albania was opposed to their reciprocal political interest. The pact was followed in February, 1927, by the conclusion of a treaty of defensive alliance. In September, 1928 Zog I was proclaimed King of the Albanians and a constitution was set up providing for a Council of Ministers (appointed by the King) and an elected Chamber of Deputies. Complete religious freedom, existing in practice, was reaffirmed.

ITALIAN INFILTRATION

Albania in those years made much progress in the educational and economic fields; schools and banks were opened, roads built, and the gendarmerie reorganized. Meanwhile, the Italians, under treaty cover, were digging themselves in with techniques now familiar; missions of various sorts, technicians, experts, and advisers, came and went.

For years Zog remained unmarried, to the regret of Albanians who desired to see the dynasty stabilized. To find a suitable alliance for a European ruler who was at the same time Muslim was not easy; but in 1938 there took place, with all the pomp that the little kingdom was able to provide, the King's marriage to a beautiful young Hungarian, Countess Geraldine Apponyi, daughter of Count Julius Apponyi and his wife *née* Miss Steuart of New York. As the King was Muslim and his bride a Roman Catholic, the marriage was necessarily a civil one. On April 5, 1939, Queen Geraldine gave birth to a son. The very next day she was dispatched by her husband to Greece and on Good Friday, after a preliminary bombardment from the sea, Italian forces landed and seized Durazzo, Santi Quaranti, Valona, and San Giovanni di Medua. A week later all serious resistance had ended and Zog joined his Queen in Greece.

From Greece Zog and his family came to England, where he lived during the Second World War, in a house near High Wycombe, Buckinghamshire. Elections in Albania in December, 1945, returned a Communist Government, and a republic was at once declared. Great Britain broke off relations with Albania, and Zog and his entourage sailed for Egypt, where his friend King Farouk placed a house at his disposal. Troubles in Egypt caused him to move to Long Island, in the United States, but he did not remain there long, and by 1955 the exiles had moved to Cannes. He is survived by his wife and their son, Leka.

April 10, 1961.

Horatius Albarda, who died in an air crash in the Swiss Alps on May 17, 1965, had been president of K.L.M. Royal Dutch Airlines since 1963. He was 61.

His presidency began when K.L.M. was losing money, and he said on taking office that he intended to retire when the company was on a sound financial footing once more.

He was mainly responsible for new policies which have brought the Royal Dutch Airline almost to break even.

Born at Leeuwarden on February 28, 1904, Albarda studied at Leyden University and took his degree as Doctor of Law in 1932. He joined the General Treasury of the Ministry of Finance, and was rapidly promoted. In 1940 he resigned, as acting treasurer general, to become a partner in a private banking firm at the Hague.

During the final year of occupation of the Netherlands, in 1944, the Council of Resistance leaders asked him to take charge of the Ministry of Finance as temporary secretary general, after liberation; he agreed and gave up his partnership.

At the end of 1945, he resigned, and became a member of the management of Nederlandsche Handel Maatschappij, one of the biggest Dutch commercial banks with interests all over the world. He held this post for 10 years. With a former Cabinet Minister, Mr. Steenberghe, he founded an Institute for the promotion of Netherlands and American industrial cooperation. He was a member of the Hirschfield Committee which advised the Netherlands Government on spending Marshall Aid.

MEMBER OF BOARD

In 1946 Albarda became a member of the K.L.M. board of directors: he had been a member of the committee of delegates since its formation. In 1956 he was appointed vice-chairman. Then at a meeting of shareholders in June, 1963, he was proposed as president of the board of directors.

He said he realized the task would be "no sinecure"; he wanted the company to complete its reorganization as quickly as possible. There would be an aggressive sales policy combined with very economical conduct of business; every attention would have to be paid to the quality of the K.L.M. product, and in particular to regularity. Albarda believed that cooperation in air transport would sooner or later be seen to be the logical consequence of technical and political development, and he encouraged economically sound forms of cooperation in Europe and elsewhere. K.L.M. reopened negotiations with Air Union, and agreements were formed with airlines in Venezuela, Spain and the Philippines.

One of Albarda's brain children was A.L.M., K.L.M.'s Caribbean subsidiary which is now self-contained and has its own management.

He was a working president, and under his leadership a positive working atmosphere and healthy labour discipline soon developed and were combined with an appreciation of modern business methods.

Albarda was married twice; his second wife, Charlotte van Poelvoorde, died with him.

May 19, 1965.

Cardinal Anselmo Maria Albareda, O.S.B., for many years Prefect of the Vatican Library, died in Barcelona on July 20, 1966, at the age of 74.

His work in the Vatican Library, to which he was appointed by Pope Pius XI, himself a famous librarian, covered the years of the World War, when Dom Anselmo rescued and housed at the Vatican a number of famous libraries. They included books and manuscripts from the abbey of Monte Cassino, destroyed by the allies during the Italian campaign, the Dante library in Rome, and the library of Eastern documents from the Basilian monastery at Grottoferrata.

An air raid was taking place in the area of the seminary where the library of the Cardinal Duke of York was housed while Dom Anselmo was superintending its removal to the Vatican. As hostilities continued he worked on the manuscripts and books, the care of which he had assumed, providing a great deal of information on them to the libraries concerned, particularly at Monte Cassino, when the collections were returned in times of peace.

Apart from this enforced protective work on archives he was responsible for the development of the scientific schemes for the preservation of books and manuscripts at the Vatican before and after the war. He created laboratories for examination, care and microfilm reproduction of the Vatican treasures, many manuscripts from which are now available in photostats and microfilms in libraries throughout the world.

Born in Barcelona on February 16, 1892, he was sent to the Benedictine Abbey of Montserrat, originally as a choir student, and entered the Abbey novitiate at the end of his schooling. He was professed a monk in 1908 and was sent in 1913 to the international college at San Anselmo, Rome, to complete his theological studies.

Ordained to the priesthood in 1915 he spent some years at Montserrat during which he wrote theses on manuscripts he had studied in the abbey library. Later, he published new research theses from the abbey, including a definitive bibliography on the Rule of St. Benedict. Meanwhile he had returned to Rome for study, partly on biblical subjects.

In 1936 he was appointed Prefect of the Vatican Library by Pope Pius XI and began a term of office in which he was supported fully by the Pope and by Cardinal Pacelli, then Secretary of State, who succeeded in 1939 as Pope Pius XII. Dom Anselmo was created Cardinal Deacon of St. Appolinaire and a titular Archbishop in 1962 by Pope John XXIII.

July 21, 1966.

Richard Aldington, the writer, died at his home at Sury-en-Vaux in central France on July 27, 1962. He had just returned with his daughter from a visit to Moscow, where he had been warmly received. He was 70.

Poet, critic, novelist, biographer, translator, Richard Aldington was nevertheless not a real man of letters. He always conveyed the impression of having a driving force greater than writing itself. He was an angry young man of the generation before they became fashionable: he remained something of an angry old man to the end.

There were times when his anger betrayed him. Then he wrote beneath his true bent. Some of his books embarrassed even his friends. Yet the tendency that sought to write him off as a discomfited railer of no consequence was wrong.

MAN'S STUPIDITY

His anger was directed at the stupidity of mankind. His ideal of what human society might be had something fine about it. And while he will probably remain best known as the author of his 1914–18 War novel—*Death of a Hero*—which has now become something of a best seller in Soviet Russia—he wrote at least one poem, *A Dream in the Luxembourg,* which was perhaps more evocative of the 1920s than much more pretentious poetry. As a critic he had great potentialities and an appreciable performance.

Edward Godfree Aldington was born in Hampshire on July 8, 1892. He was educated at Dover College, and then spent some terms at London University, though he did not take a degree. He began to write poetry at an early age, his first volume appearing when he was 17. It was as the editor of the magazine called *Egoist* that he became known as an Imagist poet. In 1913 he married Miss Hilda Doolittle, the daughter of a professor of mathematics at an American university. She signed her own poems "H.D." and was by many judged to be a better poet than her husband. Together they translated from the Greek and Latin, and in 1915 brought out a volume entitled *Images, Old and New*.

Early in 1916 Aldington enlisted in the infantry, and after having seen some of the worst fighting in France and Flanders, returned to civilian life in a shell-shocked condition, and without visible prospects. In order to live as cheaply as possible and to recover his poise, he lived abroad, chiefly in France and Italy. His mainstay for a time was reviewing, and writing of special articles for *The Times Literary Supplement*. A volume of *Greek Songs in the Manner* of *Anacreon* was inferior work: a translation of Cyrano de Bergerac's *Voyages to the Moon and the Sun* had more to recommend it. But he revealed his quality best as a critic, particularly of the minor classics and of French literature. His collections of *Literary Studies and Reviews* and *French Studies* are still worth reading. In *A Fool i'the Forest* he attempted an elaborate metaphysical poem deriving in some degree from T. S. Eliot, to whose *Criterion* he was for some years a contributor.

A SHRILL ATTACK

By the end of 1927 he had apparently thrown off the worst effects of his war-shattered condition. He began *Death of a Hero,* but set it aside for a time in order to undertake a translation of Boccaccio. The novel was published in 1929, and therefore joined the spate, which was just beginning, of a whole stream of literature that attacked the futility and beastliness of war. But it can be said that Aldington's main target was the English middle class and the things they held dear. The attack was shrill.

There followed a book of sbort stories of the war, *Roads to Glory* (1930) which was not dissimilar in temper: *The Colonel's Daughter* (1931), a satire on the feudalism, as Aldington conceived it, of English village life, that showed some of the crudity and tastelessness which was to mar some of his later works. Much better were two novels, *All Men are Enemies* (1933), which had passages of great tenderness, and *Women Must Work* (1934).

Thereafter, it could be said that Aldington's creative writing ceased. He himself was rather taken aback when another writer suggested that his true vocation was to be a literary critic, and that he was in danger of missing his way. He rebutted this strongly, but none of his subsequent writings—outside his biographies—fulfilled the promise of his earlier work. Some books, such as *Pinorman* (1954) and *Lawrence of Arabia* (1955) are better forgotten.

But Aldington himself should not be forgotten. A restless soul, perpetually seeking for some point of rest which was unattainable, he settled for a time in the United States, then returned briefly to England, and finally became an exile in France. In his later years he gained recognition with the James Tait Black Memorial Prize of 1946 for his *Life of Wellington*. But a new generation had grown up who knew little about him. There remained, however, among the middle-aged, some who still remembered gratefully the heady but justified indignation of his earlier days; others who found his writings about D. H. Lawrence the best that Lawrence's circle of acquaintances had produced; others still who by chance had picked up *A Dream in the Luxembourg*, and valued it for its naivety and charm; others who owed their own excursions into French literature to his inspiration (including an excellent *Life of Voltaire*).

Aldington's marriage to Hilda Doolittle—who died in September 1961—was dissolved in 1937, after which he married Netta, the daughter of James McCulloch.

July 30, 1962.

Lord Alexander of Hillsborough, K.G., P.C., C.H., Leader of the Labour peers in the House of Lords until the general election of 1964, died on January 11, 1965, at the age of 79. He had held many ministerial offices and, when in the House of Commons, had been First Lord of the Admiralty during five anxious years of the last war. In all he was at the Admiralty longer than any other statesman of modern times. He was created a viscount in 1950, and had previously sat in the Commons as Labour member for the Hillsborough division of Sheffield since 1922, with the exception of the period 1931 to 1935.

It was as the first Minister of Defence after the higher direction of the armed forces was reorganized in 1946 that he passed through some of the roughest political waters of his career. He never enjoyed the full support of his military advisers. Although a hard and unobtrusive worker and a conscientious administrator, he was not at home in the world of grand strategy.

NO CLEAR ADVICE

His task was made no easier by the consistent lack of clear, coordinated advice from the Chiefs of Staff, who then had no permanent Chairman. Lord Montgomery of Alamein has related in his memoirs how as Chief of the Imperial General Staff he tried to enlist the support of the First Sea Lord and the Chief of the Air Staff in asking the Prime Minister to remove Alexander on the ground that they had no confidence in him—the only recorded case, according to Montgomery, of real unanimous agreement in the Chiefs of Staff Committee.

That he survived this abortive palace revolution and later recommended Montgomery, its principal architect, to be the first Chairman of the Western Union Commanders-in-Chief is a measure of Alexander's magnanimity as well as of his political durability. He was proud of his working class beginnings, once telling the House of Lords, after a debating battle with Lord Hailsham, that he was thankful that he "did not have to go to Oxford University to learn to be a bully". He came to political prominence quite suddenly after 20 obscure years as a local government official.

Albert Victor Alexander was born at Weston-super-Mare on May 1, 1885, son of Albert Alexander, an engineer's smith, and went to the Barton Hill elementary school in Bristol. He left at thirteen, and began work as a junior clerk in the offices of the Bristol Education Committee.

TWO GREAT INTERESTS

After five years with the Bristol Committee Alexander entered the service of the Somerset County Education Committee, with which he remained for seventeen years, rising to the post of chief clerk and for some time acting as secretary of the Somerset Branch of the National Association of Local Government Officers. He had outside his routine work two great interests: a Baptist lay preacher, winning some reputation in that capacity, and incidentally gaining valuable experience in public speaking; and he became a member of the management committee of the Co-operative Society in Weston-super-Mare, and later on vice-president of the Society.

When war broke out in 1914 Alexander joined the Artists' Rifles, rising to be corporal and later to a commission. He served throughout that war, and was demobilized with the rank of captain after being in 1919 education officer to the South-Western District. In 1920 he was appointed secretary to the Parliamentary Committee of the Co-operative Congress, which coordinates the various Co-operative organizations as the T.U.C. does the unions. It fell to him the next year to lead the strenuous opposition to the proposal to tax the undistributed dividends of the societies—a fight which he found it necessary to renew in 1933. Alexander was for many years a powerful force in this national movement, playing a great part in developing its machinery, and in 1932 being one of the prime movers in the creation of a new National Co-operative Authority.

It was as a Co-operator, too, that he first entered Parliament in 1922, as M.P. for the Hillsborough division of Sheffield, winning the seat with a big turnover. Until 1924 he acted as whip to the Co-operative Party. He increased his majority in December, 1923, and was appointed Parliamentary Secretary to the Board of Trade in the first short-lived Labour Government. After the defeat of the Conservative Government at the 1929 general election Alexander, to the surprise of some observers, was made First Lord of the Admiralty in the second Labour Government.

Almost before he had had time to acquaint himself with the duties of his office and the details of the great Service over the administration of which he was thus called to preside, he found himself immersed in the intricate negotiations of the London Naval Conference. He cannot escape a share of the responsibility for the Naval Treaty of 1930 that emerged from it, the restrictive effects of which were still left by the Navy when war broke out nine years later; and, indeed, it was after he became First Lord for the second time that the shortage of destroyers and other such ships was still one of the chief causes of the immensity of the shipping losses from U-boat attack. But Alexander would not have disclaimed any of that responsibility, for he was very proud of the success of the Socialist Government in negotiating a treaty at all, and he regarded it as a good one which, without detriment to British security, promised a substantial advance towards the goal of general international agreement. He fully realized that the security of the country and of the British Empire depended on the Fleet, and he would have strenuously opposed any unilateral disarmament by Great Britain.

At the 1931 election, Alexander lost his seat, but he returned to Parliament in 1935. As a moderate socialist he opposed the "Popular Front" agitation, but he was a strong critic of the policy of non-intervention in Spain. He maintained his deep interest in the Navy and its affairs, taking a prominent part in all debates on those subjects.

Though still in opposition when war broke out in 1939, he gave full support to Mr. Churchill's administration of the Admiralty, and was kept fully informed on naval matters. Hence, when appointed to be First Lord for the second time (in the Coalition Government in May, 1940), there was complete continuity of policy.

OVERSHADOWED

Inevitably, Alexander was overshadowed in the public eye through the retention of full control over war operations by the Minister of Defence. Churchill himself—of whom he, though the most loyal of subordinates, stood in no little awe. But his solid competence, and extensive grasp of the problems of naval administration, were of high value to the country and to the Navy itself throughout the war.

Replaced at the Admiralty by Brendan Bracken for the few weeks of the "caretaker" Government, he returned there on the formation of the third Labour Government, to grapple with the Navy's task of transition from a war to a peace footing.

In October, 1946, Attlee made sweeping changes in the Government. The heads of all three Service departments were changed, and Alexander was appointed Minister without Portfolio. At the same time proposals were put forward for a Central Organization for Defence. These included plans for the appointment of a Minister of Defence, with a Ministry, and were the result of an inquiry instituted by the Prime Minister soon after he took office in the summer of 1945. Alexander was to remain in the Cabinet, and his name was to be submitted for appointment as Minister of Defence when the legislation had been passed which was necessary to establish such a Ministry.

The Ministry of Defence Act quickly reached the statute book, and on December 20, 1946, the King's approval to the appointment of Alexander as Minister of Defence was announced. In many ways the choice of the new Minister was perhaps the best that could have been made at that time.

A DOUBLE SOMERSAULT

His policy, however, was sometimes vacillating. This was particularly so in regard to the length of national service. Indeed, he was strongly criticized for performing a double somersault on this issue. First, he announced the decision of the Labour Cabinet that 18 months' service was the indispensable minimum. But a revolt of his own back-benchers stampeded him into accepting 12 months, and he himself moved an amendment to this effect during the committee stage of the National Service Bill in May, 1947. For this he was severely taken to task by Churchill and the Conservative Opposition. A few months later (in 1948) Alexander was forced by events to introduce a Bill restoring the 18 months.

TASK IN LORDS

When, after the general election of 1950, the Labour Government was returned to office with the narrow majority of six over all other parties, it was felt essential that the Minister of Defence should be in the Commons. Shinwell was therefore appointed, and Alexander (who had been elevated to the peerage in the New Year Honours) accepted the post of Chancellor of the Duchy of Lancaster. He continued to represent the Government on defence in the Upper House, and when later the Labour party went into Opposition, he made many well-informed contributions to defence debates.

In November, 1955, Lord Jowitt retired as Leader of the Opposition in the Lords. Alexander, the Deputy Leader, accepted nomination, though he was then 70 and only two weeks younger than Jowitt. He was elected unanimously. He proved a hard-working, devoted, but somewhat pedestrian leader. Conscientious in attendance, assiduous in challenging the Government, weighty in manner, what he lacked was the light touch. Yet he retained the respect of all sections of the party.

He had been a Privy Councillor since 1929, and an Elder Brother of Trinity House since 1941. He was made a Companion of Honour in that year. In 1963 he was created an Earl.

He married, in 1908, Esther Ellen, youngest daughter of the late George Chapple, of Tiverton, Devon. They had one daughter. There is no heir.

January 12, 1965.

Field Marshal Lord Alexander of Tunis, K.G., P.C., G.C.B., O.M., G.C.M.G., C.S.I., D.S.O., M.C., died on June 16, 1969, at the age of 77.

He was one of the outstanding soldiers of the 1939–45 War, particularly distinguishing himself in command of forces of mixed nationality. His personality and gift for inspiring confidence contributed markedly to this result, and he gained the trust and unswerving support of subordinates of other races to the same extent as he always obtained from those of his own countrymen. At the end of the war, when still relatively young, and with the prospect of holding the highest military offices in time of peace, he said farewell to the Army—though remaining on the active list as a field marshal—became a successful and popular Governor-General of Canada, and was later Minister of Defence from 1952 to 1954.

"Always at the back of my mind when I make plans is the thought that I am playing with human lives", he told war correspondents. "Good chaps get killed or wounded and it is a terrible thing. The proudest thing I can say is that I am a front-line soldier. I fought with my battalion of guards and was wounded three times, so I know what it means and I do not throw away lives unless it is absolutely necessary."

Alexander had a reputation as a pugnacious fighter. His slogan was "Attack, attack, attack: even if you are on the defensive." "I have always aimed at the technique of the ring and the double-handed punch", he said.

The Rt. Hon, Sir Harold Rupert Leofric George Alexander, Earl Alexander of Tunis and Baron Rideau, of Ottawa, and of Castle Derg, in the county of Tyrone, Viscount Alexander of Tunis, of Errigal, in the county of Donegal in the Peerage of the United Kingdom, was born on December 10, 1891, the third son of the fourth Earl of Caledon and of Lady Elizabeth Graham Toler, daughter of the third Earl of Norbury. He was educated at Harrow and at Sandhurst, at both of which he distinguished himself at cricket and at running. A little later, as a subaltern, he won the Irish mile championship. He entered the Irish Guards in 1911 and was promoted lieutenant in 1912.

On the outbreak of war in 1914 he went out to France with his regiment. Virtually all his war service was with fighting troops. He was promoted captain in 1915 and major in August, 1917, at the age of 25 and at the latter date he was already acting lieutenant-colonel commanding his battalion. In the course of the war he was wounded thrice, was awarded the D.S.O. (1916) and M.C. (1915) and was mentioned five times in dispatches. He was also decorated with the French Legion of Honour and the Russian Order of St. Anne with swords. In 1919 he commanded the Baltic Landwehr, affiliated to the Latvian Army, in the operations in North Russia, exercising as strong an influence over these troops, for the most part Balts of German origin and previously commanded by German officers, as he had over his own Irish Guardsmen.

RARE SENIORITY

In 1921 Alexander commanded the detachment of the Irish Guards which lined the staircase of the Belfast City Hall at the opening of the first Northern Ireland Parliament by King George V. He was promoted lieutenant-colonel in 1922 and took over command of the 1st Battalion of his regiment. He spent 1926 and 1927 at the Staff College, his seniority in the Army making him a rare figure in its records, though there have been many students of his age. He was now looked upon as likely to make the outstanding fighting commander in the Army, and though his promotion became a little slower in peacetime, it was still rapid. From 1928 to 1930 he commanded the Regiment and Regimental District Irish Guards, and in the latter year attended the Imperial Defence College. In 1931 he was given a staff appointment—a rarity for him—that of G.S.O.2 at the War Office. Next year he became G.S.O.1, Northern Command.

In 1934, Alexander was appointed to command the Nowshera Brigade in the Indian Northern Command, with the temporary rank of brigadier. He took part in the Loe-Agra and the Mohmand operations of 1935, being mentioned in dispatches for each campaign and being made C.S.I. It was noted by the experts in frontier warfare, foremost among whom was another brigadier, temporarily Alexander's superior in command. C.J.E. Auchinleck, that though he was without experience in this difficult type of operation, he was extremely efficient.

While serving in India he was appointed A.D.C. to the King. He was promoted major-general in 1937, being one of the youngest to reach that rank in the period between the two wars, and in February, 1938, took over command of the 1st Division. With this formation he went to France in 1939 on the outbreak of war. He had been made a C.B. the previous year.

During the withdrawal from Dunkirk Alexander displayed those qualities of character and leadership to be expected of him. He assumed command of the remaining troops after General (later Field Marshal) Lord Gort had come home to report, and supervised the final embarkations.

On June 2, 1940, with the senior naval officer, Alexander made a final tour of the beaches and harbour and, being satisfied that no British troops remained ashore, they left for England. After Dunkirk he drew up a memorandum dealing with the changed conditions of warfare, which resulted in the adoption of battle drill for the army and the establishment of a G.H.Q. battle school.

Later in 1940 he was promoted lieutenant-general and appointed Commander-in-Chief, Southern Command, in succession to General Sir Claude Auchinleck. He held this appointment for over a year, during which his training methods made a great impression. Early in 1942, with disaster looming in Burma, he flew out to take command in that theatre. The campaign developed into an attempt to afford India time for preparation to meet the Japanese menace. As such it succeeded, though the hope of saving Burma was early extinguished. Alexander contrived to extricate his little army, after it had undergone heavy loss and sufferings. The British and Indian troops fought well, but his subsequent public comments showed that he considered his force to have been inadequately trained and equipped for warfare of that nature. He was promoted general on April 3.

From Burma he went straight to another theatre where affairs had gone ill, but this time with better prospects of improving them. On August 18, 1942, he was apointed Commander-in-Chief, Middle East, again in succession to Auchinleck, who had recently brought the advance of Rommel and his German-Italian army to a halt at Alamein, when Alexandria had appeared to lie at his mercy. Powerful British reinforcements were now arriving in Egypt, which gave promise of turning the tables on the enemy, but Alexander's lieutenant, General (now Field Marshal Lord) Montgomery, in command of the Eighth Army, had to withstand one more serious threat when Rommel attacked him on August 31, to be repulsed after sharp fighting.

The great victory of Alamein, beginning on October 23 and won after 12 days of the hardest fighting, was Montgomery's operation, though he owed much to Alexander's constant support then and during the long pursuit across North Africa. Meanwhile. British and American forces had entered Tunisia, where they were engaged in fluctuating fighting. In February, 1943 when the Eighth Army had advanced beyond the town of Tripoli, Alexander was appointed Deputy Commander-in-Chief to the American General Eisenhower. This involved the command of the 18th Army Group comprising the Eighth Army and all the land forces in Tunisia, and responsibility for the conduct of operations. By a series of finely conducted manoeuvres and assaults he brought the campaign to an end in mid-May with the complete destruction or capture of the forces of the Axis. Over 200,000 prisoners and all the enemy's material fell into the hands of the allies. It was as decisive a victory as any in the annals of history.

Alexander conducted the invasion of Sicily and then that of Italy on the same level, with the title of Deputy (to General Eisenhower) Commander-in-Chief Allied Forces, Combined Operations, Mediterranean, in the latter part of 1943 and that of Commander-in-Chief Allied Armies in Italy in 1944. He was subjected to criticism over the handling of the earlier assaults on the strong Cassino position, which were repulsed by the enemy. In May, 1944, however, he brought off an operation of exceptional brilliance, transporting the bulk of the Eighth Army across the Appennines in secrecy and throwing it, with the Fifth which was already on the western side, into an assault which completely shattered the front.

A swift pursuit led to the capture of Rome and a rapid advance beyond the capital. At one moment, indeed, it looked as though the Germans, streaming north in disorder, could never again pull themselves together, but, aided by the defensive advantages of the country, they finally contrived to do so. Alexander became Supreme Allied Commander Mediterranean on November 27, with responsibilities extending far beyond the Italian theatre, but he continued to give it his main attention. On the same date he was promoted field marshal, the appointment being antedated to June 4.

He had to face some disappointments in Italy.

KNOCK-OUT

With the invasion of North-west Europe the Italian theatre had been relegated to a secondary position and was constantly denuded of troops just when chances arose of dealing the enemy a knock-out blow. Yet in the last days of the war with Germany, with relatively narrow allied resources, the knock-out was delivered before it could be dealt in Germany. Alexander was the first commander to take the surrender of a great German army group on the continent.

He had already received the highest military honours, the field marshal's baton and the G.C.B., the latter as far back as 1942. The United States, the U.S.S.R., Greece, and Poland had bestowed on him the highest decorations they had to give. He received also honorary degrees from universities and the freedom of London. Belfast, and Londonderry. Late in 1945 it was announced that he had been appointed Governor-General of Canada. Early the following year he was created a viscount. As Governor-General designate he was made G.C.M.G. His appointment was received with enthusiasm in Canada, and he was installed at Ottawa on April 12, 1946.

No phase of his career, not even that of victory in Italy, was more triumphant. The Canadian people, critical by nature and not prepared to accept any newcomer solely on his reputation, took to this one from the first and liked him to the last. He naturally displayed a deep interest in military matters then fresh in everyone's memory and in the returned soldiers so many of whom had fought under his command. He travelled even more widely than had Lord Byng between the wars and not only in Canada but as far afield as Brazil.

His first year of office was marked by a fresh honour when he was appointed a Knight of the Garter on December 3. His term was twice extended, but was suddenly cut short at the beginning of 1952, so that the second extension did not take effect. He left behind a great reputation and Canadians remarked that outspoken utterances, which might not have gone down well from anyone else, had always been welcome from him. Before leaving, he was awarded an earldom on January 27 and was made a member of the Privy Council of Canada on January 29.

The termination of Alexander's appointment was due to the desire of Churchill that he should become Minister of Defence at the earliest possible moment. He did not start in smooth water in March. In the House of Commons his new appointment displeased the Opposition, but this little storm was nothing to the hurricane that burst out over a very slight indiscretion on the subject of the Korean War. It is fair to say that he never fathomed the natures or motives of politicians, but he none the less became a competent Minister of Defence. His conception of the function of the Ministry was, however, different from that at present in vogue. Under his direction it was not peremptory in its demands and relied on discreet guidance and persuasion rather than hard and fast programmes.

UMPIRE ONLY

On occasion it reduced its role to that of an umpire. Yet, whatever one's opinion may be of the present attitude of the Ministry, it will probably be admitted that Alexander was right not to move too fast on the path to dictation at that time. On October 18, 1954, after two and a half years, he handed over to Macmillan.

In October, 1962, a violent controversy followed the publication of Alexander's memoirs. In his account of the campaign in the western desert, he suggested that a sentence in the published official dispatches on the campaign, frequently quoted by historians analysing the battle of Alam el Halfa, had not been included in the original typescript as drafted by Alexander himself. This suggestion that the dispatch of a commander-in-chief had been tampered with before publication drew loud demands for an official explanation. Military historians, politicians, and the general public joined in the outcry, and the War Office eventually announced, with the agreement of Alexander, that he had changed the wording of the dispatch himself and had apparently forgotten the incident. Alexander's reputation for integrity was such that this explanation was immediately and universally accepted.

Handsome and with charming manners. Alexander was an attractive personality. At one time he was hampered by shyness, but this he overcame by force of will. All who came in contact with him, whatever their walk in life, were impressed by him. His place among British commanders will assuredly remain high and honourable.

CONSTABLE OF TOWER

Alexander was her Majesty's Lieutenant of the County of London from 1957 to 1965, and of Greater London from 1965 to 1966. From 1960 to 1967 he was Grand Master of the Order of St. Michael and St. George, and from 1960 to 1965 he was Constable of the Tower of London. Alexander was a trustee of the Thomson foundation set up in 1962. In 1968 he became Governor, Securicor Ltd.: he had been a Governor of Harrow School from 1952 to 1962, and was formerly president of M.C.C. and chairman of the Churchill Scholarship Memorial Fund. He held numerous medals, foreign orders, and honorary degrees.

In 1931 he married Lady Margaret Diana Bingham, younger daughter of the fifth Earl of Lucan, and had two sons, one daughter and one adopted daughter. The heir to the earldom is Lord Rideau, born June 30, 1935.

June 17, 1969.

Patriarch Alexii, of Moscow and All Russia, Head of the Russian Orthodox Church for the past 25 years, died in Moscow in April, 1970, at the age of 92.

His real name was Sergey Vladimirovich Simansky, and he was born in Moscow in 1877. He graduated from the law faculty of Moscow University in 1899, and in 1904 from the Moscow Ecclesiastical Academy.

In 1902 he had already become an Orthodox monk with the name of Alexii and was ordained priest in 1903. For the next 10 years he held positions in ecclesiastical seminaries and, from 1911, as Father Superior of the St. Anthony Monastery. In 1913 he was ordained Bishop of Tikhvin and Vicar of the Novgorod Eparchy.

After the Russian revolution, when the position of the church was coming under attack from the Bolsheviks, Alexii was named Bishop of Yamburg and Vicar of the See of Petrograd formerly St. Petersburg. In 1925 he became Archbishop of Novgorod, in 1927 a member of the Holy Synod, and in 1932 Metropolitan of Novgorod.

IN SIEGE

In the following year he was named Metropolitan of Leningrad. He stayed in the city throughout the Second World War siege and for his courage was awarded a medal "for the defence of Leningrad". In 1944, he became temporary incumbent of the Patriarchal throne on the death of the Patriarch Sergius. Sergius had been elected in 1943 following Stalin's restoration of the Patriarchate, which had been vacant since the death of Tikhon in 1925.

Alexii continued the conciliatory attitude of Sergius towards the Communist regime, thus incurring the criticism of many Orthodox outside the Soviet Union, and under his Patriarchate the church was virtually without political influence in Russia, although allowed to function in a limited way and still claiming millions of adherents, particularly among the older generation.

By accepting that his position entailed complete and articulate loyalty to the regime, the Patriarch became involved in various activities aimed at destroying the authority of the Russian Orthodox Churches abroad which for political reasons would not submit to Moscow. He was a member of the Soviet Committee for the Defence of Peace, an instrument of official Soviet propaganda.

SUPPORT FOR INSURGENTS

He is held responsible for the dissolution of the Uniate church in Galicia and attempted to enlist the support of the Greek Orthodox Church for communist insurgents in Greece, as well as returning a Yugoslav decoration, presented to him by Marshal Tito, after the split between Belgrade (which he had visited) and Moscow. In the nineteen fifties he came out against American involvement in Korea and rearmament of west Germany, and supported Soviet government policy on nuclear disarmament.

CHURCHES IN COMPETITION

In 1961, Alexii announced that the Russian Church was willing to enter the World Council of Churches, although he had resisted the suggestion until then. The conflict with Orthodox churches abroad has been particularly sharp in America, where two rival centres of authority, one appointed by the Moscow Patriarchate, have competed for influence. In 1969, the Moscow Patriarchate made proposals for a reconciliation, but these in turn led to conflict with the Greek Orthodox Church, whose Patriarch Athenagoras wrote to Patriarch Alexii warning him of "disastrous consequences" if the conflict continued.

Alexii had met Athenagoras in 1960 when he journeyed to Jerusalem, Turkey and Greece for five weeks to visit the Orthodox patriarchates in the non-communist countries.

VISIT TO BRITAIN

In 1964, Alexii paid a five-day visit to Britain as guest of Dr. Michael Ramsey, the Archbishop of Canterbury. During his stay Alexii was presented with the Lambeth Cross, awarded to foreign church dignitaries preeminent in working for Christian unity. Last July, Alexii opened a four-day conference in Moscow of high clergymen of the world's religions. The conference, held at Alexii's initiative, was only the second of its type to be hosted by Russia in the thousand-year history of the Russian Orthodox Church. The first was in 1952.

Alexii held several Soviet orders of the Red Banner of Labour and two Second World War decorations.

April 20, 1970.

Muhammad Ali, of Bogra, Foreign Minister and former Prime Minister of Pakistan, died at Dacca on January 23, 1963.

He was comparatively little known when in April, 1953, he was dramatically called from the Embassy at Washington to replace the dismissed second Prime Minister of the new State, Khwaja Nazimuddin, who had held office some 18 months after the assassination in November, 1951, of the gifted and clear-sighted Liaquat Ali Khan.

Though without any special political following, or, indeed, with much administrative experience, his charm and zest made him one of Pakistan's most popular Prime Ministers during a period when politicians generally were under a cloud. In two years of office until his resignation in August, 1955 he tried his best to give shape and stability to the political structure of Pakistan by forwarding the work of the constituent assembly. Unfortunately the general elections over which he hoped to preside were defeated by the intrigues of the politicians and a state of emergency was declared by the Governor-General, Mr. Ghulam Mohamed in October, 1954.

After his resignation of the Premiership Muhammad Ali returned to Washington for a second term as Ambassador, remaining there until his appointment as Ambassador to Japan in 1959.

In the cabinet Muhammad Ali formed in 1953 General Ayub Khan had accepted the defence portfolio and arising from this association Muhammad Ali was brought back into political life in June, 1962, when martial law was ended and President Ayub formed a new government. He became Foreign Minister and proved a popular one, having some of the necessary flexibility to respond to the change of public opinion in Pakistan in recent months. Nevertheless, whereas during his period as Prime Minister he had used his influence in Washington to establish closer relations and get more aid, besides joining the South East Asia collective defence treaty in 1954, he had lately been taking Pakistan in the other direction in closer relations with China and a somewhat cool attitude towards the western military alliances to which the country was committed. This had caused some heartburnings in the United States where he had served for so many years as Pakistan's Ambassador and where he had certainly shown an affection for things American which sometimes made him criticized in his own country.

KEPT HIS INDEPENDENCE

Nevertheless, as Foreign Minister, he might well have made a better mark than he did as Prime Minister, a position for which he had insufficient weight and political experience, whereas his skill and charm as a diplomatist had already been proved.

Muhammad Ali was also an asset to the new government as a Bengali who had in the past stood up for the rights of East Pakistan and might now channel the political discontent which was again welling up there. However, East Pakistan opinion in the elected National Assembly demanded that no one should accept office from East Pakistan until President Ayub agreed to certain basic demands. Although a member of the assembly himself, and, before his appointment, somewhat critical of military rule. Muhammad Ali refused to be bound in this way and maintained his own independence.

LOCAL GOVERNMENT

Muhammad Ali was born at Bogra, East Bengal, in 1909 and when 21 graduated at Calcutta University. He entered public life by way of local self government. He was elected to the Bogra municipality and became its chairman. Later he filled the like office on the Bogra District Board, the Indian equivalent of an English county council. In that capacity he founded a college and became president of its governing body. He was associated with the Muslim League, and in 1937 was elected to the Bengal Legislative Assembly. In 1943 he was chosen to be private parliamentary secretary to the Prime Minister, Khwaja Nazimuddin, whom he was to replace 10 years later in a much higher position. In 1946 he was made Finance and Health Minister, and on occasions he acted as Prime Minister.

When partition came in August, 1947, Muhammad Ali was elected to the Pakistan Constituent Assembly. A few months later, on Burma gaining her independence, he was sent to Rangoon as Ambassador. In 1949 he went to Ottawa as High Commissioner in Canada. In February, 1952, he became Ambassador in Washington in succession to his old friend and mentor. Mr. M.A.H. Ispahani, who was moved to the High Commissionership in London. In Burma, Canada, and the United States, Muhammad Ali made many friends by his personal charm, his forthrightness, his keen sense of humour, and a maturity of wisdom beyond his years. Moreover, he had a happy knack of seeing the bright side of things.

A NEW START

When summoned from Washington to form a new government in April, 1953, Muhammad Ali did his best to make a new start in Pakistan. From the first he was against religious obscurantism and refused to have the country shackled by a strict Muslim orthodoxy, an attitude which made enemies among some nationalist extremists.

His vigour and foresight was also shown by seizing the opportunity for a fresh and non-recriminatory approach to the sharp controversies which had embittered relations between India and Pakistan for nearly six years. He stated that the chief task before him was the elimination of these disputes, for they carried with them the germs of war. He promptly communicated with Mr. Nehru and it was agreed that they should have preliminary talks for a settlement while in London for the Coronation and the Conference of Prime Ministers. Within five weeks of taking office the new Prime Minister was a guest of this country at Claridge's, where he and Mr. Nehru had informal talks over the breakfast table. These were later followed by more detailed discussions in Delhi and Karachi with the assistance of advisers.

January 24, 1963.

Sydney Allard, who died on April 12, 1966, at his home, Black Hills, Esher, Surrey, was chairman and managing director of the Allard Motor Co., Ltd. and designer of the sports car which bore his name. He was 55. Sydney Herbert Allard was born in London in June, 1910, educated at St. Saviour's College, Ardingly, and on leaving school became a director of the family-owned Adlards Motors Ltd., Putney. The accelerated progress of Allard from a keen motor-cycling enthusiast to the constructor of a prestige-winning sports car, was based on the principle of taking one step at a time. It began with a family passion for powered transport and Allard became a staunch member of the Streatham Motor Cycle Club together with his brothers Leslie and Dennis and his sister Mary.

Although Allard was still working for Adlards (which was owned by his father) at this time, he was fascinated by the thrill of speed and decided to obtain something more powerful than his motor-cycles. He bought a Super Sports Morgan and with this car made his competition debut at Brooklands, winning a three-lap novice handicap at his first attempt. After various unsuccessful experiments with a Talbot Special, he purchased an ex-Tourist Trophy Ford and with this set up the fastest time of the day for an unsupercharged sports car in the 1935 Brighton speed trials.

Allard's next step forward was to create his first Allard special, which was a Bugatti-tailed two-seater. It won its first event at Taunton and continued to do well in other trials and encouraged by its acceptance Allard began to build replicas for sale.

During the Second World War, Allard staffed, equipped and ran an Army auxiliary workshop at Fulham under the Ministry of Supply, with Mrs. Allard looking after the canteen and the social life of 250 employees. At the end of hostilities, he completed a body and chassis for his own new car and in 1945 formed the Allard Motor Co. Ltd., with himself as chairman—a position he also held with Encon Motors Ltd., Hilton Bros. (Coachworks) Ltd., and Adlards Motors Ltd.

YOUNG DRIVERS

The first appearance of the Allard sports car was at the Bristol Club speed trials, and thanks to the enthusiasm and dedication of its designer, who seriously believed that "racing improved the breed", each subsequent model was a refined and improved car. The Allard car, which was fitted with a variety of large and powerful engines, met with considerable success in races, rallies, hill climbs and sprints not only in Europe, but also in the United States. Many young racing drivers made their debuts on Allard sports cars, which had a reputation for their excellent construction and ruggedness. One of the most meritorious performances of the marque was in 1950, when Allard and his American co-driver Tom Cole took third place in the Le Mans 24-hours race.

In the post-war years the name of Sydney Allard was always prominent in international motoring events and wherever he went the burly, bespectacled veteran could be relied upon to produce sterling performances. In 1949 he won the British hill climb championship and in 1952 was the outright winner of the Monte Carlo Rally, a feat which earned him world-wide acclaim.

A brilliant engineer who was utterly immersed in high-performance vehicles, he was one of the very first Englishmen to realize the potential of the American sport of drag-racing. This exciting spectacle attracts millions of fans each year to the hundreds of "drag-strips" up and down the continent, where the faster cars achieve the speed of 200 miles per hour from a standing start in the space of 440 yards. In 1963, Allard visited America to learn first hand and on his return announced that he had invited the top 10 American dragsters and their drivers to a British Drag Racing Festival to be held in September/October, 1964, on certain British airfields. The festival was highly successful and during one of the meetings a car was timed at 198 m.p.h.

Although the British contenders in the festival were outmatched by the American visitors, one of the best performances was set by the Allard DragStar Dragon. Driven by his son Alan, this first British-designed dragster achieved nearly 150 m.p.h. and was the prototype of a new range of Allard cars. As the result of Allard's foresight, the British Drag Racing Association was formed with himself as president.

April 13, 1966.

Sir Carleton Allen, M.C., Q.C., noted jurist and a former warden of Rhodes House, Oxford, 1931–52, died in Oxford on December 11, 1966. He was 79.

Carleton Kemp Allen was born in Sydney, New South Wales, on September 7, 1887, the youngest son of the Rev. William Allen, Congregational minister. He received his early education at Newington College and, after graduating from the University of Sydney, went on with a leaving scholarship to New College, Oxford, in 1910, where he was the contemporary of a group of exceptionally able lawyers. His main interest outside the law lay in music and in acting; he was prominent in the O.U.D.S., with which he long retained a connexion and through which he met his first wife. He took a first in Jurisprudence in 1912, was Eldon Law Scholar in 1913, and when war came, besides being engaged in freelance journalism and coaching, he was acting as secretary to Professor Paul Vinogradoff.

He returned to journalism and coaching having been called to the Bar by Lincoln's Inn in 1919. In 1920 he was elected Stowell Fellow of University College, Oxford, where he was law tutor for the next nine years. He published a light novel, *The Judgement of Paris,* in 1924 and was for many years a regular weekly reviewer of other people's novels; he was Junior Proctor in 1925; and in 1926 Tagore Professor at Calcutta. The substance of his Tagore lectures appeared in the following year in his first serious book, *Law in the Making*, which was soon recognized as indispensable to the law student (seventh edition, 1964) and resulted in his being appointed in 1929 Professor of Jurisprudence in succession to Walter Ashburner and Sir Paul Vinogradoff. He published two other considerable books in 1931, *Bureaucracy Triumphant* and *Legal Duties* (largely collected articles), but in the same year he resigned his chair to become Oxford Secretary to the Rhodes Trustees and Warden of Rhodes House in succession to Sir Francis Wylie, who had held the appointment since 1903.

In the short tenure of his professorship Allen could not give the full measure of his capacity as a teacher and legal thinker, but he made it impossible to doubt that his retirement was a severe loss to legal science. He was a first-rate teacher, especially an admirable lecturer, his exposition combining that lightness of touch and seriousness of thought which are notable in his writings. As a legal theorist he owed much to Vinogradoff, not indeed on the technical side, for which he had an inborn gift, but in the broad sociological background which enabled him to do justice to his own native humanity. He might have gone far as a legal thinker, but his acceptance of the offer of the Rhodes Trustees in 1931 was no renunciation of a pronounced vocation. In spite of immediate and marked success, he was never wholly happy as an academic teacher, and it was only under friendly pressure that he accepted a chair which most law teachers would have regarded as a great prize. The office of warden of Rhodes House was far more congenial. He was able to maintain his scholarly interests, to contribute valuable articles to legal periodicals, and to continue to serve on the board of the Faculty of Law as a coopted member; and he remained a professorial fellow of his college.

At the same time he now found scope for his practical gifts as an administrator and director.

GUIDING SCHOLARS

His own experience of the difficulties of a young arrival at Oxford from overseas qualified him to an unusual degree to guide the Rhodes Scholars. They could have no better mentor, since he combined the keenest sympathy in their hopes and disappointments with a very shrewd commonsense which kept his sympathy free from sentimentality. Especially, he gave them an imaginative fairmindedness with an exceptional gift for standing objectively outside his own firm prejudices. His own account of his twenty-one years' stewardship is to found in his contribution—a characteristic piece of writing—to the volume published by the Rhodes Trustees in 1955, *The First Fifty Years of the Rhodes Scholarships*, edited by his colleague Lord Elton with whom, as with Lord Lothian when he was secretary of the Trust, Allen achieved a most effective working relationship.

A more artless account of the Allens' reign at Rhodes House is to be found in *Sunlight and Shadow* (1960), which his first wife wrote for her grandchildren just before her death in 1959 and which Sir Carleton (as he became in 1952) subsequently edited for publication. It reveals a singularly happy marriage—Allen married Dorothy Frances, the youngest daughter of Edward Halford of Oxford in 1922—and does not conceal that it was she who brought the open hearted buoyancy and he the quietly shrewd sympathy to what was essentially a task undertaken in unison; in which, because he had heart trouble, she would more often take the affectionate initiative. The warmth of the heartfelt response to the Allens' devotion was revealed at the Rhodes Centenary celebrations in Oxford in 1953 when they were presented by the Rhodes Scholars of all generations with a motor-car and a portrait, by Mr. Edward Halliday, of Lady Allen. The Rhodes Trustees had caused Allen himself to be painted for Rhodes House by Mr. James Gunn. Allen was knighted on his retirement and his first wife, who had already been awarded the British Empire Medal for her war-work, was made, to Allen's evident delight, an honorary M.A. of the University of Oxford.

The Allens had seen three distinct phases of the short history of Rhodes House: the spacious and well-staffed hospitality of the pre-war epoch; the exhilarating improvisations of wartime Oxford; and the return of the veterans—and their wives—while rationing still continued. To each period the Allens brought a note of enjoyment and, particularly for her part, a gift for greeting the unexpected combined with a shared sense at once of continuity and of quiet adventure. As the Wylies had done in their time, "C.K." and Dorothy Allen made Rhodes House a most welcoming home.

In addition to his full life at Rhodes House Allen continued to contribute to legal scholarship and wit, to serve on the local Bench (of which he was chairman until 1956) and, in the Second World War, upon the Appellate Tribunal for Conscientious Objectors; and to be an informed member of the Surrey County Cricket Club and a shrewd judge of Oxford cricket. He was elected F.B.A. in 1944 and F.R.S.I. in 1951. He took silk in 1945 and the honorary degree of LL.D. was conferred upon him by the University of Glasgow in 1951 (he had proceeded to his Oxford D.C.L. in 1932). He was elected an Emeritus Fellow of his College in 1952, an Honorary Fellow in 1963. He was already an Honarary Bencher of his Inn.

R.S.A. PRIZE

His *Law in the Making* was awarded the Swiney Prize of the Royal Society of Arts in 1944, his *Law and Orders* appeared in 1945 (second edition, 1956) and in 1953 he delivered the Hamlyn Lectures, published in the same year as *The Queen's Peace*. *Laws and Disorders* was published in 1954. *Administrative Jurisdiction* in 1956, *Aspects of Justice* in 1958.

Allen was essentially a believer in the individual, with the deep distrust of the good lawyer—and the good Australian—for the increasing power of the State. If in later years he came to modify his extreme distaste for some of the aspects of delegated legislation to which he was uneasily reconciled, he maintained his eagle-eyed readiness to expose, often in the correspondence columns of *The Times*, both the absurdities and the tendency to overbear to which he felt public servants were *ex officio* too liable. *Democracy and the Individual* (1943) is a good example of the flavour of his view and manner. His club was the Reform.

Allen was of short, stocky, build but impressive appearance. His strong eyes, striking nose, clipped moustache and magnificent crop of lint-white hair (he greyed early) reminded one that he had been a soldier. That he remained an Australian might be remarked at once by the way he wore his hat. If he came to absorb some (more, maybe, than he was aware) of the prejudices of the English with whom he spent most of his life, since he never returned to Australia, he retained his quizzical right to poke his own sort of fun at them.

To the delight of their many friends he married again in 1962. His new wife, Miss Hilda Mary Grose, had been Dorothy Allen's greatest friend. The second marriage was also exceptionally contented and 114 Banbury Road, Oxford, warm in its welcome to every generation.

December 12, 1966.

Margery Allingham, who died on June 30, 1966, at Colchester, Essex, at the age of 61 made her name in the great era of classical detective fiction. She ranked with Dorothy Sayers and Agatha Christie, but, unlike most of her contemporaries, she was able to adapt her style with notable success to the more sophisticated suspense genre which became fashionable after the war.

She was born in 1904. Her father, Herbert John Allingham, wrote boys' fiction and he encouraged her to start writing stories when she was only seven: a year later she edited her own magazine, *The Wagtail*. After attending the Perse High School for Girls at Cambridge she went on to the Polytechnic School of Speech Training, where she wrote a verse play about Dido and Aeneas. Her first novel, a pirate story called *Blackkerchief Dick* (1921), was published when she was 17. She liked to speak of herself as "one of the last of the real trained professional writers".

In 1927 she married Philip Youngman Carter, who became a well-known journalist and illustrator, and for 10 years they collaborated on pulp fiction. *The Crime at Black Dudley* (1928) introduced her detective, Mr. Campion, though only in a minor role: but she followed it with her first considerable success, *Mystery Mile* (1929), *Look to the Lady* (1930), and *Sweet Danger* (1933). These early Campion stories were picaresque adventures, and she felt obliged to add an apologetic preface when she promoted him to more serious detection in *Death of a Ghost* (1934). Although presented as a deliberately mild and inconspicuous figure Mr. Campion was, typically for an amateur investigator of that period, the younger son of a family of very superior social status; but he had friends at Scotland Yard. Miss Allingham's skill and Mr. Campion's character developed together. *Flowers for the Judge* (1936), *Dancers in Mourning* (1937), and *The Fashion in Shrouds* (1938) are most distinguished detective stories.

In 1940 Miss Allingham's American publishers asked her for a book about daily life in wartime England. She wrote *The Oaken Heart* (1941), a lightly disguised description of the Essex village where she lived: it was one of her own favourite books. The public, however, wanted Mr. Campion, and she brought him back in *Coroner's Pidgin* (1945) and *More Work for the Undertaker* (1949); her characterization and plotting were stronger and simpler now. This new power was shown to the full in *The Tiger in the Smoke* (1952), which is probably her best book; it is neither a detective story nor a light thriller, though Mr. Campion and his Scotland Yard colleagues appear in it, but a magnificently atmospheric tale of a murderer at once hunted and hunting through the foggy backwaters of London. In this novel, which was rather ineptly filmed, and in its successor, *Hide My Eyes* (1958), Miss Allingham stepped away from the world of Dorothy Sayers into that of the *New Arabian Nights*. If the force of her narrative can justly be compared with Stevenson's, she also shared his feeling for London as a place of dark magic and mysterious doors. *The China Governess* appeared in 1963. *The Mind Readers* in 1965.

She divided her life, like the settings of her books, between the two places she loved best: London, where she kept a flat in Bloomsbury, and Essex, where she and her husband had an old house in the village of Tolleshunt D'Arcy, barely three miles from her childhood home.

July 1, 1966.

Dr. Ernest Huie Riddall Altounyan, O.B.E., M.C., died on March 13, 1962 at Coniston, a far cry from Aleppo, in Syria, which was the home town of his family. He was 72. Altounyan was educated at Rugby, went up to Emmanuel College, Cambridge, where he was an exhibitioner, and from there to the Middlesex Hospital. He spent the greater part of his medical career practising in the hospital at Aleppo which was built up by his father, Dr. A.A. Altounyan, who was also famous in Syria as a medical practitioner.

During the First World War he served in the Royal Army Medical Corps, was wounded and was awarded the Military Cross in France for gallantry in action. He returned to Syria soon after the end of the war and apart from his medical work he played a considerable role, behind the scenes, in the political life of that country. He was liked by many of the Syrian politicians, some of whom had known him from boyhood and were therefore ready to speak more freely to him than they would have done to an official representative of Great Britain. He was a close friend of T.E. Lawrence, whom he had come to know before the First World War when Lawrence was doing archaeological work on the ruins of Carcemish on the Euphrates and used to come in to Aleppo for medical attention. After Lawrence's death Altounyan wrote the poem *Ornament of Honour*, "as a memorial embodying what I believe to be our common philosophy of life".

During the Second World War Altounyan rejoined the Royal Army Medical Corps, in which he was promoted to the rank of lieutenant-colonel. His services as an expert adviser on Middle Eastern affairs and his knowledge of languages were, however, of greater value to the allied cause than his medical skill. Nevertheless, his official role of medical officer served as a useful cover for other activities for which publicity was not desired. In 1941 he was attached to the Arab Legion and he accompanied a detachment of that force which marched into Syria under the command of General Sir John Glubb with the British and Free French forces.

There again he took an active part in the various political manoeuvres which resulted in the emergence of Syria as an independent sovereign state. The first President of Syria, Shukri Kuwatly, always treated Altounyan as a friend and sought his political advice frequently during the difficult early days of independence.

ADVICE AFTER SUEZ

When Syria broke off diplomatic relations with Great Britain in connexion with the Suez Canal affair, Altounyan's position as a man who had acted as an agent of her Majesty's Government became difficult and he thought it advisable to withdraw from Syria. His hope at that time was that this withdrawal would be temporary but, when Syria united with Egypt to form the United Arab Republic under the rule of President Nasser, it became impossible for him to return to Aleppo.

Altounyan was the son of an Armenian father and a Scots mother and he seemed to combine the best qualities of both races in his person. He had a shrewd, penetrating mind that combined with physical courage and tenacity.

He married Dora, sister of R.G. Collingwood, the Oxford philosopher. The five children of the marriage served as models for the sailing family well-known to all readers of the books of Arthur Ransome.

March 17, 1962.

Field Marshal Mohammed Abdel Hakim Amer, who committed suicide on September 14, 1967, was President Nasser's number two and close confidant for 15 years. He was 47.

Until he lost his position after the Arab-Israel war in June, his relationship with the President was a complementary one—Nasser the policy maker and Amer the executive.

Amer was placed under house arrest early in September after Egyptian authorities reported unmasking a plot by dismissed military leaders to regain power by force.

His whole career revolved round the army and ran a fairly close parallel to that of Nasser, with whom he has fought, plotted, and governed since they first met in the army.

Amer was promoted to the highest rank in the army—that of marshal—at the early age of 38.

Born on December 11, 1919, in Istal in the Minya province of Egypt, Amer went to the Military Academy in Cairo, where Nasser also trained.

In 1939 he was commissioned as a second lieutenant and graduated from the Staff Officers' College in 1948 to serve in the Palestine war that year. Both Nasser and Amer became key members of the Free Officers' Movement which seized power in 1952 and replaced King Farouk with General Neguib.

Amer became the Director of General Neguib's office at the presidency and was promoted to major general in 1953, a year which also saw his participation in the evacuation of British troops from the Canal Zone.

From 1953 to 1958 he was commander-in-chief of Egypt's armed forces and from 1958 to 1962 of the United Arab Republic Forces, during the political union between Syria and Egypt.

During this period he also became nominal head of the joint staff of Egyptian, Saudi Arabian, Jordanian, and Syrian Forces—but this was only a gesture on the part of Egypt's neighbours to demonstrate solidarity after the Suez crisis.

Syria became an important responsibility for Amer, who served as its governor in 1959 until the U.A.R. broke up in 1961.

He continued as second vice-president and Minister of War until it was suddenly announced in 1964 that he was to hold the new post of first vice-president. This carried with it power to rule for 60 days in case anything happened to the president.

Amer's other big task was to deal with the Yemen where Egypt has backed the Republicans against the Saudi Arabian-backed Royalists. As a representative of his Government, Amer travelled widely—particularly to the Soviet Union, which gives aid and arms to the U.A.R.

September 16, 1967.

General Wladyslaw Anders, commander of the Polish II Corps in the 1939–45 War, died in London on May 12, 1970, at the age of 77.

His name will always stand for one of the most heroic episodes of the last war, out of which grew the Polish Army of the Middle East, more popularly "the Anders Army". It was assembled from the wide-scattered remnants of ragged and starving Polish prisoners and deportees in the U.S.S.R. whom he brought out of that country in 1941 into Persia, thence through the Middle East to Italy. His life, wherein four times he has fought the Germans, twice the Russians, epitomises the Polish tragedy. Officially vilified in Poland he made his home in London.

Born in 1892, he studied at the University of Riga (then part of Tsarist Russia), later attending a Russian Military staff college. From 1914 to 1917 he served as Chief Staff Officer of a division of the Russian Imperial Army when he joined the First Polish Corps. In the Russo-Polish war of 1919–20 he commanded the 15th Polish Lancers, When Hitler invaded Poland in September, 1939, he was in command of the Independent Cavalry Brigade, within a matter of days finding himself fighting not only Germans, but, as the Red Army invaded from the east, Russians also. Wounded, captured by the Red Army, he was kept for some time in indescribable conditions and under constant interrogation in a prison in Lvov. Later he was transferred to the Lubianka prison in Moscow.

On the signing of the Polish-Soviet agreement in July, 1941, the Soviet Union then being at war with Germany, Anders was released. His task was to command and organize an army from among the Poles, soldiers and civilians, who under the Soviet occupation of eastern Poland had been deported in their tens of thousands to Soviet prisons and forced labour camps. Overshadowed by the tremendous events of those times, the story of this Polish "Dunkirk" has not been told too often; how in spite of their wretched physical condition—the death rate was very high—and vast distances to travel, the hazards of war, and Stalinist diplomacy, Anders somehow brought his people out, in all over 100,000. In Persia an army of 75,000 was organized.

It continued its long and arduous journey through the Middle East and in 1944–45 was fighting alongside the British 8th Army in Italy. Anders's name will always be associated with the bitter struggle for Monte Cassino.

WEEK'S ATTACK

After a heavy bombardment the attack on the monastery was launched on May 11, 1944. A week later Anders's men stormed the last battlement and hoisted the Union Jack and Polish flag side on the summit. After this notable feat of arms the Polish forces took a major part in liberating the Adriatic coast and completed their campaign with the capture of Bologna.

Not least of Anders's achievements was to maintain his soldiers' morale and keep them fighting during the bitter political setbacks to their homeland. particularly when the terms of the Yalta agreement were announced by which Russia was to annex eastern Poland. In a preface to General Anders's book *An Army in Exile*. Harold Macmillan, who had much to do with him at that time, wrote of his courage and forbearance in face of what he saw as a betrayal by allies and friends. A foreword to the book was written by Field-Marshal Lord Alexander.

Anders published two other books, one in Polish, *The Katyn Crime*, which deals with the massacre of some 10,000 Polish officers near Smolensk in 1940, and the other, *Hitler's Defeat in Russia*.

POLES' WELFARE

After the end of the war Anders settled in London to head the Polish side of the Central Coordinating Committee for Polish welfare looking after the interests of over 100,000 Polish ex-Servicemen in Britain; these included those who had served under him in Italy. In 1946 he was deprived of his nationality by the Polish Government "for activities detrimental to the state". In 1951 he won a £5,000 libel action against the Daily Worker claiming that an article published in it implied that he was a traitor and renegade. He was awarded £7,000 damages in 1960 when he sued a Polish-language newspaper, Naradowiec, which alleged that he had "believed in Hitler's victory".

Among his awards and decorations were an honorary C.B., Virtûti Militari (Polish) 3rd, 4th and 5th class: Cross for Valour; Legion of Merit 2nd class (U.S.A.): Croix de Guerre with Palms.

He was twice married.

May 13,1970.

Emily Anderson, who died on October 26, 1962, was one of those rare scholars who was completely at home in the world of action. She was 71.

Born on March 17, 1891 into the world of scholarship—her father, Alexander Anderson, was President of University College, Galway—Miss Anderson studied at the universities of Berlin and Marburg. After some years teaching, first at Queen's College. Barbados, and then at University College, Galway, she entered the Foreign Office in which she remained—apart from three years' war service from 1940 to 1943 during which she was seconded to the War Office and engaged in Intelligence work in the Middle East which led to her being given an O.B.E.—until her retirement in 1951.

Languages, however, were her pleasure as well as her profession and together with music and travel (her other pleasures) lay behind the patient achievements of scholarship which brought her a celebrity in the world of music which she managed entirely to disregard. Her first publication, in 1923, was a translation of Benedetto Croce's study of Goethe; this was followed in 1938 by the three volumes of *The Letters of Mozart and His Family*.

This work is a model for all similar collections; its translator disdains archaisms and any attempt to make either the composer or his period picturesque, but renders his eighteenth-century German into direct, impeccable English which, by its simple unfussiness, is virtually timeless. In addition to that, the world of the composer and his family, their friends, colleagues and hangers-on together with the events and personalities on which they comment are elucidated for the reader by precise, unassuming editorial annotation. The volume of work involved in either translation or in presentation is such that its combination from the hands of a single scholar occupied at the same time with a busy professional career is amazing.

Ten years' activity in retirement from official life bore fruit in *The Letters of Beethoven*, published a little over a year ago and superseding all earlier collections, German as well as English, of the composer's correspondence. Although the three Beethoven volumes may have less appeal to the general reader than those which depict the wider world of the Mozart family the qualities of precision in translation and patient editorial exactitude are present on every page. Just as nothing available in the composer's handwriting was too insignificant to escape her net, none of his puns, orthographical eccentricities or casual references seemed too elusive for her attention, and new problems revealed by the letters received the scrupulous consideration that she brought to all her work.

Whatever celebrity attached to her achievements. Emily Anderson refused to acknowledge its existence. It might well prove difficult to disentangle a genuine modesty from an equally genuine disdain in her rejection of anything that seemed likely to divert attention from her work to her personality. Brusque and by no means unformidable if she felt that an unwelcome publicity was pursuing her, impatient of merely personal considerations, she relaxed into warmth and cheerfully alert wisdom when she felt secure upon her own ground. It was as though she refused to live on the trivial level at which music and scholarship could be put aside to make room for gossip and chatter to pass the time of day.

October 29, 1962.

Princess Andrew of Greece—See under **Greece.**

Sir Norman Angell, a Nobel Peace Prize winner, author of *The Great Illusion* a book that was perhaps more widely discussed than any other of its analytical and prophetic kind during the fateful years before 1914—and afterwards—died on October 7, 1967, at Croydon. He was 94.

Norman Angell was a political commentator of acute and searching mind, who in *The Great Illusion* confronted the issue of war under modern conditions with great earnestness and with penetrating clarity also. Its essential argument—and it was the essence that mattered more than the admixture of dubious illustration—was that war could no longer pay; whatever the case might have been in the past, he maintained, in the contemporary world the consequences of war must be only a degree less disastrous to the victor than to the vanquished.

This was not intended as pacifist doctrine; rather it was an appeal to the enlightened self-interest of the potential aggressor. Inevitably, however, Angell came under the charge, in the period immediately before 1914, of conducting pacifist propaganda, and, in the war and afterwards, of having asserted that war was impossible. These misconceptions of his purpose he rebutted with strenuous and irritated insistence. Yet it is doubtful whether Angell allowed for an almost unavoidable degree of misunderstanding of his work on the part of the general public. In seeking to expose many of the political and economic fallacies which contributed to the risk of war he rested his argument for peace too largely upon pure reason, ignoring the precise circumstances in which Britain found itself in the face of German ambitions.

Norman Angell adopted by deed poll the name by which he became known as the author of *The Great Illusion*. He was born in Lincolnshire on December 26, 1872, the son of Thomas Angell Lane, J.P., of Holbeach, Lincolnshire, and was christened Ralph Norman Angell. After preparatory schooling he was sent to the Lycée de Saint Omer, in France, from which he passed on to the University of Geneva. He did not stay long there, however, but, exercising a choice which in retrospect seems an odd one for the quiet scholar, ran away to America to be a cowboy, taking cattle to and fro across the Mexican border. This was in 1891, and Angell stayed in America for seven years, during the latter part of which he engaged in journalism, writing for the *San Francisco Chronicle*, the *St. Louis Globe-Democrat*, and other papers.

In 1898 he went over to Paris as European correspondent for several American papers. The next year he became editor of *Galignani's Messenger*, an English daily published in Paris, in which after a time he acquired a controlling interest. This he tried unavailingly to sell to Lord Northcliffe. Northcliffe cherished his own vision of a continental daily paper in English and in 1905, having set to work on the continental *Daily Mail*, approached Angell with an offer of the editorship. Angell edited the continental *Daily Mail* for several years with a success which is a matter of journalistic history.

His knowledge of international affairs, which was greatly increased by these seven years in Paris, was supplemented by wide reading. Towards the end of 1909 he published, at his own expense, a small and unpretentious volume entitled *Europe's Optical Illusion*. It received almost no notice at all. The author asked Massingham, of *The Nation*, to form his own conclusions ("this book", he said, "is either pure nonsense or important"), and Massingham gave it a two-page notice. Fifty marked copies sent to businessmen and diplomatists evoked no response. Then Lord Esher sent 200 copies to leading European figures, among them the Kaiser and Sir Edward Grey. In a speech at Guildhall Grey dealt at length with the thesis of *The Great Illusion*. The book's fortune was made, and Angell's reputation with it. Some months later a revised and enlarged edition was put out under the title of *The Great Illusion*, this at the suggestion of Northcliffe. The book created what is perhaps fairly described as a sensation. During the next 30 years it sold over a million copies, being translated into some 25 languages, among them Gujarati and Tamil.

Angell was now plunged into a busy career as writer and lecturer. He spoke at clubs, to religious and political bodies, all sorts of societies—wherever, indeed, it appeared that seed might be sown. In 1912 he severed his formal connexion with Northcliffe, but was given space whenever he wished it in the *Daily Mail*, though the policies he advocated were nearly always opposed to those of the paper.

LECTURERS SENT OUT

In this same year Sir Richard Garton set up the Garton Foundation for the spread of Angell's ideas. It sent lecturers all over the country, one of the men picked out being Harry Snell, the future Labour peer. A year later some of Angell's associates founded a monthly magazine called *War and Peace*. He lectured by invitation during the same year at various German universities, and, in spite of contretemps at Berlin and Göttingen, was on the whole courteously listened to.

But so reasonable a philosophy as Angell's could not prevail in the world of 1914. In September of that year he joined with Ramsay MacDonald, E. D. Morel, and others in forming the Union of Democratic Control. He became a regular contributor to the American *New Republic* from 1916 onwards, lectured in the United States, and aroused some resentment at home by his remarks on the freedom of the seas.

He spent three months in Paris during the peace conference, and on his return took an active part in the Fight the Famine Fund movement. In *The Economic Chaos and the Peace Treaty* and *The Fruits of Victory* he assailed—somewhat too easily—the Versailles Treaty on both economic and moral grounds. He watched the dawning Soviet regime with sympathetic interest, describing it on one occasion as "the greatest political and social experiment since the foundation of Christianity".

In 1920 Angell was adopted as prospective Labour candidate for the Rushcliffe division of Nottinghamshire, but he did not enter Parliament until 1929, when he won North Bradford from the Conservatives. He retired in 1931, in which year he was knighted for political and public services, feeling that he could be more useful outside the House. From 1928 to 1931 he edited *Foreign Affairs*, the organ of the U.D.C.

PROLIFIC WRITER

International questions continued to be his main preoccupation. A prolific writer, he restated his case for peace in a variety of forms, bringing parts of the argument down from a metaphysical level to one that might carry more persuasion with the man in the street.

Before ideas of federal union had attained any wide popularity he maintained that the national state had outlived, or was fast outliving, its utility and advocated some form of federal world government. He was an early critic of the totalitarian scheme of things. In 1933 he published a new edition of *The Great Illusion* and in the same year was awarded the Nobel Peace Prize. In 1935 he stood as Labour candidate for London University without success. The darkening of the international scene gave new urgency to his warnings, but he was under no illusions regarding the Nazi menace and in December, 1939, he produced in *For What Do We Fight?* a reasoned statement of his conviction that the principle at stake in the second German war was nothing less than the preservation of the rights of man. He spent much of his time in the United States in later years. In 1947 he published *The Steep Places*, in which he brought keen insight and an equable temper to an examination of the political tendencies which separated eastern from western Europe.

In 1951 he published *After All*, an autobiography, an exhilarating compound of adventure and evangelism and, like its author, good tempered and modest.

In 1958 his book *Defence and the English-Speaking Role*, in which he argued against one-sided disarmament, and came to the conclusion that absence of sanctions would only mean anarchy, was published. Five years later, when he was 90, he went on a two-month tour of the United States, lecturing on education for the nuclear age.

Angell invented "the Money Game", a series of card games teaching the rudiments of economics, particularly of banking and currency. He was a frail, fair man of slight build, ascetic of feature and quiet and undemonstrative in manner—though when the occasion required he could be vigorous and indeed vehement enough in argument. From 1928 he had been a member of the council of the Royal Institute of International Affairs.

October 9, 1967.

Ernest Ansermet, the Swiss conductor who died in Geneva on February 20, 1969, at the age of 85, is known the world over as that of a champion of modern music—"modern" being defined as the music of the present century, other than late survivals of the romantic movement, with the iconoclasm of Stravinsky as its starting point.

But he had other claims to fame, especially in his native country in which he once taught mathematics, since he was for 45 years at the centre of a flourishing school of composition and exercised a quickening influence on the musical life of Switzerland which has had international repercussions. He created the Orchestre de la Suisse Romande, which he founded at Geneva in 1918 and has directed ever since for 40 years.

He was born at Nevey on November 11, 1883, and educated at Lausanne, where he was subsequently (1905–09) professor of mathematics. But music was already beckoning and he was studying with Denereaz at Lausanne. He went on to work at composition with Ernest Bloch at Geneva. For conducting he apprenticed himself to Francesco de Lacerda, the conductor of the Montreux orchestra, whom he subsequently succeeded, and went for advice to Nibisch and Weingartner.

In 1910 he turned over to music as a career and became conductor at Montreux for four years and then of the Geneva Symphony Orchestra from 1915 to 1918. During these years he met Diaghilev and began his association with the Russian Ballet which was to make him an international figure.

His association with Diaghilev precipitated his interest in modern music, though in fact his taste was catholic enough to enable him to give regular series of concerts with widely representative programmes in the towns of Switzerland in his early days.

To the interpretation of complex modern scores he brought the keen mind of the mathematician. The mysterious affinity of music and mathematics manifested itself on Ansermet in the clarity of his readings, and in the alert expression of his face that reflected a delight in abstract relationships, as though a score was an exercise in applied mathematics, to be realized through ardent sensibility. For many years he was the authoritative exponent of Stravinsky's music, until that composer went to live in America.

Ansermet was responsible for many pointed and just performances of music by Bach, Haydn, Mozart, Beethoven and Schubert, but throughout his career it was the later French composers and the early works of Stravinsky which gave him his special platform. It was, therefore, surprising that, as Stravinsky moved towards serialism, Ansermet became one of the most bitter critics of his later works and of all the music which grew from the theory and practice of Schoenberg.

This repudiation was based, essentially, on a traditional view of music as a means of expression, and his objection to serialism and its offshoots was that they inhibited the composer's ability to express himself because of technical demands which resulted in an obsession with compositional techniques.

For all that, it may be that the future will remember him not only as the creator of a great orchestra and as a conductor of unusual personal and interpretative qualities but also as a stimulating, highly controversial writer on his art. The clarity which eluded his work as a writer was always present in his performances. Rhythmic precision and vitality, together with clean, ordered sound, and a concentration on the text of such works as the Beethoven symphonies rather than a sympathy with the legends which have grown round them, were the special qualities which he brought to the rostrum and which remained with him throughout his active career until his retirement in 1967.

He composed a little, chiefly for voice and orchestra: *Feuilles au Printemps* was his most ambitious purely orchestral work.

He was an officer of the French Legion of Honour and of the Star of Belgium.

February 21, 1969.

Sir Edward Appleton, G.B.E., K.C.B., F.R.S., who died on April 21, 1965, had been Principal and Vice-Chancellor of Edinburgh University for nearly 16 years, and was one of the foremost physicists of his time. He won this position by his pioneering investigations into the electrical properties of the upper atmosphere, one result of which was the discovery of the electrified sheet which is known as the Appleton layer.

In 1901, when Marconi first transmitted wireless messages across the Atlantic, the fact that communication could be established between England and America caused much astonishment, since there seemed to be no adequate reason why the waves should bend round and follow the curvature of the earth to the extent necessary. In 1902 Oliver Heaviside and A. E. Kennelly independently suggested that a high layer of air endowed with the power of conducting electricity would act as a mirror for wireless waves and prevent them escaping, but for many years this was an unsupported speculation. It was Appleton who initiated and carried through a striking series of experiments which demonstrated the real existence of such conducting layers of ionized air and who followed this up by prolonged investigations into the structure and properties of this electrified region, now known as the ionosphere.

The First World War, in which he had served as a junior officer in the Royal Engineers, had made Appleton familiar with the generation and detection of wireless waves by the technique involving thermionic valves, then just being introduced, and soon after that war, when he was still in his early twenties, he began an extensive series of experiments in which he showed how these waves could be used for exploring the electrical state of the upper atmosphere. It was in 1925 that, with his student M.A.F. Barnett, he obtained interferences between waves passing along the ground and waves reflected from above, which proved the existence of the reflecting layer and enabled its height to be found. He then worked out the conditions which determined whether waves should be reflected from a layer of electrified particles in the upper atmosphere or should penetrate the layer and be lost in space, showing that the behaviour depended upon the nature and the number of particles and upon the frequency of the waves and also predicting the influence of the earth's magnetic field on the phenomena.

SUN SPOT ACTIVITY

With the aid of this theoretical knowledge he established experimentally the existence of a second layer (which was called after him), proved that the electrified particles responsible for the reflection were electrons and showed how to measure the number of electrons in a given volume. This led in 1931 to systematic work on the variation of the number of electrons present at different heights at different times of the day and at different seasons: Appleton thus inaugurated the continuous study of the electrical state of the upper atmosphere which is today carried on at a large number of stations spread all over the world. The layer structure of the ionosphere was also further analysed by Appleton and he showed the existence of lunar tides in it.

One of his most interesting findings was that the ionization in the upper layer was due to ultra-violet light from the sun; this went hand in hand with his discovery of the connexion between sun spot activity and ionization. He was also active in investigating wireless waves sent out by the sun itself.

The methods which Appleton initiated and the results which his keen physical insight won from them were not only of theoretical interest but also of great practical importance. They enable us to forecast what the conditions of reflection for wireless waves will be at different times of the day and at different seasons, and thus to predict the most suitable wavelengths to use. More important still, it was Appleton's work that really led to the use of radar for locating distant aircraft, for the detection of wireless waves reflected from aircraft was first carried out by methods which he had devised for the detection of waves reflected from the ionosphere. Appleton's work on the ionosphere brought him many scientific distinctions, including the Hughes Medal of the Royal Society in 1933, a Royal Medal of the Royal Society in 1950, and the award of the Nobel Prize for Physics in 1947. He received honorary degrees from many British and North American universities.

Appleton was also a very successful administrator. In 1939 he was appointed to the secretaryship, which is the directing post, of the Department of Scientific and Industrial Research and carried the burden of this responsible position throughout the Second World War, being prominently concerned with the organization of the development of radar and with the secret work on the atomic bomb, among many other matters. After the war he was actively associated with the development of technological research and in this capacity carried the confidence of his scientific colleagues, of industry and of the Government alike.

Edward Victor Appleton was born on September 6, 1892, at Bradford, Yorkshire, into a modest Wesleyan household. He always maintained an active affection for his native city. His family supported the ambitions for a scientific career which showed themselves towards the end of his school career, and in 1911 he entered with a scholarship St. John's College, Cambridge, of which he later became an honorary fellow. A brilliant university career, in which he achieved distinction in mineralogy, was interrupted by the 1914–18 War, after which he returned to Cambridge and began, while acting as assistant demonstrator in the famous Cavendish laboratory, the researches to which reference has already been made. At the age of 32 he had already made sufficient of a name in physics for him to be appointed as Wheatstone Professor of Physics at King's College London, where he remained for 12 years, a period during which some of his best research was carried out. In 1936 he was appointed to the Jacksonian Professorship at Cambridge as successor to the famous C. T. R. Wilson.

ACADEMIC WORLD

In 1949 Appleton returned to the academic world as Principal and Vice-Chancellor of the University of Edinburgh, a very demanding and distinguished post. He had many of the qualities necessary for success—intellectual stature, vast administrative experience, a strong determination and an eagerness to look to the future. There was no danger of a stagnant university under his guidance.

He presided over one of the largest building programmes in the history of the university. It was his misfortune that the most spectacular scheme, the George Square development, was bound to provoke controversy to the point of bitterness. There was never much chance that a square which was a unique example of one stage in the history of Edinburgh could be so substantially changed without loud protest. But the scheme was not of Appleton's authorship. Plans for the redevelopment of George Square existed some years before he went to Edinburgh. What he did was to obtain action, in spite of all opposition, on a specific project.

This incident was typical of much in Appleton's rule in Edinburgh. He could override opposition, but all too rarely could he mollify it. No doubt much of the criticism must have seemed merely destructive to a Principal who, with the responsibility of planning for expansion, could not let his policy be dictated by an impractical nostalgia. There were occasional difficulties. They are bound to occur in such a post.

CONTACT WITH STUDENTS

Sometimes his fault was more one of personal presentation than of policy. His forthright influence and mental stimulus were highly beneficial, however, among those in Edinburgh with whom he came in close contact—and he did what he could to make sure that he was in touch with as many as possible, staff and students. In this as in every other aspect of his responsibilities he was immensely conscientious. He had the dignity, the authority and the gift of expression necessary for formal occasions. But his concern went far beyond that. His enthusiasm for the development of science was more than a personal predilection: it was an example of his determination that the university should be equipped to play its full part in the modern world.

Appleton combined a profound and penetrating genius for physical research with unusual administrative ability and great natural shrewdness in all practical matters. He had in him a great appreciation of intellectual values, which made him a popular figure in academic circles, combined with a certain Yorkshire homeliness which enabled him to mix freely with the class of people who like to call themselves plain men. He made good friends and he retained them. He was a brilliant lecturer, both to general and to expert audiences, and everything that he wrote was distinguished by clarity and decision.

Early in life, in 1915, he married Jessie, daughter of the Rev. J. Longson. There were two daughters of the marriage. His wife died in 1964. He married secondly, in the month before he died, Mrs. Helen F. Allison, who had been his private secretary for some years.

April 23, 1965.

Lady Apsley, C.B.E. Conservative and National Liberal M.P. for Bristol Central from 1943 until 1945, died on January 19, 1966, at her home at Cirencester, Gloucestershire.

She was a past national chairman of the British Legion's Women's Section. Holder of a pilot's licence, Lady Apsley had taken part in motor trials, and had hunted with the V.W.H. (Earl Bathurst's) Hunt until a serious accident confined her to a wheelchair. She was Joint Master of the V.W.H. from 1946 to 1956. She wrote several books on hunting and was the compiler of *The Fox-Hunter's Bedside Book*, published in 1950.

Violet, daughter of Captain B.C.S. Meeking, married in 1923 Lord Apsley, who was killed on active service in 1942. They had two sons. Lord Bathurst and the Hon. George Bathurst.

During the First World War Lady Apsley served with a Voluntary Aid Detachment at Marsh Court Military Hospital from 1914 to 1918. She developed an early interest in politics, and became president of the Southampton Women's Conservative Association in 1924. In 1926 she became president of the Links of Empire organization.

Her husband had been elected Conservative M.P. for Southampton in 1922. He became Parliamentary Private Secretary to the Secretary of the Overseas Trade Department of the Board of Trade, and because of complaints about the treatment of "assisted" emigrants in Australia, he was sent there, travelling under an assumed name. His wife joined him later, and their experiences were recorded in *The Amateur Settlers* published in 1925, the work of both of them.

Lady Apsley received her pilot's licence in 1930—her husband had been president of the United Kingdom Pilots' Association since 1925.

ELECTED FOR BRISTOL

During the early years of the Second World War she was prominent in A.T.S. work. After her husband's death in an aircraft accident in the

Middle East she stood as a Conservative for Bristol Central in the resulting by-election. She had been president of the Bristol Women's Conservative Association since 1932.

It was a four-cornered fight, with Miss Jennie Lee standing as an Independent, and two other candidates, both of whom lost their deposits, Mr. John McNair, general secretary of the Independent Labour Party, and another Independent.

RAISED MAJORITY

Lady Apsley was returned with a majority of 1,559, slightly larger than her husband's in the general election of 1935. Under the terms of the electoral truce the Labour Party were unable to contest the seat, and at one time before nomination day seven Independent candidates had announced their intention to stand, including one describing himself as the "President of the Society of Angelic Revelations".

In the 1945 general election Lady Apsley was defeated in a straight fight by her Labour opponent with a majority of 5,676.

Later she was the unsuccessful Conservative and National Liberal candidate for Bristol North-East, contesting the seat several times between 1947 and 1951. From 1952 to 1954 she was a member of the Central Council of the Victoria League. She was made C.B.E. in 1952.

A contributor to *Country Life, Field* and *Light Car,* her other publications were *To Whom The Goddess* (with Lady Diana Shedden, published in 1932), a study of hunting and riding for women, and *Bridleways Through History* (1936), a fascinating but disjointed account of hunting from the earliest days.

January 21, 1966.

Lieutenant-General Pedro Eugenio Arámburu, whose death was announced on July 17, 1970, in Argentina, was practically unknown when a Palace coup put him into the presidential chair in November 1955. His 30 months in office as Provisional President of Argentina in the period following the overthrow of President Juan Perón showed him as a far from brilliant ruler, who alienated even many of his initial supporters. But for his small group of militantly anti-Peronist supporters known as "Gorillas", he became a symbol of a 10-year struggle against the former dictator although he played a secondary role in his ousting. He earned the hatred of Perón's supporters, however, by allowing, if not actually ordering, the summary court-martial and execution of 40 military and civilian leaders of an abortive uprising aimed at bringing the ousted president back in June 1956.

Arámburu had risen to be head of the army's sanitary department after a colourless military career when he joined the plotters planning Perón's overthrow in 1955. After a first attempt by the armed forces to oust Perón failed in June, 1955, General Eduardo Lonardi led a second uprising in the central city of Cordoba on September 16, which succeeded after three days of fierce fighting. Perón sought refuge in the Paraguayan embassy on September 19, the first step towards his current exile in Spain, and two days later General Lonardi became President with Admiral Isaac Rojas as vice-President. Arámburu was promoted to army Chief of Staff.

Arámburu on becoming provisional President immediately adopted a hard-line policy towards the Peronists, disbanding the former ruling party and banning publication or exhibition of all its symbols, including pictures of Perón and his late wife Eva. Later he had the body of Eva Perón withdrawn from the headquarters of the General Labour Confederation (C.G.T.) where it had been reverently kept since her death in 1952 pending construction of a public monument. The fate of Eva Perón's body was never made public.

Arámburu's ban on the Peronist party backfired in the 1958 general elections when Arturo Frondizi, leader of a splinter group of the left-of-centre radical party, won a landslide presidential victory mainly because of Peronist support. The outgoing President attempted a political comeback in 1963, but he trailed far behind the other five presidential contenders. The now-retired army officer played a passive role in local politics in his later years and only really came back into the news when he was kidnapped on May 29 by a group claiming to be Peronists.

July 18, 1970.

Alexander Archipenko, sculptor, painter, designer and teacher, who died at his home in New York on February 25, 1964, is important as one of the pioneers of modern sculpture and probably the first artist to translate Cubist principles into three dimensions. He was 76.

In his work the effort of the Cubist painters to break through a merely surface appearance became an organization of space, distinct from the production of a solid object. He devised rhythmical alternations of convex and concave areas anticipating the interplay of masses and voids of which Henry Moore was later to make effective use.

He also produced an equivalent of the Cubist painters' *collage* in his combinations of different materials, painted wood, metal, glass; and these, which he called *Médranos,* may be regarded as the prototype of the Constructivism, later developed by Naum Gabo and Antoine Pevsner. His work has some points of contact with Futurism in conveying a dynamic energy and in his "Archipentura" of 1924, a machine designed to set a structural assemblage in motion, he may be looked on as a precursor of the "mobile".

CUBIST INFLUENCE

Archipenko shared some general characteristics of style and aim with other sculptors influenced by Cubism. One might group together his "Boxing Match" of 1913 with Raymond Duchamp-Villon's "The Horse" and Epstein's "Rock Drill". His spatial sculpture has points of correspondence with that of Jacques Lipchitz, Henri Laurens, Umberto Boccioni and Ossip Zadkine. He was distinct, however, in a gracefulness of personal style which appeared in the rhythmic, elongated rendering of female form, the primary subject of his sculpture. The terms "blunt" and "barbarian" applied by a critic to an early exhibition of Archipenko in Berlin seem especially inept in view of the grace with which he invested so many interpretations of the figure in the most creative period of his art, from 1910 to the mid-1920s.

Alexander Archipenko, the son of an engineer, was born at Kiev in the Ukraine on May 30, 1887. He studied painting and sculpture in the Kiev art school, 1902–05. In 1906 he continued study in Moscow, taking part in a number of exhibitions, and in 1908 attended the Ecole des Beaux Arts in Paris for a short while. He held his first one-man show in Berlin in 1910 and soon after opened his own school in Paris. It was at this time that he developed, from Cubism, his characteristic departures in the "modelling of space" and unconventional use of materials.

JOINED BERLIN GROUP

His work was included in the epoch-making Armory Show in New York in 1913 and in the same year he joined the Berlin *Sturm* Group and exhibited at the Herwarth Walden gallery. He lived in Berlin from 1921 to 1923, where he had his own school, and in 1923 went to New York, opening a school there and becoming an American citizen in 1928. He taught in Washington State University, 1935–36, and in 1937 became an instructor in the new Bauhaus conducted by Moholy-Nagy at Chicago. He reopened his school for sculptors in New York in 1939, adding a summer school in Woodstock, N.Y., both being successful and highly thought of.

Though his development as an artist seems to have halted after his early phase of invention he held frequent exhibitions, and in 1948 showed a method of "modelling light" in carved plastic in the New York galleries of the Associated American Artists. Nationally and internationally he exhibited so often that in 1963 he had 138 one-man shows to his credit.

Archipenko found a rapport between sculpture and science. "I know", he wrote, "that my knowledge of science is not adequate to understand fully Einstein's theory but its spiritual implication is clear to me. . . . I think that the theory of relativity was always hidden in art, but the genius of Einstein defined it, expressing it in words and numbers." Pursuing this line of thought he once said that his art was no more Ukrainian than Chinese, or than Einstein's theory of relativity was German, American, or Jewish. However, when, in 1934, the American Ukrainians sent his sculpture" "Ma" to the Ukrainian Museum in Lvov he conceded that as "every nation has its typical psychological traits and as art is the image of the spirit" nationality in art might to that extent be said to exist.

Books on Archipenko include studies by Hans Hildebrandt (Berlin, 1923), Maurice Raynal (Rome, Valori Plastici, 1923), and Roland Schacht (Berlin, Der Sturm) 1924. His work is represented in many museums and private collections throughout Europe and America.

February 28, 1964.

Elizabeth Arden, who founded and later assumed the name of the cosmetics business, died in hospital in New York on October 18, 1966.

Who's Who in America listed Miss Arden as having been born in 1891, which would have made her 75. But a spokesman for Elizabeth Arden, Inc., said that she was in her eighty-second year. Others placed her age at nearer to 84.

A tough, self-sufficient woman who described her chosen career as the world's nastiest—"there are so many people in it, and they all just copy me"—she built up a chain of beauty salons in more than 20 cities in the United States and half a dozen countries overseas. Her company also became an international manufacturer and wholesaler of cosmetics, and she was reputed to be the biggest female money-earner as well as one of the richest women in the United States.

Born Florence Nightingale Graham in Ontario, the youngest of five children of a Scots emigrant who ran a grocer's shop, she had a sketchy education (her mother died when she was five) and experimented with a number of jobs, including nursing, before going to seek her fortune in New York.

As an assistant in a cosmetics shop, she discovered a talent for massage and became a partner in a beauty salon in 1909. Partnership did not suit her, and she set up on her own, choosing her *nom de guerre* from the title of a book and poem she liked—*Elizabeth and her German Garden* and "Enoch Arden".

She took up horse racing in 1931 and won the Kentucky Derby with Jet Pilot in 1947, although her greatest notoriety in racing came from having her horses rubbed down with Ardena Cream. A peppery and nostalgic conservative who considered society was in decline, she was nevertheless happy to accept a special award for "having made beauty attainable to all American women". She was a staunch Republican and attended several national conventions.

Miss Arden married first Mr. Thomas Lewis in 1918. He became her business manager until their divorce in 1935. In 1942 she married Prince Michael Evlanoff and in 1944 divorced him. There were no children.

October 19, 1966.

Sir Charles Arden-Clarke, G.C.M.G., died on December 16, 1962, at the age of 64.

His name will always be most closely linked with the attainment of independence by the Gold Coast, thereupon renamed Ghana. Though not the first African dependency to become independent after the War, the emergence of Ghana and its leader Kwame Nkrumah was in many ways the decisive event which released the torrent of African nationalism which has since transformed the appearance of the continent and had repercussions throughout world politics.

When Sir Charles Arden-Clarke became its governor in 1948, none of this was even dreamed of; and indeed few people anticipated independence within eight years. Nevertheless, Arden-Clarke had already received from the Labour Government which appointed him, the year after India's independence, a broad brief to channel the forces of nationalism not to thwart them. The new Governor took over with little knowledge of these forces, but considerable experience of colonial Africa.

His predecessor had been shaken by the violence which had brought the Coussey Commission into being. Sir Charles found Kwame Nkrumah planning to use the Peoples Convention Party, of which he had only recently become leader, to start a campaign of "positive action" to drive out "the imperialists", and he made use of his Colonial Secretary, Mr. Reginald Saloway, late of the I.C.S. to win Nkrumah to a "dialogue" between friendly antagonists, if not to cooperation.

ARRESTED NKRUMAH

In 1950, a strike brought violence and Sir Charles had Nkrumah arrested; he was jailed for incitement and sedition. In the ensuing elections held under the new Coussey commission, however, the C.P.P. swept the country, and the campaign was led by Kwame Nkrumah by proxy. Sir Charles accepted the situation, and when the victorious C.P.P. leaders reached Christiansborg Castle to demand their leader's release, he said "You are behind the times". He had released Nkrumah by act of grace, and called on him to form a government, as "Leader of Government Business" next day.

Sir Charles, thenceforth in partnership with Nkrumah, guided and controlled the country through the series of constitutional changes during which, as it was supposed, a swift but durable training was given to African ministers and parliamentarians in democratic government on the "Westminster Model"—which Africans then seemed to be demanding. It was an exciting experience, though one which many governors have had since then. Sir Charles once remarked that "every morning I wondered how the day would end".

In his autobiography Dr. Nkrumah records the occasion when at last the telegram arrived from London conceding full independence. "This is a great day for you. Prime Minister". Sir Charles said. "It is the end of what you have struggled for." "It is the end of what we have been struggling for, Sir Charles", Dr. Nkrumah replied.

A few months later Sir Charles was Ghana's first Governor-General: but when he left, doubts and anxieties were already saddening him, for he already saw the signs of the Nkrumahist dictatorship which he had hitherto stoutly maintained could not exist in the tribal traditions and structure of African society.

Sir Charles Noble Arden-Clarke was born at Bournemouth in 1898, the eldest son of the Rev. C. W. Arden Clarke (the hyphen was put in by deed poll), a retired South India missionary. He was educated at Rossall, and was 16 when the Great War Broke out. In 1917 he joined the Machine Gun Corps, became a captain, and was mentioned in dispatches.

BREACH OF DISCIPLINE

In Germany after the war he became involved in a breach of discipline which led to his volunteering for the allied expeditionary force to South Russia to support the "White" Russian army.

In 1920 he joined the Colonial Service, and served his first 13 years in Nigeria, where he became known as an able and authoritarian district officer.

In 1924 he married Miss Georgina Reed, and the couple had a son and two daughters.

From 1934–36 he made his mark (as rising Colonial Servants usually did) in the Secretariat in the Capital, Lagos. In 1937 he went to Bechuanaland as assistant Resident Commissioner, where he enjoyed the friendship of Tchekedi Khama, and perhaps at that time developed his first faith in the possibilities of the "African personality". From 1942 to 1946 he was Resident Commissioner of Basutoland.

Immediately after the war the reforming Labour Government took over Sarawak from the "White Rajah". Sir Antony Brooke, who had, of course, lost the territory when the Japanese seized the entire East Indian archipelago in the war: Mr. Creech Jones made Sir Charles its first Colonial Governor. Sir Charles was naturally a target for resentment, and though he worked hard and successfully to rebuild the country and develop better relations, a plot against his life as symbol of British authority only misfired because he had by then been sent to the Gold Coast: his successor was murdered.

LATER TASKS

Sir Charles's experience with African Nationalism fitted him for the great variety of tasks to which the state and unofficial bodies called him after his retirement. He was chairman of the Royal African Society and of the Royal Commonwealth Society for the Blind from 1959. In 1960, he took on the chairmanship of the National Council for the Supply of Teachers Overseas, a ponderously named but exceedingly important organization which seeks to encourage teachers to do a spell abroad and to ensure that such public spirit and adventurousness shall not impair their career prospects on return.

The recruitment of Sir Charles Arden-Clarke's wide African experience to the Monckton Commission did not save it from being boycotted by the African nationalists in the Federation of Rhodesia and Nyasaland, nor did it incline the Federal Government to be any more sympathetic to its—admittedly somewhat diverse—conclusions.

Sir Charles, however, made important contributions to its work, which, though inapplicable now, was liberal when the report appeared and might, if accepted by H.M.G. have made a difference to the present position of the Federation.

In the last two years of his life Sir Charles rounded out his experience of the High Commission territories. He was called in in 1961 as constitutional adviser to the committee working on a new constitution for Swaziland, and helped to frame proposals which will be studied by a conference that is expected to be held in London early in 1963.

December 18, 1962.

Field Marshal Abdul Salam Muhammad Arif, President of Iraq from 1963, who was killed in a helicopter crash on April 13, 1966, was an astute "political soldier" who, having seized power by opportunism, managed to retain it by skilful manoeuvring between contending factions.

In the past eight years particularly Arif lived with violence, in the sense that it repeatedly took place around him even though he did not always have a hand in it. The particular tragedy of the manner of his death is that until then he seemed to have developed a unique capacity for survival.

Born in 1921, he pursued a normal military career until 1958, when he abruptly came to prominence as the commander of the first military unit to enter Baghdad in opposition to the monarchical regime when the revolution broke out; it was he who broadcast the news of the coup and incitements to the population, all too readily heeded, to destroy the Royal Palace. General Kassim, who emerged from the revolution as Head of State, made him deputy Prime Minister, Minister of the Interior, and Commander-in-Chief of the armed forces: but within a month they had fallen out and Arif was sent abroad as Ambassador to Bonn.

He apparently found diplomatic life little to his liking, as the next month he was back in Baghdad. Here he was arrested and brought to trial before the "People's Court" on charges of conspiracy and of attempting to assassinate Kassim, being acquitted on the former count but found guilty on the latter. He remained in prison until November, 1961, when Kassim pardoned and released him and even drove him home. In February, 1963, however, another military coup resulted in Kassim's overthrow and murder, and Arif, who called upon the Army to disperse Kassim's much disliked National Guard and to occupy Baghdad, became President and Head of State, subsequently promoting himself Field Marshal.

DIFFICULT COURSE

The new President found himself obliged to steer a wary course between the advocates and the opponents of closer union with Nasser's Egypt both of whom formed factions in the Army and amongst the politicians. He allowed his first Government, under the influence of the Baath Party, the predominant political organization, to pursue a policy of rapprochement with Egypt, which in April, 1963, led to their joining with the Egyptian and Syrian Governments in a declaration of intent to federate their countries within two years. By November this project had run into difficulties and discredited the Baath, and another coup d'état, in which the Field Marshal found it expedient to connive, resulted in the exile of the Baath leaders and the assumption of power by another military junta of more nationalistic and less pro-Nasser complexion.

During the lifetime of this Government, which lasted 20 months, negotiations with Egypt under the President's aegis resulted in two further announcements of measures intended to promote an eventual Iraqi-Egyptian connexion. These, however, merely served to increase internal strains in Iraq on this issue: and although in September, 1965, the Government disintegrated because a majority of Ministers considered that the Prime Minister's attitude to Egypt was too hostile, the successor Government was in turn upset for showing itself too pro-Egyptian, and it became clear that the issue of a connexion with Egypt was dead. At this juncture the President turned to a civilian to form a new Government, and for the first time since 1958 Iraq found itself under civilian control.

April 15, 1966.

The Rev. C. M. Armitage, who died at Dymchurch on June 7, 1966, at the age of 66, was rector of St. Bride's Church, Fleet Street, from 1954 to 1962.

He gave up the precentorship of Westminster Abbey to take on the difficult tasks of supervising as incumbent the reconstruction of the war-damaged Wren church of St. Bride, Fleet Street, and of making it a lively and outstanding centre of worship.

Cyril Moxon Armitage was born on June 4, 1900, at Wakefield, Yorkshire. From Queen Elizabeth's School there he went up to St. Chad's College, Durham, where he graduated in arts in 1921 and took the Diploma in Theology the following year. He was captain of his college boat club, coxed the university crew, and was president of the university choral and orchestral society. In 1923 he was ordained as assistant curate of St. Augustine's, Kilburn, and he stayed there until 1931, when he went to the Abbey as a minor canon, being appointed precentor in 1934.

The post suited Armitage admirably, enabling him to express and widen the interest which he had had in church arts and music from an early age (his brother was Noel Gay, the composer, who died in 1954). He undertook with enthusiasm planning the music and ceremonial for many important occasions. For his part in the wedding of the Queen and the Duke of Edinburgh he was made M.V.O. He took part in the 1953 Coronation ceremony, and he was priest-in-ordinary to four Sovereigns.

The results of Armitage's researches into the organization and constitution of the Abbey were published in 1951 in *The Church of Westminster*. Although he received several offers of preferment, including a deanery, Armitage turned them all down. But in 1951, the Dean and Chapter, the patrons, offered him St. Bride's.

CHALLENGE OF WREN

This was a challenge he felt he must accept: the opportunity not merely to recreate Wren's masterpiece, which had stood roofless and forlorn since it was destroyed by fire bombs in 1940, but also to build anew a tradition of worship and music which would draw people from far away.

Immediately decisions on the reorganization of the City churches authorized the restoration of St. Bride's Armitage gathered an executive committee representative of the press generally and of trades and professions located in the parish, to guide the rebuilding effort and necessary appeal. The intention was that, with Godfrey Allen, surveyor to the fabric of St. Paul's, as architect, the church should rise again more purely Wren and more beautiful than when it was burnt down; nothing but the best in material and workmanship would do; somehow the large sum would be found to augment the "plain repair" payment of the War Damage Commission. The new church was reopened in the presence of the Queen and the Duke of Edinburgh in December, 1957.

One of Armitage's earliest acts was to revive the Guild of St. Bride, which was confirmed by writ of Edward III at the Tower of London in 1375, and the wearing by members of gowns of russet as recorded by Wynkyn de Worde. Guildsmen form the nucleus of the congregation and read the lessons and take part in the services. The idea has spread to churches of St. Bride overseas.

Armitage did much work for the Church Lads' Brigade, of which he was assistant secretary from 1931 to 1932 and general secretary and headquarters staff chaplain from 1932 to 1935. He was an R.N.V.R. chaplain from 1940 to 1946. He was president of the London central area of the St. John Ambulance Brigade from 1953 to 1954, and was sub-chaplain of the order from 1953. From 1950 to 1951 he was proctor in convocation for London. He was the author of *Courage*, a collection of war-time talks to sailors; and *Beauty for Ashes*, describing the history and rebuilding proposals of St. Bride's.

June 9, 1966.

Tommy Armour, who died at Larchmont, near New York, in September, 1968, at the age of 71, achieved success in golf on both sides of the Atlantic, being one of that select band who have won the Open championships of both countries.

Born in Edinburgh on September 24, 1896. Thomas Donaldson Armour attended the University and was drawn into the war at once. He joined The Royal Scots as a machine gunner and was later commissioned into the newly formed Tank Corps, where he temporarily lost his eyesight in a gas attack.

He won many European events as an amateur, including the French Open but soon after the war he went to live in the United States, turning professional in 1925. Two years later he won the American Open, holing from 10ft. on the last green to force a play-off with H. Cooper, whom he defeated by three strokes. The same year he won the Canadian Open and within a few years he had won several lesser championships including the P.G.A. in 1930. A year later he returned to Scotland for the Open when for the first time it was held at Carnoustie. His final round of 71, the lowest of the day, brought him in one stroke ahead of Jurado, an Argentinian.

Armour was equally successful as a teacher. He had a glorious style and was strong in every department of the game with the possible exception of his short putting. It was once said of him that he was never happy on the greens.

He eventually took a post in Florida at the Boca Raton club which he held for nearly 25 years. His two instructional books were outstanding in a highly competitive field. He enjoyed the unique distinction of having played against the United States for Britain as an amateur in an unofficial match in 1921, and against Britain for the United States as a professional in the match at Wentworth in 1926 which preceded the Ryder Cup fixture.

September 14, 1968.

Ralph Arnold, novelist, historical writer, and chairman of Constable and Co. from 1958 to 1962, died on September 23, 1970, at the age of 63. Like his former colleague, Michael Sadleir, he successfully combined a publishing career with a life of authorship.

Ralph Crispian Marshall Arnold was born at Meopham, Kent, on October 26, 1906, and educated at Loretto and Trinity College, Oxford, and from 1929 to 1934 worked on the staff of the Royal Institute of International Affairs, joining Constable's in 1936. Enlisting in 1939 as a second lieutenant in the Cameronians (Scottish Rifles), he served as personal assistant to Lord Ironside when he was C.I.G.S. and Commander-in-Chief, Home Forces, in 1939–40, of which experience he contributed some characteristically light-hearted recollections to *Blackwood's Magazine*, which formed the nucleus of an entertaining book of war reminiscences, *A Very Quiet War*. He was personal assistant to the Commander-in-Chief, Scottish Command, 1941–42; Assistant Deputy Director of Public Relations, XIV Army, 1943; and Deputy Director of Public Relations at the headquarters of South-East Asia Command, 1944. He was demobilized with the rank of colonel.

Arnold best showed his gift for light fiction in *Hands Across the Water* (1946), a clever, amusing and affectionate little comedy of English village life, and in *Spring List* (1956), a dexterous entertainment in which he used his special knowledge of the publishing profession to great advantage. He also wrote short stories, books of adventure for boys, and detective novels, notably *Fish and Company* (1951), and was a contributor of occasional reviews and light leading articles to The Times.

In his literary approach Arnold had much in common with his friend Peter Fleming, in particular an easy and characteristically English humour and a gift for readable narrative. If his fiction was influenced by Dornford Yates, whom he greatly admired, his historical writing was coloured by the romanticism of another of his heroes, John Buchan. He began as a local historian of his own county with *The Hundred of Hoo* (1947), an allusive and highly subjective account of this little-known corner of Kent.

In *A Yeoman of Kent* (1949), he concentrated on his own village of Cobham, including a description of his attractive home there, Meadow House, and drawing on the diaries of a local eighteenth-century landowner. For his next historical venture, *The Unhappy Countess* (1957), he went farther afield, discovering congenial material in the old romantic story of the Bowes Lyon family; a delightful piece of exploration. *Northern Lights* (1959) was an excursion in the same vein into the Derwentwater family history, while *The Whiston Matter* (1961) provided a skilful and entertaining reconstruction of the scandalous happenings at Rochester which gave Trollope his material for *The Warden*. *Orange Street and Brickhole Lane* (1963) completed his autobiographies and told of his time at Constables, which he stated "had a strangely endearing persona." *A Social History of England 55 B.C. to 1215 A.D.* was published in 1967.

In the long run, however, it may be that Ralph Arnold's best achievement was simply—himself. His character might with some accuracy have been deduced from his books—his humour, honesty and loyalty, his unpretentiousness with its engaging dash of self-mockery, his keen sense of the joys of literary and historical discovery, especially in eighteenth and nineteenth century biography; to Constable authors he was a constant encouragement and many became his personal friends.

Arnold was married in 1936 to Constantia Pamela, youngest daughter of the late Mark Fenwick.

September 24, 1970.

Tom Arnold, O.B.E., the producer and theatrical manager, died on February 2, 1969, in St. Mary's Hospital, Paddington, at the age of 72.

Tom Arnold was a man who for more than 40 years kept his finger firmly on the pulse of middle-class theatrical taste. From touring revues in 1922 to his management of the *Folies Bergère* at the London Palladium in 1925 and on to *Pickwick* in 1963, *Our Man Crichton* a year later and *The Solid Gold Cadillac* in 1965, he was responsible for a long string of successes ranging from Shakespeare to the circus, to several of the triumphs of the late Ivor Novello.

His activities included most types of entertainment—operas, classical plays, films, and the circus; the spectacular ice-skating pantomimes produced in London and the provinces were started through his shrewdness and enterprise. His career had been singularly free from the varying fortunes usually experienced by those who specialize in providing entertainment for the public. This was probably due to the fact that before he ventured into showmanship on a big scale in London he served a long apprenticeship in the presentation of less ambitious performances in provincial centres.

Thomas Charles Arnold was born in Yorkshire. His ambition from an early age was to become a showman, and at 18 he launched boldly on the career he had deliberately chosen. Realizing the possibilities of the touring entertainment, he formed travelling companies, whose cooperation enabled him to establish a relatively lucrative business as a promoter of many kinds of amusements. In the days when revues were a novelty even in London he took to the road with stage attractions bearing such titles as *The Showbox*, *Better and Better* and *Seeing Life*, which he sponsored in 1922 and 1923. As long ago as September, 1925, he put on a *Folies Bergère* show at the London Palladium.

Although his faith in his capacity as a promoter was justified by the experience he decided to confine his amusement activities to the provincial field and continued to finance and produce musical plays, for presentation at theatres throughout the country. Some were notable versions of originals staged in London by the late Sir Charles Cochran, then at the zenith of his career, and included such favourites as *Keep Dancing* and *This Year of Grace*. In 1933 he secured the rights to *Waltzes from Vienna,* and subsequently also toured with *Streamline, Stop Press. The Merry Widow, Anything Goes, Balalaika,* and other successful pieces featuring light music, comedy, and scenic spectacle. His first attempt at pantomime production was at Birmingham in 1933, and he was so impressed by the result, that in the following year, when, on the death of Julian Wylie, the pantomime interests of the famous manager became available, he acquired them. Arnold lost no time in exploiting his new acquisition and was soon firmly established in London, where he not only set up a new high standard in Christmas pantomimes, but also entered into theatrical association with Ivor Novello.

TALENTED COMPANIES

In spite of his many commitments Arnold went on sending talented companies round the country in musical plays which had succeeded in London, such as *Wild Oats*, *Me and My Girl*, *The Fleet's Lit Up*, and *What's Going on Here*. In March, 1939, he joined Ivor Novello in staging *The Dancing Years* at Drury Lane, and after the Second World War, toward the end of which he had acquired the lease of the Palace Theatre, the partnership was resumed and maintained until the actor's tragically sudden death. Though strikingly dissimilar in some of their characteristics, the two men had much in common in theatrical matters, and were firm friends, and Arnold's sense of loss was apparent. But he continued to extend his interests, produced pantomimes in many provincial cities, presented musical comedies and pantomimes on ice in London and Wembley, and achieved fresh distinction by establishing a Christmas circus tradition at Harringay which added to his fame year by year. Arnold's touring companies were almost as well known in South Africa and Australia as in this country. At one time his film *Waltzes from Vienna* was being shown at one New York theatre, while, as a play, it was having a record success at another.

If, in the last 10 or 15 years, Arnold's touch seemed a little less secure and some of his more ambitious ventures, like *Maggie May* and *Our Man Crichton* did not win the public's heart as they might have done a few years before, and though *The Solid Gold Cadillac,* his last big West End venture, suffered from competition with an unusually well played and effective film, *Pickwick* proved that he still knew and could provide exactly what the public wanted. There always remained a solid corps of theatregoers whose minds he understood and whose tastes he could serve with skill.

February 3, 1969.

Jean Arp, the French sculptor, painter and poet, died in Basle on June 7, 1966. He was 78.

Arp had long been considered one of the foremost modern sculptors, and one of the pioneers of abstract art. Certainly quite apart from questions of the long-term importance of his sculpture Arp's career was a key one in the formation of modern art. Humorous, polemical, sharply critical of the social scene, alternatively in the midst of public controversy and jealously guarding his isolation, he grew with modern art and his creative vigour enabled him to survive the death of the various groups he enthusiastically supported.

He was born in the Alsatian city of Strasbourg in 1887, and its dual Franco-German character no doubt made it easy for him to span these two worlds and to welcome enthusiastically the ideas of the band of rootless individuals who began Dada in Zurich in 1916. However, even before that date he had been to Paris studied painting there and met Apollinare, Max Jacob, Modigliani, Delaunay, and Picasso, met Max Ernst in Cologne, and Klee and Kandinsky in Munich, where he exhibited in the second Blaue Reiter show.

But the period of Zurich Dada, which lasted from 1916 to 1924 was probably the most vital in the whole of Arp's career. He crystallized his ideas, created sculptures, reliefs, collages and paintings and poems with a flowing day-to-day rhythm, among them some of his most slyly poetic and humorous works. "What can I do?" he said to Hans Richter after a particularly full morning's work, "it grows out of me like my toenails. I have to cut it off and then it grows again."

In 1919 Arp moved to Cologne, then to Berlin and eventually to Paris in 1920 where he met Breton, Aragon and Eluard and was taken into the fold of Surrealism.

WIFE'S PAINTING

In 1926 he settled in Meudon, near Paris, where he lived a quiet and uneventful life until his death. He married Sophie Taeuber, an artist of great strength and clarity whom he had met in Zurich. They collaborated on many projects and there is no doubt that the severity and purity of her abstract painting exercised a strong influence on his work. She died in 1948. Arp exhibited with the abstract groups "Circle and Square" and "Abstraction—Creation" in the thirties, dropping the Dada humour of his earlier works for simpler organic forms, often made in white marble or polished bronze. He occasionally worked on a large scale with great success (as in the pure white and billowing form "Shepherd of the Clouds" in the university city, Caracus) but after his work of the thirties and forties he made few stylistic changes.

To describe his art in general he used the word "concrete". He disliked the term "abstract" because he thought it disguised the natural quality of the work of art. "Art is a fruit that grows in man, like a fruit on a plant", he wrote.

Arp's work has shown an impressive continuity and consistency, an unwavering adherence to a personal vision and great fertility. It had long been an influence on the work of other sculptors and painters. He never made the formal innovations, the real transformations of the sculptural language of a Brancusi, a Gonzalez or a Gabo, but his production is one of the most lyrical and optimistic in twentieth century art—"Something peaceful and vegetative" were the words he used himself when describing his aims.

June 8, 1966.

The Right Rev. Wilfred Marcus Askwith, K.C.M.G., D.D., Bishop of Gloucester since 1954, died at Gloucester on July 16, 1962, at the age of 72.

Born on April 24, 1890, the son of Prebendary Henry Askwith, of Hereford, he was educated at Bedford School and Corpus Christi College, Cambridge, where he took a second class in the Classical Tripos in 1912 and he rowed in the Cambridge crew in the university boat race of the ensuing year. He was then ordained to a curacy at St. Helens, but some two years later returned to his old school as chaplain and assistant master, where he remained until 1920. For the next five years he was rector of Stalbridge, Dorset, and then began a seven-year ministry in Kenya, where he gained an insight into the problems of the Church overseas.

When he returned to England in 1932 it was to become vicar of Sherborne. There his first task was to complete a scheme for the restoration of the Lady Chapel of Sherborne Abbey and by his energy and personal magnetism he succeeded in raising a large portion of the cost of the work. He soon endeared himself to all classes and interests in the ecclesiastical, academic and civic life of the town and his enthusiasm for education found scope in his acceptance of places on the governing bodies of both the boys' and girls' secondary schools. He was made surrogate soon after his induction and in 1938 the conferment upon him of the Stall of Grantham Borealis in Sarum Cathedral seemed to indicate that he was destined to high preferment in the diocese. A very few months later, however, he was invited to minister in one of the most important parishes in the country, St. Peter's, Leeds. His stay at Leeds was all too short but even so his attractive personality and deep spiritual convictions left their mark in and beyond church and academic circles in the city.

His consecration as the second Bishop of Blackburn, in succession to Bishop Herbert, who had been translated to the see of Norwich, took place in 1942 and his tall, athletic figure became thenceforward a familiar sight in the densely populated diocese. Though under modern conditions a bishop's days are continually crowded with administrative matters. Bishop Askwith, clear-minded and scholarly, was determined that he should not lose sight of the main purpose of all who serve the Church, pastoral work. He was indefatigable in holding confirmation and his fine voice was often heard preaching not only in his own cathedral but in many lesser churches in his diocese. Above all, he had that higher kind of tact that does not arise from a determination to be tactful and this gift, allied to sterling qualities of heart and mind, gained him the respect and affection of his flock. In November, 1951, he was appointed Prelate of the Order of St. Michael and St. George and that same year he was made an honorary fellow of his old college.

THE SEE OF GLOUCESTER

Translated in 1954 to the See of Gloucester. Askwith was forced, largely through the strain of overwork, to move to a diocese where the demands made upon him would be lighter. In fact he found himself busier than ever, but regaining much of his health he began soon to throw himself wholeheartedly into the life of the diocese, gaining the confidence and affection of his clergy, bringing the laity much more into the counsels of the Church, and persuading them both that they must look forward, and not back. His Visitation Charges, given in 1960, were published under the title *Towards 2,000 A.D.* In fact the older he got the more he urged them to look into the future and to see there not difficulties but opportunities, and towards these he never grew tired of pointing.

If anything he grew stronger as the years went by, which sometimes quite falsely gave the impression of intolerance and insensitivity. His inner integrity shone through all the time: his infinite patience with difficult people and situations made him lovable, and the three attractive qualities—a sense of humour, an amused contempt of all pomposity, and a love and delight in flowers and children. These last lay behind all his concern for education, and his Christmas Party for the children of the clergy was one of the occasions to which they looked forward most.

These qualities all helped to make up a "real" man: a man of God and Bishop of the Church for whom many will always be thankful. He was connected with the Children's Council of the Church Assembly for a long time and was chairman of the National Society from 1960. He married in 1928 Margaret Sibyl Luis, daughter of Mr. G. W. L. Fernandez. There were no children of the marriage.

July 17, 1962.

Anthony Asquith, who did much to establish the reputation of the British film industry in the 1920s and 1930s, died in a London nursing home on February 21, 1968. He was 65.

Anthony Asquith was born in London on November 9, 1902. Son of the first Earl of Oxford and Asquith, the Liberal statesman and former Prime Minister, by his second marriage to Margot Tennant, he was educated at Winchester and Balliol; on coming down from Oxford he went to the United States with his sister for six months and studied American film-making in Hollywood. His interest in film-making had begun at Oxford or earlier—in 1925 he was one of the founder members of the Film Society—and when he returned to England he obtained a job at British Instructional Films under H. Bruce Woolfe, who was impressed by a script he submitted. At first he served his apprenticeship as a sort of general factotum around the studios, and on the first film with which he was associated, *Boadicea* (1926), it is recorded that he worked as property-master, assistant make-up man, assistant editor and stand-in for Phyllis Neilson-Terry in the more hazardous chariot scenes.

However, this arduous apprenticeship bore fruit when Woolfe gave him the chance to direct, under the supervision of A. V. Bramble, his own story, *Shooting Stars* (1928). This was a new departure in British films, a subtle and sophisticated study of life in a film studio, and the technique was remarkably assured and inventive, only very occasionally self-consciously experimental: even reseen today the film has not lost its elegance and charm.

UNDERGROUND THRILLER

It was followed by *Underground*, a thriller taking place mainly in the London Underground, which was briskly directed and excellently photographed but offered less opportunity for Asquith's sly touches of humour, which have often been the principal hallmark of his films. There followed an Anglo-German venture, *The Runaway Princess*, and then one of his biggest early successes. *A Cottage on Dartmoor*, an effective thriller which pointed the way to the future by including a brief sound sequence.

Asquith's first sound film was *Tell England*, an adaptation of Ernest Raymond's novel about Gallipoli. This scored a triumphant success at the time, and though the personal drama has sometimes dated rather badly, the free and imaginative use of sound and especially the admirably handled battle sequences (in the staging of which Asquith was assisted by Geoffrey Barkas) remain impressive. His next film, *Dance, Pretty Lady*, adapted from Compton Mackenzie's novel *Carnival*, was a great artistic success, made with real atmospheric feeling and containing some good ballet sequences, but did not achieve much success commercially: the next year, in 1932, British Instructional Films merged with British International and Asquith passed through a period of uncertainty. During the next six years, unable to find a congenial production set-up, he directed only three remakes of foreign films, *The Lucky Number* (a good light comedy). *Unfinished Symphony* and *Moscow Nights*.

Finally in 1938 he had the chance to make a worthwhile film again when he was signed by Gabriel Pascal to direct the screen version of Shaw's *Pygmalion*. This film offered ample opportunities for the exercise of his major talents: the fluid handling of long dialogue scenes, lightness of touch in comedy and a feeling for the shape and flow of the film as a whole. His direction of actors (in collaboration with Leslie Howard) also brought the best out of his cast, and the film achieved enormous success in this country and abroad, a success consolidated by his next film, *French Without Tears*. *French Without Tears* initiated a long series of collaborations with Terence Rattigan; of Asquith's next dozen or so feature films, seven were wholly or partly scripted by Rattigan.

During the war Asquith found himself involved, like many other distinguished directors, in making topical thrillers and war stories as well as occasional documentaries for the Government. Among the thrillers were *Freedom Radio*, *Cottage to Let* and *Uncensored*, all capable enough but allowing little scope for the director's individuality, and among the documentaries *Channel Incident, Rush Hour*, and the excellent *Welcome to Britain*, an informal guide to Britain for American troops. More personal, however, were the light comedy *Quiet Wedding*, the stylish period novelette *Fanny by Gaslight*, and especially *The Demi-Paradise*, a touching and wryly amusing picture of the British at war seen through the eyes of a visiting Russian (Laurence Olivier), which incidentally has a good claim to be regarded as the original of the post-war Ealing type of comedy. Asquith's last film of the war, *The Way to the Stars*, another Rattigan subject, remains for many his most moving achievement.

After the war the association of Asquith and Rattigan continued with the formation of a company, International Screenplays, to film Rattigan's plays, the first two in the series being *While the Sun Shines* and *The Winslow Boy*.

SKILFUL ADAPTATION

Asquith showed in these all his habitual skill in imparting fluidity to screen versions of stage originals, but his next film, *The Woman in Question*, from an original screenplay showing the same woman through the eyes of five different people, gave more opportunity for the development of a specifically cinematic style free from the trammels of the stage. From this film on he alternated stage adaptation with original film subjects; among the former two more Rattigan adaptations, *The Browning Version* and *The Final Test*, and a beautifully mounted version of *The Importance of Being Earnest* graced by an unusually distinguished cast: among the latter two of his most individual films, *The Young Lovers*, a tragic romance set against a background of international politics, and *Orders To Kill*, a subtle psychological study of a wartime political killing. In 1958 he renewed his collaboration with the producer Anatole de Grunwald, with whom he had worked on *The Demi-Paradise*, *The Way to the Stars* and several other films, to film *The Doctor's Dilemma* and *Libel*. His later films included Shaw's *The Millionaires*, with Sophia Loren and Peter Sellers. *The V.I.P.s* with Elizabeth Taylor and Richard Burton, and *The Yellow Rolls-Royce* with Ingrid Bergman, Rex Harrison, Shirley MacLaine, and Omar Sharif.

Perhaps at heart Anthony Asquith always remained a straightforward and old-fashioned romantic, with a romanticism which underlay his essentially kindly and good-natured comedy and came unashamedly to the surface in his dramas, from *Tell England* to *The Young Lovers*. His control over his medium was complete, to such an extent that his unusual skill and stylistic polish were often, perhaps too often, called in to produce workmanlike versions of stage plays which allowed him little freedom for personal creations. Nevertheless, a record including such films as *Shooting Stars*, *Tell England*, *Pygmalion*, *French Without Tears*, *The Demi-Paradise*, *The Importance of Being Earnest*, *The Young Lovers*, *Orders to Kill* and *The Doctor's Dilemma* could not but ensure its holder a minor but quite secure place among the world's best directors.

He was a governor of the British Film Institute and president of the Association of Cinematograph, Television and Allied Technicians.

February 22, 1968.

Lady Asquith of Yarnbury, D.B.E., better known as Lady Violet Bonham Carter, daughter of the Right Hon. Herbert Henry Asquith, first Earl of Oxford and Asquith, K.G., and one of the most distinguished Liberal spokesmen, polemicists, and orators of her age and generation died in London on February 19, 1969. She was 81. By her death English public life loses a sterling character; humane, progressive and cultural causes a gallant fighter; and an innumerable host of people of all parties a warm and generous friend.

She was patron of the United Nations Association. She had also served as a Governor of the Old Vic from 1945 onwards, as a Governor of the B.B.C. from 1941 to 1946, as president of the Liberal Party from 1944 to 1945, and subsequently as a vice-president, and as president of the Women's Liberal Federation from 1923 to 1925 and again during the six years of the Second World War.

Born on April 15, 1887, and educated in Dresden and in Paris, Helen Violet Asquith was the fourth of the five children of Asquith and his first wife, Helen Kelsall Melland, the youngest being Cyril, later Lord Asquith of Bishopstone. In September, 1891, when Violet Asquith was four, her mother died. She was five when her father became Home Secretary in the fourth and last Gladstone Ministry of 1892, and 18 when he accepted in December, 1905, the Chancellorship of the Exchequer in the Campbell-Bannerman Administration. Asquith had married Margot Tennant in 1894. In April, 1908, he achieved the Premiership in the month of his daughter Violet's coming of age.

The Cabinet crisis of December, 1916, and the incoming of a "new combination" under Lloyd George—a veritable *coup d'Etat*—provoked a 12-year internecine party warfare.

PRIDE IN FATHER

Throughout this phase, the daughter was, as always, the father's most loyal and most redoubtable partisan. "To a freakishly developed gift of expression and a verbal memory hardly inferior to her father's", averred J. A. Spender and Cyril Asquith in their *Life of Lord Oxford and Asquith*, "she adds perhaps the most devastating powers of ridicule of which her acquaintances have any experience. A being of tenacious and protective loyalties, and a born partisan, she is always prepared to mobilize these formidable gifts in defence of her friends, to whom they are worth many battalions."

Fighting on the Liberal platform beside her father, it was at Paisley that Lady Violet won her political and oratorical spurs. It was in the four Paisley contests that her speeches attained both their consummate artistry and their elegance of form, qualities which enshrined her rhetoric in the memory of her hearers long after her choice of phrase, however felicitous, had been forgotten. For indeed she conceived each address as a unit, and always felt compelled to select her speaking engagements with care.

The Coupon Election of December, 1918, had decimated organized Liberalism. Asquith, after 32 years' continuous service, was rejected by East Fife. In February, 1920, however, the electors of Paisley returned him to the House of Commons, where he forthwith took over from Sir Donald Maclean the leadership of the "Wee Frees" It was no mean triumph for the Asquithian policy of full Dominion Home Rule status for seething Nationalist Ireland and for the new and comprehensive Liberal programme on which he had fought. He contrived to hold the seat in 1922, and again in 1923. When Lloyd George spoke for him in the Free Trade Election of 1923, and opponents acclaimed the synthesis of the lion and the lamb, Lady Violet rejoined. "I have never seen Mr. Lloyd George look less voracious or my father more uneatable".

Then came the Campbell case and the Russian Treaty. Liberals reviled, on the one hand, for allowing minority Labour Government the reins of office, and on the other, for ejecting it, fell from 158 to 42. At Paisley, in spite of the "almost Prussian perfection" of the machine, and in the full knowledge that, as Lady Violet recorded in a three-page narrative for the official biography, "argument and appeal were going to play no part whatever", Asquith was decisively defeated. There is a compelling pathos in the last paragraph of this report, where she recalled the homeward journey.

MADE HIS PEACE

She asked her father, in "an agony of solicitude", whether he had in his bag a "P. G. Wodehouse", only to be assured that he had acquired "four brand new ones!" He had "made his peace with events". "My wounds were healed", she concluded, "for I knew that he was invulnerable". Such were her love and her sustenance of his cause throughout the vicissitudes of the four final years until his death in 1928.

Little by little, during the "isthmus years" between the two World Wars, Violet Bonham Carter won a reputation for international statesmanship of a high order. The late 1920s were the years of the Lloyd George ascendancy in her party. In October, 1931, she declared for the National Government, repudiated as claptrap all talk of "the clamour of bankers and financiers", demanded the maintenance of credit, and urged "an international rather than a narrowly national approach" and "a real effort to break all trade barriers between nations and thaw those frozen streams of credit, wealth, and goods which can alone bring back life to a perishing world". Two months after the passing of the Import Duties Act and three months after the promulgation of the Cabinet "agreement to differ", Lady Violet was seconding Major Gwilym Lloyd George's Free Trade resolution at the National Liberal Federation annual meeting at Clacton in April, 1932, indicating the new Protectionist "Star Chamber" and exhorting the rank and file to lead in the fiscal battle. If retaliation were effective, she sallied, Protectionist states ought to have retaliated tariffs out of existence.

"A few voices crying in the wilderness", she proclaimed in June, 1932, writing in the old *Yorkshire Observer*, "repeat the simple truths—that we can never buy security by force; that free interchange between peoples is essential not merely to the prosperity but to the peace of the world; that while charity begins at home, trade must begin abroad; that to forgive a debtor is not merely better ethics, but better policy, than to insist on a pound of flesh we shall never get". That summer brought with it Ottawa, and all that Ottawa implied, and 11 Free Trade Ministers, headed by Sir Herbert Samuel, withdrew in protest from the Government.

Meanwhile the storm-clouds had been gathering over Germany, and in May, 1933, a blasting attack by Lady Violet on Herr von Papen opened a sustained and withering onslaught on the personnel and the institutions of the Third Reich. During the thirties she was in the vanguard of the League of Nations Union crusade and its offensive for collective security as well as of Churchill's Focus for Freedom and Peace campaign. Advocacy was her forte. "What is a trade union but collective security in action?" she asked. "Let us apply it with the same loyalty and courage in the international field".

Lady Violet played a leading part, too, with Sir Archibald Sinclair (later Viscount Thurso) in the fierce and historic agitation for the creation of a Ministry of Supply and for the inclusion of Churchill in the Chamberlain Ministry, though she never ceased to deplore Mr. Churchill's acceptance of the offer of the Conservative Party leadership of the nation.

CIVIL DEFENCE

Another theme which preoccupied her in those tempestuous years was the creation of a Ministry of Civil Defence.

Ever since Count Richard Coudenhove-Kalergi had launched the Pan Europa movement in Vienna, the concept of the organic unity of Europe had captivated her generous imagination. In the postwar years, with Benelux, O.E.E.C., E.P.U., the Council of Europe, the Schuman Community, and the Common Market and Free Trade zone slowly patterning themselves into a United States of Europe, that cause was her foremost love. With her, as with others, the assassination by the French National Assembly of M. Pleven's project for an E.D.C. supranational army left its scars.

For Lady Violet the cause of freedom was one and indivisible, whether the place and the occasion be Budapest or Serowe, Johannesburg, or the House of Lords in its debate on Viscount Samuel's Rights and Liberties of the Subject Bill. In domestic politics her major interests were liberty in all its facets, family allowances (she fought alongside Eleanor Rathbone in that battle) and electoral reform (with a propensity towards the single transferable variety but a willingness, too, to experiment, *faute de mieux*, with the alternative vote). She suffered a sharp reverse in a triangular contest in Wells in 1945. She was narrowly defeated in 1951 in a bid to capture Colne Valley. Since the Second World War, Lady Violet's counsel was much sought after as one of the "Elder Statesmen" of the Liberal Party Committee (formerly the "Shadow Cabinet"). She was appointed D.B.E. in 1953.

In 1963 she delivered the Romanes lecture at Oxford, the first woman to do so.

In 1965 she published *Winston Churchill as I Knew Him*, an account of a long friendship with the great statesman.

Hers was a warm and vibrant personality. An occasional acidity in no way militated against her fundamental kindliness, lively wit and talent for friendship. She was never one to believe that loyalty and neutrality could be harnessed to each other. Even to the most casual of observers her most self-evident characteristics were a complete integrity and an undeviating fidelity, coupled with a deep awareness of the majesty of words.

She married in 1915 Maurice Bonham Carter, an old family friend, and, at that time, her father's principal private secretary. He died in 1960. They had four children. Their daughter Laura Miranda, married in 1938 Mr. Joseph Grimond, who became in 1950 Member of Paliament for Orkney and Shetland and formerly Leader of the Liberal Party.

February 20, 1969.

Nancy Lady Astor, C.H., the first woman to take her seat as a member of the House of Commons, died on May 2, 1964, at Grimsthorpe Castle, Lincolnshire. She was 84.

In any age or country Nancy Astor would have been remarkable for outstanding vitality, personality, charm and will-power. She was always a delight to the eye, small, compact, a finely drawn profile, a classic head, growing more and more exquisite with the years. She was made all of one piece, a perfect working model, always well-dressed. From the first day she entered the House of Commons in neat black with touches of white at collar, in appearance she struck the exact note and set the style for her feminine colleagues in years to come.

Nancy Witcher Langhorne was born of an old Virginian family on May 19, 1879, on the same day as her future husband, William Waldorf Astor, was born in New York. In 1897 she married Robert Gerald Shaw, of Boston, from whom she obtained a divorce in 1903 and in 1906 she married Waldorf Astor. When he succeeded to the viscounty and resigned from the representation in Parliament of the Sutton Division of Plymouth Lady Astor was elected as Unionist member on November 28, 1919. She was the first woman to sit in the House of Commons, being introduced by Balfour and Lloyd George. Countess Markievicz, who did not take her seat, had been elected by an Irish constituency in the Sinn Fein interest at a slightly earlier date. From 1919 to 1945 Lady Astor continued to represent Plymouth and most of her life and work were closely identified with the city, of which during the Second World War she was Lady Mayoress.

In Parliament she naturally devoted herself mainly to the claims of women and children, speaking with gaiety or gravity according to her mood, but never dully and always briefly and sometimes brilliantly. Her worst fault was a habit of interruption which, however tempered with wit, was apt to cause annoyance. Temperance, education, nursery schools, women police were subjects which deeply interested her.

Like Zenobia, and also in St. James's Square, Lady Astor was a famous political hostess and her house was the meeting place of distinguished visitors to the metropolis, especially Americans.

GANDHI OR GRANDI

One day it might be Gandhi, the next Grandi and the following day a batch of social workers or Cabinet Ministers or Charlie Chaplin or Ruth Draper or G.B.S. And there were from time to time the huge party gatherings comparable with those of Londonderry House or of the Devonshire House of an earlier day. On the top of the staircase, sparkling with jewels, she welcomed each guest with a bantering quip or jest and was the central figure throughout the evening.

Her energy was extraordinary. After a long day in London and in the House she would return to Cliveden about seven, change into tennis clothes and play two or even three sets of singles with one of her nieces; then down to the river (before the war) in her cream-coloured car, driven at speed; she would swim across the Thames, talking all the time about God, or advising someone on the bank about the way to live his, or usually her, life, touch the bottom on the far bank, tell the swans to go away, and swim back still talking. In earlier years she was a dashing rider and a sure shot; later golf was her favourite game. She played it well and conversationally and distinguished herself in parliamentary matches.

She had a sharp sense of the ridiculous and could have made a fortune on the variety stage. No one who saw her Christmastide impersonations in the old days at Cliveden, egged on by her sisters Phyllis and Nora, will ever forget her clever performances. Dressed in a hunting coat of her husband's and her hair hidden under a large black velvet huntsman's cap she became the little foreign visitor, here for the hunting season; or with a row of celluloid teeth worn crookedly, an upperclass Englishwoman who thought Americans peculiar. Someone once said she was a cross between Joan of Arc and Gracie Fields. She wasn't courageous, if by courage is meant mastery of fear, for she did not know about fear. She was fearless of physical dangers, of criticism, of people.

No one could be kinder, more tender, generous, comforting and swift to help in time of trouble. She loved being needed and was at her best in a crisis. She would have denied it but she had an innate sense of drama and had a flair for dealing with people *en masse*. American politicians and journalists of the old school were bewitched by her. The later, war-time journalists were scared by her outspokenness and refused to be charmed. It is recorded that Gladstone asked his wife whether she would prefer to know nothing and say anything she pleased, or to know everything and say next to nothing on matters of foreign and domestic policy. Lady Astor got the best of both worlds, knowing everything and saying anything she pleased.

Her matriarchal feelings were strong and she liked to feel in touch with the whole circle at all times. She held the family together, including nieces and nephews. Within this circle she loved to recall Virginia days, her father, Colonel Langhorne, her sisters and their beaux. During a visit to the States in 1922 she made 40 speeches, mainly in Virginia, "without a single *faux pas*" reported an American correspondent.

Her deep religious sense found its formal setting in the Christian Science Church and she was a diligent student of the Scriptures, with a strong horror of sin and a crusading spirit which spurred her to pursue reforms regardless of party divisions. There were four persons whose influence and friendship and characters she was never tired of acknowledging with gratitude and affection: Rachel Macmillan, Henry Jones, Arthur Balfour, and Philip Lothian.

After her withdrawal from Parliament in June, 1945, when she did not stand for reelection. Lady Astor continued her interest in the city she had represented so long and made regular visits while her health permitted.

On July 16, 1959, she was made an honorary Freeman of the City of Plymouth.

In the same year Lady Astor performed the launching ceremony for H.M.S. Plymouth, first ship for 250 years to bear the name, presented a diamond and sapphire necklace to be worn by Lady Mayoresses of Plymouth, and gave her home at 3, Elliot Terrace, overlooking the Hoe to the city for use as a Lord Mayor's residence. Its use was later modified to a place for the accommodation of official visitors.

She was made C.H. in 1937.

Her husband died in 1952 and she is survived by her four sons, Viscount Astor; David Astor, editor of the *Observer*: Michael Astor: Major J. J. Astor; and by her daughter, the Countess of Ancaster.

May 4, 1964.

Lord Astor, who was M.P. for East Fulham from 1935 to 1945 and for the Wycombe division of Buckingham from 1951 to 1952, died on March 8, 1966 at Nassau, where he was on holiday. He was 58.

William Waldorf Astor was born on August 13, 1907, the eldest son of the second Viscount and Nancy Astor, the first woman to take her seat as a member of the House of Commons. He was educated at Eton and New College, Oxford, where he gained a half-blue for polo and steeplechasing. His love of horses and riding remained throughout his life.

During 1931–32 he worked for the Pilgrim Trust. He had travelled extensively in the Far East for the Institute of Public Relations, and in 1932 was private secretary to Lord Lytton on the League of Nations Commission of Inquiry to Manchuria. He then spent a year working with the unemployment division of the National Council for Social Service, and accompanied the then Duke of Kent on several tours of industrial areas.

In the general election of 1935 he stood for East Fulham as one of the youngest Unionist candidates, and reversed the result of the 1933 by-election, gaining the seat with a majority of 1,054 over his Labour opponent. He was to represent the constituency for 10 years. From 1936–39 he was Parliamentary Private Secretary to Sir Samuel Hoare while he was First Lord of the Admiralty (1936–37) and Home Secretary (1937–39). In 1939 Astor was commissioned in the R.N.V.R. and served during the war in the Middle East. In 1944 he became chairman of the Council of the R.N.V.R. Officers' Association. He stood again for East Fulham in the general election of 1945, but was defeated by his Labour opponent in a three-cornered fight.

ELECTIONS AT WYCOMBE

He contested the Wycombe division of Buckingham in 1950, when he was narrowly defeated, and 1951, when he gained the seat for the Conservatives with a majority of 1,753.

He succeeded his father in 1952. This marked the end of his political career in the Commons, and he devoted himself to the management of his family's affairs and to charities. He was particularly interested in hospitals and aid for refugees.

He was a prominent member of the executive committee of the U.K. Committee for World Refugee Year 1959–1960, and since July, 1960, had been chairman of the Standing Conference of British Organizations for Aid to Refugees.

For his work in connexion with Hungarian refugees—whom he helped to rescue on the Austrian border—he was awarded the Grand Cross of Merit of the Sovereign Military Order of Malta in 1957. A member of several hospital management committees, Astor was on the board of the Great Ormond Street Hospital for Sick Children. He remained an occasional speaker in the House of Lords.

He was patron and good friend of the artist Sir Stanley Spencer and did him many kindnesses in Spencer's closing years. He guaranteed Spencer an income and invited him to finish the large picture "Christ preaching at Cookham Regatta". It was Astor who gave the address at Spencer's funeral in December, 1959, and he joined together with other friends of the painter to provide funds to convert the old Wesleyan Chapel at Cookham into the Stanley Spencer Gallery.

THE PROFUMO AFFAIR

He was tenant of Cliveden, which his father had given to the National Trust in 1942. In 1956 he first sub-let a cottage on the estate to Stephen Ward, who as an osteopath had treated Astor in the past and had become a friend. It was during a weekend in July, 1961 that Profumo, who with his wife was a guest at Cliveden, first met Christine Keeler, who was staying with Ward. The incident was described in detail in the Denning Report on the Profumo affair. Lord Denning also said that Astor had placed all records of his bank accounts and financial dealings fully before him. He held that there was no truth in the rumours that Astor had paid money to anyone in furtherance of the disappearance of Miss Keeler.

Astor did not have the success of his father

on the turf, although he won many races. He kept about 23 mares at stud. Ambiguity and Hornbeam were his best racehorses, Ambiguity winning the Oaks and Hornbeam losing the St. Leger only by three-quarters of a length. Some of the other races won by Astor's horses were the Great "Jubilee" twice, the Jockey Club Cup, the White Rose Stakes. Winston Churchill Stakes, Greenham Stakes, Great Voltigeur Stakes, and the Queen's Prize. The Cliveden Stud bred Ambiguity, Hornbeam, Counsel, and Grey of Falloden as the outstanding horses among its winners.

Among his business interests, he was a director of the North British and Mercantile Insurance Company, the *Observer*, and the Trust Corporation of the Bahamas.

He was married three times: first in 1945 to the Hon. Sarah Norton, daughter of the sixth Baron Grantley. They had one son, his heir, the Hon. William Waldorf Astor, who was born in 1951. The marriage was dissolved in 1953 and he married secondly in 1955 Philippa Victoria, daughter of Lieutenant-Colonel Henry Hunloke. They had one daughter. This marriage was dissolved in 1960 and he married, thirdly, Janet Bronwen Alun, daughter of Judge Sir Alun Pugh. They had two daughters.

March 9, 1966.

Air Marshal Sir Richard Llewellyn Roger Atcherley, K.B.E., C.B., A.F.C., died on April 18, 1970, at the age of 66. He was one of the most striking personalities the Royal Air Force has produced.

Atcherley was born on January 11, 1904, the son of Major-General Sir Llewellyn Atcherley, a former Chief Constable of the West Riding and H. M. Inspector of Constabulary.

In 1922, Atcherley entered the newly founded R.A.F. College, Cranwell, which he was to command 23 years later. After graduating in 1924 he was posted to No. 29 (Fighter) Squadron, then still partially equipped with Sopwith Snipe fighters. He took an instructor's course at the Central Flying School and became a flying instructor, first with his old squadron and then with No. 23 (Fighter) Squadron.

In 1928 while an instructor at the Central Flying School he was chosen as a member of the R.A.F. teams for the 1929 Schneider Trophy race. Atcherley flew one of the Supermarine S.6 seaplanes (designed by R. J. Mitchell), from which sprang the Spitfire fighter. Although he was disqualified for not completely rounding a pylon during the race itself, he set up a record of 331.6 m.p.h. over a distance of 100 kilometres and broke the lap record at 332.49 m.p.h. In the same year with George Stainforth he won the King's Cup race in a Gloster Grebe at an average speed of considerably less than half the Schneider Trophy times.

In 1930, and for the next few years, he was invited by the National Air Race Committee to fly in the meetings held at Chicago and Cleveland. He brought "crazy" flying to a fine art, his "props" including hunting pink, a saddle and reins and a professorial top-hat and umbrella. During this time he was normally in the Middle East serving with No. 14 (Bomber) Squadron at Amman, where his aerial exploits took on a suitably oriental aspect.

Returning home in 1934 he was posted as test pilot to the Royal Aircraft Establishment at Farnborough where he developed a system of air-to-air refuelling which was demonstrated at the 1936 R.A.F. Display.

COMMAND OF NIGHT FIGHTERS

He took the R.A.F. Staff College course in 1937 and after a spell on air staff duties at Training Command, he joined the Inspector General's department. Soon after war broke out he was given command of No. 219 Squadron, which attempted with its Blenheim night fighters to intercept German raiders off the north-east coast of England. It was unrewarding work and Atcherley responded with relief to an appointment as garrison commander to the small R.A.F. fighter force which was put into the Narvik area for the ill-starred Norwegian campaign.

Returned to the United Kingdom, Atcherley was given command of the R.A.F. fighter station at Drem. Here he applied his ingenuity and appreciation of the night-fighter pilots' problems by devising an airfield lighting system which gave much help to the pilots while denying to enemy aircraft in the vicinity the same degree of assistance. The Drem lighting system became in fact standard R.A.F. equipment throughout the war and for some years afterwards. In 1941 and 1942 he commanded other fighter stations, flying whenever his duties permitted.

INITIATIVE IN DESERT

At the beginning of 1942 he was given command of No. 211 Group in the Middle East Air Force, which held the fighter wings of the Desert Air Force. This command gave Atcherley great scope for initiative and enterprise. He had a varied mixture of units, British, American, South African, Australian and Polish. He welded them into a formation of precision, efficiency and dash, combined with a professional technique that was a pattern for future Allied tactical support. As a highly successful leader in this field he was, like others who had proved themselves in Africa, selected to prepare for similar operations in Europe by being posted in December, 1943, to the Allied Expeditionary Air Forces.

This task completed, he was called upon to use his vital experience in a narrower but highly important field. The need was apparent to have a specialized unit to study and develop fighter tactics and techniques, and in 1944, the R.A.F. Central Fighter Establishment was formed for this purpose with Atcherley as the first Commandant. The war over, he was made Commandant of the newly reopened R.A.F. College, Cranwell, in September, 1945.

NEW AIR FORCE

In 1949 he was again given the opportunity to break new ground when he was appointed Air Officer Commanding the embryo air force of Pakistan. It was an uphill struggle to build from the sketchiest of precedent, plans and resources, but the excellent qualities the Pakistan Air Force showed in later years spoke well of the foundations he laid in the two years he commanded it. He returned to become A.O.C. of No. 12 (Fighter) Group in May, 1951 responsible for the air defences of the northern and eastern part of the United Kingdom, and early in 1954 went out to Washington as Head of Air Force Staff.

In 1955, he became a Commander-in-Chief, of Flying Training Command and an Air Marshal.

Early in his Service career he became generally known as "Batchy".

From 1959 to 1961 he was co-ordinator Anglo-American Community Relations; and from 1959 to 1965 he was Sales Director Folland Aircraft Co.

Like his twin brother, Atcherley never married.

April 20, 1970.

C. T. Atkinson, Emeritus Fellow of Exeter College, died in Oxford on February 18, 1964. He was 89.

Christopher Thomas Atkinson was born on September 6, 1874, elder son of Edmund Atkinson, professor at the Staff College. From Clifton he went up to Oxford as a demy of Magdalen College in 1893. After taking a second class in Classical Honour Moderations in 1895, he went on to get a first class in Modern History in 1896 and then a second class in Greats in 1898. In 1899 he won the Lothian Prize with an essay on Michel de l'Hopital. He had already, in 1898, been elected to a Fellowship at Exeter College. Oxford, and had thus embarked upon his long and remarkably successful career as a history tutor. In 1908 he published his *History of Germany 1715–1815*, his largest and most ambitious book, besides contributing chapters to the eighteenth-century volumes of the *Cambridge Modern History*.

AT WAR OFFICE

By 1912 he had also completed, in five volumes, the *Letters and Papers relating to the First Dutch War, 1652–4*, begun by S. R. Gardiner for the Navy Records Society in 1898. In January, 1912, he married Cosotte, daughter of Major-General Sir J. F. Maurice.

Soon afterwards, the 1914–18 War caused his only prolonged absence from historical studies and teaching. In August, 1914, he was attached to the General Staff at the War Office, being transferred in March, 1915, to work under the Committee of Imperial Defence. He did not return to Oxford until 1919. For the ensuing 22 years, years saddened in mid-course by the death of his wife, he again played an active and highly useful part in the affairs of his College, the History Faculty, and the University O.T.C. Despite a heavy load of teaching over an extraordinarily wide range of periods, he found time to write a life of *Marlborough* (1921) which at once became a standard work; a *History of the Royal Dragoons 1661–1934* (1934); the *South Wales Borderers 1689–1937*

(1937); and a number of articles, chiefly on military subjects.

Retirement in 1941 and election by Exeter to an Emeritus Fellowship by no means implied the end of his activity. During the 1939–45 War he was an enthusiastic Home Guard and in the overcrowded years after the war he was pressed back into service as an examiner, while harassed college tutors turned to him often for help, and rarely in vain.

UNFASHIONABLE VIEWS

Atkinson's ackowledged preeminence as an authority on military history and his remarkable success as a teacher were both based upon the depth of his knowledge and the directness and clarity of his exposition rather than upon the fashionableness of his views. For he was not easily swayed by historical fashions and his interest, like his written style, had few frills. A certain lack of sympathy with aspects other than the political and military, which was perhaps his chief limitation as an historian, could sometimes become exasperating to pupils who were more attracted than he was towards the expanding frontiers of historical inquiry. Yet the exasperation was often provoked deliberately as a stimulus to harder thinking. For Atkinson's own common sense and clarity gave him a salutary intolerance of airy generalization or cloudy argument. Besides, he never forgot that he was teaching people as well as teaching history.

His comments, always pointed and often pungent, were sharpened by a mordant humour and enlivened from a rare fund of homely anecdote that impressed them even upon the most apathetic. But a "private hour"—to miscall it a "tutorial" was to invite prompt correction—with "the Atters" gave little chance for apathy, even for those who had negotiated a satisfactory *modus vivendi* with Pincher (a dog not unaptly named) or, later, with Perkin. His teaching, widely though it ranged, was backed by that astonishing memory and easy command of detail which enabled him to give off-hand the whereabouts of almost any unit of the British Army at any time from Marlborough's wars to the 1918 Armistice. Above all, he had that firm grasp of essentials amid the welter of detail that, as he was never tired of insisting, is the first requirement of an historian.

STRONG PREJUDICES

This clear, if in some respects limited, vision and the zest and vigour of his teaching were part and parcel of his personality. They showed themselves no less strongly in his comments upon the cricket in the Parks, which so often caused a small detour in his homeward walk from Exeter. His prejudices were numerous and strong, witness his unrelenting regret at the presence of women as members of the university. Yet these, too, were expressions of a character of rare individuality and overflowing vitality, and they could seldom wholly conceal the deep-rooted kindliness that grew more apparent the more one came to know him.

February 19, 1964.

Lord Attlee, K.G., P.C., O.M., C.H., F.R.S., who died in his sleep at Westminster Hospital on October 8, 1967, was Prime Minister for six and a half years in the third Labour Administration, the first to hold office with an independent majority in the House of Commons. His Government carried through, with unexampled speed, a comprehensive programme of nationalization and social reform. When the importance of that social revolution and the smoothness with which it was effected are set beside the surface qualities of the man who presided over it, there emerges the paradox that lurks in all assessments of his statesmanship.

Both his opponents and his more impatient colleagues were prone to underrate him as a political force. He was devoid of those external marks which Aristotle thought necessary for men of consequence—sincere and quietly impressive was the most that could be said of his public personality. More than any of his predecessors in the highest political office he was innocent of poses and deficient in the more popular arts of leadership. Much that he did was memorable: very little that he said.

The absence of these superficial qualities was a handicap in his exercise of democratic government. It contributed to the failure of his party to dispel the air of drabness that gathered over postwar socialism. But as a basis for judgment on Attlee's public life it is totally inadequate. Attlee came from a middle-class home and received a conventional education at public school and university. He was not an undergraduate socialist. His politics were grounded on his observation of life in the East End of London in the early 1900s, and were laced with local government and the "gas and water" socialism of the Webbs. He came to the leadership of the Labour Party not by the thrust of ambition but by virtue of his parliamentary competence and general acceptability. The party was still embittered by the events of 1931, its morale still shaken. Pacifists, meliorists and social revolutionaries warred within it. Attlee's influence was steadying, but not steadying enough to transform it into a convincing Opposition in the years before the war.

HONESTY OF APPROACH

"For myself", he once wrote, "I have seldom, if ever, had such a high opinion of my own judgment as to esteem it above that of the consensus of views of my colleagues. The majority are more likely to be right than I am. As a democrat I accept that position." This conceals the pertinacity with which he asserted his view when he had absolute confidence in it but it does explain his failure to conjure out of the Labour Party a consistent and acceptable alternative to the Government's policies in the period of dictatorial aggrandisement on the Continent.

By 1945 he had overcome this weakness. He had never shrunk from assuming responsibility; his post in the War Cabinet gave him experience in its exercise. He remained sensitively attuned to what his party could and could not be induced to accept. But the idea that his statesmanship began and ended in compliant chairmanship is completely wide of the mark. His role in the Labour Cabinet has often been misunderstood. He worked extremely closely with two or three senior colleagues, especially Bevin, and sometimes settled questions with them rather than with the full Cabinet. Many other Ministers in and outside the Cabinet went somewhat in awe of him, and his comments at ministerial meetings had on occasion a sharp and waspish note. Indeed, his language in private meetings and personal converse had a racy pointedness that was altogether lacking on the platform. In certain matters in which he felt confident of his own judgment—for instance, India and Abadan—he himself played a dominant part in the Cabinet. He was always ready to take upon himself clear and heavy responsibility, as in the remarkable decision that Britain should make an atom bomb in complete secrecy.

He was a guide rather than an imaginative leader, a pilot in charted waters rather than a pioneer. Yet his essentially practical mind did not exclude breadth of vision, most notably in his concept of the Commonwealth, which had occupied him from his early years in Parliament. He inspired respect more than devotion. He was a man who stood aloof and whose intimate friendship was rarely given. A steadiness of judgment, a matter-of-fact honesty of approach, and a quite uncommon degree of common sense mark him out as one of the least colourful and most effective of British Prime Ministers of this century.

He was born on January 3, 1883, the fourth of the eight children of Henry Attlee, a solicitor. He was educated at Haileybury and University College, Oxford, where he obtained second class honours in modern history. His shelves were filled with works of serious historical study, especially on the development of Parliament, many of which he managed to read even while Prime Minister. His sense of history was manifest in many of the larger political decisions that he had to make. He was called to the Bar by the Inner Temple in 1906.

GALLANT WAR RECORD

His early Conservative opinions underwent a rapid change, the result partly of personal reasoning, partly of experience of life in the East End, and parly of association with Sidney and Beatrice Webb. He joined the Fabian Society and became a member of the London School Board. After the publication of the Minority Report of the Poor Law Commission, he was appointed lecture-secretary of the organization the Webbs established for the furthering of the minority report's policy and later took the post of secretary of Toynbee Hall. In the meanwhile he and a younger brother had lived in Poplar in a workman's dwelling and also for a time he was manager of Haileybury House in Stepney. As an additional means of investigating working-class conditions of life Attlee took work at the docks. In 1911 he was lecturing at Ruskin College on trade unionism and trade union law. By now he had abandoned any intention of practising at the Bar and was giving himself to politics and social work. From 1913 to the outbreak of the First World War he was a lecturer at the London School of Economics in social science and administration and resumed the work after his return to civil life.

Attlee had a gallant record in the war. He was 31 years of age when, within a few weeks of the opening of hostilities, he joined the Inns of Court O.T.C. His first commission was in the 6th Battalion of The South Lancashire Regiment, with which in the following year he went to Gallipoli. Promotion came quickly and he was already a captain in command of a covering party at the Suvla Bay landing. Falling ill, he went to hospital in Malta. After the evacuation of Gallipoli in 1916 his battalion sailed for Mesopotamia and took part in the first and unsuccessful attempt to relieve the garrison in Kut. Severely wounded, he was invalided home. After recovery he served in the Tank Corps for a time but, returning to the infantry, and now a major, he was with the South Lancashires in France in 1918. Sickness sent him home again in the autumn and upon recovery he was discharged from the service.

In 1919 Stepney Council invited him to become Mayor. Unemployment was already a severe affliction in the East End and when an association of Labour mayors was formed to strengthen the hands of men with little administrative experience it was to Attlee that they turned for a chairman. He led a deputation of mayors on foot to Downing Street to convince the Prime Minister of the gravity of unemployment in both its social and individual consequences.

Attlee's parliamentary career began in 1922, when he stood for Limehouse and won a seat which he continued to hold till it lost its identity in the redistribution of 1948. Thereafter he sat for West Walthamstow. In the 1922 general election Labour won more seats than the Liberals and attained the status of the official Opposition. The total Labour vote had risen in 16 years from 323,000 to 4,312,000. The composition of the party also showed a marked development. Whereas formerly the trade unions had provided nearly all the Labour members, there was now a considerable admixture of middle class and professional elements. Ramsay MacDonald, returning to the House after four years' exile, was elected leader in succession to J. R. Clynes, and chose Attlee to be one of his private secretaries. The Parliament was shortlived.

Seeking a mandate for tariff reform, Stanley Baldwin appealed to the country at the end of 1923 and lost heavily, though still the leader of the largest party in the House of Commons. A combination of Labour and Liberals overthrew him and the first minority Labour Government entered upon a short and uneasy tenure of office. Attlee held the post of Under-Secretary for War (the Secretary of State being Stephen Walsh).

IN THE GOVERNMENT

In the election of 1924 Labour lost 41 seats; but Attlee's own position was unshaken, and, in opposition, he took up the task of presenting the party's case in Parliament, notably on the Electricity Bill and the Rating and Valuation Bill introduced by Neville Chamberlain—so that two experts on local government worthily crossed swords—and of building up the party in the country. Attlee was soon too much absorbed in national affairs to have time for local government. The severance came in the autumn of 1927 when he was appointed a member of the Statutory Commission on India, of which Sir John Simon was chairman. A large part of the next two years was occupied with a study of the political problems of India and the preparatory steps for the development of Indian self-government. It was in these two years that he formed the conclusions that guided his later Indian policy. He was still engaged on the work of the commission at the time of the 1929 election and for this reason had no place for several months in MacDonald's second Government.

An opening came in the spring of 1930 when Oswald Mosley, at odds with the Government on the measures necessary to combat unemployment, resigned the office of Chancellor of the Duchy. Attlee succeeded him but was not directly concerned, as Mosley had been, in the preparation of an unemployment policy. He assisted the Prime Minister with the work of the Imperial Conference which met in London in 1930 and became familiar with the wide differences on tariff policy which separated Labour Ministers from other Commonwealth Governments. He was also associated with Addison in the preparation of an agricultural policy. All this was quiet, unostentatious work. Later he was transferred to the Post Office and, being immersed in the duties of a post which was not of Cabinet rank, the ministerial crisis of 1931 found him, as it did most Ministers, unprepared and suspicious of a needless surrender. He certainly did not realize the gravity of the economic crisis.

MacDonald's formation of a coalition Government was wholly unexpected by his colleagues. Confronted with the division of opinion in the Cabinet, Attlee had no doubt of his personal decision, which was to remain with the party and go into opposition to the new Government. He had had close association with MacDonald (both in and out of office) but had retained a firm independence of opinion. In the autumn, when the coalition Government went to the country, the judgment passed on the Labour Party by a panic-stricken electorate was severe, and Labour returned with only 52 members. The National Government had the unwieldy majority of 493.

George Lansbury, the one surviving Minister of Cabinet rank, was elected leader and Attlee outrode the hurricane to become deputy leader.

ARDUOUS TIME

It was an arduous time for him. The criticism of Government policy devolved on so few, and Attlee was required to speak on a wide range of subjects and to speak often.

Attlee led his party in the general election of 1935. Only three weeks before the opening of the campaign Lansbury resigned. Attlee's succession to the leadership was challenged by Morrison and Greenwood, but he was elected after a second ballot. He stepped quietly and confidently into the vacant place. He returned to Westminster with a following of 154, and his leadership was confirmed.

The war in Abyssinia moved to its inevitable end in the absence of effective intervention by the League of Nations, Germany denounced the Treaty of Locarno, and the civil war in Spain disclosed the ominous share which Italy, Germany, and Russia were taking in the conflict, and Attlee more vehemently attacked the weakness of British policy. But a new note was heard in his speeches; he began to doubt whether the system of collective security could survive the shocks it was suffering. Continuing to accuse the Government of betraying the League, he continued also to oppose the increase of the armed forces. He now began, however, to shift the emphasis to the argument that a vote for the defence estimates implied support for the Government's foreign policy. This precarious and equivocal position began to be attacked by some of the more realistic Labour members of Parliament in the privacy of the party meeting, but it carried the support of the still large pacifist wing of the party, whose views Attlee felt he could not ignore. In the summer of 1936 he refused to support the recruiting campaign of a Government whose foreign policy he did not trust and whose armaments policy he thought futile and inept. He began to feel his way towards a more realistic and logical position. Before long the cynical disregard by Germany and Italy of the agreement on non-intervention in Spain brought him to face the contingency of war.

ATTITUDE TO HITLER

He was soon to show acute alarm at the increasing Nazi aggression and to realize the danger and even the imminence of war. Such was the ironical development of events that he had to deny that the Labour Party wanted war. Eden resigned office as foreign secretary. Austria was helplessly over-run in the March of 1938. Attlee now redefined the attitude of the Labour Party thoroughly aroused to the menace of Hitler's territorial ambitions. He posed the anxious question of whether, if we allowed the fortresses of liberty to be captured one by one, could this country survive? A few days later Chamberlain outlined his foreign policy. The Government could not accept an unconditional, automatic liability to go to war to defend an area—Czechoslovakia—where British vital interests were not directly concerned, but should war break out it was unlikely to be confined to those who had assumed such automatic obligations. Attlee's vigorous rejoinder, showing unwanted passion, was a declaration that we could not barter our freedom for peace and we could not have a peace of slavery.

Then came the Nazi pressure on Czechoslovakia. Attlee read the portents clearly and wondered for how long the world could continue to live under a militarist menace and how—sooner or later—would a war break out. It was a new experience for him—a zealous supporter of the no-more-war movement after the First World War, a steadfast believer in collective security and, almost to the end, an opposer of rearmament—to be confronted in his constituency with demonstrators who chanted in chorus "we want peace: Attlee wants war". His mind was made up and he declared that Britain and France could not in honour desert Czechoslovakia.

He was not deceived by the Munich agreement: it was but a temporary armistice and Hitler had won a tremendous victory.

The military catastrophes of the spring and early summer of 1940 compelled the formation of a National Government. Chamberlain sounded the Labour leaders on their willingness to join a reconstructed Ministry. They refused to serve under him but welcomed the opportunity to join an administration led by Churchill. Attlee became Lord Privy Seal, deputy Prime Minister and a member of the small War Cabinet. Leadership had come to him as the due of service rather than the prize of ambition, but it had made him the unquestioned head of the second largest party in the state. Now he was to reveal an unaffected readiness to disregard personal assertion, and to accept and even to seek partial effacement. Attlee was no rival of Winston Churchill's supremacy. He was an assiduous and able member of the small group of Ministers forming the War Cabinet, informed and able in council and steady in judgment. The War Cabinet itself was remarkably harmonious, and this harmony, derived in large measure from the knowledge and temper of the Labour movement, both political and industrial, which Attlee and Bevin supplied, was a powerful influence in maintaining an undistracted determination throughout the nation.

FORMING A CABINET

In 1942 while Churchill was in Washington it fell to Attlee to make one of the periodical reviews of the state of the war which Churchill had inaugurated. Hence forward he took the Prime Minister's place, in this and other ways, with some regularity as military strategy and the invasion of Europe, first from the south and afterwards from the west, more and more engrossed Churchill's time and energy. The grave turn of events in the Far East in 1942 brought an added responsibility to Attlee. Japan's drive through Malaya, Singapore, and the Dutch East Indies had caused deep apprehension in Australia and New Zealand, and they needed confirmation of the active concern of the Cabinet in London. Attlee became Secretary of State for Dominion Affairs and thus Australia, along with the other Commonwealth nations, had direct and continuous representation in the War Cabinet as well as special representation by their own Ministers when any were in London. He held the appointment for 16 months and relinquished it knowing that the unity of the Commonwealth was inviolable. He returned to the office of Lord President of the Council and was responsible for the coordination of home policy. The tide of war had turned, and the Government was preparing a social programme for application after the war. Attlee was able to say at the reopening of Parliament in November, 1943, that part of the reconstruction programme was already in legislative form.

Attlee went to the San Francisco conference in 1945 for the foundation of the United Nations organization in company with Anthony Eden, Foreign Secretary, Lord Cranborne (now Lord Salisbury), Secretary for the Dominions, and Lord Halifax, Ambassador at Washington. Victory in Europe was announced on May 8. Ten days later Churchill formally sent to Attlee a proposal that the coalition should continue until the end of the war with Japan. Churchill's letter was seen in draft by Attlee, who did not disapprove its purpose and indeed suggested an amendment likely to improve its chance of success. Churchill had proposed to say "It would give me great relief if you and your friends were found resolved to carry on with us until a decisive victory had been gained over Japan". Attlee's suggested interpolation, which Churchill embodied in his letter, was "In the meantime we should do our utmost to implement the proposals for social security and full employment contained in the White Papers which we have laid before Parliament". The Labour Party executive would not consider a prolongation of the coalition nor assent to a referendum on this single issue and the Labour members left the Government. Churchill formed a caretaker administration, Parliament was dissolved on June 15 and polling took place the following month. Labour's resounding triumph returned Attlee with 393 followers, an increase of 227, and a majority far greater than he had regarded as adequate for the socialization of the key industries and services. He became Prime Minister at the age of 62.

Attlee's first Cabinet reflected the currents of opinion and even the various moods and tempers within the party and established a convenient balance between the distinctively trade unionist and the other elements in the party structure.

BEVIN'S MOVE

The transfer of Ernest Bevin from the Ministry of Labour and National Service to the Foreign Office caused more surprise than it should have done. For the strategic posts in the van of the socialist revolution Attlee chose men of aggressive energy and debating skill. Mr. Dalton was sent to the Treasury to take charge of the nationalization of the Bank of England and to control monetary and credit policy. To the salient post of Minister of Fuel and Power for the nationalization of the coalmining and electricity industries, Attlee appointed Mr. Shinwell, while the drive and ruthless vitality of Aneurin Bevan were harnessed to the housing programme of the Ministry of Health and the inception of a national health service which was certain to encounter difficulties notwithstanding general assent to its essential principles. The development of relations between Britain and India and the consummation of Indian self-government was entrusted to the urbane, wise and tactful Pethick-Lawrence. As the Government's policy unfolded and India was found to be unready to reconcile its major communal antagonisms, Attlee's Government added to the incentive of self determination the constraint of a time limit for the continuance of the British occupation.

The Government launched its massive legislative programme, but these great plans alone did not absorb all Attlee's concern. He endeavoured to arouse the country to the imminent and grave dangers of inflation and to temper majority rule, as he would also temper the pride of victory, with regard for human qualities and rights. He strongly maintained that the one principle to save the world was the Christian principle that all men were brothers. In the autumn of the year he went to America to discuss with President Truman, and afterwards with Mackenzie King, the problems of atomic energy. The result was a tripartite declaration of willingness to share basic scientific information for peaceful ends accompanied by a refusal to spread specialized knowledge concerning the application of atomic energy until effective safeguards against its use as a war weapon had been devised. The duty of establishing safeguards was referred to the United Nations.

U.S. LOAN DWINDLING

His own and his Government's repudiation of imperialism was given practical expression in the withdrawal from Egypt and from India and from Burma and the surrender of the mandate for Palestine when it was found impossible to reconcile the conflicting claims of Jews and Arabs. Never did the nation's economic position allow him rest of mind or a happy assurance of the social security which from the first had been his political aim. When he moved the second reading of the National Insurance Bill, six months after the Government took office, he qualified his exultation with the warning that the country could afford the new service only if it employed all its resources of skill, organization, and labour, and reinvigorated its economic life. The American loan which followed the abrogation of lend-lease, dwindled rapidly and in the autumn Attlee was appealing again to his supporters and the trade union leaders to face the economic facts. The outlook was darkened in the early months of 1947 by a severe fuel shortage, which deranged the year's production estimates: and time and again within the next two years Attlee was renewing his appeals for greater output. Further generous American financial help in the form of the Marshall plan staved off immediate drastic reductions in the standard of living.

Marshall aid was no less significant in the field of foreign policy which increasingly became as pressing an anxiety for the Government as the economic situation. In facing the mounting gravity of international relations, Attlee and Bevin worked as one man. Bevin's staunch and unwavering support for the Prime Minister, whom he affectionately called "the little man", became the main pillar of Attlee's personal position, safeguarding him against attacks in the Cabinet and the party. More than once his lack of the capacity to dramatize his leadership led to widespread criticism in the press and in the Parliamentary Labour Party. On one occasion one at least of his senior colleagues seriously considered challenging Attlee's tenure of the Prime Ministership. Bevin unhesitatingly scotched the attempt.

Towards the end of 1948 there came the Berlin air-lift which was hastily improvised to counter Russia's attempt to cut off the city and starve it into surrender. In March, 1949, Attlee paid a visit to Berlin to see the air-lift in full operation with a continuous stream of British and American aircraft landing at Templehof. Meanwhile the problem arose of the method by which western Europe was to be consolidated. A federalist movement came to the fore on the Continent that wished to merge the existing states of Europe into a new political unit with central organs of government. Attlee shared Bevin's instinctive determination to preserve Britain's national identity. The Government therefore resisted the blandishments of M. Schuman and M. Spaak and incurred the charge, which was echoed by the Opposition, of "dragging its feet". The desire for European integration was, however, sincere and Bevin put his energy into the creation of inter-governmental organizations of the type of E.C.E., O.E.E.C., and the E.P.U. Neither Attlee nor Bevin had much patience with those who wished to set up the Council of Europe which they regarded as an important talking-shop that would get in the way of the real work to be done.

MIDDLE EAST SETBACKS

Another problem that soon pressed upon the Government was the rise of nationalism in the Middle East. Attlee attempted to come to terms with this force in the same manner as in India and Pakistan. But he became increasingly involved in intractable difficulties that dogged him to the end of his Prime Ministership and did much to bring about his ultimate defeat at the polls.

Against setbacks in the Middle East must be put the consolidation of the new and enlarged Commonwealth. This was a sphere of activity in which Attlee felt confident and at home and the progress made was largely his personal achievement. He quickly established relationships of trust and friendship with the other Prime Ministers of the Commonwealth and this stood him in good stead in the four Prime Ministers' meetings over which he presided with singular success. When India, Pakistan, and Ceylon attained independence it was by no means certain that they would remain in the Commonwealth; indeed to most observers the odds seemed the other way.

It was Attlee's simple and undogmatic approach to this question that largely settled it. As a matter of course he invited the Asian Prime Ministers to join their colleagues in conference before they had decided whether or not to continue in membership of the Commonwealth. Their inside view of the Commonwealth at work, their realization that it was truly an association of equal nations whose concern was to help one another, became an important factor in their decisions to remain in the Commonwealth.

Attlee's masterly handling of two crises in the Commonwealth smoothed over difficulties that might otherwise have split it asunder. Towards the end of 1948 it became clear that India would become a republic. For a time it seemed that the problem of fitting a republic into a Commonwealth whose basis was common allegiance to the Crown would be insuperable. Attlee set about the problem with care and vigour. He instituted a searching study of the question and in January resorted to the unusual device of sending personal envoys to talk the matter over with the other Prime Ministers. The Prime Ministers' meeting that assembled in April, 1949, was the most thoroughly prepared that had ever been held. It continued its discussions to the single point of India's membership as a republic and the declaration that it produced on this subject takes its place among the basic constitutional documents of the Commonwealth. The solution found was that India as a republic recognized the King as Head of the Commonwealth and that all the other members recognized India's continuing membership. All the Prime Ministers went in a body to the Palace to report the outcome to the King, who had already signified his acceptance of the formula.

KASHMIR QUESTION

The second Commonwealth crisis with which Attlee dealt occurred in January, 1951, when Mr. Liaquat Ali Khan, Prime Minister of Pakistan, announced at the last moment that he would not attend the meeting of Prime Ministers that was already assembling in London unless the question of Kashmir were placed on their agenda. Mr. Nehru's refusal to agree to this course produced a deadlock. Attlee held firm to the principle that the Prime Ministers could discuss only matters to which all agreed; that the purpose of those meetings was not to air differences but to deal with common problems. At the same time Attlee actively sought for a solution that would satisfy Pakistan. All the Prime Ministers agreed that the problem of Kashmir should be talked over in informal gatherings outside the formal and plenary sessions. The Prime Ministers met in this manner in various combinations in strenuous efforts to find an agreed solution, though without success. However, a precedent had been created that might help Commonwealth disputes to be handled more smoothly in future. Whatever other judgments may be formed on Attlee's role as Prime Minister, his place is secure in history as one of the great architects of Commonwealth.

The economic and international problems of the country seemed to have eased when Attlee decided in February, 1950, to go to the country. The Labour Party entered the election with confidence on the assumption that its establishment of the welfare state by means of the Health Service, family allowances and a comprehensive system of social insurance would win it a reduced but still considerable mandate for a second term of office. It fought the election on a policy statement entitled "Labour Believes in Britain", which was in effect a justification of the Government's policies and an appeal for their continuance.

Labour put up its vote by over 1,250,000 but saw its majority slashed to 10. This came as a great shock to the party. But Attlee decided without hesitation to continue in office. Few in the party or outside it thought that the Government could survive for more than a matter of weeks. In the event it continued for 18 months. During its course Attlee was subjected to great strain which affected his health. His judgment and leadership became less sure.

After the election he undertook a limited reconstruction of his Administration which considerably reduced its average age. Death soon struck the new Government heavy blows that deprived him of his two principal colleagues. In October, 1950, Cripps was forced under doctor's orders to resign and died 18 months later after a painful illness courageously borne. In March, 1951, Bevin, who had been kept for some time by ill-health from continuous discharge of his official duties, resigned from the Foreign Office, dying a few weeks afterwards. Bevin was the only one of Attlee's colleagues who succeeded in penetrating his reserve and getting on to terms of intimate friendship with him and Attlee was deeply affected by his loss. The whole balance of the Cabinet and the basis of Attlee's personal leadership was altered. He had managed to remain Prime Minister of a Government that contained greater and more dynamic men than himself because Bevin, Cripps, and Morrison formed a kind of triangle of forces that maintained a political equilibrium beneath Attlee's feet.

SUPPORT FOR TRUMAN

The survivor of the triumvirate, Morrison, who succeeded Bevin as Foreign Secretary, never enjoyed good personal relations with Attlee. The incompatibility and lack of full confidence between the two now came to the fore in a Cabinet that had lost its previous internal poise. Gaitskell, who replaced Cripps as Chancellor, belonged to the younger generation in the Party. Throughout his second Administration Attlee failed to establish the relations of trust and understanding between a Prime Minister and his Foreign Secretary and Chancellor of the Exchequer that are necessary to a stable and harmonious Cabinet.

In July, 1950, North Korea suddenly invaded the South. Attlee at once supported President Truman's decisions to dispatch United States forces to Korea under the authority of the United Nations. Despite the heavy commitment of British forces in various parts of the world, a brigade was sent to Korea which became the nucleus of a Commonwealth Division. Considerable British naval strength was also put at the disposal of the United Nations Command. The open communist aggression in Korea faced the Government with the crucial problem of a sharp increase in armaments expenditure. The economy was heavily overloaded when the world prices of raw materials rose very rapidly. Attlee failed to persuade the Americans of the seriousness for Britain of the rise in world prices. A number of international committees were set up to allocate raw materials, but they never worked effectively and in any case it was too late to shut the stable door; prices were already at war-scarcity levels.

The mounting economic crisis also brought strains and divisions in the Cabinet. Gaitskell, now Chancellor of the Exchequer, stuck firmly by the decision to rearm and used his Budget to help close the inflationary "gap" between the supply of, and the demands upon, national resources. This led him to impose a charge to meet part of the cost of false teeth and spectacles supplied under the National Health Service, making use of legislation earlier introduced by Bevan. Bevan strongly opposed these charges in the Cabinet, later widening the area of dispute to include the whole question of rearmament. In the midst of these discussions which became bitter and personal, Attlee fell ill and had to go to hospital for treatment of duodenal ulcers. He tried from his bedside to compose the quarrel but without success.

He returned to work in time to preside over the Cabinet held on the day before the Budget at which Bevan and Wilson, President of the Board of Trade, resigned. This was in April, 1951. The following month a new crisis broke on a shaken Government, the product once again of Middle Eastern nationalism. In May, 1951, the Shah signed decrees nationalizing the Persian oil industry and taking over the refinery at Abadan. Between that date and October, 1951, when the Anglo-Iranian Company ceased operations in Persia—a period that coincided with the remaining term of office of the Government—the Cabinet was perplexed and embarrassed. Attlee had to face again the problem of Britain's relations with nationalist forces in areas in which previously British influence had been unquestioned. His instinctive reaction was the same as it had been towards Indian independence—namely, that Britain must come to terms with nationalism.

RUN ON RESERVES

The ultimate closure of the Abadan refinery gravely increased the economic difficulties that were already pressing on the country. The run on the gold and dollar reserves began to gather perilous momentum. Attlee came to the conclusion that he needed a larger majority to face this situation. The King was due to visit Australia and New Zealand in the following year and Attlee did not want to subject him to the constant anxiety of a possible fall of Government during his absence from the country. This was characteristic of Attlee's personal consideration of others, even in matters of high party political moment and of the close and warm relations that grew up between him and King George VI. He gave some expression to these when he paid tribute to the King's memory in the House of Commons, a speech in which he displayed more emotion than was his wont.

Had Attlee gained victory in 1951 he would have been the first Prime Minister to win three consecutive elections. In fact the Labour vote increased by 700,000 and was larger in total than the Conservative poll; but Labour lost 19 seats and control of the Commons passed to Sir Winston Churchill. Attlee at once tendered his resignation to the King who conferred upon him the Order of Merit. After 11 continuous years of high office Attlee proved a less successful leader of the Opposition than in the years before the War. He seemed to miss the authority that a Prime Minister derives from the disposal of office and could not quite recapture his former touch in his relations with members of a Parliamentary Committee who owed their position to election by their fellows. The former divisions in his Cabinet had hardened into organized faction. For several years Bevan and his supporters in Parliament and the country formed a cohesive party within the party that on a number of occasions defied the authority of the leaders. Bitter and prolonged disputes broke out, all turning in reality on a struggle for the succession to the leadership of the party. Attlee assumed almost the attitude of a detached observer to the intrigues and manoeuvres that rent the party and brought it low in public esteem.

The tensions reached their high point at the 1952 conference at Morecambe at which it was doubtful till the last moment whether or not the established leaders would succeed in carrying their policy of support for German rearmament. Attlee's part in this debate lacked the vigour and clarity with which he had opposed Lansbury's pacifism in 1935. He conveyed the impression that he was not greatly concerned with the outcome and left the main burden of the battle to Morrison. The policy of the leadership was endorsed by an extremely narrow majority.

In 1954 Attlee published his autobiography, *As it Happened* in which he recounted with dry matter-of-factness the world-shaking events in which he had played so prominent a part.

SPICED WITH WIT

The book was spiced with occasional flashes of quiet wit and digs at Sir Winston Churchill. It was the unassuming self-portrait of a simple and contented man and its closing words would serve as a fitting epitaph on Attlee's life:—"Up to the present I have been a very happy and fortunate man in having lived so long in the greatest country in the world, in having a happy family life and in having been given the opportunity of serving in a state of life to which I had never expected to be called."

It was a still divided party that Attlee led in the General Election of 1955 called by Sir Anthony Eden on his succession as Prime Minister to Sir Winston Churchill. For the fifth and last time Attlee made his customary wide-ranging tour, mainly through marginal seats, driven in a small car by his wife. The calls on him were as imperative as ever and he never flinched nor spared himself physically. As in the past he would make up to eight speeches in a single day and he spoke for the party over the air. But the old assurance and deftness of stroke were no longer in evidence. No election since 1935 had been fought by the Labour Party with so little confidence in victory. The Conservatives increased their majority to 60. When Attlee appeared on television after the results of the election were known he wore the air of a weary man, no longer looking forward.

LEADERSHIP SURRENDERED

Soon after, in August, he suffered a slight stroke from which he made, in due course, a complete recovery, and his relinquishment of his post as Leader of the Opposition became widely expected. Yet the occasion came as a surprise. He made a typically brief and modest speech to a regular meeting of the Parliamentary Labour Party and then slipped quietly out of a side door from the famous Committee Room No. 14 in which he had presided over uncounted similar gatherings. That was the way he chose to end his 20 years unbroken leadership of a party that he had done more than any other of its leaders to bring to maturity and to shape as a permanent political power in the state. Next day, on December 7, 1955, the Queen conferred an Earldom upon him.

After he left office and particularly after laying down the leadership of the Party Attlee travelled widely. The most notable of his visits was his leadership of a Labour Party delegation to Russia and China.

But he also paid many visits to Europe, Asia, Africa, and North America, journeying privately, attending conferences or lecturing with his habitual terseness and restraint.

WORLD GOVERNMENT

As time went on he dwelt more and more upon the theme of world government. He also provided timely support for Hugh Gaitskell in the Labour Party conflict over unilateral nuclear disarmament, and in 1961 accepted the presidency of the Campaign of Democratic Socialism.

The other issue which provoked him to vehement controversy in his later years was the Common Market: he was an outspoken critic of Britain's application for membership.

Attlee was a successful if not a great Prime Minister. He left his mark on the great office. One of his contributions to British constitutional development was that, as the first Labour Prime Minister with a majority, he quietly and unostentatiously fitted himself into the traditional descent. After the "betrayal" by MacDonald there had been a persistent movement in the Labour Party to hamstring any future leader by subjecting his choice of Ministers, as in Australia, to the vote of the caucus or party meeting. Attlee did not hold with such notions and on taking office in 1945 he chose his own Ministers in the established manner. He also gave stable and regulated form to the Cabinet committees that had grown up during the war and thus made this system a permanent part of British Cabinet Government.

Perhaps more than any other Prime Minister he brought the atmosphere of family life into the dignified abodes of office. He abandoned the attempt to live in the state apartments at 10 Downing Street and converted the previous servants' attics into a family flat in which he led the same domestic life as previously in Stanmore. His Boxing Day parties at Chequers for the children of his ministerial colleagues and private secretaries, which followed year by year exactly the same routine, ending always with the Prime Minister himself standing by the open front door handing every departing child a bag of sweets, were perhaps the occasions when he most unbent and felt most happy.

CROSSWORD PUZZLES

He was to an extraordinary degree impervious to public criticism and political abuse. Often he failed even to look at the "popular" press and sometimes his main interest in *The Times* was the crossword puzzle, which he unfailingly solved. He delighted to pore over works of personal reference like *Who's Who*. His sturdiness of character, his unwavering resolution, his staunch but inarticulate love of British things were qualities of the highest worth in the silent revolution at home and in the Commonwealth over which he presided. His integrity was absolute.

He married in 1922 Violet Helen, daughter of the late H. E. Millar, of Heathdown, Hampstead, and they had one son, upon whom the family honours now devolve, and three daughters. His wife died in June, 1964.

October 9, 1967.

Clare Atwood, who died on August 2, 1962, at the age of 96, was a versatile painter of interiors with figures, portraits, architectural subjects, landscapes and still life, including decorative flower compositions. She was one of the comparatively few women artists to receive official commissions during the First World War.

The only daughter of an architect, Frederick Atwood, Miss Atwood was born at Richmond, Surrey. She studied under L.C. Nightingale and at Westminster and the Slade School under Professor Frederick Brown, and his influence as well as an orderliness recalling her father's profession could be traced in her work. Miss Atwood was a fairly frequent exhibitor at the Royal Academy, mostly of still life paintings, but her natural home was the New English Art Club, of which she was a member.

IN COVENT GARDEN

For some years Miss Atwood's address was the unusual one for an artist of Bedford Street, Strand. She found artistic material in Covent Garden—her painting of "St. Paul's Church Covent Garden" was in the 1932 Academy—but more to the point, one surmises, was her interest in music and the theatre. Her close acquaintance with theatrical life is recorded in "Mr. John Gielgud's Dining Room", exhibited at the Academy in 1933, and in portraits of the Terry family.

In 1919 she was commissioned by the Canadian Government to paint one of the large decorations for the Canadian War Memorial Exhibition at Burlington House, and the following year she received commissions to paint pictures for the Imperial War Museum in London. In 1940 a picture by her was purchased for the National Gallery of New Zealand.

August 4, 1962.

Mischa Auer, one of the best-known personalities in American comedy during the 1930s and 1940s, died in Rome on March 5, 1967. He was 61.

Mischa was born in St. Petersburg on November 17, 1905. He had an eventful childhood: his father was an army officer killed in action in 1916, and in the confusion of the Revolution he became separated from his mother, who found him, months later, wandering Siberia with a band of half-wild children. Making their way southwards they eventually encountered the British Expeditionary Force, and his mother worked with them as a nurse until she died of typhus.

IN NEW YORK

Finally, through the offices of family friends he managed to reach New York, where his grandfather, Leopold Auer, was a distinguished violin teacher. After completing his schooling and studying literature in New York, he decided he would like to take up acting as a career, and soon found a part in a Broadway production.

After appearing successfully in a number of Broadway plays, among them *The Wild Duck*, *Magda*, and *The Riddle Woman* he completed a tour at Los Angeles and resolved to try his luck in films, making his debut in *Something Always Happens* (1928). For several years he tended to be cast as a villain, often vaguely oriental and mysterious, appearing in such films as *Lives of a Bengal Lancer*, *Clive of India*, and De Mille's *The Crusades* before finding his niche in comedy. In 1936 he appeared in rapid succession in Mamoulian's *The Gay Desperado*, Alfred Santell's rather pretentious version of Maxwell Anderson's grim verse-play *Winterset*, and Gregory la Cava's enchanting crazy comedy *My Man Godfrey* in which he played the hypochondriac artist-protégé of the household, and did his famous imitation of a gorilla to devastating effect. There followed appearances in two Deanna Durbin vehicles, *Three Smart Girls* and *A Hundred Men and a Girl*, and then another of his most famous performances in Capra's *You Can't Take it With You*, where he played Boris Kolenkhov, the mad ex-wrestler maestro of the dance.

MAD AND SHADY ROLES

During the war he continued to play the type of role for which he was renowned—generally a rather mad, somewhat shady. Russian émigré aristocrat with more than dubious credentials (one remembers him in *Hellzapoppin* horrified at the impending revelation that he is a real aristocrat, when his livelihood depends on his being taken for an entertaining phoney). During this period he appeared in two of René Clair's American films, *Flame of Orleans* (1941) with Marlene Dietrich, and *The Ten Little Niggers* (1945), Lubitsch's *Czarina*, with Tallulah Bankhead as Catherine the Great, and the film of the Kurt Weill's musical *Lady in the Dark*. After the war he left Hollywood and returned to the stage. He came to Europe, touring the English provincial theatres before settling on the Continent, where he appeared in numerous French films such as *Frou-Frou* and *Tabarin*. In 1955 Orson Welles started shooting a colour version of *Don Quixote* with Mischa Auer as Quixote and Akim Tamiroff as Sancho Panza, but unfortunately the production had to be called off owing to lack of funds; he did, however, appear to great effect in Welles's following film, *Confidential Report*, as the sinister owner of a flea circus. He was last seen on the international screen in *Monte Carlo Story*, starring Marlene Dietrich and Vittorio de Sica.

TYPE-CASTING

For most of his career Mischa Auer was type-cast as a comic Russian, and excellently though he played the part, especially in films like, *My Man Godfrey*, *You Can't Take It With You* and *Hellzapoppin*, he was certainly capable of better things, as he clearly demonstrated whenever given the chance. It is especially to be regretted, therefore, that we never had an opportunity to see his *Don Quixote*; in lieu of that perhaps his most interesting performance was in *Confidential Report*.

March 6, 1967.

Vincent Auriol, first President of the French Fourth Republic, died on January 1, 1966, at the age of 81.

When he was elected President in January, 1947, he was an obvious choice for that high office. He was an experienced politician who had several times held ministerial rank; he had been one of the few socialists who had voted against Marshal Pétain in 1940, had been imprisoned by the Vichy regime, had escaped, worked with the Resistance and had got away—rather romantically, wearing a false beard—to London, where he had joined General de Gaulle. He had then displayed remarkable qualities of persuasion and conciliation as an acknowledged leader in the quarrelsome and inexperienced Consultative Assembly in Algiers in 1943 and 1944, had been President of the two constituent assemblies which, back again in Paris, had drawn up the new Constitution of 1946, and had been the first President of the new National Assembly. He was elected President of the Republic effortlessly, on the first ballot, and set himself with a will to the onerous duties of an office to which—he made no secret of his ambition—he had keenly aspired.

His interpretation of the Presidential role during the seven difficult years, 1947 to 1954, he held office, provoked a certain criticism in parliamentary circles. Certainly he managed to give the Presidency an importance the Constituent Assembly had intended it should not have. Both his own Socialists and the Communists, the preponderant parties, with the M.R.P., in both constituent assemblies, had wished to make the President no more than a representational puppet. But Vincent Auriol, although he saw his role as that of an arbiter, a conciliator, never intended that it should be merely passive. Thus he intervened personally and vigorously during the many and interminable political crises of his septennate, criticizing the political leaders for their intransigence, calling upon them to make concessions "as one should in a democracy".

There seems little doubt that without the President's active intervention the confused political situation during those chaotic years might have been far worse, even to the collapse of France's parliamentary institutions. None the less, the President's attitude was strongly resented by the political parties and by none more than the Socialists, who, because to some extent they held the balance of parliamentary power, were the most frequent target for his admonitions.

SON OF A BAKER

Vincent Auriol was born on August 27, 1884, at Revel, in the Haute Garonne. His father, the village baker, and a land-owner in a small way, was a keen local politician, passionately anti-clerical, and a pillar of the then very "advanced" party, the Radical-Socialists. He read political science and law at Toulouse University, and under the influence of Jean Jaurès joined the Socialist Party—a step which led to a temporary estrangement from his father. At the age of 21, while practising successfully at the Bar, he founded and edited a local party newspaper. *Le Midi Socialiste*. Like many another ambitious young lawyer, he soon turned towards the prospect of a Parliamentary career, and in 1914 was elected to the Chamber for his home constituency. He became a member of the Chamber's finance commission two years later and remained the Socialist Party's principal financial expert until 1939. Appointed in 1919 general secretary of the socialist group in the Chamber, he held that honorary office until 1936 and thus remained continuously in close touch with Léon Blum, who had been appointed party leader at the same time.

On the return of the Popular Front in 1936 Auriol became Minister of Finance. It was unfortunate that in trying to contend with the consequences of the deflationary policy of the previous Government he was made responsible, in the public mind, for the instability of the currency which followed his cautious measures of devaluation.

In June of the following year he was Minister of Justice under Chautemps, and in Blum's second and brief Government in the spring of 1938 he was entrusted with the new ministerial task of coordinating the work of the Prime Minister's department. In spite of his high reputation and political seniority he only once again held ministerial office, when he became Minister of State and Vice-Premier in the Provisional Government headed by General de Gaulle in November, 1945. But he was, of course, president of various assemblies before his election to the highest office in the land in 1947.

During Auriol's Presidency there were 14 governments and after each fell there was a "crisis" lasting from seven days to 27, 28 and even, following the overthrow of M. René Mayer's Cabinet in May, 1953, 36 days before a new Government could be formed. Most of the Prime Ministers urged into office by President Auriol were of necessity established political leaders, but he did break new ground most successfully in picking M. Edgar Faure, at the age of only 44, and then the totally unknown M. Antoine Pinay, the outstanding and most popular Premier of Auriol's septennate.

At the end of May, 1958, when France appeared to be on the brink of civil war, President Coty asked Auriol to make contact on his behalf with General de Gaulle to discuss his terms for a constitutional return to power.

ACTION AFTER REFUSAL

Auriol refused, but went to see the General on his own initiative and it was his reassurances concerning de Gaulle's intentions, given in the form of an exchange of letters between them, that did much to persuade the Socialists to vote for de Gaulle when he went before the National Assembly to seek investiture as Prime Minister. Auriol, as a former President, became an ex officio member of de Gaulle's new Constitutional Council but resigned the following year—as he did also from the Socialist Party, of which he had been a life-long member—as a protest against certain aspects of the new regime.

A friendly little man, Vincent Auriol combined a natural bonhomie with an innate distinction in a manner which made him not only one of the most widely popular of Presidents but equally at home with the distinguished guests he had to receive in the name of France. In this task he was considerably helped by his wife Michaéle, daughter of Michel Aucouturier, a Toulouse trade union leader, whom he married in 1912, a woman of great charm and elegance.

January 3, 1966.

Florence Austral, who died in Newcastle, New South Wales, on May 16, 1968, at the age of 74, was one of the many Australian singers whose gifts were put at the service of British music.

A dramatic soprano with a powerful stage personality, she was a notable exponent of heroic Wagnerian and Verdian roles and possibly the only English-speaking soprano who was a born Isolde.

Florence Wilson—the name "Austral" was adopted with a touch of national pride, at the opening of her career—was born in Melbourne on April 26, 1894. A scholarship took her to Melbourne Conservatory in 1914, and four years later she moved to New York to continue her studies.

Offered a contract by New York Metropolitan opera, she refused it, and her stage career opened in London, where she was engaged by Robert Radford for Grand Opera Syndicate's season in 1921. When circumstances made it impossible for the work of the syndicate to proceed and the season was abandoned Florence Austral became a member of its successor, the British National Opera Company, and she was first heard at Covent Garden in 1922 as Brünnhilde in *Die Walküre* and *Siegfried.*

A voice of unusual beauty and strength placed intelligently at the service of drama kept her active in English opera until 1939, when she made her final stage appearances as a guest artist with the Sadler's Wells Company. She was, too, an artist much admired in oratorio and as a concert singer (it was in this guise that the United States and Commonwealth countries knew her) whose varied concert programmes always contained a good deal of operatic music. She recognized that her gifts were for the heroic, and Santuzza, in *Cavalleria Rusticana,* was the farthest she strayed from the world of Aïda, Isolde and Brünnhilde.

Florence Austral was, off the stage, entirely Australian, simple, direct and business-like. These bracing qualities made her popular among conductors and colleagues used to the stormy, demanding temperaments which often make their home in the opera house.

May 17, 1968.

Captain Harold Auten, V.C., D.S.C., who was awarded the Victoria Cross in 1918 for conspicuous bravery and devotion to duty when in command of a "mystery ship," known later as a Q ship, died on October 3, 1964, at his home in Pennsylvania.

The notification of the award of the V.C. to Lieutenant Auten, as he then was, in the *London Gazette* of September 14, 1918, was unaccompanied by any details owing to the secrecy of the work in which he was engaged. Q ships, a variant of the old idea of decoy ships, were devised as a counter to the U-boat menace which was such a threat to the survival of Britain in the First World War. Small merchant vessels were put to sea with concealed guns and tried to lure enemy submarines within their range by a variety of stratagems—most notable among them being the practice of putting a "panic party" into the boats as soon as the enemy had opened fire, thereby creating the impression that the ship was in a desperate plight and the crew unnerved.

Harold Auten was born in 1891, the son of W.B. Auten, of Plymouth, and educated at Wilson's Grammar School. He joined the Royal Navy in 1910 and his first experience of a Q ship came in the summer of 1915 when he was serving on the staff of the captain of the Devonport Dockyard. He was appointed to the Zylpha, an old and dirty tramp of some 2,000 tons. His experiences in fitting out the ship and her crew were amusingly related in his book *Q Boat Adventures*. Over the next few years he served on a number of other Q ships and was awarded the D.S.C. in 1917.

The climax to his career in Q ships was in the summer of 1918 when he was in command of the Stockforce. In a dramatic engagement a U-boat was defeated and severely damaged—though not sunk as was thought at the time—while his own ship finally sank just before it could make its way into port. It was for this action that he was awarded the V.C.

Auten, a Younger Brother of Trinity House, served again in the Second World War and was more latterly executive vice-president of the J. Arthur Rank Organisation in the United States.

He was twice married and had one son and one daughter.

October 5, 1964.

Gladys Aylward, the little English woman whose dedicated courage as a missionary and guardian of orphans in China for 40 years found fame in the film *The Inn of the Sixth Happiness,* died in Taipei in January, 1970, at the age of 68.

Miss Aylward—popularly known as "The Small Woman" for she was only 5ft. tall—settled in Taiwan (Formosa) in 1953 after two decades of missionary work—and inn-keeping—in the primitive regions of North China.

The inn, featured in the film *The Inn of the Sixth Happiness,* starring Ingrid Bergman and based on the book *The Small Woman,* by Alan Burgess—was founded by Miss Aylward and a Scottish woman missionary on the Shansi mountain trails. Years later, Miss Aylward recalled that they took this unusual step when they realized that the local travellers were ignoring their lonely mission outpost and that the only way to spread the gospel was to attract them into an inn. "So we never did have a mission", Miss Aylward said. "We kept an inn".

After the death of her companion, Mrs. Jeannie Lawson, Miss Aylward carried on running the inn, winning the respect of the local Chinese. She made friends with the Mandarin and helped to push through a decree that the feet of Chinese girls must no longer be bound. She adopted waifs and even quelled a riot in a local prison. But her most famous exploit was during the Sino-Japanese war, in 1938, when she led a long column of nearly 100 Chinese children to safety in face of the advancing Japanese armies. Crossing mountains, travelling on foot for weeks, they survived without money or equipment and with very little food.

Born in the London suburb of Edmonton, Miss Aylward became a parlourmaid when she left school at 14 and had her first taste of missionary work some years later in the employment of two retired missionaries in Bristol.

OFF TO TIENTSIN

In 1930, at the age of 27, she took every penny of her savings, bought a railway ticket to the North China port of Tientsin—the cheapest way she could get there—and set out for the mountainous heart of China.

Her route over the Trans-Siberian railway led to the first of her adventures. The Russians and the Chinese were fighting over ownership of part of the railway and, after long delays in Siberian forests, and passport difficulties, she finally landed at Tientsin after travelling through Japan. In Tientsin she knew no one, but the principal of the Anglo-Chinese college arranged for her to join Mrs. Lawson at her lone missionary outpost at Yangcheng in Southern Shansi. In this remote Chinese community, "the small woman" set about mastering the local dialect and overcoming her shock at local customs, which included public executions with curved swords in the market place.

War with the Japanese reached Yangcheng in 1938. The province of Shansi was overrun and the little missionary had to flee—with her column of children. She threw in her lot with the Nationalists, spending the next few years dodging from cave to cave and village to village, tending the wounded and burying the dead. She was credited with carrying out espionage for the Nationalists. She returned to England in 1948, preached there for several years and then settled finally in Taiwan—to run an orphanage.

January 5, 1970.

Marcel Aymé, the French writer, died in Paris on October 14, 1967. He was 65. He will be remembered especially for his satirical novels, of which *La Jument Verte*, the tale of a village battle between Catholics and anti-clericals under the early Third Republic, is one of the best known.

Aymé was born on March 29, 1902, at Joigny (Yonne), of parents who came from the Jura. His father was a blacksmith. His mother died when he was two years old, and he was brought up first by grandparents and then by an aunt. His early life was marked by a series of unsuccessful attempts at self-improvement. After a few months of studying mathematics he went to Germany to learn the language. Then, after military service, he began studying medicine. This too was soon abandoned, and during the mid-twenties the young Aymé lived in Paris by a series of different professions, including banker, life insurance broker, journalist and clerk. His first novel, *Brûlebois,* was written in 1926 and published with the help of Jacques Reboul, the manager of *Cahiers De France*. It won the admiration of many other writers, who encouraged Aymé to continue, and it was soon followed by *Aller et Retour* and *Les Jumeaux du Diable* (1927). The author was now able to leave the export firm where he had been working for the past year, and became an accountant in the Paris Bourse.

In December, 1929, he won the Prix Théophraste Renaudot with another novel *La Table Aux Crevés.* From then on he published novels, essays, plays, and short stories in a continuous stream. Major landmarks were *La Jument Verte* (1933), *Le Passe-Muraille* (1943), and *Le Chemin des Ecoliers* (1946). In later years he also turned a number of his novels into filmscripts. He married in 1932 Mme. Marie-Antoinette Arnaud.

His death will be regretted by his friends as that rare phenomenon, a man of great wit who was none the less remarkably indulgent in his everyday personal judgments, and a hater of publicity who none the less made himself a great reputation both with the critics and with the reading public. He has been called a literary descendant of de Maupassant, and even of Voltaire.

October 16, 1967.

B

Professor Wilhelm Backhaus, the pianist, died on July 5, 1969, at the age of 85 in Southern Austria.

He was his generation's greatest surviving exponent of the classical German musical tradition fostered in the Conservatoire of his native Leipzig. He embodied the virtues of classical restraint and strict fidelity to a given text which have always been the salient principles of Leipzig teaching.

Wilhelm Backhaus was born on March 26, 1884. At Leipzig Conservatoire he studied under Reckendorf and, in 1889, became a student of Eugene d'Albert at Frankfurt-am-Main. He made his first concert tour in 1900; and at the age of 20 he became Professor of Piano at Manchester Royal College of Music. Subsequently, his career of more than 60 years—for he continued to play in public until 1969—was spent as a travelling virtuoso based, after the Second World War, on a home in Switzerland.

The career of an international pianist, Backhaus himself admitted, tended to narrow the range of music he played: Beethoven and Brahms, Bach, Schubert and Mozart became the staple of his programmes although he played other works, for example, Chopin, with a sensitivity unhampered by his refusal to indulge in extravagances or to add his own glosses to the music as he found it in print before him. The restrictions demanded by audiences who saw in him a specialist on the works of the great German masters did not, however, strike him as being in any way irksome. In the music he played, especially in the concertos and sonatas of Beethoven, he found a well of beauty and wisdom which no single pianist, however long his career, could ever exhaust. It was therefore possible for him always to avoid a performance which seemed to have reduced itself to the level of routine.

In his early years Backhaus was capable of a colourful exuberance of response to the music he played, but later in life the rigorous precision of his musical outlook led him to approach his art, which had nothing meretricious or ostentatious in it, with an entirely businesslike concentration. If he rarely seemed, as Schnabel (to whose generation he belonged) often seemed, to be recreating a great work as he played it, Backhaus was never less than a devotedly unselfish mouthpiece for the composers he served.

July 7, 1969.

Sir Edward Bailey, M.C., F.R.S., a former Director of the Geological Survey of Great Britain and the Museum of Practical Geology, and for seven years Professor of Geology in the University of Glasgow, died on March 19, 1965, at the age of 83.

One of the most distinguished and colourful geologists of his generation, he enhanced the prestige of British geology by original work and became a scholar of Clare College, Cambridge.

Complex rocks found in mountain ranges had a challenging appeal for him and their successful study was aided by his excellent physique, spartan demeanour and fertile brain. Although some of his interpretations were denied as being too imaginative even those provided stimulus to further research.

Edward Battersby Bailey was born in July, 1881. He went to Kendal Grammar School and became a scholar of Clare College, Cambridge, where he had the distinction of achieving double first class honours in geology and physics in Part II of the Natural Sciences Tripos: he also gained the Harkness Scholarship. From Cambridge he joined the Geological Survey in 1902 and was assigned to field work in Scotland, first in the Lowlands, then also in the Highlands. His studies in East Lothian and Campsie Fells soon won him a reputation as a skilled and thoughtful interpreter of the history of ancient volcanoes. In 1909, with C. T. Clough and H. B. Maufe, he recorded results of geological mapping in the neighbourhood of Glencoe which demonstrated a sunken volcano area called a cauldron subsidence surrounded by igneous intrusions described as ring dykes. Similar interpretation has since been applied to many other areas in the world. In 1910 Bailey announced his belief in the mechanism of recumbent folding and sliding of the rocks as an explanation of other geological structures in the nearby Ballachulish district of the Grampians and though subsequently he accepted criticism that he had misread the "way up" of the rocks within his groupings the concept of recumbent folds remained. Fifty-one years later he gave a reassessment of this early work in the second edition of the *Geology of Ben Nevis and Glencoe* Geological Survey Memoir.

SAND FOR GLASS-MAKING

After Glencoe Bailey's attention was diverted south-west to the geology of the Scottish Tertiary igneous complex, especially in the island of Mull where he recognized gravitational differentiation of a magma, pillow lavas, crater lakes and, again, ring dykes. This Mull work was broken into by war service with the Royal Garrison Artillery as a lieutenant: twice wounded, he received the Military Cross, the Croix de Guerre with palms and he was made a Chevalier of the Legion of Honour. Shortly after his return from the war Bailey was given charge of west Highland field work and he saw through the press the Mull map which he had helped to construct: it is one of the most beautiful and complex maps produced by the Ordnance Survey Office for the Geological Survey. Duty took Bailey in 1922 to Loch Aline, on the mainland side of the Sound of Mull, and he studied there a white sandstone of exceptional purity in silica. He inferred that this sandstone had been deposited on the desert shores of the same sea that formed the chalk of the English downlands. Chemical analysis showed the sand to be of first class quality for optical glass manufacture and during the 1939-45 War it was mined and used in quantity by the Admiralty as a welcome replacement of supplies.

In December, 1929, Bailey left the Geological Survey for the Chair of Geology in the University of Glasgow which he occupied until 1937, and during this period he announced some results of earthquakes in geological history, notably near Quebec and off East Sutherland; he also wrote *Tectonic Essays, mainly Alpine* (1935), a book which is still widely read.

SURVEY OF RESOURCES

Bailey returned to the Geological Survey in April, 1937, as its Director, but the war, which occupied six of the eight years of his directorate, caused a change of plans which he had for the survey: these are described in his book, *The Geological Survey of Great Britain* (1952). The survey's effort was diverted to appraisal of the country's underground water and mineral resources including coal, ironstone, barytes, fluorspar, mica, and tungsten. From 1940 to 1942 Bailey was Lieutenant commanding the Geological Survey and London Civil Defence Region section of the Home Guard and in 1943 he visited Malta to advise on water resources there. One achievement of his directorate was the preparation in two sheets of the 10 miles to one inch geological map of Great Britain: this was not published until 1948, whereas Bailey retired in 1945 in which year he was knighted. He continued geological work after retirement and latterly he had been working on a problem of Italian tectonic geology. He also enjoyed writing biographies of geologists and his book on Charles Lyell was published in 1962. Shortly before his death he was preparing a book on James Hutton.

WALKER AND CLIMBER

Bailey was a keen walker and climber and this led him to support the Scottish Youth Hostels' Association, which he served successively as Glasgow District Chairman, vice-president, and honorary president.

Among his awards were Fellowship of the Royal Society in 1930 and the Royal Medal in 1943: from the Geological Society of London he received the Bigsby, Murchison and Wollaston Medals and he was elected to foreign membership of the national scientific academies of Belgium, Norway, Switzerland, and the United States as well as of many geological societies. He also received honorary doctorates from the universities of Belfast, Birmingham, Cambridge, Glasgow, and Harvard.

He married Alice Meason, an endearing person, in 1914; they were devoted to each other and had a son and a daugher. Lady Bailey died in 1956, and in December, 1962, he married Miss Mary Young, who survives him.

March 20, 1965.

Lieutenant-Colonel Frederick Marshman Bailey C.I.E., died on April 17, 1967, at his home in Stiffkey, Norfolk.

In its diversity of adventure his career as soldier, explorer, linguist, secret agent and diplomatist can be compared with that of Sir Richard Burton and it included not a few incidents reminiscent of Kipling's *Kim*; Sarat Chandra Das, who examined young Bailey for his proficiency in Tibetan, was in fact the Bengali secret explorer who appears in *Kim* under the name of Hurry Chunder Mookerjee. Participants in the "great game" of obtaining information for the Government of India which would enable frontiers to be defined continually risked death from assassination, disease, starvation and the accidents of avalanches and sudden floods, and it was by unusual resourcefulness, toughness, diplomatic tact, linguistic ability and luck, all in good measure, that Bailey survived so many hazards to reach the age of 85. Curiously enough, Bailey, for all his explorations and secret service work in Central Asia, is likely to be remembered for his incidental discovery of the now celebrated Tibetan blue poppy named *Meconopsis betonicifolia baileyi*.

The eldest son of Lieutenant-Colonel F. Bailey, R.A., he was born on February 3, 1882. From Edinburgh Academy he went to Wellington College, thence to Sandhurst and the Indian Army, first with the 17th Bengal Lancers and then the 32nd Sikh Pioneers, serving with the 1903–04 Younghusband Expedition to Lhasa.

FRUSTRATED BY FIGHTING

Immediately he took part in the exploration of western Tibet. He was seconded to the Indian Political Department in 1905 and for three-and-a-half years occupied the new post of British Trade Agent at Gyantse and Chumbi in south-eastern Tibet. In 1911 he travelled from western China into south-eastern Tibet and the Mishmi Hills, being awarded the Gill Memorial by the Royal Geographical Society, but was frustrated in his main object by fighting between the Tibetans and Chinese. The results were recorded in his *China-Tibet-Assam*.

As late as 1913 geographers were still not absolutely certain that the great Tibetan river the Tsangpo flowed by way of Dihang into the Brahmaputra because its unexplored course in south-eastern Tibet cut through some of the most mountainous, difficult and inhospitable country in the world and had to be reached from India through the territory of murderous and treacherous tribes. For several years Bailey had fostered the ambition of solving the mystery of the Tsangpo gorges and had prepared himself by mastering colloquial Tibetan; he had also learnt Persian. In 1913 he and the late Captain H. T. Morshead risked official displeasure and came near to losing their lives by tracing the course of the Dihang river up into the Tsangpo.

Bailey and Morshead brought back from this hazardous journey, described in Bailey's *No Passport to Tibet* (1957), not only much valuable geographical information but also many natural history specimens, among them the blue poppy *Rhododendron baileyi*, the shrew, *Soriculus baileyi*, imperfectly known pheasants and new butterflies including *Lycaenopsis morsheadi*. The 10 miles of the Tsangpo which they were unable to survey were successfully tackled by F. Kingdon Ward and Lord Cawdor in 1924, the 1914–18 War having ended Bailey's Tibetan exploration. This work brought Bailey the award of the Royal Geographical Society's Gold Medal.

In the early part of the 1914–18 War Bailey served with the Indian Expeditionary Force in Flanders, then went to Gallipoli and was later back on the North-West Frontier. He was made a C.I.E. in 1915. In the closing stages of the war he was Political Officer in Iraq and subsequently in Persia. Soon there followed an amazing series of adventures which he laconically described in *Who's Who* as "Mission to Central Asia, 1918–20". In August, 1918, he was sent to Central Asia to assist the Allied endeavour to restore the Eastern front from the White Sea to the Persian Gulf. The collapse of that front following the Russian revolution made the danger of enemy intrigues very great, for large numbers of prisoners captured by the Russians had been kept in camps in Turkistan. In the chaotic conditions then prevailing in Russian territory the organization by the enemy of these former prisoners might have created a formidable force on the flank of Afghanistan. Various concurrent measures to meet this menace had been taken by the British. Bailey's task was to persuade the Chinese authorities in Chinese Turkistan to counter any hostile moves.

From Kashgar Bailey went to Tashkent to explore the attitude of the local Bolshevik Government in Russian Turkistan. Soon he was compelled to go "underground" owing to the increasingly hostile attitude of that regime. His adventures were amazing. He repeatedly changed his identity with remarkable skill, and attained a crowning success by securing his own recruitment as a member of a Bolshevik counter-espionage band, with the task of tracking down a British agent in the area by the name of Bailey! He was thus able to make his way to Bukhara, still a nominally independent Emirate, and eventually to travel with some refugees, who put themselves under his protection, back to Persia. For many months no news of him had come through, and there was great relief when he reached Meshed in January, 1920. He gave frequent lectures to the Royal Geographic Society and other societies but it was not until 1946, more than a quarter of a century later, that he told the full story in his *Mission to Tashkent*.

He married in 1921 the Hon. Irma Cozens-Hardy, only child of the second Lord Cozens-Hardy.

April 19, 1967.

Sir George Bailey, C.B.E., late Chairman of Associated Electrical Industries Limited, died on October 14, 1965, at his home at Compton, Buckinghamshire. He was 85.

He was for nearly half a century a prominent figure in British engineering, and had held most offices in the various organizations which watch the interests of the industry. He was especially known at home and abroad for his long career with the Associated Electrical Industries group of companies, the chairmanship of which he assumed in 1951. George Edwin Bailey was born at Loughborough, Leicestershire, in 1879, a son of Thomas W. Bailey, and was educated at Loughborough Grammar School and University College, Nottingham. He served his apprenticeship with the Brush Company at Loughborough and having completed his articles, in 1907, joined Metropolitan-Vickers Electrical Company, then the British Westinghouse Company. Thus began his long association with the company which was to culminate in his chairmanship.

In his early days at Trafford Park he was mainly concerned with the development of steam turbines and gas engines, eventually becoming chief draughtsman to the department. Moving to the production side he became works manager in 1919 and later works director. He was appointed to the board of Metropolitan-Vickers in 1927 and chairman of the company in 1944. When a group of companies was formed into Associated Electrical Industries in 1929 Bailey assumed responsibility for coordinating production. He became managing director of A.E.I. in 1945 and deputy chairman a year later.

During his time in the electrical industry he was involved in many technical developments. Among these were Metropolitan-Vickers' contribution to the axial flow type of gas turbine, and the first British gas turbines for a power station, a locomotive and for ships' propulsion. He was also concerned in the production of the first thousand radar transmitters produced at Trafford Park under conditions of extreme urgency in the early stages of the war.

He had been president of the British Electrical and Allied Manufacturers Association, of the Engineering and Allied Employers' National Federation, of the Institution of Production Engineers, the Manchester District Engineering Employers' Association, and in 1939 he was appointed to the Industrial Panel of the Ministry of Production.

Later, he became a member of the Engineering and Industrial Panel of the Ministry of Labour and National Service, and also served on the committee which considered the position of skilled men in the services (the Beveridge committee). He was created a C.B.E. in 1941 and knighted in 1944.

He married in 1910, Margaret Fanny Bolesworth, and they had one daughter.

October 15, 1965.

Professor Victor Albert Bailey, the well-known Australian physicist, who made notable contributions to the understanding of the ionosphere, died in Geneva on December 7, 1964, in his sixty-ninth year. His brilliancy of mind showed up at a very early age and remained undiminished until his death, giving another lie to the tale that scientists above 30 or so are lacking in creativeness.

Bailey was born on December 18, 1895, in Alexandria, Egypt son of William Henry Bailey. From King Edward VI Grammar School, Southampton, he went with a scholarship to Queen's College, Oxford, taking a first class in mathematical moderations in 1914. After a brief period as Pioneer Instructor in the R. E. Signals he returned to Oxford in 1918 to read engineering science: there, incidentally, he met Nevil Shute (N. S. Norway of Balliol). In 1920 with a first in engineering, he joined Professor J. S. Townsend to work in the electrical laboratory on the motion of electrons in gases, a field from which plasma physics developed. Townsend soon recognized Bailey's remarkable mathematical abilities and skill in experimental physics, as shown in several joint papers. Having taken a D.Phil. degree in 1923 Bailey, at the age of 29, was appointed to the Chair of Physics at Sydney University, which in 1936 became the Chair of Experimental Physics, a post he held until his retirement in 1960.

He set up a successful research school to study the electric properties of the ionosphere, a subject probably inspired by Appleton's work, and continued to investigate electrons in gases, particularly the halogens which, having been hit by electrons, form readily heavier negative ions. However, Bailey is best known for solving the riddle of the Luxembourg effect (1934); radio operators found that Radio Luxembourg could be received on other wavelengths than its own, a fact he explained by the interaction of an electromagnetic wave and the ionized atmosphere about 50 miles up, modulated by a second more powerful wave.

Another contribution, in 1937, was the gyromagnetic resonance in the ionosphere caused by free electrons rotating in the earth's magnetic field when the frequency of rotation is in resonance with the frequency difference of the two interfering waves. During the last war he established courses for officers of the Australian Armed Forces in radar techniques.

By assuming that stars and galaxies have a net electric charge. Bailey showed in 1960 that phenomena such as the cosmic rays of highest energy, the sun's and earth's magnetic field, and the existence and position of the outer van Allen belt can be understood. Some of his theoretical predictions of the magnetic field in interstellar space seem to have been borne out by recent results obtained from American satellite records. Bailey intended to follow up this work and was on his way to take up a visiting professorship of space science at the Catholic University of Washington, DC.

In his youth Bailey played Association football and cricket. He was fluent in Arabic, fond of music, a keen photographer and chess player, and a stimulating conversationalist whose company was always enjoyed by his many friends.

He is survived by his wife and four children.

December 24, 1964.

Norman Baillie-Stewart—"the Officer in the Tower"—died in Dublin on June 7, 1966, at the age of 57.

Baillie-Stewart, who was tried in 1946 for making wartime broadcasts from Germany, was gaoled for five years. His defence was that he was a German citizen and could not be indicted. He became known as the "Officer in the Tower" when he was held in the Tower of London before the war.

He had decided to end 20 years of silence and tell his story in a book which was due to appear in November, 1966.

Baillie-Stewart was a lieutenant in the Seaforth Highlanders when he was first arrested in 1933 and imprisoned in the Tower. He was then sentenced to five years penal servitude and cashiered for betraying secrets to Germany. During the trial he said that a German blonde called Marie Louise had given him money.

When he was sentenced in 1946 for aiding the enemy by broadcasting from Germany, Mr. Justice Oliver said: "You are one of the worst citizens that any country has ever produced." The judge hoped that as soon as matters in Germany were sufficiently settled Baillie-Stewart would be sent from Britain on licence, "because this country does not require you." Later, from his cell at Dartmoor, Baillie-Stewart asked for the judge's recommendation to be carried out. He wanted to go to Austria.

It was in the Austrian Tyrol that he was captured in 1945, wearing Tyrolean chamois shorts, white woollen stockings, embroidered braces and a forester's green jacket.

At his second trial after the war it was said that he had applied for German nationality in 1938 and became a German after war broke out. However, under British law he remained a British citizen, as change of nationality is not allowed during wartime. It was thus as a Briton that he was gaoled.

Baillie-Stewart was a general cadet in No.1—The Champion—Company at the Royal Military College, Sandhurst. While awaiting a commission he changed his name by deed-poll from Norman Baillie Stewart Wright to Norman Baillie-Stewart. His father, Lieutenant-Colonel Baillie-Wright, a man with a distinguished career, collapsed when his son was sentenced, and became an invalid.

Mr. Leslie Frewin, the publisher, said after the news of Baillie-Stewart's death: "We have Captain Baillie-Stewart's German naturalization papers and his German passport locked away at our bank.

"We negotiated with him for his life story, which was finished and delivered to us about seven weeks ago. He wrote it specifically because, he said, he wanted to clear his name for the sake of his two children".

June 8, 1966.

Lord Baillieu, K.B.E., C.M.G., who died on June 18, 1967, in Melbourne at the age of 77, was president of the Dunlop Rubber Company and its chairman from 1949 to 1957. From 1945 to 1959 he was chairman of the Central Mining and Investment Corporation, Ltd. He was a former president of the Federation of British Industries.

Clive Latham Baillieu was born in Melbourne, Australia, on September 24, 1889. His father, William Lawrence Baillieu was a prominent industrialist, who for more than 20 years was a member of the Victorian State Legislature—holding office as Leader of the Upper House.

Clive Baillieu was educated at the Church of England Grammar School, Melbourne, and entered Trinity College, Melbourne University, in 1908; two years later he went to Magdalen College, Oxford, to read History and Economics. In 1914 he was called to the Bar. A powerful oarsman, he rowed in the winning Oxford crew in 1913.

Returning to Australia early in 1914, Baillieu was called to the Australian Bar, but the outbreak of war cut across any intention of his pursuing a legal career. He served first with the Australian Forces and then with the Royal Flying Corps from 1915 to 1918. He was mentioned in dispatches, received an O.B.E., and retired with the rank of major.

He returned to Britain in 1923, and became associated with W. S. Robinson, British representative of Broken Hill Smelters, who was responsible for the freighting sale of large tonnages of concentrates and metals. This association continued until the Second World War.

Soon after the start of the war, together with Sir D'Arcy Cooper, Sir Samuel Beale, Lord Hyndley and Sir Cecil Weir, Baillieu was invited by Sir Andrew Duncan, President of the Board of Trade, to become a full-time member of the Export Council. He played an important part in the work of the council and in 1941 went to Washington as director-general of the British Purchasing Commission.

SUPPLY TASKS

At the same time he became a member of the British Supply Council in North America. From 1942 to 1943 he was also Head of the British Raw Materials Mission in Washington and British representative on the Combined Raw Materials Board.

From 1945 to 1953 he sat on the National Productivity Advisory Council on Industry. He was a member of the National Investment Council from 1946 to 1948, a member of the General Advisory Council of the British Broadcasting Corporation from 1947 to 1952—and in 1948 he led the British Trade Mission to the Argentine.

He was deputy president of the Federation of British Industries from 1944 to 1945, concerned with the task of adjusting industry to the post-War period. He was president of the F.B.I. from 1945 to 1947, a task for which he was well armed.

Baillieu was rightly proud of the part he took in the creation and organization of the Dollar Exports Board, formed in 1949.

In November, 1945, he accepted an invitation from Sir Stafford Cripps, President of the Board of Trade, to preside over a committee to "formulate detailed proposals for setting up a Central Institute for all questions connected with managements". The committee reported in March, 1946, and its recommendations were accepted by the Government. The British Institute of Management came into being the following year with an Exchequer grant of £150,000 spread over five years, after which time the institute had to be self-supporting. Lord Baillieu sat on the B.I.M. council for five years. He was the institute's first president in 1959 and was made an honorary Fellow in 1960.

He married in 1915, Ruby, daughter of William Clark. She died in 1962. They had three sons and one daughter. He is succeeded by his eldest son, the Hon. William Latham Baillieu.

June 19, 1967.

Nigel Balchin, the novelist whose best-known novels are *The Small Back Room* and *Mine Own Executioner*, died on May 17, 1970, at the age of 61.

In *The Small Back Room*, Balchin told the story of a scientist who, spurred by a sense of inferiority, becomes for the first time a man of action in dismantling an anti-personnel bomb. Through a network of personal intrigues, closely observed under the intimate conditions of office life, the climax is arrived at. This attack on wartime Civil Service bureaucracy was described by one reviewer as "witty, trim, hard and beautifully made—an accomplished and exciting entertainment". *Mine Own Executioner*, a pyschological thriller, published in 1945, two years after *The Small Back Room*, was the story of Felix Milne, a psychoanalyst and his patients. Although it became probably his most popular novel, one critic thought it disappointing. Both novels were filmed, and produced on television.

Nigel Marlin Balchin was born in Wiltshire on December 3, 1908, and educated at Dauntsey's School and Peterhouse College, Cambridge, where he was an exhibitioner and prizeman in natural science.

Balchin in his career sought "to combine business and authorship in varying proportions" and he balanced his time successfully between research work in science and industry and writing in private life. He was a psychologist in the personnel section of the War Office and later Deputy Scientific Adviser to the Army Council. His business experience not only went into novels but also into two mock treatises on industrial efficiency (under the pseudonym Mark Spade) called *How to run a Bassoon Factory* and *Business for Pleasure*. The former was Balchin's earliest published writing, appearing as a series of sketches for Punch explaining (and delightfully distorting) various phases of business.

The appeal of Balchin's novels for one critic lay in his catching the uprooted and jittery attitudes of the not-so-young generation just after the war, and packaging them into a sleek narrative skein. *Lord I was Afraid* (1947) was a "drama somewhat in the early Auden-Isherwood manner."

HONEST WRITER

His novels show the perception of a skilful writer and the story moves at a fast pace. Another reviewer praised his "accuracy of ear, the honesty of his subjects, and the abounding vitality of his characters."

Seen Dimly Before Dawn, published in 1962, was his first novel for some seven years during which he was a script-writer in Hollywood, and wrote "*The first folio edition of Cleopatra*". *Kings of Infinite Space* (1957) centres on Frank Lewis, a decent Cambridge man who is taken to Texas to become the first English astronaut. *In the Absence of Mrs. Petersen* (1966) is about an English script-writer in Hollywood.

Several of Balchin's novels were adapted to the stage or film: *A Sort of Traitors* was the basis of the film *Suspect* and also became a radio play. The play *Waiting for Gillian* was based on another of his novels; so was the television play *The Fall of the Sparrow*. Balchin himself wrote a few plays. *Miserable Sinners* and *The Leader of the House* were among them. He wrote the story and the screenplay for *Josephine and Men*, produced and directed by the Boulting brothers, in 1955.

He was twice married.

May 18, 1970.

Alhaji Sir Abubakar Tafawa Balewa, the first Prime Minister of the Federation of Nigeria, and one of Africa's outstanding statesmen, was found dead on January 21, 1966, having been kidnapped by dissident elements in the Nigerian Army uprising.

His death is particularly tragic coming as it does so soon after his greatest triumph. The Lagos Commonwealth Conference would never have been held without his initiative. That 18 other Commonwealth countries accepted his invitation at short notice was a tribute not only to the urgency of the Rhodesian crisis but also to his personal standing in the world. That the conference succeeded, in spite of many gloomy forecasts, in producing such a substantial measure of agreement was also largely his achievement. He did not dominate the conference. Mr. Lester Pearson produced the most vital ideas: Mr. Wilson enjoyed the triumph of advocacy. But it would be hard to exaggerate the value of Sir Abubakar's quiet authority and judgment in the chair. He controlled the conference with the unforced dignity of a man in a customary role—rather than as the first African ever to preside over such a gathering.

Yet while the conference was proceeding the storm was gathering outside. He had been turning too much of a blind eye to the disorders that had been disrupting life in the western region since the disputed election last October. The bland assumption that this was just a regional problem of law and order seemed increasingly unconvincing as the chaos mounted. This was the type of challenge for which his quintessential courtesy and calmness of judgment fitted him less well. His dilatoriness then proved his fatal flaw.

STRICT MUSLIM

A Northern Nigerian, though not from one of the North's aristocratic families, Sir Abubakar entered federal politics when the Federation came into being, and was its first Minister of Works in January, 1952. In a country which contained Dr. Azikiwe, Chief Awolowo and the Sardauna of Sokoto, Sir Ahmadu Bello, Abubakar was a relatively unknown figure. His choice as federal Prime Minister was a tribute to his personal standing and it was a choice well justified by events.

Although a Northerner, and a strict and sincere Muslim, he developed early a Nigerian outlook. Political supporters and opponents alike accepted him as a man of complete integrity and complete fairness.

Abubakar's background was unusual. His origins were humble. He was in fact the son of a slave who had risen in the service of the Emir of Bauchi, a remote emirate of Northern Nigeria, to the post of direct head. In spite of this, and his lack of any of the titles possessed by almost all the leading politicians in Northern Nigeria (where politics is largely an aristocrat's calling), Abubakar rose to the top.

Born in 1912 in the village of Tafawa, Balewa, a member of the Gere tribe (not of the Hausa-Fulani ruling group), Abubakar was educated at Bauchi Provincial School and then at Katsina Training College, which produced an intellectual elite in the North under British rule. He became a teacher, and a headmaster in Bauchi, and then, in 1945, won a scholarship to Britain, where he studied at the Institute of Education of the University of London. On his return he became a Native Authority Education Officer.

His first taste of politics came with membership of the Northern House of Assembly, and he then became one of the North's representatives in the House of Representatives. Three years before independence, in August, 1957, Abubakar was appointed Federal Prime Minister. On independence day, October 1, 1960, it was he who received from Princess Alexandra the constitutional instruments ending colonial rule. On this occasion he struck an unusual note, in a time of strident African nationalism, in a speech in which he said that Nigeria's pride in their independence was "tempered by feelings of sincere gratitude to all who have shared in the task of developing Nigeria politically, socially, and economically".

If he was ready to give credit to his British friends, people who saw him as a pro-western "moderate" misunderstood his standpoint. He was essentially a Nigerian, who believed deeply in democratic standards, in fairness, in free speech. But when western interests conflicted with those of Nigeria, there was never any doubt where he stood.

ELOQUENT SPEAKER

Ascetic by nature, with a scholarly interest in Islam, Abubakar was calm and dignified where other political leaders were flamboyant and florid. He did not allow himself to be hustled. He thought about problems before making up his mind, but having made it up, he stood by his decisions. For those outside he was Nigeria. His impressive figure, his flowing Northern robes, his obvious qualities of intellect and above all his beautiful voice and by any standards remarkable eloquence in the English language (which earned him in Nigeria the title "the golden voice of the North") combined to make him an outstanding personality. That this should have been true in London was not surprising; it was, however, equally true elsewhere. When he rose to speak at the Addis Ababa African summit conference in 1963, for instance, he held his audience of fellow leaders as effortlessly as he could hold his brother Commonwealth Prime Ministers.

Within Nigeria, Sir Abubakar was to some extent hamstrung by the nature of federal politics, and the need for a coalition. From independence, the Northern People's Congress and the National Convention of Nigerian Citizens were allied—but in each case the party leader was not in the Cabinet. Abubakar himself was vice-president of the N.P.C. and had to defer to some extent to the Sardauna of Sokoto, the party leader.

Relations between the N.P.C. and the N.C.N.C. deteriorated and when the general election of December, 1964, took place, the N.C.N.C. staged a boycott. President Azikiwe hesitated for some days before calling on Sir Abubakar to form a new government—the President's own sympathies being with the N.C.N.C. In the event, he followed constitutional practice, in a decision that owed much to his own sense of propriety (and feeling of Nigerian nationhood), but was due in no small measure to the calm authority of Abubakar, as usual dignified and manifestly acting not for himself but for the national good.

He was a man of courage and sound judgment and above all of patience which was often sorely tried in the frenzies of Nigerian politics. Understandably, however, he often yearned for his farm in Bauchi, and for a peaceful life studying Islam and astronomy.

He was made O.B.E. in 1952 and promoted C.B.E. in 1955. In 1960 he was knighted and promoted K.B.E. He became a member of the Privy Council in 1961.

January 24, 1966.

Lord Balfour of Burleigh, chairman of Lloyds Bank from 1946 to 1954, who died on June 4, 1967, in London, at the age of 83, was a man who touched public life at many points.

He was an indefatigable committeeman, always in demand, chairman of the Land Tax Commissioners, a former chairman of the Medical Research Council, and a former Alderman of Kensington where he had strong ties and where he will be remembered particularly for the Kensington Housing Trust which he founded and over which he presided from 1926 to 1949.

He was chairman of the Committee of the London Clearing Banks from 1950 to 1952, president of the Institute of Bankers from 1948 to 1949; and chairman of the Departmental Committee on the Export of Live Cattle in 1957. He sat on the Select Committee of the House of Lords on the Powers of the House in relation to the Attendance of its members and was also on the Committee on Administrative Tribunals and Enquiries.

CRUSADER SPIRIT

He had in him something of the crusading spirit which came out strongly when he was pursuing his campaigns for better housing, improved town planning, land use, and associated problems of our time. On these matters he spoke lucidly and with authority in the House of Lords.

The Rt. Hon. George John Gordon Bruce, 11th Lord Balfour of Burleigh, and a representative peer for Scotland from 1922 to 1963, was born on October 18, 1883, the second but only surviving son of the 10th Lord Balfour of Burleigh.

While at Eton a lung weakness compelled him to spend winters in Switzerland where he became an accomplished skater. He had no luck in the entrance examination for the Diplomatic Service and set out to make a career in the City. Joining the Alliance as a junior insurance clerk at £90 a year, he did well, was moved to Edinburgh where he widened his experience, and at 27 was back in London as manager of the West End branch.

DISLIKED CANVASSING

However he found the canvassing side of insurance not altogether to his taste and left insurance to join in a finance firm in the City. He served with distinction in the First World War in the Argyll and Sutherland Highlanders and the Intelligence Corps, was wounded at Neuve Chapelle and four times mentioned in dispatches.

After the war he returned to the City and went through some difficult years. But his natural intelligence and versatility and, above all, his capacity for hard work brought him through and he became a force in City affairs and a director of influential concerns.

His elder brother, Robert, was killed in action at Le Cateau in 1914 and in 1921 he succeeded his father.

Outside his many financial interests, as has been remarked, he found time for much social work. Until 1945 he was a member of the Central Housing Advisory Committee. He advocated the creation of regional housing authorities for the area in and around London, and public ownership for town planning purposes and the creation of satellite towns. He was President of the Royal Sanitary Institute from 1931 to 1941.

PROGRESSIVE BANKER

As chairman of Lloyds Bank (he succeeded Lord Wardington) he took a progressive line in all matters relating to banking practice, organization, and staffing and he was certainly a stimulating influence on the banking world, though none was more insistent than he that the experience and judgment of the general managers must have the decisive voice. Under his chairmanship Lloyds Bank initiated some important and valuable developments in methods of selection, grading, and promotion of staff. He was keenly interested in the bank's monthly *Review* as a forum for the expert discussion of economic subjects and as a record of current economic trends, and under his guidance and encouragement the *Review* acquired a prestige which extended much beyond the banking world itself. His annual addresses as chairman of the bank, coupled with his speeches in the House of Lords, struck a strong and individual note on general financial and economic affairs.

CRITIC OF INFLATION

He was always regarded as a very stern critic of inflation—especially the "suppressed" inflation which involved controls and which in his view made for a serious rigidity of industry and immobility of labour. While he shared the general bankers' view that excessive Government expenditure must bear much of the blame for inflation, he was one of the first to insist that the "cheap money" policy was a strong inflationary influence and that a harder monetary policy was essential if "over-employment" was to cease and the domestic economy was to be made more mobile and flexible. Not unnaturally, his views attracted much attention among left-wing critics, and he was widely accused by Labour Party speakers and others of leading a campaign for a "healthy dose of unemployment". But he insisted that he was urging no more than that there should not be such an over-demand for labour as would necessitate controls and make the economy rigid and unadaptable.

GOLF CAPTAIN

Although much of his time was occupied by his London activities he had a place in Scotland at Brucefield, Clackmannan, and was a J.P. and Deputy Lieutenant for Clackmannanshire. In 1943 he was appointed chairman of the committee on the Hill Farming Sheep Industry in Scotland.

He was captain of the Royal and Ancient Golf Club of St. Andrews in 1949.

He married in 1919 Violet Dorothy, M.B.E., younger daughter of Richard H. Done, and they had two sons and four daughters. He is succeeded by his elder son, the Master of Burleigh.

June 6, 1967.

Lorenzo Bandini, the Italian racing champion and Ferrari ace, who died on May 10, 1967, from injuries received in the Monaco Grand Prix on May 7, was one of Italy's brightest hopes.

His arrival on the international motor racing scene was widely acclaimed by his intensely patriotic countrymen, for he accepted the mantle of glory vacated by the deaths of Tazio Nuvolari, Alberto Ascari and Luigi Musso. In so doing, he helped Italian motor sport out of the doldrums and achieved a popularity as great as any star matador.

Bandini was born in Barce, Cyrenaica, North Africa, on December 21, 1935, of Italian parents and had an older sister, Graziella. The family returned to Italy in 1939 and lived in the outskirts of Florence. When Bandini was just 15 his father died and he left home to become an apprentice mechanic at the workshop of Signor Freddi in Milan. This wealthy and kindly man helped shape Bandini's career and it was through him that he made his competition debut in 1957 at the wheel of a Fiat 1100.

After gaining experience in several Italian hill climbs, Bandini attracted national publicity with a class win in the 1958 Mille Miglia Rally in a Lancia and later bought a Volpini Formula Junior car. He was placed third in the first FJ race in Sicily and said of the new formula to a friend "A new, terrible world beckons me." Bandini scored several successes in 1959 and 1960 with an FJ Stanguellini, placing fourth in the Formula Junior World Championship the latter year.

A critical year in Bandini's career was 1961.

UNHAPPY SEASON

He was bitterly disappointed when his compatriot Giancarlo Baghetti was chosen to drive a sponsored Ferrari by the association of Italian motor clubs (FISA). But Bandini had been spotted by Signor "Mimo" Dei, the team patron of Centro-Sud, and finished third in his Formula I debut at Pau. He drove in his first world championship race at Spa later that year, retiring with engine failure. During the winter of 1961-62 Bandini drove in the "Tasman" races in Australia and New Zealand and joined Ferrari in 1962. It was not a happy season, for the Maranello empire was a shadow of its former self after the World championship successes of 1961 with the new rear-engined Ferraris of Phil Hill and the late von Trips and his drives were almost on an *ad hoc* basis. Bandini did make an excellent debut in a works Ferrari in the Monaco GP and finished third.

For 1963, Bandini was retained by Ferrari for sports car races only and it was Signor Dei who again came to his rescue by buying Bandini the ex-Graham Hill BRM, which he campaigned most successfully under Centro-Sud colours.

WIN AT LE MANS

After a brilliant victory at Le Mans (with Scarfiotti) for Ferrari, Bandini was eventually promoted to the Ferrari Formula I team in the 1963 Italian GP and has been with it ever since. In 1964, he proved his ability by winning the Austrian GP, his first championship event. His other notable Ferrari victories include Clermont-Ferrand, the Nurburgring 1,000 kms., the Targa Florio and the Daytona 24-hours.

Lorenzo Bandini, Ferrari's team leader this year, was at the peak of his career. Driving the red Maranello cars he shared the winning Ferrari in the Daytona 24-hours race in February and the Monza 1,000 kilometre race on April 25. Early April, 1967, he set fastest lap and an unofficial outright circuit record at the Le Mans Practice weekend and was clear favourite to win the 24-hour French classic on June 10–11. That he died after unflinchingly disputing the lead in a major grand prix was typical of this colourful Italian.

Of medium height, with dark hair worn low on the collar and film star looks, Bandini had a great sense of humour. Although at times his forceful driving was criticized by other competitors, he was popular both on the track and off. Bandini lived at Milan and was married in February, 1964, to Margherita Freddi, the daughter of his former employer.

May 11, 1967.

Tallulah Bankhead, the actress, died in New York on December 12, 1968, at the age of 65. With long, lank hair, a husky voice and a devastating wit, she was unique in her field—a personality as much as an actress.

Miss Bankhead, who was outspoken in her likes and dislikes, was most noted for her stage performances in *The Little Foxes, Private Lives* and *The Skin of our Teeth.* Her comedy timing, haunted face with its drooping eyelids and her particular way of saying "dahling", provided impersonators with rich material and she was one of their favourite subjects.

She made her first stage appearance at the age of 16 and from that time her career was a mixed bag of hits and misses. Among the latter was a flop production on Broadway of Shakespeare's *Antony and Cleopatra* in which she appeared as the Egyptian queen. Years later, she delighted audiences of her popular radio and television shows by quoting reviews of her as Cleopatra.

Her films included Alfred Hitchcock's *Lifeboat, Tarnished Lady, Devil and the Deep* and *Royal Scandal,* in which she played Catherine the Great of Russia. Miss Bankhead, who arrived in Britain in the 20s and quickly became the "darling" of London society, started making cabaret appearances in the 1950s with her own brand of humour and glamour.

LAW SUIT

Her outspokenness in her autobiography, published in 1952, led to at least one law suit. The British publishers agreed in court to pay compensation to actress Olga Lindo because of Miss Bankhead's comments on that actress's performance as Sadie Thompson in Somerset Maugham's *Rain.* Maugham had turned down Miss Bankhead for the role of the slut Sadie. In her autobiography Tallulah said she went home, put on Sadie's costume, "gulped down 20 aspirins" and lay down after scribbling "It ain't gonna rain no more". The next day her friend Noel Coward telephoned to offer her a role in his play *Fallen Angels,* which was a big hit for her.

Tallulah Bankhead was a Southerner: her father, William Brockman Bankhead was from Alabama, and her mother was a Virginian. Tallulah was born at Huntsville, Alabama, on January 31, 1903; her father was Democratic City Attorney for Huntsville and later Solicitor General for the judicial district, and in 1917 he was elected to Congress. That same year she won a beauty prize offered by a film magazine and in 1918 she played her first parts on the New York stage and in films.

TAWNY HAIR

In 1922 she was recommended by Charles B. Cochran to Gerald du Maurier as a possible leading lady of a play due for production at Wyndham's in London. Du Maurier sent for her, then put her off, but she decided none the less to go to England: "You'll be offered a part because your hair is so beautiful", said her friend the British-born actress, Miss Estelle Winwood. Her hair was "tawny". Sure enough, when du Maurier saw her without a hat, he again changed his mind and she was engaged for *The Dancers.*

In London she at once attracted a following of "gallery girls" which grew within two years into a feminine legion of Tallulah-fans. This was hard on her as an actress, for they did not support her when she gave her best performance in Sydney Howard's *They Knew What They Wanted.* They preferred her in *The Gold Diggers,* doing the charleston and turning a cartwheel, or in *The Garden of Eden* and *Her Cardboard Lover,* semi-undressed. To prove there was more to her than all this, she appeared in *The Lady of the Camellias* in 1930, but her monotonous delivery of the lines betrayed her inexperience, and, having accepted a long-term offer from Paramount, she prepared to go home at the beginning of 1931. "Tallulah is always skating on thin ice; everyone wants to be there when it breaks", Mrs. Patrick Campbell had said of her, but the British ice had not broken.

NO LIGHTWEIGHT

Anti-climax followed. She did not establish herself as a film star in Hollywood, and on returning to the theatre in New York had no luck till 1939, when Miss Lillian Hellman's *The Little Foxes* gave her the finest dramatic opportunity of her career. After this no one could again dismiss her as a lightweight or an exhibitionist. She earned a second award from the New York critics for her comedy work in 1942 in Thornton Wilder's *The Skin of Our Teeth,* the play described by Alexander Woolcott as the nearest thing to a great American one.

ACADEMY PORTRAIT

She married in 1937 John Emery, the actor; the marriage was dissolved in 1940. Augustus John's portrait of her as a young woman was exhibited at the R.A. and is referred to in her autobiography, *Tallulah,* as her most valued possession.

December 13, 1968.

Sir John Barbirolli, C.H., who died on July 28, 1970, at the age of 70, was a virtuoso conductor in the tradition of those spell-binding artists who made the conductor the centre of popular devotion for concertgoers in the twentieth century.

A vividly colourful personality whose presence on the rostrum added its own indefinable excitements to any programme, he was at the same time a devoted, perfectionist musician indefatigable in his service of the works he chose to conduct and in his determination to mould any orchestra into an instrument producing precisely the tone colour and phrasing he required.

He was permanent conductor of the Hallé Orchestra, Manchester, from 1943 to 1958; principal conductor from 1958 to 1968 and that same year appointed Conductor Laureate for life.

John Barbirolli, the son of an orchestral violinist and grandson of an Italian musician who had settled in England, was born in London on December 2, 1899. As a child he began to learn his father's instrument but changed to the cello, and it was as a cellist that he first appeared in public, playing Goltermann's Cello Concerto with the orchestra of Trinity College of Music, where he was a student, when he was only 11 years old. From 1912 to 1917, already an experienced soloist with a considerable reputation as a child prodigy—he had made his first gramophone records before the outbreak of war in 1914—he studied at the Royal Academy of Music, and, his studies ended, after a brief period in the Army, in 1919 he became a cellist in the Queen's Hall Orchestra and played with the Kutcher and International String Quartets, augmenting his earnings by work in London theatre orchestras.

From his first appearance as a conductor, with a string orchestra he himself founded in 1924, and with the Guild of Singers and Players and the Chenil Orchestra in 1925, his ascent was rapid. In 1926 the British National Opera Company entrusted him with *Aida, Madame Butterfly* and *Romeo and Juliet*; in the following year he appeared with the Covent Garden Opera Company, extending his range to *Der Rosenkavalier* and *The Bartered Bride*; at the same time he was demonstrating unusual qualities in the concert hall and from 1933 to 1936 he conducted the Scottish and Northern Philharmonic Orchestras.

His appointment to succeed Toscanini as conductor of the New York Philharmonic Orchestra after Toscanini's retirement in 1936, though it aroused some discontent from American concertgoers who felt that an older and more internationally celebrated musician should have been appointed, showed how high Barbirolli's reputation had begun to stand beyond the world of English music, and his performances in New York entirely justified his appointment, so that discontent rapidly changed into complete satisfaction. Barbirolli himself believed, however—and history will probably endorse his view—that his greatest achievement was the revival of the Halle Orchestra in 1943. Home-sick for a beleaguered Britain—his feelings had brought him back for a 10 weeks' tour in which he conducted 34 concerts after a difficult wartime Atlantic crossing in 1942, and under pressure from the American Musicians' union to take American citizenship—he accepted the Hallé Society's invitation to become the orchestra's first permanent conductor since the retirement of Sir Hamilton Harty in 1933.

Since the formation of the B.B.C. Northern Orchestra, many of the Hallé players had worked for the B.B.C. as well as the Hallé Society, and the society's intention to reorganize the orchestra on a permanent basis at a time when all its younger musicians were in the armed forces left Barbirolli, on his arrival in Manchester, with nothing but the Hallé's tradition and prestige together with a nucleus of fewer than 30 players. The story of how, in a couple of months of endless auditions, he rebuilt the Hallé, accepting any good player whatever his musical background—he found himself with a schoolboy first flute, a school mistress hornist, and various brass players recruited from brass and military bands in the Manchester area—deservedly ranks as a wartime epic. The reborn Hallé's first concert somehow lived up to the Hallé's great reputation at a time when much English orchestral playing was understandably makeshift.

The Hallé Orchestra, however, maintains financial equilibrium only through a gruelling concert schedule which in the years immediately after the Second World War almost defied the maintaining of high standards. Not only were standards maintained but Barbirolli, exhaustive and exhausting in rehearsal, conducted up to 75 of the concerts a year. Conductorships of greater security, less demanding in their terms, were offered to him, but he used them only as levers to obtain better conditions for the orchestra to which he had given his loyalty. At the same time, in the 1950s he conducted a number of very impressive opera performances at Covent Garden, including a *Tristan and Isolde* which, though it was some distance from the German tradition, was lyrically intense and convincing. In 1960, he accepted the conductorship of the Houston, Texas, Symphony Orchestra, a post which, held in conjunction with his direction of the Hallé, took him from Manchester for 12 weeks of every year while reuniting him with American audiences.

ON TOUR

The Halle's prestige in Britain took it to many of the native festivals, and for several years it bore the main weight of the Cheltenham Festival where its style seemed to exert a good deal of influence upon the annual symphony which at the time was the central novelty to be heard. One of Barbirolli's ambitions, which he prosecuted with characteristic energy and determination, was to win the orchestra an international reputation; he conducted the orchestra on several Continental tours which won it acclaim as far away as the Athens Festival, but it remained a lasting disappointment to him that he was never able to tour the United States with his own orchestra. If, in the 1960s, the Hallé tended to become a youthful and, consequently, rather inexperienced orchestra whose members tended to move rapidly towards London, so that its performance did not always preserve the mellow, rich shine which was Barbirolli's sound ideal, in his hands it never lost the tradition, preserved from Beecham and Harty, of whole-hearted exciting playing, and Barbirolli's appearances as a guest conductor on the Continent were rapturously acclaimed. In 1949 he was knighted and in 1950 the Royal Philharmonic Society awarded him its gold medal. He was created a Companion of Honour in 1969.

CATHOLIC TASTES

If Barbirolli's choice of music was largely formed by tastes developed in youth, those tastes were remarkably catholic: he would lavish as much care on a waltz by Strauss or Lehar as on a symphony by Mozart, and was one of the few conductors not born in Vienna to whom the rhythmic subtleties of Viennese dance music came naturally. The early works of Britten, notably the *Sinfonia da Requiem*, he played splendidly, and he served Vaughan Williams (to whom he was "Glorious John") with heartfelt devotion. The music of Alban Berg, too, won richly emotional performances from him but he seemed to be unwilling to advance further along twentieth century paths. If, in the music of Haydn, Mozart and Beethoven, he seemed to demand a smooth elegance not always totally convincing in such works as the *Eroica* or the Choral symphony, he was a great conductor of the late nineteenth century masters.

He could build the patient architecture of a Bruckner Symphony with complete conviction: his Sibelius was powerfully dramatic and in Elgar he conveyed violent emotional experiences always grown from his own affection for the music. His work for Mahler—whose music he played whenever possible even at a concert in La Scala, Milan—was characteristically devoted; it grew not from the legends which have grown round the works but from a scrupulous, note by note consideration of what Mahler wrote. In the same way, he prepared himself for his first performance of the Saint Matthew Passion through study detailed enough to make his conducting score look like a new annotated edition.

MINOR SLAVERY

Barbirolli was a fascinating amalgam of Italy and England. He loved cricket and collected glass, but music left him little time for any other activities or any hobbies. A sense of showmanship, used always to project the music and never its conductor, including an almost instinctive exploitation of his smallness and deceptively frail appearance—for he was a man of enormous energy and determination—seemed to be vehicles for extrovert Italian characteristics. Orchestral musicians accepted a degree of slavery when they worked with him, but they did so with affection and admiration, knowing that he was never their taskmaster but a fellow slave driven along by an appetite for perfection in phrasing, nuance and tone colour.

Barbirolli was twice married. He married first Marjorie Parry, the singer, and this marriage was dissolved; he married secondly, in 1939, Evelyn Rothwell, the oboe player.

July 30, 1970.

Sir Alan Barlow, BT., G.C.B., K.B.E., who died on February 28, 1968, at the age of 86, was a man of great versatility, whose interests and achievements extended far beyond a very distinguished career as a civil servant.

James Alan Noel Barlow was the eldest son of Sir Thomas Barlow, Bt. (1845–1945), sometime Physician Extraordinary to Queen Victoria. The Barlows came from a family of Manchester cotton spinners, who in the industrial revolution laid the foundations of the family fortunes—a younger brother, Sir Thomas D. Barlow, G.B.E., was Director General of Civilian Clothing in the Second World War and chairman of Barlow & Jones Ltd.

Born on Christmas Day, 1881, Alan Barlow was educated at Marlborough and Corpus Christi College, Oxford, of which he was a Scholar. He took a second in Mods in 1904, a 1st in Greats. After a year as a Clerk in the House of Commons he was selected by Sir Robert Morant for a Junior Examinership in the Board of Education.

Early in the war of 1914 he was transferred to the Labour Supply Department of the Ministry of Munitions, where he was Deputy Controller and where, with the late Mr. Justice Langton, he was particularly successful in smoothing out labour difficulties and settling labour disputes. With the return of peace, Barlow was transferred to the Ministry of Labour as Principal Assistant Secretary, and put in charge of the Training Department. The success of the Ministry's Training Centres was largely due to his initiative and business capacity.

In 1933 he was appointed Principal Private Secretary to the Prime Minister (Ramsay MacDonald). The two men were not temperamentally best suited to each other, and MacDonald was not the easiest man to serve; so, the following year when changes in the Treasury left open an Under-Secretaryship, Barlow was glad of an exchange. He served in the Treasury until he retired in 1948 having then for some years been joint Second Secretary.

The varied work of the Treasury was eminently suited to a man with Alan Barlow's interests and wide range of friendships.

He came of hardy Manchester business stock and his remarkable capacity for getting straight to the heart of a question was more suggestive of the successful business man of the best type than of a product of Whitehall. His mind was less subtle than direct, and though his manner was conciliatory and good-tempered, he was no respecter of persons, however highly placed, and was certainly never afraid of them.

He had the capacity for seeking out among his innumerable friends the one who could provide accurate information or support his judgment on some difficult issue.

Small wonder then that he was in great demand to serve on important commissions and committees. The committee bearing his name which is most likely to live in history was the committee of which he was chairman appointed towards the end of 1945 to consider the policy which should govern the use and development of scientific man-power resources over the next ten years. The committee recommended doubling the scientific output of the universities.

This recommendation which was accepted and carried out, was the chief factor in the increase in the university population in the first decade after the Second World War. He was a member of the Iron and Steel Board in 1946–48 and of the court of the University of London from 1949 to 1956.

Barlow had strong interests in artistic matters and a good sympathy and understanding with scientists, a side of him which was no doubt fostered by his marriage in 1911 to Emma Nora, daughter of the late Sir Horace Darwin, K.B.E., F.R.S., of Cambridge. He served for many years on the Advisory Council on Scientific Policy.

In his years at the Treasury after the Second World War it seemed inevitable that Barlow should be asked to exercise an oversight over the Treasury's relations with all those who looked to the Exchequer for help for the Sciences, for Museums and Galleries and the Arts, and for academic Institutions. Barlow's admirable conduct of this function was perhaps made all the easier by the fact that his discussions with those concerned was carried out as often in the Athenaeum as in Treasury Chambers.

But not even all these activities could exhaust Barlow's energies. For several years he was chairman of the executive committee of the Athenaeum and for a time he was also chairman of the Savile Club. He also farmed successfully several hundred acres of Wendover. He was a keen gardener and a great collector, especially of porcelain.

The Barlow Collection of Oriental art is one of the finest in the world. Sir Alan was president of the Oriental Ceramic Society for many years and had been a collector of Oriental porcelain since he was 18. He made many generous benefactions from his collection to public galleries.

He also had a wide knowledge of modern art and literature, and a fine taste in wines. All this was done with enjoyment and in an unflurried way.

On his retirement from the public service Alan Barlow found more time for his artistic interests. For seven years he was a member of the board of trustees of the National Gallery and for three years chairman of that body.

February 29, 1968.

Sydney Barnes, one of England's greatest bowlers, died on December 26, 1967, at the age of 94. Sydney Francis Barnes turned to splendid advantage his physical advantages. Right-arm fast-medium, he made full use of his height—he stood fully six feet—and possessed a most deceptive flight, exceptional accuracy of length and command of both swerve and break. Though he generally brought the ball in from leg he could turn it either way, and could bowl for long spells without loss of effectiveness.

Up till the First World War, and for some time afterwards, two international bowlers were widely accepted as supreme: Spofforth and Barnes. Debates on which was the deadlier remained inconclusive, if only for chronological causes. Sydney Barnes, born on April 19, 1873, some 20 years after Spofforth, was the slower to prove his genius. As an amateur for Warwickshire in 1894 and 1895, he was unimpressive and revealed scarcely more promise as a Lancashire professional in 1899.

He might never have developed as he did but for the perception of A. C. MacLaren, who reimported him from League cricket into the Lancashire side for the last match of 1901, and invited him to Australia—provoking the inevitable outcry.

A raw recruit can seldom have confuted criticism more completely: five for 66 against South Australia, 12 for 99 against Victoria, and—in the first Test match—five for 65 (after a useful little 26 not out), paving the way for England's only victory. Australia's revenge at Melbourne was achieved in spite of Barnes's six for 42 and seven for 121; and 'there is no knowing what might have followed if his knee had not given way at Adelaide and incapacitated him for the rest of the tour—which was all Australia's.

THOUGHT TO BE TEMPERAMENTAL

In 1902 he played in one Test match—at Sheffield, where he took six wickets for 49. He was considered temperamental, and, in spite of 130 wickets in 1903, was liable to variations. Then a dispute with Lancashire led him to quit first-class cricket and join Staffordshire, who benefited by twice becoming Minor County Champions.

In 1907, however, he visited Australia under A. O. Jones, playing in three Test matches: in the third, at Melbourne, having taken five for 74 in the second innings, he scored 38 not out in a partnership with Fielder, giving England her solitary, one-wicket victory. He also took seven for 36 against New South Wales and 10 for 67 against Victoria.

He played in three Test matches during 1909, and his 17 wickets (average 20) suggested that he might have played in all. That year, in taking five for 22 against the Gentlemen in the first innings, his tremendous spin tore pieces out of the turf. "I have never played against finer bowling", wrote Sir Pelham Warner.

Yet his greatest achievements lay ahead—in the 1911–12 tour of Australia, perhaps the only occasion on which the famous Australian morale faltered. Domestic dissension was partly responsible, but the real reason was that Barnes had found the ideal partner in Frank Foster. Though England, deprived of P. F. Warner's captaincy by illness, lost the first Test match, the winning of the last four, under Douglas, was accomplished by a bowling partnership which brought 34 wickets to Barnes and 32 to Foster.

Foster bowled left-handed, round the wicket, in the classic manner. Barnes was a "lively medium who could make the ball do something either way", wrote Moyes. "Both were masters of their art."

There followed the rain-ruined Triangular Tournament in England in 1912. England had an inspired captain in C.B. Fry and a devastating slow left-hander in Blythe; but Barnes with 39 wickets (average 10.35) led the way decisively.

Barnes made a tour to South Africa in 1913–14. There, at 40, he moved many cricketers in three countries to proclaim him the greatest bowler who had ever lived. At Johannesburg in December he established the (pre-Laker) record of taking 17 wickets in a Test match. Admittedly the Hon. L. H. Tennyson's team outclassed their opponents, but consider that, in this series, Barnes took 49 wickets in *four* Test matches—being unable to play in the fifth.

His Test match total of 189 wickets has since been exceeded by others—but he obtained them in 27 matches.

Let us take leave of statistics and picture him bowling: "a lithe, springy run to the crease, and, with his tall, loosely knit figure, the embodiment of hostile action". He turned his leg-break at a great pace—and made it get up. Sir Pelham Warner thought that he had never played a better innings than he did against Barnes at Lord's in 1913, when he made 24. Then a leg-break of perfect length on the middle and leg stump got up like lightning, touched the thumb of his left glove, and was held by "Tiger" Smith at eye level.

As a Test match bowler Sydney Barnes ended his career in 1914, when so many great and good things ended. He continued to play for Staffordshire until 1935; but the figure that endures in our memories is that of a lithe, tall, loose-limbed man, firm-jawed, slightly hollow-cheeked, and implacably hostile to anyone who held a bat.

December 27, 1967.

The former Maharaja Gaekwar of Baroda, G.C.I.E., once the world's second richest man, died on July 19, 1968, in the London Clinic, at the age of 60. He ruled one of the most important of the Indian Princely States from 1939 until shortly after its absorption in the democratized state of Bombay. In 1951, he was deposed, and—five years before he died—he was given a £17,000 allowance from the Indian Government. At one time he ruled with almost absolute power more than 3,000,000 people with all the pomp and pageantry of an oriental court.

Farzand - I - Khas - I - Dowlat - O - Englishia, Maharaja Sir Pratapsingh Gaekwar, Sena Khas Khel Shamsher Bahadur, was known for his love of sport—racing, tennis and polo in particular—he acquired much practical experience of administration, and in the first few years after he had ascended the *gadi* in 1939 was almost a model ruler.

In April, 1951, he was given a month's notice to quit his £190,000 a year job as ruler. The order came from Pandit Nehru, who sacked him for "defying the central government".

USED RIGHT OF APPEAL

With a right to appeal against the sacking, he did so, and told friends: "My only fault, if any, has been, above all else, to act in the best and true interests of the people in my state."

In New Delhi he lived in a huge, white, stone house in the Princes Park. His neighbour was the Nizam of Hyderabad, who topped the Gaekwar, at one time as the world's richest man. At that time, the Gaekwar had a bank balance of £9m. While he was under notice to quit, his second wife flew 3,000 miles to London from New York, to phone her husband. Leaving the aircraft she explained: "I can't phone India from America so I have come over here." She was Princess Sita Devi whom he married in 1943. She smoked £10 Havana cigars—held in a ruby-studded holder. They were divorced in Bombay in 1956. His first wife was Princess Hanta Dev. They married in 1929—to a salute from gold and silver guns.

In May, 1951, he lost his appeal against his dismissal, and with it his throne, palace, many of his jewels and a £200,000 a year tax-free purse. His eldest son, the Yuvraj Fateh Singh, succeeded him.

While he lived in England, he continued to build up his string of racehorses, and in 1957 paid a record price of £29,400 for a yearling colt. At bloodstock sales at Newmarket and Doncaster, he spent close to a million pounds on animals. Shortly after this, he announced his retirement from the racing world. He had already sold his Newmarket racing stables in 1951.

Pratapsingh was born on June 29, 1908, to Rajkumar Fatesingh Rao, eldest of the three sons of the Maharaja Sayaji Rao III. Fatesingh was allowed far too much to spend during his student days at Oxford and died in young manhood. His son, Pratapsingh, was educated at the Chief's College, Rajkot, and for a time in England. In February, 1939, he came to the rule of a prosperous administrative heritage.

The Maharaja gave full and generous support to the Allied cause in the Second World War.

BOMBER SQUADRON

Its principal feature was the provision of the 124th (Baroda) Squadron of the R.A.F., which gained a notable war record in bombing attacks on Germany and repulsing enemy raids. The Maharaja took close personal interest in the welfare of the squadron, and for three years in succession allotted a Christmas gift of £500 for amenities and social reunions. The squadron crest was prepared by the College of Heralds, and a silver replica of its emblem—a mongoose—was presented to every officer pilot and member of ground staff by the Maharaja.

In pursuance of his grandfather's promotion of Hindu social reform the Maharaja assented to State legislation prohibiting polygamy. Yet at the end of 1943 he contracted a second marriage with Sita Devi, third daughter of the Maharaja of Pithipuram, one of the richest landowners of South India. She temporarily embraced the Muslim faith in order to divorce her first husband. To the strong remonstrances of his far-sighted Dewan, Sir V. T. Krishnamechari, Pratapsingh turned a deaf ear, claiming that he was not himself bound by the State Laws.

With the eager encouragement of the new spouse, Pratapsingh took up racing with enthusiasm. At the Newmarket auction in 1945, he gave the record price of 28,000 guineas for a yearling (full brother of Dante, the year's Derby winner) and later raced him under the name of My Babu. In 1952, his Aquino II won the Ascot Gold Cup.

Stories of the Maharaja's lavishness and of his being "the second richest man in the world" lost nothing in the telling in Baroda and caused growing dissatisfaction. In 1948 soon after the transfer of power, the Baroda Legislature passed a resolution calling for his abdication in favour of his eldest son. A further resolution requested the Indian Government to investigate the Maharaja's alleged misappropriation.

BRIEF REFORM

On the main issue of the Maharaja's powers, the late Sardar Patel, the States Minister, induced him to set up a system of popular government in 1948, based on a wide franchise and with ministers having full executive responsibility. But the arrangement was of brief duration, for in May 1949 orders were issued from Delhi for the State to be completely merged in the Bombay province. Though the Maharaja publicly assented to the merger, he deemed himself deeply aggrieved, alleging that he had not been consulted.

July 20, 1968.

Air Chief Marshal Sir Arthur Sheridan Barratt, K.C.B., C.M.G., M.C., a former Inspector-General of the R.A.F., died at his home in Hampshire on November 4, 1966, at the age of 75.

He served for more than 36 years in the Army, R.F.C., and R.A.F., and was an expert on army and air cooperation. As a young artillery officer in the First World War he gained his first decoration for the effective help he gave to his old corps as an air spotter for a siege battery. Between the wars he saw service in India and at Shanghai, and commanded the School of Army Cooperation. When the needs of war led to the setting up of an Army Cooperation Command within the R.A.F. in 1940, he was chosen to command it.

Arthur Sheridan Barratt, born on February 25, 1891, at Peshawar, India, was educated at Clifton, entered the R.M. Academy, Woolwich, and was commissioned as second lieutenant in the Royal Artillery in December, 1910. In June, 1914, he graduated from the Central Flying School as a pilot and was seconded to the R.F.C., with which he gained promotion to flight commander in March, 1916, and wing commander in June, 1917.

IN A GALE

For most of the time during the First World War he served with artillery spotting units, and he commanded a squadron when the Battle of Arras was fought. The official air history records that on July 23, 1915, he was observer for the 19th. Siege Battery which was attempting to destroy a long range gun which was shelling Bethune. With his assistance the battery obtained three direct hits, the last of which pierced the roof over the gun and exploded the ammunition. A gale was raging at the time. For his war services Barratt was awarded the M.C. in January, 1916, and the Belgian Croix de Guerre avec Palme. He was also made a Chevalier of the Belgian Order of the Crown in 1918 and a C.M.G. in June, 1919.

He became chief instructor at the R.A.F. Staff College, Andover. He commanded No. 1 Group at his birthplace, Peshawar, 1931–32; he then became senior air staff officer at headquarters in New Delhi, being promoted air commodore. In 1935 he was appointed Director of Staff Duties, Air Ministry, and a year later was promoted to air vice-marshal and made commandant of the Staff College.

Following his promotion to air marshal in 1939 he was selected to become A.O.C. in India, but the war intervened, and instead he went to France as principal R.A.F. liaison officer with the French Army and Air Forces. In January, 1940, he became A.O.C.-in-C., British Air Forces in France. In the retreat from Dunkirk Barratt remained on the beaches and refused to leave until he was certain that all his men had been got away. He returned to England and was promoted to K.C.B. (having been made a C.B. in 1937).

When, in December, 1940, the War Office and Air Ministry agreed to set up an Army Cooperation Command to secure the most effective working between the Army and the R.A.F., Barratt was an abvious choice for the post of A.O.C.-in-C. He held it until June, 1943, when he was appointed A.O.C.-in-C., Technical Training Command, until after the war ended. From 1945 to 1947 he held the post of Inspector-General, R.A.F., and was made an air chief marshal in January, 1946. He retired in March, 1947, and was appointed Gentleman Usher to the Sword of State. He was appointed a deputy-lieutenant for Hampshire in 1956.

Barratt was married in 1916 to Norah Lilian Crew and they were divorced in 1948. They had one daughter. In 1949, he married secondly Judith Rhoda Cartmell, widow of Terence Horsley.

November 7, 1966.

President René Barrientos Ortuno, president of Bolivia since August, 1966, died on April 27, 1969, in a helicopter crash. He was in his late forties.

Earlier in the month he had conceded that members of the C.I.A. had helped the Bolivian Army to fight the guerrillas led by the late Ché Guevara. The death of the former Cuban revolutionary in 1967, and the handling of the Communist-inspired guerrilla campaign were to have international reverberations. The sweat-stained notebook calendar in which Guevara jotted down his final guerrilla adventure was captured by the Bolivian Army; this somewhat commonplace diary, not published immediately, was handed to Minister Arguedas, for a single hour, which permitted Fidel Castro to release the text to the world—Arguedas who had been Barrientos's top security adviser had placed a photostated copy in his hands.

Barrientos survived the Arguedas affair—but not totally unharmed. He had quarrelled with his Vice-President, Luis Adolfo Siles, over the arrest of opposition legislators, and the four political parties which made up the governing front originally, and then the governing coalition, withdrew their support. Barrientos replaced his wholly civilian Cabinet with a wholly military one last year to eradicate guerrilla activities.

Barrientos, a handsome former Air Force general, was the target of many assassination attempts; and the dark-haired president carried three bullets in his body as a result of one of the attempts in 1963.

It was in the Air Force that he earned a reputation for outstanding personal bravery.

PROVED SAFE

He once attended an air show where a parachutist under his command fell to his death. In order to prove that the parachutes were not defective, he picked one out at random and jumped.

Barrientos, at the time vice-president, originally came to power as the head of the military junta which displaced the Nationalist Revolutionary Movement (N.R.M.) government of President Paz Estenssoro in a bloodless coup in November, 1964. Barrientos raised the flag of revolt on home ground in Cochabamba, Bolivia's second city. One of the reasons the new junta put forward for the coup was that Estenssoro had insisted on a second consecutive term of office. But it was also a victory for the armed forces over the miners and politicians: in 1952, the Old Guard had been beaten down by armed miners—now the army was once more in control. For a brief period in 1965, Barrientos shared the presidency with General Alfredo Ovando Candia, then resigned to take part in the elections of 1966, and was elected president.

Once at the helm Barrientos took a firm line with the miners. He banished their leaders, who were accused of plotting against the military regime. Using martial law, he broke up strike meetings, restored order, and got the strikers back to work. He sharply cut down on the number of miners (as required by the rehabilitation scheme for the miners—"Operation Triangle"), operating under a state of siege. He also proclaimed that, if necessary, he would not hesitate to use the Army to run the mines. His tough handling of the miners paid off: for the first time in some 13 years the mines showed a profit again.

Barrientos was less fortunate in his conduct of foreign affairs. Even though Bolivia rejoined the Organization of American States, the border dispute with Chile remained a source of contention. Again, in 1967, his handling of the Debray trial, and the initial mystery surrounding the death of the guerrilla Ché Guevara, was somewhat hamhanded.

Barrientos was born in 1920 in a small town near Cochabamba. His father was of Spanish descent, his mother an Indian. One of his sources of power was his close association with the poverty-stricken Indians. His father died while he was a child, and Barrientos lived in a Franciscan orphanage until he was 12: then he worked his way through high school and the military academy in La Paz.

He joined the MNR, the Paz revolutionary party, when he was about 18: he was expelled from the academy for revolutionary activity.

After the revolutionary forces won the presidency in 1952, Barrientos was sent to

America to train as a pilot. In time he became Commander-in-Chief of the Bolivian Air Force.

April 28, 1969.

Sir Gerald Barry, who died on November 21, 1968, at the age of 70, was that unusual combination a good journalist who revelled in presiding over committees.

Equally successful as an editor and as Director-General of the Festival of Britain, his versatility was based on an underlying guiding purpose—enthusiasm for all liberal causes at home and in international affairs. A flair for giving and receiving hospitality won him many friends in diverse walks of life. This talent for getting on with men and women at all levels of society helped him considerably in making good in his two careers.

Gerald Reid Barry was born on November 20, 1898, son of the Reverend G.D. Barry. Educated at Marlborough and Corpus Christi, Cambridge, he served in the Royal Flying Corps and then the R.A.F. from 1917 to 1919. Entering journalism after the war he became assistant editor of the Saturday Review in 1921 and editor in 1924. The manner of his leaving that chair in 1930 caused a sensation and won him much sympathy. He resigned the editorship when the Saturday Review was abruptly committed by its directors to support Beaverbrouk's United Empire Party. The first intimation that the editor had of this volte face policy decision was a headline in the Beaverbrook Press. The last issue of the Saturday Review brought out under Barry's control was strongly critical of the United Empire Party line. The next issue toed the Beaverbrook line. Barry's prompt repudiation of it and the support he was given by his editorial colleagues were described in The Times as a "real credit to independent journalism ... and a remarkable gesture on behalf of the profession".

PARTIES' WELCOME

Within a few days of this upset, the Weekend Review appeared, with Barry as editor, and messages of goodwill from the Prime Minister, Baldwin, and public men of all parties. The Weekend Review enlisted a distinguished team of contributors and, for several years, gave entertaining and suave coverage to politics, books, the theatre, art and music. But the tide in the thirties was running against a journal uncommitted to any ideology except a general loyalty to civilized values. So the Weekend Review was swallowed up by Kingsley Martin's New Statesman. Barry joined the board of the New Statesman and the "This England" feature which he had started was carried over from the wreckage of his venture.

His next move was into popular daily journalism; in 1936 he became managing editor of News Chronicle. This post he held during the testing period for editorial judgments of the Abdication and Munich and throughout the war. Barry never allowed bad news—and it came thick and fast as he sat at his desk in Bouverie Street—to get him down. He enjoyed attacking with zestful wit whatever was at the moment the bête noire of the left—Blackshirts in Britain, Franco in Spain, Mussolini in Ethiopia, the Japs in Manchuria. Nobody could move more adroitly than Barry among politicians, diplomatists and literary celebrities, many of them at logger-heads with one another in a hectic period. Nobody had a more sensitive ear for the murmurs and undertones of liberalism, radicalism and opinion farther to the left.

RESIGNED AS EDITOR

When he resigned the editorship in 1947 it was commonly thought that increasing difficulties with the chairman of the News Chronicle, Lord Layton, were the cause. But Barry denied this and continued his association with the paper as a director.

In 1948 he was chosen as Director-General and Chairman of a small executive committee appointed to supervise the arrangements for the Festival of Britain in celebration of the Centenary of the 1851 Great Exhibition. He entered wholeheartedly into the task, taking it as a challenge of his power of carrying out executive duties. It has been said that he got in first with the suggestion for the Festival. But John Gloag was ahead of him with a letter in The Times. Barry had followed this up on September 14, 1945, with an open letter to Stafford Cripps, then President of the Board of Trade, arguing the case for a trade and cultural exhibition.

ADVICE TO FARMERS

Knighted in 1951 Barry found that his achievement over the Festival of Britain had made him a much-sought-after public figure. His wide interests led him to be tempted by a series of posts as consultant. He served with the L.C.C. in that capacity on the redevelopment of the Crystal Palace site, advised the National Farmers' Union on public policy. He became a member of the Government committee on the scope of Town and Country Planning, was chairman of the New Barbican committee, and on Cities Redevelopment Research, and deputy chairman of a committee on Obscene Libel Laws. He was a co-founder of P.E.P. (Political and Economic Planning). In 1958 Granada TV gave him executive charge of their plans for educational television.

Whatever Barry did absorbed him for the moment. But the multiplicity of these later assignments brought him under fire for scattering his talents. Delight in travel, architecture, and as he put it—in every thing except Egyptology—remained with him to the end. The gaiety with which he had entertained between the wars in a house under the Sussex Downs with Philip Jordan as a near neighbour was never quenched.

EDITING FAVOURITES

He edited a Week-end Calendar (1933) and This England (1934), and, with Francis Meynell, Week-end Book.

Barry was married three times, in 1921 to Gladwys Williams, in 1944 to Mrs. Vera Burton, and in 1959 to Mrs. Diana Wooton Schlumberger. He had two sons.

November 22, 1968.

Dr. Karl Barth, who died on December 9, 1968, in Basle at the age of 82, was Professor of Theology at Basle University from 1935 to 1962.

He was one of the leading religious figures of our times, a Reformed theologian whose stature rivalled that of the giants of the Reformation epoch. It was said of him that he accomplished a Copernican revolution in Protestant thinking, but his influence radiated far beyond the frontiers of Protestantism itself. What gave him peculiar significance, living as he did in an age of international tumult, was his combination of relentless inquiry in the realm of pure theology with his readiness to apply positive theological principles to the social and political life of his times. He was indeed much more than a theologian, for he earned a place in the ranks of Christian prophets.

Born on May 10, 1886, at Basle, he was the son of Fritz Barth, Professor of New Testament and Early Church History there at the time of Karl's birth, but transferred to Berne three years later. After going to school at the Freies Gymnasium at Berne Karl Barth studied at the Universities of Berne, Berlin, Tübingen, and Marburg. At Berlin he attended Harnack's seminar, and at Marburg he fell under the influence of W. Herrmann and became an enthusiastic student of Schleiermacher, deeply interested in the questions of scientific method. From 1909 to 1911 he served a curacy in Geneva, and in the latter year was appointed a pastor in Safenwil (Aargau). The 10 years he spent there were the formative period in his life. Overwhelmed by the disillusionments of the First World War, not least by the collapse of the ethic of religious idealism, and by his own agonizing consciousness of the responsibilities of a minister of the Gospel to his flock, he was led to a profound questioning of the then fashionable liberalism. The first fruit of this struggle with his own soul was the publication in 1919 of his celebrated Commentary on Romans (*Der Römerbrief*) which at once established his position as a theologian with a new and arresting message.

In 1921 he was appointed professor of dogmatic theology at Göttingen, and in 1925 and 1930 was promoted successively to chairs at Münster i.W. and Bonn. During these years of exhaustive critical study of the content, method and language of theology, in an attempt to lay bare the ultimate sources for a pure theology in its own right, Barth was forced to carry through a searching theological analysis of the social and cultural amalgam of modern bourgeois Christianity and not least of the whole political theory of National Socialism with its roots deep in the romantic and anthropocentric philosophy of the nineteenth century.

INVOLVED AGAINST HITLER

This brought him into sharp conflict with all who wanted to ground Christianity upon the soil of natural existence and to bring theology into line with the new ideology that was being developed out of it. With the accession of Hitler to power in 1933 he became deeply involved in the church struggle. He was one of the founders of the so-called Confessing Church, reacting vigorously and indignantly against the Nazi ideology of "blood and soil" and race and the attempt to set up a "German Christian" Church.

The famous Barmen Declaration drawn up in 1934 was largely based on a draft which he had prepared, and gave uncompromising expression to his conviction that the only way to offer effective resistance to the secularizing and paganizing of the Church was to hold fast to the one ground of Christian security, God's self-revelation in Jesus Christ. Though a Swiss citizen Barth was not altogether immune from persecution, but his courageous stand and his refusal to take the oath of unconditional allegiance to the Führer cost him his chair in Bonn in 1935. Later still in 1939, he was stripped of his doctorate by the University of Münster; in the meantime, however, he had been forced out of Germany, and had been invited to occupy the chair of theology in his native city. From that date until the end of the war he continued to champion the cause of the Confessing Church, of the Jews, and the oppressed peoples generally.

As a theologian Barth was concerned to establish the truth that God can be known only in accordance with his nature as it is revealed in the overflowing of his life and love to creation. In his early writings he set out to stress the immense gulf between God and man in order to destroy the pantheism embedded in modern culture and let God really be God and man really be human. He attacked relentlessly all forms of religion and culture grounded upon romantic and irrational principles. His primary object was in fact to lead theology away from what he believed to be the fundamentally erroneous outlook of the religious philosophy emanating from the nineteenth century, in the identity between the Spirit of God and the religious self-consciousness or between the laws of God and the natural structures of man's life and history.

He found himself moving towards a vast positive theological construction. Drawing on the Fathers and the Reformers he demanded a return to the prophetic teaching of the Bible (Jeremiah, Paul) of which he believed the Reformers were authentic exponents. He accepted much trenchant criticism of historical Christianity from Kierkegaard, Dostoevsky and Overbeck and found positive help in Dorner, Vilmar, Kohlbrügge and the Blumhardts. The essence of the Christian message, he affirmed, was the overwhelming love of the absolutely supreme, transcendent God, who comes in infinite condescension to give himself to man in unconditional freedom and grace.

Barth expounded his doctrines in a series of sermons, addresses, lectures, and in popular expositions of the faith as well as in his more solid continuous works. Its style was vividly lit up by brilliant similes and turns of speech, and irrepressible humour. In 1922 he published the second, drastically altered, edition of *Der Römerbrief*, inaugurating what came to be called the "theology of crisis" or "dialectical theology". This was followed in 1927 by *Die Christliche Dogmatik in Entwurf*.

In 1932 he launched the *Kirchliche Dogmatik*, far and away the most original and remarkable contribution to systematic theology that the twentieth century has seen. By 1959 it reached its eleventh substantial volume (Band IV 3). During these fruitful decades his influence was spreading to other countries, and not least to Great Britain.

Barth continued to be an immensely productive writer throughout the whole of his active life.

After the war the University of Münster made amends by restoring his doctorate in 1945. He continued to interest himself keenly in current theological discussion, taking part in controversies regarding Baptism, hermeneutics, "demythologizing", &c. With his vast authority and prestige as a prophetic teacher, his words made a profound impression at the Conference of the World Council of Churches held in Amsterdam in 1948. In the sphere of the arts he was regarded as one of the foremost exponents of the music of Mozart.

After leaving Germany in 1935 Barth began to read English literature and soon became a devoted admirer of the writings of Winston Churchill and Dorothy Sayers. In the practical sphere he was much concerned with the future of Germany, declaring that, although responsible for the disasters to themselves and to the world, the Germans now needed friends to help them to become what they had never been—a free people, learning not to luxuriate in ideas but to face facts in the spirit of Christian realism. He declined to show towards communism the same kind of direct hostility he had adopted towards Nazism. In 1913 he married Nelly, daughter of Robert Hoffmann, state secretary of the canton of St. Gall. They had one daughter and four sons.

December 11, 1968.

Harry Guy Bartholomew, who died at his home in Surrey on May 4, 1962, at the age of 77, was an outstanding figure in the world of journalism in the first half of the present century. He joined the *Daily Mirror* in 1904 some two months after its foundation and on the eve of its transformation from a paper for women into the first daily picture paper in the world, and he retired as chairman in 1951.

In its original form it had been Northcliffe's first and greatest failure. When "Bart" joined it the circulation was about 25,000. When he left the circulation was 4,350.000, at that time the highest daily sale in the world. He went into the newly formed engraving department, taking with him considerable technical knowledge which helped to produce the line and half-tone blocks for the illustrations which the *Mirror* carried in its early days. But he soon transferred his energies to a broader field and secured many notable pictorial exclusives. When Cecil King paid tribute to him at the annual meeting of the Daily Mirror in 1952 he told the story of how "Bart", hastening back to Britain with the first pictures of a royal tour, set up an engraving plant in a cross-Channel steamer and made the blocks during a stormy crossing. For a time he was assistant art editor, but in 1913 at the age of 28 he was appointed a director of the *Daily Mirror*. As art director he arranged for special trains to hasten the arrival of pictures, and when aviation developed he made full use of it. At the same time he was working on a scientific method of transmitting photographs by telegraphic cable. His work was based on earlier experiments by a German professor, and with the aid of an assistant named Macfarlane he produced the Bartlane process which first transmitted pictures across the Atlantic.

In 1934 the editorial direction of the *Daily Mirror* was handed over to him at a time when the newspaper was in the doldrums with a circulation of about threequarters of a million.

"MIRROR" TRANSFORMED

He quickly transformed it. The *Mirror* as it is today owes more to his hand than to that of any other man. When he came to power it was a sober "middle-class" paper; under him it became the first of the tabloids.

Bartholomew was one of the central figures in the excitement which followed the publication in the *Mirror* in March, 1942, of a cartoon which carried the picture of a drowning merchant seaman with the caption: "The price of petrol has been increased by one penny—official". With Cecil Thomas, the editor, he was summoned to visit Herbert Morrison at the Home Office. The Home Secretary reminded them that he had closed one paper and that if the *Mirror* was closed it would be for a long time. He added that no further warning would be given and that his department would act with a speed that would surprise them. He repeated the warning in the House of Commons. Much fire and heat were generated but nothing further happened.

EXPANSION OVERSEAS

One project for which he did not perhaps receive sufficient credit, except from the Royal Navy, was the production for nearly three years of *Good Morning*, a secret newspaper for submarine crews. It was one of the happy inspirations which appealed to the armed forces and together with other *Daily Mirror* attitudes fostered the belief that the paper was looking after their interests. There is little doubt that the "anti brass-hat" attitude fostered by the *Mirror* contributed to the defeat of the coalition Government at the close of the war in Europe. It was for his work in producing *Good Morning* that he was made O.B.E. in 1946.

It was at Bartholomew's suggestion that the Mirror company bought *Reveille* which, in new hands, increased its circulation from 100,000 to three million. In 1944 he succeeded John Cowley as chairman of both the Daily Mirror and the Sunday Pictorial companies and he played a considerable part in widening their investment interests in overseas fields. This involved him in visits to Canada, Australia, and West Africa.

A chubby man with thick white hair, Bartholomew was volatile in temperament and audacious in action. If his interests were not cultured, he lacked neither ideas nor the ruthlessness to put them into effect. If he was not an easy man to work with, he had the more priceless asset of energy, and energy untrammelled by inhibitions.

May 5, 1962.

With the death of **John Bartholomew,** C.B.E., M.C., on February 9, 1962, geography and cartography lost one of their most notable figures. He was almost 72, and the fifth in family line of distinguished mapmakers, with over a century of world-wide service radiating from the offices and printing works in Edinburgh, so that the main course of his career must have been determined right at its start.

Son of the late Dr. John George Bartholomew, he received his early education at Merchiston Castle School, Edinburgh, and studied cartography at the universities of Leipzig and Paris before taking his Master of Arts degree at the University of Edinburgh. During the First World War he served with the 1st Battalion, The Gordon Highlanders and the General Staff, being thrice mentioned in dispatches and awarded the Military Cross in 1915.

At the termination of hostilities he returned to the family business and on his father's death in 1920 took over its entire management. A year later he was appointed Cartographer to King George V. In 1920 he married Marie, daughter of Professor Leon Sarolea, by whom he was to have five sons and one daughter.

The firm from its inception played an outstanding part in perfecting and advancing the science of cartography, in adapting to use new methods of projection and in employing new methods of printing, of colour layering and in the introduction of varieties of paper able to stand up to the trials of wide ranges of temperature and of humidity. John Bartholomew completed *The Times Survey Atlas* which was commenced by his father and saw the publication of a long line of atlases—*Handy Reference Atlas, Citizens Atlas of the World, Survey Gazetter of the British Isles, The Times Handy Atlas, The Advanced Atlas of Modern Geography*—and pioneered some of the newest maps called for by airline companies, anxious to sell their wares.

All the time he was giving generously of his influence and experience in advancing the cause of the science of geography. He played a notable part in the founding of the Chair of Geography in the University of Edinburgh and was early a protagonist for adequate library and laboratory facilities. He carried on the family tradition of intense active support for the Royal Scottish Geographical Society, which he served for 30 years as joint honorary secretary and subsequently from 1950 to 1954 as its greatly appreciated president. For all these years he was a most assiduous attender of its council meetings, where his kindly personality and wise comments were always welcome.

LOVE FOR SCOTLAND

His knowledge and services were ever in demand and no reasonable call was ever refused. He served on the Permanent Committee on Geographical Names, sponsored by the Royal Geographical Society, and on the National Committee on Geography under the Royal Society. His erudition on the subject of maps and early works on geography made him a valuable member of the board of trustees of the National Library of Scotland, and his love for his native land secured his election to the executive committee of the National Trust for Scotland.

Though he was by nature a shy and retiring man, latterly severely handicapped by arthritis, honours were bound to find their way rightly to him. He served for a term on the council of the Royal Society of Edinburgh. In 1956 Edinburgh University gave him an honorary LL.D. and last year he was made a C.B.E. The Royal Scottish Geographical Society awarded him its gold medal in 1954 and in 1961 the Royal Geographical Society bestowed upon him the Founder's Medal for his outstanding contributions to cartography.

A recent trip round the world not only let him see for himself many of the places he had known in atlases but provided an opportunity for university and government geographers and cartographers to show their personal appreciation of him as a man of international standing. As secretary and president of the Royal Scottish Geographical Society he knew several generations of explorers and took a kindly interest in all their doings whether they were university society beginners back from North Greenland or Hunt and Hillary and Fuchs with the accolade upon them, and not a few must treasure happy memories of warm hospitality at Inveresk. His good work is being carried on by three out of his four sons in the family firm of John Bartholomew and Son Ltd.

February 12, 1962.

Bernard Baruch, who died on June 20, 1965, in New York at the age of 94, was one of those rare men who spend half their lifetime as a legend.

As an American financier he amassed a vast fortune on Wall Street, but his reputation derived from much more than his stupendous success as a speculator. He was essentially a man of influence not of office. Although he did good work in a number of public posts, he never held Cabinet rank. He was the confidant of those in power rather than powerful himself.

As always with men whose prominence depends largely upon having the private ear of others, the precise scale of his influence is difficult to measure. What is certain is that he was the adviser of Wilson and succeeding presidents, that his friendship with Sir Winston Churchill was long and enduring, and that he was accorded the exceptional respect of his fellow countrymen. He was a man of commanding presence—six feet three inches tall—with a genial manner.

The extent of his friendship with a succession of presidents was revealed in 1964 when he presented his papers—including 1,200 letters from nine presidents and 700 communications from Churchill—to Princeton University. There, they were to form the nucleus of a study centre in twentieth-century American statecraft and public policy.

Bernard Mannes Baruch was born in Camden, South Carolina, on August 19, 1870. His father, Simon Baruch, a Jewish doctor who had emigrated from east Prussia in his teens, moved to New York when Bernard—the second of four sons—was 10. When he was 15 he entered the College of the City of New York, and graduated in 1889. His first job was that of office boy in a glassware business at three dollars a week; but his career really began when he joined the brokerage firm of A. A. Housman and Company in 1891. By the age of 25 he was a partner, and by the time he had reached 32 he was worth $3,200,000. He was one of the comparatively few people who liquidated nearly all their holdings before the 1929 stock market crash.

FRIEND OF PRESIDENT

Baruch's public career owed its origin to his friendship for Woodrow Wilson. The two were introduced in 1912 and took an instant liking to each other. Baruch in later years frequently confessed his deep respect for Wilson and his ideals. Wilson, on his side, had a particular admiration for Baruch's comprehensive and detailed knowledge of American industry, naming him "Dr. Facts". In 1916 Baruch accepted membership of the advisory commission of the Council of National Defence and when the United States entered the First World War he became chairman of the Commission on Raw Materials, Minerals and Metals and a member of the Allied Purchasing Commission. His principal contribution to the war effort was made through his chairmanship of the War Industries Board, to which he was appointed on March 3, 1918, and which he retained until the end of that fateful year.

In 1919 Baruch was one of those who accompanied President Wilson to Versailles—a crossing of the Atlantic which brought about a meeting with Winston Churchill which soon ripened into a deep and lasting friendship. Baruch served as economic adviser to the American Peace Commission. He represented the United States on the Supreme Economic Council and was chairman of its Raw Materials Division. Baruch was for mitigating the harshness of the reparations liability imposed on Germany by the Versailles Treaty, just as he inclined to more Carthaginian terms while the Second World War was running its course.

The fall of Wilson naturally diminished Baruch's possibilities for influencing the American administration, though the taste, once acquired, never disappeared. He was occasionally consulted by Coolidge and Hoover and stood out during the pre-depression decade for fairer treatment of American agriculture. With Roosevelt's inauguration Baruch's chance of resuming his role of confidential adviser to the President reappeared. Though he held no office, he was frequently summoned to Washington, and the first members of Roosevelt's brains trust included a number of "Baruch men"—the most prominent among them being General Hugh Johnson, who had been his assistant in Wall Street.

NEW DEAL EXPERIMENTS

Roosevelt was fickle in his use of advisers and it was not long before Baruch's influence waned. Though a Democrat he was of conservative hue, a friend of Alfred E. Smith and a protagonist of the political philosophy of Jefferson and Wilson. Thus while his ultimate loyalty to the party was great he disapproved of the more advanced experiments of the New Deal. He shared Roosevelt's apprehensions of the growing menace of Nazi Germany and conveyed Churchill's views on the European situation to the President. America's projection into the Second World War seemed to give Baruch the opportunity to repeat his performance in the first as the mobilizer of American industry. But he accepted no office, though acting as adviser both to Roosevelt and James F. Byrnes on economic problems arising out of the war. At the President's request he visited England in April, 1945. Baruch was less close to President Truman. However, he was United States representative to the United Nations Atomic Energy Commission from 1946 to 1951 and was the author of the American plan to control atomic weapons which was named after him.

One of Baruch's foibles was his fondness for park benches. He would sit on a bench in Lafayette Square, Washington, just across the road from the White House, and dispense advice to officers of government.

Baruch received numerous honorary degrees and similar honours. He published *A Philosophy for Our Times* (1953) and two volumes of autobiography, *My Own Story* (1958) and *The Public Years* (1961).

Baruch married in 1893 Anne Griffen and had one son and two daughters. His wife died in 1938.

June 22, 1965.

Professor R. Bassett, who died on July 9, 1962, at the age of 61, was a man of many remarkable qualities.

Politics was in his blood, and he owed his first political education to his mother, with whom, as a boy, he used to attend political meetings. He acquired strong political beliefs which led him to join the I.L.P. at an early age, and for many years he was a well known and active member. But to his partisan persuasions was added the temperament of a scholar; and on leaving school and entering a solicitor's office in Wadhurst (where business was not very brisk) he set about educating himself. A scholarship at the age of 25 took him to Ruskin College and then to New College, Oxford. For 15 years he was a lecturer under the Extra-Mural Delegacy of the University of Oxford, working mainly in his native Sussex. When in 1945, under the inspiration of Professor Tawney and Evan Durbin, the London School of Economics started a course for students drawn from the trade unions, Bassett was made tutor. Academic life suited his disposition; he soon made his mark as a teacher and in 1961 he was appointed to a Professorship in the University of London.

His great intellectual passion was for the political history of his times, to the study of which he brought a powerful memory for events, persons, and occasions, an acute political sensibility, a profound knowledge of the history and conduct of parliamentary government in Great Britain and a care for detail. For him, political history was composed neither of the sweeping movements beloved by the "intellectual" nor of the fortunes of "systems" of government, but of the footprints left by those engaged in political activity, each a moment of significance to be recognized, reflected upon, and interpreted in its context. Circumstances had something to do with the slackening of his partisan activities—in 1931 he was a MacDonaldite and ceased to be a member of a poltical party—but it was characteristic of him that the only cause which held his unwavering allegiance was that of Parliamentary Democracy, which he understood as a manner of conducting politics and reaching political decisions and not as the pursuit of a favourite policy.

PARLIAMENTARY GOVERNMENT

This appeared in his first book, *The Essentials of Parliamentary Democracy* (1935), where he was concerned to understand the conduct of parliamentary government and to take to task those (on the right or on the left) in whom he detected an attachment to their own policies greater than an attachment to the manner of governing and being governed which they had as a common inheritance. And, although deep personal loyalties were engaged, it was, in the end, his understanding of British parliamentary government which determined the view he took of the happenings of 1931.

In other circumstances Bassett might have written a remarkable history of the politics of his own times. In talk he could unfold the political realities—in Westminster—in the countryside—of the last 60 years in fascinating detail. But as it was, he spent himself on a different project. The ambition never to have deserted one's principles, the desire to discredit one's opponents and the normal course of human forgetfulness have imposed, during the last four decades, a remarkable stock of legends upon some passages in our politics, and Bassett undertook to put the record straight in respect of some of the more notable of them. *Democracy and Foreign Policy* (1952) was a study of what was thought and said during the Sino-Japanese dispute, 1931–33, and in *Nineteen Thirty-one: Political Crisis* (1958) he sought to disentangle the historical truth from the various partisan legends.

This and other studies might have lost him some of his old political friends, but, in fact (although in later years he was reluctant to "talk politics" as in former days), his clear honesty of purpose, his charm and his modesty held those who might otherwise have been repulsed. He was a man of deep loyalties, both local and personal; a devoted son of Sussex, a faithful scholar and an affectionate friend.

July 11, 1962.

H. M. Bateman, the famous comic artist, died on February 11, 1970, in Malta, at the age of 82.

His vision of a National Gallery of Humorous Art has regrettably failed to materialize and without such an institution we are denied an opportunity of remembering the man or rediscovering his comic masterpieces of the quality of "The Guardsman Who Dropped It", "The One-Note Man" or "The Man Who Lit His Cigar Before The Royal Toast".

A man of disarming simplicity, H. M. Bateman was not the slightest bit interested in politics and the social upheavals of the inter-war years passed unnoticed in his work. For him it was quite enough that people, with or without the drama of their hopes and aspirations, were enormously funny. The bulk of his output was concerned with depicting a proliferation of gaffes: lonely, embarrassed figures, having just committed some unpardonable breach of convention—throwing a snowball at St. Moritz, for example—surrounded by a dazed or outraged assembly. By ignoring passing fashions and concentrating instead on basic human failings—envy, greed, pride, rage—he appealed to all classes of people at a time when British humour was particularly class conscious. Everybody up and down the social registers could laugh, kindly, at "The Guest Who Called 'Paté de Foie Gras' 'Potted Meat'"!

Son of Henry Charles Bateman, Henry Mayo Bateman was born on February 15, 1887, at Sutton Forest. New South Wales, but he was brought to England in childhood. He was educated at Forest Hill House, London, and studied drawing and painting at the Westminster School of Art and Goldsmiths' College School of Art, New Cross. He also worked for several years in the studio of Charles Van Havenmaet.

BEGAN AT 19

He began to draw for reproduction when he was 19, and in the course of his career he contributed thousands of humorous drawings to most of the leading weekly and monthly periodicals. He also produced many cartoon series for advertisers both in Britain and America, and his theatrical posters for George Bernard Shaw's *Fanny's First Play* and *John Bull's Other Island* were highly successful.

Bateman's childhood ambition was simply a desire "to draw and make people laugh". At least it sounds simple; in practice there could be no more difficult or daunting objective in life. The laughter of some of his early work had an acidic flavour, due in some measure perhaps to the influence of the Continental artists to whom he turned for inspiration. The vitality and originality of "Caran d'Ache", a Russian born Frenchman of great comic talent, and another Russian, the sadly neglected Henry Ospovat, appealed strongly to the shy, diffident Englishman. But by 1910, to use his own words he "went mad on paper" and the energies which had been bound by his shyness found an outlet in his work. The *Sketch* billed him as "Our Untamed Artist" and his theatrical caricatures—disliked at first by his subjects, but later avidly collected—were unsurpassed.

DRAWING'S OWN HUMOUR

Bateman had no time for the "collapse of stout party" joke and, unlike most of his cartoonist contemporaries, his humour did not depend on the caption but was, instead, an intrinsic part of the drawing. By the time he reached his middle-twenties he had become one of the funniest and most widely imitated of comic draughtsmen. His influence spread to all parts of the world, particularly America, and some early New Yorker cartoons of the thirties bear a striking resemblance in idea and execution. In the pages of *Punch* he perfected the story without words—"The Boy Who Breathed on the Glass in the British Museum" is a classic example of this form—and by drawing people as they *felt* rather than as they appeared he introduced a fresh spirit and insight into comic art.

In 1919 an exhibition of 80 of Bateman's drawings was held at the Leicester Galleries. *The Times* critic of that day said that they had "a comic beauty of line, a rhythmical extravagance like that of the Ingoldsby Legends and the choruses of Offenbach". This showing displayed what was probably the high-water mark of his artistic development, although he was to grow in public popularity, and exert his influence, for many years to come.

ILL-HEALTH

Poor health kept him out of the Services in the 1914–18 War. Subject to moods of depression he often visited Dartmoor to walk, fish, rest and relax. In later years he moved to Devon where he lived simply and quietly, although he managed to travel extensively. Trout fishing with the fly was Bateman's lifelong recreation. In 1960 he published *The Evening Rise; Fifty Years of Fly Fishing*. He was helped to chose his first rod by H. T. Sheringham, the eminent angling editor of the *Field*. Another great fishing friend was William Caine, the author of one of the best-loved fishing books, *An Angler at Large*, in which the then youthful Bateman makes a fleeting appearance. Bateman was fortunate in being able to combine in an unusual degree the occupations of artist and angler. A few sheets of paper, drawing board, and his sketch-books were all he needed to turn his bedroom at a fishing hotel or riverside lodgings into a studio, and he says in his book that many of his best-known and most successful drawings at one period of his life were done in such settings.

He never lost his interest in oil and water-colours and at least on one occasion he contributed to the Royal Academy (1933), and in 1936 the Leicester Galleries held a showing of paintings resulting from a visit to Spain. But although he was a fine draughtsman and an excellent colourist, he was most at home with uninhibited exaggeration. His serious work, while technically interesting, lacked the strange inspirational spark which gave such frenetic life to his comic drawings.

GALLERY OF HUMOUR

Bateman published several collections of drawings, including *Burlesques; A Book of Drawings; Suburbia; More Drawings; Considered Trifles; Brought Forward; Colonels* and *H. M. Bateman by Himself*. In 1949 he read a paper, "Humour in Art", to the Royal Society of Arts in which he put forward his idea for a National Gallery of Humorous Art. In spite of genuine enthusiasm and subsequent committee work the project foundered, largely through a lack of suitable premises.

In 1926 he married Brenda Mary Collison Weir.

They had two daughters.

February 13, 1970.

Clifford Bax, author and playwright, died on November 18, 1962, at his London home. He was 76.

Clifford Bax was a versatile and talented writer, who brought something of poetic sentiment and a fluent elegance of style to almost everything he produced. Poetry, poetic drama, fiction, table-talk—in all these his offering was never less than gracefully acceptable. Yet he never quite accomplished what was expected of him or indeed what he expected from himself, his facility for good talk and companionship seemed to impede his powers. Even as a playwright, in which capaclty he had given greatest promise and was most often in the public eye, he fell notably short of genuine effect and of popular favour. The truth was, perhaps, that Bax's was a "literary" cultivation of mind, and as such was not of the most fruitful variety. His somewhat pessimistic turn of thought grew more marked in later years and was joined to a pervading mysticism of temper.

Born on July 13, 1886, Clifford Bax was the son of Alfred Ridley Bax and Charlotte Ellen Lea and a younger brother of Sir Arnold Bax, Master of the King's Musick. He was educated privately and, in pursuit of an early ambition to paint, studied art at the Slade School and at Heatherley's. Afterwards he lived abroad for some time, chiefly in Germany and Italy, and eventually abandoned painting for verse drama. The first piece of his to be produced in the commercial theatre in 1912, was a short rhymed play, described as an "antique pageant", *The Poetasters of Ispahan*, which with three other examples of the kind was subsequently published in volume form. Bax's earliest real opportunity, however, came in 1923, when he rewrote and reconstructed Gay's ballad-opera *Polly*, which was produced with music by Frederick Austin. In the following year came a comedy, *Midsummer Madness*—slight and rather artificial—with music by Armstrong Gibbs, and then came two more ballad-operas, both charming in their way, *Mr. Pepys* (1926) and *Waterloo Leave* (1928), each with music by Martin Shaw.

HISTORICAL THEMES

Bax did not maintain the stage promise of these early ventures in the theatre. He wrote a great many full-length plays during the next 20 years (including translations and adaptations) some of them in collaboration with another hand, but increasingly he turned towards historical themes and a dramatic rendering that favoured the pleasures of reading rather than of performance. With the years his work was produced in the commercial theatre less frequently. The most notable of his dramatic compositions are *Socrates,* a skilful attempt to abstract drama from the stuff of the socratic dialogues; *The Immortal Lady,* a brightly costumed episode of the reign of George I; *The Rose without a Thorn,* celebrating Lady Katheryn Howard—probably his most effective piece for the theatre; *The House of Borgia, The King and Mistress Shore,* and *Golden Eagle,* with Mary Queen of Scots for subject.

Among Bax's numerous other works are several volumes of graceful and discursive autobiography and reminiscence and of eager and at times wayward argument. They include *Inland Far* (1925), *That Immortal Sea* (1933), *Ideas and People* (1936), *Evenings in Albany* (1942), *Rosemary for Remembrance* (1948), and *Some I Knew Well* (1951). He also produced a volume of stories on the old Italian model, *Many a Green Isle,* and a rather over-fluent novel, *Time with a Gift of Tears,* and—in illustration of his versatility—an excellent *Essex* in the Highways and Byways series.

Nor was this the sum of his accomplishments. Bax's interests, apart from the theatre—he had helped to found the Phoenix Society after the 1914–18 War and in 1929 was elected chairman of the Incorporated State Society—included music, antiquities, Buddhism, and Eastern philosophy generally. A great lover of cricket, he published a biography of W. G. Grace in 1952. He was, finally, a very good host both in his Wiltshire manor house and in his Albany flat.

He married first, in 1910, Gwendolen Bishop (*née* Bernhard Smith), who died in 1926 and by whom he had a daughter; secondly, in 1927, Vera May Young, daughter of Colonel Claude Rawnsley.

November 19, 1962.

Dr. Norman Baynes, Professor Emeritus of Byzantine History in the University of London, died on February 12, 1961, at the age of 83.

Norman Hepburn Baynes was born on May 29, 1877, the son of Alfred Henry Baynes. He was educated at Eastbourne College and New College, Oxford. He read Greats, graduated in 1900, and almost at once began work on the history of the later Roman Empire. His gifts in the field of historical research were shown during these early years and he was awarded the Marquess of Lothian's Prize in 1901 and the Arnold Essay Prize in 1903. He was called to the Bar after reading in the chambers of R. J. Parker, afterwards Baron Parker of Waddington, a Lord of Appeal and the father of the present Lord Chief Justice, and he was until 1916 for some years tutor under the Law Society.

During the 1914-18 War he worked in Watergate House on intelligence matters and it was during these years that his connexion with University College London began. He became a Reader in the History of the Roman Empire in the University of London in 1919, and then in 1931 a Chair of Byzantine History was created for him, which he held until his retirement in 1942. One of his great interests at University College was the Evening School of History, a non-graduate diploma school with which he was associated from 1919 to 1933 and of which he was director after the retirement in 1927 of Professor A. F. Pollard.

TRANSLATING HITLER

During the war of 1939-45 he worked in Oxford for the Foreign Research and Press Service, afterwards the Research Department of the Foreign Office, where he prepared in his own scholarly and inimitable way a translation of Hitler's pre-war speeches.

Both by training and temperament Baynes

was admirably fitted for work in east Mediterranean history of classical and early Christian times. Though never primarily concerned with the medieval world he was, however, passionately interested in the Roman Empire of the early Middle Ages and did more than any English scholar of his time to bring the claims of Byzantine history (long neglected in England) before a wide public. The way had to some extent been prepared by J. B. Bury, but Baynes—unlike Bury—combined scrupulously exact scholarship with the gift of an imagination which he was not afraid to use. It is for this reason that his lectures and writings have meant so much to generations of undergraduates and others who were enabled by his bold reconstructions to understand something of Jewish, Greco-Roman and Byzantine life. For these Baynes will live not only in their memories of his lectures but in his masterly survey *The Byzantine Empire*, characteristically brought to an end at 1204, and in his two essays on Hellenistic civilization and East Rome "which tell us more than many big books".

Baynes's historical research was based on a relentless examination of all available material and those who knew his method and approach will understand (though perhaps with regret) why he did not more readily publish; even the shortest essay was accompanied by the fullest and most fascinating bibliographical notes.

ENERGY IN REVIEWS

And then much of Baynes's time and energy went into reviews which are in themselves a substantial contribution to knowledge. He put into his reviews the work that others put into their books and by the time that he had finished he was often better fitted to write the work than the author himself.

His balanced, acute and lively judgments are to be found from 1910 onwards in a number of English and foreign periodicals. His distinguished work and his unforgettable personality became as well known in continental as in English circles. His profound bibliographical knowledge, his cosmopolitan approach and his instinctive generosity were never more in evidence than when he was discussing problems of research, and so often he would produce not only the essential reference but the actual work, perhaps some vital text published in Tiflis or some rare offprint from St. Petersburg. Among Baynes's more important writings are *The Historia Augusta, its Date and Purpose* (1926), *Israel among the Nations* (1927), a *Bibliography of the Works of J. B. Bury* (1929), *Three Byzantine Saints* (with E. Dawes, 1948), *Byzantium* (edited with H. St. L. B. Moss, 1948), and various contributions to the history of the fourth century A.D. A selection of his articles and lectures was published in 1955 as *Byzantine Studies and Other Essays*; it includes one of his most characteristic orations, "The Custody of a Tradition".

CONVERSION OF CONSTANTINE

Although his interests were never concentrated exclusively upon any narrow period there was one subject which he had made his own: the Emperor Constantine the Great. In his Raleigh Lecture (1929) on "Constantine the Great and the Christian Church" and in various articles he examined afresh the problem of Constantine's conversion and considered the nature of the Roman imperial tradition. He had already contributed various chapters to the earlier volumes of the "Cambridge Medieval History" and was well qualified to become one of the editors of the last volume of the "Cambridge Ancient History" for which he himself wrote on Constantine the Great. Scholars are divided in their acceptance of Baynes's views on Constantine but none will deny the integrity and vigour and distinction with which he has marshalled his evidence. He had hoped to write on the social history of the East Roman Empire during his retirement, but to the great regret of his friends and admirers was prevented by the long illness which overshadowed his last years.

Baynes was in 1930 elected a fellow of the British Academy. The University of St. Andrews conferred on him the honorary degree of D.D., and he was an honorary doctor of letters of Oxford, Durham, Cambridge, and London.

In the University of London, and more particularly in University College and on the board of studies in history, he gave unsparingly of his time and of himself; he served the Society for the Promotion of Roman Studies as president and in many other ways, and he maintained an unflagging interest in the Historical Association. He was, as he rejoiced to proclaim, "a Victorian individualist", and he stood for the preservation of independence of judgment and "the possibility of an alternative."

February 13, 1961.

Elyesa Bazna, the spy "Cicero" who sold to the Germans photographic copies of Allied documents during part of the Second World War, was on December 24, 1970 reported to have died in Munich.

He was valet to the British Ambassador in Ankara and photographed almost daily top secret documents which the Germans were only too willing to see. During the Second World War it was the practice of the Foreign Office to keep certain embassies posted about Allied plans. Ankara, because of the key position held by Turkey, was one of those which was regularly informed of some of the most closely guarded secrets of the war, such as the business transacted at the Allied meeting at Casablanca, and of the conferences held at Moscow, Cairo and Teheran.

Bazna gave the German Embassy—it seems only right that the German Ambassador in Ankara was Franz von Papen—a great deal of extremely valuable information but the claim that has been put forward from time to time that he handed over the plans for Overlord (the name of the operation that was to be the invasion of Europe in 1944) must be treated with some scepticism. Bazna is believed to have thrown in his hand in April, 1944 at which time the operational plans for Overlord were not even completed and would not have been telegraphed. The Allies had long been pledged to invasion, the Germans knew this; what they needed to know was when, where and in what force the blow would come. This was successfully concealed from all except those directly concerned in the actual carrying out of the operation. Bazna, in his book *I Was Cicero*, written in collaboration with Hans Nogly, is frank about his motives. He professes at times that he wanted to keep Turkey out of the war, but for much of the book he is talking of money, and the money he wanted in order to cut a dash with his mistresses. Later, he had an idea of building a luxury hotel but this was only partially built when it was discovered that the £5 notes financing the project were forged.

An interesting account of the episode is given in the book *Operation Cicero*, written by a German diplomat who served in the Turkish capital.

Bazna tried for many years to get a pension from the west German Government—claiming that he had done as much for Germany as any front-line soldier.

Bazna wrote his memoirs and was anxious to star in a film about himself, but the film was made without him. James Mason took the title role.

December 28, 1970.

Cardinal Bea, President of the Vatican Secretariat for Christian Unity died on November 16, 1968, at the age of 87.

Without doubt he was the most astonishing phenomenon in the Sacred College of his day because there was no one with whom to compare him for a sudden blossoming of progressive achievement except John XXIII himself. Small, bent, and seemingly frail, he emerged from a long life devoted to scholarship to become the effective spokesman of the Roman Church's ecumenical interests and the main architect of its ecumenical policy.

Bea himself remarked once that all his life had been a preparation for his work as head of the Vatican's secretariat for Christian unity. In a sense this is true. Most of his earlier life was spent in biblical scholarship and as rector of the Biblical Institute in Rome· he gradually established many contacts with non-Catholic scholars working in the same field. Moreover the proper scriptural basis for ecumenical discussion was assured. As Pius XII's personal confessor Bea was given insight into the workings of the centre of ecclesiastical government. This must have helped him to have the measure of the conservative opponents in the Roman Curia who were later to stop at nothing, including accusations of possible heresy, to impede his more adventurous work. As a German and a Jesuit he retained a greater feeling of independence, both from the mentality likely to grow as a result of long residence in Rome and from the often unconscious restrictions of belonging to a national hierarchy.

Oxford University decided in 1968 to confer on him as honorary D.D. but because of ill-health he was unable to visit Oxford to receive the degree.

Augustin Bea was born on May 28, 1881, in the village of Riedbohringen in Baden on the edge of the Black Forest. His father was a carpenter and builder who also owned a farm. One of Bea's memories was that of being shown plans by his father and it is not fanciful to suppose that an early acquaintance with the principle of building to last with the materials available had its effect on a mind which decades later would apply just that principle to the business of bringing Christians closer together.

He was a sickly child. Indeed at the age of 11 the doctor who examined him sent him out of the room and explained to his mother that his lungs were in a condition which allowed him no more than three months to live. There was certainly a weakness in the lungs and when he went to Rome in 1924 it was against medical advice. His state of health in no way showed in the combination of hard work and gentle strength of character which were to mark his long life. When over 80 years of age he was dispatching over 2,000 letters in a year while receiving 500 visits from representatives of Christian churches, presiding over the meetings of his own secretariat, attending those of at least three Sacred Congregations as well as the biblical commission and the central steering commission of the council. Despite his gentleness of manner and sweet smile he was a determined and formidable adversary both learned and shrewd.

He went to the village school, followed by secondary education in Sasbach at Constance and, finally, the diocesan boarding school at Rastatt. At the age of 17 he was thinking about joining the Jesuits and decided to do so after a retreat with them. His father opposed the idea because the Jesuits were expelled from Germany and his son would have to go abroad. He waited four years for his father's consent. In the meantime he studied theology at Freiburg. When just short of 21 he entered the Jesuit novitiate in Holland. He was ordained in 1912 and after taking his doctorate in theology went to Berlin University to study ancient Oriental languages. He meant to follow that by going to Rome but ill-health prevented him. In 1921 he was made Provincial of the new south German province of the Jesuits. Rather more than two years later he was summoned to Rome to direct the studies of postgraduate Jesuit students. For the rest of his life Bea was closely connected with movements in the Roman Church to deepen scholarship and broaden the outlook, a labour for which the secretariat for Christian unity was to be the peak.

While directing the Institute for Higher Ecclesiastical Studies of the Jesuits Bea was also teaching at the Pontifical Biblical Institute. He moved there in 1928 and two years later became rector. The institute had been established because Catholic biblical scholarship had been inadequate to meet the Modernist crisis. It was intended to defend the Church and to encourage progress in biblical studies. Both under Bea and after his departure the institute was to meet strong attack from the traditionalists of the Curia and their friends. Though conflicts in biblical studies seldom attract great attention outside specialist circles it is sufficient to say that Bea was an indefatigable worker in improving the institute, reasonably open minded in his approach to new methods of study though theologically scarcely liberal even if insistent on gaining all necessary assistance from philology, palaeontology, archaeology and comparative cultures. He was in fact already much on the course which Pius XII was to lay down in his encyclical *Divine afflante spiritu* of 1943 which went a long way towards freeing biblical criticism so far as the prudent use of modern methods was concerned. Bea showed wisdom and balance in his direction of biblical studies.

So did he in his relations with non-Catholic scholars. He closely followed Protestant work. With Pius XII's permission he had gone in 1935 to Göttingen for a biblical conference where he formed personal ties with Protestant scholars. He was also confirming an extraordinary application to work. Bea was able to lecture in Latin, Italian, German, French, English and Portuguese. He was able to read with ease Greek, Hebrew, Syriac and Aramaic. His spoken Latin, as his speeches at the Vatican Council showed, was clear, almost vibrant. Much of the gentle ease with which he spoke, whatever the language, must have been due to the technical mastery of his subjects.

John XXIII appears to have known nothing very much about Bea except that he had been Pius XII's confessor and an eminent biblical scholar. These were two of the reasons why the Pope made him a cardinal; a gesture to the memory of his predecessor and an accolade to biblical scholars in general. To this might be added that John would have found out that the Jesuit was a sensible kind of reformer. Through Cardinal Bea the suggestion was received at the Vatican that a special organ be set up for relations with non-Catholics. Bea took the request to John who granted it, placing Bea at the head of this Secretariat for Christian Unity. In October, 1962, it was given the same standing as the Commissions of the Council. The documents for which the secretariat was directly responsible were those dealing with the principles of ecumenism, the statement on religious liberty, the statement on relations with non-Christians especially the Jews, and a part of the decree on divine revelation. All of these documents represented some new step of outstanding importance in Catholic thinking. Most of them suffered obstructions and attempts to tone down innovations. Bea fought hard to retain the sense and spirit which he believed essential and which John XXIII had specifically requested.

The secretariat was also in charge of facilities and contacts with the observer-delegates from non-Catholic Christian churches. The liaison was close. By constant personal contact the Cardinal and the staff which he had gathered gained the confidence of the observers in a striking way. What might have been a matter of form turned into a long and productive exchange of views which did not of course end when the Council ended. Any more than did Bea's persistent expression of the powers of baptism in providing a bond among Christians. His view was not new but he gave it a new importance by his insistence on it. It was simply that baptism made people members of the mystical body of Christ, even if not in the full sense understood by Roman Catholics. It was nevertheless the basis of a brotherhood truly Christian. Bea himself expressed what he meant in the following sentence: "When we speak so freely these days of 'separated brethren' it is not just a polite way of speaking but the expression of a profound Christian truth." It was the foundation of his work. Decades will have to pass before the full effect can be judged of what he hoped to do. As far as foundations go it is difficult to see how anyone could have laid them better.

Among his later publications were: The Church and the Jewish People; The Way to Unity after the Council; and The Church and Mankind.

November 18, 1968.

Sylvia Beach, who died on October 9, 1962, in Paris at the age of 75, has a unique place in the literary history of the twentieth century as the original publisher of James Joyce's *Ulysses.* Her small Left Bank bookshop, Shakespeare and Co., was a centre for literary and artistic activity of the most diverse kinds in the Paris of the nineteen-twenties and thirties.

Here, at various times, appeared T. S. Eliot, Ezra Pound, André Gide, E. E. Cummings, Paul Valéry, Ernest Hemingway, Scott Fitzgerald, Sherwood Anderson, and many other notable writers.

Sylvia Beach was born in 1887 in Baltimore, the daughter of the Rev. Sylvester Woodbridge Beach, D.D., a Presbyterian minister and the descendant of nine generations of clergymen. Her mother was the daughter of a medical missionary in India. She had two younger sisters, Holly and Cyprian. When Sylvia was about 14 years old her father took the whole family to Paris, where he had been asked to take charge of what were known as Students' Atelier Reunions. Although they later returned to America, to Princeton, the whole family had, in Miss Beach's words, "a passion for France" and they made many return visits. In 1916 Sylvia Beach was in Spain and the next year in Paris, where she soon found her way to the little French bookshop of Adrienne Monnier in the rue de l'Odeon, and was enrolled in La Maison des Amis des Livres. Her sister meanwhile got her a job with the American Red Cross and together the girls went to Belgrade.

In July, 1919, she returned to Paris and some months later with the small savings of her mother and the active help of Adrienne Monnier opened her famous bookshop in an empty laundry in the rue Dupuytren. Two years later it moved to a permanent address at number 12 rue de l'Odeon, opposite La Maison des Amis des Livres. The bookshop and library were to continue in business until 1941, when Miss Beach was removed by the Germans to a concentration camp in Vittel.

In her engaging recollections *Shakespeare and Company,* published in 1960, Miss Beach records the literary and social life that flowed in and out of her little shop, and describes its many vicissitudes; chief among them those that were the consequence of her courageous decision to print, publish and distribute *Ulysses.* Miss Beach was intensely devoted to James Joyce and his family, and she cherished his literary reputation throughout her life. On her recent visits to this country and to Ireland she won many new friends through her vivacity and charm, and the unselfconscious way she told her stories of the great figures she knew and admired in Paris between the wars.

The literary treasures which she hid during the occupation formed the showpiece of an exhibition "Paris in the Twenties" which attracted more than 15,000 visitors in the French capital in 1959 and which was transferred to London.

In June, 1962, she went to Dublin to open the James Joyce Museum in the Martello tower at Sandycove, Co. Dublin, the setting of the opening scene of *Ulysses*.

October 11, 1962.

Wilfred B. Beard, O.B.E., who died near Stockport on December 16, 1967, at the age of 75, was general secretary of the United Patternmakers' Association, one of the smallest craft unions, since 1941, and chairman of the Trades Union Congress General Council in 1955–56. He was 75.

Born in Manchester in 1892, Beard served an apprenticeship in the skilled trade of pattern making. He worked at his craft until he became a full-time official of his union which he joined in 1912. Before he was elected union general secretary, he had been a voluntary officer and then the secretary and organizer of the Lancashire and Cheshire region.

After he joined the T.U.C. General Council in 1947, he held many offices in the trade union movement and in a wider public field. He was made chairman of the T.U.C. education committee and a member of the general council of the Confederation of Shipbuilding and Engineering Unions, of which he was president from 1958 to 1959.

In 1953, Beard was the central figure in an unfortunate interlude in his union. On May 21 of that year he was appointed a part-time member of the Iron and Steel Board. Two days later, he had to announce his withdrawal because of the opposition towards the appointment on the part of his union executive, with whom apparently he had no prior consultation.

For many years Beard was a leading member of the Ford National Negotiating Committee, which represents a large number of engineering unions and has often been harassed by unofficial stoppages at the huge motor car manufacturing plant at Dagenham. He was also a member of the Railway Shopmen's Council.

An eager committee man, Beard engaged at various times in the activities of the Board of Governors of Ruskin College, Oxford, a Government commission dealing with Wages Boards, the Youth Employment Council, the Industrial Training Council, the National Production Advisory Council on Industry, the National Joint Advisory Council, the Iron and Steel Consumer's Council, the Independent Television Authority, the Transport Consultative Council, the consultative committee on the Companies Act, and the Government committee dealing with the resettlement of discharged Servicemen in civilian life.

Beard was a formidable opponent of communists, a fair but determined negotiator at the collective bargaining table and a specialist in trade union education. His rubicund complexion and silver hair made him a familiar figure at gatherings of all ranks of the engineering industry at home and abroad for many years. He had catholic interests outside the trade union movement. In his youth he was active in Manchester amateur drama and music societies.

He was married, and had a daughter.

December 18, 1967.

Infanta Beatrice of Spain—See under **Spain.**

Sir Alfred Chester Beatty, the mining millionaire who was founder and former chairman of Selection Trust, died in Monaco on January 19, 1968, at the age of 92. He was the greatest of all living figures in the mining industry, and with his passing the world has lost one of its most romantic characters.

Millionaire, philanthropist, art collector, and industrialist, Beatty contributed as much to the world as he took from it. Perhaps his greatest achievement was the development and equipment of the Zambian copperbelt. His wide engineering knowledge gained from long experience, coupled with his ability in financing and his keen insight and judgment, established the copperbelt as one of the major mineral fields of the world.

In 1935 he was presented with the Gold Medal of the Institution of Mining and Metallurgy and the citation included these words: "The diversity of his ability was well illustrated by the fact that not only had he been the outstanding figure among technical men in the development of new mineral wealth in West Africa, Serbia and Northern Rhodesia, but he had carried these companies successfully through the various stages of financing and development to productive and profitable operations. Thus, to the qualities necessary to the successful pioneer in mining he added those of the constructive organizer, the conservative financier and the able administrator."

Beatty was born in New York in 1875, and graduated as a mining engineer from the Columbia School of Mines. When he was only 28 he became consulting engineer and assistant general manager of the Guggenheim Exploration Company. With John Hays Hammond, the friend of Cecil John Rhodes, he acquired and developed many of Guggenheim's largest mines. He opened up gold and silver mines in Mexico, copper mines in the West, and prospecting concessions in what was then the Belgian Congo.

In his early days in America's wild west he travelled by stage coach, wore a Colt revolver in his boot, and experienced the roaring revelry of mining settlements on the boom. He knew the tough life of the saloons, made friends of men with six-shooters at their hips and bags of gold and silver in their hands.

On one occasion, when he was a mine superintendent, striking miners tried to kill him. They put him in a cage and dropped him down a mine shaft. He escaped death by jumping out just before the cage crashed at the bottom of the pit.

Retiring from the American mining scene in 1913, Beatty settled in England where he established the Selection Trust.

After the First World War, he again embarked on a career of developing, financing and administering mining businesses throughout the world. Selection Trust's first important mining venture under his direction was an exploration on the Gold Coast for diamonds. Then in 1925 he became interested in copper mining in Northern Rhodesia and his activities resulted in the formation of the great Roan Antelope and Mufulira copper companies.

At the same time as he was developing the copper fields of Rhodesia, Beatty became engaged in opening up the Tetiuhe mine in Siberia and others in Yugoslavia. His services to Yugoslavia in developing its mineral resources earned him the Grand Cordon of the Order of St. Sava.

He adopted British nationality in 1933 and on the outbreak of the Second World War he gave great service to Government departments active in his own field. He became engaged in work connected with economic warfare involving diamond, tungsten, and other non-ferrous metals, and many of his staff were loaned for the war effort.

In May, 1950, he retired from the chairmanship of Selection Trust and in July of that year, at the age of 75, he left England to live in Dublin. Beatty had strong views on restrictions and considered that life in Britain was regulated "sometimes beyond reason". He took with him his treasure house which has often been described as beyond value. It included priceless collections of rare eastern manuscripts; 9,000 rare books, weighing 35 tons; a stamp collection known to be the most valuable of its kind in the world; a collection of French snuff boxes and eighteenth century watches; a bible two centuries older than the Codex Sinaiticus for which the British Museum paid £100,000; and the earliest known copy of the Rubaiyat of Omar Khayam.

GENEROUS GIFTS

He was a great and a generous man, and many national and public institutions benefited from his gifts. He gave £40,000 for the establishment of the Royal Cancer Hospital in Fulham Road, London, of which he was vice-patron (formerly president).

In 1950 he gave more than 80 canvases of the Barbizon and contemporary schools, estimated to be worth about £500,000, to the National Gallery in Dublin, and in 1955 handed over to the nation a 13th century book of hours which had been on loan to the British Museum.

He was knighted in 1954 and became the first honorary citizen of the Irish Republic under the Irish Nationality and Citizenship Act of 1956. It was granted to him by the Irish government as a token of honour for distinguished service to the Irish nation.

When, early in 1961, Beatty sought to dispose

of seven Impressionist paintings he indicated that he was prepared to sell below the current market price, provided the paintings went to public art galleries in Britain. "I don't want my paintings to go to America", he said at the time. "I want them to stay in Britain. I love Britain and I'm British now."

Towards the end of 1962, 172 gold snuff boxes and watches belonging to Beatty were sold at Sotheby's for £124,029. In June the following year the second part of his collection made £100,558.

In 1965, he was presented with an address of honour on behalf of the British Academy at a luncheon to celebrate his ninetieth birthday. It was the first time the Academy had paid such a tribute. He left his library to the Eire government.

He was twice married. His second wife, the daughter of Mr. John Dunn, of New York City, died in 1952, and he handed over control of his interests to his son, Mr. A. Chester Beatty, Jnr.

January 22, 1968.

Sir Hugh Beaver, K.B.E., who died on January 16, 1967, at the age of 76, was a former president of the Federation of British Industries. He had occupied a number of important posts in business and industry, and at one time or another had been closely connected, either professionally or in an advisory role, with the new towns, clean air, the metric system, industrial engineering and colonial development.

He was a former managing director of Arthur Guinness and Co., Ltd., and it was he who, when shooting by the river Slaney in Ireland in 1954, conceived the idea of publishing the *Guinness Book of Records*, which has now sold over two million copies.

Hugh Eyre Campbell Beaver was born on May 4, 1890, the son of Hugh Edward Campbell Beaver, and was educated at Wellington College, of whose governing board he was later to become chairman.

His first thought on leaving school was to join the Indian Civil Service, and as a first step he went into the Indian Police. It was while he was on leave in England that he met Sir Alexander Gibbs, who, at that time, was establishing his firm of consulting engineers, and he gave Beaver a job as his personal assistant. Beaver had no experience of engineering, but he possessed an exceptional talent for mastering technical details and economic possibilities.

It was for the firm that he spent 1931 in Canada on problems of the Canadian national ports and, at the request of R.B. Bennett, then Prime Minister of Canada, directed the rebuilding of the harbour of St. John, New Brunswick, after its almost complete destruction by fire in June, 1931. He later became a partner in his firm and his particular interest before the Second World War was in developing the industrial engineering side of the firm—factory building and planning, industrial layout and planning &c. Thus he was closely concerned in the measures of reindustrialization of the depressed areas of South Wales, Tyneside and Durham, and West Cumberland, in which his firm acted as consultants to the Commissioner for Special Areas in planning and starting the various trading estates.

EXPLOSIVES FACTORIES

At the outbreak of the war the firm became the agents of the Ministry of Supply for the construction of the immense filling factories at Swynnerton in Staffordshire, Risley near Warrington, and Kirkby near Liverpool. In October, 1940, he was brought by Lord Reith to the Ministry of Works; he became Director General and was responsible *inter alia* for the direction of the building and construction industry and for the general planning of the whole wartime programme of works.

At the end of the war he joined Arthur Guinness Son and Co., Ltd., and he became managing director in 1946, and in 1959 joint managing director with Lord Boyd. He retired in 1960.

After the war he was a member of the Reith New Towns Committee, which laid down the pattern and principles on which the new towns have been built. He was a member of the working party on the building industry. He became a member in 1952, and from 1954 to 1956 was chairman, of the Advisory Council of the Department of Scientific and Industrial Research. He was chairman of the Committee on Power Station Construction in 1952–53 and of the British Institute of Management in 1951–54; and of the Committee on Air Pollution, 1953–54, which led to the Clean Air Act, 1956. He was a director of the Colonial Development Corporation from 1951–60; and since 1956 had been a director of Richard Thomas and Baldwins Ltd. Beaver was president of the Federation of British Industries from 1957 to 1959. He was chairman of the Industrial Fund for the Advancement of Scientific Education in Schools, which raised and distributed the sum of over £3m. to assist or expand the teaching of science in all boys' and girls' secondary schools not financed by Government funds.

From 1958 to 1963 he was chairman of the governing board of Ashridge College. He had been president of the Institute of Chemical Engineers and was chairman of the British Association's committee of inquiry into the metric system. He was knighted in 1943 and created K.B.E. in 1956.

During his years as president, the F.B.I. was faced with a full quota of economic problems; in particular there were the effects of the findings of the Radcliffe and Cohen committees to be considered. It was also during his presidency that the important *Industrial Trends Survey* was started. He did his best to strengthen the links between industry and educational bodies, for this was a subject very close to his heart. His quick intelligence and skill as an assessor of opinions were seen at their best when the reactions of industry to the Treaty of Rome were being tested.

He married in 1925 Jean Atwood, daughter of Major Atwood Beaver, O.B.E., M.D. They had two daughters. His wife died in 1933.

January 18, 1967.

The death of **Lord Beaverbrook** on June 9, 1964, at his home at Cherkley, at the age of 85, removed a personality held in affection and vehemently criticized for more than 50 years.

The young Max Aitken, fresh from Canada, puzzled Westminster before the First World War, winning a few friends, making some enemies and leaving many members of parliament suspicious of him. The brilliance he showed as a go-between in the crisis that led to the fall of the Asquith government first taught those behind the scenes that he was more than a colonial adventurer who need not be taken seriously. Then he acquired the *Daily Express* and proved, in the twenties, that his finger on the pulse of mass-circulating journalism was more sensitive than those of Northcliffe's heirs. This turned him into a household figure. He helped in this process of building up by freely allowing himself to be caricatured. The little impish figure with the eyes sometimes twinkling and sometimes steely—the image of a gnome who would be jovial company at dinner for all those round the table who had armed themselves with long spoons—was irresistible.

When in the Second War it became known that he had the friendship of Sir Winston Churchill, the image grew larger in public consciousness. Housewives cheerfully gave up their kettles to this persuasive salesman. Sober citizens, who shook their heads over his antics as a director of newspaper policies, relaxed into a chuckle at the latest story about him or against him—likely enough told by himself. He was a natural and disarming self-publicist. He once remarked:—

> Just a few days ago Churchill asked me "What are you doing?" "Writing", I replied. "What do you write about?", he asked. "Me", I answered. "A good subject", he said, "I have been writing about me for fifty years, and with excellent results."

Old age became him. He changed relatively little in appearance and not at all, except for a little mellowing, in his enthusiasm for causes, his relish for power and his sense of fun. Time will be needed to get him in perspective. The child of the manse, on whom Christianity never lost its hold, the quickly rich player of markets for whom wealth was always delightful, the politician in the long run *manqué*, make a complicated unity. But unity there was in Beaverbrook. It was his misfortune that he could not bring himself to accept that, fundamentally, he was a lightweight in public life.

RARE GAIETY

But lightweights so full of gaiety as he was are rare and he would not mind being mentioned with that fictional character who achieved great riches and remained unspoilt, Arnold Bennett's Card, and, so, identified "with the great cause of cheering us up".

William Maxwell Aitken was born on May 25, 1879, at Maple, a village, 15 miles from Toronto. He was a son of the Rev. William Cuthbert Aitken, a Presbyterian minister at Newcastle, New Brunswick, and both his parents came of Scottish Lowland stock. He was educated at the village school, and at the age of 18 entered a solicitor's office. He had a hard struggle, but not for long. Success gave him a golden handshake while he was still in his early twenties.

He became connected with successful enterprises in his own province, and a prominent figure in the Canadian financial world. He engineered several "mergers" which gave him a reputation for business acumen and power of organization. Before he was 30 he was the owner of a large fortune but in the process of making it he had failed to create the good will necessary to a successful career in Canadian public life.

BUSINESS AND POLITICS

He therefore went to England, where he had a friend in Bonar Law. On his advice he stood for Parliament and won a sensational victory in what was regarded as the Liberal stronghold of Ashton-under-Lyne in the second election of 1910. He purchased a country house in Surrey, and for some years devoted himself to politics and to a certain amount of City business. He made no particular mark in Parliament, but acquired a circle of political friends. He was knighted in 1911.

On the outbreak of the War he volunteered at once for the Canadian Expeditionary Force and was appointed "Eye-Witness" to the Canadians in 1915, and in 1916 representative at the front of the Canadian Government. He was also officer in charge of the Canadian War Records, and brought that department to a state of high efficiency.

Towards the end of November, 1916, he took a leading part in the events which led to the fall of the Asquith Government. With a natural aptitude for political tactics and gifted with conspicuous powers of persuasion as well as audacious courage, it was largely to him that Lloyd George owed his accession to the post of Prime Minister. He has himself left an account of the part he played in those hectic days and of the silence which succeeded the constant ring of his telephone—an instrument of which he made the fullest use—when Lloyd George had received the King's commission and began to form his Government.

During 1917 he took little part in public life, contenting himself with his activities at the Canadian War Records and with organizing the cinema work of the British War Office. To him was due the admirable series of war films taken on the Western front and their successful distribution throughout the world. In February, 1918, when Sir Edward Carson's resignation from the War Cabinet left the Department of Information without a ministerial head, Lord Beaverbrook was appointed Chancellor of the Duchy of Lancaster and Minister of Information. The two volumes of his *Canada in Flanders* had already appeared.

MINISTER OF INFORMATION

His work as Minister of Information showed that he possessed unusual administrative gifts. Many of his actions were attended with great success, notably the visits which he organized of large parties of representative Americans to this country and to the front. In August his health broke down, and in October he resigned his post as Chancellor of the Duchy. The Ministry of Information was closed towards the end of the year. In 1917 he was created a baronet and in the same year a peer. He took his title from Beaverbrook, the name of a small stream near his early New Brunswick home.

In December, 1925, Beaverbrook published a revealing little book, *Politicians and the Press*, which is almost an autobiography of the years from the Armistice to that time. He followed this in 1928 with a much larger book, *Politicians and the War, 1914–16*, the chief object of which was to pay a whole-hearted tribute to his old friend and benefactor, Bonar Law. When he recovered his health he devoted himself to various business activities, among them the cinema industry in Britain. But his chief interests lay in the newspaper world. He had for some years controlled the *Daily Express*, and he soon made this paper, together with the *Sunday Express*, which he founded, a leader in popular journalism. A special Scottish issue began in the autumn of 1928, and he had previously purchased the control of the *Evening Standard* and greatly increased its size and circulation. On the advice of Sir Abe Bailey he had taken up racing as a hobby, and acquired a house at Newmarket, and horses from the stable, usually bearing Canadian names, had some success.

Early in 1929 his interest in politics suddenly revived. He started a campaign for Empire Free Trade, believing that the only line of economic salvation for Britain lay in making the Empire a single economic unit like the United States, with internal free trade, and tariff barriers against the rest of the world. This creed he preached not without inconsistencies but with conviction and fervour. He urged it in the House of Lords and on platforms throughout the land, and his earnestness, combined with effective journalistic support, gave him a hearing though he won few converts. He had never been a good speaker and had always disliked the duty, but now practice and enthusiasm made him a platform draw.

His attitude involved him in conflict with the party leaders, and his active part in the promotion of independent candidatures at by-elections led to a controversy with Baldwin marked by a vituperation commoner in politics a hundred years ago than in more recent times.

EATANSWILL EXCHANGES

The prominence given to these Eatanswill exchanges in the *Daily Express* exaggerated their real significance. Public opinion was diverted rather than impressed by his presentation of economic realities in crusading terms.

During subsequent years his interventions in politics were less open and personal, though his papers were inclined to be critical of the National Government until Neville Chamberlain became Prime Minister. Lord Beaverbrook found the views and policy of that statesman more congenial. He was one of Chamberlain's supporters and up to the very eve of the outbreak of war was convinced that war could and should be avoided. When it came he did not flinch. Eight months after its declaration, he readily accepted the new post of Minister of Aircraft Production created, it is believed, at his own suggestion, in the administration formed by Mr. Churchill. He was eminently fitted for the part of a new broom. His methods made critics, but they also impressed friends. His personality was felt everywhere. The situation called for speed and improvisation and Lord Beaverbrook's qualities exactly filled its requirements. The knowledge of British feeling which his journalistic experience had given him proved invaluable. He knew when to call on the men in the factories for a special effort and when to mobilize public sympathy for gifts of aluminium saucepans and support of Spitfire funds.

PERSONAL CONTROL

But the scale of his new Ministry was such that he could also keep personal control over details and himself take steps to secure a particular worker for a particular factory. In the grim months of that autumn Lord Beaverbrook was faced with the duty of securing the utmost possible output of machines while at the same time dispersing the industry by way of protection against air attack, and his success in meeting this double emergency contributed materially to victory in the Battle of Britain.

By the spring of 1941 the crisis was past. In a broadcast delivered in March, notable for its warm tribute to a few named research workers. Beaverbrook was able to tell the nation that six new types of aircraft and five new engines had been brought into production. The department had acquired its own momentum and its head rightly felt that his best work in it had now been done. Just under a year after his appointment he vacated his office and became a Minister of State, a post created for him by the Prime Minister in order that he might bring his energies to bear upon the more general questions of policy coming before the War Cabinet. In his new post he became a member of the Defence Committee of the Cabinet and deputy chairman of its supply section.

MISSION TO MOSCOW

The new arrangement, with its divorce of responsibility for policy from executive control, proved unsatisfactory. At any rate it was abandoned within two months, and Beaverbrook, while remaining a member of the War Cabinet, took over the Ministry of Supply. Russia had just entered the war, and the new Minister threw himself into the congenial task of speeding up the production of tanks and guns. In September, after visits to the United States and Canada, he headed the British section of an Anglo-American mission to Moscow. Before he left he sent a telegram to all factories engaged in tank manufacture assuring them that the whole of their product for the following week would be sent to Russia. The mission undertook to satisfy, in the words of the communiqué, "practically every requirement for which the Soviet military and civil authorities asked." On his return he delivered a broadcast, rich in vivid detail, and calling for the production of 30,000 tanks.

On taking over the Ministry of Supply, he let it be known that he hoped to complete his work there in six months. As the year wore on the asthma from which he suffered gave him increasing trouble and it caused no surprise when in February, 1942, he was transferred to the newly created Ministry of War Production with general supervision over supplies. Within a fortnight, however, he had left the War Cabinet and, after carrying through yet another mission to the United States, he withdrew from the Government.

Eighteen months later he returned to office as Lord Privy Seal with general duties which included the supervision of civil aviation policy. Circumstances called for a cautious approach hardly to his taste and he was probably thankful when the appointment of a Minister of Civil Aviation left him free for other duties. He had secured agreement at the Empire Air Conference in 1943 and had avoided a breakdown in his discussions with Mr. Adolf Berle in the following year. Another matter to which he gave eager attention was an understanding with the United States on the difficult question of oil supplies. Here he negotiated an arrangement which it proved impossible to implement.

POST RETAINED

He retained his office after the Coalition broke up and vacated it on the Government's resignation in July, 1945.

After the war he spent less time in his English homes in Arlington Street and in Surrey and more in the south of France and the Bahamas. But he never ceased to take a close and almost a daily interest in the newspapers from which he had nominally detached himself and he kept a critical eye on the performances of successive governments. The veteran crusader rode again at the challenge of the Common Market which to him was an infidel conception—a betrayal of the principles of Commonwealth unity. His delight in hospitality—he was happy alike as host and guest—remained with him.

In recent years his talents as a political historian of his times became more widely appreciated: telling his story from the inside his works were not only immensely readable but will prove valuable material for historians in the future. Some of his earlier books were republished and in 1956 came *Men and Power 1917–18*, a sequel to *Politicians and the War*. In 1963 *Decline and Fall of Lloyd George* was published. Beaverbrook also wrote a number of a more various nature: *Don't Trust to Luck* (1954), *Three Keys to Success (*1956*)*, *Friends (*1959*)*, an account of his lifelong connexion with Lord Bennett, the former Canadian Prime Minister, and *The Divine Propagandist* (1962).

In May, 1964, a fortnight before he died, his eighty-fifth birthday was marked by a dinner given in his honour by Lord Thomson of Fleet at which more than 650 guests were present. In his speech on this occasion Beaverbrook gave convincing proof that his zest and mental energy were unimpaired.

In 1906 he married Gladys, daughter of the late General Drury, of Halifax, Nova Scotia. She died in December, 1927. They had one daughter and two sons, of whom the elder, the Hon. Max Aitken, D.S.O., D.F.C., chairman of Beaverbrook Newspapers Ltd., survives and now succeeds to the peerage. Last year Beaverbrook married secondly Marcia Anastasia, widow of Sir James Dunn, first baronet.

June 10, 1964.

Sir John Beazley, C.H. who died on May 6, 1970, at the age of 84, was the greatest Oxford scholar, in any classical field, of his generation. He was Professor of Classical Archaeology from 1925 to 1956.

Working on the foundations laid by Hartwig and Furtwaengler in Germany in the late nineteenth century, he built up the scientific study of the Attic vase painting, with a mastery of detail, and a knowledge of the comparative material and of classical literature, that make his achievement without parallel in the history of classical scholarship in England. Discoveries were being made, particularly in Italy, during the second half of his life, that added enormously to the corpus of material which concerned him. But he never failed to keep abreast of them.

John Davidson Beazley was born in Glasgow on September 13, 1885, and from Christ's Hospital went up to Balliol in 1903. After an undergraduate career outstandingly distinguished, he was elected to a studentship of Christ Church, as Mods, Tutor in 1908. Those who know the crisp and fastidious English of his learned works will not be surprised to hear that in early days he wrote, and occasionally published, poems of a quality which led his friend and Oxford contemporary, J.E.Flecker, to protest in verse against his immersion in archaeology, while T.E.Lawrence thought him the most notable English poet of his day.

DELIGHTFUL GREEK

His delightful Herodotus at the Zoo, which won the Gaisford Greek prose prize in 1907, attained the extraordinary distinction of being reprinted four years later and there is now a more modern edition published in Germany. He himself wrote books in German and Italian, and was equally at home in French.

Beazley could have made a name for himself in literary scholarship, and his command of the literary sources contributed greatly to his eminence as an archaeologist, but archaeology early became his primary interest: directed at first to gems, but soon turned mainly towards Greek red-figured vases. His first paper, on the Kleophrades Painter (1910) was followed by *Attic Red-figured Vases in American Museums* (1918), and, in 1925, by *Attische Vasenmaler des rotfigurigen Stils.* That book distinguished more than a hundred and fifty personalities, whom Beazley equipped with conventional names, and whose style he summarized in a few pithy sentences. It was followed by *Greek Vases in Poland* (1928) and by a flow of papers and reviews; and in 1942 was superseded by *Attic Red-figure Vase-Painters,* in which many new artists were distinguished and more than 15,000 vases classified.

Beazley's mastery of the scattered material is neatly illustrated in the frontispiece to his *Campana Fragments in Florence* (1933). This represents a single cup, reconstructed by means of photographs of 30 or 40 fragments dispersed among the museums of Rome, Florence, Heidelberg, Brunswick, Baltimore and Bowdoin College. The progress he achieved is shown by his work on the Kleophrades Painter, to whom, in 1910, nine vases had been ascribed by Hartwig and three more by Hauser. Beazley's paper that year raised the number to 35, his book *Attische Vasenmaler* to 72, *Der Kleophrades Maler* (1933) to 89, and *Attic Red-figure Vase Painters* (1963 edition) to over 100, over and above the 20 or more, in the Black-figure technique, included in his book on Black-figure.

In spite of the difficulties which the parochialism of directors and excavators sometimes created, his almost unequalled visual memory meant that little of importance which he had seen failed to find its place in his work, even if (as sometimes happened) he had not been allowed to make notes. *Etruscan Vase-painting* (1947) and *Attic Black-figure Vase painters* (1956) listed and assigned to artists a large proportion of the extant Etruscan and Black-figure vases; while his lectures on the *Development of Attic Black Figure,* published in 1951, show his gift for selecting from an immense mass of material, and for setting it out in readable and delightful form.

EARLY MASTERY

Though Beazley's work on vases was his primary interest, the chapters on Greek art (written in collaboration with Professor Ashmole) contributed to the *Cambridge Ancient History,* or the list of his writings published by the Clarendon Press in 1951, show a range which extends through the whole field of Greek archaeology. His mastery was recognized early, and when still a young man he was instructing students in Oxford from Germany, America and elsewhere. He was elected to his Oxford Chair in 1925.

Not perhaps until the question was raised late in his life, whether his "archive" could be acquired for Oxford University, were its comprehensiveness and the systematic quality of its compilation and annotation fully appreciated. There were some 65,000 photographs of vases alone, mounted and docketed. The essence of his achievement thus lay not only in his brilliant talent, but in his powers of industry and concentration also.

During the last 15 years of his life, deafness made it increasingly difficult for him to maintain ordinary social contacts. His deaf aid, manipulated by those delicate hands, seemed designed to give off a shrill warning note to others, rather than to convey their observations to him: he seemed sometimes to live in a world of his own, and delighted his colleagues at college meetings by breaking into gentle song, or making lively exclamations about the scholars whose works were in his mind at the moment ("what", he would ask himself aloud, "would Rumpf say to that?"), apparently oblivious to what was happening around him. Friends and pupils who were privileged to penetrate the barrier found his charm and gaiety as well as his learning undiminished. At such moments his own failures to hear what had been said would set him off on some witty and vivacious anecdote, or on one of those unassuming but brilliant displays of scholarship, which left no doubt that his real powers were in no way impaired.

He remained to the end of his life exceptionally good looking, his face sensitive and profile delicately chiselled, his blue eyes rather deeply set; and as he moved about from one pile of photographs to another in a house from which photographs, books and off-prints eventually crowded out most other things (including incidentally most of the heating apparatus), wearing as often as not a pair of cherry-coloured trousers, a heavy roll-neck jumper, and on his head, something woollen which was neither turban nor tam-o'-shanter, but partook, in the Aristotelian phrase, of the nature of both, he was a picturesque as well as a singularly handsome figure.

During those years he relied more and more on his wife, Marie, daughter of Bernard Bloomfield, whom he had married, a war widow, in 1918. She taught herself to photograph vases, but archaeology owes her a far greater debt since her care for him was the background that made the work of his later years possible. Their charming hospitality had a dash of the unconventional which in the early days of their marriage had found expression in the keeping for a few dramatic days of a goose in Christ Church, in Tom Quad. She died in 1967.

May 7, 1970.

Joe Beckett, who held the British and Empire heavyweight boxing championship from 1919 to 1923, died at Northampton on March 12, 1965.

The swarthy-skinned, muscular Joe Beckett will always be remembered more for his two swift defeats at the hands of Georges Carpentier of France than for the night of February 27, 1919, when he won the British title by knocking out Bombardier Billy Wells in the fifth round at Holborn Stadium.

The reason for this sorry reputation might well lie in the attention which the first meeting with Carpentier, at the Holborn Stadium on December 4, 1919, received from the press. Bernard Shaw was recruited to report the bout for the *Nation* and Arnold Bennett for the *New Statesman.* Both noted that the regular boxing correspondents gave Carpentier little chance. Yet the Frenchman, conceding weight and suffering from blood poisoning in his right arm, won in 74 seconds.

Bennett wrote: "Beckett was utterly outclassed. He never had a chance. The Stadium beheld him lying stunned on his face. Two minutes earlier Beckett in his majestic strength had been the idol of a kingdom. Now Beckett was a sack of potatoes and Carpentier in his might and glory was publicly kissing his chosen girl within a yard of the Prince of Wales. The English race was profoundly interested and moved and nothing less than winning the greatest war could have interested and moved it more profoundly."

FAIRGROUND YOUTH

On October 1, 1923, the Prince of Wales was again present for the return bout at Olympia—when Beckett was knocked out even more swiftly—and admitted afterwards he missed the finish. "My cigar had gone out", he explained. "I just had time to light it again and look up—and the fight was over."

Beckett was born on April 4, 1894, at Wickham, Southampton, and learnt to box in the booths of a fairground where his family worked. He had his first official contest in 1914 at the National Sporting Club when he knocked out Harry Smith in the fourth round. Four years later he gained in stature with three victories over the experienced Harry Curzon, but he was knocked out by the erratic Frank Goddard and beaten on points by Dick Smith for the vacant British light-heavyweight title in 1918.

Nonetheless Beckett looked sufficiently a good prospect when he beat Wells for the heavyweight championship for some optimists to talk of him challenging the world title held by Jack Dempsey. What they overlooked was the inferiority complex and sensitivity which sometimes led to his being so tense in vital matches. In 28 professional bouts he was beaten inside the distance six times.

Beckett at his best will be remembered for the beating he gave to the American Frank Moran at the Albert Hall in 1922. But only a year later his career was finished by the second knockout from Carpentier. Happily he invested his ring earnings wisely, and, even in recent years, regularly attended the dinners of the Boxing Writers' Club—a quiet, craggily distinguished looking man who seemed to have come to terms with the frustrations of his career.

March 15, 1965.

Sir Thomas Beecham, BT., C.H., who died on March 8, 1961, was one of the most remarkable figures in contemporary musical history. He was 81.

It is primarily as an orchestral conductor that he is celebrated. As an interpreter of a wide range of music he counts as one of the comparatively few executant geniuses this country has ever produced: continental Europe and America alike recognized him as such. In the last two decades of his life his stature was recognized as second to none among the great conductors of the world. But the work he did by shouldering the functions of the impresario, by his insistence on the highest standards of performance, can now be seen to have left a more enduring influence on the musical life of this country than was apparent in 1944, when he published what he described as "leaves from an autobiography". In *A Mingled Chime* he recounts in the form of an *apologia pro sua vita* his Sisyphean labours in the cause of opera and orchestral music. The years since the war have showed that the enterprises which seemed at the time to have foundered have proved to be foundations upon which, in changed circumstances, the remarkable vitality and vigour of our present institutions, alike in opera and in orchestral music, have been established.

Born on April 29, 1879, at St. Helens, the eldest son of the late Sir Joseph Beecham, the wealthy manufacturer of pills, Thomas was endowed not only with riches but with a quite unusual degree of musical sensibility. An ordinary schooling at Rossall, followed by a brief residence at Wadham College, Oxford, provided him with no special musical training. Yet in 1899, at the age of 20, he had founded and conducted an amateur orchestra, and seven years later, after a brief experience with a touring opera company, he created the New Symphony Orchestra, with which he gave a remarkable series of concerts at the Queen's Hall. After two years with this orchestra, another was formed and called the Beecham Symphony Orchestra.

The most important work done by Beecham during these years was the production of the works of Delius, whom he persistently championed in the face of general opposition or apathy until the composer gradually took his proper place in the scheme of things. Twenty years later his faith in Delius was reaffirmed in a triumphant festival in London in the presence of the then stricken composer and again, after the 1939–45 War in a Delius festival in 1946, and subsequently in gramophone recordings under the auspices of the Delius Trust. The biography of Delius published two years ago crowned his efforts in that it made public what no other person knew about the personality of the composer.

The writing of it was the fulfilment of a pledge made to Mrs. Zelka Delius many years ago, and though more concerned with Delius the man than with detailed, technical analyses of the works themselves, yet it nevertheless proves that man and artist were very much one.

ECLECTIC TASTES

In 1909 Beecham started upon his career as an operatic impresario, when he produced Ethel Smyth's *The Wreckers* at His Majesty's Theatre. In the following year a more ambitious season was undertaken at Covent Garden, when Strauss's *Elektra* and Delius's *Village Romeo and Juliet* were presented for the first time in England. Other seasons followed in rapid succession and among the operas produced were *Cosi fan tutte*, which had not been given in England for many years, *Fidelio*, *Salome*, and Stanford's *Shamus O'Brien*. It will be seen from this selection of titles that Beecham's tastes were thoroughly eclectic and that he kept a corner warm for the British composer. In 1911 he was instrumental in bringing to England Serge Diaghilev's Russian Ballet, an event which has had profound effects upon almost every branch of art. This innovation was followed up two years later by the importation of a Russian opera company, Chaliapin being among the singers, and *Boris Godounov*, *Khovanshchina*, and *Ivan the Terrible* were introduced to the astonished musical public of England. He was knighted for his services to music in 1916 and that same year succeeded to the baronetcy which had been conferred on his father in 1914. No other honour was given him until 1957 when he was made a Companion of Honour.

During the 1914–18 War Beecham's musical activities were unceasing. He produced opera in English and the repertory of his company ranged from Leoncavallo and Puccini to Mozart, Wagner and Moussorgsky. In the orchestral sphere he undertook the conductorship of the Royal Philharmonic Orchestra in London and of the Hallé Orchestra. Manchester had kept these two societies above water both by his enthusiasm and by financial assistance in those difficult days.

After the war he continued to give opera in English, adding, among other works, *Parsifal* and *Falstaff* to his repertory. In 1920 he gave a "grand" season at Covent Garden. His enthusiasm had, however, outrun his financial resources and possibly his discretion. For a time he had to retire from active musical work. The Beecham Opera Company was transformed into the British National Opera Company, which bravely attempted to maintain in the face of adversity the standard he had set.

UNDIMINISHED VITALITY

A few years later he reappeared as an orchestral conductor, undiminished in vitality and deepened in musical understanding. He added Handel to the number of his especial favourites among the composers, and gave performances of *Messiah* and other oratorios which astonished everyone by their vitality and their insight. In 1928 he became conductor of the Leeds Triennial Festival and in all festivals up to the outbreak of war in 1939 secured some remarkable performances—of Delius's *Mass of Life*, Verdi's *Requiem* and of the choral works of Berlioz as well as of more conventional masterpieces.

He continued his work for opera by association with various syndicates at Covent Garden and a renewal of his Russian enterprises at the Lyceum in 1931, but his attempt to found an Imperial League of Opera, which he launched in 1927, though promising well at first, failed before it could begin the large scale operations projected for it throughout the country. Another project, the founding of an orchestra which should be moulded to his style of playing, was brilliantly successful while it lasted. This was the creation of the London Philharmonic Orchestra in 1932 which was in part a counterblast to the B.B.C., with whom Beecham sometimes found it difficult to work in harmony.

From this time until the outbreak of the second German war the L.P.O. played regularly for the Royal Philharmonic Society for various serial concerts as well as for opera and ballet during the summer. Its characteristics were crisp ensemble and such an intensity of sheer singing tone that in Haydn and Mozart at any rate it sometimes seemed as though the ear was being lashed with thongs of silk. Beecham's style was essentially lyrical, though he was not always considerate to singers in his operatic performances. Wagner in his hands—he conducted *The Ring* annually at Covent Garden for a number of years—shrank a little from epic size but gained in mellifluousness, so that *Lohengrin*, for instance, became a singer's, almost an Italian, opera

PRODIGIOUS MEMORY

It was part of Beecham's eclectic taste that though not fundamentally in sympathy with the heroic element in Wagner—nor, indeed, with Beethoven—he could redress the balance of his sympathies with their other qualities, with all the elements that appealed to his acute sensibility, so that his readings of the German masters were unusual or individual, yet free from distortion. Mozart was his favourite above all others. Intellectual music made little appeal to him: the appearances of Bach or late Beethoven in his programmes were rare and his interpretation of Brahms (e.g., the C Minor Symphony) was not always convincing. His memory was extraordinary and he conducted everything, except concertos and operas, without a score, but with evident knowledge of its contents. Indeed, it was taken as a sign that he did not really know the work if a score was brought on of a purely orchestral composition. His dramatic gestures at one time gave offence—they were interpreted as an affectation and dubbed "ballet dancing"—but careful observation showed that he rarely made an insignificant gesture, and the details of his exquisite phrasing were moulded by his hands.

In 1940 he went to Australia and to America on conducting engagements, and during the 1939–45 War remained in the United States, to which he had long threatened to emigrate in disgust at artistic conditions in this country. Beecham used to give expression to his ideas of what the nation and in particular, though he was no democrat, of what the wealthier members ought to do for music, in pungent terms. In speech he was often indiscreet and took pleasure in indiscretion. He allowed his very acute wit unrestrained play and there was an imp of mischief in his make-up. He had the gift of quick repartee and his quips and sallies gave rise to many stories, more true than fabulous.

WIDELY READ

There is little doubt that his wit, which is less congenial to his fellow countrymen than humour, his benevolent dictatorship in artistic matters, and a touch of aristocratic disdain in manner contrived during his middle life to create some distrust in the minds of the British public. It was to combat what had become a liability to all his schemes for his country's good that he portrayed himself in his autobiography as a conventionally educated man of the world, a musician who could read a balance-sheet as easily as a full score, a hard-headed Lancastrian with no Celtic nonsense about him.

He was no doubt all of these things and a well and widely read man into the bargain. But these qualities were overlaid by his extraordinary sensibility, his darting wit, his prodigious memory, his idiosyncrasies and above all by his genius, to make him a legendary figure in his lifetime. The legend, like the work he did for our musical life, will survive after the laurels of the dead conductor have, inevitably, withered.

The effervescence of Beecham's personality was such that at the time most people think of retiring he returned to the scene with a remarkable outburst of new musical vigour. His eightieth year was marked by a triumphant season at the Teatro Colon in Buenos Aires, during which he conducted *Otello*, *Carmen*, *Samson et Dalila*, *Die Zauberflöte*, and *Fidelio*. This followed hard on the heels of a concert tour which had taken him to Paris, Switzerland, Vienna, Spain, Portugal, Monte Carlo, and Rome (where be directed the sound track for a musical film). In the autumn of 1958 he returned to England, and after proving that his wit was unimpaired when unveiling a bronze of himself by David Wynne at a ceremony in the Festival Hall, proceeded to direct a series of concerts which were like a tonic to the orchestra and audience alike. Not only his energies but also his range of interests increased with the years. In the recording studio he was no less active than in the concert hall as a recent issue of Bizet's Symphony in C testifies. He was to have conducted 10 performances of Mozart's *Die Zauberflöte* at the 1960 Glyndebourne festival but his health did not allow him to fulfil the engagement. There had also been discussion of a possible visit to Russia with his orchestra, the Royal Philharmonic.

Sir Thomas married first in 1903 Utica, daughter of Dr. Charles S. Welles, of New York, a descendant of Governor Thomas Welles, one of the Puritan Fathers and a member of an old Bedfordshire and Northamptonshire family, and secondly in 1943, Betty Humby, the pianist. She died in 1958 and he married thirdly, in 1959, Shirley Hudson, who is connected with the Royal Philharmonic Orchestra on the administrative side. His eldest sister Emily (Madame Helena Dolli) is a teacher of operatic dancing. He is succeeded in the baronetcy by the elder of the two sons by his first marriage, Adrian Welles Beecham, who was born in 1904.

March 9, 1961.

Brendan Behan, the Irish writer, who died at Meath Hospital, Dublin, on March 20, 1964, at the age of 41, had lived long enough to see at least one of his plays and, unofficially, himself taken to its heart by the United Kingdom, where he had once undergone eight years of Borstal training for terrorist activity on behalf of the I.R.A.

Not that he settled in England. He would appear, and as suddenly leave again; and while he was there Behan frequented, apart from the company presenting his own plays, crowds rather than individuals. It seems to have been a passion with him to be like his fellows and to do as they did; and he could gratify this most readily by mingling with them wherever they habitually foregathered to drink, gossip, play darts, and drink again. To have the reputation of a drinker meant, as Behan saw it, to be accepted as a man like others, only more so. This perhaps he was. But he exceeded his own ideal of mediocrity not through self-indulgence or through his conversation, which was sometimes no more than obstreperous or silly, but through his writing.

One of the three sons of Mr. Stephen Behan, a house-painter in Dublin, he was born on February 9, 1923, and was educated by the French Sisters of Charity in North William Street. According to the statement that he, at the age of 16, made at C.I.D. headquarters in Lime Street, Liverpool, after his arrest during the Second World War, he had come over to fight for the Irish Workers' and Small Farmers' Republic for a full and free life for his countrymen, North and South, and for the removal of British Imperialism from Irish affairs. Too young to be imprisoned he was sentenced to a period of Borstal training. An Expulsion Order being made against him eight years later, Behan returned to Dublin and published in 1958 a long chapter of autobiography under the title *Borstal Boy*. He showed in this how he had preserved his self-respect by continuing to mock at authority. The only animosity in the book is against stupidity, and even this was converted to tolerance as he found that, unperceived by anyone but himself, stupidity could be scored off, provided he kept his temper.

ANTI-HEROIC

Borstal Boy—it was banned in the Republic of Ireland and in Australia—was an anti-heroic book, and *The Quare Fellow* and *The Hostage* were anti-heroic plays. Both reached Miss Joan Littlewood at Theatre Royal, Stratford, in a much shorter form than that in which they were eventually produced there and later transferred to the West End. *The Quare Fellow*, a study of life in a prison on the eve of a hanging, was originally written in Irish, like other sketches in dramatic form by Behan, and was presented by the Gaelic League. It has been played in west Berlin, by Miss Littlewood's company at the Drama Festival in Paris in 1959, and on television, and a film made of it was shown here in 1962. Its successor *The Hostage*—the man in question being a Cockney soldier kidnapped and held in a Dublin brothel—established itself as a smash hit in the West End on its arrival there in the summer of 1959. The public, having learnt to look at life through Behan's eyes and to listen to it speaking with his voice, found the experience exciting. Things seemed to be not merely turned upside down by him, but made mellower. It was as though at curtain fall his characters shook hands, like two teams at the end of a football match, laughed, and went off to enjoy the evening together.

The Hostage was played in German for the first time in 1959, was produced on Broadway in 1960, and in the translation by M. Georges Wilson who called it a great popular *divertissement*, closer to cabaret than to didactic theatre, it was voted the best play of the season by the French dramatic critics in July, 1962.

A jazz revue entitled *Impulse*, in which an American impresario hoped to make use of Behan's talent as compère, petered out in Toronto on the pre-Broadway tour in 1961.

TWO NEW PLAYS

During that year projects for the production of two new plays of his own, *Richard's Cork Leg* at Theatre Royal, Stratford, and *Checkmate* at the Dublin International Festival, had to be shelved. A play written for radio in 1957 was given "live", at the Pike Theatre, Dublin, reappearing under the title *The Big House*—it was about the departure of an Anglo-Irish family of landlords and their replacement by a Dublin spiv in a Soho suit—at Theatre Royal, Stratford, in the opening bill of an Irish comedy season in July, 1963.

The text of this one-act play was included in *Brendan Behan's Island*, an Irish sketch-book with drawings by Mr. Paul Hogarth, which was published in October, 1962. *Hold Your Hour and Have Another*, though published in the following September with illustrations by his wife, consists of older material, which he had contributed weekly to the *Irish Press* between 1954 and 1956. In one of these articles he describes a Belfastman as an inebriate of some standing whose politics were purely alcoholic. If he too in later years might have been described as an inebriate of some standing, he was not content that his authorship should be purely alcoholic, as is shown by the use that he came to make of tape-recorders when the effort of concentrating on the act of writing, complicated by increasing ill health, grew to be too much.

His marriage to Miss Beatrice Salkeld took place in 1955. They had one daughter.

March 21, 1964.

M'Bark Ben Mustapha al Bekkai, the first Prime Minister of independent Morocco, died at Rabat on April 12, 1961.

Si Bekkai was born in 1907. He came from the tribe of Beni Snassen, formerly warlike and nomadic but within the last generation settled and grown rich. He chose a military career and became an officer in the French Army, in which he served with distinction. The war found him a captain, and he ended up with the rank of lieutenant-colonel, having been badly wounded and lost a leg.

After the war Si Bekkai became Pasha of Sefrou, but resigned in protest against the French Government's deposition and exile of the Sultan Muhammad V in 1953. He first began to take a leading part in politics by sharing in the confidential negotiations which led to the return of the Sultan in triumph two years later, and, as a patriot who had served his monarch well but who retained the confidence of the French, he was an obvious choice for Prime Minister, which he became in December, 1955.

BURDEN OF INDEPENDENCE

The final stages of independence, involving negotiations with Spain as well as with France, thus fell to a large extent on Si Bekkai's shoulders.

He remained Prime Minister of Morocco until April, 1958. It was not an easy period of office. In theory he was a non-party leader of a coalition Cabinet, but in fact he had often to act as a buffer between the Sultan (who became King in 1957) and the main political party, the Istiqlal. Eventually the Istiqlal succeeded in taking sole control of the Government, and Si Bekkai retired.

Si Bekkai looked and spoke like the French officer he had been, though there could be no doubting the strength of his nationalist feeling. He believed that geography and economics obliged Morocco to remain part of the west, and it was his hope that his country might become a fertile meeting place of European and Islamic civilizations.

April 14, 1961.

Queens—See under names of their states.

Queen Elisabeth of the Belgians, widow of King Albert of the Belgians, died on November 23, 1965. She was 89.

Hers was a life of devotion to others; a life of courage and endurance in times of great danger, of avid interest in all branches of life and thought. A woman of grace, charm and character, independent in thought as in action, she was the least conformist of Belgians.

She was endowed with decided artistic gifts, as musician, painter, and sculptor, and her sitting room at the Chateau de Stuyvenberg was a veritable museum of all her tastes and artistic achievements. She had studied the violin under Ysaye, Jacques Thibault, and Georges Enesco and had played duets with Yehudi Menuhin, and she leaves permanent memorials to her love of music in the Palais des Beaux Arts (which she established) where some of the world's leading performers can be heard and the Concours Reine Elisabeth, an international musical competition which she founded.

Her activities were not confined to the arts; she had an insatiable interest in all modern problems and trends of thought. It was this which led her in her last years to visit Yugoslavia, Poland, Russia, and China, where she was greeted with great cordiality. During one of her later visits to the Soviet Union in May, 1962, Mr. Khrushchev called on her. These visits were not uniformly applauded in Belgium; as a Catholic newspaper remarked tartly when she went to a Chopin Festival in Warsaw, the Polish Prime Minister was no longer Paderewski.

The year 1954 saw the crowning of her achievements; the Royal Academy of Belgium awarded her an honorary degree and her foundations—the Braille League for the Blind, the Anti-Polio League, the Anti-Cancer League were united in a single organization called Le Front Blanc de la Santé.

Born on July 25, 1876, she was the daughter of Duke Charles Theodore in Bavaria, known as a philanthropist and expert oculist, and of his second wife Marie Joseph of Braganza, Infanta of Portugal.

MET THE PRINCE

She first met her future husband, then Prince Albert, at the funeral of her ill-fated aunt and godmother the Empress Elizabeth of Austria in 1898, but it was not till 1900 that the betrothal took place in Paris. They were married in Munich on October 2 of the same year. There were three children, Leopold, Duke of Brabant, later King Leopold III, born in November, 1901, Charles, Count of Flanders, born in 1903, and Princess Marie José, born in 1906 and married in 1930 to the Prince of Piedmont, heir to the Italian throne.

From her first arrival with her husband she won the hearts of the Belgian people and earned their admiration for her interest in those in humble circumstances. During the reign of King Leopold II the Royal couple lived in comparative seclusion, but on King Albert's accession in December, 1909, she emerged to a life full of opportunity for the exercise of her many qualities.

The outbreak of war in August, 1914, entailed, of course, a complete severance from her own family in Germany, a trial which she loyally accepted. It plunged her adopted country into horrors which continued for four years, only to be repeated with greater fury 20 years later. The Royal Palace was at once converted into a hospital and the Queen threw herself into war work, Red Cross and care for children from ruined villages. When the King and Army were forced to withdraw she followed them, settling for some time at La Panne, a seaside village near Furnes, whence she carried on her work besides from time to time joining the King in visits to front line trenches in the neighbourhood.

In the triumphant days of November, 1918, after King Albert had returned from Le Havre (to which the Belgian Government had eventually withdrawn), she accompanied him on visits to Dunkirk, Bruges, and Antwerp and on November 22 was with the King and his five sons in the ride into Brussels in which Prince Albert, later King George VI, also took part.

PEACEFUL YEARS

The years immediately following the end of the first war were years of peaceful activity at home varied by visits with King Albert to London, Copenhagen, the Congo, Cairo, Baghdad and Syria, in which latter country they made a walking tour through the Lebanon.

This happy period witnessed the marriage in 1926 of her eldest son, Prince Leopold, to Princess Astrid of Sweden and reached its climax in the Belgian centenary celebrations in 1930 together with the birth of the first grandson, now King Baudouin.

But that cloud of tragedy which had in earlier days overshadowed the Belgian Royal Family was destined to return. In 1934 a climbing accident on the cliffs bordering the Meuse near Namur took the life of King Albert and in the following year Queen Astrid met her death in a motoring accident in Switzerland, where she and King Leopold III were touring. To the overwhelming personal blow of the sudden end of a long partnership both as husband and wife and as King and Queen was added the burden of obligations which but for the death of her daughter-in-law she would have been spared. The load was unflinchingly shouldered.

During the occupation of Belgium in the Second World War the Queen remained in seclusion at Laeken, sharing and doing all in her power to alleviate the sufferings of the people. After the military collapse in 1940 she was joined at Laeken by King Leopold, then technically a prisoner of war, until shortly before the German defeat he and his family were removed to St. Wolfgang in Tirol. She was a formidable woman and on many occasions intervened on behalf of Jews and other Belgians arrested by the Germans.

It was at the gates of Laeken that the Queen stood to greet the Guards Division on the day when they entered Brussels, the first of the allied armies of liberation.

Difficult times followed and serious problems. The release of King Leopold did not bring the expected early solution. During the ensuing vicissitudes and the long period of uncertainty up to the accession of King Baudouin in 1951 the presence behind the scenes of Queen Elisabeth, with her long-standing knowledge, influence, and experience of over 60 years, must have been of inestimable value. It was not until King Baudouin's marriage in 1960 that she was at last able to lay down her responsibilities.

November 24, 1965.

Krim Belkacem, the Algerian soldier and politician, who played a leading part in the struggle which led to France granting independence to Algeria, was found strangled in Frankfurt on October 20, 1970.

Born in 1922 in the Kabylie mountains in Algeria, he served for a time in the French Army but in 1947 joined the Algerian Nationalist movement. When in 1954 this movement broke out into open rebellion against the French authorities, he became responsible for the direction of guerrilla operations in the Kabylie region and was five times sentenced to death *in absentia* by French courts martial. In 1956 he played a prominent role in the first meeting of the "Algerian Revolutionary Committee," of which he was a founder-member, but in 1957 increasing French pressure forced him to escape to Tunis. There, when in 1958 a "Provisional Government of the Algerian Republic" was established and secured recognition by a number of Afro-Asian and Communist states, he became its "Vice-President and Minister for the Armed Forces" and was thus made responsible for the direction of all resistance operations within Algeria.

In 1960 he became "Minister for Foreign Affairs" of the Provisional Government, and in that capacity led the Algerian Delegation when peace talks with the French, which had broken down the previous year, were resumed, in May, 1961. In August, 1961, he became "Vice-President and Minister of the Interior" of the Provisional Government, but continued to lead the Algerian Delegation, which finally, at Evian in February, 1962, signed with the French a series of agreements providing for the grant of complete independence to Algeria within five months. In May, 1962, however, at a Revolutionary Committee meeting held at Tripoli, he clashed violently with the rival Algerian leader Ben Bella, who had been in a French prison while the Evian agreements were being negotiated and had now returned full of criticisms of their terms; and in July, in the struggle for power between the Algerian leaders which followed the actual acquisition of independence, he headed a group in opposition to Ben Bella's.

OPEN BREACH AVOIDED

The latter prevailed and thereafter Krim Belkacem, while avoiding an open breach with Ben Bella's regime, and contenting himself with cautious criticism of it, remained outside the political arena and spent long periods abroad.

He opposed President Boumedienne who came to power in June, 1965.

Declaring himself at open political war with the administration in Algiers, Belkacem formed the opposition Democratic Movement for Algerian renewal in Paris in October, 1967.

After an attempt against the life of the F.L.N. party leader Ahmed Kaid in 1968, Belkacem was one of six people sentenced to death in their absence for conspiracy in April, 1969. This trial took place at Oran while Belkacem was in Paris.

In later years he spent most of his time in Lausanne. He was married and father of four children.

October 23, 1970.

C. F. Bell, who died on April 3, 1966, at the age of 94, was First Keeper of the Department of Fine Art in the Ashmolean Museum, Oxford.

Charles Francis Bell had retired from the world for so long and so completely that even quite elderly people connected with the world of art and museums in which he had spent the greater part of his active life often supposed him to have been dead for many years. His links with the past were manifold. Through his mother, a daughter of Ambrose Poynter, he was connected with Rudyard Kipling, Lord Baldwin, Sir E. Burne Jones, Sir Edward Poynter, P.R.A., and only slightly more remotely with the world of the pre-Raphaelites and William Morris. Farther back his great-uncle Philip Courtney had been Wordsworth's factotum in money matters and his great-great-grandfather was Thomas Banks, R.A., the sculptor, whose life he wrote partly as an act of piety and partly from a genuine admiration for the work of this great but forgotten neo-classic. Of all this inheritance he was strongly aware so that, as was said of Alexandre Benois, the extraordinary longevity of his family had caused the past to have a special significance for him; the eighteenth century appeared quite near. As a man he was reticent and as a scholar he was scrupulous to a fault. As a consequence the volume of his writings was quite disproportionate to his encyclopaedic knowledge. With this he was most generous, especially to younger scholars, so that his monument is to be found as much in the acknowledgements in the prefaces to other people's books or the dedications of such works as Sir Kenneth Clark's *The Gothic Revival* and Sir Osbert Sitwell's *Winters of Content*, as in anything he wrote himself.

Charles Francis Bell was born on April 28, 1871, of an Anglo-Indian family, the fourth son of Robert Courtney Bell, a banker. He was a delicate child and was educated privately, picking up much of his knowledge from the clever and remarkable people who met at the house of his parents, a home charmingly described in J. A. Fuller Maitland's *A Doorkeeper of Music*. Through the chemist Sir Arthur Church, a friend of the family, he became acquainted with Dr. Drury Fortnum who recommended him in 1896 to Sir Arthur Evans as a suitable assistant to supervise the arrangement of the great collection of Renaissance art which Fortnum shortly afterwards bequeathed to Oxford.

SENSE OF SETTING

For more than 30 years thereafter the galleries of the Ashmolean gave scope to the exercise of Bell's special gifts. The university collections had only been transferred from their original home in Broad Street to their present buildings in 1894 and Bell found the rooms shabbily decorated, over-encumbered, and arranged without coherent plan. It was due entirely to his taste and sense of setting that, with very slender financial resources (sometimes supplemented from his own pocket), he gradually transformed them into one of the most attractively arranged of English museums. Indeed, the pattern he imposed on the collections is still apparent in spite of extensive changes due to later acquisitions. When the constitution of the Ashmolean was remodelled in 1908 he was appointed first Keeper of the Fine Art Department.

His earliest publication in 1901 was a catalogue of Turner's exhibited works, the forerunner of a series of essays on early English watercolours which appeared in the volumes of the Walpole Society, of which he was a founder and, at his death, the senior honorary vice-president.

It was as secretary to the committee appointed to survey and catalogue the University's vast assemblage of historical portraits that he established himself as a leading authority on English portraiture. The extremely able catalogues of the exhibitions of these held in 1903, 1904, and 1905, no doubt led to the invitation in 1910 to succeed his friend Sir Lionel Cust (with whom he had worked on the Burlington Club's exhibition of Early English Portraiture in 1909) as Director of the National Portrait Gallery. But projects for which he cared deeply were maturing at Oxford and he elected to remain there, though shortly afterwards he was appointed a Trustee of the Portrait Gallery.

On all the subjects he touched, notably his work on *The Designs for Masques by Inigo Jones* in collaboration with the late Percy Simpson, his catalogue of the Old Master drawings at Christ Church, and even in his last work, a paper on Thomas Gray and the Fine Arts published in 1945, Bell was a pioneer.

Bell was elected a Fellow of Magdalen in 1912 largely on the initiative of his friend Sir Herbert Warren. He retired prematurely from Oxford in 1931, largely on account of failing health. Nevertheless he survived for a further 35 years, thus enjoying a university pension for a longer period than he had received a salary as an active member of the university. This often caused him amusement latterly, as did many of the anomalies of a world he increasingly found grotesquely different from that in which he grew up.

April 5, 1966.

Sir Harold Idris Bell, C.B., O.B.E., who died on January 22, 1967, at the age of 87, was Keeper of the Manuscripts and Egerton Librarian at the British Museum from 1929 to his retirement in 1944. His wife died only a week before him. He was a papyrologist of world-wide authority, as well as a fine and devoted Welsh scholar. Indeed, Wales held a great part of his devotion, and somehow it seemed natural that, whereas in England he was most often referred to as "Sir Harold", in Wales he was always "Sir Idris"

Bell was born on October 2, 1879, at Epworth in Lincolnshire, the son of Charles Christopher Bell and Rachel Hughes—an English father and Welsh mother—educated at Nottingham High School, Oriel College, Oxford, and the Universities of Berlin and Halle. On his return from Germany in 1903, he joined the staff of the Department of Manuscripts at the British Museum, where he remained unitl his retirement as Keeper and Egerton Librarian in 1944, apart from a period of service at the War Office in World War I. He arrived at the museum at an opportune moment, when F. G. Kenyon needed assistance in coping with the great number of Greek papyri acquired by the museum; from their collaboration came the third volume of *Greek Papyri in the British Museum,* to which Bell later added a fourth and fifth, as well as the volume known as *Jews and Christians in Egypt,* also collaborating with others in the edition of Parts XVI and XIX of *The Oxyrhynchus Papyri, Fragments of an Unknown Gospel and other Early Christian Papyri, Magical Texts from a Bilingual Papyrus, Wadi Sarga, and* Volumes I and II of *The Merton Papyri.*

His work as an editor, supplemented by numerous papers and reviews in learned periodicals all over the world, by the notable monograph *Juden und Griechen im römischen Alexandreia,* and by his contribution to the *Cambridge Ancient History* had established him as one of the world's leading papyrologists by the thirties, and, from 1936 onwards, when C.B. was added to his O.B.E. and he was elected an honorary Fellow of his College, having the previous year been appointed University Reader in Papyrology at Oxford, honours came thick and fast: four Universities—Wales, Michigan, Brussels, and Liverpool—honoured him with their doctorate, many foreign academies elected him corresponding member, and he became president of the Society for the Promotion of Roman Studies (1937–45), of the British Academy (1946–50), of the International Association of Papyrologists (1947–55) and of the Classical Association (1955); he was vice-president, too, of the Society for the Promotion of Hellenic Studies (since 1930), the Egypt Exploration Society (since 1945), and the International Council for Philosophical and Humanistic Studies (1949–52). He was knighted in 1946.

All this time Bell was extending his authority over another, almost totally unrelated, field.

PASSION FOR WELSH

His passionate interest in the Welsh language, which he had begun to study, largely for sentimental reasons, as a young man, led to the publication of many *opera subseciva,* the best known being his *Development of Welsh Poetry,* written primarily for the benefit of English readers but bearing nevertheless the characteristic stamp of his wide scholarship. The same motive which inspired him to write this book, that of making known to those outside Wales the charm and beauty of Welsh poetry, also underlay the three volumes of translations which he published, *Poems from Welsh,* in collaboration with his father, *Dafydd ap Gwilym, Fifty Poems,* jointly with his son David, and *Welsh Poems of the Twentieth Century.*

For his work in the field of Welsh studies he was awarded the Medal of the Honourable Society of the Cymmrodorion in 1946, made its president in 1947, and afterwards its vice-president, and admitted as a Druid to honorary membership of the Welsh Gorsedd in 1949.

Even his later years, which saw the publication of two sets of University lectures on papyrological subjects, *Egypt from Alexander the Great to the Arab Conquest* and *Cults and Creeds in Graeco-Roman Egypt,* also saw the completion of his translation of Dr. Thomas Parry's *Hanes Llenyddiaeth Gymarcg,* to which he had added a comprehensive appendix on twentieth-century literature, and the appearance of a volume of essays and addresses entitled *The Crisis of Our Time,* which recalled in its broad humanism and natural charm the account, translated into Welsh 10 years before, of his search for papyri in Egypt, *Trwy Diroedd yDwyrain.*

The main ingredients of Bell's success as a scholar were his prodigious memory, his capacity for hard work and intense concentration of the job in hand, his command of foreign languages and literatures, and his mastery of the idiom and style of English prose, which he wrote with such precision and felicity that he seldom needed to correct his rough manuscript. In all that he did he maintained the highest standards of scholarship, but perhaps it is his work as editor of the last two volumes of the London Papyri and *Jews and Christians,* together with the masterly synthesis of Egypt, which shows him at his most brilliant.

The barest outline of his achievements is enough to shock the complacency of the modern specialist; yet he entitled his presidential address to the Classical Association "A specialist's apologia", a title to which the broad sweep of its contents gave the lie outright.

SECRET OF SUCCESS

Herein lay the secret of his success as a man; he was unable to see in himself anything to justify the distinctions which had been lavished on him, a completely unassumed humility which often led to reticence in committee and in discussion, for the simple reason that he was reluctant to press his views, unsought for, in the presence of others whom he considered more competent than himself. Committees were a sort of penance to him, but, characteristically again, he never refused to serve or failed to attend, as long as others thought that he had some contribution to make, and as a chairman he proved himself thoroughly businesslike with a shrewd grasp of procedure and detail. But it was in the intimate circle of his friends and his devoted family that the real man was revealed: courteous, kindly, sympathetic, of the simplest tastes, a good listener and a delightful raconteur. For all the avowed agnosticism of his middle years, he was *anima naturaliter Christiana,* and when he found his way back to the Church in his retirement, it was a homecoming which brought great joy to him and great benefit to the Church in Wales, of whose Governing Body he became a member.

Bell married, in 1911, Mabel Winifred, daughter of Ernest Ayling. They had three sons.

January 23, 1967.

Vanessa Bell died on April 7, 1961, at her home near Lewes, Sussex. She was 81.

Coming easily into the front rank of English women painters, Mrs. Vanessa Bell might be claimed as a product of, or a rebel against, academic training according to the point of view. She studied under that pillar of orthodoxy the late Sir Arthur Stockdale Cope, R.A., and at the Royal Academy schools, but she made her first appearance at the New English Art Club, though she was never a member; and it was as one of the young enthusiasts who flocked to the banner of Post-Impressionism under the wing of Roger Fry that she came into notice. Work of hers was included in Fry's second Post-Impressionist exhibition at the Grafton Galleries in 1913, she was one of his team of decorative artists at the Omega Workshops, and she was a member of the Fry contingent which joined the London Group in 1918.

Vanessa Bell came of a very distinguished family. Born in 1879, she was the elder daughter of Sir Leslie Stephen, the eminent man of letters, editor of *Cornhill* and later of the *Dictionary of National Biography,* and original of "Phoebus Apollo turned fasting friar" in Meredith's *The Egoist*; and she was the sister of Virginia Woolf, the novelist. Mrs Bell was also related to the Darwins, the Maitlands, the Symondses and the Stracheys.

After the death of Leslie Stephen in 1904 Vanessa and Virginia, who were deeply attached, with their two brothers set up house in Gordon Square, Bloomsbury, where their circle of friends included Clive Bell, T.S. Eliot, Lytton Strachey, J. M. Keynes, and other members of what came to be known as the "Bloomsbury set". In 1907 Vanessa Stephen married Clive Bell, the writer on art. They had two sons and a daughter. Her elder son, Julian, who was for some time Professor of English in a Chinese university, was killed in 1938 at the age of 28, while serving with the Spanish Medical Aid Unit during the civil war.

FRY PERIOD

In considering the work of Vanessa Bell it is impossible to ignore its affinities with that of Duncan Grant, one of her associates in the Fry period and with whom she shared several exhibitions. But any influence appears to have been reciprocal. If Mr. Grant encouraged Mrs. Bell's constructive powers it is equally certain that she had a refining and aerating effect upon his colour. Both, in their efforts to achieve plastic modulation by means of colour, derived ultimately from Cézanne; both remained characteristically English in the process.

Vanessa Bell was before everything a colourist; at the same time sound and joyous, observing both the constructive and the decorative functions of colour, but with a temperamental leaning to the decorative. She painted some good portraits and figure compositions, but her most characteristic work was in landscape and still life, flower studies in particular. Broad and flexible in style, she seemed to need some escape from regular forms for the full expression of her personality—much as a town dweller will often blossom out on an escape into the country.

In a foreword to the catalogue of an exhibition of Vanessa Bell's work at the London Artists' Association in 1930 Virginia Woolf spoke of the "inviolable reticence" of painting and said "Mrs. Bell says nothing. Mrs. Bell is silent as the grave. Her pictures do not betray her." In the sense intended of factual information about nature or herself that was true but by one of the paradoxes of art the reticence became eloquent of and fragrant with the personality diffused in the painting. That is to say in the more genial works, for every now and then, in more elaborate constructions, she did seem to drop hints about her formal ambitions. Her work, indeed, in its varying quality, was a good illustration of the truth that you find yourself by losing yourself. When Vanessa Bell lost herself in her painting she appeared to be more of an Impressionist and less of a Post-Impressionist than Fry, for example, would have approved. The constructive colour of Cézanne may have been her duty, but its atmospheric and decorative possibilities were her delight.

TATE COLLECTION

Several of Mrs. Bell's best pictures appeared in the exhibition mentioned above, including "Portrait of the Painter's Daughter", "The Foundling Hospital" and "The White Urn". The last was bought by the Contemporary Art Society, which had already presented to the Tate Gallery her "Flowers in a Jug" of 1920. Another particularly happy painting of hers was "The Garden Path", included in an exhibition at the Leicester Galleries in 1941.

Besides painting pictures Vanessa Bell did a good deal of decorative work of various kinds. She was associated with Fry in the activities of the Omega Workshops, she designed embroideries for Miss Mary Hogarth in her efforts to bring contemporary feeling into an ancient English craft, carpets for Allan Walton, pottery for Foley China, book jackets and illustrations for the Hogarth Press, and she collaborated with Duncan Grant in a scheme for the decoration of a "Modern Music Room", which was shown at the Lefèvre Galleries. In all her work she gave the impression of being an instinctive artist, gaining strength, no doubt, by discipline from outside but at her best when she forgot all about the rules and trusted to her own sensibility.

April 10, 1961.

Frederick John Bellenger, Labour Member of Parliament for the Bassetlaw division of Nottinghamshire since 1935, died at his London home on May 11, 1968. He was 73.

He will best be remembered as Secretary of State for War from 1946–47—critical years for the third Labour Government. He had previously been Financial Secretary to the War Office, and had been actively concerned with demobilization problems after the Second World War; he also had much influence on the formulation of Government plans for the post-war Army.

Bellenger was born on July 23, 1894, the son of Eugene Bernard Bellenger, and received an elementary school education. He started work at the age of 14 as a tea-packer in a Houndsditch warehouse for 6s. a week. He later became a boy-messenger in the Post Office and worked as a clerk to an export firm in the City. Among the "First Hundred Thousand" to enlist in 1914, he received his commission on the Somme and was wounded twice at Ypres. Bellenger was demobilized in 1919 after serving with the Army of Occupation on the Rhine. He then became an estate agent.

Originally a Conservative from 1922 to 1928. Bellenger represented that party on the Fulham Borough Council. He then joined the Labour Party, and at the 1935 General Election won a notable victory at Bassetlaw, defeating Mr. Malcolm MacDonald, the sitting National Labour member. This was one of the sensational results of that election, for the son of the then Prime Minister had had a majority of well over 13,000 in 1931, and the seat seemed impregnable. But MacDonald had obtained that majority when an orthodox Labour member, and the division remained loyal to Socialism. Bellenger's majority was 1,139 in a straight fight; he held the seat ever since—increasing his majority to more than 10,000.

During the Second World War, Bellenger served with the Royal Artillery—his old regiment. He was in the retreat to Dunkirk and after the evacuation went straight back to the House of Commons. For five years Bellenger ran a popular feature in a Sunday newspaper, under the heading "Voice of the Services", in which he dealt with every aspect of Service welfare.

In the House Bellenger continually asked about service problems, and his advocacy was to a certain extent responsible for some of the increases in pay conceded by the Government. He was a member of the Parliamentary committee on pay and allowances, and chairman of the Labour Party Services Committee; in January, 1945, he was one of six members to visit the allied forces in Italy.

In October, 1946, he became Secretary of State for War, and a Privy Councillor. He had to face a public outcry on the sentences for mutiny imposed on some of the men of the Airborne Division in Malaya and had the delicate task of convincing the House that it was the judge-advocate's opinion that a technical mistake had been made during the proceedings and that the men had been wrongly sentenced.

In 1965, as a member of the United Kingdom branch of the Commonwealth Parliamentary Association, Bellenger visited Australia with six other M.P.s, In 1967 he was appointed to the Select Committee to review parliamentary privilege. In December, he was the only Labour M.P. known to have deliberately abstained from supporting the Government on the Rhodesia vote, because he thought there was a risk of losing control of the Rhodesian situation by going to the United Nations.

Bellenger would not claim to be an orator. His style was unexciting, conversational and sometimes discursive. But he was that useful type of back-bencher who knew his mind and confined himself to topics on which he had something positive to contribute. Another of his enthusiasms was Anglo-German friendship, and in 1956 he was awarded the insignia of

Commander of the Order of Merit of the Federal Republic of Germany. Two days before he died he received the freedom of the Borough of Worksop.

Bellenger married in 1922 Marion Theresa, only daughter of General Konsul Karl Stollwerck, of Cologne. They had five sons and one daughter.

May 13, 1968.

Alhaji Sir Ahmadu Bello, Sardauna of Sokoto, who was assassinated by shooting outside his home near Kaduna on January 15, 1966, was one of the most powerful figures—possibly the most powerful—in Nigeria.

His political career was entirely in Northern Nigeria, of which he had been Premier since 1954, the first holder of the post. He played no formal part in federal politics. As president of the Northern People's Congress, however, he was the leader of the largest party in the Federation, which was the senior component of the Federal Government. Significantly, the Federal Prime Minister, Sir Abubakar Tafawa Balewa, has never been more than the Sardauna's deputy within the party, though the common assertion that this has made him simply the Sardauna's lieutenant in Lagos grew steadily less true as Sir Abubakar's stature increased.

Of the Sardauna's importance as ruler of the largest region of the federation there can be no doubt. The very fact that he and his ally, Chief Akintola, Premier of the West, have now been removed from the scene by assassinations confirms this.

Sir Ahmadu's power derived from the fact that he combined in his person aristocracy and high religious standing, a formidable combination in Northern Nigeria.

He was born in 1909 in Rabah in the Sokoto province. His father was district head of Rabah and Ahmadu himself later held that office from 1934 to 1938.

He was educated at the provincial school in Sokoto and then at the Katsina teacher training college, the nursery of so many of the leaders of the north. He then taught English and mathematics for three years in Sokoto before becoming district head. A rival for the Sultanate of Sokoto, he was appointed Sardauna, and for a time—many years ago now—there was friction between him and the Sultan.

Ahmadu Bello's first cautious steps towards politics proper came with his support in 1945 for the Youth Social Circle. Four years later he sat in the Northern House of Assembly as representative of Sokoto, and in the constitutional discussions in 1949 and 1950 he quickly emerged as the spokesman for Northern views—in effect the political embodiment of the emirs and sultans. When the Northern People's Congress, started as a cultural organization became a party in 1951 its leading members included Ahmadu Bello and Sir Abubakar, later Federal Prime Minister. In 1954 the Sardauna became the party's general president. In fact, if not in theory, the N.P.C. has never been a party in the usually accepted sense, at least in its regional manifestation. The cut and thrust of opposing views and decision by discussion did not mean much. The Sardauna's "divine right" to dictate policy did. Some of the more progressive politicians and officials tried with more or less success to assert their independence, but the majority still could be found regularly paying court—quite literally—at the feet of power. Some close and basically sympathetic observers had in recent years become convinced that the Sardauna had been corrupted by his power, though his services to the region and his personal qualities as a leader were worthy of great respect.

His position had been vastly strengthened in 1963, when, in his capacity as head of the Northern Nigerian Government he forced the resignation of the then Emir of Kano—his own kinsman—whose administration had been severely criticized by a one-man commission of inquiry.

Ahmadu Bello was possibly the last representative of a type of rule now obsolete in Africa. That he has met his end in the tragedy of assassination rather than by the processes of political evolution—and this in a country whose responsible leaders have been among the most outspoken critics of change by violence—is sadly ironic.

January 17, 1966.

Colonel Pavel Belyaev, the Soviet cosmonaut who circled the earth in the two-man spacecraft Voskhod-2 in 1965, died on January 10, 1970. He was 44. His comrade, Alexei Leonov, made the first historic walk in space during the 17 orbits around earth in 26 hours. During this flight Belyaev supervised and controlled Leonov's walk in space.

Belyaev, who was unofficial "dean" of Soviet cosmonauts, was known as a man of action, though of few words. He ushered in man's first historic walk in space on March 18, 1965, by tapping fellow cosmonaut Alexei Leonov on the shoulder and saying simply: "It is time."

Yuri Gagarin, the world's first man in space, who helped coordinate the Voskhod-2 flight from the ground, paid tribute to Belyaev's coolness as a spaceship commander by saying after the flight: "We had all the time heard his unruffled and calculated voice".

Belyaev was born in Chelishchevo, in the Vologda region, northeast of Moscow, in 1925. In 1941, when he was only 16, he tried to enlist in an army ski unit after Germany's invasion of the Soviet Union. As a boy he used to ski the three miles to school every day during winter. Because of his youth, he was turned down, but he learnt to work a lathe and became a turner in a war plant, before being accepted for fighter pilot training. He graduated when the war ended in Europe, but was soon flying as a navy pilot in sorties against the Japanese. He remained for 11 years with a naval air squadron in the Far East, being thought of as one of the Soviet Union's best commander pilots.

Called before a commission examining potential candidates for cosmonaut training, he feared he might be too old (at the time of the Voskhod-2 flight he was Russia's oldest spaceman and ten years Leonov's senior). But he was selected as one of Russia's original group of cosmonauts, entering space training in 1959.

Of the year's training he underwent with Leonov, Belyaev said: "We understand each other remarkably well. At times it seems as if we read each other's thoughts". He was moved by his space-flight. "We even cried with surprise when we saw a man-made satellite of the earth about a kilometre away from the ship", he said later. He wrote in a magazine article that he had no intention of overestimating the significance of his profession and casting aspersion on automation. But landings on the moon, Mars and other planets by manned spaceships "cannot be fully trusted to machines", he said,

Belyaev, who leaves a widow and two daughters, was awarded the title, Hero of the Soviet Union, for his venture into space.

January 12, 1970.

Lucienne Benitz-Reixach, better known to a whole generation of Parisians before the war under the pseudonym of La mome moineau, literally "kid sparrow", a popular singer and entertainer, and after her marriage and retirement from the stage an eccentric multimillionairess, died in Paris on January 18, 1968. She was 63. Her life followed the pattern of the Cinderella story of the poor little flower girl, who one day attracted the attention of a wealthy patron, and from then on never looked back.

She was born Lucienne Garcia, in a caravan, with which her parents travelled the roads of France to sell dry goods. Very early, she had to work herself to increase the family pittance. She sold flowers on the terrace of cafés, and at 15 had become one of the characters of Fouquet's on the Champs Élysée, with her tough command of argot and her uninhibited manner. One day, in the early 1920s, a client approached her. "How much the flowers?" he asked. "Five francs a bunch", was the reply. "I will have the flowers, the basket, and the flower girl as well", the man said. He was Paul Poiret, the fashionable couturier of the period, who led a life of eccentricity, prodigality and extravagance, even for those carefree post-war days. She became a cabaret singer, but went back to flower selling from time to time. Once, it is said, she failed to turn up for her show, and was discovered back at Fouquet's, selling flowers. "I am free, free like a bird", she explained. "Then we shall call you 'kid sparrow' ", the cabaret owner declared.

Though not especially gifted she won the favour of the public for her character and outspokenness. The story of her marriage was characteristic. In New York she went wandering off alone in Coney Island, and overcome by weariness she got into a car which happened to be open and fell asleep. The owner returned, and, undaunted, she told him to drive her back to the centre of the city. He turned out to be an extremely wealthy engineer and businessman from Puerto Rico, who married her shortly afterwards.

After a last appearance in a show with Harry

Pilcher and the Dolly Sisters in 1930, the *Mome Moineau* abandoned the stage and flower selling, and led a life of great extravagance in Paris, Deauville, Cannes, and other fashionable resorts. Her properties, yachts, cars and jewels became a by-word, and her eccentric costumes the talk of the town. She tossed her hat into the crater of Etna, offered five million dollars to the man who would find a lock of hair which fell into the sea during a cruise, challenged Mr. Onassis to a yacht race, and became cultural attaché at Santo Domingo. She always lived with the same gusto and abandon, and burned the candle at both ends.

January 18, 1968.

Constance Bennett, a film star who epitomized elegance, sophistication, and a worldly disillusion during the early days of the talking films, died at Fort Dix, New Jersey, on July 24, 1965. She was 59.

Born in New York on October 22, 1905, she was educated privately in America and in Paris, where she acquired the poise that was to stand her in such good stead in her film career. She had no previous acting experience before entering films, but acting was in her blood for she was the eldest daughter of Richard Bennett (and a sister of Joan Bennett) who was widely known on both the American and British stages before the First World War and who would have preferred her to take up the theatre as a career. Instead she chose the cinema and made her first appearance in silent films as early as 1920 in a picture called *Cytharea.* But although she soon made a name for herself as an accomplished *ingénue*, marriage (she was five times married) took her from the films, and she retired to Paris. Four years later, after a divorce, she returned to Hollywood to take up the threads of her career just as talking pictures were becoming popular.

A husky voice and natural maturity fitted her ideally for those Holywood films which dealt with the bored and opulent existence of the wealthy New York socialite, and pictures such as *Common Clay*, *Rockabye*, and *Born to Love*, with leading men such as Adolphe Menjou, Lew Ayres, and Joel McCrea, quickly established her as a film star who could present suffering and disillusion with graceful resignation.

In 1931 she played opposite Robert Montgomery in *The Easiest Way*, in which Clark Gable played the minor part of a milkman, but probably her best remembered film of the 1930s was *Topper*, the ghost story comedy in which Roland Young played the title part and in which she was alternately visible and invisible. It was succeeded by other Topper films based on Thorne Smith's comic novels. In 1944 she formed her own film company and produced and appeared in *Madame Pimpernel*, and she was responsible for several other productions in the late 1940s and early 1950s.

July 26, 1965.

Captain Eugene Paul Bennett, V.C., M.C., who won the Victoria Cross on the Somme with the Worcestershire Regiment in 1916, died in Italy on April 4, 1970, at the age of 77.

After he left the army he was called to the Bar and went into practice until he was appointed a Metropolitan magistrate in 1935. He sat at the West London Court for 11 years, and at Marlborough Street Court from 1946 until 1961 when he retired. Fifty-three West End street traders, many of whom he had fined, paid tribute to him on his retirement.

Always keen on military matters, he became a private in the Artists Rifles in 1913, and after the outbreak of the war he went to France in October 1914 with the 1st Battalion. He was commissioned as a second lieutenant in The Worcestershire Regiment in 1915.

The circumstances in which Lieutenant Bennett (as he then was) gained the V.C. were as follows. The Worcesters were ordered to attack the enemy's positions near Le Transloy on November 5, and the first wave of troops that went over the top met an intense fire and in consequence suffered very heavy casualties. The officer in command of the attack was killed and it seemed that the line was beginning to waver. Bennett took command of the second wave of troops and advanced at the head of his men. The magnificent personal example of valour he displayed, and the firm resolution he showed his men, infused into them a determination to reach their objective, which they did. But the losses had been grievous and Bennett arrived with only 60 men. At once he set about consolidating his newly won position. All the time that was being done he, in common with the other members of the little party, was under extremely heavy rifle fire and machinegun fire which the enemy poured upon him from the flanks on either side. It was not long before Bennett, who had exposed himself without a thought for his personal safety, was wounded, but in spite of that he insisted on remaining in command and directing and controlling the steps that were being taken to consolidate the position. The example of cheerfulness he gave to his men and the resolution he maintained were officially said to have been "beyond all praise"

April 8, 1970.

Lieutenant-General Gordon Bennett, C.B., C.M.G., D.S.O., who commanded the Australian Forces in Malaya at the time of the fall of Singapore, died on August 1, 1962, from a heart attack in his car near his home in Sydney. He was 73.

His conduct, in a role of immense difficulty, was exposed to some criticism. In particular his judgment was questioned for escaping from Singapore on February 5, 1942, the day of the surrender to the Japanese. After the war a judicial inquiry set up by the Australian Government found that Bennett had not been justified in relinquishing his command and that the time had not come when he had an obligation to escape. Nevertheless "he acted from a sense of high patriotism and according to what he conceived to be his duty to his country".

The escape itself was a perilous enterprise. Bennett and a party of officers escaped through the Japanese lines to the western coast of Johore where they persuaded a Chinese junk skipper to take them to Sumatra—then still in Dutch hands. Bennett believed that it was his duty to escape so that the first-hand knowledge he had gained of Japanese jungle tactics could be of value. He did indeed bring back information which was used in training the A.I.F. for jungle warfare. But he never again held operational command and he resigned from the Army in April, 1944.

Henry Gordon Bennett, the son of G. J. Bennett, was born on April 15, 1887, in Belwyn. Victoria, and trained as an accountant. He joined the Australian militia in 1912, and in the First World War he was a brigadier-general before he was 29 and commanded the 3rd Infantry Brigade in France. He was made C.M.G. in 1915, C.B. in 1918, won the D.S.O. in 1919, and was mentioned in dispatches eight times.

From 1926 to 1931 Bennett commanded the Australian 2nd Division. Between the wars he was also Civic Commissioner of Sydney, president of the Chamber of Manufacturers of New South Wales, and president of the Associated Chambers of Manufacturers of Australia.

In 1940 he was appointed to command the 8th Division, A.I.F., and in 1941–42 was G.O.C. of the Australian Imperial Force in Malaya. In 1942 he became commander of the 3rd Australian Corps with headquarters in Western Australia. After the war he became a successful fruit grower.

Bennett married in 1916 Bessie Agnes, daughter of Robert Buchanan. They had one daughter.

August 2, 1962.

Pierre Benoit, a popular novelist in the years between the two wars and a member of the Académie Française, died on March 3, 1962, at the age of 75.

He rose suddenly to fame soon after the 1918 armistice when his romantic stories, a then somewhat new mixture of adventure and sex, helped people forget the strains and perils of the war years. His popularity did not, however, survive the Second World War and his more recent works were comparative failures—although the last novel was serialized in a woman's magazine.

Ferdinand Marie Pierre Benoit was born at Albi on July 16, 1886, but was brought up in Tunisia and Algeria where his father, an officer in the French Army, was posted for long periods. He himself was called up for military service in 1906 and spent two years as an officer in the Zouaves before returning to France to complete his education. He fell in with a number of the young writers of the day—Carco, Dorgenes for example—and tried to become a poet.

His first book of poems was in fact published in 1914 but it was a failure and after being invalided out of the Army in 1915 he turned his hand to fiction. He was quickly successful. His first novel, *Koenigsmark* (1917) created no particular stir at the time, but his second, *L'Atlantide* (1918) was one of the most discussed and best selling novels of the epoch, translated into many languages and turned into films and plays. It won the French Academy's prize for novels in 1919. They were similar stories, in which the heroine's name invariably began with the letter A, the setting was exotic—and surprisingly accurate—and the hero had astonishing adventures succeeding each other at a steady rhythm.

In 1929 he became president of the Société des Gens de Lettres, and two years later was elected to the Académie Française, of which he was then the youngest member.

In the prewar years when he was so successful Benoit travelled widely, using each new place visited as the background for his next story. He remained in Paris throughout the last war and after the liberation was sentenced to some months in prison for collaboration of not too serious a nature. But this marked his eclipse and although he resumed his novel writing in 1947, he was never again to come anywhere near his early successes.

Before the war Benoit had the curious habit of going to the little town of Saint Cere in the Lot—since notorious as the home town of Pierre Poujade—and putting up at a hotel there while he wrote each of his books. He was a popular and respected citizen, and there was, in those days, a street in Saint Cere named after him.

March 5, 1962.

Itzhak Ben-Zvi, President of Israel who died on April 23, 1963, succeeded President Weizmann in 1952 and was subsequently elected to additional five year terms in 1957 and in October last year. He had practically no independent constitutional powers but he utilized his exalted position to exert a moral influence for the coalescing of the various ethnic groups and to set an example of dignified, unpretentious living befitting a pioneering society.

He initiated the delightful presidential custom of inviting to his residence a representative gathering of citizens from a different ethnic group each "Rosh Chodesh", the start of a Hebrew calendar month. He gave priority to under-privileged groups from Asian and African countries in order to boost their esteem. He also held open house during the feasts of Passover and Tabernacles and talked affably in his deep bass with callers from all walks of life.

Ben-Zvi and his family had lived for 30 years in a simple wood cabin until his election to the presidency. When the government wanted to provide an impressive mansion for his residence, he baulked and insisted upon a modest apartment. At his initiative, the hall where he received official callers was built of the same wood as had been used at the time for cheap housing for immigrants.

The President had fought stubbornly against proposals to increase his salary and when the parliamentary finance committee nevertheless voted to raise it to I£ 18,000 (£ 2,138) annually, he announced that he would contribute half for scientific research.

After his election Mr. Ben-Zvi continued to attend Sabbath services in the small synagogue where he had previously worshipped and to participate in weekly *Talmud* classes. He also worked every Friday afternoon at his old desk in the Ben-Zvi Institute for Research into the Oriental Jewish Communities.

Ben-Zvi was born Itzhak Shimshelewitz in Poltava, Ukraine. His Hebraized name means "son of Zvi". His family was exiled to Siberia for organizing a Jewish self-defence organization in Poltava after anti-Jewish pogroms of 1905 but Itzhak escaped and in 1907 reached Palestine, which was then under Turkish rule.

PARTNERED BEN-GURION

Shortly after his arrival, he began his life-long association with Mr. David Ben-Gurion, who was to become Prime Minister of Israel. The pair worked together as agricultural labourers, initiated the first Jewish illegal self-defence organization, went to the Imperial Ottoman University in Istanbul to study law, returned to Palestine when the First World War interrupted their studies and were deported to Egypt by Jemal Pasha who told them they would never be allowed to return to Palestine.

Ben-Zvi and Mr. Ben-Gurion went to America where they organized the Labour Zionist Movement and recruited volunteers for the Jewish Legion. They returned to Palestine with General Allenby's forces as soldiers in the Jewish battalion of the Royal Fusiliers.

After Britain took over Palestine, the two men helped lay the basis for the new Jewish society in the homeland by creating the *Histadrut* (General Federation of Jewish Labour) and other organizations. The late Viscount (then Sir Herbert) Samuel, the first British High Commissioner, appointed Ben-Zvi to the Palestine Advisory Council but he resigned in 1921 in protest against the restrictions imposed on Jewish immigration. He later became one of the founders of the General Council for Palestine Jews (*Vaad Leumi*), the executive body of the Jewish community, and served as chairman or president from 1931 until it was dissolved with the establishment of the State of Israel.

As a member of the Provisional Council of Government he was one of the signatories of the Proclamation of Independence.

His scientific and literary activities over half a century centred on the study of less-known Jewish communities and the ethnography and culture of the neighbouring Muslim countries. He visited Syria, Lebanon, Iraq, Iran and Egypt for purposes of research before the Arab-Jewish war of 1948 and dedicated himself later to promoting better understanding of Muslims, Christians, Druze, Circassians, Karaites and Samaratins.

He is survived by a widow, the former Rachel Yanait, and by a son who is a farmer. A second son was killed in action during the 1948 war.

April 24, 1963.

Cardinal Josef Beran, Roman Catholic Primate of Czechoslovakia, died in Rome on May 17, 1969, after a life marked by persecution and suffering. He was 80.

Beran was, with Cardinal Mindszenty (still holding out in the American Embassy in Hungary) Rome's main defence against the tide of communism in eastern Europe in the forties and fifties. Beran symbolized also the once proud resistance of the church of Rome both to fascism and communism—he spent three years in Dachau under the Nazis and 14 years in communist prisons. His freedom was negotiated in 1963—an arrangement made under Pope John's auspices when the relations of Rome with the communist world took a better turn (two years later he went into self-imposed exile in Rome).

Sir Alec Guinness's portrayal of "The Prisoner" was partly based on Beran—a film that bitterly analysed the brainwashing and phoney confession era of communist interrogation in the worst period of the cold war. His death is likely to stir the Czech people considerably, particularly in the light of the recent events there. Many Czechs hoped for his return under the liberal regime of Dubcek. His death in exile is likely to create even more bitterness against the diehards of the old order of communism. Like Cardinal Mindszenty he seemed to become a dated figure during the era of Vatican dialogue with communism. But events in Czechoslovakia have renovated his cause.

A small, somewhat emaciated man with twinkling eyes and a ready smile, Beran was named Archbishop of Prague in 1946 but in 1949 after only four years of freedom, he was jailed by the Czechoslovak Government for a "negative attitude to church laws". He was freed in 1963 to live in an old pensioners home in Bohemia, but was still barred from carrying out his priestly duties. Finally, following long secret talks between the Vatican emissaries and the Prague Government, he was allowed to leave the country in 1965 to receive his cardinal's red hat in Rome. He never returned home.

LIBERAL HOPES

Hopes for church-state reconciliation grew with the rise of Alexander Dubcek and his liberal regime in 1968, but the Czechoslovak authorities maintained their position. This was that Beran could return, but only as a private citizen. This, to him, was unacceptable.

Under the Vatican-Czechoslovak agreement Beran was allowed to retain his title as Archbishop of Prague, and a younger prelate. Monsignor Frantisek Tomasek, was later named Apostolic administrator to carry out his duties.

Under the Communist Party leadership of Mr. Alexander Dubcek secret talks were started with the Vatican towards ending the impasse between the party and the church stemming back to the Stalin era when priests were jailed, church property confiscated and church teaching stopped. The church saw the return of Beran as a prime objective in these talks. There has been no further word on the future of Vatican Party talks since Dr. Gustav Husak took over from Mr. Dubcek in April, but a number of conservative speakers have hinted at a less receptive atmosphere for the church.

The aged Cardinal, tortured with anxiety for his people and knowing that he had not long to live, last January published what has become known as his spiritual testament. In a moving broadcast to the Czechoslovak people over the Vatican Radio he appealed to them to stop a wave of suicides by fire. "Let us not use up our spiritual energies in hatred, but rather pour them into harmony, work, service to our brother, a new prosperity for our country", he said. The Cardinal expressed admiration for the heroism of Prague student Jan Palach and others who burned themselves to death in protest against the Russian occupation but said he could not approve of their gesture. He pleaded that no one else should repeat the gesture. His voice filled with emotion as he concluded "If it is not granted to me to see you again, as I desire, consider this as my testament".

Beran was born in Pilsen in 1888, studied for a time in Rome and was ordained in 1911.

May 19, 1969.

Frank Beresford, the artist, died at Rye Memorial Hospital, Sussex, on May 25, 1967. He was 85.

Beresford was well known as a painter of historic scenes. His painting of the lying-in-state of George V, called "The Princes' Vigil", was accepted by the Royal Academy, described as the Picture of the Year (1936), and bought by Queen Mary. His painting of the lying-in-state of King George VI was rejected by the Academy but drew record attendances at galleries where it was on view. His sitters included the Queen Mother and King George VI, General Gruenther (former Supreme Allied Commander, Europe), Henry Ford I, Viscount Montgomery, and Field-Marshal Smuts.

Mainly a painter of portraits and interiors, though he also painted some landscapes and animals, Beresford was extremely capable in literal representation. He was a typical product of the Royal Academy Schools of his time, with a temperamental affinity with the Dutch seventeenth-century masters, whose works he loved and of which he made careful copies.

Frank Ernest Beresford was born at Derby in 1881. When he was 14 he went to the Derby School of Art, and later to St. John's Wood Art School. From there he passed into the Royal Academy Schools, where he took the full course of five years. Beresford took a painting tour round the world on a scholarship, spending most of his time in Japan. A retrospective one-man show of his work was held at the Foyle Art Gallery in 1930 where his Japanese landscape, "Mountain Mists and Snow, Motosu", gave evidence of greater sensibility that would be suggested by the exhibition as a whole. His first picture at the Royal Academy, in 1906, was a portrait of a Japanese, for which he received from the Imperial Japanese Government an award for art. By this time he was a successful portrait painter, and it is said that during the seven months previous to the outbreak of the First World War, when he enlisted in the 19th. Territorial Company of the London Regiment he received no fewer than 40 portrait commissions.

Taking Rembrandt rather than the more solid Dutch painters for his model, he painted "Under the Dome, St. Paul's Cathedral", exhibited in 1935 and acquired by Lord Wakefield. The Dutch community in London commissioned a painting in 1938 of the special service in the Dutch Church in Austin Friars to celebrate the birth of the Dutch princess. For the Hall of the Haberdashers' Company. Beresford painted the portraits of three ex-Lord Mayors of London: Sir George Truscott, Lord Wakefield and Sir Maurice Jenks.

About 1935 he had built, in fulfilment of an old dream to have a convenient flat and studio of his own, a block of eight flats, known as "Grove Hall", in St. John's Wood. He married twice; his first wife died in 1939.

May 29, 1967.

The Rev. Dr. Sidney Berry, who died on August 2, 1961, in a London hospital at the age of 80, had for more than half a century been a Congregational minister and was for 25 years the secretary of the Congregational Union of England and Wales.

He had held some of the most important posts in the Free Churches and for 11 years had occupied the pulpit of the famous Carr's Lane Church, Birmingham, following in the footsteps of Dr. J. H. Jowett. If, as is true, he had in later years become widely known as a statesman of the Church, he had certainly remained a man of zeal and piety, expressed and practised with a genial fervour which, because of his presence and appearance, was reminiscent of the monks and friars of old.

Sidney Malcolm Berry was born at Southport on July 25, 1881, a son of Dr. C. A. Berry, and educated at Tettenhall College, Staffordshire, Clare College, Cambridge, and Mansfield College, Oxford, where he graduated. After a brilliant theological career at Mansfield, Berry was ordained to the ministry, his first charge being Oxted and Limpsfield, to which he was called in 1906. Then, for three years from 1909 he was at Chorlton-cum-Hardy, Manchester, before he accepted the pastorate of Carr's Lane. At 31 Berry found himself in the pulpit which great preachers had for two or three generations been making famous, and it says much for him and for his power of exposition and attraction that he maintained its prestige completely until, in 1923, he was called to fulfil the secretarial duties of the Congregational Union of England and Wales.

OFFICE FOR FRIENDS

His work at Memorial Hall was always on the personal side, and his office was the meeting place of friends. He held the reins there with conspicuous success until his retirement in 1948, and during his last year of office the churches honoured him by electing him to the chairmanship of the union. It was characteristic of Berry's untiring enthusiasm and zest for work that upon his retirement from the union secretaryship he agreed to become minister and secretary of the International Congregational Council, and consultant to the Central Committee of the World Council of Churches. More remarkable still is the fact that when, in the spring of 1955, it was found impracticable to fill the office of Congregational union secretary, relinquished by the Rev. Dr. Leslie Cooke, Berry cheerfully agreed, at the age of 74, to take up once more these old duties which he had left behind on his retirement seven years before, promising the union leaders that he would continue for at least 12 months.

Berry was also, from 1934 to 1940, honorary secretary of the Federal Council of the Evangelical Free Churches of England, and for three of those years he was its Moderator. He had also for some years been vice-president of the British Council of Churches. For nearly 40 years he had travelled extensively in the course of his duties, and throughout all his long life in administration he was persistently being called upon to preach in Nonconformist churches on special occasions. He wrote considerably on religious and social questions, two of the best known among his books, *The Crucible of Experience* and *Vital Preaching*, having had large sales, and he also contributed a good deal to the religious and the lay press. He played golf almost up to the end, and in earlier days, tennis. He was an honorary D.D. of Glasgow University.

Berry married, in 1907, Helen Logan, of Bedford Park, W., and they had two daughters.

August 3, 1961.

Lord Beveridge, who died on March 16, 1963, at his Oxford home at the age of 84, will be remembered chiefly for his world-famous Report of 1942 on social security. Nominally, this was an officially commissioned plan for rationalizing and extending the insurance and assistance services which provide pensions and other cash payments in periods of need. So regarded, the plan was modest enough. Though covering the whole population, the cash benefits proposed were minimal—they had been sub-minimal before the war—and pensions at these minimum rates were to be introduced only gradually during the 20 years following the war.

What gripped the public imagination was the vivid and lucid language in which these proposals were expressed; the arguments with which they were supported; the insistence on benefits as a right, payable without means test; the challenging assumptions made about the need for, and the feasibility of, abolishing unemployment and establishing a comprehensive health service and a system of family allowances; and Beveridge's masterly grasp of administrative details. The Report was, so far as Beveridge could make it, "the British people become articulate about what they want in the way of social security," the conversion into a practical programme of widely desired, but only half-formulated, social reforms.

Its emotional appeal was overwhelming to a people who in less than a decade had been plunged from the miseries of mass unemployment into the turmoil of a major war. Its outline of a "Welfare State" (as it is now called) started a debate throughout the free world about the fundamentals of social policy, eventually leading to a peaceful social revolution in Britain, but immediately leaving the Coalition Government torn between admiration and bewilderment. The "Welfare State" of today differs in many respects from the Beveridge blueprint and is evolving in ways its drafter did not foresee. Yet it may properly be described as the outcome of the "Beveridge revolution".

The Report belongs to one of the three strands discernible in Beveridge's career. The first stand, the main theme of his life, starts with the never-forgotten advice Edward Caird, then Master of Balliol, gave the young undergraduate at the turn of the century: "When you have learnt all that Oxford can teach you, go and discover why, with so much wealth in Britain, there continues to be so much poverty and how poverty can be cured." To this line of thought belongs the work whereby Beveridge (earlier and no less than Keynes) helped transform public understanding of the nature of the unemployment problem. Along this thread runs his book of 1909 significantly called *Unemployment: A Problem of Industry*; his official work of 1909–12 on the creation of labour exchanges and compulsory unemployment insurance; his booklet of 1924, *Insurance for All and Everything*; his chairmanship of the Unemployment Insurance Statutory Committee, 1934–44; the Beveridge Report; and his two postscripts thereto: *Full Employment in a Free Society* (1944) and *Voluntary Action* (1948).

ADMINISTRATIVE FLAIR

The second strand in his work came from his ability to combine intellectual brilliance with unusual administrative flair. "I have spent most of my life", he wrote in 1953, "most happily in making plans for others to carry out." During the First World War he went from the new employment services to the Ministry of Munitions, for work on organizing manpower, and thence to become chief architect of the Ministry of Food and deviser of the national rationing scheme. Mr. Churchill appointed him to the Samuel Commission on the coal industry in 1925. In the Second World War he was involved in some of the preparatory work for food control and rationing and was commissioned by Mr. Bevin to conduct various surveys into the use of manpower. In 1949 he was put in charge of the official inquiry into the future of broadcasting.

The third strand comprises his wider contributions to academic life and thought. Under his directorship from 1919 to 1937 the London School of Economics developed into an institution of world repute. He himself eventually concluded that the remaking of the school was incompatible with his intellectual ambition of remaking the social sciences on lines less *a priori* and much more empirical, fact-facing, and multidisciplinary. Tired of "spending all my time organizing opportunities for others", he was glad to accept the Mastership of University College, Oxford, from 1937 to 1944. It was then that he accomplished part of one of his academic ambitions, by completing (with various collaborators) the first volume, on prices from 1550 to 1850, of a projected history of prices and wages in England.

In Beveridge were united scholarly imagination with a practical, yet impetuous, temperament; remarkable administrative ingenuity with little acumen for the daily subtleties of politics; a noble passion for social reform, an equal passion for reason in human affairs, and a certain inability to sense other people's emotions. The evolution of his character is mirrored in his autobiography, *Power and Influence* (1953). Here he surveyed his life up to 1914 with modesty and with engaging acknowledgments of what he owed to Barnett, the Webbs, and others who moulded his reforming zeal into practical courses. Thereafter, the selectivity of his memoirs becomes gradually more apparent, modesty retreats behind the prophetic mantle, simplicity turns at times into art-lessness, especially in politics. His pride was injured by the tactless way in which the Coalition Government cold-shouldered him, after giving his Report publicity which made him world famous. He never understood what had happened, because he sought only a rational explanation of events in which feelings and personalities counted for as much as ideas. He was driven impetuously and ingloriously into politics, as a Liberal M.P. for the last six months of the war; and he finally concluded, ruefully but rightly, that, for him at least, "pursuit and exercise of power do not sort naturally with pursuit of knowledge or appeal to reason".

William Henry Beveridge was born at Rangpur, Bengal, on March 5, 1879. He was the eldest son of Henry Beveridge, an Indian civil servant, and his wife Annette, daughter of William Ackroyd, a remarkable woman who was an authority on the early Mogul emperors. Educated at Charterhouse and Balliol, he took firsts in both Classical and Mathematical Moderations and then in Greats, and then took the degree of B.C.L. From 1902 to 1909 he was Stowell Civil Law Fellow of University College, Oxford. From 1903 to 1905 he acted as sub-warden of Toynbee Hall, where he investigated casual labour and unemployment in the London docks. In 1905 he became a member of the Central (Unemployed) Body for London, becoming chairman of its committee which promoted the first London labour exchanges.

LEADER WRITER

From 1906 to 1908 he worked as a leader writer on social questions for Fabian Ware's *Morning Post*.

In 1909 he was appointed Director of Labour Exchanges and head of the Employment Department of the Board of Trade. This small organ of government, which eventually grew into the Ministry of Labour, had been started by Llewellyn Smith (the board's permanent secretary), who knew Beveridge well. Beveridge had also been introduced by the Webbs to Winston Churchill, then president of the board. He set Llewellyn Smith and Beveridge the tasks, the bulk of which fell on the latter, of creating first a national system of labour exchanges and then a compulsory unemployment insurance scheme to be operated through the exchanges. Having accomplished these duties with his characteristic energy, Beveridge moved on in 1915 to the Ministry of Munitions, with Llewellyn Smith again as his chief. In 1916 he passed on to the Ministry of Food, of which, after launching the national rationing scheme of 1918, he became permanent secretary in 1919. He was created a C.B. in 1916 and promoted to K.C.B. in 1919.

In that year, induced thereto chiefly by the Webbs, he left the Civil Service to become director of the London School of Economics. During his 18 years' leadership the school grew from a small institution with part-time teachers and adult students into a major university centre of learning—and controversy. Of his practical achievements in remaking the school—in particular the struggle for funds—there can be no question. (In 1925, for instance, he inaugurated at the school the system of family allowances for members of the staff, which has since become general in British universities.) About his influence on the school's developing intellectual life and broadening curriculum and about his relations with his academic colleagues, opinions are more divided. Though there was much that all would praise, the distinguished but heterogeneous band of scholars, both in economics and politics, whom the school attracted, held varying views on the development of studies. Many disliked Beveridge's innovating empirical approach; and he, for rather different reasons, found Laski in particular uncongenial as a colleague.

MANPOWER SURVEY

In 1926 he became Vice-Chancellor of London University for two years, and was later a member of the University Court. His services to the university were great, especially in securing the funds necessary to purchase the Bloomsbury site. In 1928 he published *British Food Control* and two years later a new version of his *Unemployment* of 1909. In 1937 he succeeded Dr. A. B. Poynton as Master of University College, Oxford.

In 1940 Mr. Bevin called him in to make a crucial survey comparing the nation's manpower resources with the demands made on them by competing departments. In 1941, when he temporarily took charge of the Military Service Department of the Ministry of Labour for five months, he produced the revised Schedule of Reserved Occupations. He also campaigned successfully for the conscription of women and led an inquiry into the use of skilled men by the Services, which resulted in the creation of R.E.M.E.

Meanwhile, since June, 1941, the committee on social insurance and allied services had been at work. Appointed in response to trade union demands for a tidying up of the uncoordinated organization of social insurance schemes, the inquiry was originally conceived as chiefly a study in administrative structure, involving no fundamental issues of policy. Hence the committee consisted of eleven officials, from the Government departments directly concerned, with Beveridge in the chair. Beveridge proceeded to change all that. In December, 1941, when the committee had finished a factual survey of existing schemes, but before any outside evidence had been heard, he laid before his colleagues memoranda outlining all the essentials of the future Beveridge Report. "The committee had their objective settled for them and discussion was reduced to consideration of means of attaining that objective." This switch (to which the Government assented), entailed turning the committee into an advisory body to their chairman, who would write the report on his sole responsibility. They did in fact learn a great deal from their witnesses, but nothing which led Beveridge to alter the fundamentals of his proposals, save on industrial injury. Most members of the committee had long cherished improvements which Beveridge was able to merge into his plan, and all gave him invaluable help on questions of methods. But the Report which emerged was unquestionably a one-man production. Its deferring of full pensions for 20 years was the result of a deal whereby Keynes undertook to support the plan, in his capacity of adviser to the Treasury, if Beveridge could so frame it that the additional charge on the Exchequer would not exceed £100m. annually for the first five years.

FIGHTING FOR HIS REPORT

Following the report's publication in December, 1942, Beveridge married Mrs. Jessy Philip Mair, O.B.E., widow of his cousin and lifelong friend David Mair. She had been his secretary at the Ministry of Munitions and had followed him to become secretary of the London School of Economics, where she remained until 1938. In 1943 Beveridge himself became his report's most effective expositor and champion. Disappointed and made suspicious by the Government's cautious response (emotions shared, rightly or wrongly, by the majority of the public), he began pressing them to take up the challenge of "Giant Idleness," by initiating some fundamental work on the prevention of unemployment after the war. There followed an unedifying competition between the authorities and Beveridge to see who could get out a statement on full employment first. The Government beat him, issuing its White Paper in the summer of 1944, so enabling Beveridge to criticize it in his longer and more thorough volume, *Full Employment in a Free Society*, published in November, 1944.

All through that year the campaign for firm decisions about the Beveridge plan, and for the appointment of a Minister to carry them out, was gathering strength. In September Beveridge was adopted by the Liberals for the vacant seat at Berwick upon Tweed, which, under the political truce, he had no difficulty in winning. When he entered the Commons in October, however, he found a Minister of National Insurance newly installed. He made no great impression on Parliament. At the general election of 1945, having given up his Mastership of University College and moved house from Oxford to Northumberland, he polled 2,000 votes fewer than his Conservative opponent in a three-sided contest.

In the following summer he was created a baron and he spent part of the next few years travelling and lecturing abroad, in Spain, Australia, New Zealand, and elsewhere. In 1947, at the invitation of the National Deposit Friendly Society, he undertook to inquire into the voluntary social services. His report, *Voluntary Action*, came out the next year.

Meanwhile he had been appointed chairman of the Development Corporation of Aycliffe, in Durham, and he later went to live there. Two years later, in 1949, he became chairman of the Peterlee Development Corporation also. In June, 1952, he was told rather harshly by Mr. Macmillan, then Minister of Housing and Local Government, that he should hand over the chairmanship of Aycliffe after another year in view of his age—he was then 73.

The report of the Broadcasting Committee, of which he was chairman, came out in 1951. It amounted to a vote of confidence in the existing arrangements for broadcasting and came out in favour of the monopoly in television as in sound.

His wife died in 1959.

March 18, 1963.

Senator Zanotti Bianco died in a Rome nursing home on August 29, 1963. His death robbed Italian life of a philanthropist and scholar whose long career was one of remarkable distinction and usefulness. His profound feeling for the sufferings of others, particularly for the impoverished south, was on the pure scale of the Greek antiquities of Magna Grecia which were one of his passions, and his integrity brought him unchallenged respect.

Umberto Zanotti Bianco was born in Crete in 1889, the son of an English mother and a Piedmontese diplomatist. Almost as soon as he had completed his studies for a law degree the great earthquake which struck Reggio Calabra and Messina in 1908 shook him from his northern origins and his studies to a deep concern for southern misfortunes. Like a number of other young men of the time faced with the shock of this catastrophe, he hurried south to do what he could to help the victims. He never forgot that first experience of ancient misery, backwardness, illiteracy and sufferings which were soon to become far better known, partly as a result of his own efforts. In 1910 he founded with some of his friends the "National Association for the Interests of the Mezzogiorno". With privately raised funds this group immediately set about trying to establish schools, courses in adult education, farmers' cooperatives and other measures for attacking, if at first on a modest scale, the wrongs which he so strongly felt should be put right.

After the First World War, in which he was both decorated and severely wounded, he found that the association's work was able to be enlarged as a result of financial help from the state. It is estimated that between October 1921 and September 1928 over 8,000 schools for adult illiterates were opened in Basilicata, Sardinia, Calabria and Sicily, with something in the region of 350,000 pupils.

The Fascists had no more time for his efforts than he had for their philosophies. Told by Starace, the Fascist Party secretary, that the regime had "solved the southern problem," and that the very name of his association was "an expression of criticism and lack of confidence in the Duce and the regime," he devoted himself more fully to archaeological exploration in the south in which he showed himself to be an amateur in the best sense of the word, with a marked instinct to back his scholarship.

As early as 1921 he had in fact founded the society "Magna Grecia" which was responsible for some notable finds before it was suppressed by the fascists. While carrying out his long and valuable explorations in the early thirties at the mouth of Sele, near Paestum, Zanotti Bianco enjoyed the odd experience of being under constant surveillance by two fascist policemen.

His philanthropy was not limited to Italy. In 1922 he was contributing aid to the Russians. In 1935 he created a village at Bari for Armenian refugees. In 1944 he became chairman of the Italian Red Cross. In 1948 the Italian Government sent him to Somalia to inquire into the causes of the Mogadishu killings.

More recently he had added to his other activities the national chairmanship of the Italianostra, the association modelled to some extent on the British National Trust, which has as its principal object the safeguarding of Italy's cultural and natural heritage.

In spite of ill-health, his work for this body was energetic and often effective. In 1952 he was made a senator for life by President Einaudi.

He remained aside from party affiliations, joining the mixed group in the Senate. His speeches there were mainly concerned with cultural matters on which he spoke with vigour and an extraordinary sense of urgency. This urgent combative style of his was in a way made more effective by his frail and delicate appearance.

August, 30, 1963.

A. D. Biddle, Junior, United States Ambassador to Spain, died in a Washington hospital on November 13, 1961, at the age of 65.

During his diplomatic career, which began in 1935, he also held the posts of Minister to Norway, Ambassador to Poland in the crucial years from 1937 to the outbreak of the Second World War, and Ambassador to a number of governments in exile in London during the war.

Anthony Joseph Drexel Biddle, a member of the well known banking family of Philadelphia, was born there in 1896. His father, who bore the same name, was well known there and in many parts of the world as author, athlete, boxing instructor, explorer, lecturer, and religious leader. His grandmother was a Drexel and both Drexels and Biddles were among the oldest and most influential families of the city. Though born in a wealthy home he was brought up in an atmosphere of constant activity and a kind of muscular Christianity which his father preached and expounded to Bible classes in many parts of the world; and at St. Paul's School at Concord, New Hampshire, the son showed considerable prowess as an athlete.

As time went on he concentrated his attention largely on tennis, winning the championship of France in 1934. He played the game chiefly in the clubs of his native Philadelphia, but also at the Racquets Clubs of Chicago and New York, in Paris and Bordeaux, being a member of the Société du Jeu de Paume et Racquète de

France, and at Queen's and Prince's Clubs in London of which he was long a member. But all forms of sport came alike to him, and he found in any kind of outdoor and indoor exercise an opportunity for enjoyment and displaying his skill. While he was American Minister to Norway and Ambassador to Poland he frequently accompanied the most adventurous spirits on hunting expeditions that were likely to thrill and afford good sport.

WAR SERVICE

During the First World War, just after he had left school he served in France as a captain in the United States Army. On his return to America he was employed for some years in shipping and in mining and though he gave much of his time to the various games for which he had a passion he never allowed them to interfere with his work for which his constant physical fitness and invariable alertness left him always ready. Among the younger generation of businessmen he was looked on as a leader.

His outlook on the industrial situation was far more enlightened and advanced than that of most men of his class and station.

He had been a friend of Franklin Roosevelt and had admired his work as Governor of New York State before the financial crisis brought him to the White House in 1933. Drexel Biddle threw in his lot with the President and did the utmost in his power to further the principles and activities of the New Deal. He took a leading part in the nomination and election of Roosevelt at the elections of 1932 and 1936, being one of the secretaries to the Democratic National Convention held at Philadelphia in the latter year. Much to the surprise of every one, Roosevelt prevailed on him to accept office in the diplomatic service. It was first intended to send him to Ireland, but the appointment did not prove acceptable to the Irish Government and instead he was sent to Oslo as Minister in 1935. In 1937 he was transferred to Warsaw. His work there was more arduous and pressing but he acquitted himself with tact and diligence. Besides reporting frequently on conditions there to his friend and chief, President Roosevelt, he was on the most intimate terms with the leaders of the Polish nation, with whom he had a common interest in every form of sport, and he was also on good terms with representatives and officials in Danzig whom he visited from time to time, doing all in his power to bring about a reconciliation with Poland by peaceful means.

His diplomatic skill served him in good stead through the war, for he was one of the busiest diplomats in the world during that time.

INTO EXILE

When the Nazis attacked Poland he followed the Polish Government into exile after travelling with it to various places in Poland. While at Angers, in France, with the exiled Polish Government President Roosevelt made him interim Ambassador to France and he accompanied that Government to Tours and then Bordeaux.

London was the next scene of his diplomatic activities, and there he was American Ambassador to many exiled governments, including Poland, Belgium, the Netherlands, Norway, Greece, Yugoslavia, and Czechoslovakia, and also from 1941 to 1944 Minister to Luxembourg. That he did a remarkable job in these varied assignments was well recognized in his native country and by the governments to which he was accredited. They all decorated him, as also did France, Mexico, Brazil, and Monaco.

But another career was ahead of him. In 1944 he left the diplomatic service and returned to the United States Army, being made a colonel and going on active duty. He remained in the Army after the war and was promoted to brigadier-general in 1951, later becoming major-general. He was attached to Shaef during the later part of the war and also served with Shape from 1951 to 1953. There followed two years with the Department of the Army in the Pentagon in Washington and later he was appointed Adjutant-General for Pennsylvania. His appointment to Spain was announced by President Kennedy in February this year. His American decorations included the Distinguished Service Medal and the Legion of Merit. He was also an Officier de l'Académie de France.

He was married three times. His first wife was Miss Margaret Duke of the American tobacco fortune, one of the wealthiest heiresses in the United States. This marriage was dissolved in 1931 and he then married Mrs. Margaret Thompson Schultze, daughter of the late Mr. W. B. Thompson, the American copper magnate. His third marriage in 1946 was to Mrs. Margaret Atkinson Loughborough.

November 14, 1961.

Jack Albert Billmeir, C.B.E. who died on December 22, 1963, was one of the most colourful personalities in British shipping. He began his career as an office boy at 8s. a week. Then with only £250 in capital (his personal savings) he graduated as a shipowner through the possession of one steam trawler to the chairmanship of an important tramp shipping company.

Four of Billmeir's ventures into shipping failed, but he succeeded at his fifth attempt and the Stanhope Shipping Company, managed by the firm which bore his name, became the source of his considerable wealth.

In a broadcast in 1944 Billmeir said that in the previous year he bought two small steamers —very small coasters—and as there seemed no possibility of ever trading with the usual cargoes he tried to find unusual ones. With these ships he delivered wine and timber, hitherto carried in big vessels, from the shipper direct to the merchant. "The idea was a great success", he said, "and soon we had so much business that it was a question of having to increase the size of my organization ten-fold."

It was during the Spanish Civil War, however, that Billmeir made his fortune. As he confessed, the trade was not without its risks, but the more Hitler and Mussolini tried to stop him trading the more venturesome did his organization become.

Billmeir himself accompanied his ships when they were sent to North Russia and he was proud of the fact that the crews were made up entirely of volunteers. His men received altogether 63 honours, including 15 Distinguished Service Crosses. He was made a C.B.E. in 1953.

Jack Albert Billmeir was born in 1900, the son of Joseph and Rosa Billmeir, and educated at St. Marylebone Central School. He began his commercial life in a shipbroker's office in the City of London in 1914. It was in 1934 that he formed the Stanhope Shipping Company. He became a member of the council of the Chamber of Shipping, and was chairman of its Intermediate Tramp Section from 1948 to 1953.

Among his other shipping interests was membership of the Shipowners' Advisory Panel of the Lighthouse Commission, of the Baltic Exchange, and of Lloyd's as an underwriting member. He was a director of several companies.

Billmeir was a generous and warmhearted man. He presented his fine collection of scientific instruments to the Museum of the History of Science at Oxford and a gift of money which enabled the stone stairway from Broad Street to the old Ashmolean Museum (which houses the Museum of the History of Science) to be reconstructed. The university honoured him in 1958 by conferring on him the honorary degree of M.A.

Billmeir married in 1921 Annie Margaret Gibbs.

December 24, 1963.

Lord Bilsland, K.T., M.C., the Scottish banker and former president of the Scottish Council, died on December 10, 1970. He was 78.

Bilsland's reputation began in industry and commerce. His early activities centered on the family concern of Bilsland Brothers Ltd., bankers in Glasgow, of which he was chairman for many years but he rapidly acquired many other business responsibilities, which he retained even though his public duties grew. He was chairman of the Union Bank and Governor of the Bank of Scotland a few years after the two merged. His interests in banking grew rather than diminished as he became older. His influence was of great importance in bringing about the merger of the two banks, and, in his later years, his work for the Bank of Scotland took up much of his attention. He was particularly active in promoting the well-being of the staff of the Bank. He had strong connexions with the Colville family, since both he and his sister married Colvilles, and he was a director of Colvilles Ltd. His other business activities included directorships of a number of investment trusts, of the Scottish Amicable Life Insurance Society, of the Burmah Oil Co. Ltd., and of John Brown & Co. Ltd.

Bilsland's major contribution to the life of Scotland began in the 1930s. He was president of the Glasgow Chamber of Commerce from 1933 to 1935. In Scotland in 1933 unemployment had taken a fearsome grip; 25 per cent of the insured population were unemployed. In Glasgow alone 130,000 men were looking for employment. Bilsland was a leader among those who began the long process of recovery. As chairman of Scottish Industrial Estates Ltd., from its inception until 1955 he led that company to its first great achievement in the opening of the estate at Hillington in 1937, and was a pioneer of the industrial estates as a means of stimulating new enterprise and new types of industry. Since the war attractively-grouped colonies of small ready made modern factories have become a familiar feature of the Scottish landscape and of Scottish industrial life and have contributed nobly to the inflow of new ideas and and of new firms. Their presence is due in no small measure to the efforts of Bilsland. He was also closely associated with the Empire exhibition held in Glasgow in 1938.

Bilsland has been regarded as the personification of the Scottish Council (Development and Industry) since its inception in 1946, and, indeed, was an influential member of both the Scottish Development Council and the Scottish Council on Industry, the two predecessors of the Scottish Council. During the first ten years of the life of the Scottish Council, Bilsland was both its president and the chairman of its executive committee. After 1955 he continued to be its president. In the formative years of the work of the Council he was its active leader and was specially influential in securing American support; he travelled widely in North America on behalf of the Council.

The only surviving son of Sir William Bilsland, a former Lord Provost of Glasgow, he succeeded to his father's baronetcy in 1921 and, in recognition of his services to Scotland, was created Baron Bilsland of Kinrara, the location of his country home in Inverness-shire, in 1950. He was a member of the Royal Company of Archers, a Justice of the Peace, an honorary Associate of the Royal Institute of British Architects and an honorary graduate of the Universities of Glasgow and Aberdeen.

December 15, 1970.

Professor Gertrud Bing, who died on July 3, 1964, after a brief illness, was the animating spirit of the Warburg Institute which she had served with singleminded devotion for more than 40 years. She was the institute's director from 1955 to 1959.

Born in Hamburg on June 7, 1892, she first turned to school teaching and then read philosophy and German literature at the Universities of Munich and Hamburg, where Ernst Cassirer was a formative influence. At the age of 30 she joined the *Kulturwissenschaftliche Bibliothek Warburg* as a librarian and found her vocation in this rich and growing collection of books. When Aby Warburg had returned to his institute after a long illness she became his assistant in 1927, and these years when the ageing scholar initiated his helpmate into his ideas and researches were decisive for her life. She accompanied Warburg on his last journeys to Florence and Rome, where she acquired that understanding of things Italian which was always appreciated by her Italian friends. After Warburg's death in 1929 she became his literary executor, and the two volumes of his *Gesammelte Schriften* richly annotated and supplemented by her are a monument to her self-effacing discipleship. Assistant Director of the Institute under Fritz Saxl's administration, she represented the element of continuity in its multifarious activities.

During the dark years of Nazism when the institute and its staff found refuge in England, Gertrud Bing revealed miraculous reserves of strength and human warmth. An ever increasing stream of homeless and bewildered scholars and refugees sought her advice, and few can have left her little office in the makeshift rooms of the expatriate library without having received comfort and solid help.

BURDEN OF OFFICE

When in 1944 the institute was incorporated in the University of London, she cheerfully shouldered the burdens of administration and public relations, thus freeing Fritz Saxl and later Henri Frankfort for their teaching and research that meant so much to her. What she achieved and also what we missed through her sacrifice may perhaps be gathered from her biographical essay on Fritz Saxl (in the volume of Memorial Essays edited by D. J. Gordon), a rare gem of literary portraiture that displays both her grasp of intellectual history and her gifts of psychological intuition. It makes one mourn the fact that apart from a memorial address given in Hamburg and published in Italy she did not complete her work on Aby Warburg, on which she had been engaged during her last years. Her years as Director and Professor of the History of the Classical Tradition (1955–59) coincided with the Institute's move to its permanent quarters in Woburn Square that consolidated her life work.

Throughout these years colleagues from the most diverse fields turned to her for help with their work; she read their books and papers in draft stages, advised and criticized, always with an eye for the essential and with a genius for sympathy. Her accuracy, her sense of style and her patience made her the ideal editor, and there can be few publications of the Warburg Institute and by its friends which do not owe a substantial debt to her interventions. But invaluable as were these tangible contributions, such as her edition of Fritz Saxl's *Lectures,* they were far transcended by the catalytic effect of her unquestioning faith in the value of scholarly pursuits and by her understanding, never obtruding, of human problems past and present. She will be missed by countless friends and scholars in many fields and many lands. Her influence will continue among the young, whom she always sought out and inspired.

July 6, 1964.

Sir Alan Birch, who died on December 13, 1961, in a London hospital, was general secretary of the 350,000-strong Union of Shop, Distributive and Allied Workers, one of the "big six" unions, and also chairman of the T.U.C. economic committee, generally regarded as the most important of the T.U.C. committees. He was 51.

In the latter capacity he was normally the spokesman for the T.U.C. in their representations on economic affairs to the Chancellor of the Exchequer and other Ministers—although ill-health had sadly curtailed his activities over the past year—and was the general council spokesman on wages and economic matters at the annual Trades Union Congress. He was a formidable critic of the Government's policy.

Birch was characteristic of the best type of modern trade union leader, relying always on quietly reasoned argument rather than eloquence to establish his points. He was also one of the most thoughtful union leaders, whose analysis of their problems was always interesting and constructive.

He believed in greater coordination of trade union policy on wages and other industrial questions, and moved a resolution on those lines which was carried by the 1959 congress but up to the time of his death he had not succeeded in carrying with him his colleagues on the General Council. Because of his illness he was unable to play his full part in the negotiations with Selwyn Lloyd over the proposed National Economic Development Council.

Politically he had moved to the right as he gained in responsibility and was a supporter of Hugh Gaitskell in the controversies over public ownership and over nuclear disarmament which split the Labour movement. Although he was unable to prevent his own union delegation opposing the official party policy on nuclear disarmament at the Trades Union Congress and Labour Party conference of 1960, he continued to support Gaitskell openly as an individual. In 1961 U.S.D.A.W. backed the party leader on the major vote on defence policy.

During his period as general secretary of his union its membership and influence grew and the range of negotiated agreements in the distributive trades, particularly with multiple stores, was greatly extended.

CLERK AT 16

John Alan Birch was born at Warrington, Lancashire, on December 20, 1909, into a labour and cooperative family. When he was 16 he became a clerk in the cooperative society's offices. He was a union member from the start and once said that it was probably his experience of a one-week strike upon a victimization issue that led him away from the sphere of management into active service within the union. As a young man he was inclined to the Left in politics and was associated with the proscribed Socialist League of Sir Stafford Cripps. He had become a branch secretary of his union at the age of 24 and in 1935 was elected a union organizer. He at once made his impress among members all over the kingdom.

In 1949, when the strength of U.S.D.A.W. was approaching the 300,000 mark, he was voted its general secretary and in the same year he joined the General Council of the T.U.C. His knowledge and capacity were at once evident in the affairs of the Council and he was a member of a special economic committee which endeavoured to pilot the Cripps wage-freeze through the T.U.C. Although primarily an economist, his colleagues elected him to the International Committee of Congress, and in 1956 he attracted attention by taking the lead within the General Council by bringing it into definite opposition to Sir Anthony Eden's Suez policy. He was elected chairman of the Economic Committee in 1957. From the very first he showed wide knowledge and competent authority in negotiations and his objective attitude to the problem of attuning wages to prices won for him the respect and the confidence of all sections of the community. He had made a special study of world conditions, and was outspoken in his support of a British expansionist policy.

For some years he sat on the Monopolies Commission, and was a member of the Devlin committee on the dock labour problem. In 1958 he was appointed a part-time member of the National Coal Board and had to face and overcome criticism in his union for accepting the position. He was frequently invited to speak at professional, commercial and labour conferences and meetings.

Birch was a keen musician and amateur photographer.

He was knighted in the Birthday Honours in June this year.

Birch married in 1940 Mildred Mary Crompton, by whom he had two sons.

December 14, 1961.

Lord Birkett, formerly a Lord Justice of Appeal and Judge of the King's Bench Division, died in London on February 10, 1962, at the age of 78. He was a very popular and distinguished member of the legal profession. Before his appointment to the High Court Bench in 1941 he had appeared in many of the famous trials, civil and criminal, of his day. A warm and kind-hearted man, and possessed of great public spirit, his name was widely known to the public apart from his legal activities.

As Mr. Justice Birkett he was the colleague of Lord Oaksey (formerly Mr. Justice Lawrence) on the International Tribunal for the trial of war criminals at Nuremberg. Possessed of great eloquence in and out of court he won his final triumph in the House of Lords two days before he died, when his motion was carried to prevent Manchester Corporation increasing their water supply at the expense of Ullswater.

NOTED DEFENDER

William Norman Birkett, the first Baron Birkett in the peerage of the United Kingdom, was one of the numerous examples of successful lawyers who owed their careers to none of the advantages of family, favour or fortune. He was a son of Thomas Birkett, of Ulverston, where he was born on September 6, 1883. He was educated at Barrow-in-Furness and then went to Emmanuel College, Cambridge, where he took a second in the Historical Tripos in 1909, and his LL.B. He was President of the Union in 1910. In 1913 he was called to the Bar by the Inner Temple. He joined the Midland Circuit and practised first as a local in Birmingham.

On the circuit he soon established a large practice and became known chiefly as a defender of prisoners, and he was especially popular in this regard among the criminal community of Leicester and Nottingham. Some time before taking silk in 1924 he had moved up to London and joined the late Sir Edward Marshall Hall in chambers, and he soon appeared frequently as junior to that leader in cases which attracted wide publicity.

A LIBERAL M.P.

In the meantime he had in 1918 contested unsuccessfully as a Liberal the King's Norton Division of Birmingham. In 1923, the year before taking silk, he was elected as a Liberal for the Eastern Division of Nottingham, but lost his seat at the general election of October, 1924, regaining it in May, 1929, and holding it until he was defeated at the general election of 1931. On the whole, Birkett's career in the House of Commons was undistinguished, though when he spoke his agreeable voice and manner and obvious sincerity attracted sympathetic attention, and his increasing practice at the Bar, carried on with no great reserve of health, was sufficient to absorb all his energies.

On taking silk he was a success from the first, and at the time of Marshall Hall's death in 1927 Birkett was fast attaining a commanding position in the same class of litigation. Without Marshall Hall's theatrical brilliancy, which occasionally could work wonders with an impressionable jury, Birkett had the more solid qualities of tact and discretion and a knowledge of legal principles; and between that date and the outbreak of war in 1939 there were few outstanding cases either at *nisi prius* or in the criminal courts with which his name is not associated. A learned Judge now long passed away is reported to have humorously said of him that his powers of persuasion were "a positive menace to the administration of justice!". But it should be added that his professional reputation stood at the highest and in the conduct of his cases he always maintained the best traditions of the Bar.

FAMOUS CASES

Among the more important of these trials, in 1928, he defended Mrs. Pace for the murder of her husband; in 1930 he defended Hatry in one of the most sensational trials of financial fraud of modern times; in 1932 he defended Mrs. Dampier, charged with the murder of G. B. Parry, and the same year two women, Zellon and Thay, for murdering Sidney Marston; in 1933 he defended Maundy Gregory in what was known as the "Honours" case; the following year he defended Mancini in the "Brighton Trunk" murder of Violette Kaye, and the same year Mrs. Brownhill for in mercy killing her invalid son; in 1936 he defended Dr. Ruxton for the murder of his wife and a nursemaid in sensational circumstances on the Lancashire Fells, and in 1931 he appeared for the Crown in the remarkable Rouse murder trial. Among the famous civil actions in which he appeared was the libel action brought by Captain Peter Wright against Lord Gladstone and his brother, for whom Birkett appeared.

But all this came to an end in 1939, and Birkett was appointed chairman of the Home Office advisory committee to deal with special cases of persons who had been interned. This work of a particularly responsible and onerous character engaged his attention week by week and he continued to assist the committee even after his promotion to the Bench. During the first months of the war, as "Onlooker", he gave broadcasts for the B.B.C., his identity being discovered only by those who recognized his voice. In more recent years he appeared in person frequently on television and radio with much success.

ON THE BENCH

No doubt, had he so wished, Birkett's elevation to the Bench might have come sooner, but it was not until the death of Mr. Justice Hawke in November, 1941, that his name was submitted to the King by Lord Simon to fill the vacancy. The appointment was received with general approbation, not only by the Bar, among whom Birkett was extremely popular, but by the general public, to whom his name (unlike the names of perhaps the most distinguished occupants of the Bench) was widely known. In October, 1942, it fell to him to try, and sentence to death, at the Central Criminal Court, Scott-Ford, a British mercantile seaman, for high treason. The tale of the Nuremberg trials has been too often told to require any special reference here. It is sufficient to say that Birkett shared in the general international approval of the extreme fairness with which the proceedings had been conducted, and on his return he was sworn a member of the Privy Council. Then, at last, he could settle down to his regular judicial duties, in the performance of which he always gave satisfaction. In matters of fact his wide experience at the Bar made him exceptionally successful as a Judge. From 1950 to 1957 he was a Lord Justice of Appeal. He was chairman of Buckinghamshire Quarter Sessions from 1946 to 1958 and was elected Treasurer of the Inner Temple in 1956.

He was much in request as a speaker at public meetings and dinners and he was fond of writing articles and reviews of a non-controversial character in the press. In 1958 he succeeded the late Lord Halifax as president of the Pilgrims.

PHONE TAPPING INQUIRY

In 1937, he had served as chairman of the Committee on Abortion appointed by the Ministry of Health. In 1957 he was chairman of a committee of three Privy Councillors appointed to inquire into the exercise of the prerogative power of telephone tapping. Two years later he won much praise for his work as independent chairman in settling the printing dispute.

Birkett was a man of wide culture, as his university career had shown, and he had been president of the National Book League.

Another of his great interests was London University, of whose Court he had been chairman since 1946.

Birkett married in 1920 Ruth, daughter of Emil Nilsson, by whom he had a son and a daughter. His son, the Honourable Michael Birkett, succeeds to the title.

February 12, 1962.

Shaikh Bishara al-Khoury, who was President of the Lebanon when it achieved full independence during the Second World War, died at Beirut on January 11, 1964.

He was born in Beirut in 1892 and, after taking a law degree at the Jesuit University there, embarked on a career at the Bar. He soon displayed outstanding ability and became one of the most prominent Lebanese advocates. Like most rising Lebanese lawyers, he also entered politics and in due course became head of the Destour (Constitutional) Party, one of two loose groupings in the Lebanese Chamber of Deputies. This party, like its rival the Unionists under Emile Eddé, was mainly occupied with personal and sectarian issues but professed slightly the more nationalistic views of the two and was therefore less favoured by the French mandatory authorities.

In 1936, possibly for this reason, Bishara al-Khoury was defeated by Emile Eddé in the Presidential election. Later that year he was a member of the all-party delegation under Eddé which signed the Franco-Lebanese Treaty of Friendship and Alliance; this document, which would have terminated the French mandate over the Lebanon but gave the French numerous and far-reaching long-term advantages, was subsequently repudiated by the French Government and became a dead letter.

Constitutional life in the Lebanon, as in Syria, was suspended by the French on the outbreak of the Second World War. In 1943 the Free French authorities who were now in control of both countries after the expulsion of the Vichy regime by British and Free French troops in 1941, decreed under British pressure a return to constitutional life and permitted elections for the Presidency and for the Chamber. In the former Bishara al-Khoury was successful, defeating his old rival Emile Eddé although (or perhaps because) the latter enjoyed the open support of the French; and the Chamber which emerged was distinctly Nationalistic in colour. Under the dynamic leadership of Riad Solh, the Moslem to whom the new President entrusted the Premiership, the new Government demanded that the independence of the Lebanon proclaimed by the Free French and endorsed by the British Government when their troops entered the country in 1941 should be made a reality; and at their instance the Chamber unanimously voted a revision of the Constitution which excluded all references to the mandate, in defiance of French contentions that no such modification could be made without their prior consent.

The French, sensitive lest after the war they be accused in liberated France of having failed to defend French interests in the Levant, reacted violently by arresting and incarcerating the President and most of his Ministers, but in face of strong British representations and a remarkable show of Lebanese resistance the Free French Committee in Algiers ordered their release and reinstatement a few days later. Between then and 1946, when by virtue of an agreement reached under United Nations auspices British and French troops were simultaneously withdrawn from the Levant, all powers remaining in the hands of the French authorities were successively transferred to the Syrian and Lebanese Governments which were thus left in the full exercise of their sovereign rights.

Bishara al-Khoury, like his colleague in Syria, gained in prestige from this successful assertion of his country's independence. Counting on this, he contrived an amendment to the Constitution which allowed him a second term of office when the first came to an end in 1948. It proved to be a misjudgment. He himself was still generally respected, but he was widely accused of having allowed members of his family to profit unduly from his status and was held responsible for a sharp decline in the efficiency and rectitude of the administration. By 1952 this criticism had become so vocal and widespread that even his Prime Minister, Sami Solh, openly joined in it, and although the President summarily dismissed him it was clear that his own position was becoming untenable. He accordingly resigned and was succeeded by Camille Chamoun on a platform of "reform" which was calculated to appeal to the electorate rather than to the outgoing President.

Five years later, when Camille Chamoun and his administration were in turn assailed by much the same criticism and a revolt broke out against them which led to serious disorders, Bishara al-Khoury was one of the few Maronites who threw in their lot with the dissidents, in the obvious hope of being called on to return to the Presidency when Chamoun had been forced out of it. This hope was not, however, fulfilled, as when the crisis ended in a compromise solution the choice of President fell on the "neutral" General Chehab, and Bishara al-Khoury retired into the background, from which he never again emerged.

Gifted with a fine legal brain, a shrewd judgment, a kindly nature and a sense of humour, Bishara al-Khoury's failure to realize all his hopes was due primarily to a certain weakness of character, but this should not be allowed to obscure his many years of faithful service to his country and the gift of friendship which he bestowed generously.

January 13, 1964.

Sir John Black, formerly chairman and managing director of the Standard Motor Company, died on December 24, 1965, at the age of 70.

Black was an outstanding personality in an industry which has never been short of individuality. Under his energetic direction the Standard company, which was in a state of decline when he joined it, was built up into a flourishing concern. During the Second World War the company operated two shadow factories for the production of aircraft engines and it was for his work in connexion with aero-engines that Black was given a knighthood.

In November, 1949, he received £25,000 of ordinary capital (worth about £100,000 at the time) from the company on condition that should his connexion with the company be severed, he would not engage, directly or indirectly, in the manufacture of cars or tractors. Six months later, retrospective legislation introduced by Sir Stafford Cripps, then Chancellor of the Exchequer, imposed a surtax on capital payments for "restrictive covenants" and in August, 1950, it was announced that Black had sold his stock to meet the 95 per cent liability on the gift.

The fourth son of John George Black, he was born on February 10, 1895, at Kingston-upon-Thames, Surrey. After studying for the law he served in the 1914–18 War with the Royal Naval Volunteer Reserve at Gallipoli and later with the Tank Corps in France, being demobilized with the rank of captain. In 1919 he joined the Hillman Motor Company, Ltd., and swiftly became joint managing director. He joined the Standard Motor Company in 1929, becoming director and general manager in the following year and managing director in 1934, when he was only 39. Under his imaginative control the company increased its output enormously. In 1940 he was appointed chairman of the Joint Aero-Engines Committee, in charge of the shadow factory group. He was knighted for his services in 1943. Two years later he was made deputy chairman of the Standard Motor Company, which continued to expand when peacetime manufacture returned.

In 1953 Black concluded a 12-year agreement with the Massey-Harris-Ferguson company under which Standard Motors continued with production of the Ferguson light tractor. The agreement also provided for Standards to manufacture a new and larger Ferguson tractor.

That same year he was appointed chairman and managing director of the company, but retired in January, 1954; he had been injured in a motor accident two months earlier and the step was taken on medical advice.

In addition to being a well-known skier he was a keen fisherman, swimmer and yachtsman.

December 29, 1965.

Lieutenant-Colonel L. V. Stewart Blacker, O.B.E., soldier, inventor and explorer, died on April 19, 1964, at his home in Hampshire. He was 76.

Latham Valentine Stewart Blacker, son of Major Latham Blacker, came of a family of soldiers who, in the early part of last century, served in India and particularly on its frontiers. He was destined to do the same in the early years of this century and to push his service over the frontiers into Afghanistan, Turkestan, and Russia. He became an aircraft pilot in 1911 with certificate No. 121, and flew some of the earliest aircraft at Farnborough. When war broke out in 1914, he travelled through Russia from India with a machine-gun company of the 3rd. Turkestan Rifles, and on arrival in England succeeded in getting himself transferred to the R.F.C., and was later shot down and wounded in France.

When his old comrades of the Indian Army arrived on the Western Front he rejoined them and succeeded to the command of the 57th. Wilde's Rifles of the Frontier Force after a gas attack in France. Wounded and invalided in August, 1915, he went back to the R.F.C. and was promptly charged with the development of fire control gear and of aircraft armament. He introduced the Constantinesco gear for firing through the propeller disc and also the Pomeroy bullet for attacks on balloons.

By 1917 he was back in the Army and again on the North West Frontier of India, commanding a training battalion of the Queen's Own Corps of Guides. In that area, before and after the 1914-18 war, he had plenty of action and adventure. Out of those years came his book, *On Secret Patrol in High Asia*. By 1962 he was engaged on writing his autobiography, progressing from operations against the tribes in 1908, to contact with the Red Army at Tashkend in 1918, to moves to repel a Russian thrust into Khorassan in 1920. Yet writing attracted him less than inventing, developing, designing and doing. In those fields his activities were unceasing and a number of the products were fully worthy of the advocacy he devoted to them in military and scientific circles.

As early as 1905 Blacker had been associated with others in developing the 3.5 infantry mortar. When his fighting days were over, he came back to infantry weapons and, during the Second World War, contributed to the invention of several, the most famous of which was the P.I.A.T. (projector, infantry anti-tank).

INVENTOR'S AWARD

The spigot for firing this could be carried on one man's shoulder and the projector on another's. During the war 115,000 Piats were made, and Blacker later received an inventor's award of £25,000.

An ancestor of his, as Surveyor General in India, had organized the first accurate triangulation and mapping of that vast land and paved the way for his assistant, Everest, to put Mount Everest properly on the map and give his name to it. As a descendant of that earlier Valentine, Blacker formed his ambition to fly over the mountain.

In association with Colonel P. T. Etherton, he got together an expedition for the first flight over the mountain in 1933. At that time, Everest had not been climbed. Lord Clydesdale (now the Duke of Hamilton) then the commanding officer of the Glasgow Auxiliary Air Force Squadron and Flight Lieutenant D. F. McIntyre, one of his ablest officers, volunteered as pilots. A committee was formed during 1932 and through the influence of Lord Clydesdale, the support of Lady Houston was gained. Two of the latest general purpose aircraft were obtained from the Westland company and arrangements were made for heated flying suits, oxygen equipment, cameras, and all the necessary apparatus.

Blacker was appointed chief observer. The R.A.F. nominated Air Commodore P.F.M. Fellowes as leader, approved the use of its airfields and landing places in India, and agreed to attach six aircraft mechanics to the expedition. The undertaking was thus given a large measure of official blessing, as likely to yield a good deal of new information about flying over mountainous terrain besides adding to the topographical knowledge of that part of the Himalayas.

On both counts the expedition justified itself. The prints of the expedition were given to the world's press in words and pictures by *The Times*, whose aeronautical correspondent was the only press representative attached to the expedition.

Blacker married in 1927 Lady Doris, only daughter of the first Earl Peel, who survives him with their two sons and two daughters.

April 20, 1964.

George Blake, the Scottish novelist, died on August 29, 1961, in Glasgow at the age of 67.

Intelligent, sympathetic, veracious, George Blake's novels constituted for the most part a lively commentary on the life and industry of Clydeside from the period of the war of 1914–18 onwards. The setting of most of his books was the small industrial town and seaport of Garvel, near Glasgow, a setting which he evoked with intimate and unsentimental feeling and which served him also as a vantage point from which to observe the changing conditions and temper of Scottish life as a whole. His human sympathies were generous and unaffected, his observation flavoured by a nice instinct for realistic comedy, and his novelist's work represents, in sum, a soundly documentary and illuminated performance.

He was a well-known and effective broadcaster and described the launching of the Queen Mary and the Queen Elizabeth and scenes at the Coronation of King George VI.

Born in Greenock in October, 1893, Blake was the fifth and youngest child of Matthew Blake, a member of the old-established firm in that city of Blake, Barclay and Company. The Clyde shipyards were apparently a favourite playground for the boy. He was educated at Greenock Academy, became an articled clerk to a firm of local solicitors with a considerable maritime and harbour practice, and was on the point of proceeding to law classes at Glasgow University when war broke out in 1914. As a subaltern in the 5th Argyll and Sutherland Highlanders he went to France in February, 1915, and to Gallipoli three months later. He was badly wounded, spent many months in hospital in Alexandria and in London, and was "boarded out" late in 1916.

BOOK REVIEWING

Blake resumed law studies and, in his own phrase, finding that he could make nothing of them, furtively took to writing. He became a book reviewer for the *Glasgow Herald*, extended his range of literary journalism, and in 1922 published a collection of *Vagabond Papers*. His first novel, *Mince Collop Close*, an attractive piece of work with an authentically Scottish background, appeared in the following year. From 1924 until 1928 Blake was acting editor of *John O'London's Weekly*; for the next two years he was with the *Strand Magazine*; and for the succeeding two years he was a director of the publishing firm of Faber and Faber. Meanwhile he had produced a series of spirited and very readable Scottish novels at intervals of rather more than a year. *The Wild Men* (1925) gave an unsentimental and persuasive picture of "red" socialism in Glasgow; *Young Malcolm* (1926) and *Paper Money* (1928), the one a story of slow conversion to a rule of practical expediency in life, the other the story of a war profiteer, both impressed by their integrity of mind and feeling; *The Path of Glory* (1929), which had Gallipoli for background, conceded little to sentiment, while *Returned Empty*, in some sort a peacetime sequel, conceded scarcely more.

CLYDESIDE STUDY

Perhaps Blake's most solid achievement—certainly it was one of his most successful books—was *The Shipbuilders* (1935), a well-conceived and vivid study of Clydeside during the depression. But all the later novels, recording various phases of the development of Garvel, particularly *The Constant Star*, had their obvious and very real merits. Apart from his fiction, which continued to appear up to his death, Blake wrote an admirable book about ships and shipbuilders on the Clyde, *Down to the Sea* (1937), a companion volume, *The Firth of Clyde* (1952), a *History of the* 52nd (*Lowland*) *Division*, the *B.I. Centenary History*, *The Ben Line*, and in 1960 the *History of Lloyd's Register of Shipping*.

He married in 1923 Ellie Malcolm Lawson. There were two sons and a daughter of the marriage.

August 30, 1961.

Dr. Alfred Blalock, one of the two Johns Hopkins Hospital doctors who developed the "blue baby" operation, died on September 15, 1964, at the age of 65. He had retired on July 1, 1964, as chairman of the department of surgery and surgeon-in-chief of Johns Hopkins Hospital.

When Blalock took over the Chair of Surgery at the Johns Hopkins Hospital the reputation of this great school had to some extent become overshadowed by the new and vigorous schools of the middle and far west. He arrived in Baltimore as a young man already known throughout the surgical world for his important work on the nature of shock, and those who were familiar with this work and who knew of his brilliant potentialities foretold for the Johns Hopkins an era of great achievement under his direction. This prophecy was soon to be fulfilled. In connexion with his medical colleague Dr. Helen Taussig Blalock interested himself in the congenital anatomical abnormalities of the great vessels issuing from the heart which led to that crippling disability popularly known as the "blue baby". Together with Dr. Taussig, he unravelled the perplexities of the diagnosis and he conceived one of the most daring operations for its correction, an operation involving at that time an entirely new technique of blood vessel anastomosis.

In 1947 Blalock first visited England and demonstrated his new operation at Guy's Hospital. His visit provided a stimulus which did much to encourage those further advances in the pathology and treatment of congenital heart disease which have since emanated from this country.

During his tenure of the Chair of Surgery

at the Johns Hopkins, Blalock trained a number of young surgeons many of whom occupy important Chairs throughout the United States.

REPUTATION RESTORED

His influence and his example have restored to the Johns Hopkins Medical School the reputation, which it enjoyed in the great days of Osler and Halsted, of being the nursery for professors throughout the American Continent.

Blalock was essentially a shy person who nevertheless graced the eminent position in the world of surgery into which his qualities had thrust him; he had a puckish sense of humour and enjoyed the company of his fellow men. In the operating theatre he spent himself emotionally, mentally and physically to the degree of exhaustion, and he commanded in his assistants a devotion and loyalty which did much to contribute to his outstanding success in one of the most difficult and taxing fields of surgery.

Alfred Blalock, son of G. Z. Blalock, was born on April 5, 1899, at Culloden, Georgia, and educated at the University of Georgia and Johns Hopkins, where he held his first hospital appointments. After a period at Vanderbilt Medical School, culminating in three years as professor of surgery, he returned to Johns Hopkins in 1941 as professor of surgery, head of the department and surgeon-in-chief.

Apart from his many important appointments in the American College of Surgeons and other public bodies and in addition to his specific contribution to technical surgery, Blalock will perhaps best be remembered for his insistence on the importance of the relation of physiology to surgery. He was a great investigator with an inquiring mind and a dogged spirit who by his performance wrote a page in surgical history which will stand as an inspiration and an example for many generations of surgeons in the future.

Some years ago he lost his first wife, Mary, who had sustained him and helped him selflessly in the early years and who acted as a kindly and generous hostess to many British surgeons on the pilgrimage to Baltimore. They had two sons and one daughter. In 1959 he married Alice Seney Waters, an old friend of his first wife whom they had both known for many years.

With her he found a new happiness and looked forward to an honoured and happy retirement.

September 17, 1964.

Sir Timothy Bligh, K.B.E., D.S.O., D.S.C., Assistant Managing Director of the Thomson Organisation since 1966, died on March 12, 1969, at Swanley, Kent, at the age of 50. He was principal private secretary to Mr. Macmillan from 1959 to 1963.

Bligh was one of the outstanding men of his generation. The characteristic which marked him out from his fellows was his courage; courage shown during an exceptional career in the Royal Navy during the war, which led him to be the hero of the small boat fleet in the Mediterranean, and brought him the D.S.O., D.S.C. and Bar; courage which made him one of the outstanding advisers to serve any Prime Minister in this century.

The son of Sir Edward Bligh, he was born on September 2, 1918. He had a conventional education at Winchester, and as a scholar of Balliol.

DASH AND DISTINCTION

On joining the Royal Navy at the age of 21, at the outbreak of war, he served with great dash and distinction in destroyers, motor torpedo boats and motor gun-boats and rose to the rank of Lieutenant-Commander. He was twice wounded and four times mentioned in dispatches.

On joining the Treasury after the war, he rapidly made his way as a Principal and served as secretary to Lord Bridges in a crucially important post. In 1959, he was appointed private secretary to Mr. Macmillan, whom he served as principal private secretary until the latter's retirement. Thereafter he worked in a similar capacity for Sir Alec Douglas-Home until he was appointed to the Ministry of Defence in 1964 as Deputy Under-Secretary of State (Air). At this point, Bligh decided to quit the public service, and to accept an offer from Lord Thomson, whose company he joined.

In his new life, Bligh did not at all abandon his interest in politics. His interest in public service led him to seek to enter the House of Commons, and he was on the short list for two Conservative held seats. In 1967 he was appointed an Alderman of the Greater London Council, where he assisted the Conservative leadership in financial matters.

Bligh became a director of the Thomson Organisation in 1964 and his main responsibility was "to concentrate on the expansion of Thomson's overseas interests in new fields and new territories". Two years later he became chairman of Thomson Newscasters. In January, 1969, it was announced that Bligh was to become chairman later in the year of Thomson Yellow Pages.

FULL LIFE

In this varied and full life, Bligh's courage carried him forward. It was combined with an exceptional sense of public duty and an enjoyment in his work which was infectious. It is one of the tragedies of life that it was difficult for him to combine his strong views on the conduct of affairs with that neutral attitude which seems necessary for the civil servant under our present system. There is little doubt that in a new Conservative administration, he would have had a most constructive part to play in or outside the House.

Apart from his official interests, Bligh was keenly interested in local affairs in Swanley, Kent, where he had been brought up and to which he returned in his later years. Cricket and amateur dramatics were his recreations, and to both of them he brought his characteristic enthusiasm. He married in 1945 Ruth Pamela Robertson. His wife, daughter and two sons gave him the pleasures of a full family life.

March 13, 1969.

Karen, Baroness Blixen, as she was generally known, died on September 7, 1962. She was 77.

She was a Dane who spent all the last years of her life at her house near Copenhagen, facing the Sound. But her reputation as well as her interests had always gone far beyond her native country. It might be said that she belonged to English literature as much as to Danish; she was in fact a citizen of the world of literature and cosmopolitan culture. Much of her work was published under the pseudonym of Isak Dinesen.

Baroness Blixen's father, Captain A. W. Dinesen, handed on to her his love of adventure and a gift for writing. His years as a trapper with Red Indians in Minnesota were described by him in a book which was popular for many years. His much more famous daughter was born in 1885, and grew up near the sea. She studied painting in Copenhagen, Paris and Rome and began writing short stories early.

In 1914 she married her cousin, Baron Blixen-Finecke, who was a cousin of King Christian X of Denmark and a well-known big-game hunter. Together they went to live on a coffee estate in Kenya, but were divorced in 1921. Karen Blixen, however, remained active in the management of her estate in Kenya until 1931, and she recorded that "to my mind the life of a farmer in the East Africa highlands is near to an ideal existence". She was, she remarked, judge, teacher and doctor to the black community there in the country where she had put down her roots.

PASSING THE TIME IN KENYA

From these years of satisfying work, acute observation, and never-failing sympathy with the Africans came, in 1937, one of the best books ever written on Africa, her *Out of Africa*. It was written originally in English, in style of great distinction, charm, and simplicity. But before this Baroness Blixen had achieved international recognition with a book of a quite different kind. This was *Seven Gothic Tales*, published in 1934—also first written in English.

Both English and American critics recognized that a new and remarkable talent had entered upon English literature. Karen Blixen once said that she was not a writer by profession and only took up her tales as a means of passing the rainy season in Kenya. But there was certainly no unsophisticated amateurishness about these stories. Their "Gothic" was romantic, eerie, horrifying, macabre, bizarre in the manner of the late eighteenth century, but with great originality, vigour and picturesqueness. Cervantes, Robert Louis Stevenson, E. T. A. Hoffmann, Anatole France, or Edgar Allan Poe were mentioned as Isak Dinesen's precursors; she had indeed provided a set of brilliant variations on old themes, but added an exotic flavour and a metaphysical and philosophical subtlety all her own. Many good judges considered that the best tale of all was *The Deluge at Norderney*, an entrancing story, or series of stories, within a story, about four strange people marooned in a terrible flood in the first half of the nineteenth century. The background was Danish, as it was also for other stories, but not by any means all.

The fame which *Seven Gothic Tales* brought their writer was amply confirmed by later collections of tales. Baroness Blixen rarely achieved a long, continuous narrative, though many of her tales were more *novellen* than short stories, some more than a hundred pages long. In 1942 came *Winter's Tales*, this time written first in Danish; *Last Tales* in 1957 and *Anecdotes of Destiny* in 1958. All were greeted with applause, now and then with the reservation that some of them were mere working to a formula, a reiteration of former work, artificiality pushed to the point of affectation. But no one has even questioned Karen Blixen's place, at her best, among the supremely gifted writers of the short story or tale—*Eyentyr* was the word in Danish, as it was for Hans Andersen's stories.

DOGGED BY ILL-HEALTH

In 1961 Kenya again provided the subject for *Shadows in the Grass*.

For many years Baroness Blixen, who had many friends in literary and artistic circles in several countries, had seemed to them to be dogged by ill-health and a physical weakness only overcome by sheer will power. Her appearance had long been grey and emaciated, though her features had a fineness and intellectual nobility that struck all who knew her. In her early fifties she came out of the personal seclusion in which both her temperament and state of health had long kept her, even at the height of her fame, and gave talks on the Danish State Radio which were a vivid portrayal of scenes of her early life, especially conditions in Denmark at the turn of the century.

These were collected in a book entitled *Daguerrotypier*, published in 1951.

In 1957 Baroness Blixen confounded the pessimists about her health by undertaking a journey to America, where she had been elected as Isak Dinesen, to the American Academy, taking her place in the highly select company of honorary members.

September 8, 1962.

Sir Robert Blundell, Chief Metropolitan Magistrate since 1960, died on June 19, 1967, at Hove, Sussex. He was 66.

He had many of the cases that made criminal history before him at Bow Street, including that of George Blake, sentenced to 42 years for spying: and the "Fanny Hill" novel case. This was in 1964 when he ruled that John Cleland's eighteenth century novel *Fanny Hill—Memoirs of a Woman of Pleasure* was obscene and ordered that 171 paper back copies of the book seized by the police should be forfeited. Blundell's decision was later criticized in an all-party motion tabled in the Commons.

He was born in 1901, the son of Robert Charles Blundell. He was educated at Westminster School and Trinity College, Cambridge, and was called to the Bar by the Inner Temple in 1924. He became a pupil of George McClure (later a Judge at the Old Bailey). His practice consisted mainly of briefs for the prosecution at the Central Criminal Court, the London Sessions and the Metropolitan Police Courts (as they were then still called).

At an early stage of his career Blundell decided that the position for which he was best suited, and which he would most like to obtain, was that of a Metropolitan Magistrate; he never changed his mind about this, although he later had some experience of other judicial work, both as Recorder of Colchester (which he became in 1947) and as an occasional Deputy Chairman at London Sessions. Meanwhile he paid at least as much attention to his social as to his professional life. An elegant, friendly, easy-going man, he was a popular guest and a gracious and discriminating host. In early entries in *Who's Who* he gave his recreation as gastronomy; this was later further defined, or refined, as deipnosophism. He was always good company—often critical but never malicious, perhaps more amusable than amusing, and with more humour than wit.

DOCKLAND CHARACTERS

Blundell became a Metropolitan Magistrate in 1949. He first sat at Thames, where he enjoyed his work among the stowaways, smugglers and other exotic characters of Dockland. In 1952 he was transferred to Bow Street, an unusually rapid promotion. He also presided for several years in the Juvenile Court. It soon became apparent that the rather old-world man-about-town picture of himself, which he had been at some pains to create, was far from being a complete portrayal of the man. He was not a profound lawyer, but he had plenty of commonsense, and he was a hard-working, conscientious magistrate—quick and self-confident in his decisions, courteous to advocates, witnesses and defendants alike, open-minded without being credulous and humane without sentimentality. He studiously avoided saying anything in Court which was funny, epigrammatic, or sensational (a habit of self-denial not universally practised by those holding judicial office). By any standards he was a success; if the excellence of a magistrate is to be measured in inverse ratio to the amount of publicity he attracts, Blundell ranked very high indeed.

Blundell's interest in his work was not confined to the court-room. Those who knew him casually would have been surprised to learn how well-read he was in criminology and legal history. He made it his business to become acquainted, by frequent visits, with conditions in approved schools, probation hostels and similar institutions, and he joined the governing body of several of them. From 1956 to 1960 he was a member of the Ingleby Committee on Children and Young Persons; his memorandum, dissenting from the proposal to raise the age of criminal responsibility, attracted some hostile attention at the time.

In 1960, the Chief Magistrate, Sir Laurence Dunne, retired, and Blundell was appointed to succeed him; in due course, in accordance with a tradition going back for two hundred years, he received a knighthood. It was a choice which had been generally predicted, and which was widely welcomed. He brought valuable assets to his new position—a handsome and dignified presence, a speedy but unhurried manner of conducting business, and an absolute refusal to play to the gallery (or even to notice that there was a gallery). Advocates found him a difficult tribunal, because he never gave any indication, by word or expression, of what was in his mind, until the time came for him to give his judgment, which was invariably terse. Among those who habitually appeared in the dock, and their associates, he became known as "The Sphinx".

INTEGRATING COURTS

In July, 1960, four months after he had become Chief Magistrate, Blundell was appointed a member of an interdepartmental committee, under the chairmanship of Judge Aarvold, to consider how the Metropolitan Magistrates' Courts and the petty sessional courts could be integrated. It therefore fell to him to participate in bringing to an end a chapter of legal and social history which had begun when Colonel Thomas De Veil, a retired soldier of fortune, "set up his Justice Shop in a street in the shape of a bent Bow close to the country fields" in 1734. With the reorganization of London local government, and of the London magistracy (which came into effect in 1965) the position of Chief Metropolitan Magistrate lost something of its unique status and importance.

It may be doubted whether Blundell, who had a strong sense of the history of the office, and who had made an intensive study of the rather inadequate records which exist concerning it, entirely welcomed the change. He certainly was convinced of the need for the continuance of the metropolitan stipendiary system; but it would have been quite out of character for him to have indulged, on the Aarvold committee or elsewhere, in any battle for the maintenance of his own position or prestige. As statutory vice-chairman of the new committee which was responsible for the administration of all magistrates' courts, lay, professional and mixed, within the Inner London area, he did every thing in his power to make the new system work smoothly and well.

June 21, 1967.

Enid Blyton, who died on November 28, 1968, was perhaps the most successful and most controversial children's author of the postwar period. Certainly she was the most productive; at her death something like 400 titles stood to her name.

Inevitably, her name is linked with her creation (or, as those who disliked her work called him) her creature, Noddy. Noddy became a household name. Though a figure of fiction, fiction could not hold him; he became a hot commercial property. At different times you could find him on the West End stage; on the back of breakfast food packets; on the handles of toothbrushes; and in the form of an egg-cup.

LOVED AND LOATHED

He was loathed by many adults—particularly librarians—and loved by many children. The antis found him odious, unwholesome and wet—he was said to weep when confronted by some intractable Toyland problem. The case for the antis was crystallized some years ago in a witty article in *Encounter*. But it is probably true to say that those children who enjoyed

Noddy were not much influenced by the knockers. They looked on the works of Miss Blyton and found them good. They could not see what all the fuss was about.

However, to judge the prolific Miss Blyton solely on the merits of the misadventures of Noddy, Big Ears and Mr. Plod would be unfair.

ENORMOUS SUCCESS

The enormous success of her Famous Five and Secret Seven series and the enduring popularity of such books as *The Island of Adventure*, *The Sea of Adventure*, and *The Valley of Adventure* was earned, for she could write a readable tale, a tale with action in it, and a tale that children, shrewd critics, found credible.

The daughter of T. C. Blyton, her early years are not easy to chart exactly; she was not one to favour the publisher's practice of printing on the dust-jacket of a book a piece about its author. She was born in the late 1890s and brought up and educated in Beckenham; she was musical, taking her L.R.A.M. at an early age. Her father wished her to become a concert pianist, but she had already decided that she would write for children and to prepare for this left home and took Froebel training.

Subsequently she was governess to a family of boys in Surrey and this experience encouraged her to open a small school of her own. By now she was writing stories, poems, and plays for her pupils—the themes and ideas for those often coming from the children—and contributing regularly to *Teachers' World*.

Her first published book, *Child Whispers*, a collection of poems, appeared in 1922. Her first stories were published by George Newnes and she was intimately connected with the popular children's magazine *Sunny Stories*. It was at Newnes' that she met and in 1924 married her first husband, Lieutenant-Colonel H. A. Pollock. After her marriage she spread her wings yet further, editing books on teaching and a children's encyclopaedia.

Later, early in the 1940s it was suggested to her by a London publisher that she should emulate Angela Brazil and write school stories for girls. She took the advice and the tales she wrote went like hot cakes. So successful were they after the Second World War when there was a continuing shortage of paper and printing facilities that it was difficult to keep them in stock. At least three publishers were taking her work. Books of all kinds flowed from her pen. She produced an abridged edition of T. A. Coward's *Birds of the British Isles and their Eggs*, a children's life of Christ, some Old Testament tales, a version of *Pilgrim's Progress*, readers for class use, books on botany and volumes of verse. These, of course, in addition to her immensely popular Secret Seven and Famous Five series. Her success was not loved by the public librarians who in some cases imposed sanctions against her books. Children asked for her books and were told they were not in stock.

"COLD WAR"

Cold war broke out. While the librarians were probably unwise to betray their prejudices so openly, Miss Blyton was perhaps wrong in contending that children should have what they liked, no matter what other books were squeezed out. Whoever was in the right, the fact remains that though Miss Blyton's writings were not great literature they were harmless, as any adult who has worked through a bout of Secret Seven or Famous Five knows.

There are many children who can read but do not read much; for instance, they find Miss Nesbit, of *The Lion, the Witch and the Wardrobe*, written by C. S. Lewis, just a little too much for them. Miss Blyton they pick up and they are away; they are better catered for now, but it was not always so. Undoubtedly she helped many a child on the frontiers of book reading to take his first step.

She did frequently get what is called a good press, and over the years became as cagey as Marie Corelli about herself and her affairs. Yet her relations with children were of the best. Many years ago she reluctantly agreed to speak at a children's book week, and arrived not noticeably well turned out. She was a huge success. On the spot it was arranged that she should appear each day. For many years after that she was a first choice at one famous book fair, and always drew packed houses.

Her second husband, Kenneth Waters, F.R.C.S., whom she married in 1943, died in 1967. She leaves two daughters by her first marriage.

November 29, 1968.

Lillian Board, M.B.E., an outstanding British athlete who won the European 800 metres title in 1969, died on December 26, 1970, after a long illness. She was 22.

She went to the Ringberg Clinic in Bavaria, west Germany, on November 7, only a few hours after the world learnt she had cancer. In the space of a few hectic years, she rose from obscurity to become a household name. She gave everything in the quest for top honours and the public loved her.

She suffered from pain, mainly in the back, and the trouble was later diagnosed as Crohn's disease—an inflammation of the intestines. Reluctantly she withdrew from Britain's probable squad for the Commonwealth Games in Edinburgh.

Then, on October 8, Lillian underwent an exploratory operation at St. Mark's Hospital, London. She was not told that she had cancer until the announcement was made. But her parents, close relatives, athletic officials and journalists had known for some time.

The decision to send her to Dr. Issel's clinic was made after watching a programme on B.B.C. T.V. featuring the doctor's techniques. Lillian maintained with all the courage that hallmarked her races that she was "going to fight—and beat the disease".

She was nominated sportswoman of the year in the Daily Express ballot in the last month of her life.

Lillian Board was a great competitor who, but for her tragic death at such a young age, would surely have gained many more successes on the track. As it is, she won an Olympic silver medal over 400 metres at Mexico City in 1968 and the next season became European 800 metres champion before anchoring the British 4 by 400 metres relay team to a second European championship. Her last race was in the 1970 Women's A.A.A. 800 metres in June when, in spite of the first signs of her illness, she bravely finished third.

After that race Miss Board, who had been suffering from a stomach complaint for several weeks, was forced to withdraw from the Commonwealth Games team for Edinburgh and eventually went into hospital.

Lillian Board, who was born in Durban, South Africa, was a talented sprinter and long jumper at school after starting in athletics under the devoted coaching of her father when she was only 12. She gained her first full international for Britain over 400 metres against France in 1966 and, even though she finished last, her great potential was obvious already. The following year, in Los Angeles, she made a major breakthrough when winning for the British Commonwealth against the United States in 52.8 sec. at only 18.

SOLE WIN FOR BRITAIN

Later, in 1967, Miss Board was the only British winner in the final of the European Cup competition and by 1968 she was already under the burden of being an Olympic hope. In the 400 metres final at Mexico City she was beaten by only one tenth of a second by the little-known Colette Besson of France after leading nearly all the way down the home straight.

The following season Lillian, who admitted that she had been annoyed by some press talk of Olympic "failure", decided to concentrate on the 800 metres following a remarkable second place over two laps in the W.A.A.A. final of 1968. In the European championships in Athens she was in complete control of the final throughout and won in 2 min. 1.4 sec., her fastest ever for a distance which she had only run half a dozen times before. On the last day of the championships the British girl excelled herself by inching past Colette Besson, her Olympic conqueror, on the final leg of the 4 by 400 metres relay.

Just as important as her victories and records, to those who knew her, was the fresh, friendly personality of a girl who captivated both sports reporters and television audiences with her honesty and sense of humour. She was much more than a champion. She was also a very loyal, affectionate friend with a great zest for life.

But for her illness she would have probably in 1970 lowered the world record for 800 metres under two minutes. But, in any case, she will be long remembered as one who epitomized the best qualities of her generation in personality.

December 28, 1970.

Dr. Thomas Bodkin, who died on April 24, 1961, at his home in Birmingham at the age of 73, was Director of the National Gallery of Ireland from 1927 to 1935, and afterwards, until 1952, Barber Professor of Fine Arts and Director of the Barber Institute in the University of Birmingham. Since 1953 he had been emeritus professor.

He was a lively and learned controversialist in artistic matters, and in later life built up also a wide popular reputation on the wireless in such features as "The Brains Trust", and on television his appearance—with snow white hair and pointed beard and twinkle of eyes—became almost nationally familiar. Wit, intolerance, scholarship, a pugnacious good humour, a certain formal politeness of manner, and a kind of vanity were inextricably mingled in his character. He himself said that it was not until he heard a recording of one of his broadcasts that he realized the rich brogue with which he spoke—yet one could not help suspecting that he made some deliberate play with it.

FLAIR FOR ACQUISITION

As a personality he might have been invented by George Birmingham; as an art gallery official and collector he was distinguished by his exacting taste. Nothing would satisfy him but the best of its kind that could be got, irrespective of the dictates of fashion, and his years at the Barber Institute in particular enabled him to give full vent to his flair for intelligent acquisition.

Thomas Bodkin, who was the eldest son of Matthias O'Donnell Bodkin, county court judge of Clare and M.P. for North Roscommon, was born in Dublin in 1887. He was educated at Clongowes Wood College and the Royal University of Ireland. Intending to follow his father's profession, he early displayed gifts as a speaker and won more than one gold medal for oratory. He was called to the Bar in 1911 and practised for five years. It was evident from Bodkin's conversation that he had thoroughly enjoyed his dialectical skill, and he told with gusto how he had secured the acquittal of a probable murderer by confusing a rural policeman in cross-examination about the position of a stile which played an important part.

After studying art principally in the galleries of Italy, France, Belgium, and Austria, Bodkin began to make a private collection of pictures by minor artists, ancient and modern, interesting to students of art history. His most extravagant purchase cost him £45 and the whole collection between £500 and £600. When it was auctioned in 1959 it realized almost £20,000. In 1927 he was unanimously elected by the governors as director of the National Gallery of Ireland to succeed Lucius O'Callaghan. Bodkin held the post until 1935, when he was appointed first professor of fine arts and director of the newly founded Barber Institute of the University of Birmingham.

As a new centre of culture, the first of its kind in the country, the Barber Institute, provided by the munificence of Dame Martha Constance Hattie Barber, wife of the late Sir William Barber, gave Bodkin unlimited scope for the exercise of his independent judgment and exacting taste.

Bodkin held several public appointments. He was a trustee of the National Library of Ireland; honorary professor of the history of fine arts at Trinity College, Dublin; member of the advisory committee of the Dublin Modern Art Gallery; and commissioner and secretary to the Commission of Charitable Donations and Bequests in the Irish Free State. As a member of the council of the commission to advise the Government of the Irish Free State on coinage design in 1926 he was mainly responsible for the choice of the animal and bird designs by Percy Metcalfe. When somebody complained that the coins bore no Christian symbols, Bodkin explained characteristically that the committee disliked the idea of images of the saints being used for gambling on public house counters, or being spat upon for luck.

The title of Bodkin's first book, *May It Please Your Lordships*, an anthology of modern French poetry, published in 1917, gracefully recalled his former profession. With *Four Irish Landscape Painters*, published in 1920, he turned to art, and in *The Approach to Painting* of 1927 (revised edition 1946), he gave the full taste of his quality as a writer on the subject.

Hugh Lane and His Pictures, published in 1933 by the Pegasus Press for the Government of the Irish Free State and rewritten in 1956, outlined Ireland's case for the possession of the Lane Pictures. *Twelve Irish Artists*, a volume of reproduction in colour with an introduction and biographical notes, came out in 1940, and in 1941 Bodkin published a delightful book of reminiscences, *My Uncle Frank*, in which, besides drawing a remarkable character, he recalls his holidays at his uncle's farm 40 years earlier. In 1945 there appeared *Dismembered Masterpieces*, his plea for the reunion of the parts of a single work, when they had become separated, or of the two portaits in a pair. Books on *Virgin and Child*, *Flemish Painters* and *The Wilton Diptych* followed.

But when all has been said about Bodkin's abilities as art critic and historian, gallery director, writer and speaker, it is as a personality, in a sense a "character", that his memory is likely to be cherished. The story of how he secured for Birmingham the bronze equestrian statue of George I, attributed to the elder Van Nost, which formerly stood in Dublin, reads almost like a parody of *General John Regan*.

With his bright and twinkling blue eyes and reddish beard, Bodkin bore some resemblance to Bernard Shaw, and like him he enjoyed trailing his coat, and he got a great deal of quiet fun out of the physical resemblance. Once when he was sitting in the lounge of a hotel he observed an American family studying him with an interest that his modesty could only interpret in one way. Sure enough, the pretty daughter of the family was presently deputed to approach him with the inevitable autograph book. After, in the true Shavian manner, reproving the young woman for this unwarrantable intrusion upon his privacy, in alleged deference to her good looks, Bodkin relented and duly forged the signature requested.

Bodkin was honorary D.Litt. of the National University of Ireland, honorary Litt.D. of the University of Dublin and a member of the Royal Hibernian Academy. He married Aileen, third daughter of Joseph Cox, M.P., and had five daughters.

April 25, 1961.

Professor Niels Bohr, the Danish physicist, who died on November 18, 1962, at the age of 77 had been widely regarded, ever since Einstein died, as the greatest physicist alive. He was the leading spirit in the development of the modern quantum theory on which our understanding of atoms is based, and he has had considerable influence on the philosophy of our time.

He was born on October 7, 1885, in Copenhagen as the eldest son of Christian Bohr, Professor of Physiology in the university of that city. His younger brother, Harold, became a famous mathematician; both acquired early fame in Danish football. Niels Bohr studied at Copenhagen University and took his Doctor's degree in 1911. Then he went to England, to work for a short time under Professor J. J. Thomson at the Cavendish Laboratory, Cambridge; in the spring of 1912 he went to the University of Manchester where Professor Ernest (later Lord) Rutherford had just discovered the atomic nucleus.

As a mathematical physicist he saw clearly the great difficulties in Rutherford's assumption that each atom is a small solar system, with several negatively charged electrons circling, like miniature planets, around their "sun", the positively charged nucleus; such a system, under the laws of classical physics, would inevitably collapse very quickly, sending out its energy in the form of radiation. But he also saw that Planck's quantum law, which said that radiation was not emitted continuously but always in finite parcels, offered a possibility of accounting for the stability of atoms and also for the numerical—and so far quite mysterious—relations between their spectral lines.

THE QUANTUM LAW

By applying the quantum law to the simplest atom of all he formulated his model of the hydrogen atom which shocked the world of physics in 1913. Its features—electrons allowed to run on specified circles only, radiation emitted only when an electron jumped from one circle to another—were frankly unbelievable; yet it accounted so accurately for so many observed facts that it had to be taken seriously. Newton's mechanics, the rock on which all physics had been built, had to be changed to fit the atomic domain, and that took about 15 years; indeed the ground of physics still quakes from the great upheaval which Bohr initiated and which he had guided ever since with indefatigable patience and penetrating insight.

Bohr saw quite early that in the atomic world we do not deal with objects that behave in a certain way whether we observe them or not. The laws of quantum theory imply that we cannot help disturbing what we want to observe. With large objects the disturbance is negligible; switching the light on in a dark room does not make the furniture jump. But an atom or electron will jump even if only a single radiation quantum acts on it; every time we "see" an atom its motion changes significantly. There is no way of telling what it does when we are not looking; all we can do is to calculate the probability that the next observation will give a certain result. Bohr stressed that it depends on the kind of observation whether the object behaves like a particle or a wave: those two aspects he called "complementary" implying that no possible observation could show both at once. This idea of complementarity between different aspects of things is an important extension of philosophical thought, and Bohr has suggested interesting applications in biology, psychology, and sociology.

The atomic nucleus—Bohr realized—did not possess the planetary structure of an atom but was more nearly like a drop of liquid in which the molecules collide all the time, and in 1936 he gave the theory of nuclei a new direction by showing how the quantum theory could be applied to such a jostling crowd. The discovery of uranium fission in 1938 showed that a large nucleus could indeed divide just as a large rain drop may get torn in two by the wind, and the drop-like behaviour of nuclei was later demonstrated by many experiments, based on the brilliant theoretical work of one of Bohr's sons, Aage Bohr.

BACK TO MANCHESTER

After a year in Copenhagen, Bohr returned to Manchester in 1914 for two years as reader in mathematical physics; but in 1916 he was appointed professor of theoretical physics at the University of Copenhagen. He was largely responsible for the creation in 1920 of an Institute for Theoretical Physics, which came to house an increasing number of experimental physicists and their instruments, including (since 1937) the first cyclotron to operate in Europe.

That institute soon became a Mecca for theoretical physicists from all over the world, and after 1933 a refuge for a good many scientists who had fled from Hitler's Germany. Their social centre was the mansion "Gamle Carlsberg", given to the nation by the founder of the well-known brewery and placed at Niels Bohr's disposal in 1932. Here, under the motherly care of Bohr's beautiful wife, Margrethe (the daughter of the mathematician, Professor Nörlund, whom he married in 1912 and by whom he had four sons), students and scholars of all nations gathered to eat and talk and listen to music, and often to sit quite literally at the feet of Bohr, trying to catch his challenging remarks, subtle comments and gentle jokes, spoken in his soft, Danish voice.

But Bohr did not hesitate to make his authority heard in wider contexts. When it became known, in 1942, that Hitler planned to terminate his so far lenient treatment of Danish Jews, Bohr (whose mother had come from Jewish stock) like many others fled to Sweden in a small boat on a moonless night; there he persuaded the King of Sweden to offer unconditional sanctuary to all Jewish refugees from Denmark. Taken to England soon afterwards, and then to the United States, he urged that thought be given to the entirely new political problems which the atom bomb—then under construction—would create; and again in 1950, when the warning of Hiroshima and Nagasaki seemed in danger of being forgotten, he addressed an eloquent appeal to the United Nations, pleading for an "open world" where no war could be prepared secretly and where mutual confidence might grow and spread.

With his heavy build and large hairy hands, Niels Bohr looked more like a peasant than a scholar; but his huge head with deep-set eyes under bushy eyebrows is not easily forgotten, nor the sudden sunny smile that seemed to deprecate what he had said, lest he be taken too seriously. The tentative character of all fundamental scientific advance was always in his mind, from the day when he first proposed his hydrogen atom, stressing that it was merely a model of something as yet beyond his grasp. He was sure that every advance must be bought by sacrificing some previous "certainty", and he was forever prepared for the next sacrifice. Whether in some ways he went too far—as some physicists believe—the future will tell.

Bohr received many honours, among them the Nobel prize in 1922; election as Foreign Member of the Royal Society in 1926; the highest Danish decoration, the Order of the Elephant; the Atoms for Peace Award in 1957; and the Sonning Prize in 1961.

November 19, 1962.

Mary Boland, the stage and film actress, who will be remembered as the plump and engaging comedienne of many a successful film comedy of the 1930s, died in New York on June 23, 1965. She was 80.

Mary Boland was born in Detroit, Michigan, but she did not make her first appearance on the stage until she was 21, when she was seen in Detroit as Elinor Burnham in *A Social Highwayman*. Her first leanings were towards tragedy, but her natural buoyancy and good humour encouraged her to take up comedy, in which field she was at once successful. In her early days she played in a number of top companies and toured the United States extensively. She was first seen in New York in the autumn of 1905 and made her London debut at the Aldwych Theatre in the spring of 1907 as Dorothy Nelson in *Strongheart*.

On her return to America she was given the part of Lady Rowena Eggington in *When Knights were Bold*. When D. W. Griffith, Thomas Ince, and Mack Sennett formed their Triangle Film Corporation in 1915, Mary Boland's name appeared on a list of famous theatrical stars who were to help launch the new film industry, and she did appear in a few silent films, and was seen as a winsome but somewhat buxom heroine opposite Robert McKim in *The Edge of the Abyss* in that year, and with the same leading man shortly afterwards in *The Stepping Stone*.

However, the cinema did not hold any strong attraction for her at this period, and she soon returned to her stage career in New York. Unlike so many of her contemporaries, she was not at once lured back to films with the coming of sound in the late 1920s, and it was not until the early 1930s that she became a Hollywood regular. Her first big success was in that memorable comedy *If I Had a Million*, in which a number of directors each played a sequence, and several of Hollywood's best known actors and comedians of the day (including Gary Cooper, Charles Laughton and W. C. Fields) played short parts.

Nearly every player in this picture became famous soon afterwards, and Mary Boland was signed up to appear in *Three Cornered Moon* with Claudette Colbert for Paramount, followed by a number of other comedies including *Six of a Kind* in 1934 with W. C. Fields and Charlie Ruggles, and *Ruggles of Red Gap* in 1935, when she again partnered Charles Laughton. She went back to New York soon afterwards to appear in a musical comedy called *Jubilee*, and although she continued to be seen in a number of film comedies thereafter, and notably in the screen version of Claire Boothe's play *The Women*, it was the stage which most attracted her in middle and old age. In 1942 she played Mrs. Malaprop in *The Rivals* and one of her last stage appearances was as the mother in *Lullaby* at the Lyceum Theatre, New York, in 1954. Her last film appearance was in *Guilty Bystander* in 1949.

June 25, 1965.

John Boles, one of the best known singing stars of the pre-war era of Hollywood musicals, died on February 27, 1969, at San Angelo, Texas. He was 68.

He started his film career some years before the sound era began, but once Hollywood launched out into the production of talking films, and above all of musicals, he became a star and played in one of the first and most famous musicals of them all—*Rio Rita*, which was made in 1929 and in which his partner was Bebe Daniels. That same year he was seen in another romantic singing role in *The Desert Song*.

Boles was born on October 27, 1900, at Greenville, Texas, and was the son of a Southern banker and cotton-broker. He was educated at the Greenville High School and at the University of Texas, with the aim of becoming a doctor. But at the end of the First World War he served for a time as an interpreter in France, and stayed on there after the Armistice, studying to become a singer. He completed his training in New York, but found difficulty in achieving any recognition. However, in 1923 he was given the part of Paul Revere in a musical comedy called *Little Jesse James*. Later he was chosen to sing opposite Geraldine Farrar in her only attempt to play in light opera. In 1926 he was seen by Gloria Swanson in a Broadway musical comedy called *Kitty's Kisses*, and she asked him to make his film debut opposite her in a silent film, *Loves of Sunya*, in which he appeared without the famous moustache. Some half-dozen silent pictures followed during the next three years. But when the great musical era began in Hollywood in 1929 with the production of *Broadway Melody*, he and Bebe Daniels were almost as successful in *Rio Rita*, and this time he wore the moustache.

The success of *Rio Rita* encouraged him to turn his whole attention to the screen and he did not return to the theatre until 1943. During this period he was kept busy in a long succession of musical films, including *The Desert Song*,

King of Jazz, Music in the Air, and several films with Shirley Temple. In 1936 he was seen in *Rose of the Rancho* with the famous Metropolitan Opera singer Gladys Swarthout, who herself failed to achieve stardom. But he did not limit himself to light romantic parts, and played in some well remembered film dramas as well including *Backstreet*, with Irene Dunne, and *Stella Dallas* with Barbara Stanwyck. His return to the stage in 1943 was made in *One Touch of Venus*, which ran in New York for over a year. Thereafter he was seen only infrequently in films, and he appeared at the London Palladium in the autumn of 1948 in a revue *Sky High*. At Los Angeles in 1950 he played Gus in *Gentlemen Prefer Blondes*. One of his last film appearances was as a portly and turbaned Arab in *Babes in Baghdad* opposite Paulette Goddard in 1952. He had latterly made a new career for himself in oil.

March 1, 1969.

James Bone, C.H., who died on November 23, 1962, at his home, Abbots Holt, in Tilford, Surrey, at the age of 90, was a Scot who made London his province and its citizens, from cabinet ministers to Fleet Street down-and-outs, his friends. No journalist of the first half of this century has held a more secure niche in the respect and affection of people in all walks of life who know the true values. Visitors to his small untidy office in Fleet Street or to his dearly loved home in King's Bench Walk, never knew in what unexpected company they might find themselves: men with famous names in politics, literature, painting, or architecture, distinguished Americans (Bone's links with New York and Baltimore were close), obscure Bohemians would be enjoying the good talk.

As a host, Bone had the knack of talking well himself and bringing the best out of his guests. But this was a relaxation—and a rich source of raw material—for a journalist who missed nothing of the London scene. At work, as away from it, he contributed himself to the matter in hand and made others reveal qualities that surprised themselves. A quick writer, he was also a scrupulous one. He hated a slovenly sentence as much as a mistake of fact. Under his guidance the London Letter of the *Manchester Guardian* had upon it the stamp of his personality, although he drew its paragraphs from a remarkably wide circle of contributors. His authority over them as an artist in his own line was absolute; he exercised it by force of example and with complete informality. Many men were devoted to him as "Jim"; no man dared to offer him shoddy stuff.

He was born in Glasgow on May 16, 1872, and spent his youth in that city during a peak period of its activity, industrial and artistic.

SON OF JOURNALIST

He was the second of the six sons of David Drummond Bone. His father was a journalist on a now defunct Scottish daily, the *North British Daily Mail*, and Bone would remark in latter years that he and his brothers were "brought up with pencils in their mouths".

They were a remarkable family group. One of them, afterwards Sir Muirhead Bone, began at the Glasgow School of Art a career that put him among the foremost artists of his day. Seafaring claimed a second brother, David, who commanded for the Anchor Line in both world wars and was knighted for his services in 1946. He has described his early days at sea in *The Brassbounder* and other books. A younger brother, A. H. Bone, went also to sea and gathered some memories of his adventures in a volume called *Bowsprit Ashore*.

Bone passed from school at 14 to the quayside office of the Laird Line. He combined his work there with writing, both for Scottishand English journals. Something of the stimulus of his Glasgow days is to be found in a rather rare little volume *Glasgow in 1901*, in which, under a pen name, he combined with Muirhead Bone and A. H. Charteris (later Professor of International Law at Sydney).

Coming south in 1901 he observed the pageants and the small change of London through the Edwardian years of peace, through two wars, and through the years between. He was an artist in catching the changing face and the varying moods of the city of his adoption.

EAR FOR THE TRUE

He could make a Coronation or a Cup-tie or an air raid come to life again. His reserves of knowledge of art and architecture—modestly hidden—were always a strength to him. His eye for colour—on the river or on the face of a building—never missed what was worth seeing. His ear was always open for the significant anecdote, the true cockney accent.

These powers were given without stint to the service of his paper—of which he was London Editor from 1912 until the end of Hitler's war. They flowed over into two books—*The London Perambulator* and *London Echoing*—which, with illustrations by his brother, Sir Muirhead Bone, will stand out unashamed on the shelves with anything written since the days of his fellow countryman and London lover, Dunbar. To Scotland's capital he did the same literary service in *The Edinburgh Perambulator*. Bone's election as an Hon. F.R.I.B.A. was a tribute to his care for good architecture—a care which led him to make himself an authority on the history and use of Portland stone.

In the great public issues with which the paper was faced, from its long campaign for women's suffrage and for an Irish settlement, to its determined stand against the dictatorships, Bone was in full accord with C. P. Scott and his successors. In 1919 he became a director of the paper.

The heavy burden of administrative work did not impair his own zest in writing. His small, sturdy figure and his perambulations (brisk in spite of a limp) up and down Fleet Street were an individual part of the scene he loved and described so well. Gaiety and curiosity never deserted him.

His friends were shocked to hear rumours of the bad state he was in when, during the war, his ship was torpedoed on her way back from America. He was an old man then and he might have been landed, after exposure in an open boat, an invalid on a stretcher at Liverpool. However much his health may have suffered, he brought back with him one of the most vivid and not over-written eye-witness reports of shipwreck that ever passed a censor.

When his home in King's Bench Walk was bombed, he allowed his friends to do the lamenting and himself settled down with unwearied zest to keep an eye on wartime London from the Strand Palace Hotel.

He retired in 1945 from the London editorship of the *Manchester Guardian* while retaining for a time his place on its board of directors. The occasion brought tributes from many friends and colleagues, in Fleet Street and out of it, to one who, in the words of Mr. Ivor Brown had "done the work of making Britain real, exciting, friendly and fascinating to all sorts of people". Bone's service to international friendship as well as to journalism was recognized in 1947 when he was made a Companion of Honour.

Messages from the Queen, President Kennedy, the Prime Minister (Harold Macmillan). Hugh Gaitskell and Jo Grimond were received at his 90th birthday party held in May 1962. President Kennedy greeted him as "the unofficial but admirable mentor of all American journalists who came to London in the years before the war".

He married in 1903 Annie, daughter of John McGavigan. She died in 1950. There were no children.

November 24, 1962.

Lady Violet Bonham-Carter—See under **Lady Asquith of Yarnbury.**

General Bor-Komorowski, who died on August 24, 1966, while out rabbit shooting at Woughton-on-the-Green, Buckinghamshire, commanded the Polish Home Army from 1943 and gave the order for the Warsaw uprising on August 1, 1944. He was 71.

In the subsequent controversy he was accused of having sacrificed thousands of Polish lives in the foolish hope of setting up a Free Polish government before the Russians arrived. He defended his position by pointing out that Moscow Radio had appealed for an uprising and that he had every reason to expect help. Instead, the Red Army waited outside Warsaw for two months while the Germans fought desperately to crush the Home Army. After two months of ferocious fighting General Bor-Komorowski and the few survivors surrendered and were taken prisoner. The Russians later entered the city and set up a Communist government. In May, 1945, the Germans released him to the American forces in Innsbruck. Since then he had lived quietly in England.

Some historians still argue that the Red Army was too extended and exhausted to enter Warsaw at the beginning of August, 1944. It is true that it was not entirely ready, but there is now sufficient evidence to show that the Russians were not reluctant to see the Home Army crushed by the Germans before it could set up an authority loyal to the London exiles. They even hindered British and American efforts to drop supplies on Warsaw. The only question is whether—with the wisdom of hindsight—General Bor-Komorowski was naive to suppose that the Russians would help to save a government they did not control, and whether, in any case, there was a chance of a truly independent Poland at that time.

In the end it may have been General Bor-Komorowski's tragic, courageous and ultimately futile uprising that finally drove home the lesson that Poland had to accept a lasting alignment with Russia. At the same time, the brief blaze of national spirit gave Poland a moment of identity and pride between the German and the Russian occupations that remains a source of inspiration.

The general's real name was Tadeusz Komorowski. He took the name Bor as a cover during his days with the underground and subsequently retained it. He was born in 1895, the son of a landowner in Lwow, in eastern Poland. The resurrection of the Polish Republic in 1918 inspired him to become a professional soldier. By the following year he was a captain in the 9th Cavalry Regiment fighting in the Russo-Polish war. A year later he commanded the 12th Regiment of Lancers of Podole. From then until the beginning of the Second World War he climbed slowly up the ladder of promotion in a series of rather dull jobs, distinguishing himself less as a soldier than as a brilliant horseman. He was successful in many contests at home and abroad.

Bor-Komorowski showed no sign of political ambition. By temperament and background he tended to be conservative, but during the war he was sufficiently responsive to the popular feeling to urge the Polish Government in London to decree the expropriation of land and the nationalization of some important industries.

When the war began, he was in command of a cavalry training centre at Grudziad. The town was quickly captured by the Germans, but Bor-Komorowski got in touch with his old friend General Sikorski, who had formed the new Polish exile government in France, and was charged with the task of forming a clandestine secret army. Resisting frequent German offers to make common cause against the Russians, he became Commander of the Home Army in the Cracow district, then Deputy Commander of the Home Army, and finally, in July, 1943, Commander. At the beginning of October, 1944, the Polish Government in London appointed him Commander-in-Chief of all Polish forces, though by that time it was a more or less honorary position.

During his underground activity in Poland the Germans put £400,000 on his head and nearly caught him many times. Once they succeeded, but he was not recognised and escaped.

His forces did valuable work in sabotage against the Germans and passing information to the Allies.

August 26, 1966.

Frank Borzage, the Hollywood film director, died on June 19, 1962, at the age of 69.

Born in Salt Lake City on April 23, 1893, he went on the stage at the age of 13 as a child actor, and soon afterwards arrived in Hollywood. He rapidly found himself acting bit-parts and later important roles in the films of Thomas Ince, whose company was at that time one of the most prosperous and prolific groups in America. Like most actors of the period he was also something of a general odd-job man, able to turn his hand to script-writing, editing or direction as the occasion required, and in 1920 he became a fully fledged director.

His first notable film was *Humoresque*, followed by *Song of Love, Secrets*, and *Lady*. As the titles suggest, he rapidly became a specialist in the "woman's film", the lush and sentimental emotional drama which retained its popularity throughout the 1920s and 1930s.

He really came into his own in 1927–28, when he found an ideal star, Janet Gaynor, and perfect subjects in *Seventh Heaven* and *Street Angel*. The first won its star and director two of the first Academy Awards ever given, and from then on Borzage was firmly established as one of Hollywood's leading directors. In 1932 he won another Academy Award for *Bad Girl*, and in the next year made what remains perhaps his best film, the first version of Hemingway's *Farewell to Arms* starring Gary Cooper and Helen Hayes, which came possibly nearer than any other film to conveying the elusive spirit of its author on the screen. Among a further succession of emotional dramas were *Green Light*, based on a novel by Lloyd Douglas, *History is Made at Night*, with its spectacular shipwreck, *Big City*, with Spencer Tracy and Luise Rainer, and *Mannequin*, a glamorously upholstered vehicle for Joan Crawford, as well as *Desire*, a sophisticated comedy with Marlene Dietrich.

FILM OF HITLER'S RISE

In 1938 he turned to something more substantial with *Three Comrades*, based on Erich Maria Remarque's novel of the First World War and graced in particular with an exquisite performance from Margaret Sullavan, who also appeared, along with Joan Crawford, in his next film, *The Shining Hour*, and in *The Mortal Storm*, which concerned Hitler's rise to power. Lloyd Douglas again provided the material for *Disputed Passage*, and Joan Crawford appeared again in *Strange Cargo*: other titles during the war years included *Smiling Through, The Vanishing Virginian, Seven Sweethearts, Till We Meet Again*, and the all-star revue film *Stage Door Canteen*. By the end of the war the type of film in which he specialized was falling from favour, and he turned, less happily, to costume drama with *The Spanish Main* and *Magnificent Doll*. In 1948 his first independent production for Republic, *Moonrise*, a chase story wedded with a subtle evocation of life in the misty and impoverished southern swamps, was a commercial failure, and he retired from film-making for 10 years, returning to make *China Doll*, a tragic romance very much in his old manner for Victor Mature. After this he was commissioned by Walt Disney to direct a spectacular biblical story, again based on a novel by Lloyd Douglas, *The Big Fisherman*.

Frank Borzage specialized in one type of film—a type not as a rule very highly thought of by serious film students—the emotional drama. He brought to the often false and confected plots of his films, however, a true romantic feeling and muted sensibility which gave many of them an effective ring of truth and sincerity.

June 20, 1962.

Phyllis Bottome, the novelist, who in private life was Mrs. A. E. Forbes Dennis, died at her home in Hampstead on August 22, 1963. She was 79.

A writer of thoughtful and sympathetic temper, conscientious in craftsmanship, she drew substance and stimulus for her most effective works of fiction from two sources—her acquaintance with Austria in the years immediately after the war of 1914–18 and her faith in the psychological doctrine and method of Alfred Adler. She had begun writing at an early age and had always displayed a marked interest in psychological theory, but it was not until she had come under the spell of Adler's teaching and personality that she attracted more than passing attention by her imaginative treatment of themes that are the special province of the alienist. She became a fervent devotee of the Adlerian school and wrote in 1939 apparently at his request, a somewhat hero-worshipping but nevertheless highly instructive biography of Adler himself. Her novels fall short, perhaps, of high or serious distinction, but the best are intelligent and accomplished and make sound reading.

Of Anglo-American parentage, the daughter of the Rev. William Macdonald Bottome of New York and Margaret Leatham of Leatham, Yorkshire, Phyllis Bottome was born at Rochester on May 31, 1884. She spent her first nine years in England, the next four in the United States, and at various times afterwards lived in Switzerland, Italy, France and Austria. Her earliest novel, entitled *Raw Material*, was published in 1905, when she was 21, and not surprisingly, in that first effort, as in the two or three books that followed soon afterwards, there was a certain immaturity of thought and style. As evidence of her interest in the new psychology of the period or at least of her leaning towards simplifications of the new psychology there is *The Common Chord*, which appeared in 1913. Not until *Old Wine*, in 1926, a carefully written clever, if also somewhat extravagant, story of the aristocracy of imperial Vienna, did she suggest she possessed real potentialities as a novelist. *The Advances of Harriet* (1933), which was unexpectedly gay comedy, stood out among her books of the following period, but only with *Private Worlds* (1934) and *The Mortal Storm* (1937) did she establish her reputation as a novelist with a sympathetic awareness of psychiatric problems.

During the war years she often lectured for the Ministry of Information. *Within the Cup*, which appeared in 1943, the story of a Viennese psychiatrist in London in wartime, was done with warmth and generosity of feeling but was also rather more sentimental and didactic in tone than she evidently meant it to be. In 1947 she offered in *Search for a Soul* a detached, entertaining, and at times touching record of her life up to the age of 18. The fiction she produced in later years has many good qualities but tends to be of declining interest. In *Under the Skin* (1950), set in the West Indies, *Against Whom?* (1954), largely confined in scene to a Swiss sanatorium, and *Eldorado Jane* (1956) she combines not too happily something of romantic appeal with a feeling for the problems of society. She also brought out two collections of short stories, of which those in *Man and Beast* (1953), dealing with the relationship of human beings and animals are done with rather more than professional competence. *Walls of Glass* appeared in 1958 and in 1962 she published another volume of autobiography, *The Goal*.

Miss Bottome married Captain A. E. Forbes Dennis in 1917.

August 23, 1963.

Air Chief Marshal Sir Norman H. Bottomley, K.C.B., C.I.E., D.S.O., A.F.C., who died on August 13, 1970, at the age of 79, was Deputy Chief of the Air Staff for the greater part of the second world war. He was a most able staff officer with a distinguished flying record in the first world war, which he enhanced in command of a group on the North-West Frontier during a period of widespread unrest among the tribes in 1937. After he had retired from the R.A.F., he was Director of Administration, B.B.C., for eight years.

Norman Howard Bottomley was born on September 18, 1891, the son of Thomas Bottomley, of Ripponden, Yorks. He was educated at Halifax Secondary School, the Borough College, London, and Rennes University, France. In 1914, he was commissioned into the 3rd Battalion, The East Yorkshire Regiment, and in 1916 seconded to the Royal Flying Corps. He served in France during 1917 as a flight commander, and in 1918-19 was a staff officer, 2nd grade, and acting major, R.A.F., with No. 1 Group at Kenley. He was awarded the A.F.C. in 1918.

After attending the R.A.F. Staff College in 1924–25, he served for over three years in the Directorate of Operations and Intelligence, and in 1928–29 commanded No. 4 (Army Co-operation) Squadron at Farnborough. Promoted to wing-commander, he was selected for the 1930 course at the Imperial Defence College, and for the next three years was an instructor at the R.A.F. Staff College.

In 1934, he went to India to command the aircraft park at Lahore, and from October 1934, to January 1938, commanded No. 1 Indian Group at Peshawar—from July 1935, as a group captain. He served with distinction in the operations in Waziristan between January and September 1937. The dispatch of General Sir Robert Cassels commended his "high example and ready co-operation", and said that under the direction of Group Captain Bottomley the R.A.F. units "played a prominent part in bringing the operations to a successful conclusion". He was made a C.I.E. in the Coronation honours list, and in 1937, was also awarded the D.S.O. He returned to become senior air staff officer in Bomber Command in February 1938, and in the following November was promoted to air commodore.

He served with Bomber Command in the war until May, 1941, first as S.A.S.O. and from November, 1940, in command of No. 5 Group.

SUCCEEDED TO MINISTRY POST

He was made an acting air vice-marshal in March, 1940, and received substantive promotion on July 1. In June, 1941, he succeeded Sir Arthur Harris as Deputy Chief of the Air Staff, and he remained at the Air Ministry until after the end of the war. When the post of D.C.A.S. lapsed he was made Assistant Chief of the Air Staff (Operations), and when there was a re-establishment of the appointment of D.C.A.S. in August, 1943, he again took it up, being granted the acting rank of air marshal. In September, 1945, he again succeeded Sir Arthur Harris, as Air Officer Commanding-in-Chief, Bomber Command. In January, 1947, he was appointed Inspector-General of the R.A.F., and held the post for a year.

In 1948, when the B.B.C. was seeking a Director of Administration, Bottomley was induced to accept the post, and left the R.A.F. to do so. It was a completely new world for him. He coped with it in his usual calm, precise, and meticulous way. He was a great believer in principles rather than in expediency. During his eight years' service with the B.B.C., he gained a reputation for absolute fairness. In his retirement he maintained friendships from both his service and civilian occupations. He was indeed a most humane and friendly man who never talked about, and rarely showed, the great responsibilities he had had.

He married, in 1927, Anne, daughter of Sir William B. Lang, and had one son and one daughter.

August 15, 1970.

Adeline Bourne, who died on February 8, 1965, at the age of 92, was well known as an actress, a suffragette, and a strenuous worker for charity who, between 1915 and 1963, was estimated to have raised more than £750,000 through her personal efforts for such causes as the Star and Garter Home, Richmond, the Elizabeth Garrett Anderson Hospital, and the Wayfarers Trust for elderly and impoverished gentlepeople.

Born in India in January, 1873, Miss Bourne was educated at Eastbourne and Blackheath before studying drama under Sarah Thorne. Her stage debut was at Chatham in 1898 as Anne Chute in *The Colleen Bawn,* and she stayed with Miss Thorne's company in Chatham and Margate until the following year. In 1901 she went to London, appearing at the Grand Theatre, Islington, in *The Little Outcast,* and later the same year joined Mrs. Patrick Campbell at the Royalty, with whom she stayed until 1903. With her she played in *Beyond Human Power, Lady Tetley's Divorce, The Joy of Living* and other pieces which for their day and age were distinctly avant-garde and occasionally feminist.

In 1904 Miss Bourne played Aphrodite at the Lyric Theatre, and for the next two years was continually engaged in West End successes until she began her long association with Forbes Robertson, touring the United States with *Caesar and Cleopatra, The Merchant of Venice,* and *Hamlet*. Nineteen hundred and eleven saw her in her most famous role, as Salome, in a production of Wilde's play at the Court Theatre. Two years later she rejoined Forbes Robertson on his farewell tour of the provinces, and went with him to America and Canada in the early years of the First World War.

Since then she has been best known for her forceful charity appeals. Her suffragette activities are commemorated in the Actresses' Franchise League, of which she was founder member, and her theatrical loyalties in the New Players' Society, which she also founded. Having served overseas as an officer in Queen Mary's Army Auxiliary Corps, she raised no less than £150,000 for the British Women's Hospital for the Totally Disabled, formerly the Star and Garter Hotel in Richmond Park.

February 10, 1965.

General Sir Alan Bourne, K.C.B., D.S.O., M.V.O., who died at Torquay on June 24, 1967, at the age of 84, served for 44 years in the Royal Marines, and as Adjutant-General of the Corps was the first Director of Combined Operations.

He was appointed to this post on June 12, 1940, immediately after the fall of France. Superseded on July 17 by Admiral of the Fleet Sir Roger Keyes, he remained as second-in-command until the end of the year, coordinating plans for the Royal Marine Commandos which later won fame in various theatres of the war.

Alan George Barwys Bourne was born on July 25, 1882, the son of the Rev. C. W. Bourne.

UNDER QUEEN VICTORIA

He was educated at Cheltenham and entered the Royal Marine Artillery in 1899. When he retired in 1943 he was the last serving officer of the Corps to have held Queen Victoria's commission.

When the 1914–18 War broke out he was attending the Staff College, Camberley, and was appointed to H.M.S. Queen and, two months later, to H.M.S. Tiger, in which he served in the Grand Fleet until 1917. Following his promotion to major he was seconded to the Army and served on staff duties in France and on the Rhine with the 3rd Army and the 8th and 34th Divisions until 1920. He received the D.S.O. in 1918, and the Italian Government made him a Cavalier of the Order of St. Maurice and St. Lazarus, and awarded him the Silver Medal for Military Valour. After the war he was brigade major of the R.M.A. at Eastney, and military instructor at the R.M. Depot at Deal. From 1927 to 1930 he served in the Plans Division, Admiralty, during which he became a lieutenant-colonel in 1929. After attending the Imperial Defence College during 1931, he was Assistant

Adjutant-General, R.M., and was promoted to colonel in 1933. He was Colonel Commandant (temporary Brigadier) of the Portsmouth Division from 1935 to 1938, and in 1937 was appointed a C.B., and A.D.C. to the King. Promoted major-general in 1938, he succeeded to the post of Adjutant-General, Royal Marines, a year later, just after the outbreak of the War of 1939–45, with the rank of lieutenant-general. At the end of 1940 he reverted to the post of Adjutant-General until 1943, when he was placed on the retired list. He was promoted K.C.B. in 1941. A keen athlete, he represented the Navy at hockey in 1909.

He married in 1911 Lilian Mary Poole, daughter of Colonel Poole Gabbett, R.A.M.C., and they had one daughter. His wife died in 1958.

June 27, 1967.

Clara Bow, one of the gayest, gaudiest and most representative stars of the American silent film, died on September 27, 1965, in Hollywood.

In 1927 she became known as the "it" girl, a phrase coined by Elinor Glyn in a moment of literary flamboyancy, and although the term was at first intended to suggest only sex appeal, Clara Bow was able to invest it with a wider meaning. With her, it came also to imply not only vitality and an enthusiasm for life but also the paradox of outward sophistication in a basic unsophisticated era.

Clara Bow belonged to the cinema and was its child, as was Jean Harlow and later Marilyn Monroe. Here was no real acting ability and no exceptional beauty but just a simple love affair with the film camera, which in return could so marvellously interpret all the moods of wayward youth and could create an almost childlike fantasy of romance. Clara Bow also belonged to the postwar era of the silent twenties. She was the flapper, the jazz girl, the dancing daughter and the bright young thing. She had bobbed hair, cupid bow lips and the comely but sturdy body of the typical young American girl.

This typicality was emphasized by her birth and upbringing. She was born in Brooklyn, New York, on August 5, 1906, and was educated at high school. She became a secretary when she reached adolescence and might well have remained one had not her bright red hair and buoyant personality won her a beauty contest in 1922, in which the prize was a part in a film called *Beyond the Rainbow*. Soon after this she went to Hollywood to appear in *Down to the Sea in Ships*. However, it was not until the arrival of Elinor Glyn in Hollywood in 1926 that stardom was thrust upon an inexperienced and unpretentious young girl. Hollywood quickly grew tired of Miss Glyn, but the film of her story It, which was made by Paramount in 1926, launched Clara Bow on a brief but meteoric career which was accompanied by some of the most brazen and ill-advised publicity campaigns of the silent cinema, and resulted in her receiving up to 20,000 fan mail letters a week at the height of her career.

Numerous films followed, including *Mantrap, Kid Boots* with Eddie Cantor, *The Plastic Age, Dancing Mothers, The Fleet's In, Dangerous Curves* (her first talking film), *Paramount on Parade, True to the Navy, Her Wedding Night, Kick In, No Limit* and many others and she also appeared unnecessarily but certainly not without impact in William Wellman's war film *Wings,* with Gary Cooper and Richard Arlen.

In 1930 she was forced to retire from the screen through illness, and in 1931 she married the film actor, Rex Bell, and was seen in only two films thereafter, but it seems doubtful whether she could have held her place in the cinema for long after the coming of sound. Her era had passed; the gay twenties were over.

September 28, 1965.

Sir Eric Bowater, chairman of the Bowater Paper Corporation Limited, died at his Surrey home on August 30, 1962, at the age of 67. He became chairman in 1927 at the age of 32, and from a small family paper merchant business Bowaters has grown under his guidance into one of the largest paper companies in the world.

Eric Vansittart Bowater was born in London in 1895, the only son of Sir Frederick Bowater, K.B.E. He was at Charterhouse and left with the ambition of becoming a professional soldier. He was, in fact, serving with the Royal Artillery at the outbreak of the 1914–18 War. He was severely wounded at Ypres and was invalided out in 1917.

After a long convalescence he joined his father and two uncles in the firm of W. V. Bowater and Sons, in the City of London, that had been founded in 1881 by his grandfather. He began with no knowledge whatsoever of the paper industry, but rapidly learnt enough to realize that the true potential of the business lay in establishing its own production.

KENTISH MILL

His father shared his view, and in spite of some opposition Eric Bowater devised the plan for the first Bowater paper mill at Northfleet, Kent. This was opened in 1926, two years after his father's death. Two years previously he had been made managing director. In 1927 he enlisted the financial support of Lord Rothermere and bought out his uncles. From that day forward he had been in full command.

In 1928 the capacity of the Northfleet mill was doubled as newspaper circulations leaped upwards and the newsprint industry strove to keep pace. One of Eric Bowater's major tasks at that time was to establish a strong team of executives, particularly on the production side, since few of the 100 or so men employed by the original firm had technical qualifications.

The Bowater policy of continuing expansion was next seen in the start of construction in 1929 of a two-machine newsprint mill at Ellesmere Port, Cheshire, to supply the growing market of the Manchester editions of the London dailies and the provincial newspapers of the north. Bowater won practical support from Lord Beaverbrook and Lord Rothermere for his venture. By the end of 1930 the mill was in production; two years later its capacity was doubled.

FREE FROM PUBLISHING

In 1932, influenced by the success of the manufacturing side of the business, the interests in Bowaters of Lord Rothermere and Lord Beaverbrook were acquired, and thus the organization freed itself permanently from any financial link with the newspaper and publishing industry.

In 1936 Eric Bowater acquired the Edward Lloyd paper mills at Sittingbourne, Kent, and the newsprint mill at Kemsley near by. The following year he bought groundwood mills in Norway and Sweden as a first move towards independence in source of supply of raw materials.

He had barely started to carry his expansionist policy across the Atlantic, with the purchase in 1938 of the newsprint and pulp mills at Corner Brook, Newfoundland, when development was halted by the 1939–45 War.

He joined the Ministry of Aircraft Production under Lord Beaverbrook in 1940, being director-general until 1943, and then deputy controller for two years until his appointment as controller in 1945. For his service there he was knighted in 1944.

From the acquisition in 1944 of a single fibreboard container plant there has grown a major concern in the booming packaging industry producing paper-based packaging of every kind and now expanding into the realm of plastics.

EXPANSION IN NORTH AMERICA

Meanwhile Bowaters pursued their expansion in the North American market with mills in Tennessee, Nova Scotia, and South Carolina. In 1956, with the Scott Paper Company, of Chester, Pennsylvania, Bowaters entered into equal partnership in Bowater-Scott Corporation Limited to manufacture and convert tissue for domestic and industrial use in Britain. This development led in turn to Bowater-Scott partnerships with Belgian and Italian paper-making companies, and to the establishment at Melbourne of the first integrated tissue manufacturing and conversion plant in Australia.

Sir Eric took the decision in 1959 to move into the promising new market of postwar Europe. He first acquired two packaging companies in Belgium, one in France and one in Italy. This was followed in 1960 by the acquisition of a paper mill at Rouen, a pulp mill at Strasbourg, and a packaging plant in Rome. Today there is a Bowater holding company, Bowater Europe S.A. in Brussels, controlling these continental interests.

An entirely new development has been the establishment in 1961 of a plant in Britain to manufacture pitch fibre pipe. Early in 1961 Bowater Philips, operating a big new corrugated case plant at Ghent, Belgium, was opened by the Belgian Prime Minister.

This vast and varied empire was created in 35 years by the vision and unrelenting energy of one man: a man who rarely took a holiday, and who maintained a day-to-day interest in every facet of its manifold activities until his death.

He farmed a 300-acre estate at his home, Dene Place, West Horsley, Surrey, where he founded a prize herd of pedigree attested Guernsey cattle in 1935.

His other business interests included directorships of Sun Alliance Insurance Limited, the Alliance Assurance Company and Lloyds Bank. He was an Officer of the Legion of Honour and a Fellow of the Royal Society of Arts.

He married in 1937 Margaret Vivian, daughter of Charles Perkins. She survives him with their son and two daughters.

August 31, 1962.

Professor F. P. Bowden, C.B.E., F.R.S., Professor of Surface Physics and Director of the Sub-Department of Surface Physics at the Cavendish Laboratory, Cambridge, died on September 3, 1968, at the age of 65.

Frank Philip Bowden, the son of Frank Posser Bowden, was born and brought up in Tasmania, and was educated there, and held for a year a demonstratorship in physics in the University of Tasmania. In 1927 he obtained an 1851 Exhibition, which enabled him to work in the Department of Colloid Science at Cambridge.

METAL BEHAVIOUR

Here he became interested in the surfaces of catalytic metals and obtained many interesting results especially in the effect of activation and of sintering on the specific surface, and also on the rates of decay of the electro-deposited monolayer of hydrogen and of oxygen.

On completion of this work he joined C. P. Snow, now Lord Snow, who had taken his degree in the laboratory at the same time, on a photochemical investigation of calciteral and ergosterol. While at first the work showed promise it was later found to be somewhat complex, with the result that Bowden returned to his early interests in the surfaces of metals and to problems connected with friction. He became a lecturer in the Department of Physical Chemistry, and Director of Studies in natural science at Caius.

After a lecture tour in the United States, he was visiting his former home in Tasmania when war was declared. In 1940 he was asked by Sir David Rivett, chairman of the Council for Scientific and Industrial Research (the forerunner of the Commonwealth Scientific and Industrial Research Organization), to set up a laboratory for the study of wartime problems associated with friction and lubrication. The group was called the Lubricants and Bearings Section and was housed in the Chemistry Department of the University of Melbourne. It grew to about 20 scientific workers and a total staff of 50 and their work rapidly expanded.

PARTS NOT AVAILABLE

Bowden's skill in blending fundamental and technological discoveries inspired the team to produce several developments of importance to the Australian war effort. Replacement parts for many aircraft engines were not available in Australia and the necessary sophisticated methods of manufacture and testing were developed. Concurrently the idea was developed that friction was caused by the fracture of minute welded junctions between the sliding surfaces and the importance of soap formation during lubrication by fatty acids was discovered. These studies have influenced all modern ideas about friction and lubrication.

An early investigation into the origin of an industrial explosion developed into a major research effort and important discoveries were made about the initiation and propagation of explosive reactions in liquid and solid explosives. His policy was to assemble a group with a wide variety of disciplines and to try to interest each member in two problems, one fundamental, the other technological. The result was a wide variety of original work. A few years after he left in 1944 the section was renamed and then became the Division of Tribophysics of the Commonwealth Scientific and Industrial Research Organization, which still continues in many essential respects the tradition established by Bowden.

After the war he continued work in the Physical Chemistry Department at Cambridge.

FRICTION STUDIES

In association with Dr. Tabor, his continuing researches were responsible for our present understanding of the nature of friction between two moving bodies, which is perhaps his best known achievement. The results of this work are embodied in the well-known book Friction and Lubrication of Solids.

In view of his interest in the practical applications of science in industry, it was natural that he should be asked in 1954 by Sir Ivan Stedeford, chairman of Tube Investments Ltd., to advise on the creation of new research facilities in support of that company. In the belief that both industry and the university would benefit by geographical proximity, a site was chosen at Hinxton Hall, 10 miles from Cambridge for a central research laboratory, where in the following years were gathered a group of active young scientists some of whom had indeed been trained in Bowden's laboratory in Cambridge.

In 1957 his Cambridge research group was made a subdepartment of the Cavendish laboratory, always referred to as "P.C.S.", or more fully "the Sub-Department for the Physics and Chemistry of Solids"; it was housed in old buildings along Free School Lane.

LOVED RESEARCH

Bowden was a man who loved the research life at Cambridge, and, apart from the war years, could not be tempted away. His election in 1965 to a chair in the Cavendish in "physics of surfaces" gave him great pleasure. He was a keen mountaineer and skier, and indeed through his study of friction made some contribution to the science of this sport.

He married in 1931 Margot Hutchison, also a Tasmanian; she and three sons and a daughter survive him.

September 4, 1968.

By the death of **Sir David Bowes-Lyon,** K.C.V.O., at Ballater in Scotland on September 13, 1961, many walks of British life suffered a severe loss. He was 59. In the City generally and in banking particularly, in the county of Hertford of which he was Lord Lieutenant, in the world of horticulture, at the British Museum, of which he had been a trustee since 1953, in Printing House Square, and in a number of other fields he was a constantly active figure. It was his nature to give devoted and whole-hearted service to any activity he took up. Great charm did not blunt an incisive mind. Working associations quickly developed into personal friendships; at the same time the good of whatever cause was being served was kept paramount.

David Bowes-Lyon was born on May 2, 1902. He was the sixth son of the fourteenth Earl of Strathmore, and was therefore a brother of Queen Elizabeth the Queen Mother and an uncle of the Queen. From Eton he went to Magdalen College, Oxford. In 1929 he married Rachel, the younger daughter of Lieutenant-Colonel the Rt. Hon. H. H. Spender-Clay. They had one son and one daughter. Lady Bowes Lyon was her husband's enthusiastic helper in all he did.

Sir David's business experience was gained in the first place as a merchant banker but after a while his interests and responsibilities covered a much wider field including as they did directorships of such other institutions as Martins Bank, Cunard, Dunlops, and The Times Publishing Co. At the time of his death he was a managing director of Lazards and sub-governor of the Royal Exchange Assurance.

He was appointed a director of The Times Publishing Company in February, 1939. He became chairman of the finance committee in June, 1955, and took an active part in the company's financial affairs. He also took a keen interest in *The Gardeners' Chronicle* and attended meetings in an advisory capacity.

During the war Sir David undertook a number of important tasks. In 1940, he was in the Ministry of Economic Warfare; later he was associated with Special Operations Executive.

WARTIME DUTIES

His outstanding contribution was made when he moved to Washington in 1942 as head of the Political Warfare Mission. His first task there was to establish relations with parallel American agencies on a basis of confidence. For this he was perfectly equipped. He not only quickly had his office on a really close and worthwhile working basis with all its transatlantic associates; he also had access to the President. Franklin Roosevelt became one of his admirers.

Much has been written about the problem of Anglo-American relationships during the war. In some spheres no doubt there were difficulties though on the whole too much has been made of them. But both at the time and in all the years that passed subsequently there was a constantly growing appreciation of what Bowes-Lyon achieved. Both the work he did and the way he did it gained substantial praise from those on both sides of the Atlantic who had had anything to do with those particular matters. Some of the work has remained secret.

Certainly Bowes-Lyon's range went much farther than his ostensible brief and beyond the terms of reference that have been made public. At one stage he took a particular interest in Far Eastern affairs as well as those in Washington. He himself never talked very much about the work he did in the war years; his colleagues remember it with both respect and warmth.

Throughout his life Sir David was passionately interested in plants and every aspect of horticulture. He spent a period of training in the Royal Botanic Gardens at Kew and at one time intended to make horticulture his career. He found great relaxation from his busy life in the City through his work for the Royal Horticultural Society, the Gardeners Royal Benevolent Society of which he was honorary treasurer from 1953 to 1960, and in his own beautiful garden at St. Paul's Walden Bury. His service to the Royal Horticultural Society began when he became a member of the council in 1934. He became treasurer in 1948, and when Lord Aberconway died in 1953 he was the obvious choice to succeed him as president. He brought to that office enthusiasm and a democratic approach which endeared him to everybody. Under his leadership many new projects were brought to fruition, the fellowship was almost doubled, and the vast improvements to the Wisley gardens were due in no small part to his drive and encouragement. He was awarded the Victoria Medal of Honour in Horticulture in 1953.

He was chairman of the Gardens Committee of the National Trust since 1953.

His interests in gardens was by no means confined to Great Britain. He was indefatigable in his zeal to project Britain overseas and he attended the great flower shows in the United States and in Europe as a representative of the Royal Horticultural Society and as a judge.

In 1957 largely through Sir David's insistence the British Committee for Overseas Flower Shows was formed and he was its first chairman.

FLORALIES SUCCESS

As a result of his efforts Britain for the first time was adequately represented at an international flower show in Europe and gained conspicuous success at the Paris Floralies in 1958 and at Ghent in 1960.

His own garden at St. Paul's Walden Bury is on a clay soil—a challenge to even the most ardent gardener. It was laid out in the style of Le Notre and the superb avenues of beeches were planted by Sir David's own hands. It is a delightful combination of the formal and informal. In the wood Sir David grew rhododendrons, azaleas, and primulas unusually well in such inhospitable soil. He also had a great fondness for peonies and roses, both the species and hybrids which he always grew himself.

He became a Justice of the Peace for Hertfordshire in 1939, Deputy Lieutenant in 1946, High Sheriff in 1950 and Lord Lieutenant in 1952.

He was created K.C.V.O. in 1959; in 1957 Belgium bestowed on him the Order of Leopold.

September 14, 1961.

Admiral Sir Denis W. Boyd., K.C.B., C.B.E., D.S.C., who died on January 21, 1965, at the age of 73, played a prominent part in naval aviation during the Second World War.

As a sub-lieutenant he was enthusiastic for aviation, and actually learnt clandestinely to fly—without the knowledge, approval or permission of the Admiralty—at the Naval Air Station at Eastchurch. But he was not one of the very few regular naval officers who were selected or allowed to specialize in flying, so that he never performed flying duty, or indeed served with the Fleet Air Arm, until he took command of the new aircraft carrier Illustrious on her completion in 1940. It was under his command that her aircraft crippled the Italian Fleet at Taranto in 1940. obtaining torpedo hits on three of the six battleships present and thereby altering the balance of naval power in the Mediterranean. Later in the war he commanded the aircraft carriers of the Mediterranean and Eastern Fleets, and from 1943 to 1945 was Fifth Sea Lord (Air). During the First World War he was decorated for service in submarines.

Denis William Boyd was born on March 6, 1891, the son of William John Boyd. He entered the Navy with the last term of Britannia cadets in 1906, joining the new R. N. College, Dartmouth, direct, as the old ship had then been discarded. He passed out and was rated midshipman in May, 1907. In 1915 he joined the Vernon to specialize in torpedoes, and six months later was appointed to the submarine depot for torpedo duties with these craft. From September, 1916, he was torpedo officer of the light cruiser Fearless, leader of the Grand Fleet submarines, with which he served for the rest of the war. The D.S.C. was awarded him in 1918. He commanded the Vivien and Valentine in 1932–33 as a division leader in the 6th Destroyer Flotilla, and then joined the Tactical Division, of which he was Director from 1934 to 1936. For the next two years he commanded the 4th and 2nd Destroyer Flotillas, in the Keith and Hardy, in the Mediterranean, during the period of the Spanish Civil War. He returned in 1938 to take command of the Vernon, torpedo school.

SAFELY TO PORT

His first command afloat in the war was the new aircraft carrier Illustrious, from which was launched in November, 1940, the attack which crippled the Italian battle fleet in harbour at Taranto. Later at Malta and on passage to Alexandria German dive bombers made strenuous efforts to destroy the Illustrious, but Boyd by his stubborn defence and skilful handling of the ship got her safely to port, though damaged. He was made C.B.E. In 1941 he was made Flag Officer (Air) in the Mediterranean. After an eventful year in the Mediterranean he was transferred to a similar command in the Eastern Fleet under Admiral Somerville, with his flag in the Indomitable, and was present at the assault on Madagascar in May, 1942. In 1943 he was appointed to the Board of Admiralty as Fifth Sea Lord and Chief of Naval Air Equipment, and held the post until April, 1945. He was made C.B. in 1943 and in 1945 was promoted K.C.B. That year he took up the new appointment of Admiral (Air) in charge of all naval air stations in the British Isles and to coordinate all flying training in the Royal Navy. In 1946 Boyd became Commander-in-Chief, British Pacific Fleet in succession to Admiral Sir Bruce Fraser, and hoisted his flag in the aircraft carrier Venerable at Singapore.

He served in the Far East until the end of 1948, was promoted to admiral in January, 1948, and retired in 1949.

To commemorate Boyd's work the Fairey Aviation Company some years ago presented the Boyd Trophy, which is awarded annually for the most meritorious feat of naval aviation.

In December, 1949, Boyd succeeded General Sir Bernard Paget as Principal of Ashridge College and held the post until 1957.

He was keen on outdoor sports, and played hockey, tennis, golf, and Rugby football. For many years he was an official Rugby football referee.

He married in 1915, Audrey Edoline, daughter of Lieutenant-Colonel A. B. Shakespear, R.M.A., and had two sons and two daughters. One son died in 1925.

January 23, 1965.

Sir Richard Boyer, K.B.E., died on June 5, 1961, at Sydney, aged 69. He was not only one of the main architects of Australian broadcasting but also one of the most distinguished Australians of his time. A devoted visitor to Britain, he was known by a wide circle on both sides of the globe and admired for his ideals and his grasp.

Boyer's life was so varied that many early periods seem unrelated to its long distinguished ending as chairman of the Australian Broadcasting Commission from 1945. However it was probably this variety together with a close and constant relation to the Australian ideal of what a man should do which prepared him for his finest work. The A.B.C. needed more than ever a liberal chief, and Boyer's liberalism, which reasserted the freedom of national broadcasting after wartime toils with the Government and set national television on a firm footing, was the tough product of English nonconformity derived from his parents, and Australian independence derived from the Bush where he worked for many years.

Soon after his appointment Boyer said it was the commission's responsibility to choose matter "which touches ethical, religious, political, and aesthetic tastes of the community. We do not regard our function as achieved if we merely keep out of trouble". The commission's job was to help to build an informed, critical, cultural democracy. Boyer never failed to lead the commission this way. In July, 1946, for example, broadcasting Parliamentary proceedings began as a regular service and in June, 1947. A.B.C.S. Independent News Service came into full operation.

Richard James Fildes Boyer was born in the country town of Taree, New South Wales, on August 24, 1891, the son of the Rev. F.C. Boyer, a Presbyterian minister from Manchester. He was educated at Newington College, Sydney, and Sydney University, where he graduated with first class honours in European History.

He was ordained a Presbyterian minister and in December, 1914, became padre at the Royal Military College, Duntroon, near Canberra. But very soon he felt impelled to go to war as lay representative of the Y.M.C.A. in Egypt whence he stowed away on a ship bound for Gallipoli, somehow becoming a private during the voyage. Subsequently he was invalided home and later returned to Duntroon as a cadet officer and rejoined the A.I.F. in France as a platoon commander. He was gassed at Passchendaele and later repatriated.

In 1920 he married his nurse, Elenor Muriel Underwood, by whom he had a son and a daughter, and went on medical advice to live as soldier-settler in the dry Outback of Queensland.

They lived for three years on a 60,000-acre property, 90 miles from Charleville, where Boyer built his own homestead. Drought and depression forced him from cattle to sheep, and it was 10 years before he prospered. Until 1937 he managed the place himself. Wider responsibilities then claimed him, but he remained in appearance and character very much of the land.

From the beginning his public life was by no means all based on country affairs. In 1939 he attended not only the World Agricultural Conference at Dresden, but also the League of Nations Assembly as Australian delegate. In 1941 he was president of the Graziers' Federal Council of Australia and was president of the United Graziers' Association of Queensland from 1941 to 1944. He led the Australian delegation to the Pacific Relations conferences at Montreal in 1942 and at Hot Springs in 1945. He was delegate to the British Commonwealth Relations Conference in London in 1945 and was president of the Australian Institute of International Affairs from 1946 to 1948. For most of the last war he was honorary director of the American division of the Australian Ministry of Information and was A.B.C. Commissioner for Queensland from 1940 to 1945.

In 1950 he visited the United Kingdom and the United States to study television there before reporting to the Government on the establishment of television in Australia. He said he welcomed television as he welcomed all new knowledge: its hazards should be faced, its rewards reaped. It was the sensible approach of a man whose life was an unusual mixture of the intellectual and the earthy.

SOCIAL ASPECTS

As Boyer's interest in broadcasting and television was always in their social implications rather than in their administrative problems or scientific possibilities he was almost as concerned about what happened in British broadcasting as in developments in Australia. He took a continuing interest in the proceedings of the Beveridge Committee in 1949–50 and appeared before them. He had during recent months taken an equally lively interest in the progress of Sir Harry Pilkington's Committee and had hoped to be able to visit Britain again during its sittings. In recent letters to friends he had said how greatly he was looking forward to yet another visit. It can be said that he had a strong care for the B.B.C.'s wellbeing. The things it had always tried to do were those he most deeply believed in. Of late years, however, his health had begun to fail, and his heart became affected.

FAILING STRENGTH

He remained the same eager, earnestly questioning, vital, diffident yet impressive figure. But it was clear that he had to harbour his strength. The old stamina was no longer there. He will be mourned by many concerned with public affairs, culture, and commerce, as well as by all who have to do with braodcasting.

Boyer was vice-president of the Australian Elizabethan Theatre Trust. He constantly refreshed himself by visiting his property in Queensland. He was made K.B.E. in 1956.

June 6, 1961.

Lord Brabazon of Tara died on May 17, 1964, at his home at Chertsey, at the age of 80. His appetite for life was only equalled by his appetite for adventure (which never noticeably diminished), and in a career which it would be trite to describe as adventurous he had been a pioneer flier and motorist, yachtsman, scratch golfer ("the best bad golfer in England," according to Mr. Roger Wethered), and champion performer on the Cresta Run.

He celebrated his 70th birthday by taking a bobsleigh ride down the Cresta Run at St. Moritz and in 1963, at the age of 79, drove a Mercedes sports car at 115 m.p.h. over Salisbury Plain.

Yet though a formidable figure in so many physical pursuits his life was not dominated by them. He sat for many years in Parliament, and had been first Minister of Transport and later Minister of Aircraft Production in Sir Winston Churchill's wartime administration.

"Brab", as he was always known among his big circle of friends, will be remembered, more for his quality of frankness and his skill in ironical wit which went on gaining him unsought platforms right to the end of his days, than for his share in a host of sporting and scientific activities or for his achievements as inventor, administrator, and servant of his chosen causes. He was brilliant as an analyst of situations and a deviser of solutions; he was industrious beyond belief in his treatment of duties and his application to tasks: he was original in the best sense and often found his way around awkward corners, especially as a politician facing emergencies.

FLYING WORLD

Until he died he remained a power in the flying world, on the touring and sporting side through the Royal Aero Club which he served as president; on the commercial and technological side through his chairmanship of the Air Registration Board, the body which is responsible for the issue of certificates of airworthiness and so lays down in effect the standards which new developments must satisfy. He made his influence felt in other ways by speaking out as a private citizen on subjects on which he felt strongly. One such subject was the use by a small minority of air lines of a form of petrol for their jet engines instead of the more general paraffin. He challenged the president of one of the lines to stand in the middle of a puddle of his fuel, and scatter lighted matches while he, Brab, did the same in a puddle of paraffin, to prove how much more dangerous in a crash the one fuel would be than the other. The challenge was not taken up but the subject gained immense publicity particularly on television screens with Brab the central figure in a series of demonstrations.

Lieutenant-Colonel the Right Hon. John Theodore Cuthbert Moore-Brabazon, P.C., G.B.E., M.C., first Lord Brabazon of Tara of Sandwich in the county of Kent in the Peerage of the United Kingdom, was born on February 8, 1884, the son of Lieutenant-Colonel J. A. H. Moore-Brabazon, of Tara Hall, co. Meath, Ireland, and his wife. Emma Sophia, daughter of Alfred Richards, of Forest Hill.

EARLY MOTORIST

He was educated at Harrow and at Trinity College, Cambridge, and while still a youth, before the turn of the century, he began to indulge in the then new-fangled pastime of motoring, starting with a seven horse-power Panhard two-cylinder. In the course of a long and enthusiastic career as a motorist he was eventually to sample more than 200 makes of car and to become chairman of the Order of the Road. Soon after leaving college he began motor racing, frequently in association with the Hon. C. S. Rolls, his friend, whom he would serve as an amateur mechanic. His biggest racing success was the winning of the Circuit des Ardennes in 1907. He drove a Minerva under the Kaiserpreis Formula and won a hotly contested race from Koolhoven by 27 seconds. At the same meeting he finished second to Porlict in the Leiderkirke Cup, again in a Minerva.

1908 FLIGHT

At this same early date Moore-Brabazon was already exploring the possibilities of aviation and built two not very effective aeroplanes. A year later, in December, 1908, he accomplished a flight of 450 yards in his own machine at Issy-les-Moulineaux, being the first Englishman to fly such a distance. He had his eye on the Channel, and if he had not lost time on the project by insisting on his machine being all-British, the honour of the first crossing might well have come to Britain instead of to France. In 1909 he won the *Daily Mail* prize of £1,000 for flying a circular mile in an all-English made aircraft at the Isle of Sheppey, the machine being a wheelless Voisin, launched by catapult. Another trophy won was the first British Empire Michelin Cup.

During the period April 30–May 2, 1909, Moore-Brabazon was at Eastchurch with his aeroplane, and on the latter date he made the first flight accomplished by any Briton in Great Britain. This claim was substantiated 20 years later (February, 1929) by a specially appointed committee of the Royal Aero Club, which weighed it against rival claims by A. H. Phillips and A. V. Roe. In 1910 Moore-Brabazon received the first pilot's certificate ever issued by the club. In the Four Years' War he served in France from 1914 to 1918 with the Royal Flying Corps (later R.A.F.), winning promotion in April 1915 from assistant equipment officer to equipment officer with the rank of captain. He was awarded the Military Cross and rose to lieutenant-colonel. His principal task in this war was the development of aerial photography; and when in June, 1926, the Royal Commission on Awards to Inventors was at work he submitted his claim to have invented the first really effective air camera.

PARLIAMENTARY CAREER

At the 1918 election Moore-Brabazon was elected to Parliament as Unionist member for the Chatham division of Rochester, and he continued to represent that division until ejected in the big Labour turnover of 1929. His knowledge of aviation was employed when he was co-opted to the first Civil Aviation Committee, Lord Weir's advisory committee, and the Air Mails Committee (of which he was chairman); and for some time he was chairman of the Royal Aero Club. In 1923–24, and again from the end of 1924 to 1927, he was Parliamentary Secretary to the Ministry of Transport, and during the latter period he nursed the Electricity Act through Parliament.

In January, 1927, he resigned from the Ministry to take up a City career. He was out of Parliament from 1929 to 1931, but in 1930–31 he served as an assessor on the commission of inquiry into the R 101 disaster. He was one of two possible candidates for a by-election at St. George's. Westminster, in March. 1931, but when Lord Beaverbrook's anti-Baldwin nominee, Sir Ernest Petter, intervened Moore-Brabazon withdrew, not wishing to fight an election on a personal issue. He was a member of the L.C.C. for St. George's in 1931–32; and at the general election of 1931 was re-elected to Parliament in the Conservative interest for Wallasey. He continued to devote a good deal of attention to aviation, and was president of the Royal Aeronautical Society in 1935. He was very outspoken in his advocacy of rapid rearmament, being one of those members who remained profoundly sceptical of "appeasement." Minor office came to him again during Sir Samuel Hoare's brief tenure of the Air portfolio in 1940, when he acted as parliamentary private secretary.

In May, 1940, Moore-Brabazon was appointed Minister of Transport, and there was a peculiar relevance in the appointment, for he was the first holder of this portfolio to have spent many years actually studying methods and problems of transport. He showed a vigorous and practical skill as administrator, bringing the provincial buses to London, introducing the "free lifts" system for private cars, and advocating an extra hour of summer-time to obviate some of the traffic dangers caused by the blackout.

LABOUR CENSURE

He became Minister of Aircraft Production in May, 1941, succeeding Lord Beaverbrook, but was obliged to resign in the spring of 1942 after a speech to a private gathering, in which he was said to have expressed the hope that the German and Russian armies would exterminate each other, had brought on him strong Labour censure. With characteristic phlegm, the author in his autobiography *The Brabazon Story* referred to this closure of his ministerial career as "rather inglorious and very silly." In March, 1942, he was raised to the peerage.

Not for long was his connexion with the air to be severed, for he was chosen to preside over the Civil Aviation Committee on Post-War Transport, known popularly as the Brabazon Committee, set up first in 1943. This recommended, *inter alia* the modification of four types of aircraft, then in current use, for post war service; they were the York, Sunderland, Halifax, and Tudor. Five new machines were proposed—among them the DH. Dove, the Airspeed Ambassador and the Bristol Brabazon, named in his honour but never fated to achieve his distinction in the air. He was president of the Royal Institution from 1948 to 1963 and at his death was honorary Professor Extraordinary.

SPORTING SKILLS

He was highly proficient at a number of sports: the hazards of the bobsleigh appealed to him and he was well known on the Cresta Run at St. Moritz, winning the Curzon Cup in 1920, 1922, and 1927 and being one of the first dozen bobsleigh riders even when past his half-century.

Through his enthusiasm for golf and through his desire to put something back into the game which had given him so much pleasure, he came to occupy the highest posts of honour on the amateur and professional side. In 1952 he drove himself in—it was not a stroke on which he later chose to dwell—as captain of the Royal and Ancient. Two years later he was elected president of the Professional Golfers' Association, and in that office he became an active figurehead, remaining aloof from petty differences but bringing dignity and humour to formal occasions both here and in America. In spite of failing health he became a cohesive force through difficult times and rendered the association service which it is not likely to forget. As a golfer he got down to scratch within a few months of taking up the game, and although there was something contrived about his swing, as a putter he was quite out of the ordinary.

GOLF UNION POST

He became president of the English Golf Union in 1938.

Moore-Brabazon was a sturdy, slcw-moving man: he might have been debited by a stranger with an indolence that was, in fact, not at all part of his temperament.

He married in 1906 Hilda, daughter of the late Charles H. Krabbé, of Buenos Aires, and two sons were born of the marriage. The younger son died in 1950.

The barony now passes to the elder son, the Hon. Derek Charles Moore-Brabazon, who was born in 1910 and who married in 1939 Henriette Mary, daughter of Sir Rowland Clegg. There is a son of the marriage.

May 18, 1964.

Bessie Braddock, former Labour M.P. for Liverpool Exchange, died in Rathbone Hospital, Liverpool, on November 13, 1970. She was 71. She was one of the most vivid and robust personalities in the Labour movement. From 1945 to 1970 she was M.P. for the Exchange Division of Liverpool, hitherto believed to be an impregnable Conservative stronghold. She was a fighter all her political life, a fearless champion of the poor, the underprivileged and the oppressed against "Toryism, capitalism and the boss-class". Her combative spirit plunged her into conflict not only with these traditional enemies of her political faith but with leftwing elements in her own party whom she suspected of seeking to erode it with Communistic influences.

Her implacable opposition to Bevanism was another facet of this deep antagonism to the left which some found so hard to understand in one who was such a natural rebel, a Socialist who constitutionally was almost incapable of detecting any saving grace in a Conservative. Before the 1955 General Election there was a move within her local party to oppose her candidature and although she was eventually readopted she had to face a rival independent Labour contestant.

The right-central position which she held for the greater part of her political career may have been a reaction from the Communism she and her husband embraced for a time after the First World War. She had been drawn into it on an idealistic, emotional impulse deriving from the socialistic ardour with which her remarkable parents, "Ma and Pa Bamber", had imbued her as a girl. But she revolted against the excessive rigidity of the Communist system and she conceived a contempt for "near-Communists" and those whose ideas on defence savoured to her realistic mind as cranky sentimentalism. She was equally impatient of those who criticized her beloved boxing as degrading and brutalizing.

MARRIED EX-BOXER

She had married a former boxer and was honorary president of the Professional Boxers' Association. The Commons much enjoyed a set-to between herself and Dr. Edith (Baroness) Summerskill on this topic. In another sense she was an ardent exponent of the art of self-defence, ever prompt to uphold her rights and principles if necessary in the courts, the council chamber and the House. She figured in one or two scenes in Liverpool City Council and she was the first woman M.P. to be suspended from a sitting of the Commons.

With her generous frame, rosy countenance and forthright north country voice and manner, she was one of those M.P.s who always created a stir of interest in the public galleries. She invariably occupied the same seat at the end of the front row below the gangway. There she would amply dispose herself, her arms along the back of the bench, contemplating with undisguised distaste the ranks opposite.

Elizabeth Margaret Bamber was born in Liverpool in September, 1899, daughter of Hugh Bamber, a working man who had embraced the then unpopular tenets of Socialism and had become a prominent exponent thereof in the city. "Bessie" was thus brought up in a political atmosphere.

Bessie left her elementary school in 1914 to become an assistant in the Liverpool Co-operative Society's store. Her parents were against the war, and the girl had her baptism of political fire as a distributor of literature at anti-war meetings which aroused angry passions.

In the early twenties, when the post-war boom had given way to depression and unemployment. Bessie began to speak at meetings of the unemployed; and about this time she married John Braddock, head of the committee formed in Liverpool to look after their interests. (He died in 1963). Mrs. Braddock was by no means content to remain a mere agitator. She took a more and more active part in the trade union, Labour and cooperative movements, and made herself knowledgeable in local government matters and municipal procedure.

The Braddocks were Communists until 1924, when they left that party for Labour. They were associated together for some years as leaders of deputations and protest meetings, and were always at the storm-centre of Liverpool politics. Their acerbity was often an embarrassment to more moderate-minded colleagues.

In 1930 Mrs. Braddock and her husband were both elected to the Liverpool City Council (he later became the first Labour leader of the council) and imported into the council chamber the fighting propensities that had been evident in street meetings. Mrs. Braddock was twice "named" and twice escorted out of the Council by the police, once for persisting in argument when she had been ruled out of order, and once for calling a fellow member a "deliberate liar" and refusing to withdraw.

She was returned to Parliament at the General Election of 1945, to the surprise of most people with a majority of 639. She soon attracted attention with her downright, forceful and somewhat truculent manner and her sturdy commonsense.

In February, 1947, she was elected to fill the vacancy on the Labour Party National Executive Committee (she was a member for 22 years) caused by the death of Ellen Wilkinson.

SCENE IN COMMONS

Some two or three months later she took part in a demonstration in the House, during the committee stage of the Transport Bill, when with other Labour members she crossed the floor to sit on the empty Conservative side. Her manner of doing so was described in a newspaper as "dancing a jig" and she brought an action for libel. The case caused much stir and petitions were presented in the House to obtain leave for the attendance of M.P.s, officials and pressmen as witnesses. She lost the case and her appeal.

The incident which resulted in her being the first woman member to be suspended from the service of the House occurred in March, 1952, during a 23 hour sitting. She was evidently suffering from a sense of injustice because after a seven-hour wait she was not called to speak when she had understood she would be. She refused to obey the Deputy Speaker's order, first to resume her seat and then to withdraw from the Chamber. The Speaker having been sent for, he formally "named" her and the motion for her suspension was carried. When she was directed to withdraw she observed that she would do so with pleasure.

Meanwhile she had come into the public eye in the slightly improbable field of fashion. She opened an exhibition of "outsize" women's clothes and acted as a model for them. Her quite serious purpose was to demonstrate that designers and manufacturers could produce dresses for stout women of slender means.

TASTE IN DRESS

Bessie herself always dressed with excellent taste. She confessed to weighing nearly 15 stone but she was a comely woman, neat and quick in her movements, and by no means the amazon she was sometimes thought to be.

During the 1950s her outspoken opposition to Bevanism caused increasing tension with members of her constituency party and it came to a head in 1954 with a proposal from within the local party that she should be asked to resign at the next election. An inquiry was ordered by the National Executive Committee who afterwards rejected the proposal. It seemed for a time that the troubles between her and her constituency party had been smoothed over but a fresh crisis blew up in the spring of 1955 which resulted in a local decision not to support her candidature. The National Executive Committee ordered an inquiry into the procedure of a meeting at which this had been decided, and advised her reinstatement. In the event a resolution for her readoption was carried, but some members of the party left the meeting before it was voted on and a number of others abstained. Later the chairman and secretary of the local party resigned and so did Councillor Lawrence Murphy who decided to oppose her in the May General Election as Independent Labour candidate. Mrs. Braddock was returned with a majority of 7.186.

Mrs. Braddock was chairman of the House of Commons Kitchen Committee (later the Catering Sub-Committee) from 1964 until 1967, when she was succeeded by Mr. Robert Maxwell. In 1970 she announced that after 25 years as Labour M.P. for Liverpool Exchange, she would retire. In February she became Liverpool's first woman Freeman.

November 14, 1970.

Lord Brain, F.R.S., D.M., F.R.C.P., former president of the Royal College of Physicians of London, and of the British Association, died on December 29, 1966, at his home in London. He was 71.

Brain was a celebrated physician with an international reputation in his chosen speciality of neurology, but he achieved distinction in many other fields, for he was a man of wide interests and great intellectual powers. By his death British medicine has lost one of its most renowned figures.

Walter Russell Brain was born on October 23, 1895, son of Walter John Brain, a Reading solicitor. He was educated at Mill Hill School and New College, Oxford. Initially he read law, but later decided to pursue a career in medicine. He became the Theodore Williams Scholar in Physiology during his pre-clinical days at Oxford, where he was a pupil of Sherrington, proceeding to the London Hospital as Price Entrance Scholar for his clinical work. His contemporaries at the London immediately marked him down as a man of great ability and outstanding maturity and character; the promise which he then displayed was amply fulfilled in a career of distinction in many fields of activity. Brain's interest in the nervous system developed at Oxford, and after qualification in 1922 he held junior appointments at the London Hospital and Maida Vale Hospital for Nervous Diseases. He was elected to the staff of the London in 1927, thus joining the talented group of physicians which included Arthur Ellis, Otto Leyton, George Riddoch, and John Parkinson. His election to the staff of Maida Vale took place in 1925. These remained his major appointments until his retirement in 1960.

FLOW OF ORIGINAL PAPERS

Brain rapidly gained a reputation as an able clinician, but in spite of the demand of practice and medico-political work he produced a steady flow of original papers and reviews dealing with a variety of neurological topics from 1924 until after his retirement. He made important contributions to clinical neurology and his writings were characterized by exceptional clarity and verbal felicity. In 1933 the first edition of his textbook, *Diseases of the Nervous System,* was greeted with some criticism from his seniors, for Brain was young to produce such a comprehensive work.

However, the book was soon accepted internationally as an authoritative work and passed through many editions.

He also published *Recent Advances in Neurology,* with the late Dr. Eric Strauss, a lifelong friend from Oxford days, *Clinical Neurology* and *Speech Disorders.* Like his distinguished predecessor at the London, Sir Henry Head, Russell Brain was attracted to the study of speech and the problem of the mind-body relationship; his writings on these subjects were remarkably clear and formed the basis of many lectures and broadcast talks. Although Brain was much interested in the philosophical aspects of neurology he was equally at home in scientific or clinical discussions. Indeed, his clinical skill alone was sufficient to win him a prominent place in his profession; he was always likely to throw new light on the elucidation of a difficult problem, so that his services as a consultant were in great demand.

EDITED JOURNAL ON BRAINS

He was editor of the neurological journal *Brain* for many years.

Brain was elected president of the Royal College of Physicians in 1950 and held the office until 1957. Until this time he had confined his medico-political activities to the hospitals where he worked and to service on various committees of the British Medical Association.

On the wider stage his talents as chairman and diplomatist found full scope for their expression. Much of his time was given to negotiations with the Ministry of Health in those early days of the National Health Service.

In retrospect it seems a pity that his abilities were necessarily employed in this way for so much of his presidency, though he made a notable contribution to the welfare of his professional colleagues through his skill as a negotiator.

Brain's professional standing was also recognized by his election to the presidencies of the Association of British Neurologists and the International Society of Internal Medicine. He was also president of the Family Planning Association.

Besides his professional distinction, Brain acquired a reputation for his activities as literary critic and philosopher, for literature and philosophy were his main delights outside his work. He used his neurological and psychiatric knowledge to good effect in exploring the works and lives of such writers as Swift, Smart and Johnson, and his various publications on these subjects were gathered together in *Some Reflections on Genius and Other Essays* (1960). As a philosopher he was especially concerned to ensure that philosophical theories on perception should pay due regard to the known philosophical facts. He was no mean poet and shared an interesting friendship with Walter de la Mare; in *Tea with Walter de la Mare* he recorded many of their conversations. In 1963 he was president of the Johnson Society of Lichfield.

COOL IN DEBATE

He published *Speech Disorders* in 1961, and in 1964 *Doctors Past and Present*.

Brain was a man of imposing appearance and bore himself with an innate unconscious air of distinction. He possessed an enviable calmness, never allowing himself to become ruffled or angry in the heat of debate or controversy. There was a certain shyness and diffidence about him so that he was not easy to know, but he strove to overcome this reserve and in later years did much to help young medical men, frequently entertaining them in his home. His advice was sought by leaders of the profession in other parts of the Commonwealth, for these men were well aware of his wisdom. His colleagues regarded him with affectionate pride, and his intimates delighted in his manysided genius. There was an idealistic aspect of his nature which was less apparent than his other qualities, except to those who knew him well; he retained this idealism throughout his life, for it was deeply ingrained, possibly derived from his dissenting radical forbears.

Membership of the Royal Commissions on Marriage and Divorce and the Law Relating to Mental Illness gave him the opportunity to use his powers in the attempted solution of two social problems which were of particular concern to him.

On retirement from hospital work, Brain continued in practice and clinical research, but much of his time was devoted to public and professional service. He was an active president of the Family Planning Association and a painstaking judicial chairman of the Merit Awards Committee. His Royal Commission report on Medical Services in Newfoundland and Labrador was completed shortly before his death. His last major service was as chairman of the Standing Committee on Drug Addiction, which reported in 1966, before he died. The recommendations of this committee were far-reaching, including notification of addicts to a central authority, establishment of treatment centres, restriction of prescribing heroin and cocaine for addicts to the medical staff of these centres, and the setting up of a permanent Standing Committee. These proposals were accepted by the Government, and Brain consented to be chairman of the new Standing Committee.

LETTER OVER CHURCHILL

Both he and his wife joined the Society of Friends, and this was a natural step for one of his temperament and outlook. In May, 1966, he wrote to *The Times* pointing out that without his knowledge Lord Moran had published in his book reports on some consultations between them on Sir Winston Churchill.

Among many honours Brain numbered honorary doctorates of three universities (Wales, Belfast and Newcastle), and honorary fellowships of three Royal Colleges and several overseas societies. Perhaps the honorary fellowship of his old Oxford college gave him most pleasure. He was a gifted speaker and was twice Manson Lecturer of the British Institute of Philosophy; he held the Rede and Riddell Lectureships at Cambridge and Durham Universities respectively, and was Harveian Orator of the Royal College of Physicians in 1959. He was knighted in 1952, created baronet in 1954, and elevated to the peerage in 1962. The following year he was president of the British Association.

His marriage to Stella, daughter of Dr. R. L. Langdon Down, was ideally happy and his wife shared his life to the full. They had two sons, of whom the elder, Christopher, succeeds to the title, and one daughter.

December 30, 1966.

Lord Brand, eminent alike as banker, public servant, and writer and speaker on economic and political affairs, died on August 23, 1963. By his death the nation lost one of its most realistic minds, the City a wise and devoted counsellor, and *The Times* a friend and colleague of many years' standing. He was 84.

He was an outstanding example of a species which has dwindled in numbers over the years—the London private banker who is also economist, philosopher, and, within a certain range, statesman, too. "The London banker", wrote Walter Bagehot in *Lombard Street*, written when the private bank was still paramount, had "especially a charmed value—he was supposed to represent, and often did represent, a certain union of pecuniary sagacity and educated refinement which was scarcely to be found in any other part of society.... Banking is a watchful but not a laborious trade. A banker, even in large business, can feel pretty sure that all his transactions are sound, and yet have much spare mind. A certain part of his time and a considerable part of his thoughts he can readily devote to other pursuits."

In Lord Brand these "other pursuits" were as important a part of his long and fruitful life as his central occupation. He joined Lazard Brothers, of which he was for many years a managing director, in 1909. Behind him at that time already lay a distinguished academic career at Oxford, a Fellowship of All Souls, and seven years with Lord Milner and Lord Selborne in South Africa. Before him lay not only a long life as a successful banker and a leader of financial thought but also a sequence of important appointments, especially during the two world wars, in the service of the British Government and a long record of notable contributions to the discussion of the economic and political problems of his time.

The Rt. Hon. Robert Henry Brand, C.M.G., first Baron Brand, of Eydon, in the county of Northampton, in the Peerage of the United Kingdom, was born on October 30, 1878, and educated at Marlborough and New College, Oxford. He achieved the honour of a Fellowship at All Souls, and his mind was widened by exceptionally interesting political experiences which hereditary aptitude—he was the son of the second Lord Hampden and the descendant of a Speaker of the House of Commons—enabled him to grasp and apply with results that have been shown in his many written and spoken words. From 1902 to 1909 he was serving in South Africa under Lord Milner and afterwards under Lord Selborne. In later years General Smuts, with whom Brand had worked for nearly a year as Secretary of the Transvaal Delegates at the South African National Conventions, which made the Constitution, referred to Brand as "the most outstanding of a very able team". This connexion laid the foundation of his passionate belief in British imperialism, in its soundest and most disinterested form.

CITIZEN OF EMPIRE

With this belief behind him he was inevitably not only a good citizen of the Empire but also saw clearly that the Empire could survive and prosper only as an influence for the welfare of the world outside and for sanity and conciliation in international affairs. This wider aspect of Britain's destiny was confirmed by his activities during the 1914–18 War, first as member of the Imperial Munitions Board of Canada from 1915 to 1918 and then as deputy chairman of the British Mission in Washington in 1917 and 1918. The Peace Conference gave him a fresh point of view as financial adviser to Lord Robert Cecil (as he was then), who was chairman of the Supreme Economic Council at Paris in 1919.

In 1920 Brand was vice-president of the International Financial Conference of the League of Nations held at Brussels; at the Genoa Conference of 1922 he was financial representative of South Africa, and in the same year he acted as a member of the expert committee which advised the German Government concerning the stabilization of the Mark. For some years after 1931 he was one of the British bankers appointed to deal with the German "standstill" arrangements. When the historic Macmillan Committee on Finance and Industry was set up in the dark and bewildering days of 1930, he was an inevitable choice for the committee and in the event he was one of its most influential members. As a man who was at once in sympathy with the liberal and progressive ideas of his fellow committee-member Maynard Keynes and at the same time fully steeped in the orthodox traditions of the City, he was uniquely fitted to find a meeting point between the more extreme views represented in the commission's membership.

Throughout the 1920s and 1930s Lord Brand was engaged largely in the practical work of a merchant banker as a director of Lazards and in making exceptional contributions to unravelling the many and difficult problems which the City faced during those years. He was one of the City's accepted leaders and often played an important part behind the scenes in the settlement of questions involving relationships between the financial world and the Government. He was on terms of close friendship with many of the most eminent Americans of his day and contributed much to the cause of Anglo-American cooperation, especially in the economic sphere.

WORK IN WASHINGTON

The outbreak of war in 1939 brought him back once again to public service, and it was the combination of his knowledge of international economic and financial problems and his close relations with leading people in the United States which decided the missions which he was asked to undertake. For over three years, from April, 1941, until May, 1944, he was head of the British Food Mission in Washington, and for a further two years until May, 1946, he was the Treasury's representative in Washington. The representation of the Treasury during those two critical years, which covered among other things the ending of Lend-Lease and the negotiation of the United States and Canadian loans and the financial and commercial agreements that accompanied them, was a position of great responsibility.

He played an important part in the negotiation of the American loans and Lend-Lease settlements, being one of the principal United Kingdom delegates throughout. He took a leading part also in the discussions which led up to the formation of the International Bank for Reconstruction and Development and the International Monetary Fund, and was one of this country's representatives at the Bretton Woods and Savannah conferences, at which these two institutions were born.

In 1946 he returned to London and to Lazards once again, and for the second time turned from overseas public service to apply himself to the problem of the rehabilitation of British finance and commerce after a great and ruinous war.

CREATED PEER

On his return a barony was conferred on him in recognition of the many services which he had given to his country, especially during the two world wars. The House of Lords opened a new field for his sage counsel, and a series of speeches in the Upper House formed one of the most penetrating and consistent contemporary commentaries on postwar economic policy. From the first he emphasized the paramount importance of the external balance of payments and the decisive contribution which must be made by monetary policy.

Few men can have held a series of appointments which carried with them wider experience of Imperial and international problems; and in Brand's case the seed of this experience was sown on ground admirably prepared by education and heredity to receive and apply it.

STORED MIND

The result was a mind stored with practical facts and considerations but wide open to new impressions and always ready to weigh the many new-fangled theories lately current and to accept them as long as they stood the test of practical possibility. In him British tolerance and readiness to see the other fellow's point of view were carried to their highest point as long as it was merely a matter of discussion; but when it came to action he never forgot that the most admirable theories simply will not do unless they can be grasped and accepted by the ordinary man of business, on whose confidence and activities we all ultimately depend for our bread and butter.

The lessons of experience were the rock on which he founded his economic philosophy, and he reinforced them with a shrewd gift of foresight and his conviction, based on all that he had seen and heard during and after the war, of the imperative need for good will between men, between classes, and between the nations. He expressed himself, both in his writings and in many addresses, in a style marked by admirable lucidity.

LITERARY WORK

Chief among his published works are his study of *The Union of South Africa*, and his *War and National Finance*. He wrote the first book after serving throughout the sittings of the Convention which framed the South Africa Act as secretary to the Transvaal delegation and so would have been exceptionally able, had he so wished, to throw light on the processes by which it was hatched. But *The Times Literary Supplement* in reviewing the work on January 6, 1910, pointed out that: "It is a great misfortune for history that statesmanship in its own interests is sometimes so discreet", and that: "Mr. Brand's discretion is absolutely above reproach." The second book contained a series of articles contributed to the *Round Table* between 1912 and 1920. In it he showed his usual foresight in the opening article, in which he observed that "at present one is almost entitled to suspect that just as the War Office will train the Territorials, so the Treasury hopes to acquire a knowledge of its (wartime) duties after and not before war has broken out".

Again, he pointed out in December, 1914, the absurdity of the then common delusion that financial difficulties would end the war in a few months, reminding his readers of the fact, brought home to them very practically later on, that "so long as a Government has a printing press it can always make 'money'". And in one of the last chapters, written in 1920, he claimed for the financial leaders in all countries that they "are the only people who understand what is happening to the world and the necessity, if our civilization is not to disappear, of cooperation by all to save it".

Apart from these major literary productions, Brand devoted the "much spare mind" which, as Bagehot has told us, bankers enjoy, to a variety of activities. His long and fruitful connexion with the *Round Table* and his valuable contributions in his later years to House of Lords debates have already been mentioned, and he was always ready to throw the dry light of his sound common sense on subjects mooted at conferences or in discussion societies.

He joined the boards of Lloyds Bank and the North British and Mercantile Insurance Company in 1916, resigned from both when he went to Washington but was later reelected.

STATE SUCCOUR

He was chairman of the North British until 1957 and remained on the board of Lloyds Bank until 1959. A year later he retired from the board of Lazard Brothers and Company having served that firm 50 years. In June, 1960, he retired from the board of The Times Publishing Company which he had joined in November, 1925, a period of service interrupted only by his sojourn in Washington.

On many occasions he had put the fruits of his ripe and varied experience before the readers of *The Times* in weighty and clearly written articles. He was president of the Royal Economic Society, of which he had for many years been a governor, from 1952 to 1953. In 1952 he was made a member of the B.B.C. General Advisory Council. Oxford, in 1937, honoured him with the D.C.L., the Vice-Chancellor hailing him as having "so often succoured both the University and the State."

In appearance he was as different as possible from the popular idea of the financier. With his mild face, deprecating manner, and gentle voice he was the embodiment of modesty. A rather pessimistic cast of mind never weakened his eager interest in life. He changed little with advancing years, and at an age when many men are set in their ways and their ideas he was still the same open-minded, inquiring philosopher, with his attention fixed on current problems and prospects and on contemporary ideas with as keen an interest as if he were still in his twenties.

He married in 1917 Phyllis, a daughter of Mr. Chiswell Dabney Langhorne, of Virginia, a sister of Nancy Viscountess Astor. She died in January, 1937, having borne him one son and two daughters. He is survived by his two daughters. His son was killed in action in 1945.

August 24, 1963.

Air Vice-Marshal Sir Quintin Brand, K.B.E., D.S.O., M.C., D.F.C., died at Umtali, Rhodesia, on March 7, 1968, at the age of 74.

With General Sir Pierre van Ryneveld he made the first flight from England to the Cape in 1920. They set out from Brooklands on February 4, 1920, and reached Wynberg on March 20. The actual flying time was about 109 hours, but the pioneers encountered some tricky weather and had several mishaps.

Silver Queen I (a Vickers Vimy bomber), the aircraft in which they set out, crashed at Wadi Halfa and was wrecked. The engines were salvaged, however, and fitted to Silver Queen II, which crashed near Bulawayo when the fliers were setting out from Pretoria. They finally reached the Cape in "Voortrekker" which the Union Government had supplied.

They received a telegram from King George V and were both knighted. In May, they were honoured at a banquet at the Savoy Hotel, London, and their health proposed by the Secretary of State for Air, Winston Churchill.

Brand, who was born at Beaconsfield, near Kimberley, on May 25, 1893, and educated at the Marist Brothers, Johannesburg, had an extremely distinguished career in the 1914–18 War in the R.F.C. and R.A.F., winning the D.S.O., M.C., and D.F.C., and being mentioned in dispatches. He shot down a German Gotha in the last raid of the war on England. He was Director General of Aviation, Egypt, from 1932 to 1936, Director of Repair and Maintenance, Air Ministry, from 1937 to 1939 and from 1939 to 1941 Commander No. 10 Fighter Group, R.A.F. He retired in 1943.

March 9, 1968.

Georges Braque, the inventor, with Picasso, of Cubism, and generally acknowledged, with Matisse, as one of the two greatest painters of his time, died at his home in Paris on August 31, 1963, at the age of 81.

In the ruling triumvirate of the School of Paris, Picasso-Braque-Matisse, Braque perhaps tended to take third place. He appeared more as a natural heir to French tradition and less of a radical creative innovator than either of the others. Picasso and Matisse, opposite yet complementary, changed the face of modern art. Braque exerted no comparable influence as an individual, being overshadowed by the personality of Matisse during his Fauve period, and by that of Picasso—who had moved from Barcelona to settle in Paris in 1904—during the short but extraordinarily close working partnership out of which Cubism was born. It was his achievement to have painted some of the most profoundly original and beautiful pictures of our time without evoking that spirit of revolution which is the most restless characteristic of "modernism". Yet the whole development of an art which seemed to reach back, by way of Cézanne, to Chardin, rested on the part he played in the revolution which was to be the most far-reaching of them all.

It is probably fruitless to discuss at length whether he or Picasso, in result, was Cubism's originator. Their experiments for a time drew them so close together as to make them virtually one artist, though they arrived at the same point by somewhat different routes—Braque by way of French art and Picasso through a typically eclectic sympathy not only with Cézanne but also with African sculpture and primitive art. Braque, however, is credited with exhibiting the first Cubist picture which may have given rise to the name. Matisse, seeing his work in 1908, is said to have exclaimed in good-humoured derision "It is Cubist!" There is some uncertainty about the identity of the painting in question and where it was exhibited, but it is on record that Matisse, meeting the critic Louis Vauxcelles, told him that Braque had sent to the Autumn Salon a picture with little cubes and by way of illustration drew on a scrap of paper two ascending converging lines with cubes between them.

Braque's "Nude" begun about December, 1907, was certainly directly inspired by the "Demoiselles d'Avignon"; his L'Estaque landscapes exhibited by Kahnweiler in November, 1908, on the other hand, anticipate by almost a year Picasso's work in a comparable idiom at Horta de San Juan, and it seems enough to say that both for a time were equal in revolutionary daring, even if the innate lyricism and painterliness of the one and the more urgent, linear style of the other made for an obvious divergence in the course of time.

STUDY IN PARIS

Georges Braque was born at Argenteuil-sur-Seine on May 13, 1882, the only son of a house-painter and decorator. As a boy he would watch his father's workmen carrying out the processes of graining and marbling, to which, later, in his still-life compositions he was to produce analogous effects. On leaving school he was for a short while apprentice to a painter-decorator at Le Havre, where his family settled, but in 1902 went to Paris to study painting. After a period at the Académie Humbert and in the atelier of Léon Bonnat at the Ecole des Beaux-Arts he began to work on his own in 1904. In the following year he was impressed by the Fauve Salon d'Automne, to which Raoul Dufy and Othon Friesz, friends he had known at Le Havre, were contributors along with Matisse, and in 1906, influenced by them, he was painting with the Fauvist freedom of colour and some reminiscence of Signac. The great change that shortly after took place in his work can be related to the Cézanne memorial exhibition of 1907 and his meeting and friendship with Picasso. Together they worked out the first stage of Cubism, now termed "analytical", in which objects and spatial relationships were resolved into an elaborate, new geometric complex and the system of construction was emphasized by reducing colour to a near-monochrome. It was followed in 1912 by "synthetic" Cubism, in which still-life objects made a recognizable appearance but were represented by flat pattern on the surface-plane of the picture without regard for the dimension of depth, a "real" element often being introduced by the addition of "papiers collés", lettering or other actual material.

During the War of 1914–18 Braque served as a lieutenant in an infantry regiment, was severely wounded and invalided out of the army in 1917. Like most of the French artists of his age he was deeply moved by the war and after 1920 his work became less intellectual and more human, less angular in style and more lyrical in feeling. The paintings produced during the next decade, usually of still-life, fruit, flowers and studio accessories, were richly decorative, full in tone and quality of pigment and exceedingly beautiful in colour with characteristic schemes of russet and olive enlivened by more positive hues and relieved with black and white lines on "graining" principles. Flowing curves and a sense of quality in material textures clearly distinguish his paintings from the Cubist stylizations of such followers of the movement as Metzinger, Leger, or Gleizes. For Diaghilev during this period Braque designed the settings and costumes for the ballets *Les Fâcheux* and *Zéphyre et Flore* and made colour-woodcut illustrations for Erik Satie's lyrical comedy *Le Piège de Méduse*.

EXTENSION OF CUBISM

Yet the still-life painting of the 1920s by no means marked the limit of his progress. In the next decade he embarked on a remarkable series of figure compositions of which "The Duet" 1937 (Musée d'Art Moderne, Paris) is an example. A late work which occupied him for a number of years between 1939 and 1955 was the series of large paintings of his studio, in which he so disposed various objects as to provide a profound and original extension of the Cubist idea. Substance and shadow in these works, which represent the crown of his career, are ambiguously interwoven, and in several of them a favourite motif of a bird in flight, seeming to detach itself from the picture represented within the picture, symbolized a life-long obsession with the mystery of pictorial space. His decorative gift showed itself in incised plaster panels and reliefs; in 1952–53 he was engaged on a ceiling decoration for the Etruscan Gallery of the Louvre, where only a few months ago an exhibition of his recent designs for jewelry was held, and in 1954 designed a series of stained-glass windows for a church at Varengeville. His graphic art included etchings and distinguished colour lithographs.

Braque did not lack appreciation in Britain. He was included in the second of Roger Fry's Post-Impressionist Exhibitions at the Grafton Galleries in 1911. One-man shows of his work were held in the 1930s at the Rosenberg and Helft, and Reid and Lefevre Galleries. In 1946 his wartime paintings were shown, with those of Rouault, at the Tate Gallery (which has works by him in its permanent collection). The full range of his art was splendidly displayed in the retrospective exhibition of 1956 at the Edinburgh Festival and Tate Gallery (Braque himself designing the catalogue cover). About the same time he was elected Honorary Academician of the Royal Scottish Academy.

Braque, a notable athlete in his youth, but always modest and retiring in disposition, is described as a grave and studious man and many of his reflections on art (some published in one form or another) are of note—"I like the rule, the discipline which controls and corrects emotion"; "reality only reveals itself when it is illuminated by a ray of poetry"; and "once an object has been incorporated in a picture it accepts a new destiny".

He married in 1912 Mlle. Marcelle Lapré.

September 2, 1963.

Dr. Heinrich von Brentano, one of the most prominent members of the Christian Democratic Union, and the first Foreign Minister of the Federal Republic, died on November 14, 1964, in a Darmstadt hospital at the age of 60. He underwent a serious operation last December, but remained parliamentary leader of the Christian Democratic Party until his death.

Heinrich von Brentano brought to German politics of the decade an element of aristocratic tradition and refinement, which the social and political upheavals of the Third Reich and the immediate post-war period had almost entirely eliminated. His urbanity, natural courtesy, and refinement, allied to a distinct stubborness, a penetrating mind, and undoubted oratorical talents, marked him out from the start in a parliamentary society rather poor in strong personalities.

RAVAGE OF WAR

This was due in part to the ravages caused by war among men of his generation; but more perhaps to the towering stature of Dr. Adenauer, which dominated the political scene increasingly during his 14 years in office. Although a devoted supporter of the Chancellor—he was often nicknamed his "young man"—even after his painfully abrupt replacement at the Foreign Ministry following the 1961 elections, Heinrich von Brentano was never a mere instrument. He retained Dr. Adenauer's confidence and respect so long because, when he felt some decision or policy to be against his convictions, he knew also how to say no.

Thus, both as chairman of his party's group in the Bundestag, and as Foreign Minister, he was able to build up for himself an independent reputation as a dedicated European and staunch supporter of Franco-German reconciliation, in which he played a leading part at the side of Dr. Adenauer. By family tradition, religion (he was a staunch Roman Catholic), upbringing and personal inclination, his sympathies tended to be first and foremost with the Latin countries.

His connexions with the Anglo-Saxon countries were a later development. If he was never drawn to Britain emotionally in the same way as he was to France, he had a deep seated respect for British parliamentary institutions and practice, which he always held up as an example for Germany. In his own parliamentary manner, he strove to introduce into the Bundestag some of the mutual tolerance and respect and the give and take between government and opposition which he admired at Westminster.

MIXED ANCESTRY

Heinrich von Brentano was born at Offenbach on the Main, near Darmstadt, on June 22, 1904, the son of Otto von Brentano di Tremezzo, a lawyer and notary, member of the Reichstag for the Catholic Centre Party, and later Minister of the Interior and of Justice in Hessen. His family, originally from Lombardy and ennobled in the thirteenth century, had played a prominent role in the liberal and intellectual movements of nineteenth-century Germany, and his forebears included Frenchmen, Greeks, Dutchmen and Austrians. He studied law at Frankfurt, Munich and Giessen, obtained his doctorate in 1929, and then set up a successful legal practice in Darmstadt, taking no interest whatever in politics. He was, however, a confirmed opponent of the Third Reich, and was repeatedly arrested, along with other members of his family, notably in connexion with the July 20 plot against Hitler.

After the collapse of Germany he turned to politics and was one of the founders of the C.D.U. in Hessen, helping to draft the constitution of that *Land*. It was at this time that he first came into contact with Dr. Adenauer and impressed him with his ability. Until 1949 he was a member of the executive committee of the Hessen C.D.U., then chairman of that party's constitutional committee for the whole of Germany. In the same year he was returned to the Bundestag and unanimously elected chairman of the party's parliamentary group upon Dr. Adenauer's obtaining the chancellorship. This post he held uninterruptedly until he was appointed Foreign Minister in 1955, a portfolio hitherto held by Dr. Adenauer himself.

He had before then already taken an active part in European politics, first as a member, then as vice-president of the Council of Europe Assembly, and as chairman of the parliamentary section of the European movement in west Germany. One of his guiding axioms was that only through European unity could Germany achieve her own unity. He often described himself as a "European by vocation".

WIDE TRAVELS

As representative of the Federal Republic at innumerable international conferences, and in personal contacts through his travels with leading statesmen in western Europe, the United States, and elsewhere, he displayed the same qualities that had enabled him within the space of 10 years to achieve political prominence at home; and he powerfully contributed to the rehabilitation of Germany abroad, and her acceptance as a full fledged partner in the western alliance. He was not content to play second fiddle to Dr. Adenauer, and his influence was perceptible on German policy, especially after the death of John Foster Dulles, in helping to keep relations with the United States on an even keel, and in removing chronic misunderstanding; he also pressed firmly for progress towards the political unity of Europe against the numbing influence of General de Gaulle. Once he became convinced that Britain was sincere in her desire to work towards European unity, he wholeheartedly backed her candidature in the Common Market.

He had frequently been spoken of as a possible successor to the chancellorship, and was reported to be Dr. Adenauer's candidate. But he lacked the popularity and common touch of Professor Erhard in his party's eyes. His resignation from the Government after the elections of 1961, one of the few occasions on which a German minister had resigned after the war, was the outcome of unseemly haggling between the Chancellor and the Free Democrats in the coalition. It earned him widespread sympathy, not only in his own party; he was reelected chairman of the C.D.U. parliamentary group by an overwhelming majority. In the last three years of his life he tended to be critical of his successor's "policy of movement" towards the communist block; and was popularly considered a staunch upholder of the so-called Hallstein doctrine, which precluded diplomatic relations with those countries which recognized the east German regime. But he had in fact already as Foreign Minister taken steps to improve relations with the eastern satellites, a policy brought to fruition after him by Dr. Schröder.

He was unmarried.

November 16, 1964.

André Breton, who died in Paris on September 27, 1966, at the age of 70, was the greatest exponent of surrealism in literature. He was the founder of the Surrealist literary movement in France and its leading theorist. Surrealism for Breton was not merely an aesthetic doctrine but virtually an ideology to which he dedicated his life. When other surrealist poets of his generation, including Aragon and Eluard, were converted to Marxism, Breton stuck firmly to his old principles. He was by any standard a remarkably gifted poet.

Breton was trained to be a doctor. He was born in 1896 at Tinchebray, in the Orne, and while he was still a medical student the First World War broke out and he found himself attached to a psychiatric unit. It was thus that he came upon the teaching of Freud and Freud was the chief, indeed one could say the only inspiration, of Breton's surrealism. Breton had always longed to be a poet and he became during the war a close friend of Apollinaire.

POETRY AND REALITY

Poetry, he believed, had always been concerned to discover a reality hidden from commonplace observation. Now, thanks to the discovery of the unconscious by Freud, the vast area of experience had been opened to literary exploitation. Thus when Breton turned from his medical work to write poetry, he had already developed his theory of literature. The method of this theory was based on that of psycho-analysis; the poet was to seek reality through the study of dreams and the use of such devices as "automatic writing". As Breton himself expressed it, his new kind of poetry was to be "dictated by the mind in the absence of any controlled exercise by reason and kept apart from any intellectual or moral preoccupations". Elsewhere Breton said: "The exploration of the unconscious life provides the only basis for a true understanding of the motives that make men act."

ANTI-BOURGEOIS

On the negative side Breton's doctrine was aggressively anti-bourgeois and attracted the sympathy of many other young writers after the Armistice when most established institutions came under fire. In 1919 he founded a review, *Littérature*, which served as a platform for the anarchistic Dada movement until Breton decided to make it more austerely and dogmatically surrealist.

Other surrealist poets of the 1920s who lacked Breton's close knowledge of psychoanalysis tended to lose interest in automatic writing or succumbed to the appeal of more rationalistic ideologies such as communism.

Breton felt obliged to publish no less than three *Surrealist Manifestos,* in 1924, 1930 and 1942, to explain and defend his theory. But as a movement French surrealism did not hold together although its influence over the present generation of dramatists shows that its ideas are not dead.

Breton himself attempted in a short novel, *Nadia* (1928), to extend his technique from poetry to fiction but his experiment was only partially a success. Among his books and poetry that are likely to be remembered are: *Mont de piété* (1919), *Ralentir Travaux* (1930) and *Flagrant délit* (1949).

September 29, 1966.

The Abbé Breuil, who died at L'Isle Adam (Seine et Oise) on August 14, 1961, devoted a lifetime to the service of prehistoric archaeology and held an unchallenged position as a pioneer and leader in this field. He was 84. To the general public he was probably best known for his work on the cave-paintings of France and northern Spain, but there was hardly any department of prehistoric studies which did not owe much to his keen insight and untiring energy.

Henri Edouard Prosper Breuil was born on February 28, 1877, and at an early age showed a taste for natural history which went beyond the normal collecting instinct of the small boy. After the usual course at the lycée of Clermont, at the age of 17 he entered the seminary of Issy-les-Moulineaux, near Paris. It was the Abbé Guibert, Professor of Natural Science at Issy, who first directed him to the study of prehistory, and d'Ault du Mesnil, who was a friend of his family, also influenced him. In 1897 he met, for the first time, Edouard Piette.

VOCATION

The sight of Piette's great collection of carved and engraved objects from the caves of the Dordogne and the Pyrenees finally determined his vocation to prehistory. After his ordination to the priesthood a few years later, he was able, with the approval of his ecclesiastical superiors, to give his whole time to his chosen science.

In 1901, in company with Capitan and Peyrony, Breuil discovered the famous Magdalenian engravings on the walls of the cave of Les Combarelles, near Les Eyzies, and a few days later Peyrony perceived for the first time the faded but magnificent paintings in the neighbouring cave of Font-de-Gaume.

LONG STUDY

This was the beginning of the long study of Palaeolithic art to which Breuil dedicated many years of his life. He was specially qualified for this work, as he was himself a skilful draughtsman, and was able to produce copies at once accurate and beautiful. At the same time a tough and wiry physique enabled him to endure the long hours of cramped discomfort entailed in making tracings of engravings and paintings often awkwardly placed in damp and tortuous caves. The intimate knowledge thus gained bore fruit in the wonderful series of monographs on the painted caves published by the munificence of Albert I, Prince of Monaco, in which Breuil set out a relative chronology, based on superpositions, discussed styles, and made illuminating comparisons with analogous engravings and paintings made by savages in various parts of the world.

LASCAUX DISCOVERIES

The discovery of the Lascaux cave-paintings in 1940 created eventually a widespread demand for a corpus on palaeolithic graphic art, which was fulfilled by the publication in 1952 of his work entitled *Four Hundred Years of Cave Art* (translated by Mary Boyle and "realized" by Fernand Windels). The controversy which arose in 1956 over the paintings in the cave of Rouflignac was rather a sad anticlimax to his great achievements in this field: his vehemently held opinion that the paintings were entirely genuine was seriously questioned by many of his colleagues.

An outstanding contribution of his early years was the recognition of the true place of the Aurignacian in the Stone Age sequence. The veteran Gabriel de Mortillet believed that the culture now known as Aurignacian was an early phase of the Magdalenian, and therefore post-Solutrean, and this was the undisputed orthodox view when Breuil began his career as a prehistorian. In 1905, at the Congress of Périgueux, the young ecclesiastic launched a bombshell with the suggestion that the stations of the type of Aurignac and the Gorge d'Enfer were pre-Solutrean, and in the following year he definitely adopted the name of Aurignacian for this culture. The separate existence and stratigraphical position of the Aurignacian are now among the commonplaces of prehistory, but at the time they aroused violent opposition among the followers of de Mortillet, and it was many years before the bitterness engendered by this controversy was finally forgotten.

For Breuil, however, the Aurignacian was only a small corner of a wider field, and he continued to work on the Upper Palaeolithic as a whole until, at the Congress of Geneva, in 1912 he produced a masterly paper, "Les Subdivisions du Paléolithique Supérieur", which still holds the field after 25 years of research in various parts of the world.

PLEISTOCENE STUDIES

In his later years Breuil turned his attention to the problems of the Lower Palaeolithic, and studied intensively the Pleistocene deposits of northern France and England, inspiring a band of younger workers in both countries. One of the outstanding results of his work was the establishment of two new cycles of culture in the Lower Palaeolithic, the Clactonian and Levalloisian, parallel to, but distinct from, the more familiar Chellean and Acheulean. Another important contribution was his insistence on the part played by the geological phenomenon known as solifluxion in the formation of terrace deposits in northern France and neighbouring countries.

In later years he extended his researches beyond Europe. In 1929 he visited South Africa as the guest of the British Association, and gave an immense impetus to the systematic study of Stone Age industries and art in that country. Indeed, the establishment of the Archaeological Survey of South Africa in 1935 with the late Professor C. van Riet Lowe as the first director was the result of Breuil's recommendations to the South African Government. He also visited China in the 1930s and it is on record that he was the first to recognize among the debris from Chou-kou-tien evidence for the use of fire by that remarkable early tool-maker *"Sinanthropus" pekinensis.*

During the Second World War he pursued his researches outside France, first in Portugal and then through the invitation of Field Marshal Smuts in South Africa, which he also visited during the early post-war years.

TREK AT 73

His extensive studies of rockpaintings in various parts of Southern Africa are being published by the Abbé Breuil Trust, constituted in London in 1953. The first volume was devoted to the White Lady of Brandberg, a remarkable fresco which he trekked across South-West Africa to study at the age of 73. He regarded the central figure as a girl of Mediterranean (Cretan?) origin, but opinions vary.

From 1906 to 1911 Breuil was Professor in the Faculty of Sciences at Fribourg in Switzerland. In the latter year he was appointed Professor at the Institut de Paléontologie Humaine in Paris, then newly founded by the Prince of Monaco. In 1929 he was elected Professor at the Collège de France, and in 1938 Member of the Institute of France, the two highest academic honours obtainable in his own country. He had many links with Britain, and among other distinctions were honorary degrees conferred on him by Oxford, Cambridge and Edinburgh. He was an honorary Fellow of the Royal Anthropological Institute and of the Society of Antiquaries of London.

HIGH HONOURS

In 1934 he was president of the Prehistoric Society. In 1935 he was awarded the Petrie medal of the University of London, in 1937 the gold medal of the Society of Antiquaries, in 1941 the Huxley Medal of the Royal Anthropological Institute, and in 1948 the Prestwich Medal of the Geological Society.

Breuil was a man of remarkable and vigorous personality, and his enthusiasm and energy stimulated all who came in contact with him. A remarkably objective judgment of people was combined with a gift for loyal and devoted friendship. To the outer world he was known as a man of brilliant scientific achievement but his intimate friends were aware that the unobtrusive, but genuine and deep, religious feeling which led to his early adoption of the priesthood was an integral part of a personality marked above all by singlemindedness and sincerity.

August 22, 1961.

Lord Bridges, K.G., P.C., G.C.B., G.C.V.O., M.C., F.R.S., one of the most eminent public servants of his time, died on August 27, 1969, at the age of 77. He was Secretary to the Cabinet from 1938 to 1946 and Secretary to the Treasury from 1945 to 1956.

Edward Ettingdene Bridges was born on August 4, 1892, the only son of Robert Bridges, O.M., the Poet Laureate, and his wife Monica, the daughter of Alfred Waterhouse, R.A., the eminent architect. He went to Eton (of which he was later a Fellow) in 1906 as an Oppidan, and in 1911 to Magdalen College, Oxford, as a scholar. He took a first class in Greats in 1914, and was elected a Fellow of All Souls in 1920. During the 1914–18 War he served in France and Italy, and was awarded the M.C.

In 1919 he entered the Treasury. While there he was secretary to three Royal Commissions, including one on the Civil Service in 1929; this gave him a knowledge and experience which he was afterwards to put to excellent effect. Apart from this he was concerned entirely with the control of expenditure and staff. In the Treasury of those days there were some who treated the spending departments as natural enemies. That was never Bridges's way: he worked by reason and trust. He laid down then the principles which, after the war, he did so much to confirm, that economy could only be achieved by a genuine partnership between the Treasury and the spending departments, and by a sense in the latter that economy was their business too, but that, when expenditure was necessary, they could count on cooperation from the Treasury.

From 1935 onwards Bridges was concerned with defence expenditure. He and Sir Warren Fisher, under whom he worked, took no narrow view of the Treasury's functions; among the civil servants of the day they were the driving force behind rearmament. In 1938 he succeeded Sir Maurice Hankey as Secretary to the Cabinet—a post which Hankey had held since its creation in 1919. This position was always a vital one, but it changed its nature when war broke out, and still more when Sir Winston became Prime Minister and worked through a strong central secretariat: Bridges was in charge of its civil side. Churchill ascribed to him the harmony which reigned between the civil and the military staffs:

"Not only was this son of a former Poet Laureate an extremely competent and tireless worker, but he was also a man of exceptional force, ability and personal charm, without a trace of jealousy in his nature. No thought of his personal position ever entered his head and never a cross word passed between the civil and military officers of the Secretariat."

The true art of a secretary is to conceal his art; Bridges played the least possible public part in the conduct of the war, since that was not his role; but he was always at the Prime Minister's side, and his aid was invaluable.

In 1945 he was made Secretary to the Treasury and Official Head of the Civil Service. He held this position till 1956—11 years of intense activity and change. This post has not since been held by one man, and even in Bridges's day one man could not give equal attention to all its aspects. Bridges kept his finger on everything that happened in the Treasury, and was at the head at all times of crisis. But he did not claim to be a financial or economic expert though on important occasions (as at the end of the negotiations for the American loan) it was his judgment on which Ministers most relied.

He made his principal contribution to the work of the Treasury in two fields. First, he was a great head of the Civil Service. He was not himself an innovator, but he was always open to new ideas; he never assumed that he knew all the answers, but listened and discussed till the moment of decision came. He preached and practised cooperation between departments. He inspired deep affection in those who worked for him, and he returned it. Above all he was trusted by everyone. As Churchill said, he had no trace of jealousy: he was accessible to everyone and devoid of pomp. All his life there was much of the boy in him. He was enthusiastic but not partisan; he found his work fun—a word he often used. He was not gregarious (he usually lunched alone at the Athenaeum) and his private life belonged strictly to his family and to his beloved North Downs, which he helped the National Trust to preserve with his hands as well as his brains. He was detached from the world of convention, though sympathetic to its needs. He thought nothing more important than human relations, but he gave the impression that much of the ordinary run of human converse came to him more by study than by instinct.

BEST POSSIBLE CHIEF

He was the best head that the Civil Service of his time could have had; and no one concerned with administration should fail to read his admirable lectures on the subject.

The other field in which he left a lasting mark was the part played by Government in science, the arts and the universities. This had long been a special responsibility of the Treasury, and he did not work alone; but the great enlargement of the state's role in this field could never have gone so smoothly without him. If the universities retained their financial independence for so long, they owed it largely to Bridges. In the field of science, his contribution was recognized in 1952 by the rare tribute, to a layman, of a Fellowship of the Royal Society. The academic honours which poured in on him were no formality, since his repute was great in the universities; and in 1959 he was made Chancellor of Reading University.

In 1956 Bridges retired from the Civil Service, still at the height of his powers. For the next 12 years, till increasing lameness restricted his activity, he took on a large number of public duties, many of which bore the mark of his special interests in the Treasury. His chairmanships included those of the British Council, in whose service he travelled indefatigably; the Pilgrim Trust; the Governing Body of the London School of Economics, a post which at times taxed his powers of administration and peacemaking to the full; and perhaps closest to his heart, the Royal Fine Art Commission: his interest in architecture was deep and he found this difficult and sometimes frustrating assignment consistently absorbing. He was an honorary F.R.I.B.A. In so full and distinguished a life one must pass over his services, important as they were, to the Gulbenkian Foundation, the Universities of Oxford, Cambridge and Reading, and to many other bodies, including several public companies of which he was a valued director. He was elected an honorary Fellow of Magdalen College, Oxford, in 1946, of University College, Cambridge in 1965 and was Fellow of All Souls College, Oxford, from 1920 to 1927 and from 1954. In 1964 he published a book on the workings of the Treasury.

Bridges, who had been knighted in 1939 and made a Privy Councillor in 1953, was raised to the peerage in 1957 and appointed as Knight of the Garter in 1965.

He married in 1922 the Hon. Kathleen Farrer, second daughter of the second Lord Farrer, who survives him, with two sons and two daughters. The heir to his peerage is his son, the Hon. Thomas Bridges.

August 29, 1969.

Senator Henry Styles Bridges, a former Governor of New Hampshire and for two decades a leading member of the Republican Party, died on November 26, 1961, at East Concord, New Hampshire. He was 63.

Styles Bridges, as he preferred to be known after dropping his first name to avoid confusion with the longshoremen's union leader, Mr. Harry Bridges, once claimed that he had never lost an election. It was an impressive boast, but he will probably be remembered as an authentic American Tory. Although the Republican Party's nomination for the Presidency was denied him in 1940, when the late Wendell Wilkie proved irrepressible, he stood with the late Senators Taft and Vandenberg as an example of much that is good, and occasionally wrongheaded, in the party.

He was of a type easily recognizable in the United States. Born in West Pembroke, Maine, on September 9, 1898, he had to earn his living from an early age. While his widowed mother taught in the local school for six dollars a week, he worked his way through the University of Maine by milking cows and doing other farmyard chores for a pittance.

NEW ENGLAND FAMILY

He was the twelfth generation of his family in New England, and possessed to a marked degree all the self-reliance and straightforwardness of that hardy region.

In 1930, after clearly associating himself with the interests of the local farming community he was appointed to the New Hampshire Public Service Commission, and four years later successfully ran for governor.

At the age of 36 he became the state's youngest governor at a time when the Democrats were sweeping the country. In one term he balanced the state's budget and improved the standards of agricultural products before being elected to the United States Senate in 1937.

In his home state at the time, Styles Bridges

was known as a liberal, but in Washington, when he was at first one of only 17 Republican senators, he quickly became known as a conservative. He was against high taxation and for a balanced budget, and in foreign affairs his approach was no less simple and straight forward. He was against foreign aid, especially to countries such as Yugoslavia, and favoured the regimes of Chiang Kai-shek and General Franco. He was a strong supporter of John Foster Dulles, and his suspicion of career diplomatists was on more than one occasion an embarrassment for the State Department.

Yet he remained a strictly honest man of the kind that helps to make the American political system work. He was perhaps best when working behind the scenes, and was a valuable member of the Senate foreign relations and appropriations committees.

He was married three times, and is survived by his widow and three children.

November 27, 1961.

Admiral Sir Patrick Brind, G.B.E., K.C.B., who died on October 4, 1963, at the age of 71, was Chief of Staff in the Home Fleet when the Bismarck was destroyed, and Assistant Chief of Naval Staff during the planning of the Normandy landings. In the concluding months of the Second World War he commanded a cruiser squadron of the British Pacific fleet which took part in the bombardment of Truk and other Japanese strongholds. From 1951 to 1953 he was C-in-C, Allied Forces, Northern Europe.

Eric James Patrick Brind was born on May 12, 1892, the third son of Colonel E. A. Brind.

AT JUTLAND

He entered Osborne College as a naval cadet in 1908, and Dartmouth College two years later. In 1916 he joined the battleship Malaya in the Grand Fleet as a watchkeeper, and was in her for over two and a half years, taking part in the Battle of Jutland. In 1918 he joined the monitor Sir John Moore for gunnery duties until after the armistice.

Serving as a captain he commissioned the cruiser Birmingham in 1938 and took her to the China Station when Japan and China were at war. The next year he went to Tsingtao to investigate the arrest of a British merchant ship by the Japanese. He took the cruiser among a fleet of Japanese heavy cruisers and aircraft carriers and went on board the Japanese flagship to say he intended to take the merchant ship away. The Japanese threatened to blow his ship and the merchant ship out of the water but the Brimingham and her protégé sailed the next day.

When Admiral Sir John Tovey became Commander-in-Chief of the Home Fleet in December, 1940, Brind was selected as Chief of Staff, with the rank of commodore, first class, until his promotion to rear-admiral in February, 1942. For his services in the operations which led to the destruction of the German battleship Bismarck in May, 1941, he was created C.B.E. From May, 1942 to August, 1944, he served at the Admiralty as an Assistant Chief of Naval Staff. He was made C.B. in July, 1944, for distinguished services in the planning of the successful landings in Normandy.

CRUISER SQUADRON

In October, 1944, he took command of a cruiser squadron of the British Pacific Fleet, in which he served until January, 1946, taking part in various operations in the concluding part of the war against Japan. He was present at the occupation of Tokyo and the Japanese surrender there. In October, 1945, he was promoted to vice-admiral. After committee service at the Admiralty he became President of the R. N. College, Greenwich, in September, 1946, for the customary two years. In December, 1948, he took up the post of Commander-in-Chief on the Far East Station, with headquarters at Singapore, and three months later was promoted to admiral. He was advanced to K.C.B., in the 1946 birthday honours. From 1951 to 1953 he was C-in-C, Allied Forces, Northern Europe.

He married in 1918 Eileen Margaret (who died in 1940), only daughter of the Rev. J. Marling Apperly, and had one daughter. In 1948 he married Edith Gordon, widow of Rear-Admiral H. E. C. Blagrove, who lost his life in the sinking of the Royal Oak in 1939.

October 5, 1963.

Pierre Brisson, chairman and managing editor of *Le Figaro* and of its literary weekly *Le Figaro Littéraire*, died in Paris on December 31, 1964, after a short illness. He was 68.

Pierre Brisson had been head of *Le Figaro* for almost 30 years, and, as *Le Monde* writes, "for the postwar generation he *was Le Figaro,* its renown and its rise". If, before the last war, *Le Figaro* was just one of several Paris newspapers, it became after its reappearance in 1944 and under the imprint of his firm, dedicated direction, incontestably the most important of the country's morning newspapers, rivalled in authority only by *Le Monde* which appears in the evening.

Of a literary family and himself, in his early days, a dramatic critic and essayist of note, he devoted himself entirely to his editorial and managerial duties—for his post as chairman combined the two—to the exclusion of all other interests. He had a quick eye for potential talent and attracted to his team, solidly based as it was on established writers, many of them Academicians, a number of excellent young writers, so that if he made *Le Figaro* rather an austere journal, he at least kept it abreast of the times. But he never compromised in an attempt to gain circulation and although *Le Figaro* might often have appeared the establishment paper *par excellence*, he never compromised his strongly held political opinions and never hesitated to attack authority if he considered it was taking the wrong path. Thus in recent months *Le Figaro* has been markedly anti-Gaullist, opposing President de Gaulle particularly in his views on Europe, for *Le Figaro* has always been strongly pro-European.

Pierre Brisson was born in Paris on June 5, 1896, the son of Adolphe Brisson, editor of *Les Annales*. He had just left the Lycée Condorcet when the First World War broke out and he joined up in an infantry regiment in September, 1914, at the age of 18, ending the war as a sub-lieutenant. After a short spell as a sub-editor on the *Annales*, he went to *Le Temps* as dramatic critic remaining there until 1934 when he joined *Le Figaro* as managing editor at the age of 38. The Second World War came and Brisson rejoined the colours. He was captured by the Germans in 1940 but soon escaped by swimming a canal.

He resumed his editorship of *Le Figaro*, first at Clermont, for Paris was then in the occupied zone of France, and later at Lyons. After two years of this somewhat precarious existence for the paper, the Germans occupied the rest of France and Brisson had the alternative of taking his editorial policy and instructions from the Germans or of sabotaging his paper. There was for him, of course, no real alternative. He closed down *Le Figaro* and joined the Resistance.

When the paper was closed Brisson wrote a letter addressed to all readers promising that once *Le Figaro* was able to resume publication they would find "from the first day *Le Figaro* faithful to its duty and living up to their expectations."

Brisson is survived by his widow and his son Jean-François, deputy editor of *Le Figaro*.

January 1, 1965.

Sir Herbert Brittain, K.C.B., K.B.E., chairman of the Iron and Steel Holding and Realisation Agency, and formerly Second Secretary in the Treasury, died in a London hospital on September 6, 1961, at the age of 67.

The son of the Rev. J. H. Brittain, he was born on July 3, 1894, and was a Lancastrian born, bred, and educated in Rochdale and Manchester University. He served in the Royal Artillery in the 1914–18 War rising to the rank of Major and being twice mentioned in dispatches. On leaving the Army he joined the Civil Service and lived in London and worked in the Treasury for close on 40 years, but in speech and outlook he stayed a Lancastrian and in his work he exhibited Lancastrian virtues such as toughness, practical good sense, and a constant desire to see business dispatched.

His handwriting matched his work, and indeed his personal appearance, for it was small and round, and it was a constant wonder that while he wrote rapidly, his writing always stayed neat and even and invariably legible.

MASTER OF FACTS

He was not blessed with an imposing presence, and being a diffident speaker was not always a success in conference. But to Ministers and to his Civil Service colleagues he was of great value as a man who could be completely relied on to organize and carry through a Government operation by his mastery of the facts and his ability to foresee the snags and provide for them.

Brittain was also a first class draftsman, not only of papers for internal consumption but also of documents for publication and speeches.

A poor speaker himself, he wrote many good speeches for delivery by others in and out of Parliament and, in doing so, showed a knack of impersonation not altogether in keeping with the rest of his character. For example, Sir Kingsley Wood, as Chancellor, did not forget that he had been a preacher and liked any speech of his to include at least one Biblical quotation. In the many speeches that he wrote for him, Brittain never failed to provide such a quotation and Sir Kingsley Wood was never known to reject his selection.

Brittain spent all the 38 years of his public service career in the Treasury. There was no period of secondment to outside Departments, and it was perhaps a defect in an otherwise distinguished career that he never had first-hand experience of controlling the expenditure of public money or of large scale organization. Of his first 10 years in the Treasury, no less than eight were spent as Private Secretary first to Sir Basil Blackett as Controller of Finance, then to Walter Guinness and his successors in the office of Financial Secretary to the Treasury.

HUMDRUM WORK

This long assignment must have had many dull and pedestrian periods, for the Financial Secretary of those days saw little of the Budget or other aspects of higher policy in the Treasury. These were reserved for the Chancellor, while the Financial Secretary looked after the more humdrum aspects of administration in the Treasury and Revenue Departments. But he was then, as he is now, the point of contact between the Treasury and Parliament in the financing and control of public expenditure. It was typical of Brittain that he made full use of these years to become the acknowledged authority on Supply procedure and to write the standard Treasury manual on the subject. Next came a period of service on external finance, before his return to the home scene on his appointment, in 1937, to be Treasury Officer of Accounts. He then was placed in charge of the Home Finance Division of the Treasury, in which post he was promoted in 1942 to be Under Secretary (the then Treasury equivalent of the Deputy head of a major public department) and continued till 1946.

ADVISED TREASURY

Perhaps these nine years, which included all the war years, saw Brittain at the height of his powers. The Treasury Officer of Accounts has a dual function. On the one hand he advises the Treasury and indeed the whole of Whitehall on public accounting practice. On the other hand he is standing counsel for the Treasury before the Public Accounts Committee and acts in this field as a channel of communication between the Executive and Parliament. In both capacities Brittain made many friends among Members of Parliament as well as in Whitehall, for he exercised his technical mastery of the subject with acceptable modesty and was well known for the readiness of his advice. In charge of Home Finance, he framed the War Damage legislation more or less singlehanded, and was responsible not indeed for the policy but for the construction and presentation of the War Budgets, as well as the business of Exchequer management and the War borrowing programmes—not forgetting the War Savings campaigns, for which he produced speeches as well as securities. His last service in this period was in the year after the war, when the first act of the new Labour Government was to nationalize the Bank of England. Whatever Brittain's views on the policy of this measure, the operation of preparing and passing the Bill was a model of efficiency, and that in a field full of historical and legal pitfalls.

SECOND SECRETARY

But then followed some years of less noteworthy activity. Brittain was transferred first to the control of Supply Expenditure and then to Overseas Finance duties. These were years of hard work, and contained some notable achievements, particularly in the financing of collective defence, initially for the Western Union Countries and later for Nato. But they must also have been years of disappointment: he was now in his fifties, serving under men who were his juniors in age and had been his juniors in rank, with no evident prospect of reaching the top of the Treasury before his retirement. Happily, however, he was promoted to Second Secretary a few months before his sixtieth birthday, and had the satisfaction of (as he said) "coming home" to his beloved Home Finance and Supply for three years before his retirement in 1957.

In his last years as Second Secretary in the Treasury Brittain had less scope for his special talents in the singlehanded planning and carrying out of specific operations. His role was more to initiate or judge the efforts of others. This he did with a charming modesty and good humour, but always with a rigour for which his subordinates in Home Finance were grateful. Characteristically however, Brittain from time to time would remove a particular operation from the departmental machine and handle it from start to finish himself. This happened on several occasions in the affairs of the Iron and Steel Holding and Realisation Agency, and it was no doubt on account of the experience he so gained, and the personal relationships he then established, that he came to be made chairman of the Agency in 1958 after his retirement from the public service the previous year. He occupied the intervening period in learning to drive a car and writing his book on *The British Budgetary System*.

It was in character that in writing this work he should steer clear of policy objectives and concentrate on an authoritative exposition of methods and systems.

RE-SALE ISSUE

During his time at the Agency the most important question at issue was the decision to resell to private investors debenture stocks and preference shares of seven denationalized companies rather than the still-nationalized Richard Thomas and Baldwins.

Brittain was married in 1920 and had one son and one daughter.

September 8, 1961.

Vera Brittain, in private life Mrs. G. E. G. Catlin, died on March 29, 1970.

Author, journalist, and public speaker, her works excited a good deal of controversy in her middle years. This was not only because she vehemently advocated controversial causes, such as feminism and pacifism, but also because she made great use of personal experience in her novels as well as in journalism and autobiography, so that the former frequently turned into what used to be called *romans à clef*, and acquaintances of hers, recognizing themselves or their friends under thinly-veiled disguises, were occasionally resentful of what they felt to be misleading portraits. A certain lack of humorous detachment, which she shared, it must be admitted, with other publicists keenly devoted to "causes", may have contributed to this, and to her comparative lack of success as a novelist; in this respect it is interesting to make comparison with her great friend Winifred Holtby, whose interest in "causes" was no less, but whose novel, *South Riding* (reissued a generation after her early death), is emotional enough, but shows a solid imaginative quality to which her friend never attained. Miss Brittain herself attached much more importance (and rightly) to her autobiographical *Testament of Youth*, which had a large sale in its time, and to her public speaking and organizational work, than to her novels as such.

She was born at Newcastle-under-Lyme, the daughter of Thomas Arthur Brittain, a businessman who subsequently moved to Burton; and educated at St. Monica's School, Kingswood, Surrey. From her earliest years she "scribbled", completing, apparently, no less than five novels before she was eleven years old, so it is not surprising that she set her heart on a university career. She succeeded in gaining an exhibition at Somerville College, Oxford, in 1914, and spent a year there before the call of war service took her into the V.A.D. as a nurse. She served in London, France and Malta. In 1919 she returned to Somerville, where like some of the men who came to the university after years of war service, she found the gulf between the "veterans" and those fresh from school rather difficult to bridge; she obtained her degree, however, and on going down took to journalism. With her college friend Winifred Holtby, with whom she lived for a time, she played a part in organizations aiming at international understanding such as the League of Nations Union, and in movements for equality between the sexes; she was much interested in the early days of Lady Rhondda's *Time and Tide*. In 1925 she married George Catlin, a brilliant Oxford prizeman who shared her political views and had in the previous year been appointed to a chair of politics at Cornell University; she then paid her first visit to the United States, in which country she made several successful lecture tours later in her career.

Shortly after leaving Oxford she published two novels, *The Dark Tide* and *Not Without Honour*, which met with only a moderate reception. Success came with the autobiographical *Testament of Youth*, published in 1933. This came out at a time when the tide of war-disillusionment, of which *All Quiet on the*

Western Front and *Journey's End* were the first signs, was still flowing fast. The book, a vivid and passionate personal record, was widely read and praised, though some thought it overstrained and others found it embarrassingly frank in the days when outspokenness was not entirely *de rigueur*. This was her high watermark as a writer, though she published a good few other books, including three novels, *Testament of Friendship* (1940), which was a portrait of Winifred Holtby, *Testament of Experience* (1957), a sketch of Lord Pethick-Lawrence (1963), and several books of historical and other essays with a strongly feminist and pacifist flavour. In 1968 she published *Radclyffe Hall: A Case of Obscenity?*

She was an honorary D. Litt, and a Fellow of the Royal Society of Literature; but in her later years though she did not cease to write, she gave the impression that her heart was more in lecturing.

She had one son and one daughter; the daughter, Mrs. Shirley Williams, entered Parliament in 1964 as M.P. for Hitchin.

March 30, 1970.

Leonard W. Brockington, C.M.G., first head of the Canadian Broadcasting Corporation, died in a Toronto hospital on September 15, 1966, at the age of 78.

Leonard Brockington was a shining example of how fruitfully the brain drain can work in both directions. A Welshman, he emigrated to Canada, made a name there as a lawyer and administrator and then returned to do yeoman service for Britain. His broadcasts during the war were in the first flight, and although cruelly handicapped by arthritis, he did not spare himself in travelling round the world as an eloquent spokesman for the Allied cause. His energy and zest for seeing a job through went with unquenchable delight in enjoying life in the company of friends. On his visits to London he was always sure of an enormous welcome, alike as a guest and a host.

He was born at Cardiff, on April 6, 1888, the son of Walter Brockington and was educated at Cardiff High School, and the University College of South Wales, Monmouthshire. After training as a teacher he taught classics from 1908 to 1912 at Cowley Grammar School at St. Helens, Lancashire before deciding that he could better his fortunes in Canada. After working in Edmonton, Alberta, for short periods on a newspaper and in the provincial Civil Service, he served his apprenticeship for the law with the leading law firm of Calgary, of which the late Lord Bennett was a senior partner, and was admitted to the Bar of Alberta.

By 1921 he was rated a good enough lawyer to be appointed city solicitor for Calgary and held this post until 1935, when he moved to Winnipeg to become general counsel for the Northwest Graindealers' Association. In Winnipeg he confirmed a reputation which he had acquired in Calgary, that he was an eloquent orator with uncommon intellectual gifts. His fame also reached Ottawa with the result that in 1936 the King Ministry chose him as the first chairman of the reorganized Canadian Broadcasting Corporation. But three years later Mackenzie King, feeling a need for competent help in the preparation of his speeches during the war, induced Brockington to join his staff as his special assistant and he gave the Prime Minister valuable help until a clash of viewpoint caused his resignation. He then went to London, where he became special adviser on press and broadcasting relations with the rest of the Commonwealth to Lord Bracken, who was Minister of Information, and in this role he visited Australia, the United States and other countries and the high quality of his broadcasts won him acclaim all over the world. After the close of the war he joined a law firm in the city of Ottawa and practised there until Lord Rank enlisted his services as president of Odeon Theatres (Canada), which controlled a chain of "movie" theatres across Canada, and J. Arthur Rank Organization of Canada. Since its head office was in Toronto Brockington moved there and became one of that city's best known public figures.

Leonard Brockington was always ready to admit a regret that his early ambition to have a great career at the Bar had not been realized, but he found ample compensation in the preeminence which he attained as an orator and broadcaster. Endowed with a very mellifluous voice, he had a great fund of knowledge about literature, art and music and he could skilfully draw upon it for the embellishment of his speeches, while he was also master of the technique of broadcasting. So during the Second World War he was frequently employed by the British Government to enlighten over the air the American public about Britain's war effort and the aims of her policy, and his valuable services were rewarded with a C.M.G. in 1945. In his later years he was the recipient of innumerable invitations to deliver speeches, but he refused most of them. All his adult life he had been crippled by arthritis, but it did not prevent him from being an indefatigable traveller and he had friends in high places all over the world.

He had honorary degrees from several universities, but an honour which pleased him particularly was his election by the undergraduates of Queen's University at Kingston as their spokesman to the governing body with the old Scottish title of Rector.

He married, in 1913, Agnes Neave Mackenzie and they had two sons.

September 17, 1966.

Dr. Max Brod, the friend and biographer of Franz Kafka, and himself an author of uncommonly versatile stamp, died in Tel Aviv on December 20, 1968, at the age of 84.

Born in Prague on May 27, 1884, he engaged in literary journalism at an early age and published his first book in 1906. He was the author of a dozen or more novels, but he was also poet, playwright, literary critic, and writer on music as well as composer of music. For some years he edited the Prager Tagblatt. As a novelist he commanded a whole range of subjects, historical and contemporary, though he wrote most frequently about Jewish characters and problems. His style reflects the German vogue of naturalism, analytical in psychology but wanting in vivid illumination, of his period. The first novel of his to make any marked impression was *Arnold Beer: Das Schicksal eines Juden*, which appeared in 1912. A close analytical study of a sensitive, introspective, brilliant, and yet somehow ineffectual personality, who is incapable of finishing anything he begins, the novel does not seem to illustrate a specifically Jewish mentality in the hero. Yet the significant thing is that Brod's portrait of Arnold Beer bears an undoubted, though admittedly only partial, likeness to Franz Kafka.

The two men were intimate friends—Brod was, indeed, the only intimate friend that Kafka permitted himself in pursuit of his strange and tormented dual existence, and for several years they saw one another daily. It was Brod who attended to the posthumous publication of *The Castle* and *The Trial*, though he had been requested by Kafka to burn all the manuscripts which the latter left behind.

INDISPENSABLE

His biography of Kafka, which first appeared, it would seem, in 1934, almost 10 years after Kafka, is an indispensable book. It does not always persuade the reader, it casts no light where at times light is most sorely needed, and its chronology is often confused and mystifying, but for all that it offers far more valuable material concerning the subject's life and character than is to be found anywhere else.

Two of Brod's most noteworthy historical novels are *The Redemption of Tycho Brahe* (1916) and *Reubeni*, the latter an arresting study, with a Renaissance setting, of a Jew translated from the scholastic piety of the ghetto in Prague to Venice and inspired by the messianic hope of transforming Israel for its own deliverance into a race of warriors. As racial intolerance settled more deeply on Central Europe during the years before 1939, Brod turned more firmly to the imaginative expression of his Zionist convictions. He was the founder and vice-president of the National Jewish Council of Austro-Hungary. Among the novels of his published in Holland during the Nazi regime were two about the problem of the Jew in Europe and also a psychological study, *Annerl* (1937), of a formidable realism.

December 21, 1968.

Sir Charles Vyner de Windt Brooke, G.C.M.G., Rajah of Sarawak, died in London on May 9, 1963 at the age of 88.

Born in London on September 26, 1874, he was the third son of Sir Charles Brooke, 2nd Rajah of Sarawak, and Margaret de Windt, Ranee of Sarawak. His elder sister Ghita, born 1870, and his twin elder brothers, James and Charles, born 1872, all died on board the P. & O. liner Hydaspes in the Red Sea while returning from Sarawak in 1873.

He was educated at Winchester and Magdalene College, Cambridge, and in 1897 entered his father's service in Sarawak, thereafter spending many years up country living among the natives, learning the various languages, dialects, and customs of all the different tribes with which he came in contact. It was this severe training in the art of native administration which stood him in great stead later and which influenced him considerably. He preferred that his own officers should be bachelors, ready to live among the natives and get to know them thoroughly rather than married men with, as the Rajah described it, "one foot back in the bungalow". In 1904 he was acknowledged successor to the Raj and in 1911 he married the Hon. Sylvia Brett, second daughter of the second Viscount Esher, by whom he had three daughters, Leonora, Elizabeth, and Valerie.

In 1912 the old Rajah, suspicious of what he called the "Esher influence", decreed Vyner's younger brother heir presumptive to Vyner if the latter had no male issue. Five years later he became 3rd Rajah of Sarawak on the death of his father. On his accession he was already thoroughly acquainted with the needs of his people, who regarded him with the greatest affection—an affection which he held to the end. Like his father he perceived the folly of thrusting western ideas and institutions on a people whose traditions were wholly alien and he was in particular intolerant of any commercial exploitation of the country. He was created G.C.M.G. in 1927 and in 1930 started the Rajah of Sarawak fund with a gift of £100,000, the majority of which was for the education of the children of colonial civil servants, and a part for the Imperial Forestry Institute.

CENTENARY OF BROOKE RULE

In May, 1941, the country celebrated the centenary of Brooke rule. The Rajah being now a man of 67 felt that it was time to divest himself of some of his autocratic powers, and this he did by handing over certain rights to a Committee of Administration. The new constitution proclaimed again that Sarawak is the heritage of the people of Sarawak, held by the Rajah in trust for them.

Seven months later Sarawak was invaded and occupied by the Japanese. The Rajah, who was in Australia at the time, was prevented from returning to his country by the military authorities. After two years in Australia he returned to the United Kingdom.

The wealth of the country, which was liberated in August, 1945, had been destroyed during the occupation and the Rajah realized that it would require millions of pounds to rehabilitate it. At the same time he was uncertain as to whether his officers, many of whom had fallen into Japanese hands, would survive their torment and be able to play their part in the necessary reconstruction.

It was therefore in 1945–46 that the Rajah decided to cede Sarawak to the Crown. The cession was strongly opposed by the Rajah's brother, and by his nephew. In February, 1946, the Rajah returned to Sarawak and informed his people of his decision. The Council of the country was convened in April that year and, although the native vote was against it, the cession to the Crown was made. Brooke left the country immediately afterwards and retired to London, where he spent his remaining years, retaining his title of "Rajah of Sarawak".

Like his father before him, the Rajah always had a strong aversion to pomp and ceremony. But when he mixed with the public—which was often and then always or nearly always in completely informal dress—one could not but be impressed by the innate dignity of the man. He was the Rajah.

Shy to a degree, he was also generous—in fact over-generous at times—a characteristic that frequently led to his being taken advantage of. Little perhaps is known to the public of this remarkable man. He has been described as inscrutable; one seldom knew what he was really thinking.

May 10, 1963.

Senator Alfred Brooks, P.C., Q.C., a former Minister of Veteran Affairs and lately the leader of Her Majesty's Loyal Opposition in the Senate, died in New Brunswick in December, 1967, at the age of 77.

Colonel Alfred Johnson Brooks was a man of many parts always loyal to all things British. He was a soldier, lawyer and schoolmaster. Born on November 14, 1890, at Gagetown, N.B., where now lies the Aldershot of the Atlantic Provinces, he graduated in law from the University of New Brunswick. As a major in the 26th Battalion C.E.F., he served overseas in the First World War. But before that he was a school principal, believed to have been the youngest at the time in his native province. After demobilization he continued in his profession while at the same time actively keeping up his old Service connexions, not only in the Royal Canadian Legion but also in the militia as the commanding officer of the New Brunswick Rangers and later the 16th Infantry Brigade. During the last war he returned to the colours almost immediately, commanding transit camps in Fredericton, N.B., and Windsor, Nova Scotia, as well as serving overseas on two occasions. Brooks also practised law; his old university made him an honorary LL.D. in 1957.

He was one of the fiercest of Tories in a region where you are, it is said, either born a Conservative or a Liberal; it was inevitable perhaps that he was attracted by political life, and so in 1922 he became party organizer for his province, a post he held for three years. Then in 1925 he was elected to the New Brunswick legislature and subsequently became its deputy speaker. He held this position from 1930 to 1935. Then in that year he entered the House of Commons as the Conservative member for the Federal Riding of Royal and was returned to Ottawa in every general election after that until he was summoned to the Senate in 1960.

When the Diefenbaker Administration came to office in 1957, no one was more fitted for the portfolio of Minister of Veterans' Affairs than Brooks. In that post he was an ardent champion of the rights of ex-Service men, particularly their pension needs. He also put forward a plan to build a national war memorial on Nepean Point, overlooking the Ottawa river, which would commemorate all military actions by Canadians from the time of the Riel rebellion to the Korean War. However, it never came about.

On entering the Senate he became the Government leader there; and after the Conservative defeat in 1963, he was the Leader of the Opposition until a few months ago.

Brooks was one of the most popular and respected members of either house and unusually warm tributes were paid to his memory by all parties in the Commons and in the Senate. A good athlete, he loved to play golf on summer weekends on a small but tricky course in the Gatimeay Valley, nearby, with his old ex-Service colleagues.

December 11, 1967.

General Sir Dallas Brooks, G.C.M.G., K.C.B., K.C.V.O., D.S.O., Governor of Victoria from 1949 to 1963, died in Melbourne on March 22, 1966.

Reginald Alexander Dallas Brooks, the son of a Naval Chaplain, was born on August 22, 1896, and duly went to Dover College where he distinguished himself as an all-round games player. With the declaration of the 1914–18 War he joined the Royal Marines as a second lieutenant on the day of his eighteenth birthday. He seved in Gallipoli in 1915, was severely wounded and was awarded the French Croix de Guerre. A year later he was back in the Grand Fleet. On April 23, 1918, he took part in the assault on Zeebrugge, was awarded the D.S.O., and was promoted brevet major.

Between the two World Wars he did all the right things which a good officer should do. He graduated at the Royal Naval Staff College in 1933 and was then appointed Staff Officer (Intelligence) on the Staff of the Naval Commander-in-Chief, South Africa. Before this there had been five happy years from 1919 to 1924 when he played cricket for Hampshire at various times and made a century against Gloucestershire at Southampton. He also captained the Combined Services against New Zealand and played for them against Australia and South Africa. At hockey he captained the Royal Navy and Combined Services and played for England against Ireland and France. At golf he also represented the Royal Navy and remained a very sound player until past middle age.

During the Second World War he became Deputy Director-General of the Political Warfare Executive where he was most useful in connexion with all military matters, more especially as General Sir Leslie Hollis, the secretary of the Chiefs of Staff, was also a Royal Marine.

Before the end of the war he returned to Corps duty in 1944 to take up the appointment of Major-General, General Staff, Royal Marines, and on May 1, 1946, he was appointed Commandant-General, Royal Marines, with the rank of lieutenant-general to be raised later in January, 1948, to full general.

On retirement from the Royal Marines in

1948 he was only 52 and was still a very fit and energetic man. Soon he was offered various jobs which did not appeal to him. But when in 1949 he was invited to become Governor of the State of Victoria he became interested and after initial misgivings accepted the post.

On two occasions the Queen accepted recommendations from the Premier that he should serve for a further term. The first recommendation came from a Labour Premier, John Cain, and the second from a Liberal Premier, Henry Bolte. In October, 1959, when Brooks entered his eleventh year of office, he set a record for Victoria. It was one which the people found most agreeable, for Brooks identified himself successfully and sincerely with all kinds of their activities, making Government House the meeting place from time to time for the humblest as well as the grandest of Victorians. In a conservative society, which cherished its Governor, his policy was a bold one. It brought the Crown closer to the people and it was a small minority who complained that he courted personal popularity. To the great majority he was a man who inspired affection. His easy manner and obvious desire to stay in Victoria, when he was after all an Englishman, endeared him to almost everyone. He did not retire until 1963. He was a keen sportsman, who enjoyed his golf and played when he could with Peter Thomson. He was an honorary member of the Bricklayers' Society and regularly attended the annual party of the Shop Assistants' Union. Several times he acted as Administrator of the Commonwealth of Australia.

Brooks married in 1924 Muriel Violet Turner, elder daughter of Turner Laing, by whom he had a daughter.

March 22, 1966.

John Brophy, who died on November 12, 1965, was a prolific novelist who devoted his life to the art of letters with the utmost single-mindedness. He reached a high level of competence in the craft of fiction, but lacked perhaps the psychological depth and philosophic breadth of outlook which contribute so much to the making of really memorable novels, though he had a particular and deserved success with *Waterfront* (1934).

He had been chief fiction critic of the *Daily Telegraph,* the B.B.C. and *Time and Tide.* During the Second World War he edited *John O'London's Weekly.*

Born in Liverpool on December 6, 1899, he was the son of John Brophy and Agnes (Bodell) Brophy, both Irish Protestants. At an early age he felt the impact of religious and political controversy, and reacted against parental influence. Educated at the Holt Secondary School (then a co-educational institution) he romantically ran away in November, 1914, gave a false age, and enlisted in The King's (Liverpool) Regiment. His subterfuge was never discovered, and he went through the war in France and Belgium. When he was demobilized he was still not 19 and was lame from trench foot. He took a degree at Liverpool University in 1922 and then spent a year in post-graduate study in the University of Durham, reading mostly psychoanalysis.

He married in 1924, Charis Weare, daughter of the Rev. J. Grundy (she had been a fellow-undergraduate at Liverpool), and went out to Egypt to teach. He spent two years there, but his wife fell ill, so he returned with her to Liverpool. At that time F. J. Marquis (later Lord Woolton) was employing selected university graduates in Lewis's, Ltd. Brophy became one of these recruits, working at his writing in what spare time was left after a day at the store. In 1928 his first novel *The Bitter End,* was published. After leaving Lewis's he joined the London Press Exchange as a copy writer and after the publication of his fourth novel found it possible to live by his pen.

Flesh and Blood (1931) showed his maturing powers but it was *Waterfront,* an excellent study of a group of people who directly or indirectly looked to the Mersey for their living, which brought him acclaim. For many years he wrote one and sometimes more books a year.

WORKS OF FICTION

His output was mostly fiction but there were occasional diversions, among them, *Songs and Slang of the British Soldier 1914–18,* which he wrote in collaboration with Eric Partridge; *Britain's Home Guard,* in which the illustrations were by Eric Kennington; *The Human Face;* and *The Face in Western Art.* Several of the novels were made into films; they included: *The Immortal Sergeant,* in which Henry Fonda and Thomas Mitchell starred, *The Day they Robbed the Bank of England, Waterfront,* and *Turn the Key Softly.*

Mr. Brophy had one daughter, Miss Brigid Brophy, the writer, wife of Mr. Michael Levey.

November 15, 1965.

George Brough, who died in Nottingham on January 12, 1970, at the age of 79, will be remembered for the legendary Brough Superior motor cycles which he designed and built in Nottingham.

Large, powerful, fast and beautifully finished, the Brough was sometimes called the two-wheeled Rolls-Royce. Being practically hand made, a Brough was not cheap, its price between the two world wars was between £150 and £200.

George Brough's father, W. E. Brough, was also a designer and manufacturer and George once rode a Brough flat-twin, belt-driven in a Scottish Six-Day trial on a single gear.

"Ixion", the notable motor-cycling journalist, recalls in his *Motor Cycle Cavalcade,* two memorable Brough ventures, a motor cycle incorporating an 800 c.c. Austin water-cooled engine and a "Golden Dream" with an embryo transverse four cylinder power unit.

Perhaps the most famous machine to come out of the Brough stable was the S.S. 100, which was powered by a 1,000 c.c. overhead valve J.A.P. vee-twin engine, super-tuned. Prospective buyers who called at the Brough factory could see it touch 100 m.p.h. on the road "possibly with the demonstrator riding with hands off". In 1937 one 1,000 c.c. model established a world speed record at nearly 170 m.p.h.

T. E. Lawrence ("Lawrence of Arabia") was a passionate admirer of the make and found immense satisfaction and consolation in riding the various Broughs he owned, as can he gathered from his correspondence with George Brough and others—as interesting to motor cycle enthusiasts as to those whose interest in Lawrence is historical or literary—which is to be found in his published *Letters.* He records many remarkable fast rides—and some crashes—and writing to E. M. Forster in 1929 mentions that some anonymous person or persons (it was, in fact, Mr. and Mrs. Bernard Shaw) had bought and sent him "a new and apolaustic Brough". He was riding one of this make when he was involved in his fatal road accident in 1935.

From 1939 to 1945 Brough's factory was devoted to sub-contracts for Rolls-Royce Merlin aircraft engines.

January 13, 1970.

Ernest Brown, P.C., C.H., M.C., who died on February 16, 1962, at the age of 80, held a series of important Ministerial posts during the years between 1931 and 1945. From 1935 to 1940 he was Minister of Labour and in 1939 became Minister of National Service as well. He was also Secretary of State for Scotland from 1940 to 1941; Minister of Health from 1941 to 1943; Chancellor of the Duchy of Lancaster from 1943 to 1945; and Minister of Aircraft Production in 1945.

A most competent and hard-working Minister, he could be counted on to render loyal and effective service and to stand his ground against either pressure or attack. In the first of his important offices he had to bear the brunt of criticism on the still high incidence of unemployment, and, at the opening of the war, to begin the formidable task, which Mr. Ernest Bevin was to carry through as his successor, of allocating the country's labour resources between industry and the Armed Forces.

Ernest Brown was born at Torquay on August 27, 1881, the eldest son of William and Annie Brown, and educated there. His father was a Baptist preacher and it was from him that he learned the art of addressing public gatherings. He himself was to be an active Baptist worker, both as a lay treasure and later as honorary treasurer of the Baptist Missionary Society. Gifted with a tremendous and far-reaching platform voice and an unusual aptness and power of persuasion, he soon found himself employing them on behalf of the Liberal cause and in due course became one of the most effective of the Liberal platform speakers, especially in the open air.

In 1914 he joined the Sportsmans Battalion—he was always keenly interested in Rugby Football—and in 1916 received a commission in the Somerset Light Infantry. He was mentioned in dispatches and awarded the Military Cross and the Italian silver star. In 1918 he was chosen as Liberal Candidate for Salisbury but was unsuccessful both in this attempt and in a second contest in the same constituency in 1922. After another effort at Mitcham in February,

1923, he was eventually elected as Liberal Member for Rugby in November of that year. Naturally enough there was some speculation as to how he would adjust his stentorian gifts to the restricted space of the Lower Chamber.

TORY SUPPORT

At first he found some difficulty in doing so; but later they were to become more amenable and permit his vocal qualities to be appreciated. Brown was defeated at Rugby in 1924, but in 1927 succeeded by a small majority in winning the Leith election for his party. It was said at the time that 3,000 Conservative electors voted for him. It was an undoubted triumph for one who was a complete stranger to the constituency. In June, 1931, Brown joined Sir John Simon and Sir Robert Hutchinson in dissociating themselves from the Liberal Party on the ground that they could no longer be "even technically responsible" for the policy which was being pursued with regard to the Socialist Administration of the time. His action in this respect received the approval of the Liberals at Leith, a seat which he continued to represent as a Liberal National until his defeat in the 1945 general election.

From 1931 to 1932 Brown filled the office of Parliamentary Secretary to the Ministry of Health and was also Chairman of the Select Committee on Procedure. In the latter year he was appointed Secretary of the Mines Department. He was to prove a vigorous and active Minister and was soon engaged in negotiations with countries of Europe for the expansion of British export trade. The Gresford disaster occurred during his term, and he showed himself well able to defend his department against criticisms of its conduct.

In 1935 Brown was appointed Minister of Labour. He was responsible for the Agricultural Unemployment Insurance Act of 1936, which extended the principle of insurance to nearly all workers in agriculture, horticulture and forestry. He was at this period subject to frequent attack: but in 1937 the Trades Union Congress without a dissentient vote passed a resolution of thanks to him for the part he had played in organizing the workers in the distributive trades. As Minister of Labour Brown had naturally a great part to play in the organization under the menace of war of National Service, and in 1939 the Ministry of National Service was added to his own.

HOUSING PROBLEMS

In May, 1940, Brown became Secretary of State for Scotland in Churchill's Cabinet. He made a special study of hill sheep farming and did much to help it by securing a subsidy for breeding ewes. His last act in this office was to frame a Bill to continue the Arterial Drainage Act of 1930, and then in early 1941 he returned to his first department as Minister of Health. Some of his chief concerns were the continuing problems of evacuation, and he claimed that an 80 per cent success had been achieved. There were other huge problems of accommodation for workers which fell within his sphere, while the housing difficulties continued to increase. In June, 1943, a group of six members of Parliament tabled a motion which amounted to an attack upon his competence for his office: but others swiftly rallied to his support. The difficulties of the time rendered his an invidious part. There was, however, no question of the sincerity and singlemindedness of his aims or of the conscientiousness with which he discharged his duties. In November, 1943, Brown was succeeded by Mr. H. U. Willink and became Chancellor of the Duchy of Lancaster, remaining in that post until his short period as Minister of Aircraft Production from May to July, 1945, in the caretaker Government formed by Mr. Churchill before the general election.

Brown became Chairman of the Liberal National Party about a decade after this party had been formed and he made an effort to bring about reunion between it and the Liberal Party then under the leadership of Sir Archibald Sinclair.

In 1935 he was sworn of the Privy Council. He was made C.H. in 1945.

From his earliest days he was interested in yachting as well as in football. He was also a keen collector of books.

As a young man Brown married Eva, daughter of R. B. Narracott, of Torquay, whom he had first met as a child at Sunday School. She shared his religious and other interests. There were no children of the marriage. For over two and a half years she had been a patient in the hospital in which he died.

February 16, 1962.

Lieutenant-General Sir Frederick Browning, G.C.V.O., K.B.E., C.B., D.S.O., whose death took place on March 14, 1965, will be remembered as the man who created and commanded the British Airborne Forces in the Second World War. It was he who raised and trained our parachute battalions and brigades and the Glider Pilot Regiment, welding them into swift-moving, far-ranging, and hard-hitting battle formations which showed themselves superior to the Germans' best in dash, courage, and tenacity. All Browning's training and qualities combined to fit him for this task, his long regimental experience, his outstanding skill in tougher forms of sport in which he delighted, and his natural genius for command. He always loved flying, and had taken his pilot's certificate in 1931.

Frederick Arthur Montague Browning was born on December 20, 1896, the son of Colonel Frederick Browning, C.B.E. He was educated at Eton and Sandhurst and was commissioned in the Grenadier Guards in 1915. A few months later he was in the fighting line in France and, before his twentieth birthday, he had won the D.S.O. and the French Croix de Guerre.

At Eton he had already begun to show promise of the great athlete he was to become. Bobsleighing, running, and sailing were all grist to the mill. He represented England in the high hurdles at the Olympic Games and won the England high hurdles three seasons in succession; he also bobsleighed for England.

Between the wars Browning's career was that of a regimental officer except for four years when he was Adjutant at Sandhurst. In 1932 he married Daphne du Maurier, the novelist, daughter of Sir Gerald du Maurier. They had one son and two daughters.

He commanded the 2nd Battalion of the Grenadier Guards from 1936 till 1939, and subsequently was Commandant of the Small Arms School, Netheravon, Commander of 128 Infantry Brigade, and Commander of the Independent Guards Brigade Group.

When the Army was being reorganized after Dunkirk the decision was taken, late in 1940, to constitute our first airborne formation of troops to be towed in gliders and dropped by parachute, and Browning was chosen to command it. In the following year his command was expanded to become the 1st Airborne Division.

His units were first used in the Mediterranean campaign, but local conditions in North Africa and Italy did not give full scope to their powers. In their first big operation, in the landing in Sicily, they met misfortune. The wind blew very hard and in addition many of the American pilots of the transport aircraft had not been properly trained and had never flown before in operations. As a result more than a third of the gliders were cast off too early, and many of the men were drowned in the sea while most of the parachutists were scattered over south eastern Sicily far from their proper objectives.

NORMANDY LANDING

Between Sicily and Normandy great strides were made in training, and by January, 1944, the airborne force had been expanded to a Corps of which Browning, now 47 years of age, was given command with the rank of Lieutenant-General.

Browning's force was allotted a vital role in the Normandy landing, that of seizing and holding the left flank of the lodgment area between Caen and the sea, the open flank upon which the counter attack of the Panzer divisions would be launched with the object of rolling up the whole bridgehead before the seaborne troops could be securely established. This duty Browning assigned to Major-General Richard Gale's 6th Airborne Division. The division was dropped soon after midnight upon its objectives along the estuary of the Orne in time to give it six hours of darkness, before the arrival of the seaborne troops, to accomplish its task of blowing up bridges, destroying the German guns, and seizing defensive positions. All this was done with skill and gallantry, and repeated enemy attacks were driven off.

In August, 1944, the American and British airborne forces were formed into the Allied Airborne Army under the American General Lewis Brereton with Browning as his deputy. The next opportunity for the employment of airborne forces came in September when Montgomery attempted the bold stroke at Arnhem which he hoped would open the way for a rapid advance in Germany. His plan was to lay a carpet of airborne troops along a corridor 50 miles long ahead of the Second British Army and so enable it to cross the canals and rivers ahead and get over the Rhine 20 miles east of the Zuyder Zee. Browning was given command of the operation. On the first two days 2,800 aircraft and 1,000 gliders were used but, owing to a shortage of transport aircraft, the initial drop was not big enough. The weather turned against us and prevented the flying in of reinforcements, food, and ammunition, and, after a week's bitter and gallant fighting, the survivors of the 1st Airborne Division, about 2,400 out of the original 10,000, were ordered back from the end of the corridor.

Browning was not present at the last big airborne operation at the crossing of the Rhine six months later, for he had been transferred to Ceylon to take up the appointment of Chief of Staff of Lord Louis Mountbatten, Supreme Allied Commander South East Asia Command. In 1946 he was appointed Military Secretary to the Secretary of State for War, in which post he served for little over a year before retiring from the Army to take up his post in the Royal Household. He was Comptroller and Treasurer to the Queen (as Princess Elizabeth) from 1948 to 1952 and from 1952 to 1959 Treasurer to the Duke of Edinburgh.

Browning was created K.B.E. in 1946 and K.C.V.O. in 1953, and was made C.B. in 1943. He was deputy-chairman of the National Playing Fields Association, and the British Olympic Association. In 1960 he was appointed a Deputy Lieutenant for Cornwall.

March 15, 1965.

John Brownlee, the Australian baritone, who died in New York on January 10, 1969, made major careers in Paris, London and New York, and was a favourite of pre-war Glyndebourne festivals.

Born at Geelong, Australia, on January 7, 1901, John Donald Mackenzie Brownlee studied singing in Melbourne and was brought by Nellie Melba to Covent Garden for her London farewell performance in 1926, when Brownlee made his debut as Marcello in the last two acts of La Bohème. He then studied further in Paris with Dinh Gilly and was a member of the Paris Opera from 1927 until 1936, making his first appearance there as Athanael in Thais, and subsequently singing a wide variety of roles in French, German and Italian operas: they included Jokanaan and Kurwenal. Brownlee did not return to Wagner until much later. In 1930 he returned to Covent Garden to sing Golaud in Pelleas et Melisande, and during that decade was much praised in London for his well-schooled, intelligent and musicianly readings of French and Italian parts.

Brownlee's qualities as a Mozartian were nurtered at Glyndebourne, where he appeared from 1935 until 1939, and again after the war. Don Giovanni was his most famous role in Britain, but his Don Alfonso in Cosi fan tutte was also delightfully urbane. One of his few German roles was that of the Sprecher in Die Zauberflöte. His years at the Metropolitan Opera in New York began in 1937 with Rigoletto and lasted until 1958, when his last part was Kothner in Die Meistersinger.

January 20, 1969.

Lord Bruce of Melbourne, P.C., C.H., M.C., F.R.S., who died on August 25, 1967, at his home in London at the age of 84, was an outstanding and idiosyncratic figure in both Australian and Imperial politics. He became Prime Minister of Australia in 1923, when he was only 39, and remained in office until 1929—a record with few parallels in Australian federal history.

Like Deakin before him, and Sir Robert Menzies later, he was an Anglo-Australian devoted almost as much to the nourishing of British Commonwealth relations as to the interests of his native country, and like them he saw no contradiction in the pursuit of these twin ideals. But Bruce exited from Australian party politics as abruptly as he had entered them, and unlike Menzies made no spectacular comeback. Instead he spent the rest of his life in London, where he continued to play a useful if somewhat isolated role as the official representative of his country not only in the United Kingdom but in the League of Nations.

This role became extremely influential during the Abdication crisis and critical during the war when he was a member of the War Cabinet and served an Australian Labour Government as conscientiously as he had earlier that of his own party. In London his patrician manners probably proved more appropriate than they had in Melbourne and Canberra, and after the war he also did valuable work as chairman of the Finance Corporation for Industry and of the World Food Council. Bruce, equally fluent in the worlds of business, politics and sport, seemed to enjoy making a precise appraisal of his achievements difficult by his own, often deceptively off-hand references to them (he claimed that his chief advantage as a politician was that he did not give a damn) but they were by any standards impressive.

The Right Honourable Stanley Melbourne Bruce, first Viscount Bruce of Melbourne, was born in Melbourne on April 15, 1883, the youngest son of John Munroe Bruce, an Irishman of Scottish origin who had swept warehouse floors on his arrival in Melbourne and, prospering, was a founder of Paterson, Laing and Bruce, one of the largest soft goods houses in Australia. Bruce, born to genteel comfort, was educated at Melbourne Grammar School where he excelled at athletics if not scholarship.

On the death of his father in 1901 Bruce went into the family business for a year, but was determined to study at Cambridge, so he borrowed the requisite money from his sister and entered Trinity Hall.

At Cambridge, as at school, Bruce shone as an athlete. In 1904 he won a place in the Cambridge crew which beat Oxford by four and a half lengths. But among oarsmen he will probably be remembered more often as a coach of the Cambridge crews in 1911 and 1914, and for the part he played in putting rowing back on a proper footing at Cambridge in 1919. He became a Steward of Henley Regatta in 1948 and was president of Leander Club from 1948 to 1952.

In 1906, now a Cambridge graduate, Bruce was called to the Bar by the Middle Temple. He practised with some success, but on the outbreak of the First World War enlisted in the Inns of Court Regiment and obtained a commission in the Royal Fusiliers. He served as a captain in Gallipoli and France and won the M.C. and Croix de Guerre. Twice he was wounded—the second time severely—and in 1917 he was invalided out of the Army.

On the death of his eldest brother, Bruce returned to Australia to take control of the family business at the Melbourne end. When he was invited in 1918 to stand for the Commonwealth Parliament in the Nationalist interest at the Flinders by-election he declared that he had no intention of embarking on a political career, but characteristically accepted all the same and was an easy winner. In the House of Representatives he duly supported Hughes, but he made no great mark until 1921, when he was travelling in Europe and was asked by the Prime Minister at short notice to represent Australia at the League of Nations. Though making no claims to oratorical gifts, his speeches, based on his own military experience, earned him respect, and a few months after his return to Australia he succeeded Sir Joseph Cook as treasurer.

AFTER A RESIGNATION

Early in 1923, when Hughes was forced to resign under pressure from Dr. Earle Page, the Country Party leader, he nominated Bruce as his successor. Ironically Bruce incurred Hughes's enmity by accepting. Thus began the Bruce-Page Administration, the most celebrated political partnership in Federal history.

Bruce afterwards confided to Lord Casey that he had felt it was rather bad luck on the Australian people that there was nothing better offering, but he also said that he believed he was incomparably the best Prime Minister available. His main attractions were that he was untarnished by the political squabbling of the previous years and, in a period of Anglo-Australian euphoria, was an Anglicized Australian war hero. But as a political leader he was untested and his aloof and polished manner, even his dapper style of dress, were a mixed blessing on the uninhibited Australian political front. Yet, though he was the youngest member of his own Cabinet, he manipulated his colleagues with aplomb and introduced an orderliness into the conduct of public business which had been absent during Hughes's reign. His good relations with Page were the master key to his success.

That may have had an element of old man's fancy in it but his tribute to Bruce's administrative abilities—"his mind was assimilative to an extraordinary degree"—was just. So was the comment that Bruce "did not always choose his colleagues with an unerring instinct, but if they failed him he dispensed with them ruthlessly". The achievements of the Bruce-Page Government ranged from the creation of a central banking system and the Australian Loan Council to the Council for Scientific and Industrial Research and the Development and Migration Commission.

Bruce himself was not only Minister for External Affairs but took at various times the portfolios of Health, Trade and Customs and the Territories. In 1923 he attended the Imperial and Economic conferences in London and, after privately consulting Lord Milner, strongly advocated the extension of Empire trade and preference. Back in Australia he expressed disapproval of the British Labour Government's decision to abandon the provision of the naval base at Singapore, and decided to develop the Royal Australian Navy, sadly depleted after the war. He it was who determined that new Australian cruisers should be built on the Clyde. In the general election of 1925 the coalition was returned with a comfortable majority, and the following year Bruce was again in London at another Imperial conference.

The Bruce-Page Ministry fell when Bruce, piqued at the failure to secure new arbitration powers in the referendum of 1926, decided in 1929 to abandon the federal arbitration system. With the help of Hughes the Government were defeated in committee by one vote, the Speaker having resisted pressure from Bruce to save the Ministry by his vote. When Latham, the Attorney General, declined Bruce's invitation to take over from him, a dissolution was unavoidable, and at the ensuing polls Bruce lost not only the election but even his own seat.

He was still, by the standards of political longevity, a young man, and being an ex-Prime Minister carried embarrassments as well as privileges. Perhaps that explains why for the rest of his life (though he retained his membership of the Melbourne Club as well as the Athenaeum) he spent so little time in Australia.

LED AT OTTAWA

In 1931, after a world tour, he regained his seat at the general election which ended the Labour Government and he agreed to serve under Lyons as Minister without Portfolio. In 1932 he led the Australian delegation to the Ottawa conference where he contributed much both to its success and the safeguards of Australian economic interests. Afterwards, he went to London as Resident Minister. Here his suave but forceful personality, at home in both Westminster and the City, proved highly effective in negotiating the conversion of Australian loans. He also became, once again, Australian representative at the League of Nations Assembly and in 1936 was president of its council, as well as president of The Montreux Conference for the revision of the Straits convention. In 1933 he took part in the World Economic Conference and served on the Economic Commission.

The same year he gave up his seat and became High Commissioner in London, a step which marked his final withdrawal from Australian party politics. In 1939 when Lyons was ailing he apparently asked Bruce (who was visiting Australia) to succeed him. Bruce agreed on condition that he took over at once, despite the fact that he did not even have a seat in Parliament. According to Bruce, Lyons accepted this strange proposal at first, but changed his mind the following day. After Lyons died Bruce was also approached by Page, who was anxious to prevent Menzies from leading the Government; but this scheme also came to nothing, and Bruce's last chance to be once again Prime Minister evaporated.

At the League of Nations, and in his reports to Canberra, Bruce favoured an appeasement policy in Abyssinia and Europe, revealing here no more and no less wisdom than most of his contemporaries. During the Abdication crisis he influenced Baldwin in the formulation of his intransigent policy.

With the outbreak of war his life in London became much less leisurely and in June, 1942, the new Labour Prime Minister of Australia, Curtin, paid him the compliment of appointing him Commonwealth representative in the United Kingdom War Cabinet and on the Pacific War Council. That year he was also appointed Australian Minister to the Netherlands Government. Disappointed to find that his War Cabinet post carried little participation in the conduct of the war, and resentful of the scant respect shown for Australian attitudes, Bruce clashed more than once with Churchill, a conflict of two unbending, sometimes overbearing men, but inevitably an unequal one.

Bruce's appointment as High Commissioner was ended by the Labour Government in 1945 and after the war he did not resume any official connexion with Australian government and politics. Instead, in 1947 he was made chairman of the Finance Corporation for Industry and contributed during the next decade to the peacetime recovery of British industry. Between 1947 and 1951 he was also chairman of the World Food Council, where he made good use of the expertise he had acquired in the thirties. But one final distinction in Australian public life was his: in 1951 he became first Chancellor of the National University at Canberra, resigning in 1961.

In 1913 Bruce married Ethel, daughter of Andrew Anderson, at Sonning-on-Thames. She died in 1967. He leaves no heir.

August 26, 1967.

Lenny Bruce, the American comedian, was found dead in his Hollywood home on August 3, 1966. For several years his "sick" humour made him the most controversial of entertainers, and his career seemed to take the form of a running fight in which he was unequally matched against authority.

Born in 1927 in New York as Leonard Alfred Schneider, Lennie Bruce served in the United States Navy until 1946 and drifted from job to job—at one time he was a cinema usher, at another he worked in a peanut butter factory—until he began to appear in a Baltimore night club, and subsequently appeared as a comedian throughout the United States. In 1961 he was imprisoned for obscenity and from then onwards was the object of ceaseless attention from the authorities wherever he performed. In April, 1962, he was seen at the Establishment Club in London, but was refused permission to land in Britain to fulfil an engagement there a year later. In Australia, he was banned after a single show in Sydney. In May, 1963, a Los Angeles court found him guilty of illegal possession of drugs.

Lenny Bruce could, when he cared to do so, command all the techniques by means of which a comedian can succeed. Against these, as against the society in which he lived, he was an inveterate rebel whose rebellion was not merely political; he opposed a world which, in his view, was given cohesion only by the repression it endured from authority. His act, an unprepared improvisation on his experience and his state of mind, sought to deal with the tensions of which he felt his audience to be as keenly aware as he was himself, and if the discussion of sex and sexual experience was an obvious way to ventilate this, it was also the most powerfully disturbing, and Bruce sought to disturb rather than amuse.

Paradoxically, he was a moralist attempting to find some sort of lasting truth from his experience of life, an experience coloured by the divorce of his parents when he was five years old and subject to the violence and brutalities of the mid-twentieth century. He claimed to be aware of human sympathy only when working before an audience, but the blackness and pessimism which he expressed exceeded the level of tolerance—often, it seemed, he set out deliberately to do so—of many prepared to listen liberally to his amalgam of sermon and comic turn.

August 5, 1966.

Dr. Heinrich Brüning, who died on March 30, 1970, in Norwich, Vermont, at the age of 84, had some hours of glorious life and an age without a name. He was German chancellor from March, 1930 to May, 1932. Before then he was unknown. Afterwards he was obscure. During the two years he held the fate of Germany and of Europe in his hand.

Brüning was born at Münster, Westphalia, in 1885, of a middleclass Roman Catholic family. He studied political science at Bonn and other universities, and had a spell at the London School of Economics. In the 1914–18 War he was at first rejected for defective eyesight, then accepted in 1915 as a volunteer and had a distinguished career as an officer in the machine-gun corps, receiving the Iron Cross (first class).

PARTY SPOKESMAN

He entered the Reichstag in 1924 on the Centre Party (Roman Catholic) list, and became the party's spokesman on social and economic questions. In 1929 he became the party's official parliamentary leader. Germany had a government at this time of "the Great Coalition", embracing both the Social Democrats and bourgeois parties, under Hermann Müller. Early in 1930 under the impact of the world depression, the bourgeois parties insisted on reductions in unemployment benefit. The Social Democrats refused. The Great Coalition broke down, and Müller resigned.

President Hindenburg was not sorry. He did not welcome Socialist Ministers and was glad to have a government further to the Right. Brüning became Chancellor with the task of facing economic difficulties, even at the cost of unpopularity. This task was congenial to him. He was a martyr by conviction and in appearance, and did not regret that the German people should suffer after the prosperity of the preceding years. Brüning increased taxes, particularly on consumption; reduced unemployment benefit; and soon reduced as well the pay of public officials—with a cry that private industry should follow the example. His financial measures were carried through on the President's authority by emergency decree.

REICHSTAG CHALLENGE

The Reichstag had the power to challenge these decrees. On July 16, 1930, it exercised this power and rejected Bruning's fiscal measures by 256 to 193. He at once dissolved the Reichstag. This was a fatal step. The old Reichstag had a majority of convinced republicans and only 12 National Socialists. Brüning hoped that the election would return a Reichstag more to the Right, and so it did, but not the respectable Right of Brüning's hope. Instead there were 107 National Socialists. Brüning had paved the way for Hitler's victory.

Brüning now found that, against his will, his government could survive only if the Social Democrats tolerated it. Brüning resented this dependence and wished to escape from it by some daring stroke in foreign policy. His Foreign Minister, Curtius, duly projected a customs-union with Austria in defiance of the treaty of Versailles. The French protested and, in retaliation, withdrew their funds from central Europe. First Austrian and then German banks closed their doors. The customs-union was abandoned, Curtius had to resign, and Brüning himself took over the conduct of foreign affairs. He visited London and Paris hat in hand, pleaded for financial aid, and was saved by the moratorium which President Hoover proposed. The Social Democrats still stood by him. On October 14, 1931, a vote of no confidence in Brüning was rejected in the Reichstag by 295 votes to 270.

He was faced by a more immediate political problem. In March 1932, Hindenburg's term of office as President would come to an end. Brüning attempted to secure prolongation by a resolution of the Reichstag. This needed a two-thirds majority, and Hitler killed the proposal. Brüning seems also to have favoured a restoration of the monarchy, but the details of this are obscure, and the fallen Emperor William II ruined the idea by insisting that no Hohenzollern could be restored except himself. Hindenburg had therefore to run for reelection. Brüning constituted himself Hindenburg's election agent and chief advocate. He did all the speaking, conducted the campaign. Hitler was Hindenburg's rival. Inevitably therefore Hindenburg, or Brüning speaking for him, had to appeal for the votes of the Left. The appeal was successful. Hindenburg was elected by a considerable majority, though only after a second ballot.

This outcome was highly displeasing to the President. He was a Field Marshal, a high conservative, a Protestant, in his own imagination a Junker. Yet he had been elected President by the votes of working-class Socialists and Roman Catholics. He turned impatiently against Brüning who had landed him in this position. Brüning believed that he was within sight of success. His economic policy was beginning to show results. He had reduced state expenditure by a third, and the unemployment figures were no longer going up. The British and French governments had indicated that they were prepared to end reparations. The British and American governments, perhaps even the French, were prepared to remove most restrictions on German armaments.

On May 29, 1932, Hindenburg told Brüning that his government was not enough to the Right. On May 30 he was dismissed after a five minutes' audience.

Failure and disillusionment silenced Brüning for life. In 1933 he did not seek reelection to the Reichstag. On June 16, 1934, he left Germany—a fortnight before Hitler's blood bath. He was a research Fellow of Queen's College, Oxford, from 1937 to 1939 and Professor of Government at the Harvard Graduate School of Business Administration from 1939 to 1952. In his later years he returned to Germany and was Professor of Political Science at Cologne University.

April 1, 1970.

Christopher Tatham Brunner, C.B.E., a managing director of Shell-Mex and B.P., and a distinguished pioneer in the study of the economics of road transport and the oil industry, died at Hull after a short illness on March 25, 1962. He was 59.

Brunner's interest in the two industries started during his postgraduate work in economics at Manchester, where he was a distinguished student. Three books, which he wrote successively between 1925 and 1930 on *The Problems of Motor Transport, Road versus Rail*, and *The Problem of Oil*, opened up the systematic study of these subjects as seen from an economist's point of view. He had become a member of the staff of Shell-Mex Ltd. in 1926, and formed its statistical department in 1927, and thereafter held a series of growingly important positions in the distributive organization of the oil industry. He was an important figure in the wartime organization of the industry, and after the war played a leading part in adapting and modernizing the marketing arrangements of the oil industry in its period of rapid growth.

In spite of the growing burden this imposed, with much travelling, he still found time for his academic interests, wrote papers of importance, and was one of the most effective advocates of road development. He was known as "Lord M.1" in some circles. An extremely kind man, he found time, too, to keep in touch with a wide circle of friends to whom his death will be a great loss.

Born at Radcliffe-on-Trent, he was a pupil at Nottingham High School before studying economics at Manchester University. He was awarded The Frances Wood Memorial Prize of the Royal Statistical Society. Before joining Shell-Mex he worked with the Metropolitan Railway for a short spell.

OIL POSTS

During the war he was secretary of the management committee of the Petroleum Board and manager of the Board's secretariat. During the closing stages of the Petroleum Board's existence he was acting secretary. After the formation of Shell-Mex and B.P. Ltd. in 1932, he had remained in charge of the Statistical Department. In 1947 he was appointed an assistant general manager of the company, becoming a director three years later. His appointment as managing director was announced on February 27, 1962.

Among the numerous papers for which he will be remembered there was "The Pattern of the Oil Industry", given as his presidential address to the Institute of Transport in 1951; while another which attracted wide attention was "Large Scale Organization and Change—A Study in Oil Marketing", which was read at the Royal Society of Arts in 1958, and for which he received the Society's Silver Medal.

In the sphere of roads and road transport he broke new ground with his paper on "The Ideal Road System and its Economy" at the Institution of Highway Engineers in 1947. For many years he took a leading part in delegations to international conferences on roads and road transport, and for 10 years was vice-chairman of the British Road Federation

At the time of his death he was chairman of the London office of the International Road Federation and of the Road Research Board's Committee on Economics of the Department of Scientific and Industrial Research. He was also a member of the Grand Council of the Federation of British Industries and chairman of the Federation's Road Panel.

Created a C.B.E. in the 1962 New Year's Honours, Brunner was also a director of the National Benzole Company Ltd., the Power Petroleum Company Ltd., and Irish Shell and B.P. Ltd.

He married Augusta Bonnard (Dr. A. Bonnard). There were no children.

March 26, 1962.

Professor Emil Brunner, for over 30 years one of the world's outstanding Protestant theologians, died on April 6, 1966, in Zurich, at the age of 76.

He was one of the earliest leaders of the revival of Systematic Theology, which took place in Germany and Switzerland after the 1914-18 War. He was a sharp opponent of the fashionable theological liberalism of the time and in a long series of works on major Christian doctrine and on ethics he strove to restate the classical Reformation teaching in ways that took full account of the modern situation. His influence was, perhaps, even greater in English-speaking countries than on the Continent.

He was born in Switzerland on December 23, 1889, and was for many years Professor of Systematic Theology at the University of Zurich, where his teaching attracted many students from all over the world. He first achieved international prominence in the 1920s as an exponent, along with Karl Barth, of what was then called "the Theology of Crisis."

Barth's *Commentary on the Epistle to the Romans* was the first great prophetic outcry of this movement, but Brunner's *The Meditator*, which appeared in 1928, may reasonably be claimed to be the first systematic exposition on a major Christian doctrine in the terms of this theology. This book, and his great work on Christian ethics, *The Divine Imperative*, which appeared a few years later, were of great influence in the transformation which has taken place in Reformed Protestant theology in the last generation and did as much as any other books to help people recover their understanding of its distinctive message. English-speaking Protestants have usually found Brunner more readily intelligible and less disturbing than Barth.

These two books were followed by a long series of volumes which tried to interpret the Christian faith with special reference to the social and cultural situation in which the Church finds itself to-day. *Man in Revolt*, *Revelation and Reason*, and his Gifford Lectures, *Christianity and Civilization*, are outstanding among them.

In recent years Brunner had not only given us two volumes of his *Dogmatic Theology* but had also written some shorter books about the Church which expressed something of the radicalism concerning the historic churches characteristic of the tradition of Zwingli, the Reformer of Zurich. In contrast, some of his later writing about society, notably his *Justice and the Social Order*, displayed a more conservative attitude.

Comparison of Brunner with the great figure of Karl Barth in the rival and neighbouring city of Basle has always been inevitable, and it has to be confessed that neither theologian had been at his best in trying to deal with the other.

FAMOUS CONTROVERSY

Barth, in particular, attacked Brunner over their disagreements with a public vehemence more appropriate to politics than theology. This was particularly apparent in their famous controversy over Natural Theology, where Brunner seemed to Barth to be imperilling the foundation of their theological enterprise. Brunner's approach was always more detached and balanced than that of Barth, and he had a much more strongly developed pedagogic sense, but his books lack the prophetic power and the religious excitement of Barth at his best. Brunner's books did not always engage the reader's interest with a closely knit continuous argument, although they are great mines of wisdom on very many matters.

On his retirement from Zurich in 1953, Brunner took up an appointment for three years at the International Christian University at Tokyo. Two of his four sons died at an early age in very sad circumstances, and this experience prompted him to write one of his most moving and impressive books, *The Eternal Hope*.

Brunner spoke English fluently and was at home in the English speaking countries. Most of his major works were translated very shortly after their appearance by Miss Olive Wyon, but his Gifford Lectures were delivered in English. As a young man he taught for a year at a high school in Leeds, and he visited America several times. He received honorary degrees from several British and American universities. Quiet and courteous in manner, and slightly built, he immediately impressed those who met him with his vigilant and lively expression.

It was not surprising that he was a notable preacher, with a large following among the general public of Zurich.

April 7, 1966.

Dr. Martin Buber, Emeritus Professor of Social Philosophy at the Hebrew University of Jerusalem, died in Jerusalem on June 13, 1965. He was 87. Philosopher and sociologist, in many of his books he was the interpreter of Judaism and Jewish history.

Martin Buber was born in Vienna on February 8, 1878. His parents were divorced when he was three years old, and the boy went to live with his paternal grandfather. Saloman Buber was a wealthy banker, leader of the Vienna Jewish community, and a rabbinic scholar of note. Much of his time was spent in Lvov in Galicia, and the boy was thus brought into contact with eastern European Jewry, with the Russian movement for Enlightenment, with Hebrew as a living language and, above all, with the vitality and enthusiasm of Hasidism.

POPULAR MOVEMENT

This was a popular movement which arose in the eighteenth century in the Jewish communities of eastern Europe. In reaction against the intellectualism of traditional Judaism, it stressed spontaneity and joy in the relations of man to his Maker. But its curious mysticism, the uncontrolled ecstasy of its worship, and its veneration for its leaders as divine emanations caused it to be despised and misunderstood by emancipated western Jews.

To Buber it had the supreme merit of being alive, in contrast to the formalism which he had felt in the synagogues of Vienna.

In 1896 he entered Vienna University, and subsequently studied also at Berlin, Leipzig and Zurich. His subjects were philosophy and the history of art. Later he was to add to his Ph.D. of Vienna and Berlin honorary degrees in Divinity, Law and Letters from many universities. At the university he came into touch with Theodor Herzl, and became an enthusiastic Zionist, finding in the Zionist ideal the living spark which was lacking in contemporary Jewish life.

In 1901 he joined the staff of *Die Welt*, the official organ of the Zionist movement, as editor in charge of cultural questions. At the Zionist Congress in the same year he took sides with the "practicals" against those who gave priority to a political solution of Jewish need.

But Zionism was never to be his main interest, and he turned from contemporary Jewish problems to seek the real meaning of life in the deeper understanding of Hasidism. In 1907 there appeared *Die Legende des Baalschem* (first published in English as *Jewish Mysticism* in 1931), and it was followed by many other works on every aspect of the movement. The outbreak of war in 1914 recalled him to the immediate problems of Jewry, and in 1916 he began the publication of *Der Jude*, a monthly which sought to clarify the spiritual destiny of the Jewish people in both Europe and Palestine. In the same year appeared the first edition of *Reden über das Judentum* in which he defined his own religious position. Already in 1913 he had redefined his philosophical standpoint in *Daniel*, a book influenced by the existentialism of Kirkegaard as well as by the mysticism of Hasidism.

Daniel provides an obvious step towards his final declaration that "life is meeting", which was expressed in his most famous philosophical work, *Ich und Du*, in 1923 (translated into English as *I and Thou* in 1937). He himself tells of a tragic incident which was of capital importance in the crystallization of this philosophy. He was already well known; many came to seek his advice; on a certain occasion, when he was preoccupied with other things, a young man came; and, though Buber received him and spoke with him, he did not "meet" him, and the younger man went away and committed suicide.

TRANSLATING SCRIPTURES

In 1923 he began teaching at the Freies Jüdisches Lehrhaus at Frankfurt, an institution created by the genius of Franz Rosenzweig, the intellectual and spiritual leader of German Jewry, whom he had met two years previously. He became its president in 1933, and continued teaching there until 1938. Until 1933, he was also Professor of Jewish Theology and of the History of Religion at Frankfurt University.

In 1925 he was asked by a publisher to undertake a German translation of the Scriptures. He made the cooperation of Rosenzweig a condition of his acceptance; and the two scholars had almost finished work on the historical books and begun on Isaiah when Rosenzweig died in 1929. The translation was completed by Buber alone.

In 1938 he left Germany and went to the Hebrew University, Jerusalem, as Professor of Social Philosophy, a chair which he occupied until his retirement in 1951. He arrived at a time of trouble, and saw it continuously deepen.

PEACE WITH ARABS SOUGHT

Nevertheless, with the late Judah Magnes, and with colleagues such as Norman Bentwich and Ernst Simon, he resolutely sought peace with the Arab population, risking a great deal of his local reputation in doing so. From 1949 to 1953, the years of the greatest mass immigration into the new state, he was also head of the Institute of Adult Education, which was concentrated on the endless problem of the cultural absorption of the new citizens.

His stature as philosopher and prophet had grown steadily throughout the world, and in 1952 he was offered and accepted the Goethe Prize of the University of Frankfurt, an invitation which was echoed in the following year by the award of the Peace Prize of the German Book Trade. In 1963 he was awarded the Erasmus prize for contributions to European culture.

In his last years he did not write new books, but he was busy to the end preparing a fresh edition of his collected works.

In Germany he was a revered spiritual guide and prophet for the Jewish youth in their years of trial. At first he could not fill that place for the young generation of Israel, partly because of his nonconformist ideas about Jewish-Arab relations and the bi-national Palestine. But as his fame grew in the large academic world, he came to be acclaimed by the Jewish population of Israel as the seer and the sage.

June 14, 1965.

Frank Buchman, who died at Freudenstadt, West Germany, on August 8, 1961, at the age of 83, was the founder and, until his death, the acknowledged though unofficial leader of a religious movement variously known as the Oxford Group, Moral Re-Armament, or, less politely, as Buchmanism.

Beginning with many of the characteristics common to revivalist movements—imitation of the moral simplicity of early Christianity, public confession, fellowship of the initiated, private illumination by the divine will—M.R.A. grew up differently. As time passed it became less not more conscious of differences of sect and even of differences of creed and religion: its programme looked beyond changing the lives of people to changing the historical development of nations: rather than create a new spiritual élite it preferred to permeate the secular élites already existing in society. What began as the enthusiasms of a coterie became, in the eyes of its adherents, a world-wide ideology, an instrument of secular salvation.

Its founder was one of the most effective and least classifiable of the revivalists to come out of America, a country which specializes in their production. His speech was devoid of prophetic eloquence, his manners owed nothing to the solemnities of the hierophant, his way of life was far removed from apostolic poverty. With jovial assurance and with the appearance of one who is scrupulous in his toilet, he operated during some of his most fruitful years from a comfortable headquarters in Brown's Hotel, W.1. It was among men and women of secure and sophisticated social backgrounds that he chiefly sowed his seed. His power to alter the course of people's lives and to lead them to make worldly sacrifices for the way of life he recommended is well attested public knowledge. But the nature of that power remains an enigma to those who were not susceptible to its influence.

Frank Nathan Daniel Buchman was born at Pennsburg, Pennsylvania, on June 4, 1878, the son of Frank Buchman and Sarah Greenwalt.

SWISS EMIGRANTS

His father's family had migrated from St. Gallen in Switzerland in 1740. He graduated at Muhlenberg College and was ordained a minister in the Lutheran Church in 1902. For the next five years his work lay among the poor in Philadelphia where he was in charge of a hospice for waifs and strays. After a disagreement with his management committee he resigned in 1907 and went abroad.

His travels brought him to Keswick in the Lake District, and there in a small country chapel—the year was 1908—he was vouchsafed a vision of the Cross, which he used to recall in his reminiscences as the turning point of his life. The full quality of that vision remains veiled; but it evidently impressed on him the need to unburden his conscience by the open admission of sin. No sooner was he back in his hotel than he took pen and paper and wrote to each of the six committee men with whom he had quarrelled: "My dear Friend, I have nursed ill-will against you. I am sorry. Forgive me?" The committee men did not respond in the same spirit of humble repentance, or indeed in any way at all. His vision also appears to have given Buchman a sense of evangelical mission. "That same day", he recorded, "God used me to change the life of a Cambridge student who at this time was studying at Keswick."

When he had returned to the United States he was given the job of Y.M.C.A. secretary at Pennsylvania State University. His success at building up attendance at Bible classes was conspicuous. He was also able to practise his experimental evangelism. This was not everywhere well received. Some years later he was barred from the campus of Princeton University, where his methods were pronounced "dangerous from medical and psychological view points".

EXTENSIVE TRAVELS

From 1916 to 1921 he held an extension lectureship under the Hartford Theological Foundation. This enabled him to travel far and wide, and he spent some time in India, Korea, Japan, China, and the Philippines. It appears to have been at Kuling, in China, that there was held, in 1918, the first of the "house parties" which later became so well known a feature of Buchman's methods. In 1920 he went to Cambridge and enrolled at Westminster College, the Presbyterian theological college, and in the following year he paid his first visit to Oxford.

The impression he made on some of the junior, and senior, members of the university has been eloquently recorded. Buchman was then 43. He was tall and well scrubbed in appearance; he was alert and radiated a rather jovial sense of well-being. His way of penetrating the armour of worldliness and puncturing the philosophical pretensions of perplexed youth had all the art of simplicity: the naive question touching a raw spot, the remark of such stunning ordinariness that it riveted attention which had wandered from the elaborations of other speakers. But his shafts were guided by psychological shrewdness of long experience and they were tipped by the steel of a dedicated and profoundly confident man. His proselytizing prospered, and in 1922 he resigned his salaried post with the Hartford Foundation and settled down to work in Oxford.

Buchman's movement in those days went by the name of the First Century Christian Fellowship. The first qualification for followers was the resolve to live by the "four absolutes" of honesty, purity, love, and unselfishness. There was the informal ceremony of "sharing" in which the penitent ran over his sins and perplexities with the rest of the group to which he was attached. And there was the acceptance of "guidance", which was founded on the belief that if a person composed his mind in a readily attainable state of receptivity he would receive from God express directions as to his behaviour.

QUIET HOUR

So his followers would enter their "quiet hours" with notebooks open and pencils poised. Buchman was fond of illustrating this part of his teaching with metaphors drawn from the field of wireless telegraphy. "Any man can pick up divine messages if he will put his receiving set in order." "A spiritual radiogram in every home." He also emphasized the importance of comparing notes on guidance received. This was some safeguard against the excesses to which private illumination may lead: it also afforded the means of imposing some central cohesion on the movement.

At first Buchman worked privately and without noise, shunning the limelight. But as word of his success got round his dislike of publicity diminished. In 1928 a team of apostles set out from Oxford for South Africa. The newspapers there coined the expression "Oxford Group" to designate the party, and the title became the subject of much controversy. Those who both disliked the movement and valued the good name of Oxford accused Buchman of deliberately fostering acceptance of the sobriquet in order to give a *cachet* to his movement. Buchman's apologists claimed that the name was attached to them without any of their doing and in any case it was appropriate since so many of the leaders came from Oxford where Buchman had chiefly concentrated his activities. In 1939 the movement lost a legacy when the courts found that the Oxford Group was not a legally identifiable body, having no constitution, location or properly constituted officers. Later that year "The Oxford Group" was incorporated under the Companies Act, 1928, having as its objects "the advancement of the Christian religion and in particular by the means and in accordance with the principles of the Oxford Group Movement". But by the time that dispute was settled the name "Oxford Group" was already giving way to "Moral Re-Armament".

The mid–1930s were the time of most acute controversy—in England at least—over Buchman and his methods. The Oxford house parties were in full swing and Buchman had resumed his travelling habits carrying the word into the United States, Canada, Scandinavia, and Holland. The churches were for the most part warily neutral. They were eager to avoid the charge of bigotry, and they were impressed by Buchman's disclaimer that it was any part of his intention to found a separate sect. He always maintained indifference as between denominations, an impartiality that came to be extended even to religions as the company at the M.R.A. foundation at Caux began to be drawn from all quarters of the globe. Moreover, churchmen were ready to admit to themselves that Buchman had awakened enthusiasm where they had not succeeded in doing so, and this led some church leaders, among them Dr. Cosmo Lang, then Archbishop of Canterbury, to pay handsome tributes to his work.

WELCOME RECRUITS

Others were not so charitable. They were repelled by some of Buchman's methods, particularly the sharing of confessions, the rawness of the movement's publicity, and the apparent eagerness to recruit the wealthy and the celebrated. They distrusted the naivety of Buchman's views on "guidance", and they were aware that the movement's successes were accompanied by failures where the last state of the spiritual patient was worse than the first.

In May, 1938, Buchman launched the campaign for moral rearmament at East Ham town hall. It was more than a change of name: it marked a change of scale, from the personal to the international, in the activities of the movement. The European nations were rearming in the literal sense, and it was Buchman's thesis that that was not enough: the lives of nations, and particularly of statesmen, must be changed so that they became "God-controlled"; only then would the peoples of the world live in peace and happiness.

The next two years were perhaps the most active of Buchman's life. The East Ham speech was followed by an M.R.A. nordic assembly in August and by the first world assembly at Interlaken in September. In 1939 he crossed the Atlantic to establish M.R.A. in the United States, and when war came to Europe he was still there. He was under some suspicion in patriotic quarters on account of his relations with some of the Nazi leaders whose lives he had at one time entertained hopes of changing, and because of an incautious reference to Hitler, for whose existence he had once publicly thanked heaven. There was also a feeling that some of the younger labourers in his vineyard would look better in uniform.

THE CAUX ASSEMBLIES

Once the United States was in the war Buchman threw himself into the cause with unimpeachable patriotic fervour. M.R.A. produced a document called "You Can Defend America", a judicious blend of Oxford Group principles and American national sentiment, which the War Department described as "probably the most challenging statement of this nation's philosophy of national defence that has yet been published". On the basis of this document Buchman and his fellow workers set about the task of fortifying the morale of the American nation.

In 1946 Buchman returned to Europe. He held the first postwar M.R.A. world assembly in that year at Caux-sur-Montreux. It was the first of an unbroken series of annual assemblies to be held at that cluster of hotels high above the Lake of Geneva, which is now in effect the international headquarters of the movement.

An American admiral once opined that the choice for his country was M.R.A. or communism. The same choice, it was later proclaimed, confronted not just America but all mankind.

AN IDEOLOGY

In Buchman's last years M.R.A. came to be presented as an ideology, the only force capable of withstanding and coming to terms with communism. Its ambitions and its claims grew larger. "Like a mighty army moves this force across the world", said Buchman in one of his birthday addresses. The eirenic work of M.R.A. in Cyprus, Kenya, Congo, Japan, Latin America, all the world over, became the chief topic of its publicity; and the favourable observations of newspapers and public men were harvested and reissued to give colourable support to these claims. The over-enthusiastic use of a press cuttings service, sometimes prompting embarrassing disclaimers, was a weakness of Buchman's propaganda. Exaggerations tended to obscure the undoubted ability of Buchman and his disciples to bring individuals of many different races, creeds, and stations to abandon their customary antagonisms and to exude good will.

WORLD-WIDE

From Caux and from his other headquarters at Berkeley Square in London and Mackinac Island in the United States, Buchman, with no visible administrative structure to assist him, continued to preside over the world-wide activities of the movement which he founded. Stouter now, stooping a little, with failing eyesight, walking with a stick, still the soul of frank geniality, still exercising his undoubted power to arrest the full stream of a man's life and divert it into the channels of sacrifice and self-examination, the aging religious leader moved about the world passing with indifferent ease through the closets of European statesmen, the tribal ceremonies of Africa, or the floral hospitality of the East.

Buchman was a chevalier of the Legion of Honour, a commander of the Order of King George I of Greece, a recipient of the German Grand Cross of Merit, and of Japanese, Chinese, Siamese, Philippine and Iranian decorations, an honorary doctor of divinity of Muhlenberg College, and an honorary doctor of laws of Oglethorpe College.

He was unmarried.

August 9, 1961.

Sir Alfred Bucknill, P.C., a Judge of the Probate, Divorce and Admiralty Division from 1935 until 1945 and a Lord Justice of Appeal from 1945 until his retirement in January, 1952, died at his London home on December 22, 1963. He was 83.

Lord Justice Bucknill was one of the many examples in the history of the Bench of the hereditary descent of the judicial ermine. He was the son of the Rt. Hon. Sir Thomas Bucknill, who had been a Judge of the King's Bench Division from 1899 to 1914. Before his elevation to the Bench the late Judge had enjoyed a large practice in the Admiralty Division. His father had also practised in that Court, though for a time during the period when Sir Charles Butt (now a very distant memory) presided there, his relations with that Judge had become so strained that he declined to appear before him. "Tommy Bucknill", as he was affectionately called, had a large general practice as well, and enjoyed great popularity at the Bar.

Alfred Townsend Bucknill was a younger son, and was born on August 15, 1880. He was educated at Cheam and Charterhouse and at Trinity College, Oxford, where in 1902 he took a first in Modern History. He was called to the Bar by the Inner Temple in 1903.

He was in chambers with that successful Admiralty advocate Butler Aspinall, and later with the future Mr. Justice Bateson, whom Bucknill succeeded on the Bench. He served in the War of 1914 in the Surrey Yeomanry, and on the Staff in France, Egypt and Ireland, and retired with the rank of Major with the Military O.B.E. His practice in the Admiralty Division and at shipping inquiries was very large. In 1928, while still a junior, he was made a Bencher of his Inn, of which he became Treasurer in 1951. He took silk in 1931. The years between the war and Bucknill's elevation to the Bench embraced the great slump in shipping and consequential decline of litigation in the Admiralty Court but death or retirement had removed several prominent leaders, and of such work as was left the largest share came to Bucknill. It was therefore no surprise when, on the death of Mr. Justice Bateson in January, 1935, Lord Sankey, then Lord Chancellor, nominated Bucknill for the vacant post, and the appointment was widely welcomed by the Bar, where his popularity was as great as had been his father's.

RIGHT TEMPERAMENT

He at once showed himself to be endowed with the true judicial temperament. Though new to the Probate and Divorce work of the Division, he absorbed the practice and procedure without difficulty.

His previous knowledge of the seamy side of life was perhaps scanty and it was sometimes said that a plausible witness could occasionally get away with a well-pitched tale that a judge more experienced in the ways of the world would have discounted.

In 1939, he first came prominently before the public when he was appointed to conduct the inquiry into the circumstances of the loss on June 1, 1939, of the submarine Thetis during her trial dive in Liverpool Bay. His conduct of the inquiry and his able and lucid report did much to enhance his already well established reputation. In February, 1942, he was President of the tribunal which inquired into the escape that month of the three German warships from Brest. The findings of the tribunal were presented in the following month, but they were never published. It was, however, stated in the House that they did not reveal that there were any serious deficiencies either in foresight, cooperation or organization. In December Bucknill was appointed a Lord Justice of Appeal to fill the vacancy caused by the death of Viscount Finlay.

In 1953 he published *The Nature of Evidence*, a valuable work which *The Times Literary Supplement* described as "a wise and in its way a gracious book".

The late Judge married in 1905, Brenda, daughter of H. P. Bulnois, Barrister-at-Law, and an Inspector under the former Local Government Board.

He leaves one son, who took silk in 1961. His wife died in 1953.

December 23, 1963.

Oliver V. S. Bulleid, C.B.E., who was the last truly original and progressive mechanical engineer of the steam locomotive era in Britain, died on April 25, 1970. He was 87.

Oliver Vaughan Snell Bulleid was born at Invercargill in New Zealand on September 19, 1882, and was brought up largely in England. In 1901, he began work as a premium apprentice to H. A. Ivatt at the Doncaster Works of the Great Northern Railway. He left the railway in 1908 to join the French Westinghouse Company, where he at last had a large enough salary to marry Ivatt's youngest daughter, Marjorie.

After a period as mechanical engineer to the Board of Trade for continental exhibitions, he returned to Doncaster in 1912 to begin the fruitful partnership with the great Sir Nigel Gresley, which survived the interruption of the 1914–18 War and lasted until 1937.

Gresley, the first Chief Mechanical Engineer of the London and North Eastern Railway, and Bulleid, his personal assistant, made a good combination. Gresley was the strong man who sat in gentle but firm judgment of Bulleid, the ideas man.

Bulleid became Chief Mechanical Engineer of the Southern Railway in 1937.

His controversial locomotive designs for the Southern need to be seen against their background. The air-smoothed "Merchant Navy" Pacifics, for instance, emerged amid the distractions of the Second World War when some materials, which would otherwise have been used, were unobtainable. In the 1940s, when these engines were built with the lighter variation on the same design, the "West Country" and "Battle of Britain" Pacifics, the primary need was for more power. This requirement was met in abundance and it was only in the 1950s, when fuel and maintenance costs had greatly increased and trains had become lighter, that British Railways were able to make out a case against running such extravagant engines in their original form.

NOVELTIES

All Bulleid's engines were full of novelties, both inward and outward, but all were designed with the consistent objective of increasing the availability of the steam locomotive so as to make it a genuine competitor with electric and diesel traction. This particularly applied to the "Leader" class which ran on two bogies and had a driver's cab at either end like any electric or diesel locomotive. The "Leader" failed through being produced with too little care in a race against the nationalization of the railways, which Bulleid opposed with all his vehemence as a right-wing Tory.

To escape from British Railways, on which he had little of the autocratic power previously allowed him, he moved to Dublin in 1949 as Consulting Mechanical Engineer and then Chief Mechanical Engineer of Córas Iompair Eireann.

April 28, 1970.

William Christian Bullitt, who died on February 15, 1967, in Paris at the age of 76, was the first United States Ambassador to the Soviet Union after President Roosevelt recognized that country in 1933.

He had a chequered career in politics, diplomacy and literature, and was something of a maverick and individualist whose views varied widely from time to time.

Thus he at first approved of the Soviet regime and later denounced it. In the same way he at first admired President Wilson and later disliked him, becoming part-author (with Sigmund Freud) of a controversial book written in 1932 but not published until 1967, in which Wilson was described as the victim of a "father complex" which accounted for his actions at Versailles and afterwards.

The book is called *Thomas Woodrow Wilson: Twenty-eighth President of the United States: A Philosophical Study*.

Born in Philadelphia, Pennsylvania, on January 25, 1891, the scion of a family which traced its line back to George Washington and Patrick Henry, Bullitt graduated from Yale in 1912, and entered Harvard Law School to train for the legal profession which had been traditional in his family for 300 years. However, his father died after he had been at Harvard for a year and his mother took him to Europe with her.

CUB REPORTER

Bullitt was in Moscow when the First World War broke out and he decided to become a journalist. Returning home, he began as a cub reporter of the *Philadelphia Public Ledger*, and was soon writing articles on European affairs, as an associate editor. During the war he acted as a foreign correspondent for the same paper and took charge of its Washington office. In that capacity he became friendly with Colonel House, President Wilson's confidant, who was a valuable source of inside information. Later Bullitt was to become known as the "Colonel House of the Roosevelt administration".

Wilson was sufficiently impressed with the talents of young Bullitt to send him as chief of a diplomatic mission to the then revolution-torn Russia, to see what could be done to resolve the many internal conflicts in that country. Bullitt negotiated a "treaty" with Lenin by which, he said, the Soviet regime recognised the independence of the Balkan States, Siberia and part of the Ukraine.

However, when Bullitt came to the Paris Peace Conference with his treaty and a recommendation that the United States recognize the Soviet regime in the Moscow-Leningrad area, both were rejected by the Big Four. Wilson refused to see him or discuss the treaty. Disgusted, Bullitt resigned in 1919, writing a letter to Wilson in which he said that "effective labour for a new world order" was no longer possible as a servant of the U.S. administration.

Not content with resigning, Bullitt went on publicly to criticize the Versailles Peace Treaty and the League of Nations. He told a Senate committee in 1919: "This is no peace. The world has been sold into another century of war." He went to the Riviera, saying he intended to "lie on the beach and watch the world go to hell."

SATIRICAL NOVEL

Bullitt's diplomatic career appeared to be ended, and in 1921 he joined the famous Players-Lasky Corporation in Hollywood. But his interest in politics and European affairs persisted. He lived for two years in Turkey, on the Bosphorus, and wrote a novel called *It's Not Done*, satirizing Philadelphia society. Later he was to write two more serious books, *Report to the American People* (1940) and *The Great Globe Itself* (1946).

After extensive travels in Europe, including Russia, Bullitt returned to Washington and resumed his war-time friendship with President Roosevelt, whom he had known as an Assistant Secretary of the Navy. When Roosevelt decided to run for President, he sent Bullitt to Europe to gather information, especially about the Soviet Union, in 1932. As one of the strongest advocates of diplomatic recognition, Bullitt was a natural choice for the post of first American ambassador to the Soviet Union, which he became in 1933, but within three years he became a vitriolic critic of that regime, saying it had broken its pledges to the United States. In 1936 he was appointed U.S. Ambassador to France.

When the Second World War started, and before the United States entered it, Bullitt became a foremost advocate of American aid to Britain. He resigned his Paris appointment and became a roving ambassador on behalf of Roosevelt. He carried out war tasks in several countries but wanted to see active service himself. Rejected twice because of his age, he joined the First French Army at the age of 44, served in several staff appointments, and was awarded the Croix de Guerre and the Legion of Honour by General de Gaulle.

In 1947 Bullitt testified before the House Committee on un-American activities, saying that Russia intended to "assault and conquer" the United States and that time was running short.

After that, he gradually faded from public life but continued to write, travel and speak publicly. His last book, written in conjunction with Sigmund Freud, amounts to a violent attack on Woodrow Wilson's character. Most critics have called it unfair. Its publication was delayed for 35 years, partly because Mrs. Wilson was living until a few years ago, and partly, there is a reason to believe, because Freud had second thoughts about the book.

Bullitt was twice married and divorced. By his second marriage he had a daughter.

February 16, 1967.

Daniel George Bunting, who died in London on October 2, 1967, was generally known by his pen name, Daniel George. He was born on January 20, 1890, in the Isle of Portland, the son of a naval man. He grew up in Southsea, left school when about 16, and in 1914 joined the Queen's Westminster Rifles, with which he served in the ranks in France. Awarded the Military Medal for a conspicuous act of bravery, he was commissioned in 1918.

After the war he rejoined an engineering firm in London, in which he rose to be general manager. While so employed he invented a spare part for motor cars which became well known, and also found time to pursue literature, his chief interest.

As a youth he had formed a library mostly of books bought second hand for less than a shilling, and he became an almost omnivorous reader, as is evident in the entertaining anthologies by which he deserves to be remembered and which indicate his amused curiosity and his particular sort of genial disillusionment. Among them were *A Peck of Troubles* (1936),

All in a Maze, edited with Rose Macaulay (1938), *A Book of Anecdotes* (1957), and *A Book of Characters* (1959). In *Lonely Pleasures* (1954) he collected miscellaneous essays and critical articles of his own; they reflect the range of his reading.

In 1940 Bunting became a reader for the firm of Jonathan Cape, with which he continued until 1963 when his health failed. Besides advisory and editorial work he undertook in later years a great deal of reviewing and was active both in the P.E.N. and The Book Society.

His activities kept him in touch with a large part of the vast output of new books, particularly fiction, and with innumerable authors, to many of whom he gave practical and often laborious help, encouragement and advice. His kind heart and quick wit made him many friends, and although sometimes sharp in repartee, he was the least spiteful of men.

In later life he became wholly absorbed in books, authors, reading and writing. Looking back, he was perhaps chagrined that in the prime of life he had only been able to devote his spare time to them. His first literary friend had been the late Holbrook Jackson, whose encouragement led to the publication by Jonathan Cape of *Tomorrow will be Different* (1932), an interior monologue in free verse about a single day in Bunting's life.

In 1914 he married Mary Margaret, daughter of the Rev. John Whittle. She predeceased him, and they had one son.

October 3, 1967.

Wilfrid Burke, former chairman of the Labour Party, died at his Middleton, Lancashire, home on July 18, 1968.

Burke was M.P. for Burnley from 1935 until retirement in 1959. During the Attlee Government he served as Assistant Postmaster General from 1945 to 1947. Burke joined the permanent staff of the Union of Shop, Distributive and Allied Workers in 1919 as an area organizer. He retired from his union post in 1954.

Wilfrid Andrew Burke was born at Liverpool in 1889. He was educated at Oulton College, Liverpool, and for some years was a teacher before entering commercial life in Manchester in 1918. He joined the trade union that later developed into the National Union of Distributive and Allied Workers, and threw himself whole-heartedly into the fight for better wages and conditions for warehouse workers engaged in the home trade. His spare time was devoted to Socialist propaganda. In 1920, when he was appointed Manchester organizer for his union, he had the solid backing of the district organization to which he was attached. A tireless advocate of Labour ideas, he served on the executive council of the Manchester Labour Party, and as a member of the city's employment committee. He enjoyed the hurly-burly of elections, and before entering Parliament as Member for Burnley had taken part in many contests, both municipal and parliamentary, having himself been Labour candidate on three occasions for the Blackley Division of Manchester.

In 1935, when he was nominated as Labour candidate for Burnley he received such support that he won back the seat from the Conservatives whose nominee, Rear-Admiral Gordon Campbell, V.C. had been successful at the previous General Election. In 1943 he was appointed a Labour Whip in the House of Commons, and after the General Election in 1945 the Prime Minister, Mr. Attlee, made him Assistant Postmaster General, under Lord Listowel, with authority to answer for his department in the House of Commons. In the following year he flew to the United States and during a month's tour saw the telecommunications systems of America and Canada at close quarters. He retained the office for two years. He was a member of the National Executive Committee of the Labour Party before becoming its chairman.

He married in 1920 Jean, daughter of Mr. D. Fleet of Orkney.

July 20, 1968.

Lieutenant-Colonel C. D. Burnell, D.S.O., O.B.E., one of the outstanding oarsmen of his day, died on October 3, 1969, at the age of 93.

Charles Desborough Burnell was born on January 13, 1876, the son of George Edward Burnell, and was educated at Eton and Magdalen College, Oxford. He rowed in the Eton eight which won the Ladies' Plate at Henley in 1894, and went straight on to row in four successive winning university crews, from 1895 to 1898. As a freshman in 1895 he also rowed in the Leander crew in the Grand Challenge Cup, which, owing to a mistake on the part of the umpire, was left at the post by Cornell University. In 1896 he rowed for Magdalen in the Stewards' and Visitors'. But it was in 1898 that the most successful period of his Henley rowing began. In that year he won both Grand and Stewards' for Leander. In 1899 he won the Grand with Leander and the Stewards' with his college. In 1900 he won both events with Leander, and in 1901 again took the Grand and lost the final of the Stewards'. In 1902, still with Leander, he lost both finals, but by this time had rowed in the finals of Henley's two senior events for five successive years winning the Grand four times and the Stewards' three times.

Burnell also rowed in the Leander crews which won the International Eights in Cork in 1902 and 1903, and six years after the close of his active career turned out again for Leander, in 1908, in the immortal "Old Men's Eight", which represented Great Britain in the first Olympic Regatta, beating the redoubtable Belgians in the final. At first criticized for an untidy style, Don Burnell, as he was known to all rowing men, was later referred to by R.P.P. Rowe, one of the strongest protagonists of orthodox rowing, as "undisputably the best heavyweight of the day", and by Steve Fairbairn, the iconoclast of orthodoxy, as the best oar he had ever seen.

Burnell became a steward and umpire at Henley in 1919, and a member of the committee of management in 1920. For some years he represented Oxford University on the Amateur Rowing Association, and he became president of Leander Club, and of the Henley Rowing Club, in 1952, holding the latter office until his death. He umpired the Boat Race from 1927 to 1930. By oarsmen he will be remembered as one who survived from the legendary golden age of Oxford and British rowing, and retained an ever youthful and progressive outlook on the sport he loved.

Although rowing was his first love, Burnell still found time for a remarkable range of activities. He joined The London Rifle Brigade in 1894, retiring as a major in 1913. In 1914 he rejoined as a captain, and went to France, where he commanded the 1st Battalion from 1917 to 1919. He was several times wounded, twice mentioned in dispatches, and gained the D.S.O. In the war of 1939–45 he served as a major in the 12th Berkshire (Upper Thames Patrol) Battalion of the Home Guard.

He was a former vice-chairman of the Walton and Weybridge U.D.C. and a former chairman of Wokingham R.D.C. He was also chairman of the Remenham Parish Council from 1919 to 1941, and church warden of St. Nicholas, Remenham, from 1926 onwards. He was appointed a Justice of the Peace for Berkshire in 1934 and in 1936 a Deputy Lieutenant. In 1954 he was created O.B.E. for public service in Berkshire.

He married, in 1903, Jessie Backhouse Hulke, and leaves two sons and two daughters.

His son R. D. Burnell rowed for Oxford and in 1948 earned another Olympic Gold medal for the family, in the double sculls, partnered by B. H. T. Bushnell. R. D. Burnell was for many years rowing correspondent of *The Times* and is now rowing correspondent of the *Sunday Times*.

October 6, 1969.

Commander Sir Dennistoun Burney, BT., C.M.G., died on November 11, 1968, in Hamilton, Bermuda, at the age of 79.

He was an early champion of naval aviation; the inventor of the paravane, a highly successful device to protect ships against mines, and was closely involved with the building of the airship R 100.

Charles Dennistoun Burney (Dennis Burney, as he was known in the Navy) was the only son of Admiral Sir Cecil Burney, Second-in-Command of the Grand Fleet at Jutland, who was created a baronet in 1921. Dennis was born on December 28, 1888. During 1909–10 he served in the destroyers Afridi and Crusader. The latter was employed on work for the Anti-Submarine Committee, of which his father was the first president.

Young Burney entered with zeal into experiments then in progress for towing explosive charges for defence against submarines. He borrowed a primitive aeroplane to discover the position of a sunken submarine, and was thereby inspired to study the new science of aeronautics. In September 1911, he went on half pay to pursue his researches at the Bristol aviation works of Sir George White. When he was later appointed to the battleship Venerable and to the cruiser Black Prince, he only remained long enough in each ship to apply for more half pay, returning each time to Bristol. In August, 1912, he was selected to specialize in gunnery. On completing the course a year later he was appointed to H.M.S. President for experimental work in anti-submarine defence and in seaplane construction. He had become convinced of the important future for aircraft in naval warfare, and an article he contributed to the *Naval Review*, produced for private circulation, in May, 1913, showed remarkable prescience. He suggested that aircraft should be used to attack submarines, and that ships should carry aircraft which should be fitted with wireless and should be used both for attack and reconnaissance. In collaboration with Mr. F. S. Barnwell at Bristol he constructed a seaplane for which the Admiralty afforded facilities for trials at Pembroke "at Lieutenant Burney's expense", until the outbreak of war in 1914 put a stop to them.

CHANNEL PATROL

When war began Burney took command of the destroyer Velox, in the Channel patrol. The Commander-in-Chief at Portsmouth, however, allowed him to be attached to the Vernon for experimental work while retaining command of the Velox. It was then that he had a large share in devising the first paravane, which was in effect a submarine aeroplane, a torpedo body fitted with a plane, to be towed outwards from the ship's side and kept below the surface at a depth unaffected by the speed of the ship, to deflect away from the ship any submarine mines in her path and cut their mooring wires so that they would come to the surface. First trials were made in the spring of 1915 and the first order placed by the Admiralty in June, in which month Burney was appointed to the Vernon to organize a new paravane department to provide ships of the Navy with the new device. Later on, merchant ships were fitted with a modified form known as an otter. During the war at least 50 examples occurred when warship paravanes cut mines, and 40 when merchant ship otters cut them, thereby saving themselves and, by disclosing the presence of mines, possibly saving many other vessels. In 1920, the Royal Commission on Awards to Inventors decided that the main credit for the invention of the paravane was due to Burney. He had neither requested nor received any pecuniary reward for the use of the invention by the Navy but had been permitted to patent it, whereby he became entitled to royalties for its use abroad or by merchant ships; and as he had received some £350,000 from patent rights no further payment as the inventor was recommended by the Commission. In the 1917 birthday honours he was made a C.M.G., an honour very rare for a lieutenant. He retired in 1920 as a lieutenant-commander, and was promoted to commander on the retired list on reaching the age of 40.

He had for long been attracted by the possibilities of the airship and now put a proposal to the Government that an Imperial Airship Service should be set up. To further his plans he entered Parliament as Unionist member for Uxbridge in 1922. He held the seat until 1929.

He was anxious to start the airship service with German Zeppelins which had been surrendered to Britain as part of the policy of reparations. At this time, Dr. Barnes Wallis, the scientist and inventor, was with Vickers at their head office in Broadway and he carried out a survey of the hulls of the German airships at Burney's request but he found them so corroded as to render them unsafe. Later, after long negotiations, Burney, in conjunction with Vickers, formed the Airship Guarantee Company, to which Wallis was appointed chief engineer, to carry out the design and construction which resulted in the R 100 being built at Howden in Yorkshire. Burney represented the builders on the R 100's acceptance flight from England to Canada and back in 1930.

In later years he turned his inventive mind to the improvement of fishing trawlers and in 1931 designed the Burney Streamline car. There was a choice of two engines, a six-cylinder Crossley and an eight-cylinder Beverley Barnes. It had independent suspension and hydraulic brakes but it was not a cheap car. The Duke of Windsor bought one but not a large number were sold.

He was the author of *The World, The Air and The Turbine*.

He married in 1921 Gladys, younger daughter of G. H. High, of Chicago. They had one son, Cecil Denniston Burney, who succeeds to the baronetcy.

November 14, 1968.

Sir Alfred Butt, first baronet, who died on December 8, 1962, at his home at Newmarket, at the age of 84, was for 14 years Unionist Member of Parliament for Balham and Tooting. In his day one of the most prominent figures in the theatrical world of London and known also as a racehorse owner, he was involved in 1936 in the matter of a leakage of Budget secrets which eventually led to his and J. H. Thomas's retirement from political life.

Alfred Butt was born on March 20, 1878, and educated in London. In his early days he was a clerk in Harrod's, but in 1898 secured employment as a secretary at the Palace Theatre. Later he became assistant manager and, in 1904, was appointed manager. In 1906 he joined the board and was managing director and chairman until 1920. He was also for a time managing director of the Gaiety, Adelphi, and Empire Theatres, in the case of the first two until 1919 and in that of the Empire until 1928. He was also for some years head of a large provincial circuit and of a syndicate which leased the Globe and Queen's Theatres.

As sole managing director and chairman of Drury Lane Theatre in the later 1920s he was responsible for many important productions, such as *Rose Marie*, *The Desert Song*, and *Show Boat*. He resigned, however, in 1931. He had also at various times a number of other theatrical interests, including the Victoria Palace, and produced many highly successful shows.

In 1917 and 1918 Butt was director of rationing at the Ministry of Food and in the latter year was knighted for his services. In 1916 he had been adopted as prospective Conservative candidate for the Walworth Division of Newington, and in 1922 was returned as Unionist Member for the Balham and Tooting Division of Wandsworth, a seat which he was to continue to represent until 1936. In 1929 he was created a baronet.

A friend of J. H. Thomas, he was in 1936 involved with him in the matter of a leakage of Budget secrets which became the subject of an investigation by a Tribunal of Inquiry. Butt gave evidence before it in which he denied that he had ever asked or received from Thomas any information in regard to the Budget or any other confidential matter, and proferred an explanation of certain insurances which he had effected.

TRIBUNAL'S FINDING

The Tribunal, however, found that there was an unauthorized disclosure by Thomas to Butt of information relating to the Budget, and that use was made of it by Butt for the purpose of his private gain. Butt reasserted his own innocence in the House of Commons and expressed his "horror" at having learnt that no opportunity to stand his trial in a Court of Justice was to be afforded him. He said that he had not intended to resign his seat but, in view of Thomas's resignation, he had decided to follow his example, and did so.

Butt was a keen racegoer as well as a familiar figure when younger at the big chemin de fer table at Deauville and other fashionable resorts. He bought the Brook stud at Newmarket to stand Orpen, and bred there the winner of the Oaks, Steady Aim, and Petition. Petition was much fancied to win the 2,000 Guineas but had an accident at the start. He had won the New Stakes at Ascot, the Gimcrack, and Champagne Stakes as a two-year-old. Later he won the Victoria Cup and Eclipse Stakes. Other well-known mares besides Steady Aim which Butt owned were Quick Arrow, Solar Flower, and Spend a Penny.

In 1902 he married Georgina Mary, daughter of Frederick Say of Norwich. She died in 1960 and later that year he married secondly, Wilhelmina Wahl. There was one son of the first marriage who now succeeds to the title.

December 10, 1962.

Professor John Everett Butt, who died on November 22, 1965, after a long illness, at the age of 59, had been Regius Professor of Rhetoric and English Literature in the University of Edinburgh since 1959. He was an authority on eighteenth-century literature and on Dickens, and General Editor of the Twickenham edition of Pope.

The son of Francis John Butt and Charlotte Butt, he was born at Hoole in Cheshire on April 17, 1906, and was educated at Shrewsbury School, and Merton College, Oxford. He had intended to read medicine on going up—he would have made an excellent family doctor—but after his preliminary year decided to transfer to the School of English Language and Literature. His choice of English introduced him to David Nichol Smith, then Goldsmiths' Reader, who acted as his tutor. He took a Second in Schools.

In the inter-war years few graduates went on

to research, but he was eager to take advantage of the newly established B.Litt. course, and to write a thesis on Thomas Tickell, the poet of Pope's times, to the canon of whose writings he was able to make interesting additions. He became a lecturer, first as a stop-gap at Leeds University, then, after a spell as Sub-Librarian of the English Schools Library at Oxford (the stipend for which was £80 per annum), at Bedford College, London (1930).

He was the sort of man a group of academics seize on to fill any vacant office—that of secretary, treasurer, or, as the years passed, chairman, for he had not only a good head and taste for practical matters but the character and personality that normally put the members of a committee on their best behaviour; there was the good thick velvet glove and, in addition, a hand inside it as flexible as it was firm. Because of gifts like these his war service, first in the Ministry of Home Security and then in the Home Office, was much liked, and when invited to stay on after the war he was sorely tempted to comply.

Fortunately for English studies and for thousands of future students he returned to his rightful groves in Regent's Park, migrating in 1946 as Professor to King's College (University of Durham), as it was then called, and from there in 1959 to Edinburgh. Meanwhile he had given much of the spare time of seven years to editing the *Review of English Studies*. In 1961 he was made a Fellow of the British Academy, and more recently had become a trustee of Dove Cottage.

VISITS TO AMERICA

He was a prince among professors, having all the qualities—intellectual, moral, practical, physical and personal—that a so-called Chair in a populous Department demands. To begin with he was a splendid lecturer. No one ever complained that he was inaudible. He spoke the King's English, and could make it ring. He declaimed passages of prose and verse (especially verse in couplets) with practised power, and for him every lecture was a concert performance of the classics and of his own elegant prose.

He had caught a few tricks from his hero. It was pleasantly amusing for his old Oxford friends to note, as time went by, the tricks of speech and the air of making mature literary judgments that he caught from Nichol Smith, and perhaps never wholly lost.

On the platform and off there was much that was boyish and sunny about him, and his gracious and as it were willowy dignity—he was six foot three in height—seemed the merely arithmetical and even sometimes slightly embarrassed total of all his other likable qualities. He was as much interested in research as in teaching, in postgraduates as in undergraduates, in writing and publishing as in talking, in students' personalities as in their brains, in plodders as in high-flyers, in students' socials as in seminars—and always in a way that was as much that of a kindly brother as of a kindly father.

As an ambassador to overseas universities he was much in demand. In particular he visited the University of California at Los Angeles for a session, and Yale 10 years later in 1962. Finally he did not forget that academic duties sometimes include the sad piety of completing—and completing promptly—the work of others broken off by death; he finished preparing the ms. of Norman Ault's edition of Pope's minor poems, and the study of Marvell by his close friend J. B. Leishman, the last book he was to publish. In 1965 other friends and admirers in America and England planned to honour his sixtieth birthday with a volume of their writings, which to their sorrow must now become a memorial.

EDITOR OF POPE

His own writings were mainly editorial and historical. His admiration for Nichol Smith had been reciprocated, and it was on the older man's judicious recommendation that at the age of 27 he was invited to become general editor of the projected Twickenham edition of Pope.

Characteristically he chose to edit the *Imitations of Horace* (1939) himself, poems deeply rooted in the lives and, as he was able to show, the politics of the time. He survived to see the end of the edition in sight, it having been decided at a late stage to add the two Homer translations to it. Meanwhile, he had done the bibliographical half of H. V. D. Dyson's *Augustans and Romantics* (1940) in the Cresset Press series, and had written *The Augustan Age* for Hutchinson's University Library. Almost up to the time of his death he was working on the final chapters of the later eighteenth century volume of the *Oxford History of English Literature*. The wide popularity of his Penguin translation of *Candide* (1947), which he followed up with one of *Zadig* and *L'Ingénu* (1964), gave him much satisfaction. It was in the English eighteenth century that he was most at home—he liked its strong appeal to our common humanity, and the public eloquence of its grand generalizations and satiric thunderbolts.

He was perhaps the very first mover of what is now moving so quickly, the interest in the historical and bibliographical particulars about mid-nineteenth-century fiction. He wanted to see the great English novels edited as he had edited the poems of Pope. Because of this he became joint general editor, along with Kathleen Tillotson, of the Clarendon Press Dickens, the first volume of which is now in the press. It is an edition dealing with the writing, revision, and printing of the novels, but his interest in the matter that would supply explanatory notes is well illustrated by his contributions to *Dickens at Work* (1957). He was a member of the advisory board of the Pilgrim Edition of Dickens's Letters, and had been invited to edit the fourth volume of it.

He married in 1941 Enid Margaret Hope, who survives him with their son and two daughters.

November 23, 1965.

Major Anthony Buxton, D.S.O., the author and naturalist, died on August 9, 1970, at the age of 88.

Buxton was one of those who took part in Horace de Vere Cole's classic hoax in 1910—a hoax which achieved national fame—when a party believed by the town of Weymouth, the railway authorities, and the Royal Navy to be the Emperor of Abyssinia and his suite were received with due pomp and ceremony in H.M.S. Dreadnought, flagship of the Home Fleet. The party, with the exception of Cole who was faultlessly dressed in top hat and frock coat, were dusky-faced, robed, beturbaned and bearded. Buxton played the Emperor, Duncan Grant and Guy Ridley bodyguards, Virginia Woolf an Abyssinian prince, and her brother Adrian Stephen, Herr Kaufmann, the German interpreter; Mr. Cholmondeley, the man from the F.O., was Cole.

Buxton, who had a quick ear and a sound classical training, and Stephen bore the burden of the day with their inspired improvisations—at one point Stephen introduced a few words of Swahili mugged up from an S.P.G. grammar in the train. Years later, Buxton remarked, drily, that they had discovered on the way down that it was perfectly easy to speak Abyssinian provided no one else present had ever heard that language.

Born in 1881, Buxton was educated at Harrow and Trinity College, Cambridge, where he took a second class in Natural Science.

He joined the Essex Yeomanry in 1905 and served with them in France from 1914 to 1918, being awarded the D.S.O. On demobilization, he joined the International secretariat of the League of Nations and lived at Geneva until 1931. For some time he was an assistant to Sir Eric Drummond, Secretary-General of the League.

He had bought the Horsey Hall estate in Norfolk in 1929 and went to live there in 1931 maintaining its large tract of Broadland and dunes as a private nature reserve in which marsh harriers, bearded tits and bitterns found sanctuary. He made over the freehold of Horsey to the National Trust in 1949.

As a boy, he had spent much time in Epping Forest, of which his father was a verderer, and made a special study of bird songs there, never forgetting a note once identified. His recreations were natural history, fishing, shooting and hunting. He wrote books on natural history, including *Sport in Peace and War* (1920), *Sporting Interludes at Geneva* (1928), *Fisherman Naturalist* (1934), *Travelling Naturalist* (1946) and *Happy Year* (1948).

He was for many years a member of the London Zoo Council and served the Norfolk and Norwich Naturalists' Society as president (1932–34) and Editor (1936–50).

Anthony Buxton never lost his youthful enthusiasm for life in the open air and took a deep interest in everything that affected the wild life at Horsey, from the spectacular sea flooding of 1938 to the coming of the coypus after the war. He made a close study of methods of sea defence in Holland and carried out experiments in land and dune reclamation on his own estate.

In 1926, he married Mary Constable-Maxwell (who died in 1953); they had one son and three daughters.

August 10, 1970.

Sir Laurence Byrne, who died on November 1, 1965, at Gosfield Hall, Essex, at the age of 69, was a Judge of the High Court from 1947 to 1960. It was he who tried the case in 1960 in which Penguin Books, Ltd., were acquitted of publishing an obscene book, an unexpurgated version of D. H. Lawrence's novel *Lady Chatterley's Lover*.

In 1945 he appeared with the Attorney General, Sir Hartley Shawcross, and Mr. Gerald Howard for the prosecution in the trial of William Joyce ("Lord Haw Haw").

Of Irish descent, he was the younger son of William Austin Byrne, and was born on September 17, 1896. He served in the First World War as a lieutenant in The Queen's Royal West Surrey Regiment and was called to the Bar by the Middle Temple in 1918. Without special interest, and having no distinguished Chamber background, he made his way at the criminal bar on his merits alone, and within 10 years of his call his merits as a defender of prisoners had attracted sufficiently the notice of the authorities as to obtain for him the appointment of Counsel to the Mint at the Central Criminal Court.

CROWN PROSECUTOR

In 1930 he was appointed Junior, in 1937 Second Senior, and in 1942 Senior Prosecuting Counsel to the Crown there. During those years there were few crucial trials at the Old Bailey in which he did not appear, and as a Crown prosecutor his merits were seen at their best.

In 1944 he refused the offer of the post of Director of Public Prosecutions on the retirement of Sir Edward Tindal Atkinson.

He was Recorder of Rochester from 1939 to 1945 and in the latter year was appointed a Judge of the Probate, Divorce and Admiralty Division of the High Court in place of Mr. Justice Henn Collins, who had been transferred to the King's Bench Division. Byrne was himself transferred to the King's Bench Division in February, 1947.

Byrne was an outstanding advocate. Invariably polite and seldom raising his voice, his grasp of detail and powers of cross-examination made him a formidable opponent.

As a Judge he soon gained a high reputation in civil as well as criminal cases, although at the Bar he had seldom, if ever, appeared in a civil court. Both at the Bar and on the Bench his outstanding characteristic was his strong sense of fairness. One of the last judgments that Byrne delivered, and certainly the most important, was the judgment of the Court of Criminal Appeal allowing the appeal of Smith from his conviction for capital murder. The House of Lords restored the conviction, holding, contrary to the judgment of the Court of Criminal Appeal, that in considering the mental element in murder a man's intentions must be judged by the natural consequences of his acts and that what he in fact intended is irrelevant.

The decision of the House of Lords roused a storm of protest in the United States and the common law countries of the Commonwealth, and surprised and shocked many members of the English Bar whose practice lay in criminal courts. It has just been announced that the Law Reform Commissioners are to consider the implications of Smith's case. There could be no better memorial to Byrne, with his lifelong concern for fair play, than the restoration by Parliament of the fundamental principle "actus non facit reum nisi mens sit rea" upon which the judgment which he delivered in Smith was based.

After his retirement he lived at Enniskerry, co. Wicklow, until last year, when he returned to live in Essex.

During his years as a Judge he was appointed chairman of a committee of inquiry, set up by the Home Secretary, Mr. Ede, into the method of taking depositions in criminal cases. After his retirement Byrne was appointed by the Jockey Club to be a member of the committee set up to review rules and procedures dealing with the administration of drugs to racehorses.

He married in 1928 Dorothy Frances, daughter of Joseph Harkness Tickell.

November 2, 1965.

C

Jean Cadell, who died on September 29, 1967, at the age of 83, excelled as an actress in portraying both in comedy and in drama verging on the tragic lop-sided or half-baked characters, such as might easily have been objects merely of ridicule or of pity. When she played them, however, they were also felt to be human beings in their own right, with dignity and integrity worthy of respect.

As a Scotswoman, Jean Cadell pronounced her surname with the accent on the first syllable, not, as is commonly done in England, on the second. The daughter of Dr. Francis Cadell, she was born in Edinburgh on September 13, 1884, but made her professional debut in London with the Stage Society at the age of 21. After some years spent on tour and as a member of the Glasgow Repertory Company, she was again seen in London in 1911 in the Scottish comedy *Bunty Pulls the Strings* and in the same play in New York, there appearing as a maiden aunt whose proposal of marriage to Bunty's father was said to be not so much a proposal as an ultimatum.

BARRIE REVIVAL

In 1914 she was in a revival in London of one of J. M. Barrie's early plays, and in Barrie's wartime playlet *The Old Lady Shows Her Medals.* Jean Cadell established herself by her performance as a Scottish charlady who pretended that a private in The Black Watch of the same name was her son. "I like the Scotch voice of you, woman: it drummles on like a hill burn", he said to her when they at last met—it would be no bad epitaph for the actress herself.

The professional co-respondent, in private life a spinster of unimpeachable rectitude, in Maugham's farce *Home and Beauty* and the caretaker in Barrie's *Mary Rose,* who knew the dismantled house to be haunted and lived in fear of seeing the ghost, were small parts that anyone who remembers her in them will always think of as Jean Cadell parts. In 1921 she played for the Stage Society what was not only a perfect Jean Cadell part but one that the whole of a full-length play depended upon: that of the most inquisitive and talkative inhabitant of a London boardinghouse in C. K. Munro's *At Mrs. Beam's.* It received only the statutory two performances, but it caused Walkley in *The Times* to apply the words masterpiece and genius to her performance in it. Two years afterwards it was revived at the Everyman, Hampstead, where she had meanwhile played the New England spinster in Eugene O'Neill's tragedy *Diff'rent,* and was transferred thence to the West End by Denis Eadie, who later presented her in Munro's new play, *Storm.* In the Theatre Guild's production of *At Mrs. Beam's,* in which the now expanded roles of the thief and his South American mistress were played by the Lunts, Jean Cadell took her old part in New York in 1926.

WILDE AND DICKENS

A very long run in *Marigold,* a comedy set in Early Victorian Scotland, was followed by her Miss Prism in Nigel Playfair's revival of *The Importance of being Earnest,* by an excursion into one of C. B. Cochran's musicals, and by her engagement as Mrs. Micawber in *David Copperfield,* adapted for the screen by Hugh Walpole by M.G.M. Walpole's own novel *The Old Ladies,* dramatized by Rodney Ackland, was the occasion of an impeccable performance by Jean Cadell as the owner of a piece of amber frightened literally to death by a greedy neighbour (Edith Evans), who coveted that one treasure of hers.

A less happy theatrical experience was her participation in Barrie's last play *The Boy David,* written for Elisabeth Bergner, which was generally thought to show signs of failing powers in the final act; but as Higgins' housekeeper she contributed to the success of Gabriel Pascal's *Pygmalion* film: and she had interesting parts in new plays by J. B. Priestley and Munro at the Malvern Festival in 1938. After an engagement in the Irish comedy *Spring Meeting* on Broadway, she reappeared in the same Priestley play in what was now wartime London, and took up her old part of the governess in Gielgud's production of *The Importance of being Earnest* in Britain during the war years and in New York in 1947. She was again associated with Wilde by her appearance as the elderly lady who orders her husband about and persistently calls one of the other men by a wrong name in *A Woman of No Importance* in 1953.

T.V. GRAND MOTHER

In her later years viewers of B.B.C., television saw her as the grandmother in episodes of the *Whiteoak* chronicle and as one of the two murderesses in the American farce *Arsenic and Old Lace.*

Jean Cadell married P. Perceval-Clark, the actor, who was also once a member of the Glasgow Repertory company and who subsequently often played with her in London. He died in 1938. John Cadell, their son, has become established in the theatre as an agent.

October 2, 1967.

Sir Alexander Cadogan, P.C., O.M., G.C.M.G., K.C.B., who was Permanent Under-Secretary of State for Foreign Affairs during the Second World War, died on July 9, 1968, in London at the age of 83. He succeeded Sir Robert Vanisttart when the latter was appointed Chief Diplomatic Adviser to the Foreign Secretary in 1938. Cadogan played an important part in the making of crucial decisions during the troubled, critical war years; and he was one of the advisers who accompanied Churchill, then Prime Minister, to Yalta and Potsdam. In 1950 Cadogan succeeded Lord Cromer as Government director of the Suez Canal Company—a post he held throughout the Suez crisis when the company was nationalized by the Egyptian Government and the directors were concerned with protecting the former shareholders' interests; Cadogan resigned in 1957.

B.B.C. CHAIRMAN.

In 1952 his appointment as chairman of the B.B.C. Governors was the subject of questions in the House of Commons—the number of the board of Governors had been increased from seven to nine at the same time. Before his term ended in 1957 he defended the curtailment of time devoted to the Third Programme.

According to one source, Cadogan at the time of the Suez crisis fought against the broadcasting of opinions contrary to the military operation which the troops could hear on the eve of battle. Cadogan argued that this would be demoralizing and dangerous. At a crucial meeting of the Governors the traditional B.B.C. point of view prevailed; its duty to inform was an overriding one and its broadcasts could not be suppressed in its overseas services whilst being allowed at home.

From 1952 to 1957 Cadogan was Britain's Permanent Representative to the United Nations.

CALM APPRAISAL

As an official, Cadogan's chief characteristic (a typically English one) was perhaps common sense and judgment carried to a point where they almost amounted to genius. In the rush of events, the quickness with which he distinguished those which were likely to be decisive, gave time for his cool and accurate mind to reach a calm appraisal of the situation and offer advice which could be counted upon to be sound, practical and sensible. He invariably commanded advice, particularly in London and at Geneva. In a tangled negotiation he was always on the look out for any positive indication, however slight, which pointed a way out of the deadlock and from which the basis of an agreement could be formed. He had a shrewd eye for scamped work, and pungent though good-tempered comment for folly and pretence, whether in men or in assemblies.

He was ambitious enough to be gratified at reaching the top of his profession, but he played his part as Chief Adviser to the Foreign Secretary without a trace of selfconsciousness or self-seeking. He gave his subordinates his full confidence and never disturbed them without need. With him at their head, the staff of the Foreign Office could work in the secure knowledge that, whatever crisis might arise, they had as their chief one who would be steady in his judgments, and in his personal dealings just and merciful. Although he had spent a considerable part of his career abroad, he never became a cosmopolitan either in his tastes or his outlook.

Alexander George Montagu Cadogan was born on November 23, 1884. He was the youngest son of the fifth Earl Cadogan, Lord-Lieutenant of Ireland at the turn of the century.

ETON DISTINCTIONS

His mother was Lady Beatrix, daughter of the second Earl of Craven. He was at A. C. Benson's House at Eton, was president of "Pop", secretary of the Musical Society and editor of the *Eton Chronicle*. He went on to Balliol College, Oxford, where he obtained a second class in modern history.

In 1908 he was nominated an attaché in the Diplomatic Service, and two years later, was promoted to Third Secretary. From 1910 to 1912 he was at Constantinople, returned to the Foreign Office in the latter year and in 1913 was sent to Vienna. On the outbreak of war he returned to London and was appointed a Junior Clerk. In 1912 he had married Lady Theodosia Acheson, daughter of the fourth Earl of Gosford.

In 1919 he was promoted a first Secretary and also became Private Secretary to Mr. Cecil (afterwards Lord) Harmsworth at that time parliamentary Under-Secretary of State for Foreign Affairs. In 1926 he was made a C.M.G., in 1928 became a Counsellor at the Foreign Office, and in 1932 received a C.B. His K.C.M.G. came in 1934; his K.C.B. in 1941. His principal preoccupation during most of his time in London was in connexion with the League of Nations and he brought devoted service and a rare enthusiasm to it. From about 1924 on he rendered invaluable help to the British Delegation to the League and his contribution to the fashioning of the British Draft Convention on Disarmament was specially noteworthy. He also did excellent work in regard to the Manchurian dispute.

SUCCESS IN CHINA

He had given such outstanding proof of his abilities that in 1933 he was appointed Minister at Peking, a difficult and most important post. He had already given considerable study to Far Eastern affairs. After arrival at Shanghai he went first to Hankow and Nanking, where he established cordial personal relations with the Chinese leaders, which he was to preserve throughout his period of office. He was a most active and successful Minister, moved about the country, and paid a visit to Hongkong. In 1935 the status of his legation was raised.

In 1936 he was appointed Deputy Under-Secretary of State in succession to Sir Victor Wellesley who had retired. In 1938 the Under-Secretary of State, Sir Robert Vansittart, was appointed to the newly created office of Chief Diplomatic Adviser to the Foreign Secretary, and Cadogan, an obvious successor, was promoted to his place.

He remained from January, 1938, till February, 1946. His tenure of this most arduous and responsible post thus covered the whole of the Second World War, the crucial 18 months before it, and the first six months of the Labour Government formed after the war. He was one of the advisers who accompanied the Prime Minister on many of the important conferences in the latter part of the war.

Cadogan played a very important part in the making of many crucial decisions in these troubled years. From his demeanour an observer would often not have known whether he was giving advice in some crisis which called for prompt and decisive action in the recasting of our foreign policy, or whether he was taking part in some more leisurely discussion on a matter of no great importance. He always seemed to be exactly the same, calm, unflurried, always able to report the facts of the situation in as short and simple a way as possible, never anxious to be first to express his own view on what should be done; yet he always seemed to have time to get to the heart of the matter and to give clear advice as to the proper course to adopt.

At time of crisis it may have seemed almost uncanny that anyone occupying such a responsible post could seem so dispassionate about what was happening. But all who were present with him day after day in the war years, ended by having a profound admiration and respect for his cool head and clear judgment; while no one who heard him on the occasions when he felt it was his duty to point out the weaknesses in some line of policy which seemed to find favour in high quarters, can have been left in doubt of his courage and common sense, or of the strength and intensity of his convictions.

Much the same qualities showed in his capacity as an administrator. He was not one of those for ever prodding the Heads of the Departments in the Foreign Office with inquiries or suggestions. He preferred to leave his staff to do their work in their own way, and only interfered when necessary.

In 1944 the Diplomatic Service, the Consular Service and the Administrative staff of the Foreign Office were united into a new combined Foreign Office. Cadogan was thus the first Permanent Head of this Service. No one could have been better fitted for the task, not only by his high professional competence, but also by his personal qualities. To others, he was considerate and scrupulously fairminded; but he himself and his own interests were entirely subordinated to the public service. He was made a G.C.M.G. in 1939, a P.C. in 1946, and O.M. in 1951.

July 10, 1968.

Roger Cambon, the former Minister and Counsellor of the French Embassy in London, who died on July 19, 1970, lived for the better part of 50 years in England, but his mind—always orderly, clarifying and gently sceptical—remained as French as his delightfully quiet and cultured voice. He was 88 when he died at his house in Thurloe Square, London.

He was in diplomacy all his life. He was the son of Jules Cambon, the famous Ambassador in Berlin; and nephew of Paul Cambon, who was Ambassador in London from 1898 to 1920.

Roger Cambon was to come to the London Embassy in 1924, only four years after his uncle left, and he remained at the Embassy until the fall of France in 1940.

With his parentage and his upbringing he was naturally and inevitably a diplomat of the old school at its very best. While at the embassy and in all his long years of retirement he gave out the wisest of advice; and very many friends went to him regularly, knowing that they would always learn from him something of value about diplomacy or politics or life.

In his view what counted first in diplomacy, before all else, was character; secondly came the power of calm judgment; and, far behind these, came intelligence and contacts. He himself had the character, the judgment and the intelligence in full measure. He had great kindness too. Perhaps his only fault was an unshakable modesty which kept him from accepting several posts after he left the embassy in 1940.

The chief failings against which a diplomat should guard himself, he used to say, were the desire to please, the temptation to be hasty, and the tendency to lower one's sights. He himself was always outstanding for the breadth and depth of the view which he took of problems.

THOUGHT IN DECADES

He thought in decades rather than days, and taught himself to see several moves ahead when foretelling the consequences of any proposed action.

He could show the verbal firmness that came from great clarity of mind; and then, typically, he would regret words which were categorical though always extremely courteous. In 1938, for example, he believed that he had deeply offended a hostess at a reception; she asked him hopefully whether he believed that war had been averted. He replied, "Madame, before Munich I thought it probable. Since Munich I know it to be quite certain". He told how his hostess turned sharply on her heels and left him.

He was equally clear when, in the terrible days when France was being defeated, he had to call on Lord Lloyd to ask, on instructions from Paris, whether more British aircraft could be sent to help in the fight in France. Lord Lloyd listened to his official request and then asked Cambon to give his personal judgment: would the operation be worthwhile? "No", replied Cambon, and he used to say that no word had cost him more effort or pain in his whole career. But his honesty would not let him fudge his reply.

After 1940 he left the Embassy and lived, with scanty means, in London. He was a French patriot above most other men, but he could not range himself with General de Gaulle; he gave advice to one or two of the little French newspapers and magazines that were being published in London. It was only after the war that he could draw on his money and then he still lived modestly.

In 1953 he married Madame Sabline, widow of Eugène Sabline, late Counsellor of the Russian Imperial Embassy in London. She died in 1966. He was made a K.C.V.O. (hon.) in 1939.

July 21, 1970.

Commander Donald Cameron, V.C., who died on April 10, 1961, in the Royal Naval Hospital at Haslar, Gosport, Hampshire, at the age of 45, won his award for one of the war's most daring exploits—the midget submarine attack on the German battleship Tirpitz in the fortified anchorage of Kaafiord, north Norway, in September, 1943.

A lieutenant at the time, he was in command of the X 6, which in company with another boat, the X 7, commanded by Lieutenant Basil Place, who also won a V.C., was towed across the North Sea by the submarine Truculent.

Having crossed the minefields safely X 6 and X 7 reached their waiting positions and spent a night charging batteries and remedying defects. Early on September 22 they set sail for Kaafiord. Place penetrated the anti-submarine boom but was then forced to dive by an enemy motor launch. He then became entangled in an anti-torpedo net and was two hours getting free. Cameron also had his troubles, since his periscope motor burnt out and he was obliged to raise and lower it by hand. Nonetheless at 7 a.m. he had got through the entrance to the Tirpitz's net defences and was within striking distance of his target.

The enemy was not yet aroused. Then at 7.7 a.m. something was seen from the Tirpitz; it was X 6 which had inadvertently broken surface after running aground. Though his periscope was out of action and his compass had failed Cameron groped his way close to the battleship, surfaced under grenade and small arms fire, released his charges and scuttled his vessel. The whole crew was picked up by motor boat and taken on board their victim.

IN THE NETS

As Place approached he fouled nets under which he was trying to pass and broke surface—only 30 yards from the Tirpitz. He dived again, struck the battleship, passed beneath her and released one of his charges. He then worked aft and released a second charge. In trying to get through the nets he again became entangled, broke free and ran into others. At 8.12 a violent explosion put him out of control. Constantly breaking surface and under heavy fire X 7 ran alongside—a gunnery target. Place and another officer were saved but the two other members of his crew were lost.

The explosion on board the Tirpitz caused "the whole great ship to heave several feet out of the water". The most serious damage was to the main turbines, all three sets being put out of action. The ship was thus immobilized.

The awards to Place and Cameron were made in 1944, the official announcement stating, "the courage, endurance and utter contempt for danger in the immediate face of the enemy shown by Lieutenant Place and Lieutenant Cameron during this determined and successful attack were supreme".

Cameron, who was born at Carluke, Lanarkshire, in 1916, entered the Royal Navy from the Merchant Service in 1939. He became a submarine officer in August, 1940.

He leaves a widow and four children.

April 12, 1961.

Professor Sir Roy Cameron, F.R.S., F.R.C.P., who died on October 7, 1966, at the age of 67, was honorary consulting pathologist to University College Hospital, and Emeritus Professor of Morbid Anatomy, University of London. He was by general consent the outstanding British pathologist of his time.

Gordon Roy Cameron was born at Victoria, Australia, on June 30, 1899, son of the Rev. G. Cameron, and was educated at Kyneton High School, Victoria, and at the universities of Melbourne and Freiburg. He graduated M.B., B.S., Melbourne (1922), and D.Sc. (1929), and was for some years a tutor at Queen's College, University of Melbourne. During 1926–28 he also held the post of assistant director of the Walter and Eliza Hall Institute for Medical Research and in 1930–33 he held a Beit Memorial Fellowship. He was appointed reader in morbid anatomy at University College Hospital Medical School in 1935 and two years later he was called to the university chair in that subject. He retired in 1964. He had been assistant editor of the *Journal of Pathology and Bacteriology* from 1935 to 1955, a member of the Agricultural Research Council from 1948 to 1956, and a member of the Medical Research Council from 1952 to 1956. He was elected F.R.C.P. London, under the special by-law, in 1941, and F.R.S. in 1946. He was the author of a book on *The Pathology of the Cell* (1952); *Chemistry of the Injured Cell* (1961); *Biliary Cirrhosis* (1962); and of numerous contributions to scientific journals. He was knighted for his services to pathology in 1957, was Royal Medallist of the Royal Society in 1960, and was elected first President of the College of Pathologists in 1962.

Cameron was immensely learned in both the substance and the history of pathology, but he wore his learning lightly and never allowed it to dim his interest in pathology as a developing subject, to which developments in related disciplines might at any time provide opportunities for advance. His training in Melbourne had provided him with a solid grounding in morbid anatomy, to which he often referred with gratitude: but it was there that he came under the influence of C. H. Kellaway, a physiologist turned pathologist and an outstanding experimentalist, whose example and teaching strengthened his own feeling that for progress in our understanding of disease the classical methods of morbid anatomy would have to be extensively supplemented by experimental techniques.

HEART OF THE MATTER

These techniques he applied with remarkable success to many problems, and particularly to the one to which he constantly returned, the responses of the liver to injury.

He was, as he himself once said, a simple-minded person, and this simple-mindedness often enabled him to go direct to the heart of a matter and to ask the simple questions that so often led to illuminating answers. But at least as important as this was his realization that developments in biochemistry made it possible to explain the changes in disease in objective biochemical terms—to show, for example, that when poisons acted on the liver, the macroscopic and microscopic changes in the liver cell were the consequence of interference with some normal biochemical characteristic of the cell—the permeability or impermeability of its external or internal membranes, or the activity of its various enzyme systems. On this application of biochemical ideas to pathological change his future fame is likely to rest.

In his early years he was a strong, healthy man of middle height, very interested in walking and mountain climbing; in his first winters in England he suffered severely from asthma.

PUCKISH HUMOUR

As he got older he became rather heavier and less active, and rather more bald, and his general appearance might have suggested undue solemnity; but he in fact possessed a puckish sense of humour, and his rather solemn face was often split by a cheerful grin as he recounted absurdities of human behaviour, past and present.

As a teacher and as a collaborator he was superb. Though well aware of his own capacity, he never struck any attitudes about it, and was only too willing to listen to, as well as to guide, the opinions of others. In an appreciation of C. H. Kellaway he refers to Kellaway's capacity for bringing on shy young men. There must be many such shy young men who owe almost everything of their scientific and much of their personal development to Cameron's understanding, kindness and generosity.

His interests were wide not only in his own subject but in the arts; he was, for instance, a considerable authority on the Renaissance Popes, and on the history of the Renaissance in Italy, a country he loved and delighted to visit.

Much of his work, and the attitudes that inspired it, have passed into the general body of pathology; a scientist can hardly hope for more. But his friends are likely to remember him at least as much for delightful conversations in his little office in the Graham Department of University College Hospital Medical School and in the lounge of the Athenaeum, where he would talk with excitement about pathology and pathologists, and with a bubbling amusement about human activity in general. He will not easily be forgotten. He was unmarried.

October 10, 1966.

Sir Sydney Camm, C.B.E., F.R.AE.S., who died on March 12, 1966, at Richmond (Surrey) Golf Course at the age of 72, was one of the most consistently successful designers the aircraft industry has ever had. He also stood alone as the only eminent designer who climbed the ladder from skilled craftsman without making a false step through all the changes from "stick and string" aircraft to the complicated metal structures of later years, from bi-planes to monoplanes, from the modest speeds of the twenties to the sonic speeds of the fifties and even at the finish, from orthodox to vertical takeoff and landing.

He had ample reason to be satisfied with the success a lifetime of devotion brought him and it made him a forceful and somewhat intolerant advocate of his own conclusions. Over the years these were proved so often to be right that Camm came to be accepted in the industry with slightly amused affection as one who was entitled to be eccentric and aggressive, particularly as those characteristics were based on solid convictions, the product of careful thinking and shrewd appraisal.

His defiant ploughing of his own furrow lasted right on to the end of his designing career. His final effort was a military aircraft to free the service from the old tyranny of the prepared airfield and so to enable it to do duty like the Army in places where none of the amenities of mechanized warfare were to be found. This was the attack aircraft known throughout its prototype period by the serial number 1127. It came into existence as a private venture but before it flew, Camm's assured eloquence reinforced by his reputation of never having been wrong won official favour for it and an order for a number of prototypes. In it he used an entirely new engine. That was in keeping with his custom. He had done the same years before in the Fury fighter and the Hart light bomber; he did it again in the Hurricane; he did it still more audaciously in the Typhoon, but in the 1127 he took a bigger risk than with any of these and, with his usual tenacity, proved it to have been a calculated risk.

DEFLECTED JETS

In that aircraft he committed himself to the dual-purpose jet engine designed to apply jet thrust for lift or propulsion or any combination of the two. This meant the rejection of the earlier system in which separate jet engines were used for lift and for forward speed. It involved deflecting the jet stream through swivelling nozzles to allow vertical take-off and also the delicate transition to ordinary flight on lift generated by the wing. Its challenge brought Camm's experience with high-performance aircraft into the relatively unexplored field of vertical flight and demanded a design suitable for high speed and yet docile and relatively stable in the low-speed range.

The airframe was ready before the new engine had reached its promised output of power and hovering tests were done with only just enough thrust to support the structure and its test pilot. When these were followed by the orthodox test flying and then by a mixture of lift and thrust and propulsive thrust, the essay in modern design was seen to have succeeded. By that time, Camm was nearly 68. His interest in aerodynamics had begun in his schooldays at Windsor, where he was born in 1893, and had endured throughout his life. While still at school, he had made model aircraft. At the age of 19 he became secretary of the Windsor Model Aeroplane Club, and two years later he made his way as a woodworker into the aircraft industry.

ATLANTIC ATTEMPT

Manufacture was on a small scale in those days and design was only just beginning to arrive at sound principles of aerodynamics and stressing so that Sydney from 1914 onwards saw the steps by which it advanced from an art to something approaching a science. By good fortune, he also found himself working in the Martinsyde company for one of the ablest designers in the industry, the late G.H. Handasyde, whose enterprise had actually led to the construction of a machine for an attempt on the Atlantic crossing in 1914, an attempt which was never started because war came.

In that atmosphere of high endeavour, Camm learnt the ways of design, advancing from craftsman and mechanic to draughtsman and finally to senior draughtsman. By 1918 he was able to qualify for the associate fellowship of the Royal Aeronautical Society and could consider himself launched on a professional career. When in 1921 the Martinsyde company had to cease production, Mr. Handasyde retained a corner of the company's works at Woking and, taking Camm with him as assistant designer, went ahead with one more aircraft. Two years later Camm had a chance to join the Hawker company as a senior draughtsman. Another two years won him full recognition so that in 1925 he became chief designer; 10 years later he was made a director as well. In the interval the Fury and the Hart (with its numerous variants) had made his name and a start had been made on what was to become the Hurricane, the first eight-gun monoplane fighter, destined to bear the main burden in the Battle of Britain.

CONFIDENCE IN HURRICANE

How much confidence he had inspired in his fellow directors was shown by their decision to put the Hurricane into production two years before the war while the Air Ministry had still not made up its mind to place an order and the Spitfire was competing for R.A.F. business. Camm was backed with equal readiness by his board when he came forward in 1958 with his proposals for a vertical take-off fighter and the authorities, though keenly interested, were committed to a less revolutionary line of V.T.O.L. development elsewhere. During the war he had also brought forward a successor to the Hurricane, designed around the Napier Sabre H-shaped engine, another example of his peculiar ability to think his way along new paths and bulldoze his way through doubts and difficulties. The Typhoon had its troubles but it succeeded.

Into the jet age after the war he came with the same sweep and assurance. His Hunter fighter was a graceful example of the single-engined fighter of the new kind.

He was elected a fellow of the Royal Aeronautical Society in 1932 and served as the society's president in the year 1954–55. He had also received the gold medal for aeronautics in 1949. From 1951 to 1953 he was chairman of the technical board of the Society of British Aircraft Constructors. He leaves a widow and a daughter.

March 14, 1966.

Donald Malcolm Campbell, C.B.E., who was killed in an attempt on the water speed record on Lake Coniston on January 4, 1967, was a worthy successor to his father, Sir Malcolm Campbell, who in his time had held world records both on land and on water. He was 45.

Those who knew Campbell closely saw him not merely as a man of unfathomable courage but as a showman, with the inherent flair that would have probably carried him to the heights of the theatrical world. His approachability and zest for communicating his feelings to all who showed interest in his ventures was perhaps equalled only by his superstitions, of which the deepest was a belief that only blue could bring him continuing good fortune. The risks which Campbell, a lover of skiing, golf and sailing, accepted were not those which his critics would have cared to take, but he possessed the nerve of one whose whole life had been spent in the world of high speed. He died involved in a task to which he was utterly and inextricably devoted, as are other men to scaling mountains and plumbing the depths of the sea.

He was born on March 23, 1921, the only son of Sir Malcolm Campbell, and was educated at Uppingham. He then served apprenticeship as an engineer and was later a director of an engineering firm at Horley. He took an active interest in his father's attempts on the world water speed record, and formed the ambition early in life of challenging his father's prowess in that dangerous enterprise. He volunteered for the R.A.F. as a pilot in the Second World War, but was invalided out after having rheumatic fever.

He made his first attempt in 1949, nine months after Sir Malcolm Campbell's death. The record then to be beaten was his father's 141 m.p.h. set up 10 years before. The attempt was made in Sir Malcolm's Bluebird, but was delayed by bad weather and foiled by engine trouble.

U.S. SUCCESS

Next year, again on Coniston Water, he came within 0.6 m.p.h. of his father's speed, but by then the record had been captured by the United States and pushed up to 160 m.p.h.

In 1951 he competed successfully for the Oltranza cup on Lake Garda. The cup, which had been dedicated by the Italian poet Gabriele d'Annunzio to the memory of Sir Henry Segrave, had only been won once in the previous 20 years on account of the difficult conditions laid down for the race. Later that year he made a third attempt on the speed record on Coniston, this time using a new "prop-riding" method of propulsion. But the Bluebird struck something in the water while travelling at speed and sank. Campbell and his mechanic, Mr. Leo Villa, were rescued from the water by a launch. The career of Bluebird II was over.

FUND FOR BOAT

No sooner was this known than Campbell announced his intention of raising the funds for a new boat. He resigned his directorship and gave his time to exploring the possibilities of jet-propulsion. At the beginning of 1955 a new Bluebird was launched on Ullswater, an all-metal hydroplane with a turbo-jet engine having a thrust of 4,000 lb. When trials were complete, in the course of which he claimed a top speed of 185 m.p.h., Campbell was ready to make yet another attempt on the speed record, now 178 m.p.h., held by the American Mr. Stanley Sayers.

NO FAILURE

In July his perseverance was rewarded. He made the two stipulated runs over the measured kilometre without failure of engine or hull, the first at 215 m.p.h., the second at 189 m.p.h., an average of 202.32 m.p.h., and thus regained the speed record for Britain as his father had done. Never one to rest on his laurels he went to the United States that autumn and on November 16 set up a new record of 216.2 m.p.h. on Lake Mead, Nevada. In September, 1956, on Lake Coniston he raised the record to 225.63 m.p.h., in November the following year to 239.07 m.p.h. and on a perfect autumn day in November, 1958, with the first snow on the fells, to 248.62 m.p.h., exceeding for the first time the magic figure of 400 kilometres an hour. He was out again on Coniston the following spring and on May 14 took Bluebird, fitted with a new stabilizer fin, to 260.35 m.p.h. achieving on one run 275 m.p.h.

NEW BLUEBIRD

For several years past it had been plain that the land speed record was something no son of Sir Malcolm Campbell could lightly disregard. John Cobb's record of 394.196 m.p.h. set up in 1947 was much in Campbell's thoughts and the thoughts gradually took concrete shape.

The project for an entirely new Bluebird car was set in train in 1955, the task of designing it being given to Norris Brothers, the consulting engineers who had been responsible for the successful hydroplane. British suppliers of components readily responded to invitations to participate—Campbell regarded it as imperative that Bluebird should be entirely a British achievement—and an advisory council composed of a representative from each company was formed.

The car, driven by a Bristol-Siddeley Proteus free-turbine engine, developed more than 4,000 b.h.p. and was designed ultimately to reach a speed of 500 m.p.h. It arrived at Boston, Massachusetts, in August, 1960, and was then taken by road to the Bonneville Salt Flats, Utah.

CRASH AT 365 M.P.H.

The following month Campbell had a remarkable escape when he crashed at 365 m.p.h. on a trial run because of a strong cross wind that edged the car off the course into soft, rough salt. The car had to be written off, but he suffered only a hairline fracture of the skull.

A new Bluebird was built, with some modifications, and a new course was selected at Lake Eyre in South Australia. The first trial run took place in April, 1963, but exceptional rain and floods caused the postponement of the record-breaking attempt for that year. There followed criticism from Sir Alfred Owen, chairman and joint managing director of the Owen Organization, which built much of Bluebird, and Campbell issued a writ against him. This was, however, subsequently withdrawn and the disagreement resolved and Campbell returned to Australia for another attempt in 1964.

On July 17 Bluebird was twice timed through the measured mile at 403.1 m.p.h. and Cobb's record was at last broken. But it was soon to be eclipsed. The reign of Art Arfons, Craig Breedlove, and the pure jet cars had begun; unlike Campbell's car they were propelled by the sheer thrust of the jet engine which was not connected to the wheels. Their high speeds were not at once recognized but recognition or not speeds rose swiftly past 500 m.p.h. and in November, 1965, Breedlove, driving "Spirit of America", returned a speed of 600.60 m.p.h.

GOLDEN ROD'S RECORD

Finally, two young Californians, Bob and Bill Summers in a "conventional" piston-engined car, "Golden Rod", driven by four Chrysler Hemi V.8 motors, overtook Campbell's highest. In November, 1965, on the Bonneville Salt Flats Bob Summers averaged 409.277 m.p.h.

Campbell now turned again to water speed records. At the end of 1964 he had beaten his own figure of 260.35 m.p.h. at Perth, Western Australia, thus breaking both land and water records in one year.

In the autumn of 1966 he returned to Lake Coniston, determined to better his own world water speed record of 276.33 m.p.h., using the Bluebird hydroplane, powered with a Bristol Siddeley Orpheus engine. His aim at the time of his death was to take the record well above 300 m.p.h.

Simultaneously, Campbell was planning a new attack on the land speed record, with a three-wheeled pure jet vehicle. His target was to take it beyond the speed of sound, to at least 800 m.p.h., a speed at which he would have been facing the unknown hazards associated with the sonic boom and pressure waves beneath the vehicle. Preliminary work on this project had been going on for the past two years, with Campbell working in close cooperation with Mr. Kenneth Norris, the engineer who designed both the Bluebird car and the turbine-powered boat.

NO MERE DARE-DEVIL

It would be wrong to picture Donald Campbell as a mere daredevil driver, a hero from a boy's magazine, waving a cheery hand and tearing off down the salt flats. He had served his apprenticeship as an engineer and knew well what he was at and the forces against which he pitted his skill and that of the engineers who built his boats and his car. Though not a scientist, he had a firm grasp of scientific principles, of what was good engineering practice and what was not; and this close acquaintance with all aspects of the ventures he set out upon and the single-mindedness he shared with his father made him a lucid and compelling speaker; he could talk fluently without notes after dinner and his enthusiasm would invariably infect his audience, even those members of it with no particular interest in the pursuit of speed. In an age where outspoken patriotism was not always fashionable and sometimes raised a titter, Campbell spoke unselfconsciously of doing things for Britain and meant it. In 1957 he was appointed C.B.E. for services to speed boat development.

He was three times married. He is survived by his third wife Tonia Bern, the cabaret singer.

January 5, 1967.

Sir Gerald Campbell, G.C.M.G., British Minister at Washington in 1941 and again from 1942 to 1945 and, from 1941 to 1942, Director-General of British Information Services in New York, died on July 4, 1964, in a London nursing home. He was 84.

Few British officials have attained so great and wide a popularity in America. In his 18 years as Consul-General in Philadelphia, San Francisco and New York he made innumerable friends and came to enjoy an almost universal confidence. He was an excellent and ready speaker much in demand on public occasions and his natural gift of humour was always perfectly attuned to his American audiences. It would, in the delicate and difficult days which preceded the entry of the United States into the war, have been hard indeed to find a more ideal chief for the British publicity organization in that country.

For all his apparently easy-going amiability, Campbell was a shrewd and sagacious realist who not only thoroughly understood the attitude of the American people towards Great Britain but seemed to know instinctively how the British case could most effectively be presented.

Gerald Campbell was born in October, 1879, the son of the Rev. Colin Campbell, of Weston-super-Mare. He was educated at Repton and at Trinity College, Cambridge, where in 1901 he took his B.A. degree with honours in Classics. Having passed a competitive examination he was appointed Vice-Consul in the consular service in 1906 and, in 1907, was posted to Rio de Janeiro. Subsequently he served in the Congo, in Venice, and in Abyssinia.

In 1920 Campbell was promoted to be Consul-General at Philadelphia and in 1922 was transferred to San Francisco. He remained there doing admirable work until 1931, when on the retirement of Sir H. Gloster-Armstrong he became Consul-General at New York, a position which he filled with great distinction until 1938.

In May, 1938, Campbell was, in succession to Sir Francis Floud, appointed High Commissioner in Canada and took up his duties in October.

PRECEDENT CREATED

In January, 1941, it was announced that he had been made a Minister at Washington. It created a new diplomatic precedent for Nevile Butler already held that position, and no British Ambassador had ever before had two Ministers under him. After a few months in office he relinquished his diplomatic post in order to become Director-General of British Information Services in the United States. The increasing demand for fuller information in regard to Great Britain's war effort and for the improvement of the supply of news from British sources demanded an extension and elaboration of the organization which existed for this purpose. Campbell took under his control both the British Press Service and the British Library of Information in New York and proceeded at once to open additional offices in Washington and Chicago. He himself took up his station in New York and directed the activities of his organization from the Rockefeller Centre.

When in December the United States entered the war, a new situation arose. Washington, already the legislative executive and press capital of the country, became in addition the controlling centre of American war effort. It was, therefore, decided early in 1942 that Campbell should once again become a Minister and control British publicity from the Washington Embassy. A little later he was succeeded in his Director-Generalship by Harold Butler, but he remained at Washington and continued to discharge certain diplomatic functions. In retirement he published *Of True Experience*.

In 1911 he married Margaret, daughter of Henry E. Juler. They had three daughters. His wife died in 1961.

July 6, 1964.

The Rt. Rev. and Rt. Hon. H. C. Montgomery Campbell, P.C., K.C.V.O., M.C., died on December 26, 1970, at the age of 83.

Henry Colville Montgomery Campbell was the son of the Rev. S. Montgomery Campbell; he was educated at Malvern and Brasenose College, Oxford; after obtaining his degree he proceeded to Wells Theological College and was ordained in 1910 and started his ministry as curate of Alverstoke. In 1915 he married Joyce, daughter of the Rev. F. N. Thicknesse. In that same year he became a chaplain to the forces; he served at Gallipoli and was awarded the M.C.

He was by nature a shy person, but behind that shyness and a certain gruffness of manner there was a depth of feeling and affection. It was not at a first casual meeting with him that he would make his deepest impression. Those who had but a slight acquaintance with him might have thought that the sardonic wit which expressed itself so pungently and frequently showed him to be one who thought lightly of things which ought not to be treated lightly, but nothing could be farther from the truth. He was an utterly devoted person; devoted to God, devoted to his work, to his family and his friends. That became quite obvious to all those who knew him. He never spared himself and he expected a high degree of self discipline and devotion on the part of those who worked with him.

He was a good judge of people: that fact came to be recognized by those who have the responsibility of making important appointments in the church. Someone said of him "He knows more about the London clergy than they know themselves." It was people that he cared for: administration was only to be tolerated as a necessary means of carrying out the task of ministering to people, making that work more effective.

His own personal religion was, if labels are used, on Catholic lines rather than Evangelical, but the story of his ministry shows that matters of ceremonial were for him of quite secondary importance. He was Vicar of West Hackney, from 1919 to 1926 and rector of Hornsey from 1926 to 1933.

In 1933 he was appointed rector of St. George's, Hanover Square, and there remained for seven years, making his mark by his obvious sincerity, goodness, and great pastoral gifts.

SUFFRAGAN BISHOP

In 1940 Dr. Fisher chose him to be Bishop of Willesden and in 1942 Bishop of Kensington. In 1949 Montgomery Campbell was appointed to the See of Guildford, a diocese still very young and facing the inevitable problems of adolescence; chief among them perhaps being the building of the new cathedral, concerning which at first he was sceptical, if not actually opposed, but later he became converted to the idea and backed it with all the power he could. His contact with many schools in the diocese was a particular delight to him.

In 1956 he succeeded Dr. Wand as Bishop of London. He was enthroned in St. Paul's Cathedral in February and, so to speak, came back home to London and set out to administer the diocese he knew so well with that loving pastoral care which had been the chief mark of his life and ministry. That quality made him the devoted and loyal friend to his clergy, and called forth the deep respect and high regard of those countless people with whom the Bishop of London comes into close touch.

"Only one in every three Bishops of London should be someone like myself," he once told a friend, "one who is no figure in public life and no scholar, but simply and solely a Father in God who goes round the parishes visiting the chaps—the only thing I am any good at." In fact he was good for a great deal more. He was a wise and discerning administrator who could quickly grasp the essentials of a situation and impart to it his own sure touch. He was at heart a man of prayer and great dedication.

During his tenure of the See of London he was Dean of Her Majesty's Chapels Royal, and Prelate of the Order of the British Empire. In 1961 he was created K.C.V.O.

His wife died in 1928. He leaves four daughters and a son.

December 28, 1970.

Leslie Cannon, C.B.E., president of the electricians' union since 1963, and perhaps the most able and aggressive of Britain's right-wing union leaders, died on December 9, 1970, at the age of 50.

A communist himself in his early years, Cannon became the most relentless opponent of communism in the British trade union movement. Working indefatigably behind the scenes, he did more than any other man to expose and expel from control the communist leaders of the Electrical Trades Union, as it was then.

Having established dominance in his own union, he built himself a high reputation in the industrial field, becoming a part-time member of the Industrial Reorganisation Corporation, one of the T.U.C. representatives on the National Economic Development Council and on its committee on management education, training and development, and a member of the National Electronics Council, of the Energy Advisory Council, and of many other industrial and educational bodies.

Born in Wigan in 1920, "Les" was one of seven children whose father was unemployed for many years. "I have been haunted by the fear of poverty and debt", he once wrote. After gaining a grammar school scholarship, Cannon became an apprentice electrician and continued his studies at Wigan and District Mining and Technical College.

He soon became active in the Electrical Trades Union—a shop steward at 20 and district secretary at 22—and joined the active group of Lancashire communists in the union led by Mr. Frank Foulkes, later to become national president until Cannon and his associates threw him out and Cannon took his place.

BALLOT-RIGGING

In 1945 Cannon was elected to the national executive committee of the union. In the ensuing years the Communists established themselves in almost complete control and in 1954 Cannon, at that time among the most volubly doctrinaire of communists, was put in charge of the union's residential college at Esher.

But after the suppression of the Hungarian uprising by the Russians in 1956, he and some other Communists, including Mr. Frank Chapple, an active member of the E.T.U. national executive, resigned from the party. Early the next year the college was closed and Cannon was dismissed.

There existed at that time some remaining resistance to communists in the union, centring round Mr. John Byrne, district secretary in Glasgow, whenever the chief officials came up for re-election, which happened every five years. Mr. Byrne was the opposition candidate and always got a substantial vote.

But as time went on people began to examine and compare branch voting figures and found what seemed conclusive evidence of ballot-rigging. These activities were repeatedly exposed in newspapers and on television.

Mr. Byrne could not openly attack the national leadership without risking his foothold in office, but Cannon, back as a working electrician, had comparative freedom of action. With his detailed knowledge of how the communist machine worked, he visited union branches up and down the country exposing their strategems and maintained close contacts with newspapermen.

He now supplied the main driving force for the anti-communist movement. When the communists disqualified him from holding office in the union for five years, this did little to restrict his activities. A bitter animosity grew up between him and his former associates in the party. He also found time in this period to read for the Bar.

POWER BEHIND SCENES

The climax came when Mr. Byrne and Mr. Chapple issued writs for alleged fraud in the 1959 election for general secretary, when Mr. Frank Haxell, the communist holder of the office, was declared to have defeated Mr. Byrne. In a High Court action in 1961, Mr. Justice Winn found that five communist leaders of the union, including Mr. Foulkes and Mr. Haxell, had conspired together to prevent by fraudulent and unlawful devices the election of Mr. Byrne in place of Mr. Haxell, and declared Mr. Byrne to be general secretary.

Mr. Byrne took over the office immediately and made Cannon his personal assistant and the power behind the scenes. Later the same year, a new executive with a non-communist majority was elected which took office on January 1, 1962, and in July expelled Mr. Foulkes from union membership. In the subsequent election for a new president, Cannon was successful by a big majority.

Cannon was elected to the T.U.C. General Council in 1965, and quickly established himself as a leading if controversial figure on it. Among positions he held, in addition to those already mentioned, were membership of the development committee of the National Joint Advisory Council for the Electricity Supply Industry, of the governing council of Ruskin College (of which he was also a Visiting Fellow), of the governing body and of the council of Atlantic College, of the Royal Society of Arts, of the council of the Industrial Society, of the Society of Labour Lawyers, of the council of management of the Ditchley Foundation, of the Foundation on Employment and Automation and of the governing body of the Imperial College of Science and Technology. He was chairman of the Unit-holders' Investment Committee of the Trades Union Unit Trust and a vice-president of Political and Economic Planning.

December 10, 1970.

Eddie Cantor, the comedy star of many elaborate and popular musical films of the 1930s, and one of the last surviving products of the Florenz Ziegfeld era of the American theatre, died on October 10, 1964, at Beverley Hills. He was 72.

It used to be said of Ziegfeld that although he had a genius for discovering comedians, he had no great interest in them, considering that their function was simply to occupy the stage while his beautiful girls were changing their clothes. Will Rogers, Fannie Brice, Ed Wynn, W. C. Fields, Walter Catlett and Eddie Cantor each owed their early success to Ziegfeld, and of these he probably had most affection for Cantor. When talking pictures arrived, he even encouraged Cantor to accept a contract from Sam Goldwyn and go to Hollywood, because he realized the opportunities this would offer to a comedian of his style and talent; and Goldwyn more than justified this expectation.

Eddie Cantor was a son of New York and a child of the theatre. He was born on the East Side on January 31, 1892, and made his stage debut at the Clinton Music Hall at the age of 14. Later he joined Gus Edwards's *Kid Kabaret,* which included Eddie Buzzell, George Jessell and Lila Lee. During 1914 and 1915 he and Lila Lee toured together as a vaudeville team. In 1917 Cantor and Will Rogers both attracted the attention of Ziegfeld, who tried out each of them in his *Ziegfeld Roof* show before promoting each of them, with great success, to his famous *Ziegfeld Follies.*

His first appearance as a star was in *The Midnight Rounders* in 1920, and his reputation as one of Broadway's leading comedians was finally made on New Year's Eve, 1923, when he opened at the Earl Carroll theatre in *Kid Boots,* which ran for three years. This was followed by another immensely successful musical, *Whoopee.* Meanwhile he had made his screen debut in 1926 in a film version of *Kid Boots,* with Clara Bow as his leading lady.

The coming of sound and the patronage of Sam Goldwyn, a film producer with a remarkable flair for furthering the talent of his players, quickly established Cantor as a film star. His perky and irrepressible exuberance, and his gay and youthful appearance, enabled him to take over the type of comedy which Harold Lloyd would have made so well had he survived the advent of talking pictures. The film version of *Whoopee,* which was one of the earliest and most successful of film musicals, was followed by *Palmy Days, The Kid from Spain, Roman Scandals, Kid Millions, Strike Me Pink, Ali Baba Goes to Town,* and *Forty Little Mothers.* These were made in the decade before the war, during which time he also became a well-known broadcaster.

In 1941 he returned to Broadway to play in *Banjo Eyes,* but thereafter his appearances on the stage and in films were rare. He entered television after the Second World War but, after a heart attack in 1953, virtually retired. He published a volume of reminiscences under the title of *My Life is in Your Hands,* and was part author of a biography of Ziegfeld. The song by which he will chiefly be remembered will be "Making Whoopee" the theme song of the film, with its pleasing melody and its wry and sardonic lyric, which he sang so well.

He married Ida Tobias in 1914 and they had five daughters. His wife, who was the "Ida of Ida, Sweet as Apple Cider", died in 1962.

October 12, 1964.

René Capitant, former French Minister of Justice, died in Paris on May 23, 1970. He was 68.

He was Minister of Education in General de Gaulle's first government in 1944 and Minister of Justice in the last, formed after the events of May-June, 1968. He was the ablest and also the most intransigent of the left-wing Gaullists who were, in many ways, closer to the General's thinking than the mass of Gaullist deputies and most of their leaders. Capitant has been called "more Gaullist than de Gaulle".

"NESTLING"

His critics described both him and his friend Louis Vallon as Socialists nestling under the shoulder of de Gaulle.

It would have been an uncomfortable shoulder to nestle under unless the General had accepted the position.

Capitant was one of the oldest Gaullists. Born in 1901, his father, Henri Capitant, was one of the most celebrated jurists of France and the author of many of the standard manuals on French law. Capitant became Professor of Law at Strasbourg University and joined the staff of the 5th French Army in 1939 and it was there that he met Colonel de Gaulle then commanding a brigade of tanks behind the

Maginot Line. The fiery professor already known for his anti-Fascist activities and the sardonic soldier liked each other. As in the case of Debré, Malraux and others, Capitant remained under the spell for the rest of his life.

RESISTANCE FOUNDER

After the defeat in 1940, Captain was one of the founders of the Resistance movement Combat. Sent by Vichy to Algiers University, Capitant was one of the few active Gaullists in the colony. He was dismissed and for a short time imprisoned by General Giraud for "anti-national" activities. When de Gaulle left power in 1946, Capitant founded the first Gaullist group and became later National President of the Rassemblement du Peuple Français, where he soon found himself, as did the General, at odds with the conservative elements who increasingly dominated the organization. With Malraux he was one of the most outspoken critics of the use of torture in Algeria. Sent to Japan by the University in 1957, he missed the revolution of May, 1958, returned in 1960 and founded the left-wing Gaullist U.D.T. (Democratic Workers' Union). From 1962 he sat in Parliament as deputy for the Latin Quarter.

After 1962, he was active in attempting to turn Gaullism leftwards, further leftwards than the official doctrine of profit sharing. During the events of May-June, Capitant thought the government was mishandling the students and when a vote of censure was before the Assembly, he resigned his seat. He stated: "Our capitalism is worm-eaten...the government must go and de Gaulle must stay ... at present all that is anti-Gaullist has taken over from Gaullism." In the Couve de Murville government, formed in July, 1968, after the triumphant general election, his appointment as Minister of Justice was as significant as that of Edgar Faure as Minister of Education. Capitant was engaged in preparing plans for worker participation, plans which were as cordially disliked by Pompidou as Faure's reforms. In keeping with his angular forthright character, he resigned immediately after the General's departure, telling the interim President Alain Poher that he could not sit in a Cabinet presided over by someone who had helped to defeat the General's referendum proposals.

May 25, 1970.

General Lázaro Cárdenas, who died on October 19, 1970, at the age of 75, had been the enigmatic strong man of Mexican politics, much hated and much loved. After six years as president, from 1934 to 1940, he was scrupulous not to intervene directly in affairs of state. Nevertheless, his almost symbolic status as a champion of the peasants gave him unsought prestige among farming and union leaders, and also among young intellectuals not only in Mexico but throughout Latin America.

The expropriation of oil and railways, the drive to implement agricultural reforms postulated by the Mexican revolution, and the befriending of Spanish republicans all gave international fame to his administration and made it—in spite of some basic errors—the first effectively revolutionary regime after the turbulent phase of fighting and assassinations had subsided.

Lázaro Cárdenas was born in the small village of Jiquilpan, in Michoacán, of peasant parentage, in 1895. Already by 1923 he had distinguished himself as a military leader. Soon he had entered politics, and by 1930 was President of the Partido Nacional Revolucionario, later to be transformed into the all-powerful and monolithic present party, the Partido Revolucionario Institucional.

President Plutarco Elias Calles favoured him, and when a series of Calles puppets ruled the country Cárdenas was made first Minister of the Interior and then of War. Calles was clearly grooming him to follow in the puppet line, but during the presidential elections of 1934 Cárdenas was already laying plans to overthrow his benefactor, whom he considered by this time a betrayer of the revolution. Cárdenas electioneered actively all over the country, as a puppet should not have done.

As president he continued compaigning against Calles. He reformed the labour laws, thus bringing the workers on his side. He made friends with Roman Catholics who had been the chief enemies of Calles, and he allowed evangelical organizations to enter the country to work among the remote Indians. At the end of two years, Cárdenas felt strong enough to stage a coup and send Calles under armed escort across the United States border. The young Cárdenas, mildly spoken, steely eyed, with a high domed forehead, gentle mouth and stubborn chin, was now in total command of the country. He could go forward with his agrarian and educational reforms and prepare the way for the expropriation of foreign oil companies in 1938. Shortly afterwards he took over the railways. These two acts aroused deep suspicion abroad but were highly popular in nationalistic Mexico. The country behaved uprightly, paid fairly for the foreign properties, and set to work, against great difficulties, to build a truly national economy.

REFUGEES SETTLED

One of the most farsighted of Cárdenas' policies was his befriending of Spanish republican refugees. About 12,000 of them, including many intellectuals and highly skilled professional workers, were settled between 1939 and 1940. They gave Mexico a boost just when the country most needed technical aid. Earlier, in 1937 he had given Leon Trotsky asylum in Mexico.

On leaving the presidency in 1940, General Cárdenas became chief of the Pacific Military Zone and later Minister of National Defence. At the end of the war he seemed to retire from active politics, and occupied himself with studies to harness the waters of the Tepalcatepec, a tributary of the west-Mexican River Balsas. As he quietly cultivated his farm in Michoacán, part of which he gave to a Unesco project for rural education, he began to earn the respect of his former enemies, the right wing. But, seemingly pricked by remorse that many of his land reforms had gone awry through the corrupt practices of agricultural banks, he began about 1960 to cultivate friendship with Russian and Chinese communists and with Fidel Castro. He lent his name to the so-called National Freedom Movement under communist auspices, made indiscreet statements in public, and was not quieted even after being appointed to head the Balsas and Tepalcatepec River Commission. In 1955 he was awarded a Stalin Peace Prize.

In spite of his espousal of left-wing causes, many younger Mexicans were disappointed with his implicit support of government action against students during the 1968 demonstrations which led to the death of many people in the capital.

He was a sincere reformer whose strict adherence to left-wing theories often went against his peasant common sense. He was well aware that his shrewd but slow peasant mind was at a disadvantage in repartee with intellectuals, and he put up a defence which made him appear stern and humourless. He was clumsy and sometimes an easy dupe in the international political game, but never deviated from his own ideals and aspirations for Mexico. More than any other single man, Cárdenas was the shaper of modern Mexico with its stability and its staunch nationalism.

October 21, 1970.

Chester F. Carlson, the inventor of xerography, which has revolutionized office copying, collapsed in New York City on September 19, 1968, and died shortly afterwards. He was 62.

Born in Seattle, Washington, he grew up in California and studied at the California Institute of Technology. He graduated as a physicist in 1930 and later joined the patent department of a New York electronics firm. He soon realized that there must be a cheaper and more convenient way of making copies of original documents and drawings than the conventional retyping and photocopying processes.

In his typically determined way he searched unswervingly for three years to find the answer, reading, researching at the public library, and working as he travelled to the office by train.

By 1937, Carlson had succeeded in filing a patent application for a process which he called electro-photography. But it was not until October 22, 1938, that in a rented room behind a beauty parlour, in the suburb of Astoria, "10–22–38 Astoria" was inked on a glass slide and transferred to paper—and the first electrostatic copy had been made.

Enthusiastically Carlson set about designing equipment to demonstrate the revolutionary process—later called xerography, from the Greek "dry writing". But the next step forward was not made until 1944 when the Battelle Memorial Institute, the non-profit making industrial research organization in Columbus, Ohio, agreed to develop the machine. Many more difficulties lay ahead before Haloid, then a small company in Rochester, N. Y. (now Xerox Corporation), became interested in the invention and provided impressive research and development funds.

The first commercial xerographic machine was large and not easy to operate but the breakthrough, for Chester Carlson, Battelle and Xerox Corporation, came in 1958 with the introduction of the automatic, push-button office copier, the 914.

Some two years earlier in 1956, Rank Xerox was formed, a company jointly owned by the Rank Organisation and Xerox Corporation. The rapidly growing success of xerography and the demand for faster and even more versatile machines capable of printing on ordinary paper brought many rewards to Chester Carlson. His inventiveness never withered away and he continued to patent his ideas.

Already Carlson's idea has had a dramatic impact on the world business scene, second only to the computer. Xerography has changed the face of graphic communications and Carlson's invention brings the science of electronics to the art of printing.

He leaves a widow.

September 21, 1968.

James Carmichael, Labour Member of Parliament for the Bridgeton division of Glasgow from 1947 until his retirement in 1961, died in hospital in Dumfries on January 19, 1966. He was 72.

Born in 1894, he lived in and served his native city of Glasgow all his life. He tried his hand at various jobs—constructional engineer in the steel industry, insurance agent, and secretary; but he never wavered in his adherence to Socialist policy and ideals. He was educated at elementary schools and the Scottish Labour College, where he was at one time a tutor.

Early in life he became an enthusiastic member of the Independent Labour Party, and was for 14 years organizing secretary of the Scottish Council. He resigned this post in 1937 to take up a business appointment. It was largely due to his organizing ability that the I.L.P. had such a strong hold in Glasgow, where at one period names like James Maxton, George Buchanan, Campbell Stephen, John Wheatley, Neil Maclean and John McGovern were household words, for they were strong and sturdy exponents in the House of Commons of the left wing Socialist faith.

In their early days the "Clydesiders", as they were known, were an uncompromising little band of would-be revolutionaries, and Carmichael did his best for a time to follow in their footsteps. As a member of the National Union of Life Assurance Workers he upheld the left wing element in the trade union movement, and for many years he was one of the "stormy petrels" on the Glasgow City Council.

His opportunity to enter the House of Commons came in the summer of 1946, when the death of James Maxton created a vacancy in the representation of Bridgeton. Maxton had held the seat ever since 1922, and had become respected and beloved by political friend and foe alike. Carmichael, who was chosen to succeed him, had a difficult task. It is no reflection on him to say that he was following a most gifted and colourful personality; one who could have risen to high office in the Labour councils had he so desired.

Carmichael had few, if any, of Maxton's talents. He appeared to be stolid, slow, and unimaginative. He was no platform orator, though conscientious, hard working and sincere.

WORKERS DIVIDED

He had a surprisingly hard fight to retain a constituency which had always been regarded as an impregnable Socialist stronghold. This was in large measure due to divided counsels among the local Labour organizers.

When nomination day came Carmichael was faced with four opponents—Labour, Conservative, Independent Scottish Nationalist, and independent Labour. He won with the somewhat narrow majority of 1,171 votes.

Carmichael had been in the House of Commons for little more than a year when he resigned from the I.L.P. and applied for membership of the Labour Party. His resignation left the I.L.P. without representation in Parliament. Of its three members returned in 1945, Maxton and Campbell Stevens had died, and McGovern had joined the Labour Party. With his entry into the official Labour camp Carmichael gradually lost his revolutionary fire, and became one of the less conspicuous of the Scottish Labour backbenchers. He had no difficulty in holding Bridgeton at subsequent general elections. In 1961 he was forced by ill-health to apply for the Chiltern Hundreds.

His son, Mr. Neil Carmichael, is Labour M.P. for Woodside, Glasgow, and his son-in-law, Mr. Hugh D. Brown, is Labour M.P. for Provan, Glasgow.

January 20, 1966.

Professor Rudolf Carnap, one of the most influential philosophers of our time and the undisputed leader of his school called "Logical positivism" or "Logical empiricism", died on September 15, 1970, at Santa Monica, California, at the age of 79.

Carnap was born in Germany, a son of deeply religious parents and studied philosophy, mathematics and physics at the universities of Jena and Freiburg. The first great and lasting influence came from Gottlob Frege, Germany's greatest logician and philosopher of mathematics. During his student days Carnap became a free thinker, largely under the influence of Wilhelm Ostwald and the "society of Monists", the opponents of mind-body dualism. The Monists were, partly, materialists and partly, under the influence of Ernst Mach, subjective idealists whose doctrines resembled those of Berkeley and Hume. Both types of monism retained a hold on Carnap throughout his life. The first World War in which Carnap served as an officer made him politically conscious; he welcomed both the Russian and the German revolutions. After the war, in 1919 Carnap studied *Principia Mathematica* by Whitehead and Russell. Under their influence he wrote his Ph.D. thesis, *Der Raum*, on the philosophy of geometry. This was the beginning of a long series of works of great importance. Carnap's lifelong friendship with the philosopher Hans Reichenbach commenced in those early years. Through Reichenbach Carnap was introduced to Moritz Schlick of Vienna and became a lecturer at the University of Vienna (1926–1931).

At that time the famous Vienna Circle—Schlick's private seminar—was already in existence. The Circle contained a number of outstanding personalities: philosophers, mathematicians and scientists, many of them with an international reputation. Schlick had succeeded Mach and Boltzmann in a chair devoted to the philosophy of science although he was originally a critic of Mach. Mach's influence grew in the Circle until the Circle discovered Wittgenstein. Carnap arrived in Vienna at a time when Wittgenstein's influence was growing and Wittgenstein's philosophy of language became another strong influence on Carnap's work, though the two did not get on well.

Carnap stayed in Vienna until 1931 and he was appointed to a chair in Prague. But he remained a member of the Circle until he went to America. Two further influences on Carnap during these years should be mentioned; Alfred Tarski, who visited the Circle first in 1930 and Kurt Gödel, a member of the Circle.

In 1934 Carnap visited England and a year later he left Prague for the United States. He taught in Chicago until 1952 and after two years spent in Princeton he went in 1954 to the University of California at Los Angeles, as successor to his friend Reichenbach who had just died. Carnap retired in 1961.

Throughout his career Carnap produced work after work, all of them devoted to logic, epistemology, and the philosophy of science. The fundamental tendency which gives unity to these works is Carnap's rejection of all speculative philosophy or "metaphysics". Much of his work was devoted to the construction of a language free of metaphysics yet rich enough for the formulation of science. The first attempt was his book *Der logische Aufbau der Welt*, in which he tried to construct the concepts of natural and social sciences on a basis which he described as "methodological solipsism". Under the influence of Otto Neurath he replaced the spaces in his *Logical Syntax of Language* by a form of materialism called by Neurath "physicalism". Carnap constructed several "model languages", some of them rich enough for the formulation of science: but later in his life, when he turned to probability theory and the theory of induction (his theory was closely related to the work of Sir Harold Jeffreys and Lord Keynes) he had to confine himself to more rudimentary model languages.

The American school of constructive language philosophy which from its beginnings stood in sharp contrast to the English school of ordinary language philosophy, founded by Moore and Wittgenstein, was almost entirely the result of Carnap's influence. This influence was based on his great constructive powers and on the unique charm of his personality.

September 17, 1970.

Primo Carnera, "the Ambling Alp," who died on June 29, 1967, in his native village of Sequals, Italy, was perhaps the most extraordinary character ever to win the world heavyweight boxing championship. Weighing 267 lb. he was the heaviest champion of all and the second tallest, measuring 6 ft. 5¾ in., compared with Jess Willard who was 6ft. 6in. Carnera weighed 19st. 1 lb., Willard 17st. 2 lb.

Carnera, who was born on October 26, 1906, began boxing in 1928 after a former French champion had found him employed in a circus. He thought that Carnera would prove a great draw in boxing but the Italian giant was not taken particularly seriously until he reached the United States, where he came under the wing of some astute managers. Carnera was hustled through a tour of the mid-west and bowled over a score of nondescript opponents. At one hectic stage there were so many managers and partners that they calculated that they owned 105 per cent of the hapless Italian.

Carnera eventually won the title by knocking out the American Jack Sharkey in 1933 and he later defended it against Tommy Loughran (who was 80 lb. lighter) and Paolino Uzcudun. In 1934, however, Carnera was beaten in 12 rounds by Max Baer. At one stage in the fight both men were on the canvas together; one from a blow and the other carried there by the force of a mistimed swing. At this point Baer, always the joker, said to Carnera, "Last man up's a sissy." After this Carnera gradually went downhill, being stopped by Joe Louis in 1935 and suffering from temporary paralysis after taking a particularly bad beating the next year. During the war Carnera stayed in Italy, being used in posters by the Fascists, but after one more disastrous entry into the ring in 1946 he went to the United States as a wrestler. Here he made far more money than he had ever gained from boxing and proved a popular figure.

Carnera, a kindly man at heart, was very much affected by the death of an opponent, Ernie Schaaf, after he knocked him out in the thirteenth round in 1932. It was said he feared to punch with his full weight again to avoid a repetition of the tragic incident.

Carnera and his wife Pina became American citizens in 1953 and he said when he arrived in Italy that he hoped to go back to the United States one day because his children were there. His son, Umberto, is completing his medical studies, and his daughter is married to an engineer.

June 30, 1967.

A. W. Carr, the former England and Nottinghamshire cricket captain, died on February 7, 1963, at his home at Leyburn, Yorkshire. He was 69.

A pugnacious batsman, he brought the game qualities of fearless aggression and uncompromising zest into his captaincy. They won him many admirers, for he was a courageous leader of men, with the ability to command and return loyalty, and a natural air of authority. But his very forthrightness was liable to involve him in controversy. As the county captain of Larwood and Voce during their greatest days he not only gave an object-lesson in the handling of fast bowlers—avoiding the obvious but subtle temptation to bowl them for too long spells—but also became embroiled in the "body-line" storm, and it was unfortunate that his distinguished career with Nottinghamshire ended under a cloud of disagreement.

For England he suffered misfortune of a different nature. He came to the captaincy in 1926, the year when England were destined to recover the Ashes after the long lean period following the First World War. But for illness, which struck him during the fourth Test at Old Trafford he would almost certainly have been in command for the memorable decisive match at the Oval.

As it was, Percy Chapman took over and performed so brilliantly that he had the England captaincy in his keeping until Carr was past his peak. Carr was to captain England again briefly against South Africa, but he never again played in a Test against Australia.

Arthur William Carr, the elder son of Phillip William Carr, in his day a well known member of the Stock Exchange, was born at Mickleham, Surrey, on May 18, 1893. He was educated at Sherborne where he was captain of all games except cricket—but his reputation as a schoolboy cricketer was still good enough to earn him his first match for Nottinghamshire at the age of 17 in 1910. Although he was not a success then, he received further chances and in 1913 made his first century for the county.

It was not, however, until after the First World War—in which he served with the 5th Lancers and was mentioned in dispatches—that he really achieved prominence. He succeeded A. O. Jones, who had died in 1914, as captain of Nottinghamshire in the first postwar season of 1919, and in 1922–23 toured South Africa under F. T. Mann. In the fourth Test of this closely contested series he made the top score of 63 in England's first innings.

In 1925 he had an outstanding season as a hard-hitting batsman, scoring more than 2,000 runs with an average of over 50. He made seven centuries and his 206 at Leicester was the highest score of his career. His selection as captain of England the following season was a popular choice.

The first Test of 1926 was largely ruined by rain and the second was also drawn. In the third at Leeds Carr himself came in for much criticism, though he was not solely to blame for such tactical mistakes as there were. Winning the toss, he put the Australians in—a perfectly reasonable decision on a doubtful wicket, except that England dropped their best bowler on a turning wicket, Charlie Parker of Gloucestershire. But that was a collective selectorial error. Even so, all might still have been well if Carr, normally an outstanding slip fielder, had not very soon dropped a chance off Macartney who went on to make one of the great centuries of Test cricket. Yet the match was drawn.

THE SELECTORS' CONFIDENCE

The selectors maintained their confidence in Carr for the next Test at Old Trafford, in the course of which he was stricken with tonsillitis. It was because he had not recovered his form after this illness that he was dropped for the fifth and deciding Test.

Carr was a Test selector the following season, and in 1929 captained England twice against South Africa as well as leading Nottinghamshire to the county championship.

At the end of the 1934 season, after much trouble over "bodyline" bowling and considerable differences within the Nottinghamshire Club, Carr was relieved of the captaincy and so ended his first-class cricket career.

During the Second World War Carr returned to the Forces to serve with the 16th/5th Lancers from 1939 to 1941.

In recent years Carr has had horses in training with S. Hall at Middleham, the best of which was Vinnie, a filly he leased, who won several races, worth £1,750 as a two-year-old, but did nothing in her second season.

Carr was married twice and his only son was killed in the last war. He leaves a widow.

Feburary 8, 1963.

Dr. Francis Howard Carr, C.B.E., who died on January 25, 1969, at the age of 94, was Chief Manufacturing Chemist to Burroughs, Wellcome & Co. from 1898 to 1914 and director and Chief Chemist, Boots Pure Drug Co., from 1914 to 1919.

He was a pioneer who contributed greatly to the creation of the industry in fine chemicals in Britain during the first half of the century. Born in 1874, the seventh of 12 children of strict Baptist parents, he was taught by his eldest sister until, at the age of 10, he went to the Whitgift Grammar School for the limited time his parents could afford to send him. At 15 he went to the Finsbury Technical College. Although illness robbed him of a certificate he left at 17 with a chemistry prize and some knowledge of engineering: the latter, a compulsory subject, proved to be a great but unforeseen benefit. He became research assistant to Dunstan first at the Pharmaceutical Society's laboratories and later at the Imperial Institute. By the age of 20 he had published several papers, mostly relating to aconitine, and was awarded a scholarship by the Salters Company.

In 1898, he was appointed by Henry Wellcome as chief chemist to the newly devoloping Dartford Factory of Burroughs Wellcome, to work out and set up the manufacture of many medicinal compounds which had not been made before in Britain. There followed, up till the outbreak of war in 1914, a very congenial time, at first taken up with designing machinery for the large-scale preparation and purification of delicate substances and then with chemical and physiological collaborations with Barger, Dale and Pyman which laid the foundations of lifelong friendships.

It was Carr's meticulousness which led to the discovery of emetine as a specific for amoebic dysentery; he found that the ipecac then used and described as free of emetine indeed contained small amounts of it and after purification the ipecac was reported to have become ineffective. The separated emetine was then tried in

India.

On the outbreak of war, Carr was acutely aware of Britain's dependence on German imports of medicinal products. He became director of Boots Pure Drug Company in Nottingham where he rapidly set up new manufactures in plant covering some five acres.

GAS ATTACKS

Very soon after the first gas attacks the chemical problems of large-scale manufacture of protective substances was tackled and later the assembly of the box gas masks, the entire supply for all the allies, was undertaken, some 250,000 masks a week. This was an achievement of technical chemistry and administration. For his services Carr was created C.B.E. He served on the Chemical Defence Research Committee for some 20 years.

In 1920 he became a director of British Drug Houses and subsequently its chairman. Among his foremost technical achievements was the invention of a large-scale process, the first in Europe, for preparing insulin. With Jewell he invented a vacuum distillation process for the isolation of vitamin A and he evolved a chemical assay of that vitamin. The firm's wide range of highly purified chemical reagents, the start of Analar standards, became perhaps indirectly his greatest contribution to medical progress.

He took a keen interest in education, serving for 28 years as a governor of The Imperial College. He succeeded his friend J. H. Badley, the founder of Bedales School, as chairman of the school's Board of Governors and served for some 40 years in all as governor, vice-president and president, bringing to the last wise counsel and a liberal influence to bear on the needs of coming generations.

His marriage in 1898 to Hilda Mary Sykes was an exceptionally happy one. They had three daughters.

January 28, 1969.

Sir Alexander Carr-Saunders, K.B.E., F.B.A., director of the London School of Economics from 1937 to 1956, died at Thirlmere on October 6, 1966, after pushing his car. He was 80.

His name was never much in the public eye, but in more than one field he was among the foremost of his generation. As a scholar he brought a training in biology to bear on human affairs, and made fundamental contributions to the study of population and the social structure. Called to academic office he proved an outstandingly successful administrator. His work for the development of higher education in the colonies was an historic achievement.

Alexander Morris Carr-Saunders was born in 1886, by some 15 years the youngest child of J. C. Saunders, a wealthy underwriter. A sister married Admiral Sir John Slade, and their younger daughter became Gandhi's disciple Mirabhai. Carr-Saunders went to Eton, but left at 16 to spend two years in Paris and the French Alps. His childhood had been lonely, and when he went up to Magdalen he was detached and old for his years. He decided to read zoology because that was the branch of science he thought capable of most development in the next half century. It meant starting from scratch, and he read deeply in philosophy meanwhile, but he took a first in 1908. He held the Naples Biological Scholarship and returned to serve for a year as a demonstrator at the Oxford laboratory. But he had come to feel that he would not make an experimental scientist. Two lifelong interests had already been formed: he had acquired skill as a mountaineer, and a love of the visual arts. His father was a trustee of the woman mountaineer, Mme. Charlet-Straton, and he used to stay with her near Chamonix, and gained a special knowledge of the Aiguilles Rouges. The first sight of Raphael's frescoes in the Vatican, he said, had opened a new world to him. Already, moreover, he was concerned with social problems. Conscious of great powers, endowed with a private income, and having scant respect for academic institutions and many who worked in them, he took Darwin and Galton as his pattern, and moved to London to pursue inquiries of his own choosing in his own way. Already his mind was busy with social problems. He studied biometrics under Karl Pearson, became secretary of the research committee of the Eugenics Education Society, and resided for a time in Toynbee Hall, where he was made Sub-Warden. He left it for a house at Wapping Old Stairs, showing in this a characteristic interest in buildings. Meanwhile he was elected to the Stepney Borough Council, and called to the Bar by the Inner Temple.

STUDY OF POPULATION

When war came in 1914 he joined the ranks of the infantry, but when men who could speak French were called on to raise their hands in order that they might be seconded to liaison duties he had to raise his: the result was a commission in the R.A.S.C. and a posting to a ration depot at Suez, where he was kept for the rest of the war. On his return he went back to help a short-handed zoology department at Oxford, but his heart at that time was in farming, and he lived outside the city, farming in partnership with Philip Morell at Garsington, and later with a Canadian agricultural economist at Tubney. In 1921 he was one of the organizers and members of the Oxford University expedition to Spitzbergen, being responsible for the marine biology at the base. At the same time he was at work on a great study of population which he had planned during the war. When *The Population Problem* appeared in 1922 it made his reputation overnight: its application of biological knowledge to human society, its breadth of learning and its cautious but pertinacious approach to basic issues made it a landmark. It has since been acclaimed as having made a fundamental contribution to social biology by its formulation of the principle of the optimum number.

In 1923, much to his own surprise, he was called to Liverpool as the first holder of the Charles Booth Chair of Social Science, and there he was to remain for 14 years. By interest and experience he was well qualified to direct a department that had grown up about good works and was extending into research. His own publications added steadily to his reputation, especially *The Professions*, a pioneering study, written in collaboration with P. A. Wilson. He took an effective part in university administration, and was friendly alike to pupils and colleagues, yet was always felt to keep his detachment, and to belong elsewhere. In 1929 he married Teresa Molyneux-Seel, and they made their home at Water Eaton manor, near Oxford. They had two sons and a daughter.

ADMINISTRATIVE CAPACITY

In 1937 he was called to succeed Sir William (later Lord) Beveridge as director of the London School of Economics. His administrative capacity was soon proved. When war came it was his exertions, meeting a generous response in Cambridge and especially in Peterhouse, that saved the school from the far-flung dispersion to which it had been consigned, and maintained not only its teaching but its corporate life until a second strenuous campaign enabled him to bring it back to its own home in October, 1945. There followed years of rapid expansion through which until his retirement in 1956 he upheld the high standards that he always took for granted, and strengthened his hold on the trust and affection of the school. He had identified himself with it completely. His authority was based on a confidence unalloyed by superiority, and on objectivity and patience in all personal dealings. He made a skilful therapeutic use of discussion, which he never sought to dominate and seldom even checked, but which in practice led to an unforced acceptance of conclusions that seldom ran contrary to his own judgment. He combined a natural interest in detail with a sense of proportion, and a foresight that obviated haste.

In 1943, when he joined the Asquith Commission on higher education in the colonies, he took up a major task to which he was to give unstinted energies that sprang from a deep and humane sense of its importance. He created and for 11 years helped direct the two central agencies for carrying out the new plans: the University of London Senate Committee which guided the development of the university colleges in East Africa, Sudan, Central Africa, Nigeria, the Gold Coast, and the West Indies; and the Inter-University Council through which the help of all the United Kingdom universities was given to the six university colleges and the universities of Malta, Hongkong, and Malaya.

DECISIVE

At two points of this development his own contribution was decisive: he was chairman in 1947 of the commission that led to the creation of the University of Malaya, and in 1953 of the commission on higher education for Africans in Central Africa that led to the foundation of the multi-racial University College of Rhodesia and Nyasaland. He was indefatigable in travel. His respect for the autonomy of the young foundations helped them to adapt themselves to their local needs and opportunities; the high academic standards he upheld ensured that all the main British dependencies were endowed with a college worthy of recognition and acceptance by the universities at home. He served on the Royal Commission on Population in 1944–49 and was chairman of its Statistics Committee. He was knighted in 1946, and made a K.B.E. in 1957.

His conduct had the consistency that flows from complete integrity, but his character was full of surprises. The mien of the saddhu masked keen powers of observation and an exceptional capacity for rapid work. No attack ever shook him, but on a public occasion he could appear diffident and dejected. His work combined great breadth with great caution and an exacting attention to detail. He seemed aloof, yet timid undergraduates found themselves at home with him, and he had a profoundly sympathetic interest in the problems of young people. In his private judgment his contempts were withering, for to him there was always something inexplicable in any departure from wisdom, but in public action he was unfailingly tolerant and unprejudiced. His temperament was sceptical and pessimistic, his activity constructive and undaunted. In his younger days he had been a Victorian rationalist; later in life he became a practising Anglican of unaffected devotion.

October 8, 1966.

Lord Carron, who died on December 3, 1969, at the age of 67, had been one of the most formidable figures in the British trade union movement since he was elected president of the one-million-strong Amalgamated Engineering Union in 1956. He held the post until his retirement in 1967.

If he did not assume the undisputed leadership of the Right, which was formerly held by Arthur Deakin, it was because the structure of the A.E.U. prevents its president from exercising a dominating influence over his own organization. Nevertheless, he gave it strong leadership, at a time when strong leadership was badly needed, and throughout his years of office held at bay the communists who were constantly at his heels.

He was not a particularly impressive figure, either personally or on the platform. Short and plump, with a disarming smile and a bald head, his speeches were plentifully sprinkled with clichés and he sometimes allowed himself extravagant flights of fancy, as on the famous occasion when he described the Communists as "werewolves rushing madly towards industrial ruin and howling delightedly at the foam on their muzzles which they accept as their guiding light".

But colleagues and opponents soon learned that he was not to be under-estimated. He was one of the shrewdest men in the business and among the most determined, even obstinate. When he had decided what was the right thing to do, he stuck to it, and was completely imperturbable in the face of criticism or ridicule.

SOLITUDE

A devout Roman Catholic, he sometimes retired into solitude for a few days when faced with a difficult situation.

His first big test came in the national engineering and shipbuilding strike less than a year after he was elected to the leadership of his union. His casting vote on the A.E.U. executive resulted in the calling off of the strike when the issue was still in doubt, an act which resulted in recrimination and hostility.

It was another casting vote by the president which decided that the A.E.U. block vote should be cast for two contradictory defence motions at the Trades Union Congress in 1960. It made the union a laughing stock, but it prevented the complete defeat of the Labour Party leadership under Hugh Gaitskell, of whom he was a staunch supporter.

Carron was a forward-looking trade union leader, believing that strikes should only be used as a last resort and that there should be cooperation between the two sides of industry. A former chairman of the British Productivity Council, he appreciated the importance of technical advance and education, but he could not always carry his union with him.

He was a member of many government committees and joint organizations of employers and workers. He was made a trustee of Churchill College, Cambridge, in 1958 and was a visiting Fellow of Nuffield College, Oxford. He was a member of the National Economic Development Council from its inception. In 1963 he was appointed a director of the Bank of England. As a mark of "his conspicuous work within the Church and constant witness to Catholic principles in everyday life", the Pope appointed him a Knight of the Order of Chivalry of St. Gregory the Great.

START IN ENGINEERING

Born at Hull on November 19, 1902, William John Carron, after working at the bench for some years in his early manhood, held many A.E.U. posts before he was elected to the national executive committee in 1950. In 1956 he defeated a Communist rival in the election for the office of president for the ensuing three years.

He repeated his success in 1959, when the period of office was lengthened to one of five years. Also in the 1950s he was elected to the national executive of the Confederation of Shipbuilding and Engineering Unions and to the T.U.C. General Council. In 1966 he became a director of Fairfields shipyard.

Carron was re-elected president of the union in August 1964, with a substantial majority over his Communist opponent Reg Birch. This victory ensured that for over three years, until his retirement, the A.E.U. came under right-wing domination and acted as a counter-weight to the left-wing Transport and General Workers' Union within the T.U.C. and the Labour Party.

Carron was a loyal and unswerving supporter of Harold Wilson's Government. If he had any private criticisms, he never voiced them in public and always adopted the attitude that trade unions must back the Labour Government at all costs. At the T.U.C. at Brighton in 1967, he swung his union's vote behind a motion supporting the Government's economic policies, to the fury of his delegation. Carron argued that he had been given blanket authority to support the Government by the A.E.U. National Committee, which was the sole arbiter of policy. There were angry demonstrations in the hall and there were accusations that Carron was a "right-wing dictator" and imposing "Carron's Law". He remained bland and smiling throughout the controversy.

He was made a Life Peer in 1967 and retired from his union in November that year. He was succeeded by the left-wing candidate Mr. Hugh Scanlon and Britain's second biggest union abruptly changed course. Carron remained on the T.U.C. General Council until September, 1968, fulfilling the role of elder statesman.

When the new A.E.U. leaders called for a national stoppage, Carron attacked them as "left-wingers determined on the economic destruction of this country".

He married in 1931 Mary Emma, daughter of John McGuire. They had two daughters.

December 5, 1969.

Douglas Carruthers, who died on May 23, 1962, at the age of 79, made a name for himself as an explorer and naturalist prior to the 1914–18 War, at the outbreak of which he was already a recognized authority on the Middle East.

Alexander Douglas Mitchell Carruthers, born on October 4, 1882, was the eldest son of the Rev. W. Mitchell Carruthers and was educated at Haileybury and Trinity College, Cambridge. From an early age he was destined to become a traveller and collector far above the ordinary, and by the age of 26 had crossed what was still called "darkest Africa", had explored rock-hewn Petra and had reached that strange capital at the back of the world—remote Bokhara. In 1904–05 he was in Syria where he was attached to the Museum of the American University at Beirut, returning home in time to join the British Museum Expedition to Ruwenzori, one of the most successful zoological expeditions which has ever left these shores. Carruthers was a wonderful collector of birds and mammals and the specimens which he sent home are in a class by themselves, so expert was he in taxidermy: the numerous appellations *Carruthersi* in scientific literature bear witness to the many new animals and birds of which he was the discoverer. At the close of the Ruwenzori Expedition in 1906, in company with A.F.R. Wollaston he crossed Africa from Uganda to the Congo mouth, making fine zoological collections en route, but it was to the great mountain ranges and deserts of Central Asia that his heart was drawn and 1907–08 found him far away in Russian Turkestan. The following January he was back in Damascus, laying plans for what was probably the most daring adventure of his life—to penetrate to the heart of Arabia in search of the White Oryx, in the quest for which he was successful. Carruthers was not only a daring hunter and collector, he was thoroughly equipped as a geographer and surveyor, and for his services to geography he received on his return from Arabia the Gill Memorial of the Royal Geographical Society.

HUNTING IN SIBERIA

There followed two years of successful exploration and hunting in Siberia, Mongolia, and

Turkestan during which time he got together an invaluable collection of zoological specimens for the British Museum (Natural History) and broke entirely new ground in the exploration of the sources of the Yenesei river, of north western Mongolia and Dzungari, surveying and mapping the region traversed with—as Lord Curzon expressed it—"the patience and thoroughness of the true geographer". For that work Carruthers received the Patron's gold medal of the Royal Geographical Society.

Early in 1913 he visited Turkey, covering the regions of the Eastern Taurus, but on that expedition no zoological collections were attempted. From the outbreak for war (1914) for six long years he was entrusted by the War Office with the exacting work of compiling the maps of the Middle East, especially that of Arabia, and in the compilation of handbooks for the Admiralty and the Arab Bureau. In 1916 he was elected honorary secretary of the Royal Geographical Society, a post which he held until 1921. He gave up active exploration on his marriage in 1915.

He possessed an easy scholarly style. Literature gained what exploration lost and his publications included *Unknown Mongolia* (two volumes, 1913), *The Desert Route to India* (Hakluyt Publishing, 1929), *Arabian Adventure —to the Great Nafud in search of the Oryx* (1935), *Northern Najd* (1938), and *Beyond the Caspian* (1949), together with his contributions to the *Geographical Journal* and *The Ibis*.

He married in 1915, the Hon. Mrs. Morrison, daughter of the first Lord Trevor. The marriage was dissolved by divorce in 1948 and he married secondly in the same year, Rosemary Arden, only daughter of Lieutenant-Colonel E. C. Clay, C.B.E.

May 26, 1962.

Lieutenant-General Sir Adrian Carton de Wiart, V.C., K.B.E., C.B., C.M.G., D.S.O., died on June 5, 1963, at his home in county Cork. He was 83.

It was to the age of chivalry that Adrian Carton de Wiart properly belonged. He saw life as a list in which honour (when nothing much was happening) and duty (when his country was in peril) engaged him automatically as a constestant. It was once said of him that in the world of action he occupied the same sort of niche that Sir Max Beerbohm occupied in the world of letters; and this was true, for he was in all things a stylist.

De Wiart's appearance was distinguished and, thanks partly to a black eye-patch and one empty sleeve, faintly piratical. He could be fierce and was intolerant of fools; but his mind had an almost feminine perceptiveness, and he was unfailingly considerate to others. He accepted, with an air of quizzical insouciance, every challenge that life offered. He might not have agreed—for he disliked empty or pretentious language—that danger has bright eyes; but he found them irresistible.

Adrian Carton de Wiart was born in Brussels on May 5, 1880. His father was a lawyer; one of his grandmothers was Irish. After a childhood spent mostly in Egypt, he was educated in England: first at the Oratory School, in those days at Edgbaston, then at Balliol. His cricket was a great deal better, and taken much more seriously, than his scholarship; and his academic career was in a fair way to being terminated by the examiners when the South African War broke out and de Wiart without a moment's hesitation enlisted in a yeomanry regiment, Paget's Horse. Trooper Carton—an alias was necessary lest this change in his educational programme should come to the ears of his father—was not in fact eligible for the British service, being under age and of foreign nationality; but he was soon in action and received the first of his many wounds. They were serious, and in hospital de Wiart's identity came to light. His father took the characteristic escapade well.

When the Boer War ended de Wiart was given a commission in the 4th Dragoon Guards, then stationed in India. Polo, pigsticking and such improbable feats as seizing a cobra by its tail as it disappeared down a hole and dispatching it with his sword alleviated but could not dispel the monotony of garrison duties, and a chance to serve as A.D.C. to the Commander-in-Chief in South Africa, Sir Henry Hildyard, was seized in 1904. Four years later he rejoined his regiment in England and was seconded to the Royal Gloucestershire Hussars as adjutant.

DANGER AHEAD

The storm-clouds gathering over Europe somehow escaped his attention, but Somaliland, where the Mad Mullah was giving trouble, seemed to offer a rendezvous with danger; three weeks before England declared war on Germany he set off to do battle with the Dervishes.

He was soon back in England, having lost an eye and gained a D.S.O. while storming a fort, and spent the rest of that war in the trenches or in hospital. As a *grand blessé* he was in a class by himself: he was severely wounded eight times and lost his left hand. He was awarded the Victoria Cross after the Battle of the Somme, when he led the 8th Battalion, The Gloucestershire Regiment, in the capture of La Boisselle. He subsequently commanded the 12th, the 105th, and the 113th Infantry Brigade. After the Armistice he led the British Military Mission to Poland, whose forces were fighting simultaneously the Germans, the Bolsheviks, the Ukrainians, the Lithuanians, and the Czechs. These minor campaigns produced many adventures—and many friends—for de Wiart. When they ended, one of the latter, Prince Charles Radziwill, lent him an estate in the Pripet Marshes, near the Russo-Polish frontier. De Wiart, who had resigned his commission after a difference of opinion with the War Office, accepted the offer with alacrity, and for most of the period between the wars made his home in a desolate but strangely beautiful region which provided some of the best shooting in Europe.

In July, 1939, he was summoned to London and appointed, once more, to lead a British Military Mission to Poland. When war broke out there was little that the mission could do save withdraw, on the heels of Marshal Smigly-Rydz, to Rumania: but de Wiart was the first senior British officer to experience the novel realities of a *Blitzkrieg*, and it may be doubted whether, on his return, the General Staff paid sufficient attention to the lessons he had learnt. He was given command of the 61st Division, but when, in the following spring, the Germans invaded Norway, he was placed in charge of the allied force destined for Namsos. Arriving in Norway ahead of his troops, by seaplane, he immediately recognized the enterprise as a forlorn hope. Whitehall at first took a rosier view of its prospects, but under a hail of bombs and an almost equally disconcerting barrage of unrealistic advice from London de Wiart remained imperturbable and when the time came extricated his dazed force with light losses. He resumed command of his division, throughout whose ranks his popularity and prestige were exceptional. It was a blow to him to be told, early in 1941, that he was too old to continue in command; but his disappointment evaporated when he was ordered, in April, to Yugoslavia as head of a British Military Mission which was to nourish Yugoslav resistance to the invading Germans. The Wellington bomber carrying him to the Middle East came down in the sea off North Africa, and de Wiart found himself a prisoner of the Italians, perhaps the last predicament which anyone would have prophesied for him. Though straitly incarcerated, he made several bold, well-planned bids for freedom.

It had been a tribute to his reputation that the British General Staff should have sent him to Poland, to Norway and to Yugoslavia; it was perhaps an even higher tribute that the Italian General Staff should, when they wished to ask for an armistice, have sent their prisoner to London to arrange matters. Disguised (in so far as disguise was possible for that conspicuous figure) and provided with a false passport, de Wiart was flown home via Lisbon, an essential intermediary in, if not—as was popularly believed—the architect of, Italy's withdrawal from the war on September 7, 1943. Three weeks later Mr. Winston Churchill asked him to go to China as his personal representative at Marshal Chiang Kai-shek's headquarters.

He spent the rest of the war in Chungking, where he made a deep impression on the Chinese. He was at the Mena Conference and in December, 1944, made, at the instance of the Prime Minister, a personal report to the Cabinet on the situation in the Far East. He also managed, characteristically, to attend a naval bombardment of Sabang. After the general election of 1945 Mr. Attlee asked him to continue at his distant post, and it was not until 1946 that he returned to England for good—and as usual on a stretcher, for he had broken his back in Singapore.

He had married in 1908 Countess Frederica, eldest daughter of Prince Fugger Babenhausen and Nora Princess Hohenlohe, and they had two daughters. His wife died in 1949, and two years later he married Mrs. Joan Sutherland. They settled in co. Cork, where the general's tireless physical activity found ample outlets in the pursuit of snipe and salmon.

June 6, 1963.

Sir Lewis Casson, M.C., the actor and producer, a dedicated member of his profession and for many years one of its leaders, died on May 16, 1969, at the age of 93.

It may have looked as though his career as an actor had been subordinated to that of his wife, Dame Sybil Thorndike: but it was as a producer-director that he had his most important contribution to make, and he could not have found worthier material than the great ability of his actress consort.

A Welshman and a socialist, he spoke his mind fearlessly on the drama, the theatre and the position of the theatre, in and out of season, throughout his long career.

Born at Birkenhead on October 26, 1875, the son of Major Thomas Casson, J.P., of Festiniog and Portmadoc, Lewis Thomas Casson went on from Ruthin Grammar School to the Central Technical College, South Kensington. Originally a teacher, then an organ-builder, he began acting as an amateur in Shakespearian productions by Charles Fry and William Poel, became a professional in 1903 and in 1904 was in Granville Barker's production of *The Two Gentlemen of Verona,* which was the starting point of the Vedrenne-Barker management. Casson worked for Barker consistently during the next three years, first at the Court, where he appeared in *Man and Superman*, *The Doctor's Dilemma*, and *The Silver Box*; afterwards at the Savoy in *The Devil's Disciple* and in *Medea*.

His career took a decisive turn in September, 1908, on his joining Miss Horniman's company at the Gaiety, Manchester, "the first repertory theatre in Great Britain." There he was allowed to try his hand at directing, and there he renewed acquaintance with his future wife. He and Sybil Thorndike were married in December of that year at Aylesford Church, in Kent. They were back in London in 1910, and they went to New York that autumn to play in Somerset Maugham's *Smith*. In 1911 Casson returned to Miss Horniman's company as director and there, at a time when the "Manchester School" was in the advanced guard of the English drama—*Hindle Wakes* and *Jane Clegg* were produced during this period—he found the opportunities he needed. When he left it was to take over the direction of the Royalty (repertory) Theatre in Glasgow.

HUSBAND-AND-WIFE LEADS

But the First World War came. Casson served from 1914 until 1919, first in the Army Service Corps, later in the Royal Engineers as an officer, being wounded and being awarded the M.C., and then began his career all over again in London. In conjunction with Bruce Winston he organized a season at the Holborn Empire, where his wife showed her true stature in Greek tragedy. Together the two were mainstays of "London's Grand Guignol" at the Little, and in 1922 were ready to enter into management, in association with Mary Moore (Lady Wyndham). At the New Casson directed his wife in the first public performance of Shelley's *The Cenci,* in *Cymbeline*, and in 1924, jointly with the author, in *Saint Joan*.

Casson played supporting parts in this and in his own productions of *Henry VIII* and *Macbeth*, but he shared the "leads" with his wife when the Old Vic Company was at the Lyric, Hammersmith, in 1927-28. A decade later, after long tours of South Africa (1928), and the Middle East, Australia, and New Zealand (1932), he entered on a further period of association with the Old Vic, directing Sir Laurence Olivier in *Coriolanus* in 1938 and, with Grenville Barker, Sir John Gielgud in *King Lear* in 1940.

In the same year Casson, together with Dame Sybil, made a sponsored tour of Welsh mining villages in *Macbeth*, and he followed this up at later stages of the Second World War by touring in *King John*, *Candida*, and *Medea*, and, with his daughter, Ann Casson, in *Saint Joan*. Also he was for two years Drama Director of C.E.M.A. and in recognition of these services he was knighted in 1945, just 14 years after his wife had been created D.B.E.

The two did a great deal of work together in the postwar period, not only in London—as the elderly professor in Mr. J. B. Priestley's *The Linden Tree*, Casson came into his own as a leading man—but also at an Edinburgh Festival, in New York, and on four tours comprising the Middle and Far East, India, Australasia, and southern and East Africa. They gave dramatic recitals on two of these and were seen in contemporary English plays on the other two. In the intervals Casson collaborated as an actor with Gielgud, Sir Donald Wolfit, and Sir John Clements in various seasons of the classics in London. In 1958 the Cassons celebrated the jubilee of their wedding by appearing in Clemence Dane's play, specially written for them, *Eighty in the Shade*.

Subsequently they were seen together in Noel Coward's *Waiting in the Wings*; in a Festival at Perth, Western Australia; in *Uncle Vanya* with Olivier during the first two seasons at Chichester; and in a revival of the American horror-comic *Arsenic and Old Lace* in 1966.

One matinee of the last named play was cancelled in order that Dame Sybil and Casson might receive dual honorary degrees of Doctor of Letters at Oxford from Harold Macmillan as Chancellor of the university.

Casson had already received the degree of Hon. LL.D. from the universities of Glasgow and Wales. He was president of Actors' Equity from 1941 to 1945, and was made a Fellow of the Imperial College of Science and Technology in 1959. His two sons, John and Christopher, and his two daughters, Mary and Ann, have all worked in the professional theatre at different times in their careers.

May 17, 1969.

General Georges Catroux, one of the oldest and most illustrious "Gaullists," who pursued honourable, enlightened, and difficult courses throughout his career, died in Paris on December 21, 1969, at the age of 92.

Governor-General of Indo-China in 1940, he was the only great French pro-consul and the only Général d'Armée to join de Gaulle in London in 1940—for which he was condemned to death by the Vichy government. There were people near to Churchill and also in the Free French movement who would have liked to see Catroux replace de Gaulle. Catroux's attitude made this out of the question (as did, in fact, those of Churchill himself and Eden, neither of whom was prepared to abandon de Gaulle). Catroux recognized, in the leader of Free France, a man with the quality of representing the growing forces of the nation and, as he wrote, "a hero in the ancient sense of the term".

De Gaulle gave Catroux the command of the French forces in the Syrian campaign in 1941 and he was later High Commissioner in the Middle East where his tact and negotiating ability took some of the edge off quarrels between the British and the Free French. In the Lebanon, in 1943, he restored calm after a disastrous Free French decision to arrest the President and the Government. In February 1943 he was the Free French representative in Algeria in the difficult negotiations with General Giraud, prior to de Gaulle's arrival in Algeria. In 1945, the Provisional Government of the French Republic sent him as Ambassador to Moscow where he remained until 1948. He took up his post in a good period of Franco-Soviet relations but soon came in for the difficulties of the beginning of the Cold War. A member of the Grand Council of de Gaulle's Rassemblement du Peuple Français, Catroux left the fast breaking up Rassemblement in 1952 because he thought it was a mistake to vote against the Schuman Plan for the Iron and Steel Community which was then before Parliament; and because he thought, though he was mistaken in this, that the Schuman government really had a serious intention of granting autonomy to Tunisia and Morocco.

Catroux remained in close contact with de Gaulle during the latter's period of retirement from politics at Colombey and, like him, protested against the exile of the Sultan of Morocco early in 1955, an illegal act carried out by the French Resident-General, Guillaume. In September, 1955, when Prime Minister Edgar Faure was undoing the work of French reactionaries and giving Morocco independence, it was Catroux who was sent to Madagascar for talks with the exiled Mohamed Vth and who brought him back to France.

OFFER TO RESIGN

His appointment as Governor-General of Algeria by the Republican Front Government headed by the Socialist leader, Guy Mollet, which came to power in January, 1956, after a general election, was taken as a sign that this government intended to seek an end to the civil war which had started in November, 1954. Catroux's reputation as a liberal and a friend of Muslims provoked an immediate outcry from the Europeans in Algeria and their supporters. Catroux offered to resign, Mollet stood firm but the French Prime Minister, after he had been pelted with tomatoes in Algiers and seen at first hand the temper of the French Algerians, then decided to accept Catroux's resignation.

The Mendès-France government of 1954 made Catroux Grand Chancellor of the Legion of Honour. He did not shirk two other highly difficult and disagreeable tasks. He presided over the inquiry into the Indo-China war in 1954 and in 1961 over the Military Court which condemned the rebel Algerian army generals, Challe, Zeller and, in absentia, Jouhaud and Salan.

Born at Limoges in 1877, the son of Colonel René Catroux, much of his youth was spent in Algeria. He went to St. Cyr and then saw most of his war service in the Middle East. His sympathy for Muslims and Muslim culture was strong. In 1930, de Gaulle, a young staff officer on a tour of duty in the Middle East, noted sardonically the general failure of French policy in Syria, its lack of imagination and inability to arouse sympathy or respect from the people. "There has been one man, and only one," he wrote, "who understood Syria and knew what to do. That was a Colonel Catroux and that is perhaps why he is not there now."

A highly intelligent man, well read, mild in manner, Catroux loved society and, in Algiers in 1943 and 1944, visitors to his house, among whom were Duff and Lady Diana Cooper, found almost the only intelligent contacts with the Arab world that it was possible to find in Algiers, in an atmosphere of a certain oriental splendour which Catroux liked.

He wrote a number of memoirs and was the holder of a great many French and foreign decorations. He was created honorary G.C.B. in 1946.

Catroux, who had been twice married and twice made a widower, married in 1963 Mademoiselle Frances Dellschaft.

December 22, 1969.

Mr. Justice Albert van de Sandt Centlivres, Chief Justice of South Africa from 1950 to 1957, died on September 19, 1966, in Capetown at the age of 79.

The peak of a long and distinguished legal career was his judgment, in November, 1952, that the High Court of Parliament Act was invalid, by rejecting the Government's appeal against the Cape Supreme Court's judgment against the validity of the Act. By this judgment the Separate Representation of Voters Act, declared invalid by the Appellate Division, was also made invalid.

The Government was forced to find other means of removing the coloured workers from the roll, and in so doing further weakened its pretentions always to act within the constitution and under the rule of law. Parliament had constituted itself a High Court of Parliament by creating senators to get the necessary majority in the upper house, but the five judges of the supreme court presided over by Dr. Centlivres unanimously ruled that the act was unconstitutional. The Chief Justice, in a long judgment, ruled that the so-called high court of parliament was not a court of law but simply parliament functioning under another name. He described as "a startling proposition" the contention of the counsel for the government that parliament sitting bicamerally could validly pass an act providing that no court should have the jurisdiction to decide whether any act had been passed in conformity with sect. 152 of the South Africa Act, which prescribes procedure for amending entrenched clauses. He rejected the contention that under such a procedure any substantive entrenched rights could remain intact, when they could no longer be enforced, which would amount to giving the individual a right of no value.

Mr. Justice Centlivres was born at Newlands, Cape Town, in January, 1887, a son of Mr. Fred Centlivres. He won scholarships at the South African College School and the College, and went as a Rhodes Scholar to New College, Oxford, where he took the B.A. degree in law and passed the B.C.L. examination. He then became a member of the Middle Temple and was called to the Bar in 1910. In 1911 he was admitted as an advocate of the Cape Provincial Division, and practised at the Cape Bar, with a short interlude in Rhodesia.

DRAFTED BILLS

In 1920 he became parliamentary draftsman and held the post for 14 years. In that period all the Union bills and statutes passed through his hands and gave him an unrivalled insight into constitutional matters, as they had to withstand the scrutiny of the courts.

He became a K.C. in 1927. He was a leading counsel in such important actions as Hofmeyr v. Badenhorst, a suit brought by a former Administrator of South West Africa for defamation uttered in an election campaign, and du Plessis v. Synod of the Dutch Reformed Church, an important heresy trial. He was also Chairman of a Commission on salaries and conditions of service of public servants.

After acting as Judge of the Cape Provincial Division, in 1935 he received a permanent appointment and in 1939 was elevated to the Appellate Division. He succeeded Mr. Edward F. Watermeyer as Chief Justice in October, 1950.

SUCCEEDED SMUTS

In the following year he became Chancellor of the University of Capetown in succession to General Smuts, an appointment he held until his death. He was an honorary D.C.L. of Oxford, and honorary fellow of New College, and honorary Master of the Middle Temple.

While fully acknowledging the powers of legislators, Dr. Centlivres believed explicitly in the rule of law in South Africa, and in 1955 at Harvard University said: "So long as the principle of government under the law is faithfully observed by the legislature and executive judiciary of any country, the liberty and dignity of the individual . . . will be reasonably safe." He strongly upheld western civilized values, and opposed apartheid in higher education.

In 1916 he married Miss Isabel Short, and they had three daughters.

September 20, 1966.

Maria Valentinovna Chaliapin, who died in Rome on June 26, 1964, in her eighty-third year, was a woman of independence and strength.

She was born in Kazan, on the Volga, where her father was keeper of the Imperial forests. Left a widow at 20 after her first marriage and with two children, she met Chaliapin when she was 28, and a devoted association of 30 years began. She saw the triumphs of the first seasons between 1908 and 1913 when Diaghilev took to Paris and London Russian ballet and Russian opera, with Chaliapin to sing Boris Godounov and Ivan the Terrible.

After the revolution the Bolshevik Government fostered the arts as much as they could and the family were spared great hardship.

RESENTED BUREAUCRATS

But Chaliapin was a fanatical perfectionist in all to do with the theatre, and he resented officialdom. His public explosions became an embarrassment to his friends and to the Government, who were reluctant to discipline an artist who was already a legend among all Slavs.

Maria Valentinovna, seeing danger to him and to their children, took the initiative by approaching Lunacharsky, the Minister of Education and Culture, and suggesting that Chaliapin might be allowed to leave Russia. The family moved to Paris in 1922, taking a few trunks of possessions and theatrical costumes, but otherwise without resources.

Chaliapin was in favour of this move which led to great artistic and worldly success, and though he was asked many times to perform again in Russia he felt it would be wrong to go back. But a deep sadness for his country pervaded his life and his work in later years. He trusted his wife for strength in moods of despair, and for balance in times of triumph. It was not easy to be the wife of an artist who seemed to be of more than human size, but until he died in 1938 they were as one.

Maria Valentinovna was the centre of a large family circle. She knew all the musicians, composers, artists, dancers of an epoch. She had simple but stately manners illuminated by the beauty which she kept into old age. She could be formidable, but she was pleased that Diaghilev labelled her "that beautiful woman", and flattered, with an understanding smile, when he declared that she was the only one he ever found attractive.

June 30, 1964.

A. P. F. Chapman, who died in a Hampshire hospital on September 16, 1961, at the age of 61. was one of the great English cricket captains.

Some may cavil that he was a persuasive charmer rather than a stern disciplinarian, that his leadership owed more to the vivacity of his personality than to the subtle study of tactics—even that he was too lighthearted. But a generation that has seen too much of unrelenting warfare on the first-class field will remember with relish the gaiety of his approach, the uninhibited vigour of his batting and the glamour of his fielding. There was sunlight in his cricket. In any case, however carefree he may have seemed on the surface, he yielded the results: in terms of matches won, there have been few more successful leaders of England.

Arthur Percy Frank Chapman was born at Reading on September 3, 1900, and educated at Uppingham where he was soon noticed as a cricketer of outstanding promise. He captained the XI, played in the representative matches at

Lord's, and in 1919 was chosen by *Wisden* as one of the five "Public School Cricketers of the Year". At that time he was also a more than useful player of Rugby and fives.

When he went up to Cambridge he won his Blue as a Freshman in 1920 and was also a member of the side for the following two seasons. This was a vintage period in Cambridge cricket with players like the three Ashton brothers, G. O. Allen, and M. D. Lyon. Yet Chapman was not outshone. In 1921 he was a member of the team assembled and led by A. C. Maclaren which, at Eastbourne, inflicted the first defeat upon Warwick Armstrong's Australians. The following year he scored a dazzling century against Oxford and followed it up with an innings of 160 for the Gentlemen against the Players at Lord's. Apart from his batting, his athletic fielding in the covers was of the highest class.

After coming down from Cambridge he played for Berkshire for a few years before qualifying for Kent. He toured Australia with Arthur Gilligan's M.C.C. side in 1924–25, but his great moment came in the final Test of 1926, at the Oval. He had played in some of the earlier Tests of the series, all of which had been drawn, but for the Oval match—on which depended the Ashes which Australia had held throughout the postwar period—he was chosen as captain. It was a surprise selection, for his experience of captaincy was virtually limited to school and minor matches. Yet he led England to a triumphant victory.

In the winter of 1928–29 he won further renown as the captain of M.C.C. in Australia.

POPULARITY

This was an immensely successful tour both on and off the field. It is doubtful if there has ever been a more popular English captain in Australia, and the team won the four Tests which they played under his command—they lost the fifth when he was unfit to play. The luck admittedly favoured him in some respects. He was opposed by an uncertain Australian team, suffering all the difficulties inevitable between the break-up of one great side and the formation of another. And while the Australians were going through a lean period, the English team was one of the richest ever in talent. It was one of those seasons when one would have expected England to win. But that should not rob Chapman of the praise for his achievement. He welded his men into a happy and united side, and nobody could say that in the Tests he allowed the generosity of his sentiments to cloud his judgment.

His performance in this country in 1930 was more suspect. He maintained his winning sequence against the Australians in the first Test at Trent Bridge, but his captaincy came in for authoritative criticism after the defeat at Lord's. This was one of the greatest of Test matches, and, whatever tactical errors he may have committed, there was nothing the matter with Chapman's play. By now a close fielder as well as an expert in the covers, he took fantastic catches to dismiss Bradman in both innings, and in the second innings he scored one of the most famous of Test centuries. England were facing ignominious defeat when he went to the wicket, and he would have been out for a "duck" if a simple catch had been held. But then he proceeded to score 121 with powerful strokes as magnificent as they were improbable.

DROPPED

The next two Tests were drawn in Australia's favour, and Chapman was dropped for the fifth and final one. Whether any other captain could have done better when faced with Bradman in such phenomenal form must remain an unanswered question—although it is interesting to note that Australia won comfortably at the Oval.

That was virtually the end of Percy Chapman's career at the highest level. In 1930–31 he led the M.C.C. in South Africa—an unsuccessful tour marred by illness and injury—but he never again captained England at home, and he never again met the Australians in Test match cricket.

Nevertheless, he captained Kent from 1931 to 1936 where he was a stimulating influence. At his best his batting had been brilliant but not reliable—his gifts were for attack, he never developed the defensive technique for really consistent success in first-class company. As he became more rotund in figure, so his batting became more erratic; but, strangely enough his fielding did not fall off noticeably, and at his best he had been one of the finest fielders ever to play for England.

A warm and convivial personality, he made a host of friends wherever he went.

His marriage in 1925 to Miss G. H. H. Lowry, daughter of a New Zealand racehorse owner and sister of a New Zealand cricket captain, was dissolved in 1942.

September 19, 1961.

Professor Sydney Chapman, F.R.S., who died on June 16, 1970, at the age of 82, was both a legend and a scientist. Up to his retirement from Oxford in 1953, he had made contributions of the first magnitude to each of stellar dynamics, terrestrial magnetism (which he renamed geomagnetism), meteorology and the kinetic theory of gases. Widely honoured and frequently consulted, he was an inevitable choice in that year as president of the Commission for the International Geophysical Year. At the same time, he took up new scientific posts at the High Altitude Observatory, Boulder, Colorado, and at the Geophysical Institute of Alaska where he had already been advisory scientific director for two years.

For more than 15 years after reaching retiring age, he remained as active and interested as ever. He was younger in spirit and pleasure than many 20 or even 25 years his junior. At 80, he delighted in getting through as much or more in a day as he had ever done. And he frankly enjoyed not only work but also world recognition, the rewards that went with it and the many stories told of him.

He was born at Eccles in Lancashire on January 29, 1888, and educated at elementary and technical schools and took an engineering degree in Manchester in 1907. His interests soon turned to mathematics and after graduating in this subject at Manchester in 1908 proceeded to Trinity College, Cambridge. He became wrangler in 1910, having sat for the mathematical tripos in his second year, and began his researches in pure mathematics under G. H. Hardy. He might have continued in this field but for the intervention of Sir Frank Dyson, Astronomer Royal, who offered him the post of Chief Assistant at Greenwich, a post which he held from 1910 until 1914, when he returned to Cambridge as a lecturer in mathematics. He was awarded the first Smith's prize in 1913, and in the same year was elected to a fellowship at Trinity College which he held until 1919. In this same year he was elected a Fellow of the Royal Society. He held professorships at Manchester (1919–24), Imperial College, London (1924–46), and Oxford (1946–53). He was Deputy Scientific Advisor to the Army Council from 1943 to 1945.

In geomagnetism he extended the work of Moos on the average characteristics of magnetic storms and showed that they could be divided into two distinct phases, the first of which is characterized by an increase in the horizontal force for a period of a few hours, the second or main phase, by a larger and more prolonged decrease lasting several hours. Taking up a suggestion of F. A. Lindemann, later Lord Cherwell, that magnetic storms and aurorae are caused by the interaction of a neutral but ionized solar corpuscular stream with the earth's magnetic field, Chapman with one of his pupils developed in 1930 a theory of magnetic storms in which their sudden commencement and first phase were ascribed to the compressions of the tubes of force of the magnetic field by the first onrush of the stream.

In seeking for an explanation of the Earth's magnetic field in periods of a lunar day and its submultiples, Chapman found that part of the origin must be sought in the atmosphere. He succeeded in tracing this to its source.

TIDE IN ATMOSPHERE

The moon must produce a small tide in the atmosphere, and the atmosphere contains charged particles. The tidal current carrying these would produce the kind of change in the magnetic field required, provided the atmospheric tide was large enough. The expected changes of pressure would be only of the order of that of a foot of air or 0.03mm. of mercury. By a discussion of an enormous number of observations, Chapman succeeded in tracing it. The analysis was carried out for many meteorological stations, but apart from its original application the results are of the first importance to the study of atmospheric motions.

Chapman's other major contribution was to the kinetic theory of gases, which, until he began his researches in 1911, was much in the same state as Maxwell and Boltzmann had left it, apart from an attempt by Lorentz in 1905 towards an accurate theory of a non-uniform gas. In 1916 Chapman published a memoir in which he was able to complete the theory of non-uniform gases so as to give exact formulae for the various transport coefficients for a simple gas. In 1917 he extended this work to a gas mixture and predicted the phenomenon of thermal diffusion, the prediction of which, unknown to Chapman, had been made by Enskog in 1911. The reality of this phenomenon was demonstrated experimentally by Dootson in 1916, and it has since found important technical applications.

Chapman was awarded the Adams Prize for an essay in geomagnetism in 1929. This was later expanded in a book, *Geomagnetism*, written in collaboration with J. Bartels. In 1939 he likewise collected his work on gases in a book written with T. G. Cowling entitled *The mathematical theory of non-uniform gases*.

INFLUENCED SCIENTISTS

It would be difficult to overestimate the great influence which Chapman exerted on the scientific world at large. His counsel was widely sought and he was an acknowledged authority on many scientific subjects. It was inevitable that, at its inception, Chapman should have been elected president of the Commission for the International Geophysical Year. He also served as president of the International Association for Meteorology (1936–48), Terrestrial Magnetism and Electricity (1948–51) and of the International Union for Geodesy and Geophysics from 1941–54, and of several learned societies, the London Mathematical, Royal Meteorological, Royal Astronomical and Physical Society.

He was elected to the United States, Indian, Norwegian, Swedish and Finnish National Academies of Science and to the Academies of Halle and Göttingen. He was made an honorary Fellow of Queen's College, Oxford (1954), of Imperial College (1956) and his own college, Trinity, similarly honoured him in 1957. The Universities of Cambridge, Alaska and Michigan conferred honorary degrees on him. His great capacity for work enabled him, on his retirement from Oxford in 1953, to take up scientific posts at the High Altitude Observatory, Boulder, Colorado, and at the Geophysical Institute of Alaska, where he had been Advisory Scientific Director since 1951.

Chapman's mild manner veiled a strong will and great determination; his tastes and habits were simple. He was an enthusiastic cyclist, swimmer and walker, and both on his visits to foreign universities or to international conferences, however varied the available modes of transport might be, Chapman could always be relied on to arrive on a bicycle. He rode from Montreal to Washington in 1939 to attend the meeting of the International Geophysical Union.

He married in 1922, Katharine Nora, daughter of the late A. E. Steinthal, of Manchester, and they had three sons and a daughter.

June 18, 1970

Sir Arthur Charles, who was shot dead by terrorists in Aden on September 1, 1965, had been Speaker of the Aden State Legislative Council and public service commissioner of the different branches of the Civil Service in South Arabia since 1959.

Arthur Eber Sydney Charles was born in 1910, son of the Rev. E. F. Charles, sometime vicar of Hampton, Middlesex. He was educated at Sherborne, where he was head of school, and Worcester College, Oxford. He played Rugby football for the university in 1932 and also represented the university at rugby fives. The following year he joined the Sudan Political Service. He was successively assistant District Commissioner of Kordofan province and deputy assistant Civil Secretary and was then seconded to the Palestine Government. He returned to the Sudan in 1941 and subsequently held the posts of District Commissioner North Darfur, Assistant Director of Establishments, Director of Establishments and from 1955 to 1957 Establishments Adviser. On his leaving the Sudan in 1957 he was appointed in Aden to be chairman of the committee for the Adenization of the Civil Service after which post he took up his appointments in the Legislative Council and Public Service Commission in which he was serving at the time of his death.

After 25 years of outstanding service in the Sudan Charles brought to the problems of Aden and South Arabia the expertise he had acquired in the Sudan. His mission was to provide the Civil Service with a precise programme of training and career guidance designed to eliminate the expatriate and to set local officers for the highest responsibilities. Every problem was to him a human one and the secret of his success in the years of toil in an austere field of work was his unvarying humanity and sympathy for the men and women, schoolboys and schoolgirls whose future in their country he planned and pondered over so lovingly. As a public service commissioner he was the personification of integrity and precision. No one could feel a doubt that his case had been fairly treated if Arthur Charles had sieved and winnowed it. As Speaker of the Legislative Council his courtesy, charm, boundless patience and good humour were an education to all who sat under his guidance.

He broke down all communal boundaries and was the enemy of partisanship. In a land which recognizes authority and is greedy for power Arthur Charles added a new dimension, that of statesmanship. His Arab and British colleagues and his multifarious friends in all communities and walks of life know that his example will bear fruit in some happier day in South Arabia when malignity and enmity have shot their bolt.

He married in 1949 Mary Elise, daughter of T. C. Sheppard.

September 3, 1965.

Hugo Charteris, M.C., writer and playwright, died on December 20, 1970, at his home in Elvington, near York, at the age of 48.

Hugo Charteris published nine novels, and a book for children. From the first *A Share of the World* in 1952, on a familiar theme of the upper class young man as an officer in war and his difficult return to life in peace, it was recognized that Charteris was a natural novelist with unusual and imaginative gifts. His values were civilized, patrician even, allied to an original technique, a great gift for dialogue and penetrating social observation.

His main characters tended to be imprisoned in their own emotions and circumstances—John Grant, the hero of *A Share of the World*—the 14 year old Etonian, Tim Loxley in *The Coat* (1966) on the loose in the Blitz with a quarter of a million in diamonds sewn in the lining of a coat—Elizabeth, the narrator and helpless observer of *The River Watcher* (1965)—a complex story not entirely of salmon poaching nor a political satire, though the portrait of Conrad Manders "one of Mosley's henchmen in the thirties" was one of the best things Charteris wrote—and Gabriel Murray the former naval V.C. who opted out of modern life into the highlands in *The Indian Summer of Gabriel Murray* (1968).

Several of the novels had Scottish backgrounds, each detail revealing unforgettable images of the country and society Charteris knew and observed so well. Much of his writing was complex, even tortuous. Underneath the wit and the brilliance there was a current of danger, death and violence, not always suppressed. Brilliant, disturbing and unpredictable, he was undoubtedly a considerable writer, and one of the few whose novels were getting better and better as the years went by.

T.V. OUTSIDERS

After 1965 Charteris built himself an impressive reputation as a writer of television plays. Probably his most popular work in this field was that B.B.C. series, Take Three Girls, which dealt with the adventures of Kate, who had the flat which she shared with the other two heroines, a baby to provide for but only a divorced husband. Kate's experiences ranged from the everyday to the semi-gothic, but it was typical of Charteris that the everyday was always viewed from an oddly oblique angle and that Kate approached life in a similarly sidelong manner. Charteris's detached plays for television firmly denied the viewer his cherished right to identify himself with an unambiguous character, for the people who interested Charteris were always outsiders, never totally at home in the modern world which he depicted with firm perspectives but unusually simplified details. The world made his dramatis personae, and hence the viewer's attitude towards them, oddly ambiguous.

Hugo Francis Guy Charteris was the son of the Hon. Guy Charteris. He was born on December 11, 1922 and educated at Eton and Oxford. He served with the Scots Guards in the Second World War in Italy and was twice wounded. He was awarded a Military Cross.

Later in the war he went to S.E.A.C. as a Public Relations officer in Malaya and Java. After the war he worked for the Daily Mail in London and Paris.

He was a brother-in-law of Ian Fleming who married his eldest sister Ann.

He married in 1948 Virginia, daughter of Colin Forbes Adam. They had two sons and three daughters. The elder son died in 1951.

December 22, 1970.

Pauline Chase, the actress who played the part of Peter Pan for eight consecutive seasons before the First World War, died at Tunbridge Wells on March 3, 1962. She was 76.

Pauline Chase was born on May 20, 1885, the daughter of a Washington dentist. She was educated at the Convent of the Society of the Holy Cross in the American capital and made her first stage appearance at the age of 13 at the Casino Theatre, New York, in *Rounders*. After playing boys' parts in *The Belle of New York* and *The Lady Slavey* she went to London and appeared with Miss Edna May in *The Girl from Up There* in April, 1901.

Back in New York she scored a success as the Pink Pyjama Girl in *The Liberty Belles*. At Christmas, 1904, she made a beautiful picture as First Twin in the original production of *Peter Pan*, and Sir James Barrie soon found that he had a potential star in his company. He gave her the part of Columbine in his play *Pantaloon*, and in this she acted before the King and Queen at both Windsor and Sandringham.

Miss Nina Boucicault had played Peter Pan in its first season and Miss Cissie Loftus in its second, and it came as something of a surprise when for the third season the part was offered to Pauline Chase, for many playgoers wondered whether the young American girl had yet had sufficient experience to play such a complex part. The critics were agreed that she had not the dramatic ability or the boyishness of Miss Boucicault. But she had a certain air of remoteness and strangeness which lent force to Barrie's whimsicalities and which, as *The Times* dramatic critic wrote, "made it easy to believe that Peter lived on the island in the Serpentine or in the Never Never Land or anywhere out of reach of real houses and real commonplace life. To see Miss Chase flying in at the window or playing her pipes after the carnage of the pirate ship is to have a sense of something not quite human, some fairy that has no soul and is gay almost without a care. The fairiness of Miss Pauline Chase added to the force of the persistent spirit of Peter Pan which fills an audience with strange promptings of "vagabondage and adventure."

Her run of eight successive Christmas seasons from 1906 was a record which stood until Miss Jean Forbes-Robertson played for eight years and once again after a few years' interval. Pauline Chase also played the part during two summer seasons in Paris. Throughout all that time she retained the same delicate grace and the same note of fragile and haunting romance. She did other work in the London theatre, although it will be for Peter that she will always be gratefully remembered. She was Ann Whitfield in a revival of *Man and Superman* at the Criterion in 1911 and she was one of the three daughters in a revival of Pinero's *The Amazons* in 1912.

In October, 1914, she married Mr. Alexander Victor Drummond, a member of the banking family.

Television viewers saw her briefly in 1958 when she was one of the friends to pay tribute to A. E. Matthews in the B.B.C. programme "This Is Your Life."

March 5, 1962.

General Lionel Chassin, who died in Marseilles on August 17, 1970, was a highly distinguished French Air Force officer but an unsuccessful politician. Born in Bordeaux in 1902, he studied at the Ecole Navale and began his career in maritime aviation before switching to the Air Force. In 1936 he was promoted captain, and in 1938 major, at the same time winning entrance to the Ecole de Guerre and a diploma at the Ecole Libre des Sciences Politiques.

One of the first French officers to join General de Gaulle in London after the armistice of June 1940, he went to North Africa in 1942 and commanded a bomber group during the fighting in Tunisia. Promoted lieutenant-colonel, he took command of a squadron in 1944 and thereafter rose steadily in the Air Force hierarchy, reaching the rank of Général d'Armée in 1957.

Among the important posts which he held after the war were those of Deputy Chief of Staff at the Defence Ministry (1946–48), Commander of the third Air Force region and of the Air Force schools (1948–51), commander of the Air Force in Indo-China (1951–53), Commander of Home Air Defence (1953–56), and Coordinator of Air Defence in Central Europe (1956–58).

Meanwhile, however, he became one of the leaders of the clandestine movement planning to end the Fourth Republic by a military coup d'état. In April, 1958, he was placed on permanent leave, and on May 13, the day of the Algiers putsch, a warrant was issued for his arrest. He escaped in time from his Paris address and went into hiding in the Loire department, where he organized an unsuccessful attempt to seize the Prefecture and the town hall of Saint-Etienne in support of the Algiers "Committee of Public Safety" led by General Salan.

On June 12, after General de Gaulle had taken over the Government, Chassin announced the creation of the "Mouvement Populaire Du 13 Mai," which was supposed to be the counterpart in metropolitan France of the revolt in Algiers.

CALL ON PATRIOTISM

In alliance with Maître Jean-Louis Tixier-Vigancour, the right-wing civilian leader, he called for a "revolution" to "demarxize" the French people by a reform of state education, the press and the radio. He called on all patriots to help General de Gaulle "not to deviate."

In September of the same year, Chassin resigned from his movement, proclaiming his support for Gaullism. But this did not prevent him from standing unsuccessfully in Bordeaux, in the ensuing general election, against the official Gaullist candidate M. Jacques Chaban-Delmas.

Thereafter he took no further part in politics, but worked as a consultant engineer, becoming chairman of a study group on aerial phenomena, a member of the Bordeaux academy, and honorary president of the Overseas Veterans' Association. His published works include *A Military History of the Second World War*, which won a prize from the Académie Française. He also founded the Revue des Forces Aeriennes.

August 20, 1970.

Admiral of the Fleet Lord Chatfield, P.C., G.C.B., O.M., K.C.M.G., C.V.O., died on November 15, 1967, at the age of 94. His death marks the passing of one of the most able and distinguished naval officers of the twentieth century. Though a gunnery specialist by profession his influence throughout the whole field of naval policy and strategy was profound, especially during the difficult period between the wars, when he served for over 12 years in various capacities on the Board of Admiralty, including five-and-a-half years as First Sea Lord and Chief of Naval Staff.

Chatfield was one of the band of brilliant young officers whom Admiral the Earl Beatty (as he finally became) gathered around himself in the Battle-Cruiser Squadron on the eve of the outbreak of war in 1914. Throughout that conflict he was Flag Captain to Beatty, in the Lion, while the latter commanded the battle cruisers, and in the Iron Duke and Queen Elizabeth, still as Flag Captain, after Beatty had taken over command of the Grand Fleet from Admiral Jellicoe in November, 1916. He thus took part in all the principal North Sea battles of the 1914–18 War—Heligoland Bight (August 28, 1914), Dogger Bank (January 24, 1915), and Jutland (May 31, 1916). The Lion sustained heavy damage in the second and third of those fights and indeed narrowly escaped destruction in both of them. Chatfield was commended in the dispatches reporting all three battles.

The reorganization of the Navy at the end of the war was not by any means the end of his association with Beatty. In June, 1919, Chatfield joined the Board of Admiralty for the first time as Fourth Sea Lord, with particular responsibility for transport and supplies. But in March, 1920, shortly after Beatty had begun his seven and a half year term of office as First Sea Lord, he transferred to the staff side as Assistant Chief of Naval Staff, being promoted Rear-Admiral in the following July.

While A.C.N.S., Chatfield conducted the preparations on the British side for the Washington Conference of 1921–22, and became a member of the team of naval experts who, under Lord Lee of Fareham, the First Lord, negotiated the Treaty for the Limitation of Naval Armaments and the other treaties which were the outcome of that conference. After Beatty had been forced to return to London to deal with other urgent business Chatfield became the senior British naval delegate. It thus came to pass that before he was 50 years old Chatfield had acquired unrivalled experience in command at sea in time of war, had become familiar with the technical, administrative and staff sides of the Admiralty's organization, and had also taken an important part in the first of the long series of international conferences by which the statesmen of the world hoped to avoid a repetition of 1914–18.

Plainly he was marked out for further distinction in his career.

After two years (December, 1922-January, 1925) in command of the 3rd Light Cruiser Squadron Chatfield returned to the Admiralty as Third Sea Lord and Controller of the Navy in April, 1925, with responsibility for the whole material side of the sea service. This was a very difficult time for the holder of that office, because the limitations in the size and armament of battleships and cruisers agreed at Washington resulted in all naval powers building ships of untried and novel design, armed with the biggest weapons permitted by the treaty. At the same time the conversion of three large cruisers to aircraft carriers was taken in hand, the first postwar cruisers and destroyers were laid down, and work was started on the Singapore base.

FIGHT FOR AIR ARM

Unhappily this was also the period when the prolonged and often acrimonious dispute between the Admiralty and the Air Ministry over the control of the Fleet Air Arm was at its height. Though it was Beatty who in general conducted the Admiralty's case, the experience left Chatfield determined to continue the struggle, even after successive governments had refused to grant the Navy its own air service. He also had to deal with a series of powerful committees appointed by the Treasury to enforce further economies and retrenchment in accordance with the deflationary fiscal policy of the day. In addition to the struggle to maintain a small but steady building programme in face of the "no war for 10 years" rule on which the Government of 1919 had ordered all service estimates to be based, and to progress the Singapore base, Chatfield was particularly concerned to build up the Navy's reserves of oil fuel, on which the mobility of the fleet depended. And, as a member of the board, he was also involved in the prolonged negotiations to prevent reduction of the greatly improved rates of pay introduced in 1919, and to procure a marriage allowance for naval officers—as was enjoyed by the Army and R.A.F. In March, 1926, Chatfield was promoted Vice-Admiral.

In April, 1929, he hoisted his flag as Commander-in-Chief, Atlantic Fleet, but just over a year later, shortly after being promoted admiral, he transferred his flag to the Mediterranean Fleet. Chatfield thus missed participation in the London naval conference of 1930.

It was during Chatfield's Mediterranean command that real progress was made in the employment of aircraft carriers and in the development of carrier air tactics. Although he was an ardent supporter of the capital ship as the dominant weapon he fully realized that in any future conflict the aircraft carrier was bound to assume great importance. On January 21, 1933, he returned to the Admiralty as First Sea Lord. He immediately set himself to progress the policies which had been left unfulfilled at the end of his previous term on the Board, and to prepare a building programme which would be started when the Washington and London treaties expired in 1936. At the same time he had to advise on the policy to be adopted when another naval limitation conference was called in 1935. His term of office was twice extended, and before he finally left the Admiralty on September 7, 1938, having meanwhile been promoted admiral of the fleet, the naval rearmament, for which he had so long pressed, had at last begun and the Admiralty had also regained full control of the Fleet Air Arm.

In appearance Chatfield was not at all the popular idea of an admiral. Of only moderate stature, and without any very striking physical presence, there was yet great force of intellect and of character, and a steely determination, behind his invariably quiet manner. Although with the wisdom generated by hindsight to guide us it is now clear that certain mistakes were made during his tenure of office as First Sea Lord and a member of the Chiefs of Staff's Committee (notably over the defence scheme for Singapore), the fact that the Royal Navy was able to meet the enormous responsibilities that fell to it between 1939 and 1942, though with scarcely any margin of safety, probably owed more to him than to any other man.

CHOSEN AS MINISTER

In the Coronation honours of 1937 Chatfield was raised to the peerage as Baron Chatfield of Ditchling, and in October of the following year, shortly after he had left the Admiralty, he went to India as chairman of the expert committee on Indian Defence. Before his return his appointment as Minister for Coordination of Defence, in succession to Sir Thomas Inskip, was announced. There had been no case since the Napoleonic War of a First Sea Lord accepting political preferment as a Minister of the Crown. In January, 1939, he was awarded the Order of Merit and, in the following month, was appointed a member of the Privy Council. But he found that in his ministerial capacity, he did not possess the powers necessary to press ahead with preparing the nation for the war which by that time he knew to be inevitable. He served on until March, 1940, by which time the War Cabinet had been formed and he considered his services could be dispensed with. After his resignation he became chairman of the committee on the evacuation of casualties in London Region hospitals.

Alfred Ernle Montacute Chatfield was born on September 27, 1873, the son of Admiral A. J. Chatfield. He received many British and foreign decorations and honours, including honorary degrees from both Oxford and Cambridge universities. He published two volumes of autobiography, *The Navy and Defence* (1942) and *It Might Happen Again* (1947). In the latter he wrote, sometimes with understandable bitterness, of the consequences of the policy adopted towards the Navy between the wars. He married in 1909 Lillian, daughter of Major G. L. Matthews, by whom he had one son and two daughters.

The heir is the Hon. Ernle David Lewis Chatfield, born in 1917, who served in the Second World War in the R.N.V.R.

November 16, 1967.

Ruth Chatterton, the American stage and screen actress, who died on November 24, 1961, at Norwalk, Connecticut, was born in New York on December 24, 1893. She first went on the stage, it is recorded, as the result of a schoolgirl dare; her bold bearding of a theatrical manager in his lair led to her being given her first role, in a play called *Merely Mary Ann*, at the age of 14, and from there on she never looked back.

She was kept busy for the next seven years or so, playing minor roles suited to her age, until in 1914 she achieved stardom in *Daddy Long Legs*, on Broadway. After this she was acting continuously on Broadway until 1928, playing in a wide variety of pieces, the most famous and successful of which were *The Little Minister*, *The Man with a Load of Mischief*, and *The Green Hat*; at this time she also tried her hand at authorship with two adaptations from the French, *La Tendresse*, in which she starred in 1922, and *The Man in Evening Clothes*.

In 1928 Ruth Chatterton finally succumbed to the lure of Hollywood, which was busily recruiting stage talent to meet the new problems of the sound cinema, and abandoned the stage until 1937. During her nine year film career she was not as fortunate as she had been on the stage, and though for a short period she became one of the screen's most popular stars, the roles she was given in cheerfully nonsensical films with titles like *Sins of the Fathers, Laughing Lady*, *Lady of Scandal*, *Anybody's Woman*, *Once a Lady* and *Female* did not enhance her reputation as an actress and before very long began to pall on the public.

By 1936 she was thought to be finished as a film star by most Hollywood producers, and it was only a brilliantly imaginative piece of casting by William Wyler which enabled her in *Dodsworth* to give one of the most astonishing and beautifully observed performances of the talking cinema as the silly, spoilt, insecure American wife giving way spectacularly to the allurements of sophisticated Europe.

After this triumph she returned to the stage, in London this time, playing the lead in a revival of Maugham's *The Constant Wife*, as well as making two British films, *A Royal Divorce* and *The Rat*. Back in America she was seen on the New York stage in *West of Broadway*, *The Affairs of Anatol*, and *Leave Her to Heaven*, but from 1940 onwards she worked almost entirely with summer stock companies in various parts of the United States, playing such roles as Amanda in *Private Lives*, Eliza in *Pygmalion*, and Regina in *The Little Foxes*. Her last appearance in New York was in 1951 when she took the part of Irene in a revival of *Idiot's Delight* at the City Centre; her most recent appearance on the stage was as Mrs. St. Maugham in *The Chalk Garden* at St. Louis in 1956. She was married three times: to Ralph Forbes, George Brent and G. Barrie Thomson.

November 27, 1961.

The Rt. Rev. Christopher Maude Chavasse, O.B.E., M.C., D.D., the first Master of St. Peter's Hall, Oxford, and from 1940 to 1960 Bishop of Rochester, died on March 10, 1962, at Oxford. He was 77.

The son of a famous evangelical Bishop of Liverpool, he was one of the outstanding leaders of the Evangelical school of thought in the Church of England. A man of deep religious convictions, very human sympathy and boundless energy, he was perhaps at his best in the pastoral sphere, whether military, parochial or academic. St. Peter's might fairly be described as virtually his creation, and during his 10 years as Master he was one of the leading influences in the religious life of Oxford, especially among the undergraduates.

Born on November 9, 1884, Chavasse was a son of Bishop F. J. Chavasse, who was Bishop of Liverpool from 1900 to 1923, and who died in 1928. He was educated at Magdalen College School, Oxford, at Liverpool College, and at Trinity College, Oxford, where he graduated in 1909. He had a distinguished athletic career, playing for Oxford v. Cambridge at lacrosse in 1905, 1906, and 1907; representing Oxford in the 100 yards and quarter mile in 1906, 1907, and 1908; and representing England in the 400 metres at the Olympic Games of 1908.

He read for the ministry at Bishop's Hostel, Liverpool, and was ordained in 1910 to a curacy at St. Helen's, Lancashire. He was domestic chaplain to his father from 1913 to 1919, when he became vicar of St. George's, Barrow-in-Furness. In 1914 he joined up as a Temporary Chaplain to the Forces and had a distinguished and gallant career. In 1916 he became Senior Chaplain to the 62nd Division and in 1918 he was appointed Deputy Assistant Chaplain General to the 9th Corps. He was wounded and was awarded the Military Cross and the Croix-de-Guerre. His twin brother, Noel Godfrey Chavasse, who had joined the Royal Army Medical Corps in 1913, was one of the very few who received the Victoria Cross with Bar. He later died of wounds. C. M. Chavasse continued his association with the Army after the Great War as a Chaplain to the Forces (Territorial Army) from 1921 to 1939, and was Senior Chaplain (T.) to the 48th (S.M.) Division from 1933 to 1937. In 1936 he was created O.B.E. (Mil).

ST. PETER'S HALL

In 1922 he was appointed rector of St. Aldate's, Oxford, and a new career began which was destined to influence the life both of the University and of the town. He remained rector of St. Aldate's for six years, resigning on appointment to the neighbouring rectory of St. Peter le Bailey, which made it possible for this church to become also the College Chapel of St. Peter's Hall.

The addition of a new college or hall to the University of Oxford is never an easy matter. It has even been described by cynics as more difficult than founding a whole new university. But the name Chavasse was one with which to conjure. The Hall was founded as a tribute to the memory of C. M. Chavasse's father, the Bishop of Liverpool, who first dreamed of the foundation of such a centre of Evangelical influence in the university, but who did not live to see his plans take tangible form. In 1929 his son was appointed the first Master and it was due to his remarkable organizing ability and powers of work that the considerable difficulties were overcome, and that it gained so rapidly the influence for which his father had hoped. It had never been the intention that the Hall should be rival to Wycliffe Hall as a training centre for ordinands. What was planned was a Hall with ordinary undergraduates in the various faculties of the university, and as such it took its place.

Meanwhile, Chavasse was busy in other directions. He took an active part in reorganizing the Oxford Evangelical pastorate. The establishment of St. Michael's House at Oxford and the removal of St. Catherine's Deaconess Training Centre there from Mildmay Park was mainly owing to his strong desire for an evangelical training institution for women workers in Oxford, as Wycliffe Hall was for clergy.

When Dr. Wilson, the Rector of Cheltenham, was appointed Bishop of Chelmsford, there was a question as to the future of the Cheltenham Conference. The suggestion was made that it should be transferred to Oxford and Chavasse accepted an invitation to become its chairman. As the Oxford Evangelical Conference it continued to meet in St. Peter's Hall each year and to attract large numbers of evangelical churchmen.

PLAIN SPEAKING

A part at least of Chavasse's success was due to his courage and vigorous plain speaking. In an Oxford that tended increasingly to question all things here was one man who knew his own mind and, in all prayerful humility, was not afraid to speak out where others were doubtfully or timidly silent. He denounced moral evils in Oxford. He defended the Thirty-nine Articles of religion against those who ascribed to them only a temporary, local and secondary importance. While expressing an earnest desire for union with the Orthodox Churches, he emphasized as a hindrance the Orthodox "placing of Tradition practically on a level with Scripture". He vigorously opposed the 1927–28 proposals for the revision of the Prayer Book and he opposed the Oxford Group Movement.

In addition to everything else he found time during this period for a good deal of writing. His publications included *The Meaning of the Lessons and of the Psalms* (1933) and *A Letter from the Catacombs* (1934). He was also a contributor to *The Atonement in History and in Life* (1929), *The Anglican Communion* (1929), *Christianity in the Modern State* (1935), and *Charles Simeon: An Interpretation* (1936).

In 1939, when Chavasse was 55 years of age, he was nominated for election as Bishop of Rochester; but almost immediately afterwards he met with an accident (while boating on a holiday in Northern Ireland) involving a compound comminuted fracture of the leg. As a result, his consecration did not take place until April 5, 1940: and in the summer of 1941 he underwent an operation, and in 1942 his leg was amputated.

THOUGHT AND STUDY

To one of his dynamic and ever youthful temperament, the enforced idleness was galling to a degree. But it produced a valuable result. It ensured for the Bishop elect a long period of meditation and study. It made him see that he must conserve his energies, relying heavily on addresses and letters to his diocese as a medium of influence; it brought a new deepening of the spiritual life to one who already had always with him the sense of the presence of God; and it produced one of the most inspiring series of pastoral messages that have been addressed in modern times by any English bishop to his diocese.

Chavasse had the defects of his qualities. He was impetuous and sometimes almost rash. In July, 1940, he startled many by authorizing clergy celebrating Holy Communion several times a day to treat the later celebrations as extensions of the earlier celebration and so not partake again themselves. When the propriety of this was questioned he himself referred to Lambeth and loyally accepted the subsequent unfavourable ruling. A more cautious man might have sought the ruling privately in the first instance, but of his loyalty there was never any question, and his action had at least the advantage of securing a weighty and valuable pronouncement from the Archbishop.

Perhaps the greatest contribution made by Christopher Chavasse in the guiding of the postwar Church was in his chairmanship of the Commission appointed by the archbishops to consider the urgency of evangelism. Chavasse gathered around him men of great distinction in this field of church activity, both clerical and lay.

CLEAR REPORT

Although the commission of 50 comprised representatives of all shades of thought in the Church of England, and although there were accordingly many differences of approach to the subject, nevertheless within two years, one report which stated the recommendations of the whole commission was presented. Scarcely ever can the Church have had put before it so cogently and with such lucidity, the nature, the need, and the purpose of evangelism. Diocesan and ruri-decanal conferences alike up and down the country, clergy and ministers' fraternals and local councils of churches, all used this report freely as a basis for "forward movement" within their own respective churches.

The Bishop's emphasis upon the inalienable rights of the laity in relation to the sphere of church government were no less insistent than his appreciation of the part laity should take in evangelism.

DIOCESAN LEADERSHIP

Yet his interest in the general problems of the Church in no wise diminished his intimate grasp of diocesan detail. His leadership here was full of freshness and vitality. Unorthodox in many of his ideas and opinions, he did not hesitate to express them plainly both at his diocesan conferences, as also in his two visitations of the diocese. Thus, honest as the day, he won the understanding, if not the support of his clergy and laity. Constantly did he stress the importance of the "family" life of his diocese and was never happier than when great services were held in his Cathedral church. In latter years, there was the epoch-making service to mark the twenty-seventh jubilee of his diocese. Also the sacred synods summoned to consider matters of grave diocesan concern. One of his last and greatest efforts was the launching of his appeal for new churches, parochial halls and the like. For this, the Bishop asked for no less than £1m. and his pastoral heart was cheered by the willing and generous response of every section of community life. He retired in 1960 and in November of that year he and his wife were handed a cheque for £5,745, a farewell gift from the diocese and outside and a contribution to the cost of a house the Bishop had bought in Oxford for his retirement.

So Christopher Chavasse retained all his enthusiasm and zeal to the very end. It is true that he was not the easiest of men with whom to work, and one could not always agree with the line he took. Perhaps he carried too great a burden upon his own shoulders, not finding it easy to delegate duties to others. Yet this twentieth century can scarcely have recorded a member of the episcopate who on the one hand was so obviously abreast of the changing moods and currents of modern thought and knowledge—his sermon on "Fundamentalism" in St. Margaret's, Westminster, a few years ago is a case in point—albeit on the other hand a man of such profound devotion and deep simple piety.

Chavasse married in 1919 Beatrice Cropper, daughter of the late William Edward Willink, J. P., of Dingle Bank, Liverpool and leaves three sons and two daughters.

March 12, 1962.

Lucy Evelyn Cheesman, O.B.E., F.R.E.S., the wellknown naturalist, explorer, broadcaster and author, died on April 15, 1969.

The second daugher of Robert Cheesman, she was born in 1881 at Westwell, near Ashford, Kent. She wanted to be a veterinary surgeon, but the profession was then closed to women, and so for a time she worked as a canine nurse. During the First World War she became a temporary civil servant, and worked with a niece of Professor Maxwell Lefroy, through whom a new field was opened when she was invited in 1920 to be Curator of the Insect House at the Zoological Society's gardens in Regent's Park.

As she had had no scientific training up till then she attended Professor Lefroy's general course on Entomology at the Imperial College of Science for two years. Then talks given to parties of children at the Zoo became so popular that they led to broadcasting in Children's Hour and so to writing books. The opportunity she was looking for came in 1924, when she was invited to join the St. George's Expedition to the West Indies, Panama, Galapagos Islands and South Pacific, as official entomologist.

At the Society Islands she left the expedition and stayed behind alone to collect insects. In this way she overstayed her leave of absence and severed her connexions with the Zoo. And when finally she returned to England she started working voluntarily at the British Museum (Natural History) on the insects she had brought back and given to the Museum.

LONE EXPEDITIONS

From now on, except for another interlude as temporary civil servant censoring letters in the Second World War, she divided her time between making solitary expeditions to islands in the South Pacific, lecturing and writing about her travels to pay for them, and working without pay as an honorary associate at the Museum. In 1953 her services to science were recognized, and her lack of means somewhat eased by the award of a Civil List Pension, and in 1953 she was given an O.B.E.

After the St. George's Expedition she visited by herself the New Hebrides in 1929–31, Papua 1933–34, the Cyclops Mountains of Dutch New Guinea in 1936, Waigeu and Japen Islands off Dutch New Guinea, and the Torricelli Mountains of Mandated territory in 1938–39.

LONE TRIPS

After the Second World War, at the age of 69, she went off alone to New Caledonia from 1949–50 and in 1954–55 at the age of 74 to the New Hebrides again to consolidate her studies there.

Between 1924 and 1960 she had had 16 books published, besides numerous papers in scientific journals. About half the books were on insects and general natural history for children, and the rest mainly popular accounts of her collecting expeditions. Her chief contributions to science were in collecting insects and other animals from the little-known fauna of islands in the South Pacific and recording them.

In *Things Worth While* (1957) she described how she had to fight against the stifling Victorian standards of her youth to be allowed to live her life her own way.

GIFTS AS TEACHER

She was a kind and friendly person much loved by those who knew her, austere though she was with herself and single-minded in her devotion to natural history. Nor was she robust, but a frail little woman and full of courage, fearless in exposing pretence or tilting at authority. Her greatest gifts were as a teacher of the young. Her understanding of children and primitive peoples enabled her to befriend and live alone with even savage cannibal tribes such as the Big Nambas of the New Hebrides. Her tastes in food and comfort were simple in the extreme. Any money from her tiny income, beyond her humblest needs, was ploughed back in such form as a gift-book to a young naturalist or a microscope to a government department.

April 17, 1969.

Colonel Robert Ernest Cheesman, C.B.E., who in the 1920s penetrated the "Empty Quarter", the Great South Desert of Arabia, died on February 13, 1962, at the age of 83.

Born in Westwell in Kent on October 18, 1878, the son of Robert Cheesman, and educated at Merchant Taylors' School and Wye Agricultural College, his first working years were spent in brewing. On the outbreak of the First World War, helped by a slight adjustment of his age, he enlisted in the 1/5th Buffs, serving in India and Mesopotamia. By January, 1916, the Buffs, like most other battalions on the Tigris, were in poor case after the battles staged in the attempts to relieve General Townshend in Kut al Amara. With a commission in the Regular Army Reserve of Officers Cheesman next spent a short period in the 1/4th Somerset Light Infantry. In 1916, when it became necessary for the Army to grow its own vegetables and crops in Mesopotomia, he was appointed by General Sir Stanley Maude to be Assistant to the Deputy Director of Agriculture. From 1920 to 1923 he was Personal Assistant to the High Commissioner in Iraq, Sir Percy Cox.

In 1921, having been granted local leave, he undertook a short expedition by sailing boat and camel into the Bay of Salwa in the Persian Gulf to search for the ruins of the Phoenician port of the spice trade, Gerra, mentioned by Ptolemy; the opportunity was taken to map the uncharted shore of Salwa Bay.

RUINS OF JABRIN

On the retirement of Sir Percy Cox in 1923 he went again to Arabia and with the help of H. H. Ibn Saud, Sultan of Najd, he penetrated into the Great South Desert of Arabia, called by western Arabists the Empty Quarter, but known to the Arabs as "The Sands". After a waterless camel journey of 150 miles from Hufuf, he reached and photographed the lost oasis and ruins of Jabrin in February, 1924. The ruins of Gerra were also discovered on the coast near Oqair, the latitude and longitude of Oqair, Hufuf, and Jabrin were fixed astronomically by theodolite, and first news of another oasis, Maquainama, 50 miles farther into the Sands was obtained from tribal information. For this journey he was awarded the Gill memorial by the Royal Geographical Society. The "Sands" were first crossed from sea to sea in 1931 by Bertram Thomas.

From 1925 to 1934 Cheesman served in the Sudan Political Service as H. M. Consul in N. W. Ethiopia with his Consulate at Dangila, south of Lake Tana, and was on duty in Addis Ababa at the Coronation of the Emperor Haile Selassie in 1931. Among his activities was the stopping of the annual expeditions of elephant poachers who had been crossing the undemarcated international boundary to hunt in the Sudan Game Reserve where the ivory was better.

During the nine years he spent in North-West Ethiopia he mapped the 500-mile canyon of the Blue Nile, cruised 160 miles by reed raft. charted the shore line of Lake Tana and visited the monasteries on the sacred islands. For these journeys he was awarded the Gold Medal (Patron's) of the Royal Geographical Society.

TRACKS MAPPED

In addition, most of the mule tracks leading through 100 miles of lowland forest from the Sudan frontier were mapped by compass traverse and compiled, and these were to prove of unexpected value in the Second World War when they were used by the Emperor Haile Selassie and his patriot troops under Colonel D. A. Sandford, Colonel Hugh Boustead and Colonel Orde Wingate and the remainder of his 16,000 camels as they fought their way back from the Sudan to Addis Ababa in 1940–41.

During his journeys in Asia and Africa Cheesman systematically collected thousands of bird and mammal skins, butterflies and moths, and these were presented to the British Museum (Natural History) and Tring Museum.

In 1934 he retired from Government service and began, with his wife, to farm in Kent, but in 1940 when war with Italy seemed inevitable, at the request of the Governor-General of the Sudan (leaving his wife to carry on the farm) he returned once more to Khartum now in the Sudan Defence Force, with the rank of Bimbashi. He was soon promoted Colonel, as head of the Ethiopian Branch of Intelligence on the Staff of General Sir William Platt.

At the end of the Italian East African Campaign, at the request of the Foreign Office he transferred from Khartum to the reopened British Legation at Addis Ababa as Oriental Counsellor until 1944 when he finally retired to his farm in Kent.

His account of the Arabian journeys in *Unknown Arabia* was published in 1926 and *Lake Tana and the Blue Nile* in 1936.

He was appointed O.B.E. in 1923 and advanced to C.B.E. in 1935. In both world wars his services were mentioned in dispatches.

He married in 1927 Catherine, daughter of W. F. Winch, of Cranbrook; she died in 1958. There were no children of the marriage.

February 15, 1962.

Ada Chesterton, O.B.E., (Mrs. Cecil Chesterton) died on January 20, 1962, in a Croydon nursing home.

Her death—in her nineties—has removed a notable woman in the world of journalism and literature as well as a pioneer in practical philanthropy. For many years she was one of the busiest contributors to the periodical press on a variety of subjects. She had strong instincts towards the drama and the theatre, but her best memorial, perhaps, is her work for the poor and the sick which had its origin in Cecil Houses (Incorporated). This was the compelling passion of her life.

She was born in London. Her father was Frederick John Jones, and her mother was Ada Charlotte Jones, and she was christened Ada Elizabeth, although in the intimate circle of her family and friends she was always known as Keith. She was, it has been said of her, practically born into the Street of Ink as the daughter, sister, aunt, and, of course, wife, of men associated with newspapers and periodicals, and her own gravitation to journalism was therefore natural. When recognition came to her she became a frequent and much sought after contributor of special articles and descriptive writing to London daily and weekly papers and magazines on topics of social, psychological, literary, and economic interest, as one of the reference books expresses it.

Sheridan was a paternal family name, and a good deal of her work in those days appeared under or above the signature "Sheridan Jones". She was assistant editor of *New Witness* (orginally *Eye Witness* when founded by Hilaire Belloc and Cecil Chesterton) during the last part of Cecil's editorship before he joined the Army and so continued when G.K.C. first became editor. She married Cecil Chesterton in 1917 before he was drafted overseas as a private in the H.L.I. Cecil Chesterton died in a military hospital in France shortly after the Armistice in 1918, and only by the unyielding persistence that characterized her life did Mrs. Chesterton break through red tape to be with her husband at his end. There followed journeys to Poland—she made the voyage on an American ship through seas still unswept for mines—and to Russia, China and Japan, later vividly described in her books.

She wrote much of the dramatic criticism which appeared in *New Witness* and later, with Ralph Neale, adapted G.K.C.'s *The Man who was Thursday* for the stage.

In 1925 she voluntarily lived the life of a down-and-out in London to find out for herself the conditions of the homeless. Her book *In Darkest London* created a furore—the Bishop of London preached a sermon on it, the Lord Mayor of London lent the Mansion House for a meeting to raise money for the Fund which sprang into existence as Cecil Houses (Incorporated) and this was followed by other Cecil Houses where for 1s. a night any homeless woman could secure a good comfortable bed, bath, and tea and bread and butter night and morning—a rare luxury in those days.

During the war the five Houses never closed, and gave shelter to the ever-increasing number of bombed-out women and children.

At the end of the war the Cecil Residential Club for Working Girls on small wages was opened by the Lord Mayor of London, and—like the Houses—became self-supporting. Once this was running smoothly all Mrs. Chesterton's energy was concentrated on starting a similar club for old age women pensioners. In spite of doubt on the part of some of her council members at the enormous amount of £100,000 to be raised for the enterprise, Mrs. Chesterton pressed ahead with her plan, and on February 4, 1953 the Lord Mayor of London opened the doors of the Cecil Residental Club in Wedlake Street, North Kensington, for 72 elderly women.

January 23, 1962.

Gabriel Chevallier, the author of *Clochemerle*, a full-blooded, uproarious farce in the Rabelaisian tradition, died in April, 1969, in Cannes, at the age of 73.

The novel, first published in the 1930s, became a best-seller and was translated into many languages. In the novel the ambitions of a politically minded mayor, the fanaticism of a schoolmaster, the love affairs of the town's prettiest women, the meddlesome zeal of an old maid—all combine with the introduction of a "public convenience" to create a series of scandals which makes Clochemerle for the moment the most notorious place in France.

Clochemerle-Babylon and *Clochemerle-les-Bains* were sequels to the book. In the former one critic thought the humour laboured and the story suffering from the lack of a central plot; in the second Gauloiserie is still rampant, carnality has lost none of its savour, and the Clochemerlin continues to dedicate himself to growing Beaujolais.

Chevallier wrote several other novels: among them *Mascarade* and *Sainte-Colline*.

April 8, 1969.

John Christie, C.H., M.C., died on July 4, 1962, at his home in Glyndebourne, a place he had made world famous.

Big, jovial, still both a boy and a schoolmaster impishly mixed together, he created in Glyndebourne opera a modern glory of music in England. People came to his comparatively small opera house from many countries, to experience an evening they could have nowhere else. It was a man of powerful character who could thus give significance to a Sussex home of 700 years.

John Christie, great-great-grandson of Daniel Béat Christie and Elizabeth Langham, was born in 1882, the son of Augustus Langham Christie and Lady Rosamond Alicia Wallop, daughter of the fifth Earl of Portsmouth. The Wallop connexion is familiar to operagors from the name given to the dining rooms at Glyndebourne.

John Christie was educated at Eton and Trinity College, Cambridge. He returned to Eton as a master teaching physics—unconventionally according to the stories told by his pupils—before he succeeded to the Glyndebourne property. He served with the King's Royal Rifle Corps in the 1914–18 War and was awarded the M.C. About 1920 he began to simplify and beautify the house, and in the next few years "exchanged fishing holidays for operatic holidays". In both enterprises he had guidance from his friends Mr. and Mrs. John Mounsey, and amateur music was frequently given before audiences of neighbours and servants in the Organ Room, which had been built before the war under the influence of Dr. C. H. Lloyd, whom he had known at Eton. The organ, a large four-manual, was built to Lloyd's specification and Christie's interest in the organ, which was subsequently to change to positive dislike, led him to acquire the business of Norman and Beard, the organ builders, who named after him the new type of instrument which they designed and built for cinemas.

The two interests of amateur music at home and opera abroad coalesced about 1930 into a scheme for local opera on a semi-amateur, semi-professional basis at Glyndebourne and plans for an opera house got as far as digging trenches for the foundations. But at this point Christie's marriage in 1931 to the opera singer, Audrey Mildmay, caused a decisive change to be made to something so ambitious that anyone who knew anything about English musical life declared it to be impossible of realization. Miss Mildmay had sung with the Carl Rosa company and so had practical and professional knowledge of what was involved in presenting opera of the highest quality. Her husband was rich and had at his disposal in the Ringmer Building Works the means of carrying out any structural plans for an ideal theatre. The Continental holidays had provided some knowledge of operatic personalities and in 1933 the Christies went to Copenhagen to ask Fritz Busch if he would be willing to direct the enterprise. He suggested that Professor Carl Ebert should be invited as producer and he in turn introduced Mr. Rudolph Bing, who was at that time a concert agent in Berlin, as manager.

The collaboration was astonishingly successful. John Christie propelled the undertaking with a single-minded devotion—a single-mindedness that was to irritate many sympathizers, to alienate Lord Keynes when larger schemes were in the air and the Arts Council was becoming a necessary agent in their realization, and to make it difficult to fit Glyndebourne into any other more comprehensive plan with the notable exceptions of the Bath and Edinburgh Festivals. But it realized the impossible. The Glyndebourne plan of ideal opera in ideal surroundings became a reality in 1934, when a first season of two of Mozart's operas was given in the newly built theatre in a hollow of the Sussex Downs.

The subsequent history of Glyndebourne with its enlarged repertory—all five of Mozart's standard operas, Verdi's *Macbeth*, and Donizetti's *Don Pasquale* had been produced by 1939—and its revival after the war, at first modestly with Gluck's *Orpheus* in 1947, and on its old scale in 1951, is a tribute, as Christie himself was foremost and most emphatic in asserting, to the value of the basic idea, which was Mrs. Christie's: that only the best was good enough, and "best", for the first time in operatic history, at any rate in Britain, included the visual and the dramatic aspects of the art on an equality with the musical.

Glyndebourne launched out into a somewhat less self-contained world when from 1947 to 1955, with the exception of one year, it was responsible for the operas at the Edinburgh Festival. This huge international event originated in an idea conceived during a tour of *The Beggar's Opera* in 1950, Glyndebourne's only production during the war, by Mrs. Christie and Mr. Bing. When the festival was launched and succeeded beyond expectation it was natural for Glyndebourne to be associated with it and John Christie was always present at the King's Theatre. In 1954 he was made a C.H., an honour which he accepted, though he had previously declined all honours, as in some way a tribute and memorial to his wife, who died in 1953.

NO COMPROMISE

He was made an honorary doctor of music of Oxford University in 1956, and he received German and Austrian decorations. In 1954 he received (the first Englishman) the Mozart Medal from the Vienna Mozart Society, and was presented at the same time with another awarded posthumously to his wife.

Christie's secret was that from beginning to end he was an implacable perfectionist. It led him at times to be a most unreasonable man. To him reason meant compromise. And where standards were concerned he would admit no compromise. He made some enemies. In his old age he tended to fight old battles over again. But to the overwhelming number of those who knew him he was a fount of inspiration and a dear friend. His sense of fun never really deserted him even when he waxed most indignant. He would suddenly laugh, deliver himself of some typically English piece of nonsense, turn his back mentally on those he thought were his opponents, and grow excited and enthusiastic about his latest venture. Few men lived a dedicated life more intensely or savoured it more.

The death of his wife—so gracious a hostess, so delightful a companion—was a blow from which he never recovered. To those who had been to her private dinner parties at Glyndebourne in their heyday together it was a sad sight to see Christie wandering about the house solitarily. It was her memory as well as the enduringly tough streak in him that caused him to drive Glyndebourne to its final financial as well as artistic success.

In 1954 he formed a trust for the perpetuation of Glyndebourne opera. There are two children of the marriage, a daughter and a son George, who succeeds, subject to the trust provisions, to the estate in Sussex and to Tapley Park in Devonshire.

July 5, 1962.

Randolph Churchill, M.B.E., son of Sir Winston Churchill, died on June 6, 1968, at the age of 57.

Despite fast deteriorating health Randolph Churchill continued to the last to operate with undiminished zest from his country retreat at East Bergholt. His chief task was, of course, the massive biography of his father, now left uncompleted, but he managed as well, in collaboration with his son Winston, to knock off a lively volume on the Arab-Israel war.

TELEVISION HITS

His television appearances were rare, but, like everything he did, usually had some bizarre twist which made them memorable. As an able, if erratic, journalist he continued to interest himself in the press, sounding his brassy trumpet (latterly in the columns of the *Spectator*) before what he considered to be Fleet Street's tottering walls. Let it also be recorded how, with characteristic chivalry, he found time and energy to champion Mrs. Jacqueline Kennedy in the controversy arising over the Manchester biography of her husband.

Randolph Frederick Edward Spencer Churchill was born in 1911, the only son of Sir Winston Churchill. His schooldays at Eton, while not as scholastically abysmal as his famous father's at Harrow, were undistinguished. At Christ Church, Oxford, likewise, he made his mark more through his social and political activities than by diligence at his studies or brilliance at examinations.

A political career was inevitable, and he seemed exceptionally qualified for one. With a handsome and attractive presence, famous name, unusual oratorical gifts, energy, courage and quickness of mind, particularly in argument, small wonder that he was called a young man of destiny, and reacted as such. At a phenomenally early age he was lecturing across America, addressing political meetings with an aplomb that could be mistaken for arrogance, and engaging in popular and well-paid journalism under the aegis of the first Lord Rothermere.

Parliament was an obvious objective, and it might have been supposed that through family influence an appropriate constituency would easily be found for him. Actually, Winston Churchill's quarrel with Baldwin over Indian policy in the thirties made the Conservative Party machine little inclined to want to please him. Randolph, at this time as throughout his life, loyally followed his father, and shared the political disabilities his attitude involved. No son could, in this respect, have been more devoted. Any aspersion on the father was bound to receive a rebuke from the son. However preposterous its terms, it was impossible not to admire the filial love and respect out of which it arose.

FAILED AS CANDIDATE

A series of attempts to get into Parliament (in one case—at the Wavertree Division of Liverpool in 1935—standing as an independent Conservative) all failed. On the need to rearm, to build up a common front with the U.S.S.R. against the menace of Nazi Germany, Randolph was wholly in agreement with Winston Churchill and his friends. He spoke with force and passion at the Oxford Union against the notorious King and Country resolution.

When, in 1940, his father at last became Prime Minister, and, in his capacity of war leader, began to exercise quasi-dictatorial powers, it might have been supposed that Randolph's moment had likewise come. He was already a serving officer with the 4th Q. O. Hussars, and was returned unopposed in a by-election as Conservative member for Preston. This seat he held throughout the war, losing it to his Labour Party opponent at the 1945 general election. Thenceforth, though he stood on numerous occasions—for instance, in Plymouth against Michael Foot—he never succeeded.

If in the war years he expected a ministerial appointment, none came his way, though his brother-in-law, Duncan Sandys, soon got his foot on the ladder of political promotion. Whatever disappointment he may have felt he kept strictly to himself, and served honourably throughout the war as an Intelligence Officer, first in the Middle East, and then in Yugoslavia. On this latter mission he was accompanied by Evelyn Waugh, who, in order to stop him talking (always difficult, and usually impossible), induced him to read through the Holy Bible: an arduous, but no doubt rewarding, undertaking. What Tito and his partisans made of these two unusual officers can only be a matter for speculation.

NOISY ARGUMENT

By this time, certain characteristics of disposition and behaviour in Randolph Churchill had become well marked. He was, for instance, an inveterate user of the telephone, over which instrument he would read to his friends, and even acquaintances, any piece of composition that he happened to be engaged on. At social gatherings he was liable to engage in heated and noisy arguments which could ruin a dinner party, and made him the dread of hostesses on both sides of the Atlantic. The tendency was exacerbated by an always generous, and occasionally excessive, alcoholic intake. His public *persona* could seem irascible and arrogant, if not absurd. Yet, however irritating, or, in certain circumstances, despicable, he might appear, his intimates knew that underneath he was a sensitive, perceptive person, easily wounded, very unsure of himself, and, ultimately, lovable and affectionate.

Though he could be seen as a failure, in his own bizarre way he made a considerable mark on his times. As a political journalist he was usually astute, and sometimes brilliant. His single-handed campaign against newspaper pornography was spirited, and, up to a point, effective. Above all, he made himself notable as a person both in this country and in the United States. He put on a unique individual performance in an age of collective enterprise and average men, in itself an uncommon achievement. People might sigh at his name, but were always eager for news of his doings and sayings. However appalling his behaviour he never lacked invitations or guests.

TWO BIOGRAPHIES

Most of his last years were spent at East Bergholt, in Suffolk, where he was engaged first on a biography of the seventeenth Lord Derby, and then on one of his father. This was to be a massive and definitive work, whose preparation required, like Sir Winston Churchill when similarly employed, relays of secretarial and research assistants.

Among the books which he did publish, his biography of Lord Derby (1960), rightly earned great approval. *The Rise and Fall of Sir Anthony Eden* (1959), while containing interesting and provocative information on the Suez crisis, was as a whole uneven and tendentious. It was hardly a full-length biography in the accepted meaning of the term. *The Fight for the Tory Leadership* (1964) was the first, though by no means definitive, work on the manoeuvres that led to the succession of Sir Alec Douglas-Home to the premiership. Although internal evidence suggested that Churchill did not lack well-placed sources of information, this book will probably be remembered more for the rejoinder from Mr. Macleod that it provoked than for itself.

He married twice but neither marriage lasted. By the first he had a son, Winston, and by the second a daughter, Arabella. He was a devoted and affectionate father, quite at his best in the company of his children.

OVERSHADOWED

Admirers and critics of Randolph Churchill are liable alike to shake their heads and say that to be the son of so remarkable a father was a hard fate in life. It is true, of course, that Randolph was to some extent overshadowed by Sir Winston, and that he often made himself pathetic or absurd (according to the mood of the observer, by copying his father's ways, echoing his rhetoric, and emulating his style). Yet, after all, had he been content just to sail along in Sir Winston's wake, he would easily have reached secure and prosperous anchorage. It was because of something original, something distinctive, perhaps clownish, in his own disposition that he failed so signally, and honourably, to profit from his father's fame and influence. This quality, this clownishness even, is what many people will miss: not the poor echo of parental braggadocio.

June 7, 1968.

Sir Winston Churchill, who died in London on January 24, 1965, led Great Britain from the peril of subjugation by the Nazi tyranny to victory; and during the last four years of his active political life he directed his country's efforts to maintain peace with honour, to resist another tyranny, and to avert a war more terrible than the last. In character, intellect, and talent he had the attributes of greatness.

An indifferent schoolboy, he was indifferent at nothing else which he attempted. Inheriting Lord Randolph Churchill's energy and political fearlessness, and being granted twice as many years, he carried to fulfilment a genius that in his father showed only brilliant promise. Leader of men and multitudes, strategist, statesman of high authority in the councils of nations, orator with a command of language that matched the grandeur of his themes, able parliamentary tactician, master of historical narrative, his renown is assured so long as the story of these lands is told.

The great war leader of his age, he lived through the fastest transformation of warfare the world has ever known, charging with the 21st Lancers at Omdurman in his youth, and in his old age arming his country with the hydrogen bomb.

He first entered Parliament in the sixty-fourth year of the reign of Queen Victoria. Sixty-four years later, in the thirteenth year of the reign of her great-great-granddaughter, he retired from it. Through more than half a century of British history there was not a year—barely a month—in which he was not actively and prominently engaged in public affairs.

Churchill's outstanding political virtue, which never deserted him, was his courage. There was the sheer physical courage which led him to seek more risks on active service before he was 25 than many professional soldiers know in a lifetime; and which gave him the will, when he was past 75, to overcome an affliction which would have laid other men low from the start. But there was moral and intellectual courage in equal degree. He served in Kitchener's Army in the Sudan—but attacked Kitchener publicly for his desecration of the Mahdi's tomb. He was returned as a Conservative in the "Khaki Election" of 1900—only to devote a passage in his maiden speech to a generous tribute to the Boers. No sooner was his maiden speech over than he shocked the Conservative front bench again by turning on one of his own party leaders, the Secretary of State for War, with a scorn which would have been startling even in a member of the Opposition.

CHANGE OF PARTY

He was still under 30 when, finding himself at odds with the tariff reform policy of Joseph Chamberlain, he crossed the floor of the House. So it continued all through his life—the habit of following his own judgment, his own intuition, and his own impulses. When he resigned from the Conservative "Shadow Cabinet" in 1931, as a protest against its attitude to India, he was acting with the same courage and independence which—they were inherited from his father—he had displayed from the very beginning. His independence frequently baffled his contemporaries, who tended to conclude, as did Margot Asquith in 1908, that he was a man of "transitory convictions". But the point is not that they were transitory but that they were his own. His mind was always restlessly surveying the political scene. He was for ever testing, courting, encouraging new ideas. No politician of this century has been less conservative and less hidebound.

This adventurousness, of course, had its disadvantages, of which his colleagues were often painfully aware. His mind never stopped roaming, and Asquith's Cabinet was described by one of its members as "very forbearing to his chatter". During the 1939–45 War—as the famous memoranda published as appendices to his history of *The Second World War* show—any question however trivial or however far removed from the central direction of the war might gain his attention. He seized on new ideas so indiscriminately that it became necessary for some of those closest to him to act as a sieve, and so prevent valuable time from being wasted on the wilder schemes. Yet, when the dross had fallen through, there remained in the sieve one or two nuggets. There is in Printing House Square a letter written early in the 1914–18 War by a high personage accusing Churchill of madness because of some impracticable scheme which he was pressing through in the face of much expert opposition. The "scheme" was the tank.

The independence of his ideas always made it difficult to define Churchill's political position. He was more of a Tory than a Conservative. The symbols of Toryism—Crown, Country, Empire, which might seem abstractions to some, were to him realities. There was, indeed, always a personal element in the service he gave to his Sovereigns, which found quite different expressions in his attitude to the abdication of Edward VIII and in the tributes he paid when George VI died and Queen Elizabeth II was crowned. But it was a Toryism infused by another abstraction which to him was equally a reality: the People. He believed deeply that the People existed—not different and warring classes of people. In an earlier age he would have stood committed to the idea of the King and the People against the great Whig magnates—the cardinal principle of Disraelian Toryism. He was, in brief, a Tory Democrat, and in a speech to the Conservative conference in 1953 he proclaimed again the creed of his father, the first prophet of Tory Democracy.

SENSE OF HISTORY

Least of all was he a "Little Englander". No statesman has ever been more aware of his country's position in the world and its responsibility to the world. It was not merely his awareness of the facts of Germany's rearmament which made him speak so clearly from the beginning of the thirties: it was, even more (as befitted a descendant of Marlborough), his fundamental assumption that Britain was a part of Europe. He could no more have talked of Czechoslovakia as a far-away country than of Blenheim and Ramillies as far-away towns.

His politics were infused with a sense of history. It was a common gibe of his opponents that he lived in the past—that he was, in the words of Harold Laski, a "gallant and romantic relic of eighteenth-century imperialism".

Nothing could be farther from the truth. He was as aware of the present, its opportunities and its challenges, as any of his contemporaries. But he drew from the past a profound conviction in the greatness of Britain, her people and her heritage. Romantic? It may be. But it was from this reserve that he drew the inspiration which he communicated to his fellow-countrymen in their and his finest hour. He was the symbol of British resistance, but of how much more as well. In his voice spoke the centuries which had made Britain as they had made him, and those who heard him in those days will never forget the echoes of Burghley, of Chatham, of Pitt, and countless more. "The last of the great orators to reach the heights."

The Right Honourable Sir Winston Leonard Spencer-Churchill, K.G., O.M., C.H., F.R.S., was born on St. Andrew's Day, 1874, at Blenheim Palace. He was the elder son of Lord Randolph Churchill and a grandson of the seventh Duke of Marlborough. His mother was the beautiful and talented daughter of Leonard Jerome, a New York businessman. Surviving her husband until 1921, she lived to see her son's fame firmly established.

SOLDIER AND JOURNALIST

The year had been an eventful one for Lord Randolph. Apart from his marriage and the birth of a son and heir, it had begun with his election as Conservative M.P. for Woodstock and included a maiden speech which drew from Disraeli, who had a good eye for a duke's son, a warm commendation. Lord Randolph's rise to power and influence was to be rapid, but his decline was even more rapid, and when he died in 1895 he left his son with memories of defeat and failure which carried a moral he was often to remember. Winston Churchill's education was conventional in its pattern; from a preparatory school at Ascot, to a small school at Brighton, to Harrow in 1888, and then, after twice failing to gain admission, to the Royal Military College at Sandhurst. But his verdict on Harrow was individual, for he left there, as he later confessed, convinced that he was "all for the public schools, but I do not want to go there again".

In 1895, soon after his father's death, he entered the 4th Hussars at Aldershot, and immediately obtained leave to go to Cuba for the *Daily Graphic* to watch the Spanish Army at work. While he was there he participated in the repulse of the insurgents who tried to cross the Spanish line at Trocham. After enjoying the London Season in 1896 he embarked for India, where he relieved the monotony of morning parades and evening polo by indulging his delight in reading. He was back in London for the Season in 1897, and then left in September to join the Malakand Field Force on the North-West Frontier of India. After being mentioned in dispatches for "making himself useful at a critical moment", he had to return to the 4th Hussars at Bangalore early in 1898, and there he occupied himself with the writing of his first history, *The Story of the Malakand Field Force*, which had considerable success at the time and is still consulted.

While he was at Bangalore he also wrote his only novel, *Savrola, a Tale of the Revolution in Laurania*, which he later urged his friends not to read. It contained, however, the sentence which seems to be as autobiographical as any he wrote: "Under any circumstances, in any situation, Savrola knew himself a factor to be reckoned with; whatever the game, he would play it to his amusement, if not to his advantage." During these early years Lieutenant Churchill, enjoying a liberty not likely to be granted nowadays to a serving officer, was able to combine the roles of a soldier and a newspaper correspondent, and it was as the representative of the *Morning Post* that at last, after three rebuffs from Kitchener, he joined the Sirdar's Army in Sudan. He reached Cairo in time to take part in the advance south into the Mahdi's country, and was present at the final victory at Omdurman.

PRISONER OF THE BOERS

The strategy, tactics, and what a later generation has learnt to call the logistics of the campaign were set out by Churchill in *The River War, an Account of the Reconquest of the Sudan*, which was immediately successful when it was published in 1899. His early military writings showed a grasp, remarkable in a man of his years, of the operations of war, which was best revealed in the clear separation of the essential from the accidental. They were also distinguished by a dogmatic self-confidence which never hesitated in its criticism of senior officers. His outspokenness did not improve his prospects and he was doubtless wise to resign his commission after wearing the Queen's uniform for only four years. Moreover, his success as a journalist had enabled him to think of giving up the Army as a career, and he had even turned his attention to politics, addressing a Conservative garden party at Bath (his first political speech) and fighting a by-election (unsuccessfully) at Oldham.

It was as a correspondent, again for the *Morning Post*, that he left for South Africa within a fortnight of the outbreak of war in the autumn of 1899. There he met with sensational adventures very much to his taste. Taken prisoner on an armoured train expedition by a Boer by the name of Louis Botha he succeeded in escaping from the prison camp at Pretoria within three weeks, "jumped" a train, and after an extraordinary journey reached Delagoa Bay. He saw the campaign out until he could reenter Pretoria with the victorious Army, and when he returned to England he was received tumultuously at Oldham, where, in the "Khaki Election" of 1900, he won the seat from Walter Runciman. He was not yet 26, and contemporary accounts record that Joseph Chamberlain sat up and nudged his neighbour on the front bench when, in his maiden speech, Churchill declared: "If I were a Boer fighting in the field—and if I were a Boer, I hope I should be fighting in the field . . ."

TARIFF REFORM

Chamberlain was right to take notice: there was an ominous smack about the words, and in his first session in the House not only did Churchill speak vehemently against the Conservative Government's plans for Army reform—and their unfortunate advocate, Mr. Brodrick—but he voted against them as well. His unorthodoxy had deep roots. He was at work on his life of his father, who had remained in a party with whose orthodox leaders he was at war and had suffered in the end only isolation and defeat. At the very beginning of his political career Churchill was in much the same position. He was as much a Tory Democrat as his father, in a party led by Balfour, who had always seemed to Lord Randolph to be the main opponent of Tory Democracy. Moreover, there was little intellectual adventure to be found in the Conservative Party of 1902, and Churchill, who always retained a great respect for the academic and cultured intellect, felt drawn to the company of Morley, Asquith, Haldane, and Grey.

Then, in the summer of 1903, Joseph Chamberlain made his great effort to revive protection—"playing Old Harry with all party relations", as Campbell-Bannerman excitedly remarked. With the Duke of Devonshire and Lord Hugh Cecil, Churchill declared himself a Unionist Free Trader, and by September, when it became clear that the Protectionists in the Cabinet had won, he was publicly exclaiming to a meeting at Halifax, "Thank God for the Liberal Party". Not unreasonably, the Oldham Conservative Association took exception to this and disowned him, and in the following year he crossed the floor of the House. How many who were there on that May 31, 1904, could foresee the irony in the incident as Churchill took his seat by the side of none other than David Lloyd George?

Before the end of 1905 Churchill had completed the life of his father. It stands, over half a century later, as one of the most brilliant political biographies of all time. The prose was perhaps never excelled by Churchill—later in his life the influence of the platform and the House of Commons made his prose too rhetorical—and the bringing to life of the political scene is so vividly and precisely done that the reader never loses his interest.

BATTLE IN PARLIAMENT

No sooner was this work of filial vindication done than Balfour—after months of trying to pacify his party and the House by "expressing no settled conviction where no settled conviction exists"—threw in his hand, and Campbell-Bannerman took office, Churchill accepted the office of Under-Secretary of State for the Colonies and was the spokesman of his department in the House of Commons. A month later, at the general election, Churchill was returned as a Liberal for North West Manchester—while Balfour was defeated in the adjacent seat. In the House it fell to him to maintain the Government's decision to grant full self-government to the annexed Boer Republics—a controversial issue—and he began to develop his parliamentary style in the thick of a major parliamentary battle. At the same time his mind was moving to a new outlook on home affairs. Before leaving the Conservative Party he had looked back to the time "when it was not the sham it is now, and was not afraid to deal with the problem of the working classes". Now he confidently declared that the Liberal Party's cause was "the cause of the left-out millions".

He was a Radical, describing the obstructive attitude of the House of Lords as "something very like an incitement to violence". In 1908, when Asquith succeeded Campbell-Bannerman, Churchill was promoted to the Cabinet as Lloyd George's successor at the Board of Trade, having turned down the Local Government Board on the ground that he refused "to be shut up in a soup-kitchen with Mrs. Sidney Webb". Under the law then still in force his promotion forced him to submit himself for reelection and a tempestuous by-election ended in his defeat by Mr. Joynson-Hicks. But he was found a seat at Dundee, and he returned to London, his official career uninterrupted, to marry Miss Clementine Hozier.

In the political field he became a less conspicuous figure in the House of Commons, but in the country was second only to Lloyd George in his advocacy of the new Liberalism. A natural association developed between these two dissimilar men. Side by side they tried to check the rising naval expenditure, for, war-leaders though they were both to be, in 1908–09 their whole interest was focused on the first experiments in the "welfare state".

BITTER ATTACK

Churchill hesitated for a moment when Lloyd George introduced his People's Budget in 1909, but then threw himself into the fight in the country. Bitterly he denounced the House of Lords—especially the backwoods peers "all revolving the problems of Empire and Epsom" —and as president of the Budget League he enthusiastically praised the social policies which had made the Budget necessary. There were Conservatives who, though they could have overlooked his treason to his party in 1904, never could forgive his treason to his class, as they saw it, in 1909. They were later to have their revenge. He was now becoming—though still only 35—one of the leading members of the Government. In Cabinet, where one of his colleagues thought him "as long-winded as he was persistent", he distributed long memoranda to the rest of the members on all subjects—however far removed from the affairs of his own department. (In the Board of Trade he was teaching his subordinates the duties which now belong to the Ministry of Labour.) "Winston", recorded Grey, "will very soon become incapable from sheer activity of mind of being anything in a Cabinet but a Prime Minister."

After the bitter general election of 1910 Churchill was promoted to the Home Office, where his interest in the future welfare of prisoners helped to launch the movement for penal reform. But the most famous episode of his term at the Home Office was the Sidney Street "siege", which he characteristically insisted on witnessing personally. Germany's intervention in Morocco had made it imperative to put a term to the controversy over the British naval programme which was dividing the Liberal Party, and Asquith took what proved to be the decisive step of inviting the First Lord of the Admiralty (Reginald McKenna) and the Home Secretary to exchange offices. Churchill went to the Admiralty, with a mandate to maintain the Fleet in constant readiness for war.

RIGHT POST

Germany's threat had completely changed Churchill's attitude to naval and military armaments, and he became (as 25 years later) a powerful advocate of preparedness, so much losing his interest in party differences and social policies that Lloyd George said he was apt to approach him with "Look here, David", and then "declaim for the rest of the afternoon about his blasted ships". In fact, the post exactly suited Churchill's temperament and gifts. His speeches in introduction of the Navy Estimates rank with Gladstone's Budgets as classical expositions of the relationship of policy to departmental practice. In the face of considerable service opposition he created a Naval War Staff. At weekends and when the House was in recess he familiarized himself with the work of the Navy, going everywhere, seeing everything, and exercising a magnificent judgment in his selection of officers.

When war came Churchill mobilized the Fleet on his own responsibility, forcing from Morley a sad reflection on "the splendid *condottiere* at the Admiralty". But two years later, when he was dismissed to satisfy the Conservative Party leaders, Kitchener took to him the personal message: "Well, there is one thing at any rate they cannot take from you. The Fleet was ready." Heads were to fall in the 1914–18 War which never should have fallen, and Churchill's was one of them.

He had carefully prepared for the Navy's first task—the carrying of the British Expeditionary Force to the Continent—and it was done well and without mishap. He had also foreseen the possibility of a German advance threatening the Channel ports, and in October it seemed that the way to them would be open unless Antwerp could be held—or, at least, not given up without a struggle. He himself organized and accompanied the expedition to Antwerp which not only delayed the fall of the city by five days, but by doing so saved the Channel ports and prevented the Germans from gaining a quick decision in the west.

Back in London Churchill took a decision which was eventually to involve him in misfortune. Although it was due to Prince Louis of Battenberg that the Fleet which was concentrated at Portland in the last fortnight of peace was not allowed to disperse, Churchill felt under the pressure of popular agitation that his name and origin deprived him of public confidence, and he suffered him to go into retirement.

THE DARDANELLES

In his place he recalled to active service Lord Fisher, a warrior after his own heart, dauntless and indefatigable, a master of every detail of the sea service. The Navy could confidently look for a direction equal to any emergency so long as these two men saw eye to eye. Together they brilliantly restored the British command of the sea, which had been compromised by the destruction of Cradock's squadron off the South American coast. But still there was no decisive victory over the main German fleet, and the shelling of Scarborough and Hartlepool brought public criticism of Churchill and the Admiralty to a focus.

He had, at the beginning of 1915, little public support—a relevant fact to keep in mind as one begins the confused story of the Dardanelles. The breach between Fisher and Churchill had come over a fundamental issue of the direction from which British sea power could make the most effective impact on the course of the war in Europe. Fisher favoured the Baltic, Churchill the Dardanelles. Few would now dispute the strategic insight underlying Churchill's conception of a swift, dramatic stroke at a vital point. Success might have been achieved by the employment of such a combination of sea and land forces as was eventually brought to bear—but only after the initial advantage of surprise had been lost.

The most important criticism of Churchill's role is that he persisted in the enterprise without securing the support of his own department and the cooperation of the War Office. The documents do not support the criticism. He was careful from the very beginning to seek and obtain the approval of those with whom he had to work, and when the idea of the operation was submitted to the War Council there was no expression of dissent. The Dardanelles did, in fact, become official policy, and the French and Russian Governments were informed of it. The two main causes of the failure were the late hour of the objections raised by the unpredictable Fisher and the War Council's inability to resolve the question of a divided command. The delays, hesitations, and postponements are in many cases directly traceable to Fisher's behaviour—he resigned shortly after the first military landings—and it was only at the very late stage of his resignation that the admirals turned against Churchill's plan.

OUT OF OFFICE

Churchill took to heart the lessons of 1915. A notable feature of his direction during the 1939–45 War was his assumption of the post of Minister of Defence. In this capacity he was able to secure uninterrupted and effective liaison between the Chiefs of Staff themselves and between them and the Cabinet which he led. The 1935–45 War was singularly free of the disputes between commands, between the Services, and between the Services and the politicians which Lloyd George never succeeded in ending between 1916 and 1918.

The political consequences of the Dardanelles were immediate—so immediate that when Churchill crossed to Downing Street to inform the Prime Minister that Sir Arthur Wilson was ready to take Fisher's place he found that others had preceded him. Now was the hour of the Conservative Party's revenge. Bonar Law had informed Lloyd George that if Fisher had resigned Churchill must depart as well. Between them—and faced with a critical debate on the Dardanelles—Lloyd George and Asquith determined on their best way out: a Coalition Government formed at the cost of the resignation of Churchill. This was a hard political decision against which there could be no appeal, and in the new Government Churchill had to be satisfied with what the Conservatives were prepared to grant him—the Chancellorship of the Duchy of Lancaster. The public, then deeply suspicious of Churchill's talents, drew obvious conclusions. Six months of idleness and frustration were sufficient, and in November Churchill resigned his sinecure and rejoined the Army.

NOT TO BLAME

Within a few days he was at the Front, attached to the 2nd Grenadier Guards. A month later, with the rank of colonel, he was given command of a battalion of The Royal Scots Fusiliers. But his thoughts remained fixed on the conduct of the war, and in the spring of 1916 he was home on leave delivering a weighty speech in which, with the magnanimity which marked him all his life, he urged the recall of Fisher to the Admiralty. Later in the year his battalion was absorbed and he returned permanently to political life. Asquith had meanwhile refused all Lloyd George's attempts to place Churchill in the Ministry of Munitions, and even when Lloyd George replaced Asquith as Prime Minister the Conservatives were still firm that they would not admit him to the Cabinet. But, in February, 1917, in spite of all Asquith's protests, Lloyd George published the report of the Dardanelles Commission, which Asquith himself had appointed.

Asquith's interest in the matter was soon apparent to the public, for it was Asquith who was severely condemned and Churchill who was exonerated. The commission could find no grounds on which to indict Churchill: his plan had been right and the delays and ill-organization had not been his fault. Churchill's stock rose immediately and, after a brilliant survey of the war situation during a secret session of May, 1917, Lloyd George (with Smuts's support) appointed Churchill Minister of Munitions. Established less than two years before, the Ministry had become the greatest directorate of industry in the country. No episode in the whole of Churchill's career is so eloquent of his exceptional capacity as a departmental head than the success with which he imposed unity and order on this vast organization and established himself as the source and controller of its multitudinous activities.

During these last months of the war Churchill became a close adviser of Lloyd George on its central direction. He was not in the War Cabinet, but Lloyd George consulted and used him frequently on matters far outside his departmental activities. Churchill's visits to the Continent, in fact, became so frequent that the backbench Conservative members, still harbouring their grudge, warned Lloyd George that he must not take the renegade into the War Cabinet.

DAMAGED REPUTATION

But Lloyd George still turned to Churchill and, after the German break-through in March, 1918, summoned him to a conference with Haig and Bonar Law. Haig found Churchill "a real gun in a crisis", and as the situation worsened Churchill slept at his Ministry so that he might be more closely in touch with the Prime Minister. He was Lloyd George's emissary at a meeting with Clemenceau, Foch, and Rawlinson—the prelude to the appointment of Foch as Supreme Commander—and at the hour of victory could feel that he had been at the heart of things, playing his part.

Churchill had entered the war as a Liberal with an enviable popular reputation. He emerged from it a Coalition Liberal with a damaged reputation. As long as Lloyd George's Coalition held together Churchill was certain of office and could hope for promotion. But after that?

PRESSING TASKS

The immediate tasks were, however, pressing. Lloyd George (who had been impressed by his departmental ability) asked him to move to the War Office (with which he combined the Air Ministry) to smooth away the friction which had at first attended demobilization. This he did in a fortnight. In this dual office Churchill became prominently involved in the question of Bolshevist Russia—eager, as he was, to continue the resistance to the Bolshevists. His appeal for a volunteer force to cover the withdrawal of British troops from Murmansk and Archangel—8,000 men were raised—lent weight to the suspicion that he was anxious to provoke a war with Russia.

Early in 1921 the growing difficulties in framing a policy suited to Britain's new position in the Eastern Mediterranean led to his transfer to the Colonial Office. In this capacity he was a member of the Cabinet Committee which in 1921 negotiated with the Irish leaders, and he played the role of peace-maker. "Tell Winston", said Collins afterwards, "we could never have done anything without him." But the pugnacity which he had kept in restraint during the Irish negotiations found new and unfortunate expression in 1922. The new Turkish state which was constituting itself under Mustapha Kemal clashed with British power in the Dardanelles.

CONFLICT AVOIDED

Thanks largely to the tact of the British Commander, Sir Charles Harington, a conflict was avoided, but Churchill's attitude, and especially his premature appeal to the Dominions, contributed to the fall of the Government and to his own defeat at the ensuing election.

The Conservatives had for some time been restless under their allegiance to Lloyd George, and at a meeting at the Carlton Club on October 19, 1922, decided to end their association with him. Lloyd George immediately dissolved Parliament, and a confused general election gave the Conservatives power for the first time since 1905. Churchill was defeated—and for the first time since 1900 was out of the House of Commons with no certain hope of returning. He was politically isolated. He had severed himself from the Asquithian Liberals. He distrusted the Labour Party. And there was still much to divide him from the Conservatives; indeed all the more when, in the autumn of 1923, Baldwin appealed to the country on the issue of Protection—the very issue on which Churchill had left the Conservative Party 20 years before. He fought and lost the election as a Coalition Liberal—a term which barely had meaning any longer.

During 1923 Churchill completed the earlier portions of *The World Crisis*, though the whole work, together with its sequel, *The Aftermath*, was not completed until 1931. The volumes were not entirely successful. The style was too rhetorical and there was not the breadth of vision that marked his history of *The Second World War*. Balfour was not far wrong when he wrote to a friend: "I am immersed in Winston's brilliant autobiography, disguised as a history of the universe." In the following year Churchill severed his last links with Liberalism, and when, in February, a by-election was pending in the Abbey Division of Westminster he stood as an Independent Anti-Socialist. There was an official Conservative candidate in the field, but Churchill had the support of many of the more independent Conservatives, including Austen Chamberlain and Birkenhead. He was defeated by only 47 votes.

CHANCELLOR OF EXCHEQUER

He fought the general election of 1924 as a Constitutionalist—and since there was no Conservative opponent was in effect the official Conservative candidate. He was returned to the House of Commons and (greatly to his surprise) was appointed Chancellor of the Exchequer. Baldwin had, in fact, decided to go outside the ranks of the safe and the orthodox: Austen Chamberlain and Birkenhead were also brought in. Even so, Churchill, as Asquith said, "towered like a Chimborazo or Everest among the sandhills of the Baldwin Cabinet". His first Budget, brilliantly introduced, contained provisions for widows' pensions, but its most conspicuous feature was the decision to return to the gold standard. This act of policy, though roundly condemned in the light of after events, was generally approved at the time by almost all except Keynes, who contributed a lively polemic entitled *The Economic Consequences of Mr. Churchill*.

Keynes's warnings proved right. The mine-owners decided that in order to retain their markets in the world they must cut down their costs, and there followed the tragic course of events which led to the General Strike in 1926. Churchill's role was not a happy one. All the evidence suggests that he was not one of the more conciliatory members of the Cabinet, and his production of the *British Gazette* from the commandeered premises of the *Morning Post*—though the object was sound: the communication of information to the public—was marred by his eagerness to turn it into a partisan anti-strikers sheet, which could only inflame feelings still more on both sides. The remaining years of the Baldwin Government were quiet. In 1929 Baldwin appealed to the country and lost the general election. Churchill, however, was again returned at Epping. Two years later the National Government was formed but Churchill was not a member, and he remained out of office until the outbreak of the 1939–45 War.

REBEL OVER INDIA

In 1930 the Simon Commission on India published its report, and the Round Table Conference was summoned the following autumn. Churchill opposed this moderately liberal policy, refusing to cast away "that most truly bright and precious jewel in the crown of the King"—an almost precise echo of a phrase used by his father, Lord Randolph. In January, 1931, he resigned from the Conservative "shadow Cabinet" as a protest against its support for the

Labour Government's Indian policy. It was a courageous act whatever one may think of the merits of his views. Churchill's conduct of the opposition to the India Bill in the House of Commons—fighting it clause by clause in committee—was perhaps his most brilliant parliamentary performance. But even weightier issues were beginning to hold his attention. In 1932 there started his seven-year struggle to halt the drift to what he later called "the unnecessary war".

His freedom from office did, however, give him time to write the biography of Marlborough, which his cousin, the Duke of Marlborough, had long urged him to do. Based on a mass of material in the muniment room at Blenheim, the work was planned and completed on an ample scale, the last of its four volumes appearing just before the Munich crisis. Never restrained in the expression of his dislikes, Churchill pursued Macaulay with a rancour excused rather than justified by family loyalty. But no one else could have so brilliantly attempted to vindicate the qualities of a man of genius from the reproaches cast by a master of invective.

THE NAZI MENACE

Wherever the balance of advantage for foresight lies between the Conservative, Liberal and Labour Parties during these years, Churchill's record is not open to even the smallest criticism. His views developed all the time—and consistently. As long as the Weimar Republic had endured he had urged the wisdom of encouraging Germany in a policy of peaceful cooperation with Europe through the revision of the Versailles clauses most obnoxious to German sentiment. Even after 1932, when he already saw that Hitler was "the moving impulse behind the German Government and may be more than that soon", he still demanded an effort to remove "the just grievances of the vanquished". But after Hitler's confirmation in power Churchill's theme changed. He sought, first, British preparedness—especially in the air—and carried on a persistent cross-examination of the Government's intentions in this respect. His warnings seemed to be dramatically confirmed by Baldwin's "confession" in 1936, and his influence in the country was steadily growing when an extraneous incident suddenly restored Baldwin's popularity and emphasized Churchill's isolation and unpredictable temperament. This was the abdication of Edward VIII.

During the crisis Churchill seemed sometimes on the verge of forming a "King's Party", and his action and public utterances stood in unhappy contrast to the steady and wise guidance offered by Baldwin. This was undoubtedly a setback, but Churchill continued his campaign for preparedness, seeking the cooperation of all who agreed with him. His views had now developed further. More and more he put the emphasis on the need for collective strength—collective security. He had never trusted the League of Nations as an instrument for general disarmament, but he looked to it now as the instrument of collective preparedness by all the non-aggressive Powers of Europe.

It was all in vain, and on September 3, 1939, Britain was again at war. Churchill returned to office as First Lord of the Admiralty—an appointment greeted with relief by the public which had for so long been heedless of his warnings—and from the first he established himself as the popular war leader. At the Admiralty he took the first steps to combat the submarine menace which later became so formidable, but the main episode of his term was the brilliant operation in which Commodore Harwood, in command of Ajax, Achilles, and Exeter, drove the Graf von Spee to its destruction. His voice meanwhile was strengthening the nerve of the British people—an invaluable task in the confusing days of the "phoney war". There was the characteristic cockiness with which he offered "to engage the entire German Navy, using only the vessels which at one time or another they have declared they have destroyed". Meanwhile he was still pursuing his concept of collective security, urging the small European neutrals to understand the danger. But they did not heed either, and in the spring of 1940 Norway, Denmark, Belgium, and the Netherlands were all invaded.

On Churchill, as First Lord, fell the responsibility for the dispatch and disembarkation of the forces sent to strengthen Norway. Once more, as in 1915, an improvised undertaking ended in failure. The debate which followed—in which Churchill manfully defended the Government—decided the fate of Chamberlain's Government, and on May 10 Chamberlain resigned and advised the King to send for Churchill. The Labour and Liberal leaders agreed to serve with him, and so the great Coalition was formed which was to remain united until victory in Europe had been won.

In the first volume of his history of the war Churchill has described his feelings on that night in words which are as moving as they are simple: "During these last crowded days of the political crisis my pulse had not quickened at any moment. I took it all as it came. But I cannot conceal from the reader of this truthful account that as I went to bed at about 3 a.m. I was conscious of a profound sense of relief. At last I had the authority to give directions over the whole scene. I felt as if I were walking with destiny and that all my past life had been but a preparation for this hour and for this trial ... I thought I knew a good deal about it all, and I was sure I should not fail."

UNDRAMATIC CONFIDENCE

This undramatic confidence—recalling Chatham's "I know that I can save this country and that no one else can"—was quickly communicated to the people of Britain. "What is our aim?" he exclaimed when he first met the House of Commons as Prime Minister. "I can answer in one word: Victory—victory at all costs, victory in spite of all terrors; victory, however long and hard the road may be; for without victory there is no survival." And then: "I have nothing to offer but blood, toil, tears, and sweat." Was ever language so matched to the occasion?

Meanwhile, attacking through country which before the days of mechanization had been regarded as unsuitable for large-scale operations, the Germans drove a wedge between the Franco-British armies advancing north-eastwards and the main French Army. Holland surrendered after five days. Belgium held out until the allied troops were cut off both from their support and from the sea. There followed the unexpected success of the evacuation from Dunkirk, which so lifted the hearts of the British people that Churchill had to warn them that "Wars are not won by evacuations". It was at this point that Churchill ended a survey of the campaign with the words: "We shall not flag or fail. We shall go on to the end. ... We shall defend our island whatever the cost may be. We shall fight on the beaches. We shall fight on the landing grounds. We shall fight in the fields and in the streets. We shall fight in the hills. We shall never surrender. And even if—which I do not for a moment believe—this island or a large part of it were subjugated and starving, then our Empire beyond the seas, armed and guarded by the British Fleet, would carry on the struggle until, in God's good time, the New World, with all its power and might, steps forth to the rescue and liberation of the old!"

FALL OF FRANCE

The agony of France was now prolonged for another three weeks, heavy with disaster, during which Churchill himself carried the whole weight of the British effort to keep France in the war. He visited the French Ministers at Tours, and crossed the Channel again a few days later after he had already made his brave offer of a solemn Act of Union between the two countries. It was too brave for the Ministers at Bordeaux, and on June 21, 1940, France surrendered, without giving Churchill an undertaking not to allow the French fleet to fall into German hands. Churchill, bowing to the logic of necessity, then took what must have been one of the hardest decisions of his life. The French warships—constituting the flower of the French fleet—were fired on, with damage and destruction, by British vessels as they tried to make their way from a North African port to Toulon.

Britain was now alone and almost unarmed. For her immediate deliverance she relied upon the chosen band of her own young men flying a few machines. Churchill neither planned nor directed the Battle of Britain on which the future of human freedom depended; but it was he who had evoked and deployed the indomitable strength behind the British airmen which now inspired their unsleeping fight against enormous odds. It was fitting that he should stamp on men's minds the character and significance of this battle in the simplest of all his phrases: "Never in the field of human conflict was so much owed by so many to so few." The bombing of London followed in September—with Churchill cheerfully calculating that "it would take 10 years at the present rate for half the houses of London to be demolished. After that, of course, progress would be much slower."

CONDUCT OF THE WAR

The organization through which every department of Government consciously worked under Churchill's superintending eye and felt the drive of his personality was built up gradually in the light of experience. When first constructed his administration was modelled on Lloyd George's

War Cabinet, and of the Prime Minister's four colleagues, Mr. Chamberlain, Mr. Attlee, Mr. Greenwood, and Lord Halifax, only the last carried, as Foreign Secretary, the burden of heavy departmental responsibilities. But three months later the intimate relationship already apparent between the issue of the war and the activities of the Ministry of Aircraft Production—itself one of Churchill's creations—led to the inclusion in the War Cabinet of its head, Lord Beaverbrook. As the war developed the Prime Minister brought in the Ministers in charge of other departments most directly concerned with its conduct, so that in its later form the War Cabinet had a membership of eight or nine, and included the Chancellor of the Exchequer and the Ministers of Labour, Production, and Home Security. Gradually, too, Churchill worked out his functions as Minister of Defence, a title which he had assumed when he became Prime Minister. It was never his intention to create a full-blown Ministry such as has now been established. His purpose was to give definition and authority to his transactions not with the service Ministers who were members of his Government but with the Chiefs of Staff, and to this end he provided himself with a small technical staff headed by General (now Lord) Ismay.

The system which Churchill created was emphatically personal in principle and was devised to give full scope both to his military knowledge and to his vast departmental experience. It worked because he was able to handle a mass of details which would have overwhelmed any other man. It was equally personal in its method of operation. Its timetable was governed by the Prime Minister's habits.

AFTERNOON REST

Churchill's practice was to go to bed and sleep soundly in the early afternoon. When he had dressed again he brought a refreshed mind to bear on the immediate business of the day. Exhilarated by his contact with practical difficulties, he went on to address himself to questions of policy, regularly called Cabinet meetings for 11 p.m., and, after they had ended, continued for some time to pour out comment and suggestion to those of his associates who could keep his hours. Nor was he merely equal to his self-imposed tasks; as Mr. Attlee said later, he set the pace.

The war surveys for which his return from his journeys often provided the occasion rank among the outstanding events of his parliamentary career. World-wide in range and profound in matter, they at once informed and inspired both the House and the country. The richness of their content was enhanced by a delivery characteristic of their author. Churchill's voice was not impressive in volume. But it was wide in compass. In his loftiest moments its somewhat metallic tones vibrated with passion, the more combative passages were given colour by the effective use of the rising inflexion and the frequent assertions of high resolve were made resonant by the accompaniment, felt rather than heard, of a sort of bulldog growl. Read over in the light of after events these speeches are notable for their masterly restraint. They revealed much but they concealed more; of the great plans which filled his mind and with the execution of which he must have been busy up to the moment when he rose in his place not a hint was allowed to transpire.

CAMPAIGN IN AFRICA

Italy's entry into the war had exercised a decisive influence upon British strategy. Her geographical position combined with her armed strength in all three elements enabled her to close the Mediterranean to all except the most heavily convoyed traffic. The main line of Britain's Imperial communications was perforce diverted round Africa and the extension greatly added to the strain on the British mercantile marine. On all counts, therefore, it was essential to counter the Italian threat to the Suez Canal. It was with special satisfaction that Churchill informed the House of Commons of the "crippling blow" struck at the Italian Fleet in harbour at Taranto and he threw all his energies into the task of building up an effective striking force in the Middle East. He realized that though the war could not be won in the Mediterranean it could be lost there, and his sensitiveness to any threat in this quarter as well as his eagerness to give aid to a small and very gallant ally induced him to move troops from Africa to Greece when Germany struck her blow in the Balkans. The wisdom of this decision may be questioned.

ROMMEL'S SUCCESSES

The reduction of British strength in Africa and the necessity, which Churchill immediately recognized, of returning the Australian troops when Japan declared war, opened the way to the successes of Rommel's Afrika Corps, whose formidable military quality was not, and perhaps could not have been, foreseen. There was less excuse, however, for allowing the lesson of Norway, that an army could not maintain itself against hostile air supremacy, to be repeated in the Aegean. It was widely felt that Crete should either have been evacuated earlier or more effectively held and its capture, after a tremendous German effort which came within an ace of failure, provided the one occasion in the whole war when Churchill's strategic judgment was seriously criticized by Parliament or public.

In the summer of 1942, while Churchill was in Washington, Rommel launched the greatest of his attacks. The British front was driven in for hundreds of miles and the crowning shock came when Tobruk, which earlier had resisted a long siege, fell almost without a fight. The blow was softened by President Roosevelt's immediate offer of American tanks to help in retrieving the position, and Westminster echoed Washington by defeating a no-confidence motion by 475 to 25. Some two months later Churchill was himself in the desert, having taken a visit to Moscow in his stride, and there effected those changes in the higher command which launched both Lord Alexander and Lord Montgomery on their great careers.

END OF THE BEGINNING

The decision to deploy American military strength in Africa was thus sufficiently in line with Churchill's stragetic thought for him to describe it as "perhaps the end of the beginning", but he was also at pains to make it clear that the plan was Roosevelt's and that he had been no more than the President's lieutenant. The two met at Casablanca early in 1943 and there proclaimed "unconditional surrender" as their aim. They decided as a first step to attack what Churchill pungently described as "the soft under-belly of the Axis" and by the following September unconditional surrender had been made by such governmental authority as was left in Italy. Churchill was again in Washington when he received the news of this complete turn of fortune's wheel. But the Germans continued to turn the country into a battlefield and as "the rake of war"—the phrase is again Churchill's—was drawn throughout the length of the peninsula, he did not conceal his pity for the Italian people. Pneumonia attacked him on his return to London after the Casablanca conference and he suffered another attack later but his determined will to live pulled him through.

From the first Churchill had looked forward to the eventual participation of the United States in the war. Deeply appreciative of the support, material as well as moral, given by the American Government while nominally neutral and determined that friction with Britain should not obstruct the evolution of American policy, he was sympathetic towards American plans for the more effective defence of the western hemisphere and was even prepared for some small cession of territory. President Roosevelt, however, asked no more than 99-year leases of land for naval and air bases, and in September, 1940, an agreement was concluded. The bases in Newfoundland and Bermuda were leased "freely and without consideration", Britain thus aligning herself with Canada in treating the defence of North America as a matter of partnership. Six bases in the Caribbean were also leased in exchange for 50 destroyers from the United States navy.

PEARL HARBOUR

The Lend-Lease Act of March, 1941, and the Atlantic Charter of the following August carried the process further, and when in December Japan attacked at Pearl Harbour Churchill gave effect to his warning, uttered a month earlier, that a British declaration of war would follow "within the hour".

Six months before Pearl Harbour Churchill had triumphantly surmounted a severer test of his appreciation of the needs of war. No man had shown fiercer opposition to the Soviet Power in its revolutionary phase, and though time and the growth of the German menace had modified his judgment, he had been a party in 1939 to plans, happily found impracticable, for the dispatch of an Anglo-French expeditionary force to aid Finland in her war with Russia. Hitler's decision in June, 1941, thus confronted him with a difficult choice. He made it without hesitation, and in the most dramatic of his broadcasts announced that every possible aid would be given to the latest victim of German aggression. The declaration had prompt results. Early in July an Anglo-Soviet agreement was signed in Moscow, and in the following month the two Governments sent troops into Persia to eradicate German influence and to secure the use of the

Trans-Persian railway for the conveyance of supplies to Russia. The operation led in September to the abdication of the Shah. Under his son and successor Persia signed a treaty with the allies. Meanwhile the American Government, which had followed these developments with sympathy, had in August itself signed an agreement with Russia, and on the joint suggestion of the President and Churchill a three-Power conference met in Moscow at the end of September. In the following May Mr. Molotov came to London and Anglo-Russian cooperation was rounded off by the signature of a treaty of alliance. Meanwhile 26 allied nations had signed a declaration committing them to fight to a finish against the Axis. The Grand Alliance was in being.

THROUGH DISASTER TO VICTORY

With Churchill's efforts from the middle of 1941 onwards to establish unity of policy and action between Britain, Russia, and the United States his war Premiership entered upon its second phase, the first, that of preparation for insular defence, having closed when Britain ceased to fight alone. At the beginning of 1942 this second phase was overlapped by the third in which British arms suffered what Churchill himself described as "the greatest disaster which our history records". The Prime Minister was under no illusions as to the probable consequences of Japan's entry into the war. The new enemy was a first-class Power whose might the British Commonwealth, already engaged in a fight to the death with Germany and Italy, could not hope to meet on equal terms. But the Japanese pressed home their advantage with a success whose rapidity and extent exceeded all expectations. In December, 1941, the Prince of Wales and the Repulse were sunk in Malayan waters. Their flanks thus safeguarded, the Japanese land forces advanced and completed their conquest by the capture of Singapore at the end of February.

The tale of misfortune was not yet complete. Rangoon was occupied early in March, and with the evacuation of Mandalay the whole of Burma, which Churchill's father had added to the Empire, passed into enemy hands. Churchill firmly refused to allow any examination of the causes of these distressing events. The House of Commons endorsed this view by a vote of 464 to 1, but it is instructive for the estimate of Churchill's attitude towards public opinion to contrast his firmness in holding the veil drawn over the loss of an Empire in the Far East with his readiness to grant an inquiry into the successful escape of the Scharnhorst, Gneisenau, and Prinz Eugen from Brest into German waters, which occurred a few days before the fall of Singapore. It is equally instructive to note his disregard of the cry for "a second front now" which began to be raised in the spring and summer of 1942 as the Germans thrust ever more deeply into Russia. Dieppe was a final warning against operations on an inadequate scale and Churchill now flung himself into the elaborate preparations which occupied two full years and constitute the fourth phase of his Premiership.

With the victories of Stalingrad and El Alamein towards the close of 1942 the "awful balance" of war began to incline towards the allies and another aspect—the fifth—of Churchill's activities became increasingly prominent.

RECONSTRUCTION

Issues of reconstruction began to thrust themselves forward, though it was not until late in 1943, the year which saw the establishment of Unrra and the preliminaries to the creation of Food and Agriculture Organization, that vital decisions were reached. After a conference of Foreign Secretaries at Moscow in October had cleared the ground and itself reached important conclusions as to the future organization of Europe, Churchill and Roosevelt met General Chiang Kai-shek at Cairo in November and there agreed to strip Japan of all her conquests during the past 50 years. President and Prime Minister then flew to Tehran, where they met Stalin.

The three statesmen declared their resolve to conclude a peace which would "banish the scourge and terror of war for many generations" and their readiness to welcome all freedom-loving peoples "into a world family of democratic nations".

There was no meeting of the Big Three in 1944. But Churchill's many journeys, apart from visits to the front, took him to Quebec in September to concert plans with Roosevelt, to Moscow in October to seek a solution of the Polish difficulty, and to Athens at Christmas in an effort to bring toleration and decency back into Greek public life. Churchill's ceaseless journeyings between 1941 and 1945 serve to emphasize that if the war was won by the collaboration of the three great Powers, he was the architect of their cooperation. He built the Grand Alliance and held it together. The most vital of all the great Power meetings came in February, 1945, at Yalta.

SEEDS OF LATER PROBLEMS

At that conference the Allies concerted their plans for the final assault on Germany, settled the terms on which Russia should enter the war against Japan, and sought agreement about a defeated Germany and about the future of the United Nations Organization. Many of the problems which later beset the world have been traced in their origins to Yalta. But references in published memoirs and the American version of the proceedings published 10 years later all bear witness to the prescience and grasp of realities Churchill brought to the conference table. Roosevelt, enfeebled by the great strain of his office and within two months of his death, believed that he could "handle" Stalin and took an optimistic view of his trustworthiness. Churchill had a juster appreciation of the uses Russia would make of the power and opportunities she possessed. His ideas on the settlement of Europe displayed an altogether deeper sense of history. Deprived this time of the President's solid support in negotiation, and placing allied unity first among the objects to be achieved, he was obliged to acquiesce in decisions about which he expressed deep misgivings.

BERLIN AND PRAGUE

In the final throes of Germany's defeat Churchill saw more clearly than ever the importance of thrusting as far eastwards as possible before the Russian armies should be drawn into the vacuum of central Europe. He pressed this view upon Roosevelt, Mr. Truman who succeeded him in April, 1945, and General Eisenhower, who commanded the allied armies on the western front. Particularly he urged that our troops should advance to Berlin and Prague when these capitals came within their grasp. As early as April 5 he warned Roosevelt that "we should join hands with the Russian armies as far to the east as possible, and, if circumstances allow, enter Berlin." But another policy prevailed in Washington.

Perhaps the best account of Churchill's part in the war was given in 1957 by Lord Alanbrooke who was Chief of the Imperial General Staff and chairman of the Chiefs of Staff committee from 1941 until the end of the war, in *The Turn of the Tide*, written by Sir Arthur Bryant and based on Alanbrooke's war diaries. Irritation at Churchill's incorrigible desire for action, which was seldom related to the resources available, is frequently expressed, and at his perpetual goadings of his staff—"I sometimes think some of my Generals don't want to fight the Germans", Churchill once remarked when his plans for a landing at Trondheim were being opposed. This was taken by some at the time to be a denigration of the great man, but the book was in fact a truthful panegyric. Churchill's greatest single contribution in Alanbrooke's view was that he carried the Americans with him—he kept together the alliance that won the war.

AT POTSDAM

Soon after the German surrender the Coalition Government broke up. Churchill after forming a "caretaker" Government was preoccupied for a while with final plans for the defeat of Japan. In June, accompanied by Attlee as his "friend and counsellor", he went to Potsdam to settle with Stalin the many matters which the end of the war had made ripe for decision and join with President Truman in a final warning to Japan. Then he returned to London to receive the election results which dismissed him from office. The conduct of Churchill during the campaign of the 1945 election will always seem one of the strangest episodes of his career. The swing against the Conservative Party, which had started before the war, was so strong that even his reputation as a national leader could be of no avail. But he could have emerged from the election with that reputation untarnished. Instead he indulged in accusations, imputations and even personal abuse against his wartime colleagues which shocked his hearers—even his friends—and embittered his opponents.

Churchill was undoubtedly dismayed and unsettled by the verdict of the election—and he had to lead a party which was just as disheartened and just as unsure of itself. In the House of Commons he was less assured than ever before, and his weekly brushes with the Leader of the House, Mr. Herbert Morrison, which came to be known as "Children's Hour", saddened many of his admirers. In his criticisms of the Labour Government's social and economic policies he never seemed able to strike the right note. He struck some of his old notes in his speeches opposing the Government's Indian policy. He was bitterly critical of the proposal to give independence to India, and when, towards the end of 1946, the Government announced their intention of granting self-government to Burma he denounced it fiercely as a policy of scuttle. In 1947 the Government fixed a date for the handing over of power to the Indians, and Churchill's opposition was even more violent.

NEW STATUS

However, he welcomed as a statesmanlike means of averting civil war the intention to confer immediate Dominion status on the two succession states likely to emerge in India and promised to facilitate the passage of the necessary legislation. For a man whose vision could be so wide Churchill appeared sometimes to close his eyes to the nature of the problems facing Britain in India. He had inherited from his father a romantic—Disraelian—attitude to India which warped his judgment. The story, nevertheless, ended on a happier note. When he again returned to office his own and his Government's relations with India were cordial, and it was his Government which supported Indian initiative on the Korean question at the United Nations.

He used the years out of office to make headway with his history of *The Second World War*. The first volume was published in 1948 and the sixth and last six years later. "In War: Resolution. In Defeat: Defiance. In Victory: Magnanimity. In Peace: Goodwill" was the motto of the work; the greatest of the war leaders, he chose with perfect aptness these ancient, simple, and resonant virtues. The work, which puts forward his personal interpretation of events, varies considerably in quality, but at its best it matches the magnificence of its theme. Churchill had moved far from his early models, Macaulay and Gibbon, and had fashioned a less studied manner of his own. His account of the battle for Crete stands comparison with the finest passages of narrative prose, and the closing chapters of the work are charged with a tragic irony that Aeschylus would have acknowledged with applause.

FULTON SPEECH

His vision did not desert him in the postwar years when he addressed himself to the problems of foreign policy. Churchill's ideas on foreign policy developed so consistently after 1945 that it is impossible to draw a line at the point in 1951 when he was again returned to power, the Conservatives under his leadership winning a parliamentary majority of 17. But it is worth noticing the precise nature of his achievement while he was in Opposition. He made a series of speeches which were as important as statements by a sovereign Government. They had a world wide influence. They were creative. They helped to form the policies not only of Britain but of the whole free world. Yet when he made them he was out of office and speaking only for himself.

It was in March, 1946, when he visited the United States at the invitation of Mr. Truman and was accompanied by the President to the town of Fulton, that he first addressed the world as its seer. The occasion, with the President of the United States present, was clearly chosen to give the speech the widest prominence —and Churchill began by offering openly his "true and faithful counsel in these anxious and baffling times". The first purpose of the speech was to present a clear picture of the change which had been wrought in the world since the end of the war. The "splendid comradeship in arms" had not continued. Instead, "from Stettin in the Baltic to Trieste in the Adriatic, an iron curtain" had "descended across the Continent".

Here, in two words, was the crystallization.

VIVID PHRASE

The phrase, the "iron curtain" only summarized a cogent argument, but it vividly painted the background against which all thinking about foreign policy had to be done. From this followed Churchill's three important conclusions: that there should be a close association between Britain and the United States—providing "no quivering, precarious balance of power to offer its temptation to ambition or adventure": that "the secret knowledge or experience of the atomic bomb" should remain largely in American hands; and that "the safety of the world requires a new unity in Europe from which no nation should be permanently outcast".

This last point was elaborated in a speech which he delivered at Zürich University on September 19, 1946. "What is the sovereign remedy", he asked, "for the tragedy of Europe? It is to re-create the European family, or as much of it as we can .... We must build a kind of United States of Europe." There followed another forward-looking proposal.

MORAL LEADERSHIP

"I am now going to say something that will astonish you. The first step in the re-creation of the European family must be a partnership between France and Germany. In this way only can France recover the moral leadership of Europe .... The structure of the United States of Europe, if well and truly built, will be such as to make the material strength of a single State less important." A United States of Europe—"or whatever name or form it may take"—to include "a spiritually great Germany"; the seeds of future policy were being sown. The next time Churchill spoke in a foreign affairs debate in the House of Commons (October, 1946) he was able to say, with perfect truth, that "what I said at Fulton has been outpaced and overpassed by the movement of events and by the movement of American opinion. If I were to make that speech at the present time and in the same place, it would attract no particular attention."

Throughout 1947 and 1948 Churchill devoted much of his energy to the concept of a United Europe. He had no very clear idea of what he meant or intended. The differences between federation and confederation baffled and did not particularly interest him. But much of the criticism of his role in these years was misplaced. Churchill was not primarily concerned with building a political structure. He himself said at a United Europe meeting at the Albert Hall on May 14, 1947, "We are not acting in the field of force, but in the domain of opinion". And he went on: "It is not for us at this stage to attempt to define or prescribe the structure of constitutions. We ourselves are content, in the first instance, to present the idea of United Europe ... as a moral, cultural and spiritual conception to which all can rally .... It is for us to lay the foundation, to create the atmosphere and give the driving impulsion."

NEGOTIATION FROM STRENGTH

When, at the Congress of Europe in May, 1948, he noticed that "16 European States are now associated for economic purposes; five have entered into close economic and military relationship", he could not hide the implication that these achievements owed something to the general concept of a United Europe. They certainly owed much to his own initiative. At the back of Churchill's ideas from Fulton onwards was the belief in negotiation from a position of strength. It was possible to deal with the Russians, he said in March of 1949, "only by having superior force on your side on the matter in question; and they must be convinced that you will use—you will not hesitate to use—these forces, if necessary, in the most ruthless manner". He found encouragement in the fact that "our forces are getting stronger, actually and relatively, than they were a year ago".

It was because of this slowly changing balance of power that in February, 1950, he threw out "the idea of another talk with Soviet Russia upon the highest level". The suggestion was made at the end of an election speech at Edinburgh and was immediately dismissed as a "stunt". At the time it seemed, even to the non-partisan, to offer few real hopes. But the idea was a natural development of his Fulton argument and not a contradiction of it.

IDEAS FOR SUMMIT

At intervals throughout the next five years the idea of "talks at the summit" recurred in Churchill's foreign policy speeches. It was taken up by the Opposition, and he was increasingly criticized for delay in bringing a meeting about. His explanation came at an unexpected moment. It was in the course of a debate on the White Paper on Defence in March, 1955. Churchill had opened the debate with a speech which can be rated among his great parliamentary orations. He held a packed House in silence while he expounded his appreciation of the world situation which had determined the Government to press forward with the manufacture of the hydrogen bomb and the means of its delivery. On its deterrent power he founded his hopes for peace. If the ability and determination to use the weapon in self-defence were well understood on both sides war might be averted. "That is why", he said, "I have hoped for a long time for a top-level conference where these matters can be put plainly and bluntly .... Then it might well be that, by a process of sublime irony, we shall have reached a stage in this story where safety will be the sturdy child of terror and survival the twin brother of annihilation."

But later in the debate when Mr. Bevan taunted him with being prevented from holding such a conference by the United States, Churchill rose to explain the reasons for delay. He would have liked, he said, to have seen a conference shortly after Malenkov took power and he had prepared to go over to see President Eisenhower to arrange for the invitation. "However, I was struck down by a very sudden illness which paralysed me completely physically, and I had to put it all off, and it was not found posssible to persuade President Eisenhower to join in that process." He went on to speak of the hopes he had entertained of a dual meeting at Stockholm or some like neutral place. "But then the Soviet Government began a very elaborate process of trying to stop the ratification of E.D.C., which I thought had been more or less accepted ... and so all this other matter has come up now and stood in the way of further general talks."

DOMESTIC POLICY

Through all the diplomatic activity of the autumn of 1954 which followed the French Assembly's rejection of the Defence Community treaty, Churchill remained in the background. It was his Foreign Secretary who described and executed British policy and who announced the Government's historic decision, reversing the policy of ages, to commit troops to the Continent for a period of some 50 years. And it was Sir Anthony Eden who went to Geneva the following summer for the long-awaited conference of heads of state.

Churchill's record in domestic affairs during the Parliament of 1951 is less impressive. This is partly accounted for by the policy of his Government, which was to repair the national economy and grant a respite from major legislation, and partly by his preoccupation with the great questions that lay unsettled between the nations. In the more controversial domestic debates it was not he but his subordinate Ministers who appeared in the front line.

WELFARE STATE

Churchill himself, in contrast to his tactics while in opposition after 1945, exerted his parliamentary talents in the mitigation of party strife. Yet it was while under his leadership that the Conservative Party revolutionized its policy, became a guarantor of the welfare state, and stole so many of its opponents' clothes; and it was while he was Prime Minister that the party gave proof of its new convictions in office. It was not too difficult a transformation for one who had been a member of the Liberal Government of 1906.

Shortly after the Coronation he became suddenly ill and was ordered a complete rest by his doctors. Though he was back at work in October rumours grew of his retirement and of incapacity brought on at last by age. His movements it was noticed were less vigorous, his uptake in the Commons less quick, but again and again he came to the dispatch box and reasserted his mastery.

His eightieth birthday on November 30, 1954, found him still in office and in full control. The occasion drew forth tributes from his countrymen and from abroad of such number and warmth as have never been accorded to any English statesman before. Both Houses of Parliament met in Westminster Hall to present him with gifts. It was an occasion with no parallel.

CLIMAX OF ACCLAIM

This was perhaps the climax of the public honour paid him during his lifetime. His resignation of the office of Prime Minister had long been preceded by rumour, and when it came on April 5, 1955, it unhappily coincided with a strike in offices of the London national newspapers which prevented their publication. Yet the public did not need to be reminded in order to be aware that the last page was turned on one of the greatest chapters of British statesmanship. Preferring to the highest honours which might have been bestowed upon him to remain a private member of the House of Commons, he presented himself again to the electors of Woodford, as he did once more in 1959. Though he was often to be seen in the chamber of the House during these last years, he took no further part in its debates. In the summer of 1962 he fell and fractured a thigh bone. About 12 months later he announced that he would not seek reelection in the next Parliament. On July 28, 1964, shortly before the dissolution of Parliament, the House of Commons accorded him the rare honour of passing a motion "putting on record its unbounded admiration and gratitude for his services to Parliament, to the nation and to the world. ..." He did not take his seat in the Chamber that day. The motion was brought to him by the party leaders at his home at Hyde Park Gate. His ninetieth birthday in 1964 was the occasion of widespread celebration.

A glowing loyalty to the Monarchy, which was fed by the romantic strain in Churchill's nature, was matched by a warm personal regard for the Sovereigns whom he served. His attachment to George VI was especially marked, and can be measured by the fact that he deferred to the King's wish that he should not, as he had planned and as he dearly wanted to, embark in a warship on D day to observe the bombardment of the Normandy coast. The panegyric which he broadcast the night after King George's death was deeply moving in its sincerity. For similar reasons the Knighthood of the Garter, conferred on him by Queen Elizabeth just before her coronation, was a source of particular gratification to him. He had declined the same honour at the hands of her father in 1945, before the restoration of the practice by which conferment of the Order is the sole prerogative of the Sovereign who does not act on the recommendation of the Prime Minister.

PRIZE IN EUROPE

In the spring of 1956 he was awarded the Charlemagne Prize for services to Europe, at Aachen. That this should have gone to the man who was above all responsible for the overthrow of the German Reich was a sign of the rapidity with which the European scene had changed in 10 years. In his speech on that occasion he cast his last stone that was to ripple the surface of international waters. He spoke, as he had so often done before, of the grand design of a united Europe. Russia, he said, must play a part in the alliance that would guarantee the peace of Europe; if that position was first achieved, it might be that the reunification of Germany would be more easily effected. In Bonn the reaction was chilly to this strategy, which did not accord with the rigorous views there held about the steps by which reunification should be accomplished. During the Suez crisis Churchill, to the disappointment of many, was silent except for two letters to his constituents, in which he intimated that the Government's actions had his full support.

OLD STORIES

He used his leisure to work at the long-projected *History of the English Speaking Peoples* in four volumes. Professional historians found much to cavil at, in spite of the assistance Churchill had from some of their number. But the public recognized in it a master hand of historical narrative, a shrewd and appreciative judgment of magnanimity, and an endearing preference for the good old stories, however "tiresome investigators" might have undermined them.

Two of his private pursuits in particular excited public interest—his horse-racing and his painting. He became a racehorse owner late in life. His racing colours were registered in 1949 and two months later he won his first race with Colonist II. It was a popular victory.

His taste for painting was of much longer standing. He began during enforced inactivity after his removal from the Admiralty in 1915. Four years later he exhibited a portrait at an exhibition of the Royal Society of Portrait Painters. But it was landscapes that he grew to prefer. "Audacity", he wrote, "is a very great part of the art of painting." And his decisive, boldly coloured, impressionistic works became familiar at the Royal Academy. His election to that body as Royal Academician Extraordinary was an honour he particularly relished, and his speeches at the annual banquets added much to the gaiety of the occasion. An exhibition of 62 of his paintings held at Burlington House in the summer of 1959 brought more than 140,000 visitors.

CROWDED HONOURS

The honours that crowded upon him towards the end of his life are far too numerous to list. First in esteem was his honorary citizenship of the United States of America, which was declared by proclamation at a ceremony at the White House on April 9, 1963—an honour that has been bestowed on no one else in the history of the union. In 1958 he was decorated by General de Gaulle with the Cross of Liberation. He was made Grand Seigneur of the Company of Adventurers of England into Hudson's Bay; he was the first non-American to receive the Freedom Award; he was Lord Warden of the Cinque Ports and Grand Master of the Primrose League: he held honorary degrees at more than 20 universities and was a freeman of some 50 towns and cities from Thebes and Cap d'Ail to Harrow. Among the minor honours in which he took special delight was the annual invitation to song night at Harrow School.

He married, as recorded earlier, Clementine, daughter of Colonel Sir Henry M. Hozier and Lady Blanche Ogilvy, and granddaughter of the seventh Earl of Airlie. From then on, he wrote in *My Early Life*, they "lived happily ever afterwards". That judgment, given in 1930, was not to be disturbed by time. Lady Churchill added grace and harmony to innumerable occasions in Sir Winston's public life, and made for him a secure and happy home at Chartwell. Three children of the marriage survive: Mr. Randolph Churchill; Miss Sarah Churchill, the actress; and Mary, wife of Mr. Christopher Soames, M.P. Diana, formerly wife of Mr. Duncan Sandys, M.P., died in 1963.

The proposal was made by Harold Laski in 1944 that a fund should be raised in token of the nation's gratitude to its Prime Minister. In thanking Laski, Churchill remarked that things of that kind were better left until a man is dead. "If, however", he added, "when I am dead people think of commemorating my services, I should like to think that a park was made for the children of London's poor on the south bank of the Thames, where they have suffered so grimly from the Hun".

January 25, 1965.

Lord Chuter-Ede, P.C., C.H., who died on November 11, 1965, in a Ewell nursing home at the age of 83, was Home Secretary from 1945 to 1951, and was Leader of the House of Commons for seven months in 1951. During the wartime Coalition, as Parliamentary Secretary to the Ministry of Education, he gave valuable service in helping to pilot through Parliament the 1944 Education Act.

He was created a life peer in 1964. Known all his life as Chuter Ede, he combined these names in his title.

Ede was one of the most sensible politicians of his generation. His wit and wisdom were a constant refreshment to the House and a salutary corrective to vagaries and vacuity. He brought to it the finest qualities of the best type of schoolmaster—patience, good humour, tolerance and an acute instinct for detecting humbug and woolly-mindedness. His sympathy for the weaknesses of humankind and his understanding of the criminal mind, derived from long experience on the bench, were invaluable assets to him as Home Secretary. But he was no sentimentalist; corrupters of youth found him an implacable foe.

The capital punishment issue plunged him into complex difficulties during the passage of the Criminal Justice Bill. His advice against suspension of the penalty was rejected by the Commons and his attempt at a compromise was spurned by the Lords.

BALANCED PERSONALITY

Ede was no puritan. He wanted his fellow citizens to enjoy life as fully as he did. Horse racing was one of his passions. Nothing would keep him from the Derby. He thought betting was folly but he saw no sin in it and he had a soft spot for the street bookmaker. Although he was a total abstainer he saw no reason to deny reasonable indulgence to others. His was indeed a remarkably balanced and well rounded personality of a quality which can ill be spared from public life.

James Chuter Ede was born at Epsom in 1882, the son of James and Agnes Mary Ede. He was educated at the Epsom National Schools, the Dorking High School, and Battersea Pupil Teachers' Centre and Christ's College, Cambridge. He was a master in Surrey elementary schools until 1914. In the First World War he served in the East Surreys and the Royal Engineers and became a sergeant. He was a member of the Epsom U.D.C. from 1908 to 1927 and again from 1933 to 1937. He was on the Surrey County Council from 1914 to 1949 and was chairman from 1933 to 1937. He was Charter Mayor of Epsom and Ewell in 1937.

Meanwhile he had moved from Liberalism to the Labour Party and had entered national politics. In 1923 Mitcham sent him to Parliament, one of the few teachers in the House at that time. He sat for South Shields from 1929 to 1931 and then continuously from 1935 to 1964. In the wartime coalition he was appointed Parliamentary Secretary to the Ministry of Education and bore much of the burden of preparing the 1944 Education Bill and guiding it through committee. His witty and well informed speeches greatly impressed the House. His liking and admiration for Mr. R. A. Butler (later Lord Butler), his chief, were mutual. In 1944 he was sworn of the Privy Council.

On the formation of the Labour Government in 1945 began his long and distinguished tenure of the Home Office—the longest by any statesman since the great Reform Act. By temperament and training he was admirably fitted for the post, and apart from his departmental activities he brought to the affairs of his party a judgment and commonsense which were of the utmost value to the Prime Minister. Many of the controversies in its inner counsels were brought to an amicable settlement by Ede's tact and patience. At the Home Office the wave of violent crime which broke out after the war gave a particular urgency to the framing of the Criminal Justice Bill. When Ede moved the second reading in November, 1947, he explained that the Government did not regard the time as opportune for including in it provision for suspending or abolishing the death penalty. But he promised a free vote on report stage. When that time came he strongly advised the retention of hanging, but the Commons decided for a five-year suspension of the penalty. Ede was much criticized in high judicial circles for announcing a decision to recommend commuting all death sentences in anticipation of a change in the law.

LEADING THE HOUSE

After the Lords had decisively reversed the Commons vote, Ede found it necessary to announce that after all each case would be considered on its merits. This was a time when the Parliament Bill was threatening a serious clash between Lords and Commons and the situation was highly complex. Ede tabled a compromise clause prescribing hanging for certain categories of murder committed with "express malice". The Commons carried it but the Lords shot it to pieces. Ede persuaded the Commons not to persist with the compromise. His shrewd mind sensed that it would be neither in the public interest nor in accordance with public opinion for the Commons to sacrifice important penal reforms merely for the purpose of expressing their disagreement with the peers. At the same time he foreshadowed an inquiry into the possibility of limiting the incidence of the death penalty, and in due course a Royal Commission was appointed. Some years later, though he doubted if the case for or against hanging as a deterrent had been proved either way, he voted in favour of its experimental temporary suspension.

During his time as Home Secretary, Ede had to decide whether or not to grant a reprieve in the case of Timothy John Evans. He decided against it and Evans was hanged. Later, in 1961, Ede was one of the sponsors of the Timothy John Evans Bill, which sought to allow Evans's remains to be transferred to his next-of-kin.

Later his own views veered toward suspension of the death penalty, but by that time he had shed Cabinet responsibility and was well established as an elder statesman. In opposition in the Commons he supported abolition, as he did in 1965 in the Lords.

In 1947 Ede was appointed deputy leader of the House and in 1951 he was for a few months its leader. His sense of humour helped a lot in tempering acerbities and he performed no mean feat in facilitating business at a time when the nominal Government majority was less than double figures.

He had a deep love for the Commons which he led with outstanding competence and tact. On the back benches he gathered an immense fund of respect for the ripe wisdom of his counsel. He was impressively knowledgeable on such subjects as local government, education and penology, but he was never didactic or pompous. A rich vein of the driest wit sparkled through the solid sense he always spoke. Members relished his sly asides, his flashes of irony and his delight in deflating the more portentous manifestations of orthodoxy.

He was president of the International Association for Liberal Christianity and Religious Freedom. He was an ardent Miltonian and could quote *Areopagitica* on the slightest provocation. One of his first reforms at the Home Office was to remove from his desk an old copy of *Crockford's Clerical Directory* and to substitute a volume of his favourite poet.

In June, 1955 he announced his decision to withdraw from the Labour Shadow Cabinet. Ede served on many public bodies, including the B.B.C. General Advisory Council of which he was chairman for seven years. He received honorary doctorates from universities and the freedom of boroughs—he was much loved in South Shields.

Ede married in 1917 Lilian Mary Stephens Williams, daughter of the late Richard Williams of Plymouth. She was for nine years a member of the Surrey County Council with him and shared his interest in education and local politics. She was stricken by chronic illness and when Ede was Home Secretary it was a familiar sight to see him pushing his wife along the terrace at Westminster. It was a crushing blow to him when she died in July, 1948.

November 12, 1965.

Mary Clare, an actress whose career spanned more than 50 years in the theatre, and who also made a name for herself in the cinema, died on August 29, 1970.

In this long and distinguished career it is not easy to name any particular highlight, but theatre-goers of the 1920s will recall, more than anything else perhaps, the scene in *The Likes of Her* at the St. Martin's Theatre in the summer of 1923 in which she played opposite the 16-year-old Hermione Baddeley and the two faced each other in a moment of bitter acrimony.

Mary Clare was born in London on July 17, 1894. She began earning her living in an office, but was able to borrow £50 for training on the stage, and made her debut in repertory in 1910. This was followed by two years touring the provinces and after going to London to play in *A Posy on a Ring* at the theatre at the Earls Court Exhibition in 1912, she made her West End debut in *Turandot* at St. James's Theatre in 1913.

From then on there were few months in any year when she was not to be seen on the West End stage. Her outstanding successes apart from *The Likes of Her* included *The Skin Game*, *White Cargo*, *The Ghost Train* and *The Constant Nymph*. In 1931 she played Jane Marryot at Drury Lane in *Cavalcade*, the play which Noel Coward is said to have written specially for her. She was seen in some English silent films during the 1920s, including *The Constant Nymph*, and made her first appearance in a sound film in *Hindle Wakes* in 1931. Thereafter she made a number of films, including the sound version of *The Constant Nymph*, *The Skin Game*, *The Passing of the Third Floor Back*, *Jew Süss*, *The Lady Vanishes*, *The Citadel*, *A Girl Must Live* and—during and after the Second World War—*Next of Kin*, *Oliver Twist* and *Ester Waters*.

One of her last screen appearances was in *The Black Rose* in 1950, with Tyrone Power and Orson Welles.

She was only seen in the theatre occasionally during the 1950s, but played the Duchess in *Alice in Wonderland* in 1956 and Almina Clare in *Waiting in the Wings* at the Duke of York's in 1960.

Miss Clare was married in 1915 to Lieutenant L. Mawhood of the Royal Inniskilling Fusiliers. He was badly wounded in the First World War, and died in 1935. She leaves a son, David, a retired Air Force officer, and a daughter, Rozanne, who appeared on stage before the last war as Anne Clare.

August 31, 1970.

Jim Clark, O.B.E., twice world champion race driver (1963 and 1965), who died when his Lotus 48 crashed in the European Formula II championship race at Hockenheim, west Germany, on April 7, 1968, will be remembered as he had already surpassed the total of 24 world championship race victories scored by five times world champion Argentine Juan Manuel Fangio.

He was leading the 1968 world championships following his victory in the South African Grand Prix in January, first round of the 1968 series.

Clark, a 32-year-old bachelor, had driven for team Lotus regularly since 1960 and was in his ninth season with the Norfolk based team founded by his patron and personal friend Colin Chapman. Clark won the Tasman championship in New Zealand and Australia in 1968 for the third time.

He was born on March 4, 1936, in Kilmany, Fifeshire, the only son of a prosperous farmer, and educated at Loretto School, Edinburgh, where he was not particularly happy and left at 16, working on his father's 1,300-acre farm for 18 months as a shepherd. He later took over his own 1,200-acre estate at Edington Mains, Berwick—one of the best Border farms in the country. At one time he had about 1,100 feeding sheep, 500 fat cattle and flocks of Suffolk and Border Leicester sheep, and as his time became more and more occupied with racing, his father made three regular weekly visits to discuss points with Clark's resident farm manager. Clark was acknowledged as an expert on cattle and pedigree sheep.

WIRY SCOT

He made his racing debut in a D.K.W. saloon at Crimond airfield, near Aberdeen, in 1956, and was later given considerable assistance by his Border farmer friends. Recognizing his natural ability, they clubbed together and sponsored him with a variety of cars with which he scored numerous victories. He had his first single-seater drive on Boxing Day, 1959, in a Gemini Formula Junior car and early in 1960 he was tested by the Aston Martin team. But he was released after failing to get a grand prix drive and signed for Colin Chapman's Team Lotus in formula junior and formula two.

Small and wiry, the Latin-looking Border Scot was ideal for the diminutive rear-engined Lotuses and after winning at Oulton Park and Goodwood, he was promoted to the Formula one team, finishing fifth in the 1960 Dutch Grand Prix. From that day on, Clark became a regular member of Team Lotus and has driven for them in Formula one cars ever since.

After giving Team Lotus its first continental race victory by winning the 1961 Pau Grand Prix, Clark shrugged aside criticism that he was running before he had learnt to walk and won the 1962 Belgian, British and United States Grands Prix. He narrowly failed to take the title, when his Lotus lost a tiny bolt while he was leading the South African G.P., allowing Graham Hill into the world championship crown. Clark showed scintillating form in 1963, however, and brilliant successive wins in the Belgian, Dutch, French and British G.P.s and went on to take his first drivers' championship. That year, he shook American racing pundits by finishing second in the Indianapolis 500 in a revolutionary Lotus-powered-by-Ford and two years later won it outright at a record average speed of 150.6 m.p.h.

Clark's other grand prix victories included 1964, Dutch, Belgian, and British; 1965, South African, Belgian, French, British, Dutch, and German; 1966, United States; 1967, Dutch, British, American, and Mexican. He can thus claim two incredible records of having won the same grand prix four years in succession, the Belgian (at Spa) and the British Grands Prix in 1962–63–64 and 1965 respectively... Fangio won the Argentine G.P. in 1954–55–56 and 1957.

Clark was equally at home in all types of machinery... formula one, formula two, formula junior (joint champion in 1960), saloon car racing.

For the 1967 season, Clark was once again with Colin Chapman and the Team Lotus and had as his team-mate Graham Hill in the powerful new Lotus fitted with an all-new Ford engine.

Clark found motor racing the utmost in pleasure and will be remembered for his immaculate driving style and lightning reactions. He was rarely headed from the starting grid and was definitely a driver who liked to control the race from the front of the pack and at a blistering pace. He seemed to be born with not only a "silver spoon" but also a charmed life, and escaped without injury in several high-speed crashes, including Aintree, Brands Hatch, and Monaco. Clark was a non-smoker who drank in moderation and rapidly became frustrated if he was not active. He played cricket at school, learnt the violin, was an excellent dancer, hockey player, sprinter, and water-skier and enjoyed rough shooting and photography.

In 1967, Clark announced that for tax reasons he would not be resident in Great Britain and only expected to make infrequent racing appearances here. He was a hard and successful businessman and was a director of his own self-promotion company, Clarksport Ltd. He was a talented private pilot and flew his own Comanche aircraft all over Europe to and from races.

Away from the cockpit, Clark's modest—even shy—manner and quiet Scottish speaking voice belied the fact that he was a double world champion in the most dangerous and demanding of all sports. It was behind the wheel of a racing car that he started to live.

April 8, 1968.

Sir Arthur Clark, K.C.M.G., C.B.E., Director of Information Services and Cultural Relations, Commonwealth Office, since 1964, and before that British High Commissioner in Cyprus, died on May 29,1967. He was 58.

Before taking up his appointment in Cyprus he had earned golden opinions as a trouble-shooter in Commonwealth affairs. In 1953 he played a leading part in healing the breach created by the dispute over the Bamangwato chieftainship in Bechuanaland, and in 1960 he successfully brought to a conclusion the negotiations over the R.A.F. base in the Maldive Islands.

As Director of Information he played a large, though unobtrusive, part in ensuring that the British public should see clearly the moral issues involved over the Rhodesian declaration of independence in 1965, and in the negotiations which followed it. He was about to leave with the Prime Minister for the British day at the Montreal Exhibition, where he had been closely involved in the British pavilion and exhibits, widely acclaimed as imaginative.

William Arthur Weir Clark, eldest son of the Rev. W. W. Clark, B.D., was born on December

5, 1908, and educated at Stewart's College, Edinburgh, Edinburgh University and Trinity College, Oxford. He was appointed to the Colonial Administrative Service in 1931 and served for eight years in Kenya after which he was seconded to the Dominions Office. He was private secretary to two successive Dominions Secretaries, Lord Attlee and Lord Cranbourne (now Lord Salisbury), and was a member of the United Kingdom delegation to the United Nations Conference in San Francisco in 1945. That same year he was appointed chief secretary to the Central African Council, an organization set up before the days of the Central African Federation to coordinate services in Southern and Northern Rhodesia and Nyasaland. This organization, always regarded with suspicion in Southern Rhodesia, where it was seen as a device for blocking federation, was dissolved some years later, and Clark was posted to the staff of Sir Evelyn Baring, then High Commissioner in South Africa. He was thus brought into contact with the territories of Swaziland, Basutoland and Bechuanaland shortly before the marriage of Seretse Khama and the English Ruth Williams and their ensuing exile.

He remained Chief Secretary to the High Commissioner until 1950 when he went to the Commonwealth Relations Office. He was given special responsibility for the settlement of the Bamangwato dispute, and for the way in which that tangle was sorted out Clark must be given much of the credit. He was an Assistant Under-Secretary of State at the Commonwealth Relations Office from 1954 to 1956 when he went out to India as Deputy British High Commissioner in Delhi.

There he went through the period in which the High Commission was completely starved of news over its own Government's intentions in the Suez crisis, and helped to repair the damage done to British-Indian good will thereafter.

In July, 1960, he was chosen to be the first United Kingdom representative in Cyprus after that country attained independence and when Cyprus joined the Commonwealth he became High Commissioner. He held the post until March, 1964, when he relinquished it for reasons of health. The new High Commissioner was Major-General W. H. A. Bishop, then director of Information Services and Cultural Relations, and it was to this appointment that Clark succeeded in May, 1964.

Sir Arthur Clark had a very pronounced "style" in his dealings with the press and his death will undoubtedly be deeply regretted and he will be remembered with affection. The husky voice which his earlier illness bequeathed to him easily commanded attention at the informal as well as the formal conferences at which he excelled. He was witty, wise, urbane, and remarkably frank within the limits any given situation imposed. He gave the impression always of wanting to say more, not less, of trusting journalists, and of understanding their problems. Among his colleagues his enthusiasm and energy were a never failing source of wonder in a man of far from robust health. He played a large part in integrating the information departments of the Colonial and Commonwealth Offices earlier this year.

He married in 1935 Margaret Jean, daughter of the Rev. W. Dobbie, by whom he had a son and a daughter.

May 30, 1967.

Air Marshal Sir Robert H. Clark-Hall, K.B.E., C.M.G., D.S.O., who was the first specialist armament officer of the Naval Wing. R.F.C., in 1913, and was largely concerned in the development of the aeroplane as a fighting as well as a reconnaissance machine, died at Christchurch, New Zealand, on March 7, 1964, at the age of 80.

He was among the small band of enthusiasts who qualified as air pilots at their own expense before the R.F.C. was formed in 1912, and later was an original member of the R.N.A.S. and R.A.F. During the Second World War he served with the Royal New Zealand Air Force, having gone to live at Christchurch after his retirement.

Robert Hamilton Clark-Hall was born at Chelsea on June 21, 1883. He entered the Britannia as a naval cadet in the spring of 1897, and was a midshipman afloat from October, 1898, on the China station. In 1900 he was landed from the Aurora for service with the naval brigade for the relief of Pekin during the Boxer rebellion. He specialized in gunnery in 1907, and in 1910 qualified as an interpreter in German. It was while serving as gunnery officer of the battleship Illustrious that he learnt to fly privately on a Bristol biplane on Salisbury Plain, his Royal Aero Club certificate, No 127, being dated August 2, 1911. His official association with aircraft began in March, 1913, when he was appointed to the R.F.C., Naval Wing, in charge of experimental work with aircraft armament.

On the formation of the R.N.A.S. on July 1, 1914, he was graded as squadron commander. Three months later, war having broken out, he was given command of the seaplane carrier Ark Royal, in which he served at the Dardanelles and was mentioned in dispatches. In December, 1915, he was promoted to commander R.N., and wing commander, R.N.A.S., and during 1916 served as assistant director in the Admiralty Air Department. From February, 1917, he commanded No. 1 Wing of the R.N.A.S. at Dunkirk until the following November, after which he served as fleet aviation officer with the Grand Fleet. He was graded as temporary colonel when the R.A.F. was formed in 1918.

DECLINED PROMOTION

Subsequently he twice declined promotion to brigadier-general, R.A.F., as he considered higher rank would impair his usefulness with the fleet. The Admiralty expressed their appreciation of his valuable services, and of the way he had "worked with absolute singleness of purpose for the advancement of naval flying". He was awarded the D.S.O. in 1918 for services at Dunkirk, and the C.M.G. and French Legion of Honour in 1919 for distinguished war service.

Following the dispersal of the Grand Fleet in April, 1919, he commanded the Scottish (No. 29) Group, R.A.F., and was granted a permanent commission. On the formation of the R.A.F. Staff College in 1922 he was made assistant commandant. From May, 1924, he commanded the Egyptian Group, and from November, 1925, to February, 1929, was A.O.C. in the Mediterranean, with headquarters at Malta. He returned home to become Director of Equipment, Air Ministry, from March, 1929, to October 1931, during which time he was promoted to air vice-marshal in July, 1929. His last appointment in the R.A.F. was as A.O.C., Coastal Area, from October, 1931, to 1934. On August 11, 1934, he retired at the age of 51, after 37 years' service, to settle in New Zealand. He was created a K.B.E. in the birthday honours of that year.

When the Second World War broke out he offered his services to the Dominion Government, and in 1940 joined the R.N.Z.A.F. as wing commander to command the air station at Harewood. In 1943 he was promoted to air commodore to command the southern (training) group, and in October, 1944 was appointed A.O.C., No. 1 Islands Group in the Pacific, where he served until the war ended.

He married, in 1919, Lillias, daughter of Colonel R. Eliott-Lockhart, of Lockerbie, and had two sons (one of whom was killed on operations with the R.A.F. in 1944) and one daughter.

March 10, 1964.

John Clerides, Q.C, the Cyprus lawyer who unsuccessfully opposed Archbishop Makarios for election to the Presidency of the Republic in 1959, died on Januray 17, 1961, in Nicosia. He was 73.

Regarded as the island's elder statesman and a valued adviser to many successive Governors, Clerides resigned from the Executive Council in 1956 to protest against the decision to exile the Archbishop to Seychelles and remained in retirement, politically speaking, until 1959 when he became, and remained, one of the most outspoken critics of the Zurich Agreement which ended the four-year emergency in Cyprus. Courage in speaking out for opinions that found little popular sanction in Cyprus was something Clerides often showed. As a moderate he opposed much that the enosis movement came to advocate and, in 1955, publicly condemned Eoka violence, subsequently receiving threats from the terrorists himself.

John Clerides was born in the Cypriot mountain village of Agros and when only nine went to Nicosia, working there in an uncle's grocery shop while attending school. His abilities soon became marked and by the time he was 20 he was a teacher. He decided subsequently for the law, however, and in 1924 enrolled at Gray's Inn, becoming the first Cypriot to qualify in England as a barrister. Returning to Cyprus he built up a large and flourishing family practice and took Silk in 1952.

He had already long been active in Cyprus politics, being a member for many years of the Executive Council formed after the 1931 disturbances. After the war he was elected Mayor of Nicosia, defeating the Nationalist candidate with the aid of left-wing votes. He remained three years in office.

URGED SELF-GOVERNMENT

With the rise of the enosis movement in the 1950s Clerides found his advocacy of an appreciable period of stable self-government for Cyprus to precede union with Greece put him increasingly in isolated positions. The forces of extremism gained the ascendancy, however, and agitation erupted into violence.

It was Clerides's view, in condemning Archbishop Makarios for finally assenting to the Zurich agreement, that Cyprus would have been better off had she accepted the Macmillan plan of 1958, which he believed would have led to eventual full self-determination, rather than what he regarded as semi-partition and a "mockery of independence" imposed under Zurich.

Shortly before the presidential elections in December, 1959, Clerides formed a new party, the Cyprus Democratic Union, with the express intention of opposing the Archbishop and enabling the people of Cyprus "to express their opposition to Zurich". He was, however, defeated at the polls by a majority of two to one.

In July, 1960, he refused to consent to the C.D.U. taking part in the elections to the island's House of Representatives on the ground that the electoral system was "undemocratic".

Since independence Clerides had remained an uncompromising political opponent of the Archbishop and had frequently expressed strong criticism of the policies of his Government in the Greek-Cypriot opposition press.

Clerides leaves a widow, two sons, and a daughter. His elder son, Mr. Glafcos Clerides, is President of the Cyprus House of Representatives.

January 18, 1961.

Vice-Admiral Sir Eric Clifford, K.C.B., C.B.E., who died on September 7, 1964, at the age of 64, served for 40 years in the Royal Navy. He had a wide and varied experience and was Deputy Chief of Naval Staff in 1954–57.

Eric George Anderson Clifford was the son of Captain W. T. Clifford, R.N.R., and was born on September 3, 1900. Like his father, he entered the Thames Nautical Training College, H.M.S. Worcester, and from January, 1917, was a midshipman, first R.N.R. and then R.N., in the Iron Duke, the destroyer Nugent, and the Colossus and Royal Sovereign in the Grand Fleet. He was selected to specialize in navigation in 1924 when serving in the destroyer Tourmaline at Gibraltar. Between 1925 and 1931 he was navigator of the sloop Magnolia in China, second navigator in the Atlantic Fleet flagship Nelson, and navigator of the cruisers Caradoc in the West Indies and Dorsetshire in the Atlantic Fleet. He then joined the staff at the Navigation School and in 1932 was selected for the course at the R.N. Staff College. In 1935–37, following his promotion to commander, he served in the Plans Division, Admiralty, and resumed sea service in 1938, in H.M.S. Kent as fleet navigator on the China station.

He served in the Kent until 1940 and then commanded the destroyers Mackay and Salisbury. From 1941 and 1943 as a captain he was naval assistant secretary to the War Cabinet and during this time served as secretary to the Anti-U-boat Committee set up by Churchill.

CONVOY PERILS

He took command of H.M.S. Diadem in 1943, as flag-captain and chief staff officer to the rear-admiral commanding one of the Home Fleet cruiser squadrons. On one occasion during a North Russian convoy operation the force led by the Diadem destroyed three out of a strong force of U-boats and shot down several aircraft. During the landings in Normandy the Diadem was one of the bombarding ships which supported the Allied armies. Clifford was twice mentioned in dispatches for his services, which included the sinking of an armed merchant ship west of La Rochelle and various other exploits. At the end of the war he served as chief staff officer to Admiral Sir Cecil Harcourt when the latter was appointed Commander-in-Chief at Hongkong. He attended the Imperial Defence College in 1946.

In 1947, he returned to the Navigation School for two years in command. He went to sea again in 1949, in command of the Illustrious, trials and training aircraft carrier, and in 1951 was promoted to rear-admiral. In February that year he became Assistant Chief of Naval Staff. In 1952–53 he was flag officer commanding the Fifth Cruiser Squadron and second-in-command, Far East. As such he was responsible for naval operations in Korean waters during the latter part of the war. In 1954, he was promoted to vice-admiral and appointed Deputy Chief of Naval Staff, serving on the Admiralty Board for three years. He was placed on the retired list in 1957.

He married in 1936 Nita Marion, eldest daughter of Edgar H. Hill, of Eastbourne, and had one daughter.

September 9, 1964.

Alec Clunes, who died on March 13, 1970, in a London hospital at the age of 57, was respected for the range of his achievements as an actor in the classics and in modern plays, and in particular for his work as manager, director and actor at the Arts Theatre, Great Newport Street, over a period of more than 10 years.

Both his parents were on the stage, but Alexander (Alec) S. de Moro Clunes, who was born in London on May 17, 1912, had experience of advertising and journalism before he became first an amateur, then a professional actor, spending two seasons at the Old Vic under Henry Cass and staying on for the beginning of a new season under Tyrone Guthrie.

He appeared at Barry Jackson's Malvern Festival in 1938, and as Petruchio (under Komisarjevsky), Aguecheek (under Irene Hentschel), Iago and, in Elizabethan costume with Roman accoutrements, Coriolanus at the Stratford-on-Avon Festival in 1939. That season was brought to an end by the Second World War, as was Shaw's play about Charles II, in which Clunes played Godfrey Kneller, in 1940, and for a while he toured the provinces with the Old Vic Company; but, in 1942, having rented the Arts Theatre in London, and founded a group of actors called after it, he began operations with Clifford Odet's *Awake and Sing*.

Having done a number of revivals of Shaw and a notable one of Farquhar's *The Constant Couple* with himself as Sir Harry Wildair, Clunes played Hamlet—a Hamlet that one young drama critic considered the best he had yet seen—and bought a lease of the Arts all in the same month of October, 1945. There, after touring western Europe on behalf of the British Council and playing at Shaw's own suggestion Higgins in *Pygmalion* at the Lyric, Hammersmith, he was seen as the discharged soldier Thomas Mendip in *The Lady's Not For Burning*, by Christopher Fry, to whom he had paid a weekly wage while he wrote that comedy.

He returned to the Old Vic, as Orsino to Peggy Ashcroft's Viola, on its reopening in 1950; presented and appeared in Fry's *The Firstborn;* and did three more productions at the Arts, the membership of which had risen to 25,000 and where he now had 132 plays to his credit, including 14 transfers to public theatres, before disposing of his lease in 1953.

SHAKESPEARE ROLES

His Claudius, one of his most highly praised performances, in Peter Brook's production of *Hamlet* at the Moscow Art Theatre, and in London, was followed by his Faulconbridge, Brutus and (again under Brook) Caliban at Stratford-on-Avon in 1957, the last of which roles he repeated, to Gielgud's Prospero, for a season at Drury Lane, though A. V. Cookman in *The Times* described his Caliban as being simply a buffoon. He took over Higgins in *My Fair Lady*, his first musical, from Rex Harrison at that same theatre and Sir Lewis Eliot in *The Affair* from John Clements at the Strand. In 1967 be played the Bishop's ascetic chaplain in a revival of Shaw's *Getting Married*, and in 1968 as the Bishop of Chichester in Hochhuth's *Soldiers* he splendidly combined fervour with reasonableness in presenting the case against the saturation bombing of Germany to John Colicos's Winston Churchill. He appeared in several films, among them Sir Laurence Olivier's *Richard III* in which he played the part of Hastings.

For all that, it is as a professor, as a man whose geniality or whose testiness alike had something professional about it, but whose true magnanimity broke through in the end, that theatregoers may first think of Clunes, the actor, when they look back. Shaw obviously considered him a natural for Higgins, and there was perhaps a touch of the purist in his recent avowal that he could find no writer whose work he liked.

Clunes was a collector of prints and drawings and was well known as a buyer and seller of books. His monograph, *The British Theatre*, was published in Cassell's *Arts of Man* series in 1964. His marriage to Miss Stella Richman was dissolved in 1954. In 1956 he married Miss Daphne Acott, by whom he had one son and one daughter.

March 14, 1970.

Louis Hervé Coatalen, a pioneer in the design and development of motor-car and aircraft engines in Britain, died in Paris on May 23, 1962, at the age of 82.

Louis Hervé Coatalen was born at Concarneau, Finistère, in 1879, the second son of J. Coatalen, and served his apprenticeship with the De Dion Bouton, Clement and Panhard et Levasseur firms before going to England in 1901 to join the Humber Company at Coventry. In 1907 he entered into partnership with William Hillman, and in 1908 drove a Hillman-Coatalen car in the Tourist Trophy race in the Isle of Man; but the partnership was short-lived, and the following year he joined the Sunbeam Motor Car Company with which his name was afterwards to be intimately connected.

LIGHT CARS' PROMISE

The 12–16 h.p. Sunbeam car, for which he was responsible, quickly distinguished itself as one of the outstanding light cars of the day, and in 1912 three somewhat modified versions of this standard model won the first three places in the two-day race for the *Coupe de l' Auto* at Dieppe for three-litre cars, the first of them being third in the Grand Prix.

Thereafter, in spite of his undoubted ability as a designer, Coatalen appears to have been rendered impatient by the success of certain of his rivals, and was somewhat prone in consequence to copy their methods rather than to adhere to his own. Sunbeam cars won the Tourist Trophy race in 1914 and 1922, but their design was based more nearly on the lines of the Peugeot and other successful French racing cars than on those which had been laid down by Coatalen himself. Similarly, the Sunbeam car which in 1923 not only scored the first British win but took all first three places in the French Grand Prix, at that time the premier Continental racing event, owed much of its inspiration to the successful Fiat racer of the previous year.

FRONT WHEEL BRAKES

During the early 1920s the Talbot-Darracq racing cars, for which Coatalen was also responsible, were as successful in light-car races as were the Sunbeams in events for larger cars. In 1923 under his general technical direction Sunbeams were one of the first English firms to adopt front-wheel brakes, which became standard on all models in 1924.

In the late 1920's he designed the engine for the first car to exceed 200 miles an hour—a 1,000 horse power Sunbeam driven by Sir Henry Segrave at Dayton in America.

During the First World War he had acquired British nationality and designed the first engine for the Short seaplanes. Later he also designed the engines for the first transatlantic airships, the R33 and R34.

In 1930 he returned to France to become chairman and managing director of Lockheed Hydraulic Brakes and later assumed the directorship of K.L.G. Sparking Plugs (France), in which he actively participated until his sudden death.

May 25, 1962.

Alvin Langdon Coburn, one of the last survivors of the heroic generation of artistic-photographers, who made their mark in the 1900s, died at his home in Colwyn Bay on November 23, 1966. He was 84.

Though he had lived in Britain since 1899, Coburn was American in origin, and came to Britain when he was 17, already equipped with a camera and an obsorbing passion for using it on anything and everything. In particular he delighted to photograph people, and before long he had made his mark in London society and got to know just about everybody worth knowing. This ease of access to the great and famous stood him in excellent stead as a photographer, since those he did not come to know in the ordinary course of social life could soon be cajoled by friends or would summon him of their own accord to photograph them.

In this way, he came to take some of the best photographs ever taken of Shaw, Chesterton, Yeats, George Meredith (despite the latter's resistance to being photographed at all in his old age), Wells and Henry James. James indeed, a notoriously difficult sitter, was so taken by his work that he got him commissioned to make a series of 24 photographic illustrations for the Definitive Edition of his Novels and Tales. The cream of his work at this time was published in two volumes of portraits, *Men of Mark* and *More Men of Mark*, but the contents of these books were only a small part of his vast collection of portraits, many of them never published. In his files are preserved amazingly acute portraits of Stravinsky, Chaliapin, Moiseiwitsch, Matisse, Ezra Pound, Annie Besant, and many others who liked—or at least respected—his view of them, not to mention some, like Yeats, who did not.

EXPERIMENTS IN COLOUR

Even at this period his work was not confined to portraiture; he also experimented with colour in a series of figure compositions, and illustrated several books with landscape photographs. Some of his most impressive landscapes were taken around 1905 of Edinburgh, to appear only in 1954 in an edition of Stevenson's *Picturesque Notes* alongside parts of another series taken as recently as 1950. During the First World War he went off for a while in a different direction; abandoning his early manner, the nearest comparison for which might be the style of some of Brangwyn's etchings, he took up instead his own kind of abstractionism, producing a series of "vortographs" somewhat suggestive of the contemporary vorticist paintings of Wyndham Lewis or such early Epstein sculptures as "The Rock Drill".

In 1923, an artist at the height of his powers, Coburn chose suddenly to retire from the world, though not by any means from photography. He settled in Wales and began to devote most of his spare time to the study of esoteric doctrine—in particular the druids fascinated him, and when he was not learning Welsh and studying the ancient books of Wales or the more dubious writings of Iolo Morganwg (he was later given a bardic title, much to his gratification) he was photographing the remains of prehistoric tombs and stone circles. His *Autobiography*, published just before he died, revealed that his active life as a photographer extended well into the 1960s, and in recent years, after 40 years of seclusion, he had again emerged as a public figure as a result of the Royal Photographic Society's one-man show of his work in 1957 and retrospective exhibitions of his photographs in Reading and New York.

The comment of George Bernard Shaw, made on the occasion of Coburn's first one-man show, also at the Royal Photographic Society, in 1905, still stands: "With the same batch of films, the same lens, the same camera, the same developer, Mr. Coburn can handle you as Bellini handled everybody; as Hals handled everybody; as Gainsborough handled everybody; or as Holbein handled everybody, according to his vision of you." Alvin Langdon Coburn remains one of the few photographers who can thus be spoken of in the same breath as great artists in other media without even the slightest feeling of absurdity or exaggeration.

November 25, 1966.

Sir Sydney Cockerell, who rendered notable service to the fine arts both as Director of the Fitzwilliam Museum from 1908 to 1937 and as an authority on illuminated manuscripts, died on May 1, 1962, at his home at Kew at the age of 94.

Sydney Carlyle Cockerell was the second son of Sydney John Cockerell, of Beckenham, and was born on July 16, 1867. His mother was a daughter of Sir John Bennett, and he was a brother of Mr. Douglas Cockerell, the bookbinder and expert on printing.

He was educated at St. Paul's School, and for some years worked in the coal-merchant's business belonging to his family, which he always regarded as a valuable training in practical affairs. He began his long connexion with artistic matters as secretary of the New Gallery and of the Arts and Crafts Society on its foundation, after which he acted for some years as secretary and assistant to William Morris. On the death of the latter in 1896 he was appointed his literary executor, together with Mr. Emery Walker, to complete the work in progress of the Kelmscott Press. This came to an end in 1898 with Cockerell's own history of the press, the last book printed at Hammersmith Mall.

ARTISTIC DISPLAY

In 1908 he became director of the Fitzwilliam Museum at Cambridge, and in 1910 was elected to an honorary fellowship at Jesus College, where he also acted for a time as bursar. Under his directorship the Fitzwilliam achieved a new standard of artistic museum display and was enormously enriched by gifts, of which the Marlay bequest, entailing the erection of new galleries which were opened in 1924, was the outstanding example. He was an honorary member of the Art Workers Guild and an honorary A.R.I.B.A., as well as a member of the Roxburghe Club. In 1936 Cockerell was appointed London adviser to the Felton Bequest to the National Art Gallery of Victoria, New South Wales, which post he held for the ensuing three years. He was best known as an authority on illuminated manuscripts and published several scholarly works, of which the chief that need be mentioned were his monographs on the *Book of Hours* of Yolande of Flanders, the *Psalter and Hours* of Isabelle of France, sister of St. Louis, the *Gorleston Psalter*, and *German Woodcuts of the Fifteenth Century*.

Cockerell, who was a grave, bearded man, was above all a "character". His slightly portentous manner concealed a dry humour, as when it pleased him to call himself a coal merchant, with reference to his occupation from 1889 to 1892. He was extremely successful in attracting gifts and bequests of works of art for his museum and his success gave rise to many, perhaps apocryphal, stories of his methods. Cockerell was literary executor not only of William Morris but also of Wilfrid Scawen Blunt and Thomas Hardy. He was in the habit of writing his diary *ambulando*, in trains, buses, and taxicabs, so that if ever his memoirs are published they should have the interest and value of a contemporary commentary.

MODEST REFUSAL

Knighted in 1934, Cockerell retired from the Fitzwilliam in 1937, and the occasion was marked by many tributes in the press. *The Times* of July 13, 1937, had a leading article inspired by the "unprecedented event" of a refusal by Cockerell of the offer of "a fine work of art" to the Fitzwilliam Museum. It was explained that the friends and supporters of the museum had wished to present to it a portrait of Cockerell in oil, but he declined to sit for such a work, preferring the more modest record of a small portrait drawing. Later in the same year, on October 1, *The Times* published a "turnover" article celebrating the Fitzwilliam's 30 years of progress under Cockerell's direction, and on January 8, 1938, it was announced that £850 had been collected for a portrait drawing of Cockerell by the late Francis Dodd. R. A., and for the travel fund which Cockerell wished to see established for the benefit of the assistants in the Fitzwilliam.

Friends of a Lifetime. Letters to Sydney Carlyle Cockerell, edited by Viola Meynell, was published in 1940. It was reviewed in *The Times Literary Supplement* under the heading "The Friend of Man", that being the name given to Cockerell by Lady Burne Jones a long time ago. Tolstoy, Ruskin, Hardy, Ouida, Octavia Hill and Charlotte Mew were among Cockerell's correspondents, and the book is full of anecdotal interest.

This was followed in 1956 by *The Best of Friends* also edited by Violet Meynell, which reproduced letters from friends who had died since 1940 or who were still alive. They included G. B. S., Sir Alec Guinness, Miss Freya Stark, Mr. Siegfried Sassoon and Mr. T. H. White. A special section of the book commemorates his long friendship with Dame Laurentia McLachlan, Abbess of Stanbrook. At Bernard Shaw's cremation in 1950 Cockerell delivered an address during which he read from *Pilgrim's Progress*, remarking that, years before, Shaw, a great admirer of Bunyan, had persuaded William Morris to publish his work.

UNIQUE COLLECTION

In the last years of his long life he disposed of some of his valuable library. In December, 1956, his unique collection of books from the Kelmscott Press, together with proof copies and a great amount of associated material, made £11,710 at Sotheby's. Four months later 19 medieval and Renaissance manuscripts realized £27,315. In May, 1958, Cockerell gave to the library of the Victoria and Albert Museum 11 volumes of autograph letters relating partly to the William Morris circle and partly to the modern revival of interest in fine handwriting and he followed this in March, 1960, with the gift to the same library of an important group of manuscripts by the calligrapher Edward Johnston (1872-1944).

In his later years, when he was able to get about less freely, he regularly invited selected groups of his literary friends to tea—and on one such occasion he spoke of when he himself had had tea with Robert Browning.

He married in 1907 Florence Kate, daughter of C. T. Kingsford. There were three children of the marriage, a son, Mr. Christopher Cockerell, inventor of the Hovercraft, and two daughters. Lady Cockerell, who was well known in artistic circles as a bookbinder and illuminator, died in 1949.

May 2, 1962.

The Rt. Rev. F. A. Cockin, Bishop of Bristol from 1946 to 1958, died on January 15, 1969 after an attack of bronchitis. He was 80.

Frederick Arthur Cockin, son of C. E. Cockin, was born on July 30, 1888, at Lea, near Gainsborough, and brought up in the Yorkshire countryside. Educated at Marlborough and University College, Oxford, of which he was a scholar, he gained a first class in classical moderations and a second class in Literae Humaniores and was awarded a Liddons studentship, graduating in 1911. He then taught for two years at St. Stephen's College, Delhi, before going to Cuddesdon. He was ordained deacon in 1915. In 1917 he became an assistant secretary of the Student Christian Movement, and served it for 12 years at a time when it was at the height of its influence under Canon Tissington Tatlow. These years were to leave their mark on the whole of his future ministry. Here he was in his métier.

With a mind alert to new thought and a life-long enthusiasm for the latest idea and person, "George", as he was known to his friends, was always at his best among students and at conferences, which positively refreshed him.

From 1929 to 1933 he was Canon Missioner and Warden of St. Saviour's, Carshalton, and was then recalled to work among students as vicar of St. Mary's, Oxford, succeeding Canon F. R. Barry, and extending further its influence as a centre of evangelism and a meeting place for both College Chaplains and students of different traditions.

TEACHER AND INTERPRETER

It was as a teacher that he excelled. Though an interpreter rather than an original thinker, he had an almost unique gift of revealing people's minds to themselves and of suggesting to them aspects of the faith which they had overlooked. Already he showed a special aptitude for commending the gospel to those on the fringe or outside the Church, a capacity which was to make him later such an effective broadcaster.

In 1938 he was appointed Canon and Precentor of St. Paul's Cathedral, where he introduced a new pension scheme for the Vicars Choral and took a keen interest in the welfare of the Cathedral staff.

It was now that he made his name as a religious broadcaster, while outside St. Paul's he organized study groups of students and teachers and was already drawing together the principals and others concerned with the Church's Training Colleges. He left St. Paul's as soon as the war was over to become secretary of their newly constituted Council and to plan their rapid expansion and development as a major part of the Church's educational policy.

In 1946 he became Bishop of Bristol. Here he was faced with the task of rebuilding the Church's life in a city which had suffered grievously from bombing, and at the same time of reorganizing parish boundaries (never a popular thing) where Churches had been destroyed or the population shifted, as well as providing spiritual ministrations for the great new housing estates which began to spring up round Bristol, Chippenham and Swindon. This he set about with characteristic tact, energy and thoroughness. A rapid and indefatigable worker himself, he made full use of others. A consummate chairman, by his lucidity of thought and expression, he rarely failed to gain support at a meeting.

TRAINING CLERGY

But teaching was still his favourite work. The annual Clergy School, attended by upwards of a hundred of his clergy, was always for him a highlight of the year, as were also his training weekends for the laity and the regular industrial conferences which he instituted. The selection, ordination and training of his clergy were matters very close to his heart and he was a radical critic of the Church's too frequent failure to relate its ministry to the needs of the day.

Increasingly evangelism became his chief interest. He took a mission for Oxford University in 1950, in which year he was made an Honorary Fellow of his college, and for the University of Bristol in the following year. He took schools of evangelism and encouraged missions throughout the diocese.

More than ever he was in demand as a broadcaster for sixth forms and in Christian forum, and as chairman of the Central Religious Advisory Council of the B.B.C. he exercised considerable influence on its policy. A stalwart champion of the Church of South India, he encouraged inter-Church cooperation no less eagerly at the local level as chairman of the Bristol Council of Christian Churches. Evangelism was to him a world issue, and the diocese was never allowed to forget the world Church and its needs. But the housing estates, with their unshepherded thousands, were his own special concern, and in 1956, as the culmination of a long process of education, he asked for £250,000 to provide churches and halls for them.

APPEAL OF INTEGRITY

Largely as a result of his personal pleading within six months the amount was guaranteed. It was his integrity and good stewardship which appealed to the business world; his fairness and unemotional sincerity to the general public; and his obvious concern for the kingdom of God to his clergy. He was not good at social gatherings and his habit of relapsing into long silent thought when considering a question at times made conversation difficult. He loved his visitors with his mind rather than his heart.

Retirement did not mean for him withdrawal from activity and policy making. Settling down in Marlborough, next to his old school, he took a keen interest and part in its religious teaching. And he broadcast as forcefully as ever. He also rewrote his book *The Holy Spirit and the Church* under the title *God in Action.* This, together with *Does Christianity make Sense*? and *Faith and Work*, a book of sermons, well represents his lucid style of writing and speaking.

In 1920 he married Olive Mary Moberly, who throughout his life was his perfect companion. She died in 1968.

January 17, 1969

Sir John Cockcroft, O.M., K.C.B., C.B.E., F.R.S., Master of Churchill College, Cambridge, and one of the world's leading scientists, was found dead at Master's Lodge at the college on September 18, 1967. He was 70. He had hoped to attend the Liberal Party Conference during the week and earlier he had accepted the party presidency for 1968–69.

He was one of the pioneers of nuclear research in Britain; head of the Atomic Energy Research Establishment at Harwell in the immediate postwar years, he became Member for Scientific Research of the Authority on its formation in 1954 and held this position until 1959 when he was appointed Master of Churchill College, Cambridge, while continuing as a part-time Member of the Authority.

His early creative scientific work on the structure of nuclei gained world renown, while those who worked in the British atomic energy field knew him as the creator of Harwell and as a great scientific leader and administrator.

John Douglas Cockcroft was born in 1897 at Todmorden (later to make him an honorary Freeman), on the west side of the Lancashire-Yorkshire border. His family owned a business. During his boyhood and young manhood the business seems not to have been specially prosperous, and he was brought up frugally. But all his life he kept the modest independence of his origins. He retained a slight, flat Lancashire intonation until he died.

He went to Todmorden Secondary School and displayed very early the astonishing all-round competence which later everyone took for granted. In a completely relaxed fashion he was good at almost everything he turned his hand to, from mathematics to cricket.

ACTIVE SERVICE

He was only 18 when he was caught up in the First World War. He was in Signals, and on active service in France during almost the whole duration. He did not miss any of the great battles from Loos and the Somme to the end of the war, and he did not get a scratch. He used to reflect on this phenomenon with impassive satisfaction.

When the war ended, with the family fortunes still not as comfortable as they became later, he entered Metro-Vic as an apprentice and was sent by the firm to Manchester University to read electrical engineering. He showed such talent that Miles Walker persuaded him—although he was now in his mid-twenties—to go up to St. John's, Cambridge, as an undergraduate. In Cambridge, with the same absence of strain, he distinguished himself at mathematics. In his own view, coping with Part II of the Tripos at a relatively advanced age was the most difficult thing he ever had to do, and of all the people who influenced his life, Rutherford included, he felt the most intimate debt to Cunningham, his mathematics teacher at St. John's. This seemed a very odd view to those who had not been taught by Cunningham, but he always insisted upon it. It is interesting that one of the greatest physicists of his time should never have taken an academic course in physics in his life. In fact, his first impact on the Cavendish was partly because he brought certain technical skills which were not possessed by physicists of Rutherford's generation nor by most of Rutherford's pupils.

RARE MATHEMATICIAN

Along with Kapitza, Cockcroft was the only member of the Cavendish in the twenties with serious engineering training. In addition he was, what was also rare, a mathematician of considerable technical power. The combination made him an invaluable addition, especially as with his relaxed, friendly, unassertive temperament he was prepared to help anyone about anything. His own personal researches, productive as they were, took up only a fraction of his time. As for the rest, he would go off, never tired, always willing, to help Kapitza with some mathematical calculations, or to design a piece of apparatus for someone who had never seen an engineering drawing—or, a little later, when he was already an international figure, to perform the useful but scarcely exciting tasks of the Steward of St. John's, such as supervising the painting of the main gate.

To his friends in the late twenties he seemed too unobtrusive and too good-natured to be true. It sometimes seemed at that time that he lacked the obsessive drive of the best of his contemporaries. He was wrapped up in his family life, and suffered a deep sorrow with the death of a beloved child. Yet in 1932 he produced one of the most dramatic discoveries of that dramatic age of physics, when he and E. T. S. Walton demonstrated that accelerated protons were able to split atomic nuclei. Cockcroft had been quietly thinking of this possibility for years. He brought to bear all his unique range of skills to design the experiment, which was a triumph of technical power outside the range of any of his colleagues. It was for this work that Cockcroft, together with Walton, was awarded the Nobel Prize for Physics in 1951.

In an address, called "Some Personal Recollections", which he gave at Rice University, Houston, Texas, in 1963. Cockcroft said: "I started work as a student in the Cavendish Laboratory in 1922 towards the end of what might be described by the irreverent as the Old Stone Age of nuclear physics".

HEAVY WATER DEAL

The atmosphere of nuclear research in the days before it became "big business" was evoked characteristically in his anecdote of a visit which he paid to the United States in 1933:—

"A letter from Oliphant asked me whilst in Berkeley to purchase or steal a gallon or so of heavy water, since it was needed desperately for dozens of experiments. He added kindly that Rutherford would willingly spend some money on it. So I collected about a gallon of 2 per cent D_2O and paid G. N. Lewis $10 for it. After passing through the Customs with difficulty, since they did not understand why I should be importing a liquid which looked very like water, I presented the heavy water and the bill personally to Rutherford, only to find that he considered the price to be too high and I should have asked his authority for purchasing it."

He was a Fellow of his old college from 1928 to 1946 and later an honorary Fellow, and 1939 to 1946 Jacksonian Professor of Natural Philosophy.

In the late thirties he was one of the first scientists brought into the secrets of what was then called R.D.F., later called radar. He played an important part in the installation of the first radar chain, and it was he who approached so many of the Cavendish scientists just before the war to ask them to work for it. He acted as Tizard's second in command on the famous visit to America in 1940, which brought American scientists into the war long before their Government. From 1941 to 1944 he was Chief Superintendent, Air Defence Research and Development Establishment, Ministry of Supply. The next major contribution, which was to determine much of the rest of his technical life, was as head of the Atomic Energy Commission, National Research Council of Canada.

In this post, and in the similar one at Harwell which he held from 1946 to 1958, he was at his best; experienced, wise, familiar with every scientific detail, devoted to the young scientists round him. Those who worked for him at that time found him a most inspiring director. One of his staff records that if he came to him with an idea, he was really keen to understand it and they would end up by working it all out on the blackboard. Only at the end of the discussion would Cockcroft say that he felt there might be neither staff nor money to implement it.

His taciturnity had begun to leave him by this point, although never in his life did he become fond of argument. Soon he was established as the father-figure of the English nuclear scientists, and became respected and loved both in his own country and all over the world.

He was knighted in 1948 and created K.C.B. in 1953; in 1957 the O.M. was conferred upon him. He had over 20 honorary degrees. In his modest, cheerful fashion he did not pretend not to like the honours that gathered round him, just as he did not pretend not to like international reclame and international travel, for which he developed what his friends thought a slightly excessive passion. All his medals and ribbons were on display in his house and this was a rather lovable characteristic of him. His little black book which he manipulated with one hand and in which he took notes of anything relevant said to him gave his friends the impression, always justified, that he listened to what they said and would help them if he could.

He had a most active and strenuous period in the early and middle 1950s, both as chairman of the Defence Research Policy Committee and as a member of the Atomic Energy Authority at the time it was determining its major policy, in which he played a leading part. He was a strong advocate of this country playing a major role in high energy nuclear physics, and took a leading part in the formation of the National Institute for Research in Nuclear Science. As usual, he brought his great gifts to bear on everything he was asked to touch. Though he enjoyed power for most respectable reasons, namely to get projects going in which he believed, he was not fond of, nor specially good at, the infighting of the high official life and it was with joy that he accepted the first Mastership of Churchill College.

His last days were singularly benign and happy. He had always loved Cambridge, he loved the young, he loved surrounding himself with clever men, and it was through him far more than through anyone else that the first Fellows of Churchill contained so much high talent. He threw himself with enthusiasm into everything the college did, cheering the boats, entertaining the undergraduates, dining with the Fellows, and was a most popular Master. He was naturally the most tolerant of men, and would put up with any displays of oddity provided there was ability behind it. He was a fine scientist, one of the most reliable and upright human beings of his time, and a man of absolute good will. As a friend, he was like a rock.

He was president of the British Association in 1962, and Chancellor of the Australian National University, Canberra, from 1961 to 1965. Since 1961 he had been president of the Manchester College of Science and Technology. He was elected president of the Pugwash conference on science and world affairs last week.

He married in 1925 E. Elizabeth Crabtree by whom he had one son and four daughters.

September 19, 1967.

Jean Cocteau died on October 11, 1963. Few figures have been so prominent for so long in French intellectual life. Or, indeed, prominent in so many spheres: as a poet, novelist, dramatist, film-maker, critic, designer—as almost anything one cares to think of connected with the arts. Regarded by many—and himself rather enjoying the reputation—as a perennial *enfant terrible*, he never ceased to surprise and startle, to undertake new tasks, to turn old conventions to new uses.

In many ways his own versatility worked against him; jack of all trades, he was most frequently castigated by critics for not really going deeply enough into any one of them, for being a "brilliant" writer, director, and designer when with more concentration he might have achieved real greatness as one or another. How much truth there is in this view time alone will tell, though even at this point of time it seems certain that he was at the least a "great" film-maker. But meanwhile his astonishingly varied gifts and the large number of substantial works in several media which he produced along with many obvious ephemera are hardly to be questioned, nor indeed is his position as a unique phenomenon of the twentieth-century artistic scene.

Jean Cocteau was born at Maisons-Lafitte, near Paris, on July 5, 1889. His father, Georges Cocteau, was a lawyer. His mother had been Mlle. Lecomte. They lived in the centre of Paris, and sent their son as a day boy to the Lycée Condorcet, close to the St. Lazare Station. It was, however, in the home that he received most of his early education as distinct from his schooling. His mother entertained, and so did his grandmother. Both liked artists, writers, and actors. From the moment Cocteau was old enough to appear in their drawing rooms—and he seems to have become old enough while still very young indeed—he met notabilities. In this hothouse atmosphere, as it may be termed in no pejorative sense, he turned into something of a prodigy. At an almost tender age he was composing verse. A first volume, *La Lampe d'Aladin*, appeared over his name while he was only 16, and he had published six volumes of poems by the time he was 30. The actor De Max—who was Mark Antony in Antoine's memorable production of *Julius Caesar*—liked the vivacious and obviously talented youth, and arranged that he should give a recital of his poems in the Fémina Theatre in Paris before he was 20. Then, soon, a more decisive influence appeared.

FRIEND OF DIAGHILEV

The Russian Ballet became the rage in the French capital, and Cocteau formed an enthusiastic friendship with Diaghilev. One night in 1912 they were crossing the Place de la Concorde with Nijinsky slightly ahead when Cocteau asked Diaghilev to tell him frankly if he considered him to be a poet. The reply made a deep impression. "Astonish me", Diaghilev said. "I shall wait till you astonish me." It was from the moment in which he heard these words that Cocteau liked to date his taking himself seriously as a writer. From that moment certainly he seems to have striven to astonish. The titles of many of his pieces of writing are enough to indicate this. If *Le Grand Écart* (1923) and *Le Coq et l'Arlequin* (1918) are reminiscent of the ballet, the titles of the plays, *Les Mariés de la Tour Eiffel* (1912) and *Les Parents terribles* (1938), and still other titles, *Vocabulaire, Le Potomak* (1919), *La Fin de Potomak* (1940), *Le Secret Professionnel, Portraits-Souvenir, L'Ange Heurtebise, Le Cap de Bonne Espérance, Le Livre Blanc, Discours du Grand Sommeil,* and *La Noce Massacrée,* all hold the promise of paradox, and invariably the promise is fulfilled.

Cocteau, nevertheless, was a good deal more than a dancer in words. Alike in his life and in his writings, he typified the smart Paris of the 20 years—1919 to 1939—which bridged the interval between the two wars. He himself shared its cosmopolitanism, its versatility, its absence of faith, its exhibitionism, its liking for opium, its insatiable eagerness for excitation and for the exotically novel in art; and all this he somehow transmuted into literature. He made fashions, not in clothes but in amusement.

OPIUM TALES

The title of a play of his, *Le Boeuf sur le Toit*, was taken over by a night club, which enjoyed so tremendous a vogue that a chronicle of the period has utilized the date of its opening as a starting point. His opium-smoking, legal offence though it was, it is impossible to ignore discreetly, for he boldly wrote about it, as he frankly paraded other vices. He claimed indeed to write in a state of semi-torpor, thereby achieving the extreme modishness of being on the margin of surrealism. Actually he worked a good deal harder than his claim would imply.

Following his efforts of early boyhood, he discovered Rimbaud and learnt to appreciate Guillaume Apollinaire and Max Jacob. He cast his net still wider. For *Le Potomak* he sought his models, he said, in the music of Satie and in the painting of Picasso. At all events it was in *Le Potomak* that he first struck upon his own proper and congenial line. Thenceforward his verse was to abound in internal rhymes, subtle plays on words, private allusions, and in all his writing the paradoxes were to coruscate like fireworks. He wrote not only poems and plays but also novels and critical essays (one was devoted to Picasso), and in 1930 he turned to a new medium for him, the cinema, writing and directing what he described with a touch of perversity as an "antisurrealist" fantasy, *Le sang d'un poète*. He also dabbled in the ballet and drew illustrations for his own and other people's books.

ENORMOUS OUTPUT

Whatever he did he insisted on regarding as poetry—hence the various labels of his works as "poésie critique", "poésie du théâtre" and even "poésie du roman". Poetry as it is more usually understood continued, however, to be a major pre-occupation throughout his career, and if in the opinion of some French critics his early volume *Plain-Chant* still stands as his first achievement in verse, others prefer the greater complexity of *L'Ange Heurtebise* (1925), *Léone* (1945), *La Crucifixion* (1947), or *Paraprosodies* (1958). His output in practically every artistic medium was enormous, to a degree which becomes self-defeating: many works, interesting enough in themselves, are likely just to get lost in the crush. It seems likely, though, that at least two of his novels, *Thomas l'Imposteur* and *Les Enfants terribles,* will continue to be read, and virtually certain that, even if his earlier plays have mostly proved ephemeral, a number of his mature dramatic works will continue to be revived from time to time.

The sheer variety of his plays alone is daunting, though these are transfigured boulevard melodramas like *Les Parents terribles* and *La Machine à écrire*; mythological tragedies like *Orphée* and *La Machine infernale*, in which classical legend is firmly bent to the uses of private fantasy; romantic costume drama in the style of a twentieth-century Victor Hugo, like *L'Aigle à deux têtes*; numerous one-act plays, among them the famous monodrama *La Voix humaine*; and such unclassifiable works as the ambitious "opéra parlé" in classical couplets *Renaud et Armide* and the Arthurian tragicomedy *Les Chevaliers de la Table Ronde*. Which of these will survive it is impossible to say, but all are, one way or another, impregnated by and draw life from their author's extraordinary personality.

MAGICIAN IMAGE

Cocteau had always been drawn to the image of the artist as magician, and it was perhaps inevitable that *Le Sang d'un poète* should not remain his only flirtation with the cinema, that magician's medium *par excellence*. During the war years he began to dabble in films again, at first tentatively, by scripting three films for other directors, two of them, Serge de Poligny's *Le Baron fantôme* and Robert Bresson's *Les Dames du Bois de Boulogne*, adaptations from given material, and the third, *L'Éternel retour*, an original and highly characteristic screen-play offering a modern variation on the Tristram and Iseult story. Though this was directed by Jean Delannoy, Cocteau's designing hand was clearly visible in it, and having held as it were a watching brief on this film he launched in 1945 on a film for which he was solely responsible as writer and director, *La Belle et la bête*. This, in spite of its nominally happy ending, captured to perfection, like his contemporary ballet *Le Jeune Homme et la Mort*, the romantic fatalism of the just postwar years, and remains visually one of the most beautiful films ever made.

He followed it with film versions of his own plays *L'Aigle à deux têtes* and *Les Parents terribles*—the second a work of extraordinary concentrated power and an object-lesson in the art of transforming theatre into cinema—then in 1949 came his cinematic masterpiece *Orphée*. A film of magisterial confidence and controlled virtuosity, *Orphée* used all the resources of the modern cinema to give definitive dramatic form to Cocteau's major obsession throughout his career: the inextricability of romantic love and death, represented in this case by the relationship between a poet who has lost his inspiration (Jean Marais) and a mysterious princess who represents his own personal death (Maria Casarès). Cocteau announced that *Orphée* was to be his last film, and broke the resolution 10 years later only for a playfully ironic after-thought, *Le Testament d'Orphée*, in which he himself played the central role.

His other works in the postwar period are too numerous to mention, except perhaps for his "spiritual autobiography" *La Difficulté d'être*, which appeared in 1947, and the products of his recent preoccupation with painting and decoration, among them such notable schemes as the chapel of Saint-Blaise-des-Simples at Milly-la-Forêt and the triptych in the French church in London. In none of his work did he fail to reflect himself, and it is the man, as he was at his apogee, with the mop of black hair, the waspish waist, the leaping step and the wild eyes in the white face, or as the impish prophet of *Le Testament d'Orphée*, and always the incomparable conversationalist, that will be most vividly remembered by all who ever knew him.

He was unmarried; his adopted son, the painter Édouard Dermit, survives him.

October 12, 1963.

Alma Cogan, who died on October 26, 1966, was a singer who, although she was only in her early thirties, followed the tradition of entertainers who never attempted to dim their brightness or to appear—as their latest generation of successors strives to appear—as ordinary as a next door neighbour. With a voice that, together with its much-publicized chuckle, was capable of brassy stridencies more familiar in the United States than in Britain, she not only made the most of her unusual good looks but acted and dressed with the magnificence and confidence of a born star.

Alma Cogan, the daughter of a haberdasher, was born in St. John's Wood and was educated at St. Joseph's Convent, Reading. It was her mother's decision and determination which made her a singer. She appeared as a child in a charity concert at the Palace Theatre, Reading, and when, after her father's death, her mother moved the family to Worthing, she won £5 in a song contest in a Brighton hotel, and, by the time she was 13, she was singing regularly with a Worthing dance band although her own ambition at the time was to be a dress designer; with this in mind she entered an art school.

Her mother's recognition of her gifts, however, won the day. When she was 16, Alma Cogan played in the chorus of *High Button Shoes*, followed that with cabaret at the Cumberland Hotel and began to be known through gramophone records which quickly became popular. It was, however, radio which made her a celebrity even where her singing was unlikely to reach. A part in Mr. Dick Bentley's show *Gently, Bentley*, and then she replaced Miss Joy Nicholls in *Take it from Here*. The show provided her with the opportunity to develop apparently unexpected gifts as a comedienne while she provided a natural and enjoyable contrast with its boisterous masculinity; it was perhaps the most popular radio comedy series of the post-*Itma* period, and it carried the artists who made it to the top of their profession.

Alma Cogan remained where it had placed her. She was said to be the most highly paid of British variety artists and was heard, now only on records, all over Europe. Since early in 1965 she had been in bad health, underwent an operation in March, 1966, and in September was admitted to hospital after abandoning a tour of Sweden which she had just begun.

October 27, 1966.

Lord Cohen of Brighton, chairman and managing director of the Alliance Building Society died in the Royal Marsden Hospital, Chelsea, on October 21, 1966. He was 69.

His death removes from the building society world one of its most colourful and controversial personalities, for it is probably in that connexion that his name was most widely known. But he was prominent and also controversial in the fields of local government and party politics, and, in addition, had wide business interests in this country and in South Africa.

Lewis Coleman Cohen was born on March 28, 1897, at Hastings, the son of Hyam Cohen, a jeweller. He was educated at Hastings and later at Brighton Grammar School, but left at the age of 13½ years to become an articled clerk (at 5s. a week) to a Brighton firm of estate agents, Reason and Tickle. This was his introduction to the world of property.

In 1928 Mr. Reason was killed on safari, Mr. Tickle retired, and Mr. Cohen, as he then was, bought out his employer. His major life's work began in 1928 when he became secretary of the Brighton and Sussex Building Society, a small local concern with assets of only £20,000. Possessed of vision and driving power he realised the potentialities of the future and soon embarked on the policy of expansion which brought the Brighton and Sussex to a national society with assets of almost £200m.—a figure surpassed by only six other societies. In 1945 the society's name was changed to Alliance, as an indication of its aims. From 1933 he had been managing director and in 1959 he became chairman as well. All this was assisted by his flair for publicity for his society but which drew a good deal of limelight on himself.

The fact that he was never a member of the council of the Building Societies' Association gave him a degree of independence of which he took full advantage—to the occasional embarrassment of his more orthodox colleagues. But he was never vindictive and was frank and ready to admit a mistake.

Cohen held strong individual views on the financing of homes. In April, 1964, at the annual meeting of the Alliance, he suggested that an arrangement might be made whereby legal costs could be added to a house buyer's mortgage and the repayment spread over the term of the mortgage. A year later he spoke of the idea of Government money being channelled to building societies at times of shortage, and in July this year criticized the size of the reserves held by building societies against losses through default. Far too much money was tied up in this way, he said.

He was elected to Brighton Town Council in 1930 and in 1956–57 was mayor. He was elected an alderman in 1964. As mayor he was active and successful in many directions and also achieved a private ambition by driving "Genevieve" in the veteran car rally of his mayoral year.

LIFE PEER

His membership of the Labour Party dated from 1914 and was firm and uncompromising. He carried his convictions (though not always his colleagues) into local government and though he sought election to parliament on several occasions, this ambition eluded him. In 1965 he was created a life peer. His advice was sought on various occasions by the government which appointed him Chairman of the Agrement Board, set up by the Minister of Public Building and Works.

For many years he was chairman of Brighton and Hove Housing Society, which provides homes for old people, and was chairman of the non-profit-making Brighton Theatre Royal Ltd. In 1965 he became a member of the council of Sussex University and chairman of the Buildings Committee.

He married in 1939 Sonya Lawson by whom he had a son and two daughters. The marriage was dissolved and he married secondly in 1961 Renie, widow of Leonard Bodlender.

Cohen was well liked as a man by his colleagues, including nearly all those who disagreed with him. Tall, extrovert, sociable, a good speaker, and talker, with a liking for public occasions, he made an agreeable companion and will be widely missed as an able man with an original mind who brought colour to life with a ready wit devoid of any kind of rancour.

October 22, 1966.

Sir Andrew Cohen, K.C.M.G., K.C.V.O., O.B.E., died on June 17, 1968, at the age of 58. He had been Permanent Secretary to the Ministry of Overseas Development since its creation in October, 1964.

He was previously, from July, 1961, Director-General of the Department of Technical Co-operation, and before that, from the beginning of 1957 until May, 1961, he was permanent United Kingdom representative at the Trusteeship Council of the United Nations. Cohen's earlier career was in the Colonial Office and from 1952 until 1957 he was Governor of Uganda.

CLASSICS STUDY

Andrew Benjamin Cohen was born in October, 1909, the son of Walter Cohen, sometime director of the Economic Board for Palestine, and of his wife, Mattie Cobb, sometime headmistress of Roedean and later principal of Newnham College, Cambridge. He was educated on the classical side of Malvern College, and proceeded to Trinity College, Cambridge.

In 1932 he passed into the Civil Service and was assigned to the department of Inland Revenue. It was the late R. V. Vernon, then serving in the Colonial Office, who suggested to Sir Charles Jeffries, then establishment officer, that it would be a good idea to try to get young Cohen transferred there. The transfer was arranged and Cohen's real career began in 1933.

He went through the usual training, including a spell as Private Secretary to Lord Rugby (then, as Sir John Maffey, Permanent Under-Secretary), and a visit to Central Africa as Secretary to a financial commission. He was selected for a Commonwealth Fund Fellowship to visit America, but his programme was cut short by the outbreak of war in 1939. In 1940 he was seconded to Malta, where he remained until 1943 organizing with great efficiency the supply of food and necessaries to the beleaguered island.

His return to the Colonial Office as head of one of the African departments was an important milestone in his life and indeed in the history of the African colonies. In 1947 he was appointed Assistant Under-Secretary of State in charge of the African Division of the Office. As such he was in a position to wield great influence, and his strong personality, high intellectual ability, and progressive outlook ensured that that influence would be felt, not only on the African territories but in the higher reaches of Whitehall and Westminster.

Many observers have been justly impressed by Cohen's dynamism and administrative efficiency; but his character had many sides and at least as important was his passion for digging out the essential questions of principle on which administrative action should be based and for encouraging the free play of ideas.

The turning point of post-war British Colonial policy is to be found outside Africa. It was the grant of independence to Ceylon in 1948 which made it only a matter of time before the African and other Colonial dependencies would follow the same road. But how much time? Many people regarded the matter as outside the "foreseeable future". Not so Cohen. He realized that the drive for independence was imminent and gave all his energies to helping the African colonies and protectorates to prepare themselves for it, so that, when political advance became inescapable, economic and social advance would not lag too far behind. In pursuing this line, he was fully in accord with the approach of his Secretaries of State, Mr. Creech Jones and, later, Mr. James Griffiths. The latter was so strongly impressed with Cohen's ability and outlook that he decided, in 1951, to transfer him to the field, and recommended his appointment as Governor of Uganda.

At first the new Governor was very successful. Drastic reforms were introduced and swift progress made on both the political and economic fronts. Unhappily his conception of a unitary State of Uganda conflicted with the aspirations of Buganda political leaders, headed by the hereditary Kabaka, for separate independence. A clash of wills developed, as a result of which the British Government, on Cohen's advice, withdrew its recognition of the Kabaka and removed him from the country at the end of 1953.

Cohen came under strong criticism from many quarters for this action, but he continued to serve as Governor and gradually regained much of the confidence he had lost. Reforms went forward, and the wisdom of Cohen's aims was increasingly recognized by the local public. With a change of Colonial Secretaries, it became possible for the Kabaka to return on mutually acceptable conditions, and when Cohen eventually left Uganda in January, 1957, the foundations of future independence were firmly laid.

Cohen's next assignment was the diplomatic post of permanent United Kingdom representative on the Trusteeship Council of the United Nations. Here, as in the Colonial Office and in Africa, his personality made itself powerfully felt, but undoubtedly a better use of his abilities was offered by the creation in 1961 of the new Department of Technical Cooperation to take over most of the non-political functions of the old Colonial Office and to develop the organization of technical and financial assistance to countries in need of it, irrespective of their political status.

Appointed as Director-General of the new Department, Cohen set about organizing it with his customary "whirlwind" enthusiasm, and substantial practical progress was made even during the early years when the arrangements were necessarily make-shift and the staff, gathered from a number of sources, was learning to settle down as a team. It was not until the Department was able to move into its present accommodation in Eland House that it could begin to work out its own tradition and corporate outlook. Transformed into the Ministry of Overseas Development, the new organization rapidly established itself, especially during a partnership between Minister and Permanent Secretary irreverently described as "the Elephant and Castle" phase, as a very efficient and effective machine for carrying out an extremely important aspect of the British Government's overseas policy in the post-colonial period.

A man so "big" in all sense as Andrew Cohen was bound to become a legend. Many years ago a journalist recorded a vision of him rushing down the Colonial Office stairs two or three at a time, with a bundle of files under each arm and his hatbrim held between his teeth. It was his habit to pace the room while dictating, and an endearing recollection is of an occasion when he quite unconsciously strode out of the room whose door had been inadvertently left open, and was last seen disappearing round the corner of a long corridor still talking and followed by an anxious secretary feverishly taking his words down on her pad as she strove to keep up with him.

It is said that on one occasion in Malta, when a delegation had called to complain about the bread, Cohen was found, during the conversation, to have eaten the sample which had been produced as a basis for discussion.

In 1949 he married Mrs. Helen Donington, by whom he had one son. He was a warm and affectionate father to his child and to his three step-children, and an immense favourite with their many friends.

June 19, 1968.

Major Sir Brunel Cohen, K.B.E., treasurer of the British Legion for 23 years and former chairman of Remploy Ltd., an organization which employs disabled people, died at his home in London on May 10, 1965. He was 78.

In 1917, at the age of 30, Cohen was badly wounded at Ypres, and had both legs amputated above the knees. Although he spent most of his adult life in a wheeled chair, he went on to become a Conservative M.P. for 13 years and served on more than 30 Government committees and voluntary bodies concerned with the welfare of ex-servicemen and women and the disabled.

Cohen was born in 1886 a son of Alderman Louis Cohen, one-time Lord Mayor of Liverpool. He was educated at Cheltenham College, and joined the 1st V.B. of the King's Liverpool Regiment in 1906. He was on the Reserve at the outbreak of war and served until wounded in 1917.

He entered Parliament as Conservative M.P. for the Fairfield Division of Liverpool in 1918, retiring in 1931.

He was a member of the original committee which framed the constitution of the British Legion in 1921, and became its first honorary treasurer that year, a post which he held until 1946, with a break from 1930–32 when he was vice-chairman.

He was connected with most of the Legion's activities, and at the time of his death was President of the Legion's village, Preston Hall.

Cohen was a past chairman of the National Advisory Council (Ministry of Labour) on employment of the disabled. In 1955 he became chairman for one year of Remploy Ltd., of which he had been vice-chairman for five years.

After the First World War, Cohen acquired a house at Ypres and presented it to the Legion as a place of rest for ex-servicemen and their families visiting the battlefield. It was named Haig House and opened in 1932.

Despite his disability, Cohen was a keen swimmer. In 1956 he published his autobiography called, characteristically, *Count Your Blessings*. He was knighted in 1943 and made K.B.E., in 1948.

He married in 1914 Vera, daughter of Sir Stuart Samuel, Bart. They had two sons and one daughter, and celebrated their golden wedding last year.

May 12, 1965.

Harriet Cohen, C.B.E., the concert pianist, who died on November 13, 1967, was for more than a quarter of a century one of the most persuasive and accomplished exponents of modern English piano music. She combined an instinctive sympathy with the works of Bax, Vaughan Williams and other English composers of their generation with a serious musicianship which was at home in a wide range of music from Bach to Debussy.

Harriet Cohen studied the piano at the Royal Academy of Music from 1912 to 1917, winning several prizes and scholarships before she moved to the Matthay School becoming, with Dame Myra Hess and Miss Irene Scharrer, one of the outstanding exponents of the then-new method, which she stayed at the Matthay School to teach after 1922. She was already known as a concert pianist in Britain when, in 1924, she played at the Salzburg Festival. From then onward, until 1948, when she seriously injured her right hand, she was frequently heard on the Continent and in the United States as a player of modern English works and of the music of Bach. Many of the English composers whose work she introduced to foreign audiences dedicated music to her. She became particularly associated with the works of Bax and after her injury he wrote and dedicated to her a "Concertino" for left hand and orchestra. The composers for whom she did so much repaid her, in 1932, with *A Bach Book for Harriet Cohen*, a set of transcriptions of music of J. S. Bach by Bantock, Bax, Lord Berners, Sir Arthur Bliss, Bridge, Eugene Goossens, Herbert Howells, Ireland, Constant Lambert, Vaughan Williams, William Walton and W. G. Whittaker. Her dedication to the memory of Bax led her to institute an annual memorial lecture at Cork University.

While Harriet Cohen played the music of Bach with great musicianship, precision, buoyancy and an emotional tact which refused ever to aim at effects outside a true Bach style, her performances of later music, such as the massive concerto of Vaughan Williams or the epic scale Second Sonata which Bax dedicated to her, were remarkable achievements for a pianist whose unusually small hands denied her the normal virtuoso concertos and display pieces; knowing her physical limitations, she based her career on the music which lay within her capacities and on extremely keen musical sensibility.

In her book *Music's Handmaid* which she published in 1936, she described the principles of interpretation which she followed in extremely simple but telling language. In 1938 she was awarded the C.B.E., for "services to British music".

Unusually beautiful in her youth, always striking in appearance and elegant in dress, Harriet Cohen was a personality, a wit and conversationalist whose friends included Shaw, Elgar, Arnold Bennett and Ramsay MacDonald.

SENSE OF DRAMA

She brought to life a sense of drama and excitement which was fed into the rhythmic precision and sense of style which marked her appearances on the concert platform.

The Harriet Cohen International Music Awards, of which Sir Arnold Bax was the founder and first president, were established to encourage performers, composers, and musicologists on a large, cosmopolitan scale.

Miss Cohen received orders from many countries—Belgium, Finland, Brazil, Czechoslovakia, France, Italy, and Spain. She was also a Freeman of the City of London. In the fifties she gave a series of concerts to raise funds for the Africa Bureau. In 1960 she announced that after two operations on her eyes together with the injury to her hands, she was retiring. That year she received an honorary doctorate from the National University of Ireland.

November 14, 1967.

Vice-Admiral Bernard St. George Collard, C.B., D.S.O., died on April 12, 1962, at the age of 86. He was the principal figure in the affair on board the battleship Royal Oak in March, 1928, which led to the most notable courts martial in the Royal Navy for many years.

An officer of proved capacity, with a distinguished record of service, his reputation as a gunnery specialist stood high. He had proved his personal courage both in command of a ship in action and as a young officer by saving life at sea, and he was known for his strength of character. As might be expected, he was also a strict disciplinarian, and when faced with an ugly situation as a lieutenant at Portsmouth Barracks by reason of the conduct of some turbulent stokers, his firmness and fortitude did much to restore order. He was, it is true, convicted of a technical error in ordering one man "on the knee", but service opinion supported his conduct and his subsequent career did not suffer.

The unfortunate imbroglio on board the Royal Oak was altogether different. The incidents there were more of a social and personal character than matters of technical proficiency. Collard, though he tried, could not cultivate cordial relations with the principal officers of his flagship, and complaints which he had a perfect right to make were not received with that spirit of unquestioning loyalty usually associated with the service. The affair was badly handled, and ought never to have been allowed to develop into such serious proportions. Quite apart from the effect upon individuals, it inflicted damage upon the prestige and reputation of the service itself. But for this Collard was not to blame. His conduct throughout was straightforward, frank, and open, and he had many sympathizers among his brother officers at this unhappy termination of his career. He bore the calamity manfully and without complaint. It was but one side of the character of this blunt and outspoken sailor which was shown in the court-martial proceedings.

LIFE SAVING AT SEA

Collard was the third son of the Rev. Canon John Marshall Collard, and was born on February 27, 1876. He was educated at Clifton and entered the Britannia as a naval cadet in July, 1890. He went to sea two years later, and subsequently won the testimonial on vellum of the Royal Humane Society for having, on August 20, 1895, at Aalesund, Norway, jumped overboard to assist in saving a man who had fallen into the sea. He decided to specialize in gunnery, and entered the gunnery school at Whale Island for this purpose in September, 1899.

In November, 1906, his name came prominently before the public in connexion with the disturbances at the Portsmouth Barracks among a number of stokers, certain of whom were tried by court martial and sentenced to terms of penal servitude or imprisonment with hard labour for endeavouring to make or join in a mutinous assembly. Although Collard himself received a technical reproof, the occurrence did not affect his subsequent career. He served afloat in other ships, and when the war broke out held an appointment in the Intelligence

Division at the Admiralty. Early in 1915 he went on active service to the Dardanelles and was commended for service in action.

In January, 1918, he became Deputy Director of the Operations Division of the Naval Staff, and served at the Admiralty for two years. After taking courses for senior officers he was given command, in September, 1921, of the Colossus, the boys' training establishment at Portland, but in the following April returned to the Admiralty as Director of the Gunnery Division, Naval Staff.

Five years later he was selected for the appointment of Rear-Admiral in the First Battle Squadron, Mediterranean Fleet, and took up his command on board the Royal Oak in November, 1927. The Flag Captain and Chief Staff Officer in the vessel was Captain Kenneth G. B. Dewar, C.B.E., and the executive officer of the ship, Commander H. M. Daniel, D.S.O. The relations between the Rear-Admiral and these officers were not happy, and the clash of temperaments unfortunately led to the termination of their service together and of Collard's career.

SERIOUS FOR DISCIPLINE

There was an unpleasant incident concerning a complaint made by Collard about the playing of the ship's band at a dance. Following this Collard remonstrated in connexion with the arrangements made for his disembarkation from the ship on the evening of March 5, and called for a report in writing. In making this Commander Daniel reflected upon what he considered to be the influence of Collard's conduct and manner upon the personnel of the ship. Captain Dewar accepted and forwarded this letter to Collard, who took a serious view of the matter from the standpoint of discipline, and passed on the complaints to the Vice-Admiral and the Commander-in-Chief. It was unfortunate that this took place on the eve of the departure of the Fleet for the annual combined exercises, and the sailing was postponed 15 hours to enable a court of inquiry to be held. On receiving their report the Commander-in-Chief suggested as a compromise that Collard should transfer his flag to the Resolution. For reasons wholly creditable to him, he preferred to leave at once, and was ordered to strike his flag and remain at Malta. The Captain and Commander were also relieved of their positions, sent home and subsequently court-martialled and severely reprimanded.

On April 17, 1928, the First Lord of the Admiralty announced in the House of Commons the decision of the Board after reviewing the proceedings of the courts martial. They were of opinion that the initial blame for what happened rested with Collard, "who dealt with trivial causes for dissatisfaction in a manner unbecoming his position, and showed himself unfit for further high command". The Board decided, with regret, in spite of his good services in the past, to place him on the retired list.

Collard was married, in 1909, to Rosamond, the third daughter of John Frederick Starkey, of Banbury, and had one son and one daughter.

April 13, 1962.

Robert Colquhoun, one of the most distinguished Scottish artists of his generation, died suddenly on September 20, 1962, while still at work on an exhibition of his drawings and monotypes due to open at a London gallery. He was 47.

Colquhoun first achieved prominence in the early 1940s when, with artists like John Minton, John Craxton, Michael Ayrton and Prunella Clough, he seemed representative of a new sensibility in British art very typical of its time. Intense and somewhat strained in manner, it was in intention both humanist and tragic, with strong elements of romantic lyricism. Colquhoun will probably be best remembered for his work of that decade, for after a marked change of style in 1947 he seemed to withdraw into himself and for several years exhibited very little. But a collection of his drawings and monotypes shown in 1957, followed next year by an impressive retrospective exhibition at the Whitechapel Gallery, indicated a renewal of confidence, and at the time of his death he seemed about to establish a new and enhanced reputation.

His theme was essentially the mute and lonely human being. Though individuals rather than generalized types, his subjects, usually women, seemed representative of a world of poverty and resignation, their ravaged faces and twisted hands expressing a mood of compassion or pathos with an occasional hint of more violent emotion. An eloquent, intensely nervous draughtsman, Colquhoun in his paintings evolved a rather mannered personal style which, owing something at first to Wyndham Lewis and afterwards to Jankel Adler, always remained somewhat taut and linear.

Born in Kilmarnock, Ayrshire, in 1914, he was encouraged to draw and paint as a child, and in 1933 won a scholarship to Glasgow School of Art. A travelling scholarship took him to France and Italy in 1938. Invalided out of the army in 1941 he went to London and shared a studio with John Minton and his fellow-student at Glasgow, Robert MacBryde, and in 1943 held his first one-man exhibition at the Lefevre Gallery, where he was to exhibit again in 1944, 1946 and 1947. The 1946 exhibition marked a climax in his career, and included three of his best and best-known paintings—"Woman with leaping cat" (Tate Gallery), "Woman with birdcage" (Bradford Art Gallery) and "Two Scotswomen" (Museum of Modern Art, New York). His work so far had been restrained in hue, with typical warm ambers and greens.

Then in 1947 he developed a more brilliant and formally contrived manner, flatter and more angular in design, with bright and often harsh colour, which may partly have reflected a growing interest in theatrical conventions. In 1951 he designed, with MacBryde, the sets and costumes for Massine's ballet *Donald of the Burthens* at Covent Garden, and in 1953 a production of *King Lear* at Stratford. Recently his work seemed to be reverting to something like his earlier manner, though with a dramatic boldness of expression in the monotypes of figures and animals.

September 21, 1962.

Pierre Comert, who during all but the last few years of its existence was one of the principal pillars of the Secretariat of the League of Nations, and who deserves to be remembered also as the editor in England during the German occupation of France, of the French daily newspaper, *France*, died in Paris in March, 1964.

Like not a few of his eminent French contemporaries in public life, Pierre Comert, born at Montpellier in 1880, was a "Normalien" who had originally made teaching his career. Appointed lecturer at Göttingen University in 1907, he entered journalism in the following year, when he became correspondent of *Le Temps* in Vienna. He stayed there for two years, after which he was transferred to Berlin, remaining there almost until the last moment before the outbreak of war in 1914. He was attached to the press bureau of the French Foreign Office in 1916 and a year later was sent to London as director of the information service of the French Mission. His unfailing tact and good sense in that capacity won for him an unusual degree of trust and the friendship of many British and allied journalists and politicians.

After the armistice he returned to Paris as a senior member of the editorial staff of *Le Temps*. But he did not stay there long. His was one of the first and most obvious names to be considered for the Secretariat at Geneva. As one of the five Directors, and being charged with responsibility for the information section, he headed a talented and expert staff from 1919 until 1933 with striking distinction, and in the result achieved larger and more practical results than is perhaps generally appreciated at the present time. He was unvaryingly alert, understanding and helpful, and exerted a real influence upon events.

When in 1933 the Secretary-General to the League, Sir Eric Drummond (afterwards Lord Perth), resigned, having been appointed British Ambassador in Rome, and was replaced by Avenol, his deputy, objections were raised, more particularly in Berlin, against the occupation of the two most important posts in the world organization by Frenchmen. Comert resigned in favour of his Dutch deputy and was made chief of the press department at the Quai d'Orsay. He held that post until 1938, never at any moment concealing his somewhat "leftish" opinions or his critical attitude towards trends in French political life which he considered dangerous—he was not an "easy" subordinate.

ESCAPE TO BRITAIN

He was then given the post of assistant director of the American section at the Quai d'Orsay. It was in that capacity that he witnessed the disastrous events of the summer of 1940.

With Pétain's assumption of power Comert resigned his office, escaped to London, and there, with the assistance of a number of friends and colleagues, started a daily French journal. Independent in tone, lending firm support to de Gaulle's war effort without endorsing what appeared to be his political creed, contending with inevitable practical difficulties, *France* was a remarkable feat of journalism. It survived the war and, on Comert's return to Paris in 1944, after the liberation, was transformed into a weekly, which bore all the marks of the good Frenchman and good European who was its editor. Its publication, which Comert for some time continued to support at his own expense, came to an end in June, 1948. His difference of opinion with de Gaulle resulted in a number of doors being closed to him in Paris, to which he had come back just when de Gaulle was in power; and, of course, his official life was at an end. In 1949 he joined the staff of *Paris-Match*.

To the end he remained an acute, if sad, observer of the political scene, greatly changed from the world which he had known and liked.

March 17, 1964.

Archie Compston, who died on August 8, 1962 in London at the age of 69, was one of the outstanding British golfers of the years after the 1914 War when the scene was dominated by such great American names as Jones, Hagen and Sarazen.

In such an era it is hardly surprising that he did not win the Open championship but he came close to doing so and carried high, along with Duncan and Mitchell, the hopes of the British public during those lean years.

At Prestwick in 1925 he was tied in second place in the championship after three rounds, but a good final round of 75 left him still one stroke behind the winner, J. Barnes, of America.

LOST LEAD

That was the year in which Macdonald Smith plunged from the lead with a final round of 82, and in 1930 Compston was to do almost exactly the same thing. A third round of 68 at Hoylake that year gave him a lead of one stroke over Jones but he slipped to an 82 and Jones's victory was another step on the way to his "grand slam".

Compston, who was strongly built, had great ability and was a real artist of the game. In spite of his height, which was well over six feet, he had a comparatively neat and orthodox style. He was also a player of great determination who practised hard. Behind a bluff exterior which never gave offence there lay a kind heart, a disposition too gentle perhaps for the very highest competitive level. Hagen once remarked that he was temperamental and he should know, for he was involved with him in one of the most memorable trials of strength in the history of the game.

SUPERB WIN

In 1928 Hagen had won the Open championship twice and the American match-play championship four years in succession, but that year he played Compston in a 72-hole match at Moor Park and was beaten 18 and 17. Compston had practised hard for this match whereas Hagen arrived at the last moment. Going out in 32 Compston was five up at the turn in the first round and never looked back. He played superbly and with a second round of 66 finished the first day's play 14 up. On the following afternoon for perhaps the first and last time in a serious encounter the match ended on the first green. Hagen repaired his reputation by winning the Open that same year—Compston finished third—but the Moor Park victory made a strong impact at a time when British achievement in the championship was at a low ebb.

Compston played four times against America. In the opening match in 1926 he was the only Briton to lose his single and in the following year, when the Ryder Cup was first played for, he was again beaten by W. Melhorn by one hole. Two years later when Britain won at Moortown he beat Sarazen but lost heavily in 1931. He twice won the *News of the World* matchplay championship and in 1930 he won the important Southport tournament. He was born at Penn, Wolverhampton, and was successively engaged at Kidderminster, where he took up his first job at the age of 16, Coventry, North Manchester, and Coombe Hill. Later he left England and settled at the Mid Ocean Country Club, Bermuda.

August 10, 1962.

Professor Arthur Holly Compton, the distinguished American physicist and a Nobel prizewinner, who did pioneer work on the first atomic chain reaction, died in Berkeley, California, on March 15, 1962. He was 69.

Compton is known to all physicists by the effect—which bears his name—concerning the behaviour of an electron struck by radiation, for which in 1927 he was awarded a Nobel Prize (it was shared with C. T. R. Wilson, inventor of the cloud chamber). He was then only 35. For nearly 20 years he was consultant to the General Electric Company of America. Thus it was not surprising that as a leading atomic physicist on good terms with his fellows and a man of considerable industrial experience he should have been closely connected in the first discussions and experimental work on the possible military application of atomic energy.

In 1942 Compton was placed in charge of a scheme based on Chicago, designed to investigate the possibilities of making plutonium, the element used in the first atomic bomb. From this came much—as was seen three years later.

The growth of the whole project, the shifts to which the scientists were put to achieve their ends, the moments of comedy and of hazard were described with admirable clarity in *Atomic Quest* which Compton published in 1956.

ATOMIC PILE

In this personal narrative, as he called it, he tells how it came about that the first atomic pile, due mainly to Fermi, was built in a squash court under the stands of the Stagg Athletic Field in Chicago, although, on account of the possibility of a cataclysmic explosion, caused by unforeseen nuclear processes, it had been planned to do the deed in the Argonne Forest. In the event the first "run" was successful and proved that plutonium could be bred in a controlled manner.

Compton's book gives a graphic account of the stages along the road at the end of which was the nuclear weapon; the bulk production of plutonium at Hanford by Du Pont's; the isolation of the uranium 235 isotopes; and the construction of the bomb at Los Alamos.

Before he was caught up in these significant and sinister concerns, Compton had had a career of great academic distinction.

His father was a professor of philosophy and his mother a doctor of law. His brother was the physicist Karl Taylor Compton.

Born on September 10, 1892, at Wooster, Ohio, and educated at its college, he went to Princeton in 1913, got his M.A. in 1914, his Ph.D. in 1916, served as assistant in physics in 1914–15, and was a Fellow in 1915–16. After two years as a research physicist in the Westinghouse laboratory he went as a National Research Council fellow to Cambridge. Subsequently he held chairs of physics at Washington University, St. Louis—of which he was later Chancellor and Professor of Natural Philosophy—and Chicago.

He was George Eastman visiting professor at Oxford in 1934–35 and at the same time a Fellow of Balliol College. He was awarded the Hughes Medal of the Royal Society in 1940.

March 16, 1962.

Dame Ivy Compton-Burnett, D.B.E., who died on August 27, 1969, had for long been regarded by some critics as one of the foremost figures in English fiction, though she was slow in attaining that prominence. She was 85.

She was an uncompromisingly "high-brow" writer who made no concession to her readers' laziness, who never departed from the novel as a form, and who restricted her own novels to a single subject; life in the closed circles of the family or the school. She never condescended to any form of self-advertisement; her only non-fiction work was her share in *A Conversation* (1945) with her friend Margaret Jourdain about her own writing, and almost her only contact with the wireless was over the broadcasting of this conversation, and of versions of some of her novels.

Though her artistic integrity was as pure as that of Jane Austen she would never have wished to be regarded as an isolated, dedicated writer. "I give very little time to writing", she used to say. And yet almost regularly, every other year, there was a new book: "I'm a biennial", she said. She found time for other things: for flowers, for keeping abreast with contemporary literature, and for her friends. Teatime was her hour, and it was a prolonged hour, for tea went, as in one of her novels, "through all its stages" in her flat in Kensington. For years she had shared it with Margaret Jourdain, the expert on English furniture; during these years, and in the lonely years that followed Miss Jourdain's death in 1951, she enjoyed seeing their literary and artistic friends, and others who belonged to neither of these categories.

She was exquisitely neat and good mannered and her chat was gossipy, cosy and amusing—though sometimes, there were pregnant silences, sharp questions and sibylline utterances. She was intensely interested in the details of other people's lives, and acutely aware of the importance of mohey in them. Her letters, short and rather formally phrased, and written in a hideous and distinctive hand, often surprised and touched the recipient by a few words of piercing intimacy and kindness. Those who loved her —and they were many—must have been stupid or self-satisfied indeed if they were quite without fear of this acute observer, this high-minded judge of human behaviour; but she was as sensitive as she was acute, and her mercy was of the quality required by that Christianity in which she did not believe. Her values were those of an enlightened, nineteenth-century, liberal agnosticism, combined with a refreshing lack of enthusiasm for any kind of "cause": she took little interest in public events except in so far as they affected her friends or herself.

NOVELS OF FAMILY TENSION

She was born at Pinner, Middlesex, on June 5, 1884, the daughter of James Compton-Burnett, a doctor. Her education was classical: "One came between brothers and shared their tutor"; later she took a degree at Holloway College. She began to write with *Dolores* (1911). "One wrote it as a girl" and it is a juvenile and sentimental work in which a daughter's self-sacrifice, in the face of paternal selfishness, is regarded as noble; in the later and mature novels such self-sacrifice would be roundly condemned. Nevertheless, there is already a great precision in phrasing, a happy eye for eccentricity, and a turn for aphorism. She published nothing else until her sketch, *Pastors and Masters* (1925), a short but entirely mature work in which, on a slight plot, she seems to have been trying out an already accomplished hand. There followed a series of novels in which parental tyranny and unhappy families were penetratingly exposed in a dialogue of ever increasing brilliance. In the first four of these, the tense family atmosphere generates crime, and violent happenings continue to occur, though less frequently in her later books. "I think", she said, in the *Conversation*, "there are signs that strange things happen, though they do not emerge. I believe it would go ill with many of us if we were faced with a strong temptation, and I suspect with some of us it does go ill."

In an interview, she once described her books as all "much of a muchness", and they are very alike in theme and range; each, however, has its own special talents. The finely integrated plots of *Men and Wives* (1931), *A House and Its Head* (1935) and *The Present and the Past* (1953) have especially attracted some readers; some most admire the grimness of *A House and Its Head* or of *Daughters and Sons* (1937), others the tenderness of *A Family and A Fortune* (1939)—for she understood the strength of the family no less well than its weakness, and the alliance between members of the same generation is as well analysed as the opposition between the generations. Particular mention must also be made of the wonderful children in *Elders and Betters* (1944), and of the scenes "below stairs" in *Manservant and Maidservant*, her one book to be successful in the United States.

Her work, from the first appreciated by a few discerning admirers, was for many years dismissed by critics and by the general public as the object of a modish cult. The bare, stylized dialogue needs a closer attention than most novel-readers are prepared to give. But the fine comedy and the deep humanity of her books in later years attained a wider recognition, of which the C.B.E., conferred on her in 1951 was an acknowledgement and the degree conferred on her by Leeds University. She was advanced to D.B.E., in 1967.

RADIO SUCCESS

The radio, for which her brilliant dialogue is eminently suited, won Miss Compton-Burnett many more adherents: several of her novels have been adapted for broadcasting, and *A Father and His Fate* (1957), originally written for that medium, was broadcast before publication. *A Heritage and its History* appeared in 1959, *The Mighty and their Fall* in 1961, and *A God and his Gifts* in 1963. In April, 1965, Mr. Julian Mitchell's stage version of *A Heritage and its History* was put on at the Playhouse, Oxford, and in May at the Phoenix Theatre, London.

Her later novels, though their finish is as beautiful as ever, and their aphoristic brilliance is undimmed, show signs of weariness and are unlikely to add to her reputation, though each of them was received with joy by her "inner circle" of readers.

Though she was grateful for the appreciation of dramatized versions of her novels *A Heritage and its History* and *A Family and a Fortune*, many of her closest friends thought this success came to her too late in life to give her much pleasure.

August 28, 1969.

Sir Arthur Comyns Carr, Q.C., who died on April 20, 1965, in London at the age of 82, had a versatile career at the Bar, with occasional diversions into politics and authorship on public affairs. His name should be specially remembered in connexion with the case that led to the final fall of Horatio Bottomley and with trials of war criminals arising out of the Second World War, in which he acted as prosecutor, both in Japan and Germany. He was a former president of the Liberal Party.

Arthur Strettell Comyns Carr was the son of J. W. Comyns Carr, one of the founders and directors of the New Gallery (later a cinema), and writer of much art criticism, and the author of a number of plays. His mother, under her maiden name of Strettell, was a novelist. He was born on September 19, 1882, and educated at Winchester and Trinity College, Oxford. He was called to the Bar by Gray's Inn in 1908, was later elected a Bencher and was Treasurer in 1950. He acquired a good "rough and tumble" practice, both civil and criminal. He was bold and persistent, fearing neither Judges nor eminent opponents, and a good cross-examiner.

Comyns Carr's greatest forensic triumph was the case that led to Bottomley's downfall, which arose out of a charge of criminal libel and attempting to obtain money by menances brought by Bottomley against Bigland, with whom he had financial transactions. It was heard at Bow Street by Sir Chartres Biron, and Comyns Carr appeared for the defence. It is sufficient to say that his cross-examination of Bottomley, in which he showed him up as a deliberate perjurer, completely broke down the charge of attempting to obtain money by menances, and it was dismissed. On the libel charge the magistrate had no option but to commit Bigland for trial, but the prosecution was subsequently withdrawn, and the last chapter in Bottomley's career, concluding with a sentence of seven years' penal servitude, was opened. Comyns Carr was not concerned in the later proceedings. Sir Chartres Biron in his book, *Without Prejudice*, pays a high tribute to Comyns Carr's conduct of the Bow Street proceedings. He took silk in 1924.

RATING SPECIALIST

Thereafter he specialized in the law of rating and local government work, about which he had learnt much in the course of his political excursions, and he appeared in a number of important rating appeals. After the Second World War he was in charge of the prosecution of war criminals in Japan, which occupied several months, and he also prosecuted in Germany Field Marshal Von Manstein, one of the last of the generals to be tried. He was appointed chairman of the Foreign Compensation Commission in 1950.

Comyns Carr was a keen Liberal in politics and had been president of the Liberal Candidates Association and a member of the council of the Policy Committee. After more than one unsuccessful attempt in various constituencies, he was elected for East Islington in 1923. At the general election of 1945 he unsuccessfully contested Shrewsbury, and at a by-election the same year, he stood as a candidate for the City of London, and was defeated by Mr. Ralph Assheton, the Conservative. He was a past president of the Institute of Industrial Administration and president of the Association of Approved Societies. From 1950 to 1958 he was chairman of the Foreign Compensation Commission. In 1930 he produced a pamphlet that attracted attention, entitled *Escape from the Dole*, and he was also part-author of a work on National Insurance, another on mining legislation, and another on Empire and World Currency. He was knighted in 1949.

He married in 1907 Cicely Oriana Raikes, daughter of the late R. R. Bromage, by whom he had three sons. His wife died in 1935.

April 21, 1965.

Maureen Connolly, the former world tennis champion, died in hospital at Dallas, Texas, on June 21, 1969, at the age of 34.

She had suffered from cancer since 1966 and earlier this month had undergone her third operation. By her death lawn tennis loses a great champion.

"Little Mo", as she was widely known, had a remarkable career in championship play that was cut short in tragic fashion with an injury in 1954. At only 16 years of age she won the

American singles title in 1951. This was the start of Miss Connolly's three years' domination of the post-war vintage era of women's tennis which brought together players like Louise Brough, Margaret Du Pont, Doris Hart, and Shirley Fry.

Entering Wimbledon in 1952, Maureen Connolly won the singles at her first attempt. From then on she was almost invincible in championship play. She won the American and Wimbledon titles three times running, the Australian singles in 1953, the French singles in 1953 and 1954. In 1953 she became the first player after Donald Budge to win all the four major singles titles in the same year.

Her rise to the top appeared in Europe to have been meteoric but it was the result of sheer hard work of an intensity that has seldom been equalled in the game. Tony Mottram who first saw "Little Mo" play when she was 14 at the South Orange Club in New Jersey remembers that her game was then already well advanced though it was in no way spectacular. She played steadily from the baseline but in comparison with her forehand and backhand drives her serving and volleying were only moderate. At this stage the quality that made one take notice, however, was her indefatigable appetite and zest for practice.

For several years she was coached by Miss "Teach" Tennant until a widely publicized difference of opinion between them during Wimbledon brought their association to an end. Miss Connolly said at the time: "This one-man task force can have only one commander." This remark underlines the self-confidence that was always clearly to be seen in Miss Connolly's play.

She applied herself with dedicated purpose to improve her game. The strengthening of her forehand drive which had been suspect on her first visit to Wimbledon was her first objective. Later she added spin and power to her service stroke and developed a net game that was effective and free from error.

Her practice sessions were prodigious feats of concentration. On a hot and humid day at Forest Hills she is remembered as having taken on several practice opponents one after the other, reducing them all to a state of exhaustion with a stream of accurate drives and volleys.

With her bounding strides across the court "Little Mo" was often likened to Suzanne Lenglen. Inevitably the question arose as to whether the American girl was the greatest player of all time. There can never be a sure answer to this but after winning her third singles title at Wimbledon in 1954 it was widely felt that Miss Connolly would reign supreme for many years. Then, only a few weeks after her return to the United States, came the riding accident that injured a leg and cruelly ended her playing career.

She married Norman Brinker, who was in the United States Olympic equestrian team. Miss Connolly maintained her interest in tennis as a coach and was back at Wimbledon as a television commentator. She remained active in coaching young players up to her death.

June 23, 1969.

Sir William Neil Connor, "Cassandra" of the *Daily Mirror*, died on April 6, 1967, at the age of 57 at St. Bartholomew's Hospital in London. He joined the *Daily Mirror* in 1935 in the period when it was being transformed from a staid pictorial paper into a radical, rumbustious tabloid.

During the whole of that time—apart from the 4½years he spent in the Army—he wrote his column four, five, or six times a week, interrupting it only to cover in his highly opinionated and vivid style some historic world event—a Nuremberg rally, the test of the British H-bomb near Christmas Island, the trial of Eichmann, the enthronement of Pope John, the funeral of Sir Winston Churchill, the Korean war. Nobody could manage the set piece better.

His pen-name was well chosen for a writer beginning his career in 1935, when every great prophecy of gloom was to come true. Connor's early background only partly explains the man. His high spirits derived from a Scottish mother and an Irish father. He was born on April 26, 1909, at Muswell Hill "exactly", he would say, "where the bricks met the grass." He was neither a happy nor a successful pupil at Board School, prep school, grammar school or the crammers to which his father, an admiralty clerk, sent him in the vain hope that he might become a naval officer. His eyesight was not good enough. His real preparation for his role in life was probably in his 10-year attendance twice each Sunday at a Presbyterian Church where scholarly Scottish ministers wrestled with the devil; men, as he described them, as full of scholarship as they were empty of doubt.

The column he was to write has been described as the "whipping posts, stocks, and ducking stool for jacks-in-office, muddling magistrates, indiscreet politicians and erring judges". It was all those things, but it was principally a pulpit of the old kind, from which the sinners could be denounced and the virtuous praised.

At 17, Connor became a clerk at a London store and drifted into an advertising agency. This constituted his training for journalism. He worked all his life for the *Mirror*, and in spite of his distinguished reporting from abroad, it will be by his column that he will be remembered. Into this he put prodigious effort. He rose early at his home at Fingest near Henley and by the time he reached the office, he had selected his subjects. Five minutes later he circulated his schedule, in order to preempt the best subjects before the editorial and feature writers had even thought of them.

CHESTERBELLOC ERA

Connor never seemed quite to belong to his own generation of journalists. In appearance, particularly when his figure became plump, his hair sparse and his face rubicund, he was of the Chesterbelloc era of Fleet Street. His tastes were of that generation too—a vast appetite for the classics, a passion for scholarly argument and invective at the public house bar, a strange affection for the elaborately contrived anecdote, preferably based on a pun. But in the office he was a man of deep kindliness to whom people went when in trouble for grave and sensitive counsel.

The young Cassandra was a fiercer customer; an early battler against Fascism, early convinced that Hitler was hell-bent on war. The *Mirror*'s criticism of the war effort aroused the wrath of Churchill, and Cassandra, as is seen in the correspondence which passed between the Prime Minister, Winston Churchill, and Cecil King, was at the centre of the storm. Churchill criticized one paragraph of Cassandra's as offensive and untrue. Another paragraph, dealing with a prospective reshuffle showed, he said, that the writer was dominated by malevolence. Cassandra had described it "as a game of musical chairs, played to a funeral march, Ours!"

When King defended Cassandra against the charge of malevolence, he described him as a hard hitting journalist with a vitriolic style".

ROW OVER CARTOON

Later Churchill retaliated that "throwing vitriol is thought to be one of the worst of crimes". He extended his attack to the *Mirror* papers generally and described them as written in a spirit of hatred and malice against the National Government. The row was brought to a head by a cartoon of Zec's based on an increase in the price of petrol. His object was to remind people that petrol cost lives as well as cash and should not be wasted.

The cartoon showed a torpedoed sailor with oil-smeared face lying on a raft in an empty sea. He wrote a caption: "Petrol is dearer now". Cassandra advised: "Bring in the penny rise. It will dramatize the whole thing." The caption became: "The price of petrol has been raised by a penny (*official*)." The Government's interpretation was that the cartoon intended to suggest that the sailor's life had been put at risk to increase the petrol companies' profits.

Churchill ordered an investigation of the *Mirror's* ownership and in the Commons Herbert Morrison threatened to suppress the *Mirror* under Defence Regulation 2 D.

He wrote his last wartime article for the *Mirror* on March 27, 1942, saying that he proposed to see whether the rifle is a better weapon than the printed word. "Mr. Morrison", he concluded, "can have my pen—but not my conscience. Mr. Morrison can have my silence—but not my self respect."

"I campaigned for Churchill", he wrote, "and my support was early and violent. But since he came to power, I have distrusted many of his lieutenants . . . and I have said so with scant respect either for their position or their feelings . . . it has seemed to me that we have never got going in this war . . . our efforts are disastrously below that which we will have to achieve to avoid defeat. Economically, we are trying to temporize with a system that is discredited, outworn and totally inadequate for the emergency. Militarily I feel that our system has not been able to absorb and utilize the gigantic civilian army that is being amassed. The government is extraordinarily sensitive. They are far too glib with the shameful rejoinder that those who do not agree with them are subversive—and even traitors.

Cassandra served in the artillery and was taken out of it to join the staff of the British Army newspapers. He rejoined the *Daily Mirror* in

August, 1946, with the words: "As I was saying when I was interrupted, it is a powerful hard thing to please all the people all the time."

RICHER STYLE

Slowly, in the postwar years, Cassandra's style became richer and mellower. He was in the radical tradition of Cobbett, Hood and Blatchford, with hints of Mencken. When praised he would say "Oh, I am the *Mirror's* fig leaf". But it is going too far to describe him as the conscience of the paper. The editorials too were boldly radical.

Cassandra found his radicalism reflected, though by no means perfectly, in the Labour Party. He always attended the Labour Party's annual conference and delighted in the saltier characters such as Shinwell, Cousins, or Ted Hill, irrespective of their views. What he despised most was humbug; what he loved most was a man with the courage of his convictions. Gaitskell at bay against the Left, Wilson in his early days as Prime Minister facing financial crisis with a majority of three, George Brown always in trouble.

Connor was a deeply spiritual man. He loved his Bible and his hymnal. About his faith he was publicly ambiguous. But he was one of those who shared Arnold's grief at the "melancholy, long, withdrawing roar" of the "sea of faith". Indeed, "Dover Beach" was part of him, as it is of other men of his generation.

Bestowed last year, Connor's knighthood was perhaps an incongruous reward for a life's work of radical protest. But it delighted his colleagues who saw it as an official amend for the events of 1942. He was named Journalist of the Year in 1954. In 1963 he was named descriptive writer of the year when the first Hannen Swaffer awards for journalism were announced. In 1967 he was chosen Columnist of the Decade. He published two books *The English at War* (1940) and *Cassandra's Cats* (1960).

When he first lay ill, he received a long handwritten letter from Mr. Wilson at No. 10 Downing Street, another from Mr. Chaplin and a characteristically opulent gift of flowers from Lady Docker. But he will be mourned too by the millions of his readers and especially those humble individuals whose private cause he championed and for whose rights he fought.

April 7, 1967.

Gary Cooper, who died at his home at Hollywood on May 13, 1961, was one of the few film stars to stay for more than 30 years at the top of the tree.

Frank James Cooper, as he was christened, was born at Helena, Montana, on May 7, 1901, the son of Charles Cooper, who had emigrated to the United States from Bedfordshire and became a judge of the Montana Supreme Court. At the age of nine he was sent to school at Dunstable, Bedfordshire, where his father had been educated, and after four years he returned to finish his education at Grinnell College, Iowa. He began in college drama, and, after working as a stunt-man and extra in films, played a number of small parts, having achieved little success in his chosen job of cartoonist and commercial artist. His first featured role came in a Vilma Banky film, *The Winning of Barbara Worth* (1925), and soon his good looks had made him one of the silent screen's leading romantic heroes in such films as *It* (with Clara Bow), *Beau Sabreur, The Texan* and *The Virginian.* He weathered without difficulty the coming of sound, and soon became associated in the public's mind with the slow-speaking man of action, though from the first he frequently showed himself fully capable of dealing with parts much more complex than the monosyllabic roles popularly assigned to him. Among his most memorable films during the thirties were Sternberg's *Morocco*, with Marlene Dietrich in her first Hollywood role, *A Farewell to Arms,* in which he showed himself the perfect embodiment of the Hemingway hero, Lubitsch's *Design for Living*, and Capra's *Mr. Deeds Goes to Town*, which gave him one of his best-remembered parts as the shy and eccentric social crusader; there were also a number of more conventional action films, such as *Beau Geste* and *The Lives of a Bengal Lancer*.

The early 1940s saw him playing another Capra hero, in *Meet John Doe*, and receiving his first Academy Award, for *Sergeant York* (1941). This helped to silence those critics who persisted in the opinion that he could not act, or at least that his talent extended only to the most elementary of action-roles. In the main, however, the 1940s were a period of consolidation in which he retained his popularity without making any notable new departures: perhaps the only films of the period which need mention are *For Whom the Bell Tolls,* a less happy return to Hemingway, *Unconquered*, a de Mille spectacular, and *The Fountainhead*, King Vidor's interesting version of a novel about an architectural genius with Nietzschean tendencies.

In 1952 he won his second Academy Award for his performance in an unusually intelligent and subtle western, *High Noon*, and began to extend his acting range quite extraordinarily; as well as superior action-films like *Vera Cruz* he appeared in rapid succession in biography (*One Man Mutiny*), sophisticated romantic comedy (*Love in the Afternoon*), comedy-drama (*Friendly Persuasion*), in which he astonished his admirers by playing a Quaker paterfamilias with strong pacifist principles, and emotional drama (*Ten North Frederick*), which produced one of his most delicate and penetrating performances as "a gentleman in an age which has no use for them".

His last films included *The Hanging Tree; They Came to Cordura*; and *The Wreck of the Mary Deare* and *The Naked Edge*, both of which he made in England under the direction of Michael Anderson.

If any one star could be said to sum up in himself the qualities most Americans would expect to see in the ideal American, it would certainly be Gary Cooper. His good looks, "romantic" in his twenties and thirties, "rugged" in his forties, "distinguished" in his fifties, and his air of being deep-thinking, slow-speaking, and, when necessary, quick-acting endeared him to several generations of film-goers as an ideal of American masculinity, an embodiment of the mythical all-American heroes of Hemingway or Capra. As a man of action he was in his element, but his quality of sterling honesty enabled him to play successfully men who thought as well as men who just acted, and while perhaps by nature a little too phlegmatic for high comedy, he had a streak of humorous good nature which stood him in good stead in the more easy-going type of comic role. As an actor he never ceased to learn, to widen his range and to probe more deeply into the characters he portrayed; his command of his craft was so easy and unobtrusive that it often went unnoticed, but any lingering doubts about his acting ability can hardly be sustained after the most cursory glance at a list of his performances. In the naturally shifting and changing realm of screen reputations he was one of the few really perennial stars, and his place will be very difficult to fill.

He married in 1933 Veronica Balfe, who survives him with a daughter of the marriage.

May 15, 1961.

Giles Cooper, O.B.E., who died on December 2, 1966, at the age of 48, was certainly the most prolific, and arguably the most original, dramatist of our mass communications. A thorough craftsman whose adaptations of novels and short stories for television were always precisely balanced between the claims of the original text and the counter claims of the medium he employed, his own work for the stage and the television screen was never less than disturbing and unusual; it was, however, the discipline of radio which stimulated his best writing, and much that he has written in this field may well survive with classic authority.

Giles Cooper was born in Ireland in 1918. Educated at Lancing College and Grenoble University, he was at first destined for the Consular Service. He decided, however, that his future lay in the theatre, and when the Second World War and military service interrupted his career he was a student at the Webber-Douglas School. Seven years mainly spent as an infantry officer in Burma rewarded him with a wealth of experience which coloured (though it is never specifically alluded to) his plays, and he returned to England intending to act rather than to write; his first attempts at authorship were the result of the periods of "resting" which interrupt most actors' work on the stage.

It was the theatre, and the appeal to a present and responsive audience, which meant most to him, and his first work to achieve any success, *Never Get Out!*—it was, incidentally, the first of his plays which he cared to remember—was seen at the Gateway Theatre in 1950; it moved, characteristically, from a world of quite solid factuality into the other world created by the imagination of its two characters. Twelve years, however, passed before he returned to the stage play as his essential medium with *Everything in the Garden*, which won enough success at the Arts Theatre to achieve more than 100 performances when it was transferred to the Duke of York's Theatre. *Out of the Crocodile*, which followed it in 1963, was less bitterly funny but more consistent in its working-out. *The Spies are Singing*, produced in 1966, at Nottingham Playhouse, was like all his work, a play which moved from normality into the private world of its characters, but with insufficient force to convince an audience that its fantasy was inevitable, and only *Happy Families*, which was seen at the Hampstead Theatre Club in May marked an achievement on the stage as definitive as he had made in the fields of radio and television drama, which had occupied him during his absence from the theatre.

Mathray Beacon, *Under the Loofah Tree*, and *The Disagreeable Oyster*, the first of his radio plays to announce the unusual quality of his imagination and the almost devastating certainty of his radio technique, were works which, by accepting the conditions of an unseen theatre of speech, are unthinkable in any other medium. They were followed by a considerable number of plays, all equally telling though some are obviously minor works, in which the radio's ability to leap from objectivity to subjectivity was exploited to the full; some of these, like *Unman, Wittering and Zigo*, *Pig in the Middle* and *Without the Grail*, stood adaptation to television, but with some loss of their original qualities of horror expressed through hilarity. Cooper was not, however, restricted to a limited view of the materials at his disposal when he wrote for radio or for television; *Loop*, seen in 1963, was science-fiction, and *Carried by Storm*, which arrived in 1964, was an incident in the Peninsular War. What, however, stimulated his mind most effectively was the investigation of meanings and motives beneath everyday normalities of action.

Between 1957 and 1964, Cooper wrote some 40 plays for radio or for television as well as providing about 50 television dramatizations. For his work on the B.B.C.s *Maigret* series he received the Guild of Television Producers and Directors' Award in 1961. His work on Evelyn Waugh's trilogy of war novels, *Sword of Honour*, is still to be seen, as is his adaptation of Hugo's *Les Misérables*.

Cooper's world was one in which the sinister and the terrifying hid behind smooth, polished surfaces of action and witty, hilarious dialogue. In *Before the Monday*, the sheer complexity of living edges his characters in suicidal despair. *Unman, Wittering and Zigo* demonstrates the corrupting influence of authority on those who wield it and those who suffer it. More recently, in *The Long House*, Cooper examined our nostalgia for life within a community only to show the community exercising the most corrupt of tyrannies. He did not, however, write directly about the ideas which underlie his plays, for he believed that a play which obviously declares such meanings as those we can deduce from his work is incompletely imagined; his art was oblique, indirect and unfailingly witty. Although he was no more than indirectly concerned with our contemporary anxieties about sex and violence, what he wrote showed an almost frightened apprehension of the modern world and its ailments. He leaves a widow and two sons.

December 5, 1966.

Admiral of the Fleet Lord Cork and Orrery, G.C.B., G.C.V.O., died on April 19, 1967, at the age of 93.

Generally known to the Navy in his younger days as "Ginger" Boyle, the Admiral and his monocle were familiar by sight or reputation to most naval officers of his time.

The Right Hon. Sir William Henry Dudley Boyle, twelfth Earl of Cork and Orrery was born on November 30, 1873, the second son of Colonel Gerard Edmund Boyle.

He entered Britannia as a naval cadet in 1887, and went to sea two years later in the battleship Monarch in the Channel Squadron. In 1890 he moved into the Colossus in the Mediterranean, in which ship he came under the influence of officers of outstanding ability, for of her seven lieutenants six attained flag rank. In 1913 he was promoted to captain and was appointed Naval Attaché in Rome, where he served until after Italy had joined the allies in the 1914–18 War.

In the autumn of 1915, he resumed duty afloat in command of the light cruiser Fox, in which he served two years in the Red Sea and Indian Ocean on escort duty. As senior officer of the Red Sea Patrol he came much into contact with Lawrence of Arabia, who paid handsome tribute to his qualities in *The Seven Pillars of Wisdom*. In November, 1917, he joined the Grand Fleet in the North Sea as Flag Captain in H.M.S. Repulse to Rear-Admiral Sir Henry Oliver, transferring in 1918 to the Lion as commodore, second class, and Chief of Staff to Vice-Admiral Sir W. Pakenham. He was appointed C.B. in 1918.

In December, 1928, he took command of the Reserve Fleet, but four months later was selected as president of the R.N. College at Greenwich, with charge of the War College for senior officers. Promoted to admiral in November, 1932, he hoisted his flag in the following September in H.M.S. Nelson as Commander-in-Chief of the Home Fleet. In 1934 he succeeded his kinsman as Earl of Cork.

When he hauled down his flag in 1935 it seemed improbable that he would be employed again, but on the premature death of Admiral Sir William Fisher in 1937 he was selected to succeed him as Commander-in-Chief at Portsmouth. He held that command for the normal two years, being promoted Admiral of the Fleet in the vacancy which occurred in 1938. From 1936 to 1938 he was First and Principal Naval Aide-de-Camp to the King.

At the outbreak of war in 1939 he was unemployed, but his energy and desire for active service being quite undiminished, he importuned the authorities for employment, and his chance came when it was under consideration to send a force to the assistance of Finland, then under unprovoked attack by Russia. Before that expedition was launched, however, the German attack on Norway had begun, and the amphibious expedition was diverted to the support of the new victim. Lord Cork was sent in command, of the military as well as of the naval force employed, retaining—somewhat to the general surprise—his full substantive rank as Admiral of the Fleet.

Thus he was senior to Admiral Sir Charles Forbes, his C-in-C., Home Fleet, who was charged with the general responsibility for the naval operations off the Norwegian coast. This division of responsibility was scarcely conducive to the efficient conduct of the hastily organized conjunct expedition.

The difficulties of the expedition were increased by an almost total lack of planning preparation or specialized equipment—Lord Cork records in his dispatch, not published until 1947, that "the General (Gen. Mackesy) and myself left the United Kingdom with diametrically opposite views as to what was required", and did not discover the discrepancy until they met in a Norwegian harbour—and, although the German invaders finally were cleared out of the area of Narvik, the whole expedition had to be withdrawn, just when they had achieved the object for which they had been sent, owing to the collapse of France and the resulting general military situation.

In 1941 he was sent, with the late Admiral Sir George Lyon, to Gibraltar, charged with the unpopular task of holding a court of inquiry into the conduct of Vice-Admiral Sir James Somerville, Commanding "Force H", in the course of an operation in which a valuable convoy was safely passed through to Malta in face of an attack by a greatly superior Italian force. In London it was apparently considered that Somerville should not have broken off the action with the enemy in order to safeguard the convoy. An inquiry was ordered before his report had even been received; but Lord Cork's court found and reported that the operation had been ably and gallantly conducted and that the admiral had displayed skill and sound judgment, so that the incident was satisfactorily closed.

He was president of the Shaftesbury Homes and Arethusa Training Ship from 1942 to 1953, and for some years a trustee of the National Maritime Museum, and president of the Royal Naval Fund.

Lord Cork was married in 1902 to Lady Florence Keppel, daughter of the seventh Earl of Albemarle. They had no children, and Lord Cork is succeeded by his nephew, Mr. Patrick Reginald Boyle.

His wife died in 1963.

April 20, 1967.

Alfred Cortot, the French pianist, died at Lausanne on June 15, 1962. He owed the distinction of his playing to the fact that he was much more than a pianist, though it was as a pianist that he was known in Britain. But his contributions to French musical life were various, as conductor, as editor, and as a dynamic force which led him in his early days to found a number of societies for the promotion of certain kinds of music that he had at heart.

Grove's Dictionary describes him as conductor and pianist in that order. For though he first appeared at the turn of the century as an exponent of Beethoven's piano concertos and quickly made a European reputation as a recitalist he was simultaneously acting as assistant to Mottl and Richter at Bayreuth. To him at the age of 24 went the credit of bringing

Götterdämmerung to Paris and of giving notable performances of *Tristan*.

Next he founded a society for the performance of choral music and soon after another for the performance of modern French orchestral works. He also regularly conducted concerts at Lille. Chamber music too came within his enthusiasms for in 1905 he formed a pianoforte trio with Jacques Thibaud and Pau Casals which continued its activities for many years and made some notable gramophone records.

WROTE ON PIANO

He edited an edition of Chopin in four volumes and in the thirties wrote a number of expository and critical books on piano technique and interpretation. Among these publications he issued in 1936 a catalogue of his personal collection of treatises on musical theory from the fifteenth to the eighteenth centuries.

His many sided mind fertilized his piano playing, for to Beethoven he added romantic music, especially Chopin, and modern music. Chopin came to him by a kind of apostolic succession, for his teacher at the Paris Conservatoire had been Descombes, one of Chopin's last disciples. Thus, scholarship, tradition, a catholic taste, and an instinctive rhythm combined to give his playing individual distinction. When he last played in London a year or two after the last war he was received with acclamation in total disregard of some political aspersions.

He was born in Switzerland on September 26, 1877, the son of a French father and a Swiss mother and had his first piano lessons from his sisters. In 1896 he won the *premier prix* at the end of his time at the Conservatoire, of which he subsequently became a professor. In 1918 he founded the École Normale de Musique in Paris and so added teaching to his other interests. He never attempted composition, but was a versatile musician with a great career.

June 16, 1962.

William T. Cosgrave, President of the Executive Council of the Irish Free State from 1922 to 1932, died on November 16, 1965, at his home in Dublin at the age of 85.

An advanced Nationalist from his earliest days he fought in the rising of 1916 and then, devoting himself to politics, became a leader of the extremist movement. On the issue of the Irish Treaty of 1921 he stood with Arthur Griffith for its acceptance, and on Griffith's death, was elected head of the government which established the new regime.

Confronted by the tremendous difficulties and fierce passions of that time he proved himself during the ensuing decade to be a statesman of resource, wisdom, and good-will. In spite of the opposition of a large and formidable section of his fellow-countrymen who regarded him as false to the true nationalist tradition he continued with persistence to seek within the Commonwealth a closer economic relationship with Great Britain. In this, however, he failed to carry his country against the force of de Valera's appeals and personality, and, once defeated, was never again returned to power.

William Thomas Cosgrave was born in Dublin in 1880. He was the son of a licensed trader there, and after education at a neighbouring Christian Brothers' School himself became an assistant in a public house. He took an active part in the formation of the Sinn Fein movement during the early years of the century, and in 1909 was selected as a Sinn Fein candidate for a seat in the Dublin Corporation.

In the rising of 1916 Cosgrave fought under Eamon Ceannt in the South Dublin Union, was taken prisoner and condemned to death, but the sentence was commuted to penal servitude for life. Of this he served one year in Portland prison and was then released under the general amnesty. Back in Ireland he devoted himself to the Sinn Fein movement, and was elected to Parliament by an overwhelming majority at a by-election in Kilkenny City, though as a Sinn Fein he refused to take his seat. Then in 1918 he was returned unopposed for North Kilkenny.

FIRST DAIL

In the following year, when the Sinn Fein members of Parliament formed their first Republican Dail Eireann, Cosgrave became Minister of Local Government and also a hunted man. He was twice imprisoned; but he succeeded nonetheless in formulating a new system on the Sinn Fein model. After the Truce he stood by Arthur Griffith who had succeeded de Valera as leader, and, resuming his old position as Minister for Local Government, faced the bitter animus which the extreme Republicans directed against those of their fellow-countrymen who accepted the Treaty.

When in 1922 the Provisional Parliament, after its confirmation by a general election, met to consider the situation which had arisen owing to the sudden deaths of Griffith and Michael Collins, Cosgrave was chosen to be President of Dail Eireann. He also accepted the portfolio of finance. As President of the Executive Council of the Irish Free State, a title which soon replaced his earlier one, he was in a position of great difficulty. His government consisted of untried men. Militant republicanism was both strong and relentless and, owing to its refusal to sit in the Dail, one-third of the country was virtually disfranchised. The whole country, moreover, was torn by the passions engendered by the civil war. But the people came together behind him, and an increased majority confirmed this.

PERIOD OF PROGRESS

He was assisted and inspired by the late Kevin O'Higgins; together they decided to bring the new Dominion into an intimate relationship with Great Britain and thus to serve the mutual interests of both countries. He became as time went on far less inclined than he had been at first to placate his Republican opponents by anti-British gestures. He continued, however, to insist on Ireland's independent status and at the two Imperial conferences at which the Free State was represented during his presidency its delegates were protagonists of Dominion independence.

The period of the fourth Dail, 1923–27, was one of great progress. The Legislature became efficient and reputable, the mechanism of local government and the judiciary was established. In the country, however, the Republicans having abandoned militancy were carrying on a vigorous propaganda campaign against the government. Cosgrave decided boldly to attack this issue and introduced the Electoral Amendment Bill, under which all candidates for an election were compelled to give a guarantee that they would take their seats. He thus presented de Valera with the alternatives of participation or political extinction. Cosgrave knew that this policy was more likely to help his opponents than himself. But he was satisfied that he would obtain a sufficient majority to carry on and took a risk in what he believed to be the national interest. Shortly before the 1927 election in which he stood for Cork, he predicted that his own party would win by 61 seats. The forecast proved exactly accurate. As a result de Valera decided to treat the oath as an "empty formula" and with his supporters entered the Dail.

Also in 1927 Cosgrave went to Geneva, where he delivered a speech in Irish. The next year he visited the United States and Canada. He was indeed at the height of his prestige; but it was not long before the foundations of his authority began to crumble. De Valera's arguments, pointed by the 1930–31 fall in British prices, exerted an increasing effect. Terrorism raised its head once more, and Cosgrave's measures against it told against him with the result that in 1932 he was defeated and de Valera's party found itself with the assistance of Labour in office.

Cosgrave's qualities were those of a sound and resourceful administrator rather than leader of an opposition. He was up against a man of a far more arresting personality than his own who understood the Irish temperament even more deeply than he. There was another election in 1933 but Cosgrave's "whirlwind" campaign failed to reverse the result.

True to the convictions of his career, Cosgrave continued to plead for a settlement with Great Britain and a relationship with the Commonwealth. With the outbreak of the Second World War, however, the attitude of Eire to the war became the absorbing political interest of her people, and, although all parties were agreed upon neutrality, de Valera, whose steadfastness on points of principle had become a legend, was generally regarded as the obvious and remained the chosen leader. The election of 1943 did reduce his majority, but it in no way brightened the prospects of his chief opponent, who also suffered a considerable loss of seats. Cosgrave, moreover, wearied by his long struggle and deeply disappointed in the hopes he had placed in the Irish people, had begun to show increasing signs of strain. His health began to fail, and in January, 1944, he retired finally from public life.

In 1919 he married Louise, daughter of Alderman Flanagan of Dublin. They had two sons. His wife died in 1959. His elder son, Mr. Liam Cosgrave, became leader of Fine Gael, the main opposition party, in April, 1965.

November 17, 1965.

Marshal Artur da Costa e Silva, former president of Brazil, died on December 17, 1969, at the age of 67. He was appointed president in 1967; in August, 1969, he suffered a stroke and several weeks later his successor was appointed.

Marshal da Costa e Silva, one of the leaders of the military coup which ousted João Goulart, the left-wing president, in 1964, succeeded Marshal Humberto Castelo Branco. Costa e Silva had been Minister of War in the revolutionary government headed by Castelo Branco.

Costa e Silva took a middle-of-the-road position in the Cabinet between hard-line right-wingers and more moderate supporters of Humberto Castelo Branco, and when the two Houses of Congress picked him as Castelo Branco's successor in 1966 he said he intended to govern democratically.

OATH AND PROMISE

After he was sworn in as president, Costa e Silva promised he would not abuse the authoritarian powers at his disposal under a new constitution, which took effect on the day of his inauguration. But in December 1968, after student and worker unrest, and a Congress-baulked bid to prosecute an Opposition deputy for an alleged insult to the armed forces, Costa e Silva dissolved Congress and assumed sweeping personal powers. Opposition deputies and left-wing journalists were arrested and some were deprived of their political rights for ten years.

Costa e Silva was once described as a "taciturn, hard-bitten, somewhat sinister-looking officer of the old school." A one-time tank commander in Italy, he used to wear dark glasses and kept aloof from the public. He played a large role in the army coup, and believed that to take care of the country is the natural function of the army.

HOST TO QUEEN

In 1968 Costa e Silva was host to the Queen during her visit to Brazil—part of the tour of South America. He spent some £2m. on two luxury B.A.C. One-Eleven jet aircraft to speed the Queen and Prince Philip round Brazil during their ten-day visit. He himself was in Britain in 1966 as Minister of War, when he met Denis Healey, the Defence Minister.

Costa e Silva was born in Rio Grande do Sul; he rose from rough and tumble beginnings to graduate from the Brazilian Military Academy in 1921. He and Castelo Branco were in the same class and were friends ever since. As a young officer, Costa e Silva took part in the suppression of the Paulista revolts in 1926, 1927 and 1932; studied at the United States Armor School at Fort Knox, Kentucky; during the Second World War served with distinction in Italy; became military attaché in Argentina after the war; did a good deal of teaching; and eventually was named commander of one of the four regional commands in the Brazilian Army (1956–58). But Goulart relieved him of this post, presumably because he would not yield to local left-wing pressure, and put him on the shelf in the war ministry.

December 18, 1969.

Sir Richard Costain, C.B.E., F.I.O.B., chairman of the Costain group of companies, died at his home at Farnham, Surrey, on March 26, 1966. He was 63.

Richard Rylandes Costain was born at Crosby, Liverpool on November 20, 1902, and educated at Rydal School and Merchant Taylors. He then trained as a building craftsman, working as a joiner and a bricklayer, and doing a course of architecture in Rome. In 1920 he joined the family firm founded by his grandfather and he became joint managing director of the group in 1927. He became chairman in 1946.

Despite the responsibility of handling the group's affairs, Costain still found time for service to the public interest and the contracting industry. Since 1950 he had been chairman of the Harlow Development Corporation and in that year he was president of the London Master Builders Association.

In 1937 the company built Dolphin Square on the Embankment, at that time the largest block of flats in Europe, and later to become Costain's home. In 1958 he sold the block for £2,500,000 to Mr. Maxwell Joseph.

It was always Sir Richard's aim to have half the company's turnover overseas. Currently the group is undertaking work in Africa, Pakistan, South America, Australia, New Zealand, Canada and Europe.

Costain was chairman of the Export Group for Constructional Industries from 1955 to 1957. He was knighted in 1954.

During the Second World War he served in the Ministry of Works, first as Deputy Director of Emergency Works and then as Deputy Director of Works. His firm was engaged in building airfields, munition factories, and Mulberry Harbour. Later his firm was responsible for building of the river wall on the South Bank of the Thames between County Hall and Waterloo Bridge, the "Dome of Discovery" for the 1951 Festival of Britain, and new government offices in Whitehall.

Costain's outstanding qualities of courage, determination, dynamism and vision were in inverse proportion to his physical size.

He was a forthright, friendly, helpful, and humorous competitor, who was incapable of any smallness, meanness or lasting anger. There was never any doubt about his reaction to a situation or proposal; people never had long to wait for a decision, and it was always positive.

BUSINESS LEADER

From a business point of view, decisiveness and leadership were perhaps his most outstanding assets.

He entered the export market early in his career during the depression. In the prewar era he successfully carried out several major civil engineering contracts under extremely difficult physical conditions in countries where the risks were much higher than normal. The only "guarantees" he had were embraced in the ability of his team and his own personal ability and judgment.

After the war, recognizing the vital necessity for Britain to materially expand her export markets, he tackled overseas construction with renewed vigour. He set up subsidiary firms and branches overseas in strategic areas and concentrated on those fields of construction where he felt his company and Britain were most likely to be at their competitive best. He travelled extensively, for he believed there was no substitution for personal knowledge and his personally knowing the client as well as he knew his own team.

However, he did not in any way neglect the home market, as is especially well known by his competitors. With his lively imaginative mind he made a considerable contribution to improving methods and organization in the construction industry at home and had many progressive "firsts" to his credit.

He freely gave of his time to many public offices. One of his greatest pleasures was in Harlow New Town, of which he was a chairman and of which he was more than justifiably proud.

He married, and had one son and two daughters.

March 28, 1966.

Billy Cotton, who died on March 25, 1969, was the last great exponent of the big-band comedy show which reached the height of its popularity in the 1930s. Having hit on the formula at that time, he continued in it throughout his career, on stage, on radio and on television, and remained a general favourite when many other, perhaps in their day more notable, bands fell by the wayside.

Born in Westminster on May 6, 1899, he took his first important step as a musician when he joined the Royal Fusiliers as a drummer at the age of 15, and saw service with them in the Dardanelles. Subsequently, by lying about his age, he joined the Royal Flying Corps, and was commissioned before returning to civilian life.

Here one job seemed obviously open to him, and in spite of his flirtations with boxing, football and motor racing, he settled rapidly as a drummer in a dance band. In this capacity he made his first broadcast in 1924, from the Wembley Exhibition; by 1928 he was to be heard on radio as the leader of his own band. Success came rapidly, and by the early 1930s he was top of the bill at Ciro's Club, the Alhambra, Leicester Square, and elsewhere throughout the country.

His band specialized in comedy songs and sketches, and were regular broadcasters throughout the war and after, when one of radio's most familiar sounds was his opening cry of "Wakey-wakey" and his signature tune "Somebody stole my gal". In 1956 he branched out into television with The Billy Cotton Band Show, and later, Wakey-Wakey Tavern. The show remained for more than seven years one of the most reliable popular draws on B.B.C. Television, with a weekly viewing figure of between 15 and 16 million, and in spite of its air of easy spontaneity was planned down to the last detail with all the old-time professionalism he acquired in his years in the theatre. He remained a theatre man at heart, at his best with a live audience, and his ability to gauge such an audience's tastes and requirements was probably the greatest single factor in his real and lasting popularity.

Asked once why he did not change his style, Cotton replied "Why change? Quite a few million people seem to like us as we are."

During his many engagements both at dance halls and for the B.B.C. he found time to indulge in his love of speed on many of the motor racing circuits. He was a familiar figure at the old Brooklands track. It was a sport he did not give up until he was 50, when he came sixth in the British Grand Prix at Silverstone.

At the age of 64 he was taken seriously ill and was off work for three months. Asked why he made his comeback, he said that he had many responsibilities, including the major one of not breaking up his band. Some of his "boys" had been with him for 30 years, Taking it easy for him meant selling his Jaguar sports car and buying a Rolls.

Shortly before his illness he was named show business personality of 1962, by the Variety Club of Great Britain. He had also made several appearances at royal command performances.

His last series was Billy Cotton's Music Hall from May to July, 1968, and his last appearance on B.B.C. Television was in *Cilla* on December 31.

There was to have been a new series for him in the spring.

Mr. Cotton was married and had two sons.

March 26, 1969.

Jack Cotton, who died at Nassau on March 21, 1964, at the age of 61, was one of the great property entrepreneurs of his generation.

From small beginnings he built up the powerful City Centre Properties group after the war, having acquired control of that company in 1947. The crowning glory to the rapid expansion of his group came with the announcement in October, 1960, of the merger with his greatest rival, Mr. Charles Clore's City & Central Investments, to form what is claimed to be the largest property complex of its kind in the world. The merging of interests between two strong individualists was not without its difficulties, and eventually led to the sell-out by the Cotton family interests of the bulk of their holdings in City Centre.

In July, 1963, Cotton gave up the chairmanship of City Centre, which he had held since 1958. On medical advice he had been told to give up all business activities for six months. He was subsequently appointed first president of the group. However, less than a month ago he severed all remaining links with the company. He gave up his seat on the board and resigned as president.

Cotton was an expansionist on the large scale. But just as significant as the rapid growth of his company to its mammoth size in less than a decade were his innovations in the area of property finance. Cotton largely pioneered the participation of City institutions, mainly the insurance companies, in the equity shareholding of property development companies. This type of financing has since been widely adopted. He was also the guiding spirit in formulating a policy of joint development with pension funds of leading industrial and trading companies, including many household names like I.C.I., Unilever, A.E.I. and the Church Commissioners. (In the City it was widely believed that this particular policy of expansion led to board room friction.)

At home, the City Centre group has been connected with many major developments including the thwarted Piccadilly Circus development, the Notting Hill Gate and the Top Site development in Birmingham. Abroad, Cotton's most ambitious venture was his company's half-interest in the $100m. Pan-American building, which straddles Grand Central Station in New York, claimed to be the largest office building of its kind.

Cotton was born at Edgbaston, Birmingham, on January 1, 1903. After attending King Edward's School, Birmingham, and Cheltenham College, he was articled to a firm of estate agents and surveyors. His quest for independence was not long delayed. On his twenty-first birthday he rented an office in Birmingham and founded the estate agent firm of Jack Cotton & Partners; he also founded a firm of architects, Cotton, Ballard & Blow, with offices in London, Birmingham, and Newcastle upon Tyne.

Cotton took an active part in the charitable work of Jewish communal life and during the last war went to the United States to help immigration into Palestine as it then was. In 1945 he was one of the delegates representing the British section of the World Jewish Congress at the Emergency War Conference. Among his numerous benefactions were the founding of chairs of: architecture and fine arts at the Hebrew University of Jerusalem; biochemistry at the Royal College of Surgeons; biochemistry at the Weizman Institute, Israel. He was patron of the London Zoological Society and creator of the "Cotton Terraces". Cotton was also a collector of impressionists. He is survived by his widow, three sons and a daughter.

March 23, 1964.

René Coty, seventeenth president of the French Republic, who retired in January, 1959, two years before the end of his septennate, to allow General de Gaulle to assume the presidency, died at Le Havre on November 22, 1962. He was 80.

Coty was completely unknown to the public at large when in the tumultuous and undignified presidential election at Versailles in December, 1953, he was chosen, after six days and 13 ballots, to succeed Vincent Auriol as Head of State. He had held none of the high offices, president of the Senate or of the National Assembly or Prime Minister, which were the traditional and almost essential stepping-stones to the Presidency, and if he had a solid parliamentary reputation, he was, at the age of 71, already in semi-retirement. He had not been a candidate and when on the twelfth ballot, with the election hopelessly deadlocked, a group of right-wing senators suddenly entered his name, it must have been entirely outside his expectations—and rather against his wishes—that he should become President of France.

France was more fortunate than she deserved to be. On the ceremonial and representational side of his duties, and they were important and onerous and, indeed, under the Constitution of the Fourth Republic constituted nine-tenths of a President's role, this courteous, charming and kindly man made an admirable First Citizen of France. But it was on the tightly circumscribed executive side of his position that René Coty was, eventually, able to render his greatest service to his country.

Throughout the four and a half years of his presidency, up till May, 1958, he had watched impotently as the Fourth Republic descended ever deeper into chaos. The Constitution limited his powers to the selection of candidates for the premiership after each succeeding political crisis, and the giving of advice to the political leaders, which might or might not be followed. But each time the choice became more difficult, the crisis longer and more dangerous. Coty, from his early days in Parliament, had been an advocate of the reform of, first, the monarchical Constitution of 1875, and then that of 1946, which he had fought steadfastly in its draft stages, so as to increase governmental stability and the authority of the state. But on being elected President, he had sworn obedience to the Constitution and he intended to respect his oath. By early May, 1958, however, it was apparent that "the system" was "hopelessly blocked" and on May 5 Coty sent his Military Secretary, General Ganeval, in secrecy to General de Gaulle's A. D. C., Colonel de Bonneval, to discover under what conditions General de Gaulle would accept return to office. Although de Gaulle agreed with Coty that the *sine qua non* of his return must be that it took place "in rigorous respect of the Constitution" there seemed insuperable obstacles, of which the most important was the utter unlikelihood of the Assembly voting the General's investiture.

Then, on May 13, the revolution broke out in Algiers. The next day the President, as Commander-in-Chief, broadcast an appeal to the Army "not to add to the country's ordeals" and ordered officers and men to do their duty. The broadcast was unheeded and conditions deteriorated rapidly. In a series of meetings with the political leaders Coty suggested that de Gaulle was the only man to end the crisis, and insinuated that the choice lay between him and that terrible bogy of French politicians, a Popular Front with the communists. As a result of his advocacy several politicians met de Gaulle, but although the General was reassuring and insisted that he would return to power only constitutionally, there was still too large and rigid a parliamentary opposition to him to allow any reasonable chance of his being acceptable to Parliament.

On May 28 Coty received reliable information that a military *coup d'état* would take place within 24 hours. He immediately issued a communiqué to the effect that he had asked the presidents of the Senate and the National Assembly to make contact with the General to examine with him "the conditions in which he would constitute the Government of the Republic". The following day he took the almost unprecedented step of sending a special message to Parliament—an action which had constitutional authority but had been taken only once before. It was the message itself which was unconstitutional, for it was that to save the country from civil war, he had called upon General de Gaulle to set up a Government of National Safety "within the framework of Republican legality" and if de Gaulle were rejected he would have no alternative to handing over his functions. It was Coty's threat—or "blackmail", according to the left wing of the Assembly—that was the decisive factor in the affirmative vote given General de Gaulle.

René Coty was born at Le Havre on March 20, 1882. His father was the proprietor and headmaster of a small private school there, where he was educated before going on to lycée and university at Caen. He took a degree in arts—philosophy—and law, and was called to the bar at Le Havre in 1902. Five years later he married Mlle. Germaine Corblet, daughter of a well-known Normandy shipbuilder, and had two children, both daughters. He became a municipal councillor in 1908, enlisted in 1914 and served throughout the war as a private soldier, winning the Croix de Guerre and the Croix du Combattant Volontaire.

He was elected a councillor-general for the Seine-Inférieure (now Seine-Maritime) in 1919 and became vice-president in 1931. In 1923, at the age of 41, he went into national politics and won the Le Havre seat in a by-election, retaining it until 1935, when he became a Senator. He took no part in politics between 1940 and 1945, was a member of both Constituent Assemblies, was again elected a Deputy in 1945, and held the post of Minister for Reconstruction and Town Planning in three successive governments, from November, 1947, until September, 1948, when he was again elected to the Conseil de la République—as the Senate had been renamed—becoming one of the four vice-presidents.

In politics he was a conservative, a member first of the Gauche Républicain and then after the war, of the Républicains Indépendants, considered then one of the extreme right parties. Coty was, however, always a moderate.

As an advocate René Coty specialized in constitutional law, but although he was recognized as an expert in that field, it is not one, in France anyway, that brings in large financial rewards.

He was immensely helped in his representational duties as President of the Republic by his wife, a large, jolly, delightful woman, loved by everyone who knew her. Her sudden death, two years after he became President, was a loss from which, at first, it seemed he might not recover.

After the approval by referendum of the new Constitution for the Fifth Republic, and the success of the neo-Gaullist U.N.R. in the general election in November, 1958, René Coty, who had still, legally, two more years to serve as President, informed de Gaulle that he would withdraw.

After he left the Elysée Palace he went to live at Le Havre with his daughters and their husbands, and 10 grandchildren.

November 23, 1962.

Piers Courage, the British racing driver, was killed on June 21, 1970. He was 28. One of the undisputed finds of Formula 3 racing in 1965, Piers Courage progressed through Formula 2 into the seat of a Grand Prix 1 machine during the 1967 season.

After winning the Longford, Tasmania, race in March, 1968, Courage drove regularly in Tim Parnell's B.R.M. placing fourth in the Italian Grand Prix and sixth in the French Grand Prix.

In 1969 he remained a leading Formula 1 privateer, driving Frank Williams' racing B.R.M. and placed eighth in the drivers' world championship after scoring stirring second places in the Monaco and United States Grands Prix. He was also a worthy contender in the European Formula 2 championship and won the Mediterranean Grand Prix at Enna.

Born at Colchester on May 27, 1942, the oldest son of Mr. R. H. Courage, the chairman of the wealthy Courage Barclay and Simonds Ltd., brewery chain, Piers became a motor racing enthusiast at Eton.

Courage first raced a Lotus Seven at Brands Hatch in 1962 and then switched to a rear-engined Merlyn sports car for two seasons of national club races. In 1964, he bought a Lotus 31 Formula 3 car, forming the Anglo-Swiss racing team with Jonathan Williams (who himself joined the Ferrari team in 1967).

PLACE ESTABLISHED

Courage gained prominence in 1965 as a member of the Charles Lucas racing team and had been at Eton with Lucas. Driving an F3 Brabham-Cosworth he won at Silverstone (3), Goodwood, Brands Hatch, Caserta, Oulton Park and Rouen and was invariably in the leading bunch in the close skirmishing of international F3 racing.

Before the 1966 European season started, Piers Courage was one of several promising young British drivers invited by five-times world champion Juan Manuel Fangio to compete in the "Temporada" series of Formula 3 races in Argentina in January/February, but crashed in practice for the first race at Buenos Aires with painful burns.

On his return, Courage was married in March, 1966, to Lady Sarah Curzon, daughter of the fifth Lord Howe, the former racing driver.

In 1966, the successful Charles Lucas team was chosen by Colin Chapman to run his F3 cars and became known as the Charles Lucas-Team Lotus.

June 22, 1970.

Edward Gordon Craig, C.H., R.D.I., who died on July 29, 1966 in Vence, was the last Victorian of the English stage and the first prophet of a new order in the theatre, an order still in the making and, some would add, incapable of being made completely in accordance with his ideas. He was 94.

When he ceased acting, for which in the judgment of his mother, Ellen Terry, he had more natural gift than anyone she had known, and began to design scenery, he wanted, to quote words used by him much later, to create a new world on the boards rather than to make an imperfect but historically accurate copy of the real one, as was the standard practice of late Victorian scene painters.

THWARTED GENIUS

According to him this new world was that imagined by the writer of a play, rediscovered and interpreted by the stage director: his project for a setting for Duse's production of *The Lady From the Sea* shows a part of what he meant by this. But according to his detractors Teddy Craig, the spoilt child of artistic Europe, wanted something quite different and when it was withheld from him, sulked, lived on his friends, and made a profession of being a thwarted genius. Craig wanted, said Bernard Shaw, a theatre to play with as Irving played with the Lyceum, in which he could frame his pictures in the proscenium and cut the play to ribbons to suit them. He did not get a theatre to play with: any effort to provide one, such as Tree initiated in 1911, the New York Stage Society shortly afterwards, and C. B. Cochran in 1930, was stillborn.

GAVE ENORMOUSLY

He did not, indeed, get anything, because, when the time came, he would not accept anything; but he gave enormously. His new world remained on paper; in his notebooks, in his woodcuts, and in his words; but these substitutes did his job for him. They opened people's eyes, they gave to readers, theatre-goers, and theatre-workers a new sense of the beauty, the grandeur, the imagination, loftiness of theatrical art. This, not acting or producing, was Craig's life-work, to which he proved to be ready to sacrifice his career, time, money and comfort, and the time, money and comfort of other people. "Genius and service don't go together", he said cheerfully in a broadcast at the age of 88; "Great Britain therefore showed good sense in not trying to make more use of 'my genius'."

The second child of Edward William Godwin, architect, and Ellen Terry, actress, he was born at Stevenage, Hertfordshire, on January 16, 1872, the year in which his friends Max Beerbohm and William Rothenstein were also born. When their parents separated he and his sister Edith remained with their mother. He appeared with her on the stage in 1878 in London and accompanied her and Irving on the latter's second American tour in 1885. In the following year he went to Bradfield College, where he was known by the name of Ellen Terry's second husband, Wardell, and in 1887 he was at school at Heidelberg. In 1888 he was christened, receiving the names of Edward, after his father, Henry after Irving, Gordon after his mother's friend Lady Gordon, and Craig after the island of Ailsa Craig.

WOOD-ENGRAVINGS

In 1889 he became a regular member of Irving's company at the Lyceum, but he decided some nine years later, in spite of his whole-hearted admiration for his chief, that acting was not an art. By then he had married, and, at the village of Denham where they all lived, had come to know William Nicholson and James Pryde. Having learnt from the former how to use a wood engravers' block and tool and print proofs, Craig made in the course of time more than 500 wood-engravings, including a great many designs for scenes and costumes, and landscape headpieces, tailpieces, and other decorations for his published texts. The collection of his proofs in the Victoria and Albert Museum is remarkable for the mingling of black, white and grey, occasioned by his varying the distances between the black lines. Etchings by him are rare, but he brought out two portfolios of work in that medium.

FIRST MAGAZINE

After 1900, a year when his first magazine *The Page* was in production, Craig had, he declared, one main thought, the theatre, and was urged on to produce, design and write by "affection and admiration" for first Irving, secondly, Nicholson, Pryde and Rothenstein, thirdly writers (Wilde, Beerbohm, Shakespeare, Montaigne), fourthly Isadora Duncan, the American-born dancer. His earliest productions, made between 1901 and 1903 in association with Martin Shaw, were of Purcell's *Dido and Aeneas*, and *The Masque of Love*, Handel's *Acis and Galatea* and Laurence Housman's *Bethlehem*, and was followed by those of Ibsen's *The Vikings* and *Much Ado About Nothing* for his mother at the since demolished Imperial Theatre. The last two were considered on the whole disappointing, but his staging of *Venice Preserv'd* in Berlin in 1904 and of *Rosmersholm* for Duse in Florence in 1906, together with the publication of his first and most important book *The Art of the Theatre*, caused a good deal of attention to be paid to him outside England, for instance by Reinhardt and Stanislavsky.

PRODUCER-DESIGNER

In his own view Craig now, in 1906, ceased to be subject to influence in the theatre and began to exert it. He did this partly through his practical work as producer-designer or teacher: in *Hamlet* at the Moscow Art Theatre in 1911; in his School for the Art of the Theatre in the Arena Goldoni in Florence, financed by Lord Howard de Walden, founded in 1913 and closed after the outbreak of World War I; and in Ibsen's *The Pretenders* at the Royal Theatre, Copenhagen, in 1926. But he did it far more... *L'Homme qui n'a rien fait* as his enemies called him, through his activities outside the theatre; through his books, his periodical *The Mask* issued at Florence between 1908 and 1929, his lectures and his broadcasts, with their charm, wit and learning; through his designs, such as those made for an edition of *Hamlet* published at Weimar in 1930 or collected in exhibitions of his graphic work in many countries, and, as he grew old, moving from Rapallo to Saint-German-en-Lave and thence to Vence; through the prestige conferred on him by longevity, by his unquenched gaiety, and by that very independence and refusal to come to terms with life which had once seemed to be his defeat and to presage his undoing.

He inherited from his mother his appearance, his grace of movement, and the Terry voice.

Women loved him throughout his life and he accepted love from many of them; of these Isadora Duncan described her association and artistic partnership with him in her autobiography. His own published works include *Ellen Terry and Her Secret Self* and a book on his old "Master" with a simpler title, *Henry Irving*. He was president of the Mermaid Theatre since 1964. He was appointed C.H. in 1956.

July 30, 1966.

Charles Creed, well-known couturier and a founder member of the Incorporated Society of London Fashion Designers, died suddenly on July 17, 1966. He was 56.

He was one of the very few modern designers to come of a family associated for several generations with high fashion. Creed's grandfather founded the famous house of Creed in the Rue Royale, Paris, where he specialized in making superb tailor-mades and riding habits, and included Queen Victoria among his distinguished international clientele. Creed's father is alleged to have designed the suit Mata Hari was wearing when she was shot.

Creed himself was clearly very strongly influenced in his work both by the emphasis on tailoring in which his family firm specialized and by his favourite hobby—that of collecting toy soldiers in vast quantities and almost invariably of historical interest, many of the Napoleonic period. Over the years those exhibited in his premises at Knightsbridge aroused considerable interest among his clients, who were not surprised to find that uniform details, often just in the cut of a collar or pockets, or the sweep of a jacket skirt, were seldom absent from his collection. His customers included the Duchess of Abercorn and the Duchess of Westminster. He once made a dress for Mrs. Khrushchev.

TRUST IN TAILORING

Creed always kept his late-day and evening dresses to a minimum number, making it clear that, even in these, tailoring was his best medium for expressing his sense of fashion. With his tailoring went a deep appreciation of high quality British woollens and a discerning eye for skilfully blended colours.

Several years ago Creed opened a wholesale fashion house specializing in knitwear. He planned to devote himself to this interest when, a few weeks before he died, he announced that he was closing his couture business and would not be showing an autumn collection. He leaves a widow, who was a former fashion editor of British *Vogue*.

July 19, 1966.

Sir Thomas Creed, K.B.E., M.C., Q.C., Vice-Chancellor of the University of London, 1964–67, and Principal, Queen Mary College, 1952–67, died on May 11, 1969. He was chairman of the Burnham Committee from 1958 to 1965; from 1936 to 1941 he had been Chief Justice of the High Court of Sudan; and from 1941 to 1947 he was legal secretary to the Sudan Government.

It is not perhaps surprising that with two brothers as dons, Creed should have been attracted to the university world when he left Sudan. In 1948 he was appointed Secretary of King's College London. The apprenticeship in the Strand proved fruitful, for in 1952 Creed was ready to accept the principalship of Queen Mary College.

BUILDING LAND

Unlike most of the institutions of the University of London, Queen Mary College possessed land on which to build, and it was not long before Creed found himself absorbed in development plans which were to come to fulfilment in almost dramatic fashion. From the day in 1956 when the foundation-stone of the first new building—for the Faculty of Engineering—was laid, Creed's principalship was marked by the start of one new major building project in every succeeding year. By 1965 there were already more than three times the prewar number of students in the college, many of them, particularly in engineering and pure science, studying in new buildings with modern equipment. The library too had been extended and new halls of residence built. New faculties of law and economics were added to the academic disciplines of the college. Even so, Creed was not satisfied and continued to apply pressure at every point for the designation and acquisition of more sites to provide a campus worthy of the college. Following the publication of the Robbins Report on Higher Education, the college expressed its readiness to expand from 1,600 to 3,000 students and Creed was not afraid to express publicly his dismay at town planning obstacles and procedural difficulties.

With characteristic modesty, Creed had turned down earlier suggestions that he should allow his name to go forward for nomination as vice-chancellor. When, however, the university was sternly enjoined in the autumn of 1963 "satisfactorily and speedily" to resolve its internal difficulties by itself, under threat in case of failure of being subjected to an outside independent inquiry, Creed could not refuse the call of duty. He was unanimously elected vice-chancellor in 1964, a position which he held for three difficult and momentous years. (He was deputy vice-chancellor from 1958 to 1961).

IMPARTIALITY

After a prolonged and searching self-examination, the university felt justified in reaching the conclusion that, though there were a number of important spheres in which changes in the existing arrangements were necessary, there was beyond doubt a general desire to maintain the federal relationship.

In the long discussions which preceded this conclusion, Creed played a leading part. As the head of a college, he appreciated fully the college point of view but his vision was wider and he was convinced of the vital importance to the colleges themselves of developing and improving the federal structure of the university.

Of all Creed's many great qualities, the one which leaves the most lasting impression is his innate fairness. He seemed to embody everything that is excellent in the law, the profession he had graced in his earlier years. He was the embodiment of impartiality; he had a deep and abiding concern for the rights of individuals; yet he was determined that decisions, once taken, should be strictly and honourably carried out. It is significant that, of all the many distinctions which came his way in the course of a long and varied career, perhaps the one which gave him the greatest personal satisfaction was his election as an honorary Bencher of Lincoln's Inn, his own Inn of Court.

CALL TO BAR

Creed entered the Sudan Political Service in 1922. After short periods as assistant district commissioner in Berber and Darfur provinces he was seconded as a District Judge to the Legal Department in 1926 and transferred to it in 1929. Meanwhile he had been reading law and had received a call to the Bar at Lincoln's Inn. His subsequent career proved that his choice was a right one, but he was the first to admit to the debt which he owed to his earlier experience of provincial administration in knowledge of the people and of the Arabic language which few of his more professionally trained colleagues could rival. In 1931 he was seconded to Iraq under the Anglo-Iraq Judicial Agreement and on his return to the Sudan in 1935 he was appointed Judge of the High Court. He became Chief Justice in 1936 and Legal Secretary with a seat on the Governor General's Council in 1941. In 1947 he was Chief Representative of the Sudan Government at the hearing of the Egyptian case at the Security Council, and in 1948, shortly before his retirement, he was appointed King's Council—the first member of the Sudan Bar to be so recognized.

As a judge Creed was above all conscientious and realistic. As Legal Secretary he was quietly firm in the administration of his department. As an advocate of the rights of the Sudanese he could be fearlessly outspoken. His letters to The Times on the 1955 Anglo-Egyptian Agreement showed him to be as formidable a critic of alleged British appeasement to Egypt as of Egyptian pretensions to Sudan sovereignty.

VARIED DUTIES

One with Creed's legal training and judicial experience was naturally in demand for a variety of duties. Ever since his retirement from the Sudan he had been one of the chairmen of the Medical Appeal Tribunal under the National Insurance (Industrial Injuries Act), work which he found particularly interesting and, strangely enough, relaxing. In 1955, when the Forestry Commission set up a committee to review the administration of the Forest of Dean, Creed became its chairman. Best known among his public work was undoubtedly his chairmanship of the Burnham Committee from 1958 to 1964, a particularly critical period in its history. His impartiality and patience earned him the respect of his colleagues. In 1961, when Oxford House, the well known social settlement in Bethnal Green. was in difficulties about its future, they turned to Creed for a chairman.

An activity of which he was particularly proud was his membership of the Education Committee of the Goldsmiths' Company of the City of London. He was jealous, too, of the close connexions between the Drapers' Company and Queen Mary College and was careful to keep the college community aware of the debt which it owed to the generosity of the Company ever since its formation. The Drapers' Company marked his service to Queen Mary College by making him a freeman of the Company in 1963. His own college at Oxford, Pembroke College, elected him an honorary fellow in 1950.

Thomas Percival Creed was born in 1897, and educated at Wyggeston School, Leicester, and Pembroke College, Oxford, where he was a classical scholar.

He served with the Leicestershire Regiment in the First World War.

In 1928 he married Margaret, daughter of A. Brewis, and they had one son and two daughters.

May 13, 1969.

General Henry Duncan Graham Crerar, C.H., C.B., D.S.O., a very distinguished Canadian soldier, who crowned a military career of unbroken success as a commander of the Canadian Overseas Army in the later stages of the Second World War, died in Ottawa on April 1, 1965. He was 76.

He was born on April 28, 1888, at Hamilton, Ontario, where his father, Peter Crerar, a Highland Scot, was a prominent lawyer, who had married Marion, widow of C.J. Ottaway, a famous English cricketer. Harry Crerar, as he was always called, was educated at Highfield School, Hamilton, and Upper Canada College, Toronto, before he passed into the Royal Military College at Kingston, Ontario. After graduating at the R.M.C. he decided, instead of taking a commission in the Canadian army, to become a civil engineer and, as an officer of the reserve, continued his military training as a lieutenant in the 4th Field Battery of the Canadian militia.

FINE RECORD

When war came in 1914 he was called up for service and, proceeding overseas as a captain in the 3rd Brigade of the Canadian Field Artillery, served with great credit until the end of the war. He was promoted to Major, Brigade-Major (Artillery) and Counter Battery Officer with the rank of Lieutenant-Colonel on the headquarters staff of the Canadian Army and his fine record of service earned him the D.S.O. in 1917.

After the war he elected to become a professional soldier and was given an appointment as an artillery staff officer in the Department of National Defence at Ottawa. Determined to rise to one of the highest posts in the Army, he became an assiduous student of military history and tactics, and after achieving promotion to the rank of G.S.O.2, was in 1925 appointed Professor of Tactics at the Royal Military College where he remained until he was brought back to Ottawa as G.S.O.1. In this post he acted as technical adviser to the Canadian delegation at the Disarmament Conference at Geneva in 1932 and at the Imperial Conference in London in 1934. Then from 1935 to 1938 he was Director of Military Operations and Intelligence and, after taking a course at the Imperial Defence College in 1937, was appointed in 1938 Commandant of the Royal Military College with the rank of Colonel.

RECRUITMENT PROBLEM

On the outbreak of the Second World War he was recalled immediately to Ottawa and appointed Senior Staff Officer at G.H.Q., where he served until he was sent in 1940 to London to assume charge of a headquarters for Canada's overseas army, which had been established there. But within a year the King Cabinet, which had great confidence in his abilities, insisted that he must return to Ottawa to serve as Chief of the Canadian Army Staff. In this post he had to grapple with the difficult problem of recruitment for the army which had been aggravated by the revival of controversy over conscription.

He chafed continually at being relegated to a desk in Ottawa and his keen desire to go go on active service was gratified in 1942, when he was given command of the 2nd Canadian division of Canada's army overseas. Promotion to command the Canadian corps in Italy followed in 1943. When in 1944 such acute friction developed between Lieutenant-General A. G. L. Macnaughton, G.O.C. of Canada's Overseas Army, and the British High Command, he was recalled. Crerar was the obvious choice as his successor. Until the end of the war, with the rank of Lieutenant-General, he was a successful commander of the Canadian forces in Europe and for a period had under his command a Polish division. For his services in the war he was appointed a Companion of Honour and Oxford University conferred an honorary degree of D.C.L. on him. He was appointed A.D.C. General to King George VI in 1948 and had this honour renewed by Queen Elizabeth in 1952.

GOOD RELATIONS

General Crerar retired from the army in 1946 and settled down to live in Ottawa for the rest of his life. He declined to accept more than one important diplomatic appointment offered to him by the St. Laurent Ministry before losing favour with it through speeches in which he argued that military conscription was essential for Canada's security.

Crerar was an even-tempered man who was always ready to consider other viewpoints than his own, and as he was a firm believer in close cooperation between Canada and Britain, he had much happier relations with British commanders like Montgomery and Alanbrooke than his predecessor ever had.

He married in 1916 Verschoyle, elder daughter of B. B. Cronyn of Toronto, and they had one son and one daughter.

April 2, 1965.

Lady Crewe, C.I., widow of the first and last Marquis of Crewe, died in London on March 13, 1967, at the age of 86.

Her husband, who died in 1945, held many of the chief offices of state: Secretary of State for the Colonies, Lord President of the Council and Secretary of State for India. From 1922 to 1928 he was British Ambassador in Paris.

A unique personality, her charm fascinated her friends drawn from the widest circle, which included all ages and interests—political, literary and artistic. Her wit was clearly inherited from her father and her gift for friendship started at a very early age. The Rev. C. L. Dodgson (Lewis Carroll) was so fond of her that he gave her a personal copy of *Alice in Wonderland* with a letter of dedication when she was a small child—and her beauty, which remained with her always, is clearly shown in the picture of her ("Lady Peggy Primrose") by Sir John Millais, painted at the age of six.

She was born on January 1, 1881, the second daughter of the fifth Earl of Rosebery, the Liberal statesman, and Hannah, only daughter of Baron Mayer de Rothschild. Her husband was the only son of Richard Monckton Milnes, first Lord Houghton, politician and man of letters and friend of Tennyson, Hallam and Thackeray; and Keats's first biographer.

The second Lord Houghton's first wife, Sibyl, daughter of Sir Frederick Grant, Bt., died in 1887 and he married Rosebery's younger daughter, Lady Margaret Etrenne Hannah, in 1899.

In her foreword to Mr. James Pope-Hennessy's life of her husband, published in 1955, she wrote: "...we met at a dinner party at the Asquiths', though I had known him at a distance as a child. We talked at dinner and the rest of the evening, and Margot Asquith said afterwards that she immediately prophesied our marriage. We became engaged at the coming-out ball of his daughter Annabel, who was eight months younger than myself, and our marriage was strongly opposed by my grandmother (the Duchess of Cleveland). She thought the difference in age and three stepdaughters were insuperable obstacles to married happiness. She did not know that age does not affect affinity..."

MARRIED AT 18

Her marriage in 1899 at the age of 18 took place soon after Lord Rosebery's premiership had ended, and this union with a rising member of the Liberal Party caught the public imagination; and the carriage, drawn by postilions, had difficulty in getting through the massed crowds in Parliament Square on the way to Westminster Abbey. The majority of sightseers wore real or artificial primroses and the *Evening News* that day was printed on sheets of primrose-yellow paper. The couple were married by Crewe's old friend and mentor, Dr. Butler, Master of Trinity.

Lady Crewe assumed the responsibility of a political hostess immediately after marriage and, wherever she lived, be it at Crewe House, Crewe Hall or at the Embassy in Paris, where Lord Crewe was Ambassador from 1922 to 1928, her parties were famed for the interesting people she invited from all walks of life. It was at a dinner party at Crewe House that Sir Winston Churchill met his future wife for the first time.

Lady Crewe's activities covered a wide field; at the outbreak of the war in 1914 she was appointed chairman of the Central Committee on Women's Training and Employment, on which—to quote from the late Miss Bondfield—all classes in society were represented. Lady Crewe's friendship with the late Mary MacArthur dated from the committee and one of her enduring interests was in the Mary MacArthur Holiday Home for Working Women, of which she was president. A lifelong Liberal, she helped the party in innumerable ways, and to the end of her life was an active member of the Liberal Society Council and its president and chairman for many years.

In the Second World War she devoted herself to the French in Great Britain Fund, of which she was chairman. Her outstanding services to the Free French were recognized by General de Gaulle, who made her a Chevalier of the Legion of Honour.

After the death of her husband, she succeeded him as chairman of the Keats-Shelley Memorial Association. She herself had a marked literary gift—a short poem she wrote was published in *The Times Literary Supplement*.

She was one of the last entrancing figures of an era that has ended.

March 14, 1967.

General Sir John Crocker, G.C.B., K.B.E., D.S.O., M.C., the foremost of the younger group of armed force leaders who followed the pioneers of the inter-war period and made their own mark on the Second World War, died in a London hospital on March 9, 1963, at the age of 67.

He rose higher in the Army than any of his predecessors and contemporaries. He was the first officer of the Royal Tank Corps and Royal Tank Regiment to command an army corps in the field, the first to become a Commander-in-Chief overseas, and the first to be a member of the Army Council. That he reached such high levels was not through "push", but due to the wide respect felt for his combination of ability and balanced judgment. Few men have gone so far while remaining modest and unassertive and with him it was not an assumed "mask of modesty". Indeed, the main criticism among his staff was that he tended to be too diffident in imposing his will or exerting the influence that he could. Few commanders have been so beloved and respected by those serving under them.

AWARD AFTER RETEAT

John Tredinnick Crocker was born on January 3, 1896. He enlisted as a private soldier in November, 1915, and was immediately transferred to that distinguished Territorial unit, the Artists Rifles, with which he served until in January, 1917, he was given a temporary commission in the Machine-Gun Corps. He went on active service in March, to France, and won the M.C. in the Third Battle of Ypres a few months later. Then, in the "March Retreat" of 1918, he won the D.S.O. while still a second lieutenant in command of a machine-gun section. In August, 1919, he was demobilized and went back to civil life, but returned to the Army in 1920 with a Regular commission as lieutenant in the Middlesex Regiment. In January, 1922, he was seconded to the Tank Corps, and when the new arm was given permanent form in 1923 as the Royal Tank Corps he was definitely transferred to it.

A HAPPY PARTNERSHIP

In 1934 the first permanent tank brigade was established, under the command of Brigadier P. C. S. Hobart, with John Crocker as his Brigade Major. He proved a very able and harmonious assistant to his dynamic commander during the next two years. Crocker was appointed G.S.O.1 of the first armoured division (then called the Mobile Division) when it was formed in 1937—initially under the command of the future Field Marshal Lord Alanbrooke. In April, 1940, he was given command of one of its two armoured brigades. Belatedly sent to France in mid-May, the division only arrived on the scene after the German armoured forces had pierced the French front on the Meuse and reached the sea near Abbeville, cutting off most of the B.E.F. along with the whole left wing of the Allied armies. On May 27 the division was launched to an assault on the German bridgeheads along the Somme, but was checked by the now well-established defence, and suffered heavy loss. After a brief rest, Crocker's depleted 3rd Armoured Brigade was called on to help in meeting the second German offensive, southward over the Somme, after the new French front had collapsed. With its flanks laid bare it had a narrow escape from being cut off by the swift exploiting drive of Rommel's 7th Panzer Division, but managed to slip back across the Seine by an oblique withdrawal to a crossing at Les Andelys, which the Germans had not reached. In the next phase of the campaign, Crocker was again left isolated by the spreading French collapse west and south of the Seine. But he succeeded in extricating his small force, and reached Cherbourg on the night of June 17 by a circuitous and very rapid retreat—his tanks having covered 175 miles in 20 hours. Crocker's force had run a desperately close race with Rommel's, and was embarked at Cherbourg only just before Rommel's spearhead reached that escape port.

Crocker's cool and competent handling of the retreat had made so good an impression that he was promoted to command the 6th Armoured Division, the first of the new series that were now raised. A year later he was put in charge of the 2nd Armoured Group, which comprised the armoured division and army tank brigades in the Eastern Command. In 1942 he was appointed to command the 9th Corps, which was earmarked to follow up the Allied landing in French North Africa, and went out there in March, 1943.

EASTWARD STRIKE

When Montgomery's Eighth Army, advancing from Tripoli, pushed northward up the Tunisian coastal plain. Crocker was directed to strike eastward through the mountains against the rear of the retreating enemy. The opening infantry attack on the flanking heights miscarried as the American division which formed his right wing failed to make any progress on the first two days, April 7 and 8.

BREAK THROUGH

Nevertheless the 6th Armoured Division, which Crocker himself had formed and trained, succeeded in breaking through the Fondouk Pass on April 9 after a hard fight, and captured the city of Kairouan, although too late to cut off the enemy's coastal retreat. His corps was then moved northward and given the principal role in the new offensive that was now mounted to capture Tunis from the west. Sadly for Crocker he was accidentally wounded when watching the test of a P.I.A.T. mortar against a tank, and the execution of the decisive stroke in the North African campaign was thus left to his successor. But, after recovery, Crocker was given command of the 1st Corps at home, which was being prepared and trained for the leading role in the coming cross-Channel attack on the German position in northern France.

On D-Day (June 6, 1944) Crocker's 1st Corps formed the left wing of the Allied landing in Normandy, the key point and pivotal sector of the invasion front. Although narrowly frustrated in his effort to capture it at the outset, the continued pressure here during the weeks that followed helped to draw and pin down there the bulk of the German panzer forces, and thus ease the way for the American breakout on the western flank in August. In the subsequent advance eastward over the Seine, Crocker's 1st Corps carried out the attack on Le Havre, and captured this fortified port within 48 hours—the most quickly successful of any of the siege assaults on the German-held ports of France.

Immediately after the war in Europe, Crocker was appointed G.O.C.-in-C. of the Southern Command at home, and in 1947 was made C.-in-C. Middle East Land Forces. At that time he was a leading candidate for the succession to Lord Montgomery as C.I.G.S., but the post went instead to Lord Slim. However, in 1950 Crocker was brought home to become Adjutant-General to the Forces and Second Military Member of the Army Council.

LED HIS OLD CORPS

He held this high post until his retirement in 1953. Meanwhile, he had become in 1948 Colonel-Commandant of his old Corps, now the Royal Tank Regiment. In 1957 he was appointed Vice-Chairman of the Imperial War Graves Commission, of which he had become a member in 1950. He had also served as an active member of the Battle Honours Committee. In 1961 he was appointed her Majesty's Lieutenant for the County of Middlesex.

He married in 1920 Hilda May, the daughter of E. J. Mitchell, and by his marriage had one son, who was killed on active service with an armoured regiment in the Second World War.

March 11, 1963.

Richmal Crompton, the woman classics teacher who created William—the freckle-faced mud-encrusted perpetual 11-year-old schoolboy who wriggled his way through at least 37 adventures, died on January 10, 1969, at the age of 78.

Richmal Crompton—born Richmal Crompton Lamburn—once admitted there was never an actual William Brown: "He was a composite boy based partly on my brother and later on my nephew, boys in the choir and all the boys I've ever known." Miss Crompton—a vicar's daughter—thought him "a little savage" whom she wouldn't want.

William made his first appearance in print in a potboiling adult short story for Home Magazine in 1921. She tried to get rid of the scruffy schoolboy rebel after writing *William and the Outlaws*, but found that he proceeded "to take things over". Encouraged by a bright woman editor, she continued to write, and after a bout of polio she gave up teaching to dedicate herself to writing. From the first book, *Just William* published in 1922, the English language sales of William books have run close to nine million.

At the time of Al Capone, came *William the Gangster*; murder fiction and the beginning of the Crime Club brought *William the Detective*. The development of broadcasting brought *William and the Brains Trust*; then with the space age came *William and the Space Animal.*

William remained essentially the same: he never swapped his two life-long ambitions—either to own a sweet shop or be an engine driver. He continued to eat ices, cream buns and doughnuts; he still hated washing. His socks always hung about his ankles, his laces trailing, and his hair "growing at all angles".

CHANGED SCENE

But his background changed with the times; in the twenties the Browns lived in a large house with library, pantry, a cook and maids and William was addressed as Master William by the servants: in the sixties, the Brown home was more modest with only a casual daily woman. Robert and Ethel, the hero's elder brother and sister have rather faded—as has the obnoxious lisping Violet Elizabeth—his self-appointed girl friend.

Although Miss Crompton wrote some forty serious adult novels—gentle tales of family and village life—her William books consistently hogged the limelight. They were translated into languages ranging from Icelandic to Czech, Portuguese to Swedish. They have been made into films and plays: and serialized on radio and television.

The daughter of the Rev. E. J. S. Lamburn, of Bury, Lancashire, Richmal Crompton was born on November 15, 1890, and educated at St. Elphin's School, Darley Dale, and at the Royal Holloway College, London. After taking her B.A. degree at London University with second class honours in Classics, she decided to make teaching her profession, and in 1915 was appointed senior classical mistress at her old school at Darley Dale. Two years later she went as senior classical mistress to Bromley High School for Girls, where she remained for seven years; but she was now beginning to write in her spare time, and sketches and stories from her pen were soon appearing in weekly and monthly papers. "William" made his bow, and the first of the series of collected stories, *Just William*, was published in 1922 (40 years later it had reached its forty-second impression).

TOLERATED BY ADULTS

The adventures of William not only became extremely popular with the children of the twenties, but were also tolerated, to a greater or lesser degree, by their elders. Many of that ever-increasing row of red volumes, taken down, perhaps, in a condescending moment from the nursery bookshelf, must eventually have been retrieved by their indignant owners from the drawing-room. There was nothing pretentious about the "William" books, or about the respectable middle-class household which was fated to suffer the escapades of that enfant terrible, but the stories showed a natural gift of observation, a keen sense of the ridiculous, understanding of the child mind, and plenty of inventive resource. There was resource, too, in the selection of the titles, which ranged from *William the Conqueror* to *Sweet William*, and from *William the Dictator* to *William and A.R.P.*

Most of her adult novels made pleasant light reading, and several had their serious moments, though when Miss Crompton turned to tragedy, as in *Narcissa* (1941), she was not convincing. Among the best of her novels were the trilogy called *The Wildings*; the story of the old family home turned paying guest house, Chedsy Place; and *Quartet*; a thoughtful study of life in a village, written with her usual careful attention to detail. Perhaps the most original of her novels was *The Old Man's Birthday* (1934)—a delightful story based on the events of a single day and planned and executed with equal skill.

January 13, 1969.

Lord Crookshank, former Minister of Health, Lord Privy Seal, and Leader of the House of Commons, died at his London home on October 17, 1961, at the age of 68.

For 32 years, as Captain Harry Crookshank, he sat in the House of Commons as Conservative member for the Gainsborough division of Lincolnshire. Although he held many ministerial offices his abilities and personality were better known at Westminster than beyond it. He was very much a House of Commons man with a mastery of parliamentary procedure which might have equipped him to fill the office of Speaker with distinction and even with a measure of greatness. His success as a chairman of committees showed that he possessed many of the qualities demanded of a Speaker, and had the choice fallen on him he might well have developed others which as Leader of the House he failed fully to reveal. He held the leadership from 1952 until his elevation to the peerage in 1956, and during that time was also successively Minister of Health and Lord Privy Seal.

The task of arranging and controlling parliamentary business requires immense tact and a delicate judgment of the exact extent to which concessions and adjustments may safely be made without imperilling the essential purposes of the Government's legislative programme. No Leader of the House can satisfy everybody, but a little give and take can often ease the Parliamentary processes and keep the House in good humour. Crookshank came in for much criticism based on the charge of interpreting his duties too narrowly. He often seemed to invite trouble by sticking with undue rigidity to the pattern he had set, and his manner of doing so irritated and angered the Opposition. He was intensely loyal to his party and brought to its cause in Opposition and in office a zestful command of the arts of political warfare.

When he first entered the House it soon discovered that his urbane and ingenuous air of rather old-fashioned Toryism concealed a rapier-sharp wit which could bite deeply into his opponents' defences. When he attained front bench rank he was much in demand for replying to debates on hotly contested issues. Nobody who heard it will easily forget the brilliance of a speech he made in November, 1951, in winding up for the new Conservative Government on an Opposition amendment to the Address.

He was never flurried, never lost his poise, seldom raised his voice. Indeed he could often infuriate his opponents with the dry, laconic, mocking manner which he brought to issues on which their feelings were passionately engaged.

REVERENCE FOR TRADITION

They suspected him of reducing fundamentals to triviality, of riding off on irrelevancies, with a tendency to dismiss too lightly matters of great moment. They were often baffled and irritated by his smooth, adroit exercise of the art of slipping out of awkward situations. He did it all with a neat economy of effort, easy charm, and sunny equanimity that could often disarm the most violent criticism. But he could also stand his ground with stubborn resolve and offer a steely edge of resistance to attempts to dislodge him. That pale, delicately chiselled countenance with the high-domed forehead could swiftly change from mellow good humour to frosty disdain. The mild voice could sharpen to stinging tartness. But his courtesy was always impeccable and he had a reverence for parliamentary tradition and usage (indeed, he was one of the few members to remain faithful to the silk hat).

He was a highly sensitive man whose essential warm-heartedness and geniality he did not always find it easy to express in public. He had outstanding gifts as an administrator and a versatile range of ability. He brought to the parliamentary scene an incisive wit and a stimulating intellectual vigour which often enlivened its deliberations and enriched the quality of its debates. In all his years at Westminster he served its interests with a high sense of duty, loyalty, and devotion.

The Rt. Hon. Harry Frederick Comfort Crookshank, P.C., C.H., first Viscount Crookshank, was born in 1893. He was the only son of the late Harry Maule Crookshank, of Cairo, and came of a long established Ulster family which had played a prominent part in the affairs of that province. He was educated at Eton, where he was a King's Scholar, and at Magdalen College, Oxford. In the First World War he served in The Hampshire Regiment, and after 1915 on the Special Reserve of the Grenadier Guards. He was in France and at Salonika, was twice wounded, and received the orders of the White Eagle and the Serbian Gold Medal for valour.

In 1919 he was demobilized with the rank of captain. He entered the Diplomatic Service as a Third Secretary, and was later a Second Secretary at Constantinople and Washington. In 1924 he resigned upon his election to the House of Commons as Conservative member for Gainsborough. He was a conscientious and hard-working representative who, owing largely to his charm of manner, was warmly regarded in the House, where as time went on he was to build a reputation for ability and soundness. He was a keen student of parliamentary history and procedure.

SECRETARY FOR MINES

In 1934 he became Parliamentary Under-Secretary to the Home Office. In the following year he received a presentation from his constituents in recognition of the fact that he was the first member for Gainsborough to serve for 10 years or to be in a Government. In 1935 he was appointed Secretary for Mines, a position which, though it offered few opportunities for spectacular performance, demanded that its occupant should have a gift for public relations and the capacity to inspire confidence. During his tenure of office the National Joint Consultative Committee was established, and relations in the industry improved.

In 1939 he became Financial Secretary to the Treasury, and was sworn of the Privy Council. He was reappointed as Financial Secretary when Winston Churchill formed the wartime Coalition Government in May, 1940. In this period of intense strain Crookshank's habit of knowing his facts at first hand stood him in good stead. As the war went on the economic and financial difficulties increased.

DEVOTED SERVICE

While the Service and Production departments bore the brunt of action, it was for the Treasury to guard their rear against the perils of inflation. Crookshank discharged his duties more than adequately and steadily increased his reputation for dependability and devoted public service. In so far as his public utterances were concerned his task was largely to remind a war-absorbed public of the financial side of the war effort and to promote increased saving. In performing it he adhered most wisely to the simple and straightforward statement. His final task at the Treasury was to visit Washington and investigate the cost of our wartime organization in the United States.

He was promoted to the office of Postmaster-General in 1943, and held this position with unobtrusive efficiency until the end of the war. In spite of the national swing to Labour at the general election in the summer of 1945, Crookshank retained his seat at Gainsborough. In Opposition he proved himself a thorn in the side of the Labour Government with his relentless questions and pertinacious criticism of their nationalization measures.

When the conservatives returned to power in October, 1951, Crookshank was an obvious candidate for high office. There was some surprise, however, at his appointment to the Ministry of Health. Many of his friends thought that he would have been better at the Treasury or the Board of Trade. But for the first time he had a seat in the Cabinet and he was made Leader of the House—at first it was announced that he would be Deputy Leader, but then it was decided that the burden of leadership would be too much for Mr. Anthony Eden (as he then was) in view of his heavy duties at the Foreign Office. In the absence of the Prime Minister and Foreign Secretary in Canada and the United States in December of that year Crookshank was chosen to preside at meetings of the Cabinet.

Though he ran into stormy waters as Leader of the House, he continued to act in this capacity. In May, 1952, he resigned from the Ministry of Health, where he was succeeded by Mr. Iain Macleod. Crookshank became Lord Privy Seal, and, thus freed from heavy departmental duties, he was able to devote more time to his work in leading the House of Commons. He continued to be a member of the Cabinet.

RETIREMENT

When Sir Anthony Eden succeeded Sir Winston Churchill as Prime Minister in April, 1955, Crookshank retained his position as Lord Privy Seal and Leader of the House of Commons, and was reappointed to these offices after the general election in May. Six months later he resigned, and a viscounty was conferred on him. It was gazetted in January, 1956. He had been created C.H. in 1955. Three years later he was appointed chairman of the Political Honours Scrutiny Committee, and in March, 1960, he became High Steward of Westminster. In June of the same year Oxford University conferred on him the honorary degree of Doctor of Civil Law.

October 18, 1961.

Sir Ronald Cross, the first baronet, P.C., K.C.M.G., K.C.V.O., Governor of Tasmania, 1951–58, and British High Commissioner in the Commonwealth of Australia, 1941–45, died on June 3, 1968, in London at the age of 72.

From 1939 to 1940 Cross was Minister of Economic Warfare, and from 1940 to 1941 Minister of Shipping. He was Unionist M.P. for Rossendale 1931–45, and Conservative M.P. for Ormskirk 1950–51. From 1935 to 1937 he was a Government Whip; and from 1950 to 1951 he was chairman of the Public Accounts Committee.

Cross was the official representative of the British Government in Australia during the anxious and arduous years in which that country was directly exposed to the menace of Japanese aggression. It was a delicate and at times a difficult position, which demanded a wide range of qualities.

Ronald Hibbert Cross was born on May 9, 1890, the son of James Carlton Cross, and was educated at Eton. In the First World War he served in the Duke of Lancaster's Own Yeomanry and the Royal Flying Corps. Having become a merchant banker, he stood in 1931 for the Rossendale Division of Lancashire as a Unionist supporter of the National Government.

In 1933, Cross was chosen to be mover of the Address in reply to the King's Speech, and two years later was appointed a Government Whip. In 1937 he became a Lord of the Treasury and then Vice-Chamberlain of H.M. Household. In 1938 he was appointed Parliamentary Secretary of the Board of Trade. Speaking in this capacity, in October of the latter year, he strongly supported Chamberlain's policy of appeasement, but held that its success depended on Great Britain being backed by a formidable armament. At this time he entertained what he called "a certain tentative optimism" in regard to the future of British trade.

In 1939 Cross was chosen to be Minister of Economic Warfare. It was an office which entailed new and highly important responsibilities, among them that of judging the legitimate trading requirements of neutral countries. He was soon in consultation with various neutral Governments with a view to simplifying the procedure of contraband control. One of his chief aims was to secure the interception of cargoes of war supplies destined for Germany, and it fell to him strongly to rebut the Nazi accusation that Great Britain was conducting an inhumane policy of starvation. German exports had also to be restricted as far as possible. Yet another of his tasks was to compete with Germany in those European countries which were beyond the reach of British seapower. He could not in those early days expect to procure the economic collapse of the enemy; but he maintained that the activities of his department were calculated to hasten victory.

Cross had served a valuable apprenticeship when in 1940 he became Minister of Shipping. It was his task to cooperate in the movement of Empire troops with the Royal Navy and in August, 1940, he was able to claim that in transporting them not a man or a ship were lost as the result of enemy action.

Cross was Minister of Shipping for a year and then became British High Commissioner in the Commonwealth of Australia. It was in accord with the policy which also sent Malcolm MacDonald to Ottawa and Lord Harlech to South Africa, and was intended to ensure the fullest possible consultation and cooperation between the United Kingdom and the great self-governing Dominions. He retained his seat in the Commons, and the Prime Minister duly furnished the certificate necessary under the House of Commons Disqualification (Temporary Provisions) Act.

In July, 1941, Cross took over his new duties and was almost immediately attacked by W. M. Hughes, the Australian Attorney General, for a remark in regard to the Russian system of Government which had been attributed to him on his arrival at Sydney. The British Government explained, however, to the Commons that he had been completely misreported or misrepresented and stated that he had their full confidence and approval. In 1940 he had been sworn of the Privy Council and shortly after his arrival in Australia he was created a baronet.

The intervention of Japan in the Pacific was naturally to add greatly to Cross's responsibilities and difficulties, and it was his task to act as the exponent of Britain's war policies to the Australian public. A lucid speaker, he could make an excellent case. In early 1944 his constituency protested at his prolonged absence, and in August he paid a short official visit to England. He lost this seat in 1945.

In 1925 he married Louise Marion, daughter of the late Walter Emmott.

June 4, 1968.

Sir Alwyn Crow, C.B.E., a pioneer in the design of rocket weapons, died in hospital in Washington on February 5, 1965. He was 70.

In 1936, when he was Director of Ballistic Research at Woolwich, he was asked by the Government to assemble a team to explore the possibilities of a rocket gun. A remote spot had to be found and early experiments in fact took place on top of a hill deep in the country. Because of the peculiarities of the English climate the final tests were carried out in Jamaica. From the research carried out then, and later when Crow was Chief Superintendent of Projectile Development and subsequently Director and Controller of Projectile Development, emerged the anti-aircraft rocket gun which was brought into action against German night bombers in 1941.

Employed then to fill the gap caused by the lack of suitable A.A. guns, the rocket, with its solid cordite propellant and fitted with varying warheads, proved extraordinarily versatile. Fitted to Beaufighters and other R.A.F. aircraft it was highly successful against enemy shipping; it was particularly potent in the "beating up" of German army headquarters, radar stations and railways; and it was used with devastating effect against German armour in Normandy and afterwards in destroying the transport of the retreating enemy.

In 1955 the Royal Commission on Awards to Inventors awarded Crow, and two other rocket scientists, Dr. H. J. Poole and Sir William Cook, £5,000.

Alwyn Douglas Crow was born in London in May, 1894, and educated at Westminster and Queens' College, Cambridge. He served with The East Surrey Regiment during the First World War and was wounded, mentioned in dispatches and made O.B.E.

From 1945 to 1946 he was Director of Guided Projectiles at the Ministry of Supply. After this he was sent to Washington as Head of Technical Services with the British Joint Services Mission. He retired in 1953 and devoted himself to rocket development on a consultancy basis, working for firms on both sides of the Atlantic.

He was advanced to C.B.E. in 1937 and knighted in 1944.

He married in 1923 Kathleen Christiana, daughter of N. C. Barraclough. She died in 1957 and he married secondly in 1958 Frances Gore Haynes.

February 6, 1965.

John William Crow, M.A., formerly Reader in English Literature at the University of London King's College, and from 1967 to 1968 Professor of English at the University of Pittsburgh, died in London on October 29, 1969, the day before his sixty-fifth birthday.

Crow—as he usually announced and signed himself, and as his friends always thought of him—was a man of considerable erudition, particularly in the field of Elizabethan and Jacobean drama and bibliography; but, largely because of his deep distrust of those who, he felt, rushed too readily into print, his published output was relatively slight. His memorial, however, lies less in such things as his Malone Society editions of John Day's *Law Tricks* or the anonymous *Jacob and Esau* than in a phrase which will be found, with small variations, in literally dozens of prefaces and footonotes: "I am indebted to Mr. John Crow for this reference."

Such brief tributes indicate his humility and his unselfish concerns for scholarship. In an entertaining but deeply serious paper, read at the Modern Language Association's 1957 meeting and entitled "Deadly Sins of Criticism: or, Seven Ways to get Shakespeare Wrong", Crow set out his critical credo: he was against arrogance, and pedantry, and over-simplification, and a self-regarding subjectivism; and towards the end of his paper he lamented that, whereas "the criticism of Shakespeare was formerly an attempt to give assistance to the young, now we are forced to use it to impress our elders. What started life as a crutch has come to maturity as a banner with a strange device. Editions of plays, allegedly for the young, are, at all events in my country, used as pass-keys for the doors of academic promotion."

If there was a trace of bitterness in his voice it was not altogether without justification. He had been appointed as a temporary assistant lecturer at the age of 41, and it was not until 17 years, later that he obtained his Readership.

LIKE FALSTAFF

But he had of course, as the last sentence implies, come very late to academic life. Crow's past was something of a mystery to his students and colleagues (it was easy enough to think of him as having always been "Crow", as having—like the Falstaff he resembled—been born "about three of the clock in the afternoon, with a white head, and something of a round belly"), and myth conglobed around him—that he had been trained as a doctor, that he had been a professional wrestler, a champion swimmer, a celebrated boxing correspondent. The remarkable thing about these myths was that most of them were substantially true. Admittedly, he had never been a wrestler, though he had the build of one; but on leaving Charterhouse he had indeed gone on to read Medicine at Guy's, and thence won an exhibition to Worcester College, Oxford (where he took his B.A., and where he was in later years a loved and honoured guest); and while at Oxford he became joint editor, with Peter Fleming, of *Isis*, and perhaps it was this bite of the journalistic bug that determined his career for the next 12 years—what he referred to as "my days as a chronicler of the Prize Ring". As New York correspondent of *Boxing* he moved in the world of Damon Runyon; he was the London correspondent of several American boxing journals, and for a while was sports editor of a London Sunday illustrated newspaper—surely the most learned man ever to have occupied such a chair.

Whether he would have continued in this way it is difficult to say. The war came and, unfit for military service, Crow took his first decisive step back towards Academe by joining the staff of Wellington College—from where, in 1945, he went to King's, thus installing himself in that area of London most appropriate for a devout Johnsonian. But he never relinquished a certain tang of journalism; when later he wrote for the *T.L.S.* and other august periodicals, he retained the pungency and economy he had cultivated as a sports writer.

November 4, 1969.

Dame Rachel Crowdy, D.B.E., who died on October 10, 1964, at the age of 80, was Principal Commandant of V.A.D.s in France and Belgium from 1914 to 1919 and from 1919 to 1931 was Head of the Social Questions and Opium Traffic Section of the League of Nations.

The only woman to be head of an administrative section of the League, her part was that of the pioneer as—with Dame Katharine Furse—it had been in the early days of the First World War when the V.A.D.s were winning golden opinions in France. Article 23 was the first charter ever framed for the regulation of social questions of common interest to every nation, though "social questions" was perhaps not the right phrase, for Rachel Crowdy was soon at grips with such decidedly anti-social matters as the international traffic in women. Article 23 was words on paper; someone had to breathe life into it and it was Rachel Crowdy who breathed.

In 1931 when her work for the League came to an end she was feted at a dinner in the Café Royal attended by 500 women (among them Lady Astor and Margaret Bondfield) and representing all the professions, many departments of the Civil Service and every sphere of social service.

Rachel Crowdy was what is now called involved; for her, the words social work and social service had a large significance; they meant more than dispensing cheap milk and a cosy chat in provincial cities, they meant no less than a concern for the lives and health of people everywhere; which was why for the rest of her life she was to be found in the four corners of the world advising on this, inquiring into that, caring for nothing but the betterment of the human race. Her record as a committee-woman is formidable; she sat on the Royal Commission on the Private Manufacture of Armaments (1935); on the Royal Commission to the West Indies (1938–39) and went with the Parliamentary Commission to the Spanish war in 1937. In 1920–21 she went with the International Typhus Commission to Poland when the epidemic was at its height. In the war of 1939–45, she was Regions Adviser to the Ministry of Information, visiting and reporting on conditions in bombed cities.

The daughter of James Crowdy, she was born in March, 1884 and educated at Hyde Park New College; her nursing training was at Guy's Hospital. One day in 1911 when the Red Cross organization was calling for volunteers to serve in case of invasion she made for the London Scottish Drill Hall to join and there struck-up with Katharine Furse. It had not been intended that the volunteer nurses should go abroad but Katharine Furse changed all that and Rachael Crowdy soon followed her. Together they set out to discover what was being done for the wounded and as a result of their investigations rest stations were set up. Within a short while Rachel Crowdy had been appointed Principal Commandant of V.A.D.s in France and Belgium. In 1919 she was made D.B.E.

She married in 1939 Colonel C. Thornhill, C.M.G., D.S.O. He died in 1952.

October 12, 1964.

The Marquis de Cuevas, owner and artistic director of the ballet company which bears his name, died in Cannes on February 22, 1961. He was born in Chile in 1886 and became an American citizen in 1940.

A long-standing interest in, and support for, the ballet finally led him in 1944 to found in America the Ballet International. It achieved some distinction before, in 1947, he moved his centre of operations to Europe and, buying the Nouveau Ballet de Monte Carlo, formed by Eugene Grunberg in 1945, combined the two companies and their repertories to make the Grand Ballet de Monte Carlo (later renamed the Grand Ballet du Marquis de Cuevas).

The company was based on Paris, but frequently toured Europe, South America and the Near East. Its repertoire included at several times most of the classics and also a number of new works, among the most notorious of which was Dali's *Mad Tristan*, seen in London during the company's first season there in 1948. Its more serious productions and distinction of its leading dancers (the company as a whole tended to be less distinguished) established it as one of the most interesting of European companies.

In 1958 de Cuevas fell out with Serge Lifar, the dancer and choreographer, over de Cuevas's right to include in the programme which his ballet were giving in a Paris theatre a ballet which Lifar was giving at the Opera. Ceremonial insults were exchanged, seconds of each party waited upon one another, and the duel, fought with épee, took place at a mill near Vernon. After de Cuevas had slightly wounded his opponent on the right forearm the duel was stopped and the two men, their differences reconciled by this honourable blood-letting, embraced.

From start to finish the affair was accompanied by the maximum publicity which neither of the two protagonists went out of his way to discourage.

February 23, 1961.

E. E. Cummings, the American poet, who died on September 3, 1962, in North Conway, New Hampshire, made a practice in his verse of printing the personal pronoun in the lower case. He may have unwittingly followed the example of Mark Akenside in this respect, but the mannerism, in conjunction with his many other typographical extravagances, helped to assert his individuality and to disguise the traditional quality of his inspiration. He was the most obviously individualistic of all the twentieth-century American poets, but one of the most talented and genuine, too, and his death is a loss to poetry. He was 67.

Edward Estlin Cummings was born in Cambridge, Massachusetts, in 1894, and educated at Harvard University, graduating in 1915. He served with an American ambulance corps in France before America entered the war, and in 1917, on being unjustly suspected of treasonable correspondence, he was confined for several months in a concentration camp by the French authorities. He used the experience in *The Enormous Room*, published in 1922, a remarkable and deservedly popular autobiographical narrative, which describes the hardships he and his fellow prisoners underwent and celebrates the virtues of individuality. It is one of the most convincing of the war books to have been written by an American.

He published his first volume of poems, *Tulips and Chimneys* in 1923 and issued further volumes regularly; a collected edition appearing in 1954. He can hardly be said to have developed as a poet, but neither did his lyrical gifts fail him, and his best poetry was always distinguished by its wit, feeling, and realism.

NATURAL WIT

The appearance of his verse on the page is often disconcerting, but if it is read aloud, using the eccentric typography as a guide, the ear quickly discerns that it is essentially a traditional—at times, conventional—and unbewildering utterance, capable of giving great pleasure, when it is not marred by sentimentality. He was awarded the Bollingen Prize for Poetry in 1957, for his "gift of natural wit and lyric imagination", a public recognition of where his strength lay.

Cummings was a skilful artist, having studied in Paris in the early 1920s, and held several exhibitions of his work. His efforts in this field, as in the other of poetry, were admirably summed up by him in one of the Charles Eliot Norton Lectures in Poetry, which he delivered at Harvard in 1952. "So far as I am concerned," he said, "poetry and every other art was and is and for ever will be strictly and distinctly a question of individuality."

September 4, 1962.

Nancy Cunard died in a Paris hospital on March 17, 1965, at the age of 69.

Born on March 10, 1896, she was the only daughter of Sir Bache Edward Cunard, third baronet, and of Lady Cunard, the brilliant hostess, conversationalist and patron of the arts, who died in 1948. Nancy Cunard had a marked literary gift and in addition to a small output of poetry produced two highly evocative volumes of literary reminiscences of two authors she had known intimately. *Grand Man*, memories of Norman Douglas, appeared in 1954, and in addition to a discerning and affectionate portrait of Douglas contains an admirable assessment of his work. *G.M.*, memories of George Moore, came out two years later. Moore, her mother's devoted friend, she first met when she was in the schoolroom but she kept up with him in the Ebury Street days and published some of his later work on her own small press in France.

Nancy Cunard was a vigorous and outspoken campaigner for coloured people's rights in the United States. In 1932 she lived in the Harlem district of New York, gathering material for a book on the colour question; she canvassed Negroes' views on race problems; and organized a protest in an attempt to help seven young Negroes sentenced to death in Montgomery, Alabama, for alleged assault on two white girls.

Later she went to Spain as a relief worker during the civil war and helped to organize food parcels from Britain.

She married in 1916 Sidney George Fairbairn, Grenadier Guards. The marriage was annulled in 1925 and the following year she resumed her maiden name of Cunard.

March 18, 1965.

Admiral of the Fleet Lord Cunningham of Hyndhope, G.C.B., O.M., D.S.O., the outstanding naval leader of the Second World War, died in London on June 12, 1963, at the age of 80. In the early part of the war he held major command at sea as Commander-in-Chief of the Mediterranean Fleet and subsequently of the Anglo-American expedition to North Africa.

Later, as First Sea Lord from 1943 to 1946, he shared responsibility for the central direction of the war.

Cunningham was an officer whose name, until he reached the highest ranks of the Navy, was hardly known outside it. Though his merits and abilities fully justified his selection for the high posts he held, actually he owed his tenure of them to a large extent to luck. After his promotion to Vice-Admiral in 1936 he was unemployed for a year, and in view of the state of the flag lists at that time he himself hardly expected to hold more than perhaps one more minor command before concluding his career by retirement. Within three years, however, owing to unexpected retirements or deaths of flag officers senior to him, he found himself, as Commander-in-Chief of the Mediterranean Fleet, holding one of the two greatest sea commands, with the acting rank of Admiral, and well in the succession for promotion to Admiral of the Fleet. He held the Mediterranean Command at the outbreak of war in 1939, and few could have been more suitable for it. Essentially a man of action rather than an administrator, it was the general feeling in the Mediterranean Fleet that their Commander-in-Chief was the man to seize every opportunity that might present itself of conducting the war with vigour; and so indeed it proved when, in 1940, Italy joined our enemies. Faced with a pronounced material superiority, he himself remarked that a vigorous offensive was the only possible policy.

It was fortunate that the command of the Mediterranean Fleet in that dark hour should be held by one who every officer and man under him could feel was the right man in the right place. Under his inspiring leadership, complete ascendancy over the Italian Fleet was quickly established, and maintained even when the loss of both north and south coasts of the Eastern Basin enabled strong German land-based air forces to dominate the narrow seas. After an interlude in Washington, Cunningham returned to the Mediterranean command in November, 1942, as Allied Naval Commander-in-Chief, when the Anglo-American recovery of North Africa redeemed the balance once more. The next year he had the satisfaction of receiving the surrender of the Italian Fleet; and when Sir Dudley Pound died in harness in 1943, there was by common consent but one officer to succeed him as First Sea Lord. A man of florid and smiling countenance, with the blue eyes of the born sailor and the genial manner of one whose naval career had been passed chiefly in small ships, Cunningham was never one to insist on rigid formalities or precedents, and though he would excuse no failure in courage or seamanship, he would ever turn a blind eye to faults arising from dash or excess of zeal.

TORPEDO BOATS

Andrew Browne Cunningham was the son of Professor D. J. Cunningham, of Dublin and Edinburgh, and brother of General Sir Alan Cunningham. He was born on January 7, 1883, and educated first at Edinburgh Academy and later at Mr. Foster's School at Stubbington. He passed into the Britannia as a naval cadet in January, 1897.

His first command, which he held from May, 1908, to January, 1910, was torpedo boat No. 14 in the Home Fleet, one of the first oil-burning ships in the Navy, known to those serving in them as the "oily wads". They were small and fast, but handy and seaworthy craft, carrying only one warrant officer besides the lieutenant in command. There could be no better training for a young officer in seamanship, self-reliance and initiative than such a command; it was hard work, but was a much sought after job. From T.b. 14, Cunningham graduated to a bigger ship, taking command of the destroyer Vulture in reserve for a year until, in January, 1911, he achieved the aim of every young destroyer officer of the day, a command in the "running flotilla", the destroyer Scorpion, of the 1st Flotilla, Home Fleet. That command he held for the very unusually long period of seven years. In 1912, on the rearrangement of the flotilla consequent on the delivery of new ships, she was transferred to the 3rd Flotilla, Home Fleet. The next year she was transferred to the 5th Flotilla, then a unit of the Mediterranean Fleet, and Cunningham was still in command of her on the outbreak of war.

In the history of the Dardanelles campaign, the name of the Scorpion is constantly occurring—she was ever in the forefront. On October 30, 1914, she and the Wolverine opened the campaign against Turkey by running into the Gulf of Smyrna and sinking a Turkish minelayer which was lying alongside the pier at Vourlah. On March 4, 1915, she was part of the force supporting the landing on the south side of the straits, and it is on record that she ran right into the mouth of the river Mendere and silenced a battery which was holding up the advance of the Marines ashore. Time and again the Scorpion was in action, supporting the flank of the Army with her fire, assisting in the landing or evacuation of troops. On June 30, 1915, Cunningham was promoted to commander, remaining in command of the Scorpion, and on March 3, 1916, he was awarded the D.S.O. for his services off the peninsula.

DOVER PATROL

In February, 1918, he transferred to the command of the Ophelia in the Dover Patrol, coming again under the command of Sir Roger Keyes, who had been Chief of Staff at the Dardanelles, and he transferred a month later to the Termagant. In her he took part in numerous engagements, including the Zeebrugge expedition, and after the Armistice he was awarded a Bar to his D.S.O. for his services. In February, 1919, he transferred to the Seafire, of the 5th Destroyer Flotilla, in which he again saw active service in the operations in the Baltic under the command of Rear-Admiral Sir Walter Cowan, commanding the 1st Light Cruiser Squadron; for this, in the next year, he was awarded a second Bar to his D.S.O. He was promoted to captain and on the conclusion of the Baltic operations returned to Rosyth with his flotilla.

In September, 1920, he was put in charge of Sub-Commission "C" of the Naval Inter-Allied Commission of Control, and in that capacity he supervised the demolition of the fortifications at Heligoland, an appointment in which his prolonged contact with German officers and officials gave him a knowledge of the people and language which was of great value to him in later years when he came to occupy a high position at the Admiralty. In 1922, he returned once more to destroyer service, becoming Captain (D) of the 6th Flotilla in reserve, transferring later to the command of the 1st Flotilla in the Home Fleet, with his pendant in the Wallace, flotilla leader. In 1924 he went ashore, but continued his connexion with the destroyer flotillas, as he was Captain-in-Charge of the destroyer base at Port Edgar, Firth of Forth, for a year and a half. Thence he returned to sea service as Flag-Captain to Sir Walter Cowan, Commander-in-Chief of the America and West Indies Station, first in the Calcutta and later in the Despatch, cruisers, for more than two years in all. In 1929 he was selected for a course at the Imperial Defence College, on the conclusion of which he took command of the battleship Rodney, one of the most sought after of captains' commands. In accordance with the practice prevailing at that time he held it only for a year, and after a few months unemployed he became Commodore of the Naval Barracks at Chatham, a command which he continued to hold for four months after his promotion to flag rank in September, 1932.

REMOTE PROSPECT

In January, 1934, he was made C.B. and took command of the destroyer flotillas of the Mediterranean Fleet—Rear-Admiral (D) with his flag in the Coventry—which he held through the period of the Italo-Abyssinian War until March, 1936. Three months later he was promoted to Vice-Admiral, and the prospects of his further employment, except perhaps in a shore-command at home, seemed remote. A year later, however, he was suddenly appointed Second-in-Command of the Mediterranean Fleet and Vice-Admiral Commanding Battle Cruiser Squadron, temporarily, in the vacancy caused by the illness of Vice-Admiral Sir Geoffrey Blake, and on that officer being invalided Cunningham's appointment was made permanent. He held it until August, 1938, and three months later was appointed Deputy Chief of the Naval Staff at the Admiralty—a post which it was generally expected would have gone to Sir Geoffrey Blake but for his enforced retirement—under Admiral Sir Roger Backhouse, who had just become First Sea Lord and Chief of the Naval Staff. In that position great responsibility was thrown on him when illness in turn incapacitated Sir Roger Backhouse early in 1939, in the middle of the international tension, which eventually developed into war. For some six months Cunningham acted as substitute for his chief on the Committee of Imperial Defence and at the Admiralty Board; and when it was finally decided that Admiral Sir Dudley Pound should succeed Sir Roger Backhouse, Cunningham, who had been promoted K.C.B. at the beginning of the year, replaced him as Commander-in-Chief, Mediterranean, in June, 1939, as an acting Admiral, to which rank he was promoted in January, 1941.

FLEET WITHDRAWN

On the outbreak of war in September, 1939, as Italy remained "non-belligerent", the Mediterranean seemed liable to prove a backwater, and practically all the Mediterranean Fleet was withdrawn for service in other seas. It was brought up to strength the following year, however, when it became clear that Mussolini was bent on war, only to be left in marked inferiority by the defection of its French contingent; on that melancholy occasion, Cunningham showed himself a skilled diplomatist as well as a war leader, and was able to secure the effective neutralization of Admiral Godefroi's squadron—which had been part of the Allied Fleet under his command—without rancour or bloodshed. Within a few weeks of Mussolini's declaration of war, Cunningham, in the Battle of Calabria, had chased a superior Italian Fleet back into the shelter of its bases; a few months later the Fleet Air Arm attack at Taranto put half the Italian Navy out of action; and in March, 1941, in the brief night action known as the Battle of Cape Matapan, three of the largest Italian cruisers were destroyed in a few minutes. The arrival of the Luftwaffe on the shores of the Mediterranean at the end of 1941, and the loss of Cyrenaica, Greece, and Crete made it impossible for the British Fleet, lacking support in the air, to operate freely or to keep the sea route fully open. When Cunningham handed over the Mediterranean Command to Sir Henry Harwood in May, 1942, to go to Washington as the British representative with the Joint Chiefs of Staff, there was little left for it to do within the Mediterranean itself until the recovery of North Africa again gave it sea room.

ALLIED COMMAND

Cunningham was away no more than six months. When the Anglo-American descent on French North Africa in "Operation Torch" of November, 1942, began the expulsion of the Axis from Africa, he returned there as Allied Naval Commander-in-Chief under General Eisenhower as Supreme Commander of the invading forces. Two months later he again took over, in addition, as Commander-in-Chief of the whole Admiral of the Fleet. He had the satisfaction of completely regaining control of the Mediterranean, and, in September, 1943, of receiving the surrender of the whole Italian Fleet. The death of the First Sea Lord, Admiral of the Fleet Sir Dudley Pound, in October brought him back to the Admiralty in his place. He was at the head of affairs for the rest of the war.

Cunningham, who retired in 1946, was created G.C.B. while holding the Mediterranan command in 1942, and baronet on relinquishing it. On the break-up of the coalition Government in 1945 he, together with his brother Chiefs of Staff, Field Marshal Sir Alan Brooke and Marshal of the R.A.F. Sir Charles Portal, was created a baron, taking the title of Lord Cunningham of Hyndhope, which he retained on promotion to a viscountcy in the New Year Honours of 1946. In the Birthday Honours that year he was made O.M.

In 1950 and again in 1952 he was Lord High Commissioner to the General Assembly of the Church of Scotland. His memoirs, *A Sailor's Odyssey*, were published in 1951.

His marriage to Nona Christine, daughter of Horace Byatt, of Midhurst, Sussex, took place in 1929.

June 13, 1963.

Admiral of the Fleet Sir John H. D. Cunningham, G.C.B., M.V.O., who died on December 13, 1962, at the age of 77, was one of the outstanding naval leaders of the 1939–45 War, although unlike his famous namesake Lord Cunningham of Hyndhope, the victor of Matapan—to whom he bore no relation—it was not his good fortune to be directly connected with the more prominent actions and he was seldom in the public eye.

After commanding a cruiser squadron in Norway, and Admiralty service as Fourth Sea Lord, he followed Lord Cunningham in the Mediterranean Command in 1943 and as First Sea Lord in 1946. He was capable and efficient and rose to the top by sheer merit, although he had never qualified in staff duties. It was unusual—if not unique—for an ex-navigating officer to become First Sea Lord. As an allied commander he inspired the devotion of his comrades of all nations by his zeal and his kindly personality. At Ankara in 1943 his welcome by the Turks was particularly cordial, and the fact that he bore a certain physical resemblance to the late Ataturk helped to endear him to them.

John Henry Dacres Cunningham was born on April 13, 1885, at Demerara, British Guiana. He entered H.M.S. Britannia as a naval cadet from Stubbington House on 1900, and was a midshipman for three years from June, 1901, in the cruiser Gibraltar, flagship on the Cape Station, where he gained the South African war medal. In his courses as sub-lieutenant he gained five "firsts" and was promoted lieutenant in October, 1905, at the age of 20. In 1906 he qualified in navigation, and after being assistant navigator in the Illustrious was navigator of the gunboat Hebe, the cruiser Indefatigable in the West Indies, and the minelayer Iphigenia in home waters. Having passed the first-class ship course in 1910 he was an instructor at the navigation school until appointed navigator of the cruiser Berwick, in the West Indies. He was in her when the War of 1914–18 broke out.

WITH THE GRAND FLEET

In 1915, he joined the battleship Russell in the Mediterranean. She was sunk by a mine off Malta in April, 1916. Two months later he became navigator of the battle-cruiser Renown, and spent the rest of the War in the Grand Fleet, in the Renown until July, 1918 (being reappointed to her on promotion to commander in 1917), and then in the Lion, flagship.

In 1919 he became the first navigator of the new battle-cruiser Hood and squadron navigator in the battle-cruiser squadron under Admiral Sir Roger Keyes. He was commander at the navigation school in 1921–23, and then joined the Queen Elizabeth as Master of the Fleet with Admiral Sir John de Robeck, until promoted to Captain in June, 1924.

In this rank between 1924 and 1936 he served on the staff of the War College, commanded the minelayer Adventure, was Deputy Director and Director of Plans, and commanded the battleship Resolution, in which he was also Flag-Captain to Admiral Sir William Fisher during the Abyssinian emergency. In October, 1936, a few months after promotion to rear-admiral, he joined the Board of Admiralty as Assistant Chief of Naval Staff, with Lord Chatfield as the First Sea Lord. Following the Government decision to transfer administrative control of the Fleet Air Arm from the Air Ministry to the Admiralty, he was appointed in August, 1937, to the new post of Assistant Chief of Naval Staff (Air), a title changed in 1938 to that of Fifth Sea Lord and Chief of Naval Air Services.

CAMPAIGN IN NORWAY

In August, 1938, he left the Admiralty to take command of the First Cruiser Squadron in the Mediterranean. This was the post he held, with his flag in the Devonshire, when war broke out again in September, 1939. He had meanwhile been promoted to vice-admiral. The squadron was brought home, and took a prominent part in the Norway campaign in the spring of 1940. Cunningham conducted the evacuation from Namsos and brought home the King of Norway from Tromsö. He was the naval commander of the expedition to Dakar in September, 1940. Six months later he returned to the Admiralty as Fourth Sea Lord and Chief of Supplies and Transport, where he served for over two years during a very difficult period of the War, especially after the entry of Japan.

NAMESAKE AS SUCCESSOR

In June, 1943, he was appointed Commander-in-Chief, Levant, with acting rank as admiral until his substantive promotion two months later. Then in October, 1943, when Admiral Sir Andrew Cunningham was brought home as First Sea Lord, his namesake succeeded him as Commander-in-Chief Mediterranean, and as Allied Naval Commander, having also under his orders United States, French, Greek, and newly-surrendered Italian ships. He remained in the Mediterranean until April, 1946, and among the important operations with which he was associated were the landing at Anzio and the invasion of southern France. Appointed C.B. at the Coronation in 1937, he was promoted to K.C.B. in 1941 and G.C.B. in 1946. His war service also brought him a host of decorations from the governments of the United States, France, Norway, and Greece. He was made a freeman of Athens and was granted the rank of corporal in the Foreign Legion, bestowed for "carrying the Legion from the Arctic to the Equator".

On May 24, 1946, he succeeded Lord Cunningham of Hyndhope as First Sea Lord and was at the Admiralty until September, 1948, having meanwhile been promoted to Admiral of the Fleet in January, 1948. From 1949 to 1958 he was chairman of the Iraq Petroleum Company.

Cunningham married in 1910 Dorothy, daughter of G. K. Hannay, of Ulverston, Lancashire. He had two sons, of whom one was lost on active service in submarine P.33 in 1941. His wife died in 1959.

December 14, 1962.

Sir William Currie, G.B.E., chairman of the P. & O. Steam Navigation Company and of the British India Steam Navigation Company from 1938 to 1960, died on July 3, 1961, at the age of 77.

Few men looked less like a "shipping magnate" or a "City tycoon" than William Crawford Currie—Sir Willie as he was known to his friends. He was short and stocky (with indeed a pleasant plumpness in his later years). He had kindly, but shrewd eyes; he spoke quietly without striving for effect, and he had a personal charm which was as gracious as it was disarming. But as an administrator and as a man of business he made his mark in both Great Britain and India. He was unquestionably one of the foremost men in British shipping. When in 1929 he was appointed president of the Chamber of Shipping of the United Kingdom he was the youngest shipowner ever to have been elected to that high office. From that time onwards his advice and counsel were sought. It is probably not too much to say that no major decision of shipping policy was ever reached without reference to his views.

As chairman of the P. & O. group for many years he was the head of the biggest shipping "empire" in the world, and he guided the fortunes of the group in the grim period of the Second World War when merchant shipping as a whole, and the P. & O. group in particular, suffered such grievous losses.

He was also largely responsible for the rehabilitation of the companies over which he presided in the difficult post-war years.

Currie was a product of Glasgow Academy, Fettes and Trinity College, Cambridge (where he gained a Rugby Blue). He was born in Calcutta on May 4, 1884, and indeed almost born into shipping, for his father served in the Indian office of the British India Steam Navigation Co. for 28 years and became a director.

LOVE FOR INDIA

The son inherited his father's love of India, but he came to Britain at an early age, and it was not until he was 26 that he returned to the land of his birth.

After leaving Cambridge in 1906, Currie joined David Strathie, a firm of chartered accountants in Glasgow. He served his articles with them and qualified four years later. The call of India must have been insistent for he left immediately for Calcutta to become an assistant in the first Lord Inchcape's firm of Mackinnon Mackenzie & Co., the managing agents of the British India Steam Navigation Company. He became a partner in this firm in 1918 and by 1922 was the senior managing partner. He soon began to take a prominent part in the public life of India. He was Sheriff of Calcutta in 1921–22 and was also elected to the Bengal Legislative Council, on which he served until he left India in 1925. A year before that he was elected president of the Bengal Chamber of Commerce and also president of the Associated Chamber of Commerce of India, Burma, and Ceylon. During his last year in India he was appointed member of the Council of State for India and received a knighthood.

The second half of Currie's business life opened on his return to this country in 1926. He became a partner in Gray, Dawes & Co., the London agents of the British India Steam Navigation Company. In the following year he became a member of the Imperial (now Commonwealth) Shipping Committee, on which he sat for four years. He was elected president of the Chamber of Shipping in 1929, when he was a director of James Nourse, Ltd.

P. & O. FLEET REBUILT

Soon after Lord Inchcape's death in 1932 he was elected a director of the P. & O. and later one of the managing directors. He became chairman in 1938 when Lord Craigmyle resigned and also of the British India Steam Navigation Company. The P. & O. lost nearly a million and a quarter tons of shipping, but even in 1945 it had enough ships to resume at least skeleton services. The reconstruction of the fleet was one of the most astonishing achievements in the records of British shipping.

From the outset of the war until it ended, Currie was a member of the Advisory Council of the Ministry of War Transport. In 1942 he became the director of the Liner Division at the Ministry, where he remained until 1945.

RED CROSS WORK

In addition to his work in connexion with shipping Currie served as a member of the executive committee of the British Red Cross Society and Order of St. John from 1942 to 1947 and also on the Red Cross Prisoners of War Committee from 1943 to 1946.

The Institute of Marine Engineers elected him their president for 1945–46 and in the following year he became High Sheriff of Buckinghamshire. From 1946 until 1948 he was chairman of the British Liner Committee which coordinates all shipping matters between London and Liverpool. He was elected Prime Warden of the Worshipful Company of Shipwrights in 1949.

Besides his directorships of the Peninsular & Oriental and British India Steam Navigation companies, Sir William was deputy chairman of Williams Deacon's Bank, an extraordinary director of the Bank of Scotland, chairman of the Marine and General Mutual Life Assurance Society, a director of the Suez Finance Company and of William Cory and Son, Ltd.

He was chairman of the honorary committee of management of the training ship Worcester, a trustee of the National Maritime Museum, a member of the council of King George's Fund for Sailors, and an honorary member of the Honourable Company of Master Mariners.

Currie was created G.B.E., in 1947 and was appointed a Commander of the Legion of Honour of France in 1953. He was appointed an Honorary Captain R.N.R. in February, 1960.

He married in 1914 Ruth Forrest, daughter of C. S. Dods, by whom he had two sons, the elder of whom, Captain William MacKinnon Currie, 45th Cavalry, Indian Army, was killed in Burma in 1944.

July 4, 1961.

Admiral Sir Alban T. B. Curteis, K.C.B., died at his home near Ellesmere, Shropshire, on November 27, 1961, at the age of 74.

He served with distinction in the two world wars, and gained promotion to commander and captain for zealous service in command of destroyers. In the Second World War he held two flag commands in the Home Fleet and one in the Western Atlantic.

Alban Thomas Buckley Curteis, born on January 13, 1887, was the second son of the Rev. Thomas Samuel Curteis, of Sevenoaks. He entered the Britannia in January, 1902, went to sea in May, 1903, and became a lieutenant in June, 1909, at which time he was serving in the King Alfred, flagship in China. During the first year of the 1914–18 War he was a watchkeeper in the cruiser Topaze and the destroyer Manly. From July, 1915, he commanded successively the destroyers Lively, Jackal, and Ulysses, all in the North Sea.

After the armistice he was appointed to the

R.N. College, Osborne, as first lieutenant-commander and physical training officer, a post he held until the College was closed in April, 1921. He then resumed sea service in command of the destroyers Winchelsea and Verity, and while in the former was promoted to commander in December, 1921. In September, 1925, he joined the staff of the Second Sea Lord, on which he served until May, 1927, during which time he was promoted to captain in December, 1926. After a few months in command of the Castor on trooping service, he joined the cruiser Despatch as Flag-Captain and Chief of Staff to Vice-Admiral Sir Cyril Fuller, Commander-in-Chief America and West Indies Station, and served there from 1928 to 1930.

For a short time in 1931 he was Director of Physical Training and Sports, and Head of the Naval Personnel Committee, but left this post in December to become Flag-Captain in the Nelson to Admiral Sir John Kelly, Commander-in-Chief, Atlantic Fleet. From 1933 to 1935 he was Captain of the R.N. College, Greenwich, and then returned to the Nelson as Captain of the Fleet on the staff of Admiral Sir Roger Backhouse. In April, 1938, he became Commodore of the Royal Naval Barracks, Devonport, and was reappointed on his promotion to rear-admiral four months later.

BISMARCK OPERATION

After remaining at Devonport during the first winter of the 1939–45 War he hoisted his flag in May, 1940, in command of the 2nd Cruiser Squadron, Home Fleet, in H.M.S. Galatea. In her he took part in various operations, including those which led to the destruction of the Bismarck on May 27, 1941. Shortly afterwards he was appointed to command the 2nd Battle Squadron, and to be Second-in-Command, Home Fleet, in succession to the late Vice-Admiral Lancelot Holland, who lost his life when H.M.S. Hood was sunk. He was made acting vice-admiral until his promotion in the following December. In June, 1942, he commanded a substantial force which was detached from the Home Fleet to cover a convoy into Malta, his flag flying in the cruiser Kenya. Two months later he was appointed to Bermuda as Senior British Naval Officer, Western Atlantic, where he served until October, 1944. He retired in December, 1944, and was promoted to admiral on the retired list in April, 1945.

Sir Alban was awarded the C.B. in 1940, and promoted to K.C.B. on January 1, 1943.

RETIRED TO FARM

He was twice married, first in 1915 to Essex Helen, daughter of Cyrus Morrall, of Plas Yolyn, Ellesmere, Shropshire, and after her death in 1940 to her sister, Freda, in June, 1941. There were a son and a daughter of the first marriage.

After retiring he started farming at Plas Yolyn and his interests outside farming were concentrated on the Ellesmere R.D.C., of which he was an energetic member.

He is survived by his widow.

November 28, 1961.

Harlow H. Curtice, former president of General Motors Corporation, died at his home at Flint, Michigan, on November 3, 1962. He was 69.

Steady and sometimes swift advances marked his career. Before becoming president of General Motors in 1952 he was an executive vice-president of G.M. for four years and general manager of Buick Motor Division for 15 years. But his rise included no magic short cuts.

Born in Michigan in August, 1893, Harlow Herbert Curtice passed his entire business life in the motor industry. He began his career with General Motors as a book-keeper for the AC Spark Plug Company in 1914. About one year later, at the age of 21, he was made comptroller. He served in the Army during the First World War, returned to AC, and in 1923 was made assistant general manager, while retaining his duties as comptroller.

Four years later Curtice became vice-president and assistant general manager, devoting his time to manufacturing management, and in 1929, at the age of 35, he was named president of the company. During his stewardship at AC he increased the product range of the division with the result that employment in AC plants was greater during the depression than it had been previously.

Although Curtice received his first training in the fields of accounting and finance, he had an expert's grasp of styling, engineering and production. More than that, he had a natural aptitude for salesmanship, making him one of the industry's most versatile executives.

Buick, the oldest division of General Motors, was at its lowest ebb in 1933 when Curtice, then head of the AC Spark Plug Division and at 40 one of the industry's most experienced executives, was chosen president and general manager. Production had slumped to 40,621 units, less than one-sixth of Buick's 1926 peak of 266,753 cars and less even than its 1915 output. The economic depression combined with a product that had failed to remain competitive tumbled Buick from its place of leadership.

BUICK REVITALIZED

There was a tradition in the automobile business that when a popular car started to drop away in sales volume it was on the road to oblivion. Many believed this fate awaited Buick, once G.M.'s leading division. Curtice did not share this gloom. He moved quickly and effectively into the job of rebuilding Buick. His prodigious energy, quiet decisiveness and zeal for perfection revitalized Buick almost overnight. Buick's sales soared, and by 1938 the company was the industry's fourth largest producer, outselling all but the three low-priced makes.

When peace returned in 1945, Curtice led Buick's reconversion programme, spending millions of dollars rebuilding, expanding and modernizing facilities to enable Buick to produce efficiently more than 500,000 cars a year.

In September, 1948, Curtice was named an executive vice-president of General Motors in charge of general staff activities. He was named acting president of General Motors on December 1, 1952, after Charles E. Wilson was granted leave of absence to serve as Mr. Eisenhower's Secretary of Defence.

On February 2, 1953, the board named Curtice president of General Motors, succeeding Mr. Wilson. He held the post until his retirement in 1958.

He was married to Miss Dorothy Biggs of Sherman, Texas in 1927. They had three daughters.

November 5, 1962.

Michael Curtiz, for many years one of the most versatile and prolific of Hollywood directors, died in Hollywood on April 10, 1962. He was 73.

He had, even for Hollywood, an unusually varied background of theatrical and cinematic experience before he arrived in the United States. He was born in Budapest on Christmas Eve, 1888, and his real name was Mihali Kertesz, which went through a number of transformations and transliterations before reaching its final American form. He was educated at the Markoczy high school, and continued his studies at the Hungarian Royal Academy of Dramatic Art before entering the theatre as an actor and producer. He early became interested in the possibilities of the film, and after the 1914–18 War he went to Vienna to direct his first films. These were two of the big historical spectacles popular at the time, *Sodom and Gomorrha* and *Samson and Delilah*. During the next few years he travelled widely, making films in Hungary, Germany, Scandinavia, France, Italy, and England. (He worked on several Anglo-German co-productions, including *Moon of Israel* and two films with Lili Damita, *Red Heels* and *The Road to Happiness*).

In 1926 Curtiz became one of the first generation of European directors to be drawn to Hollywood. His most notable American silent films were *The Mad Genius*, which included an excellent performance by John Barrymore, and another of the Biblical epics which had been his speciality in Europe, *Noah's Ark*, the flood scenes from which remain one of the screen's finest pieces of spectacle. Among his earliest assignments in the talking picture was an Al Jolson vehicle, *Mammy*, but his reputation as a director to watch dated from *Cabin in the Cotton* (1932), followed by a number of other contributions to the series of films which offered hard-hitting social comment during the depression and its aftermath, among them *20,000 Years in Sing-Sing* (which, like *Cabin in the Cotton*, featured Bette Davis), and *Black Fury*. His work was by no means confined to the social document, however: he also directed Bette Davis in lighter melodramas like *Jimmy the Gent* and *Front Page Woman*, made the excellent horror film *The Mystery of the Wax Museum*, and a number of swashbuckling adventure stories such as *Captain Blood* and *The Charge of the Light Brigade*.

After a brief flirtation with the fashionable crazy comedy (*The Perfect Specimen*) and a momentary return to the social problem picture in *Angels with Dirty Faces*, starring Humphrey Bogart and James Cagney, Curtiz concentrated almost entirely during the immediate prewar years on the costume adventure with *The Adventures of Robin Hood*, *The Sea Hawk*, *The Sea Wolf* and most interestingly *The Private Lives of Elizabeth and Essex*, in which Bette Davis gave one of her most interesting performances as Queen Elizabeth I. The war brought the expected crop of war films, among them *Mission to Moscow*, *Passage to Marseilles*, and *Casablanca*, one of the best popular films ever made, for which Curtiz won an Academy Award in 1943. Other award-winning films of this period were *Yankee Doodle Dandy*, a life of George M. Cohen, which brought James Cagney the Academy's best actor award for 1942, and *Mildred Pierce*, for which Joan Crawford won her Academy Award in 1946.

The postwar period brought an even wider variety of films from Curitz, all of them elegantly put together if without any notable signs of individual personality. There were comedies like *Life with Father* and *We're No Angels*, dramas like *The Breaking Point* (a version of Hemingway's *To Have and Have Not*, with a striking performance by John Garfield), *Flamingo Road*, *The Scarlet Hour*, and *Man in the Net*, westerns like *The Proud Rebel* and *The Hangman*, and musicals such as *Night and Day*, *Young Man of Music*, *White Christmas*, *The Vagabond King*, and *The Best Things in Life are Free*, not to mention one of Elvis Presley's most successful films, *King Creole*.

Michael Curtiz was not a great director but he was a very competent one. A superior technician, he brought an impersonal skill to all his films, especially in the directions of actors, where his stage experience stood him in good stead. None of his films was quite first-rate, but many of them were among the most entertaining products of Hollywood, and he was deservedly one of the American directors most consistently successful at the box office.

April 12, 1962.

Richard Cardinal Cushing, Archbishop of Boston from 1944 until 1970, and probably the best known and best loved dignitary of the Roman Catholic Church in the Americas, died on November 2, 1970. He was 75.

A big cheerful, impulsive man, Cushing was a fervent promoter of good works, readily approachable and of apparently limitless energy. He first made his name as a promoter of mission work, and in his later years took particular pleasure in supporting homes for handicapped or unlucky children. At the Vatican Council he professed himself restless and ill at ease in discussing refinements of doctrine—for one thing, his Latin was rusty—but he played a leading part in advocating friendship with other Christian Churches, the formal exculpation of the Jews from any special blame for the Crucifixion, and the furthering of charitable undertakings all over the world.

Cushing was not afraid of controversy, but so little disconcerted by it that he could, for example, condemn the John Birch Society one week, endorse it the next, and write off the results as "a peck of trouble". He raised almost $1 m. for the ransom of Cubans captured at the Bay of Pigs, publicly praised the evangelical labours of Dr. Billy Graham, and called for a postponement of the Statute of Limitations relating to German war criminals.

As a preacher he was resonant and emphatic, as a pastor thoroughly homespun, ready to dance a jig on St. Patrick's Day in his sixties and carve the turkey at his annual thanksgiving dinner for the poor. He was a devout Marian, composer of a celebrated prayer to Our Lady of Boston, and after the war led many pilgrimages to European shrines.

Cardinal Cushing was a close friend of the Kennedy family. During the presidential campaign of Senator John Kennedy he defended Kennedy stating his "firmly held belief that a Catholic can serve as President of the United States and fulfil his oath of office with complete fidelity and with no reservations". Cushing said a prayer at Kennedy's inauguration as president; he was present at the funeral of his infant son Patrick, and officiated at the funeral of the President himself.

Cardinal Cushing refused to condemn Mrs. Jacqueline Kennedy when she married the divorced Aristotle Onassis. This surprised many Roman Catholics, but his attitude came as no surprise to those who knew of his fierce loyalty to his friends.

FUND RAISING

Richard James Cushing, the third American-born son of Irish immigrants to become Archbishop of Boston, and the second to attain a red hat, was the third child and eldest son of a blacksmith. He was born on August 24, 1895, and went to Boston High School and Boston College, where he broke off his studies after two years to train for the priesthood. He was ordained by Cardinal O'Connell in 1921. After a year as a curate he entered the office of the director of the Propagation of the Faith and became director himself six years later. His success in raising funds and recruiting missionaries was prodigious and made the Boston Archdiocese, with a Catholic population of more than a million and ample funds, chief provider to mission work all over the world.

In 1939 Father Cushing was elevated to monsignor and then appointed auxiliary bishop of Boston in succession to Cardinal Spellman. When Cardinal O'Connell died in 1944 at the age of 84, Cushing was first appointed interim administrator and then archbishop. At the age of 48 he was the youngest archbishop in the church.

During his long tenure, Cardinal Cushing constantly enlarged the activity of the archdiocese, and became internationally celebrated long before he was elevated to the College of Cardinals in 1958. He was an officer of the Legion of Honour and the west German Order of Merit, and Prior of the Knights of The Holy Sepulchre. He held many awards for good works, and a score of honorary doctorates. He will be remembered, like Pope John XXIII, whom he liked so well, as a man of the people.

November 3, 1970.

Colonel Sir Archer Cust, C.B.E., who died in London on May 22, 1962, at the age of 65, served in both world wars, and was a member of the Palestine Civil Service for 15 years. Later as Secretary-General of the Royal Empire (now Royal Commonwealth) Society he was widely known and highly regarded throughout the Commonwealth. He was in charge of the headquarters in Northumberland Avenue during the long years required for its reconstruction and refurnishing following on the severe war damage sustained in the spring of 1941.

Lionel George Archer Cust was born on June 6, 1896, son of Sir Lionel Cust, K.C.V.O., a member of the Royal Household. Archer's uncle, Robert Needham Cust, a distinguished Orientalist, was for many years honorary secretary of the Royal Asiatic Society and one of its vice-presidents. Archer was educated at Eton College, and at the age of 19 when war had broken out was gazetted to the Royal Field Artillery. He did staff work on the Western Front and in Egypt, and was mentioned in dispatches. In 1920 Cust joined the Palestine Civil Service. In 1921–23 he was A.D.C. to the High Commissioner, Sir Herbert (now Lord) Samuel. He was secretary of the Bertram-Luke Commission on the Jerusalem Orthodox Patriarchate. In 1925 he held a like position with the Bertram-Young Commission. From 1928 to 1931 Cust was private secretary to the then High Commissioner, the late Sir John Chancellor. In 1932 he was seconded as private secretary to the Governor of Northern Rhodesia, the late Sir Ronald Storrs, and held the position for two years.

ARMY DUTIES

On his retirement from the Palestine Civil Service in 1935 Cust was selected to be Assistant Secretary of the Royal Empire Society, the headquarters of which in Northumberland Avenue had been reconstructed and greatly enlarged and opened in the previous year by the then Duke of York. Cust was promoted to the secretaryship in 1938, but on the outbreak of war in the following year he was seconded to Army duty in the Military Intelligence and Psychological Warfare branches. His services in this position were mentioned in dispatches. Meanwhile the late Sir Walter Buchanan-Smith acted for him at the headquarters of the R.E.S. Cust had already organized there a staff Warden Service and Fire and First Aid Parties, and such spare time as he had was spent in the building. It suffered successive bomb attacks and the most destructive of these occurred on the night of April 16–17, 1941. The building was severely damaged and no less than 35,000 volumes in the library and 5,000 documents were destroyed. Even in the early calculation the claims upon the war damage commission reached a total of £127,000, and as time went on serious further damage and losses were discovered. When Cust resumed the secretary-generalship he took active steps to obtain renewals of the timbers for panelling which had been provided so recently from many countries of the British Commonwealth and Empire. In this endeavour he was markedly successful.

It was not until the early summer of 1957 that the complete restoration and refurnishing of the building with structural alterations were finally completed. The following year Cust retired from office.

Throughout these long years of reconstruction with their vexatious if unavoidable delays, Cust maintained his wonted calm and directness of purpose. His exceptionally wide range of contacts was shown when problems came up to him for decision or reference to the council. He won the warm regard of the staff and his relations with successive chairmen of the Council were happy. This was notably so during the chairmanship in the middle fifties of Colonel Sir Charles Ponsonby, with whom he planned the plebiscite of the large and growing membership at home and abroad which resulted in the name of the organization being changed to the Royal Commonwealth Society. The Society's title was thus brought into line with existing realities and the frequently expressed wish of leading members of the overseas Branches.

Cust was created O.B.E. in 1939, advanced to C.B.E. in 1954, and knighted in 1959. He married in 1925 Margaret Violet Louisa, daughter of Lieutenant-colonel H. A. Clowes, of Norbury Hall. Ashbourne, and a son and two daughters were born to them.

May 23, 1962.

D

Sir Harry Guy Dain, who was chairman of the British Medical Association at the time of the setting up of the National Health Service, died on February 26, 1966, at his home in Aberdovey. He was 95.

Harry Guy Dain was born in Birmingham on November 5, 1970, and received his training and spent his whole professional life in that city. He was at Josiah Mason's College, to which, in 1892, the Medical Department of Queen's College, Birmingham, was transferred. He qualified M.R.C.S., L.R.C.P., in 1893, and took the M.B., London, in the following year. After holding appointments as resident medical officer at the Children's Hospital, Birmingham, and assistant house surgeon at the General Hospital, he settled down in general practice and became senior partner of a large partnership in the residential and growing district of Selly Oak. In Birmingham he was a member of the first insurance committee and of the first panel committee. Soon he was elected chairman of the insurance committee.

But Guy Dain, as he preferred to be known, did not confine his activity to his home town. In 1917 he became a member of the British Medical Association Insurance Acts Committee (and its successor the General Medical Services Committee), and served with distinction until he decided not to seek re-election in 1960. He was its chairman for 12 years (1924–36). For five years (1919–1924) he presided over the Annual Conference of Local Medical and Panel Committees. He was elected to the General Medical Council in 1934 by the practitioners of England and Wales as one of their direct representatives and was reelected for successive terms until he resigned in 1961. No other medical practitioner has served on the Council for such a lengthy period.

He served as a representative on the British Medical Association's Representative Body from 1919 until 1957 and was its chairman from 1937–1942. He was a member of the B.M.A. Council from 1921–1960 and was its chairman from 1943–1949.

It was during this period that the difficult negotiations with the Labour Government in connexion with setting up of the National Health Service were carried out.

It was natural, if not inevitable, that the chairman of the council of the B.M.A. should become chairman of the composite medical body representing not only the British Medical Association but the Royal Colleges and Corporations, set up to express the profession's views on the proposals for a National Health Service.

KEPT DOCTORS UNITED

But for this it is unlikely that Dain would have been chosen as the profession's principal spokesman. He was in his early seventies, an unspectacular, competent family doctor from Birmingham, better known as a steady negotiator than as a forceful leader.

In the event he was supremely successful. In spite of the strains the profession remained united for most of the time—a very considerable achievement.

It is not difficult to analyse the elements of Dain's success. He was able and modest. He remained remarkably alert both mentally and physically. In speech he was clear and logical using no platform tricks or heavily prepared phrases. He was commonsense personified. Perhaps most important of all he was as honest as he was patient, never seeking a quick platform victory at the expense of wisdom and never butting in with his conclusions before the discussion was nearing completion. The ordinariness of his appearance and his speech turned out to be advantages in many an excited medical gathering in which oratory and emotion tended to drown good sense and sound judgment.

From the medley of issues raised by both the Willink and the Bevan proposals, Dain selected those he deemed the most important and concentrated his mind upon them. They included the importance of maintaining free choice of patient and doctor, the dangers of a wholetime, salaried service and the importance of closer links between general practitioners and hospitals. Doctors' pay, on the other hand, interested him less than it did many others.

THOUGHT FOR PATIENTS

He thought more of the patient than he did of his own purse.

He never really understood Aneurin Bevan. He thought of him as primarily a politician and he believed that politicians should yield place to doctors in the creation of a medical service. The fact that Aneurin Bevan was an extremely clever politician seemed to him to make matters worse rather than better.

In 1939 he received the honorary degree of LL. D. of Aberdeen, and in 1944 the honorary degree of M.D., Birmingham. He was admitted a Fellow of the Royal College of Surgeons of England in 1945 as a member of more than 20 years standing.

A member of the B.M.A. since 1896, he was awarded the Gold Medal of the Association in 1936, and in 1951 as principal guest at a council dinner he was presented with his portrait painted by Mr. David Jagger, R.O.I. In 1957 the Trustees of the Claire Wand Fund made him the first recipient of their Award for "Outstanding Services to General Practice".

To mark his outstanding service on behalf of insurance practitioners the Dain Testimonial Fund was inaugurated in 1936. At his request the money given was used as a Trust Fund to assist the education of the sons and daughters of medical practitioners who had fallen on hard times.

Dain was created a knight in 1961, a year after he retired at the age of 90.

Dain was twice married. His first wife died in 1933. A son of that marriage, Dr. Basil Guy Dain, practises in Birmingham.

March 1, 1966.

Edouard Daladier, who was Prime Minister of France at the time of the Munich agreement and at the outbreak of war in September, 1939, and who yet went on to take an active part in the political life of the Fourth Republic, died in Paris on October 10, 1970. He was 86.

He was a better than average Third Republic political leader who never quite lived up to his early promise. But he will go down in history as France's "Man of Munich", and if his personal share of responsibility for the climax of the policy of appeasement of Germany is undeniable, it would be wanting in justice to both men to regard Daladier as, in any intellectual sense, the "opposite number" of Neville Chamberlain. Each had the support in his own country of a considerable body, perhaps the main body, of public opinion: but, whereas Chamberlain personally and confidently took the initiative in the conduct of foreign affairs, Daladier—who in the crucial period became Prime Minister only in April, 1938—was largely following in the footsteps of a rapid succession of unhappy Ministers at the Quai d'Orsay. He was, in fact, deeply in the toils of France's political weakness and instability. He did not, moreover, deceive himself into thinking that France had gained strength or reputation by concessions to Germany at the expense of Czechoslovakia. Distressed, anxious, even fearful, he was apparently taken by complete surprise, on the flight back from Munich, by the wildly cheering crowds at Le Bourget aerodrome.

Perhaps the truth is that as a politician, Daladier, who had always affected a greater strength of character than he possessed, on the occasion of Munich paid the penalty of his affectation. Shrewd, experienced, direct in manner, from the beginning of his career prone to fortify himself by a studied brevity of speech, he was both abler and more sincere than many of his fellow politicians among the Centre parties in the Chamber, but was no more fitted to play the part of the man of destiny in France's hour of need. The leader of the left wing of the Radical-Socialists, a Minister in almost a score of Cabinets, particularly popular as Minister of War, twice Prime Minister before 1938, his personal failure in face of events reflects the general debility and decay of the Third Republic between the wars.

TEACHING HISTORY

A Southerner—he was short, dark, distinctly meridional in type—Edouard Daladier was born at Carpentras, near Avignon, on June 18, 1884. His father was a baker, and the son progressed by scholarships from the local lycée to Lyons (where one of his teachers was Edouard Herriot), the École Normale and the Sorbonne. When war broke out in 1914, Daladier was lecturer in history at the Lycée Condorcet in Paris. He was mobilized as a sergeant, fought at Verdun, was mentioned three times in dispatches and awarded the Legion of Honour, and at the date of the Armistice held the rank of lieutenant. Returning to Provence he was elected mayor of his native town and in the autumn of 1919 was elected to the Chamber as Radical-Socialist deputy for the department of Vaucluse.

Although, when he chose, Daladier did not fail as a conventional type of orator, his interventions in debate were generally brief and almost coldly precise, and this somewhat unusual trait, as was to be expected, drew attention to him. His more important speeches, however, were written by a young secretary who afterwards became a well-known novelist. With the victory of the Cartel des Gauches in 1924, Herriot appointed him Minister of the Colonies. Thereafter when any Centre-Left grouping held power, Daladier was an all but certain candidate for office. He became Prime Minister in January, 1933, a day after Hitler's accession to power in Germany, and held office until the following October.

This was the last stable Government of the Third Republic. Daladier showed vigour and tenacity in pursuit of a policy of European conciliation, but the tide of events both at home and abroad was running against him. His second spell as Prime Minister at the beginning of 1934 was terminated by the Stavisky riots, and his work at the Ministry of National Defence in subsequent Administrations was fatally handicapped by the discords of French political life. He included Reynaud and Mandel in his Cabinet in 1938, but as the Czech crisis deepened he could only proclaim his trust in Hitler's peaceful intentions.

After the German occupation of Prague in March, 1939, he was given plenary powers by both Houses of Parliament and proceeded to deliver himself from time to time of appropriately stirring speeches. With the outbreak of war he formed a new War Cabinet, with himself as Minister of War and Minister of Foreign Affairs as well as Prime Minister, and enlivened the "phoney" phase of hostilities by constant professions of optimism. His leadership, however, was plainly lacking in drive, the Cabinet was bedevilled by intrigue and the play of personal ambitions, and in March, 1940, Daladier resigned, to be succeeded by Reynaud, who temporarily dropped him from the Cabinet. Daladier, however, was successively Minister of War and Minister of Foreign Affairs before the capitulation in June.

He was arrested in that month by the Vichy regime, charged with "war guilt", released and placed under house arrest until the following June, tried by a Court for Political Justice, detained in a fortress, put in the dock at the Riom trials in February, 1942—his self-justificatory bearing there was not specially impressive—and was eventually liberated from a secret prison camp in the Alps in May, 1945.

He had argued before his judges, as Reynaud and Blum had done, that France's military unpreparedness was not due to the failure of successive governments to provide sufficient credits, but to the excessive confidence parliaments had placed in the judgment of soldiers like Marshal Pétain and General Weygand. This had not prevented Daladier appointing Pétain, then 83, Ambassador to Spain in February, 1939, nor from inviting him to join the government seven months later—an invitation the aged Marshal fortunately refused.

Daladier was one of the few Third Republic political leaders, particularly those who, rightly or wrongly, had been considered in any way responsible for the 1940 debacle, who were able to resume their careers under the Fourth Republic. But he never attained the same prominence, and never again held ministerial rank. He was elected a member of the National Assembly in 1946, to the indignation of the Communists whose party he had proscribed in 1939, after the Soviet-German Pact, and whose leaders he was alleged to have persecuted, but their efforts to invalidate his election failed.

MOVE TO LEFT

He moved steadily towards the left wing of the increasingly divided Radical Party—the position he had occupied when he entered politics 30 years earlier—and became one of M. Mendes-France's active supporters. Indeed, it was during Mendes-France's stormy fight in 1955–56 to capture the administrative machinery of the Radical-Socialist Party—which was soon to discard the outdated Socialist half of its label—from the right-wing Radicals in whose hands it had been, that Daladier relived a little of his pre-war prominence. He was a member of the Commission des Sept which, under the almost nominal presidency of the old and ill Edouard Herriot, refashioned the party statutes nearer to M. Mendes-France's desire, and in 1956 he was elected president of the Radical parliamentary group. In November, 1957, he became president of the Radical Party, but resigned this and all his other offices, including the mayoralty of Avignon, in September, 1958, when he decided not to enter the first general election of the Fifth Republic. He was then 74, a thickening, red-faced, solitary man living on in a world in which even Munich was little more than a distant name.

In 1961, at the age of 77, Daladier retired finally from politics. He lived mainly at his Paris home, in the Passy district, reflecting on his past life and writing his memoirs. His visits to his native Vaucluse, where he retained considerable popularity, became rarer and rarer. But he remained a member of the bureau of the Radical Party, of which he was honorary life chairman, and only a few months ago was photographed with the party's new secretary-general, M. Jean-Jacques Servan-Schreiber.

He married twice: first Madeleine Laffont (who died in 1935) and secondly, in 1951, Jeanne Boucoiran.

October 12, 1970.

Air Marshal Sir John H. D'Albiac, K.C.V.O., K.B.E., C.B., D.S.O., who after a distinguished career in the R.A.F. became the first Commandant of London Airport, died on August 20, 1963, at the age of 69.

John Henry D'Albiac was born at Kew on January 28, 1894, the son of Charles William D'Albiac, and was educated at Seabrook Lodge, Kent, and later at Framlingham College. He joined the Army in August, 1914, and was commissioned as a second lieutenant in the Royal Marine Artillery in December. Later he was seconded to the Royal Naval Air Service, with which he served in France as an observer from 1915 to 1917. He won a D.S.O. in 1916. After the creation of the Royal Air Force he transferred on a permanent basis to that service.

In the years between the wars he held various posts in the Middle East, in India, and at home. In 1939 a course at the Imperial Defence College was curtailed by the imminence of hostilities, and D'Albiac, now an air commodore, was sent to Palestine as Air Officer Commanding. A period of strenuous activity caused by the Arab-Jewish hostilities followed, interrupted for some months in 1940 and 1941 by a move westwards across the Mediterranean to take command of the British air forces in Greece.

It was no picnic; the R.A.F. strength was seven squadrons, composed of some 80 aircraft, compared with an estimated German strength of 800 and an Italian strength of 310. Yet the offensive spirit was maintained though the weather was often abominable, the airfields few and the terrain difficult. The R.A.F. continued the battle until almost all their aircraft had been destroyed and then used the survivors to cover the evacuation of Crete. D'Albiac gained an excellent reputation for the way he handled his small force.

After the withdrawal from Greece, D'Albiac returned to his original base in Palestine, only to receive fresh orders to proceed to Habbaniyah, where the Iraq Army was in revolt. He describes his arrival at Habbaniyah as one of the warmest receptions ever accorded to an incoming A.O.C., probably because he landed in an aircraft not of the type originally scheduled for the journey!

BOMBER GROUP

In the spring of 1942, as an Air Vice-Marshal, he took command of the Air Forces in Ceylon; within a few days of his arrival, on Easter Sunday, Colombo and Trincomalee suffered a carrier-borne attack from the Japanese, which was beaten off. There followed a period of consolidation; fighter strips were cut in the jungle, a radar warning network was set up, and a programme of combined operations training was undertaken.

Then came a home posting, and D'Albiac took command of No.2 Bomber Group. His next task, from June, 1943, to January, 1944, was the formation and command of the 2nd. Tactical Air Force, then based at Bracknell, after which he was posted as Deputy Commander of the Mediterranean Allied Tactical Air Force, then under the command of General Cannon, U.S.A.F. For the rest of 1944 he worked with that command from their Italian bases at Caserta, Rome and Siena until, in December, he was appointed Director-General of Personnel (III) at the Air Ministry with which was combined, ex officio, the Presidency of the Permanent Commission Selection Board. He was created K.B.E. in 1946, and in December of that year he retired.

His connexion with flying was not, however, to terminate so abruptly; civil aviation was rapidly recovering from the restrictions of the war years, and the Royal Air Force station at Heathrow, near Hounslow, was about to become London Airport. Sir John was offered the post of Aerodrome Commandant for the Ministry of Civil Aviation, and, in January, 1947, he took up the post he held for 10 years. During his term of office the airport developed from a temporary terminal of marquees, huts and caravans into one of the best equipped air terminals in the world.

After his retirement from London Airport, D'Albiac was appointed deputy chairman of the Air Transport Advisory Council, and that body was able to benefit from his profound experience of matters aeronautical until 1961.

He married in 1933 Sibyl, eldest daughter of Robert Owen, of co. Wicklow, and had one son and three daughters.

August 21, 1963.

Sir Henry Dale, O.M., G.B.E., F.R.S., who died on July 23, 1968, in a Cambridge nursing home at the age of 93, was an outstanding leader of medical research in Great Britain.

He had an extraordinary instinct for choosing problems of importance, for planning experiments in which every detail was foreseen, for carrying them out so that no experiment was wasted, and for describing the results so that everyone could understand exactly what he had done and what conclusions could be be drawn from the results. His work covered many fields, and all his writing bore the imprint of his clarity of thought and powers of precise exposition.

He was born on June 9, 1875, and educated at The Leys School, Trinity College, Cambridge, and St. Bartholomew's Hospital. After a short time with Paul Ehrlich, he went to work with Ernest Starling, who recommended him, at the age of 29, to Henry Wellcome as director of the Wellcome Physiological Research Laboratories. During the next 10 years, as leader of a brilliant team of investigators, he did the work which established his reputation and led to his election as F.R.S. in 1914. It is now known, largely through his work, that animal tissues contain pharmacologically active substances, such as histamine and acetylcholine, which are released during life and control some of the bodily functions. These substances are widely distributed in nature, and Dale had the insight to realize their importance when he found them in an attempt to analyse the therapeutic actions of extracts of ergot; later he called this branch of knowledge autopharmacology. A large part of modern pharmacology is based on the work he did during his time on the pharmacology of drugs allied to acetylcholine and adrenaline.

In 1914 Dale joined the staff of what later became known as the Medical Research Council and was the first director of the National Institute for Medical Research. In 1921 Otto Loewi, of Graz, had shown that a substance resembling acetylcholine was liberated in a frog's heart. Dale and his colleagues followed this up in many ways, and showed that acetylcholine itself has many important functions in the body; Dale and Loewi shared the Nobel Prize in 1936 for this work.

During these years Dale, on behalf of the Medical Research Council, was actively interested in discoveries of many kinds. When insulin was discovered in 1922 he went out to Toronto and made sure that it would be standardized by sound methods. This involved the formation of an international committee, of which Dale was chairman, and which became responsible for the biological standardization of hormones, vitamins, antibiotics, and immunological products in general and has brought order in all these fields.

In the years between the wars Dale was a busy man. He was biological secretary of the Royal Society from 1925 to 1935 and was perpetually consulted on all kinds of subjects by government departments, by universities and by individual scientists. In 1940 he was invited to be president of the Royal Society. He decided he could only undertake this if he gave up something else instead, and, after some thought, decided to give up smoking. At the same time, he joined the Scientific Advisory Committee to the War Cabinet and was later its chairman.

When the war was over Dale was 70, but his formidable energy was by no means exhausted. In 1936 he had been appointed one of the trustees to administer the estate of Sir Henry Wellcome. This gave him an office and much work. Under his guidance the Wellcome Trust spent hundreds of thousands of pounds each year encouraging medical research by grants for building, apparatus, travel, publications, &c. He was chairman of the trust from 1936 to 1960.

Dale was president of the British Association in Dundee (1947), president of the Royal Society of Medicine (1948–50), and president of of the British Council (1950–55). He held over 20 honorary degrees and was an honorary member of over 20 scientific societies in different parts of the world. He gave numerous lectures and addresses on great occasions and small, crossing the Atlantic almost every year.

He married in 1904 Ellen Harriet, daughter of F. W. Hallett. She died in 1967.

July 24, 1968.

Lord Dalton, for many years a prominent figure in British political life, who held office in the wartime Coalition and in the succeeding Labour Governments, died on February 13, 1962, at the age of 74. He was Chancellor of the Exchequer from July, 1945, to November, 1947.

This son of a canon of Windsor and Old Etonian exercised a formative influence on the Labour movement, first as university teacher, writer, and economist, and later as party organizer and administrator. He was one of those intellectuals who chose to put the services of an acute, original and highly trained mind at the disposal of a primarily working-class party, and in the process often found himself at the centre of acute controversy.

His rule at the Exchequer, marked by a cheap money policy in inappropriate conditions, will also be remembered for the manner of his leaving it. He resigned after indiscreetly disclosing one of the provisions of his interim Budget to a lobby journalist a few minutes before his speech, and the news was published prematurely in a London evening paper. This was, however, no reflection upon Dalton's personal integrity.

It was under his Chancellorship that the Finance Act, 1946, empowered the Treasury in certain circumstances to accept property through the National Land Fund in payment of death duties. Under the provisions of this Act several historic houses and important art collections have come to the nation. The national parks movement, which he did much to foster, owes a great deal to his devoted work during this period. He was a great lover of the open air and of walking, and his tramps with like-minded M.P.s caught the popular imagination. One of them cost him a broken ankle.

As a personality, some may have found his booming benevolence a trifle over-whelming, but he was undoubtedly a stimulating influence on members of his party and not least upon the promising younger men whose talents he was always ready to foster. Some of them paid him the tribute of imitating the Daltonian manner, though the political expertise which they learnt from him soon gave them the wisdom to moderate its extravagances to fit their own personalities. In any case few of them had the physique which gave such a panache to his parliamentary performances. When Dalton draped himself over the Dispatch Box, to admonish or more frequently to mock his opponents, he was a figure impossible to ignore. He seldom moderated the deep organ notes of his voice, and he had a habit of showing the whites of his eyes which sometimes gave his wide smile the saturnine threat of a leer, but the exuberance of his enjoyment beguiled even those who felt the lash of his tongue.

M.P. FOR PECKHAM

The Rt. Hon. Edward Hugh John Neale Dalton, Baron Dalton, of Forest and Frith in the County Palatine of Durham, was born at Neath, Glamorgan, on August 26, 1887, the son of the Rev. J. N. Dalton, K.C.V.O., C.M.G., Canon of St. George's, Windsor. He was educated at Eton and King's College, Cambridge, and in 1911 became a research student at the London School of Economics. In 1914 he was called to the Bar by the Middle Temple, but he never practised.

During the Great War he served in the R.A.S.C. and the Royal Artillery, his most distinguished service being in Italy where he brought the last three British guns back to the allied lines after Caporetto and was awarded the Italian Medal for Military Valour. From 1920 to 1925 he was Cassel Reader in Economics at the University of London, where he gained his D.Sc. in 1921. From 1925 to 1936 he was University Reader.

Dalton was elected M.P. for the Peckham Division of Camberwell in 1924 and was Under Secretary of State for Foreign Affairs from 1929 to 1931. He fully supported the pacifist policy of that Government though his contribution was eclipsed at the time by the reputation of his chief, Arthur Henderson, for whom he had an unbounded admiration. He was the typical Labour intellectual of the period, full of generous hopes for the pacification of Europe and of equally generous illusions how to accomplish it.

After being unseated in 1931 he returned to teaching. But when he went back to the Commons in 1935 as M.P. for Bishop Auckland he found himself swimming against the prevailing current of Socialist opinion, for he realized more rapidly than some of his colleagues the fallacy of one-sided disarmament as a means to peace. With skilful personal diplomacy, however, he kept the confidence of all sections of his party, acting as a valuable mediator between trade union conservatism and the more advanced views of the Labour intelligentsia from which he sprang. He was supremely suited to the post of chairman of the National Executive, which he held from 1936 to 1937. His debating style was lucid and expository and his easy command of expert knowledge made him valuable to the party.

He had much to do with the process by which Socialism was ceasing at this time to be a political *mystique* and was becoming a practical programme. But his administrative talents were not put to the test until 1940 when he was appointed Minister of Economic Warfare in the Coaliton Government. The choice was excellent and his bustling efficiency soon lifted the ministry from the relatively subordinate role for which it had been cast into an important instrument of victory. Churchill, recognizing his qualities, entrusted him with charge of the Special Operation Executive, a newly formed, highly secret agency for sabotage and subversion of enemy machinations overseas. His success won him promotion to the Board of Trade in 1942. He handled the whole business of clothes rationing with good sense, explained the need for the production of "utility" goods and kept a watchful eye on export requirements after the war. The Location of Industry Bill which he introduced enabled him to carry out the plans he had long nurtured for aiding the special areas.

A POLITICAL MYSTERY

When he became Chancellor of the Exchequer in 1945 he was confronted with problems as grave and complex as any which his predecessors had faced. It had generally been believed that he would have preferred the Foreign Office and the reason for his appointment to the Treasury was at the time something of a political mystery. Dalton offered his own explanation in the second volume of his autobiography. According to this version, Attlee came to the decision that Herbert Morrison and Ernest Bevin were best kept apart, the one on the home front and the other at the Foreign Office. Perhaps, as Dalton later conceded, the influence of King George VI may have had something to do with it. At all events, at the last minute Bevin, who had wanted to be Chancellor, went to the Foreign Office and Dalton got the Chancellorship.

His Budget speeches were remarkably lucid and never marred by the intellectual condescension which, in his anxiety to be understood, he sometimes displayed on the platform or before a microphone. The main feature of his conduct of domestic finance was his cheap money policy. But this was a remedy for depression applied in the inflationary circumstances of the immediate postwar years. Dalton's attitude, however, was a mere reflection of of an unrealistic public opinion—and as a politician he knew how high were popular expectations aroused by the Labour victory. History must record that he acted faithfully according to his lights.

STERLING DECISION

Dalton was also strongly criticized for permitting the free convertibility of sterling which came into force in July, 1947. This was one of the conditions attached by the Americans to their loan. In the circumstances the Government had no alternative but to accept the United States terms. As it was, the loan, which was expected to last until 1951, was rapidly exhausted.

A number of critics on both sides of the House foresaw that in such circumstances a "dash to convertibility" would impose too great a strain upon sterling.

Dalton, however, remained obstinately optimistic and refused to listen to the suggestion that Britain might find the burden too heavy and should seek to be released from it by the United States. He was eventually forced to open negotiations with the United States for that purpose and in August announced that they had agreed to suspend the convertibility clause.

The day after, it became clear that this concession had been made only on condition that the rest of the loan should be frozen. Dalton's task was harder than the critics supposed, American opinion was insistent on the fulfilment of the terms of the loan and mere repudiation was therefore out of the question.

ONLY AN INDISCRETION

The circumstances of his resignation from the Chancellorship in 1947 were generally regretted. As Mr. Churchill was the first to point out, there was no suggestion of anything worse than indiscretion, and no use had been made of the information disclosed. When Dalton offered his resignation he was replaced by Sir Stafford Cripps. Though his departure was accidental it was taken to mark a fundamental change in financial policy. As a private member Dalton was scrupulously loyal and gave unqualified support to the new policy while continuing to maintain that at the time his own was right.

Dalton's restoration to Cabinet rank in June, 1948, was widely welcomed, particularly in the constituencies, where his stock had been briskly rising. The post of Chancellor of the Duchy of Lancaster to which he was appointed carried no great burden of departmental responsibility and ceased to include the administrative care of the British zones of Germany and Austria. When in 1950 he was appointed Minister of Town and County Planning he remained a senior member of the Cabinet, ranking immediately after the Chancellor of the Exchequer, though his new post formerly had not carried Cabinet status. The scope of his ministerial opportunities was extended some months later when certain functions of the Ministry of Health were transferred to him and he was given the title of Minister of Local Government and Planning. He applied himself with joyful zest to a sphere of activity which had always been of deep interest to him.

DUTY TO HEAL

Dalton never had any association with Bevanism and he conceived it his duty to help to bridge the differences between the rival factions which threatened to split the movement. One of his rewards was to lose his seat on the Executive in 1952 to a Bevanite candidate. He did not seek to regain it the next year. His growing conviction that the older men in the Labour Party should yield place to the young and vigorous impelled him in June, 1955, to set an example to his colleagues. Accordingly he wrote to Mr. Attlee announcing that he would not be a candidate for the committee of the Parliamentary Party—the "Shadow Cabinet"—when it came to be elected early in the new Parliament. There was a touch of artless mischief in the flourish with which he made this gesture of self-abnegation and invited his fellow veterans to follow suit—though not Mr. Attlee himself.

Dalton did not stand again for the Commons at the general election of 1959. In the following New Year's Honours he was made a life peer, but this did not herald a return to the active jousting of the political arena—beyond indicating his support for Mr. Gaitskell in the controversy over defence policy. For the most part he was true to his determination to leave a younger generation to fight the battles of today.

CONTROVERSIAL MEMOIRS

Yet in the autumn of his career he had achieved a new claim to public attention as the purveyor of the inner secrets of Labour Cabinets. The first volume of his memoirs, *Call Back Yesterday*, published in 1953, took the story up to the collapse of the second Labour Government in 1931. It recaptured his years at King's, his friendship there with Rupert Brooke, and it conveyed an aching sense of the loneliness suffered by the survivors of the 1914–18 War. He also gave what must be considered the definitive version of that boyhood encounter with Queen Victoria at a Windsor children's party, which provoked the royal observation: "What a loud voice that child has—just like his father." The second volume, *The Fateful Years*, however, produced not only much agreeable material for the political gossips but also a sharp challenge from Herbert Morrison as to the accuracy of a passage concerning events which followed the Labour victory of July, 1945. The third volume, *High Tide and After*, published last week, dealt with the years of the postwar Labour Governments and his subsequent political activities. Unhampered by reticence or by too respectful an attitude to his former colleagues, Dalton showed himself capable of many a snide remark at their expense.

Hugh Dalton married in 1914 Ruth, daughter of T. Hamilton Fox. Mrs. Dalton was Labour M.P. for Bishop Auckland from February to May, 1929.

February 14, 1962.

Dorothy Dandridge, the coloured singer and actress, who was the star of the films *Carmen Jones* and *Porgy and Bess*, was found dead in her Hollywood apartment on September 8, 1965. She was 41.

She was born in Cleveland, Ohio, and educated in Los Angeles. She was a gifted singer and also possessed a talent for acting which was not at first recognized. She appeared on the stage as a child and toured America with her sister Vivian in a variety act. Later she became a popular night club entertainer and a successful band vocalist. One of her first appearances in films was in *Hit Parade of 1943*, when she was seen briefly as the vocalist with Count Basie and his orchestra, and in 1945 she sang duets with Louis Armstrong in the Warner Brothers film *Pillow to Post*, in which Ida Lupino and Sydney Greenstreet were the stars.

CHANCES FOR YOUNG

Opportunities for young coloured performers in the cinema were few and largely limited to singing parts, and although she determined in her twenties to make her name as an actress as well as a singer and studied at a drama school she won few parts for herself. She was not seen in the cinema until she played the lead in a minor film of MGM entitled *Bright Road* opposite Robert Horton in 1953 and this was followed in the same year by *Remains to be Seen* in which the stars were June Allyson and Van Johnson. *Carmen Jones* gave her the one great opportunity to show her talents. It was an adaptation of the Bizet opera to a Negro setting and she was the automatic choice for the name part with Harry Belafonte as her leading man.

Produced and directed by Otto Preminger in 1954 the film was a notable success and her acting skill was formally acknowledged in Hollywood by the Academy Award which she received for it. *Island in the Sun*, made by Warners in 1957 with James Mason and Joan Fontaine, was her next film and then when Sam Goldwyn set his heart on bringing Gershwin's Negro opera *Porgy and Bess* to the screen she again became an automatic choice for the leading part playing opposite Sidney Poitier. Otto Preminger once again directed her but the film unfortunately lacked the buoyancy and inspiration of *Carmen Jones*. She later appeared in *Tamango* with Curt Jurgens, and *Terror at Sea*, neither of which was outstanding. As a singer Dorothy Dandridge may be placed almost in the same class as Lena Horne.

Her acting ability is harder to estimate for her opportunities to reveal her true talent were so few.

September 10, 1965.

Clemence Dane, C.B.E., lover of London and of the theatre, herself the author of many plays, novels, film scripts, and radio scripts, died on March 28, 1965.

Winifred Ashton, to use the name with which she began life, was born at Blackheath and educated in England, Germany and Switzerland. After a period as art student at Dresden and the Slade School she decided to try acting; and in February, 1913, under the stage name of Diana Portis she made her debut at the Criterion in H. V. Esmond's *Eliza Comes to Stay*. The First World War came, the dearth of touring companies made it harder to get engagements, and on top of this her health broke down. For a time she taught in a girls' school, but before the end of the war she had settled down to the third and lasting phase of her working life, as a writer, using the name of Clemence Dane which she borrowed from a London church. *Regiment of Women*, her first novel, dedicated to the woman friend "E.A.", who stood by her in her new venture, was followed in 1918 by *First the Blade* and in 1919 by *Legend*, a book in which the character of a dead woman-writer was reconstructed through what people said, and what they refrained from saying, about her.

Legend was acclaimed a distinguished and promising piece of work. The year 1921 brought the first production of a play by her, and with its instantaneous success she seemed as a serious writer unquestionably to have arrived.

NIGHT OF A LIFETIME

In this study of the entwined love lives of a devoted mother and daughter, entitled *A Bill of Divorcement*, and produced by Reandean at St. Martin's, Basil Dean excelled himself as a director, and his young contract players, Meggie Albanesi and Malcolm Keen, excelled themselves in the roles of the daughter and the father. "We have not for a long time seen a more moving performance", wrote A. B. Walkley in *The Times* with reference to Meggie Albanesi. It was her night, and it was that of the new playwright, "the night that can only come once to any actor or to any playwright", to use words Clemence Dane used 40 years later in an address to the English Association with regard to Mrs. Siddons's first night as Lady Macbeth at Drury Lane.

DISTINGUISHED FAILURES

Certainly no other night for Clemence Dane in the theatre equalled March 14, 1921. On the other hand what followed was not mere anticlimax. Her next play, *Will Shakespeare*, written in verse and described as An Invention, was a failure, but a distinguished one. *Granite*, a tragedy with Lundy for a setting, and *Mariners*, a study of a clergyman's unhappy marriage to an insensitive woman, were again failures and again distinguished, in both of which Dame Sybil Thorndike and Sir Lewis Casson, devoted friends of the playwright, went down with all guns firing. *Wild Decembers*, a play about the Brontés, presented by C. B. Cochran with Diana Wynyard as Charlotte fared better, but without achieving the desired follow-up of a solid success. Nor did she fully achieve it with contributions to the lighter theatre, such as *Moonlight is Silver* in which Gertrude Lawrence and Douglas Fairbanks, junior, co-starred, or her adaptation of Max Beerbohm's *The Happy Hypocrite*, with Ivor Novello and Vivien Leigh in the leads, in 1936.

Meanwhile, however, she had begun to write scripts for musicals and films, and had continued to write novels, some of which were stories of the theatre. Her partnership with Richard Addinsell, the composer, was inaugurated in *Adam's Opera*, produced under Lilian Baylis at the Old Vic in 1928, and renewed in *Come of Age* and in a new version of Lewis Carroll's Alice stories, in which Dame Sybil "doubled" the Queen of Hearts and the White Queen.

THEATRICAL HISTORY

She was first engaged as a film scenarist by Radio Pictures Ltd. in 1932 following the success of a film version of *A Bill of Divorcement* with Katharine Hepburn in the girl's part. Scenarios on which she herself worked during the 1930s included those of *Anna Karenina* for Garbo and of *St. Martin's Lane* for Charles Laughton.

In collaboration with Miss Helen Simpson she wrote two detective stories, *Enter Sir John* and *Re-enter Sir John*, the principal character in both being an actor-manager. Her own novels, *Broom Stages* and, at a much later date (1954) *The Flower Girls*, reflected on a larger scale her abiding interest in the theatre and theatrical history. History again was the source of a novel about the year of Trafalgar, *He Brings Great News*; of her *Cathedral Steps* produced by Basil Dean on the steps of St. Paul's in 1942; and of much work for sound radio including *The Saviours*, a suite of seven plays on English themes. One of these, concerned with Elizabeth I and Essex, she re-worked into a stage play intended for Dame Sybil and John Mills, which was accepted by Cochran only to be abandoned on Cochran's sudden death. For this, perhaps the worst of Clemence Dane's heartbreaks in the theatre, she had the compensations of writing for B.B.C. television a play to commemorate the four-hundredth anniversary of Elizabeth I's accession and for Dame Sybil a stage play, *Eighty in the Shade*, the production of which celebrated the fiftieth anniversary of the Casson-Thorndike marriage. Her *London has a Garden*, published in 1964, was partly a book of reminiscences, partly a history of Covent Garden, the district where she had lived for over 30 years and may almost be said to have kept open house for her friends in peace and in war. She did not collect people, nor did she use them. She welcomed them. She took it as a jolly matter of course that they should be there. The drama that she did not write, save perhaps in her first play, she found in daily living, which she shared with innumerable friends.

March 29, 1965.

Dr. Joseph Boakye Danquah, one of Ghana's leading lawyers, an important figure in the Nationalist movement, and a strong critic of President Kwame Nkrumah, died in detention on February 4, 1965. He was 69.

Danquah, with other members of the former opposition party, was taken into custody under the Preventive Detention Act on October 3, 1961. He was subsequently released in June, 1962, but was arrested again in January, 1964, on suspicion of having been involved in the second attempt made on the President's life on January 2 in Accra. He was not put on trial with those who were charged with the earlier attempt in 1962, when two of them were acquitted and the Chief Justice was dismissed in December, 1963, or when a new trial, which is continuing, was ordered in 1964. In 1962 the International Commission of Jurists released a petition, attributed to Danquah, asking for a trial of those detained, and gave it their support.

Before Ghana became a one-party state in 1964, Danquah was a fearless but careful spokesman for the opposition, and in 1960 he stood as the United Party candidate for the first Presidency of the Republic against Dr. Nkrumah. He used the campaign to reiterate his claim to have done as much as Dr. Nkrumah himself to win Ghana's independence in the early stages; until 1948 he bulked as large in the movement as Dr. Nkrumah, and went to prison with him.

He never forgave Dr. Nkrumah for his break with the United Gold Coast Convention which led to his becoming the leader of the Convention People's Party, and finally Ghana's Osagyefo (Deliverer) and virtual dictator. He strongly criticized the destruction of the parliamentary democracy, which Britain bequeathed to the country, along with the rule of law and the independence of the judiciary, all of which the C.P.P. progressively undermined. Danquah's devotion to the law continued so long as he remained a free man.

Born at Bepong, Kwahu (northern Gold Coast) on December 21, 1895, he was the son of an evangelist of the Presbyterian Church. He attended elementary school and at the age of 17 became a law clerk, afterwards joining the Government service as a clerk in the Supreme Court. In 1916 he was appointed Secretary to the Paramount Chief of Akim Abuakwa, the late Nana Sir Ofori Atta I, who was also his elder brother. While there he developed a keen interest in traditional affairs and culture. Through private studies he passed the London Matriculation Examination and in 1921 entered University College where he gained the B.A., LL.B. degrees and the John Stuart Mill scholarship in the philosophy of Mind and Logic. At the same time, he entered the Inner Temple and was called to the Bar in 1926. In 1927 he obtained his Ph.D. for which his thesis was: "The moral end as moral excellence." He visited Helsinki, Berlin, the Hague, France and Switzerland before returning home in the same year as a recognized scholar, lawyer, philosopher and traveller—but always a politician.

He was offered a post at Achimota College as Dr. Aggrey's successor but declined and set up legal practice. Within a short time he became known as the leading constitutional lawyer. He aroused the interest of his countrymen in their culture and carried out considerable research. In the field of politics, he was the leading personality and inspired the national conscience through his writings and public lectures. In 1931, he founded the daily *Times of West Africa* and for a number of years what he wrote in the columns of this newspaper had a great influence on Gold Coast affairs. Together with a few other nationalists, he founded the United Gold Coast Convention in 1947—a nationalist movement which united the various sections of the Gold Coast community. His fame and popularity soared and he was generally regarded by various Governors and Government officials as the spokesman for his people. He visited the United Kingdom as a member of several delegations and was responsible for Dr. Kwame Nkrumah's return to the Gold Coast as Secretary-General of the United Gold Coast Convention. During the Gold Coast disturbances in 1948, he and the five other leaders including Dr. Nkrumah were arrested.

When the Coussey Committee was set up in 1949 to report upon constitutional changes for the Gold Coast, Danquah was a leading member of it. Dr. Nkrumah's resignation and formation of the Convention People's Party broke the national front which had been secured by the United Gold Coast Convention. On the formation of the National Liberation Movement, Danquah was elected leader of the Colony Branch, and when the various opposition parties coalesced into a United Party in 1957, he became one of the leaders.

His contribution to Ghana's achievement of independence was significant and considerable. He argued the case for calling the Gold-Coast Ghana after carrying out research in the British Museum in London. He has to his credit a long list of scholarly writings ranging from philosophy to plays. He was a member of various organizations and legal adviser to the Akim Abuakwa State. In the Legislative Council and later the Legislative Assembly he was an astute parliamentarian.

A man of very great intelligence with an analytical mind, he was Leader of the Opposition until he lost his seat in the general election of 1954.

He was twice married.

February 5, 1965.

Jelly d'Aranyi, C.B.E., the violinist, who died in Florence on March 30, 1966, at the age of 70, spent most of her life in England and contributed greatly to our music for the 40 years during which English music emerged from its Victorian doldrums.

With her elder sister Adila Miss D'Aranyi was associated with leading English musicians, Vaughan Williams, Gustav Holst, Donald Tovey, Hugh Allen, Adrian Boult, and Myra Hess in the performance both of new music and the classics. She also kept in touch with continental musicians of her generation, Bartok, Ravel, and Casals.

Born in Budapest on May 3, 1895, she was a great-niece of Joseph Joachim, friend of Brahms, who did a good deal for chamber music in Britain at the turn of the century. She started as a pianist but turned to the violin in 1903, when she worked at the Royal Academy of Budapest with Jenó Hubay. At the age of 14 she began her professional life with an appearance in Vienna. She then went on tour and first played in London, which was to become her home, in 1909. She and her sister, Adila, made an impression here with their performance of Bach's Double Violin Concerto. They continued from time to time to play violin duets, of Purcell, Spohr, and Holst; they gave the first performance of Holst's Double Concerto in 1930. There was always much friendly comparison of the styles of the two sisters. Adila was more a chamber music player, Jelly a temperamental soloist—it was not for nothing that Ravel dedicated his "Tsigane" to her, though she was a classical exponent of Vaughan Williams's *The Lark Ascending* and *Concerto Accademico*.

Her playing had a compulsive magnetism which was harnessed to a fine taste and a cultured mind. As with artists of fiery temperament she could have an off day, when her playing became rough, but it added to the excitement of her appearances to discover her mood of the day.

Another enterprise in which the two sisters were involved was with Baron Palmstierna, the Swedish Minister to Britain, who from 1933 investigated spiritualist phenomena, in the course of which a strong injunction, was received to perform Schumann's late violin concerto which Joachim had interdicted in his will for 100 years. It was played by Jelly d'Aranyi at a B.B.C. concert in 1937 but the demonstration did not prove that Joachim's prohibition was mistaken. During 1933 she played without fee in cathedrals all over Britain to get funds for the unemployed.

Jelly d'Aranyi made her debut in America in 1927 and appeared there, as here, in sonata recitals with Myra Hess. Towards the end of her concert life she gave a series of recitals in English cathedrals with organ. She was the dedicatee of Bartok's two violin sonatas. After the last war she and her sister, Adila, now a widow, left England and settled in Italy. Adila died in 1962. Both sisters had vivid personalities which added to the gaiety of English musical life as well as enriched it.

April 1, 1966.

Helen Darbishire, C.B.E., D.LITT., Principal of Somerville College, Oxford, from 1932 to 1945, and an unrivalled authority on Wordsworth and his circle, died on March 11, 1961, at her home at Grasmere, Westmorland. She was 80.

Miss Darbishire was born at Oxford in 1881, the daughter of a well-loved doctor, Samuel Dukinfield Darbishire, and she was closely connected with Oxford for the greater part of her life. She was educated at the Oxford High School and at Somerville College, and for a time she was visiting lecturer at the Royal Holloway College. She was Fellow and Tutor in English of Somerville, university lecturer, and visiting professor for a year at Wellesley College, Massachusetts; and when in 1931 she came Principal of Somerville she continued to lecture and teach, although pressure of administrative work stood for a time in the way of her literary and scholastic pursuits. She communicated to her pupils something of her own love of literature and fine discrimination, holding up to them always the high standard of scrupulous scholarship that distinguished her published works, her editions of Wordsworth's 1807 Poems, of De Quincey's Literary Criticism, and of the manuscript of the First Book of Milton's *Paradise Lost*. Milton became her special "study and business". In 1932 appeared *The Early Lives of Milton*, and in 1952 she published an important work, the definitive edition of Milton's English Poems.

Her time of office as principal was an eventful one. Eleven years earlier women had been admitted as members of the university, and their growing share in the academic and social life of Oxford occasioned new developments in administration and policy. The East Quadrangle, the Council Chamber, and the Chapel came into being under her watchful care. The war brought new problems—some of the staff and students were called away, air raid dangers had to be met, the changing demands of war work upon women students affected their college courses. To all problems, public and personal, Miss Darbishire brought the same open mind and steady judgment. And authority never impaired her sense of every individual's freedom and her liberal appreciation of people of widely differing characters.

RETIREMENT TO GRASMERE

After Ernest de Selincourt's death in 1943 she continued his work on Wordsworth, with which she had long been closely associated. She completed and published volumes III, IV, and V of the great edition of Wordsworth on which he was engaged at the time of his death. She left Somerville in 1945 and pursued her researches in Oxford until finally she removed with her friend Vera Farnell to Grasmere. Here she continued her life as a student, as she always liked to describe herself, giving generous and untiring help to the many students and scholars who wrote to her or came to consult her from all over the world as the pre-eminent authority on Wordsworth and his circle, with whom, and especially, it seemed, with his sister Dorothy, she seemed to enjoy almost a living intimacy. The introduction to her edition of Dorothy's *Journals* (1958) owes much to the loving knowledge of the country which she shared with Dorothy herself. She was for many years a trustee of Dove Cottage and had succeeded de Selincourt as chairman. The peace and beauty in which her own cottage was set exactly suited her, and the change was in the nature of a most happy and inevitable homecoming.

Miss Darbishire was an honorary D. Litt, of London and Durham Universities and a Fellow of the British Academy, which twice awarded her the Rose Mary Crawshay Prize for works on Milton and Wordsworth. Among her notable lectures was a series of Clark Lectures on "The Poet Wordsworth" at Trinity College, Cambridge, the James Bryce Memorial Lecture on "Milton's Paradise Lost", and a lecture to the English Association on "Milton's Language".

In Helen Darbishire's personality were united fine qualities which often tend to exclude each other. Patient and perceptive scholarship never smothered or even dimmed her clear philosophic conceptions and glowing appreciation of literature. Science ran in her family.

RESEARCH QUALITY

Her brother was a brilliant biologist and investigator into the Mendelian hypothesis and her own method of research was in the best sense scientific. But she had a keen delight in music, in pictures, in travel, and above all in poetry.

Similarly in friendship her strong affection never deflected her judgment, so that she was, above all others, the friend of whom one could seek counsel on problems of life or morals. Her friendship was innocent of partisanship and she kept her ideals unfailingly before her. One phrase from her beloved and familiar Wordsworth attached itself to her: "a heart at leisure from itself."

Humour was a family characteristic. Humour and wisdom made her a wholesome and inspiring principal to her students, and many of her addresses, given at the beginning of term or on special occasions, are gratefully remembered. From middle life her somewhat delicate health, which she so wisely husbanded that even during the overtaxed war years her work never suffered, set a limit to her physical activities, but in earlier years she sculled (her father was famous as an oar) and played tennis and swam, and was the ideal companion on walking tours in the lake country, sure-footed, enduring, and a wonder with the map. Here, as on her Italian holidays and in America, wherever she had been she left friends. These friends treasure the memory of their share in a life fruitful of work and rich in joy and laughter.

March 13, 1961.

Admiral Georges Thierry d'Argenlieu, who commanded the Free French Navy during the Second World War and presided over the dissolution in Indo-China, died at Brest on September 7, 1964, at the age of 75.

His career as sailor and administrator was remarkable as much for its brevity as for the peaks he attained at a time, admittedly, when General de Gaulle was short of admirals. Some 36 years of his mature life were spent in a monastery near Fontainebleau of the Carmelite order, to which he returned in 1947, a few months after being appointed inspector-general of the French Navy.

His few eventful years as de Gaulle's First Sea Captain were marked by great dash and spirit. They were hardly equal, however, to a hopeless task when he was sent to Indo-China in 1945 as Governor and High Commissioner—a task to which he brought a mixture of conciliation and severity, and in which he was certainly not aided by Washington's policy.

Thierry d'Argenlieu came of an old Breton family and, following his father into the Navy, passed out as a midshipman at Brest in 1911. He saw service in Morocco before the First World War, during which he served in patrol boats and submarine chasers in the Mediterranean. In 1920, called to a religious vocation, he left the sea and at the age of 31 became a Carmelite friar as Père Louis de la Trinité.

ESCAPE

As a reserve officer he was mobilized in 1939 and given command of a ship of the Cherbourg station. Taken prisoner during the German advance, he escaped from a convoy and made his way to Jersey and London, where General de Gaulle made him chief of the Free French Naval Forces—in the summer of 1940 almost non-existent.

It was not long, however, before he was confirmed in his rank after the misfortunes of Admiral Muselier, and he was severely wounded during the Dakar adventure. On his recovery he had a decisive part in rallying Gabon in conjunction with troops of Colonel Leclerc, as he was then, and after organizing other naval bases in French Africa, he was sent to the Pacific with full civil and military powers.

The North African landings found him in Washington for prickly discussions with the American chiefs of staff, and he entered liberated Paris at the side of General de Gaulle with the rank of admiral and the functions of Deputy Chief of the General Staff. He had a succession of high administrative naval posts and was French delegate at the San Francisco conference; but his worldly prizes did not keep him for long from the solitude of his Fontainebleau monastery.

September 8, 1964.

Bernard Darwin, who wrote faultlessly on golf and much else, died on October 18, 1961, at the age of 85. A member of the staffs of both *The Times* and *Country Life* for many years, he delighted not only the golfing public but also a host of non-players whom his great gifts attracted with articles of singular excellence and charm.

Author also of a number of books, he was no less successful in entertaining and holding a large following. Many were on golf; others were autobiographical, lives of sportsmen and anthologies; others again were on Charles Dickens, a writer with whom he had an intense sympathy, all the stronger because he shared his hero's vein of exuberant and kindly humour. As a sportsman, he was always fair and always uninhibitedly partisan. If Eton or Cambridge were beaten, he never pretended not to regret that the gods of chance had let him down.

A first-class golfer, Darwin was the supreme showman of the game. The human friendliness born of it delighted him even more than its thrills and interest. In regard to it he was a man who, as he once said of Andrew Lang, "never for a moment lost either his sense of humour or of proportion, who restrained his affection almost austerely so that he never fell into the easy mistake of growing too lyrical, who underwrote rather than overwrote". Again in his own words he always "tried to spread the golfing butter as thinly as may be on the more general bread". It was one secret of his unparalleled success in his own sphere.

Another was his photographic memory, which enabled him to roam a crowded course, select the events which were of real importance, and, without reference to written notes, pen at an amazing speed the record of the day's play.

KNOWLEDGE OF SPORTS

His encyclopedic knowledge of sport was not confined to golf. Woe betide the challenger who took him on, in conversation, over a disputed point about the initials of the Kent wicket-keeper in 1905 or the number of goals by which Cambridge beat Oxford in Association football in any given year.

As he became less active he supplemented his information with the reports of reliable spectators and such was his insight into the game that on such occasions he never failed to read a match correctly. His perception was acute, his observations sometimes waspish, but on the rare occasions that he criticized in his articles the tone was almost invariably kind and generous. Thus his influence on the reporting of sport was profound, for he transformed it from what had often been at the beginning of the century little more than a jumble of figures at the foot of a column into a branch of literary journalism.

Bernard Darwin was born at Downe in Kent on September 7, 1876, the only son of Sir Francis Darwin, F.R.S., the botanist, and grandson of the author of the *Origin of Species*, whom he remembered faintly though, as he once wrote, "I had no notion he was a person of any save domestic consideration". He was even more vague in regard to his first attempt at golf; but there were garden courses at two of his early homes and in 1884 he was playing at Felixstowe. In 1889 he went to Eton and his recollections of its life and spirit were to glow in him through all his days. In his book on the English public schools he held that when men stick up for them "they are not so much sticking up for a particular English institution but rather for the genius and the stupidity of the whole English people."

Fróm Eton he went to Trinity College, Cambridge, where in three years he played golf for the University and in 1897 was captain. In 1903 he was called to the Bar and practised for a time. It bred in him a lively interest in famous murder trials, with many of which he became remarkably conversant, but his contact with the law was in his own words "no more than a flirtation" and he turned gladly to writing about golf in 1908, when the opportunity arose.

INTERNATIONAL PLAYER

The first of a long series of achievements in the game came to him in 1902, when he played in the first of his eight international matches against Scotland, and the climax was reached in 1922, the year in which, having accompanied the British team to the United States as the correspondent of *The Times*, he was called upon to take the place of the captain, who had fallen ill. The previous year he had reached the semi-final of the amateur championship for the second time, a feat which did not prevent his contributing long and accurate reports of other matches in the championship. He won several coveted trophies, among them the *Golf Illustrated* Gold Vase in 1919, the President's Putter in 1924, and the Worplesdon Foursomes with Miss Joyce Wethered in 1933. This last event was perhaps the one nearest to his heart. He was an ardent believer in the foursome and in that friendly atmosphere it was seen at its best. His accounts of Miss Wethered's repeated successes in it with a variety of partners evoked some of his best writing.

He was also to be captain of the Royal and Ancient Club, and successively captain and president of the Oxford and Cambridge Golfing Society, in whose activities he took a lively interest until the end. A severe critic of his own ability, he was in fact one of the best amateur golfers of his time. Essentially a swinger rather than a hitter of the ball, he was at his best on windswept courses, such as Rye, where his controlled iron-play revealed the qualities of a true golfer. He disparaged, even mocked his putting, yet in a foursome he was one of the most dependable, if exacting, of partners, and his occasional outbursts against unkind fortune were generally followed by a succession of brilliant thrusts.

In the 1914–18 War he was a lieutenant (acting major) in the Royal Army Ordnance Corps and served for more than two years in Macedonia. For some time he was D.A.D.O.S. of the 26th Division. At the beginning of 1919 he joined the staff of *The Times*. It was not his first appearance in journalism, for at one period he had written weekly articles entitled "Tee Shots" in the *Evening Standard*, and had contributed articles to *The Times* and *Country Life* since 1907. He had, however, served no regular apprenticeship, and once, when Lord Northcliffe asked him what he knew, he modestly replied: "A little about golf, murders and Dickens." The new recruit had, however, scarcely fallen into step with the paper when his true qualities appeared. One of them was his power of seizing upon any subject which interested him, taking it to himself and so enlivening and bedecking it that it was virtually impossible to resist reading him. Robert Louis Stevenson stood in his eager appreciation next to Dickens and his mind was a concordance of Borrow, Collins, Mrs. Gaskell, and many another writer of this epoch.

SAGE OF THE COURSE

After his retirement from *The Times*—which he served for 46 years—a dinner was given in his honour by the whole golfing fraternity. It was attended by peers, judges, generals, members of Parliament, and golfers from all over the country who wished to acclaim what he had done to raise the status of the game. A dinner in his honour was held at the Garrick Club, of which he was a venerable member and a life trustee.

He continued to contribute articles to *The Times* and to *Country Life* and other periodicals. It is probable that his love for the game would in any case have made him a frequent visitor to the more important events until his arthritis became too severe a handicap. He would appear from time to time, escorted to vantage points on the famous courses which carried so many memories for him. There the golfing personalities of half a century came to salute him as he sat crouched on a seat, a familiar figure in a long coat with his cap well down over his eyes. During his retirement came the last work, *The World That Fred Made*, a collection of nostalgic memories. In 1955 he moved from London to Rye to be near the club for which he had the utmost affection and of which he had been captain 50 years before. The last years of his life he spent at South Heighton, near Newhaven, the home of Mrs. Norman Mommens, one of his daughters.

EASILY BORED

Understanding, sympathy, and good humour radiated from him. His rich memory, his kindly wit, and his ability to be interested in others made him a delightful talker. The least boring of men, he was easily bored, and, after a lifetime of experience, came to regard after-dinner speeches with acute suspicion.

He had already written two books on golf when, in 1921, he and Mr. George Duncan decided each to produce one and then to publish them in a single volume entitled *Present Day Golf*. More followed from his own pen. *The Game's Afoot* (1926) was an anthology of sports. *A Dickens Pilgrimage* (1928) was a collection of articles reprinted from *The Times*. Other collections were to follow. The "Tootleoo" series of the same period, in which his wife was his collaborator and illustrator, was versified fun of the best kind. He also contributed *W. G. Grace* and *Dickens* to the Great Lives Series.

John Gully and His Times (1935), an admirable book, showed that he knew his way about some sides of social life in the first half of the nineteenth century. He had also a special and exact knowledge of English pugilism and its history. *Life is Sweet, Brother* (1940) like his earlier *Green Memories* (1928) contained personal reminiscences, *Pack Clouds Away* (1941) many desultory and happy comments, while *Tee Shots and Others*, *Golf Between Two Wars*, *Rubs of the Green*, *Playing the Like*, and *Out of the Rough* testified to his unquenchable zest for the game.

He was made C.B.E. in 1937.

He married in 1903 Elinor Mary, daughter

of W. T. Monsell, a talented woman who, the devoted companion of his life, was his collaborator in some of his lighter work. She died in 1954. One son and two daughters survive him.

October 19, 1961.

Sir Charles Darwin, K.B.E., M.C., F.R.S., the theoretical physicist who was formerly director of the National Physical Laboratory, the home of precise measurement, died at his home in Cambridge on December 31, 1962. He was 75. By his death British science lost a representative whose influence extended much beyond the fields of his published work.

As a theoretical physicist he came close to anticipating Dirac's theory of the electron. Dirac's theory having been published, it was typical that it should have been Darwin who brought "the Dirac electron" down to earth—turning it into a form in which other physicists could use it. As a man, he liked travelling, was a good host and took pleasure in having beautiful things about him. As an administrator, it was said of him that "he was such a sensible codger he would always listen". These are not the qualities of a man dedicated wholly to physics. This he never seemed to be—perhaps because he enjoyed life too much or was merely too sensible.

Born in Cambridge in December, 1887, Charles Galton Darwin was the son of Sir George Darwin, Plumian Professor of Astronomy, and of Maud Du Pay, an American by birth, and the grandson of the author of *The Origin of Species.* Following a classical education up to the age of 16 at Marlborough, he specialized in mathematics, was a major scholar of Trinity, Cambridge, bracketted fourth wrangler in 1909 and obtained a first in the Mathematics Tripos Part II in 1910. From then until the outbreak of the First World War, he was Schuster Reader in Mathematical Physics in the University of Manchester. He was one of a famous team, including Bohr and Moseley, under Rutherford's leadership during one of the most fruitful periods of Manchester's scientific history. His most important contributions in his period were in the field of X-ray diffraction.

BEHAVIOUR OF PARTICLE

While at Manchester he was one of the first to be told by Rutherford of his discovery that the atom had a dense core or nucleus. If hit by a bombarding particle, the particle might be turned back on its tracks. He helped Rutherford with the theory of these experiments while owning that Rutherford, in his own way, had already solved the problem to his satisfaction.

After service through the First War, in which he was awarded the Military Cross, and two years of which he spent in sound ranging, he was elected Fellow and Lecturer of Christ's College, Cambridge, in 1919, to which 14 years later he returned for two years as Master. For 13 of the intervening years he was Tait Professor of Natural Philosophy at Edinburgh. It was there that much of his work in the field of quantum theory and optics was done.

In 1938 he accepted the offer of the Directorship of the National Physical Laboratory, but he had not long settled down to the varied duties of this post when war broke out and brought to him additional responsibilities. In 1941–42 he was seconded to direct the British Central Scientific Office in Washington. Later in the war he gave part-time service to the War Office as Scientific Adviser to the Army Council.

VALUABLE AMBASSADOR

Darwin played a part in scientific life which it will be hard to fill. As a familiar figure at international conferences in physics he was a valuable ambassador, and his easy, friendly manner promoted good feeling. His approach to a problem was always original. He did not immediately accept the traditional point of view in academic and scientific matters; he enjoyed stirring the waters in a provocative and witty manner which was stimulating. The same spirit was evident in his work as a member of the University Grants Committee, where he was the champion of the "rare subject", the development of which, both in teaching and research, was, he argued, so often left to chance in our university system.

His work at the National Physical Laboratory brought him into contact with a wide circle of industrialists, officials, and scientists. His task during the war and immediate postwar years was one of real difficulty, but his record of achievement under conditions when unqualified success was well-nigh impossible speaks for itself. He retired from the laboratory in 1949, and went to live in Cambridge in his old family house. In retirement he took a great interest in the problems of world population. His book *The Next Million Years* took a strongly Malthusian line, as did his Rede Lecture.

His honours included the K.B.E. in 1942, honorary degrees in the Universities of Bristol, Manchester, St. Andrews, Edinburgh and Delhi, Honorary Fellowships at Trinity and Christ's Colleges, and a Royal Medal of the Royal Society.

In 1925 he married Katharine, daughter of F. W. Pember, by whom he had four sons and one daughter.

January 2, 1963.

Professor Harold Davenport, F.R.S., who succeeded Mordell as the undisputed leader of the internationally respected British school of number theory, died on June 9, 1969, in Cambridge. He was the sort of mathematician who works in terms of solving problems rather than constructing theories. Nothing is easier in number-theory than the enunciation of intractable significant problems; but Davenport had the flair for choosing significant but apparently hopeless problems which by ingenuity and hard work could just be tackled. He will be especially remembered for his contributions to the Geometry of Numbers and to Analytic Number Theory.

He was particularly successful as a supervisor of research. Many of the younger leaders of number-theory in this country are his pupils (Roth, Rogers, Baker...) and all have come under his influence. He was equally good with the less able aspirant to the Ph.D. and had the enviable gift of suggesting problems within the capacity of the pupil and yet a genuine "contribution to knowledge". He paid particular attention to presentation and not infrequently wrote out the final version himself. Indeed to the connoisseur of style his hand is indisputable in the papers of pupils long after they were internationally recognized authorities.

Harold Davenport was born in Accrington on October 30, 1907. He attended Accrington Grammar School and Manchester University, where he came under the notice of Mordell, who was to have a major influence on his development. As the custom then was, he competed as a Manchester undergraduate in the Trinity entrance scholarship examination, was easily top of the list, and went up to Cambridge in 1927 as an affiliated student with a major scholarship and a Manchester B.Sc. (which in later life he ignored, as in his entry in *Who's Who*). He had a typical successful undergraduate career and went on to research.

PRIZE OUT OF REACH

Disappointingly, he was awarded only a Rayleigh Prize (not the more coveted Smith's Prize) in 1930. Cambridge in those days was the Cambridge of Littlewood and, after he returned from Oxford in 1931, of Hardy, an exciting and stimulating milieu. In 1932 Davenport was elected to a Prize Fellowship of Trinity.

It must have been about this time that the distinguished German mathematician Helmut Hasse wrote to Mordell asking him to recommend a young mathematician who would teach him English. Davenport went, spent a year in Göttingen, and collaborated in research with Hasse. In his lecture to the Oslo International Congress Hasse records that it was Davenport's scepticism about the worth of abstract methods which impelled him to his proof of the Riemann Hypothesis for elliptic curves. Davenport remained sceptical. It was probably at this time that Davenport acquired his fluent and accurate command of German; he used to claim that Germans would accept him as a compatriot albeit with the accent of a distant province (To the Anglo-Saxon ear that province indubitably lay near the Mersey.) When his Trinity fellowship expired, Davenport went back to Manchester University, this time as assistant lecturer. Manchester must have been an exciting place in those days. Despite a small establishment and a minimal budget Mordell had managed to find a niche for surprisingly many bright young mathematicians, many of them refugees. In 1940, while still an assistant lecturer, Davenport was elected F.R.S. and in 1941 he was appointed to the vacant chair at University College of North Wales, Bangor. There in 1944 he married a fellow Lancastrian, Anne Lofthouse, on the staff of the modern languages department.

In 1945 Davenport was translated to the Astor professorship of mathematics at University College London, and in 1958 was elected the Rouse Ball Professor of Mathematics at Cambridge in succession to Littlewood and Besicovitch.

Davenport was a natural conservative. "All changes are for the worse", he used to say with complete conviction. He was entirely out of sympathy with the waves of change in the teaching of mathematics but accepted them as inevitable evil. Selective in the enjoyment of modern technology, he never entered an aeroplane, would use a lift if no alternative existed (at the International Congress in Moscow he trudged up and down the interminable stairs of Stalin's skyscraper), and preferred to send his papers for publication written in his characteristically neat hand.

He loved to travel and, surprisingly, enjoyed the United States, to which he made many visits. But he disliked postwar Germany, feeling that too much of the Nazi outlook had survived, and it was only the honour of the Gauss Visiting Professorship of Göttingen which induced him to return for a semester in 1966. He had a wide circle of mathematical friends and a stream of visitors passed through his hospitable home in Cranmer Road.

He was president of the London Mathematical Society in 1957–59, was awarded the Adams Prize in 1941 and the Sylvester Medal of the Royal Society in 1967.

June 10, 1969.

Lord Davidson, P.C., G.C.V.O., C.H., C.B., who played a prominent part in political affairs in the twenties and thirties, died on December 11, 1970. He was 81.

Lord Davidson will be best remembered for his very close association with two Prime Ministers, Bonar Law and Stanley Baldwin, both when these statesmen were at the height of their powers and throughout their lives. In the political world of those days Davidson was very much a power behind the throne, usually as a secretary who was also a close friend and influential adviser. Davidson was never an outstanding figure in the House of Commons—where he sat as Unionist member for Hemel Hempstead for 16 years—and the highest Ministerial rank he ever held was that of Chancellor of the Duchy of Lancaster.

TAKEN OVER

But his influence in politics was in inverse proportion to his achievements under the front-bench spotlights as a Minister. At the age of 21, in 1910, he was private secretary to Lord Crewe, then Secretary of State for the Colonies. He was evidently well thought of in this post and he was taken over as private secretary by the next Colonial Secretary, "Lulu" Harcourt, with whom he remained for five years. Bonar Law was the next incumbent at the Colonial Office and he, too, retained Davidson as his private secretary there. This was in 1915 when Bonar Law, although he was Leader of the Conservative Party, accepted the relatively junior office of Secretary of State for the Colonies in Asquith's first Coalition Government. It was the beginning of a partnership between the two men which lasted—with one brief interruption—until Bonar Law's death in 1923. When Asquith fell and Lloyd George formed the second Coalition Government in 1916 Bonar Law became Chancellor of the Exchequer and Leader of the House of Commons, as well as being a member of the War Cabinet. Davidson continued as his private secretary. Then, in 1920, Davidson entered the House of Commons at a by-election in Hemel Hempstead and he at once became Bonar Law's Parliamentary Private Secretary, more particularly in his chief's capacity as Leader of the House of Commons.

AT THE HEART

Through all this period Davidson was very much at the heart of affairs. He had made a niche for himself as a discreet, high-powered and very well-informed private secretary, who was an ideal aide-de-camp to people in high places. His exquisite manners, combined with great tact and discernment and a gift for modestly effacing himself while playing an important part in state business, made him generally liked. In 1920 he was already in correspondence with Lord Stamfordham, King George V's private secretary, and in a letter to him Davidson made an acid comment on the type of Government supporter that had been floated into the House of Commons at Lloyd George's "coupon" election of 1918.

In March, 1921, when Bonar Law resigned his offices and retired from politics for a time because of ill-health Davidson became Parliamentary Private Secretary to Stanley Baldwin, then President of the Board of Trade. But he continued to keep Bonar Law—who was convalescing in the south of France—well posted about all that was afoot at Westminster and about the growing resentment of the predominant Conservative Party at Lloyd George's erratic leadership. When Bonar Law became Prime Minister in 1922, after the collapse of Lloyd George's Coalition Government, Davidson again returned to his former chief as Parliamentary Private Secretary. In the following year he was given his first Ministerial post as Chancellor of the Duchy of Lancaster but even then he continued to act informally as political secretary to the Prime Minister.

Davidson was to some extent concerned in the historic affair of the choice of Baldwin, instead of Lord Curzon, to be Prime Minister in succession to Bonar Law. Bonar Law was a dying man when he resigned and on the grounds of ill-health he let the King know that he would prefer not to be consulted about the choice of his successor.

KING SAW LETTER

The King respected Bonar Law's wish not to be consulted but he was, naturally, anxious to know what the resigning Prime Minister's private views were about the succession. Bonar Law's letter of resignation was conveyed to the King by Colonel Sir Ronald Waterhouse, who had succeeded Davidson as his private secretary, accompanied by Major-General Sir Frederick Sykes, the Prime Minister's son-in-law. It was revealed in Robert Blake's biography of Bonar Law, *The Unknown Prime Minister*, that Waterhouse on this occasion also handed to the King a memorandum which, he said, "practically expressed the views of Mr. Bonar Law." A note to this effect is attached to the document in the royal archives. This memorandum, which was unsigned, strongly argued the case for the appointment of Baldwin in preference to Curzon, both on constitutional and personal grounds. Sir Frederick Sykes afterwards said that he never saw the memorandum; and other members of Bonar Law's family, his other private secretaries, and his great friend Lord Beaverbrook also disclaimed any knowledge of it. Bonar Law's biographer holds that Waterhouse misled Lord Stamfordham and the King, since he regards this memorandum as not giving an accurate expression of the resigning Prime Minister's views.

The memorandum was, in fact, written by Davidson, although he did not authorize its use by Waterhouse in the way recorded by Lord Stamfordham. Davidson disagreed with the biographer and thought that the memorandum did not misrepresent Bonar Law's opinion on the question of the succession. "It is clear", says the biography, "that the document was intended merely as an *aide-mémoire* for Waterhouse in case the King should ask him for his own opinion—a perfectly possible contingency in view of Waterhouse's past connexion with the Court as equerry to the Duke of York—and not as a considered expression of Bonar Law's own opinion".

OTHER ADVICE

Whatever weight may have been attached to this memorandum the King sought other advice. He was known to have consulted the fourth Marquess of Salisbury and also the veteran Lord Balfour, the latter of whom held strongly that it was no longer possible to have a Prime Minister in the House of Lords. Characteristically, it was Davidson who first informed Bonar Law—apparently much to his surprise—that the King had sent for Baldwin.

Davidson came to be as closely attached to Baldwin as he had been to Bonar Law. As a member of the former Prime Minister's family has recorded, Davidson and his wife were among Baldwin's closest friends and up to the end of his life he found much happiness in their society. Even when Davidson was occupied with ministerial duties himself he continued to be Baldwin's trusted confidential adviser.

John Colin Campbell Davidson, first Viscount Davidson of Little Gaddesden, was born at Aberdeen on February 28, 1889, the only son of Sir James Mackenzie Davidson, M.B., C.M.

CALLED TO BAR

He was educated at Westminster and Pembroke College, Cambridge, and was called to the Bar at the Middle Temple in 1913. This was three years after he had become private secretary to Lord Crewe. In 1919 he married Frances Joan, younger daughter of the first Baron Dickinson, P.C., K.B.E.

Having first taken office in Bonar Law's

Government in 1923 as Chancellor of the Duchy of Lancaster Davidson was appointed in the following year to be Parliamentary and Financial Secretary to the Admiralty.

SHARP TONGUE

This office he held for three years. He had a sharp tongue on occasion and it was in a constituency speech about this time that he made a blistering attack on Lloyd George. From the Admiralty Davidson was moved by Baldwin in 1926—when he was still only 37—to become chairman of the Conservative and Unionist Organization. In the three and a half years during which he occupied this post, Davidson did some valuable work for the party.

None the less it is doubtful whether Davidson was suited by temperament to the hurly-burly of being chairman of the party and he felt keenly the criticism of the party organization that was a feature of the feud that developed between Baldwin and two of the newspaper peers about that time. The Conservatives were beaten at the election of 1929 and Davidson resigned the chairmanship in 1930. He played an active part off-stage in the formation of the National Government of 1931 under Ramsay MacDonald and he again held office in this Government—as also in Baldwin's Government that succeeded it—as Chancellor of the Duchy of Lancaster. By this time Baldwin had set his hand to the India policy and Davidson was chosen in 1932 to be chairman of one of the three Committees sent out to India to prepare the way for the plan of an all-India Federation. Davidson was chairman of the Indian States Advisory Committee and with his colleagues he visited most of the principal states and discussed financial and constitutional problems with the Princes and their Ministers.

INFORMATION TASK

For a short time in the early part of the Second World War, Davidson was Controller of Production at the Ministry of Information. In 1942 he was sent on an official tour of South America. He had a wide knowledge of the Latin American countries and this was another successful mission. From that time onward he played a big part in promoting friendship and cultural and trade relations between Britain and the Latin American countries.

Davidson is survived by his widow with two sons and two daughters. The heir to the title is the Hon. John Andrew Davidson.

December 14, 1970.

Professor Charles Findlay Davidson, O.B.E. who died on November 1, 1967, at the age of 56, was best known for his work as a war-time geologist and, from 1944 to 1955, on sources of uranium.

He was as competent an organizer as he was a geologist, and had the priceless gift of distinguishing quickly between what was worth following up and what was not. From 1955 onwards he held the Chair of Geology in St. Andrews University. As late as September, 1967, he volunteered at short notice to organize an international meeting at St. Andrews for the International Association on the Genesis of Ore Deposits—after arrangements for a meeting in eastern Europe had broken down—notwithstanding that he had had earlier warnings of cardiac trouble and was supposed to be taking life more quietly. He made a first-class job of the meeting, and a week ago was elected president of the association. He had been accustomed to drive himself hard, during the war and afterwards, and he was not the man to avoid a challenge.

MILITARY GEOLOGY

The son of John Davidson, he was educated at Morgan Academy, Dundee, and St. Andrews University, where he graduated with first-class honours in geology. An investigation of the geology of South Harris, which brought him his doctorate, was a classic of its kind and is still frequently quoted. His first job was on the staff of the Museum of Practical Geology in South Kensington. Early in the war he undertook the organization of a small military geology unit to supply geological reports required by the Services Intelligence Departments.

The information provided by this unit was used in every big military operation in Africa and Europe from the first landings in North Africa. His unit's reports on underground stores for flying bombs in France governed the successful pattern of bombing of the stocks of missiles to be launched against London.

PILTDOWN EXPOSURE

Davidson had been chief geological adviser to the British Atomic Energy Organization and head of the Atomic Energy Division of the Geological Survey. In that capacity he carried out geological studies in many parts of the Commonwealth and in foreign countries. He was jointly responsible with an American for the discovery of the vast uranium resources of the Witwatersrand gold-field which has given rise to one of South Africa's greatest industries, estimated at its peak to be worth £30m. per year.

He was jointly responsible with Mr. S. H. U. Bowie for introducing a new method of estimating the age of fossil bones from the amount of uranium they had taken up from the soil in which they had lain. This was first used in the spectacular exposure of Piltdown man culminating in 1953. It has continued to be used, both to compare the ages of bones found in similar soil conditions and, more cautiously, as a way of estimating absolute age, given that the amount of uranium in the soil and water conditions are known. In the search for uranium after the war, his prospectors' handbook to uranium mineral deposits, which sold 10,000 copies in three editions, has been credited with as big a contribution as his own world-wide studies. He was made O.B.E. in 1953 and was a fellow of the Royal Society of Edinburgh and a member of the Institute of Mining and Metallurgy.

He married in 1938 Helen McLean Wallace. They had four sons.

November 3, 1967.

Clement Davies, P.C., Q.C., M.P., who died on March 23, 1962, at the age of 78, was for 11 years the leader of the Parliamentary Liberal Party in the House of Commons, where he had represented his native county of Montgomeryshire since 1929. He had announced in 1960 that he would not stand at the next general election.

Liberalism as a continuing political and an electoral force in the country owes much to the selfless devotion with which Clement Davies guided and nourished the small Liberal group at Westminster. His unwavering faith and steady fortitude won him the respect and affection of colleagues of all parties. His passion for social justice gave a depth of sincerely felt emotion to his public utterances. He was never afraid to allow sentiment to colour the eloquence with which his Welsh ancestry had endowed him.

Born on February 19, 1884, the son of Alderman M. Davies of Llanfyllin, Montgomeryshire, Clement Edward Davies was educated at Llanfyllin School and at Trinity Hall, Cambridge, of which he was a Senior Foundation Scholar. He came first in his preliminary law examination and gained a first class in the Law Tripos, Part I in 1906 and Part II in 1907. He held a Law Studentship at Trinity Hall from 1907 till 1911, and was Law Lecturer at the University College of Wales, Aberystwyth, in 1908–09. In 1909 he was called to the Bar of Lincoln's Inn, with a First Class and a Certificate of Honour in the Bar Final. He practised in the North Wales Circuit for a year, and in 1910 he transferred to the Northern Circuit.

In the years that followed he built up a considerable practice in the King's Bench and the Admiralty and Probate Divisions. He was secretary to the President of the Probate, Divorce and Admiralty Division from 1918 to 1919, and then secretary to the Master of the Rolls until 1923. He was also one of the junior counsel to the Treasury from 1919 to 1925. He took silk in 1926. The next year he was approached to stand for Montgomeryshire and reluctantly agreed to do so if no other candidate could be found before a general election took place. In 1929 he became member for this seat, which had been Liberal without a break since 1883. In spite of strong opposition he had a majority of more than 2,000 and the Labour vote fell from 7,000 to 4,000.

A LIBERAL NATIONAL

In 1930 Davies, then a leader in the Commercial Court, gave up practice to become a director of Lever Brothers. When his party divided in 1931, he became a Liberal National. In August, 1942, he returned to the Liberal Party, a position which gave him greater freedom to speak his mind. In May, 1944, the Montgomeryshire Conservative Association decided that as a result of Davies's "persistent opposition to the National Government" the association could no longer feel under any obligation to observe the political truce.

When in 1945 Sir Archibald Sinclair—later Lord Thurso—lost his seat, Davies was elected to succeed him as Leader of the Liberal Parliamentary Party. At the opening of the Liberal

Summer School a few weeks later he warned his followers against the "Tory Spider," seeking to steal Liberal votes. He was always alert to repulse any blandishments from Left or Right and refused to regard his own as a mere centre party.

Whatever differences persisted, Davies kept his little band together with a reasonable semblance of unity, and he never wavered in his own refusal to compromise with doctrinaire Socialism. Indeed the chairman of the Montgomeryshire Conservative Association advised his members that as long as Clement Davies worked for the defeat of Socialism there was no point in opposing him. In the event they refrained from putting up a candidate in the 1951 General Election. Davies himself in a straight fight was re-elected by a majority of more than 9,000.

Then came from Winston Churchill—intent on his aim of forming a "broad-based Government"—an offer to include Davies in it. The two were closeted together in London, and Davies the next day lunched with the new Prime Minister at Chartwell. But after he had consulted Lord Samuel and other Liberal leaders later in the day it was announced that Davies had felt unable to accept Mr. Churchill's offer of a place in his Ministry. At the same time the Liberals pledged themselves to support the Government in any measures clearly conceived in the interests of the country as a whole.

WORLD GOVERNMENT

In the years that followed he combined his work in the House with an increasing preoccupation with the ideals of world government. He became president of the World Association of Parliamentarians for World Government, and it was from a group of Scandinavian delegates attending the third conference in Copenhagen in 1953 that the suggestion originated which resulted in Davies's nomination in 1955 for the Nobel Peace Prize. It was advanced by more than 100 Parliamentarians in Britain, Scandinavia, France, Germany, Italy, and Bahamas, Nigeria, and Pakistan. The width of the support he received surprised even his original sponsors.

In the general election of 1955 the Liberals, with one more candidate than in 1951, polled 8,000 fewer votes. Davies's own majority fell slightly, to 8,500 over his Labour opponent. Again he had five colleagues to join him on the Liberal bench, and for another 16 months he continued to lead them. Then at the end of September, 1956, on the last day of the Liberal Assembly in Folkestone, he announced that his resignation from the leadership would come into effect on the reassembly of Parliament on October 23. His majority was reduced to 2,794 in 1959.

In his native county Davies was active in a variety of local affairs. Since 1935 he had been Chairman of Montgomeryshire Quarter Sessions. He was President of the Welsh Liberal Federation from 1945 to 1948 and had been President of the Approved Societies of Wales since 1945. From 1945 to 1946 he was Chairman of the Advisory Committee on Greater London Planning and of the Committee on the Method of Carrying out the Plan for Greater London. He had held the chairmanship of the Select Committees on Delegated Legislation and on Members' Expenses and had been a Charity Commissioner. In 1953 he was elected a Bencher of Lincoln's Inn. In November, 1961, he was appointed to succeed Lord Thurso on the Political Honours Scrutiny Committee. Among his publications were studies of Agricultural Law and the Law of Auctions and Auctioneers.

Clement Davies married in 1913 Jano Elizabeth, daughter of Morgan Davies, M.D., F.R.C.S. Of their family of three sons and a daughter one son survives.

March 24, 1962.

Sir Daniel Davies, K.C.V.O., F.R.C.P., Extra Physician to the Queen, formerly Physician to King George VI, and to His Majesty's Household, died at his home in Wimpole Street, London, on May 18, 1966. He was 66.

Daniel Thomas Davies was born in November, 1899, the son of the Rev. Dr. Mardy Davies, in one of the mining valleys of Wales, and was educated in Bridgend and at Cardiff University. These facts moulded his personality and coloured his life. He was a true son of the Welsh mountains and valleys, and did his utmost to promote the honour of his country and the welfare of his countrymen. He was a confirmed nonconformist in all the spheres of his life. Davies was Welsh speaking, and loved to converse in that language.

After a brilliant career as a student at Cardiff, Davies went to London to seek his fortune and in 1927 was appointed to work in the Pathology Department of the Middlesex Hospital as assistant chemical pathologist under his friend, Charles Dodds. From this post he became Medical Registrar at the same hospital, and worked for Sir Robert Young.

In both these posts he made a great impression. As a medical registrar his teaching was quickly appreciated by students and house physicians. The teaching was simple and direct, and was illuminated by his great knowledge of medical history and of contemporary figures of medicine that made the subject fascinating to the listener. His keen mind was always seizing on some unusual aspect of a case, and seeking an explanation for it until he found a solution.

CLASSIC RESEARCH WORK

He also conducted lines of research that today could be considered whole time occupations in themselves. These researches were concerned mainly with problems of gastric secretions and the anaemias.

His article on the "Gastric Secretions of Old Age" with Lloyd James, a great friend and co-author, was published in the *Quarterly Journal of Medicine*. It is a masterpiece of clear, concise writing and orderly research work, and is a classic which every young man embarking on research work should study.

His greatest work was undertaken with Lionel Whitby and Graham Hodgson. It was an inquiry into the use of Felton's Serum in lobar pneumonia; this was finished and published at the same time as the first reports on "Prontosil". Unhappily for the work, though happily for mankind, Prontosil and later the sulphonamides proved so successful that this article was soon forgotten.

After years of service as physician to the Royal Household, Davies was appointed physician to H. M. King George VI, and later physician to the Queen, a post that he later relinquished on his appointment as extra physician to the Queen. His connexion with the Royal Family continued, however, as he remained physician to and close personal friend of the Duke of Windsor.

Early in his medical career Davies became attached to Lord Dawson, for whom he worked hard and unsparingly almost to the time of Dawson's death. When Dawson was bombed out of his home early in the war, Davies offered him the hospitality of his own home, and for a time Dawson saw patients there. Later a close friendship developed between Davies and Lord Horder; here it was a case of two great personalities on equal terms whereas with Dawson the relationship had been that of sage and acolyte.

For 30 years Davies was Lord Beaverbrook's personal physician, a task that put considerable strain on him and probably contributed to his relinquishing his appointment as physician to the Queen. Beaverbrook was an exacting patient with a serious chronic lung complaint and this entailed repeated nocturnal visits to Cherkley and even further afield.

Davies's contribution to the Second World War was to serve as medical adviser to Beaverbrook at the Ministry of Supply. He refused to receive any remuneration for this post, in spite of the very hard work that he put into it.

REJECTED STATE SCHEME

His nonconformity was never better expressed than in his attitude to the National Health Service. He refused to accept the service and never joined it, but continued doing his everyday hospital work as before, and, of course, without any pay. At the same time he would not join any body of doctors to fight the service, and this led to some minor differences with his great friend Horder, who founded the Society for the Freedom of Medicine, but with which Davies refused to have anything to do.

Welsh education owes much to Davies, who through his connexion with rich Welshmen caused many scholarships to be endowed for the benefit of young Welshmen. For years he played a great part in the affairs of the National University of Wales.

He was always approachable and willing to help young people in any aspect of their careers. Many young doctors owe their mode of living to him, whether it was in the Services or abroad, or in general practice. His encouragement was always freely given to his friends and proteges, and his help was extended also to those outside the profession of medicine.

Davies was an omnivorous reader, and his reading extended from everything connected with Wales in English and in Welsh, to the English poets, history, and above all, contemporary history.

His delight for much of his life was to make friends and to entertain or be entertained by them as frequently as possible. He gathered his friends from all walks and strata of life. His friends had all to have one attribute, the power to sparkle in conversation. Coupled with his delight in entertaining was his enjoyment of a good story, and he himself was a great raconteur.

LOVED A JOKE

His puckish sense of humour showed itself in his enjoyment of practical joking; even jokes against himself were recounted with joy.

His greatest friend, and undoubtedly the person he admired most was Aneurin Bevan. It was a great experience to listen to a conversation between these two. When Aneurin died, he appeared to lose a little of his zest.

After 30 years on the staff of the Royal Free Hospital, and at the early age of 60 years, he decided to retire from that hospital. He retained his position at St. John and St. Elizabeth Hospital until the normal retiring age of 65 years. He was a consultant to Hounslow, Wood Green, and Southgate Hospitals in London.

He was knighted in 1951. He married Vera, daughter of J. Percy Clarkson, and they had two daughters.

May 19, 1966.

Marion Davies, an actress who made her name in silent pictures in the early 1920s and continued to appear regularly in films until after the Second World War, died on September 22, 1961, in a Hollywood hospital. She was 64.

She belonged to what may be described as the Mary Pickford school of film heroines, for her speciality was a winsome artlessness and a stylized simplicity. She was constantly being cast in the part of a none-too-attractive girl who blossomed out before the end of the picture into a glamorous beauty.

Her real name was Marion Douras. She was born in Brooklyn, New York, on January 3, 1897, and was educated at the Convent of the Sacred Heart, Hastings, New York. She appeared as a child in religious pageants at the convent, and later modelled dresses. Her first stage appearance was as a dancer at the Forrest Theatre, Philadelphia in September, 1914, and her New York debut was made at the Globe Theatre in the same piece a month later. In 1916 she won herself a part in the Ziegfeld Follies, and made her first film, *The Runaway Romany*, in 1917, scoring an immediate success.

LAUNCH BY HEARST

She continued to appear on both the stage and the screen for a further three years, but then devoted herself exclusively to the cinema.

In 1918 she was taken up by William Randolph Hearst, the newspaper magnate, who had seen her playing a small part in a musical comedy called *Watch Your Step*. He was already interested in the financial possibilities of the cinema, and he now acquired a studio in New York in order to launch her on her film career. He remained her patron throughout his life, and spent a great deal of money and effort in establishing her as a film star. Moreover, it was Hearst who insisted on her playing ingénue parts at a time when she herself, as a blonde, would have preferred to attempt some of the tough and sophisticated blonde parts to which the American cinema has always been addicted, and which so befitted an actress born in Brooklyn. As she also had a talent for light comedy, it seems probable that Hearst may well have handicapped her career as well as giving her substantial support. In the middle twenties, when Hollywood had become established as a film centre, Hearst arranged for her films to be released through the newly formed M.G.M. company, under the special aegis of Louis B. Mayer.

With such powerful backing in the film and newspaper world, there was little chance of failure. But sometimes Hearst's enthusiasm for his prodigy's talents went too far. When he tried to insist that she play the heroine in *The Barretts of Wimpole Street*, even Mayer opposed him, and the part was given to Norma Shearer; and the association between Hearst and Mayer finally ended in 1934 after Hearst had wanted Marion Davies to play the name part in *Marie Antoinette*. Her most successful films for M.G.M. were probably *Blondie of the Follies*, with Robert Montgomery, *Operator Thirteen*, with Gary Cooper, and *Peg o' My Heart*. Her later films included *Page Miss Glory*, *Cain and Mabel*, and *Ever Since Eve*. It is generally believed that Orson Welles had Hearst and Marion Davies in mind when he made *Citizen Kane*, a film which earned him the lasting antagonism of Hearst. Whatever the truth of this, there is every reason to suppose that Hearst's dominating influence over Marion Davies cut across the full development of a gay and lively talent.

September 25, 1961.

Senator W. Rupert Davies, a distinguished Canadian newspaper publisher and a former High Sheriff of Montgomeryshire, died suddenly in Toronto on March 11, 1967, at the age of 87.

A true son of Wales, William Davies was born in Welshpool, Montgomeryshire, and received his early education there before emigrating to Canada at the age of 15. Starting at the bottom rung of the ladder which was to bring him to the top of his profession in that country and to accord him honour in his land of birth, Davies became an apprentice printer with the *Brantford Examiner* and later worked as a printer in Toronto and New York.

Before entering the publishing world proper in 1908, he took over as publisher and editor of the *Thamesville* (Ontario) *Weekly Herald* which he purchased in the following year. Later he sold it and acquired the *Renfrew Mercury*, a larger weekly. In 1925, he entered the field of daily journalism with the purchase of the *British Whig* in Kingston, Ontario. Later he decided to merge that paper with the *Kingston Daily Standard* owned by the late Harry Muir. From vice-president and editor of *The Whig-Standard*, he rose to be president in 1931. Five years later that publication took over the nearby *Peterborough Examiner*. On Muir's death in 1939 Davies bought out the Muir interests in *The Whig-Standard* and the *Examiner*. Not content with only newspapers, Davies branched out into the field of local radio, establishing a company in 1941 to build and operate two stations in Kingston and Peterborough respectively. Later he added television outlets in both cities.

Having already taken an active interest in the Canadian Press Agency, a national newsgathering cooperative—he was elected to the board of the Agency in 1929—he became president at the beginning of the last war and was re-elected in 1940 and 1941. In preparation for his first term of office as president he made an extensive tour of European countries in the summer of 1939 to make himself thoroughly conversant with international news coverage.

PUBLISHING LINKS

He had already tried to strengthen the bonds between Canadian and British newspaper publishers as far back as 1924 when he organized a party of Canadian weekly newspaper editors for a tour of Britain and Europe. A little later he helped to arrange a party of British editors and publishers who visited and looked at Canada. He was a delegate to the Imperial Press Conference in Ottawa in 1920 and in London 10 years later. He attended the annual conferences of the Empire Press Union (later to become the Commonwealth Press Union) and from 1941 to 1951 was chairman of the Canadian section. Just after the war he served as vice-chairman of the sixth Imperial Press Conference in London and again at the meeting in Ottawa four years later.

Always aware of his Welsh heritage Davies owned an estate in Montgomeryshire and managed to spend many of his summers there. In 1951 he returned to the principality to serve for a year as sheriff of his native county.

PEER'S PARTNER

Although maintaining reasonably good health until the day of his death he gradually relinquished the active management of his newspaper interests to his sons. He also entered into a partnership with Lord Thomson of Fleet to manage his radio and television stations.

An active Liberal, Davies was appointed to the Senate by Mackenzie King in November, 1942.

He was honorary life member of the Canadian section of the Commonwealth Press Union, a vice-president of the Royal Welsh Agricultural Show, governor of the Royal Agricultural Show, and chairman, Council of the Order of St. John of Jerusalem of the county of Montgomery.

He is survived by his second wife, the former Margaret Esther McAdoo (of Calgary, whom he married in 1950); also by two sons, Arthur L. Davies, president and part owner of the *Peterborough Examiner* and publisher of *The Whig-Standard*, and Robertson Davies, part owner of the *Examiner* and since 1963, Master of Massey College in the University of Toronto. A third son, Fred, was killed in an automobile accident in Nassau in 1954. The Senator's first wife died in 1948.

March 13, 1967.

Lieutenant-General Fidel Dávila, a leading military commander in the Spanish Civil War, a member of the Council of the Realm, a former Minister of War, died on March 22, 1962, in Madrid. He was 83.

A soldier practically all his life, Dávila took part in the Cuban campaign of 1898 and fought in Morocco from 1918 to 1922. He held various important military posts between his service in the Moorish campaign and the beginning of the Civil War in July, 1936. He played an active part in the secret preparations which led up to the launching of the insurrectionary military movement against the Republican Government and was in Burgos when the Civil War began. He was also a member of the military junta at Burgos over which General Franco presided and which controlled affairs at the beginning of the conflict.

After General Mola had been killed in an aircraft crash in 1937 Dávila succeeded him as commander of the Nationalist forces in northern Spain. At the head of the brigades of Navarre he occupied Bilbao and then advanced westward along the Cantabrian coast to capture Santander. From Santander Dávila's Army marched on into Asturias and captured the capital, Oviedo; then Gijon and other strongpoints held by the Republicans in that mountainous country. When the National Government was constituted Dávila was appointed Minister of War but continued to command the Army of the north. Later he played a prominent part in the total occupation of Aragon and in the capture of Huesca and Teruel. He captured Lérida, fought at the important battle of the Ebro, and led his forces in the advance across Catalonia to the Pyrénées which forced the retreat of thousands of Republican troops into France.

At the end of the Civil War in 1939 he was promoted lieutenant-general and later appointed captain-general of the second military region. From this post he became chief of the headquarters staff and was again appointed Minister of War.

March 23, 1962.

Sir Robert Henry Davis, the inventor of numerous breathing, diving and escape apparatuses, and life president of Siebe, Gorman and Co., died at Epsom on March 29, 1965. He was 94.

He spent the whole of his working life with the firm, and went to the office regularly until May 1964.

When a presentation was made to Davis to commemorate the completion of 50 years' service, in 1932, it was recorded that he had "devoted his life to study of the problems confronting those who are called upon to work in irrespirable atmospheres, and had spent thousands of pounds in research and experimental work in connexion with deep-sea diving, high-altitude flying, mine research work, &c."

Robert Henry Davis was born in London on June 6, 1870, the eldest son of the late Robert Davis, a detective in the City police. When he was 11 he obtained employment in the Siebe, Gorman works in Lambeth. By a lucky chance his neat handwriting was noticed by Gorman, and he was given a place in the office. He studied hard to complete his education after office hours. While still in his twenties he was promoted assistant manager. In 1900 he married Margaret, daughter of the late William Tyrrell, of Kildare. She died in 1952. Gorman's wedding present to his gifted assistant was a house and a gold watch.

With an established position and a free hand, he became successively general manager, managing director, and governing director. Davis's inventive, yet practical, mind concentrated entirely in developing and extending the diving and other safety apparatuses in the field in which his firm had long specialized. For use in connexion with deep sea diving, Davis and Professor Leonard Hill designed a special diving bell which comprised also a decompression chamber. Davis also invented an altitude apparatus for supplying oxygen to airmen flying in rarefied atmospheres. He originated a heated dress for flying in high altitudes.

GAS ATTACKS

When in April, 1915, the country was roused by news of the first German gas attack and the sufferings of our troops, Davis immediately devised and manufactured his emergency "respirator," known as the stocking skene or veil mask. He set to work his family and relations and anybody else he could bring in; the women of Lambeth, under his direction, turned out great quantities, working in their own homes, and within 48 hours the first consignment was sent off to France. Whether by accident or by design, the firm's works received attention during a Zeppelin visit.

Davis was a member of the Admiralty Deep Sea Diving Committee, and in 1933, the deep diving decompression tables using oxygen were completed, which for the first time allowed a safe ascent from 300ft.

He worked on these tables with Professor J. B. S. Haldane, Sir Leonard Hill, and Captain G. C. Damant, the leading naval diving expert. They have been used by the Royal Navy ever since, with revision in 1962.

The Davis Submerged Escape Apparatus was first used in 1929, and was standard equipment until replaced by the BIBS (Built In Breathing System) which the firm produced in 1951 and which is now in use in all British submarines.

In 1939, after the sinking of the submarine Thetis, Davis was appointed a member of the Dunbar Nasmith Committee to investigate causes.

The Siebe, Gorman works in Westminster Bridge Road were bombed at the beginning of the Second World War, and the firm moved to its present site at Chessington.

DIVING UNIT

There, the extensive experimental facilities for diving were put at the disposal of the Royal Navy and the Admiralty Experimental Diving Unit. Davis worked with Haldane and Hill on problems of the underwater physiology of operational divers.

Among the inventions to come out of the Chessington works were human torpedoes, midget submarines, human mine-sweepers, and anti-blast clothing.

Between 1946–48 he cooperated again with the Royal Navy on deep diving experiments, and the work culminated in the Navy's record "hard hat" dive of 540ft. in 1948.

In 1906, Davis had perfected the first really practicable oxygen breathing apparatus for mining rescue, which was accepted and is still in use in a modified form.

More recently the firm helped to pioneer the use of underwater television to investigate the sinking of the submarine Affray in 1951 and the Comet airliner disasters. In 1953 they provided the oxygen breathing apparatus for the successful British Everest expedition.

Davis was appointed life president of Siebe, Gorman in 1959, when the Fairey group took over the company. It became a public company again in 1962.

For the past 50 years, Davis had been at the centre of developments in the knowledge and practice of diving. His intensive absorption in a field of experiment in which he was a supreme—though never a satisfied—expert, virtually excluded outside interests from his life. He found time, however, to write several manuals on diving. He was knighted in 1932.

March 31, 1965.

Christopher Dawson, who died on May 25, 1970, at Budleigh Salterton at the age of 80, went to Harvard as the first Chauncey Stillman Professor of Roman Catholic Theological Studies in 1958 and on his arrival there was greeted by Anne Fremantle as "the greatest living English Catholic scholar".

Few would at that time have thought the judgment a strange one. If today other rival names might suggest themselves, it is because in the last decade persistent ill health had prevented him from further writing and in particular from defining his position towards the new problems within the Church created by the Vatican Council. He must therefore stand on a more general rather than a special reputation. It was unlikely that, whatever the temporary eclipse that he may suffer, he will in the long run be the loser for that.

Dawson was born in 1889, the son of Colonel H. P. Dawson, the squire of Hartlington Hall, near Skipton in Yorkshire. The son of a military, landowning Anglican family, he was educated at Winchester and Trinity College, Oxford. He gave no early promise either of a literary and scholarly career or of the precise direction in which his scholarship was likely to lead him.

CULTURE BASED ON RELIGION

But at Trinity he won the friendship of Mr. E. I. Watkin, a friendship which he retained through life and at the age of 25 in 1914 was received into the Catholic Church. His first article did not appear until he was 32 in the Sociological Review nor his first book until he was 40. Thus his whole writing life was the product of his Catholic days.

Dawson's first book was *The Age of the*

Gods. In it he advanced the contention by which his whole writing life was dominated—the contention that religious belief and practice was the basis of every culture. In this book he illustrated this contention from the pre-Christian cultures. In his subsequent works—*The Making of Europe*: *Progress and Religion*: *Religion and the Modern State*: *Dynamics of World History*: *Movement of World Revolution*: *The Historic Reality of Christian Culture*: *The Dividing of Christendom*: *The Formation of Christendom* and others—he carried his contention forward into Christian times, argued that Christianity, which found its full form only in the Roman Catholic Church, was the creator of Europe and that Europe was inevitably doomed to decline if she abandoned her true Christian culture for the secularist alternatives by which she was tempted. "Today she (the Catholic Church) stands as she did under the Roman Empire as the representative in a changing world of an unchanging spiritual order", he wrote in *The Modern Dilemma*. In his earlier years he saw in Marxism the main secularist challenge to the religious spirit and in, for instance, the first edition of *Religion and Culture*, was ready at least to hope that Fascism might prove a genuine champion against that materialism, offering its service to a truly religious cause. It was not, however, long before he came to think of Marxism and Fascism not as antagonists but as facets of essentially the same totalitarian evil, against which hope lay only in the defence of a constitutional regime of law and order, which, if it did not in itself provide the solution, at least provided a condition of freedom within which it was possible to work for the solution. In an age in which such an assumption was not general he always with unflinching courage asserted that history, if it was not to be merely the "tale told by an idiot", must be the story of the workings of God in this world.

IMMENSE LEARNING

A scholar of immense learning, a gentleman of natural courtesy, who was always most meticulous in understanding and stating fairly all positions from which he himself dissented, he was a natural ecumenist and when Cardinal Hinsley launched the movement of the Sword of the Spirit to further more friendly relations between the denominations, he in collaboration with Barbara Ward (now Lady Jackson) was keen in his support and became the movement's Vice-President. From 1930 to 1936 he had been a lecturer in the History of Culture at University College, Exeter and in 1940 he became the Editor of the Dublin Review. But, though a charming and the most courteous of hosts to his private friends, he was the victim of intense shyness as a result of which he was not well suited to public contacts whether in a committee or on a platform.

Harvard paid to him the high honour of electing him as its visiting Professor, but his shyness and his ill health prevented him from playing there as large a part in the univeristy's social life as those who had appointed him might have hoped. He was frequently called upon to deliver important lectures—at Exeter, when he was invited to give the Forwood Lecture at Liverpool University, the Gifford Lectures at Edinburgh, or later at Harvard. The lectures when published in book form provided most stimulating reading, but in delivery his hesitating reading and uncertain voice made them difficult to follow, and he himself thought of himself as a natural recluse, made for writing rather than for speaking.

He married Valery Mary, the youngest daughter of Walter Mills, and is survived by a son and two daughters.

May 27, 1970.

Peter Dawson, the baritone, who died in Sydney on September 26, 1961, was the son of a Scottish immigrant and was born in Adelaide, South Australia, in 1882.

At the age of 20 he went to London, where he studied under Sir Charles Santley, made the first of his many gramophone records in 1904, and appeared in opera at Covent Garden for the first time in 1909.

For the greater part of a career that extended over 50 years Dawson was, however, primarily known as a concert singer whose programmes like his gramophone records (which sold over 13m. copies), ranged from standard operatic arias to popular ballads. As a singer, his work was always both polished and infectiously sincere, and the affection in which he was held by audiences was a natural response to his friendliness of manner, and his spontaneous enjoyment of his work. As "J. P. McCall" he published a number of ballads of his own composition, the most famous being a setting of Rudyard Kipling's poem "Boots." His autobiography, *50 Years of Song*, is an entertaining account of his life and work written with humour and modesty.

He married in 1905 Annie Mortimer Noble. She died in 1953. Two years later he married her sister, Constance, who survives him.

September 27, 1961.

---

de Ayala—See under **Perez de Ayala.**

Professor Frank Debenham, O.B.E., formerly Professor of Geography at Cambridge and founder director of the Scott Polar Research Institute, died in a Cambridge nursing home on November 23, 1965. He was 81.

Debenham was a survivor of Scott's last expedition. He was first and foremost a practical man, devoted to field research. Although he appreciated scholarship, he was not himself primarily a scholar, but rather an organizer and an inspirer of work.

He was born at Boural, New South Wales, Australia, on December 26, 1883. His father, the Rev. J. W. Debenham, was Vicar of Boural and also kept a flourishing private school in a district where schools were few and far between. He died in 1898, but his widow, determined to give her sons and daughter a university education, kept on the school for some years and from it Frank Debenham won a scholarship to the King's School, Paramatta. He left in 1901 to enter Sydney University. There he first took the ordinary arts course, becoming B.A. in 1904. In that year he left the university, taking a teaching post until 1907, while he saved enough money to return to Sydney and take the Honours course in science. In 1910 he took his B.Sc., specializing in geology.

In that year, the geological department of Sydney University was working on the results of the Shackleton Expedition (1907–09). It was at that time, too, that Captain Scott and Dr. Wilson, his chief of staff, passed through Sydney on their way south on their heroic but ill-fated journey to the South Pole. Scott had the scientific side of the expedition very much at heart; he particularly wished to associate Australia with his project and Debenham was the man fortunate enough to be selected from Australia. He was not the first Australian to be chosen, for Griffith Taylor, another geologist, who was ultimately to turn geographer, was among the original staff selected in England.

During the expedition Debenham suffered an injury to his knee which prevented him from taking part in the southern journey, but, after a good winter's work at the base, in the summer of 1911–12 he went as geologist on the western journey to Granite Harbour, and the surrounding district. Features of his work on this journey, worth noting from its influence upon his subsequent career, were the making of a detailed large-scale plane table map of the area traversed, and considerable experience in more exact methods of survey, partly gained in the measurement of glaciers, partly in the general survey policy of the expedition.

RESULTS OF EXPLORATION

On his return from the Antarctic Debenham was one of a small party of the Scott Expedition scientists who were given the opportunity of going to Cambridge as advanced students to work out the physical and geological results of the field explorations. A year's pleasant work there was followed by the declaration of war.

Debenham, who had joined King Edward's Horse in 1913, was in Australia with the British Association. He did not return in time to join up with his unit, but immediately entered his name as a cadet and in a few days was drafted to the Oxfordshire and Buckinghamshire Light Infantry with the rank of captain. After preliminary training, the battalion was drafted to Salonika and after some time in the trenches went into action on Horseshoe Hill, Lake Doiran, when Major Debenham, as he then was, was knocked out by a 5.9 inch shell which burst alongside him. He was sent home with severe shell shock and wounds and after a long spell in hospital returned to the depot of his regiment where he served until he was demobilized.

On his return to Cambridge he resumed work on the Scott Expedition geology. As the cartographer of the expedition had been drowned in the Hoque disaster in 1915, only Debenham possessed the local knowledge and technical skill required to complete the charts, and so cartography which had been his hobby became his chief occupation. In 1919 he was appointed Royal Geographical Society lecturer in cartography and some years later succeeded Philip Lake as Reader in Geography at Cambridge. It was largely through Debenham's efforts that the University eventually recognized the need of proper accommodation and equipment for the Department of Geography and in 1931 he was appointed as the first Professor of Geography at Cambridge.

WATER RESOURCES

He was a very successful head of a growing department and was greatly liked by both his colleagues and students. In 1936 the university found money to erect a large building adjacent to and incorporating the old Forestry School. The designing of this department and its furnishing was a task in which Debenham delighted. He retired from the Chair in 1949, but no means gave up work. Indeed, after that date he travelled extensively in Africa and wrote an important report on water resources, as well as several books on Southern Africa.

Parallel with his activities as a geographer were his interests in Polar matters. He became in 1925 the Founder-Director of the Scott Polar Research Institute, and held the post until 1946. In 1959 he published *Antarctica, the Story of a Continent*. The institute owes much to his initiative, and to few men are given the opportunity of perpetuating their memory in two important buildings in their university.

He married in 1917 Dorothy Lucy, daughter of J. T. Lemprière of Melbourne, and by her had six children.

November 25, 1965.

The Rt. Rev. Joost de Blank, D.D., a canon of Westminster since 1964, and former Archbishop of Cape Town, died on January 1, 1968. He was 59.

He had few of the physical attributes that tend to bring ecclesiastical preferment. He was small in physical stature, quiet in voice, at times almost sinister in appearance as a result of wounds received in Hitler's war. Nor was he a scholar. But he was possessed of personal qualities that made him an impressive figure in every piece of work to which he was called. Always an indefatigable and imaginative worker, a preacher of simple, yet powerful, eloquence, a facile writer with a flair for religious journalism, he developed at Stepney qualities of leadership to which in South Africa were added gifts of statesmanship, so that he became one of the most dynamic leaders in the Anglican Communion in the present century.

Joost de Blank was born on November 14, 1908, in Rotterdam, the son of Dutch parents. They later moved to England where his father had business connexions and he was educated at Merchant Taylors' School from which he proceeded to Queens' College, Cambridge, taking a second in the English tripos. He studied for ordination at Ridley Hall, an evangelical background from which he later advanced to a truly Catholic standpoint. He was made a deacon in 1931 and ordained priest in 1932. Two curacies at Walcot and Bredon in the rural diocese of Bath and Wells were followed by his first living as vicar of Emmanuel Church, Forest Gate, in the diocese of London, to which he was appointed in 1937.

CHAPLAIN WITH ROYALS

During the war he served as an Army Chaplain in the Middle East, Italy and west Europe. The military assignment he enjoyed the most was his attachment to the Royals, with which regiment he served for a considerable period of the war until serious wounds nearly cost him his life during the offensive in western Europe in 1944.

On his demobilization he became Assistant General Secretary of the Student Christian Movement. This was followed by a conspicuously successful four years as Vicar of St. John the Baptist, Greenhill, Harrow, from 1948–52, an incumbency which he describes in his book *The Parish in Action* which first brought him to the attention of a wider circle. He was consecrated Bishop of Stepney in 1952 and immediately his gifts began to make a considerable impact in London's East End.

He was in the United States when the invitation came in 1957 to succeed the late Dr. Clayton as Archbishop of Cape Town. He admitted to his friends that he would much have preferred not to leave the work in London in which he revelled and was so conspicuously successful, but after much heart-searching he agreed to accept the challenging invitation of the Church in South Africa, which was desperately in need of strong and fearless leadership at a time when the Nationalist handling of apartheid was causing much misgiving and anxiety among most Anglicans. Clause 29 of the Native Laws Amendment Bill gave the civil authority powers to exclude Bantu or coloured people from an Anglican church on the grounds that their presence constituted a nuisance. It was felt then by many that a climax in Nationalist lawgiving had been reached and that the Anglican Church must take a stand against the Government.

CHALLENGE TO STATE

Not many weeks after his enthronement in Cape Town Cathedral, at which he preached part of his sermon in Afrikaans, he issued a pastoral letter on the church and politics in which he emphatically stated: "Any Government or any political party that advocates policies which flout universally held Christian principles has stepped out of its proper province and is putting itself in the place of God. At that point the conflict between the politician and the churchman is no longer a political one but a religious one and the churchman cannot keep silence even if he would, because the honour of God Himself is at stake." From that moment the Archbishop became a figure in South African politics and a church leader to be reckoned with by the Government of South Africa, whose spokesmen frequently and vehemently criticized him.

Throughout his tenure of the Archbishopric he neglected no opportunity of telling South Africa what he thought of the ruling policy in all its ramifications, and did not fail to act in line with his own principles. He refused to preach in any church which was not open to black as well as white, including the naval dockyard church at Simonstown. He declared in 1959 that he was prepared to withdraw from the country, if Dr. Hendrik F. Verwoerd would withdraw as prime minister and return to his native land. In 1960 he came into head-on collision with the Dutch Reformed Church and called upon other churches to disassociate themselves from that Church unless it repudiated compulsory apartheid. In the same year he proclaimed that South Africa's Jubilee Celebrations were contrary to the scriptures. "This is no time for celebration, but for shame and repentance, amendment of life and change of policy, for sober self-examination and profound sorrow of heart."

The members of the Anglican Province over which he presided were not unanimous in approving of their Archbishop's outspoken ways, even though they admired his courage.

PHYSICAL STRAIN

The task of defending "the honour of God" in South Africa together with the unremitting care of all the churches at which he worked indefatigably from the early hours of each day until late at night, placed an intolerable strain on his physical powers. In September, 1962, he was ordered by his medical advisers to rest after an attack of cerebral thrombosis and he returned to England to convalesce.

He went back to South Africa towards the end of 1962, but the next year resigned on the grounds of ill-health. The pro-Government newspaper *Die Burger* commented that it was sorry his resignation had been caused by ill-health, but "we do not lament his pending departure". It went on to say that it believed "the time came long ago for him to leave, because his mission, almost from the beginning, has been a failure in the key sphere of race relations and in the related sphere of inter-church relations". Dr. de Blank became a canon of Westminster Abbey, and in January 1966, it was announced that he would become Bishop of Hongkong. Six months later on medical advice, however, he decided not to take up the appointment. He was appointed chairman of the Greater London Conciliation Committee in 1967, and became chairman of the United Kingdom committee for Human Rights Year 1968.

January 2, 1968.

Jeanne de Casalis, the actress and comedienne, who was successful on both stage and screen but who won her greatest following through her broadcast sketches, died on August 19, 1966, in St. Mary's Hospital, Paddington. She was 68.

Jeanne de Casalis was born in Basutoland on May 22, 1898, and educated in Paris.

Although she trained originally as a pianist, she turned to the theatre from the possibility of a career in music, and studied under Madame Thenard, of the Comédie Française, and with Theodore Komisarjevsky. She first appeared on the stage in Cannes, in 1919, and in the following year played Amina, in *Afgar*, at the Central Theatre, New York. London first saw her in 1921, as Clara in Sacha Guitry's *Deburau*. After a season with J. T. Grein's players, she consolidated her international success with a season as a member of the New York Theatre Guild followed by a series of parts at the Comédie des Champs Elysées, Paris. She returned to London in 1924 to play Mathilde Fay, in Ernest Vajda's *Fata Morgana*, and it was not until 1927, when she appeared in *Packing Up*, by Henry Grattan, at the Coliseum, that she was seen in one of the light comedy roles which became her speciality. Revue and a variety of plays kept her continuously occupied until the outbreak of war in 1939.

After her first film, *Settled Out of Court*, she was frequently active in the cinema.

WARTIME REVUE

During the war, she spent much of her time entertaining service men, a task which made her, during 1942 and 1943, a member of a revue company consisting of Dame Edith Evans, Miss Beatrice Lillie and Sir John Gielgud.

In 1934 she collaborated with Mr. R. C. Sherriff in writing *St. Helena*, a play based upon the closing years of the life of Napoleon, and four years later wrote and directed *Dearly Beloved Wife*. Her adaptation of *Frou-Frou*, by Meilhac and Halévy, was seen at the New Lindsey Theatre in 1951, and it was followed in 1955 by her books *Things I don't Remember*, and *Never Will She be Unfaithful*. It was, however, with her creation in 1931 of "Mrs. Feather", the hairbrained, inconsequential and cultured middle-class descendant of Dickens's Flora Finching, that she won the hearts of the vast radio audience, many of whom knew nothing of her work in the theatre. Mrs. Feather, whose adventures continued throughout the 1930s, provided a flawless reflection of the surface of life as it is lived by a particular type of woman at a particular social level, and while Jeanne de Casalis's invention did not attempt to probe the deeper mysteries of the feminine character, it gaily and truthfully surveyed social activities and attitudes. Some of Mrs. Feather's charm can be found in *Mrs. Feather's Diary*, which Jeanne de Casalis published in 1936, but the printed page does not convey the intonations, the polish, and the precision of timing and technique which she brought to her radio monologues.

MARRIED AN ACTOR

In 1929, Jeanne de Casalis married Colin Clive, the actor well remembered as Captain Stanhope in *Journey's End*. He died in 1937, and in 1942 she became the wife of Squadron Leader C. D. Stephenson.

August 20, 1966.

Dr. Lee de Forest, a pioneer in the history of radio communications, and inventor of the "audion", the elementary form of the modern radio valve, died on June 30, 1961, at the age of 87.

He was born at Council Bluffs, Iowa, on August 26, 1873, and graduated from Yale Sheffield Scientific School in 1896, receiving his Ph.D. three years later. His career of invention began almost immediately. This was soon to be a vital time in the development of radio. The problem at that stage was to raise the speech energy which declined when carried over very long distances. In 1904 John Ambrose Fleming published the results of his investigations on metallic grids in cathode valves. The following year Pupin invented the self-induction coils which were named after him.

THE AUDION

Then in 1906 came de Forest's invention of his audion, an amplifying valve that could serve as a detector. At the same time the Viennese inventor Robert von Lieben was at work on his audion.

The usefulness of these valves as generators, amplifiers, and detectors of radio waves was, however, established only slowly. It was not really until the coming of the First World War, with the great demands that it made upon radio communications, that the full value of this device was appreciated and it was manufactured in large quantities. It subsequently helped in the expansion not only of radio broadcasting, but of television, radar and electronics as well.

In 1910 de Forest was the first to broadcast the voice of Caruso, and in 1916 he put over the first radio news broadcast. It was in that year that he established a radio station. In 1902 he had formed the De Forest Wireless Telegraph Company, but after several years it failed. Although he had a number of other business ventures, including the De Forest Radio Telephone and Telegraph Company and the De Forest Phonofilm Corporation, it was essentially as an individualistic inventor that he will be remembered.

His phonofilm, to which he devoted most of his attention between 1919 and 1924, was an early development in the sphere of talking motion pictures.

Altogether he held some 300 patents in the United States and various other countries, covering the fields of aircraft-guiding beams, the wire transmission of news pictures, cosmic ray measurement and radiotherapy.

Among his numerous honours were the Cross of the French Legion of Honour, the Edison Medal, which he was awarded in 1946, the Gold Medal of the World's Fair at St. Louis in 1909, the Gold Medal at the Panama Pacific Exposition of 1915, and the Elliott Cresson Medal in 1923. He was a founder, fellow, and past president of the Institute of Radio Engineers, whose Gold Medal he won.

De Forest's publications were *Television Today and Tomorrow* and his autobiography, *Father of Radio*, apart from scientific papers.

July 3, 1961.

General Charles de Gaulle, who died suddenly on November 9, 1970, at his home at Colombey-les-deux-Eglises, played a part in world history from June, 1940, when from London and with the support of Churchill, he rallied Frenchmen to carry on the struggle against Germany after a French government headed by Marshal Pétain had asked for an armistice. "Gaullist" passed into international vocabulary much at the same time as "Quisling", with a very different connotation.

Other Frenchmen made the same decision as de Gaulle in 1940. The originality of his achievement was his insistence that La France Combattante was not an auxiliary force in the British war effort but that it represented France, which the Vichy regime could not do because it had betrayed the country by laying down its arms. The practical consequences of his claim that his movement was the legitimate custodian of France's interests led him into frequent and bitter conflicts with Churchill and Roosevelt. By 1943 it became clear that the internal Resistance in France would recognize nobody but General de Gaulle. When France was liberated in 1944 the nation was overwhelmingly Gaullist and the Provisional Government of which de Gaulle was the head was accepted everywhere. Thanks to de Gaulle France was given, though grudgingly, a place among the victorious powers.

So from the beginning of his career as a statesman, General de Gaulle based his appeal on deeper and less conscious feelings than are normally aroused by political leaders.

De Gaulle retired from power in 1946. He made, between 1947 and 1951, an unsuccessful effort to return to power in order to revise the constitution of the Fourth Republic which he considered had the grave defects of the Third, defects which had played no small part in France's defeat in 1940. This descent into the electoral arena tended to make de Gaulle into a partisan figure. But after his virtual retirement from politics in 1952, his prestige remained at the back of the minds of most Frenchmen and, in 1958, when the French Government risked being overthrown by a revolt of the Army in Algeria, President Coty could refer to him as "the most illustrious Frenchman".

MARRYING THE CENTURY

The Gaullist era properly begins from 1959 when he became President of the Republic. The new constitution which de Gaulle insisted on being given the right to draw up has never been considered perfect by a majority of the leaders of the old established parties and the provision for the election by universal suffrage of future Presidents, which was added in 1962, raised fierce resistance from politicians at the time. The President himself stretched the powers given him under the constitution. Nevertheless, in broad outline the Fifth Republic brought about a better balance between the Executive and the Legislative and it is unlikely that, if France continues to be governed by a parliamentary system, it will be substantially abandoned. Those who advocate a Presidential constitution on the lines of that of the United States tend to regard the Fifth Republic as a useful *régime de transition*.

De Gaulle's first and most important task as

President was to make France marry the century and accept decolonization. With the authority he exerted over the nation, based at first on the support of all progressive forces, Black Africa was a relatively easy task. Algeria was another matter and de Gaulle had to use all his prestige and cunning to overcome the widely shared French illusions about Algeria and also to wean the French Army in Algeria from hostility to decolonization. It was a long, bloody struggle, and not finished until July, 1962.

From 1962, until his retirement in April 1969, he strove to restore to France a place in the world which would be, given the circumstances of the post-war period, as equivalent as possible to that which she had had in the twenties. He stood against "the two hegemonies" of the U.S.S.R. and the United States, though from 1962 onwards his activities seemed to be directed mainly against the integrated structure of the Atlantic block. He encouraged a *rapprochement* with the Soviet Union and the satellite countries.

GRAND DESIGN

His grand design was a political confederation of the principal states of Europe which, as it became independent of the United States, would be able to settle outstanding differences with the Soviet Union, in particular the problem of Germany.

A believer in economic cooperation in Europe—he had advocated a West European economic block as early as 1943—de Gaulle honoured the policy of the Fourth Republic which had led France to sign the Treaty of Rome in 1957 and took France into the Common Market. But he intended that all fundamental economic decisions should remain in the hands of national parliaments. He was, therefore, opposed to the aim of most of the postwar "Europeans" in western Europe who were working for a European federation and for precisely the abolition of much of the power of the national Parliaments. There can be no federation, de Gaulle once said, without a federator—and this could only be the United States in the case of western Europe.

Continuing the policy of the Fourth Republic as regards the Common Market, though with this significant limitation, de Gaulle also carried on the policy of reconciliation with Germany begun by Robert Schuman and Adenauer after the war. Having won the friendship of Adenauer—who though a federalist put Franco-German understanding first—de Gaulle paid a spectacular visit to the Federal Republic in 1962 before the signing of the Franco-German Treaty. He did not win over the majority of German politicians to his view of world politics and the preamble to the Franco-German Treaty included a German declaration concerning the importance of obligations entered into as part of the Atlantic Alliance. German-French policy was to diverge considerably thereafter. Yet the provision for regular head of state and ministerial meetings and the programme of social and cultural exchanges seemed to put an end to the secular conflict between Teuton and Gaul.

In pursuance of the general aim of restoring French influence in the world, the first requisite of which was independence of American direction, de Gaulle virtually vetoed Britain's entry into the Common Market in 1963. He considered that Britain was too closely the ally of the United States and at that time would reinforce Atlantic forces inside the European Economic Community. His attitude aroused resentment in western Europe. His recognition of China was another step which emphasized France's independence and the growing gap between Washington and Paris. A far more conclusive step was taken in 1966 when France left Nato.

LEAVING NATO

During the first nine years of what some Frenchmen call his "reign", the years 1958 to 1967, de Gaulle's foreign policy caused some resentment in Britain and the United States but it also evoked, everywhere, a certain admiration and respect. France left Nato but not the Atlantic Alliance and still, presumably, supported the basic tenets of the Western democracies. It was remembered how unhesitatingly de Gaulle had expressed solidarity with President Kennedy during the Cuba show-down with the Soviet Union in 1962. De Gaulle's attitude towards Vietnam disarmed the distrust which the Left in all the Western countries had felt towards him. His strenuous efforts to establish French influence outside of Europe were looked on with some scepticism because France, it was felt, had not the economic strength to back her influence. But it was thought no bad thing that at least one European statesman should be admired throughout Asia, Africa and Latin America.

Above all, Europeans, even if they were federalists, considered that the General had given some added popular meaning to the concept of a United Europe and were prepared to accept de Gaulle's "imposing confederation of sovereign states" as a necessary first step towards the United States of Europe. It was felt that, in the last resort, the enlightened thinker in de Gaulle would take charge of the fervent nationalist, and that de Gaulle was aware that posterity would judge him largely on whether he had helped or had hindered the unity of Europe.

In 1967 there came a change. France's unhelpful attitude towards Britain's second attempt to enter Europe occurred when there was a general view that it was urgent to start building a political Europe. Even Herr Strauss, known as "a German Gaullist", said that there could be no political Europe without Britain.

GOOD FAITH DOUBTED

The General's behaviour over the Middle East crisis in the summer of 1967 aroused all sorts of doubts both about his good faith as a member of the Atlantic Alliance and also his attachment to the idea of making Europe. Pursuing his "independent" policy towards Israel and the Arab world, he totally failed to consult even his allies in the Six, all of whom were strongly affected by the crisis. His behaviour over Quebec still further alienated European opinion from him. People began to wonder whether the General's policies were based on long-term views or on at times brilliant, and at other times unfortunate, improvisations, often coloured by rancour against the United States.

The arbitrariness with which three policies—the Middle East, Quebec and the rejection of Britain—were carried out, emphasized France's isolation from the west. In 1963, de Gaulle had treated the British politely when virtually stopping the Brussels negotiations; this was not so in 1967. The editor of *Le Monde* could write: "Those who hoped he would lose, with age, this taste for excess (*outrance*) must admit this is not so, but the contrary. General de Gaulle will continue to interpret the 'higher interests of the nation' well or ill, but all too often in terms of his machiavellian genius and his insatiable will to dominate. Until when?"

In 1968, neither de Gaulle nor the government had foreseen the impetus behind the student revolt nor the sympathy public opinion would show for it at first, nor that it would affect a section of the working class. At one moment in May nearly nine million workers were on strike. Returning from Rumania when the crisis was at its height, he made an ineffective intervention on May 24. There came a moment in his career similar to that after the failure at Dakar in 1940 or to his abrupt resignation in 1946; he thought of retiring and admitted this in a TV interview given when he had mastered the crisis. But if nearly overthrown, the rider recovered—well before the last fence.

It had been taken for granted by many and this included a number of Gaullists that the General would go and opposition politicians intervened publicly and talked of a Provisional Government and a new President in view of the General's forthcoming departure. On May 29, de Gaulle cancelled a Cabinet meeting at the last moment and telling M. Pompidou he was going for 24 hours rest at Colombey, flew by helicopter to Baden Baden, where he talked with General Massu commanding the French forces in Germany and with his son-in-law General Alian de Boissieu.

The news leaked back before he returned to Paris that he had decided, if necessary, to use the French army in Algeria, and it much heartened the growing Gaullist defence committees in Paris and elsewhere.

Even before the General's dramatic gesture, the strikes, the mounting economic chaos had begun to produce a reaction against the revolutionaries.

PRESTIGE RESTORED

De Gaulle's call on May 30 for a return to order was completely successful and at one blow de Gaulle appeared to have recovered the prestige which had been taken away. He dissolved Parliament and at the general election which was held peacefully throughout France, the Gaullists came back with a huge majority. The new Government was formed with M. Couve de Murville as Prime Minister, M. Pompidou being dropped, though praised.

In the eyes of many Frenchmen it was M. Pompidou who had saved the Government during the crisis. For the first time de Gaulle had appeared hesitant at Cabinet meetings and at one moment had wanted to use military force against the students but had allowed himself to be overruled. M. Pompidou had been cautious, energetic, and had never believed that the students, workers and later the opposition politicians could overthrow the State. Loyal to de Gaulle, it was obvious that M. Pompidou by no means whole-heartedly believed in the General's insistence on a fundamental revision of society which was to be based on participation and which was to create a new social order, neither communist nor capitalist. De Gaulle believed that this would give youth "an ideal, an *élan* and a hope". Straight away the new government started work on fundamental reforms, first of which were those for the University which were entrusted to M. Edgar Faure. They were opposed in their initial stages by M. Pompidou and by the increasing number of conservative-minded Gaullists. M. Jeanneney and M. Capitant, the latter a strong left wing Gaullist, worked on schemes for industrial participation of workers in a regional framework and a new system of contracts between workers and employers was being drawn up. In November, 1968, de Gaulle forbade a devaluation of the franc which most French experts considered inevitable. In April, 1969, the government's referendum on regionalisation which, for reasons not convincing to most Frenchmen, included the abolition of the Senate, was defeated.

DEFEAT BY SUCCESSOR

M. Pompidou was never disloyal in word or deed to his master but many Gaullists and conservatives were convinced that he was better fitted to handle French affairs than de Gaulle. So, in a sense, de Gaulle was defeated by his successor and it became clear that the great myths had lost their attraction for many of de Gaulle's followers. He left the Élysée immediately the referendum result was known, going shortly after to Ireland for a holiday in order not to be involved in the Presidential election.

To the end, certain aspects of de Gaulle's thoughts appealed more to the Left than to the Right. Few would deny that the old man of 78 had seen something of the way a modern affluent society should adapt itself to the needs of the vigorous discontented and disorganized youth. Yet, harsh though they may be, the words used by Servan Schreiber in an interview given to *Life* were what many people felt: "de Gaulle possesses a remarkable intuition. He has understood much and launched many ideas which history will show are valid—decolonization, that Europe must cease to be the military ally of the United States, the participation of workers in enterprises. But the essence of Gaullism is a monologue and what has crumbled now is the notion of society governed by the monologue. In the present situation, de Gaulle is an ambiguity. His historic message remains but his methods are anachronistic. He no longer belongs to this age".

The French had many reasons for being grateful to him and, though this is disputed, among these may be the drastic change in French political life carried out during his lifetime, and, in particular, the rise of an important and reasonably coherent left-wing conservative party which is what the Union for the Fifth Republic really amounts to.

But three reasons for being grateful to the General are outstanding: in 1940 he saved France's honour; in 1958 he saved the Republic; and between 1958 and 1962 he managed to end the bitter conflict over Algeria, a conflict which raged in French minds as well as in North Africa. All these tasks required a man of heroic qualities who, to a large extent, had to stand above the political mêlée and look at men and politics from a great height. Accepting a hero as the head of a state has its drawbacks but also, at times, over-riding advantages.

In character, de Gaulle was a rare combination of an intellectual with a long view of history (and impatient of middle-term views it can be said) and a tough, military character. Though conventional in behaviour, with a logical mind not given at all to flights of fancy, he was susceptible to myths. He believed that he spoke for the people of France who listened to him through the hostile barrage of the politicians. Of his leaving power in 1946 he wrote "each Frenchman, whatever his political tendency, had at bottom the feeling that the General carried away with him something primordial, permanent and necessary, which he incarnated in history and which the regime of political parties could not represent. In the leader now cast aside, people continued to see a sort of designated holder of sovereignty". Like all myths, this was unverifiable: but like some, it proved to have substance. The General, to an extraordinary degree, identified himself with that supernatural being La France, whose existence is above and independent of the political divisions into which the French are so prone to fall.

Churchill, who, for all his quarrels with de Gaulle, perceived that he was a man of great stature, wrote of him during the war years:—

"I always recognized in him the spirit and conception which across the pages of history the word France would ever proclaim. I understood and admired, while I resented, his arrogant demeanour. Always when he was behaving worst he seemed to express the personality of France—a great nation with all its pride, authority and ambition."

CHOSE HIS UNIT

Charles André Joseph Marie de Gaulle was born at Lille on November 22, 1890, the son of Henri de Gaulle, a professor of philosophy and literature who taught for many years at the Jesuit College in the Rue de Vaugirard in Paris. His mother was Jeanne Maillot-Delannoy. He was sent to the College Stanislas in Paris and later in 1909 to the École Militaire de St. Cyr. In early youth his father led him to take an interest in philosophy and history which he was never to lose. When he left St. Cyr he was permitted to choose his own unit, and out of respect for its commander, Colonel Philippe Pétain, later Marshal Pétain, he selected the 33rd Infantry Regiment and joined it shortly before the war.

In August, 1914, de Gaulle was wounded at the Battle of Dinant and again in 1915 in Champagne. Promoted captain in that year, he was wounded for the third time, at Verdun, and having been too badly hurt to get away was taken prisoner. He had shown great courage and was mentioned in dispatches. For the rest of the war in spite of five attempts to escape—his great height made him easily identifiable—he remained in German hands. Disappointed at the failure of his bids for freedom he settled down to study the Germans, and on his return to his own country published the results of his observations in *La Discorde Chez l' Ennemi* (1924). After a period at St. Cyr as a professor of history he went in 1920 to Poland with General Weygand's mission and came back with a *citation* and the Polish Cross of St. Wenceslas.

CONDUCT OF WAR

From 1924 to 1926 de Gaulle was in Paris at the École Supérieure de Guerre. He had views of his own on strategy and tactics and found himself in disagreement with his head instructor, Colonel Moyrand, who shared the current belief in the superiority of the defence, which was later to find expression in the Maginot Line. He succeeded, however, when on field manoeuvres, in vindicating his own theory of free movement. Moyrand was none too pleased at so practical a refutation of his teaching; but, fortunately for de Gaulle, his achievement attracted the attention of Marshal Pétain, and he was appointed an instructor at the École Supérieure de Guerre. A little later Pétain posted him to his own staff. When, however, in 1927 Weygand became Commander-in Chief, de Gaulle went to the General Staff of the Army of the Rhine at Tours, and then became commander of the 19th Battalion of Chasseurs à'pied in the Rhineland. From 1929 to 1932 he was engaged on Government missions in the Middle East and Syria. In the latter year he published his Le Fil de l'Épée which was the text of lectures he had given in 1927, on Pétain's order, emphasizing the importance of leadership in war.

Recalled to France he was appointed to the secretariat-general of the Conseil Supérieur de la Défense Nationale, and the next year he published *Vers l' Armée de Métier*. It was a thoughtful and prophetic book in which he pointed to the defensive weaknesses of his country and emphasized the importance of the tank. He recommended a professional army as a spearhead of national resistance and held that armoured divisions should be its first important constituent. Paul Reynaud, the French Premier, agreed with him and in the Budget debate of 1935 demanded a revision of the military estimate to include six armoured divisions; but the weight of military opinion was against him.

In 1936 de Gaulle was at the Centre des Hautes Études Militaires, was promoted Colonel in 1937, and from that year until 1939 commanded the 507th armoured regiment at Metz. In 1938 he published his *La France et son Armée*.

When in September, 1939, the war broke out de Gaulle found that his own vision had been fulfilled and that the constitution of the German armoured divisions was almost the same as that which he had proposed. During the early months of the war he was deeply suspicious of the apparent inactivity of the enemy and feared that they were building up their mechanized striking power. He warned his superiors of the peril but he failed to secure action. In 1939 he had been appointed to command the 4th Armoured Brigade of the Fifth Army.

LACKING SUPPORT

In May, 1940, he was promoted to be commandant of the 4th Armoured Division and became a Brigadier-General, the youngest in the French Army. His command, which was made up of scattered elements, was not, however, equipped to act independently of the other units. It lacked air support and even petrol. He succeeded none the less by virtue of brilliant and resolute leadership in pushing back the enemy at Laon and Abbéville.

On June 6 Reynaud summoned de Gaulle to Paris and appointed him Under-Secretary of State for War and National Defence.

On June 8 he went to London, saw Mr. Churchill, and returned next day to France. On June 11, the Government having left Paris, he followed Reynaud to Tours. He was against the proposed retreat towards Bordeaux and in favour of retirement towards Britanny, where he hoped to put into effect a somewhat unrealistic plan for a "last-ditch" resistance, the *réduit breton*.

On June 15 he went to London, where he learnt of the British plan for an "indissoluble union between Great Britain and France," which he telephoned to Reynaud in Bordeaux and then flew back to France. But on June 16 the French Cabinet rejected the proposal. Reynaud resigned and de Gaulle, in danger of arrest by order of General Weygand, flew from Bordeaux with General Sir Edward Spears, Churchill's personal representative with Reynaud. He had neither troops nor money, but he was determined to fight on and on June 18 made his now historic broadcast to the people of France, calling on them to continue the fight and to join him. The next morning volunteers began to appear at the little house in Seymour Place which had been lent to him. On June 22 after the armistice terms were known he broadcast to France again. In punishment for his activities he was cashiered by General Weygand.

FLEET ATTACKED

Continuing to appeal to what he believed to be the true spirit of France, de Gaulle announced his determination to form a Provisional French National Committee and opened communication with the French commanders in Morocco, Syria, and Indo-China. On June 29 the British Government recognized him "as leader of all Free Frenchmen, wherever they may be, who rally to him in support of the Allied cause".

When in early July the French fleet at Oran was attacked de Gaulle, while expressing his grief and anger, said that he would rather know that the Dunquerque was aground than that she was shelling English ports. At the beginning of August he was condemned to death *in absentia* by a French military court. On August 26 the Governor of the Territory of Chad announced its refusal to accept capitulation and determination to fight on. A little later the Cameroons followed its example.

In October after the failure of his attempt to land at Dakar—he had had no idea of using force—de Gaulle visited the Cameroons, where there were great problems of organization to be faced, and at Brazzaville in the French Congo set up a committee for the defence of the French Empire. By December he had a force of some 35,000 men under arms, and 20 warships which were actually cooperating with the allies. He also sought to exercise political leadership by continuing to broadcast frequently, to refute the pronouncements of Vichy, and to call for the assistance of his fellow countrymen.

In April, 1941, de Gaullle flew to Egypt. His differences with the British authorities, particularly over the conduct of the campaign which threw the Axis out of Syria and Lebanon, were sharp and typical. He regarded himself as the only legitimate legatee of power in the Levant States. After his return to London in September, he created a National Committee and a National Advisory Council to share his authority, though keeping in his own hands the supreme command of the Free French Forces.

DIFFICULT ALLY

Throughout the war years, de Gaulle partly because of his aloof, inflexible character but mainly because he was intent above all on maintaining the position and prestige of his country, was the most difficult of allies. He had constant acrimonious differences of opinion with Winston Churchill, differences which, in the long run, were usually resolved but he was distrusted and disliked to the end by President Roosevelt.

From soon after his arrival in London, when he was alone except for a tiny group of other French exiles, he behaved as though he were a Head of State and an equal partner in the alliance; he appeared to be concerned, moreover, as much with reaffirming and assuring France's position as a great Power as with the immediate task of winning the war. And this attitude, intensely irritating to a British Government whose entire energies and every thought were concentrated on a life and death struggle with Nazi Germany, a struggle in which a defeated France counted for little, increased as the Fighting French forces slowly grew larger. Proud, touchy, and quick to take offence, he was also eternally suspicious of the British, who, he was convinced, were taking advantage of France's impotence to evict her from Syria and Lebanon. He was too a thorn in the flesh of allied generals to whom he issued peremptory orders on the manner in which the small French units under their command should or should not be used.

ALL FOR FRANCE

There was, however, as Churchill admitted, something admirable in his extraordinary single-mindedness, in which, then or later, there was nothing personal or self-seeking: all that he did was for France and France alone.

None the less his relations with the other allied leaders became so bad that at the time of the landings in North Africa in 1942 Churchill had to explain to him that the Americans refused to allow his forces to take part; further, Roosevelt intended that General Giraud, who had recently escaped from occupied France to Algiers, was to replace him as leader of the Fighting French—and indeed of France. After a long wrangle Churchill arranged that the two generals should meet him and Roosevelt in Casablanca. It had become obvious that de Gaulle's replacement by Giraud was impracticable, to say the least, and Roosevelt now proposed that the two generals should become joint presidents of a directorate for the Fighting French forces and administration, on equal terms with any other members but with Giraud holding the supreme military command. De Gaulle refused to entertain the proposal and returned to London. His representatives with the increasingly important French resistance movement, which he largely directed, gradually obtained the support of a majority of the local leaders, and after lengthy negotiations, with an absolutely unwavering de Gaulle becoming more and more difficult, a French Committee of National Liberation was formed, with de Gaulle and Giraud as joint chairmen, to take over the management of French interests throughout the world. Giraud was slowly evicted from the committee and de Gaulle became *de jure* as he had all along been *de facto* President of the French Government—as he tartly reminded General Eisenhower at a first prickly meeting.

De Gaulle left Algiers for London on the eve of D-Day, the exact timing of which had, to his intense anger, been concealed from him.

WELCOME FROM FRANCE

Eight days after the allied invasion of Normandy he landed in France to receive a tremendous welcome from the people. After the liberation of Paris the first act of his Government—composed of members of the Algiers Committee and of the resistance movement in France—was to abolish the authoritarian state set up by Marshal Pétain and declare that "legally the republic had never ceased to exist".

In 1945 a French constituent assembly was elected to draft a constitution for the "Fourth Republic".

In spite of difficulties with the Communists, in spite, too, of the country's economic plight—"France with her ideals and her ruins"—de Gaulle's first preoccupation, even in the summer of 1944, was to restore France to her place as a great power. He mastered the forces of disorder quickly. It was much against the views of Churchill, Eisenhower and most of his advisers, that Roosevelt persisted in refusing to recognize the French Provisional government until October: "the French Government is satisfied that the Allies have at last decided to call it by its proper name", said de Gaulle when recognition finally came.

The future of Germany was the first problem.

POLICY ON GERMANY

On this de Gaulle's thinking underwent some changes. In the autumn of 1944 the accent was on the splitting up of the Reich into a number of federal states—no Germany but no revenge and no annexations. Subsequently French policy concentrated on the occupation of the left bank of the Rhine, other safeguards, and on the economic attachment of an independent Saar to France; in the autumn of 1945 de Gaulle emphasized the importance of creating a "European family" to which Germany or "the Germanies", would belong. This last concept was percipient.

Gaullist diplomacy had some striking failures and successes. De Gaulle received Churchill in Paris in November, 1944, and failed to win the British leader's support for an Anglo-French front against the two giants. In December, he went to Moscow and succeeded in getting a Franco-Russian pact signed, without France recognizing the Lublin Committee of Polish Communists as the government of Poland. But he failed to impress Stalin with the advantages of a common front with France on Germany and, a few weeks later, Stalin supported the American view that France should be excluded from the Yalta conference. At Yalta in February, 1945, the three Great Powers agreed to respect each other's spheres of influence. Yet, largely owing to Churchill, France at Yalta was given a zone of occupation in Germany and was invited to act as one of the founder members of the United Nations, with a permanent seat on the Security Council. Although General de Lattre de Tassigny was present at the formal German surrender in May, France was excluded from the Potsdam conference in July 1945. But her loss again was more apparent than real for, at Potsdam, the victors decided that all the Peace Treaties should be the work of the Foreign Ministers of France as well as of the Three.

EMPIRE REGAINED

In May, Franco-British rivalry in the Levant flared into open crisis. France, who had in any case promised Syria and the Lebanon their independence, had to accept a compromise which de Gaulle considered humiliating. In July French troops landed in Indo-China and, by the end of the year, France had the satisfaction of having recovered all her former colonial empire. During these diplomatic struggles France, still vitally dependent on Allied supplies, military and civil, played from a weak hand. Nor did de Gaulle feel that the French people were behind him; Britain and the Americans were still popular. It was widely thought that de Gaulle put foreign policy far too much before economic recovery.

"Do you think I saved France for a handful of dried peas?" de Gaulle, it was said, retorted to complaints by his Food Minister. Returning from Yalta, the ailing Roosevelt suggested a meeting with de Gaulle in Algiers. De Gaulle refused both on the grounds that the American President had no right to invite the Head of the French State to a meeting on French soil and also because to have met Roosevelt then would be tantamount to under-writing the Yalta agreements. Roosevelt spoke of a "prima donna who from caprice had refused a useful rendezvous". De Gaulle's attitude was not well received in France and this he admits in his memoirs, writing; "Businessmen were alarmed because my gesture might jeopardize their chances of American aid and the politicians in general were inclined to believe that rich and powerful foreigners must be right."

De Gaulle's policy of making a bridge between East and West met with more favour at home than anti-Americanism. But, as de Gaulle himself perceived before 1945 was out, the behaviour of the Russians in east and central Europe was inexorably leading towards the Cold War and perhaps a hot one. Though this same policy was carried on by M. Bidault after de Gaulle's retirement, France had to come down on the side of the West.

As President of the provisional government after the war de Gaulle believed that France would never be an effective force in the world unless its political structure was completely overhauled. He called for a regime in which political power should not depend "on the vagaries of party politics".

STRONG LEAD PLANNED

De Gaulle advocated a constitution which provided for a strong central Government with a President elected by the nation and invested with authority to act. The provisional Government extended the suffrage to women, nationalized a number of industries and set up its first Monnet Plan, the precursor of subsequent French economic planning. He had secured a measure of support from the left but disagreements soon arose. He alienated the communists by refusing their demands for key ministries.

In January, 1946, he suddenly announced that the political conditions for a continuance of his work no longer existed and he resigned.

At Strasbourg on April 7, 1947, he launched his "Rally of the French People" (R.P.F.) with the object of achieving "the unity of our people in the tasks of renewal and reform of the state". He insisted that the Rally was not a new political party but a "framework for the growing feeling of a common spirit and desire for national unity above and apart from the parties".

The Rally made great strides in the municipal elections of 1947, the 1948 election for the Council of the Republic (Upper House), and the departmental elections of 1949. But the result of the general parliamentary election of 1951 came as a bitter blow to de Gaulle.

The Rally became the biggest single party in the new legislature, but it was not strong enough to carry through constitutional reforms.

PARTIES SPLIT

Its position was further weakened in 1952 by a split over the question of cooperation with other parties.

After a severe setback in the municipal elections of 1953 de Gaulle announced that the R.P.F. would "dissociate itself from political action" and all its members were free to "go their own way."

For the next five years de Gaulle remained more aloof than ever from the hurly-burly of politics. Although he kept an office in a small hotel on the left bank in Paris, to which he went at regular intervals, most of his time was spent at his house at Colombey-les-Deux-Eglises in Haute-Marne, writing his memoirs. From time to time he would emerge for a press conference, at which the habits and policies of the Fourth Republic would be castigated. Then silence again.

As the war in Algeria dragged on and the game of party politics became more complicated and less rewarding, there became increasing talk of a "crisis of the regime", which could only be resolved by the intervention of de Gaulle. The very act of de Gaulle's silence encouraged people of widely differing points of view to believe that, when the time came, they would find in him an ally. As events were to prove, he had retained friends and supporters in every party except the communists.

It was on May 13, 1958, that the long predicted crisis finally broke, when Army and settlers in Algeria set up committees of public safety, aimed not only at thwarting the new government of M. Pflimlin but also at ending "the system" altogether. "De Gaulle *au pouvoir*" became, through the prompting of Gaullist supporters, their rallying cry.

BLOODSHED AVOIDED

The days of intense excitement that followed gave the lie to those who maintained either that de Gaulle had always lacked political sense or that years of self-imposed exile had blunted his faculties. Although no doubt the impulse that swept de Gaulle into power a second time was overwhelming, it was largely thanks to the skill with which he played his cards that the transition was made without bloodshed and without illegality.

His first direct intervention came two days after the *coup* in Algiers. In a brief statement, couched in his usual elliptic prose, he declared that he "held himself in readiness to assume the powers of the Republic". This, like so many of the phrases used by de Gaulle during the crisis—and, indeed, after he had become Prime Minister—was open to a variety of interpretations. But he quickly made it clear that he was only interested in achieving power if asked by the President and endorsed by the Assembly. "Is it credible", he said, "that at the age of 67 I am going to begin a career as a dictator?"

CIVIL WAR DANGER

His wishes were granted. Warning the Assembly of the imminent dangers of civil war, President Coty said he had turned "towards the most illustrious of Frenchmen", and called on de Gaulle to form a Government of national safety "within the framework of republican legality". On June 1, more than 12 years after he had voluntarily laid down office, the Assembly voted de Gaulle back into power by 329 votes to 224.

De Gaulle's first choice of Ministers showed clearly that his contempt for the party system, as it had developed, did not extend to individuals. Together with new names, mostly civil servants and technicians, his Cabinet included three former Prime Ministers—M. Pflimlin (M.R.P.). M. Mollet (Socialist), and M. Pinay (Conservative).

TRIUMPHAL TOUR

As he saw it, the new Prime Minister's task was threefold—to reform French institutions; to restore authority and, if possible, achieve a settlement in Algeria; and to restore "the unity, integrity, and independence of France". Parliament was immediately sent on holiday until the autumn, and a committee set up to prepare a revised constitution.

ALGERIAN TOUR

On June 4 de Gaulle set out on a brief but triumphal tour of Algeria. Here once again he showed considerable political astuteness. The self-appointed authorities in Algeria had acquired the feeling that de Gaulle was largely their property. They had started the movement that had swept de Gaulle to power, and they expected him not only to endorse their actions (which he did) but also to echo their opinions which in many cases he did not. In all his speeches in Algeria, for example, he never mentioned the word "integration", which had been adopted by the Army as the heart of its Algerian policy, and only in his last speech, at Oran, did he use the magic phrase "*Algérie française*". His tart retort to the Committee of Public Safety in Algiers, when it went beyond the charter he had set it, showed quite clearly that he expected to be obeyed.

By the autumn of 1958 the Fifth Republic, endorsed by a great majority in a referendum, was firmly established. A new constitution, of the General's preferred pattern, was in operation. A new Gaullist Party, the Union for the New Republic (U.N.R.) won, with allied deputies from Algeria, 259 seats in the Assembly. A docile nation seemed ready to accept anything devised from above for its benefit.

Much was devised. The first few months of the new regime produced a flurry of legislation by decree, almost all of lasting value. Reforms which had been pigeon-holed for decades were swept through under the Government's special powers. Education, justice, rents, and criminal procedure were some of the numerous subjects tackled.

All this was good in itself but in de Gaulle's view the tidying up process was meant to serve a loftier purpose—the rehabilitation of the image of France in the eyes of the world.

MORE THAN GLORY

This was something more than the pursuit of glory, or even of power. France was not, as under Napoleon III, out for new conquests. Indeed, never has France divested herself so rapidly of so much sovereignty as during the first two years of the Fifth Republic. Without waiting for the inevitable pressure de Gaulle swiftly granted full independence to all the 13 former French colonies in Black Africa, and if in the end only four of them remained members of the French community he had planned, all, with the exception of Guinea, retained close ties of friendship with France. The goal was esteem and influence.

De Gaulle's first essay in this direction concerned Nato. In September, 1958, Notes were sent to Britain and the United States, suggesting that what looked like their dual control of the alliance should be converted into a triumvirate by the addition of France. Here de Gaulle drew blank. This failure only confirmed his belief that in politics nothing will come of nothing, and so he pressed on with the manufacture and testing of France's own nuclear weapon, with the development of an independent striking force, the *force de frappe*.

In other respects de Gaulle could point to considerable successes. Relations with Dr. Adenauer reached such a pitch of amity that people began to talk of a Paris-Bonn axis. Yet this was not an exclusive friendship. A journey to Canada and the United States at the end of April, 1960, was marked by scenes of striking cordiality. Still more remarkable was the State visit de Gaulle had paid to London earlier in the month. Few more impressive events have marked the sometimes chequered history of the Entente Cordiale than de Gaulle's address to members of both Houses of Parliament in Westminster Hall on April 7. His audience was equally touched by the matter of his speech and by the elegant fluency with which the General, now severely handicapped by eye trouble, delivered it noteless.

BARRICADES UP

In the same period of crowded diplomatic activity de Gaulle acted as host to Mr. Khrushchev. This visit, too, passed off smoothly. De Gaulle, however, had always been sceptical over the outcome of the summit meeting which followed, and could claim that the course of events justified his scepticism. Of all those involved at the abortive summit it was de Gaulle, the astute and courteous host, who alone emerged with his reputation undamaged.

It was always from another direction that cold winds blew. Algeria had raised de Gaulle to power; on more than one occasion it threatened to cast him from it. His first journey to Algeria in June, 1958, had left the advocates of *Algérie française* puzzled. When, later in the year, he offered to the rebels a "peace of the brave" and self-determination for Algeria, their worst fears seemed confirmed. Many of the *côlons* had never liked de Gaulle. Now he had shown himself not only not an integrationist, but a man who deliberately opened the door to negotiations and independence.

In January, 1960, the Algerian extremists acted. The barricades went up in Algiers.

MOST CRITICAL

This was the most critical situation de Gaulle had so far had to face. The loyalty of the Army, as well as the survival of his regime, depended on his ability to crush the revolt, and if possible to crush it without violence. On January 29, after what seemed to many a period of dangerous delay, de Gaulle appeared before the television cameras. He was in uniform, "in order to stress that I am speaking as General de Gaulle, as well as the head of the state". Without condoning rebellion or compromising his Algerian policy, he insisted that "I must be obeyed". His firmness won the day. The revolt collapsed.

His broadcast was not only an order to his Army; it was an appeal to his people, strangely moving because if de Gaulle frequently ordered, he very rarely appealed. And his "dear old country" responded wholeheartedly to his call for unity. With expert generalship de Gaulle had turned the revolt to his advantage. The logical sequence was the arrival in June at Melun of delegates from the rebel F.L.N. to discuss preliminaries for direct negotiations. It was the failure of these talks, made inevitable by the harsh inelasticity of the French approach, which ushered in a rapid decline in de Gaulle's prestige. He had always been above all the man who was to solve the Algerian problem. But by the summer of 1960 something seemed to have gone wrong. No doubt, as de Gaulle went on his series of wide presidential sweeps through the provinces, his audiences seemed almost as enthusiastic as ever. But criticism was growing.

In November de Gaulle reached the age of 70, and there were many who talked of him as a spent force. But, as Algeria became in the last weeks of 1960 once again the centre of the world's diplomatic activity, de Gaulle showed again his old physical and intellectual courage. By proposing an "Algerian Algeria", by submitting his policy to the arbitrament of a referendum, and by visiting Algeria in person he laid down a series of challenges to his enemies.

SWIFT TRIALS

At the end of March the rebels accepted an invitation to send a delegation to France to open negotiations. The date of the talks was twice postponed because of difficulties in settling the preliminaries, a bad and, it turned out, a reliable omen. And then, before the negotiations could open, came the attempted military *coup* in Algiers. This time de Gaulle neither hestitated nor delayed. The revolt broke out with brutal suddenness and, it appeared, without any hint of the plot reaching the Government, on April 22. The following day de Gaulle spoke to the nation. He was angry and inflexible. He spoke bitterly of the leaders, "*un quarteron de généraux en retraite*", forbade all cooperation with them, and called upon the nation to oppose the revolt by all means. He was followed a few hours later by the Premier, M. Debré, who appealed to the people of Paris to go out to the airfields to be ready to repel an expected landing by paratroops. There was an immediate response to the two broadcasts: in Paris and indeed throughout France there were impressive demonstrations of loyalty to de Gaulle; in Algiers the bulk of the conscripts and a few regular officers not only refused to join the revolt but were ready actively to oppose it; and as suddenly as it had flared up, it caved in.

ARMY BEATEN

De Gaulle appeared to have won a significant victory, for his Army, which, all along, had been the only effective obstacle to his plans for Algeria—the civilian *ultras*, always a small minority, had long ceased to be of any importance—had at last come out into the open to challenge him, and had been put resoundingly in its place with hardly a shot fired. He showed no clemency towards the insurgents, not even to their leader Challe, an honest if muddled patriot. Unlike the leaders of the earlier barricades revolt, who after an almost farcical trial had nearly all been acquitted, they were tried swiftly and given relatively heavy sentences. Regiments which had revolted, including part of the Foreign Legion and crack paratroop units, were disbanded and there was a far more thorough reshuffle of senior officers than had followed any previous challenge to his plans. But the real ringleaders of the *coup*, General Salan and five dangerous colonels, had escaped and de Gaulle's authority still ran so thinly in Algeria that efforts to track them down, or indeed to arrest the authors of a series of attacks by plastic bombs, which swelled up in France as well as Algeria during the spring and summer of 1961, were entirely half-hearted. The O.A.S. was able to establish itself in Algeria. Afraid, possibly, of widening the split in the Army and, as ever, disdainful of "details", de Gaulle held back at a moment when unrelenting severity in dealing with all recalcitrant servants of the state might have changed events in France.

On the political front de Gaulle took advantage of the abortive *coup* to invoke Article 16 of the Constitution, which gave the President comprehensive powers to take "measures required by the circumstances" when any threat existed to the institutions of the Republic, the independence of the nation, or the integrity of its territory. These powers he retained long after the "threat" had disappeared.

Early in September, 1961, as the police continued to round up right-wing activists, there came a first attempt on his life. A charge of explosives in the road as he drove to his home failed to go off. He shrugged it off as "*une mauvaise plaisanterie*", and within a fortnight announced his decision to relinquish the special powers he had held since April. Nevertheless his advisers constantly pressed upon him the need for greater security. In November bombs were set off in Strasbourg just before he arrived there. In February, 1962, as he recorded a television broadcast on Algerian negotiations "in full sail", the other side of the Élysée was barred to the public. The police discovered plots to assassinate him on provincial tours in May and June, and in August, as he drove by a secret route to a military airport near Paris to fly to Colombey-les-Deux-Eglises, his car was shot at. The thwarted right wing who considered he had betrayed them seemed to have good intelligence.

After the suppression of the Generals' revolt negotiations with the F.L.N. were reopened on May 20 at Evian. But they dragged on for many months and it was not until March 18, 1962, that the Evian agreement was finally signed.

TERRORIST BLIGHT

Even then terrorism by O.A.S. extremists and internal quarrels among the Algerian leaders blighted the new state's birth.

From 1962 onwards de Gaulle, rid of the Algerian incubus, intended to devote his main effort to foreign policy. But first he had to make his home base secure and, characteristically, he decided to attack the opposition rather than await attack. In 1962 he accepted M. Debré's resignation and M. Pompidou formed a Government in which M.R.P. Ministers joined the U.N.R. De Gaulle's statement at a press conference that the idea of a supranational Europe was nonsense—he called it Volapuck—caused the M.R.P. to resign. Against the spirit, if not the letter of the Constitution, a referendum was held on the Government's proposal to elect a future President of the Republic by universal suffrage, instead of by the usual electoral college. The Government was defeated in the Assembly and resigned. The result of the referendum was not a very conclusive majority for the proposals. But at the end of the year a general election gave the U.N.R. and its allies an overall majority in the Assembly—the first time any single party had won this in the Third or Fourth Republics.

In the presidential election held at the end of 1965 de Gaulle was opposed by four candidates and did not get more than half the votes cast in the first round. He was elected with 54 per cent of votes cast against M. Mitterrand in the second poll, a sufficiently impressive result after eight years rule with the political classes largely against him. He was able to ignore the divided opposition until the next test of Gaullism, the general election of 1967.

NASSAU RESENTED

In the Common Market Gaullist policy showed a firm and intransigent defence of French interests, disputes with France's partners both in 1964 and 1965 nearly leading to a breakdown, but not quite. The disputes were resolved, on the whole, in France's favour. De Gaulle largely had his way over the agricultural sector and succeeded in checking the growing power of the Community's secretariat. Along with the economic aims de Gaulle was intent that the Community should not evolve into a supranational force and that the powers of national governments should be maintained.

De Gaulle remained tough towards Britain as the negotiations for its joining the E.E.C. unfolded from October, 1961, onwards. His special concern for French agriculture, which continued to produce its seasonal unrest, had as much to do with it as his feeling that Britain, having stood apart from framing the Treaty of Rome, should accept it without conditions.

Private talks with Macmillan at Birch Grove in November and at the Château de Champs in June, 1962, gave optimists some grounds for thinking that differences of temperament, timing and national interest might by some means be resolved.

In yet another meeting between the two at Ramouillet just before Christmas there was talk of "difficulties" over Britain's membership of the Common Market, but there were also assurances that negotiations would be continued in a cooperative spirit.

All these hopes and plans, however, were blown sky high at the presidential press conference of January 14, 1963, when de Gaulle courteously but firmly put Britain in her place—outside Europe. One day, he conceded, a transformed Britain might be able to make a new and successful application, but now (and here he was clearly irked by the recent agreement on Polaris missiles for Britain reached between President Kennedy and Macmillan at Nassau) Britain's entry would be the thin end of the wedge transforming the six into "a colossal Atlantic community under American dependence and direction".

There was an instant storm of indignation. France's partners in the Six were angry and unhappy. Those in Britain who did not object to the matter of de Gaulle's remarks were furious at their effect. America gnashed its teeth. The author of all the trouble remained predictably unmoved and impenitent.

After Algeria, the French army was reorganized with the newly created *force de frappe* as its nucleus. De Gaulle suspected that the Anglo-American détente with the Soviet Union pursued in 1964 would work to the detriment of France and an independent Europe. He refused to sign the Moscow Test Ban Treaty in 1963. French nuclear weapons had been tested in the Sahara in 1961 and subsequently, and in 1966 there were international protests against tests in the Pacific. In 1966 de Gaulle withdrew French forces from Nato; and Nato headquarters and American bases left France. De Gaulle made it clear that France intended to stay in the Atlantic Alliance.

EMPIRICAL POLICY

In foreign policy proper, he seemed to be pursuing contradictory objectives and his policy was described by domestic opponents and foreign critics as empirical nationalism. The Franco-German Treaty, a result in part of de Gaulle's close friendship with Dr. Adenauer, was signed in 1963 after de Gaulle's visit to west Germany, in which he used his charm and prestige with great effect and evoked a great response from the people. The Treaty has resulted in regular Franco-German consultations and has crowned the long process of reconciliation begun after the war. On the other hand the Federal Republic has refused to sever its ties with the United States and has not supported France's efforts to form "an imposing confederation of European States" with a policy of independence of the United States.

The Federal Republic did not approve of de Gaulle's recognition of Red China in January 1964, the most important of many acts designed to increase French influence throughout the world. His visits to central and south America, the longest and most fatiguing carried out in 1964 after a prostate operation, were parts of the same determination. Much of the sympathy aroused for France in Asia and Africa was due to de Gaulle's attitude to the war in Vietnam and his advocacy of neutralization for Indo-China and the withdrawal of all foreign troops.

His Grand Design for Europe was based on a view that the Soviet Union and its satellites no longer menaced the security of west Europe and that they were becoming inevitably more liberal and akin to the rest of the continent. The policy was summed up in the sybilline phrase "peace from the Atlantic to the Urals". The rapprochement with the Soviet Union and other communist countries was marked in 1965 in economic relations. France was opposed to west Germany being given nuclear arms and Germany was to play no part in the French *force de frappe*. In June 1966, de Gaulle paid a 12-day visit to the Soviet Union. The Soviet Government took the unprecedented step of allowing a foreign visitor to make prolonged personal contacts with the crowds in the many cities visited. In political talks in the Kremlin, de Gaulle refused to recognize the Pankow Goverment and told his hosts that the United

States should not be excluded from any agreement about the future of Germany. He pointed out that he opposed an American hegemony but equally would not work for a Russian one. The Russian leaders accepted this and openly considered the conversations a success. Franco-Russian consultations on world affairs were to take place at regular intervals, important scientific and technological agreements were signed, and a special telephone link was installed between the Élysée and the Kremlin.

At the General Election in March, 1967, the Gaullist majority in the Assembly dwindled to two or three seats with the Gaullists depending, to the extent of 44 seats, on the Republican Independents. Some Gaullists considered that this result showed a decline in the General's popularity and others that the loss of seats was due to an unpopular social policy. Perhaps both of these factors existed. On the other hand, the actual percentage of votes won by the Gaullists, the U.N.R., at the 1967 election was slightly more than in the election of 1962.

ALLIANCE LOST SEATS

The loss of seats was the effect of the honouring of the electoral alliance between the Communist Party and the Federation of the Left which grouped Socialists and Radicals and which was led by M. Mitterrand.

Yet the situation was less critical for the Gaullist régime than it appeared. Strong differences existed inside the Left-Wing alliance, and also between the Federation and the anti-Communist, anti-Gaullist groups of the centre. Although the political climate had become more lively as a result of the Presidential and then of the General Election, although there was a great deal more talk of "After Gaullism" and of the Sixth Republic, an alternative government of parties or groups accepting a common programme did not exist in 1967 and seemed far away.

De Gaulle and M. Pompidou intended to govern with this in mind. There was a blunt refusal to a request from the Republican Independence that the Assembly should debate France's attitude towards Britain joining the Common Market.

QUEBEC FURORE

When the Middle East crisis began in May, 1967, de Gaulle attempted, in vain, to call a four-power conference and then proclaimed France's non-involvement in the crisis. When the six-day war began in June, de Gaulle said that Israel was the aggressor and, in July, at the United Nations, France voted with the Communist powers for a Yugoslav resolution demanding the unconditional withdrawal of Israeli troops. French public opinion was opposed to this policy and, what was even more important, prominent Gaullists had taken part in pro-Israel demonstrations and a number of leading Gaullist deputies had gone with an all-party delegation to Tel Aviv.

The General's reasons, apart from the weight he placed on the *rapprochement* with the Arab world for which he had worked since 1962, appeared to have been his fear that, if the Soviet Union was over-ridden by Anglo-American and European support for Israel, the likelihood of a third world war was brought very much nearer. But these reasons had no wide acceptance in France and, for the first time since 1958, the unity of the Gaullist party was seriously disturbed, even though the Cabinet continued to support the President without open dissent.

Then in August came the visit to Expo '67 in Canada and the General's backing of the extremists among French Canadians. The effect on European opinion was to make many experienced commentators believe that the General had lost his sense of proportion altogether and the more charitable view was to believe, in spite of the official French statement after the General's return to France, that the ageing statesman had been carried away by enthusiasm for "Frenchness". Again, the French Cabinet backed the General unanimously and indeed not to have done this would have caused an immediate and serious crisis. But it was noted that the Gaullist leaders came tardily to express public views in defence of the Quebec episode.

Later in the month, M. Valéry Giscard d'Estaing, leader of the Republican independents, agreed with Mitterrand in criticism of the General's policy in the Middle East and in Quebec. He suggested that the President of the Republic should in future consult his Cabinet before making major executive acts in Foreign Policy. He was not desirous of sapping the authority of the President, a key part of the Fifth Republic but he, and others, drew a distinction between the exercise of legitimate power by the President and "solitary" power.

WARSAW VISIT

In September, 1967, the General paid his visit to Warsaw, postponed on account of the Middle East crisis. At the political talks held in the Polish capital, the General discussed the prospects of German reunification. France accepted the Oder-Neisse Line as the permanent German-Polish frontier and also the ban on the possession of nuclear arms by Germany. He attempted to persuade the Polish Government to accept the idea that reunification should come about when the peoples of the two Germanies could agree on how to bring it about. He wanted Poland to be prepared to take a step away from Big Brother in the East, without renouncing the Russian Alliance. The Poles on their part stressed that no real détente with Bonn was possible without a general recognition of the east German Republic as a sovereign state.

If the visit did not appear to alter the European situation, it was nonetheless a triumph for the General's diplomacy and prestige. Throughout his journey in Poland he was warmly welcomed by hundreds of thousands of people and the Polish Government appeared to welcome the public exposition of French policy for the settlement of Europe. A Franco-Polish pact was agreed upon.

In September, 1967, the E.E.C. Commission had reported in favour of enlarging the community and opening negotiations with Britain. All France's partners accepted this. At a press conference in November de Gaulle dwelt on Britain's past "rooted hostility to the building of Europe" and said that now the British were using "every imaginable promise and pressure to get in". To consent, he said, would be to break up the community. Though he conceded the possibility of some "arrangement" to help British trade with the Six, France blocked the Benelux plan and proposals put forward by the Federal Republic, both of which aimed at ensuring cooperation with Britain and her eventual entry. De Gaulle had saved the customs union with its special advantages for French agriculture; but any hope of building a political Europe and a technological pool was brought to nothing.

STUDENT VIOLENCE

What appeared to be his resentment of the Anglo-Saxon powers embittered disputes in early 1968 over the international monetary system. Many who thought the French were right in asking for revision of the dollar's relation to gold were put off by the President's animus against the United States.

The student demonstrations had been growing increasingly violent and widespread in France since their beginnings at Nanterre, an annexe of the Sorbonne, in February and March. Many workers, particularly the young well-paid workers in France's most modern factories, responded to this call for "Revolution", no matter of what kind, raised by the students. The trade union leaders had been obliged, unwillingly, by pressure from below, to declare a general strike. Many factories were already occupied by the workers. De Gaulle on May 13 flew to Rumania on a state visit. He returned a little before the time arranged but, though France was on the verge of economic paralysis, he did not speak to the nation until May 24.

His proposal then for a referendum on a law providing for participation of workers in the management of industries, coupled with a threat to resign if the result was against the proposal, fell flat. Agreements, worked out at top speed between M. Pompidou and the trade-union leaders, which provided for a general wage increase, were rejected in many factories. Though treated with scant respect by the students and workers, the political Opposition leaders made an inglorious attempt to occupy the centre of the scene; they failed to reach agreement on forming a hypothetical Provisional government. But the absence of successful action against the workers and students made people think that de Gaulle might go. "I was tempted to retire", he said in a 55-minute TV broadcast made when the crisis had passed.

CRISIS HEIGHTENED

In fact, he deliberately heightened the crisis by postponing a Cabinet meeting for the morning of May 29 for 24 hours. He left Paris for Colombey but before going to his manor-house visited various Army leaders, including General Massu, at Baden-Baden and in eastern France.

On May 30, he returned, dissolved Parliament, formed a new caretaker government under M. Pompidou, announced the holding of a general election with the minimum delay, and made it plain that public order would be enforced with rigour. That night, between 50 and 60 "revolutionaries" assembled at the Charléty sports stadium; nearly a million Parisians, including numbers of workers, paraded the streets in support of de Gaulle, and similar demonstrations took place in other cities. The "revolutionary situation" was over.

The successes of the insurrectionary movement had been won largely because of the sympathy of public opinion for the students' grievances, a sympathy increased by police brutality. From the moment the movement affected the factories and led to economic stagnation, that sympathy began to die away. De Gaulle's final act had been well timed. His popularity climbed to a new height.

Though he had long neglected the latent social crisis, though the government had shown itself complacent, the electoral victory won at the end of June was not gained through the fears of the bourgeoisie alone. In his TV interview on June 7, de Gaulle found the words which appealed to many Frenchmen. He pledged himself to work for a society which was neither Capitalist nor Communist; this was credible because such an aim had long been an aspect, if a somewhat neglected one, of Gaullism. He offered youth "an Ideal, an Elan and a Hope". Of course many young Frenchmen were unconvinced that he was the man to lead French society in a new direction. But where was the man to lead it in any direction at all? For a majority he had saved France again as he had done in 1940 and in 1958. M. Fauvet wrote in *Le Monde* the day after the TV interview: "At last General de Gaulle has had the intelligence to take the French seriously. He appeared last night not like the aged politician of May 24, nor like the Tragic Hero of May 30—but simply like a Man. What an actor."

The general election gave the Gaullists an overall majority with 358 seats in the Assembly out of 485. It was, as *Le Monde* pointed out, quite as much a reflex of irritation as fear that made Socialist and Communist bastions such as the mining districts of the North, the Paris suburbs, the Dordogne and parts of Languedoc vote Gaullist. They wished their future to be decided not on the barricades but by normal processes.

The new government was headed by M. Couve de Murville, with M. Debré at Foreign Affairs. A young technician, M. Ortoli, became Minister of Finance, the other key post, the Ministry of Education, being filled by M. Edgar Faure, not a Gaullist but a Minister in the last government. M. René Capitant, a left-wing Gaullist, popular with the students whose cause he had actively sympathized with, became Minister of Justice. Gratitude has no place in politics and M. Pompidou was dropped, though praised. He remained, perhaps, De Gaulle's choice as successor to the Presidency. His hour was to come.

De Gaulle had a remarkable ability to express himself in the written and spoken word. His War Memoirs may well survive among the works posterity will read for pleasure and intellectual stimulation, as well as for the light they throw on history. His book on the French Army, published in 1934, contains some memorable passages notably those in praise of Pétain in 1916. In *Le Fil de L'Epée*, an early work, de Gaulle gave a now much quoted analysis of the ideal leader of men, including an ability at a crucial moment to disobey orders—as Nelson at Trafalgar and de Gaulle himself in 1940. He was highly conscious of his responsibility and therefore of the effect of his acts and words: he once said to Duff Cooper: "I spend five minutes every morning thinking how what I am going to do today will appear in history."

His press conferences showed a gift for lucid exposition in *le style noble* but in which humour and irony strengthened his contact with his audience. In conversation, he frequently made remarks which showed that he was fully aware of what intelligent critics were thinking and that he did not only live in a world of great designs and vast projects. His wit was biting and sometimes malicious.

Malraux's impression of de Gaulle when they first met in 1944 was of someone who was courteous in the extreme, who asked many questions and who aired certain views himself but who was, at the same time, withdrawn.

NO ABANDON

There was an inner distance not only between the General and those he spoke with but between the General and his own words. "I had met this intense and withdrawn presence" Malraux writes in *Antimemoires* "which words did not express, not in soldiers or politicians or artists but in a few intensely religious minds whose affably banal words seemed without relation to their inner life." Malraux writes later that, to his collaborators and friends, the private de Gaulle was no different from the public one except that he did not talk of affairs of of State. He allowed himself no sudden impulses in conversation nor any abandon but he was always polite and often charming and never, as did Napoleon, terrified women. For everyone but his family, he was a "courteous reflection of his legendary personage".

In his private life de Gaulle had none of the mannerisms of the great man. His family and social life remained very much that of an austere, Catholic, upper middle-class military family. Few were admitted to the intimacy of the de Gaulle family at the Élysée and de Gaulle always shunned personal publicity as rigorously as he prepared his public appearances. He married in 1921 Yvonne Vendroux, the daughter of an industrialist in the Pas de Calais who, like her husband, was uninterested in money or property. She was fully content to live as the wife of a French officer. The de Gaulles bought a small manor house at Colombey-Les-Deux-Eglises shortly before the war and it was typical of them that, although de Gaulle had been Head of the Government from August, 1944, their house damaged by the war was still not repaired in January, 1946, when de Gaulle returned to private life. The de Gaulles have a son Philippe, born in 1923, and a daughter, Elizabeth, married to Colonel De Roissieu.

A younger daughter, Anne, died shortly after the war.

November 11, 1970.

Anatole de Grunwald, who played a leading part in the development of the British film during the past 25 years, died on January 13, 1967. As a screen writer and later as a producer, his name was associated with many of the best known films of this era, and his long association with Terence Rattigan resulted in pictures such as *While the Sun Shines*, *The Winslow Boy*, *The V.I.P.s*, and *The Yellow Rolls-Royce*. He was 56.

Anatole de Grunwald was a Russian by birth, having been born in Leningrad on Christmas Day, 1910. He was educated in Paris, and later at Caius College, Cambridge, where he took a degree in modern languages. He entered the film industry shortly before the outbreak of the war, when he worked with Terence Rattigan on the film adaptation of Rattigan's first play, *French Without Tears*. This was successfully translated into a film with a cast that included Ray Milland, Ellen Drew, and Roland Culver. Throughout the war years de Grunwald was kept busy as a screen writer, working either on his own or in collaboration. His films during these years included *Freedom Radio*, *Major Barbara*, *Quiet Wedding*, *Pimpernel Smith*, *Jeannie*, and the highly successful *First of the Few*, a story of the Battle of Britain pilots with a cast that included Leslie Howard and David Niven. He also wrote the scripts for *Cottage to Let*, *Tomorrow We Live*, and *English Without Tears*.

In 1943 he became a producer and writer for Two Cities Films and as such was at once responsible for one of the best, and perhaps the best, British war films, *The Way to the Stars*, which Anthony Asquith directed and which had a strong Anglo-American cast that included Michael Redgrave, John Mills, Trevor Howard and Douglas Montgomery. It was a film which won a number of awards and was reissued a year later. In 1946 he formed International Screenplays with Terence Rattigan, to write and produce *While the Sun Shines* and *Beau Brummel*.

He then produced *Bond Street*, *The Winslow Boy*, *Queen of Spades*, and *Flesh and Blood*.

His output continued unabated during the 1950s. In 1952 he became an executive producer and made *Home at Seven* and *The Holly and the Ivy;* and in 1953 he wrote and produced *Innocents in Paris*. He was appointed a producer to M. G. M. in the autumn of 1959; for them he made at their Boreham Wood studios *The V.I.P.s*, with Elizabeth Taylor and Richard Burton, and *The Yellow Rolls-Royce* with Shirley Maclaine and Ingrid Bergman. Thus his name is linked with many outstanding British films, but *The Way to the Stars* was undoubtedly his crowning achievement, and the picture by which he would wish to have been remembered.

January 14, 1967.

Sir Howard d'Egville, K. B. E., former Secretary-General of the Commonwealth Parliamentary Association, died at Hove on January 9, 1965.

After leaving St. Catherine's College, Cambridge, where he read law, he was called to the Bar by the Middle Temple, and practised for several years on the Midland circuit. In 1911 representatives of the Parliaments of the British Empire were invited to attend the Coronation of King George V, and on the suggestion of Leo Amery it was decided to set up a permanent organization of members of these Parliaments, under the name of the Empire Parliamentary Association. Branches were formed in the United Kingdom, Canada, Australia, New Zealand, and (in 1913) South Africa and Newfoundland. Howard d'Egville was appointed secretary of the United Kingdom branch, to whose hands was entrusted the organization of the new association.

The outbreak of the First World War hindered, though it did not stop, its development, and during the war d'Egville served on the Secretariat of the Imperial War Cabinet. In 1918 he was awarded a C.B.E. for his services. He then devoted himself completely to the work of the Empire Parliamentary Association, and by 1920 had it organized on the lines on which it was to develop. The next year he had the honour of K.B.E. conferred upon him.

The activities of the association were, and still are, the holding of conferences, of which he organized a number during the years between the two world wars, in the United Kingdom, Canada, Australia, South Africa and elsewhere; the publication of two quarterlies, the *Journal of the Parliaments of the Commonwealth* and the *Report on Foreign Affairs*, started in 1920 and still continuing, which he edited; and the mutual exchange of visits and hospitality between members of the association, which he strenuously promoted. In 1937, just before the Coronation of King George VI, he conceived the idea of reviving the Coronation Feast in Westminster Hall—discontinued since the time of King George IV—by organizing a luncheon given for his Majesty in that historic building. A similar luncheon was given for Queen Elizabeth II a few days before her Coronation in 1953 attended by all the Commonwealth Prime Ministers and over 700 members of Commonwealth Parliaments.

SERVICES IN WASHINGTON

In the 1920s the membership of the association, on his initiative, was widened to include the legislatures of countries only partially independent, particularly India, and also the state Parliaments of Australia and the Parliaments of the Canadian provinces. During the Second World War Sir Howard went to Washington, where he was able to perform certain valuable political services. He restarted conferences after the war, and at that held in London in 1948 it was decided to change both the title and the organization of the association. So the following year it became the Commonwealth Parliamentary Association, with, as its governing body, a general council representative of all its branches in the Commonwealth. Sir Howard was appointed Secretary-General, a post which he held till his retirement in 1960, by which time the association had branches in no fewer than 70 Commonwealth legislatures. He organized regular biennial conferences of the C.P.A.—as it is best known—at Wellington, Ottawa, Nairobi, New Delhi, and Canberra, with council meetings in various parts of the Commonwealth in the intervening years.

In his earlier years Sir Howard wrote several books and articles mainly on Commonwealth topics. His office, just off Westminster Hall, and subsequently in another part of the Houses of Parliament, became a centre for visiting members of Commonwealth legislatures and a fount of information for members of the association on Commonwealth and parliamentary matters. He devoted himself with single-minded energy and zeal to the work of the association, and in later years was often designated "the father of the C.P.A."—an appellation richly deserved.

He was also secretary of the British-American Parliamentary Group, founded just after the last war for the purpose of promoting friendly relations between the members of the United Kingdom Parliament and the Congress of the United States. He remained in this post to the time of his death.

January 11, 1965.

Sir Geoffrey de Havilland, O. M., C.B.E., A.F.C., the distinguished aircraft engineer and designer and founder of the de Havilland Aircraft Company, died on May 21, 1965, at the age of 82.

From the de Havilland "stable" over the years emerged a string of fine aero engines and aircraft, many of them, like the Moth, Comet, Rapide and Mosquito, to become household names. Though the brilliance of the D. H. aircraft shone in both world wars—the wooden Mosquito was perhaps the most versatile war plane ever built—it is probable that Geoffrey de Havilland will be best remembered as the designer of the Moth light aeroplane, the two-seater in which thousands of civilians learnt to fly from the mid 1920s onwards and which was developed as a trainer for the R.A.F. into the Tiger Moth to serve thousands more Service pupils. The Moth was sold in many countries and, with the military trainer that followed, came to be regarded affectionately by the large numbers who took their instruction and passed their flying tests in it. For this aeroplane he had found a promising young engine designer, Major Frank Halford, and de Havilland at last was able to realize his original dream of making both airframe and engine.

Nearly all the Moths that were sold were Gipsy Moths, a special satisfaction to de Havilland, who was trained as an engineer and himself designed the engine for his first aeroplane in 1909. More than 40 years later when the first Comet jet liner flew, de Havilland was still technical director of his company, although design had long since passed into the hands of a team, and its Ghost engines too were designed and made by his company.

Born in 1882 the son of a clergyman he was educated at St. Edward's, Oxford. He was 26 when, in 1908 he abandoned good prospects as a motor engineer to devote himself, with the help of £1,000 from his grandfather, to designing aircraft. First he set himself to design the 50 h.p. engine he needed and had it made at a Willesden motor works. Then Frank Hearle, a friend, joined him in the making of an aircraft to be driven by two airscrews. Helped by one carpenter in a workshop in West London, they produced their first model and in 1909 got it briefly into the air, only to smash it. They set at once about building a stronger airframe and using only a single airscrew. In that biplane with the original engine, de Havilland taught himself to fly in 1910. It was subsequently bought by the Government for £400; de Havilland and Hearle were given posts at the Army Balloon factory at Farnborough and by 1912 de Havilland was flying with great success a tractor biplane he had also designed, the first of the B.E. (British Experimental) series. Within two years he was designing aircraft which were to bear the distinctive D.H. designation.

PLANES FOR WAR

He had left Government employment early in 1914 to become both chief designer and test pilot of the Aircraft Manufacturing Company at Hendon and quickly turned out the D.H.1 two-seat biplane fighter or scout. When the war came he was commissioned in the R.F.C. but he was soon sent back to his designing and test flying, and so built the D.H.2 single-seat fighter and later the D.H.4 general purpose biplane. Until 1918 he went on producing aircraft and had some of them adopted for production in the United States. In that work he became acquainted with men who were to remain his associates in industry for the rest of his days. C. C. Walker, W. E. Nixon, F. E. N. St. Barbe and his older friend Frank Hearle were to join with him in 1920, when the "Airco" factory closed, in forming the de Havilland Aircraft Company. Its working capital was £1,875.

It took up modest quarters at Stag Lane, Hendon, and it had a thin time until the Moth proved to be just what the flying world was waiting for. Various civil aircraft followed and with them new engines of the lower ratings; and then the company undertook in 1934 to produce a racing aeroplane for the England to Australia race. It was called the Comet. It won the race. It had applied wooden construction in new ways and when the Second World War began in 1939, it was the inspiration of a type of unarmed fast bomber, the Mosquito, which de Havilland himself "sold" after much persuasion and demonstration to the Air Staff. Before the war ended the Mosquito was serving, with undoubted success, a variety of purposes.

The small business of 1920 had now grown into a huge organization making aircraft, engines and airscrews. Geoffrey de Havilland had never bothered to become its managing director or chairman. His interests were technical. He had neither the taste nor the training for business management. After leaving school he had gone to the Crystal Palace Engineering School, and while there had designed and built a motor cycle engine that worked. He was afterwards a pupil of a steam-engine and turbine company at Rugby and later served in the drawing office of the Wolseley company at Birmingham. He had spent two promising years with the Motor Omnibus Company (later to become the London General Omnibus Company) when aeroplanes and flying claimed him. To his new love he brought a curious mixture of cautious ingenuity and intense capacity for getting quickly on with an enterprise.

He brought a typically English middle-class belief in putting all the available money and effort into the product and devoting little to appearances and the outward signs of success and prosperity. He was given to that kind of shy enthusiasm which is best rewarded by fresh opportunity and shrinks from presenting its triumphs with a flourish. He never indulged in gestures or allowed himself to pontificate. He did, by the quality of his mind and experience, dominate his business but his eminence was that of a friendly and undemonstrative personality among friends of long standing.

GETTING ACTION

When projects involving large capital investments had to be agreed in later years, the decisions and the plan of campaign were reached by the little group of friends in one of those frank, practical and unostentatious discussions such as had set the company moving in 1920. Few companies have advanced so far and accomplished such radical developments with so few changes in the directing personalities, or in the essential methods of determining policy.

By the wisdom of his original choice of associates and by his skill in encouraging his team to express new ideas in terms of good engineering and good business, Geoffrey de Havilland found himself, in post-war years, doubly famous. From the Moth after one war, he progressed to the Comet jet liner after another. He would not have pretended that he designed this second Comet, but it was conceived under his inspiration, its characteristics were settled at conferences of those old hands, the way to finance its development and to arrange its selling was their responsibility and on them, when the early Comets suffered mysterious accidents, lay the task of seeking the solution of the trouble their pioneering in jet transport had thrown up.

De Havilland felt himself personally concerned in the loss of life in those accidents and he spared no effort to arrive at the cause.

LOST SONS FLYING

Before they happened, he had made his own sacrifice in the cause of fast flying. His oldest son, as chief test pilot, had been killed in flying an experimental fighter near the speed of sound at a time (1946) when virtually nothing was known of the peculiar conditions of transsonic flying. He had earlier lost his youngest son in a collision in the air. Well past 70, he continued with work which by now had been acknowledged at home and abroad. In 1961 his company became part of the Hawker Siddeley amalgamation but he remained associated with its activities. He was knighted in 1944 and was later appointed a Royal Designer for Industry, in 1962 he was created O.M. In the United States he was elected an honorary fellow of the Institute of Aeronautical Sciences.

He married in 1907 Louie, daughter of Richard Thomas, of Chepstow, and there were three sons of that marriage. She died in 1949. In August, 1951, he married Mrs. Joan Mary Mordaunt.

May 22, 1965.

Mazo de la Roche, the novelist, creator of the Whiteoak family, than which few institutions in twentieth-century life were more solid and more permanent, died on July 12, 1961, in Canada.

The daughter of William Richmond de la Roche, she was born in 1885 and passed her childhood on her father's fruit and stock farm in Ontario, which setting she was later to turn to good account. On her father's death she, her mother, and her cousin and lifelong friend Caroline went to Toronto which Mazo, a country child by birth, upbringing, and inclination found detestable. She lived for the summers spent in a lakeside cottage and bore the winters by taking courses in English at Toronto University. On her mother's death the summer place had to go: her cousin worked in the Civil Service. Mazo, crouched over an old drawing-board, wrote. Like minds, living frugally, they kept their heads above water. Two novels and a volume of short stories were published but they brought their author little money and not much esteem though *The Times* liked both *Possession* and *Delight*.

The appearance in 1927 of *Jalna*, the first of the many Whiteoak Chronicles (unkind critics later called the series a marathon) on which she had been working off and on for several years, brought her acclaim and won the *Atlantic Monthly's* $10.000 prize. For the rest of her life she ravelled and unravelled the history of the Whiteoaks for the benefit of an eager public, *Finch's Fortune*; *The Master of Jalna*; *Wakefield's Cause*; *Young Renny*; *Whiteoak Heritage*; in all approaching a score, bore witness to the author's strong sense of family and family idiosyncrasy.

FAMOUS MATRIARCHS

Generation succeeded generation, the handsome, virile men living and marrying and going to the wars, the tart, matronly women, the children, and the animals, but Miss de la Roche's zest and invention showed no signs of flagging. To some readers she seemed to lack both style and true feeling (a Canadian critic, for one, thought her Jalna books were a triumph of journalistic rather than of literary art), but this was a lack which, if results are used as a yard-stick, did not affect a large section of the novel-reading public. By 1949 it was estimated that 2,000,000 copies of her novels, which had been translated into 15 languages, had been sold.

The Whiteoaks of Jalna survived translation to the stage, the radio, and television. No less an actress than Miss Ethel Barrymore appeared in *Whiteoaks* as the centenarian matriarch Adeline when the play was put on in the United States; and at the Little Theatre in London in 1936 the same play ran for over 800 performances, Miss Nancy Price giving a shrewd and vigorous performance in the same part.

For some years Miss de la Roche lived in England. In 1938 she was awarded the Lorne Pierce Medal for distinguished contributions to Canadian Literature, and in 1951 she was given the University of Alberta National Award in Letters.

July 13, 1961.

General Humberto Delgado, whose murdered body was discovered in Spain, south of Badajoz, on April 24, 1965, for some years led the opposition to Portugal's Prime Minister, Dr. Salazar, and in 1958 was a candidate for the country's presidency. He had lived in exile, first in Brazil and then in Algiers, since 1959.

Humberto Delgado was born in Torres Novas, some 75 miles north of Lisbon on May 15, 1906. His father was an army officer and a republican, his mother a devout Catholic. He was the only boy in a family of five children.

He studied in the military college, took an artillery course, and went on to take aeronautical observers' courses in the army school. In 1929 he began service in the Air Force, flying the one and only Breguet B.U. it possessed. In this plane he established the record for long-distance flying over Portuguese territory. From 1938 to 1939, he was a member of the overseas military mission, and in 1940 was promoted to the rank of major. In 1943 Delgado was appointed to represent Portugal at the negotiations for the concession to Britain of air bases in the Azores.

He became professor in the Army school and the staff college, and in 1944 was made Director of Civil Aviation, a post which he held until 1946.

STORMY CAMPAIGN

In that year he received the O.B.E. from the British Government, in recognition of his services during the negotiations over the Azores bases.

From 1952 to 1957 he was military and air attaché to the embassy in Washington, and head of the military mission. In 1958 he ran for the presidency of the republic, losing to the present President, Admiral Americo Tomas. It was a stormy campaign, and the first time that a free candidate representing the opposition to Dr. Salazar had actually gone to the polls.

The "American-style" campaign, in which the candidate rode through the streets in an open car, acclaimed by his supporters, was marked by public demonstrations, police charges, and shootings. When it ended General Delgado wrote to the outgoing president of the republic, Marshal Craveiro Lopes, complaining that the results (officially it was declared that Admiral Tomas gained 75.6 per cent of the votes) were faked and that he had not been allowed freedom to campaign.

DEPRIVED OF RANK

After the 1958 presidential elections the Portuguese constitution was altered: future presidents will be chosen by an electoral college and not by the vote of the people.

A little more than six months after the elections, Delgado took political asylum in the Brazilian embassy in Lisbon, claiming that he was in danger of arrest by the political police. He left for Brazil on a safe conduct that had been negotiated with the Portuguese Government by a personal representative of President Kubitschek. Once in Brazil, he began to rally round him opposition elements, to continue his fight against the Portuguese regime.

Later, he was joined by the stormy petrel of Portuguese politics, former army captain Henrique Galvão, who had escaped from hospital supervision while serving a long sentence for plotting against the state. Galvão had taken refuge in the Argentine embassy and crossed the Atlantic on a safe conduct.

Meanwhile, the Portuguese Government deprived Delgado of his army rank. Later, the Brazilian Government banned his political activities, and he left to live and make his movement's headquarters in Algiers.

Delgado claimed to be the master mind behind the capture of the Portuguese liner Santamaria in 1961. He claimed to have reentered Portugal in disguise, with a bean in his shoe to make him limp, and to have entered Britain in 1964 disguised as an Arab. He also claimed to be the man behind the attack on Beja barracks in 1961, which was to start a nation-wide revolution led by him.

For a while affairs seemed to be going well in Algiers: Delgado was luxuriously housed and surrounded by political friends. His contacts were friendly with Arab states, and he made frequent trips to such countries as Czechoslovakia.

In November 1964 a split occurred between Delgado and the other leaders of the Patriotic National Liberation Front in Algiers. Resentment of his authoritarian manner was stated to be the cause. He continued to live there, however, until early this year when he left, according to information from his followers, for a trip to Spain. His object was to contact Portuguese and Spanish opponents to the prevailing Iberian regime. In March there were reports that he was being held in Spain and late in March, 1965 three bodies were found in shallow graves near Badajoz.

May 10, 1965.

Teresa del Riego, composer of "O Dry Those Tears" and many other popular songs, died on January 23, 1968, at the age of 91. Daughter of Miguel and Clara del Riego, she was a British subject by birth and was educated at the Convent of the Sacred Heart, Highgate, and at the West Central College of Music. She developed an aptitude for musical composition at an early age, her first song being written at the age of 12. Thereafter her song production was regular and outstanding.

Among some 300 of her songs published (and sung by many famous artists, including Melba, Gervase Elwes, John Coates, Clara Butt, Eva Turner, Maggie Teyte) were: "Slave Song", "Thank God for a Garden", "Happy Song", "La Vie est Vaine", "Les Larmes", "Sing, Red Sun" and "The Reason". "O Dry Those Tears" was sung all over the world, and translated into several languages. It gave pleasure and consolation to millions. Within six weeks of publication 23,000 copies were sold. "Homing" was almost its equal in the First World War.

Many of her well-known songs have been frequently broadcast and have proved equally popular in America, Canada, New Zealand and Australia. Her orchestral works include "Lead Kindly Light", "The Unknown Warrior", "In the Wilderness", "A Southern Night", Air in "F" for violoncello and piano, and "The King's Song", which was performed at the Albert Hall Coronation concert during the week of King Edward VII's coronation and many times afterwards. For some years "The Unknown Warrior", composed from the poem written by Captain Henderson Bland, was a feature of Armistice Day celebrations.

Mme. del Riego won the gold medal in the open competition organized by the "Empire Festival" for the best song with words and music by one writer, and it was sung at the Albert Hall. She had the medal of the Society of Arts for piano, and was a member of the Incorporated Society of Musicians, and the Society of Women Musicians. She organized and took part in many concerts for wounded soldiers and for war charities during 1914–1918. In 1917 her husband, F. Graham Leadbitter, lost his life in France.

January 25, 1968.

Diane Cleopatre de Merode, one of the celebrated beauties of the "Belle Epoque," died on October 17, 1966, in Paris at the age of 91.

With her, the last of the celebrated "idols" of the 1900s, which included Liane de Pougy, Emilienne D'Alençon and "La Belle Otero", has passed into legend. She had been the toast of Parisian society, the friend of kings and American multi-millionaires in the heady atmosphere of the last years of the nineteenth century and of the beginning of the present, now nostalgically regarded by a fast disappearing generation of Frenchmen as a kind of golden age.

Cleo de Merode, as she was better known, was born in Paris on September 27, 1875, of Belgian parentage. She made her debut at the age of seven at the opera as a "rat" of the Corps de Ballet. Her outstanding beauty soon attracted attention, and as she recalled many years later in a book of memoirs, *The Ballet of my Life*, in 1896 she was chosen beauty queen in what must have been the first of now common contests, ahead of such formidable competition as Melba, Cecile Sorel, Sarah Bernhardt, Réjane, and La Vallière, whose portraits were shown in the hall of the newspaper *L'Eclair*, which organized it.

From then on she danced her way across Europe and the United States, in a trail of glory and conquests. King Leopold II of Belgium was intrigued by the illustrious name she bore—she was related to the Austrian Merodes—and was bewitched by her performance in *Aida*. The alleged relationship between the King and the celebrated beauty caused much comment at the time. She toured the United States, at the invitation of William Randolph Hearst, who persuaded her in 1899 to resign from the Paris Opera. Afterwards she danced in Vienna, Brussels, in London at the Alhambra before King Edward VII, and in Moscow. In 1924 she returned to Paris and danced at the Empire with the dancer Rupert Doone. Her last appearance on the stage was at the Alcazar in 1924.

Until her death Cleo de Merode retained the aura of an elegance and distinction of a bygone era. She lived the last 50 years of her life in the same flat surrounded by innumerable souvenirs of her triumphs both on and off stage, entertaining a devoted circle of friends. Sometimes she would be seen walking in the Parc Monceau near by, always elaborately made up and her hair done in the style of the 1900s, with brightly-coloured sunshades which signalled her from afar. In 1950 she sued the French Radio for a broadcast in which she was ranked with the celebrated demi-mondaines of her time.

October 18,1966.

General Sir Miles Dempsey, G.B.E., K.C.B., D.S.O., M.C., who died on June 5, 1969, at the age of 72 commanded 13th Corps in the invasion of Sicily and Italy and the 2nd Army in the invasion of Europe. He was in all respects an outstanding commander.

Although he commanded an Army in the field with unbroken success for nearly a year in the Second World War, he was comparatively unknown to the public. This was doubtless due to the fact that it never fell to him to hold an independent operational command. But he was also a man who never sought the limelight.

Dempsey was tall, slim and wiry, always perfectly turned out, and looked younger than his years. He was a notably friendly man, with immense charm. He had no airs, but there was no mistaking his mastery of his profession and his authority. He was prompt and resolute in taking decisions, and had the gift of inspiring confidence in others.

Miles Christopher Dempsey was born on December 15, 1896, the son of Arthur Francis Dempsey. At Shrewsbury he captained the 1st cricket eleven for three years. After a shortened course at Sandhurst, he was commissioned in The Royal Berkshire Regiment. In the First World War he served from 1916 till 1918 on the Western Front, where he commanded a company when only 19 years, was mentioned in dispatches and awarded the Military Cross. He was gassed in 1918, but, after a few months in hospital, served in the Iraq campaign of 1919–1920.

From his earliest days in the Army he was a keen student of military history, and one of his favourite occupations between the wars was to visit the Continent to study battlefields. He made a collection of carefully indexed and annotated maps, many drawn by himself, and it used to be said of him that he could make a whole landscape come alive from the map without ever having seen it. Music was a great pleasure to him, too: he played the piano and had a pleasant baritone voice. He had a phenomenal memory which he had improved by exercises on Pelman lines.

In 1939 he had been Commanding Officer of the 1st Berkshires for 18 months, and he landed with them in France in September. Later he took over command of the 13th Infantry Brigade, which played an outstanding part in the British counter-attack at Arras in May, 1940, and the critical three-day battle on the Ypres-Comines Canal, which gained valuable time for the withdrawal from Dunkirk.

He was awarded the D.S.O.

In England he played an active part in forming and training the new armies, first as Chief of Staff of the Canadian Corps, then as Commander, first of the 46th Division, and then of the new 42nd Armoured Division.

In December, 1942, six weeks after the Battle of Alamein, he was appointed Commander of the 13th Army Corps of the 8th Army. The 13th Corps was out of the line when he arrived, and Dempsey was employed in Cairo for the next seven months on the detailed planning for the invasion of Sicily.

Dempsey's was one of the two British Corps which Montgomery commanded in Sicily. It landed with little opposition near Syracuse on July 10, 1943, but its advance up the eastern coast was made against stiff resistance and it fell to Dempsey to conduct the hardest fought battle of the 38 days' campaign, at Primasole Bridge, near Catania. The landing in Sicily was of considerable military interest at the time because it was the first combined operation of any magnitude against the Germans. New and useful methods, in which Dempsey had a hand, were evolved for the landing of troops and the cooperation of airborne forces.

On September 3, 16 days after the end in Sicily, Dempsey's Corps, of the 1st Canadian and the 5th Divisions, was the spearhead of invasion in the south of Italy. The Italian armistice followed five days later, and the 8th Army, with Dempsey's Corps on the right, advanced some 300 miles in 17 days.

WINTER BATTLES

Then, as the German resistance stiffened, and as our operations began to suffer from lack of resources, due to withdrawals for the Normandy landing, Dempsey fought a score of winter battles in a most difficult country of precipitous hills and deep valleys, including the crossing of the Biferno River and the capture of Termoli by a joint land and sea-borne attack, and culminating in the breaking of the Sangro River line after some of the bitterest fighting of the war. By his masterly conduct in command of these operations Dempsey made an essential though undramatic contribution to the capture of Cassino and the fall of Rome, but, before these results were secured, he had left Italy, in January, 1944, to take command of the 2nd Army, which was making ready in England to invade western Europe.

The 2nd Army was one of the two British Armies composing Montgomery's 21st Army Group. For six months until D. Day, June 6, 1944, Dempsey was engaged in planning and in training his troops for what was to be the greatest landing operation in face of opposition ever attempted in this or any previous war.

FIERCE FIGHTING

After the disembarkation Dempsey's Army was engaged in the fierce fighting around Caen where the bulk of the German panzer divisions were committed, and where it was Montgomery's plan to keep them committed so as to allow the American Army to break out on the right. After the town was taken there followed the heavy fighting around Falaise and Mortain, which arose from the enemy's decision to fight a decisive battle south of the Seine, and in this Dempsey's Army played a leading part. After the passage of the Seine at Louviers and Vernon, the next phase of the operation was a pursuit on a colossal scale. The defeated German Armies were everywhere streaming across France and Belgium in an endeavour to reach the shelter of the Siegfried Line inside the frontiers of Germany.

As the resistance of the Germans stiffened in Belgium, and it became apparent that they had made a most remarkable recovery, the 2nd Army settled down to the deliberate operations which occupied the winter of 1944–45. King George VI, on a visit to the 2nd Army, called for a sword and dubbed Dempsey K.C.B.

By the end of March, Dempsey's Army was established on the Rhine, and all was ready for the knockout blow. Bridgeheads were established under intense artillery bombardment and air attack and by the dropping of airborne troops, and the advance to the Elbe was begun; 21st Army Group was directed eastward into the northern plains where its superiority in tanks and mechanized transport would tell most quickly, and Dempsey's Army was in the forefront of the allied advance as it moved fast towards the heart of Germany. The German retreat soon became a rout, and by May 7, when the Germans capitulated, just 11 months after the landing in Normandy, the 2nd Army was across the Elbe.

Dempsey's service with the Army came to an end at his own wish two years later when he sent in his papers at the age of 50. In the interval he had held three high commands. In September, 1945, he succeeded Field Marshal Sir William Slim as commander of the 14th Army in the Far East, and in November of the same year he again followed Slim as Commander-in-Chief of Land Forces in South East Asia. His last appointment was as Commander-in-Chief Middle East. He had been promoted general in 1946.

RIDING DUTIES

Dempsey was an exceptionally good horseman, and he loved both hunting and racing; he had bred and raced his own horses. He was chairman of the Rececourse Betting Control Board from 1947 to 1951. He remarked at the time that, as he would be attending all the race meetings he could anyhow for pleasure, it was nice to feel it was also his duty to go.

He was a D.L. for Berkshire. He was Colonel of The Royal Berkshire Regiment from 1947 to 1956, Colonel Commandant of the Corps of Royal Military Police from 1947 to 1957, and Colonel of the 1 S.A.S. Regiment from 1951 to 1960.

He married in 1948 Viola, daughter of Captain Percy O'Reilly.

June 7, 1969.

Sir Gerard d'Erlanger, C.B.E., former chairman of British European Airways and British Overseas Airways Corporation, died at his London home on December 15, 1962. He was 56.

Gerard d'Erlanger, son of a famous financial family and trained as a chartered accountant, was at least as well known in flying circles as in the City; and in the world of flying he gained his chief distinctions. He took on cheerfully the most demanding tasks, sometimes originating and defining them himself and pressing them on the authorities, veritably making a rod for his own back. In all these spheres of work he had the advantage of being a pilot himself and so of speaking with authority on flying matters inside and outside his organizations.

Gerard John Regis Leo d'Erlanger, son of Baron Emile Beaumont d'Erlanger, was born on June 1, 1906, and educated at Eton. He had become a spokesman of private flying long before the war started in 1939. He was convinced that many of his fellow pilots would not be able to qualify for service in the R.A.F. for age or sex or physical reasons and yet could be employed on duties in which their knowledge and skill would be valuable. During the year before the war he had canvassed the best of these, obtained their promises, and undertaken to see that they were suitably employed. When war came he had still not won his battle with the Air Ministry, but he continued to press for the acceptance of his detailed plan for ferrying aircraft from the makers to the squadrons and before 1939 was out it had been accepted, Air Transport Auxiliary had been formed and he had been appointed its commandant.

AMATEUR PILOTS

He began with a handful of experienced amateur pilots. He arranged to have them tested and then "converted" to the utterly different aircraft they would have to fly. Soon the Air Ministry was aware of their value. Pilots who could not get accepted by the Services were flocking to his headquarters at White Waltham, near Maidenhead, to volunteer. Among them were some of the woman pilots, who, in the end, were flying four-engined bombers.

When A.T.A. had been wound up he was appointed director in charge of B.E.A. in 1946 and a year later he became its chairman. This was the difficult time when no new commercial aircraft were coming forward, when routes in Europe had to be organized, staffs had to be recruited and sound plans for expansion had to be made. He had to be content with what he could get and he settled for Viking airliners which used some parts of the old Wellington bomber while he ran his immediate services mainly with DC-3s and wartime Dakotas. He saw that his pilots were carefully picked, made arrangements for a number of new services with facilities for handling passengers and looking after aircraft at foreign terminals, and set the new corporation on a solid business footing. In February, 1949, he resigned from this post, having been informed by the Minister of Civil Aviation, Lord Pakenham, that his appointment was not to be renewed when it expired later that year.

d'Erlanger was called back to commercial air transport as chairman of B.O.A.C. in 1956, again at a time of difficulty and readjustment. The corporation had recovered from the disasters of the first Comets, which had promised to give it a lead in jet liners, and was putting into service the later marks of Comet while its competitors now were bringing other jet liners into use. A somewhat critical period seemed to be in prospect, but he agreed to undertake the task of guiding the corporation through it. His appointment raised an outcry from trade unionists on the maintenance side, who evidently knew nothing of his record and regarded it as having a political flavour.

Throughout the period the corporation was the subject of criticism, partly because of its spending of dollars on a fleet of big jet liners which were considered necessary to meet international competition. When the term of his appointment ended in 1960 he did not seek a renewal.

d'Erlanger's interests in finance lay largely on the investment side. He joined the family merchant banking business of Erlangers Limited, of which he became vice-chairman.

BOARD MEMBER

On the merger of Erlangers with Philip Hill, Higginson and Company, Limited, he joined the board of the Philip Hill Investment Trust. He was also on the board of a number of other investment trust companies.

Those who had to work with him appreciated his readiness to trust them with responsibility and his ability to reach prompt and firm decisions. At Eton he had somehow acquired the nickname "Pop" and that stuck to him. Some of his friends in the City still called him Pop and in a wide circle his tall, slim figure and slow smile will be deeply missed.

He was made C.B.E. in 1943 and knighted in 1958. In 1937 he married Gladys Florence, daughter of H. J. Sammut, by whom he had one son and two daughters.

December 17, 1962.

---

de Rothschild—See under **Rothschild.**

Louis de Soissons, whose death took place on September 23, 1962, was one of those architects whose classical training and approach to his art left him out of sympathy with what was most forward-looking in contemporary architecture but whose work nevertheless, because of his sensitive scholarship and understanding of basic architectural principles, had a quality of dignity and sensibility that set it well above the average of period-revival design.

Louis Jean Guy de Savoie-Carignan de Soissons—to give him his full name—was a younger son of Count Louis de Soissons and was born in Montreal, Canada, on July 31 1890. He was first articled to J. H. Eastwood, the architect of Leeds Roman Catholic cathedral and subsequently studied both at the Royal Academy Schools and at the Ecole des Beaux Arts in Paris. He was an outstandingly brilliant student, winning among other awards the Royal Academy Travelling Studentship, the Title Prize, the Henry Jarvis Scholarship at the British School at Rome and three medals at the Ecole des Beaux Arts.

His early career was interrupted by the 1914–18 War, during which he served in Italy, being mentioned in dispatches and being awarded the O.B.E. and the Croce di Guerra, and being made a Cavaliere of the Order of the Crown of Italy. In 1920 he was appointed architect to Welwyn Garden City, and his most important work during the years that followed was done on behalf of that enterprise, either alone or in collaboration with A. W. Kenyon.

Although he designed many of the public buildings in the Garden City, it was as a domestic architect that his work there gave him an outstanding reputation. It was almost exclusively in brick in keeping with the Hertfordshire landscape, neo-Georgian in style; particularly successful was the skill with which houses of simple outline were grouped round the characteristic Garden City "closes". De Soissons became a leading authority on housing, and among other similar work for which he was responsible was the layout of the Wedgwood company's garden village at Barlaston, Staffordshire.

In more recent years, as senior partner of the firm of Louis de Soissons, Peacock, Hodges and Robertson, he was responsible for a great variety of work, including schools, factories, offices, churches and flats.

NASH TERRACES RESTORED

He was architect to the Duchy of Cornwall Estate and to the Imperial War Graves Commission in Italy, but the projects which brought his work most prominently before the public were the George VI memorial in Carlton Gardens (on the completion of which he was made C.V.O.) and the restoration of the Nash Terraces in Regent's Park. His knowledge and taste in matters of classical architecture made him particularly well equipped to advise on the restoration of the terraces and the present successful outcome of the efforts to bring them back to their original appearance owes much to him.

He was also the architect of the building in Regent's Park for the Royal College of Obstetricians and Gynaecologists, but this was not one of his happiest designs. An important design recently completed by his firm was for the new building to replace Nos. 5–7, Carlton Gardens which showed unexpected freshness of treatment.

PLANNING HONOURS

Louis de Soissons was elected F.R.I.B.A. in 1923, A.R.A. in 1942, R.A. in 1953, and was awarded the R.I.B.A. distinction in town planning in 1945. He was a man of courteous manners and great personal charm; never expressing himself intolerantly about work that differed fundamentally from his own, when he respected the spirit in which it was done.

He married in 1922 Elinor Penrose-Thackwell, who survives him.

They had three sons.

September 24, 1962.

Baroness de Stoeckl died on January 30, 1968, at her home at Iver, Buckinghamshire, nine days after her 94th birthday.

She was born in Paris in 1874 of Irish parents, her father being Captain Eustace Barron, of Waterford. She married in 1892 Baron Alexander de Stoeckl, son of Baron Edouard de Stoeckl, Russian Minister Plenipotentiary to the United States in 1857 and the man responsible for negotiating the sale of Alaska to the United States. After her marriage she was closely associated with the Russian Court, being a Lady to the Czarina, her husband was a Chamberlain to the Czar, and her daughter, her only child, a Demoiselle d'Honneur to the Czarina. Later, with her husband's appointment as Comptroller to the Grand Duke George she moved in Royal circles all over Europe until the Russian Revolution forced them into exile. For a period between the wars she worked as an assistant in a gown shop in Knightsbridge.

"SKELETONS"

It was not until she was 78 that, in her own words, she was "ready for the more sober enjoyments of middle-age" and was persuaded to write her memoirs; and then only to escape the "ennui of embroidery". With the title of *Not All Vanity* they had a great success when they were published in 1950 for their piquant enjoyment of a golden past. These were followed two years later by a second volume *My Dear Marquis*, which she described as "pulling back the curtains from the cupboards containing my few remaining skeletons". A third book, in 1953. *When Men had Time to Love*, was a social picture of the Empress Eugénie. Her fourth book, in 1957, was *King of the French, a portrait of Louis Philippe*, her fifth, in 1962, was *Four Years an Empress, Marie Louise Second wife of Napoleon*, and her sixth and last book, published in 1966 when she was 92, was the life of Madame Dubarry, *Mistress of Versailles*.

She was a witty conversationalist with an inexhaustible fund of amusing stories on growing up in the Paris of the great cocottes and her many broadcasts and television appearances brought her a host of correspondents from all over Europe. She was a friend of the Royal Family and spent the last years of her life in a cottage on the Duke of Kent's estate at Coppins, where she amused herself with her colony of cats. These multiplied so fast that she was forced to build them huts at the end of her garden, commenting ruefully: "I have given them their own establishments so that they can live as they wish and conduct their amours not too near the house."

January 31, 1968.

Professor Otto Erich Deutsch, the musical historian and bibliographer, died in Vienna in November, 1967.

Born in Vienna in 1883, he was educated at the universities of Vienna and Graz, and studied the history of music, arts, and literature; he worked from 1909 as a university assistant, then (after service in World War I) as a bookseller and publisher. In 1926, he became Librarian of the Hoboken Collection. His first important contribution to musical scholarship was his study of Schubert, including a documentary biography; two volumes were published in 1913–14, but it was not issued in complete form until after World War II. His Schubert studies continued with editions of several little-known compositions, then (in 1951) a thematic catalogue—the *D* numbers from which are now the accepted method of identifying Schubert's works—and finally *Schubert, Memoirs by his Friends* (1958).

RESEARCH ON HANDEL

Deutsch had to leave Austria at the time of the Anschluss, and went to England, settling in Cambridge. He was a well-known figure there during the war years, and became naturalized in 1947; but although he was comfortable in Britain the pull of Vienna was strong and he finally returned there in 1952. During his years in Britain, he did much research on Handel, producing many articles (including a critical iconography) and finally a documentary biography (1955). He was also the first editor of the British Union Catalogue, resigning that post in 1950. To the two indispensable documentaries of Schubert and Handel, he added, in 1961, a third, of Mozart's.

He had already done much research on Mozart editions and portraits, and in recent years he has edited (jointly) a pictorial re-creation of Mozart's world as a collected edition of his letters. (His Mozart research was done in association with the Neue Mozart Ausgabe.)

MUSICAL TOPICS

He edited many further volumes of musical topics, including a facsimile series "The Harrow Replicas".

His tastes were not narrow. For years, and with eventual success, he urged the Volksoper in Vienna to take into their repertory *The Mikado* and *Oklahoma*. He had a ready wit: the coining of the word "spuriosity" is one of his happy minor achievements. He held strong views of many musical topics and was often involved in musicological controversies. In his last years he received many honours and awards in recognition of his work, including, in 1960, a Doctorate of Philosophy *Honoris causa* at the University of Tübingen.

November 27, 1967.

Isaac Deutscher, who died suddenly on August 19, 1967, while visiting Rome, aged 60, was in the very forefront of all the historians and interpreters of modern Russia. In many fields no one could touch him for his power of penetrating to the heart of problems or for his ideological knowledge and understanding, or his splendid manner of exposition—never simple, never hackneyed, never unclear, always muscular.

He came to London from his native Poland before the war broke out in 1939. For a few improbable months he was in the Polish forces in Scotland. Then, over several years, the quality of his work came to be known through his writing in the *Economist* and the *Observer*, though his identity was hidden to all but a few as he wrote anonymously or, later on, under the pseudonym Peregrine.

It was in 1949, with the publication of his great work, *Stalin: A Political Biography*, that his name and fame spread in Britain, the United States, other western countries, and—by way of smuggled copies—in Russia and the eastern camp. From that time his reputation grew with his three volumes on Trotsky and his many published analyses of the successive movements and upheavals in Russia and China.

LENIN WORK UNFINISHED

The death of Stalin, the overthrow of Khrushchev, the Sino-Soviet rift—such events led to his being overwhelmed with demands for newspaper and magazine articles and for broadcast talks.

Earlier in 1967 he gave the Trevelyan memorial lectures in Cambridge, choosing as his subject the 50 years of the Russian revolution. The lectures were a quite brilliant exposition, such as would only come from a lifetime of study and a powerful intellect. They were also a great success as delivered, some of them requiring an overflow hall for the undergraduates and others who crowded round. They were published only a few weeks before he died under the title *The Unfinished Revolution*. Even more recently there appeared the new and enlarged edition of his *Stalin*.

His death is the more tragic as he was working on the large-scale biography that meant most to him and would probably have given most to our knowledge of Russian affairs—the life of Lenin, on which he had been intensively reading and thinking for several years and which should have come out in 1970.

The Oxford University Press, which published almost all his books, lately asked him to do his autobiography, taking in, of course, his childhood and his travails in Poland. Then, further in the future, there was to be a thorough history of the revolution that would have been his crowning work, a task of scholarship that would, it was hoped, have been published by the Clarendon Press.

GOOD ENGLISH

When he came to Britain in 1939 he hardly spoke a word of English. Within a few years—such was his power of application—he was writing it not only fluently but with a distinctive, rich and fluid style. The same qualities of application and concentration were shown in every part of his work. In Poland as a boy he had been brought up in Cracow according to strict Jewish tenets; he used to say that at one time he could quote any passage from the Talmud at will. But in his teens he swung to Marxism and joined the Polish Communist Party in 1926. Thereupon the independence of his thinking showed itself. He saw that Stalin was departing from Marxism and Leninism—and, as he published his belief, he was expelled from the party in 1932 for leading an anti-Stalinist opposition. The whole party was soon in trouble. Deutscher, staying on in Poland, earned his living at times as a proof-reader, but he went on with his own research the whole time.

The independent line he took in Poland remained constant with him. He kept his Marxist faith. He would respect some of Stalin's achievements, but distrusted most of what he did, and had little respect at all for his ideological thinking. He was more attracted to the brilliant Trotsky, although acknowledging his tactical mistakes. Lenin had a reverently special place for him—and the unanswered question now is how Lenin in fact would have emerged from the intense scrutiny and research on which Deutscher was engaged. Would Lenin have come out unscathed?

SCHOLARSHIP

Sometimes Deutscher was called a romantic, sometimes a prophet. The terms do not do full justice to his deep scholarship, based on his unremitting and intelligently selected reading of primary sources in Russian, Polish, German, French and, if need be, other languages—where he was helped as in all other ways, by his Polish wife Tamara, whom he married in 1947 (they had one son). What is true in the "romantic" charge is that—with all his scrupulously careful sifting of facts—he could be enthusiastic about an idea or a man. His work would not have been so invigorating, or so controversial, if he had lacked this *élan*. He thought intensively and felt passionately.

Many believed after the death of Stalin that Deutscher became too much carried away by his hopes of freer cultural life—even freer political life—in Russia. He was certainly uplifted at the time by the ferment of ideas in Russia, and wrote many long articles looking forward to a brighter future, but he always said and wrote that progress would be governed by ebbs and flows, by advances and then by periods of reaction.

Very quickly he saw that too much could not be expected from Krushchev, whom he despised as an ideologue.

SENSE OF HISTORY

He had a deep, imaginative sense of the movement of history. It showed itself in all his writings. No one wrote with a stronger sweep about the grandeurs and the miseries, the failures and the achievements, of the Russian revolutionary years—or about the consequential changes in eastern Europe. He was helped, as his writings showed, by his studies of the English and French revolutions, and his deep understanding and love for the nineteenth-century Russian revolutionaries.

It is a remarkable record for a man working alone, in London, in the country, and back in London, without a university faculty to help him in his research and thinking. He himself knew it was remarkable; he was quite sure that with his background he had something of value to put out. There was also a great modesty about him, and a splendid warmth, as well as an unfailing kindness and a touching courtesy—at times, too, hours of sheer boyish glee—in his meetings with friends. The sudden severance of his work will be felt, with a sense of heavy loss, in many countries.

August 21, 1967.

George Devine, C.B.E., the actor and artistic director of the English Stage Company, which became at the Royal Court an advanced guard of the English theatre such as there had not been since the days of the Vedrenne-Granville Barker management of the same playhouse, died in London on January 20, 1966. He was 55.

Born in London on November 20, 1910, Devine went to Clayesmore School, Winchester, and to Wadham College, Oxford, and was elected president of the O.U.D.S. in 1931. In the society's production of *Romeo and Juliet* during his term of office, Sir John Gielgud had his first experience of directing a play, Dame Peggy Ashcroft gave her first performance of the part of Juliet, and the firm of Motley received their first commission to design stage costumes.

In that same year, 1932, Devine joined the company led by Dame Peggy Ashcroft at the Old Vic and became business manager to Motley. He acted in, and Motley did designs for, important productions in which Sir John Gielgud appeared: *Hamlet* and *Noah* at the New, and a cycle of four plays, including *The Three Sisters* at the Queen's. *Noah* and *The Three Sisters* were directed by Michel Saint-Denis, and at the drama school in Islington founded by the latter Devine was manager and resident producer between 1936 and 1939.

SERVING NEW WRITERS

In 1939 he directed a professional company for the first time and married Audrey Sophia Harris, one of the original partners in the firm of Motley.

Devine was twice mentioned in dispatches while serving with the Royal Regiment of Artillery from November, 1940, until February, 1946. On being demobilized he was appointed director of the Young Vic Company and co-director with Glen Byam Shaw of the Old Vic School, but in 1951 he, Byam Shaw and Saint-Denis all resigned from the Old Vic. He then directed several productions of Shakespeare at the Memorial Theatre, Stratford-upon-Avon, and of opera at Sadler's Wells and Covent Gardens and in 1956, as artistic director of the English Stage Company, he went into action at the Royal Court with the declared purpose of making it serve the contemporary writer—and he meant writers of significance who had as yet made no, or little, contribution to the English Theatre—as the Old Vic and Stratford-upon-Avon served Shakespeare and the classics generally.

The discovery of, and collaboration with, authors capable of using the dramatic medium and the attempt to build up an audience, not to mention the training of actors and assistant directors, absorbed more of Devine's time than directing or taking parts himself. He did, however, in the course of the first five years, direct Arthur Miller's *The Crucible*, Brecht's *The Good Woman of Setzuan* and J.-P. Sartre's *Nekrassov*, as well as revivals of *The Country Wife* and *Rosmersholm*, and appear personally in Ionesco's *The Chairs* and Samuel Beckett's *End Game*. Among British playwrights, John Osborne, Nigel Dennis, Ann Jellicoe, N. F. Simpson and John Arden were introduced to London audiences during that period at the Royal Court.

THE ROYAL COURT

In and after 1947, when Sunday night "productions without decor" were inaugurated, performances were sometimes given there on seven days of the week, and the policy of running each production for a limited season only at the Royal Court, with the possibility of transfer to the West End for the outstandingly successful, allowed the company to present a wide range of new and unfamiliar drama almost without a break.

Though the council of the company included several other well-known names, Devine was the person most definitely associated with its policy and planning in the minds of audiences. He was, too, a good, if reluctant, public relations officer in the company's cause; with his informal style of dress he invited sympathy; with his prematurely grey hair he commanded respect; while in speech, whether the occasion was a lecture or a discussion, he remained cool and courteous. Nor was he dogmatic; once, characteristically, he upheld the choice of a play by saying that being committed to being committed was a dog chasing its own tail. After directing the English Stage Company for nine years, and seeing it through a difficult period of reconstruction in 1964, in January, 1965, Devine announced that he would retire from his position in September, primarily on grounds of ill-health; and he was succeeded by William Gaskill.

In July, 1965, he appeared in the premier of John Osborne's new play concerning homosexuality, *A Patriot for Me*, at the Royal Court.

January 21, 1966.

Vice-Admiral K. G. B. Dewar, C.B.E., who died on September 8, 1964, at the age of 84, was one of the central figures in the Royal Oak incidents in 1928, which culminated in courts martial at Gibraltar.

As the hearings made plain, the affair had its roots in clashes of personality between Vice-Admiral B. St.G. Collard, Rear-Admiral in the First Battle Squadron, Mediterranean Fleet (who took up his command of the Royal Oak in 1927) and the principal officers serving under him.

Collard (who died in 1962) was placed on the retired list, and Dewar, Flag Captain and Chief Staff Officer, and Commander H. M. Daniel, executive officer, were dismissed their ship and severely reprimanded. Less than six months after the court martial Dewar was given command of the Tiger.

He was a man of strong character and independent thought, given to examining perhaps rather more closely than some of his contemporaries, accepted theories. Of his inquiring mind and firmly held views he gave proof in *The Navy from Within* (published in 1939), in which his indictment of the Navy, its training, administration, system of command, discipline, and spirit was nothing if not sweeping.

Kenneth Gilbert Balmain Dewar was born in 1879 and entered H. M. S. Britannia in 1893. He specialized in gunnery and after being gunnery lieutenant of the Dreadnought was appointed to the staff of the War College. He was made a staff officer in the same year that the war staff was instituted (1912). In the First World War he commanded the Prince of Wales, the monitor Roberts in the Dover Patrol, and in 1917–18 was Assistant Director of Plans, Admiralty. He was Deputy Director of Naval Intelligence from 1925 to 1927. He retired in 1929 and was subsequently prospective Labour candidate for Portsmouth North.

He married in 1914 Gertrude, daughter of Frederick Stapleton-Bretherton, by whom he had a son.

September 10, 1964.

Dr. Otto Dibelius, former Protestant Bishop of Berlin, died in west Berlin on January 31, 1967. He was 86.

Dibelius, one-time president of the World Council of Churches, was three times in prison during the Nazi regime for writing anti-Nazi pamphlets. After the Second World War he founded the All-German Protestant Church Council, uniting all German Protestant Churches for the first time. He retired as Bishop of Berlin-Brandenburg in 1966.

He met strong criticism from west German authorities some years before, when he opposed west German rearmament. East German authorities banned him from visiting the east German communities of his see in 1957. Two years later he aroused a storm by declaring in a pamphlet that Christians were not bound to the authority of an anti-Church atheist government. After the Berlin wall was built in August, 1961, Dibelius was prevented from preaching at his main Berlin church, the Marienkirche (St. Mary's church) in east Berlin.

In the long struggle for the independent life of the Christian Church in Germany through two totalitarian regimes Dibelius of Berlin will take his place in Germany's ecclesiastical and political history, and in the ecumenical fellowship of the Christian Church his renown will always be gratefully remembered.

EDINBURGH EXPERIENCE

Born in Berlin, on May 5, 1880, the son of a government official, Friedrich Otto Dibelius studied theology in Berlin and Wittenberg and at Edinburgh University, a student experience which gave him an insight into Presbyterian churchmanship which remained with him all his life. He then went to the parish of Crossen-on-Oder in east Germany which left another formative mark on the future church leader for he became an "eastern man" with an immediate sympathy for all people beyond the Oder. It was there during the First World War, with his wife and four children drinking water and turnip juice instead of milk, that he learned some of the rigours of deprivation and the responsibilities of an active churchmanship. He began to challenge in his books the old Lutheran concept that churchmen should be politically passive, and refuted what he called "catacomb theologians" who wanted to withdraw from the inevitable compromises of social action.

In 1925 he became, at the age of 45, General Superintendent for the Kurmark ecclesiastical district in Prussia, and preached at the inaugural service of the 1933 Reichstag at the Garrison Church, Potsdam, declaring that "the dictatorship of a totalitarian state is irreconcilable with God's will". He was even more outspoken in preaching before Hindenburg in the Church of St. Nicholas, Berlin, when he warned the aged Marshal of the dangerous brink upon which Germany stood. "As soon as the state demands to be the church itself", he said, "as soon as the state strives to assume power to rule the souls of men—then we are asked by Luther's words to exercise resistance in the name of God". Unlike many of his colleagues Dibelius saw the perils of Nazism, and his courageous preaching brought the inevitable clash with Kerrl, the Nazi Minister for Religious Affairs.

The charge of sedition was never proved. Dibelius early learned how to deal with a dictatorship by being firm, polite, unruffled, always arguing on strict theological grounds.

CLANDESTINE LETTERS

During Hitler's war he lived in a damp, dark underground apartment in Berlin's Lichterfelde, and from there by visitation and clandestine correspondence kept the souls of his pastors and their people alive, and on the day following Hitler's suicide emerged as first Lutheran Bishop of Berlin-Brandenburg. One of his first public acts was to organize the Provisional Council of the Evangelical Church, which in October, 1945, drew up the Stuttgart Declaration of German Responsibility and Repentance. He lost two of his three sons in the war.

Two-thirds of Dibelius's new diecese was now in the Russian occupied zone, but he at once set himself to preserve the unity of his church by living in west Berlin and maintaining his office in the eastern sector. He kept on speaking terms with the Russian authorities, but was never afraid of saying in public what he thought about their official actions. "We must make it clear", he said in October, 1952, at Elbingerode, in eastern Germany, "that the state has no right to restrict the existence of a human being simply because he thinks and speaks in a manner which the administration of the day does not like. The Church will not be silent when things are happening which are counter to the word of God."

POPULAR PREACHER

The great churches of Leipzig and Dresden were always crowded to hear him preach on the "church struggle" as he deliberately resisted incursions of the state into family and church life. By the 1950s Dibelius had developed into a churchman of immense wisdom and cool courage who by his very presence in Germany symbolized the unity of the country. In 1948 he brought the German churches out of their isolation fully into the ecumenical movement through the World Council of Churches and in 1954 at Evanston he was elected as one of the presidents of the Council.

Sober, reserved, detached and never carried away by his emotions, Dibelius appeared on first contact to be a subtle church-statesman. He had learned to be careful and accurate in speech.

WARM HEART

But behind his shrewd and calculated utterances was the warm heart of a Christian pastor who cared especially for the rising generation of eastern Germany's youth. "When once each of these young persons has been named after Christ", he said at the height of his fight with the communists and their demands on youth in 1956, "and the new name has been written down in the Book of Life no power on earth can take away my commitment, interwoven with my responsibility." He loved his sorely stricken pastors and people in eastern Germany, and out of that tribulation he brought fresh draughts of courage to the Christian Church throughout the world which came to salute him as a great churchman and a great servant of the faith.

February 1, 1967.

Sir William Reid Dick, K.C.V.O., R.A., who died on October 1, 1961, at the age of 82, was mainly though not exclusively a sculptor of memorial statues and busts to public commission, and he showed great skill in reconciling his talent with the conventional requirements of the kind.

His most controversial work was the National Memorial to King George V at Westminster, for which Sir Giles Gilbert Scott. R.A., designed the architectural setting. The first model of the memorial was not a success, but neither sculptor nor architect was to blame for what was an addition of parts instead of a true collaboration. When the final work was unveiled by King George VI on October 22, 1947, it was greeted with general satisfaction.

Dick was born in Glasgow on January 13, 1879, and studied at the Glasgow School of Art and in London. He also had valuable experience as a stonemason's assistant. He first exhibited at the Royal Academy in 1908, was elected A.R.A., in 1921 and R.A. in 1928. In 1933 he was elected President of the Royal Society of British Sculptors—he had been awarded the silver medal of the society in 1928.

WINDSOR EFFIGY

In 1935 he was created K.C.V.O., and in 1938 King George VI approved his appointment to the office of Sculptor in Ordinary to his Majesty for Scotland. In the same year he was made a member of the Royal Fine Art Commission.

Of King George V Dick executed several portraits, including the recumbent effigy for the tomb in St. George's Chapel, Windsor. In his earlier life he produced a good many works of an ideal or imaginative kind, such as the impassioned "Man Child" and the study of a woman and serpent called "Femina Victrix" which was purchased by the National Gallery of New South Wales, but increasing public commissions left him little time for such efforts. Among his later works that which won most attention was the memorial statue to President Roosevelt in Grosvenor Square. Dick also did a certain amount of decorative work, including figures on Selfridge's and other business premises in London.

Possibly Dick's greatest artistic success was the work he did in collaboration with Sir Mervyn Macartney, then Surveyor of the Fabric, for the Kitchener Memorial Chapel in St. Paul's Cathedral, consisting of a group in the form of a pieta and figures of military saints.

MASTER OF CRAFT

Dick is represented at the Tate Gallery by a bronze mask of a man, entitled "Androdus", a Chantrey purchase of 1919, and in the National Portrait Gallery by a bust of Lord Duveen. In 1948 Dick was awarded the Albert Medal of the Royal Society of Arts "for national memorials in living stone", presented to him at Buckingham Palace by the then Princess Elizabeth.

Dick was a man of robust appearance, suggesting a typical subject for Raeburn, with quiet manners and a very soft voice. He was a sound rather than a brilliant sculptor, thoroughly master of his craft and with a good grasp of requirements and conditions, so that his selection for so many public commissions was not surprising. He married, in 1914, Catherine, daughter of William John Treadwell, of Northampton, and they had a son and two daughters.

October 2, 1961.

Richard Dimbleby, C.B.E., who died on December 22, 1965, in St. Thomas's Hospital, London, at the age of 52 had a long and distinguished broadcasting career in the course of which his voice, and later his face and figure also, became better known to the people of Britain and of the Commonwealth than perhaps those of any other person, except members of the Royal Family whose ceremonial activities he was so often called upon to describe. In spite of arduous application for a generation and more to the demands of radio and television, Dimbleby was a successful newspaper proprietor and editor, film producer, and farmer.

Richard Dimbleby was born on May 25, 1913, into a newspaper family, and was educated at Mill Hill School. His own grounding in journalism came at first with the family firm of Dimbleby & Sons, Richmond, Surrey, and afterwards with the *Southern Daily Echo* in Southampton, and with the *Advertisers' Weekly*, London. Of the latter periodical he became news editor at the age of 21. In 1936, largely on his initiative, the B.B.C. appointed him its first full-time "observer" in what was still a small and experimental news department.

There are still, in the B.B.C. library, recordings of a rather high, fresh and eager voice which quickly became nationally known in the late 1930s, describing such varied events abroad as the Spanish Civil War, including the bombing of Barcelona, the state visit to France, and the royal tour of Canada. It was with the coming of war, however, that he quickly became recognized among his British and American colleagues, and in the Armed

Services, as a correspondent of high skill and courage. After leaving in the spring of 1940 for the Middle East he was away for nearly three years, covering more than 100,000 miles in some 15 countries.

ON MANY FRONTS

In June, 1943, he transferred to the new War Reporting Unit which the B.B.C. set up for the coming of D-Day and after the long period of preparation was one of the first over, and then, in France, where he remained, off and on, until the end of the war.

Dimbleby's reaction to the rigours and exhaustions of war on so many fronts was typical of a man whose roots were deep in his native island. For several years he took an infectious pleasure in exploring it, its beauty and its scars, its customs and its characters, from end to end. Whether the formula was as invariable as *Down Your Way* in the Light Programme, or as varied as the lengthy series of talks called *Off the Record* which he did for the North American Service, as a kind of Alistair Cooke in reverse, he by now unmistakably had what is called "star quality". He could do little wrong, and his profession, and show business, and newspapers all crowded awards upon him. By this time, he had resigned from the B.B.C. so as to be freer for his newspaper interests in Richmond. He remained a freelance, without a contract, to the end of his life, though his loyalty to the B.B.C. was unswerving, and he refused many offers from commercial television.

THE NEW MEDIUM

The moment came, with the restart and rapid spread of television, when Dimbleby had to decide whether to move across to the newer medium. Already a forbidding list of casualties among radio "personalities" had piled up. Dimbleby, aided by a skilful producer, made a comparatively modest but unimpeachable beginning with a series called *London Town*. Now for the first time the public was able to identify the bulky, slightly rumpled form, and the broad face displaying a limited but unmistakable range of emotions, with the familiar voice. Within three years, Dimbleby was once again first in the field, this time on many television occasions, such as the first Eurovision relay in 1951, but he was also, for the first time, attracting criticism (inevitable, perhaps, in the larger glare, but always irritating, if not painful, to him) for being pompous, politically naive, and unduly deferential to what was coming to be called "the Establishment".

Once, however, he had settled into the chair of *Panorama* it became increasingly difficult to imagine anyone else filling it so firmly and decisively, or indeed at all.

It was, however, behind the cameras rather than in front of them that he achieved a success which was unmatched, and which made him a truly international figure from 1953, when he was the commentator at the Coronation of Queen Elizabeth II, to the autumn of 1965 when, characteristically ignoring a high fever, he described, via the Early Bird satellite the Pope's visit to the United Nations. This was no mere extension of his earlier work for radio on similar state and governmental occasions. He discovered a style of matching word to picture which developed felicitously through royal visits to the Commonwealth, Norway, Sweden, Paris, Denmark, and Italy, through the weddings of young princesses and the funerals of world statesmen. He approached each new task with unabated enthusiasm and his capacity for immensely hard work was never more strikingly displayed than in the prolonged studio spells at the time of the declaration of results in one general election after another.

PROLIFIC

In spite of all his B.B.C. engagements he took an even closer interest in his newspapers after becoming managing director of the Richmond and Twickenham Times Series in 1954 and played an active part as chairman in the production of Puritan Films and Film Partnership. He more recently became chairman of the Commonwealth Group of Unit Trusts. He found time to write a number of books during the war and shortly after it, and was always a prolific contributor to newspapers and magazines.

He is survived by his wife Dilys, who was an active partner in his enterprises, by his son David, himself a versatile broadcaster, by two other sons, and a daughter.

December 23, 1965.

Senator Everett Dirksen, who died on September 7, 1969, was one of the most colourful, complex, and confusing men in American politics. He was 73.

As Senate Minority Leader he was the Republican Lyndon Johnson, always ready to trade and swap in the legislative lobbies. He had something about him, too, of William Jennings Bryan, the great populist orator.

Considering his decisive roles in obtaining approval for the nuclear test ban treaty and the Civil Rights Bill, both measures against which Mr. Goldwater cast his vote, Dirksen's decision to place his colleague's name in nomination in 1964 came as something of a surprise. It was, however, only the last in a long series of twists and turns that had marked his 32 years in public life and given him a reputation for changing his mind. He had been at various times lawyer, dredging contractor, washing machine maker, baker, banker, isolationist, internationalist, liberal, reactionary, peacemaker, antagonist, congressman, and senator.

He was an actor manqué, had written more than 100 short stories and five novels, all of them unpublished, and had a voice which defied description by the most talented writers. It was said of him that he blew word rings like smoke and that his tonsils were marinated in honey, but he had to be heard to be believed. He had been called "oleaginous Ev", "irksome Dirksen", and "the wizard of ooze," but he was held in great affection.

His support of Goldwater recalled the fierce denunciation made at the 1952 convention of the Liberal wing of the party led by Thomas Dewey, the former Governor of New York and unsuccessful presidential candidate. During a speech on behalf of Senator Taft, Dirksen wagged his finger at Dewey and declared: "We followed you before and you took us down the path to defeat." The speech caused an uproar but did not prevent the nomination of General Eisenhower, whom Dirksen eventually brought himself to support enthusiastically.

MIND-CHANGING

He was described as utterly without principle and the Liberals in his own party challenged his election as minority leader in 1959, but while it is true that he stood on both sides of most questions at one time or another, the charge is disputed.

In 1950 a Chicago newspaper said that during his eight terms in the House of Representatives he had changed his mind 31 times on matters related to national preparedness, alternated between isolationism and internationalism 62 times, and changed his position on agricultural matters 70 times.

He both supported and opposed the late Senator Joseph McCarthy, although he voted against censuring him and supported him during the Army hearing. In 1959 he helped the South to block the passage of civil rights legislation by staying away from committee meetings: a year later, castigating the South for dilatory tactics, he was leading the fight for senate action on civil rights. In 1964 he persuaded the great majority of Senate Republicans not only to vote for the Civil Rights Bill but also to vote in favour of cutting off debate on the issue for the first time in history.

His amendments were agreed by his most avid supporters to have improved the Bill, and the National Association for the Advancement of Coloured People presented him with an award.

He at first opposed the nuclear test ban treaty in 1963 but, after receiving assurances from the joint Chiefs of Staff that it would not weaken the United States, he played a key role in its overwhelming approval. He also helped to steer through Congress the proposal in 1962 to buy $100m. worth of United Nations bonds and he stood by the Administration during the Bay of Pigs crisis. Indeed, his campaign for reelection in Illinois, where he was opposed by an ardent Kennedy supporter, posed the late President an awkward problem. Had he been defeated the President might have found it much harder to work with his successor, yet he could hardly support him publicly.

ZEPHYRS OF CHANGE

If most politicians shift with the wind, it took a zephyr to move Dirksen. There are those who criticize such flexibility but he won over many of his critics by the brilliance of his leadership in the Senate. His political antennae were among the most sharply tuned in the business, which may account for his ability to know when to hit hard, when to prevaricate and, above all, when to wait.

Dirksen strongly defended Johnson's position in Vietnam with only occasional backsliding.

Everett McKinley Dirksen was born on January 4, 1896, in the little city of Pekin,

Illinois, the son of Johann Frederick Dirksen, a decorator, and Antje Conrady. He was educated at Pekin high school and then went to work. Later however, he managed, by canvassing for newspaper advertisements and by borrowing, to enter the University of Minnesota. He was in the law school there when in 1918 he was mustered into the Army and after training went overseas with the rank of sergeant. Later after some study at Saumur in France he was commissioned and eventually found himself in the Saint Mihiel sector as a member of the observer corps of the United States Fourth Army.

Having on his return to Illinois tried his hand at several peace-time occupations, Dirksen, who had meanwhile been called to the bar of his own state, was elected Commissioner of Finance of Pekin, and after an unsuccessful attempt in 1930, was returned two years later to Congress as a Republican representative for central Illinois district; being an excellent debater he soon established himself there and took an active part in the floor tactics of the Republican minority, becoming in due course a member of the Appropriations Committee.

STIRRING APPEAL

Dirksen was until 1941 a sharp critic of the Administration. In September of that year, however, having sounded his constituents carefully, he made a stirring appeal for all-out support of President Roosevelt's foreign policy.

He had, from his entry into the House of Representatives, been a very ardent and vocal opponent of the New Deal and in the Truman administration opposed the Fair Deal. In 1948 he was threatened by the loss of his eyesight and so retired from Congress. His health improved and in 1950 he stood for the Senate and was elected, still an ardent conservative.

SUPPORTED TAFT

In 1952 he gave his support to Senator Robert Taft. He came into prominence in 1954 when he gave support to the late Senator Joseph McCarthy during McCarthy's celebrated altercation with the United States Army. However, after McCarthy was censured by the Senate, Dirksen drew sensibly closer to the Eisenhower administration, sufficiently close to secure President Eisenhower's support when he stood for a second Senate term, which he won.

September 8, 1969.

Walt Disney, the film cartoonist and creator of Mickey Mouse and Donald Duck, died on December 15, 1966, at Burbank, California, at the age of 65.

He was by no means the innovator of film cartoons, for he had been preceded in the early days of the cinema by Pat Sullivan's *Felix the Cat*, the *Out of the Inkwell* series and by *Mutt and Jeff*, but he brought to his animation of the cartoon world an individuality, a rich humour and—in many of his *Silly Symphonies* and longer works, such as *Snow White* and *Bambi*—a lyrical fantasy and a beauty of scene and of mood that was far in advance of anything attempted by his contemporaries in the cartoon field.

Walter Elias Disney was born in Chicago on December 5, 1901. His father was an Irish-Canadian, and his mother was of German-American origin. He had an elder brother, Roy, who was his staunch ally and who was destined to play an important part in the development of the Disney empire in the years to come. His childhood was spent in Chicago, where he soon revealed a talent for drawing. At McKinley High School he also became interested in photography, and learnt about cartooning from a member of the staff of the *Chicago Herald.* He served with the American Red Cross at the end of the 1914–18 War, and afterwards took up commercial art, making advertisement slides for a firm in Kansas City.

In 1923 he left Kansas and set out for Hollywood. His arrival passed unnoticed, and he and his brother Roy struggled to make a living.

HUMAN CARTOONS

He tried at first to produce a cartoon series of *Alice* pictures in which human beings appeared with cartoon figures; and one of the actresses he used in this series, Lillian Bounds, later became his wife. A period of poverty was ended by the creation in 1927 of a new series, called *Oswald the Lucky Rabbit*, which met with some success. But he soon grew dissatisfied with Oswald, and acting against the advice of his distributor, he decided to start a new series with a new central character. On a journey across the continent from New York to California, he and his wife discussed every possible idea, and finally decided that their new star should be a mouse. At first he was called Mortimer. This was later changed to Mickey, and he was given a girl-friend named Minnie.

It was the period of revolution in Hollywood, for sound films had just been born. Some of Hollywood's leading personalities were made by sound; others were destroyed by it. Disney produced two silent *Mickey Mouse* cartoons which met with no response. His third, *Steamboat Willie*, was also made as a silent, but his slender resources were just able to meet the cost of adding sound to it. *Steamboat Willie* opened at the Colony Theatre, New York on September 19, 1928, and caused a sensation. The days of poverty for Walt Disney were over for ever.

SILLY SYMPHONIES

By the end of 1929, when he signed a contract with Columbia Pictures, Disney had produced 15 *Mickey Mouse* cartoons and had also given birth to a further series called *The Silly Symphonies*, in which Mickey did not appear. The first of these was rather horrific, and Disney was advised to concentrate on Mickey Mouse. Once again he chose to ignore advice, and the cinema was greatly enriched as a result for the later *Silly Symphonies* produced some of his best work.

It was Disney's good fortune, as it was Chaplin's, to have been born into exactly the right era. Everything was now in his favour. The advent of sound had made him. The next film revolution, which was the coming of colour, was also of immense advantage to him. Colour gave him a new impetus. His first colour film, a *Silly Symphony* made in 1932 called *Flowers and Trees*, delighted both him and his audiences.

He quickly abandoned all black-and-white films.

It was customary, in the thirties, for the average film programme to consist of two full-length films. A short film was needed to separate them, and Disney was able to fulfil this need exactly. His little comedies were often the highlight of the evening, and he soon extended the range and number of his characters. Mickey Mouse (whose voice on the screen was that of his creator) was joined in his adventures by such notable cartoon personalities as Horace Horsecollar, Goofy and the faithful and long-suffering hound, Pluto. Then, with a squawk of fury, the inimitable Donald Duck burst upon the scene. Although he was said to be a conglomeration of all the people whom Disney had ever disliked, the irascible Donald Duck was soon immensely popular, for he became a symbol of unsuppressed indignation defying the frustrations of circumstances. Meanwhile, Disney continued to rely on the nursery classics for his inspiration, and his adaptation of the fable of *The Three Little Pigs* was another international success and the song featured in it, "Who's Afraid of the Big Bad Wolf" written specially by Frank Churchill, lives on still. Disney also persevered with the gentler side of his work, and his *Silly Symphonies* included some enchanting little masterpieces, such as *Water-Babies* and *The Old Mill.*

SNOW WHITE'S SUCCESS

In 1937 Disney took another major step when he decided to enter the field of full-length cartoons, and produced *Snow White and the Seven Dwarfs.* The animation of the human figures, and notably of Snow White herself, was not altogether satisfactory, but the film received a world-wide recognition (it was always the virtue of Disney's work that it could delight both old and young of any nationality), and from then on Disney was clearly committed to the production of regular full-length films. Frank Churchill's music for *Snow White* included two lasting successes, the romantic "One day my prince will come" and the Dwarfs' rousing chorus "Hi Ho! Hi Ho! it's off to work we go".

Pinocchio and *Fantasia* followed some three years later, and then came *The Reluctant Dragon*, *Dumbo* (the story of a baby elephant) and *Bambi* (the story of a deer).

Fantasia presented great music to the vast cinema public through the medium of the cartoon. The result was uneven, the method being best suited to music which was unashamedly programmatic anyhow (*The Sorcerer's Apprentice*), light enough to stand good-natured ribbing (*The Dance of the Hours*), or at least balletic in origin (moments of *The Rite of Spring* were surprisingly effective); but other sequences, such as the Pastoral Symphony featuring centaurs in assorted pastel shades, show Disney at his worst. Nevertheless the film was a remarkably daring experiment which deserves to be remembered for its successes rather than its failures.

These were the war years, during which Disney also turned his attention to the field of documentary and instructional films for the services, and in 1943 he made *Victory Through Air Power*.

After the end of the Second World War, throughout the fifties and sixties, Disney's output was immense. Films of every description flowed from his Burbank Studios.

NATURE STUDIES

He made real-life nature studies such as *The Living Desert*, cartoons of famous classics, such as *Peter Pan*, and then turned out a steady stream of non-cartoon films with living actors, turning to the pages of famous literary works such as *Treasure Island* and *The Swiss Family Robinson*. His studio also developed a remarkable ability for turning animals into actors, as was shown in his adaptation of *The Incredible Journey*, which described the journey of a Siamese cat, a labrador and an old bull terrier across Canada. In the early fifties he extended his work to television and in 1955 he initiated a bold and highly successful commercial enterprise by building an amusement park in Southern California called "Disneyland", which became a magnet for tourists from all over the world.

Although his feature cartoon *The Sleeping Beauty* failed at the box office in 1960, Walt Disney productions made a come-back five years later with the hugely successful film *Mary Poppins*, starring Julie Andrews, *That Darn' Cat*, starring Hayley Mills and a Siamese cat called "D.C.", also did well. But Disney fell foul of A. A. Milne's admirers when in *Winnie the Pooh and the Honey Tree* he "killed" Piglet and replaced him by an all-talking, all-American Gopher. However, it was stated recently that in the next Disney-Milne cartoon the Gopher has been dropped and Piglet has been picked to play.

Thus as the years passed, his empire grows ever larger and its ramifications more complex, with its financial side controlled by his brother Roy. Disney himself was a shrewd businessman who amassed a vast fortune without ever attaching any great significance to wealth. His strength as a film producer lay in the basic simplicity of his outlook, his tremendous energy and enthusiasm, his creative mind, and his dedication to the task of making films that were wholesome, warm-hearted and entertaining. He loved stories with a happy ending, but did not ignore the harsher realities of nature and of wild life.

His influence extended to every department of his studio, and his individual stamp lay on everything which it turned out. He did not become old-fashioned in his later years, and this was at once his strength and his weakness, since by constantly progressing, both in style and in technical achievement, he lost some of the simplicity of his youth. At his best he produced work of incomparable and touching beauty.

December 16, 1966.

Sir Arthur Dixon, C.B., C.B.E., formerly Principal Assistant Under-Secretary of State, Fire Service Department, Home Office, died on September 14, 1969, at the age of 88. He will be remembered as the man primarily responsible for the modernization of the Police and Fire Services.

The son of the Rev. Seth Dixon, a Wesleyan Minister, Arthur Lewis Dixon was born on January 30, 1881 and educated at Kingswood School, Bath, and Sidney Sussex College, Cambridge. He entered the Home Office in 1903. Promoted Assistant Secretary in 1917, he became an Assistant Under-Secretary of State in 1932 and Principal Assistant Under-Secretary of State in 1941.

Until 1914–18 there was no separate Police Division in the Home Office. The Home Secretary's Police responsibilities were divided between divisions which were mainly concerned with other functions. Dixon was the first head of the Police Division and over a period of 20 years he was concerned in one way or another with many of the developments of the past 40 years. The introduction of unified training systems, the standardization of conditions of service, the forensic science service making available the resources of science in the detection of crime—these are but a few of the improvements which the police service owe to him. In the middle 1930s he was charged with preparing the country's fire service, for which 1,440 separate authorities were then responsible, to deal with the threat of war. To this task, which involved the planning, recruitment and training of the Auxiliary Fire Service, organizing the production of equipment in vast quanitities with speed—the trailer pump was one result—and devising a system of regional control Dixon applied himself with characteristic drive and energy.

When the blitz of 1940–41 convinced Lord Morrison, then Home Secretary and Minister of Home Security, that the fire danger was so serious that to fight it a nationalized fire service which could operate in any part of the country without regard to local authority areas was essential, Dixon was his principal assistant in creating the N.F.S. By August, 1941, it had been established, the problem of finding men of the right calibre to take command of the large fire forces, each larger than the largest peace time fire brigade, the L.C.C., had been resolved and the Chief Regional Fire Officers were in fact in the Civil Defence regions. Before long the National Fire Service College for the training of officers of all ranks had been established. For the invasion of the continent, Dixon organized five mobile fire service columns: in the result only one of them was required abroad but its performance abroad justified the basis on which Dixon had planned.

Arthur Dixon was a shy man; this quality at times gave him an appearance of aloofness, perhaps on occasion of rudeness. He was a difficult man to get to know intimately. But those who worked with him and really got to know the kind heart and generous sympathies under the cold exterior became devoted to him. He inspired them with his enthusiasm.

September 16, 1969.

Sir Pierson Dixon, G.C.M.G., C.B., who died on April 2, 1965, at Egham Hill, Surrey, was one of the most able and agreeable diplomatists to grace the British Foreign Office. He was also an impressive individual on his own account—classical scholar, novelist, and sportsman. In all his posts he won respect for his clear intelligence, unassuming integrity and his enormous capacity for hard work. Rather slightly built and of medium height, his mild and friendly manner was in one sense a little deceptive, for he possessed great strength of character that quickly showed itself under pressure.

After the war Dixon served as ambassador to Prague, Deputy Under-Secretary of State, Permanent Representative at the United Nations and, finally, ambassador to Paris. The climax of his career was marred by the breakdown of the Brussels negotiations and the ensuing cold war between Britain and France. These were very bitter personal disappointments, and the shadows were just beginning to lift a little when he retired in February of this year.

Dixon was born in 1904 and educated at Bedford and then Pembroke College, Cambridge. He took First Class Honours in both parts of the Classical Tripos. He was also Craven scholar and won the chief classical prizes. Later, as a fellow of the college, he spent a year at the British School of Archaeology in Athens. He married Alexandra Ismene, daughter of S. C. Atchley. She is part Greek and shared her husband's interest in the country and its history.

He entered the Foreign Office in 1928. In his pocket when he took the examination was an offer of a Cambridge fellowship that would certainly have led to a distinguished academic career. Instead, he served successively in London, Madrid, Ankara and Rome. He returned to London in 1940 and the following year accompanied Anthony Eden on the mission to the Middle East, Greece and Turkey that led to the dispatch of the British Expeditionary Force to Greece. Later he became Adviser to Harold Macmillan, then Minister Resident at the Allied Forces Headquarters in North Africa.

U.N. CRISES

In 1943 Dixon became Principal Private Secretary to Eden, and went with him to the conferences at Yalta, Cairo, Quebec, Moscow, and Potsdam. On D-Day he was in the Prime Minister's train, and on VE-Day with Eden at San Francisco, where he had a hand in setting up the United Nations. They both flew back to attend the Potsdam conference. When Ernest Bevin took over after the general election Dixon provided a vital link by continuing as Principal Private Secretary. He stayed at Bevin's side through the endlessly frustrating conferences of the next two years.

In 1947 Dixon was sent as ambassador to Prague, which was then expected to become one of the key posts between east and west. Within a few weeks came the *coup d'état*. The iron curtain descended and for the young ambassador the job came to serve as a breathing space during which he produced a novel, *Farewell, Catullus*, and other writings.

Dixon returned to London in 1950 as Deputy Under-Secretary of State, first for political and then for economic affairs. In 1954 he succeeded Sir Gladwyn Jebb as Permanent Representative at the United Nations.

During his five and a half years there Dixon had to deal with a number of crises, chief among them the Suez and Hungarian affairs of 1956 and the early stages of the Congo operation in 1960.

In his handling of these issues, Dixon was a tower of strength for his country and the western world. He earned the regard of those delegates who basically agreed with the British standpoint, and the respect of those who differed from him.

In the Suez crisis especially, Dixon found himself speaking to a brief, thrust suddenly into his hands, with which he did not necessarily find himself in full sympathy. He handled himself with dignity and restraint at a time when he was being "cold shouldered" by the United States delegation headed by Henry Cabot Lodge.

In particular, Dixon remained on good terms with the then Secretary-General, Dag Hammarskjöld, whose attitude was necessarily critical of the venture, but who realized that his friendship with the British delegate was not vitiated by their official differences.

ADMIRATION FOR GENERAL

Most of Dixon's term as Ambassador in Paris, where he succeeded Lord Gladwyn in 1960, was inevitably compromised by his conflicting duties as British deputy in the Common Market negotiations. It was not merely that the time he spent commuting between Paris and Brussels—nearly two years—prevented him from seeing more of France and General de Gaulle. This dichotomy of functions sprang from the erroneous premise that the French had some interest in British membership.

As matters turned out, Dixon's two hats were quite incompatible. His task as a negotiator was bound, in French eyes, to diminish his diplomatic mission; and when General de Gaulle finally cast his veto, the Ambassador was left to pick up the pieces of the Anglo-French relationship. Looking back, he questioned whether the dual role had been a wise decision, but concluded philosophically that the clash was bound to come.

He had high admiration for the General's personal qualities, while deploring the implications of his foreign policy; the two men established a more intimate relationship than might be supposed. One of his comments on Macmillan's ill-starred visit to Rambouillet at the end of 1962 was that convincing General de Gaulle was like "trying to get through to a man wearing a suit of armour".

Dixon's quiet diplomacy, his gentle touch and manner, was severely tried by the ensuing acerbity of Anglo-French relations: it says much for his skill and perception that they were in far better shape when he departed a few weeks ago, leaving only friends in Paris. His task was not helped by the word put about in London that Princess Margaret's visit to a charity ball in Paris had been cancelled on the Ambassador's advice. Dixon ran a young and happy embassy. Living for four years or more in the elegant house that once belonged to Pauline Borghese, sister of Napoleon, he wrote a kind little book about her, and had intended to write much more. Among his other publications were: *Corcyra* (the prize Latin poem, 1925), *The Iberians of Spain* (1939), and *The Glittering Horn* (1958). He also contributed to *The Times Literary Supplement*.

He is survived by his wife, one son and two daughters.

April 3, 1965.

Lieutenant-General Sir William Dobbie, G.C.M.G., K.C.B., D.S.O., who became famous in the Second World War when he was Governor and Commander-in-Chief of Malta, during the historic siege from 1940 to 1942, died at his London home on October 3, 1964.

He was 85. Before the war he had had a distinguished career in the Army, and had been Commandant of the School of Military Engineering at Chatham, and Commander-in-Chief in Malaya.

William George Shedden Dobbie was born at Madras on July 12, 1879, the son of W. H. Dobbie. C.I.E., an Indian civil servant who became Accountant-General of the Madras Presidency. He was educated at Charterhouse, where he was a classical scholar, and the Royal Military Academy, Woolwich, from which he was commissioned in the Royal Engineers in August, 1899. During the latter part of the South African War he saw service in the Transvaal and the Orange River Colony. In 1913 he graduated from the Staff College, Camberley, and at the outbreak of the 1914–18 War he went to France as adjutant to the C.R.E. of the 4th Divisin and took part in the retreat to the Seine and the subsequent advance to the Aisne. His service in the 1914–18 War was entirely on the staff, at Divisional Corps and Army Headquarters, and finally, in 1918, he became G.S.O. 1st grade in the operations section at G.H.Q. He was awarded the D.S.O., created C.M.G., and was mentioned five times in dispatches, and received the Legion of Honour.

For the 10 years following the war, except for one year with his corps, Dobbie continued to serve on the general staff in the Rhine Army, at Aldershot, in the War Office and in the Western Command. Then in 1928 he was given command of the Cairo Brigade, a post which he held for four years. While he was in Cairo in 1929 he was called upon to deal with a serious outbreak of racial and religious hostility between the Jews and Arabs in Palestine, arising from the question of access to the Wailing Wall in Jerusalem. Riots and disorders spread all over the country, but Dobbie, acting with great energy and promptitude, surrounded hostile villages and arrested the ringleaders, and soon restored order by vigorous offensive measures. In recognition of his services he was created C.B.

His next appointment, on promotion to major general in 1932, was as Commandant of the School of Military Engineering at Chatham, and Inspector R.E. After three years in this post he was made G.O.C. Malaya at a time when the development of the Singapore base was increasing the importance of the Malayan Command. This was his last employment on the active list.

When it came to an end in August, 1939, he was retired from the Army under the age rule.

It was particularly galling to Dobbie to be put on the shelf at the outbreak of war, and for a long time his offer to serve in any capacity went unanswered. Then one day in April, 1940, he was lunching in the United Service Club in London, and there he met General Ironside, then C.I.G.S. Ironside said to him: "Will you go to Malta?" He replied: "Certainly. In what capacity?" Ironside, to his astonishment, said: "As Governor." He arrived in Malta 10 days later, a few weeks before the siege began. He was to prove the soul of the defence for the next two years.

When the war came to Malta the garrison and the defences were hopelessly inadequate. At the outset Dobbie had only five weak battalions, 16 obsolescent anti-aircraft guns and four out-of-date fighter aircraft, which were found in cases in the dockyard stores. And the problem of defence was immensely complicated by the size of the civilian population, estimated at 2,700 persons to the square mile, nine tenths of whose food had to be brought in by sea. In the desperate situation following the fall of France there was little that could be spared from home to reinforce him. The C.I.G.S. sent him a telegram "Deuteronomy, Chapter 3, Verse 22" (Ye shall not fear them: for the Lord your God he shall fight for you).

Dobbie's first act was to issue an order of the day invoking divine aid and protection, and having done this he immediately turned his practical mind to the consideration of material difficulties and dangers—the rounding up of fifth columnists, and the digging of air raid shelters (13 miles of tunnelling was done in the limestone rock), the defences of the beaches and aerodromes, institution of conscription, and a thousand and one other details. His energy and foresight proved invaluable in preparing the community to withstand the cruel ordeal that awaited them.

HEROIC ENDURANCE

The story of the heroic endurance of the people of Malta under the almost daily bombing of the next two years need not be retold. It was not until the early summer of 1942 that the Luftwaffe were finally deprived of command of the air over Malta. By that time the civilian casualties averaged 1 in 70, as a result of some 2,000 air raids. But, although the bombing of the island began to diminish, the supply convoys were still under heavy attack; the population were suffering from malnutrition, and feeding them became a critical problem. It was at this point that Lord Gort was sent out to relieve Dobbie as Governor. The long strain had worn him down, and Churchill, who had described him as "a Cromwellian figure at the key point", decided with deep regret that there was nothing for it but to bring him home. The end of his term of office was marked by the award of the George

Cross to the Island and, on his arrival in England, Dobbie was decorated by the King with the G.C.M.G. He was not bitter at being relieved, but when he went to the War Office to see the Director of Military Operations he remarked, rather wistfully: "I could have stayed perfectly well."

Dobbie's conduct of the siege was a remarkable feat of leadership. Never once did disaffection rear its head. It was his example and his courage that inspired the people of Malta, while his deep and openly expressed religious faith accorded exactly with their own tradition of piety.

In 1945 Dobbie published a little book entitled *A Very Present Help*, in which he told the story of his life. The book was designed as "a tribute to the faithfulness of God", and he wrote it in order to encourage others to rely upon the never failing help of God. It is a complete revelation of his own fine character and his mentality. Few who read the book can fail to be moved at the humility with which the author related with touching simplicity his conviction that at every step he received divine guidance.

He wrote another book in 1948, *Active Service with Christ*. He was a Colonel Commandant R.E. from 1940 to 1947 and was Bailiff G.C. of the Order of St. John of Jerusalem.

He married in 1904 Sybil, daughter of Captain Orde-Brown, R.A., and had two sons, one of whom was killed in action, and a daughter. Lady Dobbie died in 1962.

October 5, 1964.

Sir William Dobell, the Australian landscape and portrait painter, who won the Archibald Prize, Australia's leading award for portrait painting, three times, died in May, 1970, at the age of 70. In 1962, 35 of his paintings sold for some £40,000 at a sale in Sydney—the highest price (nearly £4,000) was paid for *Study for Woman in Restaurant*.

Dobell trained at the Slade School, and painted in what one commentator described as "a heavy-handed academic style which owes something to various European artists, and his moods vary from the sentimental or gloomy to the superficial or sardonic." In 1965 James Gleeson published a monograph *William Dobell*.

In 1966 Dobell was knighted for his services to art. He won the Britannica Australia art award in 1964.

May 15, 1970.

Istvan Dobi, formerly Hungarian head of state, died on November 24, 1968. He was 70.

His political career had three phases: militant support for peasant rights, as a member of the Smallholders' Party; subordination of that Party to the communists; and finally membership of the Communist Party itself.

Dobi was born in 1898 into a peasant family. Working on the land from early childhood, he had no chance of formal education. But a sense of social injustice led him first into the Social Democratic Party and later into the newly-reconstructed Smallholders' Party.

In the Second World War, Dobi served in the Hungarian army as a guard in a labour battalion for suspected anti-Nazi elements, a thankless task in which he was known for his humane attitude to his charges. Returning to politics after the war, he was elected to the National Assembly for the Smallholders' Party, which had won more than half the popular vote and now emerged as the leading party of a coalition. From this point, however, Dobi's personal success depended on that of the Communist Party more than of his own. In 1946, he was dismissed as Minister of Agriculture by the Smallholder Prime Minister, Ferenc Nagy. In May, 1947, Nagy went abroad, to be replaced by a pro-communist successor, and Dobi regained office as Minister without Portfolio. Meanwhile the arrest in February, 1947, of the leader of the Smallholders' Party, Bela Kovacs, had cleared the way for Dobi to assume the party leadership.

Having assisted the communists to power, Dobi was appointed to the premiership (as the non-communist prime minister of a communist government) in 1948, and to the chairmanship of the presidential council in 1952. He remained in this office, which made him titular head of state, until 1967.

The revolution of 1956 made little difference to Dobi. The reviving Smallholders' Party was willing to leave him in office, and at one time he sought to resume contact with its leaders; it was Dobi who conveyed the message recalling Bela Kovacs from disgrace to join Imre Nagy's short-lived government.

Apart from this, however, Dobi did little more during the revolution and its repression than swear in the successive governments of Imre Nagy and Janos Kadar. In December, 1959, he formally joined the Hungarian Socialist Workers' (communist) Party and was elected to its central committee.

November 25, 1968.

Frances Doble (Lady Lindsay-Hogg), the actress, who died in December, 1969, will be remembered by those who can look back upon the London theatre of the 1920s and 1930s, in connexion with the plays of Noël Coward, John Van Druten, Margaret Kennedy and Edgar Wallace.

Born and educated in Canada, she appeared in England first with Seymour Hicks's company in London and then for fifteen months with Barry Jackson's company at the Birmingham Repertory. Her big opportunity at Daly's, Leicester Square, in Coward's *Sirocco* was the occasion of one of the most calamitous openings and of the most celebrated *gaffes* in the theatre of 1927. The final act, which open ridicule had turned into chaos, was followed by the angriest uproar he had ever heard in a theatre when the author confronted the gallery; and finally by the curtain speech, obviously learnt by heart in hope of the play's success, of the beautiful, but inexperienced and now utterly bewildered young leading lady: "Ladies and Gentlemen, this is the happiest moment of my life."

Coward made capital out of that very speech in his next revue, and Frances Doble lived it down and enjoyed a few years of West End prominence.

As the housemaster's wife in *Young Woodley* and as the socially ambitious wife of the young composer in *The Constant Nymph*, she suffered by comparison with Kathleen O'Regan and Cathleen Nesbitt, her predecessors in those roles, but it was well within her power to make very competent heroines for Matheson Lang in one play, and, returning to the stage after an interval following his marriage, for Edgar Wallace in another.

She was kept busy for many months in Anthony Kimmins's first success, *While Parents Sleep*, in which her disrobing scene was then considered very daring, and for a much shorter period in the title role of *Ballerina*, adapted from a novel by her great friend Lady Eleanor Smith, daughter of the first Lord Birkenhead, and presented under her own management. Anyone that saw her in the court-room play *Libel* at the end of her short career in 1934, will probably remember the grace, the feminine aplomb, and the model-like assurance with which, called on to give evidence, she rose, crossed the stage and silently took her stand in the witness box. Yet she was probably sincere when, a few years later, sitting late over a dinner table, she replied to the question whether she regretted the theatre, "No, if ever I pass a stage-door in the evening, I suppose I'm glad that I don't still have to go in."

December 23, 1969.

Frank Dobson, who died on July 22, 1963, at the Princess Beatrice Hospital, London, at the age of 74, held for many years a place of eminence among British sculptors, the intrinsic merits of his work both as carver and modeller always commanding respect, even though it was to some extent overshadowed by, or at all events less spectacular than, that of some of his contemporaries.

His sculpture, while never lacking the appreciation of critics, did not provoke the controversy and intensity of public interest which attended that of Sir Jacob Epstein. In contrast with later—and also spectacular—developments of the art in Britain, it seemed far more conservative than in the 1920s, when in comparison with the academic work of that time it gave some impression of being a radical departure. He held to the conception of the human figure "in the round" as the true vehicle of the sculptor's art, best expressing his sense of mass and of purely formal beauty. Although he might exaggerate the weight or stretch of limb, he always respected the organic completeness of the figure, and from this point of view is nearer to Maillol than to Henry Moore. He was indeed much influenced by that great French sculptor and his work has a like serenity, apparent both on a monumental scale and in his small figurines in terra-cotta. His numerous busts also showed a distinguished ability in portraiture.

Born in London, on November 18, 1888, he was the son of Frank Dobson, artist, and his wife, Alice Mary Owen. He began his education at Harrow Green School and, showing a propensity for drawing, he was sent at 13 to the art department of the Leyton Technical School. He also spent a good deal of time in the studio of Sir William Reynolds-Stephen, watching the sculptor at work and gaining an idea of methods and procedure.

He next won the Stephens Scholarship to Hospitalfield, Arbroath, and completed his artistic training at the City and Guilds School, Kennington.

PAINTER AND DRAUGHTSMAN

He began as painter and draughtsman and his first exhibition at the Chenil Galleries in 1914 consisted of drawings. He never ceased to cultivate drawing for its own sake as well as a preliminary for sculpture, his figures and studies of animals and birds regularly adding distinction to the yearly graphic exhibits of the Royal Academy. He had, however, always loved the sculptor's craft and after war service, 1914–18, he pursued it with vigour. He contributed sculpture and drawings to the Group X exhibition organized by Wyndham Lewis in 1920, and held his first one-man show of sculpture at the Leicester Galleries in 1921. The following year he exhibited with the London Group, of which he was president from 1923 to 1927.

He had already gained a considerable reputation. His head of Sir Osbert Sitwell in polished brass, 1923 (Tate Gallery) attracted attention by its bold simplification. It was followed by the successful "Marble Woman" of 1924. Dobson was selected as one of the Six European Sculptors whose works were shown in America—the others being Maillol, Despiau, Bourdelle, Kolbe, and Haller. He contributed also to a number of the principal international exhibitions—Wembley, Paris, Dresden, Venice, Stockholm, Tokyo. An artist of recognized achievement, he was elected Associate of the Royal Society of British Sculptors, 1938, A.R.A., 1942, and R. A. 1953, and was made C.B.E. in 1947. He produced some portraits as official war artist in the Second World War and was professor of sculpture at the Royal College of Art, 1946–53.

Among his principal works are his figure "Truth" presented to the Tate Gallery by the Contemporary Art Society in 1930 and his decorations for Hays Wharf. His portrait busts include those of the Earl of Oxford and Asquith, Sir Thomas Lipton, Jeanne de Casalis, Margaret Rawlings, and Lydia Lopokova. There are examples in the galleries of Manchester, Glasgow, and Leeds as well as in the Tate. His art was discussed and praised in several works: Stanley Casson's *XXth Century Sculpture* (Casson also recorded a talk with Dobson in his B.B.C. Artists at Work series); E. H. Ramsden's *Twentieth Century Sculpture*, 1949, and in monographs by Raymond Mortimer 1926, and T. W. Earp, 1945.

He married in 1926 Caroline Mary Bussell, and they had one daughter.

July 23, 1963.

Sir Roy Dobson, C.B.E., for many years an outstanding figure in the aircraft industry, died on July 7, 1968, at the age of 76.

Chairman of the Hawker Siddeley Group from 1963 to 1967, he made his name with A. V. Roe Ltd., of which firm he became managing director, having started as a fitter in 1914.

He was prominently concerned with development of the four-engined Lancaster bomber (which was itself a development of the two-engined Manchester), one of the most successful aircraft of the Second World War.

The story goes that Dobson was convinced that the Lancaster was a potential winner provided it had four good engines. Lord Beaverbrook, at the Ministry of Aircraft Production, did not share Dobson's enthusiasm, but one night Dobson went out with a lorry and came back with four Rolls-Royce Merlin engines. They were fitted and the aircraft "flew round Manchester like a fighter".

Roy Hardy Dobson was born in Yorkshire on September 27, 1891. He more genuinely belonged to Manchester, where he lived with an aunt while he served his apprenticeship in a small engineering firm in that city. For barely a year he worked in London as installation engineer for James Pollock, Sons & Co., who were agents for oil engines. In that year he had become engaged to a Manchester girl and back to Manchester he went at Easter, 1914, having had his direction determined by watching the flying of Freddie Rainham (later to be Avro's test pilot) at Brooklands. The famous A. V. Roe took him on and kept his promise to release him from the drawing office after six months.

After that he never went back to design. To his skill as an engineer was early added a shrewd business sense. He landed at Avro's, a youngster of 21, just when its fruitful season was beginning.

FORCEFUL

He had experience in all its branches, including the experimental department, and he made his first solo flight in one of the Avro 504s. At the age of 27 he was works manager. He became general manager in 1934 and in 1941, when John Siddeley ceased to be managing director, Dobson succeeded him and was also made a director of the Hawker-Siddeley group. In 1958 he became managing director of the whole group. He was chairman from 1963 to 1967, when he was succeeded by Sir Arnold Hall.

Dobson was a forceful character, around whose doings stories of explosive acts and dogmatic assertions grew like legends. What the stories failed to note were his complete lack of malice and the genial friendliness which could have him laughing with any of his workpeople an hour after laying down his law to them. His strength lay in the recognition by all his employees and associates that he would as readily fight a battle for them as against them when their cause was right; in that and in his ability to do the jobs they had to do.

From time to time he took off his coat and showed his men that a particular job could be done in the time allowed and pay them well at the price fixed for it. Just as he failed to stand on ceremony in the shops, so he could treat his masters with scant courtesy when they misjudged him or denied him proper consideration.

There were stories of equally forthright outbursts in his dealings with Government departments and yet, to the finish, he had friends all over Whitehall, even after he had impishly "leaked" the news that Avro's were to build a supersonic bomber when Whitehall's security would have kept it a close secret. He was grieved to have that order cancelled subsequently but he had won his real laurels in the war with his thousands of Lancaster bombers made in England and in Canada, and he had kept Avro's in the news after the war with his development of aircraft with delta-shaped wings, leading up to the successful Vulcan bomber.

He married in 1916 Annie Smith and they had two sons and a daughter. One of the sons was lost in an air accident. His wife died in 1954.

July 9, 1968.

Sir Gerald Dodson, who died at Esher on November 2, 1966, at the age of 82, was Recorder of London from 1937 to 1959, and had thus been the longest holder of that distinguished office. Even after his retirement he often continued to sit at the Central Criminal Court as a Commissioner to help in keeping abreast of the heavy lists. In a sphere widely different from the law his name also was known to the public through his joint authorship of the successful light musical opera comedy *The Rebel Maid.*

Born on August 28, 1884, the son of the late John Dodson, J.P., a former Sheriff of Norwich, Gerald Dodson was educated privately and at Downing College, Cambridge, where he took honours in the Law Tripos of 1905, and his LL.M. He was made an Hon. Fellow in 1945. Called to the Bar by the Inner Temple in 1907 (of which he became a Bencher in 1938), he acquired a large practice in the Criminal Courts in London and on the South Eastern Circuit. In the 1914–18 War he was a Lieutenant in the R.N.V.R. Hydrophone Service. He was Counsel to the Crown at the Central Criminal Court from 1925 until 1934, and was Recorder of Tenterden from 1932 till the latter year. He then succeeded Cecil Whiteley, K. C., who had been appointed Common Serjeant, as Judge of the Mayor's and City of London Court, the holder of which office is also styled the Commissioner when sitting at the Central Criminal Court. As a Judge, Dodson made his mark at once, and it was no surprise when, in September, 1937, he was elected Recorder by the unanimous vote of the Court of Aldermen.

Attention has often been drawn to the fact that the Recordership of London is at the disposal of the votes of the City Corporation, while that of the office below—that of Common Serjeant—is made on the recommendation of the Lord Chancellor. Accordingly, the Common Serjeant at any particular time may hope, but cannot be sure, that he will be appointed Recorder on that position becoming vacant. However, as regards Dodson, it was the unanimous view of those at the Central Criminal Court, who had practised before him when Commissioner, that no better choice could have been made, and it may be said at once that as Recorder he has left the reputation of being one of the best criminal Judges of his time.

PERSONAL MODESTY

From his long experience at the Bar he had acquired a complete knowledge of criminal law and practice; but he had something more, and something that even the widest experience at the Bar does not necessarily teach, the perfect judicial temperament. He was never ruffled and never lost control of a case; his summings up were lucid and balanced, and a prisoner could rely on every point in his favour being carefully put to the jury. Though a man of great personal modesty, his Court was conducted with a dignity that compelled respect; there was no irrelevant talk; and a liberty taken would certainly not be repeated. But there lurked behind those strong judicial features a pleasant sense of ironic, but kindly humour. For instance: "It is said by your defending counsel that you have a dual personality. All that I can say is both of you will have to go to prison." Or again: "Husbands have their defects. But they are not to be remedied by wives giving them doses of disinfectants."

Dodson's publications included (jointly) *The Law Relating to Motor Cars*; *The Road Traffic Act, 1929*; and, in *Halsbury's Laws of England*, the article on The Mayor's and City of London Court.

He was a man of wide cultivation and artistic background in agreeable contrast with the atmosphere of criminal courts in which his career had been spent. For *The Rebel Maid*, with music by Montague Phillips, produced first at the old Empire Theatre in March, 1921, Dodson wrote a number of lyrics, including "The Fishermen of England", which has been sung and broadcast all over the world.

Dodson married in 1910 Emily Alice, daughter of William Chater, of Godalming. She died in 1961 and he married secondly in 1964 Marjorie Binks Heath.

November 3, 1966.

Rosie Dolly, who died on February 1, 1970, at the age of 77 had, with her twin sister the late Jennie Dolly, made a distinctive contribution to variety and revue, also to the life of what would now be called café-society, during and immediately after the First World War.

The Dolly Sisters were primarily dancers, but they also sang, posed, showed off fabulous costumes, and in fact did a little of everything. They had a personality that appeared to be, in whatever country they might be working, mysterious, "different"; in America it seemed European, in Europe and in England, American.

Born in Hungary on October 25, 1892, the daughters of Julius Deutsch, they were taken as children to New York and made their début there at Keith's Union Square Theatre in 1909. They were from the start billed as the Dolly Sisters, but continued for several years to use a Middle-European form of their first names, Roszicka and Jancsi or Yancsi.

After being seen in "vaudeville" all over the United States, they worked in musical comedy and revue on Broadway: for Florenz Ziegfeld in his *Follies* and in *A Winsome Widow*, and for the Shubert brothers in a version of *Die Fledermaus*. They then separated, Roszicka continuing her career under such managements as the Shuberts and William Brady and George M. Cohen and Sam Harris, but were reunited in 1916 in the cast of a straight farce presented by A. H. Woods.

Before the end of the First World War they had established themselves in Paris, where, like Gaby Deslys, Mistinguett and Maurice Chevalier, they appeared for Leon Volterra at the Casiono, a theatre or rather "music hall", that became a rival to the *Folies Bergère*.

Charles B. Cochran, much impressed by their vitality and professionalism, brought them back again for *The League of Notions*, a spectacular revue that was to open his reconstructed theatre in New Oxford Street.

Cochran arranged that they should go round from the New Oxford on the opening night of his next revue *Fun of the Fayre* at the London Pavilion and, as a surprise, do their "pony trot" in the final circus scene. On the night, a troupe of clowns which was making its English debut "got the bird", and all was in confusion, till the irruption of the Dollys, this time with Clifton Webb as their coachman, made the house of one mind again and brought the curtain down to applause.

They displayed equal gallantry in their association with a third show of Cochran's, *Babes in the Wood*, his first pantomime, presented that same year, 1921, at the New Oxford. The sisters played the babes. As a cover for their American accents, and as a compliment to Hollywood's Douglas Fairbanks and Mary Pickford, the boy babe (Jennie) was called Doug and the girl babe (Rosie) Mary.

It was their last appearance in London. The Dollys resumed their career in Paris, which Cochran considered their spiritual home, then returned to New York and in 1924 appeared there in *The Greenwich Village Follies*.

Jennie died in Hollywood in 1941.

February 3, 1970.

Professor Gerhard Domagk, who was awarded the Nobel Prize for medicine in 1939, died at his home in Germany on April 24, 1964, at the age of 68.

Gerhard Domagk was born in Lagow, in the province of Brandenburg, Germany, on October 30, 1895. He was trained in medicine in the University of Kiel and after postgraduate work at the Universities of Greifswald and Munster he was in 1927 appointed director of the research laboratories for experimental pathology and bacteriology at the famous Bayer dye works at Wuppertal-Elberfeld, and a year later was made professor in the University of Munster. His professional life, strongly influenced by the tradition of Ehrlich, was devoted to the discovery of chemotherapeutic agents against infections and cancer.

Before the twentieth century the only drugs known to counter infections were quinine in maleria and mercury in syphilis. In 1910 Ehrlich introduced salvarsan ("606") for the treatment of syphilis and its success stimulated a search for other anti-infective agents. But success was confined to protozoal infections such as trypanosomiasis and kala-azar but the bacterial infections resisted all direct attack.

Domagk's contribution stems from Ehrlich's attempts as early as 1891 at finding dyes which had a specific affinity for infecting organisms and destroyed them without seriously harming the infected host. The first major success in this field made at the Elberfeld laboratories was *germanin*, the most effective remedy then known against sleeping sickness (trypanosomiasis).

SUCCESSFUL TESTS

For several years Domagk and his team sifted systematically the efficacy of a variety of dyes against experimentally induced bacterial infections in mice. After testing many pure azo-compounds they added a sulphonamide group to chrysoidine and thus *prontosil*, the first chemotherapeutic agent effective against bacteria, was born. Mice given *prontosil* survived 10 times the lethal dose of streptococci. Reports of its markedly beneficial action in patients suffering from erysipelas and child-bed fever rapidly followed. It was soon shown that the effective part of *prontosil* is its sulphonamide group and by modifications of this group drugs of great potency were developed. For example, the death rate from pneumonia fell by 75 per cent and from puerperal sepsis likewise; cerebrospinal fever which without treatment had a death rate of 90 per cent had now with early diagnosis and effective treatment fallen to less than 3 per cent; and better control was secured over certain dysentery and staphylococcal infections. Before the jubilant strains which greeted these victories over disease had died away, however, the discovery of penicillin and other antibiotics of prodigious potency tended to overshadow the magnitude of Domagk's contribution to therapeutics.

In September, 1938, Domagk was nominated for a Nobel Prize but it was not until 1939 that the prize was awarded for his discovery of the antibacterial effects of *prontosil*. A tense situation ensued, for following the award of the Nobel Peace Prize in 1936 to the ardent pacifist and anti-Nazi Carl von Ossietzky Hitler was so outraged that he forbade any German national from accepting a Nobel Prize. Domagk has himself told how after the news of the award was made public he was arrested by the German secret police, gaoled for a week and forced to write a letter saying that to accept the prize would be a culpable act of disloyalty to Germany and that he therefore felt obliged to decline.

PRIZE MONEY BARRED

In 1947 the North West German Medical Association in Hamburg inquired whether it might be possible for Domagk to receive the Nobel Prize which he had been awarded in 1939 but unfortunately the regulations did not permit that he receive the prize money. However, in 1947 he attended the Nobel celebrations and in the customary ceremony he received his diploma and gold medal of a Nobel Prize winner.

He made no further discovery commensurate

with that of *prontosil* but he continued his work in chemotherapy and made valuable contributions to the treatment of tuberculosis with thiosemicarbazones and insonizid.

In 1925 he married Gertrud Strube. They had three sons and one daughter.

April 27, 1964.

The Rev. Dr. A. C. Don, K.C.V.O., Dean of Westminster from 1946 to 1959, died at Canterbury on May 3, 1966. He was 81.

Alan Campbell Don came from a family of prosperous merchants of long standing in Dundee, and was born at Broughty Ferry on January 3, 1885. He was educated at Rugby and Magdalen College, Oxford. He entered the family business but soon withdrew and took up residence at Oxford House in Whitechapel where he formed a lasting friendship with Canon H.R.L. (Dick) Sheppard.

He went to Cuddesdon and was ordained to a curacy at Redcar, Yorkshire, in 1912. He accepted the living of Norton-juxta-Malton in 1917 and in 1921 he returned to his native land and neighbourhood as Provost of St. Paul's Cathedral in Dundee, where he remained for 10 years. He retained a great affection for the Episcopal Church of Scotland, and published in 1949 a small but handsome volume on the origins of the Scottish Book of Common Prayer. On his departure from Dundee the University of St. Andrews conferred on him the honorary degree of Doctor of Divinity.

A decisive break occurred in Don's life when he went to live in London as Chaplain to Archbishop Lang at Lambeth. They had always been great friends; they shared the same views in Church matters; and, as exiles, a sentimental affection for Scotland. In the hospitality of the palace as well as in the business of the Metropolitan, he was a great asset. His appointment by Speaker Fitzroy as Chaplain to the House of Commons followed naturally enough in 1936, and no less naturally on the death of Canon Vernon Storr his nomination to the Canonry of Westminster, to which the rectory of St. Margaret's is attached, early in 1941. The new rector was assiduous under war conditions in the spiritual and material care of St. Margaret's Church.

On Low Sunday, 1946, Bishop de Labilliere, Dean of Westminster, died, and it was remarkable that the appointment of Canon Don as his successor was announced in less than a fortnight; he was so much the obvious choice. He was installed on June 6.

STONE OF SCONE REMOVED

Don's tenure of the deanery will rank among the more distinguished in the history of the Abbey. A new look was given to the constitution of the Collegiate Church by a supplementary charter abolishing the freehold of "the Inferior Officers", among whom the Minor Canons were the most conspicuous group. This should have coincided with the abolition of the special endowments attached to the various offices, which had not, in fact, been done. The change even at this late hour was opposed, but unsuccessfully.

In December, 1950, the Stone of Scone was stolen from its place beneath the Coronation chair in Westminster Abbey. In a broadcast appeal for help in the recovery of the stone, he related how the Clerk of Works rushed into his bedroom on Christmas morning and told him of the theft, which he described as a "senseless crime". The stone was later recovered in Scotland and returned to Westminster Abbey in April, 1951.

A few months later, when Don was conducting a service in St. Andrews University chapel, some students with Scottish nationalist sympathies inserted in his hymn book a copy of a song entitled: "Dean Don Done".

The Coronation of Queen Elizabeth II was performed in 1953 with the utmost solemnity. The Dean had acted as chaplain to the Archbiship at the previous Coronation, and had made for his own use a very full record of all the proceedings and preliminaries connected with it. He brought an authoritative contribution to the arrangements for the Queen's Coronation and performed the Dean of Westminster's complicated part in the ceremonies with grace and dignity.

The Dean and Chapter made a public appeal in the same year for £1m., and a sum rather in excess of this amount was actually raised. When the target was reached Don released 1,000 "thank you" balloons. A great work of restoration and cleaning was then begun with an immediate effect that struck all who saw it and will undoubtedly be a cause for grateful recognition in the years to come. The Deanery and five other official houses, which were almost wholly destroyed by enemy action during the war, were rebuilt. The services in the Abbey reached a very high standard both musically and ceremonially, and the whole period was marked by large congregations.

The Dean was eminently fitted for his post. His fine presence, his straightforward preaching aided by a remarkable voice, and his obvious sincerity made him undisputed leader in the Church, and his friendliness and charm in society commended the Abbey in every sphere of London's life. He was much liked by his Chapter, and he was diligent in business, though somewhat handicapped by his great reluctance to say "No", in consequence of which many unreasonable and unseasonable requests were made to him without meeting with the instant refusal they deserved. He was literary executor of archbishop Lang, and J. G. Lockhart wrote that Lang would have chosen Don as his biographer.

He was Dean of the Order of the Bath from 1946 to 1959 and on the Court of the Worshipful Company of Goldsmiths; in 1959 he was elected an honorary Fellow of Magdalen College, Oxford. He was Select Preacher at Oxford 1937–38. He was chaplain to the King from 1934 to 1946, and since 1959 has been Chaplain to the Queen.

He married in 1914 Muriel, daughter of William Holdsworth McConnel; they had no children. His wife died in 1963.

May 4, 1966.

Dr. Theophilus Ebenhaezer Dönges, the South African president-elect, died in Cape Town on January 10, 1968. He was 69.

It may well be that the brilliant qualities which at the outset of his political career seemed to qualify Dönges as a future Prime Minister of South Africa were the reason why he never achieved that ambition. He was a brilliant academic, a suave and persuasive writer and speaker, a brilliant advocate. But, although he had many friends, it would be hard to justify any claim that he had a following.

So that when Dr. Malan retired it was Mr. Strijdom who became Prime Minister. When Strijdom died it was Dr. Verwoerd who succeeded him. When Verwoerd was assassinated in 1966 the pattern was repeated, and Dönges was passed over in favour of Mr. John Vorster. Dönges was chosen as president in March, 1967, to succeed Mr. G. R. Swart who retired a year before his seven-year term was to end. Owing to illness Dönges's inauguration as president in May was postponed. He was admitted to the Groote Schuur hospital suffering from brain haemorrhage. In spite of an operation in June there was no marked improvement in his condition; in December his family was given powers to handle his affairs by the Supreme Court.

Theophilus Ebenhaezer Dönges was born in Klerksdorp, in the Transvaal, on March 8, 1898. His father was a Dutch Reformed clergyman. He took the B.A. degree with distinction at the University of Stellenbosch in 1918, and the M.A. degree the next year. He later became Chancellor of his old university.

After a year or two as a registrar to a judge of the Cape Supreme Court, he went to London University where he took the LL.B. degree with distinction in 1922. This was followed by the degree of LL.D. in 1925. Returning to South Africa in 1924 he joined the Nationalist newspaper *Die Burger*, and started the Nationalist Party's first English-language journal, a weekly publication called the *South African Nation*. He was thus one of the many South African politicians with journalism in his background.

He left journalism in 1927 for fulltime practice as an advocate (they are never called barristers in South Africa) becoming among other things legal adviser to the Cape Provincial Administration. He took silk in 1939. During all this time he was on the periphery of politics, taking a notable part in movements designed to strengthen the Afrikaner economically and to help in the rehabilitation of Afrikaners who had been defeated by the drought and depression of the early thirties.

Dönges stood for parliament at Kroonstad in 1938, but was defeated. When N. C. Havenga resigned from Parliament with General Hertzog in 1941 after their split with Dr. Malan, Dönges contested Havenga's seat, Fauresmith, for the Malanite Nationalists, and won it. Thereafter he was in Parliament continuously representing the Cape constituency of Worcester since 1948.

He was appointed Minister of the Interior and Minister of Posts and Telegraphs in Dr. Malan's first Cabinet. It was he who, as Minister of the Interior, piloted through Parliament some of the controversial early Nationalist legislation designed to give legal and compulsory form to the traditional segregation between the races in South Africa. Among these were the Population Registration Act, which provided the machinery for establishing a system of race classification in South Africa, and the Group Areas Act, which empowers the Government to apply residential segregation between different races and colours.

He was also responsible for the series of legislative attempts to remove the Cape Coloured voters from the common electoral roll. He became Minister of Finance in 1958, a post he held until 1966.

His budgets were popular with the press because, although long-winded, they were clear —owing, perhaps, to his experience in journalism as a young man. His occupancy of this post spanned a difficult period in South African economic affairs, including the post-Sharpville period in the early sixties when foreign investors lost confidence in South Africa and strong measures were necessary to maintain stability of South Africa's currency.

Hardly had these difficulties given place to the boom of 1964 than inflationary pressures became apparent, against which he has had to apply progressively more drastic curbs. These measures have been the conventional ones of cutting state expenditure, discouraging imports and trying to encourage private saving, notably by progressive increases in Bank rate. Towards the end of 1966 he handed over leadership of the Cape Nationalists to Mr. M. C. Botha, now Minister of Defence. Dönges married Miss Johanna Schoeman in 1926 and they had two daughters.

January 11, 1968.

Hilda Doolittle—"H.D.", the American poet—one of the leading members of the Imagist movement, died on September 27, 1961, at Zurich. She was 75.

Her early work, characterized by a freshness and freedom from abstraction and introspection, was thought by some to be the purest exposition of the Imagist creed.

She was born at Bethlehem, Pennsylvania, the daughter of Charles L. Doolittle, Professor of Mathematics and Astronomy at Lehigh University. When she was nine the family moved to Philadelphia where her father became director of the Flower Astronomical Observatory of the University of Pennsylvania. She was educated at the Gordon School, the Friends Central School, Philadelphia, and Bryn Mawr. She was first in print as a writer of stories for children in a Presbyterian paper. In 1911 she came to Europe for what was to have been a summer visit but which became a lifelong residence. She soon came under the influence of the Imagist movement, had the good fortune to meet Harold Monro, who was active in keeping poets of diverse gifts in friendly contact, and with Ezra Pound, F. S. Flint (who died in 1960) and Richard Aldington she was one of the contributors to *The Imagist Anthology*. In 1913 she married Aldington and together they began translations from the Greek and Latin bringing out (in 1915) a volume entitled *Images, Old and New*. Early the following year, when he enlisted in the infantry she took over from him the editorship of the magazine *The Egoist*. They were divorced many years later.

In addition to her poetry and her translations she published *Hippolytus*, a verse tragedy, and three novels. The last, *Bid Me to Live*, which strikingly illuminates the lives and ideals of those Imagist poets of whom she was one, has just been published.

September 29, 1961.

Jigme Dorji, Prime Minister of the Himalayan kingdom of Bhutan, who was assassinated on April 5, 1964, had reversed an ancient policy and opened his country's doors to the outside world.

Dorji always maintained that he had been elected Prime Minister of Bhutan and it was true that the Tsongdu (National Assembly) had gone through the form of electing him, but in fact Dorji inherited the office from his father and the post has hitherto been hereditary in Bhutan. He was close to the Ruler of Bhutan, the Druk Gyalpo, in age (Dorji was 45), and the two were friends, but although Dorji was punctilious in observing their relationship in rank there was little doubt that he was the initiator of policy.

In his last six or seven years Dorji had ended the closed-door policy that, added to the fast barriers that nature had left around Bhutan, had made it an almost unknown kingdom. When for generations the Rulers of Bhutan had been refusing suggestions from India that they should allow roads to be laid into their country, Bhutan suddenly sought Indian assistance to build roads to Paro and then other towns.

TUDOR STYLE

Some of the new roads have now been completed. Bhutan also began to ask for medical assistance to improve the health of the people and for teachers to begin the transformation of a kingdom that is still essentially Tudor in character. In steering Bhutan on to its new course Dorji was attracted by possibilities of obtaining assistance from countries other than India, but in that he collided with his country's treaty obligations to its neighbour. India, understandably reluctant to see other countries establishing themselves as beneficiaries of a little kingdom which lies between itself and Tibet, discouraged such inclinations, and it is an indication of Dorji's flexibility and tact that personally he remained on best of terms with Delhi.

He was a man of great liveliness and charm as much at home in Calcutta's racing world—he ran a number of horses—as on the trails and in remotest villages of his country. Educated at schools in Darjeeling and Simla he was widely read and thoughtful and made an astute and successful Prime Minister for a country undergoing the transition from primitive to modern.

He is survived by his wife and three sons, of whom one has been at school in England.

April 7, 1964.

Captain Henry Taprell Dorling, D.S.O., R.N. (RETD.), better known as "Taffrail," died on July 1, 1968, in the Dreadnought Hospital, Greenwich.

Born in 1883, the second son of Colonel Francis Dorling, of Farnborough, Hampshire, he entered H.M.S. Britannia in 1897; served as a midshipman in H.M.S. Terrible in South Africa and China, taking part in the relief of Peking in 1900; became a sub-lieutenant in 1902, was promoted lieutenant in 1904 and qualified as staff instructor in 1913. During the war of 1914–18, he served chiefly with destroyers in the North Sea, engaged for the most part in minelaying, and (having already received, in the previous years, a gold medal from the Swedish Government for saving life at sea) was mentioned in dispatches and awarded the D.S.O. in 1918. In that year he joined the plans division of the Admiralty staff, serving there until 1921, and retired from the service in 1929.

He had by that time firmly established his reputation as a lively and popular writer on ships and the sea and on life in the Royal Navy in war and in peace. After his retirement he applied himself seriously to narratives of the sea based upon Admiralty and other authoritative sources and to naval fiction, and from the start he showed himself impeccable in matters of local colour and naval atmosphere. His earliest volume, published under the pseudonym Taffrail, *Pincher Martin, O. D.*, a collection of stories and stretches of life in the Navy, was followed by books on the "little ships" in the war of 1914–18, on famous sea escapes and adventure, and on some of the great Elizabethan sea-dogs. His first novel, *Pirates*, a story—largely based on Admiralty information—of the operations of the pirates in the Canton delta and of the duties of the British gunboats involved, appeared in 1929. It was in a sound and well tried vein, and came up to all but the highest level of naval fiction. *Endless Story* (1931) was a vivid and admirably unadorned account of the work of the destroyer flotillas in the war of 1914–18; *Seventy North* (1934) was a novel of adventure about a Hull trawler within the Arctic Circle; books about the merchant navy and the minesweepers were followed by a novel about the merchant navy, *Mid-Atlantic* (1936), which was at the same time a considered and humane plea for better conditions.

RECALLED

In 1939 Dorling was recalled to the Navy, served in the Ministry of Information and afloat in all types of warships, and in 1942, after the landing in North Africa, joined the staff of the Commander-in-Chief, Mediterranean, as press liaison officer. He found time to publish, in the following year, a novel entitled *Chenies*, which gave a spirited if perhaps somewhat conventional picture of a British naval family, with two of its members at sea, in wartime. In 1944 he was made an officer of the American Legion of Merit. Dorling was an active journalist (he was appointed naval correspondent of *The Observer* in 1945) and broadcaster.

July 4, 1968.

Marshal of the Royal Air Force Lord Douglas of Kirtleside, G.C.B., M.C., D.F.C., died on October 29, 1969, at the age of 75.

In the Second World War he was successively A.O.C.-in-C. Fighter Command, Middle East Command and Coastal Command, and subsequently Air C-in-C. British Air Forces of Occupation, Germany, and Commander-in-Chief and Military Governor British Zone of Germany. After he had retired from the R.A.F. he was an outstandingly successful chairman of British European Airways.

He held this post from 1949 to 1964, his appointment being repeatedly extended. He had seen the corporation move into the 600 m.p.h. jet airliner age, to become a profit-making undertaking, and into an airline carrying nearly six million passengers a year, against just over half a million in 1949.

He was shrewd in analysis, able in making plans, proof against all temptation to go too far too quickly and yet alive to all the possibilities a situation might present and as persistent as fate when his course was set.

The same qualities as a young man had made him a skilful fighter pilot, a highly efficient officer and a good companion. To the end of his days he was "Sholto" to his old associates of two wars, the companion who could play as hard as he worked and could bring to his play the same measure of concentration with the result that it sometimes proceeded to most unusual lengths. Douglas was a wellbuilt man, with a strong chin and sharp eyes, capable of prolonged work and hard to wear down: his relaxations, however fully indulged, put no strain on his powers and served simply to keep his mind fresh.

TOUGH JUDGE

In the service he was at his best in looking squarely at circumstances and devising solutions, whether as staff officer or instructor at staff college or ultimately as commander in chief; in air transport he was equally the maker of policies and the framer of plans to carry them through. In both spheres he trusted his subordinates but was never hoodwinked by them; he was a somewhat tough judge and yet he was no driver; he took great trouble to know his subject and to arrive at realistic conclusions; and he had a sharp if slightly caustic wit with which to enliven and point discussions.

These attributes were invaluable when, as an air vice-marshal in 1938 he had to define in precise terms the characteristics of the bombers that would be needed in the years ahead; when in 1944 as C-in-C. Coastal Command, he had to make sure that the Channel between Dover and Lands End should be sealed against enemy submarines during the operations that led to D-Day; when after the war as military governor of the British zone in Germany, he had to find his way through the mazes of civil administration as well as military occupation; and at last as chairman of B.E.A., when he had to decide what aircraft and what system would best serve the expansion of commercial air transport and how his hesitant competitors in the International Air Transport Association could be persuaded to join him in aiming at low fares to encourage the business of the air lines.

William Sholto Douglas was born on December 23, 1893, the son of Robert Langton Douglas, writer and lecturer on art and sometime Director of the National Gallery of Ireland. He was educated at Tonbridge School and in 1912 won a classical scholarship at Lincoln College, Oxford. He joined the R.F.A. in August, 1914, and by December had transferred to the R.F.C. He qualified first as an observer and later as a pilot. In his first volume of autobiography, *Years of Combat*, he described how he became unit photographer, because he had been interested in cameras at school, and cut a hole in his aircraft's cockpit to take pictures.

FOUGHT GOERING

His flying career was notable. He won the M.C., D.F.C., Croix de Guerre, was wounded and three times mentioned in dispatches. He commanded Nos. 43 and 84 Squadrons and had his share of air fighting. Hermann Goering he met in the air a number of times ("undoubtedly a brave and good fighter pilot", he wrote later). Thirty years later he was to sign Goering's death warrant.

After a year as Chief Pilot of Handley Page Transport. Ltd., which ran services to Paris and Brussels (he held professional pilot's licence No. 4), he returned to the R.A.F. By 1938 he was Assistant Chief of the Air Staff.

During the Second World War, Douglas first took over Fighter Command from Lord Dowding at the end of the Battle of Britain and set in train the expansion and development of the fighter force in readiness for the more varied tasks that were to follow. Next he followed Lord Tedder as A.O.C.-in-C. Middle East and organized the heavy attacks on shipping between Italy and Tunisia, the main supply line serving Rommel's forces in Libya during 1943. At the begining of 1944 he came home to Coastal Command to apply the same technique against German shipping and to continue the Battle of the Atlantic and the approaches against enemy submarines. At the end of the war, he became A.O.C.-in-C. British Air Forces in Germany and supervised the disarmament of the Luftwaffe in the British area. He followed Lord Montgomery in 1946 as commander of British forces in Germany and military governor of the British zone. This, as he later related in *Years of Command*, was not the happiest period of his life and he escaped from it with relief.

He joined the board of B.O.A.C. in 1948 and was withdrawn in March, 1949, to become chairman of B.E.A.

Douglas was made an honorary Fellow of Lincoln College in 1941. In 1964 he became chairman of Horizon Travel, Ltd. He played Rubgy football for Tonbridge and the R.A.F. and rowed for his college.

He was thrice married. First in 1919 to Mary Howard; the marriage was dissolved in 1932. Secondly, in 1933, to Joan Leslie, daughter of Colonel H. C. Denny; the marriage was dissolved in 1954. In 1955 he married Hazel, widow of Captain W. E. R. Walker, by whom he had a daughter.

October 31, 1969.

Admiral the Hon. Sir Cyril E. Douglas-Pennant, K.C.B., C.B.E., D.S.O., who died in London on April 3, 1961, at the age of 60, was a distinguished Staff Officer who was largely concerned in the planning and execution of the landings in North Africa, Sicily and Normandy during the Second World War. He afterwards became the first Commandant of the Joint Services Staff College.

Cyril Eustace Douglas-Pennant, who was born on April 7, 1894, was the eldest son of the fifth Baron Penrhyn, who is 95, and a great-grandson of the first baron. He entered Osborne as a naval cadet in January, 1907, and was the King's medallist of his term on leaving the training cruiser Cumberland in July, 1911. In July, 1914, he was confirmed as sub-lieutenant and appointed to the destroyer Surly. This was the first of five torpedo craft in which he served during the First World War.

He was in the Lizard from November, 1914, second-in-command of the Porpoise and Mystic from October, 1915, and in command of patrol boat P. 37 from April, 1918. The D.S.C. was awarded him in March, 1918, for service in destroyers during the previous year. During 1923 he attended the Army Staff College, Camberley, and in 1924–25 the Naval Staff College, Greenwich.

From October, 1935, he was flag captain and chief staff officer in the Exeter, of the first cruiser squadron in the Eastern Mediterranean, and for a year from October, 1936, commanded the Iron Duke, gunnery training ship at Portsmouth. From 1937 to 1939 he was on the staff of the Naval War College, Greenwich.

INVASION PLANS

Shortly before the Second World War began he became Captain of the Fleet to Vice-Admiral Sir Max Horton, Commanding the Reserve Fleet, and accompanied him to the Northern Patrol. From 1940 to 1942 he commanded the cruiser Despatch and was Commodore in the West Indies. His next appointment was as chief naval staff officer to the G.O.C.-in-C. Home Forces. Later he was chief of staff to Admiral Sir Bertram Ramsay, and took a major part in planning the invasion of North Africa in November, 1942. During the landings in Sicily in July, 1943, he was chief of staff in the Eastern Task Force, and for distinguished service in the planning and execution of these operations was made C.B.E. He returned home early in 1944 to take part in the planning of the invasion of Normandy, in which he commanded one of the naval assault forces and was awarded the D.S.O. On July 7, 1944, he was promoted to rear-admiral. Four months later he was appointed deputy chief of staff to Admiral Mountbatten, Supreme Allied Commander, South-East Asia Command. He was made C.B. in December, 1945.

When the Joint Services Staff College was established at Latimer House, Buckinghamshire, in the autumn of 1946, Douglas-Pennant was selected to be its first commandant, and the successful start of this new institution owed much to him. From December, 1948, to March, 1950, he was Flag Officer (Air) and Second-in-Command in the Mediterranean, in the rank of vice-admiral, to which he had been promoted in July, 1948. From August, 1950, he was appointed Admiral, British Joint Services Mission, Washington, in the acting rank of admiral. He was created K.C.B. in the 1950 New Year honours. He was C.-in-C. The Nore in 1952–53 and retired in the latter year.

He married first, in 1917, Phyllis Constance (who obtained a divorce in 1936), daughter of Colonel Oswald Leigh, and had one daughter. Secondly, in 1937, he married Sheila, second daughter of Stanley Brotherhood, of Thornhaugh Hall, Peterborough.

April 4, 1961.

Air Chief Marshal Lord Dowding, G.C.B., G.C.V.O., C.M.G., victor of the Battle of Britain, died at his home in Kent on February 15, 1970, at the age of 87.

As Chief of Fighter Command from 1936 to 1940, he laid the plans for and directed the Battle of Britain when "the Few" won imperishable glory.

"Stuffy" Dowding, as he was always called—a nickname given him in the artillery though no one quite knew why—had grown up with the R.A.F., but that nickname, "Stuffy", completely belied his gift of charm and accessibility. One writer said of Dowding:—

"Never in history has a commander won so signal a victory and been so little thanked by his country, and even in his own service. Even the barony was belated."

Hugh Caswall Tremenheere, First Baron Dowding of Bentley Priory, in the county of Middlesex, in the peerage of the United Kingdom, was born on April 24, 1882, the eldest child of A. J. C. Dowding. From the successful preparatory school run by his parents at Moffat he followed his father to Winchester, where he was not happy. A distaste for Greek verbs led him to the army class and the Royal Military Academy at Woolwich. Failing to qualify as a sapper, he was gazetted to the Royal Garrison Artillery. He served at Gibraltar, Colombo and Hongkong before obtaining a transfer to the Mountain Artillery and spending six agreeable years in India. After many unsuccessful requests to be allowed to sit for the staff college entrance examination he was granted a year's furlough to prepare for it.

At Camberley in 1912 and 1913 Dowding was struck by the prevailing ignorance of aviation. Attracted by flying and believing that ability to fly would further his career, he qualified for his pilot's certificate on the day of his passing-out from the staff college. After a short course at the newly-formed Central Flying School he applied for transfer to the Royal Flying Corps Reserve and rejoined the garrison artillery.

On the outbreak of war, Dowding was called from his battery to command the camp from which the first squadrons of the Royal Flying Corps left for France. In October, he went to Belgium with No. 6 Squadron, hastily dispatched on the eve of the fall of Antwerp. He served briefly at Royal Flying Corps headquarters in France and was thence posted to No. 9 (Wireless) squadron, where his technical bent stood him in good stead. On the disbandment of the squadron early in 1915 Dowding, who had succeeded to the command, was sent home to form a new unit with the same designation. Later in the year he commanded No. 16 squadron at La Gorgue. Electing to fly as observer on a particularly dangerous mission during the Battle of Loos, he narrowly escaped a forced landing behind the enemy's lines.

In 1916 he served with the administrative wing at Farnborough and afterwards as commander of the ninth wing at the Somme. In the meantime he had the congenial task of putting through its final training the first squadron of Sopwith aircraft armed with guns firing through the airscrew. Command of the ninth wing brought him directly under Trenchard, with whom he had had a disagreement caused by Trenchard's misunderstanding of a technical issue. During the battle Dowding was not convinced that his chief was wise to insist on frequent patrols over the enemy's lines at the cost of heavy casualties. Characteristically, he did not hide his views. His request that one of his squadrons should be relieved was granted, but he was deprived of his command and received no further appointment in France. Employed at home in various capacities, he rose to Brigadier-General and was awarded the C.M.G. for his war services.

On the creation of the Royal Air Force, Dowding was not selected for a commission in the new service. Only after representations from his commanding officer was he granted a temporary attachment, afterwards made permanent. As a Group Commander at Kenley, as Chief of Staff at Headquarters, Inland Area, and afterwards at Baghdad, as Director of Training at the Air Ministry and later in command of Fighting Area at Uxbridge, he found limited scope for exceptional abilities. His chance came in 1929 when he was sent to report on service requirements arising from disturbances in Palestine. His observations on the spot confirmed views already formed by Trenchard, and his report found favour.

From 1930 to 1936 Dowding served on the Air Council as air member successively for supply and research and for research and development. No better choice was ever made. A fearless pilot, Dowding was never an outstanding one. But he had a good grasp of the practical side of airmanship and a rare understanding of the limitations of air power. His period of office saw the emergence of the all-metal monoplane fighter and of radar, whose possibilities he was among the first to recognize. Almost from the start he was keenly interested in the application of radar to night fighting, but he saw that defence against a massive onslaught in daylight must come first. Even had he not lived to win the Battle of Britain his work in the field of technical development would place him high among his country's saviours.

Within a month of his joining the Air Council. Dowding was asked to sanction the issue of a certificate of airworthiness to the ill-fated *R. 101.* His surrender to the insistence of others that the reconstructed ship should leave for India without full trials was a blunder due to inexperience misled by too-hopeful reports from the ship's designers.

In 1936 Dowding was picked for a new post of Air Officer Commanding-in-Chief Fighter Command, with overriding control of all branches of active air defence at home. He held it for more than four years. Passed over for preferment to Chief of the Air Staff in 1937, he was reserved for a more crucial role. In May, 1940, the Government contemplated sending to France a substantial part of his already-depleted force as a gesture of encouragement to the French. His advice that a sacrifice which could not save France would mean defeat for his own country was tendered with an authority no other airman could command. His squadrons were spared to fight the battle for which he had prepared them. A series of setbacks for the Luftwaffe culminated on September 15 in a hard-fought struggle over London which robbed the Germans of all colourable hope of achieving the right conditions for a landing in this country.

Towards the end of the battle Dowding was accused of allowing his squadrons to be used in smaller formations than some critics thought desirable.

At the same time the bombing of Britain after dark brought demands that certain day-fighter squadrons should be relegated to night fighting. He opposed them, predicting that only fighters with airborne radar would master the night bomber. Overruled on several issues, in November he was relieved of a post already held longer than the normal term. In 1941, after a visit to the United States and Canada and the writing of a brilliant report on the Battle of Britain, his name was placed on the retired list. Within a month he was recalled to suggest economies in manpower. He retired in 1942 without attaining the rank of Marshal of the Royal Air Force, then reserved for officers who had held the post of Chief of the Air Staff. Next year he received a barony. From 1937 he was Principal Air Aide-de-Camp to King George VI.

There was controversy surrounding Dowding's removal as chief of Fighter Command. Some of his admirers said it was because he had dared to question Whitehall. In 1957, the controversy was revived by the publication of Dowding's authorized biography, *Leader of the Few*, by Basil Collier, whom Dowding had helped to write the book.

"To many members of the public", Collier wrote, "Dowding's removal from his post immediately after he had won, brilliantly, a hard-fought battle, seemed an act of almost monstrous folly and ingratitude".

More recently, there has been renewed controversy over Dowding's dismissal from his command in the second week of November, 1940, just after the Battle of Britain. He should, it was suggested, have been promoted to the most senior rank of Marshal of the Royal Air Force, which would almost have doubled his income. Lord Balfour of Inchrye, wartime Under-Secretary of State for Air, pioneered a campaign pressing for Dowding's much-belated promotion to Marshal of the R.A.F. He denied that he connived to get rid of Dowding, and said that he "yielded second place to none" in his admiration of the Air Chief Marshal.

In January, 1970, Marshal of the R.A.F. Sir John Slessor, in a letter to The Times, called into question a passage in Robert Wright's book, *Dowding and the Battle of Britain*, about the removal of Dowding from his command.

Slessor referred to "the allegation attributed to Lord Dowding that just after the real Battle of Britain had been won, in the second week of November, 1940, he was summarily—and by implication unexpectedly—dismissed from his command in the course of a sudden and very brief telephone conversation by the Secretary of State for Air, Sir Archibald Sinclair (now Lord Thurso)".

While placing himself "among the many who think he was shabbily treated at the end of the Battle of Britain", Slessor suggested "that in connexion with this event, it is not impossible that Lord Dowding's memory may have let him down". Slessor stated he had consulted a number of people in recent months associated with the events in 1940, and all agreed that it was incredible that Sir Archibald Sinclair could have acted in the manner described.

Dowding wrote to The Times in reply saying that there was no "mystery" about the manner in which he was relieved of his command. In a matter as grave as that, the record of what he remembered could not fail him. But on January 20, A. J. P. Taylor wrote revealing a document indicating that Sir Archibald Sinclair had indeed met Dowding and not dismissed him on the telephone.

In September 1969, Dowding, confined to a wheelchair because of arthritis, received a standing ovation to a trumpet fanfare at the premiere of the film, *Battle of Britain*. He took his place in the stalls among 350 of the pilots he had once commanded.

After his retirement Dowding became keenly interested in spiritualism, a subject which had long dwelt in the background of his mind. A confident speaker and a lucid writer, he did much selfless work for the spiritualist movement and wrote many books and articles, mostly on occult subjects. He was also interested in animal welfare and advocated strict control of vivisection. A keen shot, he gave up field sports and became a vegetarian. In his prime he was a skier of international standing and an enthusiastic polo player.

His first marriage in 1918 to Clarice Maud, daughter of Captain John Williams, was cruelly cut short by her death in 1920. His second marriage in 1951 to Muriel, widow of Pilot Officer Maxwell Whiting, who shared his interests brought him great happiness.

To intimates Dowding revealed himself as an affectionate and kindly figure for whom no effort on behalf of those in need of help was too much trouble. In his official dealings he was not an easy man. To him slackness, hypocrisy and self-seeking were not peccadilloes but scarlet sins. During his service career he was sometimes impatient with colleagues and subordinates whom he suspected of adopting standards lower than his own. In later years he radiated loving-kindness redeemed from mawkishness by a sense of fun and an undimmed eye for human foibles. As a public servant no man deserved better of his country. Thousands who never knew him as a public servant will mourn him as a servant of mankind.

February 16, 1970.

Lynn Doyle, by which name Leslie Alexander Montgomery was better known, died on August 13, 1961, in Dublin.

He belonged to a distinguished generation of Ulster writers and artists who flourished in the early days of the Irish literary renaissance but whose fame has been obscured by the great reputation of contemporaries whose work is associated with the greener side of the Border. By any normal standards Forrest Reid, the Henrys, Lynds, Morrows, Waddells, and St. John Ervine were a remarkable generation.

Born in Downpatrick in 1873 he was educated in Dundalk and spent most of his life in the service of The Northern Banking Company Ltd. Unlike another literary banker—Kenneth Grahame—who sought in his writing to escape from the intransigence of double-entry, Lynn Doyle did not complain about the fate that chained him to an office desk. He was a genial and sensible man whose pawky humour (more Scottish than Irish) owed some of its effectiveness to an inexhaustible interest in the workaday world; and he made full use of the opportunities that a bank manager is given to study human character in its guarded and unguarded moments.

Ballygullion, a collection of short stories, published by the Talbot Press in Dublin in 1908, won its author an affectionate public which, despite changes in taste, he never lost. Later volumes, novels as well as short stories, published by Duckworth, appeared at regular intervals until a few years ago. The author once confessed that his dearest wish was to write a successful play—he had grown up in the shadow of the Abbey Theatre and the no less vigorous, if shorter lived, Ulster Theatre—but he never realized his ambition. Plot-making was not his forte; even his novels hardly show Lynn Doyle at his best. It is as a portrayer of the northern Irish character in his sketches and short stories that Lynn Doyle will be best remembered. He had a gift of homely metaphor and quaint but authentic phrase.

In his heyday he contributed regularly to English and American magazines. He published verses and essays which won the admiration of Stephen Gwynn, a friend with whose taste in wine and letters he was in perfect sympathy. His friend Paul Henry illustrated *The Spirit of Ireland*, a travel book, written when Lynn Doyle had retired from the bank to live in Malahide. On the beautiful island golf-links he was a conspicuous and popular figure, but as a golfer more a menace to himself than to his opponents (his putter never rivalled his pen). Keeping free from all controversy, his literary personality was in some ways similar to Mark Twain's. But Lynn Doyle would have been the last to press that comparison unduly.

In later life he took an active part in P.E.N. activities and became chairman of the Dublin branch. In December, 1936, he joined the Irish Board of Literary Censors but found the work uncongenial and he disapproved of the method by which that body discharged its functions. He resigned two months later.

He married Winifred Ratcliffe in 1902.

August 14, 1961.

Harley Drayton, a commanding figure in the City, died on April 7, 1966, in London at the age of 64.

Drayton had started in the world of investment trusts and investment banking but as the years passed his interests included newspapers and commercial television. For a great many years he remained an enigma, even to many of his close friends. He talked little about his background and his early days, and it was more by chance than plan that through the buying, on his behalf, of books at an historic sale at Christie's, he was revealed as a great collector and bibliophile, as well as a connoisseur of pictures. Mr. Angus Ogilvy was a director of many of Drayton's companies.

Drayton was a man of great perspicacity, able to seize at once the essential point of a financial or industrial argument. In controlling the ramifications of his business empire he was greatly helped by his gift for picking those to whom to delegate authority. He was the sponsor of the Garda Trust Company Ltd., launched in 1963 to provide extra incentives for high executives in major companies, which has been much in the news.

Harley (Harold Charles) Drayton was born in 1901 and left school at 15 to join the staff of Government Stock and Other Securities Investment Co. at a pound a week. The head of the undertaking then was the Hon. John Wynford Philipps, later Viscount St. Davids, and he had the great fortune to become associated with J. S. Austen who founded and developed great electrical and transport enterprises, after Government Stock had in 1920 acquired the British Electric Traction Co. Drayton was always handsome in acknowledging his indebtedness to Austen, many of whose attributes, as well as his business assets, he inherited upon Austen's death. One of the most important factors in Drayton's early experience was the work he was put to do in connexion with B.E.T., which was then operating tramways and electric light undertakings. The new owners at once proceeded to sell the trams and buses in the British cities and towns, and much of the detail was left to him.

With what success the company and Drayton achieved this purpose may be gauged from the fact that within a good quarter of a century the group was operating over 10,000 vehicles. Within another 10 to 15 years the number had increased to 14,000 and its bus interests were spread also over Canada, Africa, the West Indies, and other countries. In the meantime Harley Drayton, as he was generally known, had become a dominating figure in the operations of the company and in B.E.T. as well as in the various undertakings which they were absorbing.

TELEVISION SUCCESS

After the ending of hostilities in 1945 there was a further reorganization of the undertakings and their management structure, with Drayton as chairman both of B.E.T. and of the extensive investment trust companies and some half-dozen of his colleagues in directorial and chief executive positions. There was, however, something quite homogeneous about the organization, as indicated by the fact that from then onwards it became known as "the Drayton group", with the well-known headquarters in Old Broad Street as the nerve centre.

He was not infrequently criticized in the City, by friends and sometimes colleagues and associates, for the support he brought, moral and financial, to small and little-known undertakings in need of capital for expansion; in fact Drayton was rarely wrong. A striking illustration was the provision by his group in 1956 of funds for commercial television and its offshoot, Associated Rediffusion, which, after showing majestic losses, proceeded to make within a couple of years profits of more than £5m. This was, in the public mind, a success for Drayton even more striking than when, soon after the Second World War, he overcame the Clan Line in their tussle over the ownership and control of the Union-Castle undertaking, but no deal in which he engaged ever paralleled his sale of the Argentine Railways, owned mainly in the United Kingdom, for £150m. after protracted negotiations, to decide the fate of this somewhat ill-starred company.

Through his long connexion with the British Electric Traction Company he became almost automatically chairman or director of a score or more industrial and commercial undertakings, their interests ranging from nitrates to newspapers, finance and films, banking and building. He became chairman of most of these undertakings, including the Antofagasta (Chile) and Bolivia Railway Co., the British Lion Film Corporation, the Electrical and Industrial Investment Co., the English and International Trust, the Argus Press, the Argus Press Holdings, Provincial Newspapers, and United Newspapers. He had also been on the boards of the Midland Bank, the Midland Bank Executor and Trustee Co. and the Philip Hill Investment Trust.

NEWSPAPER INTERESTS

It was characteristic of Harley Drayton that in spite of all these manifold responsibilities there were some enterprises which attracted and held his interest and attention more than others. He was particularly concerned with the newspaper enterprises which he directed, and from time to time he would make a tour of the headquarters of all the nearly three score of them. He certainly scanned, if not read, every one of them, daily or weekly, and was familiar with managers and editors throughout the provinces. He became equally absorbed in the technique of television long before his company began to enjoy the fabulous profits derived from Associated Rediffusion, and he never lost sight of the human element and its value, both in commercial and in personal experience.

Apart from the City, and life at his country home, Plumton Hall, near Bury St. Edmunds, in Suffolk, where he farmed expertly 700 acres, and liked shooting and fishing, his personal interests were restricted to literature, book collecting, and the acquisition of pictures. He was, however, also a great student of bird life, and his vast collection of books, including a discriminating selection of illuminated manuscripts and first editions, had a large section of works on ornithology. It was characteristic of him, at any rate judging from his fine build and florid appearance, which suggested the typical Englishman of the countryside, that he was particularly fond of collecting books about the English scene and its people. He had a first edition of Defoe's *Robinson Crusoe*, and most of the first editions of writers like Arnold Bennett and W. H. Hudson, and in the summer of 1958 he paid £1,600, in heavy bidding against American buyers, for the Rudyard Kipling papers when they were offered at Christie's. Indoors his recreation was music, and he played the piano well. He was High Sheriff of Suffolk in 1957.

He was married, but had no family.

April 9, 1966.

Sir Matthew Drysdale died at his London home on July 30, 1962, at the age of 69.

By his death Lloyd's lost one of its most distinguished members, who was elected chairman on no fewer than six occasions and to whom more than any other man was due the far-seeing decision to move to the building in Lime Street which is Lloyd's present home.

Born on November 27, 1892, the son of Thomas and Janet Drysdale of Montrose, Matthew Watt Drysdale was educated at the Stationers Company's School and went to Lloyd's in 1908 when he joined the staff of the foremost pioneer in non-marine underwriting at Lloyd's, Cuthbert Heath.

He served throughout the 1914-18 War with the 9th Northumberland Fusiliers and afterwards went back to Lloyd's and continued his association with Heath until 1922, when he left to start a new venture with C. T. Bowring and Company. As non-marine underwriter to the Bowring syndicate he was outstandingly successful until his retirement from the underwriting chair in 1957. Sir Matthew was very proud of the fact that he was trained under two of Lloyd's most distinguished men, Cuthbert Heath and Sir Walter Hargreaves, and he freely acknowledged how much he owed to them.

He became an underwriting member in 1919 and was elected to the committee of Lloyd's in 1939. He served continuously on the committee until 1957 with the exception of the breaks of one year between each four-year term of office and was made deputy chairman in 1947. In 1949 he was elected chairman and was re-elected in 1950, 1951, and 1952 and again in 1955 and 1956. He was awarded Lloyd's gold medal for outstanding services to Lloyd's in 1952. It was soon after being elected chairman in 1949 that steps were taken to acquire the site in Lime Street on which Lloyd's new building was to be erected. The foundation stone was laid by her Majesty the Queen during his chairmanship.

Matthew Drysdale was a very human man and an inspiration to the young men of Lloyd's for whom he had a great admiration and affection. He was an accomplished after-dinner speaker, with a very keen sense of humour which led to his receiving many requests for his presence. He was a keen, though not particularly skilful golfer and he enjoyed his membership of the New Zealand Golf Club and his golfing holidays with his friends at Nairn, a favourite resort of his, which he had visited annually for many years.

He was knighted in 1953.

In 1928 he married Nesta, daughter of Hugh Lewis. She survives him with their three sons.

July 31, 1962.

William Dubilier, one of the early pioneers in wireless telegraphy, educated at the Cooper Union Institute, New York, and a friend of Thomas Edison, died at the age of 81 on July 25, 1969, in Palm Beach, Florida.

Dubilier was the holder of several hundred patents. Before the First World War, he invented the mica capacitor which replaced the glass Leyden jar. He had the full support of the British Admiralty for this invention which proved of great importance particularly where wireless communications were in close proximity to heavy guns on battleships, the recoil and blast of which would cause the glass in the Leyden jars to break, and the only satisfactory source of supply was made in Germany.

Dubilier demonstrated the mica condenser in 1913 before the British War Office Wireless Committee; two years later he established the position for his device which has many advantages. It is not fragile, like the Leyden jar, and it avoids the generation of ozone which was inseparable from the jar; it is small and compact, and it is eminently simple. Dubilier later produced an apparatus for locating submarines, and it was adopted by the British and the French in 1916. He devised and invented radio installations for aeroplane use by the British and the Americans.

Besides making important contributions to communication systems, Dubilier was a man of foresight. Shortly after Hitler came to power in the 1930s, he held a press conference in London during which he disclosed the extent of German re-armament based on what he had seen in Germany, and information he received from enemies of the regime.

In 1912, with the help of British businessmen, the Dubilier Company was formed, now still in business as the Dubilier Condenser Company (1925) Limited. He was the holder of many honorary degrees and honours; and was decorated by the United States Government for his contribution to science.

July 30, 1969.

Dr. W. E. B. Du Bois, the Negro philosopher and writer, died in Accra, Ghana, on August 27, 1963. He was 95.

Du Bois, who was born in the United States of Negro, French Huguenot and Dutch descent, spent nearly all his working life in the United States, where he was one of the founders of the National Association for the Advancement of Coloured People and for many years one of the major, if controversial, leaders of Negro thought and philosophy.

In his later years he became frustrated with

the attitudes of both Democrat and Republican parties towards the Negro, and moved towards the Communist Party, finally joining the party in 1961 at the age of 93.

His activities in left-wing affairs before this had led him into difficulties with the United States Government. In 1951 he was indicted, along with other officers of an organization called The Peace Information Centre, in New York, for failing to register as a foreign agent. He was acquitted, but the trial added to his despair of his native country and soon afterwards he began a long series of visits abroad mostly to countries behind the iron curtain.

In 1960, however, he went to live in Ghana to work on an *Encyclopaedia Africana*. In 1963, the year he died, Ghana citizenship was conferred on him. This was a fitting honour for a man who had played a leading role in the development of Pan-Africanism and who enjoyed the trust and friendship of President Kwame Nkrumah.

Du Bois's efforts in the Pan-African cause—and incidentally Dr. Nkrumah has stated that Du Bois and Henry Sylvester-Williams of Trinidad were the first to use the term itself—reached their high point in 1945. At the Pan-African Congress held that year in Manchester, Du Bois played an important part as joint-chairman and chairman of the working committee, and also as the drafter of one of the two major declarations of the Congress. Dr. Nkrumah, who was general secretary of the committee, and Mr. Jomo Kenyatta were also leading figures at this conference which must be seen, in retrospect, as a milestone in the rapid post-war political development of Africa.

THESIS ON SLAVES' FREEDOM

Du Bois had first adopted the cause of Pan-Africanism at the London conference of 1900, the first of its kind. It was on this occasion that he made the often-quoted comment: "The problem of the twentieth century is the problem of the colour line—the relation of the darker to the lighter races of men in Asia and Africa, in America and the islands of the sea."

For at least the first quarter of this century Du Bois, the intellectual of the movement, and Marcus Aurelius Garvey, the demagogue, were the dominant figures of Pan-Africanism. Opposed personally as they were to each other, and differing in many essentials of policy, they were also unlike in temperament: Garvey a rumbustious personality; Du Bois immensely sensitive to indignities.

William Edward Burghardt Du Bois was born in Massachusetts in 1868 one of 50 Negroes in a provincial town of 5,000 inhabitants. In his autobiography, *Dusk at Dawn*, he wrote that he was born "with a flood of Negro blood, a strain of French, a bit of Dutch but, thank God, no Anglo-Saxon".

In 1888 he went to Harvard where he won a doctorate of philosophy with a thesis on the suppression of the African slave trade to the United States, which eventually became the first volume published in the Harvard historical series.

After leaving Harvard he taught successively at the Universities of Wilberforce, Pennsylvania and Atlanta, resigning from the last in 1909 to become one of the founder members of the National Association for the Advancement of Coloured People and the editor of its publication, *The Crisis*. But about this time he found himself in conflict with the philosophy of Booker T. Washington, the Negro educator who had argued that the Negro should raise his own status by pulling himself up by his bootstraps, and particularly by training for industry. Du Bois believed that a "talented tenth" of the American Negro population would be enough to lead a self-sufficient Negro society in the country.

VIVID WRITING

His strongly held opinions brought him into conflict with his colleagues in the N.A.A.C.P., and in 1934 he resigned from the editorship of *The Crisis* and from the N.A.A.C.P. For 10 years he worked again at Atlanta University, then returned to the N.A.A.C.P., for a short while before resigning once more, and this time for good, over another disagreement.

In 1945 he was consultant to the United Nations upon its formation in San Francisco and head of the council of African affairs.

In 1950 Du Bois ran unsuccessfully for the United States Senate as candidate for the American Labour Party. In 1959, shortly before he applied to join the Communist Party, he was awarded the Lenin Peace Prize.

Much of his writing remains vivid and alive, particularly *The Souls of Black Folk*, which was published in 1902 and which Henry James later described as "the only southern book of any distinction published for many a year".

He married in 1896 Nina Gomer, who died in 1950, and secondly Shirley Graham, who survives him.

August 29, 1963.

Marcel Duchamp, who died on October 1, 1968, at the age of 81, was one of the seminal figures in the history of modern art. He was the last survivor of three remarkable brothers. The other two were the sculptor Duchamp Villon, gassed in the First World War, and the painter Jacques Villon, who survived into 1963. But Marcel Duchamp will probably be considered the most remarkable of the three.

The first art movement with which he was associated was the Section d'Or, which held its first exhibition in 1912. Among the members of the group were Juan Gris, Ticabia, Herbin, Metzinger, and Gleizes. The Section d'Or was subject to both Cubist and Futurist influences as can be seen from Duchamp's best known work of this period, the Nude Descending Staircase, which was the sensation of the Armory Show—the huge exhibition which introduced New Yorkers to modern art in 1913.

But Duchamp was not destined to make his reputation as a painter. He was, rather, a provocateur of an extremely special and valuable kind. He was the true father of Dadaism, and deserves, if anyone does, the credit for having the concept of "anti-art". He was already manufacturing dada objects as early as 1913, or, rather, he did not manufacture them, he simply chose them. The generic name he bestowed on these objects was that of "ready-mades". He was quite clear about what he wanted to achieve. He remarked: "The point that I very much want to establish is that the choice of these "ready mades" was never dictated by aesthetic delectation. The choice was based on the reaction of visual indifference with a total absence of good or bad taste . . . in fact a complete anaesthesia".

In fact, after 1915, when he settled in New York, Duchamp set himself the task of questioning all values. The veteran Dadaist, Hans Richter, said of him that he "reversed the sign-posts of values so that they all pointed to the void."

INVENTED THE MOBILE

Not unnaturally, his activities often caused a considerable scandal. Perhaps the most famous of these incidents was on the occasion when Duchamp submitted an ordinary porcelain urinal to the First New York Salons des Independants, signing it "R. Mutt"—the name of a firm of sanitary engineers. It was duly rejected. Duchamp pointed to the fact that this was supposed to be an independent exhibition, and ostentatiously resigned from the jury of which he was a member.

For a man whose philosophy of art was so negative Duchamp achieved a remarkable number of discoveries. Besides his interest in irony—an irony which was to crop up again and again in successive generations of modern artists—he achieved a new attitude towards the objects, which was endowed, through his procedures, with a personality of its own which has continued to haunt us. Of all modern artists Duchamp was the one who penetrated most deeply into the environment, who made the ordinary world look suddenly rare and strange. A further interest was in the idea of movement, which led him to the invention of the mobile. Duchamp was one of the pioneers of kinetic art.

It was inevitable that Duchamp should gradually move away from art, holding the ideas he did. His last major work, the "Large Glass" also known as "The Bride Stripped Bare by her Bachelors Even", occupied him from 1915 to 1923 and was a farewell to even the pretence of conventional art-activity. He remained, an influential—if smilingly detached—figure in the world of modern art. His real passion, however, was chess. He tended to disapprove of the activities of the post-war neo-Dadaists who invoked his name, saying of them: "I thought to discourage aesthetics. In neo-Dada they have taken my ready-mades and found aesthetic beauty in them."

October 3, 1968.

Roland Dudley, a pioneer of mechanized agriculture in Britain, died at his home at Linkenholt Manor, Hampshire, on July 29, 1964, at the age of 85.

Dudley was born at Gretton, near Kettering; was educated at Wellingborough; and was trained to become—and became—an engineer. He pursued that profession with distinction and profit for more than 20 years; and in 1924 he bought Linkenholt, a 1,500-acre estate, to give his family a rural background.

Four years later the tenant of the land died. Dudley, new to farming, took it in hand and applied to it his thorough—some said ruthless—approach to a challenging problem, and his mechanical instinct. At once he established himself as a pioneer—perhaps the pioneer—of mechanized agriculture in Britain.

At a time when combine harvesters had been heard of, but not used, in Britain he imported one from the States. He designed and had built one of the first grain driers. He mechanized every agricultural process he could mechanize. He tested and then applied the then new "chemical fertilizers" in large quantities. He did, a generation ago, what every progressive farmer on wide arable acres is doing today.

A friend told him in these early days that the most miserable end he could imagine would be to hang on Coombe gibbet near by and face the desolation of the stockless, mechanized Linkenholt. That, then, was the popular reaction.

As with all pioneers—and Dudley remained one to his death—he saw his work pass through the phases of popular bewilderment, criticism, and slowly growing approval, to become nearly a commonplace. Not that he ever cared what anyone thought. He had a strength of character, an individualism, that belied his urban, industrial background. He was, outwardly, an explosive eighteenth century Improving squire with twentieth century ideas; and, inwardly, a most kindly and lovable man.

He leaves one daughter. He lost his wife in 1951, one son was killed in the war, another died at school.

July 31, 1964.

Sir James Duff, former Vice-Chancellor of Durham University and former vice-chairman of the B.B.C., died on April 24, 1970, at the age of 72.

He gave notable service to the departments of education of the University of Manchester and of the former Armstrong College, Newcastle upon Tyne, to newer universities at home and to others overseas, and to the B.B.C. as a Governor. But his principal accomplishment was in diversifying the range of studies and increasing the growth of the Durham Colleges of the University of Durham, of which he was warden from 1937 to 1960. He worked closely with the Rector of King's College, Newcastle (not then a separate university), alternating with him as Vice-Chancellor of Durham University.

James Fitzjames Duff was born on February 1, 1898, the second son of J. D. Duff, Fellow of Trinity College, Cambridge. From Winchester, where he was head of the school, he joined the Royal Flying Corps, in which he served from 1916 to 1917. He went up with an open scholarship to his father's college at Cambridge, where he took a first in the classical tripos in 1920 and a second in the economics tripos in 1921.

His first university post was as assistant lecturer in Classics at Manchester, but in the following year, 1922, he moved on to Armstrong College, Newcastle, as lecturer in Education, breaking off for a while in 1925 to be educational superintendent of Northumberland County Council.

When Duff moved back to Manchester in 1927 as second-in-command of the Education Department, he made an immediate impression as a happy blend of Oxbridge and Redbrick.

STRENGTH FOR SENATE

His succession in 1932 to the headship of the department as Sarah Fielden Professor was obvious and unquestioned. He showed himself a humane and sympathetic chief, easily accessible to students and junior colleagues; and he was a friendly and welcome guest in schools throughout the area. Carrying his learning lightly, he was the very reverse of crabbed, pedantic or ponderous. He was a brilliantly successful Public Orator, and he soon became a force in Senate.

By 1935 it had become apparent that the legal and administrative structure of the University of Durham, as embodied in the Act of 1908, needed considerable amendment. A new Act, the University of Durham Act of 1935, brought the constitution up to date. It retained the federal organization in which the present Universities of Newcastle and of Durham were then combined: one university having two divisions. Each division was given a head or principal, and in Durham an old title, that of Warden, was revived. Duff took office in 1937 as the first Warden under the new constitution.

The empire he took over was a curious one—efficient in that dons were prepared to combine university administrative offices with their learning, but run chiefly by amateur skill.

UNPOPULAR MOVES

The substitution of professionals and the elimination of multiple offices earned the new Warden some unpopularity, but made later expansion possible. Duff saw clearly that effectiveness as a university could be achieved best by increasing the range of studies rather than by deliberately fostering the growth of existing departments; that growth would follow diversification.

He also saw clearly that in the other side of the university's activity—the colleges—improvement was to be sought by increasing the numbers in individual colleges. In a decade when local opinion thought the ideal size of a college to be not more than 100 members he steadily pressed towards about 300.

While still at Durham, Duff was appointed in August, 1959, to be a Governor of the B.B.C. until the end of the then current period of its charter, June, 1962. To consider the renewal of the charter, a Government Committee was appointed in July, 1960. In the same month, Duff was chosen to succeed Sir Philip Morris as vice-chairman of the B.B.C.'s Board of Governors.

His task and that of the whole board was to be an unusually heavy one, for in addition to their normal duties, the board of 1960 had the responsibility of considering and authorizing the submissions on the corporation's behalf to the Pilkington Committee. This onerous work told on the health of the chairman, Sir Arthur fforde, and Duff found himself called on more and more to deputize for fforde during lengthening periods of illlness.

The committee issued its report in June, 1962; Duff's appointment was renewed until July, 1964. The B.B.C.'s charter had been extended until this date to allow time to consider the committee's recommendations.

In January, 1964, fforde resigned because of ill health, and Duff was appointed chairman "for the time being". In May, 1964, Lord Normanbrook became the B.B.C.'s chairman and Duff once more was appointed vice-chairman until July, 1965.

Duff spared time to travel in the interests of education overseas. He was a member of the Asquith Commission on Colonial Higher Education, 1943–45, of the Elliot Commission on Higher Education in West Africa, 1943–45, of the Government of India's Universities Commission, 1948–49, and was a member of the Council and Chairman of the Academic Advisory Committee of the University of Sussex.

University and local affairs were brought closer together by his being mayor of Durham from 1959 to 1960, and Lord Lieutenant of the county. He was knighted in 1949.

April 27, 1970.

Georges Duhamel, the French writer, a member of the French Academy and a winner of the Prix Goncourt, died at his country home at Valmondois, near Paris, on April 13, 1966. He was 81.

Georges Duhamel was born in Paris on June 30, 1884, the seventh of a family of eight children. His father was a man of modest beginnings who qualified late in life as a doctor. It was through him that Duhamel discovered the vocation for medicine which was to give his literary productions their particular quality.

His studies were pursued with some difficulty. In his early twenties, he also took part in the foundation of the community of young poets known as the group of the Abbaye, because it met in a former abbey at Créteil, on the Marne. They wished to associate manual work with intellectual activities, and in June, 1906, they set up a printing and publishing enterprise. Duhamel's first volume of poetry and *La Vie Unanime*, of Jules Romains, were among the publications. The venture lasted precariously for 18 months, when the lack of commercial success brought it to an end. The story of their vicissitudes, and of their hopes and aspirations, provided Duhamel with material for *Le Desert de Vievres*, one of the Pasquier novels. The members, in addition to Duhamel and Jules Romains, included Charles Vildrac and Luc Durtain. It was at the same time that he developed his taste for music—he was a good flautist and also a cellist—and formed a trio with other friends, the painter

Vlaminck, who played the violin, and Albert Doyen, who played the piano.

AT THE FRONT

It was at the Abbaye that Duhamel met his wife, Mademoiselle Blanche Albane-Sistoli, then an actress. They were married in 1909. He qualified as a doctor in the same year. From then until 1914, he was engaged in scientific research, and in the writing of several collections of poetry, together with literary criticism, notably a study of Paul Claudel. He became responsible for the criticism of poetry in the *Mercure de France*, which he later edited for many years. Several plays were also produced in this period: *La Lumière*, *Dans l'ombre des statues*, *L'école des athletes* and *Le Combat*. They were not outstandingly successful, and Duhamel decided that his true bent lay in other directions.

The 1914–18 War was a turning point in his development, and Duhamel could say accurately: "je suis né de la guerre." Having volunteered as a surgeon he spent 50 months at the front, where his close acquaintance with human suffering and endurance made a lasting impression upon him. His observations were movingly recorded in two books: *La Vie des Martyrs*, 1916, and *Civilisation*, 1917, which was awarded the Prix Goncourt in 1918.

These books, with several others inspired by his war experiences, established Duhamel as a writer. Apart from a wide range of literary activities, his energy found expression in many varied interests, particularly in music and in constant travel. His journeys were, in later years, often made as the representative of the Academy.

TRAGI-COMIC FIGURE

They took him to the United States, Brazil, Indo-China, Russia, Egypt, and other parts of Africa, confirmed him in his outlook as a western European: he was averse to standardization and to the dominance of the modern state over the lives of individuals. His travel books included *Le Voyage de Moscou*, *Géographie cordiale de l'Europe*, and *Scènes de la vie future*, a critical valuation of the American way of life, for which he was granted a special prize by the Académie Française in 1930.

Duhamel had the distinction of creating an unforgettable character in Salavin, who was portrayed in five of his novels. The first of these, *La Confession de Minuit*, appeared in 1920. He showed much psychological insight in the delineation of this tragi-comic figure, with his idiosyncrasies, his frustrations, and his painful struggles towards self-realization and self-acceptance. These novels were followed by the volumes of the *Chronique des Pasquier*, beginning with *Le Notaire du Havre* in 1933; *La Passion de Joseph Pasquier* appeared in 1945. In this cycle Duhamel related the history of a French lower middle-class family from the nineteenth century onwards; and it is no secret to say that the family was the one in which he was brought up, and, later, the family which he himself created. The sympathetic observation of human nature, the blend of sentiment and humour, and the easy, apparently effortless quality of the style, were features which made these stories widely appreciated.

During the German occupation of France Duhamel resumed his original profession of a doctor, as he had done during the 1914–18 War, and maintained a courageous and dignified attitude. As the Germans approached Paris he was asked whether he was going to leave, and he replied: "No, I shall stay. I am occupying France, too". His services were recognized after the Liberation by his election as president of the *Comité National des Écrivains*. He later resigned from this organization, feeling that its programme of purification was being pursued with too much severity: Duhamel was anxious that retribution should not be allowed to become merely vindictive. His experiences during the years of occupation were reflected in *Chronique des saisons amères*, and *Lieu d'asile*, 1944.

Duhamel continued writing into his old age. His later works included a five-volume autobiography, *Lumière sur ma vie* and books on Japan, Turkey, and Israel.

Duhamel was elected a member of the French Academy in 1935, and soon became its *secrétaire perpétuel*. He resigned the post in February, 1946, believing that sufficient regard was not being given to the claims of younger men in the elections to the ranks of the Immortals; but he remained a member of the Academy. He was a well known lecturer, and a contributor to a number of periodicals, especially *Le Figaro*, in addition to the *Mercure de France* of which he was so long the editor.

April 14, 1966.

Sir Paul Dukes, K.B.E., who died in Cape Town on August 27, 1967, was given a secret mission to Russia during 1918–19. It is related in full in *The Story of "S T 25"*, an epic of excitement and adventure.

Paul Dukes was born on February 10, 1889, the son of the Rev. E. J. and Edith Mary Dukes.

Drawn to the study of music, he arrived in Russia in 1909 with the intention of furthering his studies. After having supported himself in the years before the outbreak of the First World War by giving English lessons, he lived during the early part of the war in Leningrad, attached to the Marinsky Theatre and studying under Albert Coates.

A member of the Anglo-Russian Commission from 1915 to 1918, Dukes carried the passport of a King's Messenger for the first six months of 1918, charged with a roving commission of investigation in European Russia.

He received a telegram recalling him to London, and as a result was in Archangel in the summer, cultivating a beard and training for the journey on foot to Leningrad.

Fortunately, that somewhat rash scheme was abandoned. Instead, it was a person speaking perfectly good Russian and with the good Ukrainian name of Afirenko, carrying a Russian passport which showed him to be no other than an agent of the Cheka, who slipped into Leningrad one autumn night across the Finnish frontier.

From November, 1918, until September, 1919, Dukes remained in Russia, constantly changing his name and his quarters, sending out reports on general conditions amid the turmoil of the revolution for as long as he possibly could.

His luck held marvellously, though on different occasions he found it expedient to join the Red Army, even the Communist Party itself, and to simulate fits of epilepsy.

FULL STORY

Finally, when it became clear that the prospect of being able to send out further reports had vanished, Dukes smuggled himself out of Russia across the Estonian border.

In a series of articles which he contributed to *The Times* at the end of 1919 he described some of his experiences and general conclusions. Not unnaturally, Dukes did not then expect the Bolshevik regime to survive.

A further, though still very cautious account of the whole remarkable adventure appeared in 1922 under the title of *Red Dusk and the Morrow*. Dukes was understandably anxious on this occasion to make it plain that he had gone to Russia to investigate and report on conditions generally, and not, as the Bolsheviks charged, to foment counter-revolutionary plots and conspiracies.

Not until 1938 did the full story, told with unaffected modesty and discretion, appear in *The Story of "S T 25"*, later republished as *Secret Agent S T 25*.

Dukes, who lectured frequently on Russia, had another and slighter spell of odd adventure in 1939, this time in Nazi Germany. He was asked to investigate the disappearance of a Czeckoslovak industrialist on the way from Prague to Switzerland. Murder at German hands was suspected, and the suspicion was virtually confirmed by the time Dukes left Germany—on September 2, 1939.

In his account of the strange and complex affair, *An Epic of the Gestapo*, he laid repeated emphasis on the likeness, as he saw it, of Soviet and Nazi methods.

Dukes, who was made K.B.E. in 1920, married in 1922 Mrs. Ogden Mills, who was the daughter of Mrs. W. K. Vanderbilt, of New York.

The marriage was dissolved in 1929. In 1959 he married Diana Fitzgerald.

August 28, 1967.

Allen Dulles, former head of the United States Central Intelligence Agency, died on January 29, 1969, in Washington. He was 75. He headed the C.I.A. from 1953 to 1961—and retired a few months after the Cuban Bay of Pigs fiasco which the C.I.A. planned. In 1963 President Johnson appointed him a member of the Warren Commission which inquired into the assassination of President Kennedy.

Allen Welsh Dulles was born in Watertown, New York, on April 7, 1893, one of a pair of remarkable brothers who dominated the administration and formulation of American foreign policy in the nineteen-fifties.

His father was a Presbyterian minister of some standing, his maternal grandfather

Secretary of State under President Harrison. As a child he was precocious, first making his mark at the age of eight when he published *The Boer War*, a ferociously anti-British tract which received favourable review in the *New York Times*.

Graduating from Princeton with a Phi Beta Kappa and an M.A. in 1916, after interrupting his studies to teach for eight months in a missionary school at Allahabad, in India, he joined the United States Foreign Service the same year, serving in Vienna and Berne, where he missed meeting Lenin and first formed a taste for secret intrigue, through his involvement at a junior level in the secret peace negotiations with representatives of Austro-Hungary. Thereafter he served on the clerical side of the United States delegation at the Conference of Versailles, rising after service in the American missions in Berlin and Istanbul to be Chief of the Near Eastern Division of the State Department in 1922.

In 1926 he left the State Department to join the famous New York law firm of Sullivan and Cromwell, after obtaining a legal degree from George Washington University. He still retained his connexion with the Department of State, however, serving as legal adviser to the American delegations to the Geneva Naval Disarmament Conference of 1927 and the World Disarmament Conference in 1932-33.

BUILT UP NETWORK

It is an ironic comment on his sense of political realities and his future career that the more chauvinistic members of the American delegation of 1927 suspected him of being in British pay at the time. Always a staunch Republican by upbringing he played no political part during the first two administratons of Franklin Roosevelt. But in 1942, after the American entry into the Second World War, he was an early and obvious recruit to the newly formed Office of Strategic Services with which the United States attempted to repair their previous lack of anything resembling a secret intelligence service. Posted to Berne to head its central European operations, he built up, with initial British aid, a remarkable network which brought him impartially into contact with S.S. promoters of a would-be negotiated peace and with representatives of the conspiracy to assassinate Hitler, as well as with excellent sources in the German Army High Command and the German Foreign Ministry. Some of these activities he revealed in 1947 in his book *Germany's Underground* written after his return to private life in 1945.

With the onset of the cold war his talents were again called on by the Truman administration and by its Republican critics. In 1947 he served as consultant to the House of Representatives Commission on Foreign Aid, and as a member of the President's Committee on the Marshall Plan. In 1947 he was also called on to give evidence to the U.S. Senate's Committee on the Armed Services which was then considering that section of the Bill to set up a National Defence Establishment which provided for the building up of a central intelligence agency, evidence which was distinguished by its hostility to "cloak and dagger" activities and its emphasis on the importance of intensive collection and collation and close analysis of information already in the public domain. When the C.I.A. was eventually set up, its first director, General Bedell Smith, appealed to him to come as his deputy.

ROLE EXAGGERATED

In 1953, on General Bedell Smith's retirement and the return of the Republicans to power, he became Director, a post which he held until 1962. Under his direction, the C.I.A. developed into an extremely large and controversial organization, especially in so far as its clandestine political and subversive activities in foreign countries were concerned. To strengthen its position with Congress in financial matters, Dulles felt obliged to allow press stories to appear which made extremely grandiose claims about its role in the overthrow of the Moussadek government in Iran and the Arbenz government in Guatemala; and from this a whole literature sprang up covering and exaggerating this side of the C.I.A.'s activities. Dulles himself laid a good deal of stress on the C.I.A.'s role in training internal security services for friendly regimes in the less settled parts of the world to combat Communist subversion. And in these developments there is something to suggest that its more orthodox intelligence gathering activities, in which American technological expertise played a very considerable part, came to take second place to these clandestine political operations.

Towards the end of his career as director of the C.I.A. a series of disasters, especially the Soviet shooting down of the U.2 high altitude reconnaissance plane over Soviet territory immediately prior to the Paris summit conference and the pitiful collapse of the C.I.A. sponsored invasion of Cuba by political exiles in April, 1961, began to provide the world of America's critics and enemies with the image of an organization at once incompetent and perilously irresponsible in every sense of the word.

An "invisible government" is the title chosen for one of the more sensational attacks upon it.

CUBAN FIASCO

The C.I.A. was investigated in detail by Robert Kennedy on his brother's instructions after the fiasco of the Cuban invasion. In August, 1961, the Defence Intelligence Agency was established within the Pentagon and the following year, at a discreet interval of time Dulles, who had proffered his resignation to President Kennedy after the Cuban debacle, was allowed to retire. During his retirement he published his general reflections on *The Craft of Intelligence*, a book whose distinguishing marks were a certain dogmatic anti-communism reminiscent of his brother, John Foster Dulles, and a repeated emphasis on the less sensational aspects of intelligence work. *The Secret Surrender*—a record of the behind-the-scenes activity leading to the surrender of the German armies in Italy in the Second World War—was published in 1967.

January 31, 1969.

Dr. Allen Du Mont, developer of the cathode-ray tube and other major ideas in television and electronics, died on November 14, 1965, in New York. He was 64.

Du Mont, one of the most ingenious and adventurous of television pioneers, once observed that he had put his discoveries on the market 15 years too soon. He resigned from a lucrative post during the depression because his employers were not developing his inventions fast enough, built up a highly successful business of his own which he began in a basement, and then found his television sets undercut by the cheaper models of his competitors. He offered, he said, the television of a decade ahead for only $50 more than they did and correctly predicted that everyone would incorporate his refinements eventually in more expensive sets.

Allen Balcom Du Mont showed an early interest in engineering. He graduated from Rensselaer Polytechnic Institute in 1924 and after two years with Westinghouse joined De Forest Radio Company as chief engineer in 1928. He already had a couple of patents to his name, and the Westinghouse Award for Outstanding Accomplishment, which normally goes to much older men. In 1929 he put out the first television programmes for De Forest in New Jersey, and two years later he resigned to pursue his applications on his own account.

The original De Forest transmitters used mechanical scanning discs. Du Mont decided that electronic scanning would be more effective, but the cathode-ray tubes then available from Germany were too expensive and short-lived to be practicable. De Forest would not support his research.

Working by himself, Du Mont developed cathode-ray tubes and in the process invented the "magic eye" radio tube which he sold to Radio Corporation of America. With the resultant profits he opened a factory in Passaic, New Jersey, where he produced his first all-electronic receivers in 1937 and put them on the market in 1938. At the same time, he maintained a regular programme on an experimental transmitter.

MILITARY ELECTRONICS

Within 10 years Allen B. Du Mont Laboratories had established a tremendous reputation and won several important contracts for military electronics during the Second World War. Du Mont served on the National Television Systems Committee which presaged the flowering of television in the United States from 5,000 receivers in 1945 to more then 80m. today. He held more than 30 patents, some of which have not yet been commercially exploited, and liked to predict that in time it would be possible to transmit electronic impulses directly to the brain which would allow the blind to "see" television pictures without any use of their eyes.

The Du Mont network was unable to withstand the competition of larger competitors with better entertainment connexions, and in 1955 reverted to local standing with stations in a couple of cities. In 1956 Du Mont resigned the presidency of his company and acted as chairman of the board until it was taken over by Fairchild in 1960. He retired from active participation next year, remaining as a consultant. He had a handful of honorary degrees, and many awards for his services to television, including the gold medal of the American Association for the Advancement of Science (1947).

Du Mont married Ethel Martha Steadman in 1926. His widow, a son and a daughter survive him.

November 17, 1965.

Patrick Duncan, a fighter against the racial laws in South Africa, who so angered the Nationalist Government that it disowned him by depriving him of his citizenship, died on June 4, 1967, in a London hospital. He was 48.

Duncan had one initial and infuriating advantage over other civil rights workers as far as the authorities were concerned: he was the son of the first South African to become Governor-General of his country, Sir Patrick Duncan, one of Lord Milner's "Kindergarten". This inevitably helped focus attention on his defiance, but it was his personal courage, his own visionary brand of liberalism, and his impulsive actions which made him someone the advocates of apartheid could not ignore. He used many of the weapons other demonstrators employed—passive resistance, outspoken articles, public speeches and "Pimpernel" escapes. In the end he deserted the Liberal Party and allied himself—one of the first white persons to do so—with the militant Pan-African Congress which had been banned in South Africa. His adoption of a policy of active violence was something the authorities faced quickly. Within a few months he was barred from his home in Basutoland. A year later he was completely disowned by the South African Government. He lost his citizenship.

Duncan was born in Johannesburg in June, 1918, the eldest son of Sir Patrick Duncan, Governor-General of South Africa, 1937–43 He was educated at Winchester, and then followed his father at Balliol College, Oxford. He was rejected by the Army as a recruit in the Second World War because of a disability which made him permanently lame; tried to run away to sea as a merchant seaman, but was hauled back; become private secretary for a year to Sir Evelyn Baring, then High Commissioner for the United Kingdom in South Africa; and finally joined the colonial service as a district commissioner in Basutoland.

When, in 1952, the African National Congress and the South African Indian Congress began a defiance campaign against six racial laws in South Africa, Duncan resigned his post and joined in. He courted arrest by entering the African location in Germiston without a permit.

DETAINED

As a result he spent a fortnight in prison, and then, on payment of a £100 fine, was released.

Duncan, a member of the Liberal Party since its inception, then became editor of its fortnightly magazine *Contact*. In 1960, he published an article about the Communist Party, was gaoled for refusing to disclose his source, and later fined £350 for contravening the emergency regulations by publishing subversive statements. He stood as a Liberal candidate in the Cape Provincial elections in 1959, but was heavily defeated.

In 1961 he was banned from attending any public meetings for five years. In 1962, he was confined to the Cape peninsula, forbidden to enter any African township, and his passport was withdrawn, but he escaped to Basutoland. In 1963, he resigned from the Liberal Party and a month later announced that he had joined the Pan-African Congress. He protested against the 90-days detention laws recently introduced by the South African Government and compared them to Hitler's Enabling Act of 1933, which gave the executive power to dispose of the lives and liberty of the citizen. An article he wrote in *The Times* was banned in South Africa.

In June, 1963, Duncan was banned from the three High Commission territories in South Africa on the grounds that he had adopted an active policy of violence against the South African Government. In July, 1964, he was deprived of his citizenship. Duncan worked as an African Nationalist delegate in Europe and the United States, and also in a relief organization in Algeria.

He leaves a widow, two sons and two daughters.

June 5, 1967.

Sir John Duncanson, who was Controller of Iron and Steel from 1942 to 1945, and commercial and technical director of the Iron and Steel Federation from 1945 to 1948, died on July 25, 1963, at his home at Hove. He was 66.

While not a dominant figure in the industry either during or after the war, he was a most able administrator. His strength lay rather in the application than the initiation of policies.

John McLean Duncanson, son of T. M. Duncanson, was born on February 4, 1897. During the First World War he served in the Queen's Own Royal Glasgow Yeomanry.

Duncanson first made his mark in the steel industry in Scotland after the great depression when in the early thirties he came into close contact with the late Sir James Lithgow, head of the great Scottish steel and shipbuilding complex. When war broke out he was asked by Sir Andrew Duncan to join the Iron and Steel Control as deputy controller. His main task was to turn paper plans for the wartime direction of the steel industry into practical terms. This he did with such success that within the short space of a year the whole diverse structure of the steel industry was under firm administrative control. In consequence the 300 or more companies comprising the iron and steel industry and all in varying degrees vital to the war effort were able to work easily together with a minimum of friction.

AN UNPRECEDENTED EFFORT

In the next phase Sir John, who was knighted in 1942, organized the allocation of supplies of steel, perhaps the greatest single element of industrial planning needed during the war. His extraordinary capacity for bringing all his energy to bear on a problem was only equalled by his capacity for stimulating his talented colleagues in times of crisis. During this period all associated with him will remember the unprecedented effort that had to be made to reorganize steel supplies when Lord Beaverbook cancelled the programme for tank production overnight and ordered concentration instead on fighter production for the R.A.F.

THIRD PHASE

The third phase came when the United States came into the war. Duncanson, who with his colleagues had already established most friendly relations with the American steel makers, bent himself to the task of securing full coordination so that as quickly as possible there was no unnecessary duplication of effort.

Following the war, after a period as commercial and technical director of the British Iron and Steel Federation, Sir John returned to steel and shipbuilding in Scotland. In 1954 he was appointed to the board of the Lancashire Steel Corporation and he also became chairman of the Rhodesian Iron and Steel Company. It was also in 1954 that he was selected to lead a mission formed by the Federation of British Industries at the request of the Government to consider the practicability of the Suez Canal base being maintained by civilian contractors.

In 1959 he was elected the first president of the Institution of Nuclear Engineers.

Jack Duncanson will be remembered by a wide circle of friends, particularly in steel and heavy engineering, as a man who combined great warmth of human understanding with the drive and energy needed for success in the top flight of industrial management.

He married in 1925 Margaret Black, and they had one son and one daughter.

July 29, 1963.

Sir Laurence Dunne, M.C., Chief Metropolitan Magistrate from 1948 to 1960, died on June 30, 1970, at the age of 76.

Laurence Rivers Dunne was born in 1893, and educated at Eton and Magdalen College, Oxford. During the First World War he served in the 60th Rifles and on the General Staff; he attained the rank of Brevet Major, was mentioned three times in dispatches, and was awarded the M.C.

He was called to the Bar in 1922 by the Inner Temple. He began his professional career as a pupil of J. D. Casswell, a notable defender in criminal (especially murder) cases. He had the good fortune to remain in the same chambers, of which Rayner Goddard, K.C., became the head, and Dunne benefited by observing at close quarters the outstanding forensic and intellectual gifts of the future Lord Chief Justice. They were Western Circuit chambers, so it was natural that he should join that circuit, and that he should practise mainly in that part of the country.

Dunne (unlike many young barristers) was never single-minded in the furtherance of his career; he was at least as interested in fly-fishing as in law, and the Test was always a formidable rival of the Temple for his affections. His advocacy was relaxed, and uninhibited by any undue servility towards the tribunal he was addressing: it was also distinguished (again, unlike that of many young barristers) by dislike of wasting time and by an almost arid economy of words. (Many years later this quality found expression in a letter of congratulation to Maxwell Fyfe on his appointment as Home Secretary, of which the text ran "Thank God"; he received a reply equally lacking in prolixity—"I have"). He acquired a good practice, especially in Wiltshire (where for some years he held a dominating position at the Quarter Sessions) and became a well-known and well-liked figure on the most sociable of circuits.

Dunne became a Metropolitan Magistrate in 1936 and sat for some years at the Marylebone Court. It was a good and popular appointment, for he proved to be a good lawyer and a clear thinker, and he was quick, courteous and shrewd. In 1941 he was transferred to Bow Street; the fact that he was well thought of by the authorities was shown by his being seconded for special wartime duties in connexion with internees; and in 1943 the Home Secretary asked him to conduct an inquiry into the panic in the Bethnal Green Tube Shelter, in which 173 people had lost their lives. In 1945 he became a deputy chairman of Berkshire Quarter Sessions.

In February, 1948, the Chief Magistrate, Sir Bertrand Watson, died at the Garrick Club during the luncheon adjournment, after finishing his morning list at Bow Street. Although Dunne was not the next senior magistrate at that court, it came as no surprise when he was appointed to fill the vacancy. In accordance with a long-standing custom, he received a knighthood.

QUICK DECISIONS

In the same year he became a Bencher of the Inner Temple.

On the Bench, and in Committee, Dunne saw the point at once and made up his mind quickly, but he was never afraid to change it if convinced by reasoned argument that his first opinion was wrong. He was almost contemptuously indifferent to criticism, whether from a newspaper or from an Appeal Court. He was an admirable occasional speaker—polished, witty and stringent—though a colleague once commented that he would have been even better if he had not given the impression that he would have preferred the company of the trout in the Test to that of his audience.

In legal and criminological matters Dunne would have placed himself among the traditionalists rather than the reformers. Like everyone else connected with the criminal law, he was alarmed by the staggering increase in crime which took place during his professional life. This he attributed mainly to a breakdown in parental and national discipline, and to a general decline in moral standards. He thought that retribution had a part to play in penal policy, and he was opposed to the abolition of capital and corporal punishment.

Dunne had to contend with intermittent ill-health during his term as Chief Magistrate, and he retired in April, 1960, at the age of 66. From then on he spent most of his time at his country house in Berkshire, and was therefore able to give adequate time and attention to his life-long interest in fly-fishing. But he continued to sit at Berkshire Quarter Sessions; having been a deputy-chairman for nearly 20 years, he was chairman from 1964 to 1966.

Dunne married, in 1922, Armorel (who died in 1967) daughter of Col. H. Le Roy-Lewis.

July 2, 1970.

Lord Dunrossil, who died on February 3, 1961, in Canberra, had been Governor-General of Australia since November, 1959, and for eight years before that was Speaker of the House of Commons.

The Rt. Hon, William Shepherd Morrison, P.C., M.C., Q.C., first Viscount Dunrossil of Vallaquie in the Isle of North Uist and County of Inverness, in the Peerage of the United Kingdom, was one of the most distinguished, commanding and popular figures to occupy the Speaker's chair at Westminster. Great dignity and warm humanity were among the many qualities which he brought to his office, and he rose swiftly and steadily to its highest demands. As Speaker he achieved the fulfilment which had appeared to elude him as a Minister.

Physically he looked the part to perfection with his towering figure and finely modelled countenance, so fitly framed in the wig. No man wore the habiliments of his office with such elegance. The Speaker's procession, with Morrison's presence to grace it, was a rewarding sight, but Morrison did not enjoy it. He once confessed that he found it an ordeal, made tolerable only by his habit of accompanying its progress by playing the bagpipes "in his mind's ear". He was the first Scot to be chosen as Speaker since Abercomby, later Lord Dunfermline, in 1835. Morrison's voice never lost its native tones. It was a magnificent organ and he managed it superbly. The rolling "r's" of his "Order, Order," could bring the House to its senses in a second. His patience was wellnigh inexhaustible, and his courtesy, even with bores, was exquisite. But he could convey with the subtlest inflection, in calling any notorious time-waster, that he knew all too well what to expect. To points of order and procedural conundrums he brought a lambent clarity, and his judgments usually commanded acceptance. But in such matters he was always meticulous in acting as one who essentially was the servant of the House. He never exceeded his powers but within the limits set to them he could be quietly insistent in their exercise—as when he abruptly halted a rowdy scene by adjourning the sitting.

He was unwearied in his endeavours to encourage brevity in speeches and questioning and to discourage the raising of fictitious points of order.

DRY HUMOUR

The tone in which he said "We must get on" had the effect of a command. Members soon learnt not to trench too deeply on his tolerance, but they knew they could always rely on his protection of their rights and of minority interests. The weapon he used with most adroit, telling and delightful effect was his dry humour. When tempers became frayed and passions threatened to engulf the House, Morrison could dissolve all the heat with a shaft of wit which had the whole House laughing at itself. It was a precious gift, not the least of those which made his Speakership so memorable and gracious. It was inevitable therefore that when in June, 1955, he rose again "to submit himself to the will of the House", the Commons' choice should be unanimous. And when in February, 1959, he announced his decision, on medical advice, not to offer himself as a candidate at the next general election, the regret was deep and universal.

He was born on August 10, 1893, the son of the late John Morrison of Torinturk, Argyll, and was educated at George Watson's College, Edinburgh, and at Edinburgh University, where he took his degree. In 1920 he was President of the Edinburgh University Union and Senior President of the Students' Representative Council. As a student his love for Shakespeare earned him the soubriquet "Shakes", which stuck to him.

Life was to take him south: but he remained a devoted son of Scotland, proud of his Scottish character and Gaelic speech. There was in him indeed more than a trace of the Highland romanticism, which when authentic, as in his case it was, intimates both spiritual depths and powers.

In the war of 1914–18 he served in France in the Royal Field Artillery. He was wounded, mentioned three times in dispatches and awarded the Military Cross. In 1919 he resigned his commission with the rank of Captain. In 1923 he was called to the Bar by the Inner Temple and at the beginning of his legal career was secretary first to the Solicitor-General and later to the Attorney-General. In 1923 and again in 1924 he stood unsuccessfully as Unionist Candidate for the Western Isles. Afterwards, however, he became prospective Conservative candidate for the Tewkesbury and Cirencester Division of Gloucestershire, and in 1929 was elected as its member. He continued to hold this seat at subsequent general elections. In 1924 he had married Alison Swan, daughter of the late Rev. Dr. William Swan, Minister of South Leith Parish Church. She was a graduate of Edinburgh University, and at the time was reading for the Bar.

NO SURPRISE

Morrison soon began to attract attention at Westminster and in 1932 was elected chairman of the Conservative Private Members' Committee. If he had sought office he probably could have had it, but he preferred to work at his practice. He took silk in 1934, and in 1935 was appointed Recorder of Walsall. Towards the end of that year, however, he accepted the Financial Secretaryship of the Treasury. He did so conspicuously well that whispers were heard to the effect that eventually he might reach the summit of political ambition. Consequently there was no surprise when, in 1936, he was appointed Minister of Agriculture.

That office proved the grave of his political hopes, however. He soon announced that he had no startling proposals for legislation. Permanence and continuity were, he contended, essential elements in a sound agricultural policy. Farmers should be protected from the effect of slumps in the agricultural production of the world; but, on the other hand, the industry must be efficient. Such legislation as he introduced was rather incidental to a process of steady development than in the nature of basic or general reform. Meanwhile the shadows were deepening over Europe, and there were suggestions that agriculture should be placed upon a war footing. He rejected them on the ground that they would entail an injurious and unnecessary disturbance, since he continued to argue that war was not inevitable. But in 1938 he announced that the Government had a plan for a switch-over to emergency production if in fact an emergency arose.

He had indeed an increasingly thankless task. The farmers were far from satisfied with the Government's performance. They wanted a general extension of price insurance instead of what they regarded as minor palliatives, and nothing less would have satisfied them. At the time, however, rearmament imposed what appeared to be a tremendous drain upon the Exchequer. It was bad luck for Morrison. He had loyally accepted his position and exerted his considerable abilities to the utmost; but his failure was conspicuous. Early in the New Year he became Chancellor of the Duchy of Lancaster. In April, 1939, he was appointed Minister of Food, and it was, therefore, among his tasks when war came to prepare the country for food rationing. In 1940 he was made Postmaster-General, a position which at that time demanded a first-class administrator. He did good but naturally unobtrusive work, though the introduction of the airgraph signalized his regime.

RETURN TO PROMINENCE

After three years Morrison was appointed Minister of Town and Country Planning, and his chief task was to pilot through Parliament the new Town and Country Act, which embodied some of the provisions of the Uthwatt report. He held this office until Labour came into power in 1945. During his years in opposition Morrison gradually faded out of the public eye, but he came back into prominence quite suddenly when, in October, 1951, after the narrow defeat of Labour at the polls, the Commons were called on to choose a new Speaker to follow Colonel Douglas Clifton Brown (later Lord Ruffside). Various names were suggested, and it was Churchill's intuition which lighted on Morrison. After abortive negotiations, for the first time since 1895 the election of a Speaker was challenged by a vote. Morrison and Major Milner, later Lord Milner of Leeds, were proposed and after Churchill had outlined the history of the negotiations, he urged the House to support Morrison. Attlee on the other side, however, preferred the claims of Milner. On a division Morrison was elected by 318 votes to 251. What might be termed a double precedent had thus been created. The House had chosen as Speaker a former Minister of the Crown, and also one who had never been in the Chair before.

Morrison seemed quickly to acquire a real genius for controlling the House, but even his abilities were strained to the utmost towards the end of 1956 during the Suez crisis. Tempers on both sides were strained almost to breaking-point, and "scenes" were frequent. Once he had to suspend the sitting for half-an-hour because of grave disorder, and many times he was forced to quell uproar by the sheer power of his generous and fearless personality.

During his term of office the House and the Speaker, who is never off duty, endured a record number of all-night sittings for one session, and the strain began to tell on him. In February, 1959, he announced that he had decided with regret that he should not offer himself as candidate at the next election. He had recently undergone a very thorough medical examination, and his advisers had told him that he would be unwise to undergo the work of another Parliament.

FAREWELL TO THE HOUSE

When the time came for him to say farewell on September 19, 1959, Morrison had held the office just 11 days short of eight years. The wit which never deserted him lightly veiled the emotions which possessed him. "We have got used on both sides", he said, "to listening to the expression of sentiments which are abhorrent to us without getting wildly excited."

In due course the House carried a motion for a humble Address to the Queen praying that she would confer some signal mark of her Royal favour on Morrison. There was no inkling then of the breeze that was to blow up a week later when it became known that the new Viscount Dunrossil had accepted nomination by Her Majesty's ministers in Australia as Governor-General. (It was first mooted to him on October 27.) On November 12 Labour backbenchers at Westminster staged a lively demonstration over a motion to grant him the customary pension of £4,000 a year. Their objections were prompted by his acceptance of a post carrying a salary of £10,000 a year. Although Mr. Butler, the Leader of the House, explained that the Bill to give effect to the pension provided that half of it would be abated while Dunrossil was Governor-General, some Labour members, for whom Mr. Charles Pannell was the vigorous spokesman, protested that the whole of the pension should go into cold storage while Dunrossil held the office. In the event Pannell's amendment to reject the Bill was defeated by 300 votes to 155, and it was given a second and later a third reading.

ADVICE ON ACCENTS

Dunrossil sailed for Australia on New Year's Day, 1960. "I am not so old", he said, "that I cannot experience a great thrill at the prospect of taking up my duties in Australia and among Australians." He arrived in Canberra a month later and was sworn in the next day. A few months later he was advising Australians to stick to their own accents. "The Queen", he said, "is Queen not only of the B.B.C., and Southern England. She is also Queen of Scotland, and she is Queen of Australia. I intend to go my own way about speaking what is called the English language and advise you to do the same." In September he was reported to be exhausted by his strenuous official duties and was ordered to rest. Since he had arrived in Australia he had visited every state capital.

Lady Dunrossil and their four sons survive him.

February 3, 1961.

Hugh Durnford, M.C., sometime Bursar of King's College, Cambridge, and the author of a famous escape story of the First World War, died on June 6, 1965, in a nursing home. He was 79.

It was during the third battle of Ypres, after more than a year's service on the Western Front, that Durnford, walking up from his battery position to a battalion in the front line, had the misfortune to find not the British infantry position but the German. Taken prisoner, he was soon moved to the Holzminden camp for officers, on the River Weser.

The escape from there formed the prototype of many other bids for freedom through tunnels, in both World Wars, and was described by Durnford in *The Tunnellers of Holzminden* (1920). Commandant at Holzminden was Reserve-Captain Karl Niemeyer, and the book is also a history of the little war carried on between him and his captives.

The ingenuity and effort required to dig a tunnel some 60 yards long without discovery was rewarded on a night in July, 1918, when Mr. Walter Butler—who died last year—cut his way through the last turf on the far side of the wire with a bread knife, and followed by 28 other officers disappeared into the night; 10 of them got across the frontier.

Bellows made out of bed boards and a pilot's leather jacket, air pipes from old biscuit tins—these and other improvisations were put to good use in later tunnels, becoming almost common-place in the Second World War. Durnford was not among the 29 who escaped, although later after transfer to another camp he crossed the frontier into Danish territory, travelling openly by train with a forged passport.

Hugh George Edmund Durnford was born on June 4, 1886, the second of four sons of Richard Durnford, C.B. He was a scholar of both Eton and King's College, Cambridge. Leaving Cambridge, he spent six years with a business firm in India, but on the outbreak of war he joined up and was commissioned in the R.F.A. in 1914. After his capture in 1917, Durnford was Camp Adjutant at Holzminden. He was awarded the M.C. after his own escape from the island of Stralsund.

At the end of the war Durnford accepted the bursarship of his old college, of which his uncle, Sir Walter Durnford, was then Provost, and he held this post from 1919 until 1935. He also acted as joint honorary secretary of the Cambridge Preservation Society from 1928–33. In 1919 he married Margaret Evelyn, daughter of General Sir William Meiklejohn, and they had two daughters. In 1938 he joined the Education Branch of the R.A.F., and during the Second World War he did intelligence work as a Squadron Leader with the R.A.F.V.R.

June 8, 1965.

Julien Duvivier, the veteran French film director, was killed in a Paris road accident on October 29, 1967. He was 71.

Duvivier was born in Lille, on October 3, 1896. He began his career on the stage, acting at the Odeon, where according to his own account he always seemed to play second valets in comedy, and at other Paris theatres. He soon became interested in the cinema, however, and joined Gaumont, working first as an assistant and then as a script-writer for Marcel L'Herbier, Louis Feuillade and others.

In 1919 he got his first chance to direct, making a film called *Haceldama*, but for a while continued to alternate directing his own films with writing other people's. He soon established himself as an all-purpose director of considerable professional competence but as yet little individuality. He tried all sorts of films, from melodrama to religious epic and from comedy to documentary, his most interesting films of the time being a spectacular if facile drama about the problems of science faced with religion, *La Tragedie de Lourdes*, which was first shown before an audience of 3,000 in his home town of Lille, and a documentary account of the origins of the cinema running some three hours, *La Machine à refaire la vie* (1924), made in collaboration with Henri Lepage.

During the twenties, Duvivier made about 20 silent films, all capable but only a few worth noting, a first version of *Poil de Carotte* (1925), a continuation of the controversial religious trilogy begun with *La Tragedie de Lourdes*, *L'Agonie de Jerusalem* (1926) (the third part, *Jésus l'Humanitaire*, never reached the public), and his last silent film, a version of Zola's *Au Bonheur des Dames*, a subject he was to take up again 30 years later. Up to 1930 he had shown no really outstanding gifts, but unexpectedly the coming of the sound film revealed his true talent: in *David Golder* he demonstrated a complete grasp of the new medium, and followed it in 1932 with his second version of *Poil de Carotte*, based on Jules Renard's story of a French country boy. This film, which had a considerable international success, was remarkable especially for its beautiful photography and the skill with which Duvivier directed his young star, Robert Lynen.

POLISHED DIRECTION

In 1934 he had another success in a very different genre with *Maria Chapdelaine*, a basically melodramatic story made interesting by polished direction and the performances of Madeleine Renaud, Jean-Pierre Aumont and Jean Gabin, then a little-known actor who was to create some of his most famous roles under the direction of Duvivier, and indeed appeared in Duvivier's next two films. *Golgotha* (1935), a straightforward and impressive retelling of the Crucifixion with Gabin as Pilate and Edwige Feuillere as Mary Magdalen which received the Grand Prix du Cinema Français, and *La Bandera*, a story of the Spanish Foreign Legion with several impressive action-scenes. An unexpected departure produced *The Golem*, with Henri Baur, a third version of the silent German classic monster-film, made in Prague, and then there was another Gabin film, *La Belle Equipe*, about a group of down-and-outs who win a lottery and what they do with the proceeds. In 1936 Duvivier directed Gabin in one of his most famous films, though not really one of his best, *Pépé le Moko*, a rather novelettish story about a romantic criminal confined to his private kingdom in the Casbah which was instantly remade in Hollywood in close imitation of Duvivier's film, but starring instead Charles Boyer, who was readier than Gabin to play with the romantic bravura the part called for.

ROMANTIC TRIUMPH

After a minor Chevalier vehicle, *L'Homme du jour*, Duvivier directed in 1937 the film which is often considered his masterpiece, *Carnet de Bal*, an episodic film about a sentimental widow who resolves to look up all the people she danced with at her first ball. The delicate romantic sequences at the beginning remain among Duvivier's most personal work, and point the way to his next film, *The Great Waltz*, which he made in Hollywood, a fictionalized account of Johann Strauss's early life which he turned into one of the great masterpieces of the romantic cinema, pervaded by the heady rhythms of the waltz, a symphony in soft-focus. Three further films in France followed before the war interrupted his career, *La Charette Fantome*, *La Fin du Jour*, and *Untel Père et Fils*.

In Hollywood he soon found his feet, forming a company with Charles Boyer to make two episodic films with all-star casts, *Tales of Manhattan* and *Flesh and Fantasy*, as well as directing *Lydia* and Jean Gabin's second Hollywood film, *The Imposter*.

Back in France after the war he shared the general uncertainty of the French film industry, attempting subjects rather on the same lines as the pessimistic prewar films of Carne and others, which seemed out of keeping with the postwar world—characteristic of this style were *Panique* (1945), *Au Royaume des Cieux* (1949) and *Sous le Ciel de Paris* (1951); more in keeping with his real talents was the exquisitely elegant and romantic version of *Anna Karenina* (adapted by Anouilh) which he made in Britain with Vivien Leigh and Ralph Richardson in 1947: a misrepresentation of the book, no doubt, but a beautiful piece of film-making. Sensing perhaps that he was in something of an impasse, Duvivier turned after *Sous le Ciel de Paris* to a very different type of subject, the broad humours of *The Little World of Don Camillo* and *The Return of Don Camillo*, which re-established him as a top box-office director and allowed him to experiment in *La Fête a Henriette* and *Marianne de ma Jeunesse*, the former a sophisticated burlesque comedy in which two script-writers quarrel about how the story should develop, the latter a subtle and stylish evocation of German romanticism made, the director said, just to please himself. In 1958 he achieved another notable success with his bitter-sweet costume comedy *Pot-Bouille*, a further instalment from Zola's chronicle of the drapery trade. *Boulevard* (1961) was concerned with a boy near the threshold of manhood.

Though Julien Duvivier was always a prolific and eclectic director, capable of turning out capable work in almost any style required and not very liable to wear his heart on his sleeve (though something of a martinet on the set, where he expected all his collaborators to be as devoted to hard work as he was himself), a persistent strain of romantic nostalgia makes itself felt. In his best and most lasting films this comes to the surface either to be happily elaborated or analysed and rejected (as in *Carnet de Bal*, where the romantic illusions of the first few minutes are systematically broken down and destroyed in a catalogue of failure and degeneration). Ultimately, however, it is his whole-heartedly romantic films which remain most vividly in the memory, and stand the most frequent re-seeing, *The Great Waltz*, *Anna Karenina* and *Marianne de ma Jeunesse* together with those of his films, such as *Poil de Carotte*, *La Fête à Henrietta* and *Le Retour de Don Camillo*, where he has added a distinctive touch of romanticism to leave his personal mark on an otherwise not specially characteristic subject. His other films could have been made by many another skilled craftsman, but in these he created something memorable and quite individual.

October 30, 1967.

Sir George Dyson, K.C.V.O., who died on September 29, 1964, at the age of 81, was Director of the Royal College of Music from 1937 to 1952. Previously he had been director of music in a succession of public schools, but alongside teaching and administration he continued to be a composer, and of his numerous compositions *The Canterbury Pilgrims* is at once his greatest and best work.

Born at Halifax on May 28, 1883, Dyson won a scholarship to the Royal College of Music in 1900 and subsequently the Mendelssohn scholarship for study abroad. To great natural gifts of a purely musical kind he added general ability of a high order. From the age of 25 to 55, interrupted by war service, he pursued the career of an academic musician at Osborne. Marlborough, Wellington and Winchester. In 1937 he was called to succeed Sir Hugh Allen at the Royal College of Music where he had himself been trained. One product of his war service was a *Manual of Grenade Fighting* officially adopted by the War Office, and another product of his diversion from music was some financial experience in a barrister's chambers.

His reign at the Royal College of Music was chiefly notable for financial and administrative reforms—thus he obtained a grant from the University Grants Commission and established a pension fund for the staff. He renovated the building and planned for its extension. The musical side of his work there was more open to criticism, since he reversed the humanistic trend that had been the ideal of the college under its three previous directors and aimed at the narrower ideal of executive craftsmanship. But his decision in 1939 to keep the college open in London and not attempt to evacuate it was salutary, since his example was followed by other institutions and continuity in musical education so preserved that standards were maintained. Though genial and accessible he had a streak of ruthless decision impervious to argument that certainly helped him to cut through the tangle of difficulties thrown up by the onset and aftermath of war, but he also lacked something in the humanity, wisdom and diplomacy which had been built by his predecessors into a valuable tradition at the Royal College of Music.

EXTROVERT TEMPERAMENT

There was a similar ambivalence in his music, due probably to the fact that great musicial skill was allied, exceptionally, with an extrovert temperament. Everything he wrote was well-made, from a simple unison song or the little suite "Won't you look out of the window?" to the symphony and the violin concerto, but he never developed a personal idiom nor engendered much emotional sap in his larger works. *The Canterbury Pilgrims* succeeds because it is descriptive music that calls for no more than shrewd observation and the traditional English feeling for vocal writing; its conclusion, depicting the departure of the pilgrims from the Tabard Inn, is, however, a stroke of genius, and the overture, named after the Tabard Inn, is a first-rate piece of the happiest invention. Dyson wrote a number of works for the Three Choirs Festivals in which he eschewed the epic, devotional or reflective elements which were not congenial to him: *St. Paul's Voyage to Melita* and *Nebuchadnezzar* are vivid though straightforward description. *Quo Vadis*, in two parts written for Hereford in 1939 and 1949, essays a more introspective and philosophical line, and if it cannot be said to plumb all the depths of the anthology of English reflective poetry which supplies its text, it does to a surprising extent take fire from Wordsworth and Herrick and shows a previously unsuspected sensitiveness to intangibles. As a conductor he could be equally surprising in that a useful but essentially prosaic efficiency could sometimes produce a reading, for example of Vaughan Williams' Pastoral symphony, on a notable occasion, of remarkable penetration.

Dyson's acuity of mind was displayed most clearly in his book *The New Music* in which he examined the technique of modern composition (1924). In his autobiography *Fiddling while Rome Burns* he sets out in direct and succinct language the creed by which he guided his professional life. "My repute is that of a good technician happy with words but not markedly original. I am familiar with modern idioms but they are outside the vocabulary of what I want to say. I am really what the eighteenth century called a Kapellmeister." This is a just estimate: he was more of an all-rounder than is commonly found in our age of specialization.

He served for many years on the committee of the Carnegie United Kingdom Trust, whose financial dispositions held no terrors for him as they would for many musicians, and after the war was its chairman. He was lacking in sentiment for the past and was correspondingly confident in making decisions about the future. He was knighted in 1941 and was created K.C.V.O. in 1953.

He married in 1917 Mildred, daughter of the late F. W. Atkey, and leaves a daughter and a son, who is an eminent mathematician.

September 30, 1964.

C. W. Dyson-Smith, the sculptor, died in London on October 25, 1961. His name is specially associated with an elegantly stylized and highly sophisticated type of female figure in which the aim, confessed in such a title as "Modern Grace", was evidently to realize the physical beauty characteristic of the women of the period.

Charles William Dyson-Smith studied at the Royal Academy Schools, the Royal College of Art and at Munich, and his visit to the Bavarian capital, the birthplace of the periodical *Jugend*, with its lingering flavour of *L'art nouveau*, is significant in view of the character of his work. Dyson-Smith did not, however, come at once to his peculiar mannerism, but from 1919, when his war service is recalled by his appearing in the catalogue as "lieutenant", he was a regular exhibitor at the Royal Academy of works in a wide range of sculpture; portrait heads and busts, ideal statues, statuettes, and groups, medals and garden figures; though what was to be his preoccupation is already hinted at by the title of "A Modern Madonna", exhibited in 1925. Except for a stone head in 1927 all Dyson-Smith's Academy works were in bronze or lead or wax, showing that he was temperamentally a modeller rather than a carver.

The bronze statue, "Modern Grace", which occupied a prominent position in the Central Hall at Burlington House in 1931, attracted a good deal of attention and gave rise to some argument. In some quarters it was hailed as an eminently "modern" piece of sculpture, but this was not strictly true, because the modernity of the work was in the type of figure represented rather than in the treatment, which, though gracefully stylized, with an elongation of the limbs, showed little sign of an interest in sculptural form in the abstract.

For this reason the place of Dyson-Smith among the British sculptors of his generation, though distinct in the matter of subject, must remain undecided on purely artistic grounds. But all his work was technically accomplished, with care for surface finish and the refinements of patination. The type of "Modern Grace" was repeated in "The Passing of the Spirit", "Silence", "Beginning", and other compositions, and it can be said unhesitatingly that Dyson-Smith, who showed at the Royal Institute of Oil Painters, the Royal Society of Portrait Painters, and the Glasgow Institute as well as at the Academy, deserves to be recorded as a sympathetic interpreter in bronze of the physical ideal of the women of his time. He is to be thought of, perhaps, as in the same category as Du Maurier and the creator of the "Gibson Girl", and his work like theirs probably had some influence on feminine fashions.

October 27, 1961.

E

Max Eastman, poet, editor, authority on Bolshevism and one of the leading radicals and intellectuals during the years before and after the First World War, died on March 25, 1969, in Bridgetown, Barbadoes. He was 86.

Eastman was for years at the centre of political and literary controversy, first as an early and and ardent radical and later as a disillusioned leftist turned conservative. Eastman will probably be best remembered as editor of the left-wing Masses, as well as for his later exposure of the Bolshevik tyranny.

He himself considered his two major contributions to be his theory on metaphor and simile in poetry, as outlined in his *The Enjoyment of Poetry*, and his theory on wit and humour, discussed in *Enjoyment of Laughter*.

His poetry was more warmly reviewed than his autobiographies. His first autobiograhy, published in 1948 and called *Enjoyment of Living*, was criticized for its "bathos" and "confusion". *Love and Revolution*, his second autobiographical volume, was published in 1965. He published *Great Companions* in 1960.

Max Forrester Eastman was born in 1883 in Ganandaigua. New York, the son of liberally minded Congregational ministers. His mother was the first woman to be ordained a Congregational minister in New York. His sister, Crystal, collaborated with him in founding the Liberator, after the Masses was closed under the Sedition Act. She and her brother were against the mounting drive toward United States participation in the First World War.

Eastman was educated at Mercersburg Academy. Pennsylvania, and Williams College. At Columbia University, where he wrote his doctoral dissertation to pass the requirements for a Ph.D. he refrained from taking it.

Eastman's point of view on the right of succession to Lenin is apparent in the study of Trotsky which he produced in 1925. On Trosky he lavished the overflow of his admiration for Lenin's practical genius, which for long he dissociated from the dire logic inherent in the events of 1917. But he had also a keen appreciation of Trotsky's superb abilities as orator and as organizer of the Red Army. Eastman translated the latter's *The Real Situation in Russia* (1928), *The History of the Russian Revolution* (1932) and *The Revolution Betrayed* (1937).

His positive and complete disillusionment with the communist idea in theory as in practice is expressed in *Stalin's Russia and the Crisis in Socialism* (1939), in which he declared that Lenin's way of seizing power must inevitably lead to a totalitarian state. This warning to all socialists to keep clear of contamination he followed up the following year with *Marxism. Is it Science*? in which he summed up the conclusions of much of his previous writing on the shady philosophical foundations of Marxism.

Eastman was twice married: first, in 1911, to Ida Rauh, by whom he had one son and from whom he was divorced in 1922; secondly, in 1924, to Eliona Krylenko. She died in 1956, and was the sister of Nikolai Krylenko, who was made commander-in-chief of the Russian armies after the Bolsheviks came to power. In 1926, when she was employed in the Soviet Embassy in Paris, her husband, attacking Stalin's dictatorship, published in New York Lenin's suppressed testament.

March 27, 1969.

Norman Ebbutt, the chief Correspondent of The Times in Berlin before the Second World War, died on October 17, 1968, at the age of 74.

During the 10 years when he was head of the Berlin Office he wrote fearlessly about the methods and policy of the Hitler regime and was accordingly expelled in August, 1937.

Professor Ernest Barker, of Cambridge, wrote at the time that he could not have had a better guide than Ebbutt for "following the developments in contemporary Germany", and many other tributes were paid to the absolute authenticity of his judgments.

Norman Ebbutt was born on January 26, 1894, the son of William Arthur Ebbutt, who was on the Daily News and later the News Chronicle. Norman Ebbutt was assistant Correspondent in Paris for the Morning Leader and the Daily News and Leader from 1911 to 1912 and then a reporter on the Standard. He joined the staff of The Times in 1914. In November of that year he became a lieutenant in the R.N.V.R. and served mainly on the Atlantic Patrol and the North America station. After the war he resumed work with The Times in the Foreign Department. He was sent to Berlin in 1925 as Assistant Correspondent, and was appointed Chief Correspondent there in 1926.

Ebbutt was chosen to attend The Hague Conferences on Reparations and the Lausanne conference, but soon settled down to an intensive study of the politics of the postwar Germany of Stresemann and Brüning and reported fully the at first gradual and then violent transition from the Germany of Locarno to that of Hitler. His complete honesty and seriousness of mind soon made him a thorn in the side of the Nazi leaders, who regarded anybody who criticized them as a dangerous intriguer.

In 1933 he became president of the Foreign Correspondents' Association in Berlin, a position which he enjoyed and took seriously, and which enhanced his influence and authority. He would sit up night after night having thoughtful discussions on international affairs with colleagues of several countries, and the late hours after a hard day's work eventually told on his health, so much so that he was given four months' sick leave in February, 1936.

This was the period of the occupation of the Rhineland by Hitler in violation of the Treaty of Locarno. The failure of the Allied Governments to react effectually undoubtedly encouraged Hitler to pursue his far-reaching aims and also to react even more violently against criticisms of his regime whether at home or by members of the foreign press. When, therefore, Ebbutt returned to Berlin the attacks on him by the servile press became more violent than they had dared to be before, and Ebbutt was accused almost daily of "endangering Anglo-German press relations". The abuse failed to make Ebbutt abstain from his criticisms, always candidly but fairly stated; and in August, 1937, the German Government requested his withdrawal within two weeks.

SECRET CONTACTS

When the request was ignored by The Times his expulsion within two days was ordered by the president of Police. He was seen off at the railway station by a large gathering of his press colleagues.

Ebbutt had gained his unique position in Berlin by his complete honesty of mind and his intense seriousness, combined with a quiet sense of humour, just as he also combined firmness of conviction with moderation of language. Knowing that his views were wholly unwelcome to the Nazis, he was scrupulously careful to avoid over-simplification: and in his writing as well as in conversation this was apt to make him qualify every statement and over-elaborate his dispatches. They were not always easy reading; but they were read by all who were anxious about what was happening in Germany. Ebbutt had particularly good contacts—necessarily secret—with many of the church leaders who were aghast at Hitler's teachings and methods; and he was in close touch with members of the former political parties. His coverage was broad and full.

To Ebbutt's mind the duty of completely accurate reporting and honest interpretation of the news imposed upon a journalist a trust of profound importance to the community. Irresponsible misinterpretations roused him to a still, despairing contempt. He was outstandingly conscientious in all he wrote.

Ebbutt never entirely recovered from the strain of his stormy last period in Berlin, and he spent most of the rest of his life quietly in the English country.

He was twice married and is survived by his widow and a son and a daughter of his first marriage.

October 19, 1968

Admiral Sir John A. S. Eccles, G.C.B., K.C.V.O., C.B.E., who died on March 1, 1966, at the age of 67, saw considerable service in the Far East, and was among the few flag officers who had qualified as interpreters in Japanese, a language he spoke fluently. He commanded an aircraft carrier with distinction in the Second World War, and was subsequently Flag Officer (Air) from 1953 to 1955, and Commander-in-Chief Home Fleet, and Allied Commander-in-Chief, Eastern Atlantic (N.A.T.O.) from 1955 to 1957.

John Arthur Symons Eccles was born on June 20, 1898, the son of Arthur Symons Eccles and was educated at Lancing, from which he passed into the Navy with a special entry cadetship at the Royal Naval College, Keyham. As a midshipman he joined the battle cruiser Indomitable in the Grand Fleet and served in her until after the end of the First World War. He qualified as a Japanese interpreter in August, 1923. In the same year he received the commendation of the Admiralty for services during the earthquake in Japan.

From 1935 to 1937 he was staff officer (intelligence) with the Commander-in-Chief, China Station. In January, 1938, he was appointed as the first executive officer of the aircraft carrier Ark Royal, then fitting out at Birkenhead. She commissioned for the Home Fleet in the November following, and Eccles continued to serve in her until February, 1940, five months after war had broken out, a period in which the German wireless continually claimed to have sunk her. His promotion to captain was dated December 31, 1939. He commanded the cruiser Durban in 1940–41, and was Director of Operations (Home) at the Admiralty in 1941–43, returning to sea in command of the aircraft carrier Indomitable until the end of 1945.

ATTACK ON OIL

While in her he was Flag Captain to the Rear-Admiral, Aircraft Carriers, Eastern Fleet, and also to the Flag Officer, 11th Aircraft Carrier Squadron, Far East. He was appointed C.B.E. for services during an attack on enemy oil installations at Palembang, Sumatra, and was mentioned in dispatches for gallantry and skill in operations performed in collaboration with the United States Fleet in the capture of Okinawa. In September, 1945, he was present at the surrender of Hongkong by the Japanese.

Returning home, he was Chief of Staff to the Commander-in-Chief, Portsmouth, in 1946–47, and Commodore of the Royal Naval Barracks at Chatham in 1948–49. Promoted to rear-admiral in January, 1949, he was lent in the following October to the Commonwealth Government as Flag Officer Commanding Australian Fleet, for the customary two years. He was promoted to vice-admiral in April, 1952, and two months later became Admiral Commanding Reserves at the Admiralty, but in January, 1953, was appointed Flag Officer (Air) Home, hoisting his flag at Lee-on-Solent. His period as administrative head of the Fleet Air Arm was an important one of development, jet and helicopter squadrons and the angled deck in aircraft carriers being among the innovations. He was made C.B. in January, 1951, while in Australia, and in July, 1953, after the Coronation naval review and the fly past of 300 aircraft of the Fleet Air Arm, he was created K.C.V.O. In 1958, the year he retired, he was made a G.C.B. He was made Deputy-Lieutenant, County of London, 1962. He married in 1929, Madeleine Cherry Macfarlane, and had one son.

March 2, 1966.

Nelson Eddy, who died in hospital at Miami Beach, Florida, on March 6, 1967, was one of the best known and best loved stars of film musical comedy during the 1930s. He was 65.

He was born in Providence, Rhode Island, on June 29, 1901, and did not seem for some time cut out to be a singer. He worked as a telephone operator, a shipping clerk, a staff artist on a newspaper and a journalist during his twenties, never apparently regarding his singing as more than a sparetime accomplishment, until the proverbial friends told him he should take it up professionally. Once decided upon a musical career he took it seriously, studying intensively before he embarked on a series of recitals and joined a touring operetta company. From this he graduated to Philadelphia Civic Opera Company, and then moved on to New York, making his debut in Berg's *Wozzeck*, of all things.

Though this seemed an unlikely background for a budding star of film musicals, he was duly discovered: his fine, stalwart physique and manly good looks probably had as much to do with this as his vocal powers. He went to Hollywood in 1933 to appear in *Broadway to Hollywood*, but after that his career moved slowly, and he had almost given up hope of film success when someone at M-G-M had the idea of countering the new-style spectacular putting-on-a-show musicals, by 1935 somewhat past their zenith, with a version of the relatively old-fashioned romantic operetta *Naughty Marietta*. This was tailored to the talents of Jeanette MacDonald, already an established film star, and in the romantic lead opposite her was cast the still relatively unknown Nelson Eddy. The film was an enormous success, and from its success a new romantic team was born.

For the next five or six years the names of Jeanette MacDonald and Nelson Eddy were linked in the public's mind almost as indissolubly as those of Astaire and Rogers or Laurel and Hardy. Their films were tuneful, romantic, comfortable, expansive, rather old-fashioned; she was always a perfect lady, even if sometimes disguised as a tomboy, while he was always a perfect gentleman, in spite of the roguish twinkle in his eye. *Maytime*, *New Moon*, *Rose Marie*, *The Girl of the Golden West*, *Bitter Sweet*. . . . The very titles exude a delicate period scent, like lavender in a long unopened drawer. In their private lives, however, in spite of persistent attempts to link their names romantically, the stars remained just good friends, and they continued to make films apart as well as together.

OTHER PARTNERS

Nelson Eddy was seen with other partners in *Rosalie*, *Balalaika* and *The Chocolate Soldier*, and continued to appear independently in films after the partnership was dissolved with *I Married an Angel*. Jeanette MacDonald died in January, 1965, at the age of 57.

By the end of the war, however, the vogue for the sort of clean-cut, lustily-singing hero Nelson Eddy represented par excellence had passed, and with few regrets he went back to the concert platform and the stage. Here he had new successes; he aged well, kept his voice in trim, and was still getting the sort of hysterical teenage reactions one normally associates only with new pop groups when he last toured Australia a couple of years ago. Latterly he was active in cabaret, and was in fact appearing at a Miami Beach hotel in cabaret when he was taken ill on Sunday. Though fashions in singing, like fashions in films, came and went, he remained the ideal male interpreter of the romantic melodies of Sigmund Romberg and Rudolph Friml, and films like *Naughty Marietta* and *Maytime*, whatever may be said against them, remain classics of their kind. When the former was revived in the West End not long ago a group of jaded film critics at the press preview, expecting perhaps to scoff, remained euphorically to reminisce about the good old days for nearly two hours after the film was over. And that, after all, is a sort of immortality.

March 7, 1967.

Ebby Edwards, one of the leading figures in the British coal industry for a quarter of a century, died at his home near Newcastle upon Tyne on July 6, 1961, at the age of 76. As a member of the National Coal Board and secretary of the National Union of Mineworkers, and before that of the old Federation, he played a most distinguished role and probably knew more about the coal industry than anyone else of his day.

For a while he represented the Morpeth constituency in Parliament and he was capable of moving a meeting in his rich North Country accent, but he will be primarily remembered as a great organizer and negotiator, as the man who got things done, and was the miners' secretary when the Bill for the nationalization of the coal industry was before Parliament. Stocky and with humorous light blue eyes, he lived simply and was the kind of man who used to enjoy playing the concertina, at one time also being a competent performer on the organ. Although perhaps towards the end of his life a good deal less intransigent than in his youth, his loyalty to the men he led was never questioned and personal ambition never had any place where it might conflict with their well-being and interests.

Ebenezer Edwards was born in 1884 at the mining village of Chevington, Northumberland, one of a family of 11 children. He never knew why he was given such a biblical name as his father was an atheist and a disciple of Bradlaugh; but he was always known as "Ebby", with which name he even signed cheques. He went down the pit just before his twelfth birthday and it was not long before he became actively interested in the trade union movement.

GAVE UP OXFORD

At 23 he won a miner's scholarship to Ruskin College, Oxford, but finding the teaching of economics there too academic and remote from the realities of the coalfields he left after 10 months and helped found a number of educational classes which were the forerunners of the National Council of Labour Colleges.

Back at the coalface he threw himself into the everyday work of his trade union branch, being elected delegate for the Ashington Miners' Lodge in 1910 and its president in 1912. In May, 1918, while still working in the pit, he fought a by-election at Wansbeck as a Socialist, anti-war candidate, and although the odds were against him he came within a few hundred votes of winning the seat. He tried again in November of that year at the coupon election but was again beaten. The following year he was elected the financial secretary of the Northumberland Miners' Association and in 1926, the year of the General Strike, to the executive of the Mineworkers' Federation of Great Britain, of which he became vice-president in 1930. During all these years he fought hard to improve the miner's lot and earned the complete trust of the men as well as a considerable reputation for his grasp of everything affecting hours, wages, pithead baths, safety precautions and all the technical aspects of mining.

In 1929 he stood again for Parliament and this time was successful, being returned for Morpeth as the Labour member, but in Labour's disastrous election in 1931 he failed to keep the seat. Although he was elected president of the federation in the same year, the annual salary was only £104 and he returned to work in the mine. But the next year he succeeded Mr. Arthur J. Cook as the federation secretary.

LITTLE FIRE

He had little of the fiery manner of his predecessor and he was far from being one of the Labour movement's dramatic figures, but he realized that what the federation badly needed was an exceptionally efficient and detailed organization if it was to be able to meet its opposite numbers on an equal footing; and to achieve this he brought a mind that was capable of rapid analysis, was not easily ruffled, possessed a remarkable flair for statistics and in fact all the qualities which go to make a good negotiator.

He stood for a policy of the utmost conciliation and every possible channel of negotiation would have to have been explored before he would begin to think in terms of the strike. At the same time he believed that no permanent worthwhile increases in wages or reduction in hours would be possible so long as the control of the mining industry remained in private hands, and when the coal royalties were nationalized he was strongly opposed to a high figure of compensation.

PITS OUT OF DATE

He was never slow to point out that in his opinion the equipment in many of the collieries was inadequate and often hopelessly out of date and that if drastic steps were not taken the whole national economy might one day be jeopardized. Among many other activities during his time as secretary he will always be remembered as one of the architects of the National Union of Mineworkers, the more integrated form of organization which replaced the old federation. In 1936 he became a member of the Royal Commission on Safety in Coal Mines.

When the war came he weighed into the campaign to raise coal production and in 1942 became a member of the advisory board for the industry to the Government. While he would defend the miners against all comers and he really knew what work at the coalface meant from his own long personal experience, his mind was far too orderly to favour unofficial strikes and chronic absenteeism. He was a member of the T.U.C. General Council and in 1944 was president of the annual congress. He acted as president of the next one as well, owing to the transference of Mr. George Isaacs to the Ministry of Labour. This accidental opportunity to occupy this most honoured position on two occasions was a happy way of marking his long service to trade unionism, which was more formally recognized when the next year he was presented with the T.U.C.'s Gold Badge.

When the long fight for nationalization was at last won, it must have been a great day for Ebby Edwards, but he was the first to realize that it would be some time before any form of reorganization would facilitate a great increase in production and that much would still have to be asked of the miners themselves.

COAL BOARD OFFICER

When he agreed to join the National Coal Board as the Labour Relations officer at its inception in 1946, he must indeed have felt it strange to be sitting, so to speak, on the opposite side of the table, but it meant that his old trade union colleagues were able to be certain that their point of view would be completely understood.

Like many of the miners' leaders he was always acutely aware that domestic politics and the problems of the coal industry transcended national frontiers. Thus he was a strong supporter of the Spanish Government in the Spanish Civil War, opposing the policy of non-intervention, and he always favoured a form of international regulation of world markets. He was a secretary and treasurer of the International Miners' Federation and a member of the Executive of the World Federation of Trade Unions. In 1944 he attended a conference of John Lewis's United Mineworkers in the United States and the next year he went to the San Francisco conference of U.N.O. where he pressed for trade union representation. At different meetings of the I.L.O. he represented the miners and the National Coal Board.
He retired from the Coal Board in 1953.

July 8, 1961.

Ness Edwards, Labour M.P. for Caerphilly since 1939, and Postmaster-General from 1950 to 1951 in the Attlee administration, died on May 3, 1968, at the age of 71. As Postmaster General Edwards reintroduced the greetings telegram; he also had the unpopular task of announcing increased postal charges.

Edwards, a former miner himself, organized the escape of Sudeten miners from Czechoslovakia in 1939 after Munich. He was Parliamentary Secretary to the Ministry of Labour and National Service from 1945 to 1950.

Edwards did much to help the resettlement of labour in the difficult years immediately after the end of the Second World War. His experience as a miner in South Wales and as a trade union official served him well, and the combination of firmness and understanding which he brought to his important task proved of great benefit to the smooth conduct of labour relations. His shorter term as Postmaster-General gave him an affection for the department which endured long after he had left it. He tackled the job with zest, but he was probably more effective later as a critic than he had been as a Minister. His fighting qualities were useful assets to his party during his nine years as Opposition spokesman on Post Office affairs. He was in the thick of the battle against Conservative policy on commercial television, and after the passage of the Television Act he resisted all attempts to erode the safeguards built into it.

Ness Edwards was born on April 5, 1897. He started work in the pit at the age of 13 covering on foot the four miles there and back.

STUDY AND PITS

At sixteen he joined the Independent Labour Party, and by 18 he had been elected secretary of his local miners' lodge.

On the outbreak of the 1914–18 War, he joined, largely under Baptist influence, the "No Conscription Fellowship". In 1917 he was arrested as a conscientious objector and spent several months in prison.

He gained a place at the Central Labour College and after two years of hard study there returned to the coalface. With a growing reputation as a worker in the miners' cause, he was appointed full-time secretary of the Penallta lodge in 1927 and miners' agent for East Glamorgan in 1932. Meanwhile he had been elected to the Gelligaer Urban District Council. He became well known in the South Wales Miners' Federation, and in 1938 was appointed their representative on the national executive of the Miners' Federation of Great Britain.

He was a vigorous opponent of the Munich settlement, and in 1939 he organized the escape of the Sudeten miners from Czechoslovakia. In the same year he was elected Labour member for Caerphilly with a majority of more than 10,000, and held the seat until his death.

He became secretary of the miners' group of M.P.s in 1942, and took a leading part in debates on such topics as the introduction of Bevin boys and the call-up of miners. At the end of the war he was one of the eight members who visited the Buchenwald concentration camps, and in June, 1945, he represented British miners at the memorial to those murdered at Lidice.

With the return of the Labour Government, he was chosen as Parliamentary Secretary to the Ministry of Labour and National Service. With the Minister, George Isaacs, he had to face the enormous task of guiding workers back to peacetime industry with the maximum speed but the least possible dislocation.

"MUDDLE AND FIDDLE"

Demands for a speed-up in the rate of demobilization meant calling up a number of skilled workers who had been in reserved occupations during the war. His handling of such ticklish problems delighted members on both sides. The relatively calm state of labour relations in that immediate postwar period, compared with conditions after 1918, owed much to Ness Edwards. He was sworn a member of the Privy Council in 1947.

He had not been long Postmaster General before he decided that it was harnessed to a "Gladstonian idea of finance", and he campaigned vigorously so to free it from Treasury control that it could stand on its own feet as a great business concern. It was some nine years after he had left the department before he could welcome any significant move in that direction. But the Telephone Bill, which he introduced in 1951, did much to remove antiquated limitations on the economics of the telephone service.

Opposition gave him fuller scope, and he was soon lashing out at the Conservative Government's policies on commercial television. In the debate of December, 1953, he accused them of having bowed to the advertisers and of having produced "a muddle to cover a fiddle". When the Television Bill came before the Commons he denounced it as a monstrosity, and he warned the Government that it would be fought line by line. That was in March, 1954, and Edwards was as good as his word.

For some time, indeed ever since the 1951 General Election, Edwards had become increasingly apprehensive about the efforts of what he called a small but influential group in the party to "emasculate the fundamental principles of the movement". By July, 1960, he had reached the decision that he could not accept the restraints which membership of the Shadow Cabinet imposed on him. Therefore he asked his chief whip to inform Mr. Gaitskell that he would not sit on the Front Bench after the summer recess. Three months later came Gaitskell's challenge to the Party Conference's decision on defence. This confirmed Edwards in the attitude he had taken.

GIBE ON COTERIE

He said that the defence issue had been used as an attempt to destroy the very democratic foundations of the party, and he had some biting things to say about the influence of the "Hampstead coterie".

He retired to a back bench, but he continued to speak his mind with characteristic force and incisiveness, particularly on industrial matters and Welsh affairs. He was one of the former Ministers who, in March, 1961, signed a letter to Gaitskell asking for the restoration of the whip to five Labour rebels who had voted against the defence estimates in defiance of the party line. In 1964 he became chairman of the Labour Parliamentary Trade Union Group. In 1968 he led the trade union group of Labour M.P.s in discussions with the Prime Minister over the proposed incomes legislation.

Edwards was the author of several books, including *A History of the South Wales Miners' Federation*, *A History of the South Wales Mines*, and works on the industrial revolution in South Wales and on the Chartist movement.

May 4, 1968.

W.J. Edwards, who died at his home at Wapping on October 15, 1964, at the age of 64, was Civil Lord of the Admiralty from 1945 to 1951, and Labour Member of Parliament for Whitechapel and St. George's from 1942 to 1950 and for Stepney from then until the dissolution in September 1964. He was not a candidate in the 1964 election.

Walter James Edwards was the first man to enter Parliament from the lower deck and the only Civil Lord who brought to that office practical experience as a stoker in the Royal Navy and as a casual labourer at the docks. There would have been every excuse for "Stoker Edwards" to have been overwhelmed and inhibited by such a dramatic turn in his fortunes. But he was made of sturdy material and he was not the man to be overawed by anybody or anything. He brought to his job the robust common-sense and humour of the cockney, and the practical efficiency of the sailor. There was a rugged honesty about him which inspired respect from all ranks. Essentially a modest man, he was completely at ease in the most exalted or the humblest company.

He was beloved by the people of the East End among whom he had lived all his life and for whom he worked devotedly in municipal and national political affairs. He was mayor of Stepney in 1944, and for many years an alderman of the borough.

ATTLEE'S CHOICE

Edwards was born in Whitechapel in 1900, and apart from his years in the Navy he lived in the district all his life. He was educated at local elementary and secondary schools and when he was 17 he found work locally as a carman. He joined the Navy and served as a stoker from 1918 to 1923. When he came out of the service there was not much work to be found and he was glad to get a job as a casual dock labourer. He joined the Labour party, became an official of the Transport and General Workers' Union and organized the dockworkers. In 1934 he was elected to the Stepney Borough Council and from 1935 to 1939 was chairman of the Whitechapel Labour Party.

Just before the outbreak of war in 1939 Edwards was recalled to the Navy as a reservist and he rose to leading stoker. In 1942 a by-election occurred in the St. George's and Whitechapel Division of Stepney and the local Labour party asked that he should be allowed to stand. The Admiralty released him and he was elected unopposed. His return was highly popular, not only among members of his own party. Much respect and admiration was aroused for a man who had come straight from service at sea to the House of Commons, and Stoker Edwards with his blunt and breezy manner became one of the best-liked back-benchers.

When the Labour Government came into power in 1945 the man who three years earlier had been serving on the lower deck was appointed Civil Lord of the Admiralty. Attlee's imaginative innovation soon proved to be fully justified. If the Admirals were startled at first, they quickly recognized the sterling qualities of this sturdy, hardworking sensible Minister, who knew his own mind and was not afraid to say what he thought. His work was primarily concerned with the dockyards, the employment of the workers there, and the housing of their families. He was made a Deputy Lieutenant of London in 1946.

With the redistribution of seats which followed the passage of the Representation of the People Act of 1948, Edwards's old division disappeared. In 1950 he was returned with an overwhelming majority for Stepney. He continued to serve in the Admiralty until the defeat of his party in the 1951 election.

SPOKESMAN ON DOCKYARDS

In the years of Opposition Edwards, with his great experience of dockyard matters, could have established himself as one of the foremost party spokesmen on them. His contributions to debate were always valued highly, but he did not seek the limelight and the House heard less from him than it could have wished in a field wherein he had made himself a practical authority. He was a first-class constituency member and this preoccupation absorbed more and more of his energies. Stepney was not an easy division for any member, with its large influx of immigrants, its communist element and its problems of commercialised vice. Edward, a doughty campaigner against prostitution, plunged headlong into the controversies over the Wolfenden Report and the subsequent Street Offences Act. He took lively issue with colleagues who deprecated the "harrying" of prostitutes, and he fully supported the Act if it would rid the East End streets of them.

He was a deeply religious man, a fervent Roman Catholic and a politician whose concern for justice and morality in public life sprang from a profound and unflinching faith in the essential decencies.

Edwards married in 1919 Catherine, daughter of Daniel O'Brien, of Wapping. Their son died on active service in 1944. They also had one daughter.

October 16, 1964.

John Eglinton, (the pen-name by which Mr. W.K. Magee was generally known), the essayist of the Dublin group of writers and the biographer of "A.E.", died at Bournemouth on May 9, 1961.

William Kirkpatrick Magee was a northern Irishman born in Dublin in 1868, the second son of the Rev. Hamilton Magee, a Presbyterian clergyman. He was educated at the High School and at Trinity College, Dublin, where he was a classical honoursman, winning four times the Vice-Chancellor's prize for "the best compositions in English, Greek, or Latin prose or verse", the examiners for which included the then redoubtable S.J.P. Mahally, R. Y. Tyrell, and Edward Dowden. On going down from T.C.D. he entered the National Library of Ireland ("much against my will") as junior librarian under T. W. Lyster, remaining there from 1895 till the treaty of 1921 when he resigned and went to live in England.

His first book, *Two Essays on the Remnant* (Isaiah's and Matthew Arnold's remnant), introducing itself to the cognoscenti by a long quotation from Epode XVI, trumpeted revolt against "artificialities" of modern life and called upon youth, the chosen people, to arise and seek the fields, the happy fields and the Islands of the Blest—a somewhat improbable work to make its appearance in Dublin, and provoking there the question whether librarianship was possibly included among the "artificialities". But Emerson and Thoreau were then still in the air, as witness Matthew Arnold's sonnet on Emerson: "A voice oracular hath peal'd today".

READERS BAFFLED

Seaman of *Punch* seized upon the book for an amusing parody and Le Gallienne sang its praises for its "style" and huge erudition: but soberer criticism, in the result, indicated that the author's generalizations were somewhat baffling for the ordinary reader, or, to put it shortly in the words of his wise old father, "Willie has no small change". It went into a second edition, however, and was followed by *Pebbles from a Brook*, a series of essays from the same stream and in much the same style, the pebbles being such subjects as "Knowledge", "Heroic Literature", "The Three Qualities in Poetry". Writing to a friend some years after their publication, Magee said: "There was a young man in the nineties into whom the very breath of Emerson and Thoreau had entered, with whose tongue he spoke (or at least in their tone of voice). Now there is a battered and somewhat incredulous person who blushes when he runs across some quotation from either book. . . . How inchoate is Irish literary history! How difficult to be so full of the subject, prose or verse, as to be able to write with authority about any period or person!" In which words Eglinton had unconsciously found a solution of one, and the chief, "difficulty", as his later books were to disclose.

In his *Anglo-Irish Essays* and *Irish Literary Portraits* he had almost abandoned the subjective line, turning his scholarly mind to the study and objective criticism of what lay under his eyes: Irish past and contemporary movements, myths, and literary personalities, including their heresiarch George Moore (whom Eglinton, as unofficial secretary to that great man, found "almost intolerably tedious about literary trifles"), Yeats, Joyce, even "A.E."

GENTLE IRONY

They all suffered under his irony—the not unkind flick of the whip of one who by education and training had learnt to be tolerant of some eccentricity in what purported to be serious literature. For the mob of literary barbarians in their various classes who had turned literature into a paying proposition he had no use. His Memoir of A.E., a difficult subject, was a notable performance, and his last book, *Letters of George Moore*, written to Eglinton, was a capital contribution to our knowledge of the novelist. And as to poetry? A few of his poems found their way into the anthologies. Requests by his friends for a few more stanzas were met with a smile and Jacques's question: "Call you them stanzos?" All said and done, and though Eglinton would not for a moment have admitted it, any future writer concerning himself with Irish literary history will find himself unable to neglect John Eglinton.

Eglinton married in 1920 Miss M. L. O'Leary, his former colleague at the National Library of Ireland. They had one son.

May 11, 1961.

Ilya Ehrenburg, who died on August 31, 1967, in Moscow at the age of 76, held a unique position in Soviet life and literature. During the Stalin period he was one of the least conformist of Soviet writers, and yet never entirely ceased to be part of the Soviet "Establishment".

Although he often openly advertised views which were unpopular with the authorities, he he did not suffer—apart from occasional attacks from some Socialist-Realist *ultras*—any kind of persecution under Stalin. Unscathed, he survived both the "Zhdanov" purge in the arts in 1946–50 and the systematic persecution of Jewish writers which reached its peak in 1948—49. If his "cosmopolitanism" did not prove fatal to him, it was partly because he enjoyed the personal protection of Stalin, who never quite forgot the unique role Ehrenburg had played as an anti-German propagandist throughout the war years. Taking advantage of Ehrenburg's popularity with numerous left-wing circles in western Europe, Stalin decided to make the fullest use of him in those Peace Campaigns the Soviet Government was then encouraging throughout the world. For Ehrenburg was not only one of the most prolific and fluent writers of his time but also an extremely effective Russian and French speaker with a brilliant gift of repartee.

Paradoxically, it was not under Stalin but under Khrushchev that he was most fiercely attacked on the official level at the height of the ideological freeze in March, 1963, first by L. Ilyichev, the propaganda chief of the Central Committee, and then by Khrushchev himself.

BOY IN PRISON

He was taken to task not only for his autobiography but even for some of the allegedly "anti-Soviet" novels he had written over 30 years before. Not until after Khrushchev's "resignation" in October, 1964, did *Novy Mir*, in its January, 1965, number, publish a further instalment of Ehrenburg's autobiography, one dealing with the immediate post-war years.

Ilya Grigoryevich Ehrenburg was born in Kiev in 1891 into a fairly prosperous Jewish family. His father was the manager of a brewery. While Ilya was still a child his family moved to Moscow; and in the biography he wrote in his old age Ehrenburg said that Moscow and Paris were the only two cities in the world where he really felt at home. According to the same biography, young Ilya, as a 15-year-old schoolboy, already became involved in revolutionary—"Bolshevik"—activities, and spent some months in various Tsarist prisons. However, in 1908 his parents managed to "wangle" a passport for him, and at the end of that year the 17-year-old youth arrived in Paris as a "political émigré".

DAZZLING CAREER

Here he was to stay till 1917. Although he met Lenin in Paris, his activities throughout the next 10 years were much more literary than political. In 1909 he began to write more or less "symbolist" poetry. With little more than the small allowance from his parents to support him he lived the life of a Montparnasse Bohemian.

Although he volunteered for the French Army in 1914 he was rejected (according to his biography) on grounds of under-nourishment. During the war he became the correspondent of the highly bourgeois *Birzhevyie Vedomosti* of St. Petersburg, thus starting what was to become one of the most dazzling journalistic careers of this century. However, by 1916, after a few visits to the front, he appears to have become a pacifist and in the summer of 1917 he returned to Russia. For several years, however, his attitude to the Bolshevik revolution was to remain highly ambiguous; 1918 already found him in German-occupied Kiev, and later, in Wrangel's Crimea; and it was not till 1920 that he returned to Moscow.

EXPELLED FROM FRANCE

Although established as a poet and as a translator of French verse, he now wanted to write a novel, and, Moscow being "unsuitable" for novel-writing, he obtained permission to return to Paris. However, he was soon expelled from France, and it was in Belgium that he wrote his first big novel, *Julio Jurenito*, a stinging "early-twenties" satire on western society, but also one which was very far from conformist in its attitude to the Soviet Revolution. It appeared in Russia, but was not allowed to be reprinted.

During the next 10 years he wrote close on 20 works of fiction, most of them now forgotten. In the 1930s, somewhat discouraged by the new reign of Socialist-Realism in Russia, he turned most of his energies to journalism, and was particularly active during the Spanish Civil War. Although he frequently went to Russia, he had lived through most of the 1920s and 1930s in Paris. After the defeat of France he finally returned to Moscow. His novel *The Fall of Paris*, with its over-sentimental sympathy for "the French people", and its denunciation of the "traitors", was written in 1940, but it was not till the spring of 1941, with the Soviet-German pact in decline, that Stalin personally allowed the book to be published.

NATIONAL FIGURE

It was not until the German invasion of Russia that "bohemian", "cosmopolitan" Ehrenburg acquired at last the status of a major national figure in the Soviet Union. His almost daily articles in *Pravda* or the Army paper, *The Red Star*, with their patriotic emotionalism (sometimes bordering on alarmism) and their pungent satirical hate-propaganda against the Germans, soon became immensely popular with soldiers and civilians alike. There was nothing to equal it, except occasional articles by Sholokhov or Alexei Tolstoy; but these were occasional, while Ehrenburg, in a frenzy of work, turned out this astonishing propaganda day after day.

After the war he returned for a time to fiction, but his long novels, such as *The Storm*, written in the dull Socialist-Realist manner, were not a great success. It was not till 1954, when he wrote *The Thaw*, a cautious but still significant criticism of "Zhdanovism", that Ehrenburg caused his first postwar sensation as a novelist. There is no doubt that ever since the end of the war Ehrenburg was, as far as circumstances would permit, a salutary and "liberal" influence in the literary and artistic life of Russia. He openly ridiculed the academic paintings of Alexander Gerasimov, Stalin's "painter-laureat", and was untiring in his propaganda of Picasso, Matisse and other western painters. In literature, after Stalin's death, he did much for the "rehabilitation" of writers like Isaac Babel and poets like Marina Tsvetayeva, who had been driven to suicide in 1941.

LITERARY EVENT

His autobiography, six volumes of which have been published in English since 1961, is a continuous plea for greater artistic freedom and, in effect, a sharp attack on Socialist Realism.

The publication of his memoirs was one of the great literary events of recent years in the Soviet Union. Their controversial content earned the disapproval of the then premier, Khrushchev, who objected to Ehrenburg's statement that he and other Soviet literary figures knew Stalin's purge victims were innocent but had to keep silent. This clashed with Khrushchev's own assertions that he and other Soviet leaders under Stalin were completely convinced of the victims' guilt. Though never, like Pasternak (whom he deeply admired and defended in adversity), a rebel in any real sense, Ehrenburg nevertheless came to be regarded by the young generation of writers as the real leader of the "liberal" wing in Soviet literature, and as a man who had often shown courage—though not reckless courage—in his advocacy of "wider horizons".

Those who, in the West, have accused him of keeping within the limits of what could he "safely" written, overlook the conditions in which Soviet writers have to work; it is only fair to say that, especially in his autobiography, Ehrenburg often went beyond the "safe" limits of non-conformism, and indeed incurred the wrath of the authorities. Ilyichev's attack on him, on March 7, 1963, with its anti-semitic innuendoes, was particularly vicious, and those who met him in Moscow during the next two years found him in a sad and depressed state.

September 2, 1967.

General Robert Eichelberger, who commanded the United States Eighth Army in the war against Japan and later during the occupation of that country, died on September 26, 1961, at the age of 75.

Robert Lawrence Eichelberger, the youngest of five sons of G. M. Eichelberger, a lawyer, was born in Urbana, Ohio, on March 9, 1886. He attended the University of Ohio from 1903 to 1905 and then entered the Military Academy at West Point where he graduated in 1909.

SIBERIAN POST

Among his appointments during the First World War was that of assistant chief of staff and chief intelligence officer of the American Expeditionary Force in Siberia. This post, which he held until April, 1920, gave him the opportunity for travel in the Far East and study of the area which proved of considerable value to him in later years.

From 1935 to 1937 he was Secretary of the War Department General Staff, and in 1940 he returned to West Point as superintendent of the Military Academy. There he adapted the training programme to the needs of modern warfare and instituted an air training course.

In 1942 he was placed in command of the First Army Corps whom he led in the New Guinea campaign. Two years later he was promoted to command of the Eighth Army and took part in many engagements in the South-West Pacific, including the Biak, Visayan, and Mindanao operations. After the liberation of the Philippines, the Eighth Army was selected to strike the main blow in the invasion of Japan.

After the sudden Japanese surrender Eichelberger assumed the command of all ground occupation troops, at first just in northern and central Japan, but throughout the country from the beginning of 1946.

He retired in 1948 and three years later published a book *Jungle Road to Tokyo,* which provided pleasing evidence of his personal humility as well as his undoubted courage.

September 27, 1961.

Luigi Einaudi died in a Rome hospital on October 30, 1961, at the age of 87. As the first President of the new republican Italy, Einaudi discharged the duties of his great office with quiet dignity and a high sense of the responsibilities of the position, even though the first place in his heart was reserved for his Piedmont home rather than for the lofty chambers of the Quirinal.

His fame was doubly assured before he ever became President, first by his international reputation as an economist and writer on economic affairs, and secondly by his achievements when, in 1947, he was given the task, as economic coordinator in the fourth De Gasperi Cabinet, of stopping the inflationary riot which marked postwar Italian economy. With his death there passes one of the last remaining direct tributaries of that brilliant stream of Piedmontese liberal opinion of which Cavour was the true source and fountainhead.

Luigi Einaudi was born near Cuneo, in Piedmont, on March 24, 1874, and until 1919, when he was nominated Senator, his career was almost entirely literary and academic.

LIBERAL EDITOR

From 1897 onwards he held various chairs of economics, industrial legislation, and financial relations at the University of Turin, the Turin Polytechnic and the Bocconi University at Milan. His connexion with the University of Turin lasted, indeed, right up to 1943, when he was elected its Rector. For 25 years, from 1900 to 1925, Einaudi was a regular correspondent on economic affairs to the *Corriere della Sera,* and for 10 years before that to *La Stampa* of Turin. In 1900, also, he became editor of the *Riforma Sociale,* a distinguished liberal weekly, which was suppressed in 1935.

After his nomination as Senator, parliamentary duties naturally took Einaudi away more from Turin, but his output of economic writings showed no sign of slackening. The best known perhaps was his *Principi di Scienza della Finanza,* as well as two books he wrote under the auspices of the Carnegie Foundation on the economic impacts of the 1914-18 war upon Italy, and his *L'Ideale di una Economista,* a series of brilliant studies. For many years between the two wars he was the correspondent for Italy of *The Economist*: Einaudi's admiration for and knowledge of England and English institutions was a constant factor in his life.

MORAL INTEGRITY

As a politician, economist, and thinker, his outlook was remarkably wide and free from prejudice, and his judgment was based upon a sure foundation of common sense and the highest degree of moral integrity. He was a member of a large number of American learned societies, as well as of the Cobden Club.

The Italian armistice in 1943 followed by a few months his election as Rector of Turin University, and Einaudi, who had always been staunchly anti-fascist but who, no doubt because of his international eminence, had hitherto remained unmolested, had to flee to Switzerland. He returned 18 months later, to be appointed Governor of the Bank of Italy, a post he held until May, 1947. Then, with post-war black market at its height and a swiftly depreciating currency endangering the very basis of the economic life of the country, he was given the newly created post of Minister of the Budget in the fourth De Gasperi Cabinet. Within a few months, he had successfully applied the deflationary measures which were the turning point in the situation in Italy after the war. In fact, though subsequent critics accused him of having caused too ruthless a deflation, his policy was perfectly orthodox and unremarkable and could not even be considered classically deflationary. It consisted of a control of the credit system, effected first by the raising of the official discount rate and secondly by quantitative control of credit, under which a minimum reserve ratio was imposed upon the banks. Anyone could have prescribed the remedy for Italy in 1947, but it seemed that Einaudi alone had the moral courage to accept the inevitable temporary recession and to withstand, for the budget, the temptation of fresh inflation.

DOUBLE RATE FOR LIRE

Only a few months later the inflation of the note issue had ceased altogether and prices had steadied, yet the volume of credit as a whole had substantially increased. Those who saw Einaudi at work during these strenuous times recall his total devotion to his cause, a devotion so great that he would refuse to leave a Cabinet meeting for any reason whatever lest in his absence, even for a few minutes, some other Minister might suggest a new expenditure which the Treasury could not cover.

On May 11, 1948. Einaudi, who was Vice-Premier as well as Minister of the Budget in the Government, was elected President of the Republic and took the oath the following day. Though, under the Italian Constitution, the President's role lacks the power and influence that it commands in, for example, France, Einaudi's wisdom and guidance were during the years that followed perpetually at the disposal of the Ministers of the Government, and in particular Signor De Gasperi, the Prime Minister, worked in close and intimate collaboration with his President. It was a curious experience to be received by him at the Quirinal where, in the great ornate rooms of the former royal palace, Einaudi's small figure and modest appearance seemed almost incongruous until he began talking, and then his deep understanding and knowledge of his country's problems and his remarkable grasp of world affairs left any visitor impressed and respectful.

DEFEAT

His seven-year term ended in 1955 but, though 81 years of age, he offered himself for reelection. In the event he was overwhelmingly defeated by Signor Gronchi.

Unfailingly supported by his devoted and charming wife, Donna Ida, the President was equally indefatigable in visiting the different provinces of Italy or in entertaining at his table the distinguished visitors who might come to Rome; among his guests in this category were Princess Margaret and, in 1951, Princess Elizabeth and the Duke of Edinburgh. His illustrious position left no impression whatsoever upon the personality of the President, who remained a simple, courteous, gentle, and lovable man.

October 31, 1961.

Lewis Einstein, formerly a member of the United States Foreign Service and a man of letters, died in the American Hospital in Paris on December 1, 1967, in his ninety-first year, and will be deeply mourned by many friends in Britain.

He showed his love of scholarship at an early age, and had published his book, *The Italian Renaissance in England* before he was appointed to the American Embassy in Paris. After acting as Secretary to the American Delegation at the Conference of Algeciras, he was *en poste* at Constantinople and Peking and in 1912 was sent as Minister to Costa Rica. There he wrote an article on the involvement of the United States in the Anglo-German War which he foresaw as more than probable.

UNSIGNED

This article he was unable to induce any American publication to accept, and it was finally published anonymously in the *London National Review* in 1913. In 1914 it was followed by another of equal weight, and after America entered the war both were published in book form with an introduction by Theodore Roosevelt.

Thereafter his reputation as a diplomatist of exceptional foresight and understanding was established; and it was reinforced by high opinions of his character and resolution. In the early days of the war, Einstein was sent as a Special Agent to the Embassy at Constantinople to exercise surveillance over Allied interests, a period which he remembered with pain to the end of his life, owing to the Armenian massacres.

Later he was transferred in the same capacity to Sofia, where he carried on a courageous and victorious guerrilla warfare with the authorities on behalf of British prisoners of war and succeeded in getting considerable improvement in their treatment.

On the return of peace, Einstein was made first head of his country's Mission to Prague, a post for which he was ideally suited. He did much to promote friendly relations between Czechs and Sudeten Germans, and he became an intimate of both Thomas Masaryk and Benes. He infused warmth and sympathy into the conventional round of diplomatic entertainment, and was long and gratefully remembered for it. But when Hoover became President of the United States in 1929 he did not renew Einstein's appointment, though it was obviously regrettable that so gifted a man should be lost to public affairs.

For the next 20 years he settled in London and devoted himself to literature, writing among other works a most interesting study of the Americans who remained in England during the War of Independence, called *Divided Loyalties*.

WIT OF VOLTAIRE

But perhaps his major achievement was to make his charming house in Great Cumberland Place a refuge where there was always to be found informed talk animated by good will.

That house was bombed in the Second World War, and his wife, the daughter of Mr. Richard Ralli, died in 1949. It was a loss to his English friends when he moved to Paris, but they were consoled when he built up in his apartment in the Rue Boissière very much the same sort of stimulating social circle and found a second wife in Mrs. Lippincott, formerly Miss Camilla Hare.

In 1964, Macmillans published Einstein's correspondence with Mr. Justice Holmes covering the 30 years of their friendship. He was correcting the proofs of his memoirs when he died.

He was the most companionable of men, and his conversation never became a monologue. He was sceptical, shrewd and discerning in judging the actions of governments and men. He had a Voltairean wit, but preserved a delightful faculty for admitting the merits of others.

MODESTY

He was essentially modest though Theodore Roosevelt compared him with such lettered American diplomats as Lowell and Motley and John Hay and Maurice Egan. He was very versatile, and his connoisseurship was so great that he composed a handbook on the Italian Pictures in the Washington National Art Gallery at the request of its director. But he was not possessive, and many museums benefited by his gifts.

His love of beautiful things and his ability to surround himself with them never obscured his sense of values and to the end he cherished a platonic hope for a perfect state where there would be no injustice and no cruelty.

December 13, 1967.

General Dwight D. Eisenhower, thirty-fourth President of the United States, who died on March 28, 1969, at the age of 78, will always be remembered in Europe as Commander-in-Chief of the allied armies of liberation in the West. The task called for qualities of mind and character which Eisenhower possessed to a unique degree and which gave him, in 1952, an easy election to the presidency.

His charm was well attested: even so harsh a critic as General de Gaulle could find no hard word to write of him. He was considerate of his allies' and colleagues' susceptibilities, and bore with equanimity the tasks laid on him by Roosevelt and Churchill.

He was quite capable of firmness: how else could he have successfully commanded Generals Patton and Montgomery? He could also be ruthless on occasion and did not always care to show delicacy towards his subordinates.

His presidency was in many respects a disappointment. Some of the crucial developments of the following decade first emerged during his time in the White House, including the space race, American involvement in Indo-China, civil rights agitation, and the détente with Russia. But it cannot be said that Eisenhower gave the lead in tackling any of them, except perhaps relations with Russia.

He took to the presidency the techniques of command he had learnt and practised in the United States Army. He established a firm chain of command and delegated his responsibilities to people he trusted. The result was that he never gave to his presidency the firm personal imprint Roosevelt, Truman and Kennedy did.

The most notable of his appointments in his first team were Secretary of the Treasury, George Humphrey, and John Foster Dulles, Secretary of State. American foreign policy in the Eisenhower years was Dulles's, not Eisenhower's, and the Administration's financial policy followed the rigidity of Humphrey's orthodoxy.

Yet whatever his weaknesses may have been as a statesman, he proved himself one of the most formidable votewinners in American politics this century. Nor was his appeal confined to his own country. His personality inspired trust and confidence among the peoples of many nations. Nobody could rival him in a good-will mission overseas. The slogan "I like Ike" was more than a publicist's gimmick; it reflected what very many people felt about this warm-hearted, friendly, idealistic man. He managed to remain above the partisan political battle for so much of his time in Washington because he was a figurehead and a symbol—a symbol of all that is best in intention in American public life.

LESSONS OF WAR

Dwight David Eisenhower was born in Texas on October 14, 1890, of a family which had left Germany for Switzerland in the seventeenth century and settled in America about a century later. When he left Abilene High School, Kansas, his family could not afford to send him to college, and young Eisenhower, who was very powerfully built, set himself to earn the necessary money by working as ditcher, cow-puncher, and baseball player. Then he received a nomination for the military academy of West Point, from which he passed out in 1915.

TWO SONS

In the following year he married Miss Mamie Geneva Doud. They had two sons, of whom one died young and the other followed his father to West Point, saw active service in the Army, and later was on the White House staff under his father.

Until he reached the rank of Lieutenant-General and Commander-in-Chief of the allied landings in North Africa in 1942, Eisenhower never commanded troops in the field. He had the professional misfortune to miss serving in Europe during the First World War, but unlike many veterans, he applied himself to study the lessons to be learnt from that war.

He rose through the Army in a series of commands. The turning point in his career was his service from 1929 to 1933, as lieutenant-colonel, in the office of the Assistant Secretary of War and later in that of the Chief of Staff, General Douglas MacArthur.

MacArthur took Eisenhower to the Philippines with him in 1935 where he served as Assistant Military Adviser to the Philippines Commonwealth.

In February, 1940, he returned to an infantry regiment in the United States, but after holding a number of brief staff appointments became Chief of the War Plans Division two years later, with the temporary rank of major-general. In June, 1942, he was appointed to command the American Army in the European theatre and promoted to the temporary rank of lieutenant-general. Before his appointment as Commander-in-Chief, North Africa, he had been comparatively little known, but the success of that operation gave him a richly deserved reputation.

Eisenhower, who won the liking and the esteem of the British soldiers, sailors, and airmen with whom he came in contact, was an excellent coordinator and a good administrator, but for operations in the field he did not at that time appear to posses the necessary experience.

SUPREME COMMAND

At the Casablanca Conference it was, therefore, decided to place him in supreme command of all allied forces of sea, land, and air, while the British General, Sir Harold Alexander (later Lord Alexander of Tunis), took command of the allied army group engaged in the actual operations, in close cooperation with a tactical air force. These measures proved entirely satisfactory, and it was under this organization that the campaign was brought to a triumphant conclusion in early May with the destruction of the whole Axis force in North Africa. In this great victory Eisenhower played an honourable and valuable part, and was awarded an honorary G.C.B.

In North Africa he inevitably became involved in the disputes between General de Gaulle and his rivals. The American Government distrusted de Gaulle and, against Eisenhower's advice, supported first Giraud, then Darlan, former Vichy Vice-Premier, who happened to be in Algiers when the landings occurred and then Giraud again when Darlan was murdered.

General de Gaulle easily out-manoeuvred Giraud and set up his provisional Government, with which the allies had to deal. It was important, and typical of the man, that Eisenhower escaped unscathed through the storms, and also survived other difficulties with de Gaulle after the Normandy landings.

In December, 1943, he was appointed Supreme Commander, Allied Expeditionary Force, with the task of carrying out the invasion of France and Germany. By this time the United States was playing so preponderant a part in the war that the appointment of an American to this post had become inevitable, and in default of General Marshall, who could not be spared from Washington, Eisenhower was the obvious choice. His appointment was well received on both sides of the Atlantic.

A heavy responsibility fell upon him with respect to the date of the invasion, which he once postponed owing to unfavourable weather and then bade go forward when the prospects were more than doubtful. However, June 6, 1944, proved a fortunate day. The passage to the Bay of the Seine was made without loss and a foothold was obtained on the coast of Calvados. The earlier operations of both American and British forces were conducted by Field-Marshal (then General) Montgomery, but in September, after the break-out and the advance to the Seine, Eisenhower himself took over direct command of the land forces. There were sharp differences between him and Montgomery over the strategy of the campaign.

Montgomery advocated an attack on a narrow front into the heart of Germany, and Eisenhower favoured a simultaneous attack all along the line. In the event, the campaigns in Europe were led to a triumphant conclusion by Eisenhower, who showed complete mastery in commanding huge armies of several nations.

LAST DISPUTE

After the Normandy landings the greatest battles were the break-out from the bridgehead and the German counter-offensive through the Ardennes in mid-winter. Eisenhower rose to the crisis, and victory on both occasions owed much to his role. The last dispute of the war was whether the western Allies should attempt to reach Berlin and Prague before the Russians or whether they should drive south to prevent any Nazi last stand in the Alps.

Eisenhower is often blamed for taking the decision, his alone, of directing Patton south, and ordering the British armies in the north to allow the Russians to finish the war in their own way. It is seldom asked what the western allies would have done with Berlin and the eastern zone had they conquered it before the Russians. The answer, almost certainly, is that they would have peaceably handed them over to their Russian allies.

Eisenhower remained for a few months as commander in the American zone of occupation in Germany, but before the end of 1945 was appointed Chief of Staff of the United States Army at Washington. His main task was now to demobilize that army, a process which his successor had to reverse owing to the threatening attitude of Russia. Early in 1948 he resigned his appointment and became President of Columbia University. On December 19, 1950, he was appointed Supreme Allied Commander, Europe.

The moment was fateful. The campaign in Korea had brought home to many who had hitherto disregarded or underrated it the menace to Europe of Russian aggression. Prolonged efforts had already been made to meet the danger, but so far they had resulted in little but plans, without performance. It was felt that he now faced an opportunity but also a responsibility as great as any that had come to him in the course of the 1939–45 War, and the work that he did was of the greatest importance in starting Shape on a sound military and diplomatic footing.

Eisenhower displayed considerable hesitancy before he finally accepted the Republican invitation to run as presidential candidate in the election of 1952. Until the last moment, indeed, he had not only the general public guessing, but most of the "inner circle" too. However, in the end he resigned his commission and accepted, to the great relief of the Republicans.

General Eisenhower believed at first, it appears, that his popularity and the widespread demand that he should stand for the presidency would make it unnecessary for him to fight for the Republican nomination or descend to partisan politics. In this he was to be disappointed. The supporters of Senator Robert Taft of Ohio were entrenched in the party machine and had no intention of giving up the prize without a struggle to a non-partisan neophyte.

WIDER RIFT

A determined attempt by the highly professional Taft forces to pack the convention failed, but the rift between Eisenhower, the party's moderate and internationally minded candidate, and the conservative and nationalist right wing of the party was widened.

For the sake of the party Eisenhower accepted the foreign policy plank drawn up by Dulles favouring "liberation" of the Soviet satellites, although his experience in Europe must have taught him that this could not be accomplished overnight without a major war and that the slogan was certain to alarm America's allies. The return to the states of tidelands oil—the resources lying under the water along the coasts—was pledged; and optimistic promises were made about balancing the Budget and reducing taxation. A meeting with Senator Taft was widely regarded as a capitulation to secure party unity, although in domestic politics Eisenhower was in fact a conservative at that time. Finally, Eisenhower promised that if he was elected he would go in person to Korea to hasten a peace.

In the election he won an overwhelming victory over Stevenson, securing a majority of six million votes, and he broke open the solid Democratic South. Meanwhile, the party's congressional candidates, whom he had been at such pains to conciliate and assist, trailed far behind, securing the barest majorities in the Senate and House.

The new President, the first Republican to enter the White House since Hoover's election in 1928, was not only inexperienced, he also held certain preconceived and rather naive notions about the presidency. The most important was an extreme version of the separation of powers.

REIGN, NOT RULE

The President, in his view, was to reign, not to rule, while Congress, if its functions were treated with respect and its members with consideration, would eagerly cooperate for the general good. This is an interpretation of the Constitution which no President has found tenable. Eisenhower was no exception, although for the first few months he found an unexpectedly able and devoted lieutenant in Congress in Senator Taft. It was particularly wide of the mark in 1953, for 20 years of opposition had nourished irresponsibility and extremism in the Republican ranks.

Inside his official family the President also favoured a wide delegation of powers and reliance on staff work which reflected his military training. Nixon, the Vice-President, was encouraged to play a more active part than had ever before fallen to a Vice-President. But the key figure was Sherman Adams, who had managed the election campaign, and then went into the White House as an assistant and almost deputy-President. This streamlining and institutionalizing of the Presidency became extremely useful when the President suffered his heart attack in 1955, but it had the obvious drawback of protecting the President from responsibilities which nobody else could carry so effectively. It also meant that he did not deal personally with all the detailed information and the clash of opinion on which decisions must be based. His sessions on the golf course became increasingly the subject for wry humour, sometimes unfairly so. And there were critics who felt the President was encouraged to spend too much time away from his desk.

PERSUADING CHINESE

Once elected, the President had lost no time carrying out his pledge to visit Korea and hasten a peace. After his retirement, he revealed in an interview that he persuaded the Chinese to conclude the armistice by letting it be known that America was contemplating resuming full-scale operations, and extending the war to include bombing Chinese bases across the Yalu and the use of tactical nuclear weapons.

In February the nationalist elements in Congress were delighted by the "unleashing" of General Chiang Kai-shek, accomplished when the President rescinded Truman's order to the fleet to prevent any landings on the mainland of China. Other pledges, however, proved more difficult to honour. There was the impossibility of peacefully liberating the captive nations of Eastern Europe. The Budget was at first intractable, in spite of cuts in military spending and foreign aid; a deficit proved impossible to avoid, and tax relief had to be postponed for another year. This was a bitter disappointment and the President's authority had to be exerted to force Reed, chairman of the House Rules Committee, to cooperate. The incident was a reminder of how few of the Republican chairmen of committees were Eisenhower men.

Instead, Congress was ruled by conservative Republicans long accustomed to working with reactionary Southern Democrats. Polite suggestions from the White House clearly would not evoke from this coalition the progressive measures on education, health, and housing which were a vital part of the President's concept of dynamic or modern conservatism. On the other hand, there was a dangerous degree of support for such a measure as the Bricker Amendment to the Constitution, which came within one vote of success in the Senate and would have crippled the authority of the President in foreign affairs.

POLITICAL SKILL

The chief continuing challenge to the Administration came, however, from Senator McCarthy, who had built up a great following as a castigator of subversive elements and who now became chairman of the permanent investigating committee. Not content to claim a monopoly in the field of security, he pressed into the foreign field, attempting to dictate policy towards China and threatening to disrupt America's relations with her allies. During Eisenhower's first year in office a sorry tale of appeasement and retreat unfolded and it became more and more puzzling why the President, with his great popularity and authority, and his known distaste for the Senator, continued to hold his hand. Fear of splitting the Republican Party and losing an apparent votegetter, unwillingness to interfere in a matter possibly best left to Congress, inexperience and reluctance for a political brawl in a President whose great gift was for compromise—all, perhaps, played their parts.

The President, however, was learning the need to assert himself. In April, 1953, he gave a speech to newspaper editors in which he laid down conditions for co-existence with the Soviet Union and promised that the United States would remain faithful to its allies. There would, he implied, be continuity in foreign policy and no surrender to isolation or to the demand that the United States should "go it alone". Moreover, in the autumn of 1953, bereft of the help of Senator Taft, who had died at the end of the preceding session, the President apparently made up his mind that pressure must be applied to Congress if the Republicans were to prove themselves worthy to govern, and that he must apply it.

NEW LEADER

The new leader in the Senate was Knowland, from California, a "bitter-ender" on the subject of China. A promising, if not decisive, counterattack was launched by the President and Dulles on Senator McCarthy after his attempt to wreck the Bermuda Conference.

The political skill and courage of which the President and his advisers were becoming capable was best demonstrated in the second session of Congress by the passage of the Bill to control agricultural surpluses, which in the past had been encouraged by high, inflexible price supports designed to maintain farm income and safeguard the farm vote.

During this session a lengthy Tax Reform Act was passed and personal income taxes were reduced. Whatever the effect on the Budget the threat of recession made this desirable from an economic as well as a political point of view. The handling of this minor slump proved a credit to the President and his advisers. Harder money, to curb the long-standing inflation, had come in with the Republicans, but the credit managers proved flexible enough to handle the decline in economic activity, while the Administration refused to be stampeded into a premature panic by the possibility of another Republican setback. In fact, the slump was officially and thankfully buried in August, 1954. George Humphrey, the Secretary of the Treasury, indeed, proved the strong man of the President's first term, although he was to be blamed in days to come for insisting that the military coat should be cut according to the Budget cloth. The new look at defence, with its emphasis on the use of atomic weapons and on increasing the Air Force for its role of "massive retaliation" at the expense of the other services, had, however, the express approval of the President, and there were few able to challenge his judgment, however uneasy the Democrats or America's allies might feel.

This anxiety had existed in some degree ever since the Republican victory, partly because of their espousal of "liberation", partly because of the impatience of the Republican right-wing with negotiation and accommodation, partly because of the replacement of General Bradley as Chairman of the Joint Chiefs of Staff by the adventurous Admiral Radford. The fear that the President might not be able to prevent the United States from stumbling, or being pushed, into a major war in Asia—and dragging the free world after it—subsided, however, during 1954 and 1955 as the President increasingly took control. As early as December, 1953, Eisenhower, in his proposal to the United Nations to share fissile materials with other nations for peaceful purposes, showed that he was freeing himself from the extremists and that he felt freer to take an imaginative initiative in foreign affairs.

BEST TERMS

The next year, when Admiral Radford and Nixon were beating the drum for intervention in Indo-China, Eisenhower evidently realized that he must step in; it was his decision that military intervention in South-East Asia would be too costly in men and money, too dangerous, and too unlikely to command the support of the American people. Instead, the best terms possible were arranged with the Communists at the Geneva Conference of 1954, although Dulles never formally signed the treaty and actually boycotted the conference for part of the time. The flare-up over Formosa in the winter of 1954–55, when the Chinese Communists seemed prepared to take the island by force, provided yet more proof that the moderation of the President was to prevail and that the United States, while prepared to defend Formosa, had no intention of going to war unless the Chinese overstepped the mark. After two years the Chinese Nationalists were back on the leash. It was not long before Eisenhower and Dulles accepted the offer of the Chinese Communists to negotiate, even though this meant leaving the Nationalists out in the cold.

This restoration of moderation and sanity in place of the rigidity and violent antipathies which had once seemed to characterize both American and foreign policy and public life, was assisted by the mid-term election of 1954 which, by returning the Democrats by a small majority, eliminated outright some of the worst extremists among the chairmen of committees, and chastened others. Even before the election the Senate, at long last, had censured Senator McCarthy, the extremist *par excellence*; the Democrats' victory cost him his committee chairmanship.

In the early days of his presidency, Eisenhower clearly found much of his burden heavy and distasteful. A novice at politics and at government, he was ill at ease. There were rumours that he would refuse to run for a second term and these naturally alarmed the Republican politicians who knew that without him the party had little hope of being returned to power in 1956. But as Eisenhower began to master his job, he seemed to find it more congenial.

HEART ATTACK

In the summer of 1955, however, while he was on holiday in Colorado, there came the President's heart attack which shocked America and the world. The newspapers, with characteristic American frankness, filled their columns with details of the President's convalescence, while the public and the doctors debated whether he could and would stand again. In the spring of 1956 the President made his decision: he would run, but he told the country frankly that he would have to reduce his activities. He promised, moreover, that if ever he was not physically up to the demands of the presidency he would retire.

The possibility that the President might not be able to complete his second term and would have to hand over his office to the Vice-President, Nixon, who had many enemies, seemed a strong argument for the election of Stevenson, who was once more the Democratic candidate. But although Eisenhower had to have a stomach operation just before the campaign, he seemed to recover his vigour as it went on and the country was enjoying prosperity at home and peace abroad.

The Democrats argued, rightly, that this was illusion. When the Suez and Hungary crises erupted during the campaign's last days, however, the mass of the electorate thought this the best possible reason for not changing helmsmen. Eisenhower was returned with a majority of nearly 10 million.

WANING APPEAL

Like Roosevelt, Eisenhower was to find his almost universal acclaim dissolving before he could taste it. Although, unlike Roosevelt, he continued to be regarded with affection which transcended party lines, Eisenhower's prestige was undermined from a number of directions during the first year of his second term. The assertion of the Republicans that they had preserved the peace had been, of course, disproved even before the election. Britain, France, and Israel, their patience with Dulles exhausted, attacked Egypt. The American public shared Eisenhower's indignation and strongly supported his demand for an immediate withdrawal. But the Democrats once more controlled Congress—for Americans, in spite of their enthusiasm for the President, still felt doubtful about his party. When the Administration proposed the Eisenhower Doctrine—an attempt to stabilize the Middle East and stave off Communist aggression by offering economic aid and promising military support to nations attacked by countries dominated by "international Communism"—it was given a rough passage. This might be attributed to politics, but events were soon to show that the Arab nations themselves had no desire to take sides in the cold war and refused to be split asunder by big Power rivalries.

The main achievement of the session was the passage of the first Bill in modern times to protect Negro voting rights. But this was due to the political skill of Lyndon Johnson, the Democratic leader in the Senate rather than to the firm leadership of the President. Eisenhower, who was in office when the Supreme Court ruled that racial segregation in the state schools was unconstitutional, had always shown a tenderness for southern feeling which seemed to go beyond the need for moderation. On the civil rights Bill he showed himself to be confused and ill-advised. Thus when the crisis at Little Rock arose a number of critics complained that Governor Faubus's rebellion had been encouraged by the infirm purpose of a part-time President.

A much sharper and more general current of dismay ran through the country when the Russians, by being the first to launch an artificial satellite, disclosed that the Soviet Union was almost certainly ahead in the race to perfect an intercontinental ballistic missile and that America was now in the front line if another war should break out. The faith of the public in Eisenhower's military judgment was shaken; suspicions that his health was not equal to the inexorable challenges of his job began to grow.

Indeed, as Eisenhower struggled to meet the severest check to the leadership, his health suddenly gave way again; he suffered a small stroke, his recovery was rapid; indeed, he seemed determined to show that he was able to meet all the demands put upon him, which, at a time of year when the legislative programme and the Budget are prepared, are particularly heavy. It was widely believed that if he had not been able to go to Paris for the meeting of the North Atlantic Council in December, he would have thought seriously of redeeming his promise to retire if his health proved unequal to his job.

The year 1958 seemed to bring Eisenhower to the very nadir of his prestige and power. The recession which had begun in the second half of 1957 caused much greater unemployment than the earlier one which the Administration had weathered; more Americans were out of work than in any year since the United States entered the war in 1941. The liberal Democrats and a good many Republicans demanded strong counter-measures, but the President's advisers persuaded him that the country would right itself without large tax reliefs or a programme of public works, either of which would further unbalance the Budget.

PERSONAL BLOW

A heavy personal blow was the departure of Sherman Adams, who had relieved the President of many cares in the domestic field. Eisenhower was reluctant to lose so useful an assistant, but Republican candidates for office insisted that his involvement in a petty scandal made him a political burden too heavy for a party which, in the early days of this Administration, had dedicated itself to cleaning up "the mess in Washington."

In the foreign sphere the dispatch of troops to Lebanon caused some doubts; it was followed by the more serious crisis over the offshore islands of Quemoy and Matsu, which created much more wide-spread misgivings. The President staunchly upheld Dulles's determination not to allow the Chinese Communists to seize these islands from the Nationalists, but many Americans felt that they had been brought close to war in the Far East and that the Administration's eventual recognition of the faults on the Nationalist side was overdue. There was a further fall in the President's popularity.

In one respect, however, the country was solidly behind the Administration; this was over the President's determination not to give in to Russian threats to Berlin. In dealing with this most serious situation, the President was weakened by the loss of his closest and ablest adviser. In February, 1959, it was learnt that Dulles's cancer had recurred and by April he had been forced to resign. This was a great personal tragedy for the President and, on top of the loss of Adams, meant that Eisenhower was on his own as he had never been before in the presidency. C.A. Herter, the untried new Secretary of State, could hardly hope to wield the power which Dulles had won through his personal influence with the President. Undoubtedly the decision, in August, to try to dissolve the deadlock over Berlin by an exchange of visits with Khruschev was the President's own. It might not have been taken, at least not at this stage, if Dulles had still been at the President's elbow. But there is reason to believe that Eisenhower had long hoped to crown his presidency with some such dramatic move to reduce ill will and increase the prospects for peace.

Meanwhile, at home, the President had won a very remarkable victory. Eisenhower's obstinate insistence, in January, that the Budget for the coming fiscal year must be balanced had not been taken seriously at first. Because of the recession and higher spending, much of it on agricultural subsidies, a deficit of nearly S13 billion was incurred in the year which ended in June, 1959. But the President felt very deeply that the country must live within its means if there was not to be a resurgence of inflation. His unexpected success in this battle was due to a number of things; perhaps most important, the voters seemed at last to be convinced—perhaps over-convinced—that inflation was the chief enemy at home. This strengthened the Democratic leaders in Congress in their demand for a responsible and cooperative attitude from their own followers. Moreover the Republican Congressional leaders were new and vigorous. Finally, on money matters, the President could count on the support of the conservative Democrats.

The President's overriding interest in the last year of his term, however, was with the problems of peace. The journeys which he undertook to convince the world of the peaceful intentions of the United States might well have taxed the energies of a younger and stronger man, and for a President they were unprecedented. Before Khruschev arrived in Washington Eisenhower visited Bonn, London, and Paris in an effort to convince America's chief allies that he would reach no agreements with the Soviet Union which affected their interests without consulting them. Tremendous crowds welcomed the President in all three countries, but there were doubts, even at the time, about whether he had scored more than a triumph of personal affection.

TIME LIMIT

Back in Washington to welcome Khrushchev, the President at Camp David did succeed at least in securing a removal of the time limit imposed by the Russians on the negotiations over Berlin; in return he agreed to repay the visit and acquiesced in a summit meeting of heads of state. In rapid succession the President then set off again, first to India, Pakistan, the Middle East and the Mediterranean allies of the United States, and then to South America. Although these visits were primarily ceremonial, there is no doubt that for Eisenhower they were something of an eye-opener. The struggles of under-developed peoples to lift themselves out of their poverty made a great impression upon him. The pity was that these trips were made so late in his presidency, too late to make any great impress on policy. Perhaps, given the President's budgetary austerity, no new departures in foreign aid were to be expected. But in the countries which he visited some feeling that they had been let down was bound to follow.

Even so, these visits, many of them to countries which had never expected to see an American President in the flesh never failed to convey a sense of American good will and idealism.

BEST AMBASSADOR

He was his country's best ambassador abroad.

In a sense he was also the world's most effective spokesman in Washington. His decision to trust Russian intentions over a moratorium on small nuclear explosions underground opened the way to an agreement to ban all nuclear tests. It involved overruling many doubters in his own Administration, particularly at the Atomic Energy Commission and in the Department of Defence. The idea of banning nuclear tests was not Eisenhower's originally, but its acceptance in the United States owed a great deal to confidence in the President's judgment.

For these very reasons, the rebuffs which he encountered in the last few months of his term of office were all the more hurtful, particularly as neither the Administration nor the President himself can be cleared of all blame for them.

The affair of the U 2—the American spy aircraft which came down deep inside Russia—gave Mr. Khrushchev the excuse which he was possibly seeking to wreck the summit conference, from which he had come to realize that he had little to gain, and to withdraw the invitation to the President to visit Russia. Bad luck played its part in this misadventure. But the Senate Foreign Relations Committee, which conducted a scrupulously non-partisan inquiry into the whole story, concluded that the timing of the flight, and the fact that it was left to the Central Intelligence Agency, was an error of judgment so close to the conference; and that the lack of coordination in the statements made by various arms of the Government made a bad business worse.

Over the second blow, the humiliating cancellation, at the last moment, of the President's visit to Japan, Herter, the Secretary of State, himself admitted that there had been a mistake in judging the violence of which the mobs were capable.

The President had been allowed to drift into a position in which it was damaging both to him and to Japan to cancel the visit.

CONFIDENCE SHAKEN

In the United States itself the effect of these two misadventures was to strengthen the advocates of greater spending on defence. Abroad they shook confidence in the firmness of American leadership.

So it was that Eisenhower's eight years in the White House came to an end in an atmosphere of anticlimax and frustrated hopes. Yet he retained his old magic as a campaigner before the American people, as he demonstrated during the 1960 presidential election—and it has been persuasively suggested that if Nixon had obtained Eisenhower's active support at an earlier stage in the campaign the result might have been different.

He retired to his farm at Gettysburg, Pennsylvania, where he remained a benevolent father-figure for the Republican Party, or at least for its rank and file. His refusal to come out clearly in support of any of the liberal opponents of Senator Goldwater in the struggle for the 1964 nomination cost him the esteem of the professionals—although they still thought his approbation worth angling for in the run-up to the 1968 election; his support went to Nixon.

CONSULTED ON VIETNAM

Lyndon Johnson made a constant practice of consulting Eisenhower, particularly when things were going badly in Vietnam and after the Pueblo affair. The former President appreciated Eisenhower's support for a bi-partisan policy, particularly since he frequently used Eisenhower's commitment to Ngo Dinh Diem as justification for American involvement. Eisenhower came to give Johnson increasing support in his stand against North Vietnam; in 1967 he called for a declaration of war against North Vietnam by Congress.

He went to London in February, 1965, for the funeral of Sir Winston Churchill.

March 29, 1969.

Gerhart Eisler, a leading east German communist who was once America's "number one" communist, died on March 21, 1968, at the age of 81.

Eisler had been chairman of the east German radio commission of the Government. He was also a member of the Central Committee of the Socialist Unity (Communist) Party. He died while leading a delegation of the state radio commission on a visit to Soviet-Controlled Armenia.

REFUSED EVIDENCE

German-born Eisler was dubbed America's communist "number one" by the House of Representatives Un-American Activities Committee in postwar investigations of communist activities in the United States. When he refused to be sworn as a witness before the committee he was sentenced to a year's imprisonment for contempt of Congress. But while free on bail pending an appeal he slipped on board the Polish liner Batory in New York Harbour—after paying 25 cents to tour it as a visitor.

British police went on board the liner at Southampton and took Eisler ashore in spite of Polish protests at Eisler being arrested on board the Batory and forcibly carried off the ship; the Home Secretary explained in the Commons that the police officers were acting under a warrant for arrest issued by a Southampton magistrate on application by the United States Embassy. Mr. Ede (later Lord Chuter-Ede) revealed afterwards that before the application he had been consulted, and arrangements had been made for representatives of the Polish Embassy also to be present at the arrest of Eisler.

COMMONS PROTEST

In May, 1949, two men created a scene in the public gallery of the House of Commons, attempting to throw pamphlets bearing the headings "End this persecution" and "Set Eisler free." Two days later questions were asked in the House as to whether there was a plot between M.I.5 and the American secret service, in which the Home Office unfortunately got embroiled.

The court refused to extradite him to the United States, the magistrate ruling he had not been convicted of perjury in the United States.

Eisler flew to Prague in May, 1949. He became the east German propaganda chief, but lost his job in 1953.

Eisler, a left-wing Jewish intellectual, born in Leipzig as the son of a professor of philosophy on February 20, 1887, started on a journalistic career as a convinced communist after serving as an officer with the Austrian Army in the First World War. In 1930 and 1931 he was political secretary with Profintern, the Far East bureau of the Communist Trade Union International in Shanghai; he went to Spain in 1936, and to France in 1939, where he was interned in 1940. When released, he left for Mexico first, before going to the United States.

March 22, 1968.

Lord Elibank, C.M.G., D.S.O., the third viscount and twelfth baron, died on December 5, 1962, at the age of 83.

He was a soldier and politician who, without ever rising to high rank, was a quiet, persistent and effective influence in political life over many years. The secret lay in his own character and in his wide circle of prominent friends.

His mind was always questing; yet it was methodical and he concentrated hard on a given line once he was convinced it was right and worth pursuing. Those who knew him or who had read his many monographs knew with what intensity he supported the integrity of the Foreign Service, its freedom from outside control, and the traditional practices of diplomacy; these were principles which he learned —it was his most formative time—when he was for four years parliamentary private secretary to Sir Edward Grey before the First World War. He tended to judge Grey's successors by the extent to which they followed his lines of policy. After both world wars he argued strongly against the revival of German military power. At the same time the exclusion of communist China from the world comity deeply offended his sense of what was diplomatically proper; members of the House of Lords will remember the very many pointed questions which he put until quite recently on commercial and diplomatic relations with China.

FRIEND OF ROOSEVELT

He had many political and business friends in Britain, the United States and elsewhere. The late President Roosevelt knew him well and, after Mr. Roosevelt's death, Lord Elibank kept up a frequent correspondence on public matters with Mrs. Roosevelt. She was only one of the many people of influence who regularly went to see him in his flat near Park Lane. Another particularly close friend—and one who, like Sir Edward Grey, schooled him in the principles of diplomacy—was the late Lord Tyrrell, former Ambassador in Paris. Lord Elibank liked nothing better than having a few friends around him for a meal and a thorough discussion of affairs. On his side he would carefully prepare for the occasion.

STRAIGHT TALK

He would have newspaper cuttings ready at hand or marked passages of the official parliamentary reports. He would, sometimes a little disconcertingly, remember exactly what a guest had said—"sitting in that very chair"—a year or two before and he would often take up the talk from there. They were good intellectual exercises. They were more; they were moral exercises, for Lord Elibank always stood, first and last, for straight dealing and straight direct talk. He was essentially a loyalist, to his country and his friends.

Arthur Murray was born on March 27, 1879, fourth son of the first Viscount. He had some of his schooling in Germany, which paradoxically bred in him a hearty detestation for the German ruling class which later experiences reinforced. He joined the Army in 1898 and saw service in the Boxer Rising in China in 1900 and later on the North-West

Frontier of India. In 1908 he followed his eldest brother into Parliament as Liberal M.P. for Kincardineshire, and was Sir Edward Grey's P.P.S. at the Foreign Office from 1910 till the outbreak of war.

As things turned out Murray himself was born too late to hold office in a Liberal Government. He served in Belgium and France from 1914 to 1916, winning the D.S.O., and in 1917–18 was in Washington as assistant military attaché. In 1919 he went to Washington with Grey on a special ambassadorial mission. He returned to a political situation which appalled him—what he later called "the Lloyd George Dictatorship". Throughout the 1918-22 Parliament he denounced repeatedly the subjugation of Curzon at the Foreign Office to the Prime Minister's direction, and was outraged to discover that Curzon acquiesced in Lloyd George's appointment of ambassadors.

In 1921 he publicly denounced Lloyd George for his "attempt to divide up and segregate the community into two camps—Socialist and anti-Socialist". In 1923 he lost his seat in the House of Commons, and from then until he succeeded to the title nearly 30 years later his trenchant and well-informed views on foreign policy had no major platform. He worked chiefly through his wide connexions. He did what he could to stem the drift of policy which to his mind passed redemption when Simon succeeded Reading at the Foreign Office in 1931.

A NATIONAL LIBERAL

He stayed Liberal when the National Government was formed that year, but joined the National Liberals in 1936 with a scathing public rebuke to his former colleagues for "their tendency to walk hand in hand with the Labour Party and with the chameleonic stunts of Mr. Lloyd George".

Of his elder brothers the first, the Master of Elibank and a famous Liberal Whip, was created a peer in his own right in 1912 and died in 1920. The second had been killed in the Boer War in 1901, and the third became Lord Elibank when their father died in 1927. Arthur Murray succeeded him in 1951. Of his books the one that is probably the best known is *Master and Brother*, an account of the part his eldest brother played in the parliamentary battles of 1910–12; it was published in 1945. He wrote some notable monographs on earlier passages in the family history, notably *The Five Sons of "Bare Betty"* (1936), and his brief and scathing pamphlet, *Reflections on Some Aspects of British Foreign Policy Between the Two World Wars* (1946), was a hard-hitting contribution to the great debate on what went wrong before 1939. He wrote, as he spoke, directly and to the point, without decoration.

The most memorable passage of his foreign policy pamphlet deals with Chamberlain "in the driver's seat of the Foreign Office coach".

FOREIGN OFFICE EFFACED

Criticizing the system which Chamberlain developed, he wrote: "Under it was established the astonishing post of Chief Diplomatic Adviser to the Government, side by side with the Permanent Under-Secretary of State.... The confusion thus created enabled...the main control of foreign policy to be taken over in the spring of 1938 by the Prime Minister, Neville Chamberlain, who had little knowledge or understanding of international problems.... It would seem incredible, were it not literally true, that neither the Foreign Secretary nor the Permanent Under-Secretary of State at the Foreign Office took any direct part in the critical meetings at Berchtesgaden, Godesberg and Munich in the month of September, 1938. The effacement of the great Department of State, the Foreign Office, was complete."

In 1908 Captain Murray, as he then was, attended the Quebec tercentenary celebrations as representative of the family of the first Governor of Canada and in 1910 he was a member of the special mission to foreign courts to announce the King's accession. He was a member of the Queen's Bodyguard for Scotland. Among his business interests were directorships of the L.N.E.R., from 1923 until nationalization, and of Wembley Stadium.

He married in 1931 Faith Celli Standing, who played in the first production of *Dear Brutus* in 1917 and was the 1918 Peter Pan. She died in 1942. The viscountcy becomes extinct: the seventeenth-century barony and baronetcy are inherited by Mr. James Erskine Murray, a great-great grandson of the seventh Lord Elibank.

December 6, 1962.

T.S. Eliot, O.M. and Nobel Prizeman, died on January 4, 1965 at his home at the age of 76.

He was the most influential English poet of his time. His work had won him a high reputation, not only throughout the English-speaking world but in all countries where the European tradition, which he himself so faithfully upheld, still flourishes. His works in verse and prose have been translated into almost every European language and have been the subject of more books and articles than have ever before been published about an author during his lifetime.

EAST COKER

Thomas Stearns Eliot came of a New England family which had emigrated in the seventeenth century from the Somerset village of East Coker—a village which gave its name to one of his most famous poems and will now give the shelter of its church to his ashes. He was born on September 26, 1888, at St. Louis, Missouri, United States, the younger son of Henry Ware Eliot and Charlotte Stearns. Apart from some schoolboy verses in the *Smith Academy Record*, the first of his poems to be printed appeared in the *Harvard Advocate* (May 24, 1907), a publication of which he was later an editor. At Harvard, Eliot was a contemporary of Ezra Pound, to whose poetic example he acknowledged a debt in the dedication of *The Waste Land*. After taking his degree, Eliot studied in the Graduate School of Philosophy, where his rare intellectual gifts were recognized by his appointment as Assistant in Philosophy (1912–13) and by his election later to the Sheldon Travelling Fellowship in Philosophy, which enabled him to spend an academic year at Merton College, Oxford, working under Bradley and Joachim. A period of study at the Sorbonne confirmed what was to be a life-long interest in French literature.

MADE NAME AS CRITIC

Eliot then made his home in England and lived in London for the rest of his life. He had been a naturalized British subject since 1928.

His literary gifts began to be noticed by a discerning few of the "Bloomsbury Group" among them Maynard Keynes and Virginia Woolf during the 1914–18 War. At this period his activities included the assistant editorship of the *Egoist* (1917–19), teaching at Highgate Junior School, lecturing to L.C.C. evening classes, and reviewing; from 1919 onwards he contributed to *The Times Literary Supplement* a memorable series of articles on the Elizabethan and Jacobean dramatists. These and some earlier reviews were collected in *The Sacred Wood* (1920), a volume which marked him out as a critic well equipped and perspicuous, provocative if something "donnish" in manner. His position in the world of letters was thus assured. His first poems to appear in book form had been printed in Pound's *Catholic Anthology* (1915); *Prufrock* was issued separately in 1917; and in 1919 some 200 copies of *Poems* were hand-printed by Leonard and Virginia Woolf at the Hogarth Press.

IN LLOYDS BANK

After the war, which ended as he was about to be commissioned in the U.S. Navy, he was employed at Lloyds Bank in Cornhill, where it was his business to prepare the bank's monthly report on foreign affairs. His City career came to an end in 1922, when he was appointed the first editor of the *Criterion*, which he directed until it ceased publication in 1939. In its first issue appeared *The Waste Land*, which announced the arrival of a major poet and, by the mingled enthusiasm and execration with which it was received, the impact of an original talent. Its presentation of disillusionment and the disintegration of values, catching the mood of the time, made it the poetic gospel of the postwar intelligentsia; at the time, however, few either of its detractors or its admirers saw through the surface innovations and the language of despair to the deep respect for tradition and the keen moral sense which underlay them.

In 1925 he joined the board of Faber's, where he was responsible during the next 40 years for the publication of much of the most important poetry of our time, and was a source of counsel and encouragement to many younger poets. His own later works included *Ash Wednesday* (1930), *Four Quartets* (1943), the poetic dramas, *Murder in the Cathedral* (1935), *The Family Reunion* (1939), *The Cocktail Party* (1950), *The Confidential Clerk* (1954), and *The Elder Statesman* (1959), and several volumes of collected essays and addresses.

It was in one of these, *For Lancelot Andrewes* (1928) that Eliot had announced his allegiance to the Church of England. He at once became a leading and influential layman of the Anglo-Catholic persuasion, engaging in vigorous, but always closely reasoned, controversy upon matters of doctrine and ritual, especially after the Lambeth and Malvern conferences and during the contentions over Church Union in South India. Eliot's attitude in ecclesiastical affairs was dogmatically, even intransigently, conservative; there was perhaps a certain intolerance here in his zealous but uncompromising defence of tradition. He was a devoted churchwarden, and an active but discreet propagandist. His most imposing work of a purely religious character appeared in 1939 as *The Idea of a Christian Society*.

ANGLO-CATHOLIC TRADITION

Of the non-literary influence which most contributed to Eliot's poetic development his religion must be put first. The fastidiousness, the moral taste, and the intellectual severity, which were a legacy of his New England ancestors, merged with the Anglo-Catholic tradition to direct his poetry ever farther in the exploration of spiritual awareness, the search for spiritual values. From *The Waste Land* and *The Hollow Men*, through *Journey of the Magi* and *Ash Wednesday*, to the *Four Quartets* there ran a steady line of development towards the positive treatment of religious experience, so that he could say in the last-named work that "the poetry does not matter" while leaving the reader in no doubt as to its strictly poetic integrity. At the same time, a long-drawn-out private tragedy which darkened his middle years left a deep impression on his poetry: the rawness, the shuddering distaste, the sense of contagion, the dry despair which emerge from certain passages of *Ash Wednesday*, for instance, and *The Family Reunion*, are traces of it. But for this emotional wound, so long unhealed, his poetry might well have been more genial, less ascetic; but, equally, it might well have been less intense.

Eliot's chief literary influences were the French Symbolists and, above all, Dante. But, both as poet and critic he drew deep from the whole European tradition which, as editor of the *Criterion*, he had sought to preserve and reinvigorate. His poetry, each poem "a raid on the inarticulate", strove incessantly towards greater purity of utterance and wider integration of experience, just as it displayed an increasing mastery of those personal rhythms, sometimes colloquial, sometimes hieratically formal, which he developed from the blank verse line. Technically, his influence over younger English poets was for many years marked and widespread. No English poet since Wordsworth had so constantly, so unequivocally or so openly insisted upon absolute self-dedication to the art, or approached it with greater humility. A critic truly said of him: "In struggling towards a discipline of spirit through a discipline of language, Eliot has reaffirmed in his own practice the value of poetry."

The quality of his writing was inseparable, to those who knew him, from the integrity of his character. In public Eliot, a stooping, sombre-clad figure, appeared to be shy and retiring, formal in his manner, which was courtly and attentive, but detached. The impertinence of the curious, the sometimes intemperate attentions of admirers, he kept alike at arm's length by a playful, evasive wit. With his intimate friends he enjoyed banter and jokes —even, in earlier days, practical jokes. Although in his earlier verse and prose, he often gave the impression of having been born middle-aged, he remained very youthful in some of his responses; children were devoted to "Old Possum", and relished his elaborate and agreeably mystifying fun, which found such ingenious and rhythmically diverse expression in *Old Possum's Book of Practical Cats*. He was, above all, a humble man; firm, even stubborn at times, but with no self-importance; quite unspoilt by fame; free from spiritual or intellectual pride.

POETIC DRAMA REVIVAL

Eliot's chief preoccupation since the mid-1930s was the revival of poetic drama. By precept and example he strove to restore to the English stage a form of writing without which, he believed, drama could never express the full range of human sensibility. His entry into the theatre was made with characteristic deliberation, step by step, each preparing for the next. His first experiment, in *Sweeney Agonistes* (1932)—two brilliant "Fragments" of an Aristophanic melodrama—was never fully exploited. Its dramatic possibilities were barely explored in *The Rock* (1934), a commissioned work, something between a conventional pageant and an ecclesiastical revue and chiefly distinguished for its liturgical choruses. *Murder in the Cathedral*, first performed in the Chapter House at Canterbury in 1935, explored these possibilities to some purpose and became a theatrical success both here and in America and later (in translation) on the Continent. The play's effectiveness as drama is attested by the number of times it has been revived, but Eliot himself considered that its verse had only the negative merit of avoiding any echo of Shakespeare.

CONVERSATION'S RHYTHM

The Family Reunion (1939), the most wholly poetic of his plays, was the first of four dramas of modern domestic life whose basic theme is derived from Greek tragedy. It was also the first in which he perfected by a masterly use of the stressed line, an instrument which successfully captured the cadence and rhythm of everyday conversation in verse and passed, without breaking its own texture, from small talk to the statement of profundities. With this instrument he fashioned *The Cocktail Party*, which in 1949 and the following year had a remarkable success on both sides of the Atlantic. *The Cocktail Party* chatter, light, easy, amusing, was gaily decorated with the sprightly extravagances that make in the theatre the effect of wit; and at the same time the play told the story of four people, emotionally interlocked, who discover their appropriate forms of salvation after the impact of a shaking experience.

Not all Eliot's followers shared the public's enthusiasm. They felt that he had adhered all too closely to his self-imposed rule to avoid poetry which could not stand the test of dramatic utility. And even those who appreciated the practical value of the rule in the existing state of the theatre still hoped that the next play might more boldly seize new ground for the poetic drama. But in *The Confidential Clerk*, which came in 1953, Eliot seemed to have relinquished some of the ground he had won at least for dramatic poetry. The poetic overtones this time were fainter, for the comedy sought to hold audiences through laughter and surprise and there were lesser demands on feeling.

IN STAGE TERMS

The falling off went unchecked in his last play *The Elder Statesman* (1959) which failed to hold the stage.

Yet no dramatist of our time has come more firmly to grips with the conditions which the theatre imposes on poetry. Verse, and prose, he saw clearly, were but means to an end—the rendering whole of an imagined reality in terms of the stage. It may well be that *Murder in the Cathedral* will come in the end to have a longer life than the later experiments. But, in spite of their weaknesses of construction and characterization, there is the precision, the personal yet exquisite and unobtrusive rhythm, of the dialogue to keep them in mind and to offset the somewhat chill sense they give of moving in a kind of emotional twilight.

After the 1939–45 War Eliot's work outside the theatre was confined to the writing of lectures and addresses for various occasions at home and abroad, many of them in connexion with the bestowal of honorary degrees, prizes, and other official tributes. He was never revisited in his later years by the inspiration that produced *Four Quartets*, his greatest poetic achievement.

MANY HONOURS

He received many honours and awards: the Order of Merit and the Nobel Prize for Literature, both in 1948: the Légion d'Honneur; the Hanseatic Goethe Prize (1954); honorary doctorates from 16 universities in Great Britain, Europe, and the United States. He was an Honorary Fellow of Magdalene College, Cambridge, and of Merton College, Oxford.

Among his many appointments he was Clark Lecturer at Trinity College, Cambridge (1925), Charles Eliot Norton Visiting Professor at Harvard (1932–33); president of the Classical Association (1942); first president of the Virgil Society (1944); president of the London Library (1952). He married in 1917 Vivienne Haigh-Wood, who died after a long illness in 1947. In 1957, his seventieth year, he married secondly Miss E. V. Fletcher. There were no children of either marriage.

January 5, 1965.

Queen Elisabeth of the Belgians—See under **Belgians.**

Mischa Elman, the Russian-born American violinist, died in New York on April 5. 1967, at the age of 76.

He was born at Tajnoy, Kiev, on January

20, 1891 and studied in Odessa at the Imperial School of Music, where his teacher was Professor Alexander Fiedelmann. In November, 1902 Professor Leopold Auer heard him play, and was so impressed by his talent that he agreed to take him as a pupil if he could get the Tsar's permission for Mischa and his family to reside in St. Petersburg, as no Jew born outside the city was allowed to live either in the then Russian capital or in Moscow. Permission was granted only when Auer threatened to resign.

On October 14, 1904 he made his debut in Berlin after playing privately before Joachim the day before, and his success earned him a concert tour all over Germany. His first London appearance followed on March 21, 1905, at the Queen's Hall when he played the Tchaikovsky concerto, a work he was going to make especially his own. He was immediately engaged for two more concerts, and in May he gave two recitals, after the first of which one critic commented, "The extraordinary thing about little Mischa is that you can listen to his playing with real pleasure without making any allowances for his youth". He next conquered Paris and New York, where he gave his first concert on December 10, 1908.

STAY IN BRITAIN

He never returned to Russia, but lived in this country for a few years before the First World War, finally settling in the United States in 1914 and becoming an American citizen in 1923, although he continued to tour around the world until the end of his life.

He was a virtuoso in the old tradition, willing to take liberties even with the classics to serve his own ends, but when those ends involved playing of the utmost refinement stylistic anomalies could often be forgiven, certainly so in the Tchaikovsky concerto, whose rich romanticism is enhanced by flexible handling. Even when his interpretations failed to be revealing, we were consoled by his rich, golden tone.

He married Helen Frances Katten in 1925 and they had two children.

April 7, 1967.

Captain Charles F. Elsey, C.B.E., the former Yorkshire trainer, died on February 14, 1966, at Malton at the age of 83. He had been in indifferent health since he suffered the amputation of a leg last November.

Captain Elsey, born on December 10, 1882, at Baumber, Lincolnshire, became assistant trainer to his father in 1905, and in 1911 he moved to Middleham and set up on his own account. His first winner was Wireworm in that year, and when he retired in 1960 and handed over his Highfield stable at Malton to his son William he had sent out in the 49 years 1,547 winners of races worth £793,341. In 1956 he realized his ambition by heading the trainers' list with 83 winners and stake money of £61,621.

Of the five classic races only the Derby eluded him, but he won the Oaks twice with Musidora (1949) and Frieze (1952), the 2,000 Guineas with Nearula (1953), the 1,000 Guineas twice with Musidora and Honeylight (1956), and finally in 1959, the year before he retired, the St. Leger with the filly Cantelo.

On the outbreak of the First World War Captain Elsey volunteered for The Royal Bucks Hussars, fought in France, and returned to training in 1919 at Ayr. In his five years in Scotland he sent out many winners, including Westmead, successful in the Ayr Gold Cup in 1924, and in 1926 he bought Highfield, probably the finest stable in the north of England, with its private gallops and covered-in circular gallops measuring nearly a furlong.

From 1926 up to his retirement in 1960 Captain Elsey enjoyed season after season of outstanding success. He brought to his task all the skill, the flair for buying yearlings, and ability to find the right race for the right horse, which had marked the career of his father and made him one of the most distinguished members of the training profession in the eighties and nineties, and the first years of this century.

GIMCRACK SEQUENCE

Besides his six classic victories, he won the Cambridgeshire in 1931 with Disarmament, the Cesarewitch in 1948 with Woodburn, the Lincolnshire Handicap in successive years with Babur in 1957 and 1958, the Gimcrack Stakes three years in succession with Eudaemon, Pheidippides, and Be Careful in 1956, 1957, 1958, and there were very few great races on the flat that do not have the words, "trained by C. F. Elsey" in the record books. In 1951 he trained Reprimand to win at Liverpool for the late King George VI.

Since the war he rarely had less than 80 horses in his care at Highfield, and for 15 years the number of winners he sent out averaged between 50 and 70. Although he headed the list only once in stake money, he invariably won more races than any of his rivals.

Beneath the great charm, unfailing courtesy, boyish enthusiasm which never deserted him up to his death and keen wit, there was an immense capacity for hard work. He probably had a wider circle of friends on and off the race courses of the north and south than any trainer, and throughout his long career he set a pattern of integrity and straight dealing that not only earned him the respect of all racegoers, owners, fellow trainers, and jockeys, but was the foundation of his outstanding success in the training of racehorses.

February 15, 1966.

Lily Elsie, perhaps the most glamorous figure of the Edwardian theatre world, whose portrayal of Sonia in Lehar's *The Merry Widow* took London by storm, died on December 16, 1962. She was 76.

Her principal assets were her beauty, charm, and personality. She had a good voice, and though not a big one, she used it with great artistry. Her grace never deserted her: much later in her career than 1907 a critic wrote "...it gave great pleasure merely to see her walk across the stage."

She was born at Wortley, near Leeds, on April 8, 1886, and first made her appearance on the stage at the age of 10, as Little Red Riding Hood at the Queen's Theatre, Manchester, afterwards appearing on the halls as a child mimic known as "Little Elsie". Appearances at the Britannia, Hoxton, at the Camden Theatre and at the Coronet Theatre followed. She then toured in *Three Little Maids*.

Her first real West End part was as "Princess Soo-Soo" in *A Chinese Honeymoon* at the Old Strand Theatre, where she made a great sucess with one of the first American "song hits", namely "Egypt". She next appeared in *Lady Madcap* at the Prince of Wales Theatre followed by *The Little Cherub* at the same theatre. In this she played one of four sisters, the others being Miss Zena Dare, Miss Gabrielle Ray, and Miss Grace Pindar. The story goes that in their "sporting number" Miss Ray (always the tomboy) egged Miss Elsie on to fool, and she kicked the football used in the number into the stalls at a matinée. Edwardes happening to be in front, she was instantly dismissed.

A little later, Edwardes met her outside Daly's one day and asked her what she was doing. "Looking for work", she said. He replied: "You can come to Daly's, there is a number at the opening of Act II in *The Little Michus* that you can sing." She did this with great success, and her next part was again at the Prince of Wales, where she created the small part of the Chinese maid in *See-See*. She made such an impression with her make-up and deportment that she was noticed by the critics. Then Edwardes sent her on tour in the name part. She next created the male part of "Lally" in *The New Aladdin* at the Gaiety because Miss Gertie Millar was ill. When Miss Millar took up the part Edwardes sent Miss Elsie to Vienna to see a new play, *The Merry Widow*. She returned, saying it was a lovely part but too difficult for her. Edwardes had such confidence in her that against the advice of others he forced her to learn the part and play it.

RAGE OF LONDON

Her success at Daly's in 1907 was electrical and she became the rage of London. Many celebrated stars have played the part of Sonia, but none with greater charm and grace than Lily Elsie. After "The Widow"came the *Dollar Princess*, in which she played "Alice", followed by a revival of *A Waltz Dream*, playing Franzi, the pathetic little leader of the ladies' orchestra. Then came the *Count of Luxembourg*, with her as Angèle. After her marriage to Mr. Ian Bullough, later dissolved, she was not seen again until she appeared with Sir Beerbohm Tree in *Mavourneen* an Irish costume play at His Majesty's. She then left the stage for a while, to reappear during the war at Palace Theatre in *Pamela* with Owen Nares. After the war in 1927 she was in *The Blue Train*, again at the Prince of Wales Theatre, and her last appearance was as leading lady in Ivor Novello's comedy *The Truth Game* at Daly's in 1929. She then retired from the stage for good.

December 18, 1962.

Maurice Elvey, who died on August 28, 1967, in a Brighton nursing home at the age of 79, was one of the few remaining veterans from the old heroic days of the early British cinema.

His professional career in films spanned some 45 years, from *Maria Marten* in 1912 to *Dry Rot* in 1956, and among the 300 films he claims to have made during that time there was to be found something of everything: comedy, drama, romance, musicals, costume films, science fiction, screen originals and adaptations. Of course, with such an enormous output, much was unremarkable and many of his films are now forgotten, no doubt deservedly. But discoveries sometimes turn up in unlikely places. Only a few months ago the eccentric highbrow French film magazine *Midi-Minuit Fantastique* was enthusing about a completely unknown fantasy film of 1929 which had turned up and been discovered in a provincial cinematheque. It was Maurice Elvey's *High Treason* and from it the magazine concluded that he was undoubtedly one of the most interesting figures awaiting reappraisal from British cinemas between the wars.

Perhaps he was not in fact quite that, but there is much in his work which has the virtues of honest craftsmanship and occasionally something more. He was born in Darlington on November 11, 1887, and educated in London; his real name was William Seward Folkard. He went on the stage early, acting in all sorts of shows, and even appearing in a pantomime chorus. Before long he decided that his talents were less for acting than for directing, and he rapidly established himself as a stage director in London and New York, before venturing in 1912 on the new medium of the film. In the cinema he soon made his mark with adaptations of such popular works as *The Elusive Pimpernel* and *The Hound of the Baskervilles*, as well as more contemporary pieces like H. G. Wells's *The Passionate Friends*, Galsworthy's play *Justice*, and Stanley Houghton's *Hindle Wakes*.

FILMED CLASSICS

He also tackled the classics with adaptations of *Dombey and Son*, *Bleak House* and *The School for Scandal*.

By the end of the silent period he was one of Britain's leading film makers, along with Herbert Wilcox and Alfred Hitchcock. To begin with he remade some of his greatest silent successes as talkies, among them *Hindle Wakes* and *The Wandering Jew*, and made two of his freshest and most charming films in *Sally in our Alley*, with Gracie Fields, and *The Water Gypsies*, after A. P. Herbert.

In general his films of the 1930s were more remarkable for their commercial success than for their artistic qualities, but with the coming of the war he seemed to hit a new creative streak, and such films as *The Lamp Still Burns*, *The Gentle Sex* (which he co-directed with Leslie Howard) and *Strawberry Roan* still retain a certain liveliness and truth of observation. In 1946 he made what remains for many his best film, *Beware of Pity*, adapted from Stefan Zweig and distinguished by an exquisite performance from Lilli Palmer.

He continued to make films until the late 1950s, latterly mostly farces like *My Wife's Lodger, Fun at St. Fanny's* and *Dry Rot*. He was also quick to see the possibilities of television: in one of the earliest film programmes he had his corner, reminiscing about the past and commenting, sometimes trenchantly, on films of the present. For the last few years he had been living in retirement. He was married twice, to Philippa Preston and to the actress Isobel Elsom, who starred for him in such silent films as *Dick Turpin's Ride to York, The Wandering Jew* and *The Love Story of Aliette Brunon*. He was a link with an age of British cinema which is rapidly becoming ancient history: as long as he lived it could not vanish utterly.

August 29, 1967.

Sir Richard Elwes, O.B.E., a Judge of the High Court of Justice from 1958 to 1966, died on September 4, 1968, at the age of 67.

He was born on May 28, 1901, the fifth son of the singer, Gervase Elwes. His youth was spent at Billing Hall, near Northampton, as one of a united and talented family, all accomplished in the arts and in country pursuits. His brother Simon became the well-known artist, his brother Val a Monseigneur in the Roman Catholic Church; and he and his five brothers all served as lieutenant-colonels in the Second World War.

Richard, after his years at Christ Church, Oxford, chose the Bar and was called by the Inner Temple in 1925. He joined the Midland Circuit, where he quickly began to acquire an extensive common law practice. As a very young man he was led by Norman Birkett prosecuting in the famous cases of the burning car (Rouse) and the abduction and murder of a child (Nodder).

Few advocates of the period had such grace and polish as Richard Elwes. His persuasiveness in mitigation before a judge or in defending a criminal before a jury were the admiration of his colleagues. His choice of phrase, his musical voice and distinguished looks, his candour and dash and good humour, his courage and good sense were powerful instruments of advocacy which he fully used. He was not perhaps at his best with laborious detail or with highly technical points of law or procedure and was the first to admit it, but in his understanding of human failings and emotions and of the principles of fairness and straight dealing, he was supreme. It was these qualities which enabled Richard Elwes to shine brightly, even on a Circuit which at that time contained Norman Birkett, two future Lord Chancellors (Manningham-Buller and Gardiner), Rodger Winn, Gilbert Paull, Jack Simon, many others who now adorn the Bench and many who might have done.

To his colleagues at the Bar Elwes was ever a good friend and willing adviser, and above all, to those in trouble or distress, a generous help.

The war of 1939 came upon him at the age of 38, when he was about to take silk. He was called up for service with the Northamptonshire Yeomanry, of which he had long been a member, but static defensive pseudo-war at home did not suit him and he quickly arranged to join the 69th Infantry Brigade in France as Staff Captain, returning sooner than he expected to this country with the rest of the B.E.F. The last years of the war he spent as an A.A.G. at the War Office in charge of matters affecting British prisoners of war in enemy hands, and exchanges. He was made O.B.E. in 1944.

During the war he turned to poetry. As he said of himself "Inter arma silent leges, cantat advocatus." His volume of poems produced in 1941 was well received and deservedly so—elegant, civilized, humane, they were pleasant solace in troubled times. Some years earlier he had collaborated, with his mother, Lady Winefride Elwes, in a life of his father.

After the war was over he returned immediately to the Bar and found restarting no easy matter. But he gradually picked up his professional progress. He became Recorder of Northampton in 1946, took silk in 1950, and became successively chairman of Quarter Sessions in the counties of Rutland, Derby and Bedford. In 1958 he was made a High Court Judge.

While Elwes' life was so closely knit to the practice and administration of the law, he had many outside interests, notably music and books, and pictures, good writing and good talk. He was a devout adherent of the Roman Catholic Church in which he had been educated and for which he had a deep loyalty throughout life. His charm and kindness were without doubt rooted deep in his religious principles.

He married in 1926 Freya, elder daughter of Sir Mark Sykes, of Sledmere. They had two sons and three daughters.

September 6, 1968.

Sir Herbert William Emerson, G.C.I.E., K.C.S.I., C.B.E., who died on April 12, 1962, at the age of 80, rose in the Indian Civil Service to be Governor of the Punjab, and later did great international humanitarian work as the administrative head of the League of Nations, and later the United Nations, organization for the relief and repatriation or settlement of war refugees.

He was born on June 1, 1881, and educated at Calday Grange Grammar School and Magdalene College, Cambridge, of which in later year he was made an honorary Fellow. He entered the I.C.S. in 1905 and was gazetted to the Punjab. In 1917 he became Assistant Commissioner and Settlement Officer a post which brought him into close touch with the hardy Punjab peasantry and their problems. He took a keen interest in the customs and folklore of the countryside, and in particular those of the primitive peoples of the Simla Hills. He was selected in 1926 to be Financial Secretary of the Punjab Government and in the following year became Chief Secretary.

In 1930 he was called to Delhi to be Home Secretary at the centre and at once had to deal with a further civil disobedience campaign. He was closely associated with the negotiations at the Viceroy's House between Lord Irwin (later Lord Halifax) and Ghandi whereby the campaign was called off and the Mahatma went to London as the sole representative of the National Congress at the Indian Round Table Conference. After an uneasy truce the non-violent resistance of authority was resumed and Emerson handled the situation with mingled firmness and perspicacity.

Early in 1933 Lord Willingdon sent Emerson to Lahore as Governor of his old province. Here he was confronted with and overcame serious communal conflicts, arising in the main out of what was known as the Shadigunj dispute. He showed strength of character as well as adaptability in guiding the Punjab's transition to autonomous government provided for in the 1935 Act. The coalition Union administration owed much to his insight and was to show greater staying power than any other provincial administration. So marked was Emerson's success that when his quinquennium was ending in 1937 he was reappointed for a further term of two years, but a prolonged spell of illness compelled his resignation in 1938.

The following year the League of Nations appointed Emerson for five years as High Commissioner for Refugees under a scheme which replaced the Nansen Office and the Office for Refugees coming from Germany. The 1939–45 War came swiftly to add enormously to the complexities and anxieties of the organization, and he was made Director of the Inter-Governmental Committee for Refugees. In the autumn of 1941 he was chosen by the Foreign Secretary, Anthony Eden, to be chairman of the Advisory Council on Aliens. By 1943 he was concerned with the repatriation of some 20 million people of different nationalities scattered over Europe. At the plenary session of the International Committee at the end of 1946 Emerson was able to report that the U.N. General Assembly had approved a draft Constitution for the International Refugee Organization to take over U.N.R.R.A.'s responsibility for the displaced persons camps. On this arrangement coming into force in 1947 Emerson retired after nine years of beneficent and devoted service.

He married, in 1906, Anne Evelyn, only daughter of Edwin Bellars, of Wisbech. There were three sons of the marriage, of whom one was killed in action in 1943.

April 14, 1962.

Empress Menen of Ethiopia—See under **Ethiopia.**

Brian Epstein, who was found dead at his home in Belgravia, London, on August 27, 1967, was born in Liverpool on September 19, 1934, the elder son of Harry and Queenie Epstein. His father, who died in July, 1967, ran a successful furniture business in Liverpool. As a child he was shy, sensitive and artistic. He was educated at seven schools in all, finally leaving Wrekin College at the age of 16 to enter the family business.

He began as a furniture salesman at £5 a week in 1950. But in 1956, at the age of 22, he gave it all up to go to R.A.D.A., mainly in order to satisfy his frustrated artistic ambitions. However, he spent just a year at R.A.D.A. when he decided to leave. He disliked actors.

He returned to the family business this time to a new branch which was being opened in the centre of Liverpool in Great Charlotte Street. Here he looked after the record department, throwing himself completely into the work. It was his determination always to please every customer, which led to the shop's success. He guaranteed to get any record which anyone wanted.

When he started there was one assistant and himself. In 1959, two years after opening, the department covered three floors and employed a staff of 30. Another branch was opened in Whitechapel, which was equally successful.

But by 1961 business success was beginning to make him feel frustrated again. He took up acting once more and began studying languages. But he felt he still had not found out what he wanted to do with life.

On October 28, 1961, there was a request for a record "My Bonnie" by the Beatles. It has been said, subsequently, that it was a flood of requests for "My Bonnie" which brought the Beatles to his attention. But up to that time there had been only one. If it had not been for his rule always to get any record requested he would never have come across them.

The record in question had been produced in Germany and was not available in Britain.

BEATLES' MAGNETISM

In tracking it down he discovered, to his surprise, that not only were the Beatles a Liverpool group, but they had returned from Germany and were now playing in a Liverpool club, the Cavern.

It was their presence, he always said, which first captivated him. They had a personal magnetism which he had never come across before. With no previous experience or knowledge of the pop world, he became their manager. It was the artistic challenge he was looking for. Brian Epstein was also the man the Beatles were looking for.

They were not unsuccessful until he became their manager. They were already one of the leading groups on Merseyside. But they had had no national experience and no record contract in England.

He always said there was no single reason for the success of the Beatles. It was an amalgam of many. But if any one man could be said to have made the Beatles, at least caused the public to be aware of them, that was Brian Epstein. Certainly until he arrived there were no visible signs of them getting out of the Liverpool clubs and ballrooms.

He helped their success not by changing them but by eliminating what at that time was considered unprofessional and undesirable. For example, he made them wear suits on stage.

He stopped them smoking, eating and swearing during their act. He explained that this was the only way to get B.B.C. producers in Manchester to take them seriously and the large ballrooms to engage them. He did not change their music in any way. What he did was make it, and them, presentable and attractive to the world.

His business efficiency also helped, transforming their system of bookings and payments. He organized their whole lives for them which no one had ever done before. For almost the first year he made little profit for himself, if any, in promoting and running them.

Most of the major record companies turned him down at first. It was assumed at the time that no one could ever make it from outside London. "They will be bigger than Elvis", he told the London record men, who just laughed.

But they were eventually taken by E.M.I. who, in October, 1962, released their first record "Love me do". This was followed by their first number one hit "Please, Please Me".

Beatlemania hit Britain in the autumn of 1963, and by the following year they were the best known people in the world. For the first time in the history of pop music, not only had Liverpool taken over from London; in the international market Britain took over from America.

Throughout the following years of triumph and unprecedented crowds in most major cities in the world, the Beatles relied completely on the judgment and guidance of Brian Epstein.

GENTLE AMATEUR

He became a major figure in the pop record business, managing groups like Gerry and the Pacemakers, and Cilla Black. More recently he returned to the theatre again, acquiring the Saville Theatre.

Brian Epstein was essentially a gentleman businessman, a gentle amateur among the Tin Pan Alley wheeler-dealers. He was in no sense a ruthless businessman, as many have imagined. He relied on his word rather than the contracts. For example, he himself never signed the contract which made him the manager of the Beatles. He felt their mutual regard for each other was enough.

Perhaps now and again he worked on intuition and feeling, a quality he shared with the Beatles, which made it difficult for outsiders to follow his mind exactly. But in all his dealings he was completely honest and trustworthy. By his presence and success in the pop world he not only transformed its power and stature, he made it more respectable.

Despite the fact that the Beatles stopped touring last year and in some senses began to go the wrong way—John Lennon acting in a film, Paul McCartney writing the music for a film—he and the Beatles were as close as they had ever been. He shared all the developments in their interests and in their music.

It was a friendship based not just on his being their manager. He was part of them. He believed in their talent, that it was something absolutely unique of its kind, and their success gave him constant pleasure, as did the success of all his artists. He had a great zest for life, he lived in style and with style, but yet he remained natural and unaffected by his power and by his fame in a world where such fame tends to turn heads.

August 28, 1967.

François Christiaan Erasmus, former South African Minister of Justice, died on January 7, 1967 while on holiday at Bredasdorp, Cape Province. He was 70.

He became Minister of Justice at the end of 1959, shortly before trouble over African pass-laws broke out in the Sharpeville township. Some 71 people died during police shooting.

Erasmus recommended declaration of a state of emergency and nearly 2,000 people of all races were detained without trial for many weeks.

François Christiaan Erasmus was born on January 19, 1896, in Merweville, Cape Province, and educated at Worcester High School and at the University of Cape Town, where he graduated in law. After practising for a short time he became Assistant Organizer of the Nationalist Party in the Cape and Chief Organizer in 1930. In 1933 he entered Parliament as Member for Moorreesburg. He was one of the first professional party organizers to enter Parliament, initiating a tendency which has steadily grown since in the Nationalist Party.

Erasmus was a strong Malan follower from the beginning of his political career and was one of a small band who opposed coalition and then fusion of Nationalists under Hertzog and the South African Party under Smuts in 1933.

In Parliament he soon disclosed a keen interest in military matters on which he became his party's chief spokesman. When the Nationalists came into power in 1948 it was natural, therefore, that he should become Defence Minister and he administered his department with obvious enthusiasm and knowledge.

Although after becoming Minister he almost wholly gave up ordinary political exchanges in debate his replacement of officers with distinguished war service by others thought to have Nationalist leanings brought constant attack on him from the Opposition. So did the steady elimination of symbols with British associations, such as the crowns on officers' "pips" which he replaced with a symbolic representation of Cape Town Castle.

Erasmus showed steadily more and more interest in naval affairs and under his administration South African naval forces grew steadily until they were weighty enough to take over the Simonstown Naval Base from the Royal Navy in 1955. Erasmus was deeply concerned about the vulnerability of South Africa—and, indeed, the whole of southern Africa—to air attack from the Middle East as well as to attack from dissident elements from within. His broad policy therefore was consistently to seek the cooperation of all other relevant powers (including especially the United Kingdom) in a common African defence system, combined with constant preparedness against internal disorder.

In furtherance of his former policy he agreed when South Africa took over the Simonstown base that close liaison should remain with the Royal Navy for seaward defence in the South Atlantic.

He was taken ill with heart trouble while in London in 1959. In July, 1961, Dr. Verwoerd appointed him Ambassador to Italy. He returned from this post in 1965.

January 9, 1967.

Fritz Erler, who died on February 22, 1967, in Pforzheim, south Germany, at the age of 53, would almost certainly have become leader of the Social Democratic Party last year if he had not succumbed to a serious blood disease. He would now be in the Cabinet exercising the practical responsibility for which he worked so hard to prepare his party. He had a first-class mind combined with a sense of realism that provided a constant check on the more utopian ideologues among his colleagues. Over many years he played a leading and sometimes decisive role formulating Social Democratic policy, particularly on defence and foreign affairs. He had many friends in Britain, and was especially close to Hugh Gaitskell, with whom he had a great deal in common.

Erler's political attitudes were best summed up in some of the statements he made while the party was debating its great reform of 1959, when much of its Marxist heritage was dropped and it set out seriously to win power in an increasingly prosperous and middle class country. The electorate, he said, would give the Social Democratic Party responsibility only if it showed "the capacity and the will to shape this state in which we live, and not some state in the distant future ... we are fighting not the state but a false policy of the government and its majority". The fact that something so obvious needed saying at that time was a sign of how much the party had to learn. Erler was one of its best teachers, and many people in west Germany will find it tragic that he could not live to enjoy the fruits of his work.

How successful he would have been as a leader is difficult to say. He was well aware that he lacked a public presence. In private conversation he was brilliant, perceptive, and wonderfully honest. On the platform he often seemed a little dry, remote, and earnest. He was too honest and too self-critical to play to the gallery, and he never won a warm public following. But his qualities were widely acknowledged and admired and it is possible that television would have given him the sort of intimate means of communication that he would have needed to win over the minds, if not the hearts, of the voters.

Without Erler, the Social Democratic Party would certainly have played a far less important and sophisticated role in the evolution of west Germany's defence policies. The party originally opposed rearmament and membership of Nato.

DOUBTS OVER NATIONALISM

Once these became inevitable Erler did a great deal to develop lines of constructive criticism, in spite of resistance from pacifist elements on the left wing. He was determined that the Bundeswehr should not become the child, and perhaps the servant, of the ruling party. Later he supported German membership of the proposed multilateral nuclear force, though he gradually became more aware of its disadvantages. His main aim was to ensure that the west German forces would remain integrated in the western alliance, and he was extremely critical of France for taking a path that would inevitably, he said, stimulate similarly nationalist aspirations in west Germany. At the party conference of 1964, when these issues were debated, Erler clearly began to emerge as the next leader of the party.

Erler was also one of the strongest proponents of reconciliation with Poland. In 1965 he called for bilateral talks with Poland clearly intended to prepare the way for recognition of the present frontiers. While he had to be careful what he said in public, there is little doubt that he privately regarded the Government's legalistic attitude towards the Oder-Neisse frontier as mistaken.

In the Bundestag, where he was a member from 1949 onwards, he was a sharp and formidable debater, with a command of both facts and issues that put him head and shoulders above many of his opponents. His combination of intellect, perception, passion, and responsibility, made him a credit and an example not only to his own party but to west German political life as a whole.

Fritz Erler was born in Berlin on July 14, 1913, the son of a worker in the graphic trade and an ardent Social Democrat. He was educated at high school and at Berlin's School of Administration, and also in Paris. He became a civil servant in Berlin. After the Nazis came to power he worked underground to maintain socialist organizations. He was arrested by the Gestapo in 1938 and sentenced to 10 years imprisonment. In 1945 he escaped as he was being transported from Kassel prison to Dachau concentration camp. He then lived in hiding until the Allies took over, when the French made him a local official in their zone of occupation.

Elected to the Bundestag in 1949, Erler became a member of the Executive of the Social Democratic Party in 1956, Deputy Floor Leader in 1957, member of the Presidium in 1958, Floor Leader in 1964, and Deputy Party Leader in the same year. He also held various appointments in European organizations, and was author of a number of books about socialism, democracy, and defence.

Erler's last important public pronouncement in the summer of 1966 was to have been delivered in the abortive debates with east Germany. When the arrangements fell through he gave his speech on television. It was a moving and urgent appeal for reconciliation between the two parts of Germany.

In 1905 Erler married Maria Fahle, who bore him three children.

February 23, 1967

General Sir George Erskine, G.C.B., K.B.E., D.S.O., who died on August 29, 1965, at the age of 66, made his name in the Second World War as commander of the famous 7th Armoured Division, the "Desert Rats", but he will be chiefly remembered for the great part he played in suppressing the Mau Mau rebellion in Kenya.

Erskine was a big man, both physically and mentally. His commanding presence was such as to give to all who served under him the greatest confidence in him as a leader. In the North African campaign Lord Montgomery, who greatly admired his calmness and resolution in action, described him as a "tower of strength". He had a keen insight into political problems, which served him well in the high appointments he held in Belgium and Germany during and after the war and, later, in Egypt and Kenya. While he carried on his campaign ruthlessly against the Mau Mau rebels, he was always conscious of the fact that the problem was essentially a political one, and his ultimate aim was that the Africans should regard his troops as friends and protectors and not as their oppressors.

George Watkin Eben James Erskine was born on August 23, 1899, the son of Major-General George Elphinstone Erskine. He was educated at Charterhouse and the Royal Military College, Sandhurst. He was commissioned in the 60th Rifles in 1918, and was on active service for a few weeks on the Western Front before the end of the First World War. Between the wars he served with his regiment and, after passing through the Staff College, Camberley, he held a number of staff appointments in India and at home. In 1940 he commanded the 2nd battalion of his regiment for six months, and was then promoted brigadier to command the 69th Infantry Brigade, which he took to Egypt with the 50th Division.

BATTLE OF ALAMEIN

Erskine took part in the fighting at Gazala and Bir Hacheim, the battles at El Alamein and the advance into Tunisia. At the second battle of El Alamein, when he was brigadier, general staff, of the 13th Corps, it fell to him to take important decisions affecting the course of operations; in the words of the citation for the D.S.O. which he won there, he was stated to have been "largely responsible for the success of the battle". When Sir John Harding was wounded at Mareth, Erskine succeeded him as commander of the 7th Armoured Division, and led it in the break-through to capture the city of Tunis. Under his command this division landed at Salerno during the critical battle which made good the foothold of the allied armies on the Italian coast south of Naples and he led it later, with equal success, in Normandy.

Then followed a series of appointments which gave him the experience of dealing with civil authorities, both friendly and unfriendly, an experience which was to prove valuable to him in his later roles. In 1945, after being head of the mission to Belgium, he became deputy Chief of Staff on the Control Commission for Germany, and was stationed in Berlin when the mere maintenance of existence of the German population was an intricate problem which he played a considerable part in solving successfully. After Berlin a term in Hongkong as G.O.C. Land Forces in China followed until, in 1948, he became director general of the Territorial Army at the War Office.

EGYPTIAN COMMAND

In January, 1949, Erskine returned to Egypt as commander of the British troops. The period of his command was a particularly difficult one. The Wafd Government was attempting to force a British evacuation of the Canal Zone and was organizing anti-foreign rioting and attacks on the garrison and their families. His handling of the situation was brilliant, and his term of command was extended until April, 1952, by which time he had restored order. For his services in Egypt he was created K.B.E. and K.C.B.

On his returning to England he was G.O.C.-in-C. Eastern Command for a year, after which he was appointed Commander-in-Chief East Africa to deal with the Mau Mau rebellion, with direct responsibility to the War Office. This proved to be his most exacting assignment.

When Erskine arrived in Kenya in June, 1953, the Mau Mau rebellion had been in progress for some eight months, during which time it had been steadily gathering force. The militant wing of the Kikuyu, and the smaller tribes who became their allies in the insurrection, was about 12,000 strong; it was supported and supplied by the majority of the Kikuyu, who numbered over a million. The area affected was a square of 120-mile sides, and included extensive forests and mountain features which greatly favoured the operations of the insurgents.

The security forces under his command numbered eventually 11 battalions, in addition to over 20,000 police and 25,000 of the Kikuyu Guard. He adopted an active strategy, the basis of which was to release the army from static police duties so far as possible and to employ them in offensive operations in the forest and the mountains, in conjunction with bombing by the R.A.F. In other areas his troops acted in support of the civil authority in rounding up rebels and suspects. A clean-up of Nairobi in Operation Anvil marked the turn of the tide.

DIVIDED POWERS

When Erskine handed over to his successor, General Sir Gerald Lathbury, in May, 1955, the back of the rebellion had been broken, although another 18 months were to pass before the operational phase of the emergency was completed.

It is no secret that Erskine did not always see eye to eye with the Governor, Sir Evelyn Baring, or with the white settlers whom he often offended by his plain speaking and robust methods. It has been argued that his task could have been more effectively performed if he had been appointed governor, as Field Marshal Lord Harding was in Cyprus during the emergency there. But the circumstances were so different, in particular because one-sixteenth only of the area of Kenya was affected, that it would have been unwise to supersede the civil administration, in spite of the inevitable strains which resulted from divided responsibility.

His last military appointment was as G.O.C.-in-C. Southern Command from 1955 to 1958, after which he retired from the Army. He was then Lieutenant-Governor and Commander-in-Chief of Jersey until 1963.

He was A.D.C. General to the Queen from 1955 till 1958 and was Colonel Commandant of the 2nd K.R.R.C. from 1956.

He married in 1929 Ruby, daughter of Sir Evelyn de la Rue, second baronet, and had two sons and one daughter.

August 30, 1965.

Lord Esher, G.B.E., died on October 8, 1963, at Châteauneuf, near Grasse, at the age of 82.

The National Trust was one of the greatest interests of Lord Esher's life. He was chairman of its general purposes committee for 25 years and historic buildings committee since its inception in 1934. Although Lord Esher resigned from the chairmanship of both these committees some years ago he was still an invaluable member of them as well as of the National Trust executive committee. He had probably done more for the trust over the past 25 to 30 years than any other person.

Among the many other posts which he had held in his long service to many good causes were the chairmanship of the Trustees of the London Museum, the Grants Committee of the Historic Churches Trust, the Friends of the National Libraries, and the Victorian Society.

COMMITTEE WORK

He was Life President of the Society for the Protection of Ancient Buildings, and had also served as president of the London Society.

His relish for the finesse of committee work and his long experience in the niceties of compromise and evasion which it often entails gave a professional smoothness to his performance at the baize table which was all the more effective for the fact that he was for the most part, and in the best sense of the word, an amateur.

As a bibliophile he was something of a phenomenon. Esher was for 20 years one of the most thoughtful, pertinacious, discriminating (one would have confidently said dedicated) collectors of English literary first editions, mainly of the nineteenth century. He printed a list of the contents of the library at Watlington Park, not for ostentation but in order that such favourite booksellers as Evans of Elkin Mathews could help him to fill the gaps. In the era of Sadleir, Parrish and Carroll Wilson his name and influence were commensurate with theirs. Yet in 1946 he quit, and sent his books to Sotheby's.

BOOKLOVERS' SURPRISE

Connoisseurs were surprised to discover that he had cared so little for fine condition; but the surprise to bibliophiles at large was that so firmly established a collector could cease to collect.

Oliver Sylvain Baliol Brett, third Viscount Esher, son of the second Viscount, was born on March 23, 1881, and educated at Eton. He was assistant private secretary (unpaid) to the Secretary of State for India, Lord Morley, from 1905 to 1910. In the general elections of January and December, 1910, he stood unsuccessfully as a Liberal for Huntingdon.

In the First World War he was attached to the War Office and retired in 1921 as a captain in the 16th Battalion, London Regiment (T.A.). He was made M.B.E. (Mil.) in 1918 and raised to G.B.E. (Civil) in 1955. He had succeeded his father in 1930.

In 1912 he married Antoinette, daughter of August Heckscher, of New York. They had one son—the Hon. Lionel Brett, the architect, who succeeds to the title—and three daughters.

October 9, 1963.

Levi Eshkol, Prime Minister of Israel, who died in Jerusalem on February 26, 1969, at the age of 73, was a mellow, affable and folksy man whose talents as a conciliator advanced him to the dome of Israel political power.

It was an irony of history that the outstanding event of his six years' tenure as Prime Minister was the 1967 war which ended with Israel ruling over more territory than under King David or any other famous Jewish warrior leader. In fact the lovable Eshkol appeared so unseemly as a war leader that in the critical days before the 1967 eruption his closest associates manifested a lack of confidence in him and compelled him to turn over his defence portfolio to General Moshe Dayan, his arch political foe. It was one of several episodes during his premiership that broke his heart. Another development during his tenure which was more consistent with his personality was the unification of three workers' parties into the new Israel Labour Party and an alignment with Mapam which created the first political faction to have an absolute majority in the Knesset. At the same time he also held together a government of national unity comprising all but a few fringe parties.

A tragic aspect of Eshkol's premiership was his bitter feud with David Ben-Gurion, the former premier who had personally chosen him as successor. Eshkol had accepted the post in 1963 with considerable reluctance, fully conscious that he faced the challenge of an Attlee following a Churchill or a Truman succeeding a Roosevelt, but he never dreamed the challenge would culminate in attempts by his patron to unseat him.

Eshkol followed the basic policies of his illustrious predecessor but deviated on secondary matters. He made concessions to political rivals which Ben-Gurion had firmly declined to consider. He thus improved the interparty climate but enraged Ben-Gurion to the point where he publicly and repeatedly declared him unfit to govern. The feud, which broke a 45-year friendship, also split the ruling Mapai party. The party split was eventually repaired but Eshkol was never able to utilize his craftsmanship as a conciliator to patch up his differences with Ben-Gurion.

Like most Zionist and Israel leaders of his generation, Eshkol came from Eastern Europe.

FEAR OF POGROMS

He was born on October 25, 1895, in Oratovo, a Ukrainian railway junction near Kiev. The family name was Shkolnik but he Hebraized it after Israel became independent. He spent his early youth studying the Bible and Talmud, part of the time behind barred doors and boarded windows for fear that the wave of anti-Jewish pogroms after the Russo-Japanese war might reach Oratovo. At the age of 16 he went to Vilna for a secondary school education, and there he met Zionist socialists and came to think of Jewish independence in Palestine as an alternative to the impotence and submission of a helpless minority in Tsarist Russia.

In 1914 he sailed to Palestine which was then under Turkish rule. He landed in Jaffa wearing the tight fitting, brass buttoned uniform of a Russian secondary school student, and his only possessions were a small valise and a pillow with a red slip his mother had given him. Eager to reclaim the soil as a true pioneer, he left the port city for Petah Tiqwa, called the "mother of Jewish colonies", walking 10 miles through sands, his shoes over his shoulders, following the stage coach because he had no money for the fare.

He obtained employment in Petah Tiqwa, building a new pumphouse for irrigation and also became active in fledgling labour organizations. However, he wanted to do something more challenging; so he joined a group which established new Jewish settlements in the eroded, gravel-studded hills near Jerusalem, clearing the soil with a pistol on his hip by day, and taking his turn guarding the fields and property at night.

When the British Army entered Palestine during the 1914–18 War, Eshkol enlisted in the 40th Royal Fusiliers of the Jewish Legion, where he began his association with Ben-Gurion and other future leaders of Israel. He won his corporal's stripes, but lost them for absence without leave, having returned to camp late from Jerusalem where he attended the laying of the corner-stone for the Hebrew University.

After the war he was one of the first settlers in Degania Beth, a collective farm in the Jordan Valley, but malaria interrupted his farming career and he was recruited for public service.

SENT TO BERLIN

Active in Hapoel Hazair, a Zionist labour party which later merged into Mapai, he was a delegate to the founding conference of the General Federation of Jewish Labour (Histadrut).

As an official of the Histadrut, he helped plan and develop the first Jewish settlements in the Jezreel Valley and Emek Hefer. He also represented his party as a delegate to various Zionist Congresses. After the Nazis rose to power in Germany, he was sent to Berlin by the Zionist Organization to help transfer people and property to Palestine. He borrowed money from German Jews, bought irrigation, industrial and agricultural equipment which he shipped to Palestine and repaid the creditors in Palestine currency, thus enabling many refugees to salvage part of their property. During that period he also bought weapons and ammunition which he shipped clandestinely to Palestine for the Hagana, the underground Jewish defence force.

In 1944 he was brought to Tel Aviv as secretary of the local Labour Council and Ben-Gurion, who was then chairman of the Zionist Executive and leader of Mapai, appointed him to the high command of the Hagana. He was responsible there for finances and founding clandestine arms factories. When Israel became independent in 1948 and Ben-Guiron became Prime Minister and Minister of Defence, he appointed Eshkol director general (equivalent of permanent under-secretary) of the Defence Ministry. During the Palestine War of 1948, when the Israel Army was in the process of organization, he was thus Ben-Gurion's chief civilian aide in defence matters.

After the war, when the period of large-scale Jewish immigration began, Eshkol was elected to the executive of the Zionist Organization which maintained responsibility for settling and absorbing the immigrants. He was in charge of land settlement, and even after he joined Ben-Gurion's Cabinet in 1951, he doubled as a member of the Zionist Executive until he assumed the premiership. During his period of service some 500 new settlements were founded.

Eshkol's first Cabinet post was agriculture and in 1952 he became Minister of Finance.

HEIR TO PREMIERSHIP

Remarkably, he gained popularity in that post at a time when taxes were heavy and economic difficulties chronic. His popularity, personal charm, and conciliatory talents were often used by Ben-Gurion to smooth over domestic political troubles, and Eshkol gradually evolved as the Prime Minister's political trouble-shooter, the Number Two man in the government and Ben-Gurion's natural heir.

Two notable events in the first years of Eshkol's premiership were the establishment of full diplomatic relations with the German Federal Republic and the abolition of the military administration of the areas inhabited by the Arabs. In the general election of 1965, the Mapai-Achdut Alignment won 45 seats, and Eshkol was called on to form a new Ministry. He broadened the coalition with Mapam and the Independent Liberals. A section of Mapai, led by Ben-Gurion and supported by the former Minister, Moshe Dayan and Shimon Perez, had seceded, and formed a splinter party which bitterly opposed Eshkol. They obtained only 10 seats in the Knesset. But when the crisis came with Egypt and Syria in May, 1967, and Israel recognized that they would have to fight once more, Eshkol, after two weeks' earnest effort to avert war, appointed Dayan as Minister of Defence to meet the popular demand, and also brought into the Cabinet Mr. Begin, the leader of the Herut opposition party. The triumphant conduct of the war justified Eshkol's restraint so long as there was a possibility of the United States and United Kingdom Governments securing the freedom of navigation in the Gulf of Aqaba.

Eshkol is survived by a widow, his third wife, and by four daughters from his previous marriage.

February 27, 1969.

By the death of the **Empress Menen of Ethiopia,** which took place in Addis Ababa on February 15, 1962, after a long illness, the Emperor Haile Selassie lost a devoted consort who for 50 years shared his burdens, his dangers, his sorrows, his joys, and, above all, his unceasing labours for his people.

The Empress was born about 1891 in the Wollo Province of northern Ethiopia. Her father was Janterer Asfaw; on her mother's side she was of royal blood being the granddaughter of Negus Mikhail of Wollo and first cousin of Lij Yasu, the uncrowned successor of the Emperor Menelik, who was deposed in favour of the present Emperor. She was first married to an Ethiopian notable and had issue. In 1911 she married the present Emperor, who at that time was still known as Ras Tafari and was Governor of Harar Province. Five years later, when Lij Yasu's Islamic sympathies led to his deposition by a junta of notables, Ras Tafari was appointed Regent in his place. His position at first was far from secure, for Lij Yasu remained at large and served as a focus of disaffection among the Muslims of the eastern deserts of Ethiopia, while the attitude of Menelik's widow, the Empress Zauditu, still the ultimate repository of power, was equivocal. But the reforming zeal and dedicated activity of the new Regent, in which his wife participated fully, gradually extended his influence throughout the country.

Lij Yasu was eventually captured; in 1928 the Regent mastered a Palace revolution against himself with the aid of his wife, who hastily collected arms for his bodyguard, and prevailed upon the Empress Zauditu to accord him the style of King: and finally, in 1930, while his wife was ill with diabetes, which was to plague her thereafter, he crushed a revolt in the north by Ras Gugsa, the Empress Zauditu's former husband, who died in battle, while the Empress died of grief at the result. Ras Tafari thereupon ascended the throne and assumed his present titles.

JOINED IN EXILE

For the next five years the new Emperor was feverishly engaged in organizing and developing his empire. Education was his chief preoccupation, and it was doubtless under his influence that the Empress founded and endowed the girls' school in Addis Ababa which bears her name and is still the most important centre of female education in Ethiopia. She on her side was active. A deeply religious woman, she contributed to the construction of several new churches and was a keen supporter of charitable organizations. But their labours were interrupted by the political crisis which resulted in the Italian invasion of Ethiopia. In the ensuing conflict the Empress was at her consort's side, collecting provisions for the troops at the front and issuing an international appeal to the consciences of the world's women to aid Ethiopia in her struggle. When the outcome was clearly hopeless the Emperor sent her and his family out of the country, and he soon joined them in exile, first in Jerusalem and then in Bath.

In 1941, not long after the Emperor had recovered his throne, the Empress rejoined him in Addis Ababa. Her health was already a source of anxiety, and she was compelled to spend much of her time at a lower altitude than the capital; and the death in 1957, in a car accident, of her much beloved second son, the Duke of Harar, deeply affected both her and the Emperor. From then on she appeared little in public, though behind the scenes she undoubtedly continued to exercise a strong influence on her family and its affairs.

ROYAL VISIT

In 1958 she rallied sufficiently to be able to receive their Royal Highnesses the Duke of Duchess of Gloucester when they paid an official visit to Ethiopia, and even to attend the banquet given at the British Embassy on the occasion, and in 1959 she made a pilgrimage to Jerusalem to attend the Easter ceremonies of the Ethiopian Church there. It was, however, evident on her return that her health had not been equal to the effort and her condition gradually worsened in the months to come. Recently it became grave enough to compel the Emperor to cut short his attendance at the African "summit" conference in Lagos, and he was with her at the end.

She bore the Emperor six children, of whom three survive, including the present Crown Prince.

February 16, 1962.

Sir Lincoln Evans, C.B.E., who died on August 3, 1970, at the age of 80, will be best remembered as the spokesman of the T.U.C. on economic affairs during the difficult period of wage restraint under the Labour government in the late forties.

T.U.C. policy then was largely controlled by a right-wing triumvirate wielding big block votes: Arthur Deakin of the Transport and General Workers' Union, Sir William Lawther, of the Miners, and Tom (now Lord) Williamson, of the National Union of General and Municipal Workers. As General Secretary of the Iron and Steel Trades Confederation, Lincoln Evans had not a comparable block vote but he was closely associated with the other three.

He had the ability, which they lacked, to expound economic policy with exceptional clarity in readily understandable terms. His persuasiveness did much to induce the trade union movement to cooperate with the Government's unpopular measures to deal with inflation in the days of Sir Stafford Cripps and Hugh Gaitskell. Many would rate him the most able chairman of the economic committee that the T.U.C. has ever had.

Like other right-wing T.U.C. leaders, Lincoln Evans was the object of constant attack by Communists and other left-wingers in the movement. This criticism culminated in a series of personal attacks after the Conservatives returned to power in 1951 with a commitment to denationalize the steel industry.

Lincoln Evans and three other members of the General Council joined the new Iron and Steel Board, with the approval of the council and their action was attacked in a resolution at the congress of 1953 by representatives of the Boilermakers and Engineers and others.

ABLE DEFENCE

Sir Lincoln made a dignified and able speech in their defence and the resolution was defeated by a majority of nearly two to one. Sir Lincoln was a full-time member and deputy chairman of the board until 1960 and after that a part-time member.

The son of a steelworker, Lincoln Evans was born in Swansea in September, 1889. He left school at 12 and worked as a barber's lather boy and as an errand boy, among other jobs, before obtaining employment in a tinplate works at the age of 17 and joining his union. He became increasingly active in the union, the Iron and Steel Trades Confederation, and was on the executive for 12 years before becoming assistant general secretary and finally general secretary in 1946.

He was a member of the T.U.C. General Council from 1945 to 1952. He was for a time chairman of the joint body of the T.U.C. and the Workers' Educational Association and sat on the National Arbitration Tribunal and several courts of inquiry. He was a member of the B.B.C. General Advisory Council.

He married in 1911 Marion, daughter of David Fender. They had a son and a daughter. His wife died in 1964.

August 5, 1970.

Dr. H. V. Evatt, P.C., a former Leader of the Opposition in Australia, who died in Canberra on November 2, 1965, at the age of 71, had a career which began brilliantly and closed in a frustration of effort and ability that disappointed both the man himself and the party and country he tried so furiously to serve.

A man of prodigious intellect and industry, Evatt faced a difficult task when in 1951 he succeeded Chifley to become the first man without a trade union background to lead the Australian Labour Party. He had behind him a brilliant record—at the University of Sydney; at the Bar; on the bench, where he had been the youngest High Court Judge in Australian history; and as Foreign Secretary. As the Australian representative at the establishment of the United Nations in 1945 he had been largely instrumental in getting more authority for the General Assembly in the Charter, and was always a staunch champion of the rights of the smaller powers. As president of the Assembly in 1948–49 he had played a considerable part in the settlement of the Berlin blockade.

Yet the haul back to office looked like being a long one for the Labour Party after the defeat of 1949. The floating vote had been frightened by Chifley's attempt to nationalize the banks and by Evatt's opposition to the Communist Party Dissolution Act. Finally the Petrov defection from the Soviet Embassy in April, 1954, meant that the election a few weeks later was held in a crisis atmosphere favourable to the Government—and it was a surprise that they retained power with a majority of only seven.

Thus far Evatt's leadership of the Labour Party had been unexceptional. It became, however, to a large extent because of this experience and also because of the influence against him during the elections of the Roman Catholic church, highly controversial and at times erratic. In October, 1954, with his eyes wide open to the long-term consequences, he deliberately precipitated the great sectarian split in the Labour Party when he declared that the political wing of Catholic Action was plotting to capture control of the party through the industrial groups. Evatt was not a Roman Catholic but even Chifley, who was a Roman Catholic, had foreseen that the split must come if Labour was to remain true to its principles, so that Evatt was able to retain the support of many Catholic members of the Labour Party, including its deputy Leader in Parliament, Mr. Calwell.

LABOUR SPLIT

However, if Evatt cannot be blamed for starting and hammering wider a split that kept Labour out of office much too long for the political health of the country, he does bear a great part of the responsibility for making the breach so bitter a personal thing between men who had once been colleagues, even friends. He did not shirk the purge that kept him from office, but he could not forgive those who had made it necessary.

All this time federal politics were bedevilled by a coldness between the Leader of the Opposition and the Prime Minister which permeated the business of Parliament and the life of the nation. Evatt saw Mr. Menzies as the unscrupulous architect of his long exclusion from office, and the Prime Minister was no doubt chagrined by having to contend so often (for example, in the case of the Communist Party Dissolution Act) with a legal mind superior in all probability to his own.

Evatt was a poor debater who generally chose to remain silent under the swingeing scorn of Mr. Menzies's oratory. Even his prepared speeches became tortuous and repetitive as they proceeded: neither wit nor humour could find a place in them, for to Evatt all that he fought for was serious and the forces against him very personal, especially when he felt justice or freedom or constitutional liberty, as John Stuart Mill understood them, to be at stake.

PASSION FOR JUSTICE

His writing betrays his philosophy: *Liberalism in Australia—an Historical Study* (1919) was followed by *Conveyancing in New South Wales* (1923), *British Dominions as Mandatories* (1934) and *The King and his Dominion Governors* (1936), a consideration of the reserve powers of the Crown in Great Britain and the Dominions, in which he argued for a closer analysis and definition. *Injustice within the Law* (1937) was a study of the case of the Dorchester Labourers. *Rum Rubellion* (1938) was an account of the overthrow of Governor Bligh in 1808 and *Australian Labour Leader* was both the story of W. A. Holman and a history of the Australian Labour Movement from 1890 to 1920. He also wrote monographs on history, political science and constitutional law. To the very end of a crowded life he read with hunger and discernment from all sources.

An abstract, altruistic passion for justice and a self-centred determination to expose the machinations of those who sought to destroy him politically sometimes impelled him into actions so naive and unwise that they could not fail to injure the public standing of the Labour Party. He would act on these occasions without consulting his colleagues. In October, 1955, they learnt for the first time during a debate in Parliament on the report of the Royal Commission on Espionage that their leader had written to Molotov to ask him if the documents brought from the Soviet Embassy in Canberra by Petrov were genuine.

His approach to foreign affairs, as Leader of the Opposition, was based on a stubborn regard for the charter of the United Nations, which he would invoke as the first remedy for all international ills. His critics, especially on the Liberal benches, were quick to point out that he condemned American and even British policies more roundly than those of Russia, and they drew the obvious conclusions.

Evatt became a prickly person, whose greatest strength and weakness lay perhaps in a sense of mission (like that of Cripps or Ernest Bevin) which he developed against the slings and arrows of a fortune that must have seemed outrageous and a chosen course both arduous and unhappy.

Herbert Vere Evatt was born on April 30, 1894, at East Maitland, N.S.W., on the edge of coalfields near the Hunter constituency which he represented from 1958. He was one of six sons of the late John Ashmore Hamilton Evatt, a storekeeper, and the late Jeanie Sophia Evatt. He was educated at Fort Street High School, Sydney, at St. Andrew's College as a scholar and at Sydney University, where he held a Government bursarship. He won prizes and scholarships in mathematics, philosophy, English literature and law; he was president of the University Union. For services to university sport he was made a life member of the Sports Union.

Evatt took his B.A. with a triple first, proceeded to M.A. with a first, won university medals in both his LL.B. and LL.D. examinations, and received his Doctorate of Laws in 1924.

FOUGHT DEPORTATIONS

He became a tutor in philosophy at St. Andrew's College and was Challis Lecture in Legal Interpretation at Sydney. At the Bar he built up a successful practice and a high reputation as a constitutional lawyer. In 1925 he became a conspicuous figure by pleading successfully against the Federal Government's attempt to deport two left-wing leaders of the Seamen's Union, Walsh and Johansen. That same year he successfully contested Balmain in the state parliament, standing as an independent Labour candidate against official Labour. In 1928 he dropped the prefix "independent". In 1929 he became K.C. and in 1930 he was appointed to the High Court by the Scullin Labour Government; there was some criticism on the ground that he had been a strong party man.

THIRD BID FOR POWER

In 1940 he resigned from the bench, just before he would have become eligible for a pension, and won from the Liberals the marginal seat of Barton in the House of Representatives. In March, 1940, with Mr. Curtin, Evatt entered the Advisory War Council and in October he became Attorney General and Minister for External Affairs in the new Curtin Ministry. His purpose soon became clear: Australia was to be the principal representative of the British Commonwealth in the Pacific. In 1942 Evatt advocated the establishment of a Pacific War Council sitting in Washington, on which Australia and the United Kingdom would speak with equal voices, and it came into being that year.

As Minister for External Affairs, from 1941 to 1949, when Labour lost office, Evatt gave the Department its first major fillip, increasing its oversea posts and enhancing its status at home. He laid rather more than mere foundations for the subsequent building of Sir Percy Spender and Mr. Casey. Ironically, Sir Robert Menzies's command of the world stage owes not a little to Evatt's advocacy of Australia's right to be heard and his insistence that the leaders of small nations may be just as wise as the leaders of the big powers.

Throughout his life Evatt's choice of men was not always fortunate and, as Minister for External Affairs, he made appointments which were open to criticism.

Towards the end of 1958 he made his third and most determined electoral bid to beat Menzies. He announced in October a "family policy" to give the taxpayer £A120m. (£96m.) worth of extra social service benefits and other concessions. About 60,000 Australians were unemployed at the time and his policy was regarded as eminently responsible. But it was remembered that he had offered to abolish the means test in 1954 and an aura of irresponsibility still clung to him, for this and other reasons.

DEFEAT WITHOUT PARALLEL

It was a dramatic campaign, in which he travelled 17,000 miles in six weeks and had to rest for ten days with bronchial pneumonia. He also made an emotional and unexpected offer to resign the leadership of the Labour Party if the Democratic Labour Party would only direct its supporters to give their second preference votes to Labour. But the offer was spurned and Evatt went down to a defeat without parallel in the history of the Commonwealth. Menzies won a record majority of 32 and broke the Senate deadlock.

In February, 1959, Evatt met the parliamentary Labour party and was reelected leader for another three years. He beat Mr. E. J. Ward by 46 votes to 32, so registering his smallest majority since 1951.

Soon rumours were rife that he would become Chief Justice of New South Wales in succession to Sir Kenneth Street who was due to retire in January, 1960, and some thought that Evatt should have resigned the leadership of the Labour Party some considerable time before the official announcement, so making it clear beyond all doubt that the appointment—finally announced early in 1960—was not a *quid pro quo* in return for his resignation. He was taken ill in March, 1962, and retired in October that year.

In 1920 he married Mary Alice, only daughter of the late Samuel Fuller Sheffer. She and a son and daughter of the marriage survive him.

November 3, 1965.

Lord Evershed, P.C., who died at the age of 67 on October 3, 1966, had been a Judge of the Chancery Division, a Lord Justice of Appeal, Master of the Rolls and a Lord of Appeal in Ordinary. In addition to the heavy and responsible duties which those important offices demanded he had also been engaged on many extra-judicial tasks.

Francis Raymond Evershed was a man of considerable energy and vitality, with a sturdy figure of medium height, a quick mind, a ready smile, as well as being a lively companion, who achieved in his profession a high degree of success which he had rightly earned. As well as being a successful lawyer at the Bar and on the Bench, Evershed was also a keen law reformer with a forward-looking mind, more particularly in the area of practice and procedure in our own courts, and with a deep interest in the legal system of other countries. But the law was not his only claim. He had a gift for handling firmly, yet with tact, good humour and urbanity, social and industrial issues.

Evershed was born at Burton-on-Trent on August 8, 1899, son of the late Frank Evershed, a solicitor. He was educated at Clifton and Balliol College, Oxford (of which he became an Hon. Fellow in 1947). During the 1914–18 War he served with the Royal Engineers. Called to the Bar by Lincoln's Inn in 1923 he took silk 10 years later, at the early age of 34. In 1938 he was made a Bencher of his Inn, and elected Treasurer for the year 1958. He was remarkably successful as a practitioner, both as a junior and as a leader, and was frequently briefed before the House of Lords and the Judicial Committee of the Privy Council.

From 1939 to 1942 he was chairman of the Central Price Regulation Committee. The strenuous and searching demands of that work, for which an elaborate machinery had to be set up for the hearing of complaints, resulted in the fixing of prices over a wide-range of consumer goods.

WAR WORK

In 1942 Evershed became Regional Controller, until 1944, of the Nottinghamshire, Derbyshire and Leicestershire coal-producing area. This task, which urged the production of coal for the front and the factories, also called for the adjustment of relations between owners and miners, sometimes a delicate operation. During that period the first nationalization of a coal mine took place, for it was on his recommendation that in November, 1942, the State took over the Clifton Colliery at Nottingham.

Meantime, in 1941, Lord Reith, then Minister of Works and Buildings, appointed Evershed as a member of the Committee on Compensation and Betterment, of which Lord Uthwatt was chairman. In the same year the President of the Board of Trade made Evershed a member of the Industrial and Export Council.

In 1944 he was appointed a Judge of the Chancery Division. While still a judge he was the chairman, from 1945 to 1946, of the Commission on Wages and Conditions of Labour in the Cotton Spinning Industry; chairman in 1945 of the Committees of Inquiry into dock wages; and in the next year chairman of the Committee which considered prices and productions of textile machinery.

In April, 1947, after only two years on the High Court Bench, he was promoted a Lord Justice of Appeal. About a fortnight later his appointment was announced as chairman of the Committee—one of the most important of recent years—to inquire into the practice and procedure of the Supreme Court and to recommend what reforms were needed to reduce the cost of litigation and secure greater efficiency and dispatch of business. A number of interim reports were issued, and the final report, published in July, 1953, might be described as a significant document. A thorough investigation was carried out of the Rules of the Supreme Court, and many reforms were advocated, and have been carried out.

CONTRIBUTIONS TO THE LAW

In May, 1949, Evershed became Master of the Rolls, and was raised to the peerage in January, 1956, with the title of Baron Evershed of Staplehill, in the county of Derby. The mental and physical strain of that distinguished office is heavy, as it also involves many extra-judicial duties. The work of the Court of Appeal is itself severe, and the burden is increased when judgments have to be reserved. Evershed's contributions to the law were considerable. But, although naturally anxious to cover adequately all the matters raised, his judgments, on some occasions, whether *ex tempore* or reserved, were very long and over-elaborate. Though it is easy to criticize, perfection in performance is not a simple matter.

In November, 1956, in the first of the Maccabean lectures, he read a paper on "The Impact of Statute Law in England". The problem, he said, whether the Judges should not be released from the constricting processes on which they were so much engaged in interpreting Acts of Parliament, and new scope given to their independence, was well worthy of close attention. Should there not be a change in the method or character of the judicial function in the interpretation of enacted law? Though "problems created by the law must still be governed by the law", he asked whether it would be possible or useful for Parliament to depart from the present practice of detailed exposition (which invited literal construction and was encouraged by it in a kind of vicious circle), and deliberately leave for the Courts a defined scope for the old "equity".

In April, 1962, Evershed wrote two articles in *The Times* on the work of Appellate Courts, after there had been an exchange of visits to England and the United States of "teams" of judges and practising and academic lawyers for the purpose of examining the working in both countries of Appellate Courts, both civil and criminal. If from these visits nothing more was hoped for than an understanding and appreciation of another country's legal system, a useful purpose was served. The Court of Appeal, however, did adopt the experiment (which it was thought that the American comments on our system justified, though it was a matter recommended in the Evershed Report) of reading, before the hearing, the pleadings, the notice of appeal, the judgment of the trial Judge and any cases to which he had referred in his judgment.

As Master of the Rolls, Evershed was made chairman of the Historical Manuscripts Commission in 1949. In 1951 he became president of Clifton College; in 1952 a trustee of the Pilgrim Trust and in 1960 chairman; in 1953 a member of the Council of Legal Education and in 1956 chairman of the Law Advisory Committee of the British Council (as such he visited India and Ceylon in 1960). Since 1950 he had been a United Kingdom member of the Permanent Court of Arbitration at The Hague. In 1965 he was succeeded by Lord Harlech as president of The Pilgrims of Great Britain. He was given honorary degrees by many universities in Britain and overseas. In 1950 he became an Honorary Freeman of the Borough of Burton-on-Trent, and a Freeman of the City of London in 1953.

After many years of strenuous and varied service—for 13 of which he was Master of the Rolls—Evershed began to feel the need to ease the heavy and continual strain under which he had worked, but not to resign from a full and active life. On the retirement in March, 1962, of Lord Simonds from his office of Lord of Appeal in Ordinary, Evershed was appointed to succeed him. He gave up this post in 1965.

In 1928 he married Joan, the daughter of the late Mr. Justice Bennett.

October 4, 1966.

F

Sir Geoffrey Faber, president of the publishing house that bears his name, died on March 30, 1961, aged 71. Geoffrey Cust Faber was born on August 23, 1889, at Malvern, and was the second son of the Rev. Henry Mitford Faber, a housemaster at Malvern College. His family, of Yorkshire origin, was associated with education and with the Church. His grandfather had been a Fellow of Magdalen College, and was a brother of Father Faber. The first Headmaster of Malvern, Canon Arthur Faber, was a first cousin of his father's. His grandmother's family (Cust) was also clerical, and also of Yorkshire stock.

From Rugby Faber went up to Oxford with a scholarship at Christ Church, where he secured a First Class in Honour Mods, and a Second Class in Greats, and also took an active part in the O.U.D.S. After leaving Oxford he qualified himself for the Bar but never took up practice. He was early attracted towards publishing—two of his Oxford friends, Michael Sadleir and John Heinemann, had preceded him into this profession—and accepted an appointment with the Oxford University Press at the beginning of 1913. He abandoned this post, and had not yet fixed on any other occupation, at the beginning of the war. After four years of service, he was demobilized in 1919, and in the same year was elected to a fellowship of All Souls College.

Faber's future field of activity was, however, not yet determined. His father's cousin, Mr. David Faber, invited him to join the brewing firm of Strong and Company, of Romsey; soon after this he married. But the brewery was not to provide a career. He abandoned this profession in 1923, shortly after having been appointed Estates Bursar of All Souls, and it was through his connexion with the college that the opportunity came for what was to be his life work. The Scientific Press was the name of a publishing firm founded by Sir Henry Burdett, which specialized in medical publications, especially those designed for the use of trained nurses; it also published a highly successful weekly paper for trained nurses, *The Nursing Mirror*. Sir Henry Burdett's daughter had married Mr. Maurice Gwyer (later Sir Maurice Gwyer and Lord Chief Justice of India) who was also a fellow of All Souls. The Scientific Press was a very profitable enterprise; the directors formed the design of enlarging the business, and employing some of the profits in general publishing. The Gwyers invited Faber to join the board and to become the chairman of a new company; and the Scientific Press was transformed into Faber and Gwyer Ltd., general publishers.

The new firm began business at the end of 1925, in the premises still occupied by its successor, Faber and Faber Ltd. Faber added two recruits of his own choosing, R. H. I. de la Mare and T. S. Eliot. For the four years of its existence under this name, the business was only moderately successful; both the original directors and the new members were inexperienced in general publishing, and only a few outstanding successes gave hope of a successful future. In 1929 the majority shareholders were the Gwyers and Faber himself. The Gwyers were ready to liquidate the business; only Faber was determined to continue. *The Nursing Mirror* was disposed of on very advantageous terms; Mr. and Mrs. Gwyer withdrew their interest; and Faber, with his own capital, transformed the firm of Faber and Gwyer into that of Faber and Faber.

Such a venture, at that moment, appeared a very risky one; but it demonstrated Faber's courage and tenacity of purpose in his chosen profession. His faith was gradually justified; and Faber himself steadily advanced to a position of high distinction in the publishing world. Through Sir Stanley Unwin, he became one of the publishers' representatives on the Joint Advisory Committee of Publishers and Booksellers, a position which he resigned in 1934 on joining the Council of the Publishers' Association. In 1937 he became treasurer of the Association; and in 1939, shortly before the outbreak of the 1939–45 War, he was made president.

The presidency of this body proved to be, under wartime conditions, a much more onerous position than could have been anticipated. At the very outset occurred a crisis of the first magnitude. At the beginning of the war Sir Kingsley Wood, Chancellor of the Exchequer, imposed the purchase tax. Faber, and a few other persons of prescience, immediately appreciated the disastrous possibilities of the application of this tax to books. The consequences would have extended much farther than merely to those engaged in writing, printing, and publishing, as Faber was one of the first to see: the whole intellectual life of the nation might have been silenced, and its communication with that of America and the Dominions broken. Upon Faber, as president of the Publishers' Association, fell the chief responsibility of marshalling the forces of protest against the imposition of this tax. There were others to help; and the Archbishop of Canterbury (Dr. Cosmo Lang) lent his powerful support. The Government was finally induced to exempt books from the purchase tax; the output of books in quantity and quality, during years when all business, especially in London, was carried out under immense difficulty, was the admiration of the world. This service alone would entitle Faber's name to perpetuity.

To be the head of an important and expanding publishing firm, with responsibility for its policy and its finance, at the same time giving constant attention to many matters of detail; to be chairman of the Publishers' Association during several of its most difficult years; to be chairman of the National Book League during a formative period; to be responsible, as the Estates Bursar of a great college, for the administration of landed property scattered throughout England (all of which had periodically to be visited); to take an active interest in public affairs (as chairman of a committee, he wrote for the Conservative Party an admirable Report on Secondary Education); all these activities combined, at a difficult period in the nation's history, would seem to be more than enough for one man. They do not, however, exhaust Faber's interests or his record.

Apart from specialized writings such as the essays and addresses collected in a volume *A Publisher Speaking*, and other compositions directed towards a special public, such as an admirably written little book on the history of the All Souls Bursarship, Faber will be remembered especially first for *The Oxford Apostles*. This is a study of the Oxford movement into which he was drawn by his interest in his great-uncle Father Faber, and is a book which will remain among the essential bibliography of that phase of Anglican history. Second, there is his monumental biography of Benjamin Jowett. This book was the fruit of years of study and reading, and *Jowett* must long remain the standard biography of the great Master of Balliol. To the preparation of this book he gave endless care and the highest standard of scholarship. It was published in 1957; the work he devoted to this book may indeed have made too heavy demands upon his strength in the postwar years.

For those who knew him, however, his volume of collected poems *The Buried Stream* will remain the most intimate expression of the author's personality. It was indeed as a poet that he would most have wished to distinguish himself; though his modesty and diffidence prevented him from estimating his own verse at its true value. In 1960 he formally resigned from the chairmanship of Faber and Faber Ltd., and was appointed to the newly created post of president.

Faber received his knighthood in the New Year honours of 1954. He married in 1919 Enid, one of the daughters of Professor Sir Erle Richards (also fellow of All Souls); and leaves, besides his widow, two sons and a daughter.

April 1, 1961.

Sir Neil Hamilton Fairley, K.B.E., F.R.S., F.R.C.P. (LONDON), F.R.A.C.P. (EDIN.) died on April 19, 1966, at his home in Sonning. He was Wellcome Professor of Tropical Medicine in the University of London from 1946 to 1949.

Fairley carried out much research on diverse aspects of tropical medicine, and made many discoveries which have played a part in preventing or eradicating disease. His earliest work was on immunity reactions in helminthic diseases, when he succeeded in devising tests for the diagnosis of infection with certain worm parasites—schistosomes and filaria—which have proved of value in making epidemiological surveys. He has made important contributions to knowledge of the ecology and treatment of tropical sprue, and of the changes which can take place in the blood in blackwater fever, a disease which, however, is now virtually non-existent as a result of his later work. He played a leading part in introducing sulphonamides for the treatment of bacillary dysentery, as a result of which the mortality rate of this disease has been reduced virtually to zero. His most important work was on the chemoprophylaxis and chemotherapy of malaria.

In June, 1943, he was made a director of the Land Headquarters Medical Research Unit at Cairns, Queensland. Here he built up a complex unit, staffed by specialists in protozoology, entomology, biochemistry and clinical medicine, in which large scale experiments were carried out on human volunteers. By means of new techniques which he devised, and by employing the most rigid controls, he produced evidence of the value of certain drugs in suppressing malarial infection which was so conclusive that he had little difficulty in enlisting the cooperation of the Australian Army General Staff and Field Commanders in the measures he proposed.

DAILY DOSES

The introduction of daily doses of atrebrin as a preventive measure—with severe penalties for defaulters—brought about a reduction in the incidence of malaria from 740 per 1,000 in 1943 to 29 per 1,000 in 1945, an achievement which had a dominating influence on the success of the campaigns in the south-eastern Pacific. Equal success followed the use of this measure elsewhere, and malaria lost most of its terrors for the army in the field. His methods were subsequently used for assessing the value of more recently synthesized antimalarial drugs, and have enabled their properties to be ascertained with great precision. Apart from these practical results, Fairley's observations threw much new light on the development of the malaria parasite.

Fairley was one of the team responsible for the discovery of the exoerythrocytic phase of the malaria parasite in the human liver, a discovery of fundamental importance which solved some outstanding problems and made possible a logical approach to the treatment of relapsing in malaria.

Fairley received many scientific distinctions and honours, outstanding among them being the Chalmers Memorial Medal for Research in Tropical Medicine, the Richard Pierson Strong Medal of the American Foundation of Tropical

Medicine, the Moxon Medal of the Royal College of Physicians, the Mary Kingsley Medal, the Manson Medal of the Royal Society of Tropical Medicine and Hygiene, the James Cook Medal of the Royal Society of New South Wales, and the Buchanan Medal of the Royal Society.

APTITUDE FOR RESEARCH

Under Fairley's quiet exterior lay shrewd insight and great commonsense. He went straight to the heart of a problem, and having found a solution pursued it with inflexible singleness of purpose. He had a great capacity for friendship, and was beloved of all who had the privilege of working with him.

Fairley was born in 1891 and educated at the Scotch College and Melbourne University, qualifying in medicine with first class honours in 1915. He volunteered for war service, and soon showed his aptitude for research in a fine piece of work on cerebrospinal fever which at that time was prevalent in the Australian forces.

In 1916, he served as pathologist, and later as senior physician in the 14th Australian General Hospital in Cairo. He immediately made use of the abundant medical material with which he was surrounded, working with astonishing zeal. Aided with a grant from the Australian Red Cross, he not only organized the pathological laboratory of this hospital on a first class basis, but engaged on a series of researches on typhus, malaria, dysentery and bilharziasis. He perfected novel methods for the diagnosis of the latter, which later enabled him to develop intra-dermal, or skin tests, for the diagnosis of several other helminthic diseases.

BILHARZIA

He went to England in 1919 and studied tropical medicine at the London School and became a Member of the Royal College of Physicians at the same time. He was appointed Tata Professor of Clinical Medicine in Bombay in 1920, and remained there for five years, working mostly at the Haffkine Institute. There he engaged upon elaborate researches on the bilharzia parasite of the water buffalo, on guineaworm, and on sprue. He returned to England, and received a grant as Commonwealth research officer in Australia to work his colleague, Professor Kellaway, on Hydatid disease in man, and snake venom at the Walter and Eliza Hall Institute at Melbourne.

His reputation in scientific research had become so high that he was elected a Fellow of the Royal College of Physicians in 1928, and made physician to the Hospital for Tropical Diseases in London and Lecturer to the newly created London School of Hygiene and Tropical Medicine.

BLACKWATER FEVER

During the next 10 years, he published many papers on sprue, malaria, blood disease, and finally on blackwater fever. In the latter, he discovered an entirely new blood pigment, and for this discovery he was awarded the fellowship of the Royal Society in 1942.

Shortly after the outbreak of the Second World War Fairley was appointed consultant to the Australian Forces with the rank of brigadier general, and served in the Middle East. There his experience proved invaluable. He was soon able to test out and publish, in association with Brigadier J. S. K. Boyd, the curative effect of the new sulphonamide-sulphaguanidine in the treatment of bacillary dysentery.

In 1942, Fairley escaped from Java by plane to Australia. There he organized and directed the Army malaria research centre at Cairns, Queensland.

He returned to England in 1946 to take up his duties as the Wellcome Professor of Tropical Medicine in London, a newly created professorship.

Fairley was a voluminous writer, contributing articles to Price's and Savill's textbooks of medicine and Taylor's *Practice of Medicine*.

He was knighted in 1950. He was twice married.

April 21, 1966.

General Alexander Ernst von Falkenhausen, who died on July 31, 1966, in Nassau, west Germany, was a professional soldier of the old Prussian school. He was 87.

Like so many of his type, he found that his professional code was no guide to conduct in the latter days of the Third Reich. Hitler gaoled him just before the assassination plot of July 20, 1944, and then sent him to Dachau. The Americans saved him, detained him, and then handed him over to the Belgians, who eventually sentenced him to 12 years imprisonment for ordering the execution of hostages while he was commander of their occupied country. Three weeks later he was released as an act of clemency, partly because the court had taken into account his attempts to mitigate the severity of German rule in Belgium by interceding on behalf of individuals, including Jews, and avoiding the indiscriminate shooting of hostages.

He wrote in the golden book of the German customs station at Aachen when he crossed back to Germany "*Ingrata Belgia, non possedebis ossa mea*" (ungrateful Belgium thou shalt not have my bones.)

IN CHINA AND JAPAN

General von Falkenhausen was born on October 29, 1878, the son of a Silesian landowner. He was educated at cadet schools and commissioned in an Oldenburg infantry regiment in 1897. He took part in the Chinese expedition of 1900–1901 and later studied at the Berlin War Academy. He joined the General Staff in 1908, and was then military attaché in Tokyo from 1910 until the outbreak of war in 1914. He served in Belgium, France, Russia, the Caucasus, Palestine, and finally in Turkey, becoming Military Plenipotentiary at the embassy in Constantinople. As a young major he was decorated with the Pour le Mérite, the German equivalent of the V.C. In 1922 he became Chief of Staff of the Sixth Division and then, after commanding a Saxon infantry regiment, head of the Reichswehr Infantry School.

He retired from active service in 1930 with the rank of Lieutenant-General but remained active in the veterans' organization *Stahlhelm*, which was taken over by the Nazis in 1933.

TASK IN CHINA

Partly in order to get away from Nazi Germany he accepted an invitation from Generalissimo Chiang Kai-shek to re-form the Chinese forces. He stayed for five years and was then summoned home by Hitler, who eventually made him Governor-General of occupied Belgium and Northern France. There he tried to restrain the Gestapo and the S.S. and was eventually suspected (correctly) of being involved in conspiracy against Hitler, though he was never a leading light in the resistance movement. He was dismissed only a few days before the assassination attempt of July 20.

His first wife, Paula von Wedderkop, died in 1950. Ten years later he married Cecile Vent, a Belgian, who was on the prison commission and met him in gaol.

August 3, 1966.

Colonel-General Nikolaus von Falkenhorst, who led the German invasion of Norway and Denmark in 1940, died on June 18, 1968, at the age of 83. According to his wish, his death was not publicly announced, but was confirmed by relatives after his burial at Holzminden.

He began his military career in 1903 and served as a German General Staff Officer in Finland during the First World War. He commanded the Wehrmacht's XXI Corps during the invasion of Poland in 1939.

In February, 1940, von Falkenhorst was picked by Hitler to prepare the forces for the invasion which began on April 9, 1940. For his success, he was promoted by Hitler from lieutenant-general to colonel-general. He was C.-in-C., German Forces in Norway from 1940 to 1944, when he was relieved of his command ostensibly for opposing the policies of the Nazi commissioner for Norway, Josef Terboven.

In 1946, a British Military Court sentenced von Falkenhorst to be shot. He had been found guilty of having handed over captured British Commando troops to Himmler's Reich security service in accordance with Hitler's order that such prisoners should not be regarded as combatants qualifying for the protection of international law. The British soldiers were subsequently executed. Von Falkenhorst's sentence was commuted to 20 years' imprisonment. In 1953 he was released for reasons of health from the prison for war criminals at Werl.

June 28, 1968.

Battista Farina—See under **Pinin-Farina.**

Giuseppe (Nino) Farina, one of Italy's foremost drivers, and world champion in 1950, was killed in a road accident near Chambéry, France, on June 30, 1966. He was 60.

After entering motor racing in the 1920s Farina later joined the Alfa Romeo works team under the masterful tutorship of Nuvolari. Farina emulated Nuvolari's audacious style and was said to drive "as if the devil was behind and the angels ahead." He was Italian champion in 1937, 1938 and 1939 and even after the outbreak of war won the 1940 Tripoli Grand Prix in an Alfa at 128 miles an hour.

Farina returned after the war to achieve even greater fame and his relaxed straight-arm style was later copied by many drivers who found that it reduced fatigue. Winner of the 1948 Monaco Grand Prix for Maserati, Farina won the newly instituted drivers' world championship in 1950, driving his scarlet Alfa Romeo to victory in the British, Swiss and Italian Grands Prix. In spite of winning the coveted title he steadfastly refused to give details of his private life to the press and remained an enigma.

After winning the 1951 Belgian Grand Prix he switched to Ferrari, taking the 1953 German Grand Prix. He crashed at speed on the 1954 Millemiglia and raced the following year in Argentina, supported by morphine shots. Tired and depressed, he was present in practice for the 1955 Indianapolis 500 race when a reserve driver was killed testing Farina's race car. Farina, who had survived numerous near-fatal accidents in his career, never raced again, but worked studiously in the coachbuilding works of his uncle, Pinin-Farina, who died earlier in 1966.

July 2, 1966.

Eleanor Farjeon, best known as a writer of children's verse and stories, in which capacity she must be counted among the happiest and most charming writers of her kind, died on June 5, 1965. She was 84.

Born on February 13, 1881, she came of a versatile and talented family. Her father, Benjamin Leopold Farjeon, in his day was a successful novelist, and her mother was the daughter of the celebrated American actor Joseph Jefferson, whose name will long be remembered in the history of the theatre, most notably perhaps for his creation of the role of Rip van Winkle. In the 1890s the Farjeons' home in Hampstead was a meeting-place for many of the eminent literary and artistic people of the period. All four children—Miss Farjeon was the only daughter—were familiar from early years with the world of letters, music, and the stage, and were encouraged to exercise their individual bent. Harry, the eldest of her brothers, was a musician; the other two, Joe (J. Jefferson Farjeon) and Herbert, became well known as writers. In a vivid, entertaining, and charmingly evocative volume of reminiscences, crammed with good stories of celebrities, *A Nursery in the Nineties* (1935), Miss Farjeon recalls her almost fabulously happy and crowded childhood.

She had, in her own words, no education except what was provided by her father's library of some 8,000 volumes. For the rest she had a great love of children, and from the start much of her work in verse and prose was directly addressed to that audience. Her first book was *Nursery Rhymes of London Town* (1916); she went on to write stories, fantasies, rhymed alphabets, and delightful verses for the instruction and amusement of nursery and schoolroom. Her gift for light verse was also exhibited for many years in her topical contributions, day after day, over the signature of "Tom Fool", to the *Daily Herald*. Selections from these were also published in book form.

But her most considered work in the years between the wars—with the important exception of one book—went into the writing of delicately fanciful novels, inspired in the first place by fairy-tale themes, but making more appeal to the adult than to the child. The exception is *Martin Pippin in the Apple Orchard*, published in 1921, which must count as her masterpiece. In that enchanting work, the scene of which is the author's well-loved Sussex, six original fairy-stories, among the most accomplished that have been produced in our time, are related by Martin Pippin, and serve his purpose of delivering the farmer's daughter, imprisoned in the well-house, from the guard of the six milkmaids, each of whom has a key to a lock that cannot be opened till all the keys are won. Into *Martin Pippin* Eleanor Farjeon put all that was most felicitous in her wit and fancy.

POETIC ENCHANTMENT

Of the novels of the early period *The Soul of Kol Nikon* (1923) is particularly endearing. But there is something of poetic enchantment in most of these fantasies and semi-fantasies of hers—and, indeed, even in those novels she wrote which seem to have a solidly realistic core. Among the best of her books are *Ladybrook* (1931), a rustic Sussex tale; *Humming Bird* (1936), in which history and fairy-tale converge upon the only fan painted by Watteau; *Miss Granby's Secret* (1940) a symposium of the simplicities and splendours of Victorian sentiment; and *Ariadne and the Bull* (1945), a gay fantasy on the theme of the Minotaur. And mention must be made of her collaboration as dramatist with her brother Herbert in the charming Victorian operetta *The Two Bouquets*, and in a play for children on the Cinderella theme, *The Glass Slipper* (repeated over the air with renewed enchantment only last Christmas, and later, with another play, *The Silver Curlew*, turned into a story).

Her children's books, however, were to prove the more lasting. During the 1940s, Eleanor Farjeon produced *The New Book of Days* (1941), an exquisite miscellany, and three books of poems for children, *Cherry-stones* (1942), *The Mulberry Bush* (1945), and *The Starry Floor* (1949), later to be gathered into one book *Then There Were Three* (1958). These gay and charming poems illustrate her perceptive imagination and her flashing awareness of beauty. She herself chose what she considered to be the best of her poetry for the collections *Silver Sand and Snow* (1951), *The Children's Bells* (1957), and *A Puffin Quartet of Poets* (1958). Her moving little poem *Mrs. Malone* (1950) which appeared in an illustrated edition in 1962, will be remembered by her friends as an expression of her own warm heart.

It was in storytelling, and particularly in the short story, that Eleanor Farjeon the craftsman was seen at her most brilliant. The most memorable of these are to be found in *The Little Bookroom* (1955), the collection that won her outstanding honours in the book world: the Library Association Carnegie Medal, the international Hans Andersen Medal, and the American Regina Medal.

NEW EDITIONS

Eleanor Farjeon lived to see her books come to a second flowering and to find herself, to her bewildered amusement, one of the most important figures in the children's literature of our day. Since 1950 all her best books for children have been reprinted in new editions: the "Martin Pippin" stories *Jim at the Corner*, *Kaleidoscope*, *Tales from Chaucer*, and *Ten Saints*, with its limpid prose and perfect storytelling, being the most notable.

In spite of the ill health of her last years, she never lost her zest for life and her zest for writing. In her seventies, she mapped out four volumes of memoirs, three of which were to take shape round key figures in her life. *Edward Thomas*: *The Last Four Years* (1958) recorded vividly and movingly one of the most important of these friendships. Her brother Herbert was to be the central figure in the second volume, on which she was at work up to a few months ago. The final book was to chronicle the events leading to her reception into the Roman Catholic Church in 1951. One of the last things she wrote was a moving foreword to her friend Robert Frost's book of poems *Come With Me*. In spite of the physical handicaps of old age, there were still blessed moments for her when "writing was bliss". Her genius for friendship, her gaiety, her fun and her quicksilver intelligence remained a constant delight to her ever-increasing crowd (circle is too limiting a word) of friends: her talk would frequently leave them aching with laughter, always filled with admiration and affection.

Eleanor Farjeon's books have been translated into many languages and are found in children's libraries all over the world. She wrote out of a creative urge that was life to her. At times its expression was too facile, but more often it was akin to genius. She has an honoured place in children's literature and in the hearts of the children themselves.

June 7, 1965.

Prince Farouk, King of Egypt from 1936 until he was forced to abdicate in 1952, died in Rome on March 17, 1965. His death at the age of 45 recalls a chapter of Anglo-Egyptian relations that is now closed. They were at their lowest level in 1920 when he was born and the struggle for independence was going on; they reached their peak with the Anglo-Egyptian Treaty of 1937 just after he succeeded as King, and they deteriorated to a new low level in 1952 when he was forced to abdicate.

His popularity in Egypt was subject to the same vicissitudes. Most people remember him in recent years as a rather gross figure, first as King (like our Henry VIII in tarbush and dark glasses) and after his abdication as a playboy in various Mediterranean resorts. An earlier generation, however, will remember him as a fair, girlish boy and then as a slim, handsome young prince in the prewar period. He was the descendant of Muhammad 'Ali, the Albanian adventurer who founded the Egyptian dynasty, through his father, King Ahmad Fuad, whom he succeeded in 1936, and through his mother, Queen Nazli, of the French Colonel Sève (better known as Sulaiman Pasha), who became a Muslim and served Muhammad 'Ali. He was also the grandson of Khedive Isma'il, who too had to abdicate.

He was brought up by English governesses and tutors until he was taken to England on a British cruiser to complete his studies at the age of 15, and he spent six months at Kenry House, Kingston Hill, preparing for entry to the Royal Military Academy at Woolwich. His tutor at this time was 'Aziz al-Masri Pasha, a former "Young Turk" colonel of pro-Axis sympathies.

His stay in this country was cut short by the death of his father King Fuad, and he returned to Egypt as King, first under a regency.

GREATLY POPULAR

A year later he took the constitutional oath and assumed full powers as sovereign (as he was then 18 by the Muslim calendar). The late king, his father, had never been popular, and had never courted popularity with the Egyptians, Farouk, whose assumption of royal power practically coincided with the Anglo-Egyptian Treaty, enjoyed an unprecedented popularity. He was young and handsome, with no murky past, a truly Egyptian prince and a symbol of the new era of independence. This popularity was increased when he married the daughter of an Egyptian. Farida Zulfiqar, who was as beautiful and charming as a fairy princess.

Farouk was now on top of the Egyptian world and might have gone on from strength to strength. Unfortunately he threw away the advantages that had been conferred upon him.

LOST FAVOUR

How far this was due to his youth and lack of experience, evil or misguided advisers or deficiency of character is hard to say. The fact remains that within a few years he had not only ceased to be popular but had become more unpopular than his father. He might have initiated reforms like the Shah of Persia, who married his sister Fawziya about this time, but he chose to play the old political game of his father with the Wafd and the British. At the same time he adopted the role of the "pious king" visiting mosques on Fridays and posing as the champion of the Muslim Faith.

It soon got round that his private life was very different from his public profession. His marriage was dissolved in 1948. The Wafd, under Nahas Pasha, representing the majority of Egyptians, were soon at loggerheads with him, and though the treaty was loyally implemented by his government when war broke out in 1939, a crisis came in 1942. British intervention forced Farouk to get rid of his Axis advisers and accept Nahas and the Wafd.

After the war the negotiations with the British for complete evacuation continued unsuccessfully, and the Wafd, who had supported the British war effort, had to prove themselves more nationalist than the King. The Palestine war was lost owing to corruption and inefficiency in high places.

WIND OF CHANGE

The sands were running out for Farouk with disaffection in the Army and the wind of change blowing through the Arab world. He married again another Egyptian girl, Narriman Sadek, who bore him a son and heir but this did nothing to restore his popularity. In January, 1952, after riots and the burning of part of Cairo he dismissed the Wafd Government and brought in the Army to restore order. But six months later he was forced to abdicate in favour of his baby son, Fuad II, by the leaders of the present regime in the July Revolution, and sailed away from Alexandria in the royal yacht never to return.

By his first marrige he had three daughters, the youngest of whom was married last month to a Russian geologist in London. His second marriage was also dissolved.

March 19, 1965.

Geraldine Farrar, the opera singer, who died of a heart attack on March 11, 1967, at her home in Ridgefield, Connecticut, at the age of 85, was the last link with the "golden age" of New York's Metropolitan Opera just after the turn of the century. Together with such stars as Enrico Caruso, Antonio Scotti, and Louise Homer, she formed part of an operatic constellation such as has not been since since.

Born in Melrose, Massachusetts, on February 28, 1882, the daughter of Sydney and Henrietta Farrar, (he was a major league baseball player known for his fiery temperament), Geraldine was encouraged to sing by her parents, both of whom were ardent church choir members. She began her lessons at the age of 12 and soon showed her talent by impersonating Jenny Lind at a carnival, where she astonished her audience by singing a self-studied aria in Italian instead of the "Home, Sweet Home" that was expected of her.

Continuing her studies in Boston and New York, Miss Farrar was fortunate enough to attract the attention of Mrs. Bertram Webb of Salem, Massachusetts, who set aside a sum of $30,000 for the young soprano to go to Europe.

PUPIL OF LEHMANN

This she did in 1899, and spent some months in Paris studying with Trabadello.

Miss Farrar made her debut at the age of 19 on October 15, 1901, at the Royal Opera in Berlin, singing the role of Marguerite in *Faust*.

The quality of her voice and its rich potential were immediately apparent. The great singer Lilli Lehmann heard her and took her as a pupil. Later she went back to Paris and studied further.

During the five years from 1901 to 1906 she sang with opera companies throughout Europe from Stockholm to Monte Carlo. It was then that she met a young Italian tenor named Enrico Caruso, and in 1906 she was Gilda to his Duke in *Rigoletto* in Berlin. That was the start of a famous partnership.

In November of 1906 Miss Farrar returned to her native America and, under the aegis of Heinrich Conreid, made her debut at the New York Metropolitan Opera in *Romeo and Juliet*.

CRITICS' PRAISE

The critics were loud in their praises, while the audiences were entranced. This was the beginning of a long and triumphant reign over American opera fans.

During the next 16 years, before she retired at the height of her fame and vocal powers, the dark-haired beautiful diva was the idolized heroine of cheering crowds. Whenever she was booked to appear at the Met, a full house was assured weeks beforehand. Her splendid voice, tempestuous nature, and romantic personality assured her of success. She had many clashes with directors and conductors, and it was said that not even the iron-willed Toscanini could intimidate her.

The role for which Miss Farrar became best known was Cio-Cio San in *Madam Butterfly*, and in her 16 years at the Metropolitan she sang it no fewer than 96 times, often opposite Caruso. Her next most popular role was Carmen which she sang 58 times. Caruso and Farrar became the most popular team in New York's operatic history. The two great singers sometimes had clashes of temperament, but they stimulated each other to heights of artistry.

ONE FAREWELL

Together they were described by Gatti-Casazza, the manager of the Met, as "the strongest box office combination of operatic history."

Between concert tours and the opera Miss Farrar made many recordings which are still collectors' pieces, and she also made a dozen films in Hollywood, including *Joan of Arc* and *Carmen*. Then, suddenly, at the age of 40, when she felt that her voice was beginning to fail, she retired without any protracted preliminary "farewell appearances." The close of her career, at the Met on April 22, 1922, when she sang the name part in Leoncavallo's *Zaza*, was a tumultuous affair. Bedlam reigned both inside and outside the house, and Miss Farrar was given a tremendous send-off. In 1938 she published an autobiography, *Such Sweet Compulsion*.

Since then the heroine of New York's golden age of opera had lived quietly in her home at Ridgefield, Connecticut, resisting all offers to stage a come-back. She was married once, in 1916, to Lou Tellegen, a handsome Dutch actor.

The marriage ended in divorce two years later.

March 13, 1967.

William Faulkner, who died on July 6, 1962, in Oxford, Mississippi, was one of the few living novelists to whom the adjective "great" could be applied without much fear of over-statement. He was 64.

He was born on September 25, 1897, in New Albany, Mississippi, the eldest of the four sons of M. C. Falkner. During the First World War Faulkner (he later changed his name) left high school to join the Canadian Flying Corps and, on his return, entered the University of Mississippi at Oxford, to which his family had moved when he was a child. He took no degree, however, and, after various jobs and trips to New York and New Orleans, settled down to a career of writing.

His first published volume was a book of poems, *The Marble Faun*, in 1924, and his first novel *Soldiers' Pay* (1926). After the lukewarm reception of his second and third novels, *Mosquitoes* and *Sartoris*, Faulkner had the idea—prompted, so legend has it, by his lawyer friend Phil Stone—of writing to please himself and not the public. The result was *The Sound and the Fury* (1929), one of his finest works.

With the publication of *The Sound and the Fury* there began that series of novels which became known as the "Yoknapatawpha Saga", since they were based on the town of "Jefferson" in the county of "Yoknapatawpha", Mississippi, of which its author once drew a map with the legend "William Faulkner, Sole Owner and Proprietor".

The best of Faulkner's novels: *The Sound and the Fury*, *As I Lay Dying*, *Light in August*, *Absalom, Absalom*! and *The Hamlet* have been located in his home state. Towards the end of his life, after the publication of the ambitious but only partially successful allegory *A Fable*, he turned even more earthily and realistically to his native soil with the publication of *The Town*, *The Mansion*, and *The Reivers*.

Throughout his life Faulkner thought and wrote of himself as a poet. He said once, in an interview given to the *Paris Review*, that when he had satisfied himself that he could not be a great poet he turned to short story writing, and that when he had, later, proved to himself that he could not be a great short story writer he turned to the novel form. His poems, certainly, were not good, tending to fancifulness or imitation; but his poetic sensibility was exploited to the full in his novel.

The difficulty of his style seems to arise from the fact that he perceived, and wished to convey for any given situation, a variety of *nuances*. Another cause of obscurity lay in his attempts to grapple with the novelist's problem of consciousness in relation to time; the same problem of how to convey the multiple events and still more multiple meanings contained in a single moment of time that Proust, Joyce, and Virginia Woolf tackled each in their individual way.

DIALOGUE REALISM

The success with which, in his best work, he managed to "hold time in his hand" is shown in *Absalom, Absalom*! and *Intruder in the Dust*. It was because he ballasted his psychological exploration with immediacy of description and realism of dialogue that his work presents such a rich—and at first bewildering—texture.

That Faulkner was a Southerner one would know from his scenes and characters, but the Southern quality was also subtly present in his style. There was something of the cracker-barrel politician in his rhetoric, something of Poe's Gothic in his atmosphere. He suited his style to his subject. When he was dealing with primitives, as in *As I Lay Dying* and the Benjy section of *The Sound and the Fury*, he could be simple and colloquial; when he was writing of sophisticates, as in the Quentin section of *The Sound and the Fury*, his style was involuted and complex. But scratch the literary craftsman, the officer-romantic with the horn of Roland in his ears, and one found an earthy countrymen. ("I'm only a farmer" he is supposed to have said when asked to look distinguished for the Nobel Prize gathering.) This "country" quality came out well in his last four novels. His favourite reading was reported to be the "Sut Lovingood" stories of George Washington Harris, and he liked nothing better than to go hunting with his friends from Oxford.

After the Second World War Faulkner's stature as a novelist was fully recognized.

OLD VERITIES

He brought to life a fictional world, the highest mark of a novelist's achievement, he developed a distinctive, unmistakable style, and, under cover of his own myth of the South, he created stories with universal implications. One has only to savour the complex, rich and subtle texture of Faulkner's writing to know that, for all the critical diatribes about his violence, his primitivism and his obsession with lust and incest, here is a great literary imagination. But it is not only that. Were it only that, Faulkner would not have been great. What made him great, to quote his own Nobel Prize address, was his single-minded concern with "the old verities and truths of the heart, the old universal truths lacking which any story is ephemeral and doomed—love and honour and pity and pride and compassion and sacrifice".

July 7, 1962.

Sir Edward Fellowes, K.C.B., C.M.G., M.C., a former Clerk to the House of Commons and chairman of the General Advisory Council of the B.B.C., died at his home at Scole, Norfolk, on December 28, 1970. He was 75.

Fellowes was in the Clerk's department of the House of Commons for 42 years and served under 12 parliaments before retiring in 1961.

Mr. Iain Macleod, then Leader of the House, said in moving a motion on the retirement of Fellowes thanking him for his long and faithful service, that Fellowes would go down in history as one of the great Clerks of the House. He said that the members of Parliament would remember most of all his courtesy and friendliness to them all. Fellowes had also been an adviser to many Commonwealth countries in which national parliaments were emerging. From 1956 to 1960 he was president of the "world trade union of clerks," an association of secretaries-general of parliaments, and his influence had been felt in the Consultative Assembly of the Council of Europe and the Assembly of Western European Union.

Fellowes, the son of a barrister, was born in London in 1895 and educated at Marlborough College. During the First World War he served in Europe in the Queen's Royal regiment and attained the rank of Captain. He won the Military Cross in 1917.

After the war, Fellowes went to the House of Commons and in 1919 became Assistant Clerk to the House, a position he held until 1937. Between 1937 and 1948 he was second Clerk-Assistant to the House, and between 1948 and 1954 Clerk-Assistant. He then became Clerk to the House until his retirement.

During the Second World War he was officer commanding the Home Guard at Westminster Palace. Fellowes was made a Commander of the Order of the Bath in 1945 and a Knight Commander of the Order in 1955. He was also a Commander of the Order of St. Michael and St. George.

In 1931, with J. W. Hills, M.P., Fellowes wrote *Finance of Government*. In 1957 he edited with T. G. B. Cocks *Sir Thomas Erskine May's Treatise on the Law, Privileges. Proceedings and Usage of Parliament*. Between 1962 and 1967 he was chairman of the General Advisory Council of the B.B.C. and of the Council of the Hansard Society for Parliamentary Government. In 1964 he became a Fellow of the Royal Society of Arts. He was vice-president of the south Norfolk Conservative association.

In 1921 he married Ella Mary, daughter of Lieutenant-Colonel Macrae-Gilstrap, and they had three daughters.

December 30, 1970.

Edna Ferber, the American author who turned out such stories as *Cimarron*, *Giant* and *Showboat*, died in New York on April 16, 1968, at the age of 80. Her novel *So Big* won the Pultzer Prize of 1924.

Edna Ferber loved America, and she wrote of it for more than four decades with enthusiasm and devotion. In short stories, novels and plays, she depicted the life of its people from shore to shore, and beyond. In the novel *So Big* she wrote of Illinois; in *Showboat* of the South; in *Cimarron* of Oklahoma; in *American Beauty* of Connecticut; in *Saratoga Trunk* of New York; in *Giant* (later made into a film with Elizabeth Taylor and James Dean), of Texas; in *Ice Palace* of Alaska.

Her books were not profound, but they were vivid and had a sound sociological basis. She was among the best-read novelists in the nation, and critics of the 1920s and 1930s did not hesitate to call her the greatest of her day.

She peopled her work with men and women of the lower-middle and middle class because, she said, they interested her more than any other American stratum. Her stories concerned department store clerks and buyers, friends with whom she had grown up, madams seeking to become respectable. The conversation of a truck driver, she maintained, she always found more vigorous and stimulating than the conversation of a Cadillac owner.

Her novels went into many editions and hundreds of thousands of copies. Her short stories brought the highest rates. Plays on which she collaborated, or which were adapted from her work, enjoyed long runs and frequent revivals. Films based on her books were box-office hits.

She was born in Kalamazoo, Michigan, on August 15, 1887, the daughter of Jacob Charles Ferber, a moderately successful Hungarian-born small businessman. When the time came for Edna to attend college the family was hard put to manage it. So she went to work, instead, at 17, as a reporter on the *Appleton* (*Wisconsin*) *Daily Crescent*.

Her newspaper career later took her to the *Milwaukee Journal*. During her reporting days she wrote her first novel, *Dawn O'Hara*, the story of a newspaperwoman in Milwaukee.

The ideas for many of her novels came from snatches of conversation that piqued her interest. The germ for the novel *Show Boat*, which in turn engendered the hit musical of the same name, came just that way.

It was during the tryout of her play *Minick*, written with George S. Kaufman, "Never mind, boys and girls", Ames the producer said after a weary day, "next time we won't bother with tryouts. We'll all charter a show boat and we'll just drift down the rivers, playing the towns as we come to them."

Her childhood love of the theatre never left her and her plays, among them *Dinner at Eight*, *The Royal Family* and *Stage Door*, all written with George S. Kaufman, were popular with more than one generation. Her autobiographical works were *A Peculiar Treasure* (1939) and *A Kind of Magic* (1963).

April 17, 1968.

J. D. Fergusson, who died at his home in Glasgow on January 30, 1961, at the age of 86, was eminent among those Scottish painters whose work gave renewed evidence in this century of the old-established and special sympathy of the Scots with France.

This sympathy might be termed an immediate inheritance from the Glasgow School of the 1880s and 1890s—it is significant that Fergusson in his youth worked for some years in association with such representatives of the School as Guthrie, Lavery, and Arthur Melville. Just as this earlier group was directly influenced by the art of Barbizon, by Monticelli, and by Whistler (as a sort of intermediary with France), so Fergusson was influenced by post-impressionism, Cézanne, and the Fauves. Somewhat like his slightly younger Scottish contemporary, S. J. Peploe (who died in 1935) he developed in the French post-Impressionist atmosphere his own characteristic breadth of style and radiance of colour. While Scottish painters more recently—Robert Colquhoun and Robert MacBryde notable among them—have pursued the modern evolution farther and into another phase, Fergusson remained a vivid personality in art and might justly be termed in his later years the doyen of modern Scottish painting.

John Duncan Fergusson was born in Perthshire in 1874 of Highland parents and educated at Edinburgh High School and Blair Lodge. In 1893 he entered the University of Edinburgh as a medical student but after two years abandoned the idea of a career in medicine and went to Paris determined to become an artist. He worked somewhat perfunctorily in the Julian and Colarossi academies and, not taking kindly to academic teaching, spent most of his time in independent effort. He returned to Scotland after some months, gaining benefit from his association with the Glasgow painters and began to exhibit at the Royal Glasgow Institute of Fine Arts and at the R.B.A. Like Melville he derived a sharpened sense of colour from a visit to Spain and Morocco in 1899 but thereafter he worked mainly in Paris and the South of France until 1914 and again after the war. Paris for many years was his real home, though, as with Peploe, Cassis and Antibes were favourite painting grounds and he frequently came to England to visit friends and arrange exhibitions. His first exhibition was at the Baillie Gallery in 1905 and subsequently he was a frequent exhibitor at the Lefevre Gallery, last showing there in 1936. His work was also exhibited at the MacLellan Gallery, Glasgow, 1948, and at Saltire House, in the Edinburgh Festival of 1952, in which year the Hazlitt Gallery in London showed a small retrospective collection of paintings, 1900–52. From 1926 onwards he held exhibitions in the United States and when in 1931 he exhibited with "Les Peintres Ecossais" at the Galeries Georges Petit in Paris one of his paintings was acquired by the state. He was elected R.B.A., 1903, in 1908 Sociétaire of the Salon d'Automne and was also made an honorary LL.D., Glasgow, in 1950.

A handsome, open-hearted man, never stinting kindly and helpful advice to young aspirants, he was popular in the British and American art colonies in Paris, and for some time was president of the Anglo-American Group of painters in the French capital. He returned to Scotland in 1939 and devoted effort to advancing art there, being one of the founders of the New Scottish Group in 1942 and producing a book on modern Scottish painting in 1943.

The international reputation he shared with Peploe was well founded. The trend of his work was towards decorative effect rather than the profounder "researches" of the post-Impressionist age but equally in figures, landscapes, and still-life he displayed a firmness and solidity recalling not only Cézanne, but the fact that he practised sculpture for a while in his early days. An especially attractive feature of his colour was the way in which he repeated its harmonies both in foreground objects and their background.

Works by him are in the Tate Gallery, City of Glasgow Art Gallery and University of Glasgow, the permanent collections of Ayr, Belfast, Edinburgh, Greenock, and Leeds, and in many private collections in Britain, France, and the United States.

January 31, 1961.

Winston Field, C.M.G., M.B.E., who was the first Rhodesian Front Party Prime Minister of Southern Rhodesia, died in Salisbury on March 17, 1969, aged 64.

He came to office after the election in December, 1962, which saw the defeat of Sir Edgar Whitehead's United Federal Party, and he remained Prime Minister until early 1964, when he was replaced, in an internal party manoeuvre, by Mr. Ian Smith.

Field failed to redeem his promises to get independence for the Rhodesians by negotiation; indeed in the negotiations with Mr. Butler in 1963 he was the loser. Field negotiated in the hope of avoiding a constitutional crisis which would affect the entire Commonwealth. In the Queen's speech in the Rhodesian Parliament in 1964, however, Britain's terms for Southern Rhodesian independence were described as "most extravagant". A stalemate seemed to have been reached in the year of the British general election which was supposed to be Field's deadline for a decision—but before that took place he was succeeded by Ian Smith, the deputy Prime Minister.

Field's coming to power was in the pattern of white politics in Southern Rhodesia in that it marked a substantial move to the right. (Sir Edgar Whitehead was defeated largely because of the "liberal" platform which he had adopted.) In the same way, Field's replacement by Smith marked a further and this time more positive move to the right—or, rather, towards an obdurate adherence to white supremacy.

After ceasing to be Prime Minister, Field became seriously ill, and would certainly have had to give up active politics in any case, though as he himself remarked, he would rather have given up in his own time. He was quite ready to admit, however, that he was not a good politician. Indeed, his character was such that he would feel this to be a point in his favour rather than the reverse. His dislike of the deviousness of politics was undoubtedly part of his undoing.

A simple, outspoken man, he was essentially a paternalist. He treated well the Africans who worked for him, and he was respected by them, but the relationship was never anything but that of master and man. Yet he was certainly not a racist. Unlike many of Rhodesia's white politicans (including some far more liberal than himself), he went to some pains to get to know politically significant Africans. He enjoyed quite cordial relations, for example, with Dr. Banda of Malawi, at a time when the doctor was not quite so popular in Rhodesia as he later became. Earlier, he had known Tshekedi Khama.

After the unilateral declaration of independence of Rhodesia in 1965 Field remained in the background, though he did join a delegation to Smith to point out the economic consequences of the British sanctions policy. Though still personally respected, Field was by then of no political importance.

Winston Joseph Field was born on June 6, 1904, in Bromsgrove. Worcestershire, one of the 10 children of a shopkeeper. He was educated at Bromsgrove School, but at the age of 17 emigrated to Southern Rhodesia and took a job on a tobacco farm. He worked hard, and became himself a substantial tobacco farmer near Marandellas.

COURT-MARTIAL

In the Second World War Field joined the Rhodesian forces, but was court-martialled for striking a private (an African, but the incident seems to have been due more to temperament than colour), and was reduced from sergeant to private. He transferred to the British Army, took part in the Normandy landings and became a major in the Durham Light Infantry.

In 1952 Field initiated the Italian Peasant Farmers Scheme, which was an unsuccessful attempt to establish numerous small white farms in the territory. In 1956 he was elected Leader of the Dominion Party in the Federation and in 1957 he won the Mrewa by-election and became Leader of the Opposition in the Federal House of Assembly. In 1960, the Dominion Party split into territorial and federal sections; and he remained Federal Leader, with William J. Harper as Leader of the Southern Rhodesian Party. Field consistently pressed for a disintegration of the Federation, with a completely white dominated independent dominion consisting of Southern Rhodesia together with the Copperbelt and "line of rail" in Northern Rhodesia as it was then. In 1962—the year before the dissolution of the Federation—Field was returned to the Southern Rhodesian Parliament for Marandellas, and was elected president of the Rhodesian Front Party the same year. He retired from politics in 1965. He resigned from the Rhodesian Front Party in 1968.

In 1947 he married Barbara Ann Hayward and they had three sons and one daughter.

March 18, 1969.

Dr. Leopold Figl, who was Austrian Chancellor from 1945 to 1953 and Foreign Minister from 1953 to 1959, died on May 9, 1965, at the age of 62. He resigned to become president of the National Assembly in 1959, and since 1962 had been governor of Lower Austria. Figl played a leading part in the establishment and consolidation of the second Austrian Republic. During his years as Chancellor he cemented the coalition between the conservative Austrian People's Party and the Austrian Socialist Party, a coalition which united and stabilized Austria, ravaged by war, during the critical period of allied occupation. Combining tenacity with patience and a sense of humour, Figl succeeded in upholding Austrian rights and interests against outside encroachments, especially from the Soviet occupier's side, while maintaining good relations with the Russian officials. His native wit and genial appearance and his love of sociable pastimes, including shooting and wine drinking, hardly less than his qualities of character and statesmanship, made him a popular public figure.

Figl was born on October 2, 1902, in Rust, Lower Austria, of a long established peasant family tracing itself back to the sixteenth century. After attending secondary school in the Lower Austrian provincial capital of St. Poelten, he graduated in 1930 at the Vienna College of Agriculture. But even before that, in 1927, his talent for organization gained him a position in the Lower Austrian branch of the Bauernbund (the Austrian Farmers' League) with which he had been associated ever since. He soon became the branch secretary, then deputy director, and finally director.

In November, 1934, he was appointed to the Federal Board of Economy and a year later became the director of the all-Austrian Bauernbund. A determined opponent of the Nazis, he was arrested by the Gestapo soon after the Anschluss and interned at Dachau concentration camp in Bavaria. During the next five years he was moved from camp to camp, suffering much hardship. He was repeatedly brought to the verge of severe illness, recovering only thanks to the efforts of numerous friends, of all political hues, whom he made in the camps. Released in 1943 he obtained employment as a construction engineer in a Lower Austrian building firm (in which Herr Raab who was Chancellor from 1953–61 and died in 1964 was also employed) and began at once clandestinely to reorganize the suppressed Bauernbund. He was rearrested in October, 1944, for these activities and sent to the notorious concentration camp at Mathausen charged with high treason; the advancing Red Army troops freed him in the spring of 1945 only a few hours before he was to be brought to trial.

Within a few weeks of the end of the war Figl succeeded in reanimating the Bauernbund, which has since become one of the pillars of the Austrian People's Party and indeed of the coalition government. In May, 1945, Dr. Karl Renner, the first postwar Chancellor, a socialist, asked Figl, now once more the director of the Bauernbund, to become State Secretary in the political department of the provisional Austrian Government. When the Federal Government took over the administration of Lower Austria, from the Russians, in the same year, Figl became its provincial Governor with the task of reconstructing the provincial administration.

COALITION GOVERNMENT

In December, 1945, Figl became Federal Chancellor in virtue of his chairmanship of the Austrian People's Party which gained half the total votes in the first postwar elections held that November. He and some political associates had already laid the foundation for this party during the Nazi administration of Austria, making it in many ways the successor of the prewar Christian Social Party. As Chancellor he headed a coalition Government comprising the People's Party, the Socialist Party, and a much smaller Communist Party, to give way in November, 1947, to the coalition of the two larger parties alone. Figl's chancellorship saw not only the political consolidation and economic revival, with American aid, of Austria, even though still divided into four occupation zones, but also the defeat of the Communist instigated strike movement of 1951, aimed ultimately at seizing power, in which the Government's unyielding stand played a vital role.

After the second postwar general election in October, 1949, Figl formed his second cabinet, which resigned following differences between the coalition partners over the budget. He then formed a third cabinet to continue government business until new elections in April, 1953. Owing to a too uncompromising attitude towards the Socialist partner, Figl was replaced as Chancellor in the next coalition government by Raab. He thereupon returned to take up the duties of director of the Bauernbund until he was appointed foreign minister in the Raab government of November 23, 1953, in place of Dr. Karl Gruber.

Though foreign affairs were not his real metier, not taking kindly to the rarefied air of diplomatic palaver, Figl distinguished himself by his courageous and resourceful stand at the 1954 Four Power Berlin Conference. In 1955 he was a member of the Austrian delegation which completed in Moscow the final negotiations for the State Treaty which on May 15, 1955, he signed in Vienna declaring that day to be the happiest of his life.

In 1959 he resigned from his post as Minister of Foreign Affairs to become President of Parliament and then, three years later, Landeshauptmann of Lower Austria. A leading figure of Austria's postwar political life, whether as Chancellor or Foreign Minister, or later as President of Parliament, Figl never lost touch with the farmers whose spokesman he remained throughout. Figl knew that his illness would not permit him a long life but he faced it with great courage.

He married in 1930 Hilde Hemala. They had one son and one daughter.

May 10, 1965.

Professor G. I. Finch, M.B.E., F.R.S., who died on November 22, 1970, at the age of 82, was Emeritus Professor of Applied Physical Chemistry, London University. He was one of the two best Alpinists of his time—Mallory was the other—and was a pioneer in the use of oxygen on Everest.

George Ingle Finch was born in New South Wales, on August 4, 1888. His father was Chairman of the Land Court of New South Wales and was an internationally-known authority on land law. Both his parents were widely travelled people of many interests and they brought him to continue his education in Europe while he was still a schoolboy.

Finch's first intention was to study medicine but after a short period at the École de Médicine in Paris he found that he preferred the physical sciences and entered the Eidgenössische Technische Hochschule in Zurich. There he won the gold medal of the diploma course and afterwards was for a time Bredig's research assistant. His discovery of an improved ammonia synthesis catalyst brought him into contact with the Badische Anilin und Sodafabrik and he spent a period as chemist in one of their chemical works. Zurich not only laid the foundation of his scientific career but it also provided an opportunity for him to develop outstanding skill in mountaineering.

In 1912 he went to England as research chemist under Sir Robert Robertson at the

Royal Arsenal. In 1913 he became a founding member of the staff of the department of chemical technology of the Imperial College of Science and Technology. He served during the First World War from 1914 to 1919 with the R.F.A. and R.A.O.D. in France, Egypt and Macedonia, and was mentioned in dispatches, and awarded the M.B.E. in 1917.

After the war he returned to Imperial College and devoted himself to building up electrochemical teaching and research, becoming assistant professor in 1927. In 1936 he was appointed to the university chair of applied physical chemistry which he held until he retired in 1952 as emeritus professor, to become director of the National Chemical Laboratory of India. He was elected to fellowship of the Royal Society in 1938. During his span of more than 30 years at Imperial College he covered a range of scientific and industrial interests of remarkable breadth. Students who entered his laboratory soon became accustomed to lending a hand with an exciting variety of investigations and problems often far removed from their main line of research—an invaluable introduction to a scientific career.

Finch's earlier work was devoted to exploring the borderland between electricity and chemistry, and he made the first systematic studies of thermionic emission from metals in gases and linked the electrical effects with chemical changes. His interest in electrical discharges led naturally to research into the complex phenomena of the spark ignition of gaseous mixtures. In 1930, shortly after the recognition of the wave-mechanical properties of electrons, he began the investigations into electron diffraction which were to form his major scientific work.

The vastly greater power of electron waves over X-rays in determining the finer details of thin films and solid surfaces gave Finch the ideal tool for exploring the chemistry and physics of these regions of matter, and one in which his great experimental skill had full scope. He invented many improvements of technique and applied them to a vast range of problems. His Guthrie lecture summarizes the work which he did on mechanical wear and lubrication, on epitaxial crystal growth, solid state reactions, and the structures of the spinel series.

He spent the year 1937–38 as Franqui Professor in the University of Brussels. In 1944 he was awarded the Hughes medal of the Royal Society. He was president of the Physical Society in 1947–48 and Guthrie Lecturer in 1950. During the years 1941–45 he was scientific adviser to the Ministry of Home Security and was specially concerned with fire defence; many of his colleagues and students have vivid memories of their experiences as members of the band of fire observers into which he enlisted them.

Finch's talent for climbing first attracted notice when he and a brother, both schoolboys, evaded their tutor to scale the walls of Notre Dame Cathedral in Paris. Study in Switzerland gave the opportunity for Alpine climbing, both in summer and winter. Few, if any, Englishmen at that time were equally skilled ice climbers. When the majority of his countrymen still employed guides, Finch made many notable guideless ascents in almost every district of the Alps. Perhaps his best known climb was the north face of Dent d'Herens in 1923.

He carried his science to mountains and in the 1922 Everest Expedition he pioneered the use of oxygen at high altitudes. Although with its aid he reached 27,300ft. (a remarkable and stormy climb in company with Geoffrey Bruce) it was many years before its use was widely accepted. Finch remained an unremitting advocate of the relatively simple "open circuit" oxygen apparatus; 30 years after Finch's first demonstration Sir Edmund Hillary used equipment of this type in the first successful ascent of Everest and it has since been used in the conquest of many major Himalayan peaks.

In 1924 Finch wrote *The Makings of a Mountaineer*, which records his varied climbing experiences in the Alps, in the Himalayas and in Corsica. Illness brought an end to strenuous climbing in middle life, but his enthusiasm for the sport remained. He devoted much energy to encouraging the younger generation of mountaineers, especially in the University of London, and he was president of the Alpine Club in the years 1959–1961.

Mountaineering was, however, only one of his outdoor pursuits. As a young man he had participated strenuously in motor racing, skiing and other winter sports and in flying. After the hills, however, the sea was his major enthusiasm and for many summers after he ceased active climbing he sailed an eight-ton cutter, usually crewed by his wife and daughters.

November 24, 1970.

Professor Herman Finer, former professor of political science at the University of Chicago, died in Chicago on March 4, 1969 at the age of 71.

He was a political scientist of international repute whose life and work spanned the period of history from the Weimar Republic to the Suez crisis and after. His reputation was made by writings on political institutions and public administration, though, unlike some works in that field, his never sought to remove political theory from the analysis of political institutions and political practices. A full political man, Finer was an enthusiast and a reformer, who on occasion, joyfully loosed off spectacular blasts against the enemy. He was not a natural controversialist but when aroused, by Mussolini's Italy, Hayek's *The Road to Serfdom* or *Dulles over Suez* his attack was the artillery barrage guaranteed to do some damage.

In *Dulles over Suez* (1964), Finer accused Dulles, Secretary of State during General Eisenhower's presidency, of "bungling" over the Suez operation. He also claimed that Mr. Ben-Gurion, Prime Minister of Israel at the time of the Suez invasion, made a secret visit to France in 1956 to discuss plans for the attack with senior British and French officials. He cited a letter sent him by M. Pineau, French Foreign Minister in 1956, as proof of Ben-Gurion's secret visit. Pineau later denied that he had written to Finer about the secret meeting. Finer also claimed that Lord Avon, then Prime Minister, and Selwyn Lloyd, then Foreign Secretary, met their French opposite numbers in Paris before Israel moved against Egypt.

This book gave rise to questions in the House of Commons in May, 1964, as he lifted the veil a little on the allegations of British involvement in the French-Israeli collusion. It was a curious book in which high quality researches of the documents and interviews with some of the leading actors were presented in the style of a rather over-conversational who-dunnit.

He should be remembered, however, not for the polemics but rather for the impressive volumes on British and foreign Governments which were the solid foundations for a whole generation of students and teachers in universities on both sides of the Atlantic. His greatest work was the two volumes on the *Theory and Practice of Modern Government* (1932). Here he sought to attack the subject of comparative government in a methodologically more sophisticated manner than that adopted by Bryce in *Modern Democracies*. His work stands in several senses midway between the liberal optimism of Bryce and the rigorous methodological concerns of the moderns. In the United States, where he lived from the end of the Second World War until his death, he was soon recognized as an important writer on the political and administrative problems of his adopted country. This is not surprising for on arrival he was already well known for his work at the L.S.E. in Harold Laski's department.

He wrote one of the first studies of the Tennessee Valley Authority and a book on the administration of nursing services; he gave a newcomer's salute to the United States in *America's Destiny*, and he took a critical look at the top level in *The Presidency, Crisis and Regeneration*, 1960. At the ward level he became an active Democrat and an adviser to his city on the problems of the Chicago Port Authority.

Herman Finer was educated at the City of London College and the London School of Economics. He took a first there in 1919 and joined the staff in 1920 as a lecturer, later reader, in public administration. He gained the degree of D.Sc. (Economics) of London University in 1924, a rare and much coveted distinction. Much of his best work was done at the School. While there he produced *Foreign Governments at Work* (1922), *Representative Government and a Parliament of Industry* (1924), *The British Civil Service* (1927), *English Local Government* (1933). *Mussolini's Italy* (1935), *and Municipal Trading* (1940).

With the L.S.E. at Cambridge during the war years in 1940 Finer, who had already held a visiting professorship at Harvard, accepted an invitation as visiting professor at the University of Chicago. He returned to England in 1941, and in 1942 he went to Canada to work with the I.L.O. At the end of the war he accepted the offer of a full professorship at the University of Chicago where he stayed until retiring in 1963. From then until his death he was a professor of political science at Northwestern University, Evanston, Illinois.

Herman Finer was a prodigious worker and

enthusiastic teacher and one who demonstrated in his academic activity the essential unity of teaching and research. Though spirited in attack (he had in his youth been a noted boxer) and possessed of great self-confidence, he was neither aggressive nor overbearing. His contributions to political science were impressive and his cheerful personality and friendliness to students will be remembered.

March 7, 1969.

Group Captain Donald Finlay, D.F.C., A.F.C., an outstanding British international athlete, died on April 19, 1970, at the age of 60.

Donald Osborne Finlay was one of the greatest athletes ever to represent Great Britain both before and after the war. His international career as a high hurdler began in 1929 and ended in 1950 and his honours included eight A.A.A. titles and a silver medal in the Olympic Games.

Finlay was born at Christchurch, Hampshire, on May 27, 1909, and educated at Taunton School. He made his career in the Royal Air Force and during the war was decorated with the D.F.C. and A.F.C. From September, 1940, to August, 1941, the squadron of which he was Wing Commander destroyed 66 enemy aircraft. After retiring from the R.A.F. he went into business.

As a hurdler Finlay was peerless. He won his first R.A.F. title in 1929, was a member of the 1930 Empire Games team and took his first A.A.A. championship in 1932, coming third in the Olympics at Los Angeles in the same year. He was Empire Games champion in 1934, Olympic silver medallist behind the American Forrest Towns at Berlin two years later and European champion in 1938.

Yet the most remarkable aspect of Finlay's athletics career was his return to international competition after the war. He took the Olympic oath on behalf of the competitors of all countries for the Olympics at Wembley in 1948 and though he failed to qualify for the hurdles final he came back the next year to win his eighth A.A.A. championship.

Later in the summer of 1949 Finlay, now 40, beat an American named Dick Attlesey, who the following year beat the world record for 120 yards hurdles with 13.5sec. Finlay, who was running as fast as ever before with 14.3sec. (though there are those who believe his 14.1sec. at Stockholm in 1937 was not, as ruled, unduly wind assisted), closed his career in 1950 by coming fourth in the Empire Games.

In spite of the high regard in which he was held by so many in the sport Finlay never played a big part in the administration of British athletics but he had strong views on the way things should be run. His hurdling success was the result of fluent style which made up for his lack of basic speed and which was the result of years of painstaking effort. In full flight he was closer to art than sport.

April 22, 1970.

Sir Ronald Aylmer Fisher, F.R.S., one of the outstanding mathematical biologists of his time, died in Adelaide on July 29, 1962, at the age of 72.

Born on February 17, 1890, the seventh child of G. Fisher, of Robinson & Fisher, auctioneers in St. James's, he was educated at Harrow and Gonville and Caius College, Cambridge, where he graduated as a wrangler in the mathematical tripos in 1913. For two years he was statistician to the Mercantile & General Investment Company and then, being excluded from military service by his extremely short sight, he was engaged in teaching at Rugby throughout the First World War. In 1919 he joined the staff of the Rothamsted Experimental Station as head of the statistical department, where he remained until 1933.

Here Fisher began the remarkable series of statistical investigations which led to the techniques described in *Statistical Methods for Research Workers* (1925, 10th edition 1946), *The Design of Experiments* (1935, fifth edition 1949), and *Statistical Tables* (published with F. Yates, 1938, third edition 1947). These works revolutionized agricultural research: for they described the methods, now used all the world over, for evaluating the results of small sample experiments and for so laying our experimental trials to minimize the disturbances due to heterogeneity of soils and the unavoidable irregularities of biological material.

In 1933 Fisher was appointed to the Galton Chair of Eugenics in University College London.

CONFLICT ENDED

As an undergraduate he had been attracted to genetics and to biometry, and had shown in 1918 that biometrical correlations between relatives were to be expected on the Mendelian theory; and during his time at Rothamsted he had carried out genetical experiments as a hobby. Bringing his great mathematical ability to bear upon these two sciences of biometry and genetics, which in the past had been largely in conflict, he played perhaps the chief part in bringing about their present unity. Already in 1930 he had published *The Genetical Theory of Natural Selection*, which went far towards reconciling the Darwinian ideas of natural selection with Mendelian theory.

His mathematical treatment of natural selection has provided the basis for most modern studies of populations. His theory of the evolution of dominance introduced the notion of the modification of gene action by selection.

NEO-DARWINISM

This marriage of Darwinism with genetics, for which Fisher was in large part responsible, is sometimes referred to as "neo-darwinism".

Fisher's mathematical approach proved particularly valuable in the difficult field of human genetics. Among many other notable contributions he was responsible for the theory that provides a basis for understanding the *Rhesus* blood groups in man which attracted so much attention during the Second World War. In 1943 Fisher accepted appointment as Arthur Balfour Professor of Genetics at Cambridge, a post which he held until his retirement in 1957.

The rise of quantitative biology, which has been so noteworthy a feature of the past 40 years, has been due above all to the work of R. A. Fisher. He combined mathematical skill with biological insight; and the theoretical and practical methods which he evolved for the planning of experiments with field crops in agriculture have spread far and wide. The younger biologists of today all make use of such methods for every kind of experimentation; indeed, their influence now extends far beyond the bounds of biology.

As a penetrating thinker Fisher was outstanding; but his writings are difficult for many readers. Indeed, some of his teachings have been most effectively conveyed by the books of others who have been able to simplify their expression. As a lecturer, also, Fisher was too difficult for the average student; his classes would rapidly fall away until only two or three students who could stand the pace remained as fascinated disciples. Nor was he particularly successful as an administrator; he perhaps failed to appreciate the intellectual limitations of the ordinary man. But with his wide interests and penetrating mind he was a most stimulating and sympathetic conversationalist.

Fisher had been a Fellow of Gonville and Caius College from 1921 to 1927. He was reelected on his return to Cambridge in 1943 and was elected President of his college in 1956. He was elected Fellow of the Royal Society in 1929, receiving a Royal Medal in 1938, the Darwin medal in 1948 and the Copley medal, the highest award in the gift of the society, in 1956. He also received the Guy medal in gold of the Royal Statistical Society. He was knighted in 1952. Many foreign universities and academies conferred honours on him; he received honorary doctorates from the Universities of Glasgow, Calcutta, Ames, Harvard, London and Chicago, and he was an honorary foreign member and fellow of the American Academy of Arts and Sciences, the American Philosophical Society, the United States National Academy of Science, the Royal Swedish Academy of Science and the Royal Danish Academy of Science. In 1957 he was honorary president of the International Statistical Institute.

CHOSEN HOME

In 1959 he retired as President of his college and it was in that year that he toured Australia as the guest of the Commonwealth Scientific and Industrial Research Organization. While there he decided that Adelaide would be a pleasant place in which to live and he returned there the following January. Since then he had been attached to the C.S.I.R. division of mathematical statistics and had lectured at Adelaide University.

He married in 1917 Ruth Eileen, daughter of H. Gratten Guinness, and had two sons (the elder was killed in action in 1943) and six daughters.

July 31, 1962.

Dr. Arne Fjellbu, former Bishop of Trondheim, died on October 7, 1962. He was 72.

His death recalls some of the most heroic episodes of the Norwegian Church's resistance to the Nazis, in which he was one of the central figures.

Arne Fjellbu was born in Iowa, where his father was a pastor to a Norwegian emigrant colony, but at the age of 10 he returned to Norway and eventually took his theological examinations at Oslo University. During the First World War from 1916 to 1919 he was Norwegian pastor in Berlin, and after returning to his home church he eventually became in 1937 Dean of Trondheim Cathedral and then Bishop.

He first came into world news in the early part of 1942 when as Dean of Trondheim he refused to officiate at a service in the cathedral at the behest of the Nazi authorities to celebrate Quisling's appointment as "Minister President" of Norway. He conducted his own service while thousands of people stood in silent protest against the Nazis.

MARKED MAN

From then on Fjellbu was a marked man. He was dismissed from his office and banished from his diocese, but continued to travel and preach in many parts of Norway. His large, burly figure became a symbol of Norwegian resistance and so powerful was his example that in 1943 the Nazis banished him to the island of Andoya, the most northerly of the Lofoten Islands. After a year there he escaped to Sweden, but after another year was back in the liberated area of East Finnmark, in North Norway, where he acted as chaplain to a contingent of the Norwegian Army which arrived from Britain and by royal decree was appointed Bishop of Halogaland, which included the liberated area.

In conditions of extreme simplicity, living in one room himself. Fjellbu travelled through the liberated region by skis and reindeer sledge. In 11 towns he found the churches destroyed by the Nazis, and in the town of Kirkenes the churchyard had been desecrated by a railway line built across it.

In April, 1945, he came to Britain to represent the Norwegian Church at the enthronement of the Archbishop of Canterbury (Lord Fisher of Lambeth), and on April 9, the anniversary of the Nazi invasion of Norway, preached at a memorial service in Westminster Abbey.

In the presence of the King of Norway and members of the Norwegian Government in London Bishop Fjellbu recalled the heroic story of Norwegian resistance, saluting the courage and fidelity of the Norwegian people during their years of trial. As bishop, patriot, and pastor Fjellbu will long be remembered in the history of Norway.

October 9, 1962.

Kirsten Flagstad, the Norwegian soprano, who died at her home in Oslo on December 7,1962, at the age of 67, was the outstanding Wagnerian soprano of the mid-twentieth century.

In the late 1930s she and her fellow-Scandinavian, Lauritz Melchior, restored German opera to popularity in New York after some two generations' neglect; and 10 years later she became one of the newly formed Covent Garden Opera Company's first and most beloved guest stars. But she had been singing in opera for 20 years and was even contemplating retirement before she found the international fame which kept her before the public for a further two decades and more.

LONG CAREER

Her singing career was a long one, by normal standards, and at the end of it, when she emerged from retirement to sing Grieg at a Promenade concert, and when she recorded *Das Rheingold* in Vienna, her voice was as rich and radiant and as effortlessly produced as ever. This was doubtless because hers was above all a natural instrument which had been allowed to grow gently and in its own time until, in her forties, it reached full and glorious bloom.

Kirsten Malfrid Flagstad was born into a family of professional musicians at Hamar, Norway, on July 12, 1895. Her father Michael Flagstad was a conductor, her mother, Marie Johnsrud Flagstad-Nielsen, a pianist, who often accompanied Kirsten in recitals, as later did her brother Lasse; another brother was a cellist, and her sister Karen Marie became a soprano singer (the two sisters can be heard together in a gramophone recording of Wagner's *Götterdämmerung*). Kirsten studied the piano as a child, but from the age of six was singing songs by Schubert, and in due course she became a vocal pupil of Ellen Schytte-Jacobsen.

Flagstad made her operatic debut, while still a student, in D'Albert's *Tiefland* on December 12, 1913, at the National Theatre in Oslo. After further study and some public appearances she married Sigurd Hall in 1919 and, following temporary retirement at the time of her daughter's birth, she found that her voice had become larger. She continued to sing as a light soprano in operetta and revue as well as opera at the Stora Theatre, Gothenburg, and by 1932 had accumulated a repertory of some 75 roles.

DEBUT IN NEW YORK

After her second marriage, in 1930, to Henry Johansen, she retired again for a while and this time discovered that her voice became heavy enough for her to undertake the part of Isolde. When Nanny Larsen-Todsen became indisposed during a season at Brussels, Flagstad took over from her the role of Isolde, and as a result was invited to sing Ortlinde and third Norn at Bayreuth Festival in 1933, and Sieglinde and Gutrune in 1934. From there she went to New York where her debut on February 2, 1935, at the Metropolitan as Sieglinde excited extraordinary enthusiasm, and she was at once engaged to sing Isolde and Brünnhilde in addition, as well as Elsa and Kundry, learning several of these roles in a very few days before undertaking them in public.

On May 18, 1936, she made her Covent Garden debut as Isolde, later singing Brünnhilde and giving a hastily arranged song recital at Queen's Hall, where she showed that although her voice was big she could sing the small songs of Schubert and Grieg because her sense of style was acute.

Hard work and deep-seated musicianship had endowed her with a rock-firm sense of rhythm, and flawless intonation, as well as the power to project grandly spacious phrases based upon wonderfully clear and incisive enunciation—it seemed that she could sustain a vocal line through any concatenation of consonants. Beneath this flow of noble tone Flagstad's presentation of Isolde, unforgettable as it was, appeared a shade cold when compared with those of other great interpreters; her Isolde suggested a sublime symbol of womanhood, rather than a woman in flesh and blood. But she was Wagner's Brünnhilde to the life, from the warrior-maden of *Die Walküre* to the grand, heroic redemptress of the Immolation Scene in *Götterdämmerung*. Beethoven's Leonore, symbol of eternal womanhood, equally found in Flagstad a dignified and moving exponent, as she showed at Salzburg in a famous postwar production conducted by Furtwängler.

MALICIOUS GOSSIP

Flagstad's international career proceeded apace in the late 1930s. After London she sang in Vienna, and concert tours took her as far afield as Australia. The outbreak of war found her in the United States, where she continued to delight Metropolitan audiences until, in 1941, she returned home to Norway. Here, despite pressure from Quislings and Nazi officials, she showed her distaste for the political situation by refusing to sing, and she emphasized her passive resistance by accepting engagements in neutral Sweden and Switzerland. Her husband had, in her absence, joined the Norwegian Nazi party, but on her return she persuaded him to resign, and the couple spent the remainder of the war in retirement at Kristianssand.

After the liberation Johansen was arrested as a collaborator, and he died while awaiting trial, but malicious gossip continued for some time to associate Flagstad too with the Nazis, and it preceded her across the Atlantic when her return to America was attended by unsavoury demonstrations. Flagstad's art and her personal courage triumphed, and in addition to her Wagner roles she made some memorable appearances at the Metropolitan in Gluck's *Alceste*, a role she later broadcast for the B.B.C. and recorded for the gramophone.

LONDON WELCOME

No such stigma accompanied her return to London in 1947. Her voice, which had once again grown in size and splendour, was welcome for itself as well as for the Wagnerian opera which, after years of Wagner short-commons, London was again able to see and hear. In 1948 Flagstad sang Isolde at Covent Garden, and also the *Walküre* Brünnhilde in English, though in subsequent seasons the original German text was restored. From then until 1951 she was London's indispensable Brünnhilde thrice over (though by now her voice had become somewhat heavy for the love duet in *Siegfried*), and an everywhere admired Isolde, Kundry, Leonore and, for a single performance in 1951, Sieglinde.

In that year she announced her intention of giving up gradually her heaviest roles, but that summer she undertook another new part, Purcell's Dido, at the little Mermaid Theatre which her friend Bernard Miles had constructed in his garden in St. John's Wood (her fee was two pints of oatmeal stout a day!). Two years later she ended a series of farewell appearances at the theatre in Oslo where her career had begun exactly 40 years before, to the day.

There were the first signs of wear and tear on her voice, at this stage, but these had disappeared when, after some rest, she began to make her last broadcasts and gramophone records, and when she donned national costume to celebrate Grieg's centenary by singing his songs at a Prom concert in 1957.

When the Norwegian State Opera was formed in 1958, Flagstad was appointed director of it and for its first production she chose D'Albert's *Tiefland* in which she had made her own debut. In 1960 illness obliged her to resign this post, and she had been in poor health for some time before she died.

December 10, 1962.

Bud Flanagan, O.B.E., a comedian so popular that he became an English institution, died on October 20, 1968, at the age of 72. As the leading partner in the double-act of Flanagan and Allen, as the leading spirit in the now legendary Crazy Gang, and, since the Crazy Gang ceased its operations in 1962, as a solo artist, Bud Flanagan provided a combination of the outrageous, the inventive, and the endearing which made him a universal favourite.

Bud Flanagan was born Robert Winthrop—his Polish Jewish father had taken the name Winthrop when he settled in England—in Spitalfields, London, in 1896. The future comedian began his working life as callboy at the Cambridge Music Hall, in the East End of London, where he became aware of the tradition of English humour of which he was to become a part. At the Cambridge he saw most of the great performers of the period, amongst them Alec Hurley, "the Coster Comedian", upon whom he modelled his stage voice. Eventually the young Winthrop ran away to America, where, after casual jobs and a career as a boxer (which, he claimed, lasted for one fight) he toured in vaudeville until he returned to England to enlist in the Army during the First World War.

It was in an estaminet at Poperinghe that he first met Chesney Allen when they were both resting out of the line, and a reunion some years later, as members of one of Florrie Forde's touring revues, led to their partnership as "Flanagan and Allen". For a time before this, Robert Winthrop had been touring as "Chick Harlem", the blackface comic; the new name, Flanagan, was in part a compliment to Florrie Forde, whose maiden name was Flanagan, and in part a good humoured revenge upon an Irish Sergeant-Major Flanagan who "didn't like Jews"; Robert Winthrop had promised the Irishman that he would make the name famous as a joke, and he spent the rest of his life doing so.

The act of Flanagan and Allen was a combination of songs with cross-talk in the tradition of the down-and-out Flanagan confronting the elegantly aristocratic Allen. It allowed both the partners room for surprising invention, and Flanagan, with his broken straw hat, enormous shabby clothes he could not possibly fill, and vast Hebraic leer, showed himself to be an extremely resourceful comedian. The act began in the provinces but soon brought the pair to London, where they started in a number of reviews at the Holborn Empire and the Palladium.

The depression of 1931 nearly drove them from the stage into full-time bookmaking, for they both were devotees of racing, but instead, with the double-act teams of "Naughton and Gold" and "Nervo and Knox", and with "Monsewer Eddie Gray" they became "The Crazy Gang" and added a new dimension to comedy in the variety theatre. Their antics did not stop at the rude interruption from the gallery or the plaintive objection from a stage box, but were likely to occupy the foyer as well as the aisles of a theatre. Popularity with the Royal Family, whom they subjected to inoffensive and usually quite respectful cheekiness, gave them a position parallel to that of a medieval court jester. Flanagan's delight in absurd periphrastic mistakes—"Goodwood" was usually "Fine timber" to him—opened a vein of surrealist fantasy which, perhaps, helped to make them favourites with the intelligentsia. As well as that, in their sixties they were all capable of acrobatic hilarities. The vulgarity of their humour—Flanagan objected to the idea that his jokes were ever "dirty" but admitted that he enjoyed what he described as "broad"—was often interrupted by his shout of "Oi!", leaving the shocking dénouement to the audience's imagination.

In all this, Flanagan was the ringleader, and his approach to comedy was entirely professional and painstaking. The anarchy which he inspired on the stage was carefully built up to a climax, just as his jokes were taken over from every possible source and then polished until they seemed entirely his own. His singing of the popular songs of four decades was a pleasure his admirers will not quickly forget, but his own "Underneath the Arches"—a salute to the down-and-outs of the Depression—is perhaps the only one of the dozens he sang to have the quality of a classic.

But Flanagan received the Order of the British Empire in 1958, and after the Crazy Gang broke up in 1962 he continued to appear in pantomime, for the idea of retirement did not appeal to him. With Chesney Allen and other of his colleagues he appeared in a number of films which did not succeed in conveying the warmth and liberating power of his personality, which dissolved inhibitions in the shortest possible time. If his humour, like his personality, had something about it which was essentially Jewish, he fed this quality into the tradition of the music hall, and he came to exciting vivid life through interplay with an audience.

October 21, 1968.

Lord Fleck, K.B.E., F.R.S., former chairman of I.C.I., died on August 6, 1968, in London at the age of 78.

Although Fleck will be best remembered as an outstanding man in the chemical industry—he was for seven years chairman of Imperial Chemical Industries, retiring in 1960—he was a man of wide interests and talents who could have achieved success in many other walks of life. It was, indeed, largely a matter of chance that he forsook a promising academic career to enter the chemical industry in 1914. In later life, his ties with the university world were reestablished. The universities of Glasgow. Durham, Oxford, London and Nottingham conferred honorary degrees upon him; the Manchester College of Science and Technology made him an honorary fellow; in 1958 he became president of the British Association for the Advancement of Science; in 1960 he was elected treasurer and vice-president of the Royal Society, to whose fellowship he had been elected in 1955. He was made an honorary fellow of the Royal Society of Edinburgh in 1957. To all these activities he brought the ability, enthusiasm and stamina that had carried him to the top in industry.

No less important, he brought to all he did a generous personality, coupled with a fine sense of humour, that inspired devotion and, indeed, affection. Of humble origin himself, he never grew away from ordinary people and their problems. He maintained a friendly interest in those with whom he had been associated, whatever their status, and it was his custom to write to them in his own hand when he learnt of major events in their lives—promotions, honours, weddings, bereavements, and so on. How he managed to do this, even in his busiest years, was astonishing. Young people, in particular, had his special sympathy, and to them he extended the same courtesy and consideration as he did to their elders. He was one of the few men who rose from the ranks to the very top yet remained quite unspoilt by success.

LAB. BOY

Alexander Fleck was born on November 11, 1889, in Glasgow, where his father was in business as a coal merchant. As a boy he was not greatly interested in coal as a commodity—though in later years he was to be very much concerned with its large-scale use as an industrial raw material—and when he left school at 14 his heart was set on a scientific career. Characteristically, he was not daunted by the practical difficulties of this, but set about achieving his ambition by the only way open to him—by entering Glasgow University as a laboratory boy. Here he came under the influence of Soddy, whose assistant he became. With great determination he achieved the Glasgow doctorate—for a thesis entitled "Some Chapters on the Chemistry of the Radio Elements"—attending first at evening classes, and then enrolling as a student. Qualified, and appointed to the university staff in 1911 he continued to work with Soddy until 1913 on the chemistry of the radioactive elements. He then joined the staff of the Glasgow Radium Committee, with a laboratory of his own for radiological work on cancer, and all seemed set for an academic career.

As with so many of his generation, however, the war caused a change in his plans. In 1917 he went to Wallsend-on-Tyne as chief chemist to the Castner Kellner Company, then manufacturing a range of chemicals for wartime industry; Fleck was particularly concerned with the manufacture of sodium, required, among other things, for making sodium cyanide for gold extraction in the manufacture of light alloys. From the point of view of his future career, the significance of the move lay in the fact that in 1916 the company had allied itself with Brunner, Mond and Co., which in 1926 joined with Nobel Industries, the United Alkali Company, and the British Dyestuffs Corporation to form Imperial Chemical Industries.

One consequence of the merger was a decision, taken in 1929, to close the Wallsend works and amalgamate it with Allhusen Works, at Gateshead, and the Cassel Cyanide Company, at Glasgow. The three works were concentrated at Billingham South, later called Cassel Works; this became one of the principal factories of I.C.I.'s General Chemicals Division. The skill with which the new dispositions were made established Fleck's name in I.C.I., and in 1931 he became managing director of General Chemicals. Six years later he was appointed chairman of I.C.I.'s Billingham Division, one of the world's great centres of chemical manufacture, and carried out with great success the very difficult task of keeping it going during the war of 1939–45; it was an important target and attracted well over a hundred high explosive bombs. In 1944, he joined the main board of I.C.I. and two years later was made deputy chairman. In 1953, at the age of 63, he reached the top on election as chairman, which office he held until his retirement in 1960

SENSE OF FUN

Such an industrial appointment is arduous indeed, but Fleck contrived to discharge all his very varied tasks, involving worldwide travel, without apparent strain. While he attended to his many duties with a proper seriousness, he never lost the sense of fun that made his company so agreeable. Despite his preoccupation with I.C.I. and its affairs, it was astonishing how much else he was able to achieve. From 1953 to 1955 he was chairman of the Coal Board Organization Committee; from 1957 to 1958 of the Prime Minister's Committee on the Windscale Accident; and from 1958 to 1965 of the Scientific Advisory Council (in 1960 renamed the Advisory Council on Research and Development). He was also chairman of a Government Committee on the British Fishing Industry, which reported in 1961.

LOVE OF HISTORY

As has been mentioned, he was president of the British Association in 1958. It was very appropriate that during the Association's annual meeting in Glasgow, Fleck should have been invited to unveil a plaque commemorating the work of Soddy there. During the same meeting he was elected an honorary fellow of the Royal Faculty of Physicians and Surgeons of Glasgow.

Among Fleck's private interests was a love of history, which found expression in a number of ways. He was, for example, much interested in the studies of Bede and the earlier English chroniclers being made at the Durham Colleges, of whose Council he was a member, and whose honorary degree he received in 1953. In 1959 he founded a trust, the income from which is divided between the Universities of Durham and Glasgow, to encourage postgraduate historical research, particularly on the history of England and Scotland between the end of the Roman occupation and the Norman conquest.

AWARDS FOR YOUNG

Again, Fleck gave much encouragement to the five-volume History of Technology, which I.C.I. sponsored over the years 1950–58, to which he contributed an important chapter on a subject very much in his mind—namely. "Technology and its Social Consequences".

For Fleck, retirement was a relative term, for he not only maintained many of his old interests but acquired new ones. Very characteristically, he marked his retirement by establishing four Fleck Awards, to be given to young people in I.C.I. who had displayed outstanding all-round merit. Almost simultaneously with leaving I.C.I., he became president of the Society of Chemical Industry (1960–62)—whose Messel Medal, its highest award, he had received in 1956. Fleck remained a director of the Midland Bank, to which he was elected in 1955. Since 1963 he was Chairman of International Research and Development Co. Ltd., and also president of the Royal Institution. From 1960 to 1965, he was chairman of the Nuclear Safety Advisory Committee.

To the recognition he gained in industry and in the academic world were added other high honours. He was made K.B.E. in 1955—for services to the Ministry of Fuel and Power—and raised to the peerage in 1961, taking the title of Lord Fleck of Saltcoats.

In 1917, Fleck married Isabel Kelly, who died in 1955. There were no children of the marriage.

August 7, 1968.

Ian Fleming, whose death at the age of 56 took place on August 12, 1964, was one of the most successful and controversial thriller writers in recent years.

Ian Lancaster Fleming was born in 1908, son of Major Valentine Fleming, M.P., D.S.O. He was educated at Eton and Sandhurst, and then at Munich and Geneva universities. In 1929, having failed to secure a place in the Diplomatic Service, he joined Reuter's at a time when the international wire services were struggling for supremacy. "Reuter's was great fun in those days" Fleming said afterwards, "a very good mill. The training there gives you a good straightforward style. Above all, I have to thank Reuter's for getting my facts right." He covered the trial of the Vickers-Armstrong engineers in Moscow in 1933, and was offered the job of Reuter's assistant general manager in the Far East. He decided instead to seek his fortune in the City; an attempt which he continued, without much success, first as a banker, then as a stockbroker, until he joined the Navy in 1939. As personal assistant to the Director of Naval Intelligence, he found the war "intensely exciting". When it was over, Lord Kemsley offered him the foreign managership of Kemsley (now Thomson) newspapers. Fleming accepted on condition that he could have two months' holiday a year to spend at his house, Goldeneye, in Jamaica, where subsequently he did most of his writing.

If his war experiences and his postwar job provided the background for his thrillers, Fleming maintained that it was his marriage to Anne Viscountess Rothermere in 1952 which spurred him to start writing. "I was in the process of getting married", he said, "which is a very painful thing to do at the age of 44; so to take my mind off the whole business, I sat down and wrote a novel." The novel was a spy story, *Casino Royale* (1953), remotely derived from a real case in the history of Soviet espionage activities in France. It introduced the handsome ruthless British agent James Bond ("007—licensed to kill"), and the various elements—a gambling scene, a torture scene, physical luxury and knowingness about the world's ways—which were to become the hallmarks of Fleming's style. It was well received and he soon followed it with other James Bond adventures, *Live and Let Die* (1954), *Moonraker* (1955) and *Diamonds Are Forever* (1956).

SOARING POPULARITY

His popularity soared: his books became fashionable and they roused fierce opposition. He was accused of trading in sex, snobbery and sadism. Fleming replied by explaining his own attitude to James Bond: "I wanted to show a hero without any characteristics, who was simply the blunt instrument in the hands of the government. Then he started eating a number of meals and dressing in a certain way so that he became encrusted with characteristics much against my will. . . . Apart from the fact that he wears the same clothes that I wear, he and I really have very little in common. I do rather envy him his blondes and his efficiency, but I can't say I much like the chap."

In 1959 Fleming left regular newspaper work to devote himself to his books and the management of what had become a very valuable literary property. By now there was already a slight flagging in his style, a tendency to repeat his effects. In *The Spy Who Loved Me* (1962) he tried the bizarre experiment of telling a James Bond story through the eyes of the heroine. He knew it was a failure, and the next book, *On Her Majesty's Secret Service* (1963), reverted to normal; but, like Holmes after the Reichenbach Falls, Bond never seemed quite the same man again. *You Only Live Twice* (1964) provoked discussion, not because it was shocking, but because it was not; two-thirds of it was mere travel writing about Japan. Fleming was finding the process of invention increasingly difficult.

HERO PARODIED

The snowball of success, however, continued quite unchecked. Each book headed the best-seller list for weeks. Paper-back editions proliferated: James Bond was imitated and parodied. President Kennedy and Mr. Allen Dulles were numbered among his admirers. The fame and profitability of the books were spectacularly enhanced by a triumphant film debut. With Mr. Sean Connery as Bond, *Dr. No* maintained a delicate balance, hovering on the edge of farce; its successor, *From Russia With Love*, was outstandingly successful: a third, *Goldfinger*, will be released shortly.

In March, 1964. Fleming struck a unique and ingenious bargain, under which he sold 51 per cent of all his future royalties, excluding film rights, to Booker Brothers, the sugar and investment company, for £100,000.

Fleming had completed, and was revising, a new novel, *The Man With the Golden Arm*, set in the West Indies, and there are several James Bond short stories which have not yet been published in book form.

He had one son.

August 13, 1964.

The Rev. Dr. Robert Newton Flew, D.D., former President of the Methodist Conference, who died on September 10, 1962, at Cambridge at the age of 76, was for many years one of the most influential theological teachers of the Methodist Church.

For almost 30 years he was a member of the tutorial staff of Wesley House, Cambridge. He was appointed Tutor in Systematic and Pastoral Theology in 1927 and held that office until his retirement in 1955, having been also Principal of the College since 1937. Wesley House is the youngest of the Methodist Ministerial Training Colleges and had already built a rich academic tradition when Flew went there. This he fostered with careful pride, and the number of old Wesley House men who have since held positions of influence in the Church is a monument to his work, which gave him great pleasure.

Flew, who was the son of a minister, the Rev. Dr. J. Flew, was born at Holsworthy, Devon, in May, 1886. His family had a long association with the Island of Portland. Educated at Christs Hospital, he entered Merton College, Oxford, where he had a distinguished career. He later studied at Marburg and Fribourg Universities.

TUTOR AND PASTOR

His first appointment on entering the old Wesleyan ministry was that of Assistant Tutor at Handsworth College, Birmingham, where he remained for three years. His first circuit appointment was at Finsbury Park, where he revealed a capacity for pastoral work which surprised those who thought that he would only be really at home in the classroom. During the 1914–18 War he volunteered for chaplaincy duty and served in Mesopotamia and Persia. Before returning to normal work he served for a time as Professor of New Testament Studies at the United College of Bangalore.

Two further terms in London circuits marked the end of his normal pastoral duties and the beginning of the Cambridge period. He was elected to the Presidency of the Conference in 1946, and some pungent presidential comments on the reporting of Methodist affairs by the press ultimately led to the formation of the Methodist Press Service.

He was keenly devoted to the fostering of better understanding between the Churches and was a member of the committee of various denominations which discussed the implication of the Archbishop of Canterbury's Cambridge sermon on the subject. It was a matter of deep satisfaction to him that, when the invitation to appoint representatives to discuss closer relations with the Anglican Church was received by the Methodist Conference of 1955, he was asked by the President to be the only speaker called formally to move acceptance.

His friendly relations with the Anglican Church in no way undermined his Free Church loyalties and he was a successful Moderator of the Free Church Federal Council in 1945–46.

Flew's scholarship was recognized by many universities and colleges. He was Murtle Lecturer at Aberdeen in 1936 and Kent-Shaffer Lecturer at Yale in 1947. In 1948 he visited Australia to give the Cato Lecture which is always one of the outstanding intellectual events in the life of Australian Methodism. He was an honorary D.D. of Aberdeen.

He was the author of a number of theological works including *The Idea of Perfection in Christian Theology*, *Jesus and His Church* and *The Catholicity of Protestantism* (in collaboration with the Rev. Rupert Davies).

He was a man of wide social sympathies and was affectionately regarded by his students. It had to be a most important engagement which prevented his attendance at the Oxford and Cambridge Rugby match, and he had a deep devotion to anything connected with cricket.

He married in 1921 Miss Winifred Garrard and had one son, Professor Anthony Flew, of the University of Keele.

September 11, 1962.

Sir William Russell Flint, R.A., who died on December 27, 1969, at the age of 89, will be chiefly remembered as a water colourist of remarkable technical skill.

Though he painted also in oils and tempera and produced a considerable number of etchings and dry-points, his most characteristic works were water colour landscapes and figure compositions, elaborately carried out and displaying great virtuosity in the gradation of a wash and a special manner of enriching its effect by taking advantage of a grained paper surface. His method was in a sense traditional, though his affinity was rather with the late-Victorian than the Early English water colourists. Some of his figure pictures, depicting undraped models idealistically posed on the edge of bathing pools, might suggest Alma-Tadema, brought up to date. If a certain resulting prettiness appeared superficial to the critical eye, it undoubtedly gained him a wide measure of popularity.

In 1962 he was given a one-man exhibition at the Royal Academy. More than 300 of his paintings and drawings were shown.

Born in Edinburgh on April 4, 1880, William Russell Flint was the eldest son of Francis Wighton Flint, artist and designer. He was educated at Daniel Stewart's College, Edinburgh and studied at the Royal Institution School of Art, Edinburgh. On leaving school he served a six years' apprenticeship to a lithographic artist. An early essay in water colour was exhibited at the Glasgow Institute of the Fine Arts in 1898 and two years later he began an independent career in London. He did various kinds of journeyman work at first, including the illustration of medical textbooks but in 1902 he was chosen by Bruce Ingram of the *Illustrated London News* to illustrate a story by (Sir) Max Pemberton and was then engaged by Ingram as a regular staff artist. After four years (1903–07) on the *Illustrated London News* Flint became a free lance once more. He had already illustrated an edition of *Thomas à Kempis* for Chatto and Windus (1905) and had a picture hung for the first time in the Royal Academy in the same year. He now applied himself to oil and water colour paintings and by the outbreak of war in 1914 had become an Associate of the Royal Society of Painters in Water Colours.

AIRSHIP OVERSEER

In the First World War Flint first held a commission as lieutenant in the R.N.V.R., he was with the Airships Section R.N.A.S. and later a captain in the Royal Air Force. In 1918–19 he was Admiralty Overseer on the airship R34. After 1918 and his return to civil life he made rapid headway as an artist, exhibiting regularly at the Royal Academy and elsewhere at home and abroad, many works being acquired by public collections. He was made Associate of the Royal Academy in 1924 and a full Academician in 1933. In 1928, then 48 years old, he had taken up drypoint engraving and the year 1933 also saw his election as Fellow of the Royal Society of Painter-Etchers and Engravers. He was elected president of the R.W.S. in 1936 and held the office until 1956.

Flint held many successful one-man exhibitions, chiefly at the galleries of the Fine Art Society. They included landscapes of English, Scottish and Provencal country and also figure compositions, with their gracefully arranged nudes and semi-nudes—attractive at first sight, but tending to become an over-sweetened formula. The defect attendant upon his skill was a lack of depth or significance, the more apparent when he attempted as serious a subject as "In Their Own Home" (Spain's Agony of Civil War, 1936–38). His drawing however was clever and his brush invariably assured. His ability to render water, sand and trees with a full control of his transparent medium was especially notable. Excellent reproductions of Flint's water colours helped to make his work appreciated by a large public. He also produced an occasional poster and in 1937 painted a number of water colours for reproduction on menu cards for the then London and North Eastern Railway.

BOOK AND TYPE DESIGN

Among his special interests were typography and book design and he illustrated a number of classics for the Riccardi Press, including an edition of the *Canterbury Tales*, though in his own typical manner and without attempted archaism or decorative convention of style.

He also illustrated and edited *One Hundred and Eleven Poems by Robert Herrick*, and produced albums of his nude studies, *Models of Propriety* and *Minxes Admonished*.

Works by the artist are in the British Museum, Victoria and Albert Museum, the Fitzwilliam Museum, and in many public galleries in Britain, Canada, Australia and the United States. Flint received a knighthood in 1947. He had lived for many years at Peel Cottage, Campden Hill, where he had a spacious and pleasant studio. A quiet, modest and unassuming man, he was entirely detached from everything that was controversial or experimental in the art of his time.

He married, in 1905, Sibylle, daughter of Fleet Paymaster J. T. Sueter, R.N. She died in 1960. Their son, Francis Murray Russell Flint is a well-known painter in oils and water colour.

December 30, 1969.

Ronald Flockhart, Scotland's leading racing driver, died on April 12, 1962, when the Mustang fighter aircraft he was to fly in his second attempt to break the 24-year-old Sydney-London air speed record crashed on a test flight. He had hoped to set up a 36-hour record for the 12,000-mile journey.

He was born in Edinburgh in 1923, and in 1961 married Miss Gillian Mary Tatlow, a B.O.A.C. air hostess, daughter of Mr. and Mrs. E. M. Tatlow, of Tettenhall, Staffordshire. Ron Flockhart's racing career went back to the V-16 B.R.M. days and beyond. He drove Grand Prix, Formula Libre, sports cars and saloons, but his greatest hobby was flying.

The only son of Mr. A. Flockhart of Greenhill Gardens, Edinburgh, and the late Mrs. Flockhart, he studied engineering at Edinburgh University and graduated as a B.Sc. in 1943. He saw active service with the R.E.M.E., being demobilized with the rank of captain in 1947. He began racing motor cycles in Army scrambles in Italy and the Middle East between 1945 and 1947, and in 1952 began motor racing with a pre-war E.R.A., soon extending his activity to the racing circuits, mostly with his E.R.A., but finishing third with a Connaught at Charterhall.

In 1954 he gave up his post with a textile business in Edinburgh to join the Owen racing organization, and raced frequently in the 16-cylinder B.R.M., winning minor races at Ibsley and Snetterton. He took part in the 1955 Mille Miglia with an Austin-Healey, but the race nearly ended in disaster for him when he skidded off a bridge and landed upside down in a river, from which he was extricated almost unscathed. In 1956 and 1957 he won the classic Le Mans 24-hour race with the Ecurie Ecosse D-type Jaguars—his biggest victories of the track. In 1956 he finished third in the Italian Grand Prix in a Connaught, and a year later won the unlimited class of the British Empire Trophy for Ecurie Ecosse, was second in his class in the Goodwood 100-kilometre race, and third at Rheims. At Rouen in 1958 he crashed while practising and crushed two bones in his spine, losing his chance of competing at Le Mans that year.

FLYING SCOTSMAN

Before beginning his recent flying tests he had completed the winter series of motor races with a Lotus Climax in Australia and New Zealand. Ron Flockhart was known as the "Flying Scotsman", his flying career beginning in 1940, when he became one of the founder-members of Edinburgh University Air Squadron. In 1948 he took up gliding, and later that year gained his pilot's licence in a Tiger Moth. Fifteen months ago, in his first attempt on the Sydney-London flying record he was beaten by bad weather and an overheated engine at Athens.

At the time of his death he was a company director and engineer in a motor business.

His flying hobby contrasted sharply with his other keen interests in walking, Scottish history, serious reading, Highland dancing, and ethnology. Although his sporting life was fast and dangerous, Flockhart was a serious-minded man, who gave any project the concentration of careful thought and practice it merited.

He is survived by his widow.

April 13, 1962.

Lord Florey, O.M., F.R.S., who died on February 21, 1968, at the age of 69, was president of the Royal Society from 1960 to 1965 and provost of Queen's College, Oxford, since 1962.

He was Professor of Pathology at Oxford from 1935 to 1962 and led the team of research workers who in 1940 obtained penicillin in a concentrated form and first demonstrated its efficacy as a chemotherapeutic agent in animals and man. For this work he was in 1945 awarded the Nobel Prize for Physiology and Medicine jointly with his colleague Dr. E. B. Chain and with the late Sir Alexander Fleming. This was only one in a succession of original and imaginative investigations into fundamental aspects of the body's reaction to disease which he pursued throughout his working life. He contributed repeatedly to the subject of his first research, the activities of the small blood and lymph vessels, their reactions to injury, and their powers of healing. He had a lifelong interest in the mucus produced in the bronchial tree and gastro-intestinal tract and greatly advanced knowledge of its mode of secretion and its possible function in defence against disease. It was this interest that led him to the study of lysozyme, a substance in mucus secretions which dissolved certain bacteria, and so to the study of other antibacterial substances, among them penicillin.

He threw light on the activities of some of the cells in inflamed tissues, and cut dead wood from widely held beliefs about the interrelationships of different cell types. When he felt that infectious diseases were coming under control through the widespread use of antibiotics, he turned to investigation of the degenerative disease that was becoming known as a great killer—arteriosclerosis with its sequel coronary thrombosis, and he performed and stimulated work on a variety of body processes that might bear on its causation.

Florey held that to support able men, not particular projects, was the key to advance in scientific research, and on this basis he made of the Sir William Dunn School of Pathology at Oxford a department of great distinction. It became something of a Mecca for young men who wanted a training in fundamental medical research, and had a world-wide influence on the growth of pathology into an active branch of experimental science. At the time of his resignation a dozen chairs in Great Britain, the United States, Canada and Australia were filled, and numerous institutes and departments were directed, by men who had worked in his laboratory, and he was succeeded at Oxford by one of his former pupils.

CLEAR ANSWERS

Florey was not only a successful experimenter; he combined great enthusiasm for research with great force of character. From the 1920s he held that advances in pathology would in future come from an experimental rather than from a purely descriptive approach, and that many reactions of the body to disease would not be unravelled until relevant normal processes were better understood. This attitude owed something to the influence of Sherrington, who directed his attention to pathology as a subject where there was scope for the application of physiological ideas and methods, and was widened by his constant appreciation of the possible application of pathology to new advances in all branches of science.

In planning experiments Florey had an instinctive preference for the simple situation which would give a clear answer one way or the other. If it was possible to observe the tissues in the living state and record their reactions directly this was his method of choice. His greatness as an experimenter lay in the combination of imagination and manual skill with a judgment so fine that significant observations and procedures that would prove fruitful were picked out with what seemed an uncanny precision. One of his staff was heard to give the advice: "If the Professor suggests an experiment always do it, for it is sure to work."

It was one aspect of his enthusiasm for knowledge that he would pass over ideas or problems on which he was currently working to younger colleagues if he felt that thereby the subject might be advanced more quickly. This generous greatness of mind lay behind some of the fine contributions made from his department.

Howard Walter Florey, son of Joseph Florey, was born at Adelaide on September 24, 1898.

MANY HONOURS

He was educated at St. Peter's Collegiate School and at Adelaide University from which, after graduating in medicine in 1921, a Rhodes Scholarship took him to Magdalen College, Oxford, where he obtained a First in the Honour School of Physiology and the B.Sc. degree, working under Professor (later Sir Charles) Sherrington. In 1924 he spent a year at Cambridge as John Lucas Walker Student, then visited America as a Rockefeller Travelling Fellow. In 1926 he was elected to a Fellowship at Gonville and Caius College, Cambridge, and was Freedom Research Fellow at the London Hospital. In 1927 he became Huddersfield lecturer in special pathology at Cambridge and obtained the Ph.D. degree, and from 1931 to 1935 he was Joseph Hunter Professor of Pathology at the University of Sheffield. In 1935 he became Professor of Pathology in the University of Oxford and a Fellow of Lincoln College, and in 1962 he resigned the Chair of Pathology in order to become Provost of Queen's.

He was knighted in 1944. He became a Commander of the Legion of Honour in 1946 and received decorations and honorary degrees in many countries. He was elected a Fellow of the Royal Society in 1941 and received the society's Royal Medal in 1951 and its Copley Medal in 1957.

In 1938, with E. B. Chain, Florey planned a systematic investigation of naturally occurring antibacterial substances, choosing three produced by moulds and bacteria for first study.

PRIORITY FOR PENICILLIN

From the published reports it could not have been predicted that penicillin, the product of the mould *Penicillin notatum*, which Fleming had described 10 years earlier, would turn out to be far and away the most interesting but when, early in 1940, this was found to be the case all the resources of the laboratory were directed to it. The crude material was purified and shown to be almost completely non-toxic to laboratory animals and, in minute doses, to cure virulent bacterial diseases induced artificially in mice. The first trials in human patients showed that it was equally effective in natural disease in man and led to the results now so well known.

Early in the work on penicillin Florey grasped its great potentialities for the treatment of infection in war wounds, and when British firms were unable because of the war to divert effort to developing it, Florey visited institutions and commercial firms in America to enlist their help. He was sometimes unjustly blamed for "giving away to America" what later became a considerable source of revenue. At that time it was traditional that any medical discovery made in an academic laboratory should be given freely to the world, and he was advised that to protect the processes used would be contrary to medical ethics. In fact, without his enterprise in awakening American interest penicillin would not have been available in quantity by D-Day in 1944, by which time there was enough, mainly from the United States, to treat all those wounded in the invasion of Europe.

Florey was a member of the Medical Research Council from 1948 to 1952 and in the years after the war he served on official bodies advising the Government on biological matters.

INFLUENCE ON POLICY

When he found himself President of the Royal Society he made it his business to exert and to increase the influence of the society on national scientific policies. The loss of British scientists to other countries at a time when they were needed at home appalled him, and as a result of his representations five Research Professorships in science to be administered by the Royal Society were established by the Government in 1962.

Florey remained an Australian in voice and vigour throughout his life, and although he never returned to his native country except as a visitor he influenced events there. He deplored the fact that many of the best academic Australians settled in Britain and America for lack of facilities and intellectual stimulus at home, and he forcibly expressed his belief in the potentialities of Australian scientists in a memorandum written for the Prime Minister, John Curtin, in 1944. This report crystallized growing feeling that Australia should build up her own academic institutions to the highest standard, and it was a prime factor in the establishment of the Australian National University, which was founded as a school of advanced studies. As one of the two academic advisers on the original Council of the A.N.U., he helped to set standards which raised the sights of academic institutions throughout Australia, and he personally laboured to start the John Curtin School of Medical Research of the A.N.U. on the right lines. He became Chancellor of the university in 1965.

Florey had many friends in the United States, and he was in demand there and elsewhere for lectures and conferences, at which his natural consideration and sense of social fitness, together with his ability to converse in several languages, made him a fine ambassador for Britain. He was a genial and entertaining colleague and an excellent host, and in personal dealings he showed great kindness. He married in 1926 Mary Ethel Reed, whom he had met as a fellow medical student at the University of Adelaide, and who collaborated with him in the first clinical research on penicillin, afterwards becoming a specialist in chemotherapy. They had a son and a daughter. His wife died in 1966 and he married in 1967 the Hon. Dr. Margaret Jennings.

February 23, 1968.

Sir Cyril Flower, C.B., formerly Deputy Keeper of the Records, died on August 9, 1961, at the age of 82.

Cyril Thomas Flower was born on March 31, 1879, son of Thomas Flower. M.R.C.S., of Warminster, Wiltshire. He was educated at Warminster Grammar School, and was proud of being a "Wiltshire Moonraker". From Warminster he went to St. Edward's School. Oxford, as a scholar. He always retained his interest in the school, and in time became one of the governors. At Oxford, he won a scholarship at Worcester College, took a first in Classical Moderations in 1899 and a second in *Literae Humaniores* in 1901. After competing in the examination for the first division of the Civil Service, he was appointed a junior clerk in the Public Record Office in 1903, and became, in due course, an assistant keeper.

On the retirement of R. A. Roberts in 1919 he was appointed legal member of the committee of Inspecting Officers formed under the Public Record Office Act of 1877 for the systematic regulation of the preservation or destruction of public records. He had been called to the Bar by the Inner Temple in 1906. He was made secretary in 1926, in succession to A. E. Stamp, whom he succeeded as Deputy Keeper of the Records in 1938. He was made C.B. in 1939 and was knighted in 1946, retiring the following year. From 1938 to 1960 he was a member of the Historical Manuscripts Commission.

The War of 1914–18 made a break in Flower's official career. He was transferred to the War Office as private secretary to the Director of Army Contracts in 1914, serving at the same time as a sergeant in the Special Constabulary. The next year he volunteered for service in the Army, being gazetted to the Royal Garrison Artillery.

ARMY CONTRACTS

He was severely wounded in France in 1916, and on recovery returned as a disabled officer to his post at the War Office, where he remained till demobilized in 1919. An amusing caricature of the Contracts Branch of the War Office may be found in the novel by his temporary colleague, Edward Shanks, *The Old Indispensables* (1919); but, though Shanks used Flower's Christian name for one of the characters, no portraiture was intended. In the War of 1939–45, although Deputy-Keeper of the Records, he found time to act as Director of the Institute of Historical Research in the University of London for the period of the war. In his official capacity he showed himself a diligent and careful scholar and a successful administrator. The transfer of the bulk of the Public Records to depositories in the country, to avert the possibility of their complete destruction at one blow, was begun in good time. It was so well planned and executed that not only were all the documents needed by public departments in their current work produced and sent to London or elsewhere with very little delay, but the retransfer at the end of the war was carried out smoothly and without the loss of a document.

COMPILED ROLLS

Of his scholarship the 13 volumes of *Curia Regis Rolls* (1922–59), edited and largely transcribed by him, are a sufficient testimony. He also compiled, as an official task, an *Analytical Index of the Acts and Ordinances of the Commonwealth.* For the Selden Society he edited *Public Works in Mediaeval Law* (2 vols., 1915–16), and *Introduction to the Curia Regis Rolls* (1944), the fruit of careful study of the Rolls of John and Henry III and full of points of law and procedure not before so fully set out. For the Canterbury and York Society he edited (with M. C. B. Dawes) *Registrum Simonis de Gandavo* (2 vols., 1934). He was elected to the Society of Antiquaries in 1921, becoming a vice-president for 1939–43, and served on the council, as he also did in the Selden Society (of which he became a vice-president), the Royal Historical Society, the Canterbury and York Society, the Pipe Roll Society and the Institute of Historical Research. He was elected to the British Academy in 1947.

In 1910 he married Helen Mary Harding, daughter of David Thompson, an Inspector of Schools in the Punjab. She and their daughter survive him.

August 11, 1961.

Lieutenant-Colonel Sir Fordham Flower, O.B.E., industrialist and Shakespearean enthusiast, died at the age of 62 on July 9, 1966, at St. Mary's Hospital, Paddington.

He had been chairman of the Shakespeare Birthplace Trustees from 1946 until 1966. When the Shakespeare Trustees planned the erection of a modern building next to Shakespeare's birthplace in Henley Street—modern to the degree of high novelty in the town—he had some difficulty in overcoming the objections of Shakespeareans, both at Stratford and in many other parts of the world, to a building which suggests a Middle or Western town of the United States. It says much for the strength of his personality and persuasion that he secured formal planning consent for the building, which provides library, administrative headquarters and study centre, as well as the good will of most of his original opponents. He was also chairman of the executive Council of the Royal Shakespeare Theatre since 1944.

Fordham Flower was born on February 15, 1904, a son of the late Sir Archibald Dennis Flower, of Stratford-upon-Avon, and was educated at Winchester and Sandhurst. The Flowers have been brewers in the Midlands for generations, and he entered the family concern after Army service—he had a commission in the Ninth Queens Royal Lancers, with which he served in Egypt, Palestine and India from 1924 until 1932. In 1939 he was back with his regiment, promoted Major in 1940 and Lieutenant-Colonel in 1944. Flower had a distinguished career throughout the Second World War; he was twice mentioned in dispatches, created an O.B.E. in 1945, and made an Officer of the Order of Orange-Nassau (with Swords) in the same year. After the war was over he was back at the breweries. In 1953 he was appointed chairman of the board of Flower & Sons Ltd.; in 1958, of Flowers Breweries Ltd.; and when the firm was taken over by Whitbread & Co. Ltd. he became a director of Whitbread.

He was appointed Deputy Lieutenant of Warwickshire in 1952 and was knighted in 1956. Flower was a considerable traveller, and also a devotee of winter sports. He married in 1934 Hersey Caroline Balfour, and they had two sons and two daughters.

July 11, 1966.

Sir Newman Flower, president of Cassell and Company, and for many years chairman, died at his Dorset home on March 12, 1964, after a long illness. He was 84.

Walter Newman Flower was born at Fontmell Magna in July, 1879, and at the age of 17 went to make his way in the London publishing world. He joined Cassell in 1906 after training under Northcliffe at the Harmsworth Press. At Cassell's, then in the doldrums, he built up a great series of magazines which dominated the market for many years. In 1912 he took over the book side of the company and revitalized their list with such notable writers as G. K. Chesterton, H. G. Wells, and Arnold Bennett. In 1915 he became literary director of the company.

After the General Strike in 1926, the magazine side of Cassell was removed to the Amalgamated Press and Newman Flower raised the money to buy Cassell's as a purely book publishing house, becoming proprietor and managing director of the new company in 1927. Three years later he was joined by his son, Desmond, now chairman of Cassell. In 1938 he was knighted for his services to literature and not long after retired from active office life though keeping his seat on the board.

On the outbreak of war he went back to take over the editorial chair from his son who had joined the Army, and continued to direct the literary affairs of the company until Desmond Flower's return in 1946. On the fortieth anniversary of his joining Cassell he retired from active work again but remained as chairman.

CHURCHILL COUP

During the war years Flower had been promised by Sir Winston Churchill that he would be offered anything Sir Winston might write on the war, and the promise was duly honoured with the delivery of the first chapters of *The Second World War*, perhaps the greatest coup of twentieth century publishing. It was followed in 1956 by the first volume of Sir Winston Churchill's *A History of the English-Speaking Peoples*, which Newman Flower had commissioned before the war. In the same year he had the pleasure of seeing Sir Winston lay the foundation stone for the new Cassell building.

Flower was not only a publisher of distinction but also an author and a great collector of Handeliana. His most important book is his life of Handel, first published in 1923 and reissued in a new and handsome format in 1959. Four years later in collaboration with Herbert Sullivan, he published his biography of Sir Arthur Sullivan, based on the composer's diaries, and in 1928 followed it with a study of Schubert. He wrote also a delightful book of reminiscences, *Just as it Happened*, in which he recalled memories of many of the writers who became his friends. He will be particularly remembered by admirers of Arnold Bennett as the editor of Bennett's Journals. Flower had long been aware that the journals existed but Bennett died before he had gone through them with the result that Flower was faced with over one million words to prepare for publication. He was twice married.

March 13, 1964.

Lucio Fontana, who died in September 1968, at the age of 69, was one of the best-known and most influential European painters since the Second World War. He was also a very popular and very respected figure in Italian artistic life: an accessible, open and gentle man who constantly encouraged younger artists.

One "type" of his painting is probably better known than his name; the slashed canvas, the white or luxuriantly monochromatic canvas opened by one or more long razor cuts. During his life Fontana extended this principle to other forms; in surfaces pierced by scattered punctures, by a single ragged dark hole, and in groups of big ball-shaped sculptures on the ground with deep cavities scooped in them. Fontana produced version after version of the slashed canvas after first introducing it in the late 1950s. Doubtless he repeated himself; but his light touch, the combination of elegance and blatancy with which he used chic colours and conventional-sized canvases, kept his work fresh and spoofed any over-solemn interpretations.

Thus the cuts and holes could not be neatly put down as symbolic of wounds and pass out of favour with the passing of post-war expressionism. Fontana's work was poised between several artistic currents of the 1950s, between expressionist, informal and concrete art. In the last few years his contributions to the big international exhibitions have been small enclosed all-white environments, like sepulchres, where one or two cuts in large canvases take on a tremendous intensity.

Fontana was born in 1899 in Santa Fé, Argentina, of Italian parents. He studied in Italy and was a member of the Abstraction-Creation group in the 1930s. From 1939–46 he taught in Argentina and was influential among young artists. There he wrote his famous White Manifesto, published in 1946, proposing the concept of "Spatialism", after which virtually all his paintings since have been named. The White Manifesto was a challenge to the international style of tachism even before tachism became established and had to wait until the mid-1950s until the beliefs Fontana expressed in an elemental art "using the very energies of matters", were taken up by artists like Piero Manzoni and Yves Klein.

Fontana settled permanently in Milan in 1947.

September 14, 1968.

Rosita Forbes, traveller, lecturer, and author, died at her home at Warwick, Bermuda, on June 30, 1967.

Few women can have travelled so widely, seen so much, or produced a survey of the globe comparable with that comprised in her long series of books. She was a keen observer, a shrewd commentator on men and races, and a forceful and interesting writer. Vital, indefatigable, and immensely courageous, she was not only one of the leading women explorers of, at the very least, her own time but one of its most picturesque and entertaining personalities.

Joan Rosita Forbes, the daughter of H. J. Torr, of Morton Hall, Lincolnshire, was born in 1893 and began to travel while still in her teens. When she was quite young she married Colonel Ronald Forbes, son of Colonel Foster Forbes, of Rothiemay Castle, Banffshire, with whom she visited India, Australia and Africa.

To one of her eager and adventurous disposition the First World War came as a challenge and the part she chose in it was that of an ambulance driver for the *Société de Secours aux blessés militaires*, a service for which she obtained two war medals. The energy which she put into it over-strained her health and she had to rest for a time. In 1917 she divorced her husband.

In the next year she set forth with a woman friend upon a lonely journey across the Pacific to the Dutch East Indies and on through the Far East. Her experiences there formed the subject of her first book, *Unconducted Wanderers* (1919). Although she had had some remarkable adventures in them, the places she had visited were familiar enough to the more enterprising of globetrotters: but there was a freshness, frankness and vigour in her writing which conveyed the abounding vitality of the authoress and immediately attracted attention.

In 1920 she was off again, first to North Africa and Arabia and then on a more hazardous venture to Kufara in Libya, a place which no European had attempted to reach since Rohlf's expedition of 1879. She had already travelled across the whole breadth of Arab Africa and in crossing Cyrenaica had come into contact with the Senussi. She had also, however, the good fortune to make friends with the all-important Shaikh, Sidi Idriss, and to obtain his help in penetrating the interior of his country.

LIFE AS ARAB

Eventually she reached Taj, when she lived the life of a veiled Arab woman: but she kept a camera under her voluminious cloak and her own observant eyes on everything. Then, instead of returning to Cyrenaica, she made her way to Egypt by a route entirely new to the geographers.

On her return from this daring and successful expedition, Rosita Forbes fell into her appropriate place as one of the greatest of women explorers. In addition to adding to the knowledge of the geographers, she had obtained much useful information in regard to the Senussi and their outlook. In London, therefore, she was the heroine of the hour. The King sent for her to hear her story at first hand; learned bodies asked for lectures; and she received a "national recognition" in the form of a book of signatures of representative people with the Prince of Wales at their head. In addition the Royal Antwerp Geographical Society gave her a gold medal. In a series of articles published in *The Times* in March, 1921, she narrated her story in broad outline and later gave fuller information in her book, *Secret of the Sahara Kufara* (1922). She also wrote a novel, *The Jewel in the Lotus* (1922), of which, under a fictitious name, she made herself the principal figure; but it was not an entirely satisfying effort. *Quest* of the same year was a romance about Arabia.

In 1921 Rosita Forbes married Colonel Arthur T. McGrath, D.S.O., who was on the General Staff at the War Office, but the following year she was off on another expedition to Asia to interview the Emir Idrissi, whom she believed to hold the key to the political situation in Western Arabia. An excellent linguist, she could speak Arabic with great fluency. Then she went off to Morocco to interview Raisuli with the intention of writing his life. "By Allah", he said at their meeting, "but I can understand why Europe has left us behind if she has women such as you." The book appeared in 1924.

From Red Sea to Blue Nile (1925) contained the story of a journey of over a thousand miles by horse or mule. On that occasion she took a camera operator with her, for her chief purpose was to take pictures. *Conflict* (1931) described experiences in Persia and on her way there through Palestine and Iraq. *Eight Republics in Search of a Future* (1933) was about Evolution and Revolution in South America. *Forbidden Road, Kabul to Samarkand* (1937) opened up yet another field of exploration. In addition to such travelogues she wrote *These are Real People* (1937) in which she described some of those she had met. *These Men I Knew* (1940) was to come later.

There was scarcely a corner of the earth which she had not seen and studied, and *India of the Princes* (1939) was as vivid as her many other works. She was, however, to approach the subject of her next books, *A Unicorn in the Bahamas* (1939) and *The Prodigious Caribbean* (1940), in a somewhat different mood, for it was in the West Indies that she had made her home at Eleuthera in the Bahamas. There, too, she wrote *Gypsy in the Sun* (1944), which contained more about people. After the Second World War she wrote three volumes of autobiography, and a biography of Sir Henry Morgan, the pirate. She was a fellow of the Royal Geographical Society and an Honorary member of several foreign ones. Her second husband died in 1962.

July 4, 1967.

Jean Forbes-Robertson (Mrs. André Van Gyseghem), the actress, died in a London hospital on December 24, 1962, at the age of 57.

Her early work had been all that was expected of a daughter of Sir Johnston Forbes-Robertson and his American-born wife, Gertrude Elliott, and that was a great deal. But having quickly reached the front rank in her profession she dropped out of it, and she brought her career in the theatre to a premature end before she was 50.

The second of her parents' three daughters, Jean Forbes-Robertson was born in London on March 16, 1905, went to school at Heathfield, Ascot, and first appeared professionally in her mother's company—her father had already retired—in South Africa in 1921. She continued working with her mother in Australia, New Zealand, and London till 1925, and in the following year was engaged by Komisarjevsky to play Sonia in the first public production in England of *Uncle Vanya*. Audiences were taken by surprise by her perfect control of this part and by the end were much moved by the distinction of her performance. When it was followed by her success as Juliet, as the "possessed" girl in *The Dybbuk*, and as Peter Pan, she found herself at 22 heir to all the good will of her septuagenarian father, who had been regarded as a "lost leader" of the profession ever since his withdrawal from it at a comparatively early age.

It may be that this inheritance with its responsibilities dismayed Jean Forbes-Robertson and at last inspired her with a wish to escape. If so, her temperament and attitude towards the theatre were mirrored in the uncanny "rightness" of her performance as "the boy who would not grow up", Peter Pan, and in her prolonged association with that part. Barrie, once he had seen her in it, handed it over to her to play as often as she might wish, and she did so for the record number of eight consecutive Christmas seasons. In the intervals she was seen at the Old Vic, in the West End, and in Regent's Park in Shakespeare—after Juliet, Viola was her best Shakespearian part—as Tessa in a revival of *The Constant Nymph*, and at the Gate Theatre in Pirandello's *As You Desire Me*.

PRIESTLEY ROLES

Later in the 1930s she took leading parts, Rebecca West and Hedda Gabler, in a season of Ibsen; played at the Abbey Theatre, Dublin, and in New York; gave a moving performance in the most stageworthy of Mr. J. B. Priestley's "time-plays" *Time and the Conways*; and returned once more to *Peter Pan*. During the Second World War she and Mr. André Van Gyseghem, her second husband, toured with their own companies and with the Old Vic, and she went on acting after the war, two of her engagements being at the York Citizens' Theatre and at the Pitlochry Festival, until 1952. Then the attempt to resume her old part in a revival of one of Mr. Priestley's plays proved too much for her and she had to give it up.

Her resemblance to her father, astonishing at moments as when she wore his Romeo costume at a ball in her youth, suggested that her career would lie in "noble" parts, as his had done; but her bent was, on the contrary, towards the "off beat". The difficulty of finding scope for this among female characters accounts perhaps for the attraction that *travesti* held for her: in addition to Peter Pan, she played on various occasions Everyman, Oberon, Puck, and Jim Hawkins in *Treasure Island*.

Her first marriage to Mr. Hamish Hamilton, the publisher, was dissolved. There was a daughter of her marriage to Mr. Van Gyseghem.

December 27, 1962.

C. S. Forester, who died on April 2, 1966, at Fullerton, California, at the age of 66, was one of the most popular internationally of contemporary English novelists—deservedly so. He was a consummate story-teller and a master of Defoesque detail that stamped his work, at least at the moment of its being read, with the seal of actuality.

He was most widely known as the creator of Horatio, Lord Hornblower, R. N., whose adventures he chronicled in a dozen novels beginning with *The Happy Return*, published in 1937. Together, they compose a splendid picture of English naval life in the time of the wars against Napoleon and must stand high among modern historical fiction. Reading of Hornblower's progress from midshipman to admiral, it is difficult not to feel that Forester knew all there was to know about life in the

Royal Navy at the turn of the eighteenth century, and, as comparison with the fiction of Marryat and Michael Scott shows, he did.

The Hornblower novels were as accurate as research could make them, and the descriptions of violent action, of war at sea, were consistently exciting. What gave these novels their life, however, was the character of Hornblower. At first sight, perhaps a little too good to be true, in that, whatever the odds against him, he always prevails, he is in fact realized as anything but a simple character. Introverted, inhibited, fastidious almost to the point of neurosis, full of self-doubt, class-conscious, devoted to the works of Gibbon, deeply disapproving of the verses of that madman Wordsworth, a fanatic about discipline and efficiency, Hornblower convinces because of his complexity.

He is a man who is himself a triumph of self-discipline and because of this is able to impose his will on the circumstances in which he finds himself. He is a truly acceptable hero, and, in his own way. Forester may be called an heroic novelist.

ORIGIN OF THE SERIES

Forester himself provided a detailed account of the origin and growth of the entire Hornblower series, and afforded a glimpse of his way of life and the vagaries of his health, in *The Hornblower Companion* (1964).

The enormous popularity of the Hornblower series tended to obscure Forester's other novels, though among them is to be found what is probably his finest work. But the emphasis on discipline, efficiency and obligation to duty remains, notably in, among others, *Brown on Resolution* (1929), an heroic tale of a young English sailor's one-man war against a German sea-raider during the First World War, *The Gun* (1933), a story of Spanish guerrillas fighting the French during the Peninsular War, and *The African Queen* (1935), an episode in the campaigns against the Germans in Africa in the First World War. Novels such as these show Forester as a writer whose imagination was fired by what might be called the contemplation of the actual, a writer fascinated by exact knowledge, by specialized crafts, techniques, the skills and disciplines by which men impose their wills on the external world, as Forester's heroes habitually do.

His finest novel was probably *The General* (1936), the life story of Lieutenant-General Sir Herbert Curzon, a general of the First World War, a cavalryman put down in warfare of a kind he has never anticipated. He is possessed of all the military virtues except imagination; as Forester says: "Innovations and charlatanry were indissolubly linked in his mind." Forester indulges in no irony at his expense and records all his admirable qualities with complete detachment. *The General* must be accounted among the best novels inspired by the First World War: Forester's achievement is to reduce, while preserving its essentials, a most complex series of events to the pattern of one man's life. His books were well received by reviewers and enthusiastically praised by fellow-writers as eminent and diverse as Ernest Hemingway and Sir Winston Churchill, but they never achieved the critical attention they deserve.

The same is true of his biographies, of which *Nelson* (1929) is generally considered the best, and his ventures into "straight" history, such as *The Naval War of 1812* (1957).

Cecil Scott Forester was born in Cairo on August 27, 1899, and educated at Dulwich College and Guy's Hospital, but, turning to writing while a student, did not complete his medical studies. His first successful novel, *Payment Deferred*, a psychological study of a murderer, he wrote when he was 24. A play version, in which Charles Laughton made his initial London reputation, was also successful; it was later filmed, as were *Captain Horatio Hornblower* starring Gregory Peck, and *The African Queen*, with the late Humphrey Bogart, and other novels. During the thirties, Forester combined the writing of fiction with journalism and was a correspondent in Spain during the Civil War and in Czechoslovakia during the Nazi occupation of Prague. He was also given facilities by the British and the United States navies to observe operations in World War II. *The Ship* (1943) describing a Mediterranean surface encounter was one outcome of this experience. The manuscript of his last novel, in which Hornblower dies, is said to be locked in a London bank vault, with instructions for publication only after the author's death. As a semi-invalid, suffering from arterio-scelerosis, Forester in his later years made his home at Berkeley, California.

He was twice married; to Kathleen Belcher, by whom he had two sons, and to Dorothy Ellen Foster.

April 4, 1966.

George Formby, O.B.E., the comedian, died in hospital at Preston on March 6, 1961, at the age of 56.

The son of the most celebrated and original of the Lancashire comedians of the old music-halls, also named George, he followed to some extent the family tradition of broad Lancashire comedy but did not model himself closely upon his father, either in make-up or style. He began his stage career as George Hoy—so that no one could say he was cashing in on his father's name—and established himself as an artist in his own right before assuming his own name. Formby's stage character was that of the good-natured, foolish (but not witless) chap with a toothy grin, a talent for singing to his own accompaniment on the ukelele and an infinite capacity for muddling in and out of a succession of scrapes.

He was the amateur of the old smoking concert platform turned into a music-hall professional of genius. He added nothing to the amateur's range, only perfected his technique. He sang with the same broad smile the same sort of broad little songs ("When I'm cleaning windows", "Chinese Laundry Blues" and "Leaning on the Lamp post") which the amateur used to effect, told the same broad tales; but his pointing of those songs was as artlessly exact as the rhythm of his ukelele playing was flawless. "I wasn't very good", he once said "but I had something the public seemed to want." He did indeed and in the 1930s and 1940s became part of the English scene, attaining immense popularity on the music-halls and on the radio.

When he turned his attention to the cinema in the 1930s he retained the same good-natured and gormless character. His first picture was *No Limit*, and thereafter he made an average of two films a year until after the end of the war, a number of them for the old Ealing Studios.

SIMPLE FILMS

These films were simple in conception and straightforward in execution, but they usually showed a good profit. Each year between 1942 and 1945 he gained a place among the top 10 money-making stars in British productions in the poll held annually by the *Motion Picture Herald*; and in common with nearly every famous screen comedian before and after him he achieved some of his most notable successes in films of Service life. During the war he raised funds for charity, entertained both British and American troops and for his services was made O.B.E. in 1946.

His smile night be vacuous, but there was no shrewder professional in his own line than Formby. He had topped the bill at the London Palladium, but time and again he turned down offers of a West End show, for he was not convinced that the South would like his particular brand of humour. It was ironic that when he was finally persuaded to come to London in a full-scale musical show, *Zip Goes a Million*, a version of *Brewster's Millions*, and scored a resounding success, he should be obliged to give up his part after a matter of months through ill health. He talked then of retiring, but though never again really fit he was to be found year after year in pantomime, up and down the country, the same George Formby singing the songs he knowingly miscalled "daft" and grinning engagingly at the world before him.

His wife Beryl, whom he married in 1924, died on Christmas Day, 1960.

March 7, 1961.

E. M. Forster, O.M., C.H., the novelist and writer whose reputation has grown steadily in his later years, died on June 7, 1970, at the age of 91.

His last novel, *A Passage to India*, was published in the twenties.

Few novelists were held in higher esteem by the connoisseur of contemporary fiction in Britain or on the other side of the Atlantic, and none received from the younger generation of writers quite such warm and admiring homage. Yet Forster had written in all no more than five novels, four of them before the First World War and the last of these when he was scarcely 30, and had long ceased to think of writing another. *Howards End* appeared in 1910, and after an interval of 14 years came *A Passage to India*. After that there was silence: it was a novelist who had ceased to write novels to whom the critics continued to pay tribute. Forster wrote and broadcast on literary subjects, he lectured on the novel, he wrote a memoir of his friend Lowes Dickinson and a biography of a great-aunt, spoke in defence of the freedom of letters, he composed pageants, collaborated in writing the libretto of an opera: but, though he printed the fragment of an uncompleted novel, he produced no more fiction. Always, however, he was spoken of as in the first place a novelist, the most civilized novelist—that was the word commonly used—of his time.

The word surely provides an obvious clue to E. M. Forster's silence. There was no Rimbaud-like renunciation of literature in his disinclination to write another novel; although he seems to have judged his own work by the most exacting standards, he had never put literature before life, and his was not, in any case, the egotism of a leaning towards the absolute.

LIBERAL MORALIST

Nor, in all probability, was there any hidden personal reason for his abandonment of novel-writing. Much of the truth may well be simply that Forster's was too sensitive and controlled an intelligence, too meditative an impulse, to thrive in the mass age which emerged from world war and its immediate aftermath.

He has been described, very justly, as a liberal moralist, and the age of European liberalism ended in 1914. Imagination—creative imagination—was checked in him by the menacing relapse from a civilizing order of values. This response to an age of illiberalism apart, there remains the effect of a pronounced emotional bias. When all is said, as a novelist Forster lacked the spur of commonplace passion, and perhaps there is no other lasting urge to creation. He looked to Italy for passion (as he looked to Greece for truth) and was constant in praise of passions, but never in any of his novels did he for a moment come near a convincing likeness of ordinary sexual passion. Perhaps that explains a certain note of melodrama in his manifestation of tragedy. He had something of the intellectual temper, the proportion and restraint that belongs to Greek thought, he had vision and irony also, and all his novels, from the earliest to the last, have a luminous humanity that delights us and should make us a little wiser. He is, indeed, a novelist of rare stamp. But the defect of what was in some ways an overcivilized temperament, one must assume, had left its mark upon him when at the age of 45 he ceased to write fiction.

Edward Morgan Forster was born on January 1, 1879, the only son of Edward Morgan Llewellyn Forster and his wife, Alice Clara. He went to Tonbridge School as a day boy and from there to King's College, Cambridge.

ENCOURAGED TO WRITE

At Cambridge he won the regard of the least conventional and most Socratic of dons, Goldsworthy Lowes Dickinson, with whom his friendship was broken only by death. The tie with Lowes Dickinson gave warmth and vivid colour to Forster's sentiment for Cambridge, which was one of the enduring elements in his cultivation of mind. Perhaps the influence of G. E. Moore's philosophy upon that part of Cambridge which was associated with what afterwards became known as "Bloomsbury" was another.

It was one of the classical dons at King's, Nathaniel Wedd, who encouraged him to write and, at the early age of 20, it appears Forster completed a first novel, which was never published. Soon after he left Cambridge he began to write short stories, some of which were printed in the *Independent Review* and elsewhere. The two English writers from whom he took most in the matter of style were, on his faintly surprising confession many years later, Jane Austen and Samuel Butler. Possessed of a small private income, he was under no compulsion to seek a formal occupation and he proceeded to travel in Europe with zest, and curiosity. In the early years of this century he went to live in Italy. Two novels came out of this experience: *Where Angels Fear to Tread* (1905) and *A Room with a View* (1908), both works of astonishing maturity, instinct with high comedy and exhibiting, together with the lightness, the sureness of touch, the almost negligent ease and informality of style which were peculiarly his, an extraordinary subtle feeling for the undertones of character. *Where Angels Fear to Tread* was presented on the London stage in 1963 and *A Room With a View* was seen on Independent television five years earlier.

Between these two Italian novels came *The Longest Journey* (1907), a more remarkable work than either, and his own favourite, in which he wrote of Tonbridge School (Sawston) and Cambridge, an unhappy marriage and a scholastic bondage. The earlier parts are autobiographical in colouring, though in colouring only; the marriage and the teaching were purely imaginative exercises. It is not a wholly consistent piece of storytelling—there is in it, besides melodrama in the recurring sense of catastrophe, something of that worship of the great god Pan which Forster could never quite harmonize with the rest—but it has an integrity of thought on "the life of personal relationships" that carries an appeal of deep and compelling intimacy.

PERSONAL RELATIONS

The life of personal relationships comes to full flower in *Howards End*. (The name disguised his own home, Rook's Nest, near Stevenage). Here was the book for which his earliest admirers had waited, for which they had not to wait long. Though the charge might be preferred against the author that he weights the scales unfairly in encompassing loss and disaster, this is a novel of singular depth and beauty, the product of a truly civilized mind and imagination. "Only connect", ran the almost too wistful motto at the head, and it was a liberal and humane code of philosophy that Forster projected in trying to reconcile the world of sensibility and spirit with the world of "telegrams and anger". *Howards End* had little of the air of a landmark in the history of the English novel, but that in a sense is what it was. For it would have been impossible a few years later for him or for any other novelist, when the liberal structure of European life and society had been shattered, to write in precisely those terms again.

The novel was received with uncommon pleasure by the more discriminating public, though its fame grew slowly. During 1911 Forster occupied himself with book reviewing and other kinds of journalism; wrote a play, *The Heart of Bosnia*, which was neither produced nor published; collected some of his early short stories, which were marked by the liveliest grace and fantasy, in *The Celestial Omnibus*; and then went on a voyage to India in the company of Lowes Dickinson. There was to be a long interval of time before he addressed himself to the Indian novel for which he now began making notes. He was at Alexandria during the 1914–18 War, doing civilian war work. There he accumulated the material for *Alexandria: A History and a Guide* (1922) and also contributed to the *Egyptian Mail* the sketches and papers, done with vivid historical imagination and brimming with wit, which were collected in *Pharos and Pharillon* (1923).

NOTES FROM INDIA

With the end of hostilities Forster was back in England, busily reviewing for several journals and periodicals. For a short period he was literary editor of the *Daily Herald*. In 1921 he went for a second time to India and made a longer stay. The occasion prompted him to take out his notes of 11 years earlier on the Indian scene, and during the next two years he worked unremittingly on *A Passage to India*. There was considerable stir and excitement when the book was announced. Was it, could it be, another *novel* by Mr. Forster? It was the publication of *A Passage to India* which secured for its author general recognition. Subtle, poetical, and serious, the book makes all the deeper impression, perhaps, for refusing to entertain any hope of real tolerance or understanding between the English and the Indians and also for posing several unanswered riddles of psychology in the story itself. It was widely acclaimed both in this country and America, and was awarded the *Femina Vie Heureuse* and the James Tait Black memorial prizes. A dramatized version by Santha Rama Rau, produced in 1960, was remarkably successful. Did all its admirers perceive the tension of spirit that lay beneath the novel's reluctant acceptance of things as they are? From the landscape of imperialism in decay came only the echo in the Marabar caves, ultimate, unvarying, devoid of meaning—Ou-boum.

In the year following came a delightful and stimulating essay on "Anonymity" in literature. Two years later, in 1927, Forster chose the subject of the novel when he was invited to deliver the Clark lectures at Cambridge, and these appeared in volume form, under the title of *Aspects of the Novel*, later in the year. The book has critical penetration, zest of a quite unacademic order, and gaiety in equal measure, and has served in some sort as a text-book for critics. It is no less stimulating for being highly personal in taste and perhaps a little contentious in judgment. In 1928 Forster collected in a volume six stories, all of them written before 1914, of which the first, "*The Machine Stops*", pictures, in Butlerian and semi-prophetic fashion, the eclipse of something of familiar humanity in a scientifically ordered scheme of existence. The stories in *The Eternal Moment*, he observed in passing, together with those in *The Celestial Omnibus*, represent "all that the writer is likely to attempt in a particular line".

During the twilit decade before the outbreak of war in 1939 Forster turned more and more insistently to the theme of liberty of thought and expression. He could not misread the totalitarian threat to culture, could not but be fearful of the symbolism of the National-Socialist burning and banning of books. The future, he thought, might belong to Communism; perhaps no other political faith would serve the new times. But he was of his generation, he said, and had inherited its habit of mind. His memoir of Lowes Dickinson, composed with unselfconscious art, appeared in 1934.

The work of his last years included a half-share in the libretto for Benjamin Britten's opera *Billy Budd*—Melville was an author close to Forster's heart; another collection of essays, reviews, lectures, and broadcasts on literary and semi-literary, semi-political subjects, *Two Cheers for Democracy* (1951)—the qualified tribute of the title hit off with demure irony, but also very precisely, the "uncommitted" element in his liberalism; *The Hill of Devi* (1953), which evoked from the letters written home during his two visits to India and from extracts from a diary of those years a vividly observant, meditative, and perhaps somewhat wilful picture of a small Mahratta state; and a delightful and instructive "domestic biography" of Marianne Thornton, his great-aunt, the daughter of the real leader of the Clapham Sect, in which, amid much nineteenth-century social history drawn from copious family records, he found a place for a chapter of early autobiography. He was a remarkably good broadcaster, and many will remember his engaging account of his experiences as a youthful tutor (his successor in this post was Hugh Walpole) in the house of Elizabeth of the German Garden.

After the war his home, and in an increasing degree his heart also, was in Cambridge, where in 1946 he was made an honorary fellow of King's.

This was the beginning of a new life for him. His mother, to whom he was devoted, had just died, and the home at Abinger was lost.

IN RESIDENCE

The college, making a special exception, invited him to come into residence. Established in Wedd's old room, he threw himself into the life of Cambridge, and of the college in particular. He made friends among the undergraduates, who were proud to entertain him and give him their confidence; and to some he gave generous financial help anonymously. On his eightieth birthday the college expressed its affection and esteem by giving him a luncheon attended both by his greatest friends and by literary figures, some of whom came from as far as Greece and California. The undergraduates also gave a concert in his honour, the programme chosen by himself (for music played a great part in his life). He, in return, presented the college with a noble family heirloom, his first edition of Blake's *Songs of Innocence and Experience*. For his ninetieth birthday *A Garland for E. M. Forster*, a volume of notes and essays, was published.

Honorary degrees were conferred on him by several universities but he remained in a sense always the elect of a minority. Hesitant in manner and somewhat untidy in appearance, the moustache a little unkempt, the expression of the eyes unfailingly alert, the curiously receding chin exaggerating the sloping planes of the face, his features were probably less well known to the reading public as a whole than those of almost any other distinguished writer of his time. Although anything but a recluse, he was a man of deep reserve of character.

June 8, 1970.

Professor Friedrich Wilhelm Förster, the German educationist and political writer, widely known before, during, and after both world wars for his unsparing criticism of German militarism, died in January, 1966, at Kilchberg Sanatorium, near Zurich. He was 96.

On his ninety-fifth birthday, June 2, 1964, a German Roman Catholic paper praised him as "the Patriarch of the Good Germany", a notable tribute, seeing that Förster had spent most of his long life condemning German foreign policy and exposing the faults of German character.

He once described how the conflict between the "good" and the "bad" Germany was illustrated in his parentage. On his mother's side he was related to the famous General Von Moltke of the Franco-Prussian War; his father's influence predominated, for he, an astronomer by profession, was a pupil of Friedrich von Humboldt, representative of that "spiritual Germany" in which Förster always expressed belief, whatever her fateful aberrations. Förster began by teaching ethics divorced from religion; with his father he edited the review *Ethische Kultur*. But gradually he came to believe that Christian belief plays an essential part in moral development. His dislike of Protestant individualism and his idealization of medieval Germany inclined him to an admiration for Catholicism, though he did not embrace that religion.

All his life Förster was consistent in holding that Bismarck, and Prussian politicians generally, had been the evil geniuses of Germany.

PRUSSIAN INFLUENCE

He deplored the exclusion of Austria from Germany, and the foundation of the German Empire on Prussian domination. His criticism of the Emperor Wilhelm II in a speech he made on the anniversary of the battle of Sedan brought him three months' imprisonment for lèse-majesty, and a complete ban on his teaching anywhere in Germany.

He went to Zurich and taught and wrote there from 1899 to 1911. An early work was *Christianity and the Class-war*. He was deeply interested in social reform, but a convinced anti-Marxist. He looked for the regeneration of Germany from a new system of education based on Christian and humanist principles. In 1913 he was appointed Professor of Pedagogy at the University of Vienna. The outbreak of war in 1914 confirmed all his forebodings, but he returned to Germany and taught for a short time, till an article by him for a Swiss pacifist paper caused a scandal and once more he went to Zurich. Förster was not a Tolstoyan pacifist; indeed he criticized the French and British Governments in 1918 for excessive willingness to disarm, and in 1934 told an audience at the Royal Institute of International Affairs in London that there was only one way to stop aggression—convince the aggressor that he would be crushed. The mood of London at the time of Munich he called "an orgy of pacifism".

BOOKS BURNT PUBLICLY

In 1933 the Hitler Government deprived Förster of his German nationality and publicly burnt his books with many others. He was able to get to the United States, where he published a succession of books and pamphlets calling on governments to apply moral principles in politics. In 1937 he published his best-known work, *Europe and the German Question*: an English edition was published in 1941. In this, beside his arguments for European federation, he revealed the talks he had had in 1918 with the Austrian Emperor Karl who, he thought, might, if encouraged, have been able to keep the Habsburg Empire together and make it the nucleus of a "United States of Europe".

Germany's calamitous defeat and humiliation in 1945, Förster thought, might bring about a change of heart, with Germany giving an example of social justice and a return to her true mission of promoting international understanding. Förster praised Dr. Adenauer's work for a Franco-German reconciliation.

His influence is not easy to assess. But his utter sincerity, his high idealism and his stand for spiritual and moral values certainly won him high respect.

All his chief writings were republished in the fifties, and he even added to them, especially his autobiography *Erlebte Weltgeschichte* in 1955, a moving book on Christianity's debt to the Jews in 1961, and in the same year *Deutsche Geschichte und politische Ethik* (German History and Political Ethics), which was a recapitulation of his life's work and comments on the past, present and future of world politics. To the end he attacked the despiritualization of society through the deification of the state and the progressive deadening of the individual conscience. He thought it would lead the world again to utter disaster unless there was a Christian counter-attack and unless, in particular, Germans could rise to the challenge and find their true mission, as he conceived it, the defence of a supranational order and the service of Christian and humanist ideals.

January 14, 1966.

Sir Cyril Fox, the eminent archaeologist, who died in a nursing home at Exmouth, Devon, on January 15, 1967, at the age of 84, was Director of the National Museum of Wales from 1926 to 1948.

Cyril Fred Fox was born at Chippenham, Wiltshire, on December 16, 1882, was educated at Christ's Hospital, and in 1912 went to Cambridge as Superintendent of the University Field

Laboratories. He owed this decisive step primarily to the intervention of the robust Dr. Louis Cobbett, who, in addition to being University Lecturer in Pathology with a public reputation, was a man of wide interests with a bias towards archaeology. Fox has himself described his first meeting with Cobbett. "I was sitting on the sea front at Worthing (where I was being taught—of all things!—the art and mystery of market gardening under glass) when he entered into conversation with me, asking about the antiquities of the district. I showed him a scale plan I had made, and happened to have in my bicycle basket, of Cissbury hill-fort, and on the next Saturday afternoon we went there together. An invitation to stay with him at Round Church Street, Cambridge, followed, and when, shortly afterwards, he became one of the pathologists to the Royal Commission on Tuberculosis and that body wanted a clerk, he offered me the job. Being thus for the first time brought into direct and continuous contact with university people and scientific humanism, I feel I owe my happy life of congenial work mainly to him."

While in charge of the laboratories Fox took up a systematic study of archaeology as a sideline, and was eventually admitted to Magdalene College as a somewhat mature undergraduate with a view to reading for the Tripos in the subject. Professor H. M. Chadwick, however, was so struck with the ability and zest of the young man that he secured permission for him, as a very exceptional case, to proceed straight to the Ph.D. degree. Of this rare privilege Fox took the fullest advantage; in 1923 he became assistant to the Curator of the University Museum of Archaeology and Ethnology, and in 1924 he was appointed a Bye-Fellow of Magdalene, which was years later, in 1953, to bestow upon him an Honorary Fellowship. In 1924 he was invited to the dual post of Keeper of Archaeology in the National Museum of Wales and Lecturer in Archaeology in the University College at Cardiff, and in 1926 succeeded to the Directorship of the Museum. There he remained until his retirement in 1948. He was knighted in 1935.

EARLY CAMBRIDGE MAN

While still at Cambridge he produced a book, based upon his academic thesis, which at once established new standards in field archaeology and secured for its author a high and permanent place in humanistic scholarship. His *Archaeology of the Cambridge Region* (1923) was more than a mere continuation of the ecological studies launched by Sir John Myres, Harold Peake, and O.G.S. Crawford before the First World War. Fox took an arbitrary slice of the countryside within bicycle-range of Cambridge and, with far-reaching implication, worked out a detailed analysis, period by period, of the relationship of human settlement there to soils, water and vegetation. As throughout his life, his preoccupation was already first and foremost with ancient man in relation to the landscape; indeed there might almost have been something prophetically symbolical about his early concern with "market gardening under glass"! Some of his conclusions in his Cambridge book have subsequently been modified both by himself and by others, but many of them are now a commonplace of archaeology and a deliberate effort has to be made to appreciate their novelty in 1923.

On arrival in Wales he proceeded to apply his methods and experience to the survey of Offa's Dyke. His reports, later (1955) collected into a monograph by the British Academy, are a model of their kind, and his interpretation of the great frontier-work in relation to contour, soil, and Cambro-Mercian politics is unlikely to be superseded in its main lines. For the first time he presented a rational explanation of the deviations and omissions in the long course of the famous dyke, thinking himself back, as always, into the living minds of its creators. Fox's capacity for reliving the past, within the bounds of essentially clear and argued thinking, was one of his outstanding qualities; it endeared him to his friends and associates, and vitalized the whole of his work.

It was from his Welsh Museum that Fox issued in 1932 the first of many editions of his now-classic *Personality of Britain*, a masterly synthesis of prehistoric cultures planned as a cavalcade upon the map of Britain. The result might be described as a study of prehistoric Britain in action, and once again Fox's ability to isolate major from minor issues and to relate them rationally to one another exhibited his preeminent powers as a collator.

CELTIC ART

In later years two subjects were uppermost in his mind: Celtic art in Britain, and the evolution and social significance of our lesser domestic architecture between the Middle Ages and the eighteenth century. Fox was always responsive to aesthetic appeal, and in both of these subjects a catholic sense of beauty constantly lightened the more prosaically objective aspects of his work. His interest in Celtic art had received a fresh impetus from the discovery of an astonishing hoard of metal-work in wartime operations in Anglesey, in 1943. The wider consequences of this stimulus were embodied in 1958 in *Pattern and Purpose*, again published by his old museum but treating England and Wales as a unit. Title of the book is explained in his foreword: "Early Celtic art is distinctive; technique and design in gold, bronze, or iron are often masterly, but there is nothing of 'Fine Art' about it; the incised patterns and the relief ornament are on purposeful things—torcs and brooches, and bracelets, weapons and drinking vessels, for example. It was not only a decorative art; useful things were well-shaped, with a sense of style, so a beautiful or well-balanced form often sufficed, satisfying the bronze-worker's critical sense, as it does us."

There was indeed a strong echo of William Morris in Fox's outlook, informing without obscuring his objective sense. Parallel qualities are evident in his *Monmouthshire Houses*, published in three parts between 1951 and 1954. This represents a long and laborious term of fieldwork in collaboration with Lord Raglan, and once more sets a standard for research of its kind. In this, as in his other books, Fox's rugged but expressive draftsmanship adds aptly to the personality of the text.

Among the honours and responsibilities which came his way were Fellowship of the British Academy, the Presidency of the Society of Antiquaries (1944–49), the Gold Medal of the Society (1952), and the Presidency of the Council for British Archaeology (1944–49).

He was twice married: first in 1916 to Olive Congreve-Pridgeon, by whom he had two daughters, and after her death to Aileen Scott Henderson, who survives him with three sons.

January 17, 1967.

Sir Lionel Fox, C.B., M.C., whose influence on the British prison system was both liberal and far-reaching, died on October 6, 1961, in a London hospital at the age of 66.

He was appointed chairman of the Prison Commissioners of England and Wales after many years' experience in posts requiring chiefly the qualifications of an efficient administrator and adviser. It was therefore not a little surprising to find him exhibiting all the fervour of the reformer and crusader when he came to direct the deliberations of the specialist body of which he had been secretary for some nine years.

BETTER LIVES IN PRISON

Originally, his zeal may have been attributable in some measure to his close association with Sir Alexander Paterson, who, in spite of his contact with the most hardened criminals as Commissioner of Prisons and Director of Convict Prisons over many years, and not a few disillusionments, never ceased to strive to make their lives in prison such as would fit them to become worthy members of the community on their release. Fox hated the old-established prison system, whose purpose seemed to him to be "rooted in the idea that the offender must be cut out of the community" by death or exile. And when he became chairman of the commission, and especially after the death of "Alec" Paterson, he carried on the tradition established by his late colleague of making prison an engine of reform rather than a menagerie for human animals. When there were escapes from the open prisons and borstals which he gradually set up, he refused to be discouraged, for he could point with pride to the large number of men and women who did not relapse into crime after release.

Lionel Wray Fox was born on February 21, 1895, the son of Sam Fox, of Halifax, Yorkshire.

STEERED PRISON SERVICE

Educated at Health Grammar School, in his native town, and later at Hertford College, Oxford, he joined the Army on the outbreak of the 1914–18 War, while still under 20 years of age, and served with the Duke of Wellington's Regiment throughout its duration, being awarded the M.C. and the Belgian Croix de Guerre, and being mentioned in dispatches. He attained the rank of captain, and on demobilization obtained a post in the Home Office. Some six years later he was appointed secretary to the Prison Commission, but in 1934 relinquished the post to take up the office of deputy receiver for the Metropolitan Police district. From 1941 to 1942 he served as acting receiver. He then became chairman of the Prison Commission until he retired in August, 1960. A serious illness robbed him of the chance to preside over the second United Nations congress for the prevention of crime and the treatment of offenders, which was held in London just before his retirement. It would have been a fit crowning point of his many activities in the international field, where he was greatly liked and respected.

His work in improving the prison system of this country may have been less generally recognized than it should have been on account of his reserved personality. Yet those who got through the defensive screen of his unexpansive manner knew him to be a highly sensitive man who understood clearly the needs of other people and who went out of his way to invite constructive criticism. He steered the prison service through the difficult post-war period, and when the number of prisoners was going up rapidly and it was impossible to obtain money for new prison buildings.

PRISONERS AND STAFF

It was not until R. A. Butler became Home Secretary in 1957 that Fox was able to begin to put some of his plans into practice. *The 1959 White Paper on Penal Practice in a Changing Society* contained, apart from the outlines of the present prison building programme, some far-reaching proposals on the reorganization of prisons. If not all of them could be adopted in the end, it is none the less true that Fox laid the foundation of a modern prison system. In particular it was he who began to encourage systematic studies of the importance of personal relationships in prisons, of the influence of prisoner on prisoner and of staff on inmate. At the same time he gave his support to practical experiments in group work and group counselling in prisons and borstals.

Fox might have risen to the highest ranks of the Civil Service. But he considered himself fortunate to be allowed to remain with the Prison Commission which he had served for so long. His book *The English Prison and Borstal Systems* was a classic, notable particularly for its courageous discussion of the basic question, "What is prison for?". He was undoubtedly one of the greatest experts in the field of penology anywhere. After his retirement, the Cambridge Institute of Criminology was quick to secure his services as adviser and lecturer on penological questions. He was preparing a book on applied penology which his wide experience, his clarity of mind and, above all, his humanity would have made an invaluable guide to all who are concerned with the treatment of offenders.

He was created C.B. in 1948 and in 1953 received a knighthood.

His marriage to Marjorie, eldest daughter of C. H. Horner, of Halifax, took place in 1921. They had one son and two daughters.

October 9, 1961.

W. A. Foyle, joint founder and chairman of the well-known bookselling business in Charing Cross Road, London, died at his home in Essex on June 4, 1963. He was 78.

The bookselling firm of W. & G. Foyle, proudly described on its note-heading as "The World's Greatest Bookshop", has been for over half a century one of the household words of British commercial enterprise. With its stock of more than four million volumes, an annual turnover of some £3m., and its shelving-space of 30 miles, its success was a joint operation of the brothers William and Gilbert.

FAILED EXAM

William Alfred Foyle was born at Shoreditch, London, on March 4, 1885, a son of William Henry Foyle, a wholesale grocer. He was educated at Owen's School, Islington, and sat for, and failed, the Civil Service entrance examination in 1900. After a short course at King's College London in 1902, he became clerk to Sir Edward Marshall Hall, K.C. A chance incident, however, altered the course of his career. He and his brother, who had also failed the Civil Service examination and had gone into the offices of Shoreditch Borough Council, decided to sell their textbooks, and advertised them in an educational journal. They had so many replies that they began to think that bookselling might be a profitable trade, and began to accumulate stock in the kitchen of their home. Before long they rented a small shop in Islington and in 1903, greatly daring, gave up their jobs to become fulltime booksellers at Peckham. Catalogues were written out by hand and prospective customers were asked to return them.

They cooked their meals at the back of the shop—sausages and mash was the staple diet—they worked on Sundays and there were no half-days. Each morning's orders were examined immediately on their arrival and the new and second-hand volumes in stock were parcelled and taken by William, on his cycle, to the City. Here the remaining books for the orders were obtained after office hours and despatched by post the same evening. Already the firm was earning a reputation for being able to supply books on even the most out-of-the way subjects.

EXPANDED BUSINESS

Later the brothers moved to 131, Charing Cross Road; by 1912 they were able to expand into much larger premises at Nos. 119 and 121; and in 1929, Sir Kynaston Studd, then Lord Mayor of London, opened the new five-floor building in Manette Street. In spite of the increasing size of the concern, it always maintained a certain informality of arrangement, more or less in line with that of the small bookshop, and "browsing" was never discouraged. The very brisk secondhand trade was, as the years went on, supplemented by the stocking of all new books of note; and the fine book department was the especial care and pleasure of William Foyle.

In 1920 they had started Foyles Educational, Ltd., a school supply service, and nine years later they opened a gramophone record department and an art gallery, and initiated a lending-library chain working through small shops all over the country. Perhaps the activity which drew most public attention was the establishment of the Foyle's Literary Luncheons. This idea came from Christina Foyle, William Foyle's daughter, who continued to be the mainstay of the function. In 1937 Foyle's Book Club was started, as well as the publishing house of John Gifford, Ltd., and a literary agency. In 1944 the firm took over the old Lecture Agency, founded in 1879. From 1949 William Foyle presented an annual poetry prize of £250. He lived at Beeleigh Abbey, Maldon, Essex, where he accumulated a fine private library of 10,000 volumes—many of them rare and precious.

He married Christina Tulloch, by whom he had a son and two daughters.

June 6, 1963.

Lord Francis-Williams, C.B.E., died at his home in Surrey on June 5, 1970, at the age of 67.

Labour Peer, advisor to Attlee on public relations when he was Prime Minister, historian of the trade union movement, editor, he was first and foremost a publicist. Millions who knew little or nothing about his writings had seen him on television. He was a born talker and his best books are conversational. While he held a number of posts he did not stay in any one long enough to make it a career.

Francis Williams was born at St. Martins in Shropshire on March 10, 1903. He was educated at the Queen Elizabeth Grammar School at Middleton and after working on a number of small papers first became noticed as a young but bright city editor of the *Daily Herald.*

He had married Jessie Hopkin in 1926. She survives him, with a son and a daughter.

EDITED "HERALD"

He became editor of the *Herald* in 1936 and held the post for four years. The split authority in the control of the *Daily Herald* between Odhams and the Trades Union Congress was always difficult. In those four years encompassing the approach and outbreak of war it became almost impossible. In 1941 Williams became Controller of News and Censorship at the Ministry of Information. This, too, lasted four years. They were as satisfying and successful as the previous four had been frustrating and disappointing. For this work he was made a C.B.E., and also awarded the U.S. Medal of Freedom.

Williams had found his real métier, talking, explaining, being a little didactic. It was a clear case of the right man being put in the right place when Attlee made him P.R.O. at No. 10 Downing Street. Fully in sympathy with the Government, having plenty to talk about in the first flush of Labour's social revolution, with valuable experience of dealing with journalists and with their confidence, he seemed in his element. Yet he stayed in the post only two years. It was the same when he became a Governor of the B.B.C. in 1951, although in that office the shortness of his tenure was not voluntary. When his office came up for renewal at the end of 1952, it is understood Attlee, who would have been consulted, passed him over. In 1956 he became editor of the Socialist weekly *Forward.* After four years the paper ceased as a separate publication, and Williams was once again without a post.

This did not matter so much because whatever appointment he had Williams was writing all the time. Indeed, it could be held that a long set job was against the inclinations and his gifts. He had not the application for a hard grind. He could get his teeth into a subject and the length of a book was about right for his volatile character. The nature of the best of his books is indicated by their titles: *Democracy's Last Battle* (1941), *Tomorrow's Politics* (1942), *Press, Parliament, and People* (1946), *The Triple Challenge, the Future of Socialist Britain* (1946).

LIFE OF BEVIN

He wrote a life of Ernest Bevin, and histories of the Labour Party and of trade unionism. In 1961 he produced a book of conversations with Earl Attlee: *A Prime Minister Remembers* is one of his best efforts because again it was what he could do best. He tried his hand at some novels; they were respectable, but not memorable.

In the fifties and sixties Williams was regularly used on television as a chairman, interrogator, and debater. Always at his ease and clearly enjoying himself, he was most successful. The more formal ways of the House of Lords could not be expected to suit him so well. Made a Labour life-peer in the spring of 1962, he did not become prominent on the Opposition benches. At his introduction he affirmed instead of taking the oath; 20 years earlier he had declared himself one "who has no formal religion and no belief in the supernatural assumptions of the Christian religion".

Nothing So Strange, his autobiography, was published not long before he died. Few knew more about the history of newspapers, and he told their story from the time when they were first published 300 years ago in his book *Dangerous Estate*. Francis-Williams forecast that the time would come when the "morning papers" were received direct by television.

Early in 1964 Francis-Williams, with three others, left Television Reporters International over a difference of opinion between commentators and the company's financial directors about company policy. The company was formed to produce television documentaries and current affairs programmes for sale both in Britain and abroad.

In 1965 he published *A Pattern of Rulers*, which included a character study of three prime ministers who between them ruled Britain from 1923 to 1940. *The Right to Know: The Rise of The World Press* appeared in 1969.

In October, 1966, he was appointed to assist the Monopolies Commission in investigating the ownership merger of The Times and Sunday Times.

June 6, 1970.

Professor James Franck, who died at the age of 81 in Göttingen on May 21, 1964, was one of the great men in the development of atomic physics.

He was born in Hamburg in 1882. He began his studies in Heidelberg and continued at Berlin where he obtained his doctor's degree in 1906. He continued at the physics department of the University of Berlin until 1918, when he became the head of the physics division of the Kaiser Wilhelm Institute for Physical Chemistry. In 1920 he moved to a chair in Göttingen, which he helped to make one of the centres of research in modern physics. On the advent of the Nazi regime he could have continued in office, in spite of his non-Aryan origin, because of war service, but he chose to resign and made his reasons known in letters to the newspapers, which brought him under strong attack.

After a year as guest professor in Copenhagen he went in 1935 to Johns Hopkins University and in 1938 as Professor of Physical Chemistry to the University of Chicago where he remained until his retirement. During the war he took part in the Chicago work on atomic energy and he was the chairman of a group of scientists who towards the end of the war wrote a report urging the United States Government not to use atomic bombs against cities but to demonstrate the power of the new weapon first as a warning.

Probably his best known work, which was started in Berlin jointly with Gustav Hertz, was the discovery of the quantum loss of energy of electrons colliding with atoms, which confirmed and extended the new Bohr picture of atomic structure. For this work he was awarded the Nobel Prize in 1925 jointly with Hertz. In the Göttingen period he was mainly interested in molecules and their reaction to light, a field in which the new discoveries in physics became of fundamental importance to chemistry. His many contributions to this subject, including the "Franck-Condon principle", are today essential parts of the physicists' and the chemists' thinking about molecules. His interest in the action of light on molecules led to a study of photosynthesis, and most of his American work was concerned with reactions of fundamental importance in biological processes.

Franck's influence on science went far beyond his own research work. His advice on personal problems and problems of policy as well as on scientific matters was always in demand, and always readily given. His wisdom and his kindly interest in people brought him the confidence of all those with whom he came into contact.

His many honours included in 1964 foreign membership of the Royal Society. After the war he was honoured again in Germany, and he died during a visit to Göttingen.

He married Ingrid Josephson in 1906 and had two daughters. After the death of his wife in 1942 he married in 1946 Hertha Sponer, a long standing collaborator and family friend (now a professor at Duke University).

May 23, 1964.

Leonhard Frank, the German novelist, died in Munich on August 18, 1961.

The son of an artisan, he was born on September 4, 1882, at Würzburg. The hardships of his early life are reflected in several of the stories that centre in Würzburg and the neighbourhood, picturesque old fashioned towns, the seamy side of which Frank knew well. His reputation as a writer was established by his *Die Räuberbande* of 1914 (The Robber Band), and in this and later stories he developed the dominant themes of his generation—the conflict between parents and children, teachers and pupils, masters and men; he was one of the first to use Freudian insights in the novel *Die Ursache* (1915).

He left Germany in 1914 in protest against the war, and was one of the German exiles in Switzerland who devoted themselves to revolutionary pacifism. *Der Mensch ist gut* (1917) is an impassioned onslaught on war and power politics, and an appeal for a new order based on "Love and Friendship"; it is in every way one of the representative works of Expressionism.

VAGUELY SOCIALIST

Several of his later books show his radical hostility to the classes possessing wealth and power and to social conformism (*Der Bürger*, 1924), but his socialism, to which he clung to the end, was always of a vague and idealistic kind.

His most successful stories were studies of intimate relations between man and woman, such as *Karl und Anna* (1927) which he dramatized and which was also filmed; his treatment of sex shows a skilful blend of delicacy and deliberate crudeness. One often feels that he avoided the more exacting implications of his theme and tended to find an easy and sometimes sentimental way out; but he wrote deftly of immediate problems and enjoyed great success abroad as well as in Germany; many of his tales are translated into English. He left Germany in 1933 when Hitler came to power and spent the latter part of his exile in the United States. After the war he lived in Munich, and in 1952 published *Links wo das Herz ist*, an account of his life and opinions, with interesting descriptions of his contemporaries.

August 24, 1961.

Pamela Frankau, who died on June 8, 1967, at the age of 59, belonged on her father's side to a gifted Jewish family. Her father was the novelist Gilbert Frankau. Her grandmother wrote novels lifted out of the ruck by their shrewd asperity; her grand aunt was the amusing journalist Mrs. Aria: her grand uncle "Owen Hall" wrote some of the musical comedies last century which had genuine fantasy. Pamela Frankau's mother was Dorothea Drummond-Black, the daughter of a Home Office departmental head, much respected in his day, a woman memorable for her charm and plaintive wit. Indeed all these people were notable wits and it is natural that Pamela Frankau should have been an explicitly funny conversationalist.

But her wit owed its satisfying character to a fundamental seriousness which was ready to overthrow the superficialities only because they were hiding reality. She often appeared careless and capricious; she was a born gambler and was the first to admit that she had an outstanding incapacity to deal with her financial affairs, though this was largely due to her own inordinate generosity. But in fact she was remarkable for her steadfastness, which was often very touching. In the Second World War she took her service in the A.T.S. with the utmost seriousness, alien as it was from her temperament, because she loved England with what she herself pointed out was the peculiarly ardent love of England that is felt by some English Jews. She brought the same seriousness to her writing, and in all the books she produced after she published her first novel at the age of 19, there are passages and characters and ideas of quite idiosyncratic merit.

The *Willow Cabin* is usually considered her best novel, though she herself preferred *The Bridge*. The trilogy she had just completed with *Over the Mountains*, recalls Galsworthy. But none of her novels, though they are better than most, was as good as she was; and this was due to the fierce accidents of her personal life. She was happy by nature, and it was easy for her to be so, for she had good looks, charm, so many accomplishments that she never needed to be bored or to bore, and, above all, deep and enduring affections. Through the years she lost her enemies and kept her friends, and she had close ties with her sister (herself an admirable novelist under the name of Mary Nicholson) and her nephew. But three of her most loved friends died painfully and prematurely; her marriage, in spite of mutual liking and respect, was dissolved; her only child died in infancy; and she had recently had years of lacerated ill health. Though nobody was more conscious of the difficulties of reconciling such events with unquestioning religious faith, she remained a truly believing member of the Roman Catholic Church, in to which she had been received a quarter of a century ago. She made the task of the devoted friend who looked after her through her long illness easier by remaining true to her religion and her wit up to her last hour.

June 9, 1967.

Mr. Justice Frankfurter, who died in Washington on February 22, 1965, at the age of 82, arrived in the United States at the age of 12 unable to speak a word of English, yet he made himself the most famous American teacher of law of his generation, became a considerable political power during Roosevelt's New Deal, and during the last 20 years of his life achieved, as a Justice of the Supreme Court, a great reputation for intellectual integrity and judicial-mindedness.

The oldest member of the court and the most hard-working, he suffered a heart attack late in 1958 but refused to retire until forced to by ill-health in late 1962. He could have done so on full salary at 70. With his New Deal past, Frankfurter was expected to become a crusading liberal on the bench. But concern for the liberty and well-being of the individual had to be reconciled with the needs of society as a whole; and the progressive sympathies with which he began were tempered by his deep reverence for the law, the federal system and the intent of Congress. In recent years, as the court swung to the left, Frankfurter exerted a restraining influence and emerged as a leader of the centre and sometimes of the right wing among the Justices. Conservatives who had feared him at the beginning of his career as a dangerous radical lauded him at the end of it as a bulwark of the Constitution.

Felix Frankfurter was born in Vienna on November 15, 1882, the son of Leopold Frankfurter and the descendant of a long line of rabbis. When he was on a business trip to the United States in 1893 Leopold Frankfurter decided to stay in the country and sent for his family to join him. He did not prosper, however, and it was only by dint of much exertion that Felix Frankfurter was able to enter first the College of the City of New York and then the Harvard Law School, from which he graduated in 1906.

"TRUST BUSTING"

In the same year Frankfurter began a fruitful association with Henry L. Stimson, subsequently Secretary of State under President Hoover, and at that time United States Attorney for the Southern District of New York. Stimson was under orders from President Theodore Roosevelt to enforce strictly his "trustbusting" policy and he applied to Harvard for an assistant: Frankfurter was recommended and the two men worked together until 1910. The association was very much to Frankfurter's taste, for his Harvard years had imbued him with a deep admiration for the aristocratic liberals of Massachusetts, of whom Stimson was one, and who were still enjoying the afterglow of their golden era. From the same class Frankfurter acquired an Anglophile outlook, which was reinforced by an early visit he paid to Oxford.

There is reason to believe that English models shaped Frankfurter's policies and methods in more than one direction. He was said to have been impressed by the way in which from 1906 onwards social reforms had been introduced into England by the process of legislation and to have devoted himself to translating English methods into American terms. He was also said to have been impressed by the English system under which men who had proved themselves in the universities serve the Administration. It is tempting to speculate whether in the role he played at Harvard, Frankfurter had in mind the influence of Benjamin Jowett, or of Milner's "Kindergarten".

This, however, is to anticipate Frankfurter's career. In 1911 Stimson became Secretary of War in the Taft Administration and took Frankfurter to Washington with him as an officer in the Bureau of Insular Affairs, then part of the War Department. Frankfurter shared house in Washington with a group of bachelors—they included Lord Eustace Percy, then attached to the British Embassy—who devoted themselves to the earnest discussions of politics, so that Mr. Justice Holmes called their house "the home of good government". After the departure of the Taft Administration. Frankfurter became Byre Professor of Administrative Law at Harvard in 1914. He returned to Government service the week after America's entry into the 1914–18 War but at the end of 1919 went back to Harvard to resume his work at the Law School, where, with one interruption, he continued until 1939.

REPUTATION AS TEACHER

As a teacher Frankfurter won for himself an outstanding reputation. He was fond of teaching by the process of question and answer, goading his students with a biting tongue. But Frankfurter's influence went far beyond that of a teacher in the narrow sense. He was once described as "a trainer of prophets who has made the Harvard Law School a sort of racing stable for liberal lawyers". He kept his students in touch with the world outside, and more important, perhaps, made it a policy to encourage brilliant pupils to enter the service of the government, whatever its political complexion, and maintained close contact with them. Even during the Republican twenties, when the liberal intellectuals ceased to command any great influence in American politics, Frankfurter managed to keep open his lines to Washington.

From the Supreme Court he continued to send out into the world a succession of brilliant young law clerks, most of whom remained deeply affected by the experience of working for him and devoted to him personally. Some of them, too, found their way into government service and eventually into President Kennedy's Administration.

Frankfurter made himself the acknowledged authority on the procedure and jurisdiction of the Supreme Court, contributing a sessional article on the cases that came before it to the *Harvard Law Review* and writing *The Business of the Supreme Court* in collaboration with James M. Landis. He also became widely known as the exponent of a government-sponsored policy of social reform.

In the twenties Frankfurter gave his help in a number of *causes célèbres* involving labour legislation, civil liberties and social welfare.

UNDER ROOSEVELT

The advent of Franklin Roosevelt as President of the United States inaugurated the period of Frankfurter's greatest influence in Washington. When he was Governor of New York State, Roosevelt frequently called Frankfurter to Albany and Frankfurter wholeheartedly supported Roosevelt's nomination as candidate for the Presidency. Frankfurter's influence from 1933 onwards was both direct, because of his friendship with Roosevelt, and indirect because of the protégés whom he was able to place in the service both of the regular departments of government and of the numerous agencies which proliferated under the New Deal. Frankfurter's contacts with Washington had been strengthened four years earlier when his old chief, Henry Stimson, had taken office under Herbert Hoover, and it was Frankfurter who suggested Thomas Corcoran as Special Counsel to the Reconstruction Finance Corporation, the instrument with which Hoover hoped to stem the tide of depression.

Corcoran acquired an influential position under Roosevelt, and he was joined by other pupils of Frankfurter such as Benjamin Cohen, John Winant, and David Lilienthal. In those days a recommendation from Frankfurter was said to be a sure passport to a position under the Administration.

"Frankfurter's whole life has been a preparation for the Supreme Court, and his appointment has an aesthetically satisfying inevitability". So wrote the New York *Nation* on January 14, 1939, a few days after Roosevelt had sent to the Senate his nomination of Frankfurter to the Bench. The appointment was confirmed without dissent although in the intense feeling which was raised against Franklin Roosevelt's policies Frankfurter had become an object of attack, personal as well as political, as a "hidden hand" that was dominating the government. It was not so very hidden. Frankfurter himself was apt to give an impression of exercising great influence, although he never sought any elective office or any public part in politics.

Frankfurter's elevation to the Supreme Court came after Roosevelt had been rebuffed in his attempt to "pack" the court, which had declared unconstitutional much New Deal legislation. (It is said, incidentally, that Frankfurter had given the President prior warning that many of these laws would never be upheld by the Supreme Court.) Apart from his obvious qualifications as a jurist, Frankfurter's appointment was designed to strengthen the liberal forces in the Court, but as has happened in other cases, his opinions at times disappointed his admirers in liberal and labour circles.

HISTORY OF SAFEGUARDS

In paying tribute to Brandeis, Frankfurter had written: "Law is not a system of artificial reason but the application of ethical ideals with freedom at the core". It was widely expected that a man holding such views would formulate and apply a broad legal philosophy when he assumed a place on the Supreme Court, which exercises so much power in the American governmental system. In fact, although Frankfurter referred often to ethical principles, he was apt to take refuge in what seemed like legal technicalities; his critics felt that a deviation from correct legal procedure was more important to him than a miscarriage of justice. Frankfurter's own reply to such criticism was that "The history of liberty has largely been the history of procedural safeguards".

With the appointment of Mr. Earl Warren to be Chief Justice, the Court took a new direction which brought down upon it attacks from the conservatives quite as bitter as those from the liberals 20 years earlier. The decision that racial segregation in tax-supported schools was unconstitutional was unanimous, and in cases involving individual rights, Frankfurter usually stood with the liberals. But as one decision followed another rebuking congressional committees, state governments and government departments for invasions of individual rights which the majority considered to be guaranteed by the Constitution, Frankfurter's more traditional conception of the court's functions led him into not infrequent dissent. In his view the Court should give wide latitude to the Government and Congress, interfering only if constitutional powers had been clearly overstepped. He was always reluctant to declare a law unconstitutional.

In one of his last and most important dissents Frankfurter defined his attitude with passionate precision. On March 26, 1962, the Court decided that voters could seek action in the federal courts to correct unfair appointment of seats in state legislatures. The evils of the existing bias in favour of rural voters were obvious but Frankfurter strenuously denied the right of the judiciary to correct them. "The Court's authority—possessed neither of the purse nor the sword—ultimately rests on sustained public confidence in its moral sanction", he wrote. "Such feeling must be nourished by the Court's complete detachment, in fact and in appearance, from political entanglements and by abstention from injecting itself into the clash of political forces in political settlements ... There is not under our constitution judicial remedy for every political michief, for every undesirable exercise of legislative power ... In this situation, as in others of like nature, appeal for relief does not belong here. Appeal must be to an informed, civically militant electorate."

STATES' RIGHTS

Frankfurter had a great respect for the federal system, with all the opportunities it offered for experimentation and initiative. Early in his career he had defended the right of individual states to experiment with progressive legislation and toward its end, in a case involving double jeopardy, he wrote a decision affirming the right of a state to try a man for a crime of which he had been acquitted in a federal court. Frankfurter did not subscribe to the idea that the Bill of Rights had been applied *in toto* to the states by the passage of the Fourteenth Amendment and argued that to deny the state's authority on this issue would be to deprive the states of their primary responsibility to fight crime and would undermine the federal system, with its division of authority. For this view he was much criticized. Even in the anti-trust cases, Frankfurter parted company with the Liberals in some instances, notably over the very controversial decision that the anti-trust law had been violated because the du Pont Company held a large block of shares in the General Motors Corporation. Towards the end of Frankfurter's life, however, the Supreme Court, to the dismay of the Liberals, seemed to be moving back toward Frankfurter's position on a number of issues.

Frankfurter was the most industrious writer of opinions on the Court. He was often chosen to write the majority opinion—he was called the "workhouse" of the Court—but even when he was not, he liked to deliver his own judgment.

DISSENT

Before his time, it had been usual for not more than two opinions to be given—a majority and a dissenting opinion. He was a sharp questioner and frequent interrupter of counsel.

As a Justice, Frankfurter did not leave the great positive mark which his brilliance led people to expect of him and if he sought to remodel the federal administrative machine by having it permanently staffed with men of high intellectual calibre, his influence was not lasting. His protégés were introduced not as civil servants but as policy-makers, and this circumstance alone deprived them of any likelihood of permanency. One must think therefore of the passing influence of Milner's "Kindergarten" in South Africa rather than of the fixed bureaucracies of England and France. Frankfurter's name, however, deserves to be remembered among the company of men who in the 1930s worked a revolution in the function of government in the United States and, above all, as one of its greatest teachers of law.

CAUSTIC TONGUE

Frankfurter had a caustic tongue, talked brilliantly, and was inclined to monopolize conversation. Of his writings one critic observed "...few scholars of the law have written a more natural, more lucid, or more readable English", while another said that his "literary style is part commonplace, part lush, and runs to the excessive use of elegant quotations".

For a short time during and immediately after the 1914-18 War, Frankfurter actively concerned himself with the Zionist movement: thereafter his interest in the affairs of his co-religionists was more remote.

In 1919 he married Miss Marion A. Denman, the daughter of a Congregationalist minister.

There were no children of the marriage. During the Second World War, Justice and Mrs. Frankfurter gave hospitality to three British children. During the whole of the war, Frankfurter was ardently pro-British and was known as an early advocate of American intervention on the Allied side. In 1933–34 Frankfurter was George Eastman Visiting Professor at Oxford, of which University he was an honorary D.C.L. He was also an honorary Bencher of Gray's Inn. In *Felix Frankfurter Reminisces*, a fascinating transcript of a series of interviews by the Oral History Research Office of Columbia Univeristy (published in Britain in 1961) he describes his year at Oxford as "the fullest year my wife and I spent—the amplest and most civilized".

February 23, 1965.

Charles Samuel Franklin, C.B.E., who was associated with Marconi in the early days of wireless and was later responsible for a number of aerial developments, died at Woodford Green, Essex, on December 10, 1964. He was 85.

Franklin designed Britain's first broadcasting station—2LO—and the aerial system for the world's first regular television service, broadcast by the B.B.C. from Alexandra Palace in north London.

Born in London in 1879 and trained under Silvanus Thompson at the Finsbury Technical College, Franklin joined Marconi's Wireless Telegraph Company (now the Marconi Company) at the age of 20 and remained with the company until his retirement in 1939. In 1902 he sailed with Marconi across the Atlantic in the liner Philadelphia and messages were received on board from the Poldhu wireless transmitting station about 1,500 miles away in Cornwall. The granite column erected at Poldhu in 1937 to commemorate Marconi's achievement also records another experiment by Franklin. In 1923 and 1924 he directed short-wave radio beam transmissions from the station to Marconi, who was in a yacht cruising in the South Atlantic, and so laid the foundation of modern long-distance radio communications.

He was responsible for the Franklin beam aerial, the fundamental invention associated with the Marconi short-wave directional radio communications system; the development of the low-loss coaxial cable for the transmission of very high frequency currents used in television and radar, and a number of improvements in the design of circuits for radio transmitters and receivers.

In 1936 Franklin was the first recipient of the James Alfred Ewing Medal, awarded by the Institution of Civil Engineers for outstanding engineering research; and in 1949 he was created C.B.E., and also awarded the Faraday Medal by the Institution of Electrical Engineers for his work in radio engineering.

December 16, 1964.

Lord Fraser of Allander, one of the leading personalities and one of the most spectacular figures in the retail distributive industries in Britain, died on November 6, 1966, at his home at Mugdock, Bearsden, near Glasgow. He was 63.

For a considerable part of his life he had been head of the great concern of House of Fraser Ltd., which at one time operated in Scotland, but which, in recent years, has practically dominated the scene in the West End of London and in various provincial centres. This storming of the great emporiums of the south which brought into his control businesses like John Barker's and Harrods, was planned and executed by Fraser himself. He was chairman of George Outram and Company Limited, publishers of *The Glasgow Herald*, and also the chairman of Scottish Universal Investment Trusts. His outside interests included the honorary treasurership of the A.A. and the treasurership of the Scottish Conservative and Unionist party.

When the historic commercial battle for the famous business and property in Knightsbridge had been finally won in 1959, it was said that he controlled a capital investment of well over £50m. That figure was, in fact, increased notably within a very few years. Altogether there were more than 60 separate stores under his control, and Fraser used to say that he knew more or less what was happening at least from week to week in all of them. He was a man of prodigious memory with the keenest eye for detail, and all his business deals were carried through, certainly in the later years, with no apparent excess of effort. It was said of him that he worked at least as hard as anybody whom he employed. In many respects, excepting perhaps in his ultimate triumphs, he was not unlike that other great *entrepreneur,* Gordon Selfridge, the exception being, of course, in the fact that Fraser to the end not only retained his wealth and prestige, but signally increased both. There was nothing of the great demonstrative tycoon about him. He never made himself obtrusive upon his occasional visits to his shops and stores, but when he talked to assistants and floor walkers, it was upon their level, and not his, and it is said that he often surprised them by the range of his knowledge about the jobs they performed. At his fine home in the hills near Glasgow he and the Fraser family lived opulently, but graciously, although in spite of his wealth he did not maintain a town house.

Hugh Fraser was born on January 15, 1903, a son of the late Hugh Fraser, head of the family concern, and of Emily Florence Fraser. He was educated at Warriston and Glasgow Academy, from which he went practically direct into the stores in Buchanan Street. There afterwards, and in the company's ever more widespread shops over England and Scotland, he spent all his active life. From 1925 until 1947 he was managing director of the parent company, Fraser Sons & Co. Ltd., and became chairman in 1941 until 1947, when he assumed both the chairmanship and managing directorship of its successor, House of Fraser Ltd. In 1952 he became also chairman and managing director of the Scottish Drapery Corporation Ltd., and a year later of Binns Ltd., which by that time had also been absorbed by Frasers. For some years he was president of the Scottish Retail Drapers' Association. He was also chairman of the board of governors of the Westbourne School for Girls, Glasgow.

TAKEOVER OPPOSED

In 1964, Fraser opposed Lord Thomson's takeover bid of nearly £5,250,000 for George Outram & Co., publishers of *The Glasgow Herald* and the *Evening Times*. Fraser's first reaction was to become chairman and take steps to defend the company against the take-over. Then, realizing that only a competitive bid could keep Thomson out, and in order to keep the paper under control, he resigned from the chairmanship and the board. Then, in his capacity as chairman of the Scottish and Universal Investments, he made a competitive bid against Thomson. In the end, Fraser won.

Fraser developed his interest in, and his work for, organizations connected with the shopping world. He had been in addition to president of the Scottish Retail Association, director-at-large of the National Retail Dry Goods Association of America, and in 1961, as president of the Retail Trades' Education Council, he gave it a substantial sum for the establishment of a secretariat, with full time secretary and education officer and staff. For years, too, he had been director of the National Bank of Scotland, and, as a lover of the Scottish scene, he was for some years an active member of the Scottish Tourist Board. He gave generously to many charities and good causes, particularly North of the Border, and he shared Lady Fraser's interest in the social work of the Salvation Army. He was a magistrate and a deputy lieutenant, and—what only a few of his intimates knew—as a keen cinema enthusiast, he was honorary treasurer of Films of Scotland. Fraser was raised to the peerage in 1964.

At home near Mugdock, in Stirlingshire, he cultivated his hobbies of horticulture and farming. He loved flowers, and had an expert knowledge of their culture; he was particularly fond of motoring, and he had a first-class knowledge of the mechanism of cars.

In 1931 Fraser married Katie Hutcheon, daughter of the late Sir Andrew Lewis, LL.D., a prominent Scottish shipowner, by whom he had a son and a daughter. The son, the third Hugh Fraser, born in 1937, who has been associated with his father in his business concerns since his late teens, now succeeds to the title.

November 7, 1966.

Lionel Fraser, C.M.G., who died at his London home on January 2, 1965, at the age of 69, was among the leading City personalities of his generation; all the more so as he made his mark entirely through the force of his own character and capabilities. His remarkable career of more than 50 years straddled the fields of banking, investment trusts, insurance, and industry.

In the City he will best be remembered as chairman of Helbert, Wagg until this house was merged with J. Henry Schroder in April, 1962. He was chairman of the Issuing Houses Association from 1946 to 1948. In industry, Fraser was for many years chairman of Babcock and Wilcox, the boilermakers and heavy engineering group, and latterly its president. He was also closely associated with the building up of Thomas Tilling as one of the major industrial holding companies in Britain whose interests range from building materials and engineering products to motor distribution and publishing (William Heinemann).

William Lionel Fraser, who was born in 1895, started working at the age of 16 in the firm of Bonn & Co., which in 1921 was absorbed by Helbert, Wagg & Company, the merchant bankers. Fraser stayed on, and in 1954 became its Chairman. In 1964 he became the first chairman of the London office of the Banque de Paris et des Pays-Bas.

In the First World War he joined the London Scottish and served in France, the Dardanelles and Egypt and was later seconded for special duties with the Naval Intelligence Division of the Admiralty. In the Second World War he served at the Treasury from 1939–1945 and for his services was awarded the C.M.G.

He was a many-sided man and amongst other things had been a member of the Chelsea Borough Council from 1945–1950, a Trustee of the Tate Gallery, a Liveryman of the Fishmongers Company and member of the committee of several clubs including the St. James's and the Garrick.

RELIGIOUS CONVICTIONS

A bald recital of his career, though it implies exceptional qualities, is inadequate to portray the man. Endowed with very good looks and a fine presence, he had a warm heart, a gift for friendship and a gay attitude to life. Immensely sensitive, no one enjoyed more than he an atmosphere of enthusiasm and success, but no one was his equal in creating it and bestowing praise on others. He was an ardent Christian Scientist and his deep religious convictions added a fundamental integrity and deep seriousness to his character. All these things made him an inspiring leader. His advice was sought intimately, and he was a formidable but fair negotiator.

He was sensitive to public opinion but his liberal mind and independent spirit led him on occasion to somewhat flamboyant advocacy for the crusade of the moment. He was a modern thinker, but because he had great respect for the traditions of the City during a period of drastically changing methods he strove to fuse the best elements of the old with the less conventional in the classically English manner.

In the same way he moved with the times in his appreciation of art and latterly had built up, with the close cooperation of his wife, a collection of abstract pictures.

His autobiography *All to the Good* was published in 1963.

He married Cynthia Elizabeth Walter in 1931 and their life together was a particularly happy one and they had a wide circle of friends in this country, in France, and in the United States. He is survived by her and two sons, but his only daughter was killed in a motor accident shortly before her marriage. His faith enabled him to bear this loss with great fortitude; and indeed the key to his life may well have been this faith which directed his sense of purpose and his determination to do right.

January 4, 1965.

Reginald P. Fraser, O.B.E., who died suddenly on February 25, 1963, at the age of 66, was a scientist, engineer and inventor of unusual versatility.

He had published some 200 scientific papers, most of them in the journals of the Royal Society and the professional institutions, and had taken out some 80 patents. Throughout his life he had been associated with Imperial College. He graduated in 1923 and then worked in the Department of Chemical Engineering, Applied Chemistry and Chemical Technology, where he founded the Jet Research Laboratory.

Before the Second World War he was concerned with measuring flame speeds and detonation phenomena with a high speed photographic apparatus which became known as the Fraser high speed camera; with this a detonation front moving at a speed of the order of 6,000 miles an hour could be arrested and studied. Present-day high-speed mirror cameras are based on his original designs. Not only did he discover experimentally the nature of spin in detonation but he also demonstrated the deflection of flames in magnetic fields which forms the basis of magneto-hydro-dynamics.

REASSEMBLING FLYING BOMB

During the war he was connected with the Petroleum Warfare and the Projectile Development Establishment. For Sir Alwyn Crow he developed flame throwers, particularly the Wasp, Adder and Salamander. He carried out classical work on the flow through rocket nozzles and was the first to assemble a V 1 engine which had partly disintegrated and fallen into the Staines reservoir. Within days he was able to fire the engine on a test bed at Imperial College in the presence of the Service chiefs. His insight into the working of rocketry enabled him and his team of co-workers to predict the ability of the Germans to send rockets to London. The feasibility study from his laboratory was in Lord Cherwell's hands well before the first V 2 made an appearance over London. He was made O.B.E. in 1945.

After the war he was active in oil firing and pioneered many developments in the fields of residual fuel-fired combustion. His atomization work was first directed to the spraying of insecticides under the auspices of the Colonial Office, and later to the burning of fuel in gas turbines and rockets.

Fraser belonged to the class of artist-engineers whose creativeness is legendary. He was a leader of men, inspiring in industry and in the academic field an ever-changing and devoted band of people who recognized in him a genius of inventiveness and a master of perfection.

He was proud of his Scottish forebears who, as so many Scots, travelled widely. His father and mother pioneered at an early age on the Canadian prairies but later returned to farm at Heathfield in Sussex, where he was born. He married Emme O'Shea (now deceased) from Skibbereen, near Cork, where many of his happiest days were spent.

March 3, 1966.

A. P. Freeman, one of the great slow bowlers of English cricket, died at his home at Bearstead, Kent, on January 28, 1965, at the age of 76.

He played in 12 Test matches and toured Australia twice, yet rarely did himself justice in this class. Because of his comparative failure against the greatest batsmen on the most important occasions he cannot be regarded as the equal of the great Australian googly bowlers—Mailey, Grimmett, O'Reilly, Benaud—yet his performances in county cricket and for the Players against the Gentlemen were legendary. Only Wilfred Rhodes has taken more wickets in first-class cricket. Nobody has taken as many in a season, and it is no daring prophecy to suggest that it will be a long time before Freeman's record of 304 in 1928 is seriously challenged. On six occasions he took more than 250 wickets in a season. Seventeen times he took 100 wickets in a season—again second only to Rhodes—twice he took 17 wickets in a match, three times he took 10 wickets in an innings, and so on. Such figures tell their own story of consistently dangerous bowling over a long period of years.

Mention of Kent cricket 30 and more years ago conjures up a picture of "Tich" Freeman bowling, Ames behind the wicket and Woolley in the slips. Over and over that tiny figure—five foot two in height—would take a few, short paces to the wicket and with his easy action maintain an accuracy remarkable in a bowler of his type. He really spun both the leg-break and the googly, and had a dangerous top-spinner as well. As a batsman his achievements were few, but he played his part in the field. It is as a wonderful county bowler, however, that he will be remembered.

Alfred Percy Freeman was born at Lewisham on May 17, 1888, and in his early days played several club and ground matches for Essex, the county for whom his elder brother, J. R. Freeman played. He moved to Tonbridge in 1912 and two years later played his first match in the Kent county side. It was not, however, until after the First World War that he came to prominence. In 1920 he took 100 wickets in a season for the first time, two years later he took 194, and that winter he went to Australia and New Zealand for the first time with A. C. Maclaren's unofficial team. In 1924–25 Freeman returned there with A.E.R.Gilligan's M.C.C. side, but played in only two Tests and had little success as a bowler. His finest Test performance on that tour was, strangely enough, as a batsman when he scored 50 not out and took part in a ninth wicket stand of 128 with Frank Woolley.

Freeman had a much more successful visit to South Africa with the M.C.C. in 1927–28, when he played in four Tests and took most wickets on the tour. The following summer at home was his greatest, when apart from his triumphs in county cricket he took most wickets in the three Tests against the West Indies. In 1928–29 he went to Australia again under Percy Chapman, but this time played in no Test. Back home again, though, he was still a dominating force in county cricket and was England's most successful bowler in the Tests against South Africa, taking seven for 71 and five for 100 at Old Trafford.

In eight consecutive seasons from 1928 to 1935 he took over 200 wickets in a season, and among his many fine performances for the Players were his 13 wickets for 144 in 1929. Altogether he took 3,776 wickets at an average of 18.42.

In 1936 Kent decided not to reengage Freeman and in view of his exceptional services made him a special grant of £250 and continued to pay his wages until the summer of 1937. He had two benefits while with Kent. He subsequently accepted an engagement as professional to the Walsall club in the Birmingham and District League.

In 1949 Freeman was one of 26 stars of the past who were elected honorary life members of M.C.C. He leaves a widow and one son.

January 29, 1965.

Sir Henry French, G.B.E., K.C.B., a former Director-General of the British Film Producers' Association, and Secretary at the Ministry of Food during the Second World War, died on April 3, 1966.

After 11 years as Director-General, he became President of the British Film Producers' Association, and he retired in 1958.

He had had in the course of a long and specially active life two quite varied careers. For nearly 47 years he was a Civil Servant and then for more than a decade he was outstanding in the British film industry.

Henry Leon French was born in 1883, the third son of the late F. E. French, J. P., of Southsea, and was educated privately and at

King's College, London. He joined the Civil Service by open competition, and in 1901 was appointed to the then Board of Agriculture and Fisheries. Promoted to the first division in 1909, he became assistant secretary in 1920, and remained in that post until 1929, when he became principal assistant secretary. Five years later he was promoted second secretary at the Ministry, and in 1936 when it was thought necessary to be prepared for war, he became director of the food (defence plans) department. In 1939 he was appointed permanent secretary of the Ministry of Food and held office until a few weeks after the war ended. He retired from the Civil Service in the following year.

He had served as secretary to Viscount Milner's committee on the Home Production of Food in 1915, joint secretary to Lord Selborne's committee on Agricultural Policy from 1916 to 1917, general secretary of the Food Production Department from 1917 to 1919.

SPOKE FOR FARMING

He represented the United Kingdom and Canada on the permanent committee of the International Institute of Agriculture at Rome from 1930 to 1934. He attended the Ottawa Conference as Departmental Adviser in 1932 and during 1939–45 paid several visits to Canada, the United States, India, Australia, New Zealand, and South Africa. Even after leaving the food ministry officially, he was from time to time called in for consultations, and he did valuable work with Unesco.

He was a most modest man, tending always to decry his own work and to give credit to others. When, for example, he reviewed, in the columns of *The Times,* Mr. R. J. Hammond's second volume on the administration and control of food as part of the second volume of the history of the Second World War, he did not once mention the part he himself had played. As chief official of the Film Producers' Association, he brought to bear upon his duties all his powers of organization, drive and quiet persistence. His early years as Director-General were greatly concerned with the vexed issue of quotas as between the display of British and foreign films, and some of the tougher American negotiators found him equally tough in his handling of the various situations which arose. He was created a K.B.E. in 1938, advanced to G.B.E. in 1946 and was also a K.C.B.

He married first Clare, daughter of the late Charles Grimes, F.R.G.S., of Southsea, and they had one daughter. He married secondly, in 1929, Violet, daughter of the late G. R. Huntley, of Streatham.

April 4, 1966.

General Lord Freyberg, V.C., G.C.M.G., K.C.B., K.B.E., D.S.O., Governor General of New Zealand from 1946 to 1952, and Commander in Chief of the New Zealand Forces in the Second World War, died on July 4, 1963. He was 74.

Freyberg was a born fighter. He was wounded in action time after time without being seriously affected physically or at all in spirit. Sir Winston Churchill likened him to a salamander because he seemed to thrive in the fire, which was perhaps why he chose two salamanders to be his supporters in his coat of arms. Churchill has recorded that one day in the 1920s, when he was staying at a country house with him, he asked him to show him his wounds. He stripped himself, and Churchill counted 27 separate scars and gashes. To these he was to add, in the Second World War, another three.

In the First World War he rose to the command of an infantry brigade, and he was continuously in the line except when incapacitated by wounds. In the Second War, as a divisional and corps commander his fighting spirit was keen as ever. In action he commanded from the front line in order, as he said, to keep his finger on the pulse of the battle. His tactical headquarters in the North African campaign were in four Stuart tanks, and he liked sitting on top of one of his tanks in an exposed position where he could get a good view, often under heavy fire. He once remarked that being on a tank gave one a feeling of security, and, to one of his brigadiers who pointed out that it was neither very amusing nor very safe to make a trip up to him, he said, "Shelling doesn't hurt anybody".

CONCERN FOR HIS MEN

He was regarded by his men as a formidable character. But he won and retained their devotion, not only by sharing their dangers and discomforts, but by his humanity and his anxiety for their welfare. In the Battle of the Orsogna one platoon of 18 men refused to attack, a thing unheard of in the New Zealand Division. They were court-martialled, and received sentence of one to two years imprisonment. Freyberg held that their offence was not their fault, but that of their leaders; he suspended the sentences except that on the officer, and sent the men to different battalions to give them the chance to redeem their characters. On one occasion he recognized a battalion commander who had fought brilliantly and was being brought back wounded from the battle line; he jumped out of his car and embraced him and announced his promotion: "You're a brigadier."

His limitations as well as his merits were recognized by the higher authorities, and he was not promoted above the level which suited him so supremely well. He took the war very seriously, and he disapproved strongly of the enemy, particularly the Italians. When he took the surrender of the commander of the Trento Division after Alamein, he refused to shake hands with him, telling him that Italy had behaved very badly in entering the war against us.

Bernard Cyril Freyberg was born in London on March 21, 1889, the son of James Freyberg, of Wellington.

He was educated at Wellington College, New Zealand. In August, 1914, he was in California, and he came at once to England to volunteer for service. He had an introduction to Sir Winston Churchill, then First Lord of the Admiralty, and he was given a commission as sub-lieutenant R. N. V. R. in the Hood Battalion of the Naval Division, which he accompanied to Antwerp, where he was wounded.

Freyberg went to Gallipoli with his battalion as a lieutenant-commander, commanding a company. When Rupert Brooke died in a French hospital ship, Freyberg was one of his friends who carried him up to an olive grove in the island of Skyros and buried him there. Two days later he was awarded the D.S.O. for a particularly gallant action. His battalion was ordered to take part in a feint attack at Bulair, in order to distract the Liman Von Sanders' attention from the landings which were taking place elsewhere. On his own suggestion Freyberg was put into the water at night, two miles from the coast, and, painted brown for concealment, he swam ashore, towing rafts with oil flares and calcium lights. He lit the flares at several points on the beaches in front of the Turkish entrenchments, reconnoitred the enemy's position, and then swam back into the darkness. He was eventually sighted by the crew of a naval cutter and was hauled on board half dead from exhaustion.

THE VICTORIA CROSS

Towards the end of the Gallipoli campaign Freyberg decided to make the Army his career, and, in May 1916, he was gazetted a captain in The Queen's Royal West Surrey Regiment, remaining, however, with the Hood Battalion which he now commanded as a temporary lieutenant-colonel. The Royal Naval Division was transferred to France in time to take part in the Battle of the Somme, and he won the Victoria Cross for his conspicuous bravery and brilliant leadership in the operations at Beaumont Hamel. He carried the initial attack through the enemy's front system of trenches under particularly heavy fire. Then he rallied and re-formed his men, and, inspiring them with his own contempt of danger, led a successful assault on the second objective, and captured many prisoners. During this advance he was twice wounded, but he again rallied his men and held his position without support, under heavy fire, until the next day, when he led yet another attack on a strongly fortified village which he captured with 500 prisoners. In this operation he was again wounded, and, later in the afternoon, he was wounded a fourth time, on this occasion severely. But he refused to be carried back on his stretcher until he had issued his instructions for holding the position he had gained.

In September, 1918, he was awarded a Bar to his D.S.O. for most conspicuous bravery and devotion to duty in the operations near Gheluvelt, the success of which was largely due to his inspiring example. In the last few minutes of the war he gained a second Bar to his D.S.O. In addition to his other honours, he was mentioned in dispatches six times and was awarded the Croix de Guerre, and, in 1919, he was made C.M.G. He had been wounded nine times.

Freyberg's exploit at Gallipoli emphasized his prowess as a swimmer, and in 1925 and 1926 he made a number of attempts to swim the Channel. His best effort was in August, 1925, when, after swimming in adverse weather conditions from Gris Nez to within 500 yards of Dover, the tide turned and robbed him of the success almost within his grasp.

From 1929 to 1931 he commanded the 1st

Battalion, The Manchester Regiment, and from 1931 to 1933 was Assistant Quarter Master General at Headquarters, Southern Command. After two years as G.S.O. first grade in the General Staff at the War Office, Freyburg was promoted major-general in 1934.

BREAKDOWN IN HEALTH

He was next posted in India to command a district, but then his health broke down and he was invalided out of the Army in 1937. However he had recovered when the Second World War broke out, and he was recalled and appointed G.O.C. Salisbury Plain Area. In November, 1939, he was chosen to command the New Zealand Forces Overseas.

In the spring of 1941 he was in action again, when the New Zealand Division was sent to Greece and took up a position on the Aliakhmon Line to oppose the German southward drive on Athens. When the collapse of Yugoslavia and the disintegration of the Greek army made withdrawal inevitable, Freyberg conducted a succession of rearguard actions with great skill and stubbornness, and inflicted severe losses on the enemy; his New Zealanders played a vital part in holding up the Germans long enough to enable the British force to pass through the Larissa bottleneck.

His division was among those evacuated to Crete and provided its principal defence. When it was decided that the Allied troops in the island should be placed under a single command, Freyberg was chosen for the post, and he conducted the fight with the greatest gallantry and determination. But the struggle was a hopeless one. Our troops had lost their guns, equipment and transport in the evacuation from Greece, and our totally inadequate air forces could provide no defence against the massive attack launched by the German 11th Air Corps, the first large-scale airborne attack in the annals of war. Nevertheless Freyberg's hard and well sustained resistance broke the structure of the German Corps, which suffered, according to their own reports, "exceptionally high and bloody losses", and it never appeared again in any effective form. With the help of the Royal Navy he managed to evacuate more than half his force of 30,000 British and Imperial troops.

When it had been reconstituted, his division next took part in Sir Alan Cunningham's offensive in the Western Desert, in the course of which the New Zealanders captured Sidi Rezegh.

HEAVY LOSSES

In this operation the division suffered such heavy casualties that it had to be withdrawn. Freyberg expressed his strong disagreement with the conduct of operations by the Desert Command under Auchinleck, and in particular with the way the New Zealand Division had been handled. Having in mind his special responsibility to the New Zealand Government, he became firmly convinced, as he has recorded, that, at that time, "the only way to safeguard the interests of New Zealand and the Division was to get the Division away from the Desert Command". At his instance it was sent to Syria to retrain and reorganize, and it spent six months there until it was drawn into the line again, in June, 1942, after the loss of Tobruk, to take a share in stemming Rommel's advance on the Delta. In the first stand near Mersa Matruh, Freyberg was severely wounded, and the division was cut off and nearly lost; but, under General Inglis, it broke out and made a daring night march through the enemy's lines, and was soon deployed at Alamein where it played a gallant part in Auchinleck's defence.

Freyberg was back, with his wound almost healed, in time for Montgomery's great attack, and he and his division were in the thick of the fighting thoughout the advance to Tunis. It was Freyberg who carried out the decisive turning movement which decided the Battle of Mareth.

In November, 1944, the New Zealanders were moved to Italy and took part in the Battle of the Sangro, which was one of the bloodiest of the whole war; on its conclusion the division was transferred from the Eighth Army to the American Fifth Army on the other side of the Apennines. Freyberg was now given the task of taking Casino, where a first attack by the Americans had already failed. For this purpose he was put in command of a specially formed New Zealand Corps which comprised, besides the New Zealand Division, an Indian Division, an American Combat Group, and, later, a British Division. The German positions were immensely strong, and the defenders, who fought with remarkable toughness, were aided by the nature of the country, which consisted of knife-edge hills, rocky escarpments and deep ravines. Freyberg's difficulties were increased by the heaps of rubble left after the bombardment of the town and monastery on which he himself had insisted and which is now generally agreed to have been a tactical mistake. He conducted two gallant slogging attacks in February and March, and, although he failed in his object, he captured key positions which were of value in the final attack, which took place in May after his corps had been withdrawn.

GOVERNOR GENERAL

In 1945 he won a third Bar to his D.S.O.

During his tenure of the New Zealand Command he had won the confidence of the New Zealand Government and of the people to a remarkable degree, and his appointment as Governor General in 1946 was a popular one. For Freyberg himself there could have been no better preparation for his new duties than his close association with the men of the overseas force. Their division was regarded by the New Zealanders as "an outstanding example of democracy in action". Every officer had come through the ranks, and Freyberg was known to have taken a special pleasure and pride in this fact. During his six-year term of office he and Lady Freyberg won the warm affection of all classes.

On his return to England in 1952 Freyberg was appointed Deputy Constable and Lieutenant Governor of Windsor Castle.

He was created K.B.E. and K.C.B. in 1942 and G.C.M.G. in 1946. He was raised to the peerage in 1951. He was honorary D.C.L. Oxford, and honorary LL.D., New Zealand. In 1922 he received the honorary degree of Doctor of Law at St. Andrews University, at the same time as Sir James Barrie, who was his best man when he married in the same year.

His wife was Barbara, widow of the Hon. Francis McLaren, M.P., and daughter of the late Colonel Sir Herbert Jekyll. His heir is his only son, Major the Hon. Paul Richard Freyberg, M.C., Grenadier Guards.

July 6, 1963.

Robert Frost, the American poet, died in Boston on January 29, 1963, at the age of 88.

He was, without question, one of the most authentic poets of his generation, a nature poet of commanding integrity, an interpreter of country life of a stamp infrequent in modern American literature. A practical farmer in New Hampshire, he knew and loved the New Hampshire countryside with a quiet passion that was proof against all the temptations of conventional poetic utterance.

The seeming casualness and colloquial ease of his verse made it necessary for him to wait many years for recognition. Not, perhaps, the casualness alone; for urban life was beyond the range of Frost's interest or comprehension, and the full acceptance of "regional" American literature waited upon an adequate appreciation of his work. It was the New Hampshire forest and hillside, its farms and people, its country sociabilities and solitudes that he cared for and celebrated in an idiom of considered simplicity, drawing from familiar scenes an image of the potential beauty which men might wring out of life in the face of a prevailing materialism.

Scrupulous in his refusal to falsify or poeticize the essential quality of what moved him, his voice was at times so subdued that the subtlety of his psychological delineation did not save him from monotony. This is specially true of some of the longer poems of his earlier period.

But again and again the slow, slumbering vitality of his verse quickens into vivid life; while the shorter lyrics almost always glow with a rare inward warmth.

Robert Lee Frost was born in San Francisco on March 26, 1874, the son of William Prescott Frost, Jr., a Harvard-educated newspaper man from an old New England family, and Isabelle Moodie Frost, a Scottish-born schoolteacher. When his father died of tuberculosis 10 years later, the boy was taken east to the New England that was to become as essential to his life work as Mississippi to William Faulkner's or Dublin to James Joyce's.

Although he was a good scholar, particularly of Latin and Greek, which he read all his life, the poet stayed less than one term at Dartmouth College and later withdrew, after one successful year, from Harvard. In each case his leaving seems to have resulted from an independence of mind allied to his early and full commitment to poetry, which he had begun writing when he was 16.

His young manhood was spent alternately in teaching and farming, chiefly at Derry, New Hampshire. When he was 21 he married his high-school classmate, Elinor White, to whom many of his most personal lyrics, early and late, were dedicated. They raised four children.

Mrs. Frost died in 1938.

In 1912 the young poet, still almost unpublished and unknown, sold his New Hampshire farm and brought his wife and children and his poems to England where for three years he wrote and farmed, first at Beaconsfield, Buckinghamshire, and later at Ledbury in Herefordshire. He associated with many of the Georgian poets and formed a close friendship with Edward Thomas. His first two books of poetry, *A Boy's Will* and *North of Boston*, were published in London in 1913 and 1914 by the widow of David Nutt, and at the age of 40, after 20 years of almost unrecognized accomplishment, the poet found himself acclaimed on both sides of the Atlantic.

INFORMAL LECTURES

Returning to the United States in 1915, Frost resumed farming briefly but was soon engaged by Amherst College in the first of a long series of academic appointments in which his widely ranging mind and a genius for good talk brought continuing success. Among the American colleges and universities that laid special claim to him over the years were Yale, Harvard, Dartmouth, Middlebury, and Amherst. In recent years his teaching had become largely a matter of informal lectures in the course of which he would "say" some of his poems—a verb he used in preference to "read" as indicating the importance he attached to the speaking tone of voice in poetry.

Almost from the beginning of his published career he made a practice of "barding around" the country, as he called it. In recent years he was undoubtedly the most widely known and loved literary figure in America. In 1961 his reading took him to Israel and to the inaugural platform of President Kennedy where he read his poem "The Gift Outright". He spoke on many subjects. Often his remarks shed light on his poetic theories, which he wrote about reticently.

One of his convictions was that the rhythm of human feeling should contend with the fixed rhythmic patterns of verse. Two stanzas from a late poem on the subject of his own death show how gracefully he could accomplish this tension:

Don't think I leave
For the outer dark
Like Adam and Eve
Put out of the park.
Forget the myth.
There's no one I
Am put out with
Or put out by.

He held an almost mystical view of the efficacy of metaphor—"every poem is a new metaphor or it is nothing", he wrote—and his most significant statements were often clothed in homely figures like this: "Like a piece of ice on a hot stove, a poem must ride on its own melting."

He had many literary and academic honours. He won the Pulitzer Prize for poetry in 1931, 1937, and 1943. Resolutions were passed by the United States Senate on his seventy-fifth and eighty-fifth birthdays and the post of Consultant in the Humanities was created for him at the Library of Congress.

Independent of literary groups and movements, he knew almost all the writers of his day. In 1958 he was instrumental in securing the release of Ezra Pound from the mental hospital in Washington where he had been detained since the end of the war as unfit to stand trial for treason. "I feel authorized to speak very specially for my friends, Archibald MacLeish, Ernest Hemingway and T. S. Eliot", he wrote. "None of us can bear the disgrace of letting Ezra Pound come to his end where he is."

Robert Frost returned to England three times, in 1928, in 1957, when he received the degree of Litt. D. from Oxford and Cambridge Universities (as Longfellow had before him), and briefly on his return from Israel in 1961.

The 10 volumes of his verse were collected in "Complete Poems" in 1949. *In the Clearing*, his final book of lyrics, was published in 1962 and was generally acknowledged to be a strong addition to his mature work.

January 30, 1963.

Ruth Fry, a member of the Society of Friends, who died in London after a long illness on April 26, 1962, at the age of 83, was the last survivor of the eight children of the Right Hon. Sir Edward Fry, G.C.B., and Lady Fry—that remarkable family group which included Roger Fry, Margery Fry, Joan Mary Fry, and Isabel Fry.

Born on September 4, 1878, at Highgate, Anna Ruth Fry had what she later considered a somewhat unsatisfactory education, mainly at home. Among her early memories was her delight at being allowed to ride on the box seat of the carriage when on "First Day" morning the family drove down from Highgate to St. Martin's Lane to the Westminster Friends Mccting, which she first attended at the age of three.

After the Boer War she supported relief work to aid distressed Boer families and in 1906 was treasurer of the Boer Home Industries. At one time she acted as secretary to her father in his important work for international law; but it was not until 1914 that the work for which she is remembered began—her honorary secretaryship of the Friends' War Victims Relief Committee, which was being organized from a basement-room office near the Angel at Islington. In the next nine years the Committee sponsored a very considerable programme of Quaker relief work, notably in France, Serbia, Holland, Germany, Poland, Austria, Hungary, and Russia.

For one who was never in robust health the responsibilities of this work were overwhelming and even shattering; but the indomitable spirit characteristic of her family carried her through a programme which involved constant travelling in Europe in conditions of maximum difficulty, seeing the needs of the work at first hand. She paid three visits to Russia during the terrible famine of the early 1920s, and at some time visited every country to which the work extended. Besides this she spoke on relief needs at meetings in all parts of the British Isles and twice visited the United States, first in 1918 and again in 1923–24; on the latter occasion she addressed nearly a hundred meetings from the east to the west of America.

Ruth Fry recorded the story of these years of service to the war-stricken in her book, *A Quaker Adventure* (1926), to which Lord Cecil contributed the preface. After this date her activities were almost entirely confined to literary work; she used to say that her health had never fully recovered from the strain of the years of her relief service.

Both in her work and in her writings she dedicated herself to activities which she felt would express and promote the spirit of peace. She was a worker for the League of Nations idea and she was treasurer from 1936 to 1947 of the War Resisters' International, the body linking together conscientious objectors in all lands. From the home which she and her like-minded friend, the late Lady Gibb, made for themselves, at Thorpeness, Suffolk, for many years, she sent out a steady stream of peace literature and pamphlets, for the production and distribution of which she made herself responsible. She had correspondents among workers in peace movements all over the world.

A Quaker Adventure appeared in German in 1933 and in Danish in 1945; during the Second World War a shortened edition was produced to help in the training of relief workers. German and Swedish editions appeared of her attractive book, *Quaker Ways*, published in 1937. Her other writings include, besides many pamphlets, *From Campian to Lawes* (1914), *Life of Emily Hobhouse* (1929), *John Bellers, Quaker, Economist and Social Reformer* (1935), *The Whirlpool of War* (1939), *Everyman's Affair: A Plea for a Sane Peace* (1941), *Victories Without Violence* (1939 and various editions subsequently, including one in Bulgarian), and *Three Visits to Russia* (1942).

April 28, 1962.

Major-General John Frederick Charles Fuller, C.B., C.B.E., D.S.O.—"Boney" to the Army—who died on February 10, 1966, at Falmouth, at the age of 87, was a soldier of original and unorthodox type.

Professionally, his outstanding contribution was to armoured warfare in the First World War, but he will be longer remembered as a writer. Had he been less testy and capricious, his influence might have been greater than it was, since he would always have been arresting. It was, however, considerable and, ironically, most of all in Germany, where it helped to shape commanders and ideas prominent in the Second World War.

His favourite general was probably the Federal leader in the American Civil War, Ulysses S. Grant, to whom he devoted a volume and whom he linked with Lee in another. In the second his prejudice, his major fault, especially if combined with interpretation, appears all too obviously; while Grant can hardly put a foot wrong Lee behaves on occasion like a fool.

His virtues were manifold. He "went into history" to exploit and expound his ideas, and this he did magnificently. His critical armoury was superb; his gift of description very good; his understanding of character shrewd—except when anger raised smoke between him and his subject. He was one of the most eminent of modern military writers, if not the most.

One quality he did not profess: kindliness in his ink. In the Second World War, when the tide had well turned, his journalism fell off; "Boney" had no more tops to whip. Over his later work, including the fine three-volume work on decisive battles, there broods something loftier and sadder than the earlier acerbity; dismay and horror, fear lest the world should be moving into the grip of a single global tyranny. Here his many-sided highmindedness took another form, that of fierce denunciation of mass slaughter. He loathed brutality. His most damning verdict was: "He is a thug". One of his last published books was *The Generalship of Alexander the Great*, an amazing effort on the part of a man who had no Greek, makes fascinating reading and was kindly received.

He was born at Chichester, the son of the Reverend A. Fuller, on September 1, 1878, and educated in Switzerland and at Malvern before entering Sandhurst. In August, 1898, he was commissioned in The Oxfordshire and Buckinghamshire Light Infantry and embarked for South Africa with the 1st Battalion before the end of 1899. There he served throughout the war, for the last six months as intelligence officer with native scouts. He was promoted to captain in June, 1905. After Volunteer and Territorial adjutancies and a spell of regimental duty, he passed into the Staff College in 1913 and was still a student at the outbreak of war in August, 1914.

His service began with junior administrative and staff appointments at home, and he did not go overseas until July, 1915, when he became G.S.O.3 on the staff of the VII Corps in France. He received his majority in September of that year. In February, 1916, he went to the 37th Division as G.S.O.2 and in July to the headquarters of the III Corps in the same capacity. At the end of the year he became G.S.O.2 of the Tank Corps, then camouflaged under the name of Heavy Section, Machine-Gun Corps, and devoted himself to tank organization and tactical training. He was in no sense one of the parents of the tank and had not even seen one before August, 1916, but was now a member of a remarkable group of relatively junior staff officers, active, intelligent, and far sighted, who accomplished great work in the cause of the new weapon. Intellectually, he may have been the foremost. Without underestimating the value of the tank in flattening wire obstacles, he regarded it as above all a moral weapon, as it became.

TRIUMPH OF THE TANK

In April, 1917, he was appointed G.S.O.1. In July, 1918, he went to the War Office as Deputy Director of Staff Duties in a special tanks section. He held that appointment for four years, the period of the triumph of the tank in war and the experiments in mechanization in the postwar Army. For services during the war he received the D.S.O. in 1917, the brevet of lieutenant-colonel in January, 1918, and the brevet of Colonel a year later, and was twice mentioned in dispatches. He reached the substantive rank of Colonel in August, 1920.

In January, 1923, Fuller came from halfpay to be chief instructor at the Staff College, where he spent three well-filled years. In February, 1926, he was selected by Sir George (later Lord) Milne, Chief of the Imperial General Staff, as Military Assistant. In this promising appointment he was, however, deeply disappointed because, largely owing to financial restrictions, the drastic changes in weapons and equipment necessary for the creation of a mechanized army such as he envisaged were not forthcoming. In April, 1927, he became G.S.O.1 at Aldershot, and then commanded brigades on the Rhine and at Catterick. In September, 1930, he was promoted Major-General. However, he rather too scornfully refused the command of the Bombay District, was not again employed, and retired in December, 1933. He had been created C.B.E. in 1926 and C.B. in 1930.

In 1935–36 he spent some months of the Abyssinian War with Italian forces. He was now in an unhappy phase of flirtation with Fascism, which seems to have been due to high-mindedness having taken a wrong turning. Thence forward for another generation books came steadily from his pen. Nearly all were historical, but he showed how brilliant he could be theoretically in *On Future Warfare*, in parts astounding as a vision of what was to come.

Fuller married Sonia, daughter of Dr. Karnatzki, of Warsaw, in 1906. He leaves no children.

February 11, 1966.

Thelma Lady Furness, who in 1930 introduced Mrs. Simpson to the Duke of Windsor, who was then Prince of Wales, collapsed and died in New York on January 29, 1970. She was 65.

The meeting, according to the Duchess of Windsor, took place at the Furness's house at Melton Mowbray. It was an introduction not without irony for Lady Furness's own friendship with the Prince, which she later described in the book of reminiscences which she and her twin sister, Mrs. Vanderbilt, published under the title of *Double Exposure*, was generally believed to be extremely close. The Duchess of Windsor in her book *The Heart has its Reasons* remarks: "I was aware that Connie's sister, Thelma Viscountess Furness, was greatly admired by the Prince of Wales and was widely reputed to be the object of his interest."

Lady Furness and her twin sister, prominent and glamorous figures in high society in London in the 1920s and early 1930s, were the daughters of Harry Hays Morgan, sometime American Consular-General at Buenos Aires. Thelma, after her marriage to James Converse had ended in divorce, married the first Viscount Furness, the shipping magnate, in 1926. His first wife had died five years earlier.

Gay, elegant, and good company, she was one of the Prince's circle in which Americans were always prominent; he was reacting from his English background in which a certain deference was bound to be present and to inhibit give and take of conversation; the Prince's American friends, among them Lady Furness, had a naturally free and easy manner which the Prince found highly attractive.

In *Double Exposure* Lady Furness describes how she met the Prince for the first time when she and her husband were guests at Londonderry House, the home of Lady Londonderry, one of the great hostesses of the time. By her account they met again at a county show when he invited her to cocktails at St. James's Palace. Subsequently they often dined and danced in London. They met again while she and Lord Furness were on safari in Africa and the Prince was staying at Government House, Nairobi; in the South of France, and at weekends at Fort Belvedere.

She was granted a divorce from Lord Furness in 1933. He died in 1940 and was succeeded by their son, the present Viscount Furness.

January 31, 1970.

G

Yuri Gagarin, the first man to make a successful flight into space, died in an aircraft crash on March 27, 1968. He was 34.

One hundred and eight minutes on April 12, 1961, in the front of the Soviet multi-stage rocket, Vostok 1, turned an unknown 27-year-old Soviet Air Force officer into "The Columbus of the Interplanetary Age" or, as Mr. Khrushchev pointedly put it at the wildly enthusiastic reception given to Gagarin in Moscow, "the first Soviet swallow in the cosmos".

Discarding their usual impersonal style, the Soviet radio and news agency mentioned Gagarin's name in the 30 words or so of the historic announcement "that the road to the planets was open". While honours and congratulations from statesmen showered on Gagarin; painters and sculptors promised to portray him; and a street and a new-born child were named after him; it was a young man with a typical Soviet *curriculum vitae* who was undergoing medical tests to ascertain the effects of his extraordinary journey.

The son of a collective farmer, he was born on March 9, 1934 in the Gzhatsk district in the Smolensk region of the Russian Federation.

GERMAN INVASION

The first two big events in his life occurred within two weeks of each other in 1941; he started school and the Germans invaded Russia.

His hometown lay directly in the path of the Nazi invaders, and three months later the future spaceman and his parents joined the stream of refugees fleeing eastwards. His elder brother and sister were less fortunate. They were deported by the Germans—but eventually freed by Soviet troops. When the war ended, Gagarin went back to secondary school, and later to a vocational school at Lyubertsy, near Moscow, where he graduated with honours as a foundryman in 1951.

From early childhood he had shown a love of adventure and of flying in particular. One of his favourite authors was the nineteenth century science fiction writer Jules Verne. As is often the case at technical schools, he also attended evening classes in arts subjects. He then entered an industrial college at Saratov on the Volga, graduating with honours in 1955.

FLYING CAREER

He began his flying career while still a student, taking a course at the Saratov aero club. After he had finished this course in 1955 he entered the air school at Orenburg. He had been a pilot since 1957.

It was at 0758 (BST) on April 12, 1961, that Tass announced that the first man had been put into space. Moscow radio interrupted its programmes to give the news. The sequence of events and the reports from Gagarin quoted by the radio were:—

0707. The spaceship weighing 4,725 kilograms (about $4\frac{1}{2}$ tons) was launched by rocket into an elliptical orbit with greatest height 187 miles and least 109 miles. The inclination of the orbit to the Equator was 65 deg. 4 min. The period of revolution was 89min. 6sec.

0722. Gagarin reported by radio that he was over South America and said: "Flight is proceeding normally. I feel well.

0815. Gagarin reported over Africa. "I am withstanding state of weightlessness well." He also reported over Asia Minor.

0825. The spaceship's braking system was put into operation and Gagarin began his descent.

0855. The spaceship landed safely and Gagarin said on landing: "Please report to the party and Government and personally to Nikita Khrushchev that the flight was normal. I feel well. I have no injuries or bruises. The completion of the flight opens new perspectives in the conquering of the cosmos".

While in flight Tass said that Gagarin carried out direct two-way "cosmos-earth" radio communications for the first time in history by means of short and ultra-short waves.

A special correspondent of *Izvestia*, who was at the landing place, reported that the landing had been an excellent one: Gagarin had not waited for a helicopter. Instead, he walked out to meet the people who had spotted him in the sky. That he seemed in prime condition was clear from the historic press conference he gave in Moscow the day after his flight had been completed. There were the customary polite remarks about the party and the government, thoughts of whom apparently kept Gagarin from feeling lonely while in the upper airs, but there was also a vivid description what it had felt like to go right round the great globe itself and what he had seen from his unique point of vantage.

Though much that he then said has since become common knowledge through succeeding space flights his impressions reread have, even in translation, a certain magic about them that suggests that though a most un-Keats-like man he felt much as Keats felt (in a very different situation) "...like some watcher of the skies when a new planet swims into his ken".

"The day side of the earth was clearly visible", he said. "The coasts of continents, islands, big rivers, big surfaces of water and structural features were clearly distinguishable.

"During the flight I saw for the first time with my own eyes the earth's spherical shape; you can see its curvature when looking to the horizon. I must say that the view of the horizon is unique and very beautiful.

"It is possible to see the remarkably colourful change from the light surface of the earth to the completely black sky in which one can see the stars. This dividing line is very thin, just like a belt of film surrounding the earth's sphere. It is of a delicate blue colour and this transition from the blue to the dark is very gradual and lovely. When I emerged from the shadow of the earth, the horizon looked different", Gagarin continued. "There was a bright orange strip along it, which again passed into a blue hue and once again into a dense black colour.

"Everything was easier to perform. Legs and arms weighed nothing." Objects swam about inside Vostok's cabin and he sat suspended above his chair in mid air, gazing in admiration at the beauty of the earth while floating in a black sky.

"I ate and drank and everything was like on earth." He said he had no feeling of loneliness, adding that he could have spent much longer in the spaceship but the duration of the flight had been fixed in advance.

After the press conference the full-scale hero's welcome in Moscow, where there was a good deal of hugging and kissing with Mr. Khrushchev and the bestowal of honours: Hero of the Soviet Union, Order of Lenin, Pilot Cosmonaut of the Soviet Union (newly minted), and Honoured Master of Sport.

LONDON WELCOME

Soon afterwards he visited Prague and Sofia and in July arrived in London to a rapturous welcome. Great crowds surrounded him wherever he went and everyone wanted to shake him by the hand. He took luncheon with the Queen, had a talk with the Prime Minister, Mr. Macmillan, and flew to Manchester to be made an honorary member of the Foundryworkers Union who presented him, a former moulder, with a gold medal inscribed: "Together moulding a better world."

On all these public occasions Gagarin, without conscious effort, won friends; he was a nice-looking young man, which was a good start, and he had an engaging manner, but at the long press conference which he held on his arrival in London and at later sessions he showed that he was no empty-pated handsome hero; he handled awkward questions skilfully and when asked about the difficulties of being a celebrity he spoke up with great feeling and sincerity: "I am still an ordinary mortal", he said, "and have not changed in any way."

The warmth of Gagarin's reception in London, the first western country he visited after his flight, caused a good deal of worried comment and criticism both at home and abroad. In America, Germany and Switzerland it was interpreted in some circles as showing moral and intellectual softness, gullibility and possible lack of the fibre necessary to meet the approaching Berlin crisis. Probably there were a number of elements behind the enthusiastic welcome. Foremost, was simple admiration for a brave pioneer; then there was his undoubted charm which went to the heart of crowds but which had not a jot of political significance. Undoubtedly there was also an element of longing which exists among ordinary people on either side of the iron curtain for opportunities to break through the rigidities of the cold war and make contact with the other side.

Gagarin visited many other countries in the years after his space flight including India, Egypt, Czechoslovakia, Canada, Argentina, Brazil and Cuba.

It is thought that he never made a second flight, though he played a major role in preparing and training other cosmonauts. He was for several years commander of the Soviet Cosmonauts' Detachment but later handed this post over to Andriyan Nikolayev, who spent almost four days in space in August, 1963, aboard Vostok 3.

Gagarin was last seen in public in Moscow in December when he attended the opening night of a Moscow season by the Royal Shakespeare Company. It was while he was training at the air school at Orenburg that he met an attractive medical student, Valentina, who later became his wife. Their second daughter, Galya, was born shortly after his first space flight.

March 29, 1968.

Félix Gaillard, the former leader of the Radical Socialist Party in France, who died in a yachting accident at sea in July, 1970, was in 1957, at the age of 38, the youngest Prime Minister under the Third and Fourth Republics. This was the crowning of a dazzling political career, which began at the age of 27, when he was elected member of parliament, and was cut short by the return to power of General de Gaulle.

Félix Gaillard was a man to whom everything in life seemed to come easily and effortlessly. He cultivated an almost Anglo-Saxon nonchalance and detachment, and was amused by the political ambition displayed by others. A brilliant pupil, he was also an exceptionally gifted student, reaping every conceivable diploma and academic distinction.

A man of profound culture, he was by instinct and conviction a conservative. In recent years, he had played a discreet role in politics, and distinguished himself as a critic of his party's attempts, within the framework of the Federation of the Left, to cooperate with the Communists. But he continued to exercise considerable influence within it as the leader of its "liberal" wing. He was not much in sympathy with the attempts of Jean-Jacques Servan Schreiber, the dynamic and controversial new secretary general of the party, to give it a new revolutionary image; but he felt his manifesto might provide the basis for a new regrouping of the non-Communist reforming forces in French politics.

Félix Gaillard was born in Paris on November 5, 1919, the son of a company director. A doctor of law by the age of 20, he also came out first in the difficult competition for the Inspection des Finances. After a distinguished career in the resistance, he became the assistant at the end of the war to Jean Monnet, then Commissioner for the State Plan. In 1946, he turned to politics and became the mayor of Barbezieux and the following year was returned to parliament for the Charent, being uninterruptedly reelected for that department until his death.

His government, in which Chaban Delmas, the present Prime Minister, held the portfolio of national defence, marked the end of the Fourth Republic. It lasted only six months, and fell in April, 1958, over the affair of American and British good offices in the bombardment by the French air force of the Tunisian village used by the Algerian rebels as a base.

The return of General de Gaulle to power in May marked the elimination of Gaillard from office and his retirement from active politics, though he became president of the Radical Socialist Party in 1958, and held the post until 1961. He took an active part in the short-lived attempt to create the "Grand Federation" of the Centre and non-Communist left under Gaston Deferre, the Socialist Mayor of Marseilles. It was inevitable that he should oppose the subsequent attempt of the Federation of the Left to achieve a working partnership with the Communists. Though he disliked the revolutionary aspects of Servan Schreiber's manifesto, especially with regard to death duties, he felt the attempt to breathe new life into the moribund party, which had dominated French political life during the first 50 years of the Third Republic, was worthy of support. He was not averse to the possibility of cooperation with the Gaullist majority.

He married in 1956 Dolores Patenôtre, a widow, by whom he had four children.

July 13, 1970.

Hugh Gaitskell, who died on January 11, 1963, at the age of 56, had been Leader of the Labour Opposition in the House of Commons since December 14, 1955.

Political integrity was the most precious quality which Hugh Gaitskell brought to the service of the Labour movement. It fortified him to endure electoral defeat, the defection of associates, and much misunderstanding over his attempts to modify the party's constitution. In particular it endowed him with the courage to master the crisis which came to him in October, 1960, when the party conference rejected the official policy on defence, and declared for the unilateral renunciation of nuclear weapons. His resolve "to fight and fight and fight again", to rescue the movement from what he deemed to be perilous courses, awoke sharp conflict within it, offering a serious challenge to his leadership. He emerged from the struggle with his authority unassailably established within a party to which he had restored cohesion and confidence. The drift to disintegration was halted. His skill and patience were rewarded by the steady reversal of the unilateralist trend, borne on a massive swing of trade union opinion. The climax came at the 1961 party conference. The earlier decision was overturned by almost a ten-fold majority, a victorious testimony to the transformation which Gaitskell had wrought. In the process he had immensely enhanced his reputation and had made a powerful impact on the public consciousness as a man possessing the authentic attributes of leadership—resolute will, robust courage, resilient spirit and wise judgment.

SWIFT RISE TO EMINENCE

His bearing throughout these testing times was a triumph of the qualities of mind and character which had carried him on his swift ascent to eminence in his party. He came to the leadership with the biggest majority ever recorded, barely 10 years after he had entered the Commons. He acceded to the office of Chancellor of the Exchequer at the age of 44, one of the youngest men to do so. Almost from the start of his political career he had displayed a rare talent for lucid exposition and swift mastery of economic subtleties, political judgment and administrative skill. All these came to steady maturity in the successive offices he held, first as Parliamentary Secretary to the Ministry of Fuel and Power, then as Minister in charge of the Department, and later as Minister of State for Economic Affairs and as Chancellor.

Seldom did Gaitskell serve his cause better than during the 1959 general election. He impressed on the public mind the image of a man of transparent sincerity, intellectual eminence, and warm humanity. The response he evoked nourished in him an optimism which was to be bitterly falsified. But the manner in which he met the crushing of his hopes was a model of dignity and fortitude. He addressed himself briskly to the task of reappraisal. More than once he had persuaded his party to expose cherished political ideas to what he called the "clean, fresh wind of hard and fearless thinking".

BOLD COUNSEL

And he embarked on the task again. He boldly counselled a reexamination of the party's 40-year-old constitution. In particular he questioned the adequacy of the familiar "Clause 4" on common ownership to express party aims in the context of modern needs and conditions. His attempts to achieve a reshaping of the clause itself were doomed to founder, and they stirred currents of misunderstanding and criticism which, with the conflict over nuclear defence, threatened to erode the position as leader which he had so steadily built up before and during the election. But he gradually reasserted the balancing control which had carried the party through many convulsions. In fair weather or foul he kept true to the ideals which had brought him into the labour movement.

Hugh Todd Naylor Gaitskell was born on April 9, 1906, the son of Arthur Gaitskell, an official in the Indian Civil service. He was educated at Winchester and New College, Oxford, where he gained a first class in Philosophy, Politics and Economics. He joined the Labour Party during the General Strike while still at the University. After he had gone down he became a W.E.A. lecturer in the Nottingham coalfield and later Reader in Political Economy at London University. On the outbreak of war he became principal private secretary to Hugh Dalton, then at the Ministry of Economic Warfare, and was also put in charge of the German Intelligence Branch. Dalton quickly recognized his qualities and took him with him to the Board of Trade. He was returned as Labour member for South Leeds in the 1945 election and was created a C.B.E. in the same year.

MINISTER OF FUEL AND POWER

Few were surprised when as early as May, 1946, he was appointed Parliamentary Secretary, Ministry of Fuel and Power. He soon proved himself a highly competent assistant to Shinwell, and the brilliant coherence of his speeches in the House established him as a parliamentarian of more than average ability. When Shinwell was transferred to the War Office in October, 1947, Gaitskell succeeded him. The miners' leaders bitterly opposed Shinwell's departure and some of them felt that his successor ought to have had practical experience at the coal face.

Gaitskell exercised an increasing influence on the economic thinking of his party, and in March, 1950, he became Minister of State for Economic Affairs. He enjoyed the equivalent of Cabinet rank and acted as Deputy to the Chancellor during Sir Stafford Cripps's frequent absences abroad. Gaitskell was on a mission to North America when Cripps's resignation was announced in October, 1950. Attlee's offer of the Chancellorship to Gaitskell and his acceptance were conveyed by transatlantic cable.

Thus at the age of 44 he became the youngest Chancellor of the Exchequer since Austen Chamberlain's appointment in the Balfour Administration of 1903. He found himself the focus of lively speculation. None could doubt his ability, but it was impossible to ignore the brevity of his ministerial experience or of his active association with party affairs. Faint misgivings at his swift accession might have been forgiven to those older men more deeply involved in the movement's early struggles, and he knew he must tread delicately. The grim economics of defence, looming against a sombre international backcloth, thrust on him the recurrent need to warn the nation of the price which might have to be exacted.

CONTROVERSIAL BUDGET

It was under these dire compulsions that Gaitskell had to frame his Budget. He may have paused to glance at a report of a speech in which Aneurin Bevan, Minister of Labour, declared he would never be a member of a Government which made charges on the National Health Service for the patient. That was on April 3. A week later Gaitskell, in a speech justly acclaimed as a remarkable parliamentary performance, had produced a Budget effecting that very thing. And within a fortnight Bevan had resigned, together with Harold Wilson, President of the Board of Trade, and John Freeman, then Parliamentary Secretary, Ministry of Supply, and even better known since as editor of the *New Statesman* and for his

"Face to Face" interviews on B.B.C. Television. The conflict extended beyond the immediate issue of the health service charges as such.

When a Conservative Government came into power in October, 1951, the facade of unity erected for electoral purposes between Bevanism and the rest did not long stand the strain of conflicting views.

Appetites for political excitement were stimulated during the summer of 1954 by the news that both Gaitskell and Bevan had accepted nomination for the treasurership of the party in succession to the late Arthur Greenwood.

BEVAN OUT

In the autumn Gaitskell was elected with 4,338,000 votes to Bevan's 2,032,000. Bevan lost his seat on the executive, of which Gaitskell now became an ex-officio member, the first time he had ever sat on it.

Dissensions still rent the party when they were faced with a general election in May, 1955. The Conservatives increased their majority from 17 to 60, and Gaitskell lost no opportunity of pressing home the lessons of the Labour defeat. Constant public attacks from within on the party's official policy and leadership, he said, were a luxury they could not afford if they were to present themselves as an alternative Government.

Gaitskell was reelected treasurer at the party conference at Margate that October with 5,475,000 votes to Bevan's 1,225,000. In another sense this conference was significant for Gaitskell, a sort of climacteric. Rarely hitherto had he commanded the power to kindle emotion or flash vivid images on the mind's eye. He had left that sort of thing to Bevan. But at Margate some warmer element in his nature found release. His account of the influences which had nourished his socialist faith and practice aroused the delegates to almost ecstatic fervour. This was the answer to any who might still confuse Gaitskell with the "desiccated calculating machines" of Bevan's oft-quoted gibe.

Early in December, 1955, Clement Attlee announced his retirement from the leadership of the party and accepted an earldom. The choice of his successor lay between Morrison, Bevan and Gaitskell. The day after Attlee's resignation was made known the political dovecotes were briskly fluttered. Bevan, at the suggestion of a group of Labour members, offered to withdraw his candidature, to permit the unopposed election of Morrison, if Gaitskell would do the same. Gaitskell, however, although he had the highest regard for Morrison, believed the party should have the chance of choosing its leader.

Their choice was Gaitskell. He topped the poll with 157 votes; Bevan got 70 and Morrison 40. Thus Gaitskell was elected on the first ballot with a clear majority over the other two. He was 49. His success reflected, apart from recognition of his merits, the desire of many who otherwise would have voted for Morrison, to place youth at the helm of a boat which had been rocked too often.

In the autumn of 1956 he was reelected leader of the party with no challenge from Bevan, who became treasurer. Meanwhile the Suez affair moved to its climax—the rejection of the ultimatum and the Anglo-French intervention. At each stage Gaitskell's forceful, challenging spokesmanship for the Opposition—and for a wide public opinion outside—enhanced his reputation. But he made a tactical move which some regarded as of doubtful political wisdom when in a broadcast he offered a remarkable pledge to Conservative M.P.s who had doubts about their Government's policy. He gave an undertaking on behalf of the Opposition to support a new Prime Minister in halting the invasion of Egypt and in complying with United Nations decisions. In the Commons he was steadily strengthening his hold on the leadership of the Labour Party by his handling of their case. This showed itself in striking manner on that November day which was to be memorable for other reasons. Some hours before Eden announced the cease-fire, Gaitskell interrogated the Government on the situation. When he had ended his questioning Labour members rose in a body to cheer him, thus discharging in public a debt which had been paid in private at a party meeting earlier in the day.

Gaitskell went to Harvard early in 1957 to deliver the Godkin lectures, a statement of Labour foreign policy later published under the title *The Challenge of Co-existence*. His stay in America was cut short by news of Sir Anthony Eden's resignation and soon he was facing a new Prime Minister with whom he was to have many encounters over summit talks with Russia and testing nuclear weapons. The activities in subsequent months of the "Victory for Socialism" group, which enjoined unilateral renunciation of nuclear weapons, forced on Gaitskell and his colleagues the need to close the ranks of the party behind a clearly defined policy commanding wide support. This he claimed for a joint Labour Party-T.U.C. statement issued in March, 1958. With a general election not too far distant, he solemnly warned his supporters that victory would be seriously jeopardized if divisions and disputes broke out again.

ELECTION DEFEAT

In the ensuing year the trend of international affairs persuaded the Labour leaders of the need to think out afresh their party's foreign policy, and the result was a new joint declaration issued in June, 1959, which advanced a plan for a "non-nuclear club" of all nations except Russia and America. It came under heavy criticism from some Labour quarters but the effect of this challenge was to consolidate all but the left-wing elements behind Gaitskell and his Shadow Cabinet.

When the date of the election of October, 1959, was announced Gaitskell was on a visit to Russia with Bevan at the invitation of the Soviet Inter-Parliamentary Group, and they returned at once. The differences between the two men had yielded to an increasingly closer accord since the days of the Suez crisis.

The enthusiasm Gaitskell encountered among party workers during his election tour convinced him that Labour were going to win. But he had misread the portents. As the results came in during the night of October 8 it became more and more plain that the tide was carrying the Conservatives home. Just before one o'clock the next morning, with many more results still to come, Gaitskell conceded victory to his opponents. It was an unprecedented gesture but a realistic one. In fact, the Conservatives won an overall majority of 100 seats. Gaitskell took his party's defeat with the same dignified composure which had carried him through the campaign. It was neither a landslide nor a disaster, he said. It was just a setback. The time for self-examination and rethinking had come, and the occasion fixed for it was a weekend party conference at Blackpool.

With characteristic courage, Gaitskell opened the debate. This was a supreme test of his leadership, and he shirked nothing—not even a suggestion for revising the party's 40-year-old constitution. Having quoted the famous passage about the common ownership of the means of production, distribution and exchange, he said that, standing on its own, it could not possibly be regarded as adequate, implying as it did that common ownership was not a means but an end. His speech chilled some delegates and infuriated others, and in succeeding weeks rumour was busily questioning whether he had endangered his personal position in the party.

By the time that Gaitskell clarified his revisionist ideas in a notable speech at Nottingham in mid-February, 1960, there had been time for resistance to develop within the party. Trade union opinion built up against any rewriting of Clause 4. The National Executive Committee bowed to the inevitable and in July decided that the clause would not be touched at the party conference.

THE DEFENCE STORM

The argument over Clause 4 had shaken party unity but a graver threat to it and to Gaitskell's leadership developed over defence. Pressure for unilateral nuclear disarmament made itself increasingly felt. By early June, according to a calculation in *Tribune*, there was a tally of 2,553,000 trade union votes against nuclear arms and 1,047,000 against unilateral nuclear disarmament. Need for a clarification of Labour defence policy had become imperative, and later in June a new policy statement emerged. Endorsement of the policy by the parliamentary party coincided with a remarkable demonstration of loyalty to Gaitskell as leader, but the antinuclear trend gathered momentum. When Labour Party delegates assembled for their conference at Scarborough that October the portents for Gaitskell and his policy looked gloomy. On the eve of the defence debate the A.E.U. delegates decided to swing the decisive weight of their vote against the official statement of policy the next day.

There seemed little doubt that Gaitskell was doomed to a resounding defeat. But when his turn came to reply to the defence debate he counter-attacked his critics with an eloquence, fire and dialectical skill which confounded those who had predicted his eclipse. He pledged his parliamentary supporters and himself to "fight, and fight, and fight again to save the party we love". There was a majority of 297,000 against the official policy statement. The Transport

Workers' motion rejecting any defence policy based on the threat of nuclear weapons was carried by a majority of 43,000 and the A.E.U. motion demanding the unilateral renunciation of the testing, manufacture, stock-piling and basing of all nuclear weapons in Britain got a majority of 407,000.

LEADERSHIP ISSUE

Gaitskell's determination to fight for the reversal of the conference decision filled some members of the party with fears that the consequence would be 12 months of "civil war". It was with the declared intention of preventing this and of preserving the unity of the party that Harold Wilson reluctantly offered himself as a candidate for the leadership, having been pressed to do so by party members of disparate views. The ballot in the parliamentary party swept Gaitskell to victory by 166 votes to 81, impressively confirming his authority in the party and giving weighty endorsement of his challenge to unilateralism.

In February, 1961, a new version of the defence policy which had been defeated at the October conference was approved by the National Executive, the T.U.C. General Council and the Parliamentary Labour Party. It was plain that the tide against unilateralism was turning. It flowed more strongly in Gaitskell's favour as the months passed. More and more trade unions turned away from their unilateralist commitments, and by mid-June the massing of votes had reached a tally which assured Gaitskell of victory. Thus he went to the party conference in October to garner the fruits of it. He saw the redrafted official policy carried by a majority of 2,770,000 votes. It was an astonishing transformation and a notable triumph of pertinacity, personality and character. Under his leadership the party which a year earlier had been divided and disheartened was mastering its dissensions and gathering its forces for more militant tactics against a Government which had run into a troublous period.

ANTI-COMMON MARKET

The issue of Britain's entry into the European Economic Community presented Gaitskell with a delicate task, and his cautious approach to it exposed him to the charge of sitting on the fence. During 1962 he steadily resisted demands that his party should declare itself for or against, and was content for many months to play a waiting game. Then in September, 1962, he delivered a nation-wide television and radio broadcast which contained the sharpest criticism he had yet permitted himself of the terms for entry so far as they were yet known. It was a highly persuasive performance, but it was eclipsed by the masterly speech with which he dominated the Labour Party conference less than a fortnight later. For all its safeguarding clauses, it left a general impression of mounting the most formidable anti-European case which had yet come from any British politician. One of his most telling points was that for Britain to go into a federal Europe would mean the end of a thousand years of history. He got a standing ovation and overwhelming support for the National Executive's policy statement as a basis for preserving party unity. But he was careful to preserve his party's freedom of movement within the context of the guarantees for which he had always contended. Gaitskell had greeted 1962 as a year of opportunity for Labour. Certainly nobody had done more to make that prospect possible.

Gaitskell is survived by his wife, Anna Dora, daughter of Leon Creditor, whom he married in 1937, and by two daughters.

January 12, 1963.

William Gallacher, from 1935 to 1950 Communist member of Parliament for West Fife, and president of the British Communist Party from 1956 to 1963, died on August 12, 1965.

Until the general election of 1945 "Willie" Gallacher, as he was known to political friend and foe alike, was the only Communist M.P. Then he was joined for five years by "Phil" Piratin, who sat for Mile End, and Gallacher thus became leader of a party of two. Both lost their seats at the general election of 1950.

In spite of his extreme views, Gallacher made few enemies. He was ordered by the Speaker more than once to withdraw from the Commons for disorderly conduct and un-Parliamentary remarks, but he left little rancour behind. He was a consistent critic of the monarchy, and on the occasion of the marriage of the Queen spoke against the motion for a congratulatory address and protested against what he termed the "lavish expenditure" involved. He had been imprisoned four times for his political activities.

For all the wildness of his oratory when he was on his feet there was much that was likable about Willie Gallacher. He had a lively sense of humour and the fanatical communist in him was agreeably leavened by this ingredient. Sometimes it was difficult to believe that this amusing little Scotsman could be at the same time a dedicated communist, as he was. Even though he often got the House of Commons by the ears he was nearly always quickly forgiven.

MELLOWED

His experience at Westminster—where he sat through two Parliaments opposite Churchill—seemed to have mellowed even Gallacher. In the end he won quite a niche for himself in the esteem of the House of Commons.

The fourth of seven children, Gallacher was born on Christmas Day, 1881, of an Irish father and a Highland mother. He was educated at Paisley Elementary School but forsook his studies at the age of 12. He had done an early-morning milk round since he was 10, but his first full-time job was that of a grocer's delivery boy. While in this employment he made his first stand against unpaid overtime. Next he became an engineer's apprentice, signed on as a ship's steward during a spell of unemployment, and was shipwrecked on his first voyage.

Gallacher's introduction to politics was through the temperance movement, but he soon passed on to the Social Democratic Federation, which, in 1921, merged into the Communist Party. He became a member of the Communist International, as well as member of the executive committee of the British Communist Party.

In 1924, and again in 1935, he served on the executive committee of the Communist International.

During the First World War he was an ardent opponent of militarism, and was vociferous in his agitation against the "capitalists" in the "class struggle". After visiting the United States and Ireland he became the leader of the workers in the Glasgow Albion Motor Works. He was elected to the executive committee of the United Brass Founders' Association, and chairman of the Clyde Workers' Committee. He told the story of the activities of this committee and the story of the struggles on the Clyde during the 1914–18 War in his autobiography *Revolt on the Clyde*.

His first term of imprisonment was in 1917, when he was sentenced to 12 months for his political activities. He also served terms of three months' imprisonment in 1918, three months in 1921, and 12 months in 1925. On the latter occasion he was charged, with other leading communists, at the Old Bailey with sedition, and served his sentence in Wandsworth Gaol.

STOWAWAY TO MOSCOW

His contacts with Russia and the Soviet leaders were close and cordial. In 1920 he went, as a stowaway, to Moscow to attend the second congress of the Communist International. There he met Lenin. On his return he took part in the final negotiations for merging a number of left wing organizations in the United Kingdom into the British Communist Party. In the 1930s he was a staunch supporter of the "hunger marchers", and paid visits to Spain in the Republican interest during the Spanish Civil War. But in the Second World War he was in some difficulty in trying to follow the vagaries of the "party line."

He was the unsuccessful communist candidate for West Fife at the general elections of 1929 and 1931, but won the seat in 1935, defeating the late "Wullie" Adamson, who had been Secretary of State for Scotland in the second Labour Government. He held the seat in 1945 with a majority of 2,056 in a three-cornered fight, but in 1950 he was at the bottom of the poll.

He was more than once refused a visa for the United States, but managed to go there in 1946. In the summer of 1963 an American visa issued for him to visit a sister who was ill in Chicago was withdrawn, but after public pressure both in the United States—the *Washington Post* was sharply critical of the State Department—and in Britain had been exerted the visa was restored. In 1948 he visited Prague, where he was awarded the Order of the Slovak Rising, first class, and he went on to Budapest, where he received the Cross and Star of the Hungarian Order of Merit.

His publications included, in addition to *Revolt on the Clyde*, *The Rolling of the Thunder*, and *The Case for Communism*.

He married, in 1913, Jean Roy.

August 13, 1965.

Amelita Galli-Curci, who died on November 26, 1963, at the age of 81, was a soprano singer who won fame and wealth by virtue of voice alone.

American authorities who knew her work at the Chicago Opera in the years between 1916 and 1932 testify that she was like Caruso in possessing a voice that even the early gramophones with acoustical horns could not prevent from sounding natural, though they also say that the beauty of her florid singing was bought at the price of faulty intonation and deficiencies of rhythm and phrasing.

She was born in Milan in November, 1882, and studied the piano at the conservatoire there to such effect as to graduate with a first prize in 1903. Her singing was self-taught—another tribute to the natural quality of her voice. She made her first operatic appearance in 1909. In 1916 she went to America where she remained for the rest of her life. The Metropolitan Opera in New York persuaded the Chicago Opera in 1925 to share her services, and she made her debut in New York in the title role of Meyerbeer's *Dinorah*. The fact that *Lakmé* was another of her favourite operas indicates by its famous "Bell Song" the kind of singer she was. London never heard her in opera. She toured Britain in 1924 and her last concert there was at the Albert Hall in 1934. By that time her singing, never very strong in characterization, had become so slick that it was all tonal charm and flexibility without shape or line, so that everything sounded much-of-a-muchness, "an agreeable but unmusical flow of liquid sound", as it was described at the time. She was thus the old-fashioned type of Italian singer with a wonderful voice and the ability to use it without effort or strain but with not much else in spite of her early musical training.

November 28, 1963.

Captain Henrique Galvão, leader of the handful of Iberian exiles who seized the Portuguese liner Santa Maria in January, 1961, and held her for a week, died in June, 1970.

Originally conceived as the beginning of a venture that was to put in revolt Spanish as well as Portuguese territories in West Africa, Operation Dulcinea, as Galvão called it, petered out in a blaze of publicity and a confusion of outrage and laughter. Galvão's account of it sold widely in several languages. But although its mixture of bravura and impudence was typical of Galvão's pawky humour and remarkable enterprise, to be remembered for this escapade alone would not do him justice. He was a talented administrator who rose to high rank before his conscience impelled him to speak out against abuses in Portuguese colonies at a time when they might have been put right without catastrophe.

Henrique Carlos de Malta Galvão was born in 1895. His father, well-connected but not well off, died when he was a child and he was brought up by his mother and paternal grandfather. A talented but difficult child, Henrique ran away from some schools and was expelled from others. He chose the army as a career as the quickest way to relieve his mother's financial troubles. At the national military school he had an outstanding academic record and a score of penalties for insubordination.

Galvão soon found an outlet for his vast energy in the colonial service in Africa. He became successively a provincial governor, director of fairs and exhibitions, director of the national radio and finally, in 1937, high inspector of colonial administration, charged especially with the study and control of native affairs.

For 10 years as high inspector he presented increasingly critical reports on native conditions, without seeing any results. The reputation he had won in 1926 put him in a strong position, but he became increasingly impatient with Salazar and the system developed in Lisbon.

VIOLENT WORDS

In 1946 he consented to be "elected" a deputy again; 11 years after he had first served as a deputy. A year later he produced at a closed session a violently worded report of conditions in Africa; a year later he covered the same ground in an interpellation to the Government—the first time any major criticism of the regime had had a public airing in Parliament. An investigation by a judge was ordered, but its findings were never published. Galvão's public career was doomed. In 1950 he completed his term as deputy and resigned from the office of high inspector. He tried to organize a legal opposition during and after the presidential election of 1951, and at the beginning of the next year he was arrested on charges of subversion and sentenced to three years' imprisonment, 15 years' loss of political rights and loss of pension. Then he spent three years in four separate prisons and a hospital while a new case was prepared against him, partly on the basis of statements he had had smuggled out of prison. In 1958, just before Delgado ran as opposition candidate for president Galvão was sentenced to 18 years' imprisonment at a secret trial in his absence. Then he escaped. In 1959, he climbed out of the bathroom window of the prison hospital, walked along the sills outside, and made his way out by the back stairs. He was at large for a month, and then turned up at the Argentine Embassy disguised as a porter, and was given asylum.

Delgado was then in the Brazilian Embassy. After he and Galvão had both been flown to South America, Galvão tried to join him, but was kept out of Brazil. He went to Venezuela instead and, although he found the émigrés there disappointing, he cooked up Operation Dulcinea with a handful who seemed to him worthy of their salt. In January, 1961, they boarded the Santa Maria at Curaçao and, although there were only 24 of them, successfully took over the ship. One ship's officer was killed, and the gaff was blown when Galvão put into port to land another man who had been injured. Surprise, essential to the west African venture, was lost. There followed a ludicrous few days while Galvão waited for the accession of the new President of Brazil, Señor Quadros, before putting into Recife, handing over the ship, and accepting asylum.

There was not much he could do after dealing this painful blow to Lisbon's prestige. He was a prohibited immigrant in Britain, the United States and half of Latin America. In November he managed to divert an airliner over Lisbon for long enough to drop leaflets urging the people to tear up their papers in the general election. He was arrested in Morocco and expelled. He was arrested again when he arrived in Brazil, where President Goulart had taken over from Quadros, and finally allowed a conditional asylum in the state of Belo Horizonte. He was turned out of Delgado's liberation movement for his "self-dramatization". In February, 1962, a special court in Lisbon added 22 years' imprisonment for the Santa Maria affair to the 17 years outstanding on his last account.

June 26, 1970.

Eric M. Gamage, chairman and managing director of A.W.Gamage, Ltd., the Holborn department store, died in a London hospital on June 10, 1964. He was 78.

He resigned the chairmanship of the firm after the closure of Gamage's new store in the West End in 1931 but was reappointed 10 years later.

He was the son of Albert Walter Gamage, the seventeenth son of a Herefordshire farmer, who with a fellow drapery assistant, Frank Spain, founded the firm by opening in 1878 a small hosiery shop in Holborn with a 5ft. window space.

Eric Muir Gamage was born in February, 1886, and educated at Bradfield. He joined the firm in 1904 at the age of 18 but it was not his father's intention that the boy should be merely "the boss's son" and so, after a spell in the stockrooms, he was sent abroad to widen his experience and his horizons. He spent some some time in factories in France and Germany before returning home.

Gamage joined the R.N.V.R. in the First World War in which he was severely wounded.

It was while serving in the Hood Battalion that he met Rupert Brooke and in a letter to *The Times* published less than a month ago he described how he and Brooke, making the most of a short leave before embarking for service in Gallipoli, walked together some 20 miles through the night to Salisbury to catch an early milk train to London. Later on Skyros, on the day before Brooke was taken seriously ill, they had luncheon in the olive grove where the poet now lies buried.

June 11, 1964.

Air Vice-Marshal Sir Philip Game, G.C.B., G.C.V.O., K.C.M.G., D.S.O., died on February 4, 1961, at his home at Sevenoaks. He was 84.

His was a distinguished and highly diversified career for he had held high rank in the R.A.F., been Governor of New South Wales, and finally Commissioner of the Metropolitan Police.

Philip Woolcott Game, the son of George Beale Game, of Barn House, Worcestershire, was born on March 30, 1876. He was educated at Charterhouse, and after passing through the Royal Military Academy, Woolwich, in November, 1895, received his commission in the Royal Artillery. He was promoted captain in 1901, and that year saw his first active service in South Africa. During the years that followed the South African War Game passed through the Staff College at Camberley, and in 1910 won the gold medal for the prize essay of the Royal United Service Institution. In 1914 he was a Major and a G.S.O.2, and in that capacity went to France; within a few months he won a D.S.O. and was promoted temporary Lieutenant-Colonel. Early in 1916 the Royal Flying Corps was undergoing reorganization. Up to that time Air Chief Marshal Sir Robert Brooke Popham had been G.S.O. 1 at the headquarters of the Corps. When he became D.A. and Q.M.G., Game was sent to him to give the benefit of his experience of staff work. The excellent work that he did in organizing the growth of the Corps revealed the administrative ability that he was later to display in very different conditions.

A.O.C. IN INDIA

He remained on the staff of the R.F.C. and was later finally transferred from the Royal Artillery to the staff of the R.A.F. and rose to be temporary Brigadier-General. Shortly before the Armistice he commanded the South-West Area of the R.A.F. with the rank of acting Major-General. He had been mentioned five times in dispatches from France and was made C.B. In 1919 he joined the Air Ministry as Director of Training and Organization, and in 1922, being then an Air Vice-Marshal, he was appointed Air Officer Commanding the R.A.F. in India. A year later he returned to the Air Ministry as Air Member for Personnel. In January, 1929, at his own request, he was placed on the retired list and was made G.B.E.

At the close of that year Admiral Sir Dudley De Chair's term of office as Governor of New South Wales expired, and Game, in his 55th year, was appointed to succeed him, and he reached Sydney in May of 1930.

The grave economic depression was beginning, and by the end of the year he found himself in conflict with the Labour Prime Minister, Mr. Lang, on constitutional matters. It is sufficient now to recall that Lang was seeking to abolish the Upper House and requested the Governor to agree to the appointment of between 40 and 50 Labour nominees to the Chamber. This the Governor refused to do on the strictly constitutional ground that no Government measure had been rejected by the Upper House. A similar request was again refused in March, 1931, on which Lang proposed to telegraph to the Secretary of State asking for the Governor's recall. Wiser counsels, however, prevailed and that proposal was shelved.

LANG'S DEFEAT

As the result of further negotiations 25 new appointments to the Upper House were made in the following November. But the quarrel broke out again with even greater violence in May, 1932, when the Lang Government issued a confidential circular to the heads of state departments instructing them not to pay money into the Commonwealth Bank in compliance with the Federal law. The Governor requested Lang to withdraw the circular, holding it to be illegal, and on his refusal peremptorily dismissed him. An attempt to challenge the Governor's action in the House of Commons met with no success, and at the General Election in New South Wales the following month it received the overwhelming support of the electors and Lang's party suffered a crushing defeat.

After this matters went more smoothly, and when in January, 1935, his term of office expired, Game left New South Wales amidst general public regret.

Game was appointed to his new office of police Commisioner in June, 1935, in succession to Lord Trenchard, and was to take over his duties on November 12 of that year, but an accident to his knee postponed this until the beginning of December. Within a few weeks came the funeral of King George V, the organization of which taxed the powers of the Scotland Yard authorities to the utmost, and (through no fault of Game's) were the subject of some criticism. On that day the Commissioner must have recalled another funeral 35 years before in which he had played a small part, too, for on February 2, 1901, as a Royal Artillery officer of 24, he had been in charge of the gun-carriage that bore Queen Victoria from Windsor Station to St. George's Chapel, when one or more of the horses became so restive that it was impossible to proceed, and the horses had to be taken out and Blue Jackets substituted.

CONTROLLING LONDON CROWDS

Game realized clearly the difficulties of the control of large crowds that modern facilities of transport bring to the Metropolis on state occasions and where the weakness of previous control lay, and as a result he at once got together the officers concerned with traffic matters and evolved with them the scheme of crush-barriers, the merits of which were demonstrated with complete success at the Coronation of King George VI the following year.

The office of Commissioner of the Metropolitan Police is perhaps one of the most difficult, and certainly one of the most thankless in the sphere of public administration, and in the history of that office there can have been few more difficult periods than the one when it was filled by Game. Apart from Fascist and Communist demonstrations and riots, the I.R.A. bombs and the shooting by one MacMahon in July, 1936, at King Edward VIII, which subsequently proved to be only an attempt (which did not succeed) to frighten him, for two years previous to the outbreak of the World War its shadow required the preparations for organizing the police on a new footing in combination with all the problems of air raid precautions.

When war came, the Commissioner himself visited the more stricken districts during the worst of the London air raids, sometimes during the raid itself, and the dangers that he was impervious to were often a source of anxiety to his subordinates. With the force he was extremely popular. Early in his Scotland Yard days he had to face the problem of the Police College at Hendon, the creation of his predecessor with the idea of attracting young men from the universities and elsewhere directly to the Police Force.

As may be supposed, the scheme was by no means popular with the rank and file, and Game saw that as then constituted it would not work. He therefore required all candidates before entry to serve for one year on the streets, but before this method had been given a fair trial war broke out and the college was closed. Another of his predecessor's reforms, the short service system, he found, for reasons too technical to be entered upon here, was not working satisfactorily and had to be abandoned. Game's very human qualities were never shown better than in his personal relations with the force as a whole. He relinquished his commissionership in 1945.

He married in 1908 Gwendolen Margaret, daughter of the late Francis Hughes-Gibb. There were of this marriage two sons and one daughter.

February 6, 1961.

Mary Garden, the operatic soprano, who died on January 3, 1967, in Aberdeen at the age of 89, had a distinguished career in America and on the Continent, though not in Britain. Indeed she was commonly regarded as an American, though she was of British birth, because her chief work was done in Chicago. Her principal claim to fame, however, was that she created the part of Mélisande in Debussy's opera *Pelléas et Mélisande* at its first production at the Opéra-Comique on April 30, 1902.

Born at Aberdeen on February 20, 1877, Mary Garden was the daughter of a Scottish doctor and an American mother. When she was six years old her parents settled in the United States, living for a time at Chicopee, Massachusetts, and Hertford, Connecticut, before moving to Chicago in 1888. Her musical training began early, for at the age of six she was learning the violin and when only 12 years old she appeared on the concert platform. She learned the piano too, and did a little amateur acting, appearing at Chicago in *Trial by Jury*. It soon became evident that she had a talent for singing.

The death of her parents proved to be a turning point in her life, for, left to get her living, she went to France to become a governess in a well known French family. While in Paris she met Gustave Charpentier, in whose opera *Louise* she was destined to make her first appearance, the success of which was so great, in spite of her defective French, that it always remained a favourite with her. She studied singing under Trabadello, Fugère and Chevalier, and made her first appearance at the Opéra-Comique in 1900. She was an artist who leapt from obscurity to comparative fame in a night for she was called upon at a moment's notice to act as substitute for Mlle. Rioton who was taken ill in the third act of *Louise*. She continued to play the part for 100 nights. Later in the same year she created the role of Marie in *La Marseil-*

laise and in 1901, that of Diane in *La Fille de Tabarine*. The following year she played at the Opéra-Comique in the revival of *Manon*. Subsequently came her appearance in *Pelléas et Mélisande*, in which she was succeeded a few seasons later by Maggie Teyte. While she was the "star" of the Opéra-Comique her other outstanding performances were in *La Reine Fiamette*, *Thaïs*, *Aphrodite*, and *Cherubin*.

NEW YORK DEBUT

Her debut in the United States was made at Manhattan Opera House, New York, in November, 1907, under Oscar Hammerstein's management, as Thaïs in Massenet's opera. She stayed at the Manhattan for three years until 1910 when she became a member of the Chicago Opera Company with which almost the whole of her subsequent career was spent.

In 1921 she was appointed general director of the Chicago Grand Opera Company with complete control over both the artistic and business sides of the undertaking. She was thus the first prima donna ever to hold such a position, from which she resigned in the following season. In 1952 she published her memoirs in association with Louis Biancolli and in 1958 at the age of 80 she made a film dealing with her career.

January 5, 1967.

Sir Alan Henderson Gardiner, the leading British Egyptologist, died at his home in Oxford on December 19, 1963, at the age of 84.

As a schoolboy at Charterhouse, Gardiner had already determined that he would devote his life to the study of ancient Egypt, and in this determination and in the steps he took to fulfil it, he revealed that single mindedness which was to distinguish his whole working life. He found encouragement for his plans in his father, Henry John Gardiner, chairman of Bradbury, Greatorex and Co., Ltd., who enabled him to spend a life fully devoted to scholarship, free from financial worries and always able to promote those schemes dearest to his heart.

After leaving Charterhouse and before proceeding to Oxford, Gardiner followed up his private study of the ancient Egyptian language by spending a year at the Sorbonne working with the eminent French Egyptologist Sir Gaston Maspero. At the Queen's College, where he was a classical scholar, he read Arabic and Hebrew, taking a first class in the Final Honours School.

Almost immediately after going down from Oxford, and after his marriage to Hedwig, daughter of Alexander von Rosen, a King's Councillor of Hungary, Gardiner went to Berlin to join in the great enterprise, organized by the Berlin Academy, of publishing a *Wörterbuch* of the Egyptian language. Until 1911 he spent the greater part of every year working in Berlin or in the great collections of Egyptian antiquities in Europe, copying texts for the *Wörterbuch*. He always looked back on this period as most important for his development as a scholar; for it was then that he learnt the importance of discipline in scholarship. He then also had the privilege of meeting and working with the great German scholars who, at that time, formed the most brilliant school of Egyptology in Europe.

During these years at Berlin Gardiner's published work was not considerable, but it indicated clearly the special interests which were to inform all his subsequent labours. In *The Inscription of Mes* (1905) he studied a difficult legal inscription, paying particular attention to precision in linguistic interpretation as well as to reasoned interpretation of the substance of the text. In *The Admonitions of an Egyptian Sage* (1909) he published a didactic text of great obscurity. This book was a landmark in the treatment of hieratic literary texts: in it new standards were set for the transcription of the hieratic script and for the careful elucidation of the meaning of words.

The special interests and techniques which he had developed in his early years were concentrated and brought to fruition in his *Egyptian Grammar* which was published in 1927. This great work, now in its third edition (1957), remains the standard study of Middle Egyptian. Gardiner adopted an approach to the language fundamentally different from that favoured by continental scholars, who concentrated on grammatical forms and neglected interpretation.

GRAMMAR STUDY

He constructed his *Grammar* as a practical, progressive study, by which the student is led to a recognition of Egyptian grammatical forms and instructed in the determination of meaning as far as it is possible to do so in dealing with a language still imperfectly understood.

Of the many books published by Gardiner after his *Egyptian Grammar*, all added to his reputation, but none more than his two volumes on the Chester Beatty papyri (literary and other texts of the New Kingdom, all but one of which are now in the British Museum), his *Wilbour Papyrus* (1941–48), a study in three volumes of a cursive hieratic administrative document in the Brooklyn Museum, and his *Ancient Egyptian Onomastica* (1947), an examination of ancient Egyptian word-lists. The last, incorporating the knowledge of a life-time, is a masterly exercise in lexicographical technique, rich in wisdom and sound common sense. His last major work, *Egypt of the Pharaohs* (1961), published when he was over 80, is an unconventional history of Egypt in which special attention is paid to written sources.

In his long and fruitful career Gardiner was actively involved in, or closely associated with, many important projects—the publication of Theban Tombs, the study of the Coffin Texts, the work on the Temple of Sethos I at Abydos, the interpretation of the Protosinaitic script (in which he made the earliest and most significant discoveries), the publication of the Tomb of Tutankhamun. He standardized the transcription of the hieratic script; he established new principles for the publication of texts. Through his father's munificence, he sponsored the making of a new and particularly beautiful hieroglyphic fount of type, first used for the printing of his *Grammar*.

Throughout his life Gardiner was inspired by an unswerving devotion to his chosen study. With a clear idea of what he wanted to achieve and a freedom of action resulting from financial independence he was able to pursue his purpose with assurance. At times his independence led him to do things which antagonized friends and colleagues but it may be said that he always acted for the good of Egyptology, as he understood it.

In his private life, on which he never allowed his studies to impinge, he was a devoted father. He loved physical exercise, being more than a competent lawn tennis player; he travelled extensively; he played the violin with enthusiasm and found much consolation in music towards the end of his life. He enjoyed good food and good wine, loved entertaining people he knew well, and had a sharp, somewhat wicked, humour. He is survived by his widow and by two sons and one daughter.

December 21, 1963.

James Garfield Gardiner, P.C., who died in hospital on January 12, 1962, was for more than 40 years a very prominent figure in Canadian politics and his name will long be remembered in western Canada.

Born on November 30, 1883, at Farquhar, Ontario, the son of Scottish parents, J. C. and Elizabeth Gardiner, who lived afterwards for a period in the United States, he received his early education at Thames Road public school in Ontario, and schools at Lincoln, Nebraska, United States, and Clearwater, in Manitoba. Choosing teaching as his profession, he attended the Normal School at Regina, Saskatchewan, before proceeding to the University of Manitoba, where he graduated B.A. in 1911.

After a spell of teaching in western schools he took up land near Lemberg in Saskatchewan and became a farmer, and, taking an active interest in politics on the Liberal side, was in June, 1914, elected in a by-election to the provincial legislature. In it he soon made his mark as a competent debater and, after being reelected in the provincial elections of 1917 and 1921, he was appointed Minister of Highways and Minister in charge of the Bureau of Labour and Industries in the provincial Government which Charles Dunning formed in April, 1922.

He became Dunning's chief lieutenant and when the former moved to Ottawa to join the Federal Cabinet there was no serious challenge to Gardiner's claim to succeed him as Premier of Saskatchewan. Taking office in February, 1926, he gave his province efficient and progressive government, but the unscrupulous methods of a powerful political machine, which he built up, and abuses in political patronage developed under it antagonized so many voters that the Gardiner Ministry was defeated in a provincial election in 1928. Thereafter he spent five years as the vigilant leader of the opposition in the provincial legislature, until he was returned to power in 1934.

Shortly afterwards, however, Mackenzie King, having regained office through the Federal election of 1935, needed to find in western Canada a new Minister of Agriculture and he induced Gardiner to resign his Premiership and join his Cabinet in this role. So, after being elected to the Federal Parliament, Gardiner during the long regime of the Liberals, which lasted for 22 years until 1957, administered the affairs of the Department of Agriculture with conspicuous success. As a practical farmer he had an informed knowledge of agricultural problems and, while some of his policies were severely criticized, he had the confidence of many of the leaders of the farmers' organizations and was a staunch supporter of the cooperative wheat pools of the prairie provinces. A resolute opponent of protective tariffs, he was regarded as the leader of the left wing of various Liberal Cabinets, but he had no liking for socialist adventures and always remained a rugged individualist.

FORMIDABLE DEBATER

A ready speaker with a fine command of forceful language, he was one of the most formidable debaters on the Liberal front bench and was the Minister who could deal most effectively with the attacks of the redoubtable Lord Bennett when the latter was leading the Opposition at Ottawa. Small in stature, Gardiner was a bundle of fire and energy and he was an unbending political partisan, who believed with Coke of Norfolk that "Tories had been born bad and grew worse", and he never forgave the C.C.F. for driving the Liberal party out of power in Saskatchewan. But, while he was never popular with his political opponents, "Jimmy" Gardiner, as he was always called, was highly respected by them as an honest public servant who treated them fairly.

From July, 1940 to June, 1941, he held a special portfolio of National War Services and he was appointed to the Imperial Privy Council in 1947 as a reward for his services. In 1948 he was a candidate for the leadership of the Liberals, when King decided to retire from the field, but the more conservative elements in the party decided Mr. St. Laurent was a better choice. Defeated in the general election of 1958, he lived quietly on his farm in Saskatchewan.

He held honorary degrees of LL.D. from the universities of Manitoba and Ottawa.

He was thrice married, first in 1912 to Etta Gardiner, secondly in 1917 to Violet McEwen, and, after her death in 1944, thirdly to Mrs. Maud Christie in 1946. From his second marriage he had two sons and two daughters, and his eldest son, Edwin, an airman, was killed in 1942 in the assault upon Dieppe.

January 13, 1962.

Erle Stanley Gardner, who died on March 11, 1970, at the age of 80, was probably the world's best-selling writer of mystery stories. More than 170m. copies of his books were bought in the United States and Canada alone.

The exploits of his lawyer-detective, Perry Mason, have been translated into at least 16 different languages and became a highly successful television series. His fortyfifth crime story, *The Case of the Amorous Aunt*, was published in Britain in 1969.

Gardner was born in 1889 at Malden, Massachusetts. His father was a mining engineer and the family soon moved West covering the mining areas from the Klondyke to northern California. Young Gardner was a keen boxer and it was a reprimand from the district attorney for taking part in an illegal prize-fight which first attracted his interest to the law.

After working, and studying court-room technique, in a succession of law offices, he was admitted to the California Bar in 1911.

His early clients were mostly local Chinese who had got into trouble with the police; in those years he learned both the tricks of his trade and his love of fighting for the under-dog. After an unsuccessful flirtation with commerce between 1916 and 1918, he opened a new law office in Ventura, California; now he had partners and a much more lucrative class of work but it was still the challenge of a trial which appealed to him.

Two years later he began writing in his spare time, a stream of Westerns, thrillers, "true confessions", hunting and fishing articles, and pieces about archery, which was his favourite hobby: but not until 1933 did he find his perfect formula. In that year be brought his publisher two books, *The Case of the Velvet Claws* and *The Case of the Sulky Girl*; their hero was a trial lawyer, Perry Mason, assisted by a faithful secretary, Della Street, and a credible private detective, Paul Drake.

Through the scores of Perry Mason stories which followed, Gardner never changed his original pattern by a hair's breadth. The best of them always had a court-room climax, most of them contained neat legal twists, none of them had much characterization or description: the illusion of fast action was created by a narrative consisting largely of curt dialogue.

Gardner produced his effects with an exemplary economy of effort and, within the popular American idiom, court-room pyrotechnics have never been more entertainingly presented.

During the 1930s, he was writing over a million words a year, while still practising law.

CRIME STORIES

Under the pseudonym of A. A. Fair, he began a second series of light crime stories about a disbarred lawyer, Donald Lam, who joined a detective agency run by the mountainous and avaricious Bertha Cool. A third series, the "D.A." books about a small-town district attorney, was rather less successful.

Everything Gardner wrote was informed with his passionate concern for fair play in the administration of justice. He followed the developments of forensic science and was a welcome member of many police associations. He was responsible for a reappraisal of evidence which saved a convicted man, William Lindley, from execution.

During a trip to Baja California Harry Steeger, the magazine publisher, asked him, if he ever again came across such a real-life drama, to investigate it on behalf of *Argosy* magazine. The two men then devised "the Court of Last Resort", a committee headed by Gardner and consisting of a specialist in forensic medicine, Dr. LeMoyne Snyder, a famous private detective, Mr. Raymond Schindler, and a polygraph operator, first Mr. Leonarde Keeler, then Mr. Alex Gregory: but the true "court" was to be the American public. This unorthodox group investigated a substantial number of cases and succeeded in remedying several serious miscarriages of justice.

Gardner was a man of very great physical energy. While getting through a vast parcel of work, he entertained generously at his ranch home and travelled widely, accompanied as a rule by a whole train of secretaries, drivers, assistants and their families.

He was married in 1912 to Natalie Talbert, who died in 1968; they had one daughter. He married secondly Mrs. Bethell, his secretary.

He gave much pleasure to an inestimable number of readers: and he stood always for those good causes, simple and democratic and individualistic, which go straight to the hearts of the American people.

March 13, 1970.

Judy Garland, the film star and singer, who made her name as a child actress in 1939 in *The Wizard of Oz*, was found dead in London on June 22, 1969. She was 47. Few stars of her era gained more, or suffered more, from the mercurial quality of their temperament. She had an infectious charm, a buoyant and irresistible vivacity and an unmistakable talent both as a singer and as a film actress; but she was in many ways neurotic, her home life was disturbed by a mother who often tried to drive her too hard, and although Louis B. Mayer, the head of M.G.M., was her mentor, and immensely proud of her, he never really understood her. Her separation from M.G.M. and Mayer in 1950 was a sad affair.

In her last years she was often seen in cabaret in London. There were some rapturous receptions but there were also times of tears and temperament and to those who remembered her in happier days she was now something of a tragic figure.

Judy Garland's real name was Frances Gumm. She was born in Grand Rapids, Minnesota, in 1922. As a child she was part of her mother's vaudeville act, billed as The Gumm Sisters. The mother played the piano, and Frances and her two older sisters sang. The performance was not very good, but in 1935 Louis B. Mayer chanced to see them and was taken by this fat little girl of 11 with the buoyant personality. Mayer, at this time, was beginning to concentrate on developing child stars (who enabled him to present his favourite theme of the homely American family), and he had already made a major discovery, in the young Mickey Rooney. Then he found Deanna Durbin, whom he decided to team with Judy Garland in a short musical film called *Every Sunday*. Both girls showed promise, but by some mischance Deanna Durbin's contract was not renewed and M.G.M. lost her to 20th Century-Fox. Mayer was so angry that he ceased to take an interest in Judy Garland, who was lent to 20th Century-Fox for a college musical called *Pigskin Parade*, in which she sang "It's love I'm after" in a snowy football stadium.

MUSICAL TRIBUTE

Little might have come of all this had not Mayer decided some time later to give a birthday party in honour of one of his favourite stars, Clark Gable. M.G.M.'s songwriter, Roger Edens who had great faith in Judy Garland's talents, decided to compose a special number for the occasion, called "Dear Mister Gable", which Judy sang at the height of the festivities. By the time she had finished it, her reputation was made. She was hurriedly given a part in the current M.G.M. production *Broadway Melody of 1938*, and then partnered with Mickey Rooney in *Thoroughbreds Don't Cry*. They made a good team, and were partnered again—this time in one of the Andy Hardy series which Mayer, with his devotion to American family life, always held to be the best thing which the studios did. In *Love Finds Andy Hardy* Judy Garland played "the girl next door" to Andy, and a delighted Mayer welcomed her into the fold of his special child stars.

But even then luck was to play an important part in her career. When *The Wizard of Oz* was first planned the producer, Mervyn Leroy, wanted Shirley Temple to play the part of Dorothy, the young Kansas farm girl who visits the wonderful land of Oz, and there encounters the Scarecrow, the Tinman, and the Cowardly Lion. But Shirley Temple was not available, and so the part was given, on Mayer's advice, to Judy Garland. Jack Haley played the Tinman, Ray Bolgar the Scarecrow, and Bert Lahr the Cowardly Lion. The film did not get off to a good start, but when a new director Victor Fleming was brought in, the elusive mood of fantasy was happily created. Judy Garland sang "Over the Rainbow" enchantingly—a number by which she will always be remembered, and one which was very nearly deleted from the film in its cutting stage.

This was at the beginning of the war. Judy Garland marked its end with another notable musical, *Meet Me in St. Louis* in which her singing of "The Trolley Song" was almost as memorable as "Over the Rainbow". The film was admirably directed by Vincente Minnelli, and the cast included Margaret O'Brien, another child star of remarkable talent.

CLASH WITH M.G.M.

The Clock, *Ziegfeld Follies*, *The Harvey Girls*, *Easter Parade* (in which she sang "Easter Bonnet" with Fred Astaire), *Words and Music*, and *Summer Stock* followed. Then came the break with Louis B. Mayer. The clash had been foreseeable for some time. Judy had suffered a serious breakdown in 1949, and had been forced to retire from *Annie Get Your Gun*, already half-completed. There had been trouble again during the filming of *Summer Stock*, with Gene Kelly, but the picture was finally finished. After this she was due to make *Royal Wedding* and *Showboat*, but by then she was a mentally sick woman, and she appeared in neither. Mayer had by now lost patience with her, and he even went so far as to quarrel violently with M.G.M.'s most promising young producer, Joseph Mankiewicz, when he tried to help Judy. The result was that Mankiewicz left M.G.M. and so did Judy Garland. The father of his studio was not a man who would tolerate being crossed.

This was in 1950, and it was not until nearly five years later that Judy Garland was seen again on the screen. Then Warner Brothers decided to remake an old classic of the 30s, the story of a film star's decline and fall entitled *A Star is Born*, which had originally rescued Janet Gaynor at a moment when her career seemed almost over. Judy Garland played the Gaynor part and James Mason that originally created by Fredric March, but the film lacked the strength and heart of the original film, and Judy herself showed that she had lost something of her youthful exuberance.

DIFFICULT AGE

Thereafter her career as a public entertainer, in films and on the stage, was episodic, although she still showed her ability to hold an audience.

In 1961 she was seen again on the screen in Stanley Kramer's dramatic assessment of war guilt entitled *Judgment at Nuremberg*, in which Judy Garland played the part of a distraught and heart-broken German girl. By now she had come a long way from the mood that had so invigorated *The Wizard of Oz*. Her first British film was *I Could Go On Singing*.

No actress can remain young for ever, but some take to middle age more easily than others. It is most difficult for those who, like Judy Garland, were once a symbol of youthfulness, gaiety, and the zest for life. These were the qualities which were discovered, fostered, and ultimately suppressed in her early and formative years under Louis B. Mayer. The burden of stardom proved too much for her.

June 23, 1969.

Professor George Norman Garmonsway, Professor Emeritus of English Language, London University, died in Toronto on February 27, 1967, at the age of 68. He retired in 1965 after 35 years in the Department of English Language and Literature at King's College.

Garmonsway was not a prolific writer but everything he wrote or edited was marked by impeccable scholarship. His outstanding works were his edition of *Aelfric's Colloquy* (1939), and his translation (1954) of the *Anglo-Saxon Chronicle* in its several forms, with an introduction which is a model for the lucid handling of intricate material.

His best-selling *Penguin English Dictionary* (1965), in which he was assisted by an ex-student, Miss Jacqueline Simpson, is likewise a triumph of economy and thoroughness, with its 45,000 main entries and its inclusion of colloquialisms and slang. That his interests were not confined to the pre-Conquest period was shown also by several articles on his medieval discoveries, and (most delightfully) by his essay on "Anna Gurney: Learned Saxonist" in *Essays and Studies, 1955*.

Born at Hartlepool, co.Durham, on May 6, 1898, Garmonsway went with a scholarship from the Henry Smith School in his native town to St. Catharine's College, Cambridge, in 1916, and after two years as a lieutenant in the R.C.A. during the First World War returned to Cambridge in 1919, did brilliantly in both parts of the English Tripos, and, on graduating in 1921, was appointed to an Assistant-Lectureship in the University College, Aberystwyth, whence he moved to a Lectureship at King's College in 1930. He was made a Reader in 1946 and raised to the rank of Professor ten years later.

Garmonsway was one of the select band of students trained by H. M. Chadwick, who did so much to foster the study of Old English in relation to Anglo-Saxon archaeology, Old Icelandic, and kindred fields. At various times he was president of the Viking Society for Northern Research, a member of the Advisory Committee for the Promotion of Scandinavian Studies, and on the committees of the Philological Society and the English Association. He was an indefatigable teacher, at his best perhaps when working with small groups.

SHREWD EYE

In making appointments and choosing postgraduate students, he had a shrewd eye for promising young scholars, many of whom have gone on to do notable work in London and elsewhere. As a colleague he was exemplary, ever helpful, and quite "unflappable." He did many little acts of kindness unremembered no doubt by him, but never forgotten by their recipients. He had a wide experience of examining at all levels for schools and universities all over the country.

In administration Garmonsway was efficient and speedy, preserving a calm which was doubtless fostered by some remarkable experiences throughout the Second World War in the Ancillary Materials Division of the Ministry of Food. He never shirked the drudgery of work on boards of studies, and he was a splendid chairman, unobtrusive, but firm when need be.

Professor Garmonsway had many admirers in the United States, where he twice spent periods as Visiting Professor, at U.C.L.A. (Los Angeles) in 1955, and the University of North Carolina in 1962. When his approaching retirement was known, he was invited to the University of Toronto for the 1965–66 session, where he endeared himself so much to his Canadian students and colleagues that he was asked to return for the present session.

He would probably have stayed on for a third year, for he hated the thought of giving up teaching.

YOUNG ENCOURAGED

He will long be remembered as a teacher and encourager of young scholars. Friends all over the world will miss him, for he was "one who loved his fellow-men."

He leaves a wife, Patricia, and a daughter, Linda.

March 4, 1967.

Sir George Gater, G.C.M.G., K.C.B., D.S.O., died on January 14, 1963, at the age of 76. His career was remarkable alike for its varied character as for its success.

After more than 20 years devoted to the cause of education in different parts of England, in 1933 he was appointed Clerk of the London County Council, and six years later, at the age of 54, he was translated from local government to the Civil Service, and at a bound given the post of Permanent Under-Secretary of State for the Colonies, which, with intermissions for special duties in the Second World War, he held from 1940 to 1947.

BRILLIANT CAREER

George Henry Gater was the son of the late W. H. Gater, and was born on December 26, 1886. He was educated at Winchester and New College, Oxford, where he took honours in Modern History. His interest in education began in his Oxford days, and the same year, 1909, in which he took his degree, he obtained also a Diploma in Education. He was a member of the Oxford Education Committee from 1911 until, in 1912, he received his first educational post as Assistant Director of Education for Nottinghamshire. His career in the 1914 War was a brilliant one. After commanding the 9th Sherwood Foresters and the 6th Lincolnshire Regiment, with the rank of brigadier-general, he commanded the 62nd Infantry Brigade and saw service in Gallipoli, Egypt, and France. He was wounded twice, was four times mentioned in dispatches, and received the D.S.O. and Bar, the C.M.G., the Croix de Guerre, and the Legion of Honour. From this brilliant military background, when the war was over, he stepped once more into the relatively more peaceful field of education, and in 1919 was appointed Director of Education under the county council of Lancashire, which post he held until 1924, when he became Education Officer of the London County Council.

EDUCATION IN LONDON

At the time of Gater's appointment in Lancashire, the Education Act of 1918 had just become law, and it fell to him, and under adverse economic conditions, to organize the machinery to work it. This he did with complete success, and the cordial relationship that he established between the Board of Education, his own council, teachers, parents and scholars, bore witness not only to his organizing ability, but to the strong and sympathetic personality that inspired it. He left Lancashire for London with the regret of all who were interested in education locally, including especially the teachers, to whom he had ever been a kindly friend and helper.

The nine years, from 1924 to 1933, that he was Education Officer of the London County Council entirely maintained Gater's reputation, and to quote from the report of the General Purposes Committee of the Council in unanimously recommending him as Clerk, were "distinguished by enthusiasm, tact and great administrative ability". He succeeded Sir Montagu Cox in that office in May, 1933. He held the post for six years until his departure for Whitehall in July, 1939, when his appointment as Permanent Under-Secretary of State for the Colonies, in succession to Sir Cosmo Parkinson, was announced and was the subject of some discussion in Parliament. It was explained by the Prime Minister (Mr. Chamberlain) as being due to the exceptional pressure on other departments at the time, which prevented any equally suitable civil servant being available. However this may have been, there is no doubt that Gater's exceptional administrative ability had impressed itself on the Government and it was justly considered that his appointment to a senior post would be a valuable reinforcement to the Civil Service in the critical situation then facing the country.

WAR-TIME POSTS

In fact, war broke out before Gater could take up his new appointment, and instead of going straight to the Colonial Office he was assigned to the newly created Ministry of Home Security as Joint Secretary with Sir Thomas Gardiner. He eventually reached the Colonial Office in January, 1940, but in the following May he went to the Ministry of Supply for a time before returning to the Ministry of Home Security, where he remained until 1942. From then until his retirement in 1947 he served at the Colonial Office. The war with Japan had brought the Office into the front line, and it was deeply involved also in the economic and political aspects of the general war effort, and in the relations of this country with the United States over such matters as the American bases in the Caribbean: all this against a background of rising nationalism and increasing international criticism of the traditional colonial system. It fell to Gater to be the chief adviser of a rapid succession of Secretaries of State in steering through these difficult waters and in putting into action the big programme of economic and social development to which this country had committed itself, by a splendid gesture, at the height of the crisis of 1940.

In his remarkable career, Gater may be said to have shown himself to be an outstanding example of the pure administrator. Though his original professional sphere was that of education, it was as an organizer and director of education, not as a teacher that he made his mark. The principles of administration which he learnt and applied in educational work were of universal validity; hence his undoubted success in filling one after the other a number of posts of the greatest importance concerned with a great variety of subjects. He could not attempt to be a master of each subject; his mastery lay in his grasp of the essential issues and his appreciation both of the indispensability of experts and of the need for providing the experts with a sound administrative organization within which they could work. Ministers and officials alike felt that his was a steady hand at the helm. As might be expected from his early war record, he had the good commanding officer's gift of personal interest in and care for the welfare of those who served under him.

After his retirement it was to educational rather than to colonial affairs that Gater's interests reverted. In 1948 he became chairman of the School Broadcasting Council for the United Kingdom, and he became a member of the B.B.C General Advisory Council in 1952. He was Warden of Winchester College from 1951 to 1959, an honorary fellow of New College and of the Royal College of Music, and a coopted member of the Oxfordshire Education Committee.

During his term of office with the London County Council he was responsible, along with Mr. E. P. Wheeler, for Volume XVIII of the council's Survey of London, comprising the Strand and the parish of St. Martin-in-the-Fields, and with Mr. F. R. Hiorns for Vol. XX, concerning Trafalgar Square and neighbourhood.

Gater was knighted in 1936, while with the London County Council. He was made a K.C.B. in 1941 and advanced to G.C.M.G. in 1944.

He married in 1926 Irene, M.B.E., daughter of the late Bowyer Nicols, by whom he had one son.

January 15, 1963.

Edward Pritchard Gee, universally known to conservationists as "E. P.", who died at Weymouth, Dorset, on October 22, 1968, was the leading authority on wildlife conservation in India, and a member both of the Survival Service Commission of the International Union for Conservation of Nature and of the Indian Wild Life Board.

Born in co.Durham in 1904, he was educated at Durham School and Emmanuel College, Cambridge, and went to India as a cadet tea planter in Assam, retiring in 1959. He served in N.E. India throughout the Second World War, rising to the rank of major. Both before and after his retirement he devoted a great deal of his time to the conservation of the wild life of India. On behalf of the Fauna Preservation Society and the S.S.C., he conducted fact-finding surveys of the status of the great Indian rhino in Nepal, the Indian lion in the Gir Forest in Gujerat, the brow-antlered deer in Manipur, the Kashmir stag at Dachigam, and the Indian wild ass in the Little Rann of Kutch. These surveys were reported in the F.P.S. journal *Oryx*. He was a fine photographer, as can be seen from the illustrations to his book, *The Wild Life of India*.

In the botanical world he was increasingly known as an expert on the orchids and rhododendrons of the Assam region, many of which grew in his garden at Upper Shillong, where naturalists were always made welcome. At the very end of his life he was much cheered by the decision of the Assam Government to make the Kaziranga Wild Life Sanctuary in Assam, home of the great Indian rhino, into a national park, a step which he had advocated for many years. It is fair to say that the survival of this fine reserve, with the world's largest remaining population of great Indian rhino, is in no small measure due to the indefatigable energy and persistence which Gee devoted to its conservation over the years.

October 30, 1968.

Catherine Geltzer, the Russian ballerina assoluta, died in Moscow on December 12, 1962.

She was born in 1876, the daughter of Vassili Geltzer, a dancer who collaborated in the original scenario of the Tchaikovsky *Swan Lake*. She was trained at the Moscow Imperial School of Ballet and graduated in 1894. Her teachers were first her father, then Johanssen, Ivanov and later Vassili Tikhomirov.

During the seasons 1909–1911, Geltzer was a guest artist with the Imperial Ballet in St. Petersburg and in 1910 Diaghilev invited her to appear with his company for his second season in Paris. Here she danced in *Les Sylphides*, and performed a *boyar* dance in the divertissement called *Le Festin*. In spite of the success she and her Muscovite partner Alexandre Volinine achieved with the Parisian public, apparently Diaghilev did not feel that her style fitted in with that of his company and her contract was not renewed. However, the following year, 1911, Geltzer appeared in the Coronation Year production of *A Dance Dream* at the Alhambra Theatre, London. The ballet was produced by Alexander Gorsky and Geltzer danced for the first eight weeks of its run, at the then considerable fee of £90 per week.

SOLE APPEARANCE

This was the only occasion Geltzer appeared before the British public.

Partnering her in *A Dance Dream* was Vassili Tikhomirov, whom she later married. After the Soviet Revolution Catherine Geltzer remained in Russia and became one of the foremost artists in the newly-founded Soviet Ballet. Her ballerina career did not finish until 1926 when she danced the leading role in Glière's ballet *The Red Poppy*. She continued to teach until the end of her life and even during the middle of the 1940s she was appearing in mime roles at Moscow's Bolshoi Theatre.

FIRST "PEOPLE'S ARTIST"

In 1921 Geltzer became the first artist ever to be called "People's Artist of the Soviet Union."

After the Soviet Revolution the majority of Russia's most celebrated ballerinas went to the west. Geltzer, by remaining in Russia, played a key part in the formation of Soviet ballet.

On the only occasion she appeared in London her press reception was not particularly enthusiastic. But in Russia she was idolized. Writing of her the leading Soviet critic Yuri Slonimsky has suggested: "She excelled in the classical dance, particularly in the *terre-à-terre* technique. Broad gestures, expressive mimicry and pathetic movements were part and parcel of her dances. But she was more than a gifted ballerina. She was an active figure in Russian Ballet and her creative endeavours did much to advance it."

December 14, 1962.

Dame Adeline Genée-Isitt, D.B.E., who died on April 23, 1970, at the age of 92, was not only one of the best and most loved dancers of her day, but through tireless effort as well as example one of the founders of British ballet as it exists today.

She was born at Hinnerup, near Aarhus, Denmark, on January 6, 1878. The survivor of twins, she was named Anina. From about the age of four she showed a love of dancing which was encouraged by her father's brother, a successful ballet master and dancer, who had taken the professional name of Alexander Genée. This uncle and his wife, a Hungarian ballerina named Antonia Zimmerman, offered to make themselves responsible for Nina's upbringing as soon as she was old enough to undertake rigorous training.

She took the same adopted surname as her uncle, who also chose for her the first name Adeline (after Adelina Patti). What she was taught was the old pure classical style of dancing which had flourished in Paris nearly a century earlier, been brought from there to Copenhagen by August Bournonville, and passed on by him to Christian Johanssen, with whom Alexander Genée studied in St. Petersburg.

She made her first public appearance at ten in a *Polka à la picarde*, but she was not encouraged to become a child prodigy. Instead, she took her place in due course in her uncle's corps de ballet, although her industry and good memory soon brought her the opportunity to dance solo roles when other members of the company were absent.

Alexander Genée's career took the family to Stettin, to Berlin, and then to Munich, where he decided to revive for his niece, then 18, what became one of her most famous ballets, *Coppélia*. Shortly afterwards came an invitation to appear in London at the Empire Theatre, and although the first offer (for Queen Victoria's diamond jubilee celebrations) had to be refused, Adeline Genée arrived there in November, 1897, with a six weeks' contract. She stayed, with only brief interruptions, for 10 years.

The ballets at the Empire were of a lighter nature than the kind Diaghilev's Russian Ballet was later to popularize. In almost all of them Genée, as the star would be seen not only in her classical solo but also in at least one dance to display her gift of characterization. One of the most famous of her solos, first given in *High Jinks* in 1904, was *Return from the Hunt*, given in full long-skirted riding kit, portraying both horse and rider, the exhilaration of the one and the nimbleness of the other.

VIRTUOSITY

In October, 1902, Genée was invited as guest artist to the Royal Theatre, Copenhagen, where she danced *Coppélia* and *Flower Festival at Genzano* with Hans Beck, and a duet by her uncle with Gustav Uhlendorff. The Danish critics found her style exceptionally refined, although "a little hard and cool", and greatly admired her virtuosity which encompassed steps not then normally attempted by women, including *entrechat six* and double *pirouettes*.

In January, 1905, Genée took part in a Command performance at Chatsworth before Edward VII and Queen Alexandra, the first time a dancer had been so honoured. In 1907 she left for her first tour of the United States, where she enjoyed a success comparable to that she had long commanded in London. By now her reputation was such that works of a more serious nature could be produced at the Empire; in 1906 she danced *Coppélia* there and in 1909 Alexander Genée mounted for her a version of the ballet scene from *Robert le Diable* which, with Taglioni in the role Genée now played, had ushered in the Romantic ballet. Genée herself also produced a number of ballets, often based on historical models.

Marriage to a successful businessman, Frank S. N. Isitt, in 1910, brought her great happiness, and after further tours in the United States and Australia, and London seasons at the Coliseum, Genée in 1914 announced her farewell season. The subscription list for a farewell present was headed by five fellow ballerinas including Pavlova and Karsavina, but with characteristic generosity Genée asked that the money raised be given to relieve the poverty of another dancer who had fallen on hard times.

In fact Genée continued dancing for a time after this season, but withdrew from regular appearances in 1917. This was not, however, to be the end of her connexion with the dance. On December 31, 1920, the Association of Teachers of Operatic Dancing in Great Britain was formed to raise standards and Genée elected its first president. The post was no sinecure; she helped draw up a standard syllabus, organized performances for the benefit of the association, personally sought the patronage of Queen Mary which was granted in 1928, and eight years later had the pleasure of seeing the association granted its charter as the Royal Academy of Dancing.

Adeline Genée's last appearances were made in *The Love Song*, a duet with Anton Dolin which she produced for a charity performance in June, 1932, repeated on the programmes of a special group of English dancers which she took to Copenhagen later that year (appearing at the Royal Theatre during the British Industries Fair), and gave for the last time in a B.B.C. television broadcast on March 15, 1933.

She was created D.B.E. in 1950 for her services to ballet. She was made an honorary Mus.D. by London University in 1946. She was proud, too, of the links she maintained with her native land and of the several honours bestowed upon her by Denmark.

Dame Adeline retired from the presidency of the R.A.D. in 1954, handing over the office to Dame Margot Fonteyn. She retained her interest in ballet, however, and in 1967 was present at the Gala performance to open a new theatre named after her at East Grinstead. Her husband died in 1939.

It was Adeline Genée's blessing to bring happiness to many thousands who admired and enjoyed her art. It was her pride to conduct herself always so that her profession should be respected. It was her self-appointed task to give that art and profession a strong foundation in her second homeland. Purity and clearness of style were hers in her life as in her dancing, and for many she left the memory of "an art with the warmth and innocence of sunshine".

April 24, 1970.

Dr. P. S. Gerbrandy, who died at The Hague on September 7, 1961, at the age of 76, was Prime Minister of the Netherlands Government in London during the Second World War. He won the affection and admiration of all who met him in London. The darkest hours for his country found him undaunted. Small in stature, venerable in appearance, he was a source of strength to his own people and a tonic to his allies.

Pieter Sjoerd Gerbrandy was born on April 13, 1885, at Goengamedien in Friesland, and educated at one of the public schools founded by the famous Dutch reformer G. O. Heldring, at Zetten in Gelderland. Gerbrandy studied at Amsterdam's Free University where he took his LL.D. In 1911 he established himself in the capital as a barrister, and practised until 1930; from 1919 to 1930 he was a member of the provincial government of Friesland. In the latter year he received, and accepted, a call to the University of Amsterdam as Professor of Commercial Law and international Private Law, and in Amsterdam he remained until, in 1939, he was appointed Minister of Justice. In the meantime he was nominated in 1937 as a president of the Netherlands Broadcasting Council.

When he accepted the post of Minister of Justice in the Cabinet, headed by Jonkheer de Geer, he did so without the consent of the Anti-Revolutionary Party of which he was a member, thus showing the stubbornness and strength of character associated with his native province of Friesland.

When Queen Wilhelmina and her Ministers took refuge in Britain, Gerbrandy was entrusted with forming a Government. He kept the portfolio of Justice until 1942 and after he had relinquished it became Minister for the Continuation of Warfare. In 1941–42 he also took on his shoulders the onerous office of Minister for the Colonies.

BROADCASTS

His capacity for work was extraordinary; and through all the years in which he carried the burden of a government at war and in exile, Gerbrandy found time enough to employ his talent as a broadcaster for the benefit of the struggle of his fellow-countrymen and their allies. Chairman of the Netherlands Broadcasting Council, he was heard over the London radio more often than any other of the foreign statesmen; and was eloquent and effective in Dutch or in English.

When Queen and Government finally went home, in 1945, and political conditions in the country enforced a change of government, Gerbrandy retired, and went to live at The Hague. Among his many publications are *Het Heemstaettenrecht* (1911), *De Overeenkonist van Londen* (1924), *Struggle for new Forms of Political Society* (1927), *Religious Socialism* (1928), and a number of other books on administrative law, radio, and television. In 1941 he delivered a Burge lecture, and in 1944 a Taylorian lecture.

The moving speech of thanks, on behalf of his Government and country, he addressed to Britain over the B.B.C. when he took his departure will be long remembered. His were the words of a warm-hearted and sincere friend who—by no means blind to our mistakes and shortcomings—undaunted by the many difficulties with which he had had to cope as a responsible statesman, felt deeply the debt owed by democracy, and by the world at large, to the men who had stood against the flood of disaster until it had turned again.

CRISIS YEARS

After the war Gerbrandy received the highest decoration in the Netherlands, when the Grand Cross of the Netherlands Lion was conferred on him. Prime Minister Schermerhorn addressing him on this occasion said: "You have helped to save the inheritance of the Kingdom of the Netherlands through nearly five years of the most severe crisis. In the midst of all storms you have never despaired about the future of our fatherland."

When, in those years after the war, what then was still called the Netherlands East Indies wanted to disconnect itself from the Netherlands, Gerbrandy was a fierce fighter for the historic rights of the Netherlands in this area. He became the president of the national committee called "Maintaining the Unity of the Realm" and conducted a strong action against the agreement of Linggadjati. These agreements, having finally been accepted by the States-General, became the basis for the transfer of sovereignty to Indonesia. After this transfer of sovereignty on December 27, 1949, Gerbrandy showed himself a strong defender of the inhabitants of Amboyna and of the Moluccas who had always been extremely loyal towards Netherlands rule. He undertook all this while an Anti-Revolutionary member of the second chamber of the States-General, membership which he held from 1948 until the elections of March 12, 1959.

September 9, 1961.

Elena Gerhardt, the great Lieder singer, died in London on January 11, 1961.

She was born at Leipzig but she made her home in London in 1934 after experience at a Bayreuth festival of what Hitler's "new Germany" was like. She made a second career in Britain as a teacher and in 1953 she published an autobiography, *Recital*, in which, with modesty and transparent sincerity, she tells how she deserted opera for Lieder and so made her unique career.

She was born on November 11, 1883, the seventh child and only daughter—her first success, as she humorously calls it—of a restaurant proprietor who was from her account a genial and musical Saxon. She developed a voice at school and was sent straight to the Leipzig Conservatoire to study, where various teachers tried, in the way singing teachers have of attempting to change students' voices, to convert her soprano into a contralto. However, Nikisch saved her and made her—he became director of the conservatoire in addition to his duties as conductor at the Gewandhaus. Gerhardt even so started on the usual course of an operatic artist, although Nikisch had accompanied her at her first Lieder recital. She sang Mignon for him in her operatic debut in 1905, but though she never regretted the experience, which enlarged her powers of expression, she soon deserted opera, and in 1906 made her first London appearances, with Nikisch, at a London Symphony Orchestra concert and at a recital in the Bechstein (now Wigmore) Hall.

LONDON CONCERTS

Thereafter, till the First World War broke the sequence, she came to England for London concerts and provincial tours annually, and, of course, sang for all the chief German concert-giving organizations. Her tours included one to Russia and one to the United States in 1912, and even the war did not prevent her moving about Europe. She returned to England with some trepidation in 1922 and immediately resumed her old place in the London concert world with Paula Hegner as her accompanist—Nikisch died early that year. In 1928 she was appointed to the staff of her old conservatoire and gave her first broadcast from the Mid German Radio at the invitation of its director, Dr. Fritz Kohl, whom four years later she married. Dr. Kohl's dismissal from his job decided them to make England their home, and in 1946 they became British citizens.

Gerhardt's voice was mezzo-soprano, of good but not outstanding beauty, that is, it was an excellent instrument for song interpretation. It had the right range, the firmness and steadiness of tone, the flexibility and tonal variety to enable her to present a song as the microcosm it is. The mood was caught and conveyed without transgressing the medium—the expression was in the voice. She could sometimes be a little dull and heavy in the earnest German way, but she could also catch fire and convey passion and excitement. She sang, as all singers should, songs in several languages and styles, but it was as an interpreter of German Lieder, the great classical tradition from Mozart and Schubert to Wolf and Strauss, that her audiences most liked to hear her. She gave a twenty-fifth anniversary recital at Wigmore Hall with Ivor Newton in February, 1932, and a fortieth anniversary recital in the same hall with Gerald Moore in January, 1946.

In March, 1947, she said farewell to the concert platform at a recital in Liverpool. From that time forth she busied herself with teaching in London.

January 12, 1961.

President Oscar Gestido, President of Uruguay, who challenged one of his former Ministers to a duel in the last month of his life, died on December 6, 1967, after a heart attack.

Gestido, who was 66, took office at the head of an 11-man Cabinet in March, 1967, for a five-year term. For the previous 14 years the country had been ruled by a Swiss-type National Council. He and his Cabinet faced formidable problems including soaring inflation and a vast and cumbersome bureaucracy when they took office.

But for a few days last month General Gestido

handed over the reins of government to Vice-President Jorge Pacheco Areco in preparation to defending his honour. He asked a court of honour to decide whether remarks made by Amilcar Vasconcellos, former Treasury Minister, had injured his honour. Vasconcellos complained that some of the President's actions lacked common sense and Gestido sent round his seconds to challenge the ex-Minister. But a court of honour later advised the President he had no grounds for issuing a challenge and he resumed the country's leadership.

Gestido had gained a reputation as an efficient and honest administrator but under his rule the country faced the severest economic and financial crisis in its history as labour and inflationary troubles multiplied. Unrest and protests affected the country's labour force from school teachers to meat packers and bank clerks. Gestido restricted certain constitutional rights in October to help solve some of the troubles. The Government took strong action against hoarders and profiteers as it struggled to keep inflation and the cost of living within reasonable limits after 50 per cent devaluation last month.

Gestido, bushy-browed, white-haired son of a Spanish immigrant bricklayer, was born on November 28, 1901. He entered a military college at 16, an education that meant many sacrifices for his poor parents. At the age of 41 he reached the rank of a colonel in the Air Force and in 1949 he became a general.

Politics came late in life to Gestido. He was picked by the Liberal Colorado (Red) Party in March, 1963, to take one of the party's three minority seats in the National Council. He resigned from it when he decided to run for president.

Gestido rarely went to bed before 2 a.m. and was usually up again at 7.30 a.m., but he always took a siesta after lunch. A non-drinker, and occasional smoker, he ate frugally—usually roast beef and fresh fruit—and frequently drank "mate", the Uruguayan national tea, through a silver straw.

Gestido was a good administrator, and on two occasions he was called in by the Government to run temporarily state-owned companies—the railways and the national airline Pluna—when they ran into economic difficulties. He was praised for honesty and enthusiasm. Senior railway executives remember how Gestido, on his first day of work, called them in for an 8 a.m. meeting. When they arrived 10 minutes late, he sent a messenger to tell them outside locked doors that "the meeting was for 8 o'clock. Come back at the right time tomorrow."

Gestido left a wife, Eliza, whom he married in 1931, and three children, two boys and a girl.

December 7, 1967.

Professor Pieter Geyl, the Dutch historian, who was professor of Dutch History at London University from 1919 to 1935, and Emeritus professor at the University of Utrecht, died on December 31, 1966, in Utrecht. He was 79.

Trained as an historian at the University of Leiden, where he took his doctorate in 1913 after a sojourn in Italy collecting material, Geyl went to London in the same year as correspondent of the *Nieuwe Rotterdamsche Courant*. The six years during which he held this appointment were to be a time of tension but also of opportunity: professionally engaged in reporting from London to his Dutch readers Geyl found himself from the start also unofficially representing Holland in his country of adoption. He set himself to master the English language, which he eventually spoke, as he did French and German, with faultless accuracy and uncanny skill, and to make every possible contact which could serve his cause.

After the First World War the Dutch Government recognized the value of maintaining in London such a cultural ambassador, and, when in 1919 the Chair of Dutch History was established at University College London, Geyl was the obvious occupant. Thus began his tenure of the chair which he was to make famous. From his platform in Gower Street, as from his house in St. John's Wood, he lectured on and publicized the history and civilization of his native land. He soon won students, several of whom went on to produce published work of importance in the field of Dutch history. It was also under his direction that there was built up the excellent library of sources for Dutch history at the Institute of Historical Research.

In his temporary exile from his country Geyl did not cease to play an active part in its affairs, not less in those of its southerly neighbour. He was a born fighter. An anti-monarchist who had had his first brush with the police while a schoolboy, he was physically—and to no small extent spiritually—a reincarnation of one of those seventeenth-century regents whom he came to know so intimately, and as a natural corollary he was anti-Orangeist.

FLEMISH MOVEMENT

As the object of his fiercest hostility, however, the Dutch monarchy yielded to the Belgian state. The 20s and 30s saw the birth of the modern Flemish Movement, with Geyl as one of its founders. Proclaiming the kinship of Flemings and Dutch—the theme which was to inspire his reinterpretation of Netherlands history—he waged war on the Government of Brussels. That did not commend him to the Government of The Hague, and when in 1935 he was proposed for the Chair of Dutch History at Utrecht there was some opposition in high quarters. The Dutch historical world was, then, still smarting under his exposure of the now-forgotten scandal attaching to the celebration of the quater-centenary of William the Silent in which Geyl's passionate desire to establish truth and expose falsehood had made him enemies. His lustre was such, however, that he received the chair, which for the next three years he made as lively a centre of debate and argument as he had done in London.

Then came the Second World War, and a period which, if it might have spelled death to Geyl, was in fact to gain him undreamt-of renown. Taken as a hostage, he was put in a German concentration camp, from which he was released shortly before the end of the war. Geyl's response to this challenge (the Toynbeeian terminology springs naturally to the mind) was characterstic: he wrote an historical masterpiece (*Napoleon, For and Against*), many poems and a detective story. Sent back to Holland, he threw himself into the Resistance movement and risked death in another form than that of a concentration camp by his services in the allied cause. The war proved to be in almost every sense the turning-point of his career. After it the lifelong rebel found himself an honoured patriarch; the scholar little known outside Holland and England found himself a figure of world fame; and in his own country he rose easily and by acclaim to the pinnacle of his profession.

UNFINISHED WORK

Yet all this was not achieved without a price: and the chief part of that price was Geyl's failure to complete what had by then become his *magnum opus*. The *History of the Dutch-Speaking Peoples* had begun as a small book in a well-known series. During the thirties it began to grow into a full-scale work, but it was to be put aside after 1945 until its author was too old to finish it. Yet it remains his historical monument, and if we may follow Namier in his definition of historical greatness, this is a great work, because no one can ever write again of the sixteenth and seventeenth centuries in the Netherlands as if it had not been written. In translation it has introduced countless non-Dutch students to the fascinating problems of Dutch history and has made Geyl's name a familiar one wherever European history is taught. Instead of finishing, or at least continuing it, Geyl yielded after the war to the twin fascinations of the essay and the controversy. True, he wrote one more book, on the American Civil War, as a result of several visits to the United States, and a very good book it is. But his delight was the essay, and above all the trenchant essay: not for nothing was the best volume of his collected essays to be entitled *Battles and Tourneys.*

EXPLODING FALLACIES

Among the many targets, Arnold Toynbee took pride of place: and exploding fallacies of the *Study of History* was to become something of an obsession with Geyl.

Prolific as he was in published work, Geyl was also a letter-writer in the grand manner. Missives poured from him in unceasing flow, and as he kept carbon copies of all that he wrote there is a copious private archive to be explored one day. Geyl had himself begun to toy with an autobiography, but it will now be left to another to chronicle the deeds of this astonishing man.

He received honorary degrees from Oxford, Harvard, and St. Andrews universities. He was awarded an honorary C.B.E. in 1959, and became a corresponding member of the British Academy in 1961. In 1941 Geyl had been elected a member of the Royal Academy at Amsterdam, and this was confirmed by Queen Wilhelmina after the liberation of the Netherlands. Since 1921 he had been a fellow of the Royal Historical Society, and later became a corresponding member. In 1957 he became an honorary member of the American Historical

Association. He was awarded the Netherlands State Prize for Literature in 1958. He also received the Order pour le mérite from Germany. He paid several visits to America as a visiting professor, and in 1963 gave the G. M. Trevelyan lectures at Cambridge University.

In public a combative and awe-inspiring figure, Geyl was in his private life a man of sensitiveness and charm, whose large heart could embrace his own family, his circle of students and an army of friends. There will be many to mourn the passing of one who was, in truth, an outsize man. He is survived by his widow, and a son and daughter.

January 3, 1967.

Gheorghe Gheorghiu-Dej, who became head of state in Rumania in 1952 and had been President since 1961, died on March 19, 1965. He was 63.

For 20 years the name of Gheorghiu-Dej had been intricately linked with the pattern of eastern Europe, yet of all the communist leaders who took power after the war he was the only one who did not rise and then fall with Stalin, the only survivor of the old guard who weathered all the storms and changes to emerge even stronger, riding high on the wave of Rumania's new nationalism.

Ten years ago he would have been described as one of Russia's most colourless satellites. Today, his name symbolizes independence of Russia and even if one can argue that the pattern of Soviet rule had changed since, that Moscow is no longer the centre from which policies could be imposed or dictated, the fact remains that he was the first eastern European leader who defied Russia and got away with it. Quietly, gradually, without any public scandal but nevertheless determinedly, he had been widening the distance between Moscow and Bucharest and when during the recent meeting of communist parties he failed to appear, no eyebrows were raised and the event passed almost unnoticed. In two years Rumanian communists have established themselves as being different and nobody was surprised by their absence. Nobody asked what would be the consequence nor what would be Moscow's reaction because everybody knows that Moscow could do nothing about it.

Prudence and political wisdom seem to have been Gheorghiu-Dej's main assets and he applied them skilfully. He had enjoyed Stalin's confidence. He had followed the twists and turns of his policy yet even in those troublesome years he carefully avoided staining his hands with Titoist scapegoats. He dealt with his party's opponents if not more leniently then certainly less cruelly. He executed Stalin's policies as if in the back of his mind he could already see the changes that lay ahead and was preparing himself for the future.

As a Rumanian, a Latin, he had no sentiment for Mother Russia. But he went along when this was required of him, preaching eternal links and traditional friendship and even trying to play down the Latin character of his nationals. As a home-bred communist his vision of communism was confined to the welfare of his own country. But when necessary he spoke of identity of communist aims and interests. Yet, the moment that he saw his own national interests threatened he rose to say that common ideologies did not always mean common national interests. Ten years ago this would have been impossible. Two years ago, when Gheorghiu-Dej took the risk of defying Russia, he knew the clock could no longer be turned back.

POVERTY AND HARDSHIP

Born in 1901 in Moldavia, his early youth and political activity followed the pattern of poverty and hardship, of discontent and political agitation, of clashes, strikes, and imprisonment. In 1932 when he was arrested and sentenced to 12 years' imprisonment for organizing a strike in the Grivita rail yards he was already a full member of the party's central committee.

The war ended, the Rumanian Communist Party—an insignificant political force so far as membership was concerned—established itself as the ruling party, and having joined the first coalition cabinet as Minister of Communications in 1944 after his escape from prison Gheorghiu-Dej became its general secretary the following year. The party, divided between the home-bred devoted agitators who represented Gheorghiu-Dej's stronghold and the Moscow-trained internationalist group which returned to the country at the end of the war, was in power but internal strife and friction continued.

With his practical experience as a communist agitator, Gheorghiu-Dej began to consolidate his position, combining instinct with political astuteness, caution with swift action, and in his early fifties when Mrs. Pauker, former Minister of Foreign Affairs, and Vassili Luka, were quietly eliminated and sent to prison, the party apparatus was firmly in his hands. He became vice-chairman of the Council of Ministers in 1948 and chairman in 1952. In 1955 he became First Secretary of the Rumanian Communist Party, and in March, 1961, President after a government reshuffle.

The changes that came to Russia after Stalin's death hardly affected the Rumanian scene. The cult of the individual did not concern them since there were no errors to be corrected nor wrongs to be put right. The main culprits having been eliminated while Stalin was still alive. Rumania could say that thanks to its wise leadership it was well ahead of Russia and everybody else. It was after the twentieth congress that Gheorghiu-Dej made a speech to this effect—a speech which was in fact the beginning of his gradual estrangement from Russia. "What happens in Russia need not necessarily affect us", has since become the standard answer in Rumania.

But it was not until June of 1962 that the first cracks began to be noted, that the first discords between Moscow and Bucharest began to emerge, that the first rumours began to circulate about Khrushchev's pressures and Gheorghiu-Dej's resistance.

NO OPEN CONFLICT

Khrushchev's journey in June, 1962, could not cover up the fact that his economic integration scheme had met with strong resistance in Bucharest and that his assurances that communism being their common aim there could be no differences was not convincing to the Rumanian leader. A prudent politician, Gheorghiu-Dej realized that this case could be won only if he avoided any move that might provoke an open conflict. A shrewd politician he realized that Russia's hands were tied by the Sino-Soviet conflict and that only by maintaining a neutral position could Rumania exploit the conflict for her own ends.

His personal relations with Khrushchev grew from bad to worse in recent years. Khrushchev tried to apply pressure to which Gheorghiu-Dej responded by extending his political and economic ties with the west. He announced a visit by his Prime Minister to Paris last summer and he dispatched his economic managers and cabinet members to western Europe to seek new economic arrangements. By the summer of last year relations between Moscow and Bucharest became so strained that Khrushchev felt compelled to seek President Tito's services. An old rebel was asked to impress upon a new rebel the risks involved in going too far and too fast.

But for once Gheorghiu-Dej was prepared to discard caution. Fortified by popular support at home, encouraged by a booming economy and realizing that Moscow had no choice but to accept the fact of Bucharest's growing independence he remained firm, and when, a few weeks afterwards, he sent his Prime Minister to Moscow relations were put back on a workable if no longer fraternal basis.

But Gheorghiu-Dej remained aloof even after Khrushchev was dismissed from office in spite of evident efforts on the part of the new Soviet leaders to put his grievances right. He went to Warsaw for the Warsaw Pact meeting, but having done that much he was at pains to get away and left immediately the meeting was over.

Thus, at the end of his rule the image of the once colourless executor of Russia's policies and of a ruthless communist leader grew into that of a national leader. His policies may have been opportunist. He may have lacked the spectacular courage of a President Tito or the honoured devotion of a Mr. Gomulka, but as a politician he knew exactly when to take action and how far to go, when to stick his neck out and when to keep quiet.

March 20, 1965.

Alberto Giacometti, the Swiss sculptor and painter, who died in hospital at Chur, south-eastern Switzerland, on January 11, 1966, was one of the most eminent modern practitioners of plastic art and one also who arrived at a form of expression in which he was so individual as to stand alone—in its elemental nature his work had an attribute of greatness. He was 64.

His thin, elongated figures often conveyed an impression of suffering and mysterious isolation, and could be regarded as the product of a romantic imagination viewing the tragic side of the twentieth century. His skeletal forms stood or stalked—Solomon Eagle-like—in the art galleries; one might think of them as prophets of despair or reminders of untoward fate; and the surfaces, punched, crumbling and deliquescent, gave emphasis to emaciation.

With so much of romantic suggestion he combined a sense of space, often setting the figures in some relation with each other which created its own spatial composition like that of a picture rather than a sculptured group closely coherent in mass. In his grey paintings and drawings there was less of this characteristic exaggeration but in these, too, space assumed a special importance, the figure materialized in it as a web of lines and touches of grey and white. If this was not a new pictorial conception, it was worked out in a unique way.

Born in Stampa, a village in the Bregaglia valley in the Italian part of Switzerland on October 10, 1901, Alberto Giacometti was the eldest son of the Swiss artist, Giovanni Giacometti, an Impressionist painter of some note. He was related also to the painter, Augusto Giacometti, who made experiments in abstract art in the early years of the century which were remarkable for their time. Alberto showed an artistic bent at an early age, drawing from nature when he was about nine.

He was already accomplished in painting and sculpture at the age of 13 and became a student at the Ecole des Arts et Métiers at Geneva when he 18. After six months there and a short period in Italy, he went to Paris.

THINGS SEEN

From 1922 to 1925 he studied under Bourdelle at the Académie de la Grande Chaumière. Early influences on his art were various. In Italy he was impressed by Byzantine mosaics, by the Grottos at Padua, by Baroque architecture, filling many sketch-books with pictorial notes of things seen.

In his early efforts in sculpture he was naturalistic but he abandoned the close pursuit of nature in 1925 and began to produce sculpture from memory, though in drawing he always continued to work from life. He felt the influence of Cubism as represented by the work of Lipchitz and Laurens in particular. Between 1925 and 1928 he produced bronzes of a massive and Cubist-inspired simplicity. The change from them to his later more tenuous conceptions started with his attachment to the Surrealist movement about 1930. He contributed "automatic" poems and other writings to the Surrealist periodicals and manifestos, and exhibited in Paris in 1930 together with Miro and Arp, his sculpture now fusing abstraction with a vein of Surrealist fantasy. His first one-man show was at the Galerie Pierre Colle in 1932, followed by a one-man show at the Julien Lévy Gallery, New York, in 1934.

It was in the 1930s that he developed the form of open cage construction, the influence of which on others could be seen at a later date in the entries for the celebrated "Unknown Political Prisoner" competition. An example is "The Palace at 4 a.m." of 1933 (Museum of Modern Art, New York) where Giacometti sets a mysterious stage within a linear framework.

From 1935 to 1940 he worked from the model regularly—a "reactionary activity" which caused him to be excluded from the Surrealist group. It was not until after the Second World War that he fully realized his personal idea of space and figuration. Between 1940 and 1945 he produced sculptured heads and figures on a miniature scale but thereafter he turned to such impressive larger works as "The Pointing Man" of 1947 (Tate Gallery) and the strange anthropomorphic forest of the "Seven Figures and a Head" of 1950. In his later period he also produced many paintings and drawings from life, his brother, Diego, frequently serving as model. Another aspect of his work was a collaboration with his brother, himself an able furniture designer, on such decorative objects of use as standard lamps, chandeliers and fire-dogs.

RETROSPECTIVE EXHIBITION

An exhibition at the Pierre Matisse Gallery, New York, in 1948 included characteristic examples of his life-size figures. He subsequently exhibited again at the Pierre Matisse Gallery in 1950, 1954 and 1961, at the Galerie Maeght in Paris in 1951, 1954, 1957 and 1961 and at the Venice Biennale in 1956 and 1962. The first complete show of his sculpture, paintings and drawings to be held in England was the retrospective exhitition organized by the Arts Council in 1955. He figured prominently again in the exhibition of Swiss art "From Hodler to Klee" arranged by the Arts Council and the Pro Helvetia Foundation of Switzerland and held at the Tate Gallery in 1959.

A large retrospective exhibition of his sculpture, paintings and drawings from 1913 to 1965, organized by the Arts Council and arranged by David Sylvester, was held at the Tate Gallery in the summer of 1965. It illustrated his entire development from the naturalistic portrait heads of his father and mother (1927) to his cubist and abstract phase as in the "Spoonwoman" (1926) the Surrealism of the "Suspended Ball" (1930–31) and the period of standing figures heralded by the "Woman walking" (1934) and "Chariot" (1942). It included some remarkable portrait heads and busts of recent date in which however the tendency to exaggerated thinness began to be less noticeable than hitherto. A similar retrospective exhibition was held at the same time in the Museum of Modern Art, New York.

Giacometti was a believer in "likeness". He remarked: "If a picture is true, it will be good as a picture; even the quality of paint will necessarily be beautiful." He said of his tendency to pare things down: "the more that is taken off, the fatter it gets"—by which he seems to have meant that the lean figure seemed to occupy and fill out the space around it the more impressively.

Giacometti travelled little after settling in Paris, though he regularly spent some time each year in his native village in the Grisons and stayed from 1942 to 1945 at Geneva. Most of his work was done in his Paris studio in the rue Hippolyte Maindrou, which he took in 1927 and where he remained. It was during his stay in Geneva that he met Annette Arm, who later became his wife.

January 13, 1966.

Sir Philip Gibbs, K.B.E., a journalist of great distinction in his time and a fluent and prolific author, died on March 10, 1962, at the age of 84. Accomplished in most branches of the profession of journalism, Philip Gibbs was most signally successful as a descriptive reporter. Observant, quick-witted, of humane temper, warm, and generous in emotional sympathy, he had an unerring eye for the human essentials of a situation and a telling gift for discovering point and significance in the seemingly commonplace.

As an official correspondent in the war of 1914–18 he stamped himself deeply upon the mind and imagination of the civilian public; his dispatches, subdued though they necessarily were to the exigencies of military censorship, had the emotional ring of an authentic human document. As a novelist he was less impressive. He attained something more than popularity with *The Street of Adventure*, one of his earliest attempts at fiction, and in later years continued to hold the regard, of a faithful public; but there was, in truth, not a great deal of art in most of the long series of journalistic commentaries on current affairs which from the 1920s onwards he cast in the form of fiction.

Philip Armand Hamilton Gibbs was born on May 1, 1877, the son of Henry Gibbs, a senior civil servant at the Board of Education, and his wife, Helen Hamilton, and was educated privately. Two brothers, Cosmo Hamilton and A. Hamilton Gibbs, were also to take to writing, and it was the elder of them, Cosmo, who eventually encouraged him to do likewise. At the age of 21 Gibbs obtained a post with the publishing firm of Cassell supervising the production of school textbooks, and himself brought out a textbook, *Founders of the Empire*, which was used in schools for a good many years.

DEAL WITH NOVELIST

Then, after a spell with a literary agency of the older type during which he was responsible for the purchase of, among other works, Arnold Bennett's *The Grand Babylon Hotel*, he applied for work to Lord Northcliffe and was given an appointment on the *Daily Mail*. This was of brief duration, however, as was also a similar appointment on the *Daily Express*, from which Gibbs transferred himself to the *Daily Chronicle*—an association which, with occasional interruptions, was to last for many years.

It was during one such interruption, when he had gone as literary editor to the ill-fated *Tribune* and seen it crash, that he made his name as a writer of fiction. Thrown out of work, Gibbs retired to a cottage at Littlehampton and wrote *The Street of Adventure*, a brisk, vivid but in some ways highly coloured novel about journalists and journalism. It was much to the public taste, though the author found himself involved in an action for libel which he settled at considerable financial cost to himself. Then followed a busy period as a free-lance, during which he also turned out several popular historical works, and then a long spell as special correspondent at home and abroad of the *Daily Chronicle*. Gibbs covered various exciting episodes such as the siege of Sidney Street, and eventually scored a major success with his exposure of the Dr. Cook who falsely claimed to have reached the North Pole. In 1911, at the request of Lord Lytton, he reported on the prisons of Portugal; in the following year he was a war correspondent in the Balkans; and in 1914, after a tour of inquiry in Germany, he paid several visits of a like character to Ireland.

In early August of that year—clad, so it was said, in a lounge suit and carrying a walking stick—he started off for France. It was a high and honourable adventure. Notwithstanding all the difficulties which met the war correspondent at that phase of the fighting, Gibbs's dispatches were a triumph of enterprise and insight. When the position was regularized he became one of the five official correspondents accredited to the B.E.F., and, in recognition of his work, was with his colleagues created K.B.E.; he was also made a Chevalier of the Legion of Honour. He returned to England much moved and affected by what he had seen—he said that the war had "utterly changed" him—and produced in *Realities of War* (1920), the fifth of his war books but the first in which he was not embarrassed by the censorship, a heartfelt summing-up of the whole experience.

Afterwards Gibbs travelled widely, lectured in the United States, brought off the unusual feat of obtaining for publication an interview with Pope Benedict XV—he was himself a Roman Catholic—paid a visit to Russia, and so on. In 1921 he became editor of the *Review of Reviews*, but soon abandoned the post and settled down to authorship, combining occasional volumes of reminiscence and travel with a steady output of fiction. His novels include essays in story-telling proper such as *The Age of Reason* (1928), but most, though skilful and sympathetic in tone, are of journalistic content only. The expert reporter reappeared in *European Journey* (1934) and again in *Ordeal in England* (1937), to which volume he committed some of his thoughts while serving as a member of the Royal Commission on the private trade in arms. Although never a pacifist, he was closely beset by a sense of the waste of war, and this is always evident in his novels of the war years 1939–45—*Sons of the Others, The Long Alert, The Interpreter* and the rest. A volume of autobiography, *The Pageant of the Years,* treating chiefly of his journalistic experiences, appeared in 1946 and was followed by *Crowded Company* (1949) and *Life's Adventure* (1958).

Slight, pale, quiet in manner, Philip Gibbs bore little resemblance to the bustling and importunate reporter or special correspondent of popular fancy. Few correspondents of his generation approached him in his mastery of his craft. In 1898 he married Agnes, daughter of the Rev. W. J. Rowland. She died in 1939. He leaves one son, Anthony Gibbs, who is also a novelist.

March 12, 1962.

William Francis Gibbs, the leading American naval architecht and maritime engineer, died in New York on September 7, 1967, at the age of 81.

He was responsible for the design of the liner United States (53,000 tons) which on her maiden voyage in the summer of 1952 made a record crossing of the Atlantic averaging 35.59 knots over the 2,942 nautical miles between the Ambrose light-vessel and Bishop Rock.

He has been credited with having contributed more than any other individual to the success of the United States Navy in the Second World War. In the 1930s he led a long and hard-fought battle in federal and shipbuilding circles to convert warship design to high-pressure and high-temperature steam, which eventually gave fighting ships the high speed and endurance that played an important part in naval operations in the war. His plans were the basis for construction of more than 2,000 Liberty ships as the work horses of the war.

Gibbs was born in Philadelphia on August 24, 1886. His father was an industrial promoter there who had made and lost several large fortunes. The son went to Harvard and then studied law at Columbia Law School in New York where he took the degree of LL.B. He did not practise the law but his knowledge proved invaluable in his later work when contracts had to be drawn for the design and construction of vessels. He was attracted to that business when the liner Empress of Ireland went down in the St. Lawrence in 1914 and he felt that such disasters could be reduced if not avoided. Later he designed a kind of automatic bulk-head which would keep a ship afloat even when struck and holed and threatening to sink. He soon found work with the construction department of the International Mercantile Marine company of New York and when the war came he and his brother Frederick found jobs with the Government's shipping control committee.

PROVED CORRECT

After the war he returned to the International Mercantile Marine company but later the brothers set up as ship designers and marine engineers on Broadway in New York, Frederick taking charge of the finances and William of the work of design.

The soundness of Gibbs's views on compartmentation was brought home dramatically to the shipbuilding industry when the new liner Malolo, designed by him for the Matson line and at that time (1927) the largest United States merchant ship afloat, was rammed at full speed by a Norwegian collier. The Malolo's accident, a broadside collision, on the engine-room bulkhead, exactly duplicated that which sent the Empress of Ireland to the bottom in 10 minutes with the loss of over 1,000 lives. The Malolo, however, not only remained afloat but was towed back to port with a list of less than five degrees.

Subsequently the brothers joined forces with D. H. Cox, well known as a designer of yachts and the firm of Gibbs and Cox was formed. But Cox was 70 and much of the work fell on William Gibbs. He built a number of ships for the South American services of the Grace Line and began designing vessels for the United States Navy. His ideas were well in advance of his time and often looked at askance by conservative naval men, but before long he was regarded as the leading naval architect and marine engineer in America.

In 1927 he married Mrs. Vera Cravath Larkins, daughter of the well known New York lawyer, Paul Cravath.

September 8, 1967.

The Very Rev. O. H. Gibbs-Smith, C.B.E., Dean of Winchester since 1961, died on September 26, 1969, at the age of 67. He had been in indifferent health for some time and the Rev. Michael Stancliffe had been appointed to succeed him.

By his death Winchester has lost a dean who stands out as one of the greatest administrators the Cathedral has ever had. It is common knowledge that when the last scholar-dean died the chapter specifically asked that they might be given someone who would be capable of looking after the business side of their affairs. Gibbs-Smith, who was very humble about his deficiencies as a scholar, certainly fulfilled precisely the special aims with which he was called to his high office.

His previous career had well fitted him for the task. Born at Colchester in 1901 he was the eldest son of Edward Gibbs-Smith, M. D., a general practitioner in South Kensington, and Ethel Harvard Watts, of Cambridge, a collateral descendant of the founder of Harvard University.

He was a chorister first at St. Paul's Cathedral and then of King's College Chapel, Cambridge. He went to Westminster School and later he became a choral scholar of Clare College, Cambridge. He received training for the ministry at Cuddesdon, was ordained in 1924 and served a curacy at Harrow. In 1927, after being an assistant master at Harrow School for two and a half years, he asked the headmaster, Sir Cyril Norwood, to release him, as he felt he was at heart a parish priest. So he went to a curacy at St. Margaret's, Ilkley, where he remained four years. Then for 10 years he was in charge of the John Keble Church, Mill Hill, on which his impress, with its special marks of the English Use, surprisingly modern, is still to be discerned. From 1941 to 1947 he was in charge of St. John's Wood, where again he left a deep impression of his own ideals in liturgy and worship.

At this time his special gifts began to receive diocesan recognition. He became closely concerned with the Bishop of London's postwar Reconstruction Appeal. His abilities in this connexion were so marked that it seemed natural for him to become Archdeacon of London when that office became vacant in 1947.

CARE OF CITY

The archdeaconry included the care of the City clergy and churches, and carries with it a residentiary canonry at St. Paul's. In both spheres Gibbs-Smith showed himself more than fully competent. He had to deal especially with the rehabilitation of the City churches after the confusion of the war period. A more difficult task could scarcely be imagined, but the novel scheme for relieving a number of the churches of all parochial responsibilities and converting them into Guild churches, each with its own particular specialization, won general support, and the City of London

(Guild Churches) Act became law in 1952.

In the meantime Gibbs-Smith had been deeply engaged in the effort to build up the spiritual life of the diocese. He organized the Episcopal Visitation of 1947, which, instead of concerning itself with the kind of administrative detail usually dealt with on such occasions, was used as a lever to start a whole new evangelistic machine moving. Its purpose was seen to be achieved in the vast Mission to London of 1949, which was followed up by the School of Religion during the Lent of 1952, and by the series of sermons and study courses emanating from the Clergy Centre at St. Margaret Pattens in 1953–54.

Altogether it was perhaps the most comprehensive scheme of material and spiritual restoration ever undertaken in a single diocese. In the whole of it Gibbs-Smith was a moving spirit, and of much of it he was the originator. In him the secretarial gift was carried to the point of genius. He was quite content not to appear in person so long as operations got started, and moved smoothly to the required end.

The same gift found expression in many well organized services in St. Paul's, especially in connexion with the Order of the British Empire, of which he was Sub-Dean and for which he acted as liaison officer with the Cathedral.

He was therefore thoroughly equipped when he went to the deanery of Winchester in 1961. His capacity was immediately recognized and he was given the full confidence of his colleagues. He repaid them by sharing with them all his most intimate hopes and plans. He was fortunately assisted by the new financial aid that the Commissioners were offering to the cathedrals. His work was begun and carried forward under the happiest auguries. He was closely involved in the launching of the £405,000 Winchester appeal fund in 1966.

He married in 1949 Nora Gregg, one of the senior nursing staff of Great Ormond Street Hospital, by whom he had one son and one daughter. It was a most happy and stimulating partnership, in which his wife contributed greatly to his work both in London and Winchester.

September 29, 1969.

Wilfrid Gibson, the poet, died in a Surrey nursing home on May 26, 1962, at the age of 83.

Wilfrid Wilson Gibson was a native of Northumbria, born at Hexham, near Newcastle, on October 2, 1878. He was educated privately, and while still a youth in the north country he made his first serious attempts at verse writing. Two early volumes, *Urlyn the Harper* and *The Queen's Vigil,* which William Lyon Phelps, the American critic, thought "worth keeping as a curiosity", were published before Gibson found his true scope. It had nothing to do with the ancient legends, peopled by romantic heroes and heroines, which were the stuff of that youthful work. He turned to the poor people of his own observation, living in humble setting, the slum, the mine, the factory, the field.

Before he was 20 he had been printed in *The Spectator*: a collection of pastoral "plays" entitled *Stonefolds* and published in 1907 was his first volume of any importance: but *Daily Bread,* three years later, made him known as "the poet of the inarticulate poor". He had not discarded his technique; he adapted it to the rhythm of a life that had stirred him deeply. But there were critics who questioned whether his chief characteristics, colloquialism and symbolism, could go together. The 18 short verse-plays in *Daily Bread* made an appeal, all the same, one of them especially. A crippled boy keeps his mother company while she sits stitching endlessly for bread, and the great crane outside the window, swinging monstrous weights through the sky, becomes an obsession as he watches it, day after day. Half-crazed in a nightmare he sees it swooping down on him, grasping his bed as he lies there, and swinging him above the sleeping slum, among the blazing stars.

GEORGIAN ANTHOLOGIES

Workless men, starving wives, and stunted children—these are the tragic heroes and heroines of Gibson's maturity. Elemental passions dominate the scene, simple in his expression of them, powerfully idiomatic, making a healthful contribution to the poetry of the pre-war era. In a contemporary tribute John Freeman wrote that "he is without imitators and almost without rivals in his poetic mode". Edward Thomas and Robert Frost came nearest, although Gibson was less reflective, more trenchant.

Sir Edward Marsh included him in the famous Georgian anthologies, and after his marriage in London he moved to Gloucestershire, maintaining the friendships made at "Eddie" Marsh's chambers in Gray's Inn—a shrine for the Georgian poets—and before the bombs fell he was one of a group who founded the short-lived poetry magazine, *New Numbers.* They included Lascelles Abercrombie, Rupert Brooke, and John Drinkwater, and when Rupert Brooke died in the First World War Gibson and Abercrombie, with Walter de la Mare, were his joint beneficiaries. American enthusiasm for the dead soldier-poet was reflected in an invitation to Gibson as a poet-lecturer, and his U.S.A. tour in 1917 was successful and prolonged. The Macmillan Company of New York published in that same year Gibson's collected poems, a compliment which was not repeated over here until 1926.

PLAYS IN VERSE

In the 10 years since 1907 Gibson had published 10 volumes mostly of narrative or dramatic verse. Always his impulse led him to attempt plays in verse. *Hoops,* a one-act melodrama, was staged at a war charity matinee at His Majesty's in 1916, together with Gordon Bottomley's *King Lear's Wife* and Brooke's *Lithuania*: and *Krindlesyke,* of similar type (1922), was followed by *Kesterel Edge and Other Plays* in 1924.

Rupert Brooke's wish that his death might bring more gain than loss to his beneficiaries came true in one sense: Gibson was enabled to write even more confidently, with a steady output, and his tally of books eventually reached more than 30. He omitted the second of his three names—Brooke had telescoped them to "Wibson"—and his titles were no longer "staccato". *Fires, Borderland, Thoroughfares, Battle, Friends, Livelihood, Whin, Home* and *Neighbours* were succeeded in 1925 and thereafter at regular intervals by *I Heard a Sailor Singing, The Golden Room, Coming and Going, The Alert, Solway Ford, Goldknuckles,* and *Within Four Walls,* his last work, published in 1950, when he was 72.

He is survived by a son and a daughter.

May 28, 1962.

General Sir George Giffard, G.C.B., D.S.O., who died on November 17, 1964, at the age of 78, was Commander in Chief in West Africa from 1940 to 1942, and Commander in Chief of the 11th Army Group in the Burma Campaign of 1943–44. He made an outstanding contribution to victory: yet he was perhaps the least known of all the British generals who held high command in the Second World War. He was a tall, good looking man with nothing dramatic about him in either appearance or speech.

George James Giffard was born on September 27, 1886, the son of George Campbell Giffard, Clerk of the Journals, House of Commons. He was educated at Rugby and the Royal Military College, Sandhurst from which he was commissioned in 1906 in the Queen's Royal Regiment. Seven years later he was seconded to The King's African Rifles, and with them he saw his first active service in 1913 and 1914, when he took part in the operations against the Mereham tribe in East Africa. He remained with the King's African Rifles throughout the First World War, and served with distinction in the operations against Von Lettow Vorbeck in East and Central Africa. At the beginning of 1918 he was made a Column Commander with the temporary tank of Colonel while still only 32 years of age. He was wounded in this campaign, was awarded the D.S.O., was four times mentioned in dispatches.

Giffard was one of the officers selected for the first course at the staff college after the war, and he later passed through the Royal Naval Staff College and the Imperial Defence College. He commanded the 2nd Battalion of the Queen's from 1931 to 1933, after which he was appointed to Aldershot as G.S.O. 1st grade of the 2nd Division. In his last year with the 2nd Division, its commander was Major-General Archibald Wavell, and he played a considerable part in framing and carrying out the novel and unconventional tactical exercises which Wavell introduced, with the object of developing the initiative of junior commanders and making their training less stereotyped.

On leaving the 2nd Division in 1936, Giffard was promoted to Major-General and appointed Inspector-General of the Royal West Africa Frontier Force and King's African Rifles, and he continued to serve in this post when its scope was enlarged to cover all the African Colonial Forces.

At the beginning of 1939 Giffard was appointed Military Secretary to the Secretary of State for War, then Hore Belisha, but, after a year at the War Office, he was posted to the Middle East where he served once more under Wavell as G.O.C. in Palestine and Transjordan. He had been there only five months when he was transferred to West Africa as Commander-in-Chief. This was a new command embracing the Gambia, the Gold Coast, Nigeria and Sierra Leone, which had been set up because West Africa had become an area of great strategic importance. It was a staging area for our convoys round the Cape and for the air route to Egypt, and it was also a source of indispensable raw materials. On the Army side a large expansion was required from the nucleus provided by the West African regiments, not only for local defence but to provide fighting formations and specialist units for dispatch to active theatres of war. Giffard was the right man to tackle this immense task, with his capacity for administration and his unique experience of African soldiers in and after the First World War.

For over two years he handled the complex politico-military problems in West Africa with consummate skill, and, when he was joined later by Lord Swinton as Resident Cabinet Minister, he worked with him in the happiest cooperation. While he was in West Africa he was promoted General in 1941.

When the Mediterranean was reopened in the spring of 1943, the strategic importance of West Africa decreased accordingly. Giffard was the only senior officer in either the British or the Indian Army with experience of fighting a first class enemy in the jungle in the First World War and, when Wavell asked for his services as G.O.C. Eastern Army in India, he was at once transferred as the best man available for the job.

Before his arrival Wavell had attempted a minor offensive in the Arakan, but it had not been successful, and the operations had shown clearly that neither the British nor the Indian troops would be able to cope with the Japanese until their confidence and morale had been restored and they had been trained in a new fighting technique.

FOUNDATIONS OF SUCCESS

One of Giffard's first tasks was to devise means for keeping the soldiers fit in very difficult conditions. Land communications were practically non-existent, and to overcome this obstacle to the operation of a modern army, a unique system of air maintenance was worked out under his direction, without which the conquest of Burma from the north could never have been accomplished. He completely reorganized the rear administrative services, and, all through his first summer there, the process of intensive training and preparation went on. His work at this time undoubtedly laid the foundations of success in the campaign of the following year.

In August, 1943, the new South East Asia Allied Command was set up with Lord Louis Mountbatten as Supreme Commander, and, under the new arrangement, Giffard was appointed Commander-in-Chief of the 11th Army Group. Under him General Slim took over direct command of the Burma front as G.O.C. 14th Army. The 11th Army Group headquarters proved in some ways a fifth wheel to the coach. It was originally intended to control and coordinate the operations of the Allied Armies in all parts of the South East Asia Command, but the war ended without operations being undertaken outside Burma. Giffard's work was therefore confined almost entirely to the support of Slim who bore the main burden of the fighting. Slim, in his book *Defeat into Victory*, paid him glowing tributes. The partnership between them was a perfect one.

The campaign opened in December, 1943, when the 14th Army and Stillwell's Chinese forces began a widespread offensive. But in February it was halted. The Japanese had also planned an offensive, and they launched a series of attacks with the object of invading Eastern India and raising the flag of rebellion against the British. By skilful infiltration they cut off our forward divisions, first in the Arakan and then on the central front at Imphal, thus forestalling our projected advance to the Chindwin. Our forces did not withdraw, as the Japanese had expected, when they were surrounded, but stood their ground in previously selected positions. Now the new system of air supply came into operation. Reinforcements were flown in by Giffard, and at Imphal alone there were, at the height of the battle, some 60,000 British and Indian soldiers engaged in all round defence.

CAMPAIGN IN MONSOON

The Japanese pressed their offensive for five months until June, and then the climax came. They had lost nearly half their fighting strength, their morale broke, and they fell back into Burma in full retreat.

The campaign was continued throughout the monsoon, and it ended triumphantly with the capture of Mandalay and Rangoon. But Giffard was not there to see the victory to which he had contributed so much. At the crisis of the Imphal battle, when the outcome was still in hazard, the Supreme Commander told him that he no longer had confidence in him. Mountbatten and he, each possessing such splendid though different qualities, were incompatible in temperament, and it is probable they had never seen eye to eye. The difficulties of cooperation between them were greatly accentuated by the distance, 1,500 miles, which separated their headquarters. To this Giffard referred in strong terms in his dispatch in which he wrote that he was "continuously hampered in commanding and administering the 11th Army Group by the decision of the Supreme Allied Commander to move his headquarters to Kandy in Ceylon."

Giffard accepted the judgment without complaint or comment, and, when he was asked to stay on for some months pending the arrival of his relief, he did so and carried on his duties with complete loyalty. By the time he was relieved in November the Imphal battle had been won and he had seen his plans vindicated. Slim has recorded that he "saw him go with grief".

He came into the public eye again in 1953 in tragic circumstances. His nephew, Miles Giffard, had murdered his parents, and was convicted and hanged. Giffard had financed his defence and appeal, and when the trial was over and the sentence had been carried out, he wrote a moving letter to *The Times* in which he gave his opinion that the conviction of the young man, who had a long history of abnormality and mental illness, was manifestly unjust, and made an appeal for the revision of the M'Naughten Rules under which the jury had found him guilty.

He was created K.C.B. in 1941 and G.C.B. in 1944. From 1945 till 1954 he was Colonel of the Queen's Royal Regiment, Colonel Commandant, Royal West African Frontier Force of the King's African rifles, and of Northern Rhodesia Regiment, and was President of the Army Benevolent Fund from 1946.

He married in 1915 Evelyn, second daughter of Mr. Richard Margerison of Winchester, and had one daughter.

November 19, 1964.

Walter Gifford, Honorary Chairman of the world's largest company, American Telephone and Telegraph, who was United States Ambassador to Britain from 1950 to 1953, died on May 7, 1966, in New York. He was 81.

In many respects Gifford was the archetype of the modern American manager. He was patient, contemplative, and shy. Professionally his main concern was how best to get a job done, and he disliked ostentation and making a business of seeming to work. As a result, in his early days with A.T. and T. he developed a flair for asking and answering sensible questions which made him a pioneer efficiency expert. As president and chairman successively for a quarter of a century he built up a staff of purposeful and steady men like himself. When he retired as active chairman in 1950 the company had assets of more than $10,000m, and operating revenues of more than $2,000m.

Away from his desk, Gifford had a long record of public service as a trustee of universities and other institutions. During both wars he held important advisory office in government. In private life he was ill at ease in large groups and preferred modest occasions and small groups of friends. He had no small talk, and for this reason and his dislike of formal speeches he hesitated to accept, when President Truman asked him to take the London Embassy.

PRACTICAL APPROACH

Gifford had been a Republican all his life, well satisfied with things American and with no time for people at home and abroad who considered that they were entitled to help without being willing to work for it. He came to London prepared to consider requests for aid only when they served American as well as British interests. This practical approach served him well. The change of government in Britain in 1951 and the Japanese peace treaty were his major challenges. "If I was not pro-British when I came", he said in 1953, "I am as I leave."

He was a member of the executive board of the Pilgrims of the U.S. and the National Board of the English-Speaking Union.

Walter Sherman Gifford was born in Salem, Massachusetts, on January 10, 1885, one of the nine children of a lumber merchant and a schoolteacher. He was one of the quietest and more moderately successful members of the distinguished Harvard Class of 1905. He joined A.T. and T. by accident—an application to General Electric was misdirected to Western Electric, an A.T. and T. subsidiary—began as a payroll clerk in Chicago and apart from an experimental six months with a copper firm in 1911 saw his career grow with the company's fortunes.

Gifford married twice—in 1916 the late Florence Pitman, whom he divorced in 1929, and in 1944 Augustine Lloyd Perry. He is survived by his wife and a son by his first marriage. An elder son was killed in the Second World War.

May 9, 1966.

With the death of **Mary Gillick,** O.B.E., on January 27, 1965, England lost a talented and sensitive sculptress. Her own deeply laid convictions and her training caused her to work in the academic tradition of the west, though she always had sympathy and understanding for what younger artists were doing so long as this was based on technical competence.

Born Mary Tutin in Nottingham in 1881, she studied at the school of art there and at the Royal College of Art under Lanteri; and it was in Nottingham she met her future husband, Ernest Gillick, whose high standards and searching criticism did much to influence her and formed the basis of an ideal working partnership.

Free-standing sculpture except occasionally on a small scale was never her *métier* and she ultimately concentrated on the medal and the portrait bas-relief. She admired and studied the work of the great renaissance medallists and from them learnt much about design, the relation of relief to background, and the distribution of accents of light and shadow. As a result, from about 1920 onwards she produced a number of medals presented on occasion by learned societies and other institutions, notably the Royal Society, the Institute of Physics, and the Royal Academy schools.

ROYAL HEADS

Of wider general interest is that she designed in 1952 the uncrowned head of the Queen for the coinage of the United Kingdom and various members of the Commonwealth which was also used for various official medals; in 1953 the joint portraits of the Queen and the Duke of Edinburgh used on medals to commemorate royal visits to certain countries; and in 1955 the portrait of the Duke of Edinburgh used on medals such as that of the College of Air Training.

Inevitably this led to the production of long series of mural memorial plaques incorporating portrait medallions. Such are the memorials to Sir Henry Welcome (1955), Sir William Bragg, Sir Henry Dale, the Bishop of Chichester (1961), and Margaret Babbington of Canterbury. To church authorities in particular such memorials came as a boon. They are dignified, permanent, can be related to the structure of a building, and yet occupy little space. Always the type and direction of lighting were carefully studied; the setting of the portrait was designed to suit its surroundings; and the lettering of any inscription was always admirably designed. For the portraits, both on medals and plaques, Mary Gillick worked from photographs and available portraits, when the subject was dead, in consultation with friends and relatives. Her aim always was to represent the subject as he or she had been at the height of their powers, and as they were best known and remembered by contemporaries. In the case of the living, she followed much the same method, adding numerous interviews with the subject, the results of these being stored up in a remarkable visual memory.

Her husband, whom she married in 1905, died in 1951.

February 1, 1965.

Dame Mary Gilmore, D.B.E., who died on December 3, 1962, at the age of 97, was for most of her life easily the best known of Australian women poets, if not the only one.

With her death one of the few remaining direct links with the great wave of radicalism which flourished in Australia at the end of the nineteenth century has faded. While her poetry had a directness and an economy which made it far from negligible, it was rather in the inspiration she gave to the following generations of younger poets and writers, many of them also radicals of a kind, that her most profound contribution to Australian letters lay. At the same time, in a hidebound provincial society, her vigorous feminism set a powerful example to her sex; she was in her early life at least a pioneer of public womanhood.

She was born in August, 1865, at Goulburn, New South Wales, of a Highland father and a mother who was an Australian of the Hawkesbury. When young she often played with aboriginal children, whom she came to like and about whose way of life she learnt much.

At 16 she began to teach, at first in the country and later in Sydney, where she made the acquaintance of William Lane. He won her support for the New Australia movement, of which she became the leading woman enthusiast and subsequently she went out to Paraguay to join the colony already established.

While living there she married W. A. Gilmore. After the colony was disbanded she made her way to Patagonia where she taught English; she later moved to Argentina and for some time wrote for Buenos Aires newspapers.

POETRY AND JOURNALISM

She returned in 1902 to Australia to become an active figure in the Labour movement; for over 20 years she edited with great success a woman's page for the Sydney *Worker* but journalism was but a small part of her literary output. She published essays, a number of stories, some of which were concerned with the life and lore of the aboriginals, and several volumes of poetry. The most outstanding characteristic of her verse is its warm, simple and sincere humanity: there is also a vigour and vitality in it not altogether common in women poets.

She was perhaps unfortunate in that so many of her admirers concentrated their praise on her first book, *Married*, by no means her best, failing to recognize her steady development as a poet and to give to her later poems the praise they deserved. Now that much of her work has been gathered into a single volume her position can more readily be judged.

She was made D.B.E. in 1937.

December 4, 1962.

Professor Morris Ginsberg, F.B.A., the most distinguished among British sociologists of his generation, died on August 31, 1970 at the age of 81.

Following the example of Leonard Hobhouse, the foremost British sociologist of the previous generation, he brought his philosophical training to bear upon a wide range of sociological problems. He was Martin White Professor of Sociology at the London School of Economics from 1929 to 1954, when he became Emeritus Professor.

Born in 1889, he attracted attention as a promising student of philosophy at University College London, carrying off numerous prizes. For eight years he served on the staff of the philosophy department of that college; while so engaged he came into touch with Hobhouse and collaborated with him and G. C. Wheeler in a book dealing with the culture and institutions of the simpler peoples which was published in 1915.

His interests turned definitely to sociology, in the first instance to social psychology, on which subject he published a small book in 1921. This book and his volume on sociology in the Home University Library which appeared in 1934 are still widely read.

Otherwise his publications took the form of essays in learned journals and of named lectures, many of which he was invited to give, including the Hubert Spencer and the Auguste Pourte lectures. To the preparation of these lectures he devoted immense care and they contain much of his most important work. In 1932 he published a collection of his essays and lectures under the title of *Studies in Sociology*; he did the same in 1947 under the title of *Reason and Unreason in Society*, and again in 1956 under the title of *Essays on Sociology and Social Anthropology: On the Diversity of Morals. Evolution and Progress* appeared in 1961; *Nationalism: a Re-appraisal* in the same year. With J. A. Hobson he collaborated in 1931 in a life of Hobhouse whom he always acknowledged as the inspirer of his life's work. In 1924 he became reader in sociology at the London School of Economics, and in 1929 he was appointed to the chair of sociology tenable at the School in succession to Hobhouse.

As subjects for his essays and lectures he chose broad topics such as the causes of war, moral progress, the unity of mankind, history and sociology. With a background of very wide reading and exact knowledge he used his remarkable powers of analysis to dissect and examine such topics. Under his careful and orderly scrutiny errors, confusions and misunderstandings were detected and essential features of the problems were brought to light. In this manner he performed a most valuable work of clarification in regard to matters too often the subject of ill informed and unprofitable discussion motivated by predilection for a particular point of view. Thus, more than anyone else in his day in Great Britain, he did much to show that the highest standards of scholarship can be maintained in a field which had come under suspicion in academic circles as failing in scholarly achievement in comparison with other disciplines.

If he had been asked which of his interests engaged most of his attention, he would probably have replied that it was the building up of a rational ethic, and he was always insisting that this task turns on questions of fact. He once wrote that "despite the diversity of moral codes, general principles are discoverable which are implicit in all of them and which come increasingly to be recognized as universally building in the course of moral development." In this, as in all his other work, he laboured to master a huge range of facts in order to elucidate the very wide and general problems to which he gave successive attention. In his discussion of these problems, including for instance anti-semitism, he maintained such strict objectivity that those who did not know him could never have guessed that he was a very sensitive man deeply moved by the tragedies of his time.

A retiring scholar who sought nothing for himself, Ginsberg was an impressive lecturer.

WELCOME IN JAPAN

He accepted a number of invitations to lecture overseas, and when he visited Japan, where his reputation had preceded him, he was welcomed as one who had done as much for sociology as anyone in recent decades. He was always solicitous for the needs of individual students, many of whom owe much to his unselfish help and encouragement.

In 1931 he married Ethel Street, who died in 1962. He was elected a fellow of the British Academy in 1953 and served as president of the Aristotelian Society in 1942–43. He received honorary doctorates from the Universities of Glasgow and Nottingham; he took a prominent part in various societies and movements connected with sociology, and his advice was widely sought on problems of organization, research and teaching in his field.

September 1, 1970.

Jean Giono, the French author, died at his home at Manosque on October 8, 1970, at the age of 75.

His death has deprived French fiction of one of the few remaining major novelists who began to publish in the inter-war period.

This son of a shoemaker who spent the bulk of his life in the small town of Manosque in the Basses-Alpes was never either a populist or a regionalist writer. A sedentary man with a dynamic imagination, his fertile mind endlessly dreamt up fictional Utopias, confined to individuals, couples or small groups. When in the 1930s he tried to make a practical application of his dream world the arrival of pilgrims seeking spiritual guidance and treating him like Tolstoy made the enterprise ludicrous.

Giono's other incursion into the public arena, the proclaiming of a pacifist stand in the late 1930s was fully serious and it landed him briefly in prison in 1939. He was again gaoled in 1945 on unfounded suspicions of sympathy with the Vichy regime. Giono was understandably embittered by these two imprisonments and the colouring, if not the central nerve, of his post-war work altered.

His earlier novels had been lyrical evocations of individuals living in an extremely close contact with their natural habitat, ruled by imperious urges to satisfy their desires. Since the Second World War Giono's novels have aimed for a drier narrative mode, consciously based on Stendhal. The nature descriptions grew less expansive, though no less highly animated; the characters began to appear skeletal and enigmatic. It was as if Giono were increasingly hugging his fictional creation to himself and belittling the rest of us in our more prosaic little worlds.

His gifts were a prodigious capacity for coining metaphors and for telling stories strongly seasoned with a genuine sense of humour. In some ways he has been more purely productive and less of a moralist than most leading French novelists. Or rather any ethics he believed in were those of the individual rather than the community. Hence the heroic, Nietzschean flavour of much of his work.

His best novels are *Le Chant du Monde*, *Que ma joie demeure*, and *Le Hussard sur le toit*, all of which have strong panic ingredients. Giono is always at his best when exhibiting people liberating themselves from all restrictions except native horse-sense. His numerous supporters must hope that the legend of desk drawers stuffed with as yet unpublished novels is true and that, like the dead body of one of its characters which helped to fertilize the soil it lay on, Giono will continue posthumously to enrich the lives of his readers.

October 10, 1970.

Dorothy Gish, who died at Rapallo on June 4, 1968, at the age of 70, was the sister of Lillian Gish, and their careers followed a very similar pattern, on the stage and in films. Both of them made their name in the cinema and then left Hollywood to return to the theatre after the coming of sound and both were brought into the limelight of the film world by that great pioneer director of the early silent films, D. W. Griffith. The two sisters appeared together in *The Orphans of the Storm*, the last of Griffith's really outstanding productions, which he made in 1922. It is a film which will always be remembered in connexion with their name.

Dorothy Gish was born at Massillon, Ohio, on March 11, 1898. She began her stage career in 1902, and made her first appearance in New York a year later, as Little Willie in *East Lynne*.

JUVENILE ROLES

By 1912 she had made a name for herself in juvenile parts, and she then joined the old Biograph Film Company, whose inspiration was D. W. Griffith, a director far in advance of his time, and one with an exceptional talent for discovering and developing young players. There is no doubt that both Dorothy and Lillian Gish owed a great deal to him.

Griffith's star began to wane soon after the completion of *The Orphans of the Storm*, but Dorothy Gish remained in films until 1928, when she decided (as her sister was to do two years later) that the time had come for her to return to the theatre. In October of that year she played Fay Hilary in *Young Love* at the Masque Theatre in New York. In the following summer she played the same part at the Arts Theatre in London.

Thereafter she devoted herself very largely to the theatre, chiefly in the United States, and unlike her sister she did not feel drawn back to the cinema late in her career.

As a film actress she never achieved quite the same distinction as Lillian, who possessed a deeper sensitivity and a wider emotional range, and who was perhaps more fortunate in the parts she was given by D. W. Griffith when he was at the height of his powers. But just as Griffith was one of the outstanding pioneers of the early silent film so were the Gish sisters pioneers in the birth of emotional and romantic acting on the screen.

June 6, 1968.

A. T. Glenny, F.R.S., who died on October 5, 1965, at the age of 83, will be remembered as a pioneer in the field of immunization.

Many of the most important principles of immunology were discovered by him. For instance in 1921, with Südmersen, he described primary and secondary stimuli in diphtheria prophylaxis, showing the importance of leaving an adequate interval between the first and second doses of a course of immunization. This discovery forms the basis of all methods of immunization in use throughout the world.

Glenny's extensive work on diphtheria made possible the success of the diphtheria immunization campaign in Britain which reduced the annual death rate from this disease from 2,400 in 1940 to five in 1960.

Educated at Alleyn's School, Dulwich, he gave up a scholarship at University College to join the staff of the Wellcome Physiological Research Laboratories (now the Wellcome Research Laboratories) at Brockwell Hall, Herne Hill, in 1899.

In 1923 he first suggested diphtheria toxoid as an immunizing agent for man. Then in 1926 came the important announcement that he and his colleagues at the Wellcome Research Laboratories, Beckenham, had found that the antigenic value of toxoid could be enhanced by the addition of alum. By 1931, with Miss M. Barr, he was able to recommend the use of this alum-precipitated toxoid as an antigen for human immunization. In 1938 he collaborated with Sir John Boyd in the introduction of tetanus toxoid for human use.

DIPHTHERIA SERUM

As early as 1904, Glenny used diphtheria toxoid for the active immunization of horses in the preparation of sera for the treatment of patients. During the two world wars Glenny's knowledge of serum production was fully engaged in the preparation of tetanus and gas gangrene antitoxins for the armed forces.

Glenny retired from the Wellcome Research Laboratories as head of their Immunology Department in 1947. His work was recognized by his election as a Fellow of the Royal Society in 1944. He was awarded the Jenner Medal of the Royal Society of Medicine, and also the Addingham Medal.

As a scientist he was a meticulous worker and would not tolerate anv slipshod methods in his staff.

As a man he was shy and retiring, never seeking the limelight and pushed into it only with the greatest reluctance.

October 8, 1965.

Peter Godfrey, who died in Hollywood on March 5, 1970, at the age of 70, was regarded in America primarily as a film director, but his reputation in England rests on his work in the 1920s and 1930s as director of a pioneering club-theatre in London, the Gate.

Born at Chislehurst in 1899, Godfrey went on the stage at the age of 16 and worked as conjuror, clown, actor and producer at repertory theatres during the next 10 years. Later he realized that his only hope of being able to direct the plays he cared about, above all the Expressionistic plays of contemporary German and American authors, lay in founding his own theatre. This was done by renting, with the combined weekly savings of himself and his first wife Molly Veness, a top floor with a seating capacity of 80 in Floral Street, Covent Garden, and using it not as a public theatre—the London County Council refused to license it as such—but as a club which he then set about forming, His production of Georg Kaiser's *From Morn to Midnight* in 1926 put the Gate Theatre Salon on the map within a few weeks of its opening.

After two seasons in Covent Garden he re-established the Gate in a new theatre designed by himself in Villiers Street. There, while he built his programme round the work of such playwrights as Simon Gantillon, O'Neill, H. R. Lenormand, Alfred Savoir and Ernst Vajda, varying it with a musical burlesque at Christmas time, it was well supported. But the programme deteriorated from 1932 onwards, membership of the club dwindled accordingly, and amalgamation with Terence Gray's Festival Theatre at Cambridge proved to be no solution. In 1934, notwihstanding distinguished productions of *As You Desire Me* and *The Lady of the Camellias* with Jean Forbes-Robertson in the leading parts Godfrey was forced to sell the lease of the Gate. He had produced over 350 plays in 9 years and had helped to bring promising young players like Flora Robson, Beatrix Lehmann, Margaret Rawlings and Eric Portman to the fore. In the middle years of the 1930s he toured with Jean Forbes-Robertson in two plays written by himself.

Godfrey directed Paul Vincent Carroll's *Shadow and Substance* on the New York stage in 1938 and four years later became a film director in Hollywood, where he worked for Columbia, R.K.O., and Warner, and for a time produced plays by Gantillon and Kaiser at a theatre named after its predecessor in London. *Hotel in Berlin* scripted by Vicki Baum, with Raymond Massey in the lead, was the first film directed by him to be seen by British audiences. His later films included *The Two Mrs. Carrolls* and, made in 1956, *Please Murder Me*.

Godfrey married Miss Renee Haal in 1941.

March 24, 1970.

His Eminence William, Cardinal Godfrey, seventh Archbishop of Westminster, and Apostolic Exarch for Ukrainians in England and Wales, died on January 22, 1963, at the age of 73.

His duties as a member of the Central Commission preparatory to the Second Vatican Council obliged him to make frequent visits to Rome in the early months of 1962. He felt then the strain of extra duties while dealing also with matters affecting his diocese and his position as permanent chairman of the Hierarchy of England and Wales. Ordered by his doctors to rest before attending the first session of the Council in Rome he still dealt personally with diocesan affairs and presided over the English and Welsh Hierarchy in Rome before the council opened.

Successively Rector of the English College, Rome, Apostolic Delegate to Great Britain and Archbishop of Liverpool, before his appointment in 1956 to succeed Cardinal Griffin, he brought to his position at Westminster an exceptional knowledge of men and affairs in the archdiocese. Many of the priests over whom he assumed authority had been students at the English College; as Apostolic Delegate and therefore the Pope's personal representative in this country, he was in close association with the hierarchies of England and Wales and Scotland, and during the last illness of Cardinal Griffin he and his fellow-Metropolitan, Archbishop Grimshaw of Birmingham, had necessarily to act on behalf of the hierarchy in matters of national interest that normally would be dealt with by the Metropolitan of Westminster as permanent chairman of the hierarchy.

A man of learning, with very wide sympathies and an evident spirituality that endeared him to pupils and, later, to his flocks, he was also an experienced administrator, who could understand difficulties, but was inflexible in upholding principles. His public addresses, sermons, and pastorals were mainly homiletic in character, but on a number of occasions they contained firmly worded expositions of Catholic doctrine with regard to matters in general discussion, always so timed and worded as to give guidance to his own communion and to give information on the Catholic position to the general public.

In his personal relations with others Cardinal Godfrey fulfilled Newman's definition of a gentleman by his gentleness. By no means tall, he had a natural dignity that made him prominent in any gathering, while his wide range of interests, in scholarship and the arts, heightened the interest he aroused in conversation. Like Cardinal Hinsley, he had the essential charity that accompanies a deeply rooted interior piety; and while he insisted properly on the deference due to his office, his innate modesty made him impatient of obsequiousness, or of undue formality on informal occasions.

DOCTORATE IN DIVINITY

William Godfrey was born in Liverpool on September 25, 1889, the younger son of George Godfrey and his wife, Maria, *née* Garvey. He was educated at Ushaw College, Durham, and at the Venerable English College, Rome, where he obtained in 1913 his doctorate in Philosophy. Completing his theology he was ordained in 1916 and remained in Rome for a further year, preparing for his doctorate in divinity.

His first appointment after ordination was as a curate at St. Michael's, West Derby Road in his native Liverpool. It was his only pastoral appointment: for in 1919 he went to his *alma mater*, Ushaw College, as professor of classics. Thereafter he held the chairs of philosophy and dogmatic theology until 1930. In that year, Mgr. (later Cardinal) Hinsley was appointed Apostolic visitor to British East Africa and Godfrey was chosen to succeed him as Rector of the English College. Pope Pius XI conferred on him a domestic prelacy, to mark his appointment, and subsequently he became a member of the Supreme Council of the Congregation for the Propagation of the Faith.

His rectorship, which was to last for nearly nine years, was as distinguished in the history of the college as that of his predecessor, with whom he was on close terms of personal friendship. It brought him also into association with the English dioceses from which he received his students, while his presence in Rome prompted his appointment to various Papal missions which enabled him to make valuable diplomatic and governmental contacts. Thus he was a member of Cardinal Lepicier's suite in the Papal Delegation to Malta in 1935, marked by the award of an honorary canonry in the Cathedral at Valletta; Counsellor in the Papal Delegation led by Cardinal Pizzardo to the Coronation of King George VI—and, in 1938, Apostolic Visitor to Catholic seminaries and colleges in Great Britain, an appointment made in connexion with the formulation of a new constitution for ecclesiastical education.

APOSTOLIC DELEGATE

When in November, 1938, the Holy See announced the establishment of an Apostolic Delegation to Great Britain, with Godfrey as Apostolic Delegate, Pope Pius XI was nearing the close of his reign, which, in fact, occurred as the new Delegate was on his way to London.

The announcement was misunderstood in some circles, particularly by militant Protestant bodies which saw the appointment as a diplomatic one. In itself the character of an Apostolic Delegation unlike that of a Nunciature is purely ecclesiastical, being concerned with affairs of the Church rather than with relations between the Holy See and the Government of the country concerned. Nevertheless a Delegate, as the personal representative of the reigning Pontiff, is likely to be consulted from time to time on matters in which the Holy See may be interested. As it happened, Godfrey became more closely linked with the Diplomatic Corps during World War II, when he was appointed Chargé d'Affaires for the Holy See to the Polish Government in exile.

The spiritual jurisdiction of the delegation extended to Gibraltar, Malta, and Bermuda, to which he could not make canonical visits until 1948. He renewed this link with Malta in July, 1960, when he attended the nineteenth centenary celebrations of St. Paul's shipwreck in St. Paul's Bay.

When Archbishop Downey, of Liverpool, died in 1953, it was assumed generally that Archbishop Godfrey would succeed him, despite the fact that prelates in the direct service of the Holy See are transferred very rarely during a period of office to residential sees. In fact, no other instance is known of appointment to a See within a Delegate jurisdiction. The appointment, when it came, was well received by the people to whom he was returning as a Lancastrian. He was in Liverpool for only three years, but during that time he introduced a number of important developments, including a drastic revision of plans for the Metropolitan Cathedral of Liverpool, designed by Lutyens, which, because of steeply rising costs, had imposed on his Province a heavy burden, hardly commensurate with the value to Liverpool archdiocese of the future building. His own successor, Archbishop Heenan, was to introduce a further change by throwing new plans into open competition, from which was chosen the design by Frederick Gibberd.

DEATH OF CARDINAL GRIFFIN

Archbishop Godfrey was appointed to Westminster, again in accordance with general expectation, after the death of Cardinal Griffin in 1956. A year later he became Apostolic Exarch for Ukrainians in England and Wales, the Exarchate following the Ukrainian-Byzantine rite; its creation provided a unique occasion in that he was solemnly enthroned as an Ordinary, for the second time, within the territory of his own diocese.

At the first Consistory for the elevation of Cardinals held by Pope John XXIII, in 1958, he was created a Cardinal Priest of the title of St. Nereus and St. Acchileus. His titular church had been held by Cardinal Pole, whom he had followed as the second personal representative of the Holy See to England since the Reformation.

In 1961 he was appointed a member of the Central Preparatory Commission for the Second Vatican Oecumenical Council.

Shortly afterwards he welcomed publicly the disappearance of an old hostility and hate between the denominations. Saying that it was the duty of all Christians to come together in friendly contact, emphasizing the things in which they could live together in harmony, he added the warning that to seek doctrinal compromise would be to defeat the purpose for which seekers of unity were striving.

MEETING AT ENGLISH COLLEGE

In the nine months before the opening, by Pope John XXIII, of the Council, he was frequently in Rome for meetings of the Central Commission, returning there in October for the actual Council sessions. He presided early in October, 1962, at the autumn meeting of the Hierarchy of England and Wales held for the first time in its history at the English College.

January 23, 1963.

Sir Victor Gollancz, publisher and writer, died on February 8, 1967, at his home in London. He was 73.

His death removes from the scene a remarkable man who for some 30 years past has impressed himself on the public imagination not only as a distinguished publisher, but also as an active and highly articulate man of the left, a socialist preaching his own brand of humanistic socialism, a begetter of movements, a champion of causes, an indefatigable controversialist, an author, anthologist, and pamphleteer. Of those who between the wars helped to prepare the ground for the introduction of the welfare state and to put the Labour Party into power in 1945, he was among the foremost.

Born on April 9, 1893, the son of Alexander and Nellie Gollancz, he was educated at St. Paul's School and New College, Oxford, where he won the Chancellor's prize for Latin prose. At the outbreak of the 1914–18 War he joined the Inns of Court O.T.C. and was commissioned to the Northumberland Fusiliers. In 1916, being judged unfit for foreign service, he became a master at Repton under the headmastership of Dr. Fisher (later Archbishop of Canterbury) and broke new ground by starting a civics class. In 1920 he joined Benn's publishing house, where he worked for eight years.

He was closely concerned with the publication of Benn's "Augustan poets", properly called the "sixpenny poets", and also with Benn's Sixpenny Library.

FIRST VENTURE

Then in 1928 he founded his own firm in an ascetic (not a scrap of carpet anywhere) office in Covent Garden. The signboard of the new publishing house was designed by his wife. Gollancz's heavy type advertisements and his bright yellow book jackets quickly made an impression. The claim he sometimes made between the wars that he could impose a book on the public was not without substance. Gollancz parties became one of the highlights of literary London. His flair for combining political propaganda with successful publishing was evidenced by his promotion of the Left Book Club.

As the years passed and the scene darkened, his sense of engagement in the human situation found active and frequent expression. He loved England and especially the English countryside, but his outlook was essentially international. In 1945 his Save Europe Now movement aimed at the relief of starvation in Germany and elsewhere; during the Arab-Israel war he organized relief for the Arabs—to name only two of the many causes he espoused. Pacifism became another. But the campaign that touches the mainspring of his energy and enthusiasm was that for the abolition of capital punishment. He founded the Association for World Peace, now War on Want, in 1951.

His passionate advocacy of these and other progressive causes found its origin primarily in his reverence for life and his profound religious sense, which in turn was rooted in the history and traditions of his race. Institutional religion held no appeal for him. But anyone reading his autobiographical volumes addressed to his grandson, *My Dear Timothy* and *More for Timothy*, and his anthologies, *A Year of Grace* and *From Darkness to Light*, could not fail to be struck not only by the width of his reading but also by his sensitiveness to spiritual values and by his belief in and awareness of the divine omnipresence.

IMMENSE ENERGY

He was a man of strong emotions, and his intellectual passion was matched by a sense of urgency and great magnanimity. His energy was immense, his personality dominating. To be in his presence was a stimulating experience. Whether as host or guest (but preferably as host) he could be relied on to hold the dinner table. He had a fund of Jewish stories, which lost nothing in the telling. In moments of fun—and there were many in his company—he would sometimes jokingly doubt if he was not a bit of an anti-semite himself. He was a great and knowledgeable lover of music, especially the opera and had some pungent things to say on music and operatic production in *Journey Towards Music* (1964) and *The "Ring" at Bayreuth* (1966). Gollancz will be remembered gratefully by readers all over the world for publishing *The Musical Companion* (edited by A. L. Bacharach) which was not only a remarkably good introduction to music but remarkably cheap too.

Yet for all his deep and genuinely held religious convictions and his actively expressed preoccupation with the sufferings of others, even his most devoted admirers, acclaiming him as a proponent of high thinking, would hardly have singled Gollancz out as an exemplar of plain living. He was no ascetic. His dinner parties, his patronage of the Savoy Grill where he was a familiar figure, his travels abroad staying at first-class hotels, the luxuries of life with which in later years he was able to surround himself—this, coupled with a shrewdness which enabled him to build a highly profitable business (carried on, it must be said, in an office that reminded one of nothing so much as a warehouse), left some people with the feeling that here was something incongruous; that between his principles and his practice, between his profession of concern with the poor and needy and his own sumptuous way of life, there was something that called for explanation. It was a feeling for which in his quieter moments he probably had a good deal of sympathy. When the point was put to him once in a "Face to Face" television programme, he admitted that his love for the good things of life was a weakness, that he had compromised too much with Mammon, and that if he were taxed with the fact before the Heavenly Tribunal he would prefer to be silent.

But to say no more of him than that with all his gifts and talents he had his share of human weakness and rather more than his share of egoism would be to misplace the emphasis. If he had in some measure flamboyance and assertive characteristics, he possessed in far greater measure and at a much deeper level the messianic qualities of a prophet in whom realism and idealism were held in delicate balance. He would have made his mark in any age.

In 1953, on his sixtieth birthday, he was decorated with the Grand Cross of the German Order of Merit, "in recognition of his great help for, and sympathy with, the German people after the war"

When Adolf Eichmann was tried in 1961, he published a booklet which set out his reasons why Eichmann should not be hanged for crimes of genocide. He said that the whole idea of hunting down Eichmann over a period of more than 15 years was "deplorable".

In 1919 he married Ruth Lowy who bore him five daughters. He was knighted in 1965.

February 9, 1967.

Alderman Edwin Gooch, C.B.E., former Chairman of the Labour Party and Labour member of Parliament for North Norfolk since 1945, died at his home at Wymondham, Norfolk, on August 2, 1964. He was 75. Although he was a journalist before entering Parliament, and never a farmworker, he was President of the National Union of Agricultural Workers from 1928 to 1961.

Edwin Gooch's long career in trade unionism and in the organization of the Labour Party was solid rather than spectacular. He was generally regarded as a moderate and a man of the centre rather than the left. But he lived to see his organization achieving much more success than might have been prophesied when he joined it.

FARMWORKERS' GAINS

His union policy consolidated the gains in status which had to be given the farmworker as a result of war exigencies and postwar developments; cooperation rather than competition with other agricultural interests gave his members an improving share in the fruits of government support to British farming. At the same time the organization became influential in trade union policies to an extent far beyond what might have been inferred from its status and membership when he first became involved with it.

His thinking, like his speech, betrayed a typical East Anglian background of unexcited radical nonconformity, firm in its convictions and determined in their pursuit—the same stock and tradition from which the backbone of the Cromwellian army came. To the end of his life he devoted as much time and energy to the affairs of his native Norfolk as he did to those beyond it. It was significant that those of his acquaintance who did not address him by his Christian name usually called him Alderman. That was an office in which he was always happy.

INTO JOURNALISM

Born on January 15, 1889, the younger son of Simon Gooch, a blacksmith, of Wymondham, Norfolk, Edwin George Gooch worked as a boy in the forge while attending school. He was then articled to printing and from the composing room migrated to the editorial department. When he was first elected to Parliament in 1945, he was chief sub-editor of the *Norwich Mercury* series of newspapers. He worked in his earlier days with that notable figure George Edwards, after whose death Gooch became the farmworkers' leader in East Anglia and was their acknowledged spokesman.

Throughout his long connexion with the National Union, Gooch's services were entirely honorary, and as both a non-farmer and an unpaid official, he could not qualify to represent the union at the T.U.C. His association with the Labour Party had, however, stretched with one or two breaks from membership of the national executive, over more than 30 years, and following the party conference at Margate in 1955, he was elected by his colleagues as party chairman. Gooch had also served as president of the International Landworkers Federation, a member of the Minister of Agriculture's Smallholdings Advisory Council, and of the Permanent Advisory Agricultural Committee of the International Labour Organization, of which he was a former chairman. He had acted as adviser to the United Kingdom delegation to a number of Food and Agriculture Organization conferences.

He entered Parliament for North Norfolk in the general election of 1945 and held the seat at all subsequent elections, although sometimes with a rather narrow majority. He had announced that he would not be standing again at the forthcoming general election.

Gooch was first elected to Norfolk County Council in 1922 and later served as vice-chairman of both the county council and the Norfolk Education Committee. Among his many other local interests he became president of the Royal Norfolk Agricultural Association.

He married in 1914, Ethel, the younger daughter of C. E. Banham, of Wymondham, and they had one son. His first wife died in 1953 and in 1960 he married secondly Mary Agatha, daughter of W. Curl, of Norwich.

August 3, 1964.

Dr. G. P. Gooch, O.M., C.H., who died on August 31, 1968, at the age of 94 held high place in a long line of eminent historians nurtured by the University of Cambridge, carrying forward into our own day the scholarly conscience, the immense learning and the enlightened liberalism of his master, Lord Acton.

His special field was the political and diplomatic history of Europe during the decades before 1914. He brought to his studies here a breadth of sympathy and a lucidity of exposition that few historians of our day could rival. No better choice could have been made, after the war of 1914–18, for the work of editing the British Documents on the Origins of the War, a formidable task and a classic achievement which he shared with Professor Harold Temperley. But Gooch had an exceptional width of interest and knowledge; he ranged over the past two centuries of European history to unfailingly instructive purpose. He was perhaps as well versed as any Englishman in the cultural tradition and political development of modern Germany. In an age which was haunted by the still unresolved menace of the German problem Gooch proved a conspicuously discerning and impartial guide and witness. No doubt his affection for the more cultivated aspects of German life and thought gave an unwitting disproportion from time to time to his views on Germany in the years immediately before 1939, but it rarely impaired his political insight.

George Peabody Gooch was born in London, of East Anglian parents, in 1873. His father, C. Cubitt Gooch, was a businessman, working in partnership with the philanthropist, George Peabody, who stood godfather to the boy and gave him his Christian names. Sent to Eton in 1885, he remained there for only three years, being withdrawn owing to his delicate health. For the next three years he studied at King's College, London.

LOVE OF HISTORY

In 1891 Gooch matriculated at Trinity College, Cambridge, where his professor was Sir J. R. Seeley. His main subject of study was ecclesiastical history, for which he won the Lightfoot Scholarship. He took a first-class in history in 1894 and remained in residence for a further year, during which his learning towards philosophy all but matched his love of history.

He won the Prince Consort's Prize at Cambridge with a study of English Democratic Ideas in the Seventeenth Century, which was published by the Cambridge University Press in 1898. The book came under the notice of Acton, who had succeeded to the Cambridge chair after the death of Seeley. The great man liked the young scholar's work, urged him to read Gierke's Althusius as the best study of modern political thought, and wrote a complimentary foreword for Annals of Politics and Culture, which appeared in 1901.

Gooch did some lecturing at Toynbee Hall, the Working Men's College, Mansfield House, and the Passmore Edwards Settlements. He came of a Conservative family, but early threw in his lot with the Liberals, lecturing to small groups on Sundays and engaging in other political work. He stood as a Liberal for Bath in 1903 without success, but was elected for the same constituency in 1906. James Bryce, Secretary for Ireland, at once made Gooch his unpaid private secretary, a post which the latter filled with efficiency until Bryce's translation to the Embassy at Washington in 1907. He was unseated in 1910, and two later attempts at Parliament were abortive. From 1911 he became editor of the *Contemporary Review* continuing in that office for 49 years, after which he continued to collaborate as consulting editor.

After attempting to combine scholarship with politics Gooch devoted himself entirely to writing. He contributed to volumes VIII, IX, X, and XII of the Cambridge Modern History, wrote for H. A. L. Fisher's Home University Library in 1911 a History of Our Time (which has sold better than any of his other works), and in 1913 brought out a survey of History and Historians in the Nineteenth Century, which attested astonishingly catholic appetite for English, French, and German historical writing and of which a second edition appeared in 1952.

In 1918 he was chosen as joint editor of the Cambridge History of British Foreign Policy, and the three volumes of a brilliantly executed and authoritative work of some 2,000 pages, representing the collaboration of a score of scholars, appeared in the course of 1922 and 1923.

FRANCE AND GERMANY

The years after the cessation of hostilities were, indeed, his most remarkable and most fruitful period of activity. In 1920 he published Germany and the French Revolution, a striking study of the repercussions of the revolution upon German thought and aspiration, and in the same year he produced a life of Lord Courtney, written at the request of Courtney's widow. He took an active part in the earliest proceedings of the Royal Institute of International Affairs, extended the range of his study of European diplomatic affairs before 1914, and in 1923 published a History of Modern Europe, 1878–1919.

At the close of the same year he issued a study of Franco-German Relations, 1871–1914; in 1925 came a sympathetic, perhaps too sympathetic, account of Germany of the modern period and a volume on The Later Correspondence of Lord John Russell; and in 1927 he enlarged upon a favourite theme in Recent Revelations of European Diplomacy. By this time, however, what must be considered as, without question, his most important work had been well begun. With Professor Temperley he devoted himself steadily to the task of editing British Documents on the Origins of the War, 1898–1914, the eleven volumes of which were completed by May, 1938.

Gooch was fully alive, as he could scarcely fail to be, to the menace of Germany after 1933. He had rested his hopes upon the League of Nations and had looked forward, in truly liberal spirit, to the promise of Locarno. With the Nazi advent to power he gave informed and realistic warning in this country of possible events to come, while maintaining his profoundly sympathetic attitude towards the German people as a whole. He continued to write steadily.

After the Second World War his output was undiminished. A notable study of Frederick the Great (1947) was followed by Studies in German History (1948) and subsequently, when he was in his eighties, in addition to his memoirs entitled Under Six Reigns he produced no fewer than four volumes, mainly of eighteenth and nineteenth-century biographical portraits. These, too, bore witness to the continued width of his reading, his warm humanity, and the felicity of his style. The veneration in which he was widely held was fittingly marked by the publication in 1961 of an important collection of Studies in Diplomatic History and Historiography in Honour of G. P. Gooch, C.H.

He presided over the Historical Association from 1922 to 1925, over the English Goethe Society, over the Sir Richard Stapley Educational Trust, and over the National Peace Council between 1933 and 1936.

September 2, 1968.

Dr. Brian Laidlaw Goodlet, O.B.E., managing director of the Brush Electrical Engineering Company, Ltd., died on October 27, 1961, at the age of 58.

Earlier in his distinguished career he had been one of the two men chiefly responsible for the design of the first British power reactors. While at Harwell he had been in charge of the design-study which led to the Calder Hall type of reactor.

The son of C. W. Goodlet, he was born in St. Petersburg on March 13, 1903, and educated in Russia, at Sheffield University, and at St. John's College, Cambridge. He had his engineering training with Vickers, Ltd., in Sheffield, and Metropolitan-Vickers Electric Company, Ltd., Manchester, with whom he was later technical assistant and research engineer.

In 1937 he went to South Africa as Professor of Electrical Engineering at the University of Cape Town. He retained this chair until 1950 with the exception of a period in the same post at Birmingham University in 1939–40 and of his war service. From 1941 to 1946 he served as a temporary commander in the South African Naval Force on Africa and East Indies stations and at the Admiralty. He was made O.B.E. in 1944.

Goodlet returned to Britain to become head of the Engineering Research and Development Division at Harwell in 1950. His various awards included the Thomas Hawksby Gold Medal by the Institution of Mechanical Engineers; Kelvin and Overseas Premiums by the Institution of Electrical Engineers; and the Trevithick Premium by the Institution of Civil Engineers.

Goodlet was a member of the team of British scientists from the Atomic Energy Authority which visited Russia after the first international conference on the peaceful uses of atomic energy in Geneva in 1955.

In 1956 he left the Atomic Energy Research Establishment to join the Brush Electrical Engineering Company as chief engineer and director, becoming managing director the following year. He was also a director of Hawker Siddeley Industries and of Hawker Siddeley Brush Turbines Ltd.

October 28, 1961.

Sir Eugene Goossens, the conductor and composer, died on June 13, 1962, in a Hillingdon hospital; he had been taken ill in Switzerland, where he had been visiting two of his five daughters. He was 69.

Three generations with the name of Eugene have been violinists and conductors, and the family has contributed many musicians of the highest eminence to the profession, of whom Léon, the oboist, and Marie and Sidonie, harpists, are still active. Eugene Goossens had a considerable tale of compositions to his credit, some of which in his younger days made an impression during the period of flux and experiment that followed the 1914–18 War, but, as other conductor-composers have found, the business of conducting other men's music induced an eclecticism which the twentieth century, for reasons sufficient or insufficient, has been unwilling to accept. The most important are the two operas, *Judith* and *Don Juan de Manara*, to libretti by Arnold Bennett, both of which had their first performances at Covent Garden in respectively 1929 and 1937. Some early string quartets, including "By the Tarn" and "Jack o'Lantern", held their place for some time, but the work most frequently performed in recent years has been the oboe concerto (1927) written for and played by his brother Léon.

By 1943 when his first symphony was performed at a Promenade concert the process of losing his individuality in other men's idioms had already gone too far to commend it on the strength of its clever musicianship. Another clue to his comparative failure as a composer in contrast to his brilliant success as a conductor is to be found, negatively, in his autobiography *Overture and Beginners*, published in 1951 but only covering, in addition to much family history, the first 20 years of his own active career. Nowhere in its pages is to be found any statement or even hint of an artistic faith or revelation of a subjective attitude to the art he served with such distinction. It is the peripatetic not the psychological aspect of music which he chronicled and this may explain why his own music is lacking in sap.

Eugene Goossens III was born in London on May 26, 1893, his father then being a violinist in the Royal Opera House orchestra. Conducting and opera, however, were absorbed from infancy, for his mother was a singer and his father was soon touring as conductor with the Moody-Manners and the Carl Rosa opera companies. He was sent to school in Bruges at the age of eight and in 1903 he took violin lessons at Bruges Conservatory—the family is Belgian in extraction and both father and grandfather had attended one or other of the Belgian schools of music.

When he returned to England the family home was in Liverpool and he continued his education, musical and scholastic, there, until in 1907 he won a scholarship in violin playing at the Royal College of Music. There he studied violin with Rivarde, and composition with Charles Wood and Stanford. He joined the Queen's Hall Orchestra and the Philharmonic String Quartet, but soon began to appear as a conductor in some of Sir Thomas Beecham's enterprises. The fish took to the water and he recounts in his autobiography how he quickly won a reputation for taking on difficult and unfamiliar scores at short notice. One of his assignments was with Diaghilev's ballet and another concurrent with it the Carl Rosa's season at Covent Garden. This was in 1921 after a busy period of symphonic conducting, introducing his own and contemporary composition and participating in the launching of *The Beggar's Opera* at the Lyric, Hammersmith.

In 1923 Goossens was invited by Eastman of Kodak to direct the orchestra he was forming at Rochester, in the United States. He stayed with it until 1931 when he changed to Cincinnati; there he remained until 1946. In 1934 he was created Chevalier of the Legion of Honour. America's gain was Britain's loss, which was only retrieved in part by the work he was able to do in Australia. In 1947 he became head of the New South Wales Conservatorium and conductor of the Sydney Symphony Orchestra, and his work with both institutions brought their standards up to the level of international comparison. Goossens resigned his Australian posts in 1956 after an unsavoury law case in which he was widely believed to have been the dupe of evil-wishers. He spent his last years as a resident of London, conducting infrequently in London but making numerous gramophone records. He had been knighted in 1955 for services to music in Australia.

Goossens began his conducting career with a marked bias towards what was then contemporary and he continued subsequently to explore the byways of the repertory. This curiosity and tolerance, for Goossens's taste cut across all fashions, is the counterpart of a certain nonchalance, by which he gave the impression of having no profound convictions of his own. His performances were always urbane, civilized and immensely professional. During the years of his sojourn abroad he made frequent visits to his native country, as when he came to conduct his operas before the last war and since when he conducted the Berlin Philharmonic Orchestra at the Edinburgh Festival of 1949 and in London in 1952.

Though his output as a composer slowed down he produced a new symphony in 1944 and an oratorio *The Apocalypse* in 1954. An engaging *pièce d'occasion*, performed at Chelsea in 1958, was a concertante work for his brother Léon (oboe and cor anglais) and his two sisters, Marie and Sidonie, as harpists, with chamber orchestra. This, like a concertino for double string orchestra in 1948, though not profoundly significant, confirmed a criticism made many years before about his Sinfonietta (1922), that behind his chromatic idiom was a neo-classical mind.

Goossens was tall, good-looking, and a commanding figure on the rostrum with a loose beat that nevertheless secured the attentive cooperation of his players. He married first, Dorothy Millar, in 1919, who bore him three daughters; then in 1930 he married Janet Lewis, by whom he had two more daughters; lastly, in 1947, he married Marjorie Fetter Foulkrod.

June 14, 1962.

Lord Gorell, who combined literature with a lively interest in affairs to a remarkable degree, died at his home at Arundel on May 2, 1963, at the age of 79.

Versatile and fluent, Lord Gorell brought a graceful and sympathetic turn of mind to all the different forms of literature he attempted. As poet his most pronounced qualities were a sincere devotion to England and the English country scene and an unaffected pity for human suffering, and with these went the quiet conviction that poetry itself was a cardinal influence upon human progress in general. His verse, lyrical and narrative, was almost always accomplished, but perhaps too seldom more than that; it lacked fire and concentration and suffered from the rather conventional poetic diction he favoured. He wrote several novels, for the most part leisurely and a little old-fashioned in manner, that commented shrewdly enough upon the social history of this century and were never less than readable, but as a novelist turned his hand more frequently to detective fiction. Concurrently with his literary work he led for a time a busy official life and was much in demand as a chairman of Government committees of investigation, whose reports frequently betrayed his practised hand.

The Right Hon. Ronald Gorell Barnes, third Baron Gorell, of Brampton, in the County of Derby, in the Peerage of the United Kingdom, C.B.E., M.C., was the younger son of the first Baron Gorell and was born on April 16, 1884. He was educated at Winchester, Harrow, and Balliol College, Oxford, and was called to the Bar by the Inner Temple in 1909. The next year he joined the editorial staff of *The Times* but left in 1915 to join The Rifle Brigade, and became adjutant of the 7th Battalion. His father had died in 1913, and his elder brother, who was unmarried, was killed in action in 1917, and he thus succeeded to the family honours. In the last year of the war he went to the War Office and joined the newly created education branch with the title Deputy Director of Staff Duties (Education). His two years' work, for he did not resign his post until 1920, are vividly described in his *Education and the Army*, published in 1921.

MINOR OFFICE

He had but one short term of minor office, as Under-Secretary of State for Air from July, 1921, to October, 1922, but though he was never again a member of any Government, his services were often in demand for Government investigations of one sort or another. Thus in 1933 and again in 1938 he was chairman of the committees for the control of private flying; similarly from 1933 to 1941 he was chairman of the Prime Minister's committee on Carlton House Terrace and other questions of a like nature and in 1946 helped to investigate the possibilities for the reconstruction of the badly damaged terraces in Regent's Park. His work at the War Office had given him an abiding interest in the problems of teaching and from 1922 to 1935 he was chairman of the Teachers' Registration Council and he was president of the Royal Society of Teachers from 1929 until 1935. He had also been chairman of King's College Hospital from 1929 to 1933, of the Royal Aero Club for two terms, first from 1933 to 1936 and again from 1944 to 1946; and of Dulwich College and Alleyn's School from 1949 to 1959; and president of the National Council for the Unmarried Mother and her Child from 1928 to 1962, and of the Royal Literary Fund from 1951 to 1962.

These varied interests notwithstanding, he remained true to his first love, literature, and it is as a literary man that he will be remembered, as author and as editor for six years from 1933 to 1939 of the *Cornhill Magazine*. His earliest volume appears to be a modest record of East African travels and impressions, *Babes in the African Wood*, published in 1911. Two years later came a novel, *Out of the Blue*, in which—and this might be thought characteristic of him—a couple shipwrecked on an island observed a code of most rigid Victorian morality, and in 1917 a book of poems, including many war poems of a gentle, contemplative character, *Days of Destiny*. After that volumes of verse and volumes of fiction alternated fairly regularly.

ALLEGORY

Among the books of verse was *The Spirit of Happiness* (1925), an allegory of human life, which was afterwards retitled *The Silver Cord*; among the novels were *Plush* (1924), described as a romance of the House of Lords, and *The Devouring Fire* (1928), a particularly ingenious detective thriller. A volume of *Collected Poems, 1904–1936*, appeared in 1937. The novel *Warrior's Way*, which appeared in 1945, was a long, leisurely and thoughtful survey of changing modes and manners during the previous half-century.

In 1954 Lord Gorell, who was a lay reader in the dioceses of Chichester, Southwark, and London from 1956 to 1960, published a life of Jesus, *He Walked in Light*. Lord Gorell's autobiography *One Man...Many Parts* appeared in 1956.

He married in 1922 Elizabeth, eldest daughter of the late A. N. Radcliffe, by whom he had two sons and a daughter. His wife died in 1954. The elder son, the Hon. Timothy John Radcliffe Barnes, now succeeds to the title.

May 3, 1963.

Sir Arthur Gouge, formerly vice-chairman and chief executive of Saunders-Roe, Ltd., died on October 14, 1962, at the age of 72.

For a quarter of a century, Arthur Gouge had been concerned with flying-boats. He began his marine aircraft work with a period of research into hull form in 1920. Six years later he was advanced to the position of chief designer at Short Brothers. At the end of another three years he became general manager and so, right through the heyday of the flying-boat, he was responsible for the most outstanding military and commercial aircraft of this class. Both the Sunderland for the R.A.F. and the Empire flying-boat for Imperial Airways were evolved under his guidance and there were half a dozen other less well-known types for which he was responsible, besides a big, three-engine float seaplane and the Stirling landplane bomber which did service during the war.

After 28 years with Short's, he left the company in 1943 to become the chief of Saunders-Roe Ltd. and there he had the satisfaction of producing a jet fighter with a flying-boat hull and the 140-ton Princess flying-boat. He also launched his company on the new enterprise of helicopter development.

By this time, the day of the flying-boat seemed to be over. It had served a most valuable purpose in the military field when Britain was still policing the world and landplane bases were relatively few. It gave British commercial air transport a great advantage at the same time when many countries hesitated to embark on heavy expenditure on airports, and presented the Empire with an air mail service at a comparatively small cost. In both respects, Gouge served his country well during the decade before war broke out. Theoretically, his specialist marine craft should have found an equally important place after the war. In fact they found no market, first because of the demand for speed and then, when the cost of runways seemed to set a limit on the size and weight of landplanes, because of new devices to shorten the take-off and landing runs of big aircraft.

SWITCH TO NEW PROJECTS

Gouge was shrewd enough to see that he could no longer concentrate on flying-boats; hence his switch to helicopters and also, in 1953, to a contract for the design of a supersonic jet landplane while his three Princess flying-boats were cocooned and put away to await suitable airscrew-turbine engines. They have been sold recently to an American firm.

Gouge was born at Northfleet in July, 1890, and was educated first in the church school at Northfleet and later at Gravesend Technical School and at Woolwich Polytechnic. He had begun work as a mechanic before the 1914–18 War. As a mechanic he became an employee of Short Brothers in 1915, when it was still a small, family concern and was about to move from Eastchurch to Rochester. Within a year the company was experimenting with duralumin as a substitute for wood in the making of wing ribs. Soon it had advanced to a system of stressed skin construction for aircraft. He became the trusted assistant in this work.

He brought intelligence as well as industry to his tasks; he welcomed responsibility; he was always ready to offer an opinion and back it with sound argument. So gradually the mechanic progressed to original work, to design and ultimately to management while the company persisted through the lean years, offering design after design which were not adopted and making omnibus bodies at a separate factory in Bedford to keep the aircraft enterprise alive. The Empire flying-boat design brought the first big flying-boat order. Gouge surprised Imperial Airways by giving better performance than had been promised in the contract and by delivering the boats ahead of contract dates. His chief, Oswald Short, magnanimously waved aside the extra payments to which this excess of virtue made the buyers liable, and the fleet of boats went forward under the happiest auspices to extend Britain's airlines over thousands of miles and to earn the affection of thousands of passengers. Out of this type of boat grew the Sunderland, which played an equally famous part in its own sphere, and also the somewhat bigger commercial boats of similar design which made the first experimental crossings of the Atlantic from Foynes on the Shannon just before the war.

WATER-PRESSURE TESTS

For the young Gouge, work at Short's was a stimulus and a challenge. The three brothers, Horace, Eustace, and Oswald, had entered the aircraft industry in 1909 after earlier work in making balloons. They had progressed from the building of Wright designs to the preparation of their own models and had already had the service of another engineer, destined to succeed in his own right, C. R. Fairey, before Gouge joined them. Gouge matured in good company and qualified by hard work and close application to make his own contribution worthy of it. He remained to the end the typical engineer, a little shy of social life and yet a good companion, a believer in thorough investigation and planning before embarking on a task, well-informed on all matters relating to his industry, and always willing to break new ground provided he had first undertaken tests to satisfy himself.

As chief executive of Saunders-Roe, he made a water-pressure test of the Princess flying-boat's passenger saloon before any company had thought of testing a supercharged cabin in that way. He also approved electrical controls for that big boat while there were still doubts about the system in other people's minds. He was a stocky, solid man, blessed with a steady common sense and the ability to push an undertaking through with vigour and a sure touch. He had been president of the Society of British Aircraft Constructors and of the Royal Aeronautical Society.

He married in 1918 Margaret Ellen Cook, who died in 1940. He leaves a son and a daughter.

October 16, 1962.

Dr. Herbert John Gough, C.B., M.B.E., F.R.S., a pioneer of research into metal fatigue, and for 10 years engineer-in-chief to Unilever, Ltd., died on June 1, 1965. He was 75.

Herbert John Gough was born on April 26, 1890, the son of Henry James Gough and Mary Anne Gillis. He was educated at University College School and London University, where he obtained an Honours degree in the Faculty of Engineering, and, later, received a D.Sc.

From 1909 to 1913 he served an apprenticeship with Vickers, Sons and Maxim, and a further year with Vickers Ltd. as designer-draughtsman on naval and military weapons and other armament.

Gough joined the scientific staff of the engineering department at the National Physical Laboratory in 1914. During the 1914–18 War he served in France and Belgium in the R.E. Signals, being awarded a commission in the field and the M.B.E., and was twice mentioned in dispatches.

Resuming at the N.P.L. in 1919 he began the work with which his name will be chiefly associated—on the fatigue of metals.

His approach to the subject was both fundamental and practical. His pioneering researches on the mechanism of fatigue failure, that is failure due to repeated application of a load much lower than that necessary to produce failure in a single application, provided a firm foundation for much of the work still in progress on this subject. This work led in 1933 to his election to fellowship of the Royal Society. At the same time he devoted himself to work of more immediately practical significance to mechanical engineering designers, in the investigation of the effects of the "stress raisers" sometimes inevitably present in engineering components. Another interest at this time was in the causes of failure of wrought iron chain and cable, a problem to which, with A. J. Murphy, he succeeded in providing a practical solution.

HEAD OF DEPARTMENT

In 1930 he succeeded Sir Thomas Stanton as superintendent of the engineering department (later division) and remained its head until 1938. During these eight years he continued his personal researches particularly in the direction of fatigue under combined stresses, but his main effort had to be devoted to directing the wide range of research work of the division. He considerably enhanced its already high reputation and it became a fruitful training ground for engineering research workers. as can be seen from the fact that, with a scientific staff never exceeding 20, at least 12 members of the staff during these eight years later became directors of research elsewhere.

In 1938 Gough was called to the War Office as director of scientific research and was director general of scientific research and development, Ministry of Supply, from 1942 to 1945. Of the many contributions to the war effort for which he was responsible perhaps the one most in the public eye was the research and development applied to bomb disposal. (In 1947 he gave the Thomas Hawksley lecture on "Unexploded Bomb Disposal.") He was awarded the C.B. in 1942.

At the end of the war he became engineer-in-chief to Unilever Ltd. and as such was responsible for developing the engineering department of the company's advisory technical division in London. He was also largely responsible for the coordination of the engineering activities of its associated companies at home and abroad.

His lasting contribution, however, was the increased recognition that he achieved within the company for the importance of engineering in all its branches, and for the status of engineers. Gough retired from Unilever in 1955.

MEDALS AND PRIZES

He received many medals and prizes from engineering institutions. He was an Honorary Fellow of the Royal Scottish Society of Arts. He became a Member of the Institution of Mechanical Engineers in 1933, a member of council in 1936, a vice-president in 1944 and was president in 1949.

Another interest during the postwar years was his membership first of the Guy Committee and then of the Mechanical Engineering Research Board. The first set up what is now the National Engineering laboratory at East Kilbride and the second until 1959 advised on its activities. Gough was for six years chairman of the board's properties and mechanics of materials committee. In 1924 he wrote a book on *Fatigue of Metals*, the first of the only two books on the subject in English for a quarter of a century; he also contributed some 90 papers to learned societies, many of which in Britain and overseas honoured him by special invitations to lecture.

He married in 1918 Sybil Holmes, and they had one son and one daughter.

June 4, 1965.

General Sir Hubert Gough, G.C.B., G.C.M.G., K.C.V.O., died on March 18, 1963, at the age of 92. He was the last of the regular cavalry officers who saw service in Victorian campaigns and held high command in the 1914–18 War. At three points in his long career—as mounted infantryman in South Africa, as brigadier at the Curragh, and for his leadership of the Fifth Army in 1918—he was under fire from critics and supported by weighty professional opinion.

He was not only a good soldier and a good sportsman but a charming personality, popular with all who came into intimate contact with him, as personal friends, superior officers, or close subordinates. He came of a family renowned in war since the days of Field Marshal Lord Gough, the conqueror of the Punjab. Four members of this family—his father, his brother, his uncle, and a cousin—won the V.C. Hubert Gough maintained the tradition of his race for personal bravery.

He was born on August 12, 1870, the second son of General Sir Charles Stanley Gough, V.C., G.C.B., of Innislonagh, co. Tipperary, his mother being a De la Poer, of Gurteen la Poer, co. Waterford, close at hand beyond the Suir. Following family custom, Hubert, after being at Buckland's, Laleham, was sent to Eton, where he boarded at Arthur James's. Lord Bridgeman, Lord Willingdon, Field Marshal Lord Chetwode, Sir Neill Malcolm, and Sir Percy Hambro were among his contemporaries. His holidays were spent in Ireland with his grandfather, George Gough, a retired Judge of the India High Court, and other kinsfolk. He rode every day and hunted whenever there was a chance. After passing through Sandhurst, he was gazetted in 1889 to the 16th Lancers. He was not only a first-class horseman but a light-weight, and now had a long series of successes on the polo ground, on the racecourse, and in the hunting field. He finished second in the regimental point to point soon after he joined and won it next year. In India he won the Army Cup twice. Unlike some of his contemporaries, however, he was not infatuated with sport, but keen on his profession and on military literature. Promoted captain with five years' service in 1894, he passed the entrance examination for the Staff College in 1897, but did not join until January, 1899, because he obtained permission to take part in the Tirah campaign of 1897–98.

In this expedition he acquired useful experience as assistant to the Supply Officer of the 2nd Brigade. The outbreak of the South African War in 1899 cut short his course at the Staff College.

Gough was employed as an intelligence officer and joined Lord Dundonald's Mounted Brigade in the relief of Ladysmith. He had quickly become celebrated for his bold reconnaissances and was rewarded in February, 1900, by command of a composite regiment of mounted infantry in the brigade. In the final stages of the relief Gough scouted ahead with his regiment, the brigade waiting at each ridge until he reported the country ahead clear. Thus he led the way for Dundonald's entry into Ladysmith.

Major Gough continued to lead his mounted infantry regiment far and wide. In September, 1901, he met with a disaster. While convoying a wagon column he encountered a Commando, which happened to be Botha's advanced guard, at Scheeper's Nek, was caught between it and Botha's main column, and captured with his whole force. He and a few others escaped after dark. Lord Kitchener telegraphed that he was "not in the least put out" and attributed no blame to Gough.

In December he was promoted to the command of a column, but was shortly afterwards wounded and sent home for six months, before the end of which period peace was signed. He was awarded a brevet colonelcy. He had acquired a reputation for daring, in which, however, some older heads detected an element of rashness.

He did not return to the Staff College, but was given the p.s.c. In September, 1902, he was appointed Brigade-Major of the 1st Cavalry Brigade at Aldershot. This post he held for 15 months only, being selected in January, 1904, as instructor in tactics at the Staff College, where Sir Henry Rawlinson was then Commandant.

He acquired great popularity with the students, but after only three years' duty was appointed to the command of the 16th Lancers at Aldershot. Four years later he was promoted to the command of the 3rd Cavalry Brigade at the Curragh.

UNDER ALLENBY IN FRANCE

Now he was in his own country, where his name became synonymous with soldiering and sport. He was regarded with affection by his command, as events were to show. In March, 1914, the Government made it clear that the use of troops against the Ulster volunteers, arming to oppose the enforcement of home rule on the North of Ireland, was under consideration. To allay the anxieties of many Irish officers the Army Council made it known—the Secretary of State, the Chief of the Imperial General Staff, and the Adjutant-General initialling the paper—that officers domiciled in Ulster would be exempted from service against their countrymen; others might resign, but their resignations would not be accepted and they would be dismissed the service. Thereupon Gough and the vast majority of his officers decided to resign. He and two of his commanding officers were immediately summoned to the War Office. Neither the threats of the Secretary of State nor the persuasion of the Chief of the Imperial General Staff moved him, and since the two military members of the Army Council stuck to their given words the incident ended with the resignation of Colonel Seely (Secretary of State), Sir John French (C.I.G.S.), and Sir Spencer Ewart (Adjutant-General). The gathering war clouds soon blotted out the Curragh incident.

The remainder of Hubert Gough's military career is fully covered by his book, *The Fifth Army*, published in 1931, and further commented on in his autobiography, *Soldiering On*, published in 1954. His brigade went to France as part of Major-General Allenby's Cavalry Division, which in the retreat from Mons covered the left flank of the B.E.F. In the Battle of the Marne the 3rd and 5th Cavalry Brigades, grouped under Gough, cooperated with and covered the exposed right flank. In the advance to the Aisne Gough's force preceded the centre.

OVER RIVER

Over the flat meadows in front of Condé bridge, which he was to have seized, it was impossible for cavalry to advance in face of opposition, so he crossed the river farther east. On September 16 his force was designated the 2nd Cavalry Division, and at 44 he became a temporary major-general. He passed again under the command of Allenby, now commander of the newly-formed Cavalry Corps.

After the transfer of the B.E.F. to Flanders, Gough's division, which now consisted of the 3rd, 4th, and 5th Cavalry Brigades, formed the right of the Cavalry Corps, which during the first battle of Ypres held the Messines ridge. Through forced back, the cavalry clung on against a threefold superiority until French reinforcements arrived. Gough even contrived to send some much-needed aid to Haig's I Corps at Ypres.

In April, 1915, Gough was transferred to an infantry division, the famous 7th, which he commanded at Festubert. In July he was promoted to command the I Corps, which was heavily engaged in September in the battle of Loos.

Before the Battle of the Somme Haig had arranged that Gough should lead the three cavalry divisions and the reserve infantry to extend northward the gap which he hoped to open. However, towards evening on July 1, 1916, it became clear that there would be no break-through. Gough then took over command of the two corps on the left wing of Rawlinson's Fourth Army. His force was officially called the Reserve Army until October, when it became the Fifth. This was the front on which there had been a complete failure. Gough was instructed to renew the attack. He belied his reputation for impetuosity by declaring, after a careful examination, that there was not the smallest prospect of success, and it was not for some time, and until he had received reinforcements, that operations were resumed.

PETAIN'S APPEAL

The slogging astride the Ancre valley was long and costly, though the final operation at Beaumont Hamel was a brilliant stroke which Lüdendorff had regarded as impossible. Siege warfare of this type was not suited to Gough's talents. His reputation with the Government and the Commander-in-Chief expanded, but it shrank with certain of his subordinate commanders especially the Australians, who considered that they were thrown in without sufficient warning or time for preparation. How much the enemy was shaken was hardly realized until, in February, 1917, he slipped away in the night—prematurely according to his programme—and fell back to the Hindenburg Line.

The unhappy attempt to breach this line at Bullecourt and then the long-drawn-out battles in the mud of "Passchendaele" brought more disapproval of Gough's methods. Few realized that he was spurred on by the higher command and practically no one knew that his plea to end the battle, after the weather had become the principal enemy, was turned down.

REGAINING COAST

In his book of 1931 Gough for the first time brought to public notice the fact that one of the main reasons for persevering with the offensive was the definite statement from the Admiralty that, unless the Belgian coast was regained, the Navy could not hold the Channel, in which case it would be useless to continue the war.

Equally unknown were Pétain's appeals to Haig to keep the Germans' hands full while he reorganized an army nearly ruined by mutiny. Gough was strongly criticized. But the story that "the troops" distrusted him is nonsense. Not one private soldier in a hundred knew whether his army commander was Gough or Plumer, and the mud was no pleasanter in either case. Still, whether justly or not, his reputation declined.

In December, 1917, Sir Douglas Haig, who on several occasions picked Gough for special missions, sent him southward to take over a new front on which he had been forced by political pressure to relieve the French. The defences were in poor condition; there was little labour available to improve them; and eight front-line divisions were strung out over 40 miles, with few reserves behind them. Gough gave due warning to G.H.Q. of the certainty of attack and of the peril of his situation, but Haig felt he could do no more than send him four more divisions. The whole front was endangered and on the right French aid had been promised to Gough in case of need.

When the tremendous blow fell on March 21, Gough's defence was broken and he could do no more than fight a series of rearguard actions. French aid did come, but slowly, and divisions arrived with no reserve ammunition and in some cases without their artillery.

REMOVED FROM COMMAND

The Fifth Army continued to yield ground under the heavy pressure of Hutier's legions, but it did not cease to fight. Had Gough been removed from command during the Battles of the Somme or of Ypres not much surprise would have been aroused. That he should now be recalled—on March 28—by Lloyd George's Government, after hard fighting against great odds, appeared the height of injustice. He was, indeed, the scapegoat for the sins of omission of the Versailles Council and its advisory bodies, whose activities in military operations were put an end to by Foch.

The only further appointment offered to Gough which could be described as military employment came when, shortly after the war, he was sent as chief of a military mission to the Baltic. This did not last long because he was, curiously enough, thought to entertain left-wing views. He was recalled, and thereupon retired from the Army at the age of 51. He did, in fact, move left of centre for a time, severely condemning the Treaty of Versailles, disliking the Russian "white" aristocracy, and toying with the notion of home rule for Ireland. In 1928 he stood as a Liberal for the Chertsey division of Surrey, but was unsuccessful, apparently to his own relief.

As the facts about 1918 gradually came out the public began to revise its opinion of the public began to revise its opinion of the Fifth Army. In 1931 Gough published a history of his command. He did so, however, in order to disperse the cloud which still hung over the good name of his troops rather than to justify himself. In 1937 he was awarded the G.C.B., and this was universally recognized as not only a reward but a reparation. In the Second World War he was an enthusiastic Home Guard officer until obliged to resign under the age limit.

Some of the criticisms of Gough may have been heightened by his testiness under the strain of war. In the tactical sense close study of the war does not often bear them out, and cases can be found in which, in discussions with superiors, he fought on the side of prudence. He possessed in good measure that "sacred fire" which marks the born commander. A more humdrum but valuable virtue was his habit of seeing everything for himself.

Sir Hubert Gough married in 1898 Louisa Nora, daughter of Major-General H. C. Lewes. She died in 1951. He leaves four daughters.

March 20, 1963.

Sir Ernest Gowers, G.C.B., G.B.E., one of the greatest public servants of his day, who served in several state departments and presided over numerous official bodies and committees of inquiry, died on April 16, 1966, at King Edward VII Hospital, Midhurst, at the age of 85. He was the author of *Plain Words*, and revised Fowler's *Modern English Usage*.

As a young civil servant he was "discovered" by Lloyd George and put in one of the key posts of the National Health Insurance scheme on its inception in 1912. For many years he had a major responsibility for official efforts to secure the reorganization of the coal industry. During the Second World War he was Regional Commissioner for Civil Defence, London Region, from 1939 to 1941, becoming Senior Regional Commissioner in 1941, and from then on bore the main responsibility for civil defence in London until the end of the war.

In this post he showed his full powers as an administrator, and indeed as a leader. Energetic, forceful, always cheerful, with an unfailing eye for the essential, he gave the impression of being master of every unexpected development and, as a result, infused confidence into all who came in contact with him, In the early years of the war his whole day was taken up with meetings with Ministers, local government officials and members of his own staff, at which he was called on to make difficult decisions at short notice on matters that had proved incapable of solution at lower levels. He did his "paper work" after supper, and his typist would arrive in the morning to find a pile of letters and minutes that he had written when other people were in their beds. Yet somehow he found time to re-read Gibbon and Professor Toynbee's *A Study of History* to "keep his perspectives right". The post of Regional Commissioner had many of the exacting duties of a commander-in-chief, responsible to the Minister of Home Security and the Cabinet for the broad policy and strategy of the "battle of London" and charged with the control of the operational machine of civil defence. He had the advantage of knowing the machine thoroughly; with his fellow Regional Commissioner, Admiral Sir Edward Evans (later Lord Mountevans), and his Chief Administrative Officer, Mr. (later Sir) Harold Scott, he had been responsible for the rapid creation of the intricate and highly efficient machine of report, rescue and repair that helped so largely to carry London through her great ordeal. It was only rarely, in 1940 and 1941, that he managed to escape to his delightful home in Hampshire for a short weekend.

During the years immediately before the war he was chairman of the Manpower Sub-Committee of the Committee of Imperial Defence and played a large part in bringing the Services and the interested departments together in a single policy that took practical shape in the famous Schedule of Reserved Occupations.

IDEAL CAPTAIN

Some observers described his handling of this sub-committee as an object lesson in the delicate art of reconciling departmental differences. For a task of this kind he had exceptional gifts. The qualities which, to departmental colleagues, made him an ideal captain of the team made him also an ideal chairman in conducting a conference or inquiry. It was no accident that governments of all political colours chose him for the chairmanship of commissions and committees of inquiry on an astonishing variety of subjects. He had a happy knack of putting the shy at their ease and of making the tongue-tied articulate. Witnesses responded to the piercing but kindly blue eyes and charm of manner that administrative colleagues knew so well. He was a very human man and had a keen sense of humour. The people around him liked him and he got the best out of all with whom he worked.

His qualities of mind and personality were exceptionally well balanced. Clarity of thought, far-sightedness, courage, sound judgment, lucidity and felicity of expression—he had all the intellectual qualities desirable in a high civil servant, including the necessary one of toughness which enabled him successfully to stand the strain of overwork and heavy responsibilities in the London blitz.

His love for and mastery of the English

language are well known. After the war he put the fruits of a life-time's thought and practice into a booklet on the use of English, *Plain Words*, which was officially recommended to the Civil Service and became a best seller. Throughout his life he retained his affection for the classics, especially Homer, whom he read and re-read frequently. He had wide interests which included birds and a close acquaintance with their song. During the war he got permission to play the organ in a Kensington church, not far from his official headquarters, and sought relief in Bach and Handel from the stress of his office.

RAPID PROGRESS

Ernest Arthur Gowers was born in 1880, the youngest son of the late Sir William R. Gowers, M.D., F.R.S., London. He was educated at Rugby and Clare College, Cambridge, where he was a scholar and passed in the first class of the Classical Tripos. He was called to the Bar in 1906. He was 23 years of age when, in 1903, he entered the Civil Service. His progress was rapid. After a spell in the Inland Revenue, he was transferred to the India Office and in the course of four years acted as private secretary to a succession of Parliamentary Under Secretaries who included Edwin Montagu. In 1911 he went to the Treasury as Principal Private Secretary to Lloyd George, then Chancellor of the Exchequer and one of the most powerful figures in the Liberal Government. Lloyd George was so impressed by the administrative ability of his young private secretary that he selected him for the post of Chief Inspector in the National Health Insurance scheme, then being started. This was in 1912 and Gowers was only 32. He held the post for five years. During the greater part of the 1914–18 War he combined his National Insurance responsibilities with special duties at the Foreign Office. In 1917 he became secretary to the Civil Service Arbitration Board, and in 1919 was appointed Director of Production at the Coal Mines Department. This was the beginning of an association with coal that was to claim many years of his labours.

In the year after his appointment as Director of Production at the Coal Mines Department he was promoted to take charge of the department as Under-Secretary for Mines. He was head of the department for seven years, a period that covered the prolonged stoppage of work at the pits in 1926. He became chairman of the Board of Inland Revenue in 1927, and when he gave up that post, in 1930, he retired from the Civil Service but not from the public service. He went back to coal, as chairman of the Coal Mines Reorganization Commission, created by the Coal Mines Act of 1930. The commission's task was to further reorganization of the industry by promoting and assisting amalgamations where they appeared to the commission to be in the national interest, and it turned out to be one of insuperable difficulty. The colliery owners had no faith in amalgamation as a cure for the industry's troubles and there was a disposition to regard the commission merely as a temporary inconvenience which need not be taken too seriously. Compulsory powers existed, but there were defects in the structure of the Act which discouraged attempts at compulsion.

Not even Gowers, a master in the art of securing cooperation, could win success for the reorganization scheme of 1930 though he spent five years in the effort. Further legislation, passed in 1938, set up a new body, the Coal Commission, to acquire the mining royalties (thus making coal a national property) and to take over the functions of the Reorganization Commission, with important alterations in the machinery by which compulsion might be applied. Sir Ernest Gowers became chairman of the Coal Commission on its creation. The outbreak of war suspended the measures that were in preparation for enforcing amalgamation schemes, but there was no interruption in the programme for the unification of royalties, and on July 1, 1942, vesting date of Part One of the Coal Act, 1938, Gowers announced that on that day all unworked coal in Great Britain had become the property of the Coal Commission.

POST-WAR ACTIVITIES

His post-war activities were numerous and varied. In October, 1945, he became chairman of a committee appointed by the Foreign Secretary to re-examine the question of the admission of women to the senior branch of H.M.'s Foreign Service. His friends knew him to be a supporter of the claims of women to greater influence in public life and education, an enthusiasm he was thought to have acquired from his wife. One manifestation of it was a long association with St. Felix School, Southwold, as its chairman. In December, 1945, he became chairman of the committee appointed by the Home Secretary to inquire into the closing hours of shops and also the provisions relating to the health, welfare and safety of employed persons at places other than those regulated under the Factories and Mines Acts.

In April, 1948, the Stationery Office published a 2s. booklet he had written at the request of the Treasury, *Plain Words*, a guide to the use of English particularly by officials. The booklet was officially recommended to training officers in Whitehall. This and its sequel *An ABC of Plain Words* of 1951 have proved useful beyond Civil Service precincts in reforming officialese, and when Fowler's *Modern English Usage*, originally published in 1926, came to be revised, it was natural that the Oxford University Press should invite Gowers to undertake the task.

TEN YEARS' WORK

He worked on it for 10 years. The revised edition was published in 1965, and it became a best seller. Though some reviewers complained that the usage of the revision was hardly that of the present day, all agreed that the marriage of Fowler's idiosyncratic approach with Gowers' own had resulted in a thoroughly well integrated and often newly amusing book.

At the end of 1948 the Chancellor of the Exchequer made him chairman of a committee appointed to consider what general arrangements might be made by the Government for the preservation, maintenance and use of houses of outstanding historic or architectural interest. He became chairman of the Harlow New Town Corporation.

CAPITAL PUNISHMENT

In January, 1949, he was appointed chairman of the Royal Commission on Capital Punishment to consider whether liability under the criminal law in Great Britain to suffer capital punishment for murder should be limited or modified and if so to what extent and by what means. The Commission heard a mass of evidence dictated by experience, reason and sentimentality, all of which Gowers handled with skill, patience and courtesy. In 1953 the commission recommended that the jury should decide, on the facts of each case, whether a sentence of death or life imprisonment should be imposed on those found guilty of murder. But the commission failed to agree on the minimum age limit below which a person could not be sentenced to death—the majority recommended it should be raised from 18 to 21 in both England and Scotland. In 1956 Gowers published his personal views on capital punishment in *A Life for a Life? The Problem of Capital Punishment*, which supported the abolitionists' case. From 1952 to 1953, Gowers was chairman of the committee investigating foot and mouth disease, and it approved of the slaughter of infected animals as the right course to eradicate the disease.

Gowers became chairman of the National Hospitals for Nervous Diseases in 1948 for nine years. He was president of the English Association from 1956 to 1957, and Gentleman Usher of the Purple Rod of the British Empire from 1952 to 1960.

He was made a C.B. in 1917, K.B.E. in 1926, K.C.B. in 1928, G.B.E. in 1945, and a G.C.B. in 1953.

He received an Hon.D.Litt. from Manchester University, and was made an honorary A.R.I.B.A. and an honorary Fellow of Clare College, Cambridge.

He married, in 1905, Constance, daughter of the late Thomas Macgregor Greer, D.L., of Ballymoney, co. Antrim. She died in 1952. They had one son and two daughters.

April 18, 1966.

General Sir Douglas Gracey, K.C.B., K.C.I.E., C.B.E., who had a long and distinguished career in the Indian Army, died at his home at Woking on June 5, 1964. He was 69.

After the partition of India he was for three years Commander-in-Chief in Pakistan. There he will be remembered for his work in building up the new Pakistani Army and also for the great part he played in preventing the dispute over Kashmir from developing into open war between the two new Dominions. In the Second World War he commanded a division in Burma with outstanding success. A marked characteristic was his personal concern for the welfare of his men, who were devoted to him; it is recorded that the Gurkha battalions in his division went into action with the cry "the General's Gurkhas charge!"

Douglas David Gracey was born on September 3, 1894, the son of H. K. Gracey, C.B.E.,

I.C.S. He was educated at Blundells and Sandhurst, and was commissioned in 1914. He first saw active service in France with the 2nd Royal Munster Fusiliers; then, in 1916, he was posted to the Ist. K.G.O. Gurkha Rifles with whom he served in Iraq, Palestine, Syria and Egypt for the rest of the First World War. He won the Military Cross and bar and was twice wounded.

From 1925 to 1927 Gracey was an instructor at the Royal Military College, Sandhurst. He returned to India in 1928, passed through the Staff College, Quetta, and then served at regimental duty with the Gurkhas and in a number of staff appointments. After the outbreak of war in 1939 he continued to serve for a time in India, first as commander of the 2/3rd Q.A.O. Gurkha Rifles, and then as Assistant Commandant at the Staff College, Quetta. But his chance to get into the war came when he was given command of the 17th Indian Infantry Brigade which was sent to Iraq when Rashid Ali, the anti-British Prime Minister, seized power by a *coup d'état* in the spring of 1941.

When the Iraq rebellion had been quelled, after nothing more than a few skirmishes, Gracey's Brigade was employed in the operations against the Vichy French in Syria. The Brigade next took part in the *opera bouffe* of the invasion of Persia which brought about the abdication of the Shah.

His next command, in 1942, was the newly formed 20th Indian Division. This was the only division in General Slim's Fourteenth Army which was trained from its inception for the special conditions of the war in Burma. And how supremely well Gracey trained it was proved when he took it into action in the Kabaw Valley in the spring of 1944, when the Japanese launched their big offensive in an attempt to invade India. Gracey's was one of the divisions of General Scoon's 4th Corps which bore the brunt of the enemy's main attack. As the Japanese advanced, the division was withdrawn with the rest of the Corps to the Imphal plateau where it fought on ground of its own choosing. After three months of bitter fighting the Japanese had lost nearly half their fighting strength and were forced to fall back into Burma.

BACK IN LINE

Gracey's division had been heavily and continuously engaged for over four months, but, after a short rest, it was back in the line in time for the beginning of the Fourteenth Army offensive for the recapture of Burma. His was the division that led the advance when, in December, 1944, it crossed the Chindwin north of Kalewa. The division was then given the role of right flank guard to the Army, and it advanced down the Chindwin to the junction of that river with the Irrawady, capturing Monywa and fighting a number of stiff actions on the way.

The division next took part in the Fourteenth Army attack across the Irrawady and established a bridgehead below Mandalay. Here they had a hard fight to hold their positions in a battle that lasted nearly a month. When they broke out at last, they created hayoc on the enemy's lines of communication, and contributed greatly to Slim's victories in the battles around Mandalay and Meiktila.

On the surrender of Japan in September, 1945, the 20th Division was chosen as one of the formations to be sent to enemy held territories to disarm the Japanese forces, re-establish control and bring relief to prisoners of war. Gracey was assigned to Indo-China where there were 75,000 Japanese troops and where fighting had broken out between the French and local nationalist forces. As head of the Control Commission he was faced with a difficult politico-military situation which he handled with great skill and firmness. Six months later his division was disbanded, and Gracey left for India to take over command of the 1st Indian Corps at Karachi.

In this command he was able to give much needed help to the new Government of Pakistan in coping with the administrative chaos which preceded partition. After partition had taken place he was chosen to be Chief of Staff, and, a few months later, Commander-in-Chief of the Pakistani Army. The task which fell to him of building up the new army was immensely complicated by the long-drawn-out dispute over Kashmir. By the end of 1948 hostilities had developed to a point when a complete breach between India and Pakistan seemed inevitable, but at this critical moment Gracey and his fellow Commander-in-Chief in India, General Bucher, persuaded their respective Governments to order a cease fire, which came into effect on January 1, 1949, and so prevented open war. In January, 1951, Gracey relinquished command of the Pakistani Army and retired from the service.

He married in 1931 Kathleen, daughter of Captain R. Spring, Royal Warwickshire Regiment, and had one son and one daughter.

June 6, 1964.

Leo Joseph Anthony Gradwell, D.S.C., who died on November 9, 1969, at the age of 70, had a distinguished and colourful career at the Bar, in the R.N.V.R. and as a Metropolitan magistrate.

The son of a Liverpool solicitor Gradwell was educated at Stonyhurst and at Balliol College, Oxford, where he was an Exhibitioner. He was called to the Bar in 1925 and entered chambers in Liverpool where he soon established himself in busy practice. He retained a lifelong interest in and affection for the Northern circuit and for the many formidable and successful practitioners there, including George Lynskey, Maxwell Fyfe and Hartley Shawcross who were his adversaries and friends.

Gradwell had been a young midshipman in the 1914–18 War. He was 40 years of age when war broke out again in 1939 but without hesitation he gave up his practice and rejoined the R.N.V.R. In 1942 in command of the Asdic trawler Ayrshire he sailed in the notorious P.Q.17 convoy bound for Murmansk and Archangel. His conduct in this desperate enterprise earned him an almost legendary reputation for valour and unconventional resourcefulness.

After the convoy had been ordered to scatter Gradwell in Ayshire collected the vessels Silver Sword, Ironclad and Troubadour and took them 20 miles into the ice in the north Barents Sea. There they stayed two days, camouflaged themselves by painting their upper works white and then continued their journey southward to reach Matochkin Strait in Novaya Zemlya safely.

ADMIRAL'S PRAISE

After his return Admiral Bevan wrote: "The more law that comes to sea the better and let litigation look after itself until there are no more P.Q. convoys". Gradwell's D.S.C. was awarded in recognition for the part he played in this operation. He returned to the Bar at the end of the war and in 1951 was appointed a Metropolitan magistrate. A few months later he had again to call upon his almost unlimited stock of courage as he was afflicted by a severe attack of polio. Gradwell refused to allow this to deter him from carrying out his duties in the position which he always wanted to occupy, and after a period of convalescence he returned to the Bench and remained there until his retirement in 1967.

He first sat at the Thames Court and later at Marlborough Street and he proved to be a competent and popular magistrate unimpressed by over-subtle legal niceties but shrewd, quick and courteous. He neyer lost on the Bench or off it the robust humour and good humour which were his well known and much admired characteristics.

In 1940 Gradwell married Jean Adamson. She survives him together with the four children of the marriage.

November 11, 1969.

Percy Grainger, the composer, died in the United States on February 20, 1961, aged 78.

In the early nineteen hundreds a young Australian of a singularly handsome countenance surmounted by an aureole of straw gold hair crashed into the solemnities of music in England. His art, his debonair manners, and his good tailoring made it impossible for Kensington to dub him a barbarian.

He had studied in Germany but his music did not sound as though he had. He was an intimate friend of Edward Grieg, and when he played Grieg's Piano Concerto it sounded like Grieg (it breathed the keen air of Norway) and not like a provincial product of the Leipzig School.

As pianist, as composer, as juggler with folksongs of the Faroe Islands. Percy Grainger took everyone by surprise, and even Queen's Hall decided that a little surprise in a symphony concert might be a welcome change.

Percy Aldridge Grainger was born in the state of Victoria near Melbourne on July 8, 1882. He had a protective mother who first taught him his music, then watched over his career perhaps a little too assiduously for his good. She travelled with him when he went to Germany to study with Kwast and Busoni. She presided over his entry into London society and helped him to become a darling of the gods.

For a few years Grainger was everywhere. The Leeds Festival of 1907, when Grieg would have conducted his own Concerto with Grainger as pianist had the composer not died just before it, was one of the pianist's triumphs. The Balfour Gardiner Concerts of 1912 were his greatest opportunity as composer.

"MOLLY ON THE SHORE"

There he conducted his spirited folksong arrangements, his dance pieces, Irish reels. "Molly on the Shore", and the like, and made everyone delight in their artful gaiety. He toured as a pianist about Europe, and pleased, not only by the brilliance of his playing, but by the easy charm of his manner. He would take his audience into his confidence, tell them what he meant to play and why he wanted to play it.

His association with Grieg fired him with interest in national music and he threw himself with characteristic enthusiasm into the movement for collecting English folk song. The 1908 Journal of the Folk Song Society contains his collection of English folk songs, including "Brigg Fair" which he brought to Delius's attention.

His setting of "Country Gardens" has made it one of the most frequently broadcast tunes of the B.B.C. From the financial proceeds of this, the most popular of his many popular settings, which include the "Londonderry Air" and "Shepherd's Hey", he generously subsidized more scholarly publications of folk song.

In 1915 Precy Grainger, still accompanied by his mother, migrated to America. She died there. He made his home there and later married Ella Viola Strom, a Swedish poetess. They had a spectacular wedding in the Hollywood Bowl, for which Grainger composed music conducted by himself before an audience of some 20,000 people.

For once the bridegroom rather than the bride was the central figure of the occasion. Of late years not so much has happened, though Grainger has continued to compose music on occasions which sufficiently interested him.

He revisited his native Australia and presented a valuable and eclectic museum to the University of Melbourne. Australia is justly proud of him as one of her musical sons who has earned international fame.

February 21, 1961.

Dr. Louis Harold Gray, F.R.S., who had been Director and Nuffield Fellow since 1953 of the Research Unit in Radiobiology established by the British Empire Cancer Campaign at Mount Vernon Hospital, died on July 9, 1965. He was 59.

Since the Second World War he had taken a large part in planning the expansion of radiobiological research.

Louis Harold Gray was born in London on November 10, 1905, and educated at Christ's Hospital. There he came under the influence of a science master who stimulated and encouraged his interest in experimental research. From Christ's Hospital he went to Trinity College, Cambridge, where he took a first in the Natural Sciences Tripos, and then joined the group of young research workers around Rutherford from 1928 to 1933.

After taking his Ph.D. on the measurement of penetrating gamma-radiation he made the decision, unusual at that time for a nuclear physicist, to transfer to medical work. He went as senior physicist, and Prophit Scholar of the Royal College of Surgeons, to Mount Vernon Hospital, Northwood, where he remained for most of his scientific career.

His early work was concerned with an exact study of the interaction of radiation with matter and the fundamental principles of radiation dosimetry. His theory of the cavity ionization chamber, which became known as the Bragg-Gray Principle, has laid the foundations for all future work in this field. Later, under the influence of colleagues such as Mottram, his interest turned to the effect of radiation on living cells, and his subsequent work was principally in this field. With his colleague, John Read, he built the first neutron generator to be used in Britain for biological research—a machine which cost £600!

WIDE FIELD OF RESEARCH

From 1946 to 1953 he was in charge of the radiobiological work at the Medical Research Council's Radiotherapeutic Research Unit in the Hammersmith Hospital, where he was latterly Deputy Director. In this position he planned and started the work on the medical cyclotron and stimulated new work with radioisotopes and autoradiographic techniques. Already in 1953 he realized the importance of oxygen as an aid to radiotherapy, a theme which was to run through his later work. His suggestions in this field were taken up throughout the world and are now applied widely in the treatment of cancer.

Then he moved back to Mount Vernon Hospital as Director and Nuffield Fellow of the new research unit in radiobiology established by the British Empire Cancer Campaign. Here he was leader of a small group of workers covering a wide field of research, from radiation chemistry to in vivo tumours in mice, and this period was perhaps the happiest of his scientific life.

He became recognized not only as an outstanding and stimulating director of his own team but as the leader of the new and rapidly developing field of radiobiology. His breadth of vision and immense knowledge, coupled with a very realistic approach to research projects, made him indispensable to the radiobiological community. He made himself approachable to the most junior of his colleagues and listened with patience to their ideas. His contacts with fellow scientists throughout the world were very wide.

Many awards and honours came his way. He was elected a Fellow of the Royal Society in 1961 and made an Honorary D.Sc. of Leeds in 1962. He was founder and first chairman of the Association for Radiation Research and president of the Second International Congress of Radiation Research held in Harrogate.

Foreign awards included the Katherine Berkan Judd Award of the Sloane Kettering Institute, and the Bertner Foundation Award of the M. D. Anderson Hospital for outstanding achievements in the field of cancer research. He held the office of president of the British Institute of Radiology and of the Hospital Physicists Association; for a number of years he was vice-president of the International Commission on Radiological Units and Measurements.

He married in 1932 Frieda Marjory Picot, who survives him with two sons.

July 13, 1965.

King Paul of Greece, King of the Hellenes, who died at the age of 62 on March 6, 1964, succeeded his elder brother, the late King George II, on April 1, 1947, the third of the sons of King Constantine to occupy the Greek throne.

Early in his reign, while his country was in the grip of a communist rebellion, King Paul gave evidence of a deep knowledge of his mission in life. He became the symbol of unity of all Greeks who had rallied to save their country from becoming a communist satellite. His willingness to share in the nation's vicissitudes, his democratic ways and political wisdom in those decisive years, brought to him and to his consort, Queen Frederika, immense popularity which carried the monarchy closer to the people and steadied one of the most restless thrones in Europe. Yet, once peace and tranquillity were restored, King Paul was exposed, like his father, King Constantine, before him, though with less reason, to the sapping influence of domestic political rivalries. The communists had not forgiven his virtual leadership of the war against them. When, with the help of a "popular front", they made a comeback into Greek politics—though the party remained officially banned—they set out to undermine this popularity. Aided by the ambitions of some nationalist Opposition leaders, and the admitted mistakes of some of those closely connected with the Court, they managed to create a feeling among many people that monarchy might, after all, be a costly luxury in a poor country such as Greece.

IN EXILE

Born in Athens on December 14, 1901, King Paul was the third son of King Constantine and Queen Sophia, the sister of Kaiser Wilhelm II. He shared to the full in the strange vicissitudes of the Greek royal family, joining his father in exile in 1917 and returning with him, after the death of King Alexander (Constantine's second son), in 1920. Together with George II, who on the abdication of Constantine in September, 1922, had become King, he left Greece in 1923, just before the proclamation of the Republic. The 12 years of exile that followed were a period of varied experience. He stayed for a time in Rumania and in Switzerland, but lived for the most part, like his brother, in England. Active in mind and body, he studied engineering as well as music and philosophy, and for a year he worked under an assumed name as a mechanic at the Armstrong-Siddeley aircraft and car factory in Coventry. On three occasions during this period, in 1925, 1934, and 1935, he visited the United States. A more secret experience was his visit, as a member of the crew of a small yacht to Greek waters and even, under the protection of a beard grown for the purpose, to his boyhood home at Tatoi, near Athens. With the restoration of the monarchy in 1935 Prince Paul, now Diadoch (Crown Prince), resumed his naval career. His betrothal to Princess Frederika Luise, daughter of the Duke of Brunswick and a great-great-granddaughter of Queen Victoria (Prince Paul was himself a great-grandchild of Victoria), was officially announced in Athens on September 27, 1937, and the marriage was solemnized in the Greek capital on January 9 of the following year.

APPEAL FOR UNITY

Having chosen the Navy as a career, Prince Paul entered the Greek Naval Academy, in which he graduated in the ordinary way, served as a midshipman in the campaign in Asia Minor in 1922, and eventually rose to the rank of commander. He qualified for his pilot's wings in 1936 and he afterwards attended an intensive staff course at both the Naval and Military Academies. During the war against fascist Italy he served with the Greek General Staff. In April, 1941, just before the entry of the Germans into Athens, he flew to Crete with the royal family and was evacuated by air to Egypt, after the German invasion of the island. He was in England in 1941 and spent much of the following year in South Africa as the guest of General Smuts. A project he formed in 1943 for leading a mission to the Greek resistance movement at home had to be abandoned after allied preparations for it were all but completed. He took little direct part in the controversy, after the liberation of Greece, on the restoration of the monarchy. The plebiscite was held early in September, 1946, and on September 27 Prince Paul returned for the third time from exile, to join King George who had arrived by air from London.

Six months later, on April 1, 1947, King George died, and that same night Prince Paul was sworn in before Archbishop Damaskinos, the former Regent, and members of the Greek Cabinet as King Paul I, King of the Hellenes. His first message as King to the Greek people was an appeal for unity.

At that time the communist rebels had overrun the countryside in a second bid after the Athens uprising of December, 1944, to seize control. The King's appeal for unity was not directed to the rebels. He was demanding unity from the loyalist politicians whose petty political squabbles were prolonging Greece's ordeal. Throughout that period King Paul gave proof of great personal courage, touring the devastated provinces to be near the people whose lives were now, after so many years of war and privation, at the mercy of the communist bands. During the three years that this bitter struggle against the rebels lasted, he paid no fewer than 48 visits to the troops in the field.

When, with the help of American military support, Yugoslavia's rift with Moscow, and the leadership of Government forces by General (later Field Marshal) Papagos, the communist guerrillas were defeated in 1949, King Paul devoted himself to the problems of recovery. Soon after ascending the throne he had founded the National Institute, a voluntary organization whose activities extended over every field of social welfare in the country. Now, after the defeat of the communists, he announced a Fund for Guerrilla Victims to help the 750,000 people who had abandoned their villages as a result of communist terror. The money collected by the fund was used to rebuild houses, schools, and churches in the stricken areas.

King Paul had a rare insight into the dangerous game of Greek politics, and was sometimes accused of taking too much part in it. Yet his judgment often averted political crises. Shortly after his accession, a government of national unity was formed under the elderly liberal statesman Themistocles Sophoulis, which put an end to the dispersal of political forces and focused the nation's effort on the war against the rebels. Some of the King's initiatives, however justified, lay outside the province of his constitutional prerogatives and were deeply resented by the politicians. The King's quarrel with the late Field Marshal Papagos, victor of the war against the rebels, when the then commander-in-chief resigned after being denied the right to interfere with military appointments to the Royal Palace, was carried into the political arena when Papagos stood for election, although unsuccessfully, in 1951. In the elections of 1952, however, Papagos swept the polls and the King realized the need to improve relations with his new Premier. Many attempts at reconciliation were made, but it was only near the time of Papagos's death, in 1955, that their relations had returned to normal.

POLITICAL WISDOM

Although an interview given by King Paul to a leading American newspaper, in the early fifties, first raised officially the issue of the union of Cyprus with Greece, King Paul, throughout the bitter dispute with Britain, never forgot the need to preserve the traditionally friendly ties between the two countries. This attitude, vindicated after the settlement of the Cyprus issue, was subject to much criticism from extremists.

The death of Field Marshal Papagos aroused fears that the newly won political and economic stability of Greece would revert to the familiar and dismal pattern of the years which followed the war. It was then that King Paul gave further proof of political wisdom. He summoned to the Palace the youthful Minister of Public Works, Constantine Karamanlis, and asked him to form a new government. His action anticipated the choice of the party caucus and drew hostile comments. His choice was confirmed by popular suffrage in the general elections which followed in February, 1956, and again in May, 1958.

In the 1961 elections, which once again gave the party of Karamanlis a striking victory, the Crown became unnecessarily involved in the political controversy which followed over the fairness and validity of the general election. This had been conducted by a caretaker Cabinet under the Chief of the King's Military Household, consisting of Ministers closely connected with the Royal Palace. This involved the throne in the Opposition's accusations of electoral fraud and intimidation. Their denunciations, which even included an attempt to charge the caretaker Cabinet with treason, developed into a straight-forward and virulent campaign against the royal family. Some actions by the Court showed an insensitivity to public opinion and were fully exploited in the Opposition press. The object was to intimidate the King with the threat that, unless he gave in to the Opposition's demand for fresh and "honest" elections, he might, like his father, lose his crown. While the nationalist Opposition parties gradually realized that the campaign was undermining the only institution which offered the country a guarantee of stability, the communists persevered on the same lines.

In May the King was taken to hospital during a state visit to Greece by President de Gaulle of France. It was then stated that he was suffering from appendicitis and that the operation had been successful. He had recovered sufficiently by July when he and Queen Frederika paid their state visit to Britain—a visit which unleashed a chain reaction on the Greek political scene with the resignation of Karamanlis, whose Administration had been in power for nearly eight years.

The evolution of the political situation in Greece reconciled him with the Liberal camp, which won the lead but not a majority at November's elections. He consented when his new Prime Minister, Papandreou, recommended new elections in the hope, which proved justified, that the Centre Union Party would gain a working majority.

The first symptoms of his fatal illness came late in December. He withstood the pain with fortitude but kept it secret in order not to create anxieties before the February 16 elections. When the new Papandreou Cabinet was sworn in after a sweeping victory in the elctrions, he attended the ceremony and greeted all new Ministers personally. He collapsed soon afterwards and had to be urgently operated on.

Tall, handsome, polished in manner, ambitious for his country and with a strong pride in it, King Paul was a man of considerable ability. He was particularly interested in philosophy and had written a treatise on Plato which may later be published. On many occasions the King gave in his speeches a clear, precise and at the same time profound definition of his thoughts on the great problems which beset humanity at the present time.

The Crown Prince Constantine, who succeeds the King, was born at Psychico, near Athens, on June 2, 1940. In January, 1963, his engagement was announced to Princes Anne Marie, youngest daughter of King Frederik of Denmark. Princess Sophia was born on November 2, 1938. Her wedding to Don Juan Carlos, Prince of the Asturias, son of the claimant to the Spanish throne, was celebrated in Athens on May 14, 1962. Princess Irene, to whom the late General Smuts stood godfather, was born in Cape Town on April 11, 1942.

March 7, 1964.

Princess Andrew of Greece, the mother of the Duke of Edinburgh and sister of Lord Mountbatten, died on December 5, 1969, at the age of 84 at Buckingham Palace.

Of the many tragedies that afflicted members of European royalty in this century, hers were perhaps among the most poignant and harrowing. She bore her vicissitudes with courage and fortitude. A lonely figure in her late age, she was noticed at her rare public appearances for the grey monastic full-flowing robe and coif she always donned, the uniform of the Christian Sisterhood of Martha and Mary which she herself had founded in 1949.

H.R.H. Princess Victoria Alice Elizabeth Julia Marie, R.R.C., was born at Windsor on February 25, 1885. She was the daughter of Prince Louis Alexander Battenburg, 1st Marquess of Milford Haven, and of Princess Victoria Alberta Elizabeth Mathilde Marie, eldest daughter of the Grand Duke Ludwig IV of Hesse by his wife Princess Alice, daughter of Queen Victoria. She was the elder sister of Lord Louis Mountbatten, now Earl Mountbatten of Burma.

She was 18 when she became engaged to Prince Andrew of Greece, the fourth son of King George I and Queen Olga of the Hellenes. The wedding took place at Darmstadt in 1903 in two ceremonies, one of the Protestant Church, then in the Russian Church in the Orthodox rite. She lived in Greece where, while her husband pursued his career in the Greek Army, she devoted herself to charities. During the Balkan Wars, in 1912, she joined the Red Cross as a nurse and raised funds in England to help hospitals.

During the 1914–18 War which brought the Greek royal family at loggerheads with the politicians, she had her share of the trials and tribulations that followed. In 1917 she followed her husband and the Greek royal family in exile in Switzerland and, after three years, when her brother-in-law was restored to the Greek throne, they returned to Greece and took up residence at Mon Repos palace in Corfu, where Prince Philip was born in 1921.

TRAGIC PERIOD

This turned out to be one of the most tragic periods of her life. Prince Andrew, who had commanded an army corps during the Greek military debacle in Asia Minor in 1922, was arrested by the politicians who were desperately seeking scapegoats for the defeat. Six former ministers were shot after summary trial, but Prince Andrew had a narrow escape thanks to the intervention of the Great Powers which sent emissaries to Athens to see that the Prince was spared. Princess Andrew left her family in Corfu and went to Athens to be near her husband during the trial. After his release and banishment, they returned to Corfu under the protection of the British Emissary, Commander Talbot, and, leaving all their possessions behind, left for London and later settled on an estate at St. Cloud, near Paris. In the same year (1923) Greece was proclaimed a republic, a short-lived interlude punctuated by coups, dictatorship and revolts, until the monarchy was restored in 1935.

She had shared her husband's indignation of the way he had been treated after several years of faithful service to the Greek Army, and agreed that their son Philip should be ensured a different life. In 1929, at the age of eight, Philip was sent to school at Cheam, in Surrey, making his home with his maternal grandmother, the Dowager Marchioness of Milford Haven, and his senior uncle, George, Marquess of Milford Haven, elder brother of Lord Louis Mountbatten who later became Philip's guardian.

In the year 1930–31 her four daughters were married. First, it was Princess Sophie who became the wife of Prince Christoph of Hesse; then Cecilia married Prince George of Hesse-Darmstadt; then Princess Margarita to Prince Gottfried of Hohenlohe-Langenburg; and last was Theodora who married the Margrave of Baden. But in 1937, Cecilia, her husband and their two children were killed at Ostend in a flying accident. Princess Sophie was widowed in 1943 and in 1946 married Prince Georg of Hanover, the brother of Queen Frederika. Princess Theodora of Baden died in 1969.

DIVIDED BY WAR

All Princess Andrew's daughters were bridesmaids at the wedding of their uncle, Lord Mountbatten, and Miss Edwina Ashley in 1922.

The Second World War found Princess Andrew in the tragic situation of having three daughters married to Germans and her son in the British Navy. She remained in Greece with her sister-in-law, the Princess Nicholas (mother of Princess Marina), throughout the Nazi occupation, from 1941 to 1944, working for the Swedish and Swiss Red Cross, helping the poor with what funds she occasionally received from relatives abroad. She lost her husband who was living in Monte Carlo just as the prospect of a postwar reunion dawned in 1944. In that year her son renounced his claims to the succession of the Greek Throne. He became a naturalized British subject in February, 1947. Later that year she went to London to attend her son's wedding to Princess Elizabeth. Since then, she used to go occasionally to London to visit her son and his growing family.

But mostly she lived alone in the seclusion of her Athens apartment, where her daughters would visit her from time to time.

FOUNDED SOCIETY

In 1949 she founded the Christian Sisterhood of Martha and Mary and assumed the life presidency of this monastic society, aimed at training sisters who were prepared to dedicate their lives to the care of poor children and the sick. She travelled to the United States to raise funds which she spent in buying two houses in a hamlet near Athens. One she converted into a home for convalescence. The purpose was that the revenue from this rest-home should pay for the Sisters' Training Home. The plan failed as she found few suitable candidates for sisterhood. She therefore converted the second home into a foundation for aged pensioners who live in, paying each according to his revenue.

December 6, 1969.

Gustavus Green, the first successful British designer of aero engines, died on December 29, 1964, at his home at Twickenham less than three months before his hundredth birthday.

Born in Hounslow on March 11, 1865, a year before the Royal Aeronautical Society was formed, he moved in 1897 to Bexhill where he established a cycle-making business. In the early 1900s he became interested in motor cars, designed one and also a water-cooled engine to go with it, and it was through his interest in engines and the fact that this particular engine was noted at a Cordingley Show in London that he later received orders from the Royal Aircraft factory to manufacture aero engines. It was in 1909 that the late Lord Brabazon won the £1,000 prize for the first circular flight of one mile by a British pilot in an all-British aeroplane. This aeroplane was then powered by a 60 horsepower Green engine.

Many other pioneers in this country used his engines: A. V. Roe, Sopwith, Graham White and Cody. One of Green's engines won the Patrick Alexander £1,000 international competition for aero engines in 1911 and in 1914 his 100 h.p. engine won the £5,000 Naval and Military Aero Engine competition. The first successful British amphibian, the Sopwith Bat-Boat, was powered by a 100 horsepower Green and it won the Mortimer Singer Prize in 1913. The famous Harry Hawker, on a Green-engined Sopwith seaplane, thrilled the country in 1913 when trying to win the £5,000 Daily Mail Round Britain Seaplane Race.

AWARD AFTER CRASH

After flying 1,000 miles Hawker crashed near Dublin through his foot slipping from the rudder bar, and was awarded £1,000 for his brave effort.

The Green engine was, unfortunately, rather heavy for the power given and in view of the successful French rotary engines which had been available since well before the First World War Green was ordered by the authorities to concentrate on the production of power plans for motor torpedo boats. Consequently Green engines did not play a great part in aviation during the 1914–18 War. In the early 1920s Green was advised to retire after the war years of concentrated work and he moved to Twickenham to indulge in his hobby of collecting old watches and clocks.

In January, 1959, the Royal Aeronautical Society awarded him an honorary companionship of the society, a rare honour.

December 30, 1964.

Professor Frederick Gugenheim Gregory, F.R.S., Emeritus Professor of Plant Physiology, at Imperial College of Science and Technology, died on November 27, 1961, after a long period of failing health. He had an almost legendary international reputation as a figure of great significance in the development of modern plant physiology. He was 67.

Born in London on December 22, 1893, the fourth of a family of eight, he was educated at

Owens School and the Royal College of Science, London. He had intended to read chemistry, but became so excited by Professor J. B. Farmer's botany lectures that he transferred his registration and graduated with 1st Class Honours in Botany in 1915. Rejected by the Army on medical grounds, he at once joined the Research Institute of Plant Physiology, which had been recently founded by the Ministry of Agriculture at the Imperial College under the direction of Professor V. H. Blackman, F.R.S. Professor Blackman had established relations with a number of the research stations and Gregory began his researches at the Cheshunt Experimental Station, moved to Rothamsted, and finally returned to work at the Imperial College.

In 1932 he became Assistant Director of the Research Institute and later succeeded Professor Blackman both as Professor of Plant Physiology and Director of the Institute.

The establishment of the research institute had begun a long and fruitful association, first with the Ministry of Agriculture and later the Agricultural Research Council. Gregory maintained the established contacts with the research stations and members of the institute could be found working at East Malling Research Station, at Rothamsted and at the Chelsea Physic Garden. During this period he served on many advisory committees, particularly those of the Agricultural Research Council, but he never allowed these duties to prevent him maintaining the closest contact and deep interest in every piece of research under his general direction.

MEDAL GIVEN TO COLLEGE

He was elected a Fellow of the Royal Society in 1941 and a Foreign Associate of the U.S. National Academy of Sciences in 1956. His career has rightly been termed meteoric and culminated in the award of a Royal Medal of the Royal Society, which on retirement he presented to the Imperial College of Science as a tangible expression of his view that in making a contribution to the advancement of science every individual depends both upon the institution where he works and the colleagues with whom he works.

Gregory had an unusual equipment in mathematics, physics, and chemistry which enabled him to see ahead of his time the enormous part that biochemistry and physics would soon play in the development of biology. This vision, coupled with his insatiable scientific curiosity, extended his studies over a remarkable range of topics and it is difficult to select one or other for particular mention. Perhaps his development of new methods of growth analysis, his studies with F. J. Richards on plant nutrition and with O. N. Purvis on vernalization have received the widest publicity, not only because they are scientific classics but because of their value to practical agriculture. To these achievements must also be added the outcome of his visit in 1928 to the Gezira Research Station of Sudan, which revolutionized our knowledge of the factors affecting cotton production.

His department was visited by plant scientists from all over the world and he could be heard exhorting them with rising enthusiasm as his imagination began to play upon the problems they brought to his attention. It is for this unique capacity for inspiring others, not only with interest in their experiments but with confidence in their own capacity to achieve something worth while, that he will as well long be remembered and honoured.

It was a source of deep satisfaction to him at the memorable dinner given in his honour when he retired to see so many of his former students assembled, many now themselves directing research both in Institutes and as professors not only in the United Kingdom but in the Commonwealth countries.

LOVE OF MUSIC

The tribute to him written at the time by W. T. Williams concluded "...inspiration depends on the personal approach; and that Gregory's approach to a scientific problem would be the reverse of cold and calculating could be deduced from his other interests. He admires the novels of Meredith, Dostoevsky, and Proust. Widely read in philosophy, he has always preferred the metaphysical speculations of Whitehead and the mellifluous prose of Santayana to the asperities of Ryle and Ayer. An enthusiastic musician, his first piano sonata may show, in its opening and closing movements, the influence of his declared admiration for Hindemith and Britten; but the slow movement reveals his affection for Mahler and Bruckner. And as in literature, philosophy, and music, so also in scientific research his approach has always been essentially romantic, in the *O.E.D.* sense that it has been 'characterized... by imagination and passion'. And whatever Gregory's current passion—a novel, a philosophy, a piece of music, a new scientific idea—he has always insisted on sharing it with his colleagues and students; and in this way, in the communication of his own enjoyment, he has taught us that the only enduring reason for doing scientific research is that one enjoys doing it. Whatever else may be forgotten, this is the one lesson that all those who have passed through his hands can never forget."

Gregory bequeathed his library to Imperial College. He was unmarried.

November 30, 1961.

David Rhys Grenfell, P.C., C.B.E., former "Father of the House of Commons," and Labour member for the Gower Division of Glamorganshire, 1922–1959, died on November 21, 1968, at the age of 87. Grenfell was Secretary for Mines at the Board of Trade in the wartime Coalition Government, holding that office during an extremely critical period, from May, 1940 until June, 1942.

In a country which does not often appoint a technical expert to the control of an appropriate department, the placing of Grenfell in charge of Mines was recognized as a happy, imaginative gesture. Not only had he gone down the pit at the age of 12 and worked there until he was 35 (bearing its marks on himself ever afterwards); he had engaged in the theoretical study of mining and allied subjects and had qualified as a colliery manager.

David Rhys Grenfell, son of a South Wales coal miner, was born at Penrheol, near Swansea, on June 27, 1881. He grew up against the grim background of the colliery region. Until he was 35 his life was that of an ordinary working miner—with this difference, that he began to read, and in his "off" hours laboriously taught himself theoretical mining technique and languages. When in 1916 he became a miners' agent there was somewhat more time for these studies.

Grenfell was an enthusiastic trade unionist, and in 1922 went into politics, being elected to Parliament in July of that year as a Labour member, doubling his party's previous majority in the Gower division.

Grenfell was a member of the Forestry Commission in 1929, and later served on the Royal Commission on Safety in Mines. Through the Labour debacle of 1931 and again in later general elections his constituents remained faithful to him. He was a member of the executive committee of the United Kingdom branch of the Empire Parliamentary Association, and as such was invited to New Zealand as a Government guest in January, 1940, to represent the association at some of the centenary celebrations.

OUT OF OFFICE

In May, 1940, when Mr. Churchill formed the war Coalition, Grenfell was appointed Secretary for Mines. The conscientiousness with which he discharged his ministerial duties was shown by his treatment of supplementary questions, which he answered in great detail where another man might have dismissed many of them more cavalierly.

In the summer of 1942 it was decided to create a Ministry of Fuel and Power, with a senior Minister in charge. This would take over all the functions of the Mines Department, and the new Minister was not Grenfell but Major Gwilym Lloyd George (now Lord Tenby).

When Labour went back to power after the war, Grenfell, to the general surprise, was not given office. He gave loyal support to the Labour Government, but, on occasions took an independent line. This was notably the case on November 1, 1947, when he and another Labour stalwart (the late Rhys Davies) moved to annul the Control of Engagements Order. Grenfell, in an eloquent speech, was able to draw on his experience as a miner to illumine the theme that a worker's pride in the skill he exercised at his chosen craft was his most precious possession—a pride which directors of labour might destroy. Rhys Davies and Grenfell were not successful in their attempt to get the much-disliked order annulled, but the Government majority fell from the nominal figure of 150 to only just over 100, and ministers did not forget the sharp lesson they had been given.

In 1951 Grenfell was sworn of the Privy Council, and in 1953, the year in which he became "Father" of the House, he was invested by M. Massigli, then the French Ambassador to Britain, with the cross of Chevalier of the Legion of Honour, in recognition of his work for Franco-British understanding.

In 1905 Grenfell married Beatrice Morgan, and they had one daughter.

November 26, 1968.

Dr. A. A. Griffith, C.B.E., F.R.S., formerly chief scientist, Rolls-Royce Ltd., died on October 11, 1963, at the age of 70.

Since his retirement he had been a consultant to Rolls-Royce for long-term projects such as propulsion for hypersonic flight.

Throughout most of his 45 years of work as scientist and engineer, Griffith kept himself out of the public eye. Only in the early fifties, when, for the first time, controlled flight was achieved without the use of wings, fixed or rotating, was his determined avoidance of publicity seriously threatened. He had devised a means of using jet thrust for lift and had embodied it in a structure so primitive in form as to underline its freedom from orthodox methods of generating lift. His lifting agent was a gas turbine directing its jet downwards; his controls were jets of compressed air set fore and aft and at the lateral extremities of a steel framework which was promptly named the Flying Bedstead by journalists. Griffith was responsible for it. Rolls-Royce had produced it and Griffith kept himself carefully in the background. Nobody ever succeeded in interviewing him or persuading him to write an article or go to a microphone. What had to be said about the developments was to be said by others, some of them his colleagues at Rolls-Royce.

Right on to the end of his working life in 1960 he refused flatly to have any invasion of his privacy. He refused his employers and his friends with equal impartiality. "Shyness" is a mild word for the repugnance he felt for any intrusion into his private world or for any assumption that he should join in any battle to push his proposals against the opposition of doubters and sceptics. In essence, this exclusion of commerical, propagandist and political considerations was an expression of his concentration on his own tasks. It betokened too a ruthless demand on himself to produce such things as by their own merit would win acceptance or to submit to the harsh discipline of disappointment if they failed.

His habit of thinking a subject right through to the end and his gift of improvising ways to arrive at new conclusions meant that he rarely did fail. As a young man in his early twenties straight out of Liverpool University he won himself a curious reputation at Farnborough.

DOUBLED WAGES

The First World War was on and he was put into the shops as a craftsman. Having been allocated a job, he inquired the rate for it and promptly devised a new way of doing it which doubled his wages. Within a year he was out of the shops and into the physics laboratory where engine subjects and materials were his principal concern.

Immediately after the war, another piece of ingenuity gained him the nickname of "Bubble Griffith" among his colleagues. He had been blowing soap bubbles as the start of an exercise in analysing stresses in metal forms of irregular shape. Having got his bubbles he used optical methods to define their shape and form and ultimately succeeded in making a sound analogy in optical terms of the stresses occurring in metals fabricated in similarly irregular shapes. He had anticipated the analogue computer; he was about to anticipate the gas turbine by at least 10 years and he was about to see his study shelved, without protest, for another 10.

As far back as 1926 he had submitted to the Aeronautical Research Council a paper recommending the development of a gas turbine to drive an airscrew. At that time Sir Frank Whittle was 19 and was just making his way as a pilot in the R.A.F. The Aeronautical Research Council was not to decide to back the gas turbine until 1937. By then Whittle had gone ahead on lines which suggested that he knew nothing of Griffith's old paper, still buried in the secret files of the council. That paper has since become famous as the charter of the jet engine. It proved, as many have since confessed, that the jet engine was possible and it foresaw nearly everything in the mechanical and aerodynamic sense about the gas turbine. It took existing turbines and showed the reasons for their relative inefficiency; it insisted that the turbine blades must be regarded as aerofoils and be so treated in design that they should not have to do their work in a stalled condition; it recommended a multi-stage compressor (and therefore an axial compressor) on the ground that a gas stream cannot be turned through an angle of more than 40 deg. without serious energy losses. Thirty years later he was to be proved right on all counts, although Whittle never did agree to abandon his original centrifugal compressor.

A little more than 20 years after that paper was written, he had been tempted out of the public service into industry to take a hand in the conceiving and improving of aero-engines.

JOINED ROLLS-ROYCE

He went to Rolls-Royce in 1939 with the strangest commission ever given to an engineer. Mr. F. W. (now Lord) Hives, then director and general manager, set him down in an office among the most pleasant surroundings at Duffield and simply told him to "go on thinking". His excuse for avoiding publicity was now as good as it had been at Farnborough. There, some of his papers had gone to the Air Ministry and those clear of security objections were published as reports and memoranda. Some had gone to the Aeronautical Research Council and the more important remained unpublished for years. He claimed no credit: he resisted recognition except on two occasions. He accepted his F.R.S. in 1941 and the silver medal of the Royal Aeronautical Society in 1955.

Both acknowledged his work on gas turbines. The first, no doubt, took account, too, of his work on materials and structures at Farnborough, but it related in particular to his definition of the principles on which the successful gas turbine must be based. The second recognized the importance of applying jet thrust to lift in the Flying Bedstead. Along similar lines his work was to continue under the convenient cloak of a great industrial organization and to this day there has been no specific revelation of his share in the remarkable developments his company undertook in those two decades. Powerful jet engines were produced. The gas turbine was adapted with great success to drive a propeller. The idea of the by-pass engine was worked out to secure a measure of fuel economy and to reduce noise. (It set designers in the United States on the track of what they call the "turbofan".) Work was started on a breed of direct lift engines capable of lifting, first eight times and then 16 times their own weight. Before Griffith retired, the first aircraft powered by these engines had flown. Beyond that, there came out of the company a set of proposals for a supersonic airliner which was to start off the long argument on the subject.

Those proposals were known to have come from Griffith although he never laid claim to paternity.

Although he was born in London (on June 15, 1893) his advanced education began at the Douglas Secondary School in the Isle of Man. From there he won a Sir W. H. Tate science scholarship at Liverpool University in 1911.

CRAFTSMAN

He qualified for his B.Eng. with first-class honours in 1914, spent another year on research and then went to Farnborough. He took his M.Eng. in 1917 and his D.Eng. in 1921, both in the same university. His employment as a craftsman in his first year at Farnborough was no concession to wartime scarcity of labour. He had made himself a craftsman at Liverpool.

He married in 1925 Constance Vera, Falkner.

October 15, 1963.

Sir James Grigg, P.C., K.C.B., K.C.S.I., who was Secretary of State for War in the Coalition Administration during the Second World War, died in a London hospital on May 5, 1964. He was 73.

A civil servant who became a Minister of Cabinet rank, and afterwards a City magnate, Percy James Grigg—or "P. J." as he was widely known among friends and colleagues—was essentially a brilliant administrator. As a young civil servant at the Treasury, he attracted the attention of Sir Warren Fisher, and speedily became Principal Private Secretary to the Chancellor of the Exchequer, a position which he held with distinction throughout five successive Chancellorships. A devoted and admiring, though not always docile, servant of such different personalities as Winston Churchill and Philip Snowden, he formed in this period the political intimacies which were to bear fruit in 1942, when Churchill invited him to become Secretary of State for War—an opportunity which scarcely ever falls to the lot of a civil servant. In accepting it, which he did without hesitation, he sacrificed his civil service future and his pension. At the same time, he refused the offer of a peerage, preferring to have a seat found for him in the House of Commons.

A man of brilliant gifts, of outstanding intellectual attainments, and of strong opinion, which he was fearless in expressing, he was perhaps not always patient of the working of minds slower than his own. In character tenacious and argumentative, with a reserved and slightly brusque manner, he was nevertheless capable of forming deep and enduring attachments, and it is clear that the statesmen whom he served as a young private secretary felt for him something far warmer than mere official esteem. Of Sir Winston, in particular, he became a lifelong friend. In his dealings with the House of Commons, he retained essentially the quality of the administrator rather than the politician. His handling of his department was supremely efficient; but for the slow grinding of the parliamentary machine he had an attitude of something like impatience, dating from the days when he sat as a spectator in the Official Gallery, and by no means abjured when he entered the House as a minister. His somewhat austere personality and the sharpness of his retorts gave at times an impression of high-handedness. Of this he was himself well aware but, if he was sometimes unbending, it was at least partly because he would not let trivial grievances divert him into losing sight of essentials, and, if he was vehement in defence of his department, it was in the belief that the Army at that time needed all the support and encouragement it could get. He cared for nothing but efficiency and was ruthless in its pursuit. A man of strongly independent mind, and no respecter of persons, he would make no popular concessions, but he gave generous admiration and intense loyalty where he recognized outstanding merit.

BRILLIANT STUDENT

Born at Exmouth on December 16, 1890, Percy James Grigg was the son of a journeyman carpenter. His early education was received at an elementary school in Bournemouth, where his parents moved soon after his birth. The headmaster, a pedagogue of the old school, and a man of strong and original character, whose influence Grigg never forgot, early marking the boy's ability, persuaded his father to enter him for a scholarship at Bournemouth secondary school. To meet the further cost of his son's education, Frank Grigg set up as a builder in 1902 and in 1909 had the satisfaction of seeing him go up to Cambridge with a senior scholarship in mathematics. His college was St. John's, which admitted him to an Honorary Fellowship in later life. A brilliant student, he was debarred by the narrowness of his means from seeing much of the social and athletic life of Cambridge. In the mathematical tripos lists of 1912 he was placed as a wrangler, and a year later he took first place in the examination for entry to the first division, Civil Service.

He was appointed to the Treasury. He had not been there long when the 1914–18 War broke out. Enlisting as a second-lieutenant, he was sent to Salonika with the R.G.A., saw service in the Struma Valley and then was brought back to England to work with other mathematicians in the Ballistics Office. There he met his future wife, Miss Gertrude Hough, a niece of the Bishop of Woolwich. On return to the Treasury he was speedily promoted, and from 1921 to 1930 was Principal Private Secretary to successive Chancellors. These years, packed with dramatic events, in which he occupied a ringside seat at the political spectacle, were to him perhaps the most interesting of his Civil Service career, and from higher posts he looked back on them with something like nostalgia. With Sir Robert Horne, Grigg attended international conferences on German reparations; with Baldwin he went to New York to discuss the settlement of the American debt, and during this period watched with deep misgiving the French occupation of the Ruhr; with Neville Chamberlain he saw the beginnings of the change of policy that led to the general election on tariffs in 1923; with Churchill he saw at first hand the debates which raged round the gold standard, and he never ceased to maintain in later life that the decision to return to gold was right; with Snowden he attended The Hague conference, and watched with a mixture of admiration and amusement his chief's characteristically obstinate stand.

From these close contacts and intimacies he was withdrawn by his promotion in 1930 to the chairmanship of the Board of Customs and Excise. From this he was transferred only a month later, at the desire of Snowden, to the chairmanship of the Board of Inland Revenue, to work out a scheme of land values in which the Chancellor was interested. At the end of 1933, he was invited to go to India for five years as Finance Member of the Viceroy's Executive Council—a position which, though ranking as a Civil Service appointment, was equivalent to the status of a Cabinet Minister at home, and which gave him in the Legislative Assembly parliamentary experience destined to be useful to him later. The India to which he went in 1934 was still the India of the Montagu-Chelmsford reforms and the diarchy, but the much wider measures of self-government soon to be embodied in the Government of India Act, 1935, had already been clearly forecast in the White Paper, and during Grigg's term of office provincial autonomy was in fact introduced.

BETTERMENT OF INDIA

In official and parliamentary activities, he was held by many to be the most challenging personality of his time at Delhi. His financial policy was directed to the betterment of the rural areas, and the development of roads and broadcasting, and he strove to obtain a larger contribution from the United Kingdom for defence. For Congress as a body he had little liking, but his relations with individual Indian leaders were cordial and friendly. A convinced believer in India's ultimate claim to Dominion status, he did not want self-government to be achieved too quickly, and Britain's postwar withdrawal was in his eyes tragically premature.

In 1939 Grigg returned to England as Permanent Under-Secretary of State for War. He joined his new department at a time of great confusion, on the eve of war, when a continental land commitment had just been accepted, the Territorial Army was in process of being doubled, and conscription had been introduced. The War Office was at that time divided into watertight compartments with little provision for coordination below Army Council level and much of Grigg's early work there was addressed to administrative reforms, designed to iron out the time-honoured division between the brass-hats and the frocks, to increase coordination, to decentralize where possible and to give the whole machine the flexibility suited to the demands of modern war.

In 1942 he became Secretary of State for War in place of Captain (later Viscount) Margesson, and a parliamentary constituency was found for him at East Cardiff, where he stood as a National candidate and had a majority of 6,719 in a straight fight with an I.L.P. candidate. Under his control the organization, training, and equipment of the new type of army proceeded apace with a competence which forestalled every need and overcame every difficulty. In the words of Field Marshal, then General, Montgomery in 1944: "I doubt if the War Office has ever sent an army overseas so well equipped as the one fighting now in Normandy."

After the secession of the Labour Party from the Coalition in 1945, Grigg remained at the War Office under the Caretaker Government. At the general election, however, he lost his seat at East Cardiff to Labour by 4,993 votes.

TOBACCO POST

No longer either politician or civil servant, he filled the succeeding years with varied activities. In 1946 he went to Washington as the first United Kingdom executive director of the International Bank for Reconstruction and Development. Returning in 1947, he became associated with the Imperial Tobacco Company, first as financial adviser, then as a director; and he also accepted directorships in other large concerns, including Prudential Assurance and the National Provincial Bank. In 1959 he became chairman of Bass, Ratcliff and Gretton, and on the merger with Mitchells and Butlers, of Birmingham, in 1961, he became chairman of the new group.

Sir James was chairman of the committee on departmental records which published its report in 1954. This resulted in the transfer of the responsibility for the public record office from the Master of the Rolls to the Lord Chancellor. In 1958 he was chairman of the Advisory Committee on Recruiting which recommended improved pensions and allowances for the armed forces.

In 1948 he published his autobiography *Prejudice and Judgment*, a vigorous and often witty account of the distinguished personalities and historic events of which his career had given him inside knowledge. His attachments were, as became a civil servant, free from party bias, and his enthusiasms ranged from Lloyd George and Winston Churchill to Philip Snowden. He had, however, exceedingly definite views, which he clothed in incisive and memorable phrases, on the trends of the age he lived in. His whole outlook was away from totalitarianism and Marxism towards freedom of the individual and sturdy self-help. The son of a poor man—in his early days his father's income rarely rose above 30s. a week—he had found no lack of opportunity, and he had little patience with the doctrines that it is praiseworthy "for a whole country to live beyond its means on its wits", and that it is possible "to make a community rich by calling a penny twopence".

His busy life left him little time for hobbies. He had, however, a passion for reading—often not gratified for years at a time—and a delight in travel, especially in Greece and the Mediterranean. Though a mathematician, he had a strong bias towards the classics, and loved to remember his first sight of the Acropolis and Hymettus "violet crowned".

His career was almost, though not quite, unique among civil servants, and his secure and confident tenure of the War Department from the dark days of the early war to the growing triumphs of the later years may well be remembered with respect and gratitude. To his admirable handling and coordination must in no small measure be ascribed the efficiency of an organization which sent out every year more men, better trained, better armed and better equipped, on the long road which led from Dunkirk through El Alamein to the Normandy beaches and final victory. He received the K.C.B. in 1932, and the K.C.S.I. in 1936. Bristol University made him an honorary LL.D. in 1946 and in 1954 he became an honorary Bencher of the Middle Temple.

He married in 1919 and is survived by Lady Grigg. They had no children.

May 7, 1964.

Serge Grigoriev, who died in mid-September, 1968, was more than any other man responsible for the preservation of some of the most famous works created for the Diaghilev Russian Ballet.

Born in 1883, he studied at the Russian Imperial ballet school in St. Petersburg and graduated into the Maryinsky Theatre company in 1900. He joined Diaghilev for his company's first season in 1909 and remained until the last in 1929, the only person to be a member of the company throughout that time.

Although Grigoriev continued to dance character parts (his most famous creation was perhaps the Russian father in La Boutique Fantasque), he soon showed a talent for conducting rehearsals and became the company's régisseur. This post demanded many qualities, apparently combining the work of a modern company manager with that of a ballet master, and those who worked with Grigoriev have almost unanimously praised his calmness, tact, application and skill.

It was his work as répétiteur and coach, however, that won him lasting fame. A phenomenal memory for detail enabled him to reproduce ballets in a manner that preserved their original inspiration, Diaghilev compared this work with that of an orchestral conductor, but Grigoriev added that the régisseur's job was harder, because he had to work from memory instead of a score, and could only prepare his cast, not actually direct them during performance.

During the 1930s Grigoriev worked as régisseur for Colonel de Basil's various ballet companies, reviving many of the ballets from Diaghilev's repertory. In 1954 Ninette de Valois invited him to stage Fokine's *The Firebird* for the Royal Ballet, and he later added to their reportory *Petrushka* and the Polovtsian Dances from Prince Igor. He also revised and improved out of all recognition the Royal Ballet's production of *Les Sylphides*, besides rehearsing the Massine ballets in their programmes. Grigoriev worked also for Festival Ballet and the company at La Scala, Milan. His book on the Diaghilev Ballet, published in 1953, is an invaluable record of the company's history.

Fortunately, it is no longer true that ballets can he preserved only by memory, and Grigoriev's productions of the four Fokine ballets at Covent Garden have all been recorded with the aid of dance notation or film. His exceptional gifts will therefore have a lasting memorial. He leaves a widow, the former dancer Lubov Tcherinicheva, who was closely associated with him in his work. He was buried in Paris.

September 13, 1968.

Dr. Walter Gropius, the architect, who died in Boston in July, 1969, at the age of 86, had been for many years one of the major world forces working towards an architecture that acknowledged and exploited modern technology. With his master, Peter Behrens, with Le Corbusier in France, Aalto in Finland, and Frank Lloyd Wright in the United States he may be classed as one of the most influential architects of modern times: and his influence was spread not only by example but by precept issuing from the Bauhaus at Dessau, that great institution which combined all the crafts in one philosophic unity and brought the work of the artist into the closest association with industry.

Gropius was nevertheless always on his guard against abstract terms like "functionalism" (which he did not scruple to call "catchwords"), and deprecated the propaganda which would make the new architecture a fashion "as snobbish as any of the older academic fashions which it aims to displace". His attitude was based not only on the frank acceptance and exploitation of steel, glass, and reinforced concrete but on the realization that the day of the individual craftsman was done. He regarded the craftsman's role, in the modern industrial age, as that of creating well conceived and serviceable building components capable of being multiplied in quantity by mass production.

This great architectural philosopher and teacher was driven from his own country by the Nazi regime. Germany's loss might have been England's gain, for Gropius lived and worked there for three years, but in the end it was America which offered him a post consonant with his status, the Chair of Architecture at Harvard.

Walter Gropius was born in Berlin on May 18, 1883, the son of an architect, Walter Adolf Gropius, and his wife Manon Scharnweber.

CUBES AND GLASS

From his formative years he determined to follow his father's profession; and after studying at the technical high-schools at Charlottenburg and Munich he worked as assistant to Peter Behrens, one of the fathers of modern architecture, and it was in this period that his originality and far sightedness began to emerge.

In 1910 Gropius set up his own office; and in the following year, working with Adolf Meyer, produced one of the most remarkable industrial buildings of prewar years. This was the Fagus shoe-last factory at Alfeld-an-der-Leine, which had the forthright cubic outline and the huge areas of glass which were later to become associated with modern factory architecture. In 1914 he designed the Hall of Machinery for the Cologne exhibition of the Deutscher Werkbund, and (with Adolf Meyer) the Administrative Building at the same exhibition. From August, 1914, he served for some three years and a half as an air observer in the war, winning the Iron Cross of the first class and being shot down on one occasion by the French. Meanwhile, in 1915, he had been granted leave to discuss with the Grand Duke of Saxe-Weimar his taking control of the Saxon Academy of Arts and Crafts from the Belgian architect Henry van de Velde, who had himself suggested Gropius as his successor.

After the war Gropius took over two schools, the Grossherzogliche Sächsische Kunstgewerbeschule and the Grossherzogliche Sächsische Hochschule für Bildende Kunst, combining these institutions in 1919 as the Staatliches Bauhaus, at Weimar. Here he gathered round him a brilliant group of instructors and began to put into effect his theories about the relationship of design to industry. But he was severely hampered by the obscurantist attitude of the Government of Thuringia, and in April, 1925, left Weimar to start afresh in the smaller town of Dessau.

JUSTIFIED IN BAUHAUS

Now began a fruitful period of teaching, experimentation, craft-work and building that was to have incalculably beneficial effects on architecture in every civilized country. The Bauhaus at Dessau has been described as "the one school in the world where modern problems of design were approached realistically in a modern atmosphere". A distinguished team of professors included Johannes Itten, Oskar Schlemmer, Wassily Kandinsky, László Moholy-Nagy, and Paul Klee.

The Bauhaus building itself, begun in autumn, 1925, and finished in December 1926, was a triumphant vindication of the principles of its architect and of the lines on which he had educated the students who worked on it. The whole of its interior decorations and fittings were produced in its own workshops.

At Dessau, as at Weimar, Gropius encountered vigorous and often ill-informed criticism from official bodies, craft organizations and so forth, and the press was full of controversy. Though he had forbidden any kind of political activity in the school it was constantly urged by his enemies that the Bauhaus was a centre of "bolshevism"; and in 1928 Gropius gave up the struggle.

Meanwhile Gropius had continued with his private practice. In 1926 he designed two houses for the Weissenhof permanent housing exhibition at Stuttgart, to which several of the most famous European architects contributed designs. In 1929 he won first prize in the Spandau-Haselhorst housing competition, and although the design was never executed it exerted considerable influence.

His most noteworthy designs of this kind in Germany actually carried out were those for the large Siemensstadt estate near Berlin. Gropius was the supervising architect for the scheme in which several others collaborated, and he was responsible for two of the blocks.

MODEL SCHEME

In this scheme he was able to put many of his theories into practice. Among the best in Europe at the time it was designed and served as a model for much subsequent work.

The rise of Nazi power brought with it hard times and hard words for modern minded artists, and in 1934 Gropius left Germany for London, along with several other architects who had become refugees from Nazi persecution.

These included the late Erich Mendelsohn and the Hungarian-born Marcel Breuer, who had taught under Gropius at the Bauhaus and was later to become Gropius's partner in America. Gropius set up in practice in London in partnership with Mr. E. Maxwell Fry. He stayed for three years, and during that period he and Fry made several interesting projects, including an influential and prophetic one for high flats in a park-like setting at Windsor, and they were the architects of several buildings including Impington Village College, Cambridgeshire (1936), which was one of the four village colleges erected by the county council in support of the late Henry Morris's educational ideas with which Gropius found himself in close sympathy. A one-storey building with single depth classrooms, fan-shaped hall and club amenities, it serves the dual purpose of a secondary school, library and local community centre.

CLASSIC SERENITY

Early in 1937 Gropius was appointed Senior Professor of Architecture at Harvard University, and the following year he became Chairman of the Department of Architecture. He quickly began work on a house for his own occupation. A modern version of the traditional New England house, it had much of the classic serenity of the houses that he had designed for himself and the Bauhaus teachers in 1926.

For the first years after his arrival he entered into partnership with Marcel Breuer, who had followed him from England. Between 1943 and 1948 Gropius resumed his experiments with standardized building elements for mass-produced housing which he had begun in Germany in 1932.

His new experiments, chiefly with houses composed of timber panels based on a module both horizontally and vertically of 40 inches, were made in collaboration with Konrad Wachsmann in Long Island, and examples were erected on a considerable scale in California.

In 1945 Gropius went into partnership with several architects of the younger generation forming a team of eight under the name of "The Architects, Collaborative". In this enterprise Gropius was the guide and leading spirit.

TEAM WORK

That he was able to work enthusiastically with so large a group demonstrates his great belief in the value of team work which he had always felt to be necessary in modern building. Buildings for which the team has been responsible include the Harvard University Graduate Centre, Cambridge, Massachusetts (1949–50), the McCormick office buildings in Chicago (1953), and the United States embassy building in Athens (1961). In recent years Gropius's name re-appeared on English building sites as a result of his agreeing to become consulting architect for several big property developments, notably that of the (still vacant) Monico site in Piccadilly Circus.

Gropius's work as a designer of buildings however, though necessary to him as a means of keeping him in touch with the practical problems of a rapidly changing profession, was not as outstanding as his great reputation might suggest; only his Bauhaus building at Dessau can claim a place among the significant buildings of this century. His reputation was due to his vision as an architectural philosopher, his understanding—far in advance of his time—of the nature of architecture's place in the industrialized world of today and his dedication and integrity as a teacher. The whole essence of the challenge that the twentieth-century architect must face was contained in the ideas he spent his life expounding and the reason why, in the past few years, his name was less frequently than hitherto on the younger architects' lips was simply that those ideas—through Gropius's efforts—had become widely accepted and were no longer revolutionary. Nevertheless, the opportunities the younger generation of architects now enjoys it owes to him more than to anyone else.

UNO TASK

Gropius was an honorary F.R.I.B.A., vice-president of the Congrès Internationaux de l'Architecture Moderne (at whose conferences he was a revered and influential figure) and an Honorary R.D.I. In 1956 he was awarded the Royal Gold Medal for Architecture. He presided over numerous international committees including those responsible for appointing and briefing the architects of the Uno building, New York, and the Unesco building, Paris. His writings include *Staatliches Bauhaus* (1923), *Internationale Architektur* (1924), *Bauhaus Bauten* (1933), *The New Architecture and the Bauhaus* (1935) and *Bauhaus 1919–28* (1939) this last edited with his wife Ilse Frank and Herbert Bayer.

July 7, 1969.

Otto Grotewohl, the east German Prime Minister who died on September 21, 1964, at the age of 70, appeared a pathetic figure when latterly he briefly attended important state and party occasions in east Germany. A sick man since November, 1960, when officially he had a heart attack while visiting the Soviet Union, his condition was known to be hopeless as a sufferer from leukemia. His duties had long been carried out by Herr Willi Stoph, officially acting Prime Minister since 1962, but the communist party persistently refused to accept his request to be released from office. Grotewohl, as chairman of the former central committee of the Social Democrat party in east Germany, was retained for his symbolic value.

Grotewohl had played the key role in the Russian-backed manoeuvres by which Herr Ulbricht sought to secure for the so-called Socialist Unity party an element of democratic sanction in 1946. Grotewohl's willingness to participate in this political tragedy left behind it a hatred, still alive today, among former S.P.D. colleagues, many of whom later fled to the west.

As if to underline the fact that Grotewohl had only been for the communists a tool, his powers were only minimal right from the start and after he had been made Prime Minister at the setting up of the German Democratic Republic in 1949. After the death of the old communist functionary Wilhelm Pieck, in 1960, Ulbricht, by uniting the first party secretaryship with the new office of chairman of the east German Council of State, eclipsed him completely. In the bitter east German context, Grotewohl had served the communist purpose as the "useful idiot" in the Dmitrov phrase.

What Social Democrats in west Germany never forgave Grotewohl for, however, was the personal ambition and blindness with which they held he actively joined in pushing through the forced union of the two parties, accompanied as it was by partially concealed and partially open political terror.

TWICE ARRESTED

Grotewohl was born on March 11, 1894, in Brunswick, the son of a tailor. After school he learned to become a printer. At 18 he joined the S.P.D., having spent two years in its youth movement. In 1918 he flirted briefly with the more radical U.S.P.D., but returned to the main party, something which the communists later held against him. His application and ability as a speaker soon made him one of the leading party officials in Lower Saxony and at 26 Grotewohl entered the Brunswick Landtag.

Two years later he was made Minister of Education and in the late 1920s he was also an S.P.D. member of the Reichstag.

After the Nazis came to power he was forced to resign office as president of the Brunswick Insurance Corporation and earned his living as a salesman. He was arrested for illegal activities by the Gestapo in 1938 but released a year later without trial. A second period of detention followed in the wave of mass arrests after the July, 1944, attempt on Hitler.

The fatal step in Grotewohl's career came shortly after the end of the war when in Berlin he was chosen chairman of the S.P.D. central committee in the Russian zone. After the fusion of the parties in April, 1946, when he received the dubious office of equal ranking party chairman, Grotewohl threw himself enthusiastically into helping to nationalize the key industries and establish the foundations of a "socialist state" in east Germany.

Ulbricht's doctrinaire course brought differences with the old Social Democrat who tried at times to advocate a less rapid communization of east Germany. A signal showing he still had a better sense of political reality came when the east Berlin building workers downed tools to start the June 1953 east German uprising.

Grotewohl was the official east German signatory to the 1950 Görlit agreement recognizing, in contrast to west Germany, the former German territories across the Oder-Neisse as Polish, inaugurating the so-called "frontier of peace".

September 22, 1964.

Professor Semseddin Gunaltay, former Prime Minister of Turkey and a distinguished historian, died on October 19, 1961, at Istanbul, at the age of 79, four days after his election as Senator in the new Turkish Parliament.

Semseddin Gunaltay, who was Prime Minister from 1948 until 1950, will be chiefly remembered as the man under whose premiership the first really free and honest elections were held in Turkey, when the Democrat Party of Adnan Menderes came to power in 1950, replacing the Republican Peoples Party which ruled Turkey for 27 years.

This election will always remain as a milestone in Turkish history, and as a consequence Gunaltay became associated in the public mind with principles of honesty and integrity in politics, and also, together with the President of the Republic at the time, Mr. Ismet Inönü, his exact contemporary, with the struggle to establish democratic government in Turkey.

Professor Gunaltay was one of the relatively few remaining figures who was a grown man at the time of Atatürk's war of independence and his reforms, and who lived through the vast changes which have taken place in the country since the establishment of the Republic. He was born in 1883 in the town of Kemaliyé, in the province of Erzincan in East Turkey. His father, Ibrahim Efendi, was a school teacher. Gunaltay was elected Deputy for Bilecik in 1915, and for many years after that taught history and comparative religion at the University of Istanbul, at the time when it was still possible in Turkey to combine both duties. He took an active part in the struggle for national independence, and his work at the university is generally recognized to have been a formative influence on Turkish youth of his day.

He was elected a member of the city council of Istanbul when Atatürk set up his first nationalist government in Ankara, and in 1923 became Deputy for Sivas, in central Anatolia. From then on until his retirement from Parliament in 1954 he was Deputy either for Sivas or for his home town in Erzincan. Gunaltay became Prime Minister in 1948 and during his period of office, apart from the famous election of 1950, was responsible for a number of fiscal and other reforms, and for the introduction of a new electoral law. His greatest achievement, paradoxically enough, remains the general election of May, 1950, which turned his Government out of office.

Gunaltay was a founder member of the Turkish Historical Society created by Atatürk in 1931, and in 1941 was elected the society's president. He held this post until his death. The author of a number of works on the history and religions of the Middle East, he was regarded as an authority on these and related subjects.

Gunaltay had the reputation of a genial man and a good talker, a little unapproachable unless one knew him well, but a gay companion with his intimate friends. His death removes one more of the "old guard" who helped Atatürk to transform Turkey into a modern European state.

He is survived by his widow and three daughters.

October 23, 1961.

Sir James Gunn, R.A., who died on December 30, 1964, in a London hospital at the age of 71, was almost exclusively a portrait painter.

It was said as long ago as 1938 that, with one possible exception, he was charging more for a portrait than any other Academy exhibitor. Whether true or not the statement is relevant because it suggests the respect with which his professional accomplishment was regarded, though his artistic reputation did not stand as high. In all that is demanded in a commission Gunn's work was careful, completely finished, and sober in feeling—generally worked out in gradations of tone rather than by oppositions of colour; where it fell short was in those qualities that distinguish the creative artist from the capable craftsman.

Gunn's merits and defects might be illustrated by a comparison between one of his best known pictures, "Conversation Piece: Hilaire Belloc, G. K. Chesterton and Maurice Baring," exhibited in the Academy of 1932 and now in the National Portrait Gallery, and "Hommage à Manet", by Orpen, now in the City Art Gallery, Manchester, in which George Moore is declaiming to an audience composed of Steer, Tonks, Sir Hugh Lane, Sickert, and McColl under the painting of "Eva Gonzales", by Manet. Gunn's picture is possibly the more accurate of the two, but it lacks the life and unity of Orpen's picture.

A drawback of Gunn's method of careful and smooth painting can be seen in his portrait of Delius exhibited in the Academy of 1933, and painted when Delius was blind and then in declining health. The formal precision of style shows the limitations of his mode of academic painting when applied to a subject of a pathetic nature and the difficulty he found in conveying feeling in conjunction with his objective accuracy of representation.

In spite of his artistic shortcomings Gunn deserved praise for his professional competency. He faithfully supplied what is generally demanded in a portrait and he had a good sense of line as well as of tone and technical skill of a high order.

He took great pains with a state portrait he painted of Queen Elizabeth and his aptitude for a work of formal and ceremonial character is shown in his portrait of Harold Macmillan when Prime Minister, in his office as Chancellor of Oxford University, completed in 1963 to the commission of Balliol men in both Lords and Commons.

The son of Richard Gunn, he was born in Glasgow in 1893. He was educated at Glasgow High School and studied art in Glasgow and Edinburgh and at Julian's in Paris. He saw service in the First World War, enlisting in the Artists' Rifles, and during the 1920s when settled in London gained a steadily increasing repute as portrait painter. From 1923 he exhibited regularly at the Royal Academy, seldom failing to have hung the three works allowed to an outsider. Most people who knew his work were surprised that he had long to wait before becoming an Academician but he was elected A.R.A. in 1953 and R.A. in 1961. Gunn also exhibited at the Royal Scottish Academy and at the Paris Salon and was President of the Royal Society of Portrait Painters from 1953. He was knighted in 1963.

He married in 1929 Pauline, daughter of A.P. Miller, by whom he had a son and a daughter.

Pauline Gunn, who died in 1950, had frequently sat for her husband.

January 1, 1965.

John Gunther, the American author and journalist, famed for his Inside reports on several continents which sought to provide the reader with a bird's eye view of the problems and the peoples he wrote about, died on May 29, 1970, in New York. He was 69.

His first Inside book dealing with Europe was published in 1936, and repeatedly revised and republished. Harold Nicolson (as he then was) welcomed the book "as a serious contribution to contemporary knowledge." Another writer thought it came "near to being a political Baedeker". Gunther himself said he was fortunate in that the book appeared at the right time "when the three totalitarian dictators took the stage and people began to be vitally interested in them". The book was finished in six months with the help of "colleagues in 20 countries." Gunther, at the time working at the Chicago Daily News's London bureau, gave the book its final title at the last moment, and it became a striking success.

Inside Asia, for which Gunther spent some two years travelling in Asia, appeared in 1939. It covered the whole continent except for Siberia and there was a chapter on the Philippines. The same year Gunther's broadcasts to the United States from Europe during the summer preceding the outbreak of war, were published under the title *The High Cost of Hitler*.

After the war Gunther published his book on the United States, for which he travelled through every state for a period of 17 months interviewing from two to 20 people a day. He made his first exhaustive inspection trip of Africa in 1952, travelling more than 40,000 miles and, despite eye cataracts, took notes on interviews with 1,500 people for *Inside Africa*.

HASTY JUDGMENTS

His comprehensive survey of Russia (titled *Inside Russia Today*) (1958) contains one chapter called "a History of Russia in Half an Hour". *Inside South America* appeared in 1966, some 25 years after his first book on the continent, which was published as *Inside Latin America*.

Some critics thought his quickly-produced Insides superficial glimpses through hotel windows. He was once dubbed "the Book-of-the-Month Club's Marco Polo". His judgments sometimes proved as hasty as his stopovers. In 1955 he predicted in his book on Africa that independence would not come soon to Morocco; but less than a year after publication of Gunther's book Morocco was independent. Gunther, however, had the gift of popularizing remote places or difficult subjects; he was skilled in communicating ideas in terms of people, and interviewed contemporary leaders ranging from Lloyd George to General MacArthur.

John Gunther was born on August 30, 1901 in Chicago. His father was a convivial drifter; his mother a teacher. Gunther went to university and in 1922 joined the Chicago Daily News as a reporter. He worked in various European capitals for his newspaper from 1924 to 1936 when he published his first Inside book. During the Second World War he was a war correspondent, and took part in the invasion of Sicily and Italy in 1943.

Among his other books are *Behind the Iron Curtain*, *Roosevelt in Retrospect*, *Eisenhower: the Man and the Symbol*, and an account of Gunther's dying son, *Death Be Not Proud*. Many of his books were translated into other languages.

He married twice.

June 1, 1970.

General Cemal Gürsel, who died in Ankara on September 14, 1966, was Head of State in Turkey after the seizure of power by the Army in May, 1960, and on October 26, 1961, was elected President of the Republic when the Army, as it had promised, handed power back to a democratic civilian government.

Gürsel thus became fourth in the line of Presidents of the Turkish Republic, following Kemal Atatürk, Ismet Inönü, and Celal Bayar, in that post. It was a period when Turkey, racked by internal strife, had great need of an impartial Head of State. This function Gursel filled, while at the same time being clearly devoted to the revolutionary aims and principles of Atatürk's Republic.

He was taken gravely ill early in 1966, and in March Cevdet Sunay was elected President in his stead.

A mature, tolerant man, with plenty of rough common sense and a good sense of humour, Gürsel symbolized in his person the double objective of revolutionary Turkey: he was convinced of the rightness of Atatürk's aim to reform Turkey in the image of modern Europe; and he was also genuinely persuaded, like many of his fellow-officers in the Turkish Army, that a western type of parliamentary democracy was the best regime for Turkey.

Cemal Gürsel was born in 1895 in the historic old fortress of Erzurum, in eastern Turkey. His father, Abidin Bey (in the days before surnames were introduced) was also an Army officer.

FALL OF EMPIRE

His mother, Zekiye, was an Istanbul lady of good family. One of a family of eight, Gürsel received a strictly military education. His youth was clouded by the fall and break-up of the Ottoman Empire, which grieved his father, who is said to have blamed the disaster on incompetent military commanders.

Gürsel graduated from the military school at Erzincan, west of Erzurum, and saw his first action at Gallipoli, where he commanded a battery of the 15th division. He fought in the battles of Seddulbahir and Anafarta. Later he was transferred to the Palestine front, and was for two years a prisoner-of-war in Egypt.

When he got home after his release Gürsel soon joined Mustafa Kemal's nationalist movement. He commanded a battery in the War of Independence. He took part in all the main battles of this famous struggle, including Sakarya, Dumlupinar, and the first and second battles of Inönü. This service was followed by an exemplary military career, culminating in 1958 with his appointment as C-in-C. Land Forces, the highest military post under the Chief of Staff. Gürsel was always very popular in the Army, where he was given the affectionate nickname of "Cemal Aga" ("Elder brother Cemal").

ARMY SEIZE POWER

A new and dramatic period now opened in Gürsel's life. This was the phase when violent factional strife between the Menderes government and the opposition led by veteran Mr. Ismet Inönü had become so acute that the Army was gradually being pushed into the position of arbiter in the struggle. The top staff generals were loyal to Menderes. Gürsel was the most senior officer in the armed forces who disapproved of the reactionary and repressive policy of the government, and it was for this reason, when the Army finally struck in May, 1960, that Gürsel came to head the revolution.

Gürsel, along with many other officers, strongly opposed Menderes's attempt to use the army to restrict the activities of the political opposition. Shortly before the *coup* Gürsel wrote a strong letter to the then Minister of Defence warning the government to give up such policies, and asking that his letter should be transmitted to President Bayar. The warning was ignored. On May 5, Gürsel was sent on "terminal leave" preparatory to his retirement in June. He issued a farewell message to the troops, urging them, ironically enough, to "keep clear of politics". Three weeks later the Army seized power.

It is uncertain how much Gürsel personally knew about the planning of the *coup*. But the younger officers who made the *coup* needed Gürsel. May 27 was a touch-and-go affair.

At the beginning most foreign observers regarded elderly Gürsel as the Turkish "Neguib" and started looking around for the "Nasser". But things worked out differently. In November, 1960, after six months of deadlock inside the military Junta, it was Gürsel who ejected the 14 "radical" officers led by Colonel Turkesh, on the ground that the Turkesh group were against democracy.

This was a crisis almost amounting to a second *coup d'état*, and Gürsel underwent a great strain. His health broke down soon after, and he suffered a stroke from which he never fully recovered. In later years his direct influence dwindled, especially after the renewed ascendancy of Mr. Inönü, who became Prime Minister after the transfer of power to a civilian government in October, 1961. His life in the President's Palace, on the hill south of Ankara, became increasingly secluded.

However, Gürsel remained at the helm through the following difficult years. These were marked by the Cyprus crisis of Christmas, 1963, and by an increasingly complex internal political situation. In February, 1965, Mr. Inönü's government was defeated in Parliament. Elections followed in October, in which the Justice Party triumphed. As the Justice Party were considered the political heirs of Menderes, the Army might have found this the excuse for another dose of direct action. It was in no small measure thanks to the moderating influence of Gürsel that the new administration took over smoothly, and Turkey continued on a democratic path.

Gürsel, said to have been a personally devout man, was always interested in the question of religious reform. He strongly advocated the translation of the Koran into Turkish and the modernization of religious schools, in order to free Turkey from the grip of fanatical priests. He always denied that Islam as a religion was incompatible with scientific progress. His message to the Turks was that no advance could be achieved without hard work. "Turks must give up sitting in the village coffee-houses and expecting everything to come from Allah", he said on one occasion.

On March 6, 1961, Gürsel met the Queen and the Duke of Edinburgh at Ankara airport, where they stopped for an hour on their way from Teheran to London. Gürsel very much liked the Queen, whom he described afterwards to bystanders as "an extraordinarily charming lady".

He is survived by his widow, Mrs. Melahat Gürsel, one son, and an adopted daughter.

September 15, 1966.

Lieutenant-General the Maharaja of Gwalior, G.C.S.I., G.C.I.E., who died on July 17, 1961, at the age of 45, at his residence in Bombay, was the last personal ruler of the important central Indian state of Gwalior.

This was one of the five princely states whose

rulers had the highest permanent salute of 21 guns. Following on the transfer of power to Indian hands in 1947, the Maharaja was selected to be Rajpramuk, in other words Constitutional President, of the newly formed Malwa Union, Madhya Bharat, comprising some 20 states, each of which up to that time had been under direct personal rule. In November, 1956, Madhya Bharat was merged into Madhya Pradesh.

His Highness Sir George Jiwaji Rao Scindia, Alijah Bahadur was born on June 26, 1916, a son of the Maharaja Madho Rao Scindia, who was then giving great support in men, money, and materials to the allied cause in the 1914–18 War. The father telegraphed to King George V asking permission to name his son and heir after his Majesty and promptly received an affirmative answer. George Scindia was educated privately and matriculated for study at the Victoria College, Gwalior. He was carefully trained for rulership by experience of revenue and settlement work in the Punjab, in administrative detail in the Bombay Presidency, and this was followed by military training in Poona, the centre of Mahratta tradition and history.

REGENCY

The Maharaja Madho Rao Scindia, who had lived strenuously in work and in sport, died in June, 1925, when his heir was completing his ninth year. The administration of the state therefore devolved upon a Council of Regency presided over by the senior widow until her death in November, 1931, when the young Maharaja's mother took charge as head of the Regency.

George Scindia was invested with full ruling powers by the Viceroy, the late Lord Linlithgow, in November, 1936.

The Maharaja repeated to the utmost extent of his resources the strenuous support of the allied cause which had been shown by his father in the previous world conflict. A central War Committee was established with branches at the headquarter town of every revenue district. Recruitment for the army was encouraged and the work of the organization included assisting families of soldiers sent on active service. He contributed substantially to the Lord Mayor of London's Fund for air-raid victims, and to other voluntary efforts to alleviate suffering from enemy action in the United Kingdom. His Highness was created G.C.I.E. in 1941 and G.C.S.I. in 1946.

As the time for the transfer of power drew near the princes had to face the unwelcome prospect of the ending of personal rule. The Maharaja took part in a Conference of the Princes with Lord Mountbatten at New Delhi in April, 1947, when a Covenant was signed whereby some 20 states in Central India were grouped into the Malwa Union. The aggregate area of the Union was 47,000 square miles and with a population of over seven million.

NEW TITLE

The only difference between this arrangement and those relating to what had hitherto been known as "British provinces" was that the Constitutional President had the title of Rajpramuk, for he was similarly required to accept the advice of a Ministry responsible to an elected Legislature. Maharaja George Scindia became the first and as it proved the only holder of the office of Rajpramuk of the Union. There was some initial difficulty as to the choice of capital for the Malwa Union, but a compromise was reached whereby Gwalior was the winter capital and Indore the summer capital.

It was soon evident that his Highness could adapt himself well to the changed conditions. He was endowed with many personal gifts of character and skill. He could ride a horse, drive a car, and handle a rifle with equal facility. He was a keen shikari (big game hunter), polo and tennis player, and he was also a book-lover.

He married, in 1941, Princess Lekha Divveshwari Devi, a member of the Rana family, which gave Nepal a succession of Prime Ministers, who were for many years the real rulers of that Himalayan state instead of the titular ruling House. In November, 1945, Maharaja George Scindia laid the foundation stone of a medical college in Gwalior in celebration of the birth of a son. There were also four daughters of the marriage.

July 18, 1961.

The Rev. R. M. Gwynn, who died in Dublin on June 10, 1962, at the age of 85, was a Fellow of Trinity College, Dublin, for over 50 years and was made an honorary Fellow on his retirement in 1957. During a long career in which he held many college offices, including that of Vice-Provost, he was known as a courageous and formidable champion of liberal causes and social reform.

The family of John Gwynn, who became a Fellow of Trinity College more than a century ago and in later life was the celebrated Regius Professor of Divinity, inherited remarkable literary and scholarly gifts, and the connexion on the mother's side with William Smith O'Brien linked it with the forward political men of action in nineteenth-century Ireland. Of the 10 children three sons were Fellows of Trinity. Lucius died young, but Edward John became Provost. The eldest, Stephen, the novelist and biographer, was for a time nationalist M.P. for Galway. One of the two surviving brothers is Major-General Sir Charles Gwynn.

GOLD MEDALS

Robert Malcolm was born in 1877 at Ramelton, in his father's parish in co. Donegal, where the late A. E. W. Mason set the earlier scenes of *The Four Feathers*. He went to St. Columba's College, and thence to Trinity College, where he was a scholar of the House and the Classical Student of his year with the old "large golds" in classics and modern literature. Fellowship came in 1906. A divinity lecturer for some years, he became Professor of Biblical Greek, in which he continued to lecture until his retirement, and he was for a time Professor of Hebrew. He was for long a tutor, and in later years served as Registrar, Senior Lecturer, Senior Tutor, and Vice-Provost of the college.

Gwynn came into the public eye at the period of the bitter industrial disputes in Dublin just before the First World War. His championship of the workers led him into the back streets of the city, and, rather to the embarrassment of the Provost, the young clergyman appeared on public platforms with Connolly and Larkin. Momentous consequences have been ascribed to an occasion when Gwynn and other speakers were debarred from the Mansion House, where they were to address a meeting designed to promote conciliation in the great strikes. On Gwynn's proposal they adjourned to his college room, though one of them suggested that a little drilling might improve the morale of the unemployed, and the formation of the Irish Citizens Army is placed to this innocent and pacific contribution to their debate. Throughout later years untiring energy went into the work of a college society among the Dublin poor, which undertook the management of tenement houses.

USED VETO

The rise of the great dictatorships involved Gwynn in another remarkable episode. No longer young, and isolated to some extent by his increasing deafness, he was always capable of decisive intervention in affairs when his strong principles were outraged. In 1937 the governing body of the college decided to confer an honorary degree upon J.L.Garvin in recognition of his work as a biographer. Garvin accepted, and the proposal went to the Senate to be ratified. Gwynn, who appeared completely out of touch and had expressed no views on the matter, attended the meeting as the Senior Master non-regent, and, to the astonishment of all, imposed the absolute veto which by historic survival is the prerogative of this officer, accompanying it with a short speech on Garvin's Abyssinian policy. It was an unheard of exercise of power.

He was a man of great vigour of body, very handsome in his younger days, and preserving into age a masculine charm which enslaved his secretarial staffs when he was a college officer, in which capacity he combined a certain amateurishness of method with a genius for successful improvisation. As an old man he looked like a saint by an Italian master, but it was a saint with a strong sense of humour, kindly but often barbed and pungent. He had been a fine cricketer, even if the story of his bowling W.G.Grace first ball should be credited to his brother Lucius, and even in his last years it was never difficult to imagine in him the manly stamina of the athlete, just as it was impossible in his writings to miss the quick wit and lively observations of a man young at heart.

Gwynn married in 1914 Eileen Gertrude Glenn, M.B. He is survived by her and by his two sons and four daughters.

June 12, 1962.

Dame Helen Gwynne-Vaughan, G.B.E., who died on August 26, 1967, at the age of 88, had a career of distinction in quite separate fields. She was Chief Comptroller of the Women's

Army Auxiliary Forces during the First World War, subsequently Commandant of the Women's Royal Air Force, and in the Second World War Chief Controller of the A.T.S.; and for many years she was Professor of Botany at Birkbeck College, University of London. She was later made Professor Emeritus.

She was born in 1879, a daughter of Captain the Hon. A. H. D. Fraser, of the Scots Guards. She was educated at Cheltenham Ladies' College and later at King's College London, graduating (B.Sc.) in Botany in 1904. Only a few years later she was awarded a higher doctorate (D.Sc.) of the University of London at the early age of 28. The artist de Laszlo attending the graduation ceremony was so struck by her beauty and distinction on that occasion that he sought and was granted permission to paint her portrait in academic robes. This fine life-size picture now hangs in the Council Room of Birkbeck College.

After taking her first degree Dame Helen turned her attention to mycology and in particular to the cytology of the sexual cycle in fungi. In this field she laboured for the rest of her scientific career. In the early years she worked in close association with Professor V. H. Blackman but soon she was to establish her own research school in fungal cytology at Birkbeck College where she became head of the Department of Botany in 1909. Later in 1921, when the College achieved the status of a School of the University of London, she became the first Professor of Botany.

In 1911 she married the palaeobotanist Professor T. G. Gwynne-Vaughan whose death in 1915 robbed British botany of one of its most distinguished workers.

ORGANIZED WOMEN'S ARMY

During the 1914–18 War her career in botanical research was interrupted. She was called upon to organize a women's army and became Chief Comptroller of the Women's Army Auxiliary Forces with the British Army in France and served in that capacity from its foundation in 1917 until near the cessation of hostilities. Later she was appointed Commandant of the Women's Royal Air Force, a position she occupied until the end of 1919. Her outstanding services to her country were recognized in 1919 by the award of the D.B.E. Her great success in developing the women's Services depended not only on her organizing ability, her distinguished presence and her clear voice of command but also on her underlying charm and intense personal interest in all those with whom she was associated.

In January, 1920, she quietly resumed her scientific work at Birkbeck College. She summarized her own attitude to mycology in a scholarly monograph, "Fungi: Ascomycetes, Ustilaginales, Uredinales", published in 1922. This was followed by a textbook on fungi written jointly with Dr. B. Barnes (with a first edition in 1926 and a second in 1930) which became a standard university textbook in Britain. A number of substantial papers appeared between 1930 and 1937 supporting her earlier conclusions on the cytology of fungi. Dame Helen was the protagonist of the theory that there are two nuclear fusions and two reductions in the life-cycle of Ascomycetes. This view she resolutely upheld for the rest of her life, and although this concept is no longer accepted by mycologists it stimulated much valuable work on the cytology of fungi in many parts of the world.

Dame Helen's standing in her subject was recognized by the award of the Trail medal of the Linnean Society in 1920, by her election as President of the British Mycological Society in 1928 and in the same year by her presidency of Section K (Botany) of the British Association.

Within the university her energies were by no means limited to her own department.

CONTROL OF A.T.S.

She was an influential personality on the University Board of Studies in Botany and served on the Senate from 1929 to 1934. Further she did not neglect public work and showed some interest in politics, contesting North Camberwell unsuccessfully in the Conservative interests at the general elections of 1922 and 1923. In 1929 she was created G.B.E.

With the outbreak of World War II in 1939 she was again called upon to serve her country, this time as Chief Controller of the A.T.S. Two years later, however, she returned to botanical work and continued to adorn the Chair of Botany at Birkbeck until her retirement in 1944. In her final two years at the college she had to work in a department heavily damaged by enemy action.

For one of her character real retirement was inconceivable. She took the view, however, that her days of botanical research were over and turned all her energies to welfare work in connexion with ex-Service men and women. She became head of the County Office in London of the Soldiers', Sailors' and Airmen's Families Association. This she ran with her customary vigour, appearing promptly at the office at 9.30 each morning.

Throughout her life Dame Helen believed in quality and exacted the highest standards from those who worked with her. She could be awe-inspiring at times, but her capacity for deep and practical friendship was very great and she could inspire affectionate admiration. It took a very exceptional character to make a major contribution in two such different fields as mycology and the Services.

August 30, 1967.

H

George Hackenschmidt, the former world wrestling champion, died in Dulwich on February 19, 1968, at the age of 90.

Hackenschmidt, known as "the Russian Lion," was once the strongest man in the world and the terror of the wrestling mat. He had been in hospital since November, when he was taken ill at his home in West Norwood.

In 1896 he picked up a milkman's horse and carried it on his shoulders, and two years later, before a large fashionable audience in St. Petersburg, he held a pair of reins in each hand while two horses were whipped in opposite directions to see if they could break his grip. They failed. He continued to keep himself fit and in good trim until late in life; at 85 he used to jump over the back of a chair 50 times once a week; a few years earlier he was still in the habit of taking a 30 or 40 minute slow run. Jumping was always one of his favourite exercises. In 1902, for a wager, he jumped over a table 100 times with his feet together.

Born in 1877 at Dorpat, Estonia (then part of the Russian Empire), Hackenschmidt was, in spite of the Germanic name, the son of a dyer of Swedish origin. At the age of 22, while being trained as an engineer's draughtsman, he became the champion weightlifter and wrestler of Russia. At Vienna in 1898 he won the world championship in the Greco-Roman style of wrestling. In 1900 he turned professional. From that year until 1911, when he retired, he was never defeated by anyone in the world in the Greco-Roman style of wrestling. In 1911 his career as a wrestler came to an abrupt conclusion. He had injured his knee and it was so plastered up that he could not wear ordinary wrestling costume. He was defeated by Frank Gotch.

"TERRIBLE TURK"

In 1902 Hackenschmidt had reached England, where he fought many bouts, continuing to throw all opponents, whatever their weight or nationality. Perhaps his most celebrated bout was at Olympia, when he was under the managership of C. B. Cochran. He twice met and beat Atonia Pieri, "the Terrible Greek," who then produced Ahmed Madrali, "the Terrible Turk," to avenge him. The Turk was over 6ft. in height and all of 16 stone.

Hackenschmidt, believing that if he fell beneath the Turk he would never rise again, did some strenuous training with a five hundredweight sack of cement on his shoulders and, on the sack, a 16-stone man. The bout lasted only 44 seconds. Madrali made a move for Hackenschmidt's waist, was seized, flung on the ground, and suffered a dislocated arm. In a return match Hackenschmidt won again.

He was a prisoner of war of the Germans in the First World War, married a Frenchwoman and became a naturalized Frenchman. In 1945 he took his wife to London, and five years later achieved a 40-year-old ambition by becoming a naturalized British subject.

Outside the ring he was a man of amiable temperament, gentle manners and ascetic habits. He used neither alcohol nor tobacco, and though in his wrestling days he was a huge meat-eater he became in later life a strict vegetarian. For some time after his active career had ended he ran a physical culture school but his interest in later years was the development of a system of personal philosophy which he had first begun to think out in the German internment camp. The principles of this code were expounded in one of his books, *Man and Cosmic Antagonism to Mind and Spirit*, which he published in 1935.

February 20, 1968.

Walter Hagen, second only to Bobby Jones in golfing achievement between the two wars and unsurpassed as a personality of the game, died in Traverse City, Michigan, on October 6, 1969. He was 76. Such a colourful personality was he that Hagen the golfer has suffered eclipse from Hagen the man. The stories that have been told about him, the epigrams which have been attributed to him, would fill a book. Not all of them would be true but he was prepared to accept them even if they were not, and the legend of his gaiety, his nerve, and his approach to gamesmanship is now solidly entrenched in the history of the game.

Much less secure is his reputation as a golfer, and the balance should be redressed because even had he never opened his mouth, even if he had dressed for the fairways in sackcloth, he would stand comparison with the best in the world. Two American and four British championships became his and even more remarkable, perhaps, five American professional championships. Four of these were consecutive and in winning them he scored 22 consecutive victories over 36 holes against the flower of American professional golf. How was it all done by a man who has so often been depicted as a happy-go-lucky spendthrift?

There have been golfers more mechanical and less prone to error but none with a temperament better suited to the game. He could break his concentration between strokes, chatting nonchalantly to spectators, without losing his grip on a match. Indeed, it was his ability to project his personality in the course of a round that played such havoc with his opponents. Bernard Darwin writing in *Golf Between the Wars* perfectly caught that quality of his game: "Hagen's demeanour towards his opponents, though entirely correct, had yet a certain suppressed truculence; he exhibited so supreme a confidence that they could not get it out of their minds and could not live against it. He had a very shrewd eye for their weaknesses, and, strictly within the limits of what was honest and permissible, he would now and then exploit them to his own advantage."

MASTER OF SHORT GAME

His use of the woods was the least impressive part of his game. One or two really crooked drives were to be expected from him in a round, but he accepted bad strokes as inevitable and instantly dismissed them from his mind. In later years this part of his game became sounder and more stylish. His long iron play was always a tower of strength but it was in the short game, more especially in the execution of delicate bunker shots, that he excelled.

In this department should also be included his powers of recovery, which not only delighted the large crowds he drew after him but which struck terror into his opponents. Day in, day out it would hardly be possible to name a better putter. His touch was velvety and his stance looked at the same time firm and comfortable. Perhaps the greatest compliment that was ever paid to his putting was the recognition by A. D. Locke of the debt he owed to Hagen on the greens.

For all his genius as a player of matches he knew failure. Over 72 holes against A. Compston at Moor Park in 1928 he lost by 18 and 17, and Duncan in one of his inspired moods beat him by 10 and 8 in the Ryder Cup match the following year. But he lost with such good humour and zest that the crowds who never deserted him loved him all the more and he usually took his revenge later. In 1928, for example, he went on to win his third championship, this time at Sandwich, and in the 1931 Ryder Cup match he played with Shute and defeated Duncan and Havers by 10 and 9. Altogether he made five appearances in Ryder Cup matches and then to crown a remarkable record was made captain in 1937. He toured the world showing countries to whom it was a new game that it was above all a game to be enjoyed, and the truculence that he barely concealed on the course he carried where necessary into those club-houses in which the professional had not yet been granted recognition, destroying for all time barriers against them as much by his charm as by his nerve.

October 7, 1969.

Professor Otto Hahn, the man who got so near to discovering the effect that made nuclear weapons and power stations inevitable that he received a Nobel award for his search, died in Göttingen on July 28, 1968, at the age of 89.

The effect was nuclear fission, the splitting of uranium nuclei into fragments of not greatly different masses when a neutron enters the uranium nucleus and causes it to divide in two as in a droplet of water. This was a completely unexpected effect. Scientists in other laboratories had done similar experiments, but had been misled by pitfalls in their evidence. Hahn and his colleague, Fritz Strassmann, sorted out the evidence correctly and carried the problem to a point when the conclusion was bound soon to be drawn. Indeed, they all but drew it themselves. Early the next year Dr. Lise Meitner and Dr. (now Professor) O. R. Frisch did it for them and quickly confirmed the conclusion by further experiment which showed directly that large amounts of energy would be released.

The implication of Hahn's discovery was passed on to Allied scientists who built the atomic bomb. Hahn himself detested the bomb. He was reluctant to allow an atomic weapon to be developed under Hitler. "If Hitler gets an atomic bomb," he is reported to have said, "I shall kill myself." Hitler's mind, fortunately, was by this time arrogantly closed against new and strange ideas. When the Postmaster-General tried to interest him in the idea, the Führer cut him short with "Here we all are racking our brains how to win the war; and now the Postmaster-General of all people is going to tell us."

Hahn was in the forefront of movements to warn the world of the dangers of atomic weapons and pleaded for peaceful uses of the atom. In 1957, he signed a declaration by 18 leading German atomic physicists who said they would refuse to cooperate if asked to work on atomic arms.

Hahn, the son of a master glazier, was born at Frankfurt am Main on March 8, 1879. He studied at Marburg and Munich, initially intending to be an industrial chemist; gained his doctorate, on a problem in organic chemistry, working under the supervision of Professor T. Zincke, and in 1904, after a period as assistant to Professor Zincke, travelled to London to study under Sir William Ramsay at University College. Here he was introduced to the new field of radioactivity. Within a year he succeeded in identifying the new radioactive species, radiothorium. Ramsay was impressed by his ability and suggested he should extend his knowledge of this new field by joining Professor Ernest Rutherford in Montreal, where he was successful in identifying radioactinium.

On Hahn's return to Europe at the end of 1906. Professor Emil Fischer, then one of the most influential German chemists, supported his appointment to a post at the University of Berlin. It is interesting to note that Fischer himself only half believed the interpretation of the new discoveries in radioactivity. In Berlin Hahn became first professor extraordinarius and later, in 1912, professor at the Kaiser Wilhelm Institut für Chemie àt Dahlem, where he remained until the latter part of the Second World War and where most of his important work was carried out. Hahn's outlook on nuclear science was always that of a chemist, but in 1907 he was joined by Lise Meitner, a physicist. Together they made a very successful partnership and they collaborated in their investigations for the next 30 years, as well as becoming close friends for the rest of their lives.

WORK ON FISSION

In 1919 they completed the identification and characterization of the new radioactive element protactinium, and in 1921 their discovery of UZ led to the idea of nuclear isomerism.

In the years between the world wars, Hahn's researches laid the foundations of a new branch of chemistry called radiochemistry. Among the more important themes of research during this period may be mentioned the study of Codeposition reactions, the development of the emanation method for the study of solids, the separation of radioactive decay products by mechanical recoil and several novel applications of radioactive tracers in physical chemistry.

Besides nearly a hundred papers recording these studies, Hahn summarized the results of his work in a book entitled Applied Radiochemistry which appeared in 1936. In 1928, he became director of the Kaiser Wilhelm Institut and in 1933 he spent a year at Cornell University, United States of America, where he was appointed George Fischer Baker visiting lecturer.

In 1935, he became interested in the effects on uranium and thorium of the recently discovered thermal neutrons. This study culminated in January, 1939, in his greatest achievement, the recognition of fission. In this work he was associated with his pupil Professor F. Strassmann. The importance of his work on fission was quickly acknowledged, indeed, seldom have the repercussions of a major scientific discovery been felt so quickly. In 1944, he was awarded the Nobel prize for Chemistry. Two years later, after the war had ended, he was appointed president of the newly established Max Planck Institute at Göttingen. He made Göttingen his home for the rest of his life, although he retired from the presidency in 1960. Two years later he published A Scientific Autobiography. In the post-war period, Hahn received many honorary degrees and other honours including foreign membership of the Royal Society; and in 1966, a share of the United States Atomic Energy Commission's Fermi award.

Hahn was an excellent teacher, so that his research school inspired a numerous progeny.

July 29, 1968.

Bishop Haigh, formerly Bishop of Winchester, who died on May 20, 1962, at the age of 74, was by common consent one of the most brilliant of the Bishops. His close personal connexion with Archbishop Davidson was continued with Archbishop Lang, and gave him an insight into the general work of Church administration at headquarters which has seldom come to a man of his age. He had been behind the scenes and knew what are the special difficulties and responsibilities of a Primate and over how wide a range his work in modern circumstances has to extend. His influence in Church affairs was wide.

Mervyn George Haigh was born in London on September 14, 1887, the son of Canon W. E. Haigh, and was educated at Clifton and at New College, Oxford, where he obtained honours in the Classical schools. After his ordination in 1911 he gained the Ellerton theological prize at Oxford. He ran against Cambridge in the cross-country event of 1908. The first four years of his ministerial work were spent in London curacies. From 1916 to 1919 he served as an Army chaplain in East Africa, being twice mentioned in dispatches. Throughout the next five years he was chaplain and lecturer to the Test School for the training of ordination candidates at Knutsford.

Then came the appointment which reshaped his career. In 1924 he was chosen by Archbishop Davidson as his resident chaplain and private secretary. There could scarcely have been a stronger contrast than that between the cautious sagacity of the Archbishop and the impetuous ardour of his chaplain. Yet if the Archbishop exerted a useful restraining influence on his young colleague, Haigh proved a most loyal and useful help to the Archbishop. Such strong testimony to that help was given by Dr. Davidson, who said of him: "There is no post in the Church of England which he could not fill with distinction", that Dr. Davidson's successor, Dr. Cosmo Lang, determined to retain him.

The work of secretary to the Archbishop is of special importance at the time of a Lambeth Conference, and at that of 1930 Haigh showed skill and tact which deeply impressed all the members. Accordingly, little surprise was felt when in the following year he was nominated to the vacant See of Coventry. There his earlier promise was fulfilled and his resourcefulness had full scope. The degree with which he had been in touch with churchmen of all schools enabled him to administer the diocese with sympathy, while his relations with the Free Churches were notably harmonious. Coventry was a diocese where church work, through both limitations and new opportunities, was immensely affected by the outbreak of war. The Bishop was at home when his cathedral and much of the city were destroyed by enemy action, and bombs fell in the near neighbourhood of his own house.

When Dr. Garbett became Archbishop of York in 1942 Dr. Haigh was translated to Winchester. As he himself said, it was a striking change to pass from a diocese mainly industrial, with a strong socialist atmosphere, to one mostly composed of villages and country houses, where the prevailing tone was conservative.

His utterances, whether in village pulpits or at diocesan conferences, were marked by a rare magic of style made all the more impressive by his striking face and figure. In the ordering of services, too, his eye for dignified and gracious ceremonial and his ear for appropriate words were of great value. Though in details of administration his judgment proved sometimes to be at fault, he revealed great wisdom in his approach to the tasks of reconstruction after the war, and took the line that the large sums of money involved would best be raised by a number of limited appeals, the success of each paving the way for the next. He had, indeed, a real flair for finance.

Throughout most of his Winchester years Bishop Haigh was chairman of the Joint Committee, which prepared what was known as the Amended Lectionary (for Sundays and Holy Days only). To this work he brought an untiring industry, often working into the small hours of the morning, and also—as the late Canon Anthony Deane put it—"in bus, train, or tube". Before this work was concluded, Bishop Haigh found himself again secretary of the Lambeth Conference, that of 1948, with all the preliminary work which this involved. There can be little doubt that this aggregation of diocesan and central duties told upon his health, which was never robust; and serious illness in 1951 caused him to resign his see in the following year. He retired to Dolgelley, to be near the mountains which he loved, and to become actively associated with the work of several organizations devoted to the preservation of the countryside. At Dolgelley, as in his earlier homes, his brilliant intellectual gifts and his personal goodness and charm made him beloved of all classes, and by all his death will be deeply deplored. Never one to keep silent when he felt strongly, he wrote to *The Times* last summer protesting against a measure concerned with clerical pensions under which the increases for the general run of clergy were to be much smaller than those for the bishops. Later he was reported as saying that he would refuse to accept the increase to his own pension.

Haigh was Chaplain and Sub-Prelate of the Order of St. John of Jerusalem. From 1944 to 1961 he sat on the council of his old school.

May 21, 1962.

Lord Hailey, P.C., O.M., G.C.S.I., G.C.M.G., G.C.I.E., who died on June 1, 1969, at the age of 97, had two careers of great distinction in public life. After spending close on 40 years as one of the most brilliant members of the Indian Civil Service of his day, he retired to take up the study of African colonial administration, and after the death of Lord Lugard was the foremost British authority on its manifold aspects. In India he had held a number of high posts culminating in the Governorship successively of the Punjab and the United Provinces. In the second phase of his public life he had a strong formative influence on the new conceptions of colonial policy which marked postwar planning.

He was born on February 15, 1872, the son of Hammett Hailey, a medical practitioner of Newport Pagnell. He was educated at Merchant Taylors' School and Corpus Christi College, Oxford, where he was elected an honorary Fellow in 1925. He took first in both Mods, and Greats, was third in the I.C.S. examination of 1894, and was posted to the Punjab. He was selected in 1901 to be Colonization Officer of the Jhelum Canal in the area which now centres round Lyallpur. The irrigation engineers having brought water to a desolate desert region, Hailey was called upon to settle immigrant colonists upon the land.

SHARE IN REFORMS

Hailey was called to the Punjab Secretariat in 1907, and a few months later was transferred to the Finance Department of the Government of India as Deputy Secretary. In 1912 he became the first Chief Commissioner of the Delhi Province. As an officer on deputation with the Reforms Committee of 1918–19 he had some share in the final shaping of the Montagu-Chelmsford Reforms.

At the end of 1919 Lord Chelmsford selected Hailey to be Finance Member of his executive. His difficulties in this thankless task were increased by the mistake of the Finance and Currency Committee sitting in London in recommending the fixing of rupee sterling exchange at 2s.—a very costly leap in the dark which was soon abandoned.

At the end of 1922 Hailey was transferred to the Home Membership, which carried the leadership of the Legislative Assembly. In this capacity he developed parliamentary gifts of a high order. Hailey was in active sympathy with ordered Indian progress, and his clear vision, his logical mind, his ripe wisdom, and his gift of subtle humour were all to be reckoned with. He knew how to be coldly logical or banteringly human, and could rise to heights of eloquence. The effect was increased by a strikingly handsome appearance.

RURAL NEEDS

Hailey showed the same realism in the Governorship of the United Provinces, for which he was chosen in 1928. His intimate knowledge of the needs of the countryside and sagacious measures to improve the lot of the peasant were probably the reason for the failure of popular support for the no-revenue and no-rent campaign of the Provincial Congress Committee.

The constitutional changes embodied in the

Indian Act of 1935 owed much to Hailey's active brain and alert knowledge. He was called to London to assist the deliberations of the Round-Table Conference in the winter of 1930–31. As liaison officer between the Indian delegates and the Home authorities, he had the trust and admiration of both sides.

He gave invaluable assistance to the Secretary of State (Sir Samuel Hoare) both in preparing and giving his evidence before the Joint Select Committee of Parliament. He returned to his Governorship at the close of 1933, but resigned a year later, and came home by way of Africa. When the Bill of 1935 was going through Parliament Hailey gave voluntary service; and night after night sat in the narrow official pen in the Commons behind the Speaker's Chair in the company of India Office officials, ready to give information or advice to Ministers.

He had meanwhile entered upon a new field of public service. In his Rhodes Lecture in 1929, Field-Marshal Smuts had suggested a comprehensive survey of conditions in Africa; a committee to carry this out was eventually set up under the auspices of the Royal Institute of International Affairs. Funds were provided by the Carnegie Trustees and later by the Rhodes Trust. Hailey undertook to be director of such a study, which it was agreed should be confined to Africa south of the Sahara. Many preparatory researches were begun before he was free to visit the vast areas within the scope of inquiry. During a year's tour in 1935–36 he saw life in remote tribal villages as well as in the townships and administrative centres in British, French, and Belgian territories.

INQUIRY EXTENDED

Accompanied by Mr. Donald Malcolm he took a journey of some 22,000 miles, mainly by car, extending from the Union of South Africa to the Sahara Desert. He soon found that the inquiry must be extended far beyond the bounds originally contemplated. The Survey, published at the end of 1938 and covering more than 2,000 pages, constituted a minute examination of current problems, and a comparison of the measures taken to deal with them by the different Governments responsible. He drew information from a wide range of expert sources but everything was submitted to his own detailed and scholarly examination and was eventually translated into his own stately and measured prose. His conclusions on a long array of carefully marshalled facts are always judicial in spirit; all reasonable views are taken into account and a judgment delivered.

He gave the Romanes Lecture at Oxford in 1941 on "Britain and her Dependencies", and also wrote *The Future of Colonial Peoples* (1943), and, in the same year, *Great Britain, India, and the Colonial Dependencies in the Post-War World*. He was, indeed, the chief architect of the policy of direct assistance from Britain in the development of colonial resources and of attempting to raise the standard of living among colonial peoples.

At an early stage the Secretary of State for the Colonies appointed him chairman of the Colonial Research Committee, and when in London he worked regularly in Whitehall. In the autumn of 1940 he headed an economic mission to the Belgian Congo and secured substantial cooperation with the allies in their struggle. Thereafter, at the request of the Secretary of State, he paid repeated visits to the African colonies. In 1947–48 he toured in the British East, Central, and West African territories to study the system of administration and the part played by Native Authorities.

The vast changes in the international field brought about by the 1939–45 War were especially significant in Africa. The necessity in these circumstances of a thorough revision of the Survey was fully recognized. Lord Hailey, when he was over 80, accepted the pressing invitation of the Royal Institute of International Affairs to bring out a completely revised second edition of his monumental work.

His task was made more difficult by the rapidity of the advances towards representative government. The revision made its appearance in the autumn of 1957, some 19 years after the issue of the original work. It was marked by the same judicial balance, the same minute scholarship as the first version.

He married in 1896 Andreina, daughter of Count Hanibale Balzani. They had a son who was killed in the Second World War and a daughter who died in 1922. His wife died in 1939.

June 3, 1969.

Professor Hans H. Halban, who died in Paris on November 28, 1964, at the age of 56, will be most widely remembered for the part he played in the early history of nuclear energy.

Austrian by birth, he was educated in Austria and Germany and attained the degree of Dr. Phil. in Physics in 1935 at Zurich University, where his father was Professor of Physical Chemistry. Halban's work in nuclear and neutron physics began in 1935 when he joined Frédéric and Irene Joliot-Curie at their laboratories at the Institut du Radium. Later, in 1937, he became a member of F. Joliot's team at the Collège de France. The fact, crucial for the possibility of liberating macroscopic amounts of energy from nuclear fission, that in every neutron-induced fission in uranium more than one secondary neutron is liberated, was first demonstrated experimentally by Halban, Joliot and Kowarski early in 1939.

The French workers not only recognized plainly that their work had possible important practical applications but also embarked immediately on a programme of research designed to achieve this liberation of nuclear energy.

WAR CONTRIBUTION

In their plans the use of heavy water as a neutron moderator was essential, and Joliot succeeded in inducing the French authorities to acquire the then world stock of that substance—about 180 litres—from Norway. This took place just before Norway was overrun by Hitler's Army and not long before France herself was conquered. When this happened Joliot himself chose to remain in France but arranged for Halban, Kowarski, and the heavy water to be conveyed to England in a hazardous last-minute voyage.

In wartime Britain Halban became the leader of that group within the atomic energy project which was concerned with controlled slow neutron chain reactions, while the central British—and American—efforts were naturally directed towards the production of the uranium bomb. At a later stage in the wartime development, when the American effort dwarfed all others, the production of plutonium in controlled slow neutron fission placed reactor construction in the centre of the wartime effort. But in the early days the idea of using plutonium for a bomb had not been accepted and it must be counted as Halban's personal achievement that the research programme mapped out in France was kept alive. Under the auspices of the Maud Committee, which at the time governed the British nuclear bomb effort, a small team of collaborators was assembled and research facilities at the Cavendish Laboratory, Cambridge, were provided.

By January, 1941, the Halban-Kowarski team could report strong experimental evidence to show that a uranium heavy water reactor should be a practical possibility. Halban had to face many frustrations both because of the difficulty of the scientific problems and because there were many political and administrative obstacles to overcome. Much of his energy had to be expended in negotiations and committee work. (He was a prominent member of the Maud Technical Committee and its successors.) Inevitably the scientific work languished at times.

In 1943 the Halban team was transferred to Montreal, where it formed a part of a greater Anglo-Canadian group of which he was the first head. Later Professor J. D. (now Sir John) Cockcroft became the Director of the project, while Halban remained as head of the Physics Division. From the Montreal laboratories the Chalk River heavy water reactors were planned and it is fair to say that they were directly descended from the devices first put to work by Halban and Kowarski at Cambridge.

DOUBLE CONFLICT

In the Allied Atomic Energy Project as a whole the existence of the early French contribution, represented to a great extent by Halban's person, had a considerable significance. Such matters as the policy over early patents taken out by the French group, the participation of a French contingent in the Canadian project, the return of Frenchmen to their homeland after liberation, had unfortunate effects on Anglo-United States relations in the nuclear energy field. On more than one occasion Halban found himself in the midst of conflicts of personality as well as policy. Although never robust in health, he was untiring in his double role as scientist and custodian of French nuclear energy interests. Halban always moved easily from the laboratory, through the ministerial office, into the board room. He stood for the urgent need to secure speedy and effective postwar utilization of nuclear energy especially in relation to the rehabilitation of a liberated France, and he pursued his aims with untiring dedication.

At the war's end it became evident that

military matters were destined to dominate national policies on nuclear energy, even in peace time. Halban's special gifts had no place in this pattern and he withdrew from the field of nuclear policy, accepting an invitation from the late Lord Cherwell to return to pure physics research work at the Clarendon Laboratory, Oxford. Here he built up a most successful and active nuclear physics team. In 1950 he was elected to an official Fellowship at St. Antony's and in 1954 was given the title of Professor. In 1956 he left Oxford to take up a post as Professor at the Sorbonne.

Halban's services to France were recognized by his being created Chevalier de la Légion d'Honneur in 1949. He was a man of remarkable personal charm and a most lavish host to a wide circle of friends.

November 30, 1964.

Dr. J.B.S.Haldane, F.R.S., who died at Bhubaneswar on December 1, 1964, at the age of 72, had for many years been recognized as one of the leading theoretical biologists in the English-speaking world, and as a public figure of outstanding originality.

John Burdon Sanderson Haldane was born on November 5, 1892, and educated at Eton where he was captain of the school. His father, Dr. J. S. Haldane, C.H., F.R.S., of Oxford, was an eminent physiologist, whose work on respiration was of great importance not only theoretically but in the practical context of mining and diving. J. B. S. Haldane was, from his early childhood, drawn into his father's experiments, first as a "guinea-pig", who eagerly agreed to subject his physiological system to a variety of unwonted stresses, and later as a fully fledged scientific collaborator.

He went down in a submarine for the first time when he was 12 and at 13 was lowered in a diving suit to test one of his father's theories; the suit, being too large, leaked, and when Haldane *fils* was pulled up, was full of water.

It was probably in these formative years that he acquired two characteristics which dominated much of his scientific life; a readiness, which often appeared an actual liking, for testing on himself even the most uncomfortable predications of his physiological theories, and a very deeply felt sympathy for those whose work involved them in hazards of a respiratory nature. During the Second World War, both interests were brought into play in research connected with diving which he carried out for the Admiralty, while his strong humanitarian feelings led him also to carry out much painful work designed to investigate the conditions likely to be met in submarine accidents, such as the loss of the Thetis in June, 1939.

At the Thetis inquiry Haldane described how he sat 14½ hours in a small steel chamber to estimate the atmospheric conditions as they were in the submarine at the time of the accident and later.

Two further important lifelong features of his career can be recognized at its very beginning. As an undergraduate at Oxford before the First World War he proceeded from a first in Mathematical Moderations to a first in Greats. This background, and his astonishingly capacious memory, made him one of the very few British scientists who could have elegantly rounded off a technical contribution on mathematical genetics, given to a symposium held in Pavia in 1953, with an impromptu peroration containing a dozen apposite verses of Dante. Between 1914 and 1919 he served as an officer in The Black Watch, being wounded at Loos and in Mesopotamia; after the latter injury he was in hospital in India, thus introducing into his life another theme to which he returned later.

BIOCHEMISTRY AT CAMBRIDGE

After the First World War, Haldane returned to Oxford as a Fellow of New College, but soon moved to Cambridge as lecturer and then reader in Biochemistry. This period, in the late twenties and early thirties, was one of the most fruitful, and probably one of the happiest, in his career. Although never a great experimentalist himself, Haldane at this time played a major role in the great efflorescence of biochemistry which took place in Hopkins' laboratory at Cambridge during those years. His mind combined exceptional rapidity of thought with a breadth of interest and profundity of knowledge which was a challenge to colleagues in many different fields.

In December, 1925, after he had been cited co-respondent in a divorce case he was arraigned before the Sex Viri of the University, found guilty of "gross immorality" and deprived of his readership. Haldane promptly exercised his right of appeal. It was heard the following year by Mr. Justice Avory, Sir W. Morley Fletcher, Dr. M. R. James, Provost of Eton, Sir William Bragg and Mr. J. J. Withers, M.P., who overturned the verdict of the Sex Viri and Haldane was re-instated. That same year he married Mrs. Charlotte Burghes (Charlotte Haldane, the author and journalist).

In 1933 he moved to London, becoming for a time head of the John Innes Horticultural Garden, where he hoped to develop the study of the biochemical action of the numerous genetic colour varieties known in plants. Although a very promising beginning on these lines was made under his direction, the work could not at that time be carried as far as he wished, and his main interests shifted from the biochemical and experimental aspects of genetics to the mathematical exploration of the theory of evolution, a subject which continued to occupy the greater part of his attention during the next quarter of a century, when he held the Chair of Biometry at University College, London. Haldane had, as early as 1924, been perhaps the first to lay the foundations of the edifice of mathematical evolutionary theory, and it is his long series of contributions to this subject which will probably prove to be his most important scientific achievement.

AIR-RAID PRECAUTIONS

Haldane played a very full, and somewhat unconventional part in the political life of his time. His wide knowledge of the history of civilization, and his appreciation of literature, together with the strong humanitarian strain in his temperament, made it impossible for him to remain contentedly within the laboratory. He always engaged actively in journalism, writing very many articles of popular science, in an idiom at once very precise and almost naive in its simplicity, which have rarely been bettered. During the thirties he became a communist. He was soon one of the most prominent "intellectuals" of the party, and for some 10 years after 1940 was the chairman of the editorial board of the *Daily Worker*, in which much of his best popular science writing appeared.

As an expositor of popular science he had few equals; he challenged the attention of his readers (and not seldom their antagonism), he was clear, factual, persuasive, always seeming to have something fresh to say.

Although he was always ready to provide a fluent and even witty exposition of Marxism as an intellectual system, it was clearly to him something more deeply felt and more personal. As he once pointed out, in one of his extraordinarily self-revealing essays, he suffered from gastritis "for about 15 years, until I read Lenin and other writers, who showed me what was wrong with our society and how to cure it. Since then I have needed no magnesia."

It was as a humanitarian turned communist that he threw himself into the left-wing activities connected with the Spanish War and agitation for adequate organization of air-raid precautions in this country. His forthright views on shelter policy, on gas protection and evacuation were expressed in a practical and highly salutary book which appeared during the Munich crisis of 1938 under the title of *A.R.P.*

The depth of his attachment to communism as a general philosophy made it extremely hard for him to face the situation within his own scientific speciality when Lysenko and his followers attacked the whole system of "western" genetics and its followers in Russia. But Haldane's fundamental honesty triumphed and he brought himself publicly to admit that communist orthodoxy was mistaken, although it must have cost him a most severe effort.

EMIGRATION TO INDIA

In 1956, with the approach of his retirement from University College, Haldane decided to emigrate to India. It was the time of Suez, not at all the kind of action likely to please him, and he delivered himself of some sharp public remarks. He left in 1957, settling first at the Statistical Institute at Calcutta, and moving later to the University of Orissa at Bhubaneswar. Although Haldane was never a man to live without some degree of turbulence going on around him his Indian years were on the whole happy ones. His own enormously wide and diversified range of learning, in many fields besides biology and mathematics, found a sympathetic background in the eclecticism of the Hindu outlook on religion and philosophy. He adopted Indian citizenship in 1960, and devoted himself whole-heartedly to assisting the development of science in his rapidly maturing country. Both in explicit teaching, and by his example, he showed that scientific excellence does not necessarily depend on elaborate and expensive instruments, but that worthwhile contributions can still be made by methods no more elaborate than visual observation and simple arithmetic. He used these methods mainly to study botany and animal behaviour, and the guidance and opportunities he provided for his young Indian colleagues may well turn out to be one of his most important achievements.

Haldane was so extraordinarily fresh, so alive, so willing to consider—and sometimes devastatingly to smash down—contributions to discussion from any quarter, that his friends will find it difficult to believe that they will never meet again the great shambling bear of a man with his big bald head, his loud booming voice which could rise to an indignant bawl at some gross inaccuracy or shocking obscurantism, his slow movements, and that remarkable memory which turned a knowledge of ancient Greek, for example, or classical English literature, into a fund of quotations to illustrate modern scientific experiments or communist theology as the case might be. He had little patience with fools or pedants, particularly the latter; but he was delightfully lucid and friendly to the young, for whom he wrote the charming fairy-story *My Friend Mr. Leakey*, whom he fascinated by his own anecdotes of acting as a human guinea-pig in the cause of scientific discovery, and whose questions and speculations he was always ready to encourage. The few papers on Human Needs which he contributed to his sister, Naomi Mitchison's outline of knowledge for the young (published two years ago as *What the Human Race is up to*) excited eager interest among its young readers.

His first marriage was dissolved in 1945 and he married secondly Dr. Helen Spurway.

December 2, 1964.

Lord Hall, who had held office as a Labour Minister in various Governments for over 13 years and was a former First Lord of the Admiralty, died in Leicester on November 8, 1965.

Hall, who sat in the Commons for 24 years before being created a peer in 1946, was an outstanding figure in the compact group of Labour M.P.s who represented coal mining constituencies. Like many of his colleagues he had himself come from the mines and was a collier for 18 years, starting work at the age of 12.

But these early experiences had in no way soured him and he was widely respected as a gentle and warm-hearted man who upheld the political causes in which he believed without extremism or rancour towards his opponents. He was not in the first rank of Labour politicians but none was better liked. Lord Attlee described Hall when he resigned from the Labour Government in 1951 as having "always been the most loyal and unselfish of colleagues".

The peak of Hall's political career was reached in the years from 1946 to 1951 when he was First Lord of the Admiralty. He had previously served two terms of junior ministerial office at the Admiralty and he came to develop a deep and personal interest in the affairs of the Royal Navy. He went to the Admiralty as First Lord in succession to Lord Alexander of Hillsborough.

The Navy was then in the painful throes of transition from war to a peace footing and the First Lord's immediate concern was to maintain the morale and efficiency of the service after this drastic run-down. He went in H.M.S. Duke of York with the Home Fleet for an autumn cruise to the West Indies and more than once visited the Mediterranean Fleet. He would occasionally address gatherings of officers and ratings to explain to them the problems with which the Admiralty were having to grapple. Apart from the reshaping of the Navy after the war and the fulfilment of peacetime commitments all over the world the service now had to begin to adapt itself to the revolutionary changes of the atomic age, with all that this meant in the introduction of new weapons and new concepts of naval strategy.

COLLIERY BOY

Hall applied himself with great diligence to his work at the Admiralty for five years. In a farewell message to the Fleet when he resigned in 1951 he said: "My profound admiration for the Royal Navy, my interest in its fortunes, my respect for its traditions and my pride in its achievements will abide with me always."

George Henry Hall was born in Glamorganshire on December 31, 1881, the son of George and Ann Hall. From an elementary school he started work as a boy at a local colliery and was a miner at the coal face for 18 years. Then, in 1911, he was appointed a checkweighman and local agent of the South Wales Miners' Federation. In 1922 he turned to politics and was elected Labour M.P. for the Aberdare division of Merthyr Tydfil. He represented this constituency continuously for 24 years. In the 1935 election of the Parliament that was to sit for 10 years he was returned unopposed. At other elections he was always reelected with a huge majority.

Hall's association with the Admiralty began in 1929, under Ramsay MacDonald's Labour Government, when he was appointed Civil Lord. He held this post for just over two years and was responsible for the works services, as well as for the conditions of service of the Admiralty's industrial employees. He next held office, in the war-time Coalition Government, as Parliamentary Under-Secretary of State at the Colonial Office from 1940 to 1942. Then he was moved back to the Admiralty for 18 months as Financial Secretary. In 1943 Hall was appointed Parliamentary Under-Secretary of State for Foreign Affairs and he held this post until the Coalition Government came to an end, two years later.

BACK TO ADMIRALTY

When the Labour Government came to power in 1945 Lord Attlee chose Hall to be Secretary of State for the Colonies, as successor to Oliver Stanley. He held this appointment for too short a time to make much of an impact on Colonial affairs but he did on a visit to West Africa in 1946 preside at the first meeting of the newly constituted West African Council (of Governors).

In October, 1946, he was transferred to become First Lord of the Admiralty. Resigning this office in 1951 he was created a peer, as Viscount Hall of Cynon Valley in the county of Glamorgan. Hall left the Admiralty after five years as First Lord because he was then 69 and in indifferent health; he felt that the time had come to make way for a younger man. Hall had spent eight and a half years there, including the terms of his previous service there, and it was with deep regret that he gave up his place at the head of the long table in the historic board room. From 1947 to 1951 he was Deputy Leader of the House of Lords.

Apart from his political career Lord Hall took an active part in local affairs in South Wales. He was a member of the Mountain Ash Council and Education Committee—having been chairman of both bodies—for 18 years. He was a Governor of Cardiff University, an honorary LL.D. of Birmingham University and of the University of Wales, and a justice of the peace for Glamorganshire. He was also a former member of the executive of the Parliamentary Labour Party and had held office in the Miners' Federation.

Hall was married first in 1910 to Margaret Jones, who died in 1941. He married secondly last year Alice Martha Walker. The heir to the viscounty is his son, the Hon. (William George) Leonard Hall, who was born in 1913.

November 9, 1965.

General Sir Lewis Halliday, V.C., K.C.B., the oldest surviving holder of the Victoria Cross, died on March 9, 1966, at the age of 95. He was Adjutant-General, Royal Marines, from 1927 to 1930.

He won the V.C. while serving with the Royal Marine Light Infantry as a member of the guard of the British Legation in Peking in the Boxer uprising of 1900. Last year in a letter published in *Globe and Laurel*, the journal of the Royal Marines, he stated that the official citation recording his exploit was "wildly incorrect." The citation described how in June, 1900, Boxers and Imperial troops had attacked the west wall of the Legation, set fire to the west gate of the south stable quarters and had taken cover in buildings near by. It went on: "A hole was made in the legation wall and Captain Halliday, in command of 20 Marines, led the way into the buildings and...engaged a part of the enemy. Before he could use his revolver, however, he was shot through the left shoulder at point blank range, the bullet fracturing and carrying away part of the lung.

"Notwithstanding the extremely severe nature of the wound, Captain Halliday killed three of his assailants and, telling his men to 'carry on and not mind him,' walked back unaided to hospital, refusing escort and aid, so as not to diminish the number of men engaged in the sortie."

In his letter last year Halliday said he felt the citation ought to be corrected. He thought that Captain B.M.Strouts, another R.M. officer, had been killed before the final draft of the citation had been made. "Actually," wrote General Halliday, "I arrived at the west wall of the legation to report to Strouts that the Japanese did not need any help. I had been sent to see Colonel Shiba (Colonel G. Shiba, Japanese Military Attaché). Strouts had had a hole made in the wall and he told me to make a sortie with five men and a corporal, not 20 men.

"I went down a narrow alley and ran into a group of five Boxers, armed with rifles. The first shot was fired without bringing his rifle to the present. I then shot him and three others. The fifth ran away.....I then told the men to carry on and I got back unaided to the wall. I was helped through the hole and Dr. Rooke helped me to the hospital. Strouts then took out 20 or 30 men and pulled down the small building and cleared the field of fire.

"He told me the next morning that my pistol had a miss-fired round so I merely had pressed the trigger at the fifth man and he had escaped. It will be seen that I was acting under orders and I think that anyone must have done as I did."

LONG SERVICE

Later in his career he displayed great ability as a Staff Officer and lecturer. He was one of the first to join the Navy War Staff, and was well known at Camberley and Sandhurst before the 1914–18 War. His severe wound in China affected his later career to some extent, and although he managed to get to France during the Great War his health broke down in the summer of 1916, and his subsequent service was all performed at home. He attended the Peace Conference, and later rose to the highest post in the Royal Marine Corps. When he retired from this office in October, 1930, he had completed 41 years' service. He was an Aide-de-Camp to the King in 1924–25. From 1933 to 1946 he was Gentleman Usher to the Sword of State.

Lewis Stratford Tollemache Halliday was born on May 14, 1870, the eldest son of Colonel Stratford C. Halliday, Royal Artillery, and grandson of Major F. A. Halliday, of the Royal Marine Artillery, who served with the Marines in the Carlist War, 1836–37. He entered the Royal Marines Light Infantry in 1889.

He married, in 1908, Florence Clara, daughter of Brigadier-General W. T. Budgen, D.S.O., by whom he had one son. After the death of his first wife he married, secondly, in 1916, Violet Victoria daughter of Major Victor Blake, by whom he had one daughter and one son. His second wife died in 1949.

March 11, 1966.

Sir William Halliday, who died on November 25, 1966, at the age of 80, was Principal of King's College London from 1928 to 1952.

William Reginald Halliday, son of Charles Hoffmeister (he took the name of Halliday in 1905), was born in Belize, British Honduras, on September 26, 1886. He was educated in England as a scholar of Winchester and of New College, Oxford, where he had a successful academic career, taking a First in Lit. Hum., a Craven scholarship, and the Charles Oldham Prize. Continuing his classical studies he spent some time at the University of Berlin. He then worked at the British School at Athens, and did some excavation work in the Levant.

His first teaching appointment was a lectureship in Greek history and archaeology at the University of Glasgow. Just before the outbreak of the 1914–18 War he was elected to the Rathbone Chair of Ancient History in the University of Liverpool. As happened to so many scholars of his generation, his work there was interrupted by war service; he was commissioned in the R.N.V.R. and served with Naval Intelligence in the Mediterranean based on Crete. He was made a Chevalier of the Order of the Redeemer (Greece) for his services, and was also mentioned in dispatches.

On his return to Liverpool the nature of his academic interests was revealed in a succession of popular books often based on special lecture courses indicative of the researches he was pursuing. These included *Lectures on the History of Roman Religion* (1922), *The Growth of the City State* (1923), *Folklore Studies, Ancient and Modern* (1924), *The Pagan Background of Early Christianity* (1925), *Greek and Roman Folklore* (1927). More technical was his work on *The Greek Questions of Plutarch* and (with T. W. Allen and E. E. Sykes) *The Homeric Hymns*. His researches tended to centre more and more on early religions and folklore, a field in which he became an acknowledged authority.

After a stay of 14 years at Liverpool he was nominated to succeed Dr. Ernest Barker as Principal of King's College in the University of London, a post which he held for the next 24 years, until his retirement in 1952. He took up his duties there at a critical time in the history of that society. In 1920 the Government had offered to the Senate of the University of London for the use of the university and of King's College a site of about 12 acres in Bloomsbury, conditional on the university giving up its quarters at the Imperial Institute, South Kensington, and of King's relinquishing its site and buildings in the Strand and moving on to the new site. Negotiations were protracted, ending so far as King's College was concerned, with the rejection in 1925 of terms which were considered inadequate for the resettlement of the college. A year later the Government's offer was withdrawn. The acrimonious debates and strenuous controversy of those years left unfortunate memories within the university, and these lingered on after Halliday came to King's. These he sought to dispel during his early years as principal. It was a work in which his own tact and wise diplomacy were admirably seconded by a former Liverpool colleague who had become Provost of University College, Sir Allen Mawer, and by the Principal of the University, Sir Edwin Dellar. Much was done by these three leaders in the next few years to ease tensions and restore good relations within the university.

The decision of the college authorities to remain on the Strand site had its consequences. The fact had to be faced that future developments there would be controlled by the limits of the space available for expansion. The principal was at one with his colleagues in believing that the ideal must be a college comparatively small in numbers, accommodated in quarters which would be little more than sufficient to make life reasonably comfortable for all. During the thirties much was done under Halliday to realize that ideal by a series of adaptations of old premises and by some new building.

With the coming of the Second World War these problems lost their urgency, for Halliday, like the other heads of London colleges, had to face the task of making arrangements for evacuation. The relations established between King's College and the University of Bristol were singularly successful, and although the principal was inclined to attribute that result to the cordial relations maintained by the staffs of the two institutions working most harmoniously under considerable difficulties, those behind the scenes were fully aware of the important part he himself played in achieving that result.

The end of the war, with the college back again in London, brought him new problems. In facing them he was seriously hampered during the next few years by ill-health, and although he made a gradual recovery he did not, during the remaining years of his official life, enjoy the physical vitality of his earlier years. Nevertheless, in spite of this handicap he faced a heavy programme, the most pressing items of which were, first, the resettlement of the college into normal conditions after the break with its traditions during the years of absence from London and, secondly, the urgent need to cope with an accommodation problem which was becoming increasingly formidable as the need for greater facilities for university education began to be more fully appreciated in the post war world, and the scale of scientific, library, and other needs made growing demands upon the universities.

The first of these problems was soon solved; the second was to prove more intractable.

SPACE PROBLEM

The obvious and most economical solution would have been an extension of the college into the neighbouring building, Somerset House, but inquiries soon showed that the conflicting needs of government departments made such a convenient plan unlikely to gain official approval. Halliday therefore explored, without success, various alternative plans for a site in the vicinity. At the same time, in spite of post war controls and shortages of labour and materials, he managed by acquiring some small additional properties and by interior alterations to make provision for a new Students Union, for a limited extension of laboratories on the site, and also for a fine hall of residence for students on Clapham Common to which the college gave his name in recognition of his services for student welfare. These were all valuable additions, but, as he well knew, they fell far short of what was needed.

By nature shy and retiring, Halliday was not at his best on formal occasions, and to strangers he often seemed aloof and rather forbidding. Among his friends, however—and he was essentially a clubbable man—he was good company, appreciated for his shrewd wisdom and dry humour, often expressed to a favoured few in bright epigrams and lighthearted verse. His standards in scholarship and in human relationships were high: he was a shrewd judge of character: and in his dealings with his colleagues and with the students under his authority he was respected for his fair dealing, sympathetic understanding and tolerance, and his profound common sense. His period of office at King's was noteworthy for the happy relations existing among those who worked there, and for much of this Halliday in his imperturbable and quiet way was largely responsible.

To the regret of his friends in London he was seen very infrequently after his retirement, for he withdrew to his family home in the West.

Halliday was knighted in 1946. He married in 1918 Edith Hilda, the daughter of Professor Macneile Dixon, by whom he had four sons.

November 28, 1966.

Carl Joachim Hambro, the veteran Norwegian Conservative politician and former president of the League of Nations, died in Oslo on December 15, 1964. He was 79. For many years he was president of the Storting (the Norwegian National Assembly).

In the thirties Hambro became internationally known as a member of the Norwegian delegation to the League of Nations, and was the League's president from 1939 to 1945. He was one of the few who warned against the dangers of Nazism and Fascism, and condemned the Munich agreement.

Following the invasion of Norway on April 9, 1940, he outmanoeuvred the Germans, who had laid plans for taking King Haakon prisoner. In the early hours of the day of invasion he arranged for an extra train to take the royal family, the government and parliament out of Oslo to the village of Elverum, 80 miles to the north-east. Here Hambro again took the initiative which resulted in decisions by parliament making it possible for the Government to continue the war against the Germans while in exile in Britain. Hambro himself went with them to spend the war years in Britain.

Born at Bergen on January 5, 1885, he had his higher education at the University of Christiania (later Oslo), from which he graduated in 1907. He had begun to contribute to the Oslo daily, *Morgenbladet*, while still a student; and though his first post on graduation was that of a master at the Oslo Commercial High School, he developed and expanded his journalistic work to such good effect that in 1913, while still short of 30, he was offered the editorial chair of *Morgenbladet*. This responsible post he accepted and held until 1921. His private writings comprised a number of books on political and economic topics, and translations into Norwegian from Victor Hugo, Dickens, Kipling and Sinclair Lewis. He had a good command of spoken, as well as of literary, English, and from time to time undertook lecture tours in the United States.

Hambro's political career began with his election to the Storting as a Conservative in 1919. He shared the high hopes for peace and disarmament that then resided in the League of Nations, and he threw himself actively into the work of various organizations designed to promote these ends. He became chairman of the Conservative party, and in 1926 President of the Storting and Norwegian delegate to the League. He remained President of the Storting until 1945, apart from a short break in 1934–45.

In 1940 he published *I Saw It Happen in Norway*, an account of the German invasion; and in 1943 *How to Win the Peace*, a forceful plea for the rights of small nations in the postwar international system.

After the war he was chairman of the League of Nations Liquidation Committee in 1946–47 and continued to serve as a member of the Storting until his retirement from public life in 1957.

He was a holder of the Grand Cross of St. Olaf's Order, his country's highest distinction and was a member of the Nobel Peace Prize Committee.

December 16, 1964.

Sir Charles Jocelyn Hambro, K.B.E., M.C., who died on August 28, 1963, at the age of 65, was a member of the distinguished banking family who, coming from Denmark, established themselves in the City in the first half of the nineteenth century and originally specialized in Scandinavian business. It was Sir Everard Hambro who may be said to have given the bank its present prominence in the City. He was a personal friend of King Edward VII and a dominant figure in financial circles. Of his family of four sons and one daughter, the eldest son was the late Sir Eric Hambro and the youngest was the late Olaf Hambro.

Charles Hambro, born in 1897, was the elder son of Sir Eric Hambro. He was educated at Eton, served throughout the 1914–18 War in France and Belgium with the Coldstream Guards; was wounded and was awarded the M.C. for conspicuous bravery. After a period of training in New York in the Guaranty Trust Co., he entered the family firm of C. J. Hambro & Son, of which he soon became secretary. He played an important part in the merger with the British Bank of Northern Commerce Ltd. which resulted in the formation of Hambros Bank Ltd., with its present title, in 1921.

BANK OF ENGLAND TASKS

In 1928 began his connexion with the Bank of England, which extended unbroken to the present day, for in that year he was first elected to the Court of Directors at the unusually early age of 30. His service with the Bank under Montagu Norman included a period in 1932–33 when, to free himself to deal with exchange problems there, he obtained leave from his own firm and other activities. On ceasing his whole-time service at the Bank he returned to his family firm and assumed several fresh duties including the deputy chairmanship of the Great Western Railway in 1934 and the chairmanship from 1940 to 1945, although by then largely occupied with war duties.

When the Second World War broke out he served in the Ministry of Economic Warfare under Ronald Cross and later under Hugh Dalton. After the fall of France he was made a colonel on the General Staff and, under that cover, he joined the Special Operations Executive which had been charged by the Prime Minister with the creation of a spirit of resistance in occupied territories followed by the organization, direction and supply of resistance groups and secret armies. In 1941 Charles Hambro became Executive Chief of S.O.E., and for his services he was appointed K.B.E. in that year.

NUCLEAR EXCHANGES

In 1942 he left S.O.E. and was sent to Washington as the United Kingdom member of the Combined Raw Materials Board and head of the British Raw Materials Mission. In that capacity he dealt with the exchange of information with the United States on the subject of the atomic bomb.

After the war he returned to the City, gradually assuming more and more responsibility for the companies with which Hambros were associated and, on the death of 1961 of his uncle, Mr. Olaf Hambro, he became chairman of Hambros Bank. Another series of interests resulted in his election in 1958 as chairman of Union Corporation, with its many and varied mining operations. He maintained the family links with Scandinavia by being a Knight Commander of the Order of Dannebrog of Denmark and a Knight Commander of the Order of St. Olav of Norway. The Hambro family has had a long connexion with the Royal National Pension Fund for Nurses and Sir Charles had been chairman of the fund.

The family home was Milton Abbey, in Dorset, and in the thirties he farmed part of the Milton Abbey estate, but later he moved to Dixton Manor, near Cheltenham. He was keenly interested in shooting and was a first-class shot.

WIDER BANK INTERESTS

By the time that he became chairman, Hambros Bank had extended its interests into almost every merchant banking activity, and to direct the course of that firm alone was a huge task. While maintaining and strengthening the traditional association with Scandinavia, he took on with characteristic energy fresh responsibilities in Africa and elsewhere. His sense of humour and his fund of technical knowledge made him an ideal colleague on any board.

He married first in 1919 Pamela, daughter of John Dupuis Cobbold and of Lady Evelyn Cobbold, eldest daughter of the seventh Earl of Dunmore. Their family consists of three daughters and one son, Mr. Charles E. A. Hambro, who is now a managing director of Hambros Bank. She died in 1932 and Sir Charles married secondly in 1936 Dorothy, daughter of Alexander Mackay. They had one daughter.

August 29, 1963.

John Henry Hambro, C.M.G., who had been chairman of Hambros Bank since 1963, died on December 4, 1965. He was 61.

Born on July 7, 1904, he was the son of the late Henry Charles Hambro and Edith Gertrude Bonsor. He was educated at Eton.

Hambros is one of the leading merchant banks in Europe, particularly famous for its associations with Scandinavia. It also plays a major role in the foreign exchange and bullion markets, handles much of the banking for the London diamond trade and has close associations with the commodity markets of the City. John Henry Hambro joined the bank in 1922, being appointed a managing director in 1931.

Initially, he was most active on the new issue and industrial side of the bank's activities.

During the Second World War he gave distinguished service in the U.K. Commercial Corporation and in 1944 was made a C.M.G. for his contribution. In 1963 he was appointed deputy chairman of the bank, and in that September became chairman on the death of Sir Charles Hambro, his cousin. Although not as well known internationally as his predecessor in the chair, Hambro had travelled a lot since his appointment, visiting all the Scandinavian countries and Iceland on the bank's business.

GREEK DEBTS

He played a very important part in bringing about a general settlement of the Greek Government's external debts, this being a traditional field of Hambros activity.

In recent months he had spoken publicly of the balance of payments and the state of sterling. In recent weeks he had taken part in a correspondence in the columns of *The Times* on the subject—his last contribution, signed also by Mr. S. G. Warburg, appearing on the day he died. He was appointed a part-time member of the National Coal Board in 1949, and at one time was a director of 24 companies, including five investment trusts, and treasurer of the Middlesex Hospital.

A very kindly and charming man, with great mental capacity, he was also a notable gardener at his home, The Hyde, near Luton, Bedfordshire.

At his job Jack Hambro—as he was always known—was the supreme technician. A master of detail, he never allowed himself to become enmeshed therein, and could always clearly discern the broader issues involved in any problem. He had to an outstanding degree the power of decision and the wisdom which comes from wide experience and a profound knowledge of human nature. All his judgments were in consequence tempered with a warm sense of humanity and he had a genius for friendship.

SENSE OF HUMOUR

His keen sense of humour made him a particularly delightful companion and the many who gained his friendship over the years never lost it.

Hambro married first in 1930 Elizabeth Theresa de Knoop. They had one son and one daughter. In 1947 he married secondly Linnet, daughter of the late Major E. M. Lafone.

December 6, 1965.

Olaf Hambro, who died on April 25, 1961 in hospital in London at the age of 75, had been chairman of Hambros Bank Limited since 1932.

He joined the family firm of C. J. Hambro & Son after leaving Cambridge in 1908. For over 50 years he was an outstanding personality in the City of London, where his humour and sharp wit were familiar.

Ronald Olaf Hambro was the son of Sir Everard Hambro and grandson of Baron C. J. Hambro, who founded the house of C. J. Hambro & Son on coming to this country from Denmark in 1839. He served in the Coldstream Guards during the First World War, and was later appointed a managing director of Hambros Bank (then styled Hambros Bank of Northern Commerce Limited) on the merger in 1920 of the family firm and the British Bank of Northern Commerce. In 1932 he succeeded his brother, Sir Eric Hambro, as chairman and remained a managing director until 1953. He was governor of the London Assurance for many years, and remained a member of the court after resigning the governorship in 1959.

As a banker he had an instinct for forward planning and great foresight in international affairs. In the City he recognized the importance of cooperation between the merchant banks and issuing houses, and he was one of the prime movers in the creation of the Issuing Houses Association and the Accepting Houses Committee. For those who knew him in the City and throughout Europe and America he symbolized the maintenance of high principles in business life and particularly the integrity for which the City of London is known.

Hambro took a leading part in the formation of the City consortium which entered the contest, unsuccessfully, for the take-over of the British Aluminium Company in January, 1959. His letter to *The Times* on that occasion has been held to mark the end of an epoch in the affairs of the City.

In 1916 he married Miss Winifred Martin Smith, who died in a boating accident on Loch Ness in 1932. In his marriage he was one of the happiest of men. Both of them were expert gardeners. The gardens of his home at Port Logan, near Stranraer, Wigtownshire, were noted for rhododendrons, azaleas and subtropical plants. There visitors would find him, in shirt sleeves and grey flannel trousers, ready to explain the name and genus of some exotic shrub.

Having been brought up at his father's home at Milton Abbey, Dorset, famous for its high pheasants, he was an expert shot, and he retained his interest in his childhood home through his chairmanship of the governors of Milton Abbey School. He had a house at Linton Park, Maidstone, and was at one time high sheriff of the County of Kent. He was also honorary colonel of the 139th Regiment, Royal Artillery. Hambro was largely responsible for the rebuilding of All Hallows Church after it had been bombed in the war.

He had three sons, the eldest of whom, Mr. Jocelyn Olaf Hambro, is a managing director of the bank.

April 26, 1961.

Robert Hamer, who died in a London hospital on December 4, 1963, after a short illness, was one of the most strikingly individual talents in the British cinema and was responsible for at least one of its masterpieces, *Kind Hearts and Coronets*. He was 52.

He was born in Kidderminster in 1911, educated at Rossall and Corpus Christi College, Cambridge, and entered the cinema in the traditional fashion as a number-boy at Gaumont-British in 1934, and then as tea-boy and general odd-job man in the cutting rooms of London Films. During the next 10 or 12 years he amassed experience of all sides of film-making, working as editor, assistant director, and script collaborator on a wide variety of films, and ending up as associate producer on two films, *San Demetrio, London* and *Fiddlers Three*. But his real ambition was to direct, and his first chance came with *Dead of Night*, a portmanteau film of ghost stories on which several young directors at Ealing were given a chance (1945). For this he directed an elegant, ironic tale of a man possessed by the malign spirit of an earlier owner of his bedroom mirror, whose background and situation it continues to reflect. His success with this led to his first big chance as a director, with a cunning piece of period re-creation based on Roland Pertwee's thriller *Pink String and Sealing Wax*. This suggested much of his real talent—an intense feeling for period, an unusual gift for visual elegance, a refined sense of style—but his next film, *It Always Rains on Sunday*, showed that he could, when he wished, turn his hand with equal success to realistic working-class drama.

In 1949, though, he was given the opportunity to make a picture entirely to his own taste, under the aegis of Ealing but shot away from the studios themselves, with their cosy but sometimes limiting emphasis on group endeavour. The result was *Kind Hearts and Coronets*, a brilliant and biting high comedy about a young man who coolly murders his way through a whole family of more or less obnoxious relatives on his way to a title; written by Hamer himself, it contained some of the wittiest dialogue ever composed for the screen, and was marked from beginning to end with his own extraordinary flair for re-creating the elegance of the Edwardian era and his talent for getting the best out of actors (Alec Guinness played eight roles superbly, but the gifts of Dennis Price, Valerie Hobson and Joan Greenwood have never been better used either).

After this he made three lesser films, *The Spider and the Fly, His Excellency* and *The Long Memory*, as well as dabbling in television, notably with a fine production of *A Month in the Country* before returning to his home ground, ironic high comedy, and his best interpreter, Alec Guinness, in *Father Brown*. This proved to be his last unqualified success; his following film with Alec Guinness, *To Paris with Love*, suffered from a feeble script; and of his two later films, *The Scapegoat* (a version of Daphne Du Maurier's novel with Alec Guinness and Bette Davis) and *School for Scoundrels*, neither reached the screen as he left it. In recent years illness had kept him increasingly absent from the studios, but at the time of his death he was due to return shortly with a new version of

Lady Windermere's Fan.

Though in his whole career he managed to make only 10 feature films, two of them, *Kind Hearts and Coronets* and *Father Brown*, were among the finest and most personal productions of the British cinema. None of the others (except perhaps *To Paris with Love*) was without at least sections of great interest, or remarkable individual scenes. What makes his loss all the more saddening is that he still had so much irreplaceable to offer British films and seemed to be on the point at last of getting a real chance to do so.

December 5, 1963.

Gerald Hamilton, who died in a London hospital on June 16, 1970, at the age of 81, was the original from whom Christopher Isherwood mainly drew the central character of *Mr. Norris Changes Trains*. Not since Alice Liddell, perhaps, has there been a figure who enjoyed more *réclame* from being turned into fiction. In 1956 he published his first volume of autobiography *Mr. Norris and I*. Isherwood contributed an introduction.

Hamilton was a true eccentric; an extravagent sensualist, a man with political views which would have seemed repellent in anyone who made less of a vaudeville of his own life. Given power under a fascist regime, he might have been a monster; as it was, he was accepted by his friends as a Chaucerian rogue.

He was born in Shanghai and characteristically suggested that "my extraordinary affection for everything Chinese may be due to the fact that I was suckled by Chinese breasts". An Irishman, he liked to describe his ancestry as "faintly ducal". In 1904 he went to Rugby, where he was in the house of Rupert Brooke's father. Brooke himself was older and "therefore not in in my set", but Hamilton recalled that the poet was deified by the masters, none of whom dared to comment on the excessive length of his hair.

After school he returned to Shanghai for a time. He affected Chinese dress; made and lost money on the Stock Exchange; fell ill and promised his nurse to become a Roman Catholic if he recovered. His father could not forgive him for his conversion, but made him a small allowance.

Hamilton returned to London. In 1913 he met Roger Casement: "My character, plastic at all times, received perhaps a greater impression from this great Irishman than from any other single individual I have ever met". Hamilton made a formal offer of his services to the Sinn Fein. His pro-German sentiments and negotiations with Casement led to his arrest in 1915. Horatio Bottomley published an article headed "Hang Hamilton!" During his internment (he was released on Christmas Eve 1918) he followed the trial of Casement with emotion.

In the 1930s, The Times engaged him as its sales representative in Germany.

War again; and again Hamilton was in trouble. He was imprisoned for illegally trying to leave the country (he decided to cross the Irish Sea disguised as a nun—a piquant suggestion of which Ronald Searle drew a cartoon, "Mr. Hamilton") and for negotiating with the Vatican to promote a peace on terms favourable to the enemy. "The Special Branch officials who drove me to Brixton attempted to console me with such remarks as 'You'll be all right. You'll be able to play tennis with Sir Oswald Mosley.'"

In view of these experiences, there was a grotesque irony in Hamilton's posing in 1955 for the body of Oscar Nemon's statue of Winston Churchill. In his last years, Hamilton lived something less than the *dolce vita* in a bedsitter above the Good Earth restaurant in the King's Road, Chelsea. "Better to be above the good earth than below it", he said. His eightieth birthday was celebrated by a luncheon given by the artist James Reeve, who had recently painted Hamilton's portrait. His second book of memoirs, *The War it was with Me*, appeared in 1969.

June 18, 1970.

Mary Agnes Hamilton, C.B.E., who died on February 10, 1962, in London, had for a number of years been out of the public eye, mainly because of failing health; but from youth to late middle age she was well-known as journalist, novelist, politician and public servant.

She was, for example, a member of the Balfour Committee on Trade and Industry (1924–29), the 1929–31 MacDonnell Royal Commission on the Civil Service, a governor of the B.B.C. from 1933 to 1937, alderman of the County of London from 1937 to 1940, and decorated in 1949 with the C.B.E. Her writing, which went on *pari passu* with her public work, included several biographies, some full-length, as well as novels; and in journalism *The Economist*, the *Review of Reviews*, the *New Leader*, and *Time and Tide* all published her work. She was thus very much of an all-rounder; and had in her heyday a wide circle of friends.

She was born in 1884, the eldest daughter of Robert Adamson, professor of logic at Glasgow and other universities and educated at Glasgow High School and Newnham College, Cambridge, where she read economics at a time when few women studied that subject. She took a first-class in her finals, but does not seem to have pursued the subject to the extent which other women "firsts" have done, for while she was still at college she became interested in home and foreign affairs; she was a lively debater and much interested in college political debate—university politics being at that time closed to females. In a volume of autobiography, published in 1944 under the title *Remembering My Good Friends*, she gave a vivid description of Cambridge before the wars as it appeared to an intelligent young woman with radical leanings. Even at that early age, she was a determined controversialist with a commanding voice, a trait shared with her sisters later, when they were living in the Hertfordshire countryside; a neighbour amusedly commented that the sound of the Misses Adamson engaged in friendly argument carried well across the valley.

Her political sympathies crystallized early. She joined the I.L.P. and was acquainted with men who were more alive than the bulk of the nation to the explosive dangers in Europe. *Dead Yesterday* (1916) which was her third novel and the first to arouse general interest, presented an unforgettable picture—which is still readable today—of the dilemma of the British intellectual before and after August, 1914. Already, by then, a recognized journalist, she had become a fluent and frequent speaker on the public platform at Labour and Socialist conferences; she joined the Union of Democratic Control in its early days, and played a considerable part in the formulation of after-war policy for the Labour movement.

She was not successful in her first attempts on Parliament, failing to get in at Chatham and Blackburn; in the 1929 election, however, she headed the poll at Blackburn, then a two-member constituency. Already she had made herself a name with the Labour Party, as had been shown by MacDonald's appointment of her to the Balfour Commission—on which she signed the minority report; and in the second Labour Government she was made parliamentary private secretary to the Postmaster-General. But her political career was not too happy, partly because her own views shifted considerably. In the early twenties she was a devoted supporter of MacDonald, of whom she wrote a sentimental short biography under a pseudonym, and took his side when the fight between right and left in the I.L.P. developed, as a result of which she was made assistant editor of the *New Leader* as a sort of watch-dog over its pugnacious left-wing editor, H. N. Brailsford—an unhappy combination which soon broke up. The failure of the Labour Government, however, to deal with the unemployment which grew so rapidly in her constituency and its surroundings, turned her into a vehement critic; in the crash of 1931 she lost her seat.

There were, nevertheless, consolations. In 1929 and 1930 she was part of the British delegation to the General Assembly of the League of Nations; she greatly enjoyed Geneva and, more than that, learnt to value deeply the work of Arthur Henderson as Foreign Secretary. She became a great friend of Henderson's, and her long biography of him, begun just after his death and published in 1938, is easily the best of her books. Five years earlier she had brought out a biography of the Webbs which the subjects of it did not greatly appreciate—and indeed she did not understand them very well; short but useful sketches of Margaret Bondfield and Mary Macarthur completed her tale of biography. In 1940, when she ceased to be a London alderman, she entered the Civil Service as a temporary. She became head of the United States section in the Ministry of Information and received the C.B.E. mentioned above as a reward. She remained in the Civil Service until 1962 and thereafter retained close connexion with American life, particularly through the English-Speaking Union, to whose journal she contributed articles for many years after ill-health had debarred her from other activities. In 1953 she published a second volume of reminiscences, *Uphill All the Way*.

February 11, 1962.

Dag Hammarskjöld, United Nations Secretary-General, died as the result of an air crash on September 17, 1961. If the nations of the world ever achieve a unified government no man would have a higher claim to count as one of its founding fathers. The possibilities as well as the perils of world organization were exemplified in the career of this resolute and indefatigable Swede.

In the eight years and a half during which he held the office of Secretary-General of the United Nations there was hardly a country which he did not visit or a Minister with whom he had not talked. He was, of course, far from pleasing all the people all the time. Belgians could rage at him over the Congo; Israelis accuse him of kowtowing to Nasser; to a large section of the British population he was deeply suspect at the time of Suez; two months before his death President de Gaulle was prepared to snub him over Bizerta; to the Russians, above all, he had in his last year become anathema, and after the death of Lumumba Hammarskjöld was for them "a man who has sullied himself with foul murder".

Such abuse is part of the hazard of activity.

HIS BIG ROLE

If Hammarskjöld had chosen a less exalted interpretation of his office he might have escaped it. But, rightly or wrongly, he believed that the chief executive of a body representing nearly a hundred countries must play a big role. He must be an initiator as well as a servant, a conscience as well as an administrator. Perhaps because he came from a small and traditionally neutral country himself, he could find instinctive sympathy with other small countries trying to be neutral. "It is not", he said last autumn in the dignified apologia with which he answered the Russian onslaught, "the Soviet Union or, indeed, any of the other big Powers who need the United Nations for their protection. It is all the others. In this sense the organization is their organization and I deeply believe in the wisdom with which they will be able to use it and guide it."

To the public in many lands "the Organization" was Mr. Hammarskjöld. And, in a sense, the opposite was true too—he seemed almost as much a machine as a man. There can have been few internationally known figures who were less personally understood. He remained a private face in a public place. Few anecdotes accumulated round him. If he became known as "Dag" or "Mr. H."—or, more appropriately, "Mr. U. N."—this was not a reflection of the warm glow given off by some world figures, still less a sign of familiarity, but a way round a name too long for the headlines in which it so often had to find a place. Mr. Hammarskjöld called himself a technician. If he had not been a brilliant administrator, if he had not preserved the standards and lessons of a civil servant, he could not have made anything of his job. But he grew with experience. In recent months he was still the man who could work seven days a week with only two or three hours' sleep a night, who could set off for the ends of the earth at a moment's notice, and whose relaxations were purely intellectual.

Yet increasingly there could be detected elements of passion in his altruism. Mr. Hammarskjöld was a man with a mission.

FAMILY TRADITION

He brought to his international post both the experience of a distinguished career in his native Sweden, and a long family tradition of public service. With an occasional man of letters among them, his forebears had been soldiers and administrators since the first Hammarskjöld was knighted by King Charles IX of Sweden early in the seventeenth century.

Born on July 29, 1905, at Jönköping, Dag Hjalmar Agne Hammarskjöld was the youngest of four sons of Hjalmar Hammarskjöld, at that time presiding judge of one of Sweden's three courts of appeal, later Prime Minister during the larger part of the First World War, and governor of Upsala province for more than 20 years. The elder Hammarskjöld, who lived past the age of 90 to see his son take over as Secretary-General of the United Nations from Trygve Lie, of Norway, is said once to have remarked: "If I had been as brilliant as Dag and had his ability to deal with people, I might have gone far."

Although only 47 years old when he was elected, in 1953, as a dark-horse compromise candidate to succeed Lie, Dag Hammarskjöld had been, in turn, Under-Secretary of the Swedish Ministry of Finance for nine years, which included the entire period of the Second World War; economic adviser and then Under-Secretary of the Foreign Office in Stockholm from 1946 to 1951; and, finally, an expert non-party member of the Swedish Cabinet as Minister of State in charge of foreign economic relations. In addition, he served from 1941 to 1948 as chairman of the board of governors of the *Riksbank*, the central bank of Sweden. In his various postwar posts he had represented his country in the European organ of the Marshall plan, the Organization for European Economic Cooperation, from the outset, and he served as vice-chairman of the executive committee of O.E.E.C. in 1948–49. His activities in this body reportedly were what brought him to the attention of the French and British Governments in their search for some man of ability sufficiently "neutral" to break the long deadlock with the Soviet Union over a successor to Trygve Lie. His nomination was put to the Security Council by France it was said at the suggestion of Gladwyn Jebb.

He had also been known, particularly to the British and Americans, as a trade negotiator. Thus, he negotiated the first Swedish-British trade agreement at the end of the war in 1945. During one brief period just before his appointment as Secretary-General, he had headed the Swedish delegation to the General Assembly, but few United Nations diplomats had come to know him personally then.

Although partly international and diplomatic in nature, his past experience had been centred in the field of economics and finance to such a marked degree that few even of his closest associates expected Hammarskjöld to take on the active political role which was to mark his handling of the Secretary-Generalship and, in the view of many, to transform and widen the scope of that office to a notable extent. Receiving his doctorate in economics at Upsala in 1934, he belonged to the so-called Stockholm school of economists, sometimes regarded as Keynesians before Keynes. He had, in fact, spent a year at Cambridge and felt the direct impact of Keynes's teaching.

But although Hammarskjöld's own early work in economics was highly theoretical and earned him a teaching post at the University of Stockholm in 1934, he never showed much inclination for an academic career. His doctoral dissertation, dealing with the theory of the business cycle, was to remain his only major work of economic scholarship. Even before it was published, he had entered government service as secretary to a royal commission on unemployment during the depression of the early thirties, and from then on his career was rapid. On his appointment as Under-Secretary of Finance in 1936, not yet 32 years old, he was the youngest man ever named to that exacting office.

TALKS WITH PEKING

Hammarskjöld took over as United Nations Secretary-General at a time of crisis for the office itself. With the McCarthy era at its height, his predecessor—disavowed by the Soviet Union since the Korean War and therefore increasingly dependent on American support—had been forced to yield to pressure from the United States and dismiss a number of American secretariat officials against whom charges of pro-communism had been levelled. These dismissals were later disapproved by the United Nations administrative tribunal. In his first year in office the task of restoring confidence in and within the secretariat dominated the activities of the new Secretary-General. He drafted a new set of staff regulations and got the General Assembly to approve them. Under these regulations, the international character of the secretariat and freedom from national influence on its members were reaffirmed.

But it was not long before purely political assignments fell to Hammarskjöld. Towards the end of 1954 the General Assembly asked him to try to obtain the release of a number of American airmen, held in China since the Korean War and sentenced to long prison terms for espionage. He immediately sent a message to the Chinese Prime Minister, Chou En-lai, proposing that he go to Peking himself to talk the matter over. He returned in mid-January of 1955 without any visible results, but later that year the prisoners were set free, and the United States Government officially credited him with having achieved this. That ostensible success, in a venture not made easier by the fact that the United Nations resolution requesting him to approach Peking had in the same breath condemned the Chinese communist behaviour as a breach of the Korean armistice obligations, became the signal for increased reliance on the Secretary-General's diplomatic abilities. Gradually, Hammarskjöld took on the task of chief negotiator for the United Nations.

With tensions rising in the Middle East during 1956, he went to all the signatories of the Palestine armistice agreements during a month-long trip at the behest of the Security Council, and got them all to renew their undertakings to observe the armistice provisions. A temporary lull followed, but when Nasser's seizure of the Suez Canal precipitated the Suez crisis, whatever gains had been made were lost again. Of Hammarskjöld's role during the crucial weeks in November, 1956, when Anglo-French intervention against Egypt had been stopped, President Eisenhower remarked that "the man's abilities have not only been proven, but a physical stamina that is ... almost unique in the world has also been demonstrated by a man who night after night has gone with one or two hours' sleep and working all day and, I must say, working intelligently and devotedly".

In retrospect, Hammarskjöld later spoke of his activities during this critical period as an example of how the Secretary-General could try to fill a "vacuum", should such appear in "the systems which the (United Nations) Charter and traditional diplomacy provide for the safeguarding of peace and security". It was largely left to Hammarskjöld to organize the United Nations emergency force in Egypt and to arrange for its development as soon as the cease-fire had been sounded, and to mount international action to clear the blocked canal for shipping, a diplomatic as well as a technical operation.

When the Middle East again became the centre of unrest in 1958, with American marines landing in Lebanon and British paratroopers in Jordan at the request of the Beirut and Amman Governments after the Kassim revolution in Iraq, the inability of the Security Council to take agreed action over the veto of the Soviet Union gave Hammarskjöld another cue for initiative of his own. Without any specific new mandate from the United Nations Powers, he strengthened, many times over, a military observer group already placed in Lebanon, and when the General Assembly was called into special session he opened it by drawing up a programme for conciliation between the opposing Arab factions which eventually was accepted by them for the time being. One element of the Hammarskjöld formula in this case was the establishment of a "United Nations presence" in critical areas, which he later applied in various other situations also. One such arose in Laos in 1959, when persistent troubles in frontier areas, recalling those in Lebanon the year before, caused the Government to call upon the Secretary-General for United Nations action. Hammarskjöld found a way to bring the matter before the Security Council without invoking his Charter powers to draw the attention of the Council to "any matter which in his opinion may threaten the maintenance of international peace and security"—and then to take it out again and, in effect, create a "presence" of the United Nations in Laos that emphasized the country's economic rather than its political difficulties but still meant that a watchful United Nations eye remained kept on the situation.

IN BLACK AFRICA

During his wider-ranging travels which followed naturally from his concept of the office, Hammarskjöld tried to establish personal contacts with as many state and government heads as possible, on occasion even ahead of the time their countries might gain admission to the United Nations. A month-long trip which took him through almost 30 countries and territories in black Africa early in 1960 was both a product of and a stimulus to his interest, on behalf of the United Nations, in the new, emerging states. He did not, on that journey, have occasion to visit the Union of South Africa, but when racial outbreaks later in the year brought the South African problems before the Security Council, its members once more asked the Secretary-General to take the matter in hand and try, in consultation with the Union Government, to achieve arrangements consonant with the purposes of the United Nations Charter. To the surprise of some, in view of the intransigent attitude of the Union Government during the Council debate, Hammarskjöld succeeded in arranging preliminary conferences in London with the Verwoerd Government in May, and later was to go to Cape Town for further talks.

Within the past 16 months, Hammarskjöld's already delicate position in the United Nations as the holder of the balance between the conflicting claims of the communists and the western world grew more difficult when he became embroiled in two controversies—over the Congo and, partly as the outcome of that, over the Soviet contention that he was not neutral and should be replaced as Secretary-General by a "troika" or triumvirate representing the communist block, the western group and the uncommitted nations.

CONGO ERUPTED

The Congo erupted into civil strife soon after it became independent in July, 1960, and its Prime Minister, Lumumba, appealed to the United Nations for its assistance in restoring order. Hammarskjöld, in the face of vague and often unhelpful directives from the Security Council and later the General Assembly, organized an international military and economic operation in the Congo which brought nearly 20,000 soldiers drawn from 18 countries and several hundred technicians to the Congo.

But the Congo conflict continued and grew worse when Lumumba was assassinated by political rivals. For this crime Hammarskjöld was held responsible by the communists who, from Khrushchev down, assailed him as "an accomplice to murder". They argued that the United Nations should have protected Lumumba against his Congolese enemies, even though he had voluntarily left the shelter he was being given by the United Nations force.

Using Hammarskjöld as an instrument in its campaign to discredit and stultify the United Nations, Russia argued that the Secretary-General had exceeded his authority, had shown himself to be partial, and therefore should be replaced by a three-man body which would reflect the three groups which, in the communist view, now composed the United Nations.

Hammarskjöld strongly contested this "troika" concept as liable to deprive the organization of effective executive direction, and in this view he was upheld by most member states. Indications were that Russia would have resumed its assault on Hammarskjöld at this forthcoming session of the General Assembly. Instead, it will probably press the claim that his post be divided between the several deputy secretaries now holding office, partly on a regional representation basis.

BORIS PASTERNAK

On taking over the post as Secretary-General, to which he was unanimously reelected in 1957 for another five-year period, Hammarskjöld relinquished all official positions he held in his home country, but when his father died he agreed to take over the vacant seat in the Swedish academy of letters, the first time since the birth of the academy towards the end of the eighteenth century that a son had thus been called to succeed his father. Since the creation of the Nobel prizes, the annual award for literature is made by the members of the Swedish Academy, and Dag Hammarskjöld is known to have taken an active interest in this task. Reportedly, he had a hand both in the selection of the Russian poet Boris Pasternak for the prize in 1958, which created an official uproar in the Soviet Union, and in drafting the citation extolling Pasternak's literary merits.

He was also connected with the winner of the Nobel prize for literature two years later, St.-John Perse, whose *Chronique* was published in Stockholm with a parallel text in Swedish by Hammarskjöld. Some critics claimed this translation entitled him to rank as a poet in his own right. Certainly modern literature, and in particular modern poetry, were his abiding interest. Proust, Joyce, Hemingway, Rilke, T. S. Eliot (especially the *Four Quarters*) were his standby as much as his relaxation. Modern painting and mountaineering were two more loves. But, though a Rouault hung in his office high up in the United Nations building in New York, the mountains of Lapland of necessity knew him less often.

Hammarskjöld never married. His closest surviving relatives are two brothers in Sweden, Bo, former governor of the province of Södermanland, and Sten, an official of the Government housing board. A third brother, Åke, was a member of the permanent International Court at The Hague when he died in 1937. Dag received honorary degrees from Oxford and Cambridge and many other universities.

September 19, 1961.

Dashiell Hammett, the American crime novelist who originated the modern school of tough thrillers, died in New York on January 10, 1961. He was 66.

In such books as *The Maltese Falcon* and *The Glass Key* Hammett took murder out of the baronet's library on to the city streets, transmuting the tradition of Sherlock Holmes with the style of Ernest Hemingway. His heroes were as tough as his villains. Hammett said that Sam Spade, his most famous "private eye" was "a dream man, in the sense that he is what most of the private detectives I worked with would have liked to have been. Your private detective wants to be a hard and shifty fellow, able to get the best of anybody he comes in contact with, whether criminal, innocent bystander, or client". Hammett's detectives and criminals were authentic—or, at least, his readers believed they were—because he had himself spent several years in Pinkerton's famous detective agency.

Dashiell was originally a French family name, de Chiel. He was born in St. Mary's County, Maryland, on May 27, 1894. When he was 14, he decided that "formal education is bunk" and left the Polytechnic Institute at Baltimore in favour of a succession of jobs as labourer, stevedore, clerk, and messenger boy. In the First World War he joined the American Medical Corps and was invalided out with the rank of sergeant. His subsequent career at Pinkerton's was undistinguished. "I would have been fired", he used to say, "except for a certain literary quality about my reports". He tried to exploit this literary quality by writing book reviews, but his first real success came in 1929 with two thrillers, *The Dain Curse* and *Red Harvest*. He followed them rapidly with *The Maltese Falcon* (1930), *The Glass Key* (1931), and *The Thin Man* (1932). Each was widely acclaimed, each earned him a lot of money; but *The Thin Man* was the last book Hammett ever wrote.

Hollywood summoned him, paid him highly, and used him, characteristically, not for writing but for tinkering with other people's scripts.

MADE CLASSIC FILMS

The films of his own books, notably *The Thin Man*, with William Powell and Myrna Loy, and *The Maltese Falcon*, with Humphrey Bogart and Sydney Greenstreet, were small classics of their kind, but they owed comparatively little to Hammett. The radio, and later the television, plays based on his characters owed even less; but the royalties kept flowing in, and Hammett saw no reason to write new stories.

He left Hollywood, a cynical, lonely man, and began to be seen among leftwing groups in Greenwich Village. His marriage to Josephine Annas Dolan, a nurse who had looked after him during an attack of tuberculosis, had ended in divorce. In 1951 he was sentenced to six months' imprisonment for contempt of court, because he refused to say who had put up bail for certain communists connected with the Civil Rights Congress of which he was a trustee. He was released after two and a half months and went to live in a cottage outside New York. His royalties dried up, blocked by the income tax authorities who were suing him for arrears. "The thing that ruined me" Hammett once said, "was writing the last third of *The Glass Key* in one sitting of 30 hours. Ever since then I've told myself: 'I could do it again if I had to.' Of course I never did."

The genre he created had long ago passed into other hands, to be developed by Raymond Chandler and brutalized by Micky Spillane. Crime stories have never been the same after that brief four-year spurt of Dashiell Hammett's creative activity. His books still hold a unique, violent life of their own; but Hammett himself, as a writer and a craftsman, was dead long before he died.

January 11, 1961.

Sir John Hammond, C.B.E., F.R.S., one of the world's leading animal scientists, who pioneered artificial insemination of cattle in Britain died on August 24, 1964, at Cambridge, at the age of 75.

He was born at Briston, Norfolk, on February 23, 1889, son of Burrell Hammond, a Norfolk farmer, and was educated at Gresham's School, Holt, and Downing College, Cambridge, where he took the tripos in Natural Sciences in 1909. Between 1912 and 1914 he was a research scholar at the Ministry of Agriculture. At the outbreak of the 1914 war he joined the 7th Norfolk Regiment, became a Captain and later served as a Staff Captain in the 201st Brigade.

At the end of the war his career in science and agriculture began with a Ministry of Agriculture appointment concerned with the reorganization of milk production, and soon after he returned to Cambridge to begin a unique career in the science of animal production that continued until his retirement in 1954. His interests covered the life cycle of animals—inheritance, reproduction, growth and maturity—and against a fundamental scientific background he developed applications to agricultural research and production in farm animals connected with fertility and the production of milk, beef, pigs and sheep that have had profound effects here and in all countries abroad in which the animal industry is important.

FIRST A.I. CENTRE

His books on his own researches include *The Physiology of Reproduction in the Cow* and *Growth and Development of Mutton Qualities in the Sheep*. His interest in genetics and his knowledge of male and female fertility led him to initiate research in this country in artificial insemination as a means of improving dairy cattle and to the formation of England's first A.I. centre at Cambridge in 1942. Today two million cattle are bred by this method annually. When in 1954 Hammond retired from his post as Reader in Agricultural Physiology at Cambridge he had for long had the strongest post-graduate school in animal husbandry in Britain and had attracted men to it from all over the world.

Hammond possessed great humility and gentleness. The impression he made on the constant stream of research students that came to him from overseas was immense and they returned home inspired by his teaching to become leaders in their own animal industries.

KNIGHTED

He was elected F.R.S. in 1933, created C.B.E. in 1949 and received a knighthood in the New Year's honours list in 1960. He was a Fellow of Downing College from 1936 to 1954 and from the latter date an honorary Fellow, and was a foreign member of agricultural academies in many countries, including Argentina, Sweden, Czechoslovakia, France and Italy. He received many honorary doctorates from universities, including Iowa, Louvain, Vienna, Copenhagen, Durham and Leeds.

He married in 1916 Frances Mercy Goulder.

August 25, 1964.

Walter Hammond, the Gloucestershire and England cricketer who shares with Sir Jack Hobbs and Sir Donald Bradman the high peak of twentieth century batting, died on July 1, 1965, in Durban, South Africa, at the age of 63.

His greatest reputation is based on the number and manner of the runs he scored, but he was a superbly gifted and versatile athlete, highly accomplished in every department of cricket, good enough to be a professional footballer, though not sufficiently interested to remain one, and able, almost casually, to play well at any ball game he essayed.

Born at Dover on June 19, 1903, Walter Reginald Hammond was the son of a regular soldier and his father's postings caused his childhood to be spent in China and Malta until the outbreak of the 1914–18 War, when he went to Cirencester Grammar School. His batting as a boy at Cirencester led to a trial for Gloucestershire in a friendly match a few days after he left school. He took the opportunity to play an innings of 60 so impressive that he was chosen to play in his first Championship match, against Lancashire, only two months after his seventeenth birthday. Thus he made his first appearance for Gloucestershire in 1920, his last was in 1951.

MANY RECORDS BROKEN

From the exultantly and aggressively eye-sure young man of 1923, through the period of majesty, to the calm, almost bored, master who, in his last English season, 1946, scored 1,783 runs at an average of 84.9 (16 more than the next batsman in the country) Hammond unconcernedly, indeed, often quite unknowingly, broke many records. He scored more runs (7,249) and took more catches (101) than anyone else in Test cricket: his 10 catches in a match—against Surrey at Cheltenham in 1928—and his aggregate (78) for the same season, have never been beaten by any fielder. In all cricket he made 50,493 runs at an average (56.10) only, and narrowly, bettered among regular English players by Ranjitsinhji (56.37), and his 167 centuries have only been exceeded by Hobbs and Hendren. An automatic choice for England from his first selection in 1927 until his peremptory retirement in 1947, he played in 85 Test matches, 20 of them as captain, and scored 22 centuries.

Hammond played as an amateur from 1920 to 1922, became a professional in 1923, an amateur again in 1938, and captain of his county from 1939 to 1946; he captained winning teams of both Players and Gentlemen at Lord's. He headed the first-class batting averages of seven seasons—1933, 1935 to 1939, and 1946.

Even when he was surfeited with runs, an innings by Hammond was memorable: he was incapable of batting less than handsomely, and when the occasion offered challenge, as when he set out to destroy the menace of Fleetwood-Smith, he could lift a match to great heights.

For a period after his retirement he reported cricket for the press. Then he went to South Africa where in 1959 he made a long and narrow recovery from injuries in a motor accident.

July 2, 1965.

Sir John Hanbury-Williams, C.V.O., formerly chairman of Courtaulds Ltd., and for many years a director of the Bank of England, died on August 10, 1965, in the London Clinic, at the age of 73.

The 17 years that he presided over Courtaulds were eventful ones in the history of the company. There was the immense task of reconstruction after the war, during which the American subsidiary company was sold in the national interest and when there had been no recruiting on any scale. There was the wide diversification of Courtaulds' interests, developing the underlying strength of the company. Then there were the years not exactly of stagnation but when the full potential for expansion was not realized. And finally there came the dramatic takeover bid from I.C.I., which was repulsed by methods somewhat different from those adopted by Hanbury-Williams throughout the body of his career.

Essentially he had the outlook of a banker rather than an industrialist. He had never run a factory or a sales team himself. He was no technical man. Therefore it was perhaps natural that he was more at home in the broad sweep of policy than in the detailed assessment of profitable activities. He had the banker's liking for large liquid reserves. Prudent rather than venturesome, the task of reconstruction suited him better than the harshly competitive climate of his later years in office. A diplomatic but forceful personality, there was never any doubt that he was in command; but he had much of the traditional Courtauld reticence about the company's affairs.

Throughout his career with Courtaulds he had always been directly and personally concerned with overseas interests, and he retained and developed his wide contacts in governmental as well as business circles after he became chairman. For these visits, as, indeed, for all more formalized occasions, he was admirably fitted—a diplomatist, a linguist, courteous in manner, with a fine presence, he retained something of the air of the cavalry officer that perhaps he always remained at heart.

John Coldbrook Hanbury-Williams, son of Major-General Sir John Hanbury-Williams, who in his later years was Marshal of the Diplomatic Corps, was born on May 28, 1892, at Henley-on-Thames and educated at Wellington. He began his business career in London and Manchester with Rice Bros., a firm of Eastern merchants. Then came the First World War in which he served in France with the 10th Royal Hussars and at G.H.Q. British Army, was mentioned in dispatches and wounded. After the war he returned to his old firm for whom he travelled widely in China and Japan.

AMERICAN SUBSIDIARY

It was in 1926 that he joined Courtaulds, one of the bright young men, socially and mentally, who were intended to complement the solid core of tough, down-to-earth businessmen who had built up the company. After working for a while in Coventry he was transferred to the head office in London where he was concerned with the company's overseas yarn trade. Soon he assumed much of the responsibility for the administration of the foreign affiliated companies. He was elected to the board of Courtaulds in 1930 and appointed a managing director five years later, with special charge of the company's export trade and overseas interests. He was personally responsible shortly before the war for Courtaulds getting into nylon, and was himself concerned in the founding of British Cellophane.

BANK DIRECTOR

In 1936 Hanbury-Williams had been elected a director of the Bank of England, on whose Court he was to serve until his retirement in February, 1963—for the last 23 years of that period as a member of the Bank's Committee of Treasury as well. For a while in 1940–41 he was specially released by Courtaulds, because of the war, for full-time service at the Bank as an executive director. In 1942 he served under Lord Selborne at the Ministry of Economic Warfare.

Back at Courtaulds, he was appointed a deputy chairman in 1943 and three years later succeeded Samuel Courtauld in the chair. The war had been particularly unkind to Courtaulds in that it had been necessary to sell their almost wholly owned American subsidiary, the American Viscose Company, to provide badly needed dollars for the nation in the days just before lend-lease. In addition, there was the need to bring many new people into the company both at board and lower levels: and not the least significant feature of the major work of reconstruction then undertaken was the quality of many of the new recruits, including a high proportion of the present board.

BACK TO U.S.A.

A development that gave Hanbury-Williams particular satisfaction was the return in strength to the United States with the establishment of Courtaulds Inc. in 1951. The new subsidiary began operations the following year at the rayon staple plant near Mobile, Alabama, in the ironic position of having the old subsidiary as its main competitor. Hanbury-Williams remained chairman of Courtaulds until after the defeat of the I.C.I. bid, retiring in the summer of 1962.

Among the many outside duties he assumed during the postwar years he was chairman of the Prime Minister's Committee on the ordering procedure for civil aircraft in 1948, honorary treasurer and subsequently a trustee of the Duke of Edinburgh's Study Conference at Oxford in 1956, president in 1959–60 of the International Association for the Protection of Industrial Property and a vice-president of the National Council for Social Service.

Hanbury-Williams, who was knighted in 1950, was a Gentleman Usher successively to George V, Edward VIII, and George VI, and an Extra Gentleman Usher to George VI and Queen Elizabeth II. From 1936 he was one of H.M.'s Lieutenants for the City of London and in 1943 and 1958 he was a Sheriff of the County of London.

In 1928 he married Princess Zenaida Cantacuzene, and they had one son and two daughters.

August 11, 1965.

Sir Henry Hancock, G.C.B., C.M.G., who died in Nigeria on July 24, 1965, was a former Permanent Secretary of the Ministry of National Insurance and from 1955 to 1958, chairman of the the Board of Inland Revenue. In 1958 he was appointed by Henry Brooke to the chairmanship of the Local Government Commission for England and Wales. At the time of his death he was chairman of the "little Neddy" for the Chocolate and Sugar Confectionery industries.

Henry Drummond Hancock was born on September 17, 1895, the only son of Percy G. Hancock of Sheffield. He was educated at Haileybury and Exeter College, Oxford. He served in the First World War in The Sherwood Foresters and the Intelligence Corps. After the war he entered the Civil Service in 1920 by the Reconstruction Examination for the Administrative Class and was appointed to the Ministry of Labour, where his first chief was Humbert Wolfe. One of his earliest jobs was to act as secretary to the Committee of Inquiry into the working of the Trade Boards Acts, under the chairmanship of Lord Cave. While still an Assistant Principal he served for a time as Private Secretary to the Permanent Secretary, Sir Horace Wilson. Following the report of the Industrial Transference Board in 1928 he was engaged on the administration of various schemes for the transference of unemployed workers from areas of heavy unemployment—mainly the mining areas—to places where industry was expanding in the south and midlands and in the development of migration overseas.

When the Labour Government of 1929 appointed J. H. Thomas as Lord Privy Seal, to serve with George Lansbury and Sir Oswald Mosley as a triumvirate to take charge of measures to relieve unemployment, Hancock was appointed as Private Secretary to Thomas.

He returned to the Ministry of Labour in 1931 when the Labour Government went out of office and was engaged on the administration of unemployment insurance and the problem of assisting those who had exhausted their rights to benefit under an insurance scheme. He had a good deal to do with the framing of the Act of 1934 which created the National Assistance Board under the chairmanship of Lord Rushcliffe who, as Sir Henry Betterton, had been the Minister of Labour responsible for the Bill. Hancock was appointed to the staff of the Assistance Board and helped to create the national organization which replaced the old Poor Law system.

COST OF CIVIL DEFENCE

His next move came after Munich when the Government called upon local authorities to put in hand a system of Air Raid Precautions, later to be known as Civil Defence. Hancock went over to the Home Office and took charge of the division which was concerned with local authorities expenditure. Here he showed a flair for financial administration, and he put on a sound footing the arrangements for meeting the cost of Civil Defence. In 1941 he was asked to go to the United States as Secretary General of the British Purchasing Commission and British Raw Materials Mission and he served in Washington in this post for two years, returning to London in 1942 to become Deputy Secretary to the Ministry of Supply. There he had three strenuous years at the hub of war production. With the end of war he was appointed Deputy Secretary of the new Ministry of National Insurance, which was created to administer the National Insurance Scheme which replaced the old schemes of Unemployment Insurance, Health Insurance and Workmen's Compensation, and was based largely on the Beveridge plan. Hancock's previous experience in the Ministry of Labour was of great value in creating this new machine which covered the whole country through regional and local offices.

After three years as Deputy Secretary he succeeded Sir Thomas Phillips as Permanent Secretary when the latter retired. In 1951 he was appointed Permanent Secretary to the Ministry of Food and continued in that office until 1935. This was a period largely of disentanglement from wartime controls and systems of state purchase and by 1955 it was possible to absorb the remaining functions of the Ministry of Food into the Ministry of Agriculture and Fisheries. Hancock then became the chairman of the Board of Inland Revenue and continued in that office until his retirement in October, 1958. Shortly after this, he was appointed chairman of the Local Government Commission for England under the Local Government Act, 1958. He was a director of Booker Bros. McConnell & Co. Ltd.

Hancock had an unusually wide experience of public administration and served in more departments than is usual for a senior Civil Servant. He had a ready grasp of new problems and a flexible mind and invention in dealing with them. He was a clear and precise thinker and speaker, always ready to listen patiently to those with a less agile mind.

He married, in 1926, Elizabeth, daughter of Engineer-Captain Henry Toop of Portsmouth, and they had one son and one daughter.

July 26, 1965.

Tony Hancock, the comedian, was found dead in a flat in Sydney, New South Wales, on June 25, 1968. He was 44.

In an age of mass entertainment, when the comedian became the servant of microphone and cameras, and the subordinate of his script writers, he created a personality and inspired a style of comedy through which he dominated the camera. What grew from his work was what we have come to regard as the classic style of television comedy.

Anthony John Hancock was born in Birmingham on May 12, 1924, and educated at Durlston Court, Swanage, and Bradfield College, Reading. His father kept a public house in Bournemouth, where theatrical people, like Stainless Stephen and Elsie and Doris Waters, used to stay, and they took him back stage.

He served in the forces throughout the Second World War, from 1942 as a member of the Air Force. Before he became a part of Ralph Reader's R.A.F. Gang Show, he had some experience as a youthful amateur entertainer, and after his demobilization in 1946 he was experienced enough to find himself continual engagements in pantomime, in summer seasons in the holiday resorts, and occasionally as a straight actor. In 1948 he became one of the line of distinguished entertainers who provided laughter to interrupt the endless displays of pulchritude which occupied the stage of the Windmill Theatre. For Hancock, as for the others, the Windmill was a stepping stone to celebrity.

In his case, however, it led first to radio and then to television. From 1951 to 1953 he added a new voice, and an unusual new personality, to radio show *Educating Archie,* a show popular enough to tour the variety theatres with Hancock as a member of its company. While he was providing a startling union of opposites by appearing with Jimmy Edwards successively in *London Laughs* and *Talk of the Town* at the Adelphi Theatre, the essential Hancock character appeared in all its bizarrerie in *Hancock's Half Hour*—a title he himself announced with a sort of triumphant, emphatic caution in pronouncing its aspirates—in 1954, first as a radio show and then, from 1956 to 1960, on television.

FAMOUS FOIL

An admirable foil—Sid James, the complete and unscrupulous materialist blind to almost everything but the main chance—and superb scripts by Ray Galton and Alan Simpson, enabled him to strike a new vein of comedy in which situations rarely too extreme for immediate conviction existed to create the deeper comedy of character.

The later re-run of many of these programmes, after a great development of television style, showed them to have lost nothing of their quality in the passage of time.

A second series, in which Hancock had no regular partner, and in some of which he was left to carry the entire weight of a half-hour's script virtually or completely alone, lost some of the easy fun which had risen from the clash between his earnestness and Sid James's easy-going carelessness, but it allowed some new and rather disturbing aspects of the character he had created to be seen. A series of programmes for Independent Television, *Hancock,* in 1963, left the Hancock *persona* to function without effective scripts or worthy partners.

INSEPARABLE

Two films—*The Rebel* in 1961, and *The Punch and Judy Man* in 1963—left the character, from which he had become as inseparable as was Chaplin from his genteel tramp, to make its way in an alien world. Appearances in pantomime, variety and cabaret, though they never lacked the unobtrusive technical skill which he had refined in the close-range work of television, seemed at the same time to leave him disorientated. Every new venture he liked to think of and announce as a new departure in style, but in escaping from his television *persona* he never became more than a skilful, amusing, but fundamentally conventional entertainer.

This was principally, it seems, because of the sheer unusualness of the character he created. If it had fewer resonances and not the universal application of Chaplin's tramp, it was nevertheless unique. "Anthony Aloysius Hancock" of radio and television was not, interviews and stage appearances showed, the Anthony John Hancock who had created him. The real man, we noticed, was prepared to work with an artist's devotion to the tasks put before him. The character he created was not—and in this itself is unusual—particularly likeable or sympathetic. Lugubrious, and lugubriously attired—a black homburg hat and an over-long black overcoat, unsuitable to his occupation and way of life but chosen, apparently, as symbols of grandeur, were the externals which manifested Napoleonic ambitions and self-importance with Napoleonic determination or will, tendencies to megolomania, social illusions, a capacity for total self-deception, and an essential loneliness; when Anthony Aloysius laughed, it was maliciously, in derision or in delight, at a trivial and short-lived victory over some unfortunate who had crossed his path. The real world had no place for him.

In Tony Hancock, much that is sadly typical of his age was crystallized and found expression.

CRAVING FOR EMINENCE

He was the chronicler of social disorientation, of submission to undigested or indigestible little ideas dressed pompously in big words, of a craving for intellectual and social eminence on the cheap. Whether by instinct or by design, these things found in him a mercilessly derisive commentator.

He left Britain for Australia in March, 1968, to work on a proposed comedy series for Australian TV. Shortly afterwards, he was taken to hospital in Sydney with an undescribed illness, but was discharged about the middle of May. In January he had spent some time in a Bournemouth nursing home with pneumonia.

He married in 1950 Cicely Romanis. The marriage was dissolved in 1965 and he married the same year "Freddie" Ross, his public relations agent. She was granted a divorce a week before he died.

June 26, 1968.

Judge Learned Hand died in New York on August 18, 1961, at the age of 89.

During the past generation the names of three American judges have been outstanding: Mr. Justice Oliver Wendell Holmes, of the United States Supreme Court, Chief Judge Benjamin N. Cardozo, of the New York Court of Appeals, and Chief Judge Learned Hand, of the United States Court of Appeals for the Second Circuit. They had much in common. They were sound lawyers whose learning in the law enabled them to build on a strong scholarly foundation, their judgments had a vivid, literary quality based on conscious artistry, and they were concerned with the law as an instrument for the achievement of social progress.

All three were on the side of judicial valour against judicial caution, in Sir Frederick Pollock's phrase, but none disregarded the necessary limits placed on the judicial function if the law was to maintain its essential stability. Above all, they were great men who caught the imagination of the people at large without ever seeking to do so. There are many who will feel that with the death of Learned Hand the golden age of the American judiciary has come to an end.

Billings Learned Hand, the son of Samuel and Lydia Colt Hand, was born in upstate New York on January 27, 1872. Later he discarded "Billings" because, he said, "it is a vastly formidable name which you can use only when you bury a man or send him to jail"; but he continued to be known as "B. Hand" to many of his older friends. The name "Learned" was popularly attributed to his Puritan ancestry, but in fact it was his mother's surname, and therefore, in accordance with common American practice, it was given to him as his middle name.

From the Albany Academy he went to Harvard University where he received his B.A. degree *summa cum laude* in 1893. He spent the next three years at the Harvard Law School, receiving his LL.B. degree in 1896. He was one of the first editors of the *Harvard Law Review*.

FAMOUS FACULTY

At that time Christopher Columbus Langdell was the Dean, and the faculty included such famous names as Thayer, Ames, and Gray. It was in this atmosphere that Hand first learnt his law. After graduation he returned to Albany, the seat of government of New York State, where he practised law for six years, but in 1902 he was persuaded to move to New York City as the opportunities there were greater. In the same year he married Frances Fincke, a brilliant and charming girl, who did much throughout their long and happy married life to encourage his interest in literature and art. They had three daughters.

In 1909 Charles C. Burlingham, a leading New York lawyer who died last year in his hundred and first year, persuaded Attorney General George W. Wickersham to recommend to President Taft that he should appoint Hand as United States District Judge for the Southern District of New York. This is the most important District Court in America because its location in New York City and its wide jurisdiction in criminal, commercial, and maritime law bring before it a large number of outstanding cases. Hand proved to be an admirable trial judge: firm, courteous, and efficient. He looked every inch the judge with his strong and crag-like features, occasionally softened by an impish smile. He was not, however, popular with all the lawyers who practised before him because he did not always suffer fools gladly. Very few of his judgments were reversed on appeal.

In 1924 Hand was raised to the Circuit Court of Appeals, becoming Chief Judge in 1939. He retired in 1951, but this did not bring his judicial career to an end, for he continued to sit with regularity until 1959.

The Circuit Court of Appeals sits as a Bench of three judges so that during his 35 years of service Hand had an opportunity to write nearly 2,000 opinions. Perhaps his best-known cases concerned freedom of speech and individual liberty. In the *Ulysses* case he held that Joyce's book was not obscene, and in a number of others he took a firm stand against the abuse of police powers. His national reputation as one of the ablest jurists in American legal history made it inevitable that whenever a vacancy on the Supreme Court occurred it was rumoured that he would be elevated to that Bench. This, however, was never done; perhaps his independence of character may have made the various Presidents hesitate to take the risk. Hand himself never showed any disappointment or regret: he probably realized that his reputation was enhanced by the work he was able to do in New York, for his judgments have been cited more frequently than have been those of almost any Supreme Court Justice.

For many years his cousin Augustus Hand also sat as a Judge of the same Circuit Court of Appeals. It was sometimes said that although Learned was the more brilliant of the two, Augustus had more common sense. Learned took great pleasure in quoting this.

In 1952 a collection of his addresses and essays was published under the title *The Spirit of Liberty*. The most famous of these was the eponymous address which he delivered to a group of foreign-born men and women who had recently become United States citizens. This has been recognized as the classic statement of the ideals which ought to guide the American people. In 1958 he delivered at Harvard the Oliver Wendell Holmes lectures entitled *The Bill of Rights* in which he considered the doctrine and scope of judicial review. He expressed the opinion that in some cases this had been extended too far, in these characteristic words: "For myself, it would be most irksome to be ruled by a bevy of Platonic guardians, even if I knew how to choose them, which I assuredly do not."

One of the greatest contributions to the law made by Judge Hand was in the leading role he played in the creation of the American Law Institute in 1923. He was one of the original members of the council which planned the form to be taken by the various Restatements, and thereafter he took an active part in preparing some of them. If it had not been for the support which he and Judge Cardozo gave to this novel project it is probable that the institute would not have attained its present success.

Learned Hand received many honours in the course of his life, but perhaps the one that gave him the greatest pleasure was the hon. LL.D. which the University of Cambridge conferred on him in 1952.

August 19, 1961.

Lord Hankey, who died on January 25, 1963, in a Surrey hospital at the age of 85, was without a counterpart in British public life. His career spanned with dramatic perfection the gap between the free and easy ways of Edwardian administration and the elaborate, expensive, and, perhaps, more efficient modern machinery. When he was taken as a young officer of Marines to the Committee of Imperial Defence, none of those who, even as early as that, spotted him as the perfect secretary could possibly have foreseen his remarkable future. He rose with the rising complication of keeping cabinet records straight to a position of the highest, though undefined, responsibility. Allowing for Greville and others he stands out unchallenged as the greatest backroom figure in our political history.

Sir Winston Churchill described him as "the far-seeing Captain Hankey" and that shrewd political soldier Henry Wilson remarked of him "If you once lose hold of Hanky-Panky you are done, absolutely done!" These tributes converge as a searchlight on the key position he held. He remained in it for so long because, knowing as he did almost all the secrets of his masters, he never betrayed them and because, having an unquenchable zest for power behind the scenes and a matchless tact, he was able to be at once unobtrusive and formidable. So conscientious was he that he would never eat after a Cabinet meeting until he had written the minutes.

The Right Hon. Sir Maurice Pascal Alers Hankey, P.C., G.C.B., G.C.M.G., G.C.V.O., LL.D., F.R.S., first Baron Hankey, of The Chart, County Surrey, in the Peerage of the United Kingdom, was born on April 1, 1877, third son of Robert Alers Hankey, of South Australia and Brighton. He was educated at Rugby (of whose governing body he was subsequently a member) and joined the Royal Marine Artillery as a second lieutenant on September 1, 1895. The Royal Naval College at Greenwich at the time he was studying there had just come under the influence of the teaching of Major-General Sir George Aston, who had been appointed Professor of Fortification.

LORD FISHER MUCH IMPRESSED

Hankey's first ship was the Ramillies, the flagship in the Mediterranean of Admiral Sir Anthony Hoskins, Commander-in-Chief, which he joined on December 22, 1898. In January, 1900, the Ramillies became flagship of the Second-in-Command, Rear-Admiral Lord Charles Beresford, owing to the arrival as Commander-in-Chief of Admiral Sir John (afterwards Admiral of the Fleet Lord) Fisher, who brought his old flagship, the Renown, from North American waters. By this time Hankey had become a captain, and was in charge of the Marine contingent in the ship. In his numerous reforms in the working of what was then the most important British naval command afloat, Fisher came into contact with, and was much impressed by, the capacity and industry of the young Marine captain. Not long afterwards, in May, 1902, Fisher left to become Second Sea Lord at the Admiralty, taking Captain Hankey with him to the Naval Intelligence Division. In April, 1907, he was appointed to the Queen, flagship of Admiral Sir Charles Drury, for duty as Intelligence Officer in the Mediterranean Fleet, but his term there was cut short by his selection, in January, 1908, as assistant secretary of the Committee of Imperial Defence, of which Rear-Admiral Sir Charles Ottley was then secretary.

On the retirement of Admiral Ottley on March 1, 1912, Asquith, largely on the recommendation of Lord Haldane, appointed Captain Hankey, at the early age of 34, to succeed him and to be secretary of the standing sub-committee, composed of highly placed representatives from the nine departments concerned, for the "coordination of departmental action on the outbreak of war." When hostilities came some two and a half years later, the functions of the Committee of Imperial Defence naturally took on a much greater importance and Captain Hankey became secretary to the War Council. It was not, however, until Lloyd George became Prime Minister in December, 1916, that the secretariat of the Committee came to take what many considered its rightful place in the conduct of the war.

Of the War Cabinet, Hankey—he had been advanced from C.B. to K.C.B. in February. 1916—was appointed secretary. An important innovation was the creation of a Secretariat to the War Cabinet, with Hankey at its head, to discharge various functions, and especially to ensure that the Government departments were kept in close touch with the policy of the War Cabinet, and conversely that the members of the latter were kept in touch with the policy and action of the various departments. Of the arduous character of the work thus involved, and for which Hankey was primarily responsible, evidence is forthcoming in the fact that the War Cabinet held more than 300 meetings in 1917. The extent also to which the policy of inviting expert assistance was carried may be judged from the fact that in its first year's working no fewer than 248 persons other than members of the War Cabinet and the Secretariat attended its meetings. It was this flexibility of composition, coupled with the wide knowledge and sound judgment of Hankey, which helped to make the War Cabinet system so successful. He had learnt to take a broad view of the conduct of war, and was possessed of keen foresight and imagination.

THE PARIS PEACE CONFERENCE

In 1947 Hankey acted as secretary during the meetings of the Imperial War Cabinet. After the Armistice he was naturally chosen as the British secretary to the Peace Conference in Paris, which opened on January 18, 1919, and continued its deliberations until the signing of peace five months later. He was a great success at Paris. It was said he was the only man there who had attended every political and inter-allied conference held during the whole of the war. Certainly his knowledge and experience were invaluable to the conference deliberations. In the awards made to the leaders in the 1914–18 War Hankey was advanced to G.C.B., and received the thanks of both Houses of Parliament with a grant of £25,000.

When the War Cabinet and Home Affairs Committee were dissolved in October, 1919, and a return was made to the older system, Hankey was appointed secretary of the Cabinet, and continued in peace-time to exercise those talents which he had displayed to such good purpose in the 1914–18 War. He was secretary to the Imperial Conference of 1921, and in November, 1922, accompanied the British delegation to the Washington Conference as secretary. In June, 1923, on the resignation at the age of 72 of Sir Almeric FitzRoy of the office of clerk of the Privy Council, the duties of that office were combined with those of the secretaryship to the Cabinet and to the Committee of Imperial Defence, and Hankey became clerk of the Privy Council, without, however, any additional remuneration. Besides being a saving of public money and a matter of practical convenience, it is interesting to note that this arrangement regularized Hankey's rather anomalous position as Secretary to the Cabinet (which is the most important committee of the Privy Council), although he had not taken the special and stately oath required of the clerk of the council; this was now administered to him.

IMPERIAL DEFENCE

His new duties were not onerous. Though the permanent head of the Privy Council Office, he was troubled with little of the routine work of its administrative side, and beyond attending the Sovereign when holding council, the secretaryship of the Cabinet and of the Committee of Imperial Defence continued to occupy in the main Hankey's busy life. He was secretary to the Imperial conferences in 1923, 1926, and 1930; secretary-general of the London Conference on Reparations in 1924 and The Hague Conferences of 1929 and 1930. He was secretary of the London Naval Conference of 1930, of the London Conference of 1931, and Lausanne Conference in 1932. In August, 1934, he went to Australia as the guest of the Commonwealth Government during the celebration of the centenary of Victoria, and during his visit in his capacity as secretary of the Committee of Imperial Defence he was invited to advise the Commonwealth on defence policy.

In July, 1938, Hankey retired from the office of clerk of the Privy Council, and his retirement brought many tributes to his administrative services, including a leading article in *The Times* which was entitled "A Prince of Secretaries." He was raised to the peerage in 1939. In the month before the outbreak of war in 1939 Hankey was appointed a member of the Mandates Commission of the League of Nations, and in September, 1939, on reconstitution of the Government, he was made a member of the War Cabinet as Minister without Portfolio. His vast experience and expert knowledge, extending back before and through the previous war, gave him a unique position in the Council of Ministers, and were utilized on numerous Cabinet committees, of which he was often chairman, of whose existence and functions the public were seldom aware. He was also chairman of the Colonial Products Research Council set up in 1943. In the meantime, in October, 1940, on the resignation of Neville Chamberlain from the Government, Churchill reconstructed it to some extent, and Hankey found himself out of the War Cabinet and took over the Duchy of Lancaster, and in July, 1941, he became Paymaster-General. The next year he resigned that office, and though he filled no other post in the Government, his time was fully occupied with his numerous committees.

FELLOW OF THE ROYAL SOCIETY

In 1942 he was elected a Fellow of the Royal Society, as having rendered conspicuous service to the cause of science, and he was appointed chairman of a Government Commission on the future development of television. In 1938 he had been appointed a Government Director of the Suez Canal Company, a post which he resigned on the outbreak of war and his assumption of office. In 1945 he was appointed a commercial director, a post that carried no age disqualification. In the same year he published his book, *Government Control in War*, with a foreword by Professor G. M. Trevelyan, taken largely from material from the Lees Knowles lectures of 1945, delivered by Hankey at Cambridge the same year. On such a subject his experience was unequalled, and as an account of the machinery employed by Government in the first and second world wars, its value to the future historian is unique. In December, 1949, he published a book which raised some controversy and received some severe criticism, *Politics —Trials and Errors*. In it he condemned roundly the policies of unconditional surrender and the trials of war criminals.

In closing the life story of this remarkable man the exact qualities that accounted for his success are, as always, difficult to define. First should be mentioned a photographic memory that was never at fault either as regards events or anything he had either heard or read. Then should be noted a tireless energy, assisted by a good physique, and a capacity for thoroughness and hard work, in which few could outmatch him. His tact and discretion made him (like his predecessor, Greville) the confidant of discordant elements that he was often able to reconcile and his complete integrity inspired universal respect. No public man of his time had been the repository of more state secrets, and his memoirs were long awaited. When they came out, in 1961 as *The Supreme Command, 1914–18*, they proved a model of how absolute discretion can be combined with the casting of valuable light on history as seen by one who actively watched it in the making.

Lord Hankey, who was sworn a member of the Privy Council in 1939, was created a G.C.B. in 1919, a G.C.M.G. in 1929, and a G.C.V.O. in 1934, and he held honorary degrees from Oxford, Cambridge, Edinburgh, and Birmingham. He married in 1903 Adeline daughter of Mr. A. de Smidt, formerly Surveyor-General of Cape Colony. Of this marriage there were three sons and one daughter. He is succeeded in the peerage by his eldest son, the Hon. Sir Robert Hankey, permanent United Kingdom representative to O.E.C.D. One of the late Lord Hankey's brothers, Donald, who was killed in the 1914–18 War, had attained some reputation as a writer by his essays, "A Student in Arms."

January 28, 1963.

Sir Patrick Hannon, for many years a prominent figure in British public life, political, commercial and social, died at his London home on January 10, 1963, at the age of 88.

He touched life at many points. A Unionist M.P. for 29 years, he became part of the public and industrial life of Birmingham; and his charm, wit, and indestructible love of work won him the esteem and affection of a crowd of friends in the most diverse and often most unexpected places.

Patrick Joseph Henry Hannon was born on March 2, 1874, the son of Mathew Hannon, of Kilfree, and in spite of the fact that he had to some extent to shape and provide for his own course in the early days, he made his way to Dublin University, to the Royal College of Science in London, and the Royal University of Ireland.

Hannon himself said in later years that he realized as a young man in his twenties that improved conditions for the Irish workers could come only out of greater prosperity among the farmers, and he thereupon set to work to promote agricultural cooperation, particularly in buying and marketing. He became assistant secretary, and later chief organizer, of the Irish Agricultural Organization Society and for his work was awarded the diploma of the Royal Agricultural Wholesale Society. For some years he was associated with the late Sir Horace Plunkett in his work which embraced schemes both for the agricultural and economic regeneration of Ireland. He was convinced that a measure of protection for the revival of agriculture was essential and formed the beginning of his subsequent long career in the campaign for tariff reform.

TARIFF REFORM

His beliefs were strengthened by his tours abroad. In 1902 and 1903 he reported on conditions in Denmark and on agricultural cooperation in France. The next year he visited the United States and Canada for the Irish Industrial Movement and in 1905 he was in South Africa, where, for a while in the Jameson Administration, he became Director of Agricultural Organization. He was then confirmed in this Cape Colony post, and held it for four years, until he returned to England to devote himself to the tariff reform campaign. In the 1910 general election he became the movement's candidate—it was by now the Tariff Reform League—for Bristol East, but was defeated. Thenceforward he threw his energies into it and from 1910 to 1914 was its vice-president.

He had also become one of the dominant figures in the Navy League. He had for some time been a member of the executive committee when, in 1911, his colleagues appointed him secretary and editor of the *Navy*, a post he held until 1918. During these years he founded, and acted as honorary secretary of its education fund. He became director of the British Commonwealth Union, a post entirely after his own heart and one in which he often crossed swords with Labour leaders. He was also joint founder of the Comrades of the Great War, and the first general secretary of the movement.

In 1921 he achieved his great ambition by securing a seat in the House of Commons, succeeding Sir Halliwell Rogers as Unionist member for the Moseley Division of Birmingham. From the year of his appearance at Westminster until 1929 he was honorary secretary of the Industrial Group in the Commons. He continued to speak, write, and travel extensively, and out of this work there developed his interest in the National Union of Manufacturers, of which he became, and for many years remained, president.

Sir Patrick was an impenitent and incurable individualist, excepting in his readiness to collaborate with others in pursuing his favourite causes. He viewed with the gravest misgiving the encroachments of state control over public effort and private life. In the Commons he was, it could fairly be said, both an institution and a phenomenon, with his fresh pink complexion, and his white hair—white for so many years before he grew old—and his twinkling dancing eyes, which suggested, quite rightly, that he was always ready for a quip or a joke.

Hannon loved the House, and was always jealous of its traditions, and it is to be recalled that he left his mark upon its furnishings, long before he left the House itself, by presenting to it fine marble busts of Sir Robert Peel and Lord Palmerston. In Birmingham, and particularly in his constituency, he was adored, and the greatest test of his popularity came in 1945; when in the Labour sweep so many of his neighbouring colleagues went down to defeat, he retained Moseley although with a much reduced majority. In 1947, with heavy commercial, industrial and other public duties upon his shoulders, he announced that he would not seek reelection in 1950.

The various offices which he held during his career were legion, and read almost like a catalogue. While in the House he had been a member of the Estimates Committee for 17 years, and for many years he sat on the National Whitley Council. He had been chairman of the National Council of Inland Waterways, a movement into which he had been drawn by his old friend Neville Chamberlain; president of the National Transport Association, of the Institute of Export, the British and Latin-American Chamber of Commerce, and the Central Chamber of Agriculture, to name only a few.

He had been a vice-president of the Federation of British Industries, a director of the Dollars Export Council and of the Ideal Benefit Society, the Midland Building Societies, member of the Court of Governors of Birmingham University, a vice-president and member of the Council of the Birmingham Chamber of Commerce, for over 20 years chairman of the Constitutional Club and for 10 years of its political committee, a like post which he also held for several years at the Carlton Club. In industry he had been chairman of Sheffields Ltd., deputy chairman of the Birmingham Small Arms Company, of the Daimler Company, and a director of James Booth and Co. (1915) Ltd.

He was a devout Roman Catholic. His religion was an essential part of his everyday life, and he was always at the service of his Church.

He was a great soccer fan, and for 35 years president of Aston Villa. He was knighted in 1936.

He was twice Master of the Worshipful Company of Pattenmakers.

He married first in 1894 Mary, daughter of Thomas Wynne, of Castlebar. She died in 1928, and he married secondly in 1931 Amy Hilda Gordon, daughter of the late James Barrett. She died in 1960.

January 11, 1963.

Steven J. L. Hardie, D.S.O., who was chairman of the Iron and Steel Corporation from 1950 to 1952, died on July 22, 1969, at the age of 83.

Hardie was little known to the public when he became chairman of the Iron and Steel Corporation of Great Britain, which was to take over, and run on a nationalized basis, a large part of the steel industry. He had been chairman of the vast British Oxygen combine, of several other companies connected with the scrap metal trade, and of George Dobie and Son of Paisley, makers of "Four Square" tobaccos.

Born at Paisley in 1885, Steven James Lindsay Hardie was the son of a mathematics and science master at Paisley Grammar School. He was educated at Paisley Grammer School and Glasgow University, and qualified as a chartered accountant in Scotland. In 1913 he set up in business for himself in Glasgow. But in August, 1914, immediately on the outbreak of the war, he took a commission in the 6th Battalion, The Argyll and Sutherland Highlanders. He was a machine-gun specialist, and was in some of the toughest fighting of the war, in France, Belgium and Germany. He was three times mentioned in dispatches, won the D.S.O., and was eventually promoted lieutenant-colonel.

Hardie returned to accountancy, and in 1922 he and a fellow ex-officer, Robert Watson MacCrone, having got together some £7,000 capital, went into the scrap metal trade, raising many sunken hulks around the British coasts and breaking up many obsolete vessels. Their firm Metal Industries Ltd., having started with one small yard, expanded so rapidly that before long it controlled one of the biggest systems of shipbreaking yards in Europe. The partners heard of a new oxygen technique in Germany, bought the rights in it, and in 1930 set up their own oxygen company. After a hard fighting with trade rivals they eventually became the controllers of British Oxygen Ltd. An immense system of ancillary overseas companies was built up. Through Metal Industries Ltd., Hardie in course of time extended his interests to electrical equipment, tug-boat ownership, industrial gases, hydraulic engineering, and ferrous and non-ferrous metal-casting.

BREEDING SHORTHORNS

In 1925 Hardie branched out into the tobacco manufacturing concern of George Dobie and Son, which produced the successful "Four Square" brands of tobacco.

Hardie began, as growing wealth permitted the occupation, to breed a herd of pedigree shorthorn cattle on his estate at Ballathie, Perthshire. He owned several other farms in Scotland and a sheep farm in Australia: and, in view of his attainments as a businessman, it is not surprising to find that this by-product of an enormous energy was as profitable as everything else that he touched.

Hardie was originally a Liberal in politics, but joined the Labour Party in 1945. He was not in the habit of making political speeches, but in 1947 did voice his opinion that industrialists would be serving the best interests of the country by working for the success of the Government. He served in the Jute Working Party in 1946–47; he was a member of the executive committee of the Scottish Council

(Development and Industry) and of the British Transport Commission, and was an independent member of the Cinematography Films Council.

A massive, slow-moving man, Hardie was known as a just but severe employer.

Hardie married Maie (who died in 1939), daughter of D. H. Nicolson, of Kirkcaldy.

July 23, 1969.

Sir Cedric Hardwicke, the stage and film actor, died in University Hospital, New York, on August 6, 1964, at the age of 71.

Although to many people he was known for his character roles in films, to the theatregoer his name will probably be remembered longest for the performances he gave as a comparatively young man in England, under Barry Jackson's management.

Cedric Webster Hardwicke was justified in entitling his autobiography *A Victorian in Orbit*, for he was born on February 19, 1893, his birthplace being Lye, near Stourbridge, Worcestershire, where his father Edwin Hardwicke practised as a doctor. When his only son, having failed in his preliminary medical examination, was accepted by Tree and Violet Vanbrugh as a student at what is now R.A.D.A., Dr. Hardwicke allowed him £2 a week to live on in London. His apprenticeship in the theatre was served under Tree and Bourchier in 1912; later as a member of Benson's Northern Company playing Shakespeare in the provinces and, at the time of the outbreak of the First World War, in Southern Africa; later still at the Old Vic. He joined the Inns of Court Officers' Training Corps at the end of 1914, landed in France as an officer in the Royal Army Service Corps Horse Transport in January, 1916, was posted to the Northumberland Fusiliers early in 1918, and was, in October, 1921, officially the last British officer to leave the war zone. In postwar England he felt himself to be a misfit till a chance visit to Barry Jackson's Birmingham "Rep" gave him, as he put it, the desire for the first time to do something worth while as an actor.

PLEASED G.B.S.

He was engaged there in January, 1922. During the next two years in Birmingham, breaking completely with his Bensonian past, Hardwicke showed promise in broad character parts, and moreover in *Heartbreak House* and in the first British production of *Back To Methuselah* he pleased Shaw. In the latter play Hardwicke returned to the London stage after 11 years on Jackson's bringing it from Birmingham to the Royal Court in January, 1924, there following it up with Eden Philpotts's *The Farmer's Wife* which contained in Churdles Ash, a 70-year-old agricultural worker, the most amusing of the character parts in Hardwicke's new line of business. This play was "nursed" into a success. Churdles Ash's sayings were quoted, and the actor's name was made, everyone finding difficulty in believing that the man behind the wonderfully comic make-up was less than half the age of Eden Philpotts's elderly woman-hater.

In his next part of Caesar in Jackson's revival of *Caesar and Cleopatra* he failed, but not as badly as to forfeit the regard of Shaw, who was now not only Hardwicke's hero but his friend. Hardwicke went on to play for Jackson in London in the first modern-dress production of *Hamlet* and in another Devon comedy, *Yellow Sands*, and then in 1929, at the end of a long engagement in *Show Boat* at Drury Lane, he was offered by Jackson the part of the urbane, wily King Magnus in Shaw's new play *The Apple Cart*, due for presentation at the Malvern Festival. With Shaw's help, Hardwicke here excelled himself. Thanks to the topicality of the play and its long run in London, his performance in it was more talked about, and for the moment his prospects seemed brighter than those of any other leading man in the West End.

DIRECTION UNCERTAIN

The Barretts of Wimpole Street with Hardwicke in the part of the father had an even longer run, and he continued working for Jackson in revivals of Shaw and in one new play by him, *Too True To Be Good*, until 1933, when he played his first part under the management of Gilbert Miller. Knighted at the beginning of 1934, he admitted that his ambitions had been achieved and that he felt uncertain as to the next step. Miller offered him a trip to the United States. Though on coming home he played for a year in *Tovarich*, Hardwicke had now reached a turning point in his career. From the end of 1936 until 1939, apart from an interlude at a Malvern Festival, he appeared in the "live" theatre in the United States, and from 1939 until 1944 he worked chiefly in Hollywood, where, in the words of the British Ambassador, Lord Lothian, the maintenance of a powerful British nucleus of older actors was of great importance to our wartime interests.

AMERICAN "PYGMALION"

He was again in England, acting, in the summer of 1944, and toured for the Entertainments National Service Association in western Europe during the following winter, but after the war ended he went back to the United States, there directing Gertrude Lawrence in *Pygmalion* and partnering Katherine Cornell in Jean Anouilh's *Antigone*. Then on his next visit to England he appeared in three plays with the Old Vic Company and in 1949 reestablished his good relations with Shaw, which the actor's turning down of a part in *Buoyant Billions* had overclouded. This meeting between the two old friends proved to be the last. Hardwicke directed some months later a successful revival of *Caesar and Cleopatra* in New York and on the day of Shaw's death, November 2, 1950, when the lights of Broadway were dimmed as a sign of mourning. Hardwicke was invited to pay tribute to him in a curtain speech. The public reading in the following year of Shaw's *Don Juan In Hell*, with Hardwicke taking the Statue's part, became a great draw in the United States, but fell flat on being presented in England. He had to wait for his next success in New York till the production in 1959 of *A Majority Of One* with himself as the Japanese suitor of a widow from Brooklyn.

Since Hardwicke's career in films dated back to 1911, it had actually begun before Cecil B. de Mille's, as he had the satisfaction of telling that maker of Hollywood epics while working for him in *The Ten Commandments*. For all that, Hardwicke's film career was not a brilliant one, though it included such roles as the title-part in *Dreyfus*, the Bishop in *Les Misérables*, Dr. Livingstone in *Stanley and Livingstone*, Dr. Arnold in *Tom Brown's Schooldays*, Senator Cabot Lodge in *Wilson*, Ralph in *Nicholas Nickleby*, and Edward IV in *Richard III*. In the 1930s there was a stimulating glimpse of Hardwicke the comic actor in J. B. Priestley's study of suburbia *Laburnum Grove*, in which he played the lip-smacking, banana-eating, good-for-nothing Bertie Baxley. Film-acting was, he declared, a director's medium. Unlike acting in the "live" theatre, which he greatly preferred, it did not need to be spun out of an actor's mind and heart; continuously, as a spider's web is spun; nor could film-acting be, in Hardwicke's sense of the word, instantaneous, that is, sparked off by immediate contact between actor and audience.

HIS OWN LIFE

His two essays in autobiography *Let's Pretend* and *A Victorian in Orbit* are chiefly interesting for their quotations from Shaw's letters and spoken advice and for the frank description of the vicissitudes of an actor's life as he worked now in this medium, now in that. His short answers to the questions "how many films have you made?" and "how many plays have you appeared in?" were, respectively, "too many" and "too few" but he developed them carefully in his Rede lecture "The Drama Tomorrow", given before the University of Cambridge in 1936.

His marriages to the English actress Helena Pickard and to the American actress Mary Scott were both dissolved. He was the father of Edward Hardwicke, the actor, by his first marriage and of another son, Michael Hardwicke, by his second.

August 7, 1964.

Lieutenant-General Shri Sir Harisinghji, Maharaja of Jammu and Kashmir, former ruler of the state, died on April 26, 1961, at Bombay. He was 65, and was born on September 30, 1895, to the powerful and ambitious General Sir Amar Singh, younger brother of the Maharaja Sir Pratap Singh, an old-style ruler whose governing powers were restricted for many years on grounds of alleged connivance in a plot against the British Resident. Hari Singh entered the Mayo College, Ajmer, in 1908 and was trained in the short-lived Imperial Cadet Corps at Dehra Dun. His uncle's desire to adopt a collateral heir was not endorsed by the British Government, and his nephew and presumptive heir became the commander of the state Forces before he was 20. His interest in its efficiency and welfare remained strong.

None of the future Maharaja's predecessors had visited Europe, and his own first experience of the West in 1924 was unfortunate. He was victimized in Paris by blackmailers with the connivance of a young A.D.C. against whose appointment to his staff he had been strongly warned. When litigation ensued over the large sum of money extracted from the young Prince it was decided "for reasons of state" to keep his identity secret in the Court under the pseudonym of "Mr. A.". As was inevitable in the circumstances, the attempt failed, and at the close of 1924 the newspapers of the world rang with the story that the victim was the heir to the *gadi* of Kashmir. The weakness he showed in not defying the blackmailers was to be repeated nearly a quarter of a century later when he vacillated on the question of Kashmir's adhesion to India or Pakistan and the long-smouldering resentment of his preponderant Muslim subjects over the domination of a Hindu oligarchy burst into flame.

The excitement over the "Mr. A." case was fresh in public memory when on September 23, 1925, he succeeded his uncle. The Maharaja was always lavish in his personal requirements—he once had for his private use an aeroplane finished in silver—and when he visited Britain for the Coronation of King George VI he brought more than two score polo ponies.

SPORT LOVER

Though then too heavy to acquit himself well at the game, he was a lover of sport, a keen *shikari*, and prominent on the turf in India. He was a delegate to the Round Table Conference in London in 1930 and always took an interest in the work of the Chamber of Princes as a member of its standing committee.

The Maharaja gave freely of his resources in the Second World War. His well-trained state troops saw much service in the field. On the economic side the timber resources of the state were put to use, and the whole available supply of walnut was earmarked for rifle manufacture. He visited London in 1944 and much enjoyed a round of visits of inspection to fighting Services and war factories.

Advances were made during his rule in the administration of the state as compared with the medievalism of the time of his predecessor. But a strain of indolence led him to disregard signs of the times and when approached by reformers he took the line that he ruled constitutionally and must act on the advice of his Ministers. The main grievances of the vastly preponderant Muslim majority were no more than partially and grudgingly met.

When the British Government decided to transfer authority to the two Dominions of India and Pakistan in 1947 it called on the Princes of India to adhere to one or other of them. He, with three-fourths of his less northerly borders abutting on Pakistan but with his personal affinities to India, was in grave perplexity and long held his hand in the hope of being independent of both Dominions. All the time the movement for his abdication was gathering fresh strength, and there began an irruption of tribesmen from the unadministered areas of the N.W.F. Province in pursuance of what they regarded as a holy war. He intimated a desire to adhere to the Indian Union and in September asked through the Governor-General Lord Mountbatten, for the help of the Indian Army. The affirmative decision was vehemently objected to by Pakistan, and the pro-Muslim League element rallied to the Azad (Free) Army representing the widespread desire for adhesion to Pakistan.

While the complicated controversy between New Delhi and Karachi on the Kashmir issue was referred to the Security Council of United Nations, while the two Dominions were brought to the verge of war, and the invading tribesmen paid scant heed to the appeal of the United Nations Commission for their withdrawal, it became more and more clear that the personal authority of the Maharaja would not be reestablished. In 1949 his son, Yuvaraj Karan Singh, was appointed regent and three years later was elected head of the state. He himself retained the title of Maharaja and a diminished share of the privy purse, living thereafter in Bombay.

April 27, 1961.

Gordon Harker, who died on March 2, 1967, at his home in Cheyne Walk, Chelsea, at the age of 81, was a finished exponent of Cockney character parts on the stage and screen. He sprang into prominence at the age of 41 and remained for years one of Britain's most popular comic actors.

He came of a family that had been associated with the theatre for three generations. His grandfather was a friend of Irving, his grandmother was an actress from childhood, and his father, Joseph C. Harker, was the most prolific scene painter of the late Victorian, Edwardian and early Georgian periods, working for Irving, Beerbohm Tree, Oscar Asche, and other actor-managers of mark, and also for George Edwardes at the Gaiety and Daly's. Gordon was born in London on August 7, 1885, one of a family of six boys and three girls. Educated at Ramsey Grammar School, he showed no special proficiency either in learning or games, and started work in his father's studio, with four of his brothers. He displayed some aptitude with the brush, but hankered after the stage itself, and for a number of years picked up what small parts he could, going back into the studio at times when none was available. His first London appearance was at the Imperial Theatre, Westminster, on May 23, 1903, when he "walked on" in the revival of *Much Ado About Nothing* directed for Ellen Terry by Gordon Craig.

From 1904 to 1913 he was with Oscar Asche and Lily Brayton, acting Shakespearian parts, mostly in Australia. In November, 1914, he was in a revival of *The Flag Lieutenant* at the Haymarket Theatre, and soon afterwards joined the Army.

Harker's unit was the 8th Hampshires. He served in Gallipoli and Palestine and was so badly wounded in 1917 that he was unfit for further service, and was invalided out in 1919. The next year saw him on the boards again, playing an Arab in *The Garden of Allah* at Drury Lane.

He was in the 1921 revival of *Quality Street*, with Fay Compton, at the Haymarket. His Jefferson Davis, in John Drinkwater's *Robert E. Lee* at the Regent two years later was one of his few serious parts; but so far he had not done anything to strike the imagination of the great public.

One day in 1926 Sir Gerald du Maurier asked Nigel Bruce whether he knew of a good Cockney actor. Gordon Harker's name came up; he was introduced to Edgar Wallace; and he was given the part of Sam Hackitt, the "old lag" in *The Ringer*, which du Maurier was directing. The first night at Wyndham's was also the first night of the miners' strike, to be followed in a few days by the General Strike; but *The Ringer* nevertheless had a great success and a long run; and to this result Harker's splendid performance contributed a great deal. He was a treasure to Wallace, who wrote a number of plays containing parts suited to Harker's technique—such as *Persons Unknown*, *The Calendar* and *The Case of the Frightened Lady*. In the first two of these Gordon was on the wrong side of the law, in the last he was its minion, but whether he was a burglar or a detective sergeant—in situations artificial enough to make moral judgments more or less irrelevant—he had the knack of winning the audience's sympathy for his own side. Among plays by other authors wherein he excelled were two of Walter Hackett's comedy-thrillers at the Whitehall, *The Frog*, adapted by Ian Hay from a novel by Wallace, and *The Phantom Light* (1938), in which he gave a rich performance as a lighthouse keeper taking over a supposedly haunted lighthouse.

Soon after the success of *The Ringer* had elevated Harker to the rank of a star he began to receive offers of film engagements. His screen career started in 1927, and he acted in large numbers of films, including *The Farmer's Wife*, *The Sport of Kings*, *Rome Express*, *My Old Dutch*, and *Hyde Park Corner*.

FEW LAUGHS

During the Second World War he appeared in the West End in *Acacia Avenue* by Mabel and Denis Constanduros, and went on tour in his old parts in several of the Wallace plays. Since then he was seen on the London stage in Frank Harvey's *The Poltergeist* (1946), as Doolittle in *Pygmalion* to Yvonne Mitchell's Eliza (1951), as P. C. George Dixon in *The Blue Lamp* (1952), and as the old waiter and supreme arbiter of the dining room in *Small Hotel* (1955).

No less histrionic actor, no more solemn-faced comedian has recently been seen on our stage than Gordon Harker, whose acting illustrated the possibilities and virtues of significant quietness and immobility. He put on hardly any make-up, very rarely laughed or made a gesture, and for the most part kept his face in the state of non-committal blankness desiderated of poker players. This sorted well with the needs of characters like Sam Hackitt, well known to the police, always in and out of gaol, whose liberty might often depend on giving nothing away when questioned. A naturally truculent-looking underlip was exaggerated for instance in his playing of Bill Walter in *Major Barbara*; occasionally, when found out in some delinquency, there was a wonderful leer. Gordon's "business," though unobtrusive, was highly finished and he could raise laughter by some simple, impudent piece of by-play, as in *Number Six*—another thriller founded on a Wallace novel—where he took a generous swig of brandy before handing it to the fainting lady.

Though Cockney types were his best, Harker's Cockneyism was far enough removed from the Albert Chevalier kind. It was a quiet, slick, cynical Cockneyism; typical of it was the apt rejoinder, as when, asked by an officer whether he knew of any organized body of persons preying on the community, he answered: "Yus, the police"—with that little slur on the "s" that is unpronounceable except by a Londoner.

He was to have appeared in 1959 as Bill the Night Watchman in a series of W. W. Jacobs's "Night Watchman" stories adapted for television, but he was injured in a fall in December, 1958, and was unable to act.

March 3, 1967.

Lord Harlech, K.G., G.C.M.G., P.C., who died on February 14, 1964, at his London home, at the age of 78, threw himself zestfully into many roles in public life, as a custodian and amateur of the arts and in business. The yeoman service he performed for the colonial empire was outstanding. But he did nothing by halves and he will be remembered as an eager, high-spirited and sometines hard-hitting personality.

William George Arthur Ormsby-Gore, fourth Baron Harlech, was born in April, 1885. He was the eldest son of George Ralph Charles Ormsby-Gore, who became the third Lord Harlech. His mother had, before her marriage, been Lady Margaret Ethel Gordon and was a daughter of the tenth Marquess of Huntly. The Gores were Irish and had a parliamentary tradition which extended over many generations. He was educated at Eton and at New College, Oxford, of which in later life he was to become an Honorary Fellow. In 1913 he married Lady Beatrice Cecil, daughter of the fourth Marquess of Salisbury. He was a Yeomanry officer before the war and joined up in August, 1914. In 1915 he went with his brigade to Egypt. After service in the Arab Bureau as an intelligence officer, he was recalled in March, 1917, at Lord Milner's request to serve on his personal staff. From 1917 to March, 1918, he was Parliamentary Private Secretary to Milner and for a period Assistant Secretary to the War Cabinet. In March, 1918, he was sent back to Egypt and became an Assistant Political Officer in Palestine.

His political career had begun in 1910 when he contested Denbigh District and was elected by a majority of eight, the only Conservative to be returned in North Wales. He continued to sit for it until in 1918 he became member for Stafford. In his early days in the House at first he was regarded as supercilious and opinionated.

RARE VISITOR

He leaned towards the Left of his party, was a member of the Social Reform Committee and adopted an independent line with regard to the Irish Question. He also interested himself deeply in Imperial matters and travelled widely in the empire. In 1922 he accompanied his friend, Lord Halifax, then Edward Wood, to the West Indies and helped him in framing his important report. In the Bonar Law Government he was Parliamentary Under-Secretary of State for the Colonies.

During the first Labour Government Ormsby-Gore was chosen as chairman of a commission to visit and report on the East African Colonies. In 1924, fortified by this experience, he returned to his former post at the Colonial Office where he remained until 1929. In 1926 he visited the British Possessions in West Africa, and in addition to many speeches about them, produced a report which came out as a Parliamentary Paper. In 1928 he went on yet another tour, to Ceylon, the Malay States and Java, and reported on it. He said at the time that until his visit not a single person in the Colonial Office had ever seen Malaya.

He was one of the most active supporters of the Empire Marketing Board, furthering its agricultural research work with especial enthusiasm. In 1931 he became, for a brief time, Postmaster General and then First Commissioner of Works, a position for which by reason of his interest in art he had special qualifications.

In 1936 he became Secretary of State for the Colonies in succession to J. H. Thomas. In view of his long apprenticeship at the Colonial Office it was regarded as an excellent appointment. He had, indeed, begun amply to justify the general confidence in him when, on the death of his father in 1938, he retired from his office. He was created a G.C.M.G. and accepted the chairmanship of the Wheat Commission.

BANKING TRADITION

At the same time he was appointed Constable of Harlech Castle. In 1940 Lord Harlech went to Portugal to lecture on behalf of the British Council, and in the same year was appointed North-East Regional Commissioner for Civil Defence, a position in which he exhibited great keenness and activity. In the following February he became High Commissioner in South Africa and for Basutoland, the Bechuanaland Protectorate and Swaziland.

The Ormsby-Gore family have a long tradition of banking. He himself, when out of office, was for many years a director of the undertaking which ultimately became the Midland Bank—out of the London Joint City and Midland Company—and then was appointed a deputy chairman. In 1952 he succeeded his old friend and colleague, the third Marquess of Linlithgow, in the chairmanship, and held that office until 1957.

He wrote *The Florentine Sculptors of the Fifteenth Century* (1930); *A Guide to the Mantegna Cartoons at Hampton Court* (1935); and *Guides to the Ancient Monuments of England* in three volumes. He was a trustee of the British Museum, the National Gallery, and the Tate Gallery. He was also—he knew Arabic—chairman of the Governing Body of the School of Oriental Studies of London University. In 1937 he received an Hon. D.C.L. from Oxford University. In 1945 he became Pro-Chancellor of the University of Wales.

His home was Brogyntyn in Shropshire where in 1938 he was compelled to sell some of his land in order to meet death duties. It had contained a number of important family muniments which he and his father transferred to the University of Wales. His widow, two sons and three daughters survive him. His eldest son was killed in 1938 in a motor accident, and his second son, Sir David Ormsby-Gore, Ambassador in Washington, succeeds to the barony.

Febuary 15, 1964.

Professor Vincent Todd Harlow, C.M.G., Beit Professor in the History of the British Commonwealth at Oxford since 1948, died in Oxford on December 6, 1961, at the age of 63.

He was born in 1898, the son of a clergyman, and educated at Durham School. On leaving in 1916 he held a temporary commission with the Royal Field Artillery and was mentioned in dispatches. After the war he read history at Brasenose and was appointed a lecturer at University College, Southampton, in 1923.

Five years later when Rhodes House Library was being formed he was appointed the first (and only) Keeper of the Library, a post which he filled with distinction for 10 years. During that period he built up a specialist library from the amorphous Bodleian stacks and left Rhodes House as the foremost library dealing with imperial and American history in the country. He impressed his staff with the grasp and understanding he showed for library administration coupled with a knowledge of the subject matter of his shelves rare among professional librarians. His readiness to share the manual work of carting books up Parks Road remained for long an inspiration to his staff. He won their affection by his struggles with Bodley's Librarian for special terms of service for library clerks whom he was training in specialist responsibilities. Since the library was quite new he saw his opportunities were not lost; and he created in its subject catalogue a tool of research and reference invaluable in the field and unique in Oxford libraries of any size. So comprehensive was his scheme that it has remained substantially without modification.

In 1930 he was elected Beit Lecturer and he established for Rhodes House a reputation as a centre for teaching and seminar work which it continued to enjoy. In 1938, however, he succeeded Professor Newton to the Rhodes Chair of Imperial History at King's College, London, where his work in graduate seminars soon acquired a wide reputation throughout the Commonwealth. During the Second World War he worked for a time in the Ministry of Information where particularly in the preparation of weekly commentaries of the news—writing under the name of "Veritas"—his remarkable powers of exposition and advocacy proved valuable. His *Origins and Purposes* was indeed a by-product of this experience and work, an attempt to explain the new significance of the Commonwealth association in a historical perspective. In 1948 he returned to Oxford to the Beit Chair and to a Fellowship at Balliol, and brought with him much useful experience and many contacts which gave new vitality to imperial history in the University.

Vincent Harlow saw historical writing as an exacting self-discipline. His demands upon himself were no less than those upon his pupils, and many left his seminars with a strange exhilaration of dedication in the search for historical truth. He had no mercy on the half-proven fact or brilliantly prejudiced judgment. His pupils were expected to test all theories with the utmost caution and to stand alert to all bias, especially within themselves. With the undergraduate Harlow had little contact, but he sought to know the groups of men from overseas who were on the fringe and somewhat isolated from college life. For Devonshire course men and oversea graduates he provided generous hospitality at his delightful old house in Old Marston, which he had so tastefully restored and where a devoted wife, Gretta—the daughter of J.C. Badcock of Yarm, Yorkshire, whom he married in 1924—gave with personal effacement the conditions for his writing and reading. Gardening and tennis were his chief recreations and he was fond of travel.

He liked to visit colonies to get a feel of the contemporary political problems, for his interest was not solely historical. He had a strong preference for dependent territories: constitutional problems of full members of the new Commonwealth he would dismiss with impatience as being too metaphysical. He served on the Colonial Social Science Research Council battling with some success against its patronage of mediocrity. He was a member of the Commission for Constitutional Reform in British Guiana in 1950–51, and he was on the governing body of the School of Oriental and African Studies, of the Imperial Studies Committee and the Royal Commonwealth Society. In 1952 he was made C.M.G., and was permitted to supplicate for a D.Litt.

BRILLIANT LECTURER

As a lecturer Vincent Harlow had few equals in the Oxford History School of his day. His lectures were exhaustively prepared and admirably delivered. He could draw and hold large crowds; some were so enthralled by his balanced (and unscripted) exposition that they sat through the performance for a second time the following year. As an administrator he had the capacity of picking upon the main points and of combining them in a fluent and powerful memorandum. He had an enthusiasm for his subject which sometimes brought him into conflict with more traditional interests in the Faculty which tended to despise his subject.

He was a gallant, if not always scrupulous fighter, and his manner in committee would sometimes tend to irritate rather than to persuade. He could be influenced easily by charlatan allies, and pride made it difficult for him to acknowledge that he did not judge men well. In discussion once his mind had been made up (and he was often jolted into spot judgments) he stood firm: unfortunately his tendency to forget his own previous stands and decisions agreed upon with others did not make for long-term consistency or an easy harmony with his colleagues. He was a difficult superior; as an adviser he was wise and stimulating, often warm but also condescending. He could bully but always with a sincerity of intention which did much to disarm criticism.

He had a tremendous capacity for work which his comparatively small output of publications does not indicate. He wrote slowly with infinite thought and modification. He scrapped and threw away liberally. It was characteristic of both his courage and his self-discipline that he was ready to re-think and re-write his *Founding of the Second British Empire* after the Second World War when he found that what he had written prior to working at the Ministry of Information was unsatisfactory to himself. He would not patch. It was because those who were close to him knew this personal discipline that they forgave his seeming harshness. He was, despite his love of playing politics, a shy man whom it was difficult to know well. But he could unbend with children (he had none of his own) who could talk gravely and seriously to him and could laugh him out of his own earnest seriousness.

In 1923 he edited the *Voyages of Captain Jackson* for the Camden series. Then, in his *History of Barbados* and *Christopher Codrington* and his edition of Raleigh's *Descoverie of Guiana* he devoted himself to West Indian history. He was a contributor to several of the volumes of the Cambridge History of the British Empire, more particularly to the South African volume, but probably his most notable piece of historical writing and synthesis was his chapter on the New Imperial System in the second volume. The changes of mood and impulse in the middle and late eighteenth century occupied him thereafter, as he was able to illustrate the shift of emphasis in a formative period from an empire of settlement to an "informal" empire of trade. With Dr. J. A. Williamson he was joint editor of the Pioneer Histories, and with Dr. Madden of a comprehensive source book of documents on *British Colonial Developments, 1774–1834.*

December 8, 1961.

William Douglas Harmer, consulting surgeon to the Throat Department of St. Bartholomew's Hospital, died on October 24, 1962, at his home in Kent at the age of 89. He was not only well known as a pioneer in the treatment of cancer of the throat by radium, but was also a distinguished surgeon and teacher of laryngology.

His inspiration and encouragement deeply influenced the numerous students and practitioners who benefited greatly from his teaching and example. The high skill of his work, backed by patience, thoroughness, human understanding and kindness, increased the admiration and respect in which he was so widely held. He was jealous of the standards of his profession and, maintaining them himself, was always disturbed should he hear of any lessening of them.

Born in August, 1873, he came of an old Norwich family. He was educated at Uppingham and King's College, Cambridge, took honours in the Natural Science Tripos, and then went on to St. Bartholomew's Hospital, where he qualified medically, and proceeded to take the F.R.C.S. England in 1900 and the Cambridge Master of Surgery in 1901. At St. Bartholomew's Hospital he taught anatomy and operative surgery, was appointed Warden of the Medical College, and eventually, in 1904, Assistant Surgeon to the hospital. At that time throat diseases were in the charge of one of the assistant general surgeons, Harmer's predecessor being D'Arcy Power, but after his appointment in charge of the Throat Department Harmer decided to devote himself to laryngology and gave up general surgery.

Harmer served in the 1914–18 War as a Captain R.A.M.C., and made an important contribution to military surgery by his study and analysis of warfare injuries of the larynx. In 1919 he served in Russia. Before the war, in 1913, he had already begun his researches on radiotherapy in diseases of the throat at St. Bartholomew's Hospital in cooperation with Dr. Finzi and Dr. Canti, and after the war he became associated with the Radium Institute and was appointed Honorary Surgeon to the Mount Vernon Hospital, Northwood. In 1931 he was appointed Semon Lecturer to London University, and his lecture on radiotherapy in the treatment of cancers of the upper air-passages, published as a monograph in the following year, was a landmark in the progress of radiotheraphy.

RADIUM NEEDLES

Harmer treated cancer of the vocal cords by means of radium needles applied through a window in the side cartilages of the larynx, and in his skilful hands a high percentage of good results—and especially a good voice—was achieved, so that he did not ever consider it necessary to remove such growths by surgery. As time went on, other radiotherapists were inclined to employ deep X-ray therapy and radium-bomb treatment in these and similar conditions. But Harmer, to the end of his active career, considered these newer methods unduly tedious and unnecessary in his laryngeal cases and he stuck to the methods which he had introduced and which experience gave him no reason to alter. He insisted on the importance of early diagnosis in malignant disease and pointed out that however far radiotherapy might develop there was still no substitute for early diagnosis.

VARIED SPORTS

Late in life he was accustomed to go up to the Radium Institute once or twice a week and his advice was eagerly sought. He was fond of country life and in later years had a pleasant country home at Littlestone-on-Sea, where his large garden gave him great pleasure. In his younger days he was an excellent sportsman, with gun and rod, on the ice—he once skated from Cambridge to Peterborough—and on skis. He also played golf with a handicap of three and with wooden clubs he made.

He married in 1906 May, the daughter of Dr. John Hedley. She died in 1954. For many years she took a prominent part in the work of the Ladies' Guild of the Royal Medical Benevolent Fund. They had three sons; one is the head of the family business in Norwich, another a surgeon, and the third a solicitor.

October 25, 1962.

Walter G. Harrap, chairman of George G. Harrap and Co., Ltd., the book publishers, and second son of the founder, died on April 16, 1967, at his home at Banstead, Surrey, at the age of 72.

Walter Harrap was a great publisher, but he would probably have been just as successful if fate had led him to some other field of commercial activity, for he had the gift of sound financial sense and indeed plain common sense to a quite uncommon degree. Very few publishing ventures would pass Walter Harrap if they did not stand up to the closest financial scrutiny. Moreover he was a man of quite remarkable industry, ready to devote himself to any scheme that promised to increase public interest in reading and further the interests of the book trade. But this did not turn him into an unapproachable tycoon, for he was vastly interested in his fellow man, and anyone who wrote to him would receive a personal reply.

RESTORED WHOLESALER

Perhaps Harrap's greatest contribution to the book trade was made through his interest in the Publishers Association. He was elected to the Council of that Association in 1937. He became an officer in 1939 and remained in office during nearly all the war years, being President in 1941–42. He was thus concerned in a great deal of negotiation with Civil Servants over such matters as paper rationing and war risk insurance, and here he was remarkably successful because his approach was always patently an honest and a common sense one. When the former firm of book wholesalers, Simpkin Marshall, was utterly destroyed by enemy action he was among those who set it up again as (at that time) a book trade cooperative. As President of the Publishers Association he did much to insist on the adoption by publishers of the war economy standards in book production; he was also largely instrumental in securing the establishment of the Moberley Pool of additional paper.

Even before his official connexion with the Publishers Association, Harrap was casting about for ways and means of extending the sale and thereby the reading of books. For instance, he was among those publishers who negotiated in 1932 with Lord Camrose, then of the *Sunday Times*, for a National Book Exhibition, thus starting a series of most successful exhibitions held under its auspices.

After the war, Harrap continued to serve the cause of books, and in the last two or three years of his life took a most active interest in the formation of the publishers' special accounts house designed to solve for them the problem of the small account and the small order. Notwithstanding all this activity, Harrap did not neglect his own business for he not only kept it on a firm financial basis but also helped build it into one of the leading education and general publishers in Britain.

During the First World War Harrap had become engaged to Ivy Wallace, a girl in the editorial department. They married in 1920, and had one son.

April 18, 1967.

Moss Hart, the playwright and director, who died on December 20, 1961, at the age of 57, had been one of the moving spirits of Broadway for more than 30 years. In England he was better known in that capacity, and therefore indirectly, as a living legend, than directly through his work, but as part-author of *The Man Who Came to Dinner* and director of *My Fair Lady* he of course duplicated his New York success in London, while his autobiographical book, *Act One*, published in Britain in 1960, gained many new friends for him among British readers.

The elder son of Barnett and Lillian Hart, he was born in the Upper Bronx on October 24, 1904, and when he first went to work in Manhattan, at the age of 12, for $4 a week had never seen Broadway, though he was already stage-struck. While employed as office boy by Augustus Pitou, junior ("King of the One-Night Stands"), he wrote a play that was actually tried out, first in Rochester, New York, then in Chicago, where the leading dramatic critic's reference to it next day was an obituary notice bordered in black and headed: "There died at the Adelphi Theatre last night. . . ."

During the next six years Hart was a social director at holiday camps in the summer; as a professional he supported the Negro actor Charles Gilpin in *The Emperor Jones*; and at the suggestion of his friend Edward Cheodorov he directed an amateur little-theatre group at the Labour Temple in New York City in the winter. He also wrote six more plays and at last, acting on the advice of a professional play-reader, he tried his hand at a comedy. The subject was Hollywood, where Hart had never been, and of which his knowledge was derived from the weekly paper *Variety*. The result was the first draft of *Once in a Lifetime*. Jed Harris liked but did not buy it. Sam H. Harris of the Music Box offered to produce it if Hart would collaborate with Irving Berlin in turning it into a musical. Hart refused, but agreed to Harris's next condition—namely, that he should collaborate with George S. Kaufman, who already had a round dozen successes on Broadway wholly or partly to his credit. So began—in Kaufman's bedroom-study on the fourth floor of his house on East 63 Street—a partnership that was responsible for some eight hilarious plays during the next 10 years, including *You Can't Take It With You*, *I'd Rather be Right*, *The Man Who Came to Dinner*, *and George Washington Slept Here*.

WIT AND HUMOUR

According to Brooks Atkinson, at that time dramatic critic of *The New York Times*, these plays, fantastic in wit and humour, compact in form and swift in tempo, contributed something distinctive to the American drama. They were loud in humour but precise in phrasing. Their attacks on stupidity had bitterness and speed to them, there was a fury in the gags. In the same critic's view it was Hart who supplied the spirit, Kaufman who provided the discipline, of the long alliance.

Hart also collaborated with Irving Berlin in *Face the Music* and *As Thousands Cheer*, with Cole Porter in *Jubilee*, and with Kurt Weill and Ira Gershwin in *Lady in the Dark*. He directed the last-named play, in which Danny Kaye shared some of the honours with Gertrude Lawrence, and, both in America and in London, *My Fair Lady*. In his ambition to write serious drama he was to be disappointed, as the reception in 1946 of *Christopher Blake*, an experimental play, showed. "My gods were Shaw and O'Neill, but there is no room on Broadway for experiment", he said. "There is only hit or flop and nothing in between."

Hart married Kitty Carlisle, the actress, by whom he had a son and a daughter. He and Kaufman were awarded the Pulitzer Prize for *You Can't Take It With You*, a farcical comedy that, sad to recall, failed utterly in London.

December 21, 1961.

Lord Harvey of Tasburgh, BT., G.C.M.G., G.C.V.O., C.B., died on November 29, 1968, at the age of 75.

On his retirement in 1954 from the Foreign Service and from being H.M. Ambassador in Paris, he told his friends that he would not join the ranks of his colleagues who wrote their autobiographies and used their diplomatic and political experiences in journalism or public appearances. It accorded with his temperament to remain aloof. Most of his distinguished career, in fact, was passed behind the scenes, so far as the general public are concerned; the main exception was his ambassadorship in France, which was the culmination of many years of service in that country, at different periods of his life.

Oliver Charles Harvey was born in 1893, son of Sir Charles Harvey, 2nd baronet. He was educated at Malvern and Trinity College, Cambridge, and served in the First World War, first in France, then in Egypt and Palestine, where he was mentioned in dispatches.

He was appointed to the Foreign Office and Diplomatic Service in 1919 and sent to the British Embassy in Rome. In 1920 he married Maud Annora Williams-Wynn. From 1925 to 1929 he worked at the Foreign Office, in the Central Department, where he had to deal with the problems of Anglo-French, Anglo-German and Franco-German relations. In 1931 he was sent to Paris. He was there for five years and gained an intimate acquaintance with French politics, and also French literature, art and social institutions. Harvey, with his spare figure and spectacles, had the look of a serious student, and his knowledge of French culture went wide and deep.

POSTS IN CRISIS

In 1936 he was recalled to London to take up the important and onerous post of Principal Private Secretary to the Secretary of State for Foreign Affairs. He held this appointment until 1939, first under Sir Anthony Eden, then in 1938 under Lord Halifax; years of crisis.

Two months after the outbreak of war he was sent to Paris as Minister, becoming second in command of the Embassy under Sir Ronald Campbell. The anxieties and frustration of the next few months are a familiar part of the history of the Second World War, and men of stronger physique than Harvey might have been expected to break under the strain. After the overthrow of France Harvey returned to London. His acquaintance with personalities such as General de Gaulle, and his knowledge of the forces which could be counted upon to maintain resistance in France qualified him to be an authoritative adviser on Government policy on France. For some time Harvey was the director of the department of the Ministry of Information which was responsible for broadcasts to France. From 1941 to 1943 he resumed his post as Principal Private Secretary to the Foreign Secretary, at Sir Anthony Eden's request, and was then appointed Assistant Secretary of State, still with a special responsibility for French affairs.

In 1946 Harvey was promoted to be a Deputy Under-Secretary of State in the Foreign Office.

MISSION TO FRANCE

The same year he went on a special mission to Paris to discuss French and British policy on Germany with the Foreign Minister, M. Bidault. Within less than two years he was sent, for the third time in his career, to Paris, as Ambassador in succession to Duff Cooper, later Lord Norwich. Here he entered upon what was perhaps the most challenging and burdensome, but also the most rewarding period of his career. All roads, all political threads, then passed through Paris, and the great Embassy in the Rue du Faubourg de St. Honore became once more a political and social centre of the first importance; it had in fact been raised to this by Duff Cooper and Lady Diana Cooper, but the Harveys maintained that high standard.

Harvey took a full share of the work of this intensely active post, and for the first time was drawn into a public life he had previously shunned, and which, one might say, he took to from a sheer sense of duty. The ties of friendship which his predecessor had renewed so successfully in Paris Harvey extended to the provinces and to North Africa, a task which made great demands on his time and strength. Academic associations, trade unions, meetings of professional organizations, all were visited.

The tributes paid to him when he left Paris and retired from the British Foreign Service were of a marked cordiality. The French Foreign Minister, Georges Bidault, presided at the farewell luncheon and bore eloquent testimony to the fact that Harvey had worthily maintained the great traditions of his Embassy.

On his retirement Harvey was created a peer but he remained the discreet, self-effacing diplomat he had shown himself to be throughout a long and arduous career. Two public offices he did take up; in 1955 he became a trustee of the Wallace Collection, and in 1956 he succeeded Lord Bessborough as chairman of the Franco-British Society. By the death of his half brother in November, 1954, Oliver Harvey became the fourth baronet, and his elder son, the Hon. Peter Charles Oliver Harvey, who was born in 1921 and served in the Second World War, succeeds as baron and baronet.

November 30, 1968.

Christopher Hassall, the author, who collapsed and died in a train on the night of April 25, 1963, first gained recognition as a poet and made a contribution to the theatre and to opera as a playwright and librettist, but he may well be remembered chiefly for his work in the field of literary biography. His book *Edward Marsh: Patron of the Arts* is a conversation piece with a procession of well-known figures set against a background of social change. His biography of Rupert Brooke and his edition of the many letters exchanged by Marsh and himself, as yet unpublished, are now awaited with interest.

Christopher Vernon Hassall, the son of John Hassall, painter and illustrator, and the younger brother of Joan Hassall, the wood engraver, was born in London in 1912 and educated at Brighton College, the school song of which he wrote, and at Wadham College, Oxford. In the Oxford University Dramatic Society's production of *Romeo and Juliet* directed by Sir John Gielgud he was chosen to play Romeo, with the result that when a financial crisis at home forced him to go down from the University prematurely, Hassall, who had already decided that he did not have a vocation for the Ministry, turned to the stage for his livelihood. For this, too, he had no vocation, and it was as a very poor and worried young man, with well founded doubt of himself as an actor and with little hope of making good as a writer, as he desired to do, that Ivor Novello, in whose play *Proscenium* Hassall was touring, introduced him to "Eddie" Marsh at Oxford in 1933.

LINK WITH NOVELLO

It was Marsh who, on being shown some of Hassall's unpublished poems, exclaimed: "Dear boy, you're a poet." It was Novello who solved the problem of how the poet was to live, for, having shown himself capable of writing words for the songs of Novello's *Glamorous Night* in 1935, Hassall became lyricist-in-ordinary to that prolific composer of long-running British musicals. It was Marsh again who, later in 1935, told John Hassall that he wished to adopt Christopher as an unofficial son, and thus opened to him a world that would be described nowadays as the unofficial Establishment of late Georgian London, in which Hassall found his feet and from which he went out fully formed, a man, a craftsman, a personality, a conversationalist, a writer who had to be taken seriously in any of the fields in which, always loyally and determinedly, he served.

His blank verse drama *Devil's Dike,* produced at St. Edmund Hall, Oxford, in 1937, with himself in the cast, was followed by a book of verse consisting of five separate narratives, *Penthesperon,* which gained the Hawthornden Prize for him at the age of 27. *Crisis*, a sequence of sonnets, came out just before the outbreak of the Second World War. *S.O.S. . . . "Ludlow"*, published in 1941 after he had joined the Royal Artillery and had experience of ack-ack, contained in addition to one narrative poem a number of witty portrayals of the English wartime scene.

After the war he brought out *The Timeless Quest*, a biography of his friend, the actor, Stephen Haggard, originally introduced to him by Marsh; and the biography of Marsh, published in 1959, was awarded the James Tait Black Memorial Prize. By then he had held the attention of audiences on the air and in the "live" theatre with the libretto of an opera for broadcasting, *Anna Kraus*, with *The Player King* at the Edinburgh Festival, with *Out of the Whirlwind* in Westminster Abbey (the first secular play to be staged there since the Reformation), and with *Christ's Comet* at the Canterbury Cathedral Festival.

T.V. OPERA LIBRETTO

He also wrote the libretto of *Tobias and the Angel* (a television opera) for Sir Arthur Bliss, of *Song of Simeon* for Malcolm Arnold, and of *Troilus and Cressida* for Sir William Walton, as well as making new translations of *The Merry Widow* and of *Die Fledermans*.

He said of *Christ's Comet* that its style, which looks so unprogressive in the light of much subsequent verse drama, came as naturally to him as breathing and that, had he written in any other fashion, the result would have been artificial. This claim could have been made for all his dramatic verse. No doubt it did come as naturally as breathing, but the "trick" of breathing had been taught him in the 1930s by Marsh and the Georgians, and he went on practising it, or trying to practise it, even when the air about him changed in pressure. By many who did not read him he will be remembered for his recitals of poetry on behalf of the Apollo Society. Not long before his death he was the chosen partner of Dame Edith Evans, who had been the Nurse to his undergraduate Romeo in 1932, at a poetry recital commemorating Dame Edith's stage jubilee.

Hassall married Miss Eve Lynett, by whom he had a son and a daughter. He was a councillor and fellow of the Royal Society of Literature and a governor of the London Academy of Music and Dramatic Art.

April 27, 1963.

Major Lewis Aloysius MacDonald Hastings, M.C., who broadcast many shrewd and pungently expressed military commentaries for the B.B.C. in the Second World War, died on May 27, 1966, at Angoulème from a stroke suffered 12 days previously. He was 85.

His life was one of high adventure and service, in South Africa, Rhodesia and Britain. Educated at Stoneyhurst and destined for a career at the Bar, he rebelled early against authority and orthodoxy, made his way to the Cape as a boy of 19, joined the Mounted Police and plunged into the varied excitement of life in southern Africa at the turn of the century. In 1913 he was appointed to command the emergency reserve during the wave of strikes and violence which shook Johannesburg, and played a distinguished and dangerous part in restoring order. Subsequently at the instigation of General Smuts he was chosen to lead a highly successful recruiting campaign for the British and South African forces. He served in the Imperial Light Horse throughout the campaign in South West Africa, and, after the German collapse, returned to Britain, transferred to the Royal Artillery, and spent the rest of the First World War in France. He was twice wounded and awarded the Military Cross.

In 1920 he married Meriel Edmonstone and two years later returned with her to Rhodesia to farm. He was one of the principal founders of the Southern Rhodesia Tobacco Growers' Association, and in 1930 was elected a member of the Rhodesian Parliament.

On the outbreak of war in 1939 he again returned to Britain to join up. For a time he served as an anti-aircraft gunnery officer, but subsequently become one of the B.B.C.'s best known war commentators, seeing action on many fronts and making his first parachute jump at the age of 63.

In his highly entertaining book of reminiscences, *Dragons are Extra*, Hastings calculated that he gave not far short of 1,000 broadcasts.

"VON TAUCHNITZ"

At one time he delivered a series of talks direct to Germany. Bored, as he said, with the everlasting quotations from Clausewitz served up by the German military commentator, Dittmar, he created his own military sage, von Tauchnitz, whose "maxims" he quoted from time to time in support of his views. At least one German missed the joke, for he took Hastings to task for quoting von Tauchnitz but not understanding him.

After the war, Hastings settled in Britain and spent the last 10 years in happy retirement with his wife at Beckington, in Somerset.

Lewis Hastings was equally well known as a writer and publicist, as a broadcaster and speaker. He had a natural gift for narrative and oratory and this combined with his wide knowledge of Africa and African people kept him active until the year of his death.

No one who knew him will forget the force of his personality, his humanity, or his great zest for life. But for all his talents his goal was neither riches nor fame but experience; and they were privileged who shared it with him. He leaves his widow, a son, Stephen Lewis Edmonstone Hastings, M.C., M.P. for Mid-Bedfordshire, and a daughter, Anne Kerrison.

May 30, 1966.

Clarence Hatry, who died on June 10, 1965, aged 76, was in 1929 the leading figure in a financial scandal unprecedented in the history of the City of London and, as punishment for his part in it, served a heavy sentence of penal servitude.

Clarence Charles Hatry was born on December 16, 1888, the son of J. Hatry, silk merchant of Hampstead. He was educated at St. Paul's School and at 23 started business as an insurance broker.

For some years before his downfall he had been prominent in the City as a company promoter and financier. He was apparently rich, indulged expensive tastes, owned racehorses and kept a large yacht. His horse Furious won the Lincolnshire Handicap in 1920. During the post-armstice boom he was very active and organized the Commercial Bank of London—afterwards known as the Commercial Corporation of London—which went into liquidation in 1923 with a heavy loss to its shareholders. He was also responsible for the flotation of British Glass Industries, a company with a huge capital which also met disaster. Then, after an interval of comparative inactivity, he came before the public in connexion with the operations of the Drapery Trust, of which the control was afterwards disposed of to Debenham.

DEALINGS SUSPENDED

On September 21, 1929, the public learned that the Committee of the Stock Exchange had, after a special meeting, decided to suspend dealings of Wakefield Corporation $4\frac{1}{2}$ per cent redeemable stock and the shares of other companies with which he had been connected. It was also reported that Hatry and some of his associates had had a voluntary interview with the Director of Public Prosecutions. In the course of the criminal proceedings which followed, the story of a remarkable conspiracy emerged. The Austin Friars Trust, one of a group of companies which they had created, promoted yet another to take over a large aggregation of interests in the steel industry. The Hatry companies were already in some difficulty, but if the new venture had been a success he would have emerged into a great prosperity. But the enterprise laboured. A large sum was raised on the value of the steel shares to be acquired. Part of it was devoted to their purchase, the rest, and more besides, was spent on maintaining the shares in which Hatry was interested against a falling market, and he had to turn elsewhere than to the anticipated profits in order to hold on against a deficiency of nearly £1 million.

At that point the frauds began. Another of his companies, Corporation and General Securities Limited, had been formed for the issue of loans to municipalities. It had taken up several, among others three corporations—Swindon, Gloucester, and Wakefield.

READY MONEY

These loans had not yet reached the stage at which the whole of the proceeds had been paid over to the corporations or at which the temporary scrip, issued by Hatry, and taken up by one of his own companies, had been converted into definitive certificates by registration and seal at the borough treasurers' offices. Dates for successive payments to the corporations and for final registration, had, of course, been agreed. In this intermediate period the temporary scrip had been fully pledged to various banks and brokers as security for advances. But until the day of registration came no one save the issuers need have known whether or not the amount of temporary scrip exceeded the authorized limits of the loan. Nor did all the companies want all the money at once. Therefore in holding the balance of the corporations' funds, printing unstinted supplies of fresh scrip to serve as securities for fresh loans, and persuading the holders not to register it Hatry saw and took his chance of obtaining ready money.

SHARES DUPLICATED

By orders to the printers the loans to Swindon and Gloucester were increased by £250,000 each and the Wakefield loan by £400,000, £789,000 was raised on spurious scrip and £822,000 represented the amount withheld from the corporations. And as this was insufficient Hatry duplicated the shares by certain companies he had promoted and staffed through yet another of his companies Secretarial Services Ltd. In this way he raised another £700,000. The whole of the pledges were, of course, to be reclaimed and redeemed as soon as the steel ship came home; but as the late Mr. Justice Avory, who sentenced him to 14 years penal servitude, said, his was the defence of any office boy who robbed a till to back a winner. Hatry appealed against his sentence but in vain.

But in February, 1938 the Home Secretary, who was believed to have taken into consideration the help that Hatry had given the authorities in clearing up some of the financial difficulties which resulted from his operations, released him after nine years in gaol. He published *Light out of Darkness*, an attempt to devise some way of escape for mankind from the burden of armaments, and held that the causes of political and economic instability lay in maldistribution of population and the interdependence of nations. As a remedy he planned to divide the world into a few large and so far as possible self-contained economic units.

June 12, 1965.

Sir Ronald Hatton, C.B.E., F.R.S., who died at his home in Benenden, Kent, on November 11, 1965, was Director of the East Malling Research Station until 1949.

He will be remembered with affection and respect, especially by those who played their part with him in the development of great fruit-growing industries, in the first half of the century in Britain, the Commonwealth, in Europe, and in America.

Born in 1886, Ronald George Hatton was educated at Exeter School and Balliol College, Oxford, later going on to the South Eastern Agricultural College, Wye, where he subsequently joined the horticultural staff.

Hatton went to the infant Wye College Fruit Experiment Station, as it then was, at East Malling to assist Wellington, the first director. On the latter's mobilization in August, 1914. Hatton was asked to carry on the work, later being appointed acting director. With such success were the early plans developed, and such was the general recognition of the importance to the developing fruit industry in south-east England of his work on rootstocks that, soon after Hatton's appointment as director, the first major steps were taken towards the development of East Malling as an independent research station. Under his guidance it grew steadily from a field of 22 acres and a hut to the established research station of 363 acres and large laboratories, manned by a large and rapidly growing research staff, that he left on his retirement in 1949.

The pattern of the station's research in its earlier days bore throughout the stamp of his personality and drive, of his insistence on sound research as the prelude and basis of applied advance, and of his ability to bring together in its interests the many strong personalities of the day concerned in the development of agricultural and horticultural science.

WARTIME RESPONSIBILITIES

Then, as the fields of research widened, there fell to him the additional task of guiding and assisting the development of leaders in a growing number of specialist fields. Across this steady growth, marked in 1938 by the acquisition of the Bradbourne estate with its additional 223 acres of land, fell in 1939 the shadow of war. Many and wider reponsibilities undertaken to assist the national effort were met only at the cost of cherished plans; in 1945, the various wartime tasks well in hand, he faced the frustrations and difficulties of the early postwar years.

BROAD OUTLOOK

Nevertheless, it was at this period, in spite of all other claims upon him, that he found time to play his part in the early plans for both the National Agricultural Advisory Service and the National Fruit Trials, to foster the establishment of a flourishing Fruit Group within the Royal Horticultural Society, and to maintain his lifelong interest in education.

But to view Hatton as the research worker changing later to administrator would be to miss much of the breadth of outlook that enabled him to play so valuable, and valued, a part in the development—almost transformation—of horticultural science during his period at East Malling. To the good fortune of the station, and of the fruit industry, his efforts were always coloured and influenced by his abiding love of the land and all that goes with it.

MANY HONOURS

His achievements did not go unrecognized. An Honorary Fellow of Wye College, created C.B.E. in 1934, he was elected a Fellow of the Royal Society in 1944, and knighted on his retirement in 1949. Learned societies at home and overseas honoured him, but of all he set greatest store by the friendship of the growers and scientists with whom he had worked and the continuing development of the station to which he had devoted his life.

Above all he was enabled to see the fruits of his work in orchards all over the world and to see the Commonwealth Bureau of Horticulture and Plantation Crops, which he had served at its foundation as director and later as consultant director, become the acknowledged centre for the collation and dissemination of the results of research on the horticultural and plantation crops of the world.

He married in 1914 Hannah Rachel, daughter of the late Henry Rigden, of Ashford, Kent. They had one son.

November 13, 1965.

Coleman Hawkins, who died in New York on May 19, 1969, at the age of 64, was one of the two or three greatest tenor saxophonists in jazz.

Born on November 21, 1904, in St. Joseph, Missouri, he joined the Fletcher Henderson Orchestra at 19 and during his 11 years with the band gained a world-wide reputation as the first man to bring character and authority to his instrument. He played in Europe from 1934 to 1939, but thereafter made the United States his base for the rest of his life, during which he toured widely as a soloist.

The hallmarks of his style were a rich vibrato, lightning harmonic reflexes, and an impetuous rhythmic attack which he used on fast numbers to accumulate overwhelming solos, and on slower performances to weave a luxurious chain of decoration. His influence in the twenties and thirties was such that only Lester Young avoided sounding like him, and although post-war tenor players tended to follow Young's path, Hawkins continued to play as well as ever and to show great sympathy with contemporary jazz developments, even recording with such players as Thelonious Monk.

His 1939 "Body and Soul" is commonly named as his greatest record, but he commented that he had played just as well outside the studio a thousand times. A truer picture of his talent emerges from the amazing consistency on records stretching from his 1929 "Hello, Lola" to the L. P. he made with Duke Ellington in the mid-sixties; his importance as a pioneer is exceeded only by his greatness as a magisterial jazz figure.

May 21, 1969.

Paul Hawkins, the Australian racing driver, was killed on May 26, 1969, when he crashed in the R.A.C. Tourist Trophy Race, at Oulton Park, Cheshire. He was 31. Hawkins brought to the European motor racing scene, where he had been driving regularly for the past nine years, the rugged toughness that marks out a man as a professional in the world's most dangerous and demanding sport.

He was born in Melbourne on October 12, 1937. His father, William Robert Hawkins, was a notable Australian racing motorcyclist and high-diving champion of Victoria, his mother a talented gymnast and athletic coach. Having won a scholarship in mechanical and electrical engineering to Queensland University, in his teens he decided to fulfil a boyhood dream of becoming a professional racing driver and forsook his degree to become an apprentice electrician and motor mechanic.

After National Service in the army, Hawkins made his competition debut at the Phillip Island circuit near Melbourne, in 1958, and although he spun off while leading on the final lap, he won his class. More races, hill-climbs and speed events convinced the burly young Hawkins that only in Europe could he really reach the top in motor sport. In February, 1960, with £30 in his pocket, he arrived in Britain. Rapidly he made the rounds of the European tracks. Within a year, he was at the wheel of an Austin Healey at Sebring, was a member of the winning Sprite team in the Silverstone Six Hours and had competed at Le Mans. In 1962, having settled in London among the young British racing set, he joined the Ian Walker team to drive a Lotus 23 sports car, in which he won his class at the circuit where later his career ended.

In the following six years, Hawkins starred on every major circuit and in almost every category of motor racing, from Formula Junior to saloons, sports cars, and Grand Prix racing. It was in 1965, when he entered the World Championship series, that he survived the most spectacular accident of the season, driving a Formula 1 Lotus in the Monaco Grand Prix. The car ran into trouble at the chicane and catapulted into the harbour. But Hawkins, in characteristically cool fashion, kept his head, switched off the ignition in mid air, extricated himself under water, and swam calmly ashore—proof enough of his implacable temperament and swimming ability.

But it was in long-distance sports car racing, at Le Mans, Daytona, Sebring and the other endurance circuits, where Hawkins really excelled and his greatest successes were at the wheel of the Ford G.T. 40. A tall, rugged, well-built man, he enjoyed water skiing, squash, music and flying when he was away from the roar of racing cars. He enjoyed life, lived it with a sense of humour and purpose and was a popular, respected sportsman among his racing colleagues throughout the world. He was a bachelor.

May 27, 1969.

Frank Hawley, a distinguished Japanese scholar and *The Times* Correspondent in Tokyo from 1946 to 1951, died on January 10, 1961, in a Kyoto hospital. He was 54.

He was born on March 31, 1906, at Stockton-on-Tees, co. Durham, the son of Albert Hawley, and educated at the universities of Liverpool, Cambridge—where he took first class honours in Modern Languages—Paris, and Berlin. He went to Japan in 1930 and in the next decade held a variety of educational posts, among them that of lecturer at the Tokyo School of Foreign Languages and the Tokyo University of Science and Literature; during this period Hawley absorbed himself in the study of the Japanese language and literature, assembling a formidable library of manuscripts and books and establishing himself as a scholar and translator of note. For three years he was editor of the Japanese English dictionaries published by the firm of Kenyusha.

From 1939 to 1941 he was Director of the British Library and a member of the information committee, Ministry of Information, H.M. Embassy. On December 8, 1941, he was arrested by the gendarmerie, spent over eight months in solitary confinement and underwent over 100 days of interrogation. This, as he later wrote, "considerably deepened my knowledge of the Japanese mentality". In 1942 he was repatriated with other members of the Tokyo Embassy but was compelled to leave behind his important library comprising some 10,000 volumes, which, subsequently, without his knowledge or consent, was confiscated by the Japanese Government and sold. After the war some part of his collection was recovered.

Back in Britain he was for a short time on the staff of London University, was employed by the B.B.C. as an adviser on the technical and linguistic side of Japanese language broadcasting and saw out the end of the war at the Foreign Office.

He was engaged by *The Times* in March, 1946, and after a few months returned to Japan in July of that year as Correspondent in Tokyo.

POSTWAR CHANGE

It was by no means an easy assignment; the country he had known intimately was now under a predominantly American influence and it was by no means clear what course events would take. He strove hard to portray to readers of *The Times* the changing face of postwar Japan and to describe the delicate situations that constantly arose. However, his reports did not on all occasions find favour with General MacArthur, who in 1950 took exception to certain passages in Hawley's reports and mentioned his displeasure to the head of the United Kingdom Liaison Mission. This action was seen by some members of Parliament as unwarranted interference with the rights of correspondents and questions were asked on several days towards the end of June in the Commons. In reply, Mr. Ernest Davies, then Under-Secretary at the Foreign Office, said that the Supreme Commander's comments had been passed on to *The Times* but that no advice had been given and there had never been a suggestion that further action should be taken.

Hawley wrote a large number of articles on Japanese history, bibliography, and literature.

January 13, 1961.

Sir John Hay, who died on May 26, 1964, at his home at Westcott at the age of 76, was one of the leading personalities of the rubber industry of his generation. He lived for that industry and for many years he guided the fortunes of some of the most important rubber-growing companies of Malaya.

Never one to mince his words, Sir John was without doubt a controversial figure. Some may feel he held on too long to the belief in the supremacy of natural rubber in face of the encroaching competition of the synthetic product; others that he was among those public company directors who found it difficult to delegate power and foster the emergence of a younger generation. Indeed only about a year before he died a sort of palace revolution within the Guthrie empire—the nucleus of Sir John's rubber interests—led to some acrimonious boardroom squabbles. But whatever frictions there may have been, and few businesses can sail along without them, there is no doubt that the death of this strong-willed Scotsman who was such a powerful influence in the development and especially in the modernization of Malaya's rubber industry, will leave a sad gap both in the City and the Far East which he knew so well and loved so dearly.

John George Hay was born on February 1, 1888, a son of Peter Hay, of Aberdeen, and it was there that he spent his boyhood and youth. He was educated privately and went to London for clerical work in the old-established company of Guthrie & Co. Ltd., whose fortunes were to become his principal concern for the rest of his career. He rose rapidly and in its service he went out to Malaya when the company was busily expanding its activities as merchants and growers through a number of subsidiary undertakings, and he soon became a personality in the peninsula.

On the death of Sir John Anderson in 1934, Hay became head of Guthries. During his long stays in the peninsula he did a good deal of work for the Association of British Malaya, and was its president in the year 1936–37.

INDUSTRIAL LEAD

Some years before that, he was, in his early forties, chairman of the Rubber Growers' Association. His leadership in the industry was confirmed by his role as the architect of the International Rubber Regulation Scheme. During the Second World War he went to the United States to negotiate with the American authorities on rubber supplies for the war. He was knighted in 1939.

Hay retired as managing director of Guthries Estates in December, 1963. Apart from his chairmanship of Guthries he was chairman of United Sua Betong and many other companies. He had for many years been on the board of the Mercantile Bank of India, of which he was at one time deputy chairman.

In private life he was a keen sportsman—a good golfer and angler—and he was a close follower, from his early days, of cricket. For some years he was president of the Aberdeenshire Cricket Club and one of its constant benefactors. In his youth he played, too, and acquired more than a local reputation as a formidable bowler.

In 1910 Sir John married Constance Maye, a daughter of Thomas Leveritt, of Bath, and they had one son and two daughters. His wife died in 1959.

May 27, 1964.

Henry Hayden, the French painter, died in May, 1970.

He was born in Warsaw in 1883 and went to the Ecole des Beaux-Arts there in 1902. He arrived in Paris in 1907 and was soon influenced by the work of Cezanne, though a visit to Britanny in 1909 revived an early enthusiasm for Gauguin.

He is best known as a Cubist and still life painter; and painted in that manner from 1912 on into the 1920s. But his first generally recognized masterpiece was The Chess Players at La Rotonde of 1913. Hayden was a friend of Juan Gris and could reproduce effects of collage with direct oil on canvas. A highly skilled but never really tricky painter, he was taken by the doctrine of Cubism and went back to the practice of it later in life. But he had doubts of any aesthetic theory and is quoted as saying: "I hope I shall not succumb under the weight of the cube. Yet what a fine death that would be."

In 1922 he turned away from formal Cubism and then made many figurative and sensuous paintings, particularly of landscape, which might be thought nearer to the tradition of Renoir. His landscape painting—of forests, of the river Marne and of rich green countryside—is still underestimated. His later still lifes with coffee pot, mandolin, melon or basket are less tense than those of his Cubist time, but still in the great tradition. He left Paris for the south in 1940, and lost many of his early paintings when the Germans wrecked his studio. There is a certain melancholy about his best work—a purity of vision without any kind of comment which has been praised by Samuel Beckett. But his landscape drawings celebrate France and have remained fresh and admirably confident in his old age.

May 15, 1970.

John Hayward, C.B.E., died on September 17, 1965, at the age of 60.

He was an anthologist, critic and editor whose enthusiasm, judgment and scholarship made him outstanding in his generation among connoisseurs of good writing and good book production. His reputation in Britain and in America was built up in the face of a crippling physical handicap—he had been gravely hit when a young man—which he never allowed to daunt him. Sociable and pugnacious, he had friends and acquaintances in many walks of life and his flat in Chelsea, looking over the river, was for long a place of pilgrimage. He shared it with T. S. Eliot, who was one of his closest friends, for some years. As a conversationalist he could be delightful or formidable as the mood took him, and—whatever it was—it expressed itself in his strong, rugged features.

He will be particularly remembered as a textual expert—he produced among other works of scholarship, admirable Nonesuch editions of Donne and Swift—and for his exceptionally wide knowledge, reflected in his editing, of English literature especially of the seventeenth and eighteenth centuries, and of French literature. Yet though discriminating to a degree and a perfectionist he was no narrow literary man out of sympathy and touch with the ordinary reader, as his *Penguin Book of English Verse* and *Oxford Book of Nineteenth Century Verse*—which came out in 1964—abundantly proved.

Contingent to his attainments as editor, anthologist and critic, Hayward had achieved over the years a position of notable authority and influence in the world of bibliophily. Himself a discerning collector since his Cambridge days, ranging from Saint Evremond to contemporary poetry (his collection of his friend T. S. Eliot's works must be unmatched), his exhibition of English poetry at the National Book League in 1947, and the exemplary catalogue thereof, set a public seal on an already distinguished reputation for bibliographical connoisseurship; while his direction of the *Book Collector* during the past dozen years made it required reading for the collectors and rare book librarians of two continents, just as a visit to 19 Carlyle Mansions was a required *acte de présence* for any bibliophile visitor to London.

Chairbound as he was, Hayward made himself a hub of a network of bibliophile news and information, American as well as European. The results were distilled, often with a dash of pepper, in his magazine; and they were privately and generously bestowed, along with wise counsel and acutely practical advice, to the wide and varied circle of collectors, scholars, and enthusiasts who had come to value his exceptional qualities, and who realized also how heavily this dauntless invalid depended on personal contacts with the world.

John Davy Hayward was born in London on February 2, 1905, the son of J. A. Hayward, M.D., F.R.C.S., and educated at Gresham's School, Holt, and King's College, Cambridge, spending a period between in France. He was created C.B.E. in 1953.

September 18, 1965.

Francis Trounson Hearle, C.B.E., chairman of the de Havilland Aircraft Company from 1950 to 1954, died on September 1, 1965, at the age of 78. He was the first associate in aviation of Sir Geoffrey de Havilland, O.M., who died in May that year.

He was born at Penryn and educated at Trevethan Grammar School, Falmouth. He left school when 13½ to be apprenticed to a firm of marine engineers and for seven years and a half worked in the yards, attending evening classes to learn engineering. Not wishing to go to sea, he took a job with the Vanguard motor bus company at Walthamstow and it was here he met Geoffrey de Havilland. They left together armed with a £1,000 loan from de Havilland's grandfather and set about building an aircraft which first flew in 1910. The story goes that Hearle, during the first short hops, had to lie on the ground and watch for daylight under the wheels.

Both men worked in the Government balloon factory at Farnborough and in 1912 Hearle was for a short while works foreman for the Déperdussin Company at Highgate. When war broke out he was with Vickers at Erith and was given the task of starting up a plant at Weybridge and building B.E.2. biplanes which de Havilland designed.

LEADER IN EXPERIMENTS

From 1917 he had charge of the experimental shop of the Aircraft Manufacturing Company Limited at Hendon where de Havilland was the chief designer, and when the new de Havilland company was formed in September, 1920, he became works manager, and, later, general manager. He was made a director in 1922, and managing director in 1938. There were many hard decisions and developments in de Havilland's formative years between the wars, and in all of them Hearle's judgment always played a vital part. Without a doubt, however, he bore a greater load in the years 1940 to 1944 than at any other time of his life. He was succeeded as managing director by W. F. Nixon in 1944 and became chairman in 1950, in which year he was appointed C.B.E.

He married Ione de Havilland, sister of Sir Geoffrey de Havilland, in 1914. She died in 1953. They had one son.

September 3, 1965.

J. W. Hearne, the England and Middlesex cricketer, died at his home at West Drayton on September 14, 1965, at the age of 74.

John William Hearne was a member of what has probably been England's most prolific cricketing family, which in this century included J. T. Hearne, the Middlesex and England fast bowler, and Alec Hearne, who opened the batting for Kent. When he entered first-class cricket, J. W. was dubbed "Young Jack", to differentiate him from J. T.

He will go down as one of Middlesex's most distinguished all-rounders, a stylish right-hand batsman with all the classic strokes at his command; an admirable fielder and a teasing slow bowler, whom batsmen found hard to get away. He and Hendren shared many a profitable partnership and their big scores earned them the title of "the Middlesex twins", long before Compton and Edrich honourably inherited it. His batting was a model of grace and efficiency and his reputation for elegant correctness was richly deserved. If he was occasionally accused of a slow approach, this may have been because he was unthinkingly compared with the gay, exuberant, and wholly unorthodox Hendren. The fact is that in temperament and style the two were perfect foils for each other.

He never enjoyed robust health and much of his career was a brave fight against frequent indisposition. His later years were devoted to coaching and in this art, aided by his patience and a quiet, friendly disposition, he excelled.

"Young Jack" Hearne was born on February 11, 1891. He was ground boy at Lord's at the age of 15; played for Middlesex at 18; and, before he was 21, was chosen to play for the England team which visited Australia in 1911–12, making 114 in the Melbourne Test match.

SOLID DEFENCE

For the next 25 years his rock-like defence and equable temperament were as valuable a feature of Middlesex cricket as the sparkling gifts of Patsy Hendren. Though they were not always on view all the strokes were there; he was a master of on-side play and an elegant cutter; and was particularly skilful in forcing the ball square off his back foot to the off boundary.

Hearne had great gifts as a bowler of googlies: as H. S. Altham put it "his pace was almost medium in the air, his quick almost rotary action made him difficult to sight early, and on pitching his leg-break would nip across the wicket as if it was alive". But he was not blessed with the strongest of constitutions and this greatly affected his record. During his second visit to Australia, with Johnny Douglas's ill-fated team in 1920–21, he was obliged to retire on the first day of the second Test match because of ill health. Nevertheless, he brought off the double of 100 wickets and 2,000 runs in three separate seasons.

Hearne was indeed a splendid all-rounder, as his figures show. When his career came to an end in 1936 he had made over 36,000 runs, taken 1,839 wickets and 329 catches. His highest score was 285. In 1938 he and Patsy Hendren were each presented with a silver tankard by Sir Pelham Warner on behalf of the Middlesex committee.

September 15, 1965.

Ben Hecht, the American author and one of the most highly paid scenario writers in Hollywood, died in New York on April 18, 1964. He was 70.

The son of Joseph Hecht and Sarah Swernofsky, Jewish immigrants from Southern Russia, Ben Hecht was born in New York on February 28, 1894. He had an adventurous boyhood and was apparently for a short time a circus acrobat. He began a journalistic career with work for the *Chicago Journal* as early as 1910, while from 1914 until 1923 he was on the *Chicago Daily News*, the author of a daily column on the world war and then, after the armistice, in charge of the paper's Berlin office. Before that, however, he had made a start as playwright; a volume of short plays written in collaboration with Kenneth Sawyer Goodman appeared in 1912. He wrote his first novel in Berlin, *Erik Dorn*, a mocking, pessimistic piece of work, at once impressive and over-flamboyant in manner. Hecht was to continue to write novels from time to time over a good many years; specially characteristic, perhaps of his talent and temper, was *A Jew In Love*, published in 1930. But it was as a playwright that he made his mark, and it was by way of the theatre that he came very much into his own as an author and producer for Hollywood.

In 1928 *The Front Page*, written in collaboration with Charles MacArthur, proved a signal success on the New York stage. There was nothing particularly novel in this drama of the methods of "yellow" journalism in the United States, but the play was shrewdly put together and invigorated by crisp, taut dialogue. Transferred to the screen, it was a still more prodigious success. Hecht, still in association with Charles MacArthur, with whom he formed a film-producing company in 1934, was responsible for the scenario of an ingenious and intelligent film entitled *Crime Without Passion* (1934), and among later films of theirs that were out of the ordinary run of Hollywood productions were *The Scoundrel*, *Angels Over Broadway*, *The Spectre of the Rose* and *Wuthering Heights*. He also collaborated with Alfred Hitchcock in several films including *Notorious* and *Spellbound.* He had a genuine instinct for the cinema and a commanding talent for film dialogue.

Hecht's writing, which was prolific and uneven, breathed vitality and a ranting kind of gusto. Yet as he showed in a remarkable volume of five short stories, *A Book of Miracles* (published in Britain in 1940), he could draw on singularly rich reserves of rhetoric, wit, and fantasy as well as upon an impassioned religious preoccupation.

This racial and religious intensity of his lay at the bottom, no doubt, of his virulent attacks upon Britain during the concluding phase of the British mandate for Palestine. An indefatigably active Zionist, Hecht gave open and vehement support to the Jewish in Palestine, campaigning against the restrictions upon Jewish immigration into the country and against the British administration generally. As chairman of the "American League for a Free Palestine", he took a hand in traducing British motives and in helping to finance illegal immigration.

His first marriage, to Maria Armstrong, was dissolved in 1925; and he married in the same year Rose Caylor. There was a daughter of each marriage.

April 20, 1964.

Jacques Heim, Paris dressmaker and president of the Chambre Syndicale de la Haute Couture Parisienne from 1958 to 1962, who died on January 8, 1967, at the age of 67, represented the second generation of a family business which began in a modest way in the rue Laffitte, Paris, where he was born in 1899. He was also official couturier to Madame de Gaulle, wife of the French President.

Monsieur and Madame Isidore Heim were furriers; and it was thanks to his knowledge of the technical side of the business and her flair for contacts that the business by the time the young Jacques came into it after the First World War was already a flourishing concern. But change was in the air; and while Monsieur and Madame Isidore still tended to think in terms of royal commands, of sable coats and ermine wraps for the Beau- and Demi-Monde, they soon sensed that the days of the master-furrier were running out. In the brittle era of prosperity that followed the war, the dress-making business in Paris was expanding fast and it was in this direction he felt that the future of the house lay. The new undertaking, reluctantly agreed to by his parents, also satisfied the boundless energy, business acumen, and spirit of adventure that were throughout his life the outstanding characteristics of this untiringly active man.

The beginnings of the Heim couture business were in a sense a compromise—fur-trimmed coats, fur-trimmed suits. The first Heim dress was shown in 1929. At the depths of the depression in 1934, Jacques Heim moved his young couture house west—to No. 50 Avenue des Champs Elysées. Two years later the house moved to its present situation at No. 15 Avenue Matignon. It was during these years of expansion that branches were opened up in London, Cannes, Biarritz. In 1939 Heim Jeunes Filles opened next door to the parent house: it is to Jacques Heim's credit that he was the first European dressmaker to recognize the need for young girls' styles as a distinct branch of fashion designing.

Another of Heim's outstanding successes was in the domain of beachwear. In 1934 he launched the first Tahitian "pareos" in brightly printed cottons inspired by the native wear of the South Sea islands. Their success was instantaneous. Not only did the Heim pareos start an exotic taste in beachwear which has been in vogue ever since but their appearance in a high fashion house launched cotton as a fashion fabric, an innovation which the American market lost no time in putting to good account.

No one has ever claimed for Jacques Heim the gift of great creative powers as a designer; he never claimed them for himself. But he had brilliant ideas, a sense of style, love of fine workmanship and fabrics and an unfailing sense of timing. Above all he was an excellent businessman. His series of houses on the Avenue Matignon—Heim Couture, Heim Jeunes Filles, Heim Actualités—the out-of-town and foreign branches and the intricate business tie-ups with American firms have always been models of administrative efficiency.

These qualities, combined with an innate gift for courtesy and friendliness which Jacques Heim managed to keep intact through the stresses and strains of a long and often difficult business career, earned for him a unique position in the international fashion industry. His four years' presidentship of the Chamber Syndicale de la Couture was one of success and achievement.

In 1966 Jacques Heim was among the keenest promoters of the swinging line—full, "tent" dresses whirling out from a high, tight neckline succeeded each other in a daze of wonderful colours. Nothing could have been more youthful than the last spring collection, which included a bathing suit of coarse net spattered with large flowers. The more classic side of the House—and its unshakable reputation for unfailing good taste and fine workmanship—is reflected in the fact that Heim was couturier to Madame de Gaulle.

He leaves a widow and two children.

January 10, 1967.

King Paul of the Hellenes—See under **Greece.**

Ernest Hemingway's death on July 2, 1961, at the age of 61, in a sense came as no surprise to his readers.

Death was always one of his principal themes as a writer, and he had himself been confronting it directly ever since he had broken away from the suburban environment in which he had been raised to volunteer in 1918 for service on the Italian front as a driver with the Red Cross field ambulances. "By my troth, I care not; a man can die but once; we owe God a death and let it go which way it will he that dies this year is quit for the next." He was fond of the quotation and used it as a touchstone of conduct.

Ernest Miller Hemingway was born on July 21, 1899, the second of the six children of Clarence Edmonds Hemingway, a doctor with a reputation as a sportsman, practising in Oak Park, Chicago, Illinois, and Grace Hall Hemingway, a devout and musical woman. He was educated at the local High School and, after volunteering for active service in 1917 and being rejected on account of an eye injury, he became briefly a cub reporter on the Kansas City *Star*. He left for Italy in May, 1918, and was badly wounded in the course of duty in July; but by October he was serving, again as a volunteer, with the Italian infantry on the Austrian front. He was twice decorated by the Italian Government for his services.

His experience of war was his initiation into manhood and, like so many who underwent it, he spent his later life in trying to understand its significance, for the individual and for his generation. He wrote about the war itself most directly and fully in *A Farewell to Arms* but in all his writings the moral and psychological problems he had been brought face to face with in action were explored, whether in the setting of later wars or civil violence, big game hunting, or bull fighting.

ROVING CORRESPONDENT

He returned from Europe to North America in 1919 and resumed journalism, this time in Toronto with the *Star Weekly*, and, later, the *Daily Star*. He wrote for these papers until 1924 but spent the greater part of the time as a roving correspondent in Europe, covering, among much else of importance, the Greco-Turkish war of 1922. He had now the bitter opportunity of seeing how the disillusionment that followed so speedily upon the 1918 Armistice brought in political chicanery and the rise of fascism. He had married Hadley Richardson in 1921; a son was born in 1923.

He went back to Toronto in August, 1923, but upon deciding to withdraw from journalism and devote himself to fiction, he resigned from his newspaper in January, 1924, and returned immediately to Paris. Once he had begun to make a reputation, his domicile abroad was widely criticized at home as unpatriotic, but he himself knew that his experience of war had so essentially identified him with Europe that it was there alone that he could develop freely.

TRUE AMERICAN

And no matter how long he lived abroad he remained at heart and in the imagination thoroughly American.

He had earlier met in Paris, among other American expatriates, Ezra Pound and Gertrude Stein, and their encouragement and criticism of his early work were to influence him deeply, though he was later to quarrel publicly with Miss Stein. His first and second books, *Three Stories and Ten Poems*, and *In our Time* (enlarged and published as *In Our Time*, New York, 1925), which appeared in Paris in 1923 and 1924, won him some praise from the critics; his third, *The Torrents of Spring* (1926), a hastily written satirical novel ridiculing Sherwood Anderson, a friend from his Chicago days, made him more widely known; and the novel, *The Sun Also Rises* (1927) (published under the title of *Fiesta* in England), a collection of short stories *Men Without Women* (1927) and, lastly, *A Farewell to Arms* (1928) brought him fame and fortune. His deliberate, skilful, economic prose, learnt under the discipline of his earlier journalism, the complex and symbolically wounded character of his typical hero, and the sharp contemporaneity of mood and action were at once recognized as highly original and promoted him to the front of living writers, a position of eminence which he never lost. "Hemingway is the bronze god of the whole contemporary literary experience in America", Alfred Kazin wrote in 1942; but his influence was felt almost as deeply abroad in Britain and on the Continent, as at home.

AT KEY WEST

After his divorce in 1927 and his marriage to Pauline Pfeiffer, by whom he had two sons, he returned to America and made his headquarters at Key West, Florida, for the next 10 years. During this time he published another collection of short stories, *Winner Take Nothing* (1933), and an uneven novel, *To Have and Have Not* (1937); but more important works were *Death in the Afternoon* (1932), a remarkable, discursive study of bull-fighting, and *Green Hills of Africa* (1935), an equally discursive account of big game hunting. The character he offers of himself in both books so closely resembles and seems often to parody the hero of his own fiction, that Edmund Wilson remarked that this Hemingway "is certainly the worst-invented character to be found in the author's work." He rapidly became a legendary figure in the eyes of the public.

When civil war broke out in Spain, he actively supported the Republicans both by purchasing ambulances for them at his own expense and by going to Spain in 1936 to write a documentary film, *The Spanish Earth*. The most lasting result of his experience of the civil war was, however, *For Whom the Bell Tolls* (1940), often held to be his best novel. A play, *The Fifth Column* had appeared earlier in 1938.

Shortly after his divorce in 1940 and his marriage to Martha Gellhorn, the novelist, he went to live at Finca Vigia, a farm outside Havana; and after America's entry into the war he kept up an anti-submarine patrol of Cuban waters in his motor-yacht, the Pilar.

PULITZER PRIZE

Tiring of this distant activity, he went to Europe as a war correspondent in 1944 and flew on several missions with the R.A.F. When the invasion of Europe started he was so hotly involved in the American advance that he was nearly court-martialled for violating the Geneva Convention on the conduct of war correspondents. He was awarded a Bronze Star. His third marriage ended in divorce in 1944, and after the war he returned to Havana with his fourth wife, Mary Welsh.

His renewed experience of war and a desire to sum up all he had learnt in his varied career inspired him to write *Across the River and into the Trees* (1950), an embarrassingly autobiographical and unsuccessful novel, in which the mannerisms and sentiment dangerously latent in some of his earlier writing rose destructively to the surface. His career as a writer seemed about to end in disgrace but he suddenly recovered himself in *The Old Man and the Sea* (1952), a nobel and allegorical account of an old fisherman's lonely struggle in the Gulf of Mexico to land a huge marlin. The tale was awarded a Pulitzer Prize in 1953. The following year his international standing as a writer was recognized with the award of the Nobel Prize for Literature.

Hemingway said himself that he tried to write prose "which would be as valid in a year or in 10 years or, with luck and if you stated it purely enough, always". The remark illustrates the devoted artist concealed in the legendary figure, and whether or not his work will read freshly for "always", no history of the literature of our time will be able to ignore his achievement or his far-reaching influence.

July 3, 1961.

Dr. Philip Showalter Hench, joint Nobel Prize winner for medicine in 1950, for his work on the use of cortisone in the treatment of rheumatoid arthritis and allied diseases, died in Rochester, Minesota, on March 31, 1965. He was 69. Hench won the prize jointly with two biochemists, Dr. Edward C. Kendall, who was working with him at the Mayo Clinic, and Professor Tadeus Reichstein of Basle.

Hench was suddenly catapulted on to the platform of world fame in 1948 when it fell to his lot to report on the first patients treated with cortisone. It was fortunate for medicine, and particularly for the victims of rheumatoid arthritis that he happened to be the clinician to whom the first batches of cortisone, produced by his biochemical colleague, Kendall, were handed new to be investigated.

The initial results were so dramatic that the world press—and not a few medical enthusiasts—hailed cortisone as "the wonder drug" that we had all been waiting for and that at long last a "cure" for one of the world's most crippling disease—rheumatoid arthritis—had been found. Hopes were raised in this field as they had never been raised before.

Hench, however, consistently maintained that there was no question of "cure". Time would need to be allowed to pass and much more intensive trials carried out before any definite conclusions could be drawn. Undoubtedly a tremendous new field of possibilities had been opened out, but to go farther than that was not justifiable.

The intervening years have amply confirmed his wisdom and caution. Cortisone and its many derivatives have proved valuable adjuncts in the treatment of rheumatoid arthritis and many other diseases, but the longed-for cure still eludes us.

It was typical of Hench's clinical acumen that, while he immediately grasped the possibilities of cortisone, he refused to allow his judgment to be affected by the acclamation that he rightly received from doctors and laymen alike throughout the world.

He was born at Pittsburgh on February 28, 1896. Educated at Lafayette College and the Universities of Pittsburgh and Minnesota as well as in Germany, he became a fellow of the Mayo Foundation in 1921. He was First Assistant in Medicine from 1921–23.

In 1928, he was appointed Instructor in the Medical School of the University of Minnesota, becoming assistant professor in 1932, and associate professor in 1935. He was appointed Professor of Medicine there in 1947.

During the Second World War, he served in the United States Medical Corps, becoming Colonel in 1945. He was appointed after the war expert civilian consultant to the Surgeon-General of the United States Forces.

From 1932–48 he was Chief Editor of the *Annual Rheumatism Reviews* published by the American Rheuumatism Association, and he contributed about 200 articles to medical journals. He was a member or chairman of numerous medical committees and received many rewards for his research. During 1949–50 he was chairman of the arthritis and rheumatism study section of the American National Institutes of Health.

Hench married in 1927 Mary Genevieve Kahler: they had two sons and two daughters.

April 1, 1965.

John Scott Henderson, Q.C., Recorder of Portsmouth from 1945 to 1962, died on November 5, 1964, at an hotel in the Wiltshire village of Sutton Mandeville. He was 69. It was for his reports to the Home Secretary in 1953 on the evidence in the Evans and Christie trials that he came into prominence before a wider public.

Born in 1895 he was educated at Airdrie Academy and London University, where he took a first in Economics. During the First World War he served with the Royal Dublin Fusiliers and the Royal Army Service Corps, was wounded twice and mentioned in dispatches. On leaving the Army Scott Henderson entered the Civil Service and was posted to the Ministry of Health, where he remained from 1920 to 1927. In 1926 he went to Paris as secretary to the British Delegation at the International Sanitary Conference and in 1927 he served as secretary to the Inter-Departmental Committee on the Optical Practitioners Bill. This grounding in the Civil Service was to serve a useful purpose in later years.

In 1927 Scott Henderson was called to the Bar by the Inner Temple and he soon acquired a large and varied practice both in London and on the Western Circuit. In 1944 he was appointed Recorder of Bridgwater and in 1945 Recorder of Portsmouth, in which year he also took silk. His services were soon called upon by the Government and in 1949 he was invited by the Home Secretary, Mr. Chuter Ede, to sit as chairman upon a committee inquiring into cruelty to wild animals. Three years later, when the country had been alarmed by the escape of Straffen from Broadmoor, Scott Henderson was appointed by the Minister of Health to be chairman of an inquiry into the adequacy of the security arrangements at Broadmoor and his valuable experience in the Civil Service must have made his task in this sort of matter a great deal less burdensome than it would otherwise have been.

Until 1953 comparatively unknown to the general public, Scott Henderson became in that year a prominent figure when the Home Secretary appointed him to examine the evidence in the Evans and Christie trials. The anxiety felt by the public and in Parliament that there had been a miscarriage of justice in the Evans trial raised stormy issues which probably influenced the later debates on the abolition of the death penalty, but for the moment Scott Henderson was at the centre of the storm. He was given very little time in which to prepare his report, indeed only a matter of a fortnight or so, and in that period a mass of evidence and many documents had to be sifted and scrutinized. This was inevitable because one of the principal witnesses before the inquiry, which was held in private, was Christie, then under sentence of death. On July 14, 1953, the report of the inquiry was published and Scott Henderson found that the case against Evans at his trial for murder of his daughter was an overwhelming one; that he was satisfied that there could be no doubt that Evans was responsible for the death of his wife and daughter; and that the statements of Christie that he was responsible for the death of Mrs. Evans were not only unreliable but were untrue.

SUPPLEMENTARY REPORT

Certain members of Parliament were, however, unsatisfied with the report and Scott Henderson made a supplementary report which was published in September the same year answering a number of allegations made in Parliament. He pointed out that he came to his conclusions upon the cogency of the evidence which was all he could consider and not upon speculations, which could not be answered. It was said against him, among other things, that he would not receive the evidence of the priest to whom Evans had confessed shortly before his execution. Scott Henderson replied that he told counsel who represented Evans's mother and sisters at the inquiry that he would not send for the priest "as being a Roman Catholic priest I did not think that he would be prepared to tell me what Evans had said to him..." Scott Henderson had already learnt from Home Office papers that the priest had been approached but that he had said he was precluded from disclosing anything said in the confessional.

This supplementary report, however, did nothing to allay the suspicions of those who doubted Evans's guilt and Scott Henderson came in for strong criticism for the manner in which he had handled the inquiry. Though pressed by Labour members in the House of Commons, the Home Secretary, Sir David Maxwell Fyfe, refused either to hold a further inquiry or to publish the evidence on which Scott Henderson had reached his conclusions.

The storm continued to rage but as far as Scott Henderson was concerned that was the end of the matter. It was inevitable that adverse comment should be made on his reports but they were compiled in the most trying conditions; the toil was enormous and the time very short. It must have been one of the most unpleasant tasks ever given to a member of the Bar.

Although the public may remember him in grim connexions, the Bar will remember Scott Henderson as a doughty fighter, quite unshakable on his feet. Those who saw him in Court will remember the broad Scots accent and the eye-glass which was firmly screwed into his eye before some particularly penetrating question was put to a witness. He was much sought after as a leader and the Western Circuit will long remember an occasion when he was making a plea in mitigation of sentence at assizes. Having reviewed the circumstances of the offence Scott Henderson concluded by asking his Lordship to take into consideration that the prisoner had been put to considerable expense in defending the case. There was then a significant pause. The brief was picked up, the eye-glass firmly placed in position, the back-sheet scanned. "Yes", announced Scott Henderson, "very considerable expense."

At one stage it was rumoured in the Temple that he was to become a High Court Judge, but it was unfortunately not to be. His health deteriorated at this time and he suffered a severe stroke. Although his friends hoped that he would take this opportunity to lay aside the burden of a heavy practice, nevertheless, he went back to the Temple when he was sufficiently recovered, and with characteristic courage took up the reins again. He was made a Bencher of the Inner Temple in 1952.

November 7, 1964.

Patsy Hendren, the former England and Middlesex batsman, who died in a London hospital on October 4, 1962, was one of the great "characters" of English cricket.

His precise place in the ranks of outstanding batsmen must remain open to dispute. There have been few more prolific scorers. Only Sir Jack Hobbs has exceeded his total of 170 centuries in first-class cricket. Only Hobbs and Woolley scored more runs throughout their career than Hendren's aggregate of 57,610 in the first-class game. His 1,765 in 1929–30 remains a record for a West Indian season.

Yet for many years it was fashionable to say of Hendren that his bag was full of runs except in the very highest company. It was alleged that he lacked the "Test match temperament" and there were certainly a number of disappointments at vital moments in his earlier Test career. He played, however, in 51 Tests in an era when England often had an embarrassment of batting riches. He toured Australia with M.C.C. three times, under Douglas, Gilligan and Chapman, as well as going to the West Indies and South Africa. Nor does his record in Tests of 3,525 runs at an average of over 47 with seven centuries suggest that the selectors were too often misled by his triumphs in the county game.

If in terms of sheer artistry or the perfection of technique he fell below the standards of the greatest masters, there has probably never been a finer hooker of fast bowling and certainly no more wholehearted player. A short, stocky man with abundant vitality and a fine range of strokes, he was a magnificent deep fielder in his younger days and later excelled close to the wicket.

Above all, he was a lovable personality who was a tonic to his team and a joy to the spectators.

It is for this, even more than for his many triumphs for England and Middlesex, that he will be remembered. His name was coupled with "Young Jack" Hearne as those of Compton and Edrich were linked in recent years. Yet in many ways Hendren and Hearne were opposites. While Hearne was the academic of the cricket field, Hendren was the supreme comedian. His wit, his gift for mimicry, his antics—such as stopping the batsmen taking another run by pretending to throw the ball in yards before he had reached it, or by batting against bodyline bowling at Lord's in a specially made cap with three peaks and lined with sponge rubber—all won the hearts of the crowd. No player so gained the affection of the tough characters on "the hill" at Sydney, of the volatile West Indians, or of spectators at home. Yet he never sacrificed the interests of his team for the sake of a laugh.

One thinks of Hendren in terms of the homely, not the majestic. He was a very human player. In his zest for the game, in his sense of fun, in his generous help for younger players, in his warmhearted approach on and off the field, he was the happy cricketer.

LORD'S GROUND STAFF

Elias Hendren—Patsy was only his nickname, though he was known by it all the world over—was born at Chiswick on February 5, 1889. He began to play cricket as a young boy and at the age of 15 appeared for the Turnham Green club. Soon his promise was heard of at Lord's; he joined the ground staff and began playing for Middlesex colts and the second eleven.

In his early days in the county team he must have owed his place largely to his brilliant fielding and his promise rather than performance with the bat. But in 1911 came his first century—against Sussex at Lord's. His batting continued to develop, but he had still not reached the very front rank when the First World War broke out and he joined the "Sportsmen's Battalion".

It was in the first postwar season of 1919, when the experiment of two-day matches was tried, that he achieved his big breakthrough.

CHOSEN FOR TOUR

Perhaps the shorter time suited his vigorous style of play. Then in 1920 he scored 2,520 runs and was an early choice for the tour of Australia the following winter. He accomplished comparatively little on this visit or in the two Tests he played in England against Warwick Armstrong's men the succeeding summer.

Against South Africa in 1924 he scored two centuries and was again chosen to tour Australia that winter. At home in 1926 he scored his first Test century against Australia at Lord's, and was in the team which won back the Ashes at the Oval. After his most successful season in England in 1928, he had his most successful tour of Australia the following winter, when he scored 169 in the first Test at Brisbane, 95 in the last Test and had other good innings.

There remained a wonderful tour of the West Indies the following winter, a visit to South Africa with Chapman's team in 1930–31, and a third Test century against the Australians at Old Trafford in 1934, his last season in Test cricket. His career in the county game came to an end in 1937 when in his last match at Lord's he scored a sparkling century and received a remarkable reception from the crowd.

After his retirement he was a successful coach at Harrow for some years; and later had a period as coach of Sussex County Cricket Club, and more recently as scorer for Middlesex.

Hendren also played as a winger in league football in his earlier days, playing in turn for Brentford, Queen's Park Rangers, Manchester City and Coventry City. He played for England in a "victory" international in 1919.

In 1949 he was among 26 former professional players who were made life members of M.C.C.

October 5, 1962.

Jimi Hendrix, the pop musician, died in London on September 18, 1970.

If Bob Dylan was the man who liberated pop music verbally, to the extent that after him it could deal with subjects other than teenage affection, then Jimi Hendrix was largely responsible for whatever musical metamorphosis it underwent in the three years to 1970.

Born in Seattle, Washington, he was part Negro, part Cherokee Indian, part Mexican, and gave his date of birth as November 27, 1945. He left school early, picked up the guitar, and hitch-hiked round the Southern States of America before arriving in New York, where he worked for a while with a vaudeville act before joining the Isley Brothers' backing band. He toured all over America with various singers, including Sam Cooke, Solomon Burke, Little Richard, and Ike and Tina Turner, until in August, 1966, he wound up in Greenwich Village, New York, playing with his own band for $15 a night. It was there that he was heard by Chas. Chandler, former bass guitarist with the Animals, who became his manager and persuaded him to travel to England. Once in London he made a trio with drummer "Mitch" Mitchell and bass guitarist Noel Redding, called the Jimi Hendrix Experience. The guitarist's wild clothes, long frizzy hair, and penchant for playing guitar solos with his teeth quickly made him a sensation.

His playing was rooted in the long-lined blues approach of B. B. King, but was brought up to date through the use of amplification as a musical device, and his solos were often composed of strings of feedback sound, looping above the free-flowing bass and drums. The whole sound of the group, loose and improvisational and awesomely loud, was quite revolutionary and made an immediate impact on his guitar-playing contemporaries.

As a singer and composer he was one of the first black musicians to come to terms with the electronic facilities offered by rock music, and his songs and voice, influenced considerably by Dylan, created perhaps the first successful fusion of blues and white pop.

TOUR BANNED

After his phenomenal success in Britain he returned to America, where he was banned from a concert tour by the Daughters of the American Revolution, who considered his onstage physical contortions obscene. That served only to increase interest in him and he rapidly became one of the world's top rock attractions. Then, at the beginning of 1969 and at the height of his fame, he disappeared and spent more than a year in virtual seclusion, playing at home with a few friends. Early in 1970 he unveiled a new trio, the Band of Gipsies, and returned to Britain in August to play at the Isle of Wight festival. In his last interview he was quoted as saying that he'd reached the end of the road with the trio format, and was planning to form a big band.

In direct contrast to the violence and seeming anarchy of his music, Hendrix was a gentle, peaceful man whose only real concern was music. His final public appearance was when he sat in with War, an American band, at Ronnie Scott's club in London two days before he died, and it was typical of the man that it was he who felt honoured by being allowed to play.

September 19, 1970.

Sonja Henie, who died on October 12, 1969, at the age of 59, was one of the great innovators of sport, for she transformed ice skating from an esoteric pursuit into a popular pastime for the millions.

She won her first world championship in front of her own compatriots at Oslo in 1927 at the age of 17 and thereafter remained supreme for a decade, captivating the spectators with her ready smile and blond good looks. She carried off three Olympic gold medals, in 1928, 1932, and 1936, as well as her 10 world championships, before yielding to the Hollywood dollar.

Sonja Henie was an enormous success as a film actress, or rather as a skater in films, for she never reached any great heights in acting itself. It was enough, however, for her merely to be there, such was her charm and superlative skill on the ice.

EARNED A FORTUNE

Her films, of course, always had a winter sports setting and so popular were they that in 1938 her name appeared among the ten most lucrative attractions at the box office, in the wake of *One in a Million*, *Thin Ice*, *My Lucky Star*, and *Sun Valley Serenade*. She earned a fortune running into many millions of dollars.

By modern standards her talent as a skater is now seen as a little exaggerated, but this is the cross that all champions have to bear. There is a mounting pyramid of endeavour and those that follow always have the advantage of hindsight. But in her day she was clearly supreme.

She was married three times, to Dan Topping from 1939 to 1946 (becoming an American citizen in 1941), to Winthrop Gardiner from 1949 to 1956, and finally to Niels Onstad from 1956 until her death. In later years she developed a passion for the arts and, having gathered together the best collection in Hollywood, she went home to Norway to open an arts centre in Oslo as a gift from her and her husband.

Sonja Henie was an original whose passing will be mourned not only by those who took a deep technical interest in ice skating but also by the simple folk in all quarters of the earth who were whisked away from their 1s.3d. seats in the gallery to a winter wonderland that in the real world was out of their reach. It was an experience that young people of today would find hard to understand.

October 13, 1969.

Emile Henriot, considered by many to be one of the greatest French literary critics of this century, died in Paris on April 14, 1961, at the age of 72.

From his earliest years a literary journalist, Emile Henriot was equally a prolific and distinguished poet, novelist, essayist, and historian. In short, he devoted his life to letters and to the furtherance of French culture. Right up to the week in which he died he contributed weekly articles of great length and profundity to *Le Monde* and was an active president of L'Alliance Française as well as being a distinguished *Immortel* of the Académie Française.

Born in 1889, son of Henri Maigrot, a well known illustrator of literary magazines, whose *nom de plume* his son was to adopt, Emile Henriot grew up in an atmosphere where literature was cherished. His first article, on Barrès, was published in *Charivari*, of which his father was editor. Before joining the newspaper *Le Temps* in 1911 he had already published three volumes of poems. In journalism he started as a reporter and covered notably the theft of the Mona Lisa from the Louvre.

HEALTH SUFFERED

The 1914–18 War, in which he served voluntarily, interrupted his career and damaged his health but characteristically he published notes of his experiences as a dragoon. In 1919 he wrote his first novel and many more were to follow, notably *Aricie Brun* or *Les Vertus Bourgeoises*, which won him in 1924 the prize of the Académie Française, *Les Occasions Perdues* and *Tout va Finir*.

He also wrote many short stories, demonstrating that his personal creative achievement was never diverted by his professional involvement in the works of others. From 1919 to 1942 he was literary critic of *Le Temps*, a post which he continued with the newly founded *Le Monde* from the liberation to the present day.

In this post he became a sympathetic historian and commentator on French literature. In the course of his weekly articles over 30 years he examined the new and the old, the famous and the ignored, always expressing the essence and looking first for the praiseworthy before condemning the bad.

His novels, most of which were written

between the wars, revealed percipient and warm understanding of people and are memorable for their vivid picture of contemporary society. His warmth and humanity were also apparent in his books of souvenirs and meditations on countries visited and people he had known.

As president of L'Alliance Française, a post which he had held since 1948, he became known personally to many people abroad. Distinguished-looking with moustaches à la Gaulloise he seemed to many the typical, elegant, cultured and amiable Parisian. He was this but much more besides, and was esteemed by all who met him.

In 1921 he married Germaine Gounod, granddaughter of the composer, who survives him, together with two sons. In 1959 he received from General de Gaulle the insignia of a Grand Officer of the Légion d'Honneur.

April 17, 1961.

Sir Basil Henriques, who devoted his life to youth work in the East End of London, died in a London hospital on December 2, 1961, at the age of 71. For 19 years until his retirement from the position in 1955, he was chairman of the East London Juvenile Court. In a bare and drab court room he presided with a warmth of understanding and sympathy that was as much constructive as judicial.

For nearly 50 years he gave wholehearted assistance to the boys' club movement. All this time—with the exception of war service and lecture tours abroad—he lived in the East End. Nor did this aspect of his work cease with his retirement from the Bench. At the time of his death he was vice-chairman of the National Association of Boys' Clubs.

Basil Lucas Quixano Henriques, who came of an Anglo-Jewish family which settled in England in the earlier half of the eighteenth century, was born on October 17, 1890, one of the several sons of David Q. Henriques, of Manchester and London. Educated at Harrow and University College, Oxford, he entered the Army on the outbreak of war in 1914, serving in the 3rd Battalion of The Buffs. After about a year's service he was seconded to the newly formed Tanks Corps, with which he served until the end of the war, rising to the rank of captain. For his services he was awarded the Italian Silver Medal and was mentioned in dispatches twice.

WORK FOR BOYS

While at Oxford Henriques decided to devote his life to public and social service, especially among boys. On coming down he set about founding the Oxford and St. George's Club, but had only succeeded in doing so when the First World War broke out. While he was on active service the clubs—a girls' club had been added—were carried on by his wife, Rose, only daughter of James H. Loewe, whom he married in 1916. Throughout the rest of his life she gave him unflagging support, helping him with his youth club work and accompanying him on lecture tours overseas. They had no children.

On leaving the Army he resumed his work in St. George's and for the next 30 years this absorbed much of his life. The club developed, thanks to the generosity of the millionaire-philanthropist Bernhard Baron, into an East End settlement, the Bernhard Baron—St. George's Jewish Settlement, and was the centre of innumerable activities. Henriques became the honorary warden. The club, which had 25 members in 1914, has today a membership of more than 3,000. One generation after another of the boys who came under his influence grew up and went out into the world, but Henriques lost touch with few of them. When the Second World War broke out there were Bernhard Baron boys and former boys in every branch of the British services everywhere and with a large proportion of these he remained in correspondence throughout. He retired as warden in 1947.

With the Oxford and St. George's Club as a beginning Henriques's influence spread into the larger Lads' Club movement, and it was not long before he was recognized as one of the leaders of the social service movement among boys and adolescents.

As a magistrate Henriques understandably confined himself to children's courts. When he retired in October, 1955, as chairman of the East London Juvenile Court he had behind him 32 years' service on the Bench, during which he had acquired an enviable reputation as an expert on the problems of juvenile crime. He served as a member of the Consultative Committee of the Home Office for London Juvenile Courts, and also for a long period of the house committee of the London Hospital.

Much of his writing was in the form of sermons and articles on boys' club work and juvenile delinquency, but he also published a number of books, including *Club Leadership* (1933), *The Indiscretions of a Warden* (1937), *The Indiscretions of a Magistrate* (1950), *and The Home Menders* (1955).

In the Jewish community, apart from his membership of the executive committee of the Jewish Orphanage and his chairmanship of its Boys' After-care Committee, Henriques's special interests were in Judaism and in Zionism. The Henriques family has for long been prominent among the advocates of reform and liberalization in the ritual and observances of their faith. Henriques went in this even beyond his predecessors and he counted among the leaders of the extreme reform movement, that of the Liberal Jewish Synagogue.

He was created C.B.E. in 1948 and knighted in 1955.

December 4, 1961.

Colonel Robert David Quixano Henriques, M.B.E., writer, broadcaster and farmer, died on January 22, 1967, in London at the age of 61. Besides two prize-winning novels, *No Arms, No Armour* and *Through the Valley*, Henriques wrote the biographies of two tycoons, Marcus Samuel and Sir Robert Waley Cohen.

In 1939 Robert Henriques published *No Arms, No Armour*, which was very highly praised. It is fair to assume that a good deal of it is autobiographical at a discreet remove, for, like its hero, he had served as a gunner officer in the Regular Army in Egypt and the Sudan and then found a new profession after several months in hospital following a riding accident. But *No Arms* was published at an inauspicious time and Henriques returned to the Army to serve with one of the early commandos and later at the headquarters of Combined Operations.

He was always an enthusiast and he found a hero large enough to satisfy his enthusiasm in that controversial figure, the American general George Patton. It is possible indeed that he did himself some disservice by letting his admiration become too widely known for he was never unduly hampered by discretion. After the war he took to farming in the Cotswolds and from a very modest beginning his new enterprise grew to an impressive size and he had some outstanding successes as a breeder of cattle. But writing remained his strongest interest and in 1950 his excellent novel *Through the Valley* was given the James Tait Black Memorial Prize.

That was followed by a powerful tale told with great assurance but never properly appreciated called *Red Over Green* and in 1951 the memorable short history of an even shorter campaign *100 Hours to Suez*. Henriques had discovered his last and perhaps his greatest enthusiasm. He had always been very conscious that he was a Jew but not until his late forties did he take pride and pleasure in his birth.

He achieved distinction as a soldier, as a writer, as a farmer. He travelled widely and talked with zest and brilliance. He knew the points of a horse, he reared pheasants and bought pictures with a fine, positive judgment. But he was not easy to please and for several years his health had been poor.

Henriques's biography of Marcus Samuel (1960), the great oil pioneer and leader of the Jewish community, was a full one: like that of Sir Robert Waley Cohen (1966) both were concerned with the foundation of the Royal Dutch-Shell group.

In 1950, Henriques contributed an essay on the Cotswold country to a series of "personal books on the English scene". His novel *A Stranger Here* (1953) was also set in the Cotswolds. His account of his journey to Darfur in the Sudan appeared as *Death by Moonlight* in 1938.

Henriques was born on December 11, 1905, and educated at Lockers Park, Rugby, and New College, Oxford. He joined the Royal Artillery in 1926, and served in Egypt and the Sudan, retiring in 1933. In the Second World War he served in the Royal Artillery, Commandos and Combined Operations Headquarters. In 1961 he was Cavendish Lecturer. He also broadcast a great deal, appearing on *Any Questions* and television debates and discussions. In 1928, he married Vivien Doris, daughter of Major W. H. and the Hon. Mrs. Levy, and there were two sons and two daughters of the marriage.

January 24, 1967.

Christian Herter, who died on December 30, 1966, at the age of 71, succeeded John Foster Dulles as Secretary of State in 1959 and remained until the end of President Eisenhower's Administration. In November, 1962, President Kennedy appointed him his special representative for the trade negotiations with the Common Market, later known as the Kennedy Round. President Johnson confirmed him in the job, which he held until his death.

As Secretary of State Herter presided over an important transitional phase in American foreign policy. The cold war confrontation with Russia was slowly giving way to a search for areas of agreement and understanding. President Eisenhower wanted to leave office as a man who had made peace more secure by seeking accommodation with Russia. The death of Dulles made the transition easier. Herter had none of the legalistic and crusading zeal of his predecessor. He was firm in his principles but flexible and pragmatic in his methods. A firm believer in the possibility of finding limited areas of agreement with the Russians, he was an early advocate of a test ban treaty and of efforts to prevent the proliferation of nuclear weapons.

While he achieved relatively little in practical terms he helped to prepare the way—both in the diplomatic world, and politically at home—for the policies of President Kennedy. Many of America's friends and allies abroad also found his gracious and gentle manner, and his intimate knowledge of Europe, provided a refreshing change from the abrupt and dogmatic manoeuvrings of Dulles. As the *New York Times* said, he "created an easier atmosphere in the top levels of the alliance".

For reasons of both temperament and conviction he was willing to leave most of the limelight to the President, which meant, among other things, that his own reputation suffered little from the failure of the Paris summit conference of 1960, particularly as he had already expressed scepticism beforehand.

TYPICAL BOSTONIAN

But if his brief tenure of the State Department was seen by many as an interlude it was in some ways at least a creative interlude.

Christian Archibald Herter was born in Paris in 1895. He was often spoken of as a typical Bostonian because of his appearance, his speech, his patrician manners, but in fact his grandfather was an emigrant to America from Stuttgart. His grandfather was an architect and in America made a considerable fortune as the designer of mansions for rich Americans.

His parents were artists who spent a great deal of time abroad, and he received his early schooling in the French capital. He did not see his home land until he was nine, by which time he was as familiar with French and German as he was with English. From 1904 to 1911 he went to school in New York and then went on to Harvard, where he took his B.A. in 1915. After that he started to follow in his grandfather's footsteps, studying architecture at Columbia University. The appeal of politics and journalism however proved much stronger than that of architecture.

In 1916 he entered the foreign service and was posted to Berlin as an attaché. The end of the First World War found him serving as secretary to the American commission which helped to draft the peace treaty of Versailles. After Versailles he served in Europe with the Hoover Relief Administration.

RETURN TO AMERICA

On returning to America he lectured at Harvard for a year on international relations and then entered journalism. He was editor of *The Independent* in Boston from 1924 to 1928 and associate editor of *The Sportsman*, also in Boston, from 1927 to 1936. It was during his journalistic career that he entered domestic politics, being elected to the Massachusetts legislature in 1931. He remained there for 12 years, four of which he served as Speaker of the House. In 1943 he ran for Congress. He was returned and remained there nine years, establishing a reputation as a liberal Republican. In 1947 he introduced a resolution which led to the establishment of a House Select Committee on Foreign Aid, which he then headed. The report produced by the committee after a tour of 18 countries did a lot to gather support and prepare the ground for the Marshall Plan.

During his fifth term he stood for the governorship of Massachusetts. He won by a narrow margin when President Eisenhower carried the State in his first presidential race, and considerably increased his majority when he won a second term. In 1956, and on another occasion, groups of supporters put his name forward as a candidate for the presidency.

Herter became a member of the President's official family in 1957 when he was appointed Under-Secretary of State, his chief being John Foster Dulles. His name appeared seldom in the press in the following two years but he worked steadily and quietly in the department. When Dulles resigned in 1959 Herter immediately became acting Secretary and then in April of that year Secretary.

In Congress his name was always linked with bipartisanship in foreign policy. He was popular on both sides of the aisle and later his appointment as Secretary of State was almost unique in that scarcely a voice was raised in in the opposition party to his appointment.

A STRIKING FIGURE

He was a striking figure despite crippling arthritis which necessitated the use of crutches through a good deal of his life. He stood 6ft. 5in., was easy going, affable and known to hundreds as "Chris". His outlook was cosmopolitan and he knew how to get along with politicians and with the Press. His voice was quiet, his eyes kindly and President Eisenhower once said of him, "When you look at him you know you're looking at an honest man".

At the end of his first year as Secretary of State he came in for praise for his work from the press. He was then described as having a receptive and retentive mind, a quick grasp of ideals, always open to fresh views and always refusing to be bound by narrow legalisms. Unlike his predecessor, he had a mind cast in the political mould, realistic, pragmatic, flexible. He was largely responsible for the President's goodwill tours to Asia and Latin America that were so successful. He took the lead in 1959 during the Geneva meeting of the Big Four foreign ministers in arranging the personal meeting between Mr. Eisenhower and Mr. Khrushchev.

Perhaps one of his major achievements was the undramatic one of reestablishing confidence and morale in the State Department, using the knowledge and experience of his associates and improving the staff work of the department. He married in 1917 Mary Caroline Pratt and they had three sons and one daughter.

January 2, 1967.

Dame Myra Hess, D.B.E., the concert pianist, died at her home at St. John's Wood, London, on November 24, 1965. She was 75.

That she was more than a distinguished pianist is attested by the honours which came to her. Honorary doctorates of Durham, London, Cambridge, Manchester, Leeds, St. Andrews, and Reading and her title, Dame of the British Empire, conferred in 1941, primarily in recognition of her establishment of daily concerts at the National Gallery as a war-emergency service, were public recognition that she gave to music more than virtuosity on her instrument, more even than many years of sane and poetical interpretation of pianoforte classics.

She was not in the least a solemn person, though she had a proper appreciation of music's significance and social value. There emanated from her presence on the platform, as from her actual performances, a combination of integrity and geniality. Her arrangement of Bach's figured chorale "Jesu, Joy of man's desiring" made her name a household word among amateurs and non-musicians.

TEACHING MODEL

Myra Hess was born in London on February 25, 1890, and began her education at the Guildhall School of Music under Julian Pascal and Orlando Morgan, but in 1902 she won a scholarship at the Royal Academy of Music and came under the late Tobias Matthay, becoming one of his earliest as well as one of his most distinguished pupils. In Matthay's textbook on muscular relaxation she and Vivian Langrish are the models for the exercises which formed the basis of his method of teaching. In 1907 she came before the London public in a Queen's Hall concert conducted by Beecham, at which she played Beethoven's fourth piano concerto, an auspicious and prophetic choice. She must have played it hundreds of times—for many years it was a highlight of the Promenade concerts—yet more than 40 years afterwards it was still a revelation every time she came to it. Her success was immediate and engagements to play concertos, to give recitals and to take part in chamber music soon made her eminent. Her devotion to chamber music was never extinguished by the greater personal and material rewards of the other forms of concert giving. When she stayed at home to establish the National Gallery concerts in 1939 instead of going off on a lucrative American tour she confessed that one of her rewards for so doing was the opportunity it gave her to take part once more in chamber music. This she did with the Menges and Rosé quartets, and with Miss Isolde Menges in duet sonatas.

LARGE REPERTORY

She had a big repertory—the result of a remarkable facility in reading and an equally remarkable memory—and at an early stage in her career laid the foundations of it with the other concertos of Beethoven; all the concertos of Mozart, which she subsequently played at the National Gallery and during the Festival of Britain, 1951; the popular Schumann and Grieg concertos, which she treated as the small lyrical pieces they are; and the two big Brahms concertos, which perhaps suited her less but were well within her intellectual capacity. Her catholic taste embraced the virginalists, the sonatas of Scarlatti and late Beethoven, Bach and the romantics, and her own contemporaries and juniors. There was in her character and in her playing alike a mixture of strength and graciousness—she could be very pertinacious—which more than technical brilliance made her an artist of international reputation. She was one of the few English artists to establish herself as a musician of the front rank not only at home but in many European countries and in the United States.

The National Gallery concerts, which ran from the autumn of 1939 throughout the war to April, 1946, formed an episode of a unique character in her career and in English musical history. She had some help from Sir Kenneth Clark, then Director of the National Gallery, and from Howard Ferguson, and encouragement from one or two other musicians, but the idea, the initiative, and the plan of giving daily lunch-hour concerts at a cheap flat rate price of admission was hers. She launched the scheme with a recital, planned the programmes, and presided over the committee which ran it.

LEADER OF MUSICAL LIFE

The concerts met an acutely felt need and immediately took their place as one of the stable features in London's disrupted life. They ran uninterruptedly all through the bombardments, nocturnal or matutinal, for six and a half years. Queen Elizabeth the Queen Mother went more than once and their value to the nation was recognized by the founder's promotion in the Order of the British Empire from Commander (conferred in 1936) to Dame. She was during that grim time the leader of our musical life. Only when, in 1946, the emergency was past and the concerts came to an end did she feel able to accept the many pressing invitations she had received to play abroad again. She continued to play for another 16 years when recurring arthritis brought about her retirement. She received affectionate tributes three years later when she celebrated her seventy-fifth birthday.

November 27, 1965.

Hermann Hesse, the novelist and poet, died on August 9, 1962, at his home in Montagnola, Switzerland. He was 85.

Born in Southern Germany but a Swiss resident since 1912 Hesse commanded a larger public in Germany than perhaps any other contemporary writer, ranking with Thomas Mann and Brecht in regard. Nevertheless, outside the German-speaking world he was little known until he won the Nobel Prize for Literature in 1946. Even in Germany he had been an outsider withholding himself from literary cliques and movements. In his work the appeal is to the solitary reader: there is a deep mutual correlation between writer and his public; an appraisal of his writing reveals at the same time certain trends of German character for, though he gave up his German nationality, he was in inheritance and mental make-up intensely German. In England he drew some distinguished attention but not wide popularity and for long little of his work was available in Britain in translation.

Born on July 2, 1877, at Calw, in Württemberg. Hermann Hesse was the son of a missionary of Estonian origins, who had spent much of his life in the East Indies. For a brief space he studied theology at Tübingen University, but, having thrown over the family tradition, he set up as a bookseller in Tübingen and afterwards at Basle. At the same time he began to write verse—his first volume, *Romantische Lieder*, appeared in 1899—and then turned to short stories and full-length novels, of which the earliest *Peter Camenzind* (1904) brought him success. He spent two years in the East, chiefly in the Indies, and the fruit of his philosophical studies and meditations there is to be found in several of his volumes, notably *Siddhartha*, which appeared in 1922.

His novels, which appeared at fairly regular intervals during the twenties and thirties, reflect a contemplative and uneasy mind, a German cast of non-political sentiment, pacifist leanings, and a miscellany of literary influences—Novalis, Dostoevsky, Hindu and Chinese philosophy. *Steppenwolf* (1927) is perhaps as fair an example of his work as any, although *Narziss und Goldmund* (1930), which pursues a not dissimilar antithesis in a vague German medieval setting, is in some ways clearer in symbolical intention and exhibits to better purpose Hesse's characteristically German feeling for the romantic aspects of Nature.

The *magnum opus* of his old age, for which he was awarded the Nobel Prize, was *Das Glasperlenspiel* (*Magister Ludi*), a long sprawling novel of 900 pages, a biography of Joseph Knecht who attains great fame in Castalia as a master of the spiritual discipline and mental stimulant known as the "Bead Game" and who ultimately rejects the game's unreal purity to investigate the corrupt outer world.

Between the wars Hesse travelled a good deal in western Europe.

He was a friend of Romain Rolland, who held him in high esteem as a man and writer, of Thomas Mann and other eminent literary figures.

August 10, 1962.

Sir Hector Hetherington, G.B.E., who died on January 15, 1965, in the Westminster Hospital, London, at the age of 76, was for quarter of a century Principal and Vice-Chancellor of Glasgow University before his retirement in 1961.

Hector James Wright Hetherington was born in Cowdenbeath in July, 1888, and brought up in Tillicoultry in the shadow of the Ochil Hills. He was educated at Dollar Academy, of which he was later a governor, and went up to Glasgow University in 1905, taking honours in classics and then in philosophy. Under the influence of Sir Henry Jones, Professor of Moral Philosophy from 1894 to 1922, education became for him a form of social service; knowledge was of value chiefly as an instrument of social betterment. One of the causes to which he long remained devoted was the Glasgow University Settlement. He was later (in 1924) to write a life of Sir Henry Jones.

Hetherington was a contemporary at Glasgow of Walter Elliot and O. H. Mavor ("James Bridie") but he was never quite of their company; he preferred the study and the library to the Union and the *Glasgow University Magazine*. From 1910 to 1914 he was lecturer in Moral Philosophy at Glasgow; from 1914 to 1915 lecturer at Sheffield; and in 1915 he went to the University College of Cardiff as Professor of Logic and Philosophy. It was, however, in his next post that he made his name as an administrator. In 1920 he was appointed Principal and Professor of Philosophy at the small University College of the South-West at Exeter, at a time when it was not yet in receipt of state aid from the University Grants Committee. Hector Hetherington used to tell with great glee how he persuaded the U.G.C. to visit Exeter and on the spot so impressed them that they decided to give Exeter official standing. He greatly appreciated the honorary degree Exeter conferred on him when it reached full university status in 1957.

PRINCIPAL AT LIVERPOOL

In 1924 Hetherington returned to Glasgow to succeed A. D. Lindsay as Professor of Moral Philosophy. But he stayed only three years and in 1927 was appointed to Liverpool as Principal and Vice-Chancellor. In 1936, the year he was knighted, he returned to his *alma mater* as principal.

Hector Hetherington was a professor at 27 and a university principal at 32. His rapid elevation prevented the major contribution to philosophy of which he was capable. He published in 1918, with J. H. Muirhead, his study *Social Purpose* and, after a spell at the end of the First World War when he was attached to the International Labour Conference, he wrote *International Labour Legislation.* Yet he was a superb writer with a markedly characteristic style, warm and evocative.

It would be hard to exaggerate the value of his work as Principal and Vice-Chancellor at Glasgow. It fell to Sir Hector Hetherington to find, in the midst of the Clydeside depression, money for a new building or two. A new chemistry building was begun, and in 1939, a delightful students' reading room was completed. It fell to him to guide the University through the six years of war, to watch over its physical safety on its all-too-identifiable eminence above the winding river, to steer its staff into the right war-time jobs, and to prepare for the new world of 1945—a world of sudden university affluence. For as students came in in great numbers, so did capital grants for building. The U.G.C. grant to Glasgow in 1938-39 was just on £100,000. Twenty years later it was just on £2m. In the years from 1946 to 1961 the site on Gilmorehill was transformed: there appeared a synchrotron, a new engineering building, a new modern languages building, a new chemistry and physics building, a virology building, a gymnasium that is one of the best in the country, to name but a few. In these physical achievements Sir Hector took great pride; as he did also in the generosity of Glasgow men to the University, not least the late Herbert Ross, the late Sir Daniel Macaulay Stevenson, of whose funds Sir Hector was principal trustee, and Sir Isaac Wolfson. He played no small part himself, as a master tactician, in this benevolence. He was, to use his own phrase of Sir Henry Jones, "an excellent beggar".

GOOD CITIZENSHIP

Yet Glasgow, if the centre of Sir Hector's world, was never its only part. He practised the good citizenship he preached. He served on many commissions, especially on unemployment and labour relations. He was chairman in 1935 and 1937 of the Board of Enquiry into Wages Agreement in the Cotton Industry, in 1939 of the board that inquired into workmen's compensation. He visited the Indian universities in 1955 to advise the Indian Government; he headed the commission in 1957 that investigated the Royal University of Malta. He was twice chairman of the committee of vice-chancellors and principals. He was for 25 years an adviser to the Leverhulme research fellowship scheme and was almost continually, from their inception in 1925 to 1957, a member of the Committee of Award of the Commonwealth (Harkness) Fellowships. He was a frequent visitor to the United States and Canada; in 1957 he was awarded the Howland Prize at Yale. As the Senior Vice-Chancellor not only of the Universities of Britain but of the Commonwealth, in 1957 he presided over the great Conference of the Universities of the Commonwealth held in Montreal. He was awarded honorary degrees by a score of universities at home and abroad. In 1948 he was created K.B.E. and in 1962 he was raised to G.B.E.

Sir Hector Hetherington had a career of rich satisfaction and of uniform success. He represented everything that was best in the Glasgow tradition: friendly, unpompous, shrewd and very wise. Although administration became his task, he never forgot that he was handling people; he knew intimately the problems and interests of his large staff both at Liverpool and Glasgow; he was a real father of his vast academic family. He could relax easily; he valued exercise, kept remarkably fit and gave all credit to golf, at which he was very expert. He was no recluse; he loved the companionship of his colleagues, and never more than when they were beating the old enemy, the Senators of Aberdeen, in the annual golf match that marked the end of the academic year.

It was, however, in his home that he was seen at his best. He married in 1914 Alison Reid, herself of Tillicoultry and a Glasgow University graduate—they were rivals as students before they merged their academic rivalry in a devoted partnership. There were two sons of the marriage, of whom the younger, Alastair, is editor of *The Guardian*.

January 16, 1965.

Professor Theodor Heuss, first President of the German Federal Republic, died at Stuttgart on December 12, 1963, at the age of 79. He had been in uncertain health since the amputation of a leg in August.

Theodor Heuss was born on January 31, 1884, at Brackenheim, a small town in the Neckar Hills of Württemberg. His early background was strongly Liberal, for not only had his grandfather fought on the barricades of 1848, but his grand-uncle had suffered long imprisonment after the failure of the revolution. Later he came under the influence of Friedrich Naumann, whose ideas were to mean much to the young student of economics and sociology, and finally as a pupil of Luio Brentano, Munich's great liberal economist. It was soon apparent that the trend of thought and action of Theodor Heuss—democratic, social reformist, religious and progressive—was clearly established when at the the early age of 21 (even before he had taken his degree in economics), he was entrusted by Naumann with editing his weekly periodical, *Die Hilfe*. This he edited until 1936, when the paper was suppressed by the N.S.D.A.P. and he himself forbidden to publish anything further. He had, in the meanwhile, been editing intermittently the liberal daily newspaper the *Neckarzeitung*, and after 1918 had been drawn into active politics in the hope that the Liberals would be able to bring into being their dreams of a new democratic Germany. Elected a member of Streseman's old party in the Reichstag, he became at the same time a lecturer and director of studies at the Deutsche Hochschule für Politik, the Berlin equivalent of Chatham House, and while in many ways unsuited to the rough and tumble of political life and unable to exercise much influence on his colleagues, he was one of the last five of his party elected in 1932 on the eve of the Third Reich.

With the four members of his party, he committed the political blunder of voting in 1933 for the law conferring extraordinary powers upon the Nazi Government—in the hope that by doing so the party would share the responsibilities of government. The N.S.D.A.P. rewarded him by having some of his books publicly burned in front of Berlin University by their stormtroopers. Deprived of his posts and his living, he and his family were saved by his wife Elli who, exploiting her gifts for publicity, ran propaganda campaigns for commercial firms interested in toothpaste, cough mixtures and the like.

She thus secured for her husband the first real spell of leisure for many years, enabling him to write books, in particular the biography of Friedrich Naumann at whose feet both he and his wife had sat in their student days. This book finally appeared in 1937. He also was the author of many other biographies notably, Justus von Liebig, the chemist, the modern German architect, Hans Poelzig, and the industrialist, Robert Bosch. For a while he contributed historical and political essays to the *Frankfurter Zeitung* under the pseudonym "Thomas Brackheim".

In 1945, the Allied armies found him in an attic in Heidelberg and at once made him the first Minister of Education for Württemberg and the licensee of a Heidelberg newspaper. Stuttgart University appointed him a professor of politics and economics and his fellow citizens elected him a member of the Württemberg-Baden Landtag. He gave up his portfolio in 1946 and a year later was one of the first German politicians to visit London. Soon afterwards he was elected chairman of the Free Democratic Party (Liberal) at *Land* level. It was in that capacity that his name came to the fore when the search began for the man, worthy and able to represent the new Federal Republic of Germany as its first President in 1949.

Of impressive stature, physical as well as moral and intellectual, his gift of expressing lofty ideals in clear practical words, and great historical learning had impressed itself upon the Bundestag so that he was called "the father of the Constitution." He will be remembered too for his informal, humorous, and humanitarian behaviour as well as his *Sauberkeit* in political relations. His appearance at Schöneberg town hall in west Berlin after his election to office will long be remembered by those who saw every man in a great crowd spontaneously bare his head when he had finished speaking. For the first time in her history, Germany has been officially represented by a democrat and a humanist in the Liberal tradition.

SAVING HUMOUR

His re-election in 1954 was not in doubt because there could hardly have been a better choice. His comfortable liberalism provided the right background for the presidential office of a country determined to re-establish itself as respectable. His appreciation of a glass of wine and a good cigar helped in creating an almost avuncular relationship with the people, and his Swabian humour smoothed relations with Dr. Adenauer.

Humour was also required by a politician occupying a position of exalted dignity but remarkably little authority. The presidency of the Weimar republic was vested with considerable power and responsibility, but in 1949 with memories of that disastrous period still fresh the presidential authority was drastically restricted to guarantee parliamentary supremacy. Indeed, during the debates on the Basic Law, it was proposed that there should be no presidential office.

This radical view was not pursued, but the present office is little more than a constitutional cypher. The limitations are severe. Orders and decrees must be countersigned by the Chancellor or appropriate Minister;

the President cannot dismiss the Chancellor or dissolve Parliament, and is liable for impeachment should he wilfully violate the constitution or any federal law.

It can be said that a more forceful man could have given more stature to the office, but not at any time during Dr. Adenauer's strong administration did events call for a presidential initiative.

Professor Heuss also had his own clear conception of how the Presidential office should evolve. As he saw it, Germany had suffered too much in the past from monarchs or presidents who could ignore or over-rule parliament. He was not misled by the occasional confusions caused by comparisons with the British and American models. He never lost sight of the fact that in a parliamentary democracy of the kind freely chosen by west Germany the Chancellor, advised by his Cabinet, responsible to the Bundestag, and answerable to the electorate, assumed authority and not the President.

As one of the chief architects of the constitution, he would not have wanted it differently but his approach to his own duties was not negative. He saw most State papers and received Dr. Adenauer regularly. Some continuity would have been maintained had there been a change in the Chancellory. As representative of the nation, he also saw his duty to associate the dignity of his office with the arts, science and any expression of the national genius requiring recognition. He worked hard in establishing this conception as the basis of future tradition, and before the end of his second and final term there were few who denied that he had laid a promising foundation for the future.

He remained true to his respect for the constitution when in his final year it was proposed that he should succeed himself for a second time. This would have required a constitutional amendment, and for this reason Professor Heuss refused. It was then suggested that his second term should be extended for two years, but again he objected to constitutional changes for party benefit. Divided and confused in the post-war years, the German people were deeply in need of a constitution commanding respect and Professor Heuss was determined to defend and enhance it.

He continued with his writing—he published more than 40 books—and his keen interest in literature provided a balance in a society primarily concerned with more immediate affairs.

Professor Heuss travelled extensively abroad during his second term, and in Bonn received Heads of State and other visiting statesmen. This he accomplished with his usual dignity and humour, and no doubt helped to re-establish abroad the standing of the German people. In 1958 he visited England, the first German head of State to do so since 1907.

After his retirement from office in 1959 he continued to travel overseas whenever he could.

In 1961 he received the honorary degree of Doctor of Civil Law at Oxford.

December 13, 1963.

Dr. Egon Hilbert, the director of the Vienna State Opera, died on January 18, 1968, in Vienna at the age of 68.

Hilbert's academic degree was not in the field of music or the arts, but in police law. He was considered important enough by the Nazis to spend most of the Second World War in Dachau. He was released from the concentration camp in 1945 by the English and went directly to Salzburg, where he began the planning of the first postwar Salzburg Festival while guns were still firing in Austria. Hilbert's lifelong passion was the theatre, particularly the operatic stage. His first postwar position in Vienna was as chief of the Austrian Bundestheaterverwaltung, in which capacity he must take the lion's share of credit in reestablishing the Vienna State Opera as a name to reckon with in the world of music.

Even Viennese commentators, at least those rare ones who were able to preserve a degree of perspective, stood with awe and respect of the 1945 to 1955 years in the Theater-an-der Wien, when the Vienna Opera, under Hilbert's often fanatical guidance, set lasting standards in the performance of Mozart's operas. Under Hilbert's leadership the Salzburg Festival began a bold programme of premières of contemporary operas: the triumph of Berg's *Wozzeck* is one case in point, the launching of Von Einem's *Danton's Tod* is another.

Hilbert was never a comfortable administrator either for artists or for the politicians who were his superiors in the Ministry of Education. The former regarded him as a dilettante, the latter as too volatile for an official. He was removed from the Bundestheaterverwaltung in the mid-fifties and sent to Rome as head of the Austrian Institute. In that capacity he was responsible for the first performances of Masses by Austria's arch-Catholic composer Anton Bruckner, in the Vatican.

In 1960 he was recalled to Vienna to bring order to the Vienna Festival which was suffering from a case of undirected elephantiasis.

CULTURAL FORCE

The Vienna Festival suddenly became a force in European culture, surpassing the Salzburg Festival, which had become a museum of historical curiosities. In 1963 Hilbert was appointed co-director of the State Opera. His artistic director was Herbert Von Karajan. By the end of the season Hilbert was completely in charge, Karajan having left in customary volcanic manner in spite of heart-rending efforts to keep him. From then on Hilbert became more and more a figure of controversy. Lately Hilbert had became increasingly loath to delegate responsibility, attempting to direct such a huge and turbulent organization as the State Opera virtually single-handed. This, together with a decline in his health, made it seem advisable to terminate Hilbert's contract two years early. After weeks of negotiation a settlement was reached on January 17. Egon Hilbert, as no other man, has determined the profile of the postwar Vienna State Opera and has created the Vienna Festival as known today.

January 20, 1968.

With the death of **Dr. Paul Hindemith** at Frankfurt on December 28, 1963, at the age of 68 twentieth-century music has lost one of its most influential figures. Younger than Schoenberg, Bartok and Stravinsky, he had yet achieved something of their status as a founding father of modern music, both through the prolific flow of his compositions in every genre and through the theoretical works in which he sought to systematize his own practice as a guide to others.

Paul Hindemith was born at Hanau, near Frankfurt, in November, 1895. In spite of the opposition of his parents, he determined on a musical career when very young; he had little formal schooling, and left home at the age of 11. Earning a living by playing in café and theatre orchestras, he pursued his musical studies at the Hoch Conservatory in Frankfurt and under Arnold Mendelssohn in Darmstadt. When he was 20 he obtained the post of leader in the Frankfurt opera orchestra, which he occupied for eight years, and he also conducted on occasion during this time. In 1921 he founded the Amar Quartet (in which he played the viola), an ensemble noted particularly for its championship of modern music. He played other instruments than the violin and viola, however, seeing it as part of a composer's duties to have an understanding based on direct experience of the technique of every orchestral instrument.

GROWING REPUTATION

During these years his reputation as a composer was growing. He was among the founders of the Donaueschingen festivals of the 1920s, and later those at Baden-Baden, where a determinedly anti-romantic musical line was followed, and he composed much of the music performed at these festivals. At this period Hindemith was widely regarded as one of the more irreverent and iconoclastic of younger composers. His earliest works show something of Reger's influence, but in the 1920s he was using a near-atonal style (not serially organized) with motoric rhythms and touches of jazz influence, and generally rejecting the late romantic traditions of emotional expression along with all they entailed in terms of musical resources. He whole-heartedly embraced the notion of *Gebrauchmusik* (Utility Music), holding firmly to the belief that a composer's social obligation was to meet a demand for music actually to be performed rather than to use artistic creation as a vehicle for emotional self-indulgence. This anti-emotional attitude found its expression in his association with youth musical movements, for which he supplied a good deal of educational music, and in the topics dealt with in certain of his operas of this time—notably the one-act operas *Das Nusch-Nuschi* (for Burmese marionettes), *Hin und Zurück* (in which the action, and the music, reverses halfway through) and most of all in *Neues vom Tage* (1929), a satire on society and particularly on the press which panders to it. A later manifestation of his convictions regarding the artist as craftsman, and indeed as a craftsman with a positive duty to society, is the series of sonatas he wrote in the late 1930s and early forties for virtually every orchestral instrument with piano.

In 1927 Hindemith was appointed to the professorial staff of the Berlin Hochschule für Musik, whereupon he resigned from the Amar Quartet. But he continued his career as conductor and viola player, and in 1929 he gave, in London, the first performance of Walton's Viola Concerto.

Under Nazi rule in Germany during the 1930s his music met with official disfavour and was severely attacked. His opera *Mathis der Maler*, which dealt with the creative artist's role in society, and in which one may detect a degree of self identification with its protagonist, the sixteenth-century painter Matthias Grünewald, was banned in 1934 on account of its political overtones and had to wait until 1938 for its first production, which took place in Zurich (the B.B.C gave a concert performance the next year). *Mathis der Maler*, and the symphony drawn from it, set the seal on Hindemith's move towards a more humanistic attitude to his art, detectable even as far back as 1924 in his song cycle *Das Marienleben* and in 1926 in the opera *Cardillac* (on a similar topic to *Mathis*), and musically evident in the warmer, more expressive and more clearly tonal style which characterizes his works from the 1930s onwards, as well as his acceptance of the normally constituted symphony orchestra. It was in the mid thirties that he produced his important theoretical work, *The Craft of Musical Composition*, in which his own harmonic practice is shown to have a basis in natural acoustical phenomena.

In 1935 Hindemith visited Turkey (the homeland of Licco Amar, leader of his former quartet) to institute, at the request of the Turkish Government, a system of musical education along western lines. He accepted an invitation to visit the United States as soloist and conductor in 1937, and after a brief period of residence in Switzerland he settled in the United States with a post in the music department at Yale University, taking American citizenship. During 1940 and 1941 he taught at the Berkshire (Mass.) Academy of Music, and in 1947 he was appointed Battel Professor of Music at Yale University. He gave the Charles Eliot Norton lectures at Harvard University in 1949–50, which were later published in book form as *A Composer's World*; and a further product of his years spent teaching in America was a series of textbooks on conventional harmony. After the 1939–45 war he declined an invitation to return to the Berlin Hochschule; in 1948 he accepted the post of Professor of Music in the University of Zurich alternating between Yale and Zurich for a time before finally leaving Yale in 1953. He continued to pursue his activities as conductor and soloist, and several times visited England in these capacities; during one such visit, in 1954, the honorary degree of Doctor of Music was conferred on him at Oxford University.

MASTER-CRAFTSMAN

In recent years the theorist, the master-craftsman conscious of his powers and responsibilities, seemed to take precedence over the naturally gifted musician, bubbling over with humour and inventive energy, of whom Paul Bekker had once remarked: "He does not compose; he just makes music". Yet it would be wrong to see in this only the waning of a youthful creative impulse. Hindemith's opera *Die Harmonie der Welt*, produced at Munich in 1957, has as its subject the life of the astronomer Johannes Kepler, and his mystical quest for the supra-human music of the spheres. As before, the protagonist stands for an aspect of Hindemith's personality, and his own quest for a musical order and logic transcending both fashion and self-expression is powerfully reflected in its pages. It will be the task of future generations to decide whether Hindemith was successful in this quest or whether it proved in the end destructive of the most personal elements in his music. Whatever the verdict, the immense list of his works certainly includes a large number, for all combinations of voices and instruments, that deserve a permanent place in the repertory for their fluent craftsmanship, their humour, their humanity, and the transparent honesty with which they assert traditional musical values in an individual but essentially traditional idiom.

December 30, 1963.

Maurice Hindus, the Russian-born American commentator on Soviet Russia, died in New York on July 8, 1969, at the age of 78.

Hindus held a special place among western interpreters of contemporary Russia by reason of his intimate sympathy with the peasant masses. He had left Tsarist Russia in 1905, as a boy of 14, and it was in the first place to his own native village in central Russia that he returned on his earliest visit to revolutionary Russia in 1923. This return to the scenes of his youth was repeated annually until 1936 and more irregularly in subsequent years. The books that Hindus wrote on Russia were thus a series of progress reports, in which the changes he recorded in the small part of the countryside he knew best crystallized the general transformation effected under the Soviet regime.

CONVERSATIONAL SKILL

As an observer he was alert, unbiased, understanding, with a marked gift for drawing out the peasant types he engaged in conversation, and conspicuous skill and fidelity in reproducing such conversation. During his later visits to the Soviet Union he seldom dwelt at length on the darker side of things; though never uncritical, like other regular visitors and foreign correspondents, obliged to keep on the right side of Soviet authority and to maintain a certain reserve in these matters. For the rest, however, he was always a truthful and illuminating witness.

Maurice Gerschon Hindus, born on February 27, 1891, was the son of a small farmer. When his father died the family migrated to the United States where they lived in extreme poverty in New York. In *Green Worlds* (1938), Hindus describes his longing as a boy in New York for the familiar ways of village life. He went to study at Colgate University, Hamilton, New York State, during 1915–16, and at Harvard in the following year, after which he engaged in free-lance journalism.

IN DEMAND

His earliest book, *Russian Peasant and Revolution*, appeared in 1920. Three years later Hindus went on a visit to Soviet Russia for the Century Magazine, and from then onwards he was always in demand in the magazines and on the lecture platform as an interpreter of life and events in the Soviet Union. *Broken Earth* (1926), the first of his volumes based upon direct testimony, is in some ways the most revealing of them all. In *Humanity Uprooted* (1929) he filled in his progress report with a survey of specific aspects of Russian life—religion, morality, the position of the Jews, and so on. *Red Bread* (1931) described the first chapter—the first chapter only—of the collectivization of agriculture and the liquidation of the *kulak* as a class, and was followed by *The Great Offensive*, in which the whole experiment of Soviet planning came under review.

Hindus tried his hand at two novels about the new verities of life and character in Soviet Russia. But he was no novelist, and *Under Moscow Skies* (1936), which has an American journalist of Russian extraction for hero, is verbose and rather tiresome, while *Sons and Fathers* (1940), is singularly guileless. In between came an excellent book in its kind, observant and faithful, *We Shall Live Again* (1939), in which Hindus, who had spent the months before the Munich agreement in Prague, described the downfall of Czechoslovakia. A visit of some months to the Soviet Union in the summer of 1942—his first since 1936—enabled him in *Mother Russia* (1943), to offer a survey of the home front and to recapitulate views and conclusions advanced in earlier books. A volume on *The Cossacks*, which appeared in 1946, was superficial and disappointing. *House without a Roof* (1962) was based on a visit to Russia in 1960.

July 10, 1969.

L. E. Hinrichs, of New York City, at the age of 87 in his fifty-second year as a staff Correspondent of *The Times* died in a Manhattan hospital on September 3, 1967, after a short illness.

His tall, thin, eager figure was familiar, especially in the Wall Street district, for more than 30 years. An Englishman's idea of a Harvard "Yankee", he had that dependable sense of proportion, elastic sense of humour, reliable stock of patience, keen response to emergency and inexhaustible fund of curiosity, combined with a thorough respect for facts, that are among the first essentials of the good journalist.

For those who worked with him his tremendous and abiding competence was only one of his virtues. He could teach a young man to laugh. Although his endurance and his zest for life carried him until his last business day, only a few weeks before his death, Hinrichs had a talent for amiable objectivity. His fund of reminiscence, constantly enriched by fresh touches of the piquant and sardonic, was presented not as personal achievement but as what he had been lucky enough to see and enjoy. Had he not been so diffident he could have written a remarkable autobiography. He was at once dignified and modest, always ready to help, a dependable and sympathetic friend.

His interests were as various as his background. His favourite author was Sir Thomas Browne, and he watched baseball on television in hospital the day he died.

In his ancestry and his career, Hinrichs personified the transatlantic community. His paternal grandfather came from Oldenburg, on the Dutch-German border, as a youth in 1831, married a Scots-Irish girl from the Appalachians and prospered as a merchant—one of his bilingual posters in English and Dutch is in the New York Historical Society Museum.

His other grandfather was an English venturer who went to New York with his formidably stable wife and daughters after a time as a coffee planter in Haiti. Young Louis inherited both the stability and diligence of his forebears and a touch of the Picaresque, as well as infinite sympathies and gratitude for the opportunities that life offered him.

ENGLISH UPBRINGING

He was born in Brooklyn in 1880, before it was swallowed up in Greater New York. He was christened Christian Felix Adolph Louis to maintain the initials C.F.A. (Charles Frederick Albert went to his elder brother). But he dropped them, and borrowed the middle name of Ernest from a maternal uncle.

His father, Charles F. A. Hinrichs junior, died when he was five, and he was brought up by his mother, born May Evelyn Pressler in Lancashire, with the help of his grandmother and two sisters.

Thus his early formation was purely English. After private schools he went to Harvard in 1901, the year of the Peace of Pekin between China and the Great Powers. When, in February, 1904, Japan declared war on Russia, Hinrichs, in the mounting excitement, obtained leave of absence from Harvard and as a freelance correspondent worked his passage from San Francisco to Yokohama in company with such friends as Richard Harding Davis and John Fox, Jr.

Unable to persuade the Japanese to afford him journalistic facilities, Hinrichs went to the Russian headquarters, only to find that Americans were again unwelcome. At Tientsin he joined Percival Phillips, a fellow American then on the foreign staff of the *Daily Express*, and went with him to Europe by way of Shanghai, Hongkong, Singapore, and Saigon.

CHOOSING CAREER

They reached the Continent and finally London, where Hinrichs stayed for a few weeks. Thus, in 1905, he made his first acquaintance with the Metropolis and, having failed to settle his future, returned to college life. After more hesitation Hinrichs joined the Harvard Medical School, but a few terms later he was persuaded by Arthur Hoe, a college friend, to consider a commercial career in his father's business—that of a printing-press manufacturer.

Hinrichs now made two discoveries: first, that he was less interested in the activity of business than in its finance; and, secondly, that Hoe's office, over on the East side of New York, was far from the centre—which had begun to engross his interest—Wall Street. He soon abandoned business in favour of investment, using as his capital the balance of a family legacy. In 1906 the San Francisco earthquake wiped out his capital and profits. Thus Hinrichs, now at the age of 26, was compelled to choose a profession. He then made his decisions and offered his services to the *Evening Sun*. This then flourishing journal placed him as an all-purpose reporter of local and national occurrences and writer on criminal and political events, while leaving him the opportunity to specialize in finance. The seven years he spent on the *Sun* introduced him to high political personalities (e.g. he reported the Baltimore convention of 1912 that nominated Woodrow Wilson for the Presidency) and great financial figures (e.g. the elder and younger J. P. Morgan, E. H. Harriman, and James J. Hill).

In 1913 Hinrichs was appointed assistant financial editor of the *New York Tribune*. Three years later he attracted the notice of Harry (afterwards Sir) Perry Robinson, formerly *The Times* War Correspondent on the Western Front, and much trusted by Lord Northcliffe. At this time the trends of the New York money market were becoming of vital importance to Great Britain. (In 1916 she was responsible for financing her Allies as well as herself.) The appointment of Hinrichs fully justified itself. His ability was recognized as outstanding after Versailles, when *The Times* initiated the first of a series of Special American Supplements with the purpose of bringing British opinion up to date in respect of the industrial, economic and financial capacity of the United States, so vastly increased since 1914 when the country became the great arsenal of the Allies. The first of these numbers, published on July 4, 1919, contained important contributions by Hinrichs on economic and financial affairs. The number was edited by Perry Robinson with the assistance of the Chief Correspondent of *The Times* in New York, W. F. Bullock (who was also the Correspondent of the *Daily Mail*), and Arthur (afterwards Sir) Willert, *The Times* Correspondent in Washington since 1910.

Until after the First World War New York ranked as only a news centre and as a source of advertising. Hardly any general American financial news was transmitted. In 1922 it was recognized in Printing House Square that *The Times* needed articles on non-economic and non-political phases of American life. The inadequacy of the arrangement by which *The Times* shared (and in the minor degree) Bullock with the *Daily Mail*, therefore, needed remedying. In 1923, when Lord Northcliffe set out on his world tour, he took with him as far as America Henry Wickham Steed (then Editor of *The Times*). Together they reorganized the New York Office. Northcliffe dispatched Hinrichs to London, where he was helped by Montagu Norman, whose confidence he won on their transatlantic crossing. Hinrichs was travelling with Sir Charles Addis, whom he had known in New York. As governor of the Bank of England, Norman once confided to Hinrichs: "I wouldn't miss your column. It is required reading at the Bank". Printing House Square was said to be daunted by its Correspondent's financial expertise, especially after he predicted the Wall Street crash. Hinrichs for his part stood in awe of the ceremonial prestige of *The Times* in his green years.)

After Lord Northcliffe's death the reorganization of the New York office was completed on the lines earlier laid down. Bullock concentrated upon the *Daily Mail* and on January 1, 1923, Hinrichs was appointed Chief Correspondent of *The Times* on the understanding that he continued to be responsible for American financial news and Wall Street comment. This arrangement continued until his partial retirement in 1952. After this Hinrichs continued to write (until his annual leave in August this year) his long-established financial commentary. It had appeared on Monday for more than 40 years. He had achieved a prime ambition, never to retire.

Hinrichs married Vera McEnery, who died in 1961. They had two sons, who survive him.

September 5, 1967.

Sir Cyril Hinshelwood, O.M., F.R.S., died at his home on October 9, 1967 at the age of 70. He had been President of the Royal Society, of the Chemical Society, of the Classical Association and the British Association. In 1956 he was joint winner of the Nobel Prize for Chemistry with Professor Semenov of Russia.

By his death Britain has lost one of the outstanding intellects of his generation. In 1958–59 he had the unique distinction of being president both of the Royal Society and of the Classical Association. His Nobel Prize in 1956 and the Order of Merit conferred on him by the Queen were the recognition of the brilliance and range of his achievements. With the wide sweep of his mind, his exquisite gift for languages and his aesthetic interests, he bridged the gap in the minds of others between science and the humanities and he maintained that natural science was today the foremost of human studies.

Born in London in 1897 he was the only child of Norman Macmillan Hinshelwood, a chartered accountant, who died in 1904. He was brought up by his mother and he often spoke of his debt to her. It was perhaps owing to their affectionate devotion to one another until her death in 1959 that he never married.

He was educated at the Westminster City School and in 1916 he went as a chemist to the Explosives Supply Factory at Queensferry, where he was soon known as the boy wonder, and in 1918 he became Assistant Chief Laboratory Chemist. At Queensferry he quickly found an outlet for his innate skill as an investigator and in his Nobel Lecture he described how the testing of the stability of explosives impressed on a young chemist the mysteries of chemical change and its dependence upon the energy and environment of the molecules.

Having won a Brackenbury Scholarship at Balliol he went to Oxford in 1919, taking with him the results of his investigations at

Queensferry in the field which was to be his life work. These were published in the *Journal* of the Chemical Society while he was an undergraduate. Having gained distinction in the shortened war degree course in 1920 he was elected to a Fellowship at Balliol. This he held only for a year, when he was elected to a Tutorial Fellowship at Trinity which he held until 1937. So for 20 years his researches were done in the cellars of Balliol and the outhouses of Trinity which had been adapted to the teaching of physical chemistry in the university.

It was a time when the mechanism of chemical change was being investigated anew in laboratories all over the world. Hinshelwood's incisive attack with his choice of promising reactions, his experimental skill and his gift for mathematical analysis, quickly made rapid progress over a wide front. The publication of his *Kinetics of Chemical Change* in 1926, based to a great extent on his researches with his pupils, was a milestone in this field as it gave a broad survey of the different types of reactions which provided the basis for a systematic attack. In his presidential address to the Royal Society, Hinshelwood spoke of the three stages through which scientific theories usually passed. His book of 1926 represents this first stage "of gross oversimplification, reflecting partly the need for practical views and even more a too enthusiastic aspiration of the elegance of form." The steadily increasing size of successive editions of this classic work reflected the second stage, to which his own work and that of his pupils contributed so much, when "the symmetry of hypothetical systems is distorted and the neatness marred as recalcitrant facts increasingly rebel against uniformity".

One of the best examples of the complexity of the mechanism of chemical reactions is described in Hinshelwood's Bakerian Lecture to the Royal Society in 1946 on the combination of hydrogen and oxygen. The simplicity of his earlier views had been left far behind, pointing to the third stage in which, "if and when this is attained, a new order emerges, more intricately contrived, less obvious and with its parts more subtly interwoven, since it is of nature's and not of man's conception".

CRITICAL ATTITUDE

The breadth of Hinshelwood's outlook and his severely critical attitude towards the ultimate value of what each generation regards as fundamental, were shown in a striking manner in his monograph *The Structure of Physical Chemistry* published in 1951. It represents his individual point of view of the structure and continuity of the whole subject and in it he insists on the limitations of the current working notions so that young chemists should not invest them with more ultimate significance than they contain. In this connexion he quoted Alice: "Somehow it seems to fill my head with ideas—only I don't know exactly what they are."

One of the great merits of his lectures was defining the limits of the known and the unknown with a clarity which was reinforced by his pithy, dry humour. There is a philosophical vein running through the pages of *The Structure of Chemistry* as they progress from the world as a molecular chaos to the growth and structure of the living cell.

In 1936 Hinshelwood entered on a new field of work, the dynamics of living processes as exemplified by the growth and characteristics of bacteria. His approach to the problem followed on his studies of chemical kinetics as the living cell is a complex assemblage of chemical reactions, each of which must be subject to the same laws. There was some criticism that a chemist should invade the bacteriologists' field which soon came to a head in Hinshelwood's investigations of the adaptability of bacteria to their environment, in which he showed how they could be gradually trained to alter their habits by successive change in their environment. This seemed perilously near the fallacy of the inheritance of acquired characteristics and the results were ascribed to the selection of mutants. Hinshelwood never disputed that mutation might occur but he showed that in some cases practically all the cells were affected and that therefore in the case of unicellular organisms with their large exposure to external influences the nature of their environment in some cases was the decisive factor. He summarized the results of his work in 1946 in *The Chemical Kinetics of the Bacterial Cell*.

NUFFIELD GIFT

In 1937, on Soddy's retirement from the Dr. Lees Professorship, Hinshelwood was his obvious successor, which made him responsible for the university teaching of inorganic and physical chemistry. Owing to the lack of accommodation he continued to work in the Balliol and Trinity Laboratory until 1941, when he moved to the new Physical Chemistry Laboratory which had been built with a generous gift from Lord Nuffield. With the new laboratory and the rebuilding of the old chemical department there was ample space for the expanding chemistry school and for the research groups who were working with the members of the staff, no less than nine of whom were F.R.S.

Under Hinshelwood's administration Oxford was making important contributions to physical chemistry and allied subjects over a very wide front. In 1948 he was President of the Chemical Society for its Centenary celebrations, when he gave a brilliant address and replied so gracefully to the delegates from abroad, each in their own tongue. He was knighted in the same year.

Hinshelwood had been elected into the Royal Society in 1929. He received the Davy and Royal Medals; in 1950 he became Foreign Secretary and President in 1955, being only the third chemist to fill this office since Humphry Davy.

The list of the honours paid to him by foreign academies is too long to repeat. He was a foreign member of many learned societies. Hinshelwood retired from his Oxford Chair in 1964 and was then elected to a Research Fellowship at Imperial College, where he continued his work on living cells. His services were also in great request as an adviser to both nationalized and private industry.

October 12, 1967.

Lord Hives, C.H., M.B.E., formerly chairman of Rolls-Royce Ltd., and one of the great engineers of his time, died in the National Hospital for Nervous Diseases in London on April 24, 1965. He was 79.

Born at Reading on April 21, 1886, Ernest Walter Hives was first employed as a boy in a local garage. He drove his first car at 14 and in 1903 got himself a garage job with C. S. Rolls & Co., then the chief motor salesmen. He moved on to another selling company for a brief spell and thence went to the Napier company, whose products were about to be challenged by the new Rolls-Royce company. After three years he moved over to Rolls-Royce and from testing cars he succeeded in becoming a driver in competitive events on the Continent. In 1911 he drove a Silver Ghost at Brooklands at over 101 m.p.h. Like Royce, he had a good ear for an engine and an acute mind in diagnosing trouble. He suited Royce. He was destined to suit Royce's greatly expanded company.

He became managing director in 1946 and chairman of the company in 1950. In 1957 he retired. He had been responsible for the development of the aero-engines which helped to win the Schneider Trophy and of the Merlin engines which proceeded from them and helped to win the Battle of Britain. He turned aero-engines into tank engines and finally took in hand the jet engine. Meanwhile he had taken charge of the building and equipping of new works in Crewe and Glasgow. During the war he arranged for his engines to be made by Ford's in England and by Packard's in the United States and as chairman of the company after the war he made a most profitable deal with another United States corporation concerning jet engines.

What Hives brought particularly to this great engineering company was a cool appreciation of the standards and methods of Sir Henry Royce and an equally cool determination to make them yield results without undue loss of time. Having imbibed the Royce gospel of perfection and proved that it could be approached without interminable delay by organizing teams of young specialists and letting intensive testing sort out their ideas, he found a special, almost mischievous, satisfaction in demanding in the field of business special terms for the privilege of having the services of his company.

ENGINES FOR TANKS

When Lord Beaverbrook asked that Rolls-Royce should undertake the production of tank engines in large numbers, Hives, already full of orders for aero-engines, replied that he would want a credit of £1m. and "no interference". His bluff was called with the credit he had asked for. Again, in a deal he did in the United States, he decided to double the sum his accountants had said he might fairly ask for the right to manufacture his engines and this time, too, his terms were accepted without a murmur. Once again a huge sum of money was involved. He never boasted of these things but when they leaked out and he was asked for corroboration he grinned happily and explained that the firm did not really need the money or want to be troubled with the responsibility.

That was only true because a good deal of foresight was exercised and immense trouble was taken to make the chosen products good; and from 1912 onwards, Hives had been in the thick of the work which produced the needed product at the right time. In the 1914–18 War, in the experimental department, he had a share in the six months of hard work that turned out the first Eagle engine which yielded a mere 225 h.p. and in the remaining three years of that war he was in charge of that department while the Eagle was developed, stage by stage, until it gave 650 h.p. He was still there when, in 1931, the first of the racing aero-engines was made in the brief space of nine months—five years' work crowded into nine months, as he said afterwards—to enable Britain to win outright the Schneider Trophy.

He was still in charge while a new engine, derived from that racing engine, was prepared. There were no orders for it but it was developed with a devotion that might have foreseen the part it was to play and Hives and his team tested it to destruction in the approved Royce fashion, until they were satisfied that it was unbeatable and yet allowed scope for development. The Merlin made its own market and more than 150,000 were made before the war ended. The making of them by the thousand was to be the chief concern of Hives for the next 10 years, for in 1936 he became general works manager and a year later a director as well.

EXPANDED COMPANY

Royce had died in 1933. Hives had been his executive officer at Derby, corresponding to his design chief, A. G. Elliott, who was attached to the ailing genius at his home at West Wittering in Sussex. Elliott became chief engineer. Hives, who had every reason to know how the engines should be made, turned his attention to organizing output, increasing its pace and expanding the company's capacity. In this, too, he arranged shrewd bargains with the Government, who paid for the new factories and leased them to the company, and in Glasgow particularly he took trouble to arrive at a friendly understanding with the trade unions. All the time his advice as a director was equally effective.

By 1942 the company had decided to undertake the full development of jet engines and its Welland engine was the first jet engine to be put into production for the early Meteor fighters. The Whittle engine had been taken over in 1943, but work was soon to proceed along different lines in response to conclusions reached in Hives's old experimental department. As managing director from 1946 onwards, Hives conformed to the traditional Royce ruthlessness in development. There was, for instance, one stage in the emergence of the Avon engine at which he had to conclude that the design was wrong. The engine was "Scrapped" and a fresh start was made after many thousands of pounds had been spent. That was a rare occurrence, yet Hives never expected success without travail and never grumbled when difficulties came.

He picked his young men and then encouraged them to specialize and then took the utmost care that they should not shut themselves up in separate compartments but should argue their way through difficulties with other specialists, under the wise eye of one who had no degree to set alongside theirs but had a vast engineering experience and a belief in trying whatever looked promising.

Hives picked his own rewards with much the same care and with the same slightly quizzical mischievousness as he challenged financial authority. He became a Companion of Honour in 1943. He accepted a peerage in 1950. He was an honorary D.Sc. of Nottingham and London and an honorary LL.D. of Cambridge.

He was chairman of the Industrial Development Board for Malta from 1957 to 1960 and had been chairman of the National Council for Technological Awards.

Hives married in 1913 Gertrude Ethel, daughter of John Warwick, by whom he had four sons and three daughters. His wife died in 1961. He is succeeded by his eldest son, the Hon. John Warwick Hives.

April 26, 1965.

President Ho Chi Minh, President of the Democratic Republic of Vietnam and Chairman of the Vietnamese Workers' (Communist) Party, who died on September 4, 1969, was one of the elder statesmen of international communism. His influence within the communist movement was, for that reason, greater than his position as leader of a small and backward state would seem to justify. Unlike most of today's communist leaders, he had served the movement since the days of Lenin, whom he knew personally.

In the last years of his life Ho remained prominent as the nominal leader of North Vietnam and the father-figure of Vietnamese nationalism in a war represented as being against the Americans. Ho Chi Minh's direct part in policy making throughout the course of this war is not easy to estimate. Some reports of his ill-health would have suggested it was small; on the other hand his name was put to all official communications, such as the appeal to the British and other governments in 1965, and replies to American proposals for negotiations, notably the letter addressed to him by President Johnson in February, 1967.

Ho was also glad to need foreign visitors to Hanoi, it being an assumption of the North Vietnamese that world oppostion to the war and especially opposition in the United States was an important factor in bringing it to an end. American correspondents, church delegations from Europe, travellers of all kinds in search of peace, were received by him. Yet there is no reason to doubt that Ho's commitment to a communist solution for Vietnam was ever modified by his nationalism. The intervention of the North in the civil war that had developed in South Vietnam was put beyond doubt at the end of 1960, and much other evidence thereafter showed that direction of the war in the south remained under the overall authority of Hanoi.

The Sino-Soviet dispute presented a difficulty to North Vietnam which Ho naturally solved by doing his best to remain neutral between the two. His own past associated him closely with both countries: so did Vietnam's needs in the war as it developed with the growing American involvement from 1964 onwards.

PROFESSIONAL REVOLUTIONARY

Ideologically it seemed that a pro-Chinese wing was dominant, but Russian aid, and later the vagaries of the cultural revolution in China modified Hanoi's commitment to Maoism. Ho probably could be more independent of both countries than most of his colleagues. Like them he was intransigent. His reply to President Johnson's appeal for negotiations made in 1967 was wooden, filled with jargon, and seemed to show no flexibility whatsover.

The major portion of his long life was spent as a professional revolutionary, in which capacity he served the Communist International, and even after he emerged as President of North Vietnam he took pains to conceal these earlier activities. Born in or about 1890—his birthday was officially celebrated on May 19 at the village of Kim-lien in Nghean province of Vietnam—he was the youngest of three children. His father, Nguyen Sinh Huy, was a minor official dismissed, according to French records, for drunkenness and cruelty, who subsequently supported himself as an itinerant healer. Ho was given the name Nguyen Tat Thanh, but used numerous aliases in adult life. Educated at a Franco-Annamite school, he became an elementary schoolteacher in 1907.

Signing on as a steward in the French liner Latouche Treville in 1912, Ho travelled to Marseilles. Thereafter he worked aboard ship, visiting several countries before finding employment in the kitchens of the Carlton Hotel in London. Towards the end of the 1914–18 War he moved to Paris, where he earned his living by retouching photographs and devoted his free time to politics. Vainly he haunted the corridors of Versailles during the armistice negotiations, seeking to meet President Wilson in order to enlist his aid in improving conditions in Vietnam. About that time he made the acquaintance of such leaders of the French political left wing as Vaillant Couturier, Andre Bertou, and Marcel Cachin. He joined the French Socialist Party and formed the Inter-Colonial Union, a body of nationalists from colonial territories living in Paris.

Under the alias which he was then using, Nguyen Ai Quoe (Nguyen the Patriot), he contributed articles to the Socialist Paper *Le Populaire* and edited the Inter-Colonial Union paper Le Paria. The turning point in his life was the 1920 Socialist Congress at Tours, where Ho voted for the Third International and subsequently became a founder member of the French Communist Party. As such he attended the Comintern Congress at Moscow in 1922 and, except for two short visits to France, remained there until 1925, studying at the Toilers of the East University. In that year he accompanied the Borodin Mission to China, ostensibly working as a translator in the Soviet Consulate at Canton under the name of Ly Thuy. There he formed the Vietnamese Revolutionary Youth League, which brought young Vietnamese nationalists for training and indoctrination by Soviet instructors at Whampoa Military Academy. Some, including a number of today's communist leaders, went to Moscow for further training.

Following Chiang Kai-shek's rupture with the communists in 1927, Ho returned to Russia but was soon back at his revolutionary work in Asia.

He founded the Vietnamese—later the Indo-Chinese—Communist Party in 1930 at Hong-Kong, but was arrested there himself the following year together with a girl, Li Sam, whom he described as a niece. She was more probably his mistress, or possibly his wife, but she disappeared without trace after her release. Defended in Hongkong by a lawyer named Roseby and in Britain by Stafford Cripps, who pleaded his case before the Privy Council, Ho was released in 1932 and was smuggled in disguise to Amoy, in spite of French demands for his extradition.

Ho's whereabouts in the late 1930s remain a mystery. His is believed to have visited Yenan but soon left, apparently finding Mao Tse-tung's personality uncongenial. From there, in 1940, he went to join Vietnamese exiles near the Tonkinese border. In 1941 at Chingsi he formed a communist-dominated political movement later to become widely known by its abbreviated title Viet Minh. Arrested by the Kuomintang in 1942, he spent a year in prison before being released at the insistence of the O.S.S., which wished to use his followers to gather intelligence about the Japanese in Vietnam. It was then that he formally adopted the name of Ho Chi Minh (Ho who seeks enlightenment).

Armed Viet Minh bands in the highlands of Tonkin, supplied by the O.S.S., awaited the defeat of Japan before occupying the capital, Hanoi. In the confused period which followed, Ho's true genius showed itself as he manoeuvred to outwit the Chinese occupation force and the returning French as well as to destroy his nationalist rivals. A keen political sense, utter ruthlessness, and inspired opportunism enabled him to sustain the newly proclaimed Democratic Republic of Vietnam under his own leadership. When his communist affiliations proved a disadvantage, he took the unprecedented step of dissolving the Communist Party at least overtly. After protracted negotiations broke down he led his followers into what then appeared a hopeless war in December, 1946, but the eight years of bitter struggle culminated in the defeat of the French at Dien Bien Phu and the convening of the Geneva Conference.

UNSUITABLE REFORMS

Bowing to strong Soviet and Chinese pressure, Ho agreed to the partition of Vietnam and the communists assumed control of the north.

Victory was made possible only by Chinese aid and Ho paid the price by having to submit to Chinese influence in carrying out Maoist land reforms totally unsuited to Vietnam. Peasant revolts resulted, and all of Ho's skill and prestige were needed to avert collapse.

Ho's talents were not for political theory but for political action, in which he outdistanced all his compatriots. He will be remembered as the founder of Vietnamese communism, the leader of his country's struggle against French rule, and the creator of the Democratic Republic of Vietnam. In the simplicity of his dress and manner he resembled Gandhi—the likeness may have been deliberately cultivated—but this mild exterior concealed a shrewd, calculating and ruthless political brain more reminiscent of Stalin. His command of foreign languages, his sense of humour, and his charm of manner were effective weapons skilfully used to disarm his opponents and to achieve his political ends. With the death of Ho Chi Minh the communist world lost a man who will rank alongside Lenin, Stalin, and Mao Tse-tung as one of the outstanding figures of the movement.

A message from him, intended to reaffirm his national image among the South Vietnamese, was broadcast in July, 1969.

He appeared in 1968 at the May Day celebrations and a poem by him promising greater victories was published for the Tet festival early in 1969. His last public appearance had been at the May Day celebrations of that year.

One of Ho's most passionate concerns—and this is another thing that distinguishes him from a man like Mao Tse-tung—was his determination to win justice for the non-white peoples of the world. Vietnam was the one part of East Asia to be colonized and it proved the most resistant from the earliest days of French rule. A rebellion in 1908 when Ho was already a young man of 18 would have fired his nationalism. But when he travelled abroad he did so not simply as a Vietnamese nationalist seeking the liberation of his country from French rule; what concerned him even more was the liberation of all non-white peoples from the contempt they suffered at the hands of their white dominators.

CHALLENGE TO WHITES

This incipient international outlook found in the October revolution a challenge to this world of white domination. It was characteristic of Ho's attitude that he consistently emphasized the anticolonial character of the communist movement and openly attacked those communist parties which were laggard in this respect.

His identification with communism as an international movement lasted until the end. Indeed, one might hazard the view that a political life confined to Vietnam and marred by the growth of the Sino-Soviet dispute must have deeply distressed him. He was not involved at all in Marxist theory. The dispute about revisionism which Mao Tse-tung initiated would not have enlivened him. He was too conscious of of China as a country—in which he had lived—ever to think that an affiliation with the Russians to the exclusion of China was possible. But the decline of communism as an international movement resulting from the Sino-Soviet dispute must have darkened his last days.

Perhaps in order to measure up to Mao Tse-tung, Ho Chi Minh's selected works were published in Hanoi in 1960. They have none of the verve of some of Mao's writings; still less of any original political thinking, but the theme of maltreatment of coloured peoples —sometimes illustrated by the treatment of Negroes in the United States which deeply influenced Ho when he was a young man in the first decades of this century—runs consistently through what he wrote.

He is not, it must be admitted, a man of whom a great deal is known. A natural tendency to secrecy and to a conspiratorial attitude flowered in his early days while working for the Communist International and never left him. He was a man of more pseudonyms than close research has been able to track down. "An old man likes to have a little mystery about himself", he told the late Bernard Fall in an interview in 1962, and he remained unwilling to the last to reveal details of parts of his revolutionary career.

September 4, 1969.

Sir Jack Hobbs, who died on December 21, 1963, at his home at Hove, at the age of 81, was recognized as the greatest batsman in the world for most of the quarter-century when he was playing. He scored 61,237 first-class runs for an average of 50.65.

John Berry Hobbs, eldest of a family of 12, was born in Cambridge on December 16, 1882. He may therefore be regarded as one of the partially privileged, since it is inconceivable that anyone as sensitive as Hobbs should not be affected in his boyhood by a place so rich in beauty and associations.

His father was professionally and temperamentally connected with cricket both at Fenners and Jesus—where Jack played his first match. It was one of the happy circumstances of his life that his mother, who long survived her husband, lived to see her son acclaimed the greatest batsman in the world.

Hobbs matured comparatively late, for he played his first match for Surrey on Easter Monday, 1905, when W. G. Grace was a member of the opposing team. However, Hobbs atoned for his late start by earning his county cap in his second match when he scored the first of his 197 centuries which remain to this day a record for first-class cricket.

FOUR GREAT PARTNERS

Hobbs would eventually have made his mark in any company. He was, however, perhaps fortunate to do so under the aegis of his fellow-townsman, Tom Hayward, the first of his four great partners and one of the few men, like Hobbs, to score over 100 centuries. An opening batsman, like a Rugby half, needs a partner to understand and support him. Hobbs was lucky enough to have four—Hayward, when he was building up confidence and experience; Wilfred Rhodes of Yorkshire (who forsook his spin-bowling for a spell to earn a place in an England side as a vintage bat); Sandham (who was unlucky not to play more Test cricket than he did, but whose trim, neat batsmanship adorned Surrey's cricket for many years after the First World War); and Sutcliffe (another—though untypical—Yorkshireman, and perhaps the greatest partner of them all, whose name, linked with that of Hobbs, became a byword in England throughout the twenties).

Hobbs's career falls conveniently into two parts; the decade before the First World War, which event left him with the ruins of a benefit match, and Surrey, after a truncated season, county champions; and from 1919 to 1934, excluding 1921 when, during a phenomenally dry and run-begetting season, Hobbs was away ill. He was never heard to complain of either the war or his appendicitis, though if either had not supervened it is unthinkable that his much-cherished target of 200 centuries would have eluded him.

As a batsman Hobbs was primarily an artist with a superb technique. The basis of his method was his offensive lift of the bat which followed strictly K. S. Ranjitsinghi's dictum on all games from cricket down to golf, that "the head of the striking implement must be supported by the wrists". He stood at the crease relaxed and comfortable, looking down the wicket from a two-eyed, two-shouldered position which the pundits of his time were wont to criticize. What some did not realize was that appreciably before the bowler delivered the ball Hobbs was balanced like a ballet dancer on his toes poised to satisfy any textbook ever written on batsmanship. Very few realized that his primary position at the crease was not that from which he attacked the bowler or defended his wicket.

MASTER OF ALL THE STROKES

He was a master of every orthodox stroke and he played many of his own. He tamed the fast bowlers with his hook shot and made them bowl to him so that he could drive and cut—his favourite strokes—to his heart's content. The strokes of his own which made him day in and day out so difficult to bowl at, were, first, his back stroke. He was in position so early that he almost invariably found a gap in the field on the leg side. Secondly, he was so nimble of foot that with no apparent movement he would be 2ft. outside the off-stump persuading the ball beyond the reach of cover point's left hand.

Wilfred Rhodes said of him as a batsman: "It were impossible to fault 'im. He got 'em on good 'uns, he got 'em on bad 'uns, he got 'em on sticky 'uns and he got 'em on the mat all over the world."

It was from Hayward that he learnt to run the first run as fast as possible, and he taught all his partners the art of running between the wickets. To be in with Hobbs was an education.

In the field he was the best cover point of his time in those days of offside play, and his record of run-outs will stand for generations.

Of his great tale of long innings it is obviously impossible to speak in detail—it may be noted in passing that, after his illness, his stamina impaired, Hobbs was wont to get himself out, except when his side were in peril, presenting his wicket to the bowler he had punished most. Certain of his innings, however—and not always the three-figure ones—demand mention.

There was his 57 in the Adelaide Test of the season 1907–08, when the pitch was suddenly destroyed by rain and Hobbs, alone of the English batsmen, attacked the Australian bowling, thereby proving himself—as he was so often to prove himself subsequently—an unparalleled batsman on bad wickets; and his 154 not out on another bad wicket in 1911, for the Players against the Gentlemen—a fixture which still had *cachet* in Hobbs's epoch and in which he retained his own personal record—an unkind critic after suggested that he should stand down for the match on his current form.

Then there were his 126, also not out, in the Melbourne Test of the season 1911–12, when Hobbs played classic cricket through the pangs of toothache; and his 226 on August Bank Holiday, 1914, at the Oval "with never a thought of war". (There must have been many in that crowd who were watching cricket for the last time. If so, one could scarcely conceive a more felicitous note on which to take their departure.)

HIS BEST INNINGS

There was the occasion when Hobbs raced rain and Kent (his old bugbear) in a whirlwind finish to his delayed benefit after the war; or when he made 134 before luncheon on a Leicester wicket so fiery that four of the opposing team were injured; and mention must be made of his 85 before his thigh muscle gave out, in the depth of Norfolk, off Gregory and Macdonald, who in 1921 were still an unknown menace, if only because Hobbs himself—surely no mean critic—was wont to describe it as "the best in my life".

Perhaps his greatest innings at the Oval was in the Test match there against Australia in 1926, when both he and Sutcliffe scored centuries on a treacherous wicket to win the Ashes.

There was his partnership with Gregory, in 1932, of 232, which caused Jardine to describe Hobbs half humorously—but the phrase stuck—as "The Master"; and his last big score when, in his fiftieth year, he carried his bat for the Players v. Gentlemen at Lord's with 161.

FEATS STILL FRESH

Hobbs's feats are still too fresh in our minds for him to need a tangible memorial. Nevertheless he has two—the Hobbs Gates at the Oval and the Pavilion on Parker's Piece at Cambridge (where he had memories of changing in a tent).

He was knighted in 1953. He never sought popularity but earned it as his right, both with the public and his many personal friends. Like most men at the head of their profession he remained quiet and modest. He was deeply religious, and did not have his head turned by success such as comes to few men.

In 1906 he married Ada Ellen, daughter of E. G. Gates, of Cambridge. They had three sons and one daughter. His wife died in March, 1963.

December 23, 1963.

Sir John Hobson, P.C., O.B.E., Q.C., former Attorney General, died on December 4, 1967, at the age of 55. Hobson went into Parliament through winning a by-election in 1957 caused by the resignation of the then Sir Anthony Eden. Hobson had held important legal positions and appeared as counsel in several *causes célèbres* during a career dating back to 1938.

John Gardiner Sumner Hobson was born on April 18, 1912, the son of the late Colonel G. W. Hobson, 12th Lancers, who fought in the South African and First World Wars.

He was educated at Harrow, where he was head of the school, and in 1931 went up to Brasenose College, Oxford, to read history. On going down, he worked for a year with the Imperial Tobacco Company in Liverpool as a trainee. Afterwards he was elected to an entrance scholarship to the Inner Temple, and was called to the Bar in 1938. During the Second World War Hobson, who was in the Northamptonshire Yeomanry, was with the British Expeditionary Force in France in 1940, and came through Dunkirk. In 1942 he went with the First Army to North Africa, and from 1943 to 1945 he served with H.Q. 21st Army Group, reaching the rank of lieutenant-colonel and being mentioned in dispatches.

On return to civilian life, Hobson specialized in common law and in criminal proceedings. He took silk in 1957, the year in which he entered Parliament, Hobson was selected from a short-list of three for the traditionally safe Conservative seat of Warwick and Leamington, on the resignation of Sir Anthony Eden.

But the majority, normally a five-figure one for the Conservatives, dropped to just over 2,000. However at the 1959 general election Hobson swung the majority back to its former level of 13,000. He served as Parliamentary Private Secretary from 1960 to 1961 to Lord Alport, the then Minister of State for Commonwealth Relations.

VIEWS ON FLOGGING

At the age of 49, Hobson became Solicitor-General. It was on this appointment that he received his knighthood. In 1961 he surprised the Conservative Party Conference at Brighton with some terse remarks about the efficacy of flogging as a punishment. He said: "If flogging doesn't reform the criminal, and if it doesn't reduce crime, it can only be justified on the basis that you want an eye for an eye and a tooth for a tooth. And if you want to go back to that pre-Christian, condemned doctrine, by all means do so."

Only five months later in Mr. Macmillan's sweeping government changes of July, 1962, Hobson became Attorney General. He succeeded the present Lord Dilhorne and held the office until the Conservative Government fell in 1964. The names of William John Christopher Vassall, the Admiralty spy. and Anthony Enahoro, the Nigerian chief, figured large during Hobson's tenure of this office. Hobson was also one of the five Ministers who in March, 1963, vetted John Profumo's personal statement to the House of Commons denying any impropriety in his relationship with Miss Keeler.

He prosecuted Vassall, who in October, 1962, was sentenced to 18 years' imprisonment after pleading Guilty at the Old Bailey to four charges under the Official Secrets Act. Hobson told the court how Vassall for six years had sold "some part of the safety and security of the people of this country for cash". After this trial, as Attorney General, Hobson played a major part in the Radcliffe tribunal which was set up as a result of the Vassall affair, and which led to the imprisonment of two journalists for refusing to name sources of information.

The Enahoro case the following year drew Hobson into the unprecedented position of being "reported" to the Inner Temple over complaints by a fellow-bencher, Mr. Reginald Paget, Labour M.P. for Northampton. Mr. Paget complained about the Attorney General's so-called "professional misconduct" over the circumstances in which Chief Enahoro was deported from Britain after a long legal battle for him to remain. The complaints—which the Masters of the Inner Bench found unfounded—were that when Enahoro applied for a writ of *habeas corpus* in his efforts to prevent his return to Nigeria to face treason charges, Hobson presented an affidavit by the Home Secretary which he knew to be false and that he failed to disclose that the chief's two counsel would be barred from Nigeria. In their statement afterwards the Masters said: "They found that both the charges were unfounded and that there are no grounds for criticism of Sir John's conduct and do acquit him of all charges made against him."

CLEAR ADVOCATE

Since the Conservatives have been in opposition, Hobson has been their chief spokesman on law matters. He had always identified himself with what are called "home office" affairs, when not a law officer, and during his parliamentary career was secretary of the Home Affairs Committee of Conservative backbenchers, a member of the Royal Commission on the Police, a member of the Executive Committee of Justice and a member of the Home Secretary's Advisory Committee on the Treatment of Offenders.

Hobson was a capable speaker at the dispatch box, rarely dramatic or compelling, almost always serious in manner and cautious, carefully choosing his words and arguments in a way that invariably commanded attention and respect. He was a lean, firm, clear and unpretentious advocate.

Hobson's industry as principal legal adviser to Edward Heath was outstanding. Hardly a Bill did not go directly or indirectly through his hands for legal analysis, and no Conservative member of a committee has ever, it is said, sought Hobson's legal advice in the political field in vain.

His understanding of the complex art of the parliamentary draughtsman was the result of years of assiduous study of law and parliamentary procedure and practice. Those who knew him personally recognized that his somewhat stringent manner concealed a warm friendly nature and a lively sense of humour. His loyalty to his friends and his ideals were profound and unmistakable. One of his ideals was the reform of the law but his suspicion of idealistic enthusiasm led him to discipline his own. None the less many of the reforming measures put through by the Conservative Administration in the field of law reform during his term as Attorney General went through with his guidance and support.

Hobson never faltered in his faith in the excellence of British justice and never tired in trying to discover ways of improving the law and its procedures. He was devoted to the Bar, believed in its future as a separate branch of the legal profession and enjoyed, as often as the pressures of his work allowed, what Stanley Baldwin called "the pleasures of the Temple".

He had been chairman of both Rutland and Bedfordshire Quarter sessions and Recorder of Northampton. For six years after the war he was a member of the General Council of the Bar.

Hobson is survived by a widow and three daughters.

December 5, 1967.

General Courtney H. Hodges, who was Chief of Infantry in the United States Army, and who will be mainly remembered for his command of the 1st United States Army in Europe from August, 1944, to April, 1945, died in hospital on January 16, 1966, at the age of 79.

In spite of frustrations in his earlier days of high command and in spite also of the reserved disposition which kept him out of the headlines, Hodges was a most skilful and successful Army commander whose troops took part in some of the most difficult and severe fighting in the north-west Europe campaign. The break-out operations from Normandy, the bitter Ardennes battles, the brilliant capture and exploitation of the Remagen bridge and the huge prize of the Ruhr were no mean achievements. A slender, soft-voiced, unemotional man of medium height, his favourite recreation was rifle shooting, and he won many distinctions for his marksmanship. He must also be remembered as an expert in infantry training. Overshadowed though he may have been by his superior commander, Bradley, his colleague, Patton, and his subordinate, Collins, Hodges by his handling of the 1st United States Army must be counted as one of the great commanders of the Second World War.

Courtney Hicks Hodges was born in Georgia on January 5, 1887, and obtained an appointment to the United States Military Academy, West Point, in 1904. But a year later, failing to pass examinations in mathematics, he was obliged to leave the academy. Determined to be a soldier, however, and not satisfied with the prospect of joining his father's newspaper business, he enlisted in the Army in 1906 as an ordinary private soldier. He served for two and a half years in the 17th Infantry, reaching the rank of sergeant, and then in 1909 was commissioned as a second lieutenant.

He was next stationed at various posts in the United States, including Fort Leavenworth and San Antonio, and also in the Philippines, before seeing his first active service with the 6th Infantry in Mexico as part of General Pershing's Punitive Expedition. When the United States entered the Great War in 1917 Major Hodges fought with the 6th Infantry in France, taking part in the battle of St. Mihiel and other offensives, of which Meuse Argonne was the one where he gained most experience of being under heavy and sustained fire. He was awarded the Distinguished Service Cross and the Silver Star for valour in action.

PREPARATIONS FOR INVASION

After serving with the Army of Occupation in Germany, Hodges returned to the United States and was still with the 6th Infantry in 1919 and 1920. By 1938 he had been promoted to lieutenant-colonel and was back at the Infantry School as assistant commandant. In 1940 he became commandant of the school with the rank of brigadier-general, and it was during this long association with Fort Benning that he laid the foundation of his great skill in infantry tactics and training.

From 1941 to 1942 Hodges was Chief of Intelligence as a major-general and was also briefly in charge of the Replacement and School Command. When the United States entry into the war had made inevitable a great expansion of the army, Hodges had among others been selected by General Marshall for future high command, and later on in 1942 he was given command of 10 Army Corps. Soon afterwards, however, in February, 1943, he assumed command of 3rd Army at San Antonio, and became a lieutenant-general, but he did not take 3rd Army overseas. In March, 1944, he handed over to General Patton, and went to England to join 1st United States Army, initially as General Bradley's deputy. Hodges was responsible for supervising the training and preparation for the invasion, and also understudied Bradley. The plan was that when Bradley moved up to take command of 12 United States Army Group, Hodges would succeed him in command of 1st Army. This is what happened, and on August 1, 1944, General Hodges took command of the Army with which he was to fight his way to the Elbe.

This was not an easy time for Hodges.

PETROL EXHAUSTED

Not only was it his first command in the field, but Bradley's other Army Commander was the dashing and colourful Patton, so that when the question of priorities for supplies between 1st and 3rd Armies arose, it was not surprising that Hodges did not always get what he wanted. As a result, at the time of the Arnhem battle in September, 1st Army was unable to give real help, but this was due more than anything to Eisenhower's broad front policy which had robbed Hodges of fighting flexibility because of supply shortages. Indeed, by the end of September 1st Army had exhausted its petrol supplies without having broken into the Siegfried Line. So that an opportunity to outflank this line may have been missed, and its place was taken by a frontal assault on Aachen which was captured by 1st Army on October 13, 1944.

The next main battle was the German Ardennes counter-offensive in December, the weight of which fell on Hodges's front. In the extremely confused situation that followed, Hodges's initially slow reaction to the German threat was due to lack of reliable information. Montgomery was given the task of coordinating the operations of the United States 1st and 9th Armies, and as no attacks could be mounted until the German advance had been stopped, 1st Army's operations were really a series of delaying actions in spite of efforts to build up a reserve under General Collins. But the Malmedy shoulder was held, and after very heavy fighting by the end of January the Bulge had been eliminated.

When the Allied advance was resumed, Hodges's Army took part in the Rhine crossing battles of March, 1945, in the areas of Cologne, Bonn and Remagen, and because of III Corps' rapid advance the Remagen bridge was captured intact, a great prize, which enabled four divisions to cross and secure the bridgehead. 1st Army's subsequent thrust from the Remagen bridge in conjunction with Patton's drive from the south began in March and resulted in the encirclement and reduction of the Ruhr by 1st and 9th Armies. On April 18, 1945, German resistance in the Ruhr collapsed and 325,000 prisoners were taken. 1st Army then pushed on farther east to the Leipzig area and the Elbe. On linking hands with the Russian armies, General Hodges's task was accomplished.

January 18, 1966.

Ralph Hodgson, whose death occurred on November 3, 1962, at his home near Minerva, Ohio, won for himself a unique position in English letters by one small book, *Poems 1917*, several pieces from which, "The Bull", "Eve", "The Bells of Heaven", and, above all, "The Song of Honour", have won a permanent place in anthologies. He was 91.

All his life he avoided publicity and when a new collection of his poems appeared in November, 1958, many of those who already knew his poetry well were surprised to hear that Hodgson had survived the First World War. The reason is not difficult to see. Between his success in 1917 and his publication in 1958, he had published in Britain only one short poem, in the magazine *Today*. His *Collected Poems* were published in one volume in 1961.

Since 1924, Hodgson more or less exiled himself from England, which contributed to the obscurity he desired. Even by the end of the 1920s he had become to the average reader of poetry a poet of a past generation—like so many of the other poets who had been published in Georgian poetry. The subjects and the style of what he had then published were largely Wordsworthian.

It was at once praiseworthy as well as surprising that he was awarded the Queen's Medal for Poetry in 1954. His 1958 book—*The Skylark and Other Poems*—showed that, although all his life he had kept outside contemporary poetic trends and, although his interests had remained the same, his poetry had developed.

Hodgson was the sternest of self critics; his artistic integrity was absolute; and he would write only when what he had to say demanded it. He wrote for himself. As a result his output was small but it speaks with a strongly personal accent, is remarkably level in quality, and truly lyrical. His reputation cannot fail to grow, as it outlives temporary fashions.

Singularly little is known of his early years. In fact in the same way as Hodgson avoided publicity for his poetry, he was almost totally reticent about his private affairs, even with those closest to him; he would avoid discussing his family, his upbringing, or his career, just as he would avoid talking to his friends about their private affairs. It is known that he was born in Darlington, co. Durham, in 1871; his descent was from pure English stock, a fact of which he was proud, and his family, he once said, were "cultured" and in his home "Matthew Arnold was discussed at the breakfast table". At 15 he ran away from school to join the "Fancy", the semi-underworld of boxing and boxers. and he lived for two years in America, returning to England in 1891.

In the 1890s he supported himself in London as an artist working for newspapers and magazines. It would have been easy for him to have found employment as a writer but he rarely, if ever, wrote for money as he believed that his gifts would be dulled by prose writing. Nevertheless, it was not until he was over 30 that Hodgson began to write poetry; his first poem was published in *The Saturday Review*, October, 1904.

In 1907 was published Hodgson's first collection of poems, *The Last Blackbird and Other Lines*. This volume was a failure and the author himself came to dislike it; but, in spite of an unevenness, it contains the seeds of his full poetic strength and some lyrics (such as "The Hammers" and parts of "Human Vanity and Big Behaviour") are almost as beautiful as anything he wrote. But these were unread or forgotten; when Hodgson's second book came out, in 1917, reviewers greeted him as a poet of whom they had hardly heard before.

ART EDITOR

Hodgson worked as an artist for various newspapers until 1912, when he became art editor of C. B. Fry's *Weekly Magazine of Sport and Outdoor Life*. In 1914 he joined up, first in the Navy and later in the Army, where he was commissioned in the Royal Artillery.

In 1913 he had founded a private press in partnership with Claud Lovat Fraser and Holbrook Jackson (each of the friends contributing £5). It was this press, "At the Sign of the Flying Fame", which first published several of his poems as chap-books and broadsides; these included "The Song of Honour" and "The Bull", for which he was awarded the £100 Polignac Prize in 1914. Each of the four yellow-covered chap-books of his poems was decorated with drawings by Lovat Fraser and sold plain (black and white) for 6d., or hand-coloured (by the artist and the author) for 2s. 6d. The editions brought a success which was not expected by the publishers, whose aim was chiefly their own pleasure; they are now rarities for the book collector.

INSPIRED CAMPAIGN

After the war, Hodgson inspired the campaign against the wholesale trafficking in birds' feathers for decorative purposes which (together with the slaughter of animals for their fur) he had passionately attacked in his poem "To Deck a Woman." This poem determined Harold Massingham to "put a stop to this abomination", and it was he who set about organizing an agitation to that end. After one failure, the Plumage Group, as the agitators styled themselves, were rewarded for their energies by the Plumage Act of 1921.

Hodgson went to Japan in 1924 as lecturer in English at Sendai University; he retired in 1937 and went to live in America. While he was in Japan he began and almost completed a long and original dramatic poem—*The Muse and the Mastiff*. This was issued in America in instalments between 1941 and 1951. A number of other poems were published at the same time, some of which were certainly written during his retirement, when his creative power, though fitful, was not extinguished.

PRIVATELY PRINTED

These later poems were included in *The Skylark and Other Poems*, originally published in a private limited edition in November, 1958 and subsequently in an ordinary edition a year later.

Hodgson was a spirited and creative conversationalist, and he possessed great energy as well as personal magnetism; he was apt to be unpredictable in his opinions and his "stalwart conviction" sometimes led to unnecessary coldness with his friends. But those who came into contact with the wealth of his mind have written that they can never forget it. For those not fortunate enough to meet him, the range of his vision, the vigour of his spirit, stand revealed in his poetry.

Hodgson was married three times; first in 1896 to Janet Chatteris, who died in 1920; in the following year to Muriel Fraser. After the dissolution of this marriage in 1932, he married Arelia Bollinger in 1933.

November 5, 1962.

Greet Hofmans, the faith healer, whose attempts to improve the eyesight of Princess Marijke, Queen Juliana's youngest daughter, led to a royal crisis in the Netherlands, died in Amsterdam on November 16, 1968, at the age of 73.

During the crisis in 1956, Dr. Drees, the Dutch Prime Minister, denied that Queen Juliana was seeking a divorce, would abdicate, or had caused a constitutional crisis through her association with Miss Hofmans. A three-man committee appointed to investigate allegations that Miss Hofmans was having an undue influence over the Queen presented their report in August that year and announced that the Queen had broken off all relations with the faith healer.

Princess Maria Christina (Marijke) was born on February 8, 1947, with defective vision; her mother had had an attack of measles during pregnancy. After an operation had failed to produce any marked improvement in the eyesight of the Princess, Greet Hofmans, then aged 61, was introduced to the court by Prince Bernhard, to whom she had been recommended by General Koot, a leader of the wartime resistance. But for publicity abroad—led by *Der Spiegel*, the west German weekly—little might have been heard of the matter.

HULLABALOO

As it was, the hullabaloo lasted from the middle of June to the end of August, 1956, with minor rumblings late into the year, and was accentuated by the absence of any clear court or Government statements and by the unduly prolonged reticence of the Dutch press. Miss Hofmans's connexion with the court was severed on the insistence (or so it was popularly believed) of Prince Bernhard. Sympathy for the Queen's feelings as a mother was not wanting, but the muddle left plenty of material for critics of the monarchy.

November 23, 1968.

Sir Milner Holland, K.C.V.O., C.B.E., Q.C., Attorney-General of the Duchy of Lancaster since 1953, died on November 2, 1969. He was 67.

The Milner Holland report on housing in Greater London published in 1965 following the Rachman scandal was a penetrating and constructive investigation into the acute housing shortage in London and the hardships suffered by tenants.

Holland had all the qualifications for high judicial office, but in an age when rates of taxation have made the acceptance of such office by fashionable counsel no longer a financial sacrifice, he preferred to remain at the Bar, and was one of the most distinguished, respected and indeed well-loved advocates of his generation.

CLASSICS PRIZES

Edward Milner Holland was born on September 8, 1902, the son of Sir Edward Holland, D.L., J.P., and was educated at Charterhouse and at Hertford College, Oxford, where as a classical scholar he won a number of scholarships and prizes. He was called to the Bar by Inner Temple in 1927, obtaining a certificate of honour in his Bar Final examinations. He practised, however, at the Equity Bar and had chambers in Lincoln's Inn, which he joined *ad eundem* in 1947. The story told, not wholly apocryphal, is that he was pressed to fill a last-minute vacancy in the Lincoln's Inn team competing at golf against the other Inns of Court for the Scrutton Cup, and having assisted them to an unexpected victory was compelled immediately to join a second inn to ratify this success.

Milner Holland, as he was generally known, rapidly acquired a large junior practice of a general Chancery nature, and was in 1931 appointed Assistant Reader in Equity to the Council of Legal Education and later in 1935 Reader in Equity. All this he at once abandoned when war broke out, and was commissioned a second lieutenant in the Royal Army Service Corps. But he was one of four junior members of the Chancery Bar who all had the distinction of ending the war as brigadiers. In his case he was appointed in 1943 Deputy Director of Personal Services at the War Office, a post which gave full scope to his talents for organization and in particular to his flair for sympathetic but penetrative understanding of his fellow men. In 1945 he was rewarded for his outstanding services by a C.B.E.

LEADING CASES

On returning to the Bar Milner Holland was soon in heavy practice again, and in 1948 he took silk. He did not take long to establish himself in the front row, and in the following years his name will be found in the reports of a large proportion of the leading cases of the day, by no means confined to the Chancery division. In particular, he established a reputation in local government inquiries and in the Parliamentary corridor. He had a famous success in 1964 in winning the Burmah Oil appeal in the House of Lords in the teeth of the advice of a former Attorney-General that his clients had no case, For the oil company it was a short-lived triumph for within a year the Government had introduced a Bill to reverse the Lords decision. Among many other celebrated cases in which he appeared were the Fitz-William Peerage case, the Bernard Shaw will case, Bollinger v. Costa Brava Wine Company, concerning the right to use the term "Spanish Champagne", the "sherry" case which established that sherry comes only from the Jerez district of Spain, and Parke v. Daily News Ltd., in which it was held that it was ultra vires for the Daily News to distribute the balance of its assets upon liquidation amongst its former staff. In 1951 he was appointed Attorney-General of the Duchy of Lancaster and in 1953 he became a bencher of Lincoln's Inn.

It is generally accepted that Milner Holland was offered and refused an appointment to the High Court bench; that he did so was not due to any lack of devotion to the public service. He was twice chairman of the Bar Council, in 1957 and again in 1962. This was an office he filled with outstanding success. His first term came immediately between those of Lord Shawcross and Lord Gardiner, and there is no doubt that these three rendered incalculable services to the Bar by their wise and vigorous leadership, which did much to restore the standing of the Bar Council. Minister Holland played a large part in committing the Bar Council to the support of the idea of common examinations for barristers and solicitors, and some think that in so doing he made a major error of judgment.

RARE LAPSE

If he did so, it was a rare lapse. His judgment was in most matters as impeccable as his urbane handling as chairman of this rather difficult body. He was appointed a member of the Pilgrims in 1957 and a member of the Council of Tribunals in 1958, in which capacity he conducted on one occasion a devastating cross-examination of the head of a Government Department. He was also a member of the Bank Rate and of the Vassall Tribunals. He was knighted in 1959 for the services which he rendered to the Bar and to the public, and some six years later was appointed a K.C.V.O.

In 1963 he undertook, at the urgent request of the Government of the day and at considerable personal sacrifice, to be chairman of a committee to report on rented housing conditions in London, following the disclosures usually associated with the name of Rachman. He produced in an astonishingly short time in relation to the nature of the task the Milner Holland Report, universally acknowledged to be well informed, politically unbiased and penetrative in its conclusions and suggestions for reform; but a report destined nevertheless to be very largely disregarded in the provisions of the Rent Act 1965, which were designed to deal with the problem he investigated.

In 1929, he made a lastingly happy marriage with Elinor Doreen Leslie-Jones. They had two sons.

Milner Holland had of course a fine mind and a great capacity for lucid organization of ideas. But his quality as an advocate did not rest primarily upon penetrative intellect. He was a man of shrewd judgment. He had a great sense of tribunal and an unerring instinct as to what would run and what would not, and just how to run it. He was above all a terribly persuasive advocate. This no doubt was due to his sensitivity to people and to his vitality and charm of manner. Like all great advocates, no trouble was ever too much for him in the preparation of a case. And he had the toughness of fibre to stand his ground when necessary without yielding an inch, and yet without ever being involved in heated exchanges. Whatever his feelings, which could be no less warm than the next man's, he never lost control of an unruffled demeanour. He was an advocate formidable on a point of law, formidable in cross examination of witnesses, but perhaps most formidable of all in his masterly deployment and persuasive presentation of complicated facts. For a number of years there was probably no advocate at the Bar whose services were so widely or so eagerly sought by solicitors.

VERSATILE

Milner Holland was not only a great advocate. He was a man of many versatile gifts. He was an excellent cook, an amateur photographer of unusual ability, an authority on rare flowers, a witty after-dinner speaker, a highly competent electrical engineer, and a keen golfer who once reached the semi-final of the Bar Golfing Tournament at Rye, and who was Captain of the Bar Golfing Society. Above all he had a genius for friendship. He liked and understood people, and suffered young fools gladly and even old fools comparatively gladly. He had no sense of his own importance. And when he was charming to his less distinguished friends, no one could feel it was part of an act. It all flowed naturally from him and from his kindness and interest in his fellow creatures. It is difficult to suppose that with all his formidable talents and firmness of purpose that he ever made an enemy. While he lived he adorned the profession which he practised, and by his death he left the sadder a vast company of admiring friends.

November 3, 1969.

Sir Sidney Holland, G.C.B., C.H., Prime Minister of New Zealand from 1954 to 1957, when he retired for reasons of health, died in Wellington on August 5, 1961. He was 67.

For nine years in Opposition Holland built and consolidated the National Party, converting it from a coalition of compromise between Reform and Liberal into a unified organization based upon clear principles. In eight strenuous years of office he endeavoured to give expression to those principles and largely succeeded. The essence of his political belief was that while the Government has a duty to lead as well as to govern, it must afford the widest scope and the greatest encouragement to individual initiative and enterprise.

Sidney George Holland was born at Greendale, Canterbury, on October 18, 1893, the fourth son in a family of eight children, and was educated at West Canterbury district high school. His father, Henry Holland, C.B.E., J.P., a Yorkshireman, was the proprietor of a haulage business in Christchurch. His mother was a native of Lancashire. On leaving school he joined a hardware firm, but when his father assumed the office of mayor of Christchurch in 1912 he went into the family business. When war started in 1914, already trained as a territorial, he enlisted with the Dominion's Field Artillery on his twenty-first birthday, first serving in the ranks and later as a lieutenant. During the battle of Messines in 1918 he was stricken by severe illness and was invalided home. After the war he started with his eldest brother the Midland Engineering Company and steadily extended his commercial interests to a number of other industries, including insurance.

WON FATHER'S SEAT

His entry on a parliamentary career was the outcome of a misfortune to his father. Holland senior had been elected a member of Parliament for Christchurch North in 1925 and his son became his organizer and secretary. In 1935 the father was incapacitated by an accident two weeks before an election was due, and his son took his place and won the seat.

It was the year when the first Labour Government of New Zealand took office with the promise of state planning and management which would banish all fear of depression. The coalition of Reform and Liberal that had held office during the difficult and depressing years of the early thirties was disorganized, without fighting leadership or a firm policy. Though a young member (he was 42 at the time) without parliamentary experience, Holland quickly established a reputation for the vigour and directness of his criticism. In 1940 he was chosen as leader of the National Party and entered at once upon the task of infusing new life into the party.

Labour had created a system of controls before and during the war and was steadily extending the scope of state benefits and state management and narrowing the area of individual freedom. Holland and the men who rallied to his leadership opposed this extension energetically, but without rancour or appeal to class prejudice. The National leader, with his abounding vitality, good humour, and optimism, quickly became a platform and radio personality, but he had to fight three elections before he achieved office. When his party gained office in 1949 Holland applied himself assiduously to construction. Here his optimism led him at times into difficulties. He had great faith in the judgment and capacity of businessmen and did not make sufficient allowance for the tendency of business to move too fast when the reins of state control were dropped. But he saw and corrected this error in time. In other directions his vision and optimism were the basis of great achievement. He called for greater production and set in motion a scheme of development to stimulate production and cope with the produce as it increased.

For five years he was his own Minister of Finance. In Parliament he led in debate and between sessions travelled widely round the country to see for himself the progress of development and to keep in touch with the people. These activities, broken often by even more strenuous missions to the United Kingdom and to other dominions, undoubtedly taxed his strength.

STRIKE TEST

One of the chief tests of his leadership was the formidable waterfront strike in 1951. He broke it by a well-judged blend of resolution and restraint, and though the losers accused him of dictation his measures in fact reflected determination to eschew class policies or the excitement of class feeling. In foreign affairs and defence he made it abundantly clear that his Government could be relied on to stand by Britain in all important matters, and his immediate approval of the British Government's Suez policy in 1956 was almost instinctive.

He retired in the autumn of 1957, apprehensive about his health and with the general good will of his people, for even those who opposed his policies liked and trusted him as a frank and friendly man. His retirement gave him the leisure he coveted to enjoy his farm at North Canterbury, where he bred Romney sheep and Polled Angus cattle. He was created G.C.B. in the year of his retirement.

He married in 1920 Florence Beatrice Drayton. There were two sons and two daughters of the marriage.

August 5, 1961.

Vyvyan Holland, O.B.E., the writer, who died on October 10, 1967, at the age of 80, was born at 16 (now 34) Tite Street, London, in November, 1886—the son of Oscar Wilde. Strangely enough, when the birth was registered neither parent could remember the exact day, so November 3 was arbitrarily chosen. This had the advantage, as Vyvyan characteristically remarked in later life, of making him "completely immune from the importunities of astrologers". He was the second son of Oscar Wilde and his wife Constance Mary (*née* Lloyd), the first son Cyril having been born 17 months before. The baby was christened Vyvyan Oscar Beresford. It was only in his early years that he knew his father—after 1895 he never saw him again—but he has left, in *Son of Oscar Wilde*, an account of how Oscar Wilde, then at the height of his fame, would go down on hands and knees to play games with his children in the nursery and would tell them wonderful fairy stories, some of which (but only some) were written down and preserved.

When Vyvyan was seven he was sent to Hildersham House, at Broadstairs, a preparatory school which is still flourishing. This was in May 1894. A year later Oscar Wilde had been tried, found guilty and sentenced to two years' imprisonment. Vyvyan was too young to understand what was happening. The elder son, Cyril, found out the reason for his father's disgrace and it cast a shadow over his short life. He was killed by a German sniper in the First World War.

The two boys, in charge of a French governess, were hurried off to Switzerland, but when the manager of the hotel at Glion found out who they were he turned them out. Their name was changed to Holland, an old family name on their mother's side. They were sent to a school at Freiburg-im-Breisgau but were expelled for unruly conduct. After the same thing had happened at another German school they were sent to a school at Neuenheim, near Heidelberg, where nearly all the boys and masters were English. The elder boy was not too unhappy there but Vyvyan was, and, at the beginning of 1897, his mother took him away and entered him at the Jesuit College at Monaco. Vyvyan liked, in later life, to remark that he was "educated at Monte Carlo", which most people dismissed as a joke.

Oscar Wilde was released from prison in May, 1897. A little more than a year later his wife died. Vyvyan left the school at Monaco and was sent to Stonyhurst, while Cyril went to Radley. After this the two brothers hardly ever met. Every effort was made to hide their whereabouts from Oscar Wilde; and when in late 1900 Vyvyan was told of his death, he said, "I thought he had died long ago". He was grown up before he learned the reason for his father's disgrace. "Is that all?" he said. "I thought he had embezzled money."

Vyvyan left Stonyhurst in 1904, and went up to Trinity Hall, Cambridge, to study law. After two years, however, this project was abandoned for a time and he went to London to work for the Foreign Office examination. He soon began to meet his father's friends: Robert Ross, Max Beerbohm, Reginald Turner, and Mrs. Ada Leverson. At Cambridge, to which he returned in 1908, he was friendly with Ronald Firbank and Rupert Brooke. He left Cambridge, after taking his degree, in June, 1909. Having been called to the Bar, he endeavoured (in his own words) "much against my better judgment, to practise as a barrister until the outbreak of the 1914 War mercifully put an end to this useless effort". He joined the Royal Field Artillery, was four times mentioned in dispatches, was awarded the O.B.E. and became a major.

LITERARY TALENT

Returning to England in 1919 he "spent the next few years in dilettantism". But he was conscious of literary talent and, but for the overpowering shadow of his father's fame, he might well have begun a career as a writer. As it was, he confined himself, almost entirely, to translations from the French, in particular of the novels of Julian Green. Among his few published works may be mentioned two opuscula he wrote for the Sette of Odd Volumes: *The Mediaeval Courts of Love* and *On Bores*. He also wrote a *History of Nineteenth Century Hand-Coloured Fashion Plates*, a subject on which he was the foremost authority. Late in life, in 1954, he brought out the moving account of his childhood which he called *Son of Oscar Wilde*. He continued the story in *Time Remembered, after Père Lachaise* (1966). His other literary activities were mostly connected with gastronomy and oinophily. He was one of the founders of the Wine and Food Society and the Saintsbury Club. His last book was *Drink and be Merry* (1967).

He was never happier than when dispensing hospitality to a few chosen friends in his house in Carlyle Square, Chelsea. Here the fortunate guests would be presented with a formidable array of prephylloxera clarets. In his time he was probably one of the dozen best judges of wine in the world. He was shy and quiet-spoken by nature, preferring to hear others talk, but he had a great sense of humour and a sly wit. He was a most lovable man.

He married in 1914 Violet Mary Craigie, who died in 1918. In 1943 he married Miss Thelma Besant, of Melbourne, Australia. There is one son of the marriage, Merlin, born in 1945.

October 11, 1967.

General Sir Leslie Hollis, K.C.B., K.B.E., who died on August 9, 1963, in Cuckfield Hospital, Sussex, at the age of 66, served throughout the Second World War as senior military assistant secretary to the War Cabinet. He was Chief Staff Officer to the Minister of Defence from 1947 to 1949 and Commandant General of the Royal Marines from 1949 to 1952.

Hollis made a considerable reputation in the War Cabinet office. He had an immense capacity for work and he had a gift for picking out the important points from diffuse documents and inconclusive meetings, and for setting them down in a few crisp sentences. His imperturbability and his keen sense of humour were assets that helped him greatly to stay the course for so many years. Everyone who worked with Jo Hollis grew to have a great affection for him. He had immense pride in and love for his corps and it was a joy to him when his career was crowned by his appointment as its Commandant General.

Leslie Chasemore Hollis was born on February 9, 1897, the son of Canon C. J. Hollis, of Worthing. He was educated at St. Lawrence College, Ramsgate, and he joined the Royal Marines Light Infantry as a probationary second lieutenant in 1914. In the First World War he served with the Grand Fleet and the Harwich Force. At the Battle of Jutland he was fortunate to be in the Duke of Edinburgh, the only surviving ship of the 1st Cruiser Squadron.

After the war he served in H.M.S. Durban on the China station and subsequently at the Royal Marine depots at Plymouth and Deal, where for a time he was instructor in small arms. He then passed the staff course and on completing it was appointed as intelligence officer to the flagship of the C-in-C. Africa station, where he served until 1932, when he was posted to the Plans Division of the Admiralty. It was in the plans division that he found his metier. At the end of his tour of duty in the Admiralty, when he was about to go back to sea, Sir Maurice Hankey, then Secretary to the Cabinet and to the Committee of Imperial Defence, chose him to be Secretary of the Joint Planning Sub-committee.

Throughout the Second World War he served as one of the two principals (the other being Sir Ian Jacob) of the military wing of the War Cabinet Secretariat which was headed by General Ismay. This secretariat, a legacy from the prewar Imperial Defence Committee, became the staff of the Prime Minister in his capacity as Minister of Defence. It was one of the hardest worked organizations concerned with the higher conduct of the war. Indeed it could be likened to an immensely efficient, nonstop computing machine into which were fed the views of Ministers, the Chiefs of Staff, and a dozen wartime committees, and out of which poured, with astonishing speed, an unending stream of memoranda on which decisions could be based.

It was Mr. Churchill's view that displacements in a sphere so intimate and so concerned with secret matters would be detrimental to the continuous and efficient dispatch of business. In conformity with this policy Hollis remained at his post, as Ismay's number two, for 11 years. During the war Hollis estimated that he attended more than 6,000 meetings of the Chiefs of Staff, not to mention innumerable meetings of the War Cabinet Defence Committee and many interallied conferences. The routine must have been killing. His day had two beginnings: one was around 7.30 in the morning when the secretariat started to deal with reports that had come in overnight, and the other at 10.30 in the evening when ministerial and defence committee meetings usually took place. The hours of work were fantastic, and the mental labour concentrated and continuous, and always under pressure against time.

EASING THE LOAD

The range of work handled by the secretariat was vast and the variety of their agenda was impressive. Although they had no direct responsibility for the plans made or decisions reached, they were called upon to crystallize and set down on paper the views of the Chiefs of Staff alike on points needing immediate decision and on broad questions of future policy. After Dunkirk the volume of work threatened to overwhelm the secretariat, and Hollis put forward proposals, which were approved and adopted, for lightening it and speeding it up.

His duties brought him into close touch with the Prime Minister, who frequently addressed his minutes to the Chiefs of Staff and to Ministries through Hollis. He accompanied Churchill on most of his trips to America, to various interallied conferences, and to the fighting fronts; and he was the sole representative of the Defence Office with Churchill during his illness at Carthage in 1943 and his convalescence at Marrakesh, during which time, when his activity was hardly abated, Churchill described him as a tower of strength.

On Ismay's departure in 1947 Hollis succeeded him as Chief Staff Officer to the Minister of Defence, A. V. Alexander, and deputy secretary of the Cabinet, and he held these posts for two years.

In 1949 he was at last released from the secretariat and was appointed Commandant-General Royal Marines. With the establishment of the wartime commandos on a permanent footing, the Royal Marines had taken on a new look since his last service with them 17 years before, but he soon adapted himself to his duties as their head, and carried them out with zest and obvious enjoyment.

He published three books, *One Marine's Tale*, 1956, *War at the Top*, 1959 (with James Leasor), and *The Captain General*, 1962, a biography of the Duke of Edinburgh. The first of these was much the best: in it he blended autobiography with sidelights on the higher conduct of the war and some good stories on Churchill.

Hollis married Rose Fraser in 1922. They had no children.

August 10, 1963.

Baliol Holloway, the actor and producer, died at his home in London on April 15, 1967, at the age of 84.

During a career which extended from 1899 until after the Second World War, he devoted himself with no less zeal than accomplishment and force of personality to the classic tradition as it is represented in the English theatre by the plays of Shakespeare and his contemporaries, the eighteenth-century masters, and Shaw.

Baliol Holloway was born in Brentwood, Essex, on February 28, 1883, and educated at Denstone College, Staffordshire. After leaving school he studied for the stage under Hermann Vezin, with whom he made his first appearance, as Leonardo, in *The Merchant of Venice*, in 1899. For several years he was a member of various touring companies, notably those managed by Jerrold Robertshaw and Edmund Tearle, which specialized in Shakespeare's plays. He made his first appearance in London at the Great Queen Street Theatre in 1903, as Jacques Barzinovsky in *The Man and his Picture*, and then returned to Shakespeare, first with Osmond Tearle's company and then, from 1907 to 1912, with Sir Frank Benson.

After a year with the Liverpool Repertory Company, he was engaged by Granville Barker for a season at the St. James's Theatre, where he played in *Androcles and the Lion* and a number of modern plays. During the First World War his roles ranged from that of Sir Thomas Seymour, in *Bluff King Hal* to *Mr. Wu*, but in 1920 he joined the New Shakespeare Company in London and Stratford-on-Avon. Two seasons at the Old Vic, from 1925 to 1927, presented him with a startling variety of leading parts from Simon Eyre in *The Shoemaker's Holiday*, to *Macbeth* and *Othello*.

In 1927, he was seen at the Guild Theatre, New York, and in 1929 he toured Canada playing leading parts in and producing a repertoire of Shaw plays. From then on his reputation was as high across the Atlantic as it had become in England. Having reached the happy position in which he could choose those engagements which appealed to him,

Baliol Holloway's subsequent roles ranged from Andrew Undershaft to Long John Silver, from Dick Phenyl in *Old Lavender* to John Worthing, and from Caliban to Cardinal Wolsey. As a producer he was no less adventurous; typical of his taste and his devotion to the then neglected masterpieces was his season of Restoration plays, in which he played leading parts, at the Ambassador's Theatre in 1932 and 1933, and his almost Quixotic affection for the Open Air Theatre.

Baliol Holloway's long career can be seen as a bridge between the lavish days of nineteenth-century Shakespearian production, with their cult of personality, and the new style which grew from the work of Granville Barker. Work with the Benson company taught him the importance of directness, clarity and vigour, and these were gifts which he never lost. At the same time, a dark, sombre-toned voice and a commanding personality (his gift of subduing it was perhaps no less notable) qualified him by nature for the great tragic roles in which he made his most striking successes.

April 17, 1967.

Professor Arthur Holmes, F.R.S., Emeritus Professor of Geology and Mineralogy in the University of Edinburgh, died on September 20, 1965, at the age of 75 at his home in Putney. His brilliant research on the wider problems of geology had earned him his place as one of the great earth scientists of the century.

Holmes was born at Hebburn, near Newcastle upon Tyne, in 1890. He graduated at Imperial College in 1910 and was a member of the staff of the geology department there until 1921 when he joined Yomah Oil Company in Burma as chief geologist. In 1924 he was appointed head of the newly created Department of Geology in Durham University which under his leadership rapidly gained an international reputation for petrological research. In 1943 he was appointed Regius Professor of Geology at Edinburgh and he retired from this post in 1956, remaining in Edinburgh as research fellow for six years after that.

Holmes exercised a profound influence on almost all branches of geology, not only through his own remarkable researches but also by his beautifully written text-books and the stimulation of the research qualities of his students. His output of publications was prodigious—nearly 200 including several leading textbooks such as *The Age of the Earth*, *Nomenclature of Petrology*, *Petrographic Methods and Calculations*, and *Principles of Physical Geology*.

He made a great number of contributions to knowledge of the geology of many parts of the world, from his home district in the north of England to Africa, India and elsewhere.

He was never a man to shun controversy and his work on the origin of the alkaline rocks of Africa and elsewhere, on the thorny problems of granites and their associates, on the origin and development of magmas, and on the role of metasomatism in rock genesis broadened the vision of petrologists all over the world.

During his early years in Imperial College, not long after the discovery of radioactivity, he was a pioneer in applying radiometric methods to the dating of rocks. Since that time he was one of the leading workers in that field and took a major part in the erection of a geological time-scale in terms of millions of years. Contributions to the geophysical aspects of geology are classic; the nature of orogenic and epeirogenic activity, convection currents in the earth's mantle, continental drift, radioactivity in geology—one could go on for a long time listing the aspects of geology to which he made major contributions.

This distinguished career received international acclaim. Holmes was made an honorary member of many foreign geological societies and academies of science. He was made a Fellow of the Royal Society in 1942, and received an honorary LL.D. in Edinburgh in 1960.

He continued his creative work until the end. The second edition (largely rewritten and greatly enlarged) of his *Principles of Physical Geology*, published in 1965, is a masterpiece and shows a breadth of vision that few men possess.

Holmes married first in 1914 Margaret Howe, who died in 1938. They had one son. In 1939 he married secondly Doris Livesey Reynolds.

September 24, 1965.

Sir Maurice Gerald Holmes, G.B.E., K.C.B., who was Permanent Secretary of the Board of Education from 1937 to 1945, died at his London home on April 4, 1964.

Maurice Gerald Holmes was born in 1885, the son of Edmund Holmes, chief inspector of the Board of Education. He was educated at Wellington, where he made a name for himself as a sprinter, and at Balliol, where he took a first in the Law finals. He served in the First World War as colonel in the R.A.S.C. Originally intended for the Bar, he decided to enter the Board of Education and his career in that department coincided with a period of unprecedented activity and progress.

After passing through the posts of private secretary and establishment officer he was chosen in 1937 to succeed Pelham as permanent secretary. Almost immediately the shadows of the Second World War involved him in difficult decisions, but it was with the removal of the department to Bournemouth in 1940 that his real task began. The issue of the Green Book prepared the way for the new policy in education embodied in the Butler Act of 1944. It can safely be said that the new policy owed everything, under the ministerial direction of Mr. Butler, to the brilliant and penetrating mind of Maurice Holmes. Returning to London in 1942 he was called on to plan the working of the Butler Act and—what was perhaps even more exacting—to adjust the educational machine without friction to the policies of Ellen Wilkinson.

RETIREMENT TASKS

In 1945 he retired and was in constant demand for tasks of all kinds. He visited the West Indies and East Africa on Government inquiries and served on a number of special committees. Perhaps it was the local inquiries for the Ministry of Transport that he specially enjoyed; his legal training and his remarkably acute judgment made him ideal for this work. In private life he was active as a governor of Wellington and as chairman of the Oxford and Cambridge Club, but much of his leisure was given first to book collecting and later to the study of the life and voyages of Captain Cook. He compiled a bibliography of Cook, and his collection of records was almost unique.

It may be that his very brilliance and a certain inability to suffer fools gladly made him appear aloof and may conceivably have prevented his reaching the highest distinctions in public life of which his abilities were fully capable. But to those who knew him well he will always be remembered as the kindest and most sympathetic of men.

Maurice Holmes married in 1917 Ivy, daughter of Brigadier-General Dunsford, and had two daughters.

April 6, 1964.

Harold Edward Holt, P.C., C.H., who had been Prime Minister of the Commonwealth of Australia since January 20, 1966, lost his life in a swimming accident on December 17, 1967.

He had succeeded Sir Robert Menzies, and after 10 years as deputy leader of the Liberal Party he was determined to make his own new administration more obviously Australian and modern. He selected his first ministry at a seaside home in Portsea, Victoria, casually dressed and attended by three charming young daughters-in-law and his vivacious wife. He was an able spear-fisherman and the first photographs flashed around the world of Australia's new Prime Minister showed him in goggles and rubber suit. The impression was immediate, of a man very different from the dominant old master whose retirement gave the much younger Holt his chance.

For many years Holt had looked uncertain, unsure even, of succeeding Menzies, let alone matching him as a political leader. But Holt was sterner than he seemed. He had outlasted several rivals, notably Sir Garfield Barwick, now Chief Justice, and John McEwen, leader of the Country Party, who looked a possible coalition leader when Menzies and Holt, then treasurer, were coping shakily with the aftermath of the credit squeeze in 1960.

In November, 1966, after a year of assiduous travel, especially in Asia, where he went conspicuously before visiting London or Washington, Holt won a record victory in his first general election as Prime Minister, beating comfortably even the best performance of his brilliant mentor. It was the reward he wanted and perhaps deserved for the assiduous attention to the ambition he held as a boy. All his life, with efficiency, charm and unobtrusive determination, Holt worked hard for supreme political office. Early in 1967 Holt was at his zenith.

But 1967 saw a steady decline in the fortunes

of the Prime Minister and of the coalition, and in November, in the Senate elections, the Government was badly shaken. Holt's successful gallop through 1966 had been based on a strong attachment to American alliance and determination to honour to the full the commitment Menzies made in Vietnam. In Washington he went on record as "all the way with L.B.J." and the President went to Australia giving his personal accolade, as it were, to the Anzus treaty which means so much to that part of the world.

BACKBENCH REVOLT

The alternative to Holt was then Calwell, with a policy of withdrawal from Vietnam. In 1967, with the Vietnam war still dragging on and the new Labour leader, Gough Whitlam, younger than Holt, the electorate was changing its mind, wondering sceptically about the strength of the Prime Minister as he coped not only with the war and tension in South-East Asia but also with mundaner small matters within Australia, and particularly within Parliament. Here Whitlam, a barrister, was quick to take advantage of backbench revolt which forced the Prime Minister to appoint a new royal commission into the loss of the destroyer Voyager and also of the controversial V.I.P. aircraft issue in which Holt's style of leadership looked indequate. Instead of deciding for himself whether to accept the resignation of Peter Howson, Minister of Air, Holt consulted the Cabinet. He always said he wanted to be captain of the team and not its master. The role suited the man and, given better colleagues, it would probably have suited Australia. But political talent within the coalition had withered under the shadow of Menzies and the kindly Holt might have been wiser to replace more of his Ministers or direct them more plainly.

However, he did much for Australia, reflecting faithfully several of the people's aspirations, especially for friendship with Asia, where his genuine, quiet unpretentious charm was usefully at work upon its leaders. He relaxed very considerably the administration of Australia's restricted immigration policy and he began to interest the Commonwealth in Aboriginal affairs throughout Australia. He was a likeable, decent man who wanted to be helpful to everyone. Perhaps he dissipated too much the limited strength he had.

Holt was born in Sydney on August 5, 1908, son of a schoolteacher who became the London director of J. C. Williamson Theatres. One of his grandfathers drove a team of bullocks in the bush, so his antecedents were thoroughly Australian but his flair may have come from the theatre and his father. After early schooling in Sydney, Holt went to Wesley College, Melbourne (Menzies' old school).

His mother died when he was 16. He expected to go to an English university but depression brought his father back from London. So young Holt went to Melbourne University, where he graduated as a Bachelor of Laws in 1930. A year at the Bar in depression days of 1932 was not rewarding, so Holt became a solicitor and got a salaried job. Then at the age of 27 he won a by-election for the federal seat of Fawkner and within four years was invited to join the first Menzies ministry.

But in March, 1940, room had to be found for Country Party leaders in the new Coalition Government and Holt was dropped. He volunteered as a private in the Australian Imperial Force destined for service overseas. However in October, 1940, three ministers were killed in an air crash and he was summoned back into government with the important portfolio of Labour and National Service. He was still only 32. Within a year Menzies' Government fell and young Holt had to decide whether to stick with his leader on the Opposition front bench or return to the A.I.F.

He stayed in Parliament, where he thought his duty lay, and found himself explaining his reasons in some detail at the general election of 1943, against a disconcerting brigadier. When Menzies swept back to power in 1949 Holt again took over Labour and National service with immigration as an extra and equally exacting responsibility. He did well and in 1956 succeeded Sir Eric Harrison as leader of the House of Representatives. Two years later he became treasurer on the retirement of Sir Arthur Fadden.

Characteristically his first budget was a cheerful affair which lopped ls. off income tax. Then came the credit squeeze and a nasty period which he bore with courage and good humour. By 1963 the economy was going well again and Menzies was back with a better sort of majority after near defeat in 1961. Holt began to prepare Australia for the decimal currency changeover coming two years later, and one month after Holt became Prime Minister.

DISENCHANTMENT

Before flying to Melbourne the day after being sworn in Holt told reporters "I will be talking to ministers and others to learn their problems and aspirations and their own sense of what they are best able to do." It was a typically considerate approach but it indicated perhaps how he was going to be troubled later on, after his first remarkably good year. He began by meeting Healey in Canberra and assurances he received then must have made him disenchanted later as British defence policy in the Far East jerked away from what he had been told. In March he announced that Australia's military force in Vietnam would be trebled. It was a surprising, bold decision. In April he was in Vietnam as the first head of government to visit troops in action. He was also in Thailand, Singapore, Malaysia. In June and July he went to Washington, New York, and London, where he spoke openly, frankly and some would say unwisely of Britain's retreat from Asia.

Holt's view was that Britain might be wrong to withdraw troops from Malaysia and redeploy them in Europe when they would be more useful in Vietnam. His argument was that the peace of the whole world was being threatened in South-east Asia not in Europe.

He returned to prepare for the general election in November which was one of the wildest in Australia for many years with conscription for Vietnam as the most stirring issue. Policy had to protect the Prime Minister and he was hit by demonstrators at several meetings, However, the result was one he wanted. He was Prime Minister in his own right at last with a record majority, almost twice as big as the one he had inherited. In January, 1967, he boldly welcomed to Canberra Air Vice-Marshal Ky, then Prime Minister of South Vietnam. The next month he was in New Zealand making the first visit by an Australian Prime Minister since 1954. It was a significant effort by Holt to bring closer two peoples who ought to be better friends but are not. Holt got on well with Holyoake as he did with most men. Indeed the man's strength and weakness both stemmed from a nature which was unusually agreeable for a politician.

In 1946 Holt married Mrs. Zara Kate Fell, a leading fashion designer in Melbourne. They had no children of their own but Holt's three step sons and their wives were very close to him.

December 19, 1967.

Sir Frederic Hooper, BT., managing director of the Schweppes group of companies, died at his London home on October 4, 1963. He was 71.

English public life owers much to those men who, in addition to successfully pursuing their own chosen avocation, have been willing to make their contribution in the widest sphere of service to the community.

Such a man was Sir Frederic Collins Hooper, for through his long and successful business career are interwoven the threads of notable service to many spheres of public life—service that was given to innumerable public causes, not in the sense of seeking the full glare of publicity or, indeed, of public estimation, but rather because here was a man who over and above his work was willing to apply his talents to many varied problems where he felt that a wide knowledge and understanding of people might enable him to make a contribution.

He was born in July, 1892, the son of F. S. Hooper, and went to Sexeys School, Bruton. Graduating at University College London in 1913, he stayed there on research work until outbreak of war in 1914. He was commissioned into The Dorset Regiment and spent most of the next four years in France, becoming in 1917 Camp Commandant and A.D.C. to Sir Regional Pinney, Commanding 33rd Division.

GROWTH OF SCHWEPPES

Demobilized in 1919, he joined the Ionian Bank in Athens but returned to England towards the end of 1921. Early in 1922 he met Mr. F. J. Marquis (later Lord Woolton), who was then managing director of Lewis' Ltd, at Liverpool. Hooper was recruited as one of the first graduate trainees to join any commercial organization in Britain, and he stayed with this company for 20 years, becoming a director in 1934 and a joint managing director in 1940. He resigned in 1942, and from that time became well known as a broadcaster, writer, and speaker on a wide range of subjects. For two years, from 1942 to 1944, he was director of the Political Research Centre in London until early in 1945 he was asked to take over as director of the Business Training Scheme planned and operated by the Ministry of Labour and National Service to assist the resettlement of returning ex-Service men. There could hardly have been anyone more suited to finding solutions to the complex human problems of the transition from Service to business life, and the success of the whole of this early resettlement scheme owed a great deal to Hooper.

With this task completed, he joined Schweppes Limited as managing director in 1948, and was the chief architect of its remarkable fortunes since that date. More than that, he was a well-beloved boss to every man and woman in that company. He was due to retire from this position at the end of 1963.

IMAGINARY COUNTY

He took personal responsibility for advertising as well as for personnel and labour relations and was closely connected with the creation of a supplementary English county—"Schweppshire". The idea was born during a game of snooker between Hooper and Stephen Potter, who later wrote the sharply observed texts for the Schweppshire advertisements.

Since 1948 he had remained a most active public servant in the true sense of the word. During 1954 he was on the committee set up to inquire into the organization of the Royal Air Force; during 1955 a deputy chairman of the committee inquiring into the servicing aspects of the R.A.F.; and in 1956 a member of the committee inquiring into the employment of National Service men. He was knighted in 1956.

Always tremendously interested in matters concerning defence, Hooper in 1957 became the chairman of the advisory board set up by the Minister of Labour to deal with Regular forces resettlement. Accepting the national policy that required the premature retirement scheme, he worked indefatigably to see that the officers and other ranks leaving the Services at this time should find the work and place in civilian industry and commerce to which their great abilities entitled them. There are many ex-Service men today who thank Frederic Hooper for the opportunities they have found in this field.

RECRUITING PROBLEMS

Later, in 1960, he became adviser to the Minister of Defence, dealing especially with the problems of man-management and recruitment facing the Services in the new climate of the 1960. The great success of the 1961–62 recruitment campaign for Regular soldiers was very largely due to his advice and imagination, and to the expert knowledge which he contributed on how best to project the image of the new Regular forces. In this work he continued most active until the day of his death. He was created a baronet in June, 1962.

In other fields of education, literature and the arts he made an equal contribution. He was for many years on the council of the English Stage Company, and, until his death, a most active chairman of the Royal Academy of Dancing, working always in close association with its president, Dame Margot Fonteyn. He was a Fellow of University College London, a governor of Ashridge Management College, and had long record of service to the Royal College of Nursing as chairman of its finance committee. Actively interested in the educational work of the Institute of Directors, he was the dynamic chairman of its education committee, and governor of the outstanding course in communication techniques now operated by that committee.

All this work he carried on without relinquishing control of the very considerable commercial empire over which he presided as its managing director. In that office he was always able to bring a fresh and vigorous mind to the problems of an expanding company, no less than to the great problems of state, and to the more personal issues that concerned the many educational and charitable causes he served.

As a television broadcaster, writer and lecturer he was known to many thousands. His book on management, *Management Survey*, first published in 1948, has been reprinted many, many times since that date. He was twice married and is succeeded by his son, Mr. A. R. M. Hooper.

October 5, 1963.

Herbert Hoover, who died on October 20, 1964, at the age of 90, will be remembered as one of the unluckiest men ever to be elected President of the United States. Had he held office at a time of normal strain his rule would probably have been noted for quiet success and smooth progress. But it was his misfortune to enter the White House only seven months before the Wall Street crash of 1929.

He had in large measure the qualities required for most tasks in public life. His previous record was excellent. He was immensely capable and hard-working. He was a superb organizer. He had a genuine regard for the national interest, and his integrity was beyond question. But his gifts were essentially those of a brilliant administrator—"efficient" is the word that must keep cropping up in any account of Herbert Hoover.

What he lacked were those two essentials for a man leading a great country at a time of unparalleled crisis: the personal magnetism that uplifts, and the capacity for really bold, imaginative thinking.

Hoover's Administration was overwhelmed by the Great Depression. He seemed to apprehend neither the real nature of the crisis nor the full extent of the remedies required. The man who could be practical and far-sighted within the limits of the orthodox could not escape from the tyranny of accepted economic doctrine. That belief in a moral imperative to balance the budget and that faith in the immutable virtues of local responsibility which still form such a strong ingredient of much American thinking today had their hold upon Hoover. They dominated the Government's actions. They undermined his remedial programme of public works; they prevented any truly effective system of hardship relief.

Inevitably, he was resoundingly defeated by Franklin Roosevelt in the election of 1932.

CRITICS BLAMED

By this time he was the victim of much bitter comment. Not only had he failed to restore prosperity, but he was accused of being insensitive to suffering. His habit of trying to restore confidence by statements of facile optimism did not help. To a good number of his compatriots at the time it seemed that he neither coped nor cared.

But this was unduly harsh. Hoover may have been grappling with events that were too big for him, but he was not alone in that. No statesman anywhere in those years had the answer, and it had to be left to his successor to pursue recovery by more novel methods.

In recent years Hoover had enjoyed something of a return to esteem and affection at home—though never again to real influence. He is remembered not only as the President of the Depression but for the magnificent relief work he did during and after the First World War and for his many years of public service. Then there was the brilliance of his earlier life as an engineer. This is the correct perspective. His career was more than the story of one great failure.

Herbert Clark Hoover was born at West Branch, Iowa, on August 10, 1874, the son of Jesse Clark Hoover, a blacksmith, by his marriage with Hulda Randall Minthorn. Both were of Quaker stock and in that faith he was brought up. As a boy he first went to a local school; but was then sent to live with his uncle John Minthorn, a country doctor in Newburg, Oregon, and studied there at the Pacific Academy. He remained at Newburg for a few years; but his parents having died and his uncle having moved to Salem, he was put in the charge of an elderly man called Miles; the arrangement did not last long for, growing discontented, he ran away first to Portland and then for a time to rejoin his uncle John at Salem.

Hoover had while still at Newburg decided that he wanted a scientific education and while at Portland had studied hard. When, therefore, examinations were held there for the new Stanford University in California he sat for them and passed. At the University he had to work at collecting the college laundry and other tasks in order to pay his way, but this did not prevent him obtaining his degree. He decided thereupon to pursue his studies in mining and became successively a mine worker, a gang foreman, and a typist in a mining office in San Francisco. In this last position his employer, discovering his abilities, advanced him and eventually recommended him to a London firm who were looking for a mining engineer to investigate the recent mining developments in Western Australia. He was accepted, did extremely well, and had the good fortune to uncover a new mine.

IN CHINA

His next field was China. The new Chinese Government wanted a Director-General of Mines and his firm recommended him for the post. He travelled to it by California and on the way married Miss Lou Henry, a friend of his college days, and took her with him. His headquarters were at Tientsin and while there he was in the thick of the Boxer troubles and took an active part in the defence of the city. Then, as time went on his work developed and eventually he had many thousands of workers under his superintendence.

In 1902 Hoover returned to London and a junior partnership in his employer's firm but England was to serve only as his base for more extended journeyings. Thus he went to Australia, Russia, and many other countries. About this time a serious defalcation by a man connected with his firm was discovered. The firm was not legally liable; but Hoover decided at the cost of his own fortune and much risk to the business, to make it good. It entailed years of struggle; but all the time he was building a high reputation in the mining world, particularly as an expert in the process of turning bad mines into sound ones. Then in 1907 he went back to America and established himself as an engineer in independent practice with offices in New York, San Francisco and London. He was still, however, to travel widely. At this period of his life he wrote or helped to write several books on mining and with his wife translated Agricola's *De Re Metallica.*

In 1913 Hoover represented the Panama-Pacific Exposition in Europe. He was in London when war broke out and on the point of returning home. There arose, however, a situation in which large numbers of Americans were stranded without the means of getting home.

BANKED ON HONESTY

Risking his own money on their honesty, he created an impromptu bureau to help them. He had great powers of organization and deep human sympathy and one thing was soon to lead to another. When, therefore, Belgium was overrun he was called upon to undertake the supplies of foodstuffs for it. It was a complex and difficult task: but the result was the formation of the American Commission for Relief in Belgium and he became its chairman.

In this work he was to sacrifice a large personal income and all business opportunities and refused to take even his expenses. Under his able leadership the work of the commission grew rapidly until its rate of expenditure was £5m. a month. Distribution was extremely difficult, for the Germans frequently hampered it; but patience and devotion found ways, and when its five years' task was accomplished and some £300m. had been spent he had to his credit the greatest and most practical system of relief which had up to that time been conceived and executed.

In May, 1917, Hoover himself was recalled to the United States and created Food Administrator. His position as he saw it was not that of a despot but of a leader of opinion who sought voluntary cooperation. His task was by no means simple, for it included on the one hand the suppression of speculation and on the other the increase of production and of fair distribution of supplies. He handled it, however, with remarkable skill, delegating wisely and building up good will both within and without his organization. Thus he became one of the great figures of the First World War and an architect of the victory in which it ended.

A few days after the armistice he left for Europe at the request of the President to direct the participation of the United States in the relief of devastated Europe and, as president of the American Relief Administration, took his third great task of organization in hand. In its performance he gave succour to some 20 countries, and his work especially in regard to child nutrition was of incalculable value in ameliorating what had been an appalling situation and in restoring at least a measure of normality.

SYMPATHY WITH WILSON

When in 1919 Hoover's responsibilities in Europe permitted him to return to his own country his political future became a matter of speculation. He had been a Republican; but he had worked with the Wilson Administration and was known to be in sympathy with many of its policies. In 1920, therefore, although he had at the time no strong political ambitions, he received some backing for both the Republican and Democratic nominations. He finally confirmed that he was still a Republican, but his time had not yet come.

Hoover was at this period far from a rich man and might well have chosen to return to business and rebuild the fortune he had lost; but in 1921 he accepted the post of Secretary of Commerce in President Harding's Administration. For seven years he served with much distinction and as a general handyman of two Administrations fulfilled a number of important tasks, including the direction of the relief measures in the Mississippi flood. A born coordinator who had none the less a driving power of his own, he enhanced a reputation already great up to the point at which he became an obvious candidate to succeed President Coolidge.

SUCCESSFUL CAMPAIGN

In February, 1928 he inaugurated his campaign as candidate for the Republican nomination. His supporters' case was that "Hoover efficiency" would safeguard "Coolidge prosperity" and they fought it strenuously. He himself was not a brilliant speaker and his reputation was based on performance in the outer world even more than in the United States. But the country seemed prosperous and his opponent, Governor Al Smith, of New York, suffered from what were then regarded as the crippling handicaps for a presidential candidate of being an Irish-American and a Roman Catholic. Hoover was elected to be the thirty-first President, with an unprecedented majority.

On taking office all the auspices were favourable, but the economic storm was soon to break. The depression, which he continued to regard as a temporary phase, could not in his view be cured by legislative action or by executive pronouncement and he was therefore content for the most part, except for trying to relieve actual distress, to allow events to take their course. In the summer of 1931, however, in order to help recovery he proposed the postponement of all payments of international debts. It did but little to assist the general situation, which was growing desperate. America's much boasted prosperity had disappeared and the unemployed list was over the 10,000,000 mark. Confronting these alarming facts he had no leadership to offer to a Congress which was already deeply discontented. In June the Republicans, who would have stultified themselves by any other course, renominated him as their candidate. His platform failed, however, to present any convincing proposals for the remedy of a situation which was going from bad to worse, and in the November election he and his party suffered an overwhelming defeat.

For two years Hoover was rarely heard on public questions; but in 1935 he reentered politics by making a bitter attack on the New Deal. In 1938 he went to Europe, visited Germany and had a talk with Hitler. His advice on his return was that the United States should not ally herself with other democratic countries against Fascism. In the summer of 1940 as head of the European Food Distribution Committee he sought to obtain Great Britain's leave to supply food to Belgium, the Netherlands, Poland and Norway. Not only, however, did he fail to appreciate the real facts of the situation but his arguments tended to be inconsistent.

A VIGOROUS OLD AGE

From 1947 to 1949 he headed the "Hoover Commission", the bipartisan committee created by Congress to make recommendations for the reorganization of the executive branch of the Government. He was chairman also of the second "Hoover Commission", when that was created in 1953, with an even broader scope than the first commission had. This second commission was to operate on the programme and policy level and examine the advisability of turning some federal functions over to state and local governments or to industry. Until recurring illnesses over his last two years, he had continued to lead a remarkably vigorous and active life for a man of his age, with a number of public engagements. Even on his ninetieth birthday in August, 1964, his vitality was such that he issued a robust declaration of faith in "our American form of civilization".

In April, 1958, while Hoover was recovering in hospital from an operation, *The Ordeal of Woodrow Wilson* was published, in the writing of which he had spent a good part of 20 years. It was not a biography but rather a record and commentary on the war and postwar years of the Wilson era. In it there was expressed unbounded admiration for Wilson's character and ideals. Among Hoover's other published work were three volumes of memoirs.

Early in 1944 his wife died. They had two sons, one of whom, Mr. Herbert Hoover, junior, is a former Assistant Secretary of State.

October 21, 1964.

Gerard Hopkins, M.C., who died on March 20, 1961, at the age of 68, was the most distinguished translator from the French in Britain and one of the best-loved men in London. His work formed an important link between English literature and that of France, which honoured him by making him a Chevalier de la Légion d'Honneur in 1951. His sympathy, wit and charm extended far beyond the field in which he was expert; his fine imposing head and gentle humorous manner symbolized a life that kept a style and set its standards with a complete absence of fuss or ostentation.

Born on April 12, 1892, the son of Everard Hopkins and Amy Sichel, and a nephew of Gerard Manley Hopkins, Gerard Walter Sturgis Hopkins was educated at Marlborough and Balliol, where he was president of the O.U.D.S. and took a second in Greats. On going down from Oxford he served with great distinction in the First World War, being awarded the Military Cross. In 1919 he joined the Oxford University Press. He early became publicity manager and, much later, editorial adviser, though his editorial advice was taken throughout his time at the O.U.P. It was at his instigation that the Press became the publishers of Christopher Fry, while he had much to do with their publication of his uncle's poems, letters and diaries. He revolutionized publicity at the Press, so that it became, in the words of *The Bookseller* on his retirement in 1957, "a Rolls-Royce among bubble-cars".

He was the author of seven novels in the 1920s and 1930s, but what was to be the major work of his life began with Jules Romain's *Men of Good Will,* of which he translated volumes 7–27. His own typically modest account of this gift was that it started when he went to the sanatorium at Marlborough with measles, and found himself reading and enjoying a book in French. He never made any formal study of French, but to a wide reading in that language and his own he added immense industry, far-ranging information and deep critical sense. After the Second World War, he undertook an English edition of the works of François Mauriac. These superb translations not only introduced the French writer to a general reading public in this country, but may also be found to have influenced our own novelists. Their success made him sought after as a translator not only for novels, but for biography, memoirs, works of information, broadcasts and plays. Among these more recent translations were some of the big André Maurois biographies and Proust's *Jean Santeuil*, the quality of which led him to be compared with Scott-Moncrieff.

In his daily work, which he kept up until a few weeks before his death, he moved with the deceptively easy rhythm of self-discipline. From each session of concentrated drafting and re-drafting he would appear relaxed and sociable, whether at home where he entertained many friends or at his much-loved club, the Garrick. Reticent about his own feelings, he inspired deep confidence in others, especially among younger people; he himself in his gusto, enthusiasm, and appreciation of life never grew old.

He was twice married, first to Mabel Muirhead and then in 1949 to Babette Johanna, widow of Peter Cornwallis and daughter of Ernest Stern, the stage-designer.

March 21, 1961.

Edward Hopper died in New York on May 15, 1967, at the age of 84.

Hopper was noted among American painters of this century as one who carried on the realist tradition and gave to his scenes of city and small-town life an individual character admired by contemporaries in the United States of all shades of opinion in art, from the most conservative to the experimentally minded.

He could be regarded as a follower of the so-called "Ashcan School," the group of painters who gained the nickname from their preference for the more squalid aspects of city life, and was a pupil of its leading member, Robert Henri. He developed a style in which architecture and figures were seen with a harsh clarity, excluding from his views of cafeterias, offices, theatres and terraces of nineteenth-century buildings any element of the anecdotal, sentimental or romantically picturesque. This detached objectivity, not perhaps without an underlying element of criticism, seems to account for the special attraction his work possessed.

Hopper was born at Nyack, New York, in 1882 and studied illustration and commercial art in New York City, continuing to work as an illustrator until 1924. He went to France, however, between 1906 and 1910 and was influenced by the colour of the Impressionists whose work he saw in Paris. For many years he did little oil painting and his only sale until 1923 was his "Corner Saloon," exhibited at the Armory Show in 1913. The success of a water-colour show in 1924 enabled him to devote himself entirely to painting.

He spent his summers on Cape Cod, where some characteristic works were painted. Retrospective exhibitions were held at the Museum of Modern Art, New York, in 1953, and in 1950 and 1964 at the Whitney Museum of American Art, where he is well represented.

May 18, 1967.

David Horne, the actor whose performances in the parts of middle-aged and elderly men had contributed to the success of many dramas and comedies, died on March 15, 1970, at his home in London. He had written and directed plays, had toured with companies of his own, and had presented plays under his management, but it was as an actor that he achieved something distinctive.

The son of a rich man the late Alderson Horne, who, under the name of Anmer Hall, was a pioneering force as a producer and manager for nearly 50 years, David Horne was born at Balcombe, Sussex, on July 14, 1898. He went to Eton and Sandhurst, and he had held a regular commission in the Grenadier Guards before he joined his father's company in 1926. He appeared under his father's management in London in plays by Turgenev and Martinez Sierra, then made his first notable success as the housemaster with whose wife a boy falls in love in Basil Dean's production of *Young Woodley*. He visited New York in 1931, there playing Claudius to the Hamlet of Raymond Massey.

On his return he was seen in several plays at a theatre recently opened under his father's management, the Westminster. He appeared twice in Shakespeare with Henry Cass's company at the Old Vic in 1934, played a bishop in St. John Ervine's *Robert's Wife*, and was the Chasuble of John Gielgud's first production of *The Importance of Being Earnest*.

During the Second World War, as a member of an Old Vic Company, he toured industrial Lancashire in *Twelfth Night* and *She Stoops to Conquer*. He also toured for E.N.S.A. and later with his own company, between-whiles running a season in Aberdeen and playing in Roland Pertwee's *Pink String and Sealing Wax* in London.

He reopened Theatre Royal, Stratford, in 1946, and appeared there together with his third wife, Ann Farrer, in a repertory of modern plays. During the 1950s he was seen in the West End as the old butler, under Peter Brook's direction, in Anouilh's *Ring Round the Moon*; as a Q.C. in Agatha Christie's *Witness For the Prosecution*; and as a picture dealer in Noel Coward's comedy *Nude with Violin*, each of which had a long run; and as Charles Piper, the London clubman, again under Brook's direction in T. S. Eliot's *The Family Reunion.* On these occasions, whether as a loyal retainer or as a leader of a profession or as a duffer—in the last part and in that of a man without charm he was a special favourite of audiences—Horne's performance was free from caricature, the necessary element of exaggeration being supplied by his plump physique and by his voice, dry in tone, with a characteristic squeak.

Horne presented three of his own plays at Theatre Royal, Stratford, and revived one of them, *Legacy*, at the Arts, Cambridge. In 1966 he joined the cast of Anouilh's *The Fighting Cock*, supporting John Clements, when it was transferred from Chichester to the West End.

His first marriage, to Miss Renée Mayer, the actress, was dissolved. He had a daughter by his second marriage to the former Mrs. Ella Reiche, and another daughter by his third marriage.

March 17, 1970.

Kenneth Horne, the comedian, who died on February 14, 1969, was one of the wittiest radio entertainers of his time.

Basically a man of commerce he drifted into entertaining during the war when he was a wing commander in the R.A.F., and became a national name when he teamed up with Richard Murdoch in *Much Binding in the Marsh,* which was centred on an R.A.F. airfield. It ran until 1950.

Horne's genial, warming presence, his acute comic timing, his easy jocularity won him large audiences in a succession of radio shows like *Beyond our Ken* and *Round the Horne*.

More recently he presided over the T. V. quiz *Celebrity Challenge*, and had his own I.T.V. series *Horne a' Plenty*. Horne had broadcast for more than 28 years. A new *Round the Horne* series was to have started on Radios 1 and 2 in March, 1969.

Educated at St. George's, Harpenden, and

Magdalene College, Cambridge, he was the son of the Rev. Silvester Horne, a leading Congregationalist and former Liberal M.P., who ministered for years at Whitefields' Tabernacle.

Kenneth Horne was an entertainer whose genial likableness hid a remarkably skilful but very personal comic technique. He was, he liked one to believe, a friendly good natured old buffer who was simply doing his best, apparently lost in wonder, at the glossier, more spectacular talents of those among whom he found himself. That was the impression he liked to create, and he created it with unobtrusive, apparently casual skill.

More than 20 years before he died, when with Richard Murdoch he bore the brunt of the remarkable happenings brought by radio from the mythical Much Binding in the Marsh, the old bufferishness was already a technique played with neat expertise; he was goodnatured, physically and mentally slow-moving, apparently elephantine in his responses. Mr. Murdoch ambled gaily round him, waiting apparently as breathlessly as the audience, for the dawn of comprehension. The trick was as individual as it was effective, and coupled with the genuinely cheerful friendliness that was always part of his personality, it became a recurrent, unfailing pleasure exploited in all his radio and television work.

MASTER OF DOUBLE-MEANING

Kenneth Horne was a master of the scandalous double-meaning delivered with shining innocence. He was, too, a master of the excruciating schoolboy pun, which he used as part of the *persona* he created. Delivered with a sort of shamefaced delight, as though he admitted its atrocity, but felt that it was the best he could do to contribute to the fun he was determined to encourage, his games with words became witty as well as outrageous.

In February, 1958, he suffered a stroke which paralysed his left side and took away his speech. During the agonies of learning to walk and speak again, he decided to give up his business interests and concentrate on show business.

He threw up his chairmanship of the Chad Valley Toy Company and of five other firms and his directorships in several more, and sold his Rolls-Royce. Although past 50 he decided on show business, although he said: "I never look upon myself as an entertainer". Using ideas he worked out on his sick-bed he started the programme *Beyond Our Ken* which, after it became established, claimed 10 million listeners on a Sunday afternoon.

He began to widen his show business interests and became the chairman of *Twenty Questions* and joined television panel game teams. He was also heard on *Woman's Hour* and *Any Questions*. When *Round the Horne* replaced *Beyond Our Ken*, he had rebuilt his career from scratch.

Round the Horne was a success with lovers of the sophisticated pun as well as appealing to those who liked a good belly laugh. Obvious jokes were mixed with clever word-juggling.

It was a far cry from his war-time efforts, *Ack, Ack, Beer, Beer*, and later *Much Binding*, which he and Richard Murdoch devised as a take-off of a fictitious R.A.F. station while they were together at the Air Ministry. The two had been at Cambridge at the same time but had never met.

After he left university, Horne became a progress clerk with the Triplex Safety Glass Co., working himself up to general sales manager and eventually becoming a member of the board as sales and advertising director.

February 15, 1969.

Arthur Horner, general secretary of the National Union of Mineworkers from 1946 until he retired in 1959, died on September 4, 1968. He was 74.

As general secretary of the National Union of Mineworkers he occupied one of the most important positions in the industrial life of Britain in the years following the war. Before this for 10 years he had been president of the South Wales Miners' Federation. From earliest days he lived the life of a revolutionary, serving several sentences for political activities. He was a prominent member of the Communist Party and sat on its National Executive. Short, plump, bespectacled, he was a genial, friendly character, with an exceptionally clear mind, and too independent always to accept the party line unquestionably. Though critical of Russian intervention in Hungary in 1956 he declared his intention of remaining in the Communist Party "as the only instrument through which genuine Socialism can be ultimately realized".

Horner was born on April 5, 1894, at Merthyr Tydfil, the son of a railway supervisor. He got his first job while still at school, earning a few coppers as a "wobbler's boy", or assistant to the local barber; later on he delivered groceries. His parents were ardent Baptists and Arthur himself was a keen student at Sunday school, at 15 proving himself to be an impressive boy-preacher. This determined him to devote his life to religion and with the aid of a scholarship and some of his father's savings he went to study at the Baptist college at Birmingham. But the money was insufficient and after a short time he returned and started work with the Standard Collieries at Ynyshir in the Rhondda. While there his Christianity began to mingle with Socialism and by fairly rapid degrees he was converted to Marxism. This theoretical conversion took on a very practical form, mainly through the I.L.P., so that he was reported to the colliery manager as being unruly, which led to his dismissal and to his name being put on the blacklist of the local colliery association which barred any colliery in South Wales from engaging him.

REFUSED TO FIGHT

With the outbreak of war in 1914 he refused to fight, declaring that the war was only a struggle between rival imperialisms and opposed to the interests of the working-classes of all countries. He accepted a variety of identities in order to get work and was eventually taken on by the pit at Mardy, a small mining community with a tradition for leftism. The police were soon on his tracks and in 1918 he went to Ireland where he worked for the "Citizens Army" under the name of "Jack O'Brien". Later in the year on the birth of his first child he returned to Wales, only to be arrested as he stepped ashore at Holyhead. He was sentenced to six months' imprisonment and on his release was rearrested for still refusing to wear the King's uniform and was this time sentenced to hard labour. While in prison he went on a hunger-strike for six days and in his absence was elected checkweighman at Mardy colliery.

When he was released he threw himself into the political life of Mardy and in the 1921 miners' strikes he played a prominent part, only to receive another gaol sentence for "unlawful assembly". During the bleak years that followed in the district and culminated in the General Strike of 1926, he never relaxed from the role of professional agitator, later receiving a further 15 months' hard labour for attempting to prevent the bailiffs from seizing a miner's furniture. He was active in the "Minority Movement" and had become a member of the newly formed Communist Party, paying several visits to the Soviet Union which impressed him deeply. He lived there for a while as secretary of the Miners' International Propaganda Committee. He stood three times unsuccessfully as the communist candidate for East Rhondda.

He fell into disgrace with the Communist Party in 1929, for failure to follow the party line, and suffered rebuke when he appealed to the Communist International. But he did penance and returned to the fold.

His position in the South Wales Miners' Federation was growing in importance and he became a member of the executive. In 1933 the anthracite miners appointed him as their full-time agent and in 1936 he succeeded James Griffiths as the S.W.M.F.'s president. He held this position for 10 years and proved himself to be a skilful negotiator, winning the loyalty of a large majority of the miners even if they did not always agree with his politics. By this time he had become one of the most prominent communists, was a member of the party's executive and had an important voice in the formation of policy. When the civil war broke out in Spain, he came out solidly on behalf of the Spanish Government, declaring that it was not merely a rehearsal ground for the next world war but an important stage in the class-struggle which transcended national frontiers. He brought all the aid he could to the International Brigade and on one occasion toured the battlefront. In general his policy was naturally the same as the Communist Party's, which he personally expressed by supporting any move which made for increased friendship with Russia and combined action to prevent aggression.

When the war came he sincerely believed that the situation had suddenly altered and that it began another pointless struggle between rival imperialist powers rather than as a fight to preserve freedom and democracy. However by 1941 and with the attack on Russia he was using all his influence to raise coal production. He attacked the Government's wartime policy of "Dual Control" of the mines which he said meant that the main responsibility for production remained with the owners, and called for the earliest possible nationalization of the whole industry and, as an important first step forward, the maximum use of the pit committees. At the same time he was careful to condemn absenteeism and unofficial strikes, saying that although the Government and the owners were usually to blame, the men should resist provocation to strike.

He was one of the first to warn that the backward state of many collieries and the unhappy history of the industry would gravely jeopardize production after the war. In 1945 the National Union gave him the additional duties of Production Director. In this capacity he laid great stress on recruiting and on the interconnexion between good conditions and higher output.

ON TIGHTROPE

In August, 1946, he was elected general secretary to the National Union of Mine workers and turned down a lucrative post with the National Coal Board. When nationalization eventually came he continued to warn that unless something radical was done about recruitment, in 10 years there would not be a miner left in the country. To make the industry more attractive he supported the five-day week and asked for special benefits for the miners, including a minimum wage of £6 per week, some exemption from income tax and preferential rations. Some of these claims met with considerable opposition from the leaders of other unions, but Horner argued that the nation's whole economy was at stake and the situation called for drastic measures.

As general secretary of a union with a firm non-communist majority on the executive, Horner had to walk a political tightrope. He was left free to express his political views as an individual, but any attempt to use his office for political purposes brought immediate rebuke from his colleagues. On at least one occasion the warning was an exceedingly stiff one.

His politics prevented him from playing the part in the wider trade union movement to which he would otherwise have been entitled by his exceptional abilities. Although his union nominated him for the T.U.C. General Council year after year, he was invariably excluded, in favour of lesser men, by the votes of the other unions.

If politically he was at odds with many of his colleagues, industrially he was not. During the presidency of Sir William Lawther, he was the union's chief spokesman at wage negotiations and at annual conferences, and there were times when he did not hesitate to oppose the official communist line put forward by other communist leaders in the union. "He is a miners' leader first, and a communist second", was a tribute more than once heard from his political opponents in the union.

That meant that the party leadership probably regarded him as an unreliable member. He lost his position on the party executive in his later years, but to have a member in such an important position was too valuable an asset for any disciplinary action to be taken against him.

To his many friends it often seemed that he was tortured by a conflict of loyalties which gave him no peace, and which perhaps accentuated the human weakness to which he was always ready to confess. If he was shocked by the revelations of communist brutality in the Stalinist regime and later in the suppression of the Hungarian uprising, he held his peace until at last the execution of Nagy and his colleagues made it impossible for him to do so any longer.

RARE OUTBURST

That was needless folly, he said in a unique outburst, which shocked and horrified him. Yet he remained a member of the Communist Party within which he had built his life.

Horner was, among union leaders, exceptional in ability and sincerity, and in warm human qualities and in loyalty to the miners whom he represented. Had he not become immersed in the communist machine in his early years, he might well have become the outstanding trade union leader of his time. He did well for his members, who have cause to be grateful to him. There was much of achievement in his life, but more of the tragedy of great potentialities unfulfilled.

He retired in 1959 and was succeeded by another South Wales communist, William Paynter. The National Coal Board presented him with a miners' lamp, inscribed "from his friends". In 1960 he published his autobiography *Incorrigible Rebel*.

September 5, 1968.

Lady Horsbrugh, P.C., G.B.E., a life peeress and former Minister of Education, who was also the first woman Conservative Cabinet Minister, died on December 6, 1969, at the age of 80.

Lady Horsbrugh, who never married, dedicated her life to politics and served for 23 years in the House of Commons before going to the House of Lords as a life peeress in 1959. An experienced observer of the Parliamentary scene said of her when she left the Commons that she was "certainly the best equipped party politician of all the women who have sat in the House". This was a fair estimate of a woman who applied a vigorous mind, good judgment, and a warm heart to the profession of politics with great zeal and thoroughness. She was spirited in controversy and never shrank from the rough and tumble of the party fight. But she was also less severe than she looked; and if her Scots mannerisms were sometimes reminiscent of a very senior school mistress, there was usually a merry twinkle in her eye.

SAT FOR DUNDEE

Born on October 13, 1889, Florence Horsburgh was educated at Lansdowne House, Edinburgh, and St. Hilda's, Folkestone. She entered politics as Conservative member for Dundee—the senior of two members—in 1931 and she held this seat continuously till she was beaten in the general election of 1945. In 1936 she was appointed chairman of the Departmental Committee on Adoption Societies and Agencies and she later promoted a private member's Bill, based on the recommendations of this Committee, which was passed into law. This was the Adoption of Children (Regulation) Act 1939—a measure that marked an important stage on the way to the major legislation to benefit deprived children which came after the war.

She achieved many victories for feminism during her career. In 1936 she made Parliamentary history by becoming the first woman ever to move the Address in reply to the Speech from the Throne, in the House of Commons at the opening of a new Session. Shortly before the Second World War began she was appointed Parliamentary Secretary to the Ministry of Health and at once played an active part in the arrangements for the evacuation of children and other priority classes from London and other big cities to escape air bombing. She held this post throughout the war and worked with great devotion at some of the unprecedented tasks of those days. On one occasion in 1944, she was injured by bomb blast during an enemy raid on London. During the later part of her service at the Ministry of Health Miss Horsbrugh did much preparatory work on the draft of the national health service scheme, which came to fruition after the war under Labour.

FREAK RE-ELECTION

In the caretaker Government she was Parliamentary Secretary to the Ministry of Food. After her defeat at Dundee in 1945 Miss Horsbrugh became Conservative candidate for Midlothian and Peebles but she was defeated by a Labour candidate there in 1950. None the less she did—by freak of circumstance—win her way back to the House of Commons at this election. The Conservative candidate for the Moss Side division of Manchester had died before polling day and the election there had to be postponed. Miss Horsbrugh, defeated in Midlothian and Peebles, was quickly nominated again as Conservative candidate for Moss Side and she was elected there by a handsome majority, a fortnight after the rest of the country had polled.

When the Conservatives returned to power in 1951 Sir Winston Churchill appointed Miss Horsbrugh to be Minister of Education. She was not at first a Cabinet Minister but was promoted to the Cabinet in 1953—the first woman to hold a Cabinet post in a Conservative Government. She was unlucky in holding office at a very difficult time, with the "bulge" beginning to burst into the schools and housing then a first priority on strained national resources of money and building materials. At best it could only be a period of marking time and consolidation. Miss Horsbrugh resigned office in 1954 and left the Government. On her resignation she was made a Dame Grand Cross of the Order of the British Empire. She was made a life peeress in 1959.

December 8, 1969.

Andrée Howard, the choreographer, who was found dead in her London home on April 18, 1968, had been active in British ballet since the first permanent companies were founded almost 40 years ago.

Born in 1910, she studied dancing under Marie Rambert and later with the famous

Russian emigrée ballerinas in Paris. She danced with Rambert's company and in 1933 joined the Ballet Russe de Monte Carlo but could not stay because it proved too exhausing for a heart condition she suffered from.

Her first ballet, *Our Lady's Juggler*, in 1933, was made in cooperation with Susan Salaman. So was the next, *Mermaid* (1934), which remained in the Rambert repertory until the 1950s and might have continued longer but for difficulties over the use of Ravel's music. This ballet revealed the simplicity, imagination, and sensitivity which were to distinguish all Howard's best work.

At times her style became attenuated, and as if in compensation she was drawn occasionally towards melodramatic themes. At its best, her work had balance, depth and poetry, most notably in *La Fête Etrange*, created for The London Ballet in 1940 and since taken into the Royal Ballet repertory.

She had also a wicked sense of humour and a gift for parody, shown in her choreography and in the guest appearances which she made from time to time with various companies. These included a wildly fantasticated performance as a witch in *Selina*, which she created at Sadler's Wells in 1948, and a memorable Ugly Sister in Ashton's *Cinderella* at Covent Garden. Her last stage appearance was in Festival Ballet's *Nutcracker* at Christmas, 1967.

Andrée Howard's ballets included many innovations. She created the first two-act British ballet (*The Sailor's Return* in 1947) and made unusual and effective use of songs in *La Fête Etrange*.

In 1945 she was appointed the first resident choreographer of the new Sadler's Wells Theatre Ballet. In 1952–53 she created two works for Covent Garden, *A Mirror for Witches* and *Veneziana*. She devoted herself with equal eagerness, however, to many smaller companies, including Metropolitan Ballet, the Walter Gore Ballet and London Dance Theatre, for all of which she mounted unusual new works.

Andree Howard's most endearing qualities were her enthusiasm and her readiness to help others. There is an ironically sad splendour about the coincidence of her death being discovered on the day that students of the Harlow Ballet Club were to dance for the first time her *Death and the Maiden* which, at her own suggestion, she had extended and produced specially for them.

April 20, 1968.

Major-General Sir Richard Howard-Vyse, K.C.M.G., D.S.O., who died on December 5, 1962, at the age of 79, played a prominent part in Allenby's Palestine campaign in the First World War as Chief of Staff of the Desert Mounted Corps. He was best known to the present generation of service men as chairman of the Prisoners of War Department of the Red Cross and St. John Organization in the Second World War and subsequently as chairman and president of the British Legion.

Both officers and men of many different types with whom he served were devoted to him. He was slightly built and he had a somewhat quizzical cast of countenance which prompted someone when he joined The Blues to call him "Wombat", a nickname that stuck to him for the rest of his life. In his younger days he was a brilliant staff officer, a popular and competent commander and trainer of troops, and a first-class horseman as well.

Richard Granville Hylton Howard-Vyse came of a family with a long military tradition—in the eighteenth century one of his forebears was a general and another a field marshal. He was born on June 27, 1883, the elder son of Howard Henry Howard-Vyse. He was educated at Eton and was commissioned in the Royal Horse Guards in 1902 under the old system of nomination by the Colonel of the Regiment. He took his profession seriously, and was the first officer of the Household Cavalry ever to graduate at the Staff College. It was a tribute to his delightful personality that this departure from the regimental tradition did not detract in the least from his popularity among his fellow officers.

In the 1914–18 War he served in France as brigade major to Sir Philip Chetwode, then commander of the 5th Cavalry Brigade, which played a notable part in covering the Retreat from Mons. In 1917 he was given the chance to serve in a theatre better suited to the cavalry arm when he was selected to be Chief of Staff to the Desert Mounted Corps in Palestine. This Corps consisted of a British Yeomanry Division, an Australian Mounted Division, an Indian Cavalry Division, and the Imperial Camel Corps. It mustered a strength of some 40,000 men and was the largest force of cavalry employed on the allied side in the 1914–18 War.

ATTACK ON BEERSHEBA

As Chief of Staff, Howard-Vyse had a great share in planning and directing the cavalry in a campaign which provided a classic demonstration of the strategical and tactical power of this arm in its final form before the advent of mechanization. In particular he was responsible for drawing up the plans for the flank attack on Beersheba, and the great sweep up the Philistine Plain at the end of 1917; he also planned the fighting in the Jordan Valley, including the raid on Es Salt and the cavalry share in the Battle of Megiddo in September, 1918. For his services with the Desert Mounted Corps he was awarded the D.S.O., made C.M.G., given the brevets of major and lieutenant-colonel, and thrice mentioned in dispatches. Before Megiddo, having served for nearly a year with headquarters, he was appointed to command the 10 Cavalry Brigade, made up of Yeomanry and Indian Cavalry. Allenby's plan was that the cavalry should push through the front on the Mediterranean side and wheel round through the Plain of Esdraelon to cut across the Turkish lines of retreat. Howard-Vyse's Brigade was in the lead. But, in the darkness, on their way through the Musmus Pass, which led to the Plain, they followed the wrong track and lost their way. Luckily the mistake was discovered within an hour or two, and the main bodies of the cavalry arrived at their destination just in time to intercept the Turkish Army. But Howard-Vyse was removed from his command and sent back to take charge of a training establishment behind the lines, where he languished for three months and so missed the triumphant end of the campaign. This must have been a bitter blow, but he never complained.

INSPECTOR OF CAVALRY

After the war he returned to his regiment and commanded it from 1922 to 1926. During these years he raised it to a higher standard of field training than it had ever reached before. He then served for a time in the War Office in charge of the branch of the general staff which dealt with the training and entry of officers, after which he commanded the Cairo Cavalry Brigade for three years from 1928 till 1930. He was next appointed Inspector of Cavalry and so automatically became Commandant of the Equitation School.

On completion of his tenure of this post he was offered the appointment of Commandant of the Staff College at Quetta, which would have been a stepping-stone to higher things had he wished to remain in the Army, but he refused it, and retired in 1935 at the age of 52.

Soon after the outbreak of the Second World War, Howard-Vyse was recalled to the Service to act as Head of the British Military Mission at the headquarters of the French Supreme Commander, General Gamelin. He regarded his role as being primarily to provide a channel of communication in the frightful emergency in which B.E.F. found itself. It is possible that his temperament and character would have made it difficult for him to exercise much influence in other ways, and when the mission lapsed after the Fall of France he returned to England and became chairman of the Prisoners of War Department of the British Red Cross and St. John.

He was a J.P. for Buckinghamshire, was High Sheriff in 1938 and was appointed Vice-Lieutenant of the County in 1957. He was Colonel of the Royal Horse Guards from 1951 and Honorary Colonel of the 99th Bucks and Herts Yeomanry Field Regiment from 1938 to 1949.

He married in 1925 Hermione, daughter of Saxham Drury and widow of the Hon. Arthur Coke. They had no children.

December 7, 1962.

Lord Howe, P.C., C.B.E., a former member of Parliament for South Battersea and Conservative Whip, died at his home in Buckinghamshire on July 26, 1964, at the age of 80. He will also be particularly remembered for his enthusiasm for motor racing, a sport which ideally suited his robust personality.

As a driver Lord Howe brought skill, courage, and enthusiasm to the sport he loved; in later years as an elder statesman he showed calm wisdom that few men could equal when dealing with the many and diverse problems that continually occur in every branch of motor sport. He was a great man and a fine sportsman whose loss is irreplaceable. Perhaps he will best be remembered for his valuable contributions to the sport of motor racing as chairman of the R.A.C. Competitions Committee and with affection as chairman of the British Racing Drivers' Club. This club, which originated in 1927, is unique. It came into being during a series of private dinner parties given by Dr. J. D. Benjafield, one of the original Bentley drivers, when notable British drivers met over his table to discuss their sport. On December 21, 1928, Howe was asked to become chairman of the British Racing Drivers' Club, an office he held until his death.

EARLIEST AMBITION

Francis Richard Henry Penn Curzon, P.C., C.B.E., fifth Earl Howe of Langar in the County of Nottingham, Viscount Curzon, Baron Curzon and Baron Howe, all in the Peerage of the United Kingdom, was born May 1, 1884, the only son of the 4th Earl Howe. His earliest ambition centred in the Royal Navy, but a lack of robust health, hardly credible to those who knew him in later life, sent him to Eton and Christ Church, Oxford. He joined the Sussex division of the R.N.V.R. (which for many years he was to command) in 1904; and in 1914, as Commander Viscount Curzon, was given the Howe battalion of the Royal Naval Division with which he fought at Antwerp. He left this force to serve in the Queen Elizabeth throughout the Dardanelles campaign and to the end of the war.

The peacetime Navy did not appeal to Viscount Curzon; in 1918 he won South Battersea as a Conservative, and until his succession to the earldom in 1929, was a vigorous, hard-working and (till he became a Whip in 1924) hard hitting member of Parliament. In 1924 he was made C.B.E. and in 1929 a Privy Councillor. In 1927 he succeeded Lord Jessel as London Whip in the Conservative Office. He later became the chairman of the Central Council of the party for 1932 and 1933.

He became keenly interested in motoring while in France during the summer of 1898, and after the First World War owned many fast cars. As Viscount Curzon he had several times been fined for speeding and it was at the suggestion of a magistrate that he took up motor racing in 1928 at the age of 44, in a type 43 supercharged Bugatti. Viscount Curzon's first motor race was the Essex Club's six hours sports car race at Brooklands in May, 1928.

In 1929 as Earl Howe, in the Double 12-hour race for sports cars at Brooklands, he again ran his Bugatti, which proved rather temperamental, and after working on the car for a long time himself was forced to retire. Shortly afterwards he bought a supercharged 2.3 litre Grand Prix Bugatti, the first of several Grand Prix machines which were to gain him wins in Brooklands handicap races. He was especially fond of Bugatti. Indeed, his fastest car was a 3.3 litre Grand Prix machine of this make that was always regarded as extremely tricky to drive; but on several occasions during 1936 he lapped at more than 135 m.p.h. and became one of the few holders of the coveted 130 m.p.h. Brooklands badge.

After the Delage Grand Prix team gave up racing in 1927, Lord Howe bought two of the cars, later embarking on several seasons of Continental racing with some degree of success until he crashed badly at Monza track in Italy during 1932; a single-seater Delage coming to rest against a tree, Lord Howe receiving few injuries and being lucky to escape with his life.

His worst crash occurred in 1937 when his E.R.A. struck a parapet at Vickers Bridge Corner, Brooklands, in the very first long distance race for Grand Prix cars over the then new Campbell semi-road circuit. The E.R.A. rolled over at speed, flinging out Lord Howe, who suffered a broken wrist, a broken rib, and smashed shoulder. In typical fashion, two months later he was back at the track, acting as an observer at the very corner where he had crashed.

Howe crowded many activities, adventures and friendships into his life. Much time was given to the painstaking tuition of novices in motor racing; many drivers of a later generation owe him gratitude for sound advice and practical demonstration, and he edited the *Lonsdale Library* volume on motor racing. Howe was also interested in the training of police drivers and in testing for driving licences. He often spoke wisely and informatively in the House of Lords debates on road safety, constituting himself the defender of the skilled motorist against the advocates of extreme restrictions.

He married first in 1907 Mary, daughter of Colonel the Hon. Montagu Curzon, and they had one son and one daughter. That marriage was dissolved in 1937 and in that year he married secondly Joyce Mary McLean, daughter of C. M. Jack, of Johannesburg, by whom he had one daughter. This marriage was dissolved in 1943, the year before his marriage to Mrs. Sybil Boyter Johnson Shafto, daughter of Captain Francis Johnson. They had one daughter. The earldom now passes to his son, Viscount Curzon.

July 27, 1964.

Sir Rupert Howorth, K.C.M.G., K.C.V.O., C.B., who died on January 4, 1964, at his home at Eastbourne at the age of 83, was Deputy Secretary (Civil) of the Cabinet from 1930, and Clerk of the Privy Council from 1938, until his retirement in 1942.

Rupert Beswicke Howorth was born on July 13, 1880, the second son of Sir Henry Howorth. K.C.I.E., F.R.S., who for many years represented South Salford in Parliament and was the versatile author of numerous works on scientific, historical and other subjects. A History of the Mongols, others on the Ice Age and the Flood, advancing as they did theories peculiar to their author, attracted attention at the time but have hardly sustained the test of more exact modern research.

Rupert Howorth was educated at St. Paul's School and New College, Oxford, where he took a second in Modern History in 1902. He was called to the Bar by the Inner Temple in 1903, and the same year he entered the Board of Education. He was transferred to the Treasury in 1915, and in 1919 was seconded to the Cabinet Office, where he was established as Deputy Secretary (Civil) in 1930. He was Administrative Secretary to the Imperial Conferences of 1923. 1926, 1930 and 1937, Secretary to the United Kingdom Delegation of the Imperial Conference at Ottawa in 1932, and to the Monetary and Economic Conference in London in 1933.

In 1938, on the retirement of Sir Maurice (later Lord) Hankey, Howorth succeeded him as Clerk of the Privy Council, retaining the post of Deputy Secretary (Civil) to the Cabinet. He was made a C.B. in 1926, C.M.G. in 1931, K.C.M.G. in 1933, and K.C.V.O. in 1942. He had many of his father's interests and was a Fellow of the Society of Antiquaries.

On attaining the age of 62 in 1942 Howorth retired and devoted himself to his duties as a Justice of the Peace in Wimbledon. He was also an active Governor of the Moorfields Eye Hospital. In February, 1945, he was recalled to official life by Lord Chancellor Simon, who appointed him Secretary of Commissions of the Peace in the place of the late Sir Leo Page. Howorth threw himself into the work of the office with zeal, and when in 1946 a committee under the chairmanship of Lord Du Parcq was appointed to inquire into the position generally of Justices of the Peace, Howorth's elaborate memorandum and evidence proved of great value.

In his long career in the Civil Service Howorth made many friends and he was well known and well liked in Whitehall. He was a genial and helpful colleague, and to his staff he was always considerate and accessible. In the years between the wars, when the Offices of the Cabinet and Committee of Imperial Defence were staffed mainly by serving officers seconded from the Armed Forces on relatively short tours of duty, it was the responsibility of Hankey and Howorth to provide the element of continuity required to ensure consistency of practice and procedure. And Howorth became a mine of information on all matters of constitutional propriety affecting the Cabinet and its proceedings. He was, in himself, the memory of the Office—carrying in his head a precedent for almost every contingency and always ready to make this knowledge available to colleagues in urgent need of advice.

Sir Rupert Howorth married in 1907 Evelyn Maria, only child of the late William Roope Ellicott, of Oporto, and he leaves one son and three daughters.

January 6, 1964.

Joan Howson, the stained glass artist, died in North Wales on June 10, 1964.

The daughter of the late Archdeacon G. J. Howson, she was born in 1885 at Overton-on-Dee. An early decision to be a violinist had to be abondoned after study in Paris and Munich, owing to her mother's illness and she returned to help her father with parish duties. She later studied textile designing in the Liverpool School of Art, taking stained glass as a craft. In 1913 she became the pupil and lifelong friend and partner of Caroline Townshend, with whom she had much in common, especially Socialism and suffragist activities. Through Caroline Townshend she met and worked with the Webbs and George Bernard Shaw.

During the First World War she worked in the French hospital at Yvetot and after being invalided home, worked with Mrs. Strachey on the Women's Suffrage Bill. She returned to France and joined the Friends' Service Unit at Sermeze where she stayed until 1920, running an embroidery industry for French women.

She and Caroline Townshend were well named "The Citizens" by their fellow glass-painter Wilhelmina Geddes. At different times between wars, she cared for refugee Austrian and Spanish children and from 1938 until the outbreak of war, they arranged for many German and Austrian refugees to reach England, while during the last war they cared for up to 75 children from Fulham and Liverpool in nurseries in North Wales, until Miss Townshend's death. In 1956, Joan Howson furnished a house in Tremadoc for Hungarian refugees, helped by fellow artists and writers in the area.

CITIZEN ACTION

And still her sense of citizenship was unabated—when she found that the sea coast at her home in Wales was about to be smothered with caravans, she bought the land and made it over to the National Trust. In 1934, she was invited by her great friend, Miss Alice Gilliatt, the Mayor of Fulham, to be Mayoress.

With all this, there was still time for her glass at which she worked for hours a day, almost until the autumn of 1973 in her Putney studio, where she expressed her abiding reverence for colour and the craft of glass. From 1945 until 1961, she executed more than 30 new windows, some of which included the setting of Victorian glass and designing new and heraldic glass in Westminster Abbey Chapter House and the Savoy Chapel for King George VI. She had a very special love for the repair of medieval glass and such work can be seen in the ante-chapel of New College, Oxford, and in the East window of the South aisle in Newark Parish Church. She was one of the original Fellows of the British Society of Master Glass Painters.

June 12, 1964.

Dr. Hu Shih died in Formosa, at the age of 70, in February, 1962.

Hu Shih was one of the leading figures in the intellectual life of China during the past 50 years, and in the world of literature, perhaps the dominant one. He was a member of that younger generation whose revolt against a stultifying and conformist tradition burst into revolutionary flame during the period known as the May 4th movement of 1919. Dr. Hu's part in this movement will be most remembered for his advocacy of a vernacular literature, based on the ordinary spoken language (*pai-hua*) in place of the old classical written language. He had begun his campaign some years before while still a student in the United States; in Peking where he returned in 1917 to be Professor of Philosophy and head of the department of English literature at Peking University, he soon became a leader in the Chinese renaissance.

In these early years of intellectual revolution, politics and literature, social and educational reforms were all confused, though fiercely debated. Among Hu's close friends at the time were Ch'en Tu-hsiu, first leader of the Chinese Communist Party, and among his admirers, the assistant clerk in the University library, Mao Tse-tung. But the common feeling among this younger generation, anxious to kick off the traces of Chinese tradition, soon broke up; there were some attracted by revolutionary politics—soon to be Marxist in its emphasis—and others who pursued an intellectual revaluation in the attempt to absorb the inrush of western ideas in a Chinese context. Hu Shih emerged as the acknowledged leader of this latter group. His aim, he was later to write, was to see "the humanistic and rationalistic China resurrected by the touch of the scientific and democratic civilization of the new world".

SOCIAL REFORM

He thus remained a liberal and a reformer, concentrating on social issues such as the emancipation of women and remaining a leader of the new movement in education. Having parted company with Marxist thinking, Hu was also unable to play any part in or bring much influence to bear on the Kuomintang Party. He preferred to remain out of politics and pursue his studies in philosophy though he was a prolific contributor to the many reviews which sprang up in China in the 20s.

He founded his own journal, *The Independent Critic*, in Peking in 1932 and remained its editor until 1937. By then his international reputation was well established. At Chicago in 1933 he delivered a series of lectures later published, *The Chinese Renaissance*, which first gave the outside world a picture of the intellectual revolution in which he had been so prominent. In China he published his autobiography until the age of 40, and several volumes of collected essays established him as the leading liberal thinker. But he had never been a political influence or sought especially to be so. With others he criticized the Nationalist Government for its temporizing against Japanese aggression and when war broke out and Peking was occupied he went to London for a time until asked to serve his country as Ambassador in Washington. After four years there he returned to the wartime capital of Chungking as an accepted figure in government circles though perhaps more accepted for his influence in America than as adviser of the inner circle of the government.

PEKING UNIVERSITY

When the war ended he went back to Peking University as its head. There he found his liberalism under fierce attack from a generation of students almost wholly communist in sympathy, and since the appointment was a government one and he was inevitably associated with the stern and sometimes brutal suppression of student political activity, he was stigmatized as a reactionary and his reputation fell along with those others associated with the Nationalist Government during its decline. The truth was that Hu Shih had then become a prisoner in a political situation which he could not control and which he did not understand. He had always rejected political life and rejected any direct association with the Kuomintang Party because he detested political factions. In spite of the fact that he weakly accepted, and often was the instrument of government repression in these postwar years—repression of a kind he had attacked most fiercely only 20 years before—Hu's intellectual stature was too big to be extinguished by his decline as a public figure. This was shown after he had left China to settle in New York. The Communists, among their many campaigns of persuasion and reorganization in China, devoted one campaign after the Korean War to an attack on Hu and his ideas, damning him mainly as a mouthpiece of American ideas, capitalism and the submission of China to westernization. Such attacks had been made from the extreme left long before the war, but it was evident that his reputation in China must still have been considerable to have occasioned this especial campaign.

He was born in Shanghai on December 17, 1891, of an established and scholarly family in Anhui province. He soon showed his brilliance at school and was selected in 1910 among the Boxer indemnity scholars to go to the United States as a student. He was thus one of that early generation of Chinese students in the west which first grasped fully the nature of western civilization, accepted most of its values, and sought to import them into Chinese society. One of his most popular books was the diary he later published of his student days in America where he proclaimed himself a pacifist and confessed that he nearly became a Christian.

FIRST INTEREST

He had begun by studying agriculture but took his degrees at Cornell (M.A. 1915) and Columbia (Ph.D. 1917) in philosophy and this remained his first interest in life. He wrote some poetry and plays in the vernacular manner but his reputation was justly earned as a writer on literary and philosophical problems, detached and sometimes magisterial in manner. He was never at home in political life—though a successful Chinese Ambassador in Washington—and retired to New York in 1950, refusing the Foreign Ministry offered to him by the Nationalist Government in Formosa. He returned to the island only in 1958 as head of the Academia Sinicia but also, it seemed, as the intellectual spearhead of an American-supported attempt to inject more liberal colouring into the government of Chiang Kai-shek. In this he seems to have had little success.

Among the many honorary degrees awarded to Dr. Hu by universities in Europe and America was the D.C.L. conferred at Oxford in 1945.

February 26, 1962.

Emrys Hughes, left-wing rebel backbencher who was Labour M.P. for the South Ayrshire Division of Ayrshire and Bute since 1946 died on October 18, 1969, at the age of 75. He was editor of *Forward*, the Scottish Socialist newspaper, from 1931 to 1946.

Hughes was a Welshman who sat for a Scottish seat and he had all the Celtic fire and passion of his race. A pacifist, and on the extreme left wing of the Labour Party, he was a law unto himself during his political career. Many of his political arguments often seemed entirely illogical for he was continually swayed by the heart rather than by the head. Nevertheless he was one of the outstanding Parliamentary personalities since the Second World War.

VOTE ON REARMING

Hughes lost the party whip more than once: in 1954, in spite of instructions to abstain, he voted against the Tory acceptance of the principle of German rearmament together with Sydney Silverman and others—although he asserted that the issue involved moral convictions, the party whip was withdrawn but restored before the 1955 general election. In 1961, he was one of five who defied the parliamentary party by voting against the Service estimates. He lost the whip and his membership of the Parliamentary Party. Two years later both were restored. In 1951 Hughes was one of five backbenchers who cross-voted on the controversial health charges which had led to Bevan's resignation; no action, however, was taken against the group since there was little Labour leaders could do to discipline either the ministers or the back-benchers who had rebelled, without causing the defeat of the government.

Hughes was a master in the art of putting supplementaries; he considerably enhanced his Parliamentary reputation by thinking up in advance witty and sometimes debunking questions. Churchill when he was Prime Minister formed a personal affection for his tormentor. Hughes was not always to be drawn: once during a Tory censure motion on the Labour Government defence policy, Hughes, a pacifist, interrupted Churchill with "Nothing doing". Mr. Macmillan once confessed how he sometimes tried to imagine the follow-up he should expect from Hughes.

RECORDING ABSTAINERS

In 1962, Hughes, a seasoned exponent of the device, asked that members who deliberately abstain should be able to see themselves in Hansard as having done so, just like the Ayes and Noes. Hughes, who became one of the backbench masters of parliamentary practice and procedure, was to raise his case for radical parliamentary reform in *Parliament and Mumbo-Jumbo*, published in 1966. He was ready to scrap ceremonies such as the Speaker's daily procession to the Chamber or the visitations of Black Rod; he advocated that the Sovereign's residual powers should be removed from the Constitution, that the initiative for dissolving Parliament should be taken from the Prime Minister, and that Ministers should be elected by party ballot rather than be appointed by the Queen on the Prime Minister's recommendation.

An ardent pacifist, Hughes was a frequent visitor to Moscow, and was a friend of Samuel Marshak, the poet who translated Burns into Russian. Hughes spent a year of the First World War in Caernarvon jail, and maintained his stand. He was anti-Nato, called for peace in Korea through negotiation rather than arms, and was one of six Labour M.P.s to vote for the removal of British bases from the Suez zone in 1954. He also took part in the anti-Polaris demonstrations in Glasgow and Holy Loch in 1961.

Hughes wrote several biographies: earlier this year he completed a biography of his friend, Sydney Silverman, a leading leftwing crusader. His book, *Macmillan, Portrait of a Politician* (1962) was described by one reviewer as a "political cartoon". His book on Shaw as a politician was commissioned by the Russians, who objected to a passage concerning Shaw's relations with Frank Harris.

He was born on July 10, 1894, the son of a former Tonypandy minister, and was educated at Abercynon Council School, Mountain Ash Secondary School, and the City of Leeds Training College. Early in life he became an enthusiastic supporter of the Labour movement and was closely associated with its founder, Keir Hardie, whose daughter he married in 1924. He was happy that his literary talents were able to be used for the Labour Party. He edited Keir Hardie's *Writings and Speeches*, and one of the great joys of his life was the completion in 1950 of the pictorial centenary biography of his distinguished father-in-law.

BOOKS ON CHURCHILL

He also wrote much about his great political opponent, Sir Winston Churchill, publishing in 1930 *Winston Churchill in War and Peace*, which he described as "a critical biography". Five years later he published in the United States *Winston Churchill, the British Bulldog*. This contained much of the material in his earlier book, and Hughes explained that it was intended "to be a corrective and an antidote to much that has been written in praise of Sir Winston". From the good-tempered exchanges that frequently passed between them at question-time, when the retorts were sharp but good-humoured on either side, no one would ever have suspected that Hughes felt so deeply. But the probable explanation is that he never forgave Churchill for what happened long years before at Tonypandy.

Hughes became editor of a Scottish edition of *Tribune* after the Second World War. He never quite saw eye to eye with Aneurin Bevan, however. He had considerable experience in local government. which stood him in good stead when he entered Parliament in 1946 as the Labour representative of South Ayrshire constituency.

The following year his wife Provost Nan died. Throughout their married life she had worked and supported him in the Labour movement, and had many of the qualities of her distinguished father. Her loss seemed to cloud Hughes's judgment, and he found himself increasingly at loggerheads with his official party leaders in the Commons. He became more and more a law unto himself, and increasingly separated from his colleagues.

He married in 1949, secondly, Dr. Martha Cleland, of Glasgow.

October 20, 1969.

Hector Hughes, Q.C., Labour member of Parliament for North Aberdeen from 1945 until just before his death, died on June 23, 1970, after being rescued from the Channel at Brighton. He was 82.

He was a lawyer of some repute, who had the unusual distinction of taking silk at both the Irish and English Bars. He was defending counsel in a number of well-known cases, including murder trials at the Old Bailey. and was the author of a number of legal works.

He was born in 1887 and educated at the Diocesan School, Dublin, and at St. Andrew's College. He was compelled, at the age of 14, to take a job as office boy in a solicitor's office, but continued with his studies. In a year or two he won, in open competitive examination, a post in the Civil Service. He became a copying clerk in a Government office and attended law lectures at Trinity.

For some years he had been an ardent worker for the Irish Labour party in association with Jim Larkin and James Connolly. He helped Larkin organize the General Strike in 1913. Five years later he became a founder member of the Irish Socialist party and in 1920 of the James Connolly Memorial College and the Irish Co-operative Press.

He was called to the Irish Bar in 1915, having shown great promise while working at King's Inns, where he had gained the highest prizes for legal practice, debate, oratory, and composition, as well as the Lord Chancellor's prize for oratory and legal debate combined.

In 1923 he was called to the English Bar at Gray's Inn, but he did not immediately practise in England. He took silk at the Irish Bar in 1927, and after this his legal commitments in both countries grew rapidly.

He became more and more immersed in British politics, and in 1929 joined the Fabian Society. Two years later he became a member of the Haldane Club of Socialist lawyers. He had a fortnight's trip to Russia in 1931, and, on his return, fought his first parliamentary election in the then Conservative stronghold of North-West Camberwell, where he was heavily defeated by James D. Cassels (later Mr. Justice Cassels).

He took silk at the English Bar in 1932. He had worked hard for this, having written no fewer than eight books on various legal subjects in 16 years. At the general election of 1935 he nearly won North-West Camberwell for Labour, reducing the Conservative majority to 813 votes.

He strongly disagreed with the attitude of his party over Munich in 1938, and resigned. But he soon came back to the fold, and in the general election of 1945 was returned to the House of Commons as Labour member for North Aberdeen. His increasing popularity locally was shown in his steadily mounting majorities. He was one of the few members of his party to increase his majority at the general election of May, 1955, when he defeated his Conservative opponent by no fewer than 16,796 votes.

Though short of stature, and somewhat pugnacious in manner at times, he was the warmest-hearted of men, having a host of friends and few enemies. He had deep religious convictions, and was for a long time on the board of the Church Army, and had taken an active part in the Salvation Army.

He was a strong believer in physical fitness, and was particularly fond of swimming. No matter what the weather he enjoyed a dip in the sea at Aberdeen at any time of the year, and took part in the Christmas Day race, at Highgate Pond, London.

June 24, 1970.

Langston Hughes, the American Negro poet and writer, who died in New York on May 22, 1967, at the age of 65, liked to recall that the grandmother who mainly brought him up was the last surviving widow of John Brown's Raid of 1859. The anecdote showed how closely Hughes was linked from the start with his people's cause in the United States.

Hughes had a rather wandering childhood, and his early manhood was equally unsettled. After a year spent at Columbia University in 1921, he worked at a variety of jobs, as a sailor on the Atlantic run, and as a cook in Montmartre until he emerged as a poet, encouraged by Vachel Lindsay. He published his first collection of poems, *The Weary Blues*, in 1925. Hughes acknowledged that Walt Whitman and Carl Sandburg were his favourite poets, and their influence as well as that of the "Blues" tradition itself is apparent in his loose, informally rhythmic lines and in his use of folk idiom. He published 10 collections of verse, the last, *Ask your Mama*, in 1961.

Hughes became a professional writer and journalist. He wrote several songs and libretti, and one of his plays, *Mulatto*, first produced in 1936, ran for almost two years on Broadway and on tour. Among his many other writings were a novel, *Not Without Laughter*, 1930, and his short stories about a Negro called Simple, which he contributed to the Chicago Negro newspaper *Defender*, and which were collected in 1950 as *Simple Speaks his Mind*. He also wrote two volumes of autobiography, and his account of the National Association for the Advancement of Coloured People, *Fight for Freedom*, came out in 1962.

His expression of spontaneous Negro evangelism in *Black Nativity* was forceful—linking the story of Mary and Joseph through ballet, traditional spirituals, and narration. In 1963 Hughes edited *Poems from Black Africa*, a collection of thirty-eight African poets, which was a sequel to his earlier *The Poetry of the Negro*. *New Negro Poets*: *U.S.A.* was published in 1965.

Hughes was generally described as one of the most eminent Negro poets of this century, and though this may not mean much in relation to the achievement of twentieth-century verse as a whole, it is a great tribute to his determination, given the odds against success among his race.

No wonder that he cherished his grandmother's link with the past.

May 24, 1967.

Claude Hulbert, the very British stage and screen comedian, died on January 22, 1964, at Sydney, Australia, on a round-the-world cruise. He was 63.

As a comedian he was something of a specialist, and was one of a vintage line which was directly descended from Bertie Wooster and was led by their chief exponent, Ralph Lynn. This was the chinless wonder brigade, elegant in appearance and affable in manner, well bred, well-to-do, and well intentioned, but absentminded and always a little weak in the intellectual stakes. Names such as Shakespeare, Napoleon, or Julius Caesar rang a faint bell in their subconscious, but they would have been hard put to it to say in exactly what connexion, for the old grey matter tended to move a trifle sluggishly under the well groomed hair. The breed is now dying out, but Mr. Harry Worth, upgraded from suburbia, would make an admirable recruit to their now failing numbers.

Claude Hulbert was inevitably overshadowed in his career by his elder brother Jack—a man of much greater buoyancy and exuberance—but both had their niche in British stage and film comedy of the thirties. Jack Hulbert bounded through his parts with unfailing zest; Claude approached his more quietly and obliquely, for the Wooster clan were never prone to excessive energy. Together the two Hulbert brothers belonged to a British film decade which was rich in comics with players such as Will Hay, George Formby, Gracie Fields, Cicely Courtneidge, Tom Walls and the Crazy Gang, whose comedy style was deceptively simple but magnificently effective.

LOST ART

Today it seems in danger of becoming a lost art.

Claude Hulbert was born in London on Christmas Day, 1900. He was educated. as was his brother, at Westminster and Caius College, Cambridge, where he was a prominent member of the Footlights Club and it was the Footlights Club which first took him to the West End in *His Little Trip* at the Strand Theatre in 1920. His first appearance as a professional was made in rather more humble circumstances at the Alhambra, Bradford, in the same year, and he later toured provincial music halls for a short period before returning to London to appear at the Queen's Theatre in 1921. His first major success was at the Winter Garden Theatre three years later as Freddy Falls in *Primrose*.

Thereafter he appeared in a number of successful stage comedies during the twenties, and towards the end of the decade he began to interest himself in both films and broadcasts. One of his earliest film appearances was under Alfred Hitchcock's direction in *Champagne* in 1929, but his screen career really started with film adaptations of the Ben Travers comedies, *A Night Like This* in 1931 and *Thark* in 1932. He appeared with his brother in *Bulldog Jack* in 1935, and continued successfully in films until 1939, when he reappeared on the West End stage at the Saville in *Worth A Million*. Towards the end of the war he had the good fortune to become a member of the Ealing team of film comedy makers, and from then on he continued to appear regularly on the stage, in films, in sound radio and on television.

Although his comedy style was restricted he showed marked versatility in the medium of its presentation. His gramophone duologues were highly successful before the war and he was equally successful on the air with his wife, Enid Trevor, and his brother Jack. Claude Hulbert was one of those comedians who spend their careers doing what appears to be very simple, while hiding from their audiences the fact that it is not.

January 24, 1964.

George Magoffin Humphrey, Secretary of the United States Treasury in President Eisenhower's first Administration, of which he was much the "strong man," died on January 20, 1970, at Cleveland, Ohio. He was 79.

Humphrey was a captain of American industry who made legends. It took daring and toughness at the onset of the 1929 depression to salvage the M. A. Hanna Company, founded at Cleveland by the notorious political boss Mark Hanna, and as president build it into a vast mining and manufacturing complex. The son of a lawyer, he joined the company in 1918 as general attorney, having taken his degree at Michigan University and practised for a few years with the family law firm at Saginaw, Michigan. At the age of 33 he was in charge of Hanna's multiple operations as executive vice-president.

Another five years saw him in the saddle, taking his fences with all the verve he showed in the hunting-field. Part of the legend would be that Humphrey rode headlong at his jumps, but always knew what lay on the other side. A measure of his creative ability in later years was the opening of the rich Labrador mines by the Iron Ore Company of Canada.

CONTEMPT FOR POLITICIANS

Humphrey was generally thought to represent the Taft wing in an Administration dedicated to precepts of sound money and a balanced budget, the essence of Washington's "new look" after the soaring deficits of war and the Democratic New Deal. Eisenhower's recourse to big business for most of his Cabinet officers, given his undisguised contempt for politicians or egg-heads, had the desired impact on fiscal and monetary policies. Humphrey consented to serve against his conviction that the businessman has no place in politics. His departure in 1957 early in the second Eisenhower term seemed in line with that belief.

His one brief association with government had been in 1948 as chairman of the industrial advisory committee that went to Germany to report on dismantling for Paul Hoffman's Economic Cooperation Administration. It was largely due to these findings that 175 Ruhr factories—all in the British zone—earmarked for reparations, were left intact in the wider interests of European recovery.

The latitude enjoyed by Humphrey, especially in pursuing the "hard money" tactics which typified his tenure, gave the Treasury the semblance of power and influence; but the President, unable to reconcile the conflicting pressures of the spending departments, never went all the way with him. The great difference between them was in their backgrounds. Humphrey, at heart an expansionist, wanted to cut taxes as a way to budget equilibrium in the simple belief, as he said, that prosperity depended more on the confidence of all the people than on any act of government other than the removal of impediments to individual initiative. Eisenhower, ever fearful of inflation, insisted on a balanced budget first.

Unexpectedly high tax yields for 1956 and 1957, both boom years, gave Humphrey the satisfaction of small budget surpluses, a great victory; but for all his vehemence in council the levels of federal spending were clearly beyond his control. Foreign aid was the unhappy field in which he, leading the so-called 4-H club, and his conservative friends in Congress, wielded the axe most trenchantly, to the President's impotent fury. If dollar diplomacy could win the cold war, as many Americans liked to think, Humphrey's Washington looked too narrow for the role.

But for all the austerity of his public image, Humphrey was a bluff, jovial man of persuasive charm. His orthodox methods may have looked dull and old-fashioned but his management of the national debt won wide admiration.

FIGHTING TAXES

His fight against high taxation, with its corrosive influence, as he saw it, on American morality and private enterprise, was carried early in 1957 to a memorable outburst over the budget. In presenting estimates of $72,000m. to the press he stunned Washington by expostulating that they would have a recession "that will curl your hair" if the Government went on taking too much money out of the economy in taxes. To have a Secretary of the Treasury attack the budget on the day it went to Congress was quite unprecedented; and this budget, the first of Eisenhower's second term, was calculated to show what was intended by "modern Republicanism", his election slogan. With the President blowing hot and cold while Congress knifed the military estimates, the extent of the ensuing recession was reflected in a budget deficit of $12½m., then a record for peace-time by which time Humphrey had gone back to Ohio in a blaze of disappointment, having reduced neither taxes nor the public debt. He had left his mark on the Eisenhower era.

January 22, 1970.

Martita Hunt, the actress, died in London on June 13, 1969, at the age of 69.

She had appeared in a considerable variety of parts, and each would probably have "come out" differently if anybody else in the profession had played it. Yet she captured the imagination in one line of parts only; those of eccentric exhibitionists like the governess in *The Cherry Orchard* and the mad woman of Chaillot in Giraudoux's play of that name. In her other line of parts, those of poised and elegant women of the world, she seemed to be on the defensive and so hindered an audience from appreciating her fine performances at their proper worth.

She was born in Argentina on January 30, 1900, and made her first appearance with the Liverpool Repertory Company. Komisarjevsky picked her for the governess in his revival of *The Cherry Orchard* at Barnes, and in 1929 she was engaged by Harcourt Williams as leading lady at the Old Vic. There, in addition to playing opposite Sir John Gielgud "heavies" like Lady Macbeth and Queen Gertrude, she had to tackle "lighter" parts such as Portia and Rosalind and if possible make audiences warm to her and smile with her, though there was nothing soft and something that was Amazonian about her looks and stage presence. "I thought Portia played with real skill and judgment", Granville Barker wrote to the producer after seeing her, "though of course she could not give the fairy-princess touch to the earlier scenes". The producer himself recorded of her Rosalind: "I fancy that queer personal fear which so often obsessed her, that she could not 'bring it off', just kept her from winning through on her brilliance".

After one season at the Old Vic she returned to the West End and there gave distinguished performances of secondary parts in plays by Dodie Smith, Ivor Novello, John van Druten and Clemence Dane. Complete success in leading parts still eluded her, until, in 1948, an American management cast her as the inspired, outrageous do-gooder in *The Madwoman of Chaillot*. She appeared in this during two seasons in the United States, and it must have been a great disappointment to her, now a star for the first time, when the play failed on being taken to London in 1951. Her next part there, which she played to hilarious effect, was the supporting one of the Grand Duchess in Terence Rattigan's *The Sleeping Prince*.

She was seen in a number of films from 1933 onwards, including *The Man in Grey*; *The Wicked Lady*; *Great Expectations*, in which she played Miss Havisham; *Anastasia*, and *Bunny Lake is Missing*.

June 14, 1969.

Sir Ellis Hunter, G.B.E., chairman of Dorman, Long and Company since 1948, died at his Yorkshire home on September 21, 1961, at the age of 69.

Ellis Hunter was born in 1892 at Great Ayton, Yorkshire, the son of William Hunter, headmaster of the village school, from whom he probably acquired the capacity for concentrated study which characterised all his activities. After leaving Middlesbrough High School he served articles with a local firm of accountants, qualifying in 1913 and becoming F.C.A. in 1927.

His first direct contact with the iron and steel industry was during the 1914–18 War, when at the Ministry of Munitions he was employed in the department concerned with iron and steelworks extensions and the limitation of profits. In 1922 he became a local partner in W. B. Peat & Co., and with the formation of Messrs. Peat, Marwick & Mitchell, Ellis Hunter became a general partner in 1928.

It was in the early thirties that he became intimately concerned with the fortunes—then at a very low ebb—of Dorman Long and in 1938 he became deputy chairman and shortly afterwards managing director of the company.

The transfer was not one gilded by financial inducement, but he left the somewhat detached world of accountancy because he was attracted by the magnitude of the task and his recognition that Middlesbrough at that time depended to an extraordinary degree upon the fortunes of Dorman Long.

The task of restoring the company to full health was considerable, and the war came before most of the plans made could be implemented. The war years were successfully weathered, but, in common with the rest of the steel industry, major development was impossible, and in the immediate period after hostilities ceased shortages of plant construction resources in this country and the necessity to recognize certain priorities in the national interest delayed still further the implementing of bold schemes of modernization and expansion which had been prepared for the company.

During the war Ellis Hunter had taken an increasing part in deliberations and activities of the British Iron and Steel Federation, and in 1945 became president at a time when the whole future of the industry was under review and political influences began to exercise marked pressure on the form of future development. He remained president until 1953, a tenure of office much beyond the traditional period of two years.

One of the first tasks he undertook as president was the drawing up of the first postwar development plan, a review produced in an exceptionally short time and one more comprehensive and far seeing than anything undertaken for any comparable industry. It marked a change of outlook in an industry essentially individualistic in its approach to its problems and established for the first time a truly corporate view, an acceptance of public accountability and a disposition, reluctant at first, to submit individual company policies to the test of national need. In achieving this change Ellis Hunter's appreciation of the probable trend of public opinion and national requirements was a significant factor.

NATIONALIZATION

There began at this time an intimate association with Sir Andrew Duncan, who had resumed his office as independent chairman of the British Iron and Steel Federation. The two men were the mouthpiece of the industry in the protracted discussions which took place with the Labour Government over the proposals to nationalize the industry. They succeeded in convincing Mr. Herbert Morrison and Mr. Wilmot, then Minister of Supply, that the industry accepted the principle of public accountability, and that transfer of ownership was not essential to the success of the Labour

Party's determination to exercise a measure of over-all control. Mr. Attlee, then Prime Minister, was disposed to accept a scheme of statutory control not unlike that which exists today, and an agreed settlement on these broad lines seemed probable when Aneurin Bevan objected and threatened resignation. Attlee, feeling unable to proceed with provisional agreements reached with the industry's leaders, proceeded with the plans for full-scale nationalization of the steel industry.

Hunter and Duncan were an ideal combination, on the one hand the experienced negotiator, and on the other an uncompromising tough personality with an exceptional knowledge of the industry, its financial structure, its history, and the character of the men who managed it. Ellis Hunter, throughout protracted and often acrimonious discussions, was generally a steel hand inside the velvet glove so skilfully used by Sir Andrew Duncan.

Never modifying his unqualified opposition to nationalization, Ellis Hunter, once Parliament had approved, was scrupulously correct in his dealings with the statutory authority placed in control of the industry. It was mainly by his insistence that all dealings between the Iron and Steel Corporation of Great Britain and individual companies were confined to communications between the chairman and secretary of the corporation and the chairmen and secretaries of the companies that little interference with detailed operations of the companies occurred.

His long period of service in London on behalf of the federation never weakened his grip on and interest in Dorman Long, the full direction of which he insisted should remain centred in Middlesbrough, where monthly Board meetings were held.

The company's £100m. development programme, after the Second World War, was successfully carried through and financed to a larger degree than usual from retained profits. Ellis Hunter's policy, which resulted in modest dividends for a number of years, provoked criticism, but he was not to be deflected. His experience of the adversity of the years between the wars no doubt strengthened his determination in this matter.

SPECIAL DIRECTORS

A feature of his administration was his consistent encouragement of the younger generation and the introduction in 1944 of special directors. In this way the chief officials of the company were brought into intimate association with the Board and assisted in the formulation of policy. Several of the first special directors have become full executive directors and their places taken by younger special directors.

A certain shyness and reserve, coupled with his pertinacity and a suggestion of dourness, often created a misleading judgment of his personality by those whose contact with him was purely formal and brief. While advancing years were accompanied by a lessening of his stern expression there had always existed a sense of humour and kindliness not far below the surface.

He confined himself to directorships in the Dorman Long Group apart from his membership of the Court of Governors of the Royal Exchange Assurance Co., Ltd. At the end of March, 1961, he resigned from all executive appointments in the Dorman Long Group.

He was knighted in 1948 and advanced to Knight Grand Cross of the Order of the British Empire in 1961.

He married in 1918 Winifred Grace Stead, by whom he had two daughters.

September 22, 1961.

Leslie Hunter, who died on December 8, 1961, in a Dorking hospital at the age of 52, had been political correspondent of the *Daily Herald* for nearly six years, during some of the Labour Party's most turbulent days of inner party strife in the 1950s. This experience provided him with the material for his controversial book *The Road to Brighton Pier*, published in 1959; and it is for this book, rather than for his journalistic writing, that he is most likely to be remembered.

Leslie David Stevenson Hunter was born on July 10, 1909. Before the Second World War he was head of the Central News parliamentary service. He joined the *Daily Herald* in November, 1951, and remained with the paper until September, 1957, holding the post of political correspondent throughout that time.

As such, he was a privileged spectator of the personal jealousies and wrangles for power that tortured the Labour Party during this period. These were set down in embarrassing detail in his book without the discretion that must inhibit a political correspondent—and without, some of his critics felt, too precise a regard for personal confidences. It was a highly readable, if not edifying, account of petty intrigues and mutual hatreds dominating the discussion of policy. There was Attlee's "implacable hatred" of Morrison—a phrase which Hunter subsequently withdrew—the machinations of Arthur Deakin, the Bevanite struggle, and the reconciliation between Bevan and Gaitskell at Brighton in 1957. Not surprisingly, however much Hunter's book may have delighted his readers, it did not endear the author to fellow members of his party.

In 1950 he married Margaret Stewart, then industrial correspondent of the *News Chronicle*.

December 9, 1961.

General Patrick J. Hurley, who served President Hoover as Secretary of War and President Roosevelt and President Truman as Ambassador to China, died at Santa Fé, New Mexico, on July 30, 1963. He was 80.

A somewhat ebullient Irishman of much personal charm, his term as Secretary of War occurred at a time when that office was not one of really major importance. He won a reputation as a vigorous administrator, and under him there was increased mechanization of the regular force and greater attention was paid to the air force, for which his department was responsible.

It was after the Second World War, however, that his forthright comments and somewhat extreme position made him a controversial figure in American public affairs. During the war he had been Roosevelt's personal representative on a number of missions overseas and had then become Ambassador to China. While at first zealously seeking to promote the prescribed American policy of effecting united action between the Chinese communists and the Kuomintang, he later became increasingly critical of what he regarded as the weakness of the American Administration's reactions to developments in China.

There were charges, repeated over a period of years, of pro-Communist sympathies among officials in the State Department and American diplomatists in the Far East. Nor did politicians escape the lash of his criticism—in particular there were attacks on Mr. Dean Acheson, Mr. Byrnes, and those who bore responsibility for the Yalta agreement, not excluding Roosevelt. Naturally enough, Hurley had resigned his ambassadorship in November, 1945.

Patrick Jay Hurley was born on the lands of the Choctaw Nation in the Indian Territory on January 8, 1883. He learnt to speak the tribal dialect from his earliest days and this was of great advantage to him in later days when members of the tribe had accumulated great wealth through the development of oil on their lands and as a lawyer he had to defend their rights in the courts. In 1905 he graduated from the Indian University, which is now known as Bacone College, and then took up the study of the law at the National University of Washington, where he took the degree of LL.B. in 1908. In that year he was called to the Oklahoma Bar. He set up practice at Tulsa, the chief city of the state, but four years later moved to Washington to carry on his work before the Supreme Court where many cases connected with the oil lands, the Indians' rights and their sale to others were constantly coming up. For five years before he left for the war in Europe he was the national attorney for the Choctaw Nation. In 1912, too, at Washington he took part in the establishment of the United States Chamber of Commerce.

During the First World War Hurley, who had been an enthusiastic officer in the Oklahoma National Guard, was among the first American troops to be sent to France. He took part in the offensive on the Aisne and the Marne in the summer of 1918, and when the American Army took over a sector of its own he led his men in the offensives in the Argonne and the St. Mihiel salient. Promoted to lieutenant-colonel, he was also awarded the United States Distinguished Service Medal.

OIL IN OKLAHOMA

After the war till he became a Cabinet Minister in 1929 and after he had retired from that office in 1933, he made his home in Oklahoma and was intimately connected with the development of the oil industry there.

Although a staunch Republican he also saw a great deal of national service under Franklin Roosevelt. Immediately after the Japanese attack on Pearl Harbour he rejoined the army and was given the rank of colonel. In 1942 he was assigned to the Far Eastern theatre, being personal representative there of the chief of staff, General George Marshall. In that capacity he ran the Japanese blockade of the Philippines between January and March, 1942. Roosevelt then appointed him Minister to New Zealand but he remained in Wellington only a short time. His next assignment was as special representative of the President on a mission which took him to the Soviet Union, Egypt, Syria, Lebanon, Iraq, Iran, Palestine, Trans-Jordan, Saudi Arabia, Afghanistan, and India.

He was a member of the American delegation to the Teheran conference in 1943 and later was promoted major-general and sent to China as Roosevelt's special representative. In 1944 he was appointed United States Ambassador to China.

In 1918 he married Ruth Wilson, daughter of Admiral H. B. Wilson of the United States Navy. They had a son and three daughters.

August 1, 1963.

Sir Cecil Hurst, G.C.M.G., K.C.B., who died at his home at Horsham on March 27, 1963, at the age of 92, was a jurist of wide learning and experience. He was for many years principal legal adviser to the Foreign Office, and in that capacity was one of the drafters of the Treaty of Versailles. In 1929 he was elected by the League of Nations to be one of the Judges of the Permanent Court of International Justice at The Hague, and served until 1946, being president from 1934 to 1936. He was also one of the United Kingdom members of the Permanent Court of Arbitration at The Hague from 1929 to 1950.

Cecil James Barrington Hurst was born on October 28, 1870, the third son of Robert Henry Hurst, of Horsham Park, Recorder of Hastings and Rye, chairman of West Sussex Quarter Sessions, sometime M.P. for Horsham; and grandson of Robert Henry Hurst, who served in the Peninsular Campaign and took part in the retreat to Corunna. Like his father and grandfather he was sent to Westminster School. Going up to Trinity College, Cambridge in 1888, he was placed in the second class in Part I and in the first class in Part II of the Law Tripos. He was called to the Bar in 1893 by the Middle Temple, took silk in 1913, and was elected a Bencher of his Inn in 1922. In 1940 he was treasurer. He was junior counsel to the Post Office on the South-Eastern Circuit, 1901–2, assistant legal adviser to the Foreign Office from 1902 to 1918, and from 1918 legal adviser to the Foreign Office.

It was a fortunate appointment, as it placed his skill as a legal adviser and a draftsman at the disposal of the Crown during prolonged negotiations at the Peace Conference which preceded the Versailles Treaty and other treaties belonging to the same period. The draftsmanship and legal thought involved were of the most arduous and abstruse kind, since lawyers and statesmen of many countries took in many ways differing views which had to be reconciled in draft after draft. He was created C.B. in 1907, K.C.B. in 1920, K.C.M.G. in 1924, and G.C.M.G. in 1926. The honours which he received in 1924 and 1926 were tributes to the great services which he rendered to successive British Foreign Secretaries in their work at Geneva.

APPLYING THE PEACE TREATIES

For the first years of its existence the time of the League was necessarily much taken up in elucidating and applying the Peace Treaties, and for these tasks no better adviser could have been found than Hurst. The part which he played grew out of all proportion to the work of his predecessors in office with the growing importance of international law. In almost every dispute before the League of Nations the legal aspect was naturally that upon which attention was chiefly concentrated, and Hurst was for five years a close and trusted collaborator with Sir Austen Chamberlain. In 1940 he was made chairman of the Committee for the Release of Enemy Aliens, and three years later he became chairman of the Commission on War Crimes, but ill-health compelled his resignation from the latter in 1945.

With Mr. Bray he dealt with Russian and Japanese prize cases in 1912 and 1913. To *The British Year Book of International Law*, of which he became editor in 1919, he contributed (1921–1922) an article collating the literature on the cancellation of treaties, in which he said "The true test as to whether or not a treaty survives an outbreak of war between the parties is to be found in the intention of the parties at the time when the treaty is concluded". He was a member of various learned legal societies and president of the Grotius Society from 1940 to 1945. In an introduction to *Information on the World Court, 1918–1928*, by J. W. Wheeler-Bennett and Maurice Fanshawe, published in 1929, Hurst outlined the growth of the idea of a real judicial International Court from the time of the first Peace Conference at The Hague in 1899. In this introduction he states "That compulsory arbitration means for every State some sacrifice of national independence cannot be denied, and for a State like Great Britain perhaps a greater sacrifice than for any other State. Nevertheless, the sacrifice is worth making if the advantages outweigh the disadvantages".

While this work was in the press, Sir Cecil Hurst was appointed, in March, 1929, one of the British delegates to the Permanent Court of Arbitration at The Hague with a view to his nomination by the British delegates as Judge of the Permanent Court of International Justice, in succession to the late Lord Finlay, who had held both posts. It happened that the French Government also had to nominate a delegate in succession to the late M. Weiss, and both their nominee, M. Fromageot, and Sir Cecil Hurst were objected to on the ground that they had been closely connected as official legal advisers, with the policies of their respective Foreign Offices, and that they had not had, as other candidates had, experience on the judicial bench. Both, however, possessed a high reputation at Geneva for their wide knowledge of international law as well as for their personal distinction and in September, 1929, Sir Cecil Hurst and M. Fromageot were duly elected Judges of the Permanent Court of International Justice by both the Council and the Assembly of the League of Nations, by absolute majorities. In 1930 and again in 1945 Hurst was re-elected for additional terms of service.

Sir Cecil Hurst married, in 1901, Sibyl, daughter of the late Judge Sir Lumley Smith, K.C.

She died in 1947. They had two sons and a daughter.

March 28, 1963.

Fannie Hurst, the American novelist, died on February 23, 1968, at the age of 78.

For many years a leading best-seller in the United States, at one time reputed to be the most highly paid woman novelist in the world, Fannie Hurst wrote with an exuberance that was possibly in close keeping with the American sense of the American way of life. It was an exuberance to which even the more critical of her readers willingly succumbed in the end. The dramatic colour in her fiction, garishly brilliant, was laid on, it seemed, as thickly as possible; she knew nothing of economy of effect or of conciseness of phrase; all was loud, violent and several times larger than life—and yet the sheer vitality of her imagination and style of sentiment was irresistible. It did not matter that her language was breathless, jerky, without rhythm or individual distinction. Fannie Hurst wrote out of a lavishness of feeling, a warmth and energy of dramatized emotion, that gave vibrating power to whatever illusion of life she chose to present. As a best-selling novelist and celebrity she was perhaps a distinctively American phenomenon.

Born in Hamilton, Ohio, on October 19, 1889, the daughter of Samuel Hurst, she was brought up in St. Louis, Missouri, in a home well supplied with books. She began to write in early adolescence, and by the time she was ready for college had apparently collected a small packet of rejection slips from—the source is significant—the *Saturday Evening Post*. She studied English at Washington University, St. Louis, took her degree there, longed for New York, proceeded to Columbia University, and bent herself more deliberately to the task of studying the magazine market for short stories. In her second year in New York the editor of *Munsey's Magazine* accepted three out of 15 manuscripts which she submitted. The tide in her fortunes had turned early.

In search of material she worked for a short spell as a waitress, as a nursemaid, on the stage, and crossed the Atlantic as a steerage passenger. Hers was, in fact, a serious enough ambition as a writer, though not an unworldly ambition; the short story might not be her true medium, but it provided her with a ready livelihood and she was beginning to make her name known. Her first collection, *Just Around the Corner* appeared in 1914, and was followed in time by three more such volumes. Not until 1921 did she write her first novel. *Star Dust*, as it was confidingly called, attracted only moderate notice, but two years later came *Lummox* and with that novel came fame and more than ordinary fortune. The all too pulsating story of a big clumsy servant girl of immigrant stock and of inarticulately poetic temperament, it is shrewdly and powerfully contrived, though the poetry in question has perhaps to be taken on trust.

Afterwards during a career of prolonged success came *Appassionata* (1925), a vast and noisy monologue of the richly impassioned female heart; *A President is Born* (1928), gaudy yet vivid in its presentation of an immigrant family in the process of being absorbed into American life; *Five and Ten* (1929), celebrating the sorrows of the plutocracy; the very, very long *Back Street* (1930) with a theme that Theodore Dreiser had handled in starker fashion; *Anitra's Dance* (1934) which had for subject the personal ordeal of musical genius. In every one of these novels Miss Hurst's tremendous emotional energy told in spite of all excess. Perhaps she did not quite maintain the prodigality of her powers in subsequent books, though she kept as shrewdly calculating a hand on the pulse of the public. *Lonely Parade* (1942) was a story of three young women in New York during the first 30 years of this century, while *The Hands of Veronica* (1937) brought into dramatic view the subject of faith-healing.

She continued until late in life to be very prolific, turning out numerous novels and short stories that were vigorously written and always highly charged with emotion. Among the later volumes were *Any Woman*, *The Man with One Head* and, in 1958, her autobiography *Anatomy of Me*.

Her appeal was universal for she was translated into twelve languages including Hungarian, Portuguese and Rumanian, and she was a best-seller in all of them. Many of her short stories and novels were made into films, some of them more than once. *Imitation of Life* for instance, filmed in 1934, was re-made with a different cast in 1959.

In 1958 she struck out in a new direction, appearing regularly on television and she was also a radio commentator. Her profession honoured her by making her President of the Authors' Guild for one year and its Vice-President for three, and the United States appointed her to a conference of the World Health Organization in Geneva.

Handsome in a somewhat opulent style, travelled, fairly widely read, an enthusiastic collector of works of art, a noted hostess in New York, she took a frank pleasure in the good things that life had given her. Her husband, Jacques S. Danielson, the pianist, whom she married in 1915, died in 1952.

February 24, 1968.

Dr. Zakir Husain, President of India, died on May 3, 1969. He was 72.

Husain was well fitted for the role; until now the presidency of India has been a non-political office. His life spanned a bitterly turbulent era for the Muslims of the sub-continent, but avoiding the main stream of politics he made his mark in the university administration and the more honorific forms of government service. From 1962 to 1967 he was vice-president, and in 1967 was elected India's third president, the first Muslim to hold that office.

Husain was the candidate of the Congress Party and especially of Mrs. Indira Gandhi, the Prime Minister, and in office he was content to fill the strictly limited duties, little more than ceremonial, which the Indian constitution gives the president. In a time of growing weakness of the central government, such as the present, an ambitious or politically committed president could undoubtedly quickly enlarge his influence, and probably soon his powers too; while Zakir Husain was president there was no chance of that happening. As a Muslim any suggestion of political interference from him would have quickly been resented and beyond that would have been wholly out of character.

Zakir Husain was born in Hyderabad in 1897, when that state was still an anachronistic enclave of the mogul style, and went for his university education to Aligarh Muslim University, which was to be the intellectual seed bed for the idea of Pakistan, a separate state for the Muslims of British India.

But Husain gave his allegiance to Gandhi and the Congress Party, with its cause of a united, secular India, in which the Muslim would have equal rights with every other citizen. Leaving Aligarh when Gandhi called on Indian youth to forswear education in state institutions, he was one of a group which founded the Jamia Millia, an Islamic college in New Delhi and became its vice-chancellor in 1927 when he returned with his doctorate from Berlin University.

Partition left Aligarh University in India, and without a cause, and Husain became its vice-chancellor in 1948, his task being to make it if possible a nationalist institution. There followed spells on various government commissions, a term in Unesco in Paris, and then he was made governor of Bihar.

That in Husain India had a Muslim first as vice-president and then as president did seem an encouraging sign, but he was in no sense a leader of the Indian Muslim community. Since partition, and the death of Maulana Azad in 1958, the Muslims of India have in fact been leaderless and although Husain was widely liked and personally respected, some felt that he should have done more for the community than his own strict interpretation of secularism allowed.

May 5, 1969.

Leslie Hutchinson, "Hutch" the singing pianist of cabaret and variety, who died on August 18, 1969, was for 40 years one of the most successful and highly prized of light entertainers.

Born in Grenada of mixed Negro, Caribbean Indian, Scottish and French ancestry, he was studying the piano in Paris, intending to become a classical concert pianist, and filling in his time by playing in Joselli's bar, in the Place Clichy, when in 1927 C. B. Cochran took him to London to play in *One Damn Thing after Another* at the London Pavilion.

From his first appearance as a pianist—singing followed a little later—Leslie Hutchinson was sensationally successful. He appeared in cabaret, notably at the Cafe de Paris and Quaglino's, and became an essential part of the parties and entertainments of society before winning equal acclaim as a variety star immovably fixed at the top of the bill. No cabaret artist has ever stayed longer in one place than he did at Quaglino's after his return there in 1954. An attack of virus pneumonia in 1967 took him to Nairobi, where he appeared, to all intents ageless and inexhaustible, in cabaret.

Fanatically devoted to cricket, with an encyclopaedic knowledge of the game's statistics, Hutchinson was an extremely civilized as well as an extremely skilful entertainer. Charm, technique and tact made a spectacular approach to the key-board and everything forceful or blatant was completely foreign to his style. He was the ideal artist for the relaxed hour after dinner but he had an unusual gift for convincing large audiences that they had dined well and were sitting at ease in opulent surroundings.

August 19, 1969.

Sir William Oliphant Hutchison, vice-president of the Royal Society of Portrait Painters and president of the Royal Scottish Academy from 1950 to 1959, died on February 5, 1970. He was 80. He had been Director of the Glasgow School of Art from 1933 to 1943.

Hutchison, a well-known portrait and landscape painter, painted portraits of the Queen for the Edinburgh Merchant Company, and the Bramshill House police college, and a portrait of Prince Philip for the Royal College of Surgeons (Edinburgh). In 1948 Hutchison was elected a member of the Royal Society of Portrait Painters. He was an associate member, later a full member, of the Scottish Academy.

Hutchison was born at Kirkcaldy in 1889, and educated at Rugby, and studied at the Edinburgh College of Art and in Paris. He owed a great deal to the guidance of the Scottish landscape painter, E. A. Walton, whose youngest daughter he married.

Though he was a staunch supporter of the Royal Scottish Academy and the Glasgow Institute, Hutchison was a regular exhibitor at the Royal Academy. He made his first appearance there in 1922 with "Katriona", which was officially purchased for the Paisley Art Gallery.

ACADEMY SELECTION

His academy pictures included portraits, "genre" subjects, such as "Reading Aloud", "Family Tennis" and "A Domestic Arrangement", and some of his Scottish and Suffolk landscapes. He also showed at the International Society, the New English Art Club, the Royal West of England Academy and the Paris Salon. Hutchison is represented in the Scottish Modern Art Collection at Glasgow.

When he began to paint, the "Glasgow School", in which his mentor, E. A. Walton, had been a moving spirit, was already well established, but some influence of both Whistler and Lavery can be traced in his figure subjects.

When Hutchison was appointed Director of the Glasgow School of Art (which is housed in a building famous as the work of Charles Rennie Mackintosh), he succeeded in bringing the teaching to a high level of efficiency. He was keenly interested in modern developments and had strong views on the need for artists with technical knowledge in industry.

In 1964 he exhibited in London; among the portraits was one of "Nancy" and among the landscapes "Snow in Richmond".

February 9, 1970.

Harold Huth, whose career in the British film industry as an actor, casting director, producer and director of feature films, and a film company director, spanned over 40 years, died on October 25, 1967.

He was 75. During the last phase of his career he was a director of the Warwick Film Company, for whom he produced some half-dozen films including *The Trials of Oscar Wilde*.

Huth was born in Huddersfield on January 20, 1892, and was educated at Dover College. He was a major with the A.S.C. in France during the 1914–18 War, and was three times mentioned in dispatches. After the war he entered the motor business, and was made a director of Warwick Wright, Ltd.

He became an actor by chance when his cousin, Roland Pertwee, took him in 1927 on a visit to the Gainsborough Studios at Islington and Huth was suddenly bitten with the desire to appear in films. His military bearing led to his being given the part of an officer in a thoroughly bad picture called *One of the Best*, but this he survived. His film career was soon given impetus by his being teamed with Joan Barry, and the two of them met with considerable success. His first appearance on the regular stage was made at the Globe theatre in 1929 in *The Truth Game*, and by the early 1930s he was an established favourite, both in the cinema and on the London stage.

POPULAR CHOICE

His most popular films were *Sally Bishop* with Joan Barry and *Rome Express* in which he played beside Conrad Veidt. But unfortunately his health broke down in middle age and he was forced to give up his acting career. He became a casting director at Gainsborough, and later with M.G.M. when he worked on such well-known prewar British films as *Goodbye Mr. Chips*, *A Yank at Oxford* and *The Citadel*. He next became an associate producer with M.G.M. and made *Busman's Honeymoon* with Robert Montgomery and Constance Cummings, and finally he turned to directing. Between 1940 and 1941 he directed *Hell's Cargo, Alias the Bulldog*, and *East of Piccadilly*, each for Associated British. In 1942 he took up acting again and was seen in *This was Paris* with Ann Dvorak and Ben Lyon, but by the end of the war he had returned to the field of film production once again with Gainsborough and M.G.M.

In 1948 he formed Burnham Productions, and later formed his own company, H. H. Productions, for whom he produced *One Wild Oat*. He then became a business director of Douglas Fairbanks Limited, which made a large number of television films for the American market. In 1956 he became a director of Warwick Films, and for them he produced, in 1960, his best film, *The Trials of Oscar Wilde*, which was directed by Ken Hughes with Peter Finch as Wilde, James Mason as Carson, and Lionel Jeffries as Queensberry. However, this involved him in a legal battle with a rival company who made *Oscar Wilde* at very much the same time. His last picture was *The Hellions* which he produced for Warwick in 1961.

October 28, 1967.

Edward Hutton, man of letters, critic of Italian literature and art, died on August 20, 1969, at the age of 94.

He spent the greater part of his long life in imparting to English readers his knowledge and love of Italy, her people, her cities, her art-treasures and her literature. Most of the books in his long list—some 36 in all—dealt with Italy in one way or another.

He was born on April 12, 1875, in London; his father was a businessman with interests in Sheffield. The son was sent to Blundell's school, Tiverton, and at an early age began to apply himself to the study of the Greek and Roman classics, and to travel in Europe, in Italy especially—though he felt the strong attraction of Mediterranean culture in general, and wrote one book on Spain and another on Greece. He called the latter *A Glimpse of Greece*, and was even known to declare Greek landscape superior to Italian. But his knowledge of and affection for Italy was always deepest; it was refreshed by constant contact, frequent visits and some years of residence.

He lived, with his wife Charlotte (née Miles), whom he married in 1898, in a villa at Settignamo, above Florence, where they were friends and neighbours with Bernard Berenson. Mrs. Janet Ross, her daughter Mrs. Lina Waterfield, Norman Douglas, Herbert Horne, Langton Douglas and Mason Perkins were also among Hutton's Tuscan friends. He contributed articles about Italy to various English periodicals, and when he was 27 he published two books, *Italy and the Italians* and *Studies in the Lives of the Saints*. The first of his several books on the different regions of Italy was devoted to Umbria, published in 1905. To his sensitive perception the religion of the Italian people made an obvious appeal. He also had Roman Catholic friends, for example Hilaire Belloc and Richard Terry, the celebrated organist and choirmaster at Westminster Cathedral where, Hutton used to declare, the rendering of polyphonic church-music at that time was unequalled anywhere else. But it was some 25 years before he was received into the Roman Catholic church, appropriately enough at the church of the Porziuncula, built over the place where St. Francis of Assisi died.

In 1908 and 1909 Hutton edited Denistoun's monumental work on the Dukes of Urbino, and that once indispensable authority, Crowe and Cavalcaselle's *History of Painting in Italy*. The home of the Huttons was for 50 years on Clifton Hill, St. John's Wood, a house where the celebrated Victorian painter Frith had lived. It contained Hutton's large library, some choice paintings, including a Caravaggio, and other treasures, such as many portrait-medals of Renaissance Popes, which Hutton was always pleased to show and discuss with his guests. A Sassetta which was in his collection went to the Kress Collection in the National Museum of Art in Washington. While living in England Hutton did much travelling also, and from it came three volumes in the *Highways and Byways* series, on Wiltshire, Somerset, and Gloucestershire.

After the outbreak of the 1914-18 War, Hutton was for a short time as an A.B. in the Royal Naval Air Service, but with his expert knowledge of Italy he was soon assigned to service under the Foreign Office. Sent by it to Italy he helped to establish the British Institute in Florence. Hutton served on the council of the institute from 1918 to 1954. Before leaving Italy in 1918 Hutton was associated with the Anglo-Italian shipping magnate, Arthur Serena in establishing the chairs of Italian at Oxford and Cambridge. For a year or so he edited the *Anglo-Italian Review*, another link between the two countries Hutton loved best. Then he resumed the publication of books. In 1922 he delivered the annual Italian lecture to the British Academy, who two years later conferred on him their gold medal. Three books connected with his Catholic religion were *The Franciscans in England* (1926), *The Life of Christ in the Old Italian Masters* (1935), and *Catholicism and English Literature* (1942). He was devout, but also catholic in the other sense; his two chief literary works were on Boccaccio and Aretino, the latter a luminous and informative study of a complex and much-disputed figure, published in 1922.

GRIEF OVER WAR

Italy's entry into the Second World War as an ally of Nazi Germany brought great grief to Hutton: still more keenly was it felt when Italy came to be a battlefield. His intimate and detailed topographical knowledge of Italy was employed in compiling several volumes about the architecture and art treasures of Italy, for use by the Allied Intelligence Corps. It was with the utmost dismay and distress that Hutton learnt of the destruction of so many precious works of art during the Allied advance up and the German retreat from the peninsula. Rome, however, came through practically unscathed, and Hutton's book on the city, first published in 1909, was reissued in a revised and enlarged edition in 1950.

In 1950 Hutton published an entirely new book, *The Cosmati*, an account of the famous thirteenth-century family of mosaic and marble craftsmen. This was a subject in which Hutton took more than a literary interest. With one or two other experts he publicly criticized certain of the modern mosaics in Westminster Cathedral, and he was appointed by Cardinal Hinsley to an advisory committee on the decoration of the cathedral. During the Second World

War Hutton designed and superintended the laying of two beautiful, cosmatesque pavements, one by the tomb of Cardinal Hinsley and the other in the Benedictine abbey of Buckfast; this latter was inspired by a fine pavement in St. John Lateran, Rome.

CONVERSATIONALIST

Hutton, shy and modest with strangers, shone as a conversationalist when with friends or people who shared his tastes. His talk then could be, like his writing, infectiously enthusiastic if he approved, pugnacious and emphatic when he condemned. His best writing was in the easy, familiar style that went well with the leisured generation of travellers in Italy; in a more restless age it may have appeared somewhat dated, but Hutton gave his travel-books as a rule a solid foundation of personally acquired knowledge that kept his work alive, and made it comparatively easy to bring up to date.

Mrs. Hutton died in 1960. In 1917 he was made a Cavaliere of the Order of the Crown of Italy in recognition of his long and distinguished service to Italian art and literature. He was created a Commendatore of the Italian Order of Merit in 1959, and in 1965 was awarded the Medaglia culturale d'oro.

August 23, 1969.

Aldous Huxley died on November 22, 1963, at his Hollywood home at the age of 69.

His death brought to an end a literary career of outstanding versatility and brilliance. His first novel, *Crome Yellow* (1921), made him famous, and was the precursor of a whole body of fiction devoted in the main to the violent demolition of Victorian and Edwardian values. The whole system of a logically developing plot was jettisoned. Most of these early works, Peacockian in structure, were in great part made up of spirited conversation between witty and highly sophisticated characters who exemplified the apophthegm of one of them—the higher their talk the lower their morals. Part of the attraction of the young Huxley for his still younger contemporaries in the early twenties is that in these early novels his presence is felt as one of his own characters—gay yet melancholy, scientifically trained yet not satisfied with science, sexually curious yet profoundly puritanical, enjoying life yet disgusted with it. These early works were those of a writer whose sophistication covered over a profound yearning for innocence.

POEMS OF LONDON

Huxley also wrote *Leda* and two other books of verse, but as a poet he was too conscious of the achievement of others altogether to avoid pastiche. His vein of poetry is best shown in the poetic descriptions of the laburnum and fogs of London in *Crome Yellow*, the Tuscan countryside in *Antic Hay*.

As the iconoclastic decade of 1920–30 went on Huxley produced essays, literary and artistic criticism, and travel books, the most notable of which, *Jesting Pilate*, describes a journey to India.

He became more ambitious in the two novels *Point Counter Point* and *Eyeless in Gaza* in which he aimed perhaps at being the English Gide. At any rate, as an experiment in playing about with time sequences *Eyeless in Gaza* seems to owe something to *Les Faux Monnayeurs*. It cannot be said though that in these long and ambitious works Huxley succeeds in inventing an imaginary fictitious world; nor was he sufficiently plunged in actual contemporary living for them to provide pictures of the times. They contain interesting and intelligent discussion of ideas, and continue that series of notable, slightly disguised portraits of contemporaries such as D. H. Lawrence, Middleton Murry, Augustus John, Lady Ottoline Morrell, and a famous British Fascist leader which had begun already with *Antic Hay*. For the reader interested in Aldous Huxley's own character they also extend his self-portrait.

Huxley saw an irreconcilable split in contemporary life between the ideal living which ought to be attainable—if not through the imagination then through reason—and the real. He was one of those who found life in all times and all places deeply unsatisfactory, a task which had somehow been botched by whatever forces had created it and he could not reconcile the ideal with the real. He himself seemed divided between a mystic idealism and a scientific rationalism. The idealism led him to the pacifist attitude of *Ends and Means*, and to the mysticism of *The Perennial Philosophy*, the rationalism to a Utopianism which could be inverted and bitter in *Brave New World*, resigned and even optimistic (though perhaps unacceptable to most readers) in his most recent *Island* (1962).

RELIGIOUS YEARNING

There was in Aldous Huxley perhaps a never fully realized religious yearning, and also perhaps a streak of credulity, not altogether unknown among men of scientific training, which led him to be too uncritical of Dr. Bates's system of eye training, so that in *The Art of Seeing* he told us, too optimistically, that he had regained normal sight, and which in his last years led him to become almost a propagandist for mescalin.

Aldous Leonard Huxley was born at Godalming on July 26, 1894, scion of a most distinguished literary line. His paternal grandfather was Thomas Henry Huxley; his maternal great-grandfather was Thomas Arnold, of Rugby; his father, Leonard, for many years edited the *Cornhill*; and Mrs. Humphry Ward was his aunt. His mother (born Julia Arnold) died when he was 17, and the literary aunt therefore acted a good deal *in loco parentis*.

He went to Eton, but at 16 developed a grave ophthalmic malady which rendered him almost completely blind. He learnt Braille and touch-typing, and continued his studies under tutors. By the age of 18 he had recovered something of his sight in one eye, began to read again with the aid of a magnifying glass, and went up to Balliol. He had hoped for a career in medicine, but his sight was too poor for the close work involved, and instead he read English Literature, graduating in 1915.

In 1919 he began work under Middleton Murry on the *Athenaeum*, and spent some years engaged on various literary tasks.

Having made some financial success with early works, Huxley was able to abandon regular journalism in 1923, and for the next seven years he lived in Italy, which he made the background of those joyous (but still satirical) novels, *Antic Hay* (1923) and *Those Barren Leaves* (1925). *Little Mexican* (1924) was a book of finely wrought short stories; and *Two or Three Graces* (1926) and *Brief Candles* (1930) carried on his progress in that kind. *Proper Studies* (1927), *Music at Night* (1931) and *The Olive Tree* (1936) established him as an essayist who could embellish all sorts of themes with lively fantasy and pointed wit. He saw much of D. H. Lawrence in that novelist's later years.

SIGHT RESTORED

He returned to America in 1938, and now occurred an event of crucial importance. In an autobiographical sketch written in 1941 he says: "... a series of lucky accidents brought to my notice the system of eye-training devised by the late Dr. W. H. Bates of New York. ... I have already obtained very striking improvement in vision ..." The full story of how he regained normal sight, without the aid of spectacles, is told in *The Art of Seeing* (1943).

As he progressed through his fifties, Huxley displayed an ever-growing interest in the phenomena of mysticism. *The Perennial Philosophy* (1946) was a significant manifestation of this new line of thought, which may have been motivated by an increasing revulsion from the life-experience of the ordinary man, especially in its physical aspect. The mystical preoccupation reached its apogee in *The Doors of Perception* (1954) and *Heaven and Hell* (1956). The first of these essays arose from his experiments with the drug mescalin, which seemed to him to give vast enrichment of experience without ill after-effects.

In 1919 Huxley married Maria Nys, by whom he had a son. His wife died in 1955 and he married the following year Laura Archera.

GAY NARRATOR

In his own personality, Huxley was not the cynic one might have expected from the early novels, nor the pious, slightly cranky, mystifying theorist whom one might have expected from the later works. He retained until the end his capacity to be a gay teller of anecdotes whose stories nearly always ended with the appeal to the listeners: "Don't you think that was extraordinary!" With his pallor, his near blindness, his look of total absorption, and of profound considerateness for others, he was the most impressive of all literary men of recent times. During the past three years he knew that he had cancer of the throat but allowed no one but his wife to know it. He faced the trials of his lack of sight, his illness and great personal losses—his home was destroyed by a fire in 1961—during recent years with uncomplaining courage.

November 25, 1963.

Camille Huysmans, who died at his home in Antwerp on February 25, 1968, at the age of 96 was a prominent member of the Socialist International in the early years of this century, and, more recently, Prime Minister of Belgium from August 1946 to March 1947.

A personal friend of Lenin as well as of most of the Socialist leaders in the years before the First World War, he devoted much of his time to trying to overcome the differences which were always breaking out between the socialist parties of that period. In recent years he was still speaking of his triumph in getting Mensheviks and Bolsheviks to form part of the same delegation to a conference in 1910.

Huysmans could be caustic, even sarcastic on occasions, but he also had that fund of rough humour often found in Flemish politicians. The Belgian socialist party never found him a compliant member and when he was dropped by them in the 1965 election he decided to stand on his own, proclaiming that he would be Belgium's first centenarian member of Parliament. He was defeated, but he remained active almost to the end of his life.

He was born in the village of Bilsen, in the Flemish province of Limburg, and followed a student course at the University of Liège. He then became a schoolmaster for a few months, before it became clear that his political views would stand in the way of his career. He became a journalist, and from there passed into the Second International, where he was the international secretary from 1905 to 1921.

It was an active time and Huysmans came into contact with the leading socialists of the day—Jean Jaurès, Wilhelm Liebknecht, Rosa Luxemburg, Keir Hardie, as well as the Russians. He tried actively to bring together all the small French socialist groups, and as international secretary was responsible for the organization of the international conferences of the time at Stuttgart in 1907, Copenhagen in 1910, Basle in 1912, Stockholm in 1917. When Jaurès was assassinated in 1914, Huysmans led a delegation sent from the international to investigate.

Between the wars he entered Belgian politics and was active both at local and at national level. He was mayor of Antwerp for a time while holding his seat in Parliament in Brussels until 1965.

He was a supporter of the Flemish movement, and backed the switch from French to Dutch at the University of Ghent in the 1930s.

PACIFIST VIEWS

His views always had a strong pacifist streak and he declared a few years ago, "It is easier to declare war than to make peace. It is only possible to have peace when there are no victors."

During the Second World War he fled to London, and broadcast from there to occupied Belgium. He returned after the liberation, and became Prime Minister. He married for the second time in 1967 and is survived by his wife. His archives, which include personal letters from Lenin and a great deal of other material from his days with the Second International, have been left to the town of Antwerp.

February 26, 1968.

Sir Robert Hyde, K.B.E., M.V.O., died on August 31, 1967, at Haslemere at the age of 88.

His name will always be associated with the industrial welfare movement in Britain—he was the founder and for over 30 years the tireless energetic director of the Industrial Welfare Society, now the Industrial Society.

The son of Robert Mettam Hyde, he was born on September 7, 1878, and after being educated privately went to King's College, London. He was in business from 1893 to 1901 and then took Holy Orders, being ordained in 1903.

Hyde was an East End parson when he was called by Seebohm Rowntree to take charge of the Boys' Welfare Department in Lloyd George's war-time Ministry of Munitions, in 1916. He had been head of the Maurice Hostel, in Hoxton, and knew all there was to know about the essential nature of the boys with whom he would have to deal. He knew and proclaimed, moreover, that their nature was no different from that of boys in any other walk of life: all that was needed was the opportunity to allow it to develop.

A born leader, humanity, kindliness, and humour shone out of him—and soon he had a band of friends and admirers among the reputedly cold industrialists and employers with whom he came into contact. These men rallied round him when, in 1918, irked by the constrictions of Civil Service procedures, he broke away from the Munitions Ministry and set up an organization of his own, the Boys' Welfare Association.

The redoubtable Sir William Beardmore (later Lord Invernairn) consented to act as its first chairman, and then—with a characteristic flash of imagination and audacity—he obtained the consent of King George V to his son Prince Albert, as he then was, being its first president. Hyde himself was styled director.

An entirely self-financing organization, supported by industry itself, and dedicated to the advancement of humanism in industry, the association, largely owing to the director's energy and powers of persuasion, was soon firmly established as both a repository of much valuable and practical knowledge and as a reliable instrument for the selection and training of the growing body of welfare practitioners. The name of the association was changed in 1919—on Royal suggestion—to that of Industrial Welfare Society, to conform with the wider responsibilities it had been urged on all sides to undertake; and it was with the I.W.S., as it became familiarly known all over the Commonwealth, that Hyde's name was principally associated.

Meanwhile between the Duke of York, as he had now become, and the Rev. Robert Hyde a very genuine friendship had developed. Each in fact had a great deal to offer to the other. Hyde was able to give the Duke an intimate understanding of the industrial and commercial life of Britain such as no previous member of the Royal Family had possessed. The Duke's friendship and his unswerving patronage were, of course, for Hyde and for the Industrial Welfare Society beyond price.

Together, they conceived and carried through the venture known as The Duke of York's Holiday Camps, where boys from industry and from the public schools met and mixed, to their great mutual benefit, at seaside camps during the summer in a completely unselfconscious and egalitarian atmosphere. The last of these camps, that of 1939, was held in the grounds of Balmoral at the express invitation of the Duke, by then King George VI.

In 1932 King George V conferred the M.V.O. upon Hyde in personal recognition of his services to his son, the Duke of York. In 1949, King George VI bestowed a knighthood upon his old friend. Sadly, this honour was the unwitting occasion of perhaps the greatest deprivation of his career—its acceptance.

CONFLICT OUR ORDERS

Hyde described later how the Archbishop of Canterbury had told him that, having accepted the knighthood he must renounce his Orders. In 1961, asked by the *Evening Standard* why he had taken this view, the Archbishop said that to receive the accolade traditionally gave a sovereign the right to call upon the recipient to take the field of battle. This a priest could not do as he was non-combatant by virtue of his Orders. A priest might accept the honour of knighthood but might not receive the accolade. Sir Robert Hyde had chosen to receive the accolade and, without pressure, had relinquished his Orders.

In 1950 he retired as director of the I.W.S. and was accorded by its council the title of Founder.

In 1918 Robert Hyde married Eileen Parker, who survives him. There were two children: a son, Michael, lost in action in 1943, and a daughter, Jean, who married and now lives in Kenya.

September 1, 1967.

Jack Hylton died on January 29, 1965, at the London Clinic at the age of 72. Flamboyance and drive are by nature essential ingredients of the life of a successful impresario and they are qualities that he never lacked.

Unlike many who venture into the business side of show business he inherited no personal fortune, nor did he belong to a family experienced in the calculated gambles of theatrical presentation. His career and achievements were in fact the epitome of the self-made man. His father, a Bolton millhand, had not been able to ensure for him a lengthy formal education—but in his Lancashire home he did have the opportunity to learn to play the piano, so that by the age of 12 he was already able to earn a living as an accompanist and vocalist with a pierrot troupe.

This engagement led to further work in the entertainment field as a conductor in touring presentations, as a cinema organist and as a musician who could turn an able hand to the orchestration of musical entertainments he happened to be connected with. The struggles of these early years, which culminated in the establishment of his famous band in the twenties, left him a tough north countryman with the self-confidence later to take on presentations in all aspects of the entertainment business. And though he established his offices in Pall Mall and his work took him all over the world and won for him in France the Légion d'Honneur he remained essentially a Lancashire man.

Perhaps it was because he did not enter the managerial field until he was nearing 50 that he dared to be so wide-ranging in his presentations over the following 24 years. He came upon the scene at a time when the insidious growth of hit-or-flop economics in the theatre tended on the contrary to demand specialization. Probably the fact that he was one of the few London theatre managers to have been for many years in direct contact with the public as a performer gave him an instinctive grasp of what audiences would and would not patronize

AMERICAN HITS

His first presentation, touring the London Philharmonic Orchestra in variety theatres to prevent its dissolution, was not to be a characteristic venture—though an isolated opera season and a tour by Gigli under his management meant that he never lost touch with the musical world. Rather, though, it was in the plural form of "musicals" that he confirmed his position in postwar theatre management with a succession of American hits—*Kiss Me Kate, Call Me Madam, Ring Out the Bells, Paint Your Wagon, Pal Joey* and *Kismet.* With English productions he showed himself determined not to be channelled into any one field of presentation: eight successive revivals of *Peter Pan* were followed by many successful years with *The Crazy Gang*. And in the over one hundred productions presented under his management, there were circuses, pantomimes, Polish, French and Japanese companies and straight plays ranging from *Anna Lucasta* to *The Moon is Blue*.

Undoubtedly one of the qualities that contributed to his success was his ability to understand the implications of technical advances in entertainment. With the arrival of recorded music he had established an interest with the gramophone companies and with the advent of television he found himself Adviser on Light Entertainment for Associated Rediffusion. He rarely theorized about entertainment or attempted to lay down what it should and should not do. Opera, ballet, revue, musicals, concerts, plays for him were all part of show business. His intuitive diagnosis of public taste was his most valuable asset.

In 1922 he married Florence Parkinson, who died in 1957. They had one son and two daughters. In 1963 Hylton married, secondly, Beverley Prowse.

January 30, 1965.

Sir Harry Hylton-Foster, who died suddenly on September 2, 1965, at the age of 60, had been Speaker of the House of Commons since October, 1959, after five years as Solicitor-General in Conservative Governments.

He first entered Parliament as Conservative member for York in 1950 and retained the same party allegiance when he was returned for the Cities of London and Westminster in 1959, but when the new Parliament met and he was elected Speaker he ceased to have a party designation. At the general election of 1964 he was adopted as "The Speaker seeking re-election", and as such retained the seat with a majority of 10,279 against Labour and Liberal opponents.

Hylton-Foster was a good Speaker, though perhaps not among the greatest. He was certainly one of the best-liked of the men who have held that lonely, exacting and often exasperating office. One of his most attractive qualities was his sunny good humour. It often rescued himself and the House from uncomfortable situations and lightened the more portentous moods in which Parliament is sometimes apt to indulge itself. He had the saving grace of refusing to take himself too seriously. Though he had no doubts about the dignity attaching to his office, he never overstrained the bounds within which it was proper to invoke its magisterial resources. If he had a difficult decision to make he never rushed into making an ill-considered one. He liked to sleep on a ticklish problem and to give time for his legal brain to get the balance of precedent and common sense right. He had no pretensions to infallibility. He was too shrewd—and essentially humble—to stick obstinately to a decision just because it was the first he had thought of.

NEVER BRUSQUE

In a Speaker that sort of temperament has its obvious limitations, and Hylton-Foster's did not escape them any more than he escaped the inevitable criticism of lack of firmness at times when the House needed fatherly restraint. His solicitude for the rights of minorities could sometimes betray him into over-indulgence—particularly, perhaps, at Question time. He never lost sight of the fact that he was the servant of the House and he relied—heavily sometimes—on its willingness to cooperate with him to facilitate the despatch of business. He had a sensitive distaste for riding rough-shod over anybody's feelings. He could be tart—rarely—but never brusque. His flashes of wit were treasured by the House and he had a ready command of the elegant phrase, invariably turned with a lawyer's deft precision.

His urbanity and charm served him particularly well during the last difficult session when the Government's narrow majority imposed strains on the House. Everybody felt the burden of long hours and wearisome party battles but to the Speaker, charged with the task of preserving as much tranquillity as it is within the power of the Chair to maintain, the ordeal cannot have been light. It is a measure of the debt that the House owes Sir Harry Hylton-Foster that he guided it through those months with such a light and deceptively adroit touch.

MADE SOLICITOR-GENERAL

The Rt. Hon. Sir Harry Braustyn Hylton-Foster, Q.C., M.P., was born on April 10, 1905, the only son of the late H. B. H. Hylton-Foster, barrister-at-law, and was educated at Eton and Magdalen College, Oxford. He was called to the Bar by the Inner Temple in 1928, and in the same year was appointed legal secretary to Lord Finlay at the Permanent Court of International Justice. He took silk 19 years later. During the last war he served in the Intelligence Branch of the R.A.F.V.R. and later became Deputy Judge Advocate in North Africa and Italy. He held a number of Recorderships—Richmond (Yorkshire), Huddersfield and Kingston-upon-Hull—and was Chancellor of the dioceses of Ripon and Durham.

His first attempt to enter Parliament was in the 1945 general election when he unsuccessfully contested Shipley. In February, 1950, he won York from Labour by a majority of 77 in a three-cornered fight. He greatly increased his majorities there in 1951 and 1955. In 1952 he took over a private member's Bill dealing with intestates' estates and eventually saw it on the Statute Book. He became well known to television audiences through his appearances in the "In the News" programme of the B.B.C.

After only four years on the back-benches he was appointed Solicitor-General in 1954 and was knighted. It was an unusually swift ascent to office, but Hylton-Foster justified it by the grace and often brilliance with which he handled complex legal niceties. His light agreeable voice, dignified presence, and great charm made him one of the most attractive performers on the Treasury Bench. A speech which greatly added to his reputation was made outside the House, when he was closing the case for the Crown in the Brighton conspiracy trial. It drew from his distinguished opponent the tribute: "He is an artist in the intellectual exercise of compiling a case against a man."

CHANGE OF CONSTITUENCY

There was some local criticism in Yorkshire of Hylton-Foster's decision in 1958 to stand for the safer seat of the Cities of London and Westminster. He was elected in 1959 with a majority of 17,188. He was elected Speaker of the Commons at its first sitting that year but not before there had been a good deal of fuss about the way the preliminaries to his election had been handled. The burden of the complaint of the Labour Opposition was that there had not been enough chance for consultation between the parties and among members and that the choice of an alternative Labour nomination to Sir Harry Hylton-Foster had been limited by the Government to Sir Frank Soskice, who turned out to be not available. There was nothing personal in all this, but the atmosphere in the Chamber tended to be over-charged when the House met to elect a Speaker. Hugh Gaitskell, the Leader of the Opposition, made it plain that if it had been in order—which procedurally it was not—the Opposition would have divided against the proposal to elect Sir Harry. This was purely because they felt that the procedure had not been what it should have been—certainly not because there was the slightest animus against Hylton-Foster himself. Indeed, Mr. Gaitskell paid him a handsome tribute.

It was Hylton-Foster himself who, after the choice had been made, most effectively dispersed the Opposition's resentment, and by his wit, charm and dignity left the House in the mood to congratulate itself on its decision. Succeeding years confirmed how right that decision had been.

Hylton-Foster married in 1931 Audrey Pellew Clifton Brown, daughter of the first Viscount Ruffside, who as Colonel Clifton Brown was a former Speaker of the House. There were no children of the marriage.

September 3, 1965.

Lord Hyndley, G.B.E., first chairman of the National Coal Board, died in London on January 5, 1963, at the age of 79.

It was his particular achievement to guide the industry safely, if not brilliantly, through the immensely difficult changeover period after nationalization. If his leadership was not vigorous, if on occasion he even gave an impression of weakness, nevertheless his caution and his shrewd political sense were the qualities needed at the time. He was adept at smoothing over troubles. He established excellent personal relations on the administrative side. He had a way of securing the confidence of the miners' leaders, who never doubted his good faith. He was on good terms with successive Ministers of Fuel and Power.

GREAT KINDNESS

Personal relations were, indeed, one of his strong points. Stocky in build, urbane in manner, easy going in temperament, he will be especially remembered by many people for his great and genuine kindness.

The Rt. Hon. Sir John Scott Hindley, G.B.E., first Viscount Hyndley and first baronet, was born on October 24, 1883, a son of the late Rev. William Talbot Hindley, of Eastbourne, and went to Weymouth College. In his teens he had determined upon an industrial and commercial career, and instead of going to a university, as had been proposed at home, he was apprenticed to mining on the engineering side, at the Murton Colliery, in County Durham.

A few years after his apprenticeship was over he began to specialize on the commercial side, and this together with his already acknowledged personal qualities led to his being called, soon after the outbreak of war in 1914, into the service of the Government. From lesser responsibilities, three years later he became a member of the Coal Controller's Export Advisory Committee, and then from 1918 to 1938, and again from 1939 to 1942 he was Commercial Adviser to what was then the Mines Department.

POSTS SURRENDERED

From 1942 to late in 1943 he was Controller-General of the Ministry of Fuel and Power, then for three years his activities were largely directed towards his principal concern outside the state service as chairman of Stephenson Clarke Ltd., the coal merchants and shippers, in which firm he had been a partner long before it became a limited company, and also as a managing director of Powell Duffryn Ltd. the South Wales coalowners, and then also as chairman of the Maris Export and Trading Co. Ltd.

He surrendered all these posts in 1946 to take up the Coal Board chairmanship. With his wide experience, particularly on the selling side of the industry, he also had the undoubted advantage for that office at that time of not being too closely associated in the eyes of the mineworkers with the private coalowners. He retired at the end of his five-year term in 1951.

After moving from the departmental control of the Fuel and Power Ministry in 1943, he had combined with his other work the chairmanship of the London Committee of the Combined Production and Resources Board, and of the Finance Corporation for Industry, until going to the Coal Board, and upon his retirement he again took up the thread of his earlier interests in the administration of the City of London.

Hyndley was knighted in 1921, became a baronet in 1927, a baron in 1931, and a viscount in 1948. He was created a G.B.E. in 1939, and he was an honorary LL.D. of Leeds University. He had, in addition, the Cross of Chevalier of the Crown of Italy, was a Commander of the Légion d'Honneur, and held the American Medal of Freedom with palm leaf, given him in 1947.

TITLE EXTINCT

He married in 1909 Vera, elder daughter of the late James Westoll, J.P., of Coniscliffe Hall, Darlington. They had two daughters, but no son, and the titles become extinct.

January 7, 1963.

I

Hayato Ikeda, Prime Minister of Japan from 1960 until his retirement in November, 1964, died in Tokyo at the age of 65 on August 13, 1965.

The least contentious and most widely approved of Japan's Prime Ministers in recent years, Ikeda deserves as much as any postwar statesman the credit for Japan's brilliantly successful economic advance. He came to power after the fall of Nobusuke Kishi in the summer of 1960, when severe rioting in Tokyo had led to the postponement of President Eisenhower's proposed visit, and although without experience in foreign affairs, it was thanks to Ikeda's efforts that relations with the United States were soon restored to their normal equanimity. At the same time, with agreements out of the way for settling reparations with those countries in south-east Asia occupied by Japan during the war years, Ikeda was able to give the image of Japan a new look; still somewhat colourless, perhaps, but with the old hostility expunged.

CHANGES INCREASED

Indeed, it may be said that the transformation of Japan, both internally and in the world's view of the country, was greater during his tenure of office than in the previous decade.

This was not achieved by any forceful attitudes on Ikeda's part though he was a blunt man and exceptionally outspoken by Japanese standards. The expression "low posture" characterized his outlook on foreign policy and in home politics. He had not been a politician from the beginning, but had shifted from the bureaucracy—an established practice in the present generation. Born in Hiroshima prefecture in 1899, the son of a comfortably off *saké* merchant, he read law at Kyoto University and entered the Finance Ministry as a civil servant in 1925. He became a specialist in taxation and his reputation was such that Mr. Yoshida brought him into his government in 1947 as Vice-Minister of Finance. He was elected to the Diet in 1949, and became Minister of Finance in 1952.

SHARP TONGUE

He soon made himself indispensable in the economic field, moving between the finance ministry and international trade and industry but he was often in difficulties from a too sharp tongue and arrogance of manner. He did not suffer fools gladly. He was slow in learning to temper his opinions to public reactions. Several times he resigned over disagreement with his colleagues. Nevertheless his abilities told in his favour, as did the respect in which he was held by Mr. Yoshida, always a powerful influence in the background of the ruling Liberal-Democratic Party.

During Mr. Kishi's term of office Ikeda's abilities in the economic field, coupled with the remarkable growth in the Japanese economy that was then apparent, began to give him a powerful position in the party so that there was no real rival when he succeeded to office in 1960. To some extent circumstances favoured him both internally and externally. He was a strong proponent of economic growth and an optimist, fully in favour of expansion—and the Japanese economy duly expanded. While no neutralist—having on one occasion to retract his words when dismissing neutralist countries as small and powerless in the international scene—Ikeda did his best to move closer towards communist China over trade matters without giving offence to the United States. In 1961 he visited South Asia—India, Pakistan, Burma, and Thailand. Another tour in 1963 took him to the Philippines, Indonesia, Australia and New Zealand. The United States he knew well. He had gone with the Japanese delegation to the San Francisco peace conference, on a mission to Washington for Yoshida in 1953, and as Japanese delegate to a conference on economic development in 1958. Not long after taking office he went on an official visit to Washington.

SUCCESS AND FAILURE

In spite of his successes, Ikeda's position within his own party was never very strong. As a member of the bureaucrats group he had no large factional following and it had been his aim so far as possible to do away with a system that had often lowered the dignity of Japanese political life. He was not successful and had to survive with such support as he could get, especially against the powerful influence of his chief rival, the present Prime Minister, Mr. Eisaku Sato. After returning to power in general elections in 1963, Ikeda narrowly retained his post as party leader in the party election in July,

1964. Ill-health had by then already inhibited his active leadership, however, and he was able to survive only long enough to see Japan act as host for the Olympic Games that autumn. In November, 1964, he was forced to resign after a longer period in office than any of his predecessors.

Full credit must go to Ikeda for Japan's astonishing economic performance during his four and a half years in office, as for the new image of Japan he was able to present to the world. Where he failed—largely owing to his difficulties in controlling his own party—was in the internal legislation needed for a country so quickly climbing away from Asian standards of living to becoming fully urbanized. Had his health allowed a longer spell in office Ikeda might have given Japan the more pivotal position in the Asian scene that he himself sketched in a speech early in 1964.

For all his devotion to building a modern economy, and bringing about the westernized Japan of today, Ikeda's upbringing and taste kept well within a Japanese orbit. His feeling for nature, his Buddhism, a certain detachment from western culture—expressed, perhaps, in a personal taste for wearing national dress when possible—were conserved by a dry personality, somewhat shy, deep-voiced, withdrawn; a respected and admired but not a popular figure. He was twice married. His first wife died young and he remarried in 1935.

August 14, 1965.

Professor Vincent Charles Illing, F.R.S., F.G.S., who died on May 16, 1969, at the age of 78, was Emeritus Professor of Oil Technology, Imperial College of Science and Technology. He was a Fellow of the college.

He was a leading petroleum geologist and in 1947 took part, on behalf of H.M. Government, in the negotiation of a settlement between the Mexican Government and the major oil companies of the problems resulting from the expropriation of the oilfields.

Vincent Charles Illing was born at Jullundur, in Pakistan, on September 24, 1890. He was educated in Pakistan and Malta, at King Edward VI Grammar School, Nuneaton, and Sidney Sussex College, Cambridge. He graduated in 1912, obtaining First Class Honours in the Natural Sciences Tripos.

OILFIELD SUBJECTS

His researches on the Cambrian faunas near his home at Hartshill, begun at Cambridge, were completed at the Geological Department of the Imperial College of Science, London, where in 1913 he was offered a post by Professor W. W. Watts. At this time a decision had been reached to start a course within the Royal School of Mines related to the oil industry, and it fell to the young graduate's lot to begin to teach, among other things, subjects which were appropriate to oilfield work. Thus began a long association with the oil technology course, through the stages of lecturer, Assistant Professor and finally Professor of Oil Technology, an appointment which he held from 1936 until his retirement from the college in 1955.

In the period 1920–22 he was engaged on exploration for oil in Trinidad. This introduced him to a part of the world with which for many years he had links as a consultant on oil geology. Under him the Oil Technology Department at the Royal School of Mines thrived and evolved, and his students moved into both the exploration and exploitation sides of oilfield operation all over the world. He initiated research on problems concerned with the origin of oilfields and built up an extensive knowledge of world geology, particularly of the oilfield areas. This, coupled with a practical outlook, imagination and a sound appreciation of economics, resulted in his being recognized many years ago as one of the world's foremost petroleum geologists.

EXPLORING FOR OIL

He acted as a consultant on oil exploration and development in Venezuela for over 40 years, also in Trinidad, the United States, Mexico, Ecuador, Canada, Nigeria, Pakistan, and in many parts of Europe and the rest of the world.

In the early days of the Second World War he had leave of absence from Imperial College to enable him to devote time to boosting the rate of oil production in Trinidad. An increase in consulting work led him to form V. C. Illing and Partners in 1950. Retirement from Imperial College did not mean retirement from working, and he continued in harness to within a short time of his death.

He is survived by his wife, Frances Jean, his son, four daughters and 15 grandchildren.

May 20, 1969.

Major-General Sir Bahadur Yeshwant Rao Holkar, third successive ruler of Indore to have his princely authority brought to an end during his lifetime, died in a Bombay hospital on December 5, 1961, at the age of 53.

Both his grandfather and his father were divested of ruling powers by the British Government on grounds of misconduct. He ceased to rule for a very different reason—that of the transfer of power in 1947 when he shared the lot of the Indian princes in general in the withdrawal of personal authority over their peoples and the substitution of constitutional rule.

His Highness Maharajadhiraj Raj Rajeshwar Sawai Shree Yeshwant Rao Holkar Bahadur was born on September 6, 1908. He had the advantage not afforded to any of his predecessors of a public school education in England and from 1923 to 1926 of undergraduate life at Christ Church, Oxford. In the latter year his father, H. H. Tukoji Rao III, chose abdication rather than acceptance of the alternative of the appointment of a commission of inquiry offered by the Viceroy, Lord Reading, after an incident over a favourite dancing girl. The young Maharaja was invested with full reigning powers in 1930 over a territory of some 9,900 square miles, and with a population of a million and a half. The dynasty had been founded in 1818 by Malhar Rao Holkar, a great warrior who had shared in the striking achievements of the Mahratta confederacy.

Impressed by the fate of his two predecessors, Yeshwant Rao sought and pursued the modernization of economic and social conditions in Indore by a consistent and much-needed policy of reform. Legislation was undertaken for the protection of the landless peasantry and the promotion of self-governing institutions. In the field of social reform there came prohibition of the marriage of minors as well as measures to limit the heavy costs of marriage ceremonies to the parents of brides, leading to recourse to unprincipled money-lenders with consequent long and often lifetime indebtedness. His Highness strove for the uplift of the depressed classes, for whom schools were opened, and he ordained that there should be no exclusions from the public service on grounds of caste or non-caste.

AID TO BRITAIN

The Maharaja was a delegate to the second sessions of the Round Table Conference on Indian Reform held in London in 1931. During the 1939–45 War he maintained the tradition of his House by giving unstinted support in men, money and materials, to the paramount power. But in 1942, with Japan menacing India by way of Burma, Yeshwant Rao took upon himself to write to President Roosevelt to join with China and the Soviet Union in arbitrating on the differences between Britain and India as to the future of the sub-continent. After the granting of independence to India and Pakistan in August, 1947, Indore was linked with Gwalior and other Mahratta States to form the Malwa Union with a ministry responsible to an elected legislature. The Maharaja of Gwalior was made Rajpramukh (Constitutional President) and the Maharaja of Indore was appointed his deputy, holding that position until 1956.

His Highness married in 1924 a daughter of the Chief of Kagal Junior, a feudatory of the Kolhapur State. She died in 1937 leaving a daughter and in 1939 he married secretly an American, Miss Marguerite Lawler. The union was dissolved in 1943. Thereupon he married Mrs. Fay Crane who bore him a son. His action, so much at variance with Hindu tradition and custom, of disinheriting his son in favour of his daughter, was confirmed by Dr. Prasad, the President of the Indian Union, after careful consideration of the constitutional and legal position. The Maharaja spent much of his time after the transfer of power in the United States, where he had a luxurious home in Connecticut.

December 6, 1961.

Lord Ingleby, P.C., who, as Osbert Peake, sat for more than 25 years in the House of Commons as Conservative member for Parliament for North Leeds, died on October 11, 1966. He was 68.

He had held a number of junior ministerial appointments, and from October, 1954, to December, 1955, had a seat in the Cabinet as Minister of Pensions and National Insurance.

The Right Hon. Osbert Peake, first Viscount Ingleby, was born on December 30, 1897. He was the eldest son of George Herbert Peake, D.L., of Sulban Hall, Thirsk, Yorkshire, by his marriage with Evelyn Mary, eldest daughter of the late Hon. John Charles Dundas. He was educated at Eton, at the Royal Military College Sandhurst, and at Christ Church, Oxford, where he took his degree. In the 1914–18 War he served for three years as a lieutenant in the Coldstream Guards and was wounded at Cambrai. Later he was a major in The Nottinghamshire (Sherwood Rangers) Yeomanry. After the war he was called to the Bar by the Inner Temple.

He was also a coalowner, and was chairman of Airedale Collieries, Ltd. This gave him a first-hand knowledge of the coal mining industry, which proved useful when in 1929 he entered the House of Commons as Conservative member for North Leeds, a constituency which always remained faithful to him. Peake had politics in his blood, for he was a great-great-grandson of Lord Grey, Prime Minister at the time of the Reform Bill of 1832.

He proved a valuable recruit to the ranks of the younger Conservatives in the House of Commons and was an effective speaker, though a slight stammer gave him some difficulty in his earlier years in Parliament. But he overcame this in time, and the quiet deliberate nature of his speeches added weight to them. He was broad-minded and liberal in outlook, and had many qualifications for his first ministerial post of Parliamentary Under-Secretary of State to the Home Office. He received this appointment only six months before the outbreak of the Second World War, and was soon immersed in all the intricacies of the Defence Regulations, especially 18B. In September, 1941, when paying a visit to the Isle of Man, where his official duties often took him, he was attacked with stones by some of the internees under 18B, but fortunately escaped uninjured.

In 1944 he was promoted to the post of Financial Secretary to the Treasury, which has often been regarded as a stepping-stone to Cabinet rank. He retained this office in the short-lived "Caretaker" Government of 1945. At the general election of that year he nearly lost his seat in the Conservative debacle. His majority was 128, but he had the distinction of being the only Conservative member to be returned for the whole of Leeds. In other elections (he fought and won six in all) his majority was never less than 8,000 and in 1931 it was over 25,000.

PENSIONS AND INSURANCE REFORM

While in Opposition Peake took a leading part in all matters affecting the Home Office and National Insurance. He had earlier urged caution in the drafting of legislation arising out of the Beveridge report, and he was now able to bring constructive criticism to bear on the Labour Government's proposals. In addition to his chairmanship of the Conservative Party's Parliamentary Committee on these matters, Peake was, from 1945 to 1948, Chairman of the Public Accounts Committee.

When the Conservatives were returned to power in 1951, he became Minister of National Insurance. In September, 1953, when a number of Government changes were made, and the Ministries of Pensions and National Insurance were merged, Peake was given charge of the combined Ministry, and in 1954 was promoted to a seat in the Cabinet. He was able to introduce much needed reforms, and to pilot useful legislation on to the Statute Book.

But after the general election of 1955 he found himself out of sympathy with his Government more than once. He was, however, loyal to his party, and took no step which could possibly embarrass Sir Anthony Eden. He left the Government in the reshuffle of December, 1955, and in January, 1956, his viscounty was gazetted by the name, style and title of Viscount Ingleby, of Snilesworth, in the North Riding of the county of York.

REASONS FOR SILENCE

Ingleby did not make his maiden speech in the Lords until November, 1957. He then apologized for the delay, and gave reasons for his silence. Among them were the fact that "throughout the unhappy events of 1956 any speech of mine could only have been critical of my former colleagues and unhelpful in its effects". He thus disclosed that he had been critical of the Suez adventure. He added that "this is the first occasion on which I feel I can give the Government wholehearted support". He was then speaking during the debate on life peerages.

In January, 1956, he was appointed chairman of the board of governors of St. George's Hospital, London, and in October of the same year he presided over the Home Office Departmental Committee on the law relating to children and young people. In 1960 he headed the Ingleby Committee relating to the treatment and punishment of offenders under 17.

In 1922 he married Lady Joan Capell, daughter of the 7th Earl of Essex. They had one son and three daughters. His heir is his son the Hon. Martin Raymond Peake.

October 12, 1966.

Sir Bruce Ingram, O.B.E., M.C., who died on January 8, 1963, at the age of 85, was editor of the *Illustrated London News* for more than 60 years.

When in 1900 he took over from Clement Shorter the editorship of the *Illustrated London News* at the age of 22, he was believed to be the youngest editor of his day of a national journal. Even when in January, 1960, he had completed his sixtieth year of service neither his colleagues on the *Illustrated London News* nor his friends in many walks of life looked upon him as an old man. He was intensely proud of the journal whose dignity and traditions he jealously maintained. He had the gift of interesting his readers in important events at home and abroad, in the arts and sciences and in archaeology.

He was never the passive proprietor. During a period of world-shaking events and great social change he preserved a calmness and sanity of outlook that were reflected in his writing as well as in his direction of policy.

Bruce Stirling Ingram was born in London on May 5, 1877, the second son of Sir W. J. Ingram, Bt., and the grandson of Herbert Ingram, founder of the *Illustrated London News.* He was educated at Winchester and Trinity College, Oxford, where he took honours in Law. When the First World War broke out he was a lieutenant in The East Kent Yeomanry. He served in the Royal Garrison Artillery on the French front from 1915 to the end of hostilities, was promoted to the rank of captain, awarded the Military Cross and O.B.E. (military), and mentioned three times in dispatches.

On two occasions as a youth he had visited Egypt with his parents and became interested in archaeology. At 20 years of age he began to collect illuminated manuscripts and having sold his collection at Sotheby's he turned his attention to the collection of paintings and drawings. He acquired 700 marine paintings by the two Van de Veldes, father and son, and to mark his eightieth birthday he presented them to the National Maritime Museum at Greenwich. When he was entertained at a private luncheon by the Duke of Edinburgh and the other trustees he took along with him other gifts including a dress sword awarded to Lieutenant Robert Williams for his conduct during the naval mutiny at Spithead in 1797, a small painting by Van de Velde, the younger, and the unique impression of Van de Velde's personal seal, which he had discovered on the back of the picture.

Many other museums were enriched by Ingram's generosity including the Birmingham Art Gallery, the Royal Scottish Museum, and the Fitzwilliam Museum at Cambridge. The lovely thirteenth-century stained-glass window which was formerly on view at the Victoria and Albert Museum, he later gave to the chapel of his old school. He was honorary keeper of drawings at the Fitzwilliam Museum where a collection of his pictures was on view in 1945. He was vice-president of the Society for Nautical Research, vice-president of the Navy Records Society, and honorary adviser on pictures and drawings to the National Maritime Museum. In 1936 Ingram edited and transcribed from the original manuscripts three sea journals of Stuart times and it proved to be a fascinating volume.

He initiated and presented to the nation the beautiful Battle of Britain Roll of Honour in the Royal Air Force Chapel in Westminster Abbey, which was opened by King George VI when he inaugurated the memorial. He was knighted in 1950. In November, 1960, Oxford University conferred on him the honorary degree of D.Litt.

Ingram was chairman of the Illustrated London News and Sketch Ltd., director of Illustrated, Sporting and Dramatic News Ltd., and president of Illustrated Newspapers Ltd.

He married in 1904 Amy, daughter of John Foy, and there was one daughter of the marriage. His wife died in 1947 and he married secondly Lily, daughter of Sydney Grundy. She died in 1962.

January 9, 1963.

Ferdinando Innocenti, a self-made leader of Italian industry, who motorized Italy with the Lambretta scooter after the Second World War, died on June 21, 1966, in Varese. He was 75.

A sombre man who combined an outspoken conservative political outlook throughout his life with the most modern and original industrial and marketing concepts, Innocenti was one of a handful of industrial leaders that included Adriano Olivetti and Enrico Mattei, who created the Italian "miracle."

His career began at the age of 16 when he started to work in a tiny workshop in Pescia, a town near Lucca, where he was born to the family of a hardware store owner. Two years later he succeeded in establishing his own mechanical workshop, and in 1922 he moved to Rome to experiment in the then new field of steel pipe. Nine years later he founded a steel pipe company in Milan which was the basis of his future expansion into other industrial areas.

His first plant at Lambrate had a meteoric success, making steel pipe, and eventually employed 6,000 persons. Innocenti was considered even then one of the most forward looking of Italian industrialists for the social and career benefits he gave his employees. During the war, however, aerial bombardment almost totally destroyed the Lambrate plant.

Characteristically, Innocenti shrugged off the loss and in 1945 began reconstruction of his company on the same site. This time, however, he had conceived of the "scooter" as a way to get Italy, where means of transportation had been almost eradicated during the war, on wheels. The new company was called *Innocenti Societa' Generale per L'Industria Metallurgica e Meccanica.*

The Lambretta became synonymous with the scooter—along with its principal rival, the Vespa—and omnipotent in the decade following the war. The scooter and the three-wheeled commercial vehicles Innocenti also built were fundamental to the industrial miracle in the 1950s, providing the transportation for workers to travel to their jobs. The scooter provided a degree of mobility the Italian nation had never known before.

With typical foresight, however, Innocenti saw the day coming when the scooter would be displaced by the small car. He reached an agreement in 1959 with the British Motor Corporation which was to have profound importance for both companies. The agreement with B.M.C. permitted Innocenti to assemble British-made parts into B.M.C. cars and market and service those cars in Italy. The cars now made there include the A-40, the Austin 1100 and most recently the Mini Minor.

The success of the Innocenti-built cars in Italy has been outstanding. Even in 1963 and 1964, when Government-imposed measures to cut back imports caused foreign car imports to plummet as much as 70 per cent, the Innocenti sales remained strong. To-day the Mini is selling exceptionally well in a booming market, causing the Italian auto giant Fiat to look with increasing irritation on Innocenti's brainchild.

Innocenti, who received an honorary degree in engineering from the Milan Polytechnic Institute in 1953, is survived by his wife, Anita Innocenti, and his son, Luigi Innocenti.

June 22, 1966.

Dr. John Ireland, who died on June 12, 1962, at the age of 82 at his home in Sussex, made a modest but distinctive contribution to English music in this century.

His public esteem fluctuated considerably during his long life, from wide and affectionate recognition as a major British composer to a recent period of excessive neglect when it was found necessary to form a society, two years ago, for the propagation of his music. He enjoyed popular success, with his piano pieces and his songs, particularly the setting of Masefield's "Sea Fever", but he never went out of his way to court popularity, and the obstinate individualism, which gave power to his best work, carried with it a fastidiousness that restricted his creative output.

The streak of musical conservatism which Stanford, his teacher, ironed into Ireland's soul may have cramped his musical development; his later works, up to the *Satyricon* overture (1946), seemed to indicate numerous new paths of expression that asked to be further explored, but they remained isolated examples, and in the last 15 years of his life Ireland completed nothing, though he did permit the John Ireland Society to give "premieres" of some prentice works from his years with Stanford, including an attractive sextet for wind and strings (1898). Although he produced music for large forces and in extended forms, his fastidious workmanship inclined him to prefer small forms and textures; he was a self-made miniaturist.

John Nicholson Ireland was born at Bowden, Cheshire, on August 13, 1879; his parents were literary folk, his father, Alexander Ireland, being editor of the *Manchester Evening Examiner,* and an intimate of Carlyle and Emerson—he had even been friendly with Hazlitt. From parental influence John Ireland acquired the nice taste and sensibility in poetry which marks out his song settings. At the age of 14 he was sent to study at the Royal College of Music in London and remained there until 1901, after which he earned a precarious living as organist, pianist, and musical coach.

His first songs date from around 1905, in which year he obtained a degree of Bachelor of Music from Durham University (where he was given an honorary Doctorate in 1932). His work as organist is reflected in two morning, two evening, and two communion service settings, as well as anthems—the motet "Greater love hath no man" is particularly fine—and some organ works. In 1906 Ireland became acquainted with the writings of Arthur Machen, and these fired an interest in magic and the unknown, which the composer has identified as "racial memory", that led him to spend much of his time in the Channel Islands and other homes of primitive man, and prompted much of his music, the best known example being the orchestral work *The Forgotten Rite*. This was composed in 1913, as was the song "Sea Fever", which found a publisher for Ireland and in due course became immensely popular.

Ireland's first great success was with the second violin sonata (1915–17) which captured attention on its first performance by Sammons and Murdoch, and proved a turning-point in Ireland's career. Ireland was now composing steadily, and as prolifically as at any time in his life, chiefly songs and piano music, but also a succession of chamber works, and from 1929 onwards a series of remarkable orchestral pieces, of which the choral *These Things Shall Be* (1937) is the largest (though perhaps the least durable), the Piano Concerto (1930) the most masterly—its adaptation of Lisztian concerto structure is quite brilliant—and *A London Overture* the most immediately winning.

His life, outside composition, was uneventful. He taught composition at the R.C.M. for a number of years, and was one of the first to recognize and encourage the talent of Benjamin Britten; in 1924 he was made Hon. R.A.M. and Hon. F.R.C.M. He appeared occasionally in public as conductor and, more frequently, pianist in his own works; latterly his appearances in the audience at Promenade concerts were greeted with vociferous applause—there was no doubt that he was revered as a Grand Old Man.

As a young man Ireland was a fellow-student of Holst and Vaughan Williams, but he did not join them in the folksong revival, and held himself apart from the English musical renascence. His music is recognizably English in flavour, founded in Brahms, *via* Stanford, influenced harmonically by Debussy and Stravinsky, but imbued nevertheless with a specifically English flavour; his melody is often modal but recalls not so much folksong as Gregorian chant, and even Stanford's "modal harmony". His pianistic prowess is reflected throughout his music for that instrument, whether solo or in songs and chamber works. It is exceptionally grateful to play, and unfailingly inventive, from the comparatively straightforward "The Towing Path" to the magnificent piano sonata (1920), a landmark in the British music of this century. Ireland's range of musical emotion was comparatively small, but within its natural limits intense and original. Understatement is its essence. The piano piece *Chelsea Reach*, the song-cycle *The Land of Lost Content*, the slow movement of the piano concerto, all express themselves unpretentiously; but they speak with perfect coherence for a period of musical history, and they communicate far more than they declare.

In 1927 he married Dorothy Phillips.

June 13, 1962.

Leslie Leroy Irvin, who invented the first practical free-fall parachute, and whose companies have made parachutes that have saved an estimated quarter of a million lives, died on October 9, 1966, at his home in Los Angeles, California, where he was born. He was 71.

Irvin founded Irving Air Chute of Great Britain Ltd., of Letchworth, Hertfordshire, in 1926, shortly after the Royal Air Force adopted his parachute and seven years after he made his historic jump at Dayton, Ohio. At the time of that jump—which made him the first person ever to open a military parachute while actually falling—he was 24. It resulted in the American Army placing an initial order for 300 of his parachutes.

Irvin promptly founded the International Irving Air Chute Group.

He did not then have sufficient money to correct an error in the name of the company when it was registered, and the name "Irving" is still part of the title of the American company and other concerns in the group.

Irvin founded the Caterpillar Club, membership of which is open only to those whose lives have been saved by parachutes of Irving air chute design. Of the approximately 250,000 who have become eligible for membership so far, 40,000 were allied airmen who baled out during the Second World War. Irvin, however, never qualified, for although he made more than 300 jumps, he never had to bale out in an emergency.

Although an American citizen, he spent the whole of the last war in Britain. During his stay he accepted, at the age of 50, a challenge to parachute into a lake from an aircraft flying at only 700 ft.

Many air forces of the world adopted the Irving parachute and today parachutes made by his factories and licensees are being used by the services and other organizations for emergency, jet aircraft braking, supply dropping, space capsule recovery and paratrooping.

At the time of his death Irvin was chairman of the Irving Air Chute Co., Inc., Lexington, and was on the board of the various other companies in the groups, including the British company, of which his old friend, Captain Cyril Turner, is chairman.

He leaves a widow and a married daughter.

October 11, 1966.

Margaret Irwin, the historical novelist, died in London on December 11, 1967.

Margaret Irwin belonged to a long and honourable tradition of romantic historical novelists. She had begun her career with stories in more contemporary settings, then extended her range, having won much praise for books such as *Fire Down Below*.

The youngest of a large family, she was born on top of Highgate Hill, where it is supposed Charles II once spent a night. Her parents died when she was still a child, and she went to live with her uncle, S. T. Irwin, who was well known as classical master at Clifton, and as the author of classical essays. On leaving school at Clifton, Margaret Irwin went to Oxford where she read English. In 1924 she published a "ghost story" that combined the eighteenth century with the present day, under the title *Still She Wished for Company*. During the next few years there followed *These Mortals*, *Knock Four Times*, and *Fire Down Below*. In 1930 *None So Pretty* was published, and won first prize in the Historical Novel Competition organized by Chatto and Windus. The news that she had won the prize reached her on her honeymoon; she had just married J. R. Monsell, the author-artist of many children's picture, song, and story books. He also designed the jackets for Margaret Irwin's books.

The success, pleasing and justified as it was, did not make her an instant best seller. She first achieved this with her long and fully authentic story, *Royal Flush*, which followed the fortunes of Minette, the favourite sister of Charles II. With this book she may be said to have found her period; the background, that of the earlier and late cavaliers in which she was most at home. A succession of stories followed, all detailed and lively, of which the best was, possibly, *The Stranger Prince*, the story of Rupert of the Rhine. Her own favourite was probably *The Proud Servant* which retold the almost incredible adventures and campaigns of James Graham, first Marquess of Montrose, fighting in the lost cause of Charles I.

Margaret Irwin in her later work went both forward and backward in time, but whenever her imagination caught fire she made her characters live. She saw them, men and women alike in the popular image but with greatly enhanced colour. Her readers came to know her for famous action, the well known phrase, truth to tradition. Very rarely indeed did she disappoint them. Her books could be read with pleasure by young and old for her outlook was full blooded, generous and healthy. She was capable of being fair in her delineation to some of those she most disliked, such as Oliver Cromwell. If she was a partisan she was also chivalrous.

Margaret Irwin was firm in her loyalties like so many of her heroes. She never forgot a kindness and she never failed to acknowledge her obligations to the scholars on whose work she depended. Some of her tributes were most graceful, all were heartfelt, never more so than those to the historian whose work she had admired perhaps most of all, her friend, Dr. C. V. Wedgwood.

Good historical novelists have never been overplentiful and there are never likely to be enough with such specialized talents as the craft demands. Margaret Irwin, after an encouraging start, grew steadily surer and she kept her mastery over a comparatively long writing life. If she became very popular the reason was that she loved her heroes and heroines deeply, brought them alive and made her readers share their trials and triumphs. As a friend she will be sadly missed. As a writer she will be judged in the long run by the high standards she followed herself.

December 12, 1967

Dr. Alick Isaacs, F.R.S., the discoverer of Interferon, and one of the world's leading virologists, died in University College Hospital, London, on January 26, 1967. He was 45.

Alick Isaacs was born and academically bred in Glasgow. At the university, from which he graduated M.B., Ch.B., in 1944, he won the John Hunter Medal in Clinical Medicine and took First prizes in Clinical Surgery and Dermatology. After a year of house jobs he was awarded the McCunn Research scholarship to study in the Department of Bacteriology, and this experience determined him in his choice of a career in the laboratory rather than in clinical medicine.

A Medical Research Council Studentship made it possible for him to spend an important formative year under Professor C. H. Stuart-Harris in the Department of Medicine in the University of Sheffield. Here his thoughts turned towards virology, and towards the possibility of studying under Macfarlane Burnet at the Walter and Eliza Hall Institute in Melbourne, then at the peak of its great reputation as a centre of virological research. A Rockefeller Travelling Fellowship in 1948–49 made it possible for Isaacs to realize his ambition, and further help from the Medical Research Council prolonged his study leave into a second year. Isaacs impressed Burnet deeply both as a man and as a scientist: "He has very rapidly fitted into our general programme of work" Burnet wrote, "and has a first rate problem of his own on hand." This was the problem of viral interference—how it is that the infection of a cell by one virus makes it refractory to infection by another—and it was in this field that Isaacs came to make his permanent contribution to medical science. In Melbourne he was joined by his fiancee from Sheffield, Susanna Gordon, now a well known and busy psychiatrist, and they married before returning home.

"Home" then and thereafter meant the National Institute for Medical Research, where Isaacs had spent a few weeks before his departure for Australia—quite long enough to convince Dr. C. H. Andrewes, the head of the Virology Division, of his high promise. During the next few years Isaacs concentrated intently on the problem of viral interference, using the inter-action of influenza and cowpox viruses.

The work on viral interference reached its climax with the publication in 1957 of a famous paper (written jointly with a Swiss guest in the Institute, Dr. J. Lindenmann) which announced the discovery of a new and naturally occurring antiviral agent. It had turned out that viral interference was mediated through the synthesis by the infected cell of a specific protein of rather low molecular weight, Interferon. Isaacs spent the rest of his life in the study of what Interferon was and how it worked; scientific guests joined him from all over the world, and other laboratories took it up; it is deeply tragic that he should not have lived to see it through.

The clinical uses of Interferon are *sub judice*, but it seems likely that until, if ever, it becomes a synthetic product, its usefulness in medical practice will be somewhat limited—as indeed the therapeutic uses of antibodies and antisera are somewhat limited. The great and lasting importance of Isaac's work is to have uncovered the existence of a new natural strategem.

When Sir Christopher Andrewes retired in 1961, Alick Isaacs succeeded him as head of the Virology Division at the National Institute. Later, to give him full opportunity to concentrate his thought without distraction, he became head of the Laboratory for Research on Interferon. He was elected F.R.S. in 1966.

Alick Isaacs was a man with a naturally happy disposition, generous and warm-hearted, and with the special kind of sociability that seems to be simply the outward extension of a happy family life.

January 28, 1967.

General Lord Ismay of Wormington, K.G., G.C.B., C.H., D.S.O., who died at his home on December 17, 1965, won a great reputation as one of Sir Winston Churchill's right hand men in the Second World War, and later as the Secretary-General of the North Atlantic Treaty Organization. By temperament as well as by experience "Pug" Ismay was well adapted for the roles which it fell to him to play for he had an almost uncanny skill for smoothing over difficulties and averting friction. His power resided in friendliness, unlimited patience, and a quick sense of humour, combined with a high degree of intelligence and a wide knowledge of the processes of government.

Hastings Lionel Ismay was born at Naini Tal in the United Province on June 21, 1887. His father, Sir Stanley Ismay, was a member of the Viceroy's Legislative Council and, later, Chief Judge of the Mysore Court, and his great grandfather was military secretary to a former Viceroy, Lord Hastings, after whom Ismay was named. He was educated at Charterhouse and the Royal Military College, Sandhurst, and, after a year's attachment to the Gloucestershire Regiment, he joined the 21st (Sam Browne's) Cavalry in 1906, and with them he saw his first active service on the North West Frontier.

In the 1914–18 War he was seconded to the King's African Rifles in East Africa, and, later, he commanded the mounted column of the Somaliland Camel Corps in the operations against the Mad Mullah. His services during these years won him two mentions in dispatches, a brevet majority and the D.S.O. He had made persistent efforts to reach a main theatre of war, but without success. He thus faced a heavy handicap in his profession, and he overcame it by becoming a bureaucrat. Soon after passing through the Staff College Quetta, he was appointed, in 1926, assistant secretary to Sir Maurice Hankey in the Committee of Imperial Defence. His five years' service in this appointment determined his subsequent career. After a few years' absence from the secretariat, in the course of which he served as military secretary to Lord Willingdon, then Viceroy of India, and then for a time in the intelligence branch of the War Office, he returned to it again in 1936, as deputy secretary. He had the choice of this appointment or the command of a cavalry brigade, and, when he decided for the former. "It was like saying goodbye to the dreams of my youth; but reason quickly banished sentiment and I never regretted my decision". He thus showed shrewd judgment in the assessment of his own talents, and he never deviated from his determination to make the secretariat his career and rise to the top of it. His spell of duty in it this time was to last 11 years.

In 1938 Lord Hankey retired, his duties were divided, and Ismay succeeded to the military part of them, becoming, after the outbreak of war, deputy secretary (military) to the War Cabinet. When Churchill became Prime Minister and Minister of Defence he made Ismay his Chief of Staff. He also made him a member of the Chief of Staff Committee, a somewhat false position, but Ismay wisely insisted on regarding himself as a member of the secretariat and studiously avoided taking a hand in matters of military policy. He conceived his role as being to run the machine which ran the war, and this he did supremely well.

STRUCTURE MAINTAINED

During the early stages of the war, when things were going badly for Britain, considerable pressure was brought to bear on the Cabinet and Defence Office machine, which had been built up over many years and had stood the pressure not only of the First World War but of the intervening years. Ismay had the difficult job of keeping together the machine which he himself had been so instrumental in creating and maintaining. In times of flux and disaster there are usually demands for changes in the management. These he resisted. He maintained the structure of the old Committee of Imperial Defence with its close relationship to the civil side of the Cabinet Office. He also had the full confidence of the Chiefs of Staff Committee.

The association between Churchill and Ismay was a remarkable one. Churchill wrote "we became hand in glove, and much more". Ismay has described his side of his relations with the Prime Minister: "My whole heart went out to him in his superhuman task, and I made a silent vow that, whatever he asked of me, I would do my utmost to give." In Ismay, Churchill found a hero-worshipping subordinate, who was not a yes-man, who kept close to his master, sitting with him into the watches of the night, listening patiently to his tirades, accompanying him on his journeys to and fro across the world. There was probably no one else who could have played such a role, which called for patience, tact, good temper, humour and last, but not least, a tough constitution.

It was Ismay who for the most part handled the flow of minutes which issued in an unending stream from No. 10. It was Ismay who removed causes of offence and misunderstanding by his deft and unobtrusive action. It was to him that everyone turned when a specially controversial proposition had to be presented either to the Prime Minister or to our American allies, for he had a special aptitude for drafting a minute. "The resolution of a problem", he used to say, "lies, more often than not, in the method of its presentation". and he had brought the method of presentation to a fine art.

POLITICALLY IMPARTIAL

He managed to remain politically impartial, and served Chamberlain, Churchill and Attlee with equal ease; and what was equally important was well thought of by the American Chiefs of Staff. At the Potsdam Conference Admiral King proposed only one toast "Pug Ismay, whose contribution to our victory could never be properly rewarded".

His role was different from that played by Hankey in the 1914-18 War in that he himself did not take such an active part in formulating policy and ideas, and he was not concerned with the political side of the secretariat as Hankey was. On the other hand, his spare energies were fully engaged by his time-consuming relationship with the Prime Minister.

After the 1945 General Election Ismay remained as Chief of Staff to Mr. Attlee, and, after the Potsdam Conference he played a large part in reorganizing the defence system and in setting up the Ministry of Defence. At the end of 1946 he retired from the Army, in which he had now reached the rank of General, and received a peerage. He planned a long holiday, but within a few weeks he was asked to go to India with Lord Mountbatten to assist with the arrangements for the transfer of power.

He returned home in the autumn of 1947, and it was not long before he was invited to take over the chairmanship of the Festival Council, in which capacity he presided over a feat of organization which he himself said raised problems no less difficult than the planning of a military campaign.

In 1951, when Mr. Churchill formed his government, he appointed Ismay Secretary of State for Commonwealth Relations. But he had hardly settled into this post when he was chosen to be the first Secretary-General of the North Atlantic Treaty Organization which he had once characterized as "all harness and no horse." From the outset he sought to emphasize that the permanent Representatives had powers of "effective decision", and was loyally resolute in repudiating any suggestion that they were only a second eleven to Ministers. By means of weekly lunches and "private" sessions, without benefit of agenda or records, he tried to develop informal consultation on common problems.

Ismay took a keen interest in press and public relations and was patience itself in meeting requests for interviews, talks and broadcasts. He became increasingly convinced that information was a field unduly neglected because of the reservations or parsimony of governments. In maintaining good working relations between the civil and military branches of Nato he gave yeoman service. His training and experience had equipped him to handle such matters with skill and ease. In respect of international political questions he had provided governments, if they wished to do so, with machinery to achieve closer political consultation, and when the Suez crisis burst, Ismay and his council "family" strove manfully to ride out the storm. But the Suez crisis, although the most spectacular, was not the only demonstration that for political consultation governments sometimes preferred an arm's length posture rather than a close embrace. Towards the end of Ismay's tenure of office this attitude was modified in some degree by the effects of the Suez crisis and the recommendations of the Committee of Three.

Ismay followed these recommendations in offering his good offices (but without effect) for a settlement of the Cyprus question, but in this and other problems he deemed it wise not to step out too boldly in a political role. He had no great relish for involved political issues and was convinced moreover that it would be a mistake to attempt to cut across national sovereignty by any assertion of "supra-national" functions for Nato.

Ismay had the gift of making friends, and few men in public life can have inspired more affection from close associates. In him geniality and tact were seasoned with shrewd common sense and touches of humour. He made no pretensions to be a master of detail, but often obtained solutions by adducing some reasonable and straightforward principle. His patience could be exemplary, and even when it failed he could carry his audience with some such appeal as "Need we torture outselves with this much longer?"

In 1960 he published his Memoirs. Although agreeable to read, they were written with such discretion that they did not contribute greatly to the history of the war or of Nato, and about his own positive contributions he remained as one reviewer put it "predictably and infuriatingly modest".

He married, in 1921, Laura Kathleen, the only daughter of H. G. Clegg, of Wormington Grange, who survives him with their three daughters.

December 18, 1965.

Lord Iveagh, K.G., C.B., C.M.G., F.R.S., who died on September 14, 1967, at the age of 93, was head of the well-known Irish family of Guinness and chairman of the great brewing business of Arthur Guinness Son and Co. Ltd. from 1927 to 1962.

His father, the first Earl, had established both in Ireland and Great Britain a tradition of wise and generous use of wealth and of public service which his son was to maintain. He was not one to bury his talent, he put it to work; his transformation of his large sporting estate in Suffolk into a fruitful agricultural unit has made history. He was said to be one of the richest men in the United Kingdom. On his father's death he shared with his brothers an estate valued at nearly £14m.

Iveagh was born on March 29, 1874, the eldest son of the first Earl, the head of the brewing firm of Arthur Guinness Son and Co. Ltd., of Dublin, by his marriage with his cousin Adelaide Maria, daughter of Richard Samuel Guinness.

ETON PROWESS

He was educated at Eton, where he distinguished himself as an oar. He won the school sculling in 1892, rowed in 1893 in the Eton Eight, which won the Ladies' Plate at Henley, and won the Diamonds at Henley in 1895 and the Diamonds and the Winged Sculls in 1896. He was said to have been one of the strongest boys who ever went to Eton, and his professional trainer declared that he had "legs like a tree". As at Eton, so throughout his life he had a perfect temper and was beloved by his friends who knew also how strong his sense of duty was. Eton was, however, unable to teach him to spell, and he was reported to have been responsible for "yph" as a variant of "wife". He was also said in one letter to have spelt the word "horse" in five different ways.

After coming down from Trinity College, Cambridge, he took an active interest in the family business. In 1896 he joined the London Rifle Brigade, eventually retiring with the rank of Captain in 1905. During the South African War he went out with the Irish Hospital, which his father had equipped, was mentioned in dispatches and created a C.M.G. In 1903 he took an active part in forming the London Division of the Royal Naval Volunteer Reserve in which he was appointed a commander and afterwards a captain, and at the Coronation of 1911 received the C.B.

In 1904 he was elected to the London County Council as member for Haggerston, and four years later was elected in the Unionist interest as its member of Parliament. He represented it for two years. From 1911 to 1913 he was a member of the London Education Committee. In 1912 he was returned for South-East Essex and in 1918 for Southend-on-Sea, a seat which he held until, in 1927, he succeeded his father.

GUINNESS TRUST

Early in the century he took charge of the Guinness Trust formed by his father to build homes for working people.

Before the First World War he established a training farm on his property near Woking for instructing youth, chiefly ex-public schoolboys, in the practical methods of Canadian agriculture. They did very well in Canada, and in 1912 he went to the Dominion to see as many of them as he could and, while there, purchased a number of farms in Nova Scotia for the benefit of future "trainees". The war interrupted the working of the scheme and when he went to Canada again in 1916 it was on a recruiting mission for the Navy.

On the death of his father he succeeded him in the chairmanship of Guinness's brewery and became Chancellor of the University of Dublin (an office he held until retirement on medical advice in 1963). In 1939 he gave his large town residence on St. Stephen's Green, Dublin, to the State of Eire. He was also liberal in his gifts to good causes in Great Britain. As Lord Elveden later after his succession he made donations amounting to nearly £100,000 in money, excluding a gift of land to the Victoria Hospital at Southend, and later presented £20,000 to St. Mary's Hospital, Paddington.

CLEAN MILK

His interest in agriculture covered more than half a century. After the 1914–18 War he became interested in the production of germ-free milk and was one of the first three producers in the country to obtain a licence to sell grade A milk. He also founded the T. T. Milk Producers' Association and was instrumental in establishing the National Institute for Research in Dairying.

Experiments on his 23,000 acre estate at Elveden, Suffolk, helped to revolutionize British agricultural methods. When he inherited the famous game preserve in 1927 much of it was heathland and rabbit-infested.

A previous owner, the Maharajah Duleep Singh, whose ambition it was to shoot 1,000 birds in a day by his own gun, got as near to this figure as 700 partridges. In the golden Edwardian days of Lord Iveagh's father it was perhaps the best shoot in the whole country and the names of Edward VII and the Duke of York, later George V, occur regularly in the game records. Earlier, when Lord Albemarle had the estate, Charles James Fox was a frequent visitor.

Most of the 23,000 acres Lord Iveagh inherited was on the arid, sandy soil of the Breck.

Figures alone do not adequately convey the size and scope of the transformation wrought on this vast estate. By 1954, a little over 9,500 acres were under crops and this area increased yearly by 200 to 300 acres. In 1953, 353,000 gallons of T. T. milk were produced. Apart from the dairy herd, the estate also supports a large herd of beef cattle and a flock of breeding ewes. Of 4,500 acres of corn in 1954, 2,000 were under barley, much of it of malting quality. It is some measure of Lord Iveagh's success that these improvements were made on land much of which has been compared to steppe; the rest was always marginal. From a home farm subordinate to the interest of a shooting estate, Elveden became the largest mixed farm unit in the country and one of the most progressive enterprises of its kind.

Before taking up farming, Iveagh was keenly interested in medical science. He encouraged the work of Sir Almroth Wright and Sir Alexander Fleming and was in 1921 appointed chairman of the Wright-Fleming Institute of Microbiology at St. Mary's Hospital, Paddington.

In 1955 Iveagh was created K.G. In 1957 he was the first recipient of the Bledisloe gold medal of the Royal Agricultural Society of England. In 1964 he was elected F.R.S.

In 1903 he married Lady Gwendolen Onslow, C.B.E., who was from 1927 to 1935 M.P. for Southend. She died in 1966. There were five children of the marriage, two sons and three daughters. The elder son died in infancy. The surviving son, Arthur Onslow Edward Guinness, Viscount Elveden, who in 1936 married Lady Elizabeth Hare, younger daughter of the 4th Earl of Listowel, was killed in action in 1945 and Lord Iveagh is succeeded by his grandson, Viscount Elveden, who inherited the Suffolk estate on his coming-of-age in 1958. He is chairman of the family firm.

The eldest of Lord Iveagh's daughters is Lady Honor Svejdar, wife of Mr. F. V. Svejdar and was formerly married to Sir Henry Channon, who died in 1958. The second daughter is Viscountess Boyd of Merton, wife of Viscount Boyd of Merton, formerly colonial secretary; the third daughter, Lady Brigid Guinness, married Prince Frederick of Prussia, grandson of the former Kaiser, in 1945. He died in 1966. She married Major Patrick Ness in 1967.

September 15, 1967.

Lady Iveagh, C.B.E., wife of the Earl of Iveagh, K.G. (see above entry), and formerly Conservative M.P. for Southend, died on February 16, 1966.

She was born in 1881 Lady Gwendolen Florence Mary, elder daughter of the fourth Earl of Onslow; her sister married the first Earl of Halifax, sometime Viceroy of India and Secretary of State for Foreign Affairs.

Lady Iveagh came of a family with a strong political tradition—three of her ancestors were Speakers of the House of Commons—and politics and political instincts were in her blood. She was of a generation brought up to give service and this she did with an engaging mixture of firmness and gaiety.

When her husband became second Earl of Iveagh in 1927 on the death of his father she was invited to stand at his old seat, Southend. She was elected in November that year and held the seat until 1935 when her son-in-law, Mr. Henry Channon, was adopted in her place and elected at the ensuing general election.

She had a first-class memory which absorbed facts and figures with great ease and this allied to a natural gift for public speaking made her a figure to be reckoned with. Her maiden speech in the Prayer Book discussions of 1927 was an excellent piece of Parliamentary speaking, dignified, sincere and quietly passionate.

Her experience of affairs began early. During her childhood she spent several years in New Zealand, where her father was Governor-General and while still in her teens she acted as her father's secretary.

She was married in 1903, and her first public speech was made during her engagement. She fought for her husband in nine parliamentary elections in addition to contests for the London County Council. It was her practical acquaintance with organization work, gained during the earlier contests, and her administrative capacity which led to her appointment in 1925 as chairman of the women's organization of the Conservative Party.

TRAINING WOMAN EMIGRANTS

As a result of a visit to Canada, Lord Iveagh founded, near Pyrford Court, a training centre for young men intending to settle in the dominion, and it was followed by a similar training centre for women, started by Lady Iveagh. Her idea was to fit women to go out to the colonies as the homemakers for their brothers or husbands. This Overseas Training School for women taught cooking, preserving, dairy work, poultry-keeping, and washing, and its aim was to prepare the students to be self-reliant and able to meet the emergencies and possible discomforts that might be found in colonial farm life.

In conjunction with Lord Iveagh, Lady Iveagh was one of the pioneers of the pure milk campaign in Great Britain. Their farm was the second to obtain a licence for the supply of certified milk, and Lord Iveagh formed an association of certified milk producers in order to assist newcomers to the movement in overcoming their difficulties. Lady Iveagh also took a lively interest in the agricultural researches which Lord Iveagh instituted. She was closely identified in later years with his remarkable transformation of the great Elveden estate in Suffolk, mostly consisting of the arid, sandy soil of the Breck and in former times a game shot's delight, into a highly progressive, highly productive mixed farm unit.

In 1956 Lady Iveagh gave Clandon Park, Surrey, with an endowment, to the National Trust.

This house, her birthplace, was built by Leoni in the eighteenth century for the second Lord Onslow.

February 17, 1966.

J

Sir Barry V. Jackson, founder and governing director of the Birmingham Repertory Theatre, died on April 3, 1961, in a Birmingham hospital at the age of 81.

He was, in the days before any subsidy was given to the serious theatre in Britain, what Bernard Shaw called one of the "private adventurers" in that field. As such he "took up the running" in London—the phrase is again Shaw's—more or less at the point where Granville Barker dropped out, and he continued into an age when the theatre was receiving aid from the state for the first time in British history.

BUILDING A THEATRE

Barry Vincent Jackson—he was named after Barry Sullivan the Irish actor—was born at Birmingham on September 6, 1879, the second son of George Jackson, who had made a fortune with Maypole Dairies. His father sent Barry to a preparatory school in Moseley and later to Geneva, would not allow him to become a professional painter, but did allow him to break off after five years his training as an architect in the Birmingham office of Frank Osborn in order to write plays and organize private performances at the family home, The Grange, Moseley. The Grange, a mission hall in Inge Street, and the Edgbaston Assembly Rooms served in turn as headquarters of The Pilgrim Players, as his amateur actors were eventually called, but in 1909 Jackson resolved to put the company on a professional basis and to build a repertory theatre—no theatre had yet been built in England to serve that particular purpose—in Station Street. He appointed John Drinkwater, who had hitherto earned his living in insurance, as secretary to the Company, and F. N. Cooke, one of his contemporaries at the Birmingham School of Art, as architect. The theatre opened on February 15, 1913, with Jackson's own production of *Twelfth Night*, he himself reading aloud a dedicatory poem by Drinkwater before the curtain rose, and Felix Aylmer as Orsino speaking the first lines to be delivered from the stage.

THE IMMORTAL HOUR

Production was maintained throughout the First World War, while Jackson served with the R.N.V.R., and in 1919 John Drinkwater's *Abraham Lincoln* was transferred to the Lyric, Hammersmith, where it had a long run under the joint management of Nigel Playfair and Jackson, but made only a small profit. Jackson began his career as an independent manager in London in 1922 with Rutland Boughton's opera *The Immortal Hour* at the Regent. This established Miss Gwen Ffrangçon-Davies and gradually won a devoted public for itself, but it lost money.

Next year, turning aside Shaw's question "Mr. Jackson, are your wife and children provided for?", he mounted at Birmingham the first performance in England of the play-cycle *Back to Methuselah*, but in January, 1924, he announced that the Repertory Theatre would, in view of inadequate support over the past 11 years, close in the following month. However, a scheme guaranteeing an audience, put up to him on what was to have been the last night by the Lord Mayor, was accepted by Jackson and a new season began in September with a Celtic folk opera composed by Granville Bantock.

Notwithstanding the crises in Birmingham he had meanwhile been active in London. Having transferred *Back To Methuselah* to the Court, not then known as the Royal Court, he went on to "nurse" there Eden Phillpotts's *The Farmer's Wife* till it grew, making the name of Sir Cedric Hardwicke into a big success, and to present Sir John Gielgud and Miss Ffrangçon-Davies in *Romeo and Juliet* at the Regent. In 1925, having decided that he theatre in Birmingham could not pay its way unless the most important productions seen at it were given a chance to draw London, too, he took the Kingsway in Great Queen Street, intending that it should serve as an outlet for his "artistic capital" accumulated in the Midlands.

HAMLET IN MODERN DRESS

At the Kingsway he put on productions in modern dress of *Hamlet*—the first Shakespeare play to be so acted in London, though *Cymbeline* in khaki had already been given at the Birmingham Repertory—and *Rosmersholm*: he continued to make experimental productions at the Court, including one of *Macbeth* in modern dress ("experiments have their failures" he admitted), but by the middle of 1928, having lost money on all but three of the productions he had been responsible for in London during 10 years, he candidly expressed his discouragement in a letter to Shaw: "Is the Birmingham Repertory Theatre to go the way of the Horniman and Larker ventures?" "I give it up", wrote Shaw at the end of a long reply: but his real reply was to offer his new play *The Apple Cart* for production at the festival that Jackson proposed to institute at Malvern in 1929.

This play, transferred from Malvern to the Queens, ran for nine months under the joint management of Sir Alfred Butt and Jackson, and *The Barretts of Wimpole Street*, transferred from the second Malvern Festival, ran even longer at the Queens under Jackson's management in his own right. With the aim of encouraging the Little Theatre Movement in Canada, which he had already tried to stimulate by lecturing there, he sent a company to tour that Dominion in the last-named play and five others during the winter of 1931–32.

Next autumn two of his important productions, Shaw's *Too True to be Good* and Mr. Somerset Maugham's *For Services Rendered*, failed in London, and in 1934 he announced that he could not undertake another season at the Birmingham Repertory: of the money it had cost him to support it for 21 years, more than £100,000 had not been recovered. Some £3,000 was now raised by subscription; Jackson and Mr. William Haywood jointly agreed to open a new season; and in January, 1935, it being provided that the policy of the theatre should remain unchanged, Jackson handed over his interest in it to the Sir Barry Jackson Trust. He himself became a trustee and governing director of the theatre, which was now exempted from entertainment tax, thereby saving £2,000 per annum.

AT STRATFORD

Jackson withdrew from the Malvern Festival in 1937, after having planned and financed nine successive programmes, but he returned to active management in Birmingham during the Second World War. He first organized at the Lord Mayor's request seasons of "Plays in the Parks", then resumed direction of the Repertory Theatre, where Margaret Leighton, Paul Scofield, and Peter Brook were among those to whom he gave opportunities between 1942 and 1946, when he was appointed Director of the Shakespeare Festival at Stratford.

His authority was now such that he was able to bring about great changes there, "staggering" the productions so as to allow adequate time for rehearsal of each, and distributing them among various specially engaged producers, and to persuade the Governors that the Director of the Festival should be made Director of the Memorial Theatre itself, with power to gear the programme of its whole year's work to that of the Shakespeare season. This was done in 1947, but his contract came to an end in 1948 and Jackson, then aged 68, was told that it would not be renewed. The producers introduced by him to the Stratford-on-Avon Festival included Nugent Monck, Michael MacOwan, Brook, Michael Benthall and his own successor as Director of the Memorial Theatre, Anthony Quayle.

Jackson's activities at Stratford-on-Avon, at the Malvern Festival—a landmark in the history of drama festivals in Britain—in London as a sponsor of Shaw and the pioneer of Shakespeare in modern dress, and first and last in Birmingham, add up to a very substantial contribution, founded not only upon great inherited wealth but also on almost unlimited enthusiasm and capacity for hard work, to the British theatre during half a century. He never married. Though a hospitable man, he was more at home in the company of his own ideas than in that of his fellows, except when his contact with them was chiefly on the plane of ideas. The late Scott Sutherland, a good actor who specialized in Shaw's comic characters and a fine musician—he supervised the orchestral and choral side of the Malvern Festival—was Jackson's closest friend among the theatre people of his generation.

He wrote farces for the Pilgrim Players in his early days and plays for children, and he adapted for production *The Marriage of Figaro*, Henri Ghéon's *The Marvellous History of St. Bernard*, and two plays by Molière. He was knighted in 1925, had previously been awarded the Gold Medal of the Birmingham Civic Society, and received the Honorary Freedom of the City of Birmingham in 1955. The degrees of Hon. M.A. (Birmingham), Hon. LL.D. (St. Andrews) and Hon. D.Litt. (Birmingham, Manchester) were conferred on him.

April 4, 1961.

Naomi Jacob, a lively, sympathetic and deservedly popular novelist, died on August 27, 1964, at her home in Sirmione, on Lake Garda, Italy. She was 80.

In spite of ill-health, she had led a busy and actively diversified life, from which she drew the knowledge of people and the "human touch" that made her fiction so pleasantly readable. Possessed of a fund of shrewd good sense and much warmth and kindliness of feeling, she excelled, in her own somewhat homely fashion, in what is commonly called character-drawing, and at her best was capable of a most engaging imaginative ease and veracity. As storyteller she found her happiest themes, as a rule, in recording the chances and changes of a Yorkshire family a generation or two ago. Her thoughts returned always to Yorkshire, in which country she was born and bred, with peculiar pride and zest.

She was born at Ripon on July 1, 1884, the daughter of Nina Ellington Collinson, who wrote novels under the name of Nina Abbott. She was educated privately and at Middlesbrough High School, and for a time was a teacher in a Church of England school. She abandoned teaching to become secretary and manager of a noted music-hall artist—she was received into the Roman Catholic Church during this period—took part in the women's suffrage movement, and, during the war of 1914–18, served in the Women's Legion and was supervisor in a munitions factory. A lengthy period of illness followed, after which, apparently with little preparation, she became an actress, making her first appearance on the stage in 1920. She was on the stage for some nine years (she returned to it at intervals during the war of 1939–45), appearing in the West End of London in many notable productions of the period. With her stage career she combined an active interest in politics; she became a strong supporter of the Labour Party, stood unsuccessfully for Labour at local elections in London, and was once adopted as Parliamentary candidate for Sevenoaks. She left the Labour Party, however, after the Second World War and a few years later became a Conservative.

LIVING IN ITALY

To the stage and politics she had for some years added the writing of fiction when, in 1930, a return of her illness led her to Italy, on the shore of Lake Garda, where for the most part she continued to live afterwards. Her earliest novel, *Jacob Ussher*, had appeared in 1926, and was followed by, among others, *Rock and Sand* (1929), *Roots* (1931), *Props* and *Young Emmanuel*, both brought out in the following year. In all of them her flow of narrative invention and unaffectedly sympathetic feeling for character produced their effect upon the reader. But it was with *Four Generations* (1934), a story of a wealthy family of English Jews in a somewhat more romantic vein than she had attempted until then, that she first tasted success. Of the novels that followed in rapid succession the most attractive are, perhaps, *The Lenient God* (1937), *This Porcelain Clay* (1939), and *They Left the Land* (1940), the last of these a solid and vivid study of three Yorkshire generations.

Miss Jacob also wrote a series of gossipy autobiographical volumes, done with an infectious friendliness—*Me, Me Again, Me in Wartime* (she joined Ensa in 1939 and was in North Africa, Sicily and Italy), *Me in the Mediterranean*, and so on. The last of these, *Me—and the Stage*, was published on her eightieth birthday a month before she died, together with a novel *The Long Shadows*. And mention must be made of her glowing and affectionate biography of Marie Lloyd—*Our Marie*, published in 1936, a book that is much more than a collection of anecdotes and reminiscences. Her later novels show some falling away from her highest standards, but are nevertheless always lively and enjoyable.

August 28, 1964

Dr. Per Jacobsson, who died in a London hospital on May 5, 1963, at the age of 69, had been chairman of the Executive Board and managing director of the International Monetary Fund since 1956. He was in his last period of office before retirement, and the Fund's annual meeting in Washington in September would have been his last appearance. He left the International Monetary Fund stronger and more flexible than he found it.

He was that rarity in the international monetary field, a man who could talk and argue with economists in their own language, and a man who in his time had been father confessor to the world's leading central bankers. Discussions on economic theory would keep him entranced into the early hours of the morning, yet he never lost sight of the practical issues that had to be sold to the politicians—usually in Washington. This twin interest in pure theory and day-to-day affairs was reflected throughout his career.

Born at Tanum, Sweden, on February 5, 1894, he took his first examination in economics before the 1914–18 War. As he himself once said: "Besides Professor David Davidson I was mainly influenced by the writings of Alfred Marshall and Knut Wicksell, thus by an Englishman who was a recognized master in his own lifetime and by a Swede whom I knew personally and who, since his death, has gradually come to be regarded as one of the most original and penetrating economists of all time. Neither of them was actually engaged in politics, though both of them were much interested in public affairs." Much the same, with more accent on public affairs, could be said of Jacobsson.

His first post was in 1917 as Assistant Secretary of the Swedish Commission on Economic Defence Preparedness. Three years later he joined the Secretariat of the League of Nations when it was preparing for the Brussels financial conference. What seemed to be a temporary post turned out to be a far longer job—he remained until 1928. After returning to Sweden for a couple of years he was finally appointed Economic Adviser to the Bank for International Settlements—a post which brought him into his own. Here was the perfect sounding post. In Basle he had the ear of Europe's leading central bankers—almost the first decision he heard was the devaluation of sterling in 1931. He used this vantage point to good purpose, using his personal influence when necessary, cultivating people as well as ideas.

His influence may be debatable. What is not in dispute is his handling of the economic department under his control and the annual report of the B.I.S. with his personal stamp writen all over it. It became a model of what an annual economic and financial report should be, combining facts and views into a coherent, lucid whole. And so it remained throughout the postwar years.

HIS GREATEST TEST

His transition in 1956 from this listening post in the centre of Europe to the head of one of the west's leading international monetary institutions faced Jacobsson with his greatest test. There were qualms in more than one financial centre. Would he have enough tact, enough political sense to influence policies as much as he could influence ideas and people? Did he also have the administrative ability? The answers should be deduced from his success in transforming the I.M.F. from an automatic dollar provider into a broadly based support for all currencies. He left much still to be done. But his achievements silenced all the earlier anxieties about his personal qualities. If he could not, or did not wish to, administer, he found people who could. His way with politicians was like that with everyone he met. Taking them by the shoulder he would stir them the way he wanted to go and this went for economists, politicians, and journalists alike. He had the grip of a huge friendly Teddy bear. His affection was catching and he used it to good purpose in Washington and elsewhere. Never did he need it in greater abundance than in September at the annual meeting of 1961 when a head-on clash between the monetary influence of the United States and continental Europe was narrowly averted. The United States, fearful for the dollar, was urging new backing for the I.M.F. Europe, in the knowledge of her renewed strength, quoted stiff terms. Jacobsson went through that week radiating confidence and optimism as though nothing untoward was really taking place behind the closed doors. By Christmas a compromise, albeit a stiff one, had been reached in Paris. Jacobsson had averted a major crisis though the aftermath will trouble his successor for many a year.

MORE FLEXIBLE APPROACH

Jacobsson's period at the I.M.F. marked the end of American dominance in world monetary affairs. Previously it had largely been a mechanism for doling out dollars. Now something more flexible was needed. The fund itself needed fresh life breathing into it. Many of its original articles were sadly out of tune with problems of the late 1950s. After the move towards convertibility by the leading European currencies (including sterling) at the end of 1958, further adjustments were needed. Jacobsson saw that more funds would be required and that a drawing from the Fund should be far more automatic than it had been so far. The question was whether changes in the Fund would be enough. Was something wider needed—a revaluation of gold, floating exchange rates, the devaluation of the pound, and so on?

Jacobsson would have none of this and, while firmly behind the efforts to bring his old institution, the B.I.S., into the short-term defence of the leading currencies, he strenuously opposed any juggling with currency exchange rates. This attitude has led to an impression that Jacobsson was simply a narrow minded banker writ large, sticking to strict monetary disciplines for their own sake. This is to fall into serious error. On several issues Jacobsson certainly came to side with many orthodox economists and bankers. But he was far from being orthodox at heart. He strongly opposed the deflationists during the financial turmoil of 1931. More recently he was the first to warn about the dangers of deflation arising from a fall in commodity prices. His was a lively mind that would be difficult to place in any easy pigeonhole.

In 1921 he married Violet Mary Nye, of Farnham, Surrey. They had three daughters, one of whom is married to Dr. Roger Bannister, the former Olympic runner and world mile record holder.

May 6, 1963.

Lieutenant-General the Maharaja of Jaipur, G.C.S.I., G.C.I.E., the first Rajpramukh (President) of Rajasthan, a state of the Indian Union, died on June 24, 1970, after collapsing while playing polo at Cirencester. He was 58.

He was born on August 21, 1911, the second son of the Thakur of Isarda, a noble belonging to the Rajawat sect of the Kachhawas of Rajputana. When a boy of 10 Sawai Man Singh was adopted by the then Maharaja of Jaipur, Sawai Sir Madho Singh, whom a year later he succeeded. He was educated at Mayo College, Ajmer, and R.M.A., Woolwich.

He was assisted in his administration of the state by a council over which he presided with the Prime Minister as vice-president. He was fortunate in 1942 in securing the services as Dewan of Sir Mirza Ismail who had gained a reputation during his premiership of the "model state" of Mysore. The pace of reform and reconstruction was quickened in the four years before Sir Mirza moved to become president of Nizam of Hyderabad's Executive Council. An outstanding achievement of those four years was the creation of the Rajputana University at Jaipur.

The Maharaja led a full and active life and followed closely the Rajput tradition of love of soldiering. He was commissioned into the Life Guards in 1939 For a time in the Second World War he was at the Staff College, Quetta, and he formed a College of Infantry, bearing his name, in his capital.

No less strong was the fidelity of "Jai", as he was familiarly known, to the Rajput tradition of sport. He was for some time president of the Indian Polo Association, and was a player of great repute.

The Maharaja was present at the conference which the last British Viceroy, Lord Mountbatten, had with a number of the Princes at Delhi in March, 1947. The transfer of power came in the following August, and in December Lord Mountbatten (for a short time Governor General of the Indian Union) and Lady Mountbatten visited Jaipur for the celebration of the Silver Jubilee of the accession of the Maharaja. The principalities of Rajastan were merged in 1949 into one of the states of the new Indian Union and for all effective purposes the direct personal rule of the Princes ended.

The Maharaja married firstly, in 1924, a sister of the late Air Vice-Marshal Sir Umed Singh, the Maharaja of Jodhpur. He married secondly in 1932 the daughter of the late Sir Sumer Singh, Maharaja of Jodhpur. Thirdly he married in 1940 the younger sister of the Maharaja of Cooch Behar. From these unions the Maharaja had four sons and a daughter.

The Maharaja between the world wars led the all-conquering Jaipur polo team playing off a handicap of ninc together with the three brothers from Jaipur, Hanut, Prighi and Abhey Singh. The Jaipur side won all the London polo championships and were unbeatable in India.

FALL AT WINDSOR

After the war, as his polo handicap was reduced with the passing of the years, the Maharaja became a staunch supporter of the Guards Polo Club and did a great deal in helping young players to learn about polo from the force of his example. A fortnight before he died he had a bad fall playing polo at Windsor and suffered concussion and bruising. Besides being one of the best polo players of his generation, Jaipur made a host of friends during his glittering career and was certainly the most respected and popular figure in the polo world of India and England of the last 40 years.

June 25, 1970.

Sir Wilson Jameson, G.B.E., K.C.B., who died in a London hospital on October 18, 1962, at the age of 77, was an outstanding figure even among those distinguished men who have occupied the position of Chief Medical Officer of the Ministry of Health or its predecessors, the Local Government Board and the Privy Council. It is a line which began with Sir John Simon and during this century had included Sir Arthur Newsholme, Sir George Newman, and Sir Arthur MacNalty.

CLINICAL TRAINING

William Wilson Jameson was born on May 12, 1885. His father was John Wilson Jameson, of Perth. Educated at Aberdeen Grammar School and the University of Aberdeen, he then came south where he studied public health at University College London. He had the cultured background of a training in the classics and was an M.A. of his university. He graduated in medicine in 1909, and had a good clinical training including resident posts in Aberdeen and at Hackney Hospital.

Jameson then turned his attention to public

health and preventive medicine. He also qualified as a barrister, being called to the Bar by the Middle Temple. He always had a flair for teaching and exposition and in 1914 was assistant and lecturer in the Department of Hygiene of University College London, under Professor Kenwood.

On the outbreak of war he joined the R.A.M.C. as a hygiene specialist and saw service in France and Italy. When he returned to civilian life he was successively Deputy M.O.H. of Stoke Newington and St. Marylebone and received his first "command" as M.O.H. of Finchley, transferring later to Hornsey. On the establishment in 1929 of the London School of Hygiene and Tropical Medicine he was appointed Professor of Public Health.

REMARKABLE TERM

It was the first whole-time Chair in this subject in England. The Dean of the school was Sir Andrew Balfour and other holders of whole-time Chairs were Major Greenwood, Leiper and Topley—a truly remarkable team which quickly gave the new school an international reputation.

On the death of Sir Andrew Balfour in 1931 Jameson succeeded him as Dean while still holding his Chair and taking an active part in teaching. The school, with which the Ross Institute was later amalgamated, had, from the beginning, given instruction in Tropical Medicine and Hygiene and undertaken research into these subjects. The Colonial, Dominions and India Offices were represented on the Governing Body. A close link was forged with the colonies, many of their medical staff having been trained, or attended refresher courses, at this school. Jameson accepted many requests to visit the colonies and advise on how the health of their inhabitants could be improved. He was knighted in 1939.

Shortly after the declaration of war in 1939, he became Medical Adviser to the Colonial Office and the following year he succeeded Sir Arthur MacNalty as Chief Medical Officer of the Ministry of Health and the Board of Education. Strenuous and exhausting years followed.

Sir Wilson threw all his energy into his new and grave responsibilities. He slept in the basement of the School of Hygiene and worked incessantly at his office. He broke down isolationism in the medical staffs of the different Government Departments, and all worked together as a team under his able leadership.

His committee and conference work took heavy toll of his time. He had to attend many international conferences on medical matters and frequently flew, in not very comfortable bomber aircraft, to and from North America. He was vice-chairman of the Minister of Health's Advisory Medical Committee and a member of the Army Hygiene Advisory Committee, the Colonial Medical Advisory Committee, the Committee of Industrial Health of the Ministry of Labour and National Service, and chairman, for a time, of a committee to consider psychiatric problems in the Services.

He had always taken a great interest in medical education. He served on the General Medical Council as a Crown nominee and advised the Minister to set up an interdepartmental committee on this subject. The chairman was Sir William Goodenough and Sir Wilson, as a member, took a prominent part in its deliberations. It is as a direct result of their report and his subsequent backing of their recommendations at the Ministry of Health that substantial progress has since then been made in the training of medical undergraduates and post-graduates.

DIPHTHERIA IMMUNIZATION

Meanwhile, the routine duties of his office were exceptionally heavy. He was concerned at the poor response of the public to take advantage of immunization against diphtheria and, in spite of his dislike of the limelight and the traditional desire of civil servants to keep in the background, he became a public figure and a household word as a result of press conferences and broadcasts at which he advocated immunization with such good results that some 75 per cent of children were immunized and the incidence and death rates from diphtheria fell remarkably. Subsequently he broke new ground by broadcasting on syphilis and the venereal diseases and the taboo against the mention of this subject in "respectable" newspapers disappeared.

But, perhaps, his greatest preoccupation during the war was the prevention of malnourishment and his recognition of the need to ensure that the most vulnerable sections of the community received their proper quota of the diminished national food supply.

Even before the war was over, he had to turn his attention to the reorganization of the health and hospital services of the country which the acceptance by the Coalition Government of the Beveridge Report made inevitable. As Chief Medical Adviser to successive Ministers of Health he played a prominent part in the preparation of the Bill which became the National Health Service Act and in the difficult and protracted negotiations which took place before the new service was inaugurated. He had the confidence of all parties who realized that he had a single-minded devotion to the need for improving the medical services of the country. After he retired from the Ministry of Health in 1950 he became medical adviser of the King Edward Fund and held that post until 1960.

He was made K.C.B. in 1943, and G.B.E. in 1949. He was also F.R.C.P. London, F.R.C.P. Canada, F.R.C.O.G., and an Honorary Fellow of the American Public Health Association. A number of universities in this country and overseas bestowed honorary degrees upon him. He received the Buchanan Medal of the Royal Society and in 1942 was the Harveian Orator of the Royal College of Physicians. In 1950 he was awarded the Bisset Hawkins Medal of the Royal College of Physicians of London.

He married in 1910 Pauline, the daughter of J. P. Helm, and had two daughters. She died in 1958 and in 1959 he married Miss Constance Dobie, who had been in charge of one of the staff colleges for nurses of the King Edward Hospital Fund for London.

October 20, 1962.

James Jarché, one of the most distinguished British press photographers, died on August 6, 1965, at his home in London. He was 74.

His career spanned nearly half a century of press history and from the modest beginnings of the decade before the 1914-18 War he saw, and played a notable part in, the immense technical advance and physical expansion of illustrative technique as applied to newspapers and magazines.

In newspapers he began, and to newspapers he at length returned, but he had a long spell of work for periodicals owned by Odhams Press, and his preference was for the carefully thought-out magazine set-piece rather than the quick shot of the daily paper. Nevertheless he produced at least one classic of daily press photography. This was in 1922, when he caught a rear view of six little boys in a state of nature on the banks of the Serpentine, taking to their heels pursued (for bathing at the wrong hour) by a massive middle-aged policeman.

Jarché was born in London in September, 1890, the son of an immigrant French photographer, and so from his earliest years was surrounded by the paraphernalia of the craft. He was giving some minor help to his father at the age of nine, and in 1907 he joined a firm called Argent Archer, which supplied pictures to weekly magazines. Another early employer was Warhurst, the pioneer of Fleet Street photography. When Jarché was only 19—in 1909—he obtained pictures of historical moment, at the landing of Louis Blériot in Kent after the first flight over the Channel.

From that time an album of Jarché's pictures might serve as an illustrative commentary on English life in the first half of the twentieth century. In 1910 there came an illicit shot of Crippen and Ethel Le Neve. In the following year he took the famous picture of a top-hatted, astrakhan-collared Winston Churchill watching the "battle of Sidney Street." The crashed Zeppelin at Potter's Bar in 1916, the fire at Madame Tussaud's in 1925, the Coronation of King George VI in 1937 and of Queen Elizabeth in 1953—these were a few of the hundreds of events of which Jarché has left records. And there were portraits of Bernard Shaw, Sir Alexander Fleming, and many other leading figures including Dr. Albert Einstein (whose aversion from being photographed he overcame). He made over 2,000 lantern slides of his work, and was much in demand as a lecturer.

Jarché had a long period with Odhams Press, and much of his best magazine work was done for *Illustrated.* He left Odhams for the Associated Press in 1953, and worked on the *Daily Mail* for six years before retiring.

August 9, 1965.

John Gibson Jarvie, who died on December 29, 1964, at his Suffolk home, Gedding Hall, Bury St. Edmunds, at the age of 81, was the architect and latterly the president of United Dominions Trust, Britain's largest credit finance house.

Gibson Jarvie will best be remembered as the

pioneer of the hire-purchase business in Britain, as an individualist combining great frankness with high financial ability. His was a business success story on classic lines possible only in a free enterprise system; a system he ardently believed in. The welfare state and many of the official postwar economic policies were anathema to him and were regular targets of his somewhat unusual annual speeches during his long reign as chairman of U.D.T.

Born at Carluke, Scotland, on October 29, 1883, the second son of John Jarvie, he left Scotland as a very young man to make his way, working as a labourer, and, for a short time, using his considerable artistic gifts painting inn signs in Holland. He was also for a time advertising manager of *The Throne and Madame*. In 1913 he went to America, where he travelled extensively and gained wide business experience. He then joined the National City Bank of New York and afterwards the Continental Guaranty Corporation, which, at the end of the 1914–18 War, sent Jarvie with a capital of £10,000 to set up a banking business in London. It proved an impracticable task, however, and he turned his attention instead to developing a hire-purchase business which he had seen in operation in the United States.

Eventually he arranged a syndicate to buy out the American interest and the company became wholly British owned. From these small beginnings he created what is by any standard a very large and influential British financial institution. In 1930 indication of the status Jarvie had already attained was recognizable in his securing a substantial and unprecedented capital investment in his company by the Bank of England. Jarvie saw the hire-purchase agreement as a simple and effective instrument of security for banking business and he was often at war with the press for what he regarded as misapprehension and derogation of the hire-purchase system. He was an expansionist and in the period of regeneration after the Second World War his aim was to widen the base of his group's activities, both geographically and intrinsically. His success, and indeed his monument, is in the world wide group of financial companies which comprise the United Dominions Trust Group, and from which he retired as chairman in March, 1963.

In 1941 in order to obtain greater coordination of the national war effort at ports, the Minister of Transport appointed Jarvie regional port director for the North-Western Region at Liverpool. The appointment, however, was not a success and his methods of administration soon aroused criticism culminating in his resignation towards the end of 1942, when an inquiry into the working of the port labour scheme and allegations of slackness in handling cargoes was opened. The thought of failure had always been intolerable to him and his time at Liverpool had a great effect upon him.

Jarvie was called to the Bar by the Middle Temple in 1926 and in 1951–52 was High Sheriff of Suffolk. He enjoyed riding, fishing, and shooting and one of his great interests away from the City was farming.

A man of personal courage, mentally and physically, Jarvie was always in danger of allowing his aggressive nature to deny tolerance and impartiality.

He married Ethel Mary Patricia, daughter of Colonel M. C. Rowland, C.M.G., of Johannesburg. They had one son and three daughters. His son, Mr. Robert Gibson Jarvie, is now joint deputy chairman of U.D.T.

December 30, 1964.

Sir Jack Jarvis, the celebrated racehorse trainer, died at his home in Newmarket on December 19, 1968. He was 80.

He had long been admired and respected as one of the greatest and most popular race horse trainers in the history of the English turf. Jack Jarvis, as he was affectionately known throughout the racing world, was knighted in 1967 and no man connected with his exacting profession could have better deserved such an honour.

A fine judge of thoroughbreds, an able administrator, an all-round sportsman, and a witty speaker, he was also a great mixer. For him there was never a dull moment and not even 66 years of riding and training could take away his appetite for enjoying life. How he found time for his varied interests will always remain a mystery, but this he somehow did and the large collection of trophies and gifts which he had at Park Lodge bear witness to his dedicated professional and public work.

The son of a famous trainer with whom he served his apprenticeship, Jack Jarvis was clearly destined to follow his father's profession, as were his two elder brothers. A six stone jockey at the age of 16 with 38 winners to start him off on his career, the leading trainer in the years 1939, 1951 and 1953, a long successful and happy association with the Rosebery family carried on from father to son, were some of the highlights in the Jarvis story. He won nine classic races and four Ascot Gold Cups. He considered Blue Peter, the winner in 1939 of the 2,000 Guineas and the Derby, to have been his best horse.

His classic victories were the 1,000 Guineas with Plack (1924), Campanula (1934), and Happy Laughter (1953); the 2,000 Guineas with Ellangowan (1923), Flamingo (1928), and Blue Peter (1939); the Derby with Blue Peter (1939) and Ocean Swell (1944) and the St. Leger with Sandwich (1931).

His favourite pastimes, apart from the routine of flat racing, were shooting, fishing, coursing, pigeon racing and cricket. When proudly showing his trophies at Park Lodge, he once confided that he caught a salmon with his very first cast. As for coursing, he won the Waterloo Cup with an entry named Jovial Judge, while he successfully raced a pigeon in the Banff-Newmarket championship race. As a shot he could hold his own with anyone, and his one-time prowess with bat and ball earned him many favourable mentions.

Newmarket owes much to Jack Jarvis for his keen interest in local affairs. At the time of his death he was no longer a member of West Suffolk County Council, on which he gave so much distinguished service. For example, he played a prominent part in the founding of the Old Folks' Home at Exning, which is a memorial to the late Lord Glanely. He was also proud of the fight he led to save the Newmarket Fire Brigade from being moved—believe it or not—in an economy drive to Bury St. Edmunds, 15 miles away.

Jack Jarvis in some respects belonged to the old school. He disliked starting stalls and considered them to be "a necessary evil". He was also strongly against a Tote monopoly, and overnight declarations, with their fines for absentees. Yet nobody in some ways could have been younger in outlook. He was interested in every detail going on around him and he was always loyal to his devoted staff. His patience, skill and enthusiasm will be sadly missed by all those who were privileged to know him and these included almost everyone who mattered in the racing world.

December 20, 1968.

Lord Jenkins, P.C., a Lord of Appeal in Ordinary (1959–63) and a Lord Justice of Appeal (1949–59), who chaired the Company Law Committee, died on July 21, 1969. He was 70.

The report of the Company Law Committee, published in 1962, was the first major inquiry into the legal structure of British industry, commerce and finance since 1945 and gave it a relatively clean bill of health. Its recommendations were mainly of a consolidating nature. The committee strongly suggested that owners of 10 per cent or more of the equity capital of a company whose shares are quoted on a recognized stock exchange should be required to notify the extent of their holdings to the company as well as any changes in these holdings.

Unassuming yet assured, Jenkins proved himself one of the greatest judges of a generation. The visible proof—before he became a Lord of Appeal—was the almost monotonous regularity with which his dissentient judgments in the Court of Appeal were followed (usually unanimously) by the House of Lords. His grasp of the law was well-nigh canny in its precision.

Called to the Bar by Lincoln's Inn, in 1923, David Llewelyn Jenkins took silk in 1938. He was Attorney General of the Duchy of Lancaster from 1946 to 1947. He was a Judge in the Chancery Division from 1947 to 1949. Jenkins was chairman of the committee of inquiry set up in 1957 to report to the Lord Chancellor on the effect on the liability of insurance companies of special conditions and exceptions in their policies.

Jenkins was educated at Charterhouse where he was a Scholar, and Balliol College, Oxford, where he was Domus Exhibitioner. He served in the First World War with the British Expeditionary Force in France. In 1922 he took a degree in Greats at Oxford. During the Second World War, he held a temporary commission in the R.A.S.C. In 1950 he became an honorary fellow of Balliol College, Oxford. He was a governor of Sutton's Hospital in Charterhouse, 1953–65. In 1959 he was granted a life barony.

July 23, 1969.

Sir Hilary Jenkinson, C.B.E., Deputy Keeper of the Records and Keeper of the Land Revenue Records from 1947 to 1954, died on March 5, 1961, in a London hospital. He was 78.

His official career was one of great significance for the Public Record Office since at every stage of it he made decisive original contributions to the organization and development of the department's activities, many of which he himself initiated. He was well known as an authoritative writer and lecturer on every aspect of the study and administration of archives (a word which owes its modern currency in Britain almost entirely to his preference for it) and much of his work either broke new ground or represented a new approach to neglected problems. Certainly he did more than most men living to raise the standards of archival work throughout the country, to improve the position of archivists, and to bind them together in a community for the permanent good of their profession.

His early environment fostered an interest in archives. His uncle, Francis Jenkinson, was familiar to generations of Cambridge men as the university librarian; and his father, William Wilberforce Jenkinson, encouraged his children, of whom Hilary was the youngest son, to inquire into all things, old and new.

Charles Hilary Jenkinson was born on November 1, 1882, and educated at Dulwich and Pembroke College, Cambridge, where he graduated with first class honours in Classics. He entered the Record Office, after open competition, on January 1, 1906, and after various promotions became Principal Assistant Keeper and Secretary in 1938 and Deputy Keeper in 1947.

During the 1914–18 War he was commissioned in the Royal Garrison Artillery, served in France and Belgium from 1916 to 1918 and was then employed in the War Office as G.S.O.3 until his demobilization in 1920. During part of the 1939–45 War he was lent to the War Office for special duties in connexion with the protection of Italian and German archives, which he carried out with conspicuous success, partly because he and several of his assistants had technical training in the Record Office and partly because of his own quickness of thought and action, since salvage delayed was never done.

His early days at the Record Office were spent in the Literary Search Room, where his wide knowledge of sources, printed and manuscript, and his friendliness to students were highly appreciated. He was later in charge of the Repository and the Repairing Department where he did what may have been his most valuable work. He had three qualities which enabled him to transform the physical appearance of the records and make them easy and safe to produce. He had the sensitive hands of a craftsman: he had a thorough knowledge of archive materials, ink, paper and parchment; and thirdly he found full scope for his abiding passion for perfection. From 1938 to 1947, as Secretary and Principal Assistant Keeper, he was mainly concerned with the preservation of the archives during the war; and it is enough to say that they emerged from that ordeal unscathed.

On becoming Deputy Keeper his first problem was storage, plans for the extension of the office, made in 1939, being indefinitely postponed; and he had also to complete the existing scheme for office reorganization. He reintroduced arrangements (in abeyance during the war) for young graduates of fellowship standard to work for two years in the office so that afterwards they could teach history with a practical knowledge of its sources. He also revived a consultative committee of historians to advise him as to problems of publication. He became acting Commissioner of the Historical Manuscripts Commission and chairman of the directorate of the National Register of Archives.

His extra-official activities were associated with his profession. From 1911 to 1935 he was the Maitland Memorial lecturer at Cambridge; and was Lecturer and later Reader in paleography and archives in London University. He also took an active part in the proceedings of the Society of Antiquaries, the Surrey Record Society and records committees.

His work for the British Records Association needs special mention. He as much as anyone was responsible for its foundation in 1932, though he owed much to the support of Lord Hanworth and to the experience of Miss Ethel Stokes. As joint secretary until 1947 and since then as vice-president he was able to foster interest in local archives with remarkable success and to bring about their registration throughout the country and the establishment of Record Offices in many counties.

In 1915, in collaboration with Charles Johnson, he published a book on the English Court Hand to the end of the eighteenth century and in 1927 a volume on the later Court Hands; and he was a frequent contributor to the *English Historical Review*, *Archaeologia* and the *Antiquaries' Journal*. His *Manual of Archive Administration*, published in 1922 under the auspices of the Carnegie Trust and revised in 1937, did much to clarify archive theory and to standardize practice and may be regarded as his apologia.

He was made C.B.E. in 1943 and was knighted in 1949; in the latter year he received an honorary doctorate of letters at Aberdeen. He retired in April, 1954, but retirement brought no lessening of his activities and he was generous with his time and his counsel; the Historical Manuscripts Commission in particular greatly benefited from his help. In 1957 Oxford University Press published and Mr. J. Conway Davies edited *Studies Presented to Sir Hilary Jenkinson*, a record of gratitude to which his colleagues and pupils contributed.

He married in 1910 Alice Violet, daughter of the late Andrew Knox Rockards, who shared his interests, being a trained historian and the author of many contributions to the Victoria History of her own county, Bedfordshire. She died in 1960. In his early days he excelled at lawn tennis and Rugby football, but as time passed, he devoted himself more and more to his profession.

Two relaxations he never forwent, his garden on the banks of the Arun and his appreciation of Provencal life and living.

March 7, 1961.

Sir Ivor Jennings, K.B.E., Q.C., Master of Trinity Hall, Cambridge, and Downing Professor of the Laws of England, died in hospital in Cambridge on December 19, 1965. He was 62.

He was a lawyer by training who attained high distinction through his contributions in the field of constitutional problems and the machinery of government while shouldering during much of his career the burdens of important academic offices, one of which, the vice-chancellorship of the University of Ceylon, kept him abroad during the 15 years 1940 to 1955.

Born in 1903 he was educated at Bristol Grammar School and St. Catharine's College, Cambridge, where he was an outstanding student carrying off a number of prizes. After a spell as a lecturer in law at Leeds he went to the London School of Economics in 1929, first as a lecturer and later as a reader in English law. During his 11 years in London he wrote seven legal treatises for the use of practitioners in such fields as the poor law, housing, public health, and local authority administration.

Three books written during this period, *The Law and the Constitution* (fifth edition 1959), *Cabinet Government* (third edition 1958) and *Parliament* (second edition 1958), brought him into the front rank of writers on the constitution. Although he approached his task from the side of a constitutional lawyer, his primary concern in these books was to describe in detail the practices of English government and political institutions. He was therefore less inclined than the classic constitutional writers who preceded him to require what he observed to conform to theory.

His view of the constitution as the developing arrangements for party government, and his view of political parties as being founded in divisions of opinion, led Jennings to continue his exposition with a trilogy under the general title of *Party Politics*. These came out in 1960–62 and were concerned respectively with the electoral system, party organization, and political ideas, issues and principles.

CEYLON UNIVERSITY

It was a logical and noble design, to move with the same descriptive and historical treatment from the Cabinet, the seat of power, to Parliament, to the electorate, to the parties, to the divisions of principle and opinion in which all the rest is rooted. And it is a pity to have to record that the nearer he came to the climax of his work the less satisfactory it became.

In 1940 he was appointed Principal of Ceylon University College founded in 1921. It had long been the intention to raise the college to the rank of university, but the change was delayed by a prolonged controversy over the site; in 1938 it was decided that the site should be at Peradeniya, near Kandy, which involved a move from Colombo over a distance of 70 miles. It thus fell to him to plan the site and undertake the move which could not begin until after the war; under his guidance full use was made of what is probably the most beautiful situation of any university in the Commonwealth. It also fell to him to design a constitution for the University of Ceylon which came into being in 1942 and of which he became vice-chancellor, and grew greatly in size and reputation during his term of office; standards, secured by the use of external examiners from Great Britain, were recognized as equal to those prevailing at home. But great as were his services to the university, his services to Ceylon in the struggle for independence were even more memorable. From 1943 to 1948 he was, to use his own words, "virtually enrolled as honorary constitutional adviser" to the Ceylonese Ministers whose complete confidence he won. He advised them on the strategy and tactics to attain independence, and he took a large part in drafting the constitution of Ceylon; after independence the political leaders retained the habit of seeking his advice.

WIDE REPUTATION

His achievements in Ceylon gave him a wide reputation as an authority in constitutional and academic matters. He was constitutional adviser to Pakistan in 1954–55 for the drawing up of whose constitution he was largely responsible. He was called upon for similar help in relation to other countries, for example in Malaya in 1956–57. His success as vice-chancellor of the University of Ceylon led to his membership of the Commission on University Education in Malaya in 1947, and to the presidency of the Inter-University Board of India in 1950. After his return to England on his election to the Mastership of Trinity Hall he was made chairman of the Royal University of Malta Commission. These experiences were the basis of books dealing with the constitution of Ceylon, the economy of Ceylon, and the constitutions of India and Pakistan, and also of three publications concerning constitutional and other problems of the Commonwealth in which he had become deeply interested. From 1955 to 1958 he was chairman of the Royal Commission on Common Land, to whose report he contributed a characteristically lucid appendix on the complicated social and legal history of the commons. From 1961 to 1963 he became vice-chancellor of the University of Cambridge.

SENSE OF PUBLIC DUTY

To his colleagues in London in the decade before the war it was a puzzle how any man could carry through and publish so much work, always of high quality, including two books which made a wide and enduring impression upon the thought of the period. This was not done at the expense of teaching and other academic duties; he was a devoted and successful teacher. This accomplishment was only possible because he allowed himself little or no time for leisure or recreation; he has in fact recorded that his recreation was "books".

He was moved by a strong sense of public duty, he never spared himself, and his unusual powers of clear thinking, concentration, logical analysis and hard work enabled him to render services of great value to his generation at home and abroad. In 1963, with his wife and a married daughter, Mrs. Dewing, he was on board the ill-fated cruise liner Lakonia which caught fire and later sank in the eastern Atlantic. After the crew in their lifeboat had given up rowing Mrs. Dewing and Mr. David Decent, a London photographer, took the oars and Jennings navigated the boat.

He was the recipient of many honours. He was a Fellow of the British Academy, a Q.C., a Master of the Bench of Gray's Inn, and an honorary graduate of many universities. He married in 1928 Helena Konsalik by whom he had two daughters.

December 20, 1965.

Douglas Jerrold died on July 21, 1964, after a long illness. He was 70.

Descended from the Douglas Jerrold and Laman Blanchard of Thackeray's circle, he was born at Scarborough on August 3, 1893, and brought up in the spacious atmosphere of late Victorian Liberalism, in which he learnt that contempt for vulgarity of thought and action which was fundamental in his outlook. The mental discipline of the Roman Catholic religion, in which he was bred, was profoundly congenial to his mind.

He was educated at Westminster, where he concluded a brilliant scholastic career by becoming Captain of the School and winning an open History Scholarship to New College in 1912. At Oxford, inevitably, he founded a paper, made many friends, and engaged in Union politics. In 1914 he was commissioned in the Royal Naval Division, whose historian he later became.

The war years were the happiest of Jerrold's life. He was to feel and to write passionately on many subjects, but on none more wholeheartedly (following Winston Churchill's strategic ideas) than on the evacuation of Gallipoli, his first battleground. His left arm was shattered in an ill-planned attack in France in 1916. In the summer of 1918 he joined the rationing division of the Ministry of Food, and as a temporary civil servant he made his mark in the transport strike of 1919. He joined the permanent Civil Service the next year, remaining at the Treasury till the end of 1923.

ENGLISH REVIEW

The last years of the Lloyd George Government, as seen from a Treasury desk, finally destroyed Jerrold's faith in Liberalism. Certain Liberal characteristics remained (he never discarded Free Trade principles); but a romantic Toryism became for him the only possible creed. He expressed his disgust of post-war materialism in the novel *The Truth about Quex* and his positive convictions in *Storm over Europe*, a Ruritanian story of the moral decline of a Liberal leader surrounded by interested men and his overthrow by a traditionalist rebel serving a spurious princess. Convinced of the derivation of all political power from God and of the freedom of the human soul, Jerrold detested and despised all theories that neglected the former or invaded the latter postulate, and was incapable of seeing even a measure of good in any action that did not proceed immediately from both.

He was inclined to view almost any compromise as *la trahison des clercs.* In this spirit he was to write his critical books—*They that take the Sword*; *The Necessity of Freedom*; and *Britain and Europe 1900–1940*.

On leaving the Treasury, Jerrold joined Sir Ernest Benn's publishing firm. Here he was associated with another former Liberal—Victor Gollancz, who was then reacting in an equal but opposite sense from his former convictions. Jerrold, with many literary friends and a keen appreciation of style, found his true *metier* in this trade. Leaving Benn's to found the publishing side of Messrs. Eyre and Spottiswoode, he increased his influence and experience. His expanding business was ultimately to include the control of other firms.

In 1930, Jerrold was appointed editor of the *English Review*. Under him, the paper became the rallying ground of intellectual Toryism in the 1930s, and as such attracted a brilliant group of writers. Unhappily, the Tory reading public was too small; and the paper collapsed in 1936. Its spirit was to revive in 1944 in *The New English Review*, again edited by Jerrold. Regular contributors included Hugh Kingsmill, Charles Petrie, and A. G. Street. In connexion with the first *English Review* venture, Jerrold founded a luncheon club at which Tory policy was formulated in a number of challenging addresses. The most prominent politician associated with this movement was the late Lord Lloyd.

THE FRANCO RISING

In Republican Spain Jerrold saw the incarnation of all the policies which he most detested—a very triumph of evil and falsehood. He was early involved in the rising of Franco. In his autobiography *Georgian Adventure* Jerrold tells of a Spaniard who walked into his publishing office to ask for 50 machine-guns and half a million rounds; and of the Savoy luncheon table request for "A man and three platinum blondes to fly to Africa to-morrow." Typically, Jerrold found the man (Hugh Pollard) and two blondes; and Franco was securely conveyed from the Canaries to Morocco. That was life as Jerrold loved it: in the Spanish war he renewed his youth, and perhaps it was only the shattered arm that held him back from Franco's fighting line. It was, however, the revolutionary in Franco that appealed to him—he had no sympathy with Fascism as a system and detested Nazism.

In the early 1930s Jerrold contemplated writing a biography of Charles I, but he abandoned the idea in favour of a one-volume History of England on the lines of Jacques Bainville's *Histoire de France*. Further reflection, however, convinced him that this could not be done, so he decided to write it in four volumes, of which the first, which closed with the loss of Normandy in 1204, appeared in 1949. During the last years of his life, and in particular since his retirement from active publishing in 1959, he had been engaged upon its successor which was to take the narrative down to the fall of Wolsey, but he was hampered by bad health. That he did not live to finish the work must be a matter of regret to all scholars, who will lament the incompletion of a highly individual and valuable contribution to history.

In 1919 Jerrold married Eleanor, daughter of Mr. Henry Arnold. There were no children of the marriage.

July 23, 1964.

Fatima Jinnah, sister of Pakistan's founder Muhammad Ali Jinnah and opponent of President Ayub Khan in the last presidential elections, died at her home in Karachi on July 9, 1967. She was 74.

Miss Jinnah, who fought alongside her brother for the creation of Pakistan, stood unsuccessfully against President Ayub Khan in the presidential election in March, 1965, as candidate for the combined opposition parties.

Miss Jinnah lived at the heart of the political turbulence that ultimately split the sub-continent of India into two nations but it was not until she was 72 that, emerging from the seclusion of over a decade, she played an important part in her own right. As the sister of Muhammad Ali Jinnah, the founder of Pakistan, and as a known critic of the regime of President Ayub, she was a natural rallying point for the disparate opposition parties that in the cause of a return to parliamentary democracy opposed him in Pakistan's first general elections, over the turn of 1964 and 1965. She brought to her campaign a burning dedication, accusing the President of betraying the memory of her brother as well as the interests of the nation, and she received huge and tumultuous welcomes wherever she campaigned. Some of those who greeted her did so because she was opposing a government that had lost popularity, others because she was the sister of the Qaid-e-Azam; but her small, wispy figure had something indomitable about it and it seemed that the great crowds were expressing affection for her too.

Miss Jinnah, who was born in 1893, was 18 years younger than her brother, and after the death of their father when she was eight she lived with him. She was educated in Bombay (where her brother had preceded her from their birth place in Karachi), at a mission school and then studied dentistry.

SOCIAL STATUS OF WOMEN

In 1929 she accompanied Jinnah to the Round Table Conference in London, and brother and sister stayed on in England for four years after that. With the reorganization and galvanization of the Muslim League on Jinnah's return to India, she joined the party and became a member of the provincial branch's working committee as well as of the League's national council. She concerned herself with women's welfare work, opposing within the League the strong forces of orthodoxy that gave its social policies their conservative character, and after the creation of Pakistan she continued to devote her energies to the social liberation of her sex.

After the death of her brother, whose side she had rarely left during his lifetime, Miss Jinnah went into secluded retirement. She emerged briefly in 1954 when she was persuaded to go to the east wing of the country to campaign there for the Muslim League, threatened by the Awamy League of Mr. Suhrawardy. Then as later she was warmly greeted by the public but was unable to sway their political inclinations on that occasion and the Muslim League was almost swept from the province. Once more she retired from the public view, to emerge at rare intervals, the anniversaries of her brother's birth or death, or other national celebrations, to issue statements on the state of the nation. After the military coup in 1958 these statements began to take on an increasingly critical note and by the early nineteen sixties it could be said that she was an undisguised opponent of President Ayub's regime.

So when the combined opposition parties began in the summer of 1964 to seek a candidate who would attract public support against the President, Miss Jinnah was an obvious choice, only her age and the seclusion of her life seeming to make it unlikely that she would choose to throw herself into an election campaign. To the general surprise and to the chagrin, if not the consternation, of the Government she agreed to stand for the presidency as the candidate of the combined opposition, responding, as she put it, to the call of the people for a leader in their struggle for political freedom.

Miss Jinnah's own opposition to President Ayub and his regime was founded in what she considered to be its oppressive ways, its rough impatience with criticism whether from politicians or the press, and its assumption that the Pakistanis were not suited or perhaps even able to conduct their affairs within the frame of parliamentary democracy. Her ideas of policy, of what a democratic government once returned should do, were never clearly expressed. She was in fact running not for office but against a system, and her intention was not to replace Field Marshal Ayub in the presidency but to do away with the sort of presidency that he had created.

President Ayub rashly described Miss Jinnah as the weakest candidate the opposition could have chosen, the truth being that she was the strongest, indeed perhaps the only candidate who could have drawn out the submerged but widespread disapproval with the regime in both wings of the country.

Miss Jinnah was a small, slight woman, her hair turned white at an early age and she wore it cut short and flaring freely round her face. She could be charming if she wished but was readier to be acidulous, and her stinging tongue made those who worked with her, not to mention those who crossed her, walk carefully.

July 10, 1967.

His Holiness Pope John XXIII, who succeeded Pope Pius XII as Supreme Pontiff in 1958, died on June 3, 1963. He was 81.

He was in his seventy-seventh year when he took possession of the see of Rome, and there was some inclination to regard him as a "caretaker", an elderly Pope destined to preside over the consolidation of the changes wrought by his predecessor. A reasonable judgment has seldom been more completely mistaken. His pontificate produced an immediate and sustained change of atmosphere inside and outside the Church, it promoted internal reform and external conciliation, and it restored to Catholicism a sense of historical movement, something which, by the nature of ecclesiastical institutions, is prone to become overlaid by a cautious conservatism.

The new impetus was derived from small acts, like the Pope's abatement of Vatican ceremonial, and great acts, like his convocation of a general council. Whether small or great they were part and parcel of his conception of the nature of his office. "Some hope to find in the Pope", he said, preaching at his coronation Mass, "a skilled diplomat and statesman; others a scholar, an organizer of public affairs, or one whose mind is in touch with every kind of modern progress. . . . They are none of them on the right track . . . the new Pope has before his mind, more than all else, that wonderful picture which St. John gives, in the words of the Saviour himself, of the Good Shepherd."

INFORMAL APPROACH

It was as a shepherd of his people, as *servus servorum Dei*, that he sought to impress on the world the sacred obligations of his office, not by hieratic solemnity or the worldly dignity of a court. In this his appearance helped: the coarse strength of his peasant features was expressive of benignity and simple humanity. His personal actions too were suited to his purpose: visits to the sick in Rome and to the prisoners in the Regina Coeli, his eagerness to dispense with ceremony, and his informal encounters. Above all, his conception of his office issued in his teaching, which had a universality of reference matching, as has not always happened, the universality of papal diction.

The principal sources of his teaching are the two encyclicals, *Mater et Magistra* (1961) and *Pacem in Terris* (1963), and his homilies concerning the second Vatican Council. In the first of these encyclicals he extended the social teaching of his predecessors Leo XIII and Pius XI, enlarging on the duties owed by a society to the underprivileged within it and by prosperous nations to those which are not. He returned to the latter question in *Pacem in Terris* in which he declared that it is "vitally important that the wealthier states, in providing varied forms of assistance to the poorer, should respect the moral values and ethnic characteristics peculiar to each, and also that they should avoid any intention of political domination".

In another passage the Pope extended the principle of subsidiarity, familiar in papal teaching on the state, to the field of international relations, arguing the necessity for "a public authority, having world-wide power and endowed with the proper means for the efficacious pursuit of its objective". This authority would not supplant individual political communities but would exist to tackle economic, social or political problems which are "posed by the universal common good" and are too large or complex or urgent to be amenable to solution by individual states.

The part of the encyclical which attracted most attention concerned relations between Catholics and others in the pursuit of public goals. Having reminded the faithful that error is not to be confused with the erring person, and that false philosophies regarding man and the universe are not identical with their associated historical movements, in which there might be patches of good (a reference which was everywhere understood to embrace communism) he went on to say that "a drawing nearer together or a meeting for the attainment of some practical end, which was formerly deemed inopportune or unproductive, might now or in the future be considered opportune and useful".

ECUMENICAL COUNCIL

Even this amber light signalling a more co-operative attitude (of which an illustration had been afforded a few weeks before by the Pope's reception in audience of Mr. Khrushchev's son-in-law) was too much for the more conservative spirits in the Curia and caused some embarrassment to the more zealous denunciators of communism and all its works; and there were not wanting those who attributed the electoral successes of the Italian Communist Party which followed to confusion sown in the minds of the faithful by the Pope's departure from rigidity.

It was, however, in his decision to summon an ecumenical council, and even more in the role he assigned to it, that the historical importance of his pontificate lay. His decision was both an initiative and a response within the quickening movement towards Christian unity. The context, that of unity in which the decision was announced led to some initial confusion. It was thought possible that, like the fifteenth-century Council of Florence, the second Vatican Council might be concerned with formal overtures to separated hierarchies or with the preparation of doctrinal formulae to which other Churches might be found to subscribe. In fact, as the Pope was soon to make clear, the council was to be more immediately concerned with the unfinished business of the Vatican Council of 1870, and its approach to unity was to be along the only road giving any promise of lasting progress namely, the preparation of Christian minds and the removal of unnecessary obstructions erected by historical prejudices and by the ubiquitous ecclesiastical gift for defining and institutionalizing differences.

He gave the chief task of the council as being concerned with the spread of the Catholic faith, the renewal of right standards of morality, and the bringing of ecclesiastical discipline into closer accord with the needs and conditions of the times. The Italian word *aggiornamento* aptly signifies the process of adaptation that was to be undertaken; and it was to be pursued, not by the traditional method of condemning the errors of others but by presenting the life and teaching of the Catholic Church in a positive form. This was to be the council's task of preparation in the cause of Christian reunion. Although the Pope did not live to see this work carried through his guidance during the preparatory and opening phases of the council meant that the work was well begun.

Angelo Giuseppe Roncalli was born at Sotto il Monte, some eight miles from Bergamo in the foothills of the Italian Alps, on November 25, 1881. The eldest son of Giovanni and Maria Roncalli, who had 12 other children, he came of a line that had farmed their own land near Bergamo for some five centuries, living frugal and independent lives.

FIRST APPOINTMENT

At the age of 11 he entered the junior seminary at Bergamo, proceeding to the major seminary and in 1900 to Rome where he took his degrees in theology. He was ordained in 1904 in Rome and said his first Mass in the Basilica of St. Peter, where in later years he sang his first Pontifical High Mass as Bishop and eventually was crowned as Pope.

The young priest's first appointment was as private secretary to Mgr. Radini-Tedeschi, newly consecrated Bishop of Bergamo, who had a profound influence on him and whom he described in later years as "the pole star of my priesthood". A man of learning and saintly life, the Bishop was a pioneer in Catholic Action, particularly with regard to the promotion of Christian social principles.

In addition to his duties as secretary, Father Roncalli taught theology in the seminary where he had studied for the priesthood and devoted what time he could spare to research into the history of his native province. His interest in research was fostered by Bishop Radini, who, during a visit to Milan, introduced him to the Librarian of the Ambrosian Library, Mgr. Achille Ratti, the future Pope Pius XI. Thus he received special facilities for his studies, during which he came upon a mass of documents concerned with St. Charles Borromeo and his visits to Bergamo, which he used as the basis of a work extending over the years to six volumes, the last one appearing after his election as Pope.

Bishop Radini died in 1914. In the same year his secretary was conscribed for military service and became a sergeant in the medical corps. Subsequently as a lieutenant he was appointed chaplain to military hospitals.

During and after the 1914–18 War Fr. Roncalli developed plans for religious training in teachers' training colleges and in secular schools, and when the seminary at Bergamo reopened he played a considerable part in its spiritual direction, without resuming his former position on the faculty. His powers of organization and his increasing popularity as a preacher marked him out for advancement and in 1921 Pope Benedict XV, in the closing months of the pontificate, summoned him to Rome to become national director of the Association for the Propagation of the Faith. Four years later Pope Pius XI appointed him to the titular see of Areopolis and named him as Apostolic Visitor to Bulgaria.

His first experience in the diplomatic service of the Vatican gave him an opportunity to study the complex problems affecting the Eastern Churches, their relations with Rome, and the position of residents in Bulgaria who were of the Latin Rite. The knowledge he acquired in Bulgaria and later in Turkey and Greece served him throughout his life and inspired in him a longing for reunion between east and west. As later, in other countries, he travelled widely as his duties permitted, gained a working knowledge of the language, and in his dealings with the Bulgarian Government made continuous efforts to establish harmony.

DELICATE ROLE IN PARIS

He was transferred in November, 1934, to Istanbul as Apostolic Delegate to Turkey and Greece and as Administrator of the Latin Rite in Constantinople. His experience of ecclesiastical relations with eastern bodies was thus greatly enlarged. Over a period of 10 years he became very widely popular and he developed personal friendships both with members of the Turkish Government and with leading members of the Orthodox Church. In Greece his term of office was remembered particularly because of his successful efforts to relieve distress caused by the German occupation and the Allied blockade.

His recall from Turkey in 1944 was followed immediately by appointment as Papal Nuncio to France. The situation in Paris, to which the provisional Government had returned after the liberation of the city, was a particularly delicate one, because of the strained relations between leaders of the resistance movement and members of the hierarchy who they thought had supported the puppet Government at Vichy or had appeared to collaborate with the German occupation. One of the first steps taken by the Government was to ask the Holy See to recall the then Nuncio and it was expected that further representations would be made for the removal of a number of bishops from their sees. The new Nuncio, therefore, was called to exercise tact and patience in examining complaints, the majority of which were withdrawn within a very short time after his arrival in Paris. The arrival itself was dramatic, for, reaching the city on New Year's Eve, he prepared hurriedly an address to General de Gaulle which he delivered the next day as dean of the diplomatic corps, the Russian Ambassador senior in time of office standing beside him and fingering the address he had expected himself to read.

In 1953, after the reception of the Red Hat, Pope Pius XII appointed him to the Patriarchate of Venice, where he instituted the custom of holding open times for any of his flock to visit him privately and began unexpected visits to churches and parishes. When Pope Pius XII died in 1958 and the Patriarch left Venice for the Conclave, someone reminded him jokingly that in 1903 Pius X had left Venice with a return ticket. The Patriarch smiled and made no reply; but it was clear from his speech to the Cardinals on his election as Pope that he knew that he was *papabile*.

It was in the eleventh ballot that Cardinal Roncalli, Patriarch of Venice, was elected, surprising the Conclavists by taking the name of John, which had been his father's name and the patronal title of the church in which he was baptized. But in stating that he would be John XXIII he assumed the title of a fifteenth-century Anti-Pope. Surprise was caused too by his immediate prolongation of the Conclave by a day in order that he might hold a private consistory before the Cardinals dispersed.

GREGARIOUS NATURE

His predecessor had reigned for 19 years and had been responsible for remarkable developments in the life of the Church, notably in the revision of the Holy Week liturgy, the introduction of Evening Mass, and the relaxation of the Eucharistic fast. His reign was marked also by administrative changes natural to his rather solitary temperament in the course of which he discontinued the routine audiences of Cardinals in Curia, dispensed for much of his pontificate with the services of a Cardinal Secretary of State and tended generally to keep the reins of government in his own hands.

The new Pope, gregarious rather than solitary by nature, had shown a strong belief, as Patriarch of Venice, in the delegation of duties to free him for more active pastoral work. He had expressed his view of government as being to see everything without seeming to see much, and to correct it without seeming to do so. While paying warm personal tribute to Pope Pius XII, going so far as to suggest a possible canonization, he immediately ordered the resumption of curial audiences and began a series of informal and unexpected visits to administrative offices in the Vatican. Immediately after his coronation, seven days after the election, he began his frequent appearances in the streets of Rome, thus clearing away the last vestiges of the conflict between the Holy See and the Italian state.

It was said at the time that these informal appearances by Pope John XXIII outside the Vatican were intended by him to emphasize his dual position as Supreme Pontiff and Bishop of Rome, a point emphasized by his convocation of a Synod of Rome and by alterations in the appointment of Cardinal Bishops to ensure the exercise of episcopal duties. Apart from the formal drive to take possession of his Basilica of St. John Lateran, he preached in 1959 from an open-air altar erected beneath the Arch of Constantine, made Christmas visits to the inmates of the Regina Coeli prison in Rome and to the sick and aged in hospitals and homes. In the same year he resumed the ancient practice by which the Pope in person took part in the lenten processions to churches named as "stations".

One of his first formal acts as Pope was the elevation of 23 new Cardinals to the Sacred College. They included the late Cardinal Godfrey, Archbishop of Westminster, and Cardinal Tardini, who thereupon received appointment as Secretary of State, and they enlarged the composition of the College to 74 members, four more than the normal complement. By 1962 he had enlarged the membership of the Sacred College by a further 12.

The Pope's natural geniality allied to his knowledge of protocol made notable the visits to him by heads of state and reigning sovereigns.

ENGLISH QUEEN'S VISIT

Particularly notable was the visit in 1961 by Queen Elizabeth and the Duke of Edinburgh, as this was the first time that an English reigning Queen had visited the Pope since the Reformation. Equally significant, for another reason, was the visit in 1960 of the then Archbishop of Canterbury, Lord Fisher of Lambeth, a visit followed in the following year by the Moderator of the General Assembly of the Church of Scotland.

These two visits were regarded as being particularly important as evidence of the Pope's personal contribution to the spread of the ecumenical movement; and they occurred shortly after the proclamation of the outstanding event of the Pontificate, the holding in St. Peter's Basilica of the Second Vatican Council, which opened in October, 1962, and adjourned in December until the following September.

Three years were devoted to the preliminary work for the council, by specially created commissions, the Pope frequently presiding at sessions of the central commission. In addition the Pope created a separate secretariat for the promotion of Christian unity, headed by Cardinal Bea, who in 1962 visited England and lunched at Lambeth Palace with the Archbishop of Canterbury. The secretariat was responsible for the invitation to other churches to send representatives as observers at the council. That the Greek Orthodox Churches declined the invitation (although two observers came from the Russian Church) must have been a personal disappointment to Pope John.

GENTLE HINT

The council had not been long in session when the Pope issued a gentle hint that the assembled fathers could with advantage speed up their deliberations and restrain their pious loquacity, and he gave the presidency new powers to control debate, which were promptly used. A more important intervention followed. The *schema* on "the sources of revelation", which had been prepared with a conservative emphasis on the distinction between Scripture and tradition and which was judged by some to pay too little regard to modern biblical scholarship, encountered strong criticism. The debate having reached deadlock a motion to postpone further discussion of the *schema* was supported by a large majority but technically defeated. Thereupon the Pope intervened in favour of the majority opinion and ordered that the document be redrafted by a commission with which Cardinal Bea's secretariat was to be associated. The intervention was welcomed, and not only by the more "liberal" prelates.

Towards the end of November the Pope was confined to his apartments by illness. An operation for a prostate disorder was rumoured. There was, however, sufficient recovery in his health to enable him to make a brief appearance at the council on the day of its adjournment until the following September; and he was soon able to fulfil his normal engagements. On May 22, however, reports of another setback were confirmed when he had to cancel his general audience in St. Peter's. Although he more than once rallied bravely his condition then declined rapidly.

June 4, 1963.

Augustus Edwin John, O.M., R.A., who died on October 31, 1961, at his home at Fordingbridge, Hampshire, at the age of 83, was known for his extraordinary promise even while a student at the Slade School. Already a legend grew up about him and it lasted through his life. Bernard Shaw has said that we in England, not really caring for art, make too much fuss about some of our artists. We have the cult of the genius, whereas Botticelli, in his own time, was simply a good craftsman. Certainly there was from the first a cult of John as a genius, and he remained a nine years wonder.

It was said, when he was a student, that he could paint or draw in any style, like a master; and he used then to produce drawings which looked as if old masters had done them. This was well enough for a student, but not serious work, and all through his life he was encouraged by admirers not to be serious like Degas or Renoir or any of the great modern artists of France. It cannot be doubted that he equalled them in natural powers; but he never learnt to take those powers for granted. One suspects that he was always, to himself, the genius unaccountable and to be indulged in all artistic whims. Thus the world remained expectant about him, always ready to applaud his work, always wondering at its promise; no modern artist was so much praised or so little helped with rational criticism. But his most judicious admirers gradually became a little impatient; they asked him not for incessant masterpieces but for a regular and steady advance; they felt the absence in him of a sense of direction; and that, with all his great natural powers, he seems to have lacked.

It may seem ungrateful thus to speak of an artist who did so many beautiful things; but he gave one always the impression of not knowing his own mind, of working from hand to mouth, of not learning from his own past. It cannot be said that he deteriorated; but in any full exhibition of his work, it is to be doubted whether the latest would seem to be by an older, more experienced, more accomplished artist than the earlier. For some years he seemed to be marking time. It is long since he surprised and delighted us with his picture of "The Smiling Woman", which was bought by the Contemporary Art Society; and perhaps he never did anything since so completely finished and of equal intensity. His large groups of gypsies and the like were as fine as any large pictures by modern English artists; they contained figures and passages of extreme beauty, but with them other figures merely stylistic and passages of impatient carelessness. He was always engaged in projects full of promise but still projects; he seemed in his largest works to say: "Thus I would paint a picture if I had the mind to."

PASSION FOR BEAUTY

Of late years John became more and more occupied with portraits, and, no doubt, he was the chief of modern English portrait-painters. But here too he did not seem to be making any consistent advance, to have any profound interest in his sitters, or to be achieving any certain method of expressing such interest. Again and again he would produce a vivid sketch of a human being; but they were nearly always sketches, with the emphasis laid triumphantly and precisely on some obvious aspect of character. And so it was in all his work; the emphasis was laid on the obvious, and what people enjoyed was the force with which it was laid. He had a passion for beauty rare in English artists, he was himself a Welshman—but the passion does not seem to have been disciplined by any intellectual passion. He pursued beauty greedily with his pencil or his brush, and would pursue the same beauty over and over again, sometimes doing violence by over-emphasis when he was tired with the repetition of it.

Perhaps his finest work was the large decoration which he did for the Arts and Crafts Exhibition at Burlington House. That looked like an improvisation, but it was complete, and it had a beauty of colour not imposed on the form as in some of his work, but at one with it. It was a picture thoroughly conceived and painted without any falling short of the conception. Seeing it, one forgot the many trifles he produced utterly unworthy of his powers, mere repetitions of each other, but eagerly bought by a public which had learnt to think of him as the great genius who could do nothing wrong.

We in England have many artists of talent, but we do not make the best of them; we spoil them, if we can, with indiscriminate praise or else ignore them. It cannot be said that John was spoiled; he kept always his passion for beauty, and the greatest things were still to be expected of him, were still possible. But his fame is not as secure as it ought to be, considering the fact that no modern Englishman has equalled his natural powers of draughtsmanship, and very few Frenchmen.

John, who was the son of a Welsh solicitor, E. W. John, was born at Tenby in 1878, and but for his early proofs of artistic talent he might have followed his father's profession. His mother, who died when he was five, was an amateur artist. After his general education at Tenby and at a private school at Clifton, John at the age of 17 entered the Slade School with a scholarship of £60 for three years which he won with his painting of "The Brazen Serpent".

SPOKE GYPSY TONGUE

He began to exhibit in 1898 at the New English Art Club, where most of his work continued to be shown until 1921, when he was elected A.R.A. He became R.A. in 1928, but in 1938 he resigned as a protest against the rejection by the selecting jury of Wyndham Lewis's portrait of T. S. Eliot—an incident that gave rise to some very lively correspondence in *The Times*. In the same year John's portrait of Bernard Shaw with his eyes closed was bought by the Queen Mother. In 1940 he was re-elected a member of the Royal Academy and two years later he received the Order of Merit. In the spring of 1954 a loan exhibit of some 450 of his works was organized at Burlington House by the Royal Academy, and perhaps what then most forcibly struck visitors was the vein of true poetry that ran through his work.

John was a man of wide general culture and, when in the mood, a brilliant conversationalist. He travelled a good deal painting in out-of-the-way places, and he had a special liking for gypsies, whose language he spoke. From time to time he produced a good many etchings, which were catalogued in 1920 by Campbell Dodgson. John is represented at the Tate Gallery by no fewer than 16 works, including "The Smiling Woman" and portraits of T. E. Lawrence, Mme. Suggia, Sir Herbert Barker, and Lord David Cecil.

The range of his portraiture was wide and his literary subjects—James Joyce, W. B. Yeats and Dylan Thomas—produced some of his most striking work.

Some of his sitters were among his sharpest critics. One, the first Lord Leverhulme, who died in 1925, commissioned a portrait of himself from John in 1920. The result incensed the subject: he cut the head from the picture and placed it in his safe, sending the mutilated canvas back to John, who not surprisingly asked for an explanation. Leverhulme, in his turn, wrote back expressing his distress and made a clean breast of the affair. Some years ago, after Lord Leverhulme, grandson of the sitter, had discussed the matter with John, the head was "regrafted" to the body of the portrait by Dr. Johann Hell and it was then placed on exhibition at the Lady Lever Art Gallery at Port Sunlight.

In the last year of his life 49 paintings which had for years been lying forgotten in a cellar were shown at Messrs. Arthur Tooth and Sons in Bruton Street, W. They included an unfinished three-quarter length portrait of Queen Elizabeth the Queen Mother begun in 1940, a self-portrait, and a number of Welsh landscapes, nudes and studies of flowers and children. John published a vivid autobiography, *Chiaroscuro*, in 1952; a second volume remains uncompleted.

A robust, swashbuckling, romantic personality, he was memorably endowed with physical attributes.

He was an Hon. LL.D. of the University of Wales.

John was twice married. His elder sister, the late Gwen John, was an artist of singular refinement. One of his sons is Admiral Sir Caspar John, First Sea Lord.

November 1, 1961.

Captain W. E. Johns, the author, creator of "Biggles," whose exploits appeared in over 80 books, died on June 21, 1968, at the age of 75.

William Earl Johns was born at Hertford on February 5, 1893, and was educated at Hertford Grammar School. When he left at 16 he wanted to become a soldier, for his family had a long association with the Army going back to the Peninsular War. His parents, however, entered him as an articled pupil to a local municipal surveyor and when he qualified he was offered an appointment in Norfolk. He lost no time in joining the Norfolk Yeomanry.

When war broke out in 1914 Johns was called up and was soon serving in the Middle East with the Norfolk Yeomanry. In 1916 he was transferred to the Royal Flying Corps and he first learnt to fly an aircraft in that year at Thetford. In France he was posted to a two-seater day bomber squadron, and detailed to make raids on Rhine towns as a reprisal for the bombing of London. During one of these raids, on Mannheim in September, 1918, Johns was shot down by a famous German air ace, Ernst Udet, and was taken prisoner.

He was tried at Strasbourg and was sentenced to death for "bombing undefended towns"

ESCAPE

He succeeded in escaping from this prison before the sentence could be carried out, but was recaptured. This time he was sent to a punishment camp in Bavaria, and there he remained until the end of the war.

After his retirement he was Air Correspondent to a number of periodicals both in London and overseas. This was Johns's first venture into writing but he made an immediate impact on the aviation world; in 1932 he founded the monthly magazine *Popular Flying* and himself became editor.

In 1932 Johns first created his celebrated airman character "Biggles" in short story form, and he continued to appear in many short stories before appearing in book form. "Biggles", said his creator, "is typical of the type of British airman I knew during the Great War. His chief characteristics are courage, loyalty and sportsmanship." He soon became widely popular and Johns's reputation grew. He wrote three books at this time which added greatly to his growing reputation; they were *The Air V.C.'s*, *Fighting Planes and Aces*, and *Milestones of Aviation*.

On the outbreak of the Second World War Johns was recruited by the Air Ministry and for some time he lectured to air cadets on a variety of subjects from combat tactics to escaping from prisoner of war camps. By now Biggles was an established character in juvenile fiction and the Air Ministry persuaded Johns to create a female counterpart for recruiting purposes, "Worrals of the W.A.A.F." Soon the War Office followed suit and this time the character was "Gimlet", a Commando.

The fundamental characteristics of Biggles never changed at any time. He became as popular abroad as he had been in Britain and was translated into a score of languages. "This proved", said Johns, "that all boys everywhere are at heart the same in their admiration of the fundamental virtues in a man. A popular hero can be popular without recourse to brutality, coarse expletives or hard liquor."

"Bill" Johns was a popular figure both in Service circles and in the book world. His stocky, bulky figure, with his well-groomed iron-grey hair and friendly smile was always greeted with chaff and enthusiasm by his wide range of friends. Professionally he was a first-class craftsman. His work was delivered on time to editors to the exact length asked for: it was always checked and rechecked for accuracy in detail.

He leaves a widow.

June 22, 1968.

Daniel Johnson, Premier of Quebec Province and a moderate French Canadian leader, died in Manicouagan on September 26, 1968. He was 53.

Johnson had planned to visit Paris in October as part of his campaign to establish greater ties between Quebec and France. Tension between France and the Federal Government in Ottawa built up after President de Gaulle had shouted "Vive le Quebec Libre" from the balcony of Montreal city hall during his state visit in July, 1967. A leading spokesman for Canada's French-speaking population, Johnson succeeded Jean Lesage as Premier of Quebec in June, 1966, after his Union Nationale party had won a narrow majority in the Legislative Assembly.

A former journalist and lawyer, Johnson took a moderate line in the French Canadian struggle for greater autonomy, but was determined to establish greater contacts with France.

In a recent interview, Johnson declared that the movement by French Canadians towards self-determination was "irreversible". "It is an illusion to believe that it can be stemmed simply by proclaiming that French is an official language throughout Canada", he added. "The rest of Canada will have to admit that there is not only a linguistic community but also a quite distinct society".

This issue was put into even sharper focus in July last year when visiting President de Gaulle shouted the rallying cry of French-Canadian separatists. The French President cut short his visit in the storm of controversy which followed and which has continued ever since. Shortly before this visit Johnson had been received in style by President de Gaulle in France.

Expressing his differences with extremist separatists, Johnson said Quebec could not afford to drift away from the rest of North America. "Whether we like it or not, we are part of the North American continent and we cannot separate ourselves from it", he said.

In his Paris visit, which was to have started on October 11, Johnson planned to transmit an invitation to the French Government, through President de Gaulle, for a summit meeting between French and Quebec leaders in Quebec City in 1969.

SEAT FOR QUEBEC

Johnson was born on April 9, 1915, at Danville, Eastern Townships, Quebec, and educated at Saint-Hyacinthe College and read law at the Université de Montreal. Following a by-election in Bagot county, he was returned to the Quebec Parliament in 1946. In 1954 he was appointed parliamentary assistant to the late Premier Maurice Duplessis and two years later he became Deputy Speaker of the Legislative Assembly. He became a member of the Quebec Cabinet as Minister of Hydraulic Resources in 1958 and was elected leader of the Union Nationale Party in 1961. Johnson was appointed a K.C. in 1950: he was sometime legal adviser to the Association of French Language Weeklies. Johnson who was active in youth and professional organizations throughout his career was also formerly vice-president of Pax Romana.

He married Reine Gagne in 1943 and they had four children.

September 27, 1968.

Edward James Johnson, the Grand Old Man of Tennis, died on June 2, 1970. at the age of 91.

The rigorous training received from his father, who was for many years the professional at the first Lord Wimborne's court at Canford, fitted him well for an early post at Prince's Club, where he encountered all the leading players of his day. A short spell followed later at the Tuxedo Club, United States, but at the age of twenty-five he was back in England to watch the building of C. T. Garland's fine court at Moreton Morrell in 1905. There he was to remain as its devoted professional for the rest of his long life.

In 1908, Ted contested the World Championship at Brighton, losing by only the narrowest of margins to the redoubtable Punch Fairs. Later he was authorized to claim the coveted title, due to the default of the then holder, Covey, but he refused to accept an honour for which he had not fought. In his prime Ted was noted for the purity of his stroke and for the grace and skill of his game. He played before royalty on many occasions and it is said that King Edward the Seventh once missed the first race at Newmarket, being unable to tear himself away from an exhibition match in which Ted was performing. "Chases before races", was Ted's laconic comment.

All who knew him will tell of his great gift of friendship, of his modesty and of his staunch sense of fair play. When in the marker's box his word was law, and woe to anyone who fished for compliments after the game. His old-world courtesy was almost a ritual, seasoned occasionally with a pinch of impish fun.

He continued to train beginners almost till he retired at the age of 91. Ball after ball would be thrown on to the penthouse and the court would reverberate with well-timed cries of "Now!" Nothing gave him greater pleasure than to see his pupils improve. He once said wistfully of a very keen but totally inept performer: "If only I could put 15 onto his game and take 15 years off mine!"

June 4, 1970.

The Very Rev. Dr. Hewlett Johnson, Dean of Canterbury from 1931 to 1963 and popularly known as the "Red Dean", died on October 22, 1966, at the age of 92.

He was a baffling, complex and controversial figure. No Dean of Canterbury aroused more hostility; no Dean of Canterbury achieved such an international reputation. His critics were apt to speak of him as a clergyman who used his official position to advocate political doctrines which were held to be incompatible with Christianity. What they did not always appreciate was the comparative lateness of his championship of the Soviet Union. As Dean of Manchester he applied for a visa to enter Moscow, and the request was refused. It was not until he had reached his sixtieth birthday and had been at Canterbury for some years that he made the visit to Russia that left such an impression upon him.

Hewlett Johnson was born on January 25, 1874, the third son of C. H. Johnson, a Manchester mill owner, and Rosa Hewlett, daughter of Alfred Hewlett, who for more than half a century worked as curate and vicar of Astely in Lancashire where he was known as the "Spurgeon of the North". Johnson was educated at King Edward's School, Macclesfield, and at Manchester University where he took a B.Sc. in 1894, winning the Geological Prize. In 1898 he became an Associate Member of the Institute of Civil Engineering. Although he was trained for a business career, his social work in the slums of Manchester, combined with his religious upbringing, led him to offer his services to the Church Missionary Society. He was accepted on condition that he studied theology at Oxford. He entered Wadham College in 1900 and, gaining second-class honours, took his B.A. degree in 1904 and his M.A. four years later. But he was no longer *persona grata* with the Church Missionary Society. His liberal interpretation of the Scriptures offended the conservative evangelicals and he was not enlisted; instead he was ordained in 1905 to the title of St. Margaret, Altrincham, becoming vicar of the parish within three years, as a result of a petition signed by the two churchwardens and a large number of parishioners. Although his outspoken social views were not appreciated by some of the wealthy industrialists in the neighbourhood, the parish flourished under his vigorous leadership, the two outstanding features of his incumbency being the crowded children's services on Sunday afternoon, and the summer camps for young people. His work was recognized by the diocese and in 1919 he became an honorary canon of Chester Cathedral, and in 1922 Rural Dean of Bowden. In the same year he was elected a Proctor in Convocation.

EVERY INCH A DEAN

One of his most interesting ventures during the Altrincham period was his editorship of a theological magazine, *The Interpreter*. "Ignorance, not knowledge, is the enemy of Christianity", said the first number, published in 1905. "We seek the fullest light from every source to reveal the firm foundations of our Faith." In this search Johnson had the support of many scholars of his generation—Swete, Driver, Burkitt, Gwatkin, Streeter, Goudge, Ottley, Kirkpatrick, Barnes, Major. During the 20 years of its history the editor was known as a progressive parish priest with a penchant for popularizing Biblical research. His studies continued. In 1917 Oxford gave him the degree of Bachelor of Divinity and in 1924, for his work on the Acts of the Apostles, the Doctorate of Divinity.

In 1924, when Ramsay MacDonald was Prime Minister, Canon Johnson was appointed, as successor to Gough McCormick, to the deanery of Manchester. He quickly proved that he possessed many of the qualities that are looked for in a dean. He preached well, looked every inch a dignitary of the Church, was keenly interested in civic affairs, and had considerable charm. Moreover, his first wife, who was much loved in Manchester, was a great help.

CORDIALITY

But his relations with the Chapter were not always cordial. He had an enhanced idea of the position and authority of a dean and was apt to make alterations on his own initiative; for instance, his enthusiasm for improvements led him to order a new altar for the Jesus Chapel, and impressive inner doors with glass panels for the west end, so that passers-by could get a magnificent view of the nave and choir. But even his critics admitted his ability to attract large congregations to his popular evening services. And although 40 years have passed, Manchester still remembers a Dean, courteous and erudite, whose love for children was such that they came in increasing numbers to the cathedral, where he personally welcomed them.

In 1931 Johnson was transferred to Canterbury. Archbishop Lang, when in the northern province, had been favourably impressed by his work in Manchester. And there is reason to suppose that Lang and Archbishop Temple suggested Johnson's name to Ramsay MacDonald. The Prime Minister had moved far to the Right and had he thought that Hewlett Johnson was to prove susceptible to communist influences it is unlikely he would have considered the nomination. But at this time the Dean's political affiliations were uncertain. He was interested in industrial conditions; he deplored unemployment; he felt the Government should do more to ease economic tensions that brought hardship to the working classes. But in so far as he favoured one solution rather than another it was the theory of Social Credit as propounded by Major Douglas. And as late as 1935 he visited Alberta to acquaint himself more fully with the Douglas doctrines.

Why did Johnson transfer his interest from Alberta to Moscow? How was it that a man of his marked intelligence and ability found it possible to applaud a regime that was avowedly atheistic? These are not easy questions to answer, because in all probability Johnson committed himself without fully realizing the implications.

Hewlett Johnson always had had a passion for foreign travel—he claimed to have visited every cathedral in Europe—and, for a long time, he had had a deep concern for social studies.

RUSSIAN VISIT

These two bents now coalesced. Although his visa had been refused by the Soviet authorities, it was inevitable that he would eventually find his way to Russia. His chance came in the mid-thirties, when the Kremlin switched to a policy of coexistence with the western democracies. Its leaders were quick to appreciate the Dean's qualities as a propagandist. They were careful to impress him favourably. They knew the things that would appeal to a Christian, a social worker, and an engineer; and they knew how to exploit the foibles of a rather vain nature.

Johnson saw, and was conquered. His writings on Soviet achievements, particularly his book *The Socialist Sixth of the World* which had an enormous sale in many languages, help to explain the man. Although other students of the U.S.S.R. would question some of his facts and dissent from many of his conclusions, the significance of the book lies in what is ignored. Having decided that Soviet communism was helping the cause of human betterment, he refused to criticize. He admitted, in general terms, that there had been mistakes, but he would never deal with individual instances; and eventually, as was evidenced by his attitude towards events in Hungary, he seemed unable, and perhaps unwilling, to discriminate. He held fast to what he wanted to believe, and dismissed from his mind anything that might shatter his illusion. In 1964, when he was 90, he went to China.

HIS OVER-RIDING DUTY

And what of his work as Dean of Canterbury? Visitors to the cathedral could not fail to be impressed by his fine presence and resonant voice, and, if they met him personally, by his courtesy and friendliness of manner. As at Manchester, he could be a charming host and an interesting guide. The beauty of the cathedral and its great tradition of dignified ceremonial and music appealed strongly to the conservative strain in his character, and his judgment and taste in aesthetic matters were sensitive and well-informed. He was a man of wide culture, with an intelligent appreciation of the arts.

PSYCHICAL RESEARCH

As a preacher he continued to be eloquent and forceful. His favourite theme was the social implications of the Gospel; but that was not his only theme and at times he preached excellent sermons of a simply pastoral or homiletic kind. Pastorally he will be remembered for many acts of personal kindness. But the factors that made him a controversial figure in the world at large had an unfavourable effect on his influence locally. At times the strain on his relations with his fellow clergy and with some of the leading citizens of Canterbury became almost intolerable. That he should be concerned with social conditions was appreciated; but what appeared to be a completely uncritical acceptance of Stalinism caused bewilderment and indignation. And the apparent inconsistency between his position as Dean and his position as chairman of the editorial board of the *Daily Worker* cut at the roots of his influence. But in fairness to Hewlett Johnson it must be said that he had so adjusted himself that he was unconscious of any inconsistency. On the contrary he thought it was his over-riding duty to humanity in general, and to the Church of England in particular, to reconcile communism and Christianity. His eminent position as Dean of Canterbury he deliberately used as a means to that end.

Towards the end of his life Johnson concerned himself with psychical research. It was not a new interest. In fact at the reception that was held at King's College after the Enthronement of Michael Ramsey he told a friend that it was psychical research that had dented his atheism as a young man. Having devoted much of his life to making people aware of what he considered to be the social implications of the Gospel he decided that his remaining years should point his hearers to another dimension of reality. And it was typical of the man that he was as enthusiastic a propagandist of a life after death as he was of the communist Utopia. And he was convinced that dedication to scientific truth would eventually lead the Marxist to a proper understanding of personal survival.

SUBTLE CHANGE

Perhaps it was this transference of interest that mellowed him, and caused some critics to have second thoughts. Be that as it may, there was a subtle change in the atmosphere and Canterbury spoke of its eccentric dean with affection and respect.

Hewlett Johnson married twice. His first wife, Mary (*née* Taylor), died without issue in 1931. By his second wife, Nowell Mary (*née* Edwards), he had two daughters.

October 24, 1966.

Louis A. Johnson, United States Secretary of Defence in 1949–50, died in hospital in Washington on April 24, 1966. He was 75.

He was appointed Assistant Secretary of War by President Roosevelt in 1937 and became known as an outspoken advocate of military preparedness at a time when this was not a policy that found favour everywhere in the United States. He called for large-scale production of the B 17 bomber—the Flying Fortress—did a good deal of preparatory work for the mobilization of industry should war come; and drew up a plan for conscription which later provided the basis for the Selective Service Act. His attitudes were not those of his chief, Harry Woodring, Secretary of War, who felt that large-scale rearmament invited war. After Woodring had resigned in 1940 many felt that Johnson would win the succession, but Roosevelt had other ideas. Just as the Republican Party was gathering in Philadelphia for its 1940 national convention the President adroitly invited two of the Grand Old Party's elder statesmen, Henry L. Stimson and Frank Knox, to join his Cabinet. Stimson was made Secretary of War and Knox Secretary of the Navy. Johnson suffered a double disappointment, for Stimson asked for his resignation and then installed in his place Judge Patterson, a Republican, as Assistant Secretary of War.

That Roosevelt had no lack of faith in Johnson's abilities was made clear in the early spring of 1942 when the President chose him to lead the important mission to India with the rank of Minister. There he worked hard to assure Indians that America was well aware that the war was a world-wide one and not a European affair with an Asiatic sideshow.

He served as chairman of the finance committee of the Democratic Party in the 1948 election campaign and at a time when Democratic prospects were not thought to be of the brightest helped to raise $1,500,000.

In March, 1949, he succeeded James Forrestal as Secretary of Defence. He was instructed to keep down the defence budget at a time when the Administration was convinced that domestic inflation was a greater danger than foreign aggression, and was also given the difficult task of enforcing the unification of the three fighting services whether it was to their taste or not.

WIDELY BLAMED

It was later held against the unfortunate Johnson that he carried out his instructions with too much zeal; instead of warning the President of the risks of over-drastic pruning, he went out of his way to assure the American people that the American fighting services were equal to any demands. That they were not was soon shown by the course of events in the Korean War. He was widely blamed for United States military unreadiness and in September, 1950, he was dropped from President Truman's Cabinet and replaced by General George Marshall.

Born in 1891, Johnson entered politics shortly after his graduation from the University of Virginia law school, running for the office of mayor of Clarksburg, West Virginia. He was defeated by a narrow margin, but soon after, when he was 26 years old, was elected to the state's legislature. He became chairman of the judiciary committee and floor leader of the Democratic Party members in the legislature. In 1924 he was a delegate to the Democratic National Convention. He was national chairman of the Veterans' Advisory Committee to the Democratic National Committee from 1936 to 1940.

He was married and had two daughters.

April 26, 1966.

Eric Johnston, president of the Motion Picture Association of America since 1945, died in Washington on August 22, 1963, at the age of 67.

He has been described as "an emissary at large for capitalism". His varied career certainly showed that he both practised and preached his belief in the free enterprise system. In fact, he once wrote: "We are too mealy mouthed. We fear the word 'capitalism' is unpopular. So we talk about the 'free enterprise' system and run to cover in the folds of the flag and talk about the American way of life."

Born in Washington, D.C., in 1896, the son of a local chemist, Johnston was a self-made man, He is said to have started work at the age of six and to have continued working throughout his high school days and at the University of Washington, where he took a degree in law in 1917. Upon graduation he joined the United States Marine Corps, becoming a captain and serving until 1922, when he settled in Spokane, Washington state, married and entered business.

He invested in a vacuum cleaner concern that had been losing money and put it on a paying basis. Then he started another company in the same line of business and built it up into one of the biggest in the north-west. Meanwhile, he had made his mark as president of the Spokane chamber of commerce and entered the national field as a spokesman for business, becoming the youngest president of the United States Chamber of Commerce in 1942. This post he held for four years. Soon he was chairman or director of a dozen concerns ranging from airlines to banks and chain stores.

WORK FOR GOVERNMENT

The Government enlisted his services in a variety of roles, such as chairman of the inter-American economic development commission and member of the economic stabilization board. His high-powered salesmanship methods led to his being chosen in 1945 as president of the Motion Picture Association of America, a post that carried a salary of more than $ 100,000 a year. In that capacity he was responsible for organizing the industry's self-censorship, succeeding the Hays office with a less rigid code. His goal, as he described it, was "to make pictures reasonably accepted by reasonable people."

A handsome, youthful-looking man, Johnston was an effective spokesman for his country in many capacities. In 1963 he became the special representative of the President of the United States with the personal rank of Ambassador to the Middle East, and he made valiant efforts to evolve a constructive policy for coping with the Palestine refugee problem. His reports on this were received with approval by many countries and by the United Nations as a whole, but they foundered on the rock of Arab intransigence. Johnston was the recipient of honorary degrees from a dozen universities.

August 23, 1963.

Thomas Johnston, P.C., C.H., died on September 5, 1965, at the age of 83.

In his day one of the ablest practical minds in the British Labour movement he was Secretary of State for Scotland in the wartime Coalition Government from 1941 until 1945, and after he he had retired from Parliament for some years chairman of the North of Scotland Hydro-Electric Board and of the Scottish National Forestry Commissioners. He was Chancellor of Aberdeen University. In recent years he was widely regarded as the elder statesman of Scotland.

Possessed of a clear and orderly mind, a man of unswerving integrity of purpose, Tom Johnston commanded the whole-hearted respect of his political opponents as well as of his colleagues in the Labour movement and all those associated with him in public affairs in his native Scotland. In one sense, perhaps, he disappointed expectations. There was a time when he seemed a possible leader of the Labour Party and destined for the highest office. But Johnston himself was almost too disinterested a Socialist, possibly too modest a person also, to aspire to the heights of political responsibility. Much of his energy was concentrated on his long and lively editorship of the Scottish Labour journal, *Forward*, which he founded in 1906 and edited for 27 years from 1919. In the Commons, which he entered in 1922, he was all the more impressive in debate for a marked absence of personal ambition. As early as 1937 he announced his intention of retiring from Parliament at the next election, giving as his reasons the physical strain of travelling backwards and forwards between Glasgow and Westminster and his desire to devote himself to writing and to research. Only the outbreak of war in 1939 made him continue in active politics for longer than he had intended.

It was fortunate for Scotland that he did change his mind, for he was to prove an outstandingly successful Secretary of State. It is doubtful if any of his predecessors or successors equalled him as a spokesman for his country, vigorous, forthright, but always practical. The case for Scotland never went by default while he sat in the Cabinet.

FORMIDABLE PROPAGANDIST

Johnston's skill in using facts and figures, which lent an engaging touch of Scots didacticism to his combative debating style, was joined to genuine moral passion. Of sincerely Puritan temperament (he was a teetotaller by principle), he was a formidable Socialist propagandist, who for many years preached the I.L.P. doctrine with seriousness and moderation; he was shrewdly and—in the 1920s—very fairly described as "a moderate extremist". In 1945 he refused the peerage that was offered him in order that he might continue a parliamentary career, and became chairman of the Scottish National Forestry Commissioners. The following April he began his major task of the postwar years when he became chairman of the North of Scotland Hydro-Electric Board. Throughout his whole tenure of office he declined to draw the salary attaching to it, just as he had declined his Cabinet Minister's salary of £5,000 a year during 1941–45. In these later years he was held in continuously growing respect in Scotland and received many marks of honour, among them the freedom of Edinburgh.

Born in Kirkintilloch, Dunbartonshire, in 1882, Thomas Johnston was educated at the Lairdsland Public School there, at the Lenzie Academy, and at the University of Glasgow, where he was the contemporary of Walter Elliot. He had some general commercial experience, but soon went into the newspaper business and realized an ambition of his early years by founding the weekly Socialist journal, *Forward*. It promptly became one of the strongest influences for Socialism north of the Tweed. Johnston was an early associate of James Maxton and his Clydeside I.L.P. group. He served for some years on the Kirkintilloch town council and inaugurated various practical experiments in Socialism, including the foundation of the first Scottish municipal bank. When in 1931 he rose to be Lord Privy Seal Kirkintilloch made him its first freeman.

In 1914, as was to be expected, *Forward* took a strongly anti-war line, and during the subsequent troubles in the Glasgow munition factories was suspended for reporting a speech of Lloyd George's against orders. Characteristically Johnston asked to see Lloyd George, put his case, and secured the removal of the ban. *Forward* was, without question, a major factor contributing to the return of the large Labour group from Clydeside in the election of 1922. Johnston himself was returned for West Stirling and Clackmannan in that year and from the first established a reputation in the House of Commons for informed, dour and occasionally sardonic criticism. The impression of dourness, it should be said, sprang in part at least from the rather unmusical quality of his voice. He lost his seat in 1924, but came back almost immediately at a Dundee by-election caused by the death of E. D. Morel.

PRIVY COUNCILLOR

In 1929 he again represented West Stirlingshire and was appointed Under-Secretary for Scotland in the second Labour administration. He did first-rate work in that office, especially in connexion with housing, medical services, agricultural research and the fishing industry. In March, 1931, he succeeded Vernon Hartshorn as Lord Privy Seal, charged in particular with employment schemes, and was sworn to the Privy Council. One of the many notable Labour casualties in the "crisis" election of that year, he returned to Parliament for his old constituency in 1935.

In August, 1939, he was appointed Regional Commissioner for Civil Defence in Scotland, and in 1941 entered the Coalition Government under Mr. Churchill as Secretary of State for Scotland. Recognition of his services in wartime—and in earlier years—to his own land and people was evidenced in a variety of distinctions conferred upon him. He was made a freeman of the City of Edinburgh in 1944; a freeman of Campbeltown, Argyll, in the following year, as a tribute to his work for the Scottish herring industry; and, in the same year, an honorary Doctor of Laws of Glasgow University and an honorary Fellow of the Educational Institute of Scotland. This last honour, rarely conferred, was a mark of appreciation not only of his concern for Scottish education generally but of his distinctively unromantic views on the teaching of history, which he first elaborated in a *History of the Working Classes of Scotland* published in 1922. In his work, after the end of the Second World War, for Scottish electricity schemes and Scottish forestry he displayed the efficiency and the practical temper that were expected of him. He will be particularly remembered for the immense benefits which the Hydro-Electric Board brought to the north of Scotland during his term of office.

He resigned from the Forestry Commission in 1948 and from the Hydro-Electric Board in 1959.

In 1958 he became president of the British Electrical Development Association. He had also served as a member of the board of governors of the B.B.C., National Governor for Scotland, chairman of the Broadcasting Council for Scotland, and chairman of the Scottish Tourist Board.

In *Memories*, published in 1952, he gave his own account of his career in public life.

He was created C.H. in 1953.

Johnston was married and had two daughters.

September 6, 1965.

Arthur Creech Jones, P.C., Labour member of Parliament for the Shipley division of Yorkshire from 1935 to 1950, and for Wakefield from 1954 until the dissolution in September, 1964, and Secretary of State for the Colonies from 1946 to 1950, died on October 23, 1964 at the age of 73. He did not stand for Parliament in the 1964 general election.

Recognized as one of the Labour Party's leading experts on colonial affairs, he was the moving spirit behind the Labour Government's schemes for the political and economic development of the colonies. A modest and unassuming man, who began his career as a trade union official, he never seemed to be quite at home in the House of Commons. He was not a forceful speaker, and was not at his best when under fire from the Conservative Opposition. But he had a wide knowledge of affairs, and his sincerity and devotion to duty won him many friends. During his period of office the decision to go ahead with self-government for Ceylon was taken, and at the end of it he was involved in difficult and reluctant negotiations with Sir Roy Welensky and Sir Godfrey Huggins which ultimately developed into the scheme, under his successors James Griffiths and Oliver Lyttelton, to set up the ill-starred Central African Federation. He opposed increasing the settlers' political power.

He was born in 1891 and at the age of 16 set out from his West Country home for London. He became interested in Socialism at an early age, being elected secretary of the Camberwell Trades Council and Borough Labour Party in 1913. During the First World War he spent nearly three years in prison as a conscientious objector. Later he was for a short time in the Civil Service, but soon became engaged on full-time work for his trade union. By 1919 he was National Secretary of the Transport and General Workers' Union, specializing in the work of the sections dealing with clerical and administrative workers, at various times also holding the posts of president of the International Federation of Commercial Employees and vice-president of the National Federation of Professional Workers.

His work on the industrial side of the Labour movement did not prevent his direct participation in political activity, and from 1921 to 1928 he was an executive member of the London Labour Party. In 1929 he unsuccessfully fought the parliamentary division of Heywood and Radcliffe.

OUTDOOR LIFE

Creech Jones enjoyed walking and climbing and he had become a founder member of the Youth Hostel Association and the Workers' Travel Association. In 1929 he left his trade union appointment to become organizing secretary of the latter body, and played an important part in arranging cheap holidays and travel abroad. Ten years later he introduced, and piloted through both Houses, the Access to Mountains Act.

At the general election of 1935 he was returned as Labour member for the Shipley division, and soon impressed the House with his knowledge of colonial matters. He was chairman of the Fabian Colonial Bureau and the "Friends of Africa", and was a member of the Colonial Office Advisory Committee on Education and of the T.U.C. Colonial Labour Advisory Committee.

In the Second World War Creech Jones set himself to study its effects on the colonial peoples, particularly with regard to native labour conditions and agricultural policy, and he developed a great admiration for Oliver Stanley, Colonial Secretary from 1942 to 1945. When Creech Jones visited West Africa in 1943 as a member of the Colonial Office Commission to inquire into the state of higher education he got to know many of the local chiefs and notabilities. He was appalled by the conditions under which many West Africans then lived, but he also came to realize the complexity of tribal differences and the problems set by climate and geography.

All this time he was serving as Parliamentary Private Secretary to his old trade union colleague Ernest Bevin, then Minister of Labour. It caused little surprise when, in 1945, after the overwhelming election victory of Labour, Creech Jones was chosen to be the Parliamentary Under-Secretary of State for the Colonies. In October, 1946, he was promoted to be Secretary of State, and thus realized a great ambition. He was also sworn of the Privy Council.

COLONIES GAIN INDEPENDENCE

Creech Jones was now busy with many matters, including the preparation of the Colonial Development Corporation's schemes. In all parts of the Colonial Empire he had to deal with countries recovering from the dislocations and strains of war, as in Cyprus where he planned a number of constitutional reforms in opposition to demands for union with Greece, and in the resettlement of Malaya, where, being opposed to federation, he advocated a Malayan Union which would grant common citizenship to all who regarded Malaya as their real home and object of loyalty. But one of the most important events of his period of office was the conferment of independence on Ceylon in February, 1948. Ceylon had long been recognized as the "premier Colony", and since 1931 had enjoyed a considerable degree of internal self-government. During the war, local opinion had moved strongly towards a demand for "Dominion status", and pressure intensified as India, Pakistan and Burma succeeded in attaining independence. It fell to Creech Jones to bring the matter to a conclusion and to present it so as to secure the full approval not only of his own colleagues and party but of the Opposition and of the Commonwealth governments. In achieving this result, his own earnestness and integrity were a decisive factor. Ceylon was the first Colony with a non-European population to become independent, and it may fairly be said that the decision for which Creech Jones was primarily responsible set the pattern for the peaceful and orderly transformation, during the next 15 years, of most of the larger colonial territories into independent members of the Commonwealth.

In the general election of February, 1950, Creech Jones lost his seat at Shipley. In a fight with three other candidates he was beaten by the Conservatives by 81 votes. He accepted an industrial appointment as a director of a company of chemical manufacturers, and from 1952 to 1954 was chairman of the British Council of Pacific Relations. In the latter year he was again returned to the House of Commons. The death of Arthur Greenwood had caused a vacancy at Wakefield, and Creech Jones was elected.

He married in 1920 Violet May, daughter of Joseph Tidman.

October 24, 1964.

Brian Jones, who died on July 3, 1969, was until the previous month guitarist with the Rolling Stones pop group. He was 25.

Lewis Brian Jones was born in Cheltenham on February 28, 1944, and educated at Cheltenham Grammar School, where he stayed until he was 18, completing both O and A levels. He went to London in 1962 and met Mick Jagger, then a student at the London School of Economics, and Keith Richard, and together they formed the nucleus of the pop group that came to be known as the Rolling Stones.

In his own words, their musical influence was formed by the imported American records of Muddy Waters, Jimmy Reed, and Chuck Berry, which they used to play by day and try to imitate by night. Jones was a talented musician who apart from playing rhythm guitar with the group, had mastered the organ, saxophone, and piano.

The three original members of the group were joined by Charlie Watts, at that time drummer with Alexis Korner, and Bill Wyman; and the Rolling Stones, as most of their fans knew them, came into existence.

From the beginning their attitude was uncompromising. While other groups were projecting a clean-cut, energetic and youthful image, the Rolling Stones were openly rebellious. Their hair was longer and their clothes apparently dirtier than their contemporaries'—it was a style which was to have a crucial influence on the development of pop music in Britain and America.

Brian Jones's wide grey-green eyes fringed by his long blond hair became an important part of the group's public image. In Europe he was almost as quickly identified as Mick Jagger.

While the group's recording career went from success to success—beginning with "Come On", their first hit record, and a reputation assured with the Lennon and Macartney composition "I Wanna Be Your Man"—their brushes with the law increased. In October, 1967, Jones himself was sentenced to nine months' imprisonment after admitting the offence of possessing cannabis and allowing his flat to be used for the purpose of smoking it. In December, after an appeal, his sentence was changed to a fine of £1,000 together with three years' probation.

In 1968, Jones was again fined after being found Guilty of unlawful possession of cannabis. Indeed Brian Jones's personal life was less settled over the past year and tensions within the Rolling Stones were growing. The group's last number one record, "Jumping Jack Flash", was released in June, 1968, and Brian Jones does not feature on their new record released a week before he died, for early in June he finally left to be replaced by another guitarist.

In the group's six years of success Brian Jones was a constant source of musical invention and ability within the group. He was also the most cooperative and talkative of the group, but over the last two years he suffered from feelings of persecution and unhappiness. He felt that his relationship with his personal brand of music was threatened and he was about to form a new group.

July 4,1969.

Jack Jones, C.B.E., the Welsh writer, author of *Rhondda Roundabout*, *Bidden to the Feast* and other well-known tales of industrial Wales, died on May 7, 1970, at the age of 85.

He was born on November 24, 1884, and grew up as one of a collier's family in Merthyr Tydfil, Glamorgan. He became a collier himself at the age of 12, and a soldier at 18. He married his first wife, Laura, in 1908, as an unusually young time-expired man, but was called to the colours in 1914 with five of his brothers, and served for the duration, being once wounded. Among his trades and skills after the war were miner, navvy, trade union official, book salesman, parliamentary candidate, lecturer and journalist, and finally after a bitter, but in no sense embittering, experience of unemployment after 1927, a playwright and novelist. He published his first book in 1934, at the age of 50, and in the next 20 years produced nine novels, three plays, three volumes of autobiography, a life of Lloyd George, and a mass of minor writings.

BOOKS FOR FUTURE

In the Second World War he lost his son, Lieutenant Lawrence Jones, M.C., killed at El Alamein, and his youngest son David who died after being invalided out of the Salerno battlefield. He himself undertook arduous lecturing tours on behalf of the war effort in Britain and America, and cheered thousands of our troops on the Continent with his incisive, heartfelt, yet humorous oratory. He was a great giver of himself always, and by 1947 had given too much, so that neither he nor his writing was to be quite the same again.

The books by which he will be known in the future are the novels *Rhondda Roundabout*, *Black Parade*, *Bidden to the Feast* and possibly *Off to Philadelphia in the Morning*; the plays *Land of my Fathers* and *Rhondda Roundabout* (adapted from the novel and produced at the Globe Theatre, 1939); and the first volume of autobiography, *Unfinished Journey*. This was an important body of work for two reasons: it was to prove one of the primary, tradition-founding contributions to Anglo-Welsh literature, that is, to the literature written by Welshmen in English, and it is likely to remain a contribution of value to English literature in its less circumscribed sense. With these books he put a region, perhaps a nation, into English literature with equal power and sincerity. By the time he wrote them he had a wide experience of many modes of living, an extensive acquaintance with men and women and a vivid memory. In addition, he had humour and charity, and above all energy.

Perhaps he was less a creator than a rememberer and marshaller of known events and characters. His best books were suffused with his own rich human qualities, his affection for his fellow men, his readiness to laugh or cry with them. In literature as in life he gave himself without stint, and sometimes uncritically, overabundantly.

He lost his first wife in 1946, and married a second time in 1954. He was created C.B.E. in 1948. He now lived quietly and happily in Rhiwbina, a suburb of Cardiff, enjoying much friendship and regard, and relishing the patriarchal role for which he unmistakably cast himself in his mid-seventies. He was a personality to the end, and delighted to be such. Life was both cruel and kind to him, and he took the best and worst it had to offer at once sanely and indomitably. Merthyr and Cardiff did right to be proud of him, and his host of friends did right to love him.

May 9, 1970.

Jack James Jones, Member of Parliament for Rotherham, who was Joint Parliamentary Secretary, Ministry of Supply, from 1947 to 1950, was killed in a car crash on the Manchester-Sheffield road at Woodhead on October 31, 1962. He was 68.

He was born on October 26, 1894, and educated at Port Talbot Central School, Rotherham, later taking a W.E.A. course at Bangor. He worked for the Lancashire Steel Corporation as a smelter until shortly after the outbreak of war in 1914, when he joined up. He rose to the rank of Regimental Quartermaster-Sergeant in the Imperial Camel Corps (East Riding of Yorkshire Yeomanry) and served in the Middle East, where he acquired a knowledge of Arabic.

Between the wars he was active in local government and served on the executive of the British Iron, Steel and Kindred Trades Federation; in 1943–44 he was a member of the T.U.C. delegation which went to the United States to study American industry in war.

Jones entered Parliament at the general election of 1945, when he and John Lewis were elected for Bolton.

It was soon apparent that Jones did not intend to be a silent member. He spoke out loudly on industrial questions when he felt that his experience gave him the right. Neither worker nor employer went unscathed. Nor was his own Front Bench immune from his opinions.

In 1946 he was one of three members of Parliament who, at the invitation of the Foreign Secretary, Ernest Bevin, visited Southern Persia to examine and consider labour conditions in the Anglo-Iranian Oil Company. On his return he wrote his impressions in an article which was published in *The Times*.

TASKS IN GERMANY

In May, 1947, he was appointed Parliamentary Private Secretary to Lord Pakenham (who then held the office of Chancellor of the Duchy of Lancaster and Minister in Charge of Administration, British Zone of Germany) and Christopher Mayhew (Parliamentary Under-Secretary for Foreign Affairs). One of Jones's first duties was to visit western Germany with Lord Pakenham, and in June, 1947, he was sent there again on a fact-finding inquiry into the iron and steel industry in the British zone. He spent many weeks of that summer in Germany.

In the autumn he was appointed Joint Parliamentary Secretary to the Ministry of Supply, and this post he held until the general election of 1950. At that election Jones stood successfully for Rotherham, where his father had been a founder of the local Labour party. He was returned at subsequent general elections.

Later in his career he took a part-time post as welfare officer with the Lancashire Steel Corporation, for whom he had once worked as a smelter. It was in 1957 while holding this post that his forthright comments brought him into the news. He objected to the bringing out on strike of certain workers at the Irlam plant owned by his employers. He believed he detected communist influence in action, said so in a torrential speech in the Commons and was later involved in a television discussion—which ended in uproar—with a union official.

There was a tragic end to the matter, for

Jones's wife (Olive Archer, whom he had married in 1919 and by whom he had four sons and two daughters) died while watching the programme.

He married secondly, in 1958, Mabel Graham, who was injured in the accident in which her husband lost his life.

November 2, 1962.

Professor O. T. Jones, F.R.S., Emeritus Professor of Geology at Cambridge, who died on May 5, 1967, at the age of 89, held a preeminent position among British geologists. He produced a steady stream of papers and memoirs for nearly 60 years, each one making an advance in geological knowledge. These publications cover a wide range and touch practically every branch of geological science; many of them are also of importance in other fields of study such as geophysics and mining.

Owen Thomas Jones, a Welsh-speaking Welshman, was born in south Cardiganshire in 1878. He was educated at Pencader Grammar School and the University College of Wales. Aberystwyth, where he was Keeling Natural Science Scholar and graduated with First Class Honours in Physics in 1900. He then went to Trinity College, Cambridge, where he was an exhibitioner, taking First Class Honours in Parts I and II of the Natural Sciences Tripos. He was Wiltshire and Harkness Prizeman in Geology and he was also awarded the Sedgwick Essay Prize.

On leaving Cambridge, Jones joined the Geological Survey of Great Britain and for some seven years he was engaged in surveying parts of the West Carmarthenshire and Pembrokeshire coalfields. He was a member of a team of distinguished geologists working in a region of special interest and complexity; this experience, as he himself recognized, was of the greatest value to him in later years. He collaborated in the Survey memoirs on the Haverfordwest and Milford districts.

In addition to his official duties on the Survey, Jones began to work on the Lower Palaeozoic rocks of Plynlimmon and his paper on this area appeared in 1909. It was thus appropriate that he should have been appointed Professor of Geology at Aberystwyth in 1910. He continued his investigations in Central Wales, particularly in north Cardiganshire, which, with the help of his students, he mapped in detail. He established the succession, making use of the graptolites contained in the rocks, and demonstrated the geological structure of a region covering many hundreds of square miles and concerning which there was previously very little information.

In 1919, Jones was invited to the Chair at Manchester. He continued even more actively his researches on the Lower Palaeozoic rocks of Wales and elsewhere; in particular, he described the classic area at Llandovery with its shelly fossils, making it a standard for reference, and enabling correlation between the shelly and graptolitic rocks of lower Silurian age. He also wrote on other subjects such as the history of the Towy drainage system, introducing methods of precision into geomorphological studies, the lead and zinc ores of North Cardiganshire and West Montgomeryshire, which remains the authoritative work on this subject, and a monograph on the Plectambonitids, a group of brachiopods in the Lower Palaeozoic, in which he initiated the study of shell-rib patterns for specific identification.

In 1930, he was elected Woodwardian Professor in Cambridge, succeeding his old professor, J. E. Marr. Here again, his researches continued unabated; he worked on the stratigraphy and structure of the Silurian rocks of the Denbighshire Moors in north Wales and explained certain contorted beds as due to contemporaneous submarine sliding, an interpretation which was soon applied in many other areas. With W. J. Pugh, he carried out detailed large scale mapping of the Builth district in central Wales, revealing a remarkable example of an ancient Ordovician shore-line with cliffs, sea-stacks and beach deposits, as well as examples of complex igneous intrusions which demonstrated the validity of Gilbert's famous laccolith concept in the western United States. These and many other studies enabled him to discuss the complexities of evolution of the Lower Palaeozoic geosyncline in this country.

His interest in geomorphological studies was sustained in his work on erosional surfaces in Wales, significant in Mesozoic palaeogeography and present-day topography, and in his investigations of the Teifi drainage system in south-west Wales. He was always interested in the application of physical methods to geological problems, as may be seen in many contributions. For example, the compaction of sediments, rock fracture, roof control in mines, and the interpretation of gravity and seismic surveys. He retired from his Chair in 1943.

Jones was a brilliant field geologist; he was at his best in the field both in pursuing his own studies and demonstrating his results to others; many will remember his clear insight and apt explanation of geological phenomena. He was always accessible to other researchers, his comments and suggestions were helpful and stimulating even if at times he could be a little impatient when others disagreed with him. His knowledge and competence in all branches of geology were remarkable; his advice and guidance were sought in scientific and industrial problems; and he had an usual intuition in assessing the value and significance of work in areas with which he was not personally familiar. He had a national and international reputation; he was the recognized authority on the Lower Palaeozoic rocks of Britian; he had close contacts with American and other geologists overseas, being particularly interested in the correlation of strata on opposite sides of the Atlantic.

Jones was elected a Fellow of the Geological Society of London in 1906, served as president on three occasions, and as foreign secretary for many years; the society awarded him the Lyell and Wollaston Medals. He was elected a Fellow of the Royal Society in 1926, served on its council and as a vice-president; and the society awarded him a Royal Medal. He was a member of many other societies in this country and overseas; and he was awarded the honorary degree of LL.D. of the University of Wales.

He was married and had two sons and a daughter; his younger son was killed in 1945 while serving with the Royal Air Force.

May 6, 1967.

Parry Jones, O.B.E., who died on December 26, 1963, at his home in London at the age of 72, was an Anglo-Welsh tenor who achieved an international reputation as singer and teacher. He was one of the survivors when the liner Lusitania was torpedoed in 1915.

He was born in Monmouthshire and trained in London at the Royal College of Music, before going off for advanced study in Italy and Germany, but he retained Welsh speech intonations and a certain quick-witted shrewdness that seemed to be as Welsh as his name.

He was not gifted, however, with the sort of soft-grained voice or easy producing that is the birthright of many Welsh tenors. Indeed, his voice, though of even quality throughout a serviceable range, was not ingratiating but rather had an incisive quality that gave firmness to his vocal line and clarity to his articulation.

SANG IN RUSSIAN

This organ was at the service of a vigorous intellect which enabled him to undertake difficult and modern music as well as a wide range of operatic roles.

He mastered several languages, including phonetic Russian, in which he once sang in Moussorgsky's *Sorochintsy Fair*, and he readily undertook to learn new music both for the International Society for Contemporary Music and for more orthodox occasions such as the first performance in Britain of Kodaly's *Psalmus Hungaricus*. Other first English performances in which he took part were those of Berg's *Wozzeck*, Schoenberg's *Gurrelieder*, Busoni's *Doktor Faust* and Milhaud's *Christophe Colomb*. His intuitive grasp of Russian opera was shown most memorably in his delineation of Shuisky in *Boris Godunov*, and in *The Queen of Spades* he contributed much to its striking dramatic verisimilitude. He was indeed an excellent character actor in a considerable range of operatic roles, for he had in his time sung for the D'Oyly Carte, the Beecham and British National Opera Companies and subsequently for the new postwar organization at Covent Garden, in which he was a tower of strength equally on the stage and behind the scenes. Besides this operatic activity he undertook most forms of concert singing.

He made his debut before the First World War (in which he served in the R.G.A.) and then went on a tour of the United States. He also toured Europe, singing in opera in Italy, Germany, Belgium and Holland, and at festivals in Oslo, Amsterdam and Copenhagen. His teaching was mainly done at the Guildhall School of Music, of which he was a Fellow.

He married in 1917 Hilda Dorothy Morris, by whom he had a son.

December 28, 1963.

Sir Roderick Jones, K.B.E., one-time principal proprietor and later chairman and managing director of Reuters, died on January 23, 1962, at the age of 84.

For many years one of the two or three leading figures in the field of world news gathering, he was a man of courage, vision, and decision. He entitled his autobiography *A Life in Reuters* and that indeed was a true epitome of his long career. It was therefore all the more unhappy that when the parting came it was virtually enforced. But though he had had nothing to do with journalism during his last two decades, the fame of his prime remained. In the history not only of Reuters but of the development of international news collection and dissemination in all continents Jones's role will always have to be told.

George Roderick Jones was born at Dukinfield on October 21, 1877. His father was Roderick Patrick Jones, a hat salesman, his mother Christina, second daughter of William Gibb of Kilmarnock. His Scottish grandfather, William Gibb (a cousin of Archbishop Tait), supervised his education and, according to Jones himself, gave it "a strong literary and biblical direction". The elder Jones died early, and the youth was sent to South Africa to live with Gibb's married daughter. It was perhaps the most decisive step in his eventful life. When he first went to the Transvaal it was still a republic; he spent the greater part of the first 38 years of his life in South Africa; events there provided him with opportunities which he seized with a skill and vigour that brought him to notice; he made friends and received influences that shaped his life.

Probably because of his upbringing, Jones had begun to write in his juvenile years. His aunt lived in Pretoria and when the time came for him to work he joined the *Pretoria Press* as a sub-editor. That was in 1895; the same year came the second decisive step that settled his whole career; he became assistant to Reuters' correspondent in the Transvaal.

FULL POWERS

With the thoroughness that was one of his abiding characteristics, the young journalist had taken the trouble to get a good command of Dutch. It helped him when his chance came in 1896. Dr. Jameson was brought to Pretoria as a prisoner after the failure of the raid; thanks to Jones's connexions with the Boers he was able to get for Reuters an interview with Jameson that went all over the world. He became a war correspondent in th Boer War, a whole-time member of the Reuter staff. In 1902 he was called to London to be Reuters' first editor of South African news. Gradually he impressed himself on Baron Herbert de Reuter. When Botha, de Wet, and the other Boer generals went to London Jones was invaluable. In 1905 he was sent as Reuters' General Manager for the whole of South Africa. The formative years of the Union brought many problems and difficulties in which Jones showed shrewdness and negotiating skill. When Baron Herbert de Reuter committed suicide on his wife's death, leaving Reuters in a parlous position, a much-harassed board eventually summoned Jones to London.

At first his position, except as some kind of *deus ex machina*, was indeterminate. By resolution and with loyal help from Mark Napier, Reuters' chairman, Jones first became executive head and then, having raised a loan of £550,000 to reconstruct the company, in 1919 he assumed full powers as chairman and managing director. He still held both these offices when he resigned in 1941.

At the same time as these stretching and intricate matters were going forward Jones did war service from 1916 to 1918 in cable and wireless propaganda, in the last year becoming chief executive and Director of Propaganda in the newly established Ministry of Information. In 1918 he was made K.B.E. Just before the armistice he had to retire because of ill-health.

It was strain more than anything else that had incapacitated him, and soon he was back at Reuters in full vigour. In 1920 he married Enid Bagnold, gaining a loyal and devoted helpmate, a wise counsellor, and one who, while she had her own busy and fruitful life as author and dramatist, was at his side in all his battles.

PRINCIPAL OWNER

The events of Roderick Jones's life between the wars were largely the history of Reuters. He threw himself whole-heartedly in the postwar reorganization of the world's greatest news service. He travelled widely, negotiating and observing. Neat, dapper—the word elegant is not inappropriate—precise of voice and urbane in manner, he had an exquisite courtesy that would yield nothing unnecessary in the toughest of negotiations.

When Mark Napier died in 1919 Jones became principal owner of Reuters. He had the wisdom to see that the only secure foundation for a great British news agency was that it should have among its owners the British Press as a whole. Accordingly, in 1925 he approached the Newspaper Proprietors' Association, representing the national newspapers, and the Press Association, representing the provincial press, with the offer that they should share 50 per cent of the shareholding in Reuters, with an option over part of the remainder. Unfortunately, some members of the N.P.A. were reluctant; the national newspapers' part in the deal came to nothing. The Press Association, with greater wisdom, were eager to go into Reuters, and became the principal shareholders.

DECISION TO RESIGN

It would have been better for Jones himself if the joint partnership could have gone through in the beginning. The Press Association were ultra-loyal and staunch partners in Reuters, but their representatives having to come from various parts of the United Kingdom for board meetings, and their outlook and ways of life not being those of London, a certain gap existed between them and their chairman and managing director at the best of times. Jones for his part tended to become something of an autocrat. Bland in manner, he was determined in purpose. He saw himself as Reuters; and a second gap grew between him and his subordinates, as well as that between him and his colleagues on the board.

There was nothing wrong in this. In any struggle Britain's whole existence would be at stake. She would have to maintain the faith of the world in her ability to survive. Reuters' role in such a task would be substantial. (The full extent of what the B.B.C. was to accomplish was not foreseen.) On its own and without some form of reinforcement Reuters was not likely to be able fully to do the task. All kinds of national activity were having to contemplate some unaccustomed truck with Government.

If there had been complete confidence between Jones and his board, if he had had the unreserved backing of all his senior staff, if he had been less prone to play a lone hand and had taken the trouble to carry his associates as far as he could with him and had heeded their justified fears against going beyond that point, all might yet have been well. But in his mind Reuters had become crystallized in his person. When some of the board finally challenged his actions there was nothing left for him but to resign.

He did so with dignity. There was neither controversy nor rancour. In his own heart he possibly knew it was time to go. It was time for a new conception of Reuters, a more dispersed effort, a yet wider field of influence, a greater strength. These things have come about. But nothing should detract from the achievements of his earlier years.

In later life Jones avoided all limelight. The affairs of his beloved South Africa occasionally drew from his pen a letter to *The Times*. He was a member of the council of the Royal Institute of International Affairs from 1927 to 1955. He was chairman on the governing council of Roedean School. He received decorations from many countries, notably France, Italy, Greece, and China. He was delegate at many international and Commonwealth press conferences, and a British delegate to the Congress of Europe at The Hague in 1948. Lady Jones and three sons and a daughter survive him.

January 24, 1962.

Professor Norman Brooke Jopson, Emeritus Professor of Philology in the University of Cambridge, died on January 12, 1969, at the age of 78.

He could converse in most of the living languages of Europe, and he had a scholar's knowledge of all the principal branches of the ancient Indo-European languages. With this unique equipment he built up a new philological method, eschewing the hypothetical forms and asterisks of the old philological school, in favour of forms attested either in ancient texts or in living speech.

He was born at Leeds on January 20, 1890, and educated at Merchant Taylors School, Crosby, and at St. John's College, Cambridge. In 1912 he was awarded First Class Honours with special distinctions in both French and German, written and oral; and in 1913 a First Class also in Sanskrit and Comparative Philology in the Oriental Languages Tripos. When war broke out in 1914 he was in Russia studying languages, and probably few are aware that this quiet student found himself for a few weeks a soldier in the Russian Army. Later, his linguistic knowledge made him a valuable servant of the War Office, the Admiralty, and the Foreign Office.

His career as an academic teacher began with his appointment in the School of Slavonic Studies in the University of London in 1923, first, as Reader in Comparative Slavonic Philology; then, in 1936, as Professor. In 1937 he was appointed to the Chair of Comparative Philology in the University of Cambridge. On the outbreak of war in 1939 he was appointed Head of the Department of Uncommon Languages of the Postal and Telegraphic Censorhip, an office which he held till 1945.

MADE HIS OWN GRAMMARS

No letter defeated him, lack of dictionaries or grammars were no obstacle: he made them himself from the texts before him, whether written in a Turkish dialect, or a West African language. He had never possessed a German dictionary while working for his Tripos at Cambridge, and it was one of his articles of faith that one must acquire one's vocabulary from reading and speaking, so as to learn at the outset the words of greatest frequency. His method of recruiting his staff was no less original and effective. He could induce elderly retired high rankers from the Indian Army or Civil Service to endure the rigours of the censorship at Liverpool, or discover by a sixth sense that someone doing chores in the office had a gift for languages, and in three months have him qualified in some "uncommon language" to pass the exacting examination compulsory for all new recruits for the censorship.

In 1939, in collaboration with Professor Boyanus, he published an impressive work entitled Spoken Russian, which was intended as a practical course on both written and spoken colloquial Russian. His own research work appeared for the most part as specialized articles, chiefly on Slavonic and East European studies, contributed to learned periodicals and encyclopedias. Undoubtedly his greatest contribution to linguistic studies was made in his work for the censorship and later in his seminars, where his lively mind and exceptional range of linguistic knowledge fascinated and stimulated all who were privileged to attend. He retired in 1955.

Jopson was unmarried. His companionship was always delightful, not least for a bubbling and almost impish sense of fun, and for certain limitations, such as an almost total ignorance of geography, somewhat unexpected in a linguist of his range. After living for three years in one set of rooms in St. John's as an undergraduate he was unable at the end to say in which direction of the compass they faced. He loved the river and he loved cycling; but his gramophone was usually playing softly in his punt, and he cycled for speed, not for the pleasure of the countryside. The passing of a charming personality and rare scholar will be felt keenly by all who knew him.

January 15, 1969.

Air Chief Marshal Sir Philip Joubert de la Ferté, K.C.B., C.M.G., D.S.O., one of the pioneers of service aviation and a distinguished commander and staff officer who became well known to the public by his regular broadcasts of war commentaries during the 1939–45 War, died on January 21, 1965, at the R.A.F. Hospital, Uxbridge. He was 77.

Joubert was never hampered by the cares of the introvert; his life was full and he knew his own mind. He was a "committed" airman who, after the First World War, sought to introduce the air view into the staff colleges of the older Services, and later strongly identified himself with those progressive ideas and developments which he believed would strengthen the hand of the air arm.

The warmth and zeal with which he did this won him the regard of his fellows if it did not always win him official approval. He was as engaging a writer as a broadcaster and the books he published—*The Fated Sky*, *The Third Service*, and *Birds and Fishes* among them —give the reader a striking impression of the making of the R.A.F. and of its time of fulfilment in war.

Philip Bennet Joubert de la Ferté was born on May 21, 1887, at Darjeeling, Bengal, the son of the late Colonel C. H. Joubert de la Ferté, M.B. of the Indian Medical Service. Educated at Harrow and the Royal Military Academy, Woolwich, he was commissioned in the Royal Artillery in 1907. Five years later he learnt to fly and was granted the Royal Aero Club certificate No. 280. After taking the course at the Central Flying School at Upavon he was attached to the Royal Flying Corps (Military Wing) as a flying officer. He was promoted temporary captain in the Corps, given command of a flight three days after the outbreak of the 1914–18 War, and went to France with No. 3 Squadron, where he was one of the two pilots to make the first aerial reconnaissance of the war. Before two months had passed he was mentioned in dispatches for the first time—he was mentioned seven times altogether during the war.

BATTLE OF LOOS

After a period in England, in 1915, where experienced officers were needed to raise new squadrons, he was promoted temporary major and given command of No. 15 Squadron. He commanded No. 1 Squadron at the battle of Loos and in 1916, after six months commanding No. 33 Squadron, he was promoted temporary lieutenant-colonel with command of No. 5 Wing, R.F.C. in Egypt. During this period he was awarded the D.S.O. In 1917, after a few months at home in command of No. 21 Wing, he took command of No. 14 Wing which, after a short time in France, he took to Italy. In 1918 he was given command of the R.F.C. in Italy. In 1919 he was made C.M.G.

On resigning his Army commission, he was given a permanent commission in the Royal Air Force as a wing commander in 1919. The following year he attended the Army Staff College at Camberley and in 1922 was promoted group captain. When the R.A.F. Staff College was opened in April of that year he was appointed an instructor. After serving as Deputy Director of Personnel and Deputy Director of Manning at the Air Ministry, he was appointed in 1926 as the first R.A.F. instructor at the Imperial Defence College. He remained there for three years and at the end of this time was promoted air commodore. For a short period he commanded No. 23 Group at Grantham. He filled a post of more than ordinary importance from 1930 to 1934 when he was Commandant of the R.A.F. Staff College.

There his at times unorthodox methods and quick brain infused a new spirit of enthusiasm and inquiry among staff and students alike.

In 1933 he had been promoted Air Vice-Marshal and on leaving the Staff College a year later was appointed Air Officer Commanding the Fighting Area of Air Defence of Great Britain, the forerunner of Fighter Command.

In this post he devoted much time to the study of air tactics then evolving gradually from those employed by the comparatively slow fighters of the day into the form they finally took in 1939.

COASTAL COMMAND

He took charge of the defences during the air exercises of July, 1934, and was chairman of the flying committee of the R.A.F. Display in 1934 and 1935. In 1936, then an Air Marshal, he became for the first time Air Officer Commanding-in-Chief, Coastal Command. He was made Air Officer Commanding R.A.F., India in 1937 and held this post until 1939. It was not then the most satisfying of appointments for a man of Joubert's outlook and abilities: the powers that be were too much wrapped up in coming events in Europe to think deeply about India, and Joubert felt frustrated by an apparent inability of his superiors to face the facts of life in the Far East. On the outbreak of war he was appointed adviser on combined operations and later an Assistant Chief of the Air Staff. As such he had charge of the development of radar in the R.A.F. and the ultimate success of the war in the air was due in no small measure to Joubert's realization at this stage of the great possibilities of this aid both in defence and to a striking force. It was during this period, too, that he gave his regular broadcast commentaries on the air war. He showed a decided talent for the medium and his commentaries, which gave a balanced picture of what the R.A.F. was accomplishing in relation to the heavy attacks on this country by the German air force, drew a large audience.

COASTAL COMMAND AGAIN

In June 1941 he was promoted Air Chief Marshal and became for the second time Air Officer Commanding-in-Chief, Coastal Command—to him, perhaps, his favourite command for Coastal Command undoubtedly claimed the major part of his affections in his service life. During the 17 months he was there much was done to reduce the U-boat menace within aircraft range of Britain, and the Bay of Biscay—an area in which U-boats could not feel safe from an attack by day or night—became an important battlefield. Joubert made full use of his great technical knowledge of radar which was invaluable during the campaign and did much to make it into an effective anti-submarine aid. He was then appointed an Inspector-General of the Royal Air Force until he retired in November 1943. He was, however, re-employed in the same month to become Deputy Chief of Staff for Information and Civil Affairs under Lord Mountbatten's command in South East Asia. He was placed on the retired list in September 1945. From June, 1946, to September, 1947, he was Director of Public Relations at the Air Ministry. He was made C.B. in 1936 and promoted K.C.B. in 1938.

Possessed of much charm of manner and a kindly understanding, Joubert was a popular commander. He was intolerant of slackness and was impatient of slowness in getting things done once a decision had been made. Indeed, if he was criticized it was often for his attempts to by-pass official channels in order, as he thought, to hurry things along.

He married, in 1915, Marjorie Denison, youngest daughter of F. J. Hall, of Sheffield, and they had two daughters. This marriage was dissolved in 1948. He married in the same year Joan Catherine Cripps.

January 22, 1965.

Lieutenant-Colonel Pierce Charles Joyce, C.B.E., D.S.O., died on February 1, 1965, at Crowthorne, Berkshire.

Born in 1878 the son of Pierce J. Joyce, he was educated at Beaumont College. He joined the Connaught Rangers in 1900 and was wounded while serving in the South African War.

During the last year of the First World War Colonel Joyce was the senior British staff officer attached to the Northern Arab Army, which was commanded by the then Amir Faisal of the Hejaz. The post was not an easy one to fill, the revolt in the desert was an independent national movement, but the military operations of its forces had to conform with the overall strategic plan which was decided by the Commander-in-Chief Cairo, General Allenby, and it was Joyce's duty to ensure as tactfully as was possible that this was done. There were brilliant amateurs with the Arab Army but Joyce was a professional soldier who had to stay at advanced headquarters and on whose shoulders rested the reponsibility for maintaining the force in the field and for seeing that the enthusiastic and adventurous schemes of his Arab and British colleagues, who included T. E. Lawrence, were coordinated and kept within reasonable bounds. The Arab forces consisted of untrained Bedouin mercenaries with whom Lawrence captured the limelight by spectacular feats; regular formations of Arab officers and men, the majority of whom were Iraqis who had once served in the Turkish Army and who were fighting for patriotic motives with the certainty of suffering death as deserters should they be captured by the enemy; and lastly small British and French detachments with aircraft, armoured cars, artillery and machine guns.

The success of the rebellion depended on the regular forces and their British and French parties, and they in turn all depended on the small group of British staff officers and technicians headed by Joyce, who saw that equipment and supplies were available when and where they were needed. Joyce was a big man, over 6ft. 4in. tall and burly. His disposition was placid, which was just as well in view of the excitable natures of the people with whom he had to work. His bulk, good nature and patent honesty gained him the respect and sometimes affection of many Arabs.

It is one of the injustices of history that credit and fame for the achievements of the Arab revolt should have gone to others who were his juniors. After the war was over Joyce was posted to the Iraq, where Faisal had become king, to advise on the creation of an Iraqi Army commanded by many of his wartime colleagues.

Joyce married in 1921 Colin, only daughter of Major-General R. H. Murray, C.B., C.M.G.

February 3, 1965.

Alphonse Juin, Marshal of France, and member of the Académie Française, died on January 27, 1967, at the age of 78.

Since the death of Marshal de Lattre de Tassigny in 1952, he had been the only living Marshal and France's most senior soldier. He had had a distinguished career as a fighting soldier, as a proconsul in North Africa, and as Commander-in-Chief, Allied Forces Central Europe. But his rough and impetuous character, his strongly held and no less forcibly expressed opinions, made him also one of his country's more obstreperous servants. He was frequently at loggerheads with governments of the Fourth Republic, whose official policies he castigated publicly, when he was still their senior military adviser.

Matters came to a head in April, 1954, when he repeatedly attacked the idea of a European Defence Community which the Laniel Government were then vainly trying to impose upon a reluctant Parliament. Even while the Cabinet were meeting to consider what action should be taken, Juin delivered another anti-E.D.C. speech. A decree in the next morning's *Journal Officiel* relieved him of all his French military offices—membership of the Permanent Military Committee and the Superior War Council—save only the inalienable title of Marshal of France and the right it gave him to sit on the Supreme Defence Council. Although his publicly expressed views were in direct conflict with the official policy of Nato, he retained his Central Europe command until 1956 mainly, it was thought, by refusing to resign until he had received an assurance that he would be succeeded by one of his compatriots.

Later, his extreme opinions on North Africa, where he had served for most of his early career and where he had immense prestige with the Army and the French settlers, brought him into collision with President de Gaulle. He had taken no part in the May, 1958, revolt, although he had often been mentioned as a possible leader, or at least a figurehead, for a military government. But as de Gaulle's intention to negotiate peace in Algeria became clear, Juin began to voice open opposition. The climax came in November, 1960, when he refused to be present at the Armistice Day celebrations and, at the same time, published an open letter criticizing de Gaulle's Algerian policy. The President's riposte was to amend the decree governing the composition of the Supreme Defence Council so as to withdraw the traditional right of marshals to membership. Juin's last official function had disappeared, and with it his staff officers and other military prerogatives.

RETIRED BY ORDER

In 1962 the O.A.S. (Organization of the Secret Army) made use of a warm personal letter he had written to General Salan, the rebel leader, and the authorities took the unusual action of placing Juin on the retired list. None the less, although they had not been on speaking terms since 1960 General de Gaulle paid Juin a visit at the Val de Grâce hospital when he was gravely ill with a cerebral seizure in 1964.

Alphonse Pierre Juin was born in Bone on December 16, 1888, the son and grandson of a gendarme. He took a perverse pride in his humble origins, and although later in his career he tended to surround himself with aristocratic staff officers, on one important social occasion he announced himself as: "Commandant Juin, son of a policeman, Monsieur le Président de la République!" He was a bright, engaging, and intelligent boy, and after schooling in Algeria went on to Saint-Cyr, where, although de Gaulle and de Lattre de Tassigny were his contemporaries, he was graduated first in his class. He was posted, at his request, to Morocco, fought in campaigns there in 1912–14, and had himself transferred to France on the outbreak of the First World War. He was seriously wounded and lost the use of his right arm, but he received five citations and the Legion of Honour. In 1918 he was sent to the War College, again with de Gaulle and de Lattre de Tassigny, and graduated in 1921 as the youngest staff captain in the French Army. He returned to Morocco, where he became one of the closest associates of Marshal Lyautey, serving as his chief of staff for several years—but managing, all the same, to obtain a good share in any fighting that was going. In 1938 he was an instructor at the War College and was promoted to the rank of brigadier-general—still one step ahead of de Gaulle and de Lattre, who were still only colonels.

In December, 1939, as a major-general, he commanded the 15th Armoured Division, fought bravely to cover the 1st Army's withdrawal from Dunkirk, was then taken prisoner by the Germans, and was liberated in 1941 at the express request of General Weygand. He refused the post of Minister of War in the Pétain Government, but became Commander-in-Chief of the Vichy forces in North Africa, in succession to General Weygand. On the allied landing in Algeria, after some slight hesitation, he threw in his lot with de Gaulle and led the French Expeditionary Forces in Italy, where he increased his reputation as a tough, fighting general. In May, 1947, he was appointed Resident-General in Morocco, to the joy of the right wing and the increasing anger of the left. In April, 1951, he became Commander-in-Chief of Allied Land Forces, Central Europe, retaining his post as Inspector-General of the French Armed Forces, and two years later became overall C.-in-C. of Nato forces in the Central Europe sector.

In 1952 General Juin was made a Marshal of France, and the same year saw his election to the Académie Française, more on account of his military prominence than his literary reputation. It was typical that his *discours de reception* was hotly controversial and contained an open attack upon François Mauriac and other academicians known for their liberal views on North Africa.

He published his first novel, *C'étaient nos frères*, which, not altogether surprisingly, principally concerned Algeria, in 1962.

Among his many honours and decorations were the Honorary Grand Cross of the Order of the Bath and the American Distinguished Service Medal.

In 1928 he married Cécile Bonnefoy, and they had two sons.

January 28, 1967.

The death of **C. G. Jung,** the distinguished Swiss psychiatrist, at his home in Kuesnacht, on June 6, 1961, at the age of 85, concluded an era of discovery and advance in psychological medicine which has revolutionized the treatment of mental illness throughout the world.

Carl Gustav Jung, the son of a protestant clergyman, was born in Kesswil on the Swiss side of Lake Constance on July 26, 1875. While he was still a child his father was appointed to a church in Basle; there he went to school, and at the University of Basle he qualified in medicine. His grandfather, a noted physician in his day, had been Professor of Medicine at Basle and had set aside beds for psychiatric patients in the town hospital. Jung himself describes how his own interest in the activities of the mind was first aroused while he was still a medical student. He and some other youngsters at a party were having a game of table-turning. One of the children, a girl of 15, to the surprise of all, began to talk in high German instead of her usual Swiss German. As the game went on it appeared that the girl was highly suggestible and adopted various roles proposed to her by the group. Jung, fascinated by this phenomenon, in vain sought an explanation for it in books on philosophy. He found the first hint of an explanation on reading the introduction to a book on mental disease by Kraft Ebing. There and then Jung determined to take up psychiatry so that he might discover "the intruders of the mind". His first appointment was as assistant on the staff of Eugen Bleuler at the Burghölzli Hospital, where the Psychiatric Clinic of the University of Zurich was held. Later he became Senior Staff Physician in this hospital and Instructor in Psychiatry to the University.

With the backing of Bleuler, Jung embarked on comprehensive methods of research into dementia praecox, the commonest illness in the hospital. His methods comprised psychological and physiological investigations. Jung gave new value to Galton's Word Association Tests by demonstrating its importance as an indicator of hidden emotional activity. He showed, too, that this emotional activity was accompanied by alterations in the respiratory and heart rates and in the psychogalvanometer reading. The constellation of activity within the unconscious he described as a *complex*—a concept accepted by all writers on psychology and familiar in everyday speech. Yet he found no satisfactory explanation for the reactions which he described until he read of Freud's theory of repression, and he was the first to prove the validity of this theory.

Jung's publications on the association tests and on the psychology of dementia praecox made his name in the psychiatric world. On more than one occasion he spoke at a medical meeting in support of Freud's approach and asked that a fair hearing should be given to it. He poured scorn on the critics who had not troubled to read Freud's articles, comparing them to those men of science who disdained to look through Galileo's telescope. Nevertheless he made it plain that he did not ascribe to the infantile sexual trauma the exclusive importance seemingly attributed to it by Freud. Freud, who had been exposed to adverse criticism for several years, appreciated the objective attitude—rare in those days—shown by Jung towards his psycho-analysis.

MEETING WITH FREUD

Freud and Jung met for the first time in 1906, when Jung accepted Freud's invitation to visit him in Vienna. For the next five or six years there was close collaboration between them. In 1909 Jung was asked to lecture at Clark University (Massachusetts) on his word-association experiments and Freud on his psychoanalytical studies. It is not generally known that during this trip to the United States they engaged in mutual analysis. But this reciprocal investigation broke down, for, to Jung's surprise, Freud declined to pursue the matter beyond a certain point.

The partnership between Freud and Jung was not always harmonious, for Freud felt that Jung's views went too far. Matters finally came to a head in 1913 following the publication of Jung's book *The Psychology of the Unconscious*, and in particular his views on symbolism which conflicted sharply with the more formalized and, as Jung thought, more circumscribed views of Freud.

Jung found the break with Freud disturbing. He had given up so much in support of Freud's work, when this was criticized almost everywhere, and it came as a shock to him to discover that the conclusions he had reached and now published, and which he regarded as an inevitable development of their common work, did not commend themselves to Freud.

The break with Freud led Jung to study the reasons for it. Briefly, his conclusions were that a constitutional difference in type inevitably led each to approach clinical and other problems from a different angle. Freud, the typical extravert, saw matters from one point of view and Jung, the typical introvert, from another. The book on *Psychological Types* in which Jung expanded his views on typology, followed these reflections. His theory of types with the exposition of the four functions (thinking, feeling, sensation, intuition) proved to be of outstanding importance and although widely accepted it was, and still is, the focus of controversy. Extraversion and introversion denote the predominant direction of mental energy in the individual, and are not meant to signify a rigid grouping of personalities. Jung's "theory of opposites" is closely linked to his typology, the chief "pair of opposites" being the conscious and the unconscious. Mental energy, (libido) is described as flowing from the conscious to the unconscious and vice versa and this contrasts sharply with other psychological systems which see the energy emanating from a source in the past. Jung's concern was with the present rather than with the past—with failure to deal with life as it is today.

IMPORTANCE OF DREAMS

Compared, for example, with the relatively simple framework of Freudian or Adlerian psychology, Jung's contributions seemed complicated. His rejoinder was that he merely recorded what he observed—collected facts—and if anyone could suggest a better method of dealing with these facts he would be delighted. We must, he would say, take nature as we find it rather than twist it to fit some preconceived theory.

Psychology was of little account when Jung began his medical career. Inevitably he was a pioneer. All along his interest centred upon the unconscious, unapprehended, background of conscious life. Hence his insistence upon the importance of dreams. The dream must be taken as a fact and on a par with any physiological fact. In the dreams of his patients he often found apparently ancient material which he could not explain in terms of the personal history of the dreamer. He determined therefore to study some less advanced people at firsthand, hoping thereby to learn something of human thought. He visited North Africa, and later, with the late Dr. H. G. Baynes, he made a field study of the inhabitants of Mount Elgon in British East Africa. In addition he conducted psychological observations on the Pueblo Indians in Arizona and New Mexico. These investigations led to the study of ethnology and of comparative religion, with special emphasis upon religious symbolism.

Jung regarded the symbol, whether found in dreams or elsewhere, as the best possible expression of something not yet fully understood. But he often noted that the symbols in the dreams of his patients, while highly charged with emotion, had no meaning for the dreamer and Jung himself could elicit little significance by associations. In his endeavour to comprehend such things Jung read the books of the medieval alchemists—an imperfectly understood field. His classical background enabled him to read the medieval Latin in which the alchemists wrote. His publications on alchemy provoked a lot of criticism and often he was called a mystic. But always he had in mind the practical aim of understanding the structure of the mind and establishing a scientific basis for treatment. He himself was often appalled at the vast continent of knowledge which was opening up before him.

Concurrently with his studies on alchemy he became interested in Chinese thought. He was fortunate in meeting Richard Wilhelm, the noted sinologist, who had translated some of the Chinese philosophical classics. Jung wrote a commentary on Wilhelm's translation of *The Secret of the Golden Flower*, one of the best known of these Chinese works.

THE COLLECTIVE UNCONSCIOUS

A distinctive feature in Jung's thought was his hypothesis of the *collective unconscious*, which later he called the *objective* or *autonomous psyche*. Over the years his research and clinical observation convinced him that the mind, like the body, had a long ancestry. The traces of our mammalian descent are plain enough in the body and Jung thought it inevitable that the mind too had its antecedents. His investigations supported this, and he was eventually able to demonstrate the patterns (archetypes) in which the collective unconscious showed itself. In his writings on the collective Jung always pointed out that he did not invent but attempted to describe what was already there; and he believed that anyone following the path of research he had taken would have reached the conclusions he reported. Perhaps more than any other of his concepts that of the collective unconscious has enriched psychological thought and saved it from the barrenness of a purely personalistic psychology.

The emphasis upon the normal and healthy in Jung's psychological system is noteworthy. He insisted that symptoms were upset and disturbed normal processes and not entities in themselves. This notion dominates his typology, which is a classification of diverse normal or average human beings. Similarly he regarded a neurosis as an interference with the healthy working of the mind; and dreams were often referred to as unrealized potentialities.

Jung was a prolific writer and his books have been translated into many languages. His publications run into well over 30 volumes and more than 100 papers in various journals. A collected edition of his work is being prepared in English and several volumes have already appeared.

SKILLED LECTURER

He was a skilled lecturer and in great demand in the United States and in England. His knowledge of languages was such that he lectured in fluent English or French as well as in German. In 1936, on the occasion of the tercentenary of Harvard University, he was one of a group of distinguished scholars invited to give an oration, and in 1937 he gave the Terry Lectures at Yale University. Jung often visited England, particularly in the 1930s, and he read papers and lectured before the various medical and psychiatric societies as well as conducting seminars for those who sought more detailed information about his teaching. He was chairman of the International Congress of Psychotherapy held at Oxford in 1938 and on this occasion he gave an important address upon the possibilities of uniting the divergent systems of thought in medical psychology. It was not until his fifties, however, that he responded to the often expressed demand that he would resume systematic teaching at university level. He was elected—with the title of professor—to the staff of the Eidgenössische Technische Hochschule, that is, the Swiss Federal Polytechnic. Later his own university of Basle created a Chair of Medical Psychology specifically for him.

Jung made no effort to systematize his work, for he felt that psychology was still in its infancy and could not be set out in a finished system. Students, however, sought teaching in what came to be called Jungian methods. The demands on his time made by visiting psychiatrists and others was so great that he and his colleagues in Zurich formed what is now known throughout the world as the C. G. Jung-Institute, where those interested in analytical psychology attend regular lectures and seminars. There is a similar institution in London, although on a smaller scale, namely, the Society of Analytical Psychology. On a less formal level analytical psychology clubs were formed many years ago, first of all in Zurich, then in England and in several centres in America. The Analytical Psychology Club in England, founded to provide a centre for lectures and the reading of papers, is one of the oldest and largest of the Jungian associations.

Many universities conferred honorary degrees upon Jung. These include first of all Clark University and, later, Harvard and Oxford as well as universities in Switzerland, India, and other countries. In 1955 the Swiss Federal Polytechnic presented him with the D.Sc. on the occasion of a complimentary dinner in his honour. He was an Honorary Fellow of the Royal Society of Medicine, London, and of the Royal Medico-Psychological Association. London University was the first university in Great Britain to provide systematic lectures on Jung's work, and these have been conducted for many years at the Institute of Psychiatry (Maudsley Hospital). He was full of regret that he was unable to accept an invitation to speak at the tercentenary of the Royal Society in 1960.

ENTERTAINING TALKER

Jung, a delightful and completely natural personality, had the capacity of giving himself entirely to those he met. He was a highly entertaining conversationalist—in at least five languages—and could be extremely witty. This facet of his personality was clearly revealed to British television viewers in his "Face to Face" programme with John Freeman on the B.B.C. in October, 1959. In his younger days he was a keen mountaineer and for many years an enthusiastic yachtsman.

Jung's eightieth birthday was celebrated in July, 1955, and a *Festschrift* consisting of a volume of essays, written for the occasion by his former pupils, was presented to him at a public reception held in Zurich.

In 1903 he married Emma Rauschenbach, and they had five children. His grand-children number 19 and some of them have children. So on his eightieth birthday Jung and his wife were able to welcome at their house the entire, unbroken and healthy family, that is, their five married children, 19 grandchildren (with their respective husbands and wives), and two great-grandchildren—there were 10 at the time of his death. His wife died in November, 1955, after a short illness.

Jung regarded his contributions on the structure and functioning of the mind as preliminary to wider knowledge and merely as his subjective contribution. The time was not ripe, he felt, for a finished and rounded off psychological system which had the answer to all of life's enigmas. Over the years his ideas have stimulated thought in many branches of knowledge as well as in his own special field of psychological medicine. Since the close of the Second World War he was delighted to welcome at his house in Kuesnacht, near Zurich, historians, novelists, and scientists, as well as physicians, all of whom felt that he had light to throw on problems which were the concern of all thinking people.

June 8, 1961.

K

Pratap Singh Kairon, former chief minister of the Punjab, who was assassinated on February 6, 1965, was the autocratic ruler of his state for nearly eight years until he was forced to step down in the summer of 1964 by charges of corruption.

He was an intense personality. Both his qualities and his failings were great and in any walk of life would have made him conspicuous. He was of the new generation of Indian leaders. Terms in British jails in the days of Gandhi did not have much to do with his rapid rise after independence. He was the spearpoint of the new power growing up in the rural areas. He was not a farmer himself but belonged to the rural caste of Jats, the most powerful among the Sikhs. His strength lay in mobilizing this new power and harnessing it to the ballot box.

PLAYING THE RULES

Ruthless in his pursuit of power, he was adept at playing off against each other the two main elements of the system, the administration and the political machine, making the rules of each work against the other. What appeared at first sight to be normal democratic interaction between the popular will and the Civil Service was in fact a carefully regulated manoeuvre to ensure the perpetuation of Kairon's power. Walpole's maxim, that "every man has his price", was applied by Kairon. He used the enormously expanded economic patronage of government to confer or withhold irregular favours and thereby destroy any incipient threat to his power. To ensure that the rules and procedures of government did not come in his way he subverted the official cadres with a carefully worked out system of rewards and punishments; obstinate officers were broken by exposing them to accusers who were put up as "spokesmen of the popular will". Where nothing else worked he could be pitiless with his strong arm methods.

PUNJAB ADVANCE

Yet behind the capture and retention of power his motives were not selfish. He was not corrupt in the ordinary sense of the word: he did not line his own pocket. His dynamism, inexhaustible energy and the vision of a modern man contributed much to the building up of the Punjab as perhaps the most advanced state in India. But he could not overcome the fact that in India power has become too diffused now to be gathered into one man's dictatorial hands. Kairon tried to gather it but no sooner would he vanquish one centre of rival power than another would crop up until even his instruments of power were blunted. Then his methods began to be employed not only by him but also by those who claimed to speak in his name, and it was their misdeeds more than Kairon's that were exposed by the Dass commission appointed by Nehru over a year before he died to investigate the charges of corruption against Kairon. But the responsibility was Kairon's and he had to resign in June, 1964. The link was clear and the opposition to him strong enough to drive the advantage home.

Kairon was born in 1901 in the Amritsar district and after schooling there went to the United States. He joined the Congress Party in 1929, suffered imprisonment a few times in the independence struggle and was elected to the Punjab Assembly in 1936. For a time he was in the semi-religious political organization of the Sikhs, the Akali Dal—whose agitations he was later to crush—but most of his public life was spent in the Congress Party and for many years he was a member of the All India Congress committee and its executive agency, the working committee. He became a Minister for the first time in 1952 and chief Minister in 1956.

February 8, 1965.

Henry J. Kaiser, the United States construction engineer and contractor, who died in Honolulu on August 24, 1967, came suddenly into international prominence during the Second World War. It was he who speeded up the construction of ships for the transport of armies, munitions and food across the seas, erecting vast yards on swamps and turning out the completed vessels in an unprecedently short time. Then he turned his attention to gigantic transport aircraft and presented to the world schemes for their construction and use which many thought fantastic and impossible.

The words fantastic and impossible had often been used before of Kaiser, his work and schemes. Even before the war when his name was little known he constructed great dams in the western states which were among the wonders of the world at that time. Before 1940 he had never seen a shipyard, much less worked in one. Yet he reduced the time for constructing a standard cargo vessel from 105 days to 46 days. In Washington he was regarded as an idle boaster when he said he could build 9m. tons of shipping in a year, but within a few months he turned out and launched 55 ships at a single yard—far more than half he had promised for a full year.

When cement was required for another of his undertakings he set out to build the largest cement works in the world in record time. When magnesium was required he built a factory whose output would exceed that of all German factories combined.

The man with all these big ideas and plans and the ability to realize them so quickly was born in very humble surroundings in New York State in 1882.

Circumstances forced him to end his schooling at the age of 11. After a round of jobs he found his proper sphere as a constructional engineer.

GREAT DAMS

Yet he was well over 50 when he entered into work on the grand scale. In a short space of time he constructed the three great American dams in the west, the Boulder, Bonneville, and Grand Coulee.

After the Second World War he turned to building motor cars and homes and the manufacture of steel. In his seventies he built the fabulous hotel called Hawaiian Village on Waikiki beach, Honolulu.

It was not until 1959, when he was 77 years old, that he relinquished some of the enormous burdens he had carried for so many years.

He was twice married, first in 1917 to Bessie Hannah Fosburg, by whom he had one son. She died in 1951 and the same year he married Alyce Chester, who survives him.

August 25, 1967.

Boris Karloff, who became famous as a monster in the era of the so-called horrific films which were a Hollywood novelty of the early 30s, died on February 2, 1969, at Midhurst, Sussex. He was 81.

As is so often the case with players who specialize in certain type of part, the actual character of the man was very different from that which he portrayed on the screen. He was quiet, gentle and reserved, with a fundamental sense of pathos. This he could not always hide, and perhaps it contributed to his success, for it added a further dimension to parts that were never subtly conceived. *Frankenstein,* which made his reputation, was little more than a horrific film about a cruel monster, and yet as perceptive a critic as John Grierson could write of "the curious beauty" with which Karloff invested the part. He may have frightened his audiences, but he also commanded their pity.

DIPLOMACY UNTRIED

Boris Karloff, whose real name was Pratt, was born in London on November 23, 1887—the youngest of nine children of a civil servant. He was educated at Uppingham, at Merchant Taylors' School, London, and at London University. He was originally intended for a diplomatic career, but went to Canada and the United States when he was 21, and a year later made his first appearance on the stage in a stock company.

He spent the next 10 years working in various American stock companies, and then turned his attention to films. He appeared in a number of Hollywood pictures of the silent era, without making his mark, and it was not until *Frankenstein* that he became famous. *Dracula,* with Bela Lugosi, started the vogue for horror films in 1931, and this was followed shortly afterwards by *Frankenstein,* which was admirably directed by James Whale, and which was highly successful. Karloff's reputation was now made, and he was thereafter destined to play in a number of horrific films, including *The Bride of Frankenstein* and *The Son of Frankenstein,* and a notable thriller of the period, *The Old Dark House,* with Melvyn Douglas and Charles Laughton.

WAR STORY

But his best film during this period was a war story—*The Lost Patrol,* which described the fate of a British cavalry patrol lost in the desert of Mesopotamia during the 1914–18 War. Brilliantly directed by John Ford, it presented Karloff as a religious fanatic who tries desperately to save the souls of his comrades.

Few of his other early films were of much account. Hollywood, having once cast him in an horrific part, was reluctant to allow him to reveal his sensitivity and sense of pathos. During the last war he appeared in several horror films produced by Val Lewton, including *The Cat People, Isle of the Dead, The Body Snatcher* and *Bedlam,* which showed a better understanding of this subject, and were made with a less obvious approach to the grotesque and the macabre.

In 1941 he achieved a notable success on the stage when he played Jonathan Brewster at the Fulton Theatre, New York, in *Arsenic and Old Lace.* In 1946 he played Gramps in *On Borrowed Time*; in 1948 Professor Linden in *The Linden Tree*; in 1949 Decius Heiss in *The Shop at Sly Corner*; and finally graduated to the Mr. Darling-Captain Hook double in a record run of Peter Pan in 1951. The part of the melancholy and misunderstood pirate was perhaps the one best suited to his talents.

During his later years he continued to appear on the screen, on television, and occasionally on the stage. In 1963 he co-starred with Vincent Price and Peter Lorre in *The Raven*—a film version of Edgar Allan Poe's poem.

RESTRAINT IN HUMOUR

More recent trends in horror films have made the early Karloff pictures seem mild and innocuous in comparison, but Karloff himself will be remembered as an actor who understood the visual requirements of the cinema, and could play an horrific part with a restraint—even a delicacy—which modern productions so frequently lack. The scene in *Frankenstein* in which the monster meets the little girl in an idyllic setting by a lakeside provided a memorable contrast in beauty and harsh reality.

February 4, 1969.

Joesph Kasavubu, first President of the Congo, who headed the country through the crisis years after independence, died on March 24, 1969. He was in his fifties.

Kasavubu was President from independence in June, 1960—when the country collapsed into near-anarchy—until September 13, 1960, when General Mobutu seized power, and again from shortly afterwards until Mobutu's second coup in November, 1965. Mobutu intervened to avert a head-on collision between Kasavubu and Patrice Lumumba the then Prime Minister after barely two months of joint rule in 1960. Kasavubu had dismissed Lumumba—Mobutu dismissed both and assumed power. But although Lumumba was killed soon afterwards, Kasavubu was reinstated. Mobutu found he needed Kasavubu's political skill and prestige. Kasavubu proved to be the most astute and durable of the Congo's politicians during its early years of independence. He gave the presidency enough prestige to make it the one stable element in his storm-tossed country.

Conservative and anti-communist, Kasavubu soon came into conflict with Lumumba, a left-wing advocate of a unitary state which ignored the Congo's tribal realities. Faced with army mutiny, general chaos and a secession attempt by Moise Tshombe's Katanga province, Kasavubu showed a remarkable ability for five years to remain in power. A succession of five prime ministers served under him during this turmoil. He left the daily management of affairs to them. Kasavubu himself asked for United Nations' peace-keeping troops to help maintain order in the first year of his rule. His relations with the force fluctuated, though, as he later called for its withdrawal, and then reconciled himself to its presence.

RULE BY DECREE

In 1963, when the National Parliament refused to discuss the drafting of a new constitution, Kasavubu dismissed the body and assumed supreme powers, ruling by presidential decree. Mobutu's bloodless coup sent Kasavubu back to his farm near Tshela, and Mobutu proclaimed himself president for five years. Just before, Kasavubu had won a long-drawn-out conflict with Tshombe, the then Prime Minister, who went into exile.

Kasavubu was the first of the Congolese leaders to demand independence from the Belgians and when the Congo finally became an independent state in June, 1960, he was elected President of the new republic. At no time, however, did he fit into the generally accepted picture of an African nationalist leader and his appearance was always more that of a traditional ruler than of either an agitator or a modern statesman. Initially, he drew his strength from the powerful Bakongo tribe which inhabits the area round Leopoldville, and his first demands for independence were made for his tribe rather than for the Congo as a whole. As the independence struggle progressed, however, and as he became better acquainted with other regions and other leaders, he seemed genuinely to accept the idea of a united Congo and opposed those of his followers who still hankered after a separate Bakongo state.

When Lumumba was appointed as Prime Minister in June, 1960, there was some doubt as to whether he and Kasavubu would be able to work together since they were not only temperamentally entirely different but had also been bitter political rivals. Initially, however, the alliance worked well, and during the mutiny which followed independence, the two were careful to sign all important documents together and travelled round the country in an attempt to calm the people. At a later date, however, great pressure was put on Kasavubu to disown Lumumba and he began to feel in addition that Lumumba was treating him with insufficient respect and failing to consult him on crucial matters affecting the state. As a result, on September 5, 1960, he announced that he was dismissing Lumumba and appointing a new Prime Minister. Though Kasavubu himself was far too intelligent to think that the Lumumbists could be permanently excluded from power and seems to have intended this action as the first move in a complex negotiation rather than anything final, other factors intervened and Lumumba was arrested and finally killed.

INTENDED FOR PRIESTHOOD

Joseph Kasavubu was born in 1917 at Tshela in the Lower Congo and he came from the Bayombe, an important sub-grouping of the Bakongo tribe. He originally intended to be a priest and attended a variety of Roman Catholic seminaries. Eventually, however, he refused ordination but emerged with a much more complete education than the majority of his contemporaries. This quickly brought him to the fore in African society in Leopoldville and in 1955 he became president of the Abako, the political and cultural society of the Bakongo. It was from this base that he began to challenge the Belgians. Though from time to time there were rumours that he was losing popularity with his tribe no other Bakongo leader seemed able to replace him, and it was his undisputed position as leader of one of the largest and most important tribes in the Congo which made it inevitable that he should play a leading role in political activities.

March 25, 1969.

The Mullah Ayatullah Abul Qasim Kashani, whose death on March 14, 1962, was reported from Teheran, was a religious leader whose violent anti-foreign preaching made him, at the height of Iran's oil crisis 10 years ago, as influential a figure as Dr. Moussadek.

In the campaign which led up to the nationalization of the Anglo-Iranian Oil Company, and in the hectic months which followed, the two nationalist leaders worked closely together. Indeed, it is probable that Dr. Moussadek could not have done so much had not Kashani been there to whip up the masses. Kashani's achievement was to interpret Dr. Moussadek's doctrines of nationalism and nationalization in terms of Islam, and thus give them universal currency. Later the two split, and since the *coup* of July, 1953, both these old fire-eaters, though not forgotten in Iran, lived lives of enforced obscurity.

Kashani was born about 81 years ago in Teheran. His father was also a mullah. When Kashani was 15 he followed the common Iranian practice of going to Najaf, one of the holy Shia cities of Iraq, to continue his religious studies. He was still in Iraq when a revolt among the tribes and towns of the Middle Euphrates against the recently imposed British mandate broke out in 1920. Father and son were both involved. The father was killed, but the son escaped to Iran, nursing a bitter hatred against all western influence, particularly British.

During the reign of Reza Shah, Kashani's opportunity for political activity was as limited as that of all Iranians. After Reza Shah's overthrow in 1941, and the Anglo-Russian occupation of Iran, Kashani intrigued with the Germans, on one occasion escaping from allied pursuit in women's clothing.

VIGOROUS MISSION

At the end of the war Kashani began to pursue his single-minded mission with vigour. Everything foreign was bad, particularly foreign oil companies. He helped to defeat the proposal for an oil concession to Russia in north Iran, and thereafter the A.I.O.C. became his natural target. After experiencing intermittent periods of gaol, banishment and exile, Kashani became a deputy for the Majlis in 1949, though out of respect to his cloth he never attended its sittings.

In March, 1951, the Prime Minister, General Razmara, was assassinated by a religious fanatic—a deed for which Kashani claimed the credit. Dr. Moussadek became Prime Minister, the exciting epoch of nationalization began, and Kashani's position in the thick of things was symbolized by his election, in August, 1952, to the presidency of the Majlis.

His quarrel with Dr. Moussadek arose in January, 1953, when he opposed the Prime Minister's demand for plenary powers. He based his opposition on respect for the constitution, and no doubt Kashani's dislike of dictatorship, which he equated with foreign imperialism, was sincere. However, the deputies voted the Bill, and in July Kashani was ejected from the speakership.

Although Kashani's influence was religious he was not a noted theologian. He was an orator and political manipulator, whose appeal to the passions of the street in Teheran could, at the height of his prestige, cow or even overthrow governments.

March 15, 1962.

General A. K. Kassim, who was executed on February 9, 1963, was unknown to the outside world until he emerged as Prime Minister of Iraq after the revolution of July 14, 1958, which overthrew the Iraq monarchy. Then for four and a half years he dominated the political life of his country, becoming increasingly incoherent and authoritarian in the process. Portraits of "the sole leader, the faithful leader of the people", with their fixed and somewhat ghastly smile, were to be seen everywhere. Kassim spoke frequently and at great length.

He gave numerous interviews to foreign journalists. Yet he was personally little known.

Except for occasional excursions through the city of Baghdad, usually, in the manner of his distinguished predecessor. Harun al-Rashid, undertaken in the middle of the night, Kassim seldom left his office in the closely guarded Ministry of Defence. Here, surrounded by innumerable portraits and busts of himself, and a glass case containing the blood-stained shirt and vest he was wearing at the time of his attempted assassination, he would work for prodigious hours, being able, so he claimed, to do with two or three hours sleep a night. His visits outside Baghdad could be counted on the fingers of two hands. He never left Iraq.

In spite of his inaccessibility Kassim retained much popularity among the masses. They respected his personal honesty. They could see the sincerity behind his passionate concern for the welfare of the poor; they were little worried by the denial of civil liberties they had never known or by the confusion of policies they did not understand. Other sections of the population grew increasingly bitter and estranged.

Kassim's decisions were personal and arbitrary. Criticism of himself was equated with sabotage of the revolution, particularly after the attempt on his life in October, 1959, from which he escaped by a seeming miracle. Nationalists and communists had early been turned into opponents. The Army was alienated by defeats at the hands of the Kurds. The intelligentsia chafed at supremely unintelligent leadership.

But who exactly was this man? Was he always at heart a simple soldier? Was he a cunning manipulator of people and parties? Was he a mystic in politics? Was he mad?

A CARPENTER'S SON

Kassim, whose father was a carpenter, was born in 1914. He joined the army, and passed through the Military College and Staff College in Baghdad. He spent six months at the Senior Officers' School in England, where his reputation was erratic. During the Palestine fighting he was Assistant Adjutant-General of the Iraq Armed Forces, and was promoted to Brigadier in 1953. He became a Major-General after the revolution and a Lieutenant-General this year. It was when the 19th Brigade, which he was commanding, was ordered to pass through Baghdad in the early hours of July 14, on its way to Jordan, that the long awaited opportunity for revolt presented itself. Kassim said subsequently that he had devoted himself to conspiracy for 20 years. Not only was he all that time successful in avoiding detection, but he was one of the young officers in whom Nuri al-Said had most confidence, undertaking, for example, a mission to Turkey in connexion with the Baghdad Pact.

In the first confusion after the republic was proclaimed it was far from clear where the true seat of power lay. Above Kassim was a three-man Council of Sovereignty and below him the ebullient Colonel Aref, who had carried out the actual attack in Baghdad on July 14. But the council faded into the background, and Aref, who had made no secret of his Nasserite sympathies, was disgraced, arrested, and finally condemned to death.

For the next year the political scene was dominated by relations between Kassim and the communists. Their influence grew as new plots of Egypt-looking nationalists were exposed—that of the former Prime Minister, Rashid Ali, in December, and of Colonel Shawwaf in Mosul in March, 1959. They gained control of a newly created militia known as the People's Resistance Volunteers, and of most of the press. Many of Kassim's closest advisers were officers sympathetic to communism. It appeared to many that Kassim himself must be a communist, or at any rate a dupe of the communists.

However, signs of an open breach with the communists began to appear when, at the end of April, their demand for seats in the Cabinet met with no response. In May one of the main parties supporting the revolution, the National Democrats, decided to suspend political activities during the "transitional period" Kassim had proclaimed. The communists showed no inclination to follow suit, and tried to organize a national front as a facade for their activities. This front was described by Kassim as founded on "an erroneous idea".

The attempt on Kassim's life on October 7, 1959, was variously blamed on Nasserists and communists. Whatever the full ramifications of the plot may have been it came near to success. Kassim was wounded in several places and his chauffeur was killed.

He remained in hospital for two months, and his return to public life was the occasion for public rejoicing.

OIL NEGOTIATIONS

By this time Kassim and his Government had become deeply embroiled in negotiations for a revised agreement with the Iraq Petroleum Company which, with its associates, held a concession for the entire country and, through the royalties paid on its operations, provided the treasury with its main source of wealth. Kassim took a leading part in the discussions himself, but the impression grew that he was not really interested in a new agreement. Whenever understanding seemed near on one point Kassim would produce a new grievance or advance a new claim. Negatiations finally broke down in October, 1961. More than 99 per cent of the companies' concession area was then taken away from them, but the benefits which the Iraqis had been told would be a consequence of this action failed to materialize.

It was on June 25, 1961, that Kassim took the strangest step of his career. In the course of a press conference he laid claim to Kuwait, which had just become fully independent, as "an inseparable part of Iraq". It is believed that not even his Foreign Minister had been advised in advance of what was going to happen. Britain and the rest of the Arab world reacted sharply, an Arab League force eventually taking over from the British troops hastily assembled for the shaikhdom's defence. Kassim made no move. He persisted at frequent intervals in asserting that Kuwait would be united with Iraq, but gave no inkling of how or when this was to be done.

A similar failure marked his policy in Kurdistan. The republic he brought into being was declared a brotherhood of Kurds and Arabs. By the end almost the whole Kurdish north was disaffected and the Iraq army had suffered severe defeats. Kassim continued in the face of the evidence to insist that the trouble was no more than the work of a few misguided highwaymen which would speedily end if not supported from outside.

An inability to look facts in the face was, indeed, Kassim's chief failing. He believed deeply in himself. He was supremely conscious of his own good intentions. He preached the brotherhood of all Iraqis, the progress of mankind, the peace of the world and the unity of the Arab nation. He smothered in a blanket of words and dreams the non-appearance of that utopia for which the July revolution was supposed to have been the signal.

February 11, 1963.

Julius Katchen, who died in Paris on April 29, 1969, at the age of 42, was one of a remarkable generation of American pianists who began to make European reputations at the end of the 1940s, astounding audiences by their cast-iron virtuosity, strength and staying power. Katchen stood out among them because, in addition to this brilliance and physical strength, his playing conveyed superior intellectual and philosophical qualities which naturally led him to specialize in the keyboard music of Beethoven and Brahms, though his musical sympathies were very broad and his repertory extended from Bach to Britten.

Katchen was born in Long Branch, New Jersey, on August 15, 1926. His parents were of Russian extraction. Many of his relatives were musical, particularly on his mother's side. He had his first piano lessons from his grandmother, enjoyed piano practice more than anything else and, at the age of 11, played in a broadcast concert conducted by Sir John Barbirolli, whereupon he was at once engaged by the Philadelphia and New York orchestras.

PARIS STUDIES

The boy was much in demand but his parents insisted that his academic education must take first place. He was therefore educated privately until he was 15, then at Haverford College where he specialized in philosophy and English literature. Graduating *summa cum laude* at 19, he was awarded a scholarship by the French government, and used it for advanced musical study in Paris which thereafter became his home and where he launched his adult career as a pianist, giving seven concerts within 11 days.

His speciality at first seemed to be Russian music—Tchaikovsky, Balakirev, Rachmaninov. Prokofiev—but he made his British debut in Beethoven's Emperor Concerto, and one of his first gramophone records was of Brahms's massive F minor sonata. Eventually he recorded the whole of Brahms's music involving the piano, and gave a series of concerts in

London devoted to the chamber music with piano. One pianistic marathon of his was a recital devoted to Beethoven's last five sonatas, with the Appassionata thrown in as an encore.

He was also a superb exponent of Mozart with a real understanding of classic Viennese style. But he played Chopin, Schumann, Liszt, and Bartok with real sympathy and vitality, had a soft spot for Gershwin, and gave memorable performances of Britten's Diversions for left hand with orchestra. Fortunately for posterity he was contracted early in his career by Decca for whom he made a great quantity of piano records.

Katchen was married in 1956. His widow Arlette and son Stefan survive him.

April 30, 1969.

George S. Kaufman, the American playwright and stage director, who died at his home in New York on June 2, 1961, at the age of 71, was in his fashion a dedicated man of the theatre, of the theatre in the sense of Broadway. As some men may be said to be by nature "off-Broadway", so Kaufman in his day—and it was a long day—was by nature "on" it. He wrote, almost always with a collaborator, with the subject of pleasing the kind of playgoer that he himself was, the playgoer who wants to laugh not so much at something new as at something topical.

George Simon Kaufman, the son of Joseph and Nettie Myers Kaufman, was born on November 16, 1889, at Pittsburgh, Pennsylvania, where he attended the public high school and afterwards half-heartedly studied law. After filling in time as clerk, stenographer, and salesman, he began in 1908 to contribute prose and verse to the column in the New York *Evening Mail*, then edited by Franklin P. Adams (F.P.A.). When the latter went to the *Tribune* in 1914 Kaufman succeeded him on the *Mail*, and soon afterwards rejoined Adams on the *Tribune*, where, and also on the *New York Times*, he brought fresh life to the Sunday theatrical page. In 1921 George C. Tyler, the producer, commissioned Kaufman and Marc Connelly to write a comedy round one of the characters regularly appearing in Adams's column in the *Tribune*. The play to which she gave her own name, Dulcy, brought wide recognition for the first time in their careers to the leading lady, henceforward a star, Lynn Fontanne, and to Kaufman.

Two more plays written in conjunction with Mr. Connelly, *To the Ladies* and *Merton of the Movies*, were produced in the following season, and between then and 1955 some 40 new plays of which he was co-author were seen on Broadway. *The Royal Family* (*Theatre Royal*) and *Stage Door* were written in collaboration with Edna Ferber; *The Channel Road* (from *Boule de Suif*) and *The Dark Tower* in collaboration with Alexander Woolcott; *Of Thee I Sing* (with a score by George Gershwin) and *Let 'Em Eat Cake* in collaboration with Morrie Ryskind; *Once in a Lifetime, You Can't Take It With You, The Man Who Came to Dinner*, and *George Washington Slept Here* in collaboration with Moss Hart; and three of his later plays in collaboration with his second wife, the British-born actress Leueen MacGrath. He directed, in addition to much of his own work for the stage, the New York production of *Of Mice and Men, My Sister Eileen*, and *Guys and Dolls*. In 1930 he added to the joke of *Once in a Lifetime* by himself playing the part in it of a Broadway playwright captive in Hollywood.

FACE FOR CARICATURE

Moss Hart, recalling their first meeting in the office of the Music Box in New York, has described Kaufman as having not a handsome face but an immensely attractive one in which each single feature—bushy hair, large nose, full mouth set at a twisted tilt—was a caricaturist's delight. "Mr. Kaufman", Hart was told, "hates any kind of sentimentality; can't stand it"; this to explain the fact that the senior partner of the new team had, foreseeing a speech of thanks on the junior member's part, just leapt to his feet and flown like a large bird frightened out of its solitude. As soon as they got down to work an element of the demoniacal showed in him, not only, Hart found, in his industry and single-mindedness, but in his indifference to food, rest, and the trivialities of social intercourse. Kaufman, this sincere, silent dedicated entertainer, was, paradoxically enough, a satirist who defined satire as "that which closes Saturday night". Satire, as he understood and practised it, did not close Saturday night, being indistinguishable from something more naive, more mellow, more fantastic, and more sentimental. He spent a lifetime in the discovery and conscientious service of it.

Kaufman's marriage to his first wife, the former Beatrice Bakrow, was dissolved. His activity as a playwright slackened of recent years, and he suffered a succession of strokes in the course of his last 18 months. Two plays of which he was part author, *Of Thee I Sing* and *You Can't Take It With You*, won Pulitzer Prizes.

June 5, 1961.

Buster Keaton, one of the great clowns of the silent screen, who will be remembered above all for his performance in *The General*, died at his home in Hollywood on February 1, 1966. He was 69.

His interpretation of comedy was unique. His was "the great stone face", In a film world that exaggerated everything, and in which every emotion was dramatized and elaborated, he remained impassive and solemn, his poker-faced inscrutability suppressing all emotion. And yet emotion *was* conveyed. Disaster might be encountered with no more than a lifting of the eyebrows; astonishment by a single blink of the eyes. But, even so, the character he portrayed never failed to arouse the sympathy of an audience. This sombre, mournful clown had a great capacity for pathos. When circumstance defeated him, it was as though some patient, kindly donkey were being beaten by a bully with a stick.

He was a comedian of many parts. A man of close observation and remarkable inventiveness, most of the best gags in his films were of his own creation. He was also a fine and fearless acrobat, who scorned a stand-in and insisted on himself carrying out all the dangerous stunts which a script might demand. He had a thorough understanding of the technique of the silent cinema, and edited his own pictures.

GOLDEN AGE OF "SILENTS"

Speech, of course, had no part in his mime, and the coming of sound robbed him of his greatness, even if it did not end his film career, which continued spasmodically for many years. But he belonged essentially to the golden era of film comedy, during the silent twenties when Chaplin, Harold Lloyd, and Laurel and Hardy were also at their peak. He differed from them in many ways, one of them being in his relationship with his heroines. Chaplin and Lloyd had to fight to win the girl in the end, but Keaton was plagued by well-intentioned young women who loved him devoutly throughout but tried him sorely by their lack of intelligence. When in *Go West*, he lifted up his bride triumphantly so that she might glimpse the promised land in front of them, she faced in the wrong direction and looked back from where they had come.

Joseph Francis Keaton was born in Pickway, Kansas, on October 4, 1896, the son of Joe H. Keaton, a well-known acrobatic comedian of the circus and vaudeville. At the age of six months he was nicknamed "Buster" by Houdini after he had fallen down a flight of stairs and been picked up unhurt. At the age of 3½ he was already part of his father's knockabout act. He was therefore a fully experienced tumbler and comedian long before he entered films.

It was Roscoe "Fatty" Arbuckle who introduced him to the screen after a chance meeting in the street. This was in 1917, and his first film was *The Butcher Boy*. He made several short comedies and then joined the army. He returned to the screen in 1919, and made many films, including one "straight part" *The Saphead* in 1920—but it was not until 1923 that he first developed his poker-faced approach to comedy.

RELIC OF ACROBATICS

Possibly the rigid unsmiling demeanour was a relic of his acrobatic days, when an intense concentration was essential. A long succession of short comedies was followed in the middle twenties by full-length silent films which were constructed with much more care. These included *Sherlock Jnr.* (1924), *The Navigator* (1935), *Go West, Battling Butler*, and *The General* (1926), *College* (1927), *Steamboat Bill Jnr.* and *The Cameraman* (1928) and *Big Shot* (1929). The best of these was undoubtedly *The General*, the story of a wonderful train chase enacted against the background of the American Civil War, in which Keaton played an engine driver of the Southern forces.

The remainder of his screen career, after the coming of sound, was an anti-climax. He made various talking pictures over a long period, including one in France and one in England; and like Laurel and Hardy he also made a tour of provincial music halls in England during the fifties—a sad affair for those with any nostalgia for the past. Billy Wilder used him in *Sunset Boulevard* in 1950; Chaplin gave him a piano-playing scene in *Limelight* in 1953, and he appeared with almost every other screen veteran in Mike Todd's *Around The World in Eighty Days* in 1956. In 1957 Hollywood made a so-called biography of his life, *The Buster Keaton Story*, an inaccurate and shabby tribute to one of its finest comedians.

More recently he appeared in *It's a Mad, Mad, Mad, Mad World*.

But as a great comedian, he belonged only to the silent screen. His solemn resolution in adversity had a certain dignity; he was the patron of the still upper lip.

He had no imitators, for his style was so essentially his own. His was a magnificent resignation in the face of inevitable disaster. Last year it was announced he was to star in *The Chase*, a silent production except for sound effects and music and a tribute to silent films. His last great triumph was in September, 1965, when he received an enthusiastic reception for his performance in a 22-minute silent film scripted by Samuel Beckett, which was shown at the Venice Film Festival. It was called simply *Film*.

February 2, 1966.

Malcolm Keen, the actor, who died on January 30, 1970, at the age of 82, was seen in his true colours during the period when he worked under such fine directors as Basil Dean, Harcourt Williams and John Gielgud. In their companies, and in plays of quality, he could be relied on to pull his weight and often made a contribution of brilliance. In less auspicious circumstances, even in a leading part, he could seem unsure of himself and out of his element.

Born at Clifton, Bristol, on August 8, 1887, he made his debut under Tree at His Majesty's and after many years on the road reappeared at that theatre in Martin Harvey's company at Shakespeare's Tercentenary in 1916. In 1919 he was engaged for the first production in London to be directed by Basil Dean, and it was under Dean's direction as the mentally disturbed husband in Clemence Dane's *A Bill of Divorcement*, in Galsworthy's *Loyalties*, in Maugham's *East of Suez*, and as the Caliph in Flecker's *Hassan* that Keen proved himself a real acquisition to the West End theatre. In those dramatic plays he enriched such diverse characters as the odd-man-out in Clemence Dane's, the plain man involved in tragedy in Galsworthy's and in Maugham's, and the despot to whom the lives of others are a spectacle for his entertainment in Flecker's, with a thought-provoking humanity that seemed to bear his individual stamp. Most of all perhaps during these years of his emergence he was identified by audiences with the man who takes things hard, who suffers uncomplainingly.

After an appearance in 1925 as the King to Constance Collier's Queen in John Barrymore's *Hamlet* he again played for Dean as the missionary in the dramatized version of Maugham's *Rain*. He ventured into a musical (by Edgar Wallace) in 1928, put on without success a play under his own management in 1929, and made his American debut as the profligate Duke to Maurice Moscovitch's Jew in *Jew Süss*.

Having played the King to two more Hamlets, Henry Ainley's and Godfrey Tearle's, Keen joined Harcourt Williams's company at the Old Vic in 1932, opening as Caesar in *Caesar and Cleopatra*—"since Keen is not thin and stringy [like Forbes-Robertson] you should have altered the text to plump and crumby," wrote Shaw—and playing Shylock under Gielgud's direction and Caliban to the Portia and Miranda of Peggy Ashcroft. He appeared as the King and the Ghost, to Gielgud's Hamlet in New York in 1936 and in the latter role in Tyrone Guthrie's production of the play in its entirety and in modern dress (uniform, for the Ghost) at the Old Vic in 1938.

During the last war he returned to musicals for a time and in 1947 again appeared with Gielgud in New York, replacing Cecil Trouncer as the father of Valentine (Gielgud) and Ben (Robert Flemyng) in *Love for Love*.

February 3, 1970.

Senator Estes Kefauver, of Tennessee, the Democratic nominee for Vice-President in 1956, died on August 10, 1963, at Bethesda Naval Hospital, Washington. He was 60.

With his Davy Crockett coonskin cap, his broad smile, his speedy handshake and his informal down-to-earth manner, Kefauver was the epitome of the hard-campaigning American politician whose strength lay at the grass roots. Indeed, only a consummate vote-gatherer could have remained as a liberal Senator for the southern State of Tennessee for 15 years. It was his strong mass appeal in primary elections that made him a serious contender for the Democratic Presidential nomination in both 1952 and 1956.

Yet with all his gifts as a campaigner he never seemed to carry the political weight of a potential president. His standing was highest away from the centres of political power. He was never a commanding figure among his fellow Senators. Even his greatest prize, the Vice-Presidential nomination in 1956, would probably not have been his had the traditional method of selection—by the Presidential candidate with the aid of a small group of party advisers—been followed. It was Adlai Stevenson's unexpected decision to throw the choice open to the Convention and so to provide—with little time for the prior organization of votes—for as near to a free vote among delegates as an American Party Convention is likely to see, that enabled Kefauver to defeat the present President John Kennedy in a thrilling photo-finish.

Carey Estes Kefauver was born on his father's farm at Madisonville, Tennessee, on July 26, 1903, the son of Robert Cooke Kefauver. After graduating from the University of Tennessee and Yale Law School, he became a successful Chatanooga company lawyer before giving up the law to embark on a political career in 1939.

He failed to win election to the State Senate but when a few months later a seat in the House of Representatives became vacant Kefauver was elected.

His career in Washington was fundamentally consistent right from the start. He was a firm supporter of all liberal policies, he won no favour with the established men in the House with what they regarded as his somewhat harsh comments, but he kept the support of the voters. He was reelected four times and then in 1948 won election to Congress.

CHAMPION OF LAW

It was in 1950 and 1951 that his big opportunity came as chairman of a special Senate committee investigating interstate crime. At a time when many people in the United States were becoming worried at the charges of corruption and vice in the national life, Kefauver appeared in the televised proceedings as the champion of law and decent conduct. So great an impression did the apparently simple sincerity of this tall heavily built man make that soon he had become a Presidential possibility. Hard campaigning turned him into the front-runner for the 1952 Democratic nomination. He defeated Mr. Truman—who later announced that he would not stand again—in the New Hampshire primary, and by demonstrating his grass roots strength in other primaries went to the convention with more pledged votes than any other candidate. After leading on the first two ballots, however, he was defeated on the third by Adlai Stevenson.

Kefauver did not give up his Presidential ambitions. In 1956 he based his tactics once again on competing in as many primaries as possible and indeed created a major stir by defeating Stevenson in Minnesota. But after Stevenson's victory in California, Kefauver withdrew his candidature and threw his support to Stevenson, whose running mate he was to be.

In the years following the Democratic defeat in 1956, Kefauver continued as the champion of the underdog and the supporter of liberal causes. An outspoken believer in equal rights for Negroes, he won a bitter battle for reelection to the Senate in 1960 against a militant segregationalist. In recent years he had been concentrating on investigations into the drug industry, where he alleged companies were charging excessively high prices, and into professional boxing, which he believed was partially controlled by criminal elements.

In 1935 he married Nancy, daughter of Sir Stephen Pigott, the Clydeside shipbuilder, and her vivacious personality was to prove a great asset in his political campaigning. They had three daughters and one adopted son.

August 12, 1963.

Dr. Joseph Keilberth, who collapsed while conducting a performance of Wagner's *Tristan and Isolde* in Munich on July 21, 1968, and died next day, was a musician better known to English audiences by his gramophone records than by his rare concerts in Britain.

His death at the age of 60 removed one of

the few remaining conductors brought up within, and entirely representative of, the classic German tradition.

Joseph Keilberth was born in Karlsruhe on April 19, 1908. The Keilberths had for some generations been musicians and, following in their footsteps, Joseph Keilberth became a coach at the Karlsruhe State Theatre when he was 17 and had within 10 years become principal conductor there.

In 1940 he was appointed conductor of the German Philharmonic Orchestra in Prague. The turmoil at the end of the Second World War found him in Dresden, where the authorities appointed him Director of the Opera and the Dresden Staatskapelle in a city without a theatre or a concert hall. Using a dance hall for his concerts and a large building in the suburbs as an improvised opera house—to the Dresdeners it became the "opera in the barn"—Keilberth revived music in the shattered city.

FIDELIO

A Beethoven concert on July 16, 1945, with a concert performance of Beethoven's *Fidelio* on August 10 in the makeshift opera house, were the first fruits of his determination.

In 1951, Keilberth became conductor of the Hamburg Philharmonic Orchestra, subsequently combining this with direction of the Bamberg Symphony Orchestra, which had grown out of the Prague German Philharmonic.

He worked, too, with the Hamburg State Opera, the Berlin Civic Opera, and the Nordwestdeutscher Rundfunk Orchestra of Cologne. From 1951 onwards he was heard frequently at the Bayreuth Festival. At the Edinburgh Festival of 1952 he conducted the Hamburg State Opera, and he appeared in London with the Dresden Staatskapelle during the orchestra's visit to England in 1957.

Keilberth's attitude to music was that which we recognize as traditionally German—conscientious, serious and intense. It was an attitude which he applied to a large repertoire. Mussorgsky and the Russian composers as well as such moderns as Stravinsky, Orff, Blacher, Prokofiev, Milhaud, and Britten were all within the range of his sympathies, though it seemed that Haydn, Mozart, Beethoven, Wagner and Richard Strauss were to him the essential composers, whose works he conducted with an obvious, unsensational sense of dedication.

July 22, 1968.

Helen Keller, who died on June 1, 1968, at the age of 87, became a symbol of hope through her long career for the millions of blind, deaf and dumb people throughout the world. The American authoress was herself left suffering from these afflictions after she contracted scarlet fever in the second year of her life. She remained blind and deaf but learnt how to speak. Her success in overcoming some of her disabilities became the subject of a Broadway play, a film hit—and earned her an honorary degree from Harvard University. Miss Keller met kings and queens, presidents and prime ministers in recognition of her untiring work for the physically handicapped. "The two most interesting characters of the nineteenth century", said Mark Twain not long before his death, "are Napoleon and Helen Keller."

Born on June 27, 1880, in Tuscumbia, Alabama, Helen Keller was descended on her father's side from a colonial governor of Virginia; her father was a newspaper editor. The severe illness that deprived her of sight and hearing at the age of 19 months did not halt her physical development, but having only the senses of touch and smell as her links with the world around her, her actions could not be controlled and she became like an unruly young animal. Shortly before her seventh birthday she was put in the care of Anne Sullivan, a young woman whose sight had been partially restored by operations and who was anxious to devote her life to educating the blind. The task of teaching Helen (the subject of a play, *The Miracle Worker*) required such strength and perseverance that Anne Sullivan was often in despair; but gradually she managed to call forth the affection of the child, and the next stage was to enable Helen to connect an object with its name spelled into her hand by the manual alphabet.

When this had been achieved, the girl developed rapidly. She mastered braille, learnt to write and type, and although the sound of a human voice was something beyond her ken she was taught to speak. She became an outstanding scholar, studied at Radcliffe College, memorizing the lectures that were tapped into her hand by Anne Sullivan, and earned a B.A. of Harvard. Her examination papers, immaculately typed, were so brilliant that they are today preserved in the Harvard museum. She had a flair for languages and spoke French and German fluently. Her Latin studies resulted in her making her own translation of the *Odes of Horace*, and she revelled in Greek literature. "I think Greek is the loveliest language I know anything about", she wrote. "If the violin is the most perfect musical instrument, the Greek is the violin of human thought." Philosophy became her special study. At the time of her death, she held doctorates of the universities of Harvard, Temple, Glasgow, Berlin, Delhi and Witwatersrand, and she was an honorary Fellow of the Educational Institute of Scotland.

During a lifetime of service, she worked in close association with the American Foundation for the Blind. By her personal efforts, she set out to raise two million dollars for the work of the foundation, and she said that the happiest day of her life was the establishment of its Department of Services for the Deaf-Blind. To raise funds she used every practical method that could be devised, even accepting an offer for a coast-to-coast vaudeville tour at a weekly fee that corresponded to £400 sterling. In all her strenuous work, she had continually at her side Anne Sullivan and Polly Thompson, the latter an ebullient and dedicated Scots girl who had joined her as secretary in 1914, later took over the role of companion and died in 1960.

The biggest crisis in Helen Keller's later life was the death in 1936 of the beloved "Teacher" who had led her out from silence and darkness into a world she could realize and interpret. It was through the genius of Anne Sullivan, who in 1904 became Mrs. John Macy, that she came into touch with so many phases of modern thought. One of her books, *Helen Keller's Journal*, reveals her intimate thoughts as she struggles to adjust herself to living without the person who had been the centre of her existence for nearly five decades. This *journal intime* discloses how she emerged from a stupor of grief and set out with courage upon new adventures in many lands in the service of others. Her books include *Story of My Life*, *Teacher*, *The World I Live In*, and *The Song of the Stone Wall.*

USED NORMAL FACULTIES

Often during her lifetime it was said that she must have possessed abnormal faculties which more than compensated for her lack of sight and hearing, and the late Sir Herbert Barker declared that she could "see" colours with her fingertips. Helen Keller was examined by specialists who left it on record that she possessed no abnormal faculties but had made full use of those she did possess. Not only had she learnt to ride on horseback, to swim, and had used the aeroplane long before air travel became popular, but she enjoyed the theatre and the cinema, following the action as details were spelled into her hand at a hundred words a minute. She even learnt to "listen" to human speech by placing her thumb on one's throat, her forefinger at the corner of the mouth, the second finger on the nostril, thus acquiring from the vibrations a representation of the spoken words—an accomplishment it took her nearly 20 years to perfect. It may indeed be said that the only abnormal thing about Helen Keller was the intensity of her efforts to make closer and more comprehending contact with a world which she could not see or hear.

To be with her was to enjoy a radiant extrovert personality. Once she was taken to a service at Westminster Abbey. Helen stood with the rest of the congregation and personally conducted all the music, getting the rhythm from reverberation, just as she did by putting her hand on the piano. She had no inhibitions and no self-consciousness. After the service she wanted to "see" the Unknown Warrior's tomb. She felt all round the railings and knelt on the floor to get shape and dimension.

Another time she was in London on her way to France and Greece to find out what was being done for the deaf and blind in these countries.

HOME DESTROYED

She heard that her home had been destroyed by fire with all her treasures from every country in the world and with the manuscript of her book, *Teacher*.

Nothing was left, but she promptly set herself to the Herculean task of rewriting this book.

Helen Keller's high spirits and humour surmounted all her physical restraints and made her a radiant companion. Her impassioned devotion to her life's work and her great achievements made her an heroic figure.

June 3, 1968.

Lord Kemsley, G.B.E., who died on February 6, 1968, in Monte Carlo at the age of 84, was chairman of Kemsley Newspapers Limited until 1959, when he and his family sold their interest to Lord Thomson.

With his brother, the first Lord Camrose, gone, with Lord Beaverbrook gone, the last of the old-fashioned Press Lords has quitted the scene. The public knew much about Beaverbrook but very little about the two Berry brothers, William and Gomer. Gomer Kemsley was, indeed, something of a misunderstood man. It was the impression in Fleet Street that, though he styled himself editor-in-chief of *The Sunday Times*, he had no feeling for journalism, was a stern unbending autocrat who forfeited the affection of his staff, and was unduly addicted to personal aggrandisement. Some of those who worked closely with him would contest the validity of such a picture.

It is true that as a journalist proprietor he was not in the same class as Beaverbrook, or his brother William, or Roy Thomson. It is true that his formality of mind and manner and his conception of himself as a magnate of great importance did not endear him to everyone. But the fact remains that when *The Sunday Times* was under strenuous competition from *The Observer* he brought the paper to a circulation of something like 850,000 and an immense lead when he sold out to Roy Thomson.

Certainly he was no mere figure-head in the scrap in the 1950s with the brilliant, up-and-coming *Observer*. He led *The Sunday Times* team, he discovered in himself a flair for bold action, he was capable of coming up with suggestions which made even the youngest and brashest of his executives blink, and at office lunches and conferences could subdue his natural stiffness of manner and become easy and avuncular.

INSPIRING

In all this he inspired his editorial and managerial team in an extraordinary fashion. He was respected and surrounded with loyalty. Three of his sons, Lionel, Neville, and Anthony, were all working in his featureless headquarters at 200 Gray's Inn Road when the battle was at its height, and they too in their different ways reinforced morale.

Of course, he was wrong about Munich, and Suez, and other great watersheds of national history, but so were many others. Politically he was a nineteenth-century primitive, yet in spheres other than politics he could display flashes of extraordinary intuition, as well as a magnanimity which would have surprised his critics. The Victorian virtues and defects (prudishness included) were equally pronounced in his character, and the combination was a formidable one. To most people, in fact, he was not a sympathetic man. At the same time, when he disappeared suddenly into retirement, and was heard of no more, there were those at 200 Gray's Inn Road who looked back with a curious affection to the time when "K" was in command of his rather ramshackle but distinctly colourful empire.

He started life without noticeable advantages. James Gomer Berry, born on May 7, 1883, was the youngest of three brothers, each of whom became a peer. Seymour, the eldest, who became Lord Buckland, was an industrialist; he was killed in a riding accident in 1928. William—who died in 1954—and Gomer formed a partnership in journalism which lasted for 35 years. When it ended in 1937 they, in association with the first Lord Iliffe, controlled the largest newspaper group in Great Britain, together with other publishing properties. The holdings were split between the three, and the portion retained by each Berry brother was still sufficient to make him a major power in the world of newspapers.

Seymour, William and Gomer were the sons of an estate agent, Alderman John Mathias Berry, of Merthyr Tydfil. William, after apprenticeship on the *Merthyr Tydfil Times*, went to London at 18 and within four years was a publisher on his own account, launching the *Advertising World* from a shared third-floor room in Fleet Street. Meanwhile Gomer, four years his junior, was educated in Merthyr. He knew nothing of journalism when William invited him to come up and help with the *Advertising World*. The partnership, which began with the second issue, was one of striking harmony from the outset.

Gomer attended, at first, to building up circulation, then to selling advertisement space. After four years the Berrys sold out at a profit, and this enabled them to found *Boxing* and other successful periodicals. In 1915 they bought their first newspaper, *The Sunday Times*, then 95 years old.

After the 1914–18 War their empire grew swiftly and enormously. In 1924 the brothers bought from the first Lord Rothermere the former Hulton group of Manchester newspapers which Rothermere himself had bought only in the previous year, and with Sir Edward Iliffe they formed Allied Newspapers Ltd. to own this group and *The Sunday Times*. Lord Rothermere at first retained two Hulton newspapers which were published in London, the *Daily Sketch* and the *Illustrated Sunday Herald*, but later these, too, were acquired by Allied. So were newspapers in Glasgow, Sheffield, Newcastle, Middlesbrough and elsewhere. The Berrys also owned a controlling interest in the *Western Mail* at Cardiff, which had been purchased by their brother Seymour.

Other acquisitions made the Berry-Iliffe alliance masters of a vast periodical publishing house, the Amalgamated Press; of Kelly's Directories; and of *The Financial Times*; and in 1927 *The Daily Telegraph* was sold to them by the second Lord Burnham.

Ten years later Lords Camrose, Kemsley, and Iliffe agreed to separate. One determining factor was that William had two sons and Gomer six, and it could not safely be assumed that the harmony which had characterized their partnership would continue into the next generation. Moreover, it can scarcely be doubted that Gomer, now in his middle fifties (and a peer since the previous year: William's peerage had come seven years earlier) did not relish the prospect of permanent junior status. William was not only chairman and editor-in-chief of *The Daily Telegraph*, he was also chairman of Allied Newspapers and editor-in-chief of *The Sunday Times*; and chairman of *The Financial Times* and of Kelly's Directories.

When the holdings were divided Lord Camrose took as his own property *The Daily Telegraph*, retaining also control of the Amalgamated Press and *The Financial Times*; Lord Kemsley bought his brother's shares in Allied Newspapers and became chairman of the company and editor-in-chief of *The Sunday Times*. He proclaimed his sovereignty by changing the name of the group to Kemsley Newspapers, and of its offices in London and the provincial centres to Kemsley House; and under the title-block of each newspaper he had the words inserted, "A Kemsley Newspaper".

Lord Kemsley steadily built up *The Sunday Times* to a position of great strength. The paper remained his great pride, but with the war over and with promising young men joining his organization he hoped to see great expansion in his regional properties. To this end, and with his increasing sense of editorial responsibility, he launched in 1947 the Kemsley Editorial Plan, a pioneer scheme for the training of journalists, accompanying this with the *Kemsley Manual of Journalism*, still a standard manual of training. He also started the Kemsley Empire Journalists scheme, for giving Commonwealth journalists experience of British affairs, and the Kemsley Flying Trust, which enabled gliding and much private flying to survive.

However, amidst the fiercely competitive conditions of the newspaper industry in the late 1940s and 1950s, and the restrictions on enterprise imposed by the continuance of newsprint rationing, the expected expansion in Kemsley Newspapers did not materialize; indeed, a shrinking process set in. The *Daily Sketch*, which he had re-named *Daily Graphic* to mark its transformation into a more "serious" paper, was sold back to the Rothermere interests and resumed its former title. The Kemsley *Sunday Chronicle* was merged with the Kemsley *Empire News*, the Kemsley *Daily Dispatch* with the Cadbury *News Chronicle*, and the Kemsley Glasgow *Daily Record* went to the Daily Mirror group.

SURPRISE AGREEMENT

All this retrenchment and disappointment threw Lord Kemsley into deeper involvement with *The Sunday Times*. It became his work and his hobby, his meat and his drink. Like the friend of Dr. Johnson who published the *Gentleman's Magazine*, he could not look out of the window without thinking of his newspaper.

Then, in the middle of 1959, came the rumour that Roy Thomson was in negotiation with Lord Kemsley, and those nearest to the editor-in-chief—including directors outside his own family—could not credit that "K" was intending to get rid of his beloved *Sunday Times*; the regional papers, maybe, but not that. But it was so. After secret negotiations lasting a fortnight, Lord Kemsley, autocratic to the last, broke the news to his directors that Roy Thomson had acquired control of Kemsley Newspapers and was to pay £5m. for the family's ordinary shares. The unbelievable had happened.

Several factors influenced his decision to sell. Though he and his family held a controlling interest the margin was only a slight one, and a takeover was not an impossibility. In addition, the family had dug deep into their reserves to acquire extra shares, and his sons now thought it better to sell. Recent labour troubles had given him much anxiety, and the prospects for the *Empire News* and *Sunday Graphic* were dark—and, indeed, they did not long survive his abdication. The change of control took effect on Friday, August 21, 1959. Two days later *The Sunday Times* carried a warm tribute to Lord Kemsley on its leader page; but on the front page "A Kemsley Newspaper" had vanished from the title-block. It was the end of a chapter in Fleet Street.

Lord Kemsley became a viscount in 1945. His first wife, Mary Lilian, daughter of Horace G. Holmes, died in 1928, having borne him six sons and a daughter. Two of the sons died, one of them in action in 1944.

In 1931 Lord Kemsley married Edith, daughter of E. N. Merandon du Plessis of Constance, Flacq, Mauritius. Theirs was a marriage of great devotion, and it is sad that in latter years Lady Kemsley's health should have given such concern to her husband. His heir is the Hon. Lionel Berry, who was born in 1909.

February 7, 1968.

Henry Kendall, A.F.C., died on June 9, 1962, in the south of France at the age of 65.

He will perhaps be best remembered by playgoers for his work in intimate revue, notably in the last years of the war and after it in *Sweet and Low*, *Sweeter and Lower* and *Sweetest and Lowest*. Here his agreeable stage presence and polished style provided an excellent foil to that of Hermione Gingold "stinging like a nettle", as one critic put it.

But revue did not represent the sum total of his activities; he had composed several songs and a musical comedy, appeared in films and was an active and successful producer and director both in the theatre and on television, where he had formed a close association with Brian Rix.

Born in London on May 28, 1897, he was educated at the City of London School. He made his first stage appearance in a walking-on part in *Tommy Atkins* at the Lyceum in September, 1914, and then went into the chorus of two musical productions. A useful nine months with Old Vic company followed, during which he played many of the juvenile Shakespearian parts. His stage career was interrupted by his war service in the Royal Air Force, which he left in 1919 with the rank of Captain and the Air Force Cross.

Soon after his return to the stage he scored a considerable success in *French Leave* and at Christmas, 1920, he was playing St. George in the annual revival of *Where the Rainbow Ends*.

Thereafter he played in Shakespeare, in Restoration comedy, in farce, in musical comedy and in revue, and the light and cheery way in which he acted always made him welcome. His greatest success came as a result of his engagement to follow Mr. Walter Crisham in the revue *Sweet and Low* at the Ambassadors. This was followed by *Sweeter and Lower* and *Sweetest and Lowest* and these productions occupied him until 1948, when he went to the Savoy for another revue, *A La Carte*.

During this period of his career and indeed until he died Kendall was in demand as a producer and the many successful London plays for which he was responsible included *The Shop at Sly Corner*, *Fit for Heroes*, *See How They Run*, and *Fly Away Peter*. He made good use of the experience which he then gained when he appeared in Philip King's comedy *On Monday Next* at the Embassy and the Comedy in 1949. With Mr. Andre Van Gyseghem he directed another of King's successful pieces, *Watch it, Sailor*.

He was one of the founders of the Repertory Players and appeared in many of their productions including *Havoc*, *Tunnel Trench*, *Wrongs and Rights*, *A Murder has been Arranged*, and *Someone at the Door*.

In November, 1959, he played in *Aunt Edwina* by William Douglas-Home, which was withdrawn after six performances and then put on again for a short run.

June 11, 1962.

Marie Kendall, who died on May 5, 1964, at her home in Clapham, was one of the most notable of the great stars of the music halls who survived into our less colourful days. She was 90.

Born in July, 1873, at Victoria Park in East London, she first appeared on the stage as Baby Chester, in the Pavilion Theatre, Mile End Road, as a child of five. During an active career of more than 60 years she worked with the great legendary artistes—Marie Lloyd, Dan Leno, Chirgwin and Lottie Collins among others—with whom she will be remembered. She worked with equal distinction in pantomime, variety and music hall, and although she was in her sixties when non-stop variety shows became a temporary West End fashion, Marie Kendall returned to the stage undisturbed by new conditions in a continuous bill; she had no fear of the strains of this new method of production. Changing fashions in music, too, seemed not to worry her, for, like all great artistes, she imposed fashion upon her audiences; at least one of the songs she made popular—"Just Like the Ivy"—has achieved the ubiquitous recognition of folksong.

When the demolition of Collins's Music Hall began a few months before she died, and the disappearing theatre was celebrated in a television programme, Marie Kendall appeared before the cameras to reminisce with charm, great dignity and a certain wistfulness about the hall, the artistes it had known and its great days.

Her death made those days seem suddenly much more distant.

The head of a family many of whose members made a career on the stage, she was the grandmother of Kay Kendall, who died in 1959.

May 7, 1964.

President John F. Kennedy, who was assassinated in Dallas, Texas on November 22, 1963, died in the fullness of his fame. Whatever qualifications there may be about some of his detailed policies—and no man could hold that awesome office without receiving his measure of criticism—he will take his place in the roll of strong Presidents. Throughout his time in office he had major difficulties with Congress, but he was the master of his own Administration, a man of decision and nerve. Had he lived he would have remained a forceful influence on international affairs for many years to come. In that sense he was still a man of promise.

President Kennedy's years in office will always be marked with distinction, above all for his handling of the Cuban crisis. It was then that he took the supreme risk, told the American people, and indeed the free world, what had to be faced, and firmly blocked the advancing convoy which was bringing medium-range rockets to sites in Cuba, from which they would profoundly have altered the strategic balance of power. The decisiveness of United States policy at this time not only won President Kennedy an abiding place among the great Presidents of the United States but leading, as it has done, to an easing of the cold war, and in July, 1963, to the nuclear test ban treaty, may well be regarded as one of the real turning-points in history.

YOUNGEST EVER

He was the youngest man ever to be elected to the White House. He was the first President to be born in the twentieth century; the first Roman Catholic, and the first of purely Irish descent. He was the first since Harding to come to the Presidency directly from the Senate. But for the most part these were mere accidents of history. He happened to be a signpost to new trends in American life and politics.

He had many of the qualities necessary to achieve greatness in the White House—a cool and practical judgment; emotional detachment from the passions of the moment; a penetrating intellect; and a keen and ruthless political sense. All these gifts were combined with enormous driving energy. He had an appetite for his job.

It is sometimes said that an American President can be effective abroad or effective at home, but not both. The range of subjects that he had to deal with makes it impossible for him to follow through problems simultaneously as a foreign minister and a politician. Kennedy from the first faced trouble in Congress. His first—the eighty-eighth—gave him a fair majority for anything but civil rights issues in the Senate but only a dubious and paper majority in the House, even under skilled democratic leadership. In the first two years he was forced to water down his measures which were introduced in bold presidential messages; in his second Congress he encountered heavy defeats as the result of the strengthening of the opposition—normal in a mid-term election. Plans which the nation seemed to need most fared worst. His plans for federal aid to education, especially higher education, ran into the difficulties of state rights. His cherished scheme for medical care for the aged fell through because of fears of socialized medicine. In strengthening the economy he met the same Congressional suspicion that the aim was to increase federal power and that the Democrats were engaged in their usual "spendthrift" finance. Unbalanced budgets are a congressional bogy, and Kennedy's plan to cut taxes fell foul of it. He was held back by the difficulties of the balance of payments from a real cheap money policy, and though he was successful in getting the support of Congress for trade expansion, the Administration was perpetually hampered in its efforts to raise demand effectively enough to absorb unemployment, perpetually being increased by technological change. President Kennedy saw what was wanted—a selective public investment aimed at bringing work to the nation's underprivileged. America was affluent enough, and Wall Street soared with a considerable measure of expansion. But affluence did not reach down far enough or fast enough to prevent the brewing upsurge of discontent by the Negroes.

THE NEGRO PROTEST

Kennedy's period of office saw the full emergence of the Negro protest, which erupted in novel forms, in violence, in clashes with two southern governors, in the use of troops. He knew it was coming. He had had the Negro vote in the presidential elections and expected to hold it. From the first, the administration's chances of getting a major civil rights bill through Congress, and its timing, were discussed. He failed, however, to gauge the impatience of the Negroes, and the extent to which it was losing support for the conservative organizations like the National Association for the Advancement of Coloured Peoples, and leaders devoted to constitutional methods like the Rev. Martin Luther King. Unemployment for the unskilled, the necessity of obtaining higher education and the difficulties for Negroes to get it, and the success of African and Asian countries in asserting their independence and dignity all combined to create an explosive racial situation. Mr. Kennedy relied heavily on his brother, the Attorney General, to set a rapid enough pace in the laborious procedure of winning Negroes the right to vote or be secured from discrimination in public places or amenities by legal action following from Supreme Court rulings. In his second and third years impatience boiled over, the freedom riders, the sit-in strikes, the determination of young Negroes to enrol in key southern universities, precipitated the riots which presented the United States in an embarrassing light. While doing everything to get his way without direct confrontation, the President had to fight when Federal power was defied. His civil rights Bill was prepared after the clash with Governor Barnett and the march on Washington, but by then the Negroes were unappeasable by gradualist measures—and he faced a hard fight in getting even a gradualist measure through—while there were ominous signs that white America was reacting adversely both in the Northern cities and in the South. The growing sentiment in the Republican party in favour of Senator Goldwater was a sign the President's sensitive political antennae could not miss, and he faced possible major party realignments as the result of the Negro question. Some observers thought that he faced some disasters for law and order in cities like Chicago and New York. In spite of legal and administrative measures to end discrimination against Negroes in the Federal field, Kennedy ended three years of power with a worse race problem than he had inherited.

WARNING TO NATION

Kennedy took office with his Administration alleging negligence in defence matters against the Republicans (and with ex-President Eisenhower warning the nation against the "technological military complex"). In three years the missile gap with which the country had started, at least in Democratic imagination, had become a vast lead in missiles over the Russians; the disadvantage which the west was felt to be in against the Russians had become a lead so great that the President and his Defence Secretary, Mr. McNamara, were talking of cutting down manpower, and a tremendous reforming operation had swept through the Pentagon, though it had not wholly subjugated the generals and admirals, in spite of their heavy losses when in revolt against White House policy and discipline.

Severe standardizing and reappraising of projects led to scrapping many of the Service favourites, like the B 70 bomber and the "Skybolt" missile, on which Britain had pinned its hopes. This military change led President Kennedy to press, in his third year, for more readiness by Europe to contribute to its own defence, with an eye to the use of American weapons like the multilateral force using Polaris submarines, and saving the much more intractable foreign exchange costs of American divisions and air force formations abroad.

PARTNER WITH EUROPE

One of the most important features of Kennedy's foreign policy was what became known as the Grand Design for the Atlantic Alliance, which was expounded most inspiringly though not for the first time, in his famous address to the conference of state governors delivered on the steps of Independence Hall, Philadelphia in July, 1962. The essence of this policy was the concept of two major equal partners—the United States on the one hand, and an enlarged European Community on the other. This broad vision was temporarily shattered by President de Gaulle's exclusion of Britain from the Common Market, but in spite of the difficulties created by French intransigence Kennedy continued to devote all his endeavours to strengthening the Alliance.

On the economic side his concept of partnership was most strikingly revealed by the Trade Expansion Act passed by Congress in the autumn of 1962, which gave him greater power to negotiate mutual tariff cuts than any of his predecessors ever possessed. To some extent, of course, this was a practical defensive measure taken for the benefit of American industry, for in a world of high tariffs the European Common Market could pose a real threat to American exports. But the passing of the Act aroused the hope of wide-ranging tariff cuts on an international basis that would be of the greatest benefit to world trade. If the Kennedy Round, as the negotiations under Gatt have become popularly known, does succeed it will be a fitting posthumous reward for an imaginative initiative that was more politically bold at the time than it may seem in retrospect.

In the Far East, the President had to face the contradictions of American policy. Laos which seemed to be threatening when he took office became more stable when it was left to local personalities to settle, and the American military and C.I.A. ceased to think they could impose their own (contradictory) solutions. In Vietnam there seemed no alternative but to pour money into the Diem regime, even though the Americans were well aware that it spent more time, energy, and American money in securing itself than on prosecuting the war with the cooperation of the people.

GENERALS' ANGER

This frustrating situation continued until the generals, with covert American approval, and angered and emboldened by the repression of the Buddhists, overthrew Diem and his brother. If it removed one of the many foreign incubi from the President, it was hardly a success for American policy on the spot.

The "Alliance for Progress" was first designed to be a model programme for American aid to the underdeveloped, and a scheme to promote the agrarian and social reform which so much aid failed to accomplish. Roughed out before the President took office, it was designed to halt the deterioration in Latin American developments. But it proved much harder than was anticipated to get Latin American establishments to see the dangers of social revolution, and some governments, like Brazil, consumed aid simply as day to day subsidies, without reforming at all. After three years of planning and conference talk, it was charitable to say that the Alliance was still in its early stages; the Administration's critics said it had failed.

John Fitzgerald Kennedy was born in the Boston suburb of Brookline on May 29, 1917, into a remarkable family that was to have an exceptional influence on his development. It was an intensely political family of Irish Catholic stock on both sides. The Kennedys had settled in the United States about halfway through the last century. John Kennedy's father, Joseph P. Kennedy, was the son of Pat Kennedy, who kept a saloon and was one of the city's Democratic bosses. John's mother, Rose, was the daughter of the Mayor of Boston, John E. Fitzgerald—or "Honey Fitz", as he was known—whose speciality was a spirited rendering of "Sweet Adeline" on political occasions. The future President was thus nurtured in the distinctive atmosphere of Boston Irish politics—with its zest, its love of intrigue, and its conception of politics as a contest to be won.

PATRICIAN INFLUENCES

At the time of his birth the family were living in a comparatively modest neighbourhood, but his father's financial fortunes were rising rapidly. Through investment banking and a number of business enterprises, including an excursion into the film industry, he was becoming a multimillionaire. The family moved from Boston to New York, with holiday homes at Palm

Beach and Hyannisport. All the perquisites of wealth were theirs—foreign travel, expensive schooling, luxuries at home—although the family were still not accepted in some social circles where the father's business methods were disliked as much as his origins.

Nevertheless, patrician influences mingled with those of the Boston Irish. Jack Kennedy attended only one Catholic school, and that for only one year. At the age of 14 he went to Choate, the exclusive private school in Connecticut, and then to Princeton—very briefly—and to Harvard. After leaving Choate he had studied for a short while at the London School of Economics, but his time there was interrupted by illness. A bright and able, though not a brilliant, student; keen on games, though again without exceptional prowess; he seems to have been generally and quietly popular.

Further opportunities to broaden his contacts overseas came with his father's appointment in 1938 as Ambassador in London. Out of this experience came Jack Kennedy's book, *Why England Slept*, originally written as a university thesis. As an examination of the British reaction to the nazi threat it was thoughtful and showed a readiness to probe beyond the most obvious answers, but it was not a remarkable work. More important in the long run was that Joseph Kennedy proved a most controversial diplomat. Believing that Britain was sure to be defeated, he became notorious as a vehement advocate of American isolationism and accordingly had to give up his post in 1940. As a result, his son, in his political career, while benefiting greatly from the family wealth found the father's political reputation a heavy liability.

Where the father's impact was most beneficial was at home. He inspired his nine children, of whom Jack Kennedy was the second son, with a vitality, a competitive instinct and a cohesion which was to be of lasting significance. He wanted them to excel in their studies and at their games. He encouraged free and fierce discussion of public affairs. Yet his devotion to the gospel of success prevented any trend towards dreamy idealism.

In September, 1941, Kennedy enlisted in the Navy and after a spell of shore duty was appointed in March, 1943, to command a motor torpedo boat in the Solomons. The following August came the incident that was to make him one of the authentic American war heroes. Suddenly one night a Japanese destroyer bore down upon the boat, cut it in half and left Kennedy to do the best he could for the survivors. After a series of adventures—which included towing a badly burned man on a three-mile swim to a neighbouring island with his teeth in the other's life jacket, and long and dangerous swims in search of assistance—they were finally rescued five days later. The ordeal, terrible as it was, demonstrated Kennedy's powers of leadership and endurance. He emerged with the greatest credit, and was awarded the Purple Heart and the Navy and Marine Corps Medal.

FAMILY SUPPORT

While Jack was still recovering from his injuries—his back, which had earlier been hurt in a football match at Harvard, was badly damaged this time—news was received in August the following year of the death on a bombing raid over Europe of his elder brother, Joe, a dominant and able young man who might well have had a bright career ahead of him. This was an event of more than personal sorrow for Jack. It meant that he was now the focus of the family ambitions.

Whether this was the cause of his entry into politics, as so many stories tell, must he very doubtful. But it followed soon after. First he had a brief flirtation with journalism. He was one of the correspondents who covered the inauguration of the United Nations at San Francisco and the British election of 1945 for the Hearst newspapers. He was, however, already looking about for some opportunity to run for political office, and when the Eleventh Massachusetts Congressional District fell vacant in November of that year he gave up whatever thoughts he may have had of a journalistic career.

It was a mixed and difficult constituency for a political newcomer, and it was a general surprise when he defeated the other candidates for the Democratic nomination the following June—which made it certain that he would win the seat in such a Democratic stronghold. But it was no fluke. Many of the features which were to mark later Kennedy campaigns were evident in this first one. He got into the contest early and spent months stumping the constituency with amazing energy and singleness of purpose. He made full use of his boyish charm and attractive appearance by meeting and letting himself be seen by as many people as possible. He built up his own political machine with great efficiency and largely independently of the official party organization. The family wealth and the active support of all the immediate members of the family were devoted to the cause. Moreover, whatever liability the family background was to be in later years, the name of Kennedy was still an asset in Boston.

YOUTHFUL APPEARANCE

During his years in the House of Representatives Kennedy did not look an embryo President. His youthful appearance and nonchalant habits did not fit the conventional view of the dignity of a Congressman. For the most part his political activities were centred on the problems facing Massachusetts. He was assiduous in looking after the interests of any constituent who approached him for help. He was a "bread-and-butter" liberal, concentrating on housing and other welfare programmes which directly and immediately affected the well-being of his constituents. Where these were concerned he could be forthright and courageous—as, for instance, when he denounced the attitude toward housing legislation of the American Legion, one of the awesome bodies of the American Way of Life. But in general he did not involve himself so much with the wider and less tangible issues of the day.

Admittedly, it was in these years that he began his keen interest in labour reform, and he was one of those to vote against the passing of the Taft-Hartley Bill—though that was not likely to weaken his position back home. Also, he dissociated himself from the blatantly isolationist views of his father and openly attacked the Far East policies of the Truman Administration on the floor of the House.

But he was far from an unswerving supporter of foreign aid and other programmes whose value would seem self-evident to an orthodox liberal. The main importance of his period in the House is that the time was spent in building an impregnable base for himself in his own state.

He gained the benefit of this in 1952 when he ran for the Senate. He had been reelected unopposed to the House in 1948 and by a very substantial margin in 1950. But two years later a further term did not attract him and he boldly challenged for the Senate seat held by the formidable Henry Cabot Lodge, Jnr., then one of Eisenhower's leading backers for the Presidency and later to be Ambassador to the United Nations and Nixon's running mate in 1960. To oust a man of such standing and ability seemed an awesome proposition. But Kennedy set to with the same technique as before—he had in fact been virtually campaigning for years by accepting an incredibly intense programme of speaking engagements up and down the state. Kennedy won by some 70,000 votes at the same time as Eisenhower was sweeping Massachusetts for the Republicans by more than 200,000. It was therefore a double triumph for Kennedy ro have succeeded in such a contest when the tide was against his party.

In his early months in the Senate Kennedy still concentrated mostly on the regional needs of New England. But two other factors were soon to take more prominence in his life: one private and the other the issue that was to dog him for years. On September 12, 1953, he was married to Jacqueline Lee, daughter of John V. Bouvier III. Her charm, her good looks and her youth were to be an asset to him in his public as well as his private life. Of the three children born to them, a son and daughter survive.

MCCARTHY ISSUE

The other development was not such a happy omen. Kennedy had remained on the sidelines as resentment and concern grew over the investigating techniques of Senator Joe McCarthy. His equivocal attitude to what became the most pressing issue in American politics raised a question mark over his integrity which took very long to obliterate in the eyes of a good number of people. How could a man of real principle, it was asked, remain as silent as Kennedy was at such a time?

It is important to note that he was never in the McCarthy camp. Although he voted for McCarthy a number of times he was not a party to McCarthy's methods and was to be found on the other side just as, if not more, frequently. But he delivered no root and branch condemnation, and when the Senate finally censured McCarthy in December, 1954, Kennedy was gravely ill in hospital and unable to vote.

There were plausible reasons why Kennedy never took an open stand against McCarthy. His father was a friend of the Wisconsin Senator and contributed to his fund. His brother Robert, whom he was later to make his Attorney-General, served for a while on McCarthy's staff in 1953. Apart from such personal inhibitions, Kennedy also had to consider the warm favour in which so many of his Irish catholic constituents held McCarthy. A vehement attack from Kennedy might have been an act of political suicide, and many a prudent man in his position would have manoeuvred with equal circumspection.

Perhaps such considerations would have convinced more people if Kennedy had not published his second book, *Profiles in Courage* early in 1956—for this study of a selection of eminent Senators who had risked their careers for some principle eulogized the very quality Kennedy had not shown in the McCarthy affair: the readiness to defy public opinion for a basic belief whatever the personal consequences. But then it would be hard to judge any author, and particularly a practising politician, by the standards of his heroes.

In general, however, the book was extremely well received—it received a Pulitzer award—and helped to strengthen a rising reputation. It was written while he was convalescing from his illness, a major spinal operation in October, 1954. So serious was his condition at one stage that his life was despaired of and the last rites were administered.

HARDENING VIEWS

Some commentators have compared the impact of this illness on Kennedy's development with Franklin Roosevelt's polio attack. Kennedy's emergence as a man of strongly liberal convictions, it has been suggested, was born of his suffering. But that would appear too emotional an interpretation for a man whose guarded liberalism was of a highly cerebral nature.

What his illness may well have done was to advance his maturity and quicken his ambition. At all events, soon after his return to Washington in May, 1955, his name was being mentioned as a possible Vice-Presidential candidate in the 1956 election. At the Chicago convention the Presidential nominee, Adlai Stevenson, took the surprising course of throwing the selection of his running mate to a vote among the delegates rather than making the choice himself. At first it looked as if Kennedy would win but there was a final dramatic swing in the balloting to Senator Kefauver, who won by the narrowest of margins.

As it proved, this was a concealed blessing for Kennedy. He had been brought into national prominence without having to suffer the subsequent stigma of defeat at the hands of the country's voters. With this start he soon began his long and brilliantly organized campaign for the highest office. His speaking engagements now ranged over the country as a whole. No longer did he put the main emphasis on the problems of New England. His liberal views began to harden so that it became easier to judge exactly what he stood for—and much of what he stood for was likely to be politically advantageous. His attitude on civil rights became firmer and was to become more forthright still. On foreign policy he was an internationalist, with an enlightened appreciation of the forces of nationalism in Africa and Asia. In July, 1957, he provoked a minor international storm by his attack in the Senate on France's Algerian policy. Where the Eisenhower Administration dwelt on the need for a stable dollar Kennedy put the emphasis more on expansion. And, of course, he had long been a believer in "bread-and-butter" liberalism—government-sponsored social welfare policies.

LABOUR REFORM

Yet while his liberal commitments became more decided, he did not renounce his sense of the practical. This was particularly evident in his handling of labour reform legislation. Hearings before the Labour Rackets Committee revealed grave abuses in some union activities. Clearly there was a case for some tightening up of the law, but there were some who wanted to make this an excuse for draconian legislation. Kennedy decided on compromise and was the co-sponsor of such a measure which passed the Senate in 1958 but was lost in the House. The following session he successfully piloted another labour reform Bill which after further compromise became law.

This may not have made Kennedy many friends—there were people on both sides who intensely disliked the final outcome—but it confirmed his position as an accomplished legislator and one of the Senate's "inner circle".

That, however, was only a limited advantage to his Presidential ambitions. Only one man had moved straight from the Senate to the White House, and the precedent of Warren Harding was not a happy one. Added to the supposed disadvantage of being a Senator, Kennedy also had to face criticism of his youth and his Roman Catholicism. The only way to overcome these obstacles was to demonstrate to the party professionals that he had massive popular backing. In other words, he had to enter and win the primaries.

He won all seven primaries that he entered, and by the time the Democratic convention assembled at Los Angeles in July, 1960, his election on the first ballot was almost a foregone conclusion. The convention also provided him with the radical programme that he wanted—particularly on civil rights and social welfare questions such as education, helath, care of the aged and housing. At the same time, he kept his shrewd political judgment by choosing the more conservative Lyndon Johnson as his running mate with the special task of keeping the southern states loyal to the Democratic cause.

Throughout the months of electioneering Kennedy was always striving to catch up the lead naturally enjoyed by Nixon through the years of publicity as Vice-President and the declared support of the incumbent President. Kennedy was helped by the historic innovation of the first televised debates between the candidates in which he showed to advantage. Yet so close was the voting that even days afterwards it still seemed possible that Nixon might win. Finally Kennedy triumphed by one of the narrowest margins on record.

He had stumped the country so arduously for such a long period that many people were surprised that his health, which had remained subject to occasional breakdowns, had stood the strain. Soon after he assumed the Presidency the fears began to be realized. He injured his back again while planting a tree at a ceremony in Canada. After his return from Europe in the summer of 1961 he had to resort to crutches for a time, and although his back seemed to improve he continued whenever possible to use the rocking-chair which eased any discomfort.

NUCLEAR TESTS

After the series of atmospheric nuclear tests by the Soviet Union in the autumn of 1961 President Kennedy was under military pressure to resume the testing of United States devices. He let it be known that he was ready to do so if necessary, but he deferred a decision for some months. On March 2 he declared that the United States would resume atmospheric testing in the latter part of April unless the Soviet Union agreed before then to sign and apply an effective treaty banning all nuclear tests. He expected the Russians to show their intentions at the disarmament conference which was about to meet at Geneva. He and Mr. Macmillan would be prepared to meet Mr. Khrushchev to sign an effective treaty, an essential condition of which was on-site inspection.

The offer was not accepted and on April 25 the United States began a new series of tests in the Pacific. Mr. Macmillan was in Washington at that time for his fifth round of conversations with the President and he found that the failure to reach an understanding with Russia about nuclear tests had not changed President Kennedy's determination to seek accommodation with Russia by patient discussion and negotiation.

The American series of tests was completed on November 4, 1962, and efforts to reach a test-ban agreement were renewed in the very different atmosphere that followed the Cuban crisis. In June agreement was made to hold high-level test ban talks in Moscow, with at last a fair prospect of success, and in July these efforts were crowned by the signing of the treaty, limited in its terms, but of the greatest significance for the future of east-west relations.

CUBAN CHALLENGES

Cuba showed him at his weakest and at his best. There could be no excuse for the original catastrophe of Cuba in the spring of 1961. He was condemned from all sides—for conniving at an armed attack upon a neighbouring country, and for failing to give the rebels the assistance to make their assault successful.

The result was that he seemed to have the worst of both worlds. Castro remained in power, perhaps even more secure than before. The free world's confidence in Kennedy's judgment was gravely undermined. To the neutral nations he seemed to have infringed his own high principles. And there was the jolt to his own self-esteem.

The second crisis of October, 1962, sudden in its arrival and decisive in its outcome, was the central event in President Kennedy's handling of foreign policy. It measured his daring judgment and determination, and had a profound effect on Russo-American relations.

Russian military interest in Cuba, and political pressures in the United States that it be terminated had been building up for months.

But the crisis when it came, came suddenly. On October 20 Mr. Kennedy broke off an election tour with a "diplomatic cold". On the 22nd he announced in a broadcast to the nation that he had ordered the blockade of Cuba to prevent all supplies of offensive military equipment from reaching the island. It had, he said, been established the previous week that offensive missile bases were being prepared on the island. The transformation of Cuba into an important strategic base constituted an explicit threat to the peace and security of all the Americas and contradicted the repeated assurances of Russian spokesmen that the arms build-up in Cuba would retain its original defensive character. "It shall be the policy of this nation to regard any nuclear missile launched from Cuba against any nation in the western hemisphere as an attack by the Soviet Union on the United States requiring a full retaliatory response upon the Soviet Union."

EMERGENCY MEETING

He was asking, the message went on, for an emergency meeting of the Security Council of the United Nations, and would call for the prompt dismantling and withdrawal of all offensive weapons, under the supervision of U.N. observers, "I call upon chairman Khrushchev to halt and eliminate his clandestine, reckless and provocative threat to world peace and to stabilize relations between our two nations."

Clear notice had been given that the United States was not prepared to tolerate the disturbance to the strategic balance that missile bases on Cuba implied; effective military measures had been taken to check any further build-up; and the immediate objective of dismantlement of the bases had been defined. Khrushchev could not proceed without engaging in a limited war in the Caribbean, which he was in no position to win, or precipitating a nuclear exchange.

By the clarity and boldness of his policy Kennedy had seized the advantage; but he was careful not to put the Russians in a position from which withdrawal would be virtually impossible and careful also to keep all diplomatic channels open especially at the United Nations. Four days later, after some initial blustering by Khrushchev, both he and the President replied in conciliatory terms to an appeal by U Thant for the suspension of arms shipments and steps to search ships. Meanwhile ships from the eastern block were reported to have turned back on approaching the area of the blockade. Later Khrushchev ordered Russian ships to stay out of the interception area, while the President assured U Thant that American vessels would do everything possible to avoid a clash. On October 28 Khrushchev agreed to dismantle the missile bases under United Nations verification, a decision which Kennedy at once greeted as a statesmanlike and constructive constribution to peace. Having come within sight of achieving the objective of his bold and carefully calculated policy, he showed no desire to extract humiliation from the Russian leader. By the beginning of November the offending bases were being dismantled. This direct confrontation between the two major nuclear powers was a turning point in postwar history; and from the insight the two leaders gained into each other's purposes and strength, they moved during the succeeding 12 months towards a less tense and insecure phase of east-west relations.

RIDING OUT TROUBLE

During his first presidential visit to Europe he failed to establish either friendly personal relations or any deep respect in his first meeting with Khrushchev at Vienna.

Yet throughout these difficulties Kennedy's calmness stood him in good stead. In spite of a reported sensitiveness to criticism, he was never panicked into making a bad situation worse by desperate measures. In his conduct of the nerve-stretching Berlin crisis he was admirably resolute and moderate—at a time when such a happy combination of virtues was not always apparent in the pressure from his allies and from opinion at home.

He had demonstrated his ability to ride out trouble and, to some extent, to grow with his job as he had done throughout his career—both essential attributes for the White House.

His last visit to Europe in summer 1963, in the course of which he had talks with Harold Macmillan at Birch Grove, was particularly notable for the sentimental visit he made to Ireland, in the course of which he won many friends, and for his rousing reception by the people of Berlin.

November 23, 1963.

Major-General Sir John Noble Kennedy, G.C.M.G., K.C.V.O., K.B.E., C.B., M.C., who died on June 15, 1970, at the age of 76, served almost continuously for 10 years from 1935 on the planning and operational side of the War Office. He was denied the opportunity of high command in the field, and by the very nature of his employment was little known to the public; but he was the right-hand man to two successive Chiefs of the Imperial General Staff, Sir John Dill and Lord Alanbrooke. In 1943–45 he was Assistant C.I.G.S. (Operations and Intelligence). After the war he was a successful Governor of Southern Rhodesia.

John Noble Kennedy was born in 1893, the eldest of the six children of the Rev. J. R. Kennedy. From his father—a fine, patriarchal, bearded figure of a type long vanished—he inherited a passion for birds and for fishing which he indulged all his life. Educated locally, he entered the Royal Navy at the age of 18 as a Paymaster-Midshipman in 1911, but when the war broke out, fearing that he might find himself on non-combatant duties, he contrived to transfer to the Royal Artillery, with whom he saw continuous service in France and Flanders. Before he was 25 he had won the Military Cross, been mentioned in dispatches, had commanded a battery and been a Brigade Major.

DILL'S MOVE

Between the wars as a student at Camberley he caught the eye of Dill, who brought him into the War Office in 1935, soon after he himself was made Director of Military Operations. In the next ten years he was to leave it only twice; for a year as a student at the Imperial Defence College, and for a brief space in 1940 when he was C.R.A. of the 52nd Division and B.G.S. in Northern Ireland. In October of that year Dill, now C.I.G.S., made him D.M.O. He had already served as Director of Plans from October 1938 till December 1939, when he had been injured in the black-out.

As D.M.O. it fell to him to reduce to detailed plans the military side of the multifarious projects which emerged from the Prime Minister's brain, as well as controlling the operational machinery of the War Office. When Dill, worn out by constant bickering with the Prime Minister, was superseded by Sir Alan Brooke at the end of 1941, Kennedy slipped easily into the new relationship. Brooke and he had in common the fact that both were gunners, and both shared the same hobbies; there was also a similar and meticulous precision of mind. In 1957 Kennedy published an autobiographical account of his long service in the War Office, based largely on notes and memoranda made at the time, which he entitled *The Business of War*.

TOO DISPARAGING

It was criticized in some quarters as being too disparaging of the Prime Minister's exhausting flights of fancy, although in the main it was lavish in praise of him. It appeared soon after the much criticized *Turn of the Tide*, which was based by Sir Arthur Bryant on Alanbrooke's papers, and which was adjudged by some to chip away unduly at the popular conception of Churchill's achievement. *The Business of War* was in fact a useful footnote to history, complementary to Alanbrooke without being collusive.

In 1946, Kennedy, who had retired the year before, was appointed Governor of Southern Rhodesia in succession to Admiral Sir Campbell Tait. He found that country in a mood of optimistic expansion under Sir Godfrey Huggins (now Lord Malvern) as its Prime Minister; and he threw himself eagerly into its aspirations.

SECOND TERM

He began a second term, in the course of which his position was eclipsed by the coming of Federation and the appointment of Lord Llewellin as Governor-General in 1953.

Kennedy was in some respects an austere man, but hospitable, kindly and friendly, with a tremendous capacity for work. Whatever he put his hand to he did with all his might; he was meticulous over detail. He was for many years a valued contributor to *The Times*. It was perhaps his misfortune, so far as fame was concerned, that he had made himself so nearly indispensable in the War Office; but he was certainly the right man in the right place, and his contribution to the war considerable.

He was twice married; in 1926 to Isabella, eldest daughter of Lord John Joicey-Cecil, by whom he had three sons and two daughters; she died in 1941, and in the following year he married Catherine, only daughter of Major J. G. Fordham. She died in 1969.

June 17, 1970.

Joseph P. Kennedy, father of the late President Kennedy and Senator Robert Kennedy, died on November 18, 1969, at the age of 81.

An immensely successful financier, he also played an active and forceful part in the politics of his own generation. As befitted a Bostonian Irishman he was a loyal Democrat and a zealous supporter of Roosevelt; but as American Ambassador in London during the early days of the Second World War he became a highly controversial figure on both sides of the Atlantic. His financial activities at home and his hard-driving personality had also made him many enemies.

Yet he deserves to be remembered as much as anything as the remarkably inspiring father of a large family. It was he who developed the intense competitiveness but fundamental cohesion of the Kennedy clan. It was he who embedded in them the fierce determination to excel.

INFLUENCE ON ELECTIONS

It was he who stimulated their interest in public affairs. It was he who decided that the boys would be better prepared for the struggles of adult life if they were not brought up at Roman Catholic schools.

If John Kennedy subsequently had cause to regret his father's political reputation, there can be no doubt that his career was advanced in many other ways by his father's help. There was the family wealth, of which Joseph Kennedy was the source. Equally important, there was the concerted family drive behind every election that John Kennedy fought. Each time it was a family operation with brothers and sisters speaking, organizing, and canvassing—while the father remained out of the public eye, but exhorting, advising (even though his advice was certainly not always taken), and still very much the centre of the family.

Joseph Patrick Kennedy was born in Boston on September 6, 1888, of Irish American parentage. His father, Patrick Kennedy, owned a saloon and was one of the local Democratic political "bosses". Joseph Kennedy attended local schools and then went to Harvard, where he graduated in 1912, having also achieved some prowess as an athlete. His first job after leaving Harvard was that of a bank examiner; then, at the age of 25 he became president of the Columbia Trust Company of Boston, having borrowed the money to gain control.

In 1914 he married Rose Fitzgerald, daughter of "Honey Fitz" Fitzgerald, Mayor of Boston. They had four sons and five daughters. His eldest son, Lieutenant Joseph P. Kennedy, Junior, was killed while on a bombing raid on Normandy in August, 1944. John Kennedy was the second son. The third, Robert Kennedy, served him as Attorney General and was assassinated like his brother. President Kennedy was murdered in Dallas, Texas, in 1963, while in office; Robert Kennedy in Los Angeles in 1968 while seeking the Democratic nomination as candidate for that office. The fourth son, Edward Kennedy, is Senator for Massachusetts. The second daughter. Kathleen, married the Marquess of Hartington, elder son of the tenth Duke of Devonshire. He was killed in action in Normandy in 1944, and she died in an air crash four years later. The third daughter is married to Sargent Shriver, appointed American Ambassador in Paris in 1968; and the fourth, Patricia, married Peter Lawford, the actor, and they were divorced in 1966.

During the First World War he was manager of the Bethlehem Steel Corporation's shipbuilding yard on the Fore River at Quincy, Massachusetts, a position which incidentally, brought him his first contacts with Franklin Roosevelt, then Assistant Secretary of the Navy in the Wilson Administration. In the postwar period Kennedy was associated first with the Boston banking house of Hayden-Stone and Company, and subsequently with a number of firms in the film industry; he also added considerably to his fortunes by active speculations in Wall Street, and when in 1930 he gave up most of his film interests to enter the world of finance he was reputed to be worth $5m.

The campaign for the 1932 presidential election found Kennedy a strong backer of Franklin Roosevelt. He is said to have made a very large individual contribution to the Democratic campaign funds and even before, at the party convention in Chicago, he had some hand in securing for Roosevelt the Democratic nomination. His Wall Street record may have stood in the way of his being rewarded with high office when Franklin Roosevelt formed his Administration in March, 1933, but in the following year Kennedy, against the misgivings of many of the liberals around the President, was appointed to the chairmanship of the Securities Exchange Commission, the body set up under the New Deal to supervise stock market issues. He became a successful example of the poacher turned gamekeeper. Kennedy retired from this body in the summer of 1935 and then concerned himself successfully in the reorganization of the Radio Corporation of America. He again actively supported Roosevelt in the 1936 presidential election—writing a book *I'm for Roosevelt*—and in 1937 took the chairmanship of the newly created Maritime Commission.

CONCERN FOR WELFARE

His liberalism and support for the New Deal was limited to a concern for welfare and social security. Wider questions of individual liberty he dismissed impatiently as abstractions. This, on top of his social background and financial operations, helped to make him something of a political anomaly and lone wolf. The liberals hated him, regarded him as a Wall Street shark, and were horrified by his appointment to the Securities Exchange Commission though some were later won over. The business community distrusted him for his association with Roosevelt and called him a political opportunist. Anglo-Saxon society, particularly in Boston, rejected him because of his Irish background, causing him once to demand angrily; "I was born here; my children were born here; what the hell do I have to do to be an American?" His driving ambition was probably stimulated by these conflicts, and his personality reflected them. He tended to display a disconcerting mixture of Irish charm and blarney, steely calculation, ruthless competitiveness, and warm humanity.

In the later thirties his opposition to some of the New Deal fiscal policies grew into open hostility but his personal friendship with Roosevelt survived, and on January 7, 1938, he was appointed Ambassador to the Court of St. James in succession to Leonard Bingham.

NOVELTY

The fact that such a position had been given to an Irish-American was itself a novelty, and Kennedy showed a talent for making himself conspicuous far beyond that of other members of the diplomatic circle of whatever nationality. His tall, broad shouldered figure, his constant smile, his friendliness of manner and great energy made a ready appeal to the British public, as did his domestic life. He recognized the importance of cultivating good relations with the press, and in addition his entrance into society was assisted by his complete identification with the appeasement policy of the British Government of the day. A speech he made at the Trafalgar Day dinner of 1938—shortly after the Munich Agreement—in which he seemed to range himself on the side of those who wished to appease the dictators evoked considerable criticism.

Franklin Roosevelt was distrustful of career diplomatists, and in any event Kennedy's standing in the Democratic Party and the personal affection with which Roosevelt regarded him gave him a position of great strength as well as a large measure of independence of the State Department; and at the outset of his term in London his reports carried great weight.

Kennedy, however, did not measure up to either the difficulties or the opportunities of his position. Too much cannot be blamed on him personally; in other countries, too, men whose aptitudes lay in the field of business were given the task of making crucial decisions in the unfamiliar sphere of foreign policy. Moreover, at the time of the Munich agreement Washington, itself, had no settled foreign policy, and them and later Kennedy could only give it the advice of an old-fashioned isolationist to whom European relations were a tangled skein of iniquity in which the United States should not get itself involved.

When war broke out in September, 1939, President Roosevelt withdrew much more from his absorption in home affairs, but in the development of his foreign policy his Ambassador in London could offer him no assistance: it did not need the defeat of France in 1940 to convince Kennedy that Britain could not win and that the United States must stay out of the war. When the Nazis did overrun Europe such a conviction ran contrary to the course in which American sentiment was moving. A president who allowed his ambassadors to bypass the State Department could also bypass his ambassadors; Roosevelt made use of ad hoc missions to ascertain the situation in Europe, and Anglo-American relations began to be evolved in Washington rather than in London, and later, when Sir Winston Churchill became Prime Minister, between Roosevelt and Churchill personally.

Kennedy resigned his post in London in 1940. In Octover he had returned to the United States, it being given out that he was doing so in order to help the President with his election campaign. A statement "democracy is dead in Britain", which he was reported to have made shortly after his return, caused as much bewilderment as resentment in Britain so far as the general public was concerned. It put Kennedy in an entirely different light from that in which he had previously stood. Rumours became current of a rift between him and Roosevelt, and he bought time on the American radio to make a statement on his relations with the President.

UNPOPULAR VIEWS

It was clear that a man with his views could not remain American Ambassador in London at such a time.

During the months before the Japanese attack on the United States Fleet at Pearl Harbour Kennedy ranged himself publicly on the side of the isolationists, making statements against United States participation in the war and the granting of lend-lease aid to Great Britain.

Early in 1943 Kennedy was known to have conferred with Roosevelt, and it was rumoured that he was to be offered an important position in the Administration. However, nothing materialized.

After the war Kennedy energetically backed the entry of his son John into politics. Well aware that he was a controversial figure, he remained discreetly in the background, particularly in the final presidential campaign, but he was liberal with money and—in the early stages anyway—with advice. He certainly influenced the future president considerably but he fell far short of imprinting all his ideas upon him and would not have expected to do so. In Congress the son frequently supported measures which his father would have opposed, such as the loan to Britain, other foreign commitments, and some domestic welfare Bills enlarging the role of the federal government. The McCarthy issue also revealed their different attitudes.

Joseph Kennedy was a friend and financial supporter of the late senator.

SOUGHT DETACHMENT

His son tried to remain detached, which cost him some liberal support, but he voted against McCarthy on certain issues and resisted the efforts of his father's friends to have McCarthy endorse him. Such political differences, however, never seemed to have the least effect on the close personal relationship between father and son.

In December, 1961, Joseph Kennedy suffered a stroke from which he never properly recovered.

Kennedy was one of the leading Roman Catholic laymen in the United States. In September, 1950, he made a gift of $2,500,000 to a Bronx Home for Roman Catholic Orphans in memory of his son killed in the war. He was Roosevelt's special representative to the Coronation of Pope Pius XII, who in 1942 conferred upon him the title of Grand Knight of the Order of Pius IX. Kennedy also received honorary doctorates from the Universities of Cambridge, Edinburgh, Manchester, Liverpool, and Bristol, as well as from the National University of Ireland.

November 19, 1969.

Margaret Kennedy, the novelist, died at Adderbury, near Banbury, on July 31, 1967. She was in her early seventies.

The overwhelming success of the novel *The Constant Nymph* in 1924 almost obscured the quality of Margaret Kennedy's personality and intellectual character. She was the daughter of Charles Kennedy, a distinguished lawyer, and in 1925 she married another lawyer, David Davies, who became a Q.C. and a county court judge. She lived in a world of intellectual austerity and this was amply demonstrated in the book she published in 1958 called *The Outlaws on Parnassus*.

This was a serious study in the art of fiction and its degeneration in public esteem during the twentieth century. It revealed her sound education in literary history, in philosophy and in social awareness, a typical product of an education at Cheltenham and Somerville acting upon an abnormally brilliant intellectual equipment. She had, as *The Constant Nymph* reveals, a lively sense of the fight for freedom not only in the arts but in life at large from the moral, social and religious points of view. The book is an examination based upon a kind of caricature of the life of Augustus John and his circle. It relates the aesthetic revolution to the austerities of moral and religious restraint. The novel was of course famous throughout the world; it was dramatized with Elizabeth Bergner in the leading part. She later wrote *Escape Me Never* for Elizabeth Bergner. Her later novel, *Troy Chimneys*, received the James Tait Black Award. This book is to be related to her biography of Jane Austen, with whom she may be compared for brilliance of *mise en scène*. It is likely that among the many brilliant women novelists of the twentieth century Margaret Kennedy will be distinguished by this hardness, gaiety and firm moral stamina.

August 1, 1967.

Alexander Kerensky, who was Prime Minister in the Provisional Government of Russia during the fateful months before the Bolshevik seizure of power in 1917, died on June 11, 1970, in New York. He was 89.

It is easier today than it was 40 years ago to recognize the causes of Kerensky's failure in face of the explosive forces released by the spontaneous upheaval in Petrograd in the previous March. The personal causes were important, though less important than those that derived from the whole character of Russian historical development. An orator, fluent and resonant in a somewhat tawdry vein of eloquence and possessed of a sincere if shallow political idealism, Kerensky was not equipped for the part of a man of destiny. Although when he emerged on the revolutionary scene in the capital in 1917 he appeared to ride the whirlwind with superb assurance and evidently saw himself (as Sukhanov, the most illuminating of witnesses, put it) as "a bit of a Bonaparte", in point of fact he lacked the strength of character which alone might have enabled him to grapple with great events. More significantly, however, in the hour of crisis the whole weight of the bias of the centuries towards authoritarian rule in Russia was against him. There was all too little support in Russian society in 1917 for the democratic transformation which he vaguely hoped to bring about, all too little practical opportunity in the unstable situation of "dual power" in Petrograd to direct into orderly and constitutional channels the pent-up hopes and passions of the masses. The Provisional Government sat in the seat of authority, but all effective revolutionary power was concentrated in the Soviets.

Not that Kerensky's hope was doomed at the outset. But he would have found himself in indubitably better case if in the first place he had truly recognized the war-weariness of a Russia bled white by her losses in war. To the Bolshevik slogan of "Peace and Bread" that triumphed in November, Kerensky offered as an alternative only an irrelevant display of rhetorical leadership in war. In seeking to keep an exhausted Russia in the war on the Allied side at a time when the country's supreme and obvious need was peace, when communications were paralysed and the entire machinery of civilian supplies had broken down, Kerensky showed a total want of realism. His motives, no doubt, were in every way creditable, while for their part the Allies themselves showed far too little understanding of his predicament.

ORATORY

But there is no substitute for realism in the politics of a developing revolution. Against the drive and demagogy of the Bolshevik denunciation of the "imperialist war", Kerensky's high-flown oratory was doubly futile.

No less unrealistic was his decision, or at least the decision in which he concurred with the Social-Revolutionary members of the successive Cabinets over which he presided, to leave the solution of the "agrarian question" to the forthcoming Constitutent Assembly. Nothing could have been plainer at the start of the revolution than that the only solution acceptable to the peasant masses was the expropriation of the private estates in their interest. Wedded to a textbook legalism in the midst of the convulsion that had overtaken Russia, Kerensky delayed positive action even after the peasantry of their own accord had begun to seize and carve up the private estates. In the last resort it was his failure to secure peasant support for the Provisional Government that enabled the Bolsheviks to seize and maintain power.

Alexander Fyodorovich Kerensky was born in the Volga city of Simbirsk (now Ulyanovsk) in 1881, a son of the headmaster of the local gymnasium, who not long afterwards numbered Lenin among his pupils. He was educated there and at the University of St. Petersburg, where he graduated in law. A successful member of the St. Petersburg Bar at an early age, his impassioned defence on a number of occasions of prisoners accused of political crimes earned him a degree of celebrity and brought him into touch with anti-Tsarist opinion of all but the less and most extreme varieties. Elected to the fourth Duma in 1912 as the member for Sarotov, his denunciation of the Government over the shooting that occurred during a bitter strike in the Lena goldfields in that year brought him further notice.

He made his appearance in the Duma as a member of the small composite Trudovik (Labour) group, which at the time represented a somewhat chastened Social-Revolutionary brand of socialism. Together with the similarly small group of Social Democrats of both factions, it constituted a more or less negligible left wing in the Chamber. Kerensky made no great stir, on the whole, in the Duma. But outside his name was sufficiently well known, and on the formation in March, 1917, of the Provisional Government, which had evolved from an unofficial committee of the Duma consisting of liberal and moderate conservative leaders, he was offered, and promptly accepted, the portfolio of Justice. He was the only Socialist in the Government and its only link with the Petrograd Soviet, of which he was a vice-president. But that link made him—in fact, if not as yet in title—the most powerful member of the Government.

TOUR OF FRONT

What followed is familiar, and by now largely uncontroversial, history. In May, after the demonstrations in the capital against Milyukov, the Foreign Minister, and Guchkov, Minister of War, both resigned and Kerensky took over both the War Office and the Admiralty. He at once went on a tour of the front, delivered himself of patriotic exhortations to the troops, and encountered the growing force of Bolshevik defeatist propaganda. He returned to the capital in a dejected and uneasy state of mind, but nevertheless seems to have entertained high hopes of the July offensive on the Galician front. In the event, after a few initial gains the demoralized Russian troops virtually refused to stir and their positions were overrun by the enemy. Kerensky, now Prime Minister in place of Prince G. E. Lvov, and head of a Government in which Socialists of one complexion or another were in the majority, was already all but completely isolated. Having fumbled the opportunity to take drastic action against the Bolshevik faction as a whole during the "July days", he had only a little further to go before he would be obliged to capitulate to the Petrograd Soviet. Clearly the next and possibly decisive stage of revolution could not be long delayed. It was hastened by the Kornilov episode in September. After Kerensky, in order to forestall Kornilov's bid for power, had in effect armed the workers—a measure which until then he had strongly opposed—his position was lost. A third coalition government under his leadership was formed towards the end of September, but by now the Bolshevik seizure of power in the name of the party and not of the Soviets was at hand.

In those 10 days that witnessed the birth of Communist Russia, Kerensky went into hiding. Months later he made his escape from Russian in a British destroyer sailing from Murmansk. He went to Britain, where he was joined some two years later by his wife and two sons, lived for a time in Czechoslovakia and then in Germany, but spent most of the years of exile before 1939 in France, where for a period he was associated with an émigré Russian journal, *Dni* (*Days*). In exile he turned inevitably to self-exculpation, seeking in rather laboured fashion to saddle others with the responsibility for his errors and misfortunes. The greater part of *The Prelude to Bolshevism* (1919) consists of his evidence before the Russian Commission of Inquiry on the Kornilov affair; in *The Catastrophe* (1927) he purported to give his own account of the Russian Revolution; while he returned once more to the theme of his own rehabilitation in *The Crucifixion of Liberty* (1933).

In 1940, almost at the final stage of the collapse of France, Kerensky was enabled to reach the United States, where he remained except for brief visits to Europe, Australia, and elsewhere.

June 15, 1970.

Jack Kerouac, the novelist who spoke for the beatniks of the 1950s, died in St. Petersburg, Florida, on October 21, 1969, at the age of 47.

Jack Kerouac, who was born in Lowell, Massachusetts, in 1922, was a startling influence on the American writing and the life-style of the American young in the 1950s. His most famous novel still remains: *On the Road* (1957), which took an old American theme—that of wandering, drifting, yearning search across the country—but tied it into the attitudes and philosophies of a new generation, fascinated with beatitudes and virtuous poverty, aimless sensationalism and constant movement. Its central character, Dean Moriarty, is half-crazed but powerful; its style was the famous "spontaneous prose" that Kerouac tried to develop to create a literature of instantaneousness. This was all to crystallize into the beat generation, of which Kerouac was the main prose writer.

His work was to a considerable extent biographical, and it helped to create the geography and the style of the movement. In fact, however, it was part of a more extended attempt at a large picaresque version of modern American life, and it is extended, in theme and technique, in his Californian novels like *The Subterraneans* (1958) and *The Dharma Bums* (1959). His larger ambitions seem to have led him more recently towards a critical attitude to the search for instantaneous revelation that his earlier work embodied. He was a classic instance of the interesting writer whose fame lies more in his general influence than in the quality of his writing; but his attempts at a new prose were not without real fascination.

In *The Dharma Bums* Kerouac wrote about a Zen Buddhist clique—the hero is a young narrator in search of visions on mountain tops, and eating wheat germ and dried vegetables on his straw mat. *The Subterraneans* has a background of the beatniks with their "subterranean hip generation tendencies to silence, bohemian mystery, drugs, beards, semi-holiness." The story is a simple one of a brief love affair between a cad and his helpless victim, and is written in monologue form with the minimum of pauses for breath. In *Big Sur*, Kerouac proclaimed himself "some Buddhist"; *Desolation Angels* is an account, told with some vividness and more self-importance, of the travels, love-making, conversations, drug-takings and readings of the Buddha in the years 1956–58 among the leading figures of America's beat generation.

Satori in Paris (1967) is a record of ten days which shook Kerouac. It is a characteristically lively account of drinking and whoring and missing planes and trains in an effort to find out the Kerouac ancestry, presumed rooted in Brittany but needing the Paris Bibliotheque Nationale to provide the clues. *Lonesome Traveller* (1962) is a collection of eight travel sketches. *Visions of Gerard* and *Tristessa* are two novellas in which Kerouac is at his most sentimental.

October 22, 1969.

Frances Parkinson Keyes, the best-selling American author, died at her home in New Orleans, Louisiana, on July 3, 1970, after a long illness. She was 84. Her husband, Henry Wilder Keyes, for many years a Senator for New Hampshire and Governor of the state in 1917–19, died in 1938. They had three sons.

The author of more than 50 books, among them the highly successful *Dinner at Antoine's*, she was always confident, professional, and readable. She never gave less than value for money. Several of her novels had a New Orleans or Louisiana background, including *Crescent Carnival*, *The River Road*, and *Once on Esplanade*.

For the material of her novels Mrs. Keyes drew upon an energetic temperament, a large assortment of interests and enthusiasms, an extensive knowledge of her own country, the experience of not a little travel in Europe, much knowledge of official or semi-official life in Washington, and a considerable fund of feminine shrewdness, of quotidian sagacity. Her novels are both rhetorical and sentimental; yet at the same time they exhibit a fundamental and saving virtue of good sense. It was this quality, no doubt, that made it possible for her readers to swallow all the rest and nevertheless feel they were keeping in close touch with life as it is lived. Her novels were almost all very long, sustained without apparent effort and giving evidence of a quite remarkable fluency, and are crammed with incident.

She was born on July 21, 1885, the daughter of John Henry Wheeler and Louise Fuller Johnson. Educated at schools in Boston, Switzerland and Berlin, she apparently wrote enormously as a child, but did not begin to write for publication until 1918, when she contributed articles to various American magazines. Her first novel, *The Old Gray Homestead*, appeared in 1919, and a couple of years later came *The Career of David Noble*. From 1923 to 1936 she was an associate editor of Good Housekeeping, and in 1937–39 editor of the National Historical Magazine.

Mrs. Keyes had a house in New Hampshire and another in Virginia and also spent much time while her husband was alive in Washington. New England, the South and Washington provide the most frequent settings for her novels, though she could range freely over scenes in America and Europe whenever she chose.

In addition to those already mentioned other well-known books by Mrs. Keyes include *Also the Hill*; *Vail d'Alvery*: *Lady Blanche Farm*; *Steamboat Gothic*; *Blue Camellia*; *the Gold Slippers*; and *The Royal Box*.

July 6, 1970.

Jan Kiepura, who died on August 15, 1966, at Harrison, New York, at the age of 64, was the first operatic tenor to become a film star. In the 1930s, adding good looks and charm of manner to an attractive voice, he won the hearts of multitudes who were neither opera-lovers nor concert-goers through his performances in the films *City of Song* and *Tell Me Tonight*.

JOINED WARSAW OPERA

Jan Kiepura was born at Sosnowiec, in Poland, on May 16, 1902, and trained in Warsaw. His first appearance was at the Warsaw Opera, as Faust in Gounod's opera. Success led him to Vienna, where he sang in Korngold's *Wunder der Heliane* and other German works effectively, but he made the deepest impression in operas by Puccini. He became equally popular at the Berlin State Opera and La Scala, Milan, and toured England as a concert singer; *City of Song* was a product of his first visit to Britain. In 1938 he made his American debut, at New York's Metropolitan Opera House, as Rudolph in *La Bohème*, and was heard at Chicago Opera and the Theatro Colòn in Buenos Aires. Although Kiepura made his home in the United States, he returned to Europe shortly after the last war for a recital tour in which he was joined by his wife, the Austrian soprano Marta Eggerth.

Prolonged absence had done nothing to disturb his popularity in England, where halls throughout the country were crowded for all his concerts.

Jan Kiepura was gifted with an extremely beautiful voice of great range; he could control it admirably. His approach to music, however, was not only emotional but wilful, and, as he left the discipline of the opera house behind him, he tended often to exploit the works he sang not so much for the sake of showing off his voice as for making easy and exciting emotional effects which delighted him no less than the audience. He enjoyed success and the adulation it brought, but it seemed always as though he was at one with the audiences he captivated.

SONGS FROM CAR ROOF

When, after his last triumphant concert in the Albert Hall, he found the stage door besieged by a vast number of his compatriots, it seemed quite natural that he should climb on to the roof of his car and from it follow a taxing programme inside the hall with an extempore recital of Polish songs in the open air, gaining from it as much pleasure as the audience that inspired it.

August 17, 1966.

Lord Killearn, G.C.M.G., C.B., M.V.O., who was widely known earlier as Sir Miles Wedderburn Lampson, died on September 18, 1964, in the Royal East Sussex Hospital, Hastings, at the age of 84. His death removed a dynamic figure, with a long and eventful diplomatic career mainly in the Far East and Egypt.

He was the second son of Norman George Lampson, and grandson of Sir Curtis Lampson, Bt. Born in 1880 and educated at Eton, he passed in 1903 into the Foreign Office. But his selection as Secretary to Prince Arthur of Connaught's Garter Mission to Japan in 1906, and to the Prince's further mission in 1912 for the Emperor's funeral, led to his spending most of his early career in the Far East, with acting rank in the then distinct Diplomatic Service. With interludes in the Foreign Office and at Sofia, he served in Tokyo and Peking and acquired a knowledge of both the Japanese and Chinese languages. In 1919 he was temporarily in Siberia as Acting High Commissioner, and he was in the British delegation at the Washington Conference of 1921.

He next became Head of the Central European Department, then probably the most exacting task in the Foreign Office. Apart from its geographical sphere, its special care was the application of the Peace Treaties with Germany and her European allies. Lampson ploughed undismayed through the complications of German reparations and the Franco-Belgian occupation of the Ruhr. After the Dawes Conference, the security question took first place and in 1925 it fell to him to coordinate, under Sir Austen Chamberlain, the negotiations leading to the Locarno Treaty.

MINISTER IN PEKING

In the autumn of 1926 he was chosen by Chamberlain to return to the Far East as Minister in Peking, a task of exceptional difficulty at that time. There was no effective Government of China. The Southern Nationalist (Kuomintang) forces, in their drive against the Northern warlords, had occupied Hankow. Anti-foreign feeling was rising.

The British Government were advocates, consistently with non-intervention, of a conciliatory policy towards the Nationalist movement, and Lampson began characteristically with a visit to Hankow by warship for friendly and informal contact with Eugene Chen, Foreign Minister in the unrecognized Kuomintang Government. The immediate effect was good, but a fortnight after Lampson's departure for Peking, the storming of the foreign Concessions at Hankow and Kiukiang by mobs touched off a crisis. The British Government ordered out naval reinforcements and a Shanghai Defence Force and, almost simultaneously, announced to both sides in the civil war some practical steps which they were ready to take towards meeting Chinese aspirations.

A settlement at long last of the Nanking incident cleared the way for the recognition in December, 1928, of the new National Government of China, of which Chiang Kai-shek had by then emerged as President. When Lampson went to Nanking for this purpose he concluded a Treaty recognizing China's tariff autonomy, subject to non-discrimination.

So passed the first five years of Lampson's mission, marred by the fatal illness in 1930 at Hongkong of Lady Lampson. She was Rachel, younger daughter of William Wilton Phipps, whom he married in 1912.

In 1934 he became High Commissioner for Egypt and Sudan. And in the same year he re-married; his second wife, who survives him, being Jacqueline Aldine, daughter of Professor Count Aldo Castellani.

In Egypt he was again faced, in a different degree, with unfulfilled national aspirations complicated by many frictions, and he had to await the opportunity for a new attempt at an Anglo-Egyptian settlement. Two main questions—Sudan and British troops in Egypt—had defied all previous efforts. But the danger to both Egypt and Sudan, portended by Mussolini's ambitions and the invasion of Ethiopia, produced the miracle of an all-party delegation with whom, after negotiations in Cairo, the Anglo-Egyptian Treaty of Alliance of 1936 was signed in London. With the ratification of that treaty, Egypt became fully sovereign and Lampson the first British Ambassador. His subsequent collaboration with the Egyptian authorities in working out the means of applying the treaty to practical requirements in the event of war proved its worth when war came.

A KEY POSITION

The establishment in Cairo in 1940 of a British Minister of State to coordinate various Middle Eastern problems left unchanged Lampson's responsibilities as H. M. Representative in Egypt. The treaty and the course of the war made his a key position in the peculiar situation where Egypt, while granting all facilities for a wartime Allied base, remained non-belligerent almost throughout the war, even when it overran her borders. The hesitant, or pro-Axis, influences which gathered round the Court, the wayward character of the young king and the chronic antipathy between the latter and the Wafd, became factors of material concern when so much turned on the solidity of Egypt in the fluctuating North African campaign. The moment came in February, 1942, when, supported by armed force, Lampson drove to Abdin Palace and delivered an ultimatum to King Farouk to recall the pro-Allied Wafd to power. Controversy still lingers round this action and its long-term repercussions. But whatever the criticisms, its supporters point to the subsequent unwavering steadiness of the Wafd in office in the all-important period preceding Alamein.

In 1943 Lampson, who in 1941 had been sworn of the Privy Council, was raised to the Peerage. As the war drew to its close, Egypt's desire for the revision of the treaty grew, but that issue had not come to a head when, in early 1946, he was appointed, though well beyond retiring age, Special Commissioner in South East Asia. This was an emergency post, based on Singapore, created to cope with the political aftermath of war in the non-British territories of that large area which the Japanese surrender had left within the British sphere of Allied military responsibility. On arrival Lord Killearn found that the defeat of famine must precede all else. The credit for success is shared by many others, in the area and in Whitehall. But the key lay in his forcible representations and personal drive.

He inherited the military and political tangle of the struggle in Indonesia against return to colonial rule. Just before the British forces were withdrawn, he was successful, as independent chairman, in guiding a Dutch Commission General and an Indonesian delegation to the point of initialling what later became the Linggadjati Agreement, embodying a pattern of relationship between the two countries within a projected Netherlands-Indonesian Union. That the hopes raised by this agreement were dashed by after events does not lessen the merit of its achievement at the time.

Killearn's deferred retirement came in 1948. It did not close his active life. Business interests took him often abroad. At home, he was assiduous in the House of Lords.

His heir is Major the Hon. Graham Lampson, late Scots Guards. He also had two daughters by his first marriage, and a son and two daughters by his second.

September 19, 1964.

Lord Kilmuir, P.C., G.C.V.O., D.C.L., LL.D., who was Lord Chancellor from 1954 to 1962, and a former Home Secretary, died on January 27, 1967, at the age of 66. A careful lawyer, a life-long Conservative, conscientious in all he undertook, he did the work by which he will be most remembered at the trial of the Nazi war criminals at Nuremberg.

As a politician he might have termed himself, as Dr. Johnson defined a lexicographer, "a useful drudge"—he was perhaps the most useful maid-of-all-work the postwar Conservative Party has had, and did not mind being used as such. As a lawyer he had an extraordinary capacity for hard work, an eye for the essence of a case, and the gift as an advocate of throwing his own Scottish honesty over even the most questionable clients. He was also in two complicated professions at a complicated period, quite simply a man of good character. It was his character which gave him weight in public life.

David Patrick Maxwell Fyfe was born at Edinburgh on May 29, 1900. His father, W. T. Fyfe, was first a schoolmaster, later a schools inspector and examiner. He was also a minor writer, his most memorable book being *Edinburgh under Sir Walter Scott*. There is no doubt David Fyfe's love of literature came from him. His mother, Isabella Campbell, was a teacher before her marriage. David went to a convent school, then to George Watson's College in Edinburgh, and to Balliol. He said that at Oxford Conservatism came first, the Union second, his work third, and games fourth. Politics absorbed so much of interest that he got only a third in his Final Schools. He plunged himself into the 1921 Transport Bill, worked at the British Commonwealth Union, passed his Bar Finals, and was called in June 1922.

He was a singularly clear-headed young man, and saw his main qualification early. When Lindsay, his tutor, asked him what he thought of doing after his poor showing in Final Schools, he said "The Bar. I think, I can get up a strange subject pretty quickly".

That, and his remarkable capacity for unremitting hard work, was the secret of his successful career. Whether as a member of the Northern Circuit, as a young politician grappling with the Transport Bill, as an experienced Minister piloting the Government's policy on Broadcasting, as Falconer Lecturer in Toronto, or as Burns speaker in Scotland, he got up every subject with the same care. Nowhere was this assiduous, lucid industry shown more effectively than at the Nuremberg trials.

ASTONISHING MEMORY

After being called to the Bar he went to Liverpool and got a place in the chambers of George Lynskey (afterwards Mr. Justice Lynskey) becoming Howard Jones's pupil. He soon had a good practice at the local bar, mainly in workmen's compensation cases, running down cases, and some criminal cases. He set up chambers of his own and one of his pupils for a short time was Hartley Shawcross. From the beginning of his career as a barrister he became famous for his astonishing memory, so that he could accurately remember decided cases on relevant subjects even to the extent of the page in the volume of Law Reports in which they were reported. He also had two other advantages: that of unruffable courtesy both to the judge and to his opponents; and that of looking older than he was.

In 1925 he married Sylvia Harrison. She devoted her life to him and his activities; even before they were married she had heard him make 70 election speeches when he unsuccessfully fought the Wigan seat. She was at his side through every vicissitude in his long career. He owed a tremendous amount to her perspicacity, especially politically.

He took silk in 1934. Shortly afterwards he was one of the counsel in the Ruxton murder case at Manchester Assizes.

He gave a picture of that industry, applied both to the law and to politics, in his autobiography. When on the Northern circuit, he said, he would confer in Liverpool from 9 to 10.30 a.m., be in the court till 5.15 p.m., catch the 5.25 p.m. train to London, be in his place in the House of Commons from 9 to 11 p.m., catch the midnight train back to Liverpool, and next morning start all over again.

In spite of his active devotion to the Conservative cause it took him 14 years to get a seat. In 1935 Sir John Sandeman Allen died and he succeeded him as M.P. for the West Derby division of Liverpool.

THE NUREMBERG TRIALS

Maxwell Fyfe was on the Army Officers' Emergency Reserve and when war broke out he wished to return to the Scots Guards in which he had served in 1918. He volunteered for Norway and for France but instead was sent to the Judge Advocate General's department. In 1942 Churchill made him Solicitor General, and three years later Attorney General. From 1945 to 1946 he was Deputy Chief Prosecutor at Nuremberg. By that time a Labour Government was in power. Fyfe had been engaged in preliminary talks with the Americans, the Russians, and the French, when the 1945 election removed him from office. When the trials opened Sir Hartley Shawcross, who had succeeded as Attorney General, became the Chief Prosecutor for the United Kingdom. He made the opening and closing speeches but inevitably, for Shawcross had political duties at home, the daily donkey-work fell upon Fyfe. It was a task for which all his gifts combined to qualify him. Nuremberg was the peak of his forensic career.

Meanwhile he had been climbing up the ladder of general political esteem. In 1943 he became chairman of the Conservative Party committee on Post-War Reconstruction; in opposition he was an untiring speaker inside and outside Westminster. He travelled all over the kingdom, to Conservative rallies, garden parties, and other engagements. In the Commons in the seven months from December, 1946, to June 1947, he made 178 speeches on the Transport Bill alone. He was a good European; was Conservative member of the Council of Europe at Strasbourg from 1949, and was bitterly disappointed when in November, 1951, Eden torpedoed his hopes of Britain moving closer to Europe. He was chairman of the National Union of Conservative and Unionist Associations in 1950. Such industry was bound to be rewarded and when Churchill returned to power in 1951 he made Maxwell Fyfe his Home Secretary. He was not outstanding but to the multifarious responsibilities of the post (perhaps wider than those of any other department) he brought his usual care. He showed it simultaneously by proving a Scot could be a most assiduous Minister for Welsh Affairs.

CLEAR-SIGHTED

When Churchill reconstructed his Cabinet in October, 1954, Fyfe became Lord Chancellor, took the title of Viscount Kilmuir, and closed a 20 years' membership of the House of Commons. He said in his memoirs that he had no ambition to be a candidate for the Prime Ministership as a *tertium quid* between Eden and Butler. Perhaps strangely he might have had a chance of being the *tertium quid* between Butler and Macmillan in January, 1957. He was a very shrewd politician. He could often see farther and more clearly than many of his colleagues more in the limelight. Yet his real ambitions and abilities both favoured law more than politics.

As Lord Chancellor he dignified the Woolsack. Once more he was patient, courteous, indefatigable—on his first Bill in the House of Lords he made 82 speeches; it was on Town and Country Planning—giving equal attention to great things and small. No one act made his tenure of the Lord Chancellorship historic. The office has been less well served by more flamboyant but less conscientious men.

Finally, so far as his political career was concerned, came the holocaust of July, 1962, when Macmillan dismissed seven of his Ministers. Why Kilmuir was one of them has remained a mystery. Kilmuir, who was created an Earl, said frankly in *Political Adventure* that Macmillan lost both nerve and judgment. He was attacked for this frankness, but nothing became him better than his treatment of Macmillan in his autobiography. He was fair to Macmillan's Prime Ministership as a whole; he was entitled to write candidly about what seemed to many an irrational episode.

Having quit politics "at seven hours' notice" Kilmuir caused some eyebrows to be raised by becoming chairman of Plesseys. He had never been a rich man; and the days when even a Lord Chancellor's pension sufficed to meet a life of imposed idleness had gone.

When in November, 1962, Lord Thomson announced the establishment of the Thomson Foundation to provide educational and vocational training facilities in the emergent countries Lord Kilmuir agreed to become the foundation's chairman.

Many honours came to him—D.C.L. Oxford; LL.D. from Liverpool and other universities; an honorary Fellowship of his old college; rectorship of St. Andrews; honorary membership of the Canadian and American Bar Associations—and they rightly meant much to him.

Lord and Lady Kilmuir had three daughters, one of whom is dead. The title lapses.

January 28, 1967.

Captain Anthony Kimmins, O.B.E., who died on May 19, 1964, at the age of 62 after a long illness at his home in Sussex, will be remembered affectionately by those who were associated with him in a number of different fields and of different places: in the Royal Navy, in the London theatre, in British and Australian film studios, and at Broadcasting House and in the United States during World War II. They will remember him as an indefatigable worker who threw himself into whatever he was doing, so that all through his career, while remaining recognizably the same man, he went on learning and growing.

Born on November 10, 1901, the younger son of the late Dr. Charles William Kimmins and the late Dame Grace Kimmins, D.B.E., Anthony Martin Kimmins was educated at the Royal Naval College, Osborne, and at Dartmouth, and served during World War One as a midshipman in H.M.S. Marlborough, in submarines, and in the newly created aviation branch. He became the youngest flight commander, but a skiing accident, which damaged his spine, put an end to his career in operational flying. While convalescing he wrote a comedy which, under the title *While Parents Sleep*, was eventually accepted for professional production in London, was directed by Nigel Playfair at the old Royalty in 1932, and which, by proving to be a smash hit, led to his retiring from the Navy in his early thirties with the rank of Lieutenant-Commander.

His second play *Night Club Queen* was produced in the following year and his third *Chase the Ace* after an interval of two more years, but Kimmins had not staked everything on the theatre, wisely, since neither of these pieces was as popular as his first. He had entered films, having originally offered his services free of charge to a film company for a period of six months, and having soon afterwards resisted the temptation of a contract with Hollywood as an actor. From directing small quota films in Britain he rose to scripting and directing a number of feature films for Fox-British and other companies, including starring vehicles for George Formby.

NEW REPUTATION

On the outbreak of World War II he rejoined the Navy, serving in the Fleet Air Arm, in Intelligence at the Admiralty and as Chief of Naval Information to the Pacific Fleet, and acquiring a new reputation as a commentator for the B.B.C. on naval operations, before retiring as a captain in 1945. On his return to films he produced and directed a version of Nigel Balchin's novel *Mine Own Executioner*, and he continued to be active in films until 1958, when his *Smiley Gets A Gun* was completed.

In 1960 the success in London of his farcical comedy *The Amorous Prawn*, with Evelyn Laye and Walter Fitzerald in leading parts, reestablished Kimmins's position in the live theatre.

He married in 1928 Elizabeth Hodges, daughter of Admiral Sir Michael Hodges, Commander-in-Chief of the Home Fleet and later Second Sea Lord—"like all really keen and ambitious naval officers I married the C.-in-C.'s daughter". There was a son and a daughter of the marriage.

May 20, 1964.

King Paul of the Hellenes—See under **Greece**;
King Peter II of Yugoslavia—See under **Yugoslavia**;
King Zog of Albania—See under **Albania**.

Charles D. B. King, who was President of Liberia from 1920 to 1930, died on September 4, 1961, at Monravia.

He was also a former Ambassador to Washington—a post of particular importance because of his country's traditionally close links with the United States—and was widely regarded as the "elder statesman" of Liberia. He was 86.

He was born and educated in Sierra Leone and held other positions in the Liberian Government, including those of Attorney General and Secretary of State, before his election to the presidency.

His conduct in that office was the subject of controversy. He certainly had some achievements to his credit. His administration was the first to make a serious attempt to bring order into the affairs of the hinterland—that part of the country inhabited by the native tribes. The coastal area, peopled mostly by the descendents of returned slaves from the United States, provides the much more advanced section of the population, but as they are greatly outnumbered by the tribes the governing of the hinterland has always been a problem. King took the initiative by convening and presiding over a great conference of chiefs in 1923. This assembly, holding daily sessions for nearly a month, eventually agreed upon basic rules and regulations for the government of the native districts.

King also inaugurated one of the first road-building programmes in the country—a very modest effort by present-day standards but not to be despised in the context of those times.

Yet there was a darker side to his rule. It was strongly suspected that his long tenure of office owed a good deal to his control of the electoral machine as well as the support of the voters. No doubt similarly convincing charges could have been brought against anybody who would have ruled Liberia in those days. Far more significant was the accusation that the administration were responsible for forced labour and slave trading, particularly with the Spanish plantations in Fernando Po. An inquiry under the auspices of the League of Nations specifically condemned the Vice-President, and although no verdict was passed against King personally the ensuing clamour forced his resignation.

September 5, 1961.

Dr. Martin Luther King, vitriolic champion of Negro civil rights in the South, Nobel Peace Prize winner, and Baptist minister who never tired of turning the other cheek, died on April 4, 1968, after being shot.

In the maelstrom of racialistic strife, King's strict adherence to non-violence struck a still-point of respect for the Negro struggle among millions. The essential dignity of the Negro remained intact; King was "a kind of modern Moses who has brought new self-respect to southern Negroes". As regards the ultimate success of the civil rights movement, King's discipline proved that unlike white extremists, Negroes could fight for their rights in a civilized way.

King's non-violence tactics were based on Gandhi's thinking. They went further: he included the Christian element of love—realizing that the reconciliation of the Negroes to the whites was just as important for his cause as vice versa. Unlike Gandhi, King was fighting for the rights of a minority. Unlike the Indian leader, King had no easily defined opponent such as an imperial overlord—he had to conquer the confused racial prejudices and fears of a white, dominant race.

Though initially apolitical, King suddenly found himself the centre of party politics after Kennedy, then a presidential candidate, had rung Mrs. King in 1960 at the height of his campaign to express sympathy for King, then imprisoned. For Kennedy the telephone call helped to swing the vital Negro vote.

For King, though he found his stature immediately one of nation-wide significance, it meant inviting the contempt from militant Negroes who now had more cause to dub him a contemporary Uncle Tom. For his followers, however, King's youth and idealism appeared remarkably akin to Kennedy's. He was also a minister who no longer preached the comforting words of the more conservative Negro ministers to reconcile their brethren to their lot. King abandoned his political neutrality in 1964—urging Negroes to shun Goldwater.

King was born on January 15, 1929, at Atlanta, where his father was a Baptist preacher, as was his maternal grandfather. Both had been involved in Negro protests against discrimination at one time or another. Twice before he was 13 King attempted suicide; in both cases jumping from a second storey window. The first time was after he thought his grandmother dead; the second after she actually died. In both instances he was unhurt.

King was a bright pupil: at the age of 15 he entered Atlanta's Negro Morehouse College, where his father had studied before him. He wanted to be a doctor or a lawyer, but two years later chose the ministry—always his father's wish. He was ordained and named assistant pastor in his father's church. After completing a degree in sociology he went to the Crozer Theological Seminary in Chester, Pennsylvania, where he was the most outstanding student of his year. There he realized the futility of protesting against racial discrimination using only the normal legal channels.

UPPER INCOME FLOCK

There, too, Hegel, Kant and Gandhi's thinking had their influence on him. In 1955 he was awarded a doctorate by Boston University. Meanwhile he had married a young soprano, Coretta Scott, and become the pastor of an upper-income church in Montgomery—Dexter Avenue Baptist Church. His thinking on racial issues still tended towards the conservative approach of the N.A.A.C.P., and the interracial Alabama Council on Human Relations of which he was vice-president.

Then, in December, 1955, he was suddenly thrust into the vortex of a struggle which had all the markings of violence. A Negro seamstress, Rosa Parks, had refused to give up her seat in a bus for a white as she was required to do under local ordinances. Her arrest triggered off a boycott of the bus service by the Negroes—which stretched out to 382 days. King presided over the boycott committee—later known as the Montgomery Improvement Association—which was at first modest in its demands to the authorities. Balked however by white organized opposition, the fight intensified, until finally—and ironically for King's demonstration tactics—a Supreme Court order imposed desegregation on the Alabama buses. Nevertheless, King emerged triumphant; despite bombing of his house, riot-thirsting followers, his own arrest, he had remained calm and courageous. More—he had managed to keep his followers under control. The fruits of victory were his—he became president of the newly founded S.C.L.C.; he was among the speakers who addressed the thousands who made the Prayer Pilgrimage to the Lincoln Monument in 1957; he was invited to the independence ceremonies of Ghana; he was Nehru's guest.

The Negro struggle however waned in its intensity. The emancipation of African colonies had its effect, but the eventual prod came from youth demonstrations in 1958 and 1959. King decided to hurl himself wholeheartedly into the civil rights movement, resigning pastorship in 1960. He strove to channel the mounting student discontent in a Student Non-violent Coordinating Committee.

In December, 1961, came a dismal turning point. King's attack on Albany, Georgia, fizzled out. He had vowed he would stay in gaol until the city agreed to desegregate public facilities. But after two days he was out—on bail. He was bitterly attacked for this fiasco.

WORKED FOR CRISIS

His next major attack on Birmingham—a centre of diehard segregationists—redeemed his reputation. He had carefully recruited non-violent demonstrators willing to be gaoled. Next he worked for the ultimate confrontation—or "crisis"—so necessary to put his cause across. His initial sally was postponed more than once: just before Easter, 1963, he declared he would lead demonstrations in Birmingham until "Pharaoh lets God's people go".

Though certain Negro clergymen thought his timing bad, King was right in sensing the tension in the Negro community there. The mass demonstrations and sit-ins had their full backing. More than 3,300, including King himself, were gaoled. It seemed as if in "Bull" Connor, the defeated mayor who had refused to relinquish office, the Negroes had met their match. Then, on May 7, the police, using dogs, fire hoses, and clubs, turned on the Negro crowds—children and all. Within hours this "crisis" was making headline news throughout the world. King had triumphed. As Kennedy put it later to him: "The civil rights movement owes Bull Connor as much as it owes Abraham Lincoln."

When King's wife heard nothing from her husband after his arrest in Birmingham, she tried to reach the President. Once before in 1960, Kennedy, then a presidential candidate, had rung her to express his sympathy. Now he rang again to offer his reassurance. Kennedy did more—a Civil Rights Bill (eventually passed after his assassination) was quickly drawn up. King was released. In gaol he had written a letter from Birmingham Jail setting out his objects. Later that summer he delivered his "I have a dream" oration, with its peroration of "let freedom ring" to the millions who marched to the Lincoln Monument.

BACK-LASH

Only a few years before, under Eisenhower, he had pleaded "Give us the ballot" in the same place. Now there was quicker desegregation in schools, in swimming pools and restaurants. *Time* magazine named King its Man of the Year. He was awarded a Nobel Peace Prize in 1964. He had now become a civil rights leader of international repute. But in the wake of the new-won rights, the ugly terrorism of the white back lash erupted.

In the centenary year of the Emancipation Proclamation which had freed the Negroes from physical slavery, King made an assault on St. Augustine, Florida. For his purposes it was a good target: a totally segregated city celebrating its 400th anniversary, and it had a strong local S.C.L.C. following, King's group fought with stand-ins, swim-ins, night mass marches—only to meet with terrorism from white reactionaries and few gains. Nothing daunted, King made an attack on Solma, Alabama, in 1965, to register more voters.

Here he was assaulted by a white reactionary, and also arrested. But this time, President Johnson called for the nation to exert moral pressure on behalf of the Negroes and threatened to send federal troops. King called for a national boycott of the state of Alabama. Segregation, he said, was on its deathbed—it was merely a matter of how expensive George Wallace, the Governor of Alabama, and others were going to make the funeral. For the Negroes, however, with the failure of the southern courts to convict in cases involving race relations, matters were reaching stalemate. In 1966 King led a march into a Ku-Klux-Klan stronghold—Philadelphia, Mississippi—where three civil rights workers had been murdered two years before.

King wrote two books: *Stride Towards Freedom*, which told the story of the Montgomery boycott, and *Why We Can't Wait*, which told of the 1963 protests.

April 5, 1968.

Commander Lord King-Hall, better known as Commander Stephen King-Hall, founder of the Hansard Society, author, playwright, broadcaster, commentator on international affairs, and a former member of Parliament, died on June 1, 1966, at the age of 73.

He will be remembered, too, as the editor of the *King-Hall Newsletter-Digest* (afterwards known as the *National News-Letter*), which at one period reached a circulation of nearly 100,000. It lasted for 23 years and it was not until February, 1959, when its circulation had dropped to 8,000, that its founder announced that publication was to cease.

Stephen King-Hall was a man of extraordinary industry and great ability. Even when disagreeing with his views it was impossible not to admire the vigour and lucidity with which he put them forward. He was an ideal educator: engaging, avuncular, and opinionated, in an acceptable way. There must be thousands of grown-up people who first learnt about the political world they live in from his wireless talks of years ago.

He came of a family which had been represented in the Navy List for some 150 years, his grandfather, father and uncle all having flown their own flags as commanders-in-chief. Born on January 21, 1893, he was the eldest son of Admiral Sir George King-Hall, K.C.B., C.V.O. He was educated at Lausanne and entered Osborne as a cadet in 1906, and then went to Dartmouth, taking his lieutenant's certificate with a first-class in 1914. He was then posted to H.M.S. Southampton, flagship of the 2nd Light Cruiser Squadron, and served in her in the North Sea until 1917, the ship being present at every encounter between the Grand Fleet and the Germans, including Jutland. From 1917 until the end of the war King-Hall was a torpedo specialist with the 11th Submarine Flotilla, based on Harwich. In 1919 he was awarded the gold medal of the Royal United Service Institution, and in that year and the next served in the Training and Staff Duties department of the Admiralty.

AT CHATHAM HOUSE

During 1920–21 King-Hall passed through the R. N. Staff College, then going out to the China Squadron as torpedo lieutenant in H.M.S. Durban till the end of 1923. The following year was passed as instructor at the Military Staff College, Camberley, and now appeared his first book, *Western Civilization and the Far East*. During 1925–26 King-Hall was intelligence officer to Admiral Sir Roger Keyes with the Mediterranean Fleet. He served in Repulse with the Atlantic Fleet in 1927–28, was promoted commander in the latter year, and transferred to the Tactical Division of the Naval Staff. Meanwhile in 1927 there had appeared a second book, *Imperial Defence*, and in 1929 King-Hall retired from the Navy to take up research on international, political and economic problems for the Royal Institute of International Affairs at Chatham House.

The production in that same year of *The Middle Watch*, a farce in which he had collaborated with a seasoned playwright, Ian Hay, inaugurated a successful combined operation in the writing of "amphibious adventures" or "tales of Naval Manoeuvres". The co-authors had two more of these on the West End stage before the Second World War—*The Midshipmaid* and *Admirals All*—and a fourth in 1947—*Off the Record*. The casts of the three prewar farces at the Shaftesbury Theatre were headed by Clive Currie, usually as an Admiral, a part sustained by Fred Kerr in the New York production of *The Middle Watch* and inherited by Hugh Wakefield in *Off the Record*.

King-Hall's two single-handed experiments in writing a serious play were unfortunate, though *B. J. One*, the climax of which was on the bridge of a cruiser at night action stations during the Battle of Jutland, was an honourable failure.

NEWS LETTER LAUNCHED

In 1935 he produced an ambitious two-volume political and economic survey *Our Own Times, 1913–1934*. This was revised and brought up to date as the years went on.

As early as 1928 King-Hall had met a member of the B.B.C. Talks department, and in December of that year had made his first broadcast, on amateur theatricals in the Navy. Encouraged by its success, he took seriously to broadcasting and from 1930 onwards became very popular.

In 1935 King-Hall retired from the staff of the Royal Institute of International Affairs and was elected to its governing council. Two years later he wrote its history, *Chatham House*. A magazine for the young, called *Mine*, launched in 1935 did not pay, but when in the following June he started the *K. H. News-Letter*, issuing it privately to subscribers, it made rapid progress, rising to a circulation of 50,000 within three years and to 100,000 by 1940. It was also distributed in German to Germans, much to the annoyance of Hitler, who insisted on regarding it as official British propaganda (which, of course, it was not).

In the autumn of 1939 King-Hall was elected to Parliament as National Labour member for the Ormskirk division of Lancashire, being returned unopposed under the wartime political truce. In June, 1940, he joined the Factory Defence section of the Ministry of Aircraft Production, and was appointed unpaid director of the section some months later. He was outspoken in his criticism of British propaganda and political warfare, and in August, 1941, published *Total Victory*, a book in which he argued that 1918 had shown that military victory was not enough: there must be total victory, obtained by destroying the enemy's will to fight.

In February, 1942, he resigned from the National Labour Party and sat in the House of Commons as an Independent National member. In August, 1942, he was appointed chairman of the Fuel Economy Publicity Committee. In 1944 he founded the Hansard Society. He was honorary director and chairman of the council from that year until 1962 and in 1963 became president.

At the general election of 1945 he was unseated at Ormskirk by Harold Wilson, coming bottom of the poll in a three-cornered fight.

In the last years of his life King-Hall became one of the most articulate and stimulating in the great nuclear voices debate. He rejected the nuclear balance of power as a dangerous gamble and campaigned persuasively for unilateral disarmament in such books as *Defence in the Nuclear Age* and *Power Politics in the Nuclear Age*. He resigned from the Campaign for Nuclear Disarmament in 1961 because he believed the parliamentary procedure should be used for unilateral nuclear disarmament, not civil disobedience. In 1960 he published a cautionary novel *Men of Destiny*, giving a terrifying and convincing picture of how a nuclear war might begin.

He was knighted in 1954 and created a life peer in January 1966.

He married in 1919 Amelia Kathleen, daughter of Francis Spencer. They had three daughters. His wife died in 1963.

June 3, 1966.

Lieutenant-Colonel A. R. F. Kingscote, M.C., who died on December 21, 1964, at his home at Woking, was England's best lawn tennis player in the years just after the First World War, in spite of the fact that he was 31 in 1919, when the Wimbledon Championships were restarted.

Algy Kingscote was born in India in 1888 and learnt the game in Switzerland where he won the Swiss Championship in 1908. He then joined the Royal Garrison Artillery and could only play tournament tennis when he could get leave. Nevertheless, by 1914 he was in the British Davis Cup team. Had it not been for the war he would almost certainly have won several Wimbledon titles. At the 1919 Wimbledon Kingscote reached the final of the All-Comers, when he was beaten by the Australian Gerald Patterson who then defeated his compatriot Norman Brookes (later Sir Norman Brookes) in the Challenge Round. In the same year Kingscote represented Britain in the Davis Cup v. South Africa and France, and was captain of Britain's challenging Davis Cup team at Sydney, Australia. He also won the Australian Singles title in 1919.

At Wimbledon 1920 was a memorable year. For 40 years American players had been trying to carry off the Singles Championship, but the high water mark of their endeavours had been in the winning of the All-Comers by McLoughlin in 1913. In 1920 they achieved their ambition when W. T. Tilden succeeded in winning the title. Tilden was 27 and Kingscote 32. They faced one another on the Centre Court on the first Saturday of the Championships. Tilden won the first set, Kingscote the second, Tilden the third and Kingscote the fourth. At three-all in the final set there was some rain and stoppage of play. Tilden won the match by the skin of his teeth. In his book *The Art of Lawn Tennis*, published in 1920, Tilden gives Kingscote generous praise as Britain's greatest player.

POCKETED THE BALL

In the same year (1920) Kingscote, partnered by the Irishman J. C. Parke, reached the final of the men's doubles at Wimbledon. In the Davis Cup match between Britain and America which was played at Wimbledon on July 16, 17 and 19, both countries fielded a two-man team. America was represented by their two greatest players of that era, "Big Bill" Tilden and "Little Bill" Johnston, the reigning American champion. Kingscote took two sets off Johnston and one off Tilden, and he and Parke only lost the doubles in the fifth set.

The first year of the present Wimbledon championships was in 1922, and the King and Queen went down to open the ground on the first day. The opening match on the Centre Court was between two British players, A. R. F. Kingscote and L. A. Godfree. The latter won the toss and served. Kingscote returned the ball into the net. Godfree dashed to the net, picked up the ball and put it in his pocket.

In 1924 Kingscote was the only Englishman to reach the last eight. But increasing years and business commitments brought an end to his active Championship lawn tennis career.

On the administrative side of the game, however, Algy Kingscote became a much loved and respected figure and remained so for the remainder of his days. His chief interest and activities lay in the International Lawn Tennis Clubs. He was captain of the British International Club in 1925, 1926, 1927, and 1932, and then Chairman of the Club from 1928–30 and 1939–60. This period of 25 years as Chairman was perhaps his most unique and worthy contribution to the game of lawn tennis. His been sense of humour, his kindliness, and his dedication to the amateur game were quite remarkable.

December 23, 1964.

Canon Felix Kir, former French resistance hero and veteran Mayor of Dijon, died on April 25, 1968, in the hospital du Bocage, Dijon, which he himself had built. He was 92.

Born on January 22, 1876, at the Burgundian village of Alise-Sainte-Reine, the son of a railwayman, Felix Kir was until the age of nearly 60 a simple parish priest. Then the Archbishop of Dijon noticed his talents as a lecturer and journalist, and called him to new work in the cathedral city. When the German troops entered Dijon in 1940, Canon Kir was a lecturer for the National Catholic Federation, and editor of a catholic newspaper. He was nominated to a "municipal delegation" which was set up on the collapse of the town council.

Within this delegation, he rapidly became known as a leading opponent of the Germans. He helped some four or five thousand prisoners to escape from internment camp nearby, and used his newspaper *Le Bien du Peuple* to give a strongly anti-German account of the occupation of Dijon. As a result he was arrested and condemned to death by a German tribunal on October 10, 1940, but pardoned and released two months later.

Undeterred he continued to organize resistance and notably to help resistants to escape to Britain. At the same time his indefatigable courage and optimism did much to restore the morale of the population, which thronged about him on his pastoral visits to hear his vigorous and contemptuous predictions of German defeat.

On October 2, 1943, he was again arrested, then again released. In January, 1944, he was machine-gunned at his home by some members of the French Auxiliary Police which worked with the Gestapo. Badly wounded, he nonetheless remained standing until his attackers took fright and fled. He was then able to reach a hiding place in the Haute-Marne, where he slowly recovered. He returned to Dijon across country and on foot, arriving there on the very day of its liberation (September 11, 1944) amid general acclamation.

In April, 1945, he was elected Mayor of Dijon, and in October, by an overwhelming majority, deputy to the National Constituent Assembly. He was to remain Deputy for Dijon until his defeat by M. Robert Poujade (now Secretary-General of the Gaullist Party) in March, 1967, and Mayor of Dijon until his death.

In Parliament he sat as an independent, and he was noted for his independence both of character and of political conduct. Supported by the communists in his constituency, he was a firm partisan of Franco-Soviet friendship. He established a twinship between Dijon and Stalingrad and became a personal friend of Khrushchev.

Canon Kir won the Croix de Guerre in both world wars, as well as numerous other French and foreign decorations, including the O.B.E. As befitted a Burgundian, he was also noted for his taste in wine, and gave his name to a popular aperitif: a mixture of white Burgundy and Crême de Cassis.

April 26, 1968.

Sir Ivone Kirkpatrick, G.C.B., G.C.M.G., who died on May 25, 1964, at Celbridge, co. Kildare, at the age of 67, was a diplomatist who never allowed the conventional values of the foreign service to blunt the independence of his mind or the forthright style in which he expressed himself. Unlike most of his colleagues he began his diplomatic career with distinguished active service in the First World War and not a university as his background. He could always be trusted to say what he thought and to fight for his point of view with an Irish delight in battle. But he always fought fair and a sharp sense of humour never deserted him.

Permanent Under-Secretary at the Foreign Office from November, 1953 until his retirement at the age of 60 in February, 1957, for a large part of his time he was closely concerned in one capacity or another with Anglo-German relations. For some years immediately before the outbreak of war he was head of Chancery at the Berlin Embassy, and was called on to translate for Neville Chamberlain in his talks with Hitler at Berchtesgaden, Godesberg, and Munich in 1938. After the war he was for a time head of the German section of the Foreign Office and later became United Kingdom High Commissioner in Germany, where he took a leading part in preparing the treaties, signed eventually at Bonn, by which Germany's sovereignty was restored to her. Kirkpatrick became well known to the public when, on a May night in 1941, he was suddenly sent north to identify Rudolf Hess (whom he had frequently met while he was in Germany) when that unexpected wartime visitor landed from the skies in Scotland.

For much of the war, Kirkpatrick was Controller of the European Service of the B.B.C. and helped to build up the great reputation and influence it exerted among the resistance groups and countless others in occupied Europe. After his retirement from the Foreign Office he was chairman of the Independent Television Authority from 1957 to 1962.

Ivone Augustine Kirkpatrick was born in February, 1897, the son of Colonel Ivone Kirkpatrick, C.B.E., of Celbridge, co. Kildare. Educated at Downside, where he proved himself a brilliant scholar, he was 17 years old when the First World War broke out and he at once joined the Royal Inniskilling Fusiliers. He saw a good deal of fighting, was twice mentioned in dispatches, was awarded the Belgian Croix de Guerre and was badly wounded at Gallipoli.

JUNIOR PEACE-MAKER

At the age of 22, his character formed and developed beyond his years by the experiences and responsibilities of the war, he found himself in the Foreign Office concerned, as a junior, with the problems of peace making. He served for a short spell at the Embassy in Rio de Janeiro, and was later chargé d'affaires to the Holy See.

It was, however, in 1933 that he first made his direct contact with German affairs. He was then a First Secretary, and he went to Berlin as head of Chancery when Sir Eric Phipps was the Ambassador. It was the year when Hitler first became Chancellor, when, a month later, the Reichstag was burned out and when the election swept the National Socialist Party to overwhelming power. For five years, until well on in 1938, Kirkpatrick was a close witness of "the Darkening Scene", as Sir Winston Churchill described it. In his professional capacity he was in frequent contact with Hitler's associates; he knew of their intrigues, their racial intolerance, and of the brutalities that ensued. Secretly he abominated these manifestations and, when coupled as they were with open and surreptitious measures of rearmament, he was entirely convinced they must lead to war. His attitude to those in power in Germany was entirely correct, but he received the confidences at that time of several Germans who held confidential positions and yet were not in sympathy with the Hitler regime. Their information was of value, and served only to strengthen his own conviction.

UNLOVED TACTICS

In his heart Kirkpatrick could have little sympathy for the tactics of his own Government and when Sir Nevile Henderson succeeded Sir Eric Phipps as Ambassador in Berlin, his advice and views were by no means always agreeable or acceptable. On his visits home and when he returned in the autumn of 1938 to the Foreign Office he found more receptive listeners.

Kirkpatrick was engaged in London throughout the war years. In the spring of 1940 the Foreign Office placed his services at the disposal of the Ministry of Information, where he succeeded Professor E. H. Carr as Director of that Ministry's Foreign Division. A few months later, following the setting up of the Political Warfare Executive, the B.B.C. in agreement with the Minister of Information (then Duff Cooper) reorganized all the overseas services, and Kirkpatrick was appointed controller of the section dealing with all enemy and enemy-occupied countries. Under his control these radio services developed in importance and extent.

One night in May, 1941, however, Kirkpatrick was called to Whitehall and urgently dispatched to Scotland to interview a lone German who had landed by parachute a few miles from Glasgow and who was making the fantastic claim that he was the Fuhrer's deputy, Rudolf Hess. Later, the German radio announced that Hess (who, it was said, had been ill) was missing, and, a few hours later, Kirkpatrick was able to telephone through to London to say that he had been able to recognize the German as Hess beyond any possibility of doubt.

During the last few months of the war Kirkpatrick went again to Germany as Deputy Commissioner (Civil) of the Control Commission (British Element), where his flair for administration had full scope. He returned after a year to the Foreign Office and in 1949 became head of the German section, which had grown into a very large organization, with the rank of Permanent Under-Secretary. In 1950, he succeeded General Sir Brian Robertson as United Kingdom High Commissioner in Germany.

Kirkpatrick's knowledge of German affairs was probably unique among British officials. He did not allow his earlier unhappy experiences of Germany to prevent him from taking up his new post with good will and a desire for friendship, but he had his own ideas about the way this could best be made manifest, and he chose to be forthright and even brutally frank in his public speeches. He spoke to many influential audiences during his term as High Commissioner, rubbing in the origins of the war, the sacrifices Britain incurred in helping Germany on to her feet again, the importance of Germany aligning herself with the western powers and of making a fair contribution to their joint defence. His period of office was certainly not without its difficulties—troubles with the Russians over zonal boundaries and other matters constantly occurred. In the meetings of the High Commission his intimate knowledge of Germany served him well; he could express himself lucidly and convincingly and he always took care to be well briefed. He was on the alert for any resurgence of Nazism, and he took a tough line when Dr. Werner Naumann and neo-Nazi associates threatened to give trouble.

He was on close and friendly terms with Dr. Adenauer for whom he had great admiration and respect, sentiments that were evidently mutual. He gained the respect and gratitude of many Germans by the fairness and speed with which he redressed many of their grievances—on Heligoland, dismantling, restrictions on ship-building and other issues.

He succeeded Lord Longford in 1963 as chairman of the National Bank, and had been British President of the Channel Tunnel Study Group since 1958. His memoirs, *The Inner Circle*, were published in 1959 and his biography *Mussolini: Study of a Demagogue* was due to appear in June, 1964.

Sir Ivone Kirkpatrick married in 1929 Violet Caulfeild, daughter of Colonel R. C. Cottell, C.B.E., and had one son and one daughter.

May 26, 1964.

Sir Cecil Kisch, K.C.I.E., C.B., died on October 20, 1961, at the age of 77. He was for many years an outstanding figure in the former India Office, particularly on the financial and economic side. He did much in the international sphere in regard to monetary policy and rendered valuable supply service in the Second World War. He showed remarkable versatility and unflagging intellectual zest.

Cecil Hermann Kisch was born on March 21 1884, the eldest son of H. M. Kisch, C.S.I., a member of the Indian Civil Service who did pioneer work in shaping relief policy during the Bengal famine of the early seventies and rose to be Postmaster-General of the Dependency. At Clifton College Kisch became head of the school. At Trinity College, Oxford, he took a double First in Mods. (1905) and Lit. Hum. (1907). He entered the home Civil Service in 1908 and after brief experience at the G.P.O. was appointed to the India Office.

At an early stage he was made private secretary to the Permanent Under-Secretary of State. He similarly served the Parliamentary Under-Secretary, the late Edwin Montagu, who included him in the official retinue when he went out to India as Secretary of State towards the close of 1917 to confer with the Viceroy, Lord Chelmsford, upon the first stages of the political advancement of the country, in accordance with the declaration Montagu had made in the House of Commons on August 20 that year. The voluminous diary which Montagu dictated night by night, later published by his widow, described Kisch as having a thirst for information, and as "growing on one". While regarding his private secretary as "sometimes wrong-headed and prejudiced", he praised him for a "consummate knowledge of many subjects". The defects of Kisch did not, he wrote, spoil his good points, and his skill and helpfulness were especially commended. Montagu also took him to the 1919 Peace Conference in Paris. He was made secretary to the Indian Currency Commission, which sought, unwisely as it turned out, to peg the exchange value of the rupee at the 2s. rate in contrast to the pre-war 1s. 6d. rate which was necessarily returned to later, after heavy losses of Indian revenue.

THE LEAGUE OF NATIONS

In 1921 Kisch was made secretary of the Finance Department, and held the position for a dozen years. In that capacity he promoted reforms and advances leading to the creation of the Reserve Bank of India. He was a member of the preparatory committee of experts which sat at Geneva to prepare the way for a monetary and economic conference for the League of Nations, and he was chosen to be a delegate for India at the conference. He was also in 1937 a British representative on the international committee on the finances of Tangier.

An extremely versatile writer and speaker, he found time to tell the sensational story of *The Portuguese Bank Note Case* (1932), in which a colossal fraud was perpetrated upon a much respected London firm of currency note printers. The book showed his gift of making a highly complicated and technical narrative understandable to the ordinary man. Kisch also wrote in collaboration with Miss W. A. Elkin a standard work on Central Banks, which by 1932 had reached a fourth edition.

Kisch became an assistant under-secretary at the India Office in 1933 and was raised to deputy under-secretary 10 years later. In 1942 he was placed on special duty in the Petroleum Warfare Department and was for three anxious years director-general for the supply of the sinew of war. He was a member of the supervisory finance committee of the League of Nations from 1938 onwards, and became a vice-president of the Board of Liquidation, which in 1946 wound up the operations of the League for it to be replaced by the United Nations. He also served from 1949 on the currency committee of the Bank of Greece.

Kisch's varied labours during the war were shadowed by much personal sorrow. He had married in 1912 Myra, youngest daughter of Marcus M. Adler. She died in 1919, after bearing him a daughter and twin sons. One of these, Captain Oliver Kisch, of the Royal Signals, was killed in June, 1943, in action at sea in the Middle East. He also lost, in the Tunisian campaign in the following year, his distinguished brother, Brigadier Frederick Kisch, C.B., C.B.E. His daughter, Miss Evelyn Myra Kisch, Lecturer in Music at the University of Durham, died young in 1945. Kisch married secondly in 1922 Rebekah Grace, daughter of L. Joseph. She shared her husband's keen thirst for knowledge and his love of travel whether for business or pleasure.

One of the pursuits of the relative leisure of later years was that of acquiring a thorough mastery of Russian. Under the title of *The Waggon of Life* he translated Russian poems into delightful English verse. He was on the governing body of the School of Oriental and African Studies, University of London, and became honorary treasurer of the school. He was also a member of the governing body of the London School of Economics.

He was created C. B. in 1919 and K.C.I.E. in 1932.

October 21, 1961.

Professor Hans Knappertsbusch, who died on October 25, 1965, will be remembered by post-war Wagnerites for the unforgettably noble and beautiful performances of Wagner's *Parsifal* which he conducted at Bayreuth from 1951 onwards. Knappertsbusch had been for many years a specialist in Wagner and Strauss, and a significant figure in German operatic life.

Hans Knappertsbusch was born at Elberfeld on March 12, 1888. He had already conducted school orchestras as a boy, but came to music after studying philosophy and had his musical training from Steinbach and Lohse in Cologne. His debut as conductor was made in 1911 at Mülheim. From there he went to posts in Bochum, his native Elberfeld, thence to Leipzig, and after a period at Dessau to the coveted musical directorship of the Bavarian State Opera which he took over from Bruno Walter in 1922. It was here that he became renowned as an interpreter of Wagner and Richard Strauss, two of the three figureheads in Munich's summer festivals.

Knappertsbusch was well established at Munich when, in 1933, the Nazis came to power. His outspoken hostility to Nazism soon made him politically unacceptable for a post on which Hitler set such store, but since he held a lifelong contract with the State Opera he refused to resign until in February, 1936, he was officially retired by the Bavarian Statthalter, General von Epp. He continued to conduct, mainly in Vienna, where he was on the strength of the State Opera, but also abroad—his only London appearance was at Covent Garden in 1937 when he directed Strauss's *Salome*.

After 1945 he reemerged as a grand old man of German music, one of the last survivors of the old school of romantic interpretation, concentrating chiefly on Beethoven, Brahms, Wagner, Bruckner and Strauss (Johann II as well as Richard). His spacious tempi, propelled with the utmost authority and a minimum of fuss, and the majestic carpet of sonority which he drew from the handpicked Bayreuth orchestra, lent lustre to the first postwar Wagner festivals when he continued to conduct in spite of his antipathy to the new-style Bayreuth productions.

Screened from the audience's view, at ease in open-necked white shirt, he could make music there to his heart's content. He was, too, a familiar figure, in the *Lederhosen*, at the famous *Eule* restaurant in Bayreuth—it was said that after music his chief interest was good food.

In 1954 he resumed the musical directorship at Munich where, in protest against the delay in rebuilding the National Theatre, he absented himself from the town for a whole year. Knappertsbusch made guest appearances, of recent years, in Wagner productions abroad, notably at La Scala, Milan, and the Paris Opera.

October 28, 1965.

Dame Laura Knight, D.B.E., R.A., well-known for her paintings of fairground and circus life and backstage at the ballet, died on July 7, 1970, at the age of 92.

She spent years moving round with circuses, watching and painting—though not living in caravans, for she was not greatly in love with housekeeping. When she was 50 she began travelling with gypsies and painting them. She and her husband, Harold Knight, had a close circle of friends: George Bernard Shaw, T. E. Lawrence, Alfred Munnings, W. H. Davies, the poet, and, above all, the incandescent Augustus John ("a marvellous physical specimen and a great draughtsman"). Sooner or later each friend's likeness was put on paper. Her portrait of Shaw was a remarkable piece of work: it was done while he acted, talked and sang snatches of opera. He entirely failed to understand why it took more than a day to complete.

In her second volume of autobiography, *The Magic of a Line*, Laura Knight described how Serge Diaghilev gave her *carte blanche* to study his ballet company both in practice and on the stage. She struck up a friendship with Pavlova, who invited her to make drawings at the classes she held at her house in Hampstead.

Laura Knight, daughter of Charles Johnson, was born at Long Eaton, Derbyshire, in 1877. She was educated at Brincliffe, Nottingham and studied at the Nottingham School of Art. It was at Nottingham that she met her future husband, Harold Knight, who later became R. A. Not long after their marriage in 1903, the young artist couple migrated to Newlyn, Cornwall, where Laura Knight's already vigorous style gave a fresh stimulus to Newlyn's colony of painters. Her first notable Academy success was "Daughters of the Sun", a large composition of girls bathing from the rocks in Mounts Bay. Somewhat recalling the work of Albert Bernard it was more successful than many later works in enveloping the figures with light and atmosphere and raised high hopes for her future.

LOVE OF CIRCUS

From Newlyn she contributed regularly to the Royal Academy, paintings of bathers and local types and landscapes of the Land's End district, at Sennen in particular, and in 1927 was elected A. R. A. After the war of 1914-18 she devoted herself chiefly to paintings of the circus: she loved the life and she entered wholeheartedly into it, gaining the affection of all its performers. Sometimes the scene represented was in the "big top" but more often in the dressing room or stables. These exhibits were varied by capable paintings of the nude, portraits and landscapes. Elected R.A. in 1936, she continued for many years to be one of the most regular of Academicians in her yearly contribution of six works to the Spring Exhibition. In landscape she favoured effects of early morning sun and winter scenes but the sawdust arena and the stage provided the themes of many of her later paintings, such as the clowns, "Sawdust and Gold Dust" of 1953 and the "Bolshoi Ballet rehearsing" of 1958. A retrospective exhibition of her work was put on at the Diploma Gallery of the Royal Academy in 1965.

Laura Knight's powers as an artist received full recognition in England and abroad. In 1929 she was created D.B.E., in 1931 she received the honorary degree of LL.D, from St. Andrew's University and in 1951 of D. Litt, from Nottingham University. In 1936, on her election as full R.A., she was entertained to dinner by the Society of Women Artists of which she was president.

July 9, 1970.

Lord Knollys, G.C.M.G., M.B.E., D.F.C., chairman of the Northern & Employers' Assurance Company, died on December 3, 1966, in London. He was 71. He was Governor and C.-in-C., Bermuda, from 1941 to 1943, and chairman of B.O.A.C. from 1943 to 1947. From 1956 to 1962 he was chairman of Vickers, Ltd.

Son of a distinguished father, he had a record of gallant service in the First World War, and having laid the foundations of a successful business career, went on to hold a series of appointments in business and public service of great variety and of exceptional responsibility.

The Right Hon. Edward George William Tyrwhitt Knollys, second Viscount and Baron Knollys of Caversham, co. Oxford, was born on January 16, 1895. His father, the first viscount, was Private Secretary to King Edward VII from 1870 to 1910, and served King George V in the same capacity from 1910 to 1913. His mother was the Hon. Ardyn Mary Tyrwhitt, elder daughter of the late Sir Henry Thomas Tyrwhitt, Baronet, and the late Baroness Berners. As a boy he was page of honour from 1904 to 1910 to King Edward VII and, from 1910 to 1911, to King George V, who was his godfather.

He was educated at Harrow and at New College, Oxford.

In the 1914-18 War Knollys served in the 16th London Regiment (T.A.) and in the R.F.C. He was awarded the M.B.E., the D.F.C., the Order of the Crown of Belgium and the Croix de Guerre. In 1924 he succeeded his father.

In 1929, having studied accountancy and worked for a few years in Barclays Bank, he was appointed local director in Cape Town of Barclays Bank (Dominion, Colonial & Overseas). In 1932 he returned to England and was appointed a director of the Employers' Liability Assurance Corporation, of which he became managing director in the following year, and with which he was closely associated for the rest of his life.

Shortly before the outbreak of the Second World War Knollys had become Deputy Commissioner, South-Eastern Region, for Civil Defence, and he held the extra responsibilities of this position for the first two years of the war. In 1941 he was appointed Governor and Commander-in-Chief of Bermuda. This was an unusual appointment, in that Knollys was the first civilian to be chosen for the post, the importance of which had at this stage of the war immensely increased. It appeared necessary to have in it a man of wide experience with a special knowledge of American ways and methods of thought, such as Knollys had acquired in frequent visits to the United States in connexion with the large insurance interests of The Employers' in that country.

In 1943, having completed a most successful term of office in Bermuda, he was offered and accepted appointment as the first whole-time chairman of the British Overseas Airways Corporation. Though the corporation had been in existence for some years it fell to Knollys to give it a new system of management, new methods of operation and new plans for development to equip it for the highly competitive and expansive postwar period. The foundations laid by him were sound and imaginatively conceived and have undoubtedly remained invaluable to the Corporation to this day.

His appointment was for four years, and in 1947 he returned to his business career.

LENT TO GOVERNMENT

He was reappointed managing director of The Employers' and resumed his seat on the Board of Barclays Bank. In 1951 and 1952 he was, however, again lent to the Government, this time to represent it as United Kingdom Representative on the International Materials Conference at Washington. On his return from this tour of duty he was appointed a director of Vickers.

In 1954 Knollys retired as managing director of The Employers' and was immediately appointed its chairman. At the beginning of the following year he became deputy chairman of Vickers and in June, 1956, succeeded to the chairmanship on the retirement of Sir Ronald Weeks. It was most fitting that, as the climax of his active business career, he should have been picked for this outstanding position, one of the most important in the British industrial world, and it was typical of him to have filled it with the utmost distinction.

In June, 1962, he relinquished the chairmanship of Vickers, remaining, however, a member of the board until 1965. He was chairman of the English Steel Corporation from 1959 to 1965. Meanwhile, The Employers' having merged with the Northern Assurance Company in 1960, he became chairman of the Northern & Employers, the holding company whose board took over responsibility for the affairs of the new group.

To certain charitable interests he freely gave

his time. Before the last war he was honorary treasurer of the Radium Institute and the Mount Vernon Hospital, and a member of the finance committee of the British Empire Cancer Campaign. Since 1953 he had been chairman of the council of the R.A.F. Benevolent Fund and a member of the council of King Edward VII Sanatorium, Midhurst.

EFFICIENCY DRIVE

The main qualities that Knollys brought to his various tasks were an immense capacity for hard work, a predilection for a busy life and intelligence of a jewel-like quality, hard and brilliant. He entered business life when it was only just beginning to be fashionable for men of his background to do so. Whatever others had as their objective, his was to become as soon as possible an expert and a professional in the field of practical finance and management, into which he was probably the first courtier's son to make his way. Since his ability was equal to his ambition, his career was marked with conspicuous successes.

He made severe demands, in the interest of efficiency, on those who worked for him, but he taxed himself hardest of all. He had a remarkable ability for dealing in a day with a programme that would have been too full for a man of normal powers, never letting his grasp fail however various might be the subjects to which he had to turn his attention. Very soon after he was taken ill in March he knew that he had no hope of recovery. It was typical of him that in the time left to him he worked as hard as ever and applied himself to resolving those problems, however onerous they might be, which needed his personal attention.

He had, particularly at first meeting, an unsentimental charm of manner that won him friends and admirers at home and in every country that he visited on his many long travels.

OUTDOOR INTERESTS

He was, and knew that he was, often unsuccessful as a public speaker. In his leisure, though he was a fair cricketer, a good golfer and a very reliable shot, his first interests were gardening and fishing, and he was probably never happier than on the days he could spare at his last country home on the Test.

In 1928 he married Margaret Mary Josephine, daughter of Sir Stuart Coats, Bt. She fully shared all his interests and accompanied him on nearly all his travels. She survives him, as also do his son, David Francis, who in 1950 married the Hon. Sheelin Maxwell, and now succeeds to the title, and his daughter.

December 5, 1966.

Sir Robert Knox, K.C.B., K.C.V.O., D.S.O., who died on October 15, 1965, had been since 1939 secretary of the Political Honours Scrutiny Committee.

After his service in the First World War Knox joined the Treasury in 1920 and in 1928 he became private secretary to the permanent secretary, Sir Warren Fisher. At that time Fisher was concerned to bring some order and regularity into the arrangements for recommending awards under the British Empire Order and it fell to Knox to help him with this task.

As time went on Knox was progressively relieved of other duties so that he could concentrate on honours work and before long he became the accepted central authority in Whitehall on all questions relating to honours. He acted as secretary of the various commitees dealing with honours, medals, and awards; and his advice and guidance on these matters was available to all departments. His sphere of influence was subsequently extended to matters of ceremonial and he acted as secretary of the commissions and committees concerned with the coronations of 1937 and 1953.

In this world of precedent and protocol he found full scope for the exercise of his individual qualities—an orderly mind and a meticulous attention to detail. His insistence on the strictest compliance with the rules of eligibility for the various degrees of honours was sometimes thought to be a little tyrannical; and his official superiors found special pleasure in recommending him in 1953 for the award of a K.C.B. for which, under the rules which he himself had formulated, he was not strictly eligible. This was a measure of their affection for him and their respect for his work.

PERFECTION OF SYSTEM

The whole of his official career was devoted to the perfection of the system which he had largely devised for scrutinizing and assessing the recommendations submitted from all quarters for the award of honours. This was for him an absorbing interest to which all his energies were applied and it was because of his single-minded devotion to this work that he continued in it for years beyond the normal age of retirement.

For 40 years he was, in his own specialized subject, a constant central figure in the changing scene of Whitehall. His death will leave a gap which will not easily be filled.

Robert Uchtred Eyre Knox was born in 1889, son of the late Alexander Knox. He was educated at Dulwich and St. John's College. Cambridge, where he was an Exhibitioner and gained a B.A. in Natural Sciences in 1911. He immediately joined the War Office, and served there from 1912 to 1914.

From 1914 to 1916 he was a Captain with the eighth battalion of the Suffolk Regiment. He gained the D.S.O. and was mentioned in dispatches, but was severely wounded. He was again attached to the War Office during 1918-19. Knox was made C.V.O. in 1933 and K.C.V.O. in 1937.

He married in 1924. Dorothy Margaret, daughter of the late James Duke Hill of Harlow, Essex, who survives him.

October 16, 1965.

Dr. Lauge Koch, Danish polar explorer and geologist, who took part in 24 expeditions to Arctic Greenland, died in Copenhagen on June 7, 1964, at the age of 71. The son of Parson Carl Koch, he was born at Kjaerbyved, Kallundborg, on July 5, 1892. From early youth his ambition was to complete the whole circuit of the coast of Greenland by Danish explorers in time for the bicentenary celebration of the landing there, in 1721, of Hans Egede, the first Danish missionary. On leaving Copenhagen University he studied glaciology in Greenland during 1913, and in 1916 accompanied Knud Rasmussen as cartographer and geologist on the Second Thule Expedition. His results were published in 1916 and 1917 in maps of Melville Bay and the De Long Fiord region. Great hardships on the return journey caused the death of Dr. Thorild Wulff, one of Koch's companions: and his own life was just saved by relief sledges which Rasmussen, hurrying ahead, brought out from the Danish settlement at Etah.

Koch next led the Bicentenary Jubilee Expedition to map the whole northern part of Greenland. Setting out in March, 1921, he reached Cape Bridgman, at the extreme north of Greenland, on May 21 and hoisted the Danish flag to mark the achievement of the aim he had set himself eight years before. A trip farther north over the pack-ice took him nearer the Pole than any Danish explorer had hitherto been, and the party then travelled along the east coast of Peary Land, against a heavy snowstorm which made hunting impossible. They were saved from absolute starvation only by killing a herd of musk-oxen after a wearying hunt. Following the south coast of Peary Land, they entered Jörgen Brönland Fiord and reached the head of Independence Fiord in July.

He established that the great depression which Peary had 28 years before mistaken for a channel was really a huge frozen valley from sea to sea, partly filled by a large lake, and separating ice-free Peary Land from ice-bound Greenland proper. This he named the Wandel Valley, and the land north of it Erlandsen Land. Crossing the inland ice of Greenland westwards he next mapped large unknown areas of the Victoria Fiord.

AFTER A REST

After a rest and replenishment of clothing and provisions, Koch continued his investigations southwards to the Humboldt Glacier: and spent the winter of 1922–23 at Upernivik, on the western coast of Greenland, leaving southwards in March, 1923, for the hitherto uncharted coast of Cape York Land, north of Melville Bay; and returning to Denmark in the summer. The complete results of the survey from 1917 to 1923 were published by the Geodetic Institute of Denmark in its *Map of North Greenland*, 1932.

Koch was now appointed leader of a Government expedition to survey the region between Scoresby Sound and Danmark Harbour, the central part of the east Greenland coast, and, together with a Danish palaeontologist, Dr. Rosenkrantz, and a Cambridge palaeobotanist, T. M. Harris, arrived at the Eskimo colony at Scoresby Sound in July, 1926. Leaving his companions at this base, Koch and several Eskimos made a sledge journey to Mackenzie Bay, existing with difficulty, as on previous occasions, by shooting musk-oxen, bear, and ptarmigan after exhausting hunts, and more than once risking death. Undaunted, Koch made in February, 1927 a second journey northwards along the coast to Danmark Harbour, making a fresh geological and economic survey, and discovering, besides fossils, many active hot springs of about the same age as those of Iceland and the Faroes; surveying many fiords, ascending several mountains, and covering in all about 2,500 kilometres by sledge.

In 1931 he led the greatest expedition yet organized by Denmark, the Triennial East Greenland Expedition, on a three years' investigation of the east coastal region, and in 1933 he discovered, during a flight lasting $9\frac{1}{2}$ hours, a chain of seven or eight mountain peaks north of Scoresby Sound, each about 13,500 ft. higher than any hitherto recorded in Greenland. Owing to unusual weather, his steamer, the Gustav Holm, was able to penetrate farther north than any ship had been for decades; and from further flights over Danmark Bay northward to Peary Land the probable existence of a number of islands between Greenland and Spitzbergen was deduced.

His greatest achievements were his practical completion of the topographical mapping of the Greenland coast, and the tracing of the continuity of the ancient Caledonian mountain system of Scotland, Norway, and Spitzbergen through Northern Greenland and the north of Ellesmere Island to Grant Land.

June 8, 1964.

Dr. Zoltán Kodály, the Hungarian composer, died on March 6, 1967, in Budapest at the age of 84. No other musician of our day has received such universal affection and veneration as he. If, as creative musician, musicologist, folklorist, critic, educationist and occasional conductor of his own music, he transformed the musical life of his homeland, where for more than a quarter of a century he was accepted as a spiritual leader, his work and personality won him almost equal regard throughout Europe and the United States.

In February the Royal Philharmonic Society had announced that Kodály had been awarded the society's gold medal and that it was hoped he would come to London to receive it. In November, 1966, the first British performance of his celebrated opera *Háry Janos* was given by the Camden Opera Group in St. Pancras Town Hall.

RAILWAYMAN'S SON

Zoltán Kodály was born in Kecskemet on December 16, 1882. His father, a railway official, was committed to a rather nomadic life during his children's early years, but both Kodály's parents were amateur musicians—his mother played the piano and his father the violin—so that their home, wherever it happened to have been, was a meeting place for amateur musicians because the father was an ardent player of string quartets.

From 1884 to 1891 the Kodály family lived in Galánta (a town later to provide the composer with material for a popular suite of dances), where the boy attended the local elementary school. A move to Nagyszombat enabled the boy to attend the city's Roman Catholic Grammar School, and he began seriously to study the piano and the violin. As a treble in the cathedral choir he regularly sang performances of the Viennese-type Mass settings of Haydn, Mozart, and their contemporaries and seized the opportunity to educate himself by eager explorations among the music in the cathedral library. He was already composing: an overture written in 1897 was played by his school orchestra, and the following year his works included a Mass for chorus and orchestra. At the same time, his father's inability to find a cellist for quartet playing led the boy to teach himself the cello sufficiently well to make good the deficiency and to reconstruct with remarkable accuracy the cello parts of Haydn's quartets, apparently lost in one of the family migrations.

A government grant for his further education took him in 1900 to the University of Sciences in Budapest, apparently feeling that his future lay in directions away from music. But in 1902 he entered the Budapest Academy of Music, combining his two fields of study until, in 1906, he took his degree of Doctor of Philosophy with a thesis on "Strophic Construction in Hungarian Folk-Song". As a student he composed a great deal of music—sonatas for violin and cello and piano, a string trio and a string quartet, as well as choral works, which, like all Hungarian music of the period, was influenced almost to the point of imitation by the German composers. As the title of his thesis shows, however, Kodály's attention had already turned to the idea of a genuinely Hungarian national style, while the later stages of his education had awakened his interest in French and Italian music and culture. Recognizing the inauthenticity of published collections of Hungarian folksong, he had begun to collect and study them himself in 1905, and began his momentous partnership with Bartok, a year his senior, in 1906. The work the two accomplished together not only enabled each of them to reach his mature style and to establish authentic texts of a vast number of songs and folk dances, but also impelled Kodály to undertake studies in all the fields connected with folksong; contributions to ethnography, ethomusicology and folklore studies in general are cogently argued from precise, detailed studies of the materials he and Bartok collected. It was not, however, until 1951 that their work bore the fruit they desired in the beginning of the comprehensive collected edition of Hungarian song which they had planned and for which they had written the necessary scholastic and critical material when proposing the collection in 1913.

Another influence upon Kodaly's mature style was the music of Debussy. His early experience of music had been almost exclusively classical, based upon his father's love of Haydn string quartets and the experience of eighteenth-century church music which came to him as a choir boy. The academic training he had received was entirely German in outlook—it left him with an unshakable devotion to the music of Bach—but did not prepare him for the music of the new composers at the turn of the century. Some months in Paris, where he attended Widor's lectures, taught him to appreciate and understand the music of the impressionists, which made a lasting impression upon his own music.

ACADEMY LINK

Kodály's appointment as teacher of theory at the Budapest Academy, in 1907, and as teacher of composition a year later, began an association which lasted for the greater part of his life and made him so influential a figure in Hungarian national life; after his retirement from the academy he was recalled in 1945 to become its director. His methods as a teacher were empirical, designed to allow each student to develop his own individuality.

His works began to reach publication, and performances outside Hungary, in 1910, so that the rest of his life story is a narrative concerned only with the development of his musical style and the spread of his fame. After 1922, his music seemed to be an invariable part of the festivals of the newly formed International Society for Contemporary Music. In 1923, the commission to write a work celebrating the fiftieth anniversary of the union of the cities of Buda and Pest resulted in the *Psalmus Hungaricus*, a vivid, powerful, direct, and at times savagely forceful setting of a sixteenth-century Hungarian paraphrase of Psalm 55. It swept aside academic doubts among his own people about the value of Kodály's music, the intensely national style and impressionistic techniques of which ran counter to the Germanic preconceptions in which Hungarian musicians were reared, and was soon heard all over the world. Two operas—*Hary Janos* and *The Spinning Room*—followed, the former yielding the vividly colourful orchestral suite which has become widely popular. The *Marassek Dances* of 1930 and the *Galanta Dances* of 1933, exploiting national idioms and rhythms in an orchestral style as pungently strong as that of *Hary Janos* became equally popular. The two hundred and fiftieth anniversary of the end of the Turkish occupation of Hungary, in 1936, was the occasion for the *Budavári Te Deum*. The Concertgebouw Orchestra of Amsterdam commissioned the *Peacock Variations* for its fiftieth anniversary in 1939, and a year later the Concerto for Orchestra was written for Frederick Stock and the Chicago Philharmonic Orchestra.

In the 1930s, Kodaly grew actively interested in methods of teaching music to the young; what, in his view, was important was to give children the excitement and pleasure of singing lively and worth-while music which did not go too far beyond their range of emotional experience. To achieve an eager participation in music making was more important than any formal or academic training, so that if solmization produced quicker results with less boredom than teaching the conventional notation, solmization was the method obviously to be used. Four volumes of *Bicinia Hungarica*, a collection of folk songs and original compositions for two voices, published between 1937 and 1942, formed the greater part of Kodály's music written for children, but the young also benefit from some of his later piano pieces and many of the vast number of choral pieces he wrote during the Second World War. These, with their entirely idiomatic settings of Hungarian words, have naturally travelled more slowly than his instrumental and orchestral works; only the *Missa Brevis* completed during the German siege of Budapest has become widely popular.

Hungary had begun to honour Kodály in 1930, when he was awarded the Hungarian Order of Merit. His record of activity during the war years, when his house was destroyed by German action and he himself did nothing which could be construed as toleration of the invasion or the Nazi doctrines imposed on occupied Hungary (although the Germans recognized his importance as a musician and national figure and treated him with genuine consideration) affirmed his patriotism and increased the honour in which he was held.

During the Hungarian uprising of 1956 Kodály was chairman of the Revolutionary Committee of Intellectuals. He was reported to have cabled Soviet composers asking them to intercede for the withdrawal of Soviet troops from Hungary. After the revolution was crushed, communist officials decided not to act against him. He remained head of the folk music department of the Hungarian academy of sciences and honorary chairman of the Hungarian Musicians' Union.

In 1910. Zoltán Kodály married Emma Sandor, who for more than 50 years was his secretary, translator, amanuensis, and enthusiastic partner in all his enterprises. She died in 1959 and he married soon after Sari Peceli, a 21-year-old music student.

March 7, 1967.

General Pierre Koenig, the Free French commander at the Battle of Bir Hakeim in 1942, died on September 2, 1970, at the age of 71.

He was a man who combined all the traditional virtues of the officer with great personal kindness and charm. His political activities of the last two decades had won him many opponents, but no real enemies. As the commander who held up Rommel's advance in the Western Desert for a crucial fortnight, and thereby restored the honour of France's armed forces after the shattering defeat of 1940, he is assured of his place in history.

Koenig was born in Caen on October 10, 1898, the son of an Alsatian organ builder. At the age of 17 he volunteered for service in the First World War, from which he emerged with the Croix de Guerre and the Médaille Militaire. He was thrice mentioned in dispatches. After peacetime service in the Chasseurs Alpins, he was transferred in 1930 to the Foreign Legion with which he saw action in Morocco. In 1940 he served with distinction with the French troops in Norway. The Armistice of June, 1940, found him in Britain. where he at once decided to join General de Gaulle, He took part in the unsuccessful attack on Dakar, and then in the Gabon campaign of the autumn. In 1941 he was sent to Syria as Chief of Staff to General Legentilhomme, and after the Acre armistice he was promoted general and put in command of the 1st Free French Brigade, which was taking part in the defence of Egypt with the British Eighth Army.

In June, 1942, he commanded the Free French Brigade which held out for over a fortnight at Bir Hakeim, N. Africa, fighting off large-scale attacks by infantry, tanks and aircraft of the Axis forces. Rommel had planned to take Bir Hakeim without much difficulty but Koenig rejected Rommel's ultimatum to surrender.

When finally ordered to withdraw Koenig was able to bring out three quarters of his force, 200 wounded men and a large number of freed Allied prisoners.

ORDERS TO THE RESISTANCE

Later he took part in the Tunisian campaign and in 1944 was appointed delegate of the Algiers Government to General Eisenhower as Commander-in-Chief of French Forces in Britain, and also Commander of the "French Forces of the Interior"—that is, the armed resistance. He had the very delicate task of imposing Gaullist directives on the internal resistance, and when General de Gaulle made him Military Governor of Paris immediately after the liberation it was generally understood that one of his functions was to keep an eye on the Communist Party.

From 1945 to 1949 Koenig served as French Commander-in-Chief in Germany. In 1951 he entered politics as Gaullist deputy for Strasbourg, becoming Minister of Defence in the Governments of M. Mendes-France and M. Edgar Faure.

He resigned from the first after a dispute over the proposed European Defence Community (for whose non-ratification he was partly responsible) and from the second in protest against the restoration of Mohammed V as Sultan of Morocco. On this occasion a fellow Gaullist remarked that he was "a better military tactician than political one".

Koenig retired from politics in 1958 and from the Army in 1959. In the last years of his life he was mainly active as chairman of the French Committee for Solidarity with Israel, and hence became an outspoken critic of General de Gaulle's Middle East policy. The Arab League tried unsuccessfully to have him removed from the boards of several French oil companies which he had joined.

September 4, 1970.

Colonel Vladimir Komarov, who died in the first known space disaster on April 24, 1967, at the age of 40, was also the first Soviet cosmonaut to make a second flight.

Before this flight he stated "I dreamt of new flights with the aim of exploring Space for the benefit of the whole of mankind." Heart trouble almost took him out of the space programme 18 months before his first flight, which was made in October, 1964. Doctors found his heartbeat was irregular and ordered him six months' complete rest. Space chiefs thought the time-lag too great to make up, but he persuaded them to give him another chance. "He decided to prove he was healthy and had a right to a seat in a spaceship" Yuri Gagarin, the pioneer cosmonaut, said later.

He was tall, dark, bushy-browed and broad-shouldered—a serious-minded man, tenacious of purpose and slow of speech. The first man to pilot a multi-seater spaceship, Voshkod 1 ("Sunrise"), in 1964, he made 16 orbits. He and his two companions were in orbit for 24 hours. After the flight they were made heroes of the Soviet Union. Two years earlier he had been stand-in for Pavel Popovich but did not get a chance to make a flight at that time.

Komarov was a man of encyclopaedic engineering knowledge and tremendous aviation experience but he had the very simple background typical of many in the Soviet professions. He was born in central Moscow in the semi-basement flat of a five-storey block surrounded by the wooden houses now being torn down. His father was "dvornik", one of those Muscovite doormen-cum-handymen responsible for sweeping and clearing the snow from the streets in front of their house. The little dark-eyed boy was known as his first assistant.

The outbreak of war caught Vladimir at school. His father was called up into the A.A. forces and Vladimir and his mother were evacuated to the Urals, where he continued his schooling while simultaneously working in a timber mill. At the close of hostilities he returned to Moscow, where he left school on V. E. Day.

Graduating from an Air Force college, he was stationed for some time in the Carpathian mountains. Realizing the importance of specialized engineering training, he pushed for a place at Zhukovsky Military Engineering Academy. One of his professors recalls that Komarov "stood out in the crowd by his erudition, thirst for knowledge, and memory".

In private life he was a quiet, home-loving man. While studying he met the girl he was to marry, Valentina, who is a librarian. They had a son and daughter.

April 25, 1967.

Zoltan Korda, second of the three Hungarian brothers who played so big a part in British film production during the 1930s, died in Hollywood on October 14, 1961. He was 66.

Inevitably the career of Zoltan was overshadowed by that of his brilliant elder brother, Alexander, the architect of the family fortunes, a born showman, and a man of great culture and intellect. Alexander always led, and the other two followed, but that is not to decry their ability.

Alexander was born in 1893, Zoltan in 1895, and Vincent, the youngest, in 1897. Their father, Henrik Keller, was bailiff to a wealthy and influential family in Turkeye, Turkeye Hungary, but he died in 1906. Alexander then went to Budapest to earn money to support his younger brothers, and later entered the film business, working first with U.F.A. in Berlin and later in Paris and in Hollywood. Zoltan, who had served as an infantry officer in the Austria-Hungary

Army in the 1914–18 War, also became interested in film production and worked as a film editor for U.F.A. in Germany and for Alexander in Hungary. Later he joined U.F.A. as a director in Berlin and Vienna. He also wrote the original story for *Women Everywhere*, which was made by Fox Films in Hollywood in 1930, and it was in 1930 that he joined Alexander in America.

FUTURE ASSURED

But Alexander Korda's reputation was not made until he directed *The Private Life of Henry the Eighth* in England in 1933, for his own newly formed company, London Films. Thereafter the future of all three Korda brothers was assured, for to Alexander's ambition had now been added substantial financial backing. In 1935 Zoltan directed Edgar Wallace's *Sanders of the River* for London Films, much of it on location in Africa. In 1937 he co-directed *Elephant Boy* with Robert Flaherty, with Sabu taking the part of Toomai; and a year later he made another Indian story, *The Drum*, also with Sabu. Africa, India, and indeed the whole of the world east of Suez, always fascinated Zoltan, and in 1939 he directed what was probably his most successful picture, *The Four Feathers* from the novel by A. E. W. Mason, with a cast that included Sir Ralph Richardson, John Clements, and Aubrey Smith. This marked his zenith; and he was never quite so successful again, although *Cry, the Beloved Country* will be remembered among his more recent films.

A quiet, self-effacing, and peace-loving man, he had none of Alexander's tremendous drive and energy. But the two of them formed a redoubtable team, and one which—surprisingly enough, since they were Hungarians—proved staunch champions of the British Empire.

October 16, 1961.

Klavdia Kosygin, wife of Soviet Prime Minister Alexei Kosygin, died in April, 1967, after a long illness.

Mrs. Kosygin, a tall stately blonde believed to be in her late fifties, had been ill for several months. In December, 1966, she did not accompany her husband on his visit to Paris, and in February arrangements for her to join him on a trip to Britain were cancelled at short notice.

As is usual with Kremlin wives, very little is known of her personal life. She is believed to have met and married Kosygin when he was sent as a young technician to work in a Consumer's Cooperative in Irkutsk, Siberia, in 1924. Even during the puritanical days of Josef Stalin, when her husband was one of the rising young men in the Kremlin hierarchy, she was always smartly dressed when other top Soviet wives were uniformly conservative in their clothing.

Mrs. Kosygin was also one of the first wives to wear make-up in public. After her husband became Premier in October, 1964, she often accompanied him on official occasions. During the visit of President de Gaulle to the Soviet Union in the summer of 1966, she was often seen chatting fluently to the wives of French officials in their own language. Some sources said that even as Prime Minister's wife she had continued taking French lessons and took great pride in her proficiency in the language. The Kosygins have one daughter, Lyudmila, wife of Dzherman Gvishiani, Deputy Chairman of the State Committee for Science and Technology. Lyudmila, a tall brunette believed to have been born in 1928, stood in for her mother on Kosygin's visits to France in December, 1966, and Britain in February, 1967.

May 2, 1967.

Frol Kozlov, who died in Moscow on January 30, 1965, at the age of 56, was, until illness caused his retirement from the political scene, widely regarded as Mr. Khrushchev's successor at the top of the Soviet state and party hierarchies. Whether or not this belief, based on Khrushchev's statement to Averill Harriman in 1959, was true, Kozlov had been one of the most important personalities in the Soviet leadership as member both of the Presidium—the supreme policy-making organ—and a secretary of the Central Committee with extensive administrative powers.

A peasant turned party *apparatchik*, the handsome, square-built Kozlov had a very similar career to Khrushchev, rising through the ranks of the Communist Party from the age of 18. However, he had little of Khrushchev's personal magnetism and none of Mikoyan's free-wheeling confidence in the company of westerners. The silver-haired square-built and usually well-dressed Kozlov had the reputation of being a tough and efficient administrator but lacking a sense of humour.

Born into a peasant family at Loshchinino near Moscow in 1908, Kozlov went to work in a nearby textile mill at the age of 15. In the same year he began his party career by joining the communist league. Three years later he was foreman and secretary of the Komsomol. In 1928 he was sent to Leningrad, where eight years later he graduated from the Polytechnical Institute as a metallurgical engineer. Moved to the Urals town of Izhevsk, Kozlov was appointed to his first important party post in 1940 as Secretary of the Izhevsk Town Party Committee.

ALERT TO SABOTAGE

As the German armies occupied the western industrial areas of the Soviet Union, Kozlov's post gained in importance. Moving to Moscow in the last year of the war Kozlov was employed by the party's Central Committee, and in 1949 transferred to the Leningrad party organization which has always played a key role in the history of the party. His obedient execution of Stalin's later policies can be seen in his vigorous calls for vigilance against spies and saboteurs shortly before the fabricated "doctors' plot" in 1953 by which it is thought that the old dictator wanted to unleash an unprecedented new purge. Demoted to Third Secretary of the Leningrad party committee after Stalin's death when the plot was declared a fabrication, Kozlov regained his position rapidly and was appointed First Secretary in November, 1953. Khrushchev attended this meeting and Kozlov's subsequent promotion was closely connected with the progress of Khrushchev's own career. In the key year 1957, when Khrushchev defeated the so-called "anti-party group", Kozlov became first a candidate member and then a full member of the Presidium of the Central Committee.

His advancement in the party hierarchy was matched with promotion in the state offices. In March, 1958, he became Prime Minister of the Russian Federation and then First Deputy Prime Minister of the Soviet Union. He left this post in May, 1960, when he was appointed to the secretariat of the Central Committee. It is believed that he began to deputize for Khruschev at this period. Widely travelled outside the Soviet Union, to Rumania, Brussels, Finland, and the Far East, he probably attracted most attention when he attended the congress of the Italian Communist Party in December, 1962. Here he criticized the Chinese for their conflict with India.

Kozlov suffered from a cardiac complaint after a heart attack in April, 1961. Two years later he had a stroke and was believed to have been incapacitated since then. His final retirement from politics was marked in November, 1964, by his replacement on the Presidium.

February 1, 1965.

Victor Kravchenko, who died on February 25, 1966, having shot himself in New York, will, above all, be remembered as one of the noisiest and most controversial figures at the height of the "Cold War" between 1946 and 1950.

His book, *I Chose Freedom*, was published in the United States in 1946 and became before long a best-seller throughout the non-Communist world, not without considerable aid and encouragement from various official and unofficial agencies. Similarly, the spectacular libel action he took in 1949 against *Les Lettres Françaises*, the French Communist weekly and, indirectly, against the French Communist Party, had been encouraged by both the American and the French authorities.

There is, of course, no doubt that there was, for all its exaggeration, a strong basis of truth in Kravchenko's autobiography, *I Chose Freedom*, with its lurid stories of the Stalin purges in the 1930s, with its harrowing accounts of the police terror in Russia and of the concentration camp system in the days of Stalin, and with its description of the widespread chaos and bewilderment produced in Russia during the first months of the German invasion.

Kravchenko, who was born into a working-class family at Ekaterinoslav in 1905, received an engineering training after the Revolution, and held a variety of industrial and administrative posts in the 1930s and during the Second World War. Although he claims to have developed an intense hatred for the system throughout those years and to have planned, long before his appointment to Washington in August, 1942, to "choose freedom", he must have kept his thoughts very much to himself. Whether, in reality, he did not decide to "break with Stalin" until he had been in America for some time is difficult to say. In any case, he escaped from the Soviet Purchasing Commission in Washington on April 1, 1944, and, two days later, he announced his decision to the American press. He also accused the Soviet Government of a "double-faced" foreign policy in relation to Britain and the United States, and denounced its failure "to grant political and civil liberties to the Russian people."

It was a time when the Red Army was winning one spectacular victory after another, and Soviet prestige was high throughout the world, and no particular attention was paid to Kravchenko's desertion at first. But once the war was over, Kravchenko could, clearly, serve a useful purpose in cold-war propaganda. *I Chose Freedom* appeared in 1964 and, although Kravchenko admitted no more than that the book had been "edited" by professional American writers, his enemies widely alleged that the bulk of the book had been written by virulently anti-Soviet ghost writers.

This allegation, as well as the denunciation of Kravchenko as a "traitor" and a "liar" caused him to start his libel action against *Les Letters Françaises*. This law suit, which was in the nature of a major political operation, went on for several weeks. Kravchenko behaved with great truculence and was awarded small damages. After the publication of his second book, *I Chose Justice,* he sank into obscurity.

February 26, 1966.

Fritz Kreisler, who died in New York on January 29, 1962, at the age of 86, was at once the most distinguished and the most popular among violinists of his day. His playing was characterized by a sweetness of tone and a charm of interpretation that could only have been the expression of his own personality. This quality of charm did not lapse into effeminacy, for his playing was vigorous and glowing with vitality. He was able to achieve the rare combination of sweetness and strength. In that lay the secret of his wide appeal.

Born in Vienna on February 2, 1875, Kreisler was the son of an eminent physician, a keen amateur of music, who early recognized the boy's talent and encouraged its development.

UNDER AGE

Fritz was admitted to the Vienna Conservatoire to study under Auer at an age far below that prescribed by the rules of the institution. He justified the exception made in his favour by winning the gold medal for violin-playing at the age of 10. Further study in Paris was crowned by a similar award. His first important public appearance was in America, where he toured with Moritz Rosenthal, the pianist. Yet fame was not lightly won, and it was not till after his period of military service, followed by one of retirement, that he made his first real mark at a concert in Berlin in 1899. Two years later he made his debut in London at a concert conducted by Richter, and since that time he had been a frequent visitor to England, which seems to have been especially congenial to him. His performances of the concertos of Beethoven and Brahms were specially appreciated here. He was awarded the gold medal of the Royal Philharmonic Society in 1904, and Elgar's violin concerto, which was dedicated to him and first performed by him at one of the society's concerts in 1910, formed a special tie with this country.

At the outbreak of the war in 1914 Kreisler was recalled to the Austrian Army, and, as an indication of the place he occupied in English esteem, we may recall the dismay with which the news that he had been wounded was received in the winter of that year. He spent the remainder of the war mostly in America, and fortunately his wound proved not to be serious. Kreisler was the first ex-enemy artist to give a concert in London after the First World War, and no one could have been a better harbinger of resumed good feelings between the artists of Austria and England. Those who were at the Queen's Hall on that occasion will not easily forget the generous acclamations with which he was received, and which moved him so deeply that he was momentarily unnerved.

In later years Kreisler was apt to take the easy course marked out for him by his great popularity, choosing his programmes from attractive, but musically trivial, pieces, which delighted the vast audience, and playing them with an ease that became almost mechanical. But there was always another Kreisler, more rarely to be heard, who could play great music in a great style. As a composer Kreisler occupied himself mainly with the composition of concert-pieces for his own performance. Some were light and elegant music written in the Viennese idiom and eminently adapted to his own style of playing, such as the "Caprice Viennois", which achieved enormous popularity, and have passed into the repertory of every violinist. Some early works were at first understood to be arrangements of trifles by old composers, and so accepted until Kreisler claimed their authorship many years after. We have not yet got used to thinking of that Introduction and Allegro of Pugnani as solely Kreisler's own. The "disclosure" caused some stir in the newspapers, which Kreisler answered by declaring that he had originally announced these works as "in the style of" the composers named, thus vindicating his own honesty of intention.

January 30, 1962.

Dr. Hans Kroll, former west German Ambassador to Moscow, died on August 8, 1967, at the age of 69 in a hospital in the Starnberg district. While bathing in the Ammersee in Bavaria near his home some weeks ago Kroll suffered a heart attack from which he did not recover.

Hans Kroll was born on May 18, 1898, in Deutsch-Pickar in Upper Silesia. After studying history he joined the Foreign Service in 1920. Three years later he was assigned to the German Embassy in the Soviet Union for the first time.

He was in the headlines when he settled the case of mutiny in which the crews of German ships in a Soviet port were involved. After four years in the United States from 1925 to 1929 he worked in the Foreign Office until 1936 when he was appointed ambassador to Ankara.

From 1943 on he was Consul-General in Barcelona where he stayed until the end of the last war.

In 1950 he went into active service for the Government again and headed the department for Western trade in the Federal Ministry of Economic Affairs. In 1953 he was assigned Ambassador to Belgrade; in 1955 to Tokyo. When the first post for a west German Ambassador to the Soviet Union was to be replaced in 1958 the Government's choice was Kroll.

Kroll went to Moscow determined to do his best to work for the improvement of Soviet-west German relations. It did not take long before he was known for being on good terms with Khrushchev, then Soviet Premier. His independent way of thinking and sometimes self-willed way of proceeding caused a certain amount of tension between him and his own government at times. It was said that he was on better terms with the Soviet than with his own superiors.

Kroll was no cool, intellectual diplomat, but a man passionately engaged in the goals he pursued; he was more like an impressive parliamentarian than a state servant who quietly carried out orders. This was bound to lead to difficulties with Government circles, which insisted more than once Kroll should be recalled.

It was typical of Kroll to say that he did not see why a civil servant should lose his backbone.

BONN DENIAL

On another occasion he stated that he did not care if some people were raising their eyebrows when he chose his own more promising methods to pursue a course.

Tension between him and Bonn reached a climax when in November, 1961, a Soviet "Germany plan" became known in which Kroll was reported to have had a hand. The Bonn Government officially declared it had nothing to do with this plan. Kroll was rehabilitated by Dr. Adenauer himself, then Chancellor, who said that the Minister had not committed any indiscretion.

Adenauer, though disagreeing with Kroll's urgent pleas for a different Eastern policy (which did not fit into the Bonn concept at the time), still held him in high esteem as a man who would speak out. The Soviets quietly intervened when Kroll was to be replaced prematurely, and he stayed on until September, 1962.

During his last year before retirement Kroll served the Government as adviser on Eastern policy—a capacity in which he might have been of greater service now than before, some political observers said yesterday.

August 9, 1967.

Dr. Hans Kronberger, C.B.E., F.R.S., Member for Reactor Development, U.K. Atomic Energy Authority, was found dead on September 29, 1970, at his home in Cheshire.

His death robbed Britain of one of its most able physicists, who at the age of 50 was still at the peak of his scientific career. Apart from being among the small number of gifted people who are able to grapple with the intricacies of the world of nuclear physics, Dr. Kronberger had another and perhaps more important gift, for he was able to distil the mathematics and abstruse theory of his discipline into a form intelligible to the laymen.

At his death Hans Kronberger was Member for Reactor Development with the Atomic Energy Authority, an organization he joined when it was formed after the war-time atomic energy project. It was in 1944 that he began work on the war-time nuclear weapons project.

He once said, "Where there is a hill, I must climb it. Not so much to get to the top, but to see what is on the other side." It was a reference to a love for climbing and outdoor pursuits. But it could well be applied to describe the progress of his personal and scientific life.

He had more than an average share of uphill challenges. Hans Kronberger was born in Linz, Austria, of Jewish parents. His father had inherited a family business of leather merchants, but it was the influence of his mother that guided their only son towards an education in classics.

The first upheaval came when he was 18, and he was the only one of his family to escape Nazi persecution and reach the safety of England, with £10 in his pocket, two suitcases and his school reports. After badgering almost every university for a free place, he eventually was accepted for a course in mechanical engineering at King's College, Newcastle—then part of Durham University. Hans Kronberger might have remained a mechanical engineer had the war not intervened.

With a German passport, he was classified under the diligent screening process of the Foreign Office as a "friendly enemy alien." During a period of internment, he met some of the other refugee scientists who were to provide the backbone of so many military and postwar research projects. This was the period when he was to find a fascination with higher mathematics.

The British authorities released him from internment in 1942, and at 22 Hans Kronberger decided to switch from mechanical engineering to physics. He completed his degree at Newcastle and a Ph.D. at Birmingham University, and toward the end of the war became one of the nuclear physicists assigned to The Project.

Dr. Kronberger moved to Harwell in 1946.

PEACEFUL PROJECTS

Later he was to become one of the members of the industrial group which laid the foundation for the peaceful applications of nuclear energy for electricity. In 1956 he became chief physicist at Risley, and two years later director of research and development.

There were a number of promotions ahead, including scientist-in-chief, which led up to his appointment as the Member for Reactor Development. He was honoured by the Royal Society in 1965 for his contribution to nuclear reactor research. He was made O.B.E. in 1957 and advanced to C.B.E. in 1966.

Some of the schemes to which he devoted much of his life's work are only just bearing fruit. One was the idea of a new method of producing cheap enriched uranium by the gas centrifuge method, instead of the gaseous diffusion process. The first centrifuge system is now a matter of a collaborative development between Britain, Holland and Germany.

When Hans Kronberger embarked on the idea in the fifties, there was little information available about centrifuges of the scale needed for a new process. Recently he told the story how he and other members of Harwell visited the Battersea Fun Fair for rides on the spinning wall, because it was the only piece of equipment that was anywhere near the size of the apparatus they wanted to build. He had a sense of the ridiculous which allowed him to tell the story punctuated by peals of laughter.

Dr. Kronberger shared with other physicists a sense of responsibility for having worked on the bomb. This seemed to lend even greater fervour to a very energetic man for pressing for the development of peaceful applications of atomic power.

In recent times he had been deeply involved in the possible use of nuclear reactors as a means of providing large-scale desalination plants which would convert brackish and salt water into drinking supplies. It had been his hope that this process would be of greatest benefit to underdeveloped areas of the world where water shortage was one of the big barriers to progress.

His greatest heartbreak came undoubtedly with the death of his wife in 1962. He had married Mrs. Joan Hanson, a scientific assistant at Harwell, in 1951. Her first marriage had ended tragically after 18 months when her husband was killed in a climbing accident. Within a year of their marriage it was discovered that Joan Kronberger had a slowly developing brain tumour. About this time Dr. Kronberger learnt at last of the death of his family at the hands of the Nazis. This perhaps provided a stronger bond, in the sense of loss that both had suffered, than is experienced by many couples. They shared 10 years of great happiness and sorrow.

He leaves a stepson and two daughters.

October 1. 1970.

Alfried Krupp von Bohlen und Halbach, last representative of the famous firm which armed Germany in two world wars, died suddenly on July 30, 1967, at his home in Essen. He would have been 60 on August 13.

On that date it had been expected that Krupp would announce plans for the future disposal of the huge Krupp industrial empire, valued at £360m. Earlier in 1967, Krupp gave up his previous sole mastery of the Krupp enterprises, which will probably become a limited company, and turn their profits over to a foundation for scientific research.

The new company, when it comes into being, will continue to be called Krupp, but the name will die out in the family itself. Herr Arndt von Bohlen und Halbach, the 29-year-old son of Alfried Krupp, renounced his inheritance of the Krupp empire at his father's wish, and will retain his own name. Thus Alfried was the last holder of the name of Krupp.

Though it had been known that Krupp was ill with bronchial trouble, his death took everybody by surprise, and has caused sorrow and anxiety among the 100,000 employees of the vast Krupp concerns. The cause of his death was officially ascribed to "acute heart failure following a short incurable illness". Reports that he died of cancer are not confirmed.

Krupp flags with the three interlocking rings which are the hallmark of the firm flew at half mast in Essen, and there have been tributes from almost all parties and personalities in public life. President Lübke, in a message to Krupp's son, said: "Your father's life and work were most intimately bound up with the fate of the Fatherland."

In the spring, after prolonged rumours that Krupp was in difficulties and had piled up colossal debts, the German banks decided to forgo credit and the crisis came to a head.

The federal government stepped in, granting export financing of £27m. to Krupp, to which the state of North Rhine Westphalia (including the Ruhr) added £13,500,000 and the banks another £9m. To the fury of his rivals, Krupp was bailed out, but "what is good for Krupp is good for Germany".

In exchange for this assistance Krupp was forced to agree to the appointment of a six-man supervisory board to assist the general manager, Berthold Beitz. The saying went round: "Krupp is back under control; this time not by the allies but by the banks."

The termination of Krupps's personal ownership of the family fortune was generally regarded as the end of an epoch in German industrial history which had lasted for well over 100 years.

The firm of Krupp was founded in 1811 and started manufacturing munitions in 1857.

GUNS FOR EUROPE

By 1870 it covered 450 acres and employed 8,000 men. By 1914 it employed 80,000 men. By this time Krupp was exporting artillery to almost every government in Europe and had made Germany the foremost military power on earth.

Alfried Krupp was born at the Villa Hügel in Essen on August 13, 1907. His mother Bertha Krupp (who died in 1957) was the heiress of the Krupp fortune. She married Gustav von Bohlen and Halbach in 1906, and both her husband and her son Alfried were granted a special licence by Kaiser Wilhelm II to take the name of Krupp.

Between the two world wars Krupp took to the making of locomotives and other "toys of peace", but when Hitler came to power in 1933 the firm once again gave the Nazis the munitions they needed for the rearmament of the German Reich.

Alfried Krupp studied engineering at Munich and in the thirties worked in a humble job in the family firm. In 1943 he succeeded his father Gustav Krupp as chairman of the Krupp concern, and in the same year, by the transfer of the property from his mother Bertha Krupp, became the sole proprietor of the Krupp empire.

In March, 1945, the Krupp factories at Essen were smashed to pieces by the heaviest raid the Royal Air Force had made on Germany up to date. After Germany's defeat Krupp was branded as a war criminal. He was arrested and two years later was tried at Nuremberg on the charge of "looting and the promotion of slave labour". He was sentenced to 12 years' imprisonment and to the confiscation of his entire fortune, and imprisoned in the fortress of Landsberg.

When the Nuremberg tribunal first sat in 1945 it was Gustav Krupp who was indicted among the major war criminals, but a medical commission found him to be suffering from senile decay and unfit to appear. Britain objected to the idea of trying Alfried in his place, but in 1947 Alfried did in fact appear in the dock, together with 11 other directors. The prosecution dwelt at length on the role played by the House of Krupp in the rise of Hitler and the preparations for war, but the tribunal eventually dismissed charges of aggressive war and conspiracy and sentenced Alfried for crimes that took place after 1943.

RELEASE

In January 1951 he was released from prison on the orders of Mr. John McCloy, the American high commissioner in Germany, and was given back most of his property. But the occupying powers only allowed him to go back to industry on condition that he sold his Coal and Steel empire by 1959.

This condition Krupp failed to keep, but he swore an oath he would never again manufacture munitions, and stuck to it.

The firm of Krupp sailed to great heights of prosperity in the boom years of the 1950s under the dictatorial management of Berthold Beitz, the 43-year-old "wonder boy" from Hamburg. The firm expanded in all directions, manufacturing everything from locomotive to sausages, from false teeth to nuclear reactors.

Then it was hit by the recession, and got into ever deeper waters, leading finally to the crisis of early this year.

SOLITARY LIFE

The blows of the past 20 years had clearly marked Herr Krupp who withdrew more and more into himself, shunning people and living an almost solitary life in his house above the lake at Baldeney. His chief pleasures were hunting, shooting, and sailing in his yacht "Germania".

Though a man of legendary wealth he was modest in his habits, and was said to have a strong sense of responsibility towards the 100,000 men who worked for him. He was tall and aristocratic looking, and rarely smiled in later years.

His son Arndt von Bohlen und Halbach, who is 29, has never shown much interest in the firm, and is well enough off because he gets an income of £90,000 a year, which will be doubled after his father's death. At present he is farming in South America.

Alfried Krupp married twice: in 1937 Annelise Bahr, the mother of Arndt, who is still alive. They were divorced in 1941. His second marriage was to Vera Baroness Hossenfeldt in 1952. This marriage was dissolved in 1956.

August 1, 1967.

Shukry Kuwatly, a former President of Syria, to whom President Nasser gave the title of "First Arab Citizen," died in Beirut on June 30, 1967. He was 76.

Born in Damascus, he early espoused the cause of Syrian Nationalism, and during the 1914–18 War was imprisoned by the Turks for complicity in the Anti-Turkish underground movement which flourished in Syria until its occupation by the Allied forces. He collaborated with the regime established by the Emir Faisal in Damascus after its capture in 1918, but did not follow the Emir into exile when he was expelled by the French in 1920 and remained in Damascus to carry on opposition to the French occupation and, later, to the French Mandatory regime which was set up in 1922 by virtue of the Conference of San Remo. In 1925 he was one of a number of Damascus politicians who participated in the Druze revolt, and after its collapse and his own flight he was condemned to death *in absentia* by the French. In 1931, having been pardoned, he returned to Syria and became the leader of the Istiqlalists, the most extreme of several groups within the main political party, the National Bloc.

In 1936 he was a member of the Syrian delegation to Paris which initialled a Franco-Syrian Treaty of Friendship and Alliance; later that year, after the block had won a sweeping victory in a general election, he became Minister of Finance and of Defence in a Government headed by Jamil Mardam. The treaty was duly ratified by the Syrian Chamber, but ran into powerful opposition in France; in a vain attempt to secure its ratification by the French Chamber Mardam consented to a series of concessions over its terms which aroused in turn strong opposition in Syria. In 1938, in protest against these concessions, Kuwatly resigned from the Government and reverted to his role of leader of the most extreme nationalist wing of the block, in which capacity he rapidly enhanced his prestige in Syria by the vehemence of his denunciations of any suggestion of compromise over the Syrian demand for full independence.

The outbreak of the Second World War brought about a suspension of constitutional life in the Levant States and also of the Franco-Syrian discussions about the Treaty, which gradually became a dead letter. Kuwatly and his group, however, continued their campaign for full independence and during the Vichy period undoubtedly had contacts with the Italian Armistice Commission in Beirut, and with visiting Nazi officials, in the hope of enlisting their support and thereby bringing pressure on the French. In 1941, therefore, when British and Free French forces liberated the country, Kuwatly found it prudent to leave it.

CHOSEN PRESIDENT

After a year's absence, during which he visited other Arab capitals and made the pilgrimage to Mecca, he was permitted by the Free French authorities to return to Damascus. There he became the main spokesman of a newly united and vigorous block, and in 1943, when the French had at length been prevailed upon to allow a return to constitutional life and elections were held, the block won another clear-cut victory and Kuwatly was elected President.

During the next three critical years steadily increasing pressure by the block for the handing over of power was met with French evasions, procrastination, or downright refusal. The block leaders were encouraged by ever-growing popular support in Syria, by passive support in other Arab States, and by the sympathy of the British officials on the spot, although the British Government's official attitude was neutral and the British forces in Syria stood aloof. In such circumstances a clash was inevitable: it came in May, 1945, after months of increasingly acrimonious discussions, strikes, shooting in the outskirts of Damascus and elsewhere, and other signs of mounting disorder which redoubled in violence on receipt of a report that military reinforcements were being sent to Syria from recently liberated France.

The Syrian attitude became openly threatening, and the French authorities, believing that the only chance of maintaining a position for France in Syria was to crush the block, suddenly ordered a "cleaning-up operation" which took the form of a fierce bombardment of Damascus and other Syrian towns and attacks on Syrian gendarmerie and caused serious loss of life.

BRITISH TROOPS SENT

Kuwatly, who was ill in bed at the time, demanded British military intervention; and three days later, after urgent representations to General de Gaulle had been unsuccessful, the British Government ordered their troops in Syria to intervene and to confine the French forces to their barracks. Next year, after the question had been debated in the United Nations, an agreement was reached under which British and French forces were simultaneously withdrawn from the Levant; and the Syrians and Lebanese were left in undisputed control of their own territories.

Kuwatly's term of office as President was due to end in 1948 and the Constitution did not permit second terms. Counting on the prestige of his success in achieving independence and on the block's control of the Chamber, he contrived an alteration of the Constitution which would allow of his own reelection. It was a sad error of judgment: the Syrians, traditionally fickle, had already had enough of him and the block, and less than a year after his reelection he was unseated and exiled by the first of three successive military coups. He sought refuge with Ibn Saud, for whom he had conceived a strong admiration, and later lived in Egypt. In 1954, after the third military dictator had himself been overthrown, Kuwatly returned to Damascus, and in 1955, in a popular revulsion of feeling against military dictatorships, he was reelected president. By then, however, his powers were beginning to fail; his mentor, Ibn Saud, was dead; and he was unable to stem or deflect the political currents which, three years later, swept Syria into union with Nasser's Egypt. Nasser accorded him the title of "First Arab Citizen" and dismissed him to a limbo from which he never returned.

July 1, 1967.

L

Alan Ladd, who died at his Palm Springs home on January 29, 1964, was one of the most important Hollywood film stars of the 1940s and throughout his career seldom if ever appeared in a film which failed to make money.

He was born at Hot Springs, Arkansas, in 1913, and first achieved notice as a swimmer, winning the West Coast Diving Championship in 1933. From this it was a short step to discovery as likely film star material, and he was enrolled in the Universal acting school, but nothing came of this except a few bit-parts, and for some years he gave up acting and worked instead as a reporter and in advertising. But eventually he arrived back in the cinema by a different route, on the technical side at Warner's and then again as a bit-part player, until he achieved a featured role in Frank Lloyd's *Rulers of the Sea* (1939).

Other film parts followed, but his real chance came in 1942 when an agent, Sue Carrol (later to become Mrs. Ladd) heard him on the radio, signed him up and got him a role as the hired gunman in *This Gun for Hire*, a version of Graham Greene's *A Gun For Sale*. This characterization at once brought him fame and established the stereotype for many of his subsequent film roles, playing off cunningly the tough, ruthless personality of the character against the actor's slight physique, smooth fair hair and amiable, all-American cast of features. Sometimes he would be on the wrong side of the law, sometimes on the right, but always he was a no-nonsense man of action, a hero-villain whom audiences, if they could not legitimately love him, would at least love to hate.

Some of his films of this period, notably *The Glass Key* and *The Blue Dahlia* (scripted by Raymond Chandler) were excellent, but he found them limiting, and gradually extended his range to include period adventure stories like *Two Years Before the Mast*, westerns like *The Badlanders*, and even romantic dramas like *Boy on a Dolphin*. Sometimes when he strayed from the thriller he was not happily cast—he was, for example, hardly anybody's idea of Scott Fitzgerald's hero in *The Great Gatsby*—but his undeniable screen presence, allied to a slightly wooden, phlegmatic quality in his acting, made him an excellent western hero, and westerns brought him several of his best later roles, among them the title-role in George Stevens's *Shane*. Latterly, also, he took a hand in the production of his own films, which were seldom pretentious but always highly efficient entertainment within their chosen limitations.

His daughter, Alana Ladd, appeared in several, and his son, David Ladd, proved an unusually acceptable child actor in his father's western *The Proud Rebel*. Alan Ladd's last film role, completed shortly before his death, was in *The Carpetbaggers*, as yet unseen.

January 31, 1964.

Sir Walter Lamb, K.C.V.O., secretary of the Royal Aacdemy of Arts from 1913 to 1951, died at his home at Northwood, Middlesex, on March 27, 1961. He was 79. Henry Lamb, R.A., M.C., the painter, who died in 1960, was his younger brother.

After his appointment in 1913 as secretary of the Royal Academy in succession to Sir Frederick Eaton, Lamb was so completely identified with that institution that he might have been supposed to have had no history outside its affairs. To say that he was devoted to the Academy would be both an understatement and a misinterpretation of motive. He did not seem to be conscious of any suppression of himself in his office or of any virtue in his loyalty. His was rather the functional devotion of the watchdog, never paraded and only evident at the suspicion of danger, when his hackles would rise with an effect of "Who said rats?"

This unquestioning acceptance of his office, and the dryness of manner which his view of its obligations entailed, laid Lamb open to some misunderstanding, and he was often spoken of by journalists and others who had professional relations with the Academy as remote. Personally, Lamb was a man of agreeable manners, always ready to give relevant information, but as secretary of the Royal Academy he was aware of both its dignity and its liability to attack, and at the least hint of criticism he was on guard. Not that he flared up or advanced his personal opinion of the matter in debate, and nothing was more characteristic of him than were his occasional letters to *The Times* when public curiosity had been excited by such incidents as the rejection of a picture or the resignation of a member.

IMPERSONAL

Then, like a wise official in the House of Commons replying to questions, instead of descending to argument, Lamb would content himself with stating the Article of the Constitution which bore on the particular case. For public purposes he did not exist outside his office, and in view of the "Royal" status of the Academy his very impersonality helped to make him the ideal secretary.

At other times invisible except by appointment, Lamb generally made a round of the galleries on press day. A comparatively small man, quiet and serious, with a scholarly stoop and a meditative expression, though quick of eye and ear, he might have been said to move stealthily if it were not so obvious that his unobtrusive progress was due to concentration upon seeing that everything, including the refreshment provided for tired critics on such occasions, was in order. Except for a murmured instruction to an attendant or a greeting to an acquaintance he said nothing unless he were asked for information, when he kept strictly to the point.

Walter Rangeley Maitland Lamb was the second son of Sir Horace Lamb, F.R.S., the distinguished mathematician, and was born on January 5, 1882, at Adelaide, South Australia, where his father was Professor of Mathematics. His mother was Irish. He was educated at Manchester Grammar School and Trinity College, Cambridge, where he was Fellow from 1907 to the year of his appointment to the Royal Academy. He did not inherit the scientific interests of his father, though the scientific habit of mind was perceptible in his insistence on accuracy, but was essentially a scholar and a man of letters. Up to 1913 he was at different times classical lecturer at King's, Emmanuel, Newnham and Girton Colleges, Cambridge, and from 1907 to 1909 he was assistant master at Clifton College, Bristol. He was secretary of the Cambridge Philological Society and in 1905–06 he edited the *Cambridge Review*.

TRANSLATED PLATO

He published *Clio Enthroned: a study of prose form in Thucydides* (1914): *The discoveries of Sir Joshua Reynolds* (1924): *The Royal Academy* (1935, 2nd edition 1951): and a translation of *Plato's Dialogues* and *Orations of Lysias* in Loeb's Classical Library.

To a broadcast programme in memory of A. E. Housman in 1936 he contributed a personal appreciation of the poet based on a friendship of 25 years, a friendship which Housman's austerity of style makes easily understandable.

He was made M.V.O. in 1925, C.V.O. in 1933 and advanced to K.C.V.O. in 1943.

In 1927 he married Rose, daughter of Samuel Brooks, of Chicago.

March 28, 1961.

The death of **Dr. Winifred Lamb** has removed from the ranks of British archaeologists a figure of distinction. She died on September 16, 1963.

She was the daughter of wealthy parents, her father, Edmund Lamb, having been Liberal M.P. for Leominster Division of North Herefordshire, and she was brought up in the stately surroundings of Lord Macaulay's home, Holly Lodge, Campden Hill. Though diffident and hesitant in manner, she possessed a very independent character. During the First World War she served in the famous Naval Intelligence Department of Admiral Hall, "Room 40." Then, after studying Classics at Newnham College, Cambridge, she chose a career in classical archaeology, when such a decision for a woman was both bold and unusual.

Admitted as a student of the British School of Archaeology at Athens in 1920, she at once joined the staff of A.J.B. Wace, then director, on his excavations of Mycenae and took a prompt share in publishing the results. At this early date she had already been appointed Honorary Keeper of the Greek and Roman Department of the Fitzwilliam Museum, Cambridge, a post to which she continued to devote herself with regularity till December, 1958.

VISIT TO TROY

In 1929 she published a popular handbook *Greek and Roman Bronzes* (Methuen), which remains an invaluable guide to the subject, not yet superseded. The same year, after a visit to the site of Troy, she decided to investigate the Early Bronze Age settlement of

Thermi on the island of Lesbos (Mytilini) and conducted excavations there most ably at her own expense in three campaigns. The results were published in 1936 (*Excavations at Thermi in Lesbos*, Cambridge University Press). In 1930 and 1936 she prepared and published two fascicules of the *Corpus Vasorum Antiquorum* devoted to the Greek pottery in the Fitzwilliam Museum. She also served for very many years on the committees of the British School at Athens and the Society for the Promotion of Hellenic Studies.

In 1935 she was back in the field as an excavator, this time on the mainland of Turkey, selecting the site of Kusura, near Afyonkarahisar, as a key to the history of the unknown Bronze Age archaeology of that area. Her work was published by the Society of Antiquaries (Archaeologia, Vol. 86, 1936) of which she became a Fellow in 1936. She was, in fact, one of the first classical archaeologists after Hogarth and Garstang to seek light on the problems of Greek archaeology from Anatolia, and this at a time when conditions of living and working in Turkey were hard and primitive, and particularly difficult for a woman. Yet she easily won the regard and affection of Turks of all classes, as she did in Greece, by her genuine modesty, sincerity, and sweetness of manner, not less than by her unusual mastery of their language. She was awarded a Doctorate of Science at Cambridge in 1940.

During the Second World War she served again by working in the B.B.C. Turkish Services on audience reaction and information, 1942-46.

ANKARA FOUNDATION

When, after the war, Professor Garstang succeeded in 1950 in founding a British Institute of Archaeology at Ankara, she was naturally indicated as a devoted ally, and became its honorary secretary until 1957. By this she had returned to her country estate at Borden Wood, Liphook, as her health gradually declined.

Her kindness, modesty, generosity and encouragement of younger people were a pattern to others. Such traits were typical of her character, which will long cause her memory to be loved.

September 18, 1963.

Maurice Lambert, R.A., who died in a London hospital on August 17, 1964, at the age of 63, was a sculptor who did not easily fit into either a typically academic or typically modern category. His early work proved him to be an artist of talent and vigorous intelligence and was already highly accomplished in craftsmanship, though critical opinion was somewhat uncertain as to the direction of his art and the extent to which a modernity of appearance in his work was more than superficial.

Lambert's first public appearance was in a mixed exhibition of works by artists "known and but little known" at the old Goupil Gallery in Regent Street, where he showed 14 pieces in a baffling variety of styles and materials, with reflections of Epstein, Dobson, Brancusi and others. At a subsequent exhibition at the same gallery his works included a remarkable head of a woman, "Ceres", carved in hard red African grit-stone, fundamentally realistic but very firmly simplified. This, though it was less superficially original than some of the other works, seemed to indicate the real direction of his powers. The impression was encouraged at an exhibition of the Seven and Five Society in 1928, and a one-man show of Lambert's work at Messrs. Tooth's Gallery in 1929 left no doubt of his ability, particularly as a carver.

VARIED MATERIALS

The exhibition included carvings in alabaster, marble, portland stone and African hardwood, as well as works in metal and in several materials combined. "Departure of Birds", in alabaster and Roman stone, "Bird of Paradise", in copper, mahogany and red sandstone, "Sea birds", in aluminium, white marble and black marble, and "Fighting Swordfish", in bronze and red concrete, were compositions which made a particularly lively impression. His later work brought into prominence the classical and lyrical elements in his art.

Born on June 25, 1901, in Paris, Maurice Lambert was the elder son of George Washington Lambert, A.R.A., the Australian painter who towards the end of his life also turned his attention to sculpture. The brother of the sculptor was Constant Lambert, the brilliant musical composer and conductor. Lambert was educated at Manor House School, Clapham, and from the age of 17 was apprenticed to F. Derwent Wood. R.A., working as his assistant for five years. Not many artists can have had his experience of finding his first work exhibited at the Royal Academy chosen as a purchase for the nation under the terms of the Chantrey Bequest. This was in 1938 when Lambert was 37. He was elected an Associate of the Royal Academy in 1941 and a Royal Academician in 1952, he was Master of the Royal Academy Sculpture School from 1950 to 1958. During the Second World War he served as a captain in the Royal Welch Fusiliers, having served earlier in the ranks of the London Welsh Regiment.

He is represented in the Tate Gallery and his bronze statue of Margot Fonteyn, which was purchased for the nation through the Chantrey Bequest in 1956, is at the Royal Ballet School, White Lodge, Richmond Park.

DUKE'S TROPHY

Among his other sculptures are a statue of Viscount Nuffield for Guy's Hospital, bronze decorations for s.s. "Queen Elizabeth", carvings in portland stone for the Associated Electrical Industries building in Grosvenor Place, London, the Duke of Edinburgh's trophy for shooting and running (a drinking cup in silver and gold), a fountain for Basildon and another for Baghdad on which he was at work until his last illness. He also modelled a number of portrait busts, including those of Lord Nuffield, Sir Arthur Bliss, Sir Gerald Kelly, and Lord Devlin. Lambert married Olga Marie Stuart Morrison.

August 20, 1964.

Lord Lambury, K.B.E., president of the British Motor Corporation (formerly Sir Leonard Lord), who died on September 13, 1967, at the age of 71, will be long remembered by his colleagues in the British motor industry and his countless friends and acquaintances throughout the world. For his lifelong services to that industry, he was awarded a barony in the New Year Honours List of 1962 and assumed the title of Lord Lambury of Northfield.

Leonard Percy Lord was born in Coventry in 1896 and was educated at Bablake School, Coventry. Leaving school at an early age, he was apprenticed to the engineering department of Courtaulds Ltd., Coventry. From there he went to the Coventry Ordnance factory, and later to the Daimler Company and other engineering firms in London and Peterborough.

From an early age, the tall, mechanically minded youth had decided to make his fame and fortune in the growing automobile industry, in which he was certain there was adequate scope for his talents. In 1922 he joined the Hotchkiss Company at Coventry and stayed there until 1927, when he was invited by W. R. Morris (the late Lord Nuffield) to take charge of the firm of Wolseley Motors Ltd., later purchased by Morris.

After successfully reorganizing the Wolseley company, Leonard Lord was appointed managing director of Morris Motors Ltd. in 1932, in which position he controlled the Morris works at Cowley, the Wolseley works at Birmingham, and also the M.G. and Riley factories at Abingdon, Berkshire.

Always a man of unflagging energy, Leonard Lord took the unprecedented step of retiring at the age of 40 in 1936 and travelled abroad extensively. But he was never truly happy unless he was working hard and in January, 1937 was appointed manager of Lord Nuffield's £2m. trust fund to aid the Special Areas. He gave up this post in March, 1938, and returned to the motor industry, becoming a member of the committee of management and works director of the Austin Motor Company Ltd. In June, 1940, Lord Beaverbrook appointed him in addition, as government controller of Boulton and Paul Ltd., to hasten production of the urgently needed Defiant night-fighter aircraft, which played a major part in eventual victory in the air.

EXPANDED PRODUCTION

In May, 1941, on the death of Lord Austin, he became deputy chairman and joint managing director of the company and was responsible for the great expansion in air-frame and aero-engine production in the company's wartime shadow factories. Mr. Lord succeeded E. L. Payton as chairman and managing director of the Austin Motor Company Ltd., in 1945 and held this post until 1952, when Lord Nuffield named him in his succession as chairman and managing director of the British Motor Corporation, the merged Austin-Nuffield group which had been created in November, 1951.

In the 1954 New Year's Honours list, Lord was designated a Knight Commander of the British Empire. In August, 1958 the offices of chairman and managing director were separated and Sir Leonard was appointed executive chairman of the whole group. He retired from his position in November, 1961, assuming the new title of vice-president of the British Motor Corporation, at which time G. W. Harriman took over the responsibilities of running Britain's largest motor manufacturing group.

Sir Leonard, as he was during his more active days in the British motor industry, was tall, bespectacled and "straight to the point". In spite of his title and considerable success during his lifetime in and around the motor industry, he never forgot that he went to the top from the factory floor . . . and was intensely proud of his humble origin.

His distinction as an industrialist was paralleled in a lesser degree by his success as a farmer. He was a well-known breeder of Hereford cattle, won numerous prizes at agricultural shows, and one of his beef steers was judged supreme champion at the Royal Show in 1949.

He lived at Warren's Gorse, near Cirencester, Gloucestershire.

September 14, 1967.

George H. Lanchester, one of the most highly regarded of British pioneers in automobile engineering, died on February 13, 1970, at the age of 95.

He collaborated with Dr. F. W. Lanchester, his eminent elder brother, in designing and building an experimental car in 1897–98, which was the precursor of the highly original automobiles produced by the Lanchester Company in the early 1900s. The outstanding inventive genius of Fred Lanchester received invaluable support from the practical engineering talents of George Lanchester in a unique partnership which enabled the brothers to solve innumerable problems of manufacture as well as design.

ARMOURED CAR

From 1905 onwards, George Lanchester played an increasingly important part in the affairs of the company, which was recognized by his appointment as chief engineer in 1909. An immediate consequence was a redesigned version of the 6-cylinder model which appeared in 1910; this was to form the basis of the Lanchester armoured car of the First World War. In 1919 he launched the Lanchester "40" which had a remarkably advanced 6-cylinder overhead camshaft engine. One of these cars, fitted with a special body in 1921, set up many long distance records at Brooklands. A straight eight model followed in 1929 but by 1931 the Lanchester company was taken over by Daimler. Lanchester became Chief Engineer of the Warfare Department of Alvis Ltd., where he played a leading part in the design and development of armoured fighting vehicles.

February 17, 1970.

Professor Lev Davidovich Landau, the distinguished Russian physicist and Nobel prizewinner, died on April 1, 1968, at the age of 60.

Tass News Agency, giving news of the death, said that it was the result of the aftermath of injuries received in a car accident in January, 1962. At the time of the accident it was reported that his injuries included 11 broken bones and a fractured skull. Later Professor Wilder Graves Penfield, the Canadian neurosurgeon, flew to Moscow to assist in the treatment of Professor Landau and, after an appeal to Sir John Cockcroft, British drugs were flown to the Russian capital. Some months later it was made known that Russian doctors had recorded "clinical death" several times but that each time Landau had been revived. In November, 1962, he was awarded the Nobel Prize for Physics for his "pioneering theories for condensed matter, especially liquid helium".

In an article in *Komsomolskaya Pravda* in 1964 he revealed that during one of Stalin's purges he was imprisoned as a suspected German spy. "I spent a year in prison and it was clear that I would be unable to live for even another half year", he wrote. He said he had been saved through the intervention of Professor Peter Kapitza, the Russian scientist, who went to the Kremlin and threatened to stop his own scientific work unless Landau was freed.

Landau was one of the most original as well as one of the most versatile of theoretical physicists, and his death is a loss to science as well as the Soviet Union. A child prodigy in mathematics, he held—and from early in his university career taught—that creative work in any part of theoretical physics should begin with a deep mastery of all departments. His own work illustrated the value of this philosophy.

His greatest impact was in the strange world revealed by the study of very low temperatures.

ORIGINAL APPROACH

It is in this world that properties determined by wave mechanics show themselves not only (as in ordinary conditions) in the behaviour of individual atoms and particles, but in the behaviour of matter in the mass. Landau's interest dates from 1937 when, at the age of 29, he moved from the Physico-technical Institute of the Ukraine, at Kharkov, where he was head of the department of theoretical physics, to the Institute for Physical Problems in Moscow. This was the institute established for Professor Peter Kapitza.

Kapitza was doing experiments at the time on one of the unexpected properties shown by liquid helium at temperatures within about two degrees of the absolute zero of temperature. The property he was working on was superfluidity shown by the ability of liquid helium (when sufficiently cooled) to climb into or out of a beaker until the levels inside and outside are the same. Landau was drawn into a theoretical attack on this abnormal, low-temperature form of liquid helium—helium II. He was not the first in the field, but made an original approach which in the end compelled attention.

Landau's theory, published in 1941, predicted a new effect—a temperature wave described as "second sound". The same effect had been predicted independently and a little earlier by a Rumanian-born American, Professor Laszlo Tisza, following an approach initiated earlier by Professor F. London. In quantitative terms the two theories led to different predictions—and it was Landau's that were correct. It was also Landau's prediction which led to the experimental discovery of "second sound" in 1944 by V. Peshkov working in Moscow.

Tisza was known personally to Landau and there was an amicable rivalry between them. It therefore seemed ironic—as well as in the best tradition of science—when, in the spring of 1950, J. R. Pellam and R. B. Scott at the United States Bureau of Standards announced measurements below 1.3° absolute which agreed with Landau's prediction that at a temperature between 1.0° and 1.1° absolute, the speed of propagation of "second sound" would fall to a minimum and would thereafter rise sharply. Tisza's theory on the other hand had predicated a progressive fall. Later in the year K. R. Atkins and D. V. Osborne, in Kapitza's old laboratory at Cambridge, confirmed a further prediction made by Landau. He had written that, as absolute zero was approached, the ratio of the speed of "second sound" to that of ordinary sound in helium II would be as 1 to 3—and this, too, fitted well with measurements.

Landau made other predictions as well, and the feeling of many physicists was summed up by Sir Francis Simon at an international conference the next year. He said that everyone always criticized Landau's theories, but it was always Landau's formula that was correct.

KNOWLEDGE AND INTUITION

While this may have been due, in a sense, to physical intuition—a quality which Landau indeed possessed—intuition began in his case from an exceptionally profound knowledge of classical physical theory, a fact evidenced by a five-volume work which he wrote with his former pupil, E. M. Lifshitz, and which was published between 1950 and 1955.

Born at Baku on the Caspian Sea on January 22, 1908, the son of an engineer, Landau entered Baku University at 14, transferred after two years to the University of Leningrad, and by 19 was engaged in research at the Leningrad Physico-technical Institute. After two years he was sent abroad. Though he visited other countries, including Britain, in the course of the next year and a half, the most important influence under which he came was that of Professor Niels Bohr in Copenhagen. During this period, at the age of 22, he developed a theory of diamagnetism of metals which was found seven years later to provide an explanation of an effect not otherwise accounted for; Landau's theory was only a part of the total story, but was still a necessary part. Among those whom he met during this time were Professor R. E. Pejerls, now at Oxford, with whom he wrote an influential joint paper in Copenhagen, and the Hungarian physicist, Professor Edward Teller, later the driving force behind the American H-bomb. Landau, then and for years afterwards, was an extremely provocative young man, who liked to shock.

On returning to Leningrad, he was appointed almost at once to the senior post at Kharkov already mentioned. Bohr's opinion of him is sufficiently shown by the fact that in May, 1934, he travelled from Copenhagen to Kharkov to attend an international conference of theoretical physics organized by this extremely young professor. Landau presided; Bohr opened the discussion on all papers; Tisza, whose scientific lines crossed later with Landau's, was one who attended. Landau, for his part, had at Bohr's invitation attended a conference in Copenhagen in 1933—and in 1934 was back again, wearing a red coat and still provocative.

RANGE OF PAPERS

During the next two years he produced original scientific papers at an average rate of one every six weeks and covered an astonishing range of subjects.

This characteristic he retained. Within four years from the 1941 paper predicting "second sound", he wrote a series of five papers on the effects of shock waves. He tackled plasma oscillations later important in thermonuclear research; contributed to the fundamental theory of particles, and remained active in low temperature physics. Here there are probably implications of his work that have still to be explored.

His personal qualities were something of an enigma. He had a flaming sincerity for—and about—science. He attracted students by his enthusiasm and evident knowledge, but to a greater age than most retained aspects of the *enfant terrible*. He could also be hot and merciless in criticism. Yet those who knew him, from Niels Bohr to the writer of a Soviet appreciation on the occasion of his 50th birthday, agreed that there was human warmth below his sharpness.

A triple Stalin prize winner and an Academician since 1946, he was a Foreign Member of both the Royal Society and the U.S. National Academy of Sciences. At the seventh International Conference on Low Temperature Physics, in Toronto in 1960, he received in absence the second Fritz London award. The address which accompanied was delivered by Professor Pellam (as he by then was) who nine years earlier had provided the first confirmation of Landau's numerical predictions about "second sound".

April 3, 1968.

Sir Allen Lane, C. H., founder of Penguin Books and creater of a publishing revolution, died on July 7, 1970. He was 67. He retired as joint managing director of the Penguin Publishing Co. in 1969.

He had been active in publishing from 1919 when, at the age of 17, he left Bristol Grammar School to be apprenticed to his uncle, John Lane, at the Bodley Head. It was not altogether an auspicious time to commence publishing with this famous house, the reputation of which had been made in the nineties with the work of Aubrey Beardsley and the *Yellow Book*.

There is not much that can be learnt about publishing at 17. When Allen Lane succeeded his uncle on the latter's death six years later, the firm was in a parlous position in a rapidly-changing publishing world. Ten years were to pass, a longer apprenticeship than had been planned, before Allen Lane found himself in a position to command his own destiny. Then qualities in him which he had shared with his uncle, sharp intelligence, instinctive good taste, and a gambler's readiness to chance all on a throw, were to provide him with an opportunity for success. By an exercise of these same talents, and a "feel" for the auspicious moment in which to plunge, John Lane had been lifted into prominence on a wave of sophisticated taste suddenly finding expression in the public. This manifestation allowed him to exchange a clerkship in the Railway Clearing Office for a position eventually as the most admired and venturesome publisher in London of the nineties. Guided by the same instincts, and borne forward on a succeeding and infinitely vaster wave of popular taste, Allen Lane was to achieve with his Penguins even greater position and renown.

FOUND RENOWN

As managing director of the Bodley Head, Allen Lane in fact had no chance against the old-established firms with their profitable back lists and their educational publishing, nor was he able to compete with the brilliant publishing instincts of a more traditional kind being profitably exercised by relatively new firms in the publishing field, notably Victor Gollancz and Jonathan Cape. In fact Allen Lane showed no particular gift for general publishing. The approaching bankruptcy of the Bodley Head drove him in 1935 to a venture which he had been considering for some time. This was the issue of successful titles by well-known authors in paperback format at a cheap price. There was nothing original in the idea except that the books were to be well-produced and printed, unlike the paperbacks that had flooded the market at the turn of the century, and were to be priced at sixpence. The difficulty was to get other publishers to agree to supply the necessary titles, and to get his fellow-directors' support for the scheme. In neither of these matters was he successful, but he succeeded in winning support from Jonathan Cape, who was always ready to lend a sympathetic ear to other publishers' troubles. He needed a dozen titles to start. Cape gave him ten of them.

PRIVATE GAMBLE

The experiment was launched as a private gamble by Allen Lane, and the other directors of The Bodley Head must have lived to regret their insistence on this.

Although the start, with ten good titles including books from Hemingway, Linklater, Maurois, and Compton Mackenzie, did not meet with much success, the advance sale being less than half the number needed to recover the outlay, three months later he issued a second ten, and six months after the start he and his two brothers formed Penguin Books Limited with a capital of £100. A few months later he resigned from the managing directorship of The Bodley Head to devote himself altogether to Penguins.

The gamble had still not come off. Indeed, after a very shaky start, it had come within an ace of failure, but one good angel having manifested in the person of Jonathan Cape, another followed in Woolworths who started to sell the books. The demand grew and washed back into the bookshops, which had so far looked with less than general enthusiasm on the scheme. Other publishers followed Cape's example of releasing some of their titles for reprint. By the spring of 1937, more than one hundred titles had been "penguinised" The corner had been turned, and the fortunate founder of the Penguin series, who for 15 years had been publishing without any notable success, and whose venture into paperbacks had been the nature of a desperate gambler's throw rather than the fulfilment of a long-planned and amply-financed project, found himself upborne to success by the turn of events in world history.

The public interest was turning towards the question of war or peace, and there was a sense of immediacy about a paperback publication that the ordinary clothbound book did not convey. Penguin Specials—new books commissioned from authors on current international affairs—enlarged the operation, and the sale of some of these exceeded a quarter of a million copies. This profitable extension of the firm's activities not only provided the much-needed working capital but, as 1937 came to be the base year taken when paper rationing was imposed during the war, Penguin found themselves as a result with an ample ration which enabled them to continue to build their list at a time when most other publishers were being forced ruthlessly to prune theirs.

UPLIFT

The development of what had been a simple reprint operation into a wide variety of original publishing, with reprints playing what is in effect a subsidiary part, and the educational, the uplift slant with which the Penguin idea is now generally associated, is probably the work of the gifted men whom Allen Lane drew in to work with him. By no means an intellectual himself, he had a high respect for learning, and he surrounded himself with men not only of great capability but of a daring originality of thought. They were not gamblers: he was that. They could apprehend the reading hungers and the needs of the age, put a plan to him, and generally be sure of his support. Once given, he did not withdraw it: he had tenacity and determination and courage, and these qualities paid off handsomely in business, as they usually do, especially when allied to a sound commercial sense. The Pelicans Penguin Classics are an example of this alliance between the scholarship of others and the devoted patronage which, with a sure instinct, he gave to these ideas, resisting the get-rich-quick methods profitably and ignobly pursued by some of the rival paperback firms.

Of a part with this was his publication of *Lady Chatterley's Lover*. Among his disciple-editors, this was a battle for freedom, a gage thrown down. It was already in the tradition that Penguin should lead the way in this battle. If the case had been lost, it would have been costly to Lane; it was won, it received enormous publicity, and within a few months Penguin "went public", shares were 160 times over-subscribed, and the young publisher who had been on the edge of bankruptcy 25 years before became a millionaire. This association of earnestness and solid wealth is perfectly caught in the painting by Rodrigo Moyniham, "After The Conference; The Penguin Editors", where Allen Lane is shown standing proudly, though plainly the leader, among a handful of famous men whose inventiveness and literary perception and communion with the new public have made the penguin symbol known and honoured.

In 1952 Lane was knighted for his services to books. He was made C.H. in 1969. His two brothers, who were associated with him in the early days of Penguin, played only small parts in the development of the company, Richard retired when the company became a public one, and the younger brother, John, was killed in the war. Lane married in 1941 Lettice, the daughter of Sir Charles Orr. He is survived by her, and by their three daughters.

July 8, 1970.

Halvard Lange, the Norwegian statesman, and Foreign Minister from 1946 to 1965, died on May 19, 1970, in Oslo at the age of 67. He was a founding father of Nato and was chairman of the Nato Council in 1960.

It was Lange more than anyone else who brought Norway into the organization, not a simple achievement with Finland unquestionably neutralized, Sweden determinedly neutral and with the frozen wastes of North Finmark giving Norway a long common frontier with Russia. Lange's efforts had a marked influence in Denmark's decision to join Nato.

Lange's policy was a reflection of a peaceful family background and a heroic maturity. He was born on September 16, 1902, the son of Christian Lange, pacifist, historian, for many years a key figure in the Inter-Parliamentary Union and, in 1921, winner of the Nobel Peace Prize. Halvard Lange's education was international. For a time the family lived in Brussels and he studied in Italy before taking a degree in Oslo. When his father became Secretary-General of the League of Nations he began to study at the University of Geneva.

REJECTED COMMUNISM

He was later at the London School of Economics and completed his education by taking an honours degree at Oslo University in 1929. From then until 1940 he taught and wrote and worked hard for the Norwegian Labour Party. In 1938 he became Rector of the Norwegian Trade Union College. He had moved away from his father's nineteenth-century liberalism, had tried communism and found it uncongenial and the Labour Party offered his practical spirit a home.

He had need both of his spirit and his practicality after the German invasion of Norway in 1940. He made illicit journeys across the Swedish border and soon became deeply involved in the Norwegian resistance movement. By August he had been captured by the Germans. His undercover activities alone were enough to make him a marked man but he had also written a book on the Nazis before the war which would scarcely have endeared him to them.

They kept him naked in a cell for four weeks without electricity, with little light and with very little food. Later he was given a blanket. He had no doubt that the Germans intended him to die. He was determined not to satisfy them. He did a great deal of P.T., repeated everything that he had ever learnt by heart and sang songs. After a while he was allowed one spoonful of cod liver oil a day; it seemed to him like cream. After a week the ration was stopped and that was the hardest cross of all to bear. Four months later, no confession forthcoming, he was released and promptly re-joined the resistance movement.

In 1942 he was again arrested and was sent to Sachsenhausen. In that dreadful place he became the acknowledged leader of the Norwegian prisoners through his unflinching defence of their rights. Despite bodily enfeeblement and every kind of discouragement he began political activity, planning with Mr. Gerhardsen, the future Prime Minister, and other imprisoned Norwegian leaders, a post-war programme for the Labour Party.

After the war when Trygve Lie was appointed the first Secretary-General of the United Nations Organization Lange succeded him as Norwegian Foreign Minister.

Initially he followed Lie's line, that of bridge-builder between East and West, but the deterioration in the international climate made this an attitude difficult to sustain. The turning point was the Communist coup in Czechoslovakia in 1948. Plans for a Nordic defensive union embracing Denmark, Norway and Sweden fell through and largely due to Lange's convincing advocacy Norway linked her fortunes with those of the other Nato powers. Denmark followed suit.

Lange resigned after the Labour Party's defeat in 1965 though he remained a member of the Storting until last year. He spent his last years engaged in political research and in writing in support of Norwegian entry into E.E.C.

May 21, 1970.

Professor Oskar Lange, Vice-Chairman of the Polish Council of State, a member of the Polish Academy of Sciences, and an economist of world renown, died in the Westminster Hospital on October 2, 1965, after a long illness at the age of 61.

Oskar Lange had a most distinguished career, both as a theoretical economist and as a man of affairs. Born in Tomaszow Mazowieckj in 1904, the son of a textile manufacturer, he graduated from the University of Cracow in the late 1920s and soon acquired an international reputation for his work in mathematical economics. He visited Britain and the United States as a Rockefeller Fellow in 1935–37 and later accepted an invitation to stay in the United States, first as Professor of Economics at the University of Michigan and later as Professor in the University of Chicago; he then became an American citizen.

While at Chicago he soon gained the reputation of the "best teacher of economics in America", and he nurtured many brilliant pupils. He was one of the founders of the new science of econometrics (he was, until his death, a member of the council and of the executive of the Econometric Society) and an early protagonist of Keynesian economics. His book *Price Flexibility and Full Employment*, published in 1944, is generally recognized as a contribution of major importance which succeeded in bridging the gap between Keynesian and neo-classical (Walrasian) economics. In this he acknowledged his debt to the techniques developed by Hicks in *Value and Capital*. This volume was the progenitor of a host of other books of which Don Patinkin's *Money, Interest and Prices* is the best known. He also made important contributions in other fields, particularly on the economics of socialism. His two famous papers "On The Economic Theory of Socialism" published in the *Review of Economic Studies* in 1937 are generally considered as the most powerful refutation of the contentions of von Mises and his school on the impossibility of a rational allocation of resources in a socialist economic system.

OLD ORTHODOXIES REEXAMINED

While still in the west he had led the intellectual movement away from the influential view that centrally planned economics were doomed to failure by the lack of rational criteria and incentives. He was foremost among those who sought to reestablish the compatibility of market criteria with a socialist system of ownership and production and he helped to create what has since come to be known as the Lange-Lerner model of decentralized socialism.

It is certain that he contributed greatly to the liberalization of economic thought whenever the political climate was favourable. His basic loyalty to the Marxian ideology never seemed in doubt, but he brought to his interpretation of it the pragmatism of a much wider experience and the flexibility of a brilliantly analytic mind. Apart from his own distinguished work in mathematical economics and econometrics he will be remembered for the support he gave to all those who sought to reexamine old orthodoxies in the light of modern techniques. Like the late Nemchinov —in many ways his Russian counterpart—it may be said of him that he lent the authority of his name to much that was new and progressive in Poland, however unfamiliar and disturbing to established ways of thought.

He brought his incisive wide-ranging intellect to bear upon a variety of Polish problems but such was the respect in which he was held he was able to exercise unchallenged a remarkable frankness and freedom of comment.

VISIT TO STALIN

Lange was, from early on, a member of the Polish Democratic Party. His public career can be said to have really begun, however, with the publication of a famous letter in the *New York Herald Tribune* in 1943 in which he urged his Polish ex-countrymen not to fall victims of anti-Russian propaganda; he considered that the survival of Poland as an independent state after the war was indissolubly linked with the maintenance of friendly relations with the Soviet Union. It was as a result of this letter that he received a personal invitation from Stalin to visit Moscow early in 1944 to discuss the future status of Poland; and, as the result of this interview (which is referred to in letters, since published, between Stalin and President Roosevelt), Lange decided to support the provisional government of Poland established in Moscow, and in 1945 became the first ambassador of the new Polish State in Washington, thereby renouncing his United States citizenship (though retaining for a time his Chair in Chicago). A year later he became chief delegate of Poland at the United Nations and it was in this latter capacity that he incurred criticism among his friends in the United States for his continued support of the Stalinist line in the Security Council. Late in 1947 he was recalled to Poland where he became (for a time) the chairman of the Parliamentary Group of the United Workers Party: however in the year immediately before Stalin's death he was under a cloud and was reported to have been under house arrest.

RESPECTED

In the post-Stalinist era Lange became one of Poland's most respected citizens. He was elected chairman of the newly created State Economic Council in 1957. He renewed his former contacts with the west, both through his contributions to econometrics and through his lecturing engagements in Oxford and Cambridge and other European universities. He was also invited as an expert by the governments of India and Ceylon and visited many other underdeveloped countries. He planned to write a major three-volume treatise on Political Economy. Only the first volume was completed and this was soon translated into eight languages: an English translation appeared in 1963. In 1964, on the occasion of his sixtieth birthday, a large *Festschrift* was published in his honour to which 42 economists and statisticians made contributions from among 16 countries.

Lange was known to his numerous friends in the west as a man of unusual wit and charm and one who, in spite of his political affiliations, remained thoroughly liberal in outlook, both as a scientist and as a philosopher and observer of world affairs. He was much admired for the spirit and fortitude with which he bore his prolonged suffering in the last seven years, much of which he spent in various sanatoria in Switzerland and Italy.

He married twice and had a son and a daughter.

October 4, 1965.

Peter Lanyon, who died on August 31, 1964, of injuries received in a gliding accident in the previous week, was one of the most brilliant members of a group of British painters, now in their forties and early fifties, whose work has increasingly attracted international attention.

These painters were among the first Europeans to recognize the importance of Amercian artists such as Pollock, Rothko, de Kooning, and Motherwell; and all were in some way or another associated with Cornwall, and especially with St. Ives, where Lanyon was born and remained all his life.

Lanyon's particular contribution was in the way in which he both gave a remarkable new life to the English landscape tradition and also took his place in the international abstract expressionist movement of the 1950s. What is paradoxical about Lanyon is that his paintings are enjoyed by those who have never set eyes on a Cornish cliff for their purely abstract virtues of design, colour, and execution. Yet at the same time anyone who knows the coasts of west Cornwall must immediately be put vividly in touch with them upon viewing these apparently abstract works. Representation and abstraction have thus been made to coexist in Lanyon's painting: and in a manner that is entirely original. What is more, from 1947 on, the basic content of his art has remained constant: an abstraction that yields a specific landscape vision to those who are in a position to read its clues aright. His work was always inspired by particular localities—north Devon, the Dorset coast, the hilly country north of Rome, and above all west Cornwall.

A PERSONAL ART

Lanyon had the intelligence to use the discoveries of twentieth-century art especially of constructivism, and he learnt much as a young man from older artists resident in St. Ives, notably Naum Gabo, Barbara Hepworth, Ben Nicholson, and Adrian Stokes. The connexion between his work and theirs was fundamental, and yet Lanyon's art was quite personal. He created a pictorial language to express his love of the landscape in which he lived, and his devotion to West Penwith, that final westernmost knob of the Cornish peninsula, was absolute.

He sought a maximum knowledge of this landscape, and was never happier than when exploring it—on foot or by bicycle as a young man, then later on motor cycle and by car. His experiences of vertigo when climbing cliffs, of enclosure when descending mine shafts, of watching waves break were all incorporated in his painting.

In later years he took up gliding, not so much as a sport, but as a means to gain an even more intimate understanding of his landscape. As the titles of some of his pictures have suggested—"Soaring Flight" (in the Arts Council collection) and "Thermal" (in the Tate Galley), for example—an aerial experience of landscape has been the inspiration of much of his work. Latterly he had begun to work on a much larger scale—with murals for Liverpool and Birmingham Universities and for an American collector friend—and he was using colour with more boldness. To his friends his work seemed to be moving into the new phase that would unquestionably have consolidated his international reputation.

Peter Lanyon was born at St. Ives, Cornwall, in February, 1918, and always lived there. He was educated at St. Erbyn's, Penzance, and Clifton College. He studied art at the Penzance Art School and later at the Euston Road School with Sir William Coldstream, setting up as a professional painter in 1938. He served in the R.A.F. during the Second World War. His first one-man show was at the Lefevre Gallery in 1949 and from 1952 onwards he exhibited regularly at the Gimpel Fils Gallery where his most recent one-man exhibition was held in 1962.

Lanyon taught at the Bath Academy of Art, Corsham, 1951–56, and his paintings at this time began to attract attention both at home and abroad. He was awarded an Italian Government scholarship in 1953, an Acquisition Marzotto Award, 1962, the British Critics' Prize in 1954, was selected for the British section of the International Guggenheim Award in 1958 and was second prize winner in the John Moores Liverpool exhibition in 1959. His work appeared in many international exhibitions; at the Pittsburgh International, 1955, the Fifth International of Japan, 1959, the Sao Paulo Biennale, 1961, where he represented Britain together with Lynn Chadwick and William Scott, Documenta 11, 1959, at Kassel, Kompass II at Eindhoven, 1962, and "Art of a Decade" at the Tate Gallery in 1964.

YOUNG PAINTERS' WORK

He was one of the seven artists included in the exhibition "Young British Painters" which toured American museums, 1957–59, and his work also figured in recent exhibitions of modern British art at the Stadt Galerie, Borkum, and the Kunsthalle, Dusseldorf. In 1963 he gave a recorded talk on tape for the British Council, illustrated with colour slides of his work and widely disseminated and he lectured in Czechoslovakia in 1964 on British painting with the sponsorship of the British Council.

His work is represented in the Tate Gallery and many other public collections in Britain, the National Gallery of Victoria, Melbourne, the Toronto Gallery, the Carnegie Institute, the Albright Art Gallery, Buffalo, and the collection of the British Council.

Lanyon leaves a widow, four sons, and two daughters.

September 2, 1964.

Lord Latham, leader of the London County Council from 1940 to 1947 and chairman of the London Transport Executive from 1947 to 1953, died on March 31, 1970.

His career provided a striking illustration of the success which so many men of his day achieved by sheer force of character and self discipline. Though he had few opportunities in early life, he soon realized the value of self-help, forming studious habits to such purpose that his escape from the restricted circumstances in which he was born was only a matter of time. His long and devoted public service had its highest reward when he was raised to the peerage in 1942 and this was followed by a further signal honour in 1945, when he was appointed Lord Lieutenant of Middlesex, an appointment he held until 1956. Yet in spite of the recognition of his worth and work which these titles represented he remained at heart a man of the people, proud of the stock from which he had descended, and with a genuine sympathy for others less fortunate than himself. The two causes dearest to his heart were, perhaps, the Labour Party, and local administration. He joined the party in 1905, and was thus a pioneer of its subsequent success, and from early manhood he was, first, a member of Hendon Urban District Council, and later for many years on the London County Council.

Charles Lathan (his original name was Lathan which he later changed to Latham) was born at Norwich on December 26, 1888, the son of a tanner. Educated at a local elementary school, which he left at 14 years of age, he confessed in later years that, so far as learning was concerned, he was "an unrelieved failure". Even figures which were later to be an important part of his stock-in-trade as an accountant, meant little to him. His mother was a descendant of Huguenot weavers, and of industrious and frugal habits, but there were nine other children besides Charles to occupy her attention, and as seven of them were older than he, his training was left largely to them. His first stimulus to make up for lost time in the matter of education came from reading a book on the French revolution.

Settling in London on his return from France (where he perfected his use of French but was unable to find a job) he filled a number of clerical posts, and at the same time attended classes at the Polytechnic. By the time the 1914–18 War broke out he was a qualified accountant. He served in the Royal Sussex Regiment and on being demobilized became, first, manager, and then a partner, in the firm for which he worked.

PARTY FOUNDER-MEMBER

He helped to found the London Labour Party in 1914, serving on its executive committee for some years, and from 1942 was treasurer of the organization.

Although his time was much taken up with local and county administration, he tried on three occasions between 1922 and 1924 to get into Parliament in the Labour interest, but each time was unsuccessful. He was an alderman of the London County Council, on which he later represented South Hackney. Following Labour's victory on the L.C.C. he became chairman of the Finance Committee being second only to Herbert Morrison (as he then was) as Leader of the Council in 1940, and remained Leader throughout the difficulties of the war years until 1948. In spite of the enormous problems posed to local administration in the capital city in those years of war, Charles Latham spent much energy on planning the peaceful reconstruction of London local government affairs in readiness for the cessation of hostilities.

He had been in his younger days a member, and afterwards president, of the National Union of Clerks. He was a member of the famous Economy Committee, of which Lord May was chairman, appointed by the Chancellor of the Exchequer in 1931, and also served on the London and Home Counties Electricity Board, and the Public Works Loan Board for a number of years.

In 1935 he was appointed a member of the London Passenger Transport Board and on the nationalization of the country's transport system in 1948 he succeeded Lord Ashfield its former chairman and became chairman of the new London Transport Executive.

As a member of the House of Lords, he maintained a lively interest in matters of local government and local administration. He was a bitter opponent of the creation of the Greater London Council. Latham resumed his association with the London County Council on his cooption to its Housing Committee in 1957 where his previous experience proved to be of great value. In 1957 he was appointed to the Metropolitan Water Board on the nomination of the L.C.C. and became chairman of the board's finance committee, an area of local administration in which he specialized.

He was keenly interested in music and was a prominent member of the Sir Henry Wood Memorial Trust. During the war he was responsible for recommending the London County Council to give financial support to the London Philharmonic Orchestra, which has been continued to the present time. From 1960 until 1962 he was a member of the Council of Europe.

In 1913 he married Maya H. Allman and there were four children of the marriage, a son (who died in 1959) and three daughters. The marriage was dissolved. In 1957 Latham married secondly Mrs. Sylvia Kennard. There were no children of the second marriage. The heir to the barony is Latham's grandson, Dominic Charles Latham.

April 2, 1970.

Sir John Latham, G.C.M.G., Q.C., who died in a Melbourne hospital on July 25, 1964, at the age of 86, was for more than 60 years an outstanding figure in Australian public life—as politician, diplomatist, jurist and patron of educational, cultural, charitable and sporting organizations. An austere, rigidly self-disciplined man, he had an amazing capacity for detailed work and his eminence at law was due as much to his great industry as to intellectual power.

His service to the community reached back to before Federation, and did not cease when he retired as Chief Justice of the High Court in 1952. To most he was a name rather than a personality; a man who was remote and aloof even as a politician; one who compelled respect, even deference, but who gained the affection only of that small circle of intimates who were able to penetrate the barrier of shyness and find behind it warm, human qualities.

John Greig Latham was born at Ascot Vale, a Melbourne suburb, on August 25, 1877, the oldest of four sons and a daughter of Thomas Latham, secretary of the Society for the Protection of Animals. From an early state school education John Latham moved to Scotch College and later to the University of Melbourne on scholarships and exhibitions, graduating with distinction in arts and, later, while supporting himself as a lecturer in philosophy and logic, in law. In his early years as a lecturer he was troubled by a nervous stutter which he had to fight to overcome. While at the university he gained tennis and lacrosse Blues and later captained Victoria at lacrosse in interstate and international matches. As an administrator and patron he continued his association with lacrosse almost until his death.

PROMISING BARRISTER

Latham was admitted to the Victorian Bar in 1904, quickly gaining recognition as a promising young barrister. With the outbreak of war in 1914 he enlisted for active service, but because of his legal qualifications was transferred for special duties with the intelligence section of the Navy department. In 1918 he went abroad as Staff Officer attached to the Naval Ministry and served in this capacity for a little more than a year. He then became a member of the staff of the Australian peace delegation.

After demobilization in 1920 Latham returned to the Victorian Bar and quickly enhanced his already solidly based reputation as a constitutional lawyer. In 1922, shortly after he took silk, he remarked to a group of legal colleagues that the best sort of man was not entering Parliament and was challenged to "have a go". Accepting the challenge, he stood for Kooyong in the Federal elections of that year as an Independent and defeated the endorsed Conservative candidate after a campaign which must have been painfully difficult for one so withdrawn from the rough and tumble of the street-meeting politics of the day.

Latham believed his return was a vindication of his faith in the capacity of the people to vote for the man and not for the party but this political naivety soon disappeared after a brief period in the House. Never personally popular, he soon came to be recognized as one of the most able men in Parliament. As a speaker he was cold, precise, inexorably logical and hopelessly dull. He joined the Nationalist (Conservative) Party and in 1925 entered the Bruce-Page Ministry as Attorney General, a post he held during the transfer of the Federal Government to Canberra in 1927 and until the Bruce-Page Government was overwhelmingly defeated in 1929.

Bruce lost his seat and Latham became leader of the Nationalists and of the Opposition when Parliament resumed. He painstakingly gathered the remnants of the Nationalists together to plan a return to power.

In 1931 a group of Labour dissidents under J. A. Lyons joined with the Nationalists to form the United Australia Party and Latham, recognizing the truth of his colleagues' belief that he did not have sufficient popular appeal to fight an election, resigned the leadership of the Opposition to Lyons, thus giving up the opportunity of the Prime Ministership, which was certainly within his grasp. In the election later that year the United Australia Party were swept into office.

Latham became Lyons's right hand man, taking up the portfolios of Attorney General, External Affairs and Industry. For the next two and a half years there were many indications that he was, in fact, the Prime Minister and Lyons the figurehead. In 1934 he resigned from Parliament for reasons which he never disclosed and his seat of Kooyong was won by Sir Robert Menzies, who has held it ever since.

In 1935 Latham was appointed Chief Justice in the face of protests by Labour sympathisers that the appointment was political, and the fulfilment of a promise made on his resignation from Parliament. Whatever the truth of the allegations, Latham was undoubtedly the most suitable and best-equipped man for the position.

IN JAPAN

In 1940 he was granted leave from the Bench to become the first Australian Minister to Japan. Australia was already at war and there were difficulties in communication with Canberra and in September, 1941, Latham left Japan to consult with the Australian Government. He fell ill during the trip and spent some time in hospital in Singapore. By the time he had reached Australia and consulted with the Government it was too late to return. Japan had entered the war.

Latham resumed the Chief Justiceship and remained in the post until April, 1952, when he retired. His postwar years on the bench saw some notable constitutional cases, the most important of them the challenge to the Bank nationalization proposals of J. B. Chifley, which the court declared unconstitutional, and the Menzies Government's Communist Party Dissolution Bill, which also was declared unconstitutional, this time by a six to one majority with Latham the dissentient.

He married in 1907 Eleanor Mary Tobin, who died in March this year. They had two sons—of whom the elder was killed on active service—and one daughter who died.

July 27, 1964.

Charles Laughton, the British-born actor who died at his home in Hollywood on December 15, 1962, at the age of 63, exchanged many years ago his position in the field of the English theatre for one hard to define, since he grew to be as well known in the United States for his readings from the Bible as for his film work in the international field.

When he was asked to interpret a single character in all its complexity whether in a play or still better in a film—Alexander Korda's *The Private Life of Henry VIII* and *Rembrandt* come to mind—Laughton was in his element.

ZEST INTACT

He was out of his element when asked to do more, to interpret not only a single character in its complexity but a play as a whole in all its moods, as a player of the greatest parts in Shakespeare and poetic drama in general has to try to do. Even there, however, the personality of the man, added to the unheroic quality of his voice and appearance, lent an extraordinary interest to his attempts. Perhaps his true claim to greatness lies in his painfully acquired sense of his limitations, which did not destroy his zest for the tasks either of acting or living as he conceived of them.

By those who saw him only on the screen Laughton will be remembered with great affection for a series of commanding performances whose impact and flavour remain undiminished. *The Private Life of Henry VIII*, which did a great deal to establish the reputation of British films abroad, and *Rembrandt*—perhaps his best film—have already been mentioned, but both before and after these there were other memorable portrayals. The debauched and decadent Nero in de Mille's *The Sign of the Cross*; Captain Bligh (hurling Laughtonian defiance at the mutineers) in *Mutiny on the Bounty*; Ruggles in *Ruggles of Red Gap*, in which he deeply impressed American audiences by his recitation of Lincoln's Gettysburg speech; Ginger Ted in *Vessel of Wrath*; Mr. Barrett in *The Barretts of Wimpole Street*; and, in his last film, which opened in London earlier in 1962, a reactionary Senator in *Advise and Consent*.

The eldest of the three sons of Robert Laughton, he was born on July 1, 1899, at the Pavilion Hotel, Scarborough, which his parents owned, and went to school at Stonyhurst. A friend described him as the ungainliest of schoolboys, very fat with a huge head. He was sent to London to study the hotel business at Claridge's and after a period of active service on the Western front, where he was gassed, in 1918, he worked at the Pavilion, Scarborough, now the Laughton family's hotel; but in 1925 he entered R.A.D.A. as a student. He there won the Gold Medal, and one of his teachers, Theodore Komisarjevsky, gave him a small part in *The Government Inspector* at Barnes in 1926. Laughton was again directed by Komisarjevsky in dramatized versions of Arnold Bennett's "Mr. Prohack" and of Hugh Walpole's "Portrait of a Man with Red Hair"; in the one he caused some supererogatory amusement by copying Bennett's own mannerisms, and in the other he made his first success in what was to be regarded for years as a Charles Laughton part: that of a neurotic, greedy for power and using cruelty as a means of holding on to it. Laughton said that he, as a very fat boy with a wish to go on the stage, suffered from his fellows' cruelty and that he now shook off his old feelings of injury by playing cruel people and giving them the qualities he most disliked. He endowed such characters as the Chicago gangster in Edgar Wallace's *On the Spot* and the squalid murderer in *Payment Deferred* with a homespun reality that made them the more sinister and frightening in their moments of excess: "play it on your intimate knowledge of everybody in the audience's meannesses and their secret desires", he wrote later to an amateur actor who had consulted him about *Payment Deferred*.

OFFER FROM HOLLYWOOD

That play introduced him to New York audiences in 1931, and in the following year he accepted a offer from Hollywood. After making six films there he returned home with the ambition of playing classical parts at the Old Vic; and having in the meantime given his uncannily fine comedy performance in *The Private Life of Henry VIII.* Laughton joined the Old Vic Company in 1933, his aim being to improve his speaking voice and to find a more profound approach to acting generally—hitherto, he declared, he had just muddled along, clowning a lot and playing with roles.

The Old Vic season, during which he came to grips with Angelo, Prospero and Macbeth, was too short to turn him from an "inspirational" into a "technical" actor. According to his director, Sir Tyrone Guthrie, Laughton's Macbeth was electrifying at the dress rehearsal, but on the opening night, when inspiration failed him, lack of resource both of voice and movement caused his performance to shrivel up.

In 1936 he had the honour of being the first Englishman to appear with the company of the Comedie Française in a scene at their annual gala. Coached by one of his old teachers at R.A.D.A., Alice Gachet, he played Sganarelle in an excerpt from *Le Médicin Malgré Lui*, and that same year he was seen in London together with his wife, Elsa Lanchester, whom he had married in 1929, in *Peter Pan*.

So far as audiences in England were concerned, there now began a long interval in Laughton's career as a "live" actor. In the United States he played in Brecht's *Galileo*, having adapted it in close cooperation with the author, and, after becoming an American citizen in 1950, in revivals directed by himself of Shaw; but his next job of work in a London theatre was in 1958, followed a year later by his appearance at Stratford-on-Avon as Bottom and King Lear. This second bout with Shakespeare, this return match with tragedy, ended in a draw. Qualities he was now able to bring to a character—a deeper kind of humanity than before, tolerance, love—made him seem worthy of the part, even if there was still none of Lear's authority in his countenance. It was no more the countenance of a suspicious, aggressive man, but that of a happy one.

December 17, 1962.

Stan Laurel, the film comedian, died at Santa Monica, California, on February 23, 1965. He was 74. He will always be remembered as a partner in the comedy team of Laurel and Hardy, and he would not have had it otherwise. The two worked as a team, and their success was indivisible. Separately they did not amount to very much. Together they seemed—despite their differences in appearance and possibly because of it—to become a single unit, an expression of well-intentioned muddle-headedness in a harsh and practical world.

Stan Laurel was small and thin. Oliver Hardy was very fat. Hardy was expansive, bland and self assured. Laurel was anxious, frail and perplexed. When Hardy attempted anything it went wrong in the end. When Laurel put his hand to it, it went wrong immediately.

Arthur Stanley Jefferson (Laurel's real name) was an Englishman, born in Ulverston, Lancashire, on June 16, 1890. He was educated at King James Grammar School in Bishop Auckland and learnt the profession of a comedian the hard way—in the circus, the music-hall and the theatre. Like Chaplin, he first saw America as a member of Fred Karno's touring company when he was still in his teens (they played together in a sketch called *Mumming Birds*), and—like Chaplin—he stayed in the

United States to play in the early silent films. Hal Roach gave him his first film part in 1917, and he made some 50 short comedies for the Hal Roach Company, and also tried his hand both as a producer and a director.

GOLDEN AGE

The partnership with Oliver Hardy started in 1926, when the silent film was at its zenith, and competition among screen comedians was acute. This was in many ways the golden age of screen comedy, which was so ideally suited to the silent films, and the competition to be faced included such great names as Chaplin, Harold Lloyd, and Buster Keaton. When sound came it was in no way a handicap to them, for their voices exactly matched their appearance—Hardy's benign and soft, Laurel's plaintive and often a little squeaky, especially in moments of anguish—and their comedies were introduced by a catchy little signature tune that became almost as well known as they themselves. The second major hurdle in their career—the full-length film—was less easily surmounted. Their first long picture was *Jailbirds* made in 1931, but although their long films were frequently very funny there is no doubt that it was within the framework of their short comedies that they were seen at their best.

Hardy died in 1957, but before that their star was on the wane.

February 24, 1965.

Jay Laurier, the comedian and Shakespearian actor, died in Durban in April, 1969. He was 89.

Born in Birmingham on May 31, 1879, he first appeared on the stage at Abertillery in 1896 in *The Arabian Nights*. For many years he was a "top-liner" on the halls, where he sang songs which combined great innocence and complete fatuity. These included "I'm always doing something silly," "Ring o' Roses," and "S'what's S'nicer than a S'nice S'ice S'ice." He was also a successful pantomime performer. He played in several musical pieces like *The Merry Widow* and *Les Cloches de Corneville*, but he always hoped to play in more serious works and in 1937 achieved his ambition.

That year he joined the Old Vic company, playing first Alfred Doolittle in Shaw's *Pygmalion* and then Pompey in *Measure for Measure*. In 1938 he acted through the Stratford season as the porter in *Macbeth*, as Sir Toby in *Twelfth Night*, as Launce in *Two Gentlemen of Verona*, as Bottom in *A Midsummer Night's Dream* and as Stephano in *The Tempest*.

STRATFORD RETURN

He made the most of these parts, and was engaged again at Stratford in 1939 playing Christopher Sly in *The Taming of the Shrew*, Touchstone and Dogberry. He was seen again as Dogberry at the Aldwych Theatre in 1946, and in 1947 as Sir Toby Belch at the Savoy. He had also appeared in numerous films.

April 15, 1969.

Leonid Lavrovsky, the Russian choreographer and former artistic director of the Bolshoi Ballet, died of a heart attack in a Paris hotel on November 26, 1967. He was in Paris in charge of a group of recent graduates from the Bolshoi Ballet School, currently touring Europe. He collapsed after returning from a performance at the Champs-Elysées Theatre by the Marseille Ballet which was preceding his own group at the Paris International Dance Festival.

Lavrosvsky was born in St. Petersburg in 1905. He trained there as a dancer and graduated into the company now known as the Kirov Ballet. Later he became one of the company's choreographers, and it was in this capacity that he transferred later to the Bolshoi Ballet in Moscow, becoming artistic director there in 1945. During the 1950s the rather monumental style he represented was attacked by Igor Moiseyev, director of a famous folk dance company and himself a choreographer, as being old fashioned and out of touch with contemporary life. Lavrovsky weathered this storm but was later replaced as artistic director by Igor Grigorovich, the leading choreographer of a younger generation, who led the move towards a less realistic style.

Lavrovsky's productions included a staging of *Giselle* which came as a revelation to western audiences when first shown in London in 1956.

WIDELY COPIED

His close attention to dramatic detail and his deeper conception of the hero's role have since been widely copied. Lavrovsky's greatest work, however, was his *Romeo and Juliet*, to Prokofiev's music, which had Ulanova as its original heroine and has since evoked notable interpretations from many other dancers. This pushed to their ultimate logical conclusion the dramatic reforms introduced earlier this century by Mikhail Fokine. After it, the reaction that deposed Lavrovsky was probably inevitable, since that vein could be mined no further, but *Romeo and Juliet*, which had been filmed, will remain as his lasting memorial. Lavrovsky's last ballet, to Prokofiev's Classical Symphony, is due to be given in London next month.

He leaves a widow, who was with him as ballet mistress of the group of young dancers. His son, Mikhail, is one of the leading dancers of the Bolshoi Ballet.

November 29, 1967.

Sir Geoffrey Lawrence, Q.C., who died on February 3, 1967, at the age of 64, became known to the public in more capacities than usually fall to a man in the course of a legal career. He achieved successive reputations as a distinguished advocate, chairman of the Bar Council, chairman of the National Incomes Commission, and High Court Judge, yet all without any talent for histrionics or publicity.

Frederick Geoffrey Lawrence was born on April 5, 1902, and was educated at the City of London School and New College, Oxford, where he failed to obtain the high academic distinctions which had been expected of him. After a period spent as a tutor, he decided upon a legal career, and was called to the Bar by the Middle Temple in 1930. After a pupillage with Eric Neve, he occupied himself during his early days of practice by devilling Opinions for busier colleagues, and it is said that clients of at least one very senior practitioner observed at this period a marked improvement in the standard of his Opinions.

His capacity for seeing clearly the point of a case, and his conscientious application to detail quickly earned him a busy general practice on the South Eastern Circuit. His advocacy was characterized by clear reasoning expressed in superb English, but even when addressing a jury, he made little appeal to the emotions.

In 1948 he became Recorder of Tenterden, an office which he held until 1951. He was a member of the Royal Commission on Marriage and Divorce which was appointed under the chairmanship of Lord Morton, and there enhanced his reputation for seizing upon the essential issue among a mass of evidence. He took silk in 1950, and within a short time his practice had become largely channelled into the specialized and remunerative fields of parliamentary and planning work. At this time, his only connexion with criminal law consisted in his appointments as Recorder of Canterbury in 1952, and as chairman of West Sussex Quarter Sessions in 1953.

MURDER TRIAL

Yet it was his appearance as a criminal advocate which first brought him to the notice of the general public when, in 1957, somewhat surprisingly, he was instructed to lead for the defence in the trial of Dr. Bodkin Adams. Dr. Adams was indicted for the murder of Mrs. Edith Alice Morrell, a patient, by administering drugs. Probably the outstanding feature of the case was Lawrence's masterly cross-examination of the medical witnesses for the prosecution, which earned him numerous letters of congratulation. After a hearing lasting 17 days, Dr. Adams was acquitted. In the following year, Lawrence was briefed to defend Chief Constable Ridge, who, together with other officers of the Brighton Police Force, was indicted for conspiracy to obstruct the course of public justice. After retiring for four and a half hours, the jury returned and announced that they were unable to agree. But after a further retirement they found the chief constable not guilty.

His conduct of these two defences led to a considerable demand for Lawrence's services in the criminal courts, but he remained happiest in parliamentary and planning work. In 1960 he became chairman of the General Council of the Bar. He did not dominate the profession as Sir Hartley Shawcross had done earlier, or Lord Gardiner later. And his term of office was not marked by the pressure for reform which confronted his successors. But Lawrence will be remembered outside the United Kingdom for his successful visits on behalf of the English Bar to other countries, and in particular for the complete conquest which he made among American lawyers, who accorded him tributes of an order rarely accorded to foreign lawyers. In 1963 he was knighted for his services as chairman.

Until 1962 his experience had lain exclusively within the field of law, but in that year he was called to a wholly different sphere of activity.

NICKY

For years the government had been confronted with the problem of rising incomes, which had outdistanced the increase in production, and with the resulting inflation. Successive attempts to control the rate of increase had failed, and in 1962 there was set up the National Incomes Commission ("Nicky"). The intention was to subject any proposed increase to a judicial inquiry, and Lawrence was invited to become the first chairman. He accepted, and threw himself enthusiastically into the work. But the commission was launched to an inauspicious beginning. The trade union movement took the view that it constituted an attempt to hold down wages and salaries without a corresponding control over dividends and commercial incomes, and declined to participate. An original proposal to submit wage dispute to the compulsory arbitration of the commission was withdrawn, and when it began to function, all that remained to it was a power to make recommendations.

AUTHORITY TESTED

It was a tribute to Lawrence's determination that, in an existence of 18 months, the commission produced four reports, and its authority was sufficient to insure that no industry was anxious to be "nicked". But the scheme failed to make the impact for which Lawrence had hoped, and with a change of government in 1964 the commission made way for the National Incomes Board. In November, 1964, the report of the independent inquiry into parliamentary remuneration, under the chairmanship of Lawrence, was published. It recommended large increases in the pay of Ministers of all grades, members of Parliament, the Lord Chancellor, the Speaker, and the English and Scottish law officers.

Lawrence returned to practice, but within a few months was appointed to the High Court Bench. As a judge he was quiet, courteous, and fair. If he lacked a capacity for epigram or a sense of the dramatic which sometimes endears judges to the public, these are failings which the profession finds it easy to forgive. His career on the Bench was relatively uneventful and his happiest hours were spent on his farm in Sussex.

In 1941 he married Marjorie Avice, daughter of Charles Angelo Jones, who survives him.

February 6, 1967.

Lord Lawson, Lord Lieutenant of the County of Durham from 1949 to 1958, and a former Secretary of State for War, died in hospital at Chester-le-Street on August 3, 1965, at the age of 83.

Jack Lawson, as he was generally known, brought to high office in the service of state and county those qualities of sturdy self-respect, natural dignity, and robust vigour which flourish in the hardy mining communities of Durham. Son of a miner, nurtured in the pits he cherished jealously his pride in that perilous craft and his regard for the men who practised it.

John James Lawson, first Baron Lawson of Beamish in the County of Durham, was born in 1881, one of ten children of John Lawson, a miner of Whitehaven, Cumberland. His stern upbringing by a father who had spent his early life on the sea and a mother who could never be undignified even when there was barely enough to eat gave him a background of reality against which he could confidently weigh the problems he came upon in later life. He began to work in a Durham coal mine at the age of 12.

WIFE'S GENEROSITY

His struggles for a formal education were rewarded in 1906 when he was offered the chance of attending Ruskin College, Oxford, for a year if he could find £26. He had just married, but his wife offered to sell up their new home. When, with the help of his parents and the vicar of the parish, the money was forthcoming she followed him to Oxford and supported herself by working in the city as a domestic servant.

At the end of his time at Ruskin several eminent men offered to help him through to graduation but he felt unable to accept. He had never intended to educate himself out of the ranks of the manual workers. His intention was rather to show that a man could be a better miner for knowing something of the world of learning. So he went back to the mine.

His work as checkweighman, a legacy of the early days of the industrial revolution when rapacious owners faced distrustful men, led him to take an increasing part in the affairs of the Durham Miners' Association and in local politics; he served on the executive and the conciliation board and was elected to the Durham County Council in 1913. Soon after his service in the 1914–18 War, as a driver in the Royal Artillery, he was adopted as Parliamentary candidate for Chester-le-Street. He was elected at a by-election in 1919. As an ex-Serviceman, he displayed considerable activity on pensions questions and was marked out for promotion when Ramsay MacDonald appointed him one of his Parliamentary private secretaries. In a matter of months, he was appointed Financial Secretary to the War Office in the first Labour Government in 1924, while Clement Attlee was Under-Secretary of State.

SECRETARY OF STATE

He visited both China and Greece as a member of Parliamentary delegations sent out at critical times in 1943 and 1945 but he did not attain office again until the Labour victory in 1945. Then, surprisingly enough, for his modest and retiring nature had tended to obscure his real claims, he was made the Secretary of State of the department in which he had held minor office 20 odd years before. His post as Deputy Regional Commissioner, Civil Defence, Northern Region, had kept him much occupied with local affairs during the war years, so that when he assumed the direction of the War Office he was largely a forgotten man. This was soon changed. Reports of discontent among the troops on distant stations now that the war in Europe was over, were read with sympathy by the Secretary of State and he determined to "talk to the boys with my coat off".

He left England on September 12 and arrived back on October 6—25 days, including travelling. He spoke to troops in India, Burma, Hongkong, and Singapore, to say nothing of large meetings in Egypt and Ceylon. He also spoke to ex-prisoners of war in Calcutta, Rangoon, Hongkong, and Singapore. For him, his visit was but the starting point for the complicated business of converting the military machine from a war-time to a peace-time basis. He had told the Prime Minister earlier in the summer that he would like to retire when the House rose, but Attlee was engaged at the time in devising a new organization for defence and persuaded Lawson to stay on until it had been completed.

FREE FROM OFFICE

By early October this had been accomplished, and Lawson was free to lay down the cares of office.

In 1949, thirty years after his election as Member for Chester-le-Street, Lawson was appointed Lord Lieutenant, the first working man to attain that office which he held until 1958. Less than six months later he accepted the vice-chairmanship of the National Parks Commission and resigned his seat in the Commons. In the Dissolution Honours of February, 1950, he was created a baron. Although he was no great orator, the sincerity of his speeches always assured him a respectful hearing. In causes on which he felt deeply, such as working conditions in the pits or serving conditions in the Army, he could convey fervour without fanaticism—was he not a Wesleyan lay preacher?—and he never lost touch with reality. Nor did he ever lose the common touch. His elevation to the peerage made no difference to his manner of life.

Lawson was the author of three books, *A Man's Life*, *Peter Lee* and *Man in the Cap*. He was an Hon. D.C.L. of Durham University and a member of the Court of the University, a K.St.J., and a Vice-Chairman of the British Council.

He married in 1906, Isabella, daughter of John Scott of Newcastle. There were three daughters of the marriage.

August 4, 1965.

Wilfrid Lawson, the actor, who died on October 10, 1966, at his home in London, aged 66, deserves to be remembered for the performances of his earlier years, forceful and often brilliant ones in dramatic parts on the stage, rather than for those of his later years in parts of more limited scope in films, on radio, and on television, though these also could be of compelling interest.

Throughout the vicissitudes of his career he retained the respect and affection of directors and fellow actors, and he had not ceased to be in demand.

Born on January 14, 1900, at Bradford, Yorkshire, where he attended Hanson School and Technical College, Wilfrid Lawson became a professional actor at the age of 16. Having served as a pilot in the R.A.F. during the last year of the First World War, he returned to the stage and played over 400 parts before appearing in London, at the old Elephant and Castle, in 1928. He was in revivals of Shaw under the managements of Charles Macdona and of Sir Barry Jackson, and in 1933 his performance as John Brown of Harper's Ferry in *Gallows Glorious* convinced audiences of his genuine power: a power which, uncanny when he was at his best, was occasionally to be diminished by contact with some neurotic alloy in his own personality.

Two years later he was reengaged by Sir Barry Jackson for a revival of *The Barretts of Wimpole Street* and for the Malvern Festival, then he visited New York where he was seen in three productions. In 1937 he made his outstanding success up to date as the rich, unhappily married businessman in J. B. Priestley's "time play" *I Have Been Here Before*. Lawson perfectly expressed this character's desperate dissatisfaction with his life and his powerlessness to change it until help came in the form of a vision of something nobler. He repeated this performance in New York, where the play failed, and was again in America in 1939, but on the outbreak of the Second World War he returned to England, rejoined the R.A.F., and for the next two and a half years served with it.

In 1940 he was offered a leading part in the Hollywood film of *How Green Was My Valley*, but was not granted an exit permit in order to take it up, a decision by the Home Secretary which was the subject of a question in the House of Commons.

STAMINA IN DOUBT

When after a post-war tour of the United States he reappeared in London in Strindberg's *The Father*, he seemed lacking in the stamina necessary for so long and highly dramatic a part. In the following year, as an old man who has become a nuisance to his children in *The Woodern Spoon*, a play set in a small Texan city, he recovered much of the ground he had lost, and his sardonic quality of voice and air of indifference to the world's opinion, already put to use in the smaller part of the cell warder in Bridget Boland's *The Prisoner* both on stage and as a film, was also effective in that of the head of the gipsy family in John Arden's *Live Like Pigs* at the Royal Court.

He was back at the Royal Court, less well suited as the sailor in O'Casey's *Cock-a-Doodle Dandy* in 1959. In 1962 he appeared with the Royal Shakespeare Company as the tramp Luka in Gorki's *The Lower Depths*, making credible the influence of that character upon the other inhabitants of the night-shelter, and later that year he played the Button Moulder to Leo McKern's Peer Gynt at the Old Vic.

His most important part in films was that of Alfred Doolittle the dustman, in Gabriel Pascal's *Pygmalion*, shown in 1938. Lawson's reputation was perhaps at its highest in that year, when he was still giving what Priestley called "a performance to make your hair stand on end" in *I Have Been Here Before*, and when James Agate's question about him "Is this a great actor?" remained an open one.

Recently he had contributed a ripe performance as Black George the gamekeeper in Tony Richardson's film *Tom Jones*, and he had just finished Don Chaffey's colour film *Viking Queen*, in which he played King Priam, before his death. On radio he was heard in two important broadcasts of Chekhov, as the Army doctor in *The Three Sisters* and as the old actor in *Swan Song*. One of his outstanding performances on television was as Flambeau, the Napoleonic veteran who becomes the mentor of Napoleon's exiled son in *L'Aiglon*. His last roles on B.B.C. Television were the King of the Beggars in *The Hunchback of Notre Dame*, Grandad in *The Likely Lads* and the Dormouse in *Alice in Wonderland*, which has not yet been shown.

Lawson was married to Miss Lillian Fenn who survives him.

October 12, 1966.

Frank Lawton, who died on June 10, 1969, at the age of 64, was an actor whose charm and ability were widely recognized at the age of 23 on his appearance in John van Druten's *Young Woodley*. He lost neither the one thing nor the other as he grew older, but they did not so renew themselves as to confirm his position as a leading actor.

His father, Frank M. Lawton, made a success with his whistling in *The Belle of New York*, when that musical play was taken to Britain in 1898, and who died in 1914. Frank Lawton Junior, who was born in London on September 30, 1904, began his career in revue at the Vaudeville. In 1925 he had the opportunity of working under the direction of Gerald Du Maurier in Lonsdale's *The Last of Mrs. Cheyney*. He remained with Du Maurier for more than two years, during which he also won good opinions in two Sunday night productions; with the result that, when Basil Dean needed a young actor for the leading part in a play about a public school which might, if it gave no offence at a Sunday night show, receive a licence for general performance in England, his eventual choice for young Woodley was Frank Lawton.

Whether or not it would be licensed depended largely on the actor's personality and his handling of the situation in which an 18-years-old boy fell in love with his housemaster's wife. Directed by Dean, Lawton made it appear natural, touching and at the same time funny, something that might happen to any boy. The verdict of the Sunday night audience was upheld, the Lord Chamberlain having meanwhile granted a licence, at the Savoy Theatre, where the piece ran for some 400 performances.

Lawton appeared in Galsworthy's last play, *The Roof*, in Milne's *Michael and Mary*, in van Druten's play of office life, *London Wall*, and as Woodley on the cinema screen. Though audiences had no fault to find with his playing of those parts, what they chiefly remembered about it was the player's cherubic face, like that of a senior choirboy and, possibly with some regret, his seeming shortness of stature.

IN HOLLYWOOD

He was called to Hollywood to play the younger son in the film of Noel Coward's *Cavalcade*, and after making his New York stage debut he took over from Freddie Bartholomew at the point in Hugh Walpole's adaptation of *David Copperfield* where the hero of the M.G.M. film grew up. Evelyn Laye, for years a close friend of his, arrived to make a musical film on an adjoining studio lot, and in December, 1934, in Arizona, Lawton married Miss Laye as her second husband.

He was in London some months later in a farcical comedy by Keith Winter, but for the next few years all his work was done in the United States. When he was again seen in London in 1938, his role in Esther McCracken's *Quiet Wedding* allowed him merely to show that he looked no older, and that he was as reliable an actor as before. He joined the Territorial Army, being posted to a company of men free to train by day but not by night, and very soon after war broke out he was called up. He served until 1945, was awarded the United States Legion of Merit, and on his release toured with his wife in *Three Waltzes*, an Oscar Strauss musical, in which she had a singing role but Lawton did not.

In the 1950s he toured with her in Daphne Du Maurier's *September Tide*, and, in Australia and New Zealand, in van Druten's *Bell, Book and Candle*. After a bout of ill-health he played opposite her in a comedy by Michael Clayton Hutton and in a revival of Coward's *The Marquise*, which he directed, but he gave a more interesting account of himself as an alcoholic who instigates a murder, not at all a Frank Lawton part, in a "psychological thriller" called *The Big Killing*. A return to comedy, jointly with Miss Laye, in a revival of Maugham's *The Circle* in 1965, hardly worked out well for him, since his conscientiously assumed air of detachment and mockery did not disguise his youthfulness of heart and essential benevolence of dispostion.

June 12, 1969.

Major General Sir Robert Laycock, K.C.M.G., C.B., D.S.O., who died on March 10, 1968, at the age of 60, was Governor of Malta from 1954 till 1959. In the Second World War he made a great reputation as a daring and resourceful leader of commandos, and he was Chief of Combined Operations from 1943 till 1947.

From his earliest days Laycock had a great love of adventure. As a schoolboy and, later, as a young officer he used to spend his holidays sailing in tramp steamers to the ports of many countries in Europe, and he once sailed round the Cape as an Able Seaman in a Finnish wind-jammer. He was a keen amateur yachtsman and a member of the Royal Yacht Squadron, and was an ardent fox-hunter. These activities naturally developed his strong personality and his qualities of initiative and self-reliance, attributes which served him well as a leader of men.

His versatility was remarkable. He was a great reader, especially of biographies and poetry, and one of his hobbies was the collection of books for his extensive library at Wiseton.

HATED FORMALITY

Among his minor accomplishments was that of hair-cutting—he gave one of his officers a Bond Street trim with a pair of nail scissors on the eve of the Salerno landing. He hated formality in all its shapes, and he had a gay and romantic quality which, allied to his genuine modesty and imperturbability, won him the affection and devotion of his subordinates.

Robert Edward Laycock was born on April 18, 1907, the son of Brigadier General Sir Joseph Laycock. He was educated at Eton and at the Royal Military College Sandhurst and was commissioned in the Royal Horse Guards in 1927.

At the beginning of the Second World War he served for a time on the staff of G.H.Q. France, but was brought home to go through the wartime Staff College at Camberley. When the first call was made for volunteers for Special Service, Laycock sent in his name, and was promoted from Captain to Lieutenant-Colonel to form one of the first commandos. His chance to get into the war came when he was given a Special Service Battalion of five commandos in the Middle East which became known as "Layforce" and with this he carried out a number of small operations, including a night raid on Bardia, an attempt to seize a bridge over the river Litani in Syria, and a rearguard action during the evacuation of Crete. In the last of these actions his headquarters was ambushed by a strong party of Germans, but Laycock jumped into an abandoned British tank and drove it at the Germans and thus escaped. He also took part in Lieutenant-Colonel Keyes's raid on Rommel's headquarters in November, 1941.

DESERT ESCAPE

Owing to bad weather he was unable to re-embark his men in the submarines from which they had landed, and most of them were eventually taken prisoner, but he himself escaped into the desert with one of his sergeants and returned, thin and wasted, after existing for 41 days behind the enemy's lines.

These early efforts of the Commandos, although comparatively unsuccessful, were productive of many useful lessons, but the casualties suffered were disproportionate to the results achieved. They had, however, provided a new spice of interest in the war news, and Laycock himself gained a name for courage and enterprise.

Early in 1942 he was back in England to take command of the Special Service Brigade with the rank of Brigadier. In this appointment he was responsible for the training and organization of all the Special Service troops in Great Britain, including American units, and for planning numerous raids on the Continent in cooperation with Mountbatten's Combined Operations Command. It was Laycock who made the Commandos what they were; he found a way to instil discipline without discouraging initiative and other battle-winning qualities.

In the following year he was back in the fighting line when he personally led one of the assault landings by Commandos in the invasion of Sicily, for which he was awarded the D.S.O. At Salerno be again led British Commandos, and also American Rangers, for 11 critical days when he successfully held bridgehead positions with only infantry equipment in face of heavy attacks by tanks, artillery, and aircraft; of his total strength of 738 on this occasion, more than half were casualties.

When Lord Louis Mountbatten was appointed Supreme Commander in South-East Asia at the end of 1943 Laycock was appointed to succeed him as Chief of Combined Operations.

AMPHIBIOUS WARFARE

He was promoted to Major-General at the exceptionally early age of 36, only four years after having been a captain. As Chief of Combined Operations, for which his experience with the Commandos had been a first-rate training, he became adviser to the Chiefs of Staff on amphibious warfare and head of a command in which officers of the three services studied and developed the technical means of making assault landings. He proved to be an ideal choice for his new post and in it he did outstanding work in training and in the development of equipment for combined operations, for which he was made C.B. in 1945.

After the war Laycock continued for two years as Chief of Combined Operations.

In 1954 he was appointed Governor and Commander in Chief of Malta in succession to Sir Gerald Creasy. His term of office, which was twice extended, coincided with the difficult period of negotiations between the island's political leaders and the British Government over the integration plan. The talks on this plan finally broke down in 1958. The United Kingdom Government suspended the constitution, for the third time in Maltese history, and Laycock governed, under emergency powers, with a non-political advisory council, until the end of his term of office in 1959. He drew up a 5-year development plan, which was under way before he left.

He married in 1935 Angela Clare Louise, daughter of the Rt. Hon. William Dudley Ward, and had two sons and three daughters.

March 11, 1968.

Lord Layton, C.H., C.B.E., who died on February 14, 1966, in Putney Hospital at the age of 81 had several distinguished careers, as economist, as editor, as newspaper proprietor, and, in both the wars, as administrator.

His heart was in politics and public affairs and his unwavering attachment to the Liberal cause prevented him from realizing that complete fulfilment that he could have achieved, without much doubt, in one of the other parties. Late in his life he played an active part in the House of Lords, where he served as Deputy, and often Acting Leader of the Liberal peers from 1952–55, and his parliamentary talents flowered in the Council of Europe at Strasbourg, of which he became one of the vice-presidents. In spite of several efforts he never succeeded in election to the House of Commons and he never held ministerial office, to which he would have been well suited.

Walter Thomas Layton was born in London on March 15, 1884. Both his parents were professional musicians, his mother being the first woman to become a Fellow of the Royal College of Organists. Walter Layton inherited this musical talent which, supplemented by a quick intelligence and a restless energy, enabled him to provide for the whole cost of his education. At the age of seven he was a chorister at St. George's Chapel, Windsor. Transferred later to the Temple Church, he received his education first at King's College School and afterwards at Westminster City School.

These years of choir work did not affect his nonconformist faith, and his first university contacts, as was proper for a dissenter, were with University College London. There followed, however, a scholarship to Trinity College, Cambridge, where Layton fell under the influence of Alfred Marshall and took his place in the brilliant array of "Marshall's young men" who, in the years before the first war, built up the Cambridge tradition of economics. His career at Cambridge proceeded through a Gresham studentship and the Cobden prize to a fellowship at Gonville and Caius College in 1909 and a University Lectureship in 1912.

Even at this time, Cambridge and academic economics could not contain all his energies. He was writing articles for *The Economist*, and later working for two days a week in that paper's office. There was political activity, too; and for many years Cambridge residents remembered the sight of Walter Layton, a Fellow of his College, pushing a pram in a suffragette procession.

MUNITIONS MINISTRY

When the war came, Layton's statistical capacity and theoretical knowledge of industrial problems made it natural that he should join the Ministry of Munitions as soon as it was set up. In spite of his youth (he was only 34 when the First World War ended) he built a great reputation at the Ministry. He was taken into the close confidence of both Lloyd George and Churchill (as their memoirs show) and was a member of both the Milner Mission to Russia and the Balfour Mission to the United States. For these services he was made a Companion of Honour and awarded the C.B.E.

After the war Layton turned his hand first to the preliminary organization of the Economic Department of the League of Nations and then to the National Federation of Iron and Steel Manufacturers, of which he was director. Neither of these posts fully engaged his talents and when the editorship of *The Economist* fell vacant at the end of 1921 he gladly accepted it. He was editor for nearly 17 years. Towards the end of that period his attention was more and more directed towards daily journalism. For the first decade of his editorship, when he was writing a great deal each week, he gave *The Economist* a new force and purpose and laid the foundations for the great growth of the journal's influence in later years. He was later chairman of The Economist Newspaper Ltd., until his resignation in 1963 when he became deputy chairman.

Layton's mind was never far from public affairs. In the twenties he was very active in the Liberal Summer School and he was the person chiefly responsible for the famous "Liberal Yellow Book". He was Financial Assessor to the Simon Commission on Indian Constitutional Reform and was knighted in 1930 for his services. In the depression years governments called on him for assistance. He led (with Mr. Charles Rist) a League of Nations mission to Austria, he was a member of the commission that drafted the statutes of the Bank for International Settlements and was British member of the Preparatory Committee for the World Economic Conference of 1933, until he resigned in disagreement with the policies of the "National" Government.

'NEWS CHRONICLE'

In the late twenties, Layton's friends of the Cadbury family asked his help (which was at first to be only on the sides of policy and finance) with the *Daily News* and *The Star*. It was entirely characteristic of Layton that he did not limit himself to the original task. He was largely instrumental in negotiating the mergers of the *Daily News*, first with the *Westminster Gazette* and later with the *Daily Chronicle*, out of which the *News Chronicle* was born.

This became his major business interest and for nearly 15 years he was the executive head of a great newspaper enterprise, considering himself as editor-in-chief as well as managing director (though in fact he never held either title). He had retired from his executive duties before the papers fell into the financial difficulties that forced their closure in October, 1960. He was still, at that time, a director of The Daily News Ltd. and though he acquiesced in the closure (to which he could see no alternative) he regarded it as a bitter personal blow, the abandonment of an enterprise to which he felt that he had given the best years of his life.

For the first nine months of the Second World War, Layton, like many others, chafed under the Chamberlain administration's apparent unwillingness to use any of the experience or apply any of the lessons deriving from the First World War. When the Churchill Government was formed in May, 1940, Layton applied for work and was sent to the Ministry of Supply, where he quickly made his mark as Director-General of Programmes and later as Chairman of the Executive Committee. He moved to the Ministry of Production when that department was set up in the spring of 1942 and was able to see his ideas of co-ordinated planning put into effect by the creation of the Joint War Production Staff which brought together representatives of all the supply departments, the service departments and the Ministry of Labour, and of which he was the first head. Unfortunately, he was now in his sixties, his health could not stand the strain and he had to leave the Ministry before the end of the war.

EUROPEAN MOVEMENT

The postwar years were busy with newspaper business (especially with the supply of newsprint, where the intricate problems of administration and negotiation were tailor-made for him) and, later, with the House of Lords. The great enthusiasm of these years was the European movement, to which Layton gave a devotion that knew no limits.

He was created a Knight Bachelor in 1930 and was raised to the peerage as Baron Layton of Dane Hill in January, 1947. He was a member of the Legion of Honour and of a number of other foreign orders. He married in 1910 Miss Dorothea Osmastor and they had three sons and four daughters.

Lady Layton, well known as a Liberal and a champion of good causes, died in 1959, only a few weeks before what would have been their golden wedding anniversary. Layton published a memoir of her, *Dorothy*, in 1961. It was the story of a partnership which began when she as a student at Cambridge met Layton —a young don lecturing in economics. The heir is their eldest son, the Hon. Michael John Layton, who was born in 1912.

For all his honours and the eminence he achieved, Walter Layton remained true to the traditions in which he was brought up of simple living and high thinking. There was not a shadow of pomposity or of state in his composition, and no one ever looked less like a nobleman. Though it was often possible to be exasperated by him (particularly by his habit, strange in a journalist, of assuming that his own clear thinking could be conveyed to other men's minds without the use of intelligible words or finished sentences) it was quite impossible to dislike anyone so patently honest and well-meaning. Layton had no hobbies and indulged in few organized means of recreation. His pleasures were in music, in conversation and, in the latter years, above all in the company of the numerous and swelling tribe of his grandchildren, in whom he took an immense and undisguised pride.

February 15, 1966.

Admiral Sir Geoffrey Layton, G.B.E., K.C.B., K.C.M.G., D.S.O., died at Portsmouth on September 4, 1964, at the age of 80.

As Commander-in-Chief in China from 1940 to 1942 and in Ceylon from 1942 to 1945 he saw the temporary eclipse of British sea power in the Far East after Japan entered the war, and played a useful part in its revival by making secure the bases in Ceylon. After the loss of Admiral Phillips and his squadron off Malaya, and the fall of Singapore, he was given command of all forces, including civil, in Ceylon at a time when the situation in the Indian Ocean was critical. Under his able command the island served as a rallying point for the allies to retrieve their fortunes in this vital theatre. When he left three years later to become Commander-in-Chief at Portsmouth, strong forces on land, sea and in the air had been built up for the final offensive against Japan. Earlier in his career he served for over 20 years, including the 1914-18 War, in or with submarines.

SWAM TO FREEDOM

His name first came before the public when, after the loss of E 13 in the Baltic, he made good his escape from internment at Copenhagen, disguished as a Danish sailor, after swimming a canal.

Geoffrey Layton was born on April 20, 1884, the son of George Layton, solicitor, of Liverpool. He entered Britannia as a cadet in May, 1899. His midshipman's time from 1900 to 1901 was spent in the cruisers Niobe, in the Channel, and Cambrian, on the south-east coast of America. He specialized in submarines immediately on completing his courses for lieutenant in 1905, and within 18 months gained his first command at the age of 22.

After five years in submarines, he went back to general service, according to custom, from 1910 to 1912, and then returned to command successively C.23, E.13, the Swordfish, K.7 and K.6, during the 1914–18 War.

When in E.13, he was ordered from Harwich to the Baltic in response to an appeal from the Russians, who had only one submarine fit for service. On the early morning of August 19, 1915, owing to a compass failure, the vessel grounded on the Danish island of Saltholm, and was shelled by a German destroyer. The Danes refloated the vessel and interned the crew, but three months later her captain made good his escape. In recognition of further war service he was awarded the D.S.O. in 1918. In the same year he became Assistant to the Commodore (Submarines). He was promoted to captain in December, 1922, after commanding the 2nd Submarine Flotilla, and among other submarine appointments he held was the command of the 1st Flotilla and the post of Chief Staff Officer to the Rear-Admiral (S). From 1927 to 1929 he was Deputy Director of Operations at the Admiralty. He attended the Imperial Defence College during 1930, and from 1931 to 1933 was Chief of Staff in China. Next he commanded the battle cruiser Renown, and in May, 1934, was made Commodore of Portsmouth Naval Barracks. From 1936 to 1938 he was Director of Personal Services at the Admiralty. In August, 1938, he took command of the Battle Cruiser Squadron, and early in 1939 transferred to the command of the 1st Battle Squadron and assumed the duties of Second-in-Command, Mediterranean Fleet, first with Sir Dudley Pound and later with Sir Andrew Cunningham.

PEARL HARBOUR

In April, 1940, he was appointed Commander-in-Chief, China Station, from the following September. The British naval force there had been much reduced to meet demands in the war theatres, but in the autumn of 1941, in view of the changed situation in regard to Japan, measures were taken to restore it. Admiral Sir Tom Phillips left England with the Prince of Wales and Repulse as an advanced wing of a new Eastern Fleet, the arrival of which, it was hoped, might deter the war party in Tokyo.

Within a week of his arrival at Singapore, Japan attacked Pearl Harbour and invaded Malaya, and three days later Admiral Phillips and his ships were lost by air attack. Layton succeeded him as Commander-in-Chief Eastern Fleet, and left Singapore to organize the Fleet from less exposed bases, "so that the allies may gain sea supremacy in the Far East as soon as possible". After the loss of Java early in March, 1942, it became necessary to take special measure for the defence of Ceylon. Sir Geoffrey was appointed Commander-in-Chief, Ceylon, all naval, military, air and civil authorities in the area being placed under his direction. When the Japanese on April 5 staged a heavy attack by carrier-borne aircraft on Colombo, they found effective counter-measures already in operation; little damage was done, and the enemy lost 27 aircraft destroyed, five probably destroyed, and 25 damaged. The attack was not renewed.

Layton remained as C.-in-C. Ceylon until January, 1945, and on relinquishing his command was created K.C.M.G. On March 1, 1945, he became Commander-in-Chief at Portsmouth, retiring in 1947. He was made C.B.E. in the New Year's Honours that year.

Sir Geoffrey was married in 1908 to Eleanor Gwladys, daughter of F. T. Langley, of Tettenhall, Wolverhampton, and had three daughters.

September 7, 1964.

Sir James Learmonth, K.C.V.O., C.B.E., who died on September 27, 1967, at the age of 72, was formerly Professor of Surgery and Regius Professor of Clinical Surgery in Edinburgh University.

An outstanding authority on vascular complaints it was he who was called in in November, 1948, to examine the serious condition of King George VI's right foot. He found that because of the obstruction to the circulation through the leg arteries there was a fear that the right leg might have to be amputated. The proposed royal tour of Australia and New Zealand was put off and on March 12, 1949, Learmonth, assisted by Professor Paterson Ross, operated on the King at Buckingham Palace. Sir John Wheeler-Bennett in his life of the King remarks that Learmonth was in almost constant attendance on his patient from November, 1948 to January, 1949, again for much of March and was later frequently consulted. "There is no doubt", wrote Wheeler-Bennett, "that his unremitting care and the wise advice which he gave to the King about the necessary change in the tempo of his life and activities were a major factor in saving his right leg from amputation. This the King appreciated."

After the final examination George VI asked Learmonth to hand him his bath robe and slippers. Then pushing forward a stool and picking up a sword, hitherto hidden, he said: "You used a knife on me, now I'm going to use one on you", and bidding him kneel bestowed upon him the accolade of knighthood.

The son of William Learmonth, he was educated at Girthon School, Kilmarnock Academy and Glasgow University where he graduated with honours and won the Brunton Medal for the most distinguished graduate in medicine for the year.

He held appointments at the Mayo Clinic, at the University of Minnesota and for seven years from 1932 was Regius Professor of Surgery in the University of Aberdeen. He was Lister Medallist in 1951 and Sir Arthur Sims Commonwealth Travelling Professor of the R.C.S. in 1954. He was formerly honorary surgeon to the Queen in Scotland and at his death was an extra surgeon to her Majesty.

He married in 1925 Charlotte Newell and they had a son and a daughter.

September 28, 1967.

Lord Leathers, P.C., C.H., Minister of War Transport from 1941 to 1945, and Secretary of State for the Co-ordination of Transport, Fuel and Power from 1951 to 1953, died on March 19, 1965, at the age of 81.

A life-time's experience had made him a recognized authority on coal and shipping, and he had exhibited gifts of organization which fully justified his appointment to the all-important office of Minister of War Transport, for which Churchill selected him. It fell to Leathers to face the immense problems not only of the external but also of the internal communications of the country at a period when its existence as well as its war effort depended on them. From the first he saw transport as a continuous process from the interior to the coast and to its overseas destinations. Indeed, the unification of the national system of transport which did so much to overcome the difficulties he encountered was primarily due to him.

When the Conservatives were returned to power in 1951, Leathers was recalled to become one of the "overlords" whom Churchill appointed to coordinate various offices. At the age of 67 he was chosen to be Secretary of State for the Coordination of Transport, Fuel and Power. He had a difficult task. The system of "overlords" was neither popular nor could it be said to be successful. His duties were not only to coordinate transport but also fuel and power production. He retired from office in September, 1953, and took up once more the threads of his many business interests. In the New Year Honours of 1954 he was raised to a viscounty, which was gazetted by the name, style and title of Viscount Leathers, of Purfleet, in the county of Essex.

Frederick James Leathers was born in 1883, the son of Robert and Emily Leathers of Stowmarket, Suffolk. His father died when he was young and at fifteen he entered commercial life in a business which was subsequently merged in William Cory & Sons, Limited, and in 1916 was appointed managing director of it. In his business career he was closely associated with the late Lord Inchcape's group of companies, and eventually became chairman or director of a large number of them as well as of other enterprises, such as collieries, shipping and cement companies. In the First World War he was associated with the Ministry of Shipping.

TRANSPORT EXECUTIVE

In May, 1940, by then a shipping expert of international repute, he joined the Ministry of Shipping as adviser upon fuel problems and also took charge of coal bunkers all over the world and of shipment of coal and fuel. In 1941 he was appointed Minister of War Transport and in that capacity head of the Departments of Shipping and Transport, then amalgamated for the first time. He was also made a member of the transport executive. Almost simultaneously he was created Lord Leathers of Purfleet.

In so far as the general public was concerned, his task, for all its vital importance, was unspectacular, and he spoke only on rare occasions. He made it clear, however, that he looked beyond the immediate emergencies of the war to the creation after it of a sound system of national transport. Not the least of his problems were the conveyance of the huge supplies furnished to the Soviets and to the British forces overseas.

He shared with his Prime Minister the secrets and burdens of every great military operation and conference, from Casablanca to Potsdam. His most anxious days were undoubtedly during the Battle of the Atlantic. The transport of the United States forces to Europe and North Africa, and the success of the Normandy invasion, depended greatly on Leathers's knowledge of shipping and his remarkable gifts of organization and improvisation. He was, in fact, the one man responsible for all the nation's communications by land and sea.

In 1907 he married Miss Emily Ethel Baxter and she, two sons and one daughter, survive him. His title passes to the Hon. Frederick Alan Leathers.

March 20, 1965.

With the death of **Le Corbusier** (Charles-Edouard Jeanneret-Gris), while swimming on August 27, 1965, the world lost one of its greatest architects and certainly the most controversial architectural figure of our time.

Le Corbusier was both a major pioneer of the modern architectural movement and a visionary who saw in the revitalizing of urban planning and in a new architecture the one hope for the future wellbeing of western man. Broadly he was convinced that our towns should be built upward instead of outward and that we should separate our pedestrians from our motor traffic leaving the land for large open spaces laid out with trees and lawns. He advocated this vision with relentless propaganda and great, even poetic eloquence setting out his faith in his many writings of which the best known are perhaps *Vers une architecture* (1923) and *La Ville Radieuse* (1935): "I have said that the materials of city planning are: sky, space, trees, steel and cement, in that order and that hierarchy." Learning from earlier pioneers like Peter Behrens, Auguste Perret and Tony Garnier, and standing in line with such modern masters as Taut, Poelzig, Oud and Mallet Stevens, he outvied them all by the reach and freshness of his imagination and the variety and inventiveness of his resource.

Le Corbusier found in ferro-concrete a new material for the entire remaking of urban life which seemed to him to be dictated by the growth of towns and populations and permitted by modern developments in engineering in such fields as lighting and heating, air-conditioning, insulation against noise, lifts, ventilation, and the manipulation of large surfaces of glass. He was a notable innovator in house construction and design, and developed a method whereby the structure hangs on concrete columns thus permitting complete freedom of planning on each floor. A common feature of much of his early domestic building is the open, or partially open, ground floor which he incorporated later in many larger buildings, and which has been widely copied throughout the world. He significantly described the house as "a machine for living in", and in *Quand les Cathédrales étaient blanches* (1937) his argument was that mankind's nostalgia for the sky, trees, and the country had, in fact, had no other result than the annihilation of large spaces of real country, the cancerous spreading of the suburb, and all the waste and fatigue of the long daily journey to and from one's place of work.

Much of Le Corbusier's design, especially in his domestic buildings, was controlled by a scale based on human proportions which he called The Modulor. This resulted in designing according to geometric principles, and by the golden section, which determined the proportions of many of his famous houses, and influenced the design of buildings like the immense block of flats at Marseilles.

VIRTUES OF FERRO-CONCRETE

Jeanneret came of a Swiss watchmaking family and was born on 6 October, 1887, at La Chaux-de-Fonds, in the Canton of Neuchatel. His mother, whose name was Perret, passed on to him her musical tastes; but, on leaving school in 1900, he entered a local school of arts and crafts, where his teacher was Charles L'Eplatenier. At 18 he headed a group of fifteen students who built a house for L'Eplatenier. There followed a period of study of early medieval art in Italy, and in 1908 Jeanneret entered the studio of Josef Hoffman, in Vienna. But he found the atmosphere uncongenial, and within a few months went to Paris to study under Auguste Perret, who taught him the virtues of ferro-concrete.

In 1910 his old school at La Chaux-de-Fonds financed a trip which began with a period of work in the studio of Peter Behrens, in Berlin, and then carried him on to Greece and Rome and the Middle East, whose "architecture of masses brought together in the sun" came as a revelation and remained as an inspiration to him all his life. From 1911 to 1914 he was in Switzerland, working as an interior designer, but during that time he built a house for his father. From 1914 to 1921 he worked in Paris as a factory manager, but kept up a brisk sideline practice as architect, painter, and journalist. Being Swiss, he was a neutral in the war. In 1916 he held a big exhibition of his water-colours at the Kunsthaus, Zurich; the following year came some abattoirs in ferro-concrete at Bordeaux, and in 1920, with Dermée and Ozenfant, he launched a review called *L'Esprit Nouveau*, which lasted until 1925.

Meanwhile in 1922 he started an architectural practice in Paris with his cousin Pierre using his maternal grandfather's name, Le Corbusier, for architecture, and painting under his own name. Working always against ultra-conservative opposition, the cousins nevertheless soon made their way by sheer force of original thought and practice. As long before as 1914 Le Corbusier had evolved the "Domino" framework for standard concrete houses. The cousins now pressed on with this device, but its use was held up by war and politics until the operation of the Loucheur Law in 1929. In their first year of partnership the Jeannerets produced for the Autumn Salon a plan and panorama for a City of Three Million Inhabitants, and at the same exhibition showed the "Citrohan House", "a house like a car, conceived and worked like a bus or a ship's cabin". This scheme was first put into practical production in the Weissenhof Colony at Stuttgart in 1925–27.

TRAFFIC AND PLANNING

In this period from 1922 onwards Le Corbusier designed, with his cousin, those houses in concrete where the structure is suspended on concrete columns, and planned to give flexibility on each floor, and designed in conformity with geometric formulae like the golden section. The most famous of these houses, such as that at Garches, near Paris (1926), and the Villa Savoye at Poissy (1931) excited interest and discussion throughout the world, and it is doubtful if any houses of the century have won greater fame.

Le Corbusier had been profoundly struck by the advance in constructional engineering during the war and by the effect of the motor car on traffic circulation and the planning of cities. Coming to the conclusion that the car was responsible for muddle and mess, he reasoned that if this point of view were put to one of the big motor manufacturers, money might be forthcoming from that source to finance a thorough exploration of the possibilities of replanning the whole of central Paris. The Peugeot and Citroen companies showed no interest, but M. Mongmeron, of Voisin, agreed to support him. Thus there came into being the Voisin Plan for Paris, shown at the International Exhibition of Decorative Art in 1925. It comprised a system of skyscrapers, "stepped" and set back, cruciform in shape, with no interior wells and occupying only 5 per cent of the total area.

This far-reaching and revolutionary plan, and others comparable to it, were held up because of the enormous expense involved and the difficulty of getting municipalities and vested interests to throw all current ideas of town planning on the scrap heap. But, apart from a healthy domestic practice, the Jeannerets, as the years went on, were entrusted with many ambitious schemes, like the Centrosoyus (Co-operative) building in Moscow, reorganization plans for Algiers, Nemours (North Africa), Antwerp, Barcelona, Stockholm, and the sixth *arrondissement* of Paris. During the thirties of the century much work was done in South America. They won first prize in 1927 for a design for the Palace of the League of Nations, at Geneva, but the scheme was later rejected. Other setbacks were the rejection of the city plans at the Paris Exhibition of 1937 and the failure of the committee for the Swiss National Exhibition, Zurich, 1939, to invite the participation of the firm.

The year 1940, with its cataclysmic events, broke up the partnership. Pierre Jeanneret settled in Grenoble. Le Corbusier, after taking refuge in unoccupied France, returned to Paris in 1942, in which year he evolved a master plan for Algiers, based on earlier studies. From 1934 onwards he had been windening his scope, by consultation with sociologists and engineers. He had from the first conceived of architecture as one element in the integration of a modern civilization, and now, during the occupation period, he founded *Ascoral* (*L'Assemblée de Constructeurs pour une Rénovation Architecturale*), which included architects, farmers, lawyers, economists, and craftsmen.

THE RONCHAMP CHAPEL

In 1945 he founded *Atbat* (*L'Atelier des Batisseurs*), in association with 25 engineers and architects, and the same year headed a cultural relations mission to the United States. This, indeed, was a fruitful year. It brought the completion of one of his most ambitious and forward-looking public buildings, the Ministry of National Education and Public Health at Rio de Janeiro, which embodied his distinctive feature, the use of *brise-soleils*, to temper excessive glare in summer and to catch as much sunshine as possible in winter. It brought also a commission to redesign the industrial town of La Pallice (heavily bombed by the R.A.F. while it was in German occupation). His notion here was to preserve the undamaged old Gothic town of La Rochelle in a green belt separating it from a new linear design for the industrial and residential twin-town of La Pallice, to the west, on the sea-coast.

In October, 1952, there was completed, at Marseilles, a "town for 1,600 people under one roof", built in the teeth of much virulent criticism and opposition, at a cost of some 350m. francs. Based on concrete piles, it contained almost every conceivable facility on the premises—shops, laundry, hospital, club rooms, creche, swimming pool, running track, gymnasium, roof garden, and had an external wall of sheer glass, with *brise-soleils*. The whole is placed in a park of eight acres.

The famous chapel at Ronchamp built in 1950–55 is a very different work from Le Corbusier's previous building and represents another side of the architect. It replaces a former chapel destroyed by bombing. The building is of concrete and stone with a very irregular plan with two towers and one wall of thick pyramidal section pierced by small irregularly placed windows admitting a small amount of light, the purpose of which is to give a religious atmosphere. Light is also admitted by a space of a few centimetres between the walls and the curved concrete roof, while the floor slopes with the natural slope of the hill. It is an organic conception yet controlled in design by the architect's "Modulor" theory. Few modern buildings have been the subject of more enthusiastic study among architectural students.

Another notable ecclesiastical building is the monastery and church for 100 Dominican Friars at Eveux-sur-Arbreste near Lyons, which was built in 1954–58. Constructed of reinforced concrete on the slope of a valley adjoining a forest it provides, on the upper floors, for individual human needs, 100 cells each with a balcony opening to the valley, and for the needs of the community on the ground floor in the church, refectory, chapter house and other smaller rooms.

NEW PUNJAB CAPITAL

Perhaps Le Corbusier's greatest town planning and building achievement is to be seen at Chandigarh, the new capital of Punjab. The first stage of this city is for a population of 150,000, but it is to be designed ultimately for a population of half a million. Building began early in the fifties and will probably continue throughout the century. It is the product of team work, but Le Corbusier had a major role for an adviser to the Government. He prepared the outline plan and directed the planning for the future growth of the city while he was appointed architect of the capital buildings and the surrounding park.

The site of Chandigarh lies at the foot of the Himalaya mountains on a vast plateau between two great rivers, which are dry for 10 months of the year. A lake was created by a dam about 66ft. high by about $2\frac{1}{2}$ miles long to irrigate the area as a first stage in building the city. Le Corbusier's plan follows the classical formal system of rectangular division with the capitol in the centre, which consists of the Parliament building, the secretariat, the Governor's palace, law courts, and a symbolic sculpture of "the open hand" all set among large pools of water in a spacious park.

Architect, engineer, mural painter, water-colourist, Le Corbusier was also a prolific author, beginning with *Vers une Architecture* in 1922, continuing with *Urbanisme* (1924), *Précisions* (1930), *La Ville Radieuse* (1935), *Destin de Paris* (1941), *Perspectives Humaines* (1946), *Propos d'Urbanisme* (1946), *Le Modulor* (1951), and *L'Unité d'Habitation de Marseille* (1952), most of which have been translated into the European languages and Japanese.

Analogies were drawn from the liner, the motor car, and the aeroplane. Standardization was insisted on in the interests of speed, cheapness, and order. Le Corbusier's prose was rhetorical, combative, and positive in statement, so that he often laid himself open to easy refutation. Yet in spite of all the criticism of Le Corbusier's ideas, there can be no question of the stimulating quality of his imagination, the bright, bold clarity of his mind, and the ingenuity, effectiveness, and beauty of many of his buildings.

Le Corbusier married Yvonne Gallis, who died in 1957. Though no seeker after national or academic distinctions he accepted the honorary degree of Ph.D. from Zurich in 1933 and the R.I.B.A. Gold Medal for architecture in 1953, but he refused the ribbon of Chevalier of the Legion of Honour. On the occasion of his seventieth birthday a comprehensive exhibition of his work was held in Switzerland, which subsequently travelled the western world. It was shown in London in 1959, the year Cambridge made him an honorary LL.D.

August 28, 1965.

Dr. Una Ledingham, who died on November 19, 1965, at the age of 65, will be remembered as an outstanding woman physician and medical teacher to whom numerous student generations of women doctors were indebted.

During the period after the 1914–18 War a number of very remarkable women doctors qualified from the London School of Medicine. Names that might be mentioned are those of Dr. Katharine Lloyd-Williams, Dr. Janet Aitken, Miss Geraldine Barry, Miss Gladys Hill, and others. At this time the position of the woman doctor was well established but women still faced great difficulties in obtaining the highest medical posts and in entering general practice, Una Ledingham, who was one of this group, through both ability and personality succeeded in overcoming these difficulties.

Una Christina Ledingham was born on January 2, 1900, the daughter of the late J. L. Garvin, C.H., editor of *The Observer*, and Christina Wilson. Brought up in a family where literature and the arts rather than science and medicine afforded the background, she early showed her independence both in her choice of career and in her marriage into the medical profession. She was educated at the South Hampstead High School and the London School of Medicine for Women (now the Royal Free Hospital School of Medicine), which until 1947 admitted only women medical students. She had a distinguished career as a student, obtaining several prizes, and she qualified M.B., B.S., London, with honours and distinction in forensic medicine in 1923.

After graduating she was first elected House Physician at the Brompton Hospital for Diseases of the Chest, and then House Physician to the Royal Free Hospital. From 1924 to 1925 she was Medical Officer to the Out-Patients at the Royal Northern Hospital, and in 1925 she returned to the Royal Free Hospital as Medical Registrar. From 1929 until 1931 she was First Assistant to the Children's Department of the Royal Free Hospital until her election to the Consultant Staff as Assistant Physician in 1931. She also held the appointment of First Fellow of the Asthma Research Council so that by the time she was elected consultant she had a wide knowledge and experience of general medicine which she later put to good use as a clinician and teacher. She obtained the M.D., London, in 1927, and the M.R.C.P., London, in 1928. She was elected F.R.C.P. in 1947.

Una Ledingham made her life's work at the Royal Free Hospital, though she was for some years Consultant Physician to the Marie Curie Hospital, and remained consulting physician after her resignation from the staff. She developed a special interest and knowledge of diabetes and was Physician-in-charge of the Diabetic Clinic at the Royal Free Hospital and the Hampstead General Hospital. She was particularly interested in the problems of the pregnant diabetic woman and found ample scope for this in the large maternity department of the hospital. During the war, in addition to her normal work, she took over the running of her husband's practice while he was absent on active service.

Her ability as a medical teacher was acknowledged by her election as a recognized teacher in the University of London. She later became an Examiner in Medicine to the University of London and also examined for the Conjoint Board and for the Diploma in Nursing. She was not a prolific writer but she made some notable contributions to literature on the subject of diabetes. She was also Reviewer in General Medicine for the *Medical Annual* from 1948 to 1956. She was a member of the board of governors of the Royal Free Hospital from 1957 to 1960, at a time when the plans for the rebuilding of the hospital on a new site in Hampstead were in a formative phase.

She married in 1925 Dr. Jock Ledingham, who survives her, together with her daughter and her son, Dr. John Ledingham, now physician to Westminster Hospital. A woman of beauty, with strong personality and a generous nature, she managed to combine a distinguished medical career with a full family and social life. In the house at the corner of Ladbroke Square where she and her husband had lived ever since their marriage, people from all walks of life, both those who owed much to her medical knowledge, and those who were just friends, were always assured of a warm welcome.

November 20, 1965.

Gypsy Rose Lee, the sophisticated stripper who disapproved of nudity, died in Los Angeles on April 26, 1970. She was 56.

Miss Lee outgrew an "ugly duckling" childhood to become the undisputed queen of burlesque, a peculiarly American phenomenon that is now on its own deathbed. She was not even old enough to attend school when she joined her mother and sister June—later to become June Havoc, the film star—on the ruthless vaudeville circuit in an act called "Dainty June and her Newsboy Songsters".

At 16, she encountered Tessie the Tassel-Twirler at Kansas City's old Missouri theatre. Dainty June and her Newsboy Songsters were out of work and the only job going was a burlesque turn. Rose grabbed it because "I was tired of starving". Tessie the Tassel-Twirler gave Rose her first lessons in the fine art of stripping, and the future duchess of striptease never forgot Tessie's early advice: "In burlesque, you've gotta leave 'em hungry for more. You don't dump the whole roast on the platter." Gypsy never did. She regarded striptease as an art form spicing her act with heady quotations from such austere thinkers as Aldous Huxley and Spinoza. And she later found the theatre's trend towards nudity not at all to her liking.

By the time she was 17 she was a star at Billy Minsky's Republic theatre in New York.

ACT AS GOSPELLER

She quickly moved into Ziegfeld's Follies. She went to Hollywood—to star, among others, as the Biblethumping gospeller Aimee Semple McPherson—and in May 1937, at the pinnacle of her fame, announced her retirement from the skin game. That year she married the first of her three husbands—in a bouncing motorboat off the California coast.

Gypsy, by now an American folk heroine, turned her considerable energies to writing: she published such best-selling thrillers as *G-String Murders*, *Mother Finds a Body* and finally *Gypsy*, an autobiography that later became a Broadway musical and a Hollywood film.

It may seem pretentious to speak of artistry in relation to her act, but it was certainly a form of entertainment which required a high degree of professionalism, in just the same way as the work of the great music-hall comedians from Dan Leno to Max Miller required an equal skill and knowledge. Of Gypsy Rose Lee it could perhaps be said that she never really took very much off except her competitors whom she knew to be vastly inferior to herself.

There was no real place for her in the cinema, and least of all in the rather prudish era of Hollywood in the 1930s, although she did make a few minor and rather halfhearted appearances, and she was seen as late as 1952 in *Babes of Baghdad*. Thus she remained for most filmgoers of the period, on both sides of the Atlantic, as little more than a naughty legend, suggestive of a union between the Folies Bergères and the honky-tonk saloons of the old West. What made her distinctive was not only her style and professionalism, but also her poise, her intelligence and her sense of humour.

Her real name was Rose Louise Hovick and she was born in Seattle, Washington, in 1914.

April 28, 1970.

John Fishwick Leeming, whose death was announced on July 7, 1965, was one of the pioneers of gliding and light aeroplane flying in Britain.

He and Bert Hinkler were the first to land an aeroplane on the summit of Helvellyn, a peak in the Lake District over 8,000 ft. high, and a plaque still marks the spot. He was responsible for much of the initial organization of the Light Aero Club movement, and was chairman of the Lancashire Aero Club from 1924 to 1928; he was also a member of the General Council of Light Aeroplane Clubs, and a member of the Royal Aero Club Racing Committee.

In the early days of the Second World War, as a squadron leader, he was flying with Air Marshal Boyd from Cairo when they were forced down over Sicily and taken prisoner. At the Villa Orsini they spent their captivity with such British military leaders as Generals Neame, O'Connor, Carton de Wiart and Gambier-Parry. By feigning madness Leeming was able to achieve repatriation, and he told the story of this part of his war service in *Always Tomorrow*.

In retirement Leeming turned more to his favourite hobby of writing and produced a series of humorous novels set in Italy, which he loved dearly and regarded almost as a second home. These were published in several languages and sold for films.

He was a keen gardener and published two books on the subject. At the time of his death he was working on an historical study of the Gunpowder Plot and had just completed a book on his pet sheep Clwyd.

His children's books—*Claudius, the Bee* and *Thanks to Claudius* were most popular, and published before the war. In 1936 he wrote *Airdays* stories of his flying experiences up to that time.

A sensitive and shy man with a deep love of the countryside, Leeming had a delightful sense of humour.

July 8, 1965.

Sir Reginald Leeper, G.B.E., K.C.M.G., whom Goebbels, the Nazi propagandist, once described as his most dangerous opponent in the Foreign Office, died on February 2, 1968, at his London home. He was 79.

As an assistant to the wartime Director General of Political Warfare, Leeper was one of those concerned in providing a counterblast to Nazi propaganda. During his career he was British Ambassador to Greece and to Argentina.

Leeper, always called Rex by his friends and colleagues, was one of that small but talented band of young Australians who joined the British Diplomatic Service in the twenties or early thirties. Another was his elder brother, Allen, whose death in 1935 at the age of 48 was a poignant grief to Rex and all who knew him, and a heavy loss to the Foreign Office.

Rex Leeper himself brought many distinctive gifts to diplomacy—an alert and inquiring mind; strong convictions which he often hid behind his unruffled, quizzical bearing; powers of concentration and analysis; a pleasant strain of humour, expressed in his light, even voice; and a great capacity for hard work without showing the strain.

Reginald Wildig Allen Leeper was born in Sydney on March 25, 1888. He was the son of Alexander Leeper, a distinguished classical scholar, and Warden of Trinity College, Melbourne. Rex was educated at Melbourne Grammar School, then at his father's college, from which he went with a scholarship to New College, Oxford. He was an excellent linguist and student of modern history and in 1916 joined the Intelligence Division of the government's Department of Information. A year later he was appointed to the Foreign Office political intelligence department and did valuable work in connexion with political problems raised in the Paris Peace Conference. His service was recognized in 1920 when he was appointed permanently to the Diplomatic Service of the Foreign Office. He joined the northern department. He had learnt Russian with the exiled Litvinov and it fell to him to negotiate the exchange of that future Soviet Commissar against Mr. (later Sir) Robert Bruce-Lockhart, the British Consul in Moscow, whom the Soviet Government had arrested and detained. Leeper was First Secretary of the British Legation in Warsaw from 1923 to 1924, and added Polish to the languages he could speak and write. He returned to this post in 1927. He had pondered on the fact that British diplomacy had concentrated on politics, then later on trade, to the exclusion of what might in general be called cultural relations. When he was transferred to the Foreign Office in 1929 he began to give practical effect to his ideas.

START OF BRITISH COUNCIL

The Government agreed to encourage the teaching of English in foreign countries, and in making known British artistic and scientific achievements. From these small beginnings grew the British Council with its large and active organization. Leeper was appointed honorary vice-president of the British Council in 1949, a recognition of his original interest.

The most active part of his career, however, was still to come. In 1933 he was promoted to be Counsellor and made head of the Foreign Office News Department, a post which he kept throughout that critical period of British history gaining the confidence and esteem of the representatives of newspapers, both British and foreign. Leeper shared the views of his friend and chief, Sir Robert Vansittart, Permanent Under-Secretary of State, that it was necessary to make it clear to the German Government that Great Britain would actively assist in repelling any unprovoked aggression. A succession of Prime Ministers and Foreign Ministers did not favour this, and Leeper was increasingly frustrated over the information and guidance he was to give to the press. He was instrumental in bringing back from his holiday in Switzerland the Foreign Secretary, Sir Samuel Hoare, to whom he made clear the uproar which the Hoare-Laval plan to give Abyssinian territory to the Italians had caused in Great Britain. When Hitler sent troops into the Rhineland, Leeper was consulted by the new Foreign Secretary, Anthony Eden, about the probable reactions of British public opinion. "I think", he replied, "they will say that Germany is on her own territory." With developments in connexion with Czechoslovakia the situation became more and more embarrassing. The Foreign Office was practically excluded from the negotiations and the Prime Minister's office dealt with the Press. Nevertheless, on Vansittart's recommendations and with Lord Halifax's approval, on September 26, 1938, he issued a communique saying that if, "in spite of the efforts made by the Prime Minister, a German attack is made on Czechoslovakia, the immediate result would be that France will be bound to come to her assistance, and Great Britain and Russia would certainly stand by France". This proved ineffective to halt the Munich compromise, and thereafter Leeper, like many of his colleagues, felt that war with Germany was inevitable.

But for the outbreak of war in 1939 Leeper would have gone to Bucharest as H.M. Minister. Instead he was put in charge of a revived Political Intelligence Department. But before long he was busy with the organization known as the Political War Executive which, from headquarters in the country, carried on radio and other propaganda and political warfare in enemy-occupied countries. Leeper had assembled an excellent team, but there were difficulties of coordination between the various authorities and in 1943 he returned to the Foreign Office. He was appointed H.M. Ambassador to the Greek Government, first in Cairo, and eventually on its return to Athens.

It was a task of the utmost complexity, and Leeper gave a frank account of it in his book, published in 1950. *When Greek meets Greek*. This was an apt title, for it was a prolonged and bitter civil war with which Leeper was confronted, between the factions who had provided the core of resistance under the German occupation. One faction was communist in politics, and lent themselves to the attempt, later encouraged by Moscow and conducted from across the Bulgarian border, to turn Greece into a Soviet satellite. There was also bitter antagonism between the monarchists and the republicans. At a critical moment Leeper secured British Government approval for the proposal that King George should appoint the widely respected Archbishop of Athens, Damaskinos, as Regent. Churchill and Eden both went to Athens to study the situation on the spot. British troops acted in support of the Government, and Leeper was publicly attacked for this. He had, however, executed the British Government's policy, maintained when Attlee succeeded Churchill, that support should be given to the restoration of civil peace and the restoration of the Greek economy. In the fighting in Athens the British Embassy was in the firing line, but order was eventually restored, and in March, 1946, free elections returned an anti-Communist, and pro-monarchist government. King George returned, but died suddenly in March, 1947. Leeper had the satisfaction of seeing the heavy burden the British had borne in restoring and maintaining order and bringing relief to a destitute people eased by the assumption of responsibility by President Truman's Administration. In 1948 Leeper was transferred as Ambassador to Argentina, where he remained for two years.

In 1916 he had married Primrose Dundas, and she shared with him all the difficulties and baffling problems of a long, exacting, and distinguished career. They had two daughters. Leeper had been made K.C.M.G. in 1945, and when he retired from the Foreign Service in 1949 he was given the Grand Cross of the Order of the British Empire.

His active mind and negotiating ability were to be employed after his official retirement. In 1950 he was appointed a director of the De Beers Consolidated Mines Company (from which he retired in 1965).

February 5, 1968.

Admiral of the Fleet Sir Michael Le Fanu died on November 28, 1970, in London. He was 57.

Le Fanu was Chief of Naval Staff and First Sea Lord from 1968 until he retired. On medical advice, Le Fanu had withdrawn his acceptance of the appointment of Chief of Defence Staff, which he would have taken up a month before he died.

He was born in 1913, and after leaving the Royal Naval College, Dartmouth, served as midshipman and then sub-lieutenant. In 1939 he joined H.M.S. Aurora as first lieutenant and gunnery officer and saw service in Norway, the Atlantic, the Arctic and the Mediterranean. He was awarded the D.S.C. for helping to destroy an Italian convoy. Towards the end of the war he was liaison officer with the United States third and fifth fleets in the Pacific.

Returning to the United Kingdom, he was experimental commander at the Gunnery school on Whale Island for two years. In 1949 he was promoted to Captain and was naval assistant to the Third Sea Lord until 1951, when he took command of the Third Training Squadron. In 1953 he returned to the Admiralty to serve on the First Sea Lord's Staff.

He became Rear-Admiral in 1958, and was Director-General, Weapons and Radio for two years before becoming Flag Officer, second-in-command, Far East station. He returned in 1961 to become a Lord Commissioner of the Admiralty and Third Sea Lord and Controller of the Navy—the youngest for 70 years.

Le Fanu became Admiral in September, 1965, and later that year, Commander-in-Chief, Middle East, in Aden. He was made Admiral of the Fleet in July, 1970.

Le Fanu became a Companion of the Order of the Bath in 1960, a Knight Commander of the order in 1963, and a Knight Grand Cross in 1968. He leaves a widow, two sons, and a daughter.

Sir Michael was a sailor's sailor who fought pedantry and protocol and took pride in his victory over both. He was called Ginger because of his red hair but the nickname could have been an appellation, indicating his independence of spirit and his hatred of red tape.

His courage in the face of leukaemia became a legend in his lifetime. Even in the last few months he led a charity walk through Richmond Park and bought a kayak canoe which he loved to paddle down river from Putney to Greenwich, then back again with the changing tide—a round trip of six hours.

His father was a naval captain and the young Le Fanu decided to join the Navy at an early age. It was sadly ironic that his term as First Sea Lord was marked by a period of naval contraction rather than expansion, and of subjugation to Whitehall economies. Perhaps one of his greatest achievements was the maintenance of a high morale throughout the senior service at such a difficult time.

A wit dubbed him "Dry Ginger" when he had to preside over the ending of the Navy's rum ration. But Le Fanu was never a dry man, and "deep distress" felt at his death was voiced by the First Sea Lord.

November 30, 1970.

Herbert Lehman, who died in New York on December 5, 1963, at the age of 85, served for 10 years as Democratic Governor of New York, for three years as the first director-general of U.N.R.R.A., and then for eight years in the Senate. Yet Lehman was one of those men whose influence in American public life far transcended the offices he held. It is as an unswerving liberal, a man of integrity and rare devotion to principle in politics that he deserves to be remembered.

As Governor of New York in the days of the New Deal he proved himself an able and imaginative administrator, and one of the most zealous and valued supporters of Franklin Roosevelt. Yet he did not hesitate to attack Roosevelt's misguided and ill-fated scheme to pack the Supreme Court, because he felt that it infringed constitutional principles. Although no hard-headed political calculator, he was an immensely successful vote-getter—he had larger majorities as Governor than either Al Smith or Franklin Roosevelt before him. As a persistent foe of racial and religious discrimination, he attracted particularly large followings among the minority groups who play such an important part in New York politics. As a persistent campaigner for civil rights he won the trust of Negroes, and as a Jew himself his appeal was obvious to the most politically important minority in New York. If he lacked the feel for that subtle form of political horse-trading that makes a man a power in the Senate, and if at times he seemed a somewhat lonely campaigner in Congress for the causes he believed in, he nevertheless retained his stature. In his later years he became an elder statesman revered by liberals throughout the United States. Outspoken in his attacks on McCarthyism at the time when that did require political courage, still fighting as doughtily as ever for reform of the Democratic Party in New York, he always lived up to his role of the practical idealist in politics.

BANKING FAMILY

Herbert Henry Lehman was born in New York City on March 28, 1878. His father had emigrated from Germany and, after being engaged in the cotton business in Montgomery, Alabama, had set up as an investment banker in New York. Herbert Lehman graduated from Williams College, Massachusetts, in 1899, and after nearly 10 years with a Brooklyn textile manufacturing firm joined the family banking business, in which he remained for 20 years and established a personal fortune, withdrawing from active participation in 1928, when he entered politics.

Two years earlier he had supported Al Smith in his campaign for election to the governorship of New York, and in 1928 he was chairman of the Democratic National Committee's finance committee in connexion with Al Smith's unsuccessful campaign for the presidency. In that election Lehman himself was elected Lieutenant-Governor under Franklin Roosevelt. This was not his first association with the future President, for during the 1914–18 War Lehman had been a civilian assistant to Franklin Roosevelt when the latter was Assistant Secretary of the Navy.

In 1932 Lehman succeeded Roosevelt as Governor of New York and retained office at subsequent elections, resigning in December, 1942. His nomination as Governor was forced upon the state Democratic Party by Roosevelt and Smith together against the wishes of Tammany. When Lehman wished to retire from the governorship in 1936 Roosevelt persuaded him to remain on account of his staunch support of the New Deal. Lehman showed himself an efficient Governor of New York. He was helped by the fact that the arrival of Roosevelt in the White House lifted the whole country out of the slough of despond into which it had fallen, but he played an important part himself in placing the resources of the state behind the implementation of measures of social reform. At the same time his record as a banker was a reassurance to the more Conservative elements.

Lehman had already declined nomination for re-election to the governorship when he resigned in order to take charge of the Office of Foreign Relief and Rehabilitation Operations. The task of organizing relief for devastated Europe was a many-sided one, and so were the difficulties.

Not least of the difficulties was that Roosevelt was no believer in great administrative tidiness and allowed Governmental agencies to multiply and compete for jurisdiction. When the Allies invaded North Africa, Lehman and his staff waited for several months seeking permission from the United States Army to begin operations. Later there were disagreements with the newly created Office of Foreign Economic Co-ordination under the State Department and the Lease Lend Administration, and Lehman's resignation was expected by many people.

IN THE SENATE

In the meantime, however, the plans on which Lehman had been working for the international organization of relief were coming nearer to maturity. On November 9, 1943, 44 countries signed an agreement constituting the United Nations Relief and Rehabilitation Administration. Lehman became the first Director-General of the new organization, and showed himself a capable and conscientious administrator, retaining office until March 12, 1946, when he resigned. He was out of the public eye until in November, 1948, he was elected to the Senate winning the seat in a contest with John Foster Dulles. He retired from the Senate, though not from active concern with public affairs, in 1957.

From his youth Lehman actively interested himself in social work. During the 1914–18 War he was one of a group of influential New York Jews who collected large sums of money for their suffering co-religionists, and, as was natural, he was identified with numerous American Jewish organizations. Among the other causes in which he interested himself were the Boy Scouts of America.

In 1910 he married Miss Edith Louise Altschul, of San Francisco. They had two sons and one daughter. The elder son was killed in the last war.

December 6, 1963.

Vivien Leigh, the stage and film actress, was found dead in bed at her London home on July 8, 1967. She was 53.

At the age of 21 she had been a beautiful girl, and, literally, an overnight celebrity; for a number of years she had been the wife and stage partner of Sir Laurence Oliver. She died when still in mid-career; until the other day she was studying a role in the forthcoming production of a play by Edward Albee; and on the night of her death all theatres in the West End extinguished their exterior lights for an hour as a sign of mourning.

As a beginner she won success in London as a girl with nothing to commend her but beauty, whom a jealous woman in Ashley Dukes' *The Mask of Virtue* made use of to entrap and ridicule her own unfaithful lover; as a young woman she became an international star with her film portrayal of Scarlett O'Hara, Southern belle and world famous heroine of the best selling novel *Gone With the Wind*; somewhat later as Blanche Du Bois in *A Streetcar Named Desire*, a woman whose wits do not survive the fading of her beauty; and later still in her last two Hollywood films, as women who obviously were beautiful and who now are obviously not young, she proved herself one of those actresses who, always themselves, are always different, always learning, always turning their looks and personality to new, scrupulously prepared dramatic account.

Vivian Mary Hartley was born in India under the British Raj, at Darjeeling on November 5, 1913, the daughter of Mr. and Mrs. Ernest Hartley, her father being junior partner in a firm of stockbrokers. She was taken to England in 1920, went to school at the Convent of the Sacred Heart at Roehampton, and entered R.A.D.A. First the marriage at the age of 18 to Vincent Leigh Holman, barrister-at-law, then the birth of their daughter Suzanne in 1933, caused her to break off her training, but she began to act professionally in 1934, and within a few months—she was now known as Vivien Leigh—her spectacular appearance in Ashley Dukes's costume-play brought her a five-year contract with Alexander Korda of London Films.

For a time she made little progress, but her ambition, sustained by "postgraduate" work on her voice under Elsie Fogerty, was reinforced by encouragement from the actor who had played opposite to her in her first film for Korda, Laurence Olivier. In 1938 she found on visiting Hollywood, where Olivier was making *Wuthering Heights*—the idea of Cathy's being played by her had been dropped—that Scarlett O'Hara was still not cast, though *Gone With The Wind* was in production. The untried English girl made tests, and the most coveted part in the world was offered to her on condition that she signed a seven-year contract with David O. Selznick. On the film's being shown in Atlanta and soon afterwards in New York, the South and the North as one man capitulated and Hollywood awarded her the first Oscar of her career.

But when Olivier and she appeared in his production of *Romeo and Juliet* in New York in 1940, it was a failure; when she hoped to join the Old Vic Company on her return to England, the director was of the opinion that her new celebrity would make it impossible for her to fit in; and when Olivier wanted her for the Princess in his film of *Henry V*, David Selznick restrained her from appearing. He attempted to do the same, but in the end gave way, when she proposed playing Sabina the maid in Thornton Wilder's *The Skin of Our Teeth*, the part originally played by Tallulah Bankhead in America, under Olivier's direction. Vivien Leigh had married Olivier in California in 1940, after her marriage to Mr. Holman and Olivier's marriage to Miss Jill Esmond Moore, the actress, had been dissolved.

Olivier was knighted in 1947. In the following year the Oliviers led an Old Vic Company on a tour of Australia and New Zealand in *Richard III*, *The School for Scandal* and *The Skin of Our Teeth*, and in 1949 brought the company back to the New Theatre, London, where Vivien Leigh's most notable performance was as Antigone in the play by Jean Anouilh. She went on to make a two-fold success as Tennessee Williams's Blanche Du Bois, first under Olivier's direction on the London stage, and again in the film directed by Elia Kazan, in which her performance gained an Oscar for her for the second time in 13 years.

At the St. James's in London, where her husband had established himself, she played Cleopatra to his Caesar in Shaw's play and to his Antony in Shakespeare's during the 1951 Festival of Britain, and when this theatre was about to be demolished six years later, she led a vigorous if unsuccessful movement to save it, interrupting a debate in the House of Lords in order to protest. She was then appearing with Olivier in London, after a tour of Europe, in *Titus Andronicus*, one of the three plays, the others being *Twelfth Night* and *Macbeth*, in which they had been seen together at Stratford-on-Avon in 1955.

Both husband and wife were in Terence Rattigan's comedy *The Sleeping Prince*, but Marilyn Monroe took over the show-girl's role in the film version, which Olivier made later, and Vivien Leigh appeared without him and under other directors in Noel Coward's *South Sea Bubble*, in an adaptation by Coward of Feydeau, and in Jean Giraudoux's last play *Duel of Angels*.

DIVORCE

While Vivien Leigh was in Giraudoux's play in New York, her intention to appeal for divorce was announced, and the divorce was made absolute in 1961. During that year and the following year she had an Old Vic Company on a tour of Australia, New Zealand and South America in *Twelfth Night*, *Duel of Angels*, and *The Lady of the Camellias*, and, in 1963, made her debut in a musical, on Broadway, in *Tovarich*, playing, singing and Charlestoning the role of a former Grand Duchess which in the prewar production in London had been played straight by Eugenie Leontovitch. A comedy in which she toured the English provinces in 1965 did not reach London, nor did London see her as the neglected Jewish wife of Ivanov in Chekhov's play of that name, for she took over the role for the American run, following the run in England, of this production, in both of which Sir John Gielgud took the title part. It had been announced that she would play opposite Sir Michael Redgrave in Albee's *A Delicate Balance* in London, when she was ordered to rest in June, and rehearsals were postponed until September. This was the third occasion since 1945 on which she had been obliged to give up work on account of illness.

She received the Knight's Cross of the Legion of Honour in 1957 and a French award for her performance as a divorced American woman in her last Hollywood film, Stanley Kramer's *Ship of Fools*. Somerset Maugham had hoped to see her play his favourite feminine character, the charming, promiscuous and kind-hearted Rosie Driffield of his own *Cakes and Ale*, and had encouraged her to play Bathsheba Everdene, the innocently vain and unstable heroine of Hardy's *Far from the Madding Crowd*, but in fact neither of those promising projects for films was carried out. It might almost be said that the roles she did not play and the opportunities that now lay behind her gathered about her lately to form an aura peculiarly her own; but if so, it was an aura surrounding a beautiful woman whose strong character, humour and wit, love of works of art and delight in their collection, had all been proved and were well known.

July 10, 1967.

J. B. Leishman, senior lecturer in English literature at Oxford University since 1947, was killed in Switzerland on August 14, 1963. He was 61.

James Blair Leishman, the eldest son of a tea merchant, was born at Thursby, Cumberland, on May 8, 1902. He was educated at Earnseal School, Arnside, Westmorland, and then went to Rydal Mount, Colwyn Bay, in 1916. At Oxford, where he matriculated from St. John's College in 1922, he was debarred from reading Classical Moderations by ignorance of Greek, but he set himself to learn the language so as to qualify himself for Literae Humaniores in which he obtained Second Class Honours in 1925. Two years later he was rewarded with a First in English Language and Literature. The prospect of an academic career was opened to him and he decided to read for the higher degree of Bachelor of Letters, submitting as his dissertation a study of the three Parnassus Plays written for performance at Cambridge at the end of the sixteenth century. He was without doubt the most able student of his year, and it was not surprising that he was appointed to the only post which fell vacant in the summer of 1928, an assistant lectureship at University College, Southampton.

During his last year at Oxford he had begun to teach himself German and to take an interest in recent German poetry. His enthusiasm for the work of Rilke led a friend to express the wish to be able to read the poet in translation, and this induced him to attempt an English version. He translated a selection of thirty-five poems and offered them to the Hogarth Press, who had already published versions of Rilke's *Duino Elegies* and his *Notebook of Malte Laurids Brigge*. The reception of this volume (1934) encouraged him to attempt the whole corpus of Rilke's poetry in English; *Requiem and Other Poems* appeared in 1935, *Sonnets to Orpheus* in 1936, *Later Poems* in 1938, and the *Duino Elegies* (translated in collaboration with Stephen Spender) in 1939. Translation of *Letters to Merline* and *Remains* were published in 1951 and 1952 respectively.

HELP FOR A FRIEND

In the meanwhile he had also translated selections from Hölderlin (1944, and 1948), and in 1956 30 odes of Horace. The latter, prefaced by a long and valuable introduction on the differences between Latin and English versification and on the poetical character of Horace, was undertaken, like the first selection from Rilke, to help a friend to some understanding and appreciation of the original. Throughout these works Leishman invites comparison with his author: a scholarly translation was his first consideration, and he taxed the rhythmic and syntactic resources of English to the utmost in his effort to obtain closeness of rendering; but he never allowed himself to forget that he was translating poetry, and he might have claimed, though he never did, that his versions were themselves poetry of a high order.

Introductions and commentaries accompanied several of the volumes, and these, no less than the translations themselves, had brought him a reputation as a German scholar both in this country and abroad. But he regarded himself primarily as an Anglicist. His post-graduate work upon the *Parnassus Plays* was completed in an exemplary edition published in 1949; but by that time his principal field of interest had become the literature of the seventeenth century. His Southampton lectures provided a basis for a valuable exposition of the poetry of Donne, Herbert, Vaughan, and Traherne (*The Metaphysical Poets*, 1934), the first chapter of which was completely revised and greatly expanded to form *The Monarch of Wit* (1951).

EXPLORING MILTON

A new, revised edition of this book appeared last year. An illuminating study of *L'Allegro* and *Il Penseroso* (1951) was designed as the first instalment of an expository study of Milton's minor poems.

But his most characteristic work was perhaps his *Themes and Variations in Shakespeare's Sonnets* (1961), where his exceptionally wide reading in Greek, Latin, French, and Italian was brought to bear on clarifying the meaning of the sonnets, and demonstrating the individuality of their writer's mind. This was especially salutary at a time when Shakespeare's work had been put to so much use in explaining the traditional nature of the Elizabethan "world picture"

In 1946 he left Southampton to take up a university lectureship at Oxford, and was eventually elected to a senior research fellowship at St. John's College. His manner of life was shaped at an early date into a fixed routine. A serious illness as a schoolboy had weakened his chest and determined him in a habit of spending every afternoon on foot or on a bicycle in the countryside. It was his custom on these expeditions to meditate and polish his translations. When asked why he had limited his translations to 30 odes of Horace, he replied that that was all that he found he could hold in his memory at one time. At his solitary meals he indulged his passion for music from a huge collection of gramophone records, some of which were specially chosen as a suitable background for his post-prandial studies. He was a bachelor and, by Oxford standards, a recluse; but those friends who sought him out were rewarded by a warmly affectionate welcome and by conversation, at once learned and playfully allusive, which ranged over a wide field of European history and literature both ancient and modern, and irrupted with explosive force whenever it turned to local or national politics.

August 17, 1963.

Dr. Rudolf Lessing, C.B.E., a consulting chemist and chemical engineer, who died on September 2, 1964, at his London home at the age of 86, was an authority on coal and its treatment, and this led to a close connexion with the problems of air pollution.

This began in 1908 when he became in effect the technical adviser to the Coal Smoke Abatement Society in London. He acted as secretary to an international smoke abatement exhibition in 1912, and was one of the founder members of a committee set up for the investigation and measurement of air pollution—a work that is now organized on a national basis under the Department of Scientific and Industrial Research. Because of his wide knowledge of the subject he was a member of the Government committee on air pollution, under Sir Hugh Beaver, set up after the London fog disaster of 1952. In the fuel world he was well known for his scientific and technical papers and for his advocacy of the cleaning of coal and of other measures to reduce the emission of sulphur dioxide into the atmosphere. The Coal Smoke Abatement Society was one of the permanent bodies on the present National Society for Clean Air, of which Lessing was president from 1956 to 1958.

He was the most senior member of its executive council and a member, and the first chairman, of its technical committee.

RESEARCH WORK

Rudolf Lessing, son of Simon Lessing, was born on April 3, 1878, and educated at the Gymnasium Bamberg and the universities of Munich, Geneva, Berlin, and Manchester. He was assistant to Professor Willstaetter at Munich from 1900 to 1902 and the following year held a research studentship at Owen's College. From 1903 to 1906 he was research chemist with the Gas Light and Coke Company, Beckton, and in 1907 became chemist and engineer with the Mond Nickel Company. He was the founder, in 1914, of the Hydronyl Syndicate Limited, of which he became managing director and later deputy chairman.

In 1912 he married Milly Fuld. They had one daughter.

September 3, 1964.

Major-General John Sydney Lethbridge, C.B., C.B.E., M.C., who was General Sir William Slim's Chief of Staff with the Fourteenth Army in Burma in 1944–45, died on August 11, 1961. He was 63.

The son of Lieutenant-Colonel Sydney Lethbridge, he was born on December 11, 1897, and educated at Gresham's School, at Uppingham, at the Royal Military Academy, Woolwich, and at Jesus College, Cambridge. He passed out from Woolwich at the top of his term in the first months of the First World War, was commissioned in the R.E. in July, 1915, and was on active service at the western front three months after his eighteenth birthday. From November, 1917, he was with the Aden Field Force in Southern Arabia for 12 months.

May, 1919, found him an acting major in the Indian Army fighting the Afghans on the north-west frontier. There followed normal appointments until his spell at the Staff College, Quetta, where he passed in 1932. He then held a number of staff appointments before the war.

AMERICAN LIAISON

Lethbridge was in France with the B.E.F. and in 1940 was C.R.E. 59th Division. In 1942 he undertook liaison duties with the Americans in London and in the United States, where he struck up a happy partnership with American soldiers, administrators, and businessmen.

The following year he led a military mission to the South-West Pacific which was composed of representatives of the three British fighting services with some American and Canadian officers. Their purpose was to study the tactics and equipment that would be best suited for fighting the Japanese in this difficult theatre of operations when a full-scale allied offensive there would be possible after the defeat of Germany.

The experience and knowledge gained in this task was of the utmost value to Lethbridge when he became Chief of Staff to the Fourteenth Army in 1944. He was extremely successful in this post of exceptional responsibility, where his performance was marked by a precise and orderly mind and a robust cheerfulness. He was also noted for his excellent cooperation with the R.A.F.

After the war he was for three years Chief of Intelligence, Control Commission for Germany and B.A.O.R., at a time when the defeat of Germany and the subsequent mopping up of Nazi elements made this a position of more than usual importance.

CIVIL DEFENCE POST

He retired from the Army in 1948 and the following year became the first commandant of the Civil Defence Staff College. Even after his retirement from his post due to ill-health in 1952 he did much work for civil defence in the south-west region.

Lethbridge had won the M.C. in 1919, been made C.B.E. in 1942, and C.B. in 1946. In 1925 he married Katharine Greville, daughter of Sir John Maynard, K.C.I.E. They had one son and two daughters.

August 15, 1961.

Sir Ernest Lever, who died on September 4, 1970, at the age of 79, started work as a clerk with the Prudential Assurance Company, became the firm's joint secretary and, after the last war, played a leading part in organizing the expansion of British steel production.

He was educated at the William Ellis Endowed School and took up employment with the Prudential Assurance Company, London, in 1907. An exceptional talent for mathematics started him well on an actuarial career, and by the age of 22 he had already qualified as a Fellow of the Institute of Actuaries. He was soon marked out for distinction in the insurance and financial worlds. When he was still in his early thirties, he was a well-known figure in the world of international finance, and took an active part in questions of German debt settlement arising from the 1914–18 conflict in which he had served in the Army. In 1931 he was appointed joint secretary of the Prudential. Nine years later, at the request of the Chancellor of the Exchequer, and of the Bank of England, he undertook the task of rehabilitating Richard Thomas & Company Limited (later Richard Thomas & Baldwins Limited), which was then in financial difficulties.

With characteristic thrustfulness, Sir Ernest re-organised the company within a relatively short period—and the Bank of England released its control. In 1945, he organised the amalgamation between Richard Thomas & Company Limited and Baldwins Limited. He was responsible for the formation of the Steel Company of Wales Limited, and was its chairman from 1947 to 1955. He was a former president of the British Iron and Steel Federation and from 1953 to 1961 was a director of Lloyds Bank.

He married in 1913 Florence, daughter of Alfred Benjamin Millington, by whom he had two sons. The marriage was dissolved by divorce in 1939 and he married secondly in 1940 Mrs. Phyllis Irene Blok.

September 5, 1970.

Dr. Reuben Levy, Emeritus Professor of Persian in the University of Cambridge, and Fellow of Christ's College, died on September 6, 1966, at the age of 75.

In 1950 he became professor when, having been lecturer in a field for which Cambridge has long been celebrated, a chair was made for him. This was received by Levy's colleagues in Cambridge with something akin to jubilation because, though a most self-effacing scholar since his arrival in 1926, his amiable manners and quiet, urbane conviviality had won the hearts of all who knew him. It was the scholar's urbanity.

He went to Cambridge after the University College of North Wales and Jesus College, Oxford, with well grounded learning in the Semitic languages and Persian and Turkish. As lecturer in Persian at Oxford, before a brief interlude in the United States, Levy had already written a small work, *Persian Literature*, still one of the best introductions to the subject. The First World War gave him practical application for his Oriental scholarship. Life in Mesopotamia and Iran made his conversation in later life vivid with recollections of first encounters with living Arabs, Turks and Persians, and the fascinating vagaries of their everyday idiom in languages formerly known only in the study. The Second World War found him again in exacting service, and this took toll of his health.

SOCIOLOGY OF ISLAM

His best work was produced in the prewar years. In 1929 *A Baghdad Chronicle* was published, an extremely well documented but eminently readable account of the Muslim Middle Ages and Abbasid Caliphate—that rarity, a "popular" book which is also the product of penetrating combing, in this case of Tabari's and Ibn al-Athir's ponderous tomes and all adjacent sources, either Arabic or Persian. The *Chronicle* must be considered as the preliminary to Levy's major, pioneering work, *The Sociology of Islam* (1931–33), which was reissued in 1957 as *The Social Structure of Islam*. This work, besides being a new approach to Muslim history, inspired perhaps by the feel for that history's human agents which Levy had discovered in himself when reading for the *Chronicle*, is a reference book of encyclopaedic comprehensiveness for the terms and nature of Islamic institutions. The year 1938 saw his first piece of large scale textual criticism in the editing of the Arabic *Ma'alim al-Qurbah*. In 1951 followed his edition of the eleventh century Persian *Qabus Nama*, a "Mirror for Princes", the happy title chosen by the professor for his highly successful translation of the work. Typical of him was his amused wonder when this translation was well reviewed in *Punch*—wonder wittily expressed in remarks on possible damage such a review, in such a place, might do to a scholar's reputation. He was twitted on this in the combination room of the college he so greatly loved and whose Robertson-Smith Oriental Library he did so much to augment and maintain.

His death is the more tragic because retirement, though marred by a bereavement, but later comforted by a second marriage, brought renewed activity. In 1959, following his first successful translation, came *The Tales of Marzuban*, a tour de force from what is stylistically a most difficult Persian original. Recently he had been working hard to complete selections from the Persian *Book of King*, the *Shahnama*.

Levy married Flora Herz in 1921, and, secondly in March, 1965, after her death, Margaret Roberts, widow of Dr. J. K. Roberts, F.R.S.

September 8, 1966.

Professor C.S. Lewis, who died on November 22, 1963, was Professor of Medieval and Renaissance English at Cambridge from 1954 until he resigned the chair last month. He was 64.

Clive Staples Lewis was born at Belfast on November 29, 1898. He was the son of A.J. Lewis and of Flora Augusta Hamilton. His father was a Belfast solicitor, his mother belonged to Anglo-Irish landed stock. He was educated privately, for a short period at Campbell College, Belfast, and then for a year at Malvern, but he always said that the most important part of his education was with a private tutor, W. T. Kirkpatrick. His ruthlessly logical use of language and argument dates from this period, as well as his love and understanding of the Classics. He received a commission in The Somerset Light Infantry towards the end of the 1914–18 War and served in France as a second lieutenant in 1918.

The same year he went up to Oxford as a classical scholar at University College; his approach to the study of English literature was to be conditioned by the fact that he came to it from Classical scholarship. His academic career was uniformly successful. He gained the first class in Honour Moderations, the first class in "Greats", the first class in the finals of the English school. He was given a lectureship at University College which in fact he held until 1946; he became a Fellow of Magdalen College. Oxford, in 1924 and stayed there as Fellow and Tutor for 30 years at one time serving as Vice-President. In 1954 he transferred to Magdalene College, Cambridge, on his election to the Cambridge Chair of Medieval and Renaissance English. He was an Honorary Fellow of University College, and of Magdalen.

He was an outstanding lecturer who filled the largest lecture halls in the University. As a tutor he exercised a close and often lasting influence on all those pupils with whom he could establish a bond of personal sympathy. On the other hand he was singularly unfitted for committee work; he detested compromise and was as incapable of negotiation as of intrigue.

But it is on his writings that his real fame rests. Christian apologist, literary historian, scholar, critic, writer of science fiction and children's books, he was one of the more prolific authors of his time. As a Christian writer his influence was marked; he caught and held the attention of those usually apathetic to religion, of lapsed churchgoers and of people who liked to think themselves agnostics; with J. B. Phillips he made religious books bestsellers and, in a nice sense, fashionable.

MEDIEVAL LITERATURE

In 1936 he published *The Allegory of Love* for which he was awarded the Hawthornden Prize. Brilliant and controversial, this is essentially a young man's book; oddly so for an author nearing 40. But it opened up a new field in the study of Medieval English literature and illustrated the great range of his reading in English, in Classical Latin and in Medieval Latin poetry. It was also a marvellously lively and penetrating account of much unjustly neglected literature; Lewis had the great power of making works he wrote about seem even more splendid than they were, and of making his readers want to read them. He "rehabilitated" large tracts of our earlier literature. This was followed in 1942 by *A Preface to Paradise Lost*, one of the sanest and most compelling introductions to Milton of recent years, and then by that acknowledged and adult masterpiece *English Literature in the Sixteenth Century* which probably brought him his Fellowship of the British Academy. Later he was to publish *Arthurian Torso* which contains his critical appreciation of the later poems by Charles Williams; in 1960 *Studies in Words*, the most characteristic of all his works, that of a classical scholar intent on a changing vernacular; and in 1961 *An Experiment in Criticism*, a personal and lively plea for a more catholic approach to literary appreciation, which suggested that the academic criticism in favour at present was becoming too narrow.

As a young tutor he had returned to Christianity and had found a secure anchorage within the Anglo-Catholic tradition in the Church of England. *The Pilgrim's Regress* of 1933 was followed by *The Problem of Pain*, *Screwtape Letters*, *The Great Divorce*, *Miracles*, *Reflections on the Psalms*, and *Four Loves*. With them should be classed his autobiographical fragment *Surprised by Joy*. His apologetic output will be judged variously. It is revealing that *Screwtape Letters* (1942) has been the most widely appreciated but also the most disliked of it all. But it will be universally admitted that he continued the tradition of Gilbert Keith Chesterton whose *Orthodoxy* had influenced him deeply and that, perhaps because of his personality, his broadcasts and his lectures to such societies as his "Socratic" were far more compelling than his printed words. As an occasional preacher he and the late Archbishop Temple shared the distinction of being the only two whose sermons filled the University Church to capacity. Lewis's sermons were collected in *Transposition* and some of his "Socratic" and other addresses in *They Asked for a Paper* (1962); his broadcast talks appeared as *Mere Christianity* in 1952.

RELIGION IN PAPERBACKS

By 1963 his paperback sales alone were in the region of one million. *The Screwtape Letters* had sold over 250,000 copies, *Mere Christianity* over 270,000, and *The Problem of Pain* almost 120,000.

Almost imperceptibly his apologetics merged into his experiments in the form of the novel. In these he was deeply influenced by Charles Williams, probably the most intimate of his many close friends. The first to appear was *Out of the Silent Planet*, 1938, and it was followed five years later by its even more memorable sequel, *Perelandra*—together "the most beautiful of all cosmic voyages and in some ways the most moving". *That Hideous Strength* (1945) showed his real debt to Williams, but the influence was scarcely apparent in *Till We Have Faces* in 1956. This was the most original and important of his experiments in technique; it is the sequel to his *The Allegory of Love*; the application of the medieval theory of allegory to a concrete situation in a sub-antique world. He was writing brilliantly imagined and exciting "science fiction" long before the term was current, and using it, as he used children's fiction, to convey a deep conviction about God and about living with a subtlety and symbolic power perhaps to be found elsewhere only in the work of his beloved Edmund Spenser.

His theory that the subject dictates the form turned his creative and allegorical inspiration in the direction of children's books and the seven *Chronicles of Narnia*, appearing annually from 1950 to 1956, captured not only the young readers for whom they were intended. In all the series, and most notably in *The Lion, the Witch and the Wardrobe* (1950), *The Voyage of the "Dawn Trader"* (1952), and the last three, *The Silver Chair*, *The Magician's Nephew*, and *The Last Battle* (for which he was awarded the Carnegie Medal), the intensity of imagining, narrative power, beauty of description, and extraordinary clarity of style, together with the allegorical significance, give them a strong appeal to adults as well as to children.

November 25, 1963.

D. B. Wyndham Lewis, F.R.S.L., for many years a brilliant and prolific humorous writer in the daily and weekly press, died in Spain on November 21, 1969, at the age of 78. He was also well known as a controversial biographer, and a considerable authority on French history and literature.

Dominic Bevan Wyndham Lewis, the eldest son of David John Wyndham Lewis, of Welsh clerical stock, was born at Liverpool in 1891 and educated at Cardiff. (He is to be distinguished from the Wyndham Lewis without initials, the American-born author and artist, with whom indeed he had little in common.) After serving from 1914 to 1918 with the Welch Regiment, he joined the *Daily Express* in 1919; for a short period he was literary editor, and he was the first to use the pseudonym "Beachcomber" which was later continued by J. B. Morton. In 1925–30 he contributed a delightful column "At the Sign of the Blue Moon" to the *Daily Mail*, perhaps his best work in humorous journalism.

SPARE TIME WORK

Wyndham Lewis was then living in Paris, historical research engaging him in his spare time, and the Action Française, whose critic he tackled in a controversy over John Gay, once referred to him as "un bon Européen"—a compliment he appreciated. In 1931 he returned to England, at the same time transferring his allegiance to "Mustard and Cress" in the *Sunday Referee*. He went back to the *Daily Mail* in 1933 but later wrote for the *News Chronicle* as "Timothy Shy." He was also for some time a regular writer on the *Bystander*, and an occasional contributor to many other journals, both in England and America.

Wyndham Lewis, who was received into the Roman Catholic Church in 1921, was strongly influenced in his historical writings by his religious views. Belloc and Chesterton were his masters. His weaknesses were his subjectivity and over-eagerness for effect. Even his dashing account of François Villon (1928) and his understanding portraits of Louis XI and certain of his contemporaries (*King Spider*, 1930) might have been improved by the omission of tendentious propaganda, and this was also the case with the studies of Charles V (*Emperor of the*

West, 1932), largely a piece of "special pleading", and of *Doctor Rabelais* (1957).

But Wyndham Lewis knew old Paris and history and literature so well, wrote so zestfully, and had such a keen sense of character, that his highly individual books will remain illuminating reading, especially for fellow Catholics.

He had, also, a happy touch in the compilation of an anthology, and his collection of bad verse *The Stuffed Owl* (made in collaboration with Charles Lee) was a distinct success; so, too, was *The Nonsensibus* (1936) and, in more serious vein, *A Christmas Book* (compiled with G. C. Heseltine). In 1954, together with Roland Searle, he wrote *The Terror of St. Trinians*. Selections from his contributions to the press appeared in half-a-dozen amusing volumes. He also published lively biographical studies of Boswell, Ronsard, Molière and Cervantes (among others), and a translation of Barbey d'Aurevilly's *Anatomy of Dandyism*. His last book *The World of Goya* was published in 1968.

Like Charles Lamb, Bevan Wyndham Lewis was afflicted by a slight stammer in conversation; like him, again, he tilted at all and sundry in print—more boisterously, be it admitted, and less gracefully than "Elia"—but was in private life genial and kind-hearted. Enjoying a gusto rare to the twentieth century, with his unusual combination of scholarly erudition and combative wit, he seemed by instinct to belong to an age at once more spacious and with warmer sympathies than that in which he found himself—and which he did so much to enliven.

November 24, 1969.

Emlyn Lewis, F.R.C.S., who died on May 14, 1969, had been surgeon in charge of St. Lawrence Hospital, Chepstow, the plastic surgery and burns centre for Wales, since it opened in 1950.

During the war he and his team performed many operations on badly-burned R.A.F. aircrew. At the end of the war he was presented with a specially inscribed book, signed by hundreds of R.A.F. patients, in recognition of his work. He was responsible for the development of St. Lawrence and in 1952 led the organization to treat 18 miners severely burned in a colliery explosion. A dynamic personality, he helped to raise thousands of pounds towards the cost of providing special amenities for the hospital.

In addition to being surgeon in charge of St. Lawrence Hospital he was consultant plastic surgeon for the United Cardiff Hospitals under the Welsh Hospital Board.

May 15, 1969.

Essington Lewis, C.H., who died on October 2, 1961, at the age of 80, was managing director of one of Australia's greatest industrial concerns, the Broken Hill Proprietary Company Limited, from 1926 until 1938, when he became chief general manager. In 1950, on the death of Harold Darling, he became chairman. In 1952, at the age of 71, he decided to accept the less onerous position of deputy chairman, which he remained for the rest of his life.

B.H.P., as the company is generally known, is the largest steel producer in the British Commonwealth, and inspired and provided the firmest base for Australia's general industrial development. Essington Lewis, from the very early days, foresaw this role for B.H.P. and fashioned it deliberately. He was a remarkable managing technician, with a splendid vision of what ought to be and what could be.

Lewis was made a Companion of Honour in 1943, on the recommendation of a Labour Prime Minister, John Curtin. The honour itself was a recognition of his work as Director-General of Munitions and Aircraft Production, but the fact of its recommendation by a Labour leader was a recognition of Lewis's humane and responsible approach to the direction of what was in fact a monopoly organization. Because of Lewis, the Australian iron and steel industry in its early, hurly-burly years had none of the bitterness of the Australian coal industry.

Lewis was always determined to make Australia industrially strong because he wanted her to be as independent as possible of oversea interests. In 1936, largely as a result of his influence with Australia's leading manufacturers, the Commonwealth Aircraft Corporation Proprietary Limited was formed, with B.H.P. a major share-holder. Within two years its first aircraft, the Wirraway, had been produced and by 1942 Australian-built aircraft, in the absence (which he also foresaw) of more effective aircraft from Australia's allies, were fighting the Japanese.

In the purely technical field Lewis was exceptional. He was a very fine production engineer, with wide practical experience. He wrote three books, at intervals of a decade, on the Australian iron and steel industry, the first in 1929, the last in 1948. He was much honoured in his own country and all over the world.

But the Australian people knew little about Essington Lewis. He disliked publicity. He disliked social occasions. He disliked anything that distracted him from the work he wanted to do, although he was sensible enough to have recreations which he thoroughly enjoyed.

FAMILY BACKGROUND

Essington Lewis was a hard man physically and his look was a little forbidding. The jaw was big and blunt, and the mouth declined at the edges. His wife, whom he married in 1910, was Gladys Rosalind Cowan, the daughter of a member of the South Australian Parliament. She was a gentle, motherly woman, who died in 1954, leaving him two sons and three daughters.

Essington Lewis was born at Burra in South Australia on January 13, 1881. His grandfather, James Lewis, had gone to Australia from Wales in 1836 to help survey the new city of Adelaide and had joined Sturt's expedition to the unexplored central Australian desert in 1844. James had 11 children, the eldest of whom, John, was Essington's father. John was a man of substance, a partner in the firm of Bagot, Shakes and Lewis, stock and station agents, president of the South Australian branch of the Royal Geographical Society and a member of the South Australian Legislative Council. He was a pastoralist, with properties in the Northern Territory. Essington, in fact, was named after Port Essington, near what is now Darwin.

In 1883, two years after the birth of Essington, deposits of silver and lead were discovered at remote Broken Hill and in 1885 the Broken Hill Proprietary Company Ltd. was formed. Essington left school at 13 and worked for a while on one of his father's cattle stations, Dalhousie, in the north of South Australia.

BACK TO SCHOOL

Within a year he was back at school, St. Peter's, Adelaide, and did not leave again until he was 17. Then, after another period with cattle, he went to Adelaide University and graduated in law. But he decided, after much family discussion, that mining offered more opportunity than the law and that he would become a mining engineer. About this time B.H.P., needing ironstone for smelting the silver-lead ores of Broken Hill, pegged leases at two hills called Iron Knob and Iron Monarch on Spencer's Gulf in South Australia.

Already, during his school holidays, Essington had worked underground at Broken Hill and at Mount Lyell in Tasmania. And in 1903 he returned to Broken Hill to work underground for 5s. a day. He was sensitive about his unusual name and called himself Dick. In 1905 he gained the diploma of the South Australian School of Mines, having become foreman of the sulphuric acid and zinc plant. He was working a 48-hour week for 7s. 6d. a day. He was sent to Port Pirie as assistant manager of the smelting plant in which B.H.P. made its first pig iron. "The experiment", said Lewis, "wasn't so good, as we had to pull the furnace down to get the iron out."

By 1911 B.H.P. had decided to commit itself to the manufacture of steel from the rich ironstone at Spencer's Gulf. This was to be taken to Newcastle, in New South Wales, where there was plenty of coal and a convenient river estuary. Essington, then 34, was sent to the mudflats of Port Waratah, near Newcastle, as production engineer for the new steel works.

FIRST STEEL PROJECT

In 1917 he was in charge of the technicians responsible for making the first steel. About this time B.H.P. began to buy its own collieries and ships and in 1920 Lewis was made assistant general manager of the company.

One year later, at the age of 40, he became general manager. In 1926, when he became managing director, there began a remarkable partnership with Harold Darling, chairman of the company and a great financier, who remained chairman until his death in 1950.

In 1938 Lewis had become chief general manager of B.H.P. On his own initiative he set up a shell-producing annexe to the company's main plant at Newcastle, which was additional to four Government munitions factories. In 1938 the Government made him chairman of its advisory panel on industrial organization and business consultant to the Department of Defence. When war came Lewis was appointed chairman of a board of business administration. Then, in May, 1940, when France was about to fall, the Prime Minister, R. G. Menzies, appointed him Director-General of Munitions, with special powers, voted by Parliament. Next year he became Director-General of Aircraft Production. By the middle of 1943 Lewis had increased the number of Government munitions factories from four to 48, and the number of private industries with specially created munitions annexes was 213. Australia was largely self-sufficient in munitions and, moreover, a useful arsenal for her allies in the south-west Pacific. Immediately the war ended in 1945, Lewis relinquished his Government appointments to devote his whole time to B.H.P., but he was determined that Australia should not forsake her strategic industrial role. He said she ought to become the arsenal of the whole British Commonwealth east of Suez.

In 1950 Lewis became chairman of B.H.P., stepping down in 1952, at the age of 71, to the less arduous position of deputy-chairman. But he remained very active in thought and action on behalf of the company and of Australia. His mind remained open and inquiring. He was no less exacting in what he expected of himself and others. In 1957 he accepted invitations to become first chairman of the Australian Council of Industrial Design and first chairman of the Australian Administrative Staff College—31 years after he had introduced a staff training scheme for the education of young B.H.P. employees. B.H.P., under Lewis, had given £A75,000 (£60,000) to Newcastle Technical College and had given generously to establish chairs of mineralogy at the Universities of Adelaide and Melbourne.

October 3, 1961.

John Lewis, former Labour M.P. for Bolton West, died in London on June 14, 1969. He was 56.

Lewis, educated at Grocers' School and the City of London College, was a rubber technologist. His father founded Rubber Improvement Ltd., of which Lewis later became chairman and managing director. He was joint inventor of a rubber substitute for cable and general rubber production.

He joined the Labour Party in 1927, and became M.P. for Bolton in 1945 and for Bolton West in 1950. During his period in Parliament he served for a time as Parliamentary private secretary to the Postmaster General. In 1950 he was a member of the Sports Television Advisory Committee and in the same year was chairman of the Empire Games Appeals Committee. He lost his Parliamentary seat in 1951.

FAMOUS LAW-SUIT

In 1963 Rubber Improvement and Lewis were awarded a record £217,000 damages for libel against The Daily Telegraph Ltd., and Associated Newspapers Ltd., owners of the *Daily Mail.* The Lords described the £217,000 damages awarded as "far too high" and "ridiculously out of proportion to the injury suffered." After a retrial was ordered by the House of Lords and the Court of Appeal, under a settlement damages were reduced to £22,000, £12,000 of which were awarded to Lewis personally.

Lewis was appointed a steward of the British Boxing Board of Control in 1949.

His marriage to his first wife, Joy, was dissolved in 1954. They had a daughter. His second wife, Stella, had been his secretary for eight years. They married in November, 1968.

June 16, 1969.

John Llewellyn Lewis, for long the most powerful labour leader in the United States, in most respects the creator of the modern American trade union, died in Washington on June 11, 1969. He was 89.

Lewis was all fire and thunder, the last of his contemporaries to have worked with Samuel Gompers. His ruthless use of the strike, undeterred by the national interest in time of war, by court order or Government seizure was essentially concerned with improving the lot of the coal miner, who in his remote valleys had been especially vulnerable to the repressive, often brutal methods of the companies. The United Mine Workers of America stood as one man behind Lewis for most of his 40 years as president, not because they revered him, as was often said, but because they knew he would never call a strike that they could not win. Sometimes it was called a voluntary holiday, or it might be a "memorial period" after a pit disaster; until he changed his tactics, the men were out every spring with the regularity of the seasons.

His nerve and lusty hatreds were of legendary scale, no less than his massive presence—the mane of hair and heavy brows, the growling, melodramatic turn of oratory full of borrowed allusions from Shakespeare, to whom his wife, a schoolteacher, may have brought him. "They are smiting me hip and thigh, and right merrily I return the blows," he said, after a Gallup poll had found him to be the most unpopular man in the country. There were times when his position of power took him into the political arena, but in general he shared the traditional detachment of organized labour in America from any narrow party allegiance. Indeed, as a Republican, contemptuous of "Marxist babble", he saw his union as a dynamic force in a free market economy operating without mercy. It was by the constant pressure of labour, he would argue, that employers were forced to be efficient. He saw increased productivity as a corollary of higher pay, and would not have dreamed of opposing the extensive mechanization of American coal mines that raised a man's output to 11 tons a day. In short, prosperity was essential to preserve the hardwon concessions to his union; his own salary was £17,000 a year, with a £10,000 allowance, a colonial-type house outside Washington and a renewable Cadillac. None of his miners would have begrudged him that.

As the son of an immigrant Welsh miner, brought up on the Bible and low wages, Lewis went down the pit in Iowa at the age of 14, but was roving as far afield as the Rockies before settling down in union employ. At 27 he was in Washington as legislative agent of the Mine Workers, and four years later sat as one of their delegates in the American Federation of Labour. As president of the Mine Workers, a post he attained in 1920, he showed no immediate promise, and was regarded by President Hoover's labour chiefs as one of the more reasonable union leaders trained in the Gompers school.

It was the advent of President Roosevelt and the New Deal that made Lewis. He was quicker than his colleagues to see the full implications of Section 7A of the National Recovery Act which, as later enshrined in the Wagner Act, put the machinery of collective bargaining into the law of the land. Under the slogan "President Roosevelt wants you to join the union", he swiftly built the United Mine Workers into a rigidly disciplined force of 450,000, over which he wielded despotic powers of expulsion and the closed shop.

Having gained Roosevelt's confidence and support, he then went forward to the most notable enterprise in American labour by organizing the millions of workers in the great mass-production industries, a course that enraged most of his A.E.I. colleagues, wedded to the conservative principles of the old craft unions. Lewis's answer was to take his union out of the Federation and, with a few other rebels, create the Committee (later the Congress) of Industrial Organizations (C.I.O.) which, as its president, made him the world's most powerful labour leader.

This was also the period of snarling chaotic strikes, with their new "sit-down" technique by which the workers retained possession of their factories, a period that cost the unions public sympathy, and effectively dispelled Roosevelt's idea that he had created a working partnership between management and labour.

ALLEGED BETRAYAL

His memorable denunciation, "A plague on both your houses", was bitterly resented by Lewis, who saw the words as a betrayal—a poor return for the $500,000 contributed from his union's funds in 1936 towards Roosevelt's second-term campaign. He became the most virulent of Roosevelt haters, but badly miscalculated his strength in 1940 by going over to Wendell Wilkie, the Republican candidate for the presidency, and staking his position in the C.I.O. on the outcome. In this situation, the workers showed unmistakably that their first allegiance was to Roosevelt, and Lewis, resigning from the C.I.O., fell out again with nearly all the old labour leaders, who refused to follow him into a personal vendetta against the President. His constant coal strikes, at disastrous cost to the national economy, made him at times the most execrated man in the land, and more than others were responsible for the wave of anti-labour legislation in Congress which, culminating in the Taft-Hartley Act, finally vitiated the conciliatory atmosphere of the New Deal.

Isolationist by instinct, Lewis refused to honour the no-strike pledges given by the unions after Pearl Harbour. He called four wartime strikes in the soft coal mines, acts widely denounced as little short of treason, possibly because he knew that he could get a better deal from the Government, once it had taken over the mines, than from the companies.

PENSION AWARD

The first of his strikes in 1946, when postwar Europe was desperately short of coal, induced the Government, indeed, to award a contract setting up a pension fund for miners; but President Truman, denouncing a "dirty political trick", was quick to resort to the courts for a restraining order when the miners came out again in the autumn, this time against the Government. For defying that order, Lewis was fined $10,000 and the union $3,500,000, reduced on appeal to $700,000—fines doubled for the 1948 strike, when Lewis was asking how many men were to die digging coal to pay them.

June 13, 1969.

John Spedan Lewis, founder of the John Lewis Partnership, died suddenly at his home at Stockbridge on February 21, 1963. He was 77.

To the last an unrepentant and indeed aggressive individualist, he yet created one of the most distinctive and successful co-partnership organizations. A man of high purpose, unbridled imagination and great courage, he was outspoken, but had in many respects the most kindly and generous disposition.

John Spedan Lewis was born on September 22, 1885, the elder son of the late John Lewis who created the Oxford Street store which bears his name and he was educated at Westminster, where he was a Queen's Scholar. At the age of 21 he entered the family business and worked as a shop assistant and shop walker. There is no doubt that it was the conditions of long hours and low wages and "living in" which he encountered which first set his mind to work upon a new system of employment involving joint ownership and management, which in later life he was himself to develop. He became a partner in John Lewis and Co., while these ideas were simmering in his mind, and, as he wrote many years afterwards in his books on the subject, they began to take form and shape between 1906 and 1910. He had, however, no opportunity of putting his ideals to the test and in order to do so exchanged in 1914 his partnership in the Lewis organization for control of Peter Jones Ltd. Fourteen years later he inherited control of the family concern, and within a short while was chairman of the John Lewis Partnership.

WORKERS' CONSENT

The trust settlement evolved, distributed all profits to the work people while paying at least standard wages, and often considerably more. By 1961 £9,500,000 had been distributed in this way. In 1950 he went a step farther. He completed his foundation of the Partnership by executing a second settlement, which extended control, among other things making the consent of the workers necessary to a voluntary liquidation. By 1962, the total Partnership numbered 16,000 and the capital had risen to £30m.

Lewis relinquished active chairmanship of the parent company in 1955 in favour of O. B. Miller, who had long been connected with the enterprises. Having been a strong wind of change for so long he found it hard to blow at something less than full strength and he continued in retirement to advance with great vigour ideas for the financial and commercial improvement of the firm. He regretted his decision to retire—and said so—made critical comments on the affairs of the Partnership and attempted, unsuccessfully, to regain an active part in the running of it. He was an all-round sportsman, an omnivorous reader, greatly interested in natural history and music, and in earlier years he was a keen angler. He was president of the Classical Association in 1957 and at the annual dinner of the association in April that year expressed a desire to endow it with £300 a year. He was an ardent supporter of the Glyndebourne Opera, and, as in all he undertook, not a passive one. In 1949 the Partnership secured the continuance of Glyndebourne by guaranteeing losses up to £12,500.

He was the author of *Partnership for All* (1948); *Fairer Shares* (1954); *Inflation's Cause and Cure* (1958).

He married in 1923 Sarah Beatrice Mary Hunter. Lewis had always been of the opinion that women graduates had an important part to play in business. He approached the heads of women's colleges and later appointed a number of women trainees. One of these became Mrs. Lewis. She died in 1953. There were a son and a daughter of the marriage.

February 23, 1963.

Ted – "Kid" – Lewis, former British holder of the world welterweight boxing championship, died in London on October 20, 1970. He was 76.

Boxing has a tendency to romanticize the past. But there can be no hyperbole about the remarkable career of Ted ("Kid") Lewis. No British boxer, including the late Jimmy Wilde, ever had more success against American opposition, for no one ever adapted himself so completely to the two-handed American style which has dominated professional boxing for the past 50 years.

Ted Lewis was born Gerlston Mendeloff on October 24, 1894, into a Jewish cabinet maker's family in London. He first boxed professionally at 16 for a few pence, and ended his career 19 years later with a knockout victory. In between he won the British featherweight title at 17 (our youngest champion ever), the European featherweight title at 18, and the world welterweight title in Boston in 1915. He lost the world welterweight championship the following year, but regained it in 1917 and held it for another year.

His opponent in all these vital world championships, and in a total of 20 bouts, was the American Jack Britton. It was said once of the two that "they winced and ducked every time they heard the other man's name."

Lewis, who had about 400 professional bouts, was also British middleweight champion, and was quite ready to take on light-heavyweights and heavyweights. In 1922 he had the audacity to challenge the renowned French heavyweight Georges Carpentier, and was having the better of the first round when the referee's intervention made him carelessly drop his hands and take a knockout punch.

In the ring Lewis was a hard man, but outside the ropes he was generous to a fault. He will be remembered not only for his fiery attack and incredible determination, but also for his dignity and modesty in old age whenever lesser men, all of us, toasted him for his deeds of long ago.

October 21, 1970.

Maurice Leyland, who died in a Harrogate nursing home on January 1, 1967, at the age of 66, was one of Yorkshire's heaven-sent gifts to England, a fighting batsman with a genially imperturbable temperament.

Born in 1900, he played all through the inter-war period and, in order to help his county in starting again, for three seasons afterwards. In all, he scored 33,660 runs, including 80 centuries, nine of them in Tests. His England caps were 41, and he made 2,764 in Tests, mostly against Australia. A sturdy left-hander, he was a forceful rather than elegant bat. On occasions he would launch into fiery hitting. At Scarborough in 1932 he and Sutcliffe scored 102 at a rate of 17 runs an over and in a Festival game on the same ground he became one of the only three batsmen—the other two were C. I. Thornton and Cecil Pepper—to hit a ball over the houses in Trafalgar Square. "Mine bounced over", said Leyland with humorous modesty. (Actually the ball fell on the ridge of the roof and proceeded on its way.) His style was rugged, but effective, and his powerful pulls and thumping square-cuts positively whistled past the fieldsmen. Though not so prolific as Sutcliffe or as sparkling as Holmes, his strength and equanimity were an immense asset to Yorkshire and England.

MAN FOR THE MATCH

He was essentially a man for the big occasion, a batsman at his best in a crisis, and his favourite game was a Roses match or an Australian Test. England's supporters often breathed a sigh of relief to see his burly figure purposefully striding to the wicket. Conversely, nothing pleased Australian bowlers better than the sight of his broad departing back. He began and ended his England career with a century, and in between much of his batting was devoted to rescue work. Yet, though he revelled in a grim situation, he was never grim himself. His defiance seemed almost friendly and to the opposition he offered disservice with a smile.

He was also a useful slow left-arm bowler, one of the early exponents of the "Chinaman". He was a good performer in the field, where his cunning, clean handling and strong throwing made him an excellent man to have round the boundary.

In 1949 he was chosen to be an honorary member of M.C.C. among a small company of retired professional cricketers, "restricted to the truly great", After retirement he became chief coach with his fellow-veteran, Arthur Mitchell, to the Yorkshire County Club, and many a youngster has owed his advance to Leyland's wise, practical and never sententious counsel.

There are countless tales of his amiable but always straight-faced humour. The best known pictures him going in when England were facing a huge Australian total and had lost two quick wickets. Stubbornly Leyland held the fort, while partner after partner faltered. By 6.15 the seventh wicket had fallen and No.9, jauntily hitting his first ball into the covers, called for a quick single. Politely Leyland waved him back. "There's no hurry, Mr. Robins. We shan't get 'em tonight."

In the 1938 Oval Test, which saw Hutton's record compilation of 364, Leyland shared with him a second-wicket partnership of 382. At the end of the day there was a rush to celebrate Hutton's tremendous achievement and Leyland was first at the pavilion bar with an order for two bottles of champagne.

"Why two bottles, Maurice?"

"One for thee, Len", solemnly replied Leyland "and one for me."

Maurice Leyland was indeed the happy warrior that every cricketer would wish to be.

January 3, 1967.

Sir Basil Liddell Hart died on January 29, 1970 at the age of 74.

Captain B. H. Liddell Hart, as he was known for much of his life, was the foremost military critic in Britain and probably in the world between the wars. While he had not the imaginative range of the other outstanding military writer of his day, Major-General J. F. C. Fuller, he had the intellectual range of a first-class scholar and in the narrower field of tactics, weapons, military training and organization, he was without equal. The basic changes in mechanized warfare to which the Army owed much of its eventual success in the Second World War had all been advocated by Liddell Hart in the 1930s.

His strength as a military critic came perhaps from his belief in the Chinese proverb, "Doubt is the beginning of wisdom." He investigated every conceivable doubt before he made up his mind, so that if he sometimes rode a good idea to death he seldom espoused a bad one.

HISTORICAL PRECEDENTS

His ideas were always tested against the precedents of military history, of which he had a formidable knowledge, and he held that the conditions of the next war could often be foretold from a really objective study of the last.

The tragedy was that it was left to the Germans to vindicate his ideas. General Guderian, who first put his ideas to the test in France in 1940, never hid his debt to Liddell Hart as the "pioneer of a new type of warfare on the greatest scale". Nor did Rommel, who wrote in 1942 that the British would have avoided most of their defeats if they had paid more attention to Liddell Hart's teachings.

The success of his theories contrasts oddly with this failure to get them accepted. Like many reformers he did not see that the reforms themselves were only half the battle. The more he was in the right the more he annoyed the soldiers at the top who alone had the power to put them into effect. Much of this bitterness at what in his *Memoirs* he calls "the grooved ways of orthodoxy" evaporated after the war and there can be few senior Army officers today who have not been influenced by his teachings.

Basil Henry Liddell Hart was born in October 1895, in Paris, and educated at St. Paul's and Corpus Christi College, Cambridge, where he was reading history when the First World War broke out. He was commissioned in 1914 in The King's Own Yorkshire Light Infantry, and served at Ypres and on the Somme as a company commander.

As with so many thoughtful soldiers of his generation, the slaughter of the Somme, and in particular the success of an attack at Mametz Wood which revived the use of surprise, strongly influenced the cast of his mind in later life. The aim of nearly all his tactical thinking thereafter was to outwit the enemy, preferably by a paralysing combination of surprise and mobility, and to avoid head-on collisions that were bound to lead to carnage. He shared the ideal of Marshal Saxe,"that connoisseur of the art of war" as he described him, who argued that a really able general might win a campaign without ever fighting a battle at all.

The immediate outcome of his experiences was a book on the Somme offensive, written while he was recovering from wounds in 1916, and his evolution of battle drill. The latter was adopted by the War Office after the war but later fell into disuse. Its value was rediscovered in 1940, and battle drill became a leading feature of all Army training in the Second World War.

After the war, at the age of 24, he was asked by General Sir Ivor Maxse to re-draft the Infantry Training Manual. Some of his innovations were removed by the War Office; but with General Maxse's backing he made considerable changes in the official doctrine. His draft of the manual included what he named the "expanding torrent" method of attack, which was a development of the infiltration tacties introduced in 1917–18. This was taken up eagerly by the Germans a decade later, and became the key pattern of the German *Blitzkrieg* in 1940.

In 1924 Liddell Hart was selected for the Royal Tank Corps, but was found unfit for general service and placed on half pay. He retired from the Army in 1927.

In 1925 he had written an essay called "The Napoleonic Fallacy" later expanded in his book *Paris or the Future of War*, which was the first challenge to the Napoleonic doctrine, then universally accepted, of total war. He argued that the war aim of a nation shouid be "to subdue the enemy's will to resist, with the least possible human and economic loss to itself", and that the destruction of the enemy's armed forces was therefore only a means towards the real objective, and not necessarily an inevitable or infallible means at that. The essay is an outstanding example of his qualities of intellectual drive, courage, and clarity of argument.

CAMPAIGN IN 'THE TIMES'

His career as a military writer began at this time, first as military correspondent for *The Daily Telegraph* after the death of Colonel Repington. In 1934, when the Government launched its rearmament programme, he was appointed military correspondent of *The Times* and principal adviser on defence.

He conducted a campaign in *The Times* for the closer coordination of defence, urging the appointment of a Minister of Defence with a combined staff drawn from all three Services. The Government did appoint a Minister for the Coordination of Defence, with a small staff, in 1936, but this fell far short of what had been advocated by *The Times*.

Much his most important work between the wars, however, was his constant advocacy of mechanization. His enthusiasm for the tank began in a way that was characteristic of his open-mindedness, when he went to the War Office to persuade Major-General J. F. C. Fuller that a certain infantry manoeuvre could defeat tanks. After half an hour's conversation he saw that he was wrong, and from that moment never wavered in his belief that armour was the key to future war. He realized that the tank, misused in the First World War, promised the soldier flexibility by allowing him to vary the direction of attack with great rapidity, and mobility by enabling him to penetrate behind the enemy's front and cut his vital arteries of supply.

Along with the handful of soldiers who were the pioneers of armoured warfare, including Fuller, Hobart, Martel, Lindsay, Broad and Pile, Liddell Hart expounded the new doctrine in all its aspects. He had been consulted about the creations of the Experimental Mechanized Force in 1927, and he continually pressed the potential value of night assaults. As early as 1932 he suggested the idea of creating artificial moonlight to help the exploitation of night attacks, which came to fruition only in the last phase of the war. He was also one of the chief advocates of armoured personnel-carriers to enable the infantry to keep up with the armour in the pursuit, which enormously enlarged the scope of infantry tactics in the war.

But the Germans were apter pupils than the British. In his history *The Tanks* (probably his finest book) he described with understandable bitterness the opposition of much of the Army, particularly the Cavalry, to the tank, and their longing to get back to "real soldiering" with horses. As he wrote in 1933, the Army's expenditure on horsed cavalry could not be justified unless the War Office had a scheme for breeding bullet-proof horses. Discreditable and stupid though this opposition was later shown to be, the advocates of the tank probably contributed to it by their own apparent fanaticism. To Liddell Hart the need for mechanization was so self-evident that he underestimated the need for tact and understanding in dealing with his opponents at the War Office.

CREATIVE AND CRITICAL

He was a complex man who combined an extraordinary appetite for creative and critical thinking with a passionate desire for fame and approbation that amounted to vanity. It was possibly this that led him to make the mistake of becoming personal adviser to Hore-Belisha, the new Secretary of State for War, in 1937. Had the collaboration been strictly sub-rosa it might have been of the greatest value, for the changes he urged were much needed: the formation of several more armoured divisions, for instance, the complete mechanization of the infantry divisions, and the expansion of our anti-aircraft forces under a single command. But his position as an *eminence grise* was so blatant and his relations with the soldiers at the top so unfortunate, that hackles were raised on all sides, until the War Minister and his C.I.G.S.(Lord Gort) ceased to be on speaking terms with each other.

The partnership with Hore-Belisha failed to push through his cherished reforms, and he withdrew from it amicably in the summer of 1938. But he was never able to forget the failure, and though he was much more philosophical about it after the war he still regarded himself as a prophet without honour in his own country.

His immediate intention on ending the partnership was to apply the spur of public criticism, as Military Correspondent of *The Times*, to further Hore-Belisha's efforts at the War Office. His health, however, was not good, and there was a difference of opinion over the British Government's guarantee to Poland, which *The Times* endorsed but which he regarded as impossible of fulfilment and as likely to precipitate war when the country's defences were still unprepared. He resigned from *The Times* in 1939.

Though much of his most important work was in the form of newspaper articles, the media most congenial to him were books, memoranda and letters. Throughout his life he was an indefatigable correspondent and kept a vast collection of indexed documents and papers. The result was that few correspondents ever got the better of him in print, where he made his points far more effectively than in conversation. He was seldom willing to commit himself to an opinion until he had mastered all aspects of the particular subject, so that when he finally came to put it on paper, even as journalist, he could hardly bear to write less than two columns. He could nevertheless turn his hand to more popular journalism, and wrote regular war commentaries for the *Daily Mail* from 1941 until the end of the war.

UNORTHODOX GOOGLIES

His interests were by no means limited to military studies. He was keen on nearly all games, and began his journalistic career as Lawn Tennis Correspondent of the *Manchester Guardian*. At his prep school he developed a googly form of bowling which undermined opposing schools until a new headmaster preferred defeat to unorthodoxy, and in later life he was a fiendish exponent of croquet.

After the war he spent much time writing his history of the tanks in the Second World War. (Altogether, he was the author of some 30 books.) He thought much about the advent of nuclear weapons, which appalled him, and the possibility of unimaginable carnage if there were a head-on collision between nuclear powers. Though highly sceptical of the credibility of nuclear threats as a deterrent, he was equally sceptical about the chances of limiting an atomic conflict once it started. He remained convinced that the only hope for the west in war would be to refrain from initiating the use of nuclear weapons and that the inherent advantages of defence over attack would materially help to redress the balance against a numerically superior aggressor.

It was natural that he should prefer a conventional strategy, because nuclear weapons, if used, threatened to negate all that he had stood for. He was affronted by brute force in any form, for to him, as to Marshal Saxe, war was above all an art.

In 1965 he published two volumes of memoirs; direct, muscular, persuasively argued and firmly stamped with the Liddell Hart impress they threw a sharp light on the military history of our times. As one critic remarked, they established beyond all doubt the superiority of the pen over the sword.

In 1969, he delivered his long-awaited one-volume history of the Second World War, after 22 years work, to his publishers.

January 30, 1970.

Trygve Lie, first Secretary-General of the United Nations, died on December 30, 1968, at Geilo, Norway, at the age of 72.

He held what he once described as "the most impossible job in the world" for the first crucial years of the world organization. He resigned in November, 1952—a political victim of the cold war. The communist countries constantly accused him of serving the interests of western imperialism. They boycotted him after he recommended United Nations intervention in the Korean War which broke out in 1950—the first such "police action" in history.

Trygve Halvden Lie was born on July 16, 1896, the son of a carpenter, in a working-class district of Oslo. The family was a poor one and when Trygve was six his father went out to the United States in search of better conditions. Mother and son stayed behind.

Precocious and clever at school Trygve showed in his early teens propensities which were a foretaste of his adult life. He was only 16 when he joined the Norwegian Labour Party, and his first job in life was in that party's offices. Once he was arrested at the National Theatre for demonstrating during the progress of a political play.

In 1914 Lie entered Oslo University as a student of law; he had to work his way through college. In 1919 he graduated, was admitted to the Bar, and secured the post of assistant to the secretary of the Labour Party, which he occupied until 1922.

From 1922 to 1935 Lie was legal adviser to the Trade Union Federation. The year 1926 saw his election to the national executive of the Labour Party.

In 1935, Lie joined the Nygaardsvold Government as Minister of Justice, choosing this post rather than the proffered Chair of Law at Oslo University. He was still under 40, and was the youngest member of the Administration. One very ticklish matter that came within his province was the question of asylum for Trotsky.

DEPORTING TROTSKY

Not without trepidation, Lie gave Trotsky permission to reside in Norway, but when the Russian was discovered to be the centre of a web of political intrigue he was deported, and took refuge in Mexico.

In 1935 Lie became a member of Parliament. In 1939 he gave up the portfolio of Justice for that of Trade, Industry, Shipping and Fisheries, and in April, 1940, he succeeded Professor Koht as Foreign Minister. After the invasion of Norway by the Germans he followed King Haakon to England in the cruiser Devonshire. He lived in London throughout the war (though the Gestapo believed he had returned to Norway by submarine and made a vigorous search for him).

Lie's skill as a negotiator was of the highest value to the Allied cause, for it was mainly through him that the Norwegian merchant fleet, 4m. tons in strength, was turned to Allied uses. As representative of his Government in London he vigorously upheld Norway's standard, and made many robust broadcasts as a counterblast to the propaganda of the traitor Quisling. He had known no English on his arrival here (though he spoke French and German), but he learnt it rapidly, and made many friends in London.

As Foreign Minister of the Norwegian Government-in-exile, Trygve Lie led his country's delegation to the San Francisco conference which opened in April, 1945, and drew up the charter of the United Nations. Lie was chairman of the committee which drafted the section on the Security Council.

In his book *In the Cause of Peace*, published in 1954 after he had resigned the post, Lie wrote: "For me, it all began not in San Francisco or London, but in a cabin high in the Norwegian mountains on Christmas Day of 1945." That was when he received a message from the United States Administration wanting to know whether he would be willing to accept election as the first president of the General Assembly. After some consideration Lie answered "yes". In the event, when the Assembly met in London the following January, M. Spaak was elected president by 28 votes to Lie's 23, in spite of the latter having the support of the Soviet Union.

BACKED AGAIN

On February 1, 1946, the Assembly met and appointed Lie as the first secretary-general of the United Nations by a vote of 46 to three. At that time Lie still had the backing of Russia, but its attitude to the west was already changing and by February 16 Russia, for the first time, used its power of veto in the Security Council against France and Britain on the issue of troop withdrawals from Lebanon and Syria.

When Lie took office the United Nations was still in its formative state and he had to build both the secretariat and its new headquarters from scratch. The present splendid edifice in Manhattan on the bank of the East River stands as a monument to Lie's practical ability. Naturally enough in the circumstances of the time, he relied a great deal on American advice.

This latter was to become an embarrassment when, in the days of the McCarthy "witch hunt", questions of loyalty to the United States or to the United Nations arose and several American staff members had to resign or be dismissed. The morale of the secretariat was badly hurt and Lie came in for a degree of merited criticism for not asserting strongly enough the independence of his office.

His biggest ordeal, however, came in the late 1940s when the "cold war" was intensified, leading to the Korean clash in the summer of 1950. Lie's efforts to promote a "20-year peace programme", never very practicable, culminated in the spring of 1950 in his "peace mission" to Moscow which proved ineffectual. His personal talents were, frankly speaking, inadequate for the world role he sought to play, and his relations with the Soviet Union steadily deteriorated.

Then came the "avalanche", as Lie described it in his book, of communist attack in Korea. Lie took the initiative of declaring North Korea an aggressor and promptly became persona non grata with the communist world. In the autumn of 1950 the question of renewing his term of office for another five years arose and Russia vetoed it in the Security Council. On the initiative of the United States, his original term was "extended" for three years by pushing through a simple resolution in the General Assembly. Russia declined to concede the legality of this and ostracized Lie, ignoring his existence and his action.

In this awkward predicament Lie found himself driven to rely more and more on his western supporters, principally the United States. It is at this time that his problems with the F.B.I. over staff loyalty questions became intense and his freedom of conscience circumscribed. His position soon became untenable. On November 10, 1952, Lie resigned from the post of secretary-general, stating that "because of the stand I took in support of United Nations action against armed aggression in Korea, five member governments [the then communist block] have refused since 1950 even to recognize me as secretary-general".

His tenure of office ended in personal failure and in a constitutional crisis which lasted several months until the great powers could agree on the appointment of Dag Hammarskjöld of Sweden. History was to repeat itself in that context also, but there was a marked difference between the two men and their approach to the task. In the words of one American diplomat who worked closely with them both, "Hammarskjöld was a statesman with a sense of philosophy. Lie was a politician with a sense of expediency". This may sound unfair, but it is a judicious assessment.

December 31, 1968.

A. J. Liebling, the Amercian journalist and critic, who was a reporter and columnist for the *New Yorker* for 27 years, died in a New York hospital on December 28, 1963. He was 59.

Liebling had an immense range of interests, from medieval Arabian history to modern pugilism, from palaeontology to good food, and he wrote about them all with wit and subtlety; his style an intricate tapestry of frequently obscure scholarship, sporting metaphors and the varied rhythms of contemporary New York street talk. Although many of his articles were printed in a number of books he never became one of the most popular writers in the United States, but his work was appreciated and enjoyed by many and particularly perhaps by his fellow writers.

Since the last war Liebling had been one of the best known figures in the New York literary world.

Abbott Joseph Liebling was born in New York on October 18, 1904. He attended Dartmouth College for a short time, but was expelled for refusing to attend chapel, and later enrolled in the school of journalism at Columbia University. He joined the *New York Times* staff and worked for a time in the sports room, his main job being to compile full details of basket ball scores, which were published by the newspaper in the greatest detail, including the name of the referee. One evening when Liebling had omitted to obtain the referee's name he put it down as "Ignoto", the Italian for "unknown". In the weeks that followed Mr. Ignoto was reported in the *New York Times* to be refereeing basket ball games all over the country, sometimes several on the same night, until the sports editor's attention was drawn to it and Liebling was fired.

He worked for a number of other newspapers before joining the *New Yorker* in 1935, first achieving prominence for the magazine as its Paris correspondent on the eve of the Second World War. During the war he frequently accompanied combat patrols in spite of being handicapped by gout, nearsightedness, and a degree of plumpness.

In 1946 he took over the column "Wayward Press", which had been first established by Robert Benchley. His biting reflections on American newspaper practices were widely followed, though not always enjoyed by his colleagues of the press.

SCHOOL FOR PUBLISHERS

In spite of the obvious enjoyment he received from covering boxing matches and some of the more unusual activities of New York life, Liebling evidently gained chief satisfaction from his writings on the press. He dedicated a book of these essays "To the foundation of a school for publishers, failing which no school of journalism can have meaning". He was preparing a study of the reaction of the southern American press to the assassination of President Kennedy when he was taken ill.

Liebling is survived by his third wife, Jean Stafford, the novelist. His first two marriages ended in divorce.

December 30, 1963.

Sir Charles S. Lillicrap, K.C.B., M.B.E., formerly Director of Naval Construction, who was associated with British naval architecture for well over half a century, died on June 17, 1966. He was 78.

Charles Swift Lillicrap was the son of Charles Lillicrap, naval constructor, and was born on November 12, 1887. He was educated at Stoke public school, and at H. M. Dockyard School, Devonport. In 1906 he gained a cadetship in naval architecture and proceeded to the naval college at Keyham and Greenwich for his higher training. He was appointed to the Royal Corps of Naval Constructors in 1910. After serving for a short time at Devonport dockyard and following service at sea in the battleship Superb he went to the Admiralty in 1914. On promotion to constructor in 1917 he began a long period of association with cruiser designs. Many of the designs for which he was responsible, including those of the 8in. gun cruisers of the Kent class, were produced under the rigorous limitations of tonnage and gun calibre imposed by the Washington naval treaty of 1922 and later international agreements.

In 1930 he made a special survey of electric welding, then a comparatively new development, and became a zealous advocate of the use of welding in shipbuilding. He was later President of the British Welding Research Association and the Institute of Welding. Following his promotion to the post of Assistant Director of Naval Construction in 1936 he was associated with submarine design, but two years later returned to the general control of cruiser design. He was appointed Deputy Director of Naval Construction in 1941, and in addition to the general duties of this office he supervised the work on capital ships, including the last of them, H. M. S. Vanguard. His appointment as Director of Naval Construction was announced in January, 1944, and he held this office until the end of September, 1951.

He was made M.B.E. in 1918, C.B. in 1944, and K.C.B. in 1947. He was also an Officer of the Legion of Honour and a Grand Officer of the Order of Orange Nassau. He had many active associations with various technical institutions in addition to those for welding already mentioned. He became a member of the Council of the Institution of Naval Architects in 1937, and a vice-president in 1945. He was also a liveryman and warden of the Worshipful Company of Shipwrights. In 1955–56 he was President of the Johnson Society. After his retirement from the Admiralty he became a director of J. Samuel White and Co., the Cowes shipbuilders, and of the Island Transport Company, Isle of Wight.

He married in 1911 Minnie Shears. She died in 1961. They had two sons and one daughter.

June 20, 1966.

Sir Patrick Linstead, C.B.E., F.R.S., who died on September 22, 1966, at the age of 64, was a scientist of the highest repute who found himself called to a career of higher administration in which he became an outstanding success.

He had all the qualities of intellectual creativeness, an analytical mind, drive and energy, good common sense, and an attractive personality, which enabled him to lead the Imperial College of Science and Technology during its period of expansion, and the preeminent position of strength which the college now holds in higher education in this country is very largely the result of his work. He was the type of man who would have risen to the top in whatever career he had happened to choose, whether in the academic world, government administration, or industry. In fact he spent a part of his life in each of these three. He himself maintained that he had never planned his own career but simply found himself confronted with a succession of steps to higher appointments which attracted him.

Reginald Patrick Linstead was born on August 28, 1902, in London. His father was a pharmaceutical chemist with Burroughs Wellcome and Company, and his elder brother, now Sir Hugh Linstead, was formerly a well known member of Parliament for Putney and secretary of the Pharmaceutical Society from 1926 to 1964. Patrick Linstead went to the City of London School, where he was first on the Classical side, and his turning to science was probably due to the influence of G.H.J. Adlam, the science master at the school. He proceeded to Imperial College, where he obtained a First Class honours degree in chemistry in 1923 and stayed to do research under Sir Jocelyn Thorpe, for which he was awarded his Ph.D. in 1926. A short period as a research chemist with the Anglo-Persian Oil Company followed. In 1929 he returned to Imperial College as a member of the staff, obtaining his D.Sc. degree in 1930, and remaining until 1938, when he was appointed Firth Professor of Chemistry in the University of Sheffield.

AWARDS FOR ACADEMIC WORK

Shortly after this he went to Harvard as Professor of Organic Chemistry, and in 1940 was elected a fellow of the Royal Society. With the coming of the war, however, he became involved in Anglo-American liaison work which brought him back in 1942 to become Deputy Director of Scientific Research at the Ministry of Supply concerned mainly with chemical warfare and explosives. At the conclusion of the war he was appointed Director of the Chemical Research Laboratory, Teddington, and in 1949 returned to Imperial College to suceed Sir Ian Heilbron as Head of the Department of Organic Chemistry, an appointment which must have given him particular pleasure. Later he became head of the whole Chemistry Department and on the death of Sir Roderick Hill in 1955 he accepted the rectorship of the college.

SCIENTIFIC WORK

His scientific work as a chemist covered a very wide field and was mainly done during his two periods at Imperial College. His contributions included studies of unsaturated acids, carbocyclic fused-ring compounds and the stereochemistry of catalytic hydrogenation. But the work with which his name will be most closely associated was on compounds of the phthalocyanine type which led to important developments in the chemistry of dyes. He also worked with B. C. L. Weedon on electrolytic synthesis and the chemistry of hydrogen transfer reactions, and with D.M. Newitt on reactions at very high pressures and with O. Krayer on the chemistry and pharmacology of unsaturated lactones. He received many awards for his academic work, including the Hoffman Medal of the German Chemical Society, the Meldola Medal of the Royal Institute of Chemistry, and the Harrison Memorial Prize, for outstanding young chemists. His period at the Chemical Research Laboratory did much to found the peace-time evolution of the department and his knowledge of government research enabled him to serve effectively on many government committees, including the committee on the technique of control of government research and development.

As Rector of Imperial College he was the mainspring of many of its academic and social developments, and it would take too long to list these. Particular mention should, however, perhaps be made of his strong support of the expansion of the Engineering departments including as a few examples only, computers, nuclear power, transport engineering, and on the non-academic side, the provision of extensive residential facilities for students and facilities for libraries, sports, & c. He took particular interest in the problem of creating a true university atmosphere at the college, both academically and socially. He was energetic in developing the fringe academic studies such as economics, sociology, and the general studies courses. Altogether his part in overcoming the many different problems of the new buildings, including the Collcutt Tower problem, and in keeping up the tempo of the rebuilding, represented a very great contribution indeed. He was able to enlist the support and efficient cooperation of many distinguished professors, some of whom he himself was responsible for appointing, and to maintain the extremely good personal relations and lack of friction at the college.

Linstead had rendered valuable service to the Royal Society as a member of council and vice-president and foreign secretary. He also served on the Senate of the University of London and on the Court of Governors of the London School of Economics and Governing Body of Charterhouse. One of his most important committee activities was his membership of the Robbins Committee on Higher Education, and he is credited with the original concept of the three Sisters.

Apart from his main work he was much interested in the arts and became a trustee of the National Gallery, and also in architecture and silver. Those who knew him well always found him extremely agreeable and with a strong sense of humour while at the same time having a capacity to stick firmly to a line of action which he thought right. He never wasted his energies on things which did not matter.

He married in 1930 Aileen Rowland (*née* Abbott) by whom he had a daughter. He married secondly in 1942 Marjorie, daughter of W. D. Walters.

September 24, 1966.

M. J. Lithgow, O.B.E., Deputy Chief Test Pilot of Vickers-Armstrong (Aircraft) Ltd., whose death occurred on October 22, 1963, was one of the first British pilots to fly at and above the speed of sound and was a former holder of the world air speed record. In September, 1953, piloting a Supermarine Swift 1.4 over the Azizio Plain, Libya, he averaged 735.7 m.p.h. over four runs. Shortly before, he had set up a London to Paris air record of a little over 19 minutes. On this occasion he was also flying a Swift. In 1948 he broke the 100km. closed circuit record when he flew a Supermarine Attacker at over 564 m.p.h.

Michael John Lithgow was born in August, 1920, and educated at Cheltenham College, where he was in the rowing VIII and was head of his house. He was the second generation of pilots in his family, for his father, Colonel E.G.R. Lithgow, R.A.M.C., had attended one of the first courses at the Central Flying School, Upavon, before the First World War and qualified in 1913.

"Mike" Lithgow—he was rarely called anything else—joined the Fleet Air Arm in 1939 as a midshipman (A) and trained on Tiger Moths, Harvards and Fairey Battles. On the completion of his training he served for three years with No. 820 Squadron in Ark Royal and Formidable, carrying out operational flights with Fairey Swordfish and Albacores.

In 1942 he returned to the United Kingdom to fly experimental aircraft; this was the start of a long and notable career as a test pilot. In 1944 he went through the Empire Test Pilots' School at Boscombe Down and on passing out was posted to the United States Naval Air Test Centre at Patuxent River as a naval test pilot to the British Air Commission. In 1945 he joined the Supermarine division of Vickers-Armstrongs, and on the retirement three years later of J. K. Quill he was appointed Chief Test Pilot. Since then he had made many first flights with new types of aircraft and had been closely connected with their development. He was the author of *Mach One* and editor of *Vapour Trails* (1956).

He was married and had two sons and a daughter.

October 23, 1963.

Sir Sydney Littlewood, for many years a prominent legal figure, president of the Law Society in 1959–60 and chairman of the Legal Aid Committee of the society from 1946 to 1952, died on September 9, 1967, at the age of 71.

He was a solicitor of distinction with a wide-ranging practice of considerable variety. Perhaps his most notable activity in his professional work was in the field of town and country planning. He was a skilful and much sought after advocate in planning cases and was often employed in that capacity in preference to leading counsel.

He was for many years a member of the council of the Law Society in which capacity he served both the public and his own profession with energy, skill and devotion. He served the office of president most acceptably but he will perhaps be longer remembered as the principal architect of the legal aid scheme. From the time of the Rushcliffe Committee, through the legislative stage, the setting up of the machinery of the administration, the negotiations with the Bar and until the scheme was established and run in he was chairman of the appropriate committee. He became the recognized expert in such matters and his advice and help were widely sought in many countries abroad. His knighthood was the recognition of his pioneering work in this field.

In addition to his busy professional life and his work for the Law Society, Littlewood found time for a great deal of public work in a variety of fields. He was much interested in the activities of "Justice" and served a term as chairman of its executive committee.

Sydney Charles Littlewood, the son of Charles Sydney Littlewood, of Southampton, was born on December 15, 1895. In the First World War he saw service with the Loyal North Lancashire Regiment and the R.F.C. and was taken prisoner. Between 1925 and 1932 he was in the 6th East Surrey Regiment (T.A.).

Admitted a solicitor in 1922, he was actively associated with public affairs and with bodies connected with his profession for much of his career. In 1944–45 he sat on the Committee on Legal Aid and Legal Advice (the Rushcliffe Committee) and from 1956 he was legal member of the Town Planning Institute. From 1961 to 1966 he was chairman of the Council for Professions Supplementary to Medicine and in 1963–64 he presided over the Departmental Committee on Experiments on Animals.

The committee was set up to consider the present control over experiments on living animals. The general effect of its recommendations was to extend protection to all animals in or destined for laboratories; to impose stricter supervision over the granting of licences; to strengthen control over the use of animals for research; and to put the care of laboratory animals on a properly organized basis. The committee also felt that the facts of animal experimentation should be made more accessible to the public.

In 1965 Littlewood was appointed president of the London Rent Assessment Panel. This was no bed of roses and in the summer of 1966 he criticized at a luncheon in London some left-wing Labour M.P.s for not understanding the Act they had passed. He said later that the new Rent Act was the first attempt to get all rents on a fair basis since the Rent Act of 1920. He had found that few people seemed to realize that the duty of the committee was to fix a fair rent; left-wing Labour members of Parliament were not the only people who did not appear to understand the Act, some valuers displayed "a surprising ignorance of the way it worked". In August this year he resigned his appointment because of ill health.

He married in 1934 Barbara, daughter of Dr. Percival Langdon-Down. They had one son. Lady Littlewood, herself a solicitor, has also taken a prominent part in public affairs. She and her husband formed together a very unusual and much respected team.

September 11, 1967.

E. M. H. Lloyd, C.B., C.M.G., died in a London hospital on January 27, 1968, at the age of 78.

Lloyd was a civil servant of immense intellectual ingenuity and with unparalleled experience, covering two world wars and from within international as well as national administrations. During the First World War his influence upon economic policy in Britain was enormous and later, especially in the period from 1936 to 1942, he contributed a great deal to the development of control and rationing of food supplies in the United Kingdom. From 1919 to 1921 he was one of the gifted team of British officials, including Lord Salter and Arthur Loveday, who worked with what nowadays would be regarded as quite inadequate resources on financial and economic problems for the League of Nations. After the Second World War he served with U.N.R.R.A. in the Balkans and with F.A.O. in Washington.

Edward Mayow Hastings Lloyd was born in November, 1889, and educated at Rugby and Corpus Christi College, Oxford. When he joined the Civil Service in 1913 he was first posted to the Inland Revenue. After the outbreak of war he was transferred to the War Office, where he served under U. F. Wintour from 1914 to 1917. The business of buying munitions and explosives in 1914 was handled for the War Office by a staff of not more than 20. When war broke out, normal routine continued. At the same time in Germany Rathenau was expressing concern that no arrangements had been made there to secure supplies of raw materials. As a young man of 25 in the War Office, Lloyd was responsible from 1914 for many of the developments in requisitioning of raw material supplies and the control of prices and margins that provided essential experience for the rationing of necessities for the whole civilian population. As F. H. Coller put it, Lloyd's "was the brain behind the throne". His influence was the greater because he had E. F. Wise as a collaborator in the War Office.

In 1917 "the whirlwind trio" of Wintour, Lloyd and Wise went over to the Ministry of Food and proceeded to apply there the experience that they had gained in the War Office.

KEY FIGURE ON DIET

Lloyd was concerned particularly with the control of meat, milk, oils and fats. Not the least of his contributions based on these days was his *Experiments in State Control*, according to A. J. P. Taylor one of the most important and stimulating of the books published in the Carnegie Series on the war.

After 1919 Lloyd's influence upon public policy continued but it was of a different kind; henceforward it was to be exerted indirectly. From the League of Nations Secretariat he went with Tallents to the Empire Marketing Board and subsequently in 1926 to the Market Supply Committee. Here he was a key figure in revealing the influence of diet upon health and physique and in encouraging the development of the science of nutrition. Lloyd's interest was sparked by his realization from wartime meat control that some people could not afford to buy even the meagre quantities of meat to which their ration entitled them. The research (for which between the wars Lloyd was responsible) into food consumption levels, and the data accumulated by the Market Supply Committee under official auspices, pointed to conclusions that Ministers wanted to avoid, and ultimately found their way into print therefore in Lord Boyd Orr's *Food, Health and Income*.

In 1936 Lloyd was appointed as Assistant Director of the Food (Defence Plans) Department and from then on he provided many of the ideas for food control that after 1939 were administered by the Ministry of Food. He was more interested in the strategy than the tactics of control and after 1919 he never found a Frank Wise to translate into practical terms the best of his inspirations. But Lloyd's suggestions were to be seen in the wartime rationing scheme, as well as in many of the commodity controls.

PREVENTING STARVATION

After 1942 Lloyd served as Economic Adviser to the Minister of State in the Middle East, where he worked closely with the Middle East Supply Centre. The background of his experience in food control enabled him to contribute effectively to the prevention of starvation during the war years, notwithstanding shortages of food in the Middle East, distribution difficulties and the impact of severe inflation. From 1947 to 1953, as an under-secretary in the Ministry of Food, Lloyd pursued his interests in nutrition and international economic collaboration. He helped with the National Food Survey and worked at O.E.E.C. and Nato on food and agriculture. In 1956 he was president of the Agricultural Economics Society. From 1958 to 1964, as a consultant to P.E.P., Lloyd concentrated on the problems arising from the Common Market for food and agriculture and illustrated that, even when he was growing old, his mind remained an inquiring and effective one.

Lloyd never pretended to be very concerned with practical detail and was not so much an architect as an inspirer of others. He could provide half a dozen solutions for any problem but tended to depend upon others to pick out and apply the best of them. Always he was generous with his ideas and he gave immense encouragement to many of his younger colleagues. In 1918 he married Margaret Russell, a granddaughter of Lord John Russell; she survives him with two sons and a daughter of the marriage.

January 29, 1968.

Sir Thomas Lloyd, G.C.M.G., K.C.B., Permanent Under-Secretary of State for the Colonies from 1947 to 1956, died on December 9, 1968, at the age of 72.

Thomas Ingram Kynaston Lloyd was born on June 19, 1896, the eldest son of J. C. Lloyd, and educated at Rossall School, the Royal Military Academy, Woolwich, and Gonville and Caius College, Cambridge. He joined the Royal Engineers in 1916, and served with the Middle Eastern Force from 1917 to 1919, being mentioned in dispatches.

In 1920 Lloyd entered the Home Civil Service under the reconstruction scheme, and was at first assigned to the Ministry of Health.

In the following year, however, he was transferred to the Colonial Office, and quickly made his mark as one of the ablest officers of his generation. In 1929 he was selected for the difficult and responsible job of secretary to the Palestine Commission, which he discharged with great efficiency. From 1930 he worked for a time in the newly formed personnel division of the office, gaining an intimate knowledge of the officers of the Colonial Service and also of the establishment problems of the office itself.

Other assignments within the office followed until, in 1938, he became secretary of the Royal Commission which, under the chairmanship of the late Lord Moyne, had been appointed to go into the complex and difficult economic, social, and political problems of the Caribbean area. He accompanied the commission through its long journeys among the islands. The supreme efficiency with which he conducted their business, his grasp of the issues involved, and his skill in marshalling the vast mass of material emerging from their inquiry won the deserved admiration of the commission and of all who had to consider their report. That report was rendered in 1939, but by then war had broken out: though it was not immediately published, it was not shelved. It was largely the basis of the Government's general plan for Colonial Development and Welfare which was promulgated in 1940, as well as the foundation document for the subsequent economic and political developments in the Caribbean itself.

IN STEP

After finishing this report, Lloyd returned to the office as head of the Colonial Service Department. In 1943 he was promoted to Assistant Under-Secretary of State with wider responsibilities. His colleagues were not surprised when he was announced as the successor to Sir George Gater on the latter's retirement from the Permanent Under-Secretaryship in 1947.

Personally, Lloyd was shy and modest, quiet in manner and of medium stature. He was known as a model of industry and method. All this was true: but these qualities alone would not have brought him to the top of the Colonial Office at the peak period of that office's responsibilities and difficulties. The years of his incumbency saw, among other things, the emergence of Ceylon, Ghana and Malaya to independence; the termination of the Palestine Mandate; the federation of the Rhodesias and Nyasaland; the preliminary stages of the federation of the Caribbean Colonies; the outbreak of terrorism in Kenya and in Cyprus; the coming of the cold war; the implementation of the Development and Welfare policy; the hectic revision of constitutions here, there and everywhere to keep step with the progress of political ideas in the oversea territories; the postwar expansion of the Colonial Service, followed by the necessity for drastic reconstruction in the light of these political changes.

CHEERFULNESS

Never can a Permanent Under-Secretary at the Colonial Office have had so much on his plate.

Yet in all this hurly-burly, Lloyd preserved an air of cheerful imperturbability which gave confidence to those above and below him, as well as to Governors and civil servants overseas. Ministers knew that they could rely on him to speak his mind and give positive counsel. He was no yes-man, though he would loyally accept a ministerial decision even if he did not agree with it. He could not and wisely did not try to direct personally all the multifarious activities of the office. He trusted his officers to do their jobs and encouraged Ministers to consult directly with the officials actually concerned with the business in hand, resisting any temptation to make his own office a bottleneck.

TOUGH CHAMPION

He was a tough champion of the interests of the Colonial Office and its staff in relation to the Treasury and other government departments. Within the office itself, he was a trusted and respected head, and despite the exceptional strain placed upon the organization by the conditions of the times, the machinery worked smoothly and efficiently under his guiding hand.

Outstanding civil servant as he was, Lloyd was by no means a slave to his work. His private preference was for a quiet life and country pursuits, and he had no urge to fill the role of elder statesman when the time came for his official career to close, which, by his own wish, was on his attainment of the age of 60 in 1956.

He married, in 1922, Bessie Nora, elder daughter of G. J. Mason, and they had two sons.

December 11, 1968.

Lord Lloyd George, second Earl Lloyd George of Dwyfor, who was the son of David Lloyd George, former Liberal Prime Minister, died on May 1, 1968, at the age of 79.

His uninhibited biography of his father showed only too plainly how he suffered from the difficulties of living in the shadow of that mercurial figure, with whom his relationship was not always of the happiest.

In his biography of his father, *Lloyd George*, published in 1960, the second Earl sought to show that his father was a great man who profoundly influenced his children and upset the family.

In 1947 the second Earl had published a biography of his mother, Dame Margaret.

PROCEEDINGS

Later that year he was involved in bankruptcy proceedings.

The second Earl was born on February 15, 1889, and educated at Dulwich College and Christ's College, Cambridge. He took a degree in 1910 and was an A.M.I.C.E. He served in the First World War as a major in the Royal Engineers. Lloyd George married first, in 1917, Roberta Ida Freeman (who died in 1966, having obtained a divorce in 1933); and secondly, in 1935, Winifred Emily Calvé.

He succeeded his father in 1945, and the heir to the title is the second Earl's son Owen, Viscount Gwynedd.

May 2, 1968.

Lady Megan Lloyd George, younger daughter of David Lloyd George and Labour M.P. for Carmarthen since 1957, died on May 14, 1966, at Criccieth. She was 64 and had been in ill health for some months.

When the women M.P.s of all parties presented a gift book to her in 1949 to mark the twentieth anniversary of her return to Parliament, a preface to the book summed up the recipient very aptly. It referred to her as "a true daughter of the Welsh Wizard: she bewitches friend and foe alike". The great personal charm, the mordant phrase, the impish, flashing smile were indeed ever present reminders of Megan Lloyd George's eminent parentage. Of all David Lloyd George's children it was his younger daughter who was most like him, both in looks and temperament, and it was she who was probably closest to her father. She inherited from him the passionate radicalism that dominated her political life, which led her eventually to spurn the Parliamentary Liberal Party—of which she had been Deputy Leader—and to join the Labour Party.

Even then she was primarily a Welsh Radical, of a very independent turn of mind, and she did not always march very precisely in step or seem completely at home with her Labour colleagues. Although a born politician, of exceptional ability, who was a member of the House of Commons for over 30 years, Megan Lloyd George never held any Government office. But that probably caused her no regrets. She undoubtedly liked best the freedom of the back benches to campaign independently for the causes she had most at heart—against privilege, the House of Lords, rural slums, Toryism, the under-payment of agricultural workers, and generally, as champion of the underdog. This fiery particle of radicalism—reared in the corridors of real power—was never tamed by the urbanities of political life in London. She had her roots in rural North Wales and always proudly belonged to her native countryside and people, among whom she mostly lived. She was sometimes the despair of party managers but she remained true to her life-long political instincts and was a charming embodiment of Wales at Westminster.

HER FATHER'S HOSTESS

Megan Lloyd George was born at Criccieth on April 22, 1902. From a child of eight until she was 22 she lived in Downing Street, first at No. 11 when her father was Chancellor of the Exchequer, and afterwards at No. 10, when he was Prime Minister. She went to school, first, at Garratt's Hall, Banstead. Until she was four years old she had spoken only Welsh. She developed into a brilliant child. Her father doted on his younger daughter and when, after the 1914–18 War, he went as Prime Minister to the Peace Conference he took her with him to Paris. She was put to school there but her father would often fetch her from school and introduce her to the glittering circle of world statesmen, diplomats and soldiers by whom he was surrounded. Sometimes he would have her act as his hostess on social occasions. At this time Megan was 17 and her father was the most powerful man in the world of those days. Nobody of her age could have had such a remarkable experience.

In 1924 she went to India and spent a year there as the guest of the Viceroy, Lord Reading. She was afterwards closely associated with her father in all his political activities and in May 1929 she herself was elected to the House of Commons as Liberal member for Anglesey. Her political campaigning then as later was usually in the Welsh language. When she made her maiden speech to a crowded House in 1930 her father was there to hear her. The subject of debate was a Government housing Bill and she made an eloquent and impressive plea for better housing for agricultural labourers and their families.

Major Gwilym Lloyd-George (later Lord Tenby), the former Prime Minister's younger son, was also an M.P. and with three members of the Lloyd George family in the House together harmony was often strained in the Parliamentary Liberal Party. The Lloyd Georges were all opposed to the holding of an early election in 1931 by Ramsay MacDonald's first National Government and the three of them fought the election as Independent Liberals. But the Lloyd Georges themselves drifted apart after the father's death and while Lady Megan moved to the Left in politics her brother moved to the Right—although there was always a bond of close personal affection between them.

DEFEAT AT ANGLESEY

During the Second World War Lady Megan was associated with war work of various kinds and during this period she was privileged to make the opening speech in the first Commons debate ever devoted exclusively to Welsh affairs. She welcomed this recognition of the distinctive problems and needs of Wales as a nation with its own language, history and culture. In 1949 Lady Megan was appointed Deputy Leader of the Parliamentary Liberal Party, as lieutenant to Mr. Clement Davies. But within a year she detected "a drift to the Right" in the policy of the party which she regarded as contrary to the old and better Radical tradition in which she had been reared. She found herself at variance with the majority of her colleagues on various policy issues and she and two other Liberal M.P.s often acted together as a Radical "ginger group". Then, at the election of 1951, Lady Megan was defeated in Anglesey by the Labour candidate, Mr. Cledwyn Hughes, who won the seat by 595 votes in a three-cornered fight. This was a blow to her after she had represented Anglesey for 22 years but she commented that she was "not of a retiring age or a retiring disposition". She thought that the "drift to the Right" in the Liberal Party was gaining momentum and in 1952 she announced that she would not stand as Liberal candidate for Anglesey again. She became president of the "Parliament for Wales" campaign.

In April, 1955, Lady Megan joined the Labour Party. In a letter to Mr. Attlee, then Leader of the Opposition, she said she was convinced that in the changed circumstances it was only in the Labour Party that she could be true to the Radical tradition. She campaigned widely for the Labour Party in the 1955 election but was not herself found a seat to contest. It was not until 1957 that she returned to the House as a Labour M.P. This was after a by-election at Carmarthen, in which she beat a Liberal candidate by 3,069 votes. She thus returned to Westminster at the age of 54 after an absence of six years.

Lady Megan Lloyd George never married. From her earliest years she was dedicated to the political life and found her fulfilment in this and in working for the many good causes which interested her. In the thirties she was president of the Women's National Liberal Federation and later she was chairman of the Welsh Parliamentary Party. She was a member of one of the broadcasting inquiries and gave much time to committee work in connexion with housing, women's interests, the British Council, the National Free Church Council and the Post Office. When the Labour Party came to power again in 1964 she was elected chairman of the Parliamentary Labour Party's specialist group of M.P.s on Agriculture, Fisheries and Food.

Whether as a Liberal or a Labour M.P. Megan Lloyd George was first and foremost a Welsh Radical and very much the unique and devoted daughter of the man described by Churchill as having been "the greatest Welshman since the age of the Tudors".

May 16, 1966.

Paul Löbe, who died on August 3, 1967, in Bonn, at the age of 91, has his place in the history of modern Germany both as the last democratic president of the Weimar Reichstag and as one of the builders of the Social Democratic Movement.

It was in tune with his fine character that he survived the Hitlerian persecution (lucky indeed to have escaped with his life) with his humanity unembittered and his likeableness unalloyed. He was born in 1875, and Theodor Heuss, first President of the Federal Republic of Germany, happily described Löbe on the 75th. anniversary of his birthday as "the eternal journeyman."

Löbe was born in Silesia, always the poorest part of Germany; his father was a joiner, and even if the family did not actually hunger, at any rate food was meagre enough for a new birth in the home to cause fears, the children fearing there would be less for them at table. Potatoes in all their guises were the main diet. At 12 Löbe began contributing to the family income: he worked in a boot shop from 6 a.m. till school time at 7 a.m., and then after school till 8 p.m.

SHILLING A WEEK

He was paid a shilling a week. Late in life, when time had softened his memories of much suffering and many privations, he recorded wryly but proudly that his "wage" played an appreciable part in balancing the family budget.

The "hard times" in Silesia frustrated his own wish to qualify as a teacher. Instead his father apprenticed him to a barber, but the son—his interest in books and politics already awakening—jibbed at the idea, and he was given his chance as a compositor and corrector of the press in a printing works. He wrote articles also. With the end of his five-year apprenticeship began his joyous *Wanderjahre*, which took him, mainly on foot, through several countries as well as his own and which broadened his mind and enriched his experience as no amount of schooling could have done.

Bebel, Liebknecht, Lassalle, and lesser leaders of the day were household words in his working-class home, and it was inevitable that he should have taken up the Social Democratic cause in dead earnest in his early years. His influence with the party followers grew. He developed into an arresting orator fired by a crusading spirit which still burned brightly throughout the closing years of his long life. His editorial articles and his political activites had to be paid for with imprisonment. His newspaper, the Breslau *Volkswacht*, widened its circles of readers. In the First World War copies of it were smuggled to Germans serving on most frontiers by land and sea.

Löbe played a constructive part in the chaotic and revolutionary events after the German surrender in 1918. He was elected to the National Assembly which drew up the Weimar Constitution. From 1920 to 1932 he was president of the new Reichstag, which he guided through many national tribulations and frequent turbulence with firmness, tolerance and good humour. It fell to him to pour oil on troubled waters. The emergence of the Nazis, however, sounded the death-knell of his own democratic rule. Göring usurped his office. It is fair to say that Göring, who admired Löbe's wit without assimilating his wisdom, sought to ease the shameful conditions to which Löbe was subjected in the concentration camp where he was incarcerated, with other comrades, after having spurned the blandishments showered on him by members of the Hitlerian regime.

There was never any question where he stood when, under Russian patronage, such plotters as Pieck and Ulbricht went to desperate lengths to coerce or to cajole the Social Democrats into joining the communists in forming the present Socialist Unity Party in Berlin. A few yielded, among them Grotewohl and Fritz Ebert, son of the first and finest president of the Weimar Republic. With Kurt Schumacher (who suffered savagely in concentration camps), Ernst Reuter, Otto Suhr, Louise Schroeder (his good companion), and many others, Löbe helped to give Social Democracy a fresh start in freedom. In the Bundestag of the Federal Republic he sat, fittingly, as one of the representatives of Berlin. There he enjoyed the esteem and good will of members of all parties. When he laid down his mandate he showed how faithful he had remained to Heuss's characterization "the eternal journeyman;" the former deputy passed from the floor of the House to the Press Gallery, where he was to be seen, pencil and notebook in hand, recording the parliamentary scene.

August 4, 1967.

Sir Robert Bruce Lockhart, K.C.M.G., diplomat, author and journalist, died on February 27, 1970, at the age of 82.

In one of his many books of autobiography

and reminiscence he spoke of his "misfortune" that the label of adventure had been attached to him. But it was not an inaccurate label; and it was certainly not meant disparagingly for, given the necessary patience and discipline, Bruce Lockhart might have become a novelist in the adventurous tradition of Joseph Conrad. But all through his long, active life, from his late teens to the end of the Second World War, he hankered after frequent changes of scene and occupation. So in turn he was rubber-planter, consular official, banker, journalist, lecturer, diplomat, and finally government servant in high positions—envoy to the Czech Government in exile, and then Director-General of the Political Warfare Executive, after which he settled once more to be the writer of most readable and successful works, maintaining the reputation he had deservedly won some 20 years before.

He was born on September 2, 1887. From his preparatory school he gained a scholarship to Fettes, and was there during the years when that school won such renown at Rugger. Robert played half-back, but also, as he gratefully acknowledges, was compelled to play some soccer. This was to come in useful when, in 1911, having had some preliminary training in France and Germany he passed the Foreign Office examination, and was sent as Vice-Consul to Moscow. Here he played soccer for the famous team of the Motozovsti, learned Russian, and though so young—the American press later dubbed him the "Boy Ambassador" —prepared himself for the responsible position he was given on the outbreak of the Russian Revolution.

Owing to the illness of his chief, he was Acting Consul-General during the war, and when diplomatic relations came to an end he was, on the suggestion of Lord Milner, sent back to the semi-official British representative with the Soviet Government. His graphic accounts of the perilous changing scene, when his despatches could get through, were greatly appreciated by Lloyd George, but the policy of intervention ruined any chance there might have been of establishing normal relations. Bruce Lockhart, in fact, was imprisoned in the Kremlin in September, 1918, to be released a few weeks later and sent back in exchange for Litvinov.

DEATH SENTENCE

His activity was characterized later on in the *Soviet Encyclopaedia* as the "Lockhart conspiracy", and he was even condemned to death *in absentia*. But in truth he never believed in the wisdom of intervention and only unwillingly acquiesced in a policy which Allied desperation made inevitable in the prevailing circumstances.

In 1920 Bruce Lockhart, still in the Foreign Service, was appointed Commercial Secretary in the British Legation in Prague, so continuing that affectionate concern with Czechoslovakia which had begun when he had persuaded Trotsky to allow the Czech Legion to return home. Devotion to the Czech people lasted all Lockhart's life, and for many years he broadcast a weekly talk from London in Czech.

In 1928 Bruce Lockhart was engaged by Lord Beaverbrook to write for his papers, and he spent some years in Fleet Street. It was Sir Harold Nicolson who persuaded him that he could escape this by turning his earlier experiences into a book. And so, in 1932, came *Memoirs of a British Agent*. It had a striking success, and continued selling for many years, a classic of its kind. As Bruce Lockhart with understandable pride, said, "it started a new fashion in personal history". But these frank self-revelations of both his personal and official life in Russia were not marred by any excessive obtrusion of his personality. He gave intimate experience, vividly recollected, of a crucial period in the history of the world, turned it into literature, immensely readable.

Bruce Lockhart made good use of the freedom which his success brought him. He went on turning his reminiscences into more books: *Retreat from Glory* in 1934, describing his experiences in Czechoslovakia and his personal contact with famous European politicians, such as the dying Stresemann, who in 1929 told him that nothing remained for Europe but "brute force". Two years later came *Return to Malaya*, a delightful account of his work, in 1908, as a rubber-planter in Negri Sembilan.

As the Nazi advance gathered impetus Bruce Lockhart was engaged by the British Council to lecture in South Eastern Europe. From this came, in 1938, *Guns or Butter*. An optimistic estimate of the development of the Balkan nations was qualified by fears of Nazi aggression. In 1940 the Foreign Office appointed him representative with the Provisional Czechoslovak Government in exile, and he renewed his close and sympathetic contact with the leaders of a people he had known and admired 20 years before. He was a particularly intimate friend of Jan Masaryk.

In 1941 Bruce Lockhart was made a Deputy Under-Secretary of State in the Foreign Office, and took over the direction of the Political Warfare Executive, which coordinated all British psychological warfare and propaganda to Germany and the Nazi-dominated countries. This exacting work occupied him till the end of the war, and in a volume, *Comes the Reckoning*, published in 1948, he described his experiences, giving some valuable sidelights on Allied policy.

At the end of the War, refusing an invitation to continue in the Foreign Service, Bruce Lockhart devoted himself almost exclusively to writing books more prolific than ever. In 1951 he published a memoir of Jan Masaryk. In other books he drew heavily and profitably on his well-filled diaries and vivid memories of great events and prominent personalities; in *My Europe* (1952), *Your England* (1955), *Friends, Foes and Foreigners* (1957), and *Giants Cast Long Shadows* (1960).

Bruce Lockhart had a host of friends in many countries. He was a loyal and stimulating friend, a delightful companion. He was always assured of an enthusiastic welcome whenever he went to lecture to foreign societies: the familiar slightly hoarse voice radiated friendliness and confidence, based on years of experience and first-rate narrative ability. The same may be said of the occasions when he gave talks over the radio.

He was twice married.

February 28, 1970.

Frank Loesser, who died in New York on July 28, 1969, at the age of 59, was the composer-producer who wrote words and music for *Guys and Dolls*, *The Most Happy Fella*, and *How to Succeed in Business Without Really Trying*.

His song, "Baby it's cold outside", from the film *Neptune's Daughter*, won the 1948 Academy Award. *How to succeed* won the Pulitzer Prize for drama in 1962. Another of his hit songs was Ray Bolger's famous number in *Where's Charley*? (1948).

For many years before that, Loesser had been piling up Hollywood credits, and enormously successful popular song titles. These ranged from the infuriating "Bloop Bleep" through the humorously appealing "Two Sleepy People", the patriotically rousing "Praise the Lord and Pass the Ammunition", the casually jaunty "I Got Spurs that Jingle, Jangle, Jingle", to the lightly romantic "Moon of Manakoora," his first big hit.

Born in 1910 in New York, Loesser took on a variety of jobs after his schooling. By 1929 he earned money writing material for radio; by 1936 he was singing songs in a night club. His performances at the night club led to a Broadway musical called *The Illustrators* for which he and Actman wrote the songs. In 1937 he wrote for Hollywood with "Moon of Manakoora" for the film *Hurricane*. Since then he heard some of his many hundreds of songs aired on the Hit Parade.

For English audiences, Frank Loesser's most effective work was probably *Guys and Dolls*, for which he wrote music which seemed to belong to the odd world—hard-heartedly sentimental—of the stories by Damon Runyon, which the show brought to the stage. The soft-heartedly sentimental world of *The Most Happy Fella*, the musical version of Sidney Howard's *They Knew What They Wanted*, seemed to be not much more than extremely efficient professional music in which the composer was less deeply engaged.

He once said; "Tunes just pop into my head. Of course, your head has to be arranged to receive them. Some people's heads are arranged so that they keep getting colds. I keep getting songs."

He was twice married.

July 29, 1969.

Adrian Albert Lombard, C.B.E., a director of Rolls-Royce Ltd., and Director of Engineering of the company's aero engine division, died suddenly on July 13, 1967, at the age of 52.

He was well known throughout the aviation world as one of the world's leading designers of aero engines. For nearly 30 years he had been closely associated with the design and development of British jet engines, including the complete range of jet, propjet and turbofan engies produced by Rolls-Royce.

Born in Coventry in January, 1915, Lombard began work in the design office of the Rover Company. Apart from a brief spell on technical work at the engine branch of Morris Motors Ltd., he remained with Rover until 1943.

His work on the design of jet engines began in April, 1940, when Rover took an interest in the Whittle jet engine. When Rolls-Royce took over the Rover interest in the Whittle jet engine in 1943 Lombard continued to work on the project and joined Rolls-Royce as chief designer (Northern Factories), where his team was responsible for the design of the Derwent, Nene and the early Avon jet engines. These engines powered most of the first generation of British jet fighters and bombers.

In 1946 he moved to the Derby headquarters of the Rolls-Royce aero-engine division as chief designer, projects, and in 1949 he became chief designer of the division. He became chief engineer in 1954, and in 1958 was appointed director of engineering, aero engine division, and became a director of Rolls-Royce. As director of engineering he was responsible for the design of all Rolls-Royce turbine engines.

He was a member of the Institution of Mechanical Engineers and was on the council of the Royal Aeronautical Society, the Air Registration Board and the Aeronautical Research Council. He was appointed C.B.E. in the Queen's Birthday Honours a month before he died, and, also in 1967, his work on jet engines was honoured when he and Dr. S. G. Hooker, technical director (aero) of Bristol Siddeley Engines, were jointly awarded the James Clayton Prize of the Institution of Mechanical Engineers.

Under Lombard's leadership Rolls-Royce developed a wide range of famous jet and propjet engines which power aircraft built in many parts of the world. Examples are the Derwent jet engine which was installed in the Gloster Meteor fighter; the Avon turbojet, which powered a complete generation of British fighters and bombers such as the Hawker Hunter and English Electric Canberra; the Tyne propjet, which powers the Vickers Vanguard and a range of military aircraft; the Conway turbofan, which is installed in a number of Boeing 707 and Douglas D.C.8 airliners, as well as the Vickers V.C.10 and Super V.C.10; and the Spey turbofan, which is today Britain's most successful jet engine and has been selected for eight types of civil and military aircraft, including three produced in the United States. Lombard was also responsible for the development of a range of lift jet engines for vertical-take-off aircraft.

July 15, 1967.

Lord Longford, who had been actively associated with the Irish theatre for many years, both as benefactor and dramatist, died on February 4, 1961.

The Rt. Hon. Edward Arthur Henry Pakenham, sixth Earl of Longford, and Baron Longford, in the peerage of England, and Baron Silchester, of Silchester, in the county of Southampton, in the peerage of the United Kingdom, was born on December 29, 1902, the elder son of the fifth Earl, of Longford and Lady Mary Child-Villiers, third daughter of the seventh Earl of Jersey. He succeeded to the family honours when his father was killed in action at Gallipoli in 1915. He was educated at Eton and Christ Church, Oxford.

His death underlines a curious fact, how much the Irish theatre owes to the landed gentry. Two Connacht landlords, Lady Gregory and Edward Martyn, pioneered the Irish National Theatre which was the forerunner of the Abbey Theatre. When the Gate Theatre, founded by Hilton Edwards and Micheál Mac Liammóir, was foundering in 1931 through lack of finance Longford ("a stout rosy-cheeked young man" as Micheál MacLiammóir recalled him) came forward and offered to buy up the outstanding shares. His association with the drama in Dublin ensured that there would always be a theatre available independent of the commercial market.

This proved all the more important in the fifties when it became obvious that the Abbey was adopting a frankly commercial outlook.

PRIVATE SUBSIDY

Longford subsidized the Gate Theatre from his private wealth. Four years ago he met a crisis in the theatre's history with typical energy and resource. Thirty thousand pounds was needed for alterations in the theatre; a public fund was opened and Longford himself gathered money in the Dublin streets, carrying a little collection box that became inseparable from his personality in the humorous anecdotage of the town. Thirteen thousand pounds has been collected to date from the public, a good deal of it subscribed from people in humble circumstances, an indication of the affection in which Longford's theatre was held by the people of the city. He always hoped to keep the Gate as a people's theatre and to this end until recently he sent his company on tour in the Irish provinces. Prices of the Gate were kept exceedingly low and there was still a shilling seat to be had there. Just before his last illness he was holding out against an alteration in admission prices proposed by an English company who were hiring the Gate for a season. Eventually he settled for 7s. 6d. as the top admission price, the amount perhaps of a theatre programme on Broadway.

The golden years at the Gate were 1931–35: Mr. Mac Liammoir as actor, set designer, and linguist was able with Mr. Hilton Edwards to bring a cohesion to dramatic art rare in the modern theatre. Mr. James Mason and Mr. Orson Welles came to act and Longford himself wrote three plays in that period, *The Melians*, *Ascendancy*, and *Yahoo*. *Yahoo*, a play about Swift, was given an enthusiastic reception when the Gate had a successful London season in 1935. He translated plays from the Irish, the French and the Greek and was a fluent Irish speaker.

In 1937 he broke with Mr. Edwards and Mr. Mac Liammóir and since then their companies have alternated at the Gate. Longford was not an especially expert judge of an actor. His extreme kindness of heart often made him reluctant to dispense with a member of the company who was without talent: this more than anything else probably led to the rift with Mr. Mac Liammóir and Mr. Edwards who were determined to raise the professional standards in Dublin.

He was a man of firm Nationalist convictions and once pulled a top hat down over a man's ears at the Dublin Horse Show because he was singing "God Save the King". He received a ducking in Oxford in 1922 after he had dissociated himself from a vote of sympathy passed at the Union for the widow of Sir Henry Wilson, who had been assassinated by two Sinn Feiners in London. In Dublin, where *un original* is revered, Longford had become accepted as a character. Occasionally one saw his enormous figure pushing through Grafton Street clad in outrageously baggy flannels and the top part of an elderly serge suit, the great head, a cross between that of a jolly friar and a Norman baron, bobbing hither and thither through the crowd. Each year at his town house he gave a party for theatrical friends, distributing cream buns and sherry and invariably singing the Polish National Anthem at 4 p.m. One associated him somehow with the eighteenth century and the tradition of Grattan's Parliament when high-minded Irishmen of noble birth used their town houses as centres for patriotic endeavour and devoted the proceeds of their estates to the betterment of their fellow countrymen. Longford was a member of the Irish Senate from 1946 to 1948. He married in 1925 Christine, daughter of Richard Trew, of Cheddar, Somerset, herself a playwright. His heir is his brother, Lord Pakenham.

February 6, 1961.

Air Chief Marshal Sir Arthur M. Longmore, G.C.B., D.S.O., who died on December 10, 1970, at the age of 85, was AO.C.-in-C. Middle East in 1940–41 and subsequently Inspector-General of the R.A.F.

He was a pioneer of naval aviation. As a young lieutenant, R.N., he was one of the first four officers selected by the Admiralty to learn to fly, and he became in turn an original member of the Naval Wing of the R.F.C., the Royal Naval Air Service, and the R.A.F. His versatility was illustrated in 1916 when, within a period of six months, he commanded an air squadron at Dunkirk, fought at Jutland as lieutenant-commander in a battlecruiser, and served as wing commander in the Air Department at the Admiralty. In 1942 he contested Grantham as a Conservative candidate for Parliament, but was unsuccessful, being defeated by a narrow margin by Mr. W. D. Kendall, Independent.

In between the wars he was a successful and much-liked Commandant of the R.A.F. College, Cranwell.

Arthur Murray Longmore was born at St. Leonards, New South Wales. Educated at Benges School, Hertford, and at Foster's Academy, Stubbington, he entered the Britannia as a naval cadet in May, 1900. In November, 1911, in a Short biplane with flotation bags and skids, he flew from Eastchurch and alighted in Sheerness Harbour, the first flight from land to water in English history.

In May, 1940, he was appointed Air Officer Commanding in the Middle East, where he displayed much energy and ingenuity in making the most of his scanty resources at difficult periods.

His commitments were large and widely spread and he often had the utmost difficulty in convincing Whitehall that, whatever the number of aircraft might be under his command, not all were suitable for the tasks demanded of them.

He returned home in 1941 and was appointed Inspector-General of the R.A.F.

He was married in 1913 to Marjorie, only child of the late Mr. W. J. Maitland, C.I.E., and had three sons (one of whom was killed in action in 1943) and one daughter. His wife died in 1959 and he married, secondly, in 1960 Enid, widow of Lieutenant-Colonel ,G. Bolster.

December 12, 1970.

Dr. Tom Longstaff, who died on June 26, 1964, at the age of 89, ranked first among the company of British mountain explorers who opened up the greater mountain ranges of the world in the first quarter of the twentieth century. By the time the first attack came to be made on Everest in 1922, he had become Britain's principal pioneer of Himalayan climbing and doyen of mountain travellers.

He was the eldest son of Llewellyn Longstaff, who made practicable the National Antarctic Expedition under Captain Scott by giving £25,000 to the fund started by the Royal Geographical Society before any assistance was granted by Government, and who afterwards gave £5,000 toward the relief expedition on board the Morning. Tom George Longstaff was born in 1875 and educated at Eton and Christ Church, Oxford, where he graduated both in arts and medicine. His hospital experience he gained at St. Thomas's.

He at once applied himself to exploration with characteristic thoroughness, not only qualifying for membership of the Alpine Club (1900) and joining the R.G.S. (1902), but quickly coming into prominence in both these bodies. He had graduated as a mountaineer in the Alps; now widening his operations he carried out an expedition to the Caucasus in 1904, making five first ascents without guides, which added much to his reputation in Alpine Club circles. His expedition of the following year brought him to the front as an explorer. He travelled a thousand miles in the central Himalaya through Kumaon, Nepal, Tibet, and Garhwal. Accompanied by Alexis and Henri Brocherel of Courmayeur, he crossed passes of 18,000 ft., stood on the rim of the Inner Sanctuary of Nanda Devi (the first men to look into it), and reached 21,000 ft.' on Nanda Kot. He then joined the Deputy Commissioner of Almora on a mission into Tibet. On his return to England he joined General (then Major) C. G. Bruce and A. L. Mumm in a plan to celebrate the jubilee of the Alpine Club by a reconnaissance of Mount Everest. Although the plan was strongly supported by the R.G.S. the political difficulties at that time proved insurmountable.

His principal objective for 1907 was the summit of Trisul, 23,360 ft.: the trident of the god Shiva. His record of that climb is one of the epic tales of exploratory mountaineering. His party was small, privately financed at low cost, ill-equipped by modern standards, but extraordinarily fast-moving. It got results. The actual ascent of Trisul was only one incident in that year's programme, and the very approach involved the forcing of the great outer curtain of the Nanda Devi Sanctuary; then the Rishi Gorge had to be crossed, Trisul reconnoitred, the route selected, and the ascent made by a party of four climbers. All this was done in little more than a month. The final climb from the last camp was 6,000 ft., done in a day. That in itself was a physical feat which few have been able to emulate in these last 50 years of Himalayan climbing.

Two years later Longstaff was again in India, exploring the Karakoram. He found and crossed the Saltoro Pass, 18,200 ft.,—an old pass known only from native report—discovered the Siachen Glacier, the largest on earth outside polar regions, and surveyed the hitherto unknown mountain of Teram Kangri (24,489 ft.). In 1910 he turned his attention to Canada and crossed the Purcell Range of British Columbia. His reputation was now at its height. In seven years he had carried out five expeditions on the great ranges and had contributed maps and papers to the R.G.S. and the Alpine Club. He was indefatigable in research. In 1908 he had been awarded the Gill Memorial of the R.G.S., and in 1911 was elected to the council of the society. In that same year he married a daughter of Bernard Scott, M.R.C.S., of Bournemouth.

On the outbreak of war in 1914, Longstaff was commissioned to the Hampshires and sent to India, where he was attached to the General Staff at Simla. In 1916, his appointment to the Gilgit Corps of Scouts as assistant commandant gave him the chance to make several journeys into the Hindu Kush.

RECONNAISSANCE OF EVEREST

The aftermath of war delayed his return to active exploratory work, but he helped to mount the first Everest reconnaissance of 1921. In the next 13 years he led, or took part in, no less than seven expeditions, twice to Spitsbergen (1921 and 1923), Mount Everest (1922), the Garhwal Himalaya (1927), thrice to Greenland (1928, 1931 and 1934), and to Baffin Land (1934). In 1928 he was awarded the Founder's Medal of the R.G.S., and during the period 1930 to 1937 served as honorary secretary and then vice-president of the society. In 1938 he married Charmian, younger daughter of Duncan James Reid, M.B. His second marriage brought him great happiness, for although his geographical explorations were now ended he remained young in heart and vigorous in mind. On the outbreak of the Second World War he served for two years with the 13th Bn. K.R.R.C., before finally retiring to live in the bare lands of Wester Ross, under the wide skies that he loved so well. There he wrote his book, *This My Voyage*, the tale of his exploratory travels. In 1947 he was elected president of the Alpine Club, an honour which he valued before knighthood. But whatever honours are conferred by man, none compare with those bestowed by Providence. Here is Longstaff, aged 32, on the summit of Trisul:

"I cut a few steps in ice up on to the cornice. Henry stood back to hold in case it gave way as I crawled to the top. I craned over on my belly to look down the astounding southern precipice. Spread below were all the middle hills we had marched through; then the foothills; then the plains with rivers winding. To the west all was clear; the whole scarp of the Western Himalaya so vast that I expected to see the earth rotating before my eyes. The western foothills gave the impression of those little waves that on a calm day are born as the sea shallows and laps gently on the shelving shore of some great bay. I was very luckly. I had not the least feeling of exultation or achievement: the reward was far greater."

Longstaff was small in stature and spare of frame. He wore a big red moustache in his younger days, and latterly a beard. He seemed almost frail—until one looked him in the eye. Instantly one knew the presence of a strong personality, possessed of energies in the measure that can make for greatness. In all dealings with men he remained at once upright and downright. The cheekbone was high, the nose thin, like a hawk's, the eyes cool, deep-penetrating if they chose, the mouth firm as a fighter's—it might have been the face of a desert Arab, but more particularly, the face of a man born to the quest, to the penetration of the unknown, whether on physical, mental, or spiritual planes. Fifty years ago he was indeed a prodigy in power and performance; yet he never aged in spirit.

June 29, 1964.

Gordon Lonsdale, the Russian master spy, who was sentenced to 25 years in 1961 at the Central Criminal Court for running the Portland spy ring, died about October, 1970, near Moscow, Soviet sources reported.

Less than three years served, at dawn on April 22, 1964 he was exchanged at a Berlin checkpoint for Greville Wynne, the Briton imprisoned by the Russians for alleged spying.

At the trial at the Old Bailey Peter and Helen Kroger, Harry Houghton and Ethel Gee were also sentenced: the Krogers to 20 years' imprisonment and Houghton and Gee to 15 years. Kroger and his wife were, like Lonsdale, central figures in the case in which Houghton and Gee, two Admiralty employees, collected details of secret naval documents, some concerning Dreadnought, the nuclear submarine.

Kroger, who posed as an antiquarian bookseller, and his wife were responsible for transmitting defence secrets from their bungalow at Ruislip.

At the trial the Lord Chief Justice, Lord Parker, said to Lonsdale: "You are clearly a professional spy. It is a dangerous career and one in which you must be prepared...to suffer if and when you are caught...yours, so far as the activities of the five of you are concerned, was the directing mind."

In sentencing the spies the Lord Chief Justice said: "You must each of you know full well the gravity of the offence and, for peacetime, this must be one of the most disgraceful cases that has come before the court." He went on: "I am satisfied that this conspiracy lasted over a matter of months and related to more than one communication."

There was evidence that after almost every meeting with Houghton and Gee, Lonsdale went to the Ruislip bungalow of the Krogers, who transmitted the secrets to the Russians. In his summing up the Lord Chief Justice said the jury might think that the link, or the hub of the wheel, was Lonsdale.

The first trace of Lonsdale, a member of the Russian intelligence service, was when he went from Canada to the United States via Niagara, and went to New York in 1955 for a few weeks before sailing for Southampton. He took a flat at the White House, Albany Street, and between June and August, 1955, went to the Continent on two tours. In October that year he began a course in Chinese at the School of Oriental and African Studies in London. His application form stated that he had been educated at schools in San Francisco and Berkeley, California, but there was no trace of his being at either school.

While attending the course in London, he began to take an interest in the automatic machine business, buying two juke boxes for £500 from the Automatic Machine Company, Broadstairs in 1958, and becoming a director in the company and manager of the London office. When the company was wound up in 1959, the Official Receiver said its failure was due to the mismanagement of Lonsdale and another director.

In 1960, Lonsdale became a director in another company to market a security switch and was concerned with that and ancillary companies until his arrest, having invested about £1,000 in the company. Entries in his passport showed that in the summers of 1956, 1957, 1959 and 1960 he made long trips abroad, ranging from five to 10 weeks.

Lonsdale, whose real name was Konon Trofimovitch Molody, known as Colonel K to the Russians, was a partisan, who at the age of 17 was parachuted behind German lines in 1943 to organize his own group at Minsk. It was there that he met Colonel Rudolph Abel, then posing as a German officer, who was later to be his boss in America. Soon Lonsdale was working in Germany itself as Abel's wireless operator—and beginning a partnership which was to last until just before Abel's arrest by the F.B.I. in 1957. Abel was later to set the pattern for the swop which set Lonsdale free. He was exchanged by the Americans for the U2 pilot Gary Powers.

Lonsdale, posing as a United States naval commander, suggested Houghton should work for United States intelligence. Soon Houghton's girl friend Ethel "Bunty" Gee, who worked at Portland as well, was also supplying secret information. The end came in January, 1961, as Gee was handing over a shopping bag full of secrets in the Waterloo Road. In 1965 Lonsdale published his autobiography *Spy*.

October 14, 1970.

Samuel Joseph Looker, a life-long champion of the works of Richard Jefferies, died on January 11, 1965, at the age of 76.

He was born in 1888 in north London, but after early manhood lived in Sussex, Staffordshire and Leicestershire. His was an active and dedicated life. After early commercial work he became a writer, lecturer, journalist and publishers' reader; in this last capacity he worked for Constable and Co. from 1923 until his death. Between 1921 and 1935 he lectured on English literature to L.C.C. evening institutes and for W.E.A. classes. He also reviewed books for *The Times Literary Supplement* under the editorship of Sir Bruce Richmond, wrote on George Crabbe for the *Nineteenth Century* and contributed other articles on W. H. Hudson, Shelley, Trelawney and Henley. He contributed to *John O'London's Weekly*, then edited by his friend, Wilson Midgly, and edited anthologies on travel, hunting, shooting, and fishing. He contributed to *The Cambridge Bibliography of English Literature* the section on nineteenth-century fiction in volume three, and wrote or edited some 50 books, including nine volumes of poetry.

He came to know and love the writings of Richard Jefferies early in life; he was 13 when he read *The Story of My Heart*. He wrote in his introduction to *The Old House at Coate*, which he edited and published in 1948: "I read every one of his (Jefferies's) books on which I could lay my hands. It was then, many years ago, that I first made the resolve that, if I lived, I would one day edit this great writer and devote all my energies to making his creative and consoling work more widely known and appreciated...."

SEARCH FOR MSS.

He described also how he sought out not only every book and every bit of information but also every scrap of Jefferies's manuscript which either came into the market or was to be had by private treaty. He pursued a long and finally successful search for the field note books and occasional nature notes of the writer and for any hitherto unpublished papers including letters and essays hidden away, often unsigned, in old magazines until he was able to claim that he owned most of the material of any importance relating to Richard Jefferies.

Much of this research was done in the British Museum Newspaper Room at Colindale where Looker spent many hours poring over old periodicals, nosing out long forgotten contributions which he recognized as the work of Jefferies. As a result of all this he was able to publish two new volumes of essays, *Chronicles of the Hedges* in 1948 and *Field and Farm* in 1957.

Previously he had edited and published a number of anthologies after the copyrights had expired in 1937 and later edited with introductions and notes nine of Jefferies's books to mark the centenary of the writer's birth. He caused Worthing, where Jefferies is buried, to become intimately conscious of its association with the writer by publishing under the Worthing Art Development Scheme several handsomely illustrated volumes containing a wealth of information about the life and work of Jefferies.

It was known that Jefferies had left 24 notebooks containing his day to day comments, descriptions and observations but of these only 16 were ever found. These Looker transcribed and published in 1948 under the title of *The Notebooks of Richard Jefferies*.

This work entailed the closest application and infinite patience, since many of the notes were hurriedly written in pencil and often in the writer's peculiar shorthand, most difficult to decipher, but Looker, in persevering thus to interpret and preserve them, has left a valuable legacy for students and readers of Jefferies.

Looker had been working for some years on what he hoped would be the definitive life of Jefferies, to be called *Richard Jefferies, Man of the Fields.* Latterly he had had the help of Mr. Crichton Porteous in preparing the book, which is due to be published in the spring.

In the midst of all this literary work Looker found time to serve from 1949 to 1954 on the Staffordshire County Council while living at Cheadle. He was chairman of the Records Committee and served on the Trent River Board until he left the Midlands.

He was a conversationalist of charm and had a great capacity for making and keeping friends, among whom he included during their lifetime the son and daughter of Jefferies.

He was president of the Richard Jefferies Society since it was founded in 1950.

Looker married Caroline Finney, and they had three children, a son and two daughters.

January 12, 1965.

Sir Percy Loraine, BT., P.C., G.C.M.G., who died on May 23, 1961, at his London home at the age of 80, was British Ambassador to Turkey from 1933 to 1939 and Ambassador in Rome from 1939 until the Italians entered the Second World War.

Percy Lyham Loraine was born on November 5, 1880, the second son of Rear-Admiral Sir Lambton Loraine, eleventh baronet, of Bramford Hall, Suffolk, and Frederica Mary, daughter of Captain Charles Acton Broke, R.E. Loraine's elder brother, who was a Captain in the Grenadier Guards, died unmarried in 1912, so that when his father died in 1917, Percy succeeded as twelfth baronet.

He was educated at Eton and boarded first at Mr. Sydney James's and then at Mr. White Thompson's, both of whom were his tutors. He went to Eton in 1893 and remained there till 1899 reaching VI Form and being Captain of his house. He played in the Eton XI of 1898 which drew with Winchester and was beaten by Harrow by 9 wickets. He was a member of the Eton Society and a keen volunteer, reaching the rank of sergeant.

In 1899 he went up to New College, Oxford, but did not remain long as he joined the Imperial Yeomanry in 1899 when war broke out and served in South Africa till 1902, receiving the Queen's Medal and five Clasps and being granted the rank of Hon. Lieut. in the Army.

When he returned to England he did not go

back to Oxford but worked for the Diplomatic Service into which he passed in 1904, a year before he reached the age limit: no mean achievement seeing that he had been on active service in the Army for nearly three years.

IN CONSTANTINOPLE

After a few months in the Foreign Office he was appointed to Constantinople, where he gained an allowance for knowledge of Turkish. Promoted to be Third Secretary, he was in 1907 transferred to Teheran, where he gained allowances for knowledge of International Law and Persian. He was made Second Secretary in 1909 and transferred to Rome, where he remained until 1911, when he went out to Peking.

In 1912 he was sent to Paris, and in the same year he was British delegate at the International Conference on Pauper Aliens. Four years later he was posted to Madrid as First Secretary and Head of the Chancery, where he remained till 1918. Loraine would, no doubt, have wished to serve again in the Army. Many of his colleagues certainly were anxious to see active service, but few were able to, for the Foreign Office, doubtless rightly, was chary of losing the services of highly trained and experienced diplomatists at a time when their services were particularly required.

After leaving Madrid in 1918 he was employed at the Paris Peace Conference and then in 1919 was appointed to the newly created Legation at Warsaw, where he acted on more than one occasion as Chargé d'Affaires. At the end of 1919 serious troubles broke out in Hungary and Sir George Clerk was sent on a special mission to Budapest as special delegate from the Supreme Council at Paris, and Loraine accompanied him. In 1921 he was created a C.M.G. and made Envoy Extraordinary at Teheran. Although it is desirable that diplomatists should serve in varied posts it is no doubt useful to them to return as Minister to a post in which they have served as Secretary, for they know the ropes, have acquaintances on the spot, and are familiar with the language. This happened to Loraine three times in his career.

His years at Teheran were not uneventful and his work was of importance, mainly coloured by the rivalry between Great Britain and Russia. Loraine remained in Persia until 1926, spent three years as Minister at Athens, and in 1929 was transferred to Cairo. Here he was faced with a difficult task. His predecessor was Lord Lloyd who had been High Commissioner for Egypt and the Sudan since 1925. Lloyd was a man of great energy and ability, and had ideas about British policy in Egypt which were not in accord with those either of the Egyptian Government or of the Socialist Government in England, and he accordingly resigned. The nature of Loraine's inheritance is thus apparent. The British connexion was unpopular in Egypt and there were insistent demands for independence. Sidky Pasha, however, managed to maintain his position, and in 1931 he visited England and succeeded in obtaining a certain amount of indirect support and the possibility of a treaty was discussed. Matters might have proceeded more rapidly had it not been for the serious illness of Sidky Pasha. Although Loraine was careful to preserve a neutral attitude and to refrain, as far as possible, from any interference in the internal affairs of Egypt, he was just as bitterly criticized as his predecessor. By his neutrality he was said to be supporting Sidky Pasha. In fact, the Opposition in Egypt wished him to be active in turning out Sidky and placing them in power. His neutrality was also criticized by the British officials who had supported Lord Lloyd. In August, 1933, Loraine was succeeded by Sir Miles Lampson (Lord Killearn), and himself succeeded Sir George Clerk at Ankara.

UNBROKEN SUCCESS

His mission to Turkey was one of unbroken success. When he went to Ankara Anglo-Turkish relations were steadily improving, the patient work of his immediate predecessor having dispelled the Anglophobia which the Great War had left behind; but there was then little promise of the cordial relationship which was to be established during Loraine's stay.

Two questions of international importance arose: the revision of the Straits Convention and the status of the Autonomous Sanjak of Alexandretta. Both were solved by negotiation in sharp contrast to the *fait accompli* procedure which had become fashionable in other countries, and it was no secret that the solving of these questions by correct procedure was partly due to Loraine's mediation and advice.

Loraine was on intimate terms with Kemal Atatürk who held him in high esteem and from the early days of his mission to Ankara he was the most prominent member of the Diplomatic Corps of which he was *doyen*. Lady Loraine too was much liked, not least by the Maltese for many of whom she found employment when they were thrown out of work by legislation which reserved small trades for Turkish citizens.

In 1939 Loraine was transferred to Rome in succession to Lord Perth. Here he was thrown into the vortex of European politics. His record at Cairo and Ankara showed that the choice of the Foreign Office was a good one, although it is probable that no Ambassador could have done anything, for in 1939 Hitler and Mussolini had made up their minds—still, if there was any chance of influencing Italy, a patient and conciliatory man like Loraine was the right selection.

In 1940 Italy came into the war and Loraine and the Mission left the country. Shortly after this he retired from the Service.

Loraine had been chairman of the Home Office Advisory Committee (Italian) since 1940 and was in 1945 appointed a Royal Commissioner for the Exhibition of 1851. In 1954 he was chosen to preside over the committee set up by the Minister of Agriculture to inquire into the policy and methods of the National Stud.

This was an appointment after his own heart for he was a keen racing man. During his time in Ankara his Turkish colleague in London was an occasional backer, On one occasion Loraine sent him a telegram advising him to back a horse of his. After the horse had won, the Turkish Ambassador declared that the real way to maintain good relations between the countries was for their respective representatives to keep racing stables!

On another occasion Loraine was offered a mare for stud for £400. He replied: "I'll pay £600 if she foals—or nothing." The mare foaled, he paid the £600 and sent a telegram: "Call her Balaclava—charge of the 600."

Sir Percy did not take up the sport until quite late in life when his duties as ambassador were coming to an end. His Queenpot won the 1,000 guineas in 1948 and his Darius was third in the Derby. Among many other races in which his horses were successful were the Eclipse Stakes and The Champagne Stakes. His filly Ambergris, owned in partnership with R. More O'Ferrall, is second favourite for the Oaks. Sir Percy Loraine's chief work in the Jockey Club was in connexion with the introduction of the photo-finish camera.

He married in 1924 Louise, elder daughter of Major-General the Hon. Edward Stuart-Wortley, who survives him.

May 24, 1961.

Peter Lorre, for many years one of the character actors most in demand for villainous roles in Hollywood films, died on March 23, 1964, at the age of 59.

He was born in Rosenberg, Hungary, on June 26, 1904. His family had no interest whatever in the theatre and, indeed, did not approve of children going to the theatre at all, but he later recalled sneaking to the theatre during his spare time after they had moved to Vienna.

LEFT HOME

He ran away from home and joined a theatrical company at the age of 17, and though after this escapade his family put him to work in a bank he soon managed to return to his first love.

After some experience on the stage he was caught up in the new talking pictures, and after a film of no interest he created a sensation in his second film role, in Lang's *M* (1931). This remarkable study of a child-killer gave him a great opportunity to create a rounded character out of what could so easily have become a two-dimensional monster, and he seized it to give us a definitive screen portrait of the psychopath, horrifying yet pathetic.

The advent of Hitler sent him, like so many other prominent figures in Germany's artistic life, into voluntary exile. His first stopping place was France, where he appeared in *De haut en bas*, a goodnatured story of life in a tenement directed by another German émigré, G. W. Pabst; then he went on to England to appear in a Hitchcock thriller, *The Man Who Knew Too Much*, in which he played for the first time a role which was subsequently to become his hallmark: the ruthless professional killer.

Hollywood offered him the role of Raskolnikov in an interesting version of *Crime and Punishment* directed by Josef von Sternberg, and succeeded, with the director's help, in conveying much of the original's flavour in spite of an over-simplified screenplay. In 1936 he returned to England to appear in another Hitchcock film, *The Secret Agent*, based on *Ashenden*, and gave a splendid performance as the agent disguised as a Mexican general, terrorising the other characters with a certain macabre good humour.

Back in Hollywood he made a series of thrillers built round a character called Mr. Moto, and various minor thrillers and horror films, until it looked as if he was doomed to descend into a premature and unmerited obscurity among the B-pictures, but in 1941 he was again offered a part in which he could show his talent, in Huston's brilliant detective story *The Maltese Falcon*; his exotic and heavily-scented crook, half cowardice and half guile, was a personal and original creation, and established him again in the public eye as a major addition to the select gallery of "the men you love to hate".

VILLAINY CONTRASTS

This film also saw him teamed for the first time with Sidney Greenstreet, whose suave and ponderous villainy provided a perfect counterpoint to the shifty and excitable brand provided by Lorre, so that the combination caught the public's fancy and was repeated in several other films, most notably that masterpiece of all-star nonsense *Casablanca*, and *The Mask of Dimitrios*, and *Three Strangers*, both directed by Negulesco from scripts by Huston.

After the war the type of thriller in which Peter Lorre chiefly shone went out of fashion, and he branched out into horror and comedy, producing a *tour de force* of insane frenzy in *The Beast with Five Fingers* and gaily caricaturing himself in a Bob Hope vehicle, *My Favourite Brunette*, as he had done earlier in Capra's version of the stage farce *Arsenic and Old Lace*. In the later 1940s he returned to Germany for the first time since the advent of the Nazis and acted on stage and in films there, most notably *Der Verlorene* (1951), which he directed himself. This film showed that he possessed outstanding talent as a director, otherwise alas unexploited, and was hailed by a number of distinguished Continental critics as the best film made in Germany since the war, but it was thought excessively daring in its study of the Nazi mentality and not widely shown. In 1953 he appeared, again with a good-natured parody of the sort of role for which he was best known, in Huston's inconsequential comedy-thriller *Beat the Devil*, and in 1956 he returned to Hollywood.

GLIMPSE OF INSANITY

There he concentrated chiefly on comedy, with the smiling hero-villain of *Congo Crossing*, the temperamental director in *The Buster Keaton Story*, and the drunken commissar in Mamoulian's musical version of *Ninotchka*, *Silk Stockings*, but his brief appearance as Nero in *The Story of Mankind* did somehow manage to triumph over its comic-strip surroundings and create a memorable glimpse of extravagant insanity.

March 25, 1964.

Queen Louise of Sweden—See under **Sweden.**

Eric Louw, the former South African Foreign Minister, died in hospital in Cape Town on June 24, 1968. He was 77. He was appointed Foreign Minister in 1956 and retired from the post in 1963.

Although the best work of Eric Louw was done in the Economics and Finance Ministeries he was best known as Foreign Minister who, especially in the last three years before retirement in 1963, saw South Africa steadily declining in popularity and influence both in the Commonwealth and in the United Nations. He himself ascribed this largely to the increased influence of the Afro-Asian nations in the world body which after his retirement he compared unflatteringly with the former League of Nations—where he had represented South Africa early in the 1930s. This development aggravated his tendency to irritability in public statements, and by the time he retired he was regarded in South Africa with affectionate exasperation as the pepperiest Foreign Minister the country had ever had.

One of his last actions as Foreign Minister was to withdraw South Africa from membership of the United Nations Food and Agriculture Organization following an F.A.O. resolution excluding South Africa from conferences, organizations and other activities. After his retirement Louw contributed a political column for a brief period to *Oosterlig*, the nationalist paper in Port Elizabeth, but he gradually withdrew himself from active public life as his health began to fail.

He was born in Jacobsdal, Orange Free State, in November, 1890, and educated in Victoria College, Stellenbosch, and Rhodes University College, Grahamstown, where he gained a fine command of the English language and the degree of Bachelor of Laws.

He was called to the Bar in Grahamstown but on the death of his father, a general merchant, in 1918, took over the family business in Beaufort West, which returned him as Nationalist member six years later when the Pact Government, led by General Hertzog in collaboration with the Labour Party, came into power.

A year later Louw was appointed South African Trade Commissioner in Canada and the United States and so began a long diplomatic career which was to lead eventually to his appointment as South African Foreign Minister.

Louw was appointed South African High Commissioner in London in 1929 and that same year inaugurated South African diplomatic representation in the United States as Minister Plenipotentiary in Washington. He served successively in a similar capacity in Italy and France and during this time twice represented South Africa at the Assembly of the League of Nations as well as at the meeting of the Mandates Commission and other international agencies. In 1937 he returned to South Africa, joined Doctor Malan's small Nationalist Party and in the following year was again returned for Beaufort West. With Malan's accession to power in 1948 Louw became Minister of Economic Affairs and in this capacity represented South Africa at a series of international economic conferences. When Strijdom succeeded Malan he made Louw Minister of Finance and later gave him also the portfolio of External Affairs.

Louw continued to hold both portfolios although the burden of foreign affairs became increasingly heavier as international criticism of South Africa swelled with the intensive application of the apartheid policy, and regular attacks on the Government's attitude to the South West Africa mandate were staged in the United Nations. Finally Louw was obliged to shed one of his offices and was left with foreign affairs only in his charge. The store of nervous energy on which he had drawn heavily since the early days of his public career did not noticeably decrease in the last years of his life and at 70 his industry was undiminished. His frequent statements to the press were often written in his own hand.

Louw's devotion to duty in all the offices of state which he held was a byword. His guidance of his country's economic affairs in the difficult period just after the war of 1939–45, when a lesser man might have seized the chance to favour his party and his colleagues, was marked by scrupulous fairness. As Foreign Minister (in which capacity he deputized more than once for his chiefs at conferences of Commonwealth Prime Ministers) his zealous championship of South Africa sometimes betrayed him into overstatements of the South African case and led him to make tactless and sometimes inaccurate charges of race discrimination and unfairness against other countries. A bitter opponent, he was nevertheless respected, even by those who disliked his policies, for the single-minded devotion he brought to the service of his country.

June 25, 1968.

Sir David Low, who died on September 19, 1963, at the age of 72, was one of the great cartoonists of the world.

His work was distinguished not only by an astute sense of political trends and values and the merriest kind of humour, but by an agile and subtle draughtsmanship that won from the connoisseur the highest respect. Creating under the stress of journalistic requirements, Low yet gave the impression that his drawings were well-considered. They were up-to-the-minute in their news value, but such was their philosophic grasp of wide political issues that they lose little of their savour with the passage of time.

BLOWS SOFTENED

A fundamental kindliness underlaid his production. He could hit hard and true; but his blows were softened, even for those who received them, by an hilarious fun which was irresistible.

Political caricature in England, from "HB" to Tenniel and Partridge, had been solid and respectable but a trifle pompous. Low accepted English influences, but he turned largely to the Continent for inspiration, assimilating something of Daumier, Steinlen, and Raemakers. He could be deeply serious and indignant, as well as sublimely frivolous. He gave back to English caricature some of the vitality, irreverence, and above all the sense of moral purpose that had been lacking since the early nineteenth century. Low chastised folly, hypocrisy, and dishonesty: yet he was not an embittered and vitriolic man, but on the contrary genial and modest, though aware of his pre-eminence in his art; only the duller of his subjects were incapable of sharing in the laughs he raised against them.

FROM NEW ZEALAND

Like that other great cartoonist, the late Will Dyson, Low came out of the southern hemisphere. Born at Dunedin, New Zealand, on April 7, 1891, he was the third son of David Brown Low and Jane Caroline (Flanagan) Low. He went to the Boys' High School, in Christchurch, and was to have been trained for the ministry, but he made his debut as a cartoonist at the astonishing age of 11, with a drawing published in the Christchurch *Spectator*. On leaving school he took up free-lance art work; and in 1911 he went to Australia, securing a staff post on the Sydney *Bulletin* and continuing to operate in the free-lance field. Collections of his early work came out as *Low's Annual* (1908), *Caricatures* (1915) and *The Billy Book* (1918).

In 1919 Low came to England and was appointed political cartoonist to the *Star*, which paper he served for some eight years, making a big reputation for himself and arousing enthusiasm or dislike according to the political colour of the observer. But in 1927 Lord Beaverbrook saw that Low had such "circulation value" that people of any political persuasion would make a point of buying a paper just to see his cartoon. Low's views were always turned leftwards; but when Lord Beaverbrook made him an offer he left the *Star* for the *Evening Standard*. There was no question of his selling his conscience; and not only did he constantly take the opposite line to the *Standard* leading articles and the whole spirit of the paper but he very frequently caricatured his own proprietor, representing him as a kind of broadly grinning gnome. He caricatured himself, too; and though in reality he was a distinguished-looking, dark-bearded man with fine hands, he showed himself in corners of his cartoons as an impertinent figure of fun.

COLONEL BLIMP

In addition to his three or four half-pages a week, Low used at one time to have an entire page in the *Standard* every Saturday devoted to his "Topical Budget", which was a racy and piquant commentary on the events of the week. One immortal character who always figured in a corner of the Budget was "Colonel Blimp", a rotund, bald, fierce gentleman with long white moustaches, who formed the mouthpiece for the most reactionary opinions, which he usually prefixed with the phrase: "Gad! Sir, Lord Beaverbrook is right ..." Low would fasten on some idiosyncrasy in a public man and flog it unmercifully. J. H. Thomas came in for his attentions over a long period, especially because of his alleged joy in dining out in full evening splendour. After Thomas's resignation Low produced a *chef d'oeuvre* showing him saying goodbye to an erect but untenanted dress shirt, with the caption: "Parting is Such Sweet Sorrow." Hitler's moustache, Goering's girth and medals, Neville Chamberlain's umbrella, and Earl Baldwin's pipe all received due attention; while Mussolini's truculent jowl (always shown dark and semi-shaven) was limned with a fierce joy.

It cannot be said that Low was never cheap; but this happened seldom, and he invariably rose to the height of great events, One of his most magnificent drawings (in the *Evening Standard* of September 20, 1939) showed Hitler and Stalin, raising caps and bowing with exaggerated politeness over the prostrate body of Poland, the German saying: "The Scum of the Earth, I presume?" and the Russian: "The Bloody Assassin of the Workers, I presume?" The caption was "Rendezvous."

Low was gifted with a remarkable degree of political prescience and with a selective power over essentials that enabled him to reduce a mass of facts, speeches, and tendencies to concrete form in a few striking touches. He used the brush in a masterly way, evolving a technique of heavy black lines and masses that won him the frequent flattery of imitation.

CARTOONIST'S DAY

He would begin his day by a thorough reading of the daily papers. At breakfast in the Golders Green home in which he lived for many years he would talk over the day's news with his wife (Madeline Grieve Kenning, whom he married in 1920) and his two daughters, after which he would go off to his studio and begin the day's work in earnest. It might be a long time before he put brush to paper. "Much pacing and squirming and pipe smoking" went on, from his own account, before he was delivered of an idea at once apposite, humorous, striking, simple, and universal in appeal.

Low's work was by no means always political, and for that for Saturday's *Standard* he often used to go out with his journalist companion, "Terry", to survey some typical aspect of English life. His afternoon in the British Museum Reading Room, for example, was a gay and memorable affair. One of his own favourite efforts, which appeared in *Punch*, was "The Golden Wedding", a large family group posed for a photograph, in which he traced with affectionate guile hereditary resemblances. He did many pure caricatures, too, that were not over-distorted and had a high sense of character, including a series of public figures for the *New Statesman*. He was a man of world-wide prestige, detested and feared in the totalitarian countries as much as the usually sterner Raemakers had been in the Germany of an earlier generation; and at one of Lord Halifax's meetings with Hitler, the German dictator is reputed to have harangued the Foreign Secretary about Low.

The most remarkable of Low's books, *Years of Wrath* (1949), a cartoon history of the years 1932–45, covering Low's heyday, contained his comments on the whole course of the European tragedy, ending with some telling sketches of the defendants in the dock at Nuremberg. Other collections of his works included *Lloyd George & Co.* (1922), *Lions and Lambs* (1928), *The Best of Low* (1930), *Political Parade* (1936), *A Cartoon History of Our Times* (1939), and *The Fearful Fifties* (1960). He published his autobiography in 1956, and for the *Britain in Pictures* series he wrote the volume on *British Cartoonists, Caricaturists* and *Comic Artists*. In 1943 a film was produced with the title of *The Life and Death of Colonel Blimp*, but the connexion with Low's hero was remote.

In 1950 Low left the *Evening Standard* and joined the *Daily Herald*. In 1953, he joined the *Guardian*, to which in semi-retirement he contributed three cartoons a week. In 1962 he was knighted. His home in his later years, after his daughters had married, was a large top-floor flat overlooking Holland Park and Kensington High Street. Low was always a keen cinemagoer, and his studio window gave him a clear view of the entrance of the local cinema, which he visited with some regularity. He was an honorary LL.D. of New Brunswick.

September 21, 1963.

Percy Lubbock, C.B.E., the author, died in Italy on August 2, 1965, at the age of 86. A fastidious writer, his prose whether lively or severe is always beautiful without obscurity or affectation. But he was much more than a writer, a humane and humorous personality responding to and in touch with all manner of men and women.

His first important work was *The Craft of Fiction*, published in 1921 when he was 41; through many editions it has continued to be regarded as holding a wealth of information about form and design in the novel.

Percy Lubbock was born in 1879, the fourth son of Frederick Lubbock and Catherine Gurney, and to his Quaker ancestry, so charmingly descirbed in *Earlham*, perhaps his best known work, he owed many of his rare personal qualities. He was educated at Eton and King's College, Cambridge.

After a brief spell at the Board of Education, when Benson became President of Magdalene College, Cambridge, Lubbock went there to join his old friend as Pepys Librarian: hence his little book on *Pepys* (1909), his second; for he had already published *Elisabeth Barrett Browning in her Letters* in 1906. These Cambridge years were very happy ones, with Lapsley and many younger men added to his amusing circle of friends; but, though seemingly suited to a semi-academic life, he was irked by its restraints.

He was now the friend of Henry James and Edith Wharton, of George Calderon and Howard Sturgis; to the first three of these he was to pay his tribute. In 1920 appeared his important critical edition of the *Letters of Henry James*, to be followed in 1921 by *The Craft of Fiction*, a work of pioneer criticism, formed from his dissection of a number of great novels, the works of Tolstoy, Flaubert, Henry James, and others.

In the same year he published his *Memoir of George Calderon*. But now, having for so long dedicated his own fine craftsmanship to criticism and biography, he gave his imagination vein in *Earlham*, the delightfully written reminiscence of late Victorian childhood days spent at Earlham Hall. It went through four impressions during 1922 and has been many times reprinted since.

By this date he was dividing his life between his home in Kent and Italy, particularly Rome and Florence, and the first fruits of his love of Italy was *Roman Portraits* (1923), where humour and observation are so delicately combined. *The Region Cloud* in 1925 was little noticed; but *Shades of Eton* in 1929 challenged its many predecessors in that line of reminiscence by attempting to "measure the effect of Eton on a boy's imagination".

SETTLED IN ITALY

In 1926 he had married Lady Sybil, younger daughter of the fifth Earl of Desart, and had settled at the Villa Medici in Fiesole, with her daughter, the Marchesa Iris Origo in the *villino* below. Lady Sybil, who died in 1943, wrote *Potrait of Zelida*, and the Marchesa has written well known books, the best *Life of Leopardi*, *War in Val d'Orcia*, *Allegra* and *Flush*.

Two more books were to appear. *The Diary of Arthur Benson* was edited from a vast quarry of notebooks, with a skill which avoided giving serious offence to the living, but necessarily omitted much of the raciest matter. The last of his tributes to his friends was *A Portrait of Edith Wharton*. In later years he had lived in the beautiful house built by Pinsent for his wife and himself on a promontory near Levici, looking across the bay of Spezia. He was as much amused as honoured by his C.B.E., in 1952, "for services to literature". When congratulated he replied, "Ah yes, but it is a grave responsibility at my time of life to undertake the command of the British Empire."

He had spent the later years of his life almost totally blind—and almost bedridden at his Italian home. But he had the satisfaction of seeing a great revival in his reputation as critic and descriptive writer.

August 3, 1965.

F. L. Lucas, scholar, critic, teacher, novelist, playwright and poet, widely known in Britain and beyond, especially between the two wars, as a literary and an anti-fascist campaigner, died at his Cambridge home on June 1, 1967. He was 72.

Frank Laurence ("Peter") Lucas was born on December 28, 1894, the elder son of F. W. Lucas, later headmaster of Colfe's Grammar School. He was educated there, at Rugby and at Trinity College, Cambridge. His university career was interrupted by the First World War, in which he served in the 7th Royal West Kent Regiment and the Intelligence Corps. He is mentioned in the Official History for a daring and resourceful reconnaissance near Miraumont. Always potentially a man of action (he was admired by T. E. Lawrence) he retained an interest in soldiering, and many will remember him as the unflagging Major of the Bletchley Park Home Guard.

As an undergraduate before and after the first war he won distinction in classics, as his Pitt Scholarship, Porson Prize, Chancellor's Medal and Browne Medal testify. In 1920 he was elected to a Fellowship at King's and thereafter taught English literature as a college lecturer, university lecturer and subsequently Reader; but his roots were in the classics, and his whole approach to English studies, as to poetic creation, was traditional.

He was an uncompromising derider of the new schools of poetry and criticism associated with such names as T. S. Eliot, Ezra Pound and F. R. Leavis. Having based his reputation as a scholar firmly on his edition of Webster, he expanded into one of the most prolific and versatile writers of his time, critic, essayist, poet, novelist, translator, anthologist, diarist, pamphleteer, travel writer, short-story writer.

Though he grew impatient of the role of critic, many will feel that in it he did much of his best work—in his *Authors Dead and Living* and *Studies, French and English*, his short but penetrating *Tragedy*, and particularly *The Decline and Fall of the Romantic Ideal*. Naturally his hostility to the moderns provoked reprisals, but if he can be accused of intolerance of novelty and experiment, at least he was above pandering to fashion.

WITTY TALK

In his novels, of which the best perhaps was *Doctor Dido*, he was apt to put his own witty conversation into the mouths of his characters and add melodramatic action as though it were an afterthought. For a time in the 1930s he turned to play writing, encouraged by success with the Newcastle Repertory Company; but neither of the two pieces that reached the West End stage ran for long.

Meanwhile he helped to keep alive the reputation of nineteenth-century poets by his broadcasts and selections with introduction; and after the Second World War he did much to familiarize the reading public with the substance of classical masterpieces by his selections in translation of Greek poetry and drama for Everyman.

His passionate love of liberty made him an early and eloquent denouncer of Fascism and Nazism: this earned him abusive letters from Ezra Pound, the gratitude of many victims of oppression, and a place in Goebbels' list of candidates for post-war extermination. By 1938 he could think of little else, as his *The Delights of Dictatorship* and *A Journal under the Terror* show, and the outbreak of war came almost as a relief. He threw himself into his important work for a branch of the Foreign Office with the zeal of a crusader, and did devoted service which was recognized by the award of an O.B.E.

Lucas was a fast and insatiable reader, who reinforced an excellent memory by keeping a commonplace-book. He was thus able to enliven his conversation with a wealth of pointed fact and anecdote, such as the last words of famous people, of which he made, with Francis Birrell, a collection entitled *The Art of Dying*; and he exploded many a pretentious generalization of the critical pundits with a salvo of signal instances to the contrary.

This faculty had, however, its dangers, and the chief fault of his style was a tendency to overload with irrelevant if witty allusions. As a teacher he had so much of interest to tell his pupils that he was apt to forget the importance of the less interesting things they might have to tell him, and he was confident in all matters of the incontrovertibility of his own opinion, so that his supervisions, instructive and entertaining though they might be, were more pedagogic than maieutic; but he did take a solicitous interest in his pupils' fortunes and helped them in many practical ways.

NATURALLY SHY

Though his wit and charm won him elect friends, he was shy by nature, and partial deafness contracted in the first war as well as indifference to the elegances and frivolities of life withdrew him from the world of parties to the writing-desk in his study. But his vitality was physical as well as intellectual and those who range Greece with that admirably informative companion *From Olympus to the Styx* may find his idea of a day's walk Procrustean to them.

Romantic by temperament, he loved wild scenery and such literature as the Icelandic Sagas. Anyone introduced to the ancient Greeks through his delightful anthology *A Greek Garland* might conclude from the epigrams selected that they too were a race of romanticists. Yet he was nothing if not rational in his philosophy, and his admiration of French literature from Ronsard onwards was keenest for the age of Voltaire.

He also published a number of stories of English works of the Age of Reason, and latterly of various dramatists, besides embarking again in his retirement on novel writing.

After his marriages with E. B. C. Jones, the novelist, and Prudence Wilkinson had been dissolved without issue, he married in 1940 Elna Kallenberg from Sweden, and thereafter his happiness was centred on their home life with their daughter and son.

June 2, 1967.

Henry R. Luce, who died on February 28, 1967, in Phoenix, Arizona, at the age of 68, rose from obscure origins to become one of the most influential and controversial figures in American journalism. Almost single-handed, he built the mighty publishing empire of Time Inc. and its associated publications, and became a multi-millionaire.

Born on April 3, 1898 in Tengchow, China, the son of an American Presbyterian missionary couple (his father was descended from one of the original settlers on Martha's Vineyard, Massachusetts), Luce spent the first 14 years of his life in China, where he attended a British boarding school, and acquired an abiding interest in Far Eastern affairs.

At the age of 14 he travelled to Europe alone and at 15 to the United States, where he attended the Hotchkiss school at Lakeville, Connecticut. He paid his way as a scholarship student by waiting on table and working after school hours. At Hotchkiss he formed a life-long friendship with Briton Hadden, who was later to partner him in his magazine ventures.

Luce showed an early talent for writing and scholarship. When he went to Yale he became a managing editor of the student newspaper, the *Yale Daily News.* Hadden was chairman of the paper. Luce was voted the "most brilliant" member of his class and Hadden the "most likely to succeed." Together they interrupted their college careers to join the U.S. Army for a year during the First World War, but although they both became second lieutenants they did not get to see active service abroad.

After graduating from Yale in 1920, Luce went to Oxford to study for a year. As he said later: "I thought it was my last opportunity to have a good time." Returning to the United States he worked for a year on the *Chicago Daily News* for $16 (then about £4) a week.

NEWS MAGAZINE IDEA

He moved to *The Baltimore News*, where Hadden accompanied him, and together they worked out their idea for "the news magazine."

Quitting their jobs, the two young men moved to New York where they set about raising the capital they needed for their new venture. They hoped to get about $100,000 from wealthy Yale alumni, but finally they managed to scrape together $86,000 from friends, relatives and an elderly philanthropic lady. With this sum, they launched the first issue of *Time* on March 3, 1923.

Luce was then 25 years old. He and Hadden paid themselves a salary of $ 30 a week and it was several years before the magazine established itself. By 1927 it showed a small profit, but after that its rise became rapid and its two founders flourished.

Time, pioneered in the concept of group journalism, emphasized personalities in the news ("Character is destiny," Luce once said), invented and developed its own vocabulary and its own writing style.

Their next step was to plan *Fortune* magazine, a more ambitious venture aimed at "big business" and selling at the then unheard-of price of one dollar a copy. Before the first issue appeared Hadden died. Luce was shaken by his death, but persevered in spite of the impact of the market crash of 1929 and the advice of his friends.

Luce then evolved the radio feature, *The March of Time*, which presented the news in dramatic form, and followed it in 1935 with the equally successful cinema programme of the same name. Both quickly won public approval.

Fortune was a success from the start. It earned profits and its circulation climbed steadily. (It is now 450,000 copies.) Next came *Life* magazine in 1936, designed by Luce as a new venture in pictorial journalism, introducing new story-telling techniques to the camera.

THREAT FROM SUCCESS

Demand was so great for the magazine's first issue that the original print order for 466,000 copies—the largest first-issue printing in magazine history to that time—soon sold at a premium. *Life's* very success nearly killed the magazine before it was a year old. Advertisers were paying for space on the basis of a circulation guarantee of only 250,000. The magazine lost $3m. in its first year until advertising contracts were adjusted to the circulation figures. Its circulation today is 7,500,000 a week.

Not content, Luce went on to found *Sports Illustrated*, also a success. Almost his sole failure was *Architectural Forum* which he took over in 1932 and later abandoned. Today, Time Inc. also has a profitable line of books on a variety of subjects.

As a young man of 25, when considering starting *Time*, Luce had said: "Most people are not well informed and something should be done." He continued all his life to "do something" about many things. Illustrative of this is the story that on the day he bought *Life*, the comic weekly, solely for its title for the sum of $85,000 his wife, Clare Luce, produced a memo dated three years before which she had sent to her then employer, the editor of *Vanity Fair*. It said: "Dear Boss,—My spies tell me *Life* is on the market.....why not buy it for the name and turn it into a picture magazine?" She said to her husband, "You paid $85,000 for it. Well, three years ago they were going to sell it to me for $20,000." His characteristic answer was, "You had the idea, but I did something about it."

He was fully conversant with all sides of his business. In the early days he and Briton Hadden exchanged jobs annually; while one was editor the other was business manager.

During his rise to affluence and influence, Luce played a considerable part in public affairs but mainly behind the scenes, not as an active politician. He started as a Wilsonian Democrat and at first admired Franklin D. Roosevelt, but later turned against him. More recently Luce was a whole-hearted supporter of Eisenhower and made large contributions to the Republican Party's campaign funds.

In foreign affairs the Luce publications are basically flag-waving and chauvinist. As an official biography of the man puts it: "Perhaps the two great touchstones of Luce's personality are his Christian faith and his special feeling of patriotism toward the United States..... This feeling is exemplified by his great regret over not having the one thing most Americans have: a native town in his own country. In a sense he has made the whole of America his home town instead."

Consistent with his background, Luce was always identified with the "China lobby" and Generalissimo Chiang Kai-shek. His interest in the country of his birth never lessened and he was always interested in projects concerning China. He organized United China Relief in 1940 when China was suffering so severely from the Japanese invasion and he was for years a trustee of The China Institute in America.

Of late his publications have stood for a hard line in Vietnam and elsewhere, to withstand communist "expansionism." Luce himself, while he tended to stammer, was a frequent public speaker on this theme.

In April, 1964, Luce resigned as editor-in-chief of Time Inc., but he continued to take a lively interest in the vast publishing concern he had founded. Perhaps the best explanation of his success was that given by a friend: "He is a dreamer with a keen sense of double-entry bookkeeping."

He served as a second lieutenant in the First World War and was decorated with the Chevalier of the Lion of Honour (France) in 1937. He was also decorated by Greece, Denmark, the Netherlands, China and the Federal Republic of Germany.

Luce was twice married, first to Lila Rose Hotz, by whom he had two sons, and, after a divorce, to Mrs. Clare Boothe Brokaw, herself a distinguished writer and congresswoman, who later became United States Ambassador to Italy. Luce's elder son, Henry R. Luce III, is head of the Time-Life office in London.

March 1, 1967.

Count Felix von Luckner, who died at Malmoe, Sweden, on April 13, 1966, at the age of 84, is remembered for his daring exploits in command of the German commerce raider Seeadler during the First World War. She was the only sailing ship so employed.

Born at Dresden on June 9, 1881, he came of a landowning family with a long tradition of military service. It was intended that he also should enter the Army; but instead he ran away to Hamburg at the age of 13½, and under an assumed name and unknown to his parents joined a Russian sailing ship as an embryo deck-hand for the long passage to Fremantle, Western Australia.

It was the first of his many voyages during the strenuous years he served before the mast in American, British, and German sailing vessels. He learnt seamanship the hard way.

In 1911, after two years' service as a junior officer in steamships, and partly through family influence, he became a reserve lieutenant in the Imperial German Navy. It happened that on five separate occasions he had saved lives from drowning at the risk of his own, a record which attracted newspaper publicity and the interest of Prince Henry of Prussia, an Admiral and brother of the Kaiser. Asked if he would like to join the regular Navy, he jumped at the chance. In 1916, he was present at Jutland in the battleship Kronprinz.

To disperse the British naval effort the Germans had fitted out ex-merchant ships to operate in the South Atlantic, Indian Ocean, and Pacific. Capable of different cunning disguises as neutrals, they mounted hidden guns and torpedo tubes and carried mines, and could approach allied merchant ships without exciting suspicion.

CONVINCING DETAIL

In 1916 there were still sailing ships on the ocean trade routes, and Luckner, one of the few German naval officers with experience in sail was appointed in command of a full-rigged ship for an independent raiding cruise. She was the Pass of Balhama, captured in prize a year earlier, which presently became the pseudo-Norwegian Irma, bound for Melbourne laden with timber. In reality she was a commissioned warship, S.M.S. Seeadler.

Fitted with an auxiliary engine, provisioned for two years, and carrying a large crew, she had a deck cargo of lumber which could be jettisoned when once through the blockade. A few small guns with rifles, ammunition, bombs and hand grenades were hidden below, and in case she was boarded the surplus crew, far larger than in an ordinary ship of her kind.

would remain concealed between decks. Nothing was left to chance. Luckner and some of his men spoke Norwegian. There were pictures of the King and Queen of Norway in his cabin; Norwegian books and magazines conspicuous in the living spaces, and photographs on the bulkheads. One man, suitably attired and wearing a blonde wig, was told off to pose as Luckner's ailing "wife" if the occasion arose.

Provided with a false log, and cargo papers with the forged signatures and stamps of the Norwegian authorities and a British consular official, the ship sailed from Wilhelmshaven on December 21, 1916. On Christmas Day, when steering westward on her way to the open Atlantic, she was stopped and boarded by the British armed merchant cruiser Avenger. After a narrow escape from discovery, fully described in Luckner's memoirs, the bluff succeeded and the Seeadler got clear away.

Having disposed of her deck cargo she sailed south, and on January 9 and 10, 1917, well out in the Atlantic west of the Straits of Gibraltar, captured and sank two British steamers. The raiders helped themselves to what stores they fancied, and the crews were transferred without casualty.

Cruising to and fro in an area around the Equator Luckner had more successes between January 21 and March 15, sinking eight large sailing ships and another steamer. None of the prisoners, which included two women, had been harmed, and once on board the Seeadler they were treated with consideration, being well fed and allowed all possible freedom.

NEW GROUND

He had reason to congratulate himself when he wrote: "We had been at sea for eight weeks and had sunk eleven ships, representing more than 40,000 tons of shipping."

The Seeadler was already overcrowded. So the next ship he captured, a large French barque, he retained. Lopping off her upper masts and yards and part of her bowsprit to delay her passage, he transferred the prisoners and sent her off to Rio de Janerio, which she reached in late March.

Rounding Cape Horn in fierce weather, Luckner steered for a new hunting ground in mid-Pacific east of Christmas Island just north of the Equator. The United States had entered the war on April 6, 1917, and between June 8 and July 8 he captured and sank three American schooners after making prisoners of their crews.

By late July the raider had been seven months at sea, and her crew were showing signs of scurvy and beri-beri. Fresh water, food, and vegetables were badly needed, and on July 29 the Seeadler came to Mopelia, one of the cluster of lonely, low coral atolls near the Society Islands. It was inhabited by three natives sent to catch the turtle with which the lagoon abounded, and there Luckner found a land of plenty, with water, green food, wild pig, and fish.

The Seeadler was anchored off the reef, and disaster came on August 2 when she was overwhelmed by a tidal wave. When they tried to start the auxiliary engine it failed. With her upper masts and yards tumbling in ruin, the ship was crashed high and dry on to the jagged coral, a total wreck.

Not a man was hurt, and salving what stores and other gear they needed from the wreck, the castaways established themselves in a home-made village ashore. They numbered about 100, and there was no risk of starvation.

Luckner had the idea of seizing the French schooner which would eventually arrive to take the dried turtle meat. But impatient at the probable delay he decided to set out in one of the Seeadler's lifeboats in the hope of finding a ship to rescue the whole party. On August 23, with five companions, he set sail from Mopelia in an 18ft. boat which had been rigged and provisioned for a long voyage. They took rifles and hand grenades, with their German naval uniforms and an ensign.

ARRESTED

After a hazardous and adventurous voyage of 2,300 miles among the Cook Islands, often in foul weather and the crew suffering from scurvy, they eventually arrived at Wakaya, a small island in the Fiji group not far from the main island of Vitilevu on September 20. It was here after more adventures that the boat was identified as German and Luckner and his companions were arrested, to be sent on to New Zealand and interned with other Germans in a camp on the island of Motuihi, near Auckland. In December with great resource and cunning, Luckner and seven others stole the commandant's motor boat and captured a schooner. They got clear away to sea, only to be recaptured after eight days of freedom. Taken back to New Zealand, Luckner remained there until March, 1919, four months after the Armistice. He finally reached Germany in July.

Back at home he was awarded more than a score of decorations by the various German states. Hailed as a popular hero he toured the country lecturing on his experiences and wrote his memoirs, which were translated into English and appeared in 1928. Having married he spent seven years touring and lecturing in the United States, being made an honorary citizen of various cities and an honorary member of many clubs and fraternities.

In the closing months of the Second World War, when the United States Army reached Halle, Saxony, Luckner, in defiance of Nazi orders, came out to meet them and surrendered the town, thus saving it from severe damage.

April 15, 1966.

Sir Harry Luke, K.C.M.G., traveller and author, who was Governor of Fiji (1938–42), died in Cyprus on May 11, 1969. He was 84.

Harry Charles Luke, son of J. H. Luke (one-time managing director of the Exploration Company) was born in London on December 4, 1884. He was educated at Eton and Trinity College, Oxford, where he took an honours degree in Modern History.

By the time he had taken his degree, his passion for travel had enabled him to acquire a wide knowledge of western and central Europe, Italy, the Iberian and Balkan peninsulas and Alaska. This he extended by a journey, largely on horseback, through the remoter vilayets of Sultan Abdul Hamid II's Empire. It occasioned the first of his travel books *The Fringe of the East* (1913) and laid the foundation of his special and continuing interest in the peoples and lands of the Mediterranean and the Near and Middle East.

In 1908, Luke joined the Colonial service as Private Secretary and A.D.C. to the Governor of Sierra Leone. In 1911 he was transferred to Cyprus. From there he was seconded, as an officer in the R.N.V.R., for service on the personal staff of Admiral Sir Rosslyn Wemyss at Mudros and subsequently on that of the Commander-in-Chief, Admiral Sir John de Robeck, at Constantinople and in the Black Sea. Early in 1920 came an interlude of service under Foreign Office as British Chief Commissioner in Georgia, Armenia and Azerbaijan which lasted until the end of the year when these Republics were absorbed into the Soviet Union.

RIOTS INQUIRY

Luke then returned to the Colonial Service as Assistant Governor of Jerusalem. While holding this post from 1920 to 1924, Luke was one of the three members of the Commission of Inquiry into the Jaffa Riots of 1921, and his knowledge of the Eastern Churches was utilized on the two Commissions set up to rescue the Orthodox Patriarchate of Jerusalem from political anarchy and financial bankruptcy. At this time he became a member of the Archbishop of Canterbury's Eastern Churches Committee which grew into the Foreign Relations Council of the Church of England.

Luke was appointed Colonial Secretary of Sierra Leone in 1924 but in 1928 he returned to Palestine as Chief Secretary. During the lull before the storm which was to begin in 1929 and gather in violence during the closing years of the British Mandate, Lord Plumer had agreed to the withdrawal of the British garrison from Palestine and the disbanding of the British Gendarmerie, with the result that on the Field-Marshal's departure Luke, as Acting High Commissioner both in 1928 and 1929, had to cope with the serious disturbances, which arose out of the "Wailing Wall incident" in the latter year, without any force at his disposal. He had protested at the outset of his acting administration against the policy of leaving Palestine denuded of troops at so explosive a time and was exonerated from blame by the Parliamentary Commission which sat in Jerusalem during the autumn of 1929. The British community registered its opinion of the Zionist propaganda, which was at that time directed against Luke in three continents, by according him a really remarkable reception at the St. Andrew's Day dinner in Jerusalem.

Like many other British officials, Luke left Palestine and its intolerances with relief when he became Lieutenant-Governor of Malta, where he served from 1930 to 1938. Even there, however, he found controversies which arose from Lord Strickland's disputes with the Vatican and from the attempts to Italianise the island made with the assistance of subsidies from Mussolini, by some members of the Nationalist Ministry which succeeded Lord Strickland's. Luke, although a lifelong lover of Italy and the Italian language realized that the latter was out of place in Malta, and did much between 1932 and 1936 to rehabilitate the Maltese language and substitute it for Italian in the law courts and schools of the island.

In 1938 Sir Harry (he had been knighted in 1933) was promoted Governor of Fiji and High Commissioner for the Western Pacific with a bailiwick extending over nine million square miles of sea and land which contained the British Solomon Islands, the Gilbert and Ellice Islands, Pitcairn Island, the picturesque little Kingdom of Tonga and the Anglo-French Condominium of the New Hebrides. It was a new world to him and by using aircraft as well as ships he was able to travel about his new command to a far greater extent than had been possible for any of his predecessors, and was therefore able to visit islands and communities which had never heard of a High Commissioner, far less seen one, before his arrival.

After the fall of France in 1940, Luke, who had a wide sympathy for French and spoke their language even better than he spoke German, Italian, Modern Greek and Turkish was able at a critical moment to play the part of *deus ex machina* in substituting the authority of Free France for that of Vichy in the island of New Caledonia, and so far reconciling the new Free French administration with its overthrown predecessor that he was able to dine peacefully at the same table as the incoming and outgone French governors, although the wife of the former was presiding as hostess over the dinner which had been ordered that morning by the wife of the latter.

Against the Japanese, however, he was unable to contend and before he left the Pacific at the end of 1942 he had the sorrow of knowing that many of his Solomon and Gilbert and Ellice Islands had been occupied by the enemy. After 35 years' service under the Colonial Office, he retired in 1943 and forthwith took up the task of organizing the work of the British Council in the Caribbean, on which he was engaged until 1946. After this, although officially retired, he continued to travel extensively about the world. His journeys included a visit to Easter Island in 1952.

HATED RED TAPE

Luke was an administrator who took a deep and personal interest in and had much affection for his charges of various races; and his happy facility in the matter of languages enabled him to gain, particularly in the Mediterranean, a real influence over many of them. Strong in the conviction of Great Britain's beneficent role as a colonizing power, Luke hated red tape and bureaucratic delays and had small patience with the official who shirked responsibility by following the line of least resistance or the theory that man was made for rules and regulations.

Luke was a prolific and felicitous writer, and a witty speaker. His many books of travel, history, autobiography (and even cookery) written both during and after his period of official service were the fruit of his familiarity with and knowledge of the countries and peoples in which he had resided either as a careful and inquiring visitor or an administrator. It was the works on the Levant in particular which won him in 1938 the Oxford D. Litt. He was a frequent contributor to *The Times*. His interests were wide and various, including, in his earlier years, squash racquets and swimming.

He wrote numerous books: *Islands of the South Pacific* (1962), *Cyprus: A Portrait and on Appreciation* (1957), *Queen Salote and Her Kingdom* (1954), and his autobiography, *Cities and Men*, were among them.

In 1918 he married Joyce, daughter of Captain J. L. Fremlin, and had two sons. The marriage was dissolved in 1949. He was made C.M.G. in 1926, Knight Bachelor in 1933 and K.C.M.G. in 1939, and was an honorary LL.D. of the University of Malta. In 1952 his old college made him an honorary fellow. As a Knight of Justice of the Venerable Order of St. John (of which he was Registrar) he undertook various missions on behalf of that Order and was instrumental in bringing about the reconciliation with the Grand Master of the Sovereign Order of Malta in Rome which ended a long estrangement in 1947.

May 12, 1969.

Patrice Lumumba, whose death took place in February, 1961, had a political career as meteoric and controversial as anything the century had seen. Almost unknown outside Belgium and the Congo 12 months earlier, he became, as the first Premier of the independent Congo, one of the world's notorious figures—the centre of the Congo debacle and the focus of the cold war in Africa. He was in office for only just over two months, but in that time he was accused by the Belgians of being a communist and a murderer, by the United Nations Secretariat of genocide, by many western observers of criminal folly, and by his Congolese opponents of all these plus treason and attempted assassination. Yet to millions of Africans he seemed a great champion in the fight against imperialism, and he enjoyed to the end the consistent support of a large number of Afro-Asian Governments and the whole of the communist block.

Whatever else may be said about him, he was certainly the one truly outstanding politician in the Congo. Even after his dismissal from the office of Prime Minister by President Kasavubu and his subsequent imprisonment, he remained, like the Ghost in *Hamlet*, one of the prime movers in the Congo scene. Nobody was ever less out of mind when out of sight. At all times he had an astonishing flair for the dramatic gesture and a hypnotic command over his fellow Congolese. More than once he literally talked himself out of arrest or imprisonment. His control of the Congolese Parliament when he was actually speaking was like that of a charmer in a snake-pit—his opponents collapsed in ignorant, open-jawed frustration before his staccato but persuasive speech, his mental agility, and his fluent use of every demagogic trick.

NATURAL ABILITY

No one who knew him could doubt that he was a man of great natural ability who might, blessed with a different temperament, have become a true leader. But equally no honest observer could doubt that he was genuinely unstable—a paranoiac for whom consistency, restraint, or moderation were impossible. And perhaps it was this combined with his violent hatred of the Belgians which gave him his supreme appeal in the Congo. His headlong rise to power and his apparent readiness to leap any fence in the world without even looking at it won him an almost super-human aura; on the drums of his native region he was known as "the man who came from heaven".

Patrice Lumumba was born in 1925 in the little village of Onolua in the northern half of the province of Kasai. His father and mother were both of the Batatele tribe and live in the village still. Patrice had his first schooling at the American Methodist Mission School at Wembo Nyama not far away and when he was expelled from there in his teens for immoral conduct he passed into a Roman Catholic school—a change of Churches that was probably awakening as well as disillusioning, revealing schisms in the European mind. Later, after a spell of Roman Catholic teacher training he entered the Civil Service as tax clerk and rose to become assistant postmaster of Stanleyville from which post he was dismissed after being convicted and sentenced for embezzlement in 1956.

Meanwhile, he had been active in trade unionism and when he came to Leopoldville in 1957 as a brewery salesman he founded the Congolese National Movement (M.N.C.), a political party dedicated to early independence and the maintenance of the unity of the Congo. In 1958 he went to the Pan-African Conference in Accra where he made what proved to be a useful and lasting alliance with Dr. Nkrumah, and he then became a full-time politician.

GAOL TO CONFERENCE

Towards the end of 1959 he was imprisoned again for provoking riots against the Belgians in Stanleyville, but he was released in order to attend the round table conference in Brussels in January, 1960. From then on he quickly established himself as the Congo's dominant political leader and in spite of quarrels with some of his colleagues and the growing hostility of the Belgians his party won such a substantial minority of the seats in the elections in May, 1960, that the outgoing Governor had no choice but to ask Lumumba to form the first independent Government. He did so, taking office on July 1 and lasting until early September in circumstances of increasing confusion and danger, the aftermath of which is still one of the world's great concerns.

February 14, 1961.

Barry Lupino, who died on September 25, 1962, in a Brighton hospital at the age of 78, was one of the best known of pantomime dames.

He was a brother of Stanley Lupino and a cousin of Lupino Lane and Wallace Lupino. There was some justification for the claim that he had spent a lifetime on the stage, for he made his first appearance as a baby in arms carried on to the stage at Drury Lane Theatre, in March,

1884, during the performance of the pantomime *Cinderella*.

Born in London on January 7, 1884, he was trained from infancy as a pantomimist, chiefly by his father, George Lupino. Educated at Blackheath, he learned dancing under Espinosa and when still in his teens became resident comedian at the then popular Britannia Theatre, Hoxton, with Mrs. Sara Lane as mentor. After several years he decided to seek wider experience and toured in Europe and America, where he appeared in *A Barnyard Romeo*. He played his first part in London in 1910 in *Aladdin* at Drury Lane, and in the following two pantomime seasons he appeared in *Jack and the Beanstalk* and *Hop O'My Thumb*, also at Drury Lane.

His long career took him all over the world—he spent five years in America—and he was seen in many kinds of show business, but he preferred pantomime to anything else, insisted on being free to accept parts in Christmas productions, and was the author or part-author of more than 50.

He was three times married.

September 27, 1962.

Former chief Albert Luthuli, Nobel Peace Prize winner for 1960, African liberation leader, and former president general of the banned African National Congress, was killed by a train at Stanger in South Africa on July 21, 1967. He was in his late sixties.

Luthuli's non-violent resistance to the apartheid doctrine of the Nationalist Government drove the latter to do all it could to make him an un-person. He was stripped of his chieftainship in 1952—for declining to resign from the African National Congress. He was among the 155 people arrested in 1956 on allegations of high treason, but was released at the end of a preparatory examination. He was confined to a small area around his home at Stanger in 1959 for five years. When he won the Nobel Prize the following year the Nationalist Government allowed him to travel to Norway to receive it but barred him from going to Sweden.

He said at the awards ceremony that he regarded the prize as "a recognition of the sacrifices made by the people of all races (in South Africa), particularly the African people who have endured and suffered so much for so long". When Luthuli was elected Rector of Glasgow University in 1962 he was not permitted to attend an installation ceremony.

His autobiography *Let My People Go*, published simultaneously in Britain and South Africa in 1962, was banned a few months later by the Nationalist Government in South Africa. Two years later when the 1959 confinement order expired, a stricter order under the Suppression of Communism Act was issued. The Minister of Justice said at the time that he was satisfied that Luthuli had engaged in "activities furthering the cause of communism". Luthuli was confined to a smaller area, warned against publishing statements, and banned from attending church services. Visitors to Luthuli were always strictly screened—and Senator Robert Kennedy, who saw him in 1966, was one of the few allowed to visit him.

Coming of good Zulu stock and proud of his tribal history (he made a spirited defence of the Shaka) he was always conscious that the religion in which he had been brought up put an obligation of honour upon him to serve his non-Christian fellow countrymen. The first part of his career was on the whole a quiet one as a teacher. But the victory of Malan in 1948, bringing with it the start of apartheid, drew Luthuli into conflict with the new white rulers of the Union. He stood out against the laws prolifically passed to keep non-whites to a separate status. At the same time he used his influence, which for a while was great, to persuade Africans that violence and other forms of extremism should be avoided.

This role of middle man of good will brought Luthuli under the displeasure of both sides. The Afrikaner authorities persecuted him because he was too independent and decent to be one of their stooges prepared to countenance a bogus tribal set-up. The younger men in the African camp saw no good results coming from his forbearance. Under this double strain Luthuli never lost his magnanimity and serenity. He remained a simple, massive figure.

Albert Luthuli was born in Rhodesia where his father had gone to serve in the forces at the time of the Matabele Rebellion. He was unsure of the exact date of his birth, getting no nearer than that it was between 1898 and 1900. His mother, Mtonya, who came of Qwabe stock, a clan renowned for its strict discipline, had spent part of her childhood in the Royal Kraal of King Ceteway. The family returned from Rhodesia about 1908 and stayed on the farm of a white adherent of the Seventh Day Adventists. After that Luthuli went to school at Groutville and proved a hard-working pupil. He was offered a bursary at Fort Hare, but refused it because he wanted to earn money at once to support his mother.

In 1928 he became secretary of the African Teachers' Association and in 1933 its president. He has recalled that he got pleasure and stimulus at this period from the friendship of Professor Matthews who was later to resign his professorship and forfeit £7,000 in gratuities rather than submit to the travesty of the Separate Universities Act.

He married in 1927 Nokukanya Bhengu, daughter of a polygamous Zulu chief. Between 1929 and 1935 she bore him seven children, of whom the first and the last two were boys. He was elected Chief of the Umvoti Mission Reserve in 1936. He made two trips abroad, the first in 1938 as one of the four African delegates to an International Missionary Conference in Madras. Ten years later he enjoyed a second reprieve from what he has described as "the tense complexity of my homeland" by accepting an invitation to lecture in the United States on Christian missions under the joint aegis of the American Board and of the North American Missionary Conference.

By then the curtain was being rung down on foreign travel for Africans or anyone *non persona grata* to the party in power in the Union. Besides, Luthuli was to have his hands full in making what stand he could against mounting injustice. His connexion with the Defiance Campaign against the Segregation Laws made him a marked man. He found himself in 1952 at the head of the resistance movement as president-general of the African National Congress. Through the 1950s bans were imposed on him and lifted and imposed again. At one time he would be free to enjoy ordinary civil rights—so far as the Nationalists allow these to Africans—then he would be gagged from public speaking and be limited in his movements to the open prison of a remote locality.

He was arrested on the charge of treason at an early stage of the notorious "Treason Trials", but subsequently released.

Afrikaner jacks-in-office insulted him and, after Sharpeville in 1960, he was assaulted by the police. His health declined under the rough treatment inflicted on him, but his resolution did not. It was characteristic of him that as a gesture of protest he burnt his pass in Pretoria at the height of the bitter feelings in March, 1960, and invited all Africans to do the same.

July 22, 1967.

Ralph Lynn, who died on August 8, 1962, at the age of 80, had a career on stage and cinema screen which covered more than 50 years.

Playgoers will remember him with special affection for the remarkable period of 11 years during which he and the late Tom Walls, supported by what was virtually a stock company, played first at the Shaftesbury and afterwards at the Aldwych in a series of 13 farces when a run of less than 200 performances was regarded as a virtual failure. But his success was not easily won, for he had played many small parts in the provinces and in the United States before his considerable abilities as a light comedian were fully appreciated by West End audiences.

Ralph Lynn, a grand-nephew of Eliza Lynn Linton, the Victorian novelist, was born at Manchester on March 18, 1882, and made his first stage appearance at Wigan in *The King of Terrors* in 1900, but it was not until the autumn of 1914 that he first played in the West End in *By Jingo if We Do* at the Empire.

TURNING POINT

The turning point of his career came with the production by Leslie Henson and Tom Walls in April, 1922, of *Tons of Money*, a sparkling farce which filled the Shaftesbury Theatre for two years. Robertson Hare was also in the company and thus a great team was created which stayed together for 11 years. With the production of *It Pays to Advertise* it migrated to the Aldwych until June, 1933, when it was disbanded partly owing to the physical exhaustion of some of its members. Ben Travers, the playwright, joined the team with *A Cuckoo in the Nest* in July, 1925. The subsequent record is shown by the following list of plays and the number of performances of each—*Tons of Money* (737), *It Pays to Advertise*

(598), *A Cuckoo in the Nest* (376), *Rookery Nook* (409), *Thark* (401), *Plunder* (344), *A Cup of Kindness* (291), *A Night like This* (267), *Marry the Girl* (195), *Turkey Time* (263), *Dirty Work* (195), *Fifty-fifty* (161), and *A Bit of a Test* (142).

Ralph Lynn played in all these productions and rarely missed a performance except for illness or accident. London took to its heart the cheerful adventurer who seemed able to find his way out of the most impossible situations with his winning smile, his prominent teeth and his ever-present eye-glass. Audiences loved him because in the most outrageous quandaries he preserved his equanimity and sweet reasonableness. By the end of the evening he was still smiling happily and his audience was almost too exhausted to laugh.

It was all great fun which Ralph Lynn seemed to enjoy as much as the audience and there was general regret when the team was disbanded in June, 1933. Thereafter he turned increasingly to films and many of the Aldwych farces were transferred to the screen. But he made a successful come back to the West End theatre in August, 1944, in *Is Your Honeymoon Really Necessary*? It was one of the worst periods of the Second World War when air raid warnings were an almost nightly occurrence. Although then over 60 years of age Lynn worked with unflagging energy and was rewarded by a run of 980 performances, the longest of his whole career. He had not the least desire for retirement and inactivity and his latter years were as busy as he could make them.

NEW PLAY

In 1947 a new Ben Travers play, *Outrageous Fortune*, brought him into partnership again with Robertson Hare with whom he appeared twice more: in 1952 in Ben Travers's *Wild Horses*, at the Aldwych, and in 1954 in *The Party Spirit* at the Piccadilly.

Latterly, still a sprightly figure, he had been touring in repertory, playing his old "silly ass" roles of the Aldwych farces.

August 10, 1962.

M

Professor Paul Maas, who died in an Oxford nursing home on July 15, 1964, had been for nearly 60 years one of the foremost figures in classical and Byzantine Greek scholarship. He was 83.

Paul Mass was born at Frankfurt-on-Main on November 18, 1880, the son of Dr. Maximilian Maas. As a student at Berlin he came early under the notice of Wilamowitz; and though on occasion he dared to stand up to the great man himself in the discussions of the seminar, Wilamowitz wrote to his father during his first year and described him as a scholar of the highest promise.

The famous article in which Maas remarked for the first time the main characteristics of Bacchylides' use of the dactylo-epitrite metre, though not published till 1904, was actually composed in 1899, while its author was a student in Wilamowitz's seminar. His doctoral thesis, published in 1902, was a valuable study of the Latin poetic plural: and in 1906 he published a remarkable review of Mommsen's edition of the Codex Theodosianus, in which he used the results of recent investigation of the clausulae to make a number of corrections in the text.

BYZANTINE EXPERT

Meantime he had made himself an expert on Byzantine literature, but as Privatdozent at Berlin in 1910 he insisted on his right to lecture on classical subjects as well.

Maas spent much of the First World War in Istanbul as a member of the medical unit attached to the German Military Mission, and was eventually repatriated to Germany by way of Odessa. Returning to Berlin, he became Professor Extraordinarius in 1920: he now became a close associate of Wilamowitz, who chose him as one of the editors of his *Kleine Schriften* and who greatly regretted his departare to Koenigsberg as Professor Ordinarius in 1930. Maas did not hold this post for long; in 1934 he was deprived of his chair because of his Jewish birth. For years he refused to leave Germany: and in 1939 he was imprisoned by the National Socialists. No doubt he would have perished in a concentration camp had not Enoch Powell flown to Germany a month before the outbreak of war and somehow managed to obtain his release.

THE CLARENDON PRESS

Arriving in Oxford, Maas was able to make contact with several friends, notably with Gilbert Murray, whom he had known since 1909. He was employed as adviser by the Clarendon Press, where at first his expert knowledge of textual criticism was used upon the Book of Common Prayer; but later he became an indispensable consultant upon all manner of classical subjects. He edited the Addenda to Liddell and Scott's Greek Lexicon; he made a notable contribution to Dr. R. Pfeiffer's great edition of Callimachus; and he regularly visited Gilbert Murray on Boar's Hill to help him to revise his text of Aeschylus. With the aid of Professor C. Trypanis he completed the task, begun years earlier, of making the first critical edition of the genuine works of Romanos, the greatest religious poet of the Eastern Church. A second volume containing the works doubtfully ascribed to him is to follow. He maintained the steady stream of his publications, kept up a vast correspondence with scholars all over Europe, and spared no effort to help the many colleagues who came to consult him.

Maas never published a large book except the Romanos; yet his influence upon the methods and principles of classical scholarship in his time has been enormous. His summary account of the principles of textual criticism (first published in 1923, and now available in English in a third edition) is acknowledged to be masterly. One of his greatest achievements in this field has been that of demonstrating that Byzantine scholars were capable of far greater proficiency as editors and critics than was once assumed.

In the field of Greek metre Maas's achievement is no less remarkable. His treatise of some 30 pages embodied the results of 10 years' intensive work. It constitutes at once the most useful handbook of the subject, full of detailed observations of great value, and a theoretical treatise of the highest importance, which exposes with the sharpest clarity the weakness of the foundations upon which all general theories of the development of Greek metres rest. Maas's unique command of the techniques of textual criticism, grammar, metre and palaeography and his close acquaintance with the principles of Greek poetic style found expression in a vast number of articles, all drafted with the same masterly conciseness and precision. Nor do his publications contain anything like all his work: for few scholars have made greater contributions to the writings of others.

Anyone who knew Maas well would agree that he was not only a great scholar, but a great man. Persecution, poverty and (in his last days) ill health did nothing to diminish an exceptional enthusiasm for scholarly pursuits. Maas was a man of wide interests, which included medicine, music and the literatures of France and England as well as Germany. In his Berlin days he was a keen agriculturist and until well over 70 he would swim every morning.

ALL RESOURCES

But he had no time for small talk: the visitor to his lodgings would be asked what problem he came to discuss, and having explained it would find all the great scholar's resources put at his disposal.

In 1951 the Clarendon Press celebrated Maas's seventieth birthday in the previous year by issuing a hand-list of his publications up to that date. Both in Britain and in postwar Germany he was honoured with the highest academic distinctions. In 1962 the German Minister in London made a special journey to Oxford to invest him with the order *Pour le Mérite*.

In 1909 he married Karen Raeder of Copenhagen, and they had three daughters, who survive him, and a son of rare musical promise, who died young. His wife died in 1960.

July 17, 1964.

Sir Malcolm McAlpine, K.B.E., died on April 12, 1967 in his 90th year.

He was born on June 19, 1877, the third son of Sir Robert McAlpine, first baronet, the famous civil engineering contractor, and himself became chairman of the family firm.

During the building of the Mallaig extension of the West Highland Railway in the 1890s, Robert McAlpine senior (known as "Concrete Bob" because of his fondness for building in mass concrete) appointed his eldest son Robert to take charge of all construction and Malcolm, then 19, was made his brother's assistant.

The hardness of the rock encountered so much reduced progress that at times the steam-driven compressors were unable to supply enough air to keep all the drills in the tunnels and cuttings working. It was Malcolm who solved the problem in a way graphically described by Mr. John Thomas in his book *The West Highland Railway* (1905). While at a dentist's in Helensburgh he noticed the drill was worked by the dentist pressing a knob on the floor with his foot. He asked about this and was told that the knob worked a valve in a water pipe causing a flow of high pressure water to impinge on a Pelton wheel which provided the rotary motion for the drill. Immediately McAlpine was struck by the idea that a water turbine might be able to provide power for the air compressors on the railway project. His idea was a good one and was developed; an engineer was called in and a dam 7ft. high was built across Loch Dubh. A 21 in. steel pipe took the water from the dam to the turbine (which revolved at 9,000 r.p.m.) and the air produced was then taken to the workings by iron pipes. The system was a resounding success, the turbine doing four times the work of the steam compressor it supplanted.

Later, while superintending a blast in a cutting, Malcolm McAlpine was seriously hurt by rock fragments, suffering a broken pelvis, broken ribs and internal injuries. Told by telegram that his son's life was despaired of, Robert McAlpine senior set off posthaste from Glasgow in a special train with the notable Glasgow surgeon Sir William MacEwen. The story goes that on reaching Craigendoran (where the West Highland left the North British line) they were told that the line was closed. McAlpine, however, persuaded the driver to carry on, saying he would take full responsibility.

NO SIGNALS

And carry on they did, allegedly "without benefit of a single tablet" (necessary for single line working) and with driver and fireman manipulating the points as they came to them. On reaching Fort William they set out on an abominable seven-hour coach journey for Lochallort, where they found Malcolm in a grave condition.

MacEwen at once operated, sat by his patient's side for four days and nights and then saw that if his life were to be saved, he must be got to Glasgow. He taught eight navvies now to bear a stretcher and they set off on a slow journey over difficult country on foot and by boat until they reached the nearest point of the railway. Here an engine and truck, loosely coupled by a chain, waited. One row of navvies sat on the locomotive buffer beam and another on the truck frame, their legs touching and braced to absorb the shocks of travel. After a further stage by steamer and a long train journey from Banavie to Glasgow Malcolm McAlpine reached Glasgow—and survived.

"NATIONAL" WINNER

He was a well-known racehorse owner, his horse Shaun Spadah winning the Grand National in 1921. He was knighted in 1921 for his services at the Ministry of Munitions.

He married in 1903 Maud Dees. They had three sons.

April 13, 1967.

General of the Army Douglas MacArthur, who died on April 5, 1964, was a brilliant general and American military hero whose defiance of the civil authority during the Korean war led to his replacement, perhaps the most controversial episode of Mr. Truman's presidency.

MacArthur believed that Asia, not Europe, was the decisive battleground between the Communists and the free world, .and he advocated an aggressive military policy. Inevitably he became the idol of the Asia-first school in the United States and the focus of Republican attacks upon President Truman's foreign policy. When the Rebublican Party chose General Eisenhower as its Presidential candidate in 1952 it finally rejected MacArthur's view of the world struggle, but even President Truman continued to proclaim his respect for MacArthur as a soldier. He will be remembered for his winning of the war against Japan, for his efforts, as military governor, to set Japan upon a democratic and pacific course, and for the energy and ability with which, as the first United Nations commander, he saved the situation in the early days of the Korean war.

MacArthur's greatest achievements came after he had retired from the United States Army. He was over 60 in 1941 when he was recalled to defend his country's interests in the Far East. Unquestionably he was the best equipped commander of his day for such immense responsibility. His ability and knowledge of the Far East were both exceptional.

He was born on January 26, 1880, at Little Rock, Arkansas, the son of Lieutenant Arthur MacArthur and Miss Mary Hardy. At 19 he was appointed to the United States Military Academy, and, with characteristic intellectual ability, graduated head of his class. Early missions in the Far East, during the Russo-Japanese war, gave him a valuable insight into Japanese methods of warfare. When in 1917 the United States went to war, MacArthur became Chief of Staff of the Rainbow Division, in which, according to his own suggestion, every state in the union was represented. In France his personal courage was outstanding. Returning to the United States in 1919, MacArthur became the youngest man to be appointed commandant at West Point; in 1930, once again the youngest man to hold so high a post, he was appointed Chief of Staff of the Army with the rank of general. His warnings about the need for preparedness were disregarded and five years later he retired at his own wish, but was detailed to assist the Philippines in military and naval affairs. In 1937 he retired with the rank of general.

In July, 1941, President Roosevelt recalled MacArthur to duty and appointed him commanding general of the Far East Command. When in December the Japanese mercilessly bombed Manila 10 hours after the attack on Pearl Harbour, all that MacArthur could hope to do was to gain time and his historic defences of Bataan and Corregidor were skilful and determined efforts to this end. Ordered to transfer his headquarters when further resistance became useless, he escaped to Australia in a motor torpedo boat. As he landed he proclaimed with a characteristic touch of egotism and flair for publicity: "I have come through and I will return."

As supreme commander of the allied naval, air and land forces of the entire South West Pacific, MacArthur became one of the greatest military figures of the war. In March, 1942, he was awarded the Congressional Medal and in 1944 he was made General of the Army. A year earlier he had been made honorary G.C.B. Once the Japanese offensive had been brought to a halt his "island-hopping" return to the Philippines began. MacArthur's strategy was to use air power to neutralize a hostile strategic base and then to seize this point in a forward bound, usually through sea-power, by-passing the Japanese forces. By October, 1944, MacArthur was able to announce at Leyte "I have returned," although it took until May, 1945, to complete the reconquest of the Islands.

The capitulation of the Japanese after the dropping of the second atomic bomb made the planned invasion unnecessary, and instead MacArthur was appointed military governor of Japan and commander-in-chief of the forces of the forces of occupation. He remained in Japan six years, hastening the transformation of a feudal society into a modern democratic state. Not all observers believed that the revolution was as far-reaching as MacArthur insisted, but his sympathetic handling of the Japanese was a great asset to the free world. His power was immense; as John Gunther wrote, "he imposes democracy like a dictator."

When South Korea was attacked in June, 1950, MacArthur enthusiastically supported President Truman's decision to go to its aid in the name of the United Nations. His letter to the Veterans of Foreign Wars in August showed, however, that he was out of sympathy with the Administration's policy of neutralizing Formosa and avoiding a conflict with Communist China which might turn into a world war. MacArthur's views alarmed the other nations resisting aggression, and endangered their unity. President Truman considered recalling MacArthur, but instead he was ordered to withdraw the message, already published.

After the brilliant landing at Inchon, which displayed MacArthur's genius at its best, President Truman, anxious to discuss future plans and to meet his formidable subordinate, flew to Wake Island for an historic encounter. MacArthur never denied that he assured the President that the Chinese were unlikely to intervene in force and that victory was at hand.

BITTER CONTROVERSY

Later, however, he insisted that the Chinese moved only because they had been assured that in Manchuria they would enjoy a "privileged sanctuary."

This refusal of the Administration to allow MacArthur to bomb bases in China became an embittered political controversy as Chinese "volunteers" poured over the Yalu and the United Nations forces were pushed back. MacArthur, frustrated by this limitation on his freedom of action, called on the United Nations to choose between withdrawal from Korea or a decision to use Nationalist troops, bomb Manchuria, and blockade the Chinese mainland. Criticisms of the Administration, leaking from his headquarters, inflamed the Republicans.

In fact, early in 1951, the tide turned and plans were made for a negotiated settlement. On hearing this MacArthur issued a threatening call to the Chinese to lay down their arms. The effect was to destroy prospects of a negotiated settlement, which MacArthur viewed as appeasement of the Communists. It was this which finally convinced the Administration that MacArthur was a threat to civilian control which could not be tolerated, although another act of insubordination soon followed: a letter to the Republican minority leader criticizing the priority given to Europe in the Administration's plans.

Despite warm invitations from President Truman, MacArthur had refused to return to the United States until he was recalled. Then he had not seen his country for 14 years. He had become steeped in the Far East and out of touch with American opinion. Moreover, surrounded by supporters of an almost fanatical devotion, he had grown increasingly impatient of criticism or advice. Visitors were struck by the self-imposed isolation of the legendary viceroy of the Pacific.

MacArthur was relieved of all his commands on April 9, 1951. His homecoming released a tidal wave of emotion. Eloquent, articulate, and histrionic, the General seemed likely to sweep the country off its feet. Congressmen wept when he addressed them; the demand for records of his speech reached two million. But the exhaustive inquiry of the Senate Foreign Relations and Armed Services committees drained the enthusiasm away. MacArthur, on the witness stand, gave cautious and evasive answers to many questions. His Republican sponsors, many of whom were isolationists, were dismayed to find that he favoured expanding rather than liquidating the Korean war. The Chiefs of Staff punctured, for most Americans, the delusion MacArthur had fostered that America could escape from the frustrations of the cold war by "going it alone" and ignoring its allies.

MacArthur wrung many hearts when he told Congress that old soldiers never die, they only fade away. The prophecy was truer than he may have expected. MacArthur plunged into politics and probably would have welcomed the Republican presidential nomination. At the Republican convention, he was regarded as a Taft man because of his opposition to General Eisenhower, although there was a world of difference between Taft's isolationism and MacArthur's pronouncement that "there is no substitute for victory." This convention in 1952, which resulted in a victory for General Eisenhower and only a handful of votes for MacArthur, closed the door on either a political or a military job. MacArthur accepted the chairmanship of Remington Rand, Incorporated; and save for the brief opening of old controversies when the Truman memoirs and the Yalta papers were published, faded out of public life.

He was twice married. By his second wife, formerly Miss Jean Faircloth, he had one son.

April 6, 1964.

Sir Alexander McColl, formerly chairman of the Vacuum Oil Company (now Mobil Oil Company) died on August 15, 1962, at the age of 84.

Alexander Lowe McColl was born on June 10, 1878, the son of Hugh Boyd McColl, and educated at Kilmarnock Academy. He began work as a paper boy with the *Kilmarnock Standard*, and then spent 13 years in the locomotive department of the Glasgow and South Western Railway Company before joining Vacuum Oil in London in 1905.

During his career with the company, which extended for more than 50 years, he was successively sales manager, director, and deputy chairman before becoming chairman in 1936. He held that office for 10 years, and then served as a consultative director until his retirement from the company in 1959.

During the First World War McColl, as a member of the Ministry of Munitions Committee, assisted in the distribution of lubricating oil. In the Second World War and in the immediate postwar period he served as chairman of the Lubricating Oil Committee of the Petroleum Board. For his services he was knighted in 1946.

Sir Alexander's business interests were not confined to the oil industry. He had been chairman of the Superheater Co. Ltd, and a director of Glenfield and Kennedy Ltd, and a number of other companies.

SCOTTISH INTEREST

Throughout his life he maintained his interest in the Scottish scene and the Scottish economy. He had been a member of the old Scottish Development Council before the war. Since its functions were taken over in 1949 by the Scottish Council (Development and Industry) McColl had served continuously until his death on the London Committee, of which he was chairman from 1954 to 1958. He was also a vice-president of the Council itself. His excellent business contacts in the United States, built up over such a long period, enabled him to play an important part in the attraction of many American enterprises to Scotland, which has been such a feature of Scottish economic development in the postwar period.

In 1950 he was appointed chairman of the Committee on the Aberdeen Fishing Industry. A past president of both the MacColl Society, and the London Ayrshire Society, he also preserved his contacts with his home town, and in 1952 he was proud to become a Burgess of Kilmarnock.

He married, in 1909, Elizabeth Brown Lightfoot, by whom he had one son and two daughters.

August 17, 1962.

Dr. John M. MacCormick, chairman of the Scottish Covenant Association and one of the leading personalities within the Scottish nationalist movement for more than 30 years, died in a Glasgow hospital on October 13, 1961, at the age of 56.

Perhaps even to speak of a "movement" in this context may be misleading, for there is much disagreement between the various groups who want Scotland to have greater control of her own affairs. But no man in the past quarter-century has done more to draw the issue to the attention of the general public on both sides of the Border.

A former Rector of Glasgow University and a Glasgow lawyer, it was he who launched the Scottish Covenant which secured more than two million signatures in the early 1950s. He was a small, spry figure with considerable charm who often made friends where he could not win allies.

John MacDonald MacCormick, the younger son of Captain Donald MacCormick, a sea captain who was a native of Mull, was born on November 20, 1904. He was educated at Woodside School, Glasgow, and at Glasgow University, where he became associated with Scottish nationalism. After a spell as secretary of the University Labour Club he founded the Nationalist Association of the University in 1927. The following year, while still a law student, he was one of the founders and the first chairman of the National Party of Scotland. When it subsequently merged with the more moderate Scottish Party, MacCormick became honorary secretary.

He held that position until the great division in the Scottish nationalist movement in 1942.

OUTVOTED OVER WAR

The clash, which may have been exacerbated by differences of personality, was centred largely on whether the party should support the Government in the war. MacCormick believed that it should, and when he was outvoted he promptly resigned and founded the Scottish Convention, which was later to be the means of his greatest propaganda success.

MacCormick stood unsuccessfully for Parliament on a number of occasions. He contested the Camlachie division of Glasgow in 1929; Inverness-shire in 1931, 1935, and 1945; and Paisley in 1948, where he had both Liberal and Conservative support. Having found from bitter experience how fruitless it was to oppose major parties at the poll, it was no doubt in search of an alternative means of gathering influence that he launched the Scottish Covenant in October, 1949. This document, guilefully phrased so as not to offend many supporters of the established parties—it sought only a federal Parliament for Scotland, with "adequate authority" in Scottish affairs—attracted eventually more than two million signatures.

That, however, was the peak of MacCormick's influence. The Covenant may have succeeded in provoking the appointment of a Royal Commission on Scottish Affairs, but it did not provide an effective springboard for further political action. Very possibly, as many of the critics suggested, it was regarded by many of its signatories as an emotional protest rather than a call for specific measures.

In 1950 he was elected Rector of Glasgow University. His installation address—when he was bombarded by flour, tomatoes, and other missiles from his audience—was a disgraceful scene. But this was no indication of his popularity with the students in general. So conscientiously did he take his duties that he soon won the respect and liking of many of those who had opposed his election. A ready speaker, who had toured the United States in 1930 with a student debating team from Glasgow, he was at home in the university atmosphere. He was made an honorary LL.D. of Glasgow in 1951.

His published works included *The Flag in the Wind*, a highly readable account of his career in Scottish nationalism; and *Catastrophe and Imagination*, a more ambitious but less successful venture into a wider literary field.

In 1938 he married Margaret Isobel Miller, by whom he had two sons and two daughters.

October 14, 1961.

General Sir Richard McCreery, G.C.B., K.B.E., D.S.O., M.C., who died in London on October 18, 1967, at the age of 69, was Lord Alexander's Chief of Staff throughout the campaigns in the Desert, Tunisia, and Sicily, and served throughout the Italian campaign, first as a corps commander and then as Commander of the famous Eighth Army in its last months.

McCreery was one of a number of cavalrymen who took quickly to the tactics of the Royal Armoured Corps. His regiment, the 12th Lancers, was one of the earliest to be mechanized and later, as an armoured divisional commander, he acquired a well-founded reputation tor handling his tanks skilfully and decisively in training exercises. It was therefore something of a misfortune for him that his commands in the field were in a theatre where the conditions precluded wide manoeuvre and were almost comparable to those of the Somme and Ypres in the First World War, among mountains instead of swamps.

McCreery was tall and thin, quiet in manner and restrained in speech. He was a fine, although not flamboyant, leader; he had the gift of inspiring affection and respect in his men, and he got on well with allies at all levels. He was a splendid horseman and he won the Grand Military Cup at Sandown twice, in 1923 and 1928.

Richard Loudon McCreery was born on Febuary 1, 1898, the eldest son of Walter McCreery, and educated at Eton. He was commissioned in the 12th Lancers from Sandhurst in 1915, serving with his Regiment in France in the First World War, was wounded and won the Military Cross. Between the two wars he graduated at the Staff College and held two Staff appointments, but his service was mainly regimental.

At the beginning of the Second World War he was General Alexander's chief staff officer in the Ist Division, with which he went to France. In the fighting before Dunkirk, he commanded a mechanized brigade with gallantry and skill and won a D.S.O. After two years in command of one of the new armoured divisions in England he was appointed Adviser on Armoured Fighting Vehicles at Sir Claude Auchinleck's headquarters in Cairo, but, when General Alexander arrived to take over the Middle East Command in 1942, McCreery returned to his old master as Chief of Staff. Lord Montgomery in his memoirs has recorded that, throughout the Desert Campaign, Alexander "never suggested what I ought to do .... All the plans for Alamein and afterwards were made at Eighth Army H.Q. ... he never commented in detail on my plans or suggested any of his own". McCreery's function as Chief of Staff was, therefore, somewhat restricted until Alexander became Deputy Commander-in-Chief to Eisenhower for the Tunisian fighting and the capture of Sicily.

Although McCreery was able to exercise so little influence upon the Eighth Army's North African campaign, he revealed, many years afterwards, that he had profoundly disagreed at the time with some of Montgomery's tactical methods, particularly in the handling of the tanks. In 1959 he set out his views in an outspoken and highly critical article which he wrote for his regimental journal and which was widely discussed in the public press. He argued that the tactics of the breakthrough at Alamein were unnecessarily costly in infantry and that, after the battle, Montgomery was overcautious in the pursuit, and so missed an opportunity to cut off Rommel at El Agheila. He criticized the replacement of Lumsden, a tank expert, by Horrocks in command of the *corps de chasse*. (A short time after his relief, Lumsden walked into his London club in uniform, wearing a bowler hat, and said "I've just been sacked because there isn't enough room in the desert for two cads like Monty and me".)

He alleged that Montgomery's intolerance and inflated ideas added greatly to the difficulties of cooperation between the First and Eighth Armies in the final advance on Tunis.

In this article McCreery also stated his opinion that veteran divisions tended to become stale and gun-shy, and that, therefore, they did not go so fast or so far as fresher divisions. This proposition gave rise to a lively correspondence in *The Times*, in which the consensus of opinion was in his favour.

Late in August, 1943, on the eve of the invasion of Italy, McCreery stepped into a sudden vacancy in the command of the 10th Corps which was standing ready for the landing at Salerno. He was now fated to spend the rest of the war in operations which were ill-adapted to the task which was set them. With her long coastline, Italy is more open to sea than to land attack.

An invader by land from the south has to advance up the entire length of the Apennines, a distance of 600 miles; moreover, every river, gully, ravine and spur runs at right angles to this central backbone, and forms a natural line of defence which has to be stormed frontally. Yet invasion by land was the course forced upon the Allies because of shortage of aircraft carriers, assault shipping and landing craft, this shortage being due to the higher priority given to operations in the Pacific and to the build-up for the invasion of Normandy.

Within the limitations imposed upon him by these conditions, McCreery proved to be a successful and enterprising Corps Commander. His first battle at Salerno was a desperate one, but his men withstood the furious counter-attacks of superior German forces, and, after some days when it was touch and go, the 10th Corps rallied and flung them back. The next phase of the operations was the advance over the plain of Naples and the attack on the Volturno line, in which McCreery's Corps was assigned the difficult front of attack through the mountains on the right. His Corps played a leading part in the attacks on the successive delaying positions occupied by the Germans, until Kesselring decided to make a more prolonged stand on the Garigliano (Cassino) line.

This position was one of the strongest in Italy, and McCreery's Corps bore a considerable share of the series of costly and hard-fought attacks which occupied the next four months.

After the capture of Rome, the Allied Armies in Italy were greatly weakened by the withdrawal of forces for operations in France and elsewhere, and the campaign was continued with increasingly inadequate means. A rapid allied advance northwards from Rome was followed by a succession of attacks on the "Gothic" line. Throughout these hard-fought operations up the length of Italy, McCreery had exploited to the utmost the opportunities, such as they were, for the employment of armour in almost impossible conditions of ground and weather, and the 10th Corps had developed a brilliant technique for the passage of mountain rivers in face of opposition.

In November, 1944, McCreery succeeded Sir Oliver Leese in command of the 8th Army.

SPRING OFFENSIVE

The winter operations, which it now fell to McCreery to conduct, made little progress owing to the difficulties of the mountainous country and the bad weather. When the spring came the offensive was resumed. The plan was for the 8th Army to attack across the river Senio west of Ravenna, and, on the left of the 8th Army, the American 5th Army was to strike from the mountains of the central front, pass west of Bologna, and join hands with the British on the river Po. British troops were to land from the sea at Menate, three miles behind the enemy, using a new type of amphibious troop carrying tank called the Buffalo. The attack opened on April 9, after heavy air attacks and artillery bombardment, and was completely successful. Thousands of Germans were trapped south of the Po, which was crossed on a broad front a fortnight later. The allied air forces made havoc along the enemy's lines of supply, and the whole offensive was a fine example of well concerted land and air effort. The German front was now effectively broken, and resistance completely collapsed. On April 27 the 8th Army crossed the Adige and headed for Padua, Treviso and Venice. On April 29 the Germans signed an instrument of surrender, and, on May 2, 1945, nearly a million Germans in North Italy laid down their arms.

These operations, in which the 8th Army had played so great a part, had contained some 25 high-class German divisions at a time when their presence was dearly needed on their home front. When the 8th Army was disbanded later in the year, McCreery was appointed G.O.C.-in-C. of the British Forces of Occupation in Austria, and British Representative on the Allied Commission for Austria. From 1946 to 1948 he was G.O.C.-in-C. of the British Army of the Rhine, and his last two years in the service, until he retired in 1949, were spent at Washington as British Army Representative on the Military Staff Committee of the United Nations.

He married, in 1928, Lettice, daughter of Lord Percy St. Maur, and had four sons and one daughter.

October 19, 1967.

Carson McCullers, who died in hospital at Nyack, New York, on September 29, 1967, at the age of 50, was one of the most talented of Southern Gothic novelists in the United States. Mrs. McCullers, who had been in hospital for six weeks, had suffered a stroke.

Her persistence and successes through private misfortune were inspiring. She knew pain most of her days. Much of her ill health could be traced to a childhood bout of rheumatic fever which doctors diagnosed as tuberculosis. Before she was 29, she suffered three strokes which left her left side paralysed.

She required recently a wheelchair to move about a Victorian-style house in Nyack. When she felt able, she tapped away on a typewriter using one finger on her good right hand—but the process was slow and painful.

Born in Columbus, Georgia, in 1917, she went to New York at the age of 17 to study music, but, oddly like one of the characters from her later novels, she lost her tuition money on the second day in the city. She developed an earlier desire to write, and published her first stories in *Story* magazine shortly afterwards.

The Heart is a Lonely Hunter, her first novel, appeared in 1940; a parable of fascism, it is centred on a deaf mute's confrontations with citizens of the Deep South. Richard Wright, the Negro novelist, was impressed by Mrs. McCullers's case and justice in portraying a Negro, rare in southern fiction at the time.

RACIAL PROBLEMS

Reflections in a Golden Eye (1941) reinforced her critical reputation and here her themes of loneliness and alienation were developed in the violence and perversion of a Southern Army post. *The Member of the Wedding,* written in 1946, dramatized in 1950 and filmed in 1952 with Julie Harries as star, portrays with sympathy and understanding the tensions and conflicts of an imaginative adolescent girl.

In 1951, *The Ballad of the Sad Cafe* brought together her shorter fiction; and her second play, *The Square Root of Wonderful*, appeared in 1958. In her last novel, *Clock without Hands* (1961), her exuberant studies of freaks and grotesques gave way to a sober dramatization of Southern racial problems, and what she once called "the cheapness of human life in the South." Never a prolific writer, her few works retain their importance as psychological fables of an oppressive region of America.

In 1959, she herself defined her inner genius with characteristic precision: "Love, and especially love of a person who is incapable of returning it, is at the heart of my selection of grotesque figures—people whose physical incapacity is a symbol of their spiritual incapacity to love or receive love—their spiritual isolation."

Both *The Member of the Wedding* and *The Ballad of the Sad Cafe,* adapted by Edward Albee, were highly successful Broadway plays. Most recently *Reflections in a Golden Eye* was filmed with Elizabeth Taylor, Marlon Brando and Julie Harris.

September 30, 1967.

Derek McCulloch, O.B.E., "Uncle Mac" for many years to listeners to B.B.C. Children's Hour, died on June 1, 1967, at the age of 69.

Derek Ivor Breashur McCulloch held a simple secret of success. It consisted of his genuine love and understanding of children, together with the happy knack of "getting into their minds." He won the admiration of adults by his courage and fortitude—he underwent nearly 60 operations as a result of war wounds and a road accident. It might almost be said that McCulloch became famous by making a noise like a sheep. He was "Larry the Lamb" from the inception of the Toytown series of sound broadcasts, one of the best loved of Children's Hour Programmes.

Derek McCulloch joined the staff of the B.B.C. as an announcer in London in 1926. He was a good announcer, despite the physical handicap—one eye gone and a lung damaged—which he brought with him from the war of 1914. He was made Children's Hour Organizer in 1933 and Children's Hour Director in 1938, though in that year he had lost a leg in a road accident. The loss of physical mobility did nothing to quench his devotion to the welcome task of tapping the expanding resources of broadcasting to ensure that the best that broadcasting could do should be made available to children.

B.B.C. POLICY

This had long been the policy and intention of the B.B.C. and of John Reith, its founding Director-General, but Mac ("Uncle Mac" in the nomenclature of those days) was a devoted, thoroughly professional instrument through whom that policy was fully realized and developed. His memorial rests in the hearts of the astonishing number of people in Britain whose first affectionate memories of broadcasting spring from listening to Children's Hour, whether as children, as parents, or as grandparents. It was a moving experience to hear speeches made, when the time came to celebrate the 40th year of the B.B.C.'s existence, in which distinguished men and women revealed, in the vividness of their own first hand experience, a wealth of affection for Children's Hour and as a matter of remembered and cherished fact, for "Uncle Mac"

In 1940 "Uncle Mac" arranged the first broadcast made by the Queen—then Princess Elizabeth—when she spoke in Children's Hour to the children of the British Commonwealth. In 1943, McCulloch sponsored the play *Queen Victoria* in Children's Hour and persuaded Anna Neagle to take the name part. He also, at this time, enlisted the services of Lady Megan Lloyd George with a talk on the House of Commons for children.

WOUNDS ON SOMME

Born at Plymouth, he enlisted at the age of 17 as a private soldier in the Public Schools Battalion in the First World War. He received wounds which through the years necessitated many operations. When asked about them he once whimsically explained that they arose out of a private battle on the Somme with four German stretcher-bearers. He had been cut off trom his company 20 yards from the German lines and one of the German stretcher bearers fired at him. The bullet destroyed McCulloch's right eye. "I wasn't quite done for", he said, "and being fearfully angry I fired my rifle and saw one of the Germans fall. Then I feigned death.

"Soon after the Germans went away, I received four shrapnel wounds in the right and left shoulders, in the thigh and the leg. My collarbone, shoulder-blade and two ribs were broken and a bullet was lodged in my left lung. I managed somehow to crawl to our lines. And then I recovered consciousness—in Hampstead". After the war McCulloch worked abroad but had to come home because the bullet was still in his lung. Eventually the bullet was removed by an eminent German doctor at Munich. In 1938 disaster struck again. McCulloch was involved in a road accident near his home at Banstead, Surrey, which cost him his left leg. When next he spoke at the microphone he was on crutches. During many broadcasts he was in great pain. During his frequent spells in hospital children used to write him letters by the thousand.

Despite his own misfortunes "Uncle Mac" was ever ready to help deserving causes. One of his radio appeals, made early in the Second World War, was for £1,500 for a mobile X-ray unit. The response exceeded £11,000. On leaving the B.B.C. McCulloch became Children's Editor with the *News Chronicle* for three years and wrote a number of children's books.

FAMOUS "GOOD-NIGHT"

In recent years he had been heard on the B.B.C's "Children's Favourites" programme.

When the B.B.C. finally dropped radio's Children's Hour in 1965 it was a sad blow for many, including McCulloch, who became so well known for his signing-off words: "Good-night children, everywhere." The decision meant the temporary disappearance of Toytown (the plays have since been revived by the B.B.C.) and McCulloch remarked at the time: "I am surprised. I would have thought a lot of children still listened to Toytown. This was my life."

He married in 1931 and there are two daughters.

June 3, 1967.

Professor George Macdonald, C.M.G., who died on December 10, 1967 at the age of 64 after a long illness borne with great courage, was internationally acclaimed as one of the world's leading exponents of the principles of preventive medicine in the complex field of tropical diseases. He brought to the study of the tropical environment ideas of great originality, and a fertile, practical mind of the first order.

Born in 1903, he was the son of J. S. Macdonald, F.R.S., Professor of Physiology in the University of Liverpool, and qualified there in 1924. He turned to tropical medicine in 1925 as Research Assistant at the Sir Alfred Jones laboratory in Sierra Leone, and went to the Malaria Survey of India in 1929, and thence to the tea area of Assam until he was appointed Assistant Director of the Ross Institute of Tropical Hygiene, at the London School of Hygiene and Tropical Medicine, in 1937. He joined the R.A.M.C. in 1939, rising to the rank of Brigadier as consultant in malaria to the Mediterranean forces. After the war he became Director of the Ross Institute (1945) and Professor of Tropical Hygiene, London University (1946).

When DDT and the other new insecticides, and the new powerful anti-malarial drugs, were introduced during and after the war. Macdonald studied and used them with energy but with deliberate care for quantitative exactness in dosages. He was attracted by the notion of eradication of malaria, the policy of W.H.O., which he helped to shape. He was not afraid to press control so far that the tropical communities might lose the immunity maintained by continued infection. Some of his contemporaries argued that this loss of immunity could lead to severe epidemics, but Macdonald was confident that, even so, we had the means to deal with them.

The complexities of diseases in which intermediate hosts of the parasites are involved—mosquitoes, snails and others—stimulated Macdonald to amplify the work of Ross and McKendrick on the mathematical analysis of the many factors involved. This he did in a series of papers which displayed his mathematical erudition to the admiration of the scientific world. He constructed mathematical models which enabled him to select quantitatively those factors which, if controlled, might lead to reduction of malaria, and later of schistosomiasis, and which could be applied to other diseases.

Macdonald influenced governments, as when he was asked to advise on the structure of the health department of Tanzania, he influenced the research policies of the British Government in relation to the tropics, and he was an active member (and chairman) of Expert Committees of W.H.O. In 1952 he led a W.H.O. mission to Korea.

His work was his fun. He enjoyed it all the time; never heavy or stereotyped, his reach was enormous but did not exceed his grasp. He took every problem in detail, with a most acute eye for factual or logical errors. If one asked his advice, he gave his whole attention the question; it was part of the make-up of his character which permitted no hasty judgment or slipshod work. And he gave his advice as an equal, not as a master.

Many honours came his way: C.M.G. in 1953, the international Darling Award in 1954, the Bernhard Nocht Medal in 1963, and the presidency of the Royal Society of Tropical Medicine and Hygiene in 1965–67. He wore them easily as he was not apt to display himself as a great man. But he had the qualities of greatness, and his friends miss him.

He married in 1932 Mary, the daughter of Sir Roger Hetherington, who survives him with one son and two daughters.

December 15, 1967.

Jeanette MacDonald, star of many musical films, died on January 14, 1965. She was 57.

The great advantage Jeanette MacDonald had over almost every other coloratura soprano to seek screen fame was that she could act as well as sing: her voice, though agreeable and well-managed, was not by operatic standards exceptional, but allied with an infectious personality and a keen comic sense it made her the perfect heroine for operetta, and for a whole generation she remained the classic exponent of the graceful melodies of Rudolph Friml and Sigmund Romberg.

She was born at Philadelphia in 1907 She soon graduated to leading roles in stage musicals, and when sound films were introduced she was one of the first musical stars to be lured to Hollywood: Lubitsch, looking for someone to play opposite Maurice Chevalier in *The Love Parade*, chanced upon an old screen-test she had made and immediately offered her the role. The film was an instant success, and Jeanette MacDonald's effervescent personality and attractive voice rapidly made her a favourite with the public. During the next few years she was on several occasions teamed again with Maurice Chevalier: in *One Hour With You* and *The Merry Widow* for Lubitsch and *Love Me Tonight* for Mamoulian—as well as appearing with Jack Buchanan in *Monte Carlo*, also for Lubitsch.

In 1935, after *The Merry Widow*, she appeared in a film of the stage success *Naughty Marietta* with a new singing star, Nelson Eddy, and the combination impressed the public so much that they became almost as inseparable in the popular mind as Fred Astaire and Ginger Rogers, appearing together in a long succession of romantic operettas, generally adapted from stage originals. Among them were *Rose Marie. Maytime. The Girl of the Golden West, Sweethearts, New Moon, Bittersweet, and I Married an Angel.* During these years, however, she did not appear exclusively with Nelson Eddy: there were also *San Francisco*, with Clark Gable and Spencer Tracy, *The Firefly*, with Allan Jones, and the musical version of *Smilin' Through*. After 1943 she returned mainly to the stage, touring in operetta, making gramophone records and appearing on television. In 1948 she made a film called *The Birds and the Bees*.

January 16, 1965.

Sir Eric Macfadyen, one of the pioneers of the world's rubber industry, especially in Malaya, died on July 13, 1966 at his home at Tonbridge. He was also, in his earlier days, well-known in politics as a Liberal of the old school.

He was M.P. for Devizes 1923–24, and after his defeat returned to industry. He knew the rubber industry well, especially in Malaya, and had come to be recognized as one of the leading authorities, not only on growing, but also on the treatment and marketing of the finished product, and held many appointments in organizations associated with the trade.

Eric Macfadyen was born in 1879, and educated at Clifton and Wadham College, Oxford, where, in 1902, he was President of the Union. He had already served for nearly two years as a trooper in the South African War, during which he was awarded the Queen's Medal with three clasps.

After leaving the University, he entered the Malay Civil Service as a cadet. With his thoroughgoing and precise methods, Macfadyen, having realized the potentialities of Malaya, set himself to master every detail of production. From 1906 until 1916 he applied himself particularly to planning and contracting, and to opening up new districts.

He became agent for most of the chief agencies, visiting Malaya, the west coasts of Sumatra and Java, and helping to establish the United Planter's Association. He was its representative on the first Federal Council of the Federated Malay States, and took an influential part in shaping the land and labour legislation which was called for by the rapid expansion of growing and employment during the boom years.

After the war, Macfadyen became associated with Harrisons and Crosfield and various other growing companies—in several of which he was chairman or vice-chairman. When he was knighted in 1943, after retiring from the Governing Body of the Imperial College of Tropical Agriculture, Trinidad (of which he became Honorary President) it was specifically for services to the science of rubber-growing.

GROWERS' LEADER

He had been chairman of the Rubber Grower's Association, of the Association of British Malaya (more than once), and of the Institution of Rubber Industry and he was also awarded the Gold Medal of the Grower's Association.

When Macfadyen retired in 1955 from the boards of Harrisons and Crosfield, and certain other produce companies, he explained that this did not mean a complete severance of his associations with Malaya and the rubber trade. Indeed, he remained a director of several companies functioning in Malaya.

He served in France as a commissioned officer Royal Garrison Artillery during the First World War, and from 1940–42 he was captain of the 21st Battalion of the Home Guard. Macfadyen married in 1920, Violet, daughter of the late E.H.S. Champneys, of Otterpool Manor, Sellindge, and they had three sons and three daughters.

July 14, 1966.

K. B. McFarlane, senior Fellow of Magdalen College, Oxford, who died on July 16, 1966, was an outstanding medieval historian. He was 62.

Born in 1903, educated at Dulwich and Exeter College, Oxford, he took a first in history in 1925. In 1927 he was elected a Fellow by Examination at Magdalen and in 1928 an Official Fellow and Tutor. He remained a college tutor all his life, holding a number of college offices with distinction and for some years also a Special Lectureship in the history faculty. He was appointed as University Reader in Medieval History recently. He was unmarried.

As a young scholar he contributed the chapter on the Lancastrian kings to the last volume of the Cambridge Medieval History and the fourteenth and fifteenth centuries in England became his chief interest. He was the first to penetrate and describe clearly the new social relationships which held the English ruling classes together during this period, overlaying the older feudal obligations of Norman and Angevin times.

His two key articles: *Parliament and Bastard Feudalism* (1943) and *Bastard Feudalism* (1947) showed in a masterly fashion how English society of the later Middle Ages worked and how it must be understood. He followed these up with studies on Cardinal Beaufort, Lancastrian finance, the fifteenth-century antiquary William Worcester, and the careers of successful soldiers and office-holders in the Hundred Years War. In 1953 he published his book: *John Wycliffe and the Beginnings of English Non-conformity*. From this list alone it can be seen that his interests were by no means confined to political and social history and it comes as only a mild surprise to find that art-historians are indebted to him for an important discovery in the chronology of Hans Memling's paintings.

To anyone who listened to his Ford lectures, given in 1953, on *The English Nobility, 1290-1530*, they seemed to spell finality but he only regarded them as a sketch for a much larger study of the subject. Much of his work for this was, and had to be pioneer. More than once he stumbled over assumptions and omissions of older authorities, which had to be remedied before anything definite could be attempted and this explains his close investigation of the descents of earldoms and the family histories and genealogies of the later medieval English nobility and gentry. Time, the heavy burden of teaching, and his never very strong constitution did not allow him to crown his masterly articles on these themes with a work of synthesis. His scholarship was exacting to a fault and he refused to advance or to accept generalizations unless he had used all the available evidence, much of it new and discovered by him as he wrote. Because of this his brief life of Wycliffe has remained his only book. It is written with a pungent, brilliant conciseness, a wry humour, and an insight into the ecclesiastical and academic world of the fourteenth century that could give little comfort to protestant firebrands. His Raleigh Lecture, *The Wars of the Roses*, published recently, shows him at the height of his powers.

McFarlane shunned social and public occasions but he possessed to a rare degree the powers needed to shape the decisions of academic bodies. His college, the Oxford history faculty, the councils of the Royal Historical and the Canterbury and York Societies, to mention only some, alike benefited from his services. His interventions in the discussions of committees tended to be few but they were all the more commanding and often also salted with irony. He could be a shrewd negotiator and his independent and utterly uncorruptible judgment often unexpectedly carried the day against heavy odds. But he treated his offices and committees as chores and it became more and more difficult to persuade him to serve.

K. B., or "the Master" as his pupils sometimes called him was an awe-inspiring man, rather withdrawn and seemingly unapproachable. His authority as a scholar and tutor made him at first acquaintance formidable to his undergraduates but he recognized merit and also honest-to-goodness effort readily, and only humbug, time-wasting and pretentiousness ran the risk of being exposed by his unhedging censure all the more damning for being coldly delivered. As a teacher he had few equals and his influence on his pupils, whether they became professional historians or not, was lasting. He believed in doing only what he could do to perfection and was no less fastidious about the spoken than about the written word. Unwilling to improvise, he usually lectured from a finely polished text in manuscript avoiding puff and repetition without losing the attention of his large audiences. For despite its elaborate finish his style lacked neither life nor grandeur.

His reserve concealed in fact a shy, compassionate, easily moved and pessimistic temperament which only his friends were allowed to know although his help, advice and often lavish generosity were available not only to them but to many others besides and to any of his pupils in difficulties.

McFarlane supervised and formed more than one generation of researchers, many of them now occupying chairs and senior academic posts. His methods and especially his prosopographical approach to the history of later medieval England have founded a school for which he invented the disciplines and the norms. His influence will continue and his critics can fault him only with weapons which he himself made. Though he never sought and sometimes even looked askance at honours, he had them conferred upon him, and was made a Fellow of the Society of Antiquaries and the British Academy.

July 18, 1966.

William McFee, the author noted for his sea stories, died at New Milford, Connecticut, on July 2, 1966, at the age of 85.

Although he became a naturalized American citizen before the First World War, it is difficult to think of McFee as other than an English novelist. His fame was greater in America than in this country; here he was always a shade neglected—more than a shade, indeed, it seemed to those who had the liveliest appreciation of his superbly illustrative, romantic and subtle art. No explanation of this relative lack of recognition seems quite adequate, though a principal contributory cause is not far to seek. It was McFee's misfortune to be shadowed in all or almost all he wrote by the greater name and example of Conrad.

Born at sea, almost within sight of the English shore, on June 15, 1881, William McFee was the child of an English merchant captain of Irish stock and a mother born in Nova Scotia. Generations of his father's family had trafficked with the sea; John Henry McFee himself was a designer, builder, owner, and master of the ship on which his son was born. The son was brought up in the East End of London, went to a grammar school in Suffolk, and at the age of 16, his father having died some years earlier, was apprenticed as a mechanical engineer to a firm in the City. He rose steadily in his calling, but in 1906 gave up his prospects on dry land and went to sea as a ship's engineer with a shipmaster uncle's line. After his appointment as chief serving engineer with the company he proceeded to the United States, spent some time in making up his mind what to do, and chose to serve in the ships of the United Fruit Company, ultimately becoming a chief engineer.

Neither of his two earliest novels, *An Ocean Tramp* (1908) and *Aliens* (1914), the latter apparently written in four weeks, created much stir, but *Casuals of the Sea*, begun in 1908, when he was in Japan, and published in 1916, was another matter. Somewhat Zolaesque in its fashion of realism and distinctly Jamesian in narrative method, this study of failure in the setting of a working-class family, though imperfectly conceived, won from several critics of note the admiring attention which it deserved.

LIKENESS TO CONRAD

A striking description of a sea voyage to the East and a succession of boiler inspections in the engine-room presaged much that was to come in later and more characteristic work. *Captain Macedoine's Daughter* followed in 1921, and here the likeness to Conrad was, without question, too obviously pronounced.

Command, published in the following year, exhibits clearly the favourite design of McFee's fiction—the ironical detachment, the romantic perception, the wicked glint in the eye of the Old Man of the Sea even as he contemplates the shaping of a tragic destiny. With Spenlove as his familiar, as a rule, McFee returned again and again to the same story-teller's statement of value—in *Pilgrims of Adversity*, *The Harbourmaster* (published in Britain in 1932), *The Beachcomber* (1935), *Derelicts* (1938), the last of these a jewel of a book, probably as good as anything he wrote. He did not, it is true, always maintain a uniform level, but neither did, let us say, Conrad. At all events he wrote little that lacked distinction. Mention must be made of *Sunlight in New Granada* (1928), a travel book of finely individual quality; *Swallowing the Anchor* (1925), a volume of literary, travel, and speculative essays written between watches in the engine-room; *Sailors of Fortune* (1930), a first-rate volume of short stories with settings in every part of the globe; an admirable life of Sir Martin Frobisher. His novels, after *Derelicts*, were *Watch Below* (1940) and *Spenlove in Arcady* (1941), the first a beautifully live and vivid chronicle, essentially autobiographical in colouring, of the golden age of steam, the other a somewhat disappointing tale of the Old Man of the Sea as landsman. *Ship to Shore*, a light novel, appeared in 1946; *Family Trouble* in 1949, *The Adopted*, an Anglo-American tale about a foundling in 1952; and *The Law of the Sea* in the same year.

July 4, 1966.

Sir Donald MacGillivray, G.C.M.G., M.B.E., who died in hospital in Nairobi on December 24, 1966, at the age of 60, was the last British High Commissioner for the Federation of Malaya; he was also the youngest man ever to have held that office, having been appointed to it at the age of 48.

Donald Charles MacGillivray was born on September 22, 1906, the son of Evan James MacGillivray. Q.C., of Ringwood. Hampshire. After completing his education at Sherborne School and Trinity College, Oxford, he was selected for the Colonial Administrative Service in 1929 and posted to Tanganyika. He was soon recognized as among the most promising officers of his generation, and in 1938 was picked out for transfer to Palestine, in accordance with the Colonial Office policy of staffing that difficult territory with some of its best administrators.

Quiet in manner, slight in build and with a lively mind and a considerable gift of humour, MacGillivray was very unlike the popular image of a Colonial administrative officer, but he was ideally suited to the tasks which faced the Colonial Service during his time. In Palestine he was successful not only as a district commissioner but in the central secretariat. Towards the end of the mandate period he was assigned to act as liaison officer with a visiting Anglo-American committee and with the United Nations commission of inquiry.

DIPLOMATIC SKILL

In 1947 he was selected for promotion to the Colonial Secretaryship of Jamaica. Political conditions in the island were in a very difficult state, with a transitional constitution in force and West Indian federation in the air. MacGillivray showed great tact and diplomatic skill in dealing with the Jamaican leaders and helping to make things work smoothly.

In 1952, after five in Jamaica, he was well in line for a governorship. At this juncture, however, General (now Field Marshal) Sir Gerald Templer was appointed High Commissioner for the Federation of Malaya where a state of emergency existed. The Secretary of State (Lord Chandos) wished to provide Sir Gerald with an experienced civilian deputy, and after reviewing the field of possible candidates he selected MacGillivray as being outstandingly suitable. The appointment was badly received in Malaya, where it was felt, both by the Rulers and by the Malayan Civil Service, that the post should not have been filled by a man with no local experience.

The Secretary of State however felt strongly that the need was for a man who would bring a fresh mind to bear on the complexities of the Malayan administrative machine.

MacGillivray's task was a heavy one. It was firstly to be responsible for all the normal administrative work falling on a High Commissioner so that Templer could devote his energies to bringing the terrorist emergency under control; and secondly to advise on the many aspects of the campaign which fell within the sphere of the civil government.

THE MAIN PROBLEMS

MacGillivray quickly gained a grasp of the main problems. He recognized that even in the grave state of affairs that existed at that time it was necessary to make plans for advances in the political field. One of his first steps was to set up local councils in the new villages, which had been established for the half-million squatters who, while still scattered over the countryside, had been an important source of supply to the terrorists. Within two years the combined efforts of the Services, the police, and the civil authorities under Templer's energetic and brilliant leadership had transformed the situation and it was decided the time had come to revert to the normal pattern of a High Commissioner from the Colonial Service. MacGillivray, who had played a major part in the success which had been achieved, was the natural choice and he took over in April 1954. Much still remained to be done to bring the terrorists to final defeat, but if the full support of the public was to remain behind the Government measures it was essential to convince the political leaders that plans for the country's independence were going forward. MacGillivray accordingly introduced elections, firstly into municipal councils, then into state and settlement councils, and finally into the federal legislative council, in August, 1955. The first federal elections were a resounding victory for the Alliance party under Tunku Abdul Rahman. Constitutional discussions in London followed in a few months and a date for independence—August 31, 1957—was fixed.

In spite of a tight timetable the date was kept and MacGillivray had the satisfaction of seeing the culmination of his work in the Merdeka celebrations and in the tributes which were paid to his work by the new ruler of the country.

On leaving Malaya when it attained independence, MacGillivray returned to East Africa, to take up farming in Kenya, but his experience of public affairs was not to be wasted. In 1958 he was appointed chairman of the Kenya Council of State, a body created as part of an interim constitution and designed to promote confidence among the various communities making up the population of the country. He was also, from 1958 to 1961, chairman of the Council of Makerere College, and from 1961 to 1964 of the council of the University of East Africa. He served also in 1960 as deputy chairman of the Advisory Commission on the Federation of the Rhodesias and Nyasaland. After service with the Kenya Meat Commission he became, in 1964, Director of the United Nations Special Fund for East African Livestock Development Survey. He was on the board of a number of companies in Kenya.

He was appointed M.B.E. in 1936 for his services in Tanganyika, C.M.G. in 1949, K.C.M.G. in 1953 and G.C.M.G. in 1957.

He married, in 1936, Louisa Mai, daughter of late Mervyn Knox-Browne, of Aughentaine Castle, Fivemiletown, co. Tyrone, and had one son.

December 28, 1966.

John McGovern, who represented the Shettleston division of Glasgow in the House of Commons for 29 years, first as an Independent Labour member and afterwards as a Labour member, died on February 14, 1968, at the age of 80.

He had a chequered career, and for a long period was regarded as the "stormy petrel" of Glasgow politics and of the Left in Parliament. He was suspended more than once, arrested twice in 1931 and once imprisoned. He was a close friend of the late James Maxton, M.P., and was one of the leaders of the "hunger marchers" of the 1930s. But in later years he mellowed greatly. From 1954 onwards he became active in the work of Moral Re-Armament, travelling thousands of miles by land, sea and air and meeting statesmen in many countries.

Born on December 13, 1887, John McGovern, who was of Irish origin, was the son of Thomas McGovern, a Glasgow steel-worker. After education at local elementary schools he was apprenticed to a plumber, before setting up on his own account as a master plumber, in 1909. During the First World War he was active in the anti-war movement on Clydeside. From 1923 to 1925 he was in Australia, but returned to Shettleston, and for a short period in 1930 was an insurance agent. He was a militant Socialist and full of civic patriotism, and served first (from 1928 to 1930) on the Glasgow Parish Council, and then from 1929 to 1931 on Glasgow Town Council.

SOON SUSPENDED

He entered Parliament in 1930 as Labour member for Shettleston, and had been in the House only a few months when the first of his suspensions took place. His offence was that he had given the lie direct to a statement and had refused to retract. In March, 1931, he got into difficulties with his local Labour party, who recommended his expulsion. This was carried out, but McGovern continued to sit as one of the four I.L.P. members, and was the centre of more stormy scenes in the Commons. He was a teller against the suspension of John Beckett for seizing the Mace from the table and rushing off with it down the floor of the Chamber.

The climax came on July 2, when he was finally bundled out of the House, kicking and struggling, by eight attendants, and the uproar became so prolonged that the Speaker (Captain Fitzroy) was compelled to suspend the sitting for a quarter of an hour. The trouble had arisen because McGovern, in protesting against what he termed a "brutal sentence" on four lay speakers who had been imprisoned for preaching without permits on Glasgow Green, had disobeyed the ruling of the Chair. He was suspended for the rest of the session. The same month, and again in October, he was brought before the Glasgow stipendiary for speaking on Glasgow Green without a permit, and for forming a disorderly mob. He was sent to prison for a short time. He was also suspended from the House of Commons in 1933, 1936 and 1937, and caused trouble in the House of Lords on one occasion by protesting against the means test just after King George V had concluded his Speech from the Throne in opening the new session.

Always a champion of the "under-dog", and tending to judge issues on the dictates of the heart, McGovern was persuaded to take part in the "hunger marches" from Glasgow to Edinburgh in 1933 and from Glasgow to London the following year. But he steadfastly refused to be made a tool of by the communist organizers of these marchers. He was a staunch Roman Catholic and had no use either for communism or for Russian Bolshevism.

During the Spanish Civil War McGovern twice visited Spain and had a narrow escape from death at the hands of the communists. He supported Neville Chamberlain's attempts for peace at Munich, exclaiming in his Commons' speech: "Well done, thou good and faithful servant." For this he was censured by his official party leaders. Throughout the Second World War he did all he could to bring about peace, but the Nazi pact with Russia made him more than ever contemptuous of Soviet methods and pledges.

JOINED OFFICIAL PARTY

For some time he was chairman of the I.L.P., but after the death of his closet friend, James Maxton, in 1946, he resigned, and in March, 1947, was admitted to membership of the Labour Party. He had no difficulty in holding his seat at Shettleston.

In the summer of 1954, McGovern spent some weeks at the World Assembly for Moral Re-Armament at Caux, Switzerland. He was in Nigeria during the visit of the Queen and the Duke of Edinburgh, and in the Commons in February, 1956, spoke of the unprecedented welcome which the royal visitors had received, and associated himself with it. As the result of his frequent visits abroad, complaints were received by the Shettleston Labour Party in 1958 about McGovern's voting record in the Commons, but the local party leaders decided to take no action. Soon afterwards he announced that he would not stand at the next election.

In May, 1959, while on a visit to Berlin, McGovern caused consternation among his Labour colleagues by stating publicly that there were 26 members of the Labour party in Parliament who were either communists or fellow-travellers. He added that if the Russians were winning, 70 more would throw off their democratic masks and go over to the communist side. Asked by Morgan Phillips, the secretary of the party to withdraw these allegations, McGovern refused to do so, adding that he had never made false statements, even about his political enemies.

He married, in 1909, Mary Fenton, of Glasgow. There were two sons and one daughter of the marriage.

In 1964, McGovern declared "I'm wholeheartedly behind Sir Alec Douglas-Home", and that he would vote Conservative. Later he said, "Give Harold Wilson power and you will live to regret it." In 1960 he had published his memoirs called *Neither Fear Nor Favour*. Two years later he decided to live in Australia which he had visited frequently. He was then 74. After his wife died, he returned to Glasgow.

February 15, 1968.

Lord McGowan of Ardeer, K.B.E., D.C.L., LL.D., honorary president of Imperial Chemical Industries, Ltd., and chairman from 1930 to 1950, died in St. Mary's Hospital, Paddington, London, on July 13, 1961. He was 88.

Lord McGowan's long and active working life was devoted to the chemical industry in which, as honorary president of Imperial Chemical Industries, he maintained an interest to the end. In his remarkable career he not only climbed the ladder from its lowest rungs—beginning about 1888 as a very junior clerk in Nobel's Explosives Company in Glasgow, where he was born on June 3, 1874—but extended the ladder above him as he rose. With Sir Alfred Mond (later Lord Melchett) he was the prime architect of Imperial Chemical Industries; its formation in 1926, by the merging of four companies, gave Britain for the first time the big industrial chemical group which was essential both for strategic reasons, as the Second World War was to demonstrate, and to compete with the great chemical combines of Germany and the United States.

While it is for this great merger that Lord McGowan will be most generally remembered, his contribution to its creation owed much to his already exceptional experience in this field. Early in the century he had become managing director in Nobel's Explosives, which had established friendly relations with the Du Pont Company in the United States. Frequent visits to Canada convinced him that the explosives industry there was less efficient than it might be, and in 1910 he contrived a merger of the major companies concerned and brought in Du Pont, whose holding had previously been small, as an equal partner in the new concern, Canadian Explosives Ltd. The firm quickly extended its interests and in 1927 was renamed Canadian Industries Ltd.

At home, in 1918, he brought about an important merger within the British explosives industry, resulting in the formation of Nobel Industries Ltd. After the 1914–18 War, this company found its South African interests—which through its constituent firms dated back to 1888—clashing with those of Cape Explosives Works, owned by De Beers, Lord McGowan saw the advantages of combination and initiated talks that in 1924 resulted in the formation of the company now known as African Explosives and Chemical Industries Ltd. He was also concerned with many lesser consolidations of interest in Europe, Australasia and South America.

It was with this experience that McGowan set about effecting the merger—the biggest in the history of the British chemical industry—that brought I.C.I. into existence in 1926. Earlier in that year an approach had been made to him asking whether Nobel Industries would take on the Government-controlled British Dyestuffs Corporation. The request was refused, Lord McGowan—then chairman of Nobel Industries—being firmly of the opinion that only a merger of wider interests could prevent Britain becoming a second-class power in the chemical industry. His proposal was to bring in also Brunner, Mond & Company and the United Alkali Company, which between them were the major British manufacturers of soda and a considerable range of related products. A preliminary approach to Brunner, Mond in July of the same year brought a promise of serious consideration of the proposal, but no decision was reached.

DETERMINATION

What followed was characteristic of Lord McGowan's great determination and energy. Returning from a visit to South Africa, he learnt that Sir Alfred Mond and several of his fellow-directors had left for an extended visit to the United States. Lord McGowan, more than ever convinced of the need for haste, sailed after them. Meetings were held in New York at the end of September, and early in the following month Lord McGowan and Sir Alfred embarked in the Aquitania to return to England. During the voyage the broad outline of the scheme to amalgamate the four companies was agreed upon, and well before the end of the year on December 7, Imperial Chemical Industries was incorporated.

The speed with which this complicated amalgamation was carried out is remarkable; nor did it depart in any major particular from the original draft drawn up on the voyage home in the Aquitania. At the first board meeting Sir Alfred Mond was elected chairman of the new comapny, and Lord McGowan became president and deputy chairman; he succeeded Lord Melchett as chairman on the latter's death in 1930. McGowan remained in this office until his retirement at the end of 1950, when he was elected honorary president. During these years he saw the enterprise that he had done so much to create thrive, meet the exacting national needs of the Second World War, and emerge from the difficult postwar period as a company of world stature.

A CLEAR VISION

Some of the personal qualities that made such a career possible have already been indicated. First and foremost, he always had a clear vision of all the factors relevant to a merger, whether it was great or small. For him, it had to do far more than offer an immediate business advantage: it had also to improve efficiency and—a point always much in his mind—protect the interests of the employees concerned. Coupled with ability quickly to discern the essentials of any problem before him were many other forceful characteristics, including his swiftness to see and seize an opportunity. He himself worked hard and thoroughly; he expected the same of others and had no use for slipshod work or thought. His admiration was not for the greatness of the job but for the way in which it was done. He was a good mixer, remaining as much at home with the factory workers whom he knew so well in his early days as in the sophisticated company of his later years.

The advancing years brought Lord McGowan many honours. He was knighted in 1918 and raised to the peerage in 1937. The university of his own city of Glasgow conferred an honorary degree upon him in 1934; this was followed by similar honours from the universities of Birmingham, Oxford, Durham and St. Andrews. In 1931 he was president of the Society of Chemical Industry.

In 1903 he married Jean Boyle Young, by whom he had two sons and two daughters. Her death in 1952 put an end to a long partnership which contributed much to his success.

July 14, 1961.

Lord Mackintosh of Halifax, who died on December 27, 1964, at his Norfolk home at the age of 73, had a bluff, easy-going exterior that belied the secret of his successes in business and Government affairs. He had an admitted flair for publicity and for persuading people to do what, but for him, they would rarely have considered undertaking. It was illustrated on a variety of occasions from the time when, after the First World War, he called on Heath Robinson, George Morrow, and other artists to enliven the sales of Mackintosh's toffees to the wartime occasion when his Wings for Victory campaign brought in millions of pounds' worth of savings. But he had something more, too. This was a determination, coupled with undoubted administrative ability, that produced results in his own toffee-making ("we make toffees not sweets") as well as in the wider field of National Savings. More than one Chancellor of the Exchequer has had to face this determination in the weeks before his Budget.

Publicity may have come easy to him. Even some of his simple jokes that occasionally fell flat were turned to good account, for his broad Yorkshire accent was instantly disarming. If anyone could build up the trust so necessary in a National Savings Movement he could—and did. He had one advantage. He believed in thrift and did his best to convince others of it. Many put his wartime efforts in persuading people not to spend their earnings as his biggest success during his 20 years as chairman of the National Savings Movement. It is an understandable view. But it is probably mistaken. For it was only after the war, when the Keynesian ideas of expenditure were beginning to seep into Whitehall thinking that savings as a national habit first came under critical scrutiny.

During several post-war recessions it was occasionally urged that the National Savings Movement might go easy for a little while. Lord Mackintosh would have none of it. He dealt with this sort of criticism wherever he met it. On one occasion Enoch Powell, in a book published while he was still a Minister, questioned the future role of the National Savings Movement. Lord Mackintosh had his reply out two days before the book was published. In fact, the Savings Movement under Lord Mackintosh's care and persuasion, in producing close on £lm. of savings a day, has undoubtedly reduced the country's taxation bill by a considerable amount. Little wonder that few Budget speeches have passed without an acknowledgement of his efforts. Reginald Maudling was speaking for many of his predecessors when in his Budget of April 1964, he referred to "that almost legendary figure Lord Mackintosh".

Harold Vincent Mackintosh was born on June 8, 1891, a son of John and Violet Mackintosh. John, later known as the "Toffee King", worked in a textile mill and his wife was a weaver in a worsted factory. To supplement the household budget Violet Mackintosh made toffee over the kitchen fire (Lord Mackintosh came across the original recipe after her death, written on the page of an exercise book). Sold initially on a market stall, it became Mackintosh's Toffee which with other Halifax-made confectionery was to achieve a national reputation and become a household name.

Harold Mackintosh was educated at the New School, Halifax, and for a while, still in his teens, he studied in Germany, but long before manhood he was at work, and it has been said of him that he did most to bring the great prosperity that John Mackintosh & Sons achieved through inducing his family to embark upon large advertising schemes. Harold Mackintosh remained a devotee of advertising to the end. As chairman of the organization which created and ran the Christian Commando Campaigns soon after the end of the Second World War, he got his colleagues to bring the full force of advertising and publicity of all kinds into effect, especially in the big Greater London scheme which had such spectacular results. His connexion with the Advertising Association started early, and from 1942 to 1946 he was its president.

It has generally been assumed that Harold Mackintosh's connexion with thrift and savings began in the early days of the War Savings Movement, but that is not correct. In fact, even his local link was not forged until 1940 or 1941, when he presided over the campaign committee which ran the War Weapons Week in his native town. But it was largely as a consequence of its success that he was elected to represent the county of Yorkshire on the national committee. After he had attended only two national meetings he was then invited by the president of the National Savings Committee, the first Lord Kindersley, to act as vice-chairman to the chairman, Lord Mottistone, whom he succeeded in 1943. In the chair he remained, and in 1958 he became also its president, although retaining the chairmanship and doing all the work, routine and otherwise, that the office entailed.

If it was not national savings which in the earlier days drew him into this orbit of thrift, then it was undoubtedly his interest, developed during the earlier years of his career, in the great building society started in his birthplace. Not merely Harold Mackintosh but his family also were keenly interested in the Halifax Building Society which by then was a flourishing institution, and for over 30 years he was one of its directors. Throughout all those years, too, he was deeply interested in the work of the small banks, and encouraged the workers to make provision for themselves through the medium of industrial insurance.

Lord Mackintosh's attachment to Nonconformity was a part of his life, and largely patterned it. Through his parentage he belonged to one of the minor and less orthodox sections of Methodism, the Methodist New Connexion Church, which was firmly established in Yorkshire in the early part of the nineteenth century; but when, in the nineteen twenties and thirties efforts towards full Methodist unity began, he warmly supported them and he was one of the first and most prominent laymen to take high office. In his early days he had been a Sunday school teacher and official, like his fellow Methodist Lord Rank, and like him, too, he never, in the midst of all his other preoccupations, lost touch with Sunday school work.

UNIVERSITY INTEREST

From 1928 onwards he was president of the World Council of Christian Education and Sunday Schools, after being president of the British National Sunday School Union.

In his later years one of his major interests was the development of the University of East Anglia in Norwich. He was chairman of a special committee, the Promotion Committee, established in 1959 to investigate the possibility of establishing a university there. In 1962, he accepted office as the first Chancellor of the university, and was to have been ceremonially installed in May. When he launched a £1,500,000 appeal on May 17, 1962, he made a bet with the Chancellor-designate of the University of York, the Earl of Harewood, that Norwich would raise more money than York by the end of that year. The stake was one of Lord Mackintosh's prize Hereford heifers from his own herd on his Norfolk farm at Thickthorn Hall, Hethersett. But Lord Mackintosh lost his bet and sent the 200 guinea heifer off to York which had raised £5,000 more than East Anglia.

RARE FAILURE

This failure, if such it can be called, was one of the few he encountered in a role where he achieved much of value. That the university appeal now stands at only a little below £1,400,000 is tribute enough to his fund-raising. But his contribution was much more than that. He was an active leader who took the chair of many committees and played his full part in all the administrative work that entailed.

Apart from his chairmanship of John Mackintosh & Sons, he had various other commercial and financial interests. He was a director of Martin's Bank (London board), Ranks Ltd., the Associated Chocolate and Confectionary Co., the First and Second Investment Companies, and he was an underwriting member of Lloyd's. Otherwise he was greatly interested in art and had a good collection of traditional English paintings at Thickthorn. He was also deeply interested in pottery and ceramics, and was the author of the valuable reference work *Early English Figure Pottery*. Mackintosh also wrote a memoir of his father.

He was a Deputy Lieutenant for the West Riding, an honorary LL.D. of Leeds University, a county magistrate, and, what perhaps gave him greatest happiness, an honorary Freeman of his birthplace—the County Borough of Halifax.

In 1916 he married Constance Emily, daughter of Edgar Cooper Stoneham, O.B.E., and they had one son and one daughter. His son, the Hon. John Mackintosh, now succeeds to the viscounty.

December 29, 1964.

Dr James M. Mackintosh, LL.D., F.R.C.P., Emeritus Professor of Public Health in the University of London, died on April 20, 1966, at the age of 75.

Born in 1891 in Kilmarnock, he was the younger son of J. D. Mackintosh, a solicitor practising in that town. Educated at Glasgow High School and University, he served in the First World War, first in the Cameron Highlanders and later in the R.A.M.C. On leaving the Army in 1920 he worked as Assistant Medical Officer in Burton and Dorset before going to Northamptonshire as County Medical Officer in 1930. His excellent work in these fields, more particularly his investigations into rural housing conditions, earned him a wide reputation and in 1937 he moved to Edinburgh for four years as Chief Medical Officer of the Department of Health for Scotland. His sensitive and yet positive personality did not perhaps fit entirely smoothly in this particular position, and in 1941 he became Professor of Public Health in the University of Glasgow, moving to a similar post in London in 1944, where for some years he was also Dean of the School of Hygiene. Here, for 12 years, he exercised a wide and inspiring influence on postgraduate students of public health from all over the world, as well as taking an active part in the affairs of many university committees and of the North-West Metropolitan Regional Hospital Board. He made many visits to the United States of America, first on the casualty aspects of Civil Defence and later teaching and lecturing in various universities, becoming a warm and understanding friend of that country, where his reputation was deservedly high. He also gave much time and energy to the work of the World Health Organization, serving on many of its committees. But above all things in his heart was teaching, and on his retirement from university work in 1956 he wrote to a friend: "...My greatest satisfaction has been to watch over a thousand students and try to guide them. ..."

LIMPID DISTINCTION

Mackintosh had a profound love of English literature, in which he was widely read and from which he could produce the apposite quotation for most occasions. He was also a competent classical scholar and in his later years turned more and more to the international language of great music, particularly to Mozart and Beethoven. He wrote with distinction in clear and limpid English on subjects in his own chosen field of medicine, of these housing and mental health being perhaps nearest his heart.

CONCEPT OF HOME

His titles—*Housing and Family Life* and *Housing and the Home* (the latter in Massey's *Modern Trends in Public Health*)—indicate very clearly his concept (which in his own family circle brought him so much happiness) of a house where a family could indeed live their individual and collective lives and produce a home—*dulce domum*—in the real sense. He was also chairman of two departmental committees which produced important reports on *Moving from the Slums* and on *Social Workers in the Mental Health Services*. On the latter subject, his essays on *The War and Mental Health in England*, published by the Commonwealth Fund of New York, contain many things, written with eloquence and feeling, of current importance. Of his other writings, his London University Heath Clark Lectures on *Trends of Opinion about the Public Health, 1950–51*, and his W.H.O. publication (1957) jointly with Professor Grundy. *The Teaching of Hygiene and Public Health in Europe*, are perhaps of most importance.

SENSITIVE PHYSICIAN

Mackintosh was a sensitive and scholarly physican who reached his full stature in the academic sphere, but who never lost touch with the wider world. This indeed was one of the sources of his strength as a teacher and many a postgraduate student has borne witness to the inspiration with which he illuminated the subjects which most interested him. Through the thousand-odd medical men and women ovei whom he watched and tried to guide, his influence on events will perisist for many years to come. To the friends privileged on occasion to join his wife and himself at the fireside, to enjoy his conversation, savour and perhaps compete with his literary allusions, and to laugh at his kindly shafts of humour, will remain the vivid memory of a sensitive, warm and lovable personality, but thinly hidden behind a slightly diffident outer shell.

April 21, 1966.

Bruce McLaren, the New Zealand motor racing driver, who was killed on June 2, 1970, when his McLaren sports car crashed at high speed at the Goodwood circuit in Sussex, was one of Europe's most popular and experienced racing drivers.

A veteran of 102 starts in world championship grand prix events since his debut in the 1958 German Grand Prix, McLaren earned the reputation of being not only a top flight driver but also a brilliant engineer and designer. Like Jack Brabham he loved fine machinery. He was 32.

McLaren was testing his new car for the forthcoming Can-Am series of races for group seven cars which start on June 14 in Canada. In the past three years McLaren cars have dominated the event with McLaren himself winning the championship outright in 1967 and 1969 and his New Zealand compatriot Denny Hulme winning in 1968 when McLaren was runner-up.

McLaren was born in 1937 in Auckland, New Zealand, the son of a garage proprietor who was a well-known motor cycle rider. At the age of 10 he had a serious horse riding accident and later contracted Perthe's disease—a deformation of the hip—and spent the next three years in hospital. It was this that left him with a permanent limp. His first circuit race was in 1954 while he was an engineering student and he then graduated through numerous sports car races and hill climbs. In 1957 his father bought him the ex-Jack Brabham 1500 c.c. sports car and in 1958 this was swapped for Brabham's 1700 c.c. formula II Cooper. Driving his new mount impressively McLaren was runner-up in the 1957-58 New Zealand drivers' championship and when the New Zealand Grand Prix Association nominated its "driver to Europe" scheme it was McLaren who won, endorsed by Brabham personally.

WEALTHY OPPONENTS

He joined the Cooper works team in 1959 and stayed with the Surbiton based factory team for seven seasons of grand prix racing. During that time he faced mixed fortunes as the independent Cooper team cars battled against far wealthier and more powerful opponents. He scored his first major victory in 1959 winning the United States Grand Prix and immediately won the 1960 Argentine Grand Prix for Cooper. His other grand prix successes were at Monaco in 1962 and at Spa in 1968—the latter success was in his self designed McLaren formula I car. He had left Cooper's at the end of 1965 to construct his own formula I, formula II and sports cars following in Brabham's footsteps as a driver constructor and the amiable New Zealander established a thriving manufacturing concern.

In 1969, McLaren's last full season as a grand prix driver, he proved that experience still counts in the top echelon of motor racing.

OFTEN PLACED

In grand prix races he repeatedly appeared in the first four and finished third in the drivers' championship. This year he took second place in the Spanish Grand Prix.

He leaves a widow and a daughter.

The R.A.C. was about to announce that he had been awarded the Segrave trophy for 1969 for his outstanding performance in winning every race in the 1969 Can-Am Challenge Cup series with cars of his own design and construction.

June 3, 1970.

Sir Robert McLean, formerly chairman and managing director of Vickers (Aviation) Ltd. and of Supermarine Aviation Works Ltd., who had earlier enjoyed a career of great distinction as a railway engineer in India, died on April 9, 1964, at the age of 80.

A son of the Rev. D. McLean, of Alloa, he was born on February 3, 1884, and educated at Edinburgh Academy, where he was Dux of the school for Latin Prose and Mathematics and won the Gloag mathematical medal, and Edinburgh University, taking a Science Degree in Engineering at the age of 19. In 1905 he joined the Indian Public Works Department as Assistant Engineer. He was engaged in the operation and maintenance of railways and the survey and construction of new lines.

MAIN LINE SCHEME

In 1915–16 he served with the British Expeditionary Force in Aden and then in Mesopotamia. He also served for a time on the Western Front. On returning to India he was made Assistant Secretary of the newly-created Railway Board, and in 1919 rose to be Secretary. In 1920 his services were lent to the Great Indian Peninsular Railway Company, first as deputy agent, and then as general manager. In that capacity he initiated and carried through the first railway electrification scheme in India. The electrification of the Bombay suburban lines was followed by the beginning of a main line electrification scheme extending in his time over some 240 miles. In 1925 McLean was elected president of the Indian Railway Companies' Association. He was knighted in 1926 and retired from India in the following year.

On returning to Britain McLean was elected to the board of Vickers Limited and in 1928 was given charge of the aviation interests of that organization.

WELLINGTON BOMBERS

In a short time McLean moved in the world of aircraft with the assurance that had marked his career in railways. He was a forward-looking man and a man of imagination. He had, moreover, the ability to marry these qualities to his high professional ability so that under his aegis great things were set on foot at Vickers. First the Supermarine Company was purchased and from this long-sighted transaction, prompted by McLean's realization of the coming vital significance of military aircraft, sprang the association with the brilliant designer R. J. Mitchell, of which a single-seater fighter aircraft, later to be known as the Spitfire, was perhaps the most famous fruit. At the same time, McLean gave crucial support to Dr. Barnes Wallis in his development of the geodetic system of construction which yielded first the twin-engined Wellesley bomber, which in 1938 made a distance record of 7,162 miles, and ultimately the Wellington bomber with which, among others, the R.A.F. began the war. McLean remained managing director of Vickers (Aviation) until 1939. From 1935 to 1937 he was chairman of the Society of British Aircraft Constructors.

He was also sometime president of the Institution of Production Engineers.

He married, in 1908, Evelyn Noel, daughter of H. E. Girard, Calcutta, and they had two daughters.

April 11, 1964.

Iain Macleod, P.C., M.P., who died on July 20, 1970, at the age of 56, had been Chancellor of the Exchequer for only a month but for nearly 20 years he had been one of the most considerable figures in British public life. He might have proved a great Chancellor. He had the imagination and the determination required to be more than the creature of the Treasury. Under him British economic policy might have been directed along more adventurous lines. But his place in British political history does not depend on what might have been.

He deserves to be remembered above all as a Colonial Secretary who pursued a historic policy with a full sense of history. He saw the need to grant independence more quickly to the British colonies in Africa and had the courage to act on this conviction. It required courage. Although Macleod had the support of Mr. Macmillan's Cabinet, or at least a majority of the Cabinet, he was defying some of the most powerful sectors in the Conservative Party.

AFRICAN GOODWILL

Except on the younger, liberal wing, party sentiment was not with him. Yet he achieved his purpose in ensuring that Britain's withdrawal from most parts of Africa was accomplished with more speed and goodwill than it would otherwise have been.

This was not an isolated example of his political courage. He further offended established opinion within his party when he refused to serve under Sir Alec Douglas-Home in 1963. Whether or not his judgment was right on that occasion, he had given an undertaking and he stuck to it when it could not possibly have been to his advantage to do so. Then two years ago he once again took an unpopular stand on principle when he voted against the Kenya Asians Bill, even though it was accepted by most of the Shadow Cabinet.

With this record of acting from conviction it must seem surprising that he earned a reputation for being devious. This reputation came partly from the bitter criticism of those who disagreed with him on policy. Partly it came from his own love of political tactics. There can be no doubt that he enjoyed the game. He was adroit and ingenious. He had an acute political ear. Some of those who were not such obvious political animals felt that this was inappropriate, even distasteful. But a gift for political manoeuvre ought not to be regarded as too black a mark against a politician. Allied to conviction, it is the stuff of statesmanship—and the sincerity of Macleod's conviction is to be measured by what it cost him.

He was an ambitious man, but even before ill-health made it impossible to consider him for the party leadership it was evident that he could never achieve it. He had the intellectual administrative and oratorical capacity. As a speaker he was superb. He was probably the finest Parliamentary debater of his generation.

TOO MANY ENEMIES

On the public platform or at party conferences he was equally effective. That rasping voice, with scorn or passion controlled, but not too much, could thrill a large assembly with biting phrases of a quality too rarely heard in political rhetoric these days. But with all these gifts the highest post was bound to be denied to him because he had made too many enemies in his party. He was not forgiven for his liberalism on race and colonial independence, or for his act of rebellion against the leader thrown up by the customary processes of his party.

It was a political failing on his part that he took so long to appreciate that he had disqualified himself for the highest office. He retained his hopes beyond the point of realism. But he had accepted his place in the Tory team and there was a certain heroic quality in his last years as progressively crippled with arthritis, he none the less prepared for office once again with all the distinctive ardour that he brought to public life.

Iain Macleod was born on November 11, 1913, and was the son of a Scottish physician practising at Skipton, in Yorkshire. Educated at Skipton Grammar School and Fettes, he graduated in history from Gonville and Caius College, Cambridge, and spent three years in the City. He was reading for the Bar when the war broke out, and he joined the Army as a private. He was commissioned in May, 1940, and was wounded in the battle of France. He was promoted major and was on Field-Marshal Montgomery's planning staff for the Normandy Campaign. He was appointed D.A.Q.M.G., 50th Division.

Like many others to whom the war had brought the first experience of real responsibility, Macleod felt the attraction of politics, and in the General Election of 1945 he decided, on an impulse, to fight the Western Isles in the Conservative interest. Honourably defeated, he joined Mr. Butler's stable in the Conservative Research Department where, in company with several other young men of promise who were eventually to achieve political distinction, he played, as head of the Home Affairs department, a prominent part in the post-war process of redefining Conservatism.

Returned to the House of Commons as member for West Enfield in 1950, he attracted attention as a leading member of the One Nation Group, a body of young, intelligent and independent-minded backbenchers who were known to have the paternal protection of Mr. Butler.

MERCURIAL RISE

Though generally regarded as progressives, the men of the One Nation Group were in fact firm enemies of the prevailing type of collectivism in British political thought. They demanded positive State action in economics and welfare, but held that this should be directed towards releasing private energies, increasing effective industrial and commercial competition, and ensuring that the resources of the State, when dispensed in the form of social services, should be concentrated on those who needed help.

A good mixer and a debater of outstanding skill, often in a most effective style of controlled, rational ferocity, Macleod's rise was mercurial, and in 1952 he was promoted straight from the back benches, to be Minister of Health, a post in which, over the next three years, he displayed an outstanding command of administrative ability and showed a valuable capacity for being prosaic in speech when the circumstances called for it. At the Ministry of Labour between 1955 and 1959 he acquired the reputation of a patient but immovable negotiator, who would brave a strike rather than make an uneconomic concession.

It was at the Colonial Office between 1959 and 1961, however, that Macleod made his greatest impact, and it was during this period also that, for the first time, he began to acquire bitter enemies in his own party. With that strategic clarity which always distinguished him, he appreciated that it was now necessary for the process by which self-government was achieved in British imperial territories in Africa to go on at a greatly accelerated pace. The old formula that Britain would continue to rule until the territories under her care were "fit for self-government" could no longer apply, if indeed it had ever applied; the forces of change were too strong and the resources of material strength and imperial self-confidence too weak to resist them. Macleod believed that Britain must neither try to resist the inevitable nor wash her hands of her responsibilities. By presiding over a process many aspects of which could not fail to alarm her, she might exercise at least some influence on the character of future African regimes, and she might even eventually succeed in bringing the emergent countries into free and meaningful partnership with the rest of the Commonwealth.

TOO CLEVER

These aims, though practical, were not ignoble, and few honest men could reject the diagnosis on which they proceeded, but their pursuit, involving the exercise of very high diplomatic and administrative gifts with which Macleod was abundantly endowed, also involved compromises and the suspicion of deception, a suspicion at times shared equally by African extremists and imperially-minded Tories, and felt acutely and constantly by the white settlers of East and Central Africa and especially those of Kenya, whose leaders proved no match for his negotiating skill.

Macleod's prowess as a bridge player (he was the author of an excellent book on the subject and a former bridge correspondent of the *Sunday Times*), once regarded as an amiable proof that he had the authentically Tory quality of living for other things than politics, was now cited by Lord Salisbury, once his firm admirer, as evidence of a Machiavellian disposition. The accusation that Macleod was "too clever by half" stuck for a long time and undoubtedly damaged his reputation with the centre as well as the right wing of the party. Macmillan, on the other hand, saluted both the courage and the ingenuity of his Colonial Secretary, and rescued him from this exposed position in October, 1961, by making him chairman of the Conservative Party and leader of the Commons, relieving him of other administrative duties by making him Chancellor of the Duchy of Lancaster.

Macleod was good as Leader of the House, and, as party chairman, had a special appeal to the young, but had his difficulties particularly with the established figures in the constituencies.

When the disastrous Profumo scandal broke, it was Macleod's misfortune to be among the five Ministers who had accepted Profumo's word, and a chance remark made off the cuff to the press when the erring Minister's confession was reported to him led unscrupulous critics falsely to attribute to Macleod a lenient, or at best a credulous, attitude in the affair.

Nevertheless, Macmillan continued to admire him, and even to favour him as a possible successor during the months of frenzied speculation which followed the Government's discomfiture. His brilliant speech at the Blackpool Conference of 1963, when all minds were preoccupied with the succession, was also well received by the Party.

But there was really no chance of his being selected and at the end, like most of the other candidates, he threw his weight behind Butler.

HONOUR WITH DANGER

That was why he declined to serve under Sir Alec Douglas-Home. It was an honourable decision but a dangerous one in terms of his own career prospects. The party faithful were even more disturbed a short while later when he published his own account of the manoeuvrings that preceded the choice of Sir Alec. On leaving the Government Macleod had become editor of the *Spectator* and it was there that he published what was in fact a lengthy rejoinder to the version of events put forward in a book by Randolph Churchill.

His appointment as editor of the *Spectator* met with some criticism, particularly from those who questioned whether an influential journal should be edited by an active politician who retained further political ambitions. In the event, Macleod ran his staff on a loose rein and in his own writing gave further proof of his lively and open approach to a range of questions that went beyond the more narrow confines of politics. Yet it was evident all the time that he was a politician visiting journalism, not a man who would ever be likely to give up his politics for journalism.

A man of outstanding personal warmth and loyalty, who continued after his withdrawal from the Government to defend its policies in the country, Macleod was now accused by some of looking for his own personal future to a defeat of his colleagues at the election. It is a charge that is always likely to be made against the party rebel.

ECONOMIC TASK

In the event, the Tories were defeated in October, 1964. Sir Alec, as Leader of the Opposition, instantly and characteristically invited Macleod to join the Shadow Cabinet. Macleod was put in charge of the Opposition's case against steel nationalization, and this was a shrewd recognition of his remarkable forensic powers.

When, in 1965, Sir Alec resigned, Macleod, in spite of a number of effective speeches, stood no chance of being elected as his successor. Wisely he did not enter the lists. Heath succeeded, and immediately resolved to restore Macleod to prominence on the front benches. As Shadow Chancellor he occupied a position of crucial importance.

Macleod acquitted himself admirably in his new role. His attacks on Callaghan's financial policy, particularly on the selective employment tax, were almost comparable in effectiveness with those of Oliver Stanley against the budgets of Stafford Cripps. Macleod now applied himself again earnestly to the redefinition of Conservatism. He threw at least some of his weight behind those who demanded a more radical revision of social service policy in the direction of greater selectivity in respect of benefits and wider choice in respect of services.

His main task, however, was naturally to prepare the economic policy of the future Tory Government. He concentrated on the reform of taxation rather than on the monetary techniques for managing the economy, and managed to produce a programme that was distinctive and adventurous without being entirely clear in all particulars. Taxation would be cut. Selective Employment Tax would be abolished and, if Macleod had his way, a Value Added Tax would take its place. This would leave further scope for reducing direct taxation in order to stimulate effort and get the economy moving again. There was also a desire to cut indirect taxes so as to hold retail prices in check. How far these various intentions could be married is still not altogether clear, but it was obviously Macleod's intention to free himself from the strict orthodoxies of Treasury policy in order to attempt a more expansionist approach based upon lower taxation. It is true that his one and only statement to the Commons just before his appendix operation a fortnight ago was widely interpreted as a surrender to the will of the Treasury. He was not an economist and was not at his best in the more complex realms of economic management. But if he had lived there can be little doubt that Iain Macleod would have been determined for good or ill to be the master of his own department. Whether or not the country has lost a great Chancellor, it has undoubtedly lost one of rare spirit.

Iain Macleod married in 1941 Evelyn, daughter of the Reverend Gervase and the Hon. Mrs. Blois of Fretherne. Gloucestershire. She and one son and a daughter survive him.

July 22, 1970.

Sir Harold MacMichael, G.C.M.G., D.S.O., who died on September 19, 1969, at the age of 86, was one of the last to survive of the great proconsuls of the British colonial empire in its heyday.

Harold Alfred MacMichael was born on October 15, 1882, the eldest son of the Rev. Charles MacMichael, Rector of Walpole St. Peter's, Wisbech, and his wife the Hon. Sophia Caroline, daughter of the fourth Baron Scarsdale. He was educated at King's Lynn and Bedford schools and in 1901 distinguished himself by winning the Public Schools Fencing Championship. He went on as a scholar to Magdalene College, Cambridge, where he took his B.A. degree in 1904. In the following year he joined the Political Service of the Anglo-Egyptian Sudan.

During the earlier part of his service he took much interest in anthropological research and carried out notable studies in connexion with the tribes of Kordofan and, later, of Darfur. In the First World War he was attached as political and intelligence officer to the expeditionary force to Darfur; he was mentioned three times in dispatches and awarded the D.S.O. In 1919 he was appointed Assistant Civil Secretary to the Sudan Government, and he was promoted to be Civil Secretary in 1926. In this capacity it fell to him to act as Governor-General on several occasions.

Meanwhile, in 1922 he published his authoritative *History of Arabs in the Sudan* (two volumes, Cambridge University Press), the first of a number of important literary works which he was to produce from time to time about the country. In 1928 he was chosen to give the Burton memorial lecture to the Royal Asiatic Society and was awarded the society's medal in recognition of his splendid pioneer work.

FAMILIAR GROUND

By the nineteen-thirties his reputation had spread well beyond the Sudan. Sir John Maffey (afterwards Lord Rugby) left the Governor-Generalship of the Condominium to become Permanent Under-Secretary of State at the Colonial Office in 1933 and he no doubt drew attention to MacMichael's eminent suitability for a colonial Governorship, and in particular for that of Tanganyika, where there was need to develop a system of indirect rule along the lines which had been laid down earlier in the territory by Sir Donald Cameron. This was familiar ground to both Maffey and MacMichael, since, in the Sudan, the latter had been engaged in building up such a system on foundations established by the former. In 1934, then, the year in which his *History of the Anglo-Egyptian Sudan* was published by Faber, MacMichael found himself Governor and Commander-in-Chief of the Mandated Territory of Tanganyika. When, in 1935, he attended the Mandates Commission of the League of Nations during its examination of the British Government's report on the territory, he could not have foreseen the long and often painful experience of the mandate system which lay before him.

PALESTINE TROUBLE

The main Colonial Office headache at this period, and for several years to come, was Palestine. The influx of Jewish immigrants, stimulated by the persecution of Jews in Central Europe, provoked reactions from the Arab inhabitants of the mandated territory which developed into armed rebellion; yet there remained hope that, with restriction of immigration and cooling of tempers when law and order had been restored, some constitutional arrangement or partition scheme could be devised which would enable the two elements to share the Holy Land in peace. As a well-tried administrator with intimate knowledge of the Arab world and experience of the working of the mandate system, MacMichael had exceptional qualifications for the post of High Commissioner. The offer of it was a challenge which he accepted.

He worked hard to keep the peace and to bring relief to the thousands suffering from unemployment, poverty and the activities of the rival terrorist gangs. It was a poor reward for all his work that, shortly before his term of office came to an end in 1944, the car in which he and Lady MacMichael were travelling was ambushed by unidentified terrorists, and he narrowly escaped with his life.

On leaving Palestine MacMichael retired from regular service, but use was still to be made of his gifts. In 1945 he was entrusted with a special mission to investigate the problems of the rehabilitation and future government of Malaya, following the liberation of the Peninsula from Japanese occupation.

In 1946–1947 MacMichael was engaged in formulating proposals for a new constitution for Malta. This was yet another situation in which the circumstances of the time made impossible for anyone, however able, to offer more than an interim solution of the problem.

Though he ceased thereafter to take an active part in colonial affairs, he retained his interest in the Sudan, and in 1954 contributed the volume on that country to the Nations of the Modern World series published by Benn.

It is indeed as an administrator of genius rather than as a political innovator that MacMichael best deserves and would most wish to be remembered. Perhaps his most outstanding characteristic was his passion for fairness. He was intolerant of injustice and humbug and could express himself with trenchant wit. This made him a rather formidable figure to those who did not know him well, but he earned the affection as well as respect of those who were close to him, and the staffs who served him loyally could not have had a kindlier or more considerate chief.

He married, in 1919, Agnes de Sivrac Edith, daughter of Canon John Otter Stephens. There were two daughters of the marriage, one now deceased.

September 22, 1969.

Daniel Macmillan, who died on December 6, 1965, in London in his eightieth year, was a scholar-publisher in the best tradition of his Highland family that came south to do such historic service to English literature.

As a boy at Eton he made his mark in the classics, which were his life-long delight and solace, and this promise was kept up at Oxford, where Patrick Shaw-Stewart, Ronald Knox and others of a brilliant Edwardian generation were his contemporaries. He was happy among them, as later he enjoyed the company alike of genial men of letters such as A. G. Macdonell, J. C. Squire, and J. B. Morton, and of austere editors of the learned classical texts which he published, and also the good fellowship of the Garrick.

It was his intellect and character, touched charmingly with some gentle idiosyncrasies of manner which made him the successful chairman and active director of a great publishing house during the difficult transitional period of the past 30 years.

Daniel de Mendi Macmillan, fourth chairman, succeeded his uncle, Sir Frederick Macmillan, president of the Publishers Association and the instigator of the Net Book Agreement, on the latter's death in 1936. Daniel, born on February 1, 1886, was the eldest of Maurice's three sons, and like his more famous youngest brother, Harold, had been in College at Eton, where he was Newcastle Scholar, and had won an open scholarship to Balliol, where he took a First in Mods and a second in Lit. Hum., and was *proxime accessit* for the Craven Scholarship.

On coming down from Oxford he joined the family firm, at that time dominated by the three brothers, Frederick, Maurice, and George, Galsworthian characters to a man. It was very much a family business, run on patriarchal lines. The three brothers met every day to discuss the firm's affairs, and instead of breaking away in the middle of the day for relaxation at their clubs, in the fashion of modern publishers, they lunched together in the office dining room.

They spent the long working day, tending their business lovingly, with great scrupulousness and infinite attention to detail, squabbling with each other over small matters but standing together and doing the right thing with a Victorian grandeur and amplitude that laid the foundations of a world-wide business.

EDUCATIONAL BOOKS

Daniel's father, Maurice, had started his working life as a schoolmaster, and it was natural that his own interest should be chiefly in the firm's school books. It is not surprising that his eldest son's own scholarly temperament, and an innate diffidence and shyness should have inclined him towards the educational side of the business, the authors of school books being accustomed to less attention as well as to lower royalties than that accorded to authors of works of the imagination.

Daniel's shyness was merely a mask adopted to hide an almost pathologically sensitive nature. When he was with friends or in the intellectual company which alone afforded him any pleasure, a more charming, witty, generous spirit could not be imagined. He was of small but strong build, with very handsome features; a small cyclone of activity, he seemed to run everywhere instead of proceeding at a normal walk. He was as quick mentally as he was physically, and was intolerant of others who could not keep up with him in either sphere. But when in a flash of revelation he saw that the other's slowness was due to some defect, and not just stupidity, his generous spirit quickened and in amends he would go to the other extreme and attract attention by the very extent of his demonstrations of sympathy.

Publishing has its dynasties and Macmillan is one of them. Under Daniel Macmillan the firm kept pace with the enormous growth in the forties and fifties of publishing turnover in Britain and America. He loved the work, and was happy in it throughout his life. The contribution he made was not as an innovator of ideas and books, but as a wise conservator of the firm's rich back list, and by bringing to any proposed additions to it tests of quality and endurability that his scholarly mind and sense of tradition could supply. His particular strength lay in directing others, in encouraging their good ideas, and in dissuading them from pursuing their bad ones. He had become a pilot of experience after so long an apprenticeship under the old uncles, and his own intellect, taste, and force of character are responsible for the fact that the reputation of the firm stands as high at his death as it did 60 odd years before, when Alexander Macmillan died. In the reorganization of the firm, which took place in January, 1964, Harold Macmillan became chairman of Macmillan and Co and Macmillan (Journals) and Daniel Macmillan became chairman of Macmillan Holdings, Ltd.

He married in 1918 Margaret Matthews. There were no children of the marriage. Her death in tragic circumstances in 1957 was a great blow, but with characteristic courage he surmounted it. Indeed in his last years a mellowness, a growing gentleness of spirit was apparent to all his friends. He grew old charmingly and he will be greatly missed in the narrow circles in which he kept the last years of his life, the Garrick and the office.

December 7, 1965.

Lady Dorothy Macmillan, G.B.E., wife of the former Prime Minister, Mr. Harold Macmillan, died on May 21, 1966, at the age of 65 at their home, Birch Grove House, Sussex. She was made Dame Grand Cross of the Order of the British Empire (G.B.E.) in 1964.

Lady Dorothy met her husband in Ottawa, Canada, where her father, the ninth Duke of Devonshire, was Governor-General of Canada. The young Harold Macmillan, badly wounded in the First World War, was his A.D.C. She was 19 when they became engaged. They were married at St. Margaret's Westminster, London, in 1920 in the presence of Queen Alexandra and Princess Victoria, among others.

Lady Dorothy helped her husband in the campaign which led to his election as M.P. for Stockton-on-Tees in 1924. Although her husband moved his constituency to Bromley in 1945, her reputation for being concerned with the people and problems of Tees-side is still talked about there.

During her husband's seven-year premiership, Lady Dorothy saw to it that number 10 lacked for nothing that would make it the relaxed and tranquil setting which he needed as the background for his work. She made it a real home, reproducing there the easy-going, intimate atmosphere of the Macmillan country home, Birch Grove House, in Sussex. She was herself perfectly "at home" in both, and also at Admiralty House, which was Macmillan's official residence during the years in which number 10 was being extensively renovated and partially rebuilt.

Born on July 28, 1900, Dorothy Evelyn spent her early childhood partly in Lancashire and London, and later partly at Lismore Castle, Waterford, her family's Irish estate, and Chatsworth, the Derby seat of the Dukes of Devonshire. Apart from her lifelong interest in her husband's political career, Lady Dorothy had many non-political interests. She was a member of the Central Executive Committee of the National Society for the Prevention of Cruelty to Children and the Executive Committee of the East Sussex District Nursing Association. She was in charge of an area in Sussex of the Women's Land Army during the last war.

Lady Dorothy was a vital and lovable person with a countrywoman's steadfastness, love of beauty and shrewd humanity. She had a deep and genuine interest in people and their problems and she saw politics not only as a set of ideals but as a means of practical service.

MAKING PEOPLE HAPPY

She had the utmost consideration for the feelings and the failings of others and succeeded brilliantly in making people feel happy and at their best in her company.

She always had a special place in her heart for the constituency workers from Stockton and from Bromley. On one occasion when speaking at the Conservative Women's conference she saw in the audience of over 2,000 an old friend from Stockton whose name was not on her guest list for that day. "Why was this so?" She knew there was probably a good reason but, "Action at once please!"

On the eve of a visit from a famous world statesman the Prime Minister's wife was seen in one of the great London stores, hair slipping out from under a head scarf, buying certain small fittings which her final inspection of the guest rooms had shown to be necessary. "Everybody's so busy and they're all so good. I just thought I'd run out and do it myself."

Or again in the London stores during the weeks before Christmas she could be seen, list in hand, peering anxiously at toys or sports equipment "just to be sure the family get what they would really like". Whatever her other commitments, the grandchildren must not be neglected. Only those who saw the distribution from the Birch Grove family Christmas tree could appreciate how superbly successful she was in this.

She loved her family, she loved her home, she loved her garden, but she enjoyed political life, too. For her own part, Lady Dorothy preferred the politics of the door-step to the politics of the platform.

Her political judgments were wise, accurate, and far seeing.

GARDENER

She was intensely proud of the achievements of her husband, to whom she was a tower of strength, and of her son, Maurice. She never spared herself and she leaves an example of kindly humour, cheerful courage, and devotion to the ideals in which she believed, which will continue to be an inspiration to all Conservatives and others who knew her and loved her.

Lady Dorothy was a keen gardener and was very proud of the grounds of Birch Grove House. She opened the grounds of Birch Grove House to the public twice a year for 15 years. Lady Dorothy was a keen and able driver—she was said to enjoy driving as much as her husband disliked it—and was constantly on duty as his chauffeuse.

The Macmillans had four children—a son and three daughters.

May 23, 1966.

General Andrew George Latta McNaughton, C.H., C.B., C.M.G., D.S.O., who died at Montebello, Quebec, on July 11, 1966 at the age of 79, served his country in a variety of high posts but failed through frailties in his temperament to achieve a record of success commensurate with his considerable abilities. He had a restless and incisive intelligence and a well stored mind but his strong personality tended to take command at times of controversy.

Born on February 25, 1887, at Moosomin, Saskatchewan, he was the son of Robert McNaughton, a prosperous storekeeper, and was educated at the local public school, Bishop's College School, Lennoxville, and McGill University, where he graduated B.Sc. in 1910 and M.Sc. in 1912. After graduation he became a lecturer in engineering at McGill and, taking a commission in an artillery unit of the Canadian militia in 1910, had risen to the rank of Major when the First World War began.

Proceeding overseas with the first Canadian contingent, he served with great credit throughout the war; he was twice wounded, won a D.S.O. and was created C.B. and C.M.G. At the end of the war he was in command of the Heavy Artillery of the Canadian corps with the rank of Brigadier and he decided to remain in the army. In Canada he held a succession of high military posts, until he was appointed Chief of the Canadian Army's staff in 1929 and he carried out some useful reforms. At that time McNaughton was a Conservative in politics and was also in high favour with Lord Bennett, who led that party. After the latter became Prime Minister in 1930, he employed McNaughton for non-military administrative duties and his assumption of them was properly criticized by the Liberals. So McNaughton, foreseeing that he would not survive long as Chief of Staff after the change of power at Ottawa, which seemed certain, resigned his post and was appointed President of the National Research Council in 1935. He held this office until 1940, when he was appointed to command a Canadian corps which had been raised for service overseas, and later he was appointed G.O.C. of the First Canadian army. But his selection for this post, when it was announced, was freely criticized by experienced Canadian officers of high rank, who had served with McNaughton in the earlier war.

WAITING FOR ACTION

McNaughton's task was no easy one. He did much to raise the standard of training of his troops, and of their zeal and desire for action there was no doubt, but, this said, there remained the matter of where the Canadians could be best employed. The delay in the answering of this question was a sore trial to all. There developed, as the war went on, a divergence of view between McNaughton and Ottawa. McNaughton, while willing to authorize operations by detachments, was strongly of the opinion that in general the Canadians should be kept together as a national fighting entity. Ottawa on the other hand was plied with reasons for getting the Canadian Army into action as soon as possible. Matters came to a head late in 1943 at the time of the campaign of Sicily and McNaughton was relieved of his command.

Colonel J. L. Ralston, the distinguished

Canadian soldier, who was Minister of National Defence, was then instructed by the Canadian Cabinet to proceed to Britain and transfer the command of the army to General Crerar. On his return he, out of kindness to McNaughton, informed Parliament that ill health had caused his retirement, but McNaughton soon after landing in Canada repudiated this explanation and declared that his health was excellent. At this time he was a bitter critic of the King Ministry, with a special animosity towards Ralston.

USE OF CONSCRIPTS

In 1944 Colonel Ralston, after an inspection of the Canadian forces in the field, decided that their need for reinforcements was so acute that the men conscripted for home defence—the so-called "zombie army"—who were eating their heads off in camps in Canada, must be sent overseas without delay. But Mackenzie King, fearful of a revolt by his French-Canadian followers, opposed this move and during a bitter controversy at a meeting of the Cabinet, dismissed Ralston from it. King had to find immediately a successor to Ralston who would undertake to raise the needed reinforcements by the voluntary system of recrutiting, and there was some surprise when he persuaded such a violent critic of his Ministry as McNaughton had been to join it. The latter was defeated in a by-election in Grey county, Ontario, but remained in the Cabinet and, when he had to admit his inability to secure the required quota of recruits, Mackenzie King had to agree to adopt Ralston's policy and send the "Zombies" overseas. McNaughton would have emerged from the episode with greater credit if, after his plan had failed, he had resigned and advised King to bring back Ralston.

But he continued in office, only to suffer in the general election of 1945 a defeat, which ended his political career. It did not, however, end a useful career in public life. He was chairman of the Canadian section of the Canada-U.S. Permanent Joint Board on Defence from 1945 to 1959, Canadian representative on the U.N. Atomic Energy Commission from 1946 to 1949 and president of the Canadian Atomic Energy Commission for the years 1946–48, and from 1950 to 1962 chairman of the Canadian Section of the International Joint Commission which deals with boundary problems between Canada and the United States. He was created C.H. in 1946.

He married in 1914 Mabel Clara, daughter of Godfrey Weir. They had three sons and two daughters. One son was killed while serving with the R.C.A.F. in the Second World War.

July 12, 1966.

Sir James M. McNeill, K.C.V.O., C.B.E., M.C., F.R.S., former deputy chairman and managing director of John Brown and Company, Clydebank, Limited, who was mainly responsible for the design of the Queen Mary and the Queen Elizabeth liners, died on July 24, 1964, in a Glasgow hospital. He was 71.

Sir James, who had been ill for some time, retired as managing director in 1959 and from the board in 1962. Apart from the two Atlantic Queens the many ships which he played a part in designing included the roval yacht Britannia.

James McFadyen McNeill, son of Archibald McNeill, was born on August 19, 1892. His association with John Browns began in 1908 when he went straight from Allan Glen's School to begin his apprenticeship as a draughtsman. He later graduated at Glasgow Univeristy in naval architecture and engineering and during the First World War served with the Royal Field Artillery, receiving the Military Cross and being mentioned in dispatches. On returning to Clydebank he was appointed assistant naval architect and in 1928 chief naval architect and technical manager. In 1934 he became a local director, managing director 14 years later and in 1953 became deputy chairman as well as managing director. He was made C.B.E. in 1950 and received his knighthood in 1954.

McNeill, who was made an honorary LL.D. of Glasgow University in 1939, was elected a Fellow of the Royal Society 10 years later.

In addition to his work for his own company, Sir James was a leading figure in the industry. He was president of the Shipbuilding Conference in 1955–57, and served on the committee of Lloyd's Register of Shipping. He was a director of the British Linen Bank and a former member of the board of governors of the Royal College of Science and Technology, Glasgow. He was also a past president of the Institution of Engineers and Shipbuilders in Scotland, and an honorary vice-president of the Institution of Naval Architects.

In 1924 he married Jean Ross, daughter of Alexander McLaughlan of Glasgow. They had one son.

July 25, 1964.

Louis MacNeice, C.B.E., the poet, playwright and B.B.C. producer, died in St. Leonard's Hospital, Shoreditch, London, on September 3, 1963. He was 55.

In the 1930s, when Louis MacNeice first really emerged as a poet, his name was often linked with those of W. H. Auden, Stephen Spender and C. Day Lewis. Yet even at that time he had less in common with those poets than they appeared (temporarily at best and perhaps only superficially) to have with each other. He was never deeply committed politically or philosophically but was from the start a broadly liberal humanist. These qualities are apparent in the character of his poetry. It is seldom intensely emotional or rhetorical and never flamboyant; but highly individual feeling and imagination are married in it to verse of amazing variety and fluency, and to technical skill of a dazzling order.

It might be said that Louis MacNeice was a poets' poet. He never sought the easy limelit road to a mass audience. On the other hand he avoided the wilfully "difficult" and esoteric. He brought a delicate and fastidious craft to the expression of a robust but equally fastidious mind. None of his poems could ever have been mistaken for another man's; few of his fellow-poets could match him in either fecundity or ingenuity. Yet all was done with such artistic tact that his sheer skill was seldom apparent except to a colleague in the art. All, however, could recognize with gratitude and enduring pleasure a body of verse in which lyricism, wryness, sharp observation, sometimes even slapstick humour, were intermingled.

Born on September 12, 1907, son of a bishop, he travelled far in his 55 years from the Malone Road, Belfast, and the rocks of Connemara. He passed, abstracted, studious but gregarious, through Marlborough and Oxford. A "First" both in Mods and in Greats was followed by a translation of the *Agamemnon* of Aeschylus, and by several years' lecturing in classics at Birmingham University and Bedford College, London. During the 30s he began to publish the poems of which *Autumn Journal* (1939) was the key which made him,—together with W. H. Auden, with whom he collaborated in *Letters from Iceland*, C. Day Lewis and Stephen Spender—a leading voice among the angry young men of his time.

B.B.C. FEATURES

The first year of the war found MacNeice lecturing in the United States at Cornel Univeristy. He returned to London in the autumn of 1940 and offered his services to the B.B.C. as a writer in support of the national cause. The feature programmes he wrote and produced during the war were brilliantly effective in clarifying the moral issues of the conflict. At the same time, they revealed to MacNeice new writing and production techniques in radio. At the coming of peace, he was ready to apply these techniques to subjects of his own choosing, but he continued to write and publish poetry and criticism. It was an important decision which has largely formed the tradition and quality of original imaginative radio writing in Britain.

Few writers of MacNeice's quality have applied themselves as wholeheartedly to the radio medium. A recurring theme in his radio work was the dilemma of the contemporary hero faced with the pressures of authority, whether those of a profession, a class or an authoritarian police state.

His work for radio received international recognition with the award of Premio Italiano for his *Prisoner's Progress* in 1954. His outstanding work for broadcasting was undoubtedly *The Dark Tower* with special music by his friend Benjamin Britten, a radio dramatic fantasy inspired by the Second World War. Works such as these proved to the contemporary literary world that a small circulation and a close critical circle are not essentials for creative success in our time.

Louis MacNeice was a cat who walked by himself. He had a quality of great stillness, as he watched, at Lord's or Twickenham, in a Delhi bazaar or a Dublin pub, but there was always a sense of restrained movement and energy conserved for the decisive spring. Actors loved the sinewy quality of his writing for speech, the sharp contemporary tang of his scholar-poet's idiom. MacNeice could work anywhere immune from the traffic of telephone and typewriter, the trivia of bureaucracy and the importunate. With sad irony his last work for radio, *Persons from Porlock*, exploded the Coleridgean theme of the artist whose inspiration is a prey to distracting intruders.

But little that happened in his world escaped his notice. He had a mind of highly sensitive quality that registered subtle inflections and overtones of meaning. He loved London, his job and his fellows with the warmth and discrimination of a true humanist.

He was twice married and had a son by his first marriage and a daughter by his second.

September 4, 1963.

René Magritte, the Belgian Surrealist painter, died in Brussels on August 15, 1967, at the age of 68. A retrospective exhibition of his paintings from 1925 to 1966 is at present running at the Rotterdam Museum Boymans-van Beuningen.

Painting up till his death in very much the same manner he formed in the mid-twenties, Magritte crystallized a number of characteristic and unforgettable images. They have become very well known—perhaps partly because their essence is not difficult to communicate and pass on verbally: the horrible face made from a woman's torso, the sitting man whose chest is replaced by a cage of birds, the pair of boots ending in human feet, and the milder images of his later painting, such as the one in which two men with bowler hats and canes are going for a walk in the summer sky. In a similar way to Delvaux, but more pointedly, Magritte combined the traditional Flemish liking for a secret airless kind of fantasy with the universal banal realities of twentieth-century life.

More perhaps than any other painter of the circle, Magritte kept throughout his life to the first principle of Surrealism: to go beyond rationalism by taking the objects of common experience out of their familiar context and putting them in new ones. With his completely inexpressive, deadpan academic handling Magritte concentrated everything on these incongruous relations. His output was large and his paintings fluctuate over the years in depth of insight. As with any other kind of art, in the best paintings the spectator is less aware of the oddities of the subject-matter than their reality, the sense of necessity behind their choice.

Magritte was born at Lessines in 1898 and was educated in the tradition of Flemish Expressionism at the Brussels Academy. The decisive influence on his development was Chirico's work which he first saw in 1922. In the early twenties he associated with the first Belgian Surrealist poets and in 1927 he went to Paris, where he met André-Breton and Paul Eluard.

MANY SHOWS

Going back to Brussels in 1930 he put out a number of Surrealist reviews and pamphlets with another Belgian, E. L. T. Mesens, and illustrated books of poetry. He took part in all the big group exhibitions of Surrealism and in the last few years he held one-man shows in many parts of the world. In 1966 a monograph by Patrick Waldberg and one by J. R. Soby were published on his work.

Magritte's "dull" handling of the painting has always been controversial. His earliest critics complained that he was not a good painter, and of course the illustrative character of much Surrealist painting has often raised the problem of its merits as *painting*. A Surrealist may appear striking in a single painting, but pall in a retrospective exhibition, where the growth of another artist's work is only properly revealed. Yet Magritte's imagery and his way of realizing it in paint are certainly unified. His flat paint suits his empty facades, his wood-graining, his suburban grass. In its context his mild blue sky with its fleecy clouds suggests a genuine liberation, and like his other images has had the power to enter the modern consciousness.

August 17, 1967.

Arthur Mailey, one of the greatest slow spin bowlers in the game, died in Sydney on December 31, 1967.

Mailey, who was born in Sydney on January 3, 1888, represented Australia 21 times, 18 of them against England, and took 99 wickets in Tests, 86 against England. His most successful series was against J. W. H. T. Douglas's touring side of 1920–21, in which, though bowling in only four Tests, he captured 36 wickets, including nine for 121 in the second innings of the fourth Test. He also took 24 Test wickets against A. E. R. Gilligan's team of 1924–25 and in his two tours of England, in 1921 and 1926, he took 146 wickets (12 in Tests) the first time and 126 (14 in Tests) on his second visit.

After 1926 his former partner, Grimmett, became his natural successor as Australia's leg-spin and googly bowler. Yet in certain respects they were almost contrasting in method: Grimmett accurate, relentless, using the slightest variations in pace and spin with the maximum of subtlety; Mailey, on the other hand, a bowler of extravagance, subject to the lapses in accuracy often associated with the wrist spinner but always willing to tempt the batsman, always a potential wicket-taker in any company on any wicket.

Mailey's bowling was once called by a colleague a mixture of "spin, flight and sheer fun". With his long, powerful fingers he could impart a break that would "bite" on any pitch and he developed the arts of flight and deception by ceaseless practice.

Besides his skill as a bowler, he was a gifted cartoonist, with a strong, satirical line of which the late Sir David Low would not have been ashamed. As a person he was an amiable eccentric rather than a rebel, and his humour was incorrigibly straightfaced. When in 1958 he wrote his autobiography, *Ten for Sixty-six and All That*—a title culled from his second innings bowling figures against Gloucestershire in 1921—he described the book as a necessary act of self-expression since nature had denied him the ability to sing in his bath.

When in December, 1926, Victoria made the record score of 1,107 against his state, New South Wales, Mailey claimed the best bowling figures, four for 362, and said he only made one mistake: he should have bowled with his coat on.

A satirical humorist though he was, he is responsible for one of the most poignant lines in cricket's recorded history. Bowling as a raw youngster against his blindly worshipped idol, the mighty Victor Trumper, he deceived him with a prodigious break and had him stumped.

"As I watched the receding figure", said Mailey, "there was no triumph in me. I felt like a boy who has killed a dove."

January 1, 1968.

William Makram Ebeid Pasha, a former Egyptian Minister whose writings did much to create the climate of opinion in that country which brought about the downfall of the Farouk regime in 1952, died in Cairo on June 5, 1961, at the age of 71.

Born at Kena in Upper Egypt on October 25, 1889, and receiving his early education at Egyptian primary and secondary schools and then at the American College at Assiut, Makram early showed great promise. In 1905 he went to Oxford and took an honours degree in jurisprudence and then went to France, where he became a Doctor of Law. An early member of the Wafdist Party, he was one of Zaghlul Pasha's most ardent supporters in the anti-British revolt of 1919 and was one of those deported with Zaghlul to the Seychelles in 1921. It is said that during the two years of their exile Makram used to teach Saad Zaghlul for six hours a day.

In October, 1927, Makram, who was undoubtedly the best organizer in the party, was elected secretary of the Wafd, and it was largely due to him that the party machine became so powerful throughout Egypt. When the Wafdists came to power in February, 1942, Makram Pasha became Minister of Finance, but within a few months he was openly accusing the Prime Minister, Nahas Pasha, of allowing large scale corruption and nepotism. Aggravated by individuals who had their own axes to grind, the quarrel between Makram and Nahas soon became acute and in July, 1942, Makram was expelled from the Wafd and resigned his Ministry. With Makram went about 40 sympathisers who formed a new party known as the Wafdist Block, or Kotla Party. Early in 1943 Makram produced a Black Book elaborating his accusations against Nahas Pasha and violently attacking the Government in Parliament. Finally, Nahas Pasha placed Makram under restraint.

When Nahas Pasha was dismissed in October, 1944, Makram was released and became Finance Minister in the coalition government of Ahmed Maher Pasha, in which post he remained when, after the assassination of Ahmed Maher, Nokrashy Pasha became Prime Minister. However, within three months he provoked three Cabinet crises which terminated with his resignation, just before that of Nokrashy Pasha. When negotiations for the revision of the Anglo-Egyptian treaty of 1936 were announced, Makram, who had been one of the signatories of the agreement, was made a member of the

Egyptian Delegation but, almost immediately, he became and remained the most intractable of the negotiators. Finally, at the end of November, 1946, he and six other delegates publicly announced their unwillingness to accept the British proposals and the delegation was dissolved by royal decree. Despite his public attitude, in private Makram freely admitted his belief in alliance and his opinion that the British proposals were reasonable.

His exposures of corruption increased dissatisfaction with the existing regime and indirectly helped to bring about the revolution of 1952. After that Makram became a member of the committee appointed by General Neguib to draft a new constitution for the country. In December, 1953, and January, 1954, he was the star prosecution witness at the trial of Fuad Serag el Din, a later secretary of the Wafd, who was sentenced to 15 years' imprisonment for corruption and abuse of power.

Had Makram Pasha been less impetuous, temperamental, and quarrelsome, he would have been a great statesman. He was a born organizer, completely honest, and undoubtedly brilliant. An excellent orator, his theatrical and emotional eloquence earned him the name of "the orator of the Revolution", but significantly, another of his names was "The Fighter" and his assertiveness and combativeness made him an almost impossible colleague. Domineering and unable to play second fiddle, Makram brought dissension and often disruption to every organization of which he was a member. He is best described in the words he used himself when he opened the debate in Parliament on his Black Book: "I am an Egyptian and an Upper Egyptian, too. When I love I worship: when I hate I destroy with every sinew in my body." Tall and of striking appearance, an interesting conversationalist, Makram understood the British better than most Egyptians. He himself appeared very "English", but, in fact, the strongest traits in his character were those usually ascribed to the Copts, of which he was one.

June 7, 1961.

Group Captain A. G. Malan, D.S.O. AND BAR, D.F.C. AND BAR, one of the great fighter pilots of the Second World War, died on September 17, 1963, at Kimberley. He was 52.

Adolph Gysbert Malan, known throughout the R.A.F. as "Sailor" Malan and to his associates as John or Johnny, won fame during the war, first as an outstanding fighter pilot and unselfish leader, next as station commander and inspirer at Biggin Hill, and finally as the commander of big fighter formations which put cover over the D-Day landing and harassed the enemy continuously during the reoccupation of Europe. In all the years of his air fighting he was never shot down, never had to use his parachute; yet he destroyed over 30 enemy aircraft and had at least 20 "possibles" to his credit. In him, as in Douglas Bader and Stanford Tuck and others of that legendary group of pilots, an aggressive spirit went hand in hand with great skill.

His immunity from disaster derived in large part from his coldly calculating attitude towards air fighting and partly from his stubborn refusal to take an easy way out of difficulty. More often than not his fine flying and shooting and his fierce yet wary offensiveness brought him victory without scars and frequently he came home with bits of debris sticking to his aircraft as tokens of infighting and viciously accurate fire. He won the affection of those he led in action—there were several who knew that the watchful Malan had saved their lives—and with the affection went admiration and gratitude for the quality of his leading, the skill in estimating a situation and fitting tactics to it, and the invariably high spirit and cold determination with which an attack was pressed.

Nobody ever doubted that Malan was a dedicated man who found immense satisfaction in doing his job. Nor did he trouble to deny the satisfaction in spite of the fear the job involved. While he was instructing he remarked that it was "better to be perpetually scared than perpetually bored". At a later date he declared that the bravest thing he ever did was to ask Mr. Churchill to be godfather of his son.

RISE TO FAME

He became "Sailor" Malan after the fashion of service nicknames because he had spent 10 years at sea before he joined the R.A.F. He was the son of a Cape farmer of Franco-Dutch descent and an English mother. He was born at Wellington on October 3, 1910. At the age of 13 he became a cadet in the South African training ship General Botha and from 1930 to 1935 he was an officer with the Union-Castle line. For two years he was a sub-lieutenant in the R.N.R. Then, in 1936, the age limit for pilots in the R.A.F. was raised. He found he could qualify and, in his mid-twenties, he trained and was given a short-service commission. As an acting pilot officer in December, 1936 he was posted to No. 74 Squadron and had reached the rank of Flying Officer by the middle of 1938. In the Battle of Britain in 1940 he rose to the rank of Flight Lieutenant and a month later to Squadron Leader. In another six months he was Wing Commander. He was withdrawn from the fighting war in August, 1941, and did not get back to it until January, 1943. He was then over 30 and he ought to have been out of practice but he was quickly back in form and as busy in the air as on the ground. Later he commanded a wing in the Second Tactical Air Force in France.

Retiring from the R.A.F. in 1946, he returned to South Africa as an assistant to Sir Ernest Oppenheimer. For a time in 1951 he led an ex-Servicemen's organization in opposition to the Bill of his distant cousin, Dr. Malan, which was to deprive the coloured electors in Cape Province of their votes. He led a "torch commando" 60,000 strong in protest against the Republic Bill, asserting that he was continuing the fight against fascism. He accepted the presidency of the War Veterans' Action group, which continued to offer opposition to the Government's policy but he soon ceased to take an active part in its work. He also left the Oppenheimer post to become a sheep farmer. For some years he had suffered from a serious affliction and periodically he visited London or went into hospital in the Union for treatment. His postwar flying was done as a passenger but he will be remembered as long as Battle of Britain pilots survive, as one of the greatest of their number.

He leaves a widow, a son and a daughter.

September 18, 1963.

Marshal of the Soviet Union Rodion Yakovlevich Malinovsky, the Soviet Defence Minister, died on March 31, 1967, at the age of 68.

Malinovsky began life in very lowly circumstances, born in 1898 into a worker's family in Odessa. In 1916 he was called up to the Imperial Russian Army, and in the following year was sent to France with the Russian brigade. This force became disaffected after the outbreak of the February Revolution in Russia and sections of it were transported for mutiny to North Africa. Among the convicts was Corporal Malinovsky, who nevertheless managed to make his escape and returned to Russia. Once home, he volunteered for the Red Army, with which he served throughout the Civil War as a junior commander. At the close of the Civil War he elected to make the Red Army his career, and in 1930 attended the Frunze Military Academy.

Having served with the Soviet contingent in Spain during the Spanish Civil War, Malinovsky returned to the Soviet Union, where he apparently escaped the tribulations of the military purge; in June, 1940, he was appointed major-general, and it was as a divisional commander that he began his wartime career, all of which (in Europe) was associated with the southern, Ukrainian, and south-westerly areas. In August, 1941, he assumed command of the 6th (formerly the Reserve) Army, fighting a more than averagely successful defensive action near Dnepropetrovsk; by the end of the year he commanded the 6th and controlled the 12th armies on the Southern Front, of which he assumed command in January, 1942. In recognition of Soviet success at Rostov, he was promoted to lieutenant-general; as such, he continued to command the Southern Front until July, 1942, when this was combined with the North Caucasus Front and put under the command of Marshal Budenny, with Malinovsky as his deputy. A month later, Malinovsky was put in command of the "Don operational group", which was an attempt to establish some effective command in a critical situation. From the North Caucasus command Malinovsky was assigned to Stalingrad where, in December, 1942, he took over the 2nd Guards Army used in the counter-offensive, and which held off a German attempt to break through the Soviet ring.

In the early summer of 1943, promoted now to full general of the Red Army, Malinovsky commanded the South-Western Front in the Kharkov-Belgorod operations, and later in the year, as commander of the 3rd Ukrainian Front, played an important part in the liberation of Zaporozh'ye, Krivoy Rog, and the southern part of the right-bank Ukraine. While Tolbukhin, for long his near neighbour, took over the 3rd Ukrainian Front, Malinovsky went to the 2nd, and in the high summer of 1944 planned and fought the Jassy-Kishinev operations. When Rumania fell out of the war on the German side Malinovsky, as Soviet plenipotentiary and representative of the Allies, signed on November 12, 1944, the agreement changing Rumania's status.

For his major successes in the south, in 1944 Malinovsky was appointed Marshal of the Soviet Union. In the winter of 1944–45, under his 2nd Ukrainian Front command, Soviet forces advanced into Transylvania on Budapest and moved into Austria, aiming at Vienna.

SENT TO FAR EAST

Malinovsky's troops operated against German forces in Czechoslovakia. At once Malinovsky, a specialist in fast long-distance movements, was transferred to the Soviet Far East, to command the tank and mobile forces of the Trans-Baikal Front, which were being readied for the "lightning war" against Japan. At the conclusion of this one and only Soviet *blitzkreig* operation, Malinovsky remained in the Soviet Far East and was in February, 1946, appointed commander of Soviet forces in this area. He remained in this vital post throughout the Korean War, and returned to Moscow in October-November, 1957, when he took over Marshal Zhukov's position as Defence Minister when the former was dismissed by Khrushchev.

Although a wartime associate of Khrushchev and a member of that obviously privileged "Southern command group" with which the former Soviet leader had been closely associated during the war, Marshal Malinovsky showed himself more than once disinclined to endorse the full implications of Khrushchev's "military radicalism" whereby missiles wholly overshadowed Soviet conventional forces. At the twenty-first Party Congress (October, 1961), Malinovsky propounded military views distinctively set off from those contained in Khrushchev's "new look" strategy, aired in January, 1960. Malinovsky accorded the nuclear missile pride of place in the initial phase of any future war, but insisted that final victory would be brought only by "the combined action" of all Soviet arms, thus contradicting Khrushchev's views on the obsolescence of conventional arms and mass armies. In addition to his resistance to extremism in the design of Soviet forces, Malinovsky in public affirmed a harder, more pessimistic line in appraising the external scene. Although Malinovsky's role in the Cuban missile crisis remains very obscure, he quickly took the first opportunity, the anniversary celebration of Stalingrad in February, 1963, to indicate disapproval of Khrushchev, and in 1964 Malinovsky spoke out for military readiness, high morale (opposing "pacifist trends"), and for adequate conventional forces.

DIFFERING VIEWS

Malinovsky clearly did not share Khrushchev's view that Soviet defences were "at a suitable level". After the fall of Khrushchev, Marshal Malinovsky was associated with the increased influence of the military, qualitative improvement to the Soviet strategic missile force, diversification of the Soviet missile arsenal, the elaboration of defensive systems, including a preliminary ABM deployment, and the renovation of the conventional forces. His last pronouncement (February 23, 1967) placed great emphasis on missile-firing submarines, as well as strategic rockets. In sum, Marshal Malinovsky resisted the lop-sided development of Soviet forces, stressed military requirements in Soviet security, and diversified Soviet capabilities.

He was a Hero of the Soviet Union, was awarded the Order of Victory and five Orders of Lenin and many other Soviet decorations. Among Soviet wartime commanders he is, in Soviet accounts, generally accorded sixth place in the list of "outstanding leaders and commanders". He married in 1925 and had two sons.

April 1, 1967.

Miles Malleson, the actor and playwright, died on March 15, 1969, in London at the age of 80.

He had a long career in the theatre and gave many notable performances, but perhaps without making that mark on the theatre, and through it on the life of his times, which he sought to make. As an actor on stage and screen he had a line in nitwits in which he was unrivalled, but as a writer his power was inadequate to express his vision of things, which was that of a Shelleyan idealist. Consequently the Malleson behind the comedian's face, the Malleson who cared sincerely for the advancement of the liberties of man, never wholly discovered himself save to those who knew him personally.

William Miles Malleson was born at Croydon on May 25, 1888. At Brighton College he was both head boy and captain of cricket, and from Cambridge, where he matriculated at Emmanuel College, he emerged B.A. and Mus. Bac. (Part I) to train as an actor at the (not yet Royal) Academy of Dramatic Art. In 1911 he first appeared as a professional at the Liverpool Playhouse, under Basil Dean, in Galsworthy's *Justice*, and in 1913 he had his first play produced in London by the Play Actors, followed three years later by his play *Youth*, produced by the Stage Society and very strongly cast. By then he had acted in London for Kenelm Foss in one of Thomas Hardy's few plays and for Granville Barker in Shaw, and had in 1915 married Lady Constance Annesley, who went on the stage under the name Colette O'Neil. After war-service in the Army, which gave him the material for two short plays *D. Company* and *Black 'Ell*, Malleson was invalided home and resumed his career as an actor under J. B. Fagan at the Court.

It was there and under Nigel Playfair at the Lyric, Hammersmith, that Malleson had the opportunity of perfecting a special brand of comic character whose dim-witted amiability contributed something very positive to the humour and humanity of a play. His simpletons with their runaway chins were silly in an earlier sense of that word than ours; they were happy, blessed, almost holy in their lack of mistrust or guile. For Fagan he played Aguecheek, Lancelot Gobbo, Peter Quince, Diggory in *She Stoops to Conquer*; for Playfair the village idiot in Ervine's *John Ferguson*; Le Beau and William in *As You Like It*; David in *The Rivals*; Filch in *The Beggar's Opera*.

PLAY KILLED BY STRIKE

For the managements of more central theatres he played during that same period, apart from Shakespeare's Snout the Tinker at Drury Lane for Basil Dean, chiefly small parts in musicals, but he continued to write, and it was unfortunate for him that the West End production of a serious study of political conflict, in which his sympathy with Labour was undisguised, should have preceded by a few weeks, during which he himself was appearing in Playfair's revue *Riverside Nights*, the General Strike of 1926. The dislocation of theatrical life and the collapse of the strike killed *Conflict*.

It would almost certainly also have killed *The Fanatics*, a play directed against the authority of the older generation and pleading in particular for greater freedom of sexual morality, had he not urged Leon M. Lion to stop rehearsals and postpone it in time. Produced in 1927 with first Nicholas Hannen and later Owen Nares as the spokesman of the younger generation, it was Malleson's most successful attempt to marry his convictions with his theatre-craft, and it ran for over 300 performances. By contrast *Four People*, less radical and less funny, aroused little interest in 1928, when Malleson himself directed it.

He acted on stage once for Lion and twice for Playfair at the beginning of the 1930s, but during that decade he was chiefly occupied with writing for the stage and, often taking small parts in them, for the films. For the stage he adapted two German plays, in one of which Werner Krauss made his only appearance in London, and, in collaboration, a Czech play by Karel Capek; he collaborated in a play about the Tolpuddle Martyrs; and for Lion he up-dated and sharpened the anti-war argument of *The Fanatics* in a new version that was actually being tried out when Hitler began the Second World War; while he wrote screenplay and dialogue for Herbert Wilcox's *Nell Gwyn* and other British historical films, he became the first chairman of the Screen Writers' Association in 1937, and collaborated in a screenplay about R. J. Mitchell, the inventor of the Spitfire plane, which Leslie Howard filmed in 1942.

BACK TO OLD VIC

Returning to the classical theatre in 1943 as old Foresight in Gielgud's revival of *Love for Love*. Malleson stayed on with Gielgud for his wartime season of repertoire at the Haymarket, appearing in Congreve, Shakespeare (as Polonius and Peter Quince) and Webster, and then joined Olivier and Richardson for the Old Vic Company's first post-war season at the New and for its ensuing guest-season in New York. He rejoined the company at the New for the 1949–50 season, playing under Tyrone Guthrie's direction the name part in his own adaptation of Molière's *The Miser*, and, after appearing in a play by Guthrie and with the Bristol Old Vic Company in another Molière, he was again with the London Old Vic Company, now re-housed in the Waterloo Road, during two consecutive seasons, in which were seen his adaptations of *Sganarelle* and *Tartuffe* and his performances as a cuckolded knight in Congreve and as Canon Chasuble, a part he had already played in Anthony Asquith's film version, in Oscar Wilde.

He acted with Olivier again in Ionesco's *Rhinoceros* in 1960, and five years later, having meanwhile played in and directed his version of *Le Bourgeois Gentilhomme* at Glyndebourne, where Strauss's opera *Ariadne auf Naxos* was given as the final scene of Molière's play, and having returned to Drury Lane as Merlyn in *Camelot*, he was engaged by Olivier for *Love for Love* at the Old Vic, where the National Theatre Company was now in the third season of its existence.

Malleson's marriages with his first wife and with his second, who as Dr. Joan Malleson, M.R.C.S., L.R.C.P., became well known as a pioneer of family planning and who died in 1956, were dissolved. He married as his third wife Miss Tatiana Lieven.

As a comedian of originality Malleson deserves a place in the gallery of verbal portraits of our Old Actors which Charles Lamb inaugurated in his well-remembered essay. An over-grown baby, an enraged sheep, a touching embodiment of stupidity, complacency and good humour, gobbling in his gullibility and gobbling in his disillusionment are phrases used by A. V. Cookman to describe him in later years. So far as authorship is concerned, Malleson did not mature as a dramatist in his own right, though he had the satisfaction of seeing *The Fanatics* and *Six Men of Dorset* revived on television in the 1960s, and came to be regarded chiefly as an adapter of Moliere. In that capacity he was probably more consistently successful than anyone who has worked in England up to date.

March 17, 1969.

Dr. J. J. Mallon, C.H., died on April 12, 1961, in hospital. By his death the country loses a very eminent social organizer, a man of shining ideals, and the personal friend of many of London's working people, who has been called "the most popular man east of Aldgate Pump".

The whole of his life was devoted to social amelioration, and for 35 years he was Warden of Toynbee Hall, in the East End, where he consolidated and expanded the work of Barnett and many later workers, including Milner, Tawney, and Attlee.

James Joseph Mallon was born in Manchester in 1875, of Irish parentage, the son of Felix Mallon, of co. Tyrone and his wife, Mary O'Hare, of co. Down. He completed his education at Owens College (later the University of Manchester), from which he graduated M.A. An honorary LL.D. was to come to him from the neighbour University of Liverpool in later years.

Social work attracted him, and he joined the staff of the Ancoats Settlement, devoted to the poor of Manchester. He soon became convinced of the crying social evil of sweated wages, and in 1906 was appointed secretary to the National League to Establish a Minimum Wage. The agitation created by this body was largely responsible for the passing, in 1909, of the Trade Boards Act, which fixed minimum wages in several industries. Mallon was a member of the first 13 trade boards to be set up. He served on the Whitley Committee and was honorary secretary to the Trade Boards Advisory Council.

Mallon moved from Manchester to Toynbee Hall in 1906. His efforts on behalf of the lower wage earner were not confined to material things. He was highly sensible of the need for improved and extended education for the working man, and took the keenest interest in the pioneering work of Dr. Albert Mansbridge in this domain. He became a member of the executive of the Workers' Educational Association, and was always a strong advocate of the raising of the school-leaving age to 15, and of continued part-time education up to the age of 18.

During the First World War Mallon was a member of various committees under the Profiteering Act and for the purpose of reconstruction. In October, 1919, he was appointed Warden of Toynbee Hall, and there he led a very active life, greatly endearing himself to the local population. Under his wardenship Toynbee became known as "the poor man's university". He was in large measure responsible for the foundation of the Toynbee Hall theatre, the Workers' Travel Association, and the John Benn club for working boys.

SERVICE ON COMMITTEES

Mallon's busy life as a teacher and social worker did not prevent him from taking part in sundry national organizations and investigations. He served on the Royal Commission on Licensing, the executive committee of the League of Nations Union, departmental committees on the Cinematographic Films Act, and on the Adoption Societies and Agencies, the executive committee of the British Empire Exhibition, and the boards of governors of the Whitechapel Art Gallery and the London Museum. He was, too, a member of the Government's Economic Advisory Council, the Aliens Deportation Advisory Committee, and was chairman of the London Council for Voluntary Occupation during Unemployment. He was a governor of the B.B.C. from 1937 to 1939 and again from 1941 to 1946.

In the summer of 1939 Mallon was created a Companion of Honour. In October, 1940, he was appointed by Lord Woolton to be adviser on the provision of food and refreshment in London air raid shelters.

He retired from Toynbee Hall in April, 1954, but retained his honorary secretaryship of the Wages Councils Advisory Council and his membership of the several trade boards connected with the clothing industry. On retirement he set to work on his autobiography, to replace a virtually completed manuscript which had been destroyed during the bombing of London. In 1955 he was awarded the Margaret McMillan Medal.

"Jimmy" Mallon, as he was called in the East End, will indeed be missed by the many who have benefited by his kindness, and by all friends of progress and education. If ever there was a life single-heartedly devoted to the service of others, such a life was Mallon's. He had not a great deal of time for writing, but published some booklets on the minimum wage and on women's work, and contributed from time to time to *The Observer*, the old *Daily News* and the *Manchester Guardian*.

In 1921 he married Stella Katherine, eldest daughter of the distinguished editor A. G. Gardiner.

April 13, 1961.

Sir Frederick Mander, who died in Luton General Hospital on February 27, 1964, at the age of 80, was general secretary of the N.U.T. from 1931 to 1947—a period of office which covered the difficult years of the depression when education was under severe financial restriction, the introduction of the 1936 Education Act, the lengthy and arduous negotiations leading up to the 1944 Education Act, and the first hectic years after the war.

Mander was a tough and resourceful negotiator, and a masterful and persuasive public speaker. He led the N.U.T. firmly and never lost a clear sight of his aims. His constituents in the N.U.T. till 1944 were, in the main, the men and women teachers in the elementary schools. Between them and the graduates in the secondary schools was a social and economic barrier, which it was Mander's ambition to bridge.

His great achievement as a union leader came after 1944 when in the first salary negotiations in the reorganized Burnham main primary and secondary committee, he fought for and won a single basic scale for all teachers. Differential payments were to be added to this according to responsibilities and qualifications, but no longer was the basic salary to be automatically calculated by reference to the school in which a teacher taught. In effect, this amounted to the up-grading of the non-graduate teachers, narrowing the differentials between them and the graduates. The measure of his skill as a negotiator is the extent to which he was, if anything, too successful, and subsequent Burnham negotiations have been concerned to reassert the differentials.

LOCAL GOVERNOR

After his retirement in 1947 he became a director of Newnes Educational Publishing Company. He extended his interests in local government and rapidly became prominent in the Bedfordshire County Council, of which he had become a member in 1944. He was chairman of the education committee from 1946 to 1952 and of the county council from 1952 to 1962. He was a member of the executive committee of the Association of Education Committees from 1947 onwards. In many ways he relished his role as poacher turned gamekeeper, and he was a frequent (and, sometimes, mischievous) contributor to the *Teachers World*.

Frederick Mander was born at Luton on July 12, 1883, and was educated at the higher grade school of his native town and Westminster Training College. After taking the degree of B.Sc. at London University, he was appointed headmaster of a Luton school in 1915, and remained there until 1931, when he became general secretary of the National Union of Teachers. The organization was then struggling for higher salaries and better conditions. Mander first rallied the membership, prepared a programme of reforms, and then concentrated on their achievement, but it was some years before the union was able to make much impression.

In 1933 Mander was elected president of the World Federation of Education Associations. He subsequently became director of the federation.

In 1911 he married Hilda Irene, daughter of T. W. Sargent, of Wakefield, and there were two sons and a daughter.

February 28, 1964.

Sir Geoffrey Mander, Liberal member of Parliament for East Wolverhampton from 1929 to 1945, died on September 9, 1962, at his home, Wightwick Manor, near Wolverhampton, at the age of 80.

During his 16 years in the House of Commons he was noted for his persistent questioning of ministers, especially in the period just before the outbreak of the Second World War when he was a strong critic of Neville Chamberlain's appeasement policy.

In 1948 he joined the Labour Party because, he said, he felt that the Liberal Party since the general-election of 1945 had no future. But he did not stand for Parliament again. He was an effective speaker, a hard worker, and a strong individualist who never found it easy to obey the party whips. Even during the three years from 1942 to 1945, when he was Parliamentary Private Secretary to the Secretary of State for Air, Sir Archibald Sinclair (later Lord Thurso) he could not resist putting questions to other Ministers, and his frequent dashes across the floor of the House, behind the Speaker's chair, and on to the Opposition benches to interrogate the Government, caused not only much amusement but also some embarrassment.

Geoffrey Le Mesurier Mander was born in 1882, the son of S. Theodore Mander and Flora, daughter of H. M. Pain, M.P., of Canada. He was educated at Harrow and at Trinity College, Cambridge. Later, he was called to the Bar by the Inner Temple.

In addition to law, he was well known in business circles as head of Mander Bros. Ltd., paint and varnish manufacturers, of Wolverhampton. In 1921 he was High Sheriff of Staffordshire. He had served as a magistrate for Staffordshire and Wolverhampton and for some years on the Staffordshire County Council. He received a knighthood in 1945.

From 1922 he made three unsuccessful attempts to enter the House of Commons before he was finally elected in 1929 for East Wolverhampton, and held the seat at the 1931 and 1935 general elections. His defeat in 1945 was the end of Mander's parliamentary career.

ATTACK ON CHAMBERLAIN

In September, 1938, he had bitterly attacked the Munich agreement. National unity was essential, he declared, but it could never be attained under Chamberlain. A new National Government should be formed, including Eden, Churchill and perhaps, Lord Baldwin, and containing also the Liberal and Labour leaders, in order to save the country and the world.

In 1941 he published *We Were Not All Wrong*, in which he sought to show from speeches of Liberal and Labour leaders, and declarations of the League of Nations Union that the foreign policy they had advocated would have been justified in the event.

Approaches were made to him in 1947 by the East Wolverhampton Association to become Liberal and Conservative candidate for the division, but Mander turned them down. The following year he joined the Labour Party, which, he said, had become "heir of the Radical tradition".

In 1937 he presented to the National Trust his house, Wightwick Manor, near Wolverhampton, together with its chief contents, 17 acres of gardens, and an endowment fund. Begun by his father in 1887, the manor was considered a remarkable example of pre-Raphaelite influence. The architect was Edward Ould, and the interior contained fine examples of Morris tapestry and wall-paper, William de Morgan tiles, and stained glass by C. E. Kempe. Mander and his family continued to live at Wightwick Manor.

He was twice married. His first wife was Florence, daughter of Colonel Caverhill, of of Montreal. He married her in 1906, and the marriage was dissolved in April, 1930. In November of that year he was married in the crypt of the House of Commons to Rosalie Glynn, daughter of A. C. Glynn Grylls. By his first wife he had one son and two daughters, and by his second wife, who survives him, a son and a daughter.

September 10, 1962.

Norman Washington Manley, Q.C., Premier (and previously Chief Minister) of Jamaica from 1959 to 1962, died on September 2, 1969. He became leader of the Opposition subsequently and in 1968 in his farewell address to his People's National Party, he praised the concept of black power.

Manley distinguished himself in everything he undertook. His abilities as a lawyer, as a politician and, in his youth, as an athlete, were outstanding. In the 1914–18 War, when serving with the R.F.A. he proved himself also a man of outstanding courage, winning the Military Medal.

By the Second World War, Manley had established himself firmly as the most distinguished advocate in the West Indies and his legal career continued on a brilliant course, both there and in occasional appearances before British tribunals, until he finally retired in 1955 to devote his time to politics on becoming Chief Minister.

Manley was born in Jamaica in 1893, partly of British, partly of coloured Jamaican descent. He was educated at Jamaica College and then won a Rhodes Scholarship to Jesus College, Oxford, where he graduated B.A. and B.C.L. He afterwards became an honorary fellow of the college.

Already in Jamaica he had held the local record for the long jump and running and at Oxford he distinguished himself as a sprinter. He was called to the Bar by Gray's Inn, of which he was Lee Prizeman in 1921, and back in Jamaica he soon became the island's outstanding advocate with the largest legal practice.

SUGAR ESTATE RIOTS

His political career began in 1938. In May of that year there were riots in Jamaica, which began in the sugar estates and quickly spread. Manley negotiated with the Governor on behalf of the disaffected workers and largely as a result of his efforts a Royal Commission was appointed. Its report was not published until after the war.

In 1938, too, Sir Stafford Cripps visited Jamaica and immediately the two men found that they had much in common. It was Cripps who urged Manley to found a political party, and he was present when the People's National Party was born.

In the elections in December, 1944, for the first time under the universal adult suffrage for which Manley had striven, he and his party were crushingly defeated by his cousin, Mr. (later Sir) Alexander Bustamante.

Manley was successful in an election for the first time in 1949, but it was not until 1955 that his party won a majority and he became Chief Minister. That success marked a turning point in his political fortunes, and in Bustamante's, and Manley remained in power to become the first Premier of Jamaica in 1959.

With the advent of federation, Manley founded the West Indies Federal Labour Party but in 1958 he announced that he would not stand for the Prime Ministership which therefore went to Adams.

He became leader of the Opposition in 1962. In 1965 he made a 10-day tour of West Indian communities in Britain, and he accused the Conservatives of raising colour as a political issue.

September 3, 1969.

Anthony Mann, who died suddenly in Berlin on April 29, 1967, when nearing completion of shooting on his latest film, *A Dandy in Aspic*, was renowned, above all, as one of Hollywood's great action directors. He was 60.

He was born in San Diego, California, on June 30, 1906. He was a child actor, and crossed the country at 16 to become a bit player in various independent New York theatre companies. For a while he was under contract to Theatre Guild as an actor, but in 1930 he left to become a stage manager and then a director. In 1934 he founded a stock company on Long Island, had a success on Broadway with *Thunder on the Left* and joined Federal Theatre, to stage several productions, among them *So Proudly We Hail*. In 1938 he was hired by Selznick as a talent scout, was casting director on *Gone With The Wind*, and then worked for a while as assistant director and editor, until in 1942 the intervention of an actor friend got him his first assignment as a film director, *Dr. Broadway*.

Twelve B-films later, he made a surprise success with *T. Men* (1947), a tough location thriller, and continued to improve his position, until in 1950 he was asked to take over direction of the Western *Winchester* 73, from which Fritz Lang had retired. This was an enormous success, and began a long series of collaborations with the star James Stewart in Western subjects, among them *Bend of the River*, *The Naked Spur*, *The Far Country*, and *The Man From Laramie*. These were made with tremendous energy and directness as well as considerable visual flair, and marked Mann out as a masculine director *par excellence*.

HISTORICAL EPICS

During the same year he made several other films with James Stewart, as various as *Thunder-Bay*, *Strategic Air Command*, and *The Glenn Miller Story*.

In 1956 Mann founded his own production company, making two films for it, *Men In War* and *God's Little Acre*, a money-making version of Erskine Caldwell's sex-ridden best seller. More interesting were the Westerns *The Tin Star* and *Man of the West*; his remake of *Cimarron*, though promising, was beset by production difficulties, and the result was disappointing. Between 1961 and 1964 most of his time was occupied by two large-scale historical epics, *El Cid* and *The Fall of the Roman Empire*, both of which managed the vast paraphernalia of the modern big-screen super production with some skill and ingenuity. His last film, *The Heroes of Telemark*, was a war story, made largely in Britain.

Though all his films were extremely competent and technically accomplished, it was, perhaps, only in his Westerns that Anthony Mann made a distinctive contribution to the American cinema. They were among the first of the anti-romantic Westerns, in which heroes and villains were virtually indistinguishable in the way they behaved, and remote from the classic code-of-the-West stereotypes. For the best of them, if nothing else, Anthony Mann will continue to be remembered.

May 1, 1967.

Sir James Mann, K.C.V.O., who had served as Director of the Wallace Collection since 1936 and as Master of the Armouries at the Tower of London since 1939, died at his home in London on December 5, 1962. He had held the post of Surveyor of the Royal Works of Art since 1946. He was 65.

James Gow Mann, son of Alexander Mann, was born on September 23, 1897, and was educated at Winchester and New College, Oxford. He served in the First World War from 1916 to 1919 on the Flanders and Italian fronts, becoming a major in the Royal Artillery and joining the Territorial Reserve of Officers (Oxfordshire Yeomanry). In 1921 he took up the appointment of Assistant Keeper in the Department of Fine Art at the Ashmolean Museum, Oxford, and in 1924 went to the Wallace Collection as Assistant to the Keeper.

When the Courtauld Institute of Art was founded in 1931 he was appointed the Deputy Director and at the same time became Reader in the History of Art at London University. His organizing ability showed itself to great advantage in the early days of the new institute. He did not, however, stay there long, for on the death of S. J. Camp in 1936 he became Keeper and subsequently Director of the Wallace Collection. The appointment was appropriate for, though Mann's range as a scholar was exceptionally wide, he made himself a special authority on arms and armour, in which the Wallace Collection is particularly rich. Under his control much advantageous rearrangement of the collection took place. Sir James Mann was knighted in 1948, and created K.C.V.O. in 1957.

He was Director of the Society of Antiquaries of London from 1944 to 1949, and president from 1949 to 1954. In a busy life his voluntary services were often in demand and generously given to public bodies connected with art and antiquarian pursuits. He was chairman of the National Buildings Record, and served on the Advisory Committee of the Royal Mint, the Archbishop's Historic Churches Preservation Trust, and the Royal Commission of Historical Monuments (England). He was keenly interested in heraldry and was a trustee of the College of Arms. He helped to organize the exhibition of British Art at Burlington House in 1934, and visited Spain with Sir Frederic Kenyon at the request of the Spanish Government to inspect and report on the measures taken to safeguard art treasures in the Civil War. In 1942 he was chairman of the Red Cross Sales Committee for Works of Art, and from 1943 to 1946 he served as honorary secretary to the British Committee for the Restitution of Works of Art in Enemy Hands.

He found time to make many journeys abroad to investigate the state of foreign art treasures, and several of his reports were published in *The Times*—notably two articles on the Hermitage Museum, Leningrad in 1935, and articles on the collection of armour in the Vienna Hofburg in 1936, and on the war losses and survivals in the Italian territory in 1944.

Mann established himself as an authority on armour by his editing and translation of Count Trapp's catalogue of *The Armoury of the Castle of Churburg*, published in 1929. His linguistic and antiquarian gifts, his tact and scholarship, were well employed on this theme and his preface contributed to the book's importance. Shortly before he died he had completed a new catalogue of the European Arms and Armour at the Wallace Collection, a work which will remain a standard one on the subject. In 1951 he had published a catalogue of the sculpture in the collection. Other publications by Mann included treatises on Italian, Spanish and German armour of various periods, and a work on English church monuments of the sixteenth century.

He married in 1926 Mary, daughter of the Rev. Dr. G. A. Cooke. She died in 1956. There was one daughter of the marriage. In 1958 he married Evelyn Aimée, daughter of the late C. R. Hughes, of Wilmslow, Cheshire, who survives him.

December 7, 1962.

The Most Rev. Daniel Mannix, D.D., Roman Catholic Archbishop of Melbourne, who died on November 5, 1963, at the age of 99, was chosen for that See in the summer of 1912. At that time his reputation was academic; during the second part of his life it became that of a political prelate, but in his diocese he will be remembered above all as a pastor.

He was born at Charleville, in County Cork, on March 4, 1864, the son of Timothy Mannix and Ellen, *née* Cagney. Eamon de Valera was born in the same village 18 years later and attended the same school conducted there by the Christian Brothers. When he was President of Maynooth, where normally the professors are all priests, Mannix appointed de Valera to teach mathematics there, and for the rest of his life he remained de Valera's follower in political matters. The cross that surmounts the central spire on the Roman Catholic cathedral in Melbourne today was a gift from de Valera to Mannix, a contribution to the additions to the cathedral which Mannix made in 1939 to mark the centenary of the first Mass in Melbourne.

After a brilliant career as a student at Maynooth, Mannix was ordained there in 1890—the first priest to be ordained in the new chapel.

BISHOPS' CHOICE

He became junior professor of philosophy in the following year, and professor of theology in 1894. In 1903 the Irish bishops unanimously chose him as President; he had held that office only a few months when he received Edward VII there, and endeared himself to the king by festooning the college in the royal racing colours. It was during his presidency that Maynooth acquired the status of a university college and began to require its students to show competence in the arts before they could embark upon theology; he became a member of the Senate of the newly created National University of Ireland, of which Maynooth became one of the constituent colleges.

In the summer of 1912 he was appointed to be titular Archbishop of Pharsalus and Coadjutor of Melbourne with the right of succession, and on October 6 he was consecrated at Maynooth by Cardinal Logue. He reached Melbourne at Easter, 1913, and succeeded to the See four years later on the death of Archbishop Carr. He had been in Melbourne for only five years when Newman College, for lay students, was opened as a constituent college of the university there; the project had been initiated by his predecessor, but it was Mannix's enthusiasm which made it possible to collect the necessary funds and erect the buildings during the war years. St. Mary's Hall, for women students, followed soon afterwards.

Difficult before Mannix arrived, the relations between the Irish and other Australians became worse after the news of the Easter Week Rising of 1916, and he became Australia's chief spokesman for Sinn Fein. He vigorously led the opposition to conscription, which was rejected in two referendums. By 1917 he was saying that the war was a trade war between rival capitalists. By the end of the war the Australian Labour Party had become largely, although by no means exclusively, a party of Irish Catholics which looked to him for leadership.

In 1920, at the height of the troubles in Ireland, Mannix left Australia to make an *ad limina* visit to Rome, travelling by way of the United States and proposing then to visit Ireland. His reputation had preceded him; large and demonstrative audiences awaited him in San Francisco and in every city he visited in a coast-to-coast progress. At Omaha he met de Valera, who accompanied him to New York and sat with him on the platform at the final meeting in Madison Square Gardens. Extraordinary scenes marked his departure from New York on the liner Baltic on July 31; "there were hisses, cheers, fist fights, and the flash of revolvers," said the *New York Times*. From London *The Times* sent a radio message for Mannix in mid-Atlantic offering a column in which to print any message he cared to send, but he made no response.

Welcoming bonfires were lighted on the Irish coast, and the lights of Queenstown, where he proposed to land, were already in sight when two destroyers ordered the Baltic to stop. A boarding party presented Mannix with two documents: one, signed by Sir Nevile Macready as Commander-in-Chief in Ireland, forbade him to land in Ireland, and the other, signed by Field-Marshal Sir Henry Wilson, Chief of the Imperial General Staff, forbade him to visit the main centres of Irish population in England—Liverpool, Manchester, or Glasgow (D.O.R.A. was then still in force).

LANDED BY DESTROYER

Put ashore at Penzance by the destroyer Wyvern, he reached London on August 9. He went to Rome the following spring, afterwards visiting Australian war-graves in France, but it was not until May, 1921, that he finally left London to return to Australia by way of China and Japan.

During nine months spent mainly in England he spoke in many places, but less often and more temperately than the Government had expected. Archbishop Kelly of Sydney, calling at Downing Street, asked Lloyd George whether the Government had not erred in its estimation of Mannix through hearing only the snippets from his speeches that had been telegraphed to London; Dr. Kelly recorded afterwards that Lloyd George agreed. In Australia, the United States, and elsewhere there were strong protests at the treatment that Mannix had received. Lloyd George was embarrassed and would have liked him to go to Ireland after all, but mistook his moderation for a change of view and made the condition that he should support the treaty that was then being sought.

"I could have been in Ireland today," said Mannix in a speech in Lancashire in the spring of 1921, "if only I were to go over on the terms laid down by Mr. Lloyd George; but that condition I am never likely to fulfil." He eventually visited Ireland in 1925, when he was received enthusiastically but made few public speeches. He remained an opponent of the Free State and of the Treaty at least until de Valera entered the Dáil in 1927.

There were rumours in 1920 that Mannix had been reprimanded by the Holy See, but Gasparri, the Cardinal Secretary of State, made it clear that that was not so. Mannix, himself, when leaving New York in 1920, remarked that no one in England had complained about the patriotism of Cardinal Mercier. "Ireland," he claimed, "has just the same right as Belgium to say what form of government she will have." He was careful, moreover, to distinguish between his views as an Irishman and his teaching as a bishop of the Catholic church, and to emphasize, for example in opposing conscription, that Catholics were not necessarily expected to share personal opinions which he had every right to uphold.

In his later years, after the Second World War, his critics charged him with losing sight of this important distinction. Australian Catholic Action had originated in his diocese of Melbourne in 1937, largely under the impulse of the Catholic Congress with which he had marked Melbourne's civic centenary in 1934; and within a short space of years he was accustomed to say that it was one of the most highly developed systems of Catholic Action in the world. He was more confident of the justice of the allied cause in the Second World War than he had been in the first, and became a leading supporter of the Food for Britain campaign.

But before the end of 1939 he was maintaining that Russia was "enemy number one," and before the end of the war he was confident that Catholic Action in Australia had a very specific task in rallying the Labour Party and the trade unions against the extensive Communist penetration. One of the original lay leaders of Catholic Action in Melbourne sought to build up a political movement in which the cooperation of non-Catholics was welcomed.

This movement came into conflict with Dr. Evatt, the leader of the Australian Labour Party, especially after the Petrov case and its revelations of Communist infiltration in the Labour Party. But Mannix, who was 80 in 1944, was less and less in touch with these developments; although he was often identified with them, as when he was caricatured as "Archbishop Malone" in the widely-read novel, *Power Without Glory*, which appeared in 1951.

The National Secretariat for Catholic Action, established under him in Melbourne, was eventually wound up in 1954, the year in which he kept his ninetieth birthday, when it had been made clear by the Roman authorities that Catholic Action must not be allowed to acquire political commitments. What came then to be directed from Melbourne as the Catholic Social Movement was finally renamed at the end of 1957 as the National Civil Action Council, so that no one could mistake it for a movement under episcopal direction or control.

DAILY WALKS

Tall, lean and erect to the end, with a flashing eye and an impressive presence, Mannix daily walked the three miles between his residence and his cathedral until he was well advanced in his nineties, giving proof not only of good health but of patience with the numerous people who had long learnt to waylay him on that well-trodden path. He was a great orator, who seldom wrote pastoral letters but whose eloquence was reported at length, week after week for nearly half a century, in the columns of his diocesan weekly. The Catholics within his jurisdiction, predominantly of Irish origin, approached half a million by the time of his death; and, although he was more of a statesman than the reports reaching England 40 years ago would suggest, it is above all as a pastor that his people in Melbourne will remember him.

November 7, 1963.

Admiral Sir Maurice J. Mansergh, K.C.B., K.B.E., died on September 29, 1966, at his London home at the age of 69. He was largely concerned in the naval planning for the Normandy invasion and after the landing became Chief of Staff to the Allied Naval Commander. Later he was Fifth Sea Lord and Commander-in-Chief at Plymouth.

Maurice James Mansergh was born on October 14, 1896, the second son of Ernest Lawson Mansergh, M. Inst. C. E. He entered Osborne as a naval cadet from a preparatory school near Nuneaton in September, 1909. During the war of 1914–18 he was a midshipman in the battleship Zealandia in the Grand Fleet and at the Dardanelles, and sub-lieutenant and lieutenant in the destroyer Rigorous. After a commission in the gunboat Dwarf in West African waters he specialized in navigation. As a commander between 1931 and 1937 he served in the Admiralty Navigation Branch, qualified at the Staff College, was staff officer (operations) with the Commander-in-Chief in the Mediterranean, and executive officer of the Rodney. On promotion to captain he was selected for the Imperial Defence College course in 1938, and in January, 1939, became Assistant Director of Plans at the Admiralty.

When the Trade Division of the Naval Staff was revived four months later he was appointed Director of it, being responsible for the final preparation of the Merchant Navy for war and for the organization of the convoy system. In November, 1941, he took command of the cruiser Gambia in the Eastern Fleet, and was present in various operations, including the second attack on Madagascar and the protection of the 7th Australian Division on its return from the Middle East to Fremantle.

In June, 1943, he joined the staff of the late Admiral Sir Bertram Ramsay, Allied Naval Commander Expeditionary Force, as Deputy Chief of Staff and head planner for the coming invasion of Normandy. Three weeks after D-day in June, 1944, he became Chief of Staff in the rank of commodore first class, and went to France when General Eisenhower and Admiral Ramsay established their headquarters outside Paris. For his services towards the liberation of Europe he was mentioned in dispatches and received the C.B., the Legion of Honour and Croix de Guerre and the American Legion of Merit. He had been made C.B.E. in 1941.

CARRIER SQUADRON

In March, 1945, he returned to sea as Commodore commanding the 15th Cruiser Squadron in the Mediterranean, taking part in the closing stages of the campaign in Italy and the occupation of Trieste. Later that year he was for a short period Commodore-in-Charge in the Levant and Eastern Mediterranean, and afterwards Senior Naval Officer at Haifa, Palestine. In April, 1946, he was appointed Naval Secretary to the First Lord. He was given command in July, 1948, of the aircraft carrier squadron forming for service in the Home Fleet, with his flag in the Theseus. In the autumn of that year he took his squadron, augmented by four destroyers, on a goodwill visit to South Africa, and early in 1949 he took part in one of the first Western Union naval exercises.

In September, 1949, he was appointed Fifth Sea Lord and Deputy Chief of Naval Staff (Air). During the two years he held this post he was responsible for the building up of naval aviation at a time of important technical and operational development.

In October, 1951, he became Commander-in-Chief at Plymouth, until November, 1953. He was promoted to K.C.B. in 1952 and retired in 1954.

He married in April, 1921, Violet Elsie, younger daughter of Bernard Hillman, of Hove. They had two sons and two daughters.

October 3, 1966.

General Sir Robert Mansergh, G.C.B., K.B.E., M.C., Commander-in-Chief, United Kingdom Land Forces from 1956 to 1959, died on November 8, 1970. From 1953 to 1956 he was Commander-in-Chief Allied Forces, Northern Europe.

He became Colonel Commandant R.A. in 1950. Colonel Commandant R.H.A. in 1957, and Master Gunner, St. James's Park in 1960.

He was born on May 12, 1900, and educated at Rondebosch, South Africa. He was commissioned in the Royal Artillery from R.M.A. Woolwich in 1920. At the beginning of the Second World War he was a major and had been employed with the Iraq Army and as a member of British Military Mission in Iraq from 1931 to 1935. During this period he saw active service in Kurdistan, winning the Campaign Medal and Clasp and the Military Cross. In 1936–37 he was an instructor at the R.M.A. and Adjutant until 1939.

From the outbreak of hostilities in 1939, Mansergh was almost continuously on active service, mainly in the Middle and Far East.

In November 1940, while commanding a battery of the Surrey and Sussex Yeomanry, he served in Eritrea and Abysinnia, and later in the Western Desert with the 5th Indian Division subsequently famous for its work in the East Indies and Burma. For a short period he commanded the R.A. Base Depot in Egypt until promoted Colonel and appointed C.R.A. of the 5th Indian Division.

At the beginning of 1945 he commanded the 11th East African Division on the Burmese frontier for a few weeks, later returning in time to lead the 5th Indian Division in the advance down the Tiddim Road and the victorious campaign which ended in the capture of Rangoon and the liberation of Singapore.

Later the same year he commanded the troops in Eastern Java and in 1946 was promoted Commander of the 15th Indian Corps and Commander-in-Chief of the Allied Forces in the Netherlands East Indies.

In January 1947 he was appointed Director of the Territorial Army and Cadets, and from April 1948 to October 1949 was Military Secretary to the Secretary of State for War. He was then appointed to be Commander British Forces in Hongkong. He became Deputy Commander-in-Chief, Allied forces, Northern Europe in 1951 and two years later succeeded Admiral Brind as Commander-in-Chief.

He was unmarried.

November 10, 1970.

Jayne Mansfield, who was killed in a road accident near New Orleans on June 29, 1967, was, if not exactly one of the outstanding screen actresses of her day, at least a notable phenomenon on the Hollywood scene during the later 1950s and constantly likable for her steadfast refusal to take her appointed role as an American sex symbol too seriously. She was 33.

She was born Jayne Palmer in Brynmawr, Pennsylvania, on April 19, 1934. Her most obvious asset as a performer was the way she looked; in an era when the average American male's prime interest in a female glamour star was the blondeness of her hair and the magnitude of her bosom, Jayne Mansfield, blonder and better built than any, had all the hallmarks of an American dream come true. Her debut was nothing if not spectacular; in George Axelrod's play *Will Success Spoil Rock Hunter?* she was cast as one of the fruits of success, a Hollywood siren such as she was very rapidly herself to become. Meanwhile the cinema offered her small roles in big pictures like *Pete Kelly's Blues*, and the female lead in one adventurous low-budget feature, Paul Wendkos's *The Burglar*.

But for a Hollywood eager to find a rival to the immense popularity of Marilyn Monroe she was a godsend. Frank Tashlin first had the right idea, casting her to burlesque the sex-symbol in his eccentric comedy *The Girl Can't Help It* and having her re-create her Broadway success in the film of *Will Success Spoil Rock Hunter?* In these films she showed at least that she had a keen sense of the ridiculous which, properly harnessed, might have made her into the Mae West of the 1960s. Unfortunately it was not to be. Her latest dramatic role in Hollywood, in Victor Vicas's version of Steinbeck's *The Wayward Bus*, was not exactly striking, but film makers persisted in trying to make her play the vamp role straight, sometimes with memorable results of unconscious absurdity like *Too Hot to Handle*. She was better used in Stanley Donen's bitter comedy, *Kiss Them For Me*, but the film was not a success, and the only later film which captured some of her real qualities was the British-made parody Western *The Sheriff of Fractured Jaw*, in which she co-starred with Kenneth More.

Latterly she had worked less in films, and more as a night club performer, singer, and all-purpose show personality. She made a number of not particularly telling films in Europe, and earlier this year she began an ill-fated tour of English clubs.

Her first two marriages, to Paul Mansfield and to Mickey Hargitay, a former "Mr. Universe", were both dissolved. She had a daughter by her first marriage, a son and a daughter by her second, and a son by her third to theatrical agent, Matt Cimber.

In her private life she believed in living up fully to the old time star image: her much publicized Hollywood house had everything possible, pink and heart shaped, from beds and swimming pool to the grand piano. Absurd, obviously; but at least she knew it, and enjoyed the joke as much as anyone else. Show business will be decidedly less colourful without her.

June 30, 1967.

Sir Philip Manson-Bahr, C.M.G., D.S.O., for many years the leading consultant in tropical medicine in London, died on November 19, 1966.

Philip Henry Bahr, the son of Louis Bahr, of Oxted, Surrey, was born in Liverpool in 1881, was educated at Rugby and at Trinity College, Cambridge, where he took the Natural Science Tripos, specializing in zoology and subsequently acting as assistant to the Regius Professor Alfred Newton, the great ornithologist. He studied medicine at the London Hospital, qualified in 1907, and remained in that hospital in house appointments until 1909. At the London Hospital he met Edith Margaret, the daughter of Sir Patrick Manson "the Father of Tropical Medicine". An invitation to her father's house soon followed. Himself a keen naturalist, Manson quickly developed a strong interest in the young medical zoologist, an interest strengthened by Bahr's marriage to his daughter in 1909. After the death of Sir Patrick's son Philip, Bahr, at his father-in-law's suggestion, assumed by deed poll the surname of Manson-Bahr.

Between 1909 and 1912 Manson-Bahr took part in two expeditions to Fiji and Ceylon, laying down the foundation of his practical knowledge of clinical tropical medicine which launched him on his long career in practice in Harley Street—a practice interrupted only by service in Gallipoli and the Middle East in the First World War. During that war he rendered outstanding service with the R.A.M.C. especially in Palestine where he organized malaria diagnosis stations. He was awarded the D.S.O. and was promoted brevet-major. After demobilization he was appointed to the staff of the Albert Dock Hospital and lecturer at the London School of Tropical Medicine. He later became physician, in 1937, senior physician and subsequently consulting physician to the Hospital for Tropical Diseases. From 1937 until 1947 he was director of the clinical division of the London School of Hygiene and Tropical Medicine.

ADVANCES

In 1921 Manson-Bahr took over the editorship of Manson's *Textbook of Tropical Diseases*. He continued to edit and rewrite that leading textbook at frequent intervals throughout his working life. In a subject which developed so rapidly and expanded so widely the task of keeping abreast of advances in all parts of the world was an almost superhuman one but Manson-Bahr's great reserves of energy and his abounding enthusiasm were always equal to task. He developed an enormous practice in Harley Street and held nearly all possible public appointments in connexion with his subject. He was consulting physician to the Colonial Office and to the Crown Agents for the Colonies, consulting physician to the Admiralty and to the Air Force. He was made a C.M.G. in 1938 and knighted in 1941.

Throughout his life Manson-Bahr maintained his keen interest in zoology in general and in ornithology in particular. He served on the council of the Zoological Society and was president of the British Ornithologists Club. An enthusiastic artist, he was able to illustrate his own books and to delight audiences with examples of watercolour studies of scenes and wild life in Africa and the Pacific. He became president of the Medical Art Society.

He was Lumleian lecturer at the Royal College of Physicians in 1941. He devoted much time and enthusiasm to building up and fostering the Manson tradition. Manson House, the Manson medal, the Manson oration and the Manson lecture all owe much to the pious endeavours and filial devotion of Philip Manson-Bahr. A born raconteur, Manson-Bahr was an entertaining lecturer, drawing material from a great wealth of clinical experience and sending his hearers away ready for more. Physically a big man, tall and heavily built, with a voice to match his frame, he will be remembered with gratitude by thousands of patients, students and friends in every corner of the globe.

Lady Manson-Bahr died in 1948. They had one son and three daughters. He subsequently married Edith Mary Grossmith.

November 21, 1966.

Juan March, the Majorcan banker and industrialist, who had been a powerful voice behind the scenes in Spanish affairs for many years, died in Madrid on March 10, 1962 from injuries received in a road accident on February 25.

He was *par excellence* the self-made man, tough, shrewd, flexible, gifted with the power and will to survive.

He was born of humble stock—it was said his father was a pig-dealer—at Palma, Majorca, in 1882, and it was generally accepted that the basis of this multi-millionaire's fortune was his early interest in the contraband traffic between North Africa and Spain which led to his acquiring a very profitable tobacco monopoly in that area. His interests throve and extended and he became the owner of ships in the Mediterranean and acquired a dominating control of complex business activities in Spain.

When he was 44 he founded the Banca March in Palma, and was elected a Deputy to the Cortes for that Majorcan constituency during the Republic. He came under bitter attacks in the Cortes where it was alleged that his tobacco monopoly in North Africa was illegal. A "Commission of Responsibilities" had Juan March put in gaol in June, 1932. He escaped from the Alcala de Henares prison in September, 1933, and dashed by car to Gibraltar, taking his guard with him.

He later lived in France and Switzerland and thereafter it was said he kept in touch with the Spanish military leaders who were conspiring against the republic. Juan March's financial support for the movement launched in July, 1936, under the leadership of General Franco was especially important. It is generally believed that this remarkable figure underwrote many of the first shipments of arms to Majorca and later to the mainland which Hitler and Mussolini supplied to the Franco side in the Civil War.

CASH FOR INDUSTRIES

Under the present regime Juan March amassed great wealth through his investments in so many concerns which have been developed in the industrialization of Spain. Shipping, mining, steelworks, construction materials, banking, tobacco, oil, refineries, motor cars and hydro-electric power are among the industries into which millions of pesetas steadily flowed from the exchequer of Spain's leading capitalist.

In 1955 the Juan March Foundation was set up in Spain under a trust established by the Majorcan banker to which he made various grants of millions of pesetas. Its object is to give annual awards to Spaniards who in their lifetime have made the greatest contribution to literature, history, art, physics, sociology, medicine, law, chemistry, science and theology. The creation of this foundation brought him the nickname of the "Spanish Rockefeller".

His latest grant to it was made in the hospital the day after the accident near Madrid in which he was seriously injured. The grant totalled 1,000m. pesetas (nearly £6m.) which brings the total capital of the Foundation to 2,000m. pesetas (some £12m.).

March 12, 1962.

Rocky Marciano, former undefeated heavyweight champion of the world, died in an aircraft crash on August 31, 1969, in Iowa. It was the eve of his 46th birthday. Marciano was the undefeated heavyweight champion from 1952 to his retirement in 1956.

No boxer had more to do with the brief revival of the sport in the 1950s after the immediate postwar boom. As the heavyweights go, so goes boxing, and Marciano, as world heavyweight champion, was such an exciting fighter, such a throwback to the days of blood and glory of Jack Dempsey, that boxing in the United States regained much of its popularity.

Marciano, born Rocco Marchegiano on September 1, 1923, in Brockton, Massachusetts, had the perfect professional record of 49 bouts and 49 victories when he retired as undefeated champion of the world on April 27, 1956, to devote himself to business interests and managing the occasional heavyweight hope.

He turned professional in 1947, but when he went to Britain after his retirement he confirmed to *The Times* boxing correspondent, Neil Allen, that he first thought of taking up the sport when he was a serviceman in Britain during the war. It was in a pub brawl that he knocked out an Australian soldier with his famed right hand punch which was later nicknamed Suzi Q.

Marciano, skilfully managed by Al Weill and trained by Charley Goldstein, was a crude fighter in his early bouts but gradually he was taught how to defend his 5 ft. 11 in., 13 st. 4 lb. frame against taller, heavier opponents.

In October, 1951, he was matched with the former world champion, Joe Louis, and though Louis was by then well past his best, the victory of the young, bull-like Italian in the 10th round made Marciano a big name in the market.

SAVAGE BOUT

After four more victories inside the distance Marciano challenged the veteran Jersey Joe Walcott for the world title on September 23, 1952. It was the most savage heavyweight championship of the last 20 years, with Marciano knocked down in the opening round and both men later suffering cuts by the eyes. But in the 13th round Marciano produced a devastating right hand to the head which left Walcott on the canvas without the title.

Subsequently Marciano defended his title against Walcott (in less than a round), Roland La Starza, Ezzard Charles twice, Don Cockell of Britain—who lasted nearly nine rounds in 1955—and Archie Moore. Marciano was taken the full distance of 15 rounds in the first bout with Charles, and was knocked down by Moore before finishing off the skilful light heavyweight champion in the ninth. But eventually there were no more worlds to conquer and a healthy bank balance and family pressure caused The Rock to retire.

It is impossible to compare the ability of boxers who never met at their best. But there are those who believe Marciano was among the greatest of heavyweight champions. Neil Allen considered Louis, Cassius Clay, Jack Dempsey and Gene Tunney at their best would have beaten him. But what one can say finally is that Marciano, vicious in the ring but the mildest of men outside the ropes, was the greatest small heavyweight. No other title-holder in this division in the last 60 years measured less than 6ft. in height. Marciano made up for lack of inches in heart.

September 2, 1969.

Sir Milton Margai, M.B.E., M.L.C., the first Prime Minister of Sierra Leone, who died on April 28, 1964, was born at Gbangbatoke in the Banta chiefdom of the Moyamba district of Sierra Leone on December 7, 1895. A Mende by tribe, he was educated first at the Evangelical United Brethren Missions Schools at Gbangbatoke and Bonthe. He was then sent to the Albert Academy, Freetown, and to Fourah Bay College, (which was then in special relation to the University of Durham) in 1917. He left for the United Kingdom in July, 1920, and entered King's College, where he graduated M.B., B.S. (Durham) in 1926, the first African from the protectorate to do so.

While in England he married, but his wife did not return with him to Sierra Leone. After a short period of private practice, he entered the Government Medical Service in 1928, and retired in 1950. He was widely known as a highly skilled doctor and his most notable achievement was the introduction of modern hygiene into the methods used by the secret woman's society, the Sande, which practices clitherectomy, and he also introduced mothercraft, baby-care and instruction in anatomy into its curriculum.

PEOPLE'S RIGHTS

He wrote a *Primer on Midwifery* and *A Catechism on Midwifery* for local use.

He had, for some time, taken an interest in politics, and in 1946 he was elected to Bonthe district council and entered the Protectorate Assembly. He was concerned to uphold the rights of the Protectorate tribes, and notably his own people, the Mende, against what he regarded as suppression by the Creole political leaders of the Colony area. The Protectorate, which was numerically far stronger, had a relatively smaller representation in the legislature.

He advised the chief to press for a bigger voice in Legco, and this led to the formation of the Sierra Leone People's Party of which Dr. Margai was and stayed the leader. In 1948 he established, at the Protectorate headquarters, Bo, the *Sierra Leone Observer*, to put out the S.L.P.P. view.

Earlier, he had founded the Sierra Leone Organization Society which, beginning as a cultural movement, became the backbone of the S.L.P.P. after merging with the Protectorate Educational Progressive Union.

CREOLE OPPOSITION

In the 1951 general election, the S.L.P.P. won a resounding victory, and Dr. Margai was elected leader of the party as well as parliamentary leader. Since then he held the portfolios of Health, Agriculture and Forestry, and in 1954 became Chief Minister. Thus, there came to power in Sierra Leone a man and a party which did not derive its primary strength, as in most African colonies, from anti-colonial movements and a discontented nationalist intelligentsia.

The counterparts of Dr. Nkrumah in Ghana or President Sékou Touré in neighbouring Guinea sat in opposition to Dr. Margai until his party gradually absorbed most of them; but the opposition is still strongly Creole.

The S.L.P.P., under Dr. Margai's leadership (which was once or twice challenged, but vainly, from within), moved towards independence with notable caution; Dr. Margai himself used to say that it was "natural" for Sierra Leone, because of its weaker economy, to be about five years in evolution behind the Gold Coast. In fact, the country became independent on July 9, 1960, with Sir Milton, who was knighted in 1959, as its first prime minister.

Sir Milton set his face against any violent changes, kept all the British civil servants he could, and in African and foreign affairs aligned himself with Nigeria and Liberia rather than Ghana.

JOIN WITH BRITAIN

He took Sierra Leone into the Monrovia Group, which existed before the Addis Ababa conference of 1963, which Sir Milton also attended. Before the failure of British efforts to enter the Common Market, he indicated that Sierra Leone would enter with Britain, at a time when Nigeria, Ghana and East Africa were opposing any alignment with the E.E.C.

In this approach, Sir Milton was criticized by his younger followers, but he maintained his grip both on the party and the country to the last. He dealt, for example, with the disorders in the northern chieftaincies, and later gaoled members of the opposition for sedition in 1962. But opposition, free speech, democracy and general elections all have survived in Sierra Leone, and "the Doctor" remained a beloved figure, if sometimes a criticized one.

As a politician he was not dynamic, but he knew his people, and was shrewd, common sensical, and diplomatic. He lacked oratorical gifts, but he knew how to choose men and what, and to whom, to delegate.

He worked closely with his able and politically more radical legal brother, Albert Margai, but also curbed his ambitions. His contribution towards the cultural life of Sierra Leone was considerable, and he gave generously of time and money in arranging exhibitions and encouraging artists and craftsmen.

He organized youth clubs and promoted sport; at 63, he still played a vigorous game of tennis, and he played the piano and violin. In manner he was deceptively mild.

Behind his relaxed manner his brain worked swiftly and ruthlessly, and he was quite unafraid of complaints that he lacked true nationalistic fervour. He was without prejudice and could be caustic over the pretensions of the great "African personalities" contemporary with himself. He was affectionately known as "The Doctor" and had a personality which time is likely to enhance.

April 29, 1964.

Lord Margesson, P.C., M.C., died at Nassau, in the Bahamas, on December 24, 1965. He was 75.

Through two decades Margesson had been an inconspicuous member of the House of Lords, attending frequently but giving the impression of observing the proceedings rather as a moderately disinterested spectator from the sidelines. But there were many there who had known him in the days of his prime as a most powerful and dominating figure in the House of Commons and also as Secretary of State for War in Churchill's wartime Coalition Government. Captain David Margesson, as he then was, will be remembered mainly as the Government Chief Whip who held that key office in the fateful years that led through the ruins of "appeasement" to the Second World War.

Lean, dark, elegant and strikingly handsome David Margesson was a man of forceful personality and he was often spoken of as having been the most powerful Chief Whip since the Master of Elibank, in the Liberal Government of 1906. He was dictatorial, even ruthless, in his methods —and although he was a man with a host of friends he also made enemies. In the military tradition that had moulded him he was a rigid disciplinarian. He always saw his duty plain as requiring him to give unstinted loyalty to the Prime Minister of the day and to see to it that the members of his party voted in the right lobby when the division bells rang.

Margesson served in the Conservative Whips' Office for about 14 years and for the greater part of that time—from 1931 to 1940—he was the Government Chief Whip. He held that post under four Prime Ministers—Ramsay MacDonald, Baldwin, Neville Chamberlain, and Churchill. It was during Baldwin's third Premiership, from 1935 to 1937, and even more so during the three succeeding years when Chamberlain was Prime Minister, that Margesson was seen at the height of his powers. Conservative M.P.s of an independent turn of mind who presumed to quarrel with Ministers about high policy were regarded by Margesson as an "awkward squad" who had to be tolerated, or, if possible, dragooned. Life was not made easier for him by the fact that he had among his flock such eminent political nonconformists as Winston Churchill and Anthony Eden.

THE INDIA BILL TUSSLE

In the Parliament of 1931–35 Margesson had to cope with the Conservative "die-hard" opposition to the Government of India Bill led by Churchill, which was of formidable dimensions. In the next Parliament the resignation of Eden (now Lord Avon) from the Foreign Office in 1938 and his subsequent association with Churchill and others as persistent critics of Chamberlain's appeasement policy confronted Margesson with new problems in maintaining adequate support for the Government. He had a sharp tongue and it was he who was thought to have dubbed the backbench Conservatives who backed Eden as "the glamour boys".

When the war came Margesson continued as Chief Whip. He loyally backed Chamberlain throughout—but even all the resources that he could deploy in marshalling men into the lobbies could not prevent the Conservative defection at the end of the Norway campaign in May, 1940, that brought down Chamberlain and led to the installation of Churchill as his successor at the head of the Coalition Government. The new Prime Minister was magnanimous to the man who had regarded him in the past as the Conservative Party's arch-rebel. Margesson was allowed to continue as Parliamentary Secretary to the Treasury and Chief Government Whip, although he now held this office jointly with Sir Charles Edwards, the former Chief Whip of the Labour Party. Six months later Churchill carried his magnanimity even farther and appointed Margesson to be Secretary of State for War, after Eden had returned to the Foreign Office. At that time Margesson was serving in such scanty leisure as he had, as a private in the Palace of Westminster Company of the Home Guard. His officers and comrades alike derived some wry amusement from the fact that it was necessary to discharge this private on his appointment as Secretary of State for War.

AT THE WAR OFFICE

The choice of Margesson for the War Office was a surprise and, as Churchill wrote in his War Memoirs, "excited some adverse comment" But Churchill knew that though he and Margesson had had many sharp passages Margesson would none the less give him the same skilful and faithful service that he had given to his predecessors; he was not disappointed.

Margesson remained at the War Office for 18 months. His period of service there coincided with further setbacks for British arms in North Africa and the eastern Mediterranean. There were uneasy rumblings in the House of Commons and a demand for some ministerial changes. Margesson was abruptly relieved of this office in the spring of 1942 and had what must have been the unique experience of being succeeded as Secretary of State by his own Permanent Under-Secretary, Sir James Grigg. On leaving the War Office Margesson was raised to the peerage as the first Viscount Margesson of Rugby. He had represented Rugby as its Conservative member in the House of Commons from 1924 to 1942. Before that he had been Conservative member for the Upton division of West Ham from 1922 to 1923.

Henry David Reginald Margesson was the son of Sir Mortimer Margesson and was born on July 26, 1890. Educated at Harrow and Magdalene College, Cambridge, he served in the 1914–18 War and won the Military Cross. He became adjutant of the 11th Hussars and retired with the rank of captain. In 1916 he married Frances, daughter of F. H. Leggett, of New York. They had one son and two daughters. In 1940 the marriage was dissolved. Margesson was first elected to the House of Commons at the age of 32 and he became an Assistant Whip in 1924. Thus began his long association with the Conservative Whips' Office in the House. He became a Junior Lord of the Treasury in 1926 and in November, 1931, under the first National Government, he succeeded Sir Bolton Eyres-Monsell (later Viscount Monsell) as Parliamentary Secretary to the Treasury and Government Chief Whip. With his departure from the War Office and his acceptance of a peerage in 1942 Margesson's political career virtually ended. He left the Commons, where he had spent nearly 20 years of his life, with real regret.

His heir is his son, the Hon. Francis Vere Hampden Margesson.

December 28, 1965.

Queen Marie of Yugoslavia—See under **Yugoslavia**
Princess Marina—See under **Princess.**

Lord Marks of Broughton, who died in London on December 8, 1964, at the age of 76, was one of the great formative influences in the social and economic life of England during the past generation. His dynamic and imaginative reform of the retail trade reached its climax coincidentally with the arrival of the welfare state and the affluent society. It was through the firm of which he was the head that the new classes, brought into being by this social revolution, were able to meet many of their needs, particularly in smart and tasteful dress at prices that they could afford. A man of wide and liberal interests, he was modest in manner, a good talker and companion.

To the man in the street he will be remembered as the real initiator of high quality, low cost clothes and, at a later stage, even food. The secret of this retail revolution, hammered out by Marks & Spencer over several years, was not so widely apparent. It was based on a simple principle: that the main function of the retailer was to tell the manufacturer what the public needed. Both he and Israel Sieff, who married each other's sisters and became life partners in business, learnt the lesson in the United States and persistently bullied, cajoled, and persuaded manufacturers to make what they knew they could sell.

Lord Marks of Broughton was born on July 9, 1888, son of Michael and Hannah Marks. He was educated at Manchester Grammar School. On the unexpected and early death of his father in 1906 he went into the family business, Marks and Spencer Ltd., and for the rest of his life a major interest was the direction and development of the firm.

Marks and Spencer Ltd. had been founded by Michael Marks in Leeds market in 1884. By the time that the young Simon Marks took over it was already a thriving chain of bazaar stores based on the principle of a fixed price.

'IT'S A PENNY'

"Don't ask the price, it's a penny" was the firm's slogan. The firm continued to prosper under its new management, but the first World War inevitably changed the whole approach to trading of this type. Simon Marks was called into the forces but was released to work with Chaim Weizmann on various Government projects. This association served to strengthen his already great interest in the cause of Zionism.

With the peace the firm again became his major interest. The fixed price principle had had to be abandoned and major changes in the philosophy of the business had to be devised. Following several visits to the United States to study merchandising methods there, in the late twenties Simon Marks began the main work of the development of a type of store new to this country and probably unique in the world. His approach was firmly based on certain principles. They were that there should be a ceiling to prices—in this case 5s.—and that it was a main function of the retailer to tell the manufacturer what was needed in the way of design and quality. This latter approach was the most fundamental change and it took many years, often in the face of opposition, to educate suppliers to accept this. By the outbreak of the Second World War the principles of specification buying were well established. Indeed, such was the value of these that some of them were adopted by the Cloth Control as specifications for the standard cloths which were introduced. In particular this was the case with certain types of rayon cloth.

Again war caused fundamental changes. The price limit principle had to be abandoned once more, and has not since returned. Since 1945 the growth of the company has been based very firmly on the principle of giving maximum value for money. These values were obtained by setting high and rigid standards of manufacture for suppliers. These standards were based on much research and testing of new products and new production methods. This applied particularly in the field of synthetic fibres and, more recently, in food manufacture. It was always Simon Marks's policy that the firm should have its own extensive research and testing facilities. Through these new developments in materials and production techniques could be translated into saleable merchandise as soon as possible. In recent years, under his inspiration, big advances have been made in the food fields where the basic principles of hygiene and quality control of materials led to the development of a range of products which have become very popular with the shopping public. The standard of shopping facilities offered to the public was always foremost in his mind and the results are shown in the present standards of Marks and Spencer stores.

Simon Marks was an inspiring leader, although he could at times be exacting. He had a genius for merchandise selection and for merchandising. He had the ability to select executives of the right calibre to carry out his ideas.

HUMAN BOSS

He was attentive to detail and was daily to be seen in one or other of the stores, discussing with the sales girls in particular the needs of the public and their reaction to the merchandise. He was the most human of employers and the welfare and other arrangements for employees was outstanding. A man of great humility, he was very proud indeed when he was given the Tobe award in 1962 for distinguished contributions to retailing, especially as this was the first time that this award had been given to a retailer operating outside the United States.

Apart from business Simon Marks's range of interests was wide. These included in particular Zionism and the State of Israel. His early association with Weizmann lasted until the latter's death. He took a most active part in all the problems involved with the new state of Israel and his contribution to industrial, commercial and scientific developments there was crucial.

Since the formation of the new State he made many visits there and his advice was always available and much sought.

His interest always included science and the application of scientific developments to practical purposes. During the Second World War he gave valuable service to the Scientific Coordination Committee. He was knighted in 1944 and created a Baron in 1961, assuming the title of Baron Marks of Broughton of Sunningdale. He was an honorary Fellow of the Royal College of Surgeons and of the Weizmann Rehovath Institute of Israel. London University granted him an honorary D.Sc. (Economics) in 1939 and Manchester made him an honorary LL.D. in 1962.

In private life he was a family man and ideal host, with an exceptional range of friends; he was particularly fond of the young, and in his later days was happiest when surrounded by his grandchildren.

BIG GIFTS

Marks was a generous and discriminating philanthropist. In 1956 he gave £52, 500, spread over seven years, to the Royal College of Surgeons. A little over a year later he gave £100,000 to the college. Other gifts included £7,000 to the R.A.F. Benevolent Fund and £50,000 to Manchester Grammar School—his old school—for new science laboratories.

He gave £60,000 towards the refectory at University College London, and later in 1962 £100,000 to University College.

The following year he arranged for the British Heart Foundation to receive gifts totalling £200,000.

He is survived by his widow, a son, and a daughter.

December 9, 1964.

The Duchess of Marlborough, C.B.E., died on May 23, 1961, at Blenheim Palace at the age of 61 after a long illness.

She was the Hon. Alexandra Mary Cadogan, fourth daughter of Henry Arthur Viscount Chelsea (1868–1908) and granddaughter of the fifth Earl Cadogan, and she was born on February 22, 1900. Queen Alexandra was one of her godmothers.

Her marriage to the Marquess of Blandford, which took place at St. Margaret's, Westminster, in February, 1920, a few days before the bride's twentieth birthday, was an occasion of some splendour. King George, Queen Mary, the Princess Royal (Princess Louise Duchess of Fife). Queen Alexandra, Princess Mary, and Princess Victoria were all present and other notable guests were Mr. Balfour, Mr. Winston Churchill (both of whom signed the register in company with the King and Queen), Mrs. Churchill, Lady Randolph Churchill, Lord and Lady Curzon of Kedleston, and Mrs. Asquith. Miss Sarah Churchill was one of the child bridesmaids.

Her husband succeeded his father as tenth Duke of Marlborough in 1934 and they made their home in a wing of the palace at Woodstock. She once said "All those who come to be connected with Blenheim feel a pride that they never really lose", and certainly she was proud that thousands of visitors came to see the historic mansion every year and proud of its use as a setting for two fashion shows in 1954 and 1958; uses which Vanbrugh, its architect, never dreamed of but which he, with his eye for effect, might well have appreciated. She organized both shows to raise money for the British Red Cross Society, an abiding interest.

HOSPITALS AND HOMES

She had joined the society as a V.A.D. member in the 1914–18 War and worked in a London hospital. She joined the Oxfordshire branch of the society in her first year at Woodstock and became its president seven years later.

In the war of 1939–45 she helped to administer eight Red Cross auxiliary hospitals and convalescent homes in the county, and found temporary accommodation for thousands of patients' relatives and houses for London children evacuated during the flying-bomb raids. She became an executive committee member of the Red Cross in 1944, a council member in 1950 and an honorary life member in 1954. For her work she was made C.B.E. in 1953.

The Duchess designed a new uniform for Red Cross women in 1958, and had the first one made for herself. She did away with the belt and military style patch pockets in favour of a slim-fitting navy blue suit, white blouse, and Red Cross brooch. Although the Red Cross and hospital work were her main interest (she was chairman of the Nuffield Orthopaedic Centre at Oxford for 23 years) she was active in local government, served as county magistrate and found time for a business career.

She was mayor of Woodstock from 1946 to 1951. As mayor she ran the British restaurant and was instrumental in ridding the town of eyesore advertisements. When Sir Winston Churchill, her kinsman by marriage, received the honorary freedom of Woodstock, it was she who presented him with the parchment. She served with her husband on Woodstock Borough Council until ill-health caused her retirement this year.

FLAIR FOR ORIGINAL

The Duchess was director of a West End firm of travel agents and was largely responsible for the organization necessary when Blenheim was opened to the public. She was not one to stand on ceremony and had a flair for the unexpected. Typically, when the new Oxford speedway track was opened in 1949, she rode round it on a pillion.

She is survived by her husband, two sons and three daughters.

May 24, 1961.

Dr. James William Slesser Marr—"Scout Marr", who died on April 29, 1965, was born at Coynachie, Aberdeenshire, on December 9, 1902. He was educated at Aberdeen Grammar School and Aberdeen University.

In 1919 he was awarded the Scout Silver Medal and the Bronze Medal of the Royal Humane Society for saving bathers from drowning. When 18 he was chosen to take part in the Shackleton—Rowett Antarctic expedition in the Quest under Sir Ernest Shackleton. He returned to Aberdeen to finish his M.A. in classics in 1924 and B.Sc. in zoology in 1925. Later that year he took part in the British Arctic Expedition in Iceland under Captain F.A. Worsley. He described the plants of West Spitzbergen, Franz Josef Land, and North-east Land in the *Journal of Botany* (1927), and described the richness of the sea bottom fauna in the zoological section of Worsley's book *Under Sail in the Frozen North*.

After a year as Carnegie scholar with the Scottish Fishery Board he was appointed zoologist in the Discovery investigations concerned with the biology and migratory habits of whales and the detailed inquiry into the natural resources of the Antarctic Ocean required for attempts to place the whaling industry on a scientific basis. In this service he took part in three expeditions to the Antarctic, in 1927–29, 1931–33 and 1935–37. He was also seconded to the British, Australian and New Zealand Antarctic research expedition under Sir Douglas Mawson in 1929–30 in charge of oceanography. He made a further voyage in a whale factory in 1939–40.

His principal war service was in Iceland, Scapa Flow, the Eastern Fleet, and South Africa. In 1943–45 he organized and commanded advance parties of the Falkland Islands Dependencies Survey in the Grahamland region of Antarctica. Although best known for his work in the Antarctic, for which he was three times awarded the Polar Medal, his achievements in marine biology are likely to prove even more remarkable.

ANTARCTIC KRILL

His infinite care with the preservation of deep sea animals made the Discovery's laboratory a treasure house of beautiful specimens. He was just as careful with the long and often arduous work of sampling the Antarctic Krill, on which the Antarctic whales feed, and the results of his work appeared in an impressive volume three years ago. It covers in detail the seasonal distribution of all developmental stages of this euphausiid which feeds the Antarctic whales, seals, penguins, other birds and fishes so that its life history is probably better known than that of any other pelagic invertebrate.

He was the first to admit that his remarkable conclusions about the way in which such enormous abundance is maintained and protected from depredation in its early stages need further observations at special times and places and he presents a clear challenge to those who will follow him. An American reviewer describes this report on krill as natural history at its best. His other publications include an account of the South Orkney Islands and of the bottom living fauna of the Antarctic continental shelf.

All his writing was done with a zest for the subject which makes it a genuine pleasure to read. Since 1949 he had continued his work as a Principal Scientific Officer at the National Institute of Oceanography.

Marr married in 1937 Dorothea Helene, fourth daughter of the late G. F. Plutte of Sydenham, who survives him with five of their six children.

May 1, 1965.

Herbert Marshall, who died on January 22, 1966, in Hollywood at the age of 75, will be remembered as one of Hollywood's leading English actors during the thirties, who also enjoyed a long and successful career in the theatre.

As a film actor in Hollywood during the early days of the sound film, Marshall enjoyed several advantages over his American rivals. He had charm, polish and a quiet assurance; a cultured and pleasant voice; and he fitted easily and naturally into any background of sophistication and gentility. He also had a flair for light comedy, which he revealed in one of his earliest talking pictures, Ernst Lubitsch's brilliant satire, *Trouble in Paradise*, in which he played opposite to Kay Francis and Miriam Hopkins. He was a romantic actor of dignity and restraint—qualities which showed up excellently under good direction, but could become a little wooden and unemotional when inspiration was lacking.

Herbert Brough Falcon Marshall was born in London on May 23, 1890. He started work with a firm of chartered accountants in the City, but deserted this career for the stage, and made his first appearance in 1911, at the Opera House, Buxton, as a servant in *The Adventure of Lady Ursula*; and his first appearance in London in 1913, when he played Tommy in *Brewster's Millions*.

He served in the First World War and lost a leg, but was able to renew his stage career in 1918. During the next 15 years, until Hollywood monopolized his services, he appeared in a large number of plays both in London and New York. His first film was an English silent picture called *Mumsie*, directed by Herbert Wilcox and with Pauline Frederick and Nelson Keys in the cast.

SOUND FILM REPEATS

In 1929 he went to Hollywood to play in a sound adaptation of Maugham's *The Letter*—and incidentally was also seen in the remake of this in 1940, when he played the husband opposite Bette Davis. He made several talking pictures in England during the early thirties, but was placed under contract to Paramount in 1932, for whom he made *Secrets of a Secretary*, *Blonde Venus*, with Marlene Dietrich, *Trouble in Paradise*, and *Evenings for Sale*. He then returned to England to appear with Madeleine Carroll and Conrad Veidt in *I Was a Spy*, one of the best of the early British sound films, but returned to Hollywood again, where he made a number of films during the next 10 years. Of these the best were probably *The Dark Angel*, a Goldwyn production with Merle Oberon and Fredric March, *A Woman Rebels*, *A Bill of Divorcement* (with Katherine Hepburn), *Foreign Correspondent*, *The Little Foxes*, under William Wyler's direction, with Bette Davis, and *The Moon and Sixpence*, with George Sanders. In *The Painted Veil* he played opposite Greta Garbo.

He was five times married: with his second wife, Edna Best, he played in many popular productions including *Michael and Mary*, *The Swan*, and *There's Always Juliet*, in both London and New York.

January 24, 1966.

Basil Kingsley Martin, who died in hospital in Cairo, after a stroke, on February 16, 1969, at the age of 71, was a natural nonconformist whose lively personality found full and complete expression in an editorial chair.

Until he had reached his middle thirties he had done nothing to show that he was different from the rank and file of dons and journalists. Then, thanks largely to the Webbs, he was appointed, in the face of stiff competition, to succeed Clifford Sharp as editor of the *New Statesman*. The timing of the choice was perfect. Kingsley Martin was just the man to interpret the apprehensive, chip-on-shoulder mood of left wingers in the thirties. He took over in 1931 (the year the *New Statesman* was amalgamated with the *Nation*) and, before the Spanish Civil War had flared up, he had proved himself to be one of the most effective editors of a weekly paper in the history of English journalism.

EASILY STIRRED

The *New Statesman* became from cover to cover a reflection of its editor as much as the Edwardian *Spectator* had been of St. Loe Strachey and the *Nation* of Massingham. Highly strung, easily moved to rage and fear, interested in all sides of life, devoted to argument, delightful in his frequent moments of gaiety, Kingsley Martin contrived to pack all of himself into his paper. He won loyal readers for it, especially among the young. He attracted, too—sure sign of a good editor—a large public that was exasperated by the points of view aired in the *New Statesman* but could not resist its compelling readability. One of his strengths was that he allowed all branches of the paper to grow. The standard of literary criticism under him was so high that it drew people who loathed its politics. War and the advent of age did not diminish Kingsley Martin's effervescence. He remained, even in retirement and after in ill-health, a vivid individual. His mobile features and restless eyes would light up as ideas were exchanged and challenged. He could listen as well as talk.

J. B. Priestley has rightly said of Kingsley Martin that this is his age: "He might have bespoke it." He was, in fact, a kind of born *New Statesman* reader writ large. It has been argued that he was obsessed by grievance and guilt. J. M. Keynes said in a letter to him that, though it would be an injustice, he had at one time felt like saying: "You seem to love a grievance and to love nothing else." There was some truth in this; indeed as one leafed through the N.S. & N. one could experience a feeling akin to that felt by Uncle Matthew in *The Pursuit of Love* after the fastidious Davy had expressed criticism, among other things, of the family collection of minerals. "Damned fella, nothing's right for him." Martin acknowledged this in some sort when he wrote: "I combined in myself most of the inconsistencies of a period which tried to reconcile pacifism with collective security and the defence of individual liberty with the necessity of working with the Communists against Fascism."

It is difficult to assess exactly the influence of the *New Statesman* under Martin, but if to reflect the views of a whole generation and to provoke and stimulate intelligent discussion is influence then he and his paper had it. In his hands the *New Statesman* became compulsory reading at Cabinet level in many western countries and in senior common rooms all over the world.

CIRCULATION TREBLED

Under Martin's editorship the circulation of the *New Statesman* rose from about 15,000 in 1931 to 30,000 in 1939 and then to about treble that figure by the end of the Second World War. He was fortunate to have behind him the robust and optimistic figure of John Roberts who was first manager and then managing director of the *New Statesman*.

He was a shrewd technical editor unmoved when people told him that they "only read the back half of the paper" beginning with the highly individual small ads about Unitarians, meetings of protest, the desire of progressives to meet other progressives and books and pamphlets of a kind not always found on public bookstalls, and working back through the competitions and reviews. He rightly guessed that these Part II readers were becoming secret *New Statesman* addicts. It was not his view that the literary side of the paper should square at all points with the Socialist doctrine of the editorials. He rightly let his brilliant writers—and they included Raymond Mortimer, Desmond MacCarthy, V. S. Pritchett, G. W. Stonier, Robert Lynd, Edward Sackville-West and T. C. Worsley—have their heads.

Born on July 28, 1897, the son of a Unitarian minister, he went to Mill Hill. During the 1914–18 War he was a conscientious objector, serving as a hospital orderly in France. Then he went up to Magdalene College, Cambridge, where he read history and became a Bye-fellow.

L.S.E. POST

G. P. Gooch encouraged him to follow an academic career and from 1923 to 1927 he held an assistant lectureship in political science at the London School of Economics. But teaching was not his true line. Nor was leader writing. This he did from 1927 until 1931 on the *Manchester Guardian*. He never fitted quite happily into the company of "M.G." men, who in those days were still of the C.P. Scott school. For Kingsley Martin traditional liberalism was a strait-jacket and it cramped him. The *New Statesman* gave him the freedom he needed.

As a writer his style was so distinctive that

it showed through anonymity. He was a master of the difficult art of turning out a weekly diary of gossip and comment. Signed Critic, it is doubtful if this feature was excelled in any other comparable periodical and for many old *New Statesman* readers it was the best thing of the week, reflecting as it did the stamp of his personality and thought. Though inevitably it touched on ideological conflict and political controversy it was never monopolized by these, for, as he said, "I was also interested in many things that were not political such as gardening, cats, people, foreign countries, chess, sex problems, prisons and the passing scene in the villages of Little Easton and Charing Cross".

He wrote several books, all of which are readable and provocative. *The Triumph of Palmerston*, 1924, republished with an additional chapter in 1963; *The British Public and the General Strike*; *French Liberal Thought in the Eighteenth Century*; *Low's Russian Sketch Book*, in collaboration with David Low; *The Magic of Monarchy*; *Propaganda's Harvest*; *The Press the Public Wants*; *Harold Laski*: a memoir; *Critic's London Diary*; *The Crown and the Establishment*; and two volumes of autobiography *Father Figures* and *Editor*.

February 18, 1969.

The Rev. William Keble Martin, who died on November 26, 1969, at his home in Woodbury, near Exeter, at the age of 92, was the author of *Concise British Flora in Colour*, published when he was 87. It sold 100,000 copies within a year and led to his receiving an honorary doctorate and providing illustrations for floral postage stamps at the age of 89. To date some 200,000 copies have been sold.

William Keble Martin was born on July 9, 1877. He became a keen botanist and entomologist during his schooldays at Marlborough, then studied botany at Oxford under Professor S. H. Vines and Dr. Church, a botanist of great artistic as well as intellectual ability, who encouraged his students to draw. Martin took his B.A. in 1899, his M.A. in 1907, went meanwhile to a theological training college and was ordained in 1902.

He was successively curate of Beeston, Ashbourne and Lancaster from 1902 to 1909, vicar of Wath-upon-Dearne from 1909 to 1921—he published in 1920 *A History of the Ancient Parish of Wath-upon-Dearne*—and rector of Haccombe in Devon from 1921 to 1934 and of Great Torrington from 1934 to 1943. During this period he devoted whatever spare time he had to studying and drawing British plants. In 1930 he became a member of the newly founded Botanical Section of the Devonshire Association, for which, together with Gordon T. Fraser, he edited the *Flora of Devon* (1939).

Little by little he built up his collection of coloured drawings of British plants made direct from living specimens. He made his first drawing for the flora—snowdrops against ivy leaves in 1899. The primary purpose of these drawings was to help identification and they were "first made in the form of pen outlines on small separate sheets". He then assembled them into plates, putting related plants together, with as many as fifteen figures assembled on one, aiming to depict an average fragment of each species with its essential features and "where possible to show white or pale coloured flowers against green foliage as in a hedge-row".

TWENTY YEARS' WAIT

As he stated, "during the years there have always been gaps on the plates, because the necessary specimens could not be obtained. Some of these gaps have waited for twenty or even twenty-four years before being filled".

Ultimately he had illustrated 1,486 species and sought publication, but this proved a disappointing experience. Exhibitions of his meticulously-drawn and beautifully-coloured little portraits of British plants won admiration for his industry, tenacity and skill. They failed, however, to convince publishers that the sales of yet another illustrated book on the British flora would justify the very high cost of reproducing his drawings in colour so as to do full justice to their delicacy and accuracy. In this they were probably right. Finally there came an appeal for subscribers which received the support of well-known British botanists.

Fortunately, his work was brought to the notice of the book designer George Rainbird, who realized that it would have an immense popular appeal if published at a sufficiently low price and that this could justifiably be achieved by accepting a lower standard of colour fidelity than the prohibitive high standard alone considered earlier. The Duke of Edinburgh gave his support to the enterprise by writing a foreword in which he paid tribute to the artist's dedicated and painstaking skill; printing was then put so quickly in hand that six months later, in May 1965, the *Concise British Flora in Colour* appeared at the remarkably low price of 35s.

BEST SELLER

It deservedly became an immediate best seller, for its 1,486 figures make it an admirable companion to standard descriptive floras of the British Isles. The intimate knowledge they display of the British flora led the University of Exeter to confer upon their artist an honorary D.Sc. Their charm led the Post Office, much more surprisingly, to use his figures of the wood anemone, viper's bugloss etc. on four 4d. stamps issued in 1967. He was rector of Combe-in-Teignhead from 1943 to 1949.

His autobiography, *Over the Hills*, published in 1968 revealed a man of strong principles and great strength of character. It also showed how hardworking a parish priest he had been, conscious that while preaching the word of God was important so also was visiting people. He was twice married.

November 28, 1969.

Father C. C. Martindale, who died at Petworth, Sussex, on March 18, 1963, was an outstanding personality as a priest, a scholar, a preacher and a writer. He was 83.

Cyril Charlie Martindale was born on May 25, 1879, the son of Sir Arthur Henry Martindale, K.C.S.I. After leaving Harrow he became a Roman Catholic and joined the novitiate of the Society of Jesus at Roehampton. From then onwards his career in its main features was the normal one followed by the members of the English Province of the Society and he taught at Stonyhurst and at Manresa House. From the beginning, however, his superiors recognized the exceptional qualities of his mind and character. He was sent in 1901 to Pope's Hall, Oxford (now Campion Hall). There he gained the reputation of being the most brilliant classical scholar of his day and a long series of successes confirmed this judgment. In addition to firsts in Moderations and *Lit. Hum.* he obtained the Hertford and Craven scholarships. He won the Chancellor's Latin Verse and Gaisford Greek Verse prizes, and, after taking his degree, he obtained the Derby Scholarship and the Ellerton Theological Essay prize. After his ordination as priest at Milltown Park, Dublin, in 1911, he returned to Oxford and lectured in the faculty of *Lit. Hum.* In 1927 he was appointed to the staff of Farm Street Church.

BRILLIANT INTELLECT

Academic successes were hardly more than an accident in Father Martindale's life. The brilliance of his intellect and the capacity for hard work, in spite of poor health of which they were a sign, were regarded by himself as nothing but tools which God had placed in his hands for the real work of his life, to save souls and to make the Church of his adoption better understood and appreciated in this country. But his great success in both these aims was primarily due to the force and attraction of his personality. No one who came into contact with him could ever forget the pale, drawn scholar's face, the high forehead, the slow, decided, and rather affected speech, the muffler untidily thrown round the Roman collar, the unexpected smile that would light up his features.

CARE OF SOULS

In spite of his enormous literary output, his constant preaching and travelling, he always found time to attend to the real object of his care, the individual soul. Thus he was popular not only with those of his own standing and education but with all sorts and conditions of men. His popular works of Roman Catholic apologetics written in novel style, *Jock, Jack and the Corporal*, *Mr. Francis Newnes*, *Albert Alfred, P.C.*, reveal how a scholar of fastidious taste can rise (as he would have put it) to the understanding of his fellow men. This power of seeing men and times in the concrete enabled him to write a long series of lives of saints which has helped to alter the art of popular hagiography. His saints, no longer colourless figures with one foot already in Heaven, were living men, rather more human than their fellows. Father Martindale's Christianity was the very opposite of Stoicism: it was a religion of love, colour, adventure, and personality, a religion that enabled a man to be more than a man. This concrete positive teaching that at times seemed almost a Christian Hellenism made him a conspicuous success in the difficult task of broadcasting undenominational sermons through the B.B.C.

STANDARD BIOGRAPHIES

Though he deliberately sacrificed scholarship to the work of the ministry, he has left important studies in comparative religion, some volumes of essays that will be remembered for the purity of their style and the beauty of their conception, and the standard biographies of Robert Hugh Benson, Bernard Vaughan, and Charles Plater. His health was never good, and it often seemed that only a nervous will-power kept him to his task.

This was particularly true during the 1939–45 War, during which he was detained in Copenhagen by the German occupation. Severe heart attacks brought him three times to imminent danger of death, yet he still was able to complete a considerable body of writing in anticipation of his return to England.

Stationed at the Jesuit House at Farm Street in London, after his return from Copenhagen, Father Martindale had opportunity of renewing his contacts with an extraordinary number of people in many spheres of life, while continuing his literary work and occasionally giving retreats or preaching. But the heart trouble from which his health had become precarious obliged his retirement to Petworth, where he celebrated his eightieth birthday in 1959, and in 1961 his golden jubilee as a priest.

It was a remarkable aspect of his work as a priest that the scholar who might have developed an academic career wrote both as a scholar and a popular apologist, and devoted a great deal of time to the federation of Catholic university societies, while assisting the development of the Apostleship of the Sea, which has established port chaplaincies throughout the world.

DIARY FICTION

As an author he preserved a reputation for scholarship with his popularity for what seemed to be more ephemeral work. He was one of the advisers appointed by the Hierarchy of England and Wales during the preparation of the Knox version of the Bible.

A few months before his death he completed a fictional diary, as a complement to his last literary work, *The Castle and the Ring*, which ranged over the possible history of the gifts of the Magi and came up to date in an English country home.

March 19, 1963.

Professor Gaetano Martino, who as Italy's Foreign Minister was one of the principal architects of the European Common Market, died on July 21, 1967, in Rome at the age of 66.

One of Italy's outstanding neuro-physiologists, he was the president of the Liberal Party and the rector of Rome University at the time of his death. A distinguished-looking and soft spoken scholar he had that rare political talent of being a good listener as well as a persuasive politician. It was his force of character that enabled him to persuade the six Foreign Ministers of the member nations of the European Coal and Steel Community to meet at Messina, the city of his birth, on June 1 and 2, 1955. From that meeting resulted the European Common Market and Euratom. Two years later, on March 25, 1957, Martino and President Segni were the Italian signatories of the Treaty of Rome at the Campidoglio in Rome.

Although an effective politician, his "Europeanism" was developed from a highly successful early eareer as a teaching doctor. Born in Messina on November 25, 1900, his father was the mayor of that city before and after the catastrophic earthquake in 1908 which killed 80,000 persons.

He graduated from the University of Rome with a degree in surgery and medicine in 1923 and studied further in Berlin, Paris, Frankfurt on Main and London.

HUNDRED TEXT BOOKS

At the extraordinarily young age of 29 he was named Professor of Physiology at the University of Messina. Shortly thereafter he directed the Medical Sciences Department at the University of the Assumption in Paraguay. Returning to Messina he was vice-rector there for 13 years and from 1957 he directed the Institute of Human Physiology until 1966 when he took over the politically sensitive post of rector of the university after his predecessor had been forced to resign by student demonstrations. The author of more than a hundred medical textbooks, his tract on human physiology is the standard text in all Italian universities.

After finishing the war as a lieutenant colonel, he launched his political career as a deputy to the constituent Government in 1946. Subsequently elected a deputy to the Chamber in 1948, 1953, 1958, and 1963, he was the vice president of the Chamber in 1948. He entered the Scelba Government in 1954 as the Minister of Public Education. After seven months, he became Foreign Minister, a position he retained in the next government headed by Signor Segni until May, 1957.

RETURN TO TRIESTE

As Foreign Minister, Martino guided the intricate negotiations which returned Trieste to Italy with the London Accord of October 1954.

A year later Italy was admitted to the United Nations and he was the first leader of the Italian delegation to the U.N.

When the European Defence Community failed in 1954 because of French opposition and the West European Union was born, he made a major contribution to resolving a serious crisis in the new W.E.U.—a summit meeting of the Foreign Ministers without aides which succeeded in overcoming their differences. A short time later he inspired the historic meeting in Messina which led to the E.E.C. He was president of the European Parliament from 1962 to 1964.

July 22, 1967.

Chico (Leonard) Marx, the film comedian, died on October 11, 1961, in Hollywood at the age of 70. He was the eldest of the five Marx Brothers (of whom Groucho, Harpo, Zeppo and Gummo comprised the other four) and was born in New York on March 22, 1891.

The biography of one of the brothers must inevitably be largely that of the others because although their styles of comedy varied considerably they shared a common heritage and an exceptional flair for music as well as for madness. Groucho was one of the best guitar players in America, Harpo—as his name implies—played the harp, Zeppo the saxophone, and Chico, whose dark, Italian appearance and somewhat broken accent suggested a refugee baritone in flight from Milan, was, in fact, a remarkable pianist, who regimented his fingers like a platoon of guardsmen and marched them up and down the keys with clockwork precision.

Some purists have complained that the Marx Brothers diluted their comedy by these excursions into music, and Chico's skill at the piano is admittedly not the talent by which posterity will chiefly remember him; it was his hallmark—no more—and distinguished him from the others. Not that such distinction was ever really necessary. Groucho, the rapid-fire talker, with the sly and slinky walk, was in sharp contrast to Harpo, who never spoke, and had the detached and mystic air of a mad angel.

CHICO'S TECHNIQUE

Chico came somewhere in between. He talked more seriously than Groucho and at less speed, but the purport of his remarks was equally at variance with all known forms of logic. One recalls in particular the scene in *A Day at the Races* in which he sold a racing tip to Groucho, together with countless bulky volumes on racing form. Groucho, for once baffled and out-generalled, was persuaded to buy them all in order to discover the key to the ultimate selection for the race. It was a triumph for Chico's subdued, diffident but none the less persistent approach.

The Marx Brothers were born to the business of entertaining the public, inheriting the urge to perform from their mother, Minnie Marx, who encouraged her five offspring with immense energy and a refusal to accept defeat in the face of unenthusiastic agents and—in their earlier days—some very disinterested audiences. Music seemed to be their forte, so she formed a musical vaudeville act consisting of herself, her sister and the four elder boys, and called it The Six Musical Mascots. Later she teamed Groucho and Gummo with a girl soprano and called them The Three Nightingales; then Chico was persuaded to join forces with the group and they became The Four Nightingales.

REARED IN POVERTY

The family of five boys was reared by this indefatigable woman in the face of poverty and hardship, and were imbued by her with that family unity which ensures survival and that sense of resolution without which no comedian can ever succeed—for comedians suffer more from the changing moods and tastes of audiences than any other type of entertainer.

Minnie had emigrated to the United States

from Germany when she was a girl of 15, and her husband, Sam Marx, had come from Alsace when he was 17. He was an honest and hard working man who had become a tailor—without, as Groucho would often remark, showing any notable aptitude for the profession.

A MULE AS RIVAL

The family was split up during the First World War. Harpo and Gummo joining the Army and Chico and Groucho entertaining the troops, but they were reunited after the armistice. It was then that their work as a comedy team began to take shape. During the twenties they toured America as a vaudeville act and the story goes (apocryphal perhaps as so many of the legends connected with them) that their first real essay into lunacy came when the audience in a samll town in Texas left the theatre as a man when a mule began to kick a cart to pieces in the street outside. Piqued by this rival entertainer the brothers went crazy on the stage and behaved in so extraordinary a manner that the theatre quickly refilled. Their film debut was in a picture called *Humorisk*, which was made in New York, was bad and was never shown. After a stage hit in *The Coconuts* they were signed by Paramount in 1929 to appear in a film version of the show.

TALENTED GUIDANCE

This was followed by *Animal Crackers* and *Monkey Business* in 1931, *Horse Feathers* in 1932, and *Duck Soup* in 1933. They later came under the guidance of that most talented of all Hollywood producers the late Irving Thalberg of M.G.M., who had a great admiration for them. He encouraged them to make *A Night at the Opera* in 1935, by which time the team consisted only of Chico, Groucho, and Harpo. However, their subsequent films, after the death of Thalberg, tended to lose a certain spontaneity of effect.

One tends to believe most of the stories concerning them, since they are all so improbable. Thus one accepts the Hollywood legend that Chico's initial marriage ceremony to Miss Betty Carb was abandoned after the officiating clergyman had walked out in anger when he saw that Groucho and Harpo were eating the leaves off his much prized rubber plant. As a comedy team both on and off the stage they represented a protest against conformity and a denial of all restrictive inhibitions. Of Chico it may be said that nonconformity was a matter of comparative tranquillity with him, while with Groucho and Harpo it was carried to the ultimate realms of social anarchy.

October 12, 1961.

Harpo (Arthur) Marx, the film comedian, died in hospital in Hollywood on September 28, 1964. He would have been 71 in the November.

Harpo was the second of a family of five boys born to Sam Marx, an indifferent tailor, and to Minnie, a woman of resolution who emigrated from Europe at the end of the past century to join the impoverished Jewish community in New York. They were a united family of indomitable spirit, spurred on by their mother, who would never accept defeat. Alexander Woollcott wrote of her in his obituary in the *New Yorker* that she was among the few people he had ever met with a quality of greatness. She not only gave birth to five comedians but she also invented them.

It may be that the historians of the film and the psychiatrists of the entertainment world have attached too much significance to the work of the Marx Brothers, a splendid team of clowns who combined individualism and originality with admirable teamwork and complete professionalism. Yet in retrospect they can also be seen as the forerunners of that mood of rebellion which is so much a feature of modern entertainment. They, too, attacked the established order and the spirit of conformity with immense gusto, but they were never spiteful in the process. They graduated from poverty without resentment and their comedy was never poisoned by bitterness.

FOLLOWING IMPULSE

Harpo (the nickname was acquired during a poker game) was the wild eyed lunatic in a wig who played the harp, blew on a motor horn, chewed thermometers and never spoke. J. B. Priestley once described him as "the unconscious at play, the ordinary citizen in dreams and with the lid off". Certainly the Marx Brothers never suffered from any inhibitions on the screen. They followed the first impulse which came into their heads, and the first impulse which usually came into the head of either Harpo or Groucho was to chase the nearest blonde. This gave no offence. It was not sex rearing its ugly head but simply the uninhibited male in pursuit of what was, in every sense of the phrase, fair game.

Groucho's hallmark was his verbal assault. Harpo, deprived of speech, seemed to inhabit a different sphere altogether. His eyes had a far away look, if also one of near lunacy. Groucho had his feet planted firmly on the ground, but Harpo dwelt in the clouds. He was a wanderer from the world of fancy. The brothers started their career vaudeville act called *The Four Nightingales*—an unfortunate title since Gummo and Groucho were only moderate vocalists and Harpo could not sing at all. Later they became the Marx Brothers, and went on tour with a schoolroom act in which Groucho played the master and Harpo was a moronic pupil, with a tousled wig improvised out of some old rope. Thus was his film character born.

In the 1920s they became stars of Broadway and later the cinema. They became a part of the Hollywood world of the 1930s, guided and encouraged by that most talented of the early film producers, the late Irving Thalberg, who after their failure in *Duck Soup* took them under his wing at M.G.M. But their era was relatively short.

Perhaps the pre-war world was not yet ready for an attack on conformity, and anyway Thalberg died young. But their place in film history is secure. They outraged convention with abandon, but always without malice.

He leaves a widow and four adopted children.

September 30, 1964.

Eric Maschwitz, who was Head of Light Entertainment on B.B.C. television from 1958 to 1961 died on October 27, 1969, at Ascot. He was 68.

Maschwitz, after joining the B.B.C. in 1926 became editor of the *Radio Times* the following year and then Director of Variety.

He resigned in 1937 and wrote many successful shows for the West End, including *Balalaika* and *Carissima*, and the lyrics for such songs as "Good Night Vienna" and "These Foolish Things". From 1961 to 1963 he was Assistant and Adviser to the Controller of Television Programmes, B.B.C.

During the Second World War he did notable work for the intelligence service.

Born in Birmingham on June 10, 1901, he was educated at Repton where he was a classical scholar and at Caius College, Cambridge. He was always attracted by the possibilities of broadcasting and one of his earliest jobs was to edit the *Radio Times* from 1927 to 1933 when he was appointed Director of Variety at the B.B.C. He held the position until 1937 and during that period the popular feature *In Town Tonight* was evolved. He then decided to resign because, as he said, after 10 years of broadcasting he felt the need of "refuelling". It was announced, however, that he would still be connected with the B.B.C. as a writer and contributor to programmes. His plan was to visit Hollywood, New York and Europe and he hoped at the end of two years to return to Broadcasting House with wider experience of stage, film and radio production.

EDITED D-DAY STORY

From 1940 to 1945, however, he served as a lieutenant-colonel in the Intelligence Corps and went on an intelligence mission to North and South America in 1941 and 1942, and he also acted as the story editor of the official D. Day film *True Glory*. It was not until 1958 that he returned to the B.B.C. and the interval was mainly occupied with the theatre. Before the war he had already gained considerable success in that field, notably with the production of *Balalaika* at the Adelphi in 1936, for which he wrote the book and the lyrics.

Balalaika ran for 570 performances and, encouraged by its success. Maschwitz turned again to eastern Europe in *Paprika* at His Majesty's in 1938. But the production did not appeal to the public. Undaunted, he brought in Binnie Hale, engaged Fred Thomson and Guy Bolton to overhaul the book and re-presented it four months later under a new title, *Magyar Melody*, which ran for 105 performances. In the folloing year he wrote the book and the lyrics for a revue, *New Faces*, and presented a revised edition a year later.

Even the least expert of his songs and sketches had pleasant touches which kept expectancy alive and every now and then something first class turned up including the number "A Nightingale Sang in Berkeley Square", which proved to be one of the big song hits of the period both in Britain and in America.

In *Waltz without End* at the Cambridge in 1942 he tried, but with indifferent success, to present Chopin as *Lilac Time* had presented Schubert. The critics felt that his romantic faith in the waltzes, the mazurkas, the crinolines and the curved hat brims of the 1830s had betrayed him into writing a story savouring too much of the pantomime. His next big success came in 1948 with *Carissima*, played nearly 500 times at the Palace. It was not a particularly good book but there were one or two delightful lyrics set to the music of Hans May which became highly popular. Eleven years later the B.B.C. brought Ginger Rogers from America to play the leading part in an elaborate television production of *Carissima* but it was impossible to disguise the fact that in the interval it had become an old-fashioned comedy.

NEW TALENT

Maschwitz was concerned with at least four other notable stage successes—*Belinda Fair* (1949), a brave beguiling tale of the golden days of Good Queen Anne; *Zip goes a Million* (1951), an adaptation of the Edwardian farce *Brewster's Millions*; *Love from Judy* (1952), a delightful musical comedy based on the novel and play *Daddy Long-legs*, and *Happy Holiday* (1954), a musical version of Arnold Ridley's thriller *The Ghost Train*. His adaptation of Marc-Gilbert Sauvajon's *Treize à Table* under the title *Thirteen for Dinner*, produced at the Duke of York's in December, 1953, however, expired after its first performance. Maschwitz then produced *Romance in Candlelight* in 1955 and *Summer Song* in 1956.

When he was appointed Head of Light Entertainment (Television) at the B.B.C. in 1958, Maschwitz announced that he intended to throw the new field of entertainment wide open to new talent. He had to face the competition of Independent Television, with its immense financial resources, but it was generally agreed that he performed his task well and satisfied, at any rate, the vast majority of viewers. He was appointed Producer (Special Projects) to Rediffusion Television in 1963.

Maschwitz wrote a number of novels starting with *A Taste of Honey* in 1924, but the most delightful of all his books was his autobiography, published at the end of 1957 under the title *No Chip on my Shoulder*. He recalled his successes and his failures with an equal charm and felicity. At the end of it he admitted that he was a happy man and he certainly had the knack of imparting his own happiness to an unsually wide circle of friends.

In 1926 he married Miss Hermione Gingold, but the marriage was dissolved and in 1945 he married Miss Phyllis Gordon. He was awarded the O.B.E. in 1936.

October 29, 1969.

John Masefield, O.M., the Poet Laureate, died on May 12, 1967, at the age of 88.

A writer of energy and versatility, he had fulfilled widely differing roles in English literary life. In his earliest days he was a writer of popular poetical narratives akin to ballads in essence if not in form. In middle life his poetry appealed to a more restricted circle. For the 37 years during which he was Poet Laureate his poetry became predominantly austere. But it could be said that while the style changed the poet and the man himself were always at heart the same. There have been few poets of Masefield's position who had so little nonsense about them and who were so generally beloved. He was a writer of fiction and drama as well as a poet. In these, too, he won popular success.

His appointment as Poet Laureate came during the Prime Ministership of Ramsay MacDonald. Robert Bridges died on April 21, 1930, and on May 10 the announcement of Masefield as Poet Laureate was made. The Order of Merit was awarded to him in the Birthday Jubilee Honours of 1935. He was an honorary D. Litt, of Oxford and honorary LL.D. of Aberdeen. His eightieth birthday in 1958 was an occasion for a surge of admiration and affection towards him that could not help touching even so simple a man.

Born at The Knapp, Ledbury, Herefordshire, on June 1, 1878, Masefield was the son of George Edward Masefield, solicitor. Left fatherless in childhood, John, with his brothers and sisters, was brought up by a relative. His boyhood at Ledbury left its mark in the knowledge and love of hunting and other country affairs that are exhibited in some of his poems; but his fancy for going to sea took him at the age of 14 from the King's School, Warwick, to H.M.S. Conway, the training ship in the Mersey of which in later life he wrote a history.

After spending several years training and winning a number of prizes for seamanship, he went as an apprentice on board a sailing ship round Cape Horn to Iquique, in Chile. A notoriously bad sailor, he was taken ill on the voyage and returned home by the next steamer. He never served again in a sailing vessel.

On leaving the sea he spent some time in New York working in a Yonkers carpet factory as a gardener and as a barman.

WIDENED CIRCLE

But one afternoon, when he was 17, a leisure hour with Chaucer's poems revealed to him his passion to become a writer. The Chaucerian quality remained ever after one of the best elements in his poetry. In 1897, having made some contributions to American newspapers, he returned to England. Here he found friends ready to encourage and help him. Within five years he was contributing to the *Outlook*, the *Academy*, and the *Speaker*, and in 1907 he began work on the *Manchester Guardian*. It was at this time that his circle of friends widened to include such men as Augustus John, Professor Reilly, W.B. Yeats, and others, who had an early influence on him.

His first volume of poems was *Salt-Water Ballads*, published in 1902. Here were nautical tales in nautical language, and sea-poems of other kinds, including two great popular favourites: "Sea Fever" (set to music by John Ireland), and the poem called "Cargoes", which Kipling himself never surpassed for effective suggestion through the names of things. In 1911 he published *The Everlasting Mercy* (which caused a stir and with its "bloodys" offended some); in 1912 *The Widow in the Bye Street*; in 1913 *Dauber and The Daffodil Fields*. These four long narrative poems—*Dauber* of life at sea, the other three of rural loves and lusts—revealed the passion and power of the young poet, his skill in story-telling, his mastery of metrical pattern and pace and the values of words, and also some insecurity of judgment and a hardiness in changes of style, caused partly by his desire to fit the language to the thought and partly by mere insensitiveness. These features were less prominent in the long poems of hunting, *Reynard the Fox* (1919), and of steeple-chasing, *Right Royal* (1920). As time went by his lyrical poetry tended to become less hearty, more elegant, and more thoughtful, qualities clearly discernible in his occasional verses on public events after his appointment as Poet Laureate.

He took his duties in this post very seriously. There were few royal occasions, whether marriages, journeyings overseas, or other significant events which he did not commemorate in verse in the columns of *The Times*. In 1965 he marked the death of T. S. Eliot with lines which he called "East Coker". It was a charming side to his character—and there can be no harm in revealing it now—that such poems were always accompanied by a stamped addressed envelope for their return if they were not acceptable.

His poetry during the Laureateship rarely had the same appeal as the great stories in verse of his earlier days. The reason was simple. John Masefield was now in his sixth decade. At the same time a poem such as "The Towerer" and a volume such as *A Letter from Pontus* showed that the old fires could on occasion be revived.

NEW GROUND

In 1959 he broke new ground with *The Story of Ossian*, an epic poem based on the body of an Irish legend surrounding Finn MacCoul, which made history by being published not in print but as a gramophone record.

In a way this was a dramatic performance and a harking back to earlier days. Before *The Everlasting Mercy* won him fame as a poet he had written several plays including *The Campden Wonder* (Court Theatre 1907) and *The Tragedy of Nan* (Haymarket, 1908). One of his best achievements and services to English literature was his promotion of the religious drama. His first adventure was *Good Friday* (1917). In 1922 he made a version of Racine's *Esther*, with a new and violent conclusion all his own. Later came *The Trial of Jesus* (1925) and *The Coming of Christ* (1928), written on the invitation of Dr. G. K. A. Bell, then Dean of Canterbury, and perfectly adapted for performance in Canterbury Cathedral at the annual festival of Friends.

His best work in fiction lies in the straightforward stories of adventure by sea in South America, or wherever it may be, in which his skill at narrative and description had uninterrupted scope. The best known are *Sard Harker* (1924) and *Odtaa*—a title made up of the initial letters of "one damn thing after another" (1926); but readers young and old have found pleasure in *Jim Davis* (1911), *The Bird of Dawning* (1933)—magnificent tale of the China clippers—*Victorious Troy* (1935), and other yarns of ships and seafaring. The Defoe-like purity of narrative of *Dead Ned* (1939) marked a return to his best form, while in later years Masefield tried his hand at historical novels of the Eastern Empire. In literary criticism his best known work was the original and individual little Home University Library volume on Shakespeare (1911, revised edition 1954). One of the most interesting of his later prose works was *Thanks Before Going* which was best described by its sub-title "With other Gratitude for Old Delight".

HOSPITAL SHIP POST

When the war of 1914–18 broke out John Masefield worked with the Red Cross in France, and was serving in a hospital ship during the campaign of the Dardanelles in 1915. His personal knowledge proved to be of high value when "at the request of two of his Majesty's Ministers" he wrote a short account of the fighting, *Gallipoli* (1916). Those who had fought there were inclined to think he made too much of the horrors; but besides helping to confute a good deal of slanderous misrepresentation which the censorship had allowed to grow unchecked he used to the full the gift for narrative and description. The same qualities in different degrees marked his book on *The Old Front Line* (1917) before the beginning of the battle of the Somme, and his *Nine Days' Wonders* (1941), the tale of Dunkirk in the summer of 1940. Early in 1916 and again in 1918 he went lecturing in the United States of America; in 1939 he undertook a long lecture tour in European countries for the British Council. He took a great interest in everything to do with literature and had been President of the Society of Authors since 1937. He was President of the National Book League from 1944 to 1949.

He married in 1903 Constance, daughter of Nicholas de la Cherois-Crommelin, late of Cushendun, co. Antrim. She died in February 1960. They had two children—a daughter Judith, who illustrated some of her father's books, and a son, Lewis Crommelin Masefield, of the R.A.M.C., who died in action in June 1942, at the age of 32.

May 13, 1967.

Vincent Massey, P.C., C.H., former Governor-General of Canada, died on December 30, 1967, in London at the age of 80.

Vincent Massey, as Prime Minister Pearson said in a tirbute to his memory, will have "a very special place in Canadian history". He was, for one thing, the first native-born Canadian to become the vice-regal representative in Canada. When he took office on the recommendation of Mr. Louis St. Laurent in February, 1952, following the successful terms of men like Earl Alexander of Tunis, the Earl of Athlone and Lord Tweedsmuir, there were some critical eyes focused on him. Mr. St. Laurent said at the time that his appointment did not necessarily mean that every subsequent incumbent of Rideau Hall should be a Canadian.

There was also the feeling at the time that the Governor-General should have "no taint" of politics about him; Massey had been appointed to Mr. King's Cabinet in the twenties but was unable to win a constituency. When the Bennett Government came to power in the early thirties Massey, who had been Canadian Minister in Washington from 1926 to 1930, found himself in the political wilderness and during the Conservative regime up to 1935 he was president of the National Liberal Federation.

Some thought that one who was born to wealth—his family being in the farm implement business—and an intellectual as well, for he was at Toronto University and Balliol, might be a little too remote for the people. But this was not to be, for although Massey never allowed any lowering of his intellectual standards merely to court popularity, he was increasingly admired by his fellow Canadians everywhere. Considering that he had been appointed as the Queen's representative in Canada in his sixty-sixth year, he did an enormous amount of travelling to the farthest corners of the land in all kinds of weather and in all kinds of transport, including dog sledge in the north. At the end of his term he had done more than 180,000-miles. In 1956 he made a 10,000-mile 17-day air tour of the Arctic, including a flight over the North Pole, the most extensive journey ever made by a Governor-General of Canada. He covered thousands of miles every year carrying the message of the Crown to every part of the nation, for he believed that the Crown was a unifying force vital to Canada.

APPEAL TO NATION

He urged Canadians to show greater awareness of national character and also a greater self-confidence, self-reliance in themselves. "We still maintain our identity", he once said, "as long as we remain loyal to our traditions and keep doing things our own way."

Massey will be remembered for his long and successful tenure in London as Canadian High Commissioner from 1935 to 1946 and also for the years between 1926 and 1930 when he was in Washington as Canada's first diplomatic representative there of ministerial rank. At that particular time these was some criticism of the appointment to the United States capital on the grounds that Canada was moving away from the Empire.

But it was perhaps his days in London that he enjoyed the most despite the ravages of war. From his Balliol days and indeed before that he had an abiding love for Britain and he was particularly proud of his being a trustee of the National Gallery and the Tate Gallery. He and his late wife, Alice, daughter of Sir George Parkin, one-time headmaster of Upper Canada College, Toronto, and a trustee of the Rhodes Scholarship Foundation, did much for Canadian servicemen at their Beaver Club in London built by the Masseys out of their own money.

During wartime he received the distinction of becoming a member of the British Privy Council; in 1925 he had been appointed to the Canadian Privy Council. Later in 1948 King George VI made him a Companion of Honour.

ADVERTISING CANADA

During his early days at Canada House he attracted considerable attention in advertising the Dominion in what he called "a Canadian calling" campaign. As a result Canadian exports such as wheat, timber and bacon became better known to the British people.

On his return to Canada he became Chancellor of Toronto University in 1947 and two years later he undertook the major task of trying to diagnose Canada's cultural problems by becoming chairman of the Royal commission on national development in the arts, letters and sciences, a task that took two years. Its main recommendation was the blue-print for the establishment of the Canada Council.

Massey, despite his frail appearance, was a man of great energy, mental and physical. He was always conscious of the vice-regal traditions and felt that the outward trappings were important. One of his last acts before retiring in September, 1959, from office after seven years of Government House (a tenure that included two extensions, the first of their kind since Earl Grey's days) was the presentation of regimental colours to the Governor-General's Foot Guards. He did much to encourage ceremonial during his stay at Rideau Hall, reviving in particular the vice-regal drive to Parliament Hill on special occasions in an open landau with an escort of Royal Canadian Mounted Police.

Yet in spite of all the ceremonial Government House during his time was not an isolated unapproachable fortress governed by pomp and privilege. To it came actors, writers, union leaders and educationists. The place hummed with activity, social and intellectual. He understood the press as a writer himself. He was a life member of the Parliamentary Press Gallery and also of what is now the National Press Club of Canada.

Since he retired to his family home at Batterwood House, near Port Hope, Ontario, Massey continued to keep a lively interest in Canadian affairs. He was a governor of the University of Toronto and in 1963 published his memoirs *What's Past is Prologue*. He was working on his fifth book when he died.

Vincent Massey was born in Toronto on February 20, 1887, the eldest son of Chester Daniel and Ann Vincent Massey. On his mother's side he was an American, while his father's forebears went back to Geoffrey Massey, who came to New Salem, Massachusetts, from Knutsford, England, in the seventeenth century.

FOUNDED FAMILY FIRM

Vincent Massey's grandfather was the founder of the Massey Harris company, the largest farm implement manufacturer in the Commonwealth. Part of that wealth found its way into various philanthropies and other aids to culture through the many foundations founded by his grandfather Hart. His brother, Raymond, went on the stage to fame on Broadway and in Hollywood.

After graduating from the University of Toronto Massey went up to Balliol and got a a second in modern history, returning to his old university to lecture on that subject. He was dean of residents at Victoria College there and directed the building of Hart House. In 1915 he was on the staff of the military district No. 2 (Canada) for three years and in 1918 was associate secretary War Committee of the Canadian Cabinet. Later he was with the

Government repatriation committee as secretary and as its director.

From 1921 to 1925 he attended to family business, being president of Massey Harris, Toronto. Then in 1926 after his unsuccessful fling in politics he went to Washington as Canadian Minister in charge of posts. When Bennett came to power in 1930 Massey, as an appointee of Mackenzie King, was recalled from the United States capital and for five years helped to revive the fortunes of the Liberal Party.

Then when King returned to power in 1935 he went to London as Canadian High Commissioner for a period of 11 years. In February, 1952, he was appointed Governor-General. He is survived by one son, Hart Massey, a distinguished Canadian architect. His elder son, Lionel, died a few years ago.

January 1, 1968.

Sir Irvine Masson, M.B.E., F.R.S., formerly Vice-Chancellor of the University of Sheffield, died on October 22, 1962, at the age of 75.

The grandson of Professor David Masson of Edinburgh and the son of Sir David Orme Masson, Professor of Chemistry and later Vice-Chancellor of the University of Melbourne, James Irvine Orme Masson was born in Melbourne on September 3, 1887. After school and university education in Melbourne he came to this country and engaged in chemical research at University College London under Sir William Ramsay who had also been his father's teacher and for whom he had unbounded admiration.

He became successively lecturer and reader in chemistry at University College, though most of the 1914–18 War was spent in research at Woolwich Arsenal. From London he went in 1924 to Durham as Professor of Chemistry and head of the Department of Pure Science and while at Durham made an outstanding contribution to the difficult constitutional problems that were the subject of the Royal Commission on that university.

From there he went to Sheffield as Vice-Chancellor in 1938 and for the next 14 years until he retired at the age limit was ceaseless in his work on behalf of the university, first through its wartime difficulties and then over the equally difficult period of rapid expansion which followed. Indeed during the war his labours were doubled for in addition to the Vice Chancellorship he directed a large research team centred on the university in explosives research, a task for which he was eminently fitted but which placed him under a great strain.

Irvine Masson was a man of unusual parts. As a scientist his work largely in physical chemistry was notable and was recognized by his election to the Royal Society in 1939. But he was also at home in the classics and was distinguished as an expert on typography and an enthusiastic bibliographer. He was a lover of books with a special passion for the old and the beautiful and his competence as a palaeographer would have done credit to a professional. His last bibliographical publication, the monograph on the Mainz Psalters and the Canon Missae (1954) is a remarkable piece of patient scientific detection.

But it is by his Vice-Chancellorship that he will probably be longest remembered. In 14 years and in face of every kind of difficulty he moulded the yet small University of Sheffield into a new, modern and expanded pattern. No matter, however small, was thought unworthy of his close attention if it bore on his main object. No labour, however great, was spared. The university was a different, more effective and happier place when he left it.

Invariably courteous and seemingly hesitant, underneath he was determined and could be outspoken. Behind a reticent almost forbidding manner, which sometimes appeared in public, lay a warmth of personality which showed itself whenever he was able to break through the inevitable isolation of a Vice-Chancellor's office. Acquaintances might find him solemn. Those who knew him well found him a lively companion and a firm friend.

Masson was made M.B.E. in 1918, and knighted in 1950.

His years of retirement were spent in Edinburgh in bibliographical pursuits and as a statutory commissioner for the University of St. Andrews. They were saddened by the long and fatal illness of his wife, Flora Lovell, daughter of Professor G. Lovell Gulland, whom he married in 1913 and who died in 1960. He leaves one son.

October 23, 1964.

Adolfo López Mateos, President of Mexico from 1958 to 1964, died on September 22, 1969, in Mexico City. He was 59.

He was born on May 26, 1910, in Atizapan de Zaragoza in the State of Mexico. He was educated at the French College in Mexico City and at the Scientific and Literary Institute in the capital of his own state, Toluca. Here he distinguished himself as an orator. For eight years he was employed in the Mexican workers' bank, and in 1946 became senator for the State of Mexico. Miguel Alemani, President of Mexico from 1946 to 1952, appointed him to lead the Mexican delegation to the United Nations Economic and Social Council in Geneva. From this post López Mateos was recalled by the succeeding President, Adolfo Ruiz Cortines, to become Secretary General of the ruling party, the Partido Revolucionario Institucional (P.R.I.) and later Minister of Labour. In the latter post he showed his conciliatory talents, and there were no serious strikes during his term of office.

Mateos was chosen as the P.R.I. candidate for the Presidency in November 1957. This was a compromise decision, the party heads having quarrelled over the nomination of more controversial figures. López Mateos was therefore an unknown quantity when he took office, although the assumption that he would follow a middle-of-the-road policy proved correct. Leading the country during Dr. Castro's regime in Cuba, and at a time when many Mexicans were beginning to ask whether the revolution of 1910–17 had not been betrayed, it was essential for him to walk a tight-rope between the vociferous extreme left wing with its communist sympathies, and the extreme right who were determined to cling to fortunes netted by Mexico's rapid economic expansion. This proved no easy task, and President López Mateos was himself surprised that some of his left-wing declarations, clearly put out for home consumption, should have aroused near-panic reaction in the United States, leading to large-scale flights of capital.

CASTRO NOT CONDEMNED

He was able later to conciliate the frightened American businessman, though he refused to be intimidated into modifying his policies of government participation in industry, continued agrarian reforms, and distribution of industrial profits to workers. Although he clearly did not like the Marxist tendencies of the Cuban revolution, he refused in spite of pressure from the United States to take an actively hostile attitude to Dr. Castro's government. It was impossible, he felt, for a Latin American country that had fought its own revolution half a century earlier, to condemn a neighbour revolution out of hand.

While maintaining his country's traditional policies of non-intervention and self-determination, he insisted that his government was "non-committed but not neutral". He encouraged Mexican participation in the Latin American Free Trade Association and in the Organization of American States. In extensive tours of Latin America, the Far East, Europe, the United States and Canada, and in the hospitality he gave to foreign heads of state, he was inclined to be unfastidious and he showed equal friendship to the democracies, the non-committed group, and iron-curtain countries. Nevertheless it was clear to observers that in any serious crisis his government would be on the democratic side. He had no qualms about throwing unruly Mexican communists into jail for "social dissolution"; and on several occasions publicly upheld such democratic principles as freedom of worship and the rights of private enterprise.

September 23, 1969.

The sudden death of **Francis Mathew** on March 29, 1965, threw a shadow over Printing House Square and beyond it. He was held in warm affection and deep respect by the Proprietors and the Directors of *The Times* and by his colleagues alike on the managerial and the editorial sides. His loss is especially sad for them. But he will be missed in many circles: in the newspaper world as a whole and among men and women in diverse walks of life who had nothing to do with his professional interests. A man of boundless energy, unquenchable optimism, and mercurial temperament, he tackled everything he undertook with zest and gaiety and gained friends wherever he went.

He combined in his working career and in a remarkable degree two abilities that are not often found together. He was a master of the intricacies of the printing trade in which he had been thoroughly grounded. He had also financial acumen and a flair for handling business matters expeditiously and fruitfully. This versatility was given unity by the integrated character of the man.

Mathew was all of a piece. Religion—he belonged to a well-known Irish Roman Catholic family—was at the roots of his conduct. The enjoyment of good things and the generous wish to share happiness with all about him made association with him at once a pleasure and a stimulus. Informal in manner and approachable, he would move briskly about the office in his shirt sleeves, dropping into rooms and doing business with a minimum of time-wasting or fuss. His wit, charm and easy conversational manner added grace to a basic seriousness of purpose.

Francis Mathew was born on November 8, 1907, the fifth son of Theobald Mathew, sometime Recorder of Margate and Maidstone, a Bencher of Lincoln's Inn, and author of the brilliant *Forensic Fables*. Law can be said to have been in his blood, for there were many distinguished lawyers among his relatives, including his grandfather, Sir J. C. Mathew, a Lord Justice of Appeal, and this was a useful asset to him in his managerial duties.

VARIETY OF ENTERPRISES

Educated at Downside, where he captained the school at Rugby football, and Grenoble University, he joined Linotype and Machinery Ltd. in 1928 as a trainee. He was soon sent out to join the sales staff in Madrid where he began to learn Spanish in which he later became fluent. He spent six months in Buenos Aires in 1931 and then returned to the London sales office of the firm. Never content with a superficial knowledge of anything on which he was engaged, he benefited from his years with Linotype by gaining a thorough grasp of the manufacture of typesetting and printing machinery. In 1935 he joined St. Clements Press where for a time he understudied the managing director and in 1939 was appointed general manager.

Throughout the Second World War he worked full strength. His firm was busily engaged in a wide variety of enterprises and contracts including the printing of Government propaganda, ration coupons and newssheets for exiled governments, notably *France* and the *Polish Daily*. He became managing director of St. Clements in 1947. From 1946 to 1948 he was works director of W. Speaight and Sons Ltd.—a firm he had done much to re-form after it had been bombed out early in the war. In 1948 he joined *The Times* with a view to succeeding the manager, C. S. Kent, who retired in 1949.

From then Mathew was a tower of strength to the paper, to which he gave himself up with complete devotion. He reorganized the whole pension arrangements, an operation involving much complicated planning which he carried through to fruition. He was responsible for the changes which led to *The Times* being printed on much better paper than had hitherto been used.

He took a leading part in the rebuilding of the office. The pulling down of the original Walter private house and the Victorian office buildings and their replacement by the present ones would not have gone through as well as it did without his guidance and initiative. The reequipment of the machine room while production continued smoothly was another triumph for him. At the same time he skilfully handled the financial aspects of this whole operation.

PROGRESS AND MODERNITY

On the promotional side of the paper, he was always for progress and modernity. He had no inhibitions about drawing public attention to the merits of the paper. The tradition, supported in some quarters, that *The Times* ought to stand aloof and above the battle of advertising received no sympathy from him. He was always looking ahead and foreseeing with confidence how the strength of the paper might be increased in the future. He had a strong nerve and to further what he believed to be right he was cheerfully prepared to run great risks. He did so without failures because of a tremendous practical shrewdness which never deserted him. While the welfare of the company was foremost in his mind, he cared deeply for the welfare of members of the staff at all levels.

In negotiation he showed himself diplomatic, sympathetic to fair claims, and resolute in standing up for his own case. Those who met him across the table found that he gave nothing away and often got the better of them. But he never lost their respect. For he was a straight fighter as well as a hard hitter.

So strenuous a professional life would have been impossible without the reserves of happiness on which Mathew drew from his family life. He married in 1938 Emma Margaret, the eldest daughter of the late Thomas Lloyd Bowen-Davies, and they had five sons and six daughters. His widow and all his children survive him. Their family setting in the National Trust property, Hatchlands, at East Clandon in Surrey was ideal for so large and so united a family. Hospitality there was generously given to visitors from home and overseas. Mathew took a delight in being a host to a small party or to a larger one, such as the Throgs Cricket Club which he entertained regularly, although he was not himself a player. He had formed, in recent years, a fine collection of typographical books concerned with his particular interest, wood engraving, modern typography and early technical processes.

March 30, 1965.

Sir Theobald Mathew, K.B.E., M.C., who died suddenly on February 29, 1964, in the Middlesex Hospital at the age of 65, was the first solicitor and the youngest man ever to be appointed Director of Public Prosecutions. During his tenure of office, which lasted some 20 years, the great influence which he wielded never disturbed his personal judgment and the function of his office, to prosecute, was safeguarded from any taint of persecution.

Theobald Mathew was born in 1898 into a distinguished legal family. His father was Charles J. Mathew, K.C., and his grandfather a Lord of Appeal. Mathew himself married Phyllis Helen, the daughter of the Hon. Cyril Russell, and leaves two daughters and a son who is in practice at the Bar. Educated at the Oratory School and later at Sandhurst Mathew served with the Irish Guards in the First World War from 1917 to 1920 and won the Military Cross. In 1919 he was appointed A.D.C. to General Sir Alexander Godley.

In 1921, following the example of his family Mathew was called to the Bar but in 1925 he turned his attention to the other branch of the legal profession and became a solicitor, entering the firm of Charles Russell & Co. In 1934 he served on the Departmental Committee on Imprisonment for Debt and thus his public career commenced.

Joining the Home Office in 1941, Mathew was head of the Criminal Division from 1941 to 1942 and in 1944 he was appointed Director of Public Prosecutions.

The main duties of the Director of Public Prosecutions are to institute, undertake or carry on criminal proceedings in the case of any offence punishable by death, in any case referred to him by a Government department in which he considers that criminal proceedings should be instituted, and in any case which appears to him to be of importance or difficulty or which for any other reason requires his intervention. It is his function to give advice either on application or on his own initiative to Government departments, clerks to Justices and Chief Officers of Police, and to such other persons as he may think right in any criminal matter which appears to him to be of importance or difficulty. The influence which a Director of Public Prosecutions can wield in the sphere of the criminal law is therefore enormous but it was notable that Mathew used his great powers shrewdly and intelligently. He did not regard himself as a guardian of public morals but as an instrument by which the criminal law was enforced. Any moral reaction which he might have had in a given situation which might have affected his office he kept to himself; he was resigned to the defects in human nature and thus preserved his most important asset, a strong sense of the proper function of his office.

OBSCENITY LAWS

The situations which caused Mathew the greatest difficulty were those in which the fields of law and personal as opposed to obviously public morals overlapped. This sort of situation is perhaps typified by the law relating to the publication of obscene matter. Mathew's view was that so far as private conduct was concerned a man might damn himself so long as he did so with discretion; he would be answerable to his own conscience and it was none of the state's business. But where a man did not use discretion and thereby came into conflict with the criminal law it was the duty of the Director of Public Prosecutions to consider whether to take action. With the law relating to obscene matter this was no easy matter to decide, for who is to say whether a particular publication tends to deprave or corrupt? The simple answer that a jury must decide these things is of no real assistance to the Director of Public Prosecutions; for it is he in the first instance in the majority of cases who has to advise on or select the particular matters to put before a jury.

Striving always, as he did, to exclude his personal opinions and views it was nevertheless necessary for him to make up his mind on some basis; he could and did take advice from Treasury Counsel but they were in the same difficulty. On the one hand the law prohibited the publication of obscene material and it was the Director's duty to act, on the other hand the public and general conception of what was immoral or obscene was in a fluid state and no one could tell the outcome. It may be that Mathew made mistakes in choosing to prosecute some particular work or in choosing some particular form of procedure but it was a measure of his courage that he did not act in such a way that he could be taken to regard the law prohibiting obscene publications as a dead letter. While recognizing that his task was well nigh impossible, Mathew nevertheless sought fairly to enforce the criminal law in the state in which it had been entrusted to him.

OFFICE REORGANIZED

Mathew was possessed of striking features, his face overwhelmed by the prominence of his eyebrows, but far from possessing a frightening exterior he was in fact a cheerful and affable man. He was a good man to work for because, although his department was relatively small, he had, during his period of office, reorganized it on modern lines, assimilating up-to-date methods of office practice; and he was able to strike a proper balance between delegation and retention of responsibility.

Expected to retire within a short time, Mathew had apparently decided to continue in office until after the general election in order to be of assistance in the field of election laws in which he had great experience. It is a tragedy that his death should have come so suddenly, but his successor will find that he has been bequeathed one of the most efficient and objective law enforcement departments in the world.

March 2, 1964.

Enrico Mattei, who was killed in an air crash on October 27, 1962, was one of the driving forces in the Italian scene. He was 56.

From the position which he established for himself as president of E.N.I., the state hydrocarbons concern, he could look back on humble origins as son of a member of the carabinieri in a small town of the Marche. His father happened to have been responsible at the turn of the century for the audacious capture of a famous bandit, and if some people have seen something of the condottiere in Enrico Mattei himself no one could deny that throughout his career he showed great audacity, whether inherited or otherwise acquired.

Born on April 29, 1906, at Aqualagna, near Pesaro, he began work at the age of 14 painting beds in a workshop at Matelica. From the start his qualities of application and resource were evident. Moving to a sweet factory, he worked his way to the managership by the time he was 19, when he had 150 employees under him. He soon abandoned a safe but limited provincial future to move to Milan, and within a short period had set up his own factory producing chemical products.

A RESISTANCE LEADER

With the outbreak of war and the German occupation Mattei entered the resistance movement and brought to it his proven administrative skill. He was twice taken prisoner and twice escaped. When the partisans rose in force against the occupiers Mattei was said to be commanding some 100,000 men. This experience was to set much of the tone of his later activities because as a Christian Democratic resistance leader he fought closely with the communists and other left-wing parties who have always given him credit since for constant anti-Fascism.

His real chance came in fact with his appointment in 1945 as commissioner in northern Italy for winding up the activities of the state company A.G.I.P., which under Fascism had failed to live up to the hopes stimulated by official propaganda of discovering oil and natural gas. Taking full advantage of the somewhat weak governmental authority at the time he completely disregarded his instructions, banking instead on his own instinct and information that methane was there to be found. Early in the following year he struck the rich deposits of the Po Valley, which, once he had gained the monopoly for his company, were to become the foundation of his economic power.

He sat as a deputy in the first Parliament of the Republic, but a straightforward political career was unsuited to his temperament. Though giving up his seat, he nevertheless maintained his political interest, exerting an influence which his opponents denounced as excessive both through his connexions with leaders of the Christian Democratic Party and by less tangible contacts in this and other parties.

LIBERAL OPPONENTS

His opponents at home were the Liberals, speaking in the name of private enterprise, and the right-wing as a whole in political affairs with, of course, private industry; abroad he clashed with the international oil companies from whom he failed to gain a place in the Persian oil consortium, replying with frequent attacks on their pricing arrangements and on the share of profits which they made over to the producer countries.

An autocrat by nature with few recreations apart from fishing, he showed little sign of a sense of humour, though he softened into laughter when describing a point scored off a rival. His delight in power was unquestioned and, if many people thought it reached dangerous proportions, his use of it was undoubtedly a formative influence in Italian policy and in internal economic development. His advanced social views were also striking and rooted in his own early experiences. He was one of the best known, most serious, most bitterly attacked, and most powerful Italians of his day.

October 29, 1962.

Somerset Maugham, C.H., died on December 16, 1965, in his villa at Cap Ferrat, at the age of 91.

For a long period, and more especially from his seventieth year onwards, he had occupied—and, in his own disillusioned way, taken pleasure in—the position of the most celebrated of English authors. No writer of his generation, indeed, graced the world of English letters with more complete or more polished assurance. There is a supreme efficiency of performance which seldom belongs to literature at its most creative but which is perhaps all the more spectacular for falling short of it. This was Maugham's achievement. As playwright, as novelist and as short-story writer, he was superbly successful. In all that he wrote during the long years of his artistic maturity the detachment and precision of his observation of men and manners, his ironic sense of the human comedy, his integrity of worldly good sense, and mastery of technical means and ends were such as to evoke unstinted admiration.

His resources of experience and craftsmanship were indeed of a remarkable order, and these alone enabled him to maintain in literature the semblance of a peculiarly disinterested attitude towards life. For, romantic in impulse though he was and possibly continued to be, sentimental though he often was through every appearance to the contrary, in putting pen to paper Maugham always sought the part of the disinterested spectator. He had his own considered philosophy, which was sincerely hedonistic, agnostic, and melancholy, and there is a deal of social and moral criticism implicit in his books and plays; but he was never deeply involved in the imaginative purposes of literature. As a novelist he would have wished for no better epitaph than: "He told stories supremely well."

CYNICAL STAMP

Success achieved, almost against his will, Maugham at one time desired passionately, as is evident in *The Summing Up*, a finely tempered essay in autobiography and one of the best books he wrote, recognition of a more serious kind. This desire, too, he outgrew, though not before it was partly satisfied. Regarded for many years by the intellectual pundits of criticism as a writer of cynical and fashionable stamp, acclaimed above all else for the glitter and artifice of his comedy and for his unfailing craftsman's skill, he was eventually saluted by the majority of older critics with sincere and handsome respect. It is doubtful whether his qualities as a novelist were justly appreciated in the early phase of his success. His astonishing economy of means apart, it was the candour of his acceptance of life as he saw it, the acute and dispassionate testimony to a mode of experience he had deliberately selected for himself, that gave substance and power to his fiction. Imaginatively Maugham from the beginning chose the way of the world.

For the illumination which he brought to his vivid statement of a materialistic ethic a reader could excuse his studied manipulation of plot and character, his recurring types, the relatively restricted range of his social observation. Yet, except in a single instance, where of set purpose he followed the bent of his emotional nature and in so doing apparently worked the romantic streak out of his literary imagination, there was another and less excusable failing in even the best of his novels. These are deeply flawed, after all, by his worldliness. What is called creative art is often imperfect, but it seldom if ever endorses the way of the world or takes its stand, as does so much of Maugham's work, on the mere accident of good fortune. A story-teller of great parts and supreme virtuosity, Maugham had nevertheless rejected almost at the outset of his career the deepest source of a writer's inspiration and, in the natural course of things, could not return to it even if he had wished to do so.

MEDICINE AND LITERATURE

William Somerset Maugham was born in Paris on January 25, 1874, the son of Robert A. Maugham, solicitor to the British Embassy there. He came of legal stock. His grandfather was one of the twin founders of the Incorporated Law Society, and a brother of the novelist became Lord Chancellor. From his mother Maugham inherited a tendency to tuberculosis. She died when he was eight, and his father died two years afterwards. In infancy Maugham had been looked after by French nurses and knew so little English that he is reported on one occasion to have exclaimed: "*Regardez, maman; voilà, un 'orse*!" After his father's death he was sent over to England to stay with an uncle, who entered him in the preparatory department of King's School, Canterbury. At the age of 13 he began work at King's School itself. He was delicate in health, much embarrassed by a stammer, and did not enjoy his schooldays. For a time the condition of his lungs gave anxiety. At 17 he persuaded his uncle to let him continue his schooling on the Riviera and at Heidelberg.

MEDICAL STUDIES

As an adolescent he had resolved to be a writer; it was, nevertheless, decided that he should study medicine, and in the autumn of 1892 he began to attend lectures at St. Thomas's Hospital. He did the minimum of work necessary for examinations; on the other hand, his private reading, in English, French and Italian, was copious and embraced much history, philosophy, and science as well as imaginative literature. In vacations he made his first Italian journeys. When the mere study of medicine gave place to the work of a house physician he began to take a lively interest in hospital routine, or at least in the spectacle of human circumstance which it presented. It was at this time that he began to fill notebooks with lists of words and phrases from his reading, with passages from Jeremy Taylor's *Holy Living and Holy Dying*, and from Dryden, Addison, Swift and others, which he committed to memory. He graduated M.R.C.S. and L.R.C.P. in 1897; but, having in hand two legacies and having published his first novel, he threw up all idea of medical practice and went to Seville to write.

Liza of Lambeth (1896), his first novel, which manages to be more than a little sentimental while displaying close study of French naturalistic fiction of the nineteenth century—Maugham always owed more to French models than to English, and to Maupassant most of all—was tepidly received and advanced him little further. He wrote his first play in Rome and had it produced, without noticeable results, in Germany; he came nearer to success as a novelist with *Mrs. Craddock* (1902); he made no great stir with a play put on for a few nights by the Stage Society in 1903, *A Man of Honour*.

SOPHISTICATED PLAYS

After hawking six full-length plays from theatre to theatre, Maugham had *Lady Frederick* put on at the Court in the autumn of 1907. The curtain came down at the end of the first performance amidst loud tumult. Here was success, here was fame, here even was history. Managers competed furiously for the rights of Maugham's plays. During 1908 he broke all records by having four plays running simultaneously in London. Their wit, their smartness, their adroit sense of the theatre at once matched and made the taste of Edwardian society in the stalls. For the next six years Maugham lived the life of a wealthy and fashionable playwright. He was much interviewed and much sought after; he was cartooned in *Punch*; he held a long lead over zealous imitators. In 1914 *The Land of Promise* was playing to full houses.

On the outbreak of war Maugham went to France as a dresser, then became an ambulance driver, but was soon given responsible intelligence work. Some of the Ashenden stories originate in this experience. He passed a year in Geneva, visited the United States, had a glimpse of the South Seas, and in 1917 was sent to Russia. But his lungs were again affected and he was required to spend several months in a sanatorium in Scotland. It was in 1915 that he published *Of Human Bondage*, of which he had written a first draft at the age of 24. This is the novel which stands out from the entire body of Maugham's work. It has a deeper sense of humanity than anything else he wrote and a sympathy with the promptings of romantic idealism which he never again sought to express. In Britain (though not in the United States) it was lost to sight in the harvest of war, though full recognition came later and was all the more generous in consequence. During these war years, too, he wrote the brilliantly successful plays, *Caroline*, *Home and Beauty*, *Our Betters* and *Caesar's Wife*, and also one of his novels, *The Moon and Sixpence*, which obliquely suggested the life of Gauguin.

During the 1920s Maugham travelled widely, visiting the South Seas, Malaya and China, and availing himself of whatever form of transport offered, from the donkey and bullock-cart to the tramp steamer and luxury liner. Human types, translated freely to the printed page, interested him more than the physical landscape, though he had an eye for that too. He filled his notebooks systematically and became specially expert in observing the ways of English people in far-off lands, acquiring material which he used to admirably calculated purpose in novels like *The Painted Veil* (1925) and *The Narrow Corner* (1932), and in collections of short stories such as *The Casuarina Tree* (1926) and *Ah King* (1933). A novel of his which has specially appealed to his warmest admirers is *Cakes and Ale* (1930), a satirical and sharp-edged portrait of English literary life of the period in which Maugham projects himself once more in the person of the novelist Ashenden.

AID FOR YOUNG WRITERS

His short stories, of which the best are faultlessly shaped and serve as models of dramatic interest, brought him considerable financial reward in America. So, of course, did his plays. But no playwright, it would seem, can hope for continuous success in the theatre, and Maugham's popularity reached its peak in the mid-twenties and then declined. *The Circle* was brilliant high comedy; *Our Betters* was wickedly glittering satire. Yet in each case *The Constant Wife* (1927), *The Letter* (1927) and *The Sacred Flame* (1929) drew from Maugham the expressed resolve to write no more plays. After *Sheppey* (1933), he did indeed abandon the theatre for good.

In 1935 Maugham made a journey to the West Indies and thence to California and began to write *The Summing Up*. The deeply controlled and contemplative statement in that book of his attitude to life and literature is of the highest interest. The book is, indeed, a wonderfully clear, honest and persuasive testament of faith. It provides, incidentally, a key to the part-confessional character of his concluding phase as novelist. This begins with the antinomian irony of *A Christmas Holiday* (1939), continues with the ripe moral paradox of a long short-story, *Up at the Villa* (1941), culminates in the mystical confection of *The Razor's Edge* (1944), and tails off in the professional artifice of *Then and Now* (1946).

Reported "missing" for a time during the fall of France in 1940, when he was living at the Villa Mauresque, a beautiful home at Cap Ferrat which he had occupied since 1928, Maugham reached Britain safely but spent the rest of the war years in the United States, where he argued Britain's cause.

In 1947 he instituted a fund for the annual award to a young British writer of outstanding promise of a prize of some £400 or £500 for the purposes of foreign travel. Years later more ambitious plans to help ill and struggling writers were announced. Nineteen forty-seven saw also another collection of his short stories, *Creatures of Circumstance*, on the commercial magazine level; the following year a novel, *Catalina*, which in a twopence-coloured historical setting pursued a light and easy vein of cynicism; the year after that *A Writer's Notebook*.

The work of his last years included stories that served as film scripts; a series of six essays, *The Vagrant Mood* (1952), of which the most instructive dealt—entertainingly, but not always kindly or perhaps fairly—with some novelists he had known; *Ten Novels and their Authors* (1954), an unexacting venture in criticism reprinted from articles in a Sunday newspaper; and *Points of View*, a further series of essays written, as he said, "for his own pleasure", which appeared in 1958.

PRODIGIOUS SALES

The sales of his books were prodigious; in the summer of 1961 he mentioned, casually, to his publisher a figure of 64 million. It is thought that perhaps 10 million copies of the novel *Of Human Bondage* have been sold.

In person he was dark, slight, and of medium stature, with a high forehead, olive skin and penetrating eyes. Maugham was a witty and sometimes disconcerting conversationalist and had also the rare virtue of being a good listener. A Commander of the Legion of Honour and an honorary D.Litt. of Oxford and the University of Toulouse, he was made a Companion of Honour in 1954. To his old school he left money for scholarships, his library of 5,000 books and money for a building to house them.

Maugham married, in 1915, Syrie, daughter of the philanthropist, Dr. Barnardo. She died in 1955. They had one daughter, who in 1948 married Lord John Hope (later Lord Glendevon).

In April, 1962, 35 of Maugham's notable collection of pictures—among them works of Gauguin, Picasso, Graham Sutherland, Renoir and Matisse—were sold in London for over £500,000. Shortly afterwards Lady John Hope secured a court order blocking the proceeds of the sale, claiming that nine of the pictures had previously been given her by her father. Towards the end of that year it was announced that Maugham intended to adopt his private secretary, Mr. Searle. In July a court at Nice, in a judgment on a suit by Lady John Hope, nullified the adoption and declared that she was Maugham's legitimate daughter. Early in 1964 a joint statement by the author and his daughter gave the news that they had settled their differences and that he had dropped his appeal against the Nice judgment.

December 17, 1965.

François Mauriac, the author who won the Nobel Prize for Literature in 1952, died on September 1, 1970, at the age of 84.

His death deprived French literary and intellectual life of one of its most distinguished figures. To his distinction as a novelist he added the virtues of complete integrity and personal independence as a social and political thinker. His *bien-pensant* upbringing and instincts did not prevent him from supporting the anti-Franco forces during the Spanish Civil War (in common with his fellow-Catholics Bernanos and Maritain). He also played an honourable and courageous role during the Occupation of France, yet generously—and characteristically—pleaded for the lives of certain collaborators condemned to death after the Liberation. He was an important, if solitary, figure—at once a liberal member of a largely conservative Church and a Catholic sympathizer with the predominantly secular Left.

Mauriac was born in Bordeaux on October 11, 1885. His family owned various properties in this area which was later to become the setting for his major novels and several plays. His literary work is dominated by the presence of this particular countryside—the pines, the heathlands, the vineyards, the shuttered houses, the sultry summer heat—and indeed Mauriac found this physical setting essential to the functioning of his literary imagination. At the same time, he was as much a critic of his native province as he was its product, portraying provincial life as characterized by deep roots, tight fists, small minds and hypocrisy.

Inevitably, Mauriac was later critical of his own upbringing in this community. He valued its strong religious sense but considered that he was subjected at an early age to false emphases which encouraged excessive scruples on minor points and inadequate scruples on essential matters. Nevertheless he accurately described himself (in 1929) as belonging to the race of those who, born within the Catholic field, have the certain knowledge that they can never leave it.

FIRST NOVEL

After a largely Catholic schooling Mauriac graduated from the University of Bordeaux in 1906 with a *licence-ès-lettres*. In the same year he entered the Ecole des Chartes in Paris, but gave up his studies after a brief period and devoted himself to literary and journalistic work. In 1909 he published his first volume of poetry, *Les Mains jointes*, which attracted the favourable attention of Barres, among others. A further book of verse, *Adieu à l'adolescence*, followed in 1911. A year later he became joint editor of a literary periodical, Les Cahiers, the aim of which was, almost predictably, to create and encourage "un art d'inspiration purement catholique".

Mauriac's first novel, *L'Enfant chargé de chaînes*, was published in 1913 and in the same year he married Jeanne Lafont. With the outbreak of the First World War he went to Salonika with a French ambulance unit but after four months was invalided out and returned to France. An intense period of self-examination followed, Mauriac's tatent matured dramatically, and in 1922 he published what he subsequently described as the first novel of which he was not later ashamed, *Le Baiser au lépreux*.

Mauriac's main career as a novelist followed with *Le Fleuve de feu* (1923), *Génitrix* (1923), *Le Désert de l'amour* (1925) *Thérèse Desqueyroux* (1927), *Destins* (1928), *Le Noeud de vipères* (1932) and *Le Mystère Frontenac* (1933). With the publication of the last of these novels Mauriac was elected to the French Academy. His fiction, with its delineation of family hostilities and its exploration of avarice, hatred, hypocrisy or sexual frustration, portrays that "univers catholique du mal", which it was Mauriac's purpose to convey to his readers.

MORAL PROBLEMS

He took his responsibilities as a "Catholic novelist" very seriously and set out the moral and technical problems resulting from this role in such works as *Le Roman* (1928), *Dieu et Mammon* (1929), *Le Romancier et ses personnages* (1933) and parts of his *Journal* (5 vols: 1934–53). However, while the earlier novels were deeply pessimistic in a general Jansenist sense, a new deepening of his Christian faith and a more charitable view of human weakness had become evident in *Le Noeud de viperes*. This emphasis was largely sustained in later major novels including *Les Chemins de la mer* (1939), *La Pharisienne* (1941), *Le Sagouin* (1951) and *L'Agneau* (1954).

The only play to achieve any marked success was *Asmodée* (1938), but Mauriac wrote biographies and essays of very great interest including studies of Racine (1928), Pascal (1931) and de Gaulle (1964), his *Mémoires intérieurs* (1959), *Ce que je crois* (1962) and the independently minded *Bloc-Notes* regularly produced since 1952 and contributed successively to *La Table Ronde*, *L'Express* and *Le Figaro littéraire*. Among other things, these articles revealed Mauriac to be a staunch supporter and ardent admirer of de Gaulle.

In 1947 Mauriac received an honorary degree of D.Litt. from Oxford University. He won the Grand Prix of the Académie Française in 1926. His death leaves a gap, which will not easily be filled, both in the French literary scene and in the ranks of liberal Catholicism.

September 2, 1970.

André Maurois, biographer, novelist, interpreter of England and the English to an older generation in France—perhaps in some degree to an older and more innocent generation than the present in Britain also—died on October 9, 1967, in Paris. He was 82.

A fluent and versatile man of letters, member of the Académie Française since 1938. Maurois was held in higher esteem in his own country before the catastrophe of 1940 than afterwards. Here he long had a special place in popular regard by virtue of his imaginative sympathy with things English and his wide if not always deep knowledge of our history and literature.

Les Silences du Colonel Bramble, his first essay in English interpretation, published in 1918, struck a shrewd, humorously discerning and by no means unflattering note that could not but endear him to the English reader. In France its effect at that time was at any rate to delight anglophil sentiment and to gratify more normal curiosity. It was, however, as a writer of biography, of English biography in the first place, that Maurois achieved general recognition, and here he possibly owed his success as much as anything to the comparative novelty of the style of the *vie romancée*. This was, or became, a widespread fashion in the 1920s, deriving largely from the simultaneous practice of Lytton Strachey in England, Emil Ludwig in Germany, and Maurois himself in

France. Maurois had neither Strachey's genuine learning nor Ludwig's inveterate habit of conviction, but his lightness and grace of fancy stood him in good stead. If, more particularly in his earlier work, he not seldom offended against imaginative good taste or displayed a marked want of proportion, it may nevertheless be fairly said of him that his intimate treatment of celebrated literary and historical figures stirred the imagination of many who would never have thought of tackling the old and more formal style of two-volume biography. He certainly did produce several good books—particularly his studies of Byron, George Sand, Victor Hugo, and the Dumas family.

A member of a Jewish family settled in Alsace, Emile Salomon Wilhelm Herzog, who assumed the name of André Maurois, was born in July, 1885, at Elbeuf, Seine-Inférieure. He was educated at the Lycée at Rouen, where he studied under Alain, performed his military service and then entered the family woollen mills, where he somewhat hesitantly remained, goaded by literary ambitions, until the outbreak of war in 1914. That dualism of impulse and calculation was characteristic of the man and was promptly translated in the writer. It was his war experience that provided the "copy" for his first book and served to accentuate an early bent towards English studies. Appointed liaison officer to the British 9th Scottish Division and afterwards sent to British G.H.Q., Maurois acquired a personal knowledge of the British officer which he put to well judged and entertaining use in *Les Silences du Colonel Bramble*.

VEIN OF LIGHT FICTION

Two further works in a similar vein of light fiction appeared in 1920, *Le Général Bramble* and *Les Discours du Docteur O'Grady*.

The success which Maurois won with these books eventually enabled him to retire from the family concern, though he was careful to retain a commercial interest in it until he felt confident that literature would maintain him. He had had one failure in 1919, a novel entitled *Ni Ange ni Bête*; but it was from failure that his first spectacular triumph sprang. The novel was founded on the life of Shelley, and after it had fallen flat Maurois recast the material in the form of a biography. *Ariel* appeared in France in 1923, and an English translation was published in the following year. The sales in France, Britain, and the United States ran into hundreds of thousands and Maurois found himself established in the front rank of popularity.

The reputation he then made was sustained by his later work, or at least by his later work as a writer of biographies. As a novelist Maurois too obviously lacked substance. The most interesting of his works of fiction is the semi-autobiographical *Bernard Quesnay* (1926)—there is a pronounced strain of autobiography in most of his fiction—a sincere and graceful effort though not a very satisfying one. The other more or less realistic novels, like *The Family Circle* (1932), make no great impression, while fantasies or semi-fantasies such as *The Weigher of Souls* (1931) and *The Thought-Reading Machine* (1938) dissipate their ingenuity in the thinnest of intellectual airs. As biographer, however, Maurois undoubtedly progressed. *Ariel* might fairly have been dismissed as a *tour de force*, clever but ill-balanced and of altogether doubtful validity in its estimate of Shelley as poet, while as regards its successor, *The Life of Disraeli* (1927), Maurois was obliged to meet sharp accusations of plagiarism. His *Byron* (1930) was another matter.

MOVE INTO HISTORY

It gave evidence of close study, finer sympathy and a better management of material than could have been looked for from the author until then. From this point onwards, Maurois took history and a great deal more in his stride along with biography. His books included studies of Lyautey and of Turgenev (both published in 1931), Voltaire (1932), Dickens (1934), and Chateaubriand (1938); an elegantly written work, here and there of serious historical value, on *King Edward and His Times* (1933) and a general account, shrewd and friendly if also defective in knowledge, of the history of England (1937); and a deal of miscellaneous literature.

He was as successful as a lecturer, speaking either in French or in English, as a man of letters, and was frequently in demand at American universities, in Switzerland and elsewhere. In 1928 he gave a course of lectures at Cambridge on *Aspects of Biography*, which later appeared in book form.

Maurois was attached to British G.H.Q. as French eyewitness in 1939–40. Many people in this country will remember the accents of entreaty and despair of his broadcasts in London while France was in collapse. His record in the United States, where he proceeded after the signature of the armistice, did him no great credit in the eyes of many Frenchmen, but he left Park Avenue, New York, for North Africa in the summer of 1943 and offered his services to the French military authorities. He published a thin and rather officially minded little book in 1940 on *The Battle of France* and another, not altogether unjust in analysis though almost painfully lacking in spirit, on *Tragedy in France*. *Call No Man Happy*, the autobiography he issued in 1943, has passages of great delicacy and often a ring of eloquent and sincere feeling, even of something more, but it contains also much idle chatter.

SUCCESS WITH BIOGRAPHY

Maurois's steady output continued after the war. In 1949 he published a comprehensive and readable *History of France*, but it was again in biography that he had his greatest success. In the space of five years, 1952 to 1957, he produced three extremely long and quite excellent biographies, *Leila or the Life of George Sand*, *Olympia or the Life of Victor Hugo*, and *Les Trois Dumas*. He acknowledged his indebtedness to his wife for a good deal of the research for these massive works, but, all the same, they were at least evidence of astonishing diligence, particularly as he wrote two or three novels during the same period. In 1959 he wrote a *Life of Sir Alexander Fleming* which was less successful.

His last years were full of activity; he wrote a life of the Marquise de La Fayette; a history of the U.S.A. from Wilson to Kennedy; a pictorial biography of Napoleon; a life of Balzac; a study of Victor Hugo and his times; a delightful parody *The Chelsea Way* or *Marcel in England*, and in May, 1967, *From Proust to Camus*.

His style was invariably clear and simple and although most of his works were translated into English—amongst many other languages—they are extremely easy to read in the original French and are thus invaluable for students, particularly as they are at the same time eminently readable.

Maurois was a divided nature, in whom the spirit of intellectual freedom contended from the beginning with a narrow and worldly family tradition. He was a spruce, alert figure, full of nervous energy and animation, and an engaging conversationalist. He received in his day various high honours from France, Great Britain, and the United States. In the war of 1914–18 he won the British D.C.M. and later became successively C.B.E. and K.B.E. Oxford, Edinburgh, and St. Andrews gave him honorary doctorates, as also did Princeton. He was twice married: first, in 1912, to Janine de Szymkiewicz, who died in 1924, leaving him two sons and one daughter, and secondly, in 1926, to Simone de Caillavet, by whom he had one daughter.

October 10, 1967.

Professor John Nicholas Mavrogordato, who died on July 24, 1970, aged 88, was the son of Nicolas Mavrogordato, the Constantinople-born descendant of the Chiote Mavrogordato, who settled in London in the seventies and pursued business in the City. From Elstree School he went to Eton as a King's Scholar. In 1901 he went up to Oxford as an open classical scholar at Exeter.

His academic record (a second in Mods and Greats) scarcely mirrored his ability, and on going down in 1905 he occupied himself for a time with private tutoring. In 1908 he joined Dent's as a publisher's reader and in 1910 added to his publishing duties the task of sub-editing *The English Review*, which had just come under the editorship of Austin Harrison.

In 1912, full of patriotic enthusiasm for the Greek cause, the young Mavrogordato went out as correspondent for the *Westminster Gazette* to cover the Balkan War, and on the termination of hostilities remained at Salonika for a year as a member of the international commission which had charge of the Turkish refugee camps. Some of his dispatches and correspondence were collected into a small volume, *Letters from Greece* (1914) which reflected his warm sympathies and quick perceptions.

Returning to London and literature in 1913, it was natural that on the outbreak of war, being unfit for active service, he should join the Anglo-Hellenic League, where he worked, under Ronald Burrows, at propaganda for the cause of Greece. He was honorary secretary from 1916 to 1918. He shared however to the full the disillusion of his generation with the course of the war and its diplomacy, and gave it expression in *The World In Chains* (1917), a passionate plea for pacifism and socialism.

After the war, experimenting for a short time at painting (for which he had a considerable talent) he developed an increasing interest in modern Greek studies. In 1919 he gave the first lecture at King's College, London, on the newly established Koraes Chair of Modern Greek Language, Literature and History. He wrote several articles on modern Greece for the twelfth and thirteenth editions of the Encyclopaedia Britannica as well as a standard general history of *Modern Greece, 1800–1931* (1931).

His introductory essay to J. H. Marshall's translations of *Three Cretan Plays* (1929) established the derivation of the Greek miracle play, *The Sacrifice of Abraham*, from the Italian *Isaac* of Luigi Groto. His own study of the *Erotokritos* (1929) was the first in English, and as well as an analysis of the poem, offers acute suggestions as to its origin and dating.

Mavrogordato had considerable gifts as a translator, and both his *Greek Folk Songs* (1927) and *The Poems of C. P. Cavafy* (1951) reproduce with singular success the lyric qualities of the originals. The Cavafy in particular combines scrupulous fidelity with sensitive poetic feeling and was mainly instrumental in winning for Cavafy his place in the esteem of the English public. *Digenes Akrites* (1956), of which he published the text with a line for line English version, showed what he could do in capturing the simplicities of the ballad-epic style; his notes and extensive introduction, which deals with both the textual and substantive problems of the poem, contribute much to its understanding.

His own lyric gift, though slight was pure. His verse play, *Cassandra at Troy*, received a performance at the Lyric, Hammersmith in 1924. *Elegies and Songs*, tinged with the Eliot pallor, but by no means lacking in feeling, was published in 1934.

In 1939 he succeeded R. M. Dawkins in the Bywater and Sotheby Chair of Byzantine and Modern Greek Language at Oxford, an appointment doubly gratifying to him since it renewed his connexion with Exeter, his old undergraduate college, and placed him in succession to a scholar whom he regarded as both mentor and friend. In spite of the fact that so much of his tenure of the chair fell in the war years, he contributed a great deal to the growth of his subject in Oxford before his retirement in 1947. His rare distinction of spirit, unfailing courtesy and generosity, his characteristic blend of youthfulness, modesty and independence won him a wide circle of friends.

In friendship, as in the arts, he was a connoisseur, but a connoisseur who practised discrimination without snobbery or vanity. Along with his delicate sensitivity went an almost boyish zest for new experience and an instant, almost quixotic, sympathy for any manifestation of the human tragedy, or, for that matter, the human comedy. He was an artist, who imposed a conscious form on even the most trivial acts of everyday living, no less than on his writing and scholarship. But the result was not a selfish preciosity, but a constant, lively sharing of delight.

He married, in 1914, Christine Humphreys.

July 27, 1970.

Constantine Mavroudi, for many years Correspondent of *The Times* in Turkey, and one of the best known personalities in Istanbul, died on October 31, 1961, at the Istanbul Club. He was 76.

He was born in Istanbul in December, 1884. Educated at the Galata Saray Lycée there, he entered the Turkish Diplomatic Service at the age of 17. He served in Athens, Belgrade, Rome, London, and Washington before leaving the service at the end of the First World War. After working in the Anglo-Turkish Mixed Arbitration Tribunal as secretary to the British Agent he became in 1929 secretary to *The Times* Correspondent in Istanbul, and later became assistant Correspondent. In 1940 he was appointed *The Times* Correspondent in Turkey, working between Istanbul and Ankara.

"Tino" Mavroudi, in his last years almost a legendary figure, was a much loved and much valued friend to a great number of people. He knew everybody; and everybody in Turkish life who mattered knew him. He retired from the active correspondent work for *The Times* in 1959, and continued as before to live at the Istanbul Club, in the heart of the city he had known all his life. Here he kept in touch as well as ever with affairs, both Turkish and international. Nobody was better informed than he.

Mavroudi was a strong personality. He had the clear mind of a Greek, but also, having worked all his life among Turks, and having served in his youth in the foreign service of the Ottoman Empire in many posts abroad and at home, he came to know all the leading figures in Turkish public life. He spoke perfect Turkish. He understood the Turkish character through and through, and it was often said of him that he "knew what the Turkish Government was going to do before it did it". His forecasts of political events, being based on such sure judgment, were almost always correct.

MODEL MESSAGES

His lucid mind made him an invaluable consultant on every kind of subject, whether it be personal or otherwise. He was one of those people who could immediately throw light on the most tortuous problems, and he had the faculty of reducing difficult matters to their essential terms. This quality, which made him much sought after, also made his reports to *The Times* models for all correspondents of how a message can be clear, concise, accurate, and comprehensive.

Mavroudi's most active period as a correspondent was during the Second World War, when Turkey was neutral, but under heavy pressure from both allies and axis. Perhaps Mavroudi's most famous dispatch was the one he sent in the summer of 1944, giving news of the passage of German warships through the straits, which led directly to the resignation of the Turkish Foreign Minister, Mr. Numan Menemencioglu.

His most difficult period of reporting, for a man who was at heart a Greek, came during the Cyprus dispute, the last big story he covered before he retired. But here, being by origin Greek, by nationality Turkish, and being the correspondent of a British newspaper, he was admirably placed to present a clear objective view of the problem, which he always did. He was a great reader, especially of history, and this added to his deep understanding of international problems.

Mavroudi was an excellent companion, full of humour, and packed with extraordinary reminiscences of his earlier days, when he represented the Ottoman Empire in all sorts of strange places, such as the Russian Caucasus. He always told a good story. A few years ago when he was so ill in hospital that they had called in the priest, Mavroudi a few hours later simply got up, put on his hat, got in a taxi, and returned to the Istanbul Club.

He was a very fine bridge player, and though in his later years his health obliged him to give up the game, he would sit at the club watching his friends play, and would get as excited about each game as if he held the cards himself. Sometimes, against doctor's orders, he would play the hand of someone who was out of the room.

November 1, 1961.

Elsa Maxwell, who died in New York on November 1, 1963, achieved considerable renown as a hostess and party giver and as a chronicler of her own and other people's social activities. She was 80.

In one of her several autobiographies Miss Maxwell wrote that she was recognized "as the arbiter of international society and the most famous hostess in the world". It is not necessary to accept this as a fair assessment to acknowledge the fact that, in the limited world she set out to conquer, she scored a remarkable success.

She was born neither wealthy, nor beautiful nor socially prominent nor, as she once agreed, with any great talent. But she had boundless energy, resourceful determination and an instinct for the art of entertaining. She knew many prominent people both in Europe and America, and claimed on her 80th birthday in May, 1963, that she had more friends than anyone else.

TO BE HOSTESS

Elsa Maxwell was born in Keokuk, Iowa, in 1883, but grew up in San Francisco, leaving school at the age of 14. Her decision to become a celebrated hostess was apparently provoked by an incident in childhood, when she was once told she could not attend a party because her parents were too poor. She resolved, she said, to give parties all over the world "to which everyone would want to come, but to which the rich would be invited only if they had something more than money".

For a time she worked as an actress in vaudeville and played the piano in a peep show. She also wrote songs—including a number of patriotic choruses for British troops in the First World War, of which her own favourite was a song called "Carry On, Carry On".

She made her reputation as a lively party goer and a somewhat eccentric hostess in Europe in the twenties, when an apparently bored society was grateful for the moments of excitement she created—such as by setting free live seals instead of serving a fish course at dinner. She welcomed the publicity these occasions brought her and further stimulated it throughout her life by some controversial books and newspaper articles on the activities of her widening circle of acquaintances. A number of these involved her in suitably sensational feuds and libel proceedings.

November 4, 1963.

J. Lewis May, author, editor and translator, who died on May 28, 1961, at the age of 87, was one of the last with personal recollections of the literary nineties.

The son of Dr. L. J. May, James Lewis May was born on August 10, 1873, and educated at University College School and in France. As a young man he was an assistant in John Lane's and he remembered Lane coming to see his father on a December evening in 1889 to announce that from bookseller he had decided to turn publisher. In later life May could look back to a memorable day in 1894 when he and a senior member of Lane's staff for the first time "filled the window of the little shop in Vigo Street—the orginal Bodley Head—with *Yellow Books,* and nothing but *Yellow Books,* creating such a mighty glow of yellow at the far end of Vigo Street that one might have been forgiven for imagining that some awful portent had happened, and that the sun had risen in the west"—as indeed it had.

May was fortunate in his chief whom he later served as reader—his career offers a parallel to that of Frank Swinnerton—literary adviser, author, and finally, and perhaps best of all, as biographer (*John Lane and the Nineties,* 1936).

LITERARY PURSUITS

All his life May was fully and happily occupied in the pursuit of literature. He was editor of the English edition of the works of Anatole France (whom he knew well and often visited); for some years he was joint editor with Henry Davray of the *Anglo-French Review;* he did a great deal of translation from the French, Latin and Italian; and he wrote studies and biographies of George Eliot, Charles Lamb (he was a vice-president of the Charles Lamb Society) and Fénélon. His study of John Henry Newman, published in 1929, which was well received and carried his name abroad, was followed four years later by *The Oxford Movement.* Soon afterwards, like some of the leaders of that movement, he himself was received into the Roman Catholic Church.

His two volumes of reminiscences, *The Path through the Wood* (1930) and *Thorn and Flower* (1935) were written with a mellow gravity that betrayed an addiction to Hazlitt and Lamb. Lewis May had the power of confessing his own thoughts with charm; he had also a keen appreciation of individuality which makes his memories of such as William Watson, Ernest Dowson, Francis Thompson, and Stephen Phillips particularly evocative.

In 1937 he was granted a Civil List pension in recognition of his services to literature.

He married in 1896 Elizabeth Hyde, by whom he had a son and a daughter.

May 30, 1961.

President Leon Mba, president of Gabon, died in Paris on November 28, 1967.

Mba had been under medical treatment in Paris, presumably for cancer, since August of 1966. Vice-president Albert Bongo ran the country in his absence since that date.

Mba was president of the Republic of Gabon from the time it became independent of France. An attempted *coup d'état* in February, 1964, failed; French reinforcements restored his regime after his deposition by Army subalterns.

A member of the dominant Fang tribe, Mba was one of the first political leaders in Gabon. He formed in 1946 the Mouvement Mixte Gabonais, the local manifestation of the Rassemblement Democratique Africain, the umbrella party which covered the then French African colonies. In 1953 Mba reorganized the M.M.G. and under its new name, the Bloc Democratique Gabonais (B.D.G.) it won a large majority of seats in the March, 1957, elections. Mba became the first vice-president of the executive council and later, under a revised constitution, its president. With full independence in 1960 he became head of state.

Born in 1902 in Libreville, the capital of Gabon, and educated in local Roman Catholic schools, Mba worked first as an accountant with the French administration, and then as a journalist. A former head man of the Libreville district, he was elected to the territorial assembly in 1952 and in 1956 became Mayor of Libreville.

Like his friend President Houphouet-Boigny of the Ivory Coast, Mba was an opponent in 1957 at the R.D.A. conference of the proposals for a federation of French West Africa. He believed rather in individual independence. Much of the political opposition to him in domestic politics, however, was due to his pro-French policies.

November 29, 1967.

Tom Mboya, who was assassinated while shopping in Nairobi on July 5, 1969, will leave a huge gap in Kenya's political life, and he is assured of a prominent place among the founding fathers of the Kenya nation still in its birth throes.

But he was not at the time of his death, as he was once considered to be, a serious contender for the presidency after *Mzee Jomo Kenyatta.* He would have been politically important in the new regime, and whatever part he might have played, his expertise and experience of foreign affairs will be sorely missed. As Minister of Economic Planning, he repeatedly went abroad with other ministerial colleagues to carry through negotiations, especially, but not exclusively, on economic matters. He was, for example, a prominent alternate to the Finance Minister. Mr. James Gichuru, in representing President Kenyatta at the Commonwealth Prime Ministers' meeting in London in January, 1969.

A member of the Luo tribe, he was virtually de-tribalized, and acquired to a greater degree than most African politicians a "western" outlook. This made him a formidable administrator and departmental minister, but it was not without its disadvantages for Mboya personally, who lacked the popular following enjoyed by his fellow Luo and great rival. Mr. Oginga Odinga. A touch of arrogance, born of his own self-confidence and knowledge of his intellectual distinction, made him unpopular with many of his less gifted colleagues also. In the ups and downs of Kenya politics. Mboya sometimes appeared to be on the way out, but in the last analysis his sheer ability kept him at the centre of events.

Born on August 15, 1930, the son of a sisal worker. Thomas Joseph Mboya was educated at the Holy Ghost College in Manju and then at the Royal Sanitary Institute's Medical Training School. He qualified as a sanitary inspector and worked in that capacity for a short time for the Nairobi City Council from 1951 to 1952.

He was quickly involved in politics and trade union affairs and in 1952 became a member of the Kenya African Union (the pre-Mau Mau nationalist party) and also national general secretary of the Kenya Local Government Workers' Union. A year later he was general secretary of the Kenya Federation of Labour, a post which he retained until 1962 (when he became a Minister) and which was in his hands a position of great power and influence. In 1960 he became general secretary of the Kenya African National Union, the ruling party of Kenya, and in this capacity performed invaluable services to his leader, Kenyatta, and to the party as a whole. He was above all a good organizer and himself well organized. Kenyatta's reemergence doomed Mboya's hopes of winning the leadership of independent Kenya at the outset, but he probably never abandoned hope of the eventual fulfilment of that ambition.

HIS SLOGAN

It was Mboya who, as an ardent pan-Africanist, produced the anti-white slogan "Scram out of Africa".

If Mboya had had the opportunity early enough—before he had become involved so deeply in politics—to attend a university, there is little doubt that he would have had a brilliant academic career. As it was, he managed with the aid of a British Workers Travel Association scholarship to spend a year at Ruskin College, Oxford, Writing about this experience in his book *Freedom and After* (1963) Mboya declared, "The year at Oxford gave me more confidence in myself; it gave me the time to read more; it taught me to look to books as a source of knowledge." Dame Margery Perham, who knew Tom Mboya in his Oxford days and after, wrote in 1965: "He had no time to work for his degree but, knowing him then and since. I would say that no African leader has an abler brain or a stronger will."

To see Mboya in the middle of a complicated

constitutional conference, or to watch him presenting his Government's policy to the British Government before independence, was to understand the truth of this assessment. He knew exactly what his long-term aim was, and he knew exactly the tactical manoeuvres that would be necessary, and effective, in approaching it. He was a master of political tactics, flexible, always ready to seize an opportunity, never permitting himself to be side-tracked. He wrote interestingly about his theories of political strategy and tactics in his book, stressing above all that in dealing with the colonial regime results could best be obtained by a policy of toughness, though he did not believe in obduracy when once the end had been achieved. To use his own phrase, the policy was "Growl now, smile later". His skill in manoeuvring the white Kenya settlers out of power was ruefully acknowledged even by themselves. He was not however in essence anti-white, though he could sound it—and anti-Asian also. In his work on the important sessional white paper on African Socialism he resolutely took a cautious line which annoyed the left wingers of all racial compositions. In 1962 Mboya married Miss Pamela Odede, daughter of one of the leading Luo of the older generation, and herself a woman of considerable personality and ability.

July 7, 1969.

Professor Dr. Lise Meitner, who died on October 27, 1968, at the age of 89, was a pioneer of radioactivity as early as 1910 and in 1939 was joint discoverer of nuclear fission.

Her name was in the news when in 1966 she shared the Fermi Award with Otto Hahn and Fritz Strassmann for their joint researches that led to the discovery of uranium fission, the basis of atomic energy. But her main contributions to physics go back to the early years of the century. Otto Hahn died in July, 1968.

Her nickname, "The German Madame Curie", was justified in so far as she did most of her work in Germany. But she was born in Austria, on November 7, 1878, the third child (out of eight) of a respected Viennese lawyer. With some reluctance he let her enrol at the University of Vienna; in 1901 that was a most unusual thing for a girl to do, and she met with ridicule and occasional unpleasantness. But the great physicist Ludwig Boltzmann gave her inspiration and encouragement, and in 1906 she graduated Dr. Phil., one of the first women to do so at the University of Vienna.

To find a job proved difficult, and in 1907 she went to Berlin to study theoretical physics with Max Planck, the founder of the quantum theory, whose infallible kindness and fairness became her guiding star. But already in Vienna she had begun to study the new and puzzling phenomenon of radioactivity. To continue her experiments she needed help with the chemical aspect of the work, and she was lucky in finding a partner in Otto Hahn, who had studied radiochemistry in England and Canada. That partnership lasted for over 30 years.

At first she worked in an old carpentry shop and was not allowed to enter the chemical laboratory where the male students worked; that restriction was lifted in 1909 when Germany admitted women to academic studies. In 1912 Hahn was made head of the Chemical Institute of the newly-founded Kaiser Wilhelm Gesellschaft, a research association supported by the German heavy industry. At the outbreak of war in 1914 Hahn, a reserve officer, was called up to active service, and Lise Meitner volunteered as an X-ray nurse in the Austrian army. But they continued work during leave periods, and in 1918 were able to announce the discovery of protactinium, a long-lived radioactive element of great importance.By then Lise Meitner had returned to the institute, no longer as a "scientific guest" but in charge of the department of radiation physics.

For a number of years Hahn concentrated on chemical applications while Lise Meitner did much to clarify the relation between the beta and gamma rays of radioactive substances, i.e, the fast electrons and the hard X-rays they send out. But in 1935 they joined forces again to study the transformation of uranium nuclei under neutron bombardment. Enrico Fermi in Rome had published some evidence that nuclei heavier than uranium were formed, "transuranic elements" which were not found in nature, and at first the results of Hahn and Meitner suported that view. But working conditions under the Nazis became difficult, and after the annexation of Austria Lise Meitner no longer felt safe from racial persecution; with the help of Dutch colleagues she escaped from Germany and found sanctuary in Sweden.

MISSED SEEING PROOF

So she was not on the spot when Hahn and Strassmann broke the web of error by showing that some of the nuclei formed from uranium, far from being transuranic, were only about half as heavy as uranium. But on hearing of this she worked out and published (with her nephew O. R. Frisch) the physical details of the process, which was named nuclear fission.

In Stockholm she continued work on nuclear physics for another 20 years, first at the Nobel Institute, then at the Atomic Energy laboratory. In 1960, having become a Swedish citizen, she retired to England, to be closer to her nearest relatives. But she still took a lively interest in physics, writing, lecturing, and travelling often to Europe and America until 1965 when her health no longer allowed her to leave Cambridge.

She made many life-long friends with colleagues and others all over the world, who appreciated her wide interests and open mindedness.

Among her friends she could be lively and witty, but she never quite lost her shyness, despite the many honours she received; numerous honorary degrees, the Planck medal, the Otto Hahn medal, and a share in the Enrico Fermi prize in 1966; and memberships of several academies, including foreign membership of the Royal Society.

October 28, 1968.

Molly Mellanby, C.B.E., died on September 16, 1962, at the age of 68.

The daughter of Henry Mellanby, of Yarm-on-Tees, she was born on November 2, 1893, and from Princess Helena College, Ealing, went up to Newnham College, Cambridge, in 1914. On coming down in 1917 she joined the staff of Tunbridge Wells High School where she remained until 1921, in which year she took up an appointment at Roedean and later became a housemistress.

In 1935 when Miss Lilian Barker was made an Assistant Commissioner of Prisons Miss Mellanby was appointed to succeed her as Governor of H. M. Borstal Institution, Aylesbury. She followed in Miss Barker's steps once more in 1943, when she was herself made an Assistant Commissioner. She became Director of Prisons and Borstals in 1950 and a year later, on the retirement of Captain R. G. Williams, was appointed a Prison Commissioner. She later became Director of Women's Establishments and retired in 1959. Two years earlier she had been made C.B.E.

September 18, 1962.

Adnan Menderes, who was executed on September 17, 1961, was Prime Minister of Turkey from 1950 until he was thrown from power by the military *coup d'état* of May 27, 1960. He will probably be remembered, when this period of Turkish history comes to be written, as an able and gifted leader whose lack of political judgment at the critical point of his career led both to his own personal downfall and, at least temporarily, to the collapse of the multi-party democratic system in Turkey which began in 1945.

In the eyes of many good judges of the Turkish situation if Menderes had resigned in the critical spring of 1960, or had decided to try to resolve the internal crisis not by repressive measures but by holding free and fair elections, the Democrat Party of which he was leader, and he himself, would have had a fair chance of being returned to power. At worst he would have had the status of a distinguished former Prime Minister. But instead, owing to his tragic misjudgment of the situation he was up against, and his apparent vacillation between tough and moderate policies, the Army struck. Together with President Celal Bayar, Menderes was seized with his whole government and the entire parliamentary majority of the ruling Democrat Party, and held on the island of Yassiada near Istanbul, where they were later put on trial on charges of having "violated the Constitution".

Menders, during the later years of his term of office, was hated and feared by the Turkish intellectuals, not only because they held he had attempted to install dictatorship in Turkey but even more because the intellectuals, for the most part ardent followers of Kemal Atatürk's secular reforms of the 1920s, believed him to have encouraged the popular reaction towards Islam in Turkey, which has been such a feature of the country since Atatürk's death, and thereby seriously to have prejudiced

Atatürk's avowed ideal to make Turkey permanently part of the western community. The intelligentsia held that Menderes, not himself a religious man, had hypocritically used the power of Islam among the people to acquire electoral support. This was to some extent true. But his encouragement of the return to religion, for which he got himself abominated by the intellectuals, made him beloved by a large part of the Turkish people, to whom Atatürk's reforms and general intentions had always remained incomprehensible, if not unacceptable.

During the enormous trials of the Menderes regime which began on the island of Yassiada on October 14, 1960, Menderes and his former colleagues faced innumerable charges ranging from petty corruption or immorality to the major political accusations of "violating" the Constitution and attempting to set up a dictatorship. During his several indictments on these charges the State Prosecutor asked eight separate times for the death sentence for Mr. Menderes, and the main weight of the indictment was directed against him, and to a lesser extent against ex-President Bayar.

As the trial went on, the accumulation of the different charges, combined no doubt with sheer physical and mental fatigue involved in the interminable sittings, more and more demoralized Menderes. Whereas in some of the earlier trials he had still spoken with something of the fire and eloquence which in his day had made him one of the best speakers in Turkey, as the end of the trial drew near he withdrew more and more into himself, appeared more and more listless, and finally almost lost the power of speech altogether. When, on July 25, 1961, he addressed the Yassiada court for the last time in his own defence, his words could hardly be heard, and his arguments were relatively weak. Never during the trial did he speak out boldly in defence of the many good aspects of his period of office, as did several of his former ministers and deputies, and, to the disappointment of his many supporters, he practically let the case go by default.

Yet in spite of his poor showing during the trial, Menderes continued to exert an almost mystical influence on his followers throughout Turkey, especially those who were most deeply attached to the Islamic tradition.

ECONOMIC PERILS

A man of great drive, an able speaker, and a shrewd politician, he saw himself as a man equipped to bring Turkey economically and culturally into full partnership with Europe and the United States while maintaining his ties in the Muslim world of the Middle East. Though his achievements were remarkable in his early period of office, latterly Turkey's parlous economic condition had been blamed on his policies. He will best be remembered for his efforts in the international field to make Turkey a strong and reliable member of military pacts to resist Communist pressure, undeterred by the proximity of his country to Soviet power.

Born in Aydin, Anatolia, in 1899, Adnan Menders was the son of a large landowner whose fortunes were based on cotton. He was educated at the American College, Izmir, where he learnt English and acquired the basis of western sympathies which he later championed in Turkey. He read law at Ankara University, but gave up a legal career to return to his estates as a progressive farmer. He had been an associate of Atatürk in the days after the First World War of Turkey's "war of liberation", but it was not until 1930 that he entered politics as a member of the opposition party which Atatürk attempted to foster. Though he then distinguished himself as an able speaker and critic of the Government it was only in 1945 that he came to the fore as chief lieutenant of Celal Bayar in the new Democrat Party.

His efforts in building this opposition party were so successful that it swept the polls in Turkey's first real election in 1950. Celal Bayar then became President and Menderes Prime Minister. An energetic man—he often walked several miles to his office from home—he set about the second stage of Turkey's modern revolution, concentrating on an investment programme which brought more material benefits than had the days of Atatürk's rule. He was a keen advocate of private enterprise and at first wanted to end some of the national enterprises set up in Atatürk's day. His party essentially represented the merchants and landowners of the coastal districts and Istanbul, and as a practical farmer himself he did much to modernize Turkey's agriculture.

In the elections in 1954 he returned to power but by then the train of criticism had set in. The Opposition claimed that he had used devious methods to get reelected. After a year of his second term of office the weak foundation of some of the economic reforms which he had so energetically promoted became apparent. The budget was unbalanced and attempts to get a large American loan failed—though much American aid had previously been given. By the end of 1955 opposition in his own party was growing but he was able to form a new Cabinet and at the same time to introduce stringent controls which stifled the opposition, notably a harsh Press law which was much criticized outside Turkey.

If he overplayed his economic hand, he could be regarded as more successful in the alliances he built up. He had been firmly in favour of Turkey's membership of N.A.T.O. and his attempts to build up alliances in the Middle East led to pacts with Pakistan and Iraq out of which the Baghdad Pact grew. Earlier he had been a strong supporter of the Balkan Pact. As Prime Minister he had travelled a good deal, visiting Great Britain as the first Turkish Prime Minister ever to do so, in 1952. In 1955 he visited Italy and had an audience with the Pope. Early in 1960 he visited the Far East and was again in London and in Bonn. His control over both home and foreign affairs was absolute, and the Turkish attitude to the Cyprus question must be attributed mainly to him. While support for this policy and for Turkish firmness against the Soviet Union and in support of his western allies was never actively opposed in his own country, the opposition to his somewhat dictatorial rule was steadily growing, promoted by the worsening economic situation. At the time of the Iraq revolution some Opposition papers drew a parallel between him and Nuri es Said.

In February, 1959, while on his way to the conference in London (Mr. Macmillan had been to Ankara five months earlier) which resulted in the Cyprus Agreement, Menderes's plane crashed in foggy weather near Gatwick airport, causing the death of 14 of his compatriots. Mr. Menderes himself, by a miracle, escaped almost unharmed. In many discussions which were held after the May *coup d'état* about the extraordinary lack of judgment which led Menderes, previously so shrewd a statesman, not to realize that with the bulk of the Army against him he could not hold on to power, it has often been suggested that the Gatwick air accident, which had been known to weigh heavily on his always hypersensitive mind, might even have affected his mental stability.

September 18, 1961.

Adolphe Menjou, a major character actor of the cinema, who grew up with it and whose film career extended over more than half a century, died in Hollywood on October 29, 1963, at the age of 73.

Few actors of his day had a longer career or appeared in more numerous and varied films. The characters he assumed ranged from hero to villain, and from elegant French sophisticate to wisecracking Broadway go-getter. His comedy, too, could range from wit and satire to the broadest farce. Some of the best-known films of both the silent and sound eras were connected with his name.

Adolphe Jean Menjou was born in Pittsburgh on February 18, 1890. He was educated at the Culver Military Academy, Indiana, and Cornell University, and gained his first experience of acting with college theatrical groups, and subsequently in vaudeville and on the professional stage in New York. After a few years of this training he went to Hollywood, where his first big film was *The Sheikh,* in 1922, in which Rudolph Valentino was the star. His good fortune in being given parts in films destined to become famous in the history of the cinema continued thereafter, and in 1923 his reputation was made when he appeared as the cynical and wealthy Parisian in Chaplin's production, *A Woman of Paris.* This was the film in which Chaplin himself did not appear, and its worldly sophistication and originality of direction caused something of a sensation at the time. Thereafter Menjou was constantly in demand and made many silent films, usually as a suave, cynical man-about-town, but this type-casting began to restrict his abilities.

A turning point in his career came soon after the advent of sound, when he was given the part of Walter Burns, the ruthless and fast-talking city editor in the Hecht-MacArthur story of newspaper life in Chicago called *The Front Page.* It was a remarkable film, and in it Menjou gave a remarkable portrait of a character that was by no means purely fictional. Soon after this Menjou appeared in another memorable film, Frank

Borzage's interpretation of *A Farewell to Arms*, in which he played Lieutenant Rinaldi opposite Gary Cooper as Frederic Henry, and Helen Hayes as Catherine Barkley.

During the 1930s Menjou made many films, but by now he was able to get away from the elegant gigolo type and to concentrate more on tougher and more realistic parts. He played a bookmaker in the Damon Runyan story, *Little Miss Marker*, opposite Shirley Temple, and then turned to broad comedy in a remake of the famous Harold Lloyd comedy about a fighting milkman, called *The Milky Way*. He played a Hollywood producer in *A Star is Born*, the film which brought Janet Gaynor back to the screen in 1937, and a similar part in *Stage Door*, with Ginger Rogers. Soon after came Clifford Odet's story of the boxing ring, *Golden Boy*, with William Holden and Barbara Stanwyck, *Roxie Hart*, with Ginger Rogers. *The Hucksters*, with Clark Gable, Deborah Kerr, and Ava Gardner, and *State of the Union*, with Spencer Tracy and Katherine Hepburn, were notable films of the 1940s in which he appeared.

In the 1950s he made fewer films, but he appeared in one of the best of the decade—Stanley Kubrick's *Paths of Glory*, with Kirk Douglas and Wayne Morris, a bitter indictment of corruption in the high command during the First World War; and once again he returned to playing the part of a worldly and sophisticated Frenchman.

Menjou remained throughout his film career a supporting actor, for he never had quite the presence or personality that makes the star, but his range was so varied and his style so polished that his presence could enhance the dramatic value of even the best of films.

October 30, 1963.

Vapal Pangunni Menon, C.S.I., C.I.E., who died on January 1, 1966, at the age of 71, will be remembered, long after most Indian administrators of his generation have been forgotten, as the author of two detailed and indispensable works of reference covering the major happenings in the subcontinent during his lifetime: *The Story of the Integration of the Indian States* (1956) and *The Transfer of Power in India* (1957), both published—and this is significant—not with the assistance of the Indian Government, but with the help of the Rockefeller Foundation.

V. P. Menon's talents raised him from the obscurity of humble origins to great power and influence; but they needed for their fulfilment either of two contingencies: the British respect for sheer capacity, executive and intellectual, or the unswerving support of an influential and fearless patron. It was "V.P.'s" misfortune that both these essentials failed him in turn while he was at the height of his powers, so that a career which for many years showed great promise terminated, through no fault of his own, in almost the same obscurity from which it had emerged.

Born on September 30, 1894, of poor parents, V. P. Menon could not aspire to the Indian Civil Service; he had to be content with a humble clerkship in his own Presidency of Madras. But his outstanding abilities enabled him by degrees to overcome the handicap with which he had started; his British superiors noticed him. He moved up the ladder of promotion stage by stage; by 1917, when Edwin Montagu, as Secretary of State, visited India, he was a marked man. He was chosen as Assistant Secretary in the new Reforms office; by 1942 he had become its head as Reforms Commissioner after 14 years of practical experience in the working of the Montagu-Chelmsford scheme and of the constitution of 1935. This experience made him invaluable to Lord Mountbatten, and he found himself in the thick of the hectic work which preceded the formal termination of British rule in 1947. His account of the process, in which painstaking scholarship is buttressed by first-hand knowledge of everything that went on, will never be superseded.

When India became independent, and the Reforms office was wound up, Menon was seized on by the dynamic Sardar Vallabhai Patel, Nehru's only rival for power and influence, to help in the process of liquidating the Indian States, which the Sardar was determined to effect as quickly as possible. As Secretary to the Government of India in the States Department, Menon attained the heights of power: he was the main instrument in bringing under the control of New Delhi an area, made up of many ancient principalities and innumerable minor jurisdictions, covering half a million square miles with a population of some 87 millions. It is not perhaps unfair to say that Menon found the task congenial. He, the ex-secretariat clerk, was in a position to enforce upon the proudest dynasties of ancient India the settlements which, in his judgment, the interests of the new India required. His decisions were invariably upheld by Sardar Patel. The bargains which he struck were most advantageous. At a cost of pensions to the ex-rulers amounting to £6m. sterling a year, he acquired for the new Indian Government territories exceeding in extent the areas lost by the creation of Pakistan, bringing in £60m. annually.

With the death of Sardar Patel in December, 1950, Menon lost at once his patron and his main defence against those whose enmity or jealousy he had aroused in the days of his power. He did indeed officiate for a short time as Governor of Orissa in 1951, and then became a member of the Finance Commission. But after 1952, he was relegated to obscurity, in which he found some consolation through the composition of the remarkable books already mentioned. The label of "Patel's man" stuck to him: at a time when other civil servants far inferior to him in ability and experience were promoted to the highest offices of state, he was suffered quietly to retire under the age-limit. Had he possessed the prescience to harness himself to the chariot of Nehru, his fate might have been happier; but the world would probably have lost two great books.

January 4, 1966.

Major-General Sir Stewart Menzies, K.C.B., K.C.M.G., D.S.O., M.C., head of Britain's Secret Intelligence Service—which became known as MI6—from 1939 to 1951, died on May 30, 1968, in London at the age of 78.

To become head of the Secret Intelligence Service in the third month of a great war, with fresh tasks and new men pouring in; with Admiralty, War Office. Air Ministry and Foreign Office pressing for attention to their needs; with sparse moneybags suddenly swelling: and enemy activity creating new problems and new opportunities almost daily that was an ordeal to test a superman, Menzies would have been the last to claim for himself such quality. Indeed, standing up to the superman who was then Prime Minister probably caused him the most wearing concern. His direct access to Winston Churchill and the Chiefs of Staff must have been a source of pride to "C"; many a brilliant offering of intelligence was he able to bring to them. But they were also exacting, critical and often quite unaware of the problems that accompany the search for secret information.

In 1939 the Secret Service, like the fighting services, had suffered for years from under-manning and under-spending. Menzies's predecessor, Admiral "Quex" Sinclair, had his work cut out to decide how to use his limited resources under governments which were seldom confident of what the right targets for intelligence should be. Certainly between the wars Germany was not the main target, and the fluctuations of British policy towards Moscow created problems of loyalty of which much has lately been heard. The swift and ruthless overrunning of the Continent by the Germans in 1940 made it necessary to start again from scratch over most of occupied Europe. True, outstanding success was won by members of the allied Secret Services, notably the Norwegian one and later by the Resistance in France and the Low Countries; but the war was to show that the agent was no longer the first arm of intelligence work and that information won by technical means—above all by the study of wireless traffic—was becoming more important and increasing the authority and scope of the Service Directors of Intelligence.

It was in this rapidly changing Whitehall that Menzies's charm and intuitive gift were so valuable; even Philby paid tribute to it. He was overloaded, like all the men then in power, with paper-work and his assistants did not, perhaps, rise to the challenge of world war. Nothing in their peace-time experience had prepared them for the tasks laid on them as first Germany, then Italy, then Japan became an enemy—and as Soviet Russia after 18 months became an ally. The brilliant men brought in from outside—scholars. writers, bankers, journalists—raised the quality of the Service's work but they did little to lighten its administrative burdens.

The pressure was at its worst in the period after summer 1940 when Churchill was searching in every direction for offensive openings. Target succeeded target in rapid sequence: Norway, the Canaries, raids on France, Madagascar, Syria. It was not understood that the channels used by Menzies and his men needed long and patient preparation. (Who in his senses had thought of Norway as an intelligent target during the period between the wars?) To meet the criticisms of the Service Directors of Intelligence Menzies accepted the appointment to his own office of their nominees who were given the rank of deputy directors. The "commissars" made little difference. The vital work was being done elsewhere, under Menzies's direction it is true, by the code-breakers and analysts working on whatever the operations of war might bring to their desks.

Menzies's retirement in 1951 passed unnoticed by the general public because newspapers were observing the Whitehall request that the head of MI6 should not be embarrassed by identification and publicity. In the past two or three years, books and articles, published in Britain and abroad, had made the convention no longer enforceable. The former chief was obliged, therefore, to hear and read critical accounts of his department's war work—some of it unfair or at least unanswerable—without being able to reply. One source, but not the only one, of this criticism was his former officer, the traitor Kim Philby; and it was the searching investigation of the Philby affair, and of its connexions with the Burgess and MacLean defections, that brought MI6 into a glaring and unfavourable light.

To a man who could rightly claim—as Professor Trevor Roper wrote recently—that the enemy intelligence services had been mastered and outwitted in war by his own this was a galling experience. The one person who could have spoken up decisively in his defence—Winston Churchill—died before the sensation began. Whether historians will ever be allowed to assess his work is highly doubtful. If they are, they will doubtless note that Britain in peace time tried to get intelligence on the cheap. It was necessary to rely extensively on personal contacts in the world of finance, shipping, the Services, the press and so on. If that network—inadequate for war—was on an old-boy basis, so are most net-works, whether in the party state or the democratic one.

As the spider in the centre of such a network Menzies was suitably equipped by birth, by education, by connexion and by first war experience. A man of different background might not have been so much liked by his staff, so approachable, so successful in working with and initiating the Americans and able to survive five years at Churchill's right hand. If his death should provoke more curiosity than respect, that is one of the penalties of holding an office in which it is impossible to answer back to critics who can never be perfectly informed.

Steward Graham Menzies was born on January 30, 1890, and educated at Eton. From 1909 to 1910 he served in the Grenadier Guards, and from 1910 to 1939 in the Life Guards. During the First World War he was mentioned in dispatches, awarded the D.S.O. and M.C., becoming Brevet Major and subsequently Brevet Colonel. Menzies was a Grand Officer of the Legion of Honour, and Grand Officer of the Order of Leopold. He was commander, Legion of Merit and a member of the Order of Polonia Restituta. Menzies was a Grand Officer Orange Nassau.

Menzies married three times: first in 1918, Lady Avice Sackville (from whom he obtained a divorce in 1931), daughter of the eighth Earl De La Warr; secondly, in 1932, Pamela (who died in 1951), daughter of the Hon. Rupert Beckett; and thirdly in 1952, Audrey, daughter of Sir Thomas Paul Latham.

May 31, 1968.

Lord Merriman, P.C., G.C.V.O., O.B.E., who died on January 18, 1962, at the age of 81, was President of the Probate, Divorce and Admiralty Division since October, 1933, and twice Solicitor-General, first from 1928 to 1929, and again from 1932 until his elevation to the Bench.

Frank Boyd Merriman was the eldest son of Frank Merriman, J.P., of Hollingford House, Knutsford. He was born on April 28, 1880, and educated at Winchester. He was called to the Bar by the Inner Temple in 1904, and became a pupil of Gordon Hewart, who later became Lord Chief Justice. He joined the Northern Circuit, early acquiring a large junior practice, as a local at Manchester and on the Circuit, where his name was known through his family association with Cheshire. At the outbreak of the First World War he was commissioned in The Manchester Regiment and his career in the army was a distinguished one; he was promoted to the rank of major, in the 22nd Battalion of the Regiment and in 1917 he was made Deputy Assistant Adjutant General. He was three times mentioned in dispatches and made O.B.E.

In 1919 he took silk, and in the following year he was appointed Recorder of Wigan. As a leader he did well on the Northern Circuit, and in time he began to appear frequently in London. The first case which brought him into public notice was the distressing litigation arising out of the defamatory statements which Captain Peter Wright made about W.E. Gladstone. In the action brought by Wright against Lord Gladstone, Merriman had the difficult and unsympathetic task of appearing for the plaintiff, which he performed with an ability, a tact and good taste which won general admiration. Thenceforth his practice steadily grew until the time he became a Law Officer.

Meanwhile, he had at the General Election of 1924, in the Rusholme Division of Manchester, beaten the late C. F. Masterman by a majority of over 5,000, which was increased to over 18,000 in 1931.

SOLICITOR-GENERAL

This constituency he represented during the whole of his Parliamentary career, which must be considered a successful one. He was popular in the House; if he was vigorous, he was always fair; and his pleasant manner would conciliate if it did not always convince an opponent. Without having attained a greater position than that of many another successful lawyer who passes through the House on his way to the Bench, he was fortunate enough, in the absence of more formidable competitors, to succeed Sir Thomas Inskip as Solicitor-General in March, 1928. The appointment was generally welcomed and it was justified in its result. He was reappointed to that office when in January, 1932, Sir William Jowitt resigned, to be succeeded as Attorney-General in the National Government by Sir Thomas Inskip, who had served under him as Solicitor-General. Merriman held the post of Solicitor-General until the autumn of 1933 when he was appointed to succeed Lord Merrivale as President of the Probate, Divorce, and Admiralty Division.

Merriman's appointment to so high an office, at the early age of 53, raised no hostile criticism, if little enthusiasm, among practitioners in that division, where Merriman had probably hardly ever held a brief. It has, however, never been possible to accommodate that very heterogeneous branch of the High Court with a President familiar beforehand with the work of all its branches, and the great Presidents of the past, such as Hannen and Gorell, owed their reputations more to their capacity to learn the practice after their elevation to the Bench than to wide previous experience—especially as regarded the probate and divorce work—at the Bar.

At the time of Merriman's appointment the Admiralty work, with the world-wide decline in shipping, was much shrunken, while the number of divorce cases had greatly increased.

In his early days on the Bench he betrayed nervousness and irritation, probably due to his unfamiliarity with divorce work, and to his anxiety to be thoroughly satisfied with all the points raised. This naturally disturbed the practitioners at that Bar, who felt that Merriman did not always accord them the trust which should exist between Bench and Bar. But with the passage of time his attitude was more tactful and his manner much more amenable.

He was not unnaturally shocked at the flagrant collusion in many of the cases that came before him, and about a year after his appointment to the Bench he delivered an address to the Law Students of Birmingham in which he pointed out with some force the unsatisfactory position when "the public were taught to expect that its Judges should be blind to a conspiracy of litigants to present a case founded on fraud".

Discussing, on one occasion, the use of the words adultery and misconduct in divorce cases, Merriman said that it was a pity that plain English was not used about these matters.

"When I say plain English," he said, "I mean that, so far as I know, ever since the tablets of stone were translated into English in the English version of the Bible, adultery has been the word, not misconduct, or intimacy or any other paraphrase of it."

The Second World War and its consequences greatly increased the work of the division over which Merriman presided. The prize cases, it is true, were much fewer—through the absence of neutrals—than in the war of 1914, and most of the work was of a more or less formal character, since the main principles of law had been so recently laid down. But the divorce work, owing to war conditions disorganizing family life, and also to the wider grounds for divorce provided by recent legislation, had grown to such an extent that Parliament and the public were seriously concerned at the arrears which were accumulating and the consequential delays involved which amounted to a denial of justice. At the time of Merriman's appointment in 1933, the number of petitions filed was under 5,000 per annum; by 1947 it was over 50,000, and the judicial strength of the division had by that year been increased from three to eight and is now 11. In 1946 a strong committee, presided over by Lord Justice Denning, was appointed by Lord Jowitt, the then Lord Chancellor, to investigate the whole subject and suggest remedies. Merriman gave evidence before the committee and produced an elaborate and ingenious scheme involving the setting up of what he called Commissions of Conciliation and Inquiry working in tribunals, which would see the parties and report their findngs to the Court. After the report, what he called "Banns of Divorce" were to be published in the district where the parties lived, and, if no objection was raised, the Court would pronounce a decree. The committee did not adopt this scheme, and, as their principal recommendation, proposed the appointment of the County Court Judges and a number of Silks of the Divorce Division as Commissioners to try divorce cases, (which recommendation was adopted), as well as a number of other reforms calculated to reduce delay and expense.

In 1927 he was made a Bencher of his Inn. In 1949 he became Deputy Treasurer, in which year King George VI was Treasurer, and the Queen (now the Queen Mother) was Treasurer of the Middle Temple, the Deputy Treasurer then being Colonel Sir Henry MacGeagh. K.C. A joint dinner of the Benchers of both Inns was held in Middle Temple Hall at which the King and Queen presided. Merriman and MacGeagh were both created G.C.V.O. in 1950.

In 1946 Merriman presided over the Bishop of London's Commission to consider the rebuilding or restoration, the abandonment or adaptation to alternative uses of the bombed churches in the City of London, which in October, 1946, issued an elaborate report.

Merriman was created a peer in January, 1941. He was an honorary member of the American and Canadian Bar Associations and an honorary LL.D. of McGill University.

In private life Merriman was much liked, and his high character and genial disposition endeared him to a wide circle of friends. He fished and he played golf, he enjoyed good wine and a good cigar. In the club which he most frequented, the Savile, he was popular.

Merriman married, first, in 1907, Eva Mary, second daughter of the late Rev. Henry Leftwich Freer. She died in 1919, leaving two daughters. In 1920 he married Olive McLaren, third daughter of Frederick W. Carver, of Oakhurst, Knutsford. She died in 1952 and he married, in 1953, Jane, younger daughter of James Stormouth, of Belfast.

January 19, 1962.

Professor Ivan Meštrovíc, the sculptor, died on January 16, 1962, at the age of 78, in Indiana.

He was the leading artist of Yugoslavia in the period when its national unity was taking shape though he was not only mainly responsible for a nationalist movement in the arts but was highly regarded as a sculptor in Europe generally. His work was noted for its technical skill in which there was a forceful and linear element and his early productions in particular were evidently inspired by a strong religious and patriotic feeling. The international developments of sculpture in the past 30 years have perhaps tended to overshadow his achievement or to emphasize by contrast its local characteristics. In Yugoslavia itself the younger sculptors have probably been more influenced by the modern internationalism of art though some were trained by him, but when all qualifications are made of his work and fame he must be accorded a highly distinguished place in twentieth-century plastic art.

Ivan Meštrovíc was born in 1883 at Vrpolje in North Dalmatia, the son of Croatian peasants. He tended sheep as a boy and was taught to carve in wood in the peasant craftsman style by his father. At the age of 15 he was apprenticed to a marble-cutter at Spalato and after three years went to Vienna where he studied at the Academy until 1904, being influenced by the ideas represented by the Vienna Secession. He soon became of note by the exhibition of his work in various European capitals and was recognized as the main power of an emergent national art in the exhibition at Zagreb in 1910 and the international exhibition in Rome in 1911. His principal patriotic achievement was his design for the Temple at Kosovo and its series of sculptured figures of Yugoslav heroes.

His work included a number of religious reliefs and carvings in wood, of which the "Deposition" in the Tate Gallery is a good example. He executed numerous portraits, among them those of President Masaryk, President Hoover, and Pope Pius XI. His bronze of Sir Thomas Beecham (1915) is in the Tate Gallery. He was greatly esteemed in England, where in 1915 an exhibition of his work was held at the Victoria and Albert Museum, and in the United States, where a full exhibition was shown in 1924 at the Brooklyn Museum. He designed for Chicago its bronze equestrian statues of American Indians. One of his main works was the Memorial Chapel to the unknown soldier on Mount Avala, Belgrade. In the carving of the single figure his masterpiece may be accounted the portrait of his mother at prayer (1925). The inclusion of his "Torso" (from the Tate Gallery) at the open-air exhibition of sculpture at Battersea Park in 1948 among works by Rodin, Epstein. Maillol and Moore was a reminder of his historical place.

He was rector of the Academy of Fine Arts, Zagreb, from 1923 to 1942, and went to the United States in 1947, becoming an American citizen in 1954.

From 1947 until 1955 he was Professor of Fine Arts at the University of Syracuse, and was appointed Professor of Fine Arts at Notre Dame University in 1955.

Many of his works are in the Yugoslav National Museum, Belgrade, but his sculptures were also bought by museums and galleries in Brussels, Budapest, Florence, and a number of American cities.

Some years of his later life were spent in Switzerland as well as the United States, though he visited Yugoslavia from time to time. He presented the Yugoslavian state in 1955 with the villa at Split which houses the gallery now known by his name and contains many of the works he made before the Second World War as well as some pieces he carved in the postwar period.

January 18, 1962.

Edmond Michelet, French Minister of Culture, who died on October 9, 1970, the day after his 71st birthday, was an outstanding example of a Christian in politics.

A fervent Catholic throughout his life, he played a magnificent part in the anti-Nazi resistance both in France and in Dachau concentration camp, and later served General de Gaulle in a series of ministerial posts. He was noted among Gaullists for his liberalism, but also for his ability to maintain friendship, in spite of unflinching honesty, with people of widely differing political opinions.

Michelet was born in Paris on October 8, 1899, the son of a prosperous grocer from Bearn. At the age of 18 he volunteered for service in the First World War. He soon joined Jacques Maritain in the Catholic Action Movement, becoming president of the Jeunesse Catholique du Béarn in 1922, and later of that of the Corrèze. In 1926 he took up residence at Brive, his wife's home town, as a grain broker. He later founded a commercial agency, and in due course became president of the National Federation of Commercial Agents. Yet he kept up his activity as a Catholic militant. In 1932 he founded the Equipes Sociales in Brive, and in 1938 he helped Francisque Gay to found the Nouvelles Equipes Françaises.

After the defeat of France in 1940, Michelet did not hesitate. He was twenty-four hours ahead of General de Gaulle in publishing a call to resistance, in the form of a quotation from Péguy who, with de Gaulle, was to remain his chief earthly source of inspiration. In 1940 he helped found the "Liberté" resistance group, and in 1942 the larger network known as "Combat". Arrested by the Gestapo in January 1943, he was held for six months at Fresnes and then transferred to Dachau, where General Delestraint, head of the secret army, named him as his successor before being shot. As chairman of the French Committee in the camp he carried out "the work of St. Bernard", although himself suffering from typhus and constantly watched by the SS. Like a ship's captain, he insisted at the liberation on being the last to leave the camp.

On his return to France he quickly found himself involved in journalism and politics, being elected in October 1945 as M.R.P. (Christian Democrat) deputy for the Corrèze. General de Gaulle made him Minister of the

Armed Forces and he retained this post in the first two governments after the General's resignation in 1946.

Expelled from the M.R.P. for predicting the probable return, to power of the general, Michelet none the less remained on friendly terms with the Christian Democrat leaders. He fought the 1951 election unsuccessfully on a Gaullist ticket, but in 1952 became Gaullist Senator for Paris, working in close personal contact with the general. In the later 1950s he was one of those few Gaullists who came out strongly against the Algerian war, and after returning to office in 1958 he worked untiringly to bridge the gap between France and the Algerian nationalists. (He was Minister of War Veterans in 1958 and Minister of Justice from 1959 to 1961—in which capacity he also introduced a number of important legal reforms.)

From 1962 to 1967 Michelet served as the General's nominee on the Constitutional Council, after which he returned to the government as Minister in Charge of the Civil Service. Finally in 1969, after the General's second resignation, he reluctantly decided to stay on in public life and took over from M. Malraux as Minister of Cultural Affairs, a post which he kept until his death in spite of ill health. "I, succeed Malraux?" he remarked with characteristic humility, "it's as if François Coppée were to replace Pindar".

Michelet is survived by his widow, seven children and more than 40 grandchildren.

October 10, 1970.

J.S. Middleton, assistant secretary of the Labour Party for 31 years until 1934, and secretary from 1934 until his retirement 10 years later, died on November 18, 1962, at his London home.

James Smith Middleton was born in 1878 at Retford, the son of the late A. E. Middleton, who was originally a printer (starting as a printer's devil) and became eventually a newspaper editor and proprietor. In 1880 A. E. Middleton, who was a Radical in politics, joined John Murdoch, the leader of the Crofter Movement, in producing the journal of the movement, *The Highlander*, at Inverness. This did not long survive and Middleton's childhood was passed in various boroughs—Whitehaven, Ipswich, and Rochdale—where his father pursued his ordinary journalistic activities. Eventually, in 1888, A.E.Middleton bought the *Workington Star*, a weekly newspaper, on which his son started work, two years later, as an office boy, later having experience as a compositor and a reporter.

He took an early interest in the activities of the Independent Labour Party and of the Labour movement generally. In 1900 he became secretary of the Workington Trades Council and shortly afterwards secretary of one of the first local Labour Representation Committees in Britain. Two years later he went to London as a newspaper compositor, and in October, 1903, became part-time assistant, and then full-time assistant, to Ramsay MacDonald, the secretary of the national Labour Representation Committee.

At first their work had to be carried out in one dingy back room of MacDonald's flat in Lincoln's Inn Fields. The following year they were able to hire two rooms in Victoria Street and MacDonald received a salary of £250 a year, out of which he had to find Middleton's pay of £100. It was in these circumstances that a long friendship and understanding between the two men was founded.

In 1906, after its successes at the general election, the L.R.C. converted itself into the Labour Party, MacDonald and Middleton continuing in their posts.

The same election had returned MacDonald to Parliament and thenceforward the administrative work of running the rapidly growing Labour Party fell largely on Middleton, for MacDonald's successor as secretary in 1911 was Arthur Henderson, also a member of Parliament. In 1934 the Labour Party decided that its secretary should in future not sit in Parliament and not aspire for Ministerial office, so Middleton was the only possible choice as successor to Arthur Henderson.

He had admirable qualities for a back-room worker. He never sought the limelight: he left that to the Parliamentary leaders of the party. He never made speeches on party policy. His name was, therefore, absent from the headlines. He was patient, hard-working, attentive to detail, and utterly loyal to his leaders and to the party he served. In his office—as he conceived its functions—there was no opportunity for making a public reputation, and he did not seek one. On his retirement in 1944, he was described by the late Professor Harold Laski, then chairman of the party, as "one of the greatest servants that the Labour movement had ever had". He was honoured by the Parliamentary Labour Party on his eightieth birthday, when he was the guest of honour at a celebratory dinner.

Middleton's first wife had died in 1911; and he married as his second wife, in 1936, Lucy Cox, daughter of Mr. and Mrs. Sidney Cox, of Keynsham, Somerset who was Labour M.P. for the Sutton Division of Plymouth from 1945 to 1951, and in whose political career he took the greatest interest and pride. In his retirement he acted as her election agent.

November 19, 1962.

Professor Ludwig Mies van der Rohe, who died on August 17, 1969, was generally acknowledged to be one of the three or four most influential architects of the twentieth century. The distinctive qualities of his work were a classical sense of form, combined with a logical expression of structure. His authority, particularly over the generation of American architects emerging from the Second World War, lay in the fact that his austere architecture, above all an architecture of law and order, could be taught like a science and practised by others with reasonable success.

Ludwig Mies was born at Aachen in 1886—Van der Rohe was his mother's surname. He attended the Cathedral School and later served an apprenticeship in his father's stone-cutting yard, where he acquired that knowledge of the mason's craft which became the hallmark of his buildings. Like many of his contemporaries he had no formal architectural training but learnt to draw as a designer for stucco decorations. In 1905 he went to Berlin where he worked for two years in the office of Bruno Paul, the furniture designer, to improve his knowledge of wood. In 1907, at the age of 21, he left to build his first commission, a highly competent house in the then popular eighteenth-century manner. At that time the influence of English domestic architecture, particularly through Hermann Muthesiu's *Das Englische Haus*, was strong in Germany and Mies, as he was later always to be known, came under this influence, even making a visit to England to see the new garden suburbs.

In 1908 he joined the office of Peter Behrens where Walter Gropius was a senior assistant and Le Corbusier was to work for a short period. Behrens, one of the most productive architects in Germany was then the designer—both of industrial products and factories—for the Allgemeine Elektricitäts Gesellschaft (A.E.G.) and much of his work showed the influence of the neo-classical architect, Schinkel. While these were to be considerable, his practical experience was also to be greatly extended by an assignment to supervise Behren's prestige German Embassy at St. Petersburg. The influence of Schinkel on his own work was seen in a project for the Bismark Monument (1912) as well as in a number of domestic designs at the time. In the years following the 1914–18 War, Mies became a champion of avant-garde art movements and publications and emerged as a strikingly original architect. Some of his most daring and paradigmatic projects including the glass skyscraper, date from these years.

In 1927 as first vice-president of the Deutscher Werkbund, an organization for the improvement of industrial design, he was responsible for the permanent housing exhibition at Stuttgart called the Weissenhof, to which many of the most progressive European architects contributed. Mies's own contribution was a crisp but modest block of flats.

As a result of this project he was commissioned at the age of 43 to design the German pavilion for the 1929 International Exhibition at Barcelona. Although unfortunately destroyed, this was one of the unquestioned and most influential masterpieces of twentieth-century architecture embodying the clearest statement of Mies's ideas of architectural space. It was for this pavilion that he designed the famous Barcelona chair. In 1930 Mies carried out his last important prewar European commission, the Tugendhat house in Brno, Czechoslovakia. As in the Barcelona pavilion space was subdivided within a single large area by free standing screens of such rich materials as ebony and onyx. All the furniture and every detail down to the handles of this immaculate building were designed by Mies.

In 1930 Mies was appointed Director of the Bauhaus at Dessau and the following year made a member of the Prussian Academy of Arts and Sciences. Under local Nazi pressure Mies moved the Bauhaus to Berlin, only to close it down in 1933. Finding it increasingly hard to work under the Nazis, he emigrated to America in 1937 and soon after was made Director of Architecture at the Armour Institute, Chicago, later to become the Illinois Institute of Technology, for which he designed a campus plan in 1940. The buildings for this campus on a cleared slum area of South-side Chicago were carried out over a period of some 15 years. They consist of a series of precise prismatic blocks disposed formally on a flat table, the overall 24ft. grid being given visual expression in the steel frame. Few groups of buildings in our time have such consistency and freedom from passing fashion. In the 1950s Mies realized two other important projects: a highly refined steel framed house with glass walls, for Dr. Edith Farnsworth on the Fox River, and two glass and metal apartment towers on Lakeshore Drive, Chicago, which recall the unrealized paper projects for glass skyscrapers of 30 years previously.

The success of these towers was followed up by a number of similar, more extensive projects in various other American cities culminating in the simple monumental bronze tower for the Seagram company on Park Avenue, New York, one of the most beautiful urban buildings of our era and certainly the ultimate statement in glass and metal skyscraper construction. Mies's "skin and bones" architecture was throughout remarkably consistent and if his narrow and austere approach did at times lead to a certain dryness, a dedicated sense of order, disciplined by his famous axiom "Less is more", has left us some of the sublimest buildings of modern times.

In 1968 together with Lord Holford, he designed a 290-ft. office block for a site opposite Mansion House. In 1959 Van der Rohe received the Royal Gold Medal from the R.I.B.A.

August 19, 1969.

Stanislaw Mikolajczyk, the former Polish peasant leader, died in Washington on December 13, 1966. He was 65.

Associated from the start of his political career with the Peasant Party, Mikolajczyk, after the military collapse of his country in 1939, was elected vice-president of the Polish National Council in exile, was then appointed deputy to General Sikorski, and, after the latter's tragic death in 1943, succeeded him as Prime Minister of the Polish Government in London. In this capacity he was greatly esteemed by the Allied representatives with whom he found himself in contact for his balanced judgment and democratic views. More clearly, perhaps, than any other member of the exiled Government, he recognized the need for establishing the closest and friendliest relations between a restored Poland and the U.S.S.R. But the restored Poland that he envisaged while the war against Nazi Germany was still to be won was, in Stalin's own phrase at the time, "strong, independent and democratic".

Mikolajczyk laboured sincerely to persuade his colleagues in exile to accept Russian terms for setting up the new Polish State, resigned as Prime Minister when he could not carry them with him, and in June, 1945, entered the Polish Provisional Government in Warsaw as Minister of Agriculture and Vice-Premier. Almost from the start, however, he was subjected to virulent press attacks and denunciations as a reactionary; his powers were curtailed; and, after the Polish elections of January, 1947, against the conduct of which he entered a strong protest, he went into opposition. In October of that year, at a time when agrarian and opposition leaders in south-eastern Europe had suffered judicial murder or long imprisonment, he "disappeared" from Warsaw. He reappeared again in the British zone of Germany—he had escaped through the Soviet zone—and left no doubt that flight had been the only alternative to awaiting a sentence of death from a Polish military court. Quite plainly he had lacked neither courage nor pertinacity in pursuit of his hopes for his country. But the whole tide of events in eastern Europe was against him.

Stanislaw Mikolajczyk was born in 1901 in a village near Poznan, in a Polish province annexed by Prussia in 1793. He was one of the 16 children of a farm labourer, who migrated to Westphalia, worked there as a miner for some 10 years, and returned with the savings he had accumulated and bought a small farm near his native village. The son, after a brief schooling and a spell of work in a sugarbeet factory, inherited the farm, took an immediate interest in general farming problems, founded a Farm Youth Union in the province, and became known as a peasant leader of active temper and moderate views. Elected to the Sejm in 1930, he became secretary of the parliamentary group of the Peasant Party, but found himself thwarted for most of the period of Pilsudski's dictatorship. It was he, however, in the absence of Witos, the exiled party leader, who largely directed the peasant strike of 1937. When war came in 1939 Mikolajczyk fought in the ranks, retreated with his unit into Hungary, and made his way to France across Yugoslavia and through Italy.

Appointed in 1941 Minister for Home Affairs in the exiled Government and, on the resignation of General Sosnkowski, Sikorski's deputy, he was well qualified two years later to continue Sikorski's work in building a new Poland on democratic lines. As the civilan leader of a coalition of four parties, indeed, he was the only figure likely to command the confidence of Poland's allies. But with the rapid advance of the Red Army into Poland his difficulties multiplied fatefully. Mikolajaczyk sought to resolve the bitter and tangled Soviet-Polish dispute by every means at his disposal. In June, 1944, he flew to Washington and saw President Roosevelt; in the following August he was in Moscow; he was again in Moscow in October, when Churchill took part in Three-Power discussions on the frontier question. After his resignation in November, Mikolajczyk continued to advocate the acceptance of the Curzon Line as Poland's eastern frontier. Dissensions in Polish circles in London grew sharper, however, and in the following June he left once more for Moscow, seeking to assist in the broadening of the Polish Provisional Government in accord with the agreement reached at Yalta. By the end of the month he had become Minister of Agriculture and one of the two Vice-Premiers.

In view of the general aims of Soviet policy in Poland and indeed throughout eastern Europe it is today obvious that Mikolajczyk was attempting an impossible task. His position became less and less tenable from month to month. The campaign of arrests and intimidation directed against his party before the elections of January, 1947, left him with no choice but to demand their annulment. Then pressure from within his own party became intensified. His flight abroad, in the company of several other members of his party, some of whom were captured, was undertaken not long after the execution of Petkov, the Bulgarian peasant leader. Mikolajczyk went to Britain, where his wife had been living for some time, and then proceeded to the United States. He had by then been denounced by the Polish Government as a traitor to the Polish state and nation and had been declared to be banished for life.

While in the United States Mikolajczyk wrote *The Pattern of Soviet Domination,* in which he denounced Russia as "a gigantic economic menace to private initiative and private enterprise". By this time Mikolajczyk's divorce from his European radical background was complete. In 1960 he paid a short visit to Britain to give evidence in a libel action.

December 14, 1966.

Max Miller, one of the most successful comedians of the declining years of the English music-hall, died on May 7, 1963, at his home in Brighton at the age of 68. He belonged essentially to London and to Brighton, and to the tradition of the individual concert-party entertainer, whose virtuosity he developed to a fine art.

It must have surprised many people who had heard that Miller's material was *risqué*—as indeed it was though saucy might describe it better—to find that he himself was not at all the vulgar, red-nosed extrovert they may have expected. In person he was distinguished and had decided attractions. Although it was understood that he was a "cheeky chappie", and a cockney at that, he triumphed with the slenderest literary material by a disarming display of diffident candour and disingenuous pathos, sustained by remarkable self-confidence and a masterly sense of timing. If his jokes rarely rose above the mildly salacious; if his songs—which he sang in a light and pleasantly modulated voice—were not notably distinguished; if the little ritual dance in his flowered plus-fours was purely frivolous, though executed with unexpected grace—all this did not matter, because Miller in his way was a genius of the music-hall.

In Miller's best period, which coincided with the Second World War and the decade preceding it, he held his vast audiences in the palm of his hand. "Ain't I got lovely blue eyes?" he would ask them wistfully, standing alone in the middle of the stage before a plain backcloth. The audience would titter doubtfully. Miller deprecated the lack of seriousness with a wave of his hand "No, no—when I open 'em up?"—and he ogled them anxiously. This personal communication, so difficult to describe, or to achieve, was essentially a thing of the music-hall, or to a lesser extent of the revue or concert-party, the last-named being the branch of entertainment in which Miller served his apprenticeship. Outside the living theatre Miller was not the same man, for he depended upon establishing an intimate relationship with an immediate audience. Although he often appeared in films, on radio or on television, his impact in these media was blunted.

Max Miller was born at Brighton, Sussex. The main stage influence of his youth was derived from that famous old music-hall performer G. H. Elliott, "the Chocolate Coloured Coon". When Elliott came to Brighton, Miller never lost an opportunity of seeing him, usually from the gallery. He learnt the rudiments of soft-shoe dancing and practised ardently after watching Elliott. Years later he was able to show his gratitude by inviting Elliott to be a "guest star" in several of his variety programmes.

It was in 1913 and 1914 that Miller first appeared at concerts in and around Brighton as a light comedian and dancer. He enlisted in the Army in August, 1914, and after preliminary training was sent to India, where he gained useful experience in concert-party work as comedian, singer and dancer. On his demobilization, early in 1919, he joined Jack Sheppard's Entertainers on Brighton Pier, and after his first season was promoted to be principal comedian in the show. In 1921, touring London and the provinces as chief comedian in revue, he developed the act that made him famous, writing his own patter and songs. He made his first impact on the music-halls as a single turn early in 1924, when he assumed the title of "the cheeky chappie" and adopted his flamboyant attire, which hinted at the cockney costermonger and served to enhance his height on the stage.

In 1925 Max Miller was "featured" at the Holborn Empire, where he appeared frequently until that theatre was bombed in September, 1940, his last appearance there being in the revue *Applesauce*! He became a great favourite —perhaps the greatest of all—at the Holborn Empire. His first appearance at the London Palladium was in 1929, and each of his subsequent visits there saw an increase in the size of Miller's billing until he was performing for 30 minutes as "top of the bill", a unique achievement for a British comedian at this theatre. Miller was chosen to appear in three Royal Variety Performances at the Palladium, in 1931, 1937 and 1955. Of his several incursions into British films, perhaps the most notable were in *Friday the Thirteenth*, *The Good Companions*, and *Educated Evans*, in which he hit off exactly the Edgar Wallace character.

Miller remained faithful to the methods that had served him well.

May 9, 1963.

Sarah Gertrude Millin, the South African novelist and biographer who was a powerful and vigorous interpreter of her country's history and customs, died on July 6, 1968. She was in her late seventies.

In clear, clenched prose, with never a word wasted (as one critic put it), Mrs. Millin illuminated the particular dilemmas which beset her fellow-countrymen. Hers was a vision which was incisive and astringent: in *God's Stepchildren* Mrs. Millin (herself descended from Jewish immigrants) used her sympathetic imagination and analytical historical outlook to portray with a tormenting immediacy the lot of those who were descended from a white missionary and a black girl. As a biographer her work tended to a romantic interpretation: her sincere opinions seemed to distort her historical perspective at times in her life of General Smuts. Her insight of Rhodes as a man and a visionary made her life of him a forceful portrait. Besides the biographies of these gigantic figures in South African history, Mrs. Millin wrote a definitive historical study *The South Africans* (later published as *The People of South Africa*), an autobiography *The Night is Long*, and many novels.

Born in 1889, the child of humble Jewish parents, Sarah Gertrude Liebson spent her early years amid the scene of the river diggings of Barkly West, near Kimberley, and the impressions of these years, as is almost always the case with an authentic novelist, gave direction and imaginative purpose to her fiction, which is peopled by the remittance men, German missionaries, mixed couples, half-caste children and oddments of humanity of the world of the diggings. She was educated at the Girls' High School, Kimberley, and apparently read greedily but without guidance of any sort.

In the very interesting volume of autobiography which she wrote at the age of 50, *The Night is Long*, she describes the circumstances in which she met Katherine Mansfield, who was the first person to talk sympathetically to her of books. Her literary tastes grew more sharply defined and with them went a mounting interest in South African affairs. In 1912 she married Philip Millin, a barrister, who became a K.C. in 1927 and subsequently a Judge of the Supreme Court of South Africa. He died in 1952.

Mrs. Millin's first novel, *The Dark River*, was published in 1920 and was followed, in successive years, by *Middle-class* and *Adam's Rest*. The accuracy of observation which she displayed in them, a directness and plainness of sentiment that seemed almost masculine in quality, and her spare and taut style evoked admiring comment. but it was not until the appearance, in 1923, of *The Jordans*, a story of struggle and loneliness in a squalid Johannesburg setting, that her powers as a realistic novelist were generally recognized. The combination in her of impassioned sympathy with a hard analytical clarity of mind is seen to still better advantage in her next novel, *God's Stepchildren* (1924), which was a bestseller in South Africa. Here, in a powerful historical story of three generations descended from the marriage of a white missionary with a black girl, Mrs. Millin illustrates the curse of "colour"—how it arises and haunts later generations—a constant force in the fashioning of South Africa's people.

A year later came another very good novel, though of a different stamp, *Mary Glenn*, a scrupulously considered study of a woman of strong will and purpose in adverse circumstances, whose type recurs in several of the later novels. (A play based upon the novel was produced in London, under the title of *No Longer Mourn*, in 1935). There followed *An Artist in the Family* (1927), the study of a conventional type of charming waster—not one of Mrs. Millin's best books; *The Coming of the Lord* (1928), a story of the racial and individual passions released by a religious revival in a small Transvaal town—marking an immediate recovery in the author's powers; *The Fiddler* (1929), a short work done with impressive simplicity and concentration; *The Sons of Mrs. Aab* (1931), a piece of sombre realism on the theme of obsession and failure; and *Three Men Die* (1934), whose central character, the devouring female type at its most ruthless, cannot but bring Thérèse Raquin to mind.

The unwontedly long interval between the two last named novels had not passed in idleness. Mrs. Millin's interest in the historical problems of the Union, stimulated by contact with leading public figures, had been signalized by a volume entitled *The South Africans*. First published in 1926 this book ran to several editions and was revised as *The People of South Africa*, a definitive study of the people and politics of South Africa. The question was now more fully, if less explicitly, posed in *Rhodes: A Life*, which came out in 1933. It is, without question, a great portrait, intimate, detailed and often fascinatingly personal in style, which should dispose finally of crude denigration of Rhodes and of the "Idea" by which he was dominated and driven. In the background of the portrait of a colossus of formidably human traits, Mrs. Millin, as though for her purpose she had made Rhodes's imagination and largeness of vision her own, set in perspective all the interrelated problems of imperialism, race conflict and the ethics of government. It was, and is, a book of the highest achievement. Three years after its appearance, having in the meantime, as she declared, spent the most interesting 20 months of her life among his papers, Mrs. Millin issued her biography of General Smuts. This, too, was a portrait that gripped the imagination. The book could not but be controversial, however. It brought out with conspicuous insight Smuts's patient and passionate striving for reconciliation and unity; but, although the facts had been revised by both Smuts himself and Hofmeyr, the opinions remained Mrs. Millin's, and not all commanded assent.

Her later works appeared at longer intervals. A novel published in 1938, *What Hath a Man?* acute in temper but somewhat lacking in immediate life, exhibited the reactions of a normally educated and sensitive mind to the pressure of events and the intellectual currents of a world on the eve of catastrophe. Catastrophe came, and Mrs. Millin stood her ground in South Africa against the forces of disruption, a vigorous and eloquent defender of the unity of the Commonwealth and of the allied cause. Another novel, *The Herr Witch Doctor*, published in 1941, held in tense narrative balance Nazi propagandist tactics in the Union in preparation for *Der Tag* of a second and more blessed consummation and the rising African consciousness. But Mrs. Millin's most distinctive writing during the war consisted of the volumes of her war diary, two of which, *World Blackout* and *The Reeling Earth*, appeared in 1944 and 1945 respectively. They were extremely good books in their kind, live, candid, by no means without humour, and lit by a fervent faith in Britain.

King of the Bastards and *The Burning Man*, two historical novels, appeared in 1950 and 1952 respectively. In the former, through a fictional biography of a little-known adventurer Coenraad Buys, she reconstructed a saga in nineteenth-century South Africa. *Two Bucks Without Hair* (1957) was a collection of stories about native murders and domestics. *The Wizard Bird* (1962) and *Goodbye, Dear England* (1965) were her last novels.

July 12, 1968.

Lord Mills, P.C., K.B.E., former Minister of Power, collapsed and died in Hornton Street, near his home in Kensington, London, on September 10, 1968. He was taken by ambulance to St. Mary Abbots hospital, but was found to be dead. He was 78.

He was Minister of Power from 1957 to 1959, Paymaster-General from 1959 to 1961 and Minister without Portfolio in 1961–62.

As Controller-General of Machine Tools for four vital years after 1940 he acquired his reputation for getting things done. In 1943-44 he was Head of Production Division, Ministry of Production. He was knighted in 1942 and in 1944 was made president of the economic half of the British part of the Control Commission for Germany. Here he was deeply involved in the crucial negotiations in the Allied Control Council over the permitted level of German steel output.

In 1951 Mr. Macmillan, then Housing Minister, who had seen something of Mills's work during the war when he was Parliamentary Secretary, Ministry of Supply, and had formed a high opinion of his business acumen, brought Mills in as adviser when the Government launched its housing crusade. Macmillan's faith was justified, for Mills played an important part in the achievement of the Conservative target of 300,000 houses a year.

From 1950 to 1955 he was chairman of the National Research Development Corporation.

It was under his direction that the war-time Bailey bridges and the electronic digital computer were developed for peacetime uses.

He was Minister of Power from 1957 to 1959 and in 1959 he was appointed Paymaster-General with the duty of advising his Cabinet colleagues on the industrial problems of which he had so wide a knowledge. From 1960 to 1962 he was Deputy Leader of the House of Lords. He became Minister without Portfolio in 1961 and during Macmillan's drastic reconstruction in July, 1962, he resigned.

Lord Mills had a reputation for toughness in negotiations in the engineering industry. He exercised this determination in his dealings with civil servants, in his treatment of the Russians in the Control Commission for Germany, and in his negotiations with the militant trade union leaders in his capacity as president of the Engineering and Allied Employers' National Federation.

He was born on January 4, 1890, and educated at the North Eastern County School, Barnard Castle. He left school in his mid-teens, studied accountancy in London and progressed so well that by the end of the First World War he was able to move to Birmingham and accept the job of personal assistant to the managing director of W. T. Avery, Ltd., manufacturers of scales and weighing machines. In five years he was general manager of the firm and, at 43, he became managing director. In 1955 he was appointed chairman. He was a director of Electrical and Musical Industries and chairman of E. M. I. Electronics, Ltd.

He was appointed K. B. E. in 1946; created a baronet in 1953, a baron in 1957 and a viscount in 1962.

He married in 1915 Winifred Mary Conaty; they had a son and a daughter. He is succeeded by his son the Hon. Roger Clinton Mills.

September 11, 1968.

Freddie Mills, who shot himself in his car on July 25, 1965, was one of the outstanding figures in the boom of British professional boxing in the years immediately after the end of the Second World War. His two bouts for the world light-heavyweight championship with the American Gus Lesnevich will be remembered for many years.

Mills was born at Parkstone, Dorset, on June 26, 1919, and had his first professional contest in 1936 at the age of 16, when he won by a knockout in the third round. But it was not until 1942, after 74 bouts, that he won the British and Empire titles by knocking the veteran Len Harvey out of the ring at White Hart Lane.

He unsuccessfully challenged Jack London for the British Empire heavyweight title in 1944, being outpointed over 15 rounds, and then went back to his natural fighting weight of 12st. 7lb. to challenge Lesnevich for the world championship on May 14, 1946. Lesnevich won through the intervention of the referee with four seconds left of the tenth round, but Mills, though down four times, showed remarkable courage and Lesnevich, with one eye closed, looked much the more battered of the two at the finish.

Again Mills tried to move up to the heavyweights where the really big purses could be obtained, but he was outpointed by Britain's Bruce Woodcock and stopped in six rounds by the American Joe Baksi who had considerable advantage in height and reach and was 2st. the heavier.

But on July 26, 1948, Mills reached the pinnacle of his career when he outpointed Lesnevich over 15 rounds to win the world light-heavyweight title in a contest in which he boxed much more coolly than usual. Mills, having taken a bad beating from Woodcock in 1949 during another attempt at the heavyweight honours, lost his world title when making his first defence by being knocked out by the American Joey Maxim in 10 rounds in 1950. After 96 professional bouts his career as a boxer was over.

Mills thereafter made something of a success as a television personality thanks to his modesty and cheerful, engaging personality. With his burly build and shaggy dark hair he looked the popular image of a pugilist but it always astonished those who had seen his swashbuckling style in the ring to find him so amiable when he was outside the ropes.

No one would ever call Freddie Mills a boxing purist. He lunged, swung and swept in against his opponents with all guns firing and seemed to care little about the risk of taking counter punches. But his courage and strength were nigh inexhaustible.

July 26, 1965.

Lord Milner of Leeds, P.C., M.C., the first baron, who died on July 16, 1967, at his home in Leeds at the age of 77, was Chairman of Ways and Means, and Deputy Speaker of the House of Commons for several years during the Second World War, and later when Labour was in office.

James Milner was born on August 12, 1889, a son of James Henry Milner, a solicitor, of Leeds and London, and for many years the Leeds City coroner. He was educated at Easingwold Grammar School, and at the University of Leeds, where he graduated LL.B. in 1911, being admitted a solicitor shortly afterwards, and joining his father in practice. On the outbreak of the First World War, he enlisted in a local regiment, ultimately becoming a major in the Royal Army Service Corps, and in the Devon Regiment, in service with which he was wounded, mentioned in dispatches, and awarded the M.C. with Bar. At the end of the war he joined the Leeds Labour Party, of which, in 1926, he became chairman. Already a member of the City Council, to which he had been elected in 1923, he was, in 1928, appointed Deputy Lord Mayor of the City. In the next year he was elected Labour Member of Parliament for the South-Eastern Division of Leeds, a seat he held until his translation to the House of Lords in 1951.

He applied himself largely to the detailed work and organization of the Labour Party in the House when it was so bereft after the 1931 general election. He became Parliamentary Private Secretary to Lord Addison, who was then at the Ministry of Agriculture, was a member of the Indian Franchise Committee of 1932, and of the Chairman's Panel of the Commons from 1935 to 1943, when he became Deputy Chairman of Ways and Means.

As Deputy Speaker he was twice involved in Parliamentary "incidents". The first was in March, 1948, when he made a "personal" statement to the House after he had acted as solicitor to Mr. Emanuel (later Lord) Shinwell. In 1949 Mr. Quintin Hogg (later Lord Hailsham) challenged his conduct in the chair during a debate on meat supplies. A select committee of the House acquitted him of any partiality in the first case, and Hogg's motion of censure in the second was negatived without a division. On May 1, 1950, Milner saved the Labour Government from defeat by his casting vote from the chair after the Government and the Opposition had tied with 278 votes each in a division on the Road Haulage Bill.

He also presided over several party and parliamentary committees, including the Labour Services Committee, which he founded, the Solicitors' Group, and the Standing Orders Committee, of which he was also chairman for several years. He was chairman, too, of the British Group of the Inter-Parliamentary Union, in which capacity he attended many conferences abroad, including those held in Oslo, Copenhagen, Cairo, Rome, and Dublin, and he led the Parliamentary Delegation which was entrusted with the Presentation of the Speaker's Chair and Mace to the new Parliament of Ceylon in 1949.

In 1957, Lord Milner (then chairman) and the board of Canadian and English Stores Ltd. refused to accept the rejection of the company's report and accounts on a show of hands by shareholders at the company's annual general meeting. The accounts had shown more than £1m. loss, after taxation. Government hire-purchase restrictions were blamed. A poll of shareholders was held to decide the matter.

Milner was at one time a member of the Court and Council of his old University of Leeds, where, incidentally, his was one of its early legal degrees, and he had been president of the Leeds Law Society. For years he was closely connected with the work of the West Riding Territorial Association, and he was a trustee of the Haig Memorial Homes, as well as of the Liverpool Victoria Friendly Society.

BUSINESS INTERESTS

His other offices included those of vice-president of the Association of Municipal Corporations, and of the Building Societies Association, and, while always remaining active as a member of the family firm of solicitors, especially interested in the commercial and industrial side of the practice, he was directly connected with financial and commercial undertakings as a director of leading textile and furniture manufacturing and supplying companies. He became a Privy Councillor in 1945, was a Deputy Lieutenant of the West Riding, and had the Territorial Decoration. In October, 1966, the Freedom of Leeds was conferred on him.

He was especially fond of travel, particularly by air, but otherwise he liked the simple things, such as gardening, a hobby which he shared with his wife at their Roundhay home. He married in 1917 Lois Tinsdale Brown and they had one son and two daughters. His heir is his son, the Hon. Arthur James Michael Milner.

July 17, 1967.

The Very Rev. Eric Milner-White, C.B.E., D.S.O., died on June 15, 1963, after a long illness. He was 79. In the succession of distinguished Deans of York none made more notable contribution.

The son of Sir Henry Milner-White, he was born on St. George's Day, 1884. After leaving Harrow he proceeded to King's College, Cambridge, to begin a long and fruitful association with this college, gaining a First in Part I of the Historical Tripos in 1905 and in Part II in 1907, and also the Lightfoot Scholarship in 1906. His theological training followed at Cuddesdon, and he was ordained at Southwark in 1908 with curacies at Newington and Woolwich, returning to Cambridge in 1912 as Chaplain to King's College, combined with a Lecturership in History at Corpus Christi.

With the outbreak of war in 1914 he became a Chaplain to the Forces, serving in France with the B.E.F. where he was awarded the D.S.O. when Senior Chaplain to the 7th Division.

He returned to his beloved King's College in 1918 as Chaplain, but also becoming Dean and fellow, so finding ample scope for the liturgical and musical gifts which he used so effectively for the rest of his life. Outside his college interests he became Superior of the Oratory of the Good Shepherd from 1923, and his literary output reflected his line of thought; these included *A Cambridge Bede Book*, 1937, joint authorship of *Cambridge Offices and Orisons*, 1921, and the editing of *Memorials Upon Several Occasions*, 1933. Milner-White gloried in the Catholic heritage of tradition and devotion but was robustly Anglican. While some Anglo-Catholics inclined Romewards with more zeal than knowledge, he as a follower of Dean Church, Bishop Gore and the *Lux Mundi* school was one of the group of scholarly writers who produced the influential volume *Essays Catholic and Critical* in 1926, to which he contributed the essay on "The Spirit and the Church in History". He entered into controversy with *One God and Father of All: a Reply to Father Vernon* in 1929, and was a contributor to *Liturgy and Worship* in 1932. Throughout these years he was enjoying and influencing the far-famed worship in King's College Chapel, making this a remarkable prelude to his work in York.

CALL TO DEANERY

The call to succeed Dean Bate came in 1941, and no more fortunate or fitting choice could have been made. It was in the darkest days of war: bombs were falling on northern cities and towns and many churches were damaged or destroyed. York lost its finest parish church, but the Minster escaped. The medieval glass, of which the Minster and other York churches contained one-third of what remains in England, had been removed to safety, so that when hostilities ceased the Dean's great opportunity came. The glass was not merely replaced but completely restored.

Previous repairs down the ages had resulted in windows having a jumble of coloured glass without pattern or meaning, but it had fallen now into the care of the greatest living authority on stained glass, and the Dean with his skilled band of glaziers set about the jig-saw, and worked the miracle of bringing back each of the great windows to their original order, beauty and splendour. This work alone is a lasting monument to Milner-White's genius and devotion.

Sir Edward Bairstow was in charge of the music, to the Dean's delight, and when Bairstow died the Dean pinned his faith in the brilliant young assistant who succeeded, and the fine tradition of York has continued. As the Metropolitan Church of the North the Minster is in excessive demand for all sorts of special services, for many of which the Dean was able to indulge his originality and his flair for felicity of phrase in composing orders of service. Among these were improved orders for enthronement of three archbishops, numerous consecrations of bishops, for royal visits, civic and county occasions, diocesan and provincial services of great variety, and for the first royal wedding in York since 1328, when the Duke of Kent married a daughter of Yorkshire. All these services came readily from his pen, and were carried out perfectly, and few can have equalled his output in quality or quantity.

The fabric of the Minster was in need of attention, and the Treasurer had the Dean's active support in the successful appeal for £250,000 in 1950; but Milner-White's peculiar contribution, apart from restoring the glass, was the transformation of the interior. He was accused of "gilding the lily" by some who preferred the Minster as they knew it before the Dean lit up the dull woodwork with gold leaf, and filled the building with a variety of beautiful objects, furniture, tapestries, pictures, plate and even more glass. He gave most liberally himself, and inspired gifts from others. The annual reports of the Friends of York Minster are records of remarkable gifts and achievement largely inspired by the Dean. With all his aesthetic gifts he combined a shrewd grasp of finance, and rarely has a dean so excelled in all the aspects of cathedral life and management, its worship, music, fabric, finance and its place in the community.

INFLUENTIAL SPEAKER

In Convocation and the Church Assembly he was listened to with respect, and he was for some years chairman of the Central Advisory Council for the Care of Churches. As chairman of the Diocesan Advisory Committee his influence was felt, his views not always popular yet invariably beneficial.

In the City of York he has left his mark. For a long time he regretted not having a university of York; he seemed to be 100 years too late. So with other enthusiasts in the York Civic Trust he established the Borthwick Institute of Historical Research in the restored St. Anthony's Hall, with its wealth of material, and the York Institute of Architectural Study in the church of St. John, Ousegate, thus using the archives and treasures of ancient York for modern purposes. The Dean saw his dream come true when York was selected for one of the new universities, and he lived to see it become a reality, and was at least able to take part in the inaugural stages and help to shape its destiny. His health had been declining for some years, but his spirit was fortified by having things to achieve. At the last Enthronement he made an heroic appearance from a sickbed. His later works included a volume of devotional work, *My God, my Glory*, and the *New English Bible* owed something to him as one of its producers.

Recognition came to him for his manifold services with the C.B.E. in 1952, honorary membership of the Worshipful Company of Glaziers with the Freedom of the City of London, and the Hon. Litt. D. of Leeds University, 1962. He was Select Preacher at Cambridge eight times and at Oxford twice. In 1952 Archbishop Fisher conferred on him a Lambeth D. D., so that this devoted son of Cambridge was able to wear the Oxford hood.

He was unmarried.

June 17, 1963.

Major General Iskander Mirza, C.I.E., O.B.E., who died on November 12, 1969, was the last Governor General and the first President of Pakistan. His services, first to the British *raj*, and later to Pakistan, were numerous and distinguished; and although his latter years were passed in enforced retirement from active affairs, he is sure of his place in history.

Syed Iskander Mirza was born on November 13, 1899, in Bombay into an aristocratic family of Persian origin long settled in India. Educated at Elphinstone College, Bombay, he was nominated to the first batch of Indian cadets to enter Sandhurst and in 1920 became the first Indian ever to be gazetted to the Army from that famous establishment. After six years of military life he was selected for the Political Service in 1926. In 1938 he was promoted to the key position of Political Agent, Khyber; three years later he became deputy commissioner of Peshawar. This long experience on the Frontier shaped the whole of his later life; he learnt there—and never forgot—how to get his own way by playing off faction against faction, and thereby reducing to impotence any opposition which threatened him. After serving for a short time as Political Agent to the Orissa States, he became joint secretary in the Ministry of Defence in New Delhi in 1946. He thoroughly enjoyed European society, and was an excellent sportsman; he made many friends in the Government of India both on the civil and the military sides.

When the subcontinent was partitioned in 1947, he opted for Pakistan, and soon found full employment for his talents for organization in the reconstitution of the Pakistan Army. But after the assassination of Liaquat Ali Khan, Iskander found that conditions were changing, and that as a civil servant he could do very little unless he could keep in the good graces of the political leaders.

In 1954 he was taken off military work and sent with full emergency powers to deal with the threatening situation which had arisen in East Pakistan. Iskander Mirza handled the crisis with vigour and imagination; he arranged for an equitable distribution of food supplies; he dealt forcefully with disorders; he won widespread popularity by his personal supervision of relief work. This experience gave him the first taste of quasi-absolute power which he had enjoyed since he had left behind his work in tribal territory; it confirmed him in a conviction that politicians were inherently a race of muddlers, who must be kept in order by trained administrators. In November, 1954, Iskander Mirza was recalled from East Pakistan to take up the important post of Minister of the Interior, States and Frontier Regions. Upon him fell the main responsibility of carrying through, in the teeth of vested interests, Ghulam Muhammad's plan for sweeping away all the provincial and state administrations of West Pakistan, and of forming that area into a single province. When, in July 1955, Ghulam Muhammad's health broke down, Iskander Mirza stepped without serious opposition into the post of acting Governor General. In October of the same year, Ghulam Muhammad resigned, and Iskander Mirza succeeded him.

Iskander Mirza seemed now in a position to realize his dream of a Pakistan administered and governed by civil servants, with himself at the head of everything. But in order to attain this, he was obliged to reduce the politicians to impotence; and, unfortunately for him, this meant fighting them on their own ground. In the process, he lost the ideals which had sustained him through so much of his career, and he began to value power for its own sake. Moreover, he became so preoccupied in retaining it, that he had little energy left for setting to rights the many shortcomings which had developed in the Pakistan administration. Gradually, his preference for using as his tools able scoundrels rather than less clever honest men led to a steady deterioration in the whole tone of public life.

While the politicians wrangled, and the state of the nation went from bad to worse, Iskander Mirza was mainly preoccupied in keeping so much power in his own hands that nothing could be done without his consent. Pakistan was steadily approaching bankruptcy; prices were rising; food was short; graft and corruption were rampant; even smuggling rings found powerful protectors in the highest places. In this crisis, some of the younger Army officers, losing patience, thought that a military *coup* on the Iraq model offered the only prospect of saving the country. But before they could take action of this kind, which would have involved much bloodshed and profited only the communists, the commander-in-chief, General Ayub Khan intervened. On October 28, 20 days after the declaration of martial law (which had already been relaxed in favour of the ordinary civil administration) President Iskander Mirza was persuaded to resign. He left Karachi on November 2, 1958, for London, where he continued to live in political retirement. His long service in India had won for him many British friends, and his retirement brought out once more many of the genial "bonhomous" characteristics which those who had known him in his Frontier days had always admired.

November 14, 1969.

J. P. Mitchelhill who, as manager of the Duchess Theatre over a period of eight years made a distinctive contribution to the London theatre of the 1930s, died in London on August 6, 1966, at the age of 87.

John Percy Mitchelhill, a Londoner by birth, was already fifty years old and unknown in the theatre except as a playgoer, when in 1930 he purchased in conjunction with the late Lieutenant-Colonel Arthur S. Halford and Cecil Halford the little Duchess Theatre in Catherine Street, with its seating capacity of 494, which had opened during the previous year. The purchase was originally made as an investment, but the decision to select and present the plays there must have been rapidly arrived at, for his first production took place on November 4, 1930. This, an English version of *Le Gendre de M. Poirer* entitled *An Object of Virtue* (with Jean Forbes-Robertson in the cast) was followed in 1932 by Clifford Bax's play about Henry VIII and Katheryn Howard, *The Rose Without a Thorn*, presented jointly with Nancy Price, with Frank Vosper and Angela Baddeley in the chief parts.

Later in the same year he enjoyed a big box-office success with *Children in Uniform*, a play set in a school for officers' daughters in Imperial Germany which moved Charles Morgan to write a deeply appreciative notice in *The Times*; and in 1933 he entered upon a long and notable association with J. B. Priestley with the production of the latter's play about a racket in English suburbia, *Laburnum Grove*, with Edmund Gwenn as the amiably equivocal leading character. Together the two associates presented Priestley's next play *Eden End* (about a doctor's family in pre-1914 Yorkshire) in 1934, and his *Cornelius* (with Sir Ralph Richardson in the name part) in 1935. *Cornelius* was immediately followed by Mitchelhill's presentation of *Night Must Fall*, which proved to be a resounding success for Emlyn Williams, then barely 30 years of age, in the dual capacity of playwright and actor.

In 1936 Mitchelhill brought T.S. Eliot's play *Murder in the Cathedral*, with Robert Speaight as Thomas Becket, from Ashley Dukes's little Mercury Theatre to the Duchess, thereby securing for the poet his first West End success and a conspicuous one. At the beginning of the 1937 season he presented joinly with the author the first and theatrically the soundest and most viable of Priestley's "Time plays", *Time and the Conways*, with Jean Forbes-Robertson perfectly cast as prematurely aging young heroine.

LAST VENTURE

His last venture at the Duchess, Mr. Norman Macowan's play about a girl-student's revolt against a totalitarian state, *Glorious Morning*—Jessica Tandy, the adolescent heroine of *Children in Uniform*, was again the leading lady—was produced in 1938. On the occasion of its transfer after more than 100 performances to the Whitehall, where he had launched St. John Ervine's comedy *Anthony and Anna* (in the stage persons of Harold Warrender and Miss Tandy) on its long career three years previously, Mitchelhill retired from the Duchess.

Later he became Chairman of the Mask Theatre Ltd. in which capacity he continued to work in association with Priestley. His career is an illustration of what it was possible for an independent producer-manager to achieve bv means of taste, enthusiasm and shrewdness in business in days not long gone bv.

August 10, 1966.

Lord Mitchison, C.B.E., Q.C., former Labour M.P. for Kettering, died on February 14, 1970, at the age of 79.

Gilbert Richard Mitchison was born on March 23, 1890, the son of Arthur Maw Mitchison and Mary Emmeline Russell. His family was well to do; and he was educated at Eton and at New College, Oxford, where he obtained a first in Greats. Disappointed in his hopes of a fellowship at All Souls, he turned to the law and in 1917 was called to the Bar of the Inner Temple. The reason for the delay was, of course, the European War: at its outbreak he joined the Queen's Bays and rose to the rank of major. He served in France, was seriously wounded in the head, from which injury he took some time to recover: he was G.S.O.2 in the British Mission to the French Forces in Italy and won the Croix de Guerre. Earlier, in 1916, he had married Naomi Haldane, the youthful sister of his Etonian contemporary the eminent geneticist J. B. S. Haldane, and after the war, when Mrs. Mitchison was beginning her successful career as an historical novelist, they settled down with a growing family in a large house on Hammersmith Mall.

LEGAL WORK

Mitchison, however, was slow to embrace politics as a career. He developed his legal practice, mainly commercial cases, in London and the provinces, up to a point; but he was not very well satisfied either with it or with his position as genial host to persons who were gaining distinction in the artistic and literary world; and though his own political inclinations were radical, they were not very definite, and he was still something of a looker-on. A change came when under the influence of G. D. H. Cole and his wife he became, in 1931, treasurer of the infant New Fabian Research Bureau which was to transform the Fabian Society and nourish so many future Labour Ministers, and entered politics through the short-lived Socialist League. He was adopted Labour candidate for King's Norton when Cole resigned his candidature, and fought unsuccessful by-elections there in 1931 and 1935.

His entry into Labour politics was thus *via* the left: in 1934 he published with Victor Gollancz a quasi-utopian account written about 1980 of *The First Workers' Government* (assumed to have taken office in 1936) which envisaged the disappearance *inter alia* of the House of Lords and the City of London. This, together with his association with Stafford Cripps and Aneurin Bevan at the time of their feud with the official Labour Party, made him slightly suspect in the eyes of the leaders. There was, however, no breach: by 1940 he was at work on Beveridge's manpower survey, and the end of the war saw him as lieutenant, for the London area, to G. D. H. Cole in his massive Nuffield Social Reconstruction Survey. Here his qualities, acquired in his legal work, for accurate and painstaking research proved very useful, and the contacts which he made with leading administrators on both sides of industry and in local government particularly deepened and widened his experience, so that he had no difficulty, when he decided to leave King's Norton, in getting himself adopted as Labour candidate for Kettering, a constituency which includes a strong cooperative movement as well as a block of Clydesiders imported to work for Stewart and Lloyds at Corby. In the election of 1945 he was returned with a handsome majority and held the seat continuously, being very highly regarded there, until, in the summer of 1964, he left the Commons for the Lords.

If he had aspirations for office—and who has not?—he concealed them well, and was surprised when, in 1955, he was elected to the Labour Parliamentary Committee at his first attempt.

In 1961 Mitchison was given the task of front bench leader on science and technology; subsequently he relinquished this post to R. H. S. Crossman and led, instead, on pensions, a subject which he did not find really congenial. By 1964, notwithstanding his age, he had became one of the leading figures in the shadow Cabinet; and in the summer of that year, at the request of his leader, he accepted a life peerage. When the Labour government came in, he was already 74, too old to take on high office without previous experience. But Mr. Wilson had the happy idea of making him one of the parliamentary secretaries to the newly-created Ministry of Land. The assignment suited his talents admirably: and in addition, as one of Labour's scanty team in the Lords, he could be put on to answer for Ministers other than his own, which he did with courtesy and aplomb. He retired in 1966.

Mitchison was given his C.B.E. in 1953. His wife survives him with three sons and two daughters.

February 16, 1970.

Dr. Joseph Moffett, Minister of Crown Court Church of Scotland—the Kirk of the Crown of Scotland in London—died in hospital on May 20, 1962, at the age of 76.

It was 45 years since he became minister at Crown Court, after having been assistant at St. Columba's, Pont Street. In all that time the strength of his preaching Sunday after Sunday did not flag, and to the end he was addressing himself to large congregations of Scottish people. It was never an easy church to run, for membership is widely dispersed around London and a good part of it tends to change as Scottish families come south for a few years and then return to Scotland. But Dr. Moffett's strong personality, his preaching, his kindliness, and his sense of administration provided the main binding force throughout two generations. Each year at Christmas and the New Year he received messages from Scots all over the world who at one time or another received inspiration and practical kindness from the Minister of Crown Court Church. During the last war he took an interest in the Polish forces and practically adopted one of the servicemen, who long remembered him after returning to Warsaw.

CHURCH BOMBED

The church itself was bombed and badly damaged, but Dr. Moffett and the congregation continued to hold services there, and he looked after the Dutch community in London, whose own church was destroyed. For his services to the Dutch people, and particularly to the Anglo-Dutch Christian Fellowship, the Order of Orange-Nassau was conferred upon him.

In the pulpit he had the appearance of a Raeburn portrait, with his lean, intellectual face, his shock of white hair, and the bright hue of his doctor's robes—St. Andrews having made him D.D. in 1948 in recognition of his long service to Scots in London. Physically he was not a strong man, and he constantly overworked, but he had great staying power. He was well versed in church government and was keenly concerned in all the many doctrinal and administrative problems which such government raises. He always looked forward to going north to the General Assembly in Scotland. Since 1919 he was clerk to both the Church of Scotland Presbytery in London and the Presbytery of the Synod in England. He was a member of the theological subcommittee of the British Council of Churches, dealing with the reception and placing of foreign divinity students in British theological halls. Scottish societies in London claimed his services, and he was honorary chaplain to several. He was vice-chairman of the Royal Scottish Corporation and honorary chaplain of the Royal Caledonian Schools.

Although most of his life was in the Church of Scotland and working with Scottish people, Joseph Moffett was born in co. Donegal, at Letterkenny, on August 25, 1885, the son of the Rev. Dr. Joseph Moffett, minister of the Presbyterian Church of Ireland. He was educated at the Royal University of Ireland (now linked with Trinity College, Dublin), Magee College, Londonderry, and Edinburgh University. Throughout his life his interests were wide.

MASONIC RANK

He rose to high rank in Masonic circles, being consecrating officer to new lodges and chapters. In 1947 he was Grand Chaplain of the United Grand Lodge of England; he was Past Deputy Provincial Grand Master, Southern Counties, of the Royal Order of Scotland. He was also a member of the Board of the Royal Masonic Hospital.

He also delved deeply into the history of the Kirk of the Crown of Scotland, which began as a chapel attached to the Scottish Embassy (before the union of the kingdoms) in old Scotland Yard. After a disastrous fire the church was moved to the present site at Covent Garden and opened in 1719.

Dr. Moffett leaves a widow, a son who is a chaplain in the forces, and a married daughter.

May 22, 1962.

Benno Moiseiwitsch, C.B.E., the famous pianist, died on April 9, 1963, in London at the age of 73.

His fame was world wide and its foundations were a consummate fluency and a natural feeling for euphony, which prevented him from forcing his tone or distorting his rhythm. He was not a particularly intellectual pianist and though his taste was fairly catholic he was predominantly a player of the romantic composers. Even so, there was a certain cool control that saved him, when playing Rachmaninov and Medtner, for whom he had a natural affinity of race and artistic sympathy, from over-indulgence in the lachrymosity of the one or the volubility of the other. The mixture of cool and romantic heart, however, worked out less well in a work like Schumann's piano concerto than in Beethoven's "Emperor" concerto.

Moiseiwitsch was born at Odessa, on February 22, 1890, and was taught at the Imperial Music Academy in that city, where he won the Rubinstein prize at the age of nine. Later he studied with Leschetitzky in Vienna. He made a successful début in England as long ago as 1908 and made his home here during the 1914–18 War: he was naturalized a British subject in 1937. He began his international tours which established his world reputation in 1919. There was a time when excess of touring spoiled the finish and the finesse of his playing, but his artistic sincerity soon prevailed and restored him to the company of great, as opposed to merely popular, pianists. During the 1939–45 War he raised considerable sums for the Aid to Russia Fund, even though he had not returned to Russia since his youth, and he was a supporter of Dame Myra Hess in the conduct of the National Gallery Concerts.

Moiseiwitsch was made C.B.E. in 1946.

He married first in 1914 Daisy Kennedy the violinist, by whom he had two daughters, one of whom, Tanya, is the well-known stage designer. His second marriage in 1929 was to Annie Gensburger, by whom he had one son. His second wife died in 1956.

April 10, 1963.

Mrs. Molotov (Polina Semyonovna Zhemchuzhina) died on May 1, 1970. She was in her mid-seventies.

In the 1930s, when Vyacheslav Molotov was riding high as Stalin's heir-presumptive and right hand. Zhemchuzhina, who for career purposes used her maiden name, shone for a time in her husband's reflected glory and held such posts as Head of the Perfume Industry and People's Commissar of Fisheries with Cabinet rank. But during the purges of the late 1930s she incurred the dictator's disfavour probably because of her Jewish origin (Zhemchuzhina is the Russian rendition of the Yiddish Perlmutter) and was exiled to Siberia. Molotov did not intercede on her behalf lest he himself thereby incur Stalin's wrath.

Early in the Second World War Zhemchuzhina was released and reunited with her husband. After his removal from high office by Khrushchev in 1957 as a member of the so-called Anti-Party Group that had tried and failed to oust Khrushchev, Zhemchuzhina shared Molotov's obscurity. She is survived by her son and daughter as well as by her husband who turned 80 in March, 1970—still hale and hearty and unswervingly true to the memory of his late boss.

May 4, 1970.

Lord Monckton, who died at his home in Sussex on January 9, 1965, will be principally remembered for his work as chairman of a commission which had a potent influence on the recasting of the political future of Central Africa and, at an earlier period, for his occupation as Minister of Labour at a time when the first Conservative postwar Government was anxious to establish its good intentions with the trade unions. In each instance, his remarkable gifts for creating confidence were extended to their utmost.

Although he held a number of political posts, it cannot be said that he was either by inclination or temperament a politician. His active parliamentary life was relatively short, and it was in those affairs which required the composing of acute differences or the exercise of a judicial function that he was most successful.

The detached canons of rectitude which Monckton had framed for himself were best exemplified in his view that many who had escaped the discipline of the law or some similar educative discipline were deficient in such things; it was, he said, good for the soul not to be at liberty to express views loosely and at large. The lawyer's role—and in this is summed up Monckton's life—was to find the common ground, and to locate the fruitful basis for cooperation.

In such a philosophy, there is much of the lawyer and little of the politician, and it is hardly surprising if in carrying it into practice as Minister of Labour he won golden opinions from the trade unions while causing a certain amount of exasperation in some quarters of the Conservative Party. In a particularly turbulent time in industrial relations, he was sometimes accused of surrendering to the unions, and perhaps particularly for "buying off" the railwaymen when they threatened to strike just before Christmas, 1953, and the engineering unions in the following year.

It is said that in the case of the railwaymen he and the Minister of Transport (then Alan Lennox-Boyd) were overruled by the Prime Minister (Sir Winston Churchill) and the Chancellor of the Exchequer (R. A. Butler). On the other hand, there is some evidence that the decisions were his, and those in close association with him at the time were inclined to believe that he was too skilful a negotiator to allow himself to fall into a position where any decision he made might be overruled. As his handling of other intricate disputes showed, he was adept in controlling the progress of discussions in this way; and certainly his management of the initial meetings of the Monckton Commission in Africa demonstrated considerable strength of mind.

As a man who was perfectly consistent throughout his life, it is reasonable to assume of him that his policies at the Ministry of Labour were largely his own; and the fact remains that within a year of his departure from the Commons, the Government's view of "Moncktonism" in industrial affairs—as it came to be known—had changed considerably, under the pressure of a formidable list of accumulated wage claims.

A devout and humane man, Monckton is believed to have refused judicial office because he would have felt lonely in a position which would have denied him the opportunity to help his fellow men directly. This personal engagement with the fortunes of men was his most endearing characteristic; and his uprightness of mind and purpose, charm, and outstanding grasp of affairs combine to leave with those who had the good fortune to know him the memory of an outstanding personality.

Sir Walter, Turner Monckton, K.C.M.G., K.C.V.O., M.C., Q.C., first Viscount Monckton of Brenchley in the County of Kent, in the peerage of the United Kingdom, was the eldest son of the late F. W. Monckton. He was born at Plaxtol, Kent, on January 17, 1891. He was educated at Harrow, for whom he kept wicket against Eton at Lord's in "Fowler's match" of 1910. Cricket remained throughout his life one of his main relaxations, and he was fond of following the fortunes of Surrey at the Oval.

MAIDEN SPEECH SUCCESS

Monckton went on to Balliol College, Oxford, and at once made a name for himself with a maiden speech in the Union, of which he became president in 1913. His education was broken off by his service as a subaltern in the Royal West Kent Regiment during the 1914–18 War. He was later promoted to captain, was awarded the M.C., and on returning from the war took his degree in 1918 and read for the Bar as a pupil of the late F. T. Barrington-Ward. He was called to the Bar by the Inner Temple in 1919, joined the South-Eastern Circuit, and soon acquired a large, lucrative, and varied practice.

In 1932, he was appointed Attorney-General to the Prince of Wales, a friend of his Oxford days; a step of great importance in view of the role which he was to play behind the scenes at the time of the Abdication. His integrity of mind and coolness of judgment made him ideal as an adviser in the negotiations between the King and the Prime Minister, and it was Monckton who wrote the statement of abdication for King Edward VIII.

He attended the marriage of the Duke and Duchess of Windsor, and remained their personal friend and legal adviser afterwards. His services to the state on this occasion were rewarded by King George VI when he knighted Monckton.

Monckton took silk in 1930. He was particularly concerned with the internal policies of Hyderabad.

In November 1941 he was appointed head of the propaganda and information services in Cairo, where Oliver Lyttelton (later Lord Chandos) had become Minister of State.

He was Solicitor-General in the caretaker

Parliament of 1945, without a seat in the House, and during the period of Labour Government returned to the Bar. In February, 1951 he was returned as the Conservative member for Bristol West. Churchill invited him to become Minister of Labour, supposedly because Monckton had no political past. Monckton answered that the Prime Minister was ensuring that he would have no political future, either.

Monckton's position was extremely delicate, but his appointment by the Prime Minister can be considered as a stroke of great political shrewdness. After a week in office Monckton proclaimed his belief in government by consultation and consent, and the T.U.C. responded with a friendly and pragmatic statement. Permanent officials at the Ministry came to regard him as the most conscientious and assiduous of Ministers, and his strict legal discipline took him into negotiations fully armed on points of detail; it had not been unusual for previous Ministers, Labour no less than others, to make blunders about the facts of a case, but Monckton never did. Union leaders fell into the habit of meeting him informally, as did some of the employers' leaders.

As a Minister, he perhaps lacked the peculiarly political gift which enables a man to stand a little apart from his work from time to time, and this imposed great strains upon him. His cast of mind was such that he would become completely identified with the problem in hand; when a big dispute was going on, he would take papers home to bed with him, and would not sleep. It was perhaps loss of sleep more than anything else which resulted several times in breakdowns and periods of enforced recuperation.

At the end of 1955 he was appointed Minister of Defence, a post which he held for only 10 months. During his term of office the Suez crisis began to loom up, and there is reason to believe that he disagreed with the Cabinet's decision to use force. Resigning from that office, he found himself, as Paymaster General, in the ironic position of coordinating the Government's information service in Egypt. When Sir Anthony Eden resigned and Macmillan became Prime Minister, Monckton left the Government and was raised to the peerage.

Becoming a director of the Midland Bank Ltd., he was swiftly elected chairman in July, 1957, and a year later became chairman of the Iraq Petroleum Co, and its associated companies. At the Midland, he was credited with the invention of the personal loans scheme, which became something of a fashion in banking, and was once more able to pay more attention to his favourite sport of cricket. He was President of M.C.C. in 1956-57. In summer, 1964, he retired from the chairmanship of the Midland Bank for health reasons.

AFRICAN TREK

In 1959 he was appointed chairman of the advisory commission on the review of the constitution of the Federation of Rhodesia and Nyasaland, a work which proved to be the most influential and important of his whole career. The report itself played its main role as an educative instrument and as a stimulus to discussion rather than as an exact blueprint for the future, but it remains of major importance.

The commission's work began in February, 1960. He himself maintained liaison with all three groups by "trekking about all over Africa", as he put it; and the skills he acquired in the adjustment of the contentious politics of India stood him in good stead in the atmosphere of suspicion and uncertainty in which the commission began its work.

STRONG IN CHAIR

His personality was such, however, that it caused trust to flower in places where trust had became rare, and in itself this was of inestimable value to the success of the commission's work. There were those in Africa who thought that he would not carry enough guns for the job. Such opinions were hastily revised after the first meetings at Victoria Falls. For all his mildness of manner, it soon appeared that he was a strong chairman and not lightly to be trifled with. Those who sought to extract a declaration from him that the question of secession should not be considered by the commission did not move him. He held out unostentatiously for *carte blanche*, and got it.

His influence was also clear in the bold, but discreet, interpretation of the terms of reference, in themselves highly charged with controversy. The final report did not hesitate to grasp the nettle of secession and drew attention to the hardship and misery which would result from the break-up of the Federation. The final drafts were hammered out in London, and there is no doubt that it was Monckton's hand which applied the final polish. To the end, he maintained a diplomatic silence about his part in the commission's work, and his public utterances in the last years of his life were restricted to economic affairs and banking. He was elected president of the British Bankers' Association in 1962.

Lord Monckton was installed as Chancellor of the University of Sussex in 1963.

In July, 1914, he married Mary Adelaide Somes, eldest daughter of Sir Thomas Colyer-Fergusson, Bt., and had a son and a daughter. Monckton's first marriage was dissolved in 1947 and in the same year he married the Hon. Bridget Helen, eldest daughter and heiress to the Scottish peerage of the 9th Baron Ruthven. She was formerly married to the 11th Earl of Carlisle. The viscounty now passes to Lord Monckton's son, Major-General the Hon. Gilbert Walter Riversdale Monckton.

January 11, 1965.

Marilyn Monroe, the film actress, died on August 5, 1962, at the age of 36.

Her career was not so much a Hollywood legend as *the* Hollywood legend: the poor orphan who became one of the most sought after (and highly paid) women in the world; the hopeful Hollywood unknown who became the most potent star-attraction in the American cinema; the uneducated beauty who married one of America's leading intellectuals.

The story thus dramatically outlined was in all essentials true. Marilyn Monroe began life as Norma Jean Baker in Los Angeles, where she was born on June 1, 1926. She was brought up in an orphanage and a series of foster homes, married first at the age of 15, obtained a divorce four years later and began a career as a photographer's model. From this, in a few months, she graduated to a screen test with Twentieth-Century Fox, a contract and the name which she was to make famous. Nothing came of this contract immediately, however, and her first appearance in a film was for another studio in 1948, when she played second lead in a not very successful B picture called *Ladies of the Chorus*. There followed a number of small roles in films such as *Love Happy* (with the Marx Brothers), *The Asphalt Jungle*, directed by John Huston, in which she was first seriously noticed, Joseph Mankiewicz's *All About Eve*, Fritz Lang's *Clash by Night* and others, until in 1952 she was given her first starring role in a minor thriller, *Don't Bother to Knock*, in which she played (improbably) a homicidal baby-sitter.

This was where she began in earnest to become a legend: during the shooting of the film it came to light that some years before she had posed nude for a calendar picture, and her career, hanging in the balance, was saved by the simple avowal that she had needed the money for the rent and was not ashamed. From then on her name was constantly before the public, even if the parts she played were not always large or important, and the advertising for her next major role, in *Niagara*, which showed her reclining splendidly the length of the Niagara Falls, established the image once and for all.

GIFT FOR COMEDY

At about this time she married the baseball star Joe di Maggio—the marriage was dissolved in 1954—and began to show signs that she had talent as well as a dazzling physical presence. In *Gentlemen Prefer Blondes* and *How to Marry a Millionaire* startled critics noticed a real gift for comedy and by the arrival of *The Seven Year Itch* there was no doubt about it; she gave a performance in which personality and sheer acting ability (notably an infallible sense of comic timing) played as important a part as mere good looks. From then on she appeared in an unbroken string of personal successes: *Bus Stop*, of which as severe a judge as Jose Ferrer has said: "I challenge any actress that ever lived to give a better performance in that role"; *The Prince and the Showgirl* in which many critics felt she outshone her director and co-star Sir Laurence Olivier; *Some Like It Hot* and *Let's Make Love*.

In 1956 Marilyn Monroe was married again—to the playwright Arthur Miller (they were divorced in 1960) and his next work, the original screen play of *The Misfits*, was written for her. This was, in the event, her last film (the most recent, *Something's Got to Give*, being shelved after her failure to fulfil the terms of the contract) and in it under John Huston's direction she gave a performance which provoked its reviewer in *The Times* to a comment which might stand for her work as a whole: "Considerations of whether she can really act seem as irrelevant as they were with Garbo; it is her rare gift just to *be* in front of the camera, and, to paraphrase the comment of her apologetic employer in an earlier, more frivolous film, 'Well, anyone can *act*'."

August 6, 1962.

Lord Monsell, P.C., G.B.E., a former Conservative Chief Whip in the House of Commons who was afterwards First Lord of the Admiralty, died on March 21, 1969, at the age of 88.

Known during the greater part of his career as Sir Bolton Eyres-Monsell, he entered politics while still a young man after having served for 11 years in the Royal Navy. In 1910 he was elected Conservative M.P. for South Worcestershire and he represented this constituency throughout his 25 years in the House of Commons. He was made a Conservative junior Whip within a year of his entering the House, and by 1923 he was Parlimentary Secretary to the Treasury and the Conservative Government's Chief Whip. He continued as Government or Opposition Chief Whip for eight years. Then, in 1931, he was appointed First Lord of the Admiralty and held this office until 1936.

Eyres-Monsell, handsome and debonair, was a highly successful Chief Whip who achieved his Government targets in the division lobbies with smooth efficiency. Any members of his Conservative flock who showed deviationist tendencies were handled with a nice admixture of polite persuasion and hints of party discipline. His naval training had made Eyres-Monsell very much of a disciplinarian but he applied the spur and bridle, when needed, with a deft touch. He was much more a sailor than a politician but when he became involved in the controversy about the Anglo-German Naval Agreement of 1935—criticized by Sir Winston Churchill as "a most surprising act"—he bore his fair share in defending the Government's policy in this matter.

This was the main incident of Eyres-Monsell's political career. It was he who signed for Britain the Anglo-German Naval Agreement and he announced it to Parliament in June, 1935. The agreement had been concluded after negotiations in London with a German team led by Ribbentrop. Its main feature was that Germany's future overall naval strength was to be limited to 35 per cent of the aggregate naval strength of the whole British Commonwealth. But the agreement also conceded to Germany the right to build submarines up to 60 per cent of the British submarine strength and, if Germany deemed the circumstances exceptional, up to 100 per cent of the aggregate submarine strength of the Commonwealth.

The French and Italian Governments, who had not been consulted, were both resentful of the way in which the agreement had been concluded and it was viewed by them as an evil precedent. Russia was also upset because of implications of the agreement for the balance of naval power in the Baltic.

The First Lord defended the agreement both in a broadcast and in a House of Commons debate. Churchill strongly criticized the agreement. He afterwards wrote in his history of the Second World War that the quota of ships allowed to Germany in relation to British strength had, in effect, removed all restraint to German naval expansion and "would set her yards to work at maximum activity for at least ten years". In the event, as he records, Germany had not built up to the permitted overall strength when the war began but she had, significantly, built U-boats in excess of the 60 per cent of British submarine strength. Eyres-Monsell's defence was that the agreement was a useful step towards achieving a new treaty of naval limitation when the Washington and London agreements expired in 1936. He also made the point that Germany had proposed the building ratio agreed upon and that the Government would have incurred even more severe criticism, if not from the same people, if they had rejected the German offer.

Bolton Meredith Eyres-Monsell, born on February 22, 1881, was the son of Lieutenant-Colonel Bolton Monsell. After training as a cadet in H.M.S. Britannia he went to sea as a midshipman in 1896 and later specialized as a torpedo lieutenant. He retired from the Royal Navy in 1906 but returned to the Service in 1914 and served at sea during the 1914–18 War.

Monsell married first, in 1904, Caroline Mary Sybil, daughter of H. W. Eyres. On his marriage he assumed the name of Eyres-Monsell. This marriage, by which he had one son and three daughters, was dissolved in 1950. Later the same year Monsell married Mrs. Essex Leila Hilary Drury, granddaughter of Field Marshal the Earl of Ypres. The heir to the viscounty is the Hon. Henry Bolton Graham Eyres-Monsell.

March 24, 1969.

Pierre Monteux, principal conductor of the London Symphony Orchestra since 1961, who died on July 1, 1964, at Hancock, Maine, at the age of 89, was one of the last active great conductors who had a close personal link with the most significant musical events of the century. Old age saw no lessening either in his powers or his activity. Each successive concert increased one's astonishment at his seemingly inexhaustible energy, at his sensitivity to orchestral nuance and colour, and his remarkable ability to draw from his players the most finely articulated playing with the minimum of gesture; no less astonishing was his extraordinarily wide range of musical sympathies.

The economy of gesture, however, was a sign of authority—for he had lived with the music he directed for more than half a century—and of masterly technical control.

THE RITE OF SPRING

Monteux was born in Paris on April 4, 1875, and he studied the violin at the Paris Conservatoire. He was 12 when he conducted his first concert, and shortly afterwards he took an orchestra on a concert tour. But at this stage the violin was still his chief study. He emerged from the Conservatoire with *premier prix du violon*, shared with Jacques Thibaud, but settled down as a viola player at the Opéra Comique, and led his section in the first performance of Debussy's *Pelléas et Mélisande*. In 1910 he obtained a post as conductor at the Dieppe Casino, and in the following year began his association with Diaghilev's Russian ballet which soon brought him international fame. Monteux was in charge of the first performances of Ravel's *Daphnis et Chloé*, Debussy's *Jeux*, and Stravinsky's *The Rite of Spring*, to name only three works of the highest and most seminal importance in later music. Monteux knew and was admired by all these composers, and during the half century that followed his interpretations of their music acquired a nonpareil authority.

During the First World War Monteux served in the French Army, but in 1916 he was able to go to America as conductor of ballet and opera (he became a specialist in Russian as well as French works). In 1919 he was appointed director of the Boston Symphony Orchestra, but resigned in 1924 to return to Europe as joint conductor, with Mengelberg, of the Concertgebouw Orchestra in Amsterdam. In 1936 America called him once more, and from then until 1952 he conducted the San Francisco Orchestra, with incalculable effect on American musical culture, but also with the opportunity to enlarge his already substantial repertory, and by gradual, natural processes to deepen his understanding of his art. He and his wife made their home at Hancock, Maine (whose university awarded Pierre Monteux an honorary Doctorate), and he became an American citizen. He left San Francisco in 1952 only to travel more extensively; his vigour and appetite for music remained amazingly youthful, and his repertory was growing all the time—at the age of 80 he learnt Elgar's Enigma Variations, conducted them from memory, and gave performances which British orchestral musicians acclaimed as closer than any other to those of Elgar himself.

ENORMOUS REPERTORY

Monteux's visits to England now began to assume a major importance in our musical life: it was not only in French and American music that he excelled, but also in the Viennese classics and, particularly Brahms, music that nationalistic prejudices had long assumed outside the full comprehension of a Latin musician. Monteux was one of a number of Latin musicians who disproved this theory altogether, and when his regular appearances with the steadily developing London Symphony Orchestra received their firm recognition with his acceptance of the orchestra's principal conductorship, England gained and welcomed a conductor whose powers of illumination extended the length and breadth of his enormous repertory.

By now he knew when to spare his strength—usually—for his occasional illnesses, learnt with pessimistic alarm, regularly proved due either to accepting too many activities, or to his love of delicious food. In rehearsal, he never spared himself, but on the platform at the concert he presided with benign tranquillity, aware that the smallest flicker of his left hand would remind his players of work thoroughly prepared in advance. His personality and his serene, expressive face were enough to inspire vitality and freshness of execution. But he continued to travel throughout Europe and America, and to lead the L.S.O. on their various foreign tours. Nor did his instrumental ability fade away. In the 1950s he took the place of the Budapest Quartet's viola player, at short notice, playing the music without rehearsal, and from memory. Monteux's longevity, and the energy that accompanied it, were amazing enough, but the strength of his musicianship was the source of his unique distinction as a conductor, and it sprang from the character of the man, not from any mere powers of physical endurance.

July 2, 1964.

Sir Henry Moore, G.C.M.G., who died at his home in Cape Town on March 26, 1964, was a distinguished colonial servant, having been Governor of Ceylon, Kenya, and Sierra Leone. He had also been Assistant Under-Secretary of State, and Deputy Under-Secretary of State for the Colonies.

Henry Monck-Mason Moore was born on March 18, 1887, the younger son of the Rev. E. W. Moore and Laetitia M. Monck-Mason. He was educated at King's College School and at Jesus College, Cambridge, where he took his B.A. in 1909. The next year he became a cadet in the Ceylon Civil Service, four years later becoming fourth Assistant Colonial Secretary. During the 1914–18 war he held a temporary commission in the Royal Garrison Artillery, serving in Salonika and the British Expeditionary Force from 1916 to 1919. In the last-named year he became Assistant Colonial Secretary, Ceylon.

In 1922 Moore was made Colonial Secretary of Bermuda, and two years later received his first African appointment as Principal Assistant Secretary of Nigeria, becoming Deputy Chief Secretary in 1927. In 1928 he was made Colonial Secretary of Kenya in succession to Sir Edward Brandis Denham, who had been chosen Governor of the Gambia, and he served in this position from 1929 to 1934, when, on Sir Arnold Hodson's appointment to the Gold Coast, Moore became Governor and Commander-in-Chief of Sierra Leone. During his term of office, which ended in 1937 when he was invited to serve for a time as Assistant Under-Secretary of State at the Colonial Office, Moore accelerated the development of the Protectorate, abolished forced labour, and introduced native administrations. He was also responsible for the building of many roads, the starting of additional sanitary and medical services, the establishment of a Government reserve, and the encouragement of the inhabitants of the protectorate to use a more nutritious diet.

In 1939 Moore was made Deputy Under-Secretary of State for the Colonies in succession to Sir John Shuckburgh, the then Governor-designate of Nigeria. Three months later it was announced that he was to succeed Air Chief Marshal Sir Robert Brooke-Popham as Governor and Commander-in-Chief of the Colony and Protectorete of Kenya. In 1943 he was promoted to G.C.M.G. (he had been made C.M.G. in 1930 and K.C.M.G. in 1935) and in the following year he returned to the country of his first appointment, Ceylon, as Governor and Commander-in-Chief—an office generally regarded in the Colonial Service at that time as the "premier Governorship".

Ceylon had enjoyed internal self-government since 1931, but the United Kingdom Government still possessed reserved powers which were exercised by the Governor. The position was accepted by the Ceylonese up to the end of the war, but as soon as hostilities were over, the demand for national independence, stimulated by events in India and Burma, became insistent. It fell to Moore, as Governor during this delicate transitional period, to cooperate with the Ceylonese leader, Mr. D. S. Senanayake, in steering the island to independence in an atmosphere of general peace and good will. The successful outcome was in large measure due to Moore's tact and wisdom, and on the achievement of Ceylon's sovereign status in 1948 he was by general consent nominated as the first Governor-General under the new order. He held this office until his retirement from the public service in 1949, after which he settled in South Africa.

"Monkey" Moore as he was affectionately called by his friends and colleagues was a first-class administrator, with a tidy mind and a fund of common sense which, allied to his gifts of integrity and approachability, gained for him the trust and respect of officials and politicians alike in the many countries which he served with so much distinction.

He married in 1921 Daphne Ione Viola, only daughter of W. J. Benson, C.B.E. There were two daughters of the marriage, of whom the younger died in 1952.

March 28, 1964.

John Moore, novelist, playwright and broadcaster, of Kemerton, near Tewkesbury, died in a Bristol hospital on July 27, 1967 after an operation. He was 59.

Educated at Malvern College, he began his working life in the family auctioneering and estate agency business at Tewkesbury, but at an early age took to writing, notably on the countryside.

He became firmly established as a novelist with *Portrait of Elmbury*, which was followed by another widely popular book, *Brensham Village*, and his last published novel, *The Waters Under the Earth*, on which he was engaged for three and a half years, has been printed in seven languages.

In 1949, he helped to inaugurate the Cheltenham Festival of Literature (as a companion event to the celebrated Music Festival, which had begun five years earlier) and he was its shaping spirit from then on. He was chairman of the Festival Committee until 1956, when he was joined as co-director by the late Robert Henriques, and even after his retirement in 1964 from a central organizing role he continued to make an important contribution as an ordinary committee member, and as a judge of the Guinness Poetry Competition. In 1956–57 he was chairman of the Society of Authors.

Moore wrote about English country life from the inside. In his work there was none of the townsman's conscious effort in writing about rural England as if it were a picturesque foreign country. If he knew his village hierarchy and vividly portrayed it in his novels, he was well aware of change in the countryside; nowhere is this more sharply realized than in *The Waters Under the Earth*.

As he remarked in *The Season of the Year*, he believed it to be a virtue in itself to do as many things as possible. It was a virtue he practised; while he could write with great truth and perception about birds and horses and flowers and fishing his life was not bounded by these things. As a young man he had been a free-lance foreign correspondent in the Spanish Civil War and later he learnt to fly. He served with distinction in the Second World War in the Fleet Air Arm, which figures in the novels *Wits End* and *Escort Carrier* and whose individual flavour he interpreted so strikingly in a short historical account of the service, *The Fleet Air Arm*.

A prolific author, he wrote plays, among them *The White Sparrow* and *The Elizabethans*; books on angling and programmes for radio and television.

Probably his best writing is contained in his country essays and country calendars, like *The Season of the Year*; *Come Rain, Come Shine*; and *The Year of the Pigeons*. It was in character that he should have published *The Life and Letters of Edward Thomas*. Constable, who also came of yeoman stock, once said: "There is room for a natural painter." Moore was a natural writer.

He married in 1944 Lucile Douglas Stephens.

July 29, 1967.

William Arthur Moore, M.B.E., a special Correspondent of *The Times* in many parts of the world, notably during the 1914–18 War, and later editor of the Calcutta *Statesman*, died on July 23, 1962, at the age of 81.

He was born on December 21, 1880, the son of the Rev. W. Moore, rector of St. Patrick's, Newry, co. Down. From Campbell College, Belfast, he went to St. John's College, Oxford, where he won a classical scholarship. He was elected president of the Oxford Union in 1904. For four years from 1904 he was secretary of the Balkan Committee and his work in this post was a useful preparation for his visit to Constantinople in 1908 as the special Correspondent of *The Times* during the Young Turk rebellion. His extensive travels included a journey through central Albania.

On appointment to the permanent staff of the paper in 1909, Moore toured Persia, and was in the 100 days' siege of Tabriz. After a spell at Printing House Square he was in Persia again for more than two years, sending home graphic accounts of the fighting in the Nationalist revolution. His experiences included in 1912 a horseback journey from Teheran to the Persian Gulf. In the same year he paid a first visit to India. He returned to the Balkans when hostilities broke out there, and he also did service for *The Times* in Egypt, Russia, Spain, and Portugal. He had tried his hand at fiction, and early in 1914 he wrote *The Orient Express*.

THE AMIENS DISPATCH

In the summer of 1914 Moore was in Albania for *The Times*. During the insurrection, when Durazzo was besieged, Colonel Thomson, Dutch Gendarmerie Officer commanding Prince of Wied's forces fell mortally wounded. A brother officer and Moore carried him under fire to a place of safety, for which he received the thanks of the Dutch Government. He was then transferred to France. Travelling by car near the end of August, 1914, he found himself among scattered remnants of the British 4th Division trying to rejoin their units after the retreat from Mons. His famous Amiens dispatch, sent from Dieppe by courier, underwent severe censorship in the office before submission to the Press Bureau, then in charge of F. E. Smith (later Lord Birkenhead), who restored with his own hand some of the deleted passages and wrote definitely requesting publication. Appearing in the special issue of Sunday, August 30, this revealing dispatch on the parlous position of the expeditionary force raised a storm of protest both in Parliament and the press, but it had the effect of awakening the country to the urgency of the need for reinforcements. Meanwhile Moore, on September 2, travelling in company with Hamilton Fyfe, was captured and interrogated by a German cavalry patrol between Beauvais and Claremont. They had anxious moments, but were allowed to proceed, and succeeded in rejoining the French retreating along the Oise.

Early in 1915 Moore was commissioned in the Rifle Brigade and attached to the Cameronians (Scottish Rifles). He served in the Dardanelles and subsequently was on the general staff at Salonika. At the close of 1917, then a lieutenant-colonel he was transferred to the Royal Flying Corps. Soon after it became the R.A.F. and he was made a squadron leader. Later in Calcutta days he founded the Bengal Flying Club, and he was sometime chairman of the Aero Club of India and Burma. On demobilization Moore returned to the service of *The Times* as special correspondent in the Middle East and Afghanistan. Persia was again in a state of turmoil and he made Teheran his headquarters for two years.

In 1924 he was appointed assistant editor of the *Statesman* with a seat on the board of directors. Two years later he entered the Legislative Assembly at Delhi as representative of the Bengal European members and in 1932–33 he was leader of the whole European group. He retired from the House in the latter year on appointment to succeed Sir Alfred Watson as managing editor of the *Statesman*. No other occupant of the chair can have exercised more fully the freedom traditionally given to the editor by the directors than the mercurial and versatile Arthur Moore. While a friend of Indian claims to increasing responsibility he incurred the disfavour of the Congress party by pressing strongly and persistently for increased expenditure on defence; and when war came he was very ready to say "I told you so". His Irish extraction came out in his trenchant criticisms on this and other grounds of both the Home and Indian Governments.

In the summer of 1941 shortly before the Japanese onslaught he made a round-the-world journey by air, and his descriptive articles were republished under the title of *This Our War*. He was for a period chairman of the Indian branch of the Empire (now Commonwealth) Press Union, and president of the Indian and Eastern Newspaper Society.

Retiring from his editorship in 1942 he did relief work with the Friends' Ambulance in the great Bengal famine. In 1944 Lord Mountbatten selected him to be Public Relations Adviser, South-East Asia Command. After a short period as adviser on newspaper and publishing matters to the Dalmia industrial group, he established in 1949 a Delhi weekly *Thought*. This was not a successful venture and he went back to the Dalmia group of newspapers, becoming a "syndicated columnist".

NEW MUSICAL TUNING

After his retirement and return to England Moore developed an idea about musical temperament that had been suggested to him by the scales of Indian music. The basis of it was a dissatisfaction with the tone of the equally tempered piano, which to his acute ear sounded muddy. He therefore began to experiment with a new version of equal temperament in which the unavoidable error, the comma of Pythagoras, was differently distributed within the octave. He worked out the mathematics of it, had tuning-forks made to his specification, and had a grand piano tuned to it, which he showed to Sir Adrian Boult, Peter Crossley-Holland, of the B.B.C., and Frank Howes, who all pronounced it purer and more silvery.

DEMONSTRATION

Not content, he went on improving to the point where he thought it could be publicly compared with the conventional tuning. At Wigmore Hall in December, 1960, he gave a demonstration, with the help of Miss Ilona Kabos, who played a variety of pieces, one of which was Beethoven's Prelude through all the keys. He had two pianos on the platform, and some two-piano music was played which at first sounded passable but as the ear became accustomed to the new tuning soon sounded a jangle. There was a public discussion, and Steinway's chief tuner pointed out the objection to making a change that would affect concerto-playing with orchestra. But as far as piano solos were concerned Moore certainly demonstrated that a cleaner, more sparkling tone was available from an instrument tuned after his specification. The last years of his life were enlivened by his patient propaganda for his new tuning.

He married in 1915 Miss Maud Eileen Maillet, the journalist Eve Adam. They had one son. She died in 1957.

July 24, 1962.

Lieutenant-General Sir Frederick Morgan, K.C.B., who died on March 19, 1967, at the age of 73, will be remembered for his fine work in preparing the plans for the invasion of Normandy in the Second World War.

Never have plans been worked out on so great a scale as those hatched in 1943 at Morgan's headquarters in London. The task he was given was a formidable one, but he never seemed to tire. He gave up everything to it, working seven days a week and sleeping beside his desk. He established the happiest relations with his Anglo-American staff, and he had the gift of getting the best out of every member of his team. When the war was over, Morgan held two important posts, first with Unrra and then in the Ministry of Supply. But it is with his great achievement in planning for Overlord that his name will always be associated.

He was tall, with a fresh complexion and blue eyes. His untidy appearance concealed one of the tidiest minds in the Army, and he was friendly and courteous to everyone. From his earliest days in the Service he was noted for strength of character, ability and competence above the average.

Frederick Edgworth Morgan was born on February 5, 1894, the eldest son of Frederick Beverley Morgan of Paddock Wood, Kent. He was educated at Clifton College and the Royal Military Academy from which he was commissioned in the Royal Artillery in 1913. In the First World War, in which he was twice mentioned in dispatches, he served in France and Belgium. Early in the war he was blown up by a shell which nearly ended his career, but he returned later to serve on the staff of the Canadian Corps. Between the wars he served with his regiment and, after passing through the Staff College, Quetta, he was on the staff at headquarters in India, and then at the War Office. In 1938, as a Major and Brevet Lieutenant-Colonel, he was appointed G.S.O. 1st grade to the 3rd Division, and he was in this post when the war broke out. In the operations before Dunkirk he commanded the Support Group of the 1st Armoured Division, and, during the years when the army was being reconstituted in the United Kingdom, he was in succession Commander of the Devon & Cornwall Division, of the 55th West Lancashire Division and of the 1st Corps.

Morgan relinquished command of the 1st Corps when he was appointed, in March, 1943, Chief of Staff to the Supreme Allied Commander (Designate)—a title which became well known in its shortened form of Cossac—with instructions to mount a plan for the invasion of north-west Europe and attack the heart of Germany with a force of 100 divisions. A number of studies for a landing on the coast of Normandy had been made by planning staffs in the years preceding Morgan's appointment, and these were inherited by him. But it was a gigantic task to convert them into a practical scheme.

Morgan assembled a staff from all three Services, British and American, and set up his headquarters at Norfolk House in St. James's Square. Brooke, the C.I.G.S., outlined the problem to him, and then added "Well, there it is. It won't work, but you must bloody well make it."

Morgan and his staff did not, in the end, succeed in making a plan that would have worked. But this was not their fault. Not only were they handicapped by the fact that the Supreme Commander was at that time non-existent, but they were restricted by the inadequacy of the means allotted to them. Pleas for the allocation of greater resources were made by Churchill and the British chiefs of staff at the Quebec Conference, but it was not until General Eisenhower and his deputy commanders were appointed at the beginning of 1944 that the Americans fully realized the magnitude of the enterprise and made proper provision for it. When the Supreme Commander got into the saddle, it was therefore inevitable that Morgan's plans should be recast. One of the most serious shortages during Morgan's *régime* had been in landing craft, which the Americans would not divert from the Pacific War until after Stalin's promise at the Tehran Conference to come to their aid against Japan once Germany was out of the way. There were also other serious shortages in ships and in aircraft for lifting airborne troops. When these were made good, the front of assault was widened and the dispositions for the advance inland considerably altered. To give time to make these changes, the date of Overlord was postponed from May to June.

Among the many novel and remarkable features of Morgan's plan was the provision for large scale maintenance from artificial harbours, a method which had never till then been attempted in war. It would have been wasteful to land more Americans in this country than the minimum needed for the advance guard. The scope of the planning therefore extended from the Straits of Dover to the United States.

In spite of the disadvantages under which the Cossac staff laboured, they had worked out, by the end of 1943, all the essentials for the greatest amphibious operation ever undertaken and had overcome practical difficulties which had defeated earlier planners. They provided the basis, in all its vast detail, without which Overlord could never have been launched in 1944.

In addition to the Overlord plan, Morgan had to prepare two other plans for earlier action, one for a feint to prevent the enemy from concentrating against the Russian and Italian fronts, and a second for a rushed return to the Continent in the event of a sudden German collapse. In 1950 Morgan published a valuable and interesting record of his work at Norfolk House in his book *Overture to Overlord*. In 1961 his autobiography *Peace and War* appeared.

When he was relieved on the arrival of the Commanders with their own chiefs of staff he was appointed Deputy Chief of Staff at Eisenhower's headquarters where he served till the end of the war. In this post he became a thorn in the side of Montgomery who has described in his memoirs how Morgan's advice to the Supreme Commander often differed from his own. "Morgan", he wrote acidly, "considered Eisenhower was a god; since I had discarded many of his plans, he placed me at the other end of the celestial ladder."

In September, 1945, Morgan was appointed to the United Nations Relief and Rehabilitation Administration as Chief of Operations in Germany, to cope with the desperate problems of displaced persons uprooted and left stranded by the war, of whom there were at least a million at that time. During the next year he brought all his qualities of drive, enthusiasm, and sympathy to this task, and he was particularly successful in his relations with the military forces and the numerous private organizations which cooperated in his splendid work. In January, 1946, he created a furore when he spoke to a press conference of his belief that a secret organization existed to further a mass movement of Jews out of Europe. He was reported as having referred to a "positive plan for a second exodus."

The future of Israel was at this time still in the melting pot, for another two years were still to pass before she became an independent state. Morgan's remarks immediately caused a world wide sensation and evoked angry protests from Jewish organizations. The Director General of U.N.R.R.A. called for his resignation, but, after Morgan had appealed to him and visited him in New York, he was reinstated. There has since been published ample evidence that illegal Jewish immigration into Palestine had been secretly organized on a large scale. But Morgan's critics held that he should not have made a public statement while he was officially concerned with provision for many displaced Jews. He never lacked courage, and doubtless he felt it to be in the public interest to speak out. The storm was over only temporarily. Six months later he again came into collision with his chiefs when he alleged that U.N.R.R.A. organizations were being used as a cover for Soviet agents who fomented trouble among displaced persons. This time he was relieved of his duties.

He now retired from the Army with the honorary rank of lieutenant-general. He came back into Government service in 1951 when he was appointed Controller of Atomic Energy in succession to Lord Portal of Hungerford. In this capacity he witnessed Britain's first atomic explosion at the Monte Bello Islands in October, 1952. When the Atomic Energy Authority was set up in 1954, Morgan became Controller of Atomic Weapons.

He was made a C.B. in 1943 and promoted to K.C.B. in 1944. He was a Commander of the U.S. Legion of Merit and of the French Legion of Honour, and held the American Distinguished Service Medal. He was Colonel Commandant of the Royal Artillery from 1948 till 1958. In 1917 he married Marjorie, daughter of Colonel T. du B. Whaite, and had a son and two daughters.

March 21, 1967.

Henry Morgenthau, who died at Poughkeepsie, New York, on February 6, 1967, at the age of 75, will be remembered chiefly for his long tenure of the office of Secretary to the United States Treasury from 1934 to 1945. He was in charge of United States financial policy during the turbulent years of the New Deal and the even more momentous wartime period. During the war he was a good and trusted friend of Britain. He played a prominent part in devising the plan by which Britain and the other allies were kept supplied with the tools of victory and the necessities of life through the Lend-Lease agreements. It was Winston Churchill who had challenged the United States with the words "Give us the tools and we will finish the job". It was Henry Morgenthau who, with President Roosevelt, devised the arrangements by which the tools were provided without repeating the First World War mistakes of chalking up vast debts in respect of these deliveries.

Morgenthau resigned two months after President Roosevelt's death in 1945. Had he still been in office at the United States Treasury after victory in Europe was achieved in July, 1945, Lend-Lease, which Winston Churchill called "the most unsordid act in the history of mankind", would probably not have been ended, as it was, by a brutal and formal notification to all recipients that they would have to pay cash, even for the goods that were then in the pipeline to their destination.

Morgenthau will also be recalled for the part he played in devising the plans for postwar monetary reconstruction finally hammered out at the Bretton Woods conference in New Hampshire in 1943. The International Monetary Fund and the World Bank were the direct descendants of this far-seeing and far-sighted plan for financial reconstruction in which he played an important role.

A less memorable initiative was his plan to "pastoralize" Germany and destroy the German industrial complex which he contended had caused and fed Germany's capacity to wage two world wars. In these ideas he was prompted by Nazi Germany's ill-treatment of the Jewish race to which he belonged. These ideas found no support in the entourage of President Truman, who refused on this account to take Morgenthau to the Potsdam Conference after Germany's surrender. Morgenthau's resignation was immediate.

Henry Morgenthau, son of a Jew who had emigrated from Germany and became a New York financier, was born in New York on May 11, 1891.

Educated at Phillips Exeter Academy, he went on to Cornell University of which he held the degree of LL.D. At first he was uncertain in regard to his career. Going first to Turkey he studied architecture, but found it did not greatly interest him. Then he tried working with his father for a time; but, falling ill, went to Texas to recuperate. While there he became interested in agriculture and went back to Cornell to learn more about it. The subject proved increasingly congenial and he therefore bought a large farm on the Hudson River and settled down as a gentleman farmer. In the First World War he served as a lieutenant in the United States Navy, and in 1922 he became publisher of the *American Agriculturist*, a Poughkeepsie journal.

At Fishkill Farms, as he named his new property, Morgenthau grew apples as his chief crop, and farmed on scientific lines. Franklin

Roosevelt was a neighbour and the two men became close friends. Morgenthau was shy, ill at ease at public gatherings, and knew nothing of politics. Nevertheless, he and the future President found much in common, and Roosevelt with his flair for human quality recognized Morgenthau's gifts. When, therefore, he ran for the Governorship of New York he sought Morgenthau's help and after the election made him chairman of the State Agricultural Advisory Commission. It was an important group and as a result of its activities several reforms were instituted and enacted.

CALLED TO WASHINGTON

In 1931 Morgenthau was appointed New York State Conservation Commissioner with jurisdiction over the State lands and in this capacity directed the early stages of a million-acre reafforestation programme. Then after the Presidential election of 1932 he was summoned to Washington, appointed chairman of the Federal Farm Board, and a little later became Governor of the Farm Credit Board. In the latter position he assisted in the preparation of the Farm Mortgage Act of 1933 and the Farm Credit Act of the same year, and was also responsible for the establishment of Farm Credit administration on a large scale. In these activities he, as a practical farmer, who was used to the handling of considerable interests of his own, showed marked capacity, and gained a wide and valuable experience.

Morgenthau was not, however, to spend more than a few months at his new duties, for in November, 1933, the President appointed him Under-Secretary to the Treasury, and a few weeks later promoted him, on the retirement of his chief, Mr William Woodin, to the secretaryship. It was a bold selection for Morgenthau had virtually no experience of finance. The author of the New Deal required, however, an honest and courageous man who was prepared to concentrate on the single aim of recovery from the economic depression and to take drastic action to this end rather than an expert. Morgenthau on the other hand was only too well aware of his own lack of knowledge; but he had plenty of determination and set to work to make good his own deficiencies.

The task of the Secretary of the Treasury in the earlier stages of the New Deal was formidable indeed and was destined, with the approach and eventual coming of war, to become more formidable still. At the time he took office the President was still battling with a financial situation which, less than a year before, had seemed desperate. The United States had paid dearly for remaining on the gold standard. Gold had flowed outwards in alarming quantities and the countries which had abandoned the gold standard before her had been capturing an increasing proportion of the world's export trade. The President, immediately after he assumed power, had closed the banks and ordered gold into the national custody. This had warded off the impending disaster, but it was not until January, 1934, that the operation of revaluing the dollar at 59.06 per cent of its former gold content was complete. Morgenthau took office, therefore, at a critical moment, and was required to supervise the launching and working of the new arrangement. In 1935 he was able to claim that the dollar was absolutely sound, that the President's monetary policy had rescued his country from chaos, and that while the fort had been held through the most trying period of the recovery programme, the way was by then open for advance. One result of the new policy was to attract gold to the United States, and therefore to build up a national reserve of that metal which became embarrassing in its size. The gold policy of the United States, as administered by Morgenthau at this period was, briefly, that of nationalizing gold, raising its price. He was also active in regard to silver, fostering an increase in its production, and reburying it.

DEFENSIVE PREPAREDNESS

In 1935 he went to France, where he saw members of the French Government and in the next year took a prominent part in securing a financial agreement with that country and Great Britain for the stabilization of international trade. In 1938 he was in France again. On top of demands of the New Deal came those for defensive preparedness. During his years of office the national debt had mounted steadily. He had no choice but to borrow freely and to tax heavily, but he was haunted by the spectre of inflation and had to resort to measures which, although frequently unpopular, he regarded as necessary to prevent it. He was by inclination economical in regard to Government expenditure; but when the national safety was at stake he was the last to stint essential supplies. Hitler, in his view, had to be beaten at all costs. He was, therefore, prepared to tap every possible source of revenue, and, in matters of taxation, though not as a rule in others, was distinctly radical. He had his own strong views, and one of his governing principles was to increase the number of the *rentier* class in order to secure wider support for soundness in Government finance.

The entrance of the United States into the war and the unprecedented expenditure entailed by its efforts and by the assistance given to its allies added, of course, greatly to his problems, though he could count on a new spirit in the country to which he could appeal. In addition, moreover, to finding the money for war, he had to preserve the essential character of the capitalist democracy he served. "If", he was known to say, "the little man can be safeguarded, capitalism is the best system we know of." He had also to sustain the structure of the world currency systems as a provision for the future.

One of the authors of the Bretton Woods monetary agreement, Harry-Dexter White, was appointed as American executive director of the International Monetary Fund in 1946. White, who had been an Assistant Secretary to the United States Treasury, resigned his position with the International Monetary Fund the next year. He died in 1948 a few hours after he had given evidence before the House Committee on un-American activities. He had been accused by a former communist agent in the Congressional spy investigation, but denied the accusations. Later, in 1953, in a party political speech, the Attorney General, Mr. Brownell, claimed that President Truman had appointed White to the International Monetary Fund while knowing that he was a Russian spy. Truman, rebutting the charge, stated that White had been retained in the Government service, in spite of accusations of disloyalty, because to do otherwise would have alarmed other suspects. Morgenthau testified to an internal security committee in 1955 that while he was Secretary of the Treasury he had no reason to suspect White's integrity or his loyalty to the United States.

HIS RETIREMENT

After his retirement Morgenthau spent a great deal of time piecing together and editing the voluminous diaries and records accumulated during his 11 years at the U.S. Treasury. Every letter he wrote was preserved. Every conversation he had, however confidential, was stenotyped by an attendant secretary, often to the dismay and annoyance of the foreign officials and Ministers to whom he was talking. Two volumes of these diaries were published after the war and aroused much criticism of their alleged indiscretion. They revealed, for example, how Morgenthau and President Roosevelt between them, in 1933 and 1934, invented the daily figure at which the price of gold should be fixed, sometimes introducing the figure 7 "for luck" and on one occasion asking "I wonder what Montagu Norman in London will say to that?"

He spent many years of his retirement in Paris. He married in 1916. His first wife died in 1949. He married two years later. He leaves a widow, two sons, a daughter and 11 grandchildren.

February 8, 1967.

Stanley Morison, typographer, scholar and historian of the press, and for many years a valued member of the staff of *The Times*, died on October 11, 1967, at the age of 78.

It was Morison who designed the new type face for *The Times* in 1932. Known as The Times New Roman it was based on novel principles of stress and balance and was at once seen to be both attractive and readable. It rightly achieved success and is now used in all parts of the world. Morison, however, was always more concerned with what ideas were communicated than with the means of communication, whether it was type or anything else. The great volume, *Printing and the Mind of Man,* the memorial of the 1963 International Printing exhibition in London, with the tribute it pays him for the volume's original conception, will remain the most fitting epitome of his life's endeavour.

Stanley Arthur Morison was born on a fitting date in 1889—the 6th of May, being the feast of St. John ante portam Latinam, the patron saint of scribes and printers. He was educated at a board school.

His earliest working years were spent in the London branch of the Société Générale Bank, but his wider interests led him to the study of typography and, in particular, of the Printing Supplement issued by *The Times* in 1912. In the following year *The Imprint*, a quarterly journal devoted to typography was founded, Morison joined the staff under Gerard Meynell and it was in the eighth number that his first published essay (*Notes on some Liturgical Books*) appeared. It was an early indication of a study to be more fully developed. *The Imprint* had a short life and Morison, after working for some time with Burns and Oates, succeeded Francis Meynell as typographer to the Pelican Press in 1918.

This period saw the appearance of Morison's first studious writing about typography: *The Craft of Printing*, printed and sold at the Pelican Press, 1921. In that year he joined C. W. Hobson and Walter Lewis (with whom he was to form a life-long friendship of affection and argumentation) at the Cloister Press at Manchester.

ADVISER ON MONOTYPE

In 1923 his position in the printing world was established by his appointment as adviser to the Monotype Corporation. From this time onwards he became the outstanding consultant in typography; at the suggestion of Walter Lewis, who had been appointed University Printer at Cambridge, he became adviser to the Press in 1923; for a time he designed books for Victor Gollancz, giving them an individual and unmistakable character; in 1929 he became typographical adviser to *The Times*.

Meanwhile, his literary output was prodigious. A large folio, *Four Centuries of Fine Printing*, was published in 1924; innumerable articles, all based on solid research, appeared in *The Fleuron* and *The Monotype Recorder*: to the fourteenth edition of the *Encyclopaedia Britannica* he contributed the articles on calligraphy, printing type, and typography.

When he joined the staff of *The Times* a new field was opened to him. In November, 1930, he produced his proposals for a revision of the typography of the paper and in later years would describe the first shock of incredulous astonishment produced by the proposed abandonment of Gothic lettering for the title. But his plans were accepted and on October 3, 1932, *The Times* appeared in its new dress and The Times New Roman was firmly established in the catalogue of the Monotype Corporation as available for general use. In *The Times* office, Morison became more than a typographer. He was fascinated by the history of journalism. When he was made Sandars Reader in Bibliography at Cambridge in 1931 he thought first of taking the Alphabet for his subject, but, having failed to find an adequate history of English journalism, he determined to write one himself and chose the English Newspaper as the subject of his lectures. He amassed far more material than he could properly deliver and the outcome was a massive folio on *The English Newspaper*, 1622–1932. From this he turned to the history of *The Times* itself and, although no author's name appears on the title-pages of the five volumes published between 1935 and 1952, it is an open secret that the greater part of it was written by Morison. Even more surprising was his appointment as editor of the *Literary Supplement* in 1945. Morison was not, fundamentally, a literary man ("I'm not interested in literature", he would say, "I want *information*"). But he was, at that time, working in intimate cooperation with the editor (Barrington-Ward) and exercised an efficient control over the *Supplement* for three years.

In spite of the variety of his interests and achievements Morison unquestionably was most proud of his position on the staff of *The Times*; and there was a particular intonation, recognized by his intimates, when he referred to "the sheet" or, in the style of an old-fashioned citizen of London, to "the House". The history of *The Times* was the bridge which brought him across from the business side of the paper to mingle with the editorial staff—a bridge erected largely by chance and in the most casual fashion.

NORTHCLIFFE AIM

The plan for a history of *The Times* had always been a favourite sideline of Lord Northcliffe's, and various tentative efforts were made to get it started. In the early 1930s, under the general guidance of R. M. Barrington-Ward, then assistant editor, and with the help of a former editor. G. E. Buckle, real progress was made. Barrington-Ward was perhaps the first to spot the particular quality of Morison—the relations between the two became especially close both inside the office and outside—and he brought him forward to help with the *History*. Morison retired from *The Times* in 1960.

Morison was possibly not a graceful writer and composition never came easily to him, but his capacity for amassing the facts, for cutting his way through the tangle of politics and personal rivalries to the truth was worthy of the professional historians and envied by them. His particular achievement in the *History* was to bring Barnes to the very front and to adjust his position in relation to Delane, who had perhaps been allowed to dwarf his predecessor. More generally he brought out the weighty foreign influence of the paper, and set it against a background of foreign politics, remarkable both in detail and capacity. Although it would be wrong to couple his name exclusively with the *History*, the solid historical and political foundations on which the whole structure rests were due to his astonishing (because it seemed to be effortless) power for research. No doubt part of the explanation of the amount he got through was his habit of starting his working day with the sun.

This absorption in the history, and the business, of newspapers did not interrupt the steady flow of reviews and monographs on such specialized topics as *The Calligraphy of Ludovico degli Arrighi*, *The Alphabet of Damianus Moyllus*, *The Writing Book of Gerard Mercator*, *The Portraiture of Thomas More*, *Talbot Baines Reed*, and many others; in a hand-list compiled in honour of his sixtieth birthday there were more than 140 items. Nor was there any weakening of his interest in liturgiology. His short book on *English Prayer Books* (1943), afterwards revised and expanded, is an admirable example both of his wide reading and his vigorous clarity of expression. Morison never did anything by halves. In his young days he was violently radical in his political and religious views. Recognizing the potential anarchy of his opinions and the consequent need for an external discipline he joined the Church of Rome and preserved the customary enthusiasm of a convert.

Socially he was a superbly good clubman. He could listen as well as talk, and the echoes of his laugh and his thigh-slapping were familiar to many members of the Garrick and other societies. Many distinctions were conferred upon him, such as the gold medal of the Bibliographical Society and of the American Institute of Graphic Arts. He was a member of the editorial board of *Encyclopaedia Britannica*. These he valued, but even more he valued his honorary degrees at Cambridge and Birmingham and his fellowship of the British Academy. For these were recognitions of scholarship and Morison was nature's scholar.

October 12, 1967.

Professor Edith Morley, O.B.E., who died on January 18, 1964, at the age of 88, was Emeritus Professor English Language, University of Reading, and devoted much of her life to the publication of the literary remains of Henry Crabb Robinson.

Edith Julia Morley was born in London in 1875, fourth of the six children of Alexander Morley, a well-known dental surgeon. The household was Jewish, and orthodox, of families long settled in England. It was the problem of the emancipation of herself and of women and their place in the professional life of the country that set the pattern for her long and useful life. She attended a day school, Doreck College, in Kensington Square, duly chaperoned. At the age of 14 she went to Hanover, where she remained for three years. Returning to London she entered the Women's Department of King's College, London, her father being willing to accept sympathetically her desire for the fullest professional education available for women; and at this time under the famous Miss Lily Faithfull that department was entering a new and more rigorous academic phase.

Here Miss Morley was prepared for the Oxford Honour School of English Language and Literature, taken externally through the Oxford Delegacy for Local Examinations. In June, 1889, she passed in the First Class. In December of 1899 she and her friend Caroline Spurgeon were the first students of the Women's Department to be admitted to the Associateship of King's College. During those years Miss Morley also attended lectures at University College, where she came, like so many, under the influence of W. P. Ker; and it was now, too, that she encountered F. J. Furnivall, from whom she learnt to scull in his Hammersmith Club. Sport was part of emancipation, and she was also proficient in cycling, swimming, and hockey. At the age of 21 she had formally ceased to profess adherence to Judaism.

In 1901, while teaching at the Women's Department, she was appointed to teach German, with some English Philology, at the College in Reading, which in 1902 was recognized as a university college preparing students for the degrees of London University. In 1903 she became Lecturer in English, and in 1908 Professor of English Language and Lecturer in English Literature. In 1926 she proceeded to the degree of M.A. at Oxford. She remained Professor of English Language at Reading until her retirement in 1940: one of the first women to hold a Chair in an English university. She is commemorated by a bursary for postgraduate work which she endowed.

Absorption in the formation of one of the new institutions of higher learning, in her teaching and in her tutorial duties, in which she was notably assiduous and generous, generous with time and more than time, did not prevent Miss Morley from playing her part in the Women's Movement: for her they were two aspects of the same thing. She became a member of Mrs. Pankhurst's Women's Social and Political Union, and, from 1906, of the Fabian Society, for which she edited in 1914 a survey of *Women Workers in Seven Professions*, with a section by herself on women at the universities and in university teaching. She was a founder member of the British Federation of University Women, for which she worked with devotion throughout her life.

In 1934 she became a Justice of the Peace, and, later, chairman of the Reading Probation Committee. She found one of the causes of her life in the care of refugees from Nazi Germany and worked untiringly for the Reading and District Refugee Committee of which she was honorary secretary from its foundation in 1938: her knowledge of Germany and of English education in all its aspects was of particular value. With the years the scope of the committee's activities altered, but, until the end of her life, she was actively associated with it and was consulted regularly on its problems.

In respect of this work the O.B.E. was conferred on her in 1950.

Miss Morley's first book was an edition of Hurd's *Letters on Chivalry and Romance* (1911). In 1912 she embarked on the *mare magnum* of Henry Crabb Robinson's papers which were to occupy her for the rest of her academic life. After a preliminary selection in 1922 she issued his correspondence with the Wordsworth circle (1927). *Henry Crabb Robinson in Germany* (1929), a *Life and Times of Henry Crabb Robinson* (1935) and finally all his relevant literary references in *Henry Crabb Robinson on Books and their Writers* (1938). It was an arduous and valuable labour and combined her two major interests, in Germany and in the English Literature of the Romantic period. One of the pleasures of her retirement was to contribute a section on the eighteenth century to the annual survey published by the English Association of which she was a founder member.

For many years of her long retirement she confronted a crippling and painful illness with a vigour and contempt that were the admiration and sometimes the alarm of her friends. She leaves many people in her debt.

January 21, 1964.

Henry Morris, C.B.E., who died in hospital on December 10, 1961, after a long illness, will be especially remembered as the creator of the Cambridgeshire Village Colleges which provide not only juvenile and adult education, but also those social and cultural activities which go to make up a healthy and progressive rural community. Morris had more than his share of architectural understanding and had the vision to commission, while he was still in Britain, Dr. Walter Gropius and his English partner, Maxwell Fry, to design the Impington Village College. The result was a building (it was erected in 1938) which had a profound influence on architecture at the time and which is one of the ancestors of the modern English school which has won so high a reputation.

Morris was one of the great educationists of our time. Not only was he the creator of the Cambridgeshire Village Colleges, of which there are now 10 in Cambridgeshire alone, but he inspired a score of young men whom he met at Cambridge to become education officers, to teach in schools and to enter other branches of the educational profession. Many of those he inspired with his own passion for education hold key positions in various parts of the country today.

His width of vision was remarkable, as can be seen in the use of colour and non-traditional materials in the building of schools which he pioneered in the first village colleges of 30 years ago. Even retirement from his post as Chief Education Officer for Cambridgeshire in 1954 did not diminish his ardour for education in its widest sense. He was the initiator of the Digswell House Arts Trust which flourishes in Welwyn New Town, and of Hilltop, "a new venture in Public Houses" which he persuaded the Ministry of Housing and Local Government and the local Licensing Justices to give him permission to erect in Hatfield New Town.

Education for Morris meant a stern mental discipline allied with enjoyment of colour, the countryside, bodily fitness, the good life in every sense. Whatever he did he accomplished with passionate energy, brushing aside opposition and seeing the job done. That was the tremendous virtue of his life—he not only had ideas and vision but he translated them into living buildings for living people to enjoy.

In spite of illness Morris opened Comberton Village College in 1960. He began his speech with the remark that he thought he had come to a youth centre there was such an air of gaiety, music, colour, and amiable chatter. The poignancy of those remarks affected his friends deeply. They knew he was dying and they knew him still to be haunted by the spectre he feared all his adult life—Time—which would rob him of one more adventure on behalf of education.

If ever one man wrought together into one life the full man of science, technology, poetry and religion, of which Alfred Whitehead—whom he idolized with Rashdall and Meredith—so often spoke, it was Henry Morris. In truth he believed he was born, not for himself, but for his fellow men.

December 12, 1961.

Lord Morrison of Lambeth, P.C., C.H., died on March 6, 1965, at the age of 77.

During a lifetime devoted entirely to politics he was leader of the London County Council from 1934 to 1940, a member of Parliament from 1923 to 1924, from 1929 to 1931, and finally from 1935 to 1959. He served as Minister of Transport under Ramsay MacDonald, as Minister of Supply, Home Secretary and Minister of Home Security under Winston Churchill during the war, and then as Lord President of the Council, Deputy Prime Minister and Leader of the House of Commons in Clement Attlee's Administration, moving for a brief period in 1951 to the Foreign Office.

Herbert Morrison was the son of a policeman and was born in Brixton on January 3, 1888. His mother had been in domestic service and, with six surviving children, the early years were hard but not marked by actual lack of the basic necessities. An accident shortly after birth deprived Morrison of the sight of his right eye, though this never appeared to be a handicap either in his school life or later on. Herbert Morrison was educated at one of the Board Schools set up under the 1870 Education Act and left to become an errand boy at the age of 14. After a spell as a shop assistant and as a telephone operator, minor journalistic efforts helped to provide a living and from 1912 to 1915 Morrison worked as circulation manager for the first official Labour paper, the *Daily Citizen*. From 1914 he became part-time secretary of the London Labour Party and thereafter politics, either as an organizer or as a member of Parliament, was his sole occupation.

There is no evidence that any other politics than those of the Labour Movement ever attracted Morrison. In his early years he took part in the local forums, heard the famous figures like George Bernard Shaw and Keir Hardie, and in 1906 joined the Brixton branch of the Independent Labour Party. Following a common trend among left-wingers in London, he found this a rather pro-Liberal, north of England or non-conformist type of organization, and preferred the more direct socialism of the Social Democratic Federation to which he transferred in 1907. To the London left, free trade, anti-landlordism and Home Rule for Ireland were all meaningless, and Morrison began his life-long preoccupation with housing, transport, health, and education as provided (or neglected) by the local authorities for the citizens of the larger towns, above all, London. Later he left the S.D.F. and rejoined the I.L.P. because he saw that it was more likely to win elections and achieve actual changes. As part of this interest, he attended the Lambeth Metropolitan Borough Council—often the sole visitor—and unsuccessfully contested the Vauxhall Ward for the Labour Party in 1912. In 1910 he had become honorary secretary of the South London Federation of I.L.P. branches, and his work led steadily to the decision of the London Trades Council to call a conference and form the London Labour Party. After he became secretary to this new organization, Morrison said less and less about political theory, though he was opposed to the First World War and to conscription.

His concern was entirely with winning elections and carrying out pragmatic reforms, whose only common feature was the remedying of social grievances in a manner which showed no prejudice against governmental action or state ownership.

MINISTER OF TRANSPORT

In many respects Morrison's greatest achievements in politics were in London between 1920 and 1940. He began by bringing his organization intact through the war, going on to win 15 out of 124 seats in the 1919 L.C.C. elections. He realized that more was gained by steady work and preparation, by mastery of the immediate subject and possibilities, than by all the street corner oratory that so delighted the older generation of socialists. This work required the finding and training of candidates not only for the L.C.C. but for the elections in 28 boroughs. Once elected, these men had to be taught how to make speeches, conduct committees and actually run the machinery of local government. In late 1919, the London Labour Party won a majority or became the largest party in 16 boroughs. Morrison became Mayor of Hackney in 1919, and a member of the L.C.C. in 1922.

Elected to Parliament in 1923 and 1929, Morrison was a strong MacDonaldite and in the second Labour Government became Minister of Transport. He was responsible for the 1930 Road Traffic Act and for the London Passenger Transport Bill of 1931. In the latter case, Morrison had been leading the Labour group on the L.C.C. in opposition to a proposal to form a privately owned monopoly of London Transport. He became Minister of Transport, just in time to prevent the Bill from passing and introduced his own measure, the creation of the London Passenger Transport Board. His other major success as a departmental minister was during the war as Home Secretary and Minister of Home Security. In large part this also arose from his close knowledge of London and Londoners as the chief task was to reassure the citizens that all possible measures were being taken to preserve them from air attack.

Herbert Morrison visited all the areas and units involved in civil defence, he created the National Fire Service to get better cooperation and more rapid action and provided a proper Civil Defence uniform. This did much for morale, as did the Morrison indoor table shelter, and he went on to institute a Fire Guard with regular fire-watching duties. In all these activities, Morrison typified the irrepressible London civilian who made a joke out of nights at the office or the factory, who rallied round after the raids and would not let any German actions depress him.

As the progenitor of the London Passenger Transport Board Morrison was a firm believer in the autonomous public corporation as the best instrument for controlling a nationalized industry. He argued the case in his book *Socialization and Transport*, 1933, which was in part a defence of his views against criticism from within the Labour Party. Other possibilities, such as workers' or joint control of an industry, or management by a Government department, had a strong traditional appeal to some socialists. By winning acceptance for his view Morrison in effect determined the form that was later given to the postwar nationalization Acts. He also used to insist on fair compensation for stock-holders, and on the obligation on the advocates of nationalization to demonstrate the advantages of it industry by industry. Because, he thought, the case had not been made out for steel nationalization he was opposed to that commitment in Labour's programme.

It was probably in the 1930s that Morrison achieved his greatest hold on the Labour Party. In part this was due simply to his personality and ability. A short, stocky figure with a quiff of hair combed back from his forehead, he was a first-rate debater and public speaker. He could put his party's view in the most reasonable, lucid and engaging manner while never suggesting weakness, always ready to counter any attacks. Also his achievements in London were a tonic to the Labour Party just when it was most needed.

COCKNEY BRASHNESS

After an exhilarating rise to power in the early 1920s, there had been the disappointing experiences of the two minority Governments, the debacle of the 1931 general election, and the defection of Ramsay MacDonald. In face of these setbacks, the capture of the L.C.C. in 1934 and the steady achievements thereafter were a most welcome sign that Labour could both win and govern, and both these qualities in London were due to Herbert Morrison. Under him the L.C.C. reformed Public Assistance, kept Poor Law officers out of the hospitals, a new Waterloo Bridge was built despite Government opposition, the Green Belt was started, and slum clearance and school building were pushed ahead.

He was, in fact, a rather unusual type of Labour leader. He had not come up through the trade union movement, nor was he one of the middle-class intellectuals who formed the other major group in the senior ranks. A working-class boy who was largely self-educated, he had risen by virtue of his organizational, tactical and argumentative skills, and he had no signs of a social inferiority complex. Indeed his bearing was a mixture of Cockney brashness and the self-confidence which arises from knowledge, competence and a solidly based political position.

A further facet of Herbert Morrison's character which emerged strongly after his re-election in 1935 was his love of the House of Commons. As might have been expected, he took pleasure in mastering its rules of procedure. He was never overawed by the Palace of Westminster, but he valued its historical traditions and became an expert at using the House of Commons as part of the machinery of government.

His absence from the Commons for four years before his return in 1935, was, however, to have a possibly crucial effect on his subsequent career. Attlee, hitherto junior to Morrison, found himself Deputy Leader of the small group of Labour M.P.s in 1931 and when the leadership fell vacant in 1935 on the retirement of Lansbury, Attlee's claims were preferred to those of Morrison or Greenwood.

In many ways the climax of his career was the Labour landslide of 1945. He had prepared the ground for it in several respects. In the actual chain of events Morrison had played a considerable part. He had insisted that the Labour Party divide the House at the end of the debate on the Norwegian fiasco, and had thus given the impetus that led to Chamberlain's resignation. As one of the small group of Labour leaders who successfully occupied high office through the war, he had shown that such men could rule most effectively. And, when Churchill asked the Labour Party to continue with the Coalition till Japan was defeated, he was instrumental in insisting that this was unsatisfactory and that the country wanted a general election.

It has often been said that Morrison constructed and managed the machine that channelled the enthusiasms of 1945 into decisive action at the ballot box. Of this there is less evidence. The Conservative Party had almost totally abandoned its organization while Transport House had kept in operation. But there was no expert electioneering on either side. As with the L.C.C. campaigns, all that was done was to provide candidates, explain the legal position, and produce a manifesto and some centrally directed propaganda. But because Morrison had done this before in London and played a large part in the similar process at a national level in 1945, he, not unfairly, received a large measure of the credit for the victory.

CONTEST FOR LEADERSHIP

Though he had many subsequent achievements and his highest offices and honours were bestowed after 1945, some aspects of his career raised doubts, and Morrison himself had disappointments, which make this period perhaps a little less happy than the previous years. There are, for instance, certain episodes which remain somewhat obscure. After the election results became known in 1945, Harold Laski as chairman of the National Executive Committee of the Labour Party wrote to Attlee as leader of the party, and suggested that he should not immediately accept the royal summons to form a Government. With a large majority, the new Labour Government would need, he said, more dynamic leadership than Attlee could provide, and he felt the new Parliamentary Labour Party should be given the opportunity to choose its leader. Herbert Morrison in his *Autobiography* denies that, in supporting this move, he was seeking the post of Prime Minister for himself. Yet Harold Laski, Edith Summerskill, and the others who were active on this occasion, were quite clear that their candidate was Morrison, and that he had given them his complete support.

Again in 1947, when Sir Stafford Cripps was alarmed about the lack of leadership on economic affairs, there is some conflict of evidence. Sir Stafford was quite open that he felt Ernest Bevin should take over from Attlee as Prime Minister, Dalton should become Foreign Secretary, and Attlee could remain as Chancellor of the Exchequer. Herbert Morrison says he never associated himself with this suggestion (which was personally and honourably put to Attlee by Cripps). But in Hugh Dalton's account, Morrison was quite prepared to join if the object was to replace Attlee with himself. He only stood aside when he discovered that the objective was to elevate Ernest Bevin.

There is a similar discrepancy over Herbert Morrison's move to the Foreign Office in 1951. This was not one of his successful periods in office and he has suggested that the post fell to him as the only member of Attlee's Cabinet with the necessary seniority and authority. There is certainly some truth in this view, as the other possibilities were either James Griffiths or some younger man, but Attlee has said that the operative factor was Morrison's adamant insistence that he must have the post.

BEVAN AND WILSON RESIGN

There is the final episode of his contest for the leadership of the party in 1956. Again in his *Autobiography* Morrison says he was not ambitious and that his weakness was his "inability to intrigue". Yet there is little evidence of intrigue on the side of the victor, Hugh Gaitskell. There is little doubt that Attlee held on to the leadership in order to prevent Herbert Morrison succeeding. He resigned only when Morrison was 68 and then after declaring that the Labour Party needed a leader who was born in the twentieth rather than in the nineteenth century. As Deputy Prime Minister from 1945 to 1951 and as Deputy Leader of the Party since then, as a man who had contested the leadership with Attlee as far back as 1935, Morrison had undeniable claims to the topmost position. There was also a definite campaign to prevent his succeeding, all of which may justify his meeting such efforts with all the resources open to a politician.

It was Lloyd George who said that "in politics there is no friendship at the top", and this appears to have been the case among some of the Labour leaders. Attlee was always on reasonable terms with Herbert Morrison but he complained that "Herbert cannot distinguish between big things and little things" and this was probably a motive behind his desire to prevent Morrison obtaining the leadership. It was while Attlee was ill in hospital in early 1951 and Morrison was presiding over the Cabinet that divisions arose and Aneurin Bevan and Harold Wilson resigned. At times, Attlee blamed Morrison for this, saying "he lost me two of my ministers" and complained that the issue was not kept open for long enough. Herbert Morrison had not got on well with Bevan, but the most publicized disharmony was between Morrison and Ernest Bevin. For some reason, possibly over trade union representation on public bodies, the massive leader of the Transport and General Workers had decided that Morrison was anti-union, and to this he added a distaste for disloyalty of which he accused Morrison in 1945 when the attempt was made to replace Attlee. While Cripps's move to oust Attlee in 1947 never riled Bevin, he continued to suspect Morrison. A major reason why Attlee placed Bevin at the Foreign Office in 1945 was the feeling that their relations were not easy enough to permit the close cooperation that would have been required had both occupied posts on the home front.

But, in spite of these frictions, not uncommon in all Governments, few would deny Morrison the credit for many of the successes of the post-war Labour Government. When he was Minister of Supply in 1940 Morrison had had some difficulty with economic problems, a field which he had not mastered as thoroughly as he had general administration and the social services. This difficulty came up again between 1945 and 1947, when he was responsible, as Lord President of the Council, for economic planning and co-ordination. In 1947 this task was given to Sir Stafford Cripps at a new Ministry of Economic Affairs, and Morrison was left to lead the House of Commons to plan and carry through the legislative programme of the Government. In this task he excelled. His experience over the London Passenger Transport Act made him the authority on all the earlier nationalization measures, particularly of transport and electricity. Experienced members of the press lobby said it was a joy to watch him introduce these Bills, picking his way through the complexities and skirting the dangers like a cat walking across a mound of cans and broken bottles.

When it came to the question of steel, he had never been adamant about public ownership, and had wanted this item omitted from the 1945 election programme. Then, when the Cabinet took up the measure, Morrison was responsible for negotiations with Ellis Hunter and Andrew Duncan, the steelmasters' leaders. They produced a plan for increasing the powers of the Iron and Steel Board and allowing it to take over any firms that were not amenable to control. Bevan, Bevin and Cripps resisted this scheme throughout the summer of 1947 (during part of which time Morrison was seriously ill). In August the Parliamentary Labour Party discovered the situation and insisted on full nationalization and the Bill was put in hand in October of that year. Though Morrison was much criticized for his "hybrid measure", it was the most that could be achieved while the cooperation of the steel-masters was retained and would have given the Government a substantial measure of control.

GOVERNMENT AND PARLIAMENT

By common consent, much of Morrison's touch, his sure-footedness in all matters of domestic policy and administration, deserted him when he moved to the Foreign Office. Even friendly critics pointed out that he knew Londoners perfectly, other English fairly well, the Scots and Welsh were strangers to him, and foreigners incomprehensible. This may not have been fair but his tenure of the Foreign Office was neither successful nor fortunate. The chief problem was the decision of Dr. Moussadek's Government to take over the British-owned oil wells at Abadan. Morrison was in favour of recovering them and admonishing the Persian Government by direct military action. It was left to Attlee to veto any such idea, pointing out that world and particularly Asian opinion would react violently, that Persia could not be denied the right to nationalize such assets, and that strong-arm action in defence of commercial interests could no longer be tolerated. Unable to act as he had wanted, Morrison's policy lacked clarity or decisiveness and this short spell at the Foreign Office did considerable harm to his political standing.

After the Labour Party lost power in 1951, Morrison remained as a leading and very effective Opposition spokesman. But he also turned to writing and in 1954 published *Government and Parliament, A Survey from the Inside*. The book was at once acclaimed as a notable account of British government and Morrison hoped it would become another Erskine May, the authoritative description which would be renewed every few years and continue long after he had died. While the book has great merits, especially in the lucid accounts of parliamentary procedure, the legislative programme and the nationalized industries, it has never attained the stature Morrison hoped for. One reason was that he lacked the academic turn of mind and, while the exposition was excellent, there was little analysis. Deeper criticisms are that the book is a first-rate description of how the system worked in theory, but that Morrison put in few of the by-ways and circumventions of practice. A brilliant intuitive politician, he did not explain how he played by ear, but set out the actual score as it was on the official music sheet.

After his defeat for the party leadership he rejected all attempts to persuade him to remain as Deputy Leader although until the end of that Parliament he was still a frequent contributor to debates, as jaunty and pugnacious as ever. In the Dissolution Honours of 1959 he was made a Life Peer and the following year extended his activities by accepting the presidency of the British Board of Film Censors.

His *Autobiography* appeared in 1960 and provided little new information or insights into the period, but it did give some interesting sidelights on the author and his relations with his colleagues.

In it, Herbert Morrison says of Attlee that "he was one of the best mayors that Stepney ever had". It would be true to say that Herbert Morrison was almost certainly the best leader the London Labour Party and the L.C.C. have ever had, but it would not be enough. He was a great parliamentarian, effective in debate, a master of legislative and administrative detail, the author of a most important account of British government, and a man whose sincere desire to create better conditions for all was recognized by everyone engaged in British politics.

Morrison married in 1919 Margaret Kent by whom he had one daughter. His wife died in 1953 and he married, secondly, in 1955, Edith, daughter of John Meadowcroft.

March 8, 1965.

Anna Mary Moses, the American farm woman famous through her paintings as "Grandma Moses," died on December 13, 1961, at the age of 101.

Her career was a remarkable illustration of the unexpected ways in which the urge to paint may come out and also of the fact that it is never too late to start.

Mrs. Moses was 70 and a widow when she began to exhibit her pictures, along with her jams and pickles, at a local fair in New England and still had her zest for art when over 100 years of age. A prevalent interest in naive painting caused her to be hailed with enthusiasm as a "modern Primitive", through this is a term to be used of her work with some reservations. She was far from being a Douanier Rousseau. Her figures were never studied with the searching precision of the typical naive genius and a sentimental element sometimes suggested a *Saturday Evening Post* cover in amateur guise. She had, however, a strong feeling for the hilly landscape of her native county and the valley of the Shenandoah, where she also lived, for their change of aspect with the seasons, for rural incident, and what she called "old-timey things" which she conveyed with a charming briskness, in the style of her own that gained a widespread popularity.

Anna Mary Robertson was born, on September 7, 1860, on a farm in Washington County, New York State, of Scots-Irish descent. After working in the country as a "hired girl", she married a farmer, Thomas Salmon Moses when she was 27. They lived for many years in Virginia, returning to New York State in 1905. (In time her surviving children and grand-children also had farms in the neighbourhood). Her husband died in 1927 and after 40 years of married life Mrs. Moses, determined she "would never sit back in a rocking chair", took to making worsted pictures and subsequently to oils, which seemed "even simpler". A New York art collector discovered examples in the window of a drugstore at Hoosick Falls in 1938; in the following year, three of her paintings were included in an exhibition of Contemporary Unknown American Painters at the Museum of Modern Art, New York. They made an instant impression, confirmed in 1940 by her first one-man exhibition, "What a Farmwife Painted", at the Galerie St. Etienne, New York.

In the years following she received a number of awards of merit, including that of the Women's National Press Club, presented to her in 1949 by President Truman; was the subject of a documentary colour film; while her work in the 1950s made a triumphal progress through Europe (it was seen in more than 200 exhibitions in the United States, Canada, Europe, and Britain). Her first London exhibition was held at the Matthiesen Gallery in 1956. A book, *Grandma Moses: American Primitive*, by Otto Kallir, was published in 1946, and her autobiography, *My Life's History*, followed in 1952. It was marked by the same intelligent simplicity as the paintings which brought her international acclaim.

December 14, 1961.

Lord Mottistone, O.B.E., F.R.I.B.A., who died on January 18, 1963, in a London hospital, was Surveyor of the Fabric of St. Paul's Cathedral and widely known as an expert on historic buildings and for his restorations of, and additions to, old buildings of many kinds. He was a partner in the architectural firm of Seely and Paget. He was 63.

The Rt. Hon. Henry John Alexander Seely, eldest son of the first Baron Mottistone, whom he succeeded in 1947, was born on May 1, 1899, and educated at Harrow and Trinity College, Cambridge. He served during the 1914–18 War with the Royal Field Artillery in Italy and in the last war he was in the Auxiliary Air Force and with the Ministry of Works as an emergency works officer.

Among the many famous buildings he restored, with his partner Paul Paget, were Eltham Palace and (after war damage) Lambeth Palace, the Deanery and canon's houses at Westminster Abbey, the Charterhouse, Eton College, and the churches of All Hallows by the Tower and St. Mary, Islington. In this work he showed painstaking skill and knowledge, but in the new buildings he designed, which were chiefly for ecclesiastical or educational purposes, though his knowledge of historic styles was again much in evidence, there was less conviction.

One of his most notable recent works, the rebuilding of the City Temple, in 1958, on the site of the ruins left by the war and behind the surviving neo-classical frontage, was functionally well thought out but internally a not very satisfactory compromise between past styles and modern simplifications.

Nevertheless, Mottistone's contribution to architectural knowledge and understanding was considerable. He was an active member of many historical and amenity societies on whose behalf he worked unsparingly, and he was always willing to speak and write in favour of worthy architectural causes. He was chairman of the London Society for many years. He was devoted to London, and particularly to the City, where he lived for many years in Cloth Fair, occupying what he believed to be the only private residence in the City to have survived the Great Fire.

SURVEYOR TO ST. PAUL'S

In 1956 he succeeded Mr. Godfrey Allen as surveyor to St. Paul's Cathedral. This involved him not only in the task of designing the chapel for the Order of the British Empire, but in several controversies concerning the cathedral and its setting. He spoke in opposition to certain aspects of Sir William Holford's plan for the surroundings of the cathedral at the public inquiry held in 1957 and produced an alternative plan of his own; his and Paget's design for a new choir-school to the east of the cathedral was rejected in 1960, and a limited competition held instead in which Seely and Paget participated unsuccessfully, and he was one of those who favoured the cleaning of the outside of the cathedral—the subject of prolonged correspondence in *The Times* in the autumn of 1962.

But whether on the winning or the losing side in any controversy, and whether in the company of those whose tastes accorded with his own or not, he was always tolerant and good-humoured and delightful company. When not residing at Cloth Fair he lived in the Isle of Wight, and in 1958 he made a gift to the National Trust of 200 acres of East Afton Down, a ridge rising from the edge of Freshwater Bay.

Mottistone was a deputy lieutenant for the County of Southampton and a lay canon of Portsmouth Cathedral. He was president of the Royal Isle of Wight Agricultural Society in 1961.

He is succeeded by his brother, the Hon. Patrick William Seely.

January 19, 1963.

Dr. Eric Balliol Moullin, Professor of Electrical Engineering, Cambridge University, until 1960, died on September 18, 1963. He was 70.

He will be mourned not only in academic engineering circles but in the wider world of the electrical engineering industry where he had many friends, some of whom had been his pupils, and where his contributions to practical sciences were deeply appreciated.

Son of A. D. Moullin, civil engineer, he was born at Sandbanks on August 10, 1893. His birthplace was a few hundred yards from the site of the first wireless mast set up in England by Marconi. His talents that were to shape his life appeared early, and in his youth he himself constructed most of, the radio receiving and sending instruments that were then known, in a workshop in the garden of a house at Swanage built by his father. He was educated privately and at home learnt the mathematics which got him a scholarship to Downing College, Cambridge. He took first class honours in the mathematical Tripos, followed by the same in the mechanical sciences Tripos. Owing to a breakdown in health he was unfit for military service and spent part of the 1914–18 War teaching at the Royal Navy College, Dartmouth and returned in 1919 to become lecturer in engineering in the university and assistant lecturer at King's College.

THE VALVE VOLTMETER

One of his best known inventions, the Moullin valve voltmeter, was perfected during the twenties and became a standard instrument in electrical laboratories. Another notable instrument was an electrical torsiometer by which the torsion in rotating shafts could be measured. On tests with this he crossed the Atlantic in the liner Franconia, spending most of his time not in the elegant saloons but in the cramped propeller tunnels in the bottom of the ship, which even the greasers on their inspections left as soon as they could; here he tended his instruments on the spinning shafts and hoped that the weather would be severe enough for the propellers to pitch out of the water.

In 1929 he moved to Oxford to become Reader in Engineering Science, where he developed a school of teaching and research in electrical engineering.

He published many scientific papers, particularly on the theory of radio-frequency measurements and transmitting aerials; his work on *Spontaneous Fluctuations of Voltage*, published in 1938, became a classic on electrical "noise". In 1939 he was the chairman of the radio section of the Institute of Electrical Engineers.

On the outbreak of the war, he went to the Admiralty Signals Establishment at Portsmouth, to join in research on the rapidly changing radio and radar devices for the Navy. In 1942 he moved to the research branch of Metropolitan Vickers, who were meeting many practical difficulties in producing these new instruments. His work here included theoretical and fundamental studies of aerial design, and development of measuring apparatus for use at very high radio frequencies.

At the end of the war he returned to Cambridge to become the first holder of the newly created Chair of Electrical Engineering, and was elected to a Professorial Fellowship at King's College. He was president of the Institute of Electrical Engineers, 1949–50.

No one could know Moullin for very long without discovering his pride in his Guernsey ancestry, so that when in 1947 he inherited the Fief des Eperons as great-great-great-grandson of Jean Rougier, he was delighted by his ancient rights and duties. As Seigneur de Fief des Eperons, should a reigning sovereign visit Guernsey, it was his duty to offer a pair of gold spurs. To his great joy he was able to pay his feudal homage when the Queen visited the island in 1957, kneeling to offer her Majesty the spurs dated 1675 on a crimson cushion.

As Seigneur he also summoned the feudal court of which he was hereditary head, consisting of a Seneschal and a Douzaine of honest men which had powers over boundaries and other matters of land in Guernsey.

His books will continue to help students in engineering for many years to come as he himself did during his lifetime. During the past 50 years, the engineering of high frequency currents and electronic devices has changed from the groping empiricism of early wireless telegraphy to the highly developed science that now is basic not only to communications but to much of industry; this rests on effective theories with their roots in full mathematical treatments. Moullin by his research, writings, and teaching, has played an important part in these changes that have been wrought in his lifetime.

September 20, 1963.

Dr. Muhammad Moussadek, who died on March 5, 1967, at Teheran, was Prime Minister and near-dictator of Persia in the disastrous period, 1951–53; he achieved sudden world-fame as the passionately nationalist statesman who, with many eccentricities of manner and method, led his country to the repudiation of its agreement with the Anglo-Iranian Oil Company, and to the very verge of national ruin. His personal amiability and probity, and the sincerity of his emotional patriotism, must be judged as atoning ill for the calamities, and the ridicule, in which he involved his country; no more singular figure has ever headed a sustained and nation-wide patriotic outburst.

Moussadek was born in 1876, the son of a wealthy, landowning commoner who had risen to become Minister of the Court, and of a "princess" related to the (then reigning) Qajar dynasty. After early schooling in Persia and France, he held minor provincial appointments before returning to Europe in 1906 for higher studies in Law at Liège and Neuchâtel; the last-named University gave him a Doctorate in Law, and he was later to write a number of now-forgotten legal works in both French and Persian. Returning home in 1914, he held a series of senior government appointments between 1917 and 1922, as Under-Secretary, Governor of Fars, Deputy in the Majlis, Governor of Azarbaijan, Minister of Justice, and in 1922 Minister of Foreign Affairs. He acquired the reputation of an honest and zealous reformer, who rejected with passion any form of "foreign interference" in Persian affairs.

His criticism of the rise of Riza Shah, the illiterate officer, to ministerial rank and then to the throne, led to the termination of his mandate as Deputy (1923–1928) and his banishment from the capital to his estates. He lived in rural obscurity from 1928 to 1939, when he was imprisoned for two years by the still rancorous Pahlevi Shah, and was thereafter condemned to *residence forcée* at Ahmadabad. After the entry of Allied troops in 1941 and the Shah's abdication, Moussadek secured election to the Majlis in March 1943, and as Deputy for Teheran showed increasing signs of personal eccentricity with the xenophobic tirades, tearful speeches and naively simulated fainting-fits which later, before world audiences, became his speciality. As leader of the small, extremist National Front, he corraborated with the well-organized Tudeh Party, itself Communist-controlled. In December, 1944, opposing the grant of an oil concession to the U.S.S.R., he secured the adoption of a Law prohibiting all further oil negotiations with foreign interests till further notice; and three years later (October, 1947) he took a prominent part in securing rejection of the recently initialled Russo-Persian oil agreement.

The revised agreement offered by Anglo-Iranian, and accepted by the Persian Cabinet in July 1949, was the object of immediate and sustained attack by Moussadek and his allies. As chairman of the Oil Committee of the Majlis he secured its rejection, in favour of his committee's own proposal to nationalize the oil industry throughout Persia. The Prime Minister, General Razmara, was murdered; and after a few uneasy weeks while the committee elaborated its proposal, his successor was dismissed in favour of Moussadek himself. The latter assumed the premiership with strong Tudeh and anti-western support, and enacted on May 1, 1951, a naive and quite impracticable Nationalization Law, replacing "the former Company" by an all-Persian Board.

Missions by Averill Harriman on behalf of President Truman, and of Richard Stokes for the British Cabinet, were doomed to failure in face of Moussadek's insistence on total unmodified application of his Nationalization Law. Himself without appreciation of the industrial (or the ethical) realities involved, he visited America, spoke, wept and fainted before the Security Council, and returned at the end of 1951 to Persia, where the disordered condition of the country was not improved by his wild utterances. British Consulates were shut, attempts by the International Bank to find a solution were unavailing. The beginnings of opposition to Moussadek and the fears of the Shah, led to the latter's rejection in July, 1952, of his demand for increased personal powers; but, after replacement for four days as Prime Minister, he was able, by the organization of wide-spread rioting, to secure reinstatement, and was helped by the verdict of the International Court in July that it had, after all, no jurisdiction in the case. Peace-making suggestions conveyed to Moussadek by President Truman and Churchill were promptly rejected, and extravagant claims preferred against the "former Company" and in the prevailing atmosphere of violent xenophobia no other fate could await further suggestions offered through the United States Ambassador.

During the first half of 1953 Moussadek (who at no time visited the oil-fields or Abadan) maintained himself with difficulty by wholesale tampering with the Army, manipulation of a frightened and improperly elected Majlis, a farcical referendum, and the adroit use of rioting and terrorism. Early in August the Shah, with Army backing, issued a decree dismissing him from the premiership in favour of General Zahedli; but Moussadek refused to yield, assumed military control of the capital, and witnessed with relief the Shah's hurried departure to Rome. He could not, however, survive the growing reaction of the wearied and disgusted public, the defection of his Tudeh friends, and the still prevailing royalist sentiment of the Army; after days of anarchy, Zahedi was able to establish himself, the Shah returned, order was restored, and Moussadek, beaten at last, emerged from hiding and surrendered. He was arraigned for treachery, *lèse-majesté* and various illegalities, and after a trial in which his personal behaviour ranged from the grotesque to the merely ridiculous he was sentenced in December, 1953, to three years confinement. This was served, in spite of reiterated appeals. He was liberated in August, 1956, and went home.

Moussadek was married, and a devoted family man. He had two sons (one a doctor) and three daughters.

March 6, 1967.

Cardinal Aloisius Joseph Muench, former Papal Nuncio to west Germany and for many years the Roman Catholic Bishop of Fargo, in North Dakota, died on February 15, 1962, at the age of 72. He was a member of the Curia in Rome.

Since the last war Cardinal Muench had become better known in Europe than he was in the United States, the land of his birth, because his work in the Diplomatic Service of the Vatican had kept him on foreign assignments. There was no doubting that he was an American, however, for he retained the charm and informality always associated with public figures from that country, and he always kept in touch with his diocese in North Dakota.

More than one European statesman has testified, after conversations with him, that they spent more time on an engaging discussion of the problems of farming communities in the American Middle West than on European difficulties which, until then, had been their total preoccupation.

Muench was born on February 18, 1889, in Milwaukee, Wisconsin, the son of German immigrants. He was educated at the seminary of St. Francis de Sales, in St. Francis, Wisconsin, and at Wisconsin University, where he obtained his Master of Arts degree, after he had been ordained in the priesthood of the Roman Catholic Church in 1913. Later, in 1921, he went to Fribourg University in Switzerland, where he obtained a doctorate in social sciences, and while in Europe he also carried out some post-graduate work at the Sorbonne, at Oxford, and at Cambridge.

In 1922 he was appointed Professor of Dogmatic Theology and Dean of the Theological Department at the Seminary of St. Francis de Sales, and seven years later became Rector. In 1934 he became Domestic Prelate to Pope Pius XI, and was appointed Bishop of Fargo less than a year later.

It was during the war that he was first chosen to perform diplomatic work for the Holy See in Europe, and though the enforced withdrawal from active contact with his parishioners was obviously keenly regretted he made much of his new fields in Germany and Austria, rising daily at 6 a.m., planning his activities with the detail of a military operation and working, his assistants have said, twice as hard himself as he expected them to work. His penchant for military planning may well have come from his close contacts with the United States Army at the close of the Second World War, when he was Apostolic Visitor between the United States Occupation Forces in Germany and the Catholic Church in the country.

From 1949 to 1951 he was Regent of the Apostolic Nunciature in Germany. He was appointed Papal Nuncio in 1951. He was elevated to the title of Archbishop *ad personam* in November, 1950, and he was nominated a cardinal by Pope John XXIII in 1959.

February 16, 1962.

Dr. Hermann Joseph Muller, winner of the Nobel Prize for Medicine in 1946, died in Indianapolis on April 5, 1967. He was 76. Muller, a geneticist, won the Nobel Prize for his work on the hereditary effects of radiation and in recent years led a crusade to warn of the dangers of radiation.

Muller won his Nobel Prize "for his discovery of the development of mutations with the help of X-rays". Two years later in 1948 he resigned from the Soviet Academy of Sciences after he was said to have accused Soviet scientists of subordinating their ideas to political necessities. In 1956 his paper—not read at the United Nations conference on the peaceful uses of atomic energy in the previous year—was published. In it, Muller argued that man's first concern in dealing with radiation must be his own protection. He warned against any considerations that man might derive long-term benefits from the application of radiation to his germ plasm.

Hermann Joseph Muller was born in New York on December 21, 1890, brought up in Harlem, and studied biology at Columbia University, having won a scholarship. He specialized in heredity. After holding a scholarship (1910-11) and then a teaching fellowship in physiology at Cornell Medical College, he finally obtained a teaching assistantship at Columbia (1912-15). In 1915 he was called to the Rice Institute of Houston, Texas, by Julian Huxley. There he began his unique studies on mutation while giving courses in biology.

He returned to Columbia as an instructor and worked out methods for the quantitive estimation of mutation rates. Partly in collaboration with Altenburg he obtained in 1918-19 the first series of definite results, including evidence of a probable effect of temperature on mutation rate.

Returning to Texas in 1920, first as associate professor, then from 1925 as professor, he continued his work on mutation rates. He formulated the chief principles governing spontaneous gene mutation as now accepted. He also put forward the conception of the gene as constituting the basis of life, as well as of evolution, by virtue of its possessing the property to reproduce its own changes.

Muller, however, was best known for the researches of himself and his pupils on the artificial induction of gene mutations and chromosome changes by X-rays. The first critical evidence was obtained in 1927. In 1932 Muller left Texas with a Guggenheim fellowship to work in Berlin with Timofeff-Resovsky. He then spent three years and a half as the senior geneticist at the Institute of Genetics of the Academy of Sciences, first in Leningrad, then in Moscow. With the defeat of Vavilov and all he stood for, Muller found he could not continue his work in the U.S.S.R.

He worked at the Institute of Animal Genetics in Edinburgh (1937-40), and at Amherst College (1942-45). In 1945 he was appointed professor of the Zoology Department of the University of Indiana. He was a past president of the International Congress of Genetics and a foreign member of the Royal Society.

April 6, 1967.

Dr. Paul Muller, who was awarded the Nobel Prize for Physiology and Medicine in 1948, died in Switzerland at the age of 66 in October, 1965.

The award was "for his discovery of the high efficacy of D.D.T. as a contact poison against several arthropods." Born in 1899, Muller continued the work of P. Läuger and his associates in the laboratories of the Swiss firms of Geigy on mothproofing textiles. While engaged on this research he was led to investigate the properties of dichloro-diphenyl-trichloroethane (now known as D.D.T.), a substance which had been described as early as 1874.

It was while experimenting with the Colorado beetle that he discovered that D.D.T. was a contact poison: certain larvae which had not consumed any of it were nevertheless paralysed.

Subsquently he showed that as an insecticide it was in a class by itself—one millionth part of a gramme was enough to kill a fly, and after spraying its effects lasted for a long time. Its most crucial early test came during a typhus epidemic which broke out in October, 1943, in Naples. In January of the next year, when D.D.T. was first used, about 60 people were falling ill each day, but when the inhabitants had been deloused, the outbreak was brought under control in three weeks. In preventing malaria and other diseases spread by arthropods, the use of D.D.T. showed its great value for some time. But by 1947 reports started to come in of insects developing resistance to it, and by 1957 American workers reported evidence of resistance in 37 species.

October 14, 1965.

Claud Mullins, a controversial Metropolitan Magistrate (1931–1947), known for his outspoken comments, died on October 23, 1968, at the age of 81.

He was a passionate advocate of law reform on which he wrote several books. He was also vice-president of the London Marriage Guidance Council and the Family Planning Association.

In his autobiography, Mullins recalled that sometimes he would hesitate to read the evening newspapers, wondering what asides had been pounced on by the press. His aphorisms, some thought, would be remembered long after the irritated objections of his more conventional fellow-magistrates. "For me", he once stated, after recording a distaste for beer and spirits, "moderation has always been a higher virtue than abstention".

To an excellent analytical mind which won him prizes at the Bar without the benefit of a university education, Mullins added the sensitivity of a boy whose deep love for his ailing sculptor-father gave him an early insight into the human heart. Mullins was one of the first London magistrates to treat offenders with a compassionate understanding designed to help them rather than to avenge society.

His moderation went hand in hand with tolerance. Thus, although he had sympathy with Dr. Marie Stopes's family planning theories, he could not put up with her extreme hatred of Roman Catholicism. Once he took his children to a Guy Fawkes party to see a bonfire. When the flames reached Guy Fawkes, Marie Stopes, he recalls, shook her fist and hissed, "And he was a Roman Catholic!"

Mullins tried in his work to be "a friend of all parties and all faiths," although he himself always had a dislike of institutional religion. Throughout his years on the bench, his object was to apply in the courts the ethical standards of Christianity, while leading an impeccable life himself. In spite of his correctness and general conformity Mullins, however, remained an individualist—he objected to many aspects of the welfare state.

Mullins once said that the English legal system needed debunking: when told by a 22-year-old waitress that she was not allowed to leave her mother's cafe, in which she was said to be working without wages, he retorted: "Bunk! Cock a snook at her and leave. She has no right to turn her family into slaves."

Mullins, the son of a sculptor, was born on September 6, 1887, and educated at University College School and Mill Hill. He became a clerk in London County Council in 1907 and he read for the Bar, to which he was called by Gray's Inn in 1913, winning the Bacon Scholarship and a Certificate of Honour.

In the First World War Mullins served in France, Mesopotamia and India, and as interpreter was a member of the British delegation to the War Criminal Trials at Leipzig, of which he wrote an authoritative and interesting account. His practice was never a large one, and in 1930 he was appointed chairman of Courts of Referees (Unemployment Insurance).

Mullins became a Metropolitan Magistrate the next year and took his seat at the North London Court, being transferred later to the South-Western.

In 1938 a Labour member introduced a motion that "this House is of opinion ... that he is not a 'fit and proper person to administer justice'"—a motion which it is not surprising the Prime Minister declined to give time to discuss. In the preparation of the Bill that became the Matrimonial Causes Act, 1937, Mullins assisted A. P. Herbert (as he was then), and subsequently became involved in an acrimonious controversy in *The Times* with him following a protest against Mullins publicly criticizing parts of the Act which he had to administer.

His published works included *In Quest of Justice*; *Marriage, Children and God*; *Wife v. Husband in the Courts*; *Crime and Psychology*; and *Why Crime?*. His autobiography *One Man's Furrow*, was published in 1963.

October 24, 1968.

Paul Muni, a distinguished actor of both stages and screen, and one of the outstanding players of character parts in Hollywood during the 1930s, died in California on August 26, 1967. He was 71.

In the cinema he will be remembered for three notable biographical studies—of Emile Zola, Louis Pasteur and the Mexican President Benito Juarez; as well as for a stark portrayal of a contemporary criminal, Scarface, which was clearly based on the career of Chicago's most infamous gangster, Al Capone.

Here was a film actor who could examine every facet of human nature, whether good or bad, and could brilliantly convey that driving force which carries a man on towards his chosen destiny.

His real name was Muni Weisenfreund, and he was born in Lemberg, Austria, on September 22, 1895. His parents were both in the acting profession, and brought him to America in 1902.

He joined the Yiddish Art Theatre in New York when still a boy, and remained on the Yiddish stage until 1926. He then made his first appearance in an English-speaking part when he played Morris Levine in the Broadway play *We Americans*. Thereafter he was seen frequently on the New York stage for the next 30 years, his successes including a notable triumph as George Simon in *Counsellor-at-Law* in 1931 and 1932, and again 10 years later. He made his first appearance on the London stage at the Scala Theatre in 1924 with the Yiddish Art Theatre Company; and was seen in London again at the Phoenix Theatre in 1949 when he played Willy Loman in *Death of a Salesman*.

Audiences outside the United States, however, knew him primarily as a film actor whose performances brought style and dignity to the Hollywood scene. His film career began in 1928 with the Fox Company, for whom he made *The Valiant* and *Seven Faces*. The film which first brought him fame was *Scarface*, one of the great cycle of gangster stories made in Hollywood during the early thirties, which also brought recognition to his contemporaries James Cagney and Edward G. Robinson. *Scarface*, being factual, was perhaps the best of this series. Directed by Howard Hawks, it traced the career of Al Capone and reconstructed the merciless St. Valentine's Day massacre.

A second indictment of the social scene in America followed soon after, when Muni appeared as a workless war veteran of the depression who is wrongfully sent to prison.

PRISON BRUTALITY

I am a Fugitive from a Chain Gang was a powerful condemnation of prison brutality, and was also one of the first Hollywood films to treat the Negro problem with seriousness and sympathy. A newspaper comedy, *Hi Nellie*, followed in 1934, followed by *Bordertown* and *Black Fury*.

The Story of Louis Pasteur was made in 1936, and was in essence a moving tribute to a great man's search for the truth. It was followed by *The Good Earth*, an elaborate M.G.M. adaptation of Pearl Buck's novel of Chinese peasant life, in which Muni played opposite Luise Rainer.

He did not reach quite the same heights thereafter. His subsequent films included *A Song to Remember*, *Counter-Attack*, *Angel on My Shoulder*, *Stranger on the Prowl*, and *Last Angry Man*. On the stage he played the great American criminal lawyer Clarence Darrow in *Inherit the Wind* in New York in 1955; and in 1958 he toured in *At the Grand*.

Paul Muni was an actor of intellect. His brain rather than his emotions governed every performance. Unlike so many of his film contemporaries, who really were always themselves, no matter what the part, Muni was never himself.

The part took over the man and submerged him completely. His technique was excellent, and he brought dignity to the American film at a time when it was badly needed.

August 28, 1967.

Dr. Ferenc Münnich, former Hungarian Prime Minister, died in Budapest on November 29, 1967, at the age of 81, after a life of fighting for the cause of communism.

Münnich, who retired from political life two years before his death, joined the communist movement in a camp in Siberia, where he was taken as prisoner in World War One. There he met detained Bolsheviks, joined the Red Army and organized propaganda campaigns. After fighting in the Urals in 1918, he returned to Hungary where he took charge of the Hungarian army. He was a member of the short-lived Communist Government led by Bela Kun soon after the First World War. When the government collapsed he fled to the Soviet Union with Kun, and was later the principal accuser in the Stalinist purge which led to Kun's execution in 1938.

In 1921 the Communist International ordered him to join the German Communist Party, but one year later he was arrested in Berlin. Münnich fought in the Spanish Civil War, where he headed a division and later the 11th International Brigade. Three years later, on his way home, he was arrested in France but later managed to reach the Soviet Union. He trained partisans there and in 1942 he was a member of the general staff of the Stalingrad army.

After the Second World War Münnich returned to Hungary where he headed the Budapest Police Forces, and later he served as Ambassador in Helsinki, Sofia, Moscow and Belgrade.

In the first days of the Hungarian 1956 uprising, Münnich was Interior Minister in the Government that eventually supported the revolt—the only phase in his career which is not included in his biography issued by the Hungarian News Agency M.T.I. But soon he changed over to support Janos Kadar, the new Soviet-backed premier, and, after Russian troops crushed the uprising, Münnich became deputy premier and armed forces minister. He reached the climax of his career in 1958 when he was appointed Prime Minister. Three years later he lost this post but became Minister of State. He retained his seat on the Party's Central Committee until 1966.

November 30, 1967.

D. L. Murray, novelist, journalist and scholar, died on August 30, 1962, in a London hospital at the age of 74.

A man of great kindness and charm of character, he will be greatly missed by his friends, who were to be found among all sorts and conditions of people, and whose diversity gives some measure perhaps of both his warmth of nature and the wide range of his interests. As journalist he had served *The Times* for a quarter of a century; he became a member of the staff in 1920 and from 1938 until 1945 was editor of *The Times Literary Supplement*.

It is natural to speak of the man first rather than of his work. Murray was a man of large frame—he put on size and weight rapidly in his middle years—and in the simplest sense everything about him was large, his generosity, his fair-mindedness, his laughter. His laughter was indeed gargantuan and extraordinarily infectious. He was marvellously good company when he chose, an irresistible raconteur, the possessor of a most engaging gift of mimicry and of a streak of lightly Rabelaisian humour.

David Leslie Murray was born in London in February, 1888, the son of Charles Murray, who as a youth went out to South Africa, prospered there and returned to Britain in the early years of this century. Murray was at Harrow, where he gained an entrance scholarship in classics and history, and Balliol, where he was a Brackenbury History Scholar, got a first in *Lit. Hum.* in 1910, and was John Locke Scholar in 1912. In that year he published his first book, a fluent yet acute little study of *Pragmatism*.

He had a passion for the theatre and acted for a time in touring companies; only shortsightedness led him to abandon the stage. From 1916 until 1919 Murray served in the Intelligence Department of the War Office and in the following year he joined the staff of *The Times*, first as sub-editor and then as a literary and dramatic critic and assistant to Sir Bruce Richmond the editor of *The Times Literary Supplement*.

As assistant and, later, as editor Murray drew upon a versatile scholarship in literature and history, philosophy and theology. He wrote with zest and a catholicity of taste. A collection of the more important articles and reviews he had contributed to the *Literary Supplement* was published in 1926 under the title of *Scenes and Silhouettes*. It had been preceded by a theological study, *Reservation: its Purposes and Methods* (1923), and was followed a year later by his "impression"—lively in style and always stimulating—of Disraeli.

As a period novelist Murray eventually achieved a high degree of popular success. But his beginnings were inauspicious, certainly from an artistic point of view, and it is easy to understand why. He lacked the story-teller's power of creation—he had not, it is fair to say, the highest type of imagination—and in its place he could offer above all else a history student's sense of period and a temperamental love of the romantic. These he had to learn to negotiate and to display to the best advantage, and it was only practice that finally brought with it the necessary degree of skill and self-confidence. The scene of his first novel, *The Bride Adorned* (1929), was laid in nineteenth-century Italy, a country which he came to know well. Workmanlike and informed in detail though the reconstruction of Papal Rome was, the story itself had too little of the breath of life. *Stardust* (1931), a tale of the circus, had a brighter gleam, and after the rattling and episodic humours of *The English Family Robinson* (1933) came in the same year *Trumpeter, Sound* a full-blooded tale steeped in the atmosphere of the Crimean period and of an almost Dickensian quality of exuberance, which showed a further technical improvement.

Then came, in 1936, *Regency*, which was in the fashionable mode of the period of *Cavalcade*. Described as "a quadruple portrait", it evoked in a manner that could be described as at once realistic and baroque four generations of fatal women, the first a mistress of the Prince Regent. He was rewarded by prompt and considerable success. The success was repeated with *Commander of the Mists* (1938), a romance of the '45; again with *Tale of Three Cities* (1940), the latter boldly styled "a novel in baroque" and exhibiting a virtuoso-like decorative sweep and yet again with *Enter Three Witches* (1942), which had for setting the raffish moneyed, bohemian London of the nineties of the last century.

He continued to write novels, generally "period" in character, up to the time of his death. *Folly Bridge* (1945) was followed by *Leading Lady*, *Outrageous Fortune*, *Come Like Shadows*, *Roman Cavalier*, and *Hands of Healing*. Though neither his professional skill nor his gift for historical reconstruction deserted him none of these can be said to have added much to his reputation nor did they achieve the popular success of his earlier books.

He married in 1928 the author Leonora Eyles, who died in 1960.

August 31, 1962.

Sir John Murray, K.C.V.O., D.S.O., senior director of the historic publishing house in Albemarle Street, now known as John Murray (Publishers) Limited, and for many years the editor of the *Quarterly Review*, died on October 6, 1967, at the age of 83. The great traditions of the firm were always safe in his hands.

Murray continued working to the last and was arriving at his office each morning at 9.15 until a few days before he died. All who knew him will long remember his humility and his uprightness.

He was its fifth head in direct succession from John Murray I, who established the firm in 1768 in the shop in Fleet Street from which he watched Dr. Johnson's funeral. The publication by his son, John Murray II, of *Childe Harold* launched Byron into fame and Murray into Albemarle Street, and from that day to this there have been few writers of distinction who have not, at one time or another, been visitors to No. 50, which has fortunately survived not only the threat of a tube station in 1904 but the worse dangers of two world wars. It was John Murray II, again, who founded the *Quarterly Review* under the editorship of Gifford, and the *Quarterly* has been continuously published by the firm of Murray ever since, the late Sir John Murray conscientiously maintaining the scholarly and dignified tradition.

John Murray V was born on June 12, 1884, the son of Sir John Murray, K.C.V.O., whom he succeeded on his death in 1928. He followed his father to Eton and to Magdalen College, Oxford, and later edited the Magdalen College *Record*. In the course of a distinguished military career he rose to the rank of lieutenant-colonel, serving first with the Scottish Horse, T.A., and commanding the 12th Battalion, The Royal Scots, 1918–19. He saw service in Gallipoli, Egypt and France, was mentioned in dispatches, and awarded the D.S.O. and Bar and the Belgian Croix de Guerre. In the Second World War he served with the Home Guard from 1940 to 1942. He was a Commander of the Order of St. John of Jerusalem, High Sheriff of London (like his father before him), and was made K.C.V.O. in 1932.

The firm of Murray nevertheless remained his chief interest throughout his life. Sir John Murray put into order and expanded the family library and publishing archives, which include a remarkable collection of manuscripts and literary treasures; and he was the only person who actually saw the whole undertaking of the nine-volume edition of Queen Victoria's correspondence through to press, with all the many problems that such a publication entailed.

He yet found time to devote himself to much voluntary work, particularly for the Great Ormond Street hospital for children. He was for many years treasurer of the Roxburgh Club, and from 1928 to 1951 treasurer of the Royal Literary Fund. All these interests he inherited from his father; and, like his father, he suffered deafness, a disability which he bore with great patience, and which is recalled by his association with the Deafened Ex-Servicemen's Fund, of which he had been chairman and treasurer.

Murray married in 1916 Lady Helen de Vere, youngest daughter of the first Earl Brassey, G.C.B. There were no children of the marriage.

October 7, 1967.

Dr. Margaret Murray, the Egyptologist, died on November 13, 1963, at the age of 100.

Margaret Alice Murray was born on July 13, 1863, in Calcutta, the daughter of J. C. Murray. She came of a Border family with some Irish ancestry on her father's side and English or Northumbrian on her mother's side (Carr). The family connexion with India went back three generations or more, for her great-grandfather on her mother's side was a Hoogley pilot, who married her great-grandmother at the age of 12. A Murray went out to India in the eighteenth century in the East India Company's army, and his descendants were brought up in Calcutta. She sailed round the Cape before she was three, spent some years in Bonn—then a quiet university town—from the age of 10, where she learnt German privately, and returned to India several times between the ages of 16 and 25, when she left it finally. She shared her mother's sympathy for the women of India and loved to visit them in their homes. At the age of 17 she was the only white woman working as acting ward sister in a Calcutta hospital.

When her only sister married, Margaret went to London, fired by her sister's urgent insistence that she should study under Flinders Petrie, about whom they had read in the press. She first went to University College as a student of Egyptology in January, 1894. Petrie was then digging at Koptos, having in the previous year electrified the learned world by his discoveries at Tell el Amarna. Dr. J. H. Walker and Mr. F. Ll. Griffith were in charge; methods of teaching were experimental; and books were few. Nothing was known of Egyptian history before the great Pyramid, except for fragments of Monetho's history, Herodotus, Josephus, and a few other ancient authors. Erman's *Egyptian Grammar* had just been published, and with its help she made quick progress in the study of the language. Petrie was quick to realize her capacity for learning, and started her on a piece of research which would daunt a more experienced' worker. "The descent of property in the early period of Egyptian history". He saw to it that her paper was published in the Proceedings of the Society of Biblical Archaeology, and from then on she contributed many studies to learned journals.

The following year Miss Murray took over the teaching of elementary hieroglyphs, at a salary of £40 a year, which she supplemented by giving Oxford Extension Lectures, and by cataloguing collections of Egyptian antiquities at the National Museum of Ireland in Dublin, The Royal Scottish Museum in Edinburgh, the University Museum in Manchester, and the Ashmolean Museum in Oxford. She could visit London only two days a week, for she was nursing her paralysed mother, and much of her work was done by the bedside. When her family responsibilities ceased Miss Murray went to London and settled near the college and took an ever-increasing share and interest in its life; first as a member of the Refectory Committee, then as secretary of the Board of Studies in Anthropology, and later as member of the Professorial Board. She was a fellow of the college, an Honorary D.Litt., and a fellow of the Society of Antiquaries of Scotland. She was personally responsible for promoting the welfare of woman students in many unobtrusive ways, knowing from her own experience how hard it was for girls with little money to make do in a university.

In 1904 she joined Flinders Petrie at Abydos and was entrusted with the excavation of the Osireion, publishing a scholarly account of her work in the following year. She had one more season at Saqqara, but by then her teaching duties, as Assistant Professor, had much increased, and more and more the work of the department fell on her when Petrie was abroad. In later years she had to be content, between 1920 and 1930, with short excavations during the summer vacation, when she turned her attention to Malta and the Balearic Islands, and published five reports.

After her retirement from the Department of Egyptology in 1932 she was again able to travel and she revised the Near East, digging at Tell el Ajjul, in Palestine and in Petra.

She wrote a number of books on Egypt which had a wide popular appeal, including *Egyptian Temple*, *A Handbook of Egyptian Sculpture*, and (when she was already 86) *The Splendour that was Egypt*. Her interest in folklore led her to investigate records of magic and witchcraft and resulted in the revolutionary *Witch Cult—Western Europe* and a more popular work, *The God of the Witches*. From 1953 to 1955 she was president of the Folklore Society.

Among her other books were *The Genesis of Religion* and her autobiography, entitled in typically challenging style *My First Hundred Years*, both published in 1963. On her hundredth birthday in July the professorial board of University College passed a special resolution placing on record their deep appreciation of the "high honour" she had brought to the college.

November 15, 1963.

Ed Murrow, who died on April 27, 1965, at his home in New York at the age of 57, was an artist in reporting and commenting on world news who made himself master of both sound radio and television.

His magnificent coverage of the wartime scene in Britain won him much richly deserved admiration. He spared no pains and cheerfully ran into dangers to see for himself what was happening by day and night in the grim period of the air raids. Mixing with men and women of all walks of life he gained an inside knowledge of the British character and interpreted it on the air with penetration and warm affection. A loyal, delightful and unaffected companion in private, he enlivened any company by a dry humour which came over the more effectively because of the handsome melancholy of Ed Murrow's appearance.

Egbert Roscoe Murrow, the youngest of three sons of a tenant farmer, was born on April 25, 1908, near Pole Cat Creek, North Carolina. The family later moved to the northwest, where his father worked as an engine driver in a logging camp, and life remained hard. Murrow had to work after school hours, but emerged from Washington State College a studious young man of academic leanings and—for the environment—with the more acceptable name of Edward.

He never worked for a newspaper, and first went to Europe as assistant director of the Institute of International Education. The Columbia Broadcasting System later appointed him as director of talks and education, and he was sent back to London in 1937 to arrange cultural programmes.

Europe was then in a political ferment, and he soon dropped what he called the "cultural stuff", and reported the Austrian Anschluss. From that time he was accepted as a foreign correspondent, and reported regularly the events and developments that led to the Second World War. He was then at his best. As London suffered nightly bombardment, his broadcasts, always beginning with the announcement "This is London", carried the thrill of Britain's finest hour across the Atlantic. Some of it came back to give Londoners a new pride.

When the war was over he was strongly placed to apply his talents to the new medium of television. "See it Now", "Person to Person", and other regular programmes were successful, but the grind of producing them week after week had its toll. Inevitably his work suffered. The old confidence and authority remained, the techniques were honed to perfection, but in a way he became captive of his own disquiet.

In 1949 he had asked, "Is it not possible that ... an infectious smile, eyes that seem remarkable for the depths of their sincerity, a cultivated air of authority, may attract a huge television audience regardless of the violence that may be done to truth or objectivity?" Murrow never did violence to truth, but inevitably as his commitments increased, and others wrote the words he repeated before the camera, his own presence and authority became more important than the content of the programmes.

Yet he still possessed the ability and the political conscience to present programmes from time to time of much more than ephemeral importance. This was demonstrated particularly by his famous attack on Senator McCarthy in March 1954, which took the form of a series of film excerpts of McCarthy in action linked by Murrow's acid editorial comments. It was a brave act in the context of the times and played a significant part in the slow process of destroying the Senator's reputation. Then in 1958 there was his interview with Mr. Macmillan, first shown in the United States and subsequently to British television viewers, which did much to illuminate the personality of the Prime Minister at a time when he was still a shadowy figure to the British public at large. It was something of a landmark in his progress towards dominance over the British political scene.

This hectic period had its material rewards. At one time he was reported to be earning $300,000 a year, and he was promoted to an executive position, a post he relinquished because he had no liking for administration. But he reversed himself in 1961 when President Kennedy asked him to become director of the United States Information Agency. He relinquished the financial rewards of popular success, and for the comparatively small salary of $21,000 a year, gladly accepted the responsibilities of administering this large organization.

At the U.S.I.A. Murrow applied techniques he had learned in commercial television, and greatly improved the morale of this much maligned agency. He worked as hard as ever, and succeeded in establishing the principle that the truth must be told even should it temporarily embarrass the country. The ill-fated invasion of Cuba was objectively reported, as was the decision to resume nuclear testing in the atmosphere. Murrow, no longer in front of a camera or behind a microphone, managed to impart some of his authority to the Voice of America.

After a lifetime of reporting events, Murrow enjoyed the opportunity of influencing them. After years of mixing with the great and powerful, he similarly enjoyed the right of access to the President and an unofficial seat in the National Security Council. His interests and energy were renewed and he began a second life as exhausting as the first. The strain, and the tension which he probably found necessary to create for greater concentration, exhausted him as it had done in the past. In 1962 he collapsed with pneumonia while visiting Teheran, and recovered only to be operated upon a year later for lung cancer. He retired early in 1964. He was appointed an honorary K.B.E. in the month before he died.

He leaves a widow and a son.

April 28, 1965.

His Highness Mutesa II, K.B.E., who died on November 21, 1969, at the age of 45, was the thirty-sixth Kabaka of Buganda, and the first President and commander-in-chief of Uganda, 1963–66.

The reign of the late Kabaka was a memorable one since it coincided with the Protectorate Government's vigorous policy of unifying Uganda by means of a popularly elected Assembly. These steps seemed to the Kabaka and his people to threaten the separate identity of Buganda, and during the years 1953-62 the late Kabaka was not only a leader and active participant in the struggles of Buganda with the Protectorate Government and the other people of Uganda, but he became the symbol of his people's national feeling.

Sir Edward Frederick William Waiugembe Mutebi Tuwangeula Mutesa was born on November 19, 1924, as the only son of his father, Sir Daudi Chwa II, 35th Kabaka of Buganda, by his Christian wife, Irene Drusila Namaganda. The young heir had an almost wholly European education. He was born in the home of a mission doctor (Sir Albert Cook) and brought up from the age of four in the home of a missionary (Canon Grace.) He was educated at the Protestant school, King's College, Budo. He succeeded his father in 1939 at the age of 15 and was installed as full Kabaka in 1942. He then spent two years at the then Makerere College, Kampala, and two years at Magdalene College, Cambridge. He held an honorary commission in the Grenadier Guards, of which he was always proud. Mutesa II had a perfect command of colloquial English and English etiquette. He was well known in London, where he later became the "King Freddie" of British journalists.

When he assumed his royal duties he appeared to be a dutiful pro-Government ruler of the type described as "progressive." His marriage in 1948 to Damali Kisosonkole showed that he was able to stand out against tradition since she belonged to a clan into which the Kabakas had not previously married. Two so-called "strikes," those of 1945 and 1949, were popular risings against unpopular and traditionalist Ministers, a law to allow the Government to acquire land for public purposes, voicing economic grievances and demands for greater representation in the Lukiiko, or Buganda parliament. These risings were in effect against the Kabaka and his Government and he supported the Protectorate Government on each occasion. He also sided with the then Governor, Sir Andrew Cohen, in the democratic reforms introduced in 1953.

Nevertheless, Mutesa II early showed his determination to exercise the traditional rights of the monarchy and to maintain control over chiefly and other appointments, and when he considered that the independence of Buganda was threatened he sided with his own parliament against the Protectorate Government. He was deported by Sir Andrew Cohen on October 30, 1953, for refusing to cooperate with the Protectorate Government by advising the Lukiiko to appoint representatives to the Legislative Assembly, a step which was essential if Uganda was to be unified.

The Kabaka returned from his exile on October 7, 1955, on the signing of a new Agreement which was intended to make him a constitutional monarch in the British sense. However, he returned with greatly increased prestige as an anti-colonial hero, as well as a traditional monarch who had maintained his position. His people willingly gave him his traditional control over all appointments and he took a leading part in the constitutional conferences in London in 1961 and 1962. Buganda had a strong bargaining position as the richest and most advanced part of Uganda and a new royalist party—Kabaka Yekka—secured all the seats but three in the Buganda Lukiiko at the election immediately preceding the final constitutional conference. By joining with the radical party led by Dr. Obote, first Prime Minister of an independent Uganda, the Baganda were able to secure the position for which they had fought, that is to say a semi-federal status to the central government.

To the surprise of many observers, the Kabaka became the first President of Uganda, when the last British governor resigned, late in 1963. During all these protracted negotiations the Kabaka showed himself to be a shrewd political bargainer and a man of great determination and even obstinacy. His role continued difficult as one of the last recognized monarchs in East Africa opposed by Pan African politicians on the ground that the presence of this kingdom made it difficult for Uganda to join a wider East African Federation.

In fact, however, it was not the Kabaka's opposition but Dr. Obote's objections, as well as quarrels between Kenya and Tanzania, that prevented East African federation in 1963 or 1964.

After Ugandan independence the difficulties of Sir Edward Mutesa's dual position as Kabaka and Head of State became manifest. Technically, he was a constitutional monarch in both jurisdictions. In fact, in Buganda he was an African ruler with all the great powers—and restrictions—that are implied in chieftainship. In Uganda itself he was non-political, yet in the central parliament there was the Kabaka Yekka Party, which was vowed to protect Buganda's interests. At first it worked in coalition with Dr. Obote's U.P.C., but while some members of it in fact took out U.P.C. cards, others went the other way, and worked with the official D.P. opposition reflecting their differences with Dr. Obote's policies.

A first trial of strength came over the "lost counties" of Bunyoro, which under the terms of the Monson Commission's recommendations were to be the subject of a plebiscite after independence. They were duly returned to Bunyoro but the Kabaka refused to sign the Act that made the transfer. The Kabaka also could not approve of the left wing and Pan-African attitudes of the Obote Government and became disgusted with them when Obote openly supported the rebels against the central Congolese Government. Nor did he accept the attacks on Britain made by Uganda over Rhodesia.

The final trial of strength became inevitable when Dr. Obote decided to overthrow the constitution by a coup of his own. Opposition had been mounting against him since allegations were made that he and his friends had been dealing corruptly in gold and ivory from Congo. It looked as if he might be rejected by his own party and the troops were under the command of men on whom he could not rely. But by moving first, and relying on the powerful "special force", he took power, imprisoned five critical ministers, and imposed a new constitution. He alleged that the Kabaka had tried to get military help from foreign embassies but the Kabaka argued that these talks were precautionary, made while Obote was out of the capital and so quite constitutional. He was deposed from the presidency and in the new constitution Buganda's vital safeguards were omitted. This was unacceptable to the Kabaka's Government, which appealed to the United Nations and in a resolution renounced the new constitution. When it requested the Uganda Government to withdraw from Buganda, Dr. Obote accepted the challenge and sent the special force to arrest the Katikiro and other Buganda leaders, seize the Kabaka and capture the palace. The Kabaka went into exile in Britain.

November 24, 1969.

Sir Guildhaume Myrddin-Evans, K.C.M.G., C.B., formerly Chief International Labour Adviser to H.M. Government and Deputy Secretary at the Ministry of Labour and National Service, died on February 15, 1964, at his London home. He was 69.

It is for his work in the field of international labour affairs that Sir Guildhaume will be particularly remembered. Three times elected chairman of the International Labour Organization and a former president of the International Labour Conference—he was indeed the first civil servant ever to hold that office—he played an important role in rebuilding the organization after the war. It was under his chairmanship that the arrangements were made for the I.L.O. becoming a specialized agency of the United Nations after the dissolution of the League. A tactful, friendly man, widely popular with his colleagues, he was acclaimed as the "elder statesman" of the I.L.O. when he retired in 1959.

The second son of the Rev. T. T. Evans, of Abertillery, Monmouthshire, he was born on December 17, 1894, and educated at Llandovery and Christ Church, Oxford, where he took a First in mathematics. During the First World War he was commissioned in The South Wales Borderers and saw service in France and Flanders before being invalided out in 1917. He then joined the Prime Minister's Secretariat and in 1919 became Assistant Secretary to the War Cabinet.

AT THE TREASURY

For the next 10 years he was in the Treasury, on a number of occasions during this period representing Britain at international conferences abroad as he was to do so often later in his career. In 1929 he moved to the Ministry of Labour, becoming Deputy Chief Insurance Officer under the Unemployment Acts in 1935. It was, however, on his appointment in 1938 to head what was then the International Labour Division of the Ministry that the major task of his career began. From then until his retirement in 1959 he led the British delegation to nearly all the international labour conferences.

During the Second World War he was lent to the War Cabinet Offices as head of the Production Executive Secretariat and to the United States Government as adviser to the War Manpower Commission. He also advised the Canadian Government on manpower, was a member of the British Government delegation to the conference at San Francisco setting up the United Nations in 1945, and to the General Assembly of the U.N. from 1946 to 1953.

In 1945 he became the British Government representative on the governing body of the I.L.O. He was chairman from that year until 1947 and was re-elected to serve again in 1956–57. In 1949 he was president of the International Labour Conference. He was made C.B. in 1945 and K.C.M.G. in 1947.

An active churchman, Myrddin-Evans was a former member of the council of the Baptist Union of Great Britain and Ireland and had served as secretary of the Bloomsbury Central Baptist Church in London.

In 1919 he married Elizabeth, daughter of Owen Watkins, of Sarn, Caernarvonshire. They had two sons.

February 17, 1964.

N

Nahas Pasha, who died in Alexandria on August 23, 1965, at the age of 89, was for more than 20 years before the revolution of 1952, as leader of the Wafd Party, a dominating figure in the Egyptian political field.

Although his nationalism was necessarily directed mainly against Britain there were two occasions when British Governments had cause to be grateful for his sturdy patriotism and for the popular support he could command. The first of these was when he headed a coalition government which signed the Anglo-Egyptian Treaty in 1936; the second when, on the insistence of the British Ambassador, he took over the reigns of government at one of the darkest periods of the war.

Nahas Pasha, like his great predecessor Saad Zaghlul Pasha, was a lawyer by profession. He was born at Samanoud, in the Northern Delta, in 1876, and after being educated in the Egyptian Government Schools at Cairo he took his degree at the Cairo School of Law in 1900, and was made a Judge in 1904. Like practically every Egyptian of the professional class he was a Nationalist, and when after the war Zaghlul Pasha and his group formed the Wafd Party he joined it immediately. Early in 1919 he was dismissed from Government service for taking part in politics. Thenceforth he devoted himself entirely to politics and soon became a leading and extremely active member of the party.

Nahas had never been timid, and it was obviously only a matter of time before he fell foul of the British military authorities in Egypt. After the breakdown of the negotiations with Adly Pasha on the military issue in 1921 Adly resigned, no successor could be found, and fresh disturbances began. Zaghlul and Nahas Pashas with three of their chief associates were ordered by the British military authorities to retire to their country estates. They refused, and were deported to the Seychelles.

In June, 1923, Nahas Pasha returned to Egypt with his chief and was elected deputy for Samanoud in the first Parliamentary elections held under the new Constitution. When Zaghlul formed his Cabinet in January, 1924, he selected Nahas as Minister of Communications, a post in which he did not see eye to eye with the British railway officials. On the resignation of Zaghlul Pasha's Ministry, after the murder of the Sirdar, Nahas combined the secretaryship of the Wafd with legal work, and was one of the Wafdist counsel who defended Mahmud Fahmy El Nokrashi Effendi and Ahmed Bey Maher in the political murder trial of 1926. In that year he was again returned to Parliament and became second Vice-President of the Chamber. On the death of Zaghlul he was elected leader of the Wafd by the Wafdist members of both Houses of Parliament.

ULTIMATUM TO EGYPT

At the time his election caused British circles and Egyptian moderates some concern. Nahas was supposed to be an extremist by the British. Some Egyptians who had watched his work as Vice-President of the Chamber considered him too quick-tempered for an eventual Prime Minister and drew unfavourable comparisons between his impetuosity in politics and debate and his careful industry as Judge and advocate. The early days of his leadership were troubled. Sarwat, who had been negotiating a treaty with the British Government, showed the draft to Nahas early in 1928 while withholding it from his colleagues in the Cabinet. Nahas made no secret of his hostility to a treaty which contained no provision for the complete evacuation of Egypt by the British Army. Sarwat consequently resigned, and Nahas became Prime Minister. He soon had to face a crisis. The British Government who considered that certain legislative proposals sponsored by the Nahas Ministry were prejudicial to the safety of foreigners, served an ultimatum on Egypt, and the offending measures were postponed. The crisis was barely over when two Cairo newspapers published documents which, if authentic, would have The early days of his leadership were troubled. seriously compromised Nahas and other Wafdists. He denied their authenticity and the intrigue against King Fuad which they purported to disclose, but the King dismissed him, appointed Mohamed Pasha Mahmud Prime Minister, and on July 19, 1928, dismissed Parliament. In October of the same year the official inquiry into the charges against Nahas Pasha found no case for a prosecution.

After 18 months in Opposition Nahas Pasha became Prime Minister for the second time, on January 1, 1930. He immediately announced his intention of opening negotiations with Great Britain to secure the real independence of Egypt and to reach agreement on the four points reserved by the British Government when they acknowledged Egyptian independence in 1922. Negotiations opened in London on March 31 and broke down on May 8 over the question of the Sudan. Nahas, who led the Egyptian delegation, certainly overplayed his hand, but his relations with his *vis-a-vis* Mr. Henderson were good and his words: "We have lost a Treaty of Friendship with Great Britain, but we have won her actual friendship, which is all-important" did not exaggerate the facts. Shortly after his return to Egypt his Government submitted two Bills for the protection of the Constitution to King Fuad. The King regarded them as invasions of his prerogative, dismissed the Nahas Ministry, and presently entrusted the Government of Egypt to Sidqi Pasha, who governed dictatorially and on the whole efficiently.

TREATY OF ALLIANCE

It was not until 1936 that Nahas's chance came. The Abyssinian crisis had emphasized the necessity of a Treaty of Alliance between Great Britain and Egypt, and the Egyptian parties had formed a united front for this purpose. The terms of Mr. Eden's offer to negotiate and King Fuad's intervention eventually led to the opening of negotiations in March, 1936, between an Egyptian all-party delegation led by Nahas and including a Wafdist majority and Sir Miles Lampson, the British High Commissioner. In the course of the negotiations a general election brought the Wafd back to power and Nahas became Prime Minister for the third time. The treaty was signed in London on August 26, 1936, and Nahas Pasha received an enthusiastic welcome on his return to Egypt in October.

Another success came to Nahas in April, 1937, when he obtained the abolition of the Capitulations at the international conference at Montreux, but thereafter he lost ground. A competent negotiator and an eloquent speaker in French as well as Arabic, he had no administrative gifts. His encouragement of the "Blue Shirts", a sort of party army, and of student demonstrators antagonized some of his party colleagues. He provoked the first of what proved to be a series of unnecessary disputes with King Farouk. He became overbearing, and finally demanded that party members should pledge unqualified obedience and loyalty to him, no matter what policy he followed. This was too much for Ahmed Maher Pasha, Nokrashy Pasha, and others who believed that the principles laid down by Zaghlul were inviolable, and they and a number of others left the Wafd and formed the Saadist Party.

RECALLED TO POWER

At the end of 1937 Nahas Pasha was once more dismissed, and in the 1938 elections the Wafd won very few seats. In opposition Nahas again turned to strong nationalism as the best means of regaining support, and in speeches between 1938 and 1941 he severely attacked the British. By the end of 1941 it had become obvious that the series of coalition Governments that had been in office since 1938 were not strong enough to enable whole-hearted Egyptian cooperation in the war effort, and on February

4, 1942, Sir Miles Lampson (later Lord Killearn), British Ambassador, insisted that the King recall Nahas and the Wafd to power. This Administration lasted 30 months. It was marked by domestic mal-administration, corruption, and nepotism, by further dissensions within the Wafd resulting in the expulsion of Makram Ebeid Pasha, the secretary and right-hand man of the party, and by a series of episodes in which the Prime Minister appeared to be challenging and even attempting to usurp some of the prerogatives of the King.

In October, 1944, an unnecessary discourtesy to the King brought matters to a head. Nahas prepared to resign and go to the country on a strong anti-British programme, but the King forestalled him by a few hours and dismissed him. Although while in office Nahas had given the allies full and loyal support, once again when in opposition he turned to ultra-nationalism. As soon as the war was over he began to demand revision of the 1936 treaty and attacked the Saadist-Liberal Government for not placing revision in the forefront of its programme. These attacks became increasingly anti-British. When the Egyptian Treaty delegation was constituted early in 1946 Nahas and the Wafd refused to participate unless he was at the head of the delegation. Also, though he himself had boycotted the 1945 elections, he claimed that the Parliament was unrepresentative and that only the Wafd represented the nation. During the negotiations with Great Britain Nahas's opposition became more and more bitter. In September, 1946, however, he consented to the Wafd joining the Government, and therefore in the negotiations, but his terms were unacceptable to the other parties.

OPPOSED ALLIANCE

Thereafter his opposition to the treaty turned into opposition to alliance of any kind—a direct reversal of the policy of Zaghlul Pasha—and he did everything to have the negotiations broken off. There can be little doubt that this opposition arose almost entirely from Nahas's anger at not being given charge of the negotiations.

After no fewer than eight attempts had been made on his life and many legal and quasi-legal proceedings had been instituted against him and his wife, with a view to crippling him financially, he again became Prime Minister in January, 1950. By 1951 he was calling on his Parliament to abrogate the treaty of 1936 which he himself had signed in 1936. He was dismissed early in 1952 and therefore played no part in the drama of the abdication of King Farouk in which Nahas's successor, Aly Maher Pasha, was the chief actor. The Wafd, facing dissolution, dropped him as leader in 1952 and since then he had lived obscurely in Alexandria. "Eyeless in Gaza", the butt of lesser men, he made one further attempt to come to terms with General Neguib and then faded from the Egyptian political scene.

Nahas Pasha's personal honesty was never seriously questioned, and though his political and administrative weaknesses were much criticized his personal character stood high. He was of rather striking appearance, tall and well built, with a cast in one eye, something of a dandy, with a flower in his buttonhole and his tarbush slightly on one side. His personality was extremely attractive and he could, more than any Egyptian except perhaps Makram Ebeid Pasha, sway an audience.

August 24, 1965.

His Highness Sir Tashi Namgyal, K.C.S.I., K.C.I.E., Maharaja of the Himalayan state of Sikkim, who died in a nursing home in Calcutta on December 2, 1963, at the age of 70 had been on the throne nearly 50 years. He was not an innovating ruler, and the changes that affected his little kingdom in the past half-century were not directed by him; but he was a man of great kindness and piety and he was held in high affection and trust by his people.

When at the death of his older brother in 1915 Tashi Namgyal became Maharaja the state had been under British administration for more than 20 years, a consequence of the unruliness of earlier rulers of Sikkim and the Raj's unwillingness to risk a deeper penetration of Tibetan influence into this corner of its marches. The British resident in Gangtok was the effective ruler of the state, but in the new Maharaja he found a man who could be trusted to be moderate, humane and responsive to guidance, and the next few years saw a gradual return of the Maharaja's powers. In 1918 he was invested with full authority of administration and the annual subsidy that had been withheld since 1889 was restored. There were never grounds to repent that act of confidence. In 1930 the British political agent in Gangtok wrote of the "personal touch and wise and beneficent rule" of the Maharaja, which had "produced happiness and contentment of his people".

British policy did not encourage the infusion of new ideas or attitudes into Sikkim, and nor did the Maharaja. He was not one of those rulers, not uncommon in the Indian princely states, who actively quarantined their people from the contagion of the modern world the better to safeguard their own privileges; but his state was tranquil and the people contented, and Tashi Namgyal was content to leave things as they were. He travelled all over Sikkim, the royal cavalcades of mules and ponies traversing the mountain paths into the State's remotest valley, welcomed wherever he went.

When in later years he took up oil painting the recurrent, almost obsessive, subject was the snows and mountains that he had seen in those travels, at first treated naturalistically, later with intense symbolism.

By nature, perhaps, the Maharaja was a constitutional ruler and so he readily acceded to the appointment of an Indian dewan (prime minister) in 1949—and, indeed, by this time he had already begun to give much of his time to the painting and Buddhist observances that fully occupied his last years, when he became a recluse. The dewan was appointed after a short and unhappy experiment with representative forms of government, demanded by some of the political groups that had emerged in Gangtok after independence had come to India.

A period of social and political change followed in Sikkim, with the Maharaja approving of reforms proposed by others, and his continued popularity with the people smoothing their implementation. The most radical change was the abolition of the system of leases which had confirmed and augmented the powers of the big land-holders.

With the death in service with the Royal Air Force in 1941 of the Maharaja's elder son (Tashi Namgyal put the resources of his state with the British cause in both world wars) the second son, Gyalsay Palden Thondup Namgyal, became Maharaj-kumar, and over the next few years took over from his father more and more of the administrative responsibilities of the state. For 10 years or more before the Maharaja's death, the Maharaj-kumar had been the de facto ruler. The Maharaja, with his painting and religious rites, was little to be seen in Gangtok, but was by no means forgotten by his people, and there were occasions when popular complaints about political developments in the state—or the lack of any development—were taken to him.

One of his last public appearances was at the beginning of 1963 when he attended the ceremonies of the marriage of the Maharaj-kumar to Miss Hope Cook of New York. Slight but upright in spite of his frailness, with his long belted Sikkimese robe and skullcap of brilliant brocade, the guests who saw him then will not forget him. He was in London for some weeks in 1963 for treatment, and was flown home in the middle of November.

In 1918, following the tradition of his house, Tashi Namgyal married a Tibetan princess, who survives him. There were three sons of the marriage and three daughters.

December 3, 1963.

Heddle Nash, the English tenor, died on August 14, 1961, in a London hospital. He was 65.

He began his career as an opera singer and at various times sang leading tenor roles, the Duke in *Rigoletto*, Tamino in *The Magic Flute*, Ottavio in *Don Giovanni*, Rodolfo in *La Boheme*, and David in *Meistersinger*, at the Old Vic, Covent Garden, and Glyndebourne, but in the later part of his active life as a singer he was the chief exponent of Gerontius in Elgar's oratorio and appeared regularly at choral concerts and festivals.

He was born in London and trained at the Blackheath Conservatory. After service with the 20th London Regiment in France, Salonika, and Palestine in the 1914 war he went for study to Giuseppe Borghatti at Milan, where he made his debut in Rossini's *Il Barbiere*. Further experience in Italian opera houses settled his style and he remained Italianate in tone-production and legato phrasing. His quality of voice was sweet and lent itself to suave delivery and he had sufficient if not heroic reserves of power. Even his faults were Italianate such as a tendency to be lachrymose in pathetic music, but he was too solidly English in simplicity and cheerfulness of character ever to pose: he successfully accommodated what he had learnt in Italy to English music and the English language. His Gerontius lacked the spirituality of Elwes, the sincerity of Coates, or the insight of Wilson and his interpretation appeared rather shallow in performances dominated by Kathleen Ferrier as the Angel. All the same he sang the part with fervour and musical understanding to most people's satisfaction for many years. He was not often heard in songs or in Bach since his mellifluous manner needed room to expand or to soar as in Handel, but a part like that of Pedrillo in Mozart's *Die Entführung aus dem Serail* which he sang at Glyndebourne in its early days gave him scope for lively characterization. His last operatic appearance was in the small part of Dr. Manette in Arthur Benjamin's *A Tale of Two Cities* at Sadler's Wells in 1957. His son, John Heddle Nash, has followed his father's career as a singer but is a baritone.

August 15, 1961.

Sir Walter Nash, P.C., G.C.M.G., C.H., who died in Wellington, New Zealand, on June 4, 1968, at the age of 86, was a veteran Labour politician and statesman.

He headed the Labour administration of 1957–60 but his most influential years were spent as a leading member of the Savage and Fraser Labour ministries from 1935 to 1949. During these years he was responsible for initiating much remarkably far reaching financial and social reforms. He pushed through Parliament the bitterly contested social security legislation of 1939 which made New Zealand a prototype welfare state. As Minister of Finance he was responsible for legislation which brought the Reserve Bank under state ownership and control, for acquisition by the state of privately owned shares of the Bank of New Zealand, and for nationalization of the major domestic airline.

Nash was tenacious and confident in politics. All his energies were devoted to his work; he drove himself relentlessly. But notwithstanding his practical grasp of success in politics Nash remained an idealist and visionary.

In later years when he felt the major work in the cause of social justice in New Zealand had been accomplished under Labour administrations he concerned himself increasingly with the welfare of the world's starving and underprivileged. From his early days in Britain Nash was fired with zeal for alleviation of suffering and the correction of economic injustice.

Nash was born in Kidderminster on February 12, 1882, and before going to New Zealand worked in a legal office, in a cycle manufacturing firm in Birmingham, and later in business on his own account. After his arrival in New Zealand in 1909, he took an interest in labour questions, and in 1919 he was elected to the national executive of the New Zealand Labour Party. He was secretary of the party from 1922 until 1932 and was elected president in 1935.

He was first elected to Parliament in 1929 as member for Hutt which he held until his death. He was appointed Minister of Finance and Customs in the first Labour Government of 1935, holding those portfolios until 1949. In 1940 Nash became Deputy Prime Minister and in 1942 he was appointed New Zealand Minister in the United States and became a member of the Pacific War Council. On the death of Peter Fraser in 1950 he became Leader of the Opposition, and following Labour's narrow victory in 1957 Prime Minister of New Zealand.

Nash reassumed the Opposition leadership after Labour's defeat at the polls in 1960, but resigned that position in 1963, when Arnold Nordmeyer succeeded him, retaining, however, the membership for Hutt.

Nash was criticized on frequent occasions for his failure to delegate responsibility; but the energy which he brought to the task was undoubtedly an important factor contributing to Labour's ability to survive for three years with a working majority of only two seats after the return to power in 1957.

Nash made many visits abroad during his career. He represented New Zealand at the 1937 Imperial Conference, was leader of his country's delegation to the International Monetary Fund (Bretton Woods) in 1944, and in later years visited many countries of the world on missions connected with trade, defence and international relations. He was acquainted with many of the leading world figures of the postwar era.

His influence upon the Labour Party and its claims to public approval was profound. The policies—particularly the fiscal policies—which the party followed while he was Minister of Finance, caused him to be regarded as a stern tax-gatherer. Some of his political opponents were not slow to seize upon his visits to the Soviet Union (he had a three-hour talk with Khrushchev in 1960) as providing evidence for labelling him as one leaning dangerously towards the extreme left. The public for the most part chose to forgive him his tax-gathering policies and to remember the uncanny success of his handling of New Zealand's wartime finances. They disbelieved the reflections cast upon his political integrity and did not respect those who had levelled them.

Probably the most valuable quality Nash possessed in the party sense was his ability to secure the good will of the electorate. Well-dressed and courteous, he was at home in any company and was capable of making an appropriate and thought-provoking speech. He gave the impression of possessing in good measure the reliable common sense that most people wish to recognize in the make-up of their politicians. He was unwavering in his belief in the value of the Commonwealth and of its influence for peace.

International affairs always appeared significant to him. In particular he considered that every effort should be made by New Zealand, and other countries, to contribute towards the well being of Asian peoples and to establish a basis for better friendship and understanding. The Colombo Plan, the Freedom from Hunger Campaign and other undertakings with similar objectives could be assured of his enthusiastic support.

After his retirement from the Opposition leadership Nash continued to be a very influential figure in Labour's ranks and a spokesman whose views commanded attention. Throughout much of his adult life he was a lay reader in the Church of England and an active member of its Men's Society. In 1946 he was appointed a Privy Councillor. In May, 1960, when in Britain he revisited his birthplace, Kidderminster, where he was given a civic dinner. In the same month he laid the foundation stone of New Zealand House in London. He was created C.H. in 1959 and G.C.M.G. in 1965.

Nash was predeceased by his wife, formerly Lotty May Eaton, of Selly Oak, Birmingham, whom he married in 1906. They had three sons.

June 5, 1968.

Admiral Sir Martin Dunbar-Nasmith, V.C., K.C.B., K.C.M.G., who won the Victoria Cross for most conspicuous bravery in command of a submarine in 1915, died on June 29, 1965, at Dr. Gray's Hospital, Elgin, at the age of 82.

Long after receiving the V.C., it was revealed that he had passed and repassed the minefields, and other dangers of the Dardanelles, and during 96 days in the Sea of Marmora, of which 47 were in one spell, he sank 101 vessels, including a battleship, a destroyer and three gunboats. "This prodigious feat", wrote Winston Churchill, "remains unsurpassed in the history of submarine warfare."

Born on April 1, 1883, Martin Eric Nasmith (he added the name Dunbar after the war) was the son of the late Martin Arthur Nasmith, of Clevehurst, Weybridge. He was educated at Eastman's, Winchester and at the Royal Naval College, Dartmouth, and entered the Royal Navy in 1897. He became lieutenant in 1905, and took first class certificates in seamanship, gunnery and torpedo work. His first association with the submarine branch was in 1904, when he was appointed to the depot-ship, Thames, for a course of instruction in the mechanism and handling of the new craft.

It was not long before Nasmith qualified for the command of a submarine, in July, 1905, but during his command the vessel sank, and the admiral in charge of the fleet congratulated Nasmith on his conduct in the rescue operations. In January, 1911, after a spell with the battle cruiser Indomitable he returned to duty with submarines in command of C 18, and in the September following became captain of the D 4.

When war was declared he was appointed immediately to the command of the submarine E 11, in which vessel he won the Victoria Cross.

In 1915 he went to the Mediterranean, where the vessel was attached to the fleet. After making a perilous passage through the Dardanelles, the E 11 surfaced to find two battleships lying near by. Unfortunately the Turks saw his periscope and opened heavy fire before torpedoes could be launched.

Constantinople was the centre of Nasmith's operations, and the first target to be sunk was a large gunboat anchored off the port. The next day a large Turkish transport was sunk, then a raid on Constantinople caused consternation in the city, and damage to storeships and the quay.

FOULED A MINE CABLE

So far, the E11 had sunk one larger gunboat, two transports, three store ships, and an ammunition boat. On the return journey another transport was sunk, and the E11 encountered perhaps the most alarming adventure of her trip: the submarine fouled a cable anchoring a mine to the sea bed. Unable to surface because of enemy ships, Nasmith had to creep forward for 11 miles "with death dangling at the bows of the ship". At last able to surface, by bringing the stern up first and going full speed astern, the mine cleared itself.

His V.C. was notified in the *London Gazette* of June 25, 1915, and in the same month he was promoted commander and made a Chevalier of the Legion of Honour. In June, 1920, he was promoted captain.

After the war Dunbar-Nasmith was appointed to the command of the Mediterranean flagship Iron Duke in 1921. In 1924 he became Director of the Trade Division of the Naval Staff and after two years he was selected for the command of the Royal Naval College at Dartmouth. In 1928, after 30 years service, Dunbar-Nasmith reached flag rank. His next appointment was to the command of the Submarine Branch of the Royal Navy as rear-admiral (s). That was in 1929, when at 45 he was one of the youngest flag officers. A few years later he became Commander-in-Chief in the East Indies.

He was made K.C.B. in 1934. From 1935–38 he was a Lord Commissioner of the Admiralty and chief of Navy Personnel, becoming Admiral in 1936. At the beginning of the Second World War, from 1938–41, he served as Commander-in-Chief, Plymouth and Western Approaches and for the rest of the war was Flag Officer in Charge, London.

From 1948–54 he served as vice-chairman of the Imperial War Graves Commission. He was Vice-Admiral of the United Kingdom and Lieutenant of the Admiralty from 1945–62. In 1955 he was made K.C.M.G.

Dunbar-Nasmith married in 1920 Beatrix Justina, daughter of the late Commander Harry Dunbar-Dunbar-Rivers of Glen Rothes. They had two sons and one daughter. His wife died in 1962.

June 30, 1965.

President Gamal Abdel Nasser, President of the Republic of Egypt since 1956, and of the United Arab Republic since 1958, died in Cairo on September 28, 1970. He was 52.

Whetever the ultimate verdict of history, he will be remembered as one of the outstanding rulers of Egypt. His most enduring memorial will be the diversion of the Nile and the High Dam, which has altered the geographical features of Egypt and northern Sudan.

His political achievements are no less notable, if more controversial, but he stands out as the man who was the driving force behind the Egyptian Revolution and the creator of the United Arab Republic and the Arab Socialist Union. Unpopular in Western Europe and America for his anti-imperialistic, anti-Israeli policies and his turning to Russia for support after the clash over the Suez Canal, he was by the same token admired by the Arabs as a whole as the great liberator and unifier, the man who was to restore their former greatness by overcoming the intrigues of the imperialists and the Israeli menace.

In Egypt he not only raised the country's prestige and the standard of living of the masses, but introduced social reforms that were long overdue. In his relations with other Arab countries he suffered from the defect of being unable to tolerate a rival in the Arab world, and he sometimes pursued antagonisms which were contrary to the interests he had at heart, actuated apparently by personal feelings rather than the general good of the Arab cause. He nurtured a particular animosity for kings but was prepared to come to terms with Arab monarchs and bury the hatchet at least temporarily for the sake of Arab unity.

In international affairs he followed a policy of non-alignment and was active in support of the Afro-Asian block. By many of his compatriots he will be judged by the measure of his success, but they cannot fail to recognize, as indeed must his bitterest foes abroad, that he was above all a sincere patriot working selflessly for a cause in which he believed and that compared with other dictators his methods were singularly mild.

Gamal Abdel Nasser was born in Alexandria on January 15, 1918, the son of a small post office official from Bani Murr, Asyut Province in Upper Egypt, and was educated at various schools in Cairo and other places in Egypt. From Ras-al-Tin Secondary School in Alexandria he went to the Military College, graduating in 1938. Born in the days of the British Protectorate and growing up at a time when Egypt was in a period of transition from partial to complete independence, he seems to have been imbued with a keen sense of patriotism and a passion for reform.

At that time the Egyptian Army was just about to be expanded from the small and largely ceremonial army it had been and made into a fighting force. The young Nasser embarked on a military career with enthusiasm and with equal gusto started to conspire with other like-minded junior officers to reform if not to overthrow the existing order. He proved himself a brave and efficient soldier, graduating from the Staff College in 1947 and distinguishing himself in the war against Israel in 1948, and was wounded at Faluja. The scandals of this war spread the discontent in the Army and Nasser and his fellow conspirators formed the Free Officers Committee which planned the *coup d'état* of July 23, 1952.

When this took place it was an efficient, bloodless revolution. King Farouk abdicated in favour of his son and left Egypt for good. As the conspirators were fairly junior it was necessary to find a senior officer to act as a figurehead and their choice fell on Major-General Muhammad Neguib. Their original object seems to have been to enforce the necessary reforms and then withdraw from politics, so that to begin with they kept very much in the background. Neguib on the other hand became a popular figurehead and began to intrigue with the old politicians, or at any rate to show sympathy for the old ways Abdal-Nasir and his friends sought to change. He was soon removed from the scene and played no further part in the drama which began to unfold.

Nasser now emerged into the limelight and replaced Neguib as the national hero. At first he was welcomed by the British Government as a more reasonable and amenable leader than Neguib and he successfully negotiated the Canal Zone agreement with Britian. But he now began to interest himself not only in domestic matters but in the Arab world. At home he introduced land reforms and suppressed the Muslim Brotherhood: abroad he opposed the Baghdad Pact of 1955 and began to look towards the Iron Curtain for arms against Israel. In spite of the violence of his radio attacks he still maintained good relations with the west, and relied on America and Great Britain to cooperate in financing the High Dam project. When the offer of help was suddenly withdrawn in July, 1956, Nasser retaliated by nationalizing the Suez Canal.

The fiasco of the subsequent invasion by Anglo-French forces and the withdrawal of the Israelis from Sinai which they occupied at the same time, left Nasser with enhanced prestige in the eyes of Egypt and the Arab world, and also with the Suez Canal, which was soon reopened to all shipping except that of Israel.

BRITISH ASSETS

He also took over the base and all British assets in Egypt. It was some years before relations with Britain were fully restored. He seemed to be at the height of his success. He had arms and help with the High Dam from the Russians, while rigorously repressing communism at home. He established the United Arab Republic of Egypt and Syria in February, 1958, which was confirmed by a plebiscite.

Six months later the revolution in Iraq overthrew his main rival, Nuri Salid, and broke up the rival Hashemite Union of Iraq and Jordan. But the new dictator of Iraq proved no more pro-Nasser or pro-Egyptian than the previous regime. Iraq left the Baghdad Pact but showed no sign of drawing any nearer to the U.A.R. In 1961 Syria seceded from the U.A.R. and though there have been advances and retreats no other Arab state has joined the union.

The Yemen revolution, started with Egyptian help in September, 1962, was only partially successful and, resulted in the tying down of an Egyptian force of 50,000 or more for several years. Relations with Saudi Arabia from which the Yemeni Royalists drew support became strained, as did those with Britain owing to the encouragement by the Egyptians of terrorism in the adjoining territory of South Arabia. He denounced the Tunisian President, Habib Bourghiba for his attitude to Israel and the refugees.

His agreement with King Faisal of Saudi

Arabia for a cease-fire and the eventual withdrawal of Egyptian forces from the Yemen in 1965 came to nothing, Egyptian forces remaining in the Yemen at about the same strength as before, until the virtual triumph of the Yemeni republicans rendered their presence unnecessary.

At home things went rather better in spite of the worsening state of the country's finances, and the drain of the Yemen war. Many socialist laws were introduced and the country was proclaimed an Arab Socialist Union. Contrary to western forebodings, Nasser avoided becoming a Soviet satellite, or being drawn into the Soviet camp, by keeping his bridges with the west open for the time being. He continued to draw on Russian help for the High Dam, which went according to plan, and for the South Arabian military venture, which did not. The Suez Canal worked well, contrary to the expectations of many people in the west, and this, with the money brought in by tourists, provided a welcome source of income. Khrushchev visited Egypt and Nasser was made a Hero of the Soviet Union when the Nile was diverted in 1964. All this friendliness with Russia, and later China, did not prevent his rigorously suppressing Egyptian communists. In the matter of Israel he was intransigent and broke off relations with west Germany in 1964 because of support given to Israel, though he split the Arab world on the issue, and probably did more harm to his own country than to west Germany.

ISRAEL PROVOKED

Israel's successful blitzkrieg in June 1967 was provoked by Nasser's request for the withdrawal of the United Nations Emergency Force from Egyptian territory, the subsequent reoccupation of Sharm al-Shaikh and the threat to close the Gulf of Aqaba again to Israeli shipping. It seems unlikely that he expected the Israeli attack (though he said later that he was prepared for an attack on his airfields within 72 hours), but rather he may have hoped to regain his prestige in the Arab world by the gesture (and as he said relieve pressure on the Syrians) since all the Arab rulers, however hostile, would be compelled to support him against Israel, the common enemy, as in fact they did. He also counted on the backing of Russia and may have thought that Israel would hesitate to strike the first blow against such a formidable array.

The swift, decisive blow of the Israelis might well have caused his downfall, but after a gesture of resignation he was acclaimed in Egypt and in the Arab world with apparently undiminished popularity. He invoked the spirit of Dunkirk and attributed the defeat to the hidden forces of Imperialism, to wit Britain and the U.S.A., whose aid to the Israeli aggressors was skilfully camouflaged. The extent of the defeat was less obvious to the Egyptian public than to the Jordanians, since the war scarcely touched the Nile Valley and losses of armament and equipment were rapidly replaced by the Russians. Memories of collusion with Israel in 1956 and the unsympathetic tone of the press in Britain and the U.S.A. lent colour to the accusation of western support for Israel, which was for a time sustained by King Husain, though France, the principal supplier of Israeli arms, was absolved from blame. As a result of this false accusation the Suez Canal was closed and an oil embargo was imposed by the Arab countries on Britain and America. In his speech on the fifteenth anniversary of Egypt's revolution. Nasser accepted personally much of the blame for what had happened, but maintained an uncompromising attitude of hostility to Israel and repeated the charges of collusion, particularly against the United States.

His health deteriorated after the events of 1967 and he paid another visit to the U.S.S.R. for medical treatment. At the same time the Russians replaced his losses in the June War, and oil was discovered in some quantity in the Western Desert. He maintained his popularity with the masses, and abortive coups d'état found no support, the middle classes preferring "the devil they knew" to any likely successor. His honesty, piety and happy domestic life appealed to many.

His recent agreement to a Middle East ceasefire and peace negotiations with Israel raised hopes for an end to the Arab Israeli conflict which has flared into warfare three times in the past 22 years.

From the British point of view it is a pity that Nasser had so little contact with this country in his early years. Both Egypt and Britain might have benefited by a closer association. He visited Russia and various Eastern countries, but never came to Britain. He was married with two daughters and three sons.

September 29, 1970.

Lord Nathan, a former Minister of Civil Aviation, died on October 23, 1963, in Westminster Hospital. He was 74.

From 1929 to 1933 he was a Liberal member of Parliament who supported the National Government on its formation, but finding later that he could no longer agree with its policy and programme he crossed the floor of the House of Commons and eventually joined the Labour party. He lost his seat in 1935, but sat from 1937 to 1940 as Labour member for Central Wandsworth and was then elevated to the peerage, which made it possible for Ernest Bevin, who had been appointed Minister of Labour in the Coalition Government, to enter the House of Commons.

He was a man of immense vitality, both physical and mental, which found fulfilment in public service; fortunate was the organization which attracted his interest for he was the best of committee-men, shrewd and imperturbable. He was an ardent supporter of work for hospitals and was chairman of the Westminster Hospital from 1948 until 1963. In 1950 he became chairman of the Committee on Charitable Trusts, which later presented what has since become famous as the Nathan Report. In 1961 he was elected chairman of the Royal Society of Arts.

The Rt. Hon. Harry Louis Nathan, first Baron Nathan, of Churt, in the County of Surrey, in the Peerage of the United Kingdom, was born on February 2, 1889, the son of Michael Henry Nathan. He was educated at St. Paul's School, and in due course became a solicitor and a member of the firm of Herbert Oppenheimer Nathan and Vandyk. As a young man he took a deep interest in the Brady Working Lads' Club, the oldest and largest of the London Jewish Lads' Clubs, and acted as its Honorary Secretary. He was also an officer in the Volunteers and one of the original officers of the Territorial Army.

In the war of 1914-18 he served with the London Regiment in Gallipoli, Egypt and France, and attained the rank of major in the 1st London Regiment. He became Chairman of the National Defence Public Interest Committee and was representative of the L.C.C. on the County of London Territorial Army and Auxiliary Air Force Association.

In 1937 he became Hon. Colonel of the 33rd (St. Pancras) Anti-Aircraft Regiment R.A. and in 1939 Hon. Air Commodore No. 906 (County of Middlesex) Balloon Squadron A.A.F. He was also President of the Jewish Hospital Committee for British and Allied Forces, and chairman of the National Defence Public Interest Committee.

In 1923 Nathan contested Whitechapel and St. George's as a Liberal, but was not elected.

CROSSED FLOOR

In 1929, however, he was returned for North-East Bethnal Green and continued to represent that seat until 1935. In 1930 he registered a strong complaint that, although the Labour Government were seeking Liberal support in the House of Commons, Labour Cabinet Ministers were attacking him in his constituency. In 1931 he supported Sir Herbert Samuel in joining the National Government, but in 1933 he decided to cross the floor and go into opposition on the ground that "judged by the state of trade, unemployment, and the well being of the people" the Government had in his view been a disaster.

In 1934 he formalized his position by joining the Labour Party and applied for the Labour Whip. There was considerable regret in the Liberal Party as he had never spared himself in its service. He had, moreover, a particular interest in international finance, and for this reason was a valuable recruit to his new party. In 1929 he had published a book entitled *Free Trade Today*.

At the general election of 1935 he contested Cardiff (South) in the Labour interest, but failed to secure election. In 1937 he was returned for Central Wandsworth. During the Second World War he was Colonel (acting) Command Welfare Officer London District.

When the third Labour Government came into office with an overwhelming majority in 1945, Nathan was appointed Parliamentary Under Secretary of State for War, and Vice-President of the Army Council—posts he held until October, 1946, when Attlee made him Minister of Civil Aviation. That office he held until June 1948, but even after leaving the Government he was still assiduous, in spite of recurrent attacks of ill health, in all his public offices and duties. He had been sworn of the Privy Council in 1946.

He was a Deputy Lieutenant for the County

of London, as well as a magistrate; a Lieutenant of the City of London; and a Fellow of the Royal Statistical and Economic Societies.

Among the many other public appointments which he had held were those of deputy chairman of the Committee on the Consolidation and Amendment of the Law of Customs and Excise, appointed by the Chancellor of the Exchequer in 1951; chairman of the Queen Elizabeth Coronation Forest; a member of the General Medical Council (Crown nominee); chairman of the executive committee of the British Empire Cancer Campaign; president of the Anglo-Israeli Club; president of the Hillel Foundation; and Trustee of the Jewish Board of Deputies. He was Master of the Patten-makers' Company from 1951 to 1953 and of the Gardeners' Company in 1955-56. From 1957 to 1960 he was president of the Old Pauline Club. From 1958 to 1961 he was president of the Royal Geographical Society.

He married in 1919 Eleanor Joan Clara, a daughter of the late C. Stettauer. Lady Nathan has had her own long career in the public service, and for the municipal year of 1947-48 she was chairman of the London County Council, becoming an alderman in 1951. There were a son and a daughter of the marriage.

October 25, 1963.

Khwaja Nazimuddin, who died in Dacca on October 22, 1964, at the age of 70, played a prominent part in the affairs of Pakistan from its creation in August, 1947, to his dismissal from the Premiership in April, 1953.

For more than a quarter of a century before partition he was active in the tangled skein of the politics of undivided Bengal, and throughout had an unsullied reputation for integrity and a patriotism unmarred by self-seeking. Generous and hospitable, he enjoyed personal popularity but when he was at the head of the Pakistan administration first as Governor-General and then as Prime Minister events showed that he had not the strength and resolution needed in the first critical and anxious post natal years.

Born at Dacca on July 19, 1894, he was a grandson of the then Nawab of Dacca, the leading landed magnate of East Bengal. He was educated at Aligarh University and at Trinity Hall, Cambridge, where he studied law. He was made an honorary Fellow of Trinity in 1951. The Khwaja entered public life in municipal work in 1922, and was for seven years chairman of the Dacca town council. He was elected to the executive council of the university of Dacca soon after its creation. In 1929 he became Education Minister in Bengal.

On the introduction of provincial autonomy in April 1937 he was made Home Minister and continued in that office until 1941. He then became leader of the Muslim League Opposition Party. A turn of the wheel in April 1943 brought him back to office as Chief Minister, and he again took charge of the Home portfolio, which included in its scope Civil Defence organization. In 1946 he was delegate to the final session at Geneva of the League of Nations, and he went to the United States, as a member of the Indian Food Mission. He had been made a C.I.E. in 1926 and was advanced to K.C.I.E. in 1934.

It was a foregone conclusion in his home town of Dacca that when partition came in 1947 he would be Premier of East Pakistan. He was immediately confronted by the great exodus of Hindus from that territory and the trek thereto of Muslim refugees from West Bengal to the accompaniment of much internicine slaughter and suffering. The importance of not allowing East Bengal—more than a thousand miles from the seat of the Central Government at Karachi—to feel neglected was recognized. Hence it was regarded as a master stroke on the death of Jinnah, the Quaid-i-Azam in September, 1946, to nominate Nazimuddin for the vacant Governor-Generalship. His influence was directed to comprehension and consolidation, and his Islamic piety was a factor in steadying extremists of the North-West Frontier. The real leadership was that of the Prime Minister Liaquat Ali Khan, who in a quiet way became something of a dictator.

On the assassination of that statesman in October, 1951, Ghulam Mahommed, then Finance Minister, became Governor-General and invited his predecessor in that office to form a Government. He did so when the great prosperity brought by the phenomenal rise in the price of the large exports of jute and cotton was rapidly declining and soon values dropped to less than half they were in the peak period. With two successive years of monsoon failure there came the painful necessity to slow down projects of industrial and agricultural development. Sectarian animosities flared up and in particular Ahmadiya community was exposed to sanguinary attacks. Little or nothing had been done to ease the strained Indo-Pakistan relations.

The Governor-General, with his background of official administrative experience in British days, viewed the situation with deepening concern. He urged the easy-going Prime Minister to dismiss some inefficient Cabinet colleagues without success. Then he pressed Nazimuddin to resign.

This repeated request having been disregarded, on April 17, 1953, he took the dramatic step of dismissing the Prime Minister who had proved so inadequate to grapple with the tremendous difficulties confronting him.

After Field Marshal Ayub took over power Nazimuddin, like other politicians of his generation, retired from the scene. Only in the two years before he died had he returned, when the Muslim League, split into pro- and anti-Ayub factions gave him a chance of lending his name to the opposition under the system of basic democracies. Nazimuddin had become leader of the Councillors' Muslim League—which claimed to be the true successor of the original body—and had thrown in his lot with other opposition parties supporting Miss Jinnah's candidature in the presidential election early in 1965.

October 23, 1964.

Jawaharlal Nehru, the first Prime Minister of the Indian Union, died on May 27, 1964, at the age of 74. Nehru called Gandhi "the father of India", but the title belongs to himself. To India's masses Gandhi was not better known or better loved than "Panditji", and Nehru returned their love with a life-time dedicated not only to their political independence but to their escape from poverty and the fetters of Hindu social practice. Nehru gave the government the stamp of his own personality, pragmatic, secular, and democratic, while in the world at large he brought India into the counsels of the nations and seemed often to be the voice of calm reason in a confused and dangerous epoch.

Like Gandhi again, Nehru lived to see some of the principles and causes to which he had devoted his life shaken or threatened. The short but disastrous border war with China in 1962 was a grave blow to the policies he had conceived for India and for 15 years had directed—and a blow too to his personal prestige and the trust in which he was held. More ominous perhaps in the long run was the loss of momentum in the Indian development effort which began to be apparent in 1963 and the deterioration in the administration of the country: for on continued progress—and not less important, on the *sense* of progress—rested all of Nehru's and India's hopes for a just and free society, rid of the curse of mass poverty.

Nehru was a Kashmiri Brahmin but his family had been some seven generations removed from their native valley and were settled in Allahabad when, on November 14, 1889, he was born. He was named Jawaharlal (Red Jewel) a name, so he said once, that he found odious.

Motilal Nehru, the father, was a prosperous lawyer, and his house a centre for the sophisticated and westernized circle of Allahabad.

ENGLISH CONTACTS

From the first the young Nehru came much into contact with things English, many of his father's friends were Englishmen and the tone of the household was in many ways more English than Indian. His education was well begun at home, largely by English tutors—Brahmin scholars were assigned to teach him Hindi and Sanskrit but managed, according to the pupil, to impart "extraordinarily little". When he was 15 Nehru's family took him to England and left him at Harrow, and after two undistinguished and apparently contented years at that school he went up to Trinity College, Cambridge, to read natural sciences in which, in 1910, he took a second class degree.

In the choice of a career for the young Nehru passing consideration was given to the Indian Civil Service, but the father's profession was chosen and from Cambridge he went to the Inner Temple and was called to the Bar in 1912. He returned to India after seven years. On his likes and dislikes he later said, "perhaps more an Englishman than an Indian ... as much prejudiced in favour of England and the English as it was possible for an Indian to be."

The young Nehru joined his father in practice in Allahabad. He seems to have found life there provincial and insipid, and made no mark in his profession. There was little of the glitter and clash of battle in Indian politics in those years: the moderates set the tone and made it one of debate rather than struggle, and Nehru's interest was caught only slowly. He joined the state Congress organization in 1913, but even then was little engaged. In 1916 his father selected a bride for him, a 17-year-old Kashmiri Brahmin named Kamala Kaul, and they were married that year in Delhi. In 1917 their only child, Indira, was born.

The climate of Indian politics changed suddenly and irreversibly in 1919, and from then on Nehru's life took to its true and undeviating path. For a little time Motilal Nehru was able to dissuade his son from commitment to the civil disobedience campaign but from 1920 the son's influence was uppermost and father and son joined the movement wholeheartedly. The young Brahmin, "a bit of a prig", as he thought himself, had dedicated his life to the political service of his country.

GANDHI'S CHOICE

In the struggle for freedom Nehru's part was always subsidiary to Gandhi's; he gave the older man his utter loyalty and when it came to an issue invariably deferred to him, although many times and deeply he believed that the tactics decreed for the movement by the Mahatma were wrong. The differences between them became apparent in 1927 when Nehru advocated complete national independence, in opposition to the vaguer concept of *swaraj* (self-rule) which was Gandhi's. But in the long campaign for independence Nehru's inclination was always towards the radical course, often towards action for its own sake, while the Mahatma's decisive influence was moderating and restraining.

In spite of their frequent differences Gandhi early chose Nehru as his successor and leader of the independence struggle—the chance first became explicit in 1929, when Gandhi supported Nehru for the Congress presidency against the senior Vallabhbhai Patel. In a sense, however, Gandhi's action was as much recognition as choice; Nehru had great strength in the party as leader of the younger generation of nationalists and this made him the natural successor.

In policy and tactics Nehru's role was secondary but in two ways his contribution to Indian nationalism was unique and irreplaceable. The natural tendency of an independence movement must be to focus attention so sharply on the objective that all perspective is lost; it was Nehru who, often to the irritation of his colleagues, insisted on Congress's relating its own problems to the currents of politics in the world outside India. When it seemed absurd for Congress to aspire to a foreign policy Nehru insisted that it was vitally necessary, and by the time he became Prime Minister of independent India he had established that policy.

Again, independence movements must be tempted to look no farther than the immediate goal, to put aside potentially divisive discussion of further objectives until the first has been reached. Nehru's second great contribution to the Indian movement was to lift the party's vision beyond the obsession with freedom itself and to make it consider what kind of society a free India should be. At length he succeeded in overcoming the powerful resistance of the conservatives and made Congress accept his own vision of India transforming itself by choice and planning into a democratic, socialist and secular society.

Nehru had his first experience of gaol in 1921, when he was imprisoned with his father, and in the quarter of a century that passed before India became independent he spent nine years behind bars. Political prisoners were well treated and Nehru compared prison life to "the dull side of family life, magnified a hundred-fold, with few of its graces and compensations". His three books, *Glimpses of World History* (1934), *Toward Freedom—An Autobiography* (1936) and *The Discovery of India* (1946), were all written while he was in prison. The first took the form of letters to his daughter and is a volume of sketches of episodes in history, seen from an Asian viewpoint and compensating for what they lack in objectivity and accuracy (it was written largely without reference works) with a sweep of vision and with a narrative flow that give it unity. The *Autobiography* is his best book, a work of lucid self-examination written with grace and passion arising from his awareness of his role in the freedom struggle. *The Discovery* is more polemical but expressive of his developed love and comprehension for the country from which his education had initially estranged him.

In 1935 Nehru was released from prison to go to his wife, who had been taken to Switzerland for medical treatment. He was with her when she died early in the next year.

During the nineteen-thirties Nehru came more into conflict with what had become the old guard of Congress. Twice (in 1936 and 1937) he was elected president of the party but the power of that office was illusory while Gandhi remained the true source of authority, and the Mahatma's influence inclined to the right: this, and Nehru's profound allegiance to the unity of the party, induced him often to give way to the conservatives, to the sharp disappointment of the progressive wing of the party which looked to him for leadership.

The Second World War was for Nehru a time of anguishing dilemmas. He had a deep and reasoned hatred for Fascism, whose face he had seen on his several visits to Europe. Emotionally and intellectually Nehru was committed to the anti-Fascist cause, and his allegiance to Gandhi's creed of non-violence, always qualified, would have given way to his sense of the need to take up arms against evil under arms—but his first loyalty was to the cause of Indian independence. He sought ways to resolve the contradiction that to the Indian nationalists appeared between the two causes, hoping for a political settlement that might enable him, in spite of Gandhi, to lead Congress into active participation in the war effort; but only British statesmanship could have resolved that contradiction, and it was wanting.

For years Nehru and the Congress had been warning that they would not be involved willy-nilly in an "Imperialist war", but on September 3, 1939, the Viceroy, Lord Linlithgow, proclaimed India a belligerent state without having made the lightest gesture towards associating Indian opinion with that step. The Congress, and Nehru as one of its chief spokesmen, sought first an unequivocal affirmation from the British Government that when victory was won India would inherit her independence; and, second, a preliminary instalment of substantive political power, as an earnest of the first. The second demand was negotiable, the first was not. Britain could not bring herself to give the unqualified assurance of independence after the war, and this soured and in the end defeated the attempts at negotiation that were made.

The first such attempts issued in the civil disobedience campaign of 1940–41. In October, 1940, Nehru was arrested as he was about to offer *satyagraha* and sentenced to four years imprisonment, but was released with other political prisoners when the campaign was called off in December, 1941. Pearl Harbour and the onrush of the Japanese made the internal situation in India a matter of more urgent concern to Britain and led to the Cripps mission, whose more generous terms and higher hopes, coming too late, were dashed in total failure. Gandhi, over Nehru's loyal but intense opposition, launched the "quit India" campaign, and with all his colleagues in Congress was promptly arrested. From August 9, 1942, until June 15, 1945, Nehru was behind bars, his longest and his last term of imprisonment.

Throughout the long years of the independence struggle the nationalist camp had been disturbed by discord and perennial violence between the Muslim and Hindu communities, and Nehru's secularism made him blind to the explosive realities that this friction expressed. By his own description a pagan, Nehru was hostile to communalism whether it appeared among Muslims or Hindus: religion as practised in India, he said, had "become the old man of the sea for us, and it has not only broken our backs but stultified and almost killed all originality of the mind". He believed that communal differences were artificial and often fomented by the British, that they would disappear in an independent India, and that therefore it would be folly to give political recognition to the Muslim League. These misjudgments played their part in the progress to partition of India.

INDEPENDENCE AT LAST

A month after Nehru was released from prison in 1945 the Labour Government took office in Britain and accelerated to a headlong rush the wayward pace that concessions to Indian independence had been taking for a quarter of a century. By that time the Muslim League had confirmed its claim to represent the mass of the Muslim community and its demand for a sovereign Pakistan was on the way to becoming an unshakable commitment rather than an arguing point with which to obtain autonomy for Muslim majority provinces. The door to a united India was still not quite closed, however, and the British Cabinet Mission's plan, which left all concerns except defence, foreign affairs and communications to the provinces, was accepted by Congress and, reluctantly, the Muslim League. At this point Nehru was re-elected to the presidency of Congress, replacing the wise and moderate Maulana Azad (who had held the office since 1939), and with a single rash and untenable statement at a press conference, to the effect that the plan was not binding on the Congress, he brought down the precarious compromise achieved by the Cabinet Mission.

An interim government including both Congress and the League was formed on the basis of the plan, with Nehru as vice-president of its executive council, equivalent to prime minister; but now Mr. Jinnah was absolute in his demand for partition and the interim government showed only that it had become impossible for Congress and the League to work together.

In February, 1947, Attlee proclaimed his government's intention of transferring power to Indian hands not later than June in the following year, and the statement was welcomed by Nehru although it can now be seen as the penultimate step to the partition which he still hoped to avoid. But since the "Great Calcutta Killing" in the previous August furies of communal strife had been rising in India and carrying with them the threat of civil war and disintegration, and when Lord Mountbatten arrived as Viceroy in March, 1947, he concluded that only partition could resolve the bloody chaos into which India was lapsing.

The last Viceroy and the first leader of independent India responded warmly to each other, and with grief Nehru was persuaded that partition was the only course.

On August 15, 1947, India, in the words of Nehru, "kept its tryst with destiny", and became an independent nation. For Nehru, the first Prime Minister, the triumph was shadowed by partition and the tide of slaughter that ran through the land and was yet to reach its height, but the years of opposition were past, and Nehru was now himself at the pinnacle of power, responsible for the transformation of a diverse and archaic society into the new India whose outlines he had envisaged for so long.

From the beginning of his political life Nehru had been demanding "full independence" for India and withdrawal from the Empire which stood, he declared, "for one part dominating over and exploiting the other". But when it was at last in his power to lead India out of the Commonwealth he declined to do so, but rather affirmed new ties of brotherly equality and by this decision did more than any other man to set the Commonwealth into its new era as a free and multi-racial association of equals. At the Commonwealth Prime Ministers' meeting of 1948, the first of many attended by Nehru, informal talks were held leading to India's continuance as a member but as a Republic. The Commonwealth tie was to come under severe strain—notably at the time of the Suez adventure—but while Nehru lived it was never in danger of snapping.

SHAPING FOREIGN POLICY

As Nehru had been the architect and sole custodian of Congress "foreign policy" before independence so it continued when he became Prime Minister and Foreign Minister of free India. To a greater extent than of any other man in a democratic government it can be said that India's policies were Nehru's policies. Some of these he had articulated long before, anti-colonialism, of course, and opposition to racialist systems; others arose from the conditions of the international society when India joined it. Non-alignment was a basic principle, deriving from the conviction that the economic progress of India could be achieved only in a peaceful world and that the cause of peace could best be served by keeping India free from either of the groups of powers whose contest threatened it.

From his first visit to Russia in 1927 he had been drawn in sympathy towards the Russian people and their aspirations, and he was a socialist: that he was never a communist may be ascribed perhaps to his innate scepticism, which prevented him from becoming a "true believer", and certainly to his aversion to violence and dictatorship. His greater sympathy towards Moscow may have been accentuated by his unhappy experience in the United States on his first visit in 1949, where he was jarred by what seemed to him a materialistic and simplistic approach to life and politics. The McCarthy years in America did not endear that country to any Indian, and during Mr. Dulles's first years as Secretary of State American policy became highly critical of India and of Nehru personally.

But this sympathetic bias towards Moscow led Nehru to apply a dual standard of judgment, which became egregious in 1956 when the promptness with which he condemned the Anglo-French action against Egypt contrasted with his reluctance to criticize Russia for the brutality with which that country crushed the Hungarian uprising. It appears, however, that he did learn from that incident and after 1956 a more dispassionate tone was discernible in Nehru's attitude to the Soviet Union. The subsequent change in American policy towards neutral Powers found Nehru responsive—as indeed he must have been, considering the steady generosity with which America was underwriting India's development.

DISPUTE WITH CHINA

Nehru's attitude to China was at the beginning friendly, helpful and trusting, and the feeling that that trust had been betrayed made for inflexibility on his side when the border dispute came to a head in the late 1950s.

The first discords came with China's gradual occupation of Tibet. Nehru's attitude to China's movements in Tibet was mixed. He was strongly sympathetic to the Tibetan desire for continued independence but was inclined also to give weight to China's case that historically Tibet was part of China.

Meanwhile, a far more serious disagreement had begun to develop over the borders between India and China—between Ladakh and Sinkiang in the west and between Tibet and the North-East Frontier Agency of India in the east. With two new republics marching in such remote and empty terrain as that of Ladakh it was only to be expected that border claims would overlap, and with frankness, coolness, and a willingness to compromise on both sides they could have been resolved. But while India was pointing out that China's map showed as Chinese territory India regarded as her own, Peking, while replying that the question of maps and borders could be taken up later, was building a road across the disputed territory of Aksai Chin, in Ladakh.

Nehru, apparently believing that the situation could be made more dangerous if public opinion was aroused, kept the conflict of claims secret as long as he could. But by 1959 his government had discovered the existence of the new Chinese road and Indian patrols sent forward to ascertain its position were held by the Chinese. The public mood in India turned almost overnight into hostility toward China and the political opposition (the communists apart) promptly accused China of aggression. Nehru at first rejected that formulation, but gradually, as evidence to substantiate India's claim was accumulated, he himself discarded all tentativeness in discussing the north-western border and began to speak and act as if India's version of that border was absolute and unchallengeable.

Once that position had been taken a clash was inevitable, as China's evacuation of the territory in Aksai Chin which Peking claimed as her own was made a precondition of negotiation of a border settlement.

Nehru accepted an Army proposal that the Indians should try the tactics of infiltration by which, it was felt, the Chinese had occupied Aksai Chin. But where China had moved into empty territory, Indian troops had to probe forward into ground which was at least sparsely occupied by China, and the "forward policy" had in it the seeds of a military confrontation between India and her far more powerful neighbour.

That came about in the autumn of 1962 when China launched heavy attacks at both ends of the border, wiping out the score or so of posts set up under the forward policy behind the Chinese claim line in Ladakh, and overwhelming the Indian army in the N.E.F.A. in thrusts that carried Chinese troops to the verge of the plains of Assam. When after four weeks of fighting China unilaterally declared a ceasefire and prepared to withdraw her forces Nehru's policies were as shattered as the Indian army. "*Hindi-Chinee bhai-bhai*" had become a bitter taunt, India had suffered a humiliation as well as a defeat, resources desperately needed for economic development would now have to go to rebuilding and strengthening the armed services. In having to ask for immediate and continued military assistance from Britain and the United States Nehru had compromised the non-alignment that had been the heart of his policy in international affairs.

After the short, fierce border war the northern borders of India remained quiet. By accepting the Colombo proposals for pacification Nehru went as far as he could to return the dispute to the conference table, but China did not meet him in that. India continued to strengthen her forces with western help but little more was heard of the intention of forcing the Chinese out of the territory India claimed, which had been the rationale of the forward policy.

While relations with China are still set in enmity (although throughout the fighting and its aftermath Nehru refused to break off diplomatic relations with Peking, so keeping a bridgehead for calmer days) it may be that a more explosive bequest and a chapter even more destructive for Nehru's policies lay in the dispute with Pakistan over Kashmir, and Nehru must have felt the bitterness at the last that he was leaving this more inflamed, as far from a solution as at any time since the fighting in the state just after independence. He died, indeed, when he may have been beginning an attempt to untie the knot of the dispute, but even had death spared him longer it was plain that he had left it too late and his flagging energies as well as his reduced political stature must have made the task beyond him. The tenor of the talks with Shaikh Abdulla, recently released, could scarcely seem to point to an acceptable solution.

While it must be said that Pakistan bears a large share of responsibility for this prolonged dispute it became apparent that for Nehru negotiations that might lead to a solution which diminished Indian sovereignty over the valley of Kashmir, the heart of the state and the dispute were intolerable. It was not that he was himself a Kashmiri, although he loved the state; but rather that his profoundest political beliefs were involved in the continuance of Muslim Kashmir within the Union. If the Kashmiris, confronted with a choice presented in religious terms, were to opt for Pakistan, what would remain of India's claim to be a secular state, and what would be the repercussions on the other 40 million Muslims in India?

INDIA'S VOICE IN THE WORLD

Nehru's greatest achievement in his direction of Indian foreign relations was undoubtedly the projection of India's voice in the counsels of the world. At first non-alignment was bitterly criticized especially in Washington, but gradually the West changed its attitude and in 1960 Nehru had the satisfaction of welcoming to Delhi in quick succession President Eisenhower and Khrushchev, both coming as respectful friends of India, eager to help her development. At moments of crisis in the world's affairs—during the Korea and Indo-China wars, when the Congo fell into chaos—the Powers turned to Nehru for help in reestablishing peace and order. In 1961 Nehru affirmed his commitment to the United Nations—and demonstrated his readiness to defy strong pressure from Moscow—by sending Indian troops to the Congo.

His reputation in the world had been deeply shadowed already, however, by India's forceful annexation of the Portuguese colony of Goa at the end of 1961. In the early 1950s when it became apparent that Portugal would not follow Britain and France in granting independence to their Indian territories, there was an outcry in India for the Government to oust the Portuguese: a march of *satyagrahis* across the borders of Goa was met with gunfire and pressure on Nehru to seize the colony became intense. He stood firm then. But in 1961 he discounted such considerations. A smoke-screen of inspired, but mendacious reports about Portugal's aggressive designs upon Indian territory and the breakdown of law and order in the colony excited jingoistic expectations in a public which had lost interest in Goa; pleading provocation and an unassuageable popular demand for "liberation" of Goa the Prime Minister gave the order to march and the Indian troops which had been massed around the borders of Goa seized the colony without difficulty.

The initiative for the Government's action against Goa did not come from Nehru, who acceded to the pressure of circumstances engineered by others; but to say that is not to relieve him of responsibility for an action that, as he had once foreseen, led some of India's friends as well as her enemies to ask whether her commitment to peaceful methods was not selfishly qualified and her preaching cant.

It is as the leader of India's forced march out of poverty and social backwardness that Nehru would have wished to be judged, and if his achievements there were incomplete it will be remembered that the tasks he set himself were vast. They were no less than to set in motion a radical social and economic revolution in a deeply conservative and impoverished society, harried by the imperative of a huge and quickly growing population, and to see it through without coercion and within a democratic polity. It can be seen now that India is on the move, and on the course charted by Nehru. The Five-Year Plans have laid the foundations for accelerating economic development and the nation is committed to their continuance; India has become for Asia a model of parliamentary government while other countries around her have given up the attempt; the ancient injustices of India's social system have been outlawed and there has been a slow movement of public opinion in the wake of the law. Nehru was the unchallenged and solitary leader of India and much of the country's progress is due to his dedicated and unflagging zeal, and to the hold that he had in its people's affections. Nehru wrote—anonymously—of himself:

> "He has all the makings of a dictator in him—vast popularity, a strong will, energy, pride ... and with all his love of the crowd an intolerance of others and a certain contempt for the weak and inefficient .... His overwhelming desire to get things done, to sweep away what he dislikes and build anew, will hardly brook for long the slow processes of democracy."

Somewhere in that warning is the resolution of the paradoxes of Nehru's character. It was true, but it was wrong: when he assumed power he was culpable more for vacillation than for Caesarism; he brooked too often not only "the slow processes of democracy" but also the failures and peculations of colleagues, the obstruction or deflection of policies which he passionately declared to be vital for India. Perhaps the very depth of Nehru's commitment to democracy, the strength of his aversion to dictatorship, did something to reduce his effectiveness as a national leader.

May 28, 1964.

Lord Nelson of Stafford, chairman of the English Electric Company Limited, died at Stafford on July 16, 1962. He was 74.

George Horatio Nelson was born in London in 1887 into a family of textile merchants with its roots in Leicestershire. He was educated at the City and Guilds Technical College in London, where he worked under one of the most distinguished teachers of that time, Professor Sylvanus Thompson, the author of a classical text book on Electricity and Magnetism. Nelson moved on with a Brush studentship to the Brush Engineering Company at Loughborough, one of the earliest nurseries in England for young electrical engineers. There he gained his first practical experience, in the drawing office and on the shop floor, in mechanical and electrical engineering.

After his time with the Brush Company he had joined the British Westinghouse Company in Manchester and made rapid progress. By 1911 he was Chief Outside Engineer and in 1914 became Chief Electrical Superintendent. Nelson had remained with the company when it became Metropolitan-Vickers Electrical, and in 1920 he was made manager of its Sheffield works which were concentrated on electric traction. He stayed there for 10 years, making many friends in the steel industry and among railway managements all over the world, until the opportunity occurred of undertaking a constructive task which was to constitute the main achievement of his life.

DRASTIC CHANGES

An important competitor, the English Electric Company, long established in the industry through its constituents and with native roots traced back to the seventies of last century, had fallen into financial trouble and had been drastically reconstructed. The bankers were able to provide a liberal injection of new money and new associations and they had invited Sir Holberry Mensforth to become chairman of the company. Mensforth had just retired from the post of Director of Government Factories and had earlier been works manager at Trafford Park and in that capacity George Nelson's immediate chief. He persuaded Nelson to join him and become managing director, and when Mensforth retired in 1933 Nelson was appointed chairman and managing director. The measure of his success is that in nearly 30 years he built up the number of the company's employees from 4,000 to 80,000 and its turnover more than proportionately.

It was largely the impact of his own knowledge and personality that brought the company through the testing period of the thirties and set it firmly on its feet. He was indefatigable, engineering was his vocation, he had a complete grasp of works management and of handling men, and when he had to fight for contracts and turnover it was soon evident that he was an accomplished salesman, in the sense of a man who sees that what he promises is carried out.

By the time rearmament became official policy Nelson had broken the back of his problem of reorganization. For many months he importuned Service Ministers and their advisers for the chance to bring his organization into play. He had an early success with the Controller of the Navy but it was only after many rebuffs that in the autumn of 1938 he was offered as a training exercise a contract for 75 Hampden bombers which he was told were already obsolete. That was the beginning of seven years' work into which Nelson and all his staff threw everything they had. The Hampdens were followed by 2,470 Halifax bombers and by 2,730 tanks. When the war ended, the development of the most successful military aircraft of its generation, the Canberra bomber, was well under way to the company's own designs.

PUBLIC ACTIVITIES

Nelson himself found time during these years for much other public work. He went to the United States and Canada in 1942 as chairman of the United Kingdom Tank Mission to hammer out with the American Army and industry a joint policy for tank development and production. He served on the Heavy Bomber Group Committee of the Air Ministry from 1939 to 1945, on the Reconstruction Joint Advisory Council in 1943-44, on the Higher Technological Education Committee in 1944-45, and was chairman of the Census of Production Committee in 1945. For two difficult years in the life of the Federation of British Industries he was its President in 1943-44. After the war although his business responsibilities were increased through the acquisition in 1946 of Marconi's Wireless Telegraph Company he was able to devote a great deal of time and thought to a cause that was always close to his heart, the improvement of technical education, both through the facilities offered by his own companies to men of promise from every part of the Commonwealth and by the work which he did for technical colleges and for the professional engineering insstitutions of which he had been a lifelong member. He served on the governing body of the Imperial College of Science and Technology, on the Court of Governors of Manchester College of Science and Technology and on the governing body of Queen Mary College in the University of London. He was President of the Institution of Electrical Engineers in 1955 and of the Institute of Mechanical Engineers in 1957-58, of the British Electrical & Allied Manufacturers Association in 1950-53, of their Research Association in 1952 and of the Locomotive & Allied Manufacturers Association in 1958-60. He served as Prime Warden of the Goldsmiths' Company in 1960.

Nelson had travelled very widely overseas. The number of his friends was legion: he forgot none of them and was distressed if when they were in England he was prevented by absence or illness from meeting them and returning their hospitality. He and Lady Nelson were admirable hosts either in London or Staffordshire. He had married in 1913 Florence Howe, a member of an old Leicestershire family, whose life from then was devoted with great skill and tact to supporting him untiringly in all his activities. They had one son and one daughter.

Nelson received a knighthood in 1943, a baronetcy in 1955 and was raised to the peerage as the first Baron Nelson of Stafford in 1960. He was made an Hon. LL.D. of Manchester University in 1957, and an honorary Freeman of Stafford in 1956. The heir to the title is his only son, the Hon. Henry George Nelson, who was born in 1915 and succeded his father as managing director of the English Electric Company in 1956.

July 17, 1962.

Sir Frank Nelson, K.C.M.G., who was responsible on the executive level for the creation of the Special Operations Executive during the Second World War, died on August 11, 1966, in Oxford at the age of 83.

Frank Nelson was educated at Bedford Grammar School and Neuenheim College, Heidelberg. As a young man he went out to India as an assistant in the firm of Symons, Barlow and Co., rising to be the senior partner, though his service was interrupted by the First World War, when he was an officer in the Bombay Light Horse. In 1922 and 1923, he was Chairman of the Bombay Chamber of Commerce, and in the latter year President of the Associated Chambers of Commerce of India and Ceylon. From 1922 to 1924 Nelson was a member of the legislative council of Bombay. In 1924 he was knighted and returned to England, being elected Conservative M.P. for Stroud division of Gloucestershire that year. He was re-elected in 1929, but resigned in May, 1931, in order to go into business, some time as joint managing director of the Lamson Paragon Supply Company.

Shortly after war broke out in 1939 he was employed as Consul in Basle, but when the Special Operations Executive was created in July, 1940, by order of the War Cabinet, with Lord Dalton as the responsible Minister, Sir Frank Nelson was appointed as its chief.

With his past experience as a member of Parliament and in international commerce, he was well qualified for the task. Although never very strong physically he threw himself into his new task with all he had to give, and it needed everything. The establishment of a new and secret department, responsible to no existing department, and with a charter of almost limitless scope, naturally aroused hostility, veiled or open, throughout the length and breadth of Whitehall. That he was able, before his retirement through ill-health in the spring of 1942, largely to overcome this inherent animosity and to get his organization accepted and recognized as an essential development in modern warfare, was due entirely to his force of character, his patent honesty of purpose, and complete unselfishness. He wore himself out in the process but left a solid base on which his successor could build.

Frank Nelson was a man of grim but unshakable determination, with a strong sense of loyalty and organization.

Nelson was created K.C.M.G. shortly after he retired from the S.O.E. in 1942, and subsequently held appointments in Washington in the Air Intelligence Branch, and later in Germany, retiring with the rank of Air Commodore in 1946. He married firstly, in 1911, Jean, who died in 1952, only daughter of Colonel Patrick Montgomerie, and they had a son; secondly, Dorothy Moira Carling, who with unfailing devotion nursed him through his last years.

August 13, 1966.

Princess Wilhelmina of the Netherlands, who until her abdication in September, 1948, in favour of her daughter, had ruled the Netherlands for 50 years, died on November 28, 1962, at the age of 82.

Princess Wilhelmina enjoyed in her country a position comparable with that of the late Queen Victoria in Britain. To the prestige of a long reign was added the affection and admiration evoked by her bravery in face of the German invasion of her country in 1940 and by the resolution and patience of the years of exile in England. These qualities, matching those of King Haakon, her contemporary in misfortune, were an inspiration to the Dutch resistance under a particularly brutal occupation and, recollected in peace, led as in Norway to a strengthening of the monarchy.

Throughout her life a woman of strong faith and sterling character, and a wise and considerate ruler, her remarkable gifts, which included business ability of a high order, did much for the material prosperity and political advancement of her people. Modesty and a true simplicity were also among her qualities. In speech and action she never failed to sustain a quiet dignity; and approachable though she was to her subjects, whom she understood so well, she met all great occasions as a Queen.

Nothing, however, in all her life exemplified her true greatness as did her conduct in the last War. An elderly woman driven from her throne to a country in which, however welcome, she was a stranger, she surrendered none of her responsibilities as the ruler of her people, and continued by every means in her power to direct and encourage them. She gained from them a reverence and love which even in the days of her full power at The Hague she had not known, and won from the world at large the homage due to one whose human courage and fidelity had, strengthened by a deep religious sense, triumphed over all adversities. These gruelling years took their toll, and in 1948, three years after her return to Holland, she abdicated in favour of her daughter. Her graceful surrender of the throne enhanced her people's esteem for her and her last quiet years were the reward of an unselfish reign.

Wilhelmina Helena Paulina Maria, Queen of the Netherlands, was born at The Hague on August 31, 1880, the only daughter of King William III by his second wife Emma, Princess of Waldeck and Pyrmont. Through her mother, the Queen was related to the Royal Family of England, for Queen Emma was the elder sister of the late Duchess of Albany.

Queen Wilhelmina succeeded her father on November 3, 1890, and Queen Emma acted as Regent for her. The child could not have had a better guardian. Under her the administration of the Dutch East Indies was recast, and at home she prepared the way for the social reforms which were to follow. For 10 years the princess had an English governess, Miss Saxton Winter, and at six began lessons with the headmaster of one of the National Schools. The favourite pastime of the future queen was driving; but she also skated and played tennis well. Gardening, farming, housekeeping, and sketching—she was always to be fond of painting—were less strenuous pleasures. True to the characteristics of the House of Orange the girl had an excellent memory, spoke English, French, and German fluently, and knew something of Russian and of the Malay tongues of her future Empire.

On August 31, 1898, Queen Wilhelmina came of age and in a brief proclamation declared herself "ready to accept the splendid but weighty task" to which she was called. On September 6 she was enthroned in the New Church at Amsterdam. Early in her reign the Boer War imposed a serious strain on Anglo-Dutch relations. In the spring of 1900 the first Boer Mission, headed by Dr. Leyds, went to The Hague, where the Queen received its members in private audience. At the end of the year Kruger sailed for Europe in the cruiser Gelderland Holland provided for him and was joyfully received by the Dutch people. The Queen decided not to refuse him an audience though with characteristic tact she made it as brief as possible and the subsequent dejection of the ex-President suggested that he had forgone all hope of intervention on her part.

Meanwhile on October 16, 1900, the Queen's engagement to Duke Henry of Mecklenberg-Schwering was announced. To the Dutch people, jealous of their popular liberties and mistrustful of foreign influences, the news was by no means pleasing. The Queen's decisiveness, however, added to the Duke's tact, overcame such difficulties as arose, and when on February 7, 1901, the wedding took place there was the same outburst of devoted loyalty which had greeted her accession. Their only child, Princess Juliana, was born eight years later on April 30, 1909.

In her speech from the Throne at the opening of the Session of the Dutch Chambers in 1915, Queen Wilhelmina declared the firm intention of the Dutch Government to maintain the country's integrity and observe the duties of neutrality. At the same time a strict vigilance was necessary during the war years and the Dutch Army and Navy kept watch under the careful eye of their sovereign.

In 1934 Prince Henry died and in August of the following year she went privately with Princess Juliana for a holiday in the Perthshire Highlands. In August, 1938, Queen Wilhelmina had been a ruling sovereign for 40 years, and her people celebrated the occasion with immense enthusiasm.

This marked the end of a spacious and even splendid epoch in the history of Holland. August 29, 1939, saw the Dutch forces mobilized, and within a few days Europe was at war. On September 19 the Queen, reassuming her attitude of a quarter of a century before, laid her own emphasis on the neutrality of her country, and added her desire to cooperate for peace. In November she and King Leopold of the Belgians reiterated their willingness to employ their good offices: but it could have come to nothing, and on May 10, 1940, she issued her "flaming protest" at German violation of the territory in which she had so long cultivated peace.

King George VI recorded in his diary how Queen Wilhelmina telephoned him from The Hague at 5 o'clock on the morning of May 13 to beg him to send aircraft for the defence of Holland—perhaps, in the words of Mr. Wheeler-Bennett, the King's biographer, the first time in history the long-distance telephone was used by one sovereign to another in a cry for help. Later that day she was in London, having been brought to Harwich in the British destroyer Hereward from Rotterdam. Forced to leave The Hague to avoid German attempts at kidnapping, she first thought to join those Dutch forces which were still resisting the Germans in Zeeland. It was only when this was manifestly impossible that she was persuaded to come to England, which her daughter had already reached with her husband and two children.

Queen Wilhelmina was followed to London by members of the Dutch Government, and for the next five years, as Queen Juliana said in a speech at Guildhall in 1950, England was "a home and a hope" for the whole Dutch nation. From her refuge the Queen continued to keep in touch with her own people by broadcast and with supreme dignity gave them her grave and inspiring counsel. In exile she was in fact as well as name, and never more truly, their sovereign. "Je maintiendrai," she said. It was, she reminded them, the motto of her famous dynasty; but *fluctuat nec mergitur* is another. To the British Government and people she was intensely grateful and said so.

In February, 1943, the Queen had a narrow escape when a bomb fell near the house in which she was staying and killed two members of her household. Then in the summer of 1944 the whole picture of the war changed and on September 3 she was able to broadcast to her people on Radio Orange:—"You know that liberation is at hand."

RETURN TO HOLLAND

Before she left this country she was invested with the Order of the Garter, an honour that no other reigning queen of a foreign state had ever received. It was July, 1945, before she returned to her official residence at The Hague, but in the months between, as Holland piece by piece was cleared of the enemy, the Queen visited the liberated areas and the fervour of her welcome showed at once the loyalty she and her House commanded. In the following year she returned to England for a visit bringing with her a gift of horses for the King and Queen whose guest she was. It provided a short break in an arduous time. The great task of reconstruction at home and the situation in the Dutch East Indies, where a new political order was beginning to evolve, claimed much of her energies, and she exerted herself unsparingly. In the end the burden became too heavy for her health. She had developed pneumonia after her return to The Hague in 1945 and in October, 1947, she felt obliged to retire for a time from her duties and to hand over the cares of state to Princess Juliana, acting as Regent. She resumed her duties two months later, but fatigue again obliged her to resort to a regency and shortly afterwards she announced her intention to relinquish her royal duties. The time chosen for her abdication, the beginning of September, 1948, immediately followed the celebrations of her golden jubilee as queen. Those 50 years had brought the Dutch people through many perils and had spared her few of the trials of royal duty. She had remained at her post long enough to see recovery well on the way after a destructive war, but complicated problems remained, and she felt that she could not bring to them the attention and energy they required. Her decision was in the best interests of her subjects and was prompted by that strong sense of public duty which had marked her whole reign.

Princess Wilhelmina lived in strict seclusion. In her retirement she interested herself in road safety, but for the most part lived for her family, her religion, and her memories. In August, 1958, she made a short broadcast speech of thanks for the popular celebrations of the centenary of the birth of her mother, Queen Emma, which had moved her deeply. Her memoirs, *Lonely but Not Alone*, published in the autumn of 1958, showed not only an old woman's return to the memories of her youth but the strong religious feeling that characterized her whole personal life.

November 29, 1962.

Walter Neurath, the Vienna-born publisher and founder of Thames and Hudson, London, died on September 26, 1967, at the age of 63.

Walter Neurath was a publisher down to his fingertips. He had an unerring eye for book production and his contribution in this respect to publishing as a whole has been considerable. His fertile imagination constantly produced ideas for new books and new series of books. His knowledge of the technical side of printing enabled him to judge what could and could not be achieved in any given medium. He had a relentless demand for quality which was so exacting that it led to an almost natural selection of staff and to the creation of a unique team around him.

After the death of his wife in 1950, he married again. His widow, Eva Neurath, was a founding director of Thames and Hudson and she ideally complemented her husband and played an important part in the development of the company.

In 1959 he launched the World of Art series that now contains over 50 volumes whose world sales exceed six million copies. Archaeologists all over the world have played a major part as contributors to the "Ancient Peoples and Places" series under the general editorship of Dr. Glyn Daniel, and more recently Sir Mortimer Wheeler has undertaken the general editorship of a new archaeological series under the title of "New Aspects of Antiquity".

Born in Vienna on October 1, 1903, he studied art and philosophy at Vienna University and went to England in 1938 after Hitler occupied Austria. He had entered publishing after leaving university and had already made a name for himself in Vienna when he had to leave Austria. In London he joined a small publishing and production company, Adprint Limited, where he was a director. He was responsible among other things for the "Britain in Pictures" series, produced during the Second World War as an effort to inform the Commonwealth and America about the English way of life.

He had for some years cherished a burning ambition to make available to a wide public scholarly, well-illustrated books which under the conditions then existing were either not buyable at all or were printed in such small editions that they were too expensive for the majority of people. It was with this in mind that in 1949 he founded Thames and Hudson.

His blueprint—one might fairly say his invention—was the concept of the international publication of such books, which enabled large editions to be printed in various languages thus reducing the unit cost and making them available to an infinitely wider audience than before. With this creed in mind Walter Neurath succeeded, from small beginnings in a High Holborn attic, in creating a distinguished publishing house.

Having been, to his occasional irritation, "type-cast" as an art book publisher, Walter Neurath was always pleased to publish important books in other fields. His own wide scholarship, supported where necessary by that of his staff, inspired a remarkable trust between his authors and himself.

He really never stopped thinking, planning and talking books. His relaxations were music and walking and talking with friends. He did not suffer fools gladly and was impatient with incompetence but extremely generous. He had known of his serious illness for several months and calmly and uncomplainingly made all his arrangements with the same thoroughness he always brought to bear on his affairs.

As well as his widow he is survived by his two children, Thomas and Constance, who are both working in Thames and Hudson and his step-son Stephen.

September 27, 1967.

Marshal of the Royal Air Force Lord Newall, G.C.B., O.M., G.C.M.G., C.B.E., who died at his London home on November 30, 1963, at the age of 77, was Chief of the Air Staff in the early part of the Second World War, and from 1941 to 1946 Governor-General of New Zealand.

During his period of office as Chief of the Air Staff from 1937 until the autumn of 1940, Lord Newall was confronted with the formidable task of making the Air Force ready to fight. In many respects the task proved to be greater than the response. The hour was already late. Nevertheless, Lord Newall's term was made historically memorable by the great victory of the Royal Air Force in the Battle of Britain. Lord Newall's part in this decisive engagement was an important one. It was he who recruited Sir Henry Tizard to the scientific service of the Royal Air Force and it was in large measure due to his support that Tizard was able to translate the theory of radar early warning into the operational procedures of Fighter Command, which saved the country in 1940.

Earlier in his career Newall had been among the pioneers of the Royal Flying Corps, having learnt to fly privately several months before it was formed in May, 1912. He was then an officer of the Indian Army, and prior to the outbreak of war in 1914 was engaged in the formation of a Central Flying School for India at Sitapur. By the time the R.A.F. was formed four years later he had risen by distinguished service, although only 32, to brigadier-general, and had established a reputation which later service enhanced.

Cyril Louis Norton Newall, first Baron Newall, of Clifton-upon-Dunsmoor, in the County of Warwick, was born at Mussoorie, India, on February 15, 1886, the son of Lieutenant-Colonel William Potter Newall, Indian Army. Educated at Bedford and Sandhurst, he was commissioned to The Royal Warwickshire Regiment in 1905, but four years later transferred to the Indian Army, and it was in that country that he took up flying. During leave in England he qualified as a pilot in a Bristol biplane on Salisbury Plain on October 3, 1911. He was among the first officers selected by the Indian Army for special flying instruction at the Central Flying School at Upavon.

When war broke out in 1914 he was posted to one of the squadrons of the R.F.C. forming at home. In 1915-16 he commanded No. 12 Squadron in France, and gained the Albert Medal for conspicuous gallantry in entering a bomb shed of the squadron which had caught alight and putting out the fire. After a few months in command of No. 6 Wing, at home he returned to France to command No. 9 Wing. In 1917 he took command of the 41st. (Bombing) Wing formed near Nancy to undertake bombing operations against German objectives. This wing was the forerunner of the Independent Air Force formed in 1918, in which he commanded the 8th Brigade. For his war service he was thrice mentioned in dispatches and was awarded the C.M.G. and C.B.E.

LEAVING INDIA

In 1919 he received a permanent R.A.F. commission as wing commander, and resigned from the Indian Army. He was soon promoted to group captain, and was Deputy Director of Personnel at the Air Ministry from 1919 to 1922. Next he commanded the School of Technical Training at Halton, and in 1923-24 was an Air Aide-de-Camp to the King. In 1925 he was appointed A.O.C., Special Reserve and Auxiliary Air Force. From 1926 to 1931 he was Director of Operations and Intelligence and Deputy Chief of the Air Staff, and in 1930 he was made an additional member of the Air Council. He also received the C.B. in 1929. After a few months as A.O.C. Wessex Bombing Area, Air Defence of Great Britain, he was appointed A.O.C., Middle East, in September, 1931, and was there three years. In January, 1935, he became Air Member for Supply and Organizaton, Air Ministry, and six months later was raised to K.C.B. In September, 1937, he succeeded Sir Edward Ellington as Chief of the Air Staff. In 1938 he was promoted to G.C.B.

His period of just over three years as C.A.S. included the first 14 months of the 1939-45 War. On October 25, 1940, he was succeeded by Air Chief Marshal Sir Charles (later Lord) Portal and was appointed Governor-General of New Zealand when the term of office of Lord Galway expired in February, 1941. On leaving the Air Ministry he was promoted to the rank of Marshal of the Royal Air Force, and was awarded the Order of Merit. He was the first R.A.F. officer to receive this honour, as it was not until the end of 1935 that the statutes of the Order were altered so that Air Force officers became eligible. He served in New Zealand for the usual five-year term, leaving for England in April, 1946. At a farewell state luncheon the Prime Minister, Mr. Fraser, voiced the feelings of all parties when he said that Sir Cyril Newall had fulfilled their very highest expectations; "in the darkest hours his faith had glowed brightly". In the birthday honours in June, 1946, he was raised to the peerage.

Newall married first in 1922, May Dulcie Weddell, who died in 1924. The following year he married, secondly, Olive Tennyson Foster, only daughter of Mrs. Francis Storer Eaton, of Boston, U.S.A., and they had one son and two daughters. He is succeeded in the peerage by his son, the Hon. Francis Storer Eaton Newall.

December 2, 1963.

Sir Alexander Newboult, K.B.E., C.M.G., M.C., who died on January 5, 1964, at his home in Cornwall, at the age of 68, had a distinguished career in the Malayan Civil Service beginning just after the end of the First World War and culminating in the chief secretaryship of the Federation of Malaya, which he held from the resumption of civil government after the defeat of Japan until his retirement.

He was Under Secretary to the Government in the former Federated Malay States during the period between 1939 and the end of the following year, when unreality vanished and the Japanese onslaught fell upon the peninsula. As Senior Liaison Officer between the Malayan governments and the United Kingdom Resident Minister in Singapore, he was on duty with Duff Cooper outside the peninsula when Singapore was captured. He was thus able to return to Malaya as one of the most senior members of the British military administration in 1945 after the Japanese surrender.

He was one of the principal people upon whom fell the heavy task of rehabilitation and in addition he was engaged in the protracted and difficult negotiations which led to the setting up of the Federation of Malaya. In these matters he showed himself to be an able and efficient administrator with the capacity for dealing with an unprecedented mass of work.

He will be remembered for what he did in these very difficult years and above all for the manner in which he assumed the even heavier responsibility of the High Commissionership when Sir Edward Gent was tragically killed in the summer of 1948. At this moment the communist insurrection had burst upon Malaya at a time when the country had barely recovered from the effects of the Japanese conquest.

Newboult had to assume the task of rallying the country and of leading it at a time of crisis, when resources were dangerously stretched, the new police force hardly trained, and there was a minimum of military force to cope with a very dangerous situation. He carried out this task well and was seen in many out of the way places, rallying the administration and encouraging planters. This was the culmination of his career, his heaviest task and for the way in which he discharged it he will be remembered as one of the foremost administrators in a great colonial service.

Alexander Theodore Newboult, elder son of the Rev. A. W. Newboult, was born on January 3, 1896, and educated at Oakwood and Kingswood Schools and Exeter College, Oxford. He served in the First World War first with the R.N.D., and then with the D.C.L.I., and was awarded the M.C. in 1918.

Newboult began his career in the Colonial Administrative Service in Malaya in 1920. After the Japanese invasion he went to Fiji as Colonial Secretary in 1942 and administered the government there the following year. He remained in that post until his return to Malaya where he served until his retirement in 1950.

In 1923 he married Nancy, daughter of the Rev. W. R. Gilbert, and they had two daughters.

January 6, 1964.

Mary Newcomb (Mrs. Alexander Higginson), the actress, who died on December 26, 1966, at the age of 69, began her career in her native country—the United States—but did her best work in London, where she made her first appearance in 1928.

Born in Massachusetts on August 20, 1897, she went on the stage in 1918 but was unknown in London when 10 years later she and Crane Wilbur, the American actor, played the only two parts in a drama adapted from the French of Louis Verneuil, *Jealousy*. Her performance in this might have been described as an exhibition bout of acting, for the man, whose part was afterwards taken over by Godfrey Tearle, was required to be merely a sparring partner for the woman. Audiences were impressed. She was, they felt, a "heavyweight", and, judging by this first bout, already in the championship class.

They thought as highly of her in the second part she took in London, that of a "Lady of the Camellias" with, in this version, a Scottish student played by Leslie Banks for her "Armand" in a piece with a titled borrowed from Thomas Carlyle, *The Infinite Shoeblack*. She had now in 1929, in spite of the failure of her third play, *Emma Hamilton*, a considerable reputation as a dramatic actress, but nothing that she did thenceforward quite lived up to it, and so, as she came to act less often, it receded into the past.

She was Portia to Ernest Milton's Shylock at the St. James's in 1932 and she held her own with Marie Tempest and Owen Nares in the strong cast of Rachel Crothers's comedy *When Ladies Meet*. But neither in Shakespeare nor in Shaw did she make an unqualified success at the Old Vic, where she was leading lady of the company during the 1934–35 season. In Shakespeare she came nearest to it when playing Beatrice to Maurice Evans's Benedick. In Shaw something was missing both from her Saint Joan, a part in which she was Dame Sybil Thorndike's immediate successor on the London stage, and from her Major Barbara, though the author rehearsed her and helped to mould her performance in both plays.

On the outbreak of the Second World War she formed the Mary Newcomb Players' Mobile Theatre for the entertainment of the Forces under Southern Command, and in 1943 their production of Eugene O'Neill's *Days without End*, in which she herself appeared, was taken to London and afterwards on a tour of Miners' Welfare Halls in South Wales. She toured western Europe for E.N.S.A. in her old success *Jealousy* during the last months of the war.

After the war she became president of the Dorset Drama League and chairman of the Dorset Music Society—her playing of the piano on stage had been a feature of her performance in *Jealousy*.

She was married twice: first to Mr. Robert Edeson, secondly to Mr. Alexander H. Higginson, of the firm of Higginson and Co. of Lombard Street, who was at one time Master of Fox Hounds in Dorset.

December 29, 1966.

Sir Frank Newsam, G.C.B., K.B.E., C.V.O., M.C., Permanent Under-Secretary of State, Home Office, from 1948 to 1957, died on April 25, 1964, at the age of 70.

Newsam's name will be remembered by the Police Service, in which he took a close interest, not least for his efforts which secured the establishment in its present home of the National Police College, of which he was for several years chairman of the board of governors. The Channel Islands will link his name with their postwar constitutional developments. But penal reform was his primary and continuing interest—understandably so in one who for nine years carried the appalling responsibility of advising the Home Secretary in the exercise of the prerogative of mercy in capital cases. Developments in the administration of prisons and borstals, advances in the fields of probation and children's services, and in the scientific study of delinquency—these are but a few of the causes which owe much to his drive and persuasive support.

Frank Aubrey Newsam, the son of William Elias Newsam, of Barbados, was born on November 13, 1893, and educated at Harrison College, Barbados, and St. John's College, Oxford. He served in the Army in the First World War, winning an M.C. and being mentioned in dispatches.

A MASTER AT HARROW

On demobilization he taught Classics at Harrow under Dr. Ford, later Dean of York, before entering the Civil Service in 1920. He quickly made his mark in the Home Office, where, after a period as Private Secretary with Sir John Anderson (Lord Waverley), he served as Principal Private Secretary to the Home Secretary from 1927 to 1933. During those six years the Home Secretaries included men of different parties and of widely different qualities and capacities—Sir W. Joynson-Hicks (later Lord Brentford). J. R. Clynes, Sir Herbert Samuel (later Lord Samuel), and Sir John Gilmour.

It was in that period that Newsam's remarkable qualities became increasingly apparent. With the departure of Sir John Anderson for Bengal and the arrival of Sir Russell Scott in the spring of 1932 Newsam was in an exceptional position, for there was nobody in the Home Office to rival his long political experience and he was in effect the right hand of Sir Russell Scott. Promoted Assistant Secretary in 1933 he was in 1938 selected to be the Principal Officer in the South Eastern Civil Defence Region, who would be Chief of Staff to the Regional Commissioner in the event of war. He took up this post in 1939 but in 1940 was brought back to the Home Office as Assistant Under-Secretary of State concerned with security matters. He was promoted Deputy Under-Secretary of State in 1941 and held that post until he succeeded Sir Alexander Maxwell as Permanent Under-Secretary of State in 1948. One of his little known activities during the war was concerned with planning the restoration of the economy of the Channel Islands against their liberation from German occupation.

Newsam was a man of outstanding gifts which could have taken him to the top in politics, at the Bar or in the business world. Nobody could be quicker at mastering a brief or at getting at the heart of a problem. At the conference table, whether it was a meeting of departmental representatives concerned with action to be taken in a national emergency, a meeting with local authority representatives on a contentious matter, or a meeting of the State Management Districts Council which advised the Home and Scottish Secretaries on the State Management Schemes in Northern England and Scotland, he shone. With his ingenious and quick mind and his remarkable gifts for lucid exposition and persuasion he was a superb "conferencier"; he could secure agreement and the right conclusion.

SUPERB IN CRISIS

In a crisis he was superb; he was a strong man and never afraid to take a decision; he saw what wanted doing and where necessary never hesitated to take executive action. He was a leader who worked as the head of a team. He had that prime quality of leadership the ability to choose men. Once he had tried and tested he trusted them and gave them their chances. There are many in responsible positions today who owe him a great debt for the opportunities he gave them of showing their qualities and capacities. He was loyal to those who worked with him, and stood by them. He was so proud of the Home Office that it was said of him that he was wedded to it; he took a very personal interest in the social and sporting activities of the staff. But his devotion to, and interest in, the department encouraged similar feelings in others, and nothing gave him greater pleasure than to see assuming greater responsibilities a new generation of men and women for whom the Home Office and its many and varied duties for law and order would mean as much as they had meant to him.

He married in 1927 Jean, daughter of James McAuslin.

April 27, 1964.

Algernon Newton, R.A., who died on May 21, 1968, at the age of 88, was a painter of quiet distinction whose work was marked by a very personal handwriting. Though the ultimate source of his style is undoubtedly to be found in Canaletto, he was no mere copyist, but rather a man who, after long exploration and meditation, found that a tight, pseudoliteral handling was best suited to his temperament. Working in a highly experimental age, he refused to be side-tracked by modern theories. Having decided on his course he kept to it, and produced a body of work consistently high in quality and individual in manner.

Born on February 23, 1880, at Hampstead, Newton was educated at Farnborough School and Clare College, Cambridge. The desire to paint was already upon him, however, so he did not proceed to a degree. After two years under Frank Calderon and six months at the Slade School he began to paint independently, first of all in London for a year, and then in other parts of the country, notably Cornwall.

In 1918 Newton settled in London, spending some two years in intensive study at the National Gallery; his work began to attract the attention of the critics. His paintings were acquired by the Tate Gallery and public collections in Liverpool, Birmingham, Brighton, Hull, Pietermaritzburg and Minneapolis, and by the National Galleries of Victoria and New South Wales. He was one of the artists chosen to collaborate in the decoration of the Queen Mary; he was much in demand as a portraitist of country houses (and especially Georgian houses, to which his style was admirably suited); and in 1936 he became A.R.A., in 1943 R.A. He was also a member of the International Society of Sculptors, Painters and Gravers.

Newton's work was landscape of a special kind, chiefly industrial townscape. He could take the most forbidding canal or group of factory buildings, and, without romanticizing or shrinking any detail, create a poetic and restful composition out of it.

His handling was dry and precise, showing no brush-marks. His palette was restrained, and he worked with the definite idea that pictures, being wall-decorations, should never vociferate, but should take their places quietly in the general scheme. His colour had a mellow, golden quality, and this, like his scrupulously drawn detail, he no doubt learnt from his master, Canaletto. Newton never did *premier coup* painting, but worked up his compositions in the studio from pencil sketches, tone notations in words or figures, and occasionally photographs, made on the spot.

May 22, 1968.

Ngo Dinh Diem, as ruler of South Vietnam from 1954 until the *coup d'état* in which he was killed on November 2, 1963, at the age of 62, was a typical and tragic example of the conflict between East Asian and western civilization.

A bitterly anti-French nationalist, exiled for a time in the United States, he was a devout Roman Catholic, a convinced anti-communist and yet a modernizer of his country. All this, even the nationalism, was the side he presented to the west. But there was the other side—the traditional Confucianist who saw loyalties in a Confucian way, who upheld the Mandarin traditions in which he had been brought up, who believed that moral instruction and political tutelage were necessary before democracy of any kind could be introduced, and who found criticism the seeds of treason.

He was energetic and devoted, fiercely independent of the Americans who had put him into power, incorruptible in a system where corruption was all too often accepted, but ruined by his willingness to listen only to the views of a limited and trusted clique of personal followers. Seeing himself as an exemplar of Confucian principle, he failed to impart to his administration any positive sense of purpose. Yet this short, reserved bachelor was an impressive figure, for all his failure ever to win any popular following. He alienated the intellectuals by his refusal to allow any criticism. He alienated officialdom by promotions based on personal favouritism. He exercised no effective control over lower grade Government officials whose exactions on the peasants often made them responsive to communist leadership.

He had shown great tenacity in his early days as Prime Minister in suppressing the independent power of the Cao Dai and Hoa Hao private armies and in overcoming the private kingdom of a lucrative underworld sustained by the Binh Xuyen gangsters. He was also active in resettling the refugees who came from the north at the time of partition. But as time passed and a new rebellion spread, led by communist guerrillas and sustained from the north, Ngo Dinh Diem's unwillingness to listen to advice and his refusal to compromise isolated him more and more.

Diem was born on January 3, 1901, in Hué, the old imperial capital, the third of six sons of Ngo Dinh Kha, a Minister of the Emperor Thanh Thai. He followed his father in Government service and soon found himself in conflict with the French.

He first came to power at American instigation just before the agreement was signed in Geneva terminating the war in 1954. The seeds of future conflict were sown when Diem, pleading that his Government had not signed the agreements, refused to act on the declaration of the conference providing for consultations with the communist Government in the north to be followed by elections.

This successful obstinacy also brought him victory in his conflict with the absent Emperor Bao Dai in 1955. He refused to go to France to see the Emperor and organized an assembly of revolutionary forces which declared Bao Dai deposed. Bao Dai responded by dismissing Diem, saying that "police methods and personal dictatorship must be brought to an end", but Diem simply stayed put and organized a referendum which duly gave him a 98 per cent vote as President of a republic in October, 1955.

Diem's asceticism, his determined suppression of gambling, opium-smoking and prostitution cleared him of any charge of personal gain from his rule. He was a man convinced that he and he alone could save his country. Though elections of various kinds were held they were never intended to do more than confirm his authority; latterly they had been based on a Government-selected list of candidates. Much worse than this shadow of democratic rule was Diem's ruthlessness in suppressing opposition.

Diem survived a *coup d'état* in November, 1960, when his palace was surrounded and Saigon brought under rebel control for a day before loyal troops arrived from the countryside. Again in 1962 aircraft machine-gunned his palace. The final crisis developed over his treatment of the Buddhists. An incident arose in Hué over the refusal to allow the Buddhists to fly their own flag during ceremonies at Hué in May, 1963. Troops fired on the assembly and there followed macabre incidents when Buddhists burned themselves alive in protest.

November 6, 1963.

Ngo Dinh Nhu, younger brother of President Ngo Dinh Diem, also lost his life in the South Vietnam *coup d'état* on November 2, 1963.

Until his part in the suppression of the Buddhists brought him to international attention in the previous few months Ngo Dinh Nhu's role in the Government of his elder brother was never very public. But it was known well enough to all those who came in conflict with the regime or found themselves accused of disloyalty, whether they were workers, students, peasants, or discontented members of the professional classes of Saigon. Ngo Dinh Nhu's main activity was to organize the mass movement known as the National Revolutionary Movement, at the core of which was a kind of secret society, the Can Lao.

This body acted as a secret security organization, reporting on disloyalty and effectively controlling the police in their political role. Nhu also used the trade union organization as a political weapon of control, and if ever trouble needed armed suppression, on any anti-communist pretext, he had at his disposal special forces which, it was recently revealed, were paid for through American intelligence sources.

Ngo Dinh Nhu, born in 1911, was a product

of a French education who saw himself as an intellectual and political philosopher. While a student in France in the 1930s he was attracted by the personalist philosophy associated with the late Emmanuel Mounier.

Described as political adviser to the President, he was thought to command more actual power through his control of various special forces. His wife was also active politically as a member of the National Assembly and a leader of the women's movement.

Ngo Dinh Nhu was content to play a role in the background, holding the strings of power, yet believing himself to be a true interpreter of a political philosophy for Vietnam. He was given to intrigue, but could be openly ruthless when necessary.

November 6, 1963.

Sir Harold Nicolson, K.C.V.O., C.M.G., who brought to a varied and notably distinguished career in literature and diplomacy and to a somewhat less impressive career in politics an individual grace of style and an uncommonly wide and much admired cultivation of mind, died on May 1, 1968, at his home in Kent at the age of 81.

Nowhere was this style and cultivation more truly reflected than in the two volumes (volume three is coming out later in 1968) of his diaries and letters, edited with skill and candour by his son Nigel, which appeared in 1966 and 1967. Full of witty and intimate pictures of the famous and immediate comments on the great events of his time, they were very much more than a record of classy hobnobbings, for few excelled Nicolson in the art of self-revelation and no lesser diarist could have made so moving and fascinating a thing of the relationship between himself and his wife, Vita Sackville-West, and his sons.

Favoured by fortune at the outset of life, the son of one of Britain's ablest and most travelled ambassadors during the remote and golden years before 1914, he entered upon his training at the Foreign Office with every advantage which an intimate knowledge of the world of diplomacy and his own intellectual endowments offered. Nicolson spent 20 years in the Diplomatic Service and for the rest of his life exhibited a singularly balanced and penetrating judgment on foreign affairs. But both the climate of diplomacy during those years, rougher and rawer than the climate his father had known, and his own temperament, which leaned always towards a speculative detachment, stood in the way of his becoming a successful public figure, and it was as an author of literary and historical biographies that he came most truly into his own. No writer in the genre of biography which Nicolson favoured was more agreeable to read. If at times what lay beneath his urbanity of style seemed a little thin, the impression was soon lost in surrender to an astonishing ease and charm.

Born on November 21, 1886, in Teheran, the son of the British Minister there, Sir Arthur Nicolson, afterwards Lord Carnock (whose life he was to write), Harold George Nicolson passed his early years in Persia, Hungary, Bulgaria, and Morocco. This childhood experience of foreign countries, of Persia most of all, he turned afterwards to excellent literary advantage; few of his experiences, indeed, were wasted upon Nicolson as author or as the most graceful of journalists. He was educated at Wellington and at Balliol College, Oxford, and in 1909 entered the Foreign Office, serving in Madrid and Constantinople before returning to the Foreign Office in 1914. In 1919 he was appointed a member of the British delegation to the Peace Conference, and this experience proved to be one of the most formative and most fruitful of his career both as a student of diplomacy and as a writer. Created a C.M.G. in the following year, he was appointed Counsellor to the Legation at Teheran in 1925 and to the Berlin Embassy in 1927.

He retired from the Diplomatic Service in 1929 and settled down to a busy and purposeful activity as author, lecturer, and journalist. He married in 1913 the Hon. Victoria Mary Sackville-West, who was to achieve high distinction as poet and novelist. He had earned a literary reputation while still a professional diplomatist. His study of Verlaine, published in 1921, exhibited a felicitous critical talent. Two years later came a volume on Tennyson, not quite so happy a piece of work, but in which once again it was the poetry that chiefly engaged him. Then followed a spirited *Byron, the Last Journey* and a judicious *Swinburne* in the "English Man of Letters" series, and in 1927 a most entertaining volume, *Some People*, consisting of nine sketches rendered in a confidential vein of autobiography and with the liveliest skill in observation. A year later he produced an easy on *The Development of English Biography*, and in 1930, the first fruits of his ampler leisure, his Life of Lord Carnock.

It is without question a first-rate piece of work, at once a biographical portrait that combines intimacy with detachment and a history of the diplomatic play of events and personalities leading up to the disaster of 1914 which is done with conspicuous balance and lucidity. The two volumes with which Nicolson rounded off the study in diplomacy begun in the life of his father are in a not dissimilar vein. *Peacemaking, 1919*, in which he prefaced his diary of the time, presented as an example of youthful error, by a brilliantly sustained analytical commentary, appeared in 1933; *Curzon: The Last Phase*, a tribute in a mood of affectionate irony, in the year following.

Though one later work possibly ranks as high as literature and won attention on an altogether wider scale, this trilogy represents Nicolson's most important achievement as a writer. But there was little he wrote that lacked value or failed to please. A selected catalogue of his books in later years must make mention of *Helen's Tower* (1937), in which the principal subject was the first Marquess of Dufferin, his uncle; an excellent little volume on *Diplomacy* in the Home University Library and a sane and temperate Penguin, *Why Britain is at War*, both belonging to the year 1939; *The Desire to Please* (1943), a study of Hamilton Rowan (his great-great-grandfather) and the United Irishmen; and *The Congress of Vienna: a Study in Allied Unity, 1812–1822* (1946).

As a politician Nicolson enjoyed not only the advantages of his experience and stored knowledge but unexaggerated independence of mind and much personal courage. He spoke well on the platform and in the House of Commons and was a practised and skilful broadcaster of the more intimate variety. But his habit of detachment—his delicately refined intellectual curiosity—left too little scope for the arts of the practical politician. In 1931 he stood unsuccessfully for the United Universities as a candidate for Sir Oswald Mosley's New Party. Four years later he was returned as National Labour M.P. for West Leicester and held that seat until the election of 1945. An earnest and at times powerful critic of the policy of appeasement towards Germany, he displayed courage and clarity of vision at the time of the Munich agreement.

He took an ironic view of Ramsay MacDonald, whose P.P.S. he once declined to be. In 1940 he was made Parliamentary Secretary to the Ministry of Information, but in the following year was appointed a Governor of the B.B.C. and permitted to retain his seat in the House. He contested North Croydon for Labour at a by-election in 1948, having formally joined the Labour Party in the previous year, and fought a losing fight almost as a curious and disinterested spectator of the vagaries of party conflict.

He was disappointed in his political ambitions but it is doubtful if his was ever the temperament of the politician. The judgment that he was not formidable enough for politics is probably a true one. His experience at the much shot-at Ministry of Information was not entirely happy.

Later in that year he was entrusted by the King with the writing of the official biography of George V and the history of his reign. The book appeared in 1952, three years after a biography of Benjamin Constant that had all the balance and the readableness to be expected of him. As an achievement in what has been called the tricky art of royal biography, *King George V: His life and Reign* is a triumph.

HOW MONARCHY WORKS

Drawing upon the royal archives at Windsor, Nicolson produced a full length, human portrait and a study of the workings of the British monarchy. The book won golden opinions, and deserved them. In the following year Nicolson became K.C.V.O.

He had an enviable capacity for work. In 1954 he published *The Evolution of Diplomatic Method*, based upon the Chichele lectures at Oxford delivered in the previous autumn, in which he exercised gifts of connoisseurship to brilliant advantage, and next year, in *Good Behaviour*, a study of types of "Civility" (that is, of civilized behaviour through the ages), proved no less stimulating as connoisseur in that capacity also. Nicolson had the habit of making an index of his own on the fly-leaf of all the books he added to his library and, thanks to the inclusion of a section under the heading of "Manners", the book is, among other things, an anthology of quotations of the most felicitous kind. His later published works included *The Age of Reason 1700–1789*; *Journey to Java*; *Monarchy*; and *Saint-Beuve*. In 1956 he stood for the Chair of Poetry at Oxford and in a controversial and keenly contested election won 192 votes. W. H. Auden, who came top, received 216.

A Fellow of the Royal Society of Literature and an honorary fellow of Balliol, Nicolson held honorary doctorates from the universities of Athens, Grenoble, Glasgow, Dublin, and Durham. He had been president of the Classical Association in 1950-51—and had delivered a notable presidential address—he was a trustee of the National Portrait Gallery, and from 1952 to 1957 he was chairman of the committee of the London Library. Always a friend of France, he was a Chevalier of the Legion of Honour.

For many years from 1939 he contributed "Marginal Comment" to the *Spectator*, casual, semi-topical essays of charm and skill: it was a much-admired feature.

His wife died in 1962. He is survived by his two sons, Benedict and Nigel.

May 2, 1968.

Ove Nielsen, secretary-general of the Inter-Governmental Maritime Consultative Organization, a specialised agency of the United Nations concerned with shipping engaged in international trade, died in London on November 20, 1961, at the age of 68. He was the first person to be appointed to this post in January, 1959, and directed I.M.C.O's activities from a small body with few staff to a growing international organization with increased responsibilities.

Ove Holger Nielsen was born in Copenhagen on February 26, 1893, and for most of his life was associated with ships and maritime matters. His father was a colonel in the Danish Army who devised the Nielsen method of artificial respiration which is used by the International Red Cross.

Ove Nielsen was educated at Ordrup Secondary School, the Copenhagen Navigation School, and the Technical University. He began his martime career at the age of 15, in sailing ships, when from 1908 to 1912 he was apprenticed on board two Danish training vessels.

He had held a master's certificate for many years, and served as an officer in sailing, steam and motor vessels. During the First World War he served in the Royal Danish Navy, having been gazetted as a lieutenant in 1917. Following his war service, he attended the Danish Polytechnic in Copenhagen.

Before his government service Nielsen worked with two private shipping concerns and with the State Icebreakers. In 1920 he was appointed as a nautical surveyor in the Danish Ministry of Commerce and Shipping and a year later as a ships inspector. In 1931 he was named as Secretary to the Minister of Commerce and Shipping, and became an Assistant Secretary in the Ministry during 1937. From 1945 to 1958, when he retired from the government service, he was Chief of the Shipping Department in the Ministry. From 1958 to his appointment as Secretary-General of I.M.C.O. he was associated with one of the largest private shipping enterprises in Scandinavia.

Nielsen was the chief of the secretariat to the Copenhagen Convention of 1958, much of whose work has now been taken over by I.M.C.O. He was chairman of the Danish Joint Maritime Board from 1937 to 1958 and a member of the Danish Merchant Navy Welfare Board from 1948 to 1958.

He was married, and before moving to London where I.M.C.O., has its headquarters, he lived in the Copenhagen suburb of Hellerup.

November 22, 1961.

Fleet Admiral Chester W. Nimitz, perhaps the greatest of the galaxy of talented flag officers produced by the American Navy during the Second World War, died on February 20, 1966, at the age of 80.

Although he had achieved flag rank only in June, 1938, 10 days after the devastating Japanese attack on Pearl Harbour on December 7, 1941, he was designated Commander-in-Chief, U.S. Pacific Fleet, by President Roosevelt. When on the last day of the year he hoisted his flag on board a submarine he was faced by a disastrous situation.

Not only was his country ill-prepared for war, but a large part of the American battle fleet, though fortunately not its aircraft carriers, had been destroyed or disabled; the capital ships of the embryo British Eastern Fleet had just been sunk off Malaya, and the survivors of that force, of the small American Asiatic Fleet originally based on Manila, and of the Dutch East Indies squadron together with some Australian warships, were soon to be almost completely wiped out in the Java Sea. Allied sea power had virtually disintegrated throughout the vast area for which Nimitz had assumed responsibility. The Japanese Navy, and especially its formidable carrier striking force, was supreme over the whole of the central and western Pacific, and was reaching down towards Australia in the south and Ceylon in the West.

But Nimitz quickly showed himself not only a resolute leader in adversity but a master of the organization of large naval forces, and a supremely successful strategist. Backed by Admiral F. J. King, the Chief of Naval Operations in Washington, in whose mind the Pacific war always held first place, and by the vast output of American industry, the American naval recovery was far more rapid than seemed possible at the close of 1941. It is true enough that Nimitz was aided in making his dispositions by virtually infallible intelligence derived from the breaking of the Japanese naval cypher; but he none the less accepted grave risks by sending two of his precious carriers thousands of miles from Pearl Harbour to meet an anticipated threat in the Coral Sea in May, 1942.

The resulting battle—the first between carriers in which the opposing ships never came within sight of each other—may be classed as a drawn fight; but the Japanese threat to New Guinea and northern Australia was eliminated. Almost exactly a month later, on June 4, the Americans won their decisive victory off Midway Island when four of the Japanese carriers were sunk and the rest of the invasion fleet intended for the seizure of the whole group of the Hawaiian islands withdrew.

If Coral Sea won Nimitz and his brilliant subordinates a breathing space, the battle of Midway transformed the whole strategic situation in a few hectic hours. Nor was Nimitz slow to take advantage of the change by assuming the offensive. From the beginning he had realized that only by the establishment of temporary advanced bases in the islands of the central and south Pacific, and by the organization of floating and mobile support and supply, could naval forces operate at the required distances from their home bases. It was also clear to him that the recovery of the lost territories could be achieved only by means of large-scale amphibious operations—always the most hazardous undertakings of war.

In August 1942, the first combined assault took place in the Solomon Islands, and in the months of very hard sea-air fighting that followed losses were heavy on both sides. At one moment, in October, 1942, Nimitz was left with only one carrier in the south Pacific, and she was considerably damaged. An appeal for help led to the British Victorious being sent out. The crisis was, however, surmounted and in November, 1943, Nimitz launched the first amphibious assault across the central Pacific—at the Japanese-held Gilbert Islands. This was soon followed by a succession of westward leaps organized, planned, and executed on the same pattern.

In the autumn of 1944 the climax came with the junction of Nimitz's central Pacific forces with those of General Douglas MacArthur from the south-west Pacific in the Philippine Sea, and the total defeat of the Japanese Navy in the battle of Leyte Gulf in October. Although from time to time units of Nimitz's fleet were detached to serve under General MacArthur the great majority remained under the Admiral's direct control throughout the campaign. For the final stages of the approach to the Japanese homeland the strategy favoured by Nimitz, to seize the islands of Okinawa and Iwo-Jima, was finally accepted. He moved his headquarters forward from Pearl Harbour to Guam and directed the vast naval forces allocated to those undertakings.

SUBMARINE SUCCESSES

Meanwhile Nimitz, himself a submarine specialist of long experience, had developed a steadily increasing offensive against Japanese merchant shipping. It was the submarine arm, fostered by him, which contributed the largest share to the blockade of Japan which, by August, 1945, had become virtually complete. At the signature of the Japanese surrender on board the U.S.S. Missouri on September 2, 1945, Nimitz represented the Government of the United States as well as his country's Army and Navy.

Apart from his outstanding gifts as a strategist and as organizer and trainer of naval combat and support forces, Nimitz won the respect and affection of sailors of all nationalities who came under his command. He was that rare person in any fighting service—a leader of commanding presence who was yet naturally and entirely modest. Whenever a British ship called at Pearl Harbour he found time to board her and, insisting that work was not to be interrupted, would walk round the decks informally, chatting to officers and men in the most winning and intimate manner. He was always most generous to the part played by the British Navy and other allied forces in his campaigns, marginal though that part was. When early in 1945 the British Pacific Fleet under Admiral Sir Bruce Fraser arrived to take part in the final phase of the war, the warmth of Nimitz's welcome was in marked contrast to the attitude of those American naval men who had not wished to see the White Ensign return to the Pacific.

Chester William Nimitz was born in Fredericksburg, Texas, on February 24, 1885, and joined the Naval Academy, Annapolis, in 1901. He graduated with distinction (seventh out of 114) in 1905, and first served in the Asiatic fleet based on Manila. Early in 1909 he joined the submarine branch, and in the same year was appointed to command the First Submarine Flotilla. He continued to serve in command of submarines, or in a tanker in which diesel engines had been experimentally installed, until August, 1917. In the latter capacity he was instrumental in adapting and modifying diesel engines for use in the United States Navy.

On his appointment as C.-in-C., Pacific Fleet, he was promoted Admiral, and when in December, 1944, Congress approved the introduction of the rank of Fleet Admiral he was one of the first officers nominated by the President to that rank. In November, 1945, his appointment as Chief of Naval Operations, in succession to Fleet Admiral E. J. King, was confirmed by the Senate for two years.

Having remained on continuous "active duty" in the Navy up to the time of his death Nimitz was frequently called in for consultation by Secretaries of the Navy and others concerned in defence problems. But his chief interest after completing his term of office as Chief of Naval Operations lay in the fields of education and international relations. From 1949 to 1954 he held the title of "Plebiscite Administrator Designate" for Kashmir. Although disagreement between the parties concerned prevented the plebiscite being held Nimitz's nomination was confirmed, and during this phase of his career he acted as roving "good-will ambassador" for the United Nations Organization, and made many speeches in explanation of its purposes and problems.

February 22, 1966.

Professor William Charles Wallace Nixon, C.B.E., died suddenly on February 9, 1966 in University College Hospital where he had been Professor of Obstetrics and Gynaecology for 20 years. He was 62. He will be mourned by men and women of different creeds and colour all over the world.

Nixon was born in November, 1903 in Malta, where his father was a professor of mathematics in the university, and was educated at Epsom College, completing his medical training at St. Mary's Hospital, London. At the early age of 31 he was appointed obstetric surgeon to this hospital, for which he always retained a deep affection. Soon afterwards he was appointed to Queen Charlotte's Hospital.

In 1935, however, he resigned these posts to become Professor of Obstetrics in Hongkong University. Just before the Second World War he returned to London and his hospital appointments now included the Soho Hospital for Women. In 1943 he went out to Turkey where he was Professor of Obstetrics at Istanbul University. Shortly after returning to England he succeeded Professor F. J. Browne as Professor of Obstetrics at University College Hospital.

Throughout his medical career William Nixon fought relentlessly for improvements in British maternity care. He was an outspoken critic of any deficiencies which he felt should be corrected. This was not easy for a man of his essential gentleness and sensitivity. It was his initiative which led to the British Prenatal Survey in 1958. This was a unique national study of maternity care which will have a most important influence on the planning of future obstetric services in this country. In his unit at University College Hospital he established a first class research department which is carrying out valuable studies into the factors that influence and control the course of labour. His unit has also established an international reputation for its special interest in the psychological problems of pregnancy and labour.

There have been striking advances in maternity care during recent years and Nixon has played a central part in their evolution.

He was very concerned about the present law related to abortion and he spoke out fearlessly in medical meetings about the need for its reform. He also wrote in the medical press about the need for increased support for medical services in the less developed areas of the Commonwealth. In London he was a most active member of the university and its many associated committees. Recently he had pleaded that the 12 London teaching hospitals should seek methods of pooling their resources, thereby establishing a more efficient use of personnel and equipment.

Besides his extensive knowledge of modern medicine his interests ranged widely over all the arts: he was a very literate and a widely travelled man. He was a wonderful ambassador for Britain in his capacity as an academician, a clinician and a most civilized and witty human being. Leading obstetricians from many countries expressed a particular anxiety to meet and talk with him again.

One of his many special qualities was that he understood what it meant to be a stranger, alone in London. Even as a very young man he befriended those who had just arrived.

VISITORS WELCOME

It was inevitable that most visitors to London went straight to his unit where a warm welcome always awaited them. To one particular American professor, London is William Nixon striding across Waterloo Bridge in the pouring rain exuding an intense enthusiasm about the river and all its associations.

In 1964, just after he had suffered a serious setback in health, he still felt it was his responsibility to give expert testimony in the High Court in the case of Dering versus Uris and Others. This case was concerned with the surgical treatment of prisoners in Auschwitz. During his evidence he defined a doctor's responsibility in terms of the Hippocratic oath. This was an oath to which he had adhered with complete consistency throughout his life as a doctor.

He died because he allowed himself too little time and gave too much to others. He loved all people and seemed to feel their pain. He possessed unique compassion and a mind truly free from bigotry of any kind.

February 11, 1966.

Professor Heinrich Nordhoff, who was appointed president of Volkswagen in 1948, and was also its managing director, died in Wolfsburg, west Germany, on April 12, 1968, at the age of 69. The building up and improving of Volkswagen cars under his patriarchal leadership is one of the great German post-war achievements. He is said on his appointment to have found the people's car a "poor thing, ugly and inefficient."

No man has wielded greater influence in the post-war motor industry—worldwide—than Heinz Nordhoff. And his influence sprang ironically enough from the decision of the British Occupation Forces in Germany immediately after the war when they offered him the opportunity to rebuild the Volkswagen factory. He took up his task in January, 1948, and when in September, 1949, the British occupation authorities handed the plant over to the Federal German Government, Nordhoff was invited to continue his activity and appointed managing director.

ENIGMATIC

But Nordhoff was perhaps the most enigmatic of motor industrialists, or indeed of any industrial captains—a man who combined natural talent for administration and far sighted planning with deep rooted kindness and understanding of people. He was never deflected from his policies, resisted many powerful pressures from experts within his own company and outside, yet, as we have seen in recent years, he shrewdly foresaw that like the Model "T" Ford his ubiquitous "Beetle" could not live on perpetuating its incredible success into infinity—so gradually the Volkswagen range of cars has been extended and already a complete replacement for the Beetle is rumoured to be well advanced. Nordhoff's personal charm could be almost captivating, combining an eloquent ability to discuss fine art, music, hunting or antiques (he was a collector of Oriental antiquities and firearms) with perspicacious observations on every aspect of car making, the motor industry worldwide, automation in production, technical design, traffic problems and human problems in relation to the whole world of motoring.

The Nordhoff authority was never disputed from the moment he took over the VW plant

His was found to be a personality of enormous influence and persuasive power. He had an ability of not merely convincing business associates of his own convictions but inspiring them to share his incredible enthusiasm. Yet Nordhoff never failed to exercise his authority and his strongest argument was quoted as: "I see to it that the facts are on my side. I would rather prove than state."

From top to bottom of his Wolfsburg empire Nordhoff managed to project peace and self control. Wolfsburg itself seemed to reflect his own peaceful neat personality. In his leisure hours there was no gap between the businessman and the private individual. He was an expert photographer and an artist of considerable talent, while one writer close to him said he thought the Nordhoff success could only be explained by the "complete harmony" of his personality. "Only a man who is so balanced, so profoundly free, could draw the right consequences from his natural gifts, his energy and assiduity."

During the time he ran Volkswagen he established it as west Germany's premier exporter. But Nordhoff had rows with the Government—in particular, defying an order from Dr. Erhard not to put his prices up. In 1966 Bonn put Dr. Josef Rust on the board with orders to get a suitable successor lined up and persuade Professor Nordhoff to retire.

AMERICAN METHODS

Nordhoff was to have retired at the end of 1968.

Nordhoff (who was born in Hildesheim on January 6, 1899) joined the Adam Opel Automobile Company in 1929 after studying engineering and serving an apprenticeship. He studied American production and sales methods in the United States and in 1963 was made a director of Opel, which was controlled by General Motors. After the United States entered the war in 1942 the Opel plant at Brandenburg was converted to military production with Nordhoff as its managing director. He never joined the Nazi Party, but he was classed by United States authorities after the war as a Nazi-affiliated industrialist and therefore unemployable. He moved to the British zone and worked as a consulting engineer in Hamburg until early in 1948.

When the policy of deindustrializing Germany was abandoned in 1948 the British occupation authorities asked Nordhoff to take charge of the rehabilitation of the Volkswagen factory.

BEETLE KEPT

By the end of 1949, when authority over the Volkswagen enterprise was turned over to the new state of west Germany, production of the beetle-shaped "people's car" had risen to 4,500 a month. Nordhoff kept the beetle shape in disregard of advisers who said it was out of date. In January 1968, he told Volkswagen dealers: "I am completely certain that our beetle will be built for a very long time to come." By the end of 1967 the giant of the German vehicle-making industry had turned out 13,500,000 cars.

April 13, 1968.

Lord Normanbrook, P.C., G.C.B., who was Secretary of the Cabinet from 1947 to 1962, died on June 15, 1967, at his London home at the age of 65. He had been chairman of the B.B.C. since 1964.

Norman Craven Brook, first Baron Normanbrook, of Chelsea, in the County of London, was born in Bristol in April, 1902, the son of an inspector of schools. He went to Wolverhampton School and won a Classical Scholarship at Wadham College, Oxford. Here he was soon recognized as a fine scholar and a man of outstanding abilities and obtained a first in Mods, and a second in Lit. Hum. Brook took third place in the examination for the Home Civil Service in 1925 and was appointed to the Home Office.

During the next 13 years (1925 to 1938) he had a varied experience in that Department, serving in the Aliens Division, the Children's Branch, as Assistant Private Secretary to two Home Secretaries (Sir Herbert Samuel—later Viscount Samuel—and Mr. Oliver Stanley), in the Criminal Division and finally as Assistant Secretary in charge of the Division dealing with civil emergencies, War Book and Defence Regulations. He is best remembered in the Home Office for the work which he did on war planning, the War Book and Defence Regulations. This was a difficult task of coordination which covered all Whitehall and it was done with all Brook's customary thoroughness and stood up well to the test of war.

Norman Brook was a man of immense authority. The first impression was of size, with a head that was large even for such a heavy frame, and a calm gaze from heavy-lidded eyes. Then came the quiet, rather slow voice. At the start it might seem casual, even lethargic. But this illusion was dispelled as his voice took on a cutting edge and he shaped the words on which he wished to pivot his thought. And whether he was given information, or advice, or instructions, his thinking was dominated by the need for good order in public affairs. Good order was also the characteristic of his personal work—the written word pared down to the minimum; the elegant, even hand; the clear desk; scrupulously punctual; responsive to the call of urgency, but never confused, never hurried.

Without imposing such good order on himself he could hardly have become the outstanding exponent of public administration in his time. And it was an imposition for there was much of the artist in the man, and his natural disposition was sensitive, warm, and even impulsive. There was in many ways a conflict between his character and the principle of good order on which he based his conduct of public business. But it was a conflict in which he always had the upper hand, and it is possible that this inner tension was the secret of his powerful personality.

WAR PREPARATIONS

From his earliest days in the Home Office, Brook was regarded by his contemporaries as certain to rise to the top. Among those who shared this view was Sir John Anderson (later Viscount Waverley), who was Permanent Under Secretary of State at the Home Office from 1922 until 1932, when he was appointed Governor of Bengal.

In 1938, soon after he returned to this country from India, Sir John Anderson accepted an invitation to join Neville Chamberlain's Cabinet as Lord Privy Seal. This carried with it responsibility for air raid precautions and for keying up the organization and arrangements. This was a task of first importance in our war preparation. Sir John appointed Brook as his Principal Private Secretary.

For the next 24 years—that is, until his retirement in 1962—Brook was employed in a succession of key posts at the centre of government. From 1938 to 1942 he served continuously with Sir John Anderson. He continued to serve as his Principal Private Secretary when Sir John exchanged offices with Sir Samuel Hoare (Viscount Templewood), and became Home Secretary on the outbreak of war. This arrangement had been decided on before the outbreak of war in order to enable the air raid precautions work to be fully integrated with the wider responsibilities of the Home Secretary.

In 1940, when Sir John Anderson became Lord President of the Council, Brook accompanied him as his Personal Assistant. In this capacity he carried out duties of a special character and of great importance. Sir John was in effect the Minister in charge of the home front and the Lord President's Committee, over which he presided, became the focus for discussion and decision on civil matters which did not need to be brought to the War Cabinet, or which needed to be predigested before being so submitted. Sir John carried out these duties with a very small staff of which Brook was the head. The partnership was a happy and successful one and there was the closest understanding and sympathy between the two men which continued throughout their lives.

In 1942, on the retirement of Sir Rupert Howorth, Brook became Deputy Secretary of the War Cabinet. It was soon evident that he excelled in this type of work. It was in this capacity that he first served closely with Sir Winston Churchill, then Prime Minister.

RECONSTRUCTION WORK

In 1943 the Prime Minister decided that a stronger impetus should be given to the work of reconstruction, and appointed Lord Woolton to be Minister of Reconstruction. Brook was appointed as his Permanent Secretary and continued in this capacity until 1945.

In 1945 Sir Edward Bridges, who had been Secretary of the War Cabinet since 1938, was appointed Secretary to the Treasury but was asked to continue for the time being as Secretary of the Cabinet. Brook was recalled to the Cabinet Office and appointed as additional Secretary to the Cabinet.

This dual arrangement did not last long. The volume of work at the Treasury made it impossible for one man to be both Secretary of the Treasury and Secretary of the Cabinet, so in 1947 he became the titular as well as the actual Secretary of the Cabinet, a post which he continued to hold until his retirement in 1962.

In 1956, when Sir Edward Bridges retired

from the public service, two Joint Secretaries of the Treasury were appointed in his place. One Joint Secretary, Sir Roger Makins (later Sir Frank Lee) was in charge of the side of the office controlling finance and expenditure, while the other was in charge of administration and personnel questions. Brook held this latter post in conjunction with the post of Secretary of the Cabinet. He also became the official Head of the Civil Service.

During this long period of 16 years—1947 to 1962—he served four Prime Ministers as Secretary of the Cabinet: Mr. (later Earl) Attlee, Sir Winston Churchill, Sir Anthony Eden (later Earl Avon), and Mr. Macmillan. It is indeed remarkable that during the period since the post of Secretary of the Cabinet was created in December, 1916, up to 1962, there had been only three holders of this very strenuous post.

Given the nature of his duties, not much is known publicly about the work done by the Secretary of the Cabinet. But it is evident that all the Prime Ministers in these 16 years relied greatly on the help and support which they received from Brook. Shortly before the end of the Labour Government it was announced officially that he would before long be leaving the Cabinet Office and would be taking up the most senior post of Second Secretary to the Treasury. This looked like a translation devised to facilitate his appointment to the post of Secretary to the Treasury when the holder of that post retired. But when Sir Winston Churchill again became Prime Minister he would have none of it, and the arrangement was cancelled.

Then again, when the Prime Minister of the day has made an official journey overseas, in recent years he has very often been accompanied by Brook. It is a fair inference from this that during his period as Secretary of the Cabinet Brook acted as Chef de Cabinet to Prime Ministers to a greater extent than was the practice in earlier regimes.

He acted as secretary to no fewer than 11 full-scale conferences of Commonwealth Prime Ministers held in London between 1946 and 1962. He was well known and much trusted in Commonwealth circles. In 1948 he visited Canada, Australia, and New Zealand on a special mission relating to the forthcoming constitutional changes in India. And in 1949 he again visited Canada as part of the discussions with Commonwealth countries as to the formula whereby India, while becoming a Republic, could remain in the Commonwealth.

Most of his career was thus spent in posts of the highest responsibility at the centre of the government machine. The type of work entailed in such a post differs from that falling on those who have perhaps a clearer measure of responsibility, but in a much more closely defined field. The Secretary of the Cabinet has to be ready to deal with the great variety of subjects, each of which is probably of the highest urgency when it arises. He must have a cool head, a clear brain and be able to piece together at short notice a reliable and accurate account of what is happening and what is at stake. He has also to deal with a large number of very senior people, Ministers and civil servants. He must secure and hold their confidence, and he will also have a hand in the processes of discussion and persuasion which enable governments to come to right decisions. All these qualities Brook had to a remarkable degree. He was a tireless worker of extreme thoroughness and patience, and endowed with massive practical sense.

It is asking a lot of any man to hold a post such as that of Secretary of the Cabinet for so long a period, and for the last six years of that period to hold it in conjunction with the Joint Secretaryship of the Treasury, an arrangement discontinued on his retirement.

It is a remarkable tribute to Brook that at the end of his official career he had not only the highest reputation as an administrator but also was so greatly liked and trusted by all his colleagues.

In retirement he was again in the news during the Profumo affair of 1963. Normanbrook had spoken to Mr. Profumo, then Secretary of State for War, in August, 1961, and suggested that he should be careful in his dealings with Stephen Ward, saying that there were indications that Ward might be interested in picking up scraps of information and passing them on to Captain Ivanov, then serving at the Russian Embassy. In his report on the affair Lord Denning stated that it had been suggested that Normanbrook here went beyond his province and that he ought to have reported to the Prime Minister, Mr. Macmillan; Lord Denning did not find this point well founded. Subsequently Normanbrook was appointed to the new standing commission on security set up by Sir Alec Douglas-Home.

In 1964 Normanbrook was appointed chairman of the B.B.C., taking up the post at a time when the corporation was faced with some financial difficulties and also with difficulties over policy. He said on his appointment that he did not regard himself as a Government strong man.

In the course of a lunchtime lecture in December, 1965, in the Concert Hall of Broadcasting House on the functions of the B.B.C. Governors, he remarked that his decision "not to renew an invitation" to Mr. Ian Smith to appear in a television programme in October was not an instance of outside intervention but editorial control at the highest level.

His work did not allow him much time for private activities. But he was fond of travel. He enjoyed a game of golf, and he also indulged at home in a craft or hobby which can only be described in literal terms as "cabinet making". He married in 1929 Ida Mary Goshawk, who survives him.

Many honours fell to him. He was made C.B. in 1942, K.C.B. in 1946, promoted to G.C.B. in 1951 and raised to the peerage in 1963. He was also appointed a Privy Councillor in 1953 on the occasion of the Coronation. He was made an Honorary Fellow of Wadham College in 1949. He was also an Honorary LL.D. of Bristol, Birmingham, and Cambridge Universities and an Honorary D.C.L. of Oxford University.

June 16, 1967.

Admiral Sir Dudley North, G.C.V.O., C.B., C.S.I., C.M.G., who died on May 15, 1961, at the age of 79, is best remembered as the officer whose treatment in the Second World War provided a close parallel to that meted out to the unfortunate Admiral Byng in the eighteenth century. Both were made the scapegoats for disasters which resulted from mismanagement in London. North was not, indeed, shot "pour encourager les autres" but merely suffered the manifest deep disgrace of being relieved of his command in war and soon afterwards placed on the retired list, although the stain on his reputation was removed by Mr. Macmillan in 1957.

He served with distinction as commander and admiral respectively in both the world wars. Between them, he had unrivalled experience as aide-de-camp or equerry to members of the Royal Family on their tours to the Dominions and foreign countries. He took part in all the Empire cruises made by the Duke of Windsor when Prince of Wales. He also accompanied the Duke of Connaught to India, and King George VI and Queen Elizabeth to Canada and the United States. His wide knowledge of other countries and their customs, and his capacity as an organizer, were of great value on these missions. In the intervals between them he pursued his naval career with diligence and held both command and staff appointments. One of the last of many foreign decorations awarded him was the United States Legion of Merit, degree of Commander, for his service as Flag Officer-in-Charge, Great Yarmouth, to the United States Army Air Force in connexion with the organization of the air-sea rescue system and in establishing hospital facilities for the injured.

Dudley Burton Napier North, the son of Colonel Roger North, Royal Artillery, was born on November 25, 1881. He was in the Britannia as a naval cadet from January, 1896, to August, 1897. His midshipman's time up to March, 1901, was spent in the Jupiter and Illustrious. As a sub-lieutenant in 1902–1903 he was in the cruiser Minerva and the destroyer Charger. From 1903 to 1914 he was a lieutenant in the cruisers Rainbow, Donegal, Powerful (flagship in Australia), and New Zealand (in which he made the world cruise in 1913 with Captain Lionel Halsey). During the 1914–18 War he served in the New Zealand up to December, 1916, taking part in the three principal North Sea actions of Heligoland (1914), the Dogger Bank (1915), and Jutland (1916). When Captain Halsey transferred to the Admiralty as Fourth Sea Lord and later Third Sea Lord, North accompanied him as Naval Assistant, continuing in that post until September, 1918, when he resumed sea service as commander of the Australia, in which Rear-Admiral Halsey hoisted his flag. For war service afloat and at the Admiralty he was made C.M.G. in June, 1919.

ROYAL EQUERRY

During the next three years, he took part in the overseas tours of the Duke of Windsor, then Prince of Wales, in the battle-cruisers Renown and Repulse, first as Naval A.D.C. and later as Extra Equerry. On his return from Canada in December, 1919, he was made

M.V.O.; on the conclusion of the Australasian tour in October, 1920, he was promoted C.V.O.; and after the tour to India and Japan, in June, 1922, he was made a C.S.I. He also served as Extra Equerry to the Duke of Connaught during his Indian tour in 1920 to 1921. He had been promoted to captain in December, 1919.

From 1922 to 1924 he commanded the cruisers Caledon, Champion and Castor. Then in 1925 he was again Extra Equerry to the Duke of Windsor on his tour in the Repulse to West and South Africa and South America. In 1926–1927 he was Flag Captain in the Revenge, Atlantic Fleet flagship, and in 1927–1929 Flag Captain and Chief of Staff in the Reserve Fleet. After a few months in command of the Tiger, he was appointed Director of the Operations Division, Naval Staff, from 1930 to 1932 until promoted to rear-admiral. His first flag appointment was as Chief of Staff to Admiral Sir John Kelly, Commander-in-Chief of the Home Fleet. Then in December, 1934, he was made Rear-Admiral Commanding H.M. Yachts, in the Victoria and Albert, and held the post until war broke out in 1939. In May and June of that year he accompanied the King and Queen on their tour to Canada and the United States. While commanding the Royal Yachts he served, from 1935, as President of the R.N. Benevolent Trust. He was created a K.C.V.O. in May, 1937, on the occasion of the Coronation naval review.

Shortly after war broke out Sir Dudley was appointed Flag Officer Commanding, North Atlantic Station, at Gibraltar, to relieve an officer whose health had broken down. He served there with distinction throughout the difficult period of the fall of France and the strained relations with that country which resulted from the British attack on the French Fleet at Mers-el-Kebir in June, 1940. After the fiasco, in September, 1940, of the expedition to Dakar of Free French Forces under General de Gaulle supported by a British squadron which sustained a number of casualties, North was called to account for not, a fortnight earlier, having taken action—which would have been contrary to the Admiralty orders under which he was acting at the time—to stop six French men-of-war from Toulon when they passed through the Straits on their way to French West Africa. He was informed that he had forfeited the confidence of the Admiralty by failing "in an emergency to take all prudent precautions without waiting for Admiralty instructions;" and he was precipitately relieved of his command. He was refused a court-martial before which he could have defended himself against the charge, or even a formal Court of Enquiry; and after a year's unemployment, during which he joined the Home Guard, he was placed on the retired list. He was later employed, in a lower rank, in the minor post of Flag Officer, Yarmouth.

CALL FOR INQUIRY

North was convinced, as were all his brother officers who knew the facts—including the Governor of Gibraltar—that he had been unjustly treated, apparently as a scapegoat for the political failure at Dakar; but holding that a personal grievance, even one so serious as his, ought not to be publicly ventilated while the war was being fought, he held his peace. After the war, however, citing the precedent from the 1914 war of Mr. Lloyd George's *amende honorable* to General Gough, he renewed his application for an inquiry into the whole episode, including not only the actual events, but also the orders under which he was acting. The full facts were made public in 1948 in an article in the *National Review*, in several debates in the House of Lords, and eventually at greater length in 1957 in a little book by Mr. Noel Monks. In the meanwhile, however, successive First Lords of the Admiralty had refused his applications for the matter to be reopened, even when a deputation of five Admirals of the Fleet, three of whom were former First Sea Lords, had waited on the First Lord—then J. P. L. Thomas, afterwards Lord Cilcennin—and presented an unanswerable case for so doing.

It remained for the Prime Minister to do in 1957 what should have been done years before, to extinguish the unjustified slur on Sir Dudley North's professional reputation. After himself examining the whole case he stated categorically in Parliament on May 23 that "Admiral North cannot be accused of any dereliction of duty. He obeyed his orders as he interpreted them, and some blame must rest on the fact that they were not drawn with complete clarity... He has nothing with which to reproach himself. He had 44 years of long, distinguished and devoted service in the Royal Navy and there is no question of his professional integrity being impugned". On this statement Lord Chatfield, one of the five Admirals of the Fleet, commented in *The Times* the next day: "The past cannot be completely thrown overboard; punishment carried out cannot be cancelled; but honour can be restored."

In 1952 North was appointed Deputy Lieutenant of Dorset. He was first married in 1909 to Eglantine, daughter of the Hon. W. R. Campbell, of Sydney, New South Wales. She died in 1917, and in 1923 he married Eilean, daughter of Mr. Edward Graham, J. P., of Forston House, Charminster, Dorset. There were a son and three daughters of the second marriage.

May 16, 1961.

John Dudley North, C.B.E., chairman and managing director of Boulton Paul Aircraft Ltd., for whom as chief engineer he designed such well-known R.A.F. aircraft as the Sidestrand, Overstrand and Defiant, died on January 10, 1968, at the age of 75.

Marine engineering was the professional starting point for North as it was for several of Britain's greatest aviation pioneers. Born on January 2, 1893, North went direct from Bedford School and a brief engineering apprenticeship into aviation. And after an equally brief period as a student with Horatio Barber's Aeronautical Syndicate at Hendon he became Grahame-White's chief engineer. From the age of 20 onwards throughout most of his life he created a succession of aeroplanes of striking originality and great variety. His aeroplane designs were indeed a reflection of his rich many-sided personality, as well as of the range of his technical prowess.

In 1913 he designed the ingenious Grahame-White Popular, a small, inexpensive runabout intended for private flyers. It was a two-seater of pusher configuration, capable of a speed of 50 m.p.h. and selling for £400. It foreshadowed the light aeroplanes which became popular after the war of 1914–18. It was for that war that North thought out his Grahame-White VI. At a time when the military purpose of aircraft was still seen as reconnaissance, this machine was planned expressly for fighting, being a pusher, with a crew of two and a forward firing gun. His Type XIII of 1914 was originally intended as a seaplane but was converted to a landplane.

It had a top speed of 85 m.p.h. and was a handsome machine although it had no success. Full success and a wide popular appeal, however, attended his Grahame-White Charabanc. This again was an example of North's farsightedness for it was in some sense a commercial, passenger-carrying aircraft. With a 62ft. wing span it carried four passengers in addition to the pilot. On one occasion, for record breaking purposes, it carried nine. At the other extreme of the size scale North designed a small single-scater which was the first British aircraft to do a loop.

The acceleration in all aeronautical work during the 1914–18 War brought further opportunities within North's reach and in 1915 he joined the Austin company at Longbridge as superintendent of the aviation department. The company was engaged on producing RE 7 and RE 8 aircraft for the Royal Flying Corps. Two years later he went as chief engineer and director to the company which was to see his most mature work, Boulton & Paul of Norwich. He became chairman and managing director.

Although North always rejected the view that the early aeroplanes were crude stick and string structures, and would often point to the brilliant solutions to engineering problems achieved by some of the pioneers, his design genius undoubtedly received a stimulus from the increases in engine power and the advances in metallurgy between the wars.

His work ranged from light aircraft such as the Phoenix exhibited at the 1929 Aero Show at Olympia, to a highly original series of twin-engined aeroplanes for the Royal Air Force. These included the Sidestrand, with two Bristol Jupiter engines and then the Overstrand which was especially notable because it had the Boulton and Paul mechanically operated gun turret, a piece of equipment which was complementary to the Boulton Paul Defiant of the 1939–45 War. (Boulton Paul Aircraft had acquired the aviation department of Boulton and Paul Ltd.)

In the Defiant, North exercised all his ingenuity to produce a fighting aircraft largely dependent for its effectiveness in battle upon a separate gunner using an enclosed, power-operated, multi-gun turret. The Defiant had many successes before and during the Dunkirk evacuation and in the early stages of the Battle of Britain; but eventually the single-seat formula, with fixed, forward firing guns, prevailed and the Defiants were withdrawn from service.

A charming personality, North could become a devastating critic when he felt criticism was needed. Tall and with a slightly hesitant manner of speech, his interests were so wide that there was scarcely a subject which he could not illuminate with some pertinent and often entertaining comment. His knowledge of such disparate subjects as cooking and the collection and cultivation of Alpine plants was encyclopaedic.

His work as a designer of aircraft and particularly his studies of metal construction—for the airship R101 as well as for his own twin-engined aeroplane designs—brought him many honours. He was elected a Fellow of the Royal Aeronautical Society in May, 1961, and created C.B.E. in 1962. He was vice-president of the Society of British Aircraft Constructors in 1941.

He was married in 1922 to Phyllis Margaret Huggins and there were two daughters.

January 12, 1968.

General Sir John Northcott, K.C.M.G., K.C.V.O., C.B., who died in Sydney on August 4, 1966, at the age of 76, was the first Australian-born governor of an Australian state, serving 11 years as governor of New South Wales. Northcott's great success from 1946 to 1957 was historic because it encouraged the appointment of other Australian-born governors.

Northcott was appointed on the recommendation of the Labour Premier W. J. McKell, who was himself appointed governor-general of Australia one year later. Northcott's appointment no less than McKell's was strongly influenced by J. B. Chifley, the Labour Prime Minister, whose decision it was to release Northcott from his post as commander-in-chief of the British Commonwealth occupation forces in Japan. His translation from Tokyo to Sydney surprised Northcott but he accepted the new responsibility as manfully as several other moves in a very distinguished military career which also had its disappointments.

He was chief of the general staff, Australian military force and allied land forces from 1942 until the end of the war. This was the pinnacle of an army career which had denied him command of any unit in battle. In 1941, for example, after two years as deputy chief of the general staff he raised and commanded the first Australian armoured division and was organizing its departure by sea for the Middle East when Japan entered the war and sailing was cancelled. Then in 1942 the Second Australian Corps was not in action during the five months it was commanded by Northcott.

Northcott was a thickset man with an orderly mind and a penchant for pipe smoking. He was honourable and perhaps a little dour. Twice, in 1951 and 1956, he was administrator of the Commonwealth of Australia.

John Northcott was born on March 24, 1890, at Dean, near Ballarat in Victoria. His father owned the general store and John was one of six children who went to the local school and helped in the shop. Later, after attending Grenville College, Ballarat, he joined the Ninth Light Horse and was commissioned in 1908. He joined the small Australian regular Army and was adjutant of a battalion at Gallipoli, where he was severely wounded by machine gun fire. Northcott was eventually invalided home after convalescence in England. It was while in England that he married his Australian wife Winifred Paton at Oxted, Surrey. For a regular soldier in Australia the years between the wars were not exactly stimulating. Northcott was a major for 14 years but his potential was recognized by frequent postings to England, including a year in 1936 on the Imperial Defence Committee. In 1938 Northcott became director of military operations and intelligence in Melbourne, and on the outbreak of war deputy chief of the Australian General Staff.

Lady Northcott died in 1960 after a long illness. They had two daughters.

August 5, 1966.

Ramon Novarro, one of the most popular stars of the silent film, was found dead in Hollywood on October 31, 1968. He was 69.

His film career was short, meteoric and greatly influenced by chance; and the good luck which brought him wealth and fame at the beginning of his screen career deserted him after the coming of sound, so that his period of success lasted for scarcely a decade.

His real name was Ramon Samaniegos, and he was born at Durango, Mexico, on February 6, 1899. He was educzted in Mexico, but his family moved to the United States when he was still young, and he first earned his living as a waiter in a Los Angeles restaurant. His latin good looks enabled him to get work as an extra in films, and one of his first pictures was The Goat, which was made by Paramount in 1919. He also appeared on the stage, and in vaudeville, and he was later given a small acting part in a picture called *The Rubaiyat of Omar Khayyam.*

Meanwhile the most famous star of the early 1920s had been discovered in the person of Rudolph Valentino, who had achieved a phenomenal success in Metro's *The Four Horsemen of the Apocalypse*, in 1921, and again in *The Sheik.* He then began to ask for a very high salary, and Rex Ingram, who was Metro's leading director, decided that he would discover a rival to Valentino, and searching around for a young player with the same Latin type of looks, he chanced to see *The Rubaiyat of Omar Khayyam.* He at once offered the young Mexican the part of Rupert of Hentzau in *The Prisoner of Zenda*, having first instructed him to change his name from Samaniegos to Novarro.

The Prisoner of Zenda was a success, and Novarro then made *Scaramouche* in the same year—1922. After this, he was hailed as Valentino's rival, and later as his successor, but this he never was, for although he showed a flair for playing the romantic lover, especially in costume, he was never gifted with Valentino's curious intensity and ability to transmit emotion through the medium of the screen.

The next major stroke of luck in Novarro's career occurred in 1924, just before the merger that produced the Metro-Goldwyn-Mayer Company. The Goldwyn Company, on the point of being absorbed, were heavily committed to a difficult and costly project—the making of *Ben-Hur*—on location in Rome, with Charles Brabin as the director, and George Walsh playing Ben-Hur. Things had not gone well, and when the company merger was complete, Louis Mayer and his right-hand man, Irving Thalberg, decided to start the film afresh with a new director and a new star. Fred Niblo succeeded Brabin, and Ramon Novarro was given the part of Ben-Hur.

The film, when completed, was almost as successful as its counterpart of 1960, and Novarro rode on the crest of a wave. *Ben-Hur* was followed by *The Student Prince*, in which he played opposite Norma Shearer, and was directed by Ernst Lubitsch. It was not a good example of Lubitsch's work, but was contrived with his customary skill, sophistication and polish, and made a great deal of money. Valentino had died in 1926, and Novarro now seemed without a rival in his own particular field of romance.

Then disaster overtook him, as it overtook so many other silent stars, when talking films began to be made. The two leading romantic players, Novarro and John Gilbert, discovered that their voices recorded badly. Moreover they had very little stage experience, and their rather exaggerated style of acting tended to look ridiculous when allied to normal dialogue. Each made a final desperate effort in the early 1930s to retain his popularity, and each had the good fortune to be given Greta Garbo as his co-star. Gilbert made *Queen Christina* with her, and Novarro made *Mata Hari.* But both failed, despite Miss Garbo's great popularity.

Gilbert retired and was soon forgotten. Novarro lingered on for a year or two with M.G.M., for whom he made *The Cat and the Fiddle*, with Jeanette MacDonald, *Laughing Boy*, with Lupe Veleez, and *The Night is Young*, with Evelyn Laye. But by 1936 Novarro, although still engaged in making minor pictures, was no longer a star, and Gilbert was dead. The coming of sound had destroyed them, as it had destroyed so many others. New stars were being created, and those of the silent era were quickly forgotten. Neither had any claim to be considered as an outstanding actor, but neither deserved to be treated quite so shabbily, by fate.

November 1, 1968.

Wilfrid Noyce died on July 24, 1962, while taking part in the British-Soviet expedition to the Pamirs.

Wilfrid Noyce was born at Simla on December 31, 1917, the elder son of Sir Frank Noyce, a distinguished member of the Viceroy's Council. After being head of the school at Charterhouse he entered King's College, Cambridge, in 1936 with a classical scholarship. Already, inspired by holidays near Festiniog, he had begun his brilliant mountaineering career, making hard new routes in Snowdonia with Dr. J. M.

Edwards. (They compiled climbing guide-books to Tryfan and Lliwedd together.) At King's began a devoted friendship with A. C. Pigou, the eminent economist and generous patron of many mountaineers, 40 years his senior; and it was on the first of many holidays at Pigou's house on Buttermere that he fell 200 feet sheer from the East Buttress of Mickledore Grooves on Scafell. Edwards's strength and skill, and one strand of rope, saved him, but he was terribly injured, especially in the face. His boyish good looks were gone, but Sir Harold Gillies's plastic surgery did marvels, and his rare personality proceeded to stamp itself on his new-made features. Next summer he was Pigou's guest in the Alps, doing notable climbs with Hans Brantschen and Armand Charlet. Back at Cambridge, he got a first in Classical Tripos Part I, and completed his degree in 1940 with a first in Modern Languages.

TEACHING AT CHARTERHOUSE

By then war had broken out, and he had spent the first autumn of it with the Friends' Ambulance Unit at Edgbaston and in East London hospitals. He now served in turn as private in the Welsh Guards, subaltern in the K.R.R.C. and (from 1942) captain in the Intelligence Corps in India.

After the war and two more terms at Cambridge he began his career as a modern languages master with four years at Malvern before returning to Charterhouse. His hesitant modesty and quiet voice were perhaps a handicap in the class-room, where Mallory too had not been at his best; but his love of good literature stimulated the more intelligent boys; and out of school his enthusiasms, his achievements and his friendship were a source of pleasure to more Carthusians than he perhaps realized. He also found time for writing, peripatetic lecturing, and useful service on Godalming Borough Council.

His climbs were now always done guideless; indeed he was one of the few British climbers who could move as fast and competently as a guide on the hardest snow and ice routes of the Alps. He made many fine ascents, including, in 1959, the formidable Furggen ridge of the Matterhorn, which had previously been climbed only three times direct. His acquaintance with the Himalayas began during the war. In 1943–44 he made two expeditions to Garwhal, and he was also chief instructor at the R.A.F. Aircrew Mountain Centre in Kashmir. But his most characteristic venture was the ascent of Pauhunri in Sikkim with Sherpa Anatharkay. With a strictly limited leave, he disregarded acclimatization, and reached this 23,385 ft. summit in just over a fortnight from Delhi. He wrote *A Climber's Guide to Sonamarg, Kashmir*.

In 1953 came the successful assault on Everest. It was Noyce who, with Sherpa Annullu, opened the route to the South Col; and he climbed to the col a second time in support of Hillary and Tensing's attack on the summit. Had a further summit party been needed, he was to have gone with Hunt. In 1957 he took part in an expedition to Machhapuchare, in western Nepal (described in his *Climbing the Fish's Tail*), but was turned back by bad weather 150 ft. below the top, having pioneered himself the entire route up this difficult peak. In 1960 he led an expedition to Trivor, a 25,000 ft. summit in the Karakoram.

A POET'S APPROACH

In the following summer he gave up schoolmastering to devote himself to writing, his last published work being *To the Unknown Mountain*, a personal account of the Trivor expedition.

Though he was a mountaineer of such accomplishment, his approach to hills was always that of a poet and a lover of natural beauty. Of his varied books *South Col* was the most successful, conveying not only what happened on Everest, but what it felt like. In his mountaineering novel *The Gods are Angry* the plot was perhaps better than the characterization; yet he always thought of people along with mountains, as can be seen from the titles of *Mountains and Men*, *Scholar Mountaineers*, *British Crags and Climbers*; and *The Springs of Adventure* was an attempt to analyse their motives. His meditative temperament also expressed itself in sincere and sensitive poetry (*Michel Angelo*, 1953; *Poems*, 1960). For he was richly endowed in mind as well as body—on returning from Everest he toured western Europe lecturing on it in French, German and Italian. But what his pupils, colleagues, and countless friends will remember is a character exquisitely blended of courage, gentleness, modesty and integrity.

He married in 1950 Miss Rosemary Davies, who survives him with two sons.

July 31, 1962.

With the death on August 22, 1963, of **Lord Nuffield,** British public life was left the poorer by the loss of a great industrialist who revolutionized the motor industry in Britain and a philanthropist whose munificent benefactions must make his name remembered with those of Carnegie and Rockefeller. By the time he was 80 it was estimated that he had given away over £27m.

In him the medical profession was bereft of its most generous friend; while the city and university of Oxford lost a citizen and an honorary *alumnus* who never tired in the elaboration of new projects for their advancement and amenity. When the youth William Morris started his little bicycle shop in Oxford in 1893 no member of the academic community could have dreamt that this humble mechanic would one day found a great postgraduate medical school and set up a new college bearing his name. Yet these things came to pass; and they arose from an extraordinary ability in mechanics and marketing which brought Morris vast wealth; from the keenest foresight on social trends and public demands; and from a deep-seated idealism which impelled the giving away of large sums for cultural and medical objects.

Having come by wealth he acknowledged the moral obligation of success by devoting the surplus of his riches to public work, insisting, at the same time according to the tradition, that the power thus to benefit humanity comes through the fructifying work of private enterprise. This declaration was made when in 1943 he launched his crowning benefaction, the endowment of the Nuffield Foundation with £10m. worth of the shares of his companies.

On the industrial side, which made possible the philanthropic activities, Morris made good by anticipating a big public demand and by satisfying it when it came. It was inevitable that the small man should want his motor car. Morris provided one which was cheap and reliable, but which looked stylish. In a few years' time his fortune was made; he acquired other engineering plants; and he started his career of public benefaction.

GREAT AND DETAILED SCHEMES

"Giving away is pleasant," said Morris, in the year of his £2m. gift to Oxford, "but the worry which comes from giving is very great . . . the idea that it is easy to give money away is the biggest fallacy in the world." The statement throws strong light on Morris's quality and method as a philanthropist. His larger benefactions were not mere sporadic gestures of impulsive generosity; they were the implementation of great schemes which he had worked out in intimate detail. He accompanied his gifts with precise and well-considered prescriptions as to their administration and use.

The Right Hon. Sir William Richard Morris, first Viscount Nuffield, of Nuffield, in the county of Oxford, in the Peerage of the United Kingdom, Bt., G.B.E., C.H., F.R.S., was born on October 10, 1877, at Worcester, his mother being the daughter of Richard Pether, of Headington, Oxfordshire. The family moved to Headington when he was three, and he received the ordinary elementary education in local schools. Since William had shown mechanical aptitude he was placed, at the age of 16, in a bicycle shop to learn the trade. He remained an employee for no more than nine months, after which on borrowed capital of £4, he opened a shop of his own in 1893. At first he hired out and repaired bicycles; then he sold and raced them (his cycling trophies were among his dearest possessions); and presently he produced a model of his own which enjoyed a considerable local sale. He followed this up with a motor-cycle of advanced design. In his first six years of bicycle manufacturing he accumulated £2,000 capital; and in the next 10 years, which brought him to the age of 33, he had doubled that amount. In 1904, after an unsuccessful venture into partnership he started on his own the Morris Garage (later Morris Garages) running as well a successful taxicab service and representing various car and motor cycle firms.

FIRST MORRIS-OXFORD CARS

In 1911 there were already some 50,000 private motorists in Great Britain, but home-produced vehicles were mostly high-powered and expensive to buy and run. Morris determined to turn out a good and cheap British car, and in 1912 after some two years of development work bought small factory premises at Cowley to begin production of 400 cars, sometimes working for 36 hours on end. His knowledge of engineering was purely empirical, but he had a real gift for design; and within a year the first few Morris-Oxford cars were on the road. In 1914, foreseeing difficulty in getting enough components for his needs, he visited the United States for the first time to place orders there. Then came the War of 1914–18, during which the Morris works were turned over to war activity, Morris acting as controller.

BACK TO NORMAL

In 1919 he returned to his normal task. So far he had sold only a thousand cars, but soon, operating a policy of better work at lower prices, he brought about considerable expansion in his business. The Morris-Cowley car, and its rather more expensive stable companion, the Morris-Oxford, were reasonably priced, reliable, and economical in running. Here was a "family car" that looked good and was good. The public responded. In 1920, when other manufacturers were talking of raising their prices, Morris reduced his by £100 on the eve of the Motor Show. In 1922 his sales were just under 7,000; by the next year he had nearly tripled them, and had bought the business of E. G. Wrigley, Ltd., of Birmingham, reconstituting it as Morris Commercial Cars, Ltd. In 1924 came the first negotiations for the merger between Morris and Austin which did not finally occur until 30 years later. Morris turned down a suggestion by Sir Herbert Austin that his company, Morris, and Wolseley Motors should combine.

OVERSEAS EXPANSION

In 1925 he sold 53,582 private cars and 6,256 utility vehicles, went to Detroit to study mass production methods (a visit that resulted in the formation of the Pressed Steel Company for the manufacture of bodies), and bought the Léon Bollée concern of Le Mans, from which he popularized the Morris-Léon-Bollée 12 h.p. model in France. By 1926, when Morris Motors (1926) was formed to absorb the 1919 company of that name as well as some of the firms he had bought himself, his factory premises covered 80 acres; he was turning out 1,000 cars a week and employing 4,000 workpeople; he had built new factories for bodies and radiators, and from Morris Garages, Ltd., had started to manufacture the M.G. sports car. This year also saw the first of his munificent gifts to the University of Oxford—a sum of £10,000 devoted to completing the endowment of the Department of Spanish. In the General Strike only a mere handful of his employees came out.

The years 1927 to 1930 covered Morris's first big donations for medicine in London and in Oxford—endowments which showed the former aspirant to medical qualifications now using his wealth to advance the study and practice that would have been his choice. £104,000 went to St. Thomas's Hospital, £25,000 to the Birmingham Hospitals, £188,000 to the Radcliffe Infirmary, Oxford, and £47,000 to the Wingfield (later Morris-Wingfield) Orthopaedic Hospital. Morris was made a baronet in 1929, and in the New Year Honours of 1934 was raised to the peerage as Baron Nuffield (the names of Morris and Cowley being already pre-empted). He was advanced to a viscounty in 1938.

A new line of business had been opened out by Morris in 1927, when he bought the Wolseley concern against American competition for £730,000. He started Wolseley Aero Engines in 1929, and was by then frequently acquiring fresh interests. So great had the value of his organizations become that in 1930 he rejected an American offer of £11m. for their purchase. In the same year he visited South Africa for market investigation. This was one of many Empire journeys he made, usually scattering largesse as he went. In 1935 he gave £35,000 for crippled children in New Zealand; in 1937 he distributed £42,000 in Australia and with £168,000 established a fund for Dominion medical graduates at Oxford.

Looking ahead to the benefits of overseas trade, he formed a new company, Morris Industries Exports Ltd. in 1933. In the same year he appointed Mr. Leonard Lord (later Lord Lambury) managing director with instructions to lay out afresh first the Wolseley plant at Birmingham and then the Morris factory at Cowley. Lord stayed with Nuffield only for three years, but the two men came together again when the Austin and Morris merger was completed in 1952, Lord having in the meantime joined Austin.

Nuffield was a keen individualist, and though not a hard or "difficult" man, he was not to be trifled with or set off his determined course by any agency, however powerful. From this trait there arose an unfortunate controversy in 1936 with the Air Council on general policy for the manufacture of aeroplanes and parts. Nuffield doubted the efficacy of the "shadow" scheme and refused to participate in it, while stating a general readiness to be of service to his country. Lord Swinton, the Air Minister of that day, created an impression of discourtesy by neglecting for over three months to arrange a meeting, and the whole episode was dealt with in a White Paper. Nevertheless in January, 1937, Nuffield set up Nuffield Mechanisations, Ltd., for the manufacture of tanks and other armaments, and in June, 1938, started an aircraft factory at Castle Bromwich. In the same month two men were apprehended on a charge of attempting to kidnap Nuffield for a ransom of £100,000, one of the accused being sentenced to seven years' penal servitude.

AT THE AIR MINISTRY

In September, 1938, Nuffield bought Riley Motors, and in December started a world tour, returning in April, 1939; a luncheon was held at Grosvenor House in the next month to celebrate the manufacture and dispatch of the millionth Morris vehicle. Soon after the outbreak of war in 1939 Nuffield was appointed Director-General of Maintenance at the Air Ministry, refusing to take any salary. In this post he was responsible for the repair of aircraft and ancillary equipment. In May, 1940, Nuffield agreed to the suggestion of Lord Beaverbrook, Minister of Aircraft Production, that in the national interest Vickers should take over the Castle Bromwich aircraft factory.

After the war Nuffield made several journeys, usually in the winter, to Australia and other parts of the Commonwealth to arrange for the overseas assembly of Morris cars and otherwise foster exports. In 1945 he bought the Victoria Park racecourse at Sydney for development by the Australian subsidiary company, and he announced that ultimately a completely Australian car would be produced.

In 1948 Nuffield entered the agricultural market by producing the Nuffield universal tractor, and in the same year an agreement was reached with the Austin company to pool the resources of the two concerns although it was decided that the time was not ripe for a merger. The merger finally took place in 1952. Nuffield became chairman of the British Motor Corporation, but retired six months later and became honorary president of the new company. In 1958 he was made a Companion of Honour.

The tale of Nuffield's public benefactions is almost endless. As his wealth increased, so did the *tempo* and quantity of his lavish gifts, which by the end of 1940 had reached the prodigious total of some £16,500,000.

MAJOR GIFTS

The major philanthropic operations may be broadly divided into five categories: (a) endowments for hospital services and medical research; (b) collegiate and other foundations for the University of Oxford; (c) assistance to the Special Areas; (d) funds for the Morris employees; (e) funds for the recreation of her Majesty's Services.

Taking these gifts in the foregoing order, and chronologically, we come first to the establishment in October, 1936, of a post-graduate medical school in Oxford, with an endowment of £1,250,000. When Congregation met in November to acknowledge the gift, Nuffield got up at the end of the meeting and calmly said that, as he had learnt that the original endowment was insufficient, he proposed to increase it to £2m. In November, 1938, impressed by the efficacy of the Both Respirator (the "iron lung") in the treatment of poliomyelitis, he gave £500,000 to provide a respirator for every hospital in the Empire that could usefully employ one. In 1939 he gave £1,250,000 for hospital regionalization in the provinces, thus laying the foundation of a coordinated national hospital service.

Among other achievements of the Nuffield Provincial Hospitals Trust, formed in December, 1939, were the endowment of chairs of Social Medicine at Oxford (1942), of Child Health at King's College, Newcastle-on-Tyne (1942), and of Psychiatry at Leeds (1944) as well as the establishment of a department of Neurology in the University of Liverpool (1944).

Coupled with great sums given to Guy's, St. Thomas's, the Radcliffe Infirmary, the Birmingham hospitals, the Hospital for Sick Children, and numerous orthopaedic schemes, these benefactions have been of capital importance to the whole science and practice of medicine in England, the Dominions, and especially in Oxford. But not only did Nuffield create at Oxford a great medical centre. He extended his benefits to specific communities and to the University in general. In October, 1937, he founded Nuffield College with £1m., designing it as a graduate institution linking up theory and practice in social work.

Nuffield took no active part in politics, though

he often spoke in favour of protection; but he showed his solicitude for the economically stricken parts of the country in 1936 by establishing the Nuffield Trust, with a capital of £2m., for assistance in the Special Areas. (In 1944 a surplus, happily not needed for the original purpose, was given to London hospitals). Towards his own workpeople he did not adopt the paternalism of a Leverhulme, rather favouring the payment of high wages and the leaving of their expenditure to the discretion of the individual. Yet he did everything he could to encourage thrift in his men. As far back as 1925 he presented 6,000 fully paid life insurance policies. In 1936 he set aside £2,125,000 in shares for all his employees earning less than £1,000 a year. His biggest gift to the Services was the sum of £1,500,000 in 1939, for the improvement of their recreational facilities.

His princely gifts, too numerous to give in detail, continued year by year into his old age. To mark his eightieth birthday in 1957 the Nuffield Foundation, which had gone from strength to strength since its early days, announced two special gifts—one of £80,000 to London University for the endowment of a chair of child surgery at Great Ormond Street and one of £15,000 to the Fiji Central Medical School to establish a department of social and preventive medicine. That same year three leading members of the medical profession, Sir Clement Price Thomas, Sir Henry Dale, and Dr. W. N. Pickles, on behalf of doctors all over the world, presented him with a pair of diamond cuff links and a cheque for over £3,500. In May, 1961, Nuffield handed over all his shares in Morris Garages, Ltd., to the Nuffield Foundation. The value of this benefaction was said to exceed £500,000.

A GOOD EMPLOYER

As an employer Nuffield was not cynical, tyrannical or exacting. It was natural that so efficient and hard-working a man (whose office hours were from 8 to 7) should expect the same qualities in his employees, but he paid high wages, established an excellent welfare scheme, started holidays with pay long before most other employers, and provided his men with elaborately equipped sports grounds. His factory organization was his own product, not modelled on that of Henry Ford—though he was always willing to glean useful detail from others. He had little sympathy with trade unionism and Socialism, feeling that if employers and men acted squarely by one another and that if political interference and extravagance could be avoided, industry would be healthy and unemployment would disappear. He himself lived simply enough at Nuffield Place, Huntercombe, near Henley-on-Thames, having no taste for luxury or the panoply of wealth. The Lord Nuffield known to public fame remained essentially that Morris who had sold bicycles in Oxford back in the nineties. His public speeches were colloquial in flavour, but the long letters accompanying his major benefactions were cogently worded and were models of their kind, not only as instruments of policy but as prose.

Nuffield was above middle height, clean-shaven, but wiry. His brow lined early in life but as an elderly man his physique was much as it had been when he was a champion cyclist. In his mid-seventies his muscles were hard and his figure trim. Nuffield was elected F.R.S. in 1939 and Oxford made him an honorary D.C.L. in 1931 and M.A. in 1937. London, Sydney, and Birmingham Universities also awarded him honorary degrees of LL.D. In 1937 he received the Albert Gold Medal of the Royal Society of Arts. He was honorary colonel of the 52nd (London) A.A. Brigade, Royal Artillery (T.A.), president of Guy's Hospital, honorary member of the B.M.A., the British Orthopaedic Association, and the British Dental Association, life governor or president of many hospitals and charitable institutions at home and in the Dominions, and president of the League of Industry. He was also an Honorary Freeman of Coventry, Worcester, Oxford, Droitwich, and Cardiff, Honorary Freeman of the Worshipful Society of Apothecaries, honorary medallist of the Royal College of Surgeons, Vice-President of the Oxford Society, and Honorary Fellow of Worcester and Pembroke Colleges. In 1929 his workpeople presented him with a portrait by the late Sir Arthur S. Cope, R.A. In 1937 a portrait by the late P. A. de László, M.V.O., was unveiled at St. Peter's Hall and another by Beatrice Enes at Guy's Hospital. There is also a bust by Mme. Ginette Bingguely Lejeune.

In 1904 he married Elizabeth Maud, daughter of Mr. William Jones Anstey, an Oxford business man. His wife died in 1959. There were no children of the marriage, so that the peerage becomes extinct.

August 22, 1963.

Lieutenant-General Sir Archibald Nye, G.C.S.I., G.C.M.G., G.C.I.E., K.C.B., K.B.E., M.C., Vice-Chief of the Imperial General Staff from 1941 to 1946, and after the war successively Governor of Madras and United Kingdom High Commissioner in India and in Canada, died on November 13, 1967, at the age of 72.

Nye rose rapidly to the high position in the Army in which he played an important part in the conduct of the Second World War. His subsequent service under the Commonwealth Relations Office was equally distinguished. His outstanding gifts were a cool clarity of mind and remarkable powers of exposition; he was also a first-class administrator and organizer. Unlike many soldiers in high places he was happy in his relations with politicians; indeed he enjoyed what was called "cabinet work". No one could outline a military problem for the benefit of the layman more clearly and cogently.

As V.C.I.G.S. he worked under the direction of Lord Alanbrooke and in perfect accord with him; Alanbrooke described him as having a first-class brain, great character, courage in his own convictions, and as a quick worker with very clear vision. It was typical of Nye's many-sided energy that he studied law while he was a junior staff officer in the War Office, passed his examinations, and was called to the Bar by the Inner Temple.

Archibald Edward Nye was born in Dublin on April 23, 1895, the son of Charles Nye. He was educated at the Duke of York's Royal Military School, Dover, and intended to qualify as an army schoolmaster. But on the outbreak of war in 1914 he enlisted in a Kitchener's Army battalion as a sergeant instructor. In 1915 he was commissioned into the Prince of Wales's Leinster Regiment. He saw three spells of active service on the Western Front, amounting in all to 18 months, was wounded in action and won the Military Cross. After the war he was adjutant of his battalion for three years. Then, when the Leinsters were disbanded in 1922, he transferred to The Royal Warwickshire Regiment, in which he was promoted to captain. After graduating at the Star College in 1925 he held a number of staff appointments at home and was for some years an instructor at the Staff College. On promotion to major he made another exchange of regiments, this time to the South Lancashire Regiment (Prince of Wales's Volunteers), and in 1937 he returned to The Warwickshire Regiment as lieutenant-colonel, to command a battalion. In 1939 he was promoted colonel and temporary brigadier and appointed to the command of the Nowshera Brigade.

In 1940 he went to the War Office as Deputy Director of Staff Duties, and became Director a few months afterwards. In the following year, when Sir Alan Brooke succeeded Sir John Dill as C.I.G.S., Nye was appointed Vice-Chief of the Imperial General Staff. The Prime Minister had taken a strong fancy to him and seriously considered making him C.I.G.S. instead of Brooke, but, although he had the qualities of brain and character for the post he would have been seriously handicapped in it by his lack of experience in high command and by the fact that the army commanders, such as Wavell, Alexander, Montgomery and Paget, were considerably senior to him. He remained at the War Office as V.C.I.G.S. until after the end of the war and was one of the trinity of Brooke's principal war lieutenants, the others being the Deputy Chief of the Imperial General Staff and the Director of Military Operations.

Alanbrooke has recorded that between him and Nye there existed complete confidence.

LOYAL AND EFFICIENT

He was loyalty and efficiency personified, and Alanbrooke felt that he could always leave his post knowing that the policies he had laid down would be followed to the minutest detail. Although he made an invaluable contribution to the conduct of the war, Nye's long spell of service in Whitehall destroyed his chances of higher promotion, and this no doubt influenced his decision to leave the Army in 1946 when he accepted the appointment as Governor of Madras, in succession to Sir Arthur Hope.

In this new post he played an active part in the Viceroy's conferences on the transfer of power, which took place little more than a year after his arrival. He quickly gained the confidence of the Indians, whose cause he advocated with almost missionary zeal, and it was a remarkable tribute to his success that he was one of the only two British governors (the other being Sir John Colville, Governor of Bombay) who were invited by Congress to stay under the new regime to help India to get off to a fresh start. In the months following the transfer he helped to cope successfully with communist machinations and divisions between Brahmins and non-Brahmins and, when his term of office came to an end in 1948, a further compliment was paid him by the Indian Government when he was appointed, at their request, High Commissioner for the United Kingdom in Delhi.

On the completion of his term of office in India, he was appointed High Commissioner in Canada, and his four years' tenure of this post was again outstandingly successful. He was forthright in telling United Kingdom manufacturers that they must be competitive and prompt in winning a place for their products in Canadian markets, and in warning Canada that to sell more in Britain she must buy more there.

On his return to England he took up a number of directorships. In 1962 he returned for a time to his old beat in Whitehall as chairman of a committee set up by the Government to study the organization of the War Office. He was created K.B.E. in 1944, K.C.B. in 1946, G.C.I.E. in 1946, G.C.S.I. in 1947, and G.C.M.G. in 1951.

He married in 1939 Colleen, daughter of General Sir Harry Knox. They had one daughter.

November 15, 1967.

O

Sir Tom O'Brien, general secretary of the National Association of Theatrical and Kine Employees (N.A.T.K.E.), and a former chairman of the T.U.C. General Council, died in London on May 5, 1970, after a long illness. He was 69.

With his death, the Labour movement has lost one of its most colourful and at times controversial characters. As the representative of a "Show Business" union, he sought to inject some of the glamour and gaiety of the entertainment world into an organization which was traditionally more noted for its subfusc sobriety than for its joie de vivre.

O'Brien was born at Llanelli on August 17, 1900. His father was Irish and his mother Welsh, and throughout his career he combined Celtic romanticism with hard-headed pragmatism. He used to enjoy recounting George Gibson's wisecrack that "Tom is an Irishman masquerading as a Welshman, who looks like a Jew and is Scotch by absorption".

He came up the hard way, having left school when he was 12½ to become a baker's roundsman. He joined the Army in 1915, deliberately over-stating his age, and served in the Dardanelles campaign when he was only 16.

On demobilization he entered the cinema industry and at once set out to organize the workers in this extremely difficult and eminently exploitable field. He was at first organizer for South Wales and the West of England, then national organizer and became general secretary in 1932. His flair for organization and his deep devotion to the trade union cause produced results. Membership of N.A.T.K.E., which had been barely 1,500 rose to about 30,000 in the mid-1950s, and only dropped during the 1960s with the decline in the fortunes of the cinema industry.

O'Brien travelled widely on behalf of his union and the T.U.C. and paid many visits to the American film industry in Hollywood. In spite of awkward political and personal relationships with the leaders of the left-wing Association of Cinematograph, Television and Allied Technicians, he succeeded in forming a good working basis and developing a common approach to the problems of the entertainment industry.

O'Brien attended his first T.U.C. in 1921 and was a continuous attender from 1933 onwards. In 1940, almost by accident, he was elected to the T.U.C. General Council and became its chairman in 1952–53. Contrary to some forecasts, he proved an excellent chairman at the Isle of Man conference, and was urbane, humorous and fair in his conduct of the proceedings.

From 1945 he sat for Nottingham West (Nottingham North-West 1950-55), but was defeated by a hair's breadth in the 1959 election, and never reentered politics. He was never really at ease in the House of Commons, possibly because he disliked the discipline imposed by the Party Whips, possibly because he had an indolent streak in him. He was not an assiduous attender, or performer in Parliament, though he was a very useful speaker whenever questions involving the entertainment industry were under discussion.

Sir Tom acquired quite a reputation for dropping bricks, and the outsider never knew how far these were deliberately dropped to attract publicity. His action in sending a goodwill telegram to Sir Winston Churchill, on the eve of Churchill's departure on a mission to the United States, led to a fierce rebuke from his colleagues. He gave an interview to the *Manchester Guardian* in 1952 which was interpreted as advocating a weakening of the links between the trade unions and the Labour party. For this, he incurred the full fury of Arthur Deakin, then general secretary of the Transport Workers' Union.

Yet O'Brien always contrived to come out on top, and to be forgiven. Some big union leaders sometimes threatened to vote him off the T.U.C. General Council, while some smaller left-wing unions and the white collar unions wanted to choose another representative for the non-manual workers' section. But O'Brien was invariably re-elected.

He was a popular figure, but behind his ebullience he had an alert mind and a sense of compassion. He was a shrewd negotiator who won considerable advances in pay and conditions for his members.

He could speak well when he took the trouble, but tended to be somewhat slapdash. He enjoyed a joke against himself, and once said that a colleague had said of him "O'Brien not only kissed the Blarney stone, he swallowed the darn thing". His favourite description of himself was the late Ian Mackay's "a combination of of Friar Tuck, Henry Irving and Sam Goldwyn". He was a bon viveur, who knew his way about the West End restaurants and wine lists, and an excellent raconteur. Industrial correspondents will long remember his spirited rendering of "The Rose of Tralee" and other sentimental ballads at annual T.U.C. parties.

To O'Brien, the labels right and left were meaningless. He was equally at ease with both wings and was very friendly with Aneurin Bevan, even when Bevan was being denounced as a wrecker and splitter of Party unity. He also got on well with the leaders of the cinema industry. He was knighted in 1953.

He married in 1922 Josie, daughter of John McKelvie of Tenby, and there were two sons and two daughters of the marriage.

May 6, 1970.

Sean O'Casey, the Irish playwright, died in a Torquay nursing home on September 18, 1964. He was 84.

A writer of acknowledged genius, his professional life was threaded with misunderstandings that brought about a neglect of his plays which never ceased to trouble the theatrical conscience. There was a time when the general public eagerly expected him to go on working indefinitely in the style of his famous Dublin trilogy—*The Shadow of a Gunman*, *Juno and the Paycock* and *The Plough and the Stars*. He insisted on his right as an artist to develop in his own way. Neither politically nor stylistically were the developments in his middle period popular.

The consequence was that, when he had mellowed politically and critics were in a position to appreciate that his real preoccupation as a dramatist had not been with the destruction of society but with the destruction of dramatic realism, it was too late. O'Casey could no longer count on getting the plays he continued to publish adequately performed, if at all. Any of his later fantasies that happened to be taken up were apt to present difficulties that might not have been there if the author's contact with theatrical conditions had remained close and constant. His superbly evocative autobiography in six volumes abounds in scenes from plays that he did not write.

CASUAL LABOURER

Shaun O'Cathasaigh, the son of Michael and Susanna O'Cathasaigh, was born on March 30, 1880, in a Dublin tenement. He was the last of 13 children, eight of whom had already died in infancy. He himself contracted a chronic eye affliction, and his early years of dire poverty and much pain were a prelude to a young manhood of deprivation and insecurity. Till he was 30 years old he worked as a casual labourer with long periods of unemployment.

He had taught himself at the age of 14 to read, and he read all that came his way, getting to know some of the English classics, steeping himself in Shakespeare and the melodramas of Dion Bouccicault. His imagination was fired by Jim Larkin, the fiery orator who organized the unskilled labourers of Dublin into the newly formed Irish Transport and General Workers' Union. O'Casey became an active member of the union and served as one of the Chief's assistants during the 1913 strike. He learnt and taught Gaelic. He became secretary of the Irish Citizenry Army in 1914. It was during the war years that he began to do a little utilitarian writing and at the same time tried his hand at one or two plays. "Your strong point is characterization," Lady Gregory told him after reading *The Crimson in the Tricolour*. *The Shadow of a Gunman* (1923) was the first of his plays to be accepted. Rather to the surprise of the Abbey's directors, it filled the theatre night after night. During its run he was still working as a labourer, making cement on a road repair job. Next year came *Juno and the Paycock*, that was to win the Hawthornden Prize of 1926. These two plays restored the failing fortunes of the Abbey and enabled the author to start his professional career as a playwright.

Though Lady Gregory made him welcome at Coole and taught him, among other things, to use "divers tools at food" the celebrity from the tenements found more to poke fun at than to admire in the city's *literati*. *The Plough and the Stars* (1926) duly provoked the riot and the subsequent newspaper controversies with which Dublin customarily greets its masterpieces, and in the midst of his turbulent success O'Casey left Ireland for England.

The three plays were widely acclaimed as masterpieces of realism. There was misunderstanding here that was to persist. The condition of Dublin at the time of the Easter Rising and during the Troubles is certainly depicted with extraordinary vividness, but the spirit of the plays is far from being realistic. The Paycock, Joxer, Fluther and the Covey use language that was never spoken by mortal tenement dwellers. These unforgettable rapscallions come, like Falstaff, out of the sea of poetry, and the natural development of their creator was not along realistic lines. In 1928 the Abbey received *The Silver Tassie*, an anti-war play which sought to achieve unity through a diversity of styles, and its rejection gave rise to a public dispute between the angry author and Yeats.

The decision not to produce this play had serious consequences alike for the author and for the theatre which lost its greatest modern playwright. In 1929 *The Silver Tassie* was put on in London and, though a commercial failure, won high critical praise as a bold experiment in theatrical method. Its symbolic middle act dominated by a great howitzer and the figure of a man, chanting, is still memorable. *Within the Gates* (1934), a modern morality set in Hyde Park, carried the method still further with even less public acceptance. Its mingling of styles was thought by some critics to open up a new country of the imagination to a theatre then shut in by rigid literalism; but the audiences that might have appreciated O'Casey's intentions had yet to come into being. *Within the Gates* was the last of his plays automatically to command production on a central stage.

During the years of neglect he published *Windfalls* (1934), a collection of early poems, short stories and one act plays; *The Flying Wasp* (1937), essays on the London theatre; and in 1939 the first volume of his autobiography, *I Knock at the Door* appeared. It was followed by *Pictures in the Hallway* (1942), *Drums under the Windows* (1945), *Inishfallen, Fare Thee Well* (1949), *Rose and Crown* (1952) and *Sunset and Evening Star* (1954).

And he continued to write plays in his own highly personal style. Of these *The Star Turns Red* (1940), a piece of communist propaganda, and *Oak Leaves and Lavender* (1946), celebrating England at war, are perhaps best forgotten, but *Red Roses for Me* (1943), a piece about a doomed Dublin idealist who sees the share of a new world in the shilling-a-week for which railwaymen are striking, was taken to London in 1946 and had some success. After visiting America in the late thirties O'Casey had settled in Devonshire, and as he grew older Ireland seemed to grow more and more real to the exile.

How far his Ireland corresponded with present-day Ireland has been hotly disputed, and after the rejection of *The Drums of Father Ned* by the second Dublin Theatre Festival in 1958 O'Casey indignantly banned the presentation of any of his plays in Dublin, a ban that was relaxed earlier in the year of his death, when he permitted the Abbey Theatre company to stage a limited run of *The Plough and the Stars* and *Juno and the Paycock* before their presentation in London.

Purple Dust (1940), *Cock-a-Doodle Dandy* (1949), *The Bishop's Bonfire* (1955), and *The Drums of Father Ned* (1958) all have an Irish setting. The first three have a common theme—the arraignment of all established institutions, the Church among them, as enemies of the free mind, especially as they are leagued together to fill youth with a superstitious dread of life and a distrust of happiness. Their interest for the student of the drama is that they show that out of his ceaseless experiments, some of them rash and stumbling, O'Casey had succeeded in evolving out of the juxtaposition of different techniques a sort of kaleidoscopic play which reintroduces the song and the dance which the drama since Ibsen has lost, and restored the flamboyance that is natural to it. Imperfect as they are, they sustain the impression of bigness of mind that is inseparable from O'Casey's tragi-comic vision of life.

He married in 1927 Eileen Reynolds (Eileen Carey), an Irish actress, and they had two sons and a daughter.

September 21, 1964.

Frank O'Connor, the Irish writer, died on March 10, 1966, at his home in Dublin. He was 64.

By his death English literature has lost a master of the short story. But Ireland is worse deprived, for incomparably he revealed to Irishmen and the world the splendour and vitality of an ancient literature known only to a handful of scholars in Irish.

A revolutionary by nature, who at 19 was fighting in the Civil War, the strange rapture and naivety of the lonely child of Cork were in him to the end. At 25, after an apprenticeship with Lennox Robinson (at that time library adviser to the Carnegie Trust), he moved from a librarianship at Cork to another in Dublin, where he soon carried on his own civil war with everyone whose ideas on literature conflicted with his. In this contest, A. E. (George Russell) was his one point of rest. Yeats's friendship was more austere, but not less appreciative of a remarkable talent for both story and verse, and persuaded him towards an Abbey Theatre directorship during a critical period. O'Connor later resigned in anger at the anti-Yeats group. Librarianship, too, he abandoned for literature. The war took him to London where he did some memorable broadcasts while working with the Ministry of Information.

His first book, *Guests of the Nation* (1931), won immediate recognition just when the short story was reaching a peak of refinement as a literary form. *Bones of Contention* (1936) and *Crab Apple Jelly* (1944) followed; but in the interval there were poetry translations for the Cuala Press; *The Big Fellow* (1937), a life of Michael Collins; and five unpublished plays of his Abbey period (three in collaboration with Hugh Hunt) which elevated the theatre he was trying hard to save. The novel, too, had excited him, but neither *The Saint and Mary Kate* (1932), nor *Dutch Interior* (1940) was conspicuously successful. He returned to the story in *The Common Chord* (1947), *Travellers' Samples* (1950), and *Domestic Relations* (1957). Later there were collected editions and volumes of selections.

A DIFFERENT KIND OF GUIDE

The academic approach of the critics to Shakespeare drove him to *The Road to Stratford* (1948), a practising writer's analysis of another's workmanship. The same inspiration produced *Mirror in the Roadway* (1956), where he examined the style and technique of some great novelists. But he was curious about every art and craft, and on "discovering" Irish architecture he mounted a bike and toured the country to see its ruined monuments. *Irish Miles* (1947) remains a refreshing and intelligent guide for the tourist in Ireland. In another guide of a different kind, *The Book of Ireland* (1958), he allowed Ireland to speak magnificently for herself in the prose and poetry of native and foreign writers since the ninth century. The story-tellers got a volume to themselves, *Modern Irish Short Stories* (1957) in the World's Classics series.

A few years of lecturing and teaching in America were terminated in the 1950s by a longing for Dublin. But the tranquillity he sought there was disturbed by the mediocrity of Irish writing and the antics of place-seekers in society whose most notable contribution to a new Ireland was the mortal wound it had inflicted on literature with a state censorship. Perhaps it is significant that he was becoming more absorbed at that time with the medieval poetry; it is certain that his reputation will be hallowed by the superb translations as by the greatest of the stories. The first collected edition, *Kings, Lords and Commons* (1961), was promptly banned for containing the seventeenth-century satire, *The Midnight Court* (1945), already proscribed by state order (1946). It was later revoked on formal and tedious submission by some friends to the Appeals Board. A second collection appeared in *The Little Monasteries* (1963).

March 11, 1966.

William F. O'Dwyer, who died in a New York hospital on November 24, 1964, at the age of 74, was a former mayor of New York, and subsequently United States Ambassador to Mexico.

Born in Ireland on July 11, 1890, he studied for the priesthood in Spain but decided that he did not have the vocation and emigrated to New York in 1910. He had only small means but he was strongly built and energetic and readily found work in various capacities—at first as a stoker and afterwards as a plasterer's helper, as a longshoreman and as a policeman. While he was a policeman he studied law at night. He then graduated from Fordham University in 1923 and gave up his policeman's job the next year.

Eight years later he was appointed a magistrate in Brooklyn. He served in that office for six years and was then appointed a county judge. In 1939 he was elected district attorney for Kings County (Brooklyn), and as such won a reputation for his vigorous prosecution of what came to be called Murder, Incorporated, a gang which committed murder for hire.

O'Dwyer first ran for mayor of New York in 1941 against LaGuardia, whom he succeeded in 1945. He held that office for five years, at first building up a reputation as an opponent of the corrupt influence of Tammany Hall. But when he resigned it was on the eve of a scandal in the police department which involved some of his associates. President Truman then appointed him Ambassador to Mexico, a position he held until the election of Mr. Eisenhower to the presidency in 1952.

Meanwhile, in the course of an investigation by the United States senate crime investigation committee he was accused by that committee of contributing during his tenure in public office "to the growth of organized crime, racketeering and gangsterism in New York City". Nevertheless, he was never charged with any actual wrongdoing in connexion with his public offices.

He married Catherine Lenihan in 1916. She died in 1946 and in 1949 O'Dwyer married, secondly, Elizabeth Sloan Simpson.

November 25, 1964.

Lieutenant-Colonel Alec Ogilvie, C.B.E., British aviation pioneer, died on June 18, 1962, at the age of 80, survived by few of his contemporaries.

Colonel Ogilvie decided in October, 1908, to take up flying seriously and, after seeing Wilbur Wright fly in France two months later, ordered a Wright biplane. It was not delivered to him till October, 1909, but meanwhile, on the advice of his friends, the brothers Wright, he had practised on a glider of similar design, mostly at Friston in Sussex, where the present Southdown Gliding Club established itself 40 years later.

Colonel Ogilvie established his flying base on Camber Sands, near Rye, where he did a large amount of unobtrusive flying during the following years, and was at one period averaging 20 hours a week. He took part in meetings at Bournemouth, Blackpool, Wolverhampton and Lanark, and in 1910 competed unsuccessfully in the Gordon Bennett contest at Belmont Park, New York. For this event he used a Wright racing model of only 20ft. span, and continued to fly this machine in England right up to 1914, remaining faithful to the Wright design in contrast to all his fellow aviators. One of his passengers in 1913 was H. G. Wells.

He was granted No. 7 British Aviators' Certificate on May 24, 1910. In October of the following year, on one of his annual visits to the United States, Ogilvie joined Orville Wright in an expedition to the sand dunes at Kitty Hawk, North Carolina, to carry out soaring experiments in a glider. On October 24, 1911, Orville put up a world's gliding duration record of 9 minutes 45 seconds, which remained unbeaten until the Germans began developing the art 10 years later. Ogilvie took his turn on the glider at Kitty Hawk and made several soaring flights of up to 65 seconds' duration.

In 1916 he took charge of an aircraft repair depot at Dunkirk, and the following year joined the newly formed Air Board, eventually becoming Controller of its technical department. The Royal Aero Club appointed him a steward at the first British soaring competition on the South Downs in October, 1922, at which a prize of £50, offered by him for the longest British flight on the opening day, was won by F. P. Raynham with a duration of one hour 53 minutes.

At his estate at Clonmore, near Ringwood, Colonel Ogilvie had a large collection of historical aviation pictures and documents, many signed by the leading aviation pioneers of the world.

June 21, 1962.

His Excellency Archbishop Gerald Patrick O'Hara, Apostolic Delegate to Great Britain, Malta, Gibraltar and Bermuda, and former Bishop of Savannah, Georgia, died on July 16, 1963, at the Apostolic Delegation in London. He was 68.

Before his appointment to the Apostolic Delegation in 1954, Archbishop O'Hara was for nearly three years the Papal Nuncio to Ireland, and before that Regent of the Apostolic Nunciature in Rumania, to which he was appointed in 1946. His period of office in Bucharest tested his diplomatic skill and patience to the utmost; for having ignored repeated applications for a visa, the Communist government in Rumania allowed him grudgingly to enter the country months after his appointment, and then began a systematic campaign against the Church. The closing of schools and seminaries and the spread of propaganda against Christian teaching was followed in 1948 by the denunciation of the Concordat with the Holy See and the mass arrest of Greek Catholic and Latin rite bishops.

Efforts were made to give authority to a puppet national church, leaders of which were excommunicated by the Holy See, and shortly afterward a chauffeur formerly employed by the Nunciature was arrested and charged with treason. The trial allowed for frequent accusations in court to the effect that the prisoner was a spy in the pay of the Vatican, the plea in mitigation being that he was the tool of an American mastermind—Archbishop O'Hara.

IRISH STOCK

The Regent's formal protests to the Rumanian Foreign Office were followed by an order of expulsion. Archbishop O'Hara returned from Buchares to Rome in 1950, the last Papel representaive in Eastern Europe, received from Pope Pius XII the title of Archbishop *ad personam*, and a year later was appointed to succeed the late Archbishop Felici as Apostolic Nuncio in Dublin.

The new Nunci came of Irish stock which itself made him popular, but his popularity would have been asured in any circumstances by the benignity and pastoral friendliness which he was to show so consistently also when he succeeded Archbisho Godfrey in London after the latter's translation in 1954 to the archiepiscopal see of Liverpoo. He travelled widely in Ireland, reached friendly understandings, not only with his fellow-Catholics but also with those of other communions and was accorded a personal, general sympathy when he came under attack once more in his position as a Papal diplomat.

This time the attack originated in America with an application to deprive him of his American citizenship, under the recently passed McCarran Act, on the grounds that he had accepted from a foreign government a post involving an oath of allegiance. The application failed to enlist support in Washington and was met by a formal declaration at his employment was not by the Vatican State but by the Holy See. Subsequently Archbish O'Hara received numerous messages of sympathy from people outside his Church both in America and in Ireland.

BISHOP OF HELIOPOLIS

Gerald Patrick O'Hara waorn in May, 1895, at Green Ridge, Scrant Pennsylvania, educated at St. Charles Borro Seminary, Overbrook, Pa., and in Rom here he was ordained to the priesthood he Lateran basilica in 1920. Subsequente took his doctorate of theology. In 1924 returned to the archdiocese of Philadelpas private secretary to the Archbish Cardinal Dougherty. Five years later he wnsecrated titular Bishop of Heliopolis auxiliary of Philadelphia. His appointment e see of Savannah-Atlanta, which since ha divided into two sees, was in 1935.

In spite of his recall to Rome fdomatic

work after the 1939–45 War he retained possession of his see in Georgia even after his consecutive appointments to Dublin and to London, until 1959, when he became titular Archbishop of Pessinus.

The Apostolic Delegation to Great Britain had been set up in December 1938 with Archbishop Godfrey later Cardinal Archbishop of Westminster as first Apostolic Delegate, the appointment being a spiritual one within the ecclesiastical government of the Church, but with an inevitable national significance, since, as personal representative of the Pope, the Apostolic Delegate was regarded as speaking with the authentic voice of the Holy See. On Archbishop O'Hara's arrival to succeed Archbishop Godfrey, he was solemnly received by Cardinal Griffin and members of the hierarchies of England and Wales and Scotland in Westminster Cathedral, where the bill of appointment was read. Among his first public addresses was one in which he paid a warm tribute to her Majesty the Queen; who "with her husband and children has given, as did her parents, a supreme example of family life". On another occasion he wondered why "Americans sometimes grow up with the idea that the British people are a bit distant, cold and stand-offish", whereas he found them a warm-hearted people.

It was known then that his words were from the heart, for he had already recalled an incident in 1918 when with five other American seminarians in Rome he visited Spain during the influenza epidemic. All were taken ill while in a Barcelona hotel. A British family resident there insisted on removing them, complete strangers, to their own home where they converted an upper oor into a temporary hospital.

In himself one of th most unassuming and approachable of men, chbishop O'Hara was known for his evident ety and thoughtfulness for others. His serms and addresses were marked not only by a ep spirituality but also by commonsense, t understanding of the position of others a by frequent flashes of humour. A person interior humility, he carried himself in off with a dignity that would tolerate no slight o is position as the Pope's representative, but rebuke were necessary it was given the mo effectively because of his inherent personal desty.

The Archbisho ttended the first session of the Second Va Council in 1962 and then returned to Lon On a subsequent visit to Milan he was ta ill, but recovered. He was in Rome at th ne of the death of Pope John XXIII, an e election of Pope Paul VI.

SUFFERED IN HE

The oppressiv eat affected him. On his return to the d tion his doctors advised him, so as to avoid gatherings, against presiding at the custon reception of the Diplomatic Corps, for the sion of the Pope's coronation. His place w aken by the Archbishop of Birmingham nior Metropolitan of the Hierarchy o land and Wales.

July 17, 19

John O'Hara, who died in Princeton on April 11, 1970, was the American novelist and short story writer whose best-known books included *Pal Joey*, *Ten North Frederick*, and *Butterfield 8*.

His first novel, *Appointment in Samarra*, published in 1934, won him immediate fame. He wrote the opening 25,000 words in a furnished room in New York, using his bed as a desk. When he had only three dollars left, he sent identical letters to three New York publishers asking for a subsidy to finish the book. Harcourt. Brace & Co. was sufficiently impressed by the letter and the incomplete manuscript to keep him in board and lodging for three months.

Many of his books were made into films. His *Pal Joey* sketches published in 1940, about night-club life and people, were only moderately successful as a book, but became a "smash hit" musical for which O'Hara wrote the libretto; the music and the lyrics were by Richard Rodgers and Lorenz Hart. It later became a film. *Butterfield 8*, O'Hara's second novel, about Gloria, a young girl of a good family, in the thirties who was an alcoholic juvenile delinquent nymphomaniac, was filmed with Elizabeth Taylor in 1960. *From the Terrace*, about a sailor returning from the wars, was filmed with Paul Newman.

A Rage to Live, about the sexual relationships of the heroine, Grace Caldwell Tate, a member of the leading county family in Pennsylvania, was also filmed.

SCRIPT WRITER

O'Hara, who also worked as a film script writer, helped write the scripts for *The best Things in Life are Free* (1956), *On Our Merry Way* (1948) and *I was an Adventuress* (1940) among others.

His short stories were generally regarded as superior in quality to his novels, the last of which *Lovey Childs*, about the sexual adventures of a rich girl, appeared in 1969. For *Ten North Frederick*, O'Hara won the National Book Award in 1956. Several critics considered that O'Hara stemmed from either F. Scott Fitzgerald, Ernest Hemingway, or Joseph Hergesheimer, or from all three. He has been described as "the voice of the hangover generation" since 1929, and Edmund Wilson pointed out shrewdly that O'Hara had a positive hatred of the generation before his. Another critic noted that he "focuses intensely on people" and is impatient with anything except taut realism. O'Hara was known for his skilful rendering of dialogue and his books, many of them set in the fictitious town of Gibbsville, Pennsylvania, form a commentary on contemporary manners and morals.

Born in Pottsville, Pennsylvania, the eldest of eight children of a well-known doctor, O'Hara was prevented from going to Yale by his father's death. Instead he worked as a ship's steward, railway clerk, gas meter reader, a labourer in a steel mill. His newspaper career was equally varied, ranging from film critic of the New York *Morning Telegraph* to football editor of the *New Yorker*.

April 13, 1970.

Sean Thomas O'Kelly, President of the Irish Republic from 1945 to 1959, died in Dublin on November 23, 1966, at the age of 84.

He was closely associated with the various patriotic movements which sprang up in Ireland at the beginning of the century. He was a keen advocate for the restoration of Irish as the language of the people, and at the same time a founder-member of Sinn Féin and a prominent worker in the separatist movement. As a politician, he lacked the dynamic personality and the gift of inspiring the worship of his followers that made de Valera such a force in politics; but the work of "Sean T.", as he was familiarly known, was a dominating factor in the successes achieved by de Valera and his party. This fact was recognized when the Fianna Fáil party came to power in 1932, and he was appointed vice-president of the Executive Council of the Irish Free State, second only to de Valera himself.

O'Kelly began his long political career in the Dublin Corporation, where he was elected, as the first member of Sinn Féin to take public office, in 1906. He was for 18 years an alderman of the city, and was especially active in housing.

HEALTH AND HOUSING

His experience in this field was responsible for his appointment as Minister for Local Government and Public Health in the first Fianna Fáil Government in 1932.

Born on August 25, 1882, in Dublin, he was still in his early twenties when he helped Arthur Griffith to found Sinn Féin, and was honorary secretary of the organization from 1908 to 1910. He was by profession a journalist, and he and Griffith, also a journalist, were responsible for the various publications that emanated from Sinn Féin. After the Easter week rising of 1916, he was lodged with other Sinn Féiners in Richmond Barracks, Dublin, and on June 1 was deported and interned at Wandsworth. The following Christmas he was released, but in February, 1917, he was again deported, and remained interned until the general amnesty in June.

But the struggle went on, and in December, 1918, he was elected Sinn Féin M.P. for North Dublin City. In common with the other candidates of his party, he had resolved not to take his seat if returned to Westminster. Instead, the illegal First Dáil Eireann (Parliament of Ireland) was summoned to sit in Dublin the following January, the members consisting of those returned at the general election. O'Kelly was chosen as Speaker, holding office until 1921. When the nations gathered at Versailles for the Peace Conference in 1919, the First Dáil sent O'Kelly to Paris to endeavour to secure recognition for the "Republic of Ireland" during the recarving of Europe. Shortly afterwards he was joined by George Gavan Duffy, the eminent barrister, whose father had been Prime Minister of Victoria; but they were unsuccessful in their mission. O'Kelly was then sent by the illegal Republican Government on a mission to Rome.

When the treaty with Britain was signed in December, 1921, O'Kelly became, officially, Envoy in Paris. But as the struggle over ratification of the treaty progressed in Dublin, his personal opinions crystallized in the direction of opposition to ratification. He was recalled, and then associated himself completely with de Valera and the anti-Treaty party in the Civil War.

Apart from a two years' mission to the United States on behalf of the Republicans from 1924 to 1926, it was not until the Republicans formed the Fianna Fáil party and decided to win the country to Republicanism by constitutional means that he again came on the political stage. He was elected a Dáil deputy for Dublin North City in 1927, became vice-president of Fianna Fáil, and when the general election of 1932 returned them to power, two of the highest posts in the Government fell to his lot.

In the following April he figured in a remarkable incident at the French Legation in Dublin. M. Alphand, the French Minister, was holding a reception and dance, and among the guests were two members of the new Government, O'Kelly and Frank Aiken. When the then Governor-General, James McNeill, arrived and the band struck up the Free State National Anthem, the two members of the Government walked out. It was the first shot in the campaign between the new Government and the Governor-General which ended in McNeill's resignation and the appointment by King George, "on the advice of his Ministers in the Irish Free State", of a Governor-General who was willing to accede to their wish that he should fulfil only the function of giving formal approval in the name of the King to Acts of the Oireachtas and Orders of the Executive Council in order to bring them into force.

In June O'Kelly took a prominent part in the Downing Street conferences over the retention by the Free State of the land annuity moneys and other sums due to the British Government that culminated in the "economic war", the imposition of penal tariffs and quotas on the imports from the respective countries, and a system of export bounties and subsidies in the Free State. The same year he went to Ottawa as the head of the Free State delegation to the Imperial Economic Conference. As Minister for Finance, a post he was appointed to shortly after the Second World War began, he was to make partial amends for the folly of the economic war when he declared that Ireland "should develop its trade and commerce with its nearest neighbour... to the fullest extent. It is necessary to have a proper understanding so that we may trade to our mutual advantage." But a speech in which he advocated "flogging John Bull right, left and centre" attracted some attention, and showed how difficult it was for the ideas of economic self-sufficiency sustained by Sinn Féin to die a quiet death.

Throughout his political career, O'Kelly contributed articles to the Irish and American press on Irish politics, and he was proprietor and editor of the *Nation*, a weekly republican journal founded in 1927, and wound up in 1931 when Fianna Fáil established its own daily newspaper. He was general secretary of the Gaelic League from 1915 to 1920, and was chiefly instrumental in inducing Dublin Corporation to vote a penny rate for scholarships to help in restoring the Irish language.

Looking back on his Presidency, O'Kelly said that the happiest moment in his life had not been when he was elected to the office, because he enjoyed the rough and tumble of political life. (It was only with some difficulty that he was persuaded to offer himself for a second term.) The highlight of his career, he said, was when he heard Pearse reading the Proclamation of the Republic in front of the General Post Office in Dublin in 1916. Nevertheless, the dry round of official duties, receiving the freedom of cities and honours from many European states, showed him to be a modest and dignified representative of his people, and he won affection wherever he went. Shortly before he relinquished office, he paid an official visit to the United States, where he addressed both houses of the U.S. Congress at a joint session, thus following in the footsteps of Parnell, the first Irishman to do so. In retirement he devoted himself to writing his memoirs, which were subsequently published in an Irish edition.

O'Kelly was married twice. In 1918 he married Mary Kate Ryan, second daughter of John Ryan, who was for many years lecturer in French at University College, Dublin, one of the constituent colleges of the National University. She died in 1934.

Subsequently, O'Kelly married her younger sister, Miss Phyllis Ryan, a public analyst, who had combined her career as a chemistry student in Dublin with active work for the Republican movement.

November 24, 1966.

Chief Festus Sam Okotie-Eboh, whose body, riddled with bullets, was found in a shallow grave 30 miles from Lagos on January 21, 1966, was killed during the Nigerian revolution. He had been the first Nigerian to hold the key portfolio of finance in the Federal Government. He became Finance Minister in 1957, three years before independence, and held the office continuously until he was kidnapped in the military *coup d'état* earlier in January.

As Finance Minister he was well known in the western world and in his search for capital investment for his country was a frequent visitor to Europe. He was himself the embodiment of capitalism, a man of great wealth.

Okotie-Eboh was born in 1912 in the old Warri province, the son of the chief of the Itsekiri people of the Western Region of Nigeria. He was educated at the Baptist School in Sapele, and after a year as a municipal clerk taught for several years. Then in 1935 he joined the Bata Shoe Company as a clerk. By 1942 he had been promoted accountant and chief clerk in Lagos and then became deputy manager of the Sapele branch. Later his company sent him to Czechoslovakia, where he studied for diplomas in business administration and, curiously, in chiropody, learnt the Czech language and witnessed the communist *coup d'état* of 1948.

Back in Nigeria Okotie-Eboh decided to go into business on his own and became a timber and rubber merchant and the owner of a chain of schools, enterprises which laid the foundations of his own personal fortune.

A long-standing friend of Dr. Azikiwe, Okotie-Eboh entered political life in 1951 when he was elected to the Western Region House of Assembly. He had already been chosen as the First Secretary of the Warri National Union and was secretary general of the Itsekiri National Society. In 1954 he moved to the Federal House as M.P. for the Warri division and in the same year became national treasurer of the National Council of Nigeria and the Cameroons (the party which later kept its initials but changed its name to National Convention of Nigerian Citizens)—which Dr. Azikiwe led before becoming Governor General and then President of Nigeria. In 1955 Okotie-Eboh was appointed Federal Minister of Labour, and in 1958, the year after taking over the finance portfolio, he succeeded Dr. Mbadiwe as leader of the N.C.N.C. federal parliamentary party.

He was a flamboyant character, attending the independence ceremonies for example in flowing garments with a train yards long. He used his money lavishly in support of political causes, and at the time of the 1959 election was ferociously attacked by Action Group newspapers and by the Action Group leader, Chief Awolowo, and accused of corruption.

Not surprisingly, in a continent where socialism in one form or another is the dominant political theme, Okotie-Eboh was the focus of bitter criticisms. A man of power and influence, with considerable financial acumen and know-how, he was inevitably increasingly removed from the masses.

January 22, 1966.

Derek Oldham, M.C., one of the best-known and most popular players on the West End stage in the years between the two World Wars, died on March 20, 1968, at the age of 75.

He won a well-deserved reputation in the Gilbert and Sullivan operas as well as in musical productions at Daly's and Drury Lane. With his delightful tenor voice, his curly hair, his cheery smile and his strikingly good looks he had practically every asset the musical comedy hero could ask for—except perhaps height.

Born at Accrington on March 29, 1892, he was first employed for a short time as a bank clerk. In 1914 he made his first stage appearance at the London Pavilion in *The Daring of Diane* and was then for a short time in a revival of *The Chocolate Soldier*. But at the end of the year he joined the Scots Guards and was commissioned in the East Lancashire Regiment. He was mentioned in dispatches in France in 1917 and in the following year was awarded the Military Cross for gallantry in Macedonia.

In 1919 he joined Rupert D'Oyly Carte who was rebuilding his company, which had languished somewhat during the war, in preparation for a West End season. In a brilliant team which included Henry Lytton, Leo Sheffield, Bertha Lewis and Nellie Briercliffe, his success was immediate and lasting.

He stayed with the D'Oyly Carte Company

until 1922 and then left it for seven years. During that part of his career he had many notable successes in musical comedy including *Madame Pompadour* with Evelyn Laye, *Rose Marie* with Edith Day, and *The Vagabond King* with Winnie Melville, whom he married, and who died in 1937. He always hankered to get back to his first love, the Savoy Operas, and he returned to the company in time for a New York season in 1934 followed by a second American tour in 1936–37. He found that President Roosevelt was a Gilbert and Sullivan fan. When the President was inaugurated in 1937 the company was appearing in Washington, and Oldham and Sylvia Cecil were withdrawn from the team for a single performance to sing "Prithee, Pretty Maiden" at the inauguration party at the White House.

A tour in Britain followed, after which Oldham finally left the D'Oyly Carte company. He toured in *Rose Marie*, *Monsieur Beaucaire* and *A Waltz Dream*, and was seen in London in revivals of *Rose Marie*, *The White Horse Inn* and *Hindle Wakes* but he never quite regained the position which, by his considerable ability and personality, he had established during the earlier period of his career.

March 22, 1968.

Dr. J. H. Oldham, C.B.E., D.D., who died on May 16, 1969, at the age of 94, had been honorary president of the World Council of Churches since 1961, an office which crowned a lifetime of work for the ecumenical movement which began with his service as secretary of the World Missionary Conference at Edinburgh in 1910. This event is rightly judged to mark the beginning of the new relationships between the Churches of which none can remain unware today.

Joseph Houldsworth Oldham was born in 1874, the son of Lieutenant-Colonel G. W. Oldham, R.E., and was educated at Edinburgh Academy and Trinity College, Oxford. His ecumenical service began with a year's work as secretary of the Student Christian Movement, followed by three years as secretary of the Y.M.C.A. at Lahore. After a period of theological study, including some time in Germany, he was appointed in 1908 secretary for the World Missionary Conference to be held in Edinburgh two years later. His original churchmanship was Presbyterian, and he was intended for the ministry. In the event his extraordinary service to the Churches was given chiefly as an Anglican layman.

The combination of Oldham's "back-room" gifts with the public powers and industry of the chairman of "Edinburgh 1910", John R. Mott, was the chief factor in making that gathering what its predecessors had not been, a *working* conference prepared for by deep and wide study and arranged to bring able minds and wide experience to bear on carefully prepared reports. This—and the fact that churchmanship was taken seriously—made the conference the starting point of the modern ecumenical movement.

Contrary to earlier expectation, a continuation committee was elected and Oldham was made its secretary. The ecumenical movement now possessed its first organization. Largely through his influence (he was a fluent German speaker) by 1921 the chasm that opened up during the 1914–18 War between the German churches and others was closed and the International Missionary Council was formed. Oldham was its secretary. He remained in this office until 1938.

In planning the first full meeting of the International Missionary Council at Jerusalem in 1928, he saw clearly that it was the rise of secularism which the Christian mission must increasingly encounter everywhere. By 1920 he was deeply aware that Africa was the emergent continent of the future and served from 1931–1938 as the administrative director of the International Institute of African Languages and Cultures. He concentrated greatly on educational questions, being a member of the Advisory Committee on Education in the Colonies from 1925 to 1936.

In the thirties he saw that totalitarianism faced the Churches with their greatest challenge. His planning of the second Life and Work conference at Oxford in 1937 was superb. Its theme was "Church, Community and State", and although German delegates were prevented by the Nazi Government from attending, conference prepared the Churches for the holocaust to come. Largely for this reason the bonds of Christian fellowship held fast in a way in which, to Oldham's tragically personal knowledge, they had not done in the 1914–18 War.

For "Oxford 1937" Oldham laid many thinkers under tribute who would not readily have thought of an ecclesiastical gathering as their natural milieu (as earlier men like R. H. Tawney had been recruited for the Jerusalem gathering). He had already discovered the originality of Paul Tillich. Oldham was *par excellence* the "midwife" of group thinking. To bring unusual groups together for creative encounter was a task which Oldham loved, as befitted an early disciple of Martin Buber. To evoke and edit contributions from very diverse thinkers in preparation for larger gatherings like that at Oxford was his particular genius.

May 17, 1969.

Sir Lancelot Oliphant, K.C.M.G., C.B., formerly Ambassador to Belgium and Minister to Luxembourg, died in London on October 2, 1965, at the age of 83.

As a junior member of the Foreign Office he carried the British declaration of war in 1914 to the German Embassy in London; but it was incorrectly worded and a second declaration was sent, this time by Mr. Harold Nicolson, as he then was.

He was born in 1881 and joined the Foreign Office (then separate from the Diplomatic Service) in 1903. It was unusual in those days for Foreign Office clerks, as they were called, to be posted abroad but Oliphant had a strong feeling for the East and was allowed two short spells in Turkey and Persia. These experiences set the pattern for his future career, and on his return to the Foreign Office from Teheran in 1911 his official life and interests were centred mainly on the countries of the Middle East for the next 28 years.

In the Eastern Department Oliphant, with his first-hand knowledge of Persia, was able to speak with authority at a moment when Russian encroachments in north Persia were giving the Foreign Office many anxious moments, and he was in due course made head of that department. Later on when he was promoted assistant Under-Secretary the Eastern Department was one of those whose work he superintended. This was not altogether a happy arrangement, for it was inevitable that Oliphant should find it difficult to delegate in a field with which he was so familiar. Even in 1936, when he was promoted deputy Under-Secretary, he still trailed his Middle East aura with him, but eventually in 1939 his long connexion with that region of the world was broken when he was appointed Ambassador to Brussels.

CAPTURED BY GERMANS

It was in the days of the phony war and at such a moment and in such a place the role of an Ambassador is a nugatory one, so that it was not surprising that Oliphant found no scope for creative work. In any case events soon overtook him and when the Germans overran Belgium he was captured by them and kept for over a year. He has described his experiences in a book entitled *An Ambassador in Bonds*. In September, 1941, he was released and joined the Belgian Government in London. When that Government returned to Brussels in 1944 Oliphant pleaded hard to be allowed to go back with them. But he was already 63 and his period of incarceration had dealt hardly with him and the Secretary of State decided that a younger man must take his place and that he should retire.

Oliphant was a perfect Victorian figure, a character out of a Whyte-Melville novel; and he would have been happy to be regarded as such. Tall, gaunt, with deep sunk eyes and hollow cheeks, sparse and wispy hair and always with exquisitely polished button boots or shoes he looked far more at ease in the frock-coat and top hat which he wore in the earlier days of his career than in the anonymous garb of Whitehall. When the play *Diplomacy* was revived in 1913 Oliphant hired one of the few remaining hansom cabs in London and arrived at the theatre in it, wearing an opera cloak and gibus and carrying a gold-headed cane. It may have looked affected but to Oliphant it was a natural and proper tribute to pay to a past age.

He was an excellent and correct official. He was accurate and meticulous—though with a sometimes intempestive insistence on the niceties of procedure—and he had dealt with most of his subjects so long that he knew them by heart. Though his mind was not a wide-ranging one and though he contributed few ideas of his own, he knew to whom it was profitable to listen and his long familiarity with Whitehall enabled him to translate their views into action. He had a sense of humour that was boyish—almost private school boyish, and many a dull official meeting, especially if it were attended by members of the fighting services for whom Oliphant always had a warm corner in his heart, was enlivened by the play of his frolicsome banter.

The story goes that when he was serving at Teheran snow blocked the passes and he was detailed to take the diplomatic bag to Baghdad. A telegram was sent "Bag coming by Oliphant". In transmission the last word became elephant and back came the reply: "Surely a camel would be cheaper".

To those whom he liked he was kindly and considerate, but he had had a stern Victorian upbringing, and though his ideals were those of a chivalrous English gentleman, he could be harsh and uncompromising if he seemed to detect in a subordinate any declension from the high standards of duty which he set and maintained for himself.

In 1939 he married Christine, widow of the first Viscount Churchill.

October 4, 1965.

Admiral of the Fleet Sir Henry Oliver, G.C.B., K.C.M.G., M.V.O., died on October 15, 1965, in his 101st year.

Oliver's name is little known outside the Royal Navy—and perhaps not as well known within it as it might be—yet his influence was immence; he was a man of few words and great achievements, modest and taciturn in an age when "top sailors" exhibited a marked tendency towards flamboyance. To the visitor expecting a seaman's richness of metaphor Oliver's conversation might seem a little disappointing; but to anyone genuinely interested in the art of war and strategy it rang like good metal; his talk might be easily digested, but it was most filling. For his taciturnity he was universally—and affectionately—known in the Navy as "Dummy Oliver"; but he was also described as the "father of modern navigation", and it was a measure of his abilities that throughout the most critical period of the 1914–18 War he held the position of Chief of the War Staff at the Admiralty, to which he was appointed on the return of Lord Fisher to office in 1914.

Henry Francis Oliver, born on January 22, 1865, entered the Royal Navy in 1878, and went to sea in 1880 on board the Agincourt, a five-masted vessel, flagship in the Channel Squadron.

In 1900 he took up the post which first made him known throughout the Navy. This was navigator of the Majestic, flagship in the Channel Squadron of Vice-Admiral (later Admiral of the Fleet) Sir Arthur Knyvet Wilson, who during the naval manoeuvres of 1901 took the Channel Fleet at high speed from the north of Ireland through the Irish Sea to the Scilly Islands in thick weather without sighting land or lights and, aided only by the sound signals from the lighthouse on the Bishop Rock, into the anchorage of St. Mary's through thick fog. When in 1903 an instructional school for navigating officers was established on board Mercury at Portsmouth Oliver was promoted to Captain and placed in command of it. Here he did great work, setting new high standards for navigating officers.

From December, 1908, Oliver was for three years Naval Assistant to the First Sea Lord, Lord Fisher. Then followed a commission in command of the battleship Thunderer, which he left in November, 1913, to become Director of Naval Intelligence. Reappointed on his promotion to Rear-Admiral in December, 1913, he was in office on the outbreak of war in 1914. In his capacity as D.N.I. he went with Winston Churchill—the First Lord—over to Antwerp, ostensibly to report on the situation for the Admiralty; but once there he proved, as Churchill recorded, a great stand-by in this time of stress. Night and day he laboured to disable the large quality of merchant shipping which lay in the Scheldt, so that the Germans might not use it for embarking troops in an attempt at invasion. Assited only by a Belgian sapper officer, four privates and a Belgian boy scout, he inserted explosive charges between the cylinders of 38 large vessels, rupturing their machinery so that not one of them was fit to go down the Scheldt during the whole of the German occupation.

In October, 1914, Oliver succeeded Rear-Admiral Hood as Naval Secretary to Churchill and some three weeks later, on Lord Fisher's return to office, was appointed in Admiral Sturdee's place as Chief of the War Staff, with acting rank as Vice-Admiral. He kept that office until February, 1918. The Chief of the War Staff, from being a purely advisory officer before the war, gradually took on executive functions under the stress of hostilities, and it was eventually assumed, when Lord Jellicoe went to the Admiralty in 1916, by the First Sea Lord himself, the former chief becoming Deputy Chief of the Naval Staff, with special responsibility for all operations except those against U-boats and in direct protection of trade.

In that period it was at Oliver's motion that the introduction of "taut-wire measuring gear" greatly increased the efficiency of the British minelaying campaign in German waters and the North Sea.

C-IN-C ATLANTIC

In March, 1918, reverting to his substantive rank of Rear-Admiral, Oliver hoisted his flag afloat for the first time in command of the First Battle-Cruiser Squadron, Grand Fleet, on board the Repulse, and in her eight months later he was present at the surrender of the German High Seas Fleet off the Firth of Forth. He remained in the Repulse until the Grand Fleet was broken up early in 1919, when he was appointed Vice-Admiral Commanding the Home Fleet, with his flag in the battleship King George V. About a year later his force was merged in the Reserve Fleet, of which Vice-Admiral Oliver assumed command, in the same flagship. In September, 1920, he became Second Sea Lord of the Admiralty, and during his four years in that office he carried out, as Chief of Naval Personnel, the drastic reductions in the officers' lists which followed the Geddes report and the Washington Conference. The special retirement scheme of 1922 was the most drastic and comprehensive, and at the same time the most liberal to those affected, ever known in the history of the Navy. In August, 1924, Oliver, who had attained full Admiral's rank in the previous November, succeeded Admiral de Robeck as Commander-in-Chief of the Atlantic Fleet, and held the command until 1927. In January, 1928, he was promoted Admiral of the Fleet in the vacancy caused by the death of de Robeck.

He married in 1914 Beryl (Dame Beryl Oliver, G.B.E.), daughter of F. E. Carnegy of Lour, who survives him.

October 18, 1965.

Sir Roland Oliver, M.C., who died on March 14, 1967, in his 85th year, was a Judge of the High Court from October, 1938, till his retirement in December, 1957.

An outstanding figure at the criminal law Bar, he enjoyed an extensive practice as a junior in that class of work. After taking silk in 1925, though he was still briefed in a number of criminal trials, he practised more frequently and with great success in the civil courts. Behind his quiet manner and soft voice there was a strong and forceful character. He possessed a clear mind, an instinct for selecting the matters which were relevant, an ability to clarify them with logical precision, and the knowledge needed to argue any issues of law which might arise. Indeed, to listen to his exposition of a complicated case was to realise that his grasp and technique were those of a master of his work. In criminal matters particularly his colleagues, whether at the Bar or on the Bench, would from time to time ask his advice when difficulties confronted them and his views would illuminate and resolve their problems with a sure touch. Although his conduct of a case was always convincing, it was necessary to get accustomed to his quiet voice, and it would have been easier for his listeners had he possessed good resonant tones which carried well. While at the criminal law Bar he worked with and against some of the foremost practitioners of that branch of our legal system.

Roland Giffard Oliver was born on May 5, 1882, the third son of Edmund Ward Oliver, of Orlestone, Ashford, Kent, and was educated at Marlborough and Corpus Christi College Oxford, where he took a second in jurisprudence. He was called to the Bar by the Inner Temple in 1909 and joined the South-Eastern Circuit. He became a pupil of, and afterwards devilled for, the late Mr. Justice Humphreys whose son, Christmas Humphreys, some years later was Oliver's first pupil.

In the 1914–18 War Oliver served with the R.F.A. and was awarded the Military Cross. On his return to practice he was appointed, in 1921, Third Junior Prosecuting Counsel for the Crown at the Central Criminal Court. Thenceforth his name was constantly before the public as appearing in most of the notable criminal trials of the time—such as the Thompson-Bywaters murder, and the criminal proceedings which followed and arose out of the civil action, Robinson v. Midland Bank, Ltd.—the "Mr. A" case.

In 1926 he was appointed Recorder of Folkestone. He was made a Bencher of his Inn in 1934. Although after taking silk his practice became less confined to the criminal courts, he still appeared in a number of important trials. In 1933 he led for the Crown in the great "Fire-Raising Case", which was heard at the Central Criminal Court before his old master, Travers Humphreys, and which occupied 30 days (in this case Leopold Harris was sentenced to 14 years' penal servitude) and in the later trial of Captain Miles, Chief of the London Salvage Corps. At almost the same time he appeared in the Consistory Court for the Bishop of Norwich in the case of the Rev. Harold Davidson, rector of Stiffkey, which lasted many days and attracted much public interest.

Davidson, who was found guilty on a number of charges brought by the Bishop against his moral character, was later deposed from Holy Orders. In July, 1937, when appearing at a Skegness amusement park Davidson was mauled by a lion in whose cage he lectured and died from his injuries.

Shortly before he was made a Judge Oliver was briefed to defend Aleck Bourne, the Wimpole Street surgeon, and was successful in securing his acquittal in a case which decided an important principle concerning the rights of doctors as regards abortion.

Among his other activities Oliver was a member of the Committee which investigated in 1936 the leakage of Budget secrets, the other members being Sir Samuel Lowry Porter and Gavin Simonds, K.C. In March, 1938, he was chairman of a Committee on the Courts-martial system. After he had been appointed a Judge he presided in 1943 over a Committee which had to inquire into and report on the treatment of men under sentence in naval and military prisons and detention barracks. The Committee was set up because of a scandal at Maidstone resulting in the conviction at the Assizes of two n.c.o.s of manslaughter.

Meanwhile, in 1938, Mr. Justice Horridge had died. The opportunity was thus presented of appointing a successor who was not only familiar with the civil side but who had a wide experience of the criminal courts and would strengthen the Bench in that aspect of its jurisdiction. Lord Maugham's recommendation of Oliver for the position met with the warm approval of the legal profession, and proved to be fully justified. Neither his character nor his method of work were of the kind to encourage publicity. After nearly 20 years of service as a Judge he retired in 1957, his last appearance in Court being at the Old Bailey. This fitting conclusion, when tributes were paid to him, was touched with a pleasing sentiment; for Christmas Humphreys then said to him: "I understand from the Lord Chief Justice (Lord Goddard) it was at your request that the closing days of your long and distinguished career on the Bench should be spent in the building where they began."

Like many men whose work calls for mental concentration Oliver found great pleasure and relaxation by the use of his hands. He was a first-class carpenter, and among the varied products of his skill were a number of model boats, including a beautiful one of the Cutty Sark. His fondness for music was mainly expressed through the violin. He practised assiduously, and his performances showed an understanding of the subject and considerable ability in execution. He was a charming and generous host to his friends, but he was not the "hail-fellow-well-met" type. He was fastidious in his tastes and particular in the choice of his friends, and remained constant in his likes and dislikes.

He married in 1923 Winifred Emily, widow of George Henry Belas and daughter of Lieutenant-Colonel Eustace Beaumont Burnaby. She died in 1959. In 1961 he married Mrs Madelaine Mary Kean.

March 16, 1967.

Vic Oliver, the comedian and musician, died in Johannesburg on August 15, 1964, at the age of 66.

His death, which was discovered when he failed to take a call in the crime play in which he was acting, removes one of the few survivors from the days before the Second World War, when charm, geniality and the power to project a personality into the remotest reaches of a theatre were important parts of the entertainer's stock-in-trade. But though Vic Oliver may well be remembered for the charm that is almost the hallmark of those born in Vienna, he was as much a musician as a comedian and, at times, nearly as much a straight actor.

BARON'S SON

Born in Vienna on July 8, 1898, the son of Baron Victor von Samek, Vic Oliver studied medicine at Vienna University but abandoned the possibility of life as a doctor for music, which had been his love since childhood; for a time he was a pupil of Mahler. After service in the Austrian cavalry in the First World War he worked for some time first as a banker and then as a textile manufacturer before returning to music and visiting the United States as a conductor and violinist in 1926. An accident demanding an apology to the audience revealed the fact that he could make audiences laugh, and music was thrust into the background by a new career as a comedian which took him all over the United States. He reached the Palace Theatre, New York, in 1929 and made his first appearance at the London Palladium two years later.

The deferential, mid-European accent that he exploited with great skill, his friendly banter and the humour that, if it mocked at all, mocked himself, became extremely popular in England and kept him continually busy in musicals, revues, variety and pantomime, as well as in occasional plays like Robert Sherwood's anti-war play *Idiot's Delight*, in the provincial tour of which, in 1938 and 1939, he played the part of Harry Van with skill, zest and sincerity. *Follow the Sun*, C. B. Cochran's 1936 revue, *Black and Blue* and *Black Velvet* were among his successes.

Throughout the Second World War he broadcast regularly in *Hi Gang* with Bebe Daniels and Ben Lyon, and was subsequently a frequent broadcaster in comedy and variety programmes. Music, however, came to occupy more and more of his time, and from the foundation of the British Concert Orchestra in 1945 he was its conductor and musical director, dividing his time between music and comedy. Latterly he planned to settle and found a touring opera company in South Africa.

His autobiography, *Mr. Showbusiness*, is the story of a serious-minded and thoughtful man enjoying the multifarious occupations which, for him, were involved in entertaining the public.

In 1936 Vic Oliver married Miss Sarah Churchill, the daughter of Sir Winston Churchill; the marriage was dissolved in 1945. He subsequently married Miss Frances Condor, who survives him. They had one daughter.

August 17, 1964.

Erich Ollenhauer, chairman of the west German Social Democratic Party, and chairman of the Socialist International, died in Bonn on December 14, 1963. He was 62.

It was Ollenhauer's doubtful privilege to take over responsibility for the Socialist Party's destinies in 1952 from the far more brilliant and tempestuous Kurt Schumacher, with whom he worked closely on its reconstruction after the years of exile and prescription of nazi rule. There could not have been two more dissimilar personalities: Schumacher, a sick man whose health was ruined by years in concentration camps, was a Prussian to the fingertips, and a politician of uncompromising, provocative manner and ideas; Ollenhauer was by temperament a man of moderation and common sense, an advocate of persuasion and the middle way, firm on socialist principles but pragmatic in their application.

He was often criticized by his opponents as a typical, rather uninspring example of the *petit bourgeois* party functionary. There was certainly nothing flashy about him, and he sedulously shunned publicity. He was not the passionate, popular tribune or fiery rabble-rouser. But under a somewhat uninspiring exterior and manner, he concealed solid personal and political gifts. His sterling honesty and his uprightness, his common sense approach to political issues, and his remarkable ability as a conciliator, earned him the respect of his fellow parliamentarians of all persuasions and of anyone who had close dealings with him.

AWAY FROM MARXISM

These gifts played a decisive part in leading German socialism smoothly and without disruption over the last few years away from the trappings and ideologies of Marxism, and from a rather strident nationalism designed to over-compensate the shortcomings of the Weimar regime, and transforming it into a mildly progressive, highly respectable, and almost bourgeois party, which ceased to be a scarecrow to the German middle class voter, and could contribute to the stability of parliamentary government, and to continuity in the essential issues of policy. By his reasonableness and fairness, Ollenhauer guided his party through the great internal transformation ushered in by the Godesberg programme and kept it together and united during the long sterile years of opposition. If any reproach could be made to him, it was that, inevitably, by helping to transform German socialism and render it somewhat innocuous he made it almost indistinguishable in many respects from the more conservative political groups.

Erich Ollenhauer was born on March 27, 1901, in Magdeburg, the son of a mason. After leaving elementary school he went into trade. His membership of the Socialist Youth Movement from 1916 onwards decided his career. Three years later he became editor of the local socialist newspaper, *Volkstimmer*, and in 1920 was elected to the executive of the Socialist Youth Movement in Berlin. Already the leftwingers in that organization had nicknamed him "*Geheimrat*", or "secret councillor", because he produced the impression of a man much older and more sensible than his years. In 1928 he became chairman of the Youth Movement, a post he held until 1948. He was forced into exile by Hitler's accession to power in 1933, having that same year been elected a member of the Social Democratic Party's national executive.

The years of exile were spent at first in Prague, then Paris, and finally London, where Ollenhauer refused to take part in anti-German propaganda and became personally acquainted with all the exiled socialist leaders of Europe—contacts which were to be invaluable to him later in reconciling many countries to the existence of a new, repentant Germany.

After the collapse of the Third Rich, he returned to Germany and was Secretary of the Socialist Party office in the western zone of occupation, with headquarters in Hanover. At the first postwar party congress, in 1946, he was elected second chairman. It was a striking demonstration of his hold on the respect and affection of his party that he was subsequently repeatedly confirmed in that position. In 1949 he entered the Bundestag as a member for Hanover, and became deputy leader of the Socialist parliamentary group.

In spite of their vastly dissimilar personalities he and Kurt Schumacher had worked closely together to build up the party and extend its network throughout the country. When Schumacher died in 1952 it was a foregone conclusion that Ollenhauer would succeed him, and he was elected at the Dortmund party congress by the overwhelming majority of 357 votes out of 366 cast. From then on he remained unopposed in that office. In spite of their profound disagreements, Ollenhauer as a parliamentarian succeeded in earning the respect of Dr. Adenauer and the C.D.U. for his fairness in debate, his unruffled courtesy, and his respect for facts and plain truth. He was not a brilliant speaker, and disdained oratorical flourishes. His aim was always much more to convince than to impress or dazzle; and many of his sharply pointed criticisms went home.

He travelled extensively after 1945, helping to soften prejudice against the Federal Republic, and successfully building up good will. These efforts bore fruit in his election in July, 1951, to the vice-chairmanship of the Socialist International and its resurrection in Frankfurt. Ten years later, he became its chairman.

REUNIFICATION PLAN

In 1957 he sent to Dr. Adenauer, before the latter's journey to Washington, his so-called "Ollenhauer plan" for the reunification of Germany on the basis of four-power negotiations. He postulated a European security system in place of the existing military blocks, and negotiations with Russia; but excluded all direct dealings with the east German communists. Two years later he came out in favour of the Rapacki plan, for controlled and balanced disengagement in Europe, which he believed acceptable to the Russians—a stand which the C.D.U. tirelessly exploited to brand their Socialist opponents as unreliable supporters of the west. He also opposed German rearmament, but later, when German socialism became reconciled to the Bundeswehr, rejected any suggestion of its possessing nuclear weapons. Later, in line with the evolution of his party's ideas on western policy, he became a staunch advocate of Nato. He supported wholeheartedly Britain's attempted entry into the Common Market, and he visited Britain in 1961. It was never his ambition to become a candidate for the Chancellorship. He preferred to play his part in the background, and in 1959 declared to a party leadership meeting that it served the socialist interests best if he went on putting all his endeavours into the work he was doing.

He married in 1922 Martha Müller, and had two sons.

December 16, 1963.

C. T. Onions, C.B.E., the youngest of the four editors of the *Oxford English Dictionary* and the oldest stipendiary fellow in Oxford, died on January 8, 1965, at the age of 91.

Charles Talbut Onions was born at Edgbaston, Birmingham, on September 10, 1873. He was educated at King Edward VI School, Camp Hill, and Mason College, Birmingham, where he was well grounded in the classics under E. A. Sonnenschein and in French under Clovis Bévenot. After a period of teaching and study Onions, in 1895, joined the staff of the Oxford Dictionary, working first under Dr. (afterwards Sir James) Murray, later with Henry Bradley. His powers as a lexicographer were early appreciated, not least by Charles Cannan, secretary of the Clarendon Press, who detached him from the Dictionary to produce his *Shakespeare Glossary*, the work which first relieved English-speaking scholars from dependence on Schmidt. In this compendium Onions's knowledge of the Warwickshire dialect enabled him to make some fresh contributions to Shakespearian lexicology. Another parergon was the revision, for successive editions, of Henry Sweet's *Anglo-Saxon Reader*. Cannan detached him also for the completion of *Shakespeare's England*, which had been begun by Sir Sidney Lee. His *English Syntax* (1904) has been in use the world over.

Onions was virtually responsible for certain sections of the alphabet edited by Bradley and Craigie, and in 1914 he became an independent editor. As such he bore the chief responsibility for the concluding volume, delayed by Murray's death, Bradley's failing health, Sir William Craigie's translation to Chicago, and (not least) by the great complexity of many words that begin with W. As a lexicographer he called himself Bradley's disciple, but he had a just view of Murray's great gifts. Bradley was a consummate philologist, but had not Murray's driving power, nor his *flair* for the practical and technological aspects of words. Onions, beside his wide and profound philological learning, had a sure grasp of idiom and a Bradleian talent for discrimination. His analytical power was well seen in such articles as *set*, *shall*, and *will*, and the interrogative pronouns. His most sensational discovery was that *syllabus* had its origin in mere error—a perversion of *sillyba*.

Onions's executive powers are nowhere better seen than in his conduct of the largescale abridgment—the "Shorter Oxford" of the great dictionary, which, taking over from William Little, he completed and revised throughout.

MASTERLY COMPRESSION

His addenda to the edition of 1944, in which, in 20 pages, he dealt with nearly 1,500 words, mostly the product of war, are a masterpiece of compression, though he depreciated his work—"I don't call that lexicography".

The crowning work of his life is the forthcoming *Oxford Dictionary of English Etymology*, which on his own admission marks an advance on the corresponding parts of the *Oxford English Dictionary*.

Oxford is not always quick to appreciate scholars in its midst who are loosely attached; and Onions was only gradually given due recognition. Phelps, of Oriel, who knew his wife's family, secured his admission to that common room, and in 1923, on Bradley's death, he succeeded him as fellow of Magdalen. There he will be best remembered for his reluctant conversation and his tenure of the office of librarian. Oxford can never have had a better college librarian.

The growing school of English Language and Literature gradually absorbed a large part of his time and energies; in 1920 he became a Lecturer and later a Reader (1927–49). In 1948, on his seventy-fifth birthday, his colleagues and other friends gave him a list of his published writings: an impressive record. From 1932 to 1956 he was editor of *Medium Ævum*, the anniversary issue of which was dedicated to him. His interest in Anglo-Norman should be recorded. He became director of the Early English Text Society on the death of Robin Flower, and remained in that post for many years.

He was a Fellow of the British Academy. He was created C.B.E. in 1934.

Onions married Angela Blythman, who died in 1941, leaving 10 children. It deserves mention that their seven sons and three daughters were more or less actively engaged in the Second World War and that all survived.

January 12, 1965.

Oliver Onions, who died on April 9, 1961, at the age of 87, was a novelist of uncommonly sensitive and original imagination and of commanding resources of craftsmanship and style, and one who had received far less recognition than was his due.

He was a writer of a retiring kind, fastidious and diffident, who had no great faith in his public and who more than once had been tempted to believe that serious novel-writing was a game not worth the candle. It is possible that, like other writers of rare capacity, he had frequently suffered the discouragement of obtuse criticism. He wrote with difficulty, even with anguish, and produced in all more than 20 novels, but there were longish intervals during which he published nothing at all.

A Yorkshireman—his surname is not uncommon in that county—Oliver Onions was born at Bradford of humble parents in 1873. He went to London as a young man to study art, found employment for a time as a draughtsman in a studio attached to the Harmsworth Press, and for some years had it in mind to become a painter. He had no special inclination, it would seem, towards literature, and his earliest book, *The Compleat Bachelor* (1901), was written in the first place in answer to a challenge by a friend. Here his ironic humour, less mordant than it became afterwards, found nice expression. The result was apparently promising enough to encourage him to go on writing.

SATIRE ON JOURNALISM

His next book, *Little Devil Doubt*, was more serious in purpose. A satirical study of the cheap journalism of the period, acutely written, but somewhat wanting in both substance and style, it marks the beginning of that critical attitude towards the methods of big business which Onions was to develop in a good deal of his later fiction. It was an attitude that gave force and point to the illustration of methods of company promotion and advertising in *Good Boy Seldom* (1911). The books that followed immediately compose a memorable trilogy. The first, *In Accordance with the Evidence* (1912), was in effect completed by a sequel, *The Debit Account*, which followed in the next year, and hard on the heels of the sequel came *The Story of Louie*, which subtly resumed the narrative already unfolded from the point of view of a character given a minor part only in the earlier two volumes. Again the central figure is a man who rises to a position of power in big business. The whole work (re-written in later years and issued under the title of *Whom God Has Sundered*) is done with stern dramatic power, with searching insight into the dark places of the mind, and with something of poetic force also. That combination of realism and poetry was always to be distinctive of Oliver Onions's best work.

INTERVAL OF SILENCE

It was not a combination that made for wide popularity. Perhaps because of this, and because writing cost him so much effort, he seemed for long periods to restrict himself to less than his highest capacity. The realism grew a little clouded by artifice and ingenuity, the satire acquired an edge of bitterness, the poetry receded or turned towards the macabre. After *A Crooked Mile* and *Mushroom Town*, both of which appeared in 1914, came an interval of silence, during most of which he was in uniform, an enthusiastic member of a volunteer body known as the Old Boys' Corps and serving at home in the Commissariat Department. Then, in 1920, he published *A Case in Camera* and, a year later, *The Tower of Oblivion*, both a shade too obviously contrived to give his powers full scope.

PLACE IN ANTHOLOGIES

During the next 10 years he produced some eight novels or volumes of short stories; although as a short-story writer he never again reached the peak of artistry achieved in the relatively early collection entitled *Widdershins* (1911), many of which attain an authentic note of horror and of the uncanny and not a few of which have deservedly found a place in subsequent anthologies.

From 1931 until 1939 he seems to have written very little. In the latter year, however, appeared *The Hand of Kornelius Voyt*, a telling study in abnormal psychology, and a year afterwards came *Cockcrow*, in which satire and a barely restrained bitterness were joined to a story of young lovers told with unaffected tenderness. Again there was a period of silence, this time until 1945, when Onions produced what for his most constant admirers must surely seem the crown of his achievement, *The Story of Ragged Rohyn*. Enchantment and awe lie close about this tale of the later part of the seventeenth century, a tale lit by a tragic and haunted sense of the world's cruelty. It was succeeded, in the following year, by *Poor Man's Tapestry*, a curiously formed tale of a journeyman goldsmith in the England of the Wars of the Roses. At once more irresolute and more stylized, the book earned the award (perhaps with *Ragged Rohyn* in mind) of the James Tait Black memorial prize. Three years later came *Arras of Youth* and, three years later still, *A Penny for the Harp*, both set in a slightly earlier period and both showing, for all their felicities of historical study and imagination, a decline in power.

RETICENCE

Although he missed their fame, Oliver Onions had a more authentic creative talent than several of his more eminent contemporaries. His was, indeed, a largely neglected achievement. He was a difficult person to know, reticent even where his special interests and knowledge were concerned; he talked very fast in a rather mumbling voice, so that it was often necessary to guess what he had said. But the strain of poetry in his nature was always recognizably unaffected and English.

He married, while she also was an art student and had not started on her career as a writer of light and popular fiction, Miss Berta Ruck. They had two sons, for whose sake he changed his name by deed poll, after 1918, to George Oliver.

April 10, 1961.

Dr. J. Robert Oppenheimer, the physicist, died on February 18, 1967, at the age of 62 at his home in Princeton. He was a German immigrant's son who became the pioneer of America's atom bomb—only to be barred later from United States nuclear secrets. He was also a member of the scientific panel which advised the 10 Government leaders on whether or not to drop the bomb on Japan without warning during the Second World War. A few years later Oppenheimer was denied access to secret documents because of alleged association with Communists. The tall, thin, physicist, a chain-smoker, spent the last months of his life in retirement, seeking "an understanding . . . of what the sciences have brought to human life".

Robert Oppenheimer was known to the general public as the man who directed the development of the first atomic weapons during the Second World War, and who got into trouble as a result of controversy over the policy on hydrogen bombs. To his colleagues he was, in addition, a theoretical physicist of stature, distinguished particularly by his deep understanding of modern physics and by his sense of proportion and of style.

J. Robert Oppenheimer was born on April 22, 1904, in New York. He grew up in a background of a well-to-do and cultured family and received his secondary education at one of New York's progressive private schools. At the age of 11 he was elected to the New York Mineralogical Society. He graduated from Harvard in 1925 and, after a year in Cambridge, obtained his Ph.D. in Göttingen at the age of 23. He made many contributions to the early development of quantum mechanics. One example of this was his work with Max Born in Göttingen on the application of quantum mechanics to the physics of molecules which, as the "Born-Oppenheimer method" is now part of any standard text on the subject. He visited other institutions in Europe, including Leiden and Zurich, before returning to an academic appointment in the United States in 1929. At first he held appointments both in the California Institute of Technology and the University of California at Berkeley, where he became a full professor in 1936. During this period he continued his own work on modern quantum theory and also developed a school of modern theoretical physics.

His pupils now hold leading positions in many universities in the United States and elsewhere. He probably exerted a stronger influence on the development of modern physics through his effect on others than through his direct contributions. He was outstanding as a guide and adviser. Talking to him about a problem was a unique experience because of the speed with which he saw the point. One usually managed to tell him half the story before he had seen the rest and was able to put it in the proper perspective. His quick understanding gave him time to keep his interests wide. Not only could he comment intelligently on problems in sciences other than his own but he was erudite in the literature of many languages, including Sanskrit, and was a connoisseur of the arts.

One important contribution he made during the Californian period is worth special mention.

When Dirac first proposed the electron "hole" theory he tried to interpret the holes as protons, but this proved an untenable hypothesis. Oppenheimer concluded that, instead, the theory called for an "anti-electron" or positron, which soon after was indeed discovered to exist.

It is not surprising that a man of his vision thought about the implications of atomic energy as soon as its release became a practical possibility, and when in 1943 the production of fissile material was imminent, he was asked to take charge of the work on the problems of weapons design. He became the Director of the Scientific Laboratory at Los Alamos, a site he helped to choose in the mountain country he knew and loved. The technical success of Los Alamos owes much to him. Besides directing the work of a large and complex scientific organization he had to form the bridge between the academic scientists and the military who, while united in a common purpose, did not always see eye to eye on ways of doing things.

KEPT THEIR CONFIDENCE

It is a tribute to his personal qualities that he was able to maintain the full confidence of both.

He well knew the implications of the work he was doing and he was involved in an advisory capacity with the decision to use atomic bombs on Japan. There is no clear record of the part he played in this decision, but he made it clear on many subsequent occasions that he realized its seriousness and the responsibility he shared.

After the end of the war he took part with enthusiasm in the drafting of the Lilienthal-Baruch plan for the international control of atomic energy—an attempt, which proved unsuccessful, to utilize the existence of atomic weapons for reducing international tension and reducing the danger of future wars of mass destruction.

He had by then returned to California, but in 1947 he became the Director of the Institute for Advanced Study in Princeton, a position for which his universality and his interest in people were singularly appropriate qualifications. He resigned as director of the Institute in June last year, saying he wanted to devote more time to research, and "to seek an understanding, both historical and philosophical, of what the sciences have brought to human life".

He remained a consultant to government agencies and, in particular, the chairman of the General Advisory Committee of the Atomic Energy Committee.

This committee at one time had to advise on the desirability of a major effort in developing thermonuclear weapons. Their advice was against this. This was in part because of their reluctance to see the development of a weapon even more powerful and even more destructive than the atomic bomb which seemed powerful enough and terrible enough at the time. In part the committee were also influenced by the technical difficulties, since the only scheme proposed at the time was an extremely complex affair of doubtful feasibility. The advice of the committee was overruled at a time when an ingenious proposal had avoided most of the technical difficulties, and soon afterwards Oppenheimer was under attack for his opposition to the development. The motives for this attack were complex—the form it took was to bar him from access to secret information on the grounds that his loyalty was in question. He chose to exercise his right to insist on a hearing, and he went through the ordeal of a hearing by a three-man board. The proceedings were supposed to be secret but in the end were published in full, going into every aspect of Oppenheimer's life, his thoughts, his associations and his contacts with various organizations in case they indicated some sympathy for communism.

The Board decided by two votes to one that his judgment about the hydrogen bomb had been at fault, and that this indicated that he was a security risk. The Atomic Energy Commission did not endorse this view of the Board; they did not support the idea that a scientist should be attacked personally because of his judgment on a technical matter, but, nevertheless, the Commission decided (one of the Commissioners, the physicist Harry Smyth, dissenting) that Oppenheimer was a security risk because of "fundamental defects in his character". This decision caused much bitterness among scientists. For Oppenheimer the one relieving factor was the warm and spontaneous demonstrations of sympathy shown to him by any group of scientists and students which he met at that time.

In 1953, Oppenheimer gave the Reith lectures on the subject of "Science and the Common Understanding".

In 1963 he was chosen for the Enrico Fermi Award, a high and official honour, in a gesture evidently intended to close this sad chapter in the relations of the United States Government with its scientists.

In 1940 he married Katherine Harrison, widow of a man who died fighting for the Republicans in the Spanish Civil War, and they had one son and one daughter. His wife's evidence in the public records of the hearings shows her as a person of great strength of character, and suggests how much support he must have received from her in times of stress.

February 20, 1967.

Admiral Rauf Orbay, who died in Istanbul on July 16, 1964, at the age of 83, was one of the heroes of the Turkish War of Independence, a former prime minister, and a popular Turkish Ambassador to London during the Second World War.

Orbay was born in 1881 in Istanbul, son of Admiral Mehmed Muzaffer Pasha, and was always destined for a naval career. He was first sent to the military college at Tripoli in Libya then part of the Ottoman Empire and later to the naval college at Heybeli Island near Istanbul. His life of adventure began early. When Italy attacked the North African provinces of the Empire in 1912 Rauf Bey quickly became engaged in running arms and supplies to the Turkish forces there. He first became famous in the Balkan Wars for an extraordinary, perhaps unique, exploit in which as a young officer in the Turkish Navy he forced the Greek blockade single-handed in the cruiser Hamidiye, and made his way against a superior Greek fleet into the Mediterranean. He was one of the most gallant and popular officers of the Turkish Navy.

WITH ATATURK

In 1917 he represented Turkey at the treaty of Brest-Litovsk which ended the war between Germany and revolutionary Russia. In 1918, as the last Minister for the Navy in the old Ottoman regime, he led the Turkish delegation to the convention of Mudros which brought to an end Turkey's part in the First World War. Rauf was one of a small but celebrated band of Turks round Ataturk in the war of independence and played a leading part in all the dramas of that episode of history. Minister of Marine in the last Ottoman Government in 1918, he slipped out of Constantinople to join Mustafa Kemal in Anatolia. He was with Ataturk at the heart of the national movement in Erzurum, at the Congress of Sivas and at the signing of the Turkish "National Pact".

In 1920 he was captured by the British along with other supporters of Ataturk in Constantinople and was imprisoned on the island of Malta. Later he became Prime Minister in Ataturk's first revolutionary government, in effect replacing the Ottoman viziers as the first Prime Minister of Turkey. He held this post till 1923, when he resigned after a quarrel with the foreign minister Ismet Pasha (Inönü) at the time of the Lausanne conference.

WELCOMED BACK

Rauf after that, along with Ali Fuat Pasha, Refet Pasha and others, moved into opposition to Ataturk's autocratic rule and formed the Progressive Republican Party which opposed the abolition of the Sultanate and Caliphate. When Ataturk became sole master of Turkey, along with others who were against his rule, Rauf left Turkey and lived for about 10 years outside the country. He returned after Ataturk's death in 1938, and was welcomed back to Turkey by Ismet Inönü who had by that time succeeded Ataturk as President of the Republic.

In 1942, at the height of the Second World War, in which Turkey remained neutral, Rauf was appointed Ambassador to London. Being a naval officer and for other reasons he was one of the most popular Ambassadors Turkey has had in Britain.

In 1945 Rauf returned to Turkey and retired.

WIDE TRAVEL

He spent the greater part of his later years in his native Istanbul. He travelled widely during his life, to most of the countries of Europe, the United States, and India.

Rauf was a man of great personal bravery, impulsive, eloquent, individualistic.

He was no match intellectually or politically for Ataturk, but he was one of the most attractive and colourful figures of recent Turkish history in which he played an important part. He was unmarried.

July 18, 1964.

Professor John Orr, F.B.A., who died on August 10, 1966, in Edinburgh at the age of 81, was Emeritus Professor in the University of Edinburgh, and the doyen and outstanding representative of Romance philology in Britain, and indeed in the English-speaking world.

Orr may be thought to have come to the subject relatively late, having begun as a Classical scholar at the University of Tasmania and reading Classical Honour Moderations upon going up to Balliol as a Rhodes Scholar in 1905. After Moderations he took the Final Honour School of jurisprudence. Although he led a very active life and rowed for the College Eight, he began to be plagued by ill-health while still at Oxford; but he gradually recovered during the two postgraduate years he spent on the Continent, was able to satisfy the requirements for the Licence-ès-Lettres (Paris) and complete his edition of the works of Guiot de Provins (presented for the B.Litt. in 1913 and published in 1915). Later in life he was to suffer two very serious breakdowns, from which he made an astonishing recovery.

Orr began his teaching career as a lecturer at the University of Manchester, where he returned as professor in 1919 after a brief period as lecturer at East London College and war service with the Admiralty and the Military Intelligence Corps. In 1933 he accepted the Chair of French at Edinburgh, which became the Chair of French Language and Romance Linguistics in 1951, when a second Chair of French was created, largely on his initiative.

He played a prominent role in university administration, having been dean of the Faculty of Arts in both universities and a member of the most important committees. He was chairman of the Edinburgh-Caen Fellowship, which was his creation and which contributed so notably to the reconstruction of the University of Caen and its present prosperity. He also took a leading part in the creation and administration of the Institut Français d'Écosse.

WORD BATTLES

His interest in the arts was reflected in his membership of the Committee of the Manchester Art Gallery and later of the board of management of the Edinburgh College of Art, and he was an honorary vice-president of the Society of Scottish Artists. He was himself a discerning collector.

As a student in Paris, Orr came under the influence of Jules Gilliéron and he remained throughout his career his fervent disciple. Language was for him a living organism whose perpetual evolution involved a struggle for survival among words, in which homonymity is the disabling pathological factor against which only the various therapeutic devices (first clearly distinguished by Gilliéron) avail. While Orr's conclusions did not always command general assent in detail, his argument never failed to interest. His articles and studies reveal a remarkably deep and intimate knowledge of the French language, and he wrote French with a propriety and elegance which caused a French reviewer of his most recent publication to hold him up as a model for French scholars to imitate.

Many of Orr's ideas and predilections found expression in the revised and enlarged English version of I. Iordan's *Introduction to Romance Linguistics* published in 1937. He was frequently led to apply his methods to the English language, for example in the articles included in his *Words and Sounds in English and French* (1953) and in his Taylorian Lecture of 1948 on *The Impact of French upon English*. His publications include critical editions of a number of Old French texts and a volume of *Contes et Poèmes* by Jules Supervielle. He was closely associated with the founding of the quarterly review *French Studies* and remained a member of its editorial board throughout. He was also Romance editor of the *Modern Language Review* for a number of years.

Orr was a stern critic, but he was never content with destructive criticism, and many of his reviews constitute substantial, original contributions to the subject.

Orr's commanding presence became a feature of learned congresses such as those of the Société de Linguistique Romane, of which he was currently president, and of the Fédération Internationale des Langues et Littératures Modernes, over whose tenth Congress he was to have presided at Strasbourg. He had also been president of the Modern Humanities Research Association and of the Association Internationale des Études Françaises.

A somewhat severe exterior masked a keen sensitivity and a genuine sociability which won him many friendships formed not only in seminars and conferences, but on the golf course. His distinction brought him many honours. He was an honorary doctor of Manchester, Caen, and the Sorbonne, and was elected a Fellow of the British Academy in 1952. He was Commandeur de la Légion d'Honneur and Knight Commander of the Orden Civil de Alfonso X, el Sablo.

Orr married, in 1910, Augusta Berthe Brisac, daughter of a French family established in St. Petersburg, who predeceased him. They had a son who was killed while serving with the Royal Air Force.

August 15, 1966.

General Albert Orsborn, C.B.E., fifth in succession to William Booth as head of the Salvation Army, died at Boscombe on February 4, 1967. He was 80.

He succeeded George Lyndon Carpenter in 1946 as international leader of the Salvation Army. He retired in 1954. The son of Salvationist pioneers—his father was twice imprisoned in the eighties for playing a cornet in the street on Sundays—he rose during nearly half a century of service with the Army from an 11s. a week captain to be its most popular and most-travelled general.

Orsborn brought to the Salvation Army a new vitality reminiscent of the three Booths. Apart from his great work as a world-wide evangelist, he will be remembered for making the Army more democratic, and as its No. 1 songwriter. More than 250 of his songs and hymns are sung by the Salvation Army today, and during the First World War his evangelical hymns were sung everywhere to such tunes as "Tipperary". Ever since the day of the Salvation Army's founder, General Booth, the Army's generalship was essentially a personal mission. All appointments were made and regulations issued under his authority. But the first thing Orsborn did after succeeding General Carpenter in 1946 was to set up an advisory council of seven top-ranking officers, although the final decisions were still his. It was a gentle democratization with Orsborn helping the Army to adapt itself to the welfare state. When King George VI received Orsborn he said: "General, your uniform is different." That was because Orsborn had simplified it by removing the froggings and braid.

Albert William Thomas Orsborn was born on September 4, 1886, at Maidstone, "into the Army", the eldest son of Albert Orsborn, who, while a court shoemaker in Chelsea, had been attracted by an open-air Army meeting. He became a soldier, and later threw up business to become a pioneer officer. Orsborn, his son, received his early education at no fewer than 12 different schools. In 1899, when he was 13, Orsborn worked as an errand boy in a Manchester chemist's shop, to help his mother maintain her six younger children. Shortly afterwards he worked as an office boy at the international headquarters of the Army in London. He was promoted to junior clerk, became a cadet, and was, as he afterwards put it, "soundly converted". In 1905 he became an officer and, after early appointments at Chelmsford, Colchester, Lowestoft and Ipswich, Orsborn was appointed to the Salvation Army's officers' training college.

During this period his native gift for verse was greatly stimulated, and a collection of his poetry was published under the title of *The Beauty of Jesus*. A number of his poems are included in the Salvation Army's own hymnary.

TRAINING POST

Following administrative responsibilities in Norfolk and South London, Orsborn returned to the training college in London and was in charge of the men's section for nine years. In 1933 he was appointed Chief Secretary for New Zealand. Three years later he returned to Britain as Territorial Commander for Scotland and Ireland, and in 1940 was installed British Commissioner, with control of all the Army's operations throughout the United Kingdom.

In May, 1946, the fourth High Council elected Albert Orsborn as General. He gave himself to the renewing of the international bonds of the movement which had been strained or broken by the Second World War. During the course of his leaderhsip, the General visited the Army's work in almost all of the 70 countries in which it works. He was considered one of the most capable public speakers ever to have emerged from the ranks of Salvation Army officership.

Immediately after his election as General, Orsborn outlined his future policy. "The Army must be more mobile", he declared. "Let us put it on wheels, and if necessary on wings, and let us go as far as other wheels and other wings travel on other business."

Campaigns in Canada, the United States,

South America and the West Indies followed. He also visited Africa, India, Australia and Europe, so that within four or five years of his election, Orsborn had a personal knowledge about the Army's work throughout the world. He decided that the Army should call an International Congress of youth. This, the first gathering of its kind in the Army's history, took place in London in 1950, and was attended by nearly 6,000 young people each session at the Albert Hall. In 1958 he published *The House of My Pilgrimage*.

Orsborn was much more the ardent speaker and preacher, the man who summoned the right type of lieutenants to his side, and saw that his orders were obeyed, than a student and theologian. But his religious faith was supported by a thorough knowledge of biblical teaching. He married three times.

February 6, 1967.

Joe Orton, the dramatist, died in London on August 9, 1967, at the age of 34.

Orton will be remembered as one of the sharpest stylists of the British new wave, and as a playwright who outdid all his contemporaries in offending the traditional West End audience. For this he was not wholly to blame. His first stage play, *Entertaining Mr. Sloane*, appeared with considerable success at the Arts Theatre Club in 1964 as an experimental production, and went on to win an *Evening Standard* award. When it transferred to Wyndham's later the same year the public, enticed with promises of a brilliant comedy, were outraged to find that the play dealt with a young criminal who murdered an old man and is blackmailed into sexual submission by a middle aged pair of predatory siblings.

What Orton's adversaries ignored was his extreme skill in counterpointing a brutally anarchic action against decorously precise dialogue. The same characteristics, developed even further, reappeared in his next play *Loot* (now running at the Criterion), a comedy dealing with police corruption and featuring a dead body as its main comic property. This time the public were prepared for Orton and he was generally compared with Wilde. The final Orton production took place in June, 1967, with the Royal Court's double bill, *Crimes of Passion*—adaptations of two slight pieces first written for radio and television.

Orton was not the most original playwright of his last 10 years and his first work leaned rather heavily on Pinter. But he was a fine engineer of farcical situations, a consummate dialogue artist and a natural anarch who saw people as "profoundly bad, but irresistibly funny."

He was born in Leicester, the son of a gardener and a machinist. After failing his 11-plus he decided to be an actor and had a short career in repertory after a course at the Royal Academy of Dramatic Art. Although his acting career failed, his ambition was not to write but to act.

Shortly before the appearance of *Entertaining Mr. Sloane* he served a six months' sentence at Brixton and Wormwood Scrubs for mutilating library books. He remained unrepentant about this. "I objected to public money going on dull, badly written books . . . I removed books . . . and substituted pictures of my own choosing for the photos of the authors on the back; then I'd smuggle them back on the shelves again. I once pasted a picture of a naked tattooed man over a photograph of John Betjeman; I think the book was *Summoned by Bells*. And another time I pasted a picture of a female nude over a photo of Lady Lewisham. It was some book on etiquette."

August 10, 1967.

Henry Oscar, the actor-producer, died in London on December 28, 1969, at the age of 78.

Henry Oscar was born at Hornsey on July 14, 1891, and was educated at Enfield Grammar School. As a youth he worked in an office in the City of London and he made his first stage appearance at the age of 20 with Sir Frank Benson at Stratford-on-Avon on September 1, 1911, as Snug in *A Midsummer Night's Dream*. In 1914 he was touring with the Edward Compton Comedy Company, and it was not until August, 1916, that he made his first West End appearance as Frank Burroughs with Miss Doris Keane in *Romance* at the Lyric. One of his proudest memories of his earlier years was that in February, 1918, at the Coliseum he played with Ellen Terry in scenes from *The Merchant of Venice*. In 1921 he organized jointly with W. Edward Stirling the London Players, which marked the start of a long career in repertory including a three months' season at the Comédie des Champs Elysées in Paris. Among the many Shakespearian parts he played were Iago in *Othello* at the St. James's (1932), Metellus in *Julius* Caesar (1920), Tybalt in *Romeo and Juliet* (1920), Don John in *Much Ado About Nothing* (1946), and Philo Canidius in *Antony and Cleopatra* (1951). But he was equally happy in modern comedy and among successes with which his name is coupled were *A Little Bit of Fluff, The First Mrs. Fraser, Potiphar's Wife, The Moonraker* and *Six Characters in Search of an Author*.

Oscar was one of the first actors to recognize the potentialities of the new media which were challenging the position of the live theatre—the films, sound radio and television. In 1922 he became the first stage player to receive a long-term contract from the B.B.C., and he temporarily gave up his stage work to produce, announce, manage the sound effects and act in some of the earliest wireless programmes. His first screen appearance was in *After Dark* in 1932 and thereafter he was seen in a large number of films while his appearances on television included *As You Like It*, *L'Aiglon* and *The Gay Lord Quex*.

Much of the little spare time he had he gave up to the welfare of the members of his profession. In 1919 he was on the Council of the Actors Association and when it was reorganized as a trade union he was one of its delegates to the Trades Union Congress. In June, 1939, he was elected to British Actors Equity and when the Second World War began in the autumn of that year he was appointed drama director of E.N.S.A., a position which he filled with great distinction for the whole war period. He was responsible for the dramatic entertainment in all the theatres of war and contributed largely to the great success which E.N.S.A. undoubtedly achieved.

Oscar was a governor of the Central School of Speech Training and Dramatic Art, where, as a teacher, his pupils included Dame Peggy Ashcroft and Sir Laurence Olivier. He later acted with Sir Laurence and Vivien Leigh.

In five years of his early stage days he played more parts than David Garrick in the whole of his career. He was in 40 television plays in two years. He was recently seen in the B.B.C.-T.V. George Robey *Omnibus* programme.

December 29, 1969.

B. L. Osler, the former South African captain and one of the most famous stand-off half backs in Rugby football, died at Cape Town on April 23, 1962. He was 60, and had been ill for a long time.

Bennie Osler may be said to have acquired two reputations. Following his outstanding displays in South Africa against the British touring side of 1924 captained by R. Cove-Smith, and, again, in 1928, after the visit of a New Zealand team of All Blacks, Osler's fame reached the heights. One knowledgeable critic, F. M. Honore—a former writer for *The Times*—described Osler as "the greatest match winning player in the world". No doubt that praise had been well earned. A further comment that Osler "sometimes kicked too much" was hardly noticed at the time, the more so as this mild criticism was submerged by the statement that "no one can effect a telling breakthrough more brilliantly".

Unfortunately for Osler's reputation in Britain, though he became credited with an ice-cool efficiency in playing up to the heaviest pack of forwards encountered there, in the new 3–4–1 formation, he came to be regarded as the very embodiment of the dreary tactics of safety first. He was even said to have ruined the tour of the Third Springboks in 1931–32 by too much tactical kicking and by showing an almost callous contempt for open play as most people understood it.

Osler even came to be denounced by some of his own party for condemning his three-quarters, who indeed included some fine players, to a slow and miserable death from neglect. Undoubtedly he did prefer to make some kind of a victory certain by relying upon his own talents as a master of the punt ahead into the awkward open spaces, knowing full well that his forwards had the pace as well as the weight to wear down the opposition by what we have come to describe as "power Rugby"

DR. DANIE CRAVEN

This tour produced for South Africa another match-winning half back admirably adapted to the exploitation of a pack which had a front row with a total weight of 45 stones. That player was Dr. Danie Craven, who at scrum half in due course developed into a tactician shrewder even than Osler was over 30 years ago, and is still the dominant influence on South African Rugby.

Benjamin Louwrens Osler was born at Aliwal North, Cape Province, on November 23, 1901, into a family passionately fond of Rugby. His father, Benjamin Osler, saw to it that his son got the feel of a Rugby ball at an early age, but it was not until the age of 11 that Bennie started his playing career.

Twelve years later, in 1924, he made his international debut for South Africa against Cove-Smith's British team, playing in all four international matches. Osler represented South Africa 17 times before he retired from international Rugby in 1933.

There is no doubt that before he took his captaincy too seriously Osler was one of the great pivotal players. Even in 1931–32, every now and then when forced to do so by circumstances, Osler did reveal his superb balance and turn of speed as a runner in midfield. His physique, $11\frac{1}{2}$ stones in weight and 5ft. 8in. in height, made him a pleasure to watch on the move. Alas that occurred all too seldom on British Rugby fields. Mostly Osler took neither personal nor team risks and preferred instead to reveal his supreme talent for dropping his punts ahead on carefully selected spots with the cruel accuracy of some old time Yorkshire length bowler.

Osler and his men on that tour won all four international matches in Britain and drew with the joint forces of Devon and Cornwall and the men of the Scottish Border, losing only one match in 26 for a total of 407 points to 124.

MISSED DEFEAT

But even in that triumph there was a certain irony. Osler could claim that he was absent when the only defeat, by a Midland XV at Leicester, occurred. British Rugbymen, however, fastened upon the fact that the play at Leicester was the most attractive and exciting of the whole tour. The South Africans were beaten by 30 points to 11 but their recovery in the second half was a magnificent effort worth half a dozen victories through the tactics of safety first.

April 24, 1962.

La Belle Otero, one of the last of the famous courtesans of the Gay Nineties, died in Nice on April 10, 1965. She was 97.

At the height of her fame in the carefree years between the dawn of the twentieth century and the outbreak of the First World War, La Belle Otero was reputedly the possessor of a sizable fortune, in addition to a fabulous hoard of jewels showered upon her by her royal and aristocratic lovers. Yet, for the past 40 or so years she had lived in more than modest circumstances in a small furnished flat in Nice, gradually selling her jewels, as she had greatly dissipated her fortune to pay her gambling debts. For, despite the many famous men who had figured in her spectacular life, the green baize tables of the casinos were her one great lasting passion.

Her origins were obscure. She was born Caroline Puentovalga in Cadiz in 1868. It is believed she was carried off at the age of 13 by a cabaret dancer, and that a year later she married an Italian tenor who quickly lost whatever fortune he possessed at the baccarat tables.

Soon after that, under the name of La Belle Otero, she made her debut as a dancer at night clubs in Monte Carlo. And, at least for the next 30 years, she never looked back. In an epoch of famous courtesans she was among the half-dozen who enriched the chronicles of the time.

STOLE A MARCH

Legend places among those who shared her favours, and contributed handsomely to her fortune, King Edward VII, the Grand Duke Nicholas, the Kaiser, King Alfonso, Aristide Briand, Gabriele d'Annunzio and many, many others. She visited St. Petersburg; she made a triumphal tour in the United States, and she was acclaimed wherever she went, not so much on account of her talent, for that was slender, but because of her beauty, her vitality and what, in these days, one would call her sex appeal.

Stories about her abound. One concerns her rivalry with another famous beauty of the day, Émilienne d'Alençon. It was the fashion for the well-known courtesans of the day to appear on special occasions—a gala at the Paris opera house for example—weighed down, as it were, by all the jewellery they possessed. It was a sort of competition. On one such night La Belle Otero waited until all her bejewelled sisters, particularly the Alençon, had taken their seats to make her entry in a simple unadorned black dress—followed at a distance by her Swiss maid carrying an immense heap of jewels on a tray.

She was indeed the idol of the nineties. A few years ago the film of her life was made: it was a poor shadow of the reality.

April 13, 1965.

Amédée Ozenfant, who died in hospital at Cannes in May, 1966, at the age of 80, was a writer as well as a painter and one of the most intellectual of the French artists who followed the call of geometrical abstraction. With the architect Le Corbusier, he founded the movement called Purism, which might be described as the logical conclusion of Cubism.

Today Ozenfant's reputation rests principally on his writings, particularly on the *Foundations of Modern Art*, first published in 1929 and still in print. In this he gave a very fresh and imaginative account of modern art's sources of inspiration, in primitive art, the modern environment and so on.

Ozenfant was born at Saint-Quentin, in Picardy, in 1886. His father, who was of mixed French and Spanish origin, was a building contractor and one of the pioneers in the use of reinforced concrete, and his mother was a china painter in the factory at Sèvres. After studying at the local art school Ozenfant went to Paris, where he associated with Segonzac, Luc-Albert Moreau, and other painters who were influenced by Cezanne. At the same time he studied mathematics and philosophy, and later travelled extensively in Europe.

Ozenfant spent three years in the Urals, and his Russian experience appears to have had some influence upon his artistic ideals; at any rate when in 1915 he founded in Paris the magazine *l'Elan*, which he conducted as an open forum for artists and writers.

THE NEW SPIRIT

In 1918, in collaboration with his friend Le Corbusier, he published *After Cubism*, in which, with satirical asides on the Cubism of Picasso and others, a system was outlined of pictorial composition on architectural principles, with some affinities with the ideas of Seurat. Purism, as it was called, was finally demonstrated in detail in an illustrated review called *The New Spirit*, which Ozenfant and Le Corbusier edited from 1920 to 1925.

Purism was defined as: "The picture is a machine for the transmission of sentiments. Science offers us a kind of physiological language that enables us to produce precise physiological sensations in the spectator: thereon Purism is founded." To quote Ozenfant again: "The mechanical object can in certain cases move us, because manufactured forms are geometrical, and we are sensible to geometry."

As if conscious of some flaws in his theory of Purism he began after 1924 to reintroduce organic elements into his paintings in the form of symbolical figures of men and women.

LOW RELIEF

At first these were modelled in low relief with a thick impasto of pigment of a single colour, as shown in "Bathers in a Grotto", painted in 1931, but later relief was obtained in the ordinary way by means of light and shade and the colour became richer and more varied. The huge "Life (biological)," begun in 1931 and intended to be followed by "Life (mechanical)", was executed in this way. In 1939 it was acquired for the Luxembourg Museum.

About 1937 Ozenfant, with an English-speaking secretary and assistant, opened an art school in London in the neighbourhood of Warwick Road. The inaugural exhibition contained several of his paintings of a kind similar to the "Bathers in a Grotto". Towards the end of 1938 he went to America, where he again opened a school which he conducted for 10 years with a good deal of success.

Ozenfant had a good deal of influence on the visual arts in general, particularly in their application to the conditions of the machine age, an influence that was reflected strongly in the 1925 Paris Exhibition of Decorative Arts.

FOUGHT WITH PEN

It has been said that he fought his battles with his pen rather than with his brush, and he was certainly a very witty writer. He was said to have the most sarcastic pen in the art world of Paris, and he never hesitated to poke fun at himself.

May 6, 1966.

P

G. W. Pabst, one of the best-known German film directors of the silent and early sound picture era, and the man who brought Greta Garbo to the fore by his sympathetic handling of her in *The Joyless Street*, died on May 29, 1967 in Vinna, at the age of 82. He lived in the United States between 1911 and the end of the Second World War and produced several anti-Nazi films and a film version of Kafka's *The Trial*.

The period immediately following the First World War in Germany produced a remarkable number of brilliant film directors—men such as Fritz Lang, Murnau, Wiene, and others who seemed peculiarly well-suited, artistically, to the medium of the cinema. The majority of them —perhaps as an aftermath of war—tended to concentrate on the fantastic, the macabre, and the grotesque. Pabst was different. Originally a theatrical producer, he turned to film-making as offering a greater scope for the factual and realistic approach, and *The Joyless Street*—or *The Street of Sorrow*, as it was also called—was only his second picture. The story was concerned with the moral and physical degradation which the effects of the war had brought about in Vienna, and Pabst had been unable to find a suitable girl to play the elder daughter of an impoverished, upper-class family until he saw Garbo in her Swedish film *Gosta Berling's Saga*. He then persuaded her manager and patron, Mauritz Stiller, to allow her to play this part.

Garbo, young and inexperienced, and very nervous, required the most delicate and sympathetic handling, and here Pabst showed his exceptional ability for getting the best out of his players.

The Joyless Street was made in 1926. He followed it by a curious work, *The Secrets of a Soul*, which was produced in collaboration with Freud and was too scientific and psychoanalytical to be effective as a story. He continued to probe into the subconscious minds of his characters, in films such as *Pandora's Box* (a study of prostitution), *Crisis*, *The Love of Jeanne Ney* (which made a star of Brigitte Helm, who played a blind girl in it), *The Diary of a Lost Girl*, and *The White Hell of Piz Palu*.

CENSORS' CUTS

Each was outspoken, and each suffered from cuts by the censor.

The coming of sound was a disaster for many a famous film director. To Pabst, it was a stimulant and challenge. It opened up a new field of exploration, and resulted in some of his best work. Three outstanding films belong to this period of the early 1930s. *Westfront 1918* was a fiercely national and starkly realistic condemnation of war; *Kameradschaft*, with dialogue in both German and French, was an impassioned plea for a better understanding between nations, and showed German coalminers going to the rescue of French miners who have been entombed; and *Die Drei-Groschen-Oper*—his version of Gay's *The Beggar's Opera* —depicted the sordidness as well as the gaiety of the underworld in Victorian London.

In 1933 Pabst made *Don Quixote*, with Chaliapine in the name part and George Robey as Sancho Panza—an original and courageous attempt at a difficult subject which was not wholly satisfactory. The touch was not sufficiently light, and the humour often forced. John Grierson once described Pabst as "the Galsworthy of the Screen", a man of deep sympathy and a profound humanity, but with a tendency to preach. This heavy-handedness when dealing with the message contained in his films sometimes lessened its effectiveness. But for all that Pabst remained a director who understood film technique, who understood actors, and who was always trying to say something that was of importance to humanity.

May 31, 1967.

Sir Earle Page, P.C., G.C.M.G., C.H., who was one of Australia's most influential and colourful politicians, died on December 20, 1961, in Sydney, at the age of 81. In 1939, on the death of J. A. Lyons he was Prime Minister for 13 days, but resigned when the United Australia Party elected Mr. Menzies as its leader. As Deputy Prime Minister in the Bruce-Page and Lyons-Page administrations he had already on several occasions acted as Premier, but he was perforce reconciled to the position of No. 2 and generally seemed at home in that difficult role. He was leader of the Country Party between 1920 and 1939 and, probably more than any other man of his party, determined the now traditional pattern of anti-Labour coalitions in the Federal Parliament.

Page, who was the Country Party member for the federal seat of Cowper for an unbroken period of 42 years, also held the portfolios of treasurer, repatriation, commerce, and health. A man with great charm and wit, he had been the centre of some notable storms in the Federal Parliament, but in recent years had enjoyed the role of an elder statesman.

Earle Christmas Grafton Page, the son of C. Page, was born in Grafton. New South Wales, on August 8, 1880. He graduated as a doctor from Sydney University at the age of 21. At the beginning of the First World War he joined the A.I.F. medical services and served as a surgeon in France.

Returning in 1919, he was elected as independent member for Cowper. He was a co-founder of the Australian Country Party, and within a year was its leader. In three years he was deputy Prime Minister and Treasurer. In the Bruce-Page Administration (1923 to 1929) his period as Treasurer was both important and turbulent. He negotiated the financial agreement between the Federal Government and the states, and established the Loan Council, the National Debt Sinking Fund and the Federal Aid Roads Fund. He placed the Commonwealth Bank under an independent board of directors. In 1929 he became a Privy Councillor.

As Minister for Commerce in the Lyons-Page Government (1934–39), he established the Australian agricultural council which gave Australia a common voice in oversea markets and arranged for the sale of export surpluses to Britain. As Minister for Health in the Menzies-Fadden Government, he introduced the first comprehensive and workable national health scheme. In crusading for national development—health, water conservation, and migration—he was a tireless traveller and covered up to 50,000 miles a year by air, road, and rail in Australia, not to mention tours oversea.

In 1938 he was knighted.

Page's speeches were often woolly and he was adroit at evading the direct question when he felt that an adequate answer required preparation. But he did not pull punches. He resented Mr. Menzies' resignation over the question of a national insurance scheme on the eve of the Second World War. In one of the bitterest attacks ever heard in the Federal House he accused Mr. Menzies of deserting the Government at a time of international tension. The incident split the Country Party and Page shortly after resigned his leadership in favour of A. W. Fadden (now Sir Arthur Fadden). Page and Mr. Menzies settled their differences and in 1940 Page became Minister for Commerce in the third Menzies Ministry. In 1941 Page was appointed Australia's special wartime representative in London. On his return to Australia in 1942 he was coopted by the Labour Prime Minister, Curtin, to the Australian Advisory War Council and the War Cabinet so that his "knowledge and experience gained as special representative of the Commonwealth on the British War Cabinet and the Pacific War Council might be available in dealing with the conduct of the war". This was a striking and amply justified compliment.

GREATEST MONUMENT

Page's greatest monument is probably the national health scheme, which he set about putting into practice immediately he assumed office as Minister for Health in 1949. In this connexion, characteristically, he travelled widely abroad looking at health services. The scheme was a modest one by British standards, but the remarkable thing was perhaps that it appeared at all. He retired from the Cabinet in 1956.

Page was a champion of the "New State Movement". He believed that there should be 20 or 30 equal partners in the federal system, at least four new states in New South Wales and five in Queensland. He visualized more cities with a population of about a quarter of a million, each supporting large rural districts.

He became a very successful pastoralist and a newspaper proprietor. On the upper reaches of Clarence river near Grafton he developed a strip of country 10 miles long and one or two miles wide, stocked parts of it with beef cattle, established half a dozen dairy farms and a sawmill. He built a school, a shop, and a post office, and other amenities followed. He also developed virgin land in Queensland. In 1955 he became first chancellor of the University of New England.

Page always claimed that his only reason for rushing around was to have more time to be lazy. He also was accustomed to test the steadiness of his hand once a month by lifting a brimming cup of tea "just to see if I could still go back to surgery". Page remarked last year that his only real surgery in 41 years in Parliament was "on political colleagues and opponents". In December, 1960, at the age of 80 he played tennis for an hour at Canberra in a temperature of 80 degrees. When his companions settled down to cool off the "Doc", as he was known, hurried away to do more work on his autobiography, which he hoped would be published in 1962.

Page's first wife, Ethel Blunt, was a nursing sister whom he met in an operating theatre when a bottle of methylated spirit flared up and required the young doctor's attention. They were married in 1906. She died in 1958. Two years ago Sir Earle married Jean Thomas, who had been his secretary for 15 years. There were three sons and a daughter of the first marriage.

December 20, 1961.

Sir Frederick Handley Page, C.B.E., who played an outstanding part in the development of British aviation from its earliest beginnings, died on April 21, 1962, at his London home. Founder and managing director of Handley Page, Ltd., he had been chairman of the company since 1948.

He made himself a power in the aircraft industry and indeed in the earlier phases of the air transport industry by combining an intense interest in aeroplanes with a shrewd business sense and a capacity for detailed application. He was an engineer by choice and training. He enjoyed both the processes of advocacy and the satisfactions that belong to good salesmanship. He took into his own business, with a certain pride, that practical knowledge which enabled him to meet all his employees on level terms throughout his life. Outside his business he devoted the same clear thinking and lively power of expression to causes associated with the aircraft industry and with technical education. He made for himself a full life and in doing with zest and success things for which he had not been trained, he found all the relaxation he needed.

Born in 1885 in Cheltenham, he had set himself to become an electrical engineer and at the age of 21 had been appointed chief designer of a well-known electrical company. The following year, a paper on the design of electrical equipment which he delivered before the Institution of Electrical Engineers attracted so much attention that he was offered a tempting position by the Westinghouse company in the United States. By that time he had become fascinated by the possibilities of the aeroplane, had joined the Aeronautical Society (not yet Royal) and was casting around for means to become a pioneer in a new industry. In 1908 he started business in a modest way as an aeronautical engineer, and a year later his first success in business advocacy led to the formation of a private company—the first of its kind in ths industry—with a capital of £10,000, some sheds at Barking as workshops and some rough ground adjoining as aerodrome. Five years later he was to be building heavy bombers, and in less than 20 years he was to be chairman of the Society of British Aircraft Constructors.

Wartime opportunity determined the special line of activity he should follow. The need of the Admiralty, when Winston Churchill was First Lord, for an aeroplane capable of carrying a goodly load of missiles led to the first two-engined bomber. Sikorsky in Russia and Caproni in Italy were working along similar lines but Handley Page, now removed to more spacious quarters at Cricklewood, was first to build a big aeroplane. It flew in December, 1915, and with better engines was turned into an improved version which became Britain's standard heavy bomber in that war. Before the war ended he had built a four-engined bomber. A fleet of 255 of these monsters (loaded weight 13 tons) was ordered in 1918 and the first three were ready to bomb Berlin when the armistice came.

NEW SAFETY DEVICE

Foreseeing the lean times that must follow the war, Handley Page turned his attention to the application of the big aeroplane to civil uses. If he had succeeded in this he would have achieved a unique position as both maker and user of aircraft. For four years another company, bearing his name and using his big aeroplanes, operated air services on the routes to Paris and Brussels. Later the Paris service was extended to Zurich. The experience proved that commercial air transport at that stage was impossible without a subsidy and when subsidy was only to be had in exchange for the merging of the principal private operators, the Handley Page line lost its identity in Imperial Airways, the forerunner of B.O.A.C. Of the 14 aircraft with which Imperial Airways began its life, nine were Handley Pages. Their maker was once more dependent entirely on orders for aircraft, but he had already begun to develop and exploit a device destined to yield him fresh distinction and his company, now turned into a public company, a steady revenue for many years.

This was the device which ultimately became the automatic slot fitted on the leading edge of an aeroplane's wing. It was essentially a safety device. It was a hinged slat, which lay flat along the leading edge in flight until, losing speed or presenting too steep an angle of attack, the wing began to stall. At that stage, acting in response to aerodynamic forces, the slat swung forward on its hinges leaving a slot between itself and the wing. This induced a faster flow of air through the slot and over the wing's surface and so temporarily restored its lift. It served both as a warning and an aid to the pilot at critical moments, but it came also to be used, in association with flaps on the trailing edge of the wing, as a lift-increaser for enabling heavily loaded aircraft to take off and land in restricted spaces. The device was spread by assiduous propaganda all over the world. Forty-five countries adopted it. The R.A.F. had all its aircraft fitted with it. Royalties in respect of its use amounted to £750,000 and kept the company going in years when other business was sparse.

During the years between the wars Handley Page had one other triumph. It was comparable with his big bomber of 1918. In 1930 he produced the world's first 40-seat airliner. With its four engines, the Heracles cruised at only about 90 m.p.h. but it afforded a wholly new standard of comfort, described justly as Pullman standard, for air passengers. Imperial Airways used this type over a peiod of 10 years and built up a remarkable record of safety with it, yet it did not attract orders from other countries and no other civil aeroplane came from the same stable until the late 1950s when a modern replacement for the old D.C.3 was launched.

BACK TO BOMBERS

While the Heracles was helping to serve the Empire's routes, its builder was busy once again with a bomber. The Halifax played a notable part in the 1939-45 War. Nearly 7,000 were built. When that war ended work was begun on a four-jet bomber of unusual design and in 1952, the Victor made its first flight. It was put into production for the R.A.F., commended with characteristic superlatives to the public, and is still in service though its military function was changed.

When in 1960, under heavy pressure by the Government, the numerous aircraft constructors began to group themselves into two main companies, Handley Page withstood every bait and compulsion with typical intransigence. By the beginning of 1962 he had become the only major constructor outside one or other of the amalgamations. In competition then with one of them for an order for short-range aircraft to serve the R.A.F., his D.C.3 replacement, the Herald, was rejected; and nothing could persuade him that this was not a retributive stroke by the Government to mark their displeasure at his refusal to toe the rationalization line.

TRAINING TECHNICIANS

Throughout his life Handley Page devoted some of his energy to affairs outside his business. He was one of the most prominent builders of the Society of British Aircraft Constructors—which he had served as honorary treasurer, chairman and president. He was concerned in the development and endowment of the Royal Aeronautical Society, whose president he had been from 1945 to 1947. Having arranged quite early a scheme for his own company under which apprentices served part of their time in the shops and part at a technical school, he gave much attention to the education of technicians and engineering scientists. He was chairman of the Council of the City and Guilds of London Institute and of the governors of the College of Aeronautics, and a governor of the Imperial College of Science and Technology. He had also been master of the Company of Coachmakers and president of the Institute of Transport. From 1937 to 1958 he had served as a vice-chairman of the Air Registration Board, which is responsible for the airworthiness standards applied to civil aircraft.

He had made himself a reputation as a character whose forthright comments were often presented with a pungent and sometimes daring wit. Few suspected that he had been brought up among Plymouth Brethren and as a young man had cultivated eloquence on behalf of that cause.

Handley Page had been made C.B.E. in 1918 and knighted in 1942. A Deputy Lieutenant of Middlesex from 1954 to 1956, he was Lord Lieutenant of the county from 1956 to 1960. In 1960 the Royal Aeronautical Society awarded him their Gold Medal, their highest honour.

He married Una Helen Thynne in 1918. She died in 1957. There were three daughters of the marriage.

April 23, 1962.

General Sir Bernard Paget, G.C.B., D.S.O., M.C., died suddenly on February 16, 1961, at his home in Hampshire at the age of 73.

He will be remembered chiefly for his fine leadership in the withdrawal of the British forces from Aandalsnes in Norway in 1940 and for the great part he played in training the British Army in the Second World War. He had a distinguished career of 40 years in the Army and after his retirement he was principal of Ashridge College for three years and governor of the Royal Hospital Chelsea for seven years. He was a man of high ideals, and a remarkable sense of duty inspired his upright and strong character.

Bernard Charles Tolver Paget was born on September 15, 1887, the third son of Francis Paget, Bishop of Oxford, and of Helen, the daughter of Dean Church of St. Paul's. He was educated at Shrewsbury and the Royal Military College Sandhurst, from which he was commissioned in 1907 in The Oxfordshire and Buckinghamshire Light Infantry. In the First World War he served on the Western Front with his regiment, as brigade major of the 42nd Infantry Brigade and on Sir Douglas Haig's staff at G.H.Q.; he was wounded twice, one wound rendering his left arm practically useless for the rest of his life, mentioned four times in dispatches, and won the D.S.O. and M.C.

In 1920 he graduated at the Staff College, Camberley. Here his gifts as a teacher of officers and trainer of troops were soon recognized, and between the wars he was given no fewer than three instructional posts. He also held four other staff appointments, which left little opportunity for command. He never had a battalion, but for two years, in 1936-37, he commanded the Quetta Infantry Brigade.

By singualr ill fortune for a professional soldier, during the whole of the Second World War Paget was fated to serve in an active theatre for only seven days. But in that eventful week he accomplished a fine feat of arms. He was commanding the 18th Division when the Germans invaded Norway in 1940 and he was taken from it to play a part in the Allied attempt to reoccupy Trondheim. A British Territorial brigade was put ashore at Aandalsnes on April 18 and was at once drawn into heavy fighting in the Gubrandsdalen, south of Dombaas, in support of the Norwegians retreating northwards from Oslo. A week later this southern column, now named "Sickleforce", was reinforced by a second infantry brigade, and Paget arrived to take command. The situation could hardly have been worse. Our troops were ill equipped for fighting in the narrow valleys and high snow-covered hills, the ship carrying their artillery and transport had been sunk, they were outnumbered by the Germans, and, even more serious, the supremacy of the Germans in the air was virtually unchallenged.

EVACUATION ORDERED

Paget brought his fresh troops into action as fast as they could be landed, and was at once involved in a succession of delaying actions which he conducted with spirit and determination. Three days after his arrival the Cabinet, unwilling to face further losses of ships and unable to provide the reinforcements and air cover for which Paget pleaded, decided to evacuate central Norway, and he was ordered to extricate his force. This he succeeded in doing after fighting five skilful rearguard actions in which he inflicted heavy damage on the Germans.

Paget's skill and resolution during this short campaign received warm praise from the Prime Minister in the House of Commons, and opened his path to high command. But he never had a fighting command again. There can be little doubt that this was a deep disappointment to him, though he never showed it. More than once he was on the point of getting an operational command. In November, 1941, he was selected as Commander-in-Chief Designate for the Far East, and, when Dill went to Washington, he was even considered as a possible C.I.G.S. But none of the proposals to employ him more actively came off. His continued employment at home was largely due to ill luck, but partly also to certain limitations of character, for, although he was so highly qualified he was perhaps over rigid, sometimes to the point of obstinacy, and perhaps somwhat narrow in his outlook.

On his return from Norway he was appointed Chief of Staff, Home Forces. When the South Eastern Command was formed in 1941, Paget was appointed to it, and later in the year he succeeded Sir Alan Brooke as Commander-in-Chief, Home Forces. In June, 1943, the 21st Army Group of 15 divisions was set up in the United Kingdom in preparation for the invasion of Normandy. Paget was appointed to command it, and he held this post until, at the end of the year, the decision was taken to entrust the landing to General Montgomery. He was thus deprived of his last chance of high command in the field.

"BATTLE INOCULATION"

In these years Paget revolutionized the system of training. He was a trainer of troops in the classic Light Infantry tradition of Sir John Moore, and he sought, by closely coordinating fire power and movement, to restore the infantry to its old pre-eminence on the battlefield. In furtherance of this object he set up a School of Infantry and divisional battle schools where the training was both realistic and imaginative, and where, as he put it, he aimed at creating "a true offensive spirit. combined with the will power which will not recognize defeat". He also introduced the practice of "battle inoculation" by the use of live ammunition in exercise. The training he gave the British Army and the high morale he inspired in the troops were Paget's great contribution to the war.

When he was relieved by the General Montgomery at the end of 1943, Paget was appointed Commander-in-Chief, Middle East, under the Supreme Allied Commander in the Mediterranean. During the two and a half years of his tenure of this command, although there was no longer any active campaigning, the aftermath of the war had left problems in plenty, all of which Paget tackled with his usual calm efficiency. Soon after his arrival there he settled a mutiny of the Greek Brigade stationed in Egypt; and in the spring of 1945, when fighting broke out between the French and Syrians, it fell to Paget to restore order.

On his return from the Middle East in 1946, Paget retired from the Army at the age of 58. In the same year he was appointed by the governors of the Bonar Law Memorial Trust to be principal of Ashridge College, which at that time was devoted to adult educaton in citizenship. Paget threw himself into the work of the college with enthusiasm and cosiderable success. But in his third year the uncertain finances of the college precipitated an acrimonious controversy between its governors and its principal, and Paget left. He was then appointed governor of the Royal Hospital Chelsea, where he remained for seven years. While he was there he was able to devote himself to his duties as colonel of his regiment, in which he was much loved.

He married in 1918 Winifred, daughter of Sir John Paget, Bt., who survives him with a son. Their younger son was mortally wounded, at the age of 20, in the Reichswald in 1945 in a particularly valiant action for which he was awarded a posthumous D.S.O.

February 18, 1961.

Herbert Palmer, the English lyric and narrative poet, died in hospital at St. Albans on May 17, 1961. He was 81.

In private life and in his books a genial and emphatically self-confident man, Palmer was an indefatigable castigator of ethical and aesthetic indecision. This imparted to his critical faculty an incisive edge which he sharpened on his peers: among whom T. S. Eliot, Professor Auden, and Dame Edith Sitwell he attacked openly, and perhaps wantonly. For these cannot be accurately described as indecisive. He was not an innovator, either in technique or in his ideas and expression of feelings. (He had learnt some metrical cadences from Beowulf, and perhaps some rhetoric from Vachell Lindsay.) John Middleton Murry, AE, Sir Desmond MacCarthy, Ernest Rhys, Sir Arthur Quiller-Couch, had all admired and praised his poetry. He would proudly tell young visitors: "When my first book was published Robert

Bridges wrote to me. He began his letter: 'My dear Poet'".

Palmer's narrative poems, upon which he believed his poetic reputation could securely rest and resist changing literary fashions, are predominantly symbolic of the devilish organic need to die, and the superhuman longing for unchanging loyalty and love and truth and beauty. Blake's books he admired before all others.

He had always "intensely disliked spiritual muddle". In his latest book *The Ride from Hell* (1958) he had defined in consistently religious themes his perception in society of spiritual bankruptcy induced by too rigorous an adherence to material values, and an amoral psychology. He suffered the rewards of prophecy: his book was not widely read. Max Plowman wrote many years ago: "Any day Herbert Palmer may write the one lyric of our age which future centuries will remember." Blake, with whom he enjoyed various complex affinities, had a similar fate among his contemporaries.

In his satire and parodies Palmer seems to have been more gay and exuberant than successful in his sniping. His criticism was voluminous and often sensitive; but flawed by his own virtues, courage, honesty. He was too partisan to be just and temperate with work which offended against all his own literary principles.

Herbert Edward Palmer was born in a Methodist Manse at Market Rasen. Lincolnshire, on February 10, 1880. In his fragmentary and fascinatingly candid autobiography *The Mistletoe Child* (1935) he described his father, a Wesleyan Methodist Minister, Andrew Palmer, as "masterful, enthusiastic, and entertaining: always very emotional". The father's family originated from Redditch. The mother's family (Coleman) has long been settled in Wolverhampton, as physicians and surgeons. In contrast to the father's family with a trading record, the Colemans rejoiced in claiming Irish ancestry and distant kinship with the defunct Howth peerage.

With one brother and a bevy of sisters, Herbert developed a faculty for introspection which remained the predominant factor in his poetry. The father's vocation exposed all the family to frequent changes of residence: from Market Rasen to Leek, to Preston, Kidsgrove, Cawden, Grassington, Redcar, and Rawmarsh. His academic education began at Cawden Grammar School and Woodhouse Grove School, Leeds (a Methodist Public School). While there his beloved sister Ethel introduced to him Harriet Emily Preston, her friend from Trinity Hall School, Southport (the gifted daughter of brilliant parents). Sixteen years later, when he was a poor proposition in every way, they married (December, 1914).

After a period as an elementary schoolteacher at Mexborough, Palmer attended Birmingham University for two years, studying under W. MacNeile Dixon, J. H. Muirhead, and Frank Roscoe. He then taught at Penrhyn, Cornwall, before running away from family, advice, instructions, to Hamburg. As private tutor and schoolmaster he visited the Baltic coast, the Rhineland, Prussia, central and southern France, Denmark, and Sweden. He concluded his youthful escapade by studying in Bonn University: but he did not graduate. Throughout life he maintained what seemed to some friends an excessive respect for academic certificates.

AT BONN

Bonn rendered him the greatest service of any: he met four men with whom he ehjoyed lifelong reciprocal friendship and admiration: Professors Hereward T. Price and Liam O' Brien; Mr. Ernest Nightingale and "my great friend and masculine comfort, Leslie W. Charley".

Colonel the Rev. L. W. Charley generously sponsored his first three books: *Two Fishers* (1918), *Two Foemen* (1920), and *Two Minstrels* (1921). An earlier manuscript collection of poems, *A Main Street Nosegay*, he had dangled before London publishers before 1914, without acceptance: the verses obviously derived from the younger James Thomson and from Verlaine. His first poems had been published in the *Leeds Mercury* (circa 1898) under his own name and the pseudonym "Roland". Others were printed in *Great Thoughts*. His earliest prose articles were printed in the *Daily News* and in the *Fishing Gazette*.

The Unknown Warrior (1924), *The Armed Muse* (1930), *Songs of Salvation, Sin and Satire* (1925), *Jonah comes to Nineveh* (1930), *Cinder Thursday* (1931) were represented also in *Collected Poems, 1918–31* (1932). *Summit and Chasm* (1934), *The Gallows-Cross* (1940), *A Sword in the Desert* (1946), *The Old Knight* (1949) followed. There were two selections published, in 1931 and 1943. A comprehensive selection from all his poetry, for which Palmer had proposed as title *Portal of Eternity*, is in manuscript. He edited Mohini Chatterji's *Indian Spirituality* (1933) and *The Greenwood Anthology of New Verse* (1948). Collaborating with L. W. Charley he translated from the German Suzanne Trautwein's *The Lady of Laws* (1929). *The Teaching of English* (1930) is an attempt to formulate a systematic primer of grammatical construction. *The Roving Angler* (1935), superbly illustrated by Robert Gibbings, records his interest in angling and some other topics. *Post-Victorian Poetry* (1935) is a miscellaneous collection of his pronouncements on contemporary English writing.

Villon, whom he first discovered with a shock of wonder and delight in 1901, was the inspiration of his play *The Judgment of François Villon* (1927). This he lately revised and rewrote as *Bones in the Wind*.

Mrs. Palmer survives him with their son.

May 19, 1961.

Sir William Palmer who died at his Wimbledon home on September 26, 1964, at the age of 81, was one of those Civil Servants who served industry after retirement with the same unerring touch as they had served their department before retiring.

Palmer was educated at Alleyn's School, Dulwich, and London University where he took his M.A. and B.Sc. He joined the Board of Trade in 1908 and was appointed to the Patent Office, where he remained until 1914. During the First World War he served in the Machine Gun Corps and was badly wounded. After leaving the Army he returned to the Board of Trade and was posted to the Industries and Manufactures Department.

It was here that Palmer first showed his hidden strength and his ability to stand up to Ministers when he considered circumstances warranted. His desire to help industry is shown by an incident just before the last war during discussions to limit the severe Japanese competition felt by the British silk industry. Talks were arranged between British and French manufacturers and Palmer lent his room at the Board of Trade for these talks to give them the aura of a semi-official blessing.

When the Second World War broke out, Palmer was lent to the Ministry of Supply to take charge of the raw materials department. He did this with his unruffled simplicity and competence, stretching procedure where necessary to get things moving. Legend has it that he successfully stood up to Beaverbrook on occasion—something few achieved, but in Palmer's case just another Minister to his tally; but he made the Beaver's production drive work and was admired as a result by his chief. In 1942 he went to the newly formed Ministry of Production as Second Secretary, returning to the Board of Trade in 1944, where he remained as Principal Industrial Adviser until he retired two years later.

Palmer received his C.B.E. in 1936, his C.B. in 1938, his Knighthood (K.B.E.) in 1941, and his G.B.E. in 1951. This last was a rare award to a Civil Servant made five years after retirement but it was an award well earned for advice which was continually being sought from more than one Government department during those five years, and characteristically freely and wisely given.

RAYON INDUSTRY

When retirement came in 1946, Palmer was appointed to succeed Sir Percy Ashley as the independent chairman of the then recently formed British Rayon Federation (now the British Man-made Fibres Federation). This post he held with tact and expertise until November, 1963, when he retired and was appointed President—an office which had lain vacant since the death of Samuel Courtauld some 16 years before.

Not only rayon, but other industries sought his help. He was appointed chairman of the Oil Consumers' Council set up in 1949 by the Labour Government as an alternative to nationalization. Heating and pottery firms pressed him to join their boards and the President of the Board of Trade appointed him to the Council of Industrial Design, on which he served from September, 1948, to January, 1955, and where his long background of industrial production was of the greatest help.

He represented the British Man-made Fibres Federation on the Federation of British Industries, where his talents, particularly in connexion with E.E.C. and Efta discussions, were freely called on.

Palmer was a great pipe smoker but his

smoking never gave offence because he did it discreetly and quietly. He used his pipe to give himself time to think out the correct reply to a question. In meetings he would let everyone have his say, appearing to be dreaming or not paying much attention; and then he would put the whole problem into a neat little packet with all the points for and against effectively tied up. He was never ruffled. He hated fuss or the putting of anyone to any trouble on his behalf. He preferred to go by tube or to walk than to bother with taxis or private cars. He was well read and had the civil servant's ability to acquire specialized technical knowledge. It was a privilege to talk with him because he had a tranquillity of mind and an ability to focus complete attention on the subject under discussion.

He leaves a widow, two sons, and two daughters.

September 29, 1964.

Sardar K. M. Panikkar, who died suddenly on December 10, 1963, in Mysore at the age of 68, made his first high reputation in the service of India's princes, but went on after his country was granted independence to become one of those rare diplomatists who exert a direct and tangible influence on the policies of their Governments.

Appointed Indian Ambassador to China in 1948, he saw the disintegration of the Kuomintang regime but stayed on to establish good relations with the communist Government and to lay the foundations for friendship between Peking and Delhi which lasted until they were ruptured by the border dispute of the late 1950s.

Born in Kerala in 1895, Kavalam Madhava Panikkar was educated in Madras and then at Christ Church, Oxford, from where he went to the Middle Temple. He returned to a lecturing post at Aligarh Muslim University (Panikar was a Hindu of the Nair community) and from there took a readership in history at Calcutta University. The first sharp change in his varied career followed when he forsook his academic career for one in journalism and became editor of *The Hindustan Times*.

Changing again, he became secretary to the Chamber of Princes, from that position moving to the personal service of the ruler of Patiala and then to that of Bikaner, serving both houses in the office of Foreign Minister. He was secretary to the delegation of Indian states at the Round Table Conference in London in 1930.

He was elected to the constitutional assembly in 1946, was a member of the Indian delegation to the United Nations in 1947, and the following year was sent to China as Ambassador.

Panikkar's understanding and sympathetic dispatches from Peking in the first years after the Chinese communists came to power did much to confirm and crystallize the latent goodwill of Mr. Nehru, Prime Minister to Asia's most successful revolutionaries. His warnings to Nehru that China would intervene in Korea if the United Nations armies approached the Yalu river, although disregarded by the west, were taken in India to show his understanding of the communist Government and his closeness to them.

Since India fell out with China Panikkar's service in Peking has come under far more critical scrutiny and only in the week before his death he had been engaged in a correspondence in the press denying the charge that he had without authority, even if inadvertently, given Peking the impression that India was prepared to recognize Chinese sovereignty over Tibet.

After he left China Panikkar served as Indian Ambassador in Egypt and then France, but in neither country did he achieve the influence he had exerted from Peking. Between his appointments in Cairo and Paris he served on the States Reorganization Commission, which proposed new boundaries for the Indian states along the linguistic divisions to which the Congress Party had long before committed itself. More recently Panikkar had been vice-chancellor of the university in Srinagar and then of Mysore University, a post he occupied until his death.

Panikkar had a quick and colourful pen and was a prolific writer. His account of his term in Peking, *In Two Chinas*, gave a fresh and valuable account of the transition from one regime and one world to another, and was his most popular work. More scholarly was *Asia and Western Dominance*, in which the nationalist's approach was disciplined by that of the historian, yielding a work whose objectivity was none the less because it was explicitly written from an Asian viewpoint. Among his other works were *Hindu Society at the Crossroads*, *Caste and Democracy*, *Survey of Indian History*, and *Geographical Factors in Indian History*.

December 11, 1963.

Pandit Govind Ballabh Pant, Indian Minister for Home Affairs, died in New Delhi on March 7, 1961. He was 73.

Pant was one of "the old guard" of the Congress Party, certainly the closest of all the country's leaders to Mr. Nehru. He was a man whose integrity no one dreamed of questioning, whose instincts and judgments were sound and fair and whose only ambition was to serve his country. In the inner counsels of the Cabinet and the Congress Party he was a source of wisdom and great strength to Nehru; in Parliament he was a tremendous figure, patient but devastating in debate and capable of marshalling ideas and facts into cogent and forceful speech.

Communists, Communialists, cranks, all dreaded the vigour of his tongue but such was his mastery of the Parliamentary form that many of them today bitterly regret his departure from the scene.

Anything which seemed to him to endanger the unity of India was anathema; as Home Minister he acted forcefully against subversion from any source. He was deeply hurt by such manifestations as linguistic riots in Assam, Congress quarrels in his home state of Uttar Pradesh and communist extra-territorial loyalties. He took an uncompromising stand against the all-India strike by Government employees in 1960 and played a major part in bringing about its rapid collapse, but it was typical of the man that once the danger was over he was well in the forefront of measures aimed at conciliation.

He made a careful study of the position arising from Chinese incursions on Indian territory and was known to be in constant touch with Nehru on the diplomatic and military steps to be taken to meet the danger. His strength, his humanity, his immense commonsense have been of incalculable value to the country.

He was born on September 10, 1887, educated at Almora and the Muir Central College, Allahabad, and studied at the School of Law, Allahabad; in 1909 he was enrolled as an Advocate of the High Court. He practised his profession at the hill station of Nani Tal, and was soon drawn into Nationalist circles by joining a provincial organization to study local problems and to seek the redress of grievances. In 1916 he was elected a member of the All-India Congress Committee. Several years later he was elected to the provincial legislature on the Swaraj (self-government) Party ticket and he was leader of the party for some seven years. In 1927 he was appointed president of the United Provinces Congress Party and presided at the annual session held at Aligarh. He was active in promoting the boycott of the Statutory (Simon) Commission appointed at the close of 1927 to study the problem of Indian advancement to self-government. He threw himself into the civil disobedience campaigns of 1930 and 1932, and was twice imprisoned in this connexion. In the interval between the two periods of detention he was chairman of a committee of the Provincial Congress Party to promote agrarian reform.

In 1934 the Pandit was made general secretary of the All-India Parliamentary Committee and in the same year was elected to the Central Legislative Council at Delhi, becoming deputy leader there of the Congress Party. When provincial autonomy came into force in 1937 Pant was appointed Premier of United Provinces. His ministry shared in the resignations of Congress Governments as war approached in the summer of 1939. Consequently the Governor (Sir Harry Haig) was called upon to administer the U.P. without cabinet or Parliament. In 1940 the Pandit underwent further imprisonment for a year. In August, 1942, like all the other members of the Working Committee of the Congress he was imprisoned for advocating obstruction of the war effort and he remained in detention until nearly the end of the war.

In 1945 he was one of the party leaders invited by the Viceroy, Lord Wavell, to attend the Simla conference on the transfer of power. Pant took part with other Congress leaders in talks with Mr. Jinnah, only to be met by the stubborn refusal of the president of the Muslim League to agree to any plan other than partition. On the return of provincial congress ministries to office the Pandit resumed the Premiership of the United Provinces. He was elected to the Constituent Assembly, which began its deliberations for the making of a Constitution before power was transferred. When the partition took effect in August, 1947, Pant again became Chief Minister in the newly styled state of Uttar Pradesh. There was a marked contrast between his austerity of life and outlook, and that of the first Governor of the state after independence, the late Mrs. Sarojini Naidu, who was renowned both for poetry and for her social gifts.

In 1954 Pant was taken to Delhi from Uttar Pradesh as Union Home Minister. He was elected to the Rajya Sabha, the Upper House, and became its Leader. His preoccupations since then included the reorganization of the States, the position of the Hindi language, the ousting of the Communist Government in Kerala and the troubles in Nagaland. In 1959 he suffered a severe heart attack and in January, 1961, he had a stroke but he continued to work up to 17 hours a day.

March 8, 1961.

Professor C. F. A. Pantin, F.R.S., M.A., SC.D., former professor of zoology in the University of Cambridge and fellow of Trinity College, died on January 14, 1967, at the age of 67. In Pantin zoologists in Britain have lost one of their foremost and best-loved colleagues, who before and since his election to the professorship at Cambridge in 1959 has always played a large part in the advance of the science. He retired from the professorship in 1966.

The first half of the present century has been a time of change in zoology. Up to about 1910 British zoologists were chiefly interested in study of the structure of animals and in deducing from the results of this study the revolutionary plan of the animal kingdom. These interests dated from the period immediately after belief in the truth of evolution was accepted, that is to say from the sixties of the last century. At the turn of the century other interests were becoming general, and after the first decade of the century dominant, chiefly under the leadership of Professor James Gray of Cambridge. Younger zoologists became more interested in study of how the animal body works, comparative physiology, and how it maintains its life in its environment. At the same time the study of inheritance, genetics, had become prominent. At the end of the First World War Pantin was one of the foremost of Professor Gray's pupils in developing this new trend in zoology. There was for a time a danger that zoologists would confine themselves to their laboratories, and perhaps one of Pantin's most valuable contributions has been that he insisted, early and late, that zoology must be a broad study of animal life, in the environment in the field as well as in the laboratory.

Carl Frederick Abel Pantin was born on March 30, 1899, at Blackheath, the eldest son of Henry Pantin, who was in business in London. Pantin was educated at Tonbridge and came up to Christ's College, Cambridge, as a scholar in 1919, after a short period of service in a Field Survey Company of the Royal Engineers, plotting the positions of enemy guns by their flashes. He took a first in the Natural Sciences Tripos (Zoology) in 1922, and in that year was given the Frank Smart Prize of the university. From 1922 to 1929 he was on the staff of the Marine Biological Association's laboratory at Plymouth. In 1929 he was elected to a fellowship at Trinity and appointed to a university lectureship in zoology. Since that time he had been on the staff of the department of zoology, being appointed Reader in Invertebrate Zoology in 1937, and elected professor on the retirement of Professor Gray in 1959. He was elected to the Royal Society in 1937, was given a Royal Medal in 1950 and gave the Croonian Lecture in 1952. He was given the Traill award of the Linnean Society in 1937, and was president of that society, 1958–61. He was president of Section D (Zoology) of the British Association in 1951. He took his Sc.D. in 1933.

There can be few zoologists in this country who have not in the past 40 years come into contact with Pantin, and certainly none who have read zoology at Cambridge who will not remember his lectures or supervisions of research with appreciation. He had always taken a large part in the work of the department and had much to do with the rebuilding of the laboratory in 1936. His own research was on various invertebrates. At Plymouth he worked on the locomotion of amoeba, and after he returned to Cambridge he produced a long series of papers on the nervous system of sea-anemones and the control of muscular contraction in crabs. His work on sea-anemones was particularly noteworthy since he was able to show that their primitive nerve-net behaved in a way fundamentally identical with the behaviour of the nervous system of higher animals and he was able as a result of this work to give an interpretation of the means by which the whole behaviour of the animal is controlled. In the crabs his results have tended rather to emphasize the differences between these arthropods and other animals, especially the vertebrates, in the mechanism of control.

Pantin had many other interests. He travelled in Brazil, New Zealand, and other countries in pursuit of his animals and to study their biology. He wrote on many subjects of general zoological interest such as the origin of life, adaptation of animals to changes in the salinity of the medium in which they live, and the theory of evolution. He had also, both before and after his election as professor, taken a large share in the work of committees dealing with the organization of science teaching in the university, especially recently on the difficulties caused by the multiplication of scientific courses. He was also active in committee work for the Royal Society. In 1936 Pantin became chairman of the trustees of the British Museum (Natural History). In later years he did much work as chairman of the Nuffield Unit of Tropical Animal Ecology in Uganda.

Pantin married in 1923 Miss Amy Smith, daughter of Dr. J. C. Smith, of Edinburgh, by whom he had two sons.

January 17, 1967.

George Papandreou, the former Prime Minister of Greece, and leader of the powerful Centre Union Party, died on November 1, 1968, a lonely and embittered figure whose half-century-long political career was abruptly terminated by martial law 18 months earlier. He was 80.

When a handful of Greek Army officers seized power on April 21, 1967, he was at the zenith of a delayed popularity. He saw the coup d'état as aimed at averting a sweeping Centre Union victory in the elections of May 1967, which were never held. His opponents, however, saw the coup as a direct consequence of his own political irresponsibility.

After the coup of April, 1967, he was arrested and confined to a military hospital and later held incommunicado at home. House arrest was lifted on Christmas Eve. It was reimposed on April 15 this year but not before he had recorded his first public proclamation denouncing the regime. He was set free again on September 23 this year, but he boycotted the regime's constitutional referendum.

Born on February 13, 1888, at Kalentzi, the son of the local priest, he studied law in Athens and, later, thanks to a grant from the Bishopric of Paris, he pursued his studies in political and economic sciences at the University of Berlin.

It was there, in 1914, that the founder of the Liberal Party, Eleftherios Venizelos, met him, and, impressed by his eloquence, appointed him the following year local governor on the island of Lesbos. His political career, punctuated by periods of exile, gaol and revolutionary activity, began in earnest in 1916 when Venizelos appointed him his principal private secretary. When the pro-Entente Venizelist revolution broke out later that year, he proclaimed the revolution against King Constantine I on Lesbos and acted as government commissioner on the island of Chios until 1920. He spent four months in prison in 1921 after being court-martialled for publishing an article urging the King to abdicate.

He took up his first ministerial post even before entering Parliament, serving as Minister of Interior in the 1923 revolutionary government of General Gonatas which deposed the monarchy.

He was an early and staunch opponent of dictators and totalitarianism. He had his first brief taste of exile when he opposed the short-lived Pangalos dictatorship in 1926. Then 10 years later, he was confined to one Aegean island with other politicians under the Metaxas dictatorship. During the enemy occupation of Greece, he was imprisoned by the Italian authorities in 1942, but was later released and managed to flee to the Middle East in April, 1944, where he was promptly appointed by the British as Prime Minister of the Greek government-in-exile.

He returned to liberated Greece in October, 1944, at the head of a government of national unity which contained the seeds of the tragedy that was yet to come—three Communist Ministers. Six weeks later the Communist uprising erupted and the British, who had taken upon themselves the responsibility of keeping Greece on the safe side of the Iron Curtain, grew more and more impatient with his vacillations. He was deposed in favour of another veteran Liberal revolutionary, General Plastiras.

Between the first postwar elections in 1946 and 1952 he served in several Cabinets, but always remained the frustrated politician who had not been given a chance to show his mettle as leader of the nation. His great ambition was to be the elected Prime Minister of Greece. But, after a brief period of Liberal government between 1950 and 1952, in which he was deputy Premier, the right wing became firmly entrenched in power, first under Marshal Papagos, then under Constantine Karamanlis.

It was only in 1961, with the prospect of a general election, that the Liberal splinters decided to reunite. He was chosen as leader of the new "Centre Union" with the ulterior motive that his advanced age—he was then 73—would not keep him for long an obstacle to the individual ambitions of the splinter leaders.

His sharp attacks against the ruling right wing after the 1961 elections (which he lost), on grounds of electoral "rigging", and his efforts to topple the Karamanlis regime which he dubbed "the unrelenting struggle", came at a psychologically propitious moment. Weary with the austerity practised by the Karamanlis Government for nearly six years, the Greeks were yearning for more economic, and often social and political freedom.

The victory of the Centre Union proved only relative—140 seats against 132—but the right wing was so mortified by its first defeat since 1952 that Papandreou soon pressed for another election that would give him a working majority in Parliament. To give the people a taste of what was to come, he soon squandered a reserve of £25m. sterling (kept by the previous government in the Treasury for economic development) in generous though unproductive grants such as doubling judges' salaries and increasing subsidies to farmers for growing unwanted wheat.

He returned to power after the elections of February, 1964, on an unprecedented 53 per cent of the vote. This time he was not alone. Obsessed by a weakness common to Greek politicians—that of seeing their name perpetuated in politics generation after generation—he induced his 47-year-old son, Andreas, to join him in Greek politics. Then, with understandable paternal affection, he set out to build him up as political heir.

The King's refusal to allow Papandreou to take over the Defence Ministry, which would have given him direct access to the Aspida inquiry (into a military plot in which his son was allegedly implicated) until the affair was cleared up, forced him to resign on July 15, 1965, on a new, powerful slogan: "Who rules Greece? the King or the people?"

Papandreou was a talented orator in a country where rhetoric was born 2,400 years ago.

The more Papandreou represented his fall as the result of an antagonism with the "sinister forces" of the palace the less the King and the right wing were willing to face an election which might turn into a plebiscite over the monarchy.

November 2, 1968.

Franz von Papen, former German Chancellor, Vice-Chancellor in Adolf Hitler's first government, and Germany's wartime ambassador in Turkey, died on May 2, 1969.

He was 89, and born on October 29, 1879, in the hamlet of Weil near Soest, the ancient capital of Westphalia. He came of a Catholic family which had been ennobled by the Emperor Joseph I in 1709. After his early education at the Rektoratschule in Weil he elected to follow the military career. In 1889 was gazetted to his father's old regiment, the 5th Westphalian Uhlans.

For the next few years von Papen lived a very pleasant life. Good-looking, with comfortable private means, charming, witty and a fine performer in the ballroom, he was regarded as *bon parti* by ambitious mothers, and in 1905 he married the daughter of the Privy Councillor von Bock-Galhau, the wealthy and influential industrialist of the Saar.

Von Papen's military career prospered though his superiors were prone to regard him as "overbrilliant", with a tendency to recklessness in judgment. The truth was that he had a political rather than a military mind and not a very good one at that. He possessed a natural flair for the devious, but in matters of politico-strategy he tended to deal in broad generalities with a lack of regard for the details and consequences entailed. Nevertheless he was attached to the General Staff in 1911 and three years later (January 1914) Captain von Papen was appointed Military Attaché to the German Embassy in Washington and to the Legation in Mexico.

In company with his naval colleague von Boy-Ed, but largely without the knowledge of his Ambassador, Count Bernstorff, he embarked upon a series of activities which brought him under the suspicion and surveillance not only of the Allied Intelligence Services but of the American authorities also. In 1916 his activities were unmasked and with von Boy-Ed, he was deported by sea to Germany with a safeconduct which covered his person but not his baggage.

In transit, his ship was stopped and searched by a British warship, and among his personal effects was discovered the details of his work with Secret Service agents in America and the counterfoils of the cheques with which they had been paid. All this material was made public by the British Government in a White paper.

Von Papen fought with conspicuous courage on the Western Front, being decorated with the Iron Cross (First Class), and was then transferred to Turkey as a general staff officer to the headquarters of Expedition F. whose commander was General von Falkenhayn. Here his ability in the field of political warfare was once again recognized. His task was to stimulate revolt against the British in the Muslim world from Abyssinia and the Sudan to Aden and the Suez Canal Zone. His plans, admirable in concept, failed in every case through faulty organization of detail and the employment of the wrong type of agent in their execution.

With the collapse of the Central Powers von Papen returned to Germany and settled down to become a model farmer and horse breeder on his family estates near Dülmen in Westphalia.

Yet he was not idle; he sought to place himself in the position of a key man. Through his wife's connections he exercised considerable influence with the big industrialists. His own interests in farming and bloodstock brought him into contact with the powerful *Landbund* of the great estate owners. His old associations with the army gave him access to Reichswehr circles and politically he kept in touch with the forces of the Right by means of his membership of the *Herrenklub* of Berlin. He expressed decided views on the evils and dangers of communism in Germany and the desirability of reaching a *rapprochement* with France, and, as a devout Catholic, a member of the nobility and a landowner, he deplored the policy of the Centre Party which under Brüning had allied itself with the Social Democrats.

It was not altogether unnatural that when in 1932 General Kurt von Schleicher, the *Feldgrau Eminenz* of the Reichswehr, who had made and broken more than one Chancellor of the Reich, was seeking for a successor to his former protege Brüning, his choice should fall on Franz von Papen. Schleicher and the President's son, Oskar von Hindenburg, brought von Papen to the Marshal who, delighted with his charm, his volatility and his political views, at once gave him a mandate to form a government.

And so, at the age of fifty-three Franz von Papen became *Reichskanzler* but, alas for his dream of a coalition of the Right, the Centre Party expelled him from membership and remained loyal to their fallen leader Brüning. The new Chancellor could command no majority in the Reichstag and formed a "Government of Barons" who represented an absurdly small fraction of the electorate. Two general elections showed conclusively that the electors did not want von Papen.

Meanwhile the Nazi vote increased and von Papen sought to find a formula whereby the National Socialists should be admitted to a coalition, but in a subordinate position under himself. Hitler proved obdurate. He would have the Chancellorship or nothing. He would enter no political coalition save as its leader.

DOWNFALL

Von Papen would have continued to bargain but General von Schleicher, realizing that the situation was acute and that his nominee was not the man to handle it, engineered his downfall in the teeth of the opposition of the President, his son Oskar and of von Papen himself. In revenge, Hindenburg forced Schleicher to take the Chancellorship but withheld from him all presidential support.

Von Papen meanwhile threw himself with all his old zeal and irresponsibility into the most fateful intrigue of his life. Believing that he could control Hitler by accepting his leadership in a coalition with the Right which would give the Nazis only three portfolios in all, he entered into negotiation with the Führer on this basis at Cologne in the house of Baron von Schroeder on January 8, 1933. Finding Hitler not unamenable, Papen then sought the agreement of the President. This too he obtained on the basis of his own assurances and, on January

30, the "Government of National Concentration" was formed with Hitler as Chancellor and Minister-President of Prussia, and Frick and Göring as Cabinet Ministers; the portfolios being held either by Nationalists or officials.

The result of his intrigue delighted von Papen. Schleicher was destroyed and he himself had succeeded in doing what all others had failed to do. He had made Hitler the hostage and prisoner of the Conservatives, with every possible guarantee against his "breaking out of the reservation". The national resurgence of Germany would now take place on conservative and reactionary lines and not on the wild principles of National Socialism, which would be modulated in the interest of German nationalism. He had destroyed the evils of Weimar and the Nazi menace at one stroke. The government of Germany would become once more a government of gentlemen.

Alas for these dreams also; within three months Göring had seized the government of Prussia from von Papen. Hitler had refused to recognize his authority as Vice-Chancellor and Goebbels, Hess and Röhm had entered the Cabinet. The Trojan Horse of National Socialism within the fortress of the Reich Government had given up its hidden hordes and taken captive the other members of the Cabinet. Papen had sold the Reich to Hitler.

Shocked at this unexpected outcome of his intrigues and genuinely horrified at the excesses of the Brown Terror which followed, von Papen sought to redeem his errors by a courageous speech of protest at the University of Marburg on June 17, 1934. All that resulted from his effort, however, was a contributory factor in the Blood Purge of June 30, in which two of the Vice-Chancellor's adjutants were murdered and he himself barely escaped with his life.

AUSTRIAN POST

Yet even now, von Papen could not bring himself to break with the man whom he had brought to power. When Hitler offered him the post of Ambassador to Vienna on the day after the assassination of Dollfuss (July 25, 1934) he accepted. For the next four years his primary purpose was to undermine the Schuschnigg regime and to strengthen the Austrian Nazi Party for the purpose of bringing about an *Anschluss* with the German Reich.

He was successful in securing the appointment of men friendly to the Nazis in the Schuschnigg Cabinet and it was he who arranged the infamous meeting of Hitler and Schuschnigg at Berchtesgaden on February 12, 1938. He did, however, urge Hitler not to occupy Austria by force in March.

After the annexation of Austria von Papen retired into private life, taking no active part in politics. From 1939 to 1944 he was German Ambassador to Turkey and had a role in "Operation Cicero".

Although cleared of war crimes at Nuremberg, he was sentenced to eight years' hard labour by the Bavarian Government denazification court in 1949, but was released immediately because of his long pre-trial detention.

His next five years were devoted to the writing of his memoirs, which proved to be a very readable apologia, written with the bravura of the Herrenreiter but, nevertheless, a classic example of "qui s'excuse s'accuse". In 1968 he published *The Collapse of a Democracy 1930–33*.

When all else about him has been forgotten Franz von Papen will be assured of his place in history as the man who held his hands for Hitler to leap into the saddle.

May 3, 1969.

Dorothy Parker, writer of disenchanted short stories, poet, script writer and legendary wit, died on June 7, 1967, in the hotel in Manhattan, New York, where she lived. She was 73.

In the 1920s. New York was enlivened by a group of talented and witty young writers who, calling themselves the Round Table Club, met weekly at the Hotel Algonquin. Many of them were to attain fame but some had already done so. Among the latter was Dorothy Parker.

Her work was characterized by brilliant humour and teasing cynicism (Alexander Woollcott once described her as a "blend of Little Nell and Lady Macbeth"), but to regard it as a mere display of pyrotechnics would be unjust. She had an acute understanding of the human predicament; of loneliness, cruelty, and stupidity. She had done her share of protesting as a young woman, reported the war in Spain in the 1930s, and 20 years on was cited by the House un-American Activities Committee. As the critic Edmund Wilson fairly said: "She has been at some pains to write well, and she has put into what she has written a voice, a state of mind, an era, a few moments of human experience that nobody else has conveyed."

Her maiden name was Dorothy Rothschild, and she was born on August 22, 1893, at West End, New Jersey, of a Jewish father and a Scottish mother. She grew up in New York City and was educated in a convent where she began to write poems. When it became necessary, because of her father's death, to earn some money she sent one of her poems to the editor of *Vanity Fair*. He was impressed by it and found temporary work for her, writing picture captions for *Vogue*. Later, he made her dramatic critic of *Vanity Fair*, but in time, the hostility of theatrical managers—she wrote with a caustic pen—forced her out of that post, and for a while she engaged in freelance journalism.

Later she became a frequent contributor to *The New Yorker* and produced some much-quoted, and often less than gentle, observations of people and life. One of the most memorable was in a review of Katherine Hepburn's performance in a play, *The Lake*, in 1933. Miss Hepburn's performance, she wrote, "ran the whole gamut of the emotions from A to B". But although she often exercised her "devastating gift for the wisecrack" in her stories and poems she frequently showed through a mask of humour the sentimental as well as the satirical side of her nature. It was said of her that in her first book of poems, *Enough Rope*, published in 1926, she established herself as "master of the cynical-sentimental *genre* with the whiplash ending" and in support of this statement there were quoted the lines:

> Dream and dance and laugh and lie,
> Love, the reeling midnight through,
> For tomorrow we may die!
> (*But, alas, we never do.*)

She early gained national recognition with short stories, of which 13 were collected under the title *Laments for the Living*; and with such books of her poems as *Not So Deep as a Well* and *Sunset Gun*. One of her stories, "Big Blonde", won the O. Henry Memorial Award in 1929 and with another, "Telephone Call", it was included in many anthologies.

Although in later life she was apt to deprecate her reputation as wit her shafts, written or verbal, endured: "That girl can speak 18 languages and can't say 'no' in any of them"; "You mean those clothes of hers were intentional? My heavens! I always thought she was on her way out of a burning building"; and perhaps the most often quoted: "Men seldom make passes at girls who wear glasses."

She wrote several scripts for motion pictures, collaborating with her second husband, Alan Campbell, an actor, whom she married in 1933. They were divorced in 1947, but remarried three years later. Her first marriage had been to Edwin Pond Parker II, in 1917 a few days before he sailed for France in the First World War. They separated when he returned and she was granted a divorce in Connecticut, but she continued to write under the name of Parker.

In 1924 she had collaborated with Elmer Rice in a play called *Close Harmony*; with Ross Evans in 1949 she wrote *The Coast of Illyria*, a play based on the life of Charles Lamb; and in 1953 a piece she had written with Arnaud d'Usseau, called *Ladies of the Corridor* had a moderately successful Broadway run. It concerned a group of widows living in an expensive hotel in the Upper East Side of New York and was one of Granada Television's plays of the week in 1960.

June 9, 1967.

Ben Parkin, Labour M.P. for North Paddington since 1953, and the man who attacked the Rachman slum empire, died on June 3, 1969, at the age of 63. Housing was one of his main interests, but he also fought against open prostitution and the drugs menace.

Parkin did much to take the lid off the Rachman case: for years he had to devise ways of being heard in the Commons on property racketeering in Paddington. In 1963 he said: "I can't remember when I first mentioned Rachman's name—long before this present row, anyway. Most of my speeches were either out of order or late at night. I had to devise ways of being heard. It was the only way of calling attention to the sorrows of Paddington."

In May, 1963, Parkin withdrew a Commons question asking the Home Secretary what conclusions he had reached from information supplied to him by Dr. Stephen Ward, the osteopath and portrait artist, and what action he proposed to take, following recent metropolitan police inquiries, "to prevent the increase of expensive call girl organizations".

It was in 1963 that he vehemently attacked what he called the "Rachman Empire" in the house, giving numerous examples of what he declared to be Rachman's activities. Rachman, he told the House, took £30,000 on a property in Bryanston Mews which was mortgaged four months before he "disappeared". "Certain factors", said Parkin, "led to the suggestion that Rachman was not dead." Rachman, Parkin maintained, had owned about 20 basement clubs which he leased out, and he called for an attack on certain kinds of property dealing.

An application by Parkin to introduce a private Bill to control slum racketeering was rejected by 208 votes to 140. Parkin said: "Housing conditions in the area of the Rachman empire produced the Notting Hill race riots." In 1968 Parkin advocated the introduction of a licensing system for landlords which would shift the onus of improving property or ensuring that it was improved from the local authority to the owner.

Benjamin Theaker Parkin was born in 1906, the son of Captain B. D. Parkin. Parkin, who was destined to play a prominent part in politics, was educated at Wycliffe College, Lincoln College, Oxford, and Strasbourg University. He commenced his career as a school master and became a flight lieutenant in the R.A.F. during the war. He was on the staff of Wycliffe College before he joined the R.A.F.

For some years Parkin was headmaster of the Stonehouse council school, Stroud (Gloucestershire). It was in 1945 that he became Stroud's first Labour M.P., when he gained Stroud from the Conservatives; he had a majority of 949 votes. In 1947 he was one of a number of Labour M.P.s who went to Russia and met Stalin. The following year, with colleagues, he flew to Nigeria to spend three weeks inquiring into the spending of £23m. allocated to the colony under the Colonial Development Act, 1945, and in 1949 he was appointed by the Minister of Pensions as a member of his Central Advisory Committee.

Parkin was one of 64 Labour M.P.s who received a letter from Maurice Webb, chairman of the Parliamentary Labour Party, and William Whiteley, Government Chief Whip in 1949, warning them of their conduct towards the Labour Party. This followed the expulsion of two M.P.s and the dismissal of four parliamentary private secretaries for having voted against the Government on the Ireland Bill.

In 1950 he lost the seat at Stroud by 28 votes, and in the 1951 election he lost to the Conservative candidate by 1,582.

When he was successful at Paddington North in 1953 it was by a majority of 2,260.

In 1954, at the invitation of the People's Institute of Foreign Affairs, he and other Labour M.P.s went to Prague, from there to Moscow, and subsequently, to China. The following year he spoke at a Communist-organized meeting held in Brussels to protest against German rearmament. A few days later there were clashes with the police outside the House of Commons when demonstrators gathered to lobby M.P.s against rearming the West Germans.

During the sitting Parking said: "A number of my constituents who have come to see me by appointment are being ridden down by mounted police, driven off the pavement outside the house, and pushed away from the building altogether."

In the 1955 general election, Parkin had a majority of 2,092 over his Conservative opponent in North Paddington.

The following year Parkin said in the House that he did not realize just how widespread a legend about his borough was until he was in Peking about 18 months before. There, when he stated that he represented Paddington, he was told: "Oh, that is where the Church owns the brothels, isn't it?" "That legend", said Parkin, "persisted a long time and it was not without a basis of truth." Later he said that what was wanted in Paddington was to get the prostitutes off the streets.

The drug menace in London was also tackled by Parkin. He asked the Government to take action to stop the peddling of purple heart tablets among teenagers. "These tablets are easily available in millions", he said. "I believe the authorities and reputable firms are being hoodwinked in the distribution of this kind of tablet." He reproached the Government for not having sufficiently studied the "Soho nerve centre" of the purple heart pill racket.

June 4, 1969.

Reg Parnell, the former motor racing driver and racing manager, died on January 7, 1964, in Derbyshire Royal Infirmary. He was 52.

Reginald Parnell was born at Derby on July 2, 1911, and educated at Gerrard Street Secondary School, Derby. His racing career, which was to extend over 23 years and cover almost every type of racing car, began in 1934. In the years before the war he established a reputation as a skilful but thrustful driver and in the early postwar years he began to build up a name that was to reach the heights of motor racing in the 1950s. In 1947 and 1948 he received the coveted Gold Star of the British Racing Drivers' Club, the major award in British motor racing, and in 1957 he won the New Zealand Grand Prix before his retirement from active motor racing.

He was well known for his early postwar performances in his own 4CLT Maserati, and at the Goodwood circuit, which he knew so well, he put up some historic performances. He was one of the selected drivers who was invited to drive a works Alfa Romeo in the British Grand Prix of 1950, in the days when top ranking British racing drivers were comparatively scarce. But it was his association with the Aston Martin sports car team that brought him perhaps his greatest reputation and popularity in the racing world. He also drove the 16-cylinder B.R.M. in its early days.

He took up the position of racing manager to the David Brown team in 1957 and actively ran the team for three full and exciting years. It was in 1959 under his guidance that Aston Martin captured the World Sports Car championship and achieved their win in that year's 24-hour race at Le Mans. When the Aston Martins withdrew from motor racing he took over management of the newly formed Yeoman Credit racing team in 1960, later to become the Bowmaker-Yeoman team. His shrewd observation of drivers, and the deep knowledge of racing tactics brought the team rapidly to the forefront of the British grand prix challengers, and it was in 1962 that he signed up John Surtees, the world motor cycling champion, for the Bowmaker-Yeoman racing team to drive with R. Salvadori and helped to develop the Lola cars, designed by Eric Broadley. As a result of this association, Surtees was spotted by Ferrari and selected for the Italian grand prix team for last season and he is now their No. 1 driver.

With the withdrawal of Bowmaker from the racing scene. Parnell established his own team last year, taking over the Lola machines which Surtees had helped to develop. His drivers for the season were C. Amon, a promising young New Zealander, and M. Hailwood, the world motor cycle champion. This year he had planned a full season of grand prix racing, again with Amon and Hailwood as his drivers, using two former works Lotus 25s and a completely new "monocoque" car, which had been code named R.P. 64, and which is being built at the team's headquarters at Hounslow, Middlesex. Parnell had foreseen that 1964 would probably be the most successful season for the team which he had built up over the past year.

His first wife, Gladys, died in 1961 and later that year he married, secondly, Betty Wilson Wright. His son, Tim Parnell, has also established a name in international motor racing in recent years.

January 8, 1964.

Professor Edgar Alexander Pask, O.B.E., one of Britain's best known anaesthetists and professor of anaesthetics at the University of Newcastle, died on May 30, 1966, at the age of 53.

Pask was the designer in 1957 of an emergency makeshift iron lung, built by his laboratory joiners in four hours, which he said could be turned out in a few minutes by manufacturers tooled for the work in the event of a large poliomyelitis outbreak. It ran off a household vacuum cleaner and was assembled from parts costing less than £2.

Edgar Alexander Pask was the son of a Cheshire businessman, and was born on September 4, 1912. He was educated at Rydal School and Downing College, Cambridge, where he obtained first class honours in both parts of the tripos, and proceeded then on a scholarship to the London Hospital. He qualified M.B. in 1937 and remained at the same hospital for a further two and a half years, after which he was appointed first assistant to Professor (Sir) Robert Macintosh at the Nuffield Department of Anaesthetics in the Radcliffe Infirmary, Oxford. Soon after the outbreak of war he joined the R.A.F., being presently posted to the Physiology Laboratory (now the R.A.F.

Institute of Aviation Medicine).

Here his work was first connected with the problems of descent from high altitude by parachute. Later, he was especially concerned with air-sea rescue, and the development of protective clothing when air crew had to come down into very cold water, and with the design of lifejackets for aviators wearing special equipment. In this work, he visited many parts of the world, often in hazardous circumstances, and took part as the subject in a number of dangerous experiments, the cumulative effect of which had much to do with the efficiency of the air-sea rescue service during the war. Some of this work was included in the film *In Which We Serve*. For this and other services he was created O.B.E. in 1944 and was awarded the Snow Medal by the Association of Anaesthetists of Great Britain and Ireland in 1946.

On release from the R.A.F. in 1947 he was appointed Reader in Anaesthetics in the University of Durham (now the University of Newcastle upon Tyne), becoming professor in 1949. From the first, he established a department with great potentialities in research, and from which much basic apparatus and information has come.

He was a member of the board of Faculty of Anaesthetists in the Royal College of Surgeons of England for 14 years from its inception in 1948. He also served on the council of the Association of Anaesthetists, having been honorary treasurer for three years. He was president of the section of anaesthetics of the Royal Society of Medicine (1964). He was an examiner for the Faculty of Anaesthetists both in the primary and final examinations, and also for the Irish Faculty of Anaesthetists, from whom he was to have received the honorary fellowship four days after his death.

LIFE JACKETS

He was a member of the committee of management of the Royal National Lifeboat Institution and his work on a floating dummy ("Seaworthy Sierra Sam") has been made use of by the British Board of Trade for the production of improved lifejackets for merchant seamen.

His visits and lecture tours in the U.S.A. made him many friends and his work at Montreal with Professor Wilder Penfield is regarded as of the first rank. For long his word carried great influence, not only in British anaesthesia but in world medicine. Latterly he gave much of his time to administrative work in his hospital, the Royal Victoria Infirmary, Newcastle upon Tyne. He was chairman of the medical advisory committee, a member of the board of governors, and chairman of the planning and buildings committee; he was also adviser in anaesthetics for the Northern Regional Hospital Board.

He leaves a widow and one daughter.

June 1, 1966.

King Paul of the Hellenes—See under **Greece.**

Jean Paulhan, the distinguished French writer and member of the Académie Française, died in Paris on October 10, 1968. He was 83.

He was born at Nimes on December 2, 1884, the son of Professor Frédéric Paulhan, a well-known philosopher of the psychological school, from whom he may be thought to have inherited his scholarly disposition and his uncompromising spirit. After a distinguished career at the Lycée Louis-le-Grand and the Sorbonne, Paulhan spent some time as a schoolmaster and also as a gold prospector in Madagascar, but at the age of 24 he returned to Paris to become Professor of the Malgache Language at the School of Oriental Studies. He then seemed destined like his father for the academic life, but after service in the trenches in the First World War, he decided to abandon the university for literary journalism. He joined the staff of the Nouvelle Revue Française as editorial secretary in 1920. He was soon appointed editor, and for many years this famous periodical bore the mark of his personal direction.

When the Germans entered Paris in 1940, Paulhan severed his connection with the N.R.F. at once. He was one of the first French intellectuals to participate in the Resistance movement as founder of the clandestine Les Lettres françaises. When the N.R.F. came to life again after the war as La Nouvelle N.R.F., Paulhan resumed the editor's chair. He was elected to the Académie Française in 1963 on the death of Pierre Benoit.

Although best known as an editor, Paulhan was also a literary critic and moralist of considerable distinction. He was not, perhaps, the most perspicuous of stylists, and his academic background left him with a certain attachment to paradox and enigma. But he knew how to arrest the reader's attention, and he often shocked people. His *Guide d'un polit voyage en Suisse* is a devastating attack on romantic ideas of nature. The prefaces he wrote to Sade's *Justine* and to the even more scandalous *Histoire d'O*. by "Pauline Réagé" (which some people—wrongly—believed Paulhan to have written), were bold affronts to traditional moral notions. At the same time, in such books as *À Demain la poésie* (1955), Paulhan showed that he could be equally unsparing towards the prevailing sentiments of the avant garde.

In addition to his work with the N.R.F. Paulhan directed the successful Bibliotheque de la Pléiade, which issued many of the French classics in attractive, scholarly editions. He won the Grand Prix of the Académie Française in 1945 and of the Ville de Paris in 1951. In the First World War he was decorated with the Croix de Guerre and in the second war with the Médaille de la Résistance.

October 11, 1968.

Konstantin Paustovsky, who died on July 14, 1968, in Moscow at the age of 76, was perhaps the most highly praised and best beloved of all living Soviet writers in both Britain and the United States.

He was born in Moscow into a lively middle-class family of Zaporozhye Cossack stock on his father's side and of Polish Catholic extraction on his mother's side. His father worked for the railways as a statistician and hence the young Paustovsky's early apprenticeship to travel, the family seldom finding itself domiciled in any one place for very long.

Paustovsky, grew up in an atmosphere of intellectual curiosity, both at home and at the classical high school in Kiev where he studied from 1902 to 1912. His father died when Paustovsky was 20 years old. By then the family was in very straitened circumstances and Paustovsky had already been paying his own way at Kiev University by giving private lessons. As a schoolboy he had written a quantity of indifferent poetry and he had his first short story published in 1912 in a Kiev journal under the pen-name of Balagin.

At the beginning of the First World War, when he rejoined his mother in Moscow, his itch to be up and doing soon got the upper hand over continuing at university. For the next 15 years Paustovsky shuttled from one job to another and from one corner of Russia to the next in an untiring quest for new and varied experience. Since these were also the formative years of Soviet Russia, spanning the misery of the First World War, the chaos of the Civil War and the literary and political ferment of the twenties, Paustovsky's quest was well rewarded.

DROVE A TRAIN

He was a train driver in Moscow, a medical orderly at the front on board a hospital train, a factory worker in the Donbass, a fisherman in Tagaarog by the Sea of Azov, a newly-fledged journalist in Moscow in 1917, an eyewitness of the operations in the Ukraine against the many and varied insurrectionary bands, a reporter again in that cradle of rogues, writers and musicians—Odessa, and then back in Moscow as an editor with the forerunner to Tass. During his wanderings Paustovsky made and kept many friends; they included Bable, Bagritsky, Gilyarovsky and Kataev. His inexhaustible curiosity brought him into contact with the beggars of Moscow's "lower depths", with priests and bandits, with prince and lighthouse keeper. He chanced upon the last of the Shuisky's in Bunin's boyhood haunts at the time of the February Revolution; he heard Lenin addressing a gathering of near-mutinous soldiers in Moscow soon after the Brest-Litovsk peace.

Paustovsky turned from journalism to writing on his own account during the early thirties. He had already had a number of short stories published but his first publication of any size was *Kara Bugaz*, an account in fictional form of the reclamation of the deserts to the east of the Caspian Sea, which came out in 1932. There followed a steady stream of short stories, punctuated by the occasional longer work, based mainly on Paustovsky's continuing travels round the Soviet Union—to the Black Sea, to Leningrad and beyond, and, above all to the secluded villages and forests of central Russia which Paustovsky had loved so much ever since his first stay as a boy with his favourite uncle deep in the Bryursk Forest. He also continued to contribute articles to the press on more topical themes.

Paustovky's wartime output was relatively small. He was himself a war correspondent with the Southern Front. It was after the war, in 1946, that the first two parts of Paustovsky's memorable autobiography—*Story of a Life*—appeared in print, to be followed between 1955 and 1964 by further instalments taking the story up to the mid-thirties. In this work Paustovsky's sheer love of life and of Russia captivates the wariest of readers by its lyricism and by the immediacy of the portrayal of persons, places and events. Though some critics found Paustovsky's memoirs cloying and others questioned their accuracy, the memoirs rapidly won wide acclaim inside the Soviet Union, as also in this country when publication of an English language edition started in 1964. Volume II appeared in 1965, Volume III in 1967 and Volume IV is due to appear this autumn. Volume V is expected in 1969. They remain the outstanding miniaturist portrait of the Soviet period in which politics is only the canvas for the vicissitudes of everyday existence.

Like several of his colleagues Paustovsky had a phenomenal memory. He also had an unbounded appetite for life wherever he found himself—in Russia or abroad; at his dacha in the country town of Yarusa, a three-hour train journey to the south of Moscow, or at literary gatherings in the capital. Paustovsky was one of the most beloved and respected writers in the Soviet Union. If his *Story of a Life* failed to win a Lenin Prize when it was submitted for one in 1964, this was not for want of literary support or general popularity.

Paustovsky contributed to Soviet literature an acute, visual perception: of the lilac and chestnut blossom in Kiev in the spring; of the banks of the Oka and the streets of Paris. Time and space dwindle in importance as they might do on a Russian train journey. His compassion for his fellowmen and his wry perception of their shortcomings brought his characters vividly to life. He himself was impatient only of resignation and introspection. With his romantic temperament and his love of beauty, he remained young at heart.

Paustovsky was more than a brilliant memoirist and versatile short story writer. His fellow writers have lost a good friend and a stout champion. He had posthumously protected Aleksandr Grin against his detractors. He had spoken up in defiance of *Not By Bread Alone* when its author, Dudintsev, was first under attack. The anthology, *Pages From Tarusa*, piloted by him into print in 1961, was one outward indication that more than one young writer was indebted to him for help.

At the time of the trial of Daniel and Sinyavsky he was one of three senior Russian literary figures who offered depositions in favour of the two men. In June, 1967, he was one of the 79 writers who supported the reading of the letter by Alexander Solzhenitsyn which was presented at the Fourth Soviet Writers' Conference in which Solzhenitsyn put in a plea for the lifting of literary censorship in Russia. Finally, in February, 1968, he was one of 22 writers who appealed to Russian leaders for a review of the trial a month earlier of Yuri Galanskov and three other young intellectuals.

He was married twice and had a stepdaughter by his second marriage.

July 16, 1968.

Dr. J. L. Pawsey, F.R.S., Assistant Chief of the Division of Radiophysics at the Commonwealth Scientific and Industrial Research Organization since 1951, died on November 30, 1962. He was 54.

Pawsey was one of the pioneers of the postwar science of radio astronomy. During the war his work in Australia on radar introduced him to the use of highly sensitive radio receivers and as soon as the war ended he applied these to investigate those naturally occurring radio waves which impinge upon the earth from outer space. With the support of the Commonwealth Scientific and Industrial Research Organization he rapidly built up the radio-physics laboratory in Sydney and attracted to it a very able and enthusiastic team of workers. For several years this team shared with those of Ryle and Hey in England in making a series of fundamental discoveries which form the basis of the science of radio astronomy.

One of the team's early successes arose from their use of an aerial on the top of a cliff, which, together with its hypothetical image in the surface of the sea, formed an "interserometer" capable of measuring an angle of elevation of a source of radio waves. This apparatus was used first to observe radiation, from the sun, and later to show that two well-known visible nebuli were emittors of radio waves. Later the interserometric principle was developed in a different way to show that the sun sometimes emits bursts of radio waves from comparatively small regions in which the emitting disturbance is travelling outwards with velocities about one-tenth of the velocity of light.

In another application the interserometric principle was applied to make use of two long aerial rays, laid out on the ground in the form of a cross called after its originator a Mills Cross. With this apparatus it has been possible to locate and measure a large number of those naturally occurring sources known as "radio stars".

INSPIRING LEADER

The Radio Physics Laboratory has produced a number of world famous research workers of whom Bracewell, Christiansen, Kerr, Mills, and Wild are perhaps the best-known. It has also produced a number of important publications which can be numbered amongst the classical papers of radio astronomy. Although only a few of these bear the name of Pawsey it is common knowledge that he played a detailed part in developing the ideas of the team and in planning what should be done. There is little doubt that as leader he inspired the work of the team in a way which is rare and that he was never anxious for his own name to appear on the resulting publications.

Joseph Lade Pawsey was born on May 14, 1908, the son of J. A. Pawsey. He was educated at Wesley College, Melbourne, and Melbourne University, and in 1931 went to the Cavendish Laboratory, Cambridge, where he was awarded a Ph.D. degree for work on the propagation of radio waves through the ionosphere.

From Cambridge he joined the research laboratories of Electric and Musical Industries, where he worked on improving the performance of the original television transmitting aerial at Alexandra Palace. Soon after the start of the war he returned to Australia and started his work on radar.

In 1954 he was elected to the fellowship of the Royal Society. He had been chairman of Commission 40 of the International Union of Astronomy, where his ability and sincerity played a valuable part in solving some serious difficulties of procedure. He was also a leading member of Commission 5 of the International Union of Scientific Radio.

In 1935 he was married to Greta Lenore Nicoll of Saskatchewan. His widow, two sons, and a daughter survive him.

December 3, 1962.

Jack Payne, former band leader, broadcaster and West End impresario, died on December 4, 1969, at his home in Kent. He was 70.

Jack Payne—"Golden Boy" of the B.B.C. and the darling of the nation in the thirties—was a band leader at the Hotel Cecil in the Strand, London, in 1924. Four years later he went to join the B.B.C. as a broadcaster. When bands swamped the dance halls in the late 1930s he changed to running a theatrical agency. With the outbreak of war in 1939 he formed another band and began entertaining the troops.

FAMOUS NAME

In the early, heroic days of radio, Jack Payne's name was a household word, and with his band, the big-scale dance band of the period, he was one of the most familiar stars of the new medium, which he reached before the advent of Henry Hall and his B.B.C. Dance Band. To the dance music of the late 1920's and the 1930's Jack Payne and his players gave a convincing English accent. Their playing achieved cheerfulness with a certain emotional reserve. Other bands, following Transatlantic examples, sought to whip up enthusiasm by suggesting an almost hysterical abandon to the rhythm of the music they played, but Jack Payne made boisterous, cheerful or sentimentally easy-going music in a way which managed to be polite, noisly high-spirited and light-hearted.

In the last ten years Jack Payne continued to make occasional appearances on television. His *Words and Music* was seen as a series in 1959 and returned for two successive years, he was a frequent member of the early *Juke Box Jury* and in 1960 was seen in *It's a Square World* and *A Pair of Jacks*.

In March 1966, an issue of *Late Night Line-Up* allowed him to return in memory to his great early broadcasting days.

December 5, 1969.

Sir Edward Peacock, for many years an outstanding leader of the financial world, died on November 19, 1962, in a London hospital. He was 91.

Formerly a director of Baring Brothers and Receiver General of the Duchy of Cornwall, he was a close friend and trusted adviser of three successive Governors of the Bank of England, of which he was for more than 20 years a director. He occupied a position in many ways unique, and there was probably no one to whom even the highest in the financial world turned so readily or so often for advice and help.

As a Canadian born, with much general and business experience in Canada in his youth, who had risen to the highest eminence in the City of London and made his home in this country, he played an influential part in Anglo-Canadian relationships of many kinds. Among the important civic responsibilities which he had discharged were those of Treasurer to the King Edward Hospital Fund and of a trustee of the Rhodes Trust.

Sir Edward Robert Peacock, G.C.V.O., was born on August 7, 1871, the son of a presbyterian minister in Glengarry County on the eastern border of Ontario—in a district which was a Scottish highland settlement in which many still spoke the Gaelic tongue. "Little Ed. Peacock", as he was known to the countryside, was one of a large family and was brought up in hard surroundings, conditioned to hard winters and to austere living at home.

A HARD EDUCATION

His father died when he was still a boy, and it was only by the proverbial scraping that his mother managed to look after his education and send him in due course to the Presbyterian University, Queen's, at Kingston, not far away from his home. There, he knew what it meant to work hard and subsist on little. In part he "worked his way through college", doing many jobs from time to time, including those of farm-hand and secretary of a local fair. But meanwhile he was an industrious and talented student and took a leading place in his classes, particularly those in English, history, and economics.

In those early days he wrote two small books which gave a hint of his natural leanings. One was on Canada, the love of which he never lost even after he settled in London. The other was *Trusts, Combines, and Monopolies*, which showed that even then his financial bent was asserting itself.

Sir Edward himself recalled that his first job after graduation was that of a motorman on a street car. But it was not long after he left the university that he was appointed English master at Upper Canada College, in Toronto, a public school after the English model. He was a successful schoolmasfer, and in 1897, after he had been at the college two years, he was made senior especially qualified by his popularity with the boys and his ability to share in their play as well as their work.

He continued at the college for another five years and might well have achieved eminence as an educator. But various circumstances induced him to accept an appointment with Dominion Securities Corporation, a Toronto financial company, when it was offered to him in 1902. His natural financial talent was quickly apparent to E. R. Wood the founder and president of the company, and he was given quick promotion. In 1907 he was sent to London to take charge of the firm's newly-formed European office, and in this way his abilities became known to the financial communities on both sides of the Atlantic.

ORDER OUT OF CONFUSION

Dominion Securities Corporation had been interested in the group of electric power and traction companies in Spain, Mexico and Brazil, headed by Dr. Pearson, and when Dr. Pearson was drowned in the sinking of the Lusitania in 1915, Peacock was appointed, at the instance of banks and others who had interests involved, to important positions in this group in the well-justified expectation that he would bring order out of some of the confusion caused by Dr. Pearson's death. He became president of the Mexican Light and Power Company, vice-president of Brazilian Traction Light and Power, and chairman of the Barcelona Traction Light and Power Company. For nearly 10 years—until 1924—he devoted most of his time and attention to the administration of these companies, and his success therein drew attention to his outstanding abilities.

One of the first to be impressed by these abilities was, Montagu Norman and in 1921 Peacock was appointed a director of the Bank of England, the first Canadian ever to serve on the Bank's Court. This was certainly one of the decisive events in his career. From the first he was one of the most active members of the Court, and in his many years as a director he probably played a more influential part in central financial affairs than did any ordinary non-executive director of the Bank before or since.

In 1924 he acceded to the request of Lord Revelstoke, another who had been deeply impressed by his ability, that he should become a director of the eminent merchant banking firm of Baring Brothers. As Lord Revelstoke was himself a director of the Bank of England, and it was a rule that two directors of the same firm should not serve on the Court simultaneously, he had to resign his bank directorship when he took up his headquarters with Barings. In 1929, however, when Lord Revelstoke died, he was immediately invited to resume his place on the Court, and after this he remained a director continuously until 1946.

IN MANY SPHERES

In the meantime his high qualities were being recognized and his services requested in other spheres. Shortly after his move to Baring Brothers he became a member of the Council of the Duchy of Cornwall; later he became Receiver General of the Duchy. In recognition of his many services to the Duchy he was created a Knight Grand Cross of the Royal Victorian Order in 1934. In 1929 he became Treasurer of the King Edward Hospital Fund and chairman of its financial committee, thus handling the vast sums of money appropriated each year for the many hospitals in London. He also became Rhodes Trustee and a Lieutenant of the City of London. He received the honorary degree of D.C.L. of Oxford University in 1932 and that of LL.D. of Edinburgh University in 1938. He was already M.A. and LL.D. of Queen's University, Kingston.

In 1926 he was appointed European Director of the Canadian Pacific Railway Company, and this was one of various appointments which led him into many activities in a field which had a special appeal for him—that of Anglo-Canadian relations. Another appointment in this field was to the board of the Hudson's Bay Company in 1931, and he served on this board until 1952.

He handled many special negotiations and missions, financial and otherwise, between this country and Canada, and his services were often called on also in matters relating to the United States; as, for example, when he went to the United States in 1941 on behalf of the Treasury to handle the delicate question of this country's direct investments in the States and the extent to which they should be used in financing wartime dollar expenditure. One of his special activities during the 1939–45 War was with the Canadian National War Services Funds Advisory Board, in which it was his responsibility to supervise the financing of the welfare agencies for the Canadian forces overseas.

After his reelection to the Court of the Bank of England in 1929, his responsibilities and special duties as a director of the Bank became heavy once again. He shouldered particularly heavy responsibilities in the difficult months during the autumn of 1931, when the Governor, Montagu Norman, fell ill, and he was called on to take a large share in the duties that had to be redistributed during Norman's absence. But at all times his services were in constant request at Threadneedle Street, and he contributed much to many of the most important financial developments and policies of his time. Until very late in life age seemed to have little effect on him—except for a deafness which he seemed to be able to shake off when some vital occasion demanded—and he was already in his eighty-second year when he played an active part in the formation of the Bank-sponsored Commonwealth Development Finance Corporation.

INTELLECT AND INTEGRITY

The qualities which gave him such an influential and respected position in the financial world were simple and easily recognized. He combined an exceptional clarity of intellect with an absolute integrity of conscience and an unfailing readiness to give a decision and stand by it. He was never hasty. He formed his judgment after studying and understanding clearly the issues that were at stake. But, once formed, he gave it clearly and definitely. Ambiguity and obscurity had no place in Sir Edward Peacock's world. His tall and robust figure, clear eyes, and firm features were of a piece with his mind and his character, and his bell-clear and even voice matched the measured clarity of his ideas. His mind and manner had, in the best sense, a judicial quality. Probably he would have made a great judge. In practice, he was certainly a great arbitrator—

and was constantly being asked to act in this capacity on important occasions.

In 1912 he married Katherine Coates, and her death in 1948 after a long and happy married life was a hard blow to his later years. His family life with her and their two daughters amply filled his private life and leisure. Beyond his work and his family, his interests were the conventional relaxations of the man of affairs—golf, which was his main outdoor recreation and which he played enthusiastically; bridge, which he played less seriously; and books. He was a keen reader when time permitted, and by ordinary standards was certainly a well-read man despite his busy life. He was ever an interesting and entertaining companion in leisure hours, and he had something of a talent for the light after-dinner speech. Seriously and conscientiously though he took his many and heavy responsibilities, and hard though he worked in their discharge, he was never weighed down by them; and that, no doubt, was why he always remained much younger than his years.

November 20, 1962.

Sir Kenneth Peacock, formerly chairman and managing director of Guest Keen and Nettlefolds, died on September 6, 1968, at the age of 66.

He was born at Walsall, in February, 1902, the only son of Tom Swift Peacock who was deputy chairman of Guest, Keen & Nettlefolds Ltd. from 1933 until his death in 1946. After leaving Oundle he devoted the whole of his active life to the G.K.N. Group which he joined in May, 1920, working his way through all sections of various companies in the Midlands and becoming a director in July, 1933; he was made a managing director of G.K.N. Ltd. in January, 1936, and in August, 1950, was appointed deputy chairman and managing director, eventually succeeding Mr. J. H. Jolly as chairman in 1953, from which date he held the joint post of chairman and managing director until January, 1964, when he relinquished the managing directorship. He remained executive chairman of the group until his retirement in August, 1965, when he was elected president.

Throughout his career, he travelled extensively and was the chief negotiator in the purchase of many companies that are now well-established members of the G.K.N. Group.

Because of his close connexion with the G.K.N. steel works at Cardiff, Brymbo, and Scunthorpe, and allied companies in South Wales, he was a member of the executive committee of the British Iron and Steel Federation for 21 years, was a member of the B.I.S.F. Council and served on many of their other committees.

He was a director of Lloyds Bank Ltd. from 1949–66, of the Steel Company of Wales Ltd. from 1957–66, and of the United Steel Companies Limited from 1955–66. In 1963 he was awarded a knighthood for services to industry.

In his earlier days, Peacock was a keen amateur racing driver and between 1929 and 1934 competed in the R.A.C. Tourist Trophy Races in Ireland and the 24-hour races at Le Mans, often as a member of the Lea-Francis, Riley and Aston Martin teams. Among many others, he won the Rudge-Whitworth Cup and the Index of Performance at Le Mans in 1934. Horse riding was one of his favourite pursuits, and formerly he hunted with the North Cotswold Hounds, the Devon & Somerset Stag Hounds and the Exmoor Foxhounds.

He married in 1925 Hilaria, daughter of Sir Geoffrey Syme, by whom he had a daughter. His wife died in 1926 and he married secondly in 1934, Norah, daughter of Norman Rigby. They had two sons.

September 9, 1968.

Lieutenant Colonel Frederick Gerard Peake (Peake Pasha), founder of the Arab Legion, died on March 30, 1970.

Lieutenant-Colonel Peake was one of the most romantic figures in the history of the Middle East. His name is written large across the story of the political and social development of the state of Transjordan.

A friend and former colleague of Lawrence of Arabia, he went to Transjordan in 1921 when Britain accepted the mandate over the territory.

The new state was then one of the worst trouble spots in that turbulent area, but before he left in 1939 his wise administration and courageous leadership had brought law and order to the people.

Peake Pasha, as he was known throughout the Middle East, raised and commanded the Arab Legion and at the same time accepted responsibility for security and much of the administration.

His force was made up of Kurds, Arabs, Circassians and Turks, under the command of a handful of British officers. Yet he welded them into a force which quickly won respect.

Born in 1886, the son of Lieutenant-Colonel W. A. Peake, of Melton Mowbray, Peake Pasha began his military career in the Duke of Wellington's regiment and served in India until 1913. He was then seconded to the Egyptian Army and posted to the Camel Corps in the Sudan where he served in the Darfur expedition of 1916.

He fought with Lawrence in the Hedjaz and later went to Salonika with the R.A.F.

He was awarded the C.B.E. in 1926 and was created C.M.G. in recognition of his services in Transjordan.

April 1, 1970.

Drew Pearson, the Washington columnist, died in Washington on September 1, 1969. He was 71.

An upright man, Andrew Russell Pearson could have passed for a nineteenth-century English gentleman, but he was from a very old American mould, the son of a Methodist minister who became a Quaker. Pearson was an ardent defender of what is known in the United States as the Puritan ethic.

He was a self-appointed watchdog, especially of Congress. If he was occasionally led astray by his indignation he was a worthy successor to men such as Lincoln Steffens who established the honourable if ruthless tradition of muckraking journalism at the beginning of the century.

Born in Evanston, Illinois, on December 13, 1897, Pearson was educated at Phillips Exeter academy and Swarthmore, and graduated in 1919 as a member of Phi Beta Kappa. He was with the American Friends Service Committee in the Balkans, and taught briefly at the University of Pennsylvania. He then worked his way around the world as a seaman before turning to journalism.

While working for the *Baltimore Sun*, he met Robert Allen of the *Christian Science Monitor* and together they wrote a book on politics in the nation's capital entitled *Washington Merry-Go-Round*. This led the two of them to write a syndicated daily column with that title, which was eventually published by about 700 papers.

The partnership broke up when Allen joined the armed forces in 1942, and Pearson carried on alone until be invited one of his legmen, Jack Anderson, to share the column. Anderson, a Mormon and teetotaller, was well-equipped to support the older man.

They specialized in investigative journalism. Accused frequently of slapdash methods and little regard for the truth, they did in fact reveal much that was unsavoury in American political life. Pearson made many enemies, and one of his bitterest feuds was with the late Senator Joseph McCarthy.

He sued the Senator and others for 5.1m. dollars, charging that they plotted to discredit him. The alleged plot led to the loss of a sponsor for his radio news programme.

The role of plaintiff was a novel one. Pearson was more accustomed to being the defendant, and was involved in, and usually won, numerous libel suits. The most recent lawsuit was brought by Senator Thomas Dodd who, Pearson alleged, had used campaign funds personally.

The Senate was finally compelled to create an ethics committee, which recommended that Senator Dodd be censured. The motion was subsequently passed by the Senate, one of the rare occasions when the chamber took action against one of its own members. The Senator recently said, "Drew Pearson is a liar. He is a monster. Those associated with him are thieves, liars and monsters. His business is lying. He is a devil!"

Pearson revelled in this crude give-and-take, and prospered mightily. As his crusading reputation was established, discontented or outraged government officials and congressional assistants kept him informed of their masters' behaviour.

The columnist did not mellow as he grew older. He worked from a lovely house in Georgetown, and travelled the world to meet political leaders, but essentially he remained outraged by corruption and injustice. He was an ardent supporter of civil rights, and a contributor to worthy charities concerned with poor boys.

September 2, 1969.

Hesketh Pearson, the author, who produced a series of spirited and entertaining biographies, died on April 9, 1964, at the age of 77.

Born on February 20, 1887, in Hawford, Worcestershire, Hesketh Pearson was the son of T. H. G. Pearson and Constance Biggs. Biography, he once declared, had been his chief interest in life at the age of 14, but he had a varied career as actor and journalist among other things before he turned to the writing of biographies. After leaving Bedford Grammar School he spent two years in a City shipping office; then, having inherited a little money by the death of an aunt, went off to Mexico. On his return to this country he gravitated towards the stage and played minor parts under the management of Tree, Granville Barker and George Alexander. He enlisted as a private in 1914, served three years in Mesopotamia and Persia, and was mentioned in dispatches before concluding his war service in the rank of captain. After demobilization he returned to the stage, but also travelled and engaged in journalism and authorship.

He put his encounters with various stage celebrities and others to lively use in *Modern Men and Mummers* (1921), and two years later produced in *A Persian Critic* a collection of brief literary discussions in ingenious form, a few of which originally appeared in *The Times*. Two more volumes followed and then, in 1930, Pearson published the first of his full-length biographical portraits, a study of Erasmus Darwin, the grandfather of Charles. It was a vivid, animated and very readable piece of work, shrewdly put together rather than stylish, and its success confirmed Pearson in his decision to abandon the stage. A quick worker and fluent writer, he produced, in succeeding years, volumes on *The Smith of Smiths* (the Rev. Sydney Smith—a good subject for him), *The Fool of Love* (Hazlitt), Gilbert and Sullivan, Labouchere, *The Swan of Lichfield*, Tom Paine, *The Hero of Delhi* (John Nicholson)—a somewhat intemperate essay in adulation—Bernard Shaw (done with nice candour and an admirable sense of proportion), Conan Doyle (again a good subject for the author's pen), and Oscar Wilde. Pearson also wrote a volume of reminiscences, *Thinking It Over* (1938). and in the forties collaborated with Hugh Kingsmill in several lively and amusing volumes of English travel and gossip.

WIDELY POPULAR

In the last 15 years of his life Pearson remained what one reviewer called "an industrious husbandman in the vineyard of genius". His later biographies, of Johnson and Boswell; W.S. Gilbert, Walter Scott, Dickens ("Anyone but Dickens will be a comedown after Shakespeare and G.B.S." said G.B.S.), Beerbohm Tree and Charles II did not perhaps throw much fresh light on the characters and careers of their subjects but they were always competently done and widely read. The library ticketholder with a liking for biography, if attractively presented, took home Pearson's *Dizzy* where he would not even lift down Monypenny and Buckle's monumental Life of Queen Victoria's Prime Minister.

He was a gay talker and in earlier years of somewhat volatile temperament, and on one occasion was involved in no little embarrassment and difficulty. In 1926 a volume was published entitled *The Whispering Gallery*, which purported to be written by a "well-known diplomat of 30 years' standing". Various conversations in the book attributed to notable political figures were indignantly repudiated by them (Lloyd George called the whole thing "imaginative balderdash"), the book was withdrawn from circulation, and Pearson—who was the author—was tried in the following year on a charge of obtaining by false pretences a cheque from the publishers and was found not guilty.

He married, in 1912, Gladys Rosalind Bardili, by whom he had a son. She died in 1951 and he married secondly Dorothy Joyce Ryder.

April 10, 1964.

Lady Peck, Winifred Peck the novelist, wife of Sir James Peck, formerly Permanent Secretary, Scottish Education Department, died on November 20, 1962, in Edinburgh.

She was born in 1882, the daughter of the Rt. Rev. E. A. Knox, sometime Bishop of Manchester, and thus a sister of E. V. Knox and Monseigneur Ronald Knox. She was educated at Wycombe Abbey, where she was one of the first 40 pupils, and Lady Margaret Hall. She came from a gifted and cultivated family, shared her brothers' sharp wit and lively minds, and was well able to hold her own in complicated verse games they played among themselves. It was the family custom to spend the summer holiday in a furnished house, generally a rectory, where they amused themselves tracing the life of the absent incumbent as revealed in the photographs that were hung about his walls. In such stimulating and imaginative company she had every inducement to become a writer, where much of the material the novelist needs lay to her hand.

In a long series of novels which included *Let Me Go Back*, *A Garden Enclosed*, *Winding Ways*, *House Bound*, *There is a Fortress*, *Tranquillity*, *The Skies are Falling*, she showed a marked talent for sharp characterization, amusing dialogue and an ability to condense a life history into the minimum number of words; in this respect she had more than a little in common with Angela Thirkell. Of her own childhood and upbringing she wrote two entertaining books, *Home for the Holidays* and *A Little Learning*.

November 22, 1962.

Air Chief Marshal Sir Richard E.C. Peirse, K.C.B., D.S.O., A.F.C., died on August 5, 1970, at the age of 77.

Peirse served in the R.F.C., R.N.A.S., and R.A.F. from 1913 to 1945, and thus was concerned in the development of British air power from its small beginnings to the great force attained in the Second World War. Referring to the overseas work of the R.N.A.S. in 1914, the official history describes how "Flight Lieutenant Peirse, in an old, inefficient machine which climbed badly, made many flights over the coast (Belgium), and was wounded by shrapnel in air over Antwerp," Twenty-five years later he was Deputy Chief of the Air Staff in another world war, in which he also held three of the principal air commands.

Richard Edmund Charles Peirse, the only son of Admiral Sir Richard Peirse, Commander-in-Chief, East Indies, in the First World War, was born on September 30, 1892. He was educated at Monkton Combe, in H.M.S. Conway, and at King's College London. After learning to fly on a Bristol biplane at Brooklands, he took his pilot's certificate in 1913, and was commissioned as sub-lieutenant, R.N.R. for service in the R.F.C. Naval Wing.

During the First World War Peirse saw much service on the Belgian coast, and made repeated attacks on the submarine bases at Ostend and Zeebrugge. He gained the D.S.O. in 1915, was promoted to flight commander a month later, and to squadron commander in 1916. After a period at Cranwell, he was appointed to Dover as acting wing commander, and from 1918 served in Italy and the Adriatic. In 1919 he was awarded the A.F.C. and a permanent commission as squadron leader.

In 1922–23, as a wing commander, he attended the first course at the R.A.F. Staff College. Andover, and after commanding the base at Gosport was on staff duties at the Air Ministry in 1926–27. Next he attended the first course held at the Imperial Defence College, and then had three years in the Middle East and Palestine on staff duties and in command at Heliopolis. Peirse was appointed Deputy Director of Operations and Intelligence in 1931. From 1933 to 1936 he was A.O.C. in Palestine and Transjordan. In 1936 he was made an air vice-marshal and C.B. In 1937 he became Director of Operations and Intelligence and Deputy Chief of the Air Staff.

In 1939, Peirse was made an additional Member of the Air Council and promoted acting air marshal. From April, 1940, his post was redesignated Vice-Chief of the Air Staff. From October, 1940, to January, 1942, he was A.O.C.-in-C., Bomber Command, and planned the great expansion of this force which resulted from the decision of the Cabinet in 1941 "to hit Germany 50 times harder and increase Bomber Command's bomb-lift 10 times". He was relieved by Air Marshal Sir Arthur Harris in order to become Allied Air Commander in the Abda Area when it was set up under Lord Wavell. The rapidity of the Japanese advance and the fall of Singapore led to the dissolution of this area before it had got into proper working order, and Peirse then became A.O.C.-in-C., India. In 1943, he became A.O.C.-in-C. in the South-East Asia Command under Lord Mountbatten as Supreme Commander, where he served for about a year. He retired in 1945, as air marshal, and was permitted to retain the acting rank of air chief marshal which he had held since 1942.

He numbered among his foreign decorations that of Commander of the American Legion of Merit, the second class of the Polish Order of Polonia Restituta, the Grand Cross of the

Netherlands Order of Orange Nassau, and the Special Necklet of the Chinese Order of the Cloud and Banner.

Peirse was married in 1915 to Mary Joyce, daughter of Armitage Ledgard, and they had one son and one daughter. The marriage was dissolved in 1945, and in the following year he married secondly Jessie, daughter of Alexander Stewart.

August 6, 1970.

Dame Lillian Penson, who died on April 17, 1963, was an outstanding personality in the field of higher education, in Britain and overseas, and her career was one of unusual distinction.

She was born in 1896 and entered the University of London as student in 1913, first at Birkbeck College and later at University College. She remained attached to the University of London for the rest of her working life apart from the period between 1917 and 1919 when she joined the Department of Labour Supply in the Ministry of National Service and was later transferred to the War Trade Intelligence Department, where she took part in editing the series of Peace Handbooks for use at the Paris Conference.

HONOURS DEGREE

She had obtained the degree of B.A. in History with honours in 1917 and in 1919 she turned to research in the history of the West Indies, which earned the degree of Ph.D. for her in 1921. She was appointed a part-time Lecturer at Birkbeck College in that year and held a similar post at East London College (now Queen Mary College) from 1923–25. She was promoted to a full-time lectureship at Birkbeck College in 1925 and, five years later, was appointed to the Chair of Modern History at Bedford College at the remarkably early age of 34.

Lillian Penson's earliest interest was in colonial history, but the main body of her research was in diplomatic history, for which she acquired a remarkable knowledge of foreign as well as British archives in the century before the First World War. She did a great deal to establish this subject in the University of London in both undergraduate and post-graduate work. Her first book, on Colonial Agents in the West Indies (1924), an early paper on the Board of Trade, and her contributions to the *Cambridge Histories of the British Empire and India* still command respect. She cooperated with Dr. G. P. Gooch and the late Harold Temperley in the massive series of British documents on the origins of the First World War (1898–1914); and with Temperley in *A Century of British Blue Books* (1938), a most valuable technical aid to the research student; and in *Foundations of British Foreign Policy* (1938), an admirably conceived source book on the period 1792–1902, in which the commentaries on particular documents are masterpieces of explanation—brief, pointed, incisive, and clear. Her revision and continuation of Grant and Temperley's *Europe in the Nineteenth and Twentieth Centuries* (1952) added considerably to the value of a justly esteemed general text book.

She was invited by the University of London to give the Creighton lecture for 1961, an honour which she greatly valued. This lecture "Foreign affairs under the third Marquis of Salisbury", which she was unfortunately unable to deliver, was fully prepared, and published by the Athlone Press. It well exemplified how she was at once skilled in detailed investigation and a master of the broad exposition of fundamental principles.

In addition to her historical work, Lillian Penson had been acquiring more than her fair share of administrative duties, particularly at university level where she became Dean of the Faculty of Arts in 1938, a member of the Senate in 1940, chairman of the Academic Council in 1945, and a member of the Court of the University in 1946. The culmination of this aspect of her career came in 1948 when she was unanimously elected Vice-Chancellor in succession to Professor Sir David Hughes Parry. She discharged the onerous duties of this post for three difficult years in a manner which won universal admiration. It was not the fact that she was the first woman to become Vice-Chancellor of a University in the Commonwealth which attracted attention but rather her vigorous, purposeful, and clear-headed approach to the many problems with which the University of London was then faced.

It was her constant endeavour to bring together in a coordinated manner the vast resources of the University of London, particularly on the postgraduate side in the field of the humanities, and her lifelong connexion with the Institute of Historical Research fortified her in this belief. She took a leading part in the creation of the Institute of Commonwealth Studies and the development of the Courtauld Institute, the Warburg Institute, and the School of Slavonic and East European Studies owed much to her interest and support, as did the School of Oriental and African Studies.

HONORARY DEGREES

As Vice-Chancellor, she automatically became a member of the Committee of Vice-Chancellors and Principals and she conquered that citadel of male exclusiveness with ease, being recognized and welcomed from the outset as an equal. She was a founder member of the United States Educational Commission in the United Kingdom and held office on that body from 1949 to 1956. But her greatest contribution was made to the development of higher education in the underdeveloped parts of the Commonwealth.

Here her early historical researches had provided her with a unique foundation on which to build. She was a member of the Asquith Commission on Higher Education in the Colonies and, immediately after the publication of that committee's report in 1945, she embarked in the company of Sir Alexander Carr-Saunders on the task of persuading the University of London to modify its external degree system to meet the needs of the university institutions which were developing in the overseas parts of the Commonwealth.

Once her intrinsic merits and outstanding ability were generally recognized, honours began to be showered on her. The University of Cambridge, when it finally decided in 1948 to confer degrees on women, chose as the first recipients after the Queen, now Queen Elizabeth the Queen Mother, Dame Myra Hess and Dame Lillian Penson. She also received honorary degrees from the Universities of Oxford, St. Andrews, Leeds, Sheffield, Southampton, Belfast, McGill, and Western Ontario. She was created a D.B.E. in 1951.

Her greatest reward, however, was the multitude of friends she made. She had a happy knack of getting to know people quickly which was almost transatlantic in its efficacy. She was an excellent judge of wine and loved good company. Behind a manner which could on occasion be brusque and even intimidating was hidden a wealth of genuine kindness, as many know who approached her in time of trouble.

April 20, 1963.

Harry S. Pepper, who died on June 26, 1970, in his 75th year, was one of the great innovators in entertainment broadcasting.

A list of the radio programmes which he created includes *The Kentucky Minstrels*; *Monday Night at Seven* (later *Monday Night at Eight*); *Hi Gang; Band Waggon* and *Garrison Theatre.* His great contribution to radio was his introduction of styles, techniques and content which broke away entirely from the purely "theatre" methods of the early thirties and laid the foundations for much that is standard practice in radio (and television) today. For instance *Monday Night at Eight* contained the first broadcast quiz (*Puzzle Corner*) and the first detective thriller series (*Inspector Hornleigh Investigates*); *Band Waggon*, in its creation of the imaginary flat at the top of Broadcasting House inhabited by Arthur Askey and Richard Murdoch, their charwoman Mrs. Bagwash and her daughter Nausea, led to what is known as "situation comedy" today.

Harry Pepper was born into the world of entertainment. His father was the owner and producer of a well-known seaside concert party of the time known as *The White Coons* (a title that would create severe problems in the seventies). Harry Pepper, at the age of 15, was playing the piano for the productions, looking after the box-office and generally learning the rudiments of the profession to which he later contributed so much.

In the early part of his career he concentrated mainly on the writing of music and lyrics mainly for theatre productions. Probably his best known song (for which he wrote both words and music) was believed by many people to be a traditional "spiritual". It was "Carry Me Back to Green Pastures" recorded so successfully by Paul Robeson and by his own *Kentucky Minstrels.*

He had an especial gift for writing the English lyrics for continental songs. In this field he wrote all the English lyrics for Lehar's *Frederica* as well as for such songs as "Hear My Song Violetta" and "Drink Brothers Drink."

In the 1920s he joined the famous *Co-opti-*

mists concert party which had such a startling success in the London theatre and in the early thirties he began working for the B.B.C.—mainly composing songs and playing piano duets with Doris Arnold, whom he later married. He was invited to join the B.B.C. as a producer in 1936 and he eventually became production supervisor in the (then) Variety Department, retiring in 1951.

His quiet dignity, integrity, deep professional knowledge, and creative strength were an inspiration to all the younger producers who worked with him. He never fully recovered from the shock of the sudden death of his wife, Doris Arnold, in October, 1969, and he died peacefully after a long illness.

June 27, 1970.

Lieutenant General A. E. Percival, C.B., D.S.O., O.B.E., M.C., who died on January 31, 1966, at the age of 78, commanded the land forces in what was perhaps the most disastrous campaign in the history of British arms.

Few soldiers have been given a more hopeless assignment than the one given to him when he was sent out to take command in Malaya in the spring of 1941. The seeds of failure had been sown years before when successive British Governments adopted defence policies which did not make proper provision for war against Japan. When Japan entered the war, Britain's position in the Far East was lamentably weak, and any faint hope that Singapore might survive as a base of operations there faded with the French collapse, and disappeared entirely when the American Fleet was destroyed at Pearl Harbour. The shock of the fall of Singapore was all the greater because the public had been led to believe that the place was impregnable.

Arthur Ernest Percival was born on December 26, 1887, the son of Alfred Percival. He was educated at Rugby and, on leaving school became a clerk in a City office. When the First World War broke out, he enlisted as a private, but within a month he was given a temporary commission in The Essex Regiment. Between July 1915 and the Armistice, despite a wound which incapacitated him for some months, he saw two and a half years' active service in France and Belgium. He won the D.S.O., the M.C. and the French Croix de Guerre and was twice mentioned in despatches.

When the Second World War broke out, he accompanied Dill to France as Brigadier, General Staff of the 1st Corps. But he missed the retreat to Dunkirk through being posted to England in February, 1940, to command the 43rd Wessex Division. His next appointment was as Assistant C.I.G.S. at the War Office, but, after a few months in this post, he asked to be transferred to a field formation and was given another home command as G.O.C. 44th Home Counties Division. Here he remained until his appointment in May, 1941 as G.O.C. Malaya with the acting rank of lieutenant-general.

When he arrived in Malaya, the entry of Japan into the war was still six months away. The problem which confronted him of preparing for the outbreak of hostilities was a formidable one, but he tackled it with energy and resolution.

The security of the Singapore base rested upon the ability of the British Navy to control the sea approaches. The garrison only had to be sufficient to hold off the enemy until the Fleet arrived. But by 1940 the situation had completely altered. The Japanese were now established in southern China and Hainan, and Indo-China was also available to them as a base of attack owing to the fall of France. The penetration of the Japanese into south-east Asia, as well as the increase in the range of aircraft had made it necessary for Britain to establish airfields on the mainland of Malaya, hundreds of miles north of Singapore, and these had to be protected. Moreover, the fleet was so fully committed in the west that an adequate naval force could not be spared for the Far East.

When the Japanese attacked everything hinged on air superiorty. But Britain had in Malaya only 158 aircraft against the 582 considered necessary by the commanders on the spot, and many of these were obsolete and fit only for the scrap heap. The land forces were also far below strength. Moreover, most of the troops were raw and untrained in jungle tactics, and were unfit for employment in a theatre of war; they had no tanks and were inadequately supported by artillery.

CRIPPLED DEFENCES

It was obviously a tactical mistake to attempt to defend the whole Malayan peninsula with such scanty forces. But, if our airfields were to be protected, Percival had no choice but to accept wide dispersion in the hope of early reinforcement.

Fighting began on December 7, 1941. the day of the attack on Pearl Harbour. On that day the Japanese crossed from French Indo-China into the Kra Isthumus, and made a series of landings along the northern coast of the Peninsula. On December 10 there was the disaster of the sinking of the Prince of Wales and the Repulse. Thus the defence was crippled from the outset of the operations. Profiting from their decisive command of the sea and the air, as well as from their superiority in equipment, in jungle lore and in toughness, the Japanese pressed their attacks vigorously. By the end of January, they had destroyed or captured a great part of Percival's force and compelled the remainder to withdraw across the narrow Johore Straits into Singapore Island.

The 18th Division, which had been on the way to the Middle East, was diverted to Singapore, and landed with some other reinforcements at the last moment. The other allied fronts were already so weak that it had been impossible to denude them further. It was obvious that Singapore was doomed before the Japanese delivered their final assault on February 8. A week later they were in possession of the reservoirs in the centre of the island and cut off the water supply to the city. There were only a few days' reserves of food, ammunition, and petrol, and counter-attack was beyond the capacity of the defenders. Percival cabled on February 15 that he was unable to continue the fight, and, in the evening of that day, with Wavell's concurrence, he surrendered unconditionally, just 70 days after the first shots had been fired. Some 85,000 British, Australian, and Indian troops, of whom more than half were non-combatants, were taken prisoner, and Singapore passed into the possession of the enemy.

In 1947 Percival published a book, *The War in Malaya*, in which he gave a fair and sober account of this calamitous campaign. During his captivity he showed both courage and devotion in safeguarding the interests of his troops, and more than once suffered starvation and solitary confinement when he refused to comply with unreasonable orders. But, after some months, he was moved with other senior officers first to Formosa and then to Manchuria, where he remained till the end of the war. On his release in August 1945, he was flown by General MacArthur's instructions to Yokohama in order to be present at the ceremony of the formal surrender of Japan, and subsequently at a similar ceremony in the Philippines. Here he met again his old opponent, General Yamashita, who had taken his surrender in Singapore. "As Yamashita entered the room, I saw one eyebrow lifted and a look of surprise crossed his face—but only for a moment. His face quickly resumed that sphinx-like mask common to all Japanese, and he showed no further interest."

Percival returned to England in September, 1945. His experience had indeed been a bitter one. He felt keenly the injustice of the stigma which the failure at Singapore had inevitably fixed upon the soldiers in the minds of a public who had not realized that the insurance premium for the defence of Malaya had never been paid before the war. But his friends rallied to him, and he was given strength to bear unmerited blame when the King sent for him soon after his return and told him of his sympathy and understanding.

Percival retired from the Army in 1946 with the honorary rank of lieutenant-general. He was made C.B. in 1941. He was Colonel of The Cheshire Regiment from 1950 to 1955.

He married in 1927 Margaret, daughter of Thomas MacGregor Greer. She died in 1953. They had one son and one daughter.

February 2, 1966.

Colonel Lord William Percy, C.B.E., D.S.O., who died on February 8, 1963, at his home at Norwich at the age of 80, was a man of brilliant ability and outstanding personality. He was widely known as an ornithologist, but his countless friends the world over will remember him as one of the most remarkable and fascinating men who ever came into their lives.

He was born on May 17, 1882, the son of the seventh Duke of Northumberland, and was educated at Eton and Oxford. He was called to the Bar by the Inner Temple in 1905. The prospects were bright, and he seemed destined for a legal career. But he left the Bar in disgust after a difference of opinion with a judge whom Percy believed to be in the wrong, not so much for his judgment in a murder case as for the reasons on which it was based. He never returned again to the law except during the 1914–18 War, when, after being severely wounded with the Grenadier Guards at the Battle of Neuve Chapelle, he served as deputy advocate general and assistant adjutant general to the Egyptian Expeditionary Force under Lord Allenby.

He had a passion for travel. In the course of his life he made many expeditions to the Middle East, to Siberia, to North and South America, and to Africa, mainly with the object of observing, and, in his youth, of collecting birds. At one time he possessed perhaps the best collection in the world of duck skins, but he disappointingly disposed of it to the various museums without writing the expected monograph, which he could have done supremely well.

The only records of his vast and exact ornithological knowledge are contained in a few articles in scientific journals and other periodicals and in a rather slight book on Norfolk waterfowl, *Three Studies in Bird Character* published in 1951. He also contributed some beautifully written essays to Dr. Bannerman's *Birds of the British Isles*. One of these was an account of Steller's Eider Duck, "the most fascinating of all ducks in the Old World or the New", based upon observations made during an expedition to North East Siberia which he had undertaken to find another duck, the Spectacled Eider, then believed to be extinct. But it was Africa that he loved most, and he travelled widely all over the continent from his early youth. He returned to it again and again, and in old age one of his great interests was the discussion of its many human and political problems.

He had an intense interest in a wide diversity of subjects—everything was grist to his penetrating, analytical mind. His devotion to the principles in which he believed was unswerving and complete. He loved talk, and in conversation he was a formidable debater.

With such gifts as his he might have achieved much in almost any field he chose. That he did not make his mark in any career was certainly not due to a failure in personality, or to any lack of determination, courage, or ability. It seems likely that his complete lack of worldly ambition stemmed rather from theological principles and from the influence exercised upon him in his youth by the tenets of the Catholic Apostolic Church, of which his parents were adherents. A direct descendant through his father of Henry Drummond, one of its original "apostles" who collaborated with Edward Irving in producing its liturgy, he was raised in a religious tradition which looked for an imminent Second Advent and which stressed the transitory nature of this world. His knowledge of theological matters was considerable, his interest in them was lifelong and profound, and there was an immense spirituality in his outlook.

For his services in the 1914–18 War he was made C.B.E., won the D.S.O., and was twice mentioned in dispatches. He retired from the Army with the rank of colonel in 1919. For some years he was a member of the Council of the National Parks in the Belgian Congo.

He married in 1922 Mary, daughter of Captain George Swinton. They had two sons.

February 11, 1963.

Don Ramón Pérez de Ayala, one of Spain's foremost novelists, journalists and poets, who died on August 5, 1962, in Madrid, was 81. He was formerly the Republican Ambassador in London. A penetrating thinker, humanist, and classical scholar, he had always been known for his liberal outlook and often expressed his defence of the written and spoken word.

He was born on August 9, 1880, at Oviedo, the capital of Asturias, and had his early education at a local Jesuit school, later studying law at Oviedo University. Since then his career had been marked by varying fortunes.

He reached full stature as a writer when the anguished soul-searching characteristic of the generation of 1898 had somewhat spent itself, and in the serener atmosphere of a Spain now intellectually alert was more of an artist in the novel than either Unamuno or Baroja. Richly endowed with the Asturian gift of humour and holding art to be independent of moral preoccupations, he was in the true tradition of Spanish literature as a detached observer of the human scene unconcerned to praise or blame. The title of *Troteras y Danzaderas* (1913) stems directly from the fourteenth-century satirist, Juan Ruiz. *Belarmino y Apolonio* (1921) is a delightful study of two intellectual cobblers, one an instinctive philosopher in search of understanding, the other a dramatic poet in search of expression. *Tiger Juan* and its sequel *El Curandero de su Honra* (1926), a modern variant on the old Spanish theme of the point of honour, constitute perhaps his masterpiece. The earlier *Prometeo* (1916) is a collection of three short stories that figure among the finest in modern Spanish letters.

These novels reveal a progressive concern with the play of ideas, which gradually predominates over the earlier realism until his characters become symbols charged with Freudian subtlety. They show the author as one of the acutest Spanish minds of his generation. He was also a poet of some distinction again in an intellectual vein, and a critical essayst of note, particularly on dramatic themes. He will have his niche, too, in Spanish letters as a stylist.

In the political sphere Don Ramón Pérez de Ayala was soon playing a prominent role. He supported the establishment of the Republic in April, 1931, though later he expressed his nonconformity with some of that ill-starred regime's actions. He was the last of the three eminent intellectuals who signed the famous document entitled *Delenda est Carthago* early in 1931, with its harsh attack on the monarchy of the late King Alphonso XIII which contributed to the latter's downfall.

On the establishment of the Republic in April, 1931, Don Ramón Pérez de Ayala was appointed Spanish Ambassador to the Court of St. James. His addresses to the Foreign Press Association in London aroused much interest. It was during his first year as Spanish Ambassador that an uproar broke out in a Madrid theatre on the opening night of a dramatic version of one of his early works called *A.M.D.G.* This dealt with life in a Jesuit college and some indignant Roman Catholics staged a noisy demonstration. Following the triumph of General Franco's movement and the collapse of the Republic, Don Ramón Pérez de Ayala spent some years in South America, especially at Buenos Aires, writing for various newspapers.

In 1949 he returned to Spain and since then had lived a quiet life in Madrid. He did not produce any more the freely written works of the type which made him famous. However, he had managed to keep his pen active by confining his writing to erudite articles on the classics and other topics of a non-political nature which regularly appeared in the *A.B.C.* and could not offend the Ministry of Information censors. In 1960 he was awarded a literary prize worth about £3,000 by the Juan March Foundation.

From time to time Don Ramón Pérez de Ayala joined with other intellectuals, academicians, playwrights, scientists, and Spaniards of different ideological convictions in signing appeals to the authorities on behalf of freedom of expression. He was one of 240 intellectuals who signed a petition to the Ministers of Information and Education in November, 1960, appealing for an easing in the censorship.

August 7, 1962.

Frances Perkins (Mrs. Paul Wilson), former United States Secretary of Labour, who died on May 14, 1965, at the age of 83, was the first American woman to hold Cabinet rank.

An enthusiastic and indefatigable social reformer of wide sympathies and advanced views she had established a great reputation in New York as an expert upon social problems when President Roosevelt decided to include her in his first Cabinet she was one of the chief architects of the New Deal and was successful in securing a number of far-reaching reforms.

She had, too, many outstanding personal qualities. In all her work she was guided by plain common sense, a natural shrewdness and a true sense of justice and humanity.

Frances Perkins was born at Boston, Massachusetts, on April 10, 1882, the daughter of Frederick W. Perkins by his marriage with Miss Susan Wight and came of a long line of Puritan ancestry. She was educated at Mount Holyoake College and at the universities of Pennsylvania and Columbia. In 1910 she became executive secretary of the Consumers League of New York and a little later lectured in sociology at Adelphi College.

In 1911 Miss Perkins saw from a window in Washington Square, New York, the disastrous fire in the Triangle Shirt-waist factory in which 146 girls lost their lives. The experience deeply moved her and intensified the desire she had already felt to secure improvement in the Labour legislation of her country. Shortly afterwards she was appointed executive secretary of the New York Committee of Safety, a position which she held for five years, and in the same year director of investigations of the New York State Factory Commission. Thus she became a leading spirit in a campaign for the reforms she sought.

In 1913 she married Paul Caldwell Wilson—who died in 1952 at the age of 77—by whom she had one daughter. He was at the time employed at the City Hall and in order not to embarrass him she agreed to retain her maiden name, and continued for the rest of her life to be known by it.

Miss Perkins's numerous activities in New York naturally brought her into contact with Franklin D. Roosevelt who from 1929 to 1933 was Governor of the state, and after his election to the Presidency, he made her Secretary of Labour in his first Cabinet. She thus became the first American woman to hold Cabinet rank, a distinction which was held by great numbers of Americans to be a due recognition of her long and active career as a social reformer.

PERSONAL CONTACT

As head of a great department Miss Perkins displayed efficiency as well as energy and courage. Her knowledge of social questions had been gained in direct personal contact with men and women of all classes and before long she had put through a remarkable number of reforms. Child labour was soon abolished throughout the United States, and in 1935 she crowned her earlier successes with the Social Security Act which gave the American worker the benefits of unemployment insurance and health services.

At Washington she had her critics. Some accused her of lack of economic knowledge, others of inability to handle the press. Now and then demands for her resignation came from powerful organizations.

She had positive though not generally recognized achievements to her credit in the planning and launching of many New Deal projects and was a pioneer in public works planning. In 1938 on her way back from the International Labour Conference at Geneva she visited Great Britain where she made a brief study of conditions and returned full of ideas. In 1941 on the proposal of Mr. Ralph Assheton. M.P., she was elected chairman of the International Labour Organization's Conference in New York.

Shortly after her resignation from the Secretaryship of Labour in June, 1945, Miss Perkins was appointed by President Truman to be a member of the Civil Service Commission, the body which draws up rules governing examinations for those positions in government service which Congress places in the classified Civil Service. She served on that commission until 1952, when she retired from government service.

Between her work as Secretary of Labour and on the Civil Service Commission she wrote a warm-hearted and admiring book *The Roosevelt I Knew*, which was published in 1946. She was also the author of several books on fire hazards, maternity care, women as employers, and other problems in which she was interested.

May 17, 1965.

Frank Perkins, who built a huge business on diesel engines for cars and lorries, died at his home, Alwalton Hall, near Peterborough, on October 15, 1967. He was 78.

He founded the firm of which he was honorary president—the Perkins Engines Group—in a Peterborough back street with four men in 1932. In 1934 he drove a car powered by one of his new engines to Moscow on a sales promotion trip and the following year claimed the world's speed record for a diesel engine with a 100 m.p.h. run on the old Brooklands track. The Perkins Engines Group, a subsidiary of Massey-Ferguson, now employs 7,000 workers in Peterborough.

Francis Arthur Perkins was born on February 20, 1889, and was educated at Rugby and Cambridge University, where he took an engineering degree. He then joined the firm of Barford and Perkins, Ltd., road roller manufacturers, at Peterborough. On the outbreak of war in 1914 he was commissioned in the Royal Engineers and served in the Dardanelles and Palestine campaigns. In 1928 he was appointed managing director of Aveling and Porter Ltd., and in June, 1932, he started business for himself by founding the company of F. Perkins Ltd., at Peterborough, to manufacture high-speed diesel engines from his own patents. These engines were widely used by the Admiralty and the R.A.F. for air-sea rescue launches during the Second World War. Foreseeing a world-wide demand for diesel engines after the war, he constructed a new factory at Peterborough and his company became one of the largest manufacturers of lightweight diesel engines.

In 1959, eight years after the company was made public, it was taken over by Massey-Ferguson, which offered £4,500,000 for the share capital. Perkins retained the office of chairman until 1962 when he was elected honorary president.

He devoted much time to the affairs of the Society of Motor Manufacturers and Traders, first as a member of the Accessory and Component Manufacturers' Section in 1936 and afterwards as chairman of the Engine and Unit Component Manufacturers' Section in 1945. He became a member of the Council and Management Committee in 1944, was appointed a vice-president for 1955–56, and elected president for the year 1956–57. He was also interested in the National Youth Movement and as president of the Peterborough Council of Boys' Clubs he launched a £20,000 appeal to provide funds for new clubs in the area. He was High Sheriff for Cambridgeshire and Huntingdonshire for the years 1956 and 1957. He became a freeman of Peterborough in 1962.

October 16, 1967.

Lord Pethick-Lawrence, Secretary of State for India and Burma from 1945 to 1947, died on September 10, 1961, in a London hospital at the age of 89.

One of the most distinguished veterans of Labour Party, an expert in financial matters, a sincere friend of India, shrewd and genial in political counsel generally, and an historic figure in the campaign for women's suffrage early in the century, he gave devoted service to his country and to the causes in which he believed. He sat in the House of Commons for a period of 18 years in all, a barony being conferred upon him on his appointment to the India Office.

The Right Hon. Frederick William Lawrence (he prefixed his wife's name on marriage to his own), the first Baron Pethick-Lawrence, of Peaslake, in the County of Surrey, in the Peerage of the United Kingdom, was born in London on December 28, 1871. He was the youngest of the four children of Alfred Lawrence, whose father, a Cornish carpenter, had founded a prosperous firm of building contractors in the capital. "Freddie" was sent to Eton, where he was apparently happy enough, though somewhat detached in spirit, and was captain of the Oppidans in 1891. He went up to Trinity College, Cambridge, and achieved brilliant distinction there: he took a double first and was fourth Wrangler, second Smith's Prizeman, President of the Union, Adam Smith's Prizeman for Economics, and made his mark at lawn tennis and billiards at the same time. In 1897 he was elected to a fellowship at Trinity. But academic life did not greatly attract him, and immediately afterwards he set out on the grand tour, travelling at once to the Far East.

On returning to England he studied law and it was while he was thus engaged that he turned to social work in the East End of London. He became treasurer and a moving spirit of Mansfield House, the Nonconformist settlement in Canning Town, where his economic studies were broadened by personal investigation into local wage conditions and his Labour sympathies ripened. It was there that he met an evangelist Sister of the West London Methodist Mission, Miss Emmeline Pethick, whom he married in 1901. This was a partnership of a singularly harmonious character.

Although he had come out in unqualified opposition to the war in South Africa, Pethick-Lawrence's political interests were for some years largely confined to domestic affairs. At the time of his marriage he had acquired a controlling interest in the *Echo*, the earliest of the halfpenny evening newspapers, and from 1902 until 1905 he was its editor. When publication ceased he paid the staff and the creditors out of his own pocket. During the next two years he was editor of the *Labour Record and Review*. Then came the era of militancy in the women's suffrage movement, and with it a social crisis prolonged until the outbreak of war in 1914. As joint editors of *Votes for Women*, Pethick-Lawrence and his wife threw themselves heart and soul into the campaign of the Women's Social and Political Union. He assumed what was virtually complete financial responsibility for its activities—in all he stood bail, he calculated afterwards, for more than 1,000 woman militants—and did not waver in principle even under the dictatorial rule of Mrs. Pankhurst. In 1909 his wife was arrested and imprisoned and in 1912, after a famous demonstration marked by extensive window-breaking in the West End of London, he was arrested, together with his wife and Mrs. Pankhurst, on a charge of conspiracy and sentenced to nine months' imprisonment. All three went on hunger strike; Pethick-Lawrence and his wife were forcibly fed and were released after five weeks, after which they went to Canada to recuperate. By way of political protest he refused to pay the costs of the trial and was adjudged bankrupt upon the petition of the Director of Public Prosecutions—an order annulled in the following year.

Like many other Labour supporters, Pethick-Lawrence in 1914 was under the sway of pacifist ideas and was critical of Britain's participation in the European conflict. He was a prominent figure in the propagandist activities of the Union of Democratic Control, and in April, 1917, he contested South Aberdeen as a "peace by negotiation" candidate. He stood unsuccessfully for South Islington in 1922, but entered the House of Commons in the following year as the Labour member for one of the Leicester constituencies, his opponent on that occasion being Mr. Winston Churchill, who was making his last stand as a Liberal. Pethick-Lawrence held that seat until 1931. He was not, perhaps, outstandingly impressive on the Labour benches and was lacking in effect even as a financial expert; as a parliamentary speaker he was handicapped by a defective delivery—his dry and jerky manner was in odd contrast with his wife's natural eloquence. He was irreverently dubbed in the press gallery "Pathetic" Lawrence. Nevertheless his appointment as Financial Secretary to the Treasury in 1929 was soundly practical in the circumstances, since his abilities were undeniable. The financial crisis of 1931, in his view, could have been overcome without excessive difficulty or disturbance; he held that there was no need for this country to give way to the pressure of foreign governments or foreign banks, and that what we should have done in the first place was to mobilize in support of sterling the full resources of foreign capital held by British subjects. He wrote extensively on this and other topics during his long life.

Pethick-Lawrence, like so many of his ministerial colleagues, lost his seat in the 1931 election, but he came back to the House in 1935 as member for East Edinburgh. In opposition he gained increasing respect for the breadth of knowledge and sympathy he displayed in the debates on India. He had been a member of the Indian Round Table Conference in 1931, having appealed for precisely such an effort of statesmanship on both sides after a visit to India a few years earlier. He was sworn of the Privy Council in 1937, acquired something of the character of a Labour elder statesman but did not hold office again until Mr. Attlee selected him, after the Labour victory of 1945, for the post of Secretary of State for India and Burma. Political India, though it would have preferred to see the abolition of the India Office, warmly welcomed the appointment; both Congress and the Muslim League, though for different reasons, looked to him expectantly for action which would end the Indian deadlock.

The Indian deadlock remained intractable and in March, 1946, the Secretary of State headed the historic Cabinet mission, with Sir Stafford Cripps and A. V. Alexander as his colleagues. A chapter of his fervid contribution to *Mahatma Gandhi* (1949) in collaboration with H. S. L. Polak and H. N. Brailsford is devoted to the story of the mission without disclosing much inner information. The mission reached New Delhi on March 24, and with the Viceroy (Lord Wavell) at once began its prolonged discussions with the party leaders and the Chancellor of the Chamber of Princes. The nominal head of the mission was well aware that Sir Stafford Cripps supplied the driving force and was most sought after by the political leaders. A contributory cause of this preference was a measure of irresolution in the Secretary of State and his disinclination to reach clear-cut decisions. Moreover the Prime Minister and Sir Stafford Cripps in Downing Street had taken matters of high policy in respect to India very much into their own hands, sometimes with scant regard to the views of the India Office.

DAILY SWIM

In physical and mental energy the veteran nearing 75, in spite of a tremulous hand and head, seemed the equal of his colleagues, and never missed his early morning swim. Apart from a weekend in Kashmir and a few days of conference at Simla the mission spent rather more than three months in the sweltering heat of Delhi, and the ordeal took considerable toil of the indefatigable senior member. He was deeply disappointed by the failure of the mission to secure acceptance of its compromise plan of regionalism for the purpose of meeting Muslim League claims, leaving the centre to have powers only over defence, foreign relations and communications. The visit to London together at the end of 1946 of Nehru and Jinnah for discussions in Downing Street was also barren of tangible result. Attlee's announcement in the middle of February, 1947, of a fixed date for British withdrawal and of the replacement of Lord Wavell by Lord Mountbatten was followed early in April by the resignation of Pethick-Lawrence. As he had foreseen the pace quickened, and withdrawal was antedated by 10 months to August, 1947. He gave his utmost support to the Indian Independence Act in its rapid passage through Parliament, and thereafter, while strongly inclined to the site of the Indian Union, did all in his power to ingeminate good will between the two new Dominions. His interest in the lands formerly constituting the Indian Empire remained unabated and he was for some time chairman of the East and West Friendship Council.

Lord Pethick-Lawrence was a not uncommon type in English political life, a man of high and humane principle who employed his fortunate personal circumstances in the discharge of a scrupulous sense of public responsibility. His autobiography, *Fate Has Been Kind*, published in 1943, when he was 72, leaves an impression of unaffected warmth and simplicity of spirit and of fundamental and undeviating moral purpose. He was much travelled, but was never so happy as in his house in Surrey, where the friendliness and courtesy of nature which he revealed to his friends gave light and warmth to the personality exhibited in parliamentary debates.

His first wife died in 1954. In 1957 he married secondly Helen Millar, daughter of Sir John Craggs and the widow of Duncan McCombie.

September 12, 1961.

Egon Petri, who died on May 27, 1962, at Berkeley, California, at the age of 81, was a pianist in the grand tradition that derived from Liszt. He himself was a pupil of Busoni and the foremost interpreter of that great pianist's compositions, such as the huge concerto and the Fantasia Contrappuntistica. John Ogdon, who had a period of study with Petri at Basle, is the present representative of their leonine style in which masculine power and extreme finesse are combined in a prodigious technical control.

Petri was an international figure who lived an international life, though not that of an ever wandering virtuoso. He was a German of Dutch descent, born at Hanover on March 23, 1881; he studied with Busoni in Dresden, Weimar and Berlin, where he also studied philosophy; he made his debut in Holland and played in practically every European country, including Poland, where he made his home for a time between the wars; he lived from 1905 to 1911 in Manchester where he taught the piano at the Royal Manchester College of Music and made many friends. Subsequent teaching appointments were at the Berlin Hochschule; in addition he held master classes and summer schools of the kind formerly conducted by Busoni. In 1923 he gave recitals in Russia, the first foreign artist to appear before the Soviet people and win their acclamations. From 1939 onwards he worked in America at Cornell and at Oakland, California.

His father, Henri Petri, was a violinist who held an appointment at Dresden, where Egon had his general education and began his musical studies as a violinist. He also studied composition, organ and horn and was for a time second violin in his father's string quartet. It was not till he was 20 years of age that he decided that the piano was his true vocation, a decision supported by Busoni and justified by his immediate success. He became co-director of Busoni's edition of Bach's keyboard works and organ transcriptions. Busoni's way with Bach is not in favour with the scholarly purism of today, but of a recital which Petri gave in London in 1939 *The Times* admitted that though it might not be Bach it was certainly magnificent. His grand romantic style also caught the diabolism as well as the poetry of Liszt. He did not compose much, but he wrote a *Konzertstuck* and transcribed for piano a number of Busoni's larger works. Manchester University remembered its former colleague by conferring on him an honorary doctorate in 1938.

May 29, 1962.

William Edward Willoughby Petter, C.B.E., who died in France at the age of 59 in May, 1968, was an aircraft designer of high distinction. In his earlier days, he produced the Lysander which became famous in its association with resistance movements on the continent during the war; the Whirlwind two-engined fighter which was the first in its class to mount four cannon; and the Welkin high-level fighter developed at great speed for feared high offensives which never took place.

In his post-war years, having moved from Westland Aircraft to English Electric, he designed and built the Canberra jet bomber which was so successful that several hundred went into service with the R.A.F. and the type was also produced in the United States for the U.S.A.F. Then, once again, he changed the scene of his labours, moving in 1950 to Folland Aircraft. There he produced the Gnat supersonic fighter, capable of carrying normal fighter armament and equipment but only about one-third the loaded weight (and therefore one-third the price) of the standard types of fighter.

In the late 1950s he found current trends within the aircraft industry were not to his liking. He spoke his mind, as was his wont, and left Follands, retiring to the Continent and severing all connexions with the design and manufacture of aircraft.

Born on August 8, 1908, he had been designated to succeed his father, Sir Ernest Petter, of the famous oil engine firm, and, after Marlborough, had gone to Cambridge to take the Mechanical Sciences Tripos. The old Petter company had been drawn by the Admiralty into aircraft construction during the First War and had decided to add aircraft to its work when the war ended. In due course, Westland Aircraft had been hived off from the parent company. When Petter had been two years at Cambridge, giving an oil-engine bias to his studies, he was advised to give special attention to aerodynamics and aircraft engineering. That he did in his final year and left Cambridge with a good first.

There followed two and a half years of hard preparation for the young master in the Westland machine and assembly shops; then a spell as assistant to Robert Bruce, the managing director, who was as good an engineer as he was business man; and at last, in 1935, appointed technical director of Westland Aircraft Ltd., he was launched on his career as designer and production engineer. His first type was a fighter about which the Air Staff later changed its mind. Then came the Lysander, looking like a splay-footed butterfly. It was as promising as it was unorthodox and the R.A.F. had long years of valuable service from the 1,300 that were built.

His next design was the Whirlwind two-engined fighter, mounting four cannon, which, according to his view, missed service in the Battle of Britain because it had not been pressed forward vigorously enough by his masters.

HIGH-LEVEL FIGHTER

He went on to the design of a high-level fighter, the Welkin, at the request of the Air Staff and made a good job of it but it was never needed in quantity because the anticipated attacks at great heights failed to arrive.

Towards the end of the war he decided to move. He took his troubles and his ideas to Sir Wilfrid Freeman, who knew the industry from top to bottom, and on his wise advice offered his services to English Electric Ltd. He had two designs in the early stage. By agreement, he left one with Westland's and took the other as his stock-in-trade to his new employers. That was the design of the Canberra two-jet bomber. He had personally to "sell" that design to the R.A.F., for on paper it appeared to violate the principles of a high-level bomber. In the end it was a complete success.

In his new sphere, still a young man, Petter appeared to have found conditions to suit him, but in 1950 he left English Electric.

Within a year, he made a new arrangement with Folland Aircraft, was gathering together a new design team and filling it with his own enthusiasm for the light-weight fighter which, with his shrewd capacity for foreseeing trends, he was sure the smaller nations would need. His design of the Gnat was sound aerodynamically and full of clever weight-saving ideas based on intensive experience of the cumulative effect in aircraft structures of careful attention to detail. Judged from the engineering standpoint alone, the Gnat was as ingenious a piece of work as any Petter had turned out.

Production Gnat Mark I fighters were supplied to the Ministry of Aviation, to India, Finland and Yugoslavia. The Hawker Siddeley Gnat Trainer, a tandem two-seater trans-sonic aircraft, a development of the fighter, subsequently became standard equipment in R.A.F. Flying Training Command.

Among people in the industry who did not know him intimately Petter gained a reputation of being likable but difficult. Among those who worked with him, he was regarded only with affection and admiration. He led his teams brilliantly. He brought to full development some design workers who would never have been given a chance without his help. He was made C.B.E. in 1951.

May 27, 1965.

Dr. Robert Pferdemenges, the Cologne banker and politician, who died in a Cologne hospital on September 29, 1962, at the age of 82 after a prolonged illness, was one of the most influential personalities of the political scene of postwar Germany.

He owed his position as much to his own gifts as to an intimate friendship with Dr. Adenauer, which lasted unbroken through good days and bad over some 40 years. He was acknowledged to be one of the very restricted circle of persons whom the Chancellor trusted and consulted regularly, not only on economic questions but on general political and even personal problems as well, all the more readily perhaps because Pferdemenges worked entirely behind the scenes, and never asked for anything in return—not even, as he said himself once, for a decoration.

His influence was acknowledged by all parties to have generally been inspired by a desire for conciliation, and a pursuit of enlightened common sense. His sound judgment and independence of mind were generally praised. He by no means always agreed with Dr. Adenauer; and would tell him so openly, if he thought the occasion demanded it. He strongly urged the Chancellor, for instance, to retire to the presidency of the Federal Republic in 1959, and again in 1962 he counselled him to resist the temptation of yielding to sectional interests, in defending the German economy against the dangers of inflation.

Although he had much in common with the Chancellor—both men had a liking for the typically Rhenish brand of humour—Pferdemenges showed more sympathy for his fellow human beings; and was never tempted to overestimate his own importance. He was born on March 27, 1880, in Munchen Gladbach, the son of a textile manufacturer, and opted for a banking career. He was sent in 1904 to London for 10 years by one of the leading banking establishments in Germany at the time. In 1919 he became a member of the board of directors of a Cologne banking house, which was partly owned by the well-known Cologne banker Solomon Oppenheim, with whom he was to be associated for the rest of his life. It was then that he became acquainted with Dr. Adenauer, at the time burgomaster of Cologne.

ANTI-HITLER PLOT

With the coming to power of the National Socialists he retired from many of his directorships; but he remained a member of the advisory board of the Reichsbank, where he was closely connected with Dr. Schacht, and upon whose recommendation he had become adviser to Dr. Brüning, the Reichs Chancellor at the time. He refused, however, to enter the party. After the July, 1944, plot against Hitler, he was arrested, but later released and forbidden any activity. He played an important part in the foundation of the Christian Democratic party after the war, as a political party grouping all confessions. In 1946 he became president of the newly reformed Chamber of Commerce and Industry of Cologne but was dismissed a short while after by the British occupation authorities. During the Nazi era he had helped Dr. Adenauer to go into hiding, and assisted him in many other ways. It was he who after the end of the war advised the future Chancellor to transfer his activities to national politics. Only on the strong urging of his friend was he persuaded to stand for the Bundestag and elected in 1949.

He played a key part in the 1948 currency reform, and it was characteristic of his painstaking and thorough method that he only approved the project after a year of study. In 1950 he took over the chairmanship of a coordination committee to prepare the introduction of the Schumann Plan, and ranked as one of its fathers in west Germany.

By some irony of fate, one of his aunts had married a younger brother of Friedrich Engels.

October 1, 1962.

Edward Joseph Phelan, Director-General of the International Labour Office from 1941 to 1948, died at his home near Geneva on September 15, 1967. He was 79.

Born at Tramore, co. Waterford, Ireland, in 1888, the son of a master mariner, he was educated at St. Francis Xavier's College and Liverpool University, where he took his B.A.

and B.Sc. with honours in physics. He joined the British Civil Service in 1911. He began his career in the National Health Insurance Commission, but after a few years was transferred to the Labour Department of the Board of Trade and hence automatically became a member of the staff of the Ministry of Labour when it was formed in 1917.

Here the discerning eye of Harold Butler, Assistant Secretary, noted his capacity, and he was sent to Russia with the first British delegation to visit that country after the Revolution. On his return, Butler took him to the Peace Conference in 1919, and later to the first International Labour Conference, as a result of which the International Labour Office was set up at Geneva.

After this it was almost inevitable that, when Butler became Deputy Director of the I.L.O. under its first Director, Albert Thomas, Phelan should go with him, and in 1920 he became Chief of the Political Division.

Subsequently he had a distinguished career in the I.L.O., becoming Assistant Director in 1933, Deputy Director in 1938; and finally, when J. G. Winant relinquished his post as Director to become United States Ambassador to Great Britain in 1941, Phelan took his place and guided the organization safely through the remaining years of the war, so that it emerged ready to carry on its work as before when peace came—the only remnant of the League of Nations that survived.

Phelan came of Liverpool Irish stock, and to first-rate abilities as an organizer and administrator he added a capacity to influence, to persuade to manipulate all the intangibles in any situation, which found wide scope in the international field, and especially at international conferences. He published a biographical study of Albert Thomas in 1936. He was awarded several honorary degrees and was an honorary citizen of Mexico City.

September 16, 1967.

André Philip, a prominent personality among the generation of French political figures who came to maturity during the German occupation or in the first flush of liberation, a leader of the French Christian Socialist movement, and as Minister of Finance or Minister of National Economy in three post-liberation Cabinets the leading exponent of a policy of *dirigisme*, died at the age of 68 in July, 1970.

A staunch "European" he was France's representative on various international conferences in the post-war years. From 1950 to 1964, he was chairman of the Socialist Movement for the United States of Europe and since 1967 had been the president of the O.E.C.D. Development Centre designed to promote increased cooperation between the industrialized nations and the developing countries.

There was something of the zealot in André Philip. A professor of economics in his earlier years, an acute and widely travelled student of problems of industrial management and labour organization, he held fast to a Socialist doctrine of the superior virtues of a wholly managed economy with unshakable conviction. His was a logic that too frequently sought to counter the realities of France's economic situation by ignoring them; knowledgeable and conscientious though he was, he seemed too little capable of learning from experience in his Ministerial application of *dirigiste* principles in 1946 and 1947. This marked lack of flexibility went with, and possibly arose from, a highly emotional nature.

The politico-economic logician was also a man of peculiarly fervent Christian sentiment, a Protestant lay preacher (an unusual figure in French political life), and a rather complicated human personality generally.

Born on June 28, 1902, at Pont Saint-Esprit (Gard department) André Philip came of an old Huguenot family which had settled in Scotland at the beginning of the seventeenth century and returned to France in the next century. He left the Lycée de Marseilles at the age of 18 for Paris, where he studied law and also attended courses at the Ecole des Sciences Politiques. He paid his earliest visit to this country for the purpose of studying English institutions and English economic literature, and on his return to France published his first book *Guild Socialism and Trade Unionism.*

LABOUR PROBLEMS

Then, having graduated as a doctor of law of Paris University he proceeded to Columbia University with a Rockefeller fellowship and eventually brought out a volume, *The Labour Problem in the United States*, which was very well received in France and in translation was for some years almost a standard work in the United States itself.

On his return to France in 1926, Philip was appointed professor of political economy at the faculty of law of Lyons University and proved not only a highly popular teacher but an inspiring force in the Student Christian movement.

Two notable books by him which appeared in the thirties are *The Crisis of Managed Economy* (1935) and *Syndicalism and Trade Unionism* (1936).

He had joined the Socialist Party as early as 1920. In 1936 he was elected deputy for a working-class district, La Guillotière, of Lyons.

He was in the United States at the beginning of 1940 and returned to serve in the campaign of May and June as liaison officer with the British forces in Flanders. He opposed capitulation, withdrew from public affairs under the Vichy regime and resumed his lectures at Lyons University. In the summer of 1942, he reached England and joined de Gaulle. As Commissioner for the interior in the French National Committee in London during 1942–43 he had the task of coordinating the work of the underground resistance bodies in France. He kept that post for a time in the Committee of National Liberation set up in Algiers, but did not again come to the fore until he was appointed Minister of Finance and National Economy in the Gouin Cabinet (1946). He was reappointed to that office in the short-lived Blum Government towards the end of the year, and in spite of the chastening practical test to which his theory of controls had been submitted was made Minister of National Economy (the Finance Ministery was given to Schuman) under Ramadier in January of the following year. He served in that capacity until October, by which time the policy of *dirigisme* had apparently received its quietus. He was expelled from the Socialist Party in 1958. He had been a sharp critic of the party's Algerian policy.

July 7, 1970.

Godfrey Phillips, C.B.E., a former managing director of Lazard Brothers and a former director of The Times Publishing Company, died in London on October 24, 1965, aged 65. He was a man of exceptional quality, quality immediately apparent to anyone who knew him or did business with him. Throughout a remarkable career he never lost his simplicity of character or disinterested purpose. No man could have contributed wisdom more modestly.

George Godfrey Phillips was born on June 7, 1900. His parents were Dr. George Charles Phillips, of Grantley, Wotton-under-Edge, Gloucestershire, and Ethel Nancy Phillips. He was educated at Harrow and Trinity College, Cambridge, where he took first class honours in the Law Tripos. He was also President of the Union. Many of his contemporaries at Trinity regarded him as the leading all-round man of his year. Called to the Bar, he showed brilliant promise. But the almost obsessive desire for financial security which pursued him all his life deflected him from what would certainly have been a very successful legal career. He left the Bar to be Town Clerk of Stafford; but he soon found this much too limited a field for his talents and, yielding to the desire for adventure which was always in conflict with his fear of financial insecurity, he went off with his family to Shanghai, 34 years old, to play his part in history. Lionel Curtis, who selected him, said after the meeting, "What an extraordinarily good face he has." Above it was an extraordinarily good mind.

In 1932 he had married Betty Mary, daughter of Trevor Bright. They had two sons and a daughter. His wife was a constant support to him throughout his varied career. He rejoiced in a most happy family life.

Phillips was appointed Secretary of the Shanghai Municipal Council in 1936 and Commissioner General in 1940. Before the end of 1941 Great Britain was at war with Japan and Phillips had to face almost intolerably difficult problems as Commissioner General of the International Settlement in Shanghai. In 1942 he returned to England and that year he took charge successfully on behalf of the British Government of negotiations for the exchange of British and Japanese nationals who had been interned after Pearl Harbour. In 1943, the British Government, oppressed by weightier matters, bestowed a C.B.E. upon him—most inadequately, in the light of his achievements.

In Shanghai during those years 1934–42 Godfrey Phillips came into his own and the rest of his life, although successful and active, was something of an anti-climax. The Shanghai International Settlement, a remarkably successful experiment in international government, entered its final crisis in the 1930s. The administration was based upon a partnership—British, American, and Japanese—with the British considerably the largest shareholder both by tradition and by the actual weight of their financial and trading stake. The partnership had stood the test of Chinese Nationalist pressure and had managed to keep intact a remarkably efficient and honest administration during successive periods of civil war and crisis in China. But in the early 1930s the Japanese embarked upon their programme to control and dominate China and their interest in Shanghai became directly opposed to the interest of the other two partners in the administration of the International Settlement. As tension between China and Japan grew and developed into actual hostilities the Japanese came increasingly to resent the neutrality of the International Settlement and felt that they must have a major if not a sole voice in the government of Shanghai.

During this era of tension Godfrey Phillips was a key figure. He won and held the respect of all those concerned—British, American, and Japanese—to a quite remarkable degree. In crisis after crisis he quietly guided and controlled the complex machine of international government—through the Japanese attack on Shanghai in 1937 and through the outbreak of the Second World War, which found Great Britain as a belligerent, America as a neutral and a large German community living in Shanghai side by side with the British and claiming the protection of the international administration.

ESCAPED ASSASSINATION

Phillips once escaped assassination almost miraculously when two Chinese gunmen stopped his car and poured bullets into it at point-blank range. He was a brave man. He had no vanity, no sentimentality, no looseness of thought. But he was also a warm man and his charm was disarming. His ascendancy in Shanghai was due to a combination of moral and intellectual qualities—courage, absolute honesty, great industry, exceptional quickness of mind and a clear, good brain. He proved himself a first-class international administrator. In different circumstances his training and character would have fitted him almost ideally as a United Nations administrator.

After 1943 Phillips led a full and diversified life. He went to the War Cabinet Office, then returned to the Bar and at 46 decided to become a solicitor. He became a partner in Linklater and Paines and took part in many important transactions such as advising the Anglo-Iranian Oil Company in Teheran and Cable and Wireless when that great company was nationalized. He became a managing director of Lazards, a director of *The Times*, chairman of the Equity and Law Life Assurance Society, and joined the boards of several great industrial companies. He became a governor of Harrow School, where he had been Head Boy.

Whatever he did he did well. He worked at speed, and on paper he had a great gift of brevity. He was original and humorous and superbly honest. He was a most charming companion, his indestructible naturalness won him a host of friends. Those friends had watched his increasing physical distress with concern. He himself showed no self-pity. He was indomitable to the end.

October 25, 1965.

Professor Montague Fawcett Phillips, F.R.A.M., F.R.C.O., British composer and Professor of Harmony and Composition in the Royal Academy of Music, died at Esher on January 4, 1969. He was 83.

Phillips achieved fame in the light opera *The Rebel Maid*, which was produced at the Empire Theatre in 1921 and achieved wide popularity, since the subject was taken from English history of the year 1688, the treatment romantic and the orchestration imaginative. Strangely enough Phillips made no other attempt on the theatre but wrote mostly concert music, including two piano concertos. He was in his early days a fairly prolific composer of songs, which had a vogue in the last days of the royalty ballad.

His talent, which had been trained at the Royal Academy of Music, was for music in lighter vein, so that his symphonic poem Boadicea, his unpublished orchestral works and the two concertos have never established either themselves or the composer's claim to be regarded as a serious musician, though his skill was unquestioned. In one or two overtures and a Shakespearian Scherzo, an Empire March, played at a Prom in 1942 and a Sinfonietta broadcast in 1946, matter and manner were more favourably adjusted. Born in 1885 he was essentially a composer in the salon tradition of the late nineteenth century to which his musical idiom belonged.

January 6, 1969.

Morgan Phillips, former general secretary of the Labour Party, died on January 15, 1963, in a London hospital. He was 60.

His career was halted at a time when his standing in the party was at its highest and seemed to be still growing even though the party itself was at its lowest ebb since the war. Although he returned to his desk at Transport House he never recovered full effectiveness after a stroke which he suffered in Glasgow in August, 1960. His official retirement was announced in December, 1961.

It was an odd circumstance that the defeat in 1959 of the party, of which he was chief officer, should have been followed by a rise in his own reputation. Exactly the opposite happened after the defeat in 1955, when the tendency was to blame faults in organization for which he was held responsible. Perhaps partly because of that, much of the conduct of the 1959 campaign was entrusted to other hands, but Phillips's daily press conference was by common accord one of the outstanding successes of the election.

No one on the Labour side, save perhaps Hugh Gaitskell himself, so enhanced his reputation. Morgan Phillips was the man who presented to the national executive clear analyses of what had happened and constructive proposals for the future. Early in 1960 his status was raised from that of secretary to general secretary, with an administrative officer to take much of the detailed work off his hands.

While the political leaders were absorbed in acrimonious disputes, he was strengthening the organization and making plans for the future, many of which were brought together in his paper, *Labour in the Sixties*.

He was an able organizer, quick and unambiguous in his decisions. He seldom wasted words. He was a model conductor of press conferences. With an understanding of journalists as of most classes of people with whom he came in contact, he was aware that there is nothing they like less than listening to platitudes. He answered questions or refused to answer them, with admirable conciseness, and he took transparent pleasure in scoring a point against a hostile questioner, as he frequently did.

The whole of Phillips's career had been in the service of the Labour Party. A miner's son, he was born one of six children in Aberdare, South Wales, in June, 1902. He left school to work at the pit surface when he was only 12.

RAPID PROMOTION

As a youth he began to take an active share in the local activities of the Labour Party and the South Wales Miners' Federation. When but 18 he was a member of the Caerphilly divisional Labour Party and three years later he was secretary of the party in Bargoed. At the age of 24 came the opportunity to improve his education in economic and social subjects by a two-year residential course at the Labour College in London. The removal from South Wales, and the course of study on which he embarked, diverted him completely from trade unionism to politics. His personal abilities were developed, the scope to exercise them enlarged and, at the close of his college training, besides continuing in Labour Party organization as secretary and agent of the party in West Fulham and later in Whitechapel, he gained experience in local government by three years of membership of the Fulham borough council and chairman of its finance committee.

Another stage in his career was reached in 1937 when he went to the party headquarters as propaganda officer. His steps upward in the organization were rapid. In the following year he became secretary of the party's research department and was closely concerned with the policy and reconstruction work which was at that time being done. In 1944 he reached the highest post of all when he succeeded J. S. Middleton as secretary. He had a majority of two votes over the late Maurice Webb.

The first two secretaries of the party had been dominant personalities. As framers of policy and controllers of the party machine both Ramsay MacDonald and Arthur Henderson had had a large part in directing the party's development and its destinies. They were followed by a man of another type in J. S. Middleton who, knowing the office routine from a lifelong experience of it, was yet an official rather than an officer. At the time of his retirement there was no party leader who desired to take over the administrative work and the executive was not, in fact, looking for such a man. It had been decided that the secretary must renounce parliamentary ambitions and devote himself entirely to the secretarial office. Looking for a man of proved adminstrative capacity they turned to Morgan Phillips. He brought to the office the ability desired. The headquarters machine was quietly overhauled, several internal changes were made, administrative routine was perceptibly quickened and a higher efficiency attained.

Morgan Phillips fitted adaptably into the party constitution. He was prepared to leave the shaping of policy to the programme makers, chief of whom was Herbert Morrison, with Hugh Dalton specializing on international affairs; he was content to combine with the business of party management in the country the duty of disseminating the policy already determined.

He played a very important part in the re-creation of the Socialist international. He presided over a succession of conferences called by the International Socialist Committee from 1944 onwards and was chairman of the Socialist International from its formation in 1951 to 1957, when he resigned in spite of general protest.

At first his personal fortunes began to wane with the party, however, and the period from 1955 must have been a frustrating one for him.

ALTERNATIVE VOICE

Some in the party began to discuss the possibility of appointing a full-time chairman to become the voice of the party, leaving to the secretary merely administrative responsibilities. His relations with Gaitskell never seem to have been close. He was no longer asked to speak for the executive at the annual conference. His thoughts began to turn towards a new career in Parliament. He had been a prospective candidate 20 years earlier, but had never stood in an election.

In 1959 he made several tentative efforts to secure nomination for a safe seat, interrupted by his illness, which ended with his failure to secure nomination for North-East Derbyshire constituency. That was perhaps his low water mark.

He married in 1930 Norah, only daughter of William Lusher. They had one son and one daughter.

January 16, 1963.

Sir Thomas Phillips, G.B.E., K.C.B., formerly Permanent Secretary of the Ministry of Labour and National Service, died on September 21, 1966, at the age of 83.

He was one of the men who developed the Ministry of Labour from small beginnings into a great department. He spent 25 years in the Ministry, and in all but four of those years he was either the Deputy Secretary or the Permanent Secretary. The Ministry was created in 1917 during the 1914–18 War, taking over from the employment department of the Board of Trade responsibility for the employment exchanges, unemployment insurance, the work of the trade boards, and industrial conciliation and arbitration.

The Ministry owes a great deal of its present-day prestige to his work, and especially to his unobtrusive but extremely efficient leadership in tackling the new tasks that came with the 1939-45 War.

NEW TASKS

While nearly all government departments had additional duties thrust upon them by the war, the Ministry of Labour and National Service carried a specially heavy burden. It had the responsibility of mobilizing the nation's man and woman power for the forces and the production of munitions, a gigantic task that brought the Ministry closely into touch with every industry, trade, profession, and form of occupation in the country. Unemployment functions shrank, but training and placing work increased enormously, and welfare activities inside and outside factories and workshops expanded. The Permanent head of the department through all the important and sometimes exciting developments of policy and organization during the war was Sir Thomas Phillips.

Thomas Williams Phillips was born on April 20, 1883, in Cemmaes, Montgomeryshire, and was educated at Machynlleth county school and Jesus College, Oxford. He had a brilliant record at Oxford; first class honours in classics and mathematics, moderations and literae humaniores, and winner of the Gaisford prize for Greek prose. He entered the Civil Service in 1906 and went to the Board of Trade where for a number of years he had a special responsibility for copyright questions. He was joint secretary of the British delegation to the international copyright conference in Berlin, 1908; secretary of the copyright committee, 1909; and joint secretary of the Imperial Copyright Conference, 1910. He was called to the Bar by Gray's Inn in 1913.

FIVE YEARS' RISE

In a period of five years he rose from the rank of principal to the deputy secretaryship of a Ministry. In 1919, on being transferred to the Ministry of Labour, he was promoted assistant secretary, and was immediately afterwards promoted principal assistant secretary. Five years later he became Deputy Secretary of the Ministry, a post which he continued to hold until the end of 1934, when he succeeded Sir Francis Floud as Permanent Secretary. He left the Ministry of Labour and National Service at the end of 1944 to become Permanent Secretary of the new Ministry then being formed to launch the new scheme of national insurance. This was, of course, a subject with which he was familiar, the Ministry of Labour having had charge of unemployment insurance for many years. He was at the Ministry of National Insurance for four years.

From 1949 to 1959 he was chairman of the Central Land Board and the War Damage Commission. He had also served as chairman of the Building Industry Working Party, of the Committee on Economic and Financial Problems of Provision of Old Age, and the War Works Commission.

A shrewd judge in dealing with complexities, and an able draftsman, he was a valued counsellor to a long line of Ministers.

He married in 1913 Alice Hair, daughter of F. M. Potter. They had two sons and a daughter.

September 24, 1966.

Edith Piaf, the well-known French singer and entertainer, died on October 11, 1963, aged 47.

She was born in Paris on December 19, 1915. Her real name was Edith Giovanna Gassion, and her father was the famous acrobat Jean Gassion. After leaving the Ecole Primaire at Bernay she decided to follow the family tradition by going into show business, and set out to made her living by singing. Her beginnings in this field could hardly have been more humble, or more practical: she started by singing in the streets.

From this she progressed fairly rapidly to music-hall and cabaret, where she was soon noticed and taken up by the more intellectual critics, becoming rapidly something of an institution. In spite of this, her approach to her material always remained direct and unspoilt, though by no means without subtlety; an undertone of nostalgia and regret gave an individual flavour to even her most extrovert pieces. She made famous a number of songs—among her most familiar were "Le Voyage du Pauvre Nègre" "Mon Légionnaire", and "Un monsieur m'a suivi dans la rue"—some by herself, some by poets like Prévert, some the ordinary commercial product, but all interpreted in her own, very personal style.

Her activities were not confined to the singing of popular songs: she had experience of the theatre with *Le Bel Indifférent* (written specially for her by Jean Cocteau) and *La P'tite Lili*; she appeared in a number of films, among them *Montmartre-sur-Seine*, *Paris chante toujours*, *Les Amants de demain*, and most notably Renoir's *French-Cancan*; and she made several tours of Europe and the United States by herself or with some of her numerous discoveries (she was an indefatigable seeker after new talent), such as Les Compagnons de la Chanson. She was perhaps not so well known in Britain as elsewhere, since she was not much seen in person there, and her best-selling records in Britain, "*La Vie en Rose*" and "*Les Trois Cloches*", were not among her most characteristic. Her autobiography, *Au Bal de la Chance*, was published in 1958.

After a period of severe illness she returned to the stage in 1961 in a show of her own and again established herself triumphantly as one of the greatest artistes in the interpretation of French popular song, before a further collapse forced her withdrawal and the end of the show's run. Since then she had more than once been in hospital.

In October, 1962, she married M. Theo Sarapo.

October 12,1963.

Professor Auguste Piccard died at Lausanne on March 25, 1962, at the age of 78. Formerly Professor of Physics at the University of Brussels, he was far better known as a pioneer balloonist, an indefatigable investigator of the upper air and of the deep waters of the ocean.

Auguste Piccard was one of twin sons born at Basle on January 28, 1884, to Jules Piccard, head of the Department of Chemistry at the University of Basle by his wife Hélène (*née* Haltenhoff). The other twin, christened Jean Félix, has likewise won distinction in science; and over considerable periods of their lives the careers of the brothers ran parallel. Both had their schooling at the Ober Realschule, Basle; both went, in 1902, to the Swiss Institute of Technology, at Zurich, and both graduated in 1907—Auguste in mechanical engineering and Jean Félix in chemical engineering. Both brothers stayed on at the institute to carry out research for the degree of D.Sc. Auguste remained there as a teacher until 1922, and for the last two years as Professor of Physics.

Both Auguste and Jean became keenly interested in the possibilities of lighter-than-air flight, and in 1913 they made together a 16-hour flight from Zurich by balloon, passing over large areas of Germany and France.

CHOSE BALLOONS

In 1915, mobilized for service in the Swiss army, they chose the balloon section. Auguste gave up his post at the Swiss Institute of Technology in 1922 on appointment as Professor of Physics at the Institut Polytechnique in the University of Brussels. He kept in close touch with his brother (who, after teaching at Munich and Lausanne, continued his professorial career in the United States). As early as 1926 Auguste had conceived the idea of a high balloon ascent, to be undertaken for the purpose of making scientific observations, and within the next few years he began to make experiments for the production of the best type of gondola.

During 1930 Auguste Piccard evolved an airtight gondola, lifted by a hydrogen-filled balloon, and by May of the following year all was ready for an attempt on the stratosphere. On the 27th, with an assistant, Paul Kipfer, he took off from Augsburg, Bavaria, and achieved a height of 15,281 metres, easily beating the existing record, and descended safely at Ober-Gurgl. A further and more elaborate attempt followed quickly. This time Piccard used an aluminium globe-shaped cabin, with oxygen equipment, furnishing it with the necessary apparatus for the making of scientific observations, the total weight being 850lb., lifted by a gas-filled balloon of 33 yards diameter. On August 18, 1932, Piccard, accompanied by his Belgian collaborator, Max Cosyns, ascended from Zurich to more than 16,201 metres. These flights not only showed that it was possible to travel in the stratosphere, but furnished valuable scientific data concerning radioactivity, atmospheric electricity, and the cosmic rays. They led Piccard to make the prophecy of very fast stratospheric flights between Europe and America, and the Belgian Aero Club recognized his achievement by the award of its gold medal.

Piccard escaped the onrush of the Germans in 1940 and during the period of the Second World War worked in the Swiss aluminium industry, designing precision instruments for physicists. When the war was over he returned to his chair at Brussels, and he now turned his attention from the upper air to the ocean. His ambition was to beat William Beebe's 1934 record of 3,028ft. for an oceanic descent, to investigate conditions at great depths, to take photographs, and, if possible, to catch some of the fish which live at the deep levels. He designed a special form of diving bell which he called a "bathyscaphe". It consisted of a steel, water-tight cabin hung from a box-shaped hydrostat filled with heptane, a form of aviation petrol. He planned to descend by the weight of scrap metal and to raise the bathyscaphe again by the use of the heptane. An attempt was made near Dakar, West Africa, in October, 1948, but Piccard found great difficulty both in launching and recovering the sphere, and had to abandon the project without having carried out his aims.

Five years later, however, Piccard and his son Jacques, a former assistant professor of economics at Geneva, took the bathyscaphe, Trieste, down 1,732 fathoms (10,392 ft.)—then the greatest depth ever reached by a living man—in the Tyrrhenian pit off Capri.

This record was beaten early in 1954 by two French naval officers who went down more than 2,200 fathoms (13,200 ft.). But in January, 1960, the record was regained in a bathyscaphe of his design which was piloted by Jacques Piccard and Lieutenant Don Walsh, an American submarine officer, to a depth of 35,800 ft. in the Marianas Trench off Guam.

In 1956 Auguste Piccard's account of his various exploits was published in English, *In Balloon and Bathyscaphe*. He had retired from his chair in Brussels in 1954.

In 1920 Piccard married Marianne Denis. There were one son and four daughters of the marriage.

March 26, 1962.

Professor Jean F. Piccard, the physicist and balloonist, and Professor Emeritus of Aeronautical Engineering at Minnesota University, where he held the chair for many years, died on January 28, 1963, at his home in Minneapolis. It was his seventy-ninth birthday.

Though he spent most of his life engaged in chemical research and in teaching, Piccard was widely known for his balloon flights into the stratosphere. In 1934 he ascended with his wife, Jeanette, to a height of nearly 11 miles, and from experiments conducted on this and other flights he devised many improvements in balloon equipment.

Jean Félix Piccard was born on January 1884, in Basle, Switzerland, into a family that has since become renowned for its exploratory and scientific achievements. His twin brother, Auguste, who died last March, was even better known for his flights into the stratosphere, and it was with him that Jean made his first balloon ascent in 1913. Auguste's son, Jacques, in 1960, descended 37,800ft. to the bottom of the Pacific in the bathyscaphe, Trieste.

Jean Piccard was educated in Basle and received a degree in chemical engineering at the Swiss Institute of Technology in 1907, and the degree of Doctor of Technology in 1909. After a period at Munich University, he travelled to the United States to join the Faculty of Chicago University. He returned to Switzerland briefly to teach at Lausanne University and then in 1926 returned to the United States, where he became a naturalized citizen in 1931.

Piccard once said that he regarded ballooning as a recreation, although the prime purpose of his flights, like those of his brother, was scientific research into the stratosphere. It was from Detroit that he and his wife made their 11-mile high ascent in 1934, a height which was exceeded by two miles in the following year. In 1936 Piccard joined the staff of Minnesota University, and a year later made a test flight in a spherical metal gondola carried by 100 balloons. Later he developed a frost-resistant window for balloon gondolas and an electronic system for emptying ballast bags which could be controlled from within a closed gondola.

Colleagues at the university, where he served as Professor of Aeronautical Engineering until his retirement in 1952, regarded Piccard as a mild and brilliant man who gave freely of his scientific knowledge. He worked, as he once said, for the thrill of revealing the unknown.

He is survived by his widow and three sons.

January 29, 1963.

Lord Piercy, C.B.E., died suddenly in Stockholm on July 7, 1966, where he was attending a meeting of the Kuwait International Advisory Committee, of which he was a member. He was 80.

Lord Piercy, the son of Augustus Edward Piercy, started his career as a lecturer on Public Administration and Finance at the London School of Economics, where he was one of a distinguished generation, including Clement Attlee, Hugh Dalton and Josiah Stamp.

In the 1914–18 War he was one of the architects of the Munitions Levy, which financed a high proportion of the capital expenditure for war purposes. He was then lent to the Ministry of Munitions and the Inland Revenue, and in 1917 spent some time in the United States as a member of the Allied Provisions Export Commission. For this work he was created C.B.E.

After the 1914–18 War he became Trading General Manager of Harrison and Crosfield, and later became a director of Pharaoh, Gane and Co., where he dealt with the financing and marketing of timber and plywood and played a large part in building up the Russian timber business in Britain. He joined the Stock Exchange in 1934 and was a member until 1942. During this time he was an expert on investment trusts.

In the war of 1939–45 he was at the Export Credits Guarantee Department, where he designed the All-in War Emergency Guarantee. He then became head of the British Petroleum Mission in Washington, and later head of Programmes for the British Supply Council and joint secretary for the Combined Production and Resources Board. For two years subsequently he was personal Economic Adviser to Mr. Attlee. He became Baron Piercy, of Burford in 1945, the year in which he was appointed chairman of the Industrial and Commercial Finance Corporation Ltd. (I.C.F.C.), a position he held until July, 1964. He retired as a director two days before he died. He was a director of the Bank of England from 1946–1956, president of the National Institute of Industrial Psychology from 1946–1963, and chairman of the Wellcome Trust from 1960–65.

BUILDING UP I.C.F.C.

In an address to the Economics Society of Swansea University College in 1952 he suggested the setting up of an investment trust to ease the burden of death duties on shareholders of private companies. The Estate Duties Investment Trust (E.D.I.T.) was formed for this purpose. At the time of his death Piercy was its chairman, and was also chairman of the Ship Mortgage Finance Company Ltd., a member of the Court and Senate of the University of London, a Governor of the University of Birmingham and of the London School of Economics.

Piercy was an economist of repute and possessed a shrewd and fertile financial brain. He took an active part in promoting the Unit Trust movement before the Second World War. Perhaps his best known achievement was his building up of I.C.F.C. from scratch to a company with assets of some £70m. and which had lent over £120m. to small and medium sized businesses when he vacated the chair in 1964. The formation of E.D.I.T. also broke fresh ground.

Piercy was a man of great personal charm, and his wit, humour, and discerning comments on men and affairs made him a most entertaining companion.

He was twice married. In 1915 he married Mary Louise Pelham, O.B.E., daughter of the Hon. Thomas Pelham, C.B., by whom he had one son and three daughters. She died in 1953. In 1964 he married Veronica, younger daughter of Mrs. Ann Warham. He is succeeded by his son, the Hon. Nicholas Piercy.

July 9, 1966.

Henri Théodore Pigozzi, founder of the Simca Motor Company, died on November 18, 1964, at Neuilly at the age of 66.

A Piedmontese, he arrived in Paris in the 1920s without capital or influence. His first business venture, initially a profitable one, was the purchase of Saar coal for resale in Italy but it came to an end when Italian duties were increased. In 1926 he acquired the Fiat agency in France and when—again—customs hit the business he began to assemble Fiat cars at a small factory near Paris. In the next seven years 32,000 cars rolled off the assembly line. He set up on his own account in 1934, acquired the motor factory at Nanterre of a firm which had failed and within a short space of time launched the "Simca-5." However it was with the "Aronde" of 1951 that the firm really arrived.

A four-seater with a good turn of speed and not too greedy for petrol it "took" at once and, with various modifications, Arondes in hundreds of thousands were sold over the years.

In 1960 Simca split into Simca Automobiles, which continued to build cars, and Simca Industries, which took over the building of tractors, lorries, and farm equipment. After the Chrysler group took on control of the firm in 1963, by acquiring 63 per cent of the capital, Pigozzi was succeeded as president of Simca Automobiles by Georges Hereil, creator of the Caravelle aircraft.

In 1954 Pigozzi negotiated a merger with Ford whereby Ford got a 15 per cent interest in Simca and agreed not to enter the French market on its own account for at least seven years. Simca took over the Ford production lines at Poissy and the main Ford model, the Vedette, powered by the Ford V8 engine.

November 20,1964.

Sir Gonne St. Clair Pilcher, M.C., a Judge of the Probate, Divorce and Admiralty Division from October, 1942 to 1951, and of the Queen's Bench Division from that year until his retirement in 1964, died on April 3, 1966 at his home in Somerset. He was 75.

Though his chosen profession was the law, he came from a military background, his father being the late Major-General Thomas David Pilcher, C.B., and his mother the younger daughter of the late Colonel T. Gonne, of the 17th Lancers.

Born on September 19, 1890, he was educated at Wellington College and Trinity College, Cambridge, where he took honours in the Mediaeval and Modern Languages Tripos in 1911. His debonair manner, well-dressed figure and good carriage were characteristic of him throughout his life. He was called to the Bar by the Inner Temple in 1915. He served in the 1914–18 war in France and Belgium, winning the dispatches.

After the war he went for a time into the Chambers of Sir William Jowitt (later Lord Jowitt, Lord Chancellor). He subsequently changed to Admiralty chambers and soon became one of the busiest juniors briefed in the work of that Division. From 1935–36 he was junior counsel to the Admiralty, and in the latter year took silk. As a leader he was equally successful. In 1938 he was appointed deputy chairman of Somerset Quarter Sessions. During the Second World War, from September, 1939, to October, 1942, he was an attached officer at the War Office.

In the Long Vacation of 1942 Mr. Justice Langton, a judge of the Probate, Divorce and Admiralty Division, died. Pilcher was appointed to succeed him in the following Michaelmas term, October, 1942. Owing to the number of judges then holding office, this appointment was made pursuant on address from both Houses of Parliament. With the Admiralty work of the Division he was already thoroughly familiar. Like other judges before him, and since, he had to learn the other business carried out by that Division. Though mainly occupied with the Admiralty side, he carried out all his duties with high satisfaction and proved himself to be a capable judge who was always courteous to those who appeared before him. After nine years in the Probate, Divorce and Admiralty Division he was transferred to the Queen's Bench Division until his retirement in 1961.

While still a judge, he carried out a number of extra-judicial tasks. From 1947 he was the vice-president of the Comité Maritime International, and from 1950 President of the British Maritime Law Association. He was also chairman of the committee appointed to inquire into whether any changes were desirable in the administration of justice under the court-martial system, based on the Naval Discipline Act; the sittings of the committee were held in 1950–51. In May, 1952, September, 1958, and May, 1961, he headed the United Kingdom delegation to the important Brussels Diplomatic Conference on International Maritime Conventions.

Pilcher was an enthusiastic horseman and found his main recreation in hunting. He was also a member of the Pegasus Club and in his earlier years rode regularly in the Bar point-to-point races.

In 1918 he married Janet, elder daughter of the late Allan Hughes, of Lynch, Allerford, Somerset. They had one son who was killed on active service in 1941, and one daughter.

April 4, 1966.

Dr. Gregory Goodwin Pincus, who helped give the world the birth-control pill, died in hospital in Boston on August 22, 1967. He was 64.

Pincus worked With Dr. M.C. Chang and Dr. John Rock to develop a safe and simple oral contraceptive which has revolutionized family planning in recent years in many parts of the world. He was research director of the Worcester Foundation for Experimental Biology, where he worked with hormones.

Pincus, who is assured of a place in the history of scientific achievement for his part in the introduction of the oral contraceptive pill (the "Pincus Pill"), has been in the forefront of the development of mammalian reproductive physiology for more than 35 years. Some of his first contributions, in the early 1930s, had to do with processes involved in fertilization of the egg. Later, when knowledge of steroid hormones began to develop in the late thirties and early forties, his attention became increasingly focused on the roles these substances had to play in reproduction, and he was able to show that the steroid hormone progesterone, present in much increased amounts during pregnancy, prevented the occurrence of ovulation while pregnancy was in progress. In the early 1950s powerful new orally active synthetic progesterone-like compounds were introduced and here Pincus saw the opportunity that these presented for the development of an oral ovulation-inhibiting agent.

With his colleagues at the Worcester Foundation for Experimental Biology, Shrewsbury, Massachusetts (of which for many years he was the director), he tested some 200 compounds for their ovulation-inhibiting properties and, having selected three which seemed most likely to be suitable for human use, he and Dr. John Rock carried out the first clinical trials in 1954. The extension of these soon showed that the method was outstandingly successful and far superior in contraceptive efficacy to any method hitherto available. The oral contraceptives, in increasingly widespread use since that time, are based on the concepts put forward and shown to be valid by Pincus. The magnitude of this innovation lies not only in the fact that it was the first scientific advance in birth control, but also in that here, at the first attempt, a virtually 100 per cent effective chemical agent had been introduced, a situation almost, if not completely, without parallel in pharmacological history.

When, in 1963, the International Planned Parenthood Federation formed its Oral Advisory Group, not unnaturally Pincus was elected its first chairman.

Pincus's interests in the direction of control of reproductive processes continued throughout his scientific career and in 1965 he produced *The Control of Fertility*, an outstanding review volume citing over 1,400 references selected from more than twice that number examined. Among his other major contributions to scientific literature are his editorship of the long and important *Recent Progress in Hormone Research* and, jointly, of the five volumes of *The Hormones*, the first of which appeared in 1948 and the last two in 1964. Along with his scientific achievements Gregory Pincus will long be remembered, by all who knew him, as a charming and endearing character, who always had a merry twinkle in his eye, a friendly greeting, and usually an amusing anecdote.

Gregory Pincus was born at Woodbine, N.J., on April 9, 1903, and took a bachelor's degree in science at Cornell University in 1924. He went to Harvard University where he took a master's degree and a doctorate in science. In 1929 Pincus travelled to Europe and studied at Cambridge University, and at the Kaiser Wilhelm Institute in Berlin. He was a fellow of the National Research Council from 1927 to 1930. Pincus became a lecturer in biology at Harvard in 1930, and the following year was appointed assistant professor. From 1937 to 1938 he was a visiting research student at Cambridge University, and from 1939 to 1945 he was visiting professor in experimental zoology at Clark University. Pincus became professor of physiology at Tufts Medical School in 1944, a post he held until 1951 when he was appointed research professor of biology at Boston University. He was chairman of the endocrine panel of the National Cancer Chemotherapy Service Center from 1956 to 1960.

He was also a member of the Fulbright fellowship committee, 1958–60.

Pincus married Elizabeth Notkin in 1924, and they had two children.

August 24, 1967.

Battista Pinin-Farina, the Italian car designer and stylist, died in Lausanne on April 3, 1966. He was 70.

Born in Turin in 1895, practically together with the motor car, Giovan Battista Farina was the industrialist, craftsman and artist who unquestionably wielded the greatest influence on car design the world over. In Great Britain, Pinin-Farina styling is to be seen throughout the current range of the British Motor Corporation's cars.

Son of a carpenter and the youngest of 10 children, Giovan Farina—nicknamed "Pinin", the little one—began work at the age of 12 for his father. While still a boy he followed his elder brother Giovanni, from the Alessio Coachworks, where he had learnt the rudiments of the art, into the small motor car body workshop that was to become the Farina works. In this setting, Pinin received his first education in coach building, encouraged by an instinctive curiosity and a passionate interest in the newly developing motor car and aeroplane.

During the First World War he devoted much attention to aircraft—an experience later to influence his design—and in 1918 went to Detroit on his first visit to the United States. By 1928, with Fiat and Lancia already buying bodies from the workshop, he tired of the conventional approach and landed a Lancia contract which enabled him to found his own business—the Pinin Farina company, in which, having sensed the need to drop the old craftsman system, he rapidly developed assembly line techniques for the design and construction of special car bodies.

Applying his inborn artistic talent and knowledge of aerodynamics to land vehicles, he earned universal recognition and respect from car manufacturers throughout the world. The flowing, elegant Farina line was soon as recognizable in vehicle body work as the hand of the Paris couturier in the fashion world, for he was probably the first automobile designer who really analysed and understood the relationship between form and function in industrial design. A car styled under his direction had to be not merely aerodynamic but complete and unostentatious.

EXACT DETAIL

He gave an overwhelming demonstration of his inventiveness by solving problems of design, production, and habitability of the car from a typically industrial point of view, but without abandoning an independent artist's clarity of design. Each of his models bore an aesthetic coherence, neatness, often boldness and invariably beauty—but never mere decoration. He calculated in exact detail yet emphasized the real technical and formal requirements of a car with a highly individual style.

Among the earliest cars styled by Pinin-Farina were the 1932 Lancia Dilambda coupé, the Fiat Zero and the highly advanced Lancia Aprilia aerodynamic coupé of 1937. In 1947 came the Cisitalia, which started what the Americans called the "European line" and the *Gran Turismo* formula in sports saloons. Six years later Farina was called on to create a model using an American chassis with British engine—the Nash-Healey—which was one of his masterpieces, earning him an ovation in Detroit, where it was launched by the Nash-Kelvinator Corporation, but his deepest interest and influence lay in sports cars, and Farina-bodied Lancias. Alfa Romeos and Ferraris have captured some of the world's most coveted racing awards. His passion for high speed cars helped to forge a long personal friendship with Enzo Ferrari, Farina himself invariably driving one of his own specially styled Ferraris. In high performance design his works ranged from streamlined record breaking machines to the exotic Ferrari "Superamerica Superfast", and the latest Alfa Romeo Spider, unveiled at the Geneva Motor Show in March, 1966.

TURIN WORKS

In 1949, he was building one car a day at his Turin works, but nine years later he set up a large new £2m. plant on the outskirts of the city, where, by 1963, he was employing 1,600 skilled workers to build 15,000 cars a year—with the prospect of doubling this within five years. Although he did business with almost every car maker in the world, his most significant and important contract was the long term agreement with the British Motor Corporation, beginning in the late 1950s, with the Farina-styled Austin A40, then following through the entire range to include the 1100 and the latest 1800 front wheel drive series. B.M.C., Fiat, Peugeot, Lancia, Ferrari, and Alfa Romeo all had long term contracts with Farina when, in the early 1960s, he officially adopted the name "Pinin-Farina" for the business and progressively handed over the reins to his son, Sergio, and son-in-law Renzo Carli, the company's technical director. Pinin-Farina was not only an artist-coachbuilder, a shrewd business executive and man of great personal charm. He was a Cavaliere del Lavoro, an honorary member of the Royal Society of Arts and president of the Turin Circolo degli Artisti. He was the recipient in 1957 of the Gran Premio Nazionale La Rinascente Compasso d'oro, and many other national and international design awards.

August 4, 1966.

Panayotis Pipinelis, Foreign Minister of Greece, whose diplomatic acumen and stark realism were instrumental in averting a senseless Greek-Turkish war over Cyprus in November, 1967, died in Athens on July 19, 1970, at the age of 71. He was briefly Prime Minister in the summer of 1963.

He was the only old-time politician who volunteered his services to the present military regime, and did so just in time to handle the explosive Cyprus crisis which had led Greece to the brink of war. His strongest ambition, yet unfulfilled, was to bring about a peaceful and realistic settlement of the Cyprus dispute which for some 15 years had undermined Greek-Turkish relations and endangered peace in the Eastern Mediterranean.

Born in Piraeus on March 21, 1899, he studied law and political sciences in Switzerland and entered the Greek Diplomatic Service in 1922. He first came in contact with politics in 1933 when he served as diplomatic adviser to the Tsaldaris government for two years. He was later Minister in Budapest and Sofia where he remained until the eve of the German invasion of Greece in 1941.

He followed the Greek Government in exile and was appointed its ambassador in Moscow in 1941, and in 1943 he was Greek ambassador to the free governments of Poland and Belgium in London. In 1945 he was appointed Chief of the Political Bureau of King George II in London, at a critical moment for the Greek monarchy, as the King's return to his throne was open to question.

His counsel to the late King largely contributed to his success in the ensuing referendum on the monarchy, an institution which, he was deeply convinced, was particularly suited to Greek circumstances.

It was his long devotion to the monarchy that weighed in his appointment as Prime Minister on June 17, 1963, at a turning point in Greek domestic politics. Mr. Karamanlis had just resigned after eight years in power, ostensibly after disagreement with King Paul's plan for a scheduled state visit to Britain in defiance of communist threats to mar the visit. Pipinelis escorted the King and Queen during their London visit.

His tenure was short-lived, seeing that King Paul, giving in to pressure from the Liberals and the left, agreed by September that a non-political premier rather than he should organize the general elections of November, 1963, which ultimately ended 12 years of right-wing rule in Greece.

Before his entry into Greek politics he had served as permanent undersecretary for foreign affairs from June, 1947, to January, 1950, at a time when Greece was trying to convince the world at large that the communist rebellion in Greece was aided and abetted by her communist neighbours in the north.

In 1950 he served as Foreign Minister in a caretaker Cabinet, and later went to Paris, in 1952, as Greek Permanent Representative to Nato. He resigned from the diplomatic service in 1953.

He was not as successful in politics as he had been in diplomacy. He failed twice as a candidate for Athens on the ticket of the National Radical Union, the party of Mr. Karamanlis. But in view of his unquestionable talents he was appointed in 1961 Extra-Parliamentary Minister of Trade. He held this post until he was nominated Prime Minister in 1963.

PRIVILEGED ELECTION

He was elected for the first time in Parliament in the 1963 and then the 1964 elections, but only because of the special privileges accorded to former Prime Ministers. He was Minister of Economic Coordination in the short-lived Kanellopoulos Cabinet which was deposed by the military coup of April 21, 1967.

Through these years he continued to act as trusted unofficial adviser to the Greek Crown. He had confided to friends that he had agreed to join the revolutionary Cabinet as Foreign Minister only in order to hold in check the anti-Royalist tendencies of some of the ruling officers. He was bitterly disappointed that King Constantine had failed to seek his advice before staging the abortive countercoup of December 13, 1967, which took place while he was in Brussels for the Nato ministerial meeting.

None the less, he continued to act as a liaison between the King, now in exile in Rome, and the regime leaders, and exercised his influence to preserve—as he thought best—the monarchy's prestige and its chances of survival in Greece.

Being exposed more than any other regime Minister to foreign pressures for the return of democracy in Greece, he had managed to obtain from the Prime Minister last summer a time-table for the abolition of several emergency measures by December, 1970, in an effort to avert Greece's suspension from the Council of Europe. The time-table, however, was rejected because it ended short of pledging a date for Parliamentary elections. He walked out of the Council's December, 1969, meeting announcing Greece's withdrawal to forestall an expulsion.

In his last weeks he appeared concerned that while the regime was honouring the time-table, it refused to commit itself beyond the end of 1970. He felt the regime was powerful enough to be able to hold general elections within 1971, but this view was not evidently shared by the ruling officers.

He is survived by his widow.

July 20, 1970.

Orovida Pissarro died on August 8, 1968, at the age of 74.

She made an early artistic sensation with her paintings and etchings of horses, tigers and other animals in the Oriental manner, and preferred to be known simply as "Orovida." She was the only child of Lucien Pissarro, who became a naturalized British subject in 1916, and therefore granddaughter of Camille Pissarro (1830–1903), the great Impressionist. Two of her paternal uncles were also painters, so that her family name of Pissarro would have been as much a practical handicap as her heredity was an artistic advantage.

Orovida Camille Pissarro was born at Epping on October 8, 1893. She was educated at Norland Place School and tried several art schools (for not more than one term) before deciding to study alone with the occasional advice of her father. Whether or not deliberately, however, she turned aside from the family tradition of Impressionism and astonished artistic London with decorative compositions of Mongolian hunters and similar subjects that looked plausibly as if they had been executed by an Eastern artist.

Orovida took up etching in 1914. Her paintings were generally in the form of large decorative panels executed in tempera on silk in the Far Eastern manner, the similarity being increased by the use of strips of figured silk in mounting. She took to this style of work in 1924, with the technical assistance of a Japanese friend. From 1933 onwards, many of these panels, generally two at a time, under such titles as The Tiger Hunt, The Archers' Return and Fighting Cocks, were exhibited in the South Rooms of the Royal Academy, where, with their calligraphic style of drawing, strongly marked linear rhythms and flat decorative contour, they formed a welcome relief to rather humdrum surroundings.

Later, Orovida applied her method to contemporary English subjects, such as The Popular Cafe, exhibited in 1939. On the scale of the panels her drawing was somewhat lacking in character, but she made up for this with decorative appeal.

Allowing for the circumstances that Orovida began life with a passionate adoration for tigers, and studied ancient Chinese art with diligence in her girlhood, something was slightly uncanny about her "Orientalism".

It was her treatment of horses that raised the most tantalizing question. A good many of her decorative panels were of Mongolian hunters in pursuit of tigers and other wild animals, and an expert on breeds of horses has declared that she realized to perfection not only the type of the Tartar horse but also the characteristic seat of the rider, though she had never been out of Europe.

Orovida exhibted regularly at the Royal Academy, and also at the new English Art Club, the R.B.A., and Women's International Art Club. She first had a one-man exhibition in London in 1919 and this was followed by seven others, at the Redfern, Leicester and O'Hana Galleries. An exhibition entitled "Three Generations of Pissarro" at the Leicester Galleries in 1943 included her work with that of her father and grandfather (who, it is recorded, saw great promise in her drawings at the age of seven). Her knowledge of the career and work of Lucien Pissarro proved of much value when the Arts Council organized its survey of Lucien's art in 1963.

Her last exhibition was a retrospective of paintings and etchings at the Leicester Galleries in 1967. Her works, more especially her etchings, figure in many public collections, including the British Museum, Victoria and Albert Museum, New York Public Library, Riiksmuseum, Amsterdam, and the Municipal Galleries of Glasgow and Dublin. Her portrait was painted by Carel Weight.

Orovida, a heavily-built woman who had been ailing latterly and little capable of movement, was tended during this period by several devoted friends.

August 13, 1968.

Sir Julian Pode, chairman of the Steel Company of Wales Ltd., from 1962 to 1967 and managing director from 1947 to 1962, died on June 11, 1968, at the age of 65. He was a former president of the British Iron and Steel Federation.

He was born in Sheffield on June 26, 1902, and educated in H.M.S. Conway. During the First World War he served in the Royal Navy. By profession a chartered accountant, he was a Fellow of the Institute of Chartered Accountants and a Fellow of the Chartered Institute of Secretaries. In 1965 he received an honorary award of the Joint Diploma in Management

Accounting Services.

Pode entered the steel industry in 1926, when he joined the staff of Guest. Keen & Nettlefolds Ltd., at the Dowlais Works, as district accountant. In 1930, when the heavy steel interests of that company were amalgamated with those of Baldwins Ltd., to form Guest Keen Baldwins Iron and Steel Co., Ltd., he was appointed secretary of the new company. Later, in 1938, he became secretary and joint commercial manager. In 1943 he was appointed assistant managing director, and in 1945 managing director.

When, in September, 1947, the steel Company of Wales Limited was formed, for the purpose of modernizing the sheet steel and tinplate industries of South Wales, he was appointed managing director of the new company. For 15 years, in this role, he guided the company through one of the biggest development projects ever carried out in the steel industry, raising ingot steel output from 500,000 to 3m. tons per year. In May, 1961, he was appointed deputy chairman in addition to his position as managing director. In February, 1962, he was appointed chairman of the company.

He had many interests outside his own company and played a leading part in the affairs of the British Iron and Steel Federation. He was a member of the council and of the executive committee from 1945 and, in addition to serving on a number of other federation committees, was appointed in March, 1966, to the development coordinating committee under the chairmanship of Sir Henry Benson. Sir Julian was appointed president of the federation for three successive years, in 1962, 1963 and 1964.

He was an honorary vice-president of the Iron and Steel Institute, chairman of the National Industrial Fuel Efficiency Service, a member of the Grand Council of the Confederation of British Industry and was chairman of the F.B.I.'s Standing Committee on Fuel and Energy for a number of years. From 1959 to 1966 he was chairman of the managing committee of the Athlone Fellowship Scheme, and for a number of years was a member of the United Kingdom Commonwealth Scholarship Commission.

He was chairman of Wm. France, Fenwick & Co., Ltd., Prince of Wales Dry Dock Company, Swansea, Limited, and of North Sea Marine Engineering Construction Company Ltd., and deputy chairman of the Hodge Group Ltd. He was also a director of a number of other companies, including Guest, Keen and Nettlefolds Ltd., the Steetley Company Ltd., and the Iron Trades Employers' Insurance Association Ltd.

In addition, he was a director of Lloyds Bank Ltd, and chairman of their South Wales District Committee.

In 1948 he was a High Sheriff of Glamorgan and a Justice of the Peace from 1951 to 1966. He was made an Honorary Freeman of the Borough of Port Talbot, 1957. He was knighted in 1959.

He married in 1930 Jean Finlay, daughter of F. Finlayson. They had a son and a daughter.

June 13, 1968.

Nikolai Pogodin, the Soviet playwright died on September 19, 1962. Widely known for his plays about the life of Lenin, he was also notable for his dramatic works depicting the effects of de-Stalinization.

Born at Gundurovskaya on the Don 62 years ago, he started his professional life as a journalist. Roving correspondent of *Molot* and a number of provincial newspapers, he eventually became a special correspondent of *Pravda*. His first play, called *Tempo*, like a number of subsequent works was devoted to a topical Soviet theme. *Tempo* was about new construction; *Poem about an Axe* (1931), and *My Friend* (1932), were attempts to portray a "positive hero" in Soviet life. *After the Ball* (1934) represents simple people as the heroes of their time and the intelligentsia as Philistines. *The Aristocrats* (1935), dealing with rehabilitation and delinquency, shows criminals as basically talented and energetic people, capable of conscientious work, who have only taken a wrong path in life.

The first of his two plays about Lenin, *Kremlin Chimes*, was produced for the twentieth anniversary of the revolution. The *Third Pathetique* appeared in 1958 and both plays were performed in the Kremlin Theatre during the Communist Party congress of autumn, 1961.

Petrarch's Sonnet and *Three to the Virgin Lands* appeared in 1956, the year of Khrushchev's "secret speech" in which he revealed some of the abuses of authority in the party during the Stalin period. *Petrarch's Sonnet* deals with the uncalled-for meddling by the party in a love affair of a platonic nature and its moral is that the better part of the party stands for justice and fights careerists and bureaucrats. The manner in which he presented the motives of the young people volunteering to go out to Siberia in *Three to the Virgin Lands* brought upon him the severe criticism of *Pravda*. Accusing him of presenting only the "negative and dark" side of the movement to develop the virgin soil areas, *Pravda* stated that his play lacked "a striking, optimistic mood and a heroic foundation." Pogodin is understood to have recognized his error at a meeting of writers.

Pogodin was editor of the magazine *Teatr* and a member of the presidium of the Union of Writers. He held the Order of Lenin.

September 20, 1962.

Millie Graham Polak, who died on May 5, 1962, lived for a number of years in South Africa under the same roof as Mahatma Gandhi and his wife.

Some time after the Boer War Gandhi was about to travel from Johannesburg to Durban when Henry Polak, a Jewish friend who eventually went to prison with him, threw a copy of Ruskin's *Unto This Last* into the railway compartment. The book impressed Gandhi so deeply that he began to lead a simpler life. He cut his own hair, starched his stiff collars and was dismantling most of the furniture in his house in Johannesburg when he insisted that Henry Polak and his bride must live with him. Gandhi, though only 35, had been married 20 years, and his wife awaited the arrival of a young English girl with excusable dread.

Mrs. Polak's first battle with Gandhi was for curtains and floor-coverings. Gandhi protested that the view from the naked windows was more beautiful than any picture. "I do not understand why you want to shut it out." "Some lace curtains or thin muslin", Mrs. Polak replied, "will not shut it out." Though she won her way, the victory was short-lived.

Tolstoy was now exerting a spell over Gandhi even greater than Ruskin's, and he decided to live a more ascetic life by moving to Phoenix Farm, where Mrs. Polak and Mrs. Gandhi slept in the same bare room. On the first night the two women grumbled so openly that Gandhi entered the room and promised to make whatever improvements were really necessary; but, as Mrs. Polak pointed out in her short and amusing biography, *Mr. Gandhi: the Man*, there was always a heavy emphasis on the word "necessary". Gandhi, however, allowed her to keep a dog. He proudly attributed its sturdiness to a vegetarian diet until neighbours traced it down as the thief which was raiding their meat safes.

Whatever the difficulties and exasperations of their communal life on Phoenix Farm may have been, the Polaks never regretted the experiment, and their friendship with Gandhi was broken only by his death. Between the wars they kept an open house in South Kensington for all who had close ties with India. Their simple hospitality was greatly appreciated by many delegates, Indian and British, at the time of the All India Round Table Conference.

May 12, 1962.

Serge Poliakoff died on October 12, 1969, in Paris at the age of 63.

His death deprives European art of a master whose painting, icon-like or, in recent years, of an ethereality and luminous force still invigorated by a passion for the concentrated sturdiness of those structures of belief, was without parallel in our time.

The intensity and spiritual grace of Poliakoff's best work share common ground only with the glowing canvases of Rothko, a fellow Russian in America. In the years to come, Poliakoff's resonantly individual achievement in constructing an art in which contemplation and repose are continually brought to life, by shifting light and varying atmospheric densities, will be increasingly cherished and comprehended. The constant factor throughout his work is a richly personal awareness of the emotional and spatial connotations of colour; darkly smouldering reds and cool blues, the drama of black, translucent greens and irridescent greys in Poliakoff's hands took on a fresh significance, wholly personal and active in abstract terms, yet always humanly experienced and inhabited as emblematic states of experience and, finally, existence.

Like Brancusi—or Rothko—Poliakoff's work is best apprehended in isolation; it demands absolute conditions of space and occasion for its slow magic to work; the paintings gain tremendously in impact and sequential registration when gathered together.

Poliakoff worked in series after series of formal variations with harmonic, tonal, and textural undulations of the utmost subtlety. Each inflexion was charged by a compressed, unrhetorical eloquence: the cumulative effect of a large and representative assembly of his paintings has an almost religious solemnity; but Poliakoff, with all his awareness of the past, created an ambience that speaks of some future ritual as well as the process of becoming, of formation. Free of piety, the painting retains always an innate gravity enlivened by a luxuriously sensual concern for beautiful surfaces.

He was born in Moscow in 1906. His mother came from a family of landowners; his father bred horses for the Russian Army, and kept a racing stable. Poliakoff inherited from his mother a gift for music, and learnt to play the guitar as a boy. He was also exposed to the formal as well as to the religious connotation of icons from his earliest years through daily visits to church with his devout mother. Following the Revolution, Poliakoff finally settled in Paris in 1923, after sojourns in Belgrade, Sofia and Vienna. He did not find his vocation as a painter until around 1930, when he studied at the Grande Chaumiere as well as taking private instruction. At this time, to earn money, he played the guitar each night behind the scenes for two years for the Paris production of *Tovarich*. He enjoyed the experience.

Later, in 1935, Poliakoff spent two years studying in London at the Chelsea School of Art and at the Slade: he remained always an Anglophile and regarded this period of his life as radically formative. In 1936 he married Marcelle Perreur-Lloyd of Irish and French parentage, and this gallant, generous, warmhearted lady shared the many years of struggle and poverty which lay ahead with unassertive devotion and high spirit. Later, in the mid-fifties their apartment in the rue de Seine was to become a cosmopolitan centre for many visitors where hospitality was given with gaiety and ease; but Poliakoff was inclined to intransigence in his dealings with the art world; with many of the traits of the gambler in his optimistic handling of money and material affairs. His success and esteem were real, and remain constant, but the affluence of an artist who retained a not wholly successful racehorse and, affectionately, employed an aging Russian compatriot as a chauffeur for his ancient Rolls-Royce car, was at once exaggerated and misunderstood by a public which read the gossip columns at a certain period and did not understand the comical side of Poliakoff's romantic and impulsive nature.

Befriended by Kandinsky and Delaunay as a young man, Poliakoff was also close to de Staël until that artist's tragic death in the early fifties, but his work has little to do with the geometry of expressionism adapted by de Staël, which he later transformed into a new art of simplified figuratura.

Poliakoff stayed inside an invented world, consistently, in which intellect was balanced by great feeling and whose solid identities of form, and their convergence or dispersal, were contained by the more evanescent and transistory pressures or liberations of space.

Many will recall his retrospective exhibition at the Whitechapel Gallery, initiated by John Russell, an ardent supporter, and the radiance of that interior when his work was installed there.

October 14, 1969.

Colonel George Paton Pollitt, D.S.O., who died on March 9, 1964, at the age of 85, will be remembered as one of the pioneers of the new chemical industry which arose after the First World War.

He was born in 1878 at Mellor in Lancashire, went to school in Belgium and then studied chemistry at Owens College, Manchester, where he obtained an Honours Degree, and later did research at Zurich Polytechnic for a Ph.D. About 1900 on returning to England he joined the firm of Brunner Mond at Northwich which manufactured soda ash. At this time Sir John Brunner and Dr. Ludwig Mond, who had started the ammonia soda process in Cheshire, were still active directors of the firm.

When war broke out in 1914 Pollitt joined the Army as a motor cyclist in the intelligence corps. Later when the Germans used chlorine gas in an offensive a British gas corps was formed and he was transferred to it. Three officers and 15 other ranks were hastily got together and shipped to France within 48 hours as a special branch of the Royal Engineers to use gas as an offensive weapon and Pollitt was given a command with the rank of lieutenant-colonel. His principal work was the projection of gas into the enemy trenches from mortars. Later he transferred to the infantry and was given command of a service battalion in The Lancashire Fusiliers. He was wounded altogether four times and taken prisoner just before the Armistice.

He was awarded the D.S.O. with two bars and mentioned in dispatches four times.

INTENSIVE FARMING

After the war Pollitt returned to Brunner Mond and became chairman of the branch which the company formed at Billingham for the manufacture of nitrogen compounds, for use as fertilizers. He was one of the main inspirations of the planning and building of what became the largest chemical works of its kind in England. In 1927 when I.C.I. was formed he became one of its original directors. He had bought an estate in Shropshire which he farmed intensively and during the 1939 War he threw himself into Home Guard activities and became a zone commander, being granted the honorary rank of colonel, a fact which gave him profound satisfaction. In 1945–46 he was High Sheriff of Shropshire.

In 1947 he sold his farm where he had bred pedigree Herefords with great success and emigrated to Southern Rhodesia where he farmed 2,800 acres with the help of his two nephews. In 1952 he returned to England to undergo a throat operation which affected his speech. However, he bought a house at St. Mawes in Cornwall where he enjoyed life in sailing and fishing and watching the racing which is such a feature of the place. Pollitt was unmarried.

He made many contributions to agricultural research and his book *Britain Can Feed Herself*, published in 1942, made quite a stir at the time. He leaves behind him many happy memories.

March 12, 1964.

Erich Pommer, one of the dominating influences in the German cinema during the 1920s, died in Hollywood in May, 1966, at the age of 76. He joined the U.F.A. company soon after the end of the First World War, and was responsible for such famous German films as *The Cabinet of Doctor Caligari*, *The Last Laugh*, *Vaudeville*, *Dr. Mabuse*, *Metropolis*, *The Blue Angel* and *Congress Dances*.

"In any survey of the major movies of Germany," wrote C. A. Lejeune, more than 30 years ago, "this single name confronts us again and again."

Pommer was a cornerstone of the German film industry in the formative years between 1925 and the coming of sound, when it was in danger of losing its best players and directors to Hollywood. He was, in his way, something of a dictator, but this was at a time when a dominating influence was urgently needed in the German film industry. Later in his career he turned to direction but without great success, and it was always as an originator of films, and a supervisor of their production, that his talent was revealed to its best advantage. His business outlook ensured the films he produced were commercially acceptable, but he had the great producer's flair for recognizing talent and developing it. He was at once an artist and a man of business.

Erich Pommer was born on July 20, 1889, in Hildesheim, Germany, and was educated there and at Göttingen College. He joined the French Gaumont organization as a young man, but worked only on the business side, where he rose rapidly.

In 1913 he joined the French Eclair company, but returned to Germany at the outbreak of war in 1914. He fought with the German Army and was seriously wounded in 1916.

MANAGER-PRODUCER

He then founded the German Eclair company and later merged it with other companies, and in 1919 he produced one of the most remarkable of all German silent films—*The Cabinet of Dr. Caligari*, with Werner Krauss and Konrad Veidt. In 1921 he joined the U.F.A. board of directors and became a manager-producer, for at this time he was still looked upon as being primarily a businessman; and it was not until he made *Vaudeville* in 1925 that his obvious flair for production persuaded him to forsake the purely business side of film-making. *Vaudeville* was directed by A. E. Dupont, with Emile Jannings in the leading part, and both director and player rose above their normal high standards under Pommer's supervision.

The same thing happened in 1926 when Pommer went for a short time to Hollywood, and produced *Hotel Imperial* for Paramount, when he conjured their best work out of the director, Mauritz Stiller, and the star Pola

Negri. He returned to Germany and there produced the most famous of the early German sound films, *The Blue Angel*, in which he contrived to live on amicable terms with the temperamental star, Marlene Dietrich, and its even more temperamental director, Josef Von Sternberg.

In the early 1930s he returned to Hollywood and then went to England in 1936 to produce *Fire over England* and *Troopship* for Alexander Korda. In 1937 he formed Mayflower Productions with Charles Laughton, and for them he produced *Vessel of Wrath, St. Martin's Lane*, and *Jamaica Inn*. He went to Hollywood in 1940 and returned to Germany in 1947.

May 13, 1966.

Dr. A. L. Poole, formerly President of St. John's College, Oxford, died on February 22, 1963, at Ticehurst, Kent. He was 73.

Austin Lane Poole was born on December 6, 1889, the second son of the late Reginald Lane Poole, and a member of a family which has won distinction in the most widely separated fields. His mother, formerly Miss Rachel Malleson, had many personal links with the literary and educational movements of the Victorian period and became a distinguished writer on the history of art.

Educated at Magdalen College School and at Corpus Christi College, where he was a history scholar he took a first class in Modern History in 1911 and in the following year, with an essay on Henry the Lion, carried off the Lothian Prize which his father, the most eminent Oxford Medievalist in the generation after Stubbs, had won 33 years before.

In 1912–13 he was a lecturer at Selwyn College, Cambridge, and made many lasting friendships in that university; but in 1913 he was elected a Fellow of St. John's College, Oxford. On the outbreak of war in the following year he joined the 8th Service Battalion of the Gloucester Regiment, and in 1915 went with his battalion to France.

During the war he married Vera, daughter of Dr. Arthur Dendy, Professor of Zoology at King's College, London. Mrs. Poole was a painter and his marriage brought him a fresh circle of friends among artists.

After the conclusion of the war St. John's very naturally elected him a Fellow and tutor. He served the college with single-minded devotion, and, as he combined a rare understanding of young men with fine scholarship and business capacity he showed from the first the qualities of the best traditional type of the Oxford college tutor. He held the usual offices: and from 1931 he was Senior Tutor, an office which in St. John's entailed a very large share in the management of college affairs. In 1947 he succeeded Sir Cyril Norwood as President of the College; but a grave illness from which he only partially recovered compelled him to resign in 1957.

His former college, Corpus, elected him an Honorary Fellow; the Merchant Taylors Company, which has close associations with St. John's, conferred its freedom on him, and he received the Legion of Honour for his services to French studies in Oxford.

In 1924–25 he was Senior Proctor, and his prompt and energetic but good-humoured efficiency at once made him much sought after for university offices. He was a curator of the University Park from 1924: for six years he was on the council of Somerville College; for seven years on the General Board of the Faculties; he served as chairman of the Board of the Faculty of Modern History; he was an indispensable member of the Hebdomadal Council from 1924 to 1931 and again from 1935 to 1957. As a delegate of the University Press, and chairman of its finance committee, he rendered valuable services in the difficult period during and after the war of 1939–45. From 1948 to 1957 he was a Pro-Vice-Chancellor.

In controversial matters his attitude was generally that of an open-minded conservative; and in his earlier years at St. John's he was an active member of the Conservative Party in university parliamentary politics; but as time went on he freed himself from party ties.

JUDGMENT RELIABLE

Everyone in the university put unreserved confidence in his judgment.

As an historian he was slow to publish, but he worked steadily with scrupulous standards of method and especially with a wide knowledge of Continental scholarship. His Ford lectures published as *Obligations of Society in the Twelfth Century* showed his mastery of feudal practice. He contributed the chapters on German history in three of the volumes of the *Cambridge Medieval History*, and a volume of the *Oxford History of England* with the title *From Domesday Book to Magna Carta*. His last scholarly work was to edit the revised edition of *Medieval England*, which was published by the Oxford University Press in 1959.

From 1932 to 1936 he served on the Council of the Royal Historical Society, and he took a full share in the business of the historical world. As a reviewer, as a delegate of the University Press, and as an examiner in many universities he did much to maintain scholarly standards.

In 1952 he was elected a Fellow of the British Academy.

He will be remembered not only for his work but above all for his incomparable gifts of friendship and hospitality. From his boyhood he had intimate links with the Costwold country.

In the President's Lodgings at St. John's, one of the most beautiful houses in Oxford, full of beautiful and historical possessions, he was never for long without visitors. Old pupils, or colleagues, foreign scholars, artists, cousins and neighbours, were always welcome.

In all this Poole's gifts found a perfect complement in those of his wife. Some years after the 1914–18 War a dark shadow fell on their lives when their son and one of their daughters died in childhood within a few days of one another. They are commemorated by a mural tablet in the chapel of St. John's College. Mrs. Poole, with one daughter, survives her husband.

February 25, 1963.

Pope John XXIII—See under **John.**

A. E. Popham, C.B., F.B.A., formerly Keeper of the Department of Prints and Drawings in the British Museum, died on December 8, 1970, at the age of 81.

Arthur Ewart Popham was born in Plymouth on March 22, 1889, and was educated at Dulwich, at University College, London, and at King's College, Cambridge, where he came to know many of the younger generation of the "Bloomsbury Group" and their friends. He took his degree in the Classical Tripos in 1911 and in the following year joined the staff of the British Museum Print Room, where he remained, except for the period of the First World War in which he served with the R.N.A.S. and the R.A.F., until his retirement in 1954, becoming Deputy Keeper in 1933, and in 1945 Keeper of the Department in succession to A. M. Hind.

Popham was one of the most respected scholars of his time in the field of Old Master drawings. Perceptive, scrupulous and erudite, he combined a fastidious taste and a balanced critical appreciation of aesthetic quality and historical evidence with a very wide acquaintance with the whole range of western graphic art. His work on Italian drawings forms the major part of his achievement, but in the years following the first war his studies were largely devoted to the early Netherlandish schools.

FLEMISH DRAWINGS

In 1926 he published a brief but valuable general study of the *Drawings of the Early Flemish School*, followed in 1932 by his first official publication, the exemplary catalogue of the Museum's Fifteenth and Sixteenth-Century Dutch and Flemish drawings.

By this time, however, he had catalogued the drawings in the Burlington House Italian exhibition of 1930—a superb selection of the greatest achievements of Italian draughtsmanship—and soon afterwards was invited by T. Fitzroy Fenwick to compile a catalogue (issued privately in 1935) of the large and miscellaneous collection of drawings, mostly by the secondary Italian masters of the sixteenth and seventeenth centuries, formed by the celebrated bibliophile Sir Thomas Phillipps. Thus when, on the outbreak of war in 1939, the British Museum's Italian drawings were evacuated under his charge to the University Library at Aberystwyth, Popham was well equipped to lay the foundation of the long-projected Italian catalogue. In this he greatly benefited by the presence in Aberystwyth, at various times during the war years, of three of the most distinguished scholars then active in the Italian field, the late Johannes Wilde, the late Frederic Antal, and Philip Pouncey, to all of whom he made generous acknowledgment in the preface to his Windsor catalogue.

LEONARDO MONOGRAPH

The fruits of Popham's wartime activity were a monograph on the drawings of Leonardo (1946) followed in 1949 by a catalogue of the important collection of Fifteenth and Sixteenth-

Century Italian drawings in the Royal Library at Windsor (published jointly with Wilde who had undertaken the section dealing with Michelangelo) and in 1950 by one, written in collaboration with Pouncey, of the Fourteenth and Fifteenth-Century Italian drawings in the British Museum; a work which set entirely new standards of thoroughness and completeness in the technique of cataloguing drawings, and which was also much praised for the admirable moderation and balance with which controversial points of attribution were discussed, and the conclusiveness with which many of them were finally settled.

Popham's particular interest was in the Sixteenth-century School of Parma, and it was to this that his later studies were chiefly dedicated. In 1953 he published a monograph on the drawings of Parmigianino, and in 1957 another, more elaborate and detailed in scope, on the hitherto confused and unexplored subject of the drawings of Correggio. In this notable work—his most important single contribution to the history of Italian art—he scrutinized and sifted the great mass of drawings attributed over the centuries to Correggio and established for the first time a definitive basis for this important aspect of his activity.

PARMA SCHOOL

His catalogue of drawings by artists of the Sixteenth-century School of Parma in the British Museum, completed in draft before his retirement but later extensively revised, appeared in 1967, and in 1970 he completed the great corpus of the drawings of Parmigianino to which he had devoted his last years.

The chief acquisition of the Printroom during Popham's Keepership was that of the Phillipps-Fenwick Collection of some 2,000 drawings, secured in 1946 through the generosity of an anonymous benefactor and after lengthy negotiations, involving much patient diplomacy on Popham's part. Single drawings which he acquired included fine examples of Leonardo, Hieronymus Bosch, Correggio, Raphael and Rembrandt, and he was also instrumental in securing a large and carefully chosen group of engravings from the Liechtenstein Collection—a wise and far-sighted purchase at a time when prints were still out of fashon and often neglected even by scholars.

In 1960 he was invited to succeed the late A. P. Oppé as European adviser on the purchase of drawings for the National Gallery of Canada. In 1965 he produced, in collaboration with Miss Kathleen Fenwick, the Gallery's Curator of Prints and Drawings, a catalogue of the European (other than British) drawings in the collection.

With the open-mindedness and modesty of the true scholar Hugh Popham (as he was always known to his friends) combined absolute integrity of mind and great generosity and kindness of heart. Even as an undergraduate he had a very quiet, seemingly depressed manner; and this, combined with his slow, rather drawling voice, gave those who did not know him a misleading impression of melancholy. His manner with strangers could be shy and reserved, but his friends knew him as a genial, at times even convivial companion, with a gently ironic appreciation of the ludicrous and a vein of dry, disillusioned wit—"cynical" would be too strong a term—the effect of which was enhanced by his way of speaking; and which occasionally, and very discreetly, he permitted to enliven some passage of abstruse argument or exposition in his writing.

He was twice married. First in 1912 to Brynhild, daughter of Lord Olivier, by whom he had two sons and a daughter, and secondly in 1926 to Rosalind, daughter of Sir Hamo Thornycroft, R.A.

December 9, 1970.

Cole Porter died on October 15, 1964, at the age of 71. He was one of the most distinguished survivors among the great generation of American popular song writers who came to prominence in the early 1920s, and was unique among them in his double eminence as composer and lyric-writer.

Where Cole Porter gained in the inevitable competition of popular composers for the ear of the public was in his extraordinary combination of abilities as both composer and lyric-writer. Simply as a musician Gershwin was undeniably his superior in lyrical invention and technical resource, while just as a lyric-writer he never quite equalled Lorenz Hart, but as a good second to these in their respective fields, he must be placed on the merits of his combined achievement, far in advance of any other single man in popular music both by the standard of public approval and in the esteem of fellow musicians, "classical" as well as popular. Many of his songs have become part of the folklore of the modern world.

He was born on June 9, 1893, at Peru, Indiana, and, coming of a prosperous and distinguished family, did not have to undergo any of the picturesque early hardships which usually form part of the American composers' success stories, though he did a characteristically exotic touch to the story of his early life by enlisting in the French Foreign Legion in 1917 after a distinguished but fairly conventional academic career which included periods at Yale and Harvard (first in the Law School and later in the Music).

Before embarking on his short-lived military career, however, he had in 1916 contributed songs to the stage musical *See America First*, and though he did not heed this title's admonition, settling in Paris in 1919, his interest in popular song writing was thoroughly aroused, so that his first action after the war was to enrol in d'Indy's harmony and counterpoint classes at the Schola Captorum to improve his musical technique (he was one, incidentally, of the few song-writers of his generation who could read and write music without difficulty). His passion for France and all things French remained constant throughout his life, so that it perhaps is not surprising that among the first musicals he wrote on his return to America were *Paris* (1928) and *Fifty Million Frenchmen* (1929)—in fact, even among his very latest scores at least three—*Can Can*, *Silk Stockings*, and *Les Girls*—were written for books set in Paris.

Throughout his career Cole Porter was enormously prolific, and the list of his most famous and best-loved songs extends in time from the early 1920s to the late 1950s, but perhaps his most exciting and productive period came during the 1930s, when popular taste was perfectly suited to the civilized, astringent wit of his lyrics and the harmonic and rhythmic sophistications of his music, while in such stars as Gertrude Lawrence and Fred Astaire he found ideal interpreters, whose natural elegance and style provided the perfect counterparts to his own. From these years date such admirable scores as *The Gay Divorce*, *Nymph Errant* and *Anything Goes* (the last arguably his finest show, including such classic songs as "Anything Goes", "I Get a Kick out of You", "All Through the Night" and "You're the Top") and such inescapable popular "standards" as "Begin the Beguine", "Night and Day", "Love for Sale", "Let's Do It", "Easy to Love", and "In the Still of the Night". At this time too the leading characteristics of his style—the infinitely resourceful variations on the basic formula of the list which produce many of the most delightful touches in his lyrics, the weakness amounting almost to a passion for insidious beguine rhythms which haunts his music—became firmly established,

During the war years a newly robust and extrovert style of popular composition came into vogue—a fashion, one would have supposed, unsympathetic if not quite inimical to Cole Porter's most characteristic virtues, yet at this time he wrote at least one of his most popular songs, summing up the feeling of the moment in the simple imperative "Don't Fence Me In", as well as, on a rather more sophisticated level, turning his hand to Orson Welles's spectacular and ill-fated stage version of *Around the World in Eighty Days*, and the famous revue *The Seven Lively Arts*, in which his "Every Time We Say Goodbye (I Die a Little)" rubbed shoulders with ballet music by Stravinsky and seemed not a whit put out by the comparison.

Kiss Me Kate in 1949 brought him another major hit in the theatre, and the book, part-adaptation, part-parody of *The Taming of the Shrew*, gave full rein to his gifts of parody and burlesque (sometimes a little above his audience's head, it seems, since the song which everyone knows from the show "Wunderbar" was intended as a parody of Viennese operatta, but achieved great success as a serious romantic duet). His later shows perhaps showed occasional signs of strain: *Can Can* had possibly the weakest score he had composed since very early days, and it is difficult not to see the hit-song of his film *High Society*, "True Love", as a deliberate concession to the more mawkish side of public taste, but *Silk Stockings*, a stage musical based on *Ninotchka*, allowed a little more acid to be mixed with the honey with results almost wholly beguiling. The pantomime *Aladdin*, for which he wrote the music and lyrics, was put on in London in 1959.

His wife, Linda Lee Thomas, whom he married in 1919, died in 1954.

October 17, 1964.

Lord Portman, the 8th viscount, died in the Westminster Hospital, London, on November 3, 1967, at the age of 64.

Gerald William Berkeley Portman was a director of the Alliance Assurance Company, and lived at Burley House, Beaconsfield, Buckinghamshire. When he succeeded his father in September, 1948, the Portman estates were the second largest property in London, covering 190 acres. They included five squares, Portman, Bryanston, Manchester, Montagu and Dorset.

Death duties from the estate of the 7th Viscount Portman were the largest known to that time.

In 1950, Portman sold his 3,800 acre estate in Dorset. The family home since the seventeenth century, it was sold to the Commissioners of Inland Revenue for his father's death duties. Two years later he sold 26 acres of the Portman London estate, including 221B Baker Street, the legendary home of Sherlock Holmes. Later that year he sold more of the estate in St. Marylebone to help pay the death duties, which were £7,582,119. In 1955 a Portman family trust valued at about £4m. was created. Portman, who had no children, leaves a widow. His heir is his nephew, Edward Henry Berkeley Portman.

November 4, 1967.

Eric Portman, who died at his home in Cornwall on December 7, 1969, at the age of 66, was an actor of strong individuality whose work ranged from Shakespeare and Shaw to modern plays as diverse as *White Cargo*, Robert Bolt's *Flowering Cherry* and Eliot's *The Elder Statesman.* He was, too, a very effective actor on both the cinema and television screens.

Eric Portman was born in Yorkshire on July 13, 1903, and educated at Rishworth School. For a time he worked as a shop assistant in a store in Leeds and consoled his leisure with membership of the Halifax Opera Society, but in 1923 he joined Robert Courtneidge's Shakespeare Company while it was playing at the Grand Theatre, Leeds, played his first speaking part with the company at the Victoria Theatre, Sunderland in 1924, and reached London, as Antipholus of Syracuse, in *The Comedy of Errors*, in the same year.

In 1925 he moved from classical drama to win a great success as Worthing, in *White Cargo*, and exploited his new interest in modern plays until 1927, when he joined the Old Vic Company, for which his parts included Romeo, Charles Surface, Edmund in *King Lear*, Arcité in *The Two Noble Kinsmen* and Strength, in *Everyman*.

Portman's success as Undershaft, in Shaw's *Major Barbara*, at Wyndham's Theatre in 1929 first revealed his understanding of Shavian drama, which provided a splendid outlet for his gift of quiet, remorseless energy. Between then and the outbreak of war he played leading roles in a remarkable number of plays, both new and classical, in England and New York. The unrelenting determination he could give to any role capable of accepting it was exploited in a number of wartime films—*49th Parallel*, *One of Our Aircraft is Missing*, *We Dive at Dawn*, and *Millions Like Us*.

Not all the many roles he played in London and New York after the war until early 1968, when ill-health forced him to retire while playing in Galsworthy's *Justice*, were able to give him the stimulus his gifts needed. It will, however, not be easy to forget his playing of the crippled priest in Graham Greene's *The Living Room*, or Crocker-Harris, the disappointed schoolmaster of Rattigan's *The Browning Version* and Major Pollock in the same dramatist's *Separate Tables*. In the New York production of Robert Bolt's *Flowering Cherry* his playing of the pathetic, self-deluding Bob Cherry was, critics noted, as fine as any of his earlier work.

Portman brought to all his major roles a quality of relentless, driving integrity. The ruthless U-Boat commander of *49th Parallel*, making his way across Canada to the still-neutral United States, was typical of his power to raise the audience's admiration for courage and determination through a role that was never amiable.

He gave a moving performance as an aging criminal in *Deadfall*, his last film, which was shown in London in 1968.

December 8, 1969.

Stephen Potter, the author who invented Gamesmanship, Lifemanship, One-Upmanship and Supermanship, died on December 2, 1969, at the age of 69.

Potter invented, as Fowler's *Modern English Usage* acknowledges, "the conceit of making facetious formations by treating manship as the suffix". His humorous ploys were based on the pregnant phrase: "If you're not one up (Bitzleisch) you're one down (Rotzleisch)"—and the art of one-upness was once described as projecting a fifth-column microbe from one's own mind into that of the other person—the eternal opponent—causing him to "feel that something has gone wrong, however slightly". Lifemanship was illustrated in the film *School for Scoundrels*, in which Alastair Sim played the part of the Principal of the College at Yeovil, and Ian Carmichael the eager student who routs Terry Thomas on the tennis court by means of Gamesmanship tactics, and courts Miss Janette Scott successfully by standard Woomanship tactics.

Few writers have achieved the distinction of devising a suffix which, though subject to infinite variations, has created an entirely new concept. It was in March, 1931, in a letter to Francis Meynell regarding a forthcoming tennis match against two difficult opponents, that Stephen Potter first used the word Gamesmanship. The suffix did not come into common use, however, until after the war when his deadpan treatises and his B.B.C. programmes enlarged the concept from the Art of Winning Games Without Actually Cheating to such wider forms as Lifemanship and One-Upmanship. Thereafter it spread throughout the English-speaking world until, in the time of Foster Dulles it achieved international status in the form of Brinkmanship.

Potter was born on February 1, 1900 and was educated at Westminster School and Merton College, Oxford. After taking honours in English Language and Literature in 1923, he worked for a time as secretary to the dramatist, Henry Arthur Jones, until in 1926 he was appointed Lecturer in English Literature at London University. During the next few years, after the obligatory first novel (*The Young Man*, 1929), he published studies of D.H. Lawrence and S. T. Coleridge, and edited the letters of Mrs. Coleridge (*Minnow Among Tritons*, 1934) and the admirable *Nonesuch Coleridge*. He summed up his experiences as a lecturer in English Literature in *The Muse in Chains*, 1937. He was dramatic critic of *The New Statesman* in 1945.

In the following years he joined the B.B.C. as a writer-producer, and specialized in literary programmes: to which were added, during the war, a number of war documentaries. After the war ended, the creation of a separate Features Department and the advent of the Third Programme gave him fresh opportunities, happily symbolized by his jeu d'esprit (with Joyce Grenfell) "How to Listen", which initiated the Third Programme in September, 1946.

The "How" series, which began during the war as occasional semi-serious programmes on techniques, was transformed, after one hilarious programme by Potter and Joyce Grenfell, into a new radio form which proved highly successful. "How to be Good at Games" was broadcast in 1947, the year that saw the publication of *Gamesmanship*, and was later followed by the *Lifesmanship* lectures on the B.B.C. and by other published works in the same vein. Other notable achievements in broadcasting were the series of "New Judgments" of which he was the originator and editor; several outstanding Professional Portraits; and the broadcasting of Professor Nevill Coghill's version of *The Canterbury Tales*.

In 1956 he published *Potter on America*; *Supermanship* appeared in 1958; his autobiography *Steps To Immaturity* in 1959; *Anti-Woo* in 1965; and *The Complete Golf Gamesmanship* in 1968.

After leaving the B.B.C., Potter became for a time a magazine editor (*The Leader*); but he preferred the life of a free-lance, and, no less, that of a clubman. His friends at the Saville and the Garrick will miss his agreeable and stimulating company.

His first marriage to the painter Mary Potter was dissolved in 1955; he later married Mrs. Heather Jenner. By his first marriage he leaves two sons, and one by his second.

December 3, 1969.

Francis Poulenc, the French composer, who died on January 30, 1963, in Paris aged 64, was described by one authority as a musical personality unique in musical history.

Beginning as one of Les Six, who after the First World War were in reaction alike from romance and the ultra-refinement of the French impressionist composers, he became as he grew older increasingly concerned with serious themes. Yet the light touch, the feeling for unusual textures, the easy melodic invention of the incomparable musical jester were continued *mutatis mutandis* into the religious music, which was written even before the German occupation of France in 1940 had put a filament of steel into his large compositions. The wit who had gone to the circus, the fairground, and the music-hall for inspiration later on tackled surrealist texts and chamber music, not to mention the tragedy of the opera *Dialogues des Carmelites* (composed for La Scala and first produced—and warmly received—there in 1957 and produced at Covent Garden the following year). His music is very French but it is also very personal: it has its roots firmly in traditional harmony but was modern in feeling at least until the iconoclasts of the fifties made it seem by comparison old-fashioned.

FAVOURED INTERPRETER

He was born in Paris on January 7, 1899, received a classical education and no systematic musical training. He learnt the piano, however, from Ricardo Vines and became an accomplished pianist, rather as his friend Benjamin Britten has done. English audiences probably knew him well as the accompanist of the baritone Pierre Bernac, who is the favoured interpreter of his songs, as Peter Pears is of Britten's songs. He took composition lessons from Charles Koechlin but military service in 1918 interrupted his studies, so that he was largely self-taught. Even in 1918 some of his music was heard at a concert organized by Erik Satie and the charming "Mouvements perpetuels" for piano, which are played and enjoyed by amateurs everywhere, belong to the same year. Then came his association under Satie's influence with Les Six, out of which came settings of Apollinaire's *Bestiare* and Cocteau's *Cocardes*. The vein of freakishness, irony, and parody was continued in *Les Biches*, which he wrote for Diaghilev's Russian Ballet in 1923, and on into the extravaganza *Les Mamelles de Tiresias* (also Apollinaire), which is as late as 1944. In the piano music and the songs something nearer to sentiment and a very marked charm is stirred into the mixture.

His miniatures, such as the suite for piano, *Les Sources de Nazelle*, are fanciful in the way that Couperin's suites capture the charm and picturesqueness of pretty titles. There are more substantial keyboard works, including a concerto for two pianos, a concerto for harpsichord and a concerto for organ. This last was played at the opening recital of the Festival Hall Organ. The cheerful inconsequence of styles in the first was once realized in the same hall by the composer and Britten as duettists and its attractions have made it relatively popular in this country. Poulenc mixed the sweet with the tart, the lyrical with the humorous—he set *Barbar the Elephant*—the chic with the simple, in a way entirely his own. He was a perfectly serious musician, but some of what he did most conscientiously was flippant, funny or gaily entertaining. His choral work was mostly religious and includes a Mass, an *Exultate Deo*, *Stabat Mater* and other motets for unaccompanied choir. His chamber music was mostly for wind, though he wrote a string quartet in 1946.

But in the final reckoning he was above all a song writer and in his songs these diverse traits can find their several expressions in a field that is bounded by the sentiment of Massenet, the lyricism of Fauré and the wit of Ravel. From it he produced one set of songs after another for more than 40 years—Apollinaire and Vilmorin were his favourite poets—and in them is mirrored a very sincere and very likable musical personality.

January 31, 1963.

Dr. Roscoe Pound, who died on July 1, 1964, at Cambridge, Mass., at the age of 93, was considered by some to be the greatest living authority on law, even though he never took a legal degree. Both jurist and educator, he was a leading exponent of the reform of judicial administration. He was a versatile man with interests ranging from botany to baseball, and from Lucretius to linguistics. He knew 10 languages, among them Sanscrit and Chinese.

A portly man with a bushy white moustache, and a prodigious memory, Pound was an institution at Harvard University, where he was dean of the law school from 1916 to 1936. In 1937 he became Harvard's first "university professor" with licence to teach in any faculty of the university. He spent the next decade lecturing on a wide variety of subjects but remaining always accessible to students, who loved him for his kindly nature.

A native of Nebraska—and he remained a Middle Westerner all his life—Pound was born on October 27, 1870, at Lincoln, where his father was a judge. His mother, who came from New York, taught him at home because she was not satisfied with the local public schools. Her teaching was so successful that he entered the University of Nebraska before he was 14 and took a degree in botany when he was 18.

In 1889 Pound went to Harvard to study law but could not afford to stay more than a year. Returning to Nebraska he was admitted to the Bar in 1890 without a law degree and he practised at Lincoln for some years.

DEAN OF LAW SCHOOL

However he was more interested in the pedagogic side of his profession and became successively assistant professor of law and dean of the law department at Nebraska University.

In addition to his teaching duties he also directed the botanical survey of the state and edited *The Flora of Nebraska*. An honour in which he took particular pride was the naming after him of a rare lichen: *Roscoepoundia*.

In 1910 Pound was summoned to Harvard, to begin what has been described as one of the most illustrious law professorships of all time. Within three years he was given the coveted Carter professorship of law, and in another three years he was made dean of the Harvard law school. He became a prolific writer, with a score of weighty works to his credit, among them his great five-volume work on *Jurisprudence*.

Pound retired as dean after 20 years in the post, but stayed at Harvard as a "roving professor" until 1946 when he went to China on the invitation of the Nationalist Government to reorganize its judicial system. He had two long spells in China, during which he learnt the language and finished the task entrusted to him. He finally returned to the United States in 1949 highly critical of his country's China policy. He charged the United States with aiding the communists in putting pressure on the Nationalist regime.

His "theory of social interests" did much to change American concepts of law and exerted a strong influence on New Deal social and economic reforms. Later, however, he became a critic of the New Deal and a strong opponent of the welfare state which he called "the service state". He said its advocates refused to "look all the facts in the face" and had got perilously close to the Marxist doctrine of "to each according to his needs, from each according to his ability".

July 3, 1964.

With the death of **Dora Powell** (Mrs. Richard Powell) on May 23, 1964, at East Grinstead at the age of 90 one of the few remaining links with Elgar in his early days is snapped. She was Dorabella of the Enigma Variations.

Mrs. Powell was born Dora Penny, a daughter of the Rector of Wolverhampton, and she recalled first meeting Elgar in December, 1895, when "she had not left school very long". In 1936 she published her intimate recollections of the composer under the title *Edward Elgar: Memories of a Variation*, but after the passage of 10 years and the war she issued a second edition in which some matter that had discreetly been omitted was restored.

She has a chapter on the enigma that has defeated all commentators since the Variations were published in 1899. In it she confidently affirms that the other and larger theme that goes with it but is not played is a tune and not a concept, as some writers have desperately suggested. Her own husband at one time suggested that the tune might be in "Auld Lang Syne" and the theme friendship, which accords with the dedication "To My friends pictured within". But this has not gained acceptance and Mrs. Powell, although very close to Elgar when the Variations were being written, has not resolved Elgar's deliberate mystification. Her own Variation, it will be recalled, reproduces by a fluttering, stuttering figure on strings and woodwind a characteristic stammer of her speech in those days. Elgar borrowed her nickname from *Cosi fan tutte* and the fragrance of his friendship with the young girl who used to turn over his music for him at the piano comes from the pages of her book still 30 years after his death.

May 26, 1964.

Sir Maurice Powicke, who died on May 19, 1963, at the age of 83, was one of the greatest medieval historians ever produced in Britain. His writing added profoundly to understanding of the springs of action and thought in the Middle Ages. His personality inspired younger men and women over more than half a century. Scholarship was blended in him with a humanist delight in life. He will be remembered for the eager way in which he used a sharply cutting mind and for his kindliness and friendly charm.

Frederick Maurice Powicke was born at Alnwick on June 16, 1879. The son of a Congregational minister, the Rev. F. J. Powicke, a skilled historian and the principal authority on Richard Baxter, the Puritan divine, he inherited from his father much of his interest in religious thought and his independence of religious outlook. The elder Powicke having been transferred to Hatherlow near Manchester, the boy was sent to the Stockport Grammar School, then to Owens College, Manchester, the first constituent of the old Victoria University, where the influence of T. F. Tout and of his colleague James Tait (then responsible for ancient history) was making itself felt in the nascent history school—never, as Powicke later pointed out, in early days exclusively a preserve of medievalists. He took a first class in history during the summer of 1899, and passed from Manchester to Balliol College, Oxford, to repeat the performance in the Modern History School during 1903. From 1902 (a year before he left Balliol) till 1905 he was Langton Fellow at Manchester, a position which gave him facilities for his first major piece of research on the history of Normandy in the twelfth and early thirteenth century. One of his external examiners at Manchester had been J. M. Mackay, who secured him for Liverpool as assistant lecturer during 1905–6. In 1906 Powicke returned to Manchester as an Assistant Lecturer in the History Department and was there till 1908, when Merton College elected him a Fellow. He was in continuous residence there for the next year while he was at work on his *Loss of Normandy*. In 1909, when barely 30, he accepted the Chair of Modern History at Belfast.

MANCHESTER SCHOOL

Powicke was by nature and training a Manchester historian. He had both the flair for discovering from the original records how government worked, the facts of day-to-day administration, and an interest in the history of ideas that might be expected from the university of Henry Roscoe, A. S. Peake, and Samuel Alexander. Actually he had been appointed Lecturer in Economic History at Manchester the year in which he elected to go to Belfast. Norman and Angevin history in the twelfth century was his first main field; each year during his tenure of the Belfast chair he published in periodicals excellent articles and reviews on Anglo-Norman judicial and military administration; but he took his later history seriously, as some of his reviews and his little book on *Bismarck and the Origin of the German Empire* (1914) show; and afterwards (1941) he thought enough of his study on the Reformation in England to reprint it from Mr. Eyre's *European Civilization: its Origin and Development*. His first major work, *The Loss of Normandy (1189–1204); Studies in the history of the Angevin Empire* appeared at the Manchester Press in 1913 (a second edition appeared in 1961). In it he followed, to some extent, the line which C. H. Haskins was taking at Harvard; in a deliberate attempt to examine the reactions of Norman upon English studies he was trying, he says, "to point out some ways in which the history of England under Henry II and his sons is modified and assisted by an examination of Norman evidence".

After this notable beginning it was no surprise that in 1919 Powicke should have been recalled as Professor of Medieval History to his old university at Manchester, where with Tout, Unwin, James Tait, and A. G. Little he added to the prestige of the Honours School by his writing and his conduct of his own special subject class. He was now advancing well into the thirteenth century, although the Rylands paper on Ailred of Rivaulx and his biographer Walter Daniel (he was to edit Daniel's Ailred in the Medieval Classics series, 1950) showed his interest in the Cistercian north of the twelfth. The new studies began with Stephen Langton, the subject of the Ford lectures of 1928, and extended into the period of baronial reform and rebellion, 1258–85, his articles and reviews on which were the precursors of his main works on Henry III and Edward I.

NEW WORK

If the two chapters in the *Cambridge Medieval History*, vol. VI (1929), "England: Richard and John" and "The Reigns of Philip Augustus and Louis VIII of France" admirably consolidated his earlier researches, the new work on Langton and on the ideas behind the baronial movement were a profound and searching examination of the moral and legal bases of English political development in the thirteenth century.

In both, his realism and his critical use of record and narrative sources foreshadowed the greater work to come.

When Tout, his colleague and former teacher, retired from Manchester in 1925 Powicke became the effective head of the department and was fortunate in having among his research pupils medievalists like R. F. Treharne, N. B. Lewis and Beryl Smalley. He did not reign for long. In 1928 Powicke accepted the Regius Professorship at Oxford, and began the final and most fruitful period of his life. To Oxford he went from a centre of advanced historical study to find the History School, so far as the actual curriculum went, much as it was in 1900. He felt that there was room within the tradition of the school for a closer relation between the study of the undergraduate in his last year and advanced study; and that there was a more immediate need for a closer organization of advanced teaching backed up by closer cooperation and agreement, upon a common policy, between the supervisors of advanced students. To the development of these studies his tenure of the chair made a noteworthy contribution. When on his retirement in 1947 his friends presented him with a volume of essays written in his honour, they testified to the effect of teaching as "an influence above the hatreds and distractions of our present time". A master of atmosphere (never consciously pursued) his writing and his lectures often displayed an imaginative vein, which sometimes mystified his more pedestrian colleagues.

PROLIFIC

His penetrating and subtle mind is reflected in the prolific output of his later Oxford years; notably in *The Christian Life in the Middle Ages and other Essays* (1935), the Riddell Memorial lectures which he called *History, Freedom and Religion* (1938), and *Medieval England* (Home University Library, 1931). The period is notable for the studies in university history which were to culminate in the new edition (with A. B. Emden) of Rashdall's *Medieval Universities* (1939). Already in 1931 Powicke had published *The Medieval Books of Merton College*, his study of the growth of a notable theological and philosophical library, of the donations it received and of the way in which its contents were circulated to, and read by, the medieval college. This was part of the discipline that underlay his re-handling of Rashdall. He decided not to rewrite any of the text, but to prefix a critical introduction, which is a model of its kind, and to make corrections and additions by bracketed foot-notes. The work on universities did not deter him from his main task, to write anew the history of the reigns of Henry III and Edward I. and this was accomplished in two stages. The cartoons for the picture were drawn, so to speak, in *Henry III and the Lord Edward* (1947); the finished work was the thirteenth-century volume of the *Oxford History of England* (1953, second edition 1962). He also published two volumes of essays and papers: *Ways of Medieval Life and Thought* (1950); and *Modern Historians and the Study of History* (1955).

Powicke was knighted in 1946. He was an honorary doctor of many universities, including Caen and Harvard, where he had lectured at the Tercentenary Conference of Arts and Sciences (1937). His contacts with American scholars were of the closest. At one period he spent some months working upon the Hastings manuscripts in the Huntington Library. The *Institut de France* made him a Foreign Associate (1951) and the Royal Irish Academy an Honorary Member in 1949. He was an Honorary Fellow of Merton from 1932, of Balliol since 1939 and of Oriel since 1947.

He married in 1909 Susan Irvine Martin, daughter of Dr. T. M. Lindsay, D.D., of Glasgow. They had one son, who died in 1936, and two daughters, one of them the devoted wife of the late Professor Richard Pares. Their gracious and friendly hospitality, whether in Fallowfield or in Oxford, and the constant and eager interest they showed in their friends all over the world are not likely to be forgotten: at their cottage in Eskdale they seemed a kindly and essential part of Lakeland.

May 21, 1963.

Lieutenant-General Sir Henry Pownall, K.C.B., K.B.E., D.S.O., M.C., died on June 9, 1961, at the age of 73.

His earlier career (including his service in the Four Years War) was bound up with the artillery, but in his middle forties he branched out into wider fields as Deputy Secretary of the Committee of Imperial Defence; and at 51 he was Director of Military Operations and Intelligence at the War Office. Over and above his reputation as a sound strategist and a gallant soldier, Pownall was well known for his wide reading in military history and theory; and had a deep knowledge of military law.

He gave great assistance in military matters to Sir Winston Churchill in the preparation of *The Second World War*.

Henry Royds Pownall was born on November 19, 1887, second son of Charles Assheton Whately Pownall, of Blackheath, who built the principal Japanese railways. As an infant of three, Henry was taken out by his mother to Japan, and learnt the language concurrently with English during a stay of five years, after which he was sent home for preparatory schooling. Later he went to Rugby (where his father had been educated) and from there to the Royal Military Academy, Woolwich, whence he was commissioned into the R.F.A. in 1906, passing out among the first 15 students of his year. From 1906 to 1914 he was at various stations in England and India, and his first foreign service was with the R.H.A. at Lucknow.

From 1914 to 1919 Pownall served continuously in France and Belgium, acting as brigade major to the Royal Artillery, 17th Division, in 1917–18. He was twice mentioned in dispatches, and was awarded the M.C. and D.S.O., finishing the war with the rank of major. In 1924–25 he was Brigade Major at the School of Artillery, and from 1926 to 1929 G.S.O.2 at the Staff College, Camberley.

IMPERIAL DEFENCE

In 1931 he won a bar to his D.S.O. in action on the North-West Frontier of India. Thereafter Pownall began work with the Committee of Imperial Defence, to which he was successively Military Assistant Secretary, Senior Assistant Secretary, and Deputy Secretary (1933–36). From 1936 to 1938 he served as Commandant of the School of Artillery, Larkhill, with the rank of brigadier.

In 1938 Pownall was promoted to the first of what was to prove a long series of highly responsible appointments, becoming Director of Military Operations and Intelligence at the War Office. This appointment crowned a remarkable series of promotions and represented a jump of more than a hundred places in seniority; moreover, in the five years preceding the outbreak of war Pownall was promoted no less than five times. On the outbreak of the Second World War he went to France with the B.E.F. as Chief of the General Staff; and his admirable work during the Battle of France earned him mention in dispatches and a K.B.E. When the Local Defence Volunteer Forces were formed, Pownall, as Inspector-General, was their first chief; and though he shortly gave place to General Eastwood—to the annoyance of Mr. Churchill, who had thought that a man of Pownall's reputation at their head would hearten the volunteers—when nominated C-in-C. British forces in Northern Ireland, he was still able to oversee the work of the Home Guard while acting as Vice-Chief of the Imperial General Staff in 1941.

TO FAR EAST

In November, 1941, General Sir Alan Brooke replaced General Sir John Dill as C.I.G.S. and in the accompanying reshuffle it was announced that Pownall had been selected for a special appointment. The nature of this was not made public until over a month later when the War Office announced that he had arrived in Singapore and assumed the appointment of C-in-C. Far East in succession to Air Chief Marshal Sir Robert Brooke-Popham.

In January, 1942, he became Chief of Staff to General Wavell in the South-West Pacific Command; as Sir Winston Churchill has written:—"But for this he would have been called upon to bear the terrible load which fell upon the shoulders of General Percival". He was promoted Lieutenant-General, and then in April took over the Ceylon Command. This he held until March, 1943, when he became C-in-C. Persia-Iraq (succeeding Sir Henry Maitland Wilson) and later Chief of Staff to Lord Louis Mountbatten, Supreme Allied Commander, South-East Asia Command. In November, 1944, ill-health obliged Pownall to relinquish the appointment and he retired from the Army in 1945. That year he was created K.C.B. From 1942 to 1952 he was Colonel Commandant, Royal Artillery.

He was appointed Chief Commissioner of the St. John Ambulance Brigade in 1947—in succession to General Sir Clive Liddell—Vice-Chancellor of the Order of St. John in 1950 and Chancellor a year later. He was chairman of Friary Meux Ltd. and a member of the committee of Lloyds Bank.

Pownall's service covered areas and periods of extreme military and political difficulties for British arms: but in the most difficult situations he was well known for his unruffled imperturbability. He had a first-class brain which was seen at its best in his Staff work.

CLEAR MIND

Quiet and precise in manner, he was an energetic worker who brought to the task in hand a clear, well-ordered mind. He was a thoughtful and careful strategist, who, having evolved his plan, explained it with force and clarity to his subordinates. From those under his command he expected an equal faculty for quick and precise exposition, but to each and all of them he was a quiet, courteous and sympathetic chief. He had a remarkable memory, and was a masterly writer of minutes and reports. Off duty Pownall's relaxations were skiing, fly-fishing and golf.

He was a conversationalist of delightful but unobtrusive wit.

He married in 1918 Lucy Louttit Gray, youngest daughter of William Henderson, of Aberdeen. She died in 1950.

June 10, 1961.

John Cowper Powys, who died on June 17, 1963, at Blaenau Festiniog at the age of 90, ranks with Hobbes, Landor, and Bernard Shaw among the longest-lived of English writers. He must also be considered one of the most prodigal and most versatile.

He began with two volumes of poetry as long ago as 1896 and 1899; his epic poem, *Lucifer*, written in 1905, was first published exactly half a century later. His work as a lecturer led him to literary criticism, his *Visions and Revisions* (1915) being followed at intervals by volumes of essays culminating in *The Pleasures of Literature* (1938) and the later, longer studies of *Dostoievsky* (1947) and *Rabelais* (1948). His lifelong speculations about the meaning of life inspired many volumes of philosophy, from *The Complex Vision* (1920) and *The Religion of a Sceptic* (1925), *A Philosophy of Solitude* (1933) and *The Art of Happiness* (1935), to *The Art of Growing Old* (1944) and *In Spite Of* (1953). Finally his philosophical speculations found artistic expression in the many huge novels by which he became most widely known, the greatest of which, *A Glastonbury Romance*, appeared in 1933.

Powys was the eldest of the II gifted children of the Rev. Charles Francis Powys by his marriage to Mary Cowper Johnson, whose family was allied with those of the poets Donne and Cowper. Among his brothers were Theodore Francis (1875–1953), the Dorset novelist; Llewelyn (1884–1939), the philosopher and essayist, whose life was an epic struggle against tuberculosis; and Albert Reginald (1881–1936), a distinguished architect. His eldest sister, Gertrude Mary Powys, was a portrait-painter; another sister, Marian Powys-Grey, became a world authority on old lace.

Powys was born on October 8, 1872, at Shirley in Derbyshire, but during his childhood his father's work as a clergyman took him first to Weymouth and then to Montacute, so that the Powys brothers belong almost equally to Dorset and Somerset. On leaving Corpus Christi College, Cambridge, he decided against entering the Church and seeking a means of livelihood least likely to interfere with his "secret life of imaginatized and poetized sensations", he became a university extension lecturer.

INSPIRED LECTURES

An inspired lecturer, so "full of life, full of beliefs, full of the power to communicate his abundance", he found enthusiastic audiences in the growing public of the United States hungry for culture. For 30 years from his first visit in 1904, he spent every winter in lecture tours that took him to every town of importance there. His business manager, G. Arnold Shaw, was also his first New York publisher.

Until the 1914–18 War prevented his summer visits to England, he was too busy talking to find time for writing, but the continual urging of his brother Llewelyn opened the flood-gates for the spate of books that flowed unabated throughout the latter half of his long life. His first novel, *Wood and Stone* (1915), showed the influence of Thomas Hardy, the earliest of his friends among eminent writers; his second, *Rodmoor* (1916), set in Norfolk, which was his mother's home, was a first attempt at interpretation of "all the feverish struggles, all the frantic wrestlings with the mystery of life" that supply the substance of all his novels, all his poetry, all his volumes of philosophy.

FAMILY COLLABORATION

His share in *Confessions of Two Brothers* (1916), written in collaboration with his brother Llewelyn, offers an introduction to his *Autobiography* (1934), which has been compared to Rousseau's *Confessions* in the candour of its self-revelation and itself supplies an introduction to the fullest understanding of the mind mirrored in his novels. For he was always an equally subjective and intensely imaginative writer, projecting something of his own experience into his characters; the reader of his novels has no sooner identified one character as a self-portrait, than he detects a different manifestation of the same ubiquitous consciousness emerging in another character. So, in *A Glastonbury Romance*, such diverse characters as John Crow and Johnny Geard, Sam Dekker and Owen Evans, each reflect some aspect of their creator.

Before Grant Richards published *Ducdame* in 1925, most of Powys's books were published only in America, where his genius was recognized for a decade before *Wolf Solent* in 1929 began establishment of his reputation in England. On its simultaneous publication in both countries in 1933, *A Glastonbury Romance* was acclaimed—in J. D. Beresford's words—as "one of the greatest novels in the world, to be classed with Tolstoy's *War and Peace*". In the following year, at the age of 62, Powys abandoned his lecturing career and returned to England to earn a living by his writing.

By his marriage in 1896 to Margaret Lyon he had an only son, Littleton Alfred, who became a priest and died in 1954. To his wife, who died in 1947, and son Powys had given a generous share of his income from lecturing, as well as his patrimony, and his means were modest. His novel, *Maiden Castle* (1936), was written in lodgings over a greengrocer's shop in Dorchester and, unable to find a suitable home in Dorset, he settled in a bungalow on the hill above Corwen—his home for 20 years before in 1955 he moved to a small granite cottage looking across to the mountains from Blaenau Festiniog.

A "WELSH ABORIGINAL"

So far from regarding the land of his remote Welsh ancestors as his adopted country, he described himself as a "Welsh aboriginal" in his essays, *Obstinate Cymric*, published at Carmarthen in 1947. His imaginative appreciation of the history and spirit of the Welsh people inspired two of his greatest novels, *Owen Glendower* (1941) and *Porius* (1951), the latter reconstructing the state of Britain after the Roman evacuation and conceiving the average man's problems in a world of disintegrating values to have been much the same as those of today. After *Porius* a year rarely passed without publication of a new work, and the products of his old age included a long romance of the Middle Ages, *The Brazen Head* (1956), little inferior to his finest work, and the results of his Homeric studies, *Atlantis* (1954) and *Homer and the Aether* (1959).

In 1962 the University of Wales conferred on him an honorary D.Litt.

Admirers came from all over the world to his modest cottage in North Wales, like pilgrims to a seer in his mountain fastness, to be impressed as much by his goodness as by his genius. He was particularly delighted when a great man little his junior, Augustus John, went to sketch the portrait reproduced in his *Letters to Louis Wilkinson* (1958), and when in 1958 the German novelist, Rolf Italiaander, personally presented him with the plaque awarded by the Hamburg Free Academy of Arts.

For many years a close companion of Powys was Miss Phyllis Playter, a charming and talented woman to whom several of his books are dedicated. He once described his faith as "an acceptance of our human life in the spirit of absolutely undogmatic ignorance". The Holy Grail of Arthurian romance—the heroine of *A Glastonbury Romance*—represented for him the elusive mystery of life, of which he wrote: "Whether we shall find the beyond-life of which it is a symbol when we perish, or whether we shall vanish with it into oblivion, we know not and perhaps will never know."

June 19, 1963.

Dr. Rajendra Prasad, first President of India and one of the last intimates of Gandhi, died on February 28, 1963, at Patna. He was 78.

He was born in the Saran district of Bihar on December 3, 1884, to a landowning family of modest but sufficient means. His upbringing was entirely orthodox; in his Hindi autobiography *Atmakatha*, written when he was imprisoned along with other Congress leaders from 1942 to 1944, he has left a charming account of how, at the age of 11, he went with a marriage procession to fetch a seven-year-old bride whom he had never seen. This child grew up to be his inseparable companion, a home-maker of the true Indian type, who lived to become first lady of the land, and to preside in Rashtrapati Bhawan, the President's official residence in New Delhi, over a large joint family of the orthodox Hindu pattern.

From a very early age Rajendra Prasad displayed acute intelligence, which, buttressed by an infallible, "card index" memory, won for him distinction after distinction in his educational career. As a student in Calcutta University he was outstanding even among his ablest contemporaries, and as soon as he had taken his M.A. he was given university teaching posts in economics and history. Before long legal studies claimed him; he took an LL.D. degree and taught on the staff of the Calcutta Law College. He was anxious to join an Inn of Court in England, but, with the modesty and self-effacement which were to characterize his entire career, he bowed to the orthodox scruples of his family and refrained from crossing "the black water". This sacrifice did not prevent him from building up a rising practice in the Calcutta High Court, and when Bihar became a separate province and a High Court was set up at Patna in 1916 he transferred his practice there. He founded and edited the *Bihar Law Weekly*, and began also to write for the press on topics connected with the Indian nationalist movement. He joined the Congress, and soon won a reputation as a potential leader. But when Gandhi went to Bihar in the middle of the 1914–18 War to head a campaign to remove the grievances of the peasant cultivators of indigo in the Champaran district Rajendra was captivated by the personality as well as by the ideas of the Mahatma.

ACTIVE JOURNALIST

When the first non-cooperation was inaugurated Rajendra gave up his practice and from that time onwards was one of Gandhi's most devoted and closest followers. He became an active journalist in the nationalist interest, writing for *Searchlight* in English and founding and editing the Hindi weekly *Desh* ("Country"). Although his writings in English were of a high quality, they hardly compare with his masterful Hindi prose. He became one of the foremost living exponents of Hindi, claiming for it preeminence as *the* national language of India.

Rajendra Prasad was no mere academic figure. He was a born administrator, a first-rate debater, and an excellent negotiator. While his own views were firmly grounded and clearly held, he had the knack of putting them forward without exciting antagonism even among those who differed from him most profoundly. Everyone who met him came to love him as well as to respect him; he became leader of the Congress organization throughout Bihar, then a member of the Working Committee, and finally thrice President of the Congress.

Like almost everyone who took part in Gandhi's successive campaigns of passive resistance, Rajendra underwent several short terms of imprisonment for breaches of the law. His only long term of imprisonment, ironically enough, came about through a turn of Congress policy with which he personally disagreed. He thought that the danger to India in the Second World War was a real one; and he would have preferred Congress to participate in the war effort instead of increasing Britain's difficulties. But when Congress decided in 1942 to throw all its influence into the campaign of "open rebellion", he was too loyal to sever his connexion with it, and, with the rest of the Working Committee, he was imprisoned for more than two years.

RELATIONS WITH JINNAH

He took an active part in the negotiations with the British Government which occupied the closing years of the war; and, unlike most of his colleagues, assigned far more than merely nuisance-value to the Muslim campaign for a separate Muslim homeland. He came to believe that partition might become inevitable, and pleaded for fairness and justice on both sides in effecting it. Orthodox Hindu though he was, he was well liked by the Muslims of Bihar, and his reputation with them helped him in preserving good relations with Jinnah and those who were working for Pakistan.

As Member for Food and Agriculture in Lord Wavell's interim national government, which was set up in 1946, Rajendra proved so successful that he retained the same portfolio after independence; but before long, to his own great surprise, he was elected to preside over the Constituent Assembly which for nearly three years was engaged in drafting the lengthy and complicated constitution for the new India. He was even more startled when, in 1950, he was unanimously elected President of the new sovereign democratic Republic of India, which was proclaimed on January 26. After the first general election, held in the spring of 1952, he was again chosen by an overwhelming majority of the new electoral college.

In the unaccustomed splendours of the former Viceroy s House, now renamed Rashtrapati Bhawan, Rajendra Prasad, or "Rajen Babu", as he was affectionately known all over India, bore himself with a simple, unaffected dignity which deeply moved foreigners as well as his own countrymen. He wore homespun and the Gandhi cap; he remained a strict vegetarian; his household was organized by his faithful companion of so many years, Shrimati Rajbansi Devi, on orthodox lines. Yet he never dreamed of begrudging the formalities which surrounded his high office; he was never remiss in discharging the ceremonial duties incumbent upon him as Head of State; his punctuality and his dignity set an example to all around him. He maintained his bodyguard in all its traditional splendour; he entertained, and received his guests with high-bred courtesy. On one thing, however, he did insist—his simple way of living made his official salary of Rs. 10,000 a month excessive and it was more than once substantially reduced on his urging.

HOW MUCH INFLUENCE?

Until the archives of the new Government of India are thrown open to the scrutiny of historians, no one can know the practical extent of the influence which Rajendra Prasad exerted over his famous, brilliant, but temperamental Prime Minister, Jawaharlal Nehru. A diverting cartoon in *Shankar's Weekly* (the *Punch* of India) published at the time of the visit of Queen Elizabeth II in 1961, showed Rajendra asking the Queen from behind his hand "And what exactly are your powers?" while Nehru looks suspiciously on from a distant corner. It is at least clear that in certain matters upon which Rajendra's mind was set—for example, the pride of place accorded to Hindi—the President got his own way against the half-hearted opposition of the Prime Minister. Moreover, when the second general election made it necessary to choose a President again in 1957, it was generally believed throughout India that Nehru would have preferred the then Vice-President, the famous philosopher Sarvapalle Radhakrishnan, as Head of State. But "Rajen Babu", insisting on standing again, was again triumphantly elected. On his retirement last year, however, he was succeeded by Dr. Radhakrishnan.

All the evidence at present available goes to show that Rajendra Prasad was no mere honorific cypher as President; and that in fact his intellectual powers, his knowledge of the world, and his administrative expertise combined to make him a very real factor in the shaping of his country's policies both at home and abroad. In this connexion, it may be significant that in 1958, 1959, and 1960 he began to follow the example of world-travelling set by other Heads of State. He paid state visits in turn to Japan, Burma, Ceylon, and the Soviet Union; and in 1961 accepted the Queen's invitation to visit Britain—although illness actually prevented his making the visit. Those who accompanied him on these occasions have said that the President enjoyed them greatly and made an admirable impression upon his widely differing hosts.

His wife died in September, 1962.

March 1, 1963.

Dr. E. J. Pratt, C.M.G. who died in a Toronto hospital on April 26, 1964, at the age of 81, was by far the most considerable of Canadian writers of this century. In his ambition he tried to reflect the greatness of his country, historical and geographical, and in his achievement he expressed the national genius more finely and richly than ever before. As a Newfoundlander he could be thought of as a recent Canadian citizen, but it was the country as a whole to which he gave his allegiance and took into his scope.

Edwin John Pratt was born in Western Bay, Newfoundland, on February 4, 1883, the son of a Methodist minister. He was educated in the High School at St. John's, before entering Victoria College in the University of Toronto. The seas and wildernesses of his native home were never forgotten and affected his whole imagination, leading him again and again to describe man locked in conflict with nature and to celebrate the virtues of courage, endurance and reverence, accompanied by a robust good humour. He was intended for the ministry, and after ordination he began to teach in the Department of Philosophy and Psychology in his college, taking a Ph.D. in 1916. While he was studying, he supported himself in several ways, among them by selling books on commission in Western Canada during the summer months, an experience which brought him into wide contact with rural life. In 1918 he married Viola Whitney, a devoted and warmly understanding companion. They had one daughter.

In 1920 he was appointed to the Department of English in Victoria College, where he taught until his retirement in 1953.

Pratt developed slowly as a poet and it was not until 1923 that his first volume of verse, *Newfoundland Verse*, appeared. He displayed his abilities fully three years later in *The Witches' Brew*, an exuberant extravaganza, marked by a delight in language and general high spirits. From then on his reputation was secure, and he confirmed and increased it by regular publications across the following 30 years. He issued a collected edition of his poems in 1944, several times reprinted and enlarged.

Many of Pratt's shorter poems are good, but it was in narrative verse only that he found the room he needed for the proper exercise of his powers. His poem on the loss of the *Titanic* (1935), for instance, is full of reminiscences of the dread Newfoundland seas, and the transition from the opening theme of gaiety on shipboard to the harrowing disaster is conducted with great subtlety and a mounting sense of impending doom. But the poem which rises above all the others is *Brébeus and his Brethren* (1940), an account of the martyrdom of the early Jesuit missionaries to Canada by the Iroquois.

Pratt will be remembered in future as a poet who maintained his own unusual and rewarding course in the face of all vagaries of fashion, but his many friends will think of him now as first of all a most generous and lovable man—as Ned Pratt, as he was always known. He liked nothing better than to give dinners and, after the excellent food and wine, to settle back and talk. He had a fund of anecdotes and stories, and as he told them the vitality and humour, which were so much a part of his poetry, made extraordinary the adventures which had once befallen him or his fellow Newfoundlanders. A neat tough figure, with an attractive voice, he could keep the attention of the most convivial audience. He was shrewd but quite without malice, even when he was on a favourite theme, the absurdities of literary celebrities from abroad. He was one poet of reputation whom it was not a disappointment to meet, and his death is a loss to Canadian letters which can ill be spared.

April 28, 1964.

George Ward Price, who died on August 22, 1961, called his autobiography, *Extra-special Correspondent*, and during his long association with the *Daily Mail* he had seen history in the making in all parts of the world. He was 75.

The son of the Rev. H. Ward Price, he was educated at St. Catharine's College, Cambridge, and was at first undecided as to what profession to enter. Encouraged by the publication of some of his articles in the schoolboys' magazine *The Captain*, he wrote to the Editor of the *Daily Mail* telling him of his intention to walk across Europe during the Long Vacation. He asked that the newspaper should pay his expenses in return for a series of descriptive articles.

His letter reached the editor, Thomas Marlowe, on the day that Lord Northeliffe had told him that there must be more young men in training for the future staff. Ward Price was told that the *Daily Mail* was not interested in his proposed journey but after an interview he accepted Marlowe's suggestion that he should become a reporter to be paid by results. Twelve months later he was given a five-year contract.

At the end of 1910 he was sent to Turkey to cover the first Balkan War and at the age of 26 he was appointed the *Daily Mail's* Paris Correspondent. He stayed in Paris until shortly before the outbreak of the First World War going to Vienna just after the assassination of the Archduke Ferdinand. He was back in the French capital when war was declared and in 1915 he was unanimously selected to represent the national newspapers represented in the Newspaper Proprietors Association on the

Dardanelles campaign. His account of the evacuation of Anzac and Suvla filled several columns of *The Times*. In 1917, feeling that the Salonika front had reached the stagnation stage he asked the Newspaper Proprietors Association to transfer him to some other sector of the Allied Front, was posted to the headquarters of the Italian Army at Udine and witnessed the nightmare retreat from Caporetto. When he was offered the C.B.E. at the end of the war he asked permission to decline it saying that until all the fighting men had been decorated there was no reason for decorating the war correspondents.

Ward Price covered the meetings in Paris at the beginning of 1919 to prepare the peace treaties and secured a four column interview with Marshal Foch. He attended the Cannes and Genoa conferences in the early months of 1922 and was at Lausanne in the following November.

In 1933 he accompanied the French Foreign Legion on its campaign in the Atlas Mountains in Morocco. He repeatedly interviewed Hitler and Mussolini, was present when Hitler entered Vienna, reported Chamberlain's visit to Berchtesgaden and was in the Sudetenland when German troops took it over. In July 1939 he published his book *Year of Reckoning* and by then had altogether abandoned his earlier faith in the prospects of conciliation.

In the Second World War he was in the first group of official war correspondents approved by the War Office, but after waiting for three idle months at Arras where there was nothing to record except the ordinary routine of military life on a peaceful footing he made a tour of south-eastern Europe which included Turkey, Rumania, Yugoslavia, and Italy. He did not become a war correspondent again until November, 1942, when he was allotted to the group of journalists who were to cover the North African campaign.

He was enjoying a quiet Sunday on the Muskoka Lawes in Ontario in 1950 when a message came that the South Korean Army was in full retreat pursued by 60,000 North Koreans and a hundred Russian-built tanks. He left at once for the scene of what he thought might well be the start of a third World War. He never married.

August 23, 1961.

Nancy Price, C.B.E. (Mrs. Charles Maude), who died on March 31, 1970, at the age of 90, will be remembered primarily as an actress and as the moving spirit of the Peoples' National Theatre in London, but she was also remarkable for the fullness and activity of her life as a whole and for her love and knowledge of the English countryside, its people, animals, and birds.

Born at Kinver, Worcestershire, on February 3, 1880, Lilian Nancy Bache Price was still a pupil at school at Malvern Wells when she went for an audition in Shakespeare with F. R. Benson, at the Theatre Royal, Birmingham. She joined his company at the end of her school term, on the same day as Henry Ainley from Yorkshire, in September, 1899, and first appeared in London in the following year, during Benson's season at the Lyceum. At His Majesty's in 1902 she was one of two young actresses—Constance Collier was the other—to make a success in Tree's production of Stephen Phillip's *Ulysses*, and in 1903 she had the satisfaction of earning a special "call" from the first-night audience of Pinero's *Letty*. In this, in the secondary part of a Cockney mannequin, she spoke with a drawl contracted from the aristocratic customers of a West End dressmaker: "every sentence rings phonographically true", wrote Max Beerbohm in his notice. A sense of humour such as was wanted here, a deflationary sense of humour, was probably the making of her as an almost first-rate actress, since it could also take the form of a stoical dryness, an anti-heroic heroism, that served her well in serious parts.

In her youth she must have had considerable grace at her command. Irving had wanted her to play Portia to his Shylock in his farewell season at Drury Lane, and in 1910, when the part of Ethel Irving's rival in Henri Bataille's *Dame Nature* needed someone who could look like a Parisian society-woman and wear "ruinously simple" gowns designed by Margaine-Lacroix, Nancy Price was chosen for it. It was afterwards taken over by Lilian Braithwaite.

FOUNDED THEATRE

Audiences certainly did not associate Nancy Price with society women as she grew older. She spent much time working for the blind and on tour during and immediately after the First World War, and though she was seen in notable plays by Pirandello, the chief part in the London Production of his *Naked* being created by her, by Ibsen, and by Zola in the course of the 1920s, the younger generation hardly discovered her until 1930. She then founded the People's National Theatre in conjunction with J. T. Grein and launched its first season at the Fortune.

Grein withdrew some months later, but Nancy Price as Honorary Director carried on the enterprise at various theatres for 11 seasons until 1950, producing and appearing in many of the plays. Of these *The Insect Play* was in her view the most significantly timely, and *Whiteoaks*, with herself playing the grandmother with her own parrot Boney perched on her shoulder, and *Lady Precious Stream* had the longest runs, but *The Silver Box* and *Nurse Cavell* with their anti-heroic heroines were perhaps the occasions of her finest performances.

NATURE LOVER

She was appointed C.B.E. in 1950 and retired from the stage and from films two years later. She was faithful thereafter to her other passion, for Nature, keeping more or less a diary of the course of this true love by editing and contributing to a periodical, successor to the former *People's Theatre Magazine*, called *Pedlar's Pack*.

This side of her life was the subject of nearly all her published books. They numbered over 20.

She had many pets—a common devotion to dogs had made it possible for her and Mrs. Patrick Campbell to work together in Ibsen in 1928, and she herself was a founder of the Council of Justice to Animals.

She married in 1907 the actor Charles Maude, grandson of Jenny Lind, the "Swedish Nightingale". He did not resume his career after serving in the Army in the First World War, and died in 1943. Miss Joan Maude and Miss Elizabeth Maude, the two daughters of the marriage, both adopted their mother's profession.

April 1, 1970.

The Duke of Primo de Rivera, a former Spanish ambassador to London, died in Madrid on May 8, 1964, after a long illness. He was 60.

He was a son of General Primo de Rivera, dictator of Spain from 1923 to 1930, and a brother of José Antonio de Rivera, founder of the Falangist party, who was executed at Alicante in 1936. The Duke, an original member of the Falange, took his degree at Madrid University and was later called to the Spanish Bar. Like his brother, he was arrested before the outbreak of the Civil War and was ultimately sent for trial at Alicante, where he was given a life sentence. He was released in 1939 when an exchange (in which the British Government played a significant part) was arranged and taken to safety by a British cruiser. On one occasion during his imprisonment the intervention of the British consul saved his life when a mob broke into the gaol in which he was lodged and murdered all the other political prisoners in reprisal for a bombing raid.

The Duke was Minister of Agriculture in 1941–45 and had been Civil Governor of Madrid.

He arrived in London in 1951 to take up his appointment as Spanish Ambassador, the first to be appointed since the reversal of the United Nations decision of 1946 to withdraw diplomatic missions in Madrid.

In January, 1958, he resigned and in November of that year Major Anthony Greville-Bell was granted a decree of judicial separation on the ground of the adultery of his wife, Mrs. Helen Rosemary Greville-Bell, with the Duke during 1957. In 1959 Mr. Greville-Bell was granted a decree *nisi*.

May 9, 1964.

Prince Farouk of Egypt—See under **Farouk**
Princess Andrew of Greece—See under **Greece.**

Princess Marina, Duchess of Kent, who died on August 27, 1968, at the age of 61, was greatly admired for her personal beauty, and respected and loved for her high sense of duty, her modest charm, her dignity in sorrow, and her devotion to her family.

Princess Marina was the most recent of a long line of foreign princesses to marry into the British Royal house, and none of her predecessors was more successful in winning the affection of the British public. She was the youngest of the three daughters of Prince Nicholas of Greece and a granddaughter of the Danish prince who became King George I of Greece in 1863. She was thus a great-niece of Queen Alexandra, of whom she reminded many older folk when first she came to England as a bride. Her mother was the Grand Duchess Helen Vladimirovna of Russia.

She was born at Athens on December 13, 1906. The Greek royal family was neither wealthy nor pretentious; and though as a child Princess Marina had glimpses of the splendour of the Imperial Russian Court, her own upbringing was simple and strict. Her parents approved of well-disciplined children and entrusted their daughters to an English governess of the old school, Miss Fox, to whom, for all her sternness, they remained devoted. The family usually spoke English together; and English was Princess Marina's first language, though she always spoke it with an attractive foreign intonation. But the children were taught to be good linguists, and they never forgot that they were Greek princesses. To the last Princess Marina was a sincere member of the Orthodox Church; and her intense love for her native country survived all its political upheavals.

The first of these upheavals occurred in 1917, when Prince Nicholas and his family went into exile for four years, spent mainly in Switzerland.

FINISHING SCHOOL

They returned to Greece in 1921, but soon had to leave again, and in 1924 settled in Paris, where Princess Marina was already at a finishing school. Their financial circumstances were not easy. Prince Nicholas, who would have much preferred to be a painter rather than a prince, devoted himself to his favourite but unprofitable pastime, while Princess Nicholas spent all the money that could be spared in helping Russian refugees in worse circumstances. Princess Marina shared in both her parents' ploys. She assisted her mother in her good works, and she worked seriously to develop her own natural talent for painting. At the same time she acquired a practical knowledge of dressmaking, which, with her instinctive good taste, enabled her to be all her life one of the best dressed women of the time. She was a real trend-setter; "Marina green" became all the rage.

The family was closely knit; and it was with mixed feelings that she welcomed the marriages of her sisters. Princess Olga had married Prince Paul in Yugoslavia in 1923; and early in 1934 Princess Elizabeth married the Bavarian Count Toerring, a nephew of Queen Elisabeth of the Belgians.

Her summers were spent mainly in Yugoslavia with Princess Paul. It was there, in August, 1934, that she became engaged to her distant British cousin, Prince George. The engagement was warmly welcomed by King George V and by Queen Mary; and the British public, to whom she had been unknown, was at once enchanted by her radiant beauty and her obvious happiness. Her wedding to the Duke of Kent, as Prince George was created in October, 1934, took place at Westminster Abbey on November 29 that year.

The new Duchess of Kent was at once plunged into a series of public engagements, which she performed with great grace and growing confidence. They were interrupted only by the births of her elder son, the present Duke of Kent, in October, 1935, and of her daughter, Princess Alexandra, on Christmas Day, 1936. She and the Duke were a striking and popular couple, with their good looks, their wide interests and their zest for living. Both had artistic tastes, and together they transformed Coppins, the somewhat ugly Victorian house near Iver which the Duke had inherited from his aunt, Princess Victoria, into a charming home; and their house in Belgrave Square was a meeting place for men and women in public life, for distinguished and interesting foreigners and for representatives of the arts and the stage. The only untoward incident during these years was in June, 1939, when a welder's assistant, a New Zealander, with a history of mental illness, fired a gun in the direction of a car in which she was a passenger as it left Belgrave Square.

MANY SORROWS

The outbreak of war in 1939 was to cause her many sorrows. Her father had died early in 1938, and her mother had retired to Athens, where she was caught by the Nazi invasion of Greece. Of her sisters, Countess Toerring was living in Germany and Princess Paul was in exile in South Africa after the collapse of Prince Paul's regency of Yugoslavia in 1941. In spite of her private worries the Duchess was entirely devoted to the cause of her husband's country. She trained herself as a V.A.D. under the name of "Sister Kay"; but her services were chiefly given to the W.R.N.S. of which she became Commandant in 1940. Her taste and influence were rumoured to be responsible for the W.R.N.S. being allotted a more attractive uniform than any of the other Women's Services. Her activities were interrupted early in 1942, when she prepared for the birth of her younger son, Prince Michael, which occurred in July, 1942. One of the child's godfathers was President Roosevelt.

The following month, on August 25, the Duke of Kent was killed in a flying accident in northern Scotland, when on his way to inspect R.A.F. units in Iceland. It was a terrible blow to the Duchess, only slightly mitigated by the kindness of King George VI, who insisted that her sister, Princess Paul, should be allowed to come from South Africa to visit her. As soon as was possible she returned to her public duties, helped by the genuine sympathy of the public. The end of the war increased their number, and many of them were of the highest importance. In 1952 she made an extensive tour of the Far East, visiting Ceylon, Malaya, Borneo and Hongkong, visiting the Royal West Kent Regiment, of which she was Colonel-in-Chief, during its operations against the rebels in the Malayan jungle. In 1957 she represented the Queen at the Independence celebrations in Ghana. Other journeys took her to Mexico and South America and to Australia. On all these tours she proved a highly successful ambassadress.

Her life was not altogether easy. After the death of her husband, neither she nor her children received a penny from the civil list; and it was not always easy for her to perform her duties in a suitable style, as well as to educate her children. The end of the war enabled her to see her mother and sisters freely. But in 1955 Countess Toerring suddenly died, and Princess Nicholas died in 1957. Her children were, however, a continual pleasure to her. She was delighted by the marriages of the Duke of Kent and of Princess Alexandra to British spouses; and she was immensely proud of Princess Alexandra's popularity. After her son's marriage she made her home at Kensington Palace, in apartments which she furnished beautifully, and where she loved to entertain her friends.

Of her public duties Princess Marina was particularly interested in the Royal National Life-Boat Institution, of which she was for many years President. In that capacity she visited many small harbours round the British coasts to launch lifeboats. She took enormous pleasure in being President of the Lawn Tennis Association and was present almost daily at Wimbledon during the championship matches. She was very proud of being the first Chancellor of the University of Kent, and greatly valued the honorary degrees given her by a number of universities. Her interest in painting and music was genuine and eager. She was warm-hearted and generous, always a little diffident and to the last nervous before she had to make a public speech or even a public appearance, but perfectly controlled. She was a fiercely loyal friend and a delightful companion, full of interest and of humour, with natural dignity but no self-consciousness of her rank.

August 28, 1968.

The Princess Royal died on March 28, 1965, at the age of 67.

The Princess Royal was by habit of life a true Englishwoman. Unlike the princesses of an earlier generation she was never destined for a dynastic alliance in Europe. As a girl brought up at Sandringham and Marlborough House, and later at Buckingham Palace, she lived a quiet domestic life—the favourite companion of her father George V. She inherited the shyness and reserve of her mother Queen Mary. When she married Lord Lascelles, a wealthy landowner from the West Riding, she fitted gracefully and naturally into the social and sporting life of the Yorkshire countryside—first at Goldsborough Hall, near Knaresborough, and then at Harewood. Her knowledge of racing and enjoyment of a race meeting were outstanding and to the end of her life she was assured of an honoured and distinguished welcome at the York races. Queen Mary invariably spent part of the summer with her in Yorkshire and often accompanied by Tancred Borenius they would explore the antiquities and curiosities of the north. As became her mother's daughter the Princess Royal had a fine knowledge of the arts and of history, knowledge which she put to great effect in the arrangement of the treasures at Harewood. Her natural reserve made her public duties (especially in earlier life) more onerous than was the case with many members of the Royal Family; but she overcame this and served the nation especially in Yorkshire where she was dearly loved with a constant and rare fidelity.

Princess Victoria Alexandra Alice Mary was born at York Cottage, Sandringham, on April 25, 1897, the year of Queen Victoria's Diamond Jubilee. She was the third child and the only daughter of King George V and Queen Mary, then the Duke and Duchess of York. It was suggested that Diamond should be one of her names, but Victoria was taken instead. At the christening in Sandringham Church by the Archbishop of York (Dr. Maclagan), Queen Victoria was one of the godparents of her great-granddaughter, the others being the Duchess of Teck (Princess Mary of Cambridge), the Empress Marie of Russia, sister of Queen Alexandra, Princess Victoria, King George of Greece, and Prince Francis of Teck.

She was only four when the Duke and Duchess of Cornwall and York were obliged to part from their children and go on their tour of the Dominions in the Ophir. King Edward did his best to make up to the children for their parents' absence, and he would go constantly to York Cottage to tell them stories and to read to them the long letters which arrived regularly from the chief cities of the Empire. In November, 1901, the Duke of Cornwall and York was created Prince of Wales, and moved with his family from York House to Marlborough House.

FIRST STATE APPEARANCE

Princess Mary's early education, conducted under her mother's superintendence by Mme. Bricka and Mlle. Dussau, was indeed a case of learning without tears. Geography was taught by large-scale models, and history was made real by visits to the Tower, Hampton Court, and other monuments of the past. These were her favourite subjects, and she also became, like her mother, fluent in French. For some time she had all her lessons together with her brothers. Riding was her chief open-air delight, and having begun early, first on a much loved donkey, and then on an equally cherished pony, she became an expert horsewoman, and hunting was later her favourite sport. She was also a skilful "whip", a fair angler, a good swimmer, an average lawn tennis player, and able to handle a small boat. Her physical education was completed by a course of Swedish drill.

For botany she had an early enthusiasm, and made a remarkably full collection of the plants and also the seaweed indigenous to the district around Sandringham. For music she had a natural taste, inherited no doubt from her mother, and possessed a clear mezzosoprano voice. Her favourite reading as a child was boys' adventure stories, Ballantyne and Rider Haggard, as well as Defoe and R. L. Stevenson. She early became an expert needlewoman, and showed both taste and originality in dressing her dolls. She had a collection of them wearing each the national costume of some foreign country, reproduced with great accuracy. She also helped in making garments for Queen Mary's Needlework Guild.

The Princess's first state appearance in public was at the Coronation in 1910. She was confirmed by the Archbishop of Canterbury (Dr. Davidson) on March 17, 1913, in the chapel at Buckingham Palace.

THE 1914–18 WAR

When war broke out in 1914 Princess Mary was only 17. In all Queen Mary's activities on behalf of the wives, mothers, and children of the men on service she was her mother's chief assistant. Early in the war she wished to send a personal gift out of her private income to every combatant. This was found to be impracticable, but she issued an appeal for a Christmas gift to every sailor afloat and every soldier at the front. The £100,000 asked for was soon subscribed, and the boxes containing tobacco or cigarettes, a pipe, and a tinder lighter each bore Princess Mary's portrait.

In 1917 she made her first official appearance as deputy for her mother at an entertainment in aid of the Mesopotamia Comforts Fund, and this was followed by many similar appearances in support of various forms of national effort. She took an active part in promoting the Girl Guide movement, the V.A.D.s, and the "Land Girls". She did canteen work at a munitions factory. She became herself a V.A.D., working with great energy, and passing the advanced nursing course with honours.

Soon after the Princess came of age in 1918 she was allowed to do what she had long desired—namely, to enter the Hospital for Sick Children in Great Ormond Street as a V.A.D. "probationer". There she trained for two years. Afterwards she became president of the hospital and presented a portrait of herself in V.A.D. dress.

On November 22, 1921, the King in council consented to a contract of matrimony between the Princess and Viscount Lascelles.

Lord Lascelles was the eldest son of a Yorkshire nobleman, the Earl of Harewood. He had distinguished himself in the war, winning the D.S.O. and bar and the French Croix de Guerre, and being thrice wounded. He was an old friend of the Royal Family, and Princess Mary shared with him a true Yorkshire love of horses, both in hunting and in racing. The bridegroom was rich, having inherited a great fortune from his great-uncle, Lord Clanricarde, and was also the heir of his father.

The wedding was in Westminster Abbey on February 28, 1922. The honeymoon was spent partly in England and partly in Italy, and then Princess Mary and Viscount Lascelles settled down in their new homes, Goldsborough Hall, Yorkshire, and Chesterfield House, Mayfair. They also visited Lord Lascelles's Irish seat, Portumna Castle, co. Galway.

Princess Mary's early training had amply qualified her for her position as the mistress of large households, but she continued from time to time to fulfil the social and ceremonial engagements in accordance with her rank. On February 7, 1923, her elder son, George Henry Hubert, now Earl of Harewood, was born; and on August 21, 1924, her second son, Gerald David, was born. In 1929 Lord Lascelles, who had been created a K.G. on his marriage, succeeded his father as sixth Earl of Harewood. On January 1, 1932, the King declared in Council that Princess Mary, Countess of Harewood, should bear the title of the Princess Royal.

Early in 1937 the Princess Royal went with Lord Harewood to stay with the Duke of Windsor at Enzesfeld Castle, near Vienna, whither he had gone after the abdication. It was not often then that she went abroad, for her interest and affections were chiefly centred in her English home and she took greater pleasure in the country life of Yorkshire than in travelling.

A.T.S. CONTROLLER

The outbreak of war in 1939 brought, of course, a host of additional duties, and she threw herself into them with characteristic energy and conscientiousness. Controller of the Auxiliary Territorial Service she was promoted in early 1940 to Chief Controller, a position which entailed a number of inspections. None of the appointments she held was a sinecure, and, in spite of the insistent demands of her war activities, she preserved her earlier interest in, for instance, the Guides Association, of which she had become the president. In addition to all the rest of her preoccupations, she found opportunities for visiting numbers of canteens and undertakings of the kind and for broadcasting from time to time on behalf of important war objects. In August, 1941, she was promoted again, this time to Controller-Commandant of the Auxiliary Territorial Service, and on the death of her brother, the Duke of Kent became president of Papworth. For her the war period was strenuous indeed, and nobly as well as graciously did she fulfil its obligations. She had, too, her own anxieties as a mother. Her elder son Viscount Lascelles was wounded and taken prisoner in Italy in June, 1944, and her younger son, the Hon. Gerald Lascelles, was serving in The Rifle Brigade.

The end of the war in Europe saw her united again with her elder son and she was able to play her full part in the ceremonies organized to celebrate victory. As Colonel-in-Chief of the Royal Corps of Signals she accepted in the summer of 1946 a fifteenth-century Japanese sword taken in Malaya after the surrender of Japan. She was one of the Counsellors of State appointed to serve while her brother, King George VI, made his tour of South Africa early in 1947, but later in the year a chill prevented her attendance at the wedding of the Queen, then Princess Elizabeth, to the Duke of Edinburgh.

Her husband underwent a serious internal operation in 1945 and died on May 24, 1947, about three months after he and the Princess Royal had celebrated their silver wedding anniversary.

The introduction of military ranks in the W.R.A.C. in 1950 caused her as Chief Controller and Controller-Commandant to become a major-general, while Dame Mary Tyrwhitt, as Senior Controller and Director, W.R.A.C., became a brigadier. In November of that year she was appointed Air Chief Commandant of Princess Mary's Royal Air Force Nursing Service.

TIES WITH YORKSHIRE

Her ties with her adopted county became ever closer. In November, 1948, she had been elected president of the York Georgian Society and almost exactly a year later she was sworn in as an honorary member of the ancient Guild of Merchant Adventurers of York. She was unanimously elected Chancellor of Leeds University in the summer of 1951 and was installed in November. She was given the freedom of Harrogate in the same year and the freedom of York was conferred upon her in the newly restored Palladian Assembly Rooms in the following year.

For the remaining years of her life the Princess Royal continued unobtrusively to carry out her public duties and travelled extensively. She was in France in 1956, visited Paris and Lille (where she was given an honorary degree), Nigeria in 1957, and in 1960 undertook a four-month tour of the West Indies.

She was again in Trinidad in 1962 as the Queen's representative at the independence celebrations.

In September, 1964, she went to Newfoundland and made a private visit to the Royal Newfoundland Regiment, of which she was colonel-in-chief, for the fiftieth anniversary of the re-forming of the regiment in 1914. In October she went to Lusaka to represent the Queen at the independence celebrations during which Northern Rhodesia became Zambia.

One of the Princess's last official engagements was to represent the Queen at the funeral of Queen Louise of Sweden in Stockholm in early March, 1965.

March 29, 1965.

Princess Wilhelmina of the Netherlands—See under **Netherlands.**

Camille Prior, who for close on 50 years was dynamic in every kind of dramatic activity in and round Cambridge died on March 16, 1970, at the age of 86.

She was born at Hampton Hill on November 23, 1883, the daughter of a Protestant French banker named Mottu who later became naturalized and of a Swiss mother with whom she always spoke French. A year in Germany following school gave her German also and a most valuable education in music. In 1906 she married a Rugby master, Oliver Prior (their only son Bob was also to become a master there). Among the boys she got to know was Donald Beves, who as a Fellow of King's was to be her lifelong friend and dramatic partner.

In 1919 her husband became Professor of French at Cambridge. Memorable dinner-parties resulted from his connoisseurship of wine and her expertise in cuisine. She played a leading part in the University's French Society, entertaining distinguished visitors, organizing dramatic productions by the Compagnie du Vieux Colombier, and herself producing and acting in a French play almost every year.

Meanwhile she rendered constant services to the Marlowe Society and the A.D.C. On the memorable occasion when the Marlowe was flown into a Berlin cut off by the Russians, she went as wardrobe-mistress and played minor parts. She also produced Spanish plays for Professor J. B. Trend, and was most helpful with costumes and make-up for the triennial Greek plays. During the war she organized and took part in dramatic and concert parties for the services, with Donald Beves, which gave over two thousand performances, sometimes to quite small outposts; and they drove anything up to 40 miles in the blackout to be there. When peace returned she was persuaded to continue such productions, which brought Town and Gown together, under the name of "Pop's Priorities" (her nickname was "Pop"). She also did much for village drama around Cambridge, originally through the Women's Institutes.

But her greatest work was for musical drama, at a time when Edward Dent was providing fresh ideas and the University Musical Society was directed by Cyril Rootham and later by Boris Ord, with Gwen Raverat sometimes designing the costumes. She was the producer in a memorable series of Handel oratorios staged as operas at the Cambridge Guildhall, *Samson*, *Jephthah* and *Saul* before the war and *Solomon* after; and of *Susanna*, produced first on the Back Lawn at King's, then at the Arts Theatre, where she was also producer for pioneering presentations of Vaughan Williams's *The Poisoned Kiss* and *Riders to the Sea* and for the revival of Mozart's *Idomeneo*, long neglected in the professional repertories. Later in life, as a member of the Advisory Committee on Amateur Opera, she produced for several years at its operatic summer school. Then there were all those musical pageants at Cambridge, historical ones in the open air in long vacations, religious ones at Candlemas in King's Chapel, or in her own church, Little St. Mary's, which she was still directing as an octogenarian.

March 18, 1970.

P'u Yi, the last emperor of the Manchu Dynasty of China, and the puppet emperor of Manchuria during the Japanese occupation, died in Peking on October 17, 1967.

He was born in Peking in 1906. His father was Prince Ch'un, the younger brother of the nominally reigning Emperor Kuang Hsü. His mother was a daughter of the Manchu soldier Jung Lu, who had throughout his career been one of the Empress Dowager's most trusted henchmen. Since the failure of the ill-fated attempt at constitutional reform in 1898. Kuang Hsü had been a prisoner in the hands of the terrible Dowager, and at his death without offspring on November 14, 1908, she proclaimed the child P'u Yi as his successor in the hope of retaining power during his minority. In fact she died herself the following day, and it was Prince Ch'un, as head of a council of Manchu princes, who exercised the regency on behalf of his son.

After the successful revolution at the end of 1911 P'u Yi's abdication was announced on February 12, 1912. It was provided that he should continue to live in the Forbidden City, and that the Republic would accord him the courtesies due to a foreign monarch together with an annual subsidy of four million dollars. The boy emperor, separated from his own mother, was brought up under the supervision of five imperial widows, the relicts of the last two emperors.

In the confusion after Yuan Shihkai's death in June, 1916, there was a brief attempt at a Manchu restoration. For 12 days in July, 1917, a general seized control of Peking, put P'u Yi back on the throne and declared the Republic at an end. The *coup* which was limited to the capital was quashed with few casualties and the Court reverted without republican reprisals to its former status. Yet that this fiasco had not ended monarchical hopes was shown a couple of years later when in March, 1919, the British Colonial Office permitted one of its staff, Reginald Fleming Johnston, to become P'u Yi's English tutor.

Johnston, who had started his career in Hongkong in 1898, was a passionate admirer of the old China and detested everything, from Christian missions to modern nationalism, which seemed to threaten what he loved. Yet when he entered the palace his first step was to bring the emperor's traditional upbringing into line with western ideas. He insisted that the myopic boy of 13 should be treated by an American oculist and equipped with glasses, and little by little introduced notions of games and exercise. The English lessons were not very successful, apart from leading the Emperor to choose the name of Henry, but a genuine friendship sprang up between teacher and pupil and during Johnston's five years' tenure of his post P'u Yi's self-confidence developed so far that in 1923 he dismissed almost the entire force of Eunuchs from his service. Expelled from the Palace in the following year by one war lord for fear that he might be used as a puppet by another, P'u Yi, on Johnston's advice, put himself under Japanese protection in the Japanese Concession at Tientsin.

On September 18, 1931, there occurred the celebrated Mukden Incident, when a bomb exploded on the railway line outside that place.

JAPANESE ACTION

This was the signal for the Japanese forces to go into action, and soon all the cities of Manchuria had passed into their hands, while among local Chinese of standing enough were found willing to form a puppet administration. Within a few weeks a summons had gone to Tientsin to recall P'u Yi to the land of his ancestors, first as Chief Executive of an independent republic, and then, in a couple of years, if things went well, as ruler of an empire.

By chance Johnston, who was now professor of Chinese in London, was visiting Tientsin at the time and in his *Twilight in the Forbidden City*, published in 1934, described the happy excitement at the refugee Court. Early in November, 1931, P'u Yi left Tientsin for Manchuria. The following February the Republic of Manchukas came into existence, and soon afterwards, in his capacity of Head of State, P'u Yi had the delicate task of receiving in audience Lord Lytton and his fellow investigators from the League of Nations. Their report, though very mild, made it clear that the regime was wholly of Japanese manufacture. In 1934, the puppet-masters kept their word, and P'u Yi ascended the throne of the Empire of Manchukuo.

The Japanese had shown from the start that there was to be no question of a restoration of the Manchu Dynasty, and even after their invasion of China in 1937 they never permitted the limits of P'u Yi's nominal empire to extend south of the Great Wall.

Treated as a marionette in public, he was able in the seclusion of his palace to amuse himself by plying the pasha. When he was still a youth of 16, in 1922, he had been married to two girls. The old dynastic prohibition was still potent enough to ensure that neither of these was Chinese. The Empress proper, the lady Wan-iung, who liked to be called Elizabeth, was of Mongol race, while the Secondary Consort Wenhsiu was Manchu.

ESCAPE

The latter, unable to bear the wretchedness of such a union, ran away in Tientsin and obtained legal divorce. By the time of the emigration to Manchuria Elizabeth had become an opium addict and before long was kept in semi-confinement.

The Russian intervention in the Pacific War on August 9, 1945 seems to have taken P'u Yi by surprise. He and his family and government fled to a remote district near the Korean border where on August 17 he announced his abdication, and the return of the territory to Chinese authority. A few days later he and his brother abandoned the women and tried to escape to Japan but fell into Russian hands and were taken to Siberia. Here they remained nearly five years, except for a trip to Tokyo which P'u Yi made in 1946 to testify for the prosecution before the War Crimes Tribunal. He left a deplorable impression on the Court. The defence naturally produced evidence of his willing collaboration with their clients, citing Johnston's book in particular, whereupon he burst into vituperation against his old tutor.

In 1950, to P'u Yi's extreme terror he and his brother were handed over by the Russians to the Chinese Communist authorities. Both of them expected to be put to death, and indeed there is little doubt that such would have been their fate under the Nationalists. Instead, on their arrival at Mukden they were welcomed at a teaparty and informed they were to be sent to school for political indoctrination. The course, which was given in various Manchurian prisons, lasted till the end of 1959 when they were released.

After his release, P'u Yi was treated with indulgence by the People's Government and was often seen as a guest at official parties.

CULTURAL POST

He was given a post in a cultural bureau in the compilation of historical records. In 1962 P'u Yi was married to a Miss Li of Hangchow, who was ideally suited for such a husband, being a professional nurse. Thus properly looked after, and with work to occupy his mind, he was no doubt to be believed when he said that he had found contentment for the first time in his life. His autobiography *From Emperor to Çitizen* was published in two volumes in 1965.

October 19, 1967.

Q

Leon Quartermaine, the actor, died in hospital in Salisbury on June 25, 1967, at the age of 90.

During his long stage career, which extended over more than 50 years, he played a remarkably wide range of parts. Of striking appearance and with a delightful speaking voice, he was immensely popular. He was something more than a born actor: he took real pains to perfect his work from every possible angle.

He inspired by the modesty and the meticulous study on which his craft was based. A radio script which he had annotated was something that younger actors treasured for the sake of the accents which he placed on words for his own guidance.

TWO STUDIES

From whom had he learnt to do this? Possibly from Granville Barker. Forbes Robertson had introduced him to the West End and to New York but it was surely Barker's Shakespearian productions at the Savoy and seasons of repertory at the St. James's before the First World War that formed and set his standards for the rest of his acting career.

Though his Mercutio, and his Buckingham in *Henry VIII*, are collectors' pieces he is not remembered mainly as a Shakespearian actor; nor, though he was the original Emperor in *Androcles and the Lion*, for his performances in Shaw; nor yet, though he was the first Englishman chosen by Komisarjevsky to play Uncle Vanya, for those in Chekhov. Two authors each of whom he interpreted once only supplied him with the material for two imaginative human studies as the poet Ishak in James Elroy Flecker's *Hassan* and as the Nobleman's Man in Ashley Dukes's *The Man with a Load of Mischief*. And what could be more expressive of his sense of character and style than the small part of Lane, a bachelor's servant in *The Importance of Being Earnest* in the Gielgud production of 1939?

COMEDY PARTS

Born at Richmond, Surrey, on September 24, 1876, the son of Fred Quartermaine, Leon was educated at Whitgift Grammar School, Croydon, and made his first appearance at Sheffield before he was 18. It was not until 1901 that he first played in the West End under the management of Forbes Robertson, after gaining valuable experience by touring with Ben Greet, George Alexander, and Martin Harvey. He remained with Forbes Robertson for two years and played in America with him in *The Light that Failed.* Among his notable performances in the next few years were the Clown in *The Winter's Tale*, Sir Andrew Aguecheek and Flute.

In the autumn of 1913 he was at the St. James's under the Granville Barker-Lillah MacCarthy management, playing not only the Emperor in *Androcles and the Lion* but the Hero in *Harlequinade*; Hjalmar Ekdal in *The Wild Duck;* Dr. Blenkinsop in *The Doctor's Dilemma*; and Jones in Galsworthy's *The Silver Box.*

In the early months of the 1914–18 War he was playing in America in *My Lady's Dress* but returned to England and joined the Cadet Corps of the Royal Flying Corps in 1916. He did not return to the theatre until three years later when he gave particularly good performances as Charles Surface in *The School for Scandal*, and as Mercutio in *Romeo and Juliet*. His portrait was hailed as a real joy, and it was in striking contrast with his delicate work in Sutro's modern comedy *The Choice*, which followed. Then came his most notable work as Harry and Simon Blake in *Mary Rose*. In 1924 he gave his admirable performance as the Nobleman's Man in the Stage Society production of *The Man with a Load of Mischief*, which he repeated when the play was put on at the Haymarket. A successful revival of *Mary Rose* followed and then for more than a year he played the part of Lieutenant Osborne in the New York production of *Journey's End*. Before he returned to London in 1932 he was also seen as Malvolio in *Twelfth Night* and as Horatio in *Hamlet*. He was again in America in 1935 to play in *Escape Me Never*, in which he also appeared in the film version. There was a memorable season at the Queen's Theatre and then came his association with Marie Tempest in Dodie Smith's *Dear Octopus*.

For over a year in 1943–44 he played the part of Scandal in *Love for Love* at the Phoenix and when he joined John Gielgud's repertory company at the Haymarket in the autumn of 1944 he appeared not only in *Love for Love* but as the Ghost in *Hamlet*, Theseus in *A Midsummer Night's Dream* and the Cardinal in *The Duchess of Malfi*. In 1949 and again in 1950 he was a member of the Stratford Memorial Theatre company.

He was three times married: firstly to Aimée de Burgh; secondly to Fay Compton, with whom he appeared in many successful productions; and thirdly to Barbara Wilcox.

June 27, 1967.

Salvatore Quasimodo, the Italian Nobel prize-winning poet and author, died in Naples on June 14, 1968. He was 66.

It had been expected that the 1959 Nobel Prize for Literature would be awarded to an Italian but there was some surprise—and jealousy—when Quasimodo's name was announced since he was perhaps the least known of the probable candidates who included Ignazione Silone and Alberto Moravia.

He was born in Syracuse, Sicily, in August, 1901, the son of a station-master, and spent his childhood in that sheltered corner of Sicily. He was sent to Veneto to read for an engineering degree and later went to Milan to study Greek and Latin. He was a fine classical scholar and his translations from the *Odyssey*, from Catullus and from the *Georgics* were widely praised. For some years he was in the Genio Civile (State civil engineering service) but after being posted to Milan he resigned and became secretary to Signor Cesare Zavattini in the publishing house of Mondadori. He was appointed Professor of Italian Literature at the Conservatory in

Milan in 1941.

Though he had lived for over 30 years in Milan it was his native Sicily which provided him with much of the inspiration for his verse. His first volume of poetry *Water and Earth* appeared when he was 29. His other works include *And Suddenly it's Evening*; *Day after Day*; *Life is not a Dream*; *The False Green and the Real*; and *The Matchless Earth.* A collection of his essays, articles and introductions appeared in 1967, and in 1965 Penguin published a selection of his poems.

He made no claim to have been an active member of the Italian Resistance during the Second World War but he used the Resistance as a prominent theme of his poetry in which his aversion to war also features strongly. For a time after the war he was a member of the Communist Party but later fell out with them. Though generally seen as a man of the left he rejected any idea that political considerations accounted for his success in Communist countries.

June 15, 1968.

Queen Elisabeth of the Belgians—See under **Belgians**
Queen Louise of Sweden—See under **Sweden**
Queen Marie of Yugoslavia—See under **Yugoslavia**
Queen Salote of Tonga—See under **Tonga**
Queen Victoria Eugenie of Spain—See under **Spain.**

Henri Queuille, a distinguished Radical politician who was three times Prime Minister of France, under the French Republic, died on June 15, 1970, at the age of 86.

His record of service to his country was outstanding, for between the years 1920 and 1953 he held ministerial office on no less than 30 occasions. He will go down in French history, however, as *le Père de l'immobilisme*, a slightly unfair title bestowed on him during his long Premiership in 1948–49, when his Government established a Fourth Republic record, which was to stand until 1957, by remaining in office for 13 months, mainly by avoiding all positive action.

In fact, in the circumstances there was little any Prime Minister could hope to do but maintain the cohesion of his uneasy coalition of Radicals, Catholic Popular Republicans, and Socialists against the assaults of the Communists and the Gaullists—then the R.P.F.—and give the country some semblance of political stability, which had been sadly lacking since the war. It is significant that his "immobility", which was to some extent calculated and sprang neither from weakness nor indecision did much to hasten the disruption of the R. P. F.; while his quiet determination and the unstinted support he gave his Minister of the Interior, the Socialist Jules Moch, allowed the serious wave of strikes accompanied by violence, by which the Communists then attempted to gain their political ends, to be mastered far more easily than had seemed possible: real governmental weakness at that moment could have led France to disaster.

FRAIL AND FRIENDLY

Not a physically impressive figure—he was short, frail-looking, somewhat quavering of voice—he was a friendly, kindly man and genuinely democratic. It was no pose that when he was Prime Minister he refused to live in the official residence, the Matignon Palace, but went home each day to his modest apartment in Montparnasse, but because official splendour was alien to his nature. And it was almost natural to *le bon docteur* Queuille that the accident in 1942 which obliged him ever after to carry a walking-stick was the exceedingly democratic one of falling off a bicycle—his habitual means of transport, even in Paris.

Born at Neuvie d'Ussel, Correze, on March 31, 1884, Henri Queuille adopted medicine as a career and was in practice in the years before 1914. Like so many other notabilities of his party, he maintained a close link with local politics, being elected Mayor of Neuvic in 1912 and serving also on the council of the Corrèze Department, for which he was elected deputy in 1914. He served during the war years as a medical officer in the army, was awarded the *Croix de Guerre*,and on returning to civilian life renewed his interest in agriculture, expressing concern for the depopulation of the rural areas and urging the need for electric power in the countryside. At the age of 36 he obtained his first ministerial appointment, as Under-Secretary for Agriculture in Millerand's Government in 1920.

SERVICE RECORD

He was then 20 times a minister under the Third Republic, holding usually the portfolio of agriculture, as he did under Herriot, Poincaré, Paul-Boncour, Daladier, Sarraut, Chautemps and Doumergue, with occasional sallies into the fields of public health and public works. Interrupted by the Vichy regime, during which he returned to his native Correze and subsisted as a small timber merchant, his governmental career resumed when he joined General de Gaulle in 1943. He was appointed *commissaire d'état* and in de Gaulle's absence from Algiers in 1943 and 1944. Queuille served as acting president of the *Comité Français de la Libération Nationale.* During the Fourth Republic he established a memorable record by serving either as a minister or as premier from July, 1948 to June, 1954 without a break—being a member or head of 12 successive governments.

It cannot be said that he made any particular mark in any of them, except possibly during his first, long premiership. He was moderate, conciliatory and cautious but could be firm and almost decisive when the need arose—but it had to be a pressing need.

June 16, 1970.

R

Julius Raab, the former Austrian Chancellor, who died in Vienna on January 8, 1964, was the "strong man" of the right-wing Austrian People's Party and the grand old man of Austrian politics. He was 72.

Since 1957, when he suffered from a slight stroke, he underwent several hospital treatments, and by 1961 when he finally relinquished the Chancellorship he was already a very sick man suffering from serious liver and diabetic conditions. This, however, did not prevent him from continuing to exercise an important, even dominant, inflence upon the Austrian political scene. A shrewd and flexible politician, he remained the strongest authority in his own party, and even after his recent unsuccessful run for the presidency, a political error which must have been a blow to his prestige, his influence, though diminishing, could still be felt.

A firm believer in the coalition Government, Raab had enjoyed confidence and respect both in his own party and in the rival Socialist Party. He became Chancellor in 1953 and relinquished his post because of ill-health in 1961.

He presided over the coalition Government of People's Party and Socialist Party which saw the signing of the Austrian state treaty in May, 1955, and was associated, together with Dr. Kamitz, the People's Party Minister of Finance, in the so-called Raab-Kamitz economic policy, based on the use of orthodox methods to maintain stability of the currency, which brought Austria its postwar prosperity.

FROM THE MIDDLE CLASSES

Raab was born in St. Pölten, Lower Austria, on November 29, 1891, of a family of local builders, and he never lost the Austrian provincial middle class stamp.Though an adequate speaker when affairs of party or state called for this, Raab was in private an economizer of words, as many an interviewing journalist has experienced to his disappointment; but he was known for his talent for repartee and his delivery, almost under his breath, of humorous quips in Lower Austrian dialect. Solid, hard-working, unshakable when his mind was made up, even stiff-necked as his coalition partners viewed it, these qualities rather than brilliance or urbanity were his most telling characteristics.

Raab was educated in a provincial secondary school and gained an engineering degree at the Vienna Institute of Engineering in 1922. He finished the First World War as a lieutenant and the commander of an infantry company, having served with some distinction. After the war he developed the interest in politics which he had already shown while a student, joining the Christian Socialist Party (as the anti-Marxist party was then called) to be elected deputy in 1927 for his home constituency to the Lower House of the Austrian Parliament.

NEW ACTION

He continued in Parliament until it was dissolved by Dollfuss in 1934. He did not then abandon politics, preferring instead to approach it from a different direction, from the side of business, with which he was always closely connected. Between 1934 and 1938 Raab founded a trade corporation, and as a member of the federal economic council instigated a number of reforms in the state trading system which were subsequently recognized as exemplary.

He was made Minister for Trade and Transportation in the Schuschnigg Cabinet in January, 1938, only two months before Austria was annexed by Hitler. If Raab was criticized by political opponents for his membership of Prince Starhemberg's private "Heimwehr" army, though it was submitted that he opposed his fascist tenencies and eventually fell out with Prince Starhemberg, there is no question of his total rejection of the Anschluss. He gave up politics altogether and joined a Viennese road construction firm as a technical engineer, soon making it a refuge for persons being persecuted by the nazis for political or racial reasons. These included Dr. Figl, later to be Chancellor, who was given work in the firm after being released from a concentration camp.

After the liberation of Austria in early 1945 Raab was made Minister of Public Works and Reconstruction in Dr. Karl Renner's provisional all-party Government set up when the Russians entered Vienna. Thereafter Raab's political career developed rapidly. A Lower Austrian constituency sent him to the new Parliament after the first postwar general elections in November, 1945. At that time he also held the position of deputy chairman of the newly formed conservative Austrian People's Party as well as that of president of the Austrian Businessmen's Association and floor leader of the People's Party deputies in Parliament.

RESTORING ECONOMY

In these positions he was able to make the most of his business experience and talent for economics in the reconstruction of Austria's crippled economy. He developed the Austrian Businessmen's Association (one of the three economic associations sponsored by the People's Party) and as floor leader in Parliament he played a leading role in drafting rehabilitation legislation for Austria's economy in the difficult days of four-Power control. He was also instrumental in the formation of the Federal Chamber of Trade and Industry.

Raab became Chancellor in the Austrian coalition Government of April, 1953, for reasons connected with internal developments within his own party. For the first time he had to turn his attention seriously to the conduct of foreign affairs, in the sphere of which lay Austria's principal aspirations, to obtain a state treaty.

His natural feeling for bargaining and compromise was given a chance with the relaxation of Soviet policy towards Austria in summer 1953, which he did the most to exploit, even at the expense of causing anxiety among the western Powers, whose advice he did not always take. His policy, based on the precept, as he himself put it, of "not tweaking the bear's tail unnecessarily" and acting like a well brought-up bourgeois and saying "please" and "thank you" when you were given something, though criticized as appeasement by his opponents, probably did contribute to the further easing of the situation and in gaining more concessions from the Russians. When it came finally to the signing of the treaty in 1955, Raab led the Austrian delegation to the Moscow talks which preceded them and played a leading part in sponsoring the notion of Austria's military neutrality.

He earned recognition even from his political opponents not only for his skill as a politician and negotiator, but also for his integrity and his modest and unassuming way of life. The few hours of free time at his disposal—he worked 14 hours a day—he preferred to spend in his library reading political, economic or historical works. He was married but there were no children.

January 9, 1964.

Sir Gordon Radley, K.C.B., C.B.E., Director-General of the General Post Office from 1955 to 1960, died on December 16, 1970, at the age of 72.

The span of Radley's career in the Post Office, from a junior Research Engineer to Director-General, is a measure of his characteristics and ability. In each phase of his career he left an enduring influence. His early engineering work on interfering reactions between high voltage power transmission and telecommunications systems stands as a basis for much of today's work. His contributions over a wide range of telecommunication techniques to air, sea and land warfare enabled forces to be kept under control. His leadership of teams developing national and international telecommunications in the immediate postwar period paved the way for the national and global networks of today.

But in a very real sense his period as Director-General in the late fifties enabled his comprehensive grasp of the possibilities of science and engineering, his uncanny clarity of mind, together with an instinctive flair for decision taking to be brought to bear on the basic problems of the role of the Post Office for the future. For, under his guidance, the White Paper on Post Office Development and Finance of 1955 was prepared. It was this that presented the dilemma of a government department operating commercial services. It recaptured the spirit of "Bridgeman" and ended the role of the Post Office as a mere "revenue department" capable of being used as an instrument of general taxation. This delicately negotiated principle paved the way for a train of events, foreseen by Radley, encompassing the 1961 Act, which separated the Post Office financially from the Exchequer, and culminated in the setting up of the Post Office as a corporation in 1969.

Though he steered the administration and business of the Post Office with freshness, energy and incisiveness he remained at heart an engineer, Facts first, problem second; not to be magnified out of proportion, but to be simplified so that an elegant, uncomplicated straightforward solution could emerge, that decisions could be taken and courses set.

In his role as an outstanding engineer, he was elected president of the Institution of Electrical Engineers having served its council and committees over two decades. His counsel was sought by industry and government on the role of the engineer and scientist in administration and government. His advice and his actions predated "Fulton". Indeed, if he erred, it was that in many of his decisions he was ahead of his time having failed to give full weight to inertia of organization or to the relative slowness of major technological innovations.

After his retirement he entered industry and held important posts with Marconi's and English Electric Computers. He also sat on several important technical committees.

His kindliness and sometimes enigmatic twinkle made staff feel wanted, evoked loyalty and response, and made them stretch themselves willingly in trying to match up to his seemingly endless energy.

Typical of his Christian faith and compassion was his service for the British Council of Churches, his work as a vice-president of the Crusaders Union for a decade and in his later years, his fine work for the housing of old people; he was at one time chairman of the National Council of the Abbeyfield Societies and at the time of his death a regional chairman.

December, 19, 1970.

Claude Rains, who enjoyed a long and successful career both on the stage and in films died at Laconia, New Hampshire, on May 30, 1967.

His theatrical career began in August, 1900, at the Haymarket Theatre, when he played a small child in *Sweet Nell of Old Drury*. His debut in the cinema occurred 33 years later, when he played the title role in Hollywood's adaptation of H. G. Wells's fantasy, *The Invisible Man*.

Claude Rains was born in London on November 10, 1889. After his initial appearance at the Haymarket, he became call-boy at His Majesty's Theatre, and gradually thereafter prompter and assistant stage manager. In the years before the First World War he toured widely throughout the world, acting and working as stage manager. He was in the Army during the war, and resumed his stage career in 1919. His early successes included Klestakoff in *The Government Inspector* in 1920, and Daniel Arnault in *Daniel* in 1921. He was by then an established actor on the English stage, and appeared in a large variety of parts. In 1926 he appeared in New York as Roberto in *The Constant Nymph*, and later went on tour with it, playing Lewis Dodd.

His debut in films, in 1933, was a curious one, since although he played the leading part in *The Invisible Man*, his face was never seen by the audience. However, his performance was of a standard to ensure his future in the cinema. He played an unscrupulous lawyer in *Crime Without Passion*, an unprincipled District Attorney in *They Won't Forget*, and a corrupt Senator in *Mr. Smith Goes to Washington*. The District Attorney was probably the best part he ever played, and *They Won't Forget* the best film in which he ever appeared. A damning indictment of prejudice and race hatred, it was adapted from Ward Green's novel, *Death in the Deep South*, and expertly directed by Mervyn LeRoy. At the close of the film, the District Attorney, after obtaining a conviction for murder on doubtful evidence, is left to ponder idly on the possibility of a miscarriage of justice, disinterestedly and without a trace of conscience. It was a cold, cynical, and brilliant performance. In 1943 he appeared in *Casablanca*, with Humphrey Bogart and Ingrid Bergman, and also in a re-make of *The Phantom of the Opera*.

In 1920 Rains had played Casca, and later Cassius, in *Julius Caesar* on the English stage. In 1944 he returned to England to play Caesar himself in Shaw's *Caesar and Cleopatra*, one of Arthur Rank's most ambitious film productions up to that time. It was made under considerable difficulties at Denham, and directed by Gabriel Pascal, with whom Rains did not always see eye to eye, but his performance was impressive. Vivien Leigh played Cleopatra.

In 1950 Rains reappeared on the legitimate stage, after 16 years absence, in *Darkness at Noon*, first at Philadelphia and later in New York, and for the next decade he divided his time between stage and cinema. In 1962 he played Mr. Dryden in the film *Lawrence of Arabia*, and under David Lean's direction presented a dry and sardonic study of the calculating political mind. In the cinema the political field tended to monopolize his attention, and it was left to his theatrical career to provide far wider opportunities for a considerable acting talent.

May 31, 1967.

Dr. Ludwik Rajchman, who was the first director of the health section of the League of Nations—parent of the present World Health Organization, died at Chenu in France in July, 1965.

He was appointed as first director by Sir Eric Drummond in 1921. Later, he was one of the founders of Unrra, and inspired the creation of Unicef. His original thinking has led to many of the programmes undertaken in the field of child health and welfare in the past 50 years.

Born in Warsaw in 1881, he qualified as a doctor at the University of Cracow in 1906, and then served for two years as assistant bacteriologist at the Pasteur Institute in Paris. After a period as lecturer in bacteriology at his old university, he went to London as Chief Bacteriologist at the Royal Institute of Health. From then until his return to Poland in 1919, he was a research fellow at King's College London and for the Medical Research Council. In Warsaw he became general director of the National Institute of Health, and served as Polish member of the League of Nations Epidemics Commission in 1920 and 1921. His abilities had become known outside his own country largely as a result of the League Health Conference in Warsaw in 1921 and his work on the commission set up to meet the threat of the typhus epidemic which was then causing terrible losses in Russia and beginning to spread westward.

Rajchman was a scientist of brilliant intelligence, imagination and administrative ability, besides being a linguist who could discuss in English, French, German and Russian just as clearly as in Polish.

The Health Organization of the League—by common consent one of its most notable successes—was to a large extent his creation. He fought for and won the support and collaboration of the chief Health Ministries, including the British Ministry of Health. Thus firmly based, he was able by various means—such as special contributions from various governments and, especially, the generosity of the Rockefeller Foundation—to overcome the handicaps of official penuriousness and diplomatic indifference.

CHINA'S HEALTH SERVICE

Rajchman remained director of the Health Organization until 1939, and his second major achievement during this time was in building up a strong connexion between the League Secretariat and the Kuomintang Government in China. He visited Japan and China during the winter of 1925–26, and in succeeding years went back to China each year by invitation, becoming the trusted counsellor not only of the new Health Ministry but also of Chiang Kai-shek and of T. V. Soong, his powerful Finance Minister. In building up an efficient national health service in the country he saw how League institutions—disinterested and not painful to China's amour-propre—could help in the creation of other desperately needed services, in particular those of flood control, communication and education.

During the thirties, when political tensions forced changes on the social and economic activities of the Leauge, he played an important part in its work on nutrition, housing and other problems connected with health in a more general sense—the beginnings of the Economic and Social Council of the United Nations.

LEAGUE REALITY

During his directorship the membership of the health committee increased from 10 to 20 countries and its work made the League a reality in places where otherwise it was no more than a name.

From 1939 to 1943 he was adviser to the National Government of China. A founder of Unrra, as a member of the Polish delegation he proposed its continuation in the field of help for children—thus he inspired the creation of Unicef.

Rajchman was the first chairman of its executive board. His interest in the welfare of the world's children led him to found in 1950 with Professor Robert Debré the international children's centre in Paris—set up to study medical, social and psychological problems.

He leaves a widow.

July 24, 1965.

Paul Ramadier, a leading figure among the French Socialists, who held ministerial office on several occasions between 1936 and 1957, and was Prime Minister from January, 1947, until the following November, died on October 14, 1961, at the age of 73.

A socialist of practical and independent temper, who frequently found himself at odds with the main and more doctrinaire body of French socialist opinion, Ramadier in his years of office after the liberation of France stood close to Blum and not seldom looked to the latter for political guidance. There was some surprise when Vincent Auriol invited him, in January, 1947, to form the first government under the new Constitution, for he had previously held only minor offices. But the President's choice, based on a shrewd assessment of Ramadier's character and qualities, was fully justified by the new Premier's handling of a particularly difficult political and economic situation. General de Gaulle, whose newly founded Rally of the French People added to the Government's troubles, had a high opinion of Ramadier, who was, he said, "endowed with the exceptional quality of—obstinacy".

This was not sufficient, however, to keep the Government together in face of increasing misunderstandings with his own party colleagues, who accused him of being a "lukewarm Socialist", not appreciating that the economic policy they disliked was dictated by the fact that Ramadier was Prime Minister of a coalition in which his own party, the Socialists, were in a minority. (This was a disability inflicted upon all Fourth Republic Prime Ministers, whatever their party.) Ramadier was Minister of Defence in the first Queuille Government, in September, 1948, but did not hold office again until he became Minister of Finance and Economic Affairs in the Government formed by Guy Mollet after the 1956 general election. He was, like so many other notable Fourth Republic politicians, defeated in the 1958 general election and retired from national politics.

UNDER LEON BLUM

Born at La Rochelle on May 17, 1888, of a good bourgeois family, Paul Ramadier studied economics and law at Toulouse University and the Sorbonne, and in youth was captured by the force and sincerity of Jaurès. His legal work at the Court of Appeal lay principally with the cooperative societies, on whose problems he became a recognized authority. He was elected mayor of Decazeville, a small industrial town in the south-west in 1919 and continued in that office until his death, and was first elected to the Chamber of Deputies in 1928, for Villefranche-de-Rouergue, which he represented until 1940, and after the war was Deputy for Aveyron from 1946 until 1951 and again from 1956 to 1958.

By the time he obtained his first Government appointment, an under-secretaryship in the Blum Administration in 1937, Ramadier was moving steadily to the right of the majority of his Socialist colleagues, and indeed broke away with Renaudel, Marquet, and a few others to form a neo-Socialist splinter group. This did not prevent him, in June, 1940, from being one of the 30 Socialist Deputies who voted against the granting of full powers to Marshal Pétain and the Vichy regime. It was thus that after the war he was at once accepted back into the fold and was appointed by General de Gaulle to the thankless post of Food Minister in the second Provisional Government in November, 1944. He was Minister of Justice in Leon Blum's stop-gap, all-Socialist Government in December, 1946, and the following month, when the new Constitution came into force, headed the first Government of the Fourth Republic, the only Government to have included representatives of all parties in the National Assembly, from Communists to Independents, but which was dominated by the tripartite coalition of Socialists, M.R.P., and Communists which had held power since the Liberation.

THE COMMUNISTS OUSTED

The bonds which united the three partners were visibly weakening, to break completely four months later when the communist Ministers publicly disassociated themselves from the Government's economic policy. Ramadier displayed notable skill and patience in disembarrassing himself of the communists, who steadily refused to resign and hoped instead to bring down the Government. After they had gone—Maurice Thorez, their leader, stamping out of the Cabinet room in a fine fury—Ramadier reshuffled his team and carried on doggedly amid mounting industrial unrest, economic difficulties and dissensions within the Cabinet and between the Cabinet and Parliament, for another six months before resigning.

During his Premiership there had been an amusing incident which throws light on one aspect of Paul Ramadier's character—his modesty. The Government had decided to award the Médaille Militaire to Winston Churchill. It is France's highest military honour but is reserved for privates and n.c.o.s. or generals who already hold the Grand Cross of the Légion d'honneur. The Cabinet thought it would be an excellent gesture to have the medal handed to Churchill by a French n.c.o. who himself held it. There was discussion in the Cabinet as to ways of finding a suitable sergeant when the Prime Minister, until then silent, intervened to say: "Why go to all that trouble? I was a sergeant in the 1914 war. I hold the Médaille Militaire. Won't I do?" His colleagues had no idea of his distinguished military record.

THANKLESS BURDEN

Ramadier lost his seat at Aveyron in the 1951 general election, but regained it in the election of January, 1956, and was appointed Finance Minister in the Government formed by the Socialist leader Guy Mollet. Once again Ramadier had taken on a thankless burden, for the Algerian war was steadily increasing the country's grave economic difficulties. He did his best, as a good Socialist, to maintain the purchasing power and keep prices and wages stable, but it was at the cost of increased taxation and a dangerous dis-equilibrium in the balance of payments. The situation he handed on to his successor was critical.

It is probable he would not have accepted the post and certain that he would have followed a different policy had he not received assurances, given with cynical recklessness, that the Algerian war was nearing its end. He introduced one new tax which will be lastingly associated with his name. To provide funds to increase payments to *économiquement faibles* old age pensioners, he put a graded horse-power tax on all motor vehicles, popularly called, after the title ticket, given as a receipt, the "Vignette Ramadier". It was much resented and there was, later, an organized campaign for its abolition, many motorists sticking a poster "Non à la Vignette" on the rear windows of their cars.

In 1948 he was nominated France's representative on the Administrative Council of the International Labour Office at Geneva, and served in that capacity until March, 1961, when he resigned. He was described, on his resignation, as having been for 12 years "a tower of strength to the organization".

When the crisis of the Fourth Republic occurred in May, 1958, Ramadier, with the courage and sense of republican responsibility that had marked his career, opposed the return of General de Gaulle. In a moving speech in the National Assembly on the critical night of May 27 he called upon the Prime Minister, M. Pflimlin, not to abandon his post. "If we wish to demonstrate the country's will to achieve its own salvation", he said, "we will remain within the normal play of its institutions."

It was the culminating point of his career; soon after General de Gaulle's return he retired to Decazeville, of which he had for so long been a popular and efficient mayor. One of the least pushful of politicians, he was not publicly appreciated at his full worth, not even in his own Socialist Party. But President Auriol, who was in a position to judge, said of him when he resigned the Premiership in 1947: "I shall not easily find another man as conscientious, as knowledgeable, and as generally qualified to be Chief of Government." His benign, professorial appearance masked a strong and intelligent determination.

In 1914 he married Mlle, Marguerite Cerri, and leaves a widow and two sons.

October 16, 1961.

Sir C. P. Ramaswami Aiyar, K.C.S.I., K.C.I.E., jurist, statesman, scholar and wit, who died suddenly in London on September 26, 1966, was one of the outstanding Indians of his day. He was 86.

Edwin Montague in *An Indian Diary* on his tour in 1917–18 as Secretary of State for India described him as one of the cleverest men he had ever met, and added that in discussion "he tied us completely into knots". At the time the ambitious "C.P.", as he became generally known, had much farther to go in a brilliant career.

Chetpat Pattabhirama Ramaswami Aiyar was born on November 12, 1879, the son of a Brahmin lawyer who rose to be Judge of the Madras City Court. He was educated at the Wesleyan High School, the Presidency College, and the Law School, Madras. He joined the High Court Bar in 1903 and rose quickly to leadership of the Original side. He was for some years a member of the Madras Corporation, and also identified himself with the activities of the National Congress, serving as an All-India secretary in 1917–18. He won country-wide renown by his defence in the action brought by Mrs. Annie Besant against the *Hindu*, but later he became her staunchest supporter in the Home Rule movement as well as her legal adviser.

Lord Willingdon, made Governor of Madras in the spring of 1919, was soon attracted by the wit and wisdom of C.P., and in the following year selected him to be Advocate-General.

TALKS ON REFORM

In February, 1923, he made him Law Member of Government. C.P. was a representative of India at the Assembly of the League of Nations in Geneva in 1926 and 1927, was a delegate to the several sessions of the London Round Table Conference on Indian reforms in 1930–31 and was associated with the Joint Parliamentary Committee which followed and prepared the way for the India Act of 1935. In 1931 Lord Willingdon, then Viceroy, called him twice to Delhi for short periods as acting member of the Executive Council first as Law and then as Commerce Member.

In 1932 he accepted the whole time post of Legal and Constitutional Adviser in the Travancore State and in 1936 was appointed Dewan (Prime Minister).

In 1942 C.P. left Trivandrum for Delhi to become Information Member of the Viceroy's Executive Council. He found that the wartime atmosphere contrasted with that of the time of his patron Lord Willingdon. He promptly resigned and within 18 days was back again in Travancore as Dewan. When Indian independence was drawing near C.P. took a stand against Travancore, like the States in general, being virtually forced to merge with the Indian Union. He claimed for her a special relationship with Britain, somewhat akin to that sought by the Nizam of Hyderabad. But the currents were too strong for this southernmost State to remain high and dry above the flood. As soon as Indian partition had taken effect in August, 1947, he resigned his post after 16 years of fruitful service to Travancore.

The Maharaja in a communication of warm praise and admiration to his Dewan wrote that Travancore "has achieved an international reputation as a result of his unremitting and devoted labours". A few weeks earlier the Minister had been wounded in the face by an assailant with a sword stick, and it was a long time before he recovered from his wounds.

His public life in India after independence was largely in the academic world. He served for some years on the standing committee on university education and on the university grants committee and was appointed Vice-Chancellor of Annamalai University and Banaras Hindu University. In 1955 he led an Indian university delegation on a visit to China.

He celebrated his sixtieth birthday by giving away all his immovable and other inherited properties to members of his family and poor relations. He also made charitable gifts totalling £37,500.

He arrived in London in September 1966, to begin research on a two volume book to be called *The History of Our Time*.

He married Sitammal, youngest daughter of C. V. Sastri, the first Indian to be appointed a Judge of the Madras High Court, and had three sons.

September 27, 1966.

Dr. Karl Rankl, who died in Austria on September 6, 1968, at the age of 69, will always retain a place in British musical history for his work as the first musical director of Covent Garden Opera Company from the time of its inauguration in 1946 until his retirement from the post in 1951.

When a permanent Covent Garden opera company became a certainty rather than a dream, after the war, Rankl was an obvious choice to build up the company and repertory, since his multifarious experience in Germany had given him enviable knowledge of the needs and hopes for such an organization, as well as of a large operatic repertory.

He built up a large company of British singers and proceeded to present a diligently varied repertory of English, French, German, Italian, and Russian operas. Bizet's Carmen was the first, to be followed by Verdi, Puccini, Massenet, Mussorgsky, Wagner, Strauss. Rankl's policy was based on German repertory practice of singing operas in the language of the country.

Guest stars from abroad were occasionally engaged—a significant moment brought Kirsten Flagstad and Hans Hotter to join a British cast in Die Walküre, sung in English by them as well as their colleagues. During the same 1947–48 season, Wagner's Tristan was sung in German, which seemed more conducive to high standards in Wagner, though some other of his operas continued to be sung in English.

FOREIGN GUESTS

Elisabeth Schwarzkopf, Ljuba Welitsch and Paolo Silveri were other foreign guests who spent extended periods with the company, singing numerous roles in English under Rankl's direction. Rankl conducted the first production of Bliss's first opera, The Olympians, and took Britten's Peter Grimes into the Covent Garden repertory. A Boris Godunov with Mussorgsky's own original scoring was a landmark of his period with the company and there was a notorious, but in retrospect splendid, production of Strauss's Salome with Welitsch in the title role, decor by Dali, and production by Peter Brook.

Rankl's greatest achievement without doubt, was the complete cycle of The Ring in 1950, if only because it established this masterpiece as an annual necessity for London operagoers.

September 9, 1968.

Arthur Ransome, C.B.E., who died on June 3, 1967, at the age of 83, had an enterprising and versatile record as author and journalist. He became one of the most felicitous of English writers of children's stories—*Coot Club, Swallows and Amazons, Peter Duck* and the rest.

Arthur Ransome was a person of diverse gifts and accomplishments and of exceptionally wide cultivation of mind. He was much travelled, he was of an adventurous temper, he had a passion for boats and water and a fisherman's recondite philosophy, he was a student of folklore, and he wrote with unfailing grace and zest and with a touch of poetic imagination always in reserve. Children—not in this country alone—knew him for the very distinctive stories he wrote for them, a story almost every year for many years until the Second World War. Others had previously known Ransome for his fantastic and slightly macabre tales, or for his critical and biographical literary studies, or as the translator of Aksakov on fishing, or as a witness of the Russian Revolution in 1917.

PRINCE OF STORY-TELLERS

To his intimates he was always, among other things, a prince of oral storytellers—the creator, for instance, during his years in Russia, of the "Nancy stories", so called because these Negro folktales, delivered in the manner of an old black nurse talking to a little white girl, always began "My dear Nancy".

Born on January 18,1884, the son of Cyril Ransome, professor of history at Leeds University, Arthur Ransome went to school at Rugby. Books, fishing and sailing absorbed him in youth. From Rugby he went in a very junior capacity into the publishing firm of Grant Richards, this serving as an introduction of sorts to the life literary. His recollections of living in a still truly Bohemian Chelsea in the the first years of this century were delightfully vivid. He engaged in journalism, contributed notes on angling to various journals; and during the years 1909 to 1912 published *A History of Story-Telling,* a study of Poe, a collection of semi-fantastic tales, *The Hoofmarks of the Faun,* and a book on Wilde.

After the publication of this book a libel action was brought against Ransome by Lord Alfred Douglas, who complained that the book implied that he had been responsible for the public disgrace and infamy of Wilde and that after Wilde came out of prison he had lived with him and on him, abandoning him when Wilde's allowance was stopped. The case came up in 1913 before Mr. Justice Darling and a jury, who found that the words complained of constituted a libel but were true. Judgment was given for Ransome with costs. A document which played a significant part in the case was the original manuscript of Wilde's *De Profundis,* which Robert Ross had deposited in the British Museum. The unpublished part, until produced in court, had been seen by nobody but Ross and Wilde.

RUSSIAN STAY

In 1913 he proceeded to Russia; he needed Russian, he decided, in order to complete his studies in folk-lore. *Old Peter's Russian Tales,* published in 1916, was one of the direct results. Another and more indirect result was that he served as correspondent in the capital of the *Daily News* and, in the turmoil of Russia in revolution, of the *New York Times* also. Ransome was one of the two British correspondents in Russia who were anxious that the Bolshevists should be given their chance and who strongly deprecated the idea of foreign intervention.

In 1919, after his return to Britain availing himself of the friendly relations he had established two years earlier with some of the Bolshevist leaders, he spent six weeks in Moscow and Petrograd (he travelled from Stockholm in the company of Litvinov and Vorovsky) for the *Manchester Guardian,* and published an objective and not unsympathetic record of his impressions. Two years later, in *The Crisis in Russia,* he entered a fuller defence of the Russian Revolution, pleading for a more objective judgment of Bolshevist aims.

STORY OF CRUISE

He was a member of the Royal Cruising Club and produced in *Racundra's First Cruise* (1923) a spirited and expert account of a 500-mile voyage that he made in the Baltic in a 30-ton ketch which had been built in Riga to his specifications. A journey to Egypt for the *Manchester Guardian* was followed by a visit to China for the same newspaper, and on this occasion ill-luck pursued him. He became very ill and on his return to this country was obliged to live very carefully for a considerable time.

This circumstance helped to turn his mind while he was living in the Lake District towards the writing of *Swallows and Amazons,* published in 1930, the first of his series of authentic children's stories. Neither this book nor its successor, *Swallowdale,* was immediately successful, but in 1932 came *Peter Duck,* which handsomely established Ransome's reputation with the young. *Winter Holiday* and *Coot Club* followed in successive years, and further books appeared at intervals of a year or more almost until the end.

The author provided, as a rule, his own illustrations.

REAL NOVELIST

Ransome was not a writer of "juveniles" but a genuine novelist for children. It was personal experience and a profound watery lore that he liked to draw upon. He took his readers seriously, that is, and they, in turn, could not fail to return the compliment. His world of children and boats and lakes and islands was indeed fascinatingly real to them—and, in the particular matter of boats and water, fascinatingly instructive. The books were translated into several European languages. He was created C.B.E. in 1953

Ransome married in 1909 Ivy Constance, daughter of George Graves Walker, by whom he had a daughter. He married secondly in 1924 Evgenia, daughter of Peter Shelepin, who survives him.

June 6, 1967.

Adam Rapacki, Polish Foreign Minister from April, 1956, (when Stalinism lost its iron grip on Poland and a free atmosphere prevailed with the return to power of Wladyslaw Gomulka) until 1968, died on October 10, 1970. He was 60.

He held this office throughout a period when his Government was cautiously evolving an independent policy within the narrow limits permitted to any country in the Soviet orbit. No country in Europe has suffered as much as Poland from great power rivalries and within a year of taking office Rapacki used his country's greater independence from Moscow to try to prevent another collision. It was with this object in view that he developed and a year after his accession to office proposed to the United Nations and the world his famous "Rapacki Plan", aiming to prohibit the "presence and production of all atomic weapons in any part of Central Europe."

Adam Rapacki was born in 1909 at Zwierzyniec, near Lwow (now Lvov and, since its incorporation into the U.S.S.R., the capital of Western Ukraine). His father, who was killed in the Warsaw rising, was one of the founders of the "Cooperative" movement in Poland, a movement very close to the Polish Socialist Party of which Rapacki was a leading member until its merger with the Communist Party in 1948, when the two parties became the United Polish Workers' Party dominated by the communists.

After studying in Lwow, Rapacki graduated at the Academy of Commerce in Warsaw where he worked for a number of years as a research fellow in the Scientific Institute for Cooperatives. It was while working in the Institute that he came into contact with Boleslaw Bierut, later first President of Communist Poland, who recommended him to the Party Central Committee in 1949 and afterwards to the post of Minister of Shipping.

P.O.W. LIBERATED

When the war broke out in 1939 Rapacki joined the Army and served for a brief period as second lieutenant. He was captured by the Germans, remaining a prisoner of war until liberated by the Western Allies in 1945. He returned and joined up with the Polish Socialist Party which then was led by Mr. Cyrankiewicz, later Premier of Poland. He was elected a member to the National Council and later to Sejm where he displayed a keen interest in foreign affairs.

He is believed to have worked closely with the left wing of the party to bring about its fusion with the Communist Party. When this was accomplished in December, 1948, Rapacki was elected to the Politburo of this new Polish United Workers' Party (P.L.R.P.).

While strongly pro-Russian he never lost sight of his country's traditional historic affinity with the West and particularly of the fact that Poland is a strongly nationalistic and Catholic country with millions of Poles living abroad. Nearly 10 million Poles, he once emphasized, live in the United States, Canada, Great Britain, and other countries in the West. In the past these millions have been a source of strength to Poland in her fights for independence and freedom. This role they can still play and it was therefore necessary for any Polish Foreign Minister to follow a line of policy which could retain this valuable source of good will and support. During his first years in office Rapacki on several occasions made it clear to the Russians that Poland must be careful not to alienate the millions of her people living abroad and should not be forced, therefore, always to follow blindly Kremlin policy in all respects, but especially in the field of religion. As Minister of Foreign Affairs Rapacki was also instrumental in founding numerous communities for cultural cooperation with foreign countries, above all with those in the West. He himself travelled more widely in the free world than any of his predecessors in office.

His liberal views were of particular importance and, as generally admitted, of benefit to Poland during his terms of office as Minister of Higher Education, a post he held from 1950 until he became Foreign Minister. He was strongly against "forcing" youth into communism. Having introduced Marxism as a subject in all universities, he resisted Party efforts to compel students to join the movement. "This is a matter for voluntary decisions," he argued "The Party stands only to lose and not to benefit by forcing Polish youths to join." "There are more Polish boys and girls in the churches on one Sunday than in the ranks of the Party," is a saying coined which still holds good, thanks partly to the wise policy of Adam Rapacki.

LEADERS' WRATH

As was to be expected, this brought upon him the criticism and even wrath of the more fanatical section in the Party leadership. This resulted in a temporary loss of his seat on the Central Committee. But he soon regained it when appointed Foreign Minister. In July, 1956, he was reelected a full member of the Politburo and since then remained on the side of the more liberal and pro-Western wing in the Executive.

The failure of his plan to denuclearize Central Europe was a great disappointment to him and, according to his friends, brought about his first heart attack. When he first proposed an atom-free zone between Russia and the Great Powers in the West he had many reasons to be proud of his scheme, the main being that although it was approved by Moscow in principle, the details were all his own. In spite of allegations made by some observers at the time when he submitted it to the United Nations that it was "Kremlin made", those near him knew that the conception and details were genuinely his own creation. He may have been a figurehead for the Kremlin in many respects, but he also showed that he could stand up to Moscow as, for instance, in the negotiations which made the Soviets agree to make Russian troops stationed in Poland, and their families, subject to Polish law. It was Rapacki also who played a decisive part in removing Marshal Constantin Rokossovsky, whom the Poles regarded as a traitor, from the post of Chief of the Polish Armed Forces and Defence Minister in Poland. It was therefore a great disappointment to him when the West, including Great Britain, rejected his plan. He had, he once said, reason to believe that the West would be forthcoming. Even when he modified his plan in 1958, offering a system of aerial and ground inspection, it was strongly criticized by General Norstad and later by others in the West as inadequate and turned down. This brought about his second heart attack, necessitating a long rest.

But although he failed to win support in the West few would deny him the credit that he was genuinely interested in helping the cause of peace. He saw that relaxation of international tension, peaceful coexistence between the great powers, and stabilization of peace are the most vital conditions for Poland's existence and survival. Rapacki also sought to reduce the possibilities of Germany seeking a revision of the Oder-Neisse borderline. If the threat of atomic weapons could be removed from this area, Rapacki argued, Poland's frontiers and peace would be more secure. The western proposals for an Atlantic or Multilateral Nuclear Force caused him anxiety and he expressed his apprehensions to the British Government during his short visit to Britain in December, 1964. In a variant of his plan to freeze nuclear arms in central Europe in 1964 he had sought to bar west Germany from a mixed-manned fleet. He proposed that countries maintaining forces in the area should undertake not to transfer arms to other parties. Rapacki saw the dangers of nuclear proliferation and offered the possibility of inspection as a first step to disarmament. He saw his own proposal as a stepping stone to a wider agreement and suffered bitterly when this failed to gain support.

October 12, 1970.

Basil Rathbone, the actor, died in New York on July 21, 1967, aged 75. Although to the younger generation he was better known through his film roles, notably as Sherlock Holmes, between the two world wars he was seen in many notable productions in the West End.

He was born in Johannesburg on June 13, 1892, educated at Repton and then entered an insurance office. But after a year he pleaded with his cousin, Sir Frank Benson, to give him a trial as an actor. He was engaged for Benson's Number Two company and made his first appearance as Hortensio in *The Taming of the Shrew* at Ipswich in 1911. A succession of small parts followed while he gained invaluable experience. Benson realized his possibilities, and when he went to America in 1912 took Rathbone as a member of his company.

As a result Rathbone did not appear on the London stage until two years later, when he played in *The Sin of David* at the Savoy. In 1915 he toured with Benson and appeared with him as Lysander in *A Midsummer Night's Dream.* He then joined the London Scottish as a private, was commissioned in the Liverpool Scottish and was awarded the Military Cross in September, 1918.

After demobilization he joined the new

Shakespeare Company, and in the summer season of 1919 was seen at Stratford as Romeo, Cassius and Florizel. As a result of his work there Constance Collier engaged him for the part of Peter Ibbetson, but she was unable to obtain a theatre. Henry Ainley then offered him the part of Cassius in his production of *Julius Caesar*, but a week before the production was due Miss Collier's search for a theatre was successful, Ainley released him from his contract, and Rathbone was always grateful to him for his kindness. Two other notable performances followed in *East of Suez* at His Majesty's and in *R.U.R.* at the St. Martin's. Towards the end of 1923 he went to America.

His success in New York both in Shakespearian and modern plays was such that it was nine years before he returned to London and then only for a brief spell which is best remembered for his striking performance in a revival of *Diplomacy* at the Prince's Theatre. He rejoined Katharine Cornell's company in the United States and in 1934 in New York played Romeo to her Juliet—one of the most memorable productions of the play in the history of the American theatre. By this time he was also busily occupied with the cinema and he was seen in many successful American productions. His work in the theatre was reduced, but he found time to play in America in two successful British plays, *The Winslow Boy* and *The Gioconda Smile*.

The only regret of British play-goers was that they saw far too little of his stage work. Films brought him to the attention of a wider audience, and as often as not his dark, handsome face was ideally cast in a sinister role. His films included *After the Ball, One Precious Year, Loyalties, The Last of Mrs. Cheney, A Notorious Affair, Sin Takes a Holiday, David Copperfield, Anna Karenina, A Tale of Two Cities, The Last Days of Pompeii, Captain Blood. Frenchman's Creek, House of Fear, Casanova's Big Night, Black Sheep,* and *Tales of Terror*.

His most famous role was that of Sherlock Holmes in a series of films that started in 1939 and included *Sherlock Holmes Faces Death* and *Sherlock Holmes in Washington*. He was so completely identified with Conan Doyle's detective that he played him in many radio plays too.

In 1951 he tried his hand at something new, and went on a lecture tour in which he gave dramatic readings.

His first marriage, to Ethel Marian Forman, was dissolved. His second wife, Ouida Bergere, a writer, and their daughter Cynthia, survive him.

July 22, 1967.

Canon Charles Raven, D.D., who died at his Cambridge home on July 8, 1964, at the age of 79, was Regius Professor of Divinity in the University of Cambridge from 1932 to 1950, Master of Christ's College from 1939 to 1950 and Vice-Chancellor of the University in 1947–49. He was one of the outstanding personalities of his generation of Cambridge men.

At the outset of his academic career, he had been Dean and Fellow of Emmanuel at a time when that College was something of a vortex of theological controversy in the University, and for much of his life he was himself a somewhat controversial figure. Not only his theological liberalism, but also his pacifist opinions (though it should be remembered that he had been a chaplain to the forces in 1917–18) his identification with C.O.P.E.C. (Conference on Christian Politics, Economics and Citizenship), his association with the Modern Churchmen's Union, and his championship of such causes as the ordination of women, caused him to be regarded as "erratic" by the ecclesiastical authorities of the Church of England. There was a time when he felt frustrated because he was not made a bishop: but even his best friends realized that he would have felt even more frustrated if he had been made a bishop, for his great gifts were essentially prophetic, and by temperament he was sensitive, enthusiastic, eloquent, and impulsive. As against this, there is no other case in modern times of a Regius Professor of Divinity at Cambridge being elected Master of his College and Vice-Chancellor of the University.

After Charles Raven's retirement from his Chair and from his Mastership in 1950, his activities became more far-ranging and he became a less prominent figure in the Cambridge scene; but on both sides of the Atlantic his devotion to the task of bringing science and religion to understand each other made an effective impact. He was concerned that, since the death of Bishop Barnes, no bishop of the Church of England was, or deserved to be, a Fellow of the Royal Society.

CRUSADER

The troubled waters in which he had periodically found himself immersed were not his natural element. He had indeed a crusading spirit, but, unlike many crusaders, he never accepted disillusion, nor became soured by disappointment. With intellectual gifts of uncommon quality and range, he was a man of almost reckless moral courage combined with great generosity of mind and heart and with a ready and eager sympathy: although sometimes fired to indignation, mostly on behalf of others, he was incapable of bearing malice or cherishing a grievance. As a preacher he was, at his best, incomparable; and the engaging and endearing qualities which he so artlessly revealed in his autobiography, *A Wanderer's Way*, published in 1928, characterized him to the end.

Charles Earle Raven was born on July 4, 1885, the son of a barrister. While at Uppingham he laid the foundations of his classical scholarship and developed a taste for natural history in the particular form of moth hunting. In due course he won an entrance scholarship in Classics at Gonville and Caius College, where in later years he was to be elected to an Honorary Fellowship, and in 1907 was placed in the First Class in the Classical Tripos Part I. For his second Tripos he chose Part II Theology, not because of any deep religious convictions or any intention to seek Holy Orders, but largely because of the scope which this choice would give to his classics. He took the Tripos in 1908, and was again placed in the First Class. He had a flair for writing, and during his undergraduate career he edited both his college magazine and the *Granta*.

While still an undergraduate he became engaged to Margaret E. Buchanan Wollaston, a niece of the Master of his college. Their marriage in 1910 was the beginning of a singularly happy home into which a son and three daughters were subsequently born.

Having finished his theological tripos he proposed to be for a time at least a lay student of theology, but he was almost immediately offered an appointment as assistant secretary for secondary education under the Liverpool City Council. Office routine was a valuable discipline, and his association with the management of a large boys' club brought him two useful contacts. The boys brought him face to face with the problems of poverty and social inequality and awakened his interest in "Christian Socialism", while the club workers, whose motive and dynamic was Christian, deepened his conviction of the reality of religion. According to his own account the event which was the turning-point in his life was a vivid experience of the presence of Christ while on a visit to a clergyman friend.

His love of nature led to an interest in the biological sciences, and this gave him another approach to religion. For him there was never any incompatibility between these two activities of the human spirit. Although he had now passed from an interest in religion to the experience itself, he sat very loosely to orthodoxy and was critical of the Church. In October, 1909, he was offered and accepted the office of Dean and Theological Lecturer at Emmanuel College, Cambridge. The acceptance involved the decision to take Holy Orders; he was ordained in December, and began his work in January, 1910. Here he found himself precipitated into an acute religious controversy.

MASTER'S ACTION

The Master, William Chawner, who had all his life been a regular attender and communicant at College Chapel, not only suddenly ceased the practice, but circulated to undergraduate members of the college a somewhat controversial pamphlet which created a rather difficult situation for the new Dean. Raven was well equipped by training and experience to deal with the situation, but unfortunately the controversy got into the press; parents became exercised, prospective candidates for admission to the college were withdrawn and a crisis was only averted by the death of the Master with tragic suddenness during the Easter Vacation.

At the outbreak of war in 1914 Raven went to Tonbridge as an assistant master, but later volunteered for service abroad as a Chaplain. His front line experiences made a deep impression on him. He returned to Emmanuel for a brief period, was appointed Chaplain to the King, and was presented to the Rectory of Bletchingley in 1920 and became Canon of Liverpool in 1924. Here he gave much of his time to building up an informal evening service in the cathedral, and succeeded not merely in bringing together large congregations, but in creating a real sense of fellowship.

His election to the Regius Professorship of Divinity at Cambridge in 1932 came as a surprise, even to his friends. Not that they underrated his theological scholarship, but he was not the "safe" type so often sought for theological professorships. But the choice was a good one. His breadth of scholarship was considerable, his own religious experience was real and vital, and his presentation of his subject in formal lectures and otherwise was stimulating and challenging. He had always a large following of students in the University, and he influenced a very wide circle whose interests were in no way theological. He was elected to a Fellowship at Christ's College shortly after his return to Cambridge, and became Master of the College in 1939, a position which he held until his retirement in accordance with the College Statutes in 1950. He was immediately able to serve the University for a further period of four years as Warden of Madingley Hall. He had just previously filled the office of Vice-Chancellor with great tact and distinction during the academic years 1947 to 1949, a difficult period of post-war readjustment. In 1950 he was appointed a trustee of the British Museum and his versatile accomplishment also earned for him the presidency of the Botanical Society of the British Isles for the period 1951 to 1955.

BOOKS ON BIRDS

As a naturalist, Charles Raven showed several facets. His three bird books of the 1920s are perhaps seldom read now, as they were of the stream of enthusiasm rather than original works: but they disclose a relentless camper, photographer and traveller and a thoughtful conservationist. His important books, published by the Cambridge University Press in 1942 and 1947—*John Ray Naturalist : His Life and Works*, and *English Naturalists from Neckam to Ray*—were contributions to the history of science of a high order, distinguished by depth and variety of analysis. Raven had a peculiar facility for interpreting the personalities and identifying the drivers of Turner, Caius, Mouffet, Merret, Willughby, Ray and the other early great explorers of nature. He enjoyed them and their work as one scholar enjoys another and doubtless understood them and brought them to life so well through having followed the same paths in field, library and academic discipline.

In the years of pacifist controversy which followed the War of 1914–18, he had gradually come to the conviction that for him the renunciation of war was an inevitable part of his Christian witness. He became national Chairman of the Fellowship of Reconciliation, was associated with George Lansbury in promoting Embassies of Reconciliation and joined Dick Sheppard in starting the Peace Pledge Union, of which he became a Sponsor. During the 1939–45 War his association with the pacifist movement brought him a certain amount of isolation and unpopularity, but he worked very hard to allay bitterness and to preserve the deeper unity of Christians whatever position they might be led by conscience to take.

Always an interesting and arresting speaker he was greatly in demand for sermons, addresses, lectures and speeches of all kinds. He gave the Donellan Lectures at Trinity College, Dublin in 1919; the Hulsean Lectures at Cambridge 1926–27; the Noble Lectures, Harvard 1926; the Alan Robertson Lectures, Glasgow 1927; the Halley Stewart Lectures. London 1934; the Riddell Memorial Lectures, Durham 1935; the Herbert Spencer Lectures, Oxford 1945; the Hobhouse Lectures, London 1946; the Gifford Lectures, Edinburgh 1950–52.

Yet he never allowed the quality of his spoken word to deteriorate, and he maintained an output of written work which many a man of greater leisure must have envied. Among his published works may be noted: *What Think Ye of Christ*? (1916), *Christian Socialism* (1920), *Apollinarianism* (1932), *Our Salvation* (1925), *The Creator Spirit* (1927), *A Wanderer's Way* (1928), *Jesus and the Gospel of Love* (1931), *Is War Obsolete*? (1935), *Evolution and the Christian Conception of God* (1936), *War and the Christian* (1939), *Science and Religion* (1953), the Gifford Lectures published under the title *Natural Religion and Christian Theology*, and *Science, Medicine and Morals*.

His first wife died in 1944. In 1954 he married Mrs. E. P. Moors, who died in the same year, and in 1956 he married Mme. N. Hélène Jeanty.

July 10, 1964.

Admiral Sir Bernard Rawlings, G.B.E., K.C.B., who died on September 30, 1962, at the age of 73, had a distinguished record of service in the Second World War.

He spent five of the six years in commands on foreign stations, chiefly the eastern Mediterranean and the Far East—a record probably unique. Though his merits as admiral of a squadron in war were known to his seniors and to those who served under his command, he was of modest disposition and shunned any sort of personal publicity; and it was not until 1945 that his name became well known to the public as the Vice-Admiral Commanding the British Task Force in Japanese waters and in the bombardments of the Tokyo area. He was familiar with Japan from three years' residence as Naval Attaché at Tokyo.

After his distinguished services in the British Pacific Fleet he might well have aspired, in his turn, to the highest post the Navy had to offer, but, modest as ever, and feeling that his abilities were more in active service afloat than such as were needed in peacetime administration, he preferred to retire and leave the field to younger men.

Henry Bernard Hughes Rawlings, the son of William John Rawlings, of Downes, Hayle, Cornwall, was born on May 21, 1889. He entered the Britannia as a cadet in January, 1904, went to sea as midshipman of H.M.S. Goliath in May, 1905, and was made a lieutenant in January, 1910. In October, 1914, he gained his first command, that of torpedo boat No. 11 in the Nore Flotilla. In February, 1915, he joined the Vernon to specialize in torpedoes, and was afterwards torpedo officer in the cruisers Antrim, Undaunted and Coventry. From March 1919, he was liaison officer with the British Military Mission to Poland and for this service was made O.B.E. in 1920.

He was promoted captain in December, 1930. During the next four years he was in the Mediterranean, in command of the Active and a division of the Third Destroyer Flotilla, and as Flag-Captain in the Curacoa and Delhi, of the Third Cruiser Squadron. During 1935 he attended the Imperial Defence College. This was followed by three years as Naval Attaché at Tokyo.

WITHDRAWAL FROM CRETE

Shortly before hostilities began in 1939 he was appointed to command the cruiser Norfolk, but received instead a war appointment to command the battleship Valiant. In the autumn of 1940 he was made an acting rear-admiral in the First Battle Squadron, Mediterranean, and after promotion to substantive rank as rear-admiral in January, 1941, he took over command of the Seventh Cruiser Squadron on that station. He was largely responsible for the successful withdrawal of the British forces from Crete. In April, 1942, he joined the Admiralty as Assistant Chief of Naval Staff (Foreign), but from March, 1943, was again on foreign service as Flag Officer Commanding, West Africa. In November, 1943, he was transferred to the Levant and Eastern Mediterranean as Flag Officer Commanding, and conducted various operations in the Aegean. In the 1944 Birthday honours he was created K.C.B.

When towards the end of 1944 the British Pacific Fleet was created he was appointed to it as Second-in-Command. He commanded the Task Force which in 1945, in cooperation with the Americans, advanced into the forward area, operated against the Japanese strongholds in the Ryu-Kyu islands and finally shelled the Japanese mainland. On the occasion of the surrender of Japan he was specially appointed as K.B.E. "for good services rendered while in command of the British Task Force operating in Japanese waters". In the 1946 Birthday honours he was promoted to G.B.E. He retired in July, 1946, and was made an admiral on the retired list in September of that year. He was Deputy Lieutenant for Cornwall and was High Sheriff of the county in 1950.

He married, in 1922, Eva Loveday, daughter of William Hastings Beaumont, of Pickenhanger, Esher, and had two sons and one daughter.

October 2, 1962.

Samuel Taliaferro Rayburn, Speaker of the United States House of Representatives, who died on November 16, 1961, at Bonham, Texas, at the age of 79, always seemed a permanent fixture on the Washington scene.

He was one of those rare phenomena in politics—a dedicated man who aimed at one job, got it, and remained in a continuous love affair with it for an immense length of time. He went to Congress in 1913 as a young man of 30 and thus saw more than a quarter of its history so far. He became Speaker in 1940 and, except for two years when the Republicans held the majority (1947–48), he remained in the job until he died. He served longer than anyone else had done before, both as Speaker and as a member of the House. His power remained vast until the first session of President Kennedy's Congress this year, when he became ill and seemed to lose some of his grip.

The significance of the Speaker's position in American politics is not always appreciated abroad. He does a great deal more than exercise general control over debates and procedures. He is a leading politician of the majority party with great influence over the passage of legislation and the behaviour of his party. He decides what business is taken up, and when and how. He appoints members to the committees which confer with the Senate; he has a big say in appointments to standing committees. He also takes over the Presidency if the President and the Vice-President are both incapacitated. His power has declined since the early years of the century but he remains a figure with whom Presidents as much as Congressmen must reckon all the time. It is rare that a Bill will pass against his wholehearted opposition.

Sam Rayburn will certainly be remembered as one of the most respected and distinguished Speakers the House has known. He presided in the chamber with fairness, moderation and an expert knowledge of the 11,000 or so rules and precedents of the House. In the offices and corridors of the Capitol he earned the affection of most and the respect of all.

HONESTY AND FIRMNESS

A smallish, stocky, bald man, he was essentially shy. He married briefly in his youth and then became a confirmed bachelor. His hobbies were fishing, farming, reading, and cooking. To the public he appeared as tough and rather dour. Only in Congress—the world he knew and in which he felt secure—did he reveal the warmer and more human side of his nature. Even so, he preserved a slightly old-fashioned reserve and self-discipline among his heartier, back-slapping colleagues. He entertained modestly, and had a good sense of humour, but he disliked conviviality. He also showed his conservatism in strenuously and successfully resisting powerful pressure to allow television cameras into committee hearings.

He rarely addressed the House on important legislation and never sponsored an important Bill. He worked best behind the scenes, not with brilliance, but with sense and the benefit of long experience. Some regarded him as a rather stubborn old man and he had occasional flashes of temper. Strangers used to be warned: "When Sam's face gets red, beware; if the red overspreads his bald head, start running." However, generally he had an even disposition and was popular, even loved. He had many friends and was greatly respected for his honesty, firmness, and ability to keep his word. He took endless pains to help new members and to talk things out with anyone in trouble. Having reached the pinnacle of his own ambition he was above the petty jealousies and rivalries of many of his colleagues. He refused the Vice-Presidential nomination which President Roosevelt offered him in 1944, and it went to Mr. Truman instead. He never even tried to get elected to the Senate. For him the House was his life, and the good will that he accumulated was demonstrated when he had to step down to a Republican in 1947 and thus lost the use of the official car. Fellow Democrats clubbed together to buy him a car of his own. A small plate was affixed inside which read: "To our beloved Sam Rayburn—who would have been President if he had come from any place but the South."

SUPPORT FOR NEW DEAL

In the position he held his Texan background was actually helpful, for, as a southerner with moderately liberal beliefs, he was in a position to keep the Democratic party from splitting too deeply and dangerously. Campaigning in 1948 he helped prevent the south from defecting altogether and did a lot to get President Truman reelected. It was this moderate and middle position, coupled with his reluctance to stake his reputation on either side of much controversial legislation, that was responsible for a good deal of his effectiveness. Among other things it helped him to keep a Democratic Congress running reasonably smoothly under the Republican presidency of Mr. Eisenhower. Working closely with Senator Lyndon Johnson, the majority leader in the other chamber and also a Texan, he concentrated on encouraging responsibility, thus avoiding the paralysing collisions this situation might otherwise have produced. It was not only his nature to do so; he believed it paid off with the electorate. He was very much a party man at heart and could be as fiercely partisan as the best of them when the occasion demanded or when nettled by Republican election tactics. He could also fight hard for something he felt strongly about. For instance, in 1941, four months before the United States entered the last war, there was wide public agitation against a Bill to prevent the release of more than one million men from the Army. Rayburn worked feverishly to sway a few undecided Congressmen in favour of the Bill, which eventually passed by one vote, with an obvious effect on the subsequent war effort.

His personal political beliefs emerged mostly in the form of support for the existing Administration. He helped to nominate Roosevelt and supported his New Deal. He was a personal friend of President Truman and supported most of his Fair Deal, though probably with some reservations on civil rights—he was never a racist but he had his constituency to think of.

SPEECH FOR BRITAIN

He also got on well with President Eisenhower. He was always a strong advocate of the Hull reciprocal trade treaties. In 1957 he came out strongly for the Eisenhower doctrine and urged Congressional leaders to approve its military authorization. Much earlier, in 1946, he spoke strongly in favour of the financial loan to Britain, saying: "If we are not allied with the great British democracy I fear somebody will be, and God pity us when we have no ally across the Atlantic, and God pity them too. America has the challenge and the ability to listen to voices throughout the world".

The Kennedy Administration found him helpful in spite of his illness, but he seemed uninterested in federal aid to education and medical care for the aged under social security and this contributed to their failure in the first session of the 1961 Congress. Undoubtedly some of the liberal ideas of the new men were a little in advance of his own thinking; a new generation and a new type of man had entered the White House.

Rayburn was born on January 6, 1882, in Tennessee, the eighth of 11 children of a farmer who five years later moved to Texas to raise cotton. At an early age Sam told visitors that he would some day be Speaker of the Texas Legislature and would go to Congress. He worked his way through school, studied law at the University of Texas and set up a law practice in his home town of Bonham, Texas, in 1905. Within two years he had been elected to the State House of Representatives, where he sat until 1913. For the last two years he was Speaker. He was then elected to Congress for the Fourth Texas District and held the seat thereafter. He learnt many of the tricks of his trade under "Cactus Jack" Garner, one of the most powerful Speakers there has ever been, who ran famous daily sessions known as the "Bureau of Education" where talk and drink flowed in equal abundance. This, it is said, helped inspire him with a special pride in the power of the House as the holder of the national purse strings.

In his later years he was regularly chairman of the Democratic nominating conventions and conducted these mass meetings with unmatched skill. In the 1960 convention he renounced the job in order to be able to nominate his friend Lyndon Johnson for the Presidency.

November 17, 1961.

Ernest Read, C.B.E., who died suddenly in a London hospital on October 9, 1965, devoted the whole of his long life to the service of musical education. He was 86.

The Ernest Read Children's Concerts, the London Junior and Senior Orchestras which he founded and conducted were known and appreciated by amateurs and professionals alike. Many musicians afterwards eminent in their profession passed through his hands either at the Royal Academy of Music—where he became professor and examiner in 1914—or in one or other of the organizations which he devised for amateurs.

He was born at Guildford on February 22, 1879 and educated at the Royal Academy of Music, of which he afterwards became a Fellow.

PIONEER

He was a pioneer of musical appreciation and joint author with his own teacher, Stewart Macpherson, of text books on that subject and on aural training. As a professor at the Royal Academy of Music he taught these aspects of general musicianship and conducted choirs and orchestras. He served for many years on the associated board of the Royal Schools of Music.

But his more public activities were with young orchestral musicians, for whom he founded the London Junior Orchestra in 1926. In it players who had learnt their instruments at school found an opportunity to continue playing among friends learning the orchestral repertory. The organization flourished so much that by the outbreak of war in 1939 there were three such junior orchestras and also the London Senior Orchestra, formed in 1931, which differed from them less in age-group than in proficiency. Here the amateurs were joined by young professionals and teachers who liked to keep their hand in.

INFECTIOUS ENTHUSIASM

The war disrupted these orchestras, but opened out to Read another possibility—orchestral concerts for schoolchildren on the lines already established by Sir Robert Mayer. These concerts for musical appreciation were continued after the war and the London Junior and London Senior Orchestras were put on their feet again. To supplement them Read organized two summer schools, one for school children and one at Queenswood for players of the standard of his London Senior Orchestra, who received coaching from the most eminent instrumentalists.

The National Youth Orchestras of Wales and of Great Britain owe their inception to ideas kindled by Read's work. He was not a great conductor, but he had a way with him, as the success of his various ventures amply testified, and was an excellent trainer, whose enthusiasm was inexhaustible and infectious. He was for more than a quarter of a century director of music of Queenswood School for Girls and for a long time one of the committee of management of the Royal Academy of Music. From 1944 he was president of the Music Teachers' Association.

In the past 20 years Read's orchestras have gone from strength to strength; in 1947 a concert in the Albert Hall celebrated the twenty-first birthday of the London Junior Orchestra. Each year there was a season of concerts for children, usually with Read himself conducting and educating his audience in his inimitable way. In 1955 he became president of the London Schools' Symphony Orchestra. In 1956 the award of the C.B.E., coincided with the thirtieth birthday of the London Junior Orchestra.

In 1959 his two orchestras presented him with a concert to celebrate his eightieth birthday.

EMINENT PLAYERS

The orchestra was composed almost entirely of past members of the London Junior and Senior who had reached high positions in their profession. And in February, 1964, Read conducted *Messiah* in the Festival Hall, celebrating yet another anniversary—the twenty-first birthday of his Special Choir of 500 singers. This and all the other organizations making up the Ernest Read Music Association have become a well-established and well-known part of London musical life.

Read married first in 1906 Dorothea Johanna, daughter of the Rev. Canon G. Jackson, and they had one son and one daughter. In 1923 he married secondly Helen Frieda, daughter of W. F. Webster.

They had two daughters.

October 11, 1965.

Sir Herbert Read, D.S.O., M.C., died on June 12, 1968, at the age of 74.

By the nature of his ideas rather than by personal choice Herbert Read was predestined to succeed Roger Fry as the interpreter in England of specifically modern art. The mental differences between them corresponded to their succession in time. Fry, a painter, stopped short with the Post-Impressionists; Read, who was not a painter, was tied less to a particular aesthetic and technical standpoint. He found no difficulty in carrying on the defence and exposition of modern art, through all its later divergencies, from Cubism to Surrealism and thence to the various abstract forms of present-day painting and sculpture.

Like Apollinaire, he was a poet, who valued what was new as the product of the creative mind and always supported those who, in Apollinaire's phrase, "fight on the frontiers" of culture. If he was ever too credulous about certain manifestations of modern art, the consistency with which he pursued the conception of a new age as revealed by art gave a special force to all his writings and raised him to a position of philosophic authority.

People who met him for the first time, struck by his delicate and sensitive appearance and shy manner, were likely to be surprised on looking him up in a book of reference to find his name followed by the letters, "D.S.O., M.C.".

COLD COURAGE

The anomaly however was a matter of looks and manner only, for a brief acquaintance with Read's work was enough to show that one of his most pronounced characteristics was the cold courage of the "resolute soldier" as a reviewer once described him, which more often than spectacular gallantry is recognized in the military distinctions named.

Read, who was the eldest of the three sons of a Yorkshire farmer, Herbert Read of Muscoates Grange, Kirbymoorside, was born on December 4, 1893. In *The Innocent Eye,* published in 1933, and again in *Annals of Innocence and Experience,* 1940, he gives vivid glimpses of his childhood and youth, to the general effect that he was happy on the farm but broken-hearted when he went to school—"No wild animal from the pampas imprisoned in a cage could have felt so hopelessly thwarted". Left an orphan at an early age, he was educated at Crossley's School. Halifax, where he preferred books to games and soon discovered a taste for writing. At 16 he was a clerk in the Leeds Savings Bank but he did not mean to stop there and by way of evening schools and the public library he prepared himself for Leeds University. It was while reading for matriculation that he awoke to poetry and began to write verses. Tennyson was his first inspiration and then came Blake "like an apocalypse" to be followed by Nietzsche, who for some years dominated his philosophical thinking.

The permanent effects of Read's childhood on a farm are suggested by a passage in *Poetry and Anarchism,* published in 1938. "In spite of my intellectual pretensions, I am by birth and tradition a peasant. I remain essentially a peasant. I despise the whole industrial epoch—not only the plutocracy which it has raised to power but also the industrial proletariat which it has drained from the land. The only class in the community for which I feel any real sympathy is the agricultural class including the genuine remnants of a landed aristocracy."

It is not perhaps altogether easy to discern the peasant in this intellectual personality but the passage is interesting for more than one reason. It gives the exact turn of Read's "left-ward" inclination in politics, towards Tolstoy rather than Marx. It may also help to explain why Read, though he wrote about art and industry, did not seem to be very enthusiastic about the artistic possibilities of the machine.

From Leeds University Read entered the Army, holding a commission in The Yorkshire Regiment (Green Howards) and rising to the rank of captain. He served in France and Belgium from 1915 to 1918, winning the M.C. in 1917 and the D.S.O. in 1918 and being mentioned in dispatches. His war experiences, including the death of one of his brothers in France as recorded in the collection of sketches, *Ambush*, published in 1930, saddened him but did not warp his judgment, his view being well expressed in the remark that it was possible to be a pacifist in theory but not in practice; and such a poem as "The End of a War" (which Yeats included in the *Oxford Book of Modern Verse*) had its note of optimism.

Read left the Army to become an assistant in the Department of Ceramics at the Victoria and Albert Museum. His books, it may be noted, include technical works on "English Stained Glass", "Staffordshire Pottery Figures", and "English Pottery", the last with Bernard Rackham. In 1931 he was appointed professor of fine art at Edinburgh University. He was Sydney Jones Lecturer in Art at the University of Liverpool, 1935–36, and for several years edited the *Burlington Magazine*, relinquishing the post on his appointment as director of a proposed Museum of Modern Art, which the outbreak of war prevented. In the same year he joined the board of directors of the publishing house of Routledge and Kegan Paul, his first task being to edit a series of monographs on "English Master Painters".

BOOKS AND JOBS

Subsequently he held a number of educational appointments in England and the United States, being Leon Fellow in the University of London, 1940–42, Charles Eliot Norton Professor of Poetry at Harvard, 1953–54, and A. W. Mellon Lecturer in the Fine Arts, Washington, 1954.

From 1931 onwards he produced many books—there are at least 30 titles to his name—comprising poetry (his *Collected Poems* appeared in 1946), fiction, literary criticism, art criticism and exposition, autobiography and studies in the value of art in education. As a poet he ranged himself rather deliberately with the moderns, subordinating the sensuous element to the intellectual appeal of imagery. It might be going too far to say that his powers were critical rather than creative but the remark of a reviewer that he was a poet by "taking thought" is broadly true. But he had real imagination and his philosophical romance, *The Green Child*, published in 1935, was a work of extreme delicacy with the streak of crystalline hardness which seemed to be a spiritual characteristic of his.

As a critic of literature Read ranked with the best of his time. From *Reason to Romanticism* (1926) to *Collected Essays in Literary Criticism* (1938) (several of which had appeared in *The Times Literary Supplement*), all his critical writings excited controversy; but the qualities of mind evident in them—keen sensibility, steadiness in thinking, complete integrity and unflinching honesty in following an agrument—were universally recognized. Read's prose style, unornamented and a trifle stiff in movement, gave pleasure by the closeness with which it followed the lines of thought.

Arguably it was in literary criticism that Read reached his highest level; but the accident that the subject was more "in the news" made him more widely known as a writer on modern art and the champion of its most extreme and controversial forms, his criterion of modernity being that of Klee "the intention not to reflect the visible but to make visible". He was sometimes accused of being an erudite theorist without sensuous response to aesthetic values, but in introducing his "Critic's Choice" of paintings at Messrs. Tooth's Gallery in 1956 (all tending towards "abstraction") he stated with emphasis "I *like* this kind of art—it gives me a directly sensuous and profound enjoyment". It was, however, in a clear and systematic analysis and exposition of aims and trends that he excelled in his writings. In this respect his *Art Now*: *An Introduction to the Theory of Modern Painting and Sculpture*, first published by Faber and Faber in 1933 and now a standard work and his *Concise History of Modern Painting*, published by Thames and Hudson in 1959, are works that could hardly be bettered.

ADULT PLAY-CENTRE

Other notable studies were his account of Henry Moore's sculpture and *The Art of Sculpture*, 1956. Read exerted influence also as President of the Institute of Contemporary Arts, which in association with Mr. Roland Penrose he launched in 1947. When introducing the inaugural exhibition of "Forty Years of Modern Art" at the Academy Hall in London he said that the I.C.A. was intended to create "not another museum, another bleak exhibition gallery... but an adult play-centre...a source of vitality and daring experiment." He became a leading supporter of the "Ban the Bomb" movement and sat down in Trafalgar Square.

He published *Henry Moore*: *A Study of his Life and Work* in 1965; and *Art and Alienation* in 1967.

Read was knighted in 1953. A lanky man of few but solemn words and an apparent timidity which once caused him to be compared to "an amiable tortoise", he was far from being timid, as his war record shows, and for all his solemnity he had a keen sense of fun. When his eyes narrowed with inward laughter the "tortoise" became very much more like a faun.

His personal qualities were of value both to the British and to the international art world. During the 1930s, for instance, when he lived in Hampstead, within easy calling distance of Henry Moore, Ben Nicholson, and Barbara Hepworth, he was constantly on hand during one of the crucial episodes in the history of modern British art. It was at that time that his stature as a pioneer interpreter of new ventures in art was first fully revealed. (He was, moreover, one of the few people who managed to remain on good terms with both the surrealist group and the pure-abstraction group). After the war he was much in demand as an elder statesman of art, and on many occasions he represented Great Britain abroad: on juries and committees of all kinds his meaningful silences and occasional brief bursts of eloquence turned out to be immensely effective. His foreign colleagues came, in fact, to ascribe an almost Delphic importance to his interventions: "When Read does at last open his mouth", one of them said, "you know there's nothing more to be said". Read was liked and respected by a great many artists, important and unimportant, and his seventieth birthday was marked in private by tributes unusual in their whole-hearted acknowledgement of all that he had done on their behalf.

He was twice married, first in 1919 to Evelyn, daughter of Arthur Roff, by whom he had a son; and in 1936 to Margaret, daughter of Charles Ludwig, of Aberdeen, by whom he had three sons and a daughter.

June 13, 1968.

Sir Frederick Rebbeck, K.B.E., formerly chairman and managing director of Harland and Wolff, died on June 27, 1964, at his home in Belfast. He was 86. He had a life-long association with the shipbuilding firm of Harland and Wolff and, at a time when many men would have been thinking of retirement, he threw himself with vigour into aircraft production when the firm of Short Brothers and Harland was reconstituted and removed from Kent to Ulster soon after the ending of the Second World War.

Frederick Ernest Rebbeck was born in 1877 near Swindon, Wiltshire, and was educated privately. He served his apprenticeship to engineering in the Midlands, and had early experience at the works of Victor Coates and Co., of Belfast, and at the yards of Harland and Wolff long before there was any apparent likelihood of his becoming head of the company. For a while he was with British Westinghouse at Manchester, but later returned to Harland and Wolff, made a protracted tour of the Continent, and then went to Glasgow as general manager of the Harland and Wolff Clyde engineering branch. Only a little more than four years after rejoining the company, he was made a managing director. Later on he assumed complete charge of both the Belfast and Glasgow branches.

It was largely the result of his mastery of the mechanical side of engineering that the company made such great strides in the output of marine diesel engines as well as of gas engine compressors and other compressor units for use in the oilfields and oil refineries of the world. This latter undertaking, under licence from the Cooper-Bessemer Corporation of Mount Vernon, Ohio, United States, was welcomed when it was signed in 1950, as an example of what can be attained by cooperation between engineers on each side of the Atlantic in the matter of design and output. His contribution to the company, and to the ship-building industry generally, was not technical alone. For several years between the two wars and particularly in the thirties at the worst of the depression, Rebbeck contrived to keep a considerable proportion of the building yards and the engineering shops at work, and to attract commissions for the company's other depots in England and Scotland.

Perhaps the greatest test of his career came in 1941 when the German air raids wiped out more than half the operating capacity on Queen's Island at a moment when the output of ships and engineering was needed more acutely than at any time in British history.

UNDERSTOOD WORKERS

It was in no small part due to his immense driving force, and his understanding of the mentality of the Ulster workers, that this great blow to the Northern Ireland industry was repaired, and the resources remobilized so quickly. His labour relations, and indeed his impact upon Northern Ireland generally were, considering the fact that he had been, as he himself once put it, "imported" to Ulster, the more remarkable. But he had much in common with the Ulster people—the capacity for hard sustained work, complete honesty in his dealings, and outspokenness. He devoted his time and energies almost entirely to his business interests. He had a proper sense of the importance of higher education, especially vocational and technical. When, in 1946, he was given the honorary degree of Doctor of Science by Queen's University, it was recalled that it was largely due to his interest, and the facilities he provided, that science graduates of the university were enabled to do two years' post-graduate training at the Queen's Island yards. He retired from the chairmanship of Harland and Wolff in 1962, being succeeded by his son, Dr. Denis Rebbeck.

For many years he had been a Belfast Harbour Commissioner, and a member of the general committee and joint chairman of the technical committee of Lloyd's Register of Shipping, and he had been president of the Institute of Marine Engineers and the Shipbuilding Employers' Federation. He was knighted in 1941.

He married in 1907 Amelia Letitia, daughter of the late Robert Glover, and they had two sons and three daughters. His wife died in 1955.

June 29, 1964.

Professor T. F. Reddaway died on October 26, 1967, after a long illness. By his death University College London and the study of London history have suffered a severe loss.

Thomas Fiddian Reddaway was born in 1908, the eldest son of the late W. F. Reddaway, the distinguished Cambridge historian. He graduated at the University of Cambridge in 1930, and after a period in London returned to Cambridge in 1935 as director of Studies in History at Clare College, a post he held until the outbreak of war. After a notable war career in which he reached the rank of major he returned to academic work in 1946, as Reader in London History in the University of London, being appointed professor in 1967.

Professor Reddaway soon became well known as the leading historian of London in the country and his services were called upon by numerous bodies within the city, the county and elsewhere. He played a part in the scholarly researches of a number of London Livery companies and his relations with the Goldsmiths' Company, of which he was a member, were particularly close.

As an historian of London he followed in the tradition established at University College by Miss Eliza Jeffries Davis. In 1940 he made his reputation by *The Rebuilding of London After the Great Fire*—still the standard book on the subject. His more recent work, conducted in the face of war injury and continued ill-health, and often written up from his sick bed consisted principally of a study of the early history of the Goldsmiths' Company (virtually completed in the last days of his life). He also wrote a study of the topography of London in the 1660s, the results of which will appear in a forthcoming edition of *Pepys's Diary*, of which he was an associate editor.

All that he wrote was marked by exact scholarship and a sensitive regard for the English language. As a teacher, he did much to encourage undergraduate and postgraduate study of London history in all periods; and he played a leading part in the work of the societies serving the interests of his subject—The London and Middlesex Archaeological Society, the London Topographical Society and the London Record Society. He was greatly in demand as a lecturer and was prodigal in his benefactions and services to numerous causes. He had been hon. treasurer of the Royal Historical Society since 1949.

He owed much to the devotion of his wife, Edith Margery Jay, daughter of Sir Alan Edgar Horne, whom he married in 1944. She survives him with six children of the marriage.

October 27,1967.

Arthur Reece, formerly a well-known music hall singer, died on April 2, 1964, at the Variety Artists' Benevolent Fund Home at Brinsworth, Middlesex. He was 94.

A Cockney, he was a contemporary of Marie Lloyd and Marie Kendall and was in his prime in the golden days when an artist might play at five halls in an evening, travelling from theatre to theatre by brougham.

Reece's chief claim to remembrance is as the original singer of "Sons of the Sea", of which, dressed in naval officer's uniform, he gave a rousing performance. This is perhaps the best of a not always admirable type—the patriotic chorus song of "the halls"—and its vigorous words and swinging tune gave it a long hold upon popular affection. It is recorded that on the eve of the outbreak of war in 1914 Reece, standing with thousands of others outside Buckingham Palace, was suddenly thrilled with pride to hear the vast crowd around him break spontaneously into his own song. Even in the war of 1939–45 "Sons of the Sea" remained, in the minds of Londoners, the fitting chorus with which to greet news of a naval victory—as those who then worked in the printing office of *The Times*, for example, well remember.

Reece's chief music hall career lay before the 1914–18 War. In the 1920s he was already a veteran, appearing with a combination of old stars. In recent years he had lived in retirement, but occasionally emerged, as a representative of the old school of performers, on such occasions as the jubilee performance at the Metropolitan Music Hall in 1947. He was King Rat of the Grand Order of Water Rats in 1905.

April 3, 1964.

Sir Stanley Reed, K.B.E., who died on January 17, 1969, at the age of 96, was editor of *The Times of India*, published in Bombay, from 1907 until 1923. He was Conservative member for the Aylesbury division of Buckinghamshire from 1938 until the general election of 1950, when he retired from politics.

He was born in Bristol on January 28, 1872, and educated privately. He joined the staff of *The Times of India* in 1897, and first came into prominence when, as the correspondent of that journal and of the *Daily Chronicle*, he travelled through the famine districts in 1900.

He accompanied King George V and Queen Mary, when Prince and Princess of Wales, through their Indian tour in 1905, and his articles describing the tour were regarded as so complete that, with the permission of the Prince, Sir Walter Lawrence (Chief of the Staff) abandoned his intention of writing an official record and contributed instead the preface to the volume in which Reed's dispatches were republished. In the years before 1907, when Reed took over the editorship of *The Times of India*, he had in the service of that newspaper toured India extensively, and probably there were few Englishmen more familiar with its problems or better informed as to what the future was likely to bring forth.

Under his editorship the newspaper became not only one of the two most influential journals in India, but its general conduct and make-up challenged comparison with any English-speaking journal in the world. For 16 years Reed occupied the editorial chair, and after his retirement and settlement in England he continued to serve it as its London correspondent. Apart from his position on *The Times of India* he played an important part in the life of India. He represented Western India at the Imperial Press Conference in 1909 and 1930. He was vice-president of the Central Publicity Board, and in the war of 1914-18 he was Director of Publicity to the Government of India. In 1929 he unsuccessfully contested as a Conservative the Stourbridge Division of Worcestershire, but at a by-election in May, 1938, he was elected in the Aylesbury Division of Buckinghamshire with a majority of nearly 11,000. His voice was often heard in the House and listened to with respect and interest, as he always knew his facts and displayed an independence of view that perhaps was not always congenial to the party Whips. In 1928 he published, in conjunction with Sir Patrick Cadell, *India*: *The New Phase*, at the time a valuable little book, presenting in a lucid form a summary of the reforms introduced into India by the Act of 1919. He was the founder of the Indian Year-Book.

January 18, 1969.

Ada Reeve, one of the gayest of the Gaiety Girls, died on September 25, 1966, in a London hospital at the age of 92.

Her death removes from the world of entertainment a well-nigh legendary figure who could boast with pride that her stage career covered a span of 74 years and that, if film, television and sound boradcasting were included, she had retained her affectionate hold on the public for more than 80 years. Much of her success was due to the fact that she could get her magnetic personality and her cheery optimism across the footlights.

She was born in London on March 3, 1874, her parents being members of an obscure touring company. Her first stage appearance was on Boxing Day in 1878 at the Whitechapel Pavilion in a *Red Riding Hood* pantomime. Two years later she had her first speaking part as "Little Willie" in *East Lynne* and won the cheers and tears of her audiences for that most pathetic of stage children. The result was that she played many child parts before she appeared in the music halls as a light comedy artist.

In his history of the Gaiety Theatre Mr. Macqueen Pope has told of an evening at the Metropolitan which changed the whole course of her life. In 1894 George Edwardes was looking for a new leading lady for the Gaiety for a revival of *Little Jack Sheppard* and went one night to the Metropolitan to see Ada Reeve, a young lady who was already something of a variety star. After her performance he invited her to play the leading part in the burlesque which had been created by Nellie Farren. To his surprise she rejected the offer. She explained that everyone had seen Nellie Farren and would inevitably make comparisons. It would be bad for her but it would also be bad for Mr. Edwardes. He appreciated her point and then offered her the leading part in a new type entertainment, a "musical comedy" called *The Shop Girl*, which he was soon to present. She leapt at the chance and Edwardes's faith in her was completely justified.

When *The Shop Girl* was produced in November, 1894, she made an enormous success as the beautiful assistant in the "Royal Stores" playing opposite Seymour Hicks as a medical student and Teddie Payne as a shopwalker. It ran for more than 500 performances, a long life in those days, and thereafter she appeared in many other musical comedies including *All Abroad* and *The Gay Parisienne*, to be followed later by *Floradora*, *San Toy*, *Kitty Grey*, and *Three Little Maids*. She toured South Africa in 1906, 1911, and 1913 and was in Australia in 1897, 1914, from 1922 to 1924 and from 1929 to 1935.

When she returned in 1935 her friends imagined that it was to a quiet retirement but that was never her idea. She made her first appearance in cabaret at the Trocadero and then proceeded to embark upon the final stage of her varied career by proving that she had few rivals in "eccentric old woman" parts. Her energy and vitality were amazing and at the age of 70 she was scoring success after success. She played in J. B. Priestley's "theatrical tract", *They Came to a City*, with that other great veteran, A. E. Matthews. In *The Shop at Sly Corner*, Edward Percy's "thriller" at the St. Martin's in 1945 she contributed a largely irrelevant but none the less endearing sketch of a tipsy valetudinarian charwoman, playing the part for more than a year. In the revival of *The Dubarry* at the Prince's in 1947 she was deservedly acclaimed for her spirited management of the scene which presented with extremely genteel touch the home of the ladies of easy virtue, and in *Don't Listen Ladies*, an adaptation of a Sacha Guitry comedy, at the St. James's in 1948 she gave a charming performance. To celebrate her eightieth birthday she took part in a B.B.C. programme, and in 1954 appeared at the Players Theatre in songs from her repertory. She even found time at the end of 1954 to publish her autobiography under the title of *Take it for a Fact*.

She was twice married.

September 26, 1966.

Dr. Fritz Reiner, who died in New York on November 15, 1963, at the age of 74, was one of the great orchestral trainers of our day, and an outstanding interpreter of German music, and particularly opera, between Beethoven and Richard Strauss. A Hungarian by birth, he made his home in the United States after the First World War and paid very infrequent visits to Europe.

Reiner was born in Budapest on December 19, 1888, and graduated in law as well as music in 1908. His first musical post was as coach at the Budapest Opera, and then in 1910 he obtained the first conductorship at Laibach (Ljublana) Landestheater. He returned to the Hungarian capital in 1911 as conductor at the Volksoper, and in 1914 was called to Dresden, where he remained as chief conductor until 1921, being responsible among other things for the German premiere of Strauss's *Die Frau ohne Schatten*.

After making guest appearances in Spain and Italy, Reiner crossed the Atlantic and was in charge of the Cincinnati Symphony Orchestra from 1922 until 1931, when he took office as head of the orchestral department at the Curtis Institute of Music in Philadelphia. During his time there Reiner resumed his operatic career in conjunction with the Philadelphia Grand Opera Company. Here, as at San Francisco in the years immediately before the Second World War, he was in charge of German opera.

In 1936 Beecham engaged Reiner to conduct at Covent Garden (he had given one symphony concert there in May, 1924), and during this season Reiner directed the *Tristan und Isolde* in which Kirsten Flagstad made her London debut. In the Coronation season of 1937 Reiner made one rare excursion outside German opera when, at very short notice, he took over Gluck's *Orphée* from Beecham.

In 1938 Reiner was appointed to the Pittsburgh Symphony Orchestra, succeeding Dr. Klemperer. For three years he combined this post with his teaching duties at Philadelphia, but in 1941 he retired from the Curtis Institute and devoted his time to Pittsburgh until 1948, when his debut at the Metropolitan Opera House, New York, led to regular engagements there for five seasons, mainly in German opera but also including Mozart, *Die Fledermaus*, and Verdi's *Falstaff*. In 1953 Reiner was obliged to leave the Metropolitan in order to assume direction of the Chicago Symphony Orchestra, which, over a period of nine years, he moulded into one of the most brilliant and finely disciplined orchestras in the world. In 1955 he was invited to conduct *Die Meistersinger* in the inaugural celebrations for the reopening of the Vienna State Opera. In 1956 and 1958 he paid further visits to Europe, conducting at the Salzburg and Lucerne festivals.

Reiner's specialities were Wagner and Strauss, and his characteristic sound, which he implanted in three great American orchestras, had an extraordinary richness and grandeur that sometimes cloyed, though brilliance and precision most usually kept it fresh and invigorating. His ear and eye for a score were legendary in his profession.

November 18, 1963.

Franz Reizenstein, the composer and pianist, died in London on October 15, 1968, at the age of 57. German by birth, he lived almost all his adult life in England and brought to English music some of the earnestness and atmosphere of high, philosophical importance which surrounds the art in Germany.

Franz Reizenstein was born in Nuremberg on June 7, 1911. He studied at the College of Music there and at the State Academy of Music in Berlin, where Hindemith was his composition teacher and Leonid Kreutzer his piano teacher. As a Jew Reizenstein was compelled to leave Germany in 1934, and he made his home in London, continuing his studies at the Royal College of Music. In later life, he felt that Vaughan Williams, his composition teacher in London, had exerted a greater influence both musically and spritually than had Hindemith, though his earlier works reflect not only the meticulous craftsmanship he learnt from his German master but also a tough intellectualism like Hindemith's.

Reizenstein's piano teacher in London was Solomon, and throughout his time in England, except for a period during the Second World War when he worked in a railway office, he was prominent as a piano recitalist and a chamber music pianist. Though his rare appearances as a player of other composers' concertos did not show him at his best, he was a fine exponent of his own Piano Concertos, both of which are exuberant virtuoso works with virtuousity put to the service of complex musical designs and processes.

As a composer, Reizenstein's range was very wide; as well as his two Piano Concertos he composed a Cello Concerto in 1936 and a Violin Concerto in 1953, a good deal of chamber music for wind instruments and several ensemble works with piano. In spite of his German origin, he developed a great sensitivity to the rhythms and inflections of the English language, and this showed itself in his oratorio *Genesis*, first heard at the Three Choirs Festival in 1958, as well as in the better-known *Voices of the Night*, a cantata, written in 1951, which won a good deal of popularity in Britain after its first London performances in 1956.

Reizenstein shared Hindemith's rejection of atonality and serialism, as methods of composition which disregarded relationships that he believed to be fundamental to the nature of music, but his own style, rhetorical and emotional, is uncompromisingly modern within a liberal sense of tonality. Though fundamentally a deeply serious musician, both as a man and as a composer he was capable of humour and geniality. These showed in the cheerful Wagnerian parody he contributed to one of the late Gerard Hoffnung's early concerts.

October 17, 1968.

Erich Maria Remarque, the author, died on September 25, 1970, in Locarno. He was 72.

He became famous with his first novel, about the First World War, *All Quiet on the Western Front* (*Im Westen Nichts Neues*), and his fame proved lasting. A new paper-back edition was produced in English in 1964, which seemed to prove that the novel did not depend for its popularity on the circumstances in which it was first published in 1929.

The novelist, who once protested that he was neither a Frenchman nor a Jew, came of a family remotely of French origin. He was born in Osnabruck in 1898. His first ambition was to make a career in music, which he had taught himself, but on the outbreak of war in 1914 he enlisted and fought throughout, being twice wounded. Frustrated in his original ambition, after the end of the war he turned to several casual occupations which gave him a livelihood —racing car driver, pedlar, elementary schoolteacher, eventually taking up sporting journalism. He discovered he had a facility for writing, and in 1929 he produced his novel of life in the trenches. It took him, he said, four weeks to write, and was clearly written from deep impressions of his own soldiering, and with passionate sincerity. It made a powerful appeal to all who had suffered. A million copies were sold in Germany soon after publication, and it was translated into 32 languages, becoming a best-seller everywhere. It was turned into an impressive film which, outside Germany at least, reinforced the pacifist emotion so widely generated by the book. In Germany there was a strong nationalist reaction against both the book and the film, brought about by the Nazi party, and particularly noticeable among those who had been too young to experience the war but were impressed by militarist propaganda. There was such violent opposition to the film in both Germany and Austria that it was prohibited. This aroused many counter-protests, and at length it was permitted with some of the scenes cut out. When the Nazis came to power it was, of course, suppressed, and the novel was among those burnt publicly in Berlin in 1933.

Remarque continued writing and when he was deprived of German citizenship in 1938 moved to Switzerland. In 1931 he produced a sequel to his first novel entitled *The Road Back*, but it lacked the spontaneity of its predecessor. Once he had got the war out of his system, Remarque said, he wanted to turn to other subjects. But in most of his later novels he dealt with the Nazi tyranny or the consequences of both the First and Second World Wars.

In 1947 Remarque was granted United States citizenship, and, alternating between residence in America and Switzerland, he produced a steady succession of novels. *Spark of Life* (1952) depicts conditions in the Nazi concentration camps—though it is doubtful whether his fiction could make as much impact as the reality brought to light in the Nuremberg trials. In 1956 Remarque's first play, *The Last Station*, was produced in Berlin. It depicted frightened people under the Nazi terror and had a most enthusiastic reception. In the same year Remarque wrote the script of his first film, entitled *Ten Days to Die*, dealing with the last days of Hitler's life in the Berlin underground shelter. The production by Pabst was masterly in conveying the lunatic, horrific atmosphere of this grim episode. The novel *A Time to Love and a Time to Die* (1954) took the reader to the German army retreating on the Russian front, and to Berlin under Allied bombing. *The Black Obelisk* (1957) was an entertaining story of the great German inflation of the twenties, comic, earthy, rather laboured at times, but a reminder that Remarque could, as even his most famous novel showed, provide humorous relief. In *Heaven has no Favourites* (1961) the writer harked back to his experience as a poor demobilized soldier and portrayed a young girl, a chronic invalid, desperately in love with a racing car driver. *The Night in Lisbon* was published in 1964.

September 26, 1970.

André Renard, the leader of the Walloon Popular Movement and organizer of resistance and of strikes of metal workers during the occupation of Belgium, died on July 20, 1962, at Liège. He was 51. He had been taken to hospital on July 7 after he had been affected by congestion of the brain at his office at the newspaper *La Wallonie*.

Born at Valenciennes, in northern France, Renard became a metallurgist in the Liège industrial area. He took part in the Belgian campaign in May, 1940, and was taken a prisoner of war. On the grounds of ill-health he was released in 1942, and after his return to Liège he organized an underground trade union movement.

After the war he emerged as a leader of the left wing of the Belgian Socialist Party, became president of the Metalworkers' Union in the Liège province, deputy secretary general of the Socialist Trade Union Federation, regent of the Belgian National Bank, delegate to the European Coal and Steel Community and delegate to various commissions. Besides being manager and editor of the daily newspaper *La Wallonie* he sponsored the founding of the weekly *La Gauche*, the equivalent of the British *Tribune*, and last year started the publishing of a federalist weekly, *Combat*.

His aim to become general secretary of the Federation of Socialist Trade Unions was foiled by the leaders of the Socialist Party and of the Flemish trade unions which distrusted his extremism. In December, 1960, when the Socialist Party opposed the austerity Bill which was introduced in Parliament by the Eyskens Government, Renard precipitated a general strike which caused serious disturbances and was followed only half-heartedly by the Flemish trade unions. In the conviction that nationalization and socialist planning would be realized only in the Walloon region, Renard then started a campaign for federalism which threatened the unity of the Belgian Socialist Party.

His Walloon Popular Movement at the outset attracted the majority of the Walloon socialist members of Parliament and trade union leaders. To devote himself entirely to that movement Renard resigned as deputy general secretary of the Trade Union Federation, as regent of the National Bank and from several other posts. Before his death, however, his movement receded and several socialist members of Parliament withdrew their support.

July 23, 1962.

Sir Patrick Muir Renison, G.C.M.G., who died on November 11, 1965, in a London hospital at the age of 54, was Governor of Kenya from 1959 to 1962. In this post he succeeded Sir Evelyn Baring (Lord Howick), who had been Governor throughout the Mau Mau period. Renison's task was of a totally different order. He had to prepare Kenya for what proved to be the rapid transmission from colonial status—and crisis—to independence under an African government.

His efforts were honest and selfless as would be expected from a man with his long record of devoted public service. Before this, however, he had not served in Africa. When appointed to Kenya he had been Governor of British Guiana for four years, and before that, from 1952 to 1955, Governor of British Honduras. In these posts he had been a great and acknowledged success, but significantly they were relatively small governorships. When Renison arrived in Nairobi, to take control of a country large in size and complex in its tribal loyalties and animosities, the wind of change was already blowing strongly. At this moment, Kenya's essential need was for strong leadership and by someone who recognized, even if he did not like, the realities of developing African leadership.

Renison's approach was typified by his attitude to Jomo Kenyatta. Early in 1960, when Iain Macleod as Colonial Secretary had already presided over the constitutional conference which was to launch Kenya on the road to independence, Renison broadcast to the nation about Jomo Kenyatta, then still in restriction. He described him as "the African leader to darkness and death". Not many months later Kenyatta held senior office in an executive council over which Renison as Governor presided. Kenyatta's magnanimity and Sir Patrick Renison's natural courtesy and sense of propriety made a relationship possible, but it could hardly have been expected to produce the trust and understanding essential as Kenya covered the final delicate and much disputed stages before independence.

Renison's replacement was widely expected after the constitutional conference in the spring of 1962 but he returned and tried to hammer out the details of the "white elephant" constitution there evolved. His removal from the governorship was sudden and brutal. In spite of assurances in Whitehall that there had been no disagreement between Renison and Duncan Sandys it was apparent in November, 1962, that Renison had been sacked to make way for a successor able to provide the dynamic leadership which he by temperament could not offer.

Sir Michael Blundell, in his book *So Rough a Wind*, sums him up well. "He was one of the most sincere, honest, and likeable of men. . and he had only one idea and that was to serve Kenya to the best of his ability." But as Sir Michael adds, "Renison was never, I thought, really at ease with the political leaders of Kenya. He was essentially a civil servant. . . ."

Born on March 24, 1911, he was educated at Uppingham and Corpus Christi College, Cambridge, of which he became an honorary fellow in 1959. He entered the Colonial Administrative Service in 1932 and was seconded to the Colonial Office until 1935, when he went to the Ceylon Civil Service. There he remained until 1944 when he returned for four years to the Colonial Office, thus having an unusually extensive experience both of work in the field and in Whitehall. From 1948 until 1952 he was Colonial Secretary in Trinidad and Tobago.

On leaving Kenya he was for a time in 1963 adviser to Lord Hailsham on sport and physical recreation. From 1964 he had been joint vice-chairman of the British Red Cross Society, and he was a member of the governing body of Queen Elizabeth House, Oxford. He was made C.M.G. in 1950, K.C.M.G. in 1955, and G.C.M.G. in 1962.

Renison married in 1936 Eleanor Hope Gibb. They had one daughter.

November 12, 1965.

Sir Charles Renold died in Manchester on September 7, 1967, at the age of 83.

He was born on October 29, 1883, the eldest son of Hans Renold, founder of the Renold Group. After his schooldays at Abbotsholme, he went to America, and graduated Master of Engineering at Cornell University. He joined Hans Renold Ltd., in 1905, and in 1906 became a director.

In 1910 he introduced a personnel department, then called "the Employment Department", a startling industrial innovation at the time. In the same year a beginning was made in holding "management meetings". He revisited the United States in 1912 to study the work of F.W. Taylor, the American pioneer of modern factory production methods, and on his return persuaded his father to introduce time-and-motion study, an event then remarkable in the British engineering industry.

In the First World War the Renold works was chiefly occupied with munitions making. This brought management problems, and he began to study the whole subject of what he came to call "Constitutional Management" in the company, and its evolution is told in detail in his book *Joint Consultation over Thirty Years*, published in 1950, a book he was bringing up to date at his death.

In 1928 he succeeded his father as chairman of Hans Renold but his first period of office was short, because of the success of his own efforts in negotiating a merger with Coventry-Brampton into a single company which then became Renold and Coventry Chain Company Ltd., of which he was the first managing director as well as deputy chairman. He left the chair and ceded the appointment in the new organization to Arthur Brampton, the leading figure of the Coventry and Brampton directors. In 1945 he resumed his former place as chairman. Thereafter he presided over the affairs of the company as it evolved successively into Renold Chains Limited, and Renold Limited.

In 1946 he was appointed the first chairman of the British Institute of Management and on relinquishing the chairmanship in 1951 he became its first vice-president.

He gave notable service to the Manchester College of Science and Technology (now the University of Manchester Institute of Science and Technology) and the Manchester University, which in 1960 made him an honorary LL.D.

September 8, 1967.

Walter Reuther, for many years a dominating figure in the American trade union scene, was killed on May 9, 1970, when his executive jet aircraft crashed near Pellston, Michigan. He was 62.

For long the leader of the United Automobile Workers, he was a man of wide horizons. Informed, intelligent and shrewd, to him leadership was never limited to getting a few cents more an hour for his "boys". Rather he sought to involve labour not only in industrial production, planning and profit-sharing but also in the great social and political movements of the nation.

In 1955 he was the moving spirit behind the merging of the two largest labour organizations in America, the Congress of Industrial Organizations and the American Federation of Labour, Until then there had been bitter feuds, behind the craft unions and the industrial unions. Reuther led the C.I.O. and George Meany, the other outstanding American union leader, the A.F.L. The honeymoon was short lived; C.I.O. unions refused to merge on local levels with their A.F.L. equivalents and vice versa. Meany was president of the new body and Reuther vice-president and there was no love lost between them. Meany was the social conservative, the "avenging angel" against communism and left-wingers; Reuther was a horse of quite another colour, a champion of civil rights and an outspoken opponent of the war in Vietnam and a proponent of the philosophy that the next job of organized labour in America was to eliminate poverty.

Finally in 1967 Reuther resigned as vice-president and in 1968 took the U.A.W. out of the A.F.L.C.-C.I.O. he had helped to weld, claiming that the parent leadership was smug and satisfied and content "to sit on its status quo".

MOTOR INDUSTRY VETERAN

He was the veteran of some monumental wage and benefit negotiations with the mammoth American motor industry including the famous agreement of 1955 when United Automobile Workers compelled the two largest automobile companies, Ford and General Motors, to sign a revolutionary type of labour agreement for a guaranteed annual wage. Reuther's death will be bound to have a profound effect on the next round of three-year contract negotiations which are due to begin in July, 1970.

He always steadily maintained that labour must accept the uncomfortable effects of technological improvements, provided that it also shared in their benefits. Though the antithesis of the conventional picture of the American union leader, complete with loud tie, cigar and Cadillac (he neither smoked nor drank, and took a smaller salary than his union offered), Reuther had a close acquaintance of the tough life at shop-floor level. He had experienced violence; there had been an attempted kidnapping, an attempted assassination which left one of his arms partially paralysed, and a severe beating during the "Battle of the Overpass" at Fords.

He was born in Wheeling, West Virginia, in 1907. Both his father and his grandfather were union organizers. He left school when he was 15 to become an apprentice tool-maker but was later discharged for trying to organize a protest against Sunday work. For seven years he worked in Detroit as a tool-maker until he was sacked by Ford's for his trade union activities. Unable to get another job he and his brother Victor travelled extensively through Europe on bicycles. For more than a year Walter worked in the Ford-built plant in Gorki, but he found nothing in either the communist system or the working conditions of the motor workers that made him want to stay. Back in America he moved rapidly up the ranks of the U.A.W., organizing an important and significant strike in the Detroit industry and negotiating a contract with General Motors—the forerunner of many more.

In the year after the Second World War Reuther rid his own union of a strong communist faction in its leadership. He was elected president of the U.A.W. in 1946.

He played an active part in the creation of the International Confederation of Free Trade Unions in 1949, carved out of the communist-dominated World Federation of Trade Unions.

So uncompromising was his anti-communist stand that he was often the prime target of attack from Moscow—especially in October, 1959, after he crossed swords with Khrushchev during the Soviet Prime Minister's visit to the United States. The two men had a heated argument, with Reuther saying that Khrushchev's interest in the workers was mainly theoretical and accusing the Soviet Union of using its aid to underdeveloped countries to further the aims of the cold war.

May 11, 1970.

Count Eduard Reventlow, former Danish Ambassador to the Court of St. James's, who died on July 26, 1963, was one of the best known and most respected figures in the Diplomatic Corps in London during and after the Second World War. He was 79.

Ably seconded by his charming wife, he represented his country with quiet dignity and distinction and, during two World Wars, got to know the British character, British institutions, and the social life of the capital with a thoroughness and a shrewdness which his modesty and diffident manner often disguised from those who did not know him well.

He was born on November 28, 1883, son of Count Christian Reventlow, who held a Court appointment and had a close knowledge of the Danish monarchy which was continued in his son. As was usual with Danes destined for a diplomatic career, Eduard Reventlow took his degree in law and in 1909 entered the Ministry of Foreign Affairs. The following year he married Else, daughter of Kammerherre (Chamberlain) Admiral Bardenfleth. In 1913 they went to London, and there Eduard served until 1919, under Count Preben Ahlefeldt-Laurvig. On his return to Copenhagen he advanced step by step in the Ministry, and in 1922 became Permanent Under-Secretary, a responsible position which he held for 10 years. He was then appointed Minister in Stockholm, and in 1938 returned as Minister to London, succeeding his former chief, who told him he could look forward to a pleasant, smooth-running post. Anglo-Danish relations presented few difficulties at that time apart from a few complications over Danish exports to Great Britain. Politically and socially the sky was serene.

A DIFFICULT POSITION

It was, of course, seriously overclouded by the German invasion and occupation of Denmark in April, 1940. Countess Reventlow was in Denmark at the time, visiting her children, one of whom was Lady in Waiting to Princess

Ingrid, later Queen Ingrid of Denmark. But Countess Reventlow managed to rejoin her husband in London and remained the whole course of the war. Count Reventlow's position was made especially difficult by the British Government's appeal to Danish merchantships to enter Allied ports. A large number responded and served loyally with the British Mercantile Marine. It was therefore expected by many Danes and British friends of Denmark that Count Reventlow would, like certain of his colleagues in other capitals, at once repudiate his Government under German control and unequivocally support the Allied cause. Count Reventlow's reasons for not following this course were given in his autobiography, published in 1957, *I Dansk Tjeneste* (In the Service of Denmark). He offered no protest when informed by the Foreign Office that Iceland and the Faroes would be occupied by British forces, but decided he could best serve his King and Government by not repudiating them, but by remaining quietly in London, where the Foreign Office recognized him informally as "charged with the protection of certain Danish interests not under enemy control".

Gradually this anomalous position was abandoned. Reventlow, whose strong pro-British sympathies were never in doubt, associated himself publicy with the praise given to the courageous Danish merchant-seamen, many hundreds of whom gave their lives serving the Allied cause. Towards the end of 1941 he made Denmark's enforced adherence to the Anti-Comintern Pact the occasion for breaking with the Copenhagen Government, though reaffirming his personal loyalty to the King, whose intimate friend he had been for some years. Reventlow's declaration, published on December 3, 1941, was followed in March, 1942, by his formal "dismissal" from the Danish Foreign Service. But by then Reventlow had himself, with his staff, joined the Free Danish Movement, of which he became Honorary Chairman.

This was approved by the British Government, and when the time came to organize the administration which it would be necessary to install in Denmark on the defeat of Germany Reventlow and members of his Legation gave much assistance in settling the details beforehand.

PROMOTED TO AMBASSADOR

On Denmark's liberation in May, 1945, and the establishment of a free, legitimate Danish Government, Reventlow was reinstated in his position in London, and when in 1947 the Legation was raised to an Embassy, he was appointed the first Danish Ambassador to Great Britain. He continued to serve until his retirement, under the age rule, in 1953. After 1945 there had been several ques ions at issue between Denmark and Great Britian; the renewal of the all-important commercial relations,the agitation of the Danes in South Sleswig, under the British occupation, the tremendous burden of the German refugees who had fled to Denmark before the Russian advance. With great patience and imperturbable friendliness Reventlow made his contribution to a solution of these and other problems and Anglo-Danish relations assumed once more their accustomed cordiality. Count Reventlow was awarded the Coronation Medal, and, with Countess Reventlow, played a prominent part in the State Visit to London in 1951 of their Majesties King Frederik IX and Queen Ingrid. On this occasion he was awarded the Grand Cross of the Victorian Order.

On his retirement Reventlow took the title of Lensgreve, as head of the Reventlow family, and went to live in Denmark, chiefly at his country house near Tisvilde, in Northern Zealand.

July 29, 1963.

Paul Reynaud, who was Prime Minister of France when disaster came in June, 1940, and who became the only political personality of the Third Republic to continue to play an important role not only during the Fourth but also in President de Gaulle's Fifth Republic, died in Paris on September 21, 1966, at the age of 87.

Looking back on the main events of Paul Reynaud's brief but fateful Premiership in 1940 it is still not easy to pass a confident verdict upon him. Of his extraordinary abilities of mind, his clarity and logical temper, his honesty of purpose—even, in a measure, his courage—there can be no question. It was with the reputation of having been consistently right, as events proved, in the policies he had advocated during the years before the outbreak of war in 1939 that this small, dapper, sharp-featured man assumed charge of France's destiny in March of the following year; to not a few observers he seemed, indeed, in some degree a French counterpart of Churchill in Britain. The accuracy of his diagnosis of France's economic and financial position apart, Reynaud had been right in giving warning of Nazi Germany's aggressive designs; right in opposing, over several years, such men as Flandin, Bonnet, and Laval; right in urging, in support of the views of General (then a little-known Colonel) de Gaulle, the reorganization of the French Army and the creation of a professional striking force to supplement the conscript body; right in questioning Daladier's capacity for leadership. He had been unfailingly right, too, in preaching in season and out the need for a moral and material regeneration in France. That he was also the loyal supporter and friend of the British connexion was, in the 1930s, evidence of additional statesmanship.

Yet with all this there remains his share of responsibility for the events which led to the capitulation at Bordeaux. It is a responsibility that can be accounted for but never glossed over. The truth is, perhaps, that Reynaud was not the man of destiny in France's hour of greatest crisis because he lacked the personal qualities of a man of destiny. He cannot be blamed for France's military defeat, since no man in the space of a month or two could have repaired the divisions, or undone the folly and neglect of the years between the wars; but he undoubtedly contributed by his own blunders to the crowning catastrophe. Travelled, cultivated, a patriot, a formidable logician, always an accomplished and polished debater in the Chamber, he nevertheless lacked judgment. It was this lack of judgment, among other things, that led him to introduce Pétain and Weygand into his Cabinet and thus permitted defeatism to triumph.

SCHOLARLY INTERESTS

Born in 1878 of a farming family in the French Alps, Paul Reynaud started his career as a barrister. He married a daughter of the celebrated advocate Maître Robert and rapidly built up a lucrative practice, which enabled him to pursue a diversity of tastes and scholarly interests, among them a connoisseur's taste for Chinese art—he himself had something of the Chinese in his appearance. After serving in the War of 1914-18, during which he was twice decorated, he was elected a Right-Centre deputy for the Basses-Alpes and, after being out of the Chamber during 1924-28, for one of the Paris *arrondissements*. It was not until 1930, when he was 52, that he was appointed Minister of Finance in the Tardieu Cabinet. He held the portfolio for the Colonies under Laval in the following year and that of Justice under Tardieu once more a year later, but thereafter was in opposition during six years of embittered controversy and progressive national decline. In foreign policy he was a conspicuous champion of unpopular causes; it was his opposition to French support for Italy in Abyssinia and his demand for immediate action when Germany reoccupied the Rhineland that paved the way for his denunciation of the Munich agreement.

In April, 1938, he had been made Minister of Justice in the Daladier Cabinet, but Munich brought a change of office together with his resignation from his group in the Chamber, the so-called Alliance Démocratique, led by Flandin.

As Minister of Finance from November, 1938, until March, 1940, Reynaud had his opportunity to put into effect the financial views he had long professed, and in the result he undoubtedly enabled the country, though at some political cost, to take a step towards economic recovery.

The manoeuvres that preceded the replacement of Daladier as Prime Minister by Reynaud told further upon Cabinet unity, and in the prosecution of the war Reynaud, the unerring critic, came close to failure as a strong man. He switched his Cabinet responsibilities two or three times before final disaster; his inclusion of Pétain in the Government from May onwards led directly to the majority vote for capitulation at Bordeaux, although Paul Reynaud later insisted that he refused to take part in the capitulation or to ask for the armistice, which Pétain, Weygand and others advised.

On September 6 the Vichy Government, at the dictation, he believed, of the Germans, arrested him, together with Georges Mandel, who had been his Minister of the Interior and had also been opposed to the armistice. They were brought to trial a month later, at the same time as Léon Blum, Daladier and others; and in 1941 they were condemned by Pétain to life imprisonment in a fortress. He and Mandel were handed over to the Germans on November 20, 1942, and were imprisoned in Oranienburg, where Reynaud suffered five months' solitary confinement, and afterwards in Tirol. They were both given back to the custody of the Vichy Government in July, 1944; and Paul Reynaud believed that Hitler had not only issued strict orders that they be not allowed to escape but had given Pétain instructions that they be assassinated by the Vichy militia. Mandel was so assassinated; but Paul Reynaud was spared, and was eventually liberated by the arrival of the American Army on May 4, 1945. He had been in prison for nearly five years in all. But he had retained his health and all his intellectual alertness.

He was elected in 1946 to the new Assembly of the Fourth Republic, gave strongly condemnatory evidence at the trial of Pétain, and in 1947 produced in the two bulky volumes of *La France a Sauve l'Europe* a deal of interesting matter thickly and often rather tediously overlaid by advocacy; he had been, it seemed, right in everything—which was surely to claim to be right in too much. Others of his books of the same kind, published since the war, were *Mes Luttes*, *S'unir ou Périr*, and *Au Coeur de la Mêlée*. Another volume of memoirs appeared in 1964.

EUROPEAN UNITY

It was in July, 1948, after a lapse of eight years, that he again obtained ministerial rank. He was appointed Minister of Finance and Economic Affairs in the short-lived coalition Cabinet of André Marie, a not particularly inspiring Radical leader. After this interlude Paul Reynaud devoted himself for a time to what was to remain one of his principal preoccupations—European unity. He failed to form a government in 1953 when asked by Vincent Auriol, then President, but served as Vice-Premier in the government that was eventually formed by Joseph Laniel.

Throughout the confused and sorry remaining years of the Fourth Republic Paul Reynaud continued to play a prominent part in the work of the Assembly, mainly in the financial and economic fields. His lucid contributions to the often turgid debates, delivered in his piping little voice, invariably brought the House, if only momentarily, back to reality. As one of the leaders of the moderate wing of the heterogeneous group of right wing parties which had joined together to form the *Groupe des Indépendants et Paysans d'Action Sociale*, usually known more conveniently merely as *Indépendants*, he helped to exert a restraining influence in issues such as the Algerian problem on which passions were already riding high. Although by no means hostile to General de Gaulle, in the May crisis of 1958 Paul Reynaud took the stand that the Pflimlin Government, the legal government of France, must remain in office and must be obeyed whatever the consequences. Despite this, when the crisis subsided and General de Gaulle became Prime Minister, it was Paul Reynaud he asked to preside over the committee supervising the preparation of his new Constitution. In the general election of November, 1958, for the first National Assembly of the Fifth Republic, when the majority of the leading personalities of the Fourth Republic were swept into obscurity, Paul Reynaud, last remaining political survivor of the Third, was triumphantly reelected. And despite strong opposition from the monolithic neo-Gaullist Union for the New Republic he was once again elected President of the Assembly's Finance Committee.

Reynaud strongly supported President de Gaulle's self-determination policy for Algeria through all its phases but later he had strongly criticized French foreign policy and opposed the plan for a French nuclear force.

Reynaud had seemed not only politically and nationally but also physically indestructible. Physical fitness was indeed one of his passions and right to the closing months of his long life he exercised regularly in a gymnasium he had had constructed in his apartment in the Place du Palais Bourbon, just behind the National Assembly. His first wife having died, Paul Reynaud, in 1949 at the age of 71, married Mlle. Dolores Mabire, who bore him three children, the youngest of whom was born when Reynaud was approaching 80.

September 22, 1966.

Gerald Reynolds, P.C., Minister of Defence for Administration since 1967, died on June 7, 1969, in London at the age of 41. He had been Labour M.P. for Islington, North, since 1958.

The very few ministerial colleagues who knew Reynolds lay in hospital incurably ill spoke of the courage with which he accepted his sentence. Other politicians will now recall the speech he made in the Commons in April, 1960, when he called for the Health Service to provide improved clinical research into the treatment of kidney diseases. Reynolds told the House how, as a boy of 14, suffering from acute nephritis, he was discharged from hospital and given about three months to live.

Reynolds was an admirable example of the younger generation of working-class Labour politicians who on merit have been moving up the rungs of leadership. He was educated at Acton County School and then, with an enormous appetite for learning, went to evening classes at the Ealing School of Art. He joined the Labour staff at Transport House in an unimportant post, then made his name as a specialist in local government research, first as an assistant and then as local government officer in the years between 1952 and 1958. Meanwhile he served as secretary of the Labour Party committee which, under the late Hugh Gaitskell, produced the party policy statements "Homes of the future" and "National Superannuation". By the time he entered the Commons as M.P. for Islington, North, at a by-election in 1958, he had made a considerable mark in Labour local government circles. He was elected a member of the Acton Borough Council in 1949 and continued to serve until 1965. He was Mayor of Acton in the year 1961–62.

At Westminster he was from the beginning closely allied with George Brown (later Lord George-Brown) whose lieutenant he became. He shared Brown's sturdy views on defence in years when they were the subject of bitter party controversy, and long before Labour came to power he was publicly calling for a rationalization of Britain's defence to make it more cost-efficient.

When Denis Healey became Secretary of State for Defence in October, 1964, Reynolds joined him as an Under-Secretary, and they had been closely associated ever since in evolving and carrying out the policies of unifying the Ministry, rationalizing the three services, and reducing commitments to keep down defence spending to a budget of £2,000m. a year at 1964 prices. From 1965 to 1967 he was Minister of Defence for the Army.

In January, 1967, Reynolds was promoted to be No. 2 in the Ministry in the key post of Minister of Defence (Administration).

He married in 1949 Dorothy F. Budd. They had two daughters.

June 9, 1969.

Quentin Reynolds, the American journalist, who died at the age of 62 in California on March 17, 1965, was a widely travelled foreign correspondent who first became well known to the British public in the early part of the Second World War through a Sunday night B.B.C. "Postscript" (afterwards known as the "Schicklgruber broadcast"), in which he condemned Hitler and Hitler's methods in good round terms and thereby gave considerable satisfaction to British listeners.

This was before Pearl Harbour and not all American journalists were seen to be so sympathetic to the British cause. It was not a case of winning popularity by hissing more loudly than the rest at the villain; Reynolds, as a correspondent for the International News Service, had served in Germany in the 1930s and seen with foreboding the rise of the Nazis and the fall of freedom.

He was born in New York in 1902 and, while working as a sports reporter for the old *New York World*, he studied at Brooklyn Law School, graduating in 1931. He joined the International News Service in 1932 and became its Berlin correspondent the following year. In 1934, he became an associate editor of *Collier's Weekly* and served as a war correspondent for the magazine throughout the Second World War. Associate editor he may have been but he was content to be thought of as a reporter. Somewhere in his books there is a line about reporters not being allowed to "soften into journalists".

For a reporter Europe with a war on was the place to go, and he went to Britain in a freighter by way of Halifax, Nova Scotia.

With his extrovert bonhomie, garrulousness, and taste for the dramatic, he was the Englishman's idea of an American journalist; he identified himself whole-heartedly with the British war effort, with an enthusiasm which was liable to reach gale force. He travelled up and down the country talking to those with much authority and to those with none at all, asking questions, and writing reports, which, like his books, were vivid, chatty, discursive, full of the foreign correspondent's small change, readable, and widely popular.

He did not remain in London, but followed the war round the world; he was strafed in France, dive-bombed at Dieppe, and covered operations from North Africa to the Pacific. Perhaps his philosophy is best conveyed in the titles of some of his books, *Don't Think It Hasn't Been Fun*; *Only the Stars are Neutral*; *The Wounded Don't Cry*, and (his autobiography) *By Quentin Reynolds.*

March 18, 1965.

Dr. Syngman Rhee, who died in Honolulu on July 19, 1965, at the age of 90, was the first President of the Korean Republic, and the symbol of its independence, for which he had fought all his life.

He had in him the very stuff of greatness, but his shortcomings were on the same generous scale as his virtues. None could impugn the sincerity and steadfastness of his beliefs, to which he remained true in the face of all compromise and reasonableness. A paternalist at heart, called upon to become his nation's first democratic chief of state, he continued to believe to the end that he knew what was good for Korea better than the Koreans did themselves.

In the end his obstinacy proved his downfall. His readiness to maintain his rule by corrupt political methods—which made the police one of the most-hated elements in Korean life—culminated in the flagrant managing of the elections in March, 1960. In the following month student demonstrations in Seoul and other towns soon began to express popular feeling. The forces of suppression proved powerless against students and teachers combined. When the Army showed its sympathy for the students and the Americans withdrew their support, his regime crumpled. By May, Syngman Rhee had resigned and left his country. Since then what has come to be known as "the April revolution" has erased, temporarily at least, unhappy memories of Rhee's latter days of power.

Any judgment on Rhee must take into account the exceptional circumstances which faced him in the latter part of his life. He finally came to office in his seventies in a nation physically and spiritually diminished by 40 years of occupation. He inspired it through a devastating civil war which left it divided and prostrate under constant fear of renewed invasion from the north. He found a people accustomed to the tyranny either of their own or foreign rulers, inured to violence, and as fierce in their passions as himself. A weaker man, less convinced that he was his country's chosen instrument, might well have failed.

"I have been an agitator all my life", Rhee was fond of saying. He was born in Hwanghae Province on March 26, 1875. His father was a typical scholar of his day, steeped in genealogy and the tradition of Chinese literature.

In 1894 he joined the Independence Club, an association which sought to bring about reforms in the incredibly corrupt and inefficient administration of the Korean rulers, and he founded the *Independence*, the first newspaper in Korean and by Koreans to appear in his country, for the propagation of reformist ideas. The Japanese at this time were systematically infiltrating the country, and preparing to seize control of the Government. Rhee sensed the danger and tried to ward it off by urging popular reforms. The King continually vacillated between renovation and reaction; but the activities of the Independence Club gained such renown and became so widespread that they were feared as revolutionary. In an attempt to free himself from foreign influence and reassert his control over the situation, the King determined to crush the reformist movement. Rhee was arrested with some of his companions; others fled. He was sentenced to life imprisonment.

For six months he was subjected to unbelievable tortures which left permanent scars on his hand. During his six years in prison he became a convert to Christianity. With the complicity of warders he succeeded in organizing classes for his fellow prisoners in religion, economics and English and in conducting religious services. The 1904 amnesty of political prisoners released him from imprisonment.

Then began for Rhee over 40 years of ceaseless endeavour to bring the plight of Korea annexed outright by Japan before the public opinion in the world and especially in the United States. He remained in close contact with the independence movement in Korea and played an important part in the organization of the Mansei Revolution of 1919.

Though the revolution failed, 1919 saw the creation by delegates from all over Korea secretly assembled in Seoul of the Korean Provisional Government. Rhee was unanimously elected President and a Declaration of Independence adopted.

TRUCE DENOUNCED

Pearl Harbour and the entry of the United States into the war against Japan brought new hopes to the exiles, though their attempts at recognition and their offers of guerrilla assistance were alike spurned by the State Department, which seems to have had doubts about the degree of popular support Rhee, after years of exile, actually enjoyed in his own country. He had considerable difficulty in returning there in 1945, after its liberation.

In the elections to the Assembly which were held in the south in 1948, Rhee's followers secured an overwhelming majority. And on July 20, at the age of 73, he was chosen President of the Korean Republic by 180 votes to 16.

Then came the aggression of June 25, 1950. When the possibility of an armistice arose, he steadfastly maintained that none should be discussed unless the unification of Korea was guaranteed. He opposed with the same singleness of purpose the armistice talks at Kaesong and Panmunjom. The truce he denounced with all the passionate obstinacy of a man convinced that a grave injustice was being perpetrated on his country. He gave forcible expression to his hostility by releasing 27,000 North Korean prisoners in June, 1953, seriously compromising the armistice talks and incurring a severe rebuke from President Eisenhower.

Elections held during the war revealed plainly Rhee's prescription of authoritarian, paternalistic democracy. The Assembly was forced under duress to amend the constitution and relinquish in the people's interest the right of electing the President. Martial law, intimidation and police pressure were liberally used, and Rhee was overwhelmingly reelected for a second term. The Constitution was again amended in 1954 to allow him to run for as many terms as he wished.

Rhee's rule came suddenly to an end in the spring of 1960. In the March elections he triumphed—without an opponent—and secured the election of his nominee as vice-president, but no one sincerely believed that the result represented an expression of popular will and early on April 11 the Democratic Party filed a suit with the Supreme Court asking that the elections be declared null and void. A few days later violent rioting, in which many people were killed and injured, broke out and in Seoul and four other cities martial law was proclaimed on April 19. Two days later all 12 members of Rhee's Cabinet submitted their resignation in a gesture of atonement for the unrest and bloodshed of the past few days. Rhee himself made no such large gesture; in an effort to ride the storm he resigned as leader of his Liberal Party but declared his intention to remain chief executive of the republic; it was not enough. Further rioting broke out and this time Rhee's home was threatened by demonstrators who called for the old man to go. However, popular anger was transformed into jubilation when on April 26 Rhee announced at last his willingness to go—if it were the wish of the people. Of this there could be no two opinions and after 12 years in office Rhee became once more a private citizen. A month later, with his wife, he left for Hawaii.

He married in 1934 Francesca Donner, an Austrian. His only son by an earlier marriage died in 1915. In 1957 he adopted, in accordance with Korean practice, the eldest son of Lee Ki Poong, the Speaker of the National Assembly and then a close political friend. Shortly after Rhee's fall, the young man shot his parents and then killed himself.

July 20, 1965.

Juliet Lady Rhys Williams, D.B.E., widow of Sir Rhys Rhys-Williams, BT., Q.C., who died on September 18, 1966, in the National Hospital for Nervous Diseases, London, at the age of 65, will be remembered as a person of abounding energy who found the time to make a worthwhile contribution in a number of widely differing fields. In medical welfare, in economics, in politics as an active Liberal for some years, in the European movement—in these and in other spheres she won admiration for her zest and the originality of her mind. In spite of her range she was much more than a dilettante. She was an all-rounder of a type too rarely seen nowadays.

The younger daughter of Elinor Glyn, the novelist, and her husband Clayton Glyn, she was born on December 17, 1898 and educated at The Links, Eastbourne. In 1914, not yet 16, she refused to return to school, put her hair up and joined the V.A.D.

In the last year of the war she became private secretary to the Director of Training and Staff Duties, Admiralty, and in 1919 assistant secretary, War Cabinet Demobilization Committee. Later that year she was appointed private secretary to the Parliamentary Secretary, Ministry of Transport. This was Rhys Williams, who had been returned unopposed as a Coalition-Liberal for Banbury at the general election of 1918 and who was later made a baronet. As Parliamentary Secretary, Ministry of Transport he drafted the Bill for unifying the principal railway systems but soon after he resigned following a difference of opinion with his Minister, Sir Eric Geddes. Rhys Williams and Juliet Glyn were married in February, 1921.

In 1924 she went out to Hollywood with her husband in an attempt to impose some kind of order on her mother's business affairs—Elinor Glyn's career in film-making had been both successful and lucrative, but financial acumen she lacked and it was said of her that she would sign any contract laid before her. A company called Elinor Glyn, Ltd. was formed with members of her family as directors and Juliet Rhys Williams as secretary. That same year Elinor Glyn's second film for M.G.M., *His Hour*, was produced; King Vidor directed it, John Gilbert was one of the stars—and Elinor Glyn's daughter wrote the continuity. Its competence should not have surprised the director (as it did) for she had always a fluent pen.

In the 1930's she did valuable work for the maternity services. For some years she ran a scheme in South Wales for maternal and child welfare. For her part in the drafting and passing of the Midwives Act, 1936, she was created D.B.E. And as chairman of the National Birthday Trust Fund she was active for many years in organizing medical research, especially the nation-wide survey which produced the Perinatal Mortality Survey Report 1963.

While mainly concerned with medical welfare in the interwar period, she was already showing a keen interest in economics, attending study groups such as the Economic Research Council.

Her book called *Something to Look Forward To* published in 1943 can be regarded as a well worked out scheme for social security, rival to the more famous plan of Lord Beveridge.

STRANDS OF THOUGHT

This was followed by a number of other publications of which *Taxation and Incentive* was perhaps the best known. Her central thought contained three strands: 1. Every citizen, whether in employment or not, should receive, as of right, a basic allowance to cover subsistence; this to be supplemented by liberal family allowances, on which she was always very keen. 2. As an offset, income tax on earned income should be applied at the full standard rate from the bottom upwards, the purpose being to make every citizen feel in his own purse the cost of greater Government expenditures and thus to enhance his sense of responsibility. 3. A further objective was to provide a stronger incentive to seek employment; since the basic allowance would be paid, whether one was in employment or not, one would suffer no deduction on gaining employment. Unemployment insurance would become redundant.

Taking the three points together, she argued that her scheme, including the universal subsistence allowances, would not involve any increase in general taxation. She became a great expert on national income statistics, and critics found it very hard to trip her up. She also had a natural flair for economics, and often saw the likely effects of proposed measures more quickly than professional economists.

EUROPEAN UNITY

After the war she threw herself with great vehemence into the cause of European unity. She was an honorary secretary of the Congress at The Hague (1948). From that time forward she was the secretary and mainstay of the European League for Economic Cooperation. Her efforts to interest distinguished British personages and make them work were untiring, and her enthusiasm and idealism were infectious. She attended its frequent meetings regularly, did much of the organization on the British side, and became a familiar and much loved figure on the Continent.

She was not a mere secretary. She often took a line of her own, always having a weather eye for British interests and sometimes fearing that the Continentals might not in their plans pay sufficient regard for social welfare, her lifelong interest. She also scented deflationary tendencies in Continental thinking, deflation being her particular bugbear. In spite of her ardent advocacy of European unity, she was opposed to Britain joining the Common Market in 1962 on any terms likely to be obtainable.

She twice stood unsuccessfully for Parliament as a Liberal: at Pontypridd in 1938 and at Ilford North in 1945. She was chairman of the party's Publications and Publicity Committee from 1944 until her resignation in 1946 after a disagreement on policy with the party leaders. A governor of the B.B.C. from 1952 to 1956, she was also a former chairman of the Cwmbran Development Corporation in South Wales.

DYNAMO

She was a tremendous dynamo. Her life was bound up with the causes that she had at heart. Although so earnest, she was always gay easy and companionable in conversation, and she was supremely brave in the last period of declining health.

Her husband died in 1955. They had two sons (one of whom was killed in action in Tunisia in 1943) and two daughters.

September 19, 1964.

Elmer Rice, American playwright, producer, novelist and tireless supporter of civil liberties, died on May 8, 1967, in Southampton General Hospital. He was 74.

When he first burst on the New York stage in 1914 with *On Trial*, complete with flashbacks, close observation of life and the technical facts of the law, and a disturbing social message, Rice made his name overnight as leader of modern American drama. He was to go on writing for the stage for almost 50 years– *Love Among the Ruins* came out in 1963—although his last notable success was with *Dream Girl*.

He exploded the tragedy of the great depression with *We, the People* (1933). His *Judgment Day* (1934) dealt with Hitler's rise to power and *Between Two Worlds* (1934) depicted a hypothetical war between the United States and the Soviet Union. His last play produced on Broadway was *Cue for Passion*, a modern treatment of the tragedy of Hamlet.

NOTABLE PLAYS

The Adding Machine (1923), *Street Scene* (which won a Pulitzer prize in 1929), *The Left Bank* and *Counsellor-at-Law* (1931) were probably his most successful, influential and distinguished plays. He wrote 29 altogether, as well as a couple of novels—*A Voyage to Purilia* (1930), a skit on the film industry, and *Imperial City* (1939), a sharp and thoughtful study of contemporary life in New York. In his later years he wrote two books on the theatre and an autobiography characteristically called *Minority Report* (1963).

His career was determined by three abiding principles: a concern with social justice which often had him in the thick of controversy, a sense of professionalism in theatrical technique, which he felt must develop with other techniques of modern life and moderate their impact on humanity, and a violently expressed mistrust of any form of censorship or exploitation of office.

He was a lifelong member of the American Civil Liberties Union, and his last and perhaps greatest *cause célèbre* was his resignation from the Playwright's Television Theatre in 1951 when an actor was refused a part because of left-wing connexions. "I have repeatedly denounced the men who sit in the Kremlin for judging artistes by political standards", he said. "I do not intend to acquiesce when the same procedure is followed by political commissars who sit in the offices of advertising agencies or business corporations."

SUCCESS AND MARRIAGE

Born Elmer Reizenstein in New York in 1892, he took a law degree with highest honours at night while working as a clerk during the day.

He submitted *On Trial* to a producer by post, married on the strength of its success (about $100,000) and worked for several years in amateur and experimental theatre before the theatre guild put on *The Adding Machine*.

He held various posts in professional bodies, including honorary membership of the League of British Dramatists, and taught occasionally in the universities of New York and Michigan. He had two children by his first marriage to Hazel Levy in 1915 and three by his second to Betty Field, the actress, in 1942. Both marriages ended in divorce.

May 9, 1967.

Professor Sir Albert Richardson, K.C.V.O., P.P.R.A., died on February 3, 1964, at the age of 83.

When all his professional distinction is taken into account—his scholarship and ability as a writer; his gifts as a teacher; his talent as an architect; and his zeal as a preservationist—it is probable that Richardson will still be most generally remembered for his personality as the complete Georgian. He had an enthusiasm for all that belonged to the period that brought him into the glorious company of the English—or Irish—eccentrics. One of the most congenial of his many activities must have been his deputy chairmanship of the Georgian Group, and he was said to be so completely wedded to the eighteenth century that at his house at Ampthill, Bedfordshire, designed by Henry Holland, he wore eighteenth-century dress and read eighteenth-century newspapers.

The anecdote wherein Richardson is supposed to have confessed to having "accidentally struck a Bow Street Runner" while gesticulating outside Somerset House after the inaugural meeting of a preservation society is possibly apocryphal, or at least *ben trovato*: but it is certain that whenever he entertained a friend at Brooks's Club (also by Holland) he would illuminate his hospitality with an excited history of the place and its associations, sending for the betting-book and other relics of the past, with a dissertation on each.

Richardson's anachronism was not an assumed attitude or pose—he seemed genuinely to live and think "in period"—and although he held sound views on the essentials of architecture as being basically a matter of order and proportion, he seemed progressively to blind himself to the possibility of such principles applying equally to the newer trends and methods of construction, or to the less stylistic architecture emerging from them.

TEACHING QUALITIES

The fact is that Richardson was prominently among the last, and most colourful, of a generation of architects in whose lifetime the pendulum had swung from an over-preoccupation with bygone modes to an interest in meeting the aesthetic challenge inherent in the use of new functions and techniques. Looking chiefly towards the past, Richardson, like others of his school of thought, proceeded to justify this instinctive rather than rational preference with arguments which were given wide popular currency by the press and, later, broadcasting. These, perhaps more than conversational indiscretions easily condoned by friends, tended occasionally to strain the affection and indulgence in which Richardson was held by a younger generation of architects convinced of the need for a more realistic approach to architectural problems than the ritual exchanges of verbal broadsides in the "battle of the styles" in which Richardson loved to engage. Nevertheless, the respect in which he was held by his many past pupils showed that his qualities as a teacher far outweighed the limitations his opinions set on the subjects he taught.

Richardson's value as Professor of Architecture, first at University College London, and subsequently, until 1956, at the reconstituted Royal Academy Schools, was universally recognized. As a writer on the architecture of the period which inspired him he also stood in the front rank. At least one of his books, *Monumental Classical Architecture in Great Britain and Ireland during the Eighteenth and Nineteenth Centuries*, ranks as a standard work. Other publications included *London Houses* and *Regional Architecture in the West of England* (both with C. Lovett Gill), *The Old Inns of England*, *The Smaller English House* (with H. D. Eberlein), and *The Art of Architecture* (with Hector O. Corfiato).

EXPLOSIVE UTTERANCES

Much of Richardson's architectural work before the war was done in partnership with Charles Lovett Gill, with whom he was joint architect to the Duchy of Cornwall Estate in Devon. Among the buildings for which they were responsible were the Public Schools Club, Berkeley Street; New Theatre, Quay Street, Manchester; Southampton Hall, Holborn; Moorgate Hall, Finsbury Pavement; the facade of Regent Street Polytechnic; the Jockey Club, Newmarket; and St. Margaret's House, Wells Street, for which the firm received the 1931 R.I.B.A. Bronze Medal, together with several country houses and the reparation of churches and other ancient buildings.

After the war Richardson worked in partnership with E.A.S.Houfe (his son-in-law). Their commissions included the restoration of war-damaged St. James's Church, Piccadilly; the Church of the Holy Cross, Greenford; the altar for the Battle of Britain Memorial; the Far East War Memorial at Elston Church, Bedfordshire; the *Financial Times* building near St. Paul's Cathedral; and the rebuilding of Merchant Taylors' Hall in Threadneedle Street.

Richardson, who was born in 1880, was knighted in 1956 after he had become president of the Royal Academy. Among his memberships, as well as that of the Georgian Group, were the Standing Commission on Museums, the Royal Commission on Historical Monuments (England), the Royal Fine Art Commission, the Central Council for the Care of Churches, and the diocesan advisory committees of London, St. Albans, Ely, and Southwark.

Richardson was a short, stoutish, vivacious man who might pardonably have been mistaken for an actor. The cream of Richardson was best to be appreciated at first hand rather than quoted, when he was on his feet and his own ground, his rapid and explosive utterance giving point to a witty choice of expression whose extravagance was readily "discounted for" by those who knew and loved him. Occasional over-statement and inconsistency in attacking what did not conform to his preferences did not lessen his value as a fighter on the side of the angels, if perhaps more trenchantly and constructively in the field of preservation than in the newer one of an architecture serving contemporary social needs.

He married Elizabeth, daughter of John Byers, of Newry, county Down, and had one daughter. His wife died in 1958. He became F.R.I.B.A. in 1913, receiving the Institute's Gold Medal in 1947, was elected A.R.A. in 1936 and R.A. in 1944. He was also F.S.A., Hon. M.A. (Cantab.), Hon. Litt.D. (Dublin), and Hon. R.W.S.

February 4, 1964.

Sir Bruce Richmond, who joined the staff of *The Times* in 1899 and was for 35 years editor of *The Times Literary Supplement*, died on October 1, 1964, at the age of 93.

It is Bruce Richmond's work for *The Times Literary Supplement* that must be mentioned first: for that work absorbed his fullest energies and deepest interests. And tribute to him may well begin with a description of his methods as editor. On his retirement in 1937 an old colleague wrote of him that all through the 35 years he had been "an editor in the truest and fullest sense ... He has always kept his contributors in order. He has never let them go unscrutinized to say exactly what they fancied; still less has he been in the habit of consigning whole departments of literature to a single reviewer .... The right man for the right book has been his rule. Again he has been a persistently reading editor—a diligent reader of books old and new for his own profit and for the sake of his public.... In the matter of English style few editors have been more particular .... Hard work, in fact, quite as much as fine taste, wide sympathy, and a just capacity for criticism has gone into Sir Bruce's *Supplement* all these years."

To that tribute may be added a phrase or two of the address of the Public Orator at Oxford University in 1930, when the honorary degree of Doctor of Letters was conferred upon Richmond. Passing swiftly from "*vir ab artis suae ostentatione aversus*" to the "*opus quod informavit atque expolivit*", the late A.B. Poynton returned before the close of his speech to reveal through that life's work the spirit of the "exemplar humanitatis" who had been for so long "iuvenum litteris studentium hortator, comes, dux".

Bruce Lyttleton Richmond, born at 11, Stafford Terrace, Kensington, on January 12, 1871, was the only child of Douglas Close Richmond, who from 1900 to 1904 was Comptroller and Auditor-General in the Exchequer and Audit Office, and his first wife, Margaret Cecilia Bruce, eldest daughter of the first Lord Aberdare of Duffryn. From his preparatory school, Radcliffe's at Fonthill, he was elected in 1884, at the head of the roll, to a scholarship at Winchester College. In his last year at Winchester, 1889-90, he was Prefect of Hall; and among the prizes he won was that for Greek Prose. In 1889 and 1890 he was in Lord's Eleven. In 1890 he won a Winchester scholarship at New College. In 1892 he took a first in Classical Moderations and in 1894 a second in *Lit. Hum.* At Oxford instead of games he cultivated music, his love of music having been fostered at Duffryn as well as at Winchester. All his life Richmond was devoted to music; for many years he was a member of the Council and Executive Committee of the Royal College of Music.

On leaving Oxford he read for the Chancery Bar, and was called by the Inner Temple in 1897. But his legal career was cut short when in March, 1899, he was invited, much to his surprise, to offer himself for trial on the editorial staff of *The Times*. In the following month he was engaged as an Assistant Editor for a year. He held that appointment for 16 years and remained in the service of *The Times* till the end of 1937.

In the editorial room he found himself with George Earle Buckle (another Wykehamist), the Editor, and the first Assistant Editor, John Brainard Capper. To Richmond politics were no strange field, but he had his special contributions to bring to the editorial room—his lively interest in games and sport, in music, in the drama and the other arts. As he gained the confidence of his seniors, he was given more and more say in the treatment of these subjects and in the choice of writers about them. It is certainly not a coincidence that Richmond joined the staff of *The Times* in the spring of 1899 and that Walkley began to contribute dramatic criticism in the following September.

OBVIOUS SUCCESSOR

With his friend, John Cam Bailey, he had worked hard at Oxford upon the classics and English. When the *Literary Supplement* was started at the beginning of 1902 Richmond was early associated with it; and when it grew to be a permanent weekly feature of *The Times* he was the obvious member of the staff to take over from (Sir) John Thursfield, who shortly withdrew from direction of the journal. So long as the increasing demands of the *Supplement* allowed, he kept on his other editorial work; but from the autumn of 1915 till his retirement the assistance he gave to any other department was advisory, not official.

To the tributes already quoted it might be added that Richmond never wrote an article in his own *Supplement* (he maintained, indeed, that he "could not write"), and that his power of impressing his standard of judgment and taste on every column was combined with a contempt for the high-handed style which regards contributors' work as raw material for editorial rewriting. His desire was for well-founded and durable judgment, urbanely though fearlessly expressed: and he was resolved to make his journal so good that writers of the highest eminence should be willing to write in it anonymously, and (following the tradition of *The Times*) almost in secret.

How well he succeeded can be judged by the files of the journal he directed so ably and from the tribute paid to him on his ninetieth birthday by T.S. Eliot: "For Bruce Richmond we wanted to do our best. Good literary criticism requires good editors as well as good critics. And Bruce Richmond was a great editor; fortunate those critics who wrote for him."

OTHER ENTERPRISES

The *Supplement* apart, he could always find time to advise or help on other enterprises. The Royal Literary Fund found in him a staunch and vigorous supporter, and made him a Vice-President in 1939. In the autumn of 1922 the University of Leeds, and in the spring of 1930 his own University of Oxford, conferred upon him the honorary degree of Doctor of Letters. A higher recognition still was awarded to the journal and its director when the honour of knighthood was conferred upon Richmond in 1935. During the early months of the 1939–45 war he compiled *The Pattern of Freedom*, an anthology of prose and verse, designed to show freedom as the tradition of the west has conceived it. The book had an immediate and enduring welcome.

In 1913 he married Elena, daughter of William G. Rathbone. She brought notable gifts of taste and spirit to enrich the homes which they delighted to make together and to share with their many friends. Few men, perhaps, have combined Richmond's subtlety and refinement of taste with his genial lack of superciliousness: and in his London house, among his flowers and his beloved birds in a garden near Robertsbridge, and, after his retirement, in his beautiful home near Salisbury, which had previously belonged to Sir Henry Newbolt, and later in Oxford, he was always full of life and the best of good company.

October 2, 1964.

Sir Ian Richmond, C.B.E., Professor of the Archaeology of the Roman Provinces in the University of Oxford, and Fellow of All Souls College, died in Oxford on October 4, 1965, at the age of 62.

His life-work was the study of Roman antiquities, particularly those in Britain. His early training as an ancient historian, his innate archaeological genius and his flair for the elucidation of earthworks and architectural remains marked him out early in life as the obvious successor of F. J. Haverfield and R. G. Collingwood in this field of study.

Ian Archibald Richmond was born in 1902, the son of Daniel Richmond, M.D. From Ruthin School he went to Corpus Christi College, Oxford, where he graduated with second class honours in Greats in 1924. But already his abiding passion was archaeology. When convalescing from a serious illness during his last year at school a book of Haverfield's inspired in him an interest in Romano-British studies, so that, though to his great regret he never met Haverfield (who died in 1919), he spent more time than his tutors wished in reading archaeology, and was a prominent member of the University Archaeological Society.

On leaving Oxford he spent two years at the British School at Rome holding in succession the Gilchrist Scholarship of the School and the Craven Fellowship and Goldsmiths Senior Studentship of his university. His subject of research was the City Wall of Imperial Rome (his book on which was published in 1930) and on this he worked in very close touch with Thomas Ashby, Director of the school, whose wide knowledge of the architecture of Rome enabled him to give Richmond the greatest encouragement and assistance. He became Ashby's friend as well as his pupil and, on Ashby's premature death in 1931, undertook to see Ashby's unfinished book *The Aqueducts of Ancient Rome* (1935) through the press.

Returning from Rome in 1926 Richmond was Lecturer in Classical Archaeology and Ancient History at Queen's University, Belfast, until 1930, when he went back to Rome to be Director of the school. His work on the City Wall, published that very year, made his claim to the post paramount, and his appointment a foregone conclusion.

In 1935 the appointment as Lecturer in the University of Durham at King's College in Newcastle upon Tyne gave him the opportunity he needed to concentrate on those Romano-British studies in which his life's work was to lie. He remained at King's College, becoming Reader in 1943 and Professor in Romano-British History and Archaeology in 1950, until he was invited in 1956 by the University of Oxford to become its first Professor of the Archaeology of the Roman Empire, which carried with it a Fellowship of All Souls. This invitation he gladly accepted, though not without much regret at leaving Newcastle, where he had worked with consummate success for 21 years building up, with Eric Birley's help, a "school" of Romano-British frontier studies in the University of Durham whose importance was universally recognized.

Richmond was a masterly lecturer whose lucid exposition of even the most difficult and complicated subject never failed to grip his audience; he was also a good and painstaking teacher of those who had the will to learn; but he was above all the most skilled of excavators who could tackle with equal competence the quick selective excavation or the total clearance, layer by layer, of a complicated site. The list of sites with which his name will always be coupled is a lengthy one: Cawthorn, Chester, Lincoln, Carrawburgh (temple of Mithras), South Shields, Hod Hill, Fendoch, Inchtuthil are but some of the more important, and his work on numerous sites on Hadrian's Wall and in southern Scotland in collaboration from time to time with F. G. Simpson, R. G. Collingwood, J. P. Gillam and others, has rewritten the story of the Wall itself and of the military campaigns behind and beyond it of Agricola and succeeding Roman generals.

HADRIAN'S WALL

Nor did he fail to publish the results of all this work year by year within the shortest possible time. His list of publications begins with at least three written before or just after graduation, including a major contribution to the story of the Romans in Yorkshire, *Huddersfield in Roman Times* (1925). Thereafter scarcely a year passed without at least one, and often many, articles appearing from his pen, each one of them crystal clear and concise and, where necessary, illustrated with his own photographs and his own carefully surveyed and beautifully drawn plans and sections. He also completely revised Collingwood Bruce's *Handbook to the Roman Wall* for its tenth (1947) and eleventh (1957) editions. Nor did he neglect to produce general statements incorporating archaeological evidence he had obtained: such were *Roman Britain* (Britain in Pictures, 1947)

Archaeology and the After-life in Pagan and Christian Imagery (1950), the Pelican history of *Roman Britain* (1955), and the revision of R. G. Collingwood's *The Archaeology of Roman Britain*, on which he was still working.

A wise and careful counsellor, both in public and in private, he was in much demand on committees both in his own universities and in London and Edinburgh, and no trouble was too great, and no journey too long for him to take, if a call for advice and assistance, which he felt he should accede to, reached him. The Royal Commissions on Historical Monuments for England and Scotland (of both of which he was a member since 1944), the Society for the Promotion of Roman Studies (of which he was president, 1958–61), the Ancient Monuments Board for England (of which he became a member in 1959), the British Academy, the Society of Antiquaries of London, and many other bodies have reason to be grateful to his sense of public spirit.

His gift for lecturing and public speaking brought him not only the Public Oratorship at Durham (1949–51), but also invitations to deliver the Rhind lectures at Edinburgh (1933), the Dalrymple at Glasgow (1938 and 1956), the Riddell at Durham (1948), the Ford at Oxford (1950), the Gray at Cambridge (1941), the Cadbury at Birmingham (1952) and the Reckitt at the British Academy (1955). He was Vice-President of the Society of Antiquaries of London from 1945–49 and 1957–59, Director 1959–64, and President from last year. He was elected a Fellow of the British Academy in 1947 and was Hon. LL.D. of Edinburgh. Hon. Lit.D. of Leeds and Hon. D.Lit. of Belfast and of Manchester as well as being a corresponding Fellow of the German Archaeological Institute. He was created C.B.E. in 1958, and received his knighthood in the Birthday Honours, 1964.

In 1938 he married Isabel Little and had one son and one daughter.

October 6, 1965.

Major-General Hjalmar Riiser-Larsen, who died in Copenhagen on June 3, 1965, was one of the most outstanding Norwegians of his time, a pioneer of civil aviation, an explorer of the Arctic and Antarctic regions and during the Second World War chief of the Royal Norwegian Air Force. He was 74.

His father was a ship's capitain, and from an early age Riiser-Larsen was trained for the sea. He was commissioned as a naval officer in 1912. When the Norwegian Naval Air Arm was created in 1915 he was among the first pilots to be trained, and later he held the first airline pilot's licence in Norway.

In 1919, when the Norwegian Navy established its own aircraft factory at Horten, Riiser-Larsen was appointed the first director. In 1921 he came to England to train as a dirigible captain, and was the first Norwegian to hold a licence as a qualified dirigible pilot. From 1921 to 1927 he was chief secretary for the Aviation Council of the Norwegian Ministry of Defence.

It was in 1925 that he made his first polar exploration, captaining one of the two seaplanes in which Roald Amundsen and Lincoln Ellsworth tried to reach the North Pole. At 88 degrees North the expedition had to make a forced landing. Abandoning one aircraft, the party cleared an emergency air-strip in the ice, and it was Riiser-Larsen who piloted the aircraft which eventually brought all members of the expedition safely back to Spitsbergen. The following year, undaunted by this experience, he was chief pilot of the dirigible Norge, which under the combined leadership of Amundsen, Ellsworth, and Nobile crossed the North Pole. A heavy snowfall made conditions difficult, but the Norge made a successful forced landing on the far side of the Polar basin at Nome in Alaska.

AMUNDSEN'S FATE

In 1928 he led the expedition which went to search—unsuccessfully—for Amundsen, who had disappeared in a flying boat over the Arctic Ocean while looking for Nobile in his dirigible Italia. The Italia and its crew were found, but of Amundsen there was no trace except for a float from his aircraft, picked up off the Norwegian coast in September, 1928.

During the next two years, Riiser-Larsen led expeditions to the Antarctic, and some of the new territory discovered then forms part of Queen Maud Land under Norwegian sovereignty. When the Norwegian airline was formed in 1933 he was appointed president of the company, and held this position until the outbreak of war. He then went as Naval Attaché to Washington, and the following year became commanding officer of the Royal Norwegian Air Force, in England.

He left this command in 1946, and returned to civil aviation. During 1947 he was attached to the head office of the Scandinavian Airlines System in Stockholm, with the special task of planning the new Scandinavian air routes to South Africa and the Far East. In 1948 he was appointed president of the reorganized Norwegian Air Lines, which forms one of the three companies of S.A.S., the Scandinavian Airlines System.

Riiser-Larsen was awarded many Norwegian and foreign honours and medals, including the David Livingstone Medal, and he was a Knight Commander of the Order of the Bath.

June 5, 1965.

Douglas Ritchie, who broadcast during the Second World War as "Colonel Britton," died at his home near Dorking on December 15, 1967, at the age of 62.

Ritchie went on the air in 1941 giving advice and instructions to the resistance forces in occupied Europe. He introduced the V for Victory slogan and urged people to tap out the sign in Morse whenever a German came into a restaurant, and V signs were painted on walls all over Europe. He broadcast names of collaborators and told his listeners: "Now is the time to deal with them". He spoke in English, French, and German to his audience for nearly a year.

In May, 1942, he told the occupied countries: "I shall not speak again until the moment comes to indicate a particular line of action which is needed." It was two years before he was heard once more. Then it was as an unnamed spokesman for the Allies before D-Day.

Born in London on March 26, 1905, the son of Ernest Ritchie, he was educated at the City of London School and was a chorister at the Temple Church. He spent some years farming in the Orange Free State, the Transvaal and Cape Province before serving on the staffs of the *Rand Daily Mail* and the *Johannesburg Sunday Times* as a reporter. Later he contributed literary, musical and dramatic criticism to South African papers and covered the tour of the Duke of Kent in 1934. On his return to Britain in 1935 he joined the staff of the *Daily Telegraph.* He went to the B.B.C. European Service in 1939, was assistant Director of European Broadcasts in 1941–44, and from 1944 to 1946 Director of the European News Department. After three years in America on secondment to the British Information Services, New York, as Director of the Press and Radio Division, he returned to London as general overseas service organizer. In 1950 he was appointed head of B.B.C. Publicity. Five years later he had a stroke. In a book called *Stroke*, published in 1960, he described with great candour and detail the onset and progress of his illness and his battle for recovery.

He married in 1933 Evelyn, daughter of James Bissett. They had one son and one daughter.

December 16, 1967.

Margaret Ritchie, who died on February 7, 1969, stood out among English soprano singers of her generation for the purity of her voice, her impressive command of many musical styles from Elizabethan madrigals to operas by Benjamin Britten, and for the intelligence and charm which enhanced the value of her singing and, in recent years, her gifts as a teacher of singing.

Margaret Willard Ritchie was born at Grimsby on June 7, 1903, and educated partly in Italy, partly in this country where her teachers included Agnes Nicholls, Plunkett Greene and Sir Henry Wood. While still a student at the Royal College of Music she won praise as Pamina in a production there of Mozart's *The Magic Flute*, and during the 1930s (under the name Mabel Ritchie) her performances with the Intimate Opera Company developed her natural operatic talent though her neatly schooled voice was never large enough for grand opera. Her sense of classic style and excellent florid technique were already then serving her well in Handelian oratorio and other concert music, and when interest in other pre-classical music, notably Monteverdi and Purcell, began to arise Margaret Ritchie (she had now reverted to her baptismal name) was much in demand. In 1944 she appeared with Sadler's Wells Opera, most notably as Dorabella in the famous production of *Cosi fan tutte*, and it was for her voice that Benjamin Britten wrote the roles of Lucia in *The Rape of Lucretia* and Miss Wordsworth (an unforgettable impersonation) in *Albert Herring*. She could be impressive too in song recital often displaying unexpected musical sympathies, for example with the songs of Liszt. Of recent years she gave more time to teaching than to singing in public: in 1960 she started a summer school in Oxford for singers, and she gave master classes in London.

February 8, 1969.

Duke of Primo de Rivera—See under **Primo de Rivera.**

Air Chief Marshal Sir James Robb, G.C.B., K.B.E., D.S.O., D.F.C., A.F.C., who died on December 18, 1968, in a nursing home at Bognor Regis, was Deputy Chief of Staff (Air) to General Eisenhower in 1944–45, Vice-Chief of Air Staff in 1947–48 and from 1948 to 1951 C.-in-C. Air Forces, Western Europe.

He was born on January 26, 1895, at Hexham, the third son of the late James Thomas Robb, and was educated at George Watson's School and Durham University. In the First World war he served in the Northumberland Fusiliers and the Royal Flying Corps, and was twice wounded. He became a brilliant pilot, and won a D.F.C. for his war services, which included a personal "bag" of seven enemy aircraft.

He was given a permanent commission in the R.A.F. while serving with 92 Squadron in the Army of the Rhine in 1919. From 1922 to 1925 he was stationed in Iraq, and took part in operations in Kurdistan, where as Officer Commanding a bomber squadron he won the D.S.O. After his return from Iraq, Robb spent some years in training work as Chief Flying Instructor at the Central Flying School.

YEARS WITH NAVY

He spent the next five years with the Royal Navy. He began by passing through the Royal Naval Staff College in 1932, and was then appointed Senior Air Force Officer in the carrier H.M.S. Eagle, served with her on the China Station, and returning to Europe was Fleet Aviation Officer to the C.-in-C. Mediterranean Fleet from 1935 to 1936.

He returned in 1936 to England and to the Central Flying School at Upavon, now as Commandant. At this time the R.A.F. was switching over from biplanes to monoplanes, and the flying characteristics of the new aircraft were tested at the C.F.S., and the results embodied in notes for service pilots. They included Blenheims, Hurricanes, Spitfires and Wellingtons. As a firstclass pilot he was able to assess the characteristics of these aircraft with a sure capability which was invaluable as they came into squadron service. In 1938 he went to Canada to plan with the Canadian Government the expansion of Flying Training and soon after the outbreak of the 1939–45 War he went out again to Canada as a member of Lord Riverdale's mission which founded the Commonwealth Air Training Scheme. He commanded No. 2 Bomber Group in 1940 and the next year No. 15 Group in Coastal Command.

When in 1942 Lord Louis Mountbatten took over the post of Chief of Combined Operations, Robb was appointed his Deputy Chief, and took part in the planning of several important operations. Armed with this experience he went out to North Africa at the close of the year, and early in 1943 was appointed Deputy Commander of N.W.African Air Forces, and was also in command of the Royal Air Force in that theatre. After the Tunisian campaign he was concerned with the air support in the assaults on the island of Pantellaria, on Sicily, and finally on Italy itself. With the reformation of the command in this theatre of war, Robb was appointed to the Headquarter's Staff, Mediterranean Allied Air Forces. He did not hold this position for long; General Eisenhower had been so impressed by Robb's abilities that when he returned to Britain to prepare for the invasion of France, he specially requested Robb's services, and the latter came home to be appointed Deputy Chief of Staff (Air) at Supreme Headquarters Allied Expeditonary Force. He was one of the Supreme Commander's representatives to receive the German surrender.

In May, 1945, he was appointed A.O.C.-in-C. Fighter Command. He still flew whenever he could and when the High Speed Flight under his command was achieving the world's absolute speed record in 1946 he kept touch by flying to Tangmere in a Meteor jet fighter. Sir James returned to the Air Ministry at the beginning of 1948 to serve under Lord Tedder as Vice-Chief of the Air Staff. The new appointment was a happy one but Western Union was developing its military organization and as its equipment and operational practice in the air was inevitably to be started on British lines the commander was naturally British too. With his experience as a senior Allied officer in the Mediterranean and at Supreme Headquarters Allied Expeditionary Force no better choice could have been made as Commander-in-Chief, Air Forces Western Europe, than Robb.

He was appointed Inspector General of the R.A.F. in 1951.

December 19, 1968.

Sir Alfred Roberts, C.B.E., who died in a London hospital on November 18, 1963, was one of those few quiet, competent, lucid leaders of fairly small trade unions who are always the backbone of the T.U.C. General Council. None of them can have served the British trade union movement longer or more effectively than he did.

Without the block-vote power or the spectacular qualities of the leaders of the biggest unions, he nevertheless made his influence felt at home and abroad by his mastery of the subjects in which he specialized, by his strength of character and by his persuasive ability.

From 1948 for 10 years he was chairman of the T.U.C. social insurance and industrial welfare committee and with C. R. Dale, the secretary, formed a combination so able and well-informed that they commanded the attention and respect of Government departments and employers for trade union views on every social issue.

For much of this time he was also the British workers' representative on the International Labour Organization, where he became leader of the workers' group and vice-chairman of the governing body during the long period in which the three knights—Sir Alfred for the workers, Sir Guildhaume Myrddin-Evans for the Government, and Sir Richard Snedden for the employers—added to Britain's prestige abroad.

A portrait of Roberts paid for by the workers' group was presented to the governing body of the I.L.O. in 1961.

COTTON REORGANIZATION

Eventually these and other commitments, entailing long absences abroad, evoked protests from his own cotton union, the National Association of Card, Blowing and Ring Room Operatives, of which he was general secretary from 1935 to 1962, and Roberts withdrew from some of his commitments. But he then became chairman of the T.U.C. international committee, a position which he held until his retirement from the T.U.C. General Council in September this year.

He was a moderate, a supporter of the labour establishment almost always, but though he could speak forcefully on occasion he did not play a big part in major controversial issues, preferring to concentrate on the subjects on which he was the undisputed authority.

He was chairman of the T.U.C. General Council in the year 1950–51 and became a director of the Bank of England in 1956. In 1948 he became a member of the Cotton Board.

LOWLY START

In Lancashire he will be remembered for the part he played in the reorganization of the cotton trade during the late nineteen-fifties.

Son of a Bolton coal carter, Alfred Roberts was born on November 30, 1897, and was educated at Chalfont Street Council School, which he left at the age of 13 to work for 5s. a week as a builder's office boy. He then went into a cotton factory. He was soon immersed in trade union activities and by 1930 had become the card-room amalgamation's Preston secretary.

Among committees on which he served in later years were the national insurance advisory committee. In 1953 he became a member of the committee formed to review raw cotton buying.

He served in the Royal Navy during the First World War. In 1950 he was made C.B.E. and four years later received the honorary degree of M.A. from Manchester University. He was knighted in 1955. In 1921 he married Gladys Bertha McEntyre. They had two daughters.

November 20, 1963.

G. D. Roberts, Q.C., O.B.E., former Recorder of Bristol, who died on March 7, 1967, at the Catholic Nursing Home, Lambeth, London, at the age of 80, had in his day enjoyed one of the largest practices at the criminal Bar and was also widely known as a sportsman.

Geoffrey Dorling Roberts was the son of Charles Tanner Kingdom Roberts and was born on August 27, 1886. He was educated at Exeter School and St. John's College, Oxford, where he took honours in the law school. He was called to the Bar by the Inner Temple in 1912, but he had hardly started to practise before the First World War. He fought for four years in France, first in The Devonshire Regiment and then on the Staff, and was awarded the Military O.B.E. On returning to practice he became associated with the best class of criminal practice under the auspices of the late Sir Richard Muir and the future Mr. Justice Humphreys. In due course he was appointed a prosecuting Crown Counsel at the Central Criminal Court, and when he decided to take silk in 1937 he was the senior of the team.

In appearance Roberts ("Khaki" as he was universally and affectionately known because of his brick dust complexion), with his height and massive appearance, seemed to suggest the typical Old Bailey barrister of fiction; but there was nothing of the bully about him, and behind his formidable manner lay a sound knowledge of the principles of the criminal law and an acute mind that could assimilate all the most subtle points of a case. He was a first-rate cross-examiner, a master of tactics and quite fearless in his client's cause when he felt that a Judge was openly displaying bias.

On one occasion when he was leading for the defence, fearing that the Judge's obvious view of the case would get the better of him when summing up, Roberts began his final speech to the jury in this fashion: "Members of the jury, I shall now address you on behalf of the prisoner; when I have done, counsel for the prosecution, and his Lordship, will then address you on behalf of the Crown."

NUREMBERG TRIAL

He frequently appeared before the Judicial Committee of the Privy Council in criminal appeals, and for many years, before Indian appeals ceased to be brought to the Committee, he was counsel to the Indian Government in criminal cases.

He was one of the English counsel for the prosecution at Nuremberg, prosecuting, among others, Field Marshal Milch, the former second in command of the Luftwaffe.

Roberts was a man of great charm, sardonic wit and with an abundance of energy. He played cricket for his college, lawn tennis for Oxford, and Rugby football for Devon, Harlequins, Oxford and England. In 1957 he published a volume of reminiscences, *Without My Wig*, which unfortunately, because he was still in practice, did not give any account of what he described as his "triumphs and disasters in the forensic field". In 1964, *Law and Life* appeared. He was Recorder of Exeter from 1932 to 1946 and Recorder of Bristol from 1946 to 1961. In the latter year he retired from the Bar and as Leader of the Western Circuit, a position he had held for many years.

He married first in 1915, Margaret Petrie, who died in 1944, leaving three daughters; secondly, in 1947, Margot Sandys (*née* Von der Mühlen), widow of Captian C.J.Sandys. That marriage was dissolved in 1953, and in that year he married thirdly Louise Mary Orford (*née* Maxwell).

March 8, 1967.

Sir Sydney Roberts, Master of Pembroke College, Cambridge, from 1948 to 1958 and Vice-Chancellor of the university in 1949–51 who died on July 21, 1966, in Addenbrooke Hospital, Cambridge, gave outstanding service to his university and college during the two parts of his distinguished career. His humanity, his unspoiled enjoyment of life, and his humour will long be remembered with gratitude by a far wider company of friends in the academic and literary worlds. He was 79.

Sydney Castle Roberts was the son of Frank Roberts, M.Inst.C.E., and was born at Birkenhead on April 3, 1887. From Brighton College he entered Pembroke College, Cambridge, in 1907 as a scholar, and the value and happiness which he then found in collegiate society inspired the devoted service which he was to give to his college and which was to be rewarded later in life by his election to office as its Master. He was placed in the First Class in the Classical Tripos, Part I, in 1909; and in the Historical Tripos, Part II, in 1910; and in the following year he was appointed assistant secretary at the University Press and so began the first stage of his career. Under A. R. Waller, he was grounded in scholarly and educational publishing until the 1914–18 War called him, first to drill on Parker's Piece (the motley and academic disunity of which he used to recall with amusement) and then to commissioned service in The Suffolk Regiment. He was wounded at Ypres in 1917 and in convalescence he turned to Boswell and to his first book about Dr. Johnson; and 1919 saw him back at the University Press and *The Story of Dr. Johnson* in its list.

In 1922 upon Waller's death he was appointed secretary to the Syndics of the Press and for 26 years, with Walter Lewis as University Printer for most of them, he was the leader of a publishing and printing team which gave to the press a progressive publishing policy, an up-to-date financial and commercial organization and a typographical renaissance. In publishing his interests were wide, with a predisposition towards the eighteenth century idea of a book; books of many kinds were the better for his criticism and some revision from his pen. In 1921, on the occasion of the quadringenary of the first Cambridge printed book, he wrote the History of the *Cambridge University Press* and for the Sandars Lectures in Bibliography which he delivered in 1954 he took as his theme three episodes in the history of Cambridge publishing.

He entered actively into affairs and interests of the London publishing world and served on the council of the Publishers' Association. His position as head of a University Department which was also a considerable business organization led the Board of Trade to ask him to be its representative when Cambridge was made the headquarters of the Eastern Region in 1940. In publishing, too, as in his other activities Roberts had a gift for making friends and the ways of many Cambridge authors were the pleasanter for his humour. Was not Previté (-Orton) the soul of Whitney? The success which was gained for the books of Eddington, Jeans, and Whitehead made a notable chapter in his time as secretary, and his personal friendship with Jeans was an example of his sympathetic understanding of a very reserved man. Among his most successful writings were, indeed, the memoirs of Cambridge authors—Quiller-Couch, Jeans, T. R. Glover—which he contributed to posthumous volumes of their works.

Roberts was a firm believer in the collegiate system as an essential part of the full university life and his continued interest in the welfare of Pembroke was rewarded by his election as a Fellow in 1929. He acted as temporary bursar during an emergency in 1935–36, and in 1948 upon the retirement of Sir Montagu Butler he was elected Master, an honor as deserved as it was popular among old members of the college. He brought to the office of Master a wide knowledge of affairs and of men and great qualities as a host. He was Vice-Chancellor of the University from 1949 to 1951 and, with characteristic wit, reported that the duties of the office consisted of taking the chair all day and replying for the visitors every night.

JOHNSON AND BOSWELL

His literary interests lay chiefly in the eighteenth century. He was the author or editor of several volumes of Johnsoniana and Boswelliana, contributing *Dr. Johnson* to the "Great Lives" series and in 1944 taking him as the subject of his British Academy lecture on a master mind; he was also the author of two volumes of essays, *An Eighteenth Century Gentleman and other Essays* and *Samuel Johnson, Moralist*. He was to be read at his happiest as a parodist, of Boswell, Max Beerbohm, and Conan Doyle, and as a pioneer in the application of the principles of sound scholarship and textual criticism to the life of Sherlock Holmes and the baffling problem of Waston's second marriage. His introduction to the selection of Sherlock Holmes stories in the World's Classics was a tour de force of delightful solemnity.

St. Andrew's University conferred on him the honorary degree of LL.D. and he was an Associate Fellow of Calhoun College, Yale University, vice-president of the International Association of Universities, a member of the U.S. Educational (Fulbright) Commission, and trustee of several foundations, including Shakespeare's Birthplace. Among his more exacting public duties was the Chairmanship of the British Film Institute from 1952 to 1956 and of the Cinematograph Films Council from 1954 to 1964; and when in 1957 the Minister of Education instituted the inquiry into the Public Library services, Roberts (a former President of the Library Association) was his natural choice for Chairman of the Committee, whose report indeed came to be known as the Roberts Report. He was knighted in 1958.

He married, first, Irene, daughter of A. J. Wallis, Fellow of Corpus Christi College. She died in 1932, and in 1938 he married Majorie, widow of Dr. M. B. R. Swann. By his first marriage he had a son and two daughters.

July 22, 1966.

Sir Dennis Robertson, C.M.G., one of the foremost academic economists of our time, died on April 21, 1963, at the age of 72. He spent most of his working life in Cambridge, where he had held a Fellowship of Trinity almost continuously since 1914, and where he was Professor of Political Economy from 1944 to 1957.

Youngest son of the Rev. James Robertson, Headmaster of Haileybury, Dennis Holme Robertson was born on May 23, 1890, at Whittlesford, near Cambridge, where his father then held a country vicarage. At Eton he had an outstanding school-boy career, and in later life his election to a Fellowship of Eton meant very much to him. He went up to Trinity College, Cambridge, with a major scholarship in Classics; and there, in addition to a First Division of the First Class in Classics, won the Craven Scholarship and the Chancellor's Medal for English Verse. He also achieved distinction in other spheres, being President both of the Union and of the Amateur Dramatic Club. He was an outstanding amateur actor, and his performances as Subtle in *The Alchemist* and Philocleon in *The Wasps* before the First World War, Pandarus, Shallow and Menenius after it, have long been remembered. He excelled in humorous parts, and never over-acted.

Robertson turned from classics to economics in his third year at Cambridge, and was placed in the First Class in Part II of the Economics Tripos in 1912. He was just too late to have heard Marshall lecture; hence his active teachers were Pigou, Keynes and Walter Layton; through them it was the Marshallian tradition that was the formative influence of his mind. He remained in Cambridge to write a Fellowship Dissertation. This first work, *A Study in Industrial Fluctuation*, has become a classic.

For Robertson, as for so many others of his Liberal friends, the outbreak of war in 1914 brought an agonizing conflict of conscience. An active pacifist to the final moment, he felt it none the less his duty to join up on August 4. After serving principally in Egypt and Palestine, he returned to teach economics in Cambridge in 1919.

ASSOCIATION WITH KEYNES

His first postwar book was *Money*, which was in its essentials a brilliant exposition of traditional Cambridge ideas inherited from Marshall and Pigou. His most original work was to be found in a slim volume which succeeded it in 1926 called *Banking Policy and the Price Level.* Here Robertson, working so closely with Keynes that (in his own words) "I think neither of us now knows how much of the ideas therein contained is his and how much is mine", achieved one of those intellectual "break-throughs" which start a wholly new line of thought. He asked in effect what is the function of saving, how is it generated and what are the effects of monetary supplies on its volume. It was this short work which, more than any other single piece of thinking, initiated what has often been called the Keynesian revolution in economic thought.

IN CONFLICT

What was begun in harmonious and fruitful collaboration was, however, lost in dispute.

Keynes continued to evolve his ideas through the *Treatise on Money* to the *General Theory*; but there came a point where, in developing his new ideas, he found himself in irreparable conflict with Robertson. It seemed to Keynes that Robertson was wilfully closing his eyes to the big and revolutionary thing at which he was driving; while Robertson was convinced that Keynes was guilty of exaggerations and misrepresentations which were liable to discredit much that was true and important in past thinking. The partnership was dissolved, and Robertson retreated into a negative and critical attitude towards the upsurge of the new Keynesian doctrines.

In 1939 he accepted the offer of a Chair at the London School of Economics. But with the outbreak of war he quickly found himself in the Treasury, serving there and on the Treasury staff in Washington. His duties covered many of the difficult problems of wartime financial relations as well as the wartime conferences and discussions regarding postwar economic plans; in particular he played a highly important part in the historic conference at Bretton Woods. For his very distinguished services he was made C.M.G.

In 1944 he was elected as Pigou's successor to the Cambridge Chair and filled it with great distinction until his retirement in 1957. The years of his professorship were, however, by no means free from stress and strain. In Cambridge he found himself back among colleagues who were divided among themselves: there were those who supported him wholeheartedly, while others, devoted and loyal disciples of Keynes, believed with the utmost sincerity that Keynesian economics needed to be taught rather than merely subjected to a constant stream of criticism on points often of subsidiary importance. Differences arose over teaching and other questions of policy; and his position as head of the Faculty was sometimes a difficult one, the more so because of his own extreme sensitiveness.

EPIGRAMMATIC WRITING

To the last Robertson got much pleasure, as he had as a younger man, from the society of the young. He was at his best and happiest among a chosen group of the ablest of the younger economists. These he knew intimately and with them, unaffected by doctrinal divisions, he could be wholly natural and at his ease. The pick of the postwar generations of undergraduate economists gave him both their respect and their affection.

A life-long bachelor, he made his Trinity rooms, with the cat-hole in the door and his collection of fantastic animals on the mantelpiece, his home. In vacations, with pupils past and present, he liked, until age forbade, to find relief in strenuous walks over the hills.

After the 1930s Robertson never again wrote anything so original as *Banking Policy and the Price Level*, though his writings remained as brilliant, as penetrating and as epigrammatic as ever. But they were principally directed to the destruction of exaggerations and to the puncturing of over-ambitious and over-simplified generalizations by the more mathematically minded model makers of his subject, with whom he had little patience and sympathy.

This intolerance of exaggerations affected also Robertson's attitude to the more practical applications of economic policy. He had never felt any keen desire to be as close to policy making as Keynes had been. When his services were demanded he gave them reluctantly but very conscientiously. Among the exaggerations of which he was especially suspicious were the tendency after 1945 to regard the maintenance of full employment as a paramount objective of economic policy and the tendency to abandon traditional monetary methods of control for budgetary or more direct physical methods. Both in public utterances and as a member of the Cohen Council on Productivity, Prices and Income from 1957 to 1959 he did much to modify official thinking about both these issues. But Robertson's underlying philosophy that an economy requires from time to time a stiff dose of very unpalatable medicine, involving a sufficiency of unemployment to steady it, was inevitably antipathetic to left-wing thinking, and the reports of the Cohen Council, which had been conceived as essays in persuasive reasonableness, became the red rags of political debate.

April 22, 1963.

E. Arnot Robertson, the novelist, who in private life was Lady Turner, was found dead at her Hampstead home on September 21, 1961.

At her best a writer of witty and ironical accomplishment, pointedly unromantic in temper, Miss Arnot Robertson seemed at one time likely to develop into a novelist of considerable comic substance and power. The illuminated exposure of the jungle-released personalities of *Four Frightened People*, which appeared as far back as 1931, had a telling edge of comedy and gave the highest promise for the future. Yet although there was generally entertainment enough in the books that followed, the range of comedy in them progressively narrowed and something even of didacticism crept into the author's play of fancy. Worse still, the intervals between the novels were all too long. Miss Robertson occupying herself in the later period with film criticism to the apparent exclusion of other interest.

Eileen Arnot Robertson was born in 1903, the daughter of Dr. G. A. Robertson. She completed her education in Paris and in Switzerland. In 1927 she married Henry E. Turner, general secretary of what was then called the Empire Press Union. They had one son. Her first novel, *Cullum*, appeared in the following year, a study of the philandering and unscrupulous male charmer and egotist, who in this case also happened to be a young novelist—not a wholly original theme, but handled with a most engaging liveliness and a brisk, witty candour. In *Three Came Unarmed*, a more ambitious book, which was published a year later, the author's imaginative motive seemed to lack definition, but then came *Four Frightened People*, which is still her most enjoyable novel and a remarkable feat of vivid fancy as well as of ruthless psychological dissection.

The high level she reached there was very nearly sustained in her next novel, *Ordinary Families*, two years later. This was a rich, lightly malicious comedy of family affections in a setting of boats and sailing off the Suffolk coast—sailing had long been a passionate recreation with Miss Robertson. In *Thames Portrait* (1937), illustrated with photographs by her husband, she described very happily the exploration of the river which she and her husband made in a launch that apparently resembled an ice-cream barrow. The novels that came afterwards were *Summer's Lease* (1940), accomplished in manner but just a little bit dull, *The Signpost* (1943), a more genuinely entertaining though not quite harmonious essay in Anglo-Irish comedy dedicated to "the good friends I am about to lose in Eire", *Devices and Desires* (1954), and *Justice of the Heart* (1958). With none of these latter four books did she do much to add to her reputation as a writer of fiction. However, in 1959 her talents were displayed in another guise with the publication of *The Spanish Town Papers*, which was the fruit of loving research into the decomposing records of the Vice-Admiralty Court which sat to condemn as prizes ships captured by the Royal Navy and by its auxiliary Privateers during the War of American Independence. As in *Thames Portrait*, the illustrations were from photographs by her husband. Sir Henry Turner (he was made C.B.E. in 1935 and knighted in 1951) was drowned in April, 1961, after falling from a cabin cruiser into the Thames.

LIBEL ACTION

A well-known film critic, in 1946 Miss Robertson was involved in a libel suit against the Metro-Goldwyn-Mayer Film Corporation, who informed the B.B.C. that in their judgment she was "completely out of touch with the tastes and entertainment requirements of the picture-going millions...and her criticisms are, on the whole, unnecessarily harmful to the film industry". They stated their intention of not inviting her to review their films in future and asked the B.B.C. to cooperate in restraining her doing so in broadcasts. Awarded £1,500 damages in the High Court on the grounds of libel and defamation, she suffered a reversal of the verdict on appeal and then carried the case unsuccessfully to the House of Lords. Nevertheless, she retained the support of the B.B.C.; an appeal on her behalf for funds to meet legal costs brought forth more than £7,000; and she was widely regarded as having achieved something of a moral triumph.

The first of her many broadcasts was a 1935 programme called "Travel and Yachting on English Rivers". In recent years her lively mind and striking personality were a welcome contribution to the programme, "The Critics", and to the television and radio game, "My Word".

September 23, 1961.

Sir Howard Robertson, who died in London on May 5, 1963, at the age of 74, was a past-president of the Royal Institute of British Architects, a Royal Academician, a Royal Gold Medallist, and a past-president of the Architectural Association. As Principal, and later Director of Education, at the A.A. school for 15 years from 1920 to 1935 he was responsible for the training of many of today's best known British architects. Although Sir Howard's architecture was traditional rather than modern his teaching was the most progressive of its time in this country, so that the A.A. school was producing architects for the modern movement many years before any other British school.

The firm of Stanley Hall, Easton and Robertson (now Easton Robertson, Cusdin, Preston and Smith) built up a high reputation for sound middle-of-the-road architecture between the wars for all manner of buildings, and although many of their buildings were designed jointly each partner had his own particular speciality.

Robertson's leaning towards a steadily developing traditional form was almost certainly due to his training at the Ecole Supérieure des Beaux Arts in Paris. There seemed, however, a curious division between his teaching and his practice. Always lively, young in spirit, and aware of what was going on—he had an interesting collection of modern paintings—he was widely travelled and had more than a passing interest in music. Nevertheless his buildings on the whole lacked the life force of great architecture. His best work was done before the war. The information gained on his extensive travels when head of the A.A. school, which he often undertook with F.R.Yerbury, then secretary of the A.A. and one of the foremost architectural photographers of the day, did much to bring the image of modern architecture to this country.

A slow-speaking man, with twinkling eyes, Sir Howard was an admirable chairman and a witty after-dinner speaker. His voice to the end of his life bore traces of his American origin. He was deeply interested in young people and students, but the faith of the young in him as an architectural leader was sadly blighted by the bitter criticism which his last and largest work, the Shell building on the South Bank, received from almost all architectural critics. This design was seen as Robertson's final rejection of modern methods of cladding and fenestration. He maintained that stone was the true facing material for London buildings and turned to the tradition of early American sky-scrapers. The last word has not been said on the Shell building but even his oldest friends, and strongest supporters, have been hard put to it to find much to say in its favour and this had been, lately, the cause of much unhappiness.

SENSE OF HUMOUR

A man with a rich sense of humour, Sir Howard used to tell, with relish, a story connected with his more than passing resemblance to the late George Robey. One day, set down at his door by a taxi whose driver appeared to know him, Sir Howard asked the man who he thought he was. "Oh", replied the cabby. "some sort of an old actor."

Howard Morley Robertson was born in Salt Lake City, Utah, on August 16, 1888, the son of Casper Ludovic van Uytrecht Robertson, of Liverpool, and Ellen Duncan, of Ohio. He was educated at Malvern College. He served in the First World War, was awarded the M.C., the Legion of Honour and made an officer of the order of the Etoile Noire. He also received the United States Certificate of Merit. He was president of the R.I.B.A. in 1952–54 and was knighted in 1954.

Among his many buildings were the British Government Pavilions at a number of international exhibitions, culminating with the New York World's Fair of 1939. He also carried out extensive alteration schemes for the Savoy Group of Hotels and later became a director of that company. A new printing works for the Bank of England and buildings for the Faculty of Letters at Reading University were among his later works. Undoubtedly his best building, which he designed with his partner, John Murray Easton, also a Royal Gold Medallist, was the New Royal Horticultural Hall in Westminster. He was author of four well known books on architectural design.

In 1927 Robertson married a former pupil, Doris Adeney Lewis, of Melbourne, who survives him.

May 6, 1963.

Norman Robertson, formerly Under-Secretary of State for External Affairs and a former Canadian High Commissioner in London, died on July 16, 1968, at the age of 64.

Norman Robertson was the man, more than any other, who made the Canadian diplomatic service one of the very best in the world in the years of the Second World War and during all the succeeding time of peace-making, cold war, and co-existence. London knew his quality during his two terms as High Commissioner at Canada House, first 1946–49 and then 1952–57. Even during the war, before his first term, he had been a visitor with Mr. Mackenzie King and had been a quiet persuasive force at many of the highest meetings.

Everyone who met him in those years gained a heightened respect for Canada, for the profession of diplomacy, and for Norman Robertson himself. The description often applied to Canada—a middle power—took on real meaning as he spoke; indeed, it was Canada's special position that determined its policy in the world. Between the United States and the Commonwealth, between the big and the little powers, and possessing a cool, dispassionate, reconciliatory and imaginative diplomacy, Canada became very largely the spokesman for the middle powers—and often a guide for the larger powers as well.

For years on end, in Ottawa, in London, in Washington, at the United Nations, and at most of the international conferences, Norman Robertson was at the heart of this policy. Many of the Canadian initiatives grew out of his brain. He shared to the full Mackenzie King's and Lester Pearson's view of the Commonwealth as an association that could do good in the world by not trying to be an exclusive, self-centred partnership but by acting as an example of the right kind of association—in a sense, as a kind of leaven—in the whole world.

To think of Norman Robertson as only a Canadian representative although he was a superb one—is less than half the truth. He was a diplomatist of world rank with world-wide interests. Cabinet Ministers in Ottawa, London, and Washington would like to talk over every kind of problem with him.

Norman Alexander Robertson was born in Vancouver on March 4, 1904. From his father Lemuel F. Robertson, for many years Professor of Classics at the University of British Columbia, and his mother, *née* Flora MacLeod, both natives of Prince Edward Island, he obtained a rich inheritance of Highland Scottish blood.

RHODES SCHOLAR

Educated at local schools he matriculated at his father's university, where he was such a youthful prodigy that he obtained first-class honours at the age of 19. His excellent academic record won him a Rhodes scholarship which took him to Balliol, where it is said he just missed a first in Greats by offending one of the examiners at his *viva* by admitting that he had not read a certain book in whose authorship that examiner took great pride.

After leaving Oxford in 1926 he did postgraduate work at Brookings in Washington, D.C., and at Harvard. In 1929 Robertson was a successful candidate for entrance to the Department of External Affairs and was appointed third secretary and posted to Washington. Soon afterwards he was to accompany, as his secretary, Sir Robert Borden, formerly Prime Minister of Canada, when that Canadian statesman represented his country at the Assembly of the League of Nations. Borden formed such a high opinion of Robertson's abilities that when they returned to Ottawa he advised the late Lord Bennett, who was Minister of External Affairs, as well as Conservative Prime Minister, to make use of this young man.

The authorities at Harvard had formed a similar opinion of him and they offered Robertson a lectureship in political science with the promise of a full professorship within five years. Robertson was at that time trying to support a wife and child on a very modest salary in Ottawa, and Harvard's offer seemed too attractive to turn down. However, Dr. O. D. Skelton, the Under-Secretary of State for External Affairs, did not want to see Canada lose such a promising young officer and he managed to persuade him to take leave of absence in the hope that life in the United States would prove uncongenial to him.

After his departure to Harvard in 1933 Lord Bennett missed him greatly but was told that he could only persuade him to return from that university by offering him a decent salary. The Prime Minister then proceeded to break the rules about promotion in the Civil Service and Robertson returned to the department of external affairs as first secretary in 1934, to begin an unbroken career of success in it leading to the post of Under-Secretary of State.

In 1946 he went to his first major post abroad, that of Canadian High Commissioner in London, where he was held in great esteem. Returning to Ottawa three years later he was appointed Clerk to the Privy Council and Secretary to the Cabinet. In 1952 he again went back to London to take over Canada House and stayed there until 1957, when he became Canadian Ambassador in Washington. He was there a year and then returned to Ottawa as Under-Secretary of State.

When Lester Pearson became Prime Minister he asked Robertson to lead the Canadian delegation at Geneva for the Kennedy Round negotiations. However, before he could get to Geneva cancer struck him and he entered hospital where a lung was removed. After recuperating he went on to Geneva, where he participated in the negotiations. But by late 1965 he was tiring and asked to be relieved of his arduous duties. He went into partial retirement and became the first director of the new School for International Studies at the University of Carleton in Ottawa.

He is survived by his wife and two daughters.

July 18, 1968.

J. W. Robertson Scott, C.H., founder of *The Countryman*, died on December 21, 1962, at at the age of 96.

John William Robertson Scott was born at Wigton in Cumberland in April, 1866, and educated at grammar and Quaker schools. His parents were lowland Scots who had moved a little south across the Border and he was himself to go much farther south to be the student, publicist, and champion of country life, first in Essex and later and longer in the Cotswolds. In mid-Victorian Cumberland he was brought up amid the tough and independent farmers whom his father met in the flour trade: the home atmosphere was strictly religious with strong drink regarded as the peril and plague of the market towns where farmers met.

Before he settled down to his work for rural causes he had a full taste of urban and office life. At 20 he was working for the *Birmingham Daily Gazette*: but he was soon in London, where he was on the staff of the *Pall Mall Gazette* from 1887 to 1893, of the *Westminster Gazette* from 1893 to 1899, and of the *Daily Chronicle* in 1899. He was one of the Radicals who broke with the so-called Liberal Imperialism and opposed the Boer War. This meant leaving Fleet Street for the farmlands where his affections were rooted, a countryman returning to the field. He settled in Essex and became an industrious free-lance journalist and author of books with the problems of the countryside his usual theme. In 1910 he resumed work with the *Daily Chronicle*, as travelling "rural commissioner". He also undertook long and strenuous public service as on the Government's Rural Housing Advisory Committee.

A drastic change in his life occurred when he spent four years in Japan. In 1906 he had married Elspet Keith, a gifted writer whose sister Elizabeth was a gifted artist. The two women made the journey east together and set up a rewarding partnership in authorship and illustration of books about Japan: of these *Eastern Windows* and *Old Korea* were the best-known. Robertson Scott was himself also busy with books and journalism in his new surroundings; he successfully founded and edited the review called *New East*.

UNEXPECTED SUCCESS

Some years after his return and his settling at Idbury Manor, near Kingham, on the Oxfordshire flank of the Cotswolds, he decided to create a quarterly review of rural life. In 1927 he founded *The Countryman*, which he owned for the next 16 years. Nobody, except Robertson Scott himself, could foresee any future for such a venture with no large backing or distributive machinery.

His faith was justified by his own hard work. With his wife he did all the editing at Idbury while he made frequent journeys to London where at first he did his own canvassing for advertisements.

General interest in the economy, apart from the sports of country life, was growing. The increasing strains and monotonies of town life were providing an urban public ready for the news and views of the countryside and in *The Countryman* they found a new interest as well as an escape, while the countrymen themselves were glad to find out and learn about their own way of life and of making a living. In 10 years the green covers of *The Countryman* were a familiar sight and the review had so thriven as to produce an issue of 432 pages, of which over 200 pages were advertisements.

PUBLIC WORK

In 1943 Messrs. Bradbury, Agnew, Ltd., the proprietors of *Punch*, acquired the shares. The editor remained in charge with full independence for four years: he was then succeeded by his assistant, John Cripps. Meanwhile he had been constantly engaged in local affairs as a justice of the peace, county councillor, and school governor. Those who think of the English countryside in terms of bucolic heartiness, blood sports, and high feeding found none of these in Robertson Scott, who was teetotal, a non-smoker, and found that an avoidance of meat most assisted his work. He was opposed to the traditional sports of the Costwolds, hunting, shooting, fishing, and even racing; brought up in Puritanism he went over to rationalism.

He had been fascinated by, but not uncritical of W.T.Stead, his first London editor. He published in 1950 *The Story of the Pall Mall Gazette, of its first Editor, Frederick Greenwood, and of its Founder, George Murray Smith*. In the earlier stage of his long career Robertson Scott watched the development of what Matthew Arnold had first called "The New Journalism", and the office of the *P.M.G.* was a most suitable place from which to see it. Later, at the *Westminster Gazette*, he was the spectator of more traditional methods and the assistant of another great, but very different editor in Spender. The W.G. was said to "sell on its leading article", whereas the *P.M.G.* sold on far more than that. Stead was known as "The Father of the Interview". To be his colleague was to gain a wide and exciting experience.

Other books written by Robertson Scott in his eighties were *The Life and Death of a Newspaper* (1952) and *"We" and Me* (1956), in which he studied the relations of employers and editors, with special reference to Massingham and Spender, deciding that editors "should be easily sackable but highly pensionable". His largest sales were for an earlier book, *England's Green and Pleasant Land*.

He was made a Companion of Honour in 1947 and was awarded the degree of M.A., *honoris causa*, by Oxford University in 1949. His wife died in 1956. She had been his helpmate in all. It was a union in confidence about the future as well as service of the present, with the principal purpose of giving townsmen a full knowledge of rural economy instead of the older sentimental and patronizing view of farm and village life as something picturesquely remote and pleasantly quaint.

December 24, 1962.

R. W. V. Robins, the former England and Middlesex cricket captain, died on December 12, 1968. He was 62.

He was one of the liveliest players and thinkers in modern cricket, a gifted all-rounder and an exuberant captain of Middlesex. Both as captain and selector his deep concern for the game and the people who watch it was evident.

Wisden once called him the most active cricketer of the 1930s. He was likely to take batting guard a foot outside his crease, bowled leg-breaks and googlies, was prodigal of spin, was erratic of length and was deadly at cover.

He played in 19 Tests and captained England in the 1937 series against New Zealand in addition to serving as vice-captain under G. O. Allen in the 1936–37 team which toured Australia.

He made his county debut in 1925 while still at school, and gained a Blue for Cambridge as a freshman, playing three times against Oxford University. He also gained a soccer Blue and afterwards played for the Corinthians.

In the last of the University cricket matches in 1928 he scored 53 and 101 not out and took eight wickets for 151, this performance gaining him selection for the Gentlemen against the Players for the first of many appearances.

Robins captained Middlesex three times, from 1935 to 1939 when he retired after leading the team to second place in the championship table for the fourth successive year. He returned after the war in 1946, and helped to reorganize the county team. After a season of experiment he steered the county to the championship title in 1947, the famous summer during which the Middlesex "terrible twins", Denis Compton and W. J. Edrich, both scored over 3,000 runs.

Robins returned for a third time as captain in 1950 for one season, after which the captaincy was shared by Compton and Edrich. He then served as a Test selector before being appointed manager of M.C.C. for their 1959–60 tour of the West Indies.

He was appointed chairman of the Test Selection Committee at the start of the 1962 season, and succeeded G. O. Allen. He was succeeded as chairman by D. J. Insole in March, 1965.

His Test career brought him 612 runs at 26.60, his highest score being his 108 against South Africa at Old Trafford in 1935. This innings occupied just over two hours despite the threat of an England collapse. He collected 64 wickets at 27.46 with a best analysis of six for 32 against West Indies at Lord's in 1933.

December 13, 1968.

Emmott Robinson, the Yorkshire all-rounder, died on November 17, 1969.

Emmott Robinson was 35 before he first played cricket for Yorkshire. Between 1919 and 1931 he scored nearly 10,000 runs and took just over 900 wickets, helping to form, with Rhodes, Waddington, Macaulay, Kilner and E. R. Wilson, one of the two strongest county attacks in cricket history. In such a powerful side his chances of shining were limited, yet year after year he would bat creditably and take his 60 or 70 wickets, never quite achieving the double, but coming near to it several times, notably in 1928, with 926 runs and 113 wickets. In 1926 he shared with Leyland Yorkshire's record sixth-wicket partnership of 276 and for a dozen seasons he fielded with prehensile audacity in the close positions.

Though not a cricketer of princely rank, like Hirst or Rhodes, Sutcliffe or Hutton, he was as true a Yorkshireman as any; indeed, the Yorkshire terrier might have been his symbol; tenacious, belligerent and slightly shaggy. For him the smoking chimneys of Bramall Lane were as happy a background as were the green trees and bright bannerets of Canterbury for Frank Woolley. To him Yorkshire cricket was everything; victory for Yorkshire was a law of life; defeat an outrage. He tried with heart and soul to capture a wicket with every ball he bowled and from his fine grey head to his turned-in toes, he was Yorkshire incarnate.

North-country crowds knew him well and savoured his image with a kind of wry affection; his concertina trousers, the Christopher Robin hoppity-hop in the middle of his run-up, the wicked outswinger that took the batsman's breath (and bails) away. They chuckled over his uncanny judgment of a wicket's texture, which enabled him to advise his captain on matters of declaration in terms of minutes rather than hours. ("No, Mr. Wilson, not twenty-five past—twenty past.")

He held high place in Yorkshire's long line of rich comedy characters, which stretches from Tom Emmett to Freddie Trueman. Anecdotes of his pugnacity are innumerable and, even when apocryphal, highly characteristic. Fielding at suicidally silly mid-off, he was warned by a dashing but humane batsman to step back out of mortal danger. "Thee get on with thi lakin, Mr. Foster" said Emmott austerely, "and I'll get on with mine".

A Cambridge batsman, after a few flashing hits, was bowled by a superlative ball which pitched on the leg-stump and whipped away his off-bail. "By jove", he murmured, as he passed on his way out of history, "that was a beauty".

"It was an' all", said Emmott. "It were wasted on thee."

In his later playing years he nobly served the game by the encouragement and cunning coaching he gave to the youthful Bowes and Verity. Not for them the cinema in the evening; in their hotel bedrooms, with the aid of shaving sticks and tooth-brushes, Emmott would demonstrate just how badly they had bowled that day. To refrain from obloquy was his only praise. And they loved him for it.

November 19, 1969.

W. S. Robinson, who died on September 13, 1963, in Queensland at the age of 86, was perhaps the most constantly influential Australian, within his own country and abroad, of the past 40 years.

"W.S.", as he was almost invariably called, retired in 1951 from the presidency of the Consolidated Zinc Corporation, 22 years after receiving from the Institute of Mining and Metallurgy in London its Gold Medal and the Platinum Medal of the Institute of Metals in recognition of the work he had already done for the development of mineral resources in the British Commonwealth. But Robinson was much more than a great mining engineer, financier, and administrator. His advice and action were sought, and carefully given, by Australian and British Governments in both World Wars, he was well known in New York, and his business interests ranged from mining at Broken Hill and in Burma to the pastoral industry in tropical Australia and the introduction of Santa Gertrudis cattle from Texas.

Robinson refused all honours, apart from purely professional and academic ones, and he refused them, one would think, because he remained to the end unsure of the effect upon him of publicity. His mind was keen, his character and judgment good; humbly, as befitted a man of Presbyterian faith, he wanted to keep them that way.

However, in 1949 he permitted himself one departure from an otherwise inflexible rule. He accepted, on behalf of his old school, Scotch College, Melbourne, a Baskerville Bible inscribed jointly by Winston Churchill and Brendan Bracken with these words: "In the six relentless years of war that preceded the victory of 1945 the services manifold of William Sydney Robinson to the British Commonwealth were beyond computation. There is no token more fitting to commemorate the work of this man of unquenchable faith. . . ."

He was born in Melbourne on October 3, 1876, one of five sons of Anthony Bennett Robinson, who became financial editor of *The Age*, Melbourne. After leaving Scotch College Robinson went to Longeronong Agricultural College, where he won a diploma. He farmed for several years before entering journalism in 1896 and succeeded his father on *The Age* only three years later. In 1908 he went to London to join his brother's stockbroking firm of Lionel Robinson, Clark & Co., and was a member of the London Stock Exchange until 1914. He played an important part in developing a community of investment interest in Australian non-ferrous mining between London and Melbourne.

BROKEN HILL'S FUTURE

Earlier, before leaving for London, he had convinced himself that the suspect lead-zinc-silver mining field of Broken Hill, which had been worked for 22 years, had a stable, long-term future. With W. L. Baillieu he became associated with a renewal of interest in the field. From neglected areas at the southern end they developed two of the world's major lead-zinc mines, owned by the Zinc Corporation and New Broken Hill Consolidated.

Robinson played a major part in stimulating the search for an economic process to recover zinc ores which, as mining advanced into deeper sulphide zones, were being discarded. In the development of mineral separation by flotation processes Broken Hill led the world. The Zinc Corporation was formed in 1905 initially to recover zinc minerals discarded in the millions of tons of lead residues.

Robinson happened to be in Australia when war broke out in 1914 and was soon involved, with W. L. Baillieu (with whose son Clive, Lord Baillieu, W.S. was also always very closely associated), in trying to secure lead and zinc smelting facilities for the allies. A meeting was arranged between Robinson and W. M. Hughes, Attorney-General of the Commonwealth and within months Prime Minister. It was the beginning of a long and close relationship between the two men. In November, 1914. Hughes made him an adviser to the Government, and especially to the Prime Minister. Robinson controlled the production and distribution of all Australian non-ferrous metals. At Port Pirie, South Australia, the largest single lead smelting plant in the world was established.

In 1916 Hughes sent him to London, where he directed, for four years, Australia's trade in non-ferrous metals. He represented Australia on the Committee of Non-Ferrous Metals and helped to form the British Metal Corporation at the end of the war. Robinson's association with the growth of zinc smelting in Britain continued until his retirement in 1951.

In 1935, with the late Harold Darling and Essington Lewis of the Broken Hill Proprietary Company Ltd., he was instrumental in getting the Lyons Government to set up the Commonwealth Aircraft Corporation, against the opposition of the British aircraft industry, which was supported by the British Government. The Australian Aluminium Company was established near Sydney to fabricate aluminium for aircraft.

When war broke out Robinson travelled continuously between Britain, the United States, and Australia; he was adviser to both the Curtin and Chifley Labour Governments. He accompanied Dr. Evatt on missions to London and Washington in 1942–43 and did much to secure for his country the use of certain American aircraft, which were urgently needed against the Japanese.

Robinson did much to establish the uranium mining centre of Rum Jungle in the Northern Territory and he encouraged his friend Robert Kleberg, owner of the King Ranch in Texas, to invest in cattle properties in Queensland and the Northern Territory.

He was twice married.

September 14, 1963.

George Lincoln Rockwell, who was shot and killed by a sniper on August 25, 1967, in Arlington, Virginia, was famous beyond his abilities as the founder and leader of the American Nazi party which claims chapters in New York, Los Angeles, New Orleans and other cities.

Among the avowed aims of the party were the deportation of all Negroes to Africa, the liquidation of the Jews through sterilization and the confiscation of their property, and the hanging of "traitors" such as former Presidents Truman and Eisenhower and the Chief Justice of the United States, Earl Warren.

Rockwell maintained that Hitler's mistake was in not trying to conquer the world to prevent the triumph of "Jewish bolshevism" and to save western civilization and the white race. In his biography, *This Time the World*, published in 1962, he argued that what happened in Germany between 1918 and 1933 was occurring on a world-wide scale at the time of his writing, and that when national socialism won "there will be nobody left to pull the Jews' chestnuts out of the fire". His motto was that "The Jews are through in 1972", by which time he would be elected President of the United States, and the "power of the Jew communists and race-mixers" would be destroyed.

Although Rockwell had taken over Hitler's flag, salute, uniform, and platform, he did not look or sound at all like Hitler. He was just over six feet tall, had a dark complexion and dark, wavy, close-cropped hair.

In 1962, Rockwell was deported from England after he had addressed a camp held by the British National Socialist Movement at Guiting Power, Gloucestershire. The Home Secretary, Henry Brooke, had signed a deportation order after Rockwell's presence at the camp, attended by Colin Jordan and others, had been confirmed by photographs taken there. The camp had been raided by local residents, and after the fracas the campers moved out of the district. Rockwell, who had entered Britain by way of Ireland, at first eluded the countrywide police hunt for him, which took in airports and seaports. But he was soon detained in London, and deported. Although his admission to Britain had not been specifically prohibited at the time of his arrival, the Home Office instructed immigration officers to refuse foreigners coming to attend the rally permission to enter the country.

Rockwell, who was the son of a vaudeville performer, attended Brown University in Providence, Rhode Island, briefly but dropped out in 1940 to enlist in the Navy. He became a pilot, flew in the Pacific during World War Two and left the Navy at the end of the war with the rank of commander. After the war he studied commercial art and was a partner for a time in an advertising agency in Portland, Maine, though he failed to make a success in this enterprise.

From 1956 until he formed the "world union of free Enterprise Socialists" in 1959 he organized a number of short-lived right-wing groups. After the formation of the Nazi party he lived in Arlington, making numerous trips across the country to enlist supporters and to demonstrate against Negroes and Jews.

In 1966, Rockwell was arrested in Chicago a short time before he was to lead a march of white people through the Negro section as a counter-demonstration. The march went on—but with only about 200 instead of the 2,000 Rockwell had promised. At one point, Negroes threw acid on the marchers, many of whom wore shirts bearing swastikas or the counter-slogan "white power". In 1961, Rockwell was sentenced to 60 days imprisonment, and fined, together with nine other followers, after they had picketed the film *Exodus*. The same year he had won an appeal in the New York State of Appeals.The court upheld the decision of the lower court that Rockwell had wrongly been refused permission to speak in a public park. Rockwell had been married twice.

August 26, 1967.

Theodore Roethke, who died at Seattle on August 1, 1963, at the age of 55, was possibly the most distinguished American poet of the generation, roughly corresponding to W. H. Auden. His death in his middle fifties, following some years of indifferent health, which did not, however, affect either his fundamental sense of the sacredness of life or his creative gifts, is a sad loss to the poetry of the English language. Since 1948 he had been Professor of English at the University of Washington.

Born in Saginaw, Michigan, in May, 1908, Roethke made a continuous use throughout his poems of early memories of green-houses, seedlings, and the art of the horticulturist. "Green" is one of the most frequently recurring words in his poems. His first volume, *Open House*, which came out in 1941 when Roethke was in his early thirties, was hailed with enthusiasm by Auden.

Roethke's life was typical of the modern American poet's, in that it had behind it a solid formal education, including early law studies at Michigan and a year at Harvard, and in that he earned his living by teaching English in various universities, though at one time he worked in a pickle factory. It was perhaps difficult also in the alternation of various prize awards and fellowships with illness and distress.

Roethke was a poet who praised life and nature, with a sharp particularity of observation akin in some ways to Hopkins's, but also with a cryptic dry humour that was very American. He had no metaphysics, no transcendental beliefs, but his love of nature was almost mystical. This is well expressed in the last two lines of one of his strongest poems, "First Meditation":—

In such times, lacking a god,
I am still happy.

In 1961, Roethke visited England and Ireland and British poets who met him were moved and charmed by the natural gaiety that broke through physical ill health and recurrent moods of depression. His poems rather similarly are a statement of faith in life, more moving because it is made through and against considerable experience of pain. For English readers, the best selection of his poems is *Words for the Wind*, which was a Poetry Book Society Choice in 1957.

In 1954 he was awarded the Pulitzer Prize for poetry.

August 3, 1963.

Professor Lambert Charles Rogers, Professor of Surgery in the University of Wales, died suddenly in Cardiff on October 10, 1961, at the age of 64.

Professor Rogers was born on April 8, 1897, in Melbourne, Australia, and at the age of 18 joined the Australian Naval Transport Service, in which he served until 1917, when he resumed his interrupted medical education at the Middlesex Hospital, London. In 1918 he became a Surgeon Probationer in the Royal Naval Volunteer Reserve and served with the Grand Fleet until demobilization. He often used to remind his friends that he first saw Cardiff, the scene of his life's work, when the destroyer on which he was serving docked there in the First World War.

His student days, in spite of the interruption of war, were distinguished and brought him prizes in anatomy and physiology and histology. At qualification in 1920 he was awarded a certificate of distinction as a prosector in anatomy by the University of London and he became house surgeon to Sir John Bland-Sutton, whom he often quoted later in life in his student teaching. Although the first five years after qualifying were spent in general practice, as a ship's surgeon, and in visiting clinics in America and Europe, his heart was set on an academic career, and his real life work began when in January, 1926, he was appointed the first full-time assistant in the surgical unit of the Welsh National School of Medicine.

In June 1929 he was appointed the first senior assistant in the same unit and subsequently became assistant director of the surgical unit serving under Professor A. W. Sheen, the first occupant of the Chair of Surgery in the Welsh National School of Medicine. During this period he was honoured by the Royal College of Surgeons of England with a Hunterian Professorship of the College. In 1934 Professor Rogers left Cardiff for a year to work at the British Postgraduate Medical School in Hammersmith under Professor Grey Turner, for whom he had a high regard and who became a life-long friend.

SPINAL TUMOURS

In 1935 Lambert Rogers returned to Cardiff and succeeded Professor Sheen as Professor of Surgery and Director of the Surgical Unit, an appointment which he held till the time of his death; and in which he won most of his many surgical distinctions and achieved world-wide fame. In his early days in the Chair of Surgery his interest was drawn to neurosurgery and he established this specialty in Cardiff and within it achieved great distinction and became a close friend of many of its pioneers. It was a source of satisfaction to him when one of his own students was appointed neurosurgeon to the United Cardiff Hospitals. His own special interest was the surgery of spinal tumours, in which he acquired an unrivalled experience and became the acknowledged authority in this country. His interest in surgical conditions of the spine continued to the end of his life and in very recent years he devised and perfected a new operation for the treatment of cervical spondylosis.

He was the most methodical of men and this, combined with a great capacity for hard work, enabled him to contribute very extensively to medical literature. He always took the greatest care over anything he wrote and often rewrote it a dozen times before he was satisfied that what he had to say had been said in the best way. His love for the sea and ships led him to volunteer again for service in the Royal Navy in the Second World War and he served throughout the war with great distinction as a surgeon captain, in this country and in the Pacific, before returning to his work as Professor in Cardiff in May, 1946.

The reputation which he enjoyed among British surgeons is shown by the many honours which were accorded him. He was elected a member of the Council of the Royal College of Surgeons and became a vice-president, and was at different times president of the Association of Surgeons of Great Britain and Ireland, the Society of British Neurological Surgeons and the Surgical Section of the Royal Society of Medicine. His international reputation was equally great and is reflected in the many honorary degrees and diplomas which were bestowed on him. None of them afforded him more pleasure than the M.D. (Melbourne) (his birth-place), which was conferred on him when he visited Australia on a honeymoon trip shortly after his marriage in 1954 to Barbara Ainsley, by whom he had one daughter. He was appointed Vice-President of the International Society of Surgery at its Congress in Dublin and had been invited to act as chairman of the forthcoming Rome Congress.

UNFAILING COURTESY

As Lambert Rogers the surgeon, writer, and surgical teacher he was known and respected by surgeons everywhere and his name was a certain introduction to any surgical gathering; but, as Lambert Rogers the man, he was known and loved by a far wider circle. His innate kindliness and unfailing courtesy gained for him not only the implicit trust and affection of his patients but also of his colleagues and a wide circle of friends from many walks of life. It led him to give unsparingly of his time and substance to many charitable causes, and he was for many years the County Medical Officer of the Glamorgan branch of the British Red Cross and was recently appointed an Honorary Life Member of the Society. He was a man of strong Christian convictions which he practised as well as preached. A staunch churchman himself he was of wide Christian sympathies and was a welcome speaker at meetings of many dominations.

October 13, 1961.

Major-General Sir Leonard Rogers, K.C.S.I., C.I.E., F.R.S., died on September 16, 1962, in a Truro hospital at the age of 94.

His name ranks high among the pioneers of tropical medicine who in the early years of this century performed research work of first-class importance in India, contributing greatly to the health and well being of its people. The foundation and endowment of the School of Tropical Medicine in Calcutta which was due to his initiative, stands as a perennial memorial to his name.

Born on January 16, 1868, the son of Captain Henry Rogers, R.N., he was educated at Plymouth College and St. Mary's Hospital, London. Distinguished as a student by uncommon zeal and assiduity he obtained the Fellowship of the Royal College of Surgeons in 1893, and entered the Indian Medical Service in the same year destined to become one of its most distinguished members.

He held many appointments in India and at one time was Professor of Pathology in Calcutta, but for the most part his talents were directed towards teaching and research. In the late "nineties" he commenced research on snake venom and was able to make valuable contributions on its nature, in the course of hazardous experiments, and to improve methods of the production of antivenene. He engaged too in an inquiry on Kala-azar, or "Dum-Dum" fever, a mysterious disease which at that time was ravaging Assam, though at first he was not successful in identifying the parasite, which was found by Leishman and Donovan in 1903; later he was able, in 1904, by a brilliant piece of work, to predict the development of the Leishman-Donovan body (as it was called) outside the blood of man.

Still more important was his discovery in 1912 of the curative action of emetine, the alkaloid of ipecacuanha, in amoebic dysentery, a discovery which has since been abundantly confirmed and which has rendered his name famous throughout the world. Soon, in 1915 he made yet another therapeutic advance in the treatment of kala-azar by intravenous injections of tartar emetic, which in time led to the employment of various compounds of antimony in a variety of diseases.

TREATMENT OF CHOLERA

He next turned his attention to cholera, and showed that the mortality of this terrible disease could be substantially reduced by the intravenous injections of hypertonic salt solution combined with potassium permanganate by the mouth, and in 1911 he travelled to Palermo to test out his methods in the great epidemic which raged in that city at that time.

For many years Rogers was deeply interested in the treatment of leprosy and perhaps his most popular memorial will be in his strenuous efforts to better conditions in India for the unfortunate victims. He devised many improvements in the methods of treatment with chaulmoogra oil and eventually his work in this direction culminated in the formation of the British Empire Leprosy Relief Association. In 1926 he returned from India, was created Major-General in the Indian Medical Service, became President of the Medical Board of the India Office and was elected physician to the Hospital for Tropical Diseases and lecturer to the London School of Hygiene and Tropical Medicine. He became a fellow of the Royal Society in 1916 and president of the Royal Society of Tropical Medicine and Hygiene, 1933–1935. He received many honours including the Fothergillian Medal of the Medical Society of London and the Moxon Gold Medal of the Royal College of Physicians, of which he was also Croonian lecturer in 1924. He was awarded the Laveran Medal in 1956. Rogers, a prolific writer possessed a clear style. His standard works were on dysenteries and bowel diseases, fevers in the tropics, and leprosy (with E. Muir), and a textbook on tropical medicine in conjunction with his friend and colleague, Major-General Sir John Megaw.

Rogers retained his interest in the study of tropical disease into extreme old age. From his home in Cornwall he contributed articles to medical journals and one of these—on his speciality, cholera—appeared in the *Lancet* on his ninetieth birthday in January, 1958.

TROPICAL DISEASES

Rogers will be remembered by his friends for his forceful, active and energetic disposition as well as for his striking personality which made itself felt in any gathering. He was an incisive and vigorous lecturer, thereby exerting a memorable influence on his students, by whom he was held in great affection. He was moreover of a most upright and kindly disposition and ever helpful to his friends.

He married in 1914 Una Elsie (who died in 1951), daughter of C. N. McIntyre North, by whom he had three sons, one of whom is Professor Ambrose Rogers, F.R.S.

September 16, 1962.

Marshal of the Soviet Union Konstantin Konstantinovich Rokossovsky, K.C.B., top Soviet wartime general and postwar Defence Minister of Poland, died in Moscow on August 3, 1968, at the age of 71.

His military career spanned two regimes in Russia, the Tsarist and the Soviet. In the span of 30 years, from 1914 to 1944, he rose from cavalryman in the Imperial Dragoons to Marshal of the Soviet Union. At the outbreak of the Soviet-German War, in 1941, he represented not only the survivors of Stalin's military purge of the mid 1930s but also the promising formation commanders who were about to be put to the acid test. From the outset he displayed ability and personal courage, and went on to join that relatively small group of senior Soviet commanders with whose names the growing Soviet successes came to be associated: Moscow 1941, Stalingrad 1942, Kursk 1943, Byelorussia 1944 and the final triumphs of 1945. His wartime career was the foundation of his reputation, while his postwar activity was linked more with the phase of the Stalinist domination of eastern Europe, in particular Poland. His career as a "political soldier" came to an abrupt end in 1956; with the displacement of Marshal Zhukov in 1957 his own service began to draw to a close and ended in an extended phase of semi-retirement, a respected veteran of Stalin's great war.

In spite of widespread and officially fostered stories about his "Polish origins", Rokossovsky was born in 1896 in Velikiye Luki; his father was a railway worker, and the young Rokossovsky went to work as a stone-cutter in his youth. At the outbreak of the 1914–18 War he was called up to the Imperial Russian Army.

CAVALRY CAREER

Tall and well-built, he was assigned for this reason to the Dragoons, serving with the 5th Dragoon Regiment, and thereby beginning his long connexions with the cavalry, an extended introduction to his work with mobile forces.

At the time of the outbreak of the Russian Revolution and the disintegration of the Imperial Russian Army, he attained the rank of junior N.C.O.; in October, 1917, Rokossovsky joined the pro-Bolshevik para-military organization, the Red Guard, and entered the Red Army when it was formally established in 1918. Rokossovsky's membership of the Communist Party dated back to 1919, by which time he was a section commander with the 30th Cavalry Division on the Eastern Front, operating against Admiral Kolchak. For the remainder of the period of the Russian Civil War, Rokossovsky continued to serve in the eastern theatre, against Admiral Kolchak in Siberia, against Ataman Semenov's forces and finally in Outer Mongolia against the troops of Baron Ungern-Sternberg. By this time he was a regimental commander.

At the close of the Civil War, Rokossovsky continued to serve with the Red Army as a regular officer (or "commander", the term "officer" being as yet rigorously eschewed) and proceeded, in the company of many more Civil War veterans, to undergo formal military education, attending the Frunze Military Academy and the "Higher Red Banner Cavalry Courses" in Leningrad. With the activation and reinforcement of the Special Far Eastern Army (O.D.V.A.) for operations in 1929 against the Chinese promoted by the dispute over Soviet rights in the Chinese Eastern Railway, Rokossovsky was sent back to the Soviet Far East where he assumed command of an independent cavalry brigade, and with which he fought in the brief operations in November, 1929, in the area of Manchouli. He remained with the Special Far Eastern Army, commanded by Blyukher, and by 1932 commanded the 5th Cavalry Division which was stationed in the valley of the Dauriya. At this time the Soviet Far Eastern forces were experimenting with tanks and Rokossovsky is reported to have had his first experience of them.

When, in 1938, the military purge finally broke over the Soviet Far Eastern command, Rokossovsky was a corps commander; he was arrested, extremely roughly handled and his "case" investigated. (According to the most exact Soviet account, Rokossovsky did not "confess" and the "case" while being further probed by the NKVD, was finally dropped.) He was "rehabilitated" and returned in the winter of 1938–39 to command a mobile formation in the west, which subsequently took part in the "liberating drive" into Byelorussia and eastern Poland in September, 1939. In June, 1940, with the restoration of formal senior ranks into the Soviet command, Rokossovsky became a major-general and was posted to the Kiev Special Military District where he assumed command of the 9th mechanized Corps, which he helped to form and train.

With this formation, he fought in the first engagements of the Soviet-German War (Great Patriotic War), proving himself from the outset a competent commander and a cool head.

ON WESTERN FRONT

He was transferred in August, 1941, to the crucial Western Front, where he commanded the 16th Army covering the Minsk-Moscow highway. For the remainder of 1941 he fought on this front, first in the defensive battles before Moscow and then in the successful Soviet counterstroke which saved the capital. These successes identified him with the rapidly rising Soviet commanders whose ability was proved. In the spring of 1942, Rokossovsky went to the Bryansk front, and in October to the Don front, which was vitally associated with the successful Stalingrad counter-offensive; in January, 1943, together with Voronov, he signed the ultimatum to Field Marshal Paulus and the encircled German Sixth Army. During the gigantic battles of 1943, where the German offensive against Kursk was broken, he commanded the central front (Kursk-Orel).

During the next great period of Soviet success and advance (the "ten decisive blows" of 1944), Rokossovsky took command of the 1st Byelorussian Front for Operation Bagration, the plan to destroy the German Army Group Centre; in June, 1944, he was appointed Marshal of the Soviet Union and by August, 1944, his forces had reached the Vistula. He was, of necessity, implicated in the failure of the Red Army to support the Warsaw Rising

(1944). Having finally moved into Warsaw, his forces in the winter of 1944–45 entered East Prussia and in February, 1945, Rokossovsky's "East Prussian" campaign, one characterized by speed and swift mobile thrusts, opened; in April, he took command of the 2nd Byelorussian Front for the final phase of the operations against Berlin, covering Zhukov's flanks.

At the end of the war, Rokossovsky, now much advertised as "Polish" in origin, remained to "co-ordinate" Polish forces; in 1949, he was formally transferred to Poland, becoming Polish Defence Minister, Commander-in-Chief of the Polish forces and a Marshal of Poland, In addition, he was elected to the Polish Politburo and was a deputy to the Sejm. One more extension of his role came in 1955 when he was appointed a deputy commander of the Warsaw Pact organization. During the Polish excitements of 1956, however, he was removed from his position in the Polish armed forces and in Polish political life by Mr. Gomulka, and he returned to the Soviet Union where he was reinstated in his Soviet Marshal's appointment, and made a deputy Defence Minister, under Marshal Zhukov. In October, 1957, he was posted away from Moscow as commander of the Trans-Caucasus Military District, and his last official military appointment was that of January, 1958, as a deputy Defence Minister, this time under Marshal Malinovsky. From 1960 onwards he lived in semi-retirement, prominent only as a Deputy of the Supreme Soviet (to which he was first elected in 1946).

He was a Hero of the Soviet Union, was awarded the Order of Victory, several Orders of Lenin and all major Soviet military decorations, and the decoration Builder of People's Poland.

Rokossovsky had the reputation of being cool-headed, personally brave, and loyal to the Communist Party. His speciality was the rapid mobile thrust and he became one of the foremost Soviet exponents of this, and his reputation has continued to grow as a wartime commander. Rokossovsky, who was more than six feet tall, was known to his men as "The Hammer of the Huns".

August 5, 1968.

Sir Charles Romer, P.C., O.B.E., who died at his home in Kent on February 15, 1969, at the age of 72, was a Lord Justice of Appeal from 1951 to 1960, and chairman of the committee of inquiry into the circumstances connected with the Portland Spy case trial.

The law is proverbially the home of tradition, though even there it is rare to find that three generations in direct descent have had the honour of wearing the judicial ermine. Charles Romer was the third generation in his family to do so.

Charles Romer was born on January 19, 1897, the son of Lord (Mark) Romer, a Lord of Appeal in Ordinary from 1935 to 1944, and grandson of Sir Robert Romer, a Lord Justice of Appeal. Besides this direct descent, two of Charles Romer's uncles by marriage were Viscount Maugham, who had been Lord Chancellor, and who had married Lord Romer's sister, and the second, Lord Russell of Killowen, a Lord of Appeal. Apart from this strong legal influence, a literary flavour also came into the family, for Charles Romer's great-grandmother, the mother of the Lord Justice, was a daughter of Mark Lemon, the first editor of Punch, who had himself married a Miss Romer in 1839.

Charles Romer, like his father, was educated at Rugby, where he went in 1910 to Mr. Wilson's house. He saw service in the First World War in the King's Royal Rifle Corps, and was promoted captain, was wounded, was twice mentioned in dispatches and was awarded the military O.B.E.

He was called to the Bar in 1921 by Lincoln's Inn, of which he later became a Bencher.

LARGE PRACTICE

Though his important legal connexions offered the promise of an encouraging start, his own great natural ability brought him a large junior practice in the Chancery Courts. And his success continued and developed when he took silk in 1937.

On the death in 1944 of Lord Atkin, Lord Justice Goddard was appointed a Lord of Appeal in Ordinary (later becoming Lord Chief Justice) and Mr. Justice Morton went to the Court of Appeal from the Chancery Division. It was not unexpected that Lord Simon, then Lord Chancellor, should recommend Romer for the vacancy in that Division, and he took his seat on the Bench in October, 1944.

Just as he was a success at the Bar so he was as a Judge. And apart from his high qualities as a lawyer he was always patient and courteous to those who appeared before him. In 1951 he was promoted to the Court of Appeal and, again following custom, he was sworn of the Privy Council on his appointment as a Lord Justice of Appeal. Though he was a valuable addition to the Court of Appeal his health, after some years, began to trouble him, and after completing 15 years on the Bench he resigned in 1960. He retired to his home at Littlestone in Kent, a place where a number of well-known lawyers have lived and the relief from the previous heavy burden of his work was most beneficial in bringing an improvement in his health. He kept alive an active interest in the law by becoming a member of the local magisterial bench.

Although he was not one to court publicity, and he was not particularly well-known to the general public, his name received prominence when in March, 1961, he was persuaded to come temporarily out of retirement to be chairman of a committee which, in June, 1961, reported on their inquiries into breaches of security at the Underwater Detection Establishment at Portland as revealed by an official secrets trial in March of that year. It was stated that the Government had accepted the report.

Romer was twice married; first, to Lorna Buchanan, of which marriage there was one daughter; and, secondly, to Frances Evelyn Lebeau Kemp, of which marriage there were two sons.

February 17, 1969.

Eleanor Roosevelt, the widow of President Franklin Roosevelt, who died at the age of 78 on November 7, 1962, was perhaps the most distinguished of all the First Ladies who have graced the White House. It is true that Mrs. Wilson, the second wife of President Woodrow Wilson, exerted more direct political power for a short period. But Mrs. Roosevelt was more of an influential personality in her own right. To the men and women of America she became a figure of legendary earnestness, simplicity and devotion to the public good.

Her prominence derived in the first place, of course, from her husband. She had done more than most wives to help him in his political development, and her services to him were not curtailed when he achieved the Presidency. She was a charming and gifted hostess, interesting and interested in the many and varied guests whom it was her duty to entertain. But she was much more than that. She became the eyes and ears of a crippled man who could not move about as much as he would have wished. To him she presented the information and the views she acquired during her wide travels. As time went on she became herself a public commentator on the news in print and speech—and it must be confessed that on occasion her outspokenness proved a political embarrassment for her husband.

Her independent standing, however, was proved when she did not lapse into an honoured twilight of oblivion after Franklin Roosevelt's death. Indeed, her personal political influence became enhanced with the passage of years. In a country where politics is so often regarded as a race for the spoils she stood out for her sense of *noblesse oblige*. Among a people where political manipulation is often considered one of the higher arts she was remarkable for her undeviating devotion to principle. She became the conscience of the Democratic Party.

Inevitably, she had the failings of her virtues. She may sometimes have been earnest to the point of the didactic. So uncompromising were her ideals that she lacked her husband's political skill. So unquestioned was her own righteousness that on occasion she did not notice her own prejudices. But overall she made a noble and healthy contribution to the public life of more than one American generation.

SHELTERED YOUTH

Anna Eleanor Roosevelt was born in 1884, the daughter of Elliot Roosevelt, a younger brother of President Theodore Roosevelt, by his marriage with Anna Hull. In 1892 her mother died and she went to live with her maternal grandmother. Two years later her father, to whom she was devoted, died also. Both her parents had belonged to affluent families of high social standing in New York and she had a sheltered and very careful upbringing. Her earlier youth was spent at her grandmother's homes in New York and the country. On occasion she stayed with her uncle Theodore at Oyster Bay. Lacking playmates of her own age she learned to amuse herself and became an omnivorous reader. Her mother had wished her to acquire part of her education in Europe, and in 1899 she went with an aunt to England, where she was placed at Mlle. Souvestre's School at "Allinswood", near Wimbledon Common, frequently spending her holidays on the Continent.

Returning to New York, where she found herself somewhat out of touch with the younger generation, she was launched by her relations as a *debutante*. Soon, however, she met her distant cousin Franklin Delano Roosevelt, who was still at college. In 1903 he proposed to her and on St. Patrick's Day, 1905, they were married. After a tour in Europe Mrs. Roosevelt and her young husband returned to a New York house and, in due course, to the care of a growing family. (Their first child, a daughter, was born in 1906, and they also had five sons.) Then, however, with her husband's entry into politics, there came a new home in Albany and the dual existence of a politician's wife which was to continue through many active and crowded years. From girlhood she had had high ideals and one of them was that a wife should share her husband's interests.

In 1913 the future President became Assistant Secretary of the Navy, and the inevitable move to Washington ensued. It meant many social activities, into which she threw herself with characteristic energy. Then came the war and work for the Red Cross and in the Navy Hospital. After the armistice she was able to go with her husband to Europe. By that time his political future seemed assured, and in 1920 he was nominated for the Vice-Presidency.

A TURNING POINT

The election was lost and the following year he suffered the attack of infantile paralysis that was to be a turning-point in his life. This was a period of stern trial for a devoted wife. She responded with superb courage and calm. One of the greatest services she ever rendered to him was in encouraging his determination some day to resume his political career in the active world. His mother would have had him lead the existence of an elegant invalid: his wife would have none of it. During his long convalescence she began to take an increasing interest in affairs, and after his election to the Governorship of New York a new field of public life opened for her.

In 1932 Franklin Roosevelt was elected President of the United States and Mrs. Roosevelt became first lady in the land. She had immense energy and both enthusiasm and ability. The hesitancy of her earlier years had vanished and she threw herself into her new duties with vigour. She travelled immense distances, and was here, there and everywhere.

MANY INTERESTS

Everything interested her. She talked with everybody she met, asked questions, examined everything. There was a cartoon of miners in the bowels of the earth looking with astonishment over their shoulders and exclaiming "Here comes Mrs. Roosevelt". By this time she was a practised speaker and lecturer, and made speeches and broadcast. She also wrote books and in 1935 started her column, "My Day", which before long was reaching millions of readers. In it she was informal, chatty and friendly and the women in small homes absorbed her observations easily and felt they knew her. The profits she derived from her activities amounted to a large annual sum and she distributed it among her favourite charities.

Even if Mrs. Roosevelt had played a less ambitious role her work would have been immense. Sacks of correspondence and endless gifts came as a matter of course to the President's wife. There was also the White House—she was soon to renovate its offices—and all its entertaining to look after. She seemed, however, to take her normal duties in her stride and to be always moving on to wider interests. In such spare moments as she had, however, she reverted to the kindly matriarch and knitted for grandchildren. Naturally she was a contentious figure and the political opponents of her husband did not spare her—"Nor Eleanor either" was a hostile slogan in one of his Presidential campaigns. But criticism she accepted as the natural lot of public life, and in spite of it she became and remained a great national figure.

STAY AT PALACE

In the war, kindly always in her recollections of her early days there, she proved herself a sympathetic friend towards Britain. She sent encouraging messages and adopted an East End boy for the duration of hostilities. In October, 1942, she flew across the Atlantic and stayed at Buckingham Palace. Her visit was full of incident. She saw the bombed areas and went to Dover, she visited American troops, the R.A.F., and the women's services and paid special attention to the work of women in the war. She also crossed to Ulster to see the American troops there and travelled to Scotland. Everywhere she went she radiated encouragement and created an admirable impression. From England, moreover, she broadcast to her own country. In the summer of 1943 she went to New Zealand and Australia to be again a welcome and honoured guest. The next year she was in the West Indies.

ROLE IN POLITICS

At the President's death, in April, 1945, she was 60 but a whole new life and career and even more travel lay ahead of her. She continued her daily column of comment, "My Day", published several more books, was for years a delegate to the United Nations, visited half the countries of the world, and played an important role in American party politics.

Eight months after her husband's death President Truman asked her to be a delegate to the United Nations General Assembly meeting in 1945. The following year she was chairman of the Commission on Human Rights in Unesco. Thereafter she was constantly a delegate to the United Nations General Assembly meetings until the Democratic Administration gave way to the Republicans after the defeat of 1952. Even then she continued to be active in the American Association for the United Nations.

In 1948 she went to London at the invitation of the King and Queen to unveil the statue of her husband in Grosvenor Square. She had visited Germany immediately after the 1945 meeting of the General Assembly in London and thereafter she crossed the ocean so many times she described herself as a harassed commuter across the Atlantic. In addition to Britain, France and Germany her travels included Russia (as far as Samarkand and Tashkent), Yugoslavia, Greece, Turkey, Lebanon, Syria, Jordan, Israel, India, Pakistan, Burma, Siam, Indonesia, Hongkong and Japan. On these travels she continued writing her daily column for various American newspapers and interviewed, as a newspaperwoman, important people around the world, including an interview with Khrushchev at Yalta.

WORK IN U.N.

At home she remained pretty well aloof from domestic politics while she was representing her country at the United Nations although she did support Adlai Stevenson for President in the 1952 campaign. He inspired her, as he did so many other people of deep liberal convictions, with the belief that he would have made a President of outstanding calibre. She remained his devoted supporter. In 1956 she campaigned for him in his fight for the Democratic nomination and in his contest for the Presidency itself. Nothing would have pleased her better than for him to be the Democratic standard-bearer once again in 1960.

It was not to be, but Mrs. Roosevelt did not reconcile herself immediately to the choice of Kennedy. Her doubts were occasioned not only by disappointment over the rejection of Stevenson: she was disturbed by Kennedy's ambiguous record on McCarthyism and questioned whether he had the basic conviction and faithfulness to principle necessary for the highest responsibility. Eventually she did declare herself for him and campaign on his behalf, but there was always the suspicion that she was moved less by confidence in him than by concern at the thought of Nixon in the White House.

Throughout these years, however, she was not preoccupied by national politics. Some of her most valuable work at this time was at the level of New York state affairs. In company with Herbert Lehman and others she played a major part in freeing Democratic politics in the state from the control of Tammany Hall.

MORAL PRINCIPLES

It was on such an issue as this, where moral principles were closely involved, that she was at her best. Her popularity with people transcended parties and politics. Many times during her widowhood she was voted, in annual polls by the Gallup organization, the most popular woman in America.

In addition to her political labours, her travel and her daily journalism and her work for many charities, she found time to write a number of books of reminiscence. They included *This is My Story*, *My Days*, *If You Ask Me*, *This I Remember*, *India and the Awakening East*, and *On My Own*, this last the story of her life and activities following her departure from the White House in 1945. In the early thirties she had also published books for children and women, including, *When You Grow up to Vote*, and *It's Up to the Women*. She also edited various books including *The Moral Basis of Democracy*.

November 8, 1962.

Lord Rootes, G.B.E., died on December 12, 1964, at the age of 70. By his death the motor industry loses one of its best known landmarks and British industry one of its most outspoken characters. "Billy" Rootes, it was widely believed, could have sold anything to anyone. He certainly sold a lot of cars. But it was as a kind of super-salesman of British goods in general that he will be remembered in New York. When dollars were short, he earned Britain more than most as head of the Dollar Export Board and its successors. And his own firm, the Rootes Group, fared remarkably well in the American market too. He had more than enough energy for both jobs, as he had for most things he undertook. It was typical of his independent outlook that his company should have stood out so long against the rising encroachment of the larger groups in the motor trade. His round, ruddy countenance, seen at its friendliest at the head of so many industrial dinners and meetings since the war, rarely hid the determination that lay behind.

William Rootes was born in Kent on August 17, 1894, son of William Rootes, cycle and motor engineer. After education at Cranbrook School he went into the family workshop, and then, in 1913, to Singer Cars, Coventry. He worked long hours, but found time to engage in motor cycle track racing, at which he won valuable prizes. In 1915 he volunteered for war service as a pupil engineer in the R.N.V.R. He was moved in 1917 to the flying section, then the R.N.A.S., which was to become merged in the R.A.F. in 1918.

HILLMAN MINX

He got down to motor trading as soon as he was demobilized and used his great persuasive powers on his younger brother Reginald to quit his Civil Service post at the Admiralty and join in with him. Together, and with a £1,500 loan from their father, they started a car business in Maidstone, but soon extended to Long Acre, London, and then to the new Devonshire House, Piccadilly, when it was built in 1926. But Billy had set his mind on manufacturing and exporting motor cars, not just dealing in them, and, with financial help arranged by Sir George May, of the Prudential, the Hillman and Humber factories were acquired in 1929. New models with an export appeal were planned, first to come being the Humber Snipe with its challenge to the American type of car. In 1931 the Hillman Wizard, sub-titled "The Car for the Roads of the World", arrived and was launched at a great luncheon party held in the Albert Hall. Comparatively few British cars were then being exported, but W.E. Rootes lent his full weight to this side of the business; his brother Reginald went to Argentina and founded a branch of the firm there at the time of the 1931 British exhibition in Buenos Aires. A new small car destined to set a fashion in its class appeared in 1932—the Hillman Minx—which W. E. R. personally tested on roads abroad before it was announced. Its success was immediate and its name remains well known to motorists to this day.

All through the thirties further acquisitions of large concerns took place. Karrier Motors were added in 1934, Singer Cars, Clement Talbot, Ltd., and Sunbeam Motor Car Co., Ltd., in 1935 (these becoming Sunbeam Talbot Ltd., in 1938), and in 1937 the general process of manufacture was rounded off by the purchase of British Light Steel Pressings, Ltd., of Acton, makers of car and lorry bodies and fittings.

All this development consisted of administrative and financial mergers. The aim was not to produce a "Rootes car" but to continue the manufacture of well-tried and well-known models, each under its own name and each preserving its distinctive character. But by an all-over rationalization scheme, by the centralization of sundry manufacturing processes, and by the standardization and interchangeability of many components and assembly systems, the brothers secured a great increase in efficiency and a considerable reduction in production and service costs.

In view of the range and breadth of William Rootes's interests it is not surprising that he was from time to time asked to serve on various central or official bodies. In 1931-34, and again in 1939-40, he was a member of the Board of Trade Advisory Council; in 1933-49 he served on the Overseas Trade Development Council, and in 1933-34 as member of the Committee on the Education and Training of Students from Overseas. He served on the delegation to British Week in Finland, 1933, and on the United Kingdom Trade Mission to Poland, 1934. When, in 1936, the threat of war brought about the formation of the Joint Aero Engine Committee (shadow industry) Rootes became a member, and in 1940-41 acted as chairman. The Rootes Group was among the first to enter, in 1936, the Government aircraft scheme for the volume manufacture of airframes and aero engines. Soon after the war started Rootes was appointed chairman of the aircraft shadow industry which later became linked with Lord Beaverbrook's Aircraft Production Ministry. In 1941 he was chairman of the Motor Vehicle Maintenance Advisory Committee and in1941-42 chairman of the supply council, Ministry of Supply. He was made K.B.E. in 1942.

DOLLAR EXPORTS

After the war the Rootes Group embarked on a great programme of expansion and conversion of wartime plant to peace-time uses. Several millions were laid out, and the production capacity of the group was more than doubled. Export on a large scale now became vital, and Sir William's intimate knowledge of the American market stood the concern in good stead. He set up departments for service and parts on Long Island and in Chicago and Los Angeles, and in April, 1950, was the prime mover in organizing, at the Grand Central Palace, New York, the first British car and motor cycle exhibition to be held in that city.

In June, 1951, he became chairman of the new Dollar Exports Board, and at once initiated a vigorous campaign, urging British manufacturers to "think big" and to adopt transatlantic standards of sales and service. His insatiable desire to get things moving served his country as well as his firm. His chairmanship of the Dollar Exports Council, as it became, was lively and successful; he travelled widely on trade missions and his travels rarely failed to benefit the Exchequer. In 1960 the council's name was changed once again, this time to the Western Hemisphere Export Council. Rootes retained the chairmanship for another four years, retiring in March, 1964.

In his middle sixties he remained unquestioned head of the Rootes dynasty as the costly but triumphant stand during the Acton strike of 1961 showed. As an independent manufacturer, however, Rootes was small by current standards and in June this year a link was announced whereby Chrysler, the American car firm, took a £12m. interest. The management control of Rootes remained unchanged, but the company benefited both from the extended network for exports and from the enlarged capital for investment.

He was advanced to G.B.E. in 1955 and created a baron in 1959. In January, 1964, it was announced that he was to be Chancellor of the new Warwick University.

Rootes farmed extensively both in the south of England and in Scotland and was a notable breeder of pedigree stock. He was devoted to country pursuits—shooting, riding, and farming.

In 1916 Rootes married Nora, daughter of the late Horace Press. There were two sons of the marriage, both of whom became leading figures in their father's business concerns. The marriage was dissolved in 1951 and Rootes married the same year, Ruby Joy Ann, formerly wife of Sir Francis Henry Peek. His first wife died in September this year. His elder son, the Hon. William Geoffrey Rootes, succeeds him.

December 14, 1964.

Flight Lieutenant "Tommy" Rose, D.F.C., formerly test pilot for Miles Aircraft Ltd., and winner of the King's Cup race in 1935, died on June 20, 1968, in Alderney, at the age of 73. He was for many years a well-known figure in flying circles.

The race of 1935 was a two-day event and the final was a triumph for the designs of that pioneer of light aircraft, F.G. Miles. Rose, in a Falcon Six, won at 176.28 m.p.h., followed by two Hawk Trainers.

The following year, in the same aircraft, he flew to the Cape in three days 17 hr. 37 min., bettering Amy Mollison's solo time which had remained unapproached since 1932.

Rose, who was born on January 27, 1895, at Chilbolton, Hampshire, served with distinction during the 1914-18 War, first with the Royal Flying Corps and later in the R.A.F. He accounted for more than 12 enemy aircraft and won the D.F.C. After leaving the service he flew all over the world as a commercial pilot. He had a long flying association with Phillips and Powis Aircraft, Limited, of Reading, who built many of F.G. Miles's designs, and later with Miles Aircraft Ltd., testing in the course of his career a large number of new light machines. From 1947 to 1949 he was general manager of Universal Flying Services Ltd.

June 21, 1968.

Sir James Ross, K.B.E., C.B., who died on October 2, 1961, spent over 40 years in the Civil Service after coming down from Balliol, where he had had a brilliant career as Warner Exhibitioner and took a first in Classical Moderations. His career stretched over several Ministries but he will be remembered chiefly for his long administrative work at the War Office, and for some years before his final retirement with the Ministry of Health, in connexion with the formation of the National Health Service.

The first three or four years of his retirement were spent in writing his book, *The National Health Service in Great Britain: an Historical and Descriptive Study*, which quickly became the acknowledged authoritative work on the subject. It was characteristic of Sir James and his sense of public service that years after his retirement he came out of it to assist in the working out and the application of the National Health Service scheme, and that after having held some of the highest positions at the War Office and at the Air Ministry, he assumed the comparatively modest task at the Health Ministry of working as a Regional Officer—and that when approaching his seventies.

James Stirling Ross was born on August 3, 1877, a son of the late John Ross, V.D., F.E.I.S., of Edinburgh. From the Royal High School, Edinburgh, he went to Edinburgh University, where he was Baxter Scholar and took first-class honours in Classics, before proceeding to Balliol. Coming down from Oxford he went to the War Office in 1900 and within four years was appointed private secretary to the Chief of the General Staff. In 1905 he began a period of several years' service with the Aldershot, Scottish, and Northern Commands—in that order—but in 1912 he was recalled to Headquarters, and there he remained until the end of the First World War in 1918. Several other posts at the War Office followed, until he went as deputy to the assistant Financial Secretary at the Air Ministry. In 1921 he became Director of Accounts there, and in 1930 Principal Assistant Secretary. That post he held until 1934, when he was appointed Deputy Secretary.

He assumed this post at the time when the Government's first expansion programme for the Air Force was introduced, and during the next four years had heavy responsibility for the financial and administrative side of the expansion programmes. Before he retired in 1938 he had seen a firm basis laid for the growth of the R.A.F. for its coming task in the war.

THE AIR MINISTRY

On the outbreak of hostilities in 1939 he rejoined the Air Ministry for war services, and was its representative in South Africa and Southern Rhodesia from 1940 to 1943. At the end of the latter year he returned to London to join the Air Ministry Secretariat and Planning Executive and served until February, 1946, when he became Chairman of the Selection Board of the Allied Control Commission in Germany. It was at his own request that in August of that year he was relieved of these duties in order to go to the Ministry of Health, and there he served until 1949.

In earlier years he had been Vice-Chairman of the Bacon Development Board and a member of the Board of Trustees for eight years of the Imperial War Museum. From 1938 to 1948 he was chairman of the Aldershot and West Surrey Hospital League, within the area of whose activities he lived at Merrow, near Guildford.

Sir James was an M.A. of Oxford and was created C.B.E. in 1919. He became a Companion of the Bath in 1928, and a Knight Commander of the Order of the British Empire in 1937. He married first in 1904 Christina MacDonald Ross, M.A., who was a Scholar of Newnham, and a daughter of John Ross, M.A., Rector of Arbroath High School. By her he had two sons and one daughter. In 1928 he married, secondly, Henriette Wilson, daughter of J. P. Halket, of Woodside Park Road, N.12.

October 3, 1961.

Mark Rothko, one of the most distinguished American painters of his generation, was found dead in his studio in New York on February 25, 1970. He was 66.

Rothko, a pioneer of abstract expressionist painting, painted monumental works, in which simple rectangles of bright colours seem to float on the canvas. Avant-garde critics acclaimed Rothko, but the more conservative voiced alarm over the increasing size and emptiness of his pictures in his later years.

Rothko's art might be termed a process of elimination in which the artist sought to remove "all obstacles between the painter and the idea". The obstacles in his view were what he described as the "swamps" of memory, history and geometry which for him merely complicated the issue. The Surrealist imagery appearing in his early work was thus excised in favour of large rectangular forms subtly shading one into another. These however, far from being static, seemed to expand before the eyes or suggest a power of expansion and changes. His drastic simplification might appear to leave little for the spectator to look at but on a large scale (which certainly helped their effect) his horizontal shapes gained an extraordinary force and individuality.

Rothko, the son of a Jewish pharmacist, was born in 1903 at Dvinsk in Russia, and taken to the United States when he was 10, growing up in Portland, Oregon. He began painting in 1926, studying in New York. Like a number of other American painters in the 1930s and the early war years, Rothko was influenced by such European Surrealists as Max Ernst, André Masson and Marcel Duchamp whose wartime presence in America, together with that of André Breton, gave the movement there a living actuality. The "Art of this Century" gallery of Peggy Guggenheim was a rallying point for him and others, but a main factor in the creation of a new phase of American art seems to have been a like-mindedness in a number of painters working towards the same end, or in a relation of mood, though not necessarily in the same style. For many Europeans, Jackson Pollock probably is the *chef d'école*, though Rothko was closer in spirit to William Baziotes, Robert Motherwell, and Barnett Newman, with whom in 1948 he founded the school in New York, "Subjects of the Artist", and with whom he was later associated in the avant-garde meetings of "The Club".

Rothko's importance in American painting was marked in 1961 when he was accorded the rare distinction for a living artist of having a retrospective exhibition of his works shown at the New York Museum of Modern Art. The honour had previously been reserved for Picasso and Miro.

Rothko taught in San Francisco and New York but his influence was not confined to the United States and his works made a deep impression when shown on the continent of Europe and in London in the exhibitions of the "New American Painting" organized by the Museum of Modern Art. A big one-man show of his work was seen at the Whitechapel Gallery in 1961. In 1962 and 1963 he exhibited in Paris; and in 1964 in London. He is represented in American museums and at the Tate Gallery.

February 27, 1970.

Anthony Gustav de Rothschild, who died on February 5, 1961, in a London hospital at the age of 73, was for many years the senior partner in Messrs. N. M. Rothschild and Sons, Merchants and Bankers, of New Court, St. Swithin's Lane.

Born on June 26, 1887, he was the third and youngest son of Leopold de Rothschild by his wife Marie, daughter of Achille Perugia, of Trieste. He was educated at Harrow, where he was head of the school, and at Trinity College, Cambridge, where he gained a first in both parts of the historical tripos. He represented the university at tennis. The First World War rang down the curtain on the brilliant social scene in which his family appeared among the leading actors. Anthony de Rothschild served with the Bucks Yeomanry from 1915 to 1918, rising to the rank of Major. He was wounded at Gallipoli and mentioned in dispatches.

His father and two uncles who had brought such high prestige to the House of Rothschild during the Edwardian era passed away during the First World War. Of the next generation, the second Lord Rothschild was not identified with business, while his brother Charles died at an early age in 1923. Evelyn, second son of Leopold de Rothschild, had been killed in action and it therefore remained to Lionel and Anthony to carry on the family business, under strange conditions and on heavily depleted capital, during the inter-war years. Anthony de Rothschild became senior partner of the firm on the death of his brother Lionel in 1941. He was for many years a director and in 1949 became chairman of the Alliance Assurance Company.

Though disinclined to assume the role of leadership in the affairs of the Jewish community that was open to him, Mr. de Rothschild held office in a number of Jewish organizations. He was president of the Jewish Orphanage and of the Jews' Free School, chairman of the Central

British Fund for Jewish Relief and Rehabilitation, and, for a time, a vice-president of the Anglo-Jewish Association. Outside of the Jewish community he was chairman of the Four per cent Industrial Dwellings Company, a pioneer in the field for providing clean and comfortable houses for the working classes, and from 1948 to 1956 chairman of governors of St. Mary's Hospital.

Apart from his public and business life, de Rothschild interested himself in art and racing. In both he proved himself a public benefactor. In January, 1938, he gave Van Dyck's "The Abbe Scaglia adoring the Virgin and Child" to the National Gallery, and in 1946 gave the Palace House, at Newmarket, to the Jockey Club, of which he was a member and a trustee, "in the hope that it would be used by the Royal Family when they attend the races". While his active interest in racing continued, de Rothschild won the Grand Prix de Paris and the 1,000 Guineas.

de Rothschild married, in 1926, Yvonne eldest daughter of Baron Robert Cahen d'Anvers, of Paris, by whom he had a son and two daughters. In 1950 he and his wife gave their collection of oriental porcelain and pictures—including a fine Hogarth, two Rubens, two Gainsboroughs, and a magnificent Stubbs—to the National Trust together with the house and grounds of Ascott, Buckinghamshire, in which they continued to live.

February 6, 1961.

Captain H. J. Round, M.C., a pioneer of electronics, died at Bognor Regis on August 17, 1966, at the age of 85.

Henry Joseph Round was born on June 2, 1881, at Kingswinford, Staffordshire. His early education took place at Cheltenham and he later studied at the Royal College of Science, London, gaining first class honours.

In 1902 he joined the Marconi Company and was sent to the United States where he worked at the American Marconi Company's training school for wireless operators at Babylon, Long Island. Here, as spare-time activities, he investigated wireless propagation problems, experimented with dust-core tuning inductances and devised the elements of direction finding. In 1907, in a letter to *Electrical World*, Round gave notice of his discovery that the application of an electric potential across silicon carbide could affect the generation of light. (This was re-discovered in 1923 and is now known as the Lossey Effect. It has recently seen practical fruition in semiconductor lasers).

About this period Round constructed one of the first arc radio telephones, which on his recall to England he demonstrated to Marconi, to whom he became a personal assistant. In 1910-11 he greatly improved the performance of the Clifden (Ireland) high power transatlantic transmitter and followed this in 1912 with a brilliant feat of engineering at two stations on the upper reaches of the River Amazon which were not achieving the contract guarantee by reason of heavy signal attenuation across the jungle. Round virtually redesigned the stations *in situ* to operate on 4,000 metres by day and 2,000 metres by night, a masterpiece of ingenuity since no spares were immediately to hand.

On his return Round did considerable work on the thermionic valve and was among the first to discover that it could generate continuous wave oscillations. By 1913, he was demonstrating valve radio telephony and in 1913-14 patented important valve improvements, including the indirectly heated cathode.

DIRECTION FINDERS

At the outbreak of the First World War he was seconded to Military Intelligence with the task of building a network of valved direction-finding stations to cover the entire Western Front. These stations which Round had developed just prior to the onset of war, were so successful in pinpointing the location of enemy transmitters that he was recalled to England to supervise the construction of a second network there. In May, 1916, in the hours before the onset of the Battle of Jutland, the system detected a seven-mile change of position of the German fleet 300 miles away at Wilhelmshaven, and this led to the deduction that it was about to put to sea. For his services to the country Captain Round was awarded the Military Cross.

In 1919 he developed new types of transmitting valves and in March of that year directed the installation of a telephony transmitter at Ballybunion, Ireland, which became the first European station to span the Atlantic with telephony. Further experimental telephony work at Chelmsford followed which led, via the early broadcasts from the Marconi 2MT station at Writtle to the establishment of the original London broadcasting station 2LO at Marconi House, for which Round designed the transmitting equipment.

He was appointed Chief of the newly formed Marconi Research Group in 1921 and soon his inventive genius was in full flood. In addition to invaluable work on short-wave telephony he was responsible for the "Straight Eight" receiver, a gramophone recording system, a large-audience public address system, the artificial echo system for broadcasting studios, new types of microphone, the screened grid and r.f. pentode valves, gramophone pickups, amplifiers, sound recording systems, aerial systems and a great many other devices and circuits.

SOUND ON FILM

In 1930 he patented a method of recording sound on film, a method which superseded the existing synchronized gramophone record for talking films.

In 1931 he resigned from the Marconi Company to set up in private practice as a research consultant, returning to the company in an advisory capacity in 1937 for work on echo sounding. During the Second World War he worked on ASDIC for the Admiralty, continuing with this until 1950. In 1952 he was presented with the Armstrong Medal by the Radio Club of America.

August 19, 1966.

Dr. Peyton Rous, a pioneer in cancer research, died on February 16, 1970, in New York at the age of 90. The importance of his contribution has only comparatively recently been generally recognized. Thus it was 56 years from his discovery that a virus could cause cancer in fowls till the recognition of his work by the award of a Nobel prize in 1966.

Peyton Rous (he disliked and never used his first name, Francis) was born on October 5, 1879. He received his medical education at Johns Hopkins Hospital in Baltimore, qualifying in 1900, and obtaining his M.D. in 1905. After a residency, he was for two years an instructor in pathology at the University of Michigan. Then Simon Flexner, director of the Rockefeller Institute in New York, needed someone to continue a programme of cancer research, and Rous was persuaded, much against his will, to accept the position. Within a few weeks he had succeeded in transplanting to other fowls a naturally occurring connective-tissue tumour, now universally known as the Rous sarcoma. He was soon able to show that it could be transmitted by means of cell-free filtrates. This afforded the first evidence that a virus could cause cancer. True, Ellerman and Bang in Denmark had, shortly before this, transmitted a leukaemia of fowls with a filtrate, but the observation had not been followed up. Not unexpectedly, Rous's discovery was received with scepticism and even hostility: orthodox pathologists argued either that Rous's virus was not really a virus or that the tumour was not a true tumour. However, with J. B. Murphy and other collaborators, he patiently proceeded to demonstrate the true nature of the growths and of the causative agent. He was deeply disappointed that, even then, the significance of his discovery was not appreciated, and for some years he left the field of cancer research.

Yet many important discoveries of his date from this period. He did important work on the liver, throwing light on the function of the gall-bladder. A little later he showed, by injecting litmus and other indicator dyes into living animals, how different was the acidity of various tissues. During the 1914-18 War he found out how blood could be preserved for a number of weeks, and this knowledge proved of very great value.

In 1933 Dr. R. E. Shope discovered a warty growth in rabbits, often progressing to cancer. Rous eagerly took up its study and was happily back again in cancer research. A very productive period followed. In particular he showed in a number of ways that when chemical carcinogens (cancer-inducing substances) and a tumour-virus acted together, tumour production was speeded up and enhanced. He was also the first to show that carcinogenic action occurred in two stages: initiation, conferring malignant potentialities on a cell, and promotion, allowing these potentialities to be expressed in actively growing cancer.

He published many scientific papers on cancer and gave many important addresses on its pathology. In recent years he had received many well-deserved honours, including honorary degrees from the Universities of Cambridge, Michigan, Yale, Birmingham, McGill, Chicago and Zurich. He was elected a foreign member of the Royal Society.

His whole scientific life after 1909 was spent at the Rockefeller Institute, of which he became member, later emeritus member and professor, and where he continued in active work until well into his eighties. For 36 years he was the chief editor—and an exacting one—of the Journal of Experimental Medicine. He had spent some time in Cambridge and had many ties with this country, especially after one of his daughters married Professor Alan Hodgkin. F.R.S., who also became a Nobel Laureate.

February 17, 1970.

Lord Rowley, of Rowley Regis, P.C., Q.C., who as Arthur Henderson was Labour member of Parliament for Rowley Regis and Tipton, 1950-66, and a former Secretary of State for Air, died in London on August 28, 1968. He was 75.

Sons of distinguished statesmen not uncommonly tend to react to the political pattern of their paternity, but Arthur Henderson never diverged from the beliefs and ideals in which he had been nurtured by his father, an outstanding Foreign Secretary and one of the most influential, respected and beloved figures in the Labour movement. "Young Arthur" inherited many of his father's characteristics. He stood in the true line of that central, moderate socialism which drew its strength from old-fashioned non-conformist radicalism.

Unlike some modern heirs of that tradition Rowley was faithful to it throughout his life. He was a practising Wesleyan whose religion was the mainspring of his political beliefs. It was the inspiration of his passion for world peace and of his work in the cause of world government which he saw as the ultimate aim of all endeavours towards international accord. But his idealism was tempered with a shrewd sense of political realism. A soldier in two wars, he had no illusions about the need for adequate defences to safeguard peace. He became chairman of the Parliamentary Group for world government, and all his political life he stood for the concept of a united states of Europe. He was one of the first to see in the Common Market the nucleus of such an arrangement though he always counselled caution in negotiating terms of entry.

Rowley was born in 1893 at Newcastle upon Tyne. He was educated at the Central School, Darlington, at Queen's College, Taunton, and at Trinity Hall, Cambridge, where he gained honours in law and economics and was chairman of the Labour Club. After service in the 1914-18 War he was called to the Bar by the Middle Temple in 1921. Two years later he was returned as Labour member for South Cardiff. He failed to get reelected in 1924 but succeeded in 1929. When the National Government obtained their mandate in 1931 Rowley suffered the fate of many of his Labour colleagues, but in 1935 he was returned for the Kingswinford division of Staffordshire. He soon made his mark as one of the most reliable debaters among the younger Labour members and was for some years standing counsel to the party. He joined up on the outbreak of war and served until March, 1942, on the Army General Staff, with the rank of captain and later major. In that year Churchill appointed him Joint Parliamentary Under-Secretary of State for War, and 12 months later Financial Secretary to the War Office.

Rowley had proved himself a conscientious and efficient Minister and when Labour came to power after the war Clement Attlee made him Under-Secretary of State for India and Burma. His experience in this office at an historic juncture was to prove particularly valuable two years later, when, as Minister of State for Commonwealth Relations, he was called upon to assist the Secretary of State in the conduct of relations with India and Pakistan in their new status as independent dominions. It was largely a winding-up process which lasted only about two months. In October, 1947, Rowley was promoted Secretary of State for Air. He had been sworn a member of the Privy Council in January of that year.

Rowley's qualities found full scope in his new office. He was an air-minded Minister and he took an informed interest in all the details of the service, and not least those which concerned the well-being of the men. He was constantly preoccupied with the need to match western resources to the build-up of Soviet air power. He threw himself with zest into the task of building the R.A.F. into a balanced force, and the expansionist programme on which the Government embarked got a valuable impetus from his zeal for reequipment and recruiting. At the 1950 election he had been returned for Rowley Regis and Tipton on the disappearance of his old seat; he held the seat until 1966. That year he was created a life peer and took the title Lord Rowley of Rowley Regis.

His speeches were always factual. He permitted himself no flight of oratory. But there was a workman-like, sensible solidity about his contributions to debate which compelled the House to take him seriously and he was always given an attentive hearing. He could often command a wide measure of agreement from both sides of the House, and Ministers who suffered so much from his relentless probing treated him with deference.

He did not take much part in the internal affairs of his party and certainly he could not be described as a smoking-room type of politician. But he was a good House of Commons man, a worthy son of his father, a man of dogged tenacity, immense capacity for hard work, and inflexible integrity

Rowley, who took silk in 1939, collaborated with Sir Henry Slesser in a work on trade unions and the law. He wrote a treatise on industrial law and was joint author of a work on housing law.

He shared his interest in foreign affairs—and much else—with his brother, Lord Henderson, with whom for many years he occupied a bachelor establishment in Westminster. Arthur moved only a short distance to a neighbouring flat when, in 1958, he married Mrs. Mary Elizabeth Gliksten, of Miami, Florida, widow of Mr. Harold Gliksten.

August 29, 1968.

Helena Rubinstein, whose world-wide chain of cosmetics factories, laboratories and beauty salons grew from her manufacture of a few jars of face cream in an old family formula, died in New York on April 1, 1965.

She was born in Cracow, Poland, on Christmas Day, 1882. Her father was a food merchant, descended from a family of doctors, and persuaded his daughter to enrol as a medical student at Cracow University. But after a short period there and at Zurich, deciding that medicine could not be her future, Helena Rubinstein left for Australia.

On her arrival there in 1902, she had no definite plans and little money. With her she had brought 12 jars of face cream. Soon her friends, admiring the way she preserved her complexion in the hot, dry climate, were asking for more of it. Helena Rubinstein wrote to her mother for more, but the demand grew and she sent home for the formula.

Soon she was manufacturing it on a larger and larger scale: she leased an office and hired staff, and at the same time took university courses in dermatology and allied subjects.

MOVE TO EUROPE

She took regular advertisement space in newspapers, and soon the original Valaze cream—which still sells under another name—was supplemented by other beauty aids of her invention.

In 1904 she left Australia with the beginnings of a fortune, and started the first Helena Rubinstein enterprise in Europe, leaving two of her seven younger sisters to continue the business in Melbourne.

In 1908, her first salon was opened in London—in Mayfair—and was an immediate success; a second followed in Paris in 1912, and a third in New York in 1915. Branches soon opened in almost every major city of the world, and after the First World War, Helena Rubinstein started to sell her products wholesale as well as through the salons.

Early on, she set up special schools to educate sales girls in the science of skin analysis and the correct application of cosmetics. Helena Rubinstein personally controlled the vast chain of laboratories and factories throughout the world. Her special interest remained the scientific development of new products.

Her art collection of paintings, glass, furniture, and African sculpture was distributed among her several homes. She herself was painted by Graham Sutherland.

She married first Edward Titus, an American journalist, by whom she had two sons, and second Prince Artchil Gourielli-Tchkonia.

April 2, 1965.

Lord Rugby, G.C.M.G., K.C.B., K.C.V.O., C.S.I., C.I.E., sometime Chief Commissioner of the N.W. Frontier Province of India, later Governor-General of the Sudan, and in and after the war years United Kingdom representative in Dublin, died on April 20, 1969, at the age of 91.

John Loader Maffey was born on July 1, 1877. He was educated at Rugby and Christ

Church, Oxford, of which later he was an honorary Student. He passed the I.C.S. examination in 1899.

He began his service in the United Provinces. In 1905 he was transferred to the Political Service and began a quarter of a century's experience in the then newly created North-West Frontier Province and its hinterland. Three years later he was attached to the Mohmand Field Force, and the medal with clasp he was awarded was the first of his many decorations. For three years from 1909 he was Political Agent in the Khyber, and next he was in charge of the Peshawar district. When in the middle of the 1914-18 war Lord Chelmsford was appointed Viceroy he chose Maffey to be his principal private secretary, and the selection was a fortunate one. When the temperamental Secretary of State, Edwin Montague, went out to confer with the Viceroy on projected political reforms Maffey did much to smooth relations between his sensitive chief and the thrustful Cabinet emissary.

All the time his real *métier* was among the tribesmen whose language and outlook he understood so well. So in 1921 he went back to Peshawar, this time as Chief Commissioner. His firmness, combined with a keen sense of humour; his tall, upright, debonair figure, his cool steady judgment; his tact and moral courage; all made a deep impression on the tribesmen, and saved the Government from much expenditure and anxiety.

In 1923 his was the directing hand in the rescue of Miss Mollie Ellis. Miss Ellis, a girl of 17, was carried off into the wild Tirah territory by a gang of tribesmen who in a raid had killed her mother. Mrs. Starr, of the Peshawar Medical Mission, was asked by the Chief Commissioner, who realized that a military pursuit might mean Miss Ellis's death, to go 30 miles into that dangerous region to intercede for the return of the girl, who was being held for a ransom Maffey stoutly refused to give. She succeeded in her quest and restored Miss Ellis unhurt.

IMPERIAL AIRWAYS

Maffey resigned at the end of 1924 and took up work in the City. In 1926 he was appointed Governor-General of the Sudan. On retirement in 1933 Maffey was selected to be Permanent Under-Secretary for the Colonies. He left the Colonial Office in 1937 and became a governor of Imperial Airways.

In 1939 he was chosen to be the United Kingdom representative in Eire. Few diplomatic posts in the 1939-45 War could have been more testing and exacting. Irish neutrality meant the presence in Dublin of representatives of both Germany and Japan, and Maffey was conscious of the consequent leakage of news to the enemy. From the first the anxieties of Ulster and the possibility of Britain, later joined by America, demanding the use of the Eire ports, had to be kept in mind. Throughout Lord Rugby maintained cordial relations with Mr. De Valera personally and with all sections of Irish society. He was always himself—an English gentleman and an uncompromising Protestant—and this caused him to be respected and held in affection even by extreme anti-British Irishmen. Yet he never forfeited the confidence and esteem of Ulster. He came creditably through this severely testing time, and fully merited the barony conferred upon him at the beginning of 1947. He left Dublin in 1949.

He married in 1907 Dorothy, daughter of Mr. Charles L. Huggins. They had two sons and a daughter. The heir to the barony is the Hon. Alan Loader Maffey.

April 21, 1969.

Lord Runcorn, P.C., former Conservative Minister of Health, died in Westminster Hospital London, on January 20, 1968, at the age of 52. Runcorn was chairman of the Supplementary Benefits Commission since 1966, and of the National Assistance Board 1964–66. He was M.P. for the Runcorn Division of Cheshire 1950–64.

Dennis Forwood Vosper was born on January 2, 1916, the younger son of Gerald Vosper, and grandson of the late Sir William Forwood, K.B.E.

He was educated at The Leas, Hoylake, Marlborough College, and Pembroke College, Cambridge, where he took an honours degree in natural science and political economy. In 1938 he took a position with the firm of Wilson, Vosper and Coltart, ships' store and export merchants of Liverpool.

He joined the Territorial Army in the spring of 1939, was called up in the summer of that year and served through the war in the Cheshire Regiment, becoming adjutant and second in command of the 5th Battalion. He was demobilized in 1946 with the rank of major, and then took up a political career. He became Conservative agent for the Knutsford Division of Cheshire, where Colonel Bromley-Davenport was the member. When redistribution cut the division in half in 1949 Vosper took over the Runcorn side of it, and was returned at the 1950 general election. He held the seat without difficulty at subsequent elections until he resigned his seat in 1964.

Vosper lost little time in making his mark in the House of Commons He was appointed a Conservative whip in November, 1950, and, when the Conservatives were returned to power in 1951, became, as a Lord Commissioner of the Treasury, one of the Government whips. In October, 1954, he was appointed Parliamentary Secretary to the Ministry of Education. When Mr. Macmillan succeeded Sir Anthony Eden as Prime Minister in January, 1957, Vosper was promoted to the important office of Minister of Health. He took over at a difficult time, having to turn his attention at once to the dispute with the doctors, and to take steps to check the rising costs to the taxpayer of drugs. He was relatively young for a Minister—only 41 years old—but he made a most promising start.

However, he had been in office for only a few months when he was obliged to undergo an abdominal operation. That was in June, 1957. His hopes of a rapid and complete recovery were not realized and in September he resigned.

He was gradually restored to health and after the general election of October, 1959, the Prime Minister appointed him Joint Parliamentary Under-Secretary of State at the Home Office. He later became Minister of State, Home Office. Here he gave valuable assistance to R.A.Butler during a period when a number of important reforms were carried through. From 1961 to 1963 he was the first Secretary for Technical Cooperation. In 1964 he was appointed chairman of the National Assistance Board, and at the same time was made a life peer.

Vosper, who was one of the tallest men in Parliament (he stood at six feet five inches in his shoes) was widely popular. Though his political career took him mainly into the realm of home affairs his interests and his knowledge were not limited to domestic matters. In 1951 he was a member of the British Parliamentary Delegation to Israel, he went to Turkey in 1953, and in the same year was appointed the first honorary secretary of the Anglo-Turkish Society. He was leader of the British Parliamentary Delegation to the West Indies in 1958.

He married in 1940 Margaret Eva, only child of Sidney and Ada Ashford, of Gayton, Cheshire. His marriage was dissolved in 1966.

January 22, 1968.

Sir Peter Runge, chairman of the British National Export Council since 1968, died in a London hospital on August 19, 1970. He was 61.

At the time of his death he was joint vice-chairman of Tate and Lyle with whom he began his career. An ardent and articulate believer in the benefits of free enterprise he was a leading figure in the "Mr. Cube" campaign which was mounted to oppose the nationalization of sugar.

He combined an interest in the exact disciplines of mathematics and chemistry with a great sense of humour and warmth of understanding for human relationships, in his personal life, his business career, and public service. He showed this ability as president of the Federation of British Industries (1963–65) where his humanity and human touch were vital in bringing about the merger which resulted in the Confederation of British Industry. His long associaciation with the Industrial Society, which he had served as chairman, was evidence of his keen appreciation of the vital importance of good communication, good management, and good labour relations.

He became deeply involved with education, management education, and improved relationships between schools, universities, and industry.

His family background was very much concerned with sugar. Both his grandfather and father, J. J. Runge, were sugar brokers,the latter being a director of Tate and Lyle from the amalgamation in 1921 until his death in 1935.

Runge's relish for public affairs may well have been inherited from his mother who was Unionist M.P. for Rotherhithe from 1931 to 1935 and formerly deputy chairman of the

L.C.C.

Born on May 11, 1909, he was educated at Charterhouse and Trinity College, Oxford, where he took a degree in chemistry. He then spent some time at the Paris laboratory of the Sugar Manufacturers' Syndicate. He joined Tate and Lyle in 1931 as trainee manager with the Allscott Sugar Beet Factory. Later he moved to Thames Refinery (Silvertown, E.16), where he was appointed director in charge in 1936.

His interests were wide-ranging and included the Foundation for Management Education, the Administrative Staff College, the British Industrial and Scientific Film Association, the Duke of Edinburgh's first Study Conference, the London International Youth Science Fortnight, and the Royal Commonwealth Society for the Blind.

As an international figure, he will be missed in many lands, particularly the Commonwealth and the West Indies which he loved so dearly. He was a man of great courage, with a big heart and a well-furnished and capable mind, broad in his approach, yet never missing essential details. He was intolerant only of hypocrites, a defender of private enterprise, and of the right of the small man personified in his Mr. Cube.

He was knighted in 1964.

He married in 1935 Fiona, elder daughter of the first Lord Strathcarron.

August 21, 1970.

Sir Henry Rushbury, K.C.V.O., C.B.E., R.A., Keeper of the Royal Academy from 1949 to 1964, died on July 5, 1968. He was 78.

One of the few Royal Academicians whose work was almost exclusively graphic, Rushbury produced excellent water colour drawings and etchings in a traditional English style. His favourite medium was a combination of pencil or brown ink and wash, well suited to his landscape and architectural subjects and a certain restraint and refinement of touch prevented them from being prosaically topographic. One might say his art was that of the piccolo in the academic orchestra, not bearing direct competition with the brass and heavier instruments of the practitioners of oil, but possessing, when listened to in solo, an attractive clarity of its own.

Henry George Rushbury was born on October 28, 1889, at Harborne (then still a country village outside the city limits of Birmingham). The trend of his work may perhaps be dated back to boyhood visits to old churches and castles made with his father, who had a keen taste for architecture. At 14 the young Rushbury won a scholarship to the Birmingham School of Art, then directed by Catterson Smith, a teacher of stimulating and unconventional method. He prescribed the use of tempera rather than oil colour and directed the life class to draw from quick memory notes of figures in movement or going about their usual occupations rather than from the posed model.

After training of this kind, Rushbury worked in the Cotswolds for five years as assistant to Henry Payne, R.W.S., making designs for stained glass and helping with a series of tempera paintings for Earl Beauchamp in the chapel at Madresfield Court, Worcestershire. In 1912, with his friend Gerald Brockhurst (later R.A.), who had been a fellow pupil under Catterson Smith, he went to London and settled in Chelsea. He was encouraged to etch by Francis Dodd, who saw him drawing one day in Essex Street, Strand, and became interested in the young man's work. Muirhead Bone, whom he first met in an etching-printer's work shop, and Campbell Dodgson of the British Museum, were others who discerned and appreciated his talent. Rushbury was elected a member of the New English Art Club in 1915. During the 1914–18 War his draughtsmanship found specialized use, when he served in the infantry and R.A.F., in the form of demonstration drawings and diagrams; and as an official war artist he also drew the funeral of Nurse Cavell in London and made other records of the time now in the Imperial War Museum.

After the war Rushbury travelled much on the Continent, his visits to France and Italy (where in 1922 he witnessed the fascist entry into Rome—an event he recorded in an etching) providing him with many subjects. He had a series of successful exhibitions and the vogue of etchings in the 1920s directed special attention to this aspect of his activity, an illustrated album of his etchings and drypoints appearing in *The Studio's* "Masters of Etching" series. He was made C.V.O. in 1955 and advanced to K.C.V.O. in 1964. Small, sturdy, rubicund, silvery-haired, as one might say, a John Bull in little, Rushbury was a genial figure at all the Academy functions, and while the range of his own art was limited he was broadminded enough to welcome the appearance of L'Ecole de Paris at the Academy Exhibition of 1951.

He married Florence, daughter of Mr. H. Lazell, and they had two daughters.

July 6, 1968.

Lord Russell, O.M., F.R.S., **(Bertrand Russell)** died on February 2, 1970, at his home, Plas Penrhyn, Merionethshire. He was 97.

Bertrand Russell's claim to be remembered by history rests securely on his work in mathematical and symbolic logic and in philosophy, on which his influence was pervasive and profound. The story of symbolic logic and of the philosophy of mathematics in the twentieth century is the story of the expansion of the edifice which Russell and Frege founded. There have been major reconstructions, but they are reconstructions from within. In general philosophy, when we think of G. E. Moore and Ludwig Wittgenstein as shapers of the thought of our half-century, we are thinking of men who were fired by Russell and themselves gave Russell fire. There exist no disciples of Russell. Instead there exist scores of inquiring philosophers driven by questions which Russell was the first to ask. For Russell not only combined the hardihood of the extremist with the candour of the artist; he also had a lively sense of the ridiculous. So, if there were logical absurdities latent inside his own abstract constructions, he exposed them with cheerful callousness. The incongruities which he would not hide have become the cruces of philosophy.

Russell looked every inch a Russell and had all the "crankiness" of a Russell. He spoke his mind with Olympian disregard of the censure he might incur from established persons or received opinions or for that matter the law, which twice committed him to prison. He was throughout his life an ornament and an acquisition to a variety of public causes, generally of an unpopular kind. Into the last and for him the greatest of these, unilateral nuclear disarmament, he threw himself, now in his mid-eighties, with unabated fervour, seized with the mission of rousing his fellow men to the peril in which they stood. He was obsessed by the enormity of the evil of which these weapons could be the instrument. In the intensity of his denunciation and the galvanic activity of his failing powers there came to be less and less room for sober assessment of the political means of deliverance from the doom so vividly before his mind.

He was the intellectual in the twentieth century who, perhaps, before all others in this country, solved the problem of communications. Russell found a way of communicating with ordinary men, and explored it to the full, especially, and deliberately, in his later life. There was nothing new in the method. He merely expressed lucid thoughts in a lucid style. But how few of the thinkers or artists who were contemporary with him could do half as much!

Equally important, he could use not just terms of language but terms of reference which were intelligible to ordinary men and women, because they were inside their experience. Here was a man of uncommon ancestry, uncommon intellectual brilliance, uncommon habits of mind and behaviour, who yet was at ease in addressing common men—and they were at ease in listening to him. The answer is to be found in the paradox that he yet shared with them a common ancestry. His thought was English to the core. He dallied with Hegelianism when he was at Cambridge, but no one with his roots as firmly in English thought and in England—Whig England at that—could have long remained an apostle of Hegel.

The Right Honourable Bertrand Arthur William Russell, third Earl Russell, was born at Ravenscroft, near Tintern, in Monmouthshire, on May 18, 1872. He was the second son of Viscount Amberley and grandson of Lord John Russell, who had been created Earl Russell at the end of his long political life.

RUSSELLS AND STANLEYS

His mother was Katherine, daughter of the second Lord Stanley of Alderley. He was as much a Russell as his elder brother, the second Earl, was a Stanley. In his appearance, his artistic qualities, and his versatility the Russell genius found expression. Russell would have been the first to admit that much of his life was determined by his early years, which were not calculated to produce a conventional citizen. His father and mother had moved from orthodoxy to agnosticism before his birth. But his mother died when he was two, his father when he was three, and he was placed under the care of his grandmother, "a Puritan with the moral rigidity of the Covenanters", as he called her, who maintained a gloomy theism at Pembroke Lodge. His father had directed that the two children should be brought up agnostics and had appointed two free-thinkers as guardians, but the direction was set aside in court and the children made wards in Chancery.

Until he went to Cambridge, Bertrand Russell lived (not very happily) and was educated by governesses and tutors, at home. Cambridge was his first release into the outside world, "a new world", as he said, "of infinite delight", and of friends such as Lowes Dickinson, Dr. Trevelyan, McTaggart, and G. E. Moore.

CAST THEIR SPELL

The last two cast their spell over him. Under J. M. F. McTaggart's influence he became for some time a Hegelian, or, more precisely, a Bradleian, but Moore, whose influence on the whole of that Cambridge generation was so profound and so fortunate, broke Hegel's spell. Russell had gone to Trinity College as a scholar in 1890, but was only bracketed seventh Wrangler in 1893. His relatively low position may be explained by the fact that mathematics interested him not so much for its own sake as for being an example of certain knowledge; his interest was philosophical. The following year he took a First Class in the Moral Science Tripos with exceptional distinction. On going down from Cambridge he spent some months as honorary attaché at the British Embassy in Paris, and later made in Berlin a study of social and economic questions which bore fruit early in 1896 in six lectures on German Social Democracy for the London School of Economics. But the political career which seemed marked out for him by his heritage was abandoned—if he had ever seriously considered it—in favour of the greater interest of laying afresh the foundations of mathematics, and his later resumptions of political interest were always, until nearer the end of his life, rather desultory.

In 1895 he had been elected a lecturer at Trinity, and in 1896 he lectured in America on non-Euclidean geometry. He published an *Essay on the Foundations of Geometry*, and then his training in mathematics and philosophy led him to study the thinker in whom their union was most perfectly exemplified. His *Critical Exposition of the Philosophy of Leibniz*, a work of great distinction, was published in 1900—his first major work. It set a higher estimate on Leibniz's thought than was usual at the time—an estimate he never altered, describing Leibniz, in his *History of Western Philosophy*, as "one of the supreme intellects of all time". Russell's judgment was, of course, founded on his recognition of Leibniz as "a pioneer in mathematical logic, of which he perceived the importance when no one else did". This was the field in which Russell was to do his most revolutionary work, and in outlook as well as in achievement he resembled Leibniz closely.

In 1900, at a mathematical congress in Paris, Russell drew attention to the works of Peano, and in 1903 to those of Frege—at the time the two most immediate influences on his thought. It was their explorations and those of Leibniz which led him in 1903 to give to the world his *Principles of Mathematics*, whose purpose was "first, to show that all mathematics follows from symbolic logic, and, secondly, to discover, so far as possible, what are the principles of symbolic logic itself". The *Principles of Mathematics* was intended to be a first volume to be followed by a second giving a deductive exposition of results. This task was in fact carried out in a separate work in collaboration with A. N. Whitehead. Their *Principia Mathematica* was begun in 1900 and completed 10 years later in three volumes, which were published in 1910, 1912, and 1913 respectively. It was republished, with a new introduction, in 1925 and in succeeding years. The Royal Society, into whose Fellowship Russell had been admited in 1908, made a grant towards publication from the Government fund. Of its composition Russell later wrote: "My intellect never quite recovered from the strain. I have been ever since definitely less capable of dealing with difficult abstractions than I was before."

Principia Mathematica is one of the decisive books in the history both of mathematics and of logic. More completely and satisfactorily than in any previous work, the reduction of mathematics to a branch of logic was effected.

NEW SYMBOLISM

In the course of the reduction a new symbolism, of great logical power in skilled hands, was developed. It was the use of this power which was Russell's most enduring contribution to philosophical thought and the most constant feature of all his philosophical writings. He himself termed his contribution "Logical Atomism", and it is a term which does justice to his skill and perception in logical analysis—his attempt to break down complex ideas into, if not simple, at least irrefutable components.

The details of Russell's achievement, which allows one, without the least exaggeration—in terms of British thought at least—to talk of pre-Russell and post-Russell philosophy, are the concern of the student of philosophy. But even the layman can comprehend the value of freeing logical analysis from the tyranny of ordinary grammar or syntax. "The utility of philosophical syntax in relation to traditional problems is very great"—such was his own modest estimate of his achievement late in his life.

The point is best illustrated by a summary of one of his most important discoveries, the theory of descriptions, first developed in *On Denoting*, published in *Mind* in 1905. Such phrases as "The present President of the United States" have caused a lot of fruitless distress to philosophers trying to find the meaning of existence. "Suppose I say 'The golden mountain does not exist', and suppose you ask 'What is the golden mountain?' It would seem that, if I say 'It is the golden mountain,' I am attributing some sort of existence to it." In the two phrases "The golden mountain does not exist" and "The round square does not exist" the only difference lies in the words "The golden mountain" and "The round square", implying that the one is one thing and the other another. although neither exists. It was this problem which Russell sought to meet by the theory of descriptions. The statement "Scott was the author of *Waverley*" is, by this theory, interpreted as saying: "There is an entity *c* such that the statement 'x wrote *Waverley*' is true if *x* is *c* and false otherwise; moreover *c* is Scott." Thus "The golden mountain does not exist" means: "There is no entity *c* such that '*x* is golden and mountainous' is true when *x* is *c*, but not otherwise." "Existence", therefore, can only be asserted of descriptions. Russell was scarcely putting his claim too high when he said of the theory that it "clears up two millennia of muddle-headedness about 'existence', beginning with Plato's *Theoetetus*".

In 50 years of philosophical writing Russell used the destructive power of this logical technique to examine the traditional problems and traditional philosophies, and the mere use of the technique, however acceptable or unacceptable his conclusions, was a source of clarification and enlightenment, particularly in his analysis of relations, classes, continuity, infinity, and language forms.

His progressive extension of methodological doubt into every field of philosophical inquiry is his most lasting monument. The incorporation of mathematics and the development of a powerful logical technique were, as he himself said, what distinguished his modern analytical empiricism from that of Locke, Berkeley, and Hume. Empirical knowledge and deductive knowledge were the only two kinds of knowledge which Russell was prepared to admit.

NO OTHER WAY

He sought answers to the problems of philosophy which had "the quality of science rather than philosophy". He admitted that there might be problems to which science and the intellect could not find the answers, but he refused to admit that there was any other way, intuitive or otherwise, by which the answers could be found.

Russell's empiricism is perhaps the most valid quality in his erratic and usually "popular" intrusions into political philosophy. He was no political philosopher. But a man born with the blood of the Russells in his veins could hardly avoid carrying the spirit of Locke in his head. "The only philosophy", he wrote in *Philosophy and Politics* in 1947, "that affords a theoretical justification of democracy, and that accords with democracy in its temper of mind, is empiricism. Locke, who may be regarded...as the founder of empiricism, makes it clear how closely this is connected with his views on liberty and toleration." From this, Russell argued that "the essence of the Liberal outlook lies not in what opinions are held but in how they are held: instead of being held dogmatically, they are held tentatively". It cannot be said that he himself followed this precept in all his public utterances.

In 1907 he stood unsuccessfully for Parliament as a woman suffrage candidate at Wimbledon. But it was the 1914–18 War which was to find an outlet for his unsatisfied impulse to do good. Without hesitation he flung himself wholeheartedly into the pacifist campaign. The unhappy results made him a national storm-centre and need be only summarily recalled. In *The Times* he avowed the authorship of a pamphlet for the No-Conscription Fellowship and was duly fined £100 at the Mansion House and removed, with petty illiberality, from his lectureship at Trinity College. His library there was seized to pay the fine. In the autumn of that year, 1916, he was due to lecture at Harvard, but it was made known to the Harvard authorities that the British Government did not consider it in the public interest to issue a passport enabling him to leave the country.

In September of the same year he was forbidden from entering any prohibited area and a little later a book, *Justice in Wartime*, in which he likened the warrings of nations to the fighting of dogs angered by each other's smell, caused great resentment. Finally, in February, 1918, he was sentenced at Bow Street to six months imprisonment for having, in the organ of the No-Conscription Fellowship, made comments on the American Army "intended and likely to prejudice his Majesty's relations with the United States". On appeal the sentence was ordered to be served in the first instead of the second division. It was while he was in prison that he wrote his *Introduction to Mathematical Philosophy*.

After the war he allowed his mind to range over almost the whole gamut of human studies. A visit to Russia in 1920 with the British Labour delegation left him unimpressed by the "military dictatorship" of the Bolsheviks. He immediately uttered his first warning of what Bolshevism really was in his *Practice and Theory of Bolshevism*—and he remained a critic of Soviet communism even during the 1939–45 War, when Russia's popularity was at its height. His *Analysis of Mind* was the book form of some lectures given in London, and was published in 1921. Meanwhile, in 1920, he went to China for a brief period as Professor of Philosophy at Peking. It led to the publication of *The Problem of China*, a peg on which he hung his animus against western and Japanese civilization. On returning from China he stood unsuccessfully, in 1922 and 1923, as Labour candidate for Chelsea. Between *A.B.C. of Atoms* (1923) and the *A.B.C. of Relativity* (1925), both beautifully lucid expositions, was sandwiched *The Prospects of Industrial Civilization*, written in collaboration with his second wife.

BOOKS ON EDUCATION

In 1927 their interest in education led them to establish near Petersfield a school where a great measure of licence was allowed to the children; in 1934 his wife removed it to Hertfordshire. He wrote two books on the subject: *On Education* in 1926 and *Education and the Social Order* in 1932; in them modern tendencies were carried to exaggerated lengths. Between books appeared *The Analysis of Matter*, a magnificent review of modern physics, with more questionable metaphysical deductions. Other books followed: *An Outline of Philosophy*, *Sceptical Essays*, *Marriage and Morals*, and the *Conquest of Happiness*. In his books on social and ethical questions Russell mixed with his sometimes revolutionary ethic some wise advice. He could not write a chapter which, however unacceptable his conclusions, did not contain some provoking, stimulating, or penetrating observation. He certainly, in such offerings, often wrote trivially on weighty matters, throwing away sense for the sake of a jest or a paradox. But they had a more serious intent and the perceptive reader could usually find and profit by it.

In 1934 he published his most considerable work outside the realms of logic and philosophy. *Freedom and Organisation* traced the main causes of political, economic, and social change in Europe and America during the nineteenth century. It foreshadowed his monumental *History of Western Philosophy* by its attempt to see ideas in the context of the age which gave them birth. But it was quite different in construction from the later work, being more of a synthesis than an analysis, and it contained some of his most sparkling writing.

Russell, during the thirties, was being profoundly influenced by the rise of Hitler, confessing to a Fabian gathering that it had almost persuaded him to become a Christian. But though the success of such an irrational force as Hitlerism shook, as with so many others, so many of his rationalist predispositions, and made him abandon pacifism, and although he sought (but failed) to analyse the nature of *Power* in a popular book, he lacked the political equipment to reach a satisfactory statement of the twentieth-century's political problem. This was apparent in the Reith lectures which he delivered in 1948–49 on *Authority and the Individual*. He chose the wrong subject on which to speak, but he left no doubt of his ability to relate complex ideas to ordinary men's everyday experience.

During the later years of his life Russell was in some danger of becoming a popular, a revered, even a respectable figure. He was awarded the Nobel Prize for Literature in 1950, and the year before had been given the O.M.

NO SERENE OLD AGE

In 1953 the man who had once been judicially pronounced unfit to hold an academic chair at a certain American university was elected an honorary associate of the New York National Institute of Arts and Letters. His could have been the serene old age of a tame philosopher, a domesticated sage, publicly honoured, listened to with affection and respect, vouchsafing the occasional quip often enough and sharp enough to keep alive the legend of the rebel.

He chose otherwise. There still echoes in the memory a broadcast he gave in 1954 after the explosion of the first hydrogen bomb, his thin, sing-song voice charged with the detached intensity of a prophet: "Remember your humanity and forget the rest. If you can do so, the way lies open to a new paradise: if you cannot, nothing lies before you but universal death." It was the warning he was to reiterate, with a rising pitch of stridency, until the end of his life.

He assisted at the birth of the Campaign for Nuclear Disarmament in February, 1958, and became its president. Before and after that he strove to mobilize the opinions of scientists in support of his views. In September, 1960, impatient of the law-abiding methods of C.N.D., and finding its chairman, Canon Collins, "impossible to work with", he branched out with the Committee of 100 "for civil disobedience against nuclear warfare". The disobedience proved to be of a fairly orderly kind, and Russell, who was then 88, continued to speak, for the campaign up and down the country, to issue urgent statements to the press, and to stage public demonstrations to the extent that his health allowed. He also made a practice of sending admonitory telegrams to world leaders, notably at the height of the Cuban crisis in October, 1962.

His defiance of authority again led to imprisonment. In September, 1961, he was summoned with others of the Committee of 100 for inciting members of the public to commit a breach of the peace—a forthcoming sit-down demonstration in Parliament Square. Having refused to be bound over to be of good behaviour, he was sentenced to two months' imprisonment, a term which the magistrates reduced to seven days after representations by Russell's counsel. He served the sentence in Brixton prison, with which he had become acquainted 43 years before.

At the beginning of 1963 Russell resigned the presidency of the Committee of 100, stating among his reasons that he had become occupied with work of a different kind, though directed towards the same end. And later in the year he announced the launching of two foundations, the Bertrand Russell Peace Foundation and the Atlantic Peace Foundation, whose purpose was to develop international resistance to the threat of nuclear war. In his last years he lived in growing isolation at Plas Penrhyn, his country home in North Wales.

BIZARRE TRIBUNAL

His dealings with the outside world were conducted by his secretary, Ralph Shoenman; while his public undertakings to which he attached his name became increasingly bizarre—like his international war crimes tribunal, in which a bench of celebrated intellectuals were to try the United States in absentia on charges arising out of its policies in Vietnam. After some difficulty over a venue, the tribunal held its first session in Stockholm, and returned a unanimous verdict of Guilty.

These controversial activities, inspiring to some, misdirected or ridiculous to others, obscured in his final years the extraordinary achievements of his long life; his influence on philosophy and, something the general public had better reason to remember, his genius as a popularizer of unfamiliar or difficult ideas. He retained the style which puts him in the company of Berkeley and Hume, who adorned literature as well as philosophy. Whether he wrote in symbols or in words he was equally dextrous and equally happy. His clear-cut antitheses, his magnificent self-assurance, his polished ruthlessness of argument, his dazzling paradoxes, his wit and gaiety are the envy of all others who try to write. When passion intruded, when the Whig possessed the philosopher, his writing must be ranked with the noblest in the language. He was equally a master of the microphone and gave several memorable series of broadcasts after the war. His vignettes of some of his eminent contemporaries, crisp, witty, half-mocking, half-sympathetic, recalled the succinct vivacity of John Aubrey's sketches. In 1967 the first part of his autobiography was published, 1872–1914. It had been delivered to the publishers 10 years before. Though rather sketchy in his provision of conventional biographical material Russell, taking relish in his candour, is unusually informative about his love affairs in and out of marriage.

FOUR MARRIAGES

Russel was four times married: first to Alys Whitall Pearsall, daughter of the late Robert Pearsall Smith. The marriage was dissolved in 1921, and in the same year he married Dora Winifred, daughter of the late Sir Frederick Black. The marrage was dissolved in 1935, and in 1936 he married Patricia Helen, daughter of Mr. Harry Evelyn Spence. The marriage was dissolved in 1952, and in the same year he married Edith, daughter of Mr. Edward Bronson Finch, of New York. By his second marriage Russell had two children, John Conrad, the Viscount Amberley, and Lady Katherine Jane Russell. By his third marriage he had a son, the Honourable Conrad Sebestian Robert Russell. He is succeeded in the peerage by Viscount Amberley, who was born in 1921 and married in 1946 Susan Doninhan, daughter of the late Vachel Lindsay, by whom he has two daughters.

February 3, 1970.

Sir John Russell, O.B.E., F.R.S., who died on July 12, 1965, in a nursing home at Goring-on-Thames, played an important role in the development of British agriculture through nearly half a century. He was 92. He made many notable contributions to the literature of agriculture.

Edward John Russell, who was born at Frampton, in Gloucestershire, in 1872, was the son of a clergyman. He was educated at the University College of Wales, Aberystwyth, and at Victoria University, Manchester, becoming a lecturer in chemistry there from 1898 to 1901. For the next six years he occupied the position of head of the Chemical Department of the Wye Agricultural College during the period when Daniel Hall was Director, and one outcome of this association was their production of *The Soils and Agriculture of Kent, Surrey and Sussex*, which was published in 1911, and was at once recognized as a model of local agricultural survey.

Hall became Director of Rothamsted Experimental Station in 1902 and Russell followed him there as soil chemist in 1907. When Hall retired in 1912 Russell succeeded him as Director, and retained this position until 1943. An able and pleasing lecturer, Russell was also a prolific writer, his best known work being *Soil Conditions and Plant Growth.* This book passed through many editions and grew from a slim volume of 160 pages in 1912 to a ponderous tome of over 600 in the course of some 20 years.

Under his aegis the Rothamsted Station expanded greatly and the raising of the Centenary Fund and replacement of the cramped quarters of the old building by new and spacious laboratories was mainly due to Russell's initiative and energy. His eminence as a scientist was recognized by his election to the Royal Society in 1917 and his services to agriculture during the 1914–18 War by his knighthood in 1922. He also received honorary degrees from a number of universities both at home and abroad and was a corresponding member of various foreign learned societies. He was awarded the Messel Medal by the Society of Chemical Industry, and the Albert Medal by the Royal Society of Art.

WORLDWIDE ADVISER

Russell, for whom modern languages were a hobby, was particularly fond of travelling, and there were indeed few important agricultural regions in the world that he had not visited. It was perhaps unfortunate for Rothamsted that Russell's services as an adviser were so much in demand overseas, although the institution and agriculture generally benefited by his ever-growing experience. Not long after his retirement from the directorship of Rothamsted Russell suffered a severe illness which incapacitated him for more than a year, but he made a remarkable recovery and was able to accept the presidency of the British Association for the 1949 meeting at Newcastle, devoting his address to food production and the growing world population.

During the concluding years Russell devoted himself almost entirely to writing. In 1954 he published *World Population and World Food Supplies*—a remarkable mass of data on food production and consumption in the countries of the world, and the measures being taken to increase production. His conclusion on the world's ability to feed its fast-growing population was one of "tempered optimism". In this volume in particular he showed his remarkable knowledge of agriculture throughout the world. In 1956 was published an autobiographical volume under the title of *The Land Called Me* and in the following year there appeared a volume in the "New Naturalist" series *The World of the Soil*, which provided for the general reader an admirable account of our modern knowledge of the soil.

HISTORICAL WORK

However, his main preoccupation for some years had been a work on the history of agricultural science in Great Britain, a subject for the treatment of which the exceptional breadth of his agricultural knowledge and experience peculiarly fitted him. This book he managed to finish before he died.

For his contributions to the literature of agriculture Russell will, no doubt, be most widely remembered, but he also played an important role in other directions, as, for example, his pioneer work on partial sterilization of the soil.

He married Elinor, youngest daughter of the late Walter Oldham, of Manchester, in 1903. She died early in 1965. They had three sons and two daughters.

July 14, 1965.

Hugh Ruttledge, who led the Mount Everest expeditions of 1933 and 1936, died on November 7, 1961, at Stoke, Plymouth, at the age of 77.

On neither of these two expeditions was the luck with Ruttledge; the climbers of 1933 failed to reach the summit (though they got to within 1,000ft. of it) or to reduce any cardinal bulwark that had defied their predecessors; on the other hand they may be said to have consolidated their gains and when struck by weather capricious even by Everest standards, and Ruttledge gave the order for withdrawal, there were none of those grim losses which in the earlier assaults suggested that there were unknown elements among the risks accepted.

The expedition of 1936 fared no better, for the climbers were immobilized by the arrival of the monsoon at a date so early as to be without precedent.

On those expeditions Ruttledge took men of the highest calibre, the late Frank Smythe, Eric Shipton, H. W. Tilman, Professor L. R. Wager, and Sir Percy Wyn Harris, who together in 1933 reached 28,000ft. in the first assault, Jack Longland and T. A. Brocklebank among them.

Ruttledge, the son of Lieutenant-Colonel E. B. Ruttledge, I.M.S., was educated at Dresden, Lausanne, Cheltenham College, and Pembroke College, Cambridge, and joined the Indian Civil Service in 1909.

His period of service as Deputy Commissioner at Lucknow covered the anxious year of communal trouble, 1924. The strain was great but Ruttledge succeeded in holding the balance between the Muslim and Hindu elements. In 1925, to give him a chance to recruit his health, he was given the appointment of Deputy Commissioner of the hill district of Almora, the biggest in the Kumaon division.

He had begun serious mountaineering during leave in 1921, among other excursions making the ascents of the Matterhorn and Zinal Rothorn; now at Almora, he greatly increased his experience and his knowledge of the Himalaya. When the time came for him to lead in the assaults on Everest he had climbed widely, had travelled with all forms of Himalayan transport including Yak caravans in Tibet and was at home with Gurkhas, Tibetan and Sherpa porters. In his own hills he was welcome in every village. Spare of build, keen of mind, steadfast in character, he was the most modest of men.

He retired from the Indian Civil Service in 1932. The Royal Geographical Society awarded him its Founder's Medal in 1934. The fruit of his experience appeared in two books—*Everest 1933* and *The Unfinished Adventure*.

His marriage to Dorothy Jessie Hair Elder took place in 1915. They had one son and two daughters.

November 9, 1961.

Prince Louis Rwagasore, of Urundi, was assassinated on October 13, 1961. The bullet ended the short and stormy political career of the 32-year-old eldest son of the Mwami (King) of Urundi.

Less than a month earlier Prince Rwagasore had won a sweeping victory in the elections at the head of his Union and Progress National Party (U.P.R.O.N.A.), and with his Cabinet took the oath before his father on September 29.

Louis Rwagasore was sent by his father, a pro-western ruler of many years' standing, to Antwerp for his education where he studied political and administrative sciences. About two years ago, however, he returned home, imbued with the spirit of nationalism that was sweeping Africa. His nationalism attracted to him a mass of "Lumumbist" supporters.

He began then, and continued in his party policy, a demand for immediate independence, and was generally thought of as anti-Belgian. On taking power he seemed to be making efforts to correct the adverse impression his views were making in western eyes. On October 4, for instance, he said in a speech "like my father I have always believed that foreigners...are necessary, above all in the economic sector". As well as the prime ministership, he held the portfolio of community affairs, which was concerned with relations between Ruanda and Urundi. He saw Urundi's future as an independent state, perhaps in a confederal relationship with Tanganyika, and enjoying economic links with Ruanda.

Ruanda has been the trouble spot of the two trust territories, and it is ironical that it is the Prime Minister of Urundi who has been assassinated. At his inauguration he said his Government would not seek danger, since the road ahead was difficult enough. In the event danger has quickly sought him.

October 16, 1961.

Paul Rykens, honorary K.B.E., who died in Amsterdam on April 19, 1965, was chairman of Unilever N.V. and vice-chairman of Unilever Limited until his retirement in December, 1955. After this date he was an advisory director to the board of Unilever N.V. He was 76.

Paul Rykens was born on September 14, 1888, in Rotterdam and began his career with Van den Bergh's Limited, Rotterdam, in 1910. Three weeks after joining the firm he was transferred to their London office as assistant to the chief accountant and financial expert, Joost de Blank. Accounts, finance and organization were his special forte from that time. He returned to Holland in 1913 and became a director of the various associated companies of Van den Bergh's Limited.

In 1919 all non-British Empire interests of Van den Bergh's Limited were transferred to a new holding company in Holland—Van den Bergh's Fabrieken N.V., and an equalization agreement between these two companies was entered into: Rykens became a director of Van den Bergh's Fabrieken N.V. from its inception. Upon the amalgamation of the Van den Berghs and Jurgens companies in 1927 he became a director of the Margarine Union Limited in London and of Margarine Unie N.V. in Rotterdam. He settled in England in 1929 at the time of the merger of the Margarine Union Limited with Lever Brothers Limited and became a director of Unilever Limited in London and of Unilever N.V. in Rotterdam as from the date of the amalgamation.

He was appointed chairman of Unilever N.V., Rotterdam, in 1937, resigned at the outbreak of war and was reappointed as chairman in July, 1945.

Rykens played a decisive part in shaping the destiny of Unilever. As one of the first generation of salaried managers, he helped to look after the interest of the Van den Bergh family business during the allies' coastal blockade in the First World War; to ride the runaway inflation in Germany; to hold their position in the Scandinavian national combines; to establish personal contact with the "arch enemy" Anton Jurgens; to get one move ahead of Jurgens in the relationship with Schichts in central Europe; and finally to persuade the Van den Bergh family that Anton Jurgens was right in proposing a complete merger as the only way out of cut-throat competition and endless litigation.

Rykens helped to put the Margarine Union on a solid footing in 1927. Almost immediately he became their principal representative in the negotiations with Lever, which led to the formation of Unilever in 1929. The equalization agreement which ensures equal rights to the shareholders of Unilever Ltd. and Unilever N.V., was modelled on a prototype which the young Rykens had devised for Van den Bergh's Ltd. and Van den Bergh's Fabrieken as early as 1919, the year he was made a director of the latter company.

BILDEBERG CONFERENCES

In the 25 years he spent in London after 1929, Rykens, with his patience, tact, intelligence, and obvious honesty, became one of the main architects of unity in the Unilever organization. He possessed a happy combination of personal and intellectual qualities which enabled him, for the lasting benefit of the business, to fulfil his objectives and make friends at the same time.

Matters of public interest in the Netherlands and in Europe, particularly since his retirement took up much of his time. He took an active part in the Bildeberg conferences over which Prince Bernhard of the Netherlands presides. At these conferences prominent people from Europe and America discuss problems of political importance. In 1964 the conference was held in Williamsburg, United States, and this year the Duke of Edinburgh, Lord Mountbatten, and Denis Healey were among those attending the conference at Lake Como. Rykens also took an active interest in the political affairs between his own country and Indonesia, and when there was a deadlock between the two governments over New Guinea, he was among those who tried to bring the two governments together again.

Rykens was a member of the Special Advisory Council to the Dutch Government in exile in war-time London. Later he presided over the Dutch Study Group for Reconstruction and over the mission which sent Dutch children to Britain to recover from malnutrition suffered during the occupation. He was a Knight of the Order of the Netherlands Lion, and Commander in the Order of Oranje Nassau. In 1948 he received the honorary degree of Doctor of Economics of the Netherlands School of Economics in Rotterdam.

In 1959 he was appointed an Honorary Knight Commander of the Order of the British Empire (K.B.E.), in recognition of his work in the interest of Anglo-Dutch relations and, particularly, for his activities leading to the formation in 1958 of the Anglo-Dutch Trade Council.

Rykens was one of the founders of the Fondation Européenne de la Culture. Until a few years ago he was curator of the Rijksuniversiteit (State University) of Groningen and until recently he was a curator (member of the board of supervisors) of the Nederlandsche Economische Hoogeschool (Netherlands School of Economics at Rotterdam).

April 21, 1965.

S

Eero Saarinen, a leading modern architect, died on Septemer 1, 1961. His death at the age of only 51 deprived American architecture of one of its most versatile and energetic figures at a time when many years of creative work should still have lain before him.

He was one of the undisputed leaders of what might be termed the second generation of modern American architects, and one of his principal achievements was to translate into terms of large-scale, especially of industrial, practice those principles that had been established in the United States in the 1930s and 1940s by the earlier generation of pioneers mostly refugees from Central Europe. For example, his General Motors building at Detroit was among the first, and certainly the most distinguished, application of the ideas of Professor Mies van der Rohe to the needs of American industry. Saarinen, too, was of European origin, having arrived as an immigrant from Finland with his already famous architect father when a schoolboy of 14.

In his later work he displayed a versatility of style verging upon the eclectic, to which such various buildings as those he designed for American universities, for air transport and for the State Department overseas bear witness. But unlike many eclectic designers he was not concerned only with external characteristics. He was a thorough and meticulous craftsman, and each new material or structural method that he exploited he studied and mastered down to its every detailed implication. This quality of being a perfectionist saved his architecture from superficiality.

It is unfortunate for his reputation in England that he is represented there by the United States Embassy building in Grosvenor Square.

CARE FOR DETAIL

This building also benefited greatly from his meticulous attention to detail, but it suffers from attempting to give a monumental presence to what is functionally little more than an office block and from a misconceived anxiety to conform to English urban traditions.

Saarinen's own personality was sincere and warm. He was an immensely hard and conscientious worker who lived for architecture, for which he dispensed an infectious enthusiasm.

He was born in Kirkkonummi, Finland, on August 20, 1910, the son of the famous Finnish architect, Eliel Saarinen. It was an intellectually lively home, which soon stimulated the boy's talents. At a very early age his gifts for drawing became apparent. In 1923, however, his father settled in the United States with his family after winning second prize in the competition for the *Chicago Tribune* tower. Eero Saarinen graduated from Yale in 1934 and received the Charles O. Matcham fellowship for travel in Europe over the next two years. In 1940 he became a naturalized American citizen.

By this time his professional reputation was rising. There was no doubting his versatility—his skill was lavished on housing projects, churches, opera houses, university buildings. He designed the elegant law school for Chicago University and the embassy office at Oslo, which have been described as a less elaborate version of his design for the London Embassy. Whatever the task he always worked with the same furious energy and complete absorption. He never spared either himself or his colleagues.

He was twice married. His first marriage in 1939 to Lilian Swann was dissolved. In 1954 he married secondly Aline Louchheim.

September 2 & 6, 1961.

Shaikh Sir Abdullah as Salim as Sabah, Ruler of Kuwait, died at his palace on November 24, 1965. He was 70.

A true friend of Great Britain, he was a wise and kindly patriarch whose authority, exercised unobtrusively from the background, was of inestimable value to the people of Kuwait at a critical period of their development.

The eldest son of Shaikh Salim al Mubarak, Ruler of Kuwait from 1917 to 1921, he was born in 1895 into the ruling caste of a small and remote Arab society in which trade, pearling, and seafaring provided the main interests and Islam the main influence, and the basic characteristics of which had remained virtually unchanged through the years.

His education was wholly Koranic and although he became an accomplished Arabic scholar he learnt no foreign language and travelled no farther afield than Cairo or Bombay. For the first 55 years of his life he remained wholly absorbed in the small-town life of Kuwait with no more experience of public affairs than he gleaned from the management of its finances and supplies with which he was entrusted during the Second World War.

In 1950 he succeeded his cousin as Ruler on the latter's death. His accession coincided with the spectacular increase in state revenues which was brought about by the expansion of the operations of the Kuwait Oil Co., followed by the exploitation by other companies of the oil-resources of the Kuwait Neutral Zone and, later, of the offshore sea-bed. Within a few years these combined sources provided the little state with the highest income a head of any country in the world, which under its traditional autocratic system of government was theoretically the monopoly of the Ruler. The Shaikh could thus have indulged in luxury exceeding even that of his mainland neighbours; and it is to his immense credit that, instead of doing so, he from the first sought and followed the advice of his British protectors on the most beneficial ways of utilizing the ever-increasing flow of dollars.

As a result, Kuwait was in the next few years endowed with one of the most modern and lavishly equipped hospitals in the world, with equally fine schools, with roads, a port, public buildings, and with water-resources obtained from the sea. At the same time many millions of pounds were invested in the sterling area and provided an assurance against any future diminution of oil-revenue.

But the wealth, though it brought material benefits, also brought difficult problems in its train. Adventurers of all sorts found in this evolving economy an irresistible attraction; and while those seeking merely personal gain could be dealt with, those who came from other parts of the Arab world to provide educational or technical skills which the Kuwaitis still lacked presented a greater danger, for they brought with them the ideas of Arab Nationalism and social reform which were already becoming familiar through the out-pourings of Cairo radio and which were liable to disrupt the formerly tranquil pattern of Kuwaiti life.

The chief target of the Nationalists was inevitably the protection extended over Kuwait by her Majesty's Government by virtue of treaties extending back into the last century, which had led to a virtual British monopoly of advisory and technical posts and, it was claimed, to preferential opportunities for British firms in the numerous lucrative contracts arising from the new development. The Ruler never wavered in his loyalty to the British connexion, but Nationalist sentiment waxed to a point where it could not be denied, and was in fact rewarded in 1961 by the recognition by Great Britain of Kuwait's full independence.

LIFE-LONG FRIENDS

Ironically, however, this concession to Kuwaiti Nationalism brought about an immediate threat to Kuwait's new-found independence, for its territory was promptly claimed by the Qassim regime in Baghdad as an integral part of Iraq, and Iraqi troop-concentrations on the Kuwait border indicated an imminent intention on the part of the half-mad dictator of Iraq to seize Kuwait and its oil wealth by a *coup de main*.

At this moment of crisis the Ruler did not hesitate to turn for help to his life-long friends the British, and the timely dispatch of a British force safeguarded the integrity of Kuwait until the Arab League, horrified at the possibility of an inter-Arab conflict, could organize a token buffer force to confront Qassim. The latter's deposition and murder in 1963 removed the threat at least for the time being and Kuwait was left to pursue its evolution in peace.

Through all these years the Ruler, while thus lavishing benefits on his people, continued himself to lead a life of exemplary simplicity, his chief delight being still to embark on the waters of the Persian Gulf on long fishing expeditions. His long absences, and his apparent reluctance to accept responsibility for the leadership of his people, at times came in for criticism; but it seems probable that his frugality and modesty in fact appealed to the majority of his subjects and served as shields against the attacks of agitators posing as social reformers. The widespread grief which his recent illness had called forth bears eloquent testimony to the respect and affection in which he was held.

He was created an honorary C.I.E. in 1938, K.C.M.G. in 1952, and G.C.M.G. in 1960. He is succeeded by the Crown Prince, Sabah Salim Sabah.

November 25, 1965.

Sabu, the Indian film actor who, as a boy of 12, was taken out of the elephant stables of the Maharaja of Mysore and made into a star, died at his home in Hollywood on December 2, 1963. He was 39.

His real name was Sabu Dastagir, and he was born in the Karapur jungle on January 27, 1924. As a child he was penniless and illiterate, an orphan who became an elephant boy in the Maharaja's stables as his father had been before him. He might well have remained there all his life had not Alexander Korda in England decided in 1935 to make a film of a Kipling short story in *The Jungle Book* called *Toomai of the Elephants*. Robert Flaherty, the famous documentary director, was put in charge of the film, and the hunt throughout India for a suitable boy to play the lead was begun. Sabu was finally discovered by Osmond Borrodaile, the cameraman of the production. After the shooting of the exteriors in India, Sabu was brought to England for the studio scenes, and was sent to school at Beaconsfield. He was an eager, intelligent and athletic boy, of great charm and grace, who quickly learnt to act, and whose naturalness before the camera made his ultimate success certain. Moreover, he had the one great qualification that the story demanded—he understood elephants.

Korda quickly put him into a second film, *The Drum*, a stirring story of an out-post of Empire, in which a new star, Valerie Hobson, made her debut in a cast which also included Roger Livesey and Raymond Massey. *The Thief of Bagdad* followed, but this had not been completed on the outbreak of war, and so Korda sent his cast to California to film the exteriors. This film was made in colour, as was *The Drum,* and as Sabu was by this time a star in his own right, with an obvious flair for eastern parts, it was not surprising that he was persuaded to remain in Hollywood. Later he became an American citizen, and saw service as a sergeant with the U.S.A.A.F., winning the D.F.C. Before this, however, he appeared in *The Jungle Book* for Korda, *White Savage* and *Cobra Woman.* After being demobilized in 1946, he returned to England to play in *Black Narcissus,* with Deborah Kerr, followed by *The End of the River*. Later he returned to Hollywood to make further pictures there.

His story is perhaps one of the most dramatic in the colourful history of the cinema. No other child actor has achieved such a remarkable transformation from obscurity to international fame. His good fortune in the first place was due to his knowledge of elephants and to the fact that one of the finest of all film directors, Robert Flaherty, guided him through his first film.

December 4, 1963.

Lord Sackville, the fourth Baron, K.B.E., C.B., C.M.G., died on May 8, 1962, at Knole Park, Sevenoaks. He was Major-General Sir Charles John Sackville-West, and succeeded his brother in 1928.

He was perhaps best known to the general public as the former owner of Knole, which he transferred to the National Trust in 1946, one of the largest private houses in England, with its 365 rooms, its art treasures and fine early English furniture. His military career, however, was of particular interest both before and during the First World War.

The son of Colonel the Hon. W. E. Sackville-West, Grenadier Guards, he was born on August 10, 1870. From Winchester he went to Sandhurst and he was commissioned in The King's Royal Rifle Corps in 1889. He first saw active service with the 4th Battalion of his Regiment in the Manipur expedition of 1891, when he was mentioned in dispatches. This was followed by the operations in Burma and the Chin Hills, 1891-92. In 1898 he was appointed A.D.C. to Sir Redvers Buller, then commanding at Aldershot and himself an old officer of the 60th.

After the outbreak of the South African War he accompanied his chief to the Cape and was with him during the Natal campaign which eventually relieved Ladysmith. When Sir Redvers came home at the beginning of 1901 and returned to Aldershot, Sackville-West, who had received a brevet for his services in South Africa besides being mentioned three times in dispatches, was still with him as his A.D.C. He graduated from the Staff College in 1904. He came to the War Office in 1905 as a staff captain, afterwards G.S.O.2. in the Military Training directorate under Major-General Douglas Haig, but in 1906 was selected to join the teaching staff at the Staff College, where Brigadier-General H. H. Wilson (the future field marshal) was Commandant. To Wilson's friendship and influence "Tit-Willow", as the students called him, was to owe much during his later career.

TRENCH WARFARE

In 1910 he joined the Military Operations directorate at the War Office under Wilson, receiving the brevet of lieutenant-colonel in 1912. He returned to regimental duty with the 2nd K.R.R.C. in November, 1913, and was promoted lieutenant-colonel in the following April when he assumed command of the 4th Battalion in India.

Almost immediately after the outbreak of the Great War he received a staff appointment, going to the Indian Corps as G.S.O.1 in September, 1914. In this capacity he saw the year out in trench warfare in Flanders. He was then brought home to become G.S.O.1 of the 12th Division of the First New Army, accompanied the division to France, and was with it through the Battle of Loos, September, 1915. He was created C.M.G. and at the end of the year got his first command in the field when he was appointed G.O.C. 21st Brigade in the 30th Division. He led the brigade during the early stages of the Battles of the Somme, 1916, when it stormed the German defences south of Montauban on July 1, fought at Trones Wood a week later, and attacked Guillemont towards the end of the month. Requiring a rest he relinquished his command in August, but in October was given the 190th Brigade in the 63rd Division.

Less than a week later he was wounded in the jaw by a shell in the trenches near Hamel, and when fit for service, in March, 1917, was given the 182nd Brigade in the 61st Division.

When the Supreme War Council was instituted in November and Sir Henry Wilson was appointed British Military Representative he secured Sackville-West in the face of a rather unwilling War Office as his Chief Staff Officer. After Wilson had become Chief of the Imperial General Staff in February, 1918, and Rawlinson, who succeeded him at Versailles, had left at the end of March to command the Fifth Army, Major-General Sackville-West—he was promoted to the permanent rank in January, 1919—became British Military Representative in his turn.

Sackville-West was created K.B.E. in 1919 and C.B. in 1921. His war services were five times mentioned in dispatches. He remained in Paris as Military Attaché from 1920 to 1924 and in 1925 he was appointed Lieutenant-Governor of Guernsey and Alderney, retiring from the Army in 1929. He had succeeded his brother, the third Baron Sackville, in 1928.

LEASE RETAINED

Knole Park, as has been already stated, and 52 acres of the property were transferred to the National Trust in 1946 but under the terms of the transfer Lord Sackville and his family retained a lease of part of the house.

He married in 1897 Maude Cecilia, daughter of Captain Mathew John Bell, Bourne Park, Kent. His wife died in 1920 and in 1924 he married Anne, daughter of William Meredith and formerly wife of Stephen Bigelow. She died in 1961. There were two children of the first marriage, a son, the Hon. Edward Sackville-West, who is the heir, and a daughter.

May 9, 1962.

Lord Sackville, the fifth Baron, only son of the late Major-General Lord Sackville, died suddenly on July 4, 1965, at his home at Clogheen, co. Tipperary. He was 63.

Edward Charles Sackville-West was one of the most fascinating and distinctive personalities of his generation. He is best described as a "Dilettante" in the original and splendid sense of the term: that is to say, as a man who, for pure love of them, devoted himself to the arts—especially literature and music—and whose very contribution to them was tinged with the colour of an odd and vivid individuality. He was educated at Eton, where he became famous as a boy pianist of extraordinary precocity; he was the pupil of Irene Scharrer, the wife of his house master, S. G. Lubbock.

Sackville-West proceeded to Christ Church, Oxford. Here literature began to rival music as his main interest. He also became a popular member of a brilliant circle of friends including Sir Maurice Bowra, Sir Roy Harrod, and Mr. L. P. Hartley. His health was always delicate and he engaged in no regular profession but settled down after the university to cultivate his favourite interests and extended his circle to become friendly with the Bloomsbury group.

In the following years he published a number of novels: *The Ruin; Piano Quintet; Mandrake Over the Water-carrier; The Sun in Capricorn;* and *Simpson,* a book about an old-fashioned children's nurse in which his talent showed itself at its best. He also wrote a notable biographical study of De Quincey entitled *A Flame in Sunlight*, which won him the James Tait Black Memorial Prize. In addition to these he reviewed frequently both music and fiction for the weekly papers.

During the Second World War he joined the B.B.C. as an arranger and director of programmes.

STORY WITH MUSIC

It was during this time that a retelling of the story of Odysseus's return, entitled *The Rescue*, was broadcast. This original and inventive version of the story was written by Sackville-West with music by Benjamin Britten. After his father's death in 1962 he divided his time between Ireland, where he bought himself a house, and Dorset, where he shared a home with his old friends, Raymond Mortimer, Eardley Knollys and Desmond Shawe-Taylor. Meanwhile he had joined the Roman Catholic Church, of which he became a deeply devout member. For some years he was an active and valuable member of the board of Covent Garden.

Edward Sackville-West's musical ability, notably as a pianist, became evident while he was still at Eton. In later life he sometimes played the piano publicly, in two-piano duets with Benjamin Britten, for example. But his outstanding gifts as a writer and discriminating judge, supported by an encyclopaedic knowledge of music and thirst for fresh musical experience, drew him inevitably into music criticism. His weekly music articles in the *New Statesman and Nation* during the war years were distinguished not only for their command of the jewelled phrase but for their zealous propagation of young British composers—Britten, Tippett, Berkeley, for instance—and of lesser-known but stimulating composers of other times or other countries. His tastes were catholic but severe, and he demanded as much from his own pen as from any musician about whom he wrote.

Sackville-West's huge collection of gramophone records was famous, and his passion for the gramophone found expression not only in the columns of the *New Statesman and Nation* but also in a brilliant quarterly commentary contribution to *The Gramophone*. A more permanent and extensive testimony to his critical powers was *The Record Guide*, written in collaboration with Desmond Shawe-Taylor and published in 1951, with two later supplementary volumes and a much larger revised edition in 1955.

INFLUENCE ON COLLECTORS

This remarkable volume was not only a *catalogue raisonné* of all available records of serious and semi-serious music but a handbook to the music itself and its composers, enlightened, fastidious, reliable and compulsively readable. *The Record Guide* had wide influence on the taste of record collectors, and English musical people in general, during the early 1950s. Its method and intentions have been imitated subsequently, but the fastidiousness and the attractive literary personalities of Sackville-West and his collaborator have proved inimitable.

All his life his health was weak: perhaps because of this he never wholly fulfilled his talents. His books reveal curious inequalities. But they are always original; blending sharp-eyed humorous observation with a strain of mysterious Gothic fantasy.

These qualities appeared more fully and completely in the man. Frail, pale and slight, like a portrait by El Greco, he was possessed of a nervous temperament which showed in an uncompromising fastidiousness and in occasional fits of intense melancholy. But he faced life with courage, with a great power of enjoyment and with spiritual faith. He was an admirable friend and a delightful companion, always interested in other people's views and warmly appreciative of their gifts. Over all his talk played the mingled light of a romantic imagination and a delicate sense of fun.

He is succeeded by his cousin, Captain Lionel Sackville-West.

July 6, 1965.

Victoria Sackville West, C.H., who died at Sissinghurst Castle on June 2, 1962, at the age of 70, was a child of the Kentish Weald whose love of the countryside in which she had her roots found expression in poetry of Virgilian charm and prose rich in evidence of close and familiar attachment to the land. Drawing strength from these pastoral roots, she enjoyed and analysed the *douceur du vivre*—and the frustrations—of a privileged Edwardian girlhood and, as the wife of Harold Nicolson, took in with no less perceptive an eye the foreign vistas opened up by travel in the Diplomatic Service.

The daughter of the third Baron Sackville and Lady Sackville and the granddaughter of the wholly fascinating Spanish dancer, Pepita, whose portrait she drew in delightful detail as a companion piece to the no less felicitous and absorbing portrait of her mother in a volume expressively entitled *Pepita*, the Hon. Victoria Mary Sackville-West was born in March, 1892, at Knole. Throughout her life she had the atmosphere and the historical and literary associations of Knole in her bones, and with it all a pervading sense of family tradition.

She grew up at Knole, read omnivorously and began to write poetry and fiction at an early age. She married Harold Nicolson, then a young man in the Diplomatic Service, in 1913.

Most of her earliest published work consists of fiction; from *Heritage* onwards she brought out for a time a new novel almost every year. In style and mood her work ranged from a symbolical realism (*The Dragon in Shallow Waters*, 1921) to the fanciful and high romantic (*Grey Wethers*, 1923), though in each instance the writer's impulse plainly derived from a strong poetical sensibility. This was specially in evidence in the volume of short stories that came between these two books, *The Heir*, which echoed some of the stylistic preoccupations at that time of Virginia Woolf, with whom Miss Sackville-West then and afterwards was on terms of close sympathy.

In that same year, 1922, she brought out *Knole and the Sackvilles*. For all her devotion to historical fact it was here that her most distinctive imaginative quality was revealed for the first time. Compounded of lyrical fancy and a resolute feminine sobriety, it illuminates a delicately conceived short novel, *Seducers in Ecuador* (1924), plays happily on fragments of experience and speculation in two volumes of Persian travel, *Passenger to Teheran* (1926) and *Twelve Days* (1928), and mingles with a beautiful serenity in her long poem, *The Land*, a lovely description of familiar scenes of the Kentish countryside composed in temporary exile with her husband in Persia. The poem, published in 1926, was awarded the Hawthornden Prize for that year. A volume of *Collected Poems* appeared in 1933 and confirmed the impression of unaffected strength of sensibility and clarity of thought produced by *The Land*. But Miss Sackville-West was more generally appreciated at this phase of her career as a novelist.

In 1930 she brought out *The Edwardians*, a graphic and pointed study, in the context of a decade of history, of the smart set in Edwardian society. A year later she published what is probably her best and is certainly her most enjoyable work of fiction, *All Passion Spent*. Here, in a gallery of portraits of eminent figures surrounding the portrait of the heroine, who in public life had played the part allotted to the wife of Viceroy and then of Prime Minister, the world of great affairs casts its light and shade upon the life of personal emotions. Lively and at times glowing in style, the novel is done with an unselfconscious sense of social values and with quick and admirably controlled feeling.

GARDENING THEMES

More fiction and more poetry followed, and then, in *Saint Joan of Arc*, published in 1936, Miss Sackville-West showed that she could write biography. It is a fine piece of work, beside which most English portraits of Joan (including Bernard Shaw's) seem superficial or merely plausible. *Pepita* appeared next year, when, with *Some Flowers*, she began the first of a series of books on gardening themes—a slight work in some respects, but touched in description by a characteristic integrity of observation. She gardened with passion during the war years and afterwards, brought out two or three volumes of *Country Notes* in which she drew upon a practical working knowledge of rural husbandry for her evocation of the countryside around her home at Sissinghurst Castle not far from Knole, wrote a novel, *Grand Canyon* (1942), in which she imagined a German victory in the war, and in the following year produced another admirable work of interpretative biography, *The Eagle and the Dove*, in which the genius of Saint Teresa of Avila shines with all the greater splendour by contrast with Teresa of Lisieux.

Her later work lost nothing of variety. It includes an anthology, composed jointly with her husband, *Another World Than This*, more poetry, a delightful essay on *Nursery Rhymes*, *The Easter Party* (1953), a novel produced after an interval of 10 years, which retains many of her felicities of style but is rather wayward in impulse, a life of La Grande Demoiselle, entitled *Daughter of France*, worthy to stand beside her *Saint Joan of Arc*, and more gardening books composed for the most part of weekly journalism. The year 1961 saw the end of a long series of gardening articles in the *Observer*; it saw also the publication of her last novel, *No Signposts in the Sea*.

Two years earlier a dramatic adaptation of *The Edwardians* was put on at the Saville Theatre.

Miss Sackville-West was a Fellow of the Royal Society of Literature and an honorary D.Litt. of Durham and Newcastle. She was a J.P. for Kent. In 1948 she was appointed C.H. The two sons of her marriage to Sir Harold Nicolson are Mr. Benedict Nicolson, editor of the *Burlington Magazine*, and Mr. Nigel Nicolson, the publisher, formerly M.P. for Bournemouth East and Christchurch.

June 4, 1962.

Loudon Sainthill, who died on June 9, 1969, in London, at the age of 50, was for nearly 20 years a leading figure in London stage design. Though he always tried to avoid being typed, he was probably identified in the minds of most theatre-goers primarily with the sort of flamboyant, romantic, highly decorative sets which first made his name, such as those for the 1951 Stratford production of *The Tempest*.

In fact he was much more versatile than that as might be expected perhaps from his rather incongruous background. He was born in Tasmania, and spent his childhood amid horses and, he alleged, in the constant expectation of his parents that he would become a jockey, until he grew too tall. His first experience of theatre was at school in Melbourne; he then took up painting and nearly went to Britain with the de Basil company in 1939. The war prevented that, but after the war he went to Britain and began designing for the theatre there with *The Tempest*. From then on he was seldom absent from the London stage, sometimes with luxurious settings like those for the 1953 production of *A Woman of No Importance*, sometimes with very simple, basic designs for early productions of the English Stage Company, such as *Moon on a Rainbow Shawl*. Much of his happiest work was betwixt and between: his mouldering southern interior for Tennessee Williams's *Orpheus Descending*, the meticulously assured slice of Midland suburbia in David Turner's *Semi-Detached*, the lightly suggested Edwardian fantasy of *Half-a-Sixpence*. He was an excellent designer for ballet—the Covent Garden *Golden Cockerel* was his own favourite among his designs—and proved surprisingly at home in the different, but equally fantastic world of the pantomime with *Aladdin* in 1959, and *Cinderella* in 1960. His most recent success was with *The Canterbury Tales* for the costumes of which he won a New York Tony award recently.

June 11, 1969.

Earl St. John, the former Pinewood Studios executive producer, died suddenly while on holiday in Torremolinos, Spain, on February 26, 1968. He was 76. Mr. St. John—often referred to as the Earl of Pinewood—retired four years earlier from his job as the Rank Organisation's executive producer. He was the longest serving resident American in the British film industry and was responsible for such box office successes as *Genevieve* and *Doctor in the House*.

Born in Baton Rouge, La., he peddled films for his uncle as a teenager. Chaplin's comedies and that classic religious film *From Manger to Cross* were among the pictures in the carpet bags he carried across Mexico.

He came into the British film industry 49 years ago after service in the First World War—a "dough-boy" who never made it back up the gangplank—though he never subsequently took out British nationality. As an independent exhibitor at the Ardwick Green Picture House, Manchester, he began to wonder why 19 out of every 20 films shown were American. In 1924 his prewar boss in America, John Cecil Graham, offered him the job of head of exploitation for Paramount.

In 1926 he opened the Plaza, London, followed by the Carlton, Haymarket, and started to enlarge the Paramount circuit. When Odeon theatres bought out Paramount Theatre in the United Kingdom they took over Earl's contract and in 1939 he became personal assistant to John Davis, chairman and chief executive of the Rank Organisation. He was appointed production adviser to the Rank Organisation in 1947 and from 1951 until his retirement four years ago was their executive producer.

Other films which he produced were *Above Us the Waves*, *The Purple Plain*, *The Card*, *The Million Pound Note*, *A Town Like Alice*, *The Battle of the River Plate*, *The One that Got Away*, *A Tale of Two Cities*, *The Wind Cannot Read* and *A Night to Remember*.

The anecdotes that surrounded this immaculately-dressed, grey-haired producer were legion. Many were undoubtedly true, such as the occasion he turned away the Prince of Wales from the box office of a half empty cinema in order to get publicity that would indicate the film was playing to full houses. It was also fatal to remark to him that it was a nice day. With an eye on the cinema queues he would invariably rejoin: "I hope it rains like blazes." As executive producer on 131 films, he proved that despite the English climate British studios could still turn out films in a superior fashion to their Hollywood counterparts.

He leaves a widow.

February 28, 1968.

Dr. Antonio Salazar, Prime Minister of Portugal from 1932 to 1968, died on July 27, 1970. He had been succeeded by Professor Marcello Caetano in September, 1968, when he suffered a stroke.

Salazar, who was Minister of Finance for four years before he became President of the Council of Ministers in 1932, was the dominating figure in the Portuguese government for several decades. Twentieth-century Europe can produce no similar example of enduring personal ascendancy, except that of Stalin in Russia, and it may be necessary to go back four centuries to another Iberian ruler, Philip II of Spain, to find an autocrat who governed his people with so remote, austere and detailed a devotion to what he considered his duty and their welfare.

Doctor Salazar had the gifts of an administrator and the temper of a moralist. On rare occasions he would emerge from what he called "the semi-isolation of my work" and treat a favoured audience to an excursus on the nature of society, the frailties of humanity or the perils of the times—all related, of course, to the particular vision for Portugal in which he devoutly believed. These speeches impressed rather than stirred his hearers. The Professor of Economics at Coimbra had excited his pupils by the lucidity and boldness of his lecture-room expositions; the Prime Minister of Portugal scorned to adapt his style when addressing the nation. As a leader Salazar was accordingly respected rather than loved, and in the latter years of his reign, as problems mounted and his standard solutions seemed less and less able to deal with them, he came increasingly to be feared. Was it the professor Prime Minister who had grown out of date or the Portuguese people who had grown restless and ungrateful? Whatever the explanation, in Salazar's closing years the gulf between ruler and ruled ceased to be bridged by mutual sympathy. Instead of gradually divesting himself of power Salazar in his seventies reinforced it by greater reliance on the secret police. Abortive revolts at home, slaughter in Portugal's African territories, the loss of Goa, and mounting international criticism embittered the twilight of the Salazarist era.

Yet the dawn of the era had been bright. In one of his rare broadcasts, on December 9, 1934. Salazar contrasted the state of Portugal before and after the intervention of the Army in 1926, which prepared the way for his own period of office. "There was then permanent agitation, *coups d'état*, street fighting, anxiety, anarchy, inadequate public services, insecurity of life and property, discredit, economic ruin, general retrogression, and many revolutions, but yet no Revolution. Then came the Dictatorship, which established peace, assured order, purified the moral atmosphere, added dignity to political action, elevated public morality, confirmed the credit of the State, awoke the national conscience, directed the progress of the nation's economy, raised the standard of living of the rural population, apportioned work, organized the nation's material and moral interests for the common good, and created a worldwide prestige. In addition to all this it assured equal liberty, peace, and work to friend and foe alike."

Probably there were then few Portuguese who would have quarrelled with this judgment. But Salazar was not content to replace chaos by order. His aim was to work out within the confines of the Portuguese state the social doctrines of modern catholicism as expressed especially in *Leo XIII's Rerum Novarum*. The world, he said, was sick at heart. It was following false gods. Was it not possible that in one corner of Europe, one country—small, no doubt, and poor, but shown by history to be capable of leadership—might blaze a better path? It was with this not unworthy aim that Salazar tried to shelter a generation of Portuguese from the dangerous political winds blowing through the outside world.

António de Oliveira was born on April 28, 1889, in Vimieiro, near Comba Dão, in Upper Beira. He was the only son among four children of António de Oilveira, the keeper of a small inn, and his wife, Maria do Resgate Salazar.

YEARS IN SEMINARY

At the age of 11 he entered the seminary of Vizeu and remained there for eight years, taking minor orders, though he eventually decided against the priesthood. At 21 he went to the University of Coimbra and studied law. After graduating in 1914 he joined the teaching staff of the university, and in 1917 became Assistant Lecturer in Economics. The full professorship followed a year later.

As a young student Salazar was attracted by the nationalist ideal of a Portuguese revival, and during the 1914 War he was connected with the formation of the Catholic Centre Party and wrote articles on its behalf. In 1921 he was, in fact, elected a Centre Deputy to Parliament, but resigned his seat almost immediately and returned disillusioned to the university. When, however, in 1926 the Army, exasperated by the wrangling and corruption of the politicians, revolted under General da Costa, the military committee of Lisbon, believing that a Professor of Economics must be able to practise what he taught, offered Salazar the portfolio of finance. In all diffidence he refused. But they insisted, and he became Minister of Finance, holding the office for five days, until, on a reshuffle of the Ministry, he found himself back once again in Coimbra. Short though his first term of office had been, he left a deep impression behind him in Lisbon.

After the first stage of the revolution General

Carmona succeeded General da Costa. An able and foreseeing man he realized that only the most drastic reorganization of Portugal's finances could save the country from disaster. Salazar was approached but he refused responsibility unless he were given absolute discretion. When this was withheld he retired once more to his university. Efforts were then made to obtain a loan from the League of Nations, but these failed and Carmona once again turned to Salazar. This time his conditions were accepted. He was given supreme control over the expenditure of every department, with the right to veto any measures likely to affect the budget.

Such had been the maladministration of Salazar's predecessors that in 1928, while the rest of the world prospered, Portugal was sunk in an unparalleled depression. However, by ruthless retrenchment he eliminated the budget deficit, which had come to be regarded as inevitable. Salazar then turned to the floating debt, and in five years the nation's assets for the first time in Portuguese history exceeded its liabilities. Then came the turn for the banks. It was on this basis of financial orthodoxy that economic development became possible, in the colonies as well as in the mother country.

In July, 1932, President Carmona appointed Salazar Prime Minister. The following year saw the introduction of the *Estado Novo*, the new constitution for Portugal for which Salazar was primarily responsible. His aim was to construct a social and corporative system which should correspond to the natural structure of society. The use by the regime of the words "corporative" and "dictatorship" inevitably promoted comparison with fascism. While Salazar had sympathy with anyone who, like Mussolini, had turned his back on the great fallacy of nineteenth century liberalism, he insisted that the Portuguese revolution was no imitation. It was not a totalitarian regime that he was constructing, for totalitarianism, with its deification of the state, he regarded as essentially pagan. His new state was Christian; his nucleus the family. Private ownership was respected.

LABOUR DIGNITY

An attempt was made to give labour a dignity which Salazar believed could not be found in the excesses of either capitalism or bolshevism.

In addition to the corporations the *Estado Novo* provided other discreet outlets for political Portuguese men. There was the National Union, not intended as a party or even as a substitute for the old parties which had been swept away, but as "an institution to include the greatest number of citizens and associations prepared to accept, acclaim, and defend the gospel of national renaissance". There was also the National Assembly, which regularly assembled, though the Government, as Salazar blandly remarked, was "indifferent" to whether it had the Assembly's confidence. Indeed, in a moment of rash prophecy in 1935 he showed his estimate of its value by expressing a doubt whether in 20 years' time there would be any legislative assemblies left in Europe.

It was, perhaps, Salazar's greatest failing that he underestimated the strength of liberal instincts in an educated society, or rather that he identified these instincts with the decayed caricature of parliamentary democracy which brought postwar Portugal to the brink of disaster. As young men advocating catholic ideals Salazar and some fellow students were once set upon by roughs—" it was a regime of liberty", was his bitter comment later. Indeed, in his mouth the word "liberty" became synonymous with licence and had an almost indecent sound.

BETTER LINK

Salazar was convinced that a benevolent supply of accurate statistics, budgets, reports and plans was a better link between government and governed than the talking shop of a parliament or the scandalmongering of a free press.

The regime consolidated during the thirties, but the growing shadow of war and an actual war raging across the frontier in Spain put a brake on the evolution of political forms. In 1936 the international outlook was so threatening that Salazar took over the portfolio of Foreign Affairs, which he retained until 1947. (In addition he kept the post of Minister of Finance from 1928 to 1940, was acting Colonial Minister in 1930, and acting Minister of War from 1936 to 1944. When the fighting in Angola began he took the Ministry of Defence into his own hands, but gave it up at a Cabinet reshuffle in December, 1962.) In July, 1937, he had a narrow escape from death when a bomb was thrown at him as he was on his way to attend Mass in Lisbon.

When war came to Europe Salazar's policy was directed at keeping it out of the Iberian peninsula. Portugal's neutrality was immediately proclaimed. Salazar fostered good relations in particular with Spain—in 1942 a meeting in Seville with General Franco led to the formation of the "Iberian block"—with Brazil, and with Portugal's traditional ally, Britain. Salazar had many times referred in warm terms to the ancient alliance, though showing distress at criticism of it—and of his regime—in left-wing circles in Britain. He sought a "necessary and useful collaboration", though in the early stages of the war there could be no question of activating the alliance. After prolonged negotiations an agreement was signed in October, 1943, whereby Britain was granted facilities in the Azores for the protection of allied shipping in the Atlantic.

Soon after the end of the war Salazar, realizing that authoritarian regimes were at a discount internationally, took tentative steps towards allowing more political freedom. Elections were due in November, 1945, and it was announced that opposition candidates could come forward and new parties be formed. As was to happen on later occasions, notably in the presidential election of 1958, once the lid was lifted a little the pot was found to be unexpectedly near the boil. Quickly the lid was clamped down again.

As the years passed the anti-Salazarist forces emerged from their anonymity. The world was introduced to names such as Delgado and Galvao, though the strict internal discipline of Portugal made it hard to tell how widespread was the support they enjoyed.

Delgado, who led the opposition to Salazar for some years, stood unsuccessfully for the presidency in 1958, later leaving the country because he believed himself in danger of arrest. In the spring of 1965 a bludgeoned corpse, later identified as that of Delgado, was found in a shallow grave near Villanbueva del Fresno, south of Badajoz.

The outbreak in 1961 of African revolts in Angola, fanned by winds from neighbouring Congo, had at first the effect of rallying public support behind Salazar. However, the loss at the end of 1961 of Goa, where an heroic defensive was promised and none was seen, seriously damaged the regime. An abortive uprising at Beja on New Year's Day, 1962, was the immediate consequence. In September of the same year 50 leading members of the Opposition, including former Ministers, handed in a petition to the President demanding a new Prime Minister. The regime, they bluntly stated, "finds no echo in the national mind".

On January 3, 1962, Salazar once more addressed the National Assembly, though a throat complaint compelled him to leave the reading of his speech to the Assembly's President, while he sat, visibly moved. His theme was the loss of Goa and the decline of international reality. He spoke with some bitterness of the ancient alliance with Britain, which had proved unable to alter the course of events in Goa, and declared the intention of his Government to study "what positive content" still remained in the treaty.

The hue and cry after Portugal, which spread in Afro-Asian circles and at the United Nations, did not surprise Salazar. It was the apparent readiness of supposedly friendly countries, particularly Britain and America, to adopt a position of neutrality or even to side with Portugal's enemies which shocked him. Latterly it almost seemed as though General Franco (whom he met again in May, 1963) and the South Africans were the only people left with whom he could agree.

The simplicity of Salazar's private life was a legend. In Lisbon he occupied a small set of rooms in the Sao Bento palace, the official residence of the Prime Minister. He was happiest, however, when he could retire to the small farm he had bought in his native Vimieiro, where he could cultivate his vineyard in the plain peasant surroundings which had always seemed to him ideal for a man's labour. Except for journeys to Spain to confer with General Franco, Salazar had never travelled abroad, not even to those Portuguese colonies which he had made legally integral parts of the motherland. He never married, but had adopted two orphan girls from his village.

July 27, 1970.

Major Salah Salem, who died in hospital in Cairo on February 18, 1962, at the age of 41, was one of the earliest members of the Free Officers movement which brought about the Egyptian revolution of July, 1952. In the early years of the revolution, as Minister of National Guidance and spokesman for the regime, Major Salem was almost as well known abroad as Gamal Abdul Nasser or General Neguib. Latterly, however, ill health had kept him out of the limelight.

Major Salem and his brother, Wing Commander Gamal Salem, who also was an early recruit to the Free Officers, were, like General Neguib, born in the Sudan. Two years younger than Nasser, Salem belonged to the same generation of young unprivileged officers who felt bitterly what they regarded as the humiliation of King Farouk at the hands of the British in 1942, and their own humiliation —for which in turn they blamed Farouk— during the Palestine fighting of 1948. It was about this time that the Salem brothers became conspirators, their job in July, 1952, being to secure the support for the revolution of the first Infantry Division in Sinai—a mission which they successfully accomplished.

The post to which Salem was then appointed —Minister for National Guidance and Sudanese Affairs—seemed appropriate in view of his qualities of eloquence and energy and the fact that Sudan was his birthplace. It was on one of his visits to the Sudan, during an entertainment in his honour given by tribesmen in the course of the 1953 election campaign, that Salem received the nickname of "the dancing major", through having been photographed joining in a dance stripped to his under-clothes.

Subsequently he differed from Nasser on details of Egyptian policy towards the Sudan, though he was one of Nasser's stoutest supporters in the struggle for leadership with Neguib which divided the Army and country at the beginning of 1954. Nor did Salem confine his outside interests to the Sudan. He travelled to most other Arab countries, and though a visit to Damascus in March, 1955, was successful in producing a unified military command between the two countries, an earlier visit to Iraq was the source of much confusion. Did Nuri Pasha on this occasion promise that Iraq would never join a non-Arab military alliance? Or did Major Salem give approval to Iraq's alignment with Turkey and Pakistan? Out of this misunderstanding grew the bitter feud over the Baghdad Pact which turned the Egypt of Nasser and the Iraq of Nuri into deadly enemies.

Salem resigned office in September, 1955, becoming editor of *Al Shaab*, for which newspaper he visited London as special correspondent at the time of the Suez crisis in August, 1956. Subsequently he became head of the state publishing house, Dar al Gumhouria.

Major Salem leaves a widow, a son, and three daughters.

February 19, 1962.

Frank O. Salisbury, C.V.O., who died in London on August 31, 1962, at the age of 87, won renown as a painter of portraits, of murals, and above all of state and ceremonial occasions.

Born at Harpenden on December 18, 1874, son of H. Salisbury, he proved delicate in youth and so was educated at home. He showed early facility with crayon and brush, and began his formal art education under his eldest brother. H.J.Salisbury, the stained glass artist, at St. Albans. After three years he went to Heatherley's School, whence he proceeded, with a scholarship, to the Royal Academy Schools. There he spent five years and won various medals and other awards, including the Landseer Scholarship, which enabled him to make an Italian journey in 1896.

By the turn of the century he had already acquired considerable reputation, and in 1899 he first exhibited at the Academy—a portrait of Alice Maude Greenwood, the lady who, in 1901, became his wife. He was thereafter a consistent exhibitor at the Academy (which, however, never offered him membership) at the Paris Salon, and at various Bond Street galleries.

Child portraiture was always one of Salisbury's keen interests, and he spent one whole year on the advice of George Haité, painting his own twin daughters, Sylvia and Monica. This resulted in a great gain in dexterity, a quality without which Salisbury could never have produced the enormous body of work that was to come from his brush. Early murals included "The Nativity", in Harpenden parish church and "Great Artists of Chelsea", for Chelsea Town Hall. In 1907 he undertook a grandiose composition (measuring 15ft. by 5ft.) on "The Passing of Queen Eleanor", which gave scope for that love of pageantry which he had evinced from his youth up. Shown at the 1908 Academy, this huge decoration found no resting place until 1918, when Alderman A. Faulkner presented it to the Abbey of St. Albans.

MURAL FOR LORDS

It was this picture which led to Salisbury's first big commission in the ceremonial kind, a rendering of "The Trial of Katharine of Aragon" for the corridor of the House of Lords. There followed murals at the Royal Exchange, Liverpool Town Hall, and elsewhere.

It was Salisbury's manifest ability in the decorative handling of large crowds, while at the same time producing good portraits of the principal figures, which caused him to be chosen as the recorder of events of state. He depicted the visit of the King and Queen to France in 1917. This was followed by a painting of the National Peace Thanksgiving Service at St. Paul's in 1919, by "The Signing of the Register" at the wedding of the Princess Royal, by the ceremony of the Order of the Bath at Westminster Abbey, and by "The Burial of the Unknown Warrior" in the Abbey on November 11, 1920. Another Thanksgiving Service—for the jubilee of King George V—was also placed on record by Salisbury. Entitled "The Heart of the Empire", it was exhibited at the Royal Academy of 1936, and reproduced in colour collotype by *The Times*, the proceeds from the sale of reproductions being devoted to King George's Jubilee Fund. "The Coronation of H.M. King George VI" was another enormous canvas, which dominated the third gallery of the Academy in 1938. It was presented to the King by the Dominions and India "in token of love and loyalty".

In the portraiture of distinguished sitters Salisbury was perhaps more constantly employed than any of his contemporaries except Philip de László. He painted all the senior members of the Royal Family and men of eminence in many walks of life.

Salisbury worked not only in oils but also in stained glass, and was master of the Worshipful Company of Glaziers in 1933-34. He produced some competent, economical landscapes as vacation work.

If fitness for purpose be the criterion by which a work of art is to be judged, Frank Salisbury may in the long run claim higher worth than the many critics who spoke unfavourably of his superficial slickness and photographic quality would grant him. He was a clever portraitist, not only in capturing a likeness but in his decorative disposition of figures—well seen, for example, in the delightful circular group of "The Sen Sisters". He had a decorative ability suited to the tasks he undertook and his huge compositions of state ceremony, the result of many preliminary studies in charcoal, were grouped with unfailing efficiency. As the recorder of historic scenes he has a special niche.

In 1944 Salisbury published his memoirs under the title of *Portrait and Pageant*.

His wife died in 1951.

September 1, 1962.

Marshal of the Royal Air Force Sir John Salmond, G.C.B., C.M.G., C.V.O., D.S.O., died on April 16, 1968, at Eastbourne at the age of 86.

With the death of Jack Salmond, aviation loses a pioneer, the Royal Air Force a great officer and many older Air Force officers a beloved and deeply respected friend.

Salmond was never one to court the limelight. To some extent he was overshadowed throughout his career by the man whom he relieved as commander of the R.A.F. on the Western Front in 1918, and again as Chief of the Air Staff in 1930. It is never an easy job to take over from a great man—from an historical character. It must be admitted that his job as C.A.S. was made no easier by Trenchard's insistence, when he left the Air Ministry in 1930, on launching his "Last will and Testament"—his proposals for a wide measure of substitution of air forces for land and sea forces—as a Cabinet Paper, instead of leaving it as a guide for his successor on the development of air power, which was the original intention Jack Salmond had hoped to spend some fruitful years quietly building up the house of which his great predecessor had so truly laid the foundations; and those who served under him on the Air Staff know how little he relished the role that was forced upon him—that of a protagonist in the sometimes bitter controversies with his opposite numbers in the older services.

He was a pioneer in many fields of British air power—as a squadron commander with the old B.E.F. in 1914, as Henderson's successor on the Army Council responsible for Military Aeronautics; as Air Force Commander in France and as Commander in Chief, Air Defences of Great Britain from 1925 to 1929. But perhaps he will be specially remembered as the man who, in Iraq from 1922 to 1924, laid the foundations of the system known as Air Control which was applied so effectively in subsequent years to the control of turbulent tribesmen in the Middle East and on the N.W. Frontier of India. Jack Salmond knew how to apply the right sort of force in the right way according to varying conditions; he knew that the Air Control method could often get results quickly and with great economy in lives—both of our own men and of a tribal enemy; but he never hesitated to use ground forces, and use them well, when they were more suitable for the job in hand, as in Kurdistan in 1923.

John Maitland Salmond came of a distinguished military family. He was the son of Major-General Sir William Salmond, R.E., who died in 1932 at the age of 92. His elder brother, Air Chief Marshal Sir Geoffrey Salmond, died in 1933. John was born on July 17, 1881, was educated at Wellington and Sandhurst, and entered The King's Own Royal Regiment in 1901. In the South African War he served in the Transvaal and was awarded the Queen's Medal with three clasps. He became a captain in 1910. Two years later he took up flying, qualifying as a pilot on a Grahame-White biplane at Hendon. His Royal Aero Club certificate, No. 272, was dated August 13, 1912. He was seconded to the newly formed Royal Flying Corps and on November 12, 1912, was appointed an instructor as a flight commander.

The 1914-18 War, coming so soon after the formation of the R.F.C., provided great opportunities for its young officers, for whom it was also a searching test. Salmond was equal to all the calls made upon him, and in four years rose from major to major-general, a rank he attained at the early age of 36. He took No. 3 Squadron to France in August, 1914, and early won the D.S.O. After commanding successively a wing and a brigade he was appointed in June, 1917, to command the Training Division, R.F.C., in England. In the following October he became Director-General of Military Aeronautics, with a seat on the Army Council. In February, 1918, as acting major-general, he took command of the R.F.C. in the field. When the R.A.F. was formed in 1918, he was graded as major-general, and commanded the force in France until after the end of hostilities.

He was one of the first air vice-marshals, and in 1920 became A.O.C., Inland Area, on his return from commanding the R.A.F. with the Army of the Rhine. In October, 1922, he became the first air officer to command the combined British Forces in Iraq, and held a temporary Army commission as major-general in addition to his R.A.F. commission for purposes of discipline over Army personnel. He was promoted to air marshal in June, 1923. His next task was to organize the Air Defence of Great Britain, a new command formed to control the air forces of the United Kingdom, of which he became A.O.C.-in-C, in January, 1925. During 1928 he was temporarily detached from this post, at the request of the Australian Government, for a mission to advise on the air defence of the Commonwealth. On his return he joined the Air Council in January, 1929, as Air Member for Personnel, and at the same time was promoted to air chief marshal. A year later he succeeded Sir Hugh (afterwards Lord) Trenchard as Chief of the Air Staff and so achieved the highest post in his profession at the early age of 48. On April 1, 1933, he was due to be succeeded by his brother, Sir Geoffrey Salmond, and was appointed a Government director on the board of Imperial Airways. Sir Geoffrey, however, was taken seriously ill before he could assume office, and died on April 27. Sir John, who was transferred to the half-pay list on March 31, returned to the Air Ministry to act in his former post until Sir Edward Ellington became Chief of the Air Staff at the end of May. He had been promoted to the rank of marshal of the Royal Air Force in January, 1933, the second officer to hold it, the first being Lord Trenchard. During the 1939-45 War he served for the first two years as Director of Armament Production in the Ministry of Aircraft Production.

He was married in 1913 to Helen Amy (who died in 1916), fourth daughter of J. Forbes Lumsden, of Johnstone House Aberdeen, and had one daughter. He married secondly, in 1924, the Hon. Monica Grenfell, elder daughter of Lord Desborough. There were a son and daughter of the second marriage.

April 17, 1968.

Queen Salote of Tonga—See under **Tonga.**

The Right Hon. Lord Samuel, G.C.B., O.M., G.B.E., P.C., statesman, administrator, and philosopher, who died on February 5, 1963, was one of the most eminent Liberals of his day, one of the two surviving members of Campbell-Bannerman's great Liberal administration (the other is Sir Winston Churchill), leader of the Liberal Parliamentary Party during 1931–35, leader of the Liberal Party in the House of Lords from 1944 until 1955, and for the past 20 years or more an elder statesman of Liberalism, as widely respected for his record of public service as for his integrity of political purpose.

He could look back with undiminished pride at the transformation encompassed by those reforms won by the Liberals of an earlier day in which he himself had had so notable a part. Yet, the last thing he would have dreamed of was to rest on his laurels—to live in the past. His alert and penetrating mind reached ever forward and in old age he pressed for reforms of both Houses of Parliament to make them more truly representative. The well-deserved success he achieved in broadcasting—in which he by no means confined himself to politics—demonstrated the breadth as well as the adaptability of his lucid, profound and ingenious mind.

Of judicious and humane temper, with a commanding grasp alike of principle and detail, Lord Samuel possessed intellectual and organizing abilities of a rare order. As an administrator he was enlightened, flexible, unfailingly thorough. During his first spell of office, as Under-Secretary to the Home Office, he left what was unmistakably his own mark upon the Workmen's Compensation Act of 1906, while the Children Act of 1908, known as "The Children's Charter," was his own conception. Appointed to the Post Office in 1910, he was afterwards described by a celebrated postal reformer, Sir John Henniker Heaton, as "the greatest Postmaster General England has ever had". First High Commissioner in Palestine (as good a choice as could have been made for that delicate and arduous post), he proved himself, among other things, a conciliator of exceptional quality. Chairman in 1925 of the Royal Commission on the coal industry, he presented a remarkable and dispassionate report, which was followed, after the dispute in the industry had burst into flame, by the no less remarkable "Samuel Memorandum". Cabinet office was to fall to him once more—in 1931—though for a brief space only: afterwards the variousness of his public service was not appreciably diminished. All things considered, few of his contemporaries strove to serve the interest of the nation with more transparent sincerity or with greater consistency, ability, and devotion.

FAITH IN REASON

As a political leader, more especially as a leader in Opposition in the House of Commons, he must be judged in the light of the disheartening and peculiarly onerous circumstances in which he found himself. Samuel was a wholehearted and uncompromising Liberal at a time when the fortunes of his party were declining rapidly, when the essential missionary labour of Liberalism had indeed been brought to fruition. It is doubtful whether any other leader who had equally felt it his duty to defy the tide of events, seeking to resist the force of world changes which had shifted the entire basis of the country's historic fiscal policy, for instance, would have achieved much more than he; for he fought his position bravely and with unquestionable skill.

Never wanting in subtlety of mind, he had neither the personal magnetism nor the demagogic gifts of some of his contemporaries. Faith in reason, which is perhaps the essence of the Liberal standpoint, he preserved until the last. For the rest, he was by nature steadfast in doctrine, and those Liberals who remained faithful to him felt that with him as leader they knew where they stood, and that the noblest traditions of their party were safe in his hands.

The Right Hon. Sir Herbert Louis Samuel, first Viscount Samuel, of Mount Carmel, and of Toxteth, Liverpool, was born in that city on November 6, 1870. His father, Edwin Louis Samuel, was a banker and was brother of the first Lord Swaythling; his mother was Clara, daughter of Ellis Samuel Yates. He came, therefore, of a well known and long established Anglo-Jewish family, which on both sides had settled in Liverpool towards the end of the eighteenth century. Orphaned at the age of six, and under the guardianship of Lord Swaythling, he was educated at University College School and at Balliol, where in 1893 he took his degree with first-class honours in history. He was elected an honorary Fellow of his college in 1935.

At Oxford Samuel was president of the Russell, the University Liberal Club. From the beginning, it might fairly be said he was a Liberal not least by temperament. On leaving

Oxford he became a prominent member of the Rainbow Circle, a small debating society of Radicals and Socialists, of which Ramsay MacDonald was secretary, and was on terms of friendship with Graham Wallas, Bernard Shaw, and other early Fabians. But he was never seduced by the intellectual persuasions of Fabianism. As an undergraduate he had taken a hand in neighbouring Oxfordshire villages in forming an agricultural labourers' union, and this had drawn the attention to him of the South Oxfordshire Liberals, who in 1895 asked him to contest the seat on their behalf. Defeated, he nevertheless reduced the Conservative majority; defeated again in the "khaki election" of 1900, when the Conservatives swept the country, he brought the majority against him down to 114. Two years later he was chosen to fight a by-election in the Cleveland division of the North Riding, and was not only returned but succeeded in holding the seat until the Liberal debacle of 1918. Shortly after his election he published *Liberalism: Its Principles and Proposals*, to which Mr. Asquith contributed an introduction and which was of some considerable influence at the time.

Samuel made an immediate impression in the House; his amendment to the Address on the subject of the employment of Chinese in the Transvaal proved the start of a memorable agitation. He was clearly marked for office. On the return of his party to power in 1905 he became Under-Secretary to the Home Office, where in the next four years he brought a humane purpose and striking administrative efficiency to a large and varied volume of legislation. His success with the Children Act of 1908 was recognized, in the following year, by his promotion to the Cabinet as Chancellor of the Duchy of Lancaster and, a year later still, by his appointment as Postmaster General. In this office, too, his record was outstanding. He effected a considerable reduction in cable rates, was responsible for the much criticized nationalization of the telephone service, and secured greater Post Office efficiency by, among other things, recognition of the postal trade unions. Not less notable, perhaps, than these services to the administration was the assistance which Samuel gave in the preparation of the Budget of 1909 and of the financial part of Asquith's Home Rule Bill.

HOME SECRETARY

In 1914, having latterly been occupied with preparing a housing and town-planning programme and with a new system of local rating, he was transferred, as successor to John Burns, to the Local Government Board. There he almost at once became responsible for the reception of the vast number of Belgian refugees who poured into England. On the formation of the Coalition in May, 1915, he returned for a time to the Post Office, but in the following year, on the resignation of Sir John Simon, he crowned an unbroken spell of 10 years of office by becoming Home Secretary. The circumstances of that office in 1916 were difficult and delicate, but Samuel showed excellent judgment and good sense.

He did not hesitate, although Lloyd George pressed him to stay, to follow Asquith into political exile in December—a step in strict accord with every principle he had professed and one which was to be decisive for the rest of his political career. He continued actively to support the war effort, and in 1917 and 1918 did valuable work as chairman of the Select Committee of the House of Commons on National Expenditure. It was at this period, too, that he wrote a widely circulated statement of the British case under the title of "The War and Liberty".

Rejected in 1918 by the electors of the Cleveland division, for which he stood as an Independent Liberal, he bore his disappointment with philosophy. Early in 1920 he was asked by Lord Allenby to visit Palestine, which was then under military administration, and to advise upon questions of administration there. The sequel, a few months later, was his appointment as first High Commissioner to that country—a position of supreme difficulty which he was to fill for five years with the highest distinction. His initial task was to establish a civil administration in Jerusalem; his next to set it working smoothly. Wisely he sought to enlist all the supplementary aid he could. When he left Palestine Samuel had achieved vastly more in the way of order and prosperity for the country than had seemed possible. On the one hand, agriculture, industry, and commerce all gave promise of continued steady expansion; on the other, no opportunity had been neglected of promoting a spirit of harmony, of effective practical cooperation, between the different religious communities in the Holy Land.

Almost immediately on his return to England Samuel agreed to turn his mind to the most intractable industrial problem of the day by accepting the chairmanship of the Royal Commission on the coal industry. Its report, which rejected nationalization but argued for thoroughgoing reform, is thought to have been largely of his own writing, and certainly that remarkable document bears unmistakable evidence of his personal qualities of lucid analytical statement and balanced decision. It was widely accepted at the time as laying down the essential lines on which peace and efficiency in the industry could best be secured, and for a time it seemed that the Baldwin Government were willing to give conditional approval to some of its recommendations in order to secure a settlement. The approval was more apparent than real, the gulf between the parties to the dispute widened, the Government did nothing, and the disaster which threatened inevitably overtook the industry. Samuel was abroad when the pits closed down, but he at once returned and, on his own initiative, established contact with the T.U.C. leaders.

As a result he drew up the "Samuel Memorandum" which was accepted by them though not by the Miners' (later the Mineworkers') Federation. His was a timely and valuable intervention, and the pity is that it was not more happily consummated.

IN NATIONAL GOVERNMENT

In 1927 Samuel (who had in the previous year been created G.C.B., having received the G.B.E. in 1920) returned to active politics as chairman of the Liberal Party organization. Once again he was required to demonstrate his powers of conciliation. He had the trust of all sections of the party, and he directed his exceptional administrative gifts to overhauling and strengthening the party machinery. In spite of all his efforts, however, only 59 out of the 500 Liberal candidates in the General Election of 1929 were returned. He himself was successful in the Darwen division of Lancashire and returned to the Commons after an absence of more than 10 years. In December he resigned his chairmanship of the party organization owing to the pressure of his parliamentary duties. In the House he addressed himself with vigour to the increasingly protectionist trend of Conservatism; the steadily deepening depression was itself proof, he maintained, that a policy of economic nationalism offered no effective remedy against large-scale unemployment. When the crash came in August, 1931, Samuel, as acting leader of the Liberal Party in the absence through illness of Lloyd George, played a leading part in the negotiations which led to the formation of the National Government, and himself accepted the office of Home Secretary. He did not favour the holding of the October election. But Darwen, in spite of the insistence of the local Conservatives upon putting forward their own candidate, returned him by a good majority.

As Home Secretary again and leader of the Liberal Parliamentary Party, Samuel made his attitude in the National Government and in the House reasonably clear. He was prepared, as he had said during the election campaign, in the national interest to cooperate with all parties and to preserve an open mind; he was not prepared to forgo his Liberalism—more especially, to abandon the principle of free trade. By the beginning of the new year, however, he was conscious of an inescapable dilemma. As an alternative to resignation he accepted a suspension of the rule of the collective responsibility of Ministers. He countered Neville Chamberlain's scheme of a general tariff with a reasoned plea for an industrial commission. He even half-committed himself to a measure of protection while assailing the Government's import duties. In the end, however, the Ottawa agreements in the autumn proved the last straw for him, and he and other Liberal Ministers withdrew from the Government, though without crossing the floor of the House. In one respect at least his going was for him a cause of sincere regret, for he was planning at the time an extensive penal reform Bill.

ACTIVE IN DEBATE

For three more years he continued as leader of the Liberal Parliamentary Party. Its membership in the House of Commons was small, but Samuel was upheld by the belief that a relative handful of members nevertheless represented a vast body of public opinion which adhered to neither of the other parties. In this faith he acted with dignity and unassuming confidence, bringing a subtle and well-stored mind to bear upon the problems of the day and fulfilling most of the duties of an active Opposition. He had travelled extensively in earlier years, and he now took the opportunity to visit Canada and the United States as leader of the United Kingdom delegation to the Pacific Relations Conference. In June, 1935, Oxford conferred on him an honorary D.C.L. In the general election of the following November he was defeated at Darwen.

It was from this moment, perhaps, when he was no longer in the House of Commons, that his qualities as an elder statesman became most clearly apparent. Two years later he was created a viscount: he was introduced on the same day as Lord Baldwin. Samuel had declined a peerage 20 years before, and had consistently rejected the hereditary principle as a method of constituting a second chamber: but he was realist enough to welcome the opportunity of contributing his wide knowledge and ripe experience to the conduct of the nation's affairs. He was for long one of the members in most constant attendance in the Lords, one of the most active and influential in debate.

After Munich, it appears, Neville Chamberlain offered him a seat in the Cabinet, but Samuel hesitated for a day or two only. Towards the end of August, 1939, however, a speech he delivered in the Lords demonstrated to eloquent purpose his sense of the nation's unity and resolve. In January, 1940, he visited Palestine and the Middle East. He had a special reason for this visit. In part it sprang from the desire to serve the Jewish victims of National-Socialism in Germany. His interest in Palestine and the Jewish National Home after he had left the country in 1925 was shown in his presidency of the Friends of the Hebrew University and his chairmanship of the Palestine Electric Corporation; but a deeper sympathy was called out in him as first chairman of the Council for German Jewry.

In April of the following year he became deputy leader of the Liberal Party in the Lords, and later succeeded Lord Crewe as leader.

PHILOSOPHIC CAST

His interventions in debate were invariably distinguished by breadth of experience and truly philosophic cast of mind. He took an active part in the general election of 1951 and when it was over pressed the Government to consider a scheme to make both Houses of Parliament more truly representative. In June, 1955, at the age of 84, amid general regret, he retired from Liberal leadership in the Lords. In 1958 the Order of Merit was conferred upon him.

It remains to say something of Herbert Samuel the philosopher. To describe him merely as an exponent, however distinguished, of the English "common-sense school" of philosophy is to do less than justice to the moral idealism that moved him. He sought, it is true, to prove that the man in the street had a fundamental stake, as it were, in the philosophical thought of his time, and he returned again and again to a pragmatic statement of value. But his empirical judgments almost always acquired depth and illumination from a pervading humanist metaphysic. *Philosophy and the Ordinary Man*, an address which he published in 1932, and *The Tree of Good and Evil*, in the following year, expressed a luminous reasonableness, which guided him throughout the work, incorporating these and other fragments, which was issued under the title of *Belief and Action* (1937). Here, as in the earlier volume on *Practical Ethics* (1935), he took up a comprehensive "meliorist" position, joining to it a quickened sense of the need for a synthesis of religion, philosophy, and science. It is this intellectual liberalism which lends character to the important and revealing volume of memoirs which he issued in 1945. *In Search of Reality* appeared in 1957 and in 1961 *A Threefold Cord*, a dialogue on philosophy, science and religion with Professor Herbert Dingle. From 1931 to 1959 he was president of the Royal Institute of Philosophy. He was president also of the Royal Asiatic Society during 1940–43 and a past president of the Royal Statistical Society. He had also been president of the English Association and the Classical Association.

In 1897 he married his cousin Beatrice, younger daughter of the late Ellis A. Frankin, by whom he had three sons and a daughter. His wife died in 1959. The eldest son, the Hon. Edwin Herbert Samuel, C.M.G., who now succeeds to the title, is principal of the Institute of Public Administration in Israel. He married, in 1920, Hadassah, daughter of J. Grasovsky, of Tel Aviv, by whom he has two sons.

February 6, 1963.

Carl Sandburg, the American poet of the Middle West, who also wrote a vivid and deeply studied six-volume Life of Abraham Lincoln, died at his farm at Flat Rock, North Carolina, at the age of 89, in July, 1967.

As a poet Sandburg stemmed directly from Whitman. His verse exhibits a whole-hearted and realistic acceptance of "Americanism", of the verities of life on the prairies and in the industrial cities of the Middle West; and one of his short poems, "Chicago—Hog Butcher for the World"—is as well known abroad as any other American poem.

His poetry has an impassioned sincerity, which seeks to capture the novelty, the vitality and the promise of the quotidian American scene, and in the attempt adds substance and support to an authentically American tradition of poetry. The slow, even monotony of the plains, the smoke and bustle of the cities—these he evoked in a mood of Whitmanesque wonder and praise, distilling from the scene a heartfelt sympathy with the commonplaces of American aspiration. Intensity of poetic emotion is, perhaps, too often lacking; the residue of journalism in his verse, which is of bulky proportions, is large. But his is a saving truth to common American experience and common American values.

Born in Galesburg, Illinois, on January 6, 1878, the son of August Sandburg and Clara Anderson, who were newly settled in those parts, Carl Sandburg left school at 13 and took up many varied jobs before serving for a spell as a volunteer in the war with Spain in 1898. Afterwards, he entered Lombard College in Galesburg and upon graduating in 1902 he engaged in journalism in various towns in the Middle West, was secretary to the mayor of Milwaukee during 1910–12, was appointed to the staff of a Chicago magazine for business men, spent some months in 1918 as a newspaper correspondent in Stockholm, and then joined the *Chicago Daily News.* He had begun to write verse in his youth, but the poems that first attracted any attention appeared in 1914, in Harriet Monroe's famous review, *Poetry*. His first book of poetry, *Chicago Poems*, appeared in 1915 when he was 37. Then came *Cornhuskers* (1918), a companion volume treating of rural life, which won a special Pulitzer award, *Smoke and Steel* (1920) and *Sunburnt West* (1922), and Sandburg's merits as a poet were widely and gratefully recognized.

He continued to produce books of poetry, but for many years his principal energies were devoted to a careful and elaborate biography of Abraham Lincoln. This proved to be a singularly impressive feat of historical portraiture. The first two volumes, *The Prairie Years*, were published in 1926, and in spite of initial impressions that there was nothing very remarkable about the work, it became apparent that the author's intimacy with the prairie setting of Lincoln's early years and his gift of poetic insight had stood him in wonderfully good stead. These two volumes constituted, in fact, a masterly study of character, which was sustained at the same high level in the four volumes of *The War Years*, published in 1939. *The War Years* was awarded a Pulitzer Prize. An abridgment of all six volumes came out in 1954.

Sandburg was deeply interested in the popular song and toured the country on several occasions reciting his own poetry and accompanying his singing of folk songs on the guitar. He published a very successful collection of ballads and songs, *The American Songbag* in 1927. A collection of his poems, *Complete Poems*, appeared in 1950 and was awarded a Pulitzer Prize. Among several prose works, which included stories for children, novels and autobiography, he wrote a life of Edward Steichen, the famous photographer (1929), whose sister, Lillian, he had married in 1908.

July 24, 1967.

Lord Sandwich died at his home at Hinchingbrooke, Huntingdon, on June 15, 1962, at the age of 87. A former Conservative member of Parliament, his was a career largely devoted to the public service on the local as well as the national scene. He was also well known as an art collector.

George Charles Montagu, the ninth Earl of Sandwich, was the eldest son of Rear-Admiral the Hon. Victor Alexander Montagu and his wife, formerly Lady Agneta Yorke, daughter of the fourth Earl of Hardwicke, and was born on December 29, 1874. He succeeded his uncle, the eighth earl, in June, 1916.

He went to Winchester in 1888, to the Rev. J. T. Bramston's House, and later to Magdalen College, Oxford, where he graduated in 1897. His first post in the public service was that of assistant private secretary to the President of the Board of Agriculture, Mr. Walter (afterwards Viscount) Long, from 1898 to 1900. From 1900 to 1903 he was private secretary (unpaid) to Henry Chaplin and to his successor, Lord Sandwich's former chief, Walter Long. In 1900 he entered Parliament for South Huntingdonshire, and this seat he held until 1906, after which he did not seek reelection.

Thenceforth he devoted himself largely to the local affairs of his native county, Huntingdonshire. In 1916, he was elected an alderman of its county council and was chairman from 1933 to 1946. He was Lord Lieutenant and Custos Rotulorum of the county from 1922 to 1946. He had also been chairman of the Huntingdon Territorial Army Association, of the Bishop's Advisory Committee of the Diocese of Ely, and of the Central Prisoners of War Committee in the First World War. From 1902 to 1961 he was a director of the Exchange Telegraph Company.

Apart from his interest and work in public affairs, Lord Sandwich was a prominent figure in the art world. The family collection of pictures is widely known, and has often contributed to exhibitions of old masters. He also made his own collection of Impressionist and Post-Impressionist works, including works by Derain, Modigliani, Cezanne, Renoir, Matisse, Vuillard, and Segonzac, as well as portraits, pastels and drawings by Paul Maze, Henry Tonks, and Augustus John. Together with Lord Ivor Churchill, he was a pioneer in the collection of French Impressionist pictures in England.

YOUNG CRIMINALS

He served as a member of the Committee of the Contemporary Art Society and had been responsible for many of the purchases by that body. From 1934 to 1941 he was a Trustee of the Tate Gallery, and from 1937 to 1946 of the National Maritime Museum at Greenwich.

With a deep sense of duty and a charm of manner and kindness that endeared him to his friends, he also had a great interest in various branches of social work and especially in the reclaiming of young criminals of both sexes.

In 1951 he published his autobiography in verse, *Boyhood.* Among his other published works were: *Ten Years of Locomotive Progress*; *Windows; The Bridle-Way; In a Green Shade; Flowers of Fancy, Gleanings*; and *British and Foreign Medals relating to Naval and Maritime Affairs,* which was first published in 1937, had a supplement in 1939, and ran to a second edition in 1950. Many of these books were also in verse.

The late earl married in 1905 Alberta, daughter of William Sturges, of New York, by whom he had two sons and two daughters. He is succeeded in the peerage by his elder son, Viscount Hinchingbrooke, Conservative member of Parliament for South Dorset. His younger son, the Hon. William Drogo Sturges Montagu, was killed in a flying accident in January, 1944, while serving wiih the R.A.F. Lord Sandwich's first wife died in 1951 and in 1952 he married secondly Ella, daughter of George Sully.

June 18, 1962.

Margaret Sanger, one of the founders of the birth control movement in the United States, died on September 6, 1966, aged 82.

She was born in 1883, the daughter of a sculptor of gravestones and was one of 11 children. Very early in life she was initiated into the hardships of the working-class woman's life. Her career as a nurse followed a sketchy education, but a great deal of human experience, and early in life she determined on the course she would follow.

She was indicted in 1915 for violation of a postal regulation which prohibited the sending of information about birth control through the post (such material was for long classified as a type of pornographic literature) but the case was dropped after protests by doctors, social workers, and others to President Wilson. In 1916 she was arrested for conducting a birth control centre at Brooklyn and was found Guilty. In her autobiography published in England in 1939 she states that she was imprisoned in all eight times.

She was twice married, first to William Sanger and secondly to J. Noah H. Slee.

Margaret Sanger agitated for women's suffrage and mixed with revolutionaries from an early age. As a nurse in the immigrant slums of New York she was early introduced to the seemingly limitless fecundity of the poor and to their desperate efforts to get rid of unwanted pregnancies. Their appeals for help to midwives and doctors went unanswered even though the rich clearly knew how to plan their families, and Margaret Sanger started out on her quest to help them. Unable to learn much from the medical profession in her own country she travelled abroad, and in France found that married women there knew all there was to know about contraception as well as the act of love handed on from mother to daughter. Returning to the United States she began the long and lonely battle against the constant harrying and persecution of Comstock, who bitterly fought her at every turn, by writing pamphlets, answering thousands of individual letters and in inspiring others (including Marie Stopes) by defiantly opening the first birth control clinic in 1916 in the United States (though the very first clinic had been opened in Holland by Dr. Aletta Jacobs in 1882).

SUPPORT WON

She continued all her efforts in spite of attempts to silence her and at long last others began to join her in the struggle though it was not until she was supported by progressive doctors, particularly Dr. Dickenson and Abraham Stone, who were prepared to cooperate with birth control clinics launched under lay auspices. Yet even when the brunt of the battle was over in her own country she turned her attention to international propaganda and brought together leading demographers, scientists, sociologists, and physicians. Two scientific organizations emerged, the International Union for the Scientific Study of Population and the International Medical Group for the Investigation of Contraception.

Years later she helped to form the international committee on parenthood (later the International Planned Parenthood Federation) of which she was the federation's founder and president emeritus. With all the forces of church and orthodox Christian morality and professional prejudices against lay interference the courage of the pioneers in this field was outstanding, and Margaret Sanger, who continued her campaign for 50 years, is undoubtedly one of the foremost. Against formidable odds she stuck to the goal she had set herself to enable poor women to control their fertility, and that she managed at the same time to enlist the help of progressive elements in the medical profession and encourage scientific and social study of the problem on an international scale was an amazing achievement.

September 8, 1966.

Sir Donald Sangster, K.C.V.O., who was Prime Minister of Jamaica from the previous February, died in Montreal on April 11, 1967. He was 55.

When the Jamaica Labour Party was swept back into power in the general election of February, 1967, winning 33 out of 53 seats, it was Sangster as acting Prime Minister who led the party to victory. This was the first election to be held in Jamaica since independence in 1962, and it was difficult to deny Sangster the Prime Ministership in succession to Sir Alexander Bustamante, who had retired from active politics after a protracted illness. Thus on February 22, 1967, Donald Sangster took the oath as Prime Minister and was formally invited to form a government.

For nearly two years he had acted as Prime Minister during Bustamante's illness, and though it was generally conceded that he had done a good job, it was also felt that he was lacking in thrust, indecisive and unsure of himself. The answer may simply have been that with the powerful figure of Bustamante in the background, who was still Prime Minister on paper, Sangster had always to be looking over his shoulder. In addition he also had to be on the qui vive for intensely ambitious rivals in the party's hierarchy.

For example, at the party's annual convention in December, 1966, when Sangster sought reelection as the party's first vice-chairman, he was challenged by Robert Lightbourne, the Minister of Trade. Sangster, however, triumphed and won by three votes to one. It was realized then that Sangster had much more support in the rank and file of the party than was generally known. This internal party episode was to have a significant effect on his fortunes.

Donald Burns Sangster was born in Jamaica on October 26, 1911. He was a solicitor who looked like a solicitor—the sort of family friend who would think and think again before acting. He was educated at Munroe College, Jamaica, where he represented the school at cricket, football, athletics, gymnastics and boxing. He was admitted as a solicitor of the Supreme Court of Jamaica in 1937. Sangster, who devoted nearly all his life to public service, was first elected to the Jamaica House of Representatives in 1949, and was Minister of

Social Welfare from 1950 to 1953. Later he was appointed Minister of Finance and Leader of the House from 1953 to 1955. The Jamaica Labour Party lost the elections in 1955, but returned to power in 1962 to lead Jamaica into independence in August that year and Sangster was Minister of Finance.

In 1964 when Bustamante fell ill and Sangster was appointed to act he was at the same time acting as Minister of External Affairs and Defence in addition to his substantive post as Finance Minister. On four successive occasions he represented Jamaica at meetings of Commonwealth Prime Ministers—in London in 1964 and 1965, at Lagos in 1966 and again in London in 1966.

He was an able parliamentarian who was sincerely devoted to the principles of parliamentary democracy. He was for years a leading figure in the Commonwealth Parliamentary Association—and was chairman in 1962 when the association held its tenth conference in Jamaica.

In his unspectacular, but quietly efficient manner he was a major figure in Jamaica politics, who had grown enormously in stature in the years when he acted as Prime Minister, probably more so abroad than at home. He was a great believer in the Commonwealth, and in his own unpretentious manner had become a Commonwealth statesman.

April 12, 1967.

Sir Malcolm Sargent, who died on October 3, 1967, in London, at the age of 72, was of all British conductors in his day the most widely esteemed by the lay public.

Among musicians he was admired for his versatility and his practical, eminently businesslike approach to the preparation of musical performances. He was a fluent, attractive pianist, a brilliant score-reader, a skilful and effective arranger and orchestrator of other composers' music; while as a conductor his stick technique was regarded by many as the most accomplished and reliable in the world. As a public figure he was celebrated for his sartorial elegance, and his seemingly infallible ability to converse knowledgeably and wittily on all manner of topics.

Harold Malcolm Watts Sargent was born on April 29, 1895. While still a schoolboy he obtained his diploma as Associate of the Royal College of Organists. In 1914 he took his degree as Bachelor of Music and obtained his first musical appointment, as organist of Melton Mowbray parish church, a post which he held until 1924, though it was interrupted by war service with the 27th Durham Light Infantry.

In 1919 Sargent became the youngest Doctor of Music in the country. Composition and pianism (he was a pupil of Moiseiwitsch) shared his musical energies with the organ and the church choir. One of Sargent's orchestral compositions, *Impressions on a Windy Day,* found a place in the 1921 season of Henry Wood Promenade Concerts, and the composer was invited to conduct it. The success of the composition encouraged Wood to include a Nocturne and Scherzo by Sargent in the 1922 Promenade syllabus; but it was the conductor who made the principal impression.

Sargent held the post of conductor to the Leicester Symphony Orchestra and Choral Society from 1922 until 1939. In 1923 he was appointed to the teaching staff of the Royal College of Music. In the following year Sargent's career as a conductor made two significant strides; he was invited to become conductor and introducer of the Robert Mayer concerts for children, a function which he discharged brilliantly and unchallenged until 1939; and he conducted the first performances, for the British National Opera Company, of Holst's *At the Boar's Head* and Vaughan Williams's *Hugh the Drover*. He was hitching his wagon, challengingly, to the emergent constellation of new British composers. When in 1925 Sargent was engaged by the Royal Philharmonic Society he chose an all-British programme with Bax, Howells, Ireland, Vaughan Williams, and Berners.

In 1926 he began his famous association with the D'Oyly Carte company. Sargent insisted on having access to Sullivan's full orchestral scores, and by his deft, sympathetic handling of their music showed how much they deserved the admiration of musicians. He remained with the D'Oyly Carte company for three seasons, rejoined them during the Festival of Britain season in 1951, and made occasional guest appearances in recent years, as well as conducting complete recordings of Savoy operettas.

Sargent's powers in choral music obtained him in 1928 the posts of musical director to the Bradford Festival Choral Society and to the Royal Choral Society in London, whose annual performances under his conductorship, of *Messiah*, *The Dream of Gerontius*, and Christmas carols have remained among the most popular of London's musical events. In 1931 he was engaged to conduct the first performance of Walton's *Belshazzar's Feast* at the Leeds Triennial Festival; his completely persuasive direction of this has passed into the history of British amateur choralism, and his association with the Leeds festivals was regular until the 1950s. From 1932 Sargent also held the musical directorship of the Huddersfield Philharmonic Choir, the most famous of all the crack Yorkshire choral bodies.

CONCERT CLUB

In 1928 Sargent had collaborated in founding the Concert Club. The Courtauld-Sargent concerts, which grew out of it, continued until the outbreak of the Second World War, and gave rise in 1932 to the formation of the London Philharmonic Orchestra, an enterprise in which Sargent was joined by Sir Thomas Beecham, who become the orchestra's principal conductor. Sargent remained closely associated with the L.P.O. for many years; it was he who took the orchestra on a tour of the country, performing in music-halls and cinemas during the war.

Sargent's activity during the 1930s was interrupted by treatment for tuberculosis. He made a complete recovery, and during this decade made guest appearances in Palestine, Australia and New Zealand and at home with the Hallé Orchestra, and with the Liverpool Philharmonic Orchestra whose musical directorship Sargent was to hold between 1942 and 1948.

In 1936 he made his Covent Garden debut conducting Charpentier's *Louise*. He did not reappear at Covent Garden until 1954, when he conducted the first performances of Walton's *Troilus and Cressida*.

The suspension during wartime of some of Sargent's musical activities seems hardly to have left him less busy. Apart from his post in Liverpool he made many guest appearances—including, extra-musically, a number with the B.B.C. Brains Trust.

With the end of the war, Sargent resumed those tours abroad which caused him to be dubbed unofficially Britain's Ambassador of Music.

WORLD-WIDE CONDUCTING

He was frequently to be found conducting throughout Europe and the Commonwealth, in America, and the Far East; more recently he took British orchestras to Russia and other Soviet territories. At home he continued to introduce new British work—Vaughan Williams's sixth and ninth symphonies, Rawsthorne's second piano concerto, Britten's Young Person's Guide to the Orchestra (in the original film version of which Sargent also spoke the commentary)—but the single step which sealed his national fame was his principal conductorship of the Promenade concerts from 1950, a task in which he assumed, both personally and musically, the mantle of Henry Wood, who had died in 1944. He had returned to the Proms, as a guest in 1947, the year in which he was knighted. In time, he became the matinee idol of thousands of youthful promenaders, among others.

In 1950 the conductorship of the B.B.C. Symphony Orchestra fell vacant and Sargent accepted the post which he held until 1957. It was in this capacity that he conducted the concerts which opened the Royal Festival Hall in 1951. After 1957 Sargent held no major orchestral post, though in that year he was made president of the National Youth Orchestra, which he frequently trained and conducted.

In April, 1966, he went to Melbourne to spend two months as principal conductor of the Melbourne Symphony Orchestra. He was back for the start of the Proms in July—the opening concert was the 500th Promenade concert he had conducted, and the B.B.C. gave him an etching by Rembrandt to mark the occasion. In December, Sargent was in hospital with back trouble and jaundice. He returned to the rostrum in March, 1967, to conduct Beethoven's *Missa Solemnis* at the Albert Hall. In July a recurrence of gastroenteritis prevented him from conducting the opening promenade concert—he was operated on. He made a surprise five-minute appearance at the last-night promenade concert in September, to a loud ovation.

As a musical interpreter Sargent was sometimes the victim of his own versatility and his passion for efficiency—and of his taste, which was moulded by the Victorian cathedral tradition into which he was born. This last was more clearly perceptible in his readings of Handel and Bach than in nineteenth-century music (*Elijah* for example), where his vigour avoided any suspicion of sanctimoniousness.

The same could sometimes be felt in his readings of standard classic and romantic works; Sargent had prepared his interpretations down to the last detail, but after several decades the vitality of the music tended to become hardened and unexuberant. He became impatient, too, of music from which he could not at once draw an effect; this led him to retouch the scores of the past with a self-will which scholarly musicians could not condone. Repetition did not stale his communicable understanding of the music composed within his lifetime: his performances of Elgar, Holst, Vaughan Williams and later British composers remained lucid and continually compelling.

Sargent was married in 1923 to Eileen Laura Harding, by whom he had one son and one daughter.

October 4, 1967.

Sir Orme Sargent, G.C.M.G., K.C.B., formerly Permanent Under-Secretary of State for Foreign Affairs, died on October 23, 1962, in a Bath nursing home. He was 77.

Almost the whole of his official career was spent in the Foreign Office, and he became its leading expert on Europe. During the 1914-18 war he was sent to the listening post of Berne, and as his career ripened, he acquired not only knowledge and experience but also an understanding of policies and persons, movements and tendencies, that made a great impression on all with whom he came in contact. He had a gift for "atmosphere", and his colleagues learnt to attach the utmost importance to his prescience, which, though he had a slight tendency to pessimism, was generally confirmed by events. He was a man of great sensitivity, with a warm heart and a multitude of friends.

Orme Sargent was born on October 31, 1884, the son of H. Garton Sargent. He was educated at Radley and entered the Foreign Office in 1906. In the early part of the 1914-18 war he was in the department that dealt with the blockade, and there got a good training in commercial and economic affairs. He was at the Berne Legation from 1917 to 1919, when he went to Paris with the British Delegation to the Conference of Ambassadors. Their discussions ranged over all the problems of Europe, and gave Sargent a memorable introduction to many of the new influences, hopes and fears occasioned by the disintegration of pre-1914 Europe. In 1926 he was transferred back to the Foreign Office to take over the Central Department, which covered at that time Italy, Austria, Hungary, Yugoslavia and the Balkans. Later on he became an Assistant Under-Secretary of State and was in charge of German, Polish, French and other Western European affairs.

He remained in the Foreign Office for the rest of his career. He never had doubts about the significance of Hitler's rise to power in 1933, and he took every opportunity that came his way of emphasizing the reality of the menace. It was no surprise to his colleagues that the public rejoicings over Munich should provoke him to say, "Anybody would think that we were celebrating a major victory instead of the betrayal of a minor ally." During the war, and until he succeeded Sir Alexander Cadogan as Permanent Under-Secretary of State early in 1946, his special subjects were Italy, the Balkans, Turkey, Scandinavia and Russia. He was Deputy Under-Secretary at this time, and took charge of the Foreign Office when Cadogan was away with the Foreign Secretary, Mr. Eden, or the Prime Minister, Mr. Churchill.

THE NEW FOREIGN SERVICE

One of the big subjects he had to deal with as Permanent Under-Secretary was Eden's reorganization of the Foreign Service after the war, when the old diplomatic and consular services were amalgamated and when all the clerical and subordinate personnel were admitted to full membership of the Foreign Office. The preparation of this scheme developed in Sargent a keener interest in the administrative side of his work than had been customary in the days of his predecessors, and his great contribution to the welfare of the personnel is remembered with gratitude. He retired in 1949, having in the previous year been raised to G.C.M.G. He had been created K.C.M.G. in 1937. In 1936 he had been made C.B. and been raised to K.C.B. in 1947.

He had few interests outside his profession, but he was a connoisseur of art and furniture, and after his retirement lived in his beautifully redecorated Georgian house in Bath, where with his penetrating intelligence and genially cynical talk he was delightful company to his many friends. He took a lively interest in the Holburne of Menstrie Museum of which he became chairman, and he was successful in retaining 10 of the pictures lent to the museum by the late Thomas Cook, many of which were dispersed after Mr. Cook's death.

In 1949 he became a Justice of the Peace for Bath, and he was a Church Commissioner in 1952.

Sargent suffered from poor health during the last years of his life, which, however, he did not allow to interfere with his cheerfulness and hospitality. He was unmarried.

October 24, 1962.

Albert Sarraut, a politician of note and an authority on French colonial questions under the Third Republic, who had held Cabinet Office more than a score of times and was twice Prime Minister, died on November 26, 1962, in Paris at the age of 90. He had been for long a principal influence on the *Dépêche de Toulouse*, perhaps the most distinguished Liberal newspaper in France, at any rate until the 1939 War.

Born in Bordeaux on July 28, 1872, Albert Sarraut graduated at the university of his native town and adopted the law as a career. His practice at the Bar was joined to political ambitions, which were assisted by his cooperation on the staff of the *Dépêche*, then and for many years afterwards managed by his brother Maurice. In 1902 he was elected deputy for the Department of the Aude, soon made his influence felt in the Chamber, and was appointed Under-Secretary of State for the Interior in the Sarrien Government of 1906. He held the same post for a time in the succeeding Government of Clemenceau, was Under-Secretary of State for War in Briand's Ministry of 1909–10, and was, in 1911, made Governor-General of Indo-China, a somewhat unexpected appointment for a man under 40. Three years of uneventful administration there were followed by his return to France soon after the outbreak of war in 1914. He entered Viviani's Cabinet as Minister of Education, spent some months in the trenches as an infantry company commander and, in 1916, returned to Indo-China, where he remained until 1919.

From his return to France until the summer of 1924 Sarraut held the post of Minister of the Colonies in the two Administrations of Briand, and also under Leygues and Poincaré. During his tenure of office, an unusually long one in the France of the twenties, he drew up much-needed schemes of development for French overseas possessions and in general applied himself to the task of coordinating French colonial policy. He went as Ambassador to Ankara in 1925, and in the following year, when he had exchanged his seat in the Chamber for membership of the Senate, returned to office at home as Minister of the Interior under Poincaré. Thereafter he sat in five more Cabinets before leading a Ministry of his own for a few weeks towards the end of 1933.

DIVIDED AND WEAK

His second Premiership, during the first six months of 1936, was more important, for it was attended by the German reoccupation of the Rhineland; Sarraut himself was under no illusion as to the probable consequences, but he was faced by a divided Cabinet and a country all too conscious of its weakness.

He continued to hold office in every Government of a predominantly Centre or Socialist-Radical character, and was Minister of the Interior under Daladier when war broke out in September, 1939. When Reynaud took over in March, 1940, Sarraut was transferred to the Ministry of Education. Disaster in the summer of that year found him wanting—it is perhaps fairest to say—in single-mindeness. He withdrew into the background of events under the Vichy regime, and, on assuming control of the *Dépêche* after Maurice Sarraut had been killed by pro-Nazi terrorists in 1943, was arrested and deported to Germany. Liberated in 1945, he found the newspaper in communist hands and was obliged to conduct a prolonged legal battle to recover possession of it. The paper was then renamed the *Dépêche du Midi* and continued to wield considerable influence in south-west France. But Albert Sarraut was 75 years of age and had retired from active participation in politics, and the direction of the *Dépêche* passed into the hands of his son-in-law Jean Baylet. Sarraut was made a member of the Assembly of the French Union when that body was founded in 1947 and two years later was elected its President, an office he held with distinction. When, in December 1958, at the age of 86, and with the coming of the Fifth

Republic, he felt he had to give up all public duties, he was nominated Président d'Honneur of the Assembly which, however, with so many of its member states achieving independence, was allowed two years later quietly to disappear.

Sarraut was commonly described as "Pickwickian" in appearance. His was a somewhat florid style of oratory, though this did not prevent him from being an unusually hard worker. A member of the Institut de France—Académie des Beaux-Arts—Sarraut had for many years encouraged young or little known artists and had gradually assembled what is believed to be one of the finest private collections of paintings in France.

November 27, 1962.

Siegfried Sassoon, C.B.E., M.C., died on September 1, 1967, at his home Heytesbury House, Wiltshire. He was 80.

English letters has lost by his death one of its most dedicated sons; he became known to the public in 1916, as one of the soldier poets who stirred the emotions and consciences of his countrymen, and his reputation grew after the war with quicker prose and poetry. His best known work—*The Memoirs of a Fox-Hunting Man*—will assuredly always rank as a classic; it is more than a biography; it is an elegy. Sassoon, except in his war poems and a few others, wrote reflectively; he was never tied to contemporary fashion and all his work bears his own special and personal stamp.

His style might mislead people to think that he was an amateur; but this was far from the truth; in spite of the apparent ease with which he wrote some of his work, this was the art that conceals art. Though traditional and unadventurous in form and in subject, his work will always appeal to those who see the value of enriching life by a sensitive and humorous contemplation of it.

Sassoon was born on September 8, 1886. Much of his life and especially the early part of it has been described by himself, but he spoke in his books (as in his conversation) less of his father's than of his mother's family.

Sassoon's paternal background was complex; his father, Alfred, was a nephew of Reuben Sassoon (perhaps the Prince of Wales's closest friend), and son of Sassoon David Sassoon, who had moved to England in 1858. Alfred died in 1895 and his son Siegfried (then aged nine) had not seen very much of "Pappy" as he had lived apart from his wife since his son was five.

Sassoon's mother, Theresa Thornycroft, came from the family of distinguished Victorian sculptors and was herself an able amateur artist. Of her two brothers Hamo was also a sculptor and John was the eminent marine engineer. It was she who first encouraged her son's literary talent (at the age of 11 he had presented her with a volume of poems) and when he was about 24 introduced him to Edmund Gosse, one of her old friends. In 1913 Gosse introduced Sassoon to Edward Marsh and this proved a turning point in his career.

Until this time his talent had revealed itself sluggishly. He went to Marlborough College where, according to his own account, he did not show promise of doing anything out of the ordinary, "... seems unlikely to adopt any special career", was his final report. He started to read Law at Clare College, Cambridge (later to make him an honorary fellow), with a view to being called to the Bar, but changed to History. He competed for the Chancellor's Medal with a poem on Edward I but was not successful, and after this he went down without taking a degree. With a small private income he lived as a country gentleman; while he hunted and played cricket, he was also writing (as well as book collecting) and between 1906 and 1912 he published nine small volumes of poems—some in private editions. All the time he "muddled along, making corrections" (to his poems). "I had no one to whom I could show any poems in MS. and (my own publications) were a sort of private hobby", he wrote in 1932. At the age of 27 he was asking himself "was it really worth while to put one's poetic ambitions before everything else?"

After the appearance of *The Daffodil Murderer*, 1913 (which had begun as a parody of Masefield but had ended as a serious poem), "Eddie" Marsh gave him the encouragement he needed; Marsh not only advised him on his poetry but introduced him to a wider circle of literary friends (including Rupert Brooke).

But war interrupted his adopted career as a poet. He joined The Royal Welch Fusiliers and was posted to France. There his name became a byword for bravery, and he was nicknamed "Mad Jack"—Robert Graves, a brother officer, has written of how he calmly read *The London Mail* before the crucial attack at Fricourt. In the spring of 1916 he won the Military Cross for bringing in under heavy fire a wounded lance-corporal who was lying close to the German lines. A year later, after capturing single-handed some German trenches in the Hindenburg Line, he remained in the enemy position reading a volume of poems oblivious of the danger, and as a result was recommended for the Victoria Cross; but as the campaign eventually ended in a reverse, he only received a bar to his Military Cross.

SACRIFICED

Sassoon had himself been wounded during the fighting in the Hindenburg Line and after he had been invalided home he had an opportunity to reflect upon the human butchery that was taking place; he resolved to protest and the outcome was *A Soldier's Declaration* (July, 1917), attacking the "political errors and insincerities for which the fighting men are being sacrificed . . . also I believe that I may help to destroy the callous complacency with which the majority of those at home regard the continuance of agonies which they do not share, and which they have not sufficient imagination to realize". He expected a court martial but did not get one. His M.C. ribbon he threw in the river Mersey.

His was the pacifism of courage not of cowardice; in reply to a question in the House of Commons the Secretary of State for War put it down to shell shock and Sassoon was sent to hospital. He decided that he would be more effective if he returned to the front and after a brief spell in Palestine he rejoined his former battalion in France, where he was again wounded.

Sassoon had by this time established his reputation as a poet. He had been publishing poems about the war in the *Cambridge Magazine* and other periodicals since 1916: in May, 1917, these were collected in *The Old Huntsman*, and a second collection followed—*Counter Attack*—13 months later. Fifty-two of the poems from these two volumes that specifically dealt with the war were republished in 1919 as *War Poems.* These poems showed how his anger at the war and his lack of faith in its purpose had grown over the years and that *A Soldier's Declaration* had been a natural culmination, not a sudden impulse. They also revealed a new depth in his poetry. The poems that leave one most disgusted with the horrors of the war such as "They", "The Hero", "Base Details" and "The Glory of Women" have a bitter satirical intensity, and the depth of tragic feeling in them was not surpassed by any of the other war poets.

In 1928 *The Memoirs of a Fox-Hunting Man* appeared. At first it came out anonymously but it was in fact based upon Sassoon's early life, lovingly recalled—a way of life that the war had shattered not only for him but for everybody. Hunting and cricket, of course, continued after 1919 but Sassoon reminded us that the remote rural life of England before 1914 had disappeared: this sense of something lost—not actually stated, but implied—adds edge to what would otherwise be only a charming pastoral life.

CHARACTER SKETCHES

It had a well-deserved success and Sassoon followed it with other prose works that are either directly autobiographical or (like their precursor) near autobiographical—and that take his career up to 1920. *The Old Century* (1938), *The Weald of Youth* (1942), *Memoirs of an Infantry Officer* (1930), *Sherston's Progress* (1936), and *Siegfried's Journey* (1945)—there are wonderfully evocative passages in all of these, in particular some of the character sketches of his friends and contemporaries; but *The Memoirs of a Fox-Hunting Man* (for which he had been awarded the Hawthornden Prize in 1929) will remain his most notable.

Sassoon was writing poetry throughout his life—periodically every few years a volume would appear either in a public or a private edition—but his style altered after the 1914–18 War. At times he still displayed a satirical edge, for instance he attacked society in *Satrical Poems* (1926) and he attacked war in *The Road to Ruin* (1933). But these poems lack the passion of his earlier ones. His angry *War Poems* had been the first to make him famous and he never quite achieved their pungency again, for his poetry was at its best when he described an actual experience.

The dichotomy in his character as a young man—the poet who had been fond of sport and horse-flesh—continued as he grew older in an altered form. While he needed to participate in life to write about it, by nature he only wished to witness or reflect upon it; he himself would refer to this as his Enoch Arden complex. The approaching War of 1939 and also the unsympathetic attitude of the new generation of writers had made Sassoon more of a recluse than before, and at times (as in *The Tasking*, 1954) he revealed a melancholy and a desire for spiritual assurance.

He joined the Roman Catholic Church in 1957 (the same year as he was awarded the Queen's Medal for Poetry). *The Path to Peace* (1960) was published in a finely printed and limited edition; some of these poems were written after his conversion and they demonstrate how complete and successful it had been. All his life he had been deeply spiritual: and when he discovered a means of expressing a faith, fortunately for him it did not drive him from the world but brought him into it. More than ever was he happy to see—indeed he had always been at his best with—one or two chosen friends.

His looks were striking and throughout his life he had seemed younger than his years when he became animated over some poem or reminiscence; even in his old age his lean body and bright eyes would seem like those of a youth. The remarkable physique that he had possessed as a young man also remained with him, and in his seventies his movements were as swift as those of a man half his age. His interest in cricket never flagged and not many years before his death he had been able to keep up a week's annual cricket with The Ravens.

His conversation had a pleasing liveliness especially when he was recalling the past, and he would usually match his animation with fidgety, nervous movements of his arms and legs. His wit is obvious in his books and he spoke as he wrote, using puns and sporting metaphors, of a kind more likely to be heard in a pub over a pint than from a poet.

He was married in 1933 to Hester Gatty, who survives him with one son

September 4, 1967.

Sir Victor Sassoon, BT., G.B.E., died on August 12, 1961, at Nassau, Bahamas, where in recent years he had made his home. He was 79.

Best known in Britain, perhaps, as a winner of classic races, Victor Sassoon attained distinction in three different fields of activity, in public life, in commerce and on the Turf. The prosperous Jewish family from which he derived had emigrated from Baghdad via Bushile to Bombay about 130 years ago. His great grandfather, David Sassoon, who was a great philanthropist, started a firm bearing his own name in Bombay and in 1867 the well-known firm of E. D. Sassoon & Co., merchants and bankers, was established as an entirely independent concern by his grandfather, Elias David Sassoon, with headquarters in Bombay and with branches in India, the Far East, Baghdad and Basra. It rapidly progressed into a vast business. An important group of cotton mills in Bombay was under the firm's control. In the course of its development E. D. Sassoon & Co. acquired large interests in Shanghai, which Sir Victor actively promoted after the First World War.

Sir Jacob Sassoon, Victor's uncle, an outstanding man of business and head of the firm in his day, was famed for the many public and charitable institutions such as hospitals and schools he set up in Bombay. He was created a baronet in 1909 with special remainder to his brother Edward, who died in 1924 and who had married Leontine, daughter of A. Levy, of Cairo. She survived until 1955. Their family consisted of four, Victor, the subject of this memoir, a younger brother, Hector, who died in 1923, and two sisters. There is no heir to the title, which after Sir Jacob's death in 1916 had passed to his brother Edward, and on his death in 1924 had been inherited by his son, the present baronet, who in 1959 married Evelyn Barnes, of Dallas, United States. On his succession to the baronetcy his second name, Victor, was preferred to his first name Ellice, a variant of Elias, often found in the Sassoon family.

Victor was born on December 30, 1881.

INTEREST IN FLYING

He was educated at Harrow and Trinity College, Cambridge. His early interest in aviation led him in 1912 to compete in the Grand Prix of the Aero Club of France. In the First World War he served in the R.A.F., retiring with the rank of captain. In the course of service he met with an accident, by which he was to some extent physically incapacitated, though he was still able to ride and swim. Victor's interest in aviation revealed itself in his being one of the original sponsors of civil aviation in India.

He was a member of the Indian Legislative Assembly in 1922–23 and again in 1926–29. He served on the Royal Commission (1929) for the study of labour conditions in Indian industrial undertakings, on the health and standard of living of the workers and on the relations between employers and employees. He was a pioneer in promoting welfare and health among the mill operatives working under the Sassoon management and in encouraging other mill owners to do likewise.

Another question of great public importance which occupied Sassoon's attention was Government currency policy which was directed to stabilizing the exchange value of the rupee at 1s. 6d. To oppose this policy, which at the time roused strong feelings in India, especially among the commercial community, the Indian Currency League was created with Sir Victor as Founder-President.

When the First World War ended, Sir Victor, who showed exceptional business aptitude, had already taken over the active charge of the vast interests of E. D. Sassoon & Co. with its far-flung chain of branches. These he made a practice of visiting each year. In 1920 E. D. Sassoon & Co. was incorporated as a private company in India with a substantial capital. In 1930 E. D. Sassoon Banking Co. Ltd. was registered in Hongkong with a capital of £1m. This organization took over the banking interests of E. D. Sassoon & Co. in London, Manchester and Hongkong and later also those in Shanghai.

This concern later became the main direct interest of Victor in the East and at one time he lived in Shanghai. He also held some outside directorships—for example, in insurance. He contributed liberally to the relief of the victims of political persecution and arranged to take into his offices in India and China as many Jewish refugees from Germany as could possibly be absorbed. Political developments caused him much anxiety. He gradually reduced his financial interests in India and had also to cope with grave difficulties in China, where, though he managed to salve much, the Communists appropriated a good deal of his property in Shanghai. He transferred his personal headquarters to Nassau, from which centre he had eventually conducted his diverse activities now extending to South America.

ON THE TURF

Sassoon's keen interest in horse-racing and horse-breeding was of long standing. He bought his first racehorse in 1924, and went on to win the Derby four times—with Pinza in 1953, Crepello in 1957, Hard Ridden in 1958, and St. Paddy in 1960. His horses won all the other English classic races, and he was twice the leading owner. There were few owners who had more horses in training during the past 30 years, and some of the greatest names on the Turf were closely connected with him.

Steve Donoghue rode—and later trained—for him. He gave Sir Gordon Richards his only winning ride in the Derby, and Lester Piggott his third, on St. Paddy, Noel Murless trained for him and so did Fred Darling. A year after buying his first racehorse, Sir Victor Sassoon spent 58,750 guineas on bloodstock, but he had to wait until 1937 for his first classic win, with Exhibitionist in the 1,000 Guineas and the Oaks. In 1928 he gave £11,000 for the mare Comedienne. In 1936 he bought the French Derby and Grand Prix winner Mieuxce for stud—and in his first season the stallion sired the Oaks winner Commotion.

BRED AT NEWMARKET

Crepello, for whom Sir Victor turned down a large American offer after he had won the 1957 2,000 Guineas and the Derby, was bred at his Eve stud, Newmarket. The 1957 season put Sir Victor second in the owners' table to the Queen, with £58,522. The following year Hard Ridden—bought for only 270 guineas as a yearling at the Dublin Sales—won the Derby by five lengths. St. Paddy made it four in 1960, then went on to win the St. Leger and to earn £71,256 in one season—a record for English racing exceeded only by Tulyar. He also put Sir Victor at the head of the list of winning owners for 1960—£90,069 from 15 horses entered in 29 races. This was almost three times as much prize money as his nearest rival, and nearly double his winnings of £58,579 in 1957, when he was also leading owner. Sassoon had his last winner on the day he died, when in a sensational finish to the Phoenix Stakes at Phoenix Park his Prince Poppa, a 20 to 1 chance, won by a short head from Shandon Belle and Arctic Storm, who dead heated.

August 14, 1961.

The former **King Saud of Saudi Arabia,** who died in Athens on February 23, 1969, was an unfortunate example of the son of an illustrious father succeeding to a great position which he was unfitted by character or ability to fill.

He was the second son of Ibn Saud, creator of Saudi Arabia, and was born in 1902. He grew up in the purely Beduin atmosphere of his father's entourage, where raiding and hunting were the principal occupations, where courage and endurance of hardships were the most prized virtues, and where education was confined to the precepts of the Quran and Islamic Law.

Unhappily, although he became as tall as his father, he suffered from indifferent health and weak eyesight, and these handicaps, combined with a limited intelligence, probably accounted for a diffidence of manner and judgment which he never lost. Nevertheless he was always at his father's side, both in his *diwan* or Council Chamber and in the field, and notably during the campaign of 1921, when his father by expelling the family of Ibn Rashid from their northern stronghold of Hail consolidated his hold over the whole of Nejd, and that of 1926, when Ibn Saud expelled King Husain of the Hashemites from the Hejaz and himself assumed the protection of and control over the Holy Places of Islam. At this time Ibn Saud appointed him Viceroy of Nejd, his younger brother and main rival Faisal becoming Viceroy of the Hejaz; and in 1933, Ibn Saud, having combined his dominions into the Kingdom of Saudi Arabia, nominated Saud as Crown Prince and Heir.

From 1950 onwards, as Ibn Saud's sight failed, Saud acted as his titular Regent, and on his death in 1953 duly acceded to the Throne with Faisal as his Crown Prince.

The state of the vast country over which he was called to rule was far from healthy. Within 20 years it had been brought from poverty to wealth by oil revenues which had by now reached $250m. per annum; but these revenues were vested in the Royal Family, and Ibn Saud, for all his shrewdness and unique authority, had made no real attempt to control how his numerous progeny disposed of them. The extravagance of the Saudi princelings had become a byword, and the former Wahhabi austerity was being forgotten, with smoking openly practised and a brisk blackmarket developing in the formerly forbidden alcohol.

OSTENTATIOUS

Saud, no better equipped administratively than his father and lacking the respect which he had inspired, was in no position to check these tendencies; indeed he contributed to their intensification by displays of personal self-indulgence and ostentation, notably in the building of palaces. Before long, reports were circulating that, incredible though it might seem, the Saudi finances were shaky.

Ibn Saud's consistent policy had been to keep on good terms with the British and the Americans and to avoid too deep an involvement in the increasingly complex politics of the Middle East. In 1955, however, Saud took so hard a line with the British over the possession of a remote oasis, Butaimi, which was claimed by both Saudi Arabia and by the British protégés, the Shaikh of Abu Dhabi and the Sultan of Muscat, that the relations between the two countries were strained almost to breaking point: and in 1956, after the Suez affair, he adopted the more extreme Egyptian line by breaking off relations altogether. Meanwhile he had in 1955 allowed himself to be drawn into a five-year mutual defence pact with Egypt and Syria, in overt opposition to the the Western-sponsored "Baghdad Pact" signed the same year, and in 1957 joined with Egypt and Syria in undertaking to pay to Jordan the same annual subsidy as she had forfeited by denouncing the Anglo-Jordan Treaty of Alliance—and, alone of the three guarantors, actually paid one instalment. By now, however, he had become suspicious and resentful of the arrogance and pretensions of President Nasser of Egypt, so that in 1958 he refused an invitation for Saudi Arabia to join Nasser's "United Arab Republic" formed by the union of Egypt and Syria; and an allegation that he had at this point paid $2m. by cheque to bring about a military revolt in Syria and the assassination of Nasser, though denied by all the parties concerned, was never formally disproved and was widely believed. As a result, Saudi Arabia became largely isolated in the Arab world, while the administration and finances were going from bad to worse.

At this juncture Saud was persuaded—presumably by his abler and more experienced brother Faisal—of the absolute necessity to take positive action in both the internal and the external fields. Accordingly he promulgated a decree which in effect handed over legislative and financial control to a Council of Ministers, which his father had established in 1953 but the functions of which had hitherto been ill-defined so that it had never operated effectively.

FULL POWERS

As Faisal was its President, this in effect meant that full powers devolved upon him. Friction between the two brothers, however, rendered Faisal's efforts to cleanse the Augean stables nugatory, and in 1960 Saud himself took over the office of Prime Minister, and formed a Cabinet composed of four Royal Princes and six commoners, which somewhat eased the restrictions which Faisal, in the interests of economy, had imposed. During this term of office Saud was prevailed upon to cancel, for political reasons, the lease of a military base at Dhahran, which his father had granted the United States Government, despite his country's dependence on American oil revenues. By 1962, however, it had become clear that the country was again sliding downhill, and an internal crisis resulted in Faisal emerging once more as the effective head of the Government. He was able to bring about a renewal of diplomatic relations with Great Britain, and to institute a series of effective reforms which both gave promise of restoring stability and consolidated his own position; and Saud, finding the role of figurehead distasteful, began to spend more and more time abroad. In March 1964 the Council of Ministers officially granted Faisal full powers in all fields, and the following November they pronounced the deposition of Saud, who accepted his dismissal and, on January 4, 1965, pledged allegiance to Faisal.

From then onwards his life was in decline. He wandered aimlessly about Europe until, late in 1966, he unexpectedly arrived in Cairo and in effect threw himself on the mercy of his former adversary President Nasser. He was received with an ostentatious display of hospitality; and it soon became clear that Nasser had perceived in him an instrument to be used in his own long-drawn-out struggle with Faisal for the leadership of the Arab world, as in April, 1967, during a visit to the Republican regime in the Yemen, and again in May through Cairo radio, Saud gave vent to venomous attacks on his brother. It was, however, generally known in the Middle East that not only his health but his mental powers were rapidly deteriorating, so that these outbursts caused little more than pitying comment.

February 24, 1969.

Vinayak Damodar Savarkar, who died in Bombay on February 26, 1966, at the age of 83, is a reminder of period of Indian politics that now seems distant and faint, the period of sporadic terrorism against the British which was largely extinguished as Gandhi's influence took hold of the independence movement. But Veer Savarkar, as he was called (Veer means hero), stood for something far more lasting; he was among the first and most influential articulators of Hindu nationalism and could be called the father of Hindu communalism as a political force. His slogan was "Hinduize all politics and militarize Hindudom".

Born in a Brahmin family in what is now Maharashtra, Savarkar is said to have sworn at the age of 12 to carry on the work of two brothers who had been hanged for killing a British official. He went to England in 1906 on a scholarship arranged by Indian revolutionaries living there (his patron was Tilak, the extremist politician), and four years later when he was still in England—he had been admitted to Gray's Inn—he was implicated in the murder of the collector of Nasik, a town near his native village. He was arrested and put on a ship for return to India but when it stopped at Marseilles he escaped through a porthole and swam ashore. He was chased, caught and taken on board, an act that caused public indignation in France and later led the French Government to demand his return. The case went to The Hague Court, which found in favour of the British Government.

Savarkar was convicted and sentenced to transportation for life on two charges, the sentences to run consecutively and thus adding up to 50 years. He was taken first to the penal colony in the Andamans but was taken back after several years to a prison in Bombay state whence he was released by the New Congress Provincial government in 1937.

Savarkar's long imprisonment had kept him, but not his ideas, out of politics. He had written two books, one an interpretation of the Indian Mutiny as *The Indian War of Independence*, a book that was banned in India until 1946;

and *Hindulya* (Hinduness), which was published in 1923. In that little book can be found the basic ideology of Hindu communalism, the other side to the coin of the Muslim League. Like Jinnah, and years before him, Savarkar asserted that the Hindus and Muslims of what was then India were two separate nations. But unlike Jinnah, Savarkar did not wish to see them separated into two states, "the motherland vivisected".

The influence of Gandhi and Nehru was so powerful for so long that "Indian nationalism" has come to mean secular nationalism, which separated religion from politics; but there was always another strain, long submerged beneath Congress dominance, in which Indian nationalism was felt and expressed as Hindu nationalism—there are signs that this strain may be in resurgence today.

During Savarkar's long imprisonment his ideas had taken on a political form and as soon as he was released he was made President of the Hindu Mahasabha, the all India Hindu communist party that had been formed in 1915. The Mahasabha, opposed with equal bitterness to the Muslim League and to the Congress Party, gained in influence in the years preceding independence (Savarkar represented it at the talks with the Cripps Mission in 1942), but there was a great public revulsion against the party and all that it stood for after the murder of Gandhi in January, 1948. Savarkar, who had resigned the presidency of the Mahasabha in 1943, was one of the eight men charged with the murder of Gandhi but he was acquitted. For years after that he was more or less forgotten or ignored, but in the past three years or so, as the Hindu communal forces have been going through a process of what might be called respectabilization, he was sometimes remembered and this weekened his death has been widely noted in India.

February 28, 1966.

Lord Scarbrough, K.G., P.C., G.C.S.I., G.C.I.E., G.C.V.O., former Grand Master of English Freemasonry, who after considerable experience in Parliament was Governor of Bombay in the anxious years of attempted appeasement of Germany and the greater part of the world war which followed, died on June 29, 1969. He was 72.

As Lord Chamberlain, he was in the public eye as stage censor. During the first few years of office his blue pencil was often in use with plays dealing with homosexuality. But in 1958 he ended the ban on such plays provided they were "sincere and serious". Theatre managers also found that fewer swear words were being cut, and outspoken remarks which would previously have been banned were getting through. But he still maintained a tight grip over plays dealing with sexual deviations.

In 1966, he was made a member of the Joint Committee on Theatre Censorship, which was to report to the Government on whether the censorship exercised by the Lord Chamberlain should be abolished.

Sir Lawrence Roger Lumley, eleventh Earl of Scarbrough, Viscount and Baron Lumley, of Lumley Castle, co. Durham, in the peerage of England, Viscount Lumley, of Waterford, in the peerage of Ireland, was born on July 27, 1896, being the second and only surviving son of Brigadier-General the Hon. Osbert Lumley and a grandson of the ninth earl.

He was educated at Eton, the R.M.C. Sandhurst and Magdalen College, Oxford.

SERVED WITH HUSSARS

In 1916 he interrupted his studies to serve on the Western Front with the 11th Hussars, and 20 years later he wrote the history of that famous regiment. He was wounded in the fierce German drive of March, 1918. He returned to Magdalen and duly graduated.

In 1922, soon after graduation, Lumley contested and won for the Conservatives the Hull East division and he kept the seat until the landslide which overwhelmed his party in 1929. Two years later he reentered the House of Commons as member for York, his native city, which he represented until he went out to Bombay in 1937. He had little chance of prominence in debate, as he soon joined the silent, watchful ranks of parliamentary private secretaries. In this honorary capacity he served a succession of Ministers, all of them close personal friends—Major Sir Archibald Boyd-Carpenter at the Labour Office; Mr. Ormsby-Gore (later Lord Harlech) at the Colonial Office; Sir Austen Chamberlain when Foreign Secretary; Mr. Walter Elliot when he was Financial Secretary to the Treasury; Sir John Gilmour at the Home Office and finally Mr. Eden again at the Foreign Office. He accompanied the last-named chief on some of his official visits abroad, and also travelled independently.

In August, 1942, the Congress High Command announced their intention of proclaiming non-violent non-cooperation unless independence was granted immediately. The Viceroy and his advisers reached the conclusion that the Congress leaders were planning revolutionary sabotage of the war effort and decided to prevent this action by arresting Congress leaders throughout India. The All-India Congress committee were in the Bombay presidency and it fell to Lumley to order the arrest of Gandhi and the other leaders.

It was largely due to the Governor's initiative and the warm personal regard in which he was held that, despite Congress opposition, the contribution of the province to the war effort, both in recruitment of the services and voluntary help in war charities and the provision of comforts for the troops, was so considerable.

In all these efforts he was zealously assisted by Lady Lumley, whom he married in 1922—Katharine Isobel, daughter of the late Robert Finnie McEwen. Lady Lumley's rest-houses and canteens for the troops, Indian and British, were known throughout India; and her activities included the furtherance of the curative work of hospitals, and convalescent depots and the care of nurses and women workers.

Lumley had been home from his governorship rather less than two years when he succeeded his uncle, the tenth Earl of Scarbrough, in a peerage going back to the seventeenth century. He had rejoined the Yorkshire Dragoons, which he first entered in 1921, and he rose to be acting major-general. For two months in 1945 he had a taste of ministerial office, as Under-Secretary of State for India and Burma in Churchill's Caretaker Government.

In February of that year Eden, the Foreign Secretary, selected Scarbrough to preside over an inter-departmental commission to examine the facilities available in this country for the study of the languages, histories and cultures of oriental, Slavonic, East European and African lands. This was no light task seeing that these countries contain seven-eighths of the population of the globe. The report, published at the close of the following year, showed the marked inadequacy of provision for such studies in view of British responsibilities and interests in the international field. Not only were the recommendations accepted: they were acted upon.

Scarbrough was Lord Chamberlain of the Household (1952–63); and a permanent lord-in-waiting from 1963.

In 1948 Scarbrough became Lord Lieutenant of the West Riding of Yorkshire and custos rotulorum, and in the same year was made a Knight of the Garter. He was an honorary D.C.L. of Durham university; in 1958 he became chancellor of the university.

A life-long freemason, he was for some years deputy Grand Master of the United Grand Lodge of Freemasons in England. In 1951 he became Grand Master of English Freemasonry; and in 1967 pro Grand Master. His installation at the Albert Hall in 1951 was attended by several thousand freemasons from almost every one of the 6,000 lodges in England and Wales, and also deputations from the Grand Lodges of Scotland and Ireland and of 25 Grand Lodges overseas.

Lord Scarbrough is succeeded by his only son, Viscount Lumley.

June 30, 1969.

Dr. Hjalmar Schacht, who died on June 4, 1970, at the age of 93, was one of the outstanding men of his generation in Europe.

The services which, as president of the Reichsbank, he rendered to Germany after the First World War, by helping to conjure monetary order out of chaos, deservedly gave him an international reputation. After the advent of Hitler in 1933 he accomplished a similar feat, almost single-handed, in the realm of national finance. Whatever may have been the indirect consequences or the ultimate outcome of these achievements, only a man of exceptional ability and force of character could have played such a decisive part in times of financial trouble and political upheaval.

Horace Greeley Hjalmar Schacht was born in 1877, on the borders of Denmark, the son of a naturalized American who had lately returned to Germany after marrying into the old Hamburg family of Eggers. He thus inherited a western outlook which he was to retain for the rest of his life. He owed his first two Christian names to his father's veneration for the

American Democrat and publicist who is credited with the advice: "Go west, young man..." After following his father into journalism, the young Schacht besides attending several universities and taking his doctor's degree, was at pains to perfect his English and French by visits to London and Paris, before joining the Dresdner Bank at the age of 26. He rose by rapid promotion to an executive position in the amalgamated Danat Bank and was selected, soon after the outbreak of war in 1914, to be one of the banking administrators in occupied Belgium. From then onwards he became a leading figure in national and international finance.

In the desperate days of 1923, when Germany was struggling against the collapse of her currency, he was appointed Reich Currency Commissioner, and in December of that year president of the Reichsbank. It was said that he could have become Finance Minister if he had wished. As Currency Commissioner and Reichsbank president he shared with the Finance Minister, Dr. Luther, the credit for the stabilization of the German Mark, and he worked harmoniously under the Dawes Plan with Mr. Parker Gilbert, the American Agent General for Reparations in Berlin. By 1928 his financial reputation stood very high and his re-election as president of the Reichsbank followed as a matter of course. But a break came in 1929, when he was Germany's chief representative on the Young Committee on German Reparations in Paris. He signed the Young Plan reluctantly, but never approved of it, and shortly afterwards resigned.

He had already engaged in some severe criticism of the financial and economic policies of the German Government. Among other things he had alleged that the Young Plan was "falsified" after he had signed it and had accused the Government of rashness and irresponsibility in their budget policy. After his departure from the Reichsbank he was outspoken. As a free-lance banker, publicist, and to all appearances an aspiring politician, he poured scorn in lectures abroad and in platform speeches and newspaper articles at home on the economics of the German Democratic regime.

LECTURE CAMPAIGN

A long lecture tour in the United States formed part of this campaign. How far his political ambitions went it is hard to say, but his aggressive campaign was not unnaturally welcome to the Nationalists, with whom he had become in some ways closely associated. He took part in the "Nationalist Opposition Front" demonstration at Harzburg in 1931 and attacked the Government strongly in a speech on that occasion. In private he told people on many occasions that he thought the parliamentary regime was doomed

At any rate he became *persona grata* not only with the right-wing Nationalists but to a large extent with the Nazis themselves, and in 1933, when the Nationalist hold on the Government had strengthened and the Nazis were on the verge of their complete triumph, he was brought back to be president of the Reichsbank once again. There then began the six years of his work as the principal director of the economy of Hitler's Germany. By a whole series of special devices, many of which were looked at askance by orthodox international financial opinion, he succeeded in financing a vast programme of rearmament and public works and in providing work and wages for a huge army of unemployed. Few people thought in advance that this would have been possible without external insolvency and peril to the German currency. That he succeeded was not unnaturally everywhere regarded as a masterpiece of financial ingenuity, to which the word "wizardry" was not infrequently applied, but it did not come altogether as a surprise to those who, from his work in the 1920s, had taken the full measure of his brilliant and imaginative financial brain.

His policy during that period became associated with a system of bilateral trade applied through able diplomatic negotiators to a series of smaller countries which could not afford to neglect their commercial and political relations with Germany. The net result of the system generally was that these countries found themselves unwilling creditors of Germany in terms of specified goods which proved not to be available without considerable delays. This led to the system being impugned as amounting to something very like sharp practice backed by *force majeure*. Technical objections, arguable but basically sound, were voiced by economists, and political objections were silently charged up against Dr. Schacht, who was not averse from being regarded as only begetter of the system. He was not at a loss for a reasoned reply and, in effect, pleaded guilty to having rendered a signal service to his country by means which foreign critics and rivals had not been clever enough to think of. But this attitude did not stand him in good stead at Nuremberg.

TRIED FOR HIS LIFE

He was arrested and imprisoned at the end of the war and was in due course put on trial for his life along with Goering and other Nazi leaders. The gravamen of the charge against him was that by his financial and economic work he had made possible Hitler's vast rearmament and had been aware of the sort of purpose to which it was likely to be put. It was imputed that his resignation in 1939 was a matter of personal pride and did not reflect any real disagreement over the policy of the regime. But Schacht never had a moment's doubt that he would be acquitted and the court duly acquitted him—with the essential implication that nothing had really been proved against him except his success and skill as a financial and economic administrator. It was accepted that he had not been privy to Germany's aggressive intentions and that he had, in fact, argued strongly against the extent of German rearmament expenditure in the later 1930s.

Moral judgment must work on its own standards. Like some other patriotic Germans, he no doubt hoped originally that a Nationalist-Nazi coalition would merely be Nationalist in a civilized if somewhat authoritarian way. But, as time went on, a man as perspicacious as he can hardly have mistaken the real nature of the movement he was serving.

His relations with the Nazi party were, inevitably, both delicate and dangerous. Membership was foisted upon him, after repeated refusals, and could never be more than a label to a man of his fundamentally liberal outlook. He took the Jews in the Reichsbank under his personal protection, and in 1937 he dispatched Dr. Gördeler with a message to friends in the City of London to the effect that, with moral support, the Hitler regime could be upset. He was not in any sense a trimmer, but he was most emphatically a German patriot. He liked to think of himself as a man of strict and unbending principle, but he would not have denied that he was always ambitious, and those who had occasion to negotiate with him knew that he was also a casuist of no mean order.

He was later forced to submit himself several times to the courts of his own country, but the results were the same. What could not be rectified was that he had spent some two years in prison and been deprived of almost everything he possessed. With characteristic courage—expressed with characteristically sardonic impudence in the title of his autobiography: *My First Seventy-six Years*—he decided to make a fresh start. He founded his own bank, under his own name, at Düsseldorf and by way of bread and butter business, seized a number of opportunities to exploit his reputation for financial wizardry by acting as special consultant to Persia, Syria, Egypt and Indonesia successively.

June 5, 1970.

Dr. Adolf Schärf, President of Austria, died in Vienna on February 28, 1965, at the age of 74. A moderate and able politician whose whole life had been intricately linked with Austria's socialist movement, he was a firm supporter of the country's post-war coalition system. Whether as the socialist Vice-Chancellor or later as President of the Republic, the office he had occupied since 1957, he worked for the continuation of this political partnership.

More recently, when growing disagreements between the two major parties were threatening to break up the coalition he used the authority of his office to act as mediator. A slightly built, unobtrusive man, his personal charm and graceful manners belonged more to the nineteenth-century world of Viennese waltzes and the old empire but his political ideas and his political activity were very much concerned with the twentieth century.

Born in Nikolsburg, now Mikulov, in Monvia, on April 20, 1890, the son of a Viennese glass-blower, Schärf began his political activity as a young university student in Vienna where he founded the first socialist youth association. Thus Vienna and the socialist movement became intricately linked with his entire life and even during the troubled years when socialists were being persecuted and the party banned he continued his political activities as a lawyer and underground worker. In 1933 he was elected to the Federal Council of the first republic but the following year after the February clashes he was arrested together with many of his socialist friends and associates. Political persecution did not discourage him from continuing and he took up his law practice in order to defend his socialist friends.

Having spent some time in Hitler's concentration camps Schärf resumed his political life after the war and took part in the rebuilding of Austria's shattered parliamentary system.

As the first socialist Vice-Chancellor in the post-war coalition government he used all his authority to restore confidence between right and left. Throughout 12 years as Vice-Chancellor he remained one of the most ardent supporters of the coalition. Even after the Austrian State Treaty was signed and Austrian parliamentary democracy was no longer threatened by communists, Schärf continued to support the coalition despite growing opposition from both sides and despite opinions that the coalition, as a marriage of convenience, should come to an end.

As chairman of the Socialist Party until he resigned to become President of the Republic in 1957 Dr. Schärf had also been his party's chief ideologist and he has left numerous books on Austrian politics and socialism, the best-known being *Between Democracy and People's Democracy*.

In May of 1957 he was for the first time elected President of the Republic and he was returned to the office in the elections that took place in 1963 with an even larger majority: out of a total of some 4,500,000 electors, more than 55 per cent voted for Schärf.

He married in 1915 Hilde Hammer, who died in 1956 at the age of 72.

March 1, 1965.

Joseph Schenck, who died at Beverly Hills, California, on October 22, 1961, at the age of 78, was one of the great founding fathers of the American motion picture industry.

He was born in Russia on December 25, 1882, and emigrated to New York with his family at the age of 10. After a brief flirtation with pharmacy (he began as an errand boy and worked his way up to owning, with his brother Nicholas, two drug stores) he made his way into the cinema by the classic route of fairground showmanship; in 1908 he and his brother built an amusement park, Paradise Park, near New York, and four years later they expanded, transferring their activities to Palisades Park, Fort Lee, New Jersey, where for the first time they entered into business partnership with Marcus Loew. This association of the Schencks and Loews was to bear important fruit subsequently when the partnership developed into Loew's Consolidated Enterprises (one of the enterprises being the ownership of cinemas) and later still into the vast and powerful Loew's Incorporated, controller of M.G.M. and until the branches were legally separated, of chains of cinemas and many other associated enterprises.

Long before most of this had happened, however, Joseph Schenck left the company to found his own independent film production group, though the ties of friendship and business interest between him and his brother Nicholas, who stayed on with Loew's, remained close. Among the stars brought to prominence by Joseph Schenck's company or later employed by him were Fatty Arbuckle, Norma and Constance Talmadge, and Buster Keaton (at that time Schenck's brother-in-law), and by 1924 Schenck was prominent enough to be offered the chairmanship of the newly formed United Artists Corporation; after bringing his experience of the exhibition side of the film industry to bear on the formation of a corresponding chain of cinemas for the company he became its president in 1927.

In 1933 he left United Artists and with finance from his brother became one of the three founders and first president of the new Twentieth Century film-production company, which two years later, after an amalgamation, became Twentieth Century-Fox. He was chairman of the company from 1935 to 1941, when he and his brother were accused of bribing racketeers in the stagehands' unions to keep their respective companies, Twentieth Century-Fox and Loew's, in active film production and their affiliated cinemas running in spite of threatened strikes. Joseph Schenck was actually sentenced to a year's imprisonment for his part in the affair, but because of the aid he gave the Government in prosecuting the racketeers was paroled after four months and later pardoned.

In 1943 he returned to Fox as executive head of production, and remained in that position for 10 years, only resigning in 1953 to join Mike Todd in the organization of the Magna Corporation to promote developments in widescreen film processes—developments which ultimately produced Cinestage and Todd-AO. At the same time he returned to United Artists, but this time solely on the exhibition side, as chairman of the board of United Artists Theatres.

October 24, 1961.

Dr. Bela Schick, who developed a test for diphtheria, died in New York on December 6, 1967, at the age of 90.

He was taken ill with pleurisy in November while on a South American cruise with his wife. He was taken off the ship to a Rio de Janeiro hospital and reached New York on November 30.

Schick made a major contribution to twentieth-century medicine when, as a pediatric researcher in Vienna before the First World War, he announced his diphtheria test. Remarkably accurate and simple, the test determined whether a person was vulnerable to the disease.

Born at Boglár, Hungary, on July 16, 1877, he was for a short time a staff member of the clinic of internal medicine and the clinic for children's diseases at Graz in Austria and then served under Escherich and von Pirquet at the clinic for children's diseases in Vienna where in 1918 he was appointed professor of pediatrics.

Schick discovered that those immune to diphtheria could be detected by their skin reaction to injections into the skin of small amounts of diphtheria toxin, the so-called Schick test.

Schick made fundamental contributions in the field of allergy, a word he coined with Dr. Clemens von Pirquet. He also studied complications following scarlet fever, infantile tuberculosis, the metabolism of infectious diseases and nutrition of the newborn.

Much of his work was accomplished in New York, where he was chief pediatrician of Mount Sinai Hospital from 1923 to 1942. After his retirement at the age of 65 he was pediatric director at Beth-el Hospital in Brooklyn, consultant at Mount Sinai and a teacher in the Bela Schick Department of Pediatrics at the Albert Einstein College of Medicine in the Bronx.

December 8, 1967.

Dr. Paul Schmidt, former chief interpreter for Adolf Hitler, died in Munich on April 21, 1970, at the age of 70.

Known, to his chagrin, throughout the diplomatic world of Europe and America as "Hitler's Interpreter", Schmidt was in fact a remarkable example of a way of doing business older and subtler than the Nazi methods. His later celebrity, enhanced by the book he wrote about his experiences (*Statist auf diplomatischer Buehne 1949*), owed not a little to the astonishing contrast between on the one hand the Adolf Hitler of the mass rally and the wireless oration, and on the other the quiet-spoken, composed Herr Hitler whom foreigners met when Schmidt was present.

The calm manner of the man, his tall bulky figure, his almost Pecksniffian air and not unfriendly poker face saved not only Hitler, but also Ribbentrop and Goering, from some ugly scenes. Indeed, Schmidt liked after the war to tell those to whom he taught the art of interpreting in Munich how he had probably prevented Ribbentrop and Sir Nevile Henderson from coming to blows in 1939 by going on writing quietly while they breathed wrath at one another over his head.

It was in the days of Briand and Stresemann, Austen Chamberlain and Locarno, Ramsay MacDonald and the League, that Schmidt made his reputation and learned to be not only a translator but also an interpreter. His jump in 1923 from fourth to first German interpreter during a conference was occasioned, he used to say, by his senior bringing out most emphatically in translation a demand to discuss the departure of the French from the Ruhr. This the German representative had promised Herriot to slip in quite inconspicuously for the record. The interpreter was the victim of the ensuing newspaper furore and Schmidt was the beneficiary.

Nine years later his place at Hitler's side was ensured once he had been heard in action. Indeed, at many of the most important meetings of the 'thirties Schmidt was the only member of the Foreign Office present and therefore the only keeper of the record. Perhaps the strangest and most embarrassing moment of his career came early on the morning of September 3, 1939, when he was ordered by Ribbentrop to receive from the British Ambassador a warning that war would be declared in a few hours if German troops were not withdrawn from Poland.

Paul Schmidt, born in 1899, was the son of a Prussian railway official of the modest middle-class. He was caught briefly by the Kaiser's war and then made his mark as a student of languages. His first opportunity came when he was offered work in the office of the International News Agency.

He took a Foreign Office training course and joined the service. By 1924 he had already established a reputation, both in French and English, in spite of having never lived abroad. His part in building up confidence between Briand and Stresemann—the personal friendship on which Franco-German reconciliation was based—was considerable. In old age he would recount with tears in his eyes the warmth with which Germany was received as a member of the Council of the League of Nations in 1926. After the death of his two heroes the prospects in Europe deteriorated and Schmidt took part in the economic conferences in which statesmen vainly tried to prevent and repair the crash of 1931.

It is curious and surprising that Hitler, so distrustful and contemptuous of the old regime, should give his complete trust to this man of Geneva and disarmament and reconciliation.

LATE NAZI MEMBER

Yet not until 1943 was Schmidt obliged to join the National Socialist Party, and then only to protect him from the suspicions of Himmler's office. It fell to him to frighten his Leader in September, 1938, with Chamberlain's threat to leave Berchtesgaden on hearing (through Schmidt) that Hitler was determined to settle with the Czechs once for all and in one way or another. It was Schmidt who had, through Goering, to reassure Halifax about the impression left by Hitler in their interview. It was Schmidt again who helped to explain to a startled Mussolini on July 20, 1944, how Hitler two hours before had narrowly escaped Stauffenberg's bomb. He and the two dictators then continued their conversation at the table in the shattered headquarters.

Schmidt took very seriously the art of interpreting. He believed simultaneous translation to be wrong and misleading; he held that any statesman is entitled to make what impression he can by the tone and manner of his utterance and should not be subjected to the indignities of multi-lingual listening. He held too that it was not always wise that a personal statement should be reproduced as such. If the Fuehrer said "I demand" Schmidt thought it better that this should appear as "the Reichschancellor emphasizes"; he saw interpretation as part of the process of diplomacy when, as in his case, the same interpreter was used by both sides. Whereas we believe in the "hot line", Schmidt saw himself as a cooling tube. He regarded as quite ludicrous the use of women "with their bird-like noises" to interpret for statesmen—for businessmen, and all the other people who go to international congresses, yes, but not otherwise.

Schmidt was arrested by the Americans in 1945 but soon released on the strength of his clean record. He became an important witness at Nuremberg and did much work for the occupation authorities in inquiries and trials.

Schmidt as an old Berliner would have preferred to live in London, happy though he was in a flat overlooking the Tergernsee. He had got to know England through its language and its study became a work of devotion

In 1969 Schmidt revised his book and was the subject of a long documentary programme on the B.B.C. which showed him to be a most valuable witness of the disaster that overcame Germany between 1929 and 1945. He could say, like the Abbé Siéyès, "j'ai vécu".

April 23, 1970.

Helmut William Bruno Schroder, honorary president of Schroders Ltd. since 1966, and formerly chairman of J. Henry Schroder & Co., the merchant bankers, died on June 18, 1969.

Helmut Schroder was a deeply conscientious man, and where he saw his duty, his courage was boundless. To those who worked long and closely with him in the family firm, his greatest contribution was made in the late thirties. The standstill agreement of German debt in 1931 had a crippling effect on Schroder business; and to many in the City, the war when it came in 1939 must have looked like a knock-out blow. But Helmut Schroder fought stubbornly and mobilized all resources to continue the business. For years it was a dour struggle which might not have been won, had the head of the firm not possessed the outstanding qualities of courage and devotion to duty.

In 1926 Schroder joined the bank as a young man of 25. After Eton and Oxford, he had spent a few years abroad studying business methods and improving his languages in Hamburg. He became a partner in the family firm of J. Henry Schroder & Co.

During his first few years at Leadenhall Street, business was very brisk and profitable, and Schroder enjoyed that period of his business life immensely. Soon it was succeeded by a long stretch of difficult years. The international crisis hit Germany very hard, and a large amount of the firm's money there was tied up for nearly two decades.

The immediate pre-war years were gloomy and frustrating enough. Yet these years of difficulty brought out the fighting qualities in Schroder. During the Second World War, the firm was virtually on a "care and maintenance" basis. Schroder set about husbanding resources and asserting successful claim to the foreign assets of the firm's German debtors.

After the war, Schroder, who became senior partner, took on himself the responsibility of reviving the firm's fortunes. From the early fifties, the courage shown in facing the firm's German troubles began to see its reward. The economic miracle of post-war Germany appeared and repayments to the bank followed shortly.

He was a deeply religious man, whose strong convictions influenced his character and his life. His warm-hearted kindliness and understanding of others never failed to awaken not only his sympathy but his immediate helpful response.

He was kind, fair, with a deep sense of responsibility and integrity, excellent judgment and an ability to see points that matter clearly and simply. He possessed a most remarkable ability to select first-class men for his company both in London and in New York.

The Grosse Verdienstkreuz of the Federal Republic of Germany was given for his substantial charitable work sponsoring various German charities in Great Britain.

Schroder enjoyed shooting and fishing, and took an interest in farming and forestry. He married in 1930, Margaret, daughter of Colonel Sir Lionel Edward Hamilton Marmaduke Darell, the sixth baronet.

June 20, 1969.

Dr. Rudolf Alexander Schröder died on August 22, 1962, at the age of 84. By his death the world of letters suffered a great loss

The son of a German merchant, he was born in the old Hansa city Bremen on January 26, 1878. On the occasion of his 70th birthday in 1948 his native town made him an honorary citizen. In the same year the R.A. Schröder Society was founded. As a young student he took to graphic art and architecture, and it is perhaps not well known that he, the recreator of the German Protestant song and renowned translator of Homer, Virgil, Racine, Shakespeare, T. S. Eliot and Dutch and Flemish writers, also distinguished himself in artistic projects of interior decoration, architectural design, and plans for furnishing houses and castles. In 1913 he received the Grand Prix at Ghent.

In England, Schröder became famous as a translator of T.S.Eliot's *Murder in the Cathedral*, of Shakespeare and as the co-founder of the internationally reputed journal *Die Insel* (1899–1902), out of which Die Insel Verlag was created. Later on, with Hugo von Hofmannsthal and Rudolf Borchardt, he founded the bibliophile Bremer Presse, a rare treasure among booklovers.

Schröder, like his friend von Hofmannsthal, is one of the last strongholds of humanism in our collective age. His roots lie deep in European culture. Among his models were Sophocles, Dante, Michaelangelo, Shakespeare, and in German particularly Goethe, Schiller, Novalis, and Hölderlin. His poems *Geistliche und Weldliche Gedichte*, based on our classical and Christian heritage, bear testimony to the continuity and unity of European literature. But, at the same time, he kept in touch with contemporary movements. His literary contacts led him to France and Italy, until in 1934 he finally chose Bergen in Upper Bavaria as his tusculum for life.

When before the last war, he fell into disfavour because his religious poems revealed criticism of the Hitler regime, he had to confine his public lectures and talks to religious gatherings. His support of the Una Sancta movement reflected a cosmopolitan attitude which is above all narrowly religious or party political allegiances.

NUMEROUS HONOURS

Schröder became one of the most celebrated German authors of his age. Numerous honours were conferred upon him: the honorary degrees of the Universities of Munich, Frankfurt, Tubingen. In Hamburg he was awarded the Lessing prize and he also won the German Longfellow prize and the order of Pour le Mérite. Moreover his international reputation was marked by his election to the presidency of the German Society of the Romain Rolland Friends and of the German Shakespeare Society.

On the occasion of his 75th birthday the Suhrkamp Verlag published his Collected Works in five volumes. It is no coincidence that in the recent edition of *Die Grossen Deutschen* he chose for his essay theme the poet Friedrich Rückert with whom he had certain affinities as a poet and above all as a translator of foreign meters; but perhaps his deeper love went to Hölderlin and the last line in Hölderlin's poem "Remembrance" might well serve as an epitaph to Rudolf Alexander Schröder's own life and work: "What the poets bestow remains".

August 24, 1962.

Robert Schuman, one of the leading French political figures of the Fourth Republic and father of the so-called "Schuman Plan," the European Coal and Steel Community, precursor of the present European Economic Community, died on September 4, 1963, at his country home near Metz. He was 77.

Schuman had a spell as Prime Minister from November, 1947, until July, 1948, but his period of decisive influence came during the four and a half years he was France's Foreign Minister under 10 successive governments down to January, 1953. This was a time when the peoples of the continent of Europe, emerging from the aftermath of the Second World War, provoked by an exacerbated nationalism, were eager for political solutions offering hope of the forging of a United Europe; it was Schuman's fortune to bring forth this deep-seated longing in France in the company of his Christian Democrat colleagues, Dr. Konrad Adenauer in western Germany, and Alcide De Gasperi in Italy.

In the chronic political instability which was the hallmark of the Fourth Republic, Schuman enjoyed a period of individual stability accompanied by continuity of policy which, in retrospect, seems almost incredible. It was an extraordinary but highly important turning point in French foreign policy whose influence is still being strongly felt today. Schuman was far-sighted. He realized that Germany would sooner or later reemerge as a major European power and that there could be no peace or stability in Europe until the old enmity between France and Germany had been ended, and he tackled the problem through its economic rather than its political aspects

In May, 1950, Schuman introduced into the National Assembly his proposals for a European coal and steel pool, an association of France, west Germany, and four other European nations, in a supranational organization designed to lead ultimately to a united Europe. The organization, the ground work for which had been laid by another great champion of united Europe, Jean Monnet (subsequently to be the Community's first president), became known as the European Coal and Steel Community, and led on, through Euratom, the European atomic energy pool, to the European Common Market of today. There was widespread approval of the coal and steel pool, which was considered France's first major and imaginative initiative in foreign policy for a very long time. It was enthusiastically backed by the centre parties in the French Parliament but opposed by the two extremes, and discussions continued until the following spring. The draft treaty was signed by the six Foreign Ministers on April 18, 1951, and was ratified by the National Assembly on December 13 after a debate lasting one week.

STRASBOURG ACCLAIM

In November, 1950, Schuman, in conjunction with René Pleven, the Defence Minister, launched the proposal for an integrated European army as a means of allowing a rearmed Germany to play its part in the defence of Europe and yet of keeping German militarism under close control. At the time this plan, too, was welcomed, but hostility to it, led by the Gaullists but fed from all sides of the Assembly, became so great that when Mayer succeeded Pinay as Prime Minister in January, 1953, Schuman at last left the Foreign Ministry. He was for a time without portfolio, but became Minister of Justice in the Faure Government in 1955, shortly after the defeat of the European Defence Community proposals in the National Assembly.

When the new European Parliamentary Assembly, consultative body of the Economic Community, met at Strasbourg in March, 1958, for the first time, Schuman was elected president by popular acclamation. He relinquished that post in March, 1960, and was then made honorary president. He remained a member of the European Parliament until February, 1963, when he announced his withdrawal from its activities. His vigour had been diminished after a serious accident in January, 1961, in which, after falling in a country road near his home, he lay all night on the ground in the rain before he was found

Born on June 29, 1886, in Luxembourg, Schuman came of an old and prosperous Lorraine family and grew up in Metz, then under German rule. He studied in Luxembourg and at the universities of Bonn, Munich and Berlin, first made law his career, and was practising at the Court of Appeal at Metz when war broke out in 1914. After the war, with the restoration of Alsace-Lorraine to France, he became a P.D.P. (le Parti Démocrate Populaire) deputy in 1919 for the Moselle, which he continued to represent uninterruptedly in all general elections until 1962, when he did not stand again

In the Chamber he made finance his special subject and attracted the notice in particular of Reynaud, with whom he was soon on friendly terms. But recognition of his abilities did not come until March, 1940, when Reynaud appointed him an Under-Secretary of State charged with the welfare of the refugees from eastern France. It was while grappling with his burden of responsibility during the disastrous events of May and June that Schuman was led to make the blunder that almost proved fatal to his political career. Taking his place among those who voted full powers to Pétain, he retained his under-secretaryship in Pétain's first Cabinet and resigned only in the middle of July, after which he returned to Metz. In September he was arrested by the Germans and taken to Neustadt. He escaped in the following year, went to Lyons, and took a hand in French resistance activities, although for the most part he led a secluded existence, chiefly in monasteries, until the liberation.

Schuman had been little known to the general public in France during the years between the wars. It was only with the emergence of the Mouvement Républicain Populaire, after 1945, as one of the three main parties in the state that he came into view as a Catholic politician of progressive views and conspicuously pragmatic temper.

He was Minister of Finance under Bidault from June until December, 1946, and again under Ramadier from January until November, 1947. Allowing for the orthodoxy of his views on methods of combating inflation and his general *anti-dirigiste* bias of mind, it was the weakness and disunity of the coalition governments of the post-liberation era rather than any lack of firm purpose or administrative ability on his own part that accounted for Schuman's failure to deal effectively with the mounting problem of the franc.

That his personal qualities had impressed themselves upon the Assembly was proved, however, by the combined vote of almost all the non-communist deputies for his election as Prime Minister after the resignation of Ramadier. Again, the financial reforms he attempted to set in motion were thwarted by party divisions. But it was the general dissatisfaction felt in France over the London agreement on western Germany that finally precipitated the fall of Schuman's Government in July, 1948.

SECOND TERM

He became Foreign Minister under his successor as Prime Minister, Marie; was invited six weeks later to form a second government of his own, entered upon the task, but was defeated in the Assembly within three days. He then began his long spell at the Quai d'Orsay under Queuille.

In the orthodoxy of his approach to financial problems Schuman belonged to the conservative wing of the M.R.P., but in almost all other respects he kept to the middle of the road and showed himself a sincere believer in the necessity of compromise. A man of high principle, inspired by devout Roman Catholic sentiments, immensely conscientious and hard-working, Schuman was a curiously lonely man, frugal and indeed spartan in his daily life, whose one passion was his books. He was a fluent but rather bad speaker, and although it would be inaccurate to suggest that he was loved, he was greatly esteemed even by those who were bitterly opposed to his policies. Jacques Fauvet, in his book on the Fourth Republic, said indeed of Schuman: "A Luxembourger by birth, German by education, Roman Catholic for ever, and French at heart, he was destined to be one of the princes of Europe."

He was unmarried.

September 5, 1963.

Dr. Albert Schweitzer, O.M., died on September 5, 1965, at Lambaréné, at the age of 90.

Rarely has any man excelled in so many branches of learning and spent his days in such unselfish ministry. Eminent as a philosopher, theologian, musician, doctor, the relief of suffering was, in his own view, the main purpose of his life, and the hospital he founded and maintained for so many years on the edge of an African forest will be his chief memorial. Men may not accept his reasoning, disagree with his criticism, or challenge his exposition of Bach; but everyone can appreciate his desire to serve humanity. Great as were his achievements in other spheres, it is as a medical missionary that Dr. Schweitzer would prefer to be remembered.

Born on January 14, 1875, at Kayserberg, Upper Alsace, where his father was pastor, Albert Schweitzer was a son, grandson, and nephew of the manse. His mother, Adèle Schillinger, was a minister's daughter. He was six months old when his father was transferred to another Alsatian charge at Günsbach, where he served as vicar for nearly half a century till his death in 1925. His mother was killed accidentally in 1916. But both were spared long enough to rejoice in the successes of their brilliant son. After a year in the gymnasium at Münster Albert Schweitzer went to the High School in Mülhausen, from which he entered Strasbourg University. It is typical of him that during his year of military service he carried his Greek New Testament with him and prepared for an examination on the Synoptic Gospels. At Strasbourg he specialized in philosophy and theology and in 1898 gained a scholarship which took him to Paris for a winter, and to Berlin the following summer. In the same year he received the degree of D. Ph. for a thesis on Kant's Philosophy of Religion.

The autumn of 1899 saw him back at Strasbourg as curate at the Church of St. Nicolaus. In 1901 he published *The Problem of the Lord's Supper* and *The Secret of Jesus's Messiahship*, two brilliant analyses which contained the seeds of much of his later work in New Testament criticism. Then in 1906 came the epoch-making work *Von Reimarus zu Wrede*, published in English as *The Quest of the Historical Jesus*. In this work he effectively shattered sceptical attempts to disprove the historical existence of Jesus, by showing that he could not be explained as a personality originating in a myth arising out of later religious consciousness, but he also shattered attempts by liberal scholars to detach the historical Jesus from his eschatological setting in the New Testament presentation by showing that all such attempts could only yield an unhistorical "Jesus" dressed up in modern ethical ideas.

DEVOTION TO BACH

The argument of this book gained Schweitzer great prominence in the ranks of New Testament scholars, for it rehabilitated the historical significance of St. Mark's Gospel by proving that Jesus's involvement in late Jewish eschatology completely and firmly rooted him in the period where it placed him, and showed that Jesus's claims to authority demand not merely recognition but obedience. This was to have a decisive significance for Schweitzer's own life, for when he found he was unable, with his critical tools, to establish in *theory* connexion between this Jesus and Christology he determined to establish connexion with Jesus by *action*. Armed with the principle of "reverence for life" and "tuned in to the Spirit of Jesus", he resolved to give himself to the service of his fellows in healing and saving life.

As early as his fifth year he began to learn the piano under the care of his father. He was only nine when he was permitted to play the organ at Günsbach and occasionally to act as substitute for the regular organist. In his teens he played the organ in a performance of Brahms's *Requiem* at Mülhausen, an experience he looked back upon as one of the greatest joys of his life. Afterwards he went to Paris and studied under Widor. He specialized in Bach, of whom he wrote a critical study in French before he was 30. He rewrote and enlarged it in a German edition and further enlarged it for an English translation made by Ernest Newman in 1911. The doctrine of this book, that Bach's imagination was fundamentally pictorial, stood unchallenged for 40 years and still with some modification holds the field. His *German and French Organ Construction* (1905) is said to have saved many an old organ from the dustheap, and led to the reconsideration of the so-called baroque organ years before its vogue spread across Europe.

All this time he continued his duties at Strasbourg, ministering to his congregation and becoming Professor, afterwards Principal, of the Theological College of St. Thomas. Recognized as a scholar with a growing reputation, everything seemed to point to an increasingly brilliant career in Europe. But Schweitzer had already formed other plans. As his later autobiographical books reveal, pain to him was the great mystery. Even as a schoolboy he often wondered why he should be happy and others suffer. In his twenty-first year he decided that life must mean more than living for self. "One brilliant summer morning at Günsbach during Whitsuntide holidays (1896)" he determined to devote himself till he was 30 to science and art in order that from that time he might give himself "to the direct service of humanity".

HOSPITAL IN RUINS

In 1906, therefore, he resigned his offices at Strasbourg. At first he thought of social service among children and the poor. But one day his eye fell upon a paragraph in the magazine of the Paris Missionary Society pointing out the need for men in the Congo. At once he set about preparing for his new task by taking a course in medicine, the cost of which he defrayed from the procceds of his organ recitals, and in 1913 he graduated in medicine. His thesis was entitled "The Psychiatrical Estimate of Jesus". In it he controverted the position of those who classed Christ as a self-deluded enthusiast. He also found time to write *Paul and his Interpreters*, which he expanded 18 years afterwards.

On Good Friday, 1913, he sailed for French Equatorial Africa accompanied by his wife, Helen Bresslau, whom he married in 1912. She had already trained as a nurse. Their destination was Lambaréné in Gabon, 800 miles up the river Ogowe, where the Paris Missionary Society gave him land on which to build a hospital at his expense. Beginning in a few huts, they dealt with 2,000 cases in the first nine months. Dysentery, ulcers, sleeping sickness, leprosy were the chief diseases. For four and a half years they toiled incessantly. After his release from a short internment in France in 1917 he spent some time in Europe preparing the first two volumes of his monumental work on *The Philosophy of Civilization* outlining the stupendous scheme of the moral basis of civilization. In 1921 he wrote in German the book which in its English form, *On the Edge of the Primeval Forest*, did most to bring his name before the British public. It contains no ideal picture of the African or of the hospital; but gives a plain, often repellent view of reactions to his beneficent care, as well as some graphic descriptions of the social problems, the difficulties of administrators and the question of black and white. Christianity for the Negro, he felt, was the Light that shone amid the darkness of his fears, assuring him he was not in the power of spirits or fetishes. He calls himself "the brother but the elder brother": but the natives dubbed him "Oganga", which means fetishman.

It was 1924 before he got back to Lambaréné, this time without his wife, whose health prevented her accompanying him. He found his hospital in ruins, but this gave him the opportunity of erecting a better building on a site higher up the river, with rooms for whites as well as blacks; 1927 and 1928 saw him once more in Europe to raise more funds and to recover his own strength. He gave organ recitals in London, Birmingham, Bristol, Oxford, and Cambridge. At the end of 1928 he set out again for Lambaréné with an increased staff, and in 1931 issued *More from the Primeval Forest*. When he returned to Europe in 1932 he left behind him 10 doctors and nurses. New hospital buildings were put up and in 1933 appeared the English edition of his second autobiographical volume entitled *My Life and Thought*.

NOBEL PEACE PRIZE

Schweitzer gave the Hibbert and Gifford lectures while in Britain in 1934 and paid a brief visit to his home at Günsbach in 1939, but he sensed the imminence of war, felt that he should be at his post at Lambaréné, and returned to Africa by the same boat that had brought him to Europe, without even unpacking his luggage.

He continued to work there, without a holiday, for the next 10 years—a remarkable feat for a man of his years—and did not return to Europe until February, 1949. Schweitzer was then 74, and the hospital which he had begun so modestly 25 years before had expanded into a large establishment housed in about 50 buildings.

That same year he went to the United States to address the Goethe bicentenary festival at Aspen, Colorado, and later took part in the celebrations at Frankfurt, where he was warmly welcomed. The seal of international approval was set on Schweitzer's life and work by the honours that were bestowed on him in his last years. Together with General George Marshall he was awarded the Nobel Peace Prize for 1952 and was given an enthusiastic reception when he went to Oslo in 1954 to receive the gold medal and the diploma of the award. It was characteristic of Schweitzer that he used part of the Nobel monetary prize for reroofing the houses occupied by lepers at Lambaréné. In 1955 the Queen appointed him an honorary member of the Order of Merit and in the autumn of that year he went to Buckingham Palace to be invested by her Majesty with the insignia of the order. The same day he paid a visit to the Prime Minister at 10, Downing Street, and before he left Britain the honorary degree of Doctor of Law was conferred upon him by Cambridge University. Earlier that year he had been elected to the west German order, Pour le Mérite. In 1957 his wife died.

During his later years Schweitzer's life and work were brought to the attention of a wide public by the publication of some half-a-dozen books. Not all were favourable. In works by Gerald McKnight and others, Schweitzer has been accused of egotism and authoritarianism in his dealings with his colleagues at Lambaréné, while his hospital has been criticized for inefficiency by the standards of modern medicine.

MAN OF ACTION

With regard to the first of these accusations, it should be remembered that Schweitzer, like Livingstone, was primarily a man of action, and that without a high degree of self-reliance, strength of will and power of command, he would not even have been able to begin the task he set himself. With regard to the second, it should be stressed that when he went to the Congo he found the Africans quite unprepared to accept the conditions and discipline of the European-type hospital. He decided, therefore, to make life in the hospital as much like life in the village as was practicable. He allowed the patients to bring their families and even their pets with them, and devised a routine which was as much a lesson in communal living as a course of medical treatment. If, today, Africans are more ready to trust modern doctors and their techniques, this is partly due to the imaginative approach of Schweitzer's original experiment, to describe which as mere "paternalism" is a most misleading distortion.

These criticisms, however, are those of only a small minority. For most people Schweitzer became a twentieth-century archetypal figure of the Christian in action, and one, moreover, who was viewed sympathetically even by those who no longer professed the Christian faith. For his love of humanity, his "reverence for life", his years of self-sacrificing service and his passion for music, all represented what, for many, still seems to be most valuable in the Christian tradition. If his theology is now less revolutionary than it appeared to be 50 years ago, his achievements as scholar, musician, doctor and missionary remain a challenge to the conscience and ambition of the world.

September 6, 1965.

Lieutenant-General Sir Ronald Scobie, K.B.E., C.B., M.C., who died on February 23, 1969, at the age of 75, was commander of the Tobruk Fortress at the time of its relief in 1941, G.O.C. in Malta during the siege, and G.O.C. in Greece in the critical year after the liberation, when he played an outstanding part in saving that country from communism.

He was a first-class staff officer as well as a competent commander. As a young man he was a Rugby international, and played for Scotland against England, Ireland and Wales. He was a delightful man with a quiet, pleasant, sincere manner, and he inspired confidence and affection wherever he served. He had a special gift for getting on with foreign troops.

Ronald MacKenzie Scobie was born on June 8, 1893, the son of Mackay John Scobie and educated at Cheltenham and the R.M.A., Woolwich, from which he was commissioned in the Royal Engineers in 1914. In the 1914-18 War, in which he served with his Corps and as brigade major of an infantry brigade, he was wounded, won the M.C., was twice mentioned in dispatches and received a brevet majority.

IN THE FIELD

In 1939 he was serving in the adjutant-general's department at the War Office, and on the outbreak of war he was made deputy director of mobilization. He held this appointment until he was posted in the following year to the Middle East, where he served first as deputy adjutant-general on General Wavell's headquarters, and then as brigadier general staff in the Sudan. His first employment in the field came in October, 1941, when, a month before Sir Claude Auchinleck launched his "Crusader" offensive against Rommel, he was sent into Tobruk to take command of the 70th Division and the other troops, including the Polish Carpathian Brigade, which formed the garrison of the fortress. In the opening battle it was the task of the right wing of the 8th Army to attack the enemy investing Tobruk, and the garrison was to make a sortie. The fighting was fierce and confused, and it was not for a week that the relieving forces succeeded in making contact with Scobie's troops, and then only for a few hours before the Germans broke through the freshly opened corridor. Tobruk was again a besieged fortress, with barely 48 hours of artillery ammunition left. Scobie kept up his attacks while the battle of Sidi Rezegh raged to the south, and in another fortnight Tobruk was finally disengaged. By its vigorous action, Scobie's force had created a threat to the enemy's flank and rear, and so contributed materially to Rommel's defeat.

In 1942 he was posted to Malta to take over command of the garrison under Lord Gort. His arrival coincided with the running in of Admiral Syfret's convoy, with a loss of nine merchant ships out of 14, at a time when supplies were desperately needed to enable the island to hold out.

On the conclusion of the North African campaign Scobie returned to Cairo as chief of staff to General Sir Henry Maitland Wilson, who had been appointed C.-in-C. Middle East, and here he was concerned till the end of 1943 with the maintenance of the 8th Army, the mounting of the attack on Sicily, and the amphibious operations which were carried out against the islands in the Aegean.

KEEPING ORDER

When the Germans evacuated Greece in 1944 British troops were sent in to demobilize the guerrilla organizations and to keep order until a constitutional administration could be established. Scobie was put in command of the force, which consisted initially of a parachute brigade and an armoured brigade acting as infantry, supported by the Navy and the Air Force. The country was in a state of complete disorder, and a real danger of civil war arose when the members of the National Liberation Front resigned from the newly formed cabinet, and the guerrillas of the People's National Army of Liberation seized the port of Piraeus, and occupied most of Athens, in an endeavour to set up a communist government. The British troops were soon involved in heavy fighting and were, for a time, in danger of being overwhelmed. An additional division had already been sent in and now another was landed, with a corps commander to take over operational control under Scobie as overall commander.

After five weeks of bitter fighting a military truce was signed, order was restored, and the disarmament of the guerrillas and the creation of regular forces put in train.

It would hardly have been surprising if Scobie, as commander of a foreign force engaged in such a task as his, had become a much hated man. But the firmness, good sense, and fairness with which he carried it out were such that he not only gained the high esteem and even affection of the Greek authorities, but became extremely popular with the public.

POPULAR CRIES

They greeted him in the street, whenever he appeared, with tremendous cheering and continual cries of "Scobie, Scobie, Scobie ! " In 1945 he received the freedom of Athens and the grand medal of the municipality, and was decorated with the grand cross of George I of Greece. He remained in command until 1946 and retired from the Army the following year.

He was Lieutenant of the Tower of London from 1951 to 1954, and Colonel Commandant, R.E., from 1951 to 1958.

He married in 1927 Joan, daughter of W.H. Sidebotham, of Farnham, Surrey. They had one daughter.

February 25, 1969.

Sir Harold Scott, G.C.V.O., K.C.B., K.B.E., Commissioner of Police for the Metropolis from 1945 to 1953, died on October 19, 1969. He was 81.

Harold Richard Scott was born in Banbury in 1887, and educated at Sexey's School, Bruton, and Jesus College, Cambridge, of which he was a Scholar, and where he took three Tripos—Natural Science, History and Medieval and Modern Languages. He was elected an honorary Fellow of his college in 1950. His short autobiography *Your Obedient Servant* gives a touching and affectionate account of the efforts which his parents and the headmaster of his Grammer School made to launch a very clever boy, with no social advantages, upon a career worthy of his gifts.

He took a respectable place in the competition for the Upper Division of the Civil Service in 1910, and was assigned to the Home Office when Mr. Churchill was Home Secretary. Thirty years were to pass before Scott had his next interview with Churchill—when he was Chief Administrative Officer of London Region in 1940.

On the outbreak of war in 1914 Scott sought permission to join the Army. This was refused in accordance with the practice of the time, and before long he was transferred to the Trading with the Enemy Department which had been set up under (Sir) Harold Butler (afterwards head of the International Labour Office and himself a Home Office man). In 1916 Scott was moved to the Foreign Trade Department, and in 1918 to the Ministry of Labour to help Butler with the plans for demobilization. In 1919, at the express request of Sir Edward Troup, then the Permanent Under-Secretary of State, he returned to the Home Office. The next 12 years were spent in the Aliens Department and the Criminal Division—among the causes célèbres with which he was closely concerned were the Art O'Brien case, the Zinoviev letter, and the Arcos raid.

The year 1932 saw his appointment as chairman of the Prison Commission, in succession to Sir Alexander Maxwell. For the next six years his task, with the help of (Sir) Alexander Paterson, Dame Lilian Barker (who, under Scott, was the first woman to be appointed an Assistant Prison Commisioner) and (Sir) Lionel Fox (eventually Scott's successor as chairman), was to develop the plans and reforms which Maxwell and the same team had set on foot. It was an uneasy time, and Scott may have found his natural impatience tested by the need for going step by step. However this may be, he undoubtedly found his métier again when, in 1938, he was made Principal Officer, London Civil Defence Region and, in 1939, Chief Administrative Officer. Here he was confronted with the problem of formulating and then developing an effective A.R.P. organization for Greater London. By the time Regional Commissioners came to be appointed, Scott's immense energy and powers of quick (often violent) decision had created the organization, and almost equally important, had encouraged those personal contacts, at weekly meetings and at visits, on which the mutual confidence and trust which withstood the trials and exhaustions of the blitz was based.

On the outbreak of war Scott found himself working with two Regional Commissioners—Sir Ernest Gowers and Admiral Sir Edward Evans (Lord Mountevans)—and, in the course of time, such other diverse personalities as Captain Euan Wallace, Sir Warren Fisher, Mr. Charles Key, and (Sir) Henry Willink. Not all of these made very comfortable bedfellows and it is a great tribute to Scott's executive capacity and to his knack of handling people, that the organization which he created was kept working in the London Region with great efficiency and good temper. He had a miscellaneous and very varied team for his own staff—civil servants, local authority officers, bank clerks, people from every imaginable walk of life—but there is testimony that whether they were working at the centre or in an outstation, they were not only an effective but a happy family.

Scott returned to Whitehall in 1941 as Deputy Secretary of the Ministry of Home Security, and shortly afterwards became Secretary in succession to Sir George Gater.

In 1943, to the surprise of Whitehall, he was selected to succeed another rather unorthodox civil servant, Sir Archibald Rowlands (on his appointment as Finance Member of the Council of India) as Secretary of the Ministry of Aircraft Production. There, by all accounts, he worked with industrialists and trade unionists as readily and as successfully as he had worked with public servants and members of local authorities. But the greatest surprise of his career came in 1945 when Lord Morrison of Lambeth, then Home Secretary, invited Scott to be the Commissioner of Police of the Metropolis. Not within living memory had a civilian with no direct police experience been appointed to the most important police post in Britain.

Lord Morrison must have considered that the problems of the post-war London would call for unusual qualities, and that they would best be found in an outstanding civilian administrator with long experience, from the other side of Whitehall, of one of the end-products of police work, namely the convicted criminal. Whatever doubts may have been expressed at Scott's appointment, there was no doubt at all, when after the Coronation he retired, that it had been fully successful. He himself clearly enjoyed his time as Commissioner and in retirement wrote a useful book on *Scotland Yard* which had much popular success.

Scott used to say of himself that he was slapdash and unorthodox. There may have been a note of complacency in this but it was not inconsistent with his belief that a good decision quickly and vigorously followed up is better than the ideal decision long delayed. Throughout his official life he did what he could to discourage the clichés of officialdom and to insist on clear, precise and terse English. He was never a man for wasting time on paper. His arguments for and against were marshalled concisely and the action to be taken clearly indicated.

He married in 1916 Ethel Golledge and they had a son and two daughters.

October 20, 1969.

Stewart Scott Hall, C.B., who died in Melbourne on August 4, 1961, was head of the United Kingdom Defence Research and Supply Staff in Australia, and scientific adviser to the High Commissioner. His death at the age of 56 has robbed the aviation world of a personality well known and well liked on both sides of the Atlantic, and more recently in Australia.

Born in March, 1905, Stewart Scott Hall was educated at Eastbourne College and the Imperial College of Science and Technology, where he was Busk Memorial Scholar for 1925-26. In 1927 he started a long career as a professional civil servant, joining the Aerodynamics Department of the Royal Aircraft Establishment, Farnborough, as a Junior Scientific Officer. The hazards of experimental flying were soon brought home to him forcibly when a curious experimental aircraft in which he was taking observations got out of control, and he and his pilot had to take to their parachutes.

In 1929 Scott Hall moved to the Aeroplane and Armament Experimental Establishment at Martlesham Heath, staying there until 1933 and publishing a book, written in conjunction with Squadron Leader T.H. England, on Aircraft Performance Testing. From 1933 to 1937 he was the Air Ministry's Resident Technical Officer at Vickers-Supermarine Ltd., and saw the initiation of the Spitfire.

From 1937 to 1939 Scott Hall was in charge of the Air Ministry Ballistics Laboratory at Orford Ness, and after a brief spell as Technical Assistant to the Director-General of Aircraft Production at the Ministry of Aircraft Production he returned to the R.A.E. Farnborough in 1941 as Head of the Armament Department.

SPECTACULAR RISE

His next post, in 1944, was at the A. and A.E.E. again, now at Boscombe Down, as Superintendent of Performance Testing, and in 1946 he had a rapid and spectacular promotion to become the Principal Director (later Director General) of Technical Development (Air) at the Ministry of Supply, a post which he filled with distinction for some seven years. In 1950 he was made C.B.

In 1953 Scott Hall was appointed Head of the Ministry of Supply Staff at the British Joint Services Mission in Washington, where he did much to help Anglo-American Liaison. While there he was elected a Fellow of the Institute of Aeronautical Sciences of the United States. He returned to England in 1956 to become Scientific Adviser to the Air Ministry, and in 1959 he was sent to Australia to take up the post which he held up to his death.

Aviation was Scott Hall's primary interest throughout his life, and he showed a zest and enthusiasm for all its aspects which few have equalled. He learnt to fly in the late 1920s, became a Fellow of the Royal Aeronautical Society, which he had joined as a student in 1922, and served on its council. He was an active member of the Royal Aero Club for many years and chairman of its Records and Racing Committee in 1957–59. He was a Founder Member of the British Gliding Association. He was a familiar figure at aviation gatherings of all kinds, from race meetings to scientific symposia, and his frequent contributions at conferences were always pertinent and were put forward with clarity and conviction.

In his work, his approach to a problem was direct and vigorous, and in argument he was effective and convincing. He had a pleasant and friendly manner but did not suffer fools gladly and had no time for petty bureaucracy. Sometimes small matters seemed to worry him unduly, but on the larger issues his judgment was usually sound. He had a strong sense of personal dignity and of the status of the professional civil servant. Outside aviation, Scott Hall's interests ranged from sailing to entomology.

He was building up a high reputation in Australia, where he had hoped to settle on his retirement, when in 1960 he had a serious illness involving a long period in hospital. He recovered well from this and returned to his post towards the end of the year. Then, late in June, he had a recurrence of his illness from which he never recovered.

He married in 1940 Margaretta, daughter of Captain J. C. Watson, R.N. (retired), who survives him.

August 7, 1961.

Natalya Ivanovna Sedova, widow of Leon Trotsky, who died on January 23, 1962 was born in 1881 on the farm of a Ukrainian Cossack family which was a mixture of Ukrainian Cossacks and the Polish small gentry.

She lost her parents early in childhood and was brought up by a relative. Many of the family had been involved in the Russian revolutionary movement as members of populist circles, suffragettes in the 1880s, and there were always some members leaving for exile in Siberia and some coming back from it. In a girls' high school at Kharkov she herself was already active in a clandestine political organization and staged a political demonstration in the classroom. She then studied at the universities of Geneva and Paris first botany and then literature. In Geneva she joined the social democratic group of which the famous Plekhanov was the centre. In 1903 she met Leon Bronstein (as he was still called) in Paris. He had just assumed the pen name Trotsky when he joined the editorial staff of Lenin's and Plekhanov's *Iskra* and he was rapidly gaining fame as publicist, literary critic and speaker. He had already been married but his first marriage was dissolved and Natalya Sedova became his second wife.

SECRET MISSIONS

She exercised a considerable influence on him, as he himself testified in his autobiography, especially by getting him interested in the arts, and turned his attention to modernistic trends in painting and sculpture. But she went on doing her revolutionary work and several times she went on secret missions to Russia smuggling revolutionary literature and taking up contacts with clandestine party organizations.

The revolutionary year of 1905 brought her and her husband back to Russia but after the ebb of the revolution they went back into exile and settled for seven years in Vienna. They were expelled from Austria at the outbreak of the First World War, went to Switzerland and then to Paris, from were they were expelled in 1916 for anti-war activities. They found themselves in the United States but no sooner had they settled a little in New York than the Russian February Revolution broke out and they returned with their two children, Leon and Sergei, to Petrograd.

During the stormy months that followed, while her husband joined Lenin and prepared the October insurrection, Natalya was a propagandist and educational officer in the trade unions in the Russian capital. After the October Revolution she was appointed head of the arts department in the first Soviet Commissariat of Education under Lunacharsky. In this office she displayed her avant garde taste in the arts at a time when Russian painting was teeming with the "isms" that were to be suppressed later: constructivism, suprematism, formalism, futurism, &c.

The family now lived in the Kremlin, sharing a bathroom and a dining room with Lenin and his wife. These were the happiest years in the life of the Trotskys. Then came the grim period of her husband's struggle with Stalin after which she went with him into exile, first to Alma Ata on the Russo-Chinese border, then to the Prinkipo island, then to France and to Norway. In Norway she and her husband were, at the demand of the Soviet Government, interned by the Norwegian socialist Government at the time of the first great purge trial in Moscow, the trial of Zinoviev and Kamenev in the summer of 1936.

BRAVERY AND FORTITUDE

These were exasperating months during which they could not answer the charges levelled against them from Moscow. Eventually they left for Mexico. The nightmare of the great purges was made for Natalya even more terrible by the imprisonment of her younger son in Russia and the death of her older son in mysterious circumstances in Paris. In this most depressing time of her life she behaved with extraordinary bravery and fortitude and when her husband's truly titanic will power sometimes seemed to flag it was she who raised him back to his feet, as his British biographer gathered from their unpublished intimate correspondence. In 1940 during one of several attempts on Trotsky's life, when a gang of armed men broke into their house in Coyoacana, a suburb of Mexico City, and machine-gunned them, Trotsky escaped death only because she, with great presence of mind, removed him from the attackers' view and covered him with her own body. But it was not for long that she saved his life. A few months later on August 20, 1940, he was assassinated.

In the 21 years by which she survived her husband she guarded his memory and waited for history to do him justice. She lived to see the eviction of Stalin's body from the mausoleum in Moscow and she made two open appeals to Khrushchev urging him to explain what had happened to her son Sergei, of whom she had heard nothing since 1936, and demanding also a full and unequivocal rehabilitation of Trotsky and his comrades. To her appeals there was no answer from Khrushchev. Natalya Ivanovna was undoubtedly a very observed and gifted writer—some of the most vivid paragraphs in Trotsky's autobiography are those which he quotes from his wife's diary. She has left behind a beautiful and moving description of her husband's last days. But she wrote little for she put herself completely in her husband's shadow and devoted all her energy to helping him in his work while he was alive and guarding his memory after his death.

January 24, 1962.

Sir Walford Selby, K.C.M.G., C.B., C.V.O., formerly Ambassador at Lisbon and Minister in Vienna, died on August 7, 1965, at Salisbury, Southern Rhodesia, at the age of 84.

Very much a diplomatist of the old school, and always highly respected within the Foreign Service, it was only at the end of his career that he held wider public attention. This delayed recognition was largely caused by the circumstances of his career: he was never at any great mission at a time of crisis, and as private secretary to several Foreign Secretaries he obviously had to remain in the background. The publication of his memoirs, *Diplomatic Twilight 1930–1940*, in 1953, however, not only caused something of a furore but also created immediate respect for the pungency of his views and the rigour of his analysis. He was opposed both to the policies of appeasement and, perhaps even more strongly, to the methods of diplomacy which had brought them about. He believed that diplomacy should be left to diplomatists, that just as much as economics the art of diplomacy has its rules and precepts which are broken at peril. Consequently, he argued that the weakening of the authority of the Foreign Office between the wars through the activities of Sir Warren Fisher as head of the Civil Service was a major error.

Walford Harmood Montague Selby was born in 1881, son of Charles Edward M. Selby of Brighton. He was educated at Charterhouse and Christ Church, Oxford, where he was a contemporary of two future Secretaries of State for Foreign Affairs, Lord Halifax and Sir Samuel Hoare. In 1904 he entered the Diplomatic Service as an attaché, but transferred shortly afterwards to the Foreign Office as a clerk. In 1906 he exchanged temporarily into the Diplomatic Service and served as an acting third secretary at Berlin and then at The Hague in 1907.

Returning to the Foreign Office in 1908 he was appointed to be secretary to the Government Hospitality Fund. At the Coronation of King George V he occupied the important post of secretary to the Coronation Committee, a body presided over by the Earl Marshal and comprising representatives of all Government departments.

In 1911 he became assistant private secretary to Sir Edward Grey and in 1915 private secretary to Lord Robert Cecil, who became Parliamentary Under-Secretary of State and

Minister of Blockade. Selby's ambition was to get away from the Foreign Office and join the Army, but he found the Foreign Office very loath to allow this. They had no wish to let their trained diplomatists go. However, at last he obtained permission and joined the Grenadier Guards in August, 1918, but his service was of short duration, for directly the armistice was concluded the Foreign Office reclaimed him.

During his short absence on military service he had been promoted to be an assistant clerk and a year later became First Secretary and Head of the Chancery at Cairo. Here he remained for a couple of years, gaining an allowance for knowledge of Arabic. He returned to the office in 1922 and two years later began his long career as principal private secretary to the Secretary of State. The Labour Government came into power in January, 1924. Ramsay MacDonald became Foreign Secretary as well as Prime Minister, and he selected Selby to be his private secretary. Altogether he served in this capacity four Foreign Secretaries besides MacDonald—Sir Austen Chamberlain, Arthur Henderson, Lord Reading and Lord Simon.

Selby was an excellent linguist, and there is no doubt that he well deserved the confidence placed in him by so many Ministers. He was offered, but declined, the post of Under-Secretary of State, preferring to take an appointment abroad. He had been made a C.V.O. in 1924, a C.B. in 1926 and a K.C.M.G. in 1931.

In 1933 he succeeded Sir Eric Phipps as Minister at Vienna. In 1933 it was one of the most important posts of observation in Europe and Selby made good use of his opportunities, supplying valuable information to his Government, especially in regard to German action, which entirely supported the reports of Sir Eric Phipps in Berlin. In 1937 there occurred the abdication of King Edward VIII, who went to Vienna as Duke of Windsor and remained there until his marriage. He was frequently at the legation and the Selbys attended the wedding in France.

Shortly after this event Selby was promoted to be Ambassador at Lisbon, not without regret on his own part, and that of the Austrians, for the Selbys were very popular in Vienna. Schuschnigg, who was then Chancellor, and a large crowd of both officials and non-officials saw them off.

During his first two years in his new post no events of major importance occurred, but with the outbreak of war in 1939 Lisbon became one of the most important posts in Europe. Selby's period of appointment terminated in 1940.

Selby married in 1914 Dorothy, daughter of William Orme Carter of Hurst Green, Sussex. There were two sons and one daughter of the marriage.

August 9, 1965.

David O. Selznick, who died in Hollywood on June 22, 1965, will no doubt be best remembered as the producer of *Gone with the Wind*, but his career as a film producer spanned nearly 30 years, and included in particular a number of the most notable Hollywood films of the 1930s.

He was born in Pittsburgh on May 10, 1902, in a family of Ukrainian extraction. His father was a businessman who had drifted into the cinema as a financier and made a lot of money from producing and distributing films with Clara Kimball Young, the Talmadge sisters and other early stars. David O. Selznick (the "O" was added to give the name distinction) began in his father's business in his teens, and had a firm grounding in film commerce before his father's company was overtaken by financial ruin. In 1923 he produced his own first film, a short about Jack Dempsey, and after various jobs in film he entered M.G.M. as a reader, graduated to associate producer on some small-budget westerns, moved on to Paramount, and became a fully fledged producer by the time he was 28.

At this time he married Irene Mayer, daughter of Louis B. Mayer, a connection promising nepotism which in fact did more to hinder than help his career, since his father-in-law initially did all he could to prevent Selznick achieving his ambition of an independent production unit. However, he was taken on by R.K.O. as executive producer on an ambitious series of films, the most familiar of which are *A Bill of Divorcement* and *King Kong*. His record, in fact, was so remarkable that Louis B. Mayer finally relented and offered him a job at M.G.M., where his first production was *Dinner at Eight* (1933), an all-star film which used most of the company's top performers and made the biggest profit, relative to its cost, of any film up to then in the company's history. He followed this with, among others, *Viva Villa, David Copperfield*, the Garbo *Anna Karenina*, and *A Tale of Two Cities*.

In 1935, feeling that he required more independence to produce his own films in his own way than even his position at M.G.M. could offer, he formed his own company, Selznick-International, and produced for it such films as *Little Lord Fauntleroy, The Garden of Allah*, the Janet Gaynor version of *A Star is Born, Nothing Sacred* and *The Adventures of Tom Sawyer,* as well as Ingrid Bergman's first American film, *Intermezzo*.

GONE WITH THE WIND

But by far the biggest and most famous of his films at this time was *Gone with the Wind*. He bought film rights of the book in 1936, for a record sum, and spent much of the next three years setting the film up, supervising casting and scripting, and then working closely with the three directors during the shooting. The film, in fact, marked the climax of his career as a producer, along with *Rebecca*, Hitchcock's first Hollywood film, on which he began work before *Gone with the Wind* was completed. In 1942 difficult wartime conditions compelled him to liquidate his own company, and dispose of several films he had in preparation, among them *Jane Eyre* and *The Keys of the Kingdom*, as packages to other companies.

From this time on, in fact, he more often figured behind the scenes of films, selling them as packages or participating in them by virtue of having the star or director under contract, than as an active producer. His only wartime film was *Since You Went Away* (1944), an emotional drama starring Jennifer Jones, whom he married in 1949. Among the other films he set up and sold as packages at this time were *The Spiral Staircase*, Hitchcock's *Notorious*, and *The Farmer's Daughter*; in 1945 he himself produced another Hitchcock film, *Spellbound*, and in 1948, before Hitchcock's contract with him finally ran out, *The Paradine Case*.

His major film of the period was King Vidor's *Duel in the Sun*, a psychological western conceived primarily as a vehicle for Jennifer Jones, who also starred in the last two films he produced personally, *Portrait of Jenny* (1948) and *A Farewell to Arms* (1957), as well as the last film in which he was involved as deviser and organizer, *Tender is the Night*. During the postwar period he was also one of the first American producers to venture into coproduction deals with European film makers; among the films in which he had a hand this way were *The Third Man, Gone to Earth*, and Vittorio de Sica's *Indiscretion*, in the last two of which Miss Jones also starred.

The later course of David O. Selznick's career, after his spectacular success with *Gone with the Wind* and *Rebecca*, is very curious. He was clearly an acute businessman, and his habit of selling prepackaged productions to other companies or hiring out the services of artistes he had under personal contract instead of using them himself was no doubt profitable. And yet he was not merely a businessman with no creative interest in the films he made: *Gone with the Wind* is clearly more his film than anyone else's, and he could seldom be dissuaded from interfering with every aspect of the films he produced himself, particularly in the writing: he had a hand, credited or uncredited, in the script of virtually every film he produced himself, and many more.

June 24, 1965.

Lord Sempill, A.F.C., who devoted the greater part of his life to the cause of British aviation, died on December 30, 1965, at the age of 72.

In the 1920s and early 1930s, when he was the Master of Sempill, he made the headlines time and again by his dashing flights generally in very small aircraft: a 70-mile sea crossing to Dublin in a D.H. Moth in 1925; Land's End to John o' Groats in something over eight hours in 1926; a tour round the coasts of the United Kingdom in a Blackburn light seaplane in 1928; Norway to Scotland in a Puss Moth two years later; and in 1936 a flight from Croydon to Berlin and back in a B.A.C. Drone powered by a specially adapted motor-cycle engine, an exercise in which the petrol and oil cost him 15s. going and rather less coming back. Two years earlier he had successfully flown to Australia in a Puss Moth. His enterprise and spirit caught the popular imagination and for years he was something of a household name.

The Right Honourable Sir William Francis Forbes-Sempill, nineteenth Baron Sempill, a representative peer for Scotland from 1935 to 1963, and a baronet of Nova Scotia, was the only son of the eighteenth peer and was born on September 24, 1893. He was educated at Eton, where he was in Mr. E. W. Stone's house, and then served an engineering apprenticeship. His interest in aviation began as early as 1912 and, on the outbreak of war in 1914 he joined the Royal Flying Corps. In 1916 he transferred from the R.F.C., in which he had reached the rank of captain, to the Royal Naval Air Service as flight commander. Two years later he transferred to the R.A.F., from which he retired in 1919. In 1921 he led a mission which assisted in the organization and equipment of the Japanese Naval Air Service; in 1926 he was invited to advise on the reorganization of the Greek Naval Air Service; and for three years from 1927 to 1930, he was president of the Royal Aeronautical Society, bringing a body which had lost some of the life of its early days into a condition of much greater vitality.

He returned to the Naval Air Service in 1939 and retired in 1941.

In the years between the two wars he worked with enthusiasm to increase the popularity of flying: he organized races for cheap, light aircraft with 6 h.p. engines and he urged upon municipalities the need for providing landing grounds for the coming great expansion of aircraft. His great keenness and long experience of flying led him to be tacitly accepted as one of the chief representatives of the British flying owner, though for some time he bore no official credentials. It was not long, however, before he was associated with and held important executive positions in almost all the organizations which had as their object the promotion of aeronautics.

He generally flew himself wherever he needed to go and many of his journeys were made in his own light machines. He competed at least seven times in the King's Cup Air Race. Sempill was a great believer in airships, established close contact with Hugo Eckener and worked hard to raise capital to ensure British participation in transatlantic airship services.

In 1931 he hired the German Graf Zeppelin, and made arrangements for 30 people to enjoy a 24-hour cruise around England.

He married first in 1919 Eileen Marion, only daughter of the late Sir John Lavery, R.A., and there were two daughters of this marriage, one of whom was killed on duty in 1941. His first wife died in 1935, and in 1941 he married Cecilia Alice, elder daughter of Mr. B. E., Dunbar-Kilburn, by whom he had three daughters. The barony passes to the only surviving daughter of his first marriage, the Hon. Mrs. Stuart Chant.

December 31, 1965.

Tullio Serafin, who died on February 2, 1968, at the age of 89, was, since Toscanini abandoned Italy, the grand master of Italian operatic conducting. His career opened in Ferrara in 1899: sixty years later he conducted the performance of *Lucia di Lammermoor* which set the seal on Joan Sutherland's fame, and until 1966 he still appeared fairly regularly in Italy.

Tullio Serafin was born on December 8, 1878. He studied at Milan Conservatoire and for a time was a violinist in the orchestra of La Scala opera. Further studies led to his first appearance as conductor, and in less than seven years he had, in the usual Italian way, ascended from Ferrara's relatively obscure Teatro Comunale to the Augusteo theatre in Rome. In 1909 he became conductor at La Scala. The musical directorship of the Rome Opera followed, and, from its beginning in 1933 Serafin was one of the architects of the Florence Maggio Musicale festival.

His interests were primarily in Italian music, and it was as an exponent of Italian opera from Rossini to Puccini, Montemezzi and Respighi that he was most in demand outside Italy. He conducted frequently in Covent Garden, where he was responsible for the first English performance of *La Forza del Destino* in 1931, and, from 1924 to 1933, he was engaged to open every season at the New York Metropolitan Opera. Serafin introduced American audiences to *Turandot*, Montemezzi's *L'Amore di Tre Re* (the first performance of which he had conducted in 1913) and *Simon Boccanegra*. He was not, however, stylistically restricted to Italian works, and in New York he conducted the first performances of Deems Taylor's *The King's Henchman* and *Peter Ibbetson*, and of Louis Gruenberg's *The Emperor Jones* (a work he subsequently introduced to Italy in a performance at Rome Opera with Eugene O'Neill's fable adapted to an ancient Roman setting). Stravinsky's *Le Rossignol* and Mussorgsky's *Sorochintzy Fair* also had their American premieres with Serafin conducting. In Milan, he was responsible for the first Italian performance of *Der Rosenkavalier* in 1911, and he conducted the first Italian production of Berg's *Wozzeck* in Rome, in 1940. Serafin was, in many respects, a "singer's conductor"; there are few great singers of Italian opera from Rosa Ponselle to Madame Callas and Miss Sutherland with whom he did not work, and his stylistic influence on the singers of *bel canto* opera was profound. He had the true Italian gift, indispensable to conducting in nineteenth-century opera, of floating a singing melody over an unobtrusive accompaniment in such a way that its inflexions and phrasing were matters of great tension and rich expressiveness.

February 6, 1968.

Ben Shahn, a prominent American artist known for his social realism and his support of liberal causes, died in New York on March 14, 1969, at the age of 70.

His art was animated by a non-conformist spirit (in the secular sense of the term) which gave a strongly individual character to his work. His own words "I like stories and people" indicate his distance from the abstract and non-figurative tendencies of painting in the United States. In his paintings of the "American scene", however, he was also distinct, combining subject with an expressiveness of form which derived ultimately from the School of Paris. He profited by the study of Rouault and Dufy and in the placing of figures in space in some works, his "Handball", 1939, being an example. He seemed to aim at a surrealist strangeness of effect. He did not hesitate, however, to make use of photography also. In subject matter his nonconformity is definable as "social realism", a protest that is against what he considered abuses or injustice and containing an element of satire: this tendency being most strongly marked in the 1930s. His later paintings showed a more personal preoccupation with imaginative theme and style and his originality in both phases gained him an international esteem.

Ben Shahn was born in Kovno (Kaunas), Lithuania, September 12, 1898, and was taken to the United States in 1906, becoming naturalized in 1918. In his early years in Brooklyn he was apprenticed to a lithographer and he continued the practice of commercial lithography until 1930, being still ready, subsequently, when his fame as a painter was established, to turn his hand to the political poster. After leaving New York University and the City College of New York he began to study art in 1922 at the National Academy of Design and between 1925 and 1929 visited France, Italy, Spain and North Africa, being impressed in Paris by the work of the modern school.

The first paintings that brought him into notice concerned instances of social injustice.

INSPIRED BY DREYFUS

A series of water colours inspired by the Dreyfus case was followed by the series for which he is most widely known on the notorious Sacco-Vanzetti case. The execution of the two Italian-American anarchists in 1927, after years of weighing in the balance the very dubious evidence of their having committed murder, seemed to him "a crucifixion". While his leftist sympathies were engaged he was not unmindful of the way in which the old Italian masters had treated the theme of martyrdom. He said once that Taddeo Gaddi was for him "a secret standard of excellence" and his paintings of the Lowell Committee of Investigation and the victims themselves combined a photographic circumstantiality with a clear-cut linear style distantly reminiscent of the Italian "primitive".

A broader view of American life was stimulated by the mural paintings which next occupied him between 1933 and 1942, first under the guidance of Diego Rivera at the Rockefeller Centre and afterwards as part of the Federal Works of Art Project and other administrative schemes, though he continued to paint easel pictures and these were the main index of his subsequent progress.

A number of incisive works were inspired by the ruinous aftermath of war, a moving example being the "Liberation" of 1945 in which children play amid the wreckage. A later imaginative strain sometimes recalling his Russian origin is exemplified in the "Allegory" of 1948. In one of the papers collected in his book *The Shape of Content* (1957) he describes how this picture of a red fabulous beast took shape in his mind from the memory of a Chicago fire. In this form of evolution of image from idea, of which "City of Dreadful Night", a forest of television aerials, was another example, he consciously moved from a social to a personal realism.

Shahn was a teacher and lecturer of note and gave some lectures at the Tate Gallery as well as in many American educational centres. He was Charles Eliot Norton Professor at Harvard University, 1956-57. Among the many exhibitions of his work, the retrospective held by the Museum of Modern Art, New York, and the Arts Council of Great Britain, 1947, and the special displays at the Sao Paulo Biennial, 1953, and Venice Biennale, 1954, may be mentioned, while an exhibition of his graphic art was held in London at the Leicester Galleries in 1959.

March 17, 1969.

Moshe Sharett, who died on July 7, 1965, in Jerusalem at the age of 70, made his imprint on Israel history mainly as the man responsible for his country's foreign relations for 23 years, including the most critical period of Israel's revival. His premiership between 1953 and 1955 was an interlude, and his chairmanship of the World Zionist Executive anticlimactic.

In 1933, the year Hitler rose to power in Germany, Sharett became the virtual Foreign Minister of the Shadow Cabinet of the embryo Jewish state, when he was elected head of the political department of the Zionist Executive. When the Israel Government became official in 1948 he slipped easily into his new position of Foreign Minister. His years in the Zionist Executive were years of frustration and heartache. There were rare occasions of encouragement to lighten the pain of the White Paper of 1939 which limited Jewish immigration and land acquisition in Palestine or the anguish of watching British destroyers patrolling the coast to guard against the landing of fugitives from the Nazi gas chambers. Yet Sharett did not lose his sense of proportion, and in that difficult period he dedicated himself to recruiting Jews for the British forces and he strove to form a Jewish Brigade Group to fight Hitlerism.

Those largely unhappy years ended in a blaze of triumph with the United Nations vote in 1947 to partition Palestine into Arab and Jewish states. Sharett was a national hero when he flew to Tel Aviv from the United Nations to sign the Proclamation of Independence in 1948. Cheering crowds followed him from the Tel Aviv Museum after the historic ceremony when he walked to the home of his aged mother near by. His prestige was then at its peak.

As Foreign Minister of sovereign Israel, he continued to experience frustrations as representative of a small country that belonged to no block, but there were also moments of elation such as when he saw the Jewish flag rise at the United Nations and country after country sent envoys to the state of Israel. That happier period ended abruptly in heartache and humiliation. Ben-Gurion, who had relinquished the premiership to Sharett in 1953 and returned to office in 1955, soured on his moderate and temperate Foreign Minister. He served notice that one or the other must go and Sharett resigned. Thus, at 62, Sharett became an elder statesman and he filled the part with statesmanship and dignity. He retained his Knesset seat and was active in Mapai Party deliberations, but assiduously declined august state appointments. He became head of "Am Oved", the General Federation of Labour's publishing house.

In 1959 he became chairman of the World Zionist Executive and applied himself to that post with zeal. He attempted to breathe new life into the movement that had been flagging since its goal of establishing a Jewish State had been achieved. Sharett travelled to many countries trying to persuade Jews that the Zionist movement still had a vital function, endeavouring to recruit fresh, young blood and promoting Hebrew education in the Diaspora. At the time of his death he was chairman of the executive of the Jewish Agency.

WITH THE TURKISH FORCES

Sharett was born in Kherson in the Ukraine in October, 1894, and was taken to Turkish-ruled Palestine when he was 12 years old. His father, Yaakov Tchertok, belonged to the *Bilu* movement, which was dedicated to agricultural colonization in Palestine. Accordingly, the family's first home was a farm in a remote Arab village in the hills of Ephraim. The venture failed but the experience enabled the teenager to master Arabic, study the morals and customs of his neighbours and gain knowledge that was to influence his career. The family name was changed in Palestine from Tchertok to Shertok and after the establishment of Israel it was hebraized to Sharett. After the failure of the farming venture they moved to Tel Aviv, where Sharett attended Herzlia Gymnasium. He joined a quasi-clandestine society whose idealistic members pledged to choose occupations which would benefit the Jewish community of Palestine. Sharett was chosen to study law in Istanbul and to equip himself to defend Palestine Jews against abuses by corrupt Ottoman officials.

The 1914-18 War interrupted Sharett's law studies and he had to decide between going underground, risking detention as a Tsarist subject or becoming a Turkish citizen and joining the army. He chose the Turkish orientation and was commissioned an officer in the army. In view of his extraordinary linguistic abilities, he was assigned as interpreter to a high ranking German officer commanding Turkish forces. In that post he travelled widely and became familiar with the region. After the Armistice and the Balfour Declaration Sharett decided to resume his studies in Britain and he enrolled in the London School of Economics and Political Science. He worked his way through school by giving Hebrew lessons and working as a translator. He was also active in Zionist affairs.

FRIEND OF KING ABDULLAH

He returned to Tel Aviv in 1925 to join the staff of *Davar*, a daily newspaper started by the General Federation of Labour (Histadrut). *Davar* initiated an English-language supplement in 1929 and Sharett became editor. His work attracted the notice of Haim Arlosoroff, head of the political department of the Zionist Executive, and Sharett joined his staff in 1931. Because of his background he was Arlosoroff's righthand man in dealings with Arabs. He developed a warm friendship with the late King Abdullah and a Persian rug presented to him by the Arab ruler was one of his proudest possessions. After Arlosoroff was murdered in 1933 the Zionist Congress chose Sharett to succeed his mentor. Thus, at 39, he entered the front rank of Zionist leadership.

Apart from the mark he made in shaping Israeli history, Sharett left an imprint on the Hebrew language. Scores of words which he coined are now in pupular use. He utilized the prestige of his official positions to spread the use of his and other people's creations. Linguistics was his hobby and he was fluent in Hebrew, English, French, German, Russian, Turkish, Arabic, and Yiddish. He translated poetry into Hebrew from several languages and wrote several books.

He is survived by his wife, whom he married when both of them were students in London, two sons and a married daughter.

July 8, 1965.

Professor E. P. Sharpey-Schafer, Professor of Medicine at London University, died on October 23, 1963, at the age of 55. His sudden and tragic death removed one of the leading researchers in modern medicine and a personality whose impact on the academic medical scene and his hospital, St. Thomas's, was incalculable. His life was devoted to the physiological understanding of the circulation in health and disease and the maintenance of a standard of thinking where nothing but the first-rate was tolerated.

Edward Peter Sharpey-Schafer, son of Commander John Sharpey-Schafer and grandson of Sir Edward Sharpey-Schafer, Professor of Physiology at the University of Edinburgh, was born on September 22, 1908. He became a scholar of Winchester and an Exhibitioner and Kitchener Scholar of King's College, Cambridge, and at University College Hospital was successively house physician to Sir Thomas Lewis and house surgeon to Mr. William Trotter.

His interest in the human circulation began when he was working at the Postgraduate Hospital, Hammersmith, during the war. He, with Professor J. McMichael, was the first person to use cardiac catheterization in Britain and with this and other techniques a great harvest of knowledge was obtained which put him immediately in the international front rank as a scientist. He had an intuitive "feel" for the circulation and for the next 20 years continued to work on problems of low blood pressure and heart failure with constant originality and brilliance. The writings communicating his findings were characteristically lucid and brief and spiced with wit. His output was remarkable and he was still in full flood of original work when he died.

He was appointed to the chair of medicine at St. Thomas's Hospital in 1948. His impact was immediate and characteristic; the first day he arrived his apparatus was assembled and an observation of blood pressure was made. From this moment he exerted a profound influence over the whole hospital. He was not loquacious, but by his example the experimental method and rigorous attention to fact as opposed to theory became the way of thinking of everyone who came near his unit. This unit was a remarkable creation in which many people interested in all parts of the human organism worked, the only rule being that you worked. In recent years three of his readers became professors of medicine in other centres, a unique achievement. He was also a most far-sighted and valuable force in the hospital and medical school, perhaps the most progressive member on the staff and certainly the one in whose hands the future seemed to lie.

As a man Professor Sharpey-Schafer dwarfed his colleagues in his intellectual capacity and his wholeness: the truth was all that mattered and personal consideration never. His great talents were broadly based. The essential gift was that of a naturalist; he found something to interest him in all natural phenomena, and physiological research, photography, wild life, and his fellow beings were all grist to his mill. He never worked through delegation, but always directly; with his technician he would be daily recording and discussing new observations. He was intolerant of all disguise or secrecy so that to some he appeared brusque, but essentially he was always humorous and kind once a certain shyness had gone. He was rarely known to give a formal lecture, but his informal talk with diagrams drawn on cigarette packets was his chosen means of communication, and in this way his ideas permeated a whole generation.

There were two daughters of his marriage to Sheila Howarth.

October 26, 1963.

Lal Bahadur Shastri, who died in Tashkent on January 11, 1966, succeeded Jawaharlal Nehru as Prime Minister of India by virtue of his quiet effectiveness as an administrator and political leader and the high popularity and respect in which he was held by his colleagues. Before he became Prime Minister he was barely known in the country outside the Congress Party organization and he was the first Indian politician to rise to a position of great influence in national affairs on the strength solely of his service in government and party after independence. He was a transitional figure, too, as at a time when the balance of Indian politics was shifting from the centre to the states he owed nothing to the support in his native Uttar Pradesh; he was a man of the Congress Party and may be seen to have been the last Indian politician to rise to eminence without having a strong base in one of the states.

Shastri's first disappointment, soon after succeeding as Prime Minister, was the heart attack that prevented him from attending the Commonwealth Prime Ministers' conference. It was unique to find an Indian leader of this eminence who had never been to Britain, and it was not until December, 1964, when the Labour Government was in office that he was able to go.

He had, however, taken his own initiatives in foreign affairs nearer home. Relations with Nepal, with Burma, and with Ceylon—all of them unsatisfactory in Nehru's day—were taken in hand. A conference of non-aligned nations in Cairo gave him his first opportunity in following Nehru's own role and he acquitted himself well.

Nevertheless rising prices, food shortages and other disappointments at home lowered Shastri's reputation after his first nine months in office. He seemed too mild, content to be the sympathetic observer rather than the purposeful leader. He remained firmly in power only because his rivals cancelled each other out.

From the first Shastri had shown his sincerity in trying to reach an understanding with Pakistan. His naturally pacific tendencies were exemplified in his hostility to India's developing nuclear weapons for which there was growing agitation. Yet paradoxically, it was his firmness in standing up to Pakistan that restored his declining reputation. The Rann of Kutch dispute brought the two countries to blows in this barren wasteland.

SETTLEMENT PRAISED

The settlement which Britain mediated brought Shastri much credit. Then followed a period of travels to Moscow, to London for the Commonwealth conference and to Canada.

Then came the fresh and testing assault in Kashmir, the Pakistan drive to cut off the state from India, and India's reply across the Pakistan frontier in early August. By now Shastri's position as a national leader had been confirmed. Although anxious to maintain the closest relations between India and Russia, he was at first cautious when Kosygin suggested the meeting that has now been held in Tashkent.

Relations with the United States had been rather less happy. An intended visit in the spring of 1965 had been cancelled by President Johnson but by the end of last year the invitation had been renewed and Shastri was expected in Washington soon after the Tashkent meeting. The way had been prepared by a generous American offer of aid for India's seriously threatening famine.

It might be said that Lal Bahadur's greatest political asset was a gift for not making enemies which made him uniquely fitted to play the role of compromiser or arbitrator in the Congress Party's multiplex feuds of faction or region. But there was much more to him than that. Physically diminutive, almost sparrowlike, there was a warmth to his personality, a deep considerateness for others that had nothing in it either of the patronizing or the subservient, which combined with his unquestioned reputation for probity to give him the respect not only of the Congress Party but of all elements of Indian politics.

Lal Bahadur was born in 1903 in the then princely state of Benares into a poor family of Kyasth Caste (Shastri is an appellation usually associated with Brahmins he later earned by study). His father without much success kept a village shop. His early education was scanty but the boy was bright and diligent and when after temporarily forswearing education at the call of Mahatma Gandhi he resumed his studies he was admitted to Kashi Vidyapith at Benares, a nationalist college where he met many men who would later be his companions in the Uttar Pradesh and Central Governments. He joined the Servants of the People Society and worked for the uplift of untouchables, serving in Allahabad where he first came into association with Nehru. In 1937 he was elected as Congress member to the first United Provinces Legislative Assembly; he resigned with all his party in 1939, offered Satyagraha in 1941 and went to gaol—where he had previously served several terms for political agitation.

After independence Shastri—he gradually came to be known by the title—began the slow rise through the ranks of the Congress Party that after 17 years took him to the Prime Ministership. He came to the attention of Pandit Pant, the first Chief Minister of Uttar Pradesh and in 1947 became his Parliamentary Secretary. A year later he became Minister of Police in the State Cabinet and in 1951 with his appointment as general secretary of the Congress Party he moved into the arena of central politics.

Congress's metamorphosis from independence movement to ruling party came to a focus in the preparations for the first general elections and Shastri played a large but discreet role. The "high command" (as the central leadership of the party is called) was then at the height of its powers, the drain of authority to the states being still a decade in the future, and as general secretary Shastri was again and again called to intervene in the state capitals in the all important matter of distribution of party nominations. This experience left him with a close knowledge of the working of the party in the states as well as the centre and he performed his often invidious task so tactfully and wisely that with the party's overwhelming victory in 1952 his reputation suddenly enlarged. He developed such a firm grip—albeit one discreet and modest—on the party's inner working that even before he became Prime Minister few if any important decisions were taken without consulting him. As a reward for this service and recognition of his capabilities Shastri was taken into the central Cabinet after the elections as Minister for Railways.

UNSUITED TO HIS TALENT

That portfolio did not suit Shastri's abilities and it might be said that nothing in his tenure distinguished him more than his manner of leaving it. In 1956 he resigned after a disastrous railway accident, a gesture which still stands as a record rather than a precedent in Indian political life and which gained him much respect. Freed from Ministerial responsibilities he was ready to take charge again of the party's preparations for the second general elections. By then change in the nature of the Congress Party was further advanced, with new men, rank and file, and even the cadets of the independence movement beginning to make their way to positions of power in the state capitals and once again this experience was valuable for Shastri as well as for the party.

After the elections Shastri was recalled to the Cabinet first as Minister of Transport and Communications; then, after a year, as Minister for Commerce and Industry. These technical portfolios did not really suit Shastri's abilities but he left them with a good reputation among civil servants as a Minister who knew his own mind, would take decisions and stand by them and as a man immune from temptations of patronage and power. But in 1961, on the death of his friend and patron, Pandit Pant, Shastri took over in the Home Ministry, a portfolio that perfectly suited his experience and talents. Under the Indian constitution much of the executive responsibility of the Home Ministry must be exercised through the state governments and the Minister plays a large role in establishing the tone of the relations between states and centre. Except for brief periods in Kerala all state governments in this period were of Congress Party, and Shastri's experience as general secretary and organizer had left him a familiar and trusted figure throughout the party's rambling structure. To that advantage another was added—knowledge that Shastri was the trusted friend of the Prime Minister, Nehru, and therefore he shared some of the Prime Minister's then absolute authority in party matters.

Ideologically Shastri was more or less neutral, belonging naturally to the broad centre of his party but acceptable to the Left because of his close association with Nehru.

CHOSEN TO QUIT

Shastri's penultimate step towards the Prime Ministership was taken paradoxically in an opposite direction. He was one of those chosen by Nehru to quit the Cabinet in 1963 under the so-called Kamaraj Plan, surrendering office to devote full time and energies to the regeneration of the Congress Party organization whose decrepitude was by then becoming apparent. The importance of this somewhat deceptive plan to Shastri lay in the fact that it also removed from the Cabinet Morarji Desai who was then second to Nehru in seniority and therefore first claimant to the succession. When a few months later Nehru suffered a mild stroke and Shastri was recalled to the Cabinet as Minister without Portfolio, the circumstances more than the act made him the Prime Minister's heir apparent.

Still Nehru kept his position rather uncertain and it was not until a strenuous attempt by Desai had been deflected after Nehru's death that Shastri was elected leader of the party and called to form a government. Shastri had been the party's natural candidate by virtue of his position in the centre and of the wide respect and affection in which he was held. After the towering figure of Nehru there seemed much about Shastri that was deficient for the Prime Ministership but, in spite of that apparent discrepancy, there was a general feeling of confidence and even pride in the unassuming figure of Shastri who seemed to symbolize so well the qualities of matter-of-fact dedication, of honesty and effectiveness that would be demanded in India's next difficult phase.

Shastri is survived by his widow and six children.

January 11, 1966.

E. O. Shebbeare, Conservator of Forests in India, transport officer to two Mount Everest expeditions and chief game warden in Malaya, died on August 11, 1964, at his home in Oxfordshire. He was 80.

Edward Oswald Shebbeare was born in 1884, the son of the Rev. C. H. Shebbeare, vicar of Wykeham, Yorkshire. Educated at Charterhouse, he joined the Indian Forest Service in 1906 and served in a number of posts retiring in 1938 as Chief Conservator of Forests in Bengal. He then became chief game warden in Malaya and was a prisoner of war in Singapore from 1942 to 1945, resuming his post after the war until his retirement to England in 1947.

In a varied life in the East his name became a byword. He would disappear for periods into the forests he loved and the results would appear in technical papers on forestry, on the fishes of northern Bengal, on botany, and on zoology. He was transport officer with the 1924 Mount Everest Expedition (an inspired choice by General Bruce) and in 1929 and 1931 he acted similarly for the attempts on Kangchenjunga by the Bavarian mountaineers under Dr. Paul Bauer, who to this day remember him with affection. In 1933 again he was transport officer for Hugh Ruttledge's expedition to Mount Everest. By now over 50, against the express orders of Ruttledge, he managed to achieve a secret ambition to reach the North Col at 23,000ft. That evening he was down at his tent in camp 3 blandly reading old copies of *The Times* at the door of his tent in the setting sun. He had a remarkable gift for accomplishing things with no fuss and infinite good humour.

There was no stopping Shebbeare; not even three years as a prisoner of war in Singapore. Straight from his prison camp he proceeded to Darjeeling (which he approached on foot from Teesta Bridge to the "tenth milestone" from Darjeeling) which involves an ascent of several thousand feet. This he managed to do in shorter time than ever before, and he merely put it down to his being many pounds lighter than in earlier days.

A TIGER SHOOT

At Darjeeling he was then soon enlisted as the best person to organize a tiger shoot on the Nepal frontier for Lord Casey, at that time Governor of Bengal, who has himself recorded that Shebbeare's dress consisted of a bush shirt, very old shorts, no socks and a pair of boots commandeered from a Japanese guard at the moment of liberation. On the day of the actual shoot he was thus attired, but with socks too. Asked why the socks Shebbeare replied: "Well, you know, on these occasions you have to cut a bit of a dash."

On retirement in England he published in 1958 a remarkable book, *Soondar Mooni,* the life of an elephant based partly on inference and partly on the facts of a particular elephant story. His knowledge of forest and animals in India was here displayed in the most charming and scholarly way. But he is remembered above all by colleagues in India and by travelling companions as a man of wide knowledge, sympathies and generosity.

In 1916 he married Miss A. Cameron, who died in 1962. They had one daughter.

August 14, 1964.

Sir Thomas Sheepshanks, K.C.B., K.B.E., who died on February 1, 1964, at the age of 69, was Permanent Secretary, Ministry of Housing and Local Government from 1951 to 1955 and previously Permanent Secretary, Ministry of Town and Country Planning.

Born in January, 1895, he was the youngest son of Bishop Sheepshanks of Norwich and proudly related that for many years he had held the distinction of being the only son born to a diocesan bishop in his palace. He and his four brothers were scholars of Winchester.

Sheepshanks did not return to Trinity College, Oxford, after the war in which he served first with the Royal Norfolk Regiment and later in France with the Suffolk Regiment, but took the reconstruction examination and was assigned to the Ministry of Health in 1919. In that department his progress despite his abilities was, as was then quite usual, slow and he did not become an assistant secretary until 1936. But the threat of war and the decision to start air raid precautions and to organize them through local authorities made necessary the addition to the Home Office of a senior official of the Ministry of Health with wide experience of the local government machine and of the grant system. Sheepshanks was selected for this post and in 1937 joined the Home Office in which his elder brother had served before he joined the Army in the first war, in which he was killed.

STRONG CHARACTER

Sheepshanks quickly made his mark in the Home Office, where his very considerable experience of legislation was of the greatest assistance. When Sir John Anderson, as Lord Privy Seal, was in charge of the Bill for the Civil Defence Act, 1938, Sheepshanks was his right-hand man. The war saw Sheepshanks carrying ever-increasing responsibilities in the Ministry of Home Security, of which he was made Principal Assistant Secretary on its establishment in 1939, Under-Secretary in 1941, and Deputy Secretary in 1942. Regional commissioners and their staffs, as well as local authorities, found in him a counsellor to whom they could turn in the knowledge that they would always receive sage advice and wise counsel and be helped to solve their problems.

In 1943 he was seconded to the Ministry

of Reconstruction, where he played a most important role with Sir Thomas Phillips in working out the practical application of Lord Beveridge's report on social insurance and allied services. If Lord Beveridge was the begetter of our scheme of social security, Tom Sheepshanks was certainly one of its *accoucheurs*. His next assignment was in the Ministry of National Insurance; then he went to the Treasury from 1945 to 1946. He was transferred in 1946 to the Ministry of Town and Country Planning as deputy secretary; after a few months he was appointed Permanent Secretary. He held that post during a period of great activity until 1951, when he was transferred to the Ministry of Housing and Local Government, where he was Permanent Secretary until his retirement in 1955.

Sheepshanks was a man of strong character, high intellectual qualities, and great administrative ability. He was outstandingly successful as a negotiator, particularly with local authorities and their associations with whom he did business over many years. They knew that his was not a closed mind. He had their confidence and they trusted him; they knew where they stood with him. He was a skilful draftsman and many Ministers in a variety of departments owed much to that extra sense which seemed to suggest to him what was and was not possible in the atmosphere of Parliament. In his latter years, possibly as a result of the exceptional burdens he carried during and after the war when he was involved in so much legislation and in so many fields, his health left something to be desired.

He and his wife—Elizabeth Creemer, daughter of James Calvert—suffered two heavy losses in the death on active service of one of their sons and later of their daughter. These were all the more heavy for Sheepshanks and his wife to bear for both took a special pride in their family.

February 4, 1964.

Sir John Sheppard, M.B.E., Provost of King's College, Cambridge, from 1933 to 1954, died in London on May 7, 1968. He was 86.

John Tresidder Sheppard was born at Peckham in 1881, the son of a wool brokers' clerk. He was educated at Dulwich College, of which he was afterwards a governor. He was taught by A. C. Pearson, who in 1921 stood successfully against his former pupil for the Regius Professorship of Greek. When he went up to King's College, Cambridge, in 1900, E. M. Forster was already in residence, and Stephen Gaselee and Maynard Keynes arrived in the following years, while Lytton Strachey was at Trinity.

As a classical scholar he carried all before him, winning the Porson and Craven Scholarships, the Porson Prize, and the Chancellor's Classical Medal, as well as being mentioned for the Chancellor's English Medal. He was placed in the First Class in Part I of the Tripos in 1902, and in the Second Class in Part II in 1904. He was eminent as an actor, and as a debater at the Union, of which he was President; he also rowed in his college boat, an activity which confirmed his distaste for all forms of exercise. Indeed his life was a successful contradiction of the principle that physical exertion is necessary to health; and his indifference to the beauties of nature, especially in their more spectacular forms, spared him all temptation to indulge in superfluous movement. When he travelled it was usually to Monte Carlo, though he was a wellknown figure on Hellenic Travellers' Tours. In retirement he divided his time between Cap-Martin and King's. In his later years he travelled extensively in the countries of the Commonwealth and did much to forward the establishment at King's of studentships for graduates from certain of their universities.

At King's, under the influence of Oscar Browning, and of Wedd and Walter Headlam, he acquired the two passions which dominated and directed his life, his devotion to the college, the purpose of a college being above all to educate, and his devotion to Greek; and he was enabled happily to combine the two on his election to a Fellowship in 1906, and still more when he became a college lecturer in 1908. He had already taught for a short time at Emmanuel. Henceforward for many years he took an ample share in the work of the classical staff and was frequently called upon by the university to act as an examiner; he also did important service to the university as a member of his Faculty Board, of which he was chairman in 1931 and 1932: and in the latter year he was appointed Brereton Reader in Classical Literature.

His most serious work of scholarship, an edition of the *Oedipus Tyrannus* of Sophocles (1920), was notable for its shift of emphasis away from the traditional pursuit of ever purer texts and more precise grammatical analysis to the deeper study of form and content, a shift which was not due to any lack on Sheppard's part of the technical equipment of a scholar. In 1922 he produced *The Pattern of the Iliad*, an account of Homer's methods of construction which was, perhaps, less convincing in print than when urged in lecture or conversation with the persuasiveness of which he was a master and with the enthusiasm which sometimes mastered him. But his was not without influence on the approach of subsequent scholars to Homer. Besides a book on Aeschylus and Sophocles in the "Our Debt to Greece and Rome" series and some minor works, he wrote a number of verse translations of Greek plays remarkable for their pure and distinguished diction.

But it was as a lecturer and a producer of plays that Sheppard made his greatest contribution to the study of Greek. His fine and expressive voice, his command of language, and his immense personality combined to make him an outstanding lecturer. There could be no better testimony to his powers than his success in holding the attention of the audiences, composed largely of those ignorant of and, to begin with, little interested in Greek who flocked year after year to his open lectures on Greek and English poetry. Many owe to him their first realization of the truth that poetry exists to be enjoyed, and many, but for him, might never have realized it at all. Nor did he deny himself the mannerisms to which genius is entitled. As he warmed to his work, especially if he felt his audience to be with him, he would perch on chair or desk in postures of ever more perilous disequilibrium, which continually threatened a disaster that never came.

For many years the triennial Cambridge Greek plays were produced by him, at first in conjunction with Mr. Burnaby, later alone; the most triumphant of them was probably the *Oresteia* of 1921.

All the time, however, his main work was in King's, where he influenced deeply many generations of undergraduates; his "Sunday evenings" inherited from the O.B., to which anyone might go, and at which anything might be said, for long provided education in its most exciting form. In 1929 he became Vice-Provost, and in 1933 Provost, and Senior Fellow of Eton; and after this he was much occupied with administration, and it at last ceased to be possible for undergraduates engaged in the pursuit of elusive forms of truth to forget that their vivacious, white-haired companion in the chase was not, after all, their contemporary. In the conduct of affairs he displayed a shrewdness which surprised many who had supposed him an unpractical person, but rapidity in the transaction of business was hardly to be combined with his love of discursive conversation. He gave up the Provostship in 1954, having held it for two years beyond the normal retiring age. The final years of his office were made notable by the visit of King George VI and Queen Elizabeth to celebrate the restoration of the chapel to its full glory.

He received a knighthood in 1950. He was an honorary Litt.D. of the Universities of Manchester, Melbourne, and New Zealand, an honorary LL.D. of St. Andrews, and a Knight Commander of the Order of the Redeemer. He was an honorary Fellow of New College, Oxford, and Queen Mary College, London.

May 9, 1968.

Henry Sherek, producer and man of the theatre, who died on September 23, 1967, at the age of 67, will be remembered as a power in the British theatre. Since 1937, he was responsible for the production of a large number of plays of various styles and intellectual weights, all of which had something to contribute to the pleasure of audiences and to the well-being of the theatre itself. If as a skilful business man he was the architect of many theatrical successes and the reputations of several dramatists and actors, he had no interest in the trivial play tailored to meet popular success. His great successes were all intelligent, if not often intellectual, theatre.

Henry Sherek was born in London on April 23, 1900, and educated in Germany and Switzerland. The end of the First World War found him as a member of the Rifle Brigade and he completed his education at St. John's College, Cambridge. Between 1936 and 1939, Sherek was responsible for nearly a dozen revues at the Dorchester Hotel, and he began his career of management in the theatre in 1937 with *The Orchard Walls* at the St. James's Theatre. His adventurous taste and his determination to support his belief in plays with something of value to say were demonstrated in the following year by his production of Robert E. Sherwood's passionately outspoken anti-war play, *Delight*, at the Apollo Theatre.

From 1941 until 1944, when he was invalided out of the Forces, Henry Sherek returned to the Rifle Brigade. Nevertheless, he was responsible with H. M. Tennant for the production or Sherwood's *The Petrified Forest* at the Globe Theatre in 1942. After the war, he ranged widely; he was responsible not only for revivals of *Hamlet*, Shaw's *Pygmalion* and *You Never Can Tell*, and Bridie's *The Sleeping Clergyman*, but also for a number of new plays—the topical *Desert Rats*, Norman Ginsbury's *The First Gentleman*, *Edward My Son* by Robert Morley and Noel Langley, and Reginald Beckwith's Borstal drama *Boys in Brown* were among them.

Sherek was also the guide to and controlling power over drama at the Edinburgh Festival for several years, and it was his determination that theatre at the Festival should be no less impressive and adventurous than the music offered there. Deeply moved by T. S. Eliot's *The Cocktail Party*, Sherek put on its first production at the Edinburgh Festival of 1949 at a time when nothing could suggest that a play by so forbidding a poet might become a great popular success, but *The Cocktail Party* delighted and moved audiences in London no less than those who had seen it at the Festival. Eliot's two later plays, *The Confidential Clerk* and *The Elder Statesman* both were brought to the stage by Sherek in productions which moved London after giving lustre to the theatre at the Edinburgh Festival. A similarly adventurous determination to win attention for work in which he believed led him to present Dylan Thomas's *Under Milk Wood* on the stage.

At Edinburgh, too, he was responsible for productions of Shaw's *Fanny's First Play* and Synge's *The Playboy of the Western World*.

If as a manager Sherek led popular taste with a good deal of courage, his enormous pleasure in the theatre as it is, made plain in his autobiography, *Not in Front of the Children*, led him to produce only what satisfied an eclectic but sensitive and educated sense of the stage. The same pleasure informed all he did; as a familiar figure at theatrical occasions, and as an occasional speaker and broadcaster, he was flamboyantly larger than life, going about the world with inexhaustible gusto. His friends remember his wit, his dazzling swiftness of repartee and his endless kindness. Everything he did from turning T. S. Eliot from a remote poet into a popular dramatist, to amusing children with conjuring tricks and driving at terrifying speeds was done with delight.

In 1937, Henry Sherek married the Hon. Kathleen Mary Pamela Corona Boscawen, who was his business associate and helper all through his career in the theatre.

September 25, 1967.

Clare Sheridan—sculptor, writer, journalist, traveller, friend of many great figures of her time—who died on May 31, 1970, at the age of 84, was a woman of varied talents which, throughout a long life, she developed with uninhibited zest and success.

Adventurous in spirit, with a lively curiosity and capacity for action, she had above all a talent for life itself. Having lived it to the full, she came, in her later years, to regard death with evergrowing interest. For her it was to be the supreme adventure, and she prepared for it with the same vitality which had impelled her on other journeys over the face of the Earth.

Born on September 9, 1885, the only daughter of Moreton Frewen of Brede Place, Sussex, and Clara Jerome of New York, she was given a conventional upbringing on her father's country estates until her aunt, Lady Randolph Churchill, launched her into London society with plenty of good advice: "Every morning while she breakfasted I had to read aloud to her the leader in *The Times*, and submit to a short political lecture, in order that I might not appear too ignorant when I dined out ... I was reminded that it was not for my personal amusement that I was invited, but to contribute to the entertainment of a party".

Chosen as a friend for Princess Margaret of Connaught she became the first recipient of the news of the Princess's engagement to Prince Gustaf of Sweden, and the royal family were amused at the meticulous manner in which she fulfilled the Princess's written instructions to tell her friends, "This is not a *mariage arrangé*. We are in love."

UNLIKELY FRIENDS

While spending a winter with Princess Margaret in Stockholm she added Axel Munthe to a circle of friends then considered very unusual for a young girl to choose. It included Robert Hichens, George Moore and Henry James.

In 1910 she married Wilfred Sheridan, of Frampton Place, Dorset, the great-great grandson of Richard Brinsley Sheridan. In 1915 he was killed in action, while serving as a Captain in the Rifle Brigade, leaving his widow with a small son and daughter. She had already been disturbed by sorrow, for a third child had died young and in her efforts to model a weeping angel for the small grave she had discovered her own talent as a sculptress. Within four years she was holding exhibitions, and orders for portrait busts poured in from many countries. Asquith, F. E. Smith and her cousin Winston Churchill were among her first sitters: "While Winston painted me I modelled him." But they found it impossible to keep still for each other and when Ambrose McEvoy tried to paint both artists at work the experiment dissolved.

In 1920 Krassin and Kameneff, the first Russian Soviet delegates to visit London, asked her to do their busts which caused a sensation at Agnews. They invited her to return with them to Moscow to do portraits of Lenin and Trotsky. In spite of the fact that the Civil War was still on Mrs. Sheridan travelled to the heart of Bolshevik Russia. For two months she was lodged in the Kremlin. While at work it intrigued her as an artist to provoke Lenin "for then I aroused a certain expression". Trotsky proved harder to sculpt than the other Russian leaders, "there were such subtleties in his face. Such contradictions". He invited her to accompany him to the front or to set up a permanent studio in Russia, but as the winter snow began to fall she thought of her children waiting in London and returned to them "half starved and lacking in vitality", to meet with a reception from the English world, compounded, as she put it, of "praise, blame, compliments, abuse, eulogy and criticism". But her fame as a sculptor had grown worldwide. On her return the *New York Times* asked to publish her Russian diary, of which excerpts appeared in *The Times*, and soon she found herself, distinctly ahead of her time, a woman journalist of repute.

NOTED INTERVIEWS

While working as European correspondent for the *New York World* she covered the Irish Civil War, the Turco-Greek War, and the terrible evacuation of refugees from Smyrna. Her interviews with Kemal Ataturk, Mussolini, King Boris of Bulgaria and the delegates of the Geneva Peace Conference hit notes which had never been reached in American newspapers. At intervals of gathering news she continued to sculpt, wrote travel books, and a volume of autobiography, *Nuda Veritas*, which survives as a vivid and authentic picture of these times. When European political intrigues grew less dramatic Mrs. Sheridan left the studio overlooking the Bosphorus, in which she had settled, to drive across South Russia with her brother on a motor bicycle named Satanella. This jaunt to Kiev and Tartary resulted in *Across Europe with Satanella*. Later came *A Turkish Kaleidoscope* and *Arab Interlude*, describing her subsequent life on the edge of the Sahara, at Biskra, where she created for herself and her two children a house and garden of unusual beauty.

There followed in 1938, *Redskin Interlude*, written while she spent six months on a reservation carving Indian portraits out of tree stumps. In the previous year, tragedy had struck for the third time. Her son, Richard Brinsley Sheridan, who had sailed before the mast on a Finnish wind-jammer around both Cape and Horn, died at the age of 21. From this blow his mother never recovered. But even her grief she accepted creatively. She never looked back, only forward to the time she felt sure she would see him again. The story of her attempts to establish communication with him was published as *Without End* in 1939 and the discovery of her powers to carve oak derived from her time among the Redskins and developed as she hewed her son's memorial for Brede Church.

Mrs. Sheridan spent the last war at her family home in Sussex, living as quietly as was possible for one of her temperament. She described this period in *My Crowded Sanctuary* (1945). At intervals between gardening and milking goats, she carved trees into church statuary. For one week in the middle of the V bombs she visited Downing Street to do another bust of her illustrious cousin Winston Churchill (he proved a better sitter reading his war papers than when trying to paint his sculptress twenty years before).

In 1947 Mrs. Sheridan while visiting Assisi became a Roman Catholic. In 1957 she brought her autobiography up to date in *To The Four Winds*, which proved a best seller in two continents.

The life she made for herself as an intrepid woman traveller was more novel to her generation than now. But as a human being she must rank as unique. Her vitality never diminished. No one could be more stimulating to talk to. Her sudden, clear laugh, her intense interest in mankind, her discarding of the commonplace, her curiosity and her passionate love of the beautiful will in time be forgotten. Even her busts of famous people—names burnt into history—Lenin. Trotsky, Mussolini, Churchill—may be relegated to museum attics. But Clare Sheridan's religious works of art, the madonnas and angels in cherrywood, oak and pear, which ornament many English churches, will remain to delight the future.

June 2, 1970.

Ronald Shiner, an actor in the great tradition of cockney humorists, died on June 29, 1966, at the age of 63. He had been in poor health since his collapse at the end of a broadcast recording in 1963.

Ronald Shiner was born in London on June 8, 1903, and educated at St. Aloysius's School, Highgate. Before his first appearance on the stage as the Bos'un in *Dr. Syn*, at the Margate Hippodrome in 1928, he had been an insurance clerk, a bookmaker's clerk, a member of the North West Mounted Police, a grocery salesman, a soldier and a milkman. During the 1930s he played a variety of smaller parts in London, ranging from that of Henry Straker, in *Man and Superman* (which remained his favourite role), to Oakie in *The Amazing Dr. Clitterhouse*. From 1929 to 1931 he was stage director for the Stage Society and from 1931 to 1934 stage manager of the Whitehall Theatre.

Although he served as a full-time special constable from 1940 to 1943 Shiner was able at the same time to make a number of films—he first appeared on the screen in 1934 and by the end of his career he had acted in over 200 films—and to consolidate a reputation as a radio comedian. He returned to the stage in 1943 as Sergeant Austin in *Something in the Air* and then as A.C.2 Sam Porter in *Worm's Eye View* (which he also directed). This was his first great personal triumph; after its provincial tour, the then topical account of the sufferings of aircraftmen billeted in a provincial boarding house ran in London for 1,700 performances. He followed this with an equally effective role, that of A.B. Badger in *Seagulls over Sorrento*, which had 1,551 London performances and which he followed by similar parts in *My Three Angels* and *Reluctant Heroes*, another great box office success. In his television series, *Send for Shiner*, he showed an equally sure touch.

Ronald Shiner's success was based on the very varied experience of the world and the equally varied experience of the theatre which he had enjoyed before the Second World War. Somehow, he seemed not only to reflect but to embody and realize everybody's notion of the archetypal cockney—inquisitive (a long, apparently probing nose assisted him in this), quick witted, brilliant in improvisation when trouble threatened, and ready to face difficulties with an aggression that was always obviously compounded of equal quantities of bluff, self-reliance, and desperation.

In 1934, Ronald Shiner married Gladys Winifred Lester-Jones. He leaves a widow and one son.

July 1, 1966.

Brigadier Adib Shishakli, perhaps the ablest of the series of military leaders who seized power in Syria after the last war, was assassinated at Ceres, Brazil, on September 28, 1964. His ultimate failure illustrated the inherent difficulty of governing the volatile Syrian people.

He was born in 1901 in Hama, and enlisted in the French-officered "Troupes Spéciales" during the Mandatory period, but in 1945 deserted to the Syrian Army. In 1949 he participated in the first military *coup*, that of Husni Zaim, but then quarrelled with his leader and was dismissed. Zaim was soon afterwards ousted in a second *coup* by General Hinnawi, who reinstated Shishakli; but later the same year the latter joined forces with the Socialist leader Akram Haurani and, on the pretext that Hinnawi was planning to unite Syria with Iraq, ousted him in turn and took over the Government.

He seems to have recognized the danger of Army interference in politics and to have been sincerely anxious to restore a Parliamentary regime; under his auspices a general election was held and a new Constitution drafted. When, however, after 18 months, confusion continued to reign and stability appeared as far off as ever he lost patience, suspended the Chamber, dissolved all political parties, and assumed supreme power. In 1953 he enacted a new American-style Constitution, under which he was elected without opposition to the Presidency while his newly formed Arab Liberation Movement won 72 out of 82 seats in the new Assembly.

MISSED STABILITY

Under his firm rule Syria was quieter than for many years before or after, and had the professional politicians, who had held aloof from his party but who retained a preponderant influence among the electorate, been prepared to sink their personal ambitions and rivalries and collaborate with him, the country would have had at least a fair chance of attaining stability. They preferred, however, to intrigue against him, with the result that his rule inevitably became more and more arbitrary and repressive and thus intensified opposition. It was therefore no surprise when, in 1954, dissident elements in the Army revolted and drove him into exile. After a spell in France he retired to Brazil.

September 30, 1964.

Oswald Short, honorary Life President of Short Brothers and Harland Ltd., died at the age of 86 on December 4, 1969.

Hugh Oswald Short was the youngest of the three brothers from a Derbyshire family who helped to found the British aircraft industry and were associated with the earliest movement towards establishing sound technological standards for the light form of construction demanded by aircraft. All three were of an enterprising character. The eldest, Horace, was probably a genius who would have done great things in engineering if he had not died at an early age. The other two, Eustace and Oswald, broke into balloon making in the early years of the century, with a workshop under the railway arches at Battersea and actually made a balloon for Mr. J. T. C. Moore-Brabazon (later Lord Brabazon) in 1903.

By 1908 they had moved to Shellbeach on the Isle of Sheppey. Horace, lost to his family for several years as a rolling stone, was traced to Mexico where he was managing a mine, and was persuaded to join his brothers in the new undertaking. After a few attempts at design, they arranged with the Wright Brothers to build their type under licence and after production on the first six had begun were again approached by Mr. Moore-Brabazon for a British aircraft on which he could try to win the prize offered by the Daily Mail for the first Englishman to fly a circular mile on a British machine. That aircraft was largely a copy of the Wright machine but it won the prize and Short Brothers were launched.

Oswald thus came to maturity as an aircraft constructor in the best possible company. Shellbeach and later Eastchurch were from the first the resorts of the wealthy experimenters in aeronautics (at one period Moore-Brabazon's repairs bill ran at the rate of £300 a month) and they became the centres of the earliest scientific approach to the mysteries of the new art. The company was run on modest lines.

SUCCESS WITH SEAPLANES

It was ready to experiment. As early as 1911 it produced a twin-engined biplane; but it was not disposed to be adventurous and plodded along with the development of float aircraft; and although it had no spectacular representatives in the fighting between 1914 and 1918, its destiny had been cast. It was to succeed particularly with seaplanes and Oswald was to be early in the field with the use of aluminium alloys and to lead the way in stressed skin construction.

By 1924 Horace was dead. The R.A.F. was beginning to recognize the need for flying-boats. The two remaining brothers decided to specialize and found a site alongside the Medway at Rochester to which they moved. There they settled down seriously to flying-boat design in metal while some others were still building in wood. In 1932, Eustace died suddenly in the cockpit of a small float seaplane after landing it perfectly on the Medway, and Oswald found himself in sole conrol. He had been joined by an able designer, Arthur Gouge, and between them the work went forward. Oswald was responsible for the Singapore military boat and for the Sarafand which followed it. Thereafter he was increasingly concerned with the business side of the firm; and the design of the extremely successful commercial boats, the Calcutta, the Empire and the Golden Hind, which were to spread Britain's air mail system throughout the Commonwealth and across the Atlantic, fell more into the hands of Gouge and his team. Out of the Empire boat came the Sunderland, which the R.A.F. flew during the last war and went on flying until 1960.

December 6, 1969.

Sayed Siddik al-Mahdi, the Imam of Ansar, died on October 2, 1961. He had been the president of the former Umma Party which formed the Government before General Ibrahim Abboud's military coup in November, 1958, after which Sudanese political parties were dissolved.

A grandson of the Great Mahdi, who led the Dervish revolt in 1882, Sayed Siddik was born in 1911 and succeeded his father, Sayed Sir Abdel Rahman al-Mahdi, who died in March, 1959, as head of the powerful Ansar religious sect. He was thus the spiritual leader of several million Muslims in addition to being in charge of the commerical and financial side of the Ansar movement. He inherited great wealth from his father who had vast cotton estates south of Khartum and interests in Britain and elsewhere.

The death of Sayed Siddik al-Mahdi has removed from the Sudan political scene a figure of great potential importance. He shared with Sayed Ali el Mirghani, his father's great rival, the power to create a serious threat to the supremacy of the present military dictatorship, and the incident at the Moulid al Nebi ceremonies in the summer of 1960, when police fired on and inflicted casualties on a body of Ansar youths marching from the tomb of the Mahdi to the Moulid ground must have sorely tempted him to set the Mahdists in the Army a choice between their religious and secular allegiances. He seems to have decided that the preservation of a tradition of non-violent political change in the Sudan must be preserved at almost all costs. Sayed Siddik was a quieter character than his famous father. He came into prominence as a boy in the twenties by heading a strike in the Gordon College against proposed changes in the conditions of the Civil Service, but he was content thereafter to remain a little in the background, acting always as his father's representative rather than his heir.

Englishmen tended to regard him as being rather reserved but he was a very friendly and pleasant person to those who got to know him.

October 4, 1961.

Sir Percy Sillitoe, K.B.E., Director-General of the Security Service, more commonly known as M.I.5, from 1946 to 1953, died at his home in Eastbourne on April 5, 1962. He was 73.

Percy Joseph Sillitoe was educated at St. Paul's Cathedral Choir School. Before he was 20 he went abroad to serve in the British South Africa Police; if it was a life of adventure that he wanted he found it. In a broadcast talk he compared the lot of the B.S.A. trooper with that of the Canadian Mountie: nature was as much an adversary as the wanted man. Time and again in his experience it became a case of "him or me": to catch your man was one thing; to bring him back alive was quite another. Nevertheless, it was experience which Sillitoe never undervalued.

When war broke out in 1914 he had been gazetted in the Northern Rhodesia Police, but after British forces had occupied a considerable part of German East Africa he was one of the officers sent to administer it. After a period in the Ilundi district, where many of the natives had seldom if ever seen a European he transferred to the Administrative service in Tanganyika.

It was a serious attack of rheumatic fever—curiously forecast by a tribal usurper with whom Sillitoe had crossed swords—which brought him back to Britain and police work. His rise in the provincial police forces was rapid. He was Chief Constable of Chesterfield at 35 and three years later was made Chief Constable of Sheffield.

BEATING THE GANGS

In the late 1920s Sheffield was troubled by large gangs of gamblers and ruffians and in certain areas of the city the public were in such dread of them that it was hard to get witnesses when arrests were made. The new Chief Constable met force with force. He had no need of tear gas and machineguns; fists and very occasionally "detective batons" (smaller than the constable's truncheon) sufficed. The principal factor in breaking up the gangs, however, was not so much force as the spirit in which it was used and which gave the police confidence in their chief.

In 1931 he went to Glasgow where his qualities as an officer of the law were severely tested but where patient and courageous work triumphed as in Sheffield. There was corruption in the corporation and magistracy of the city and there were gangs but the police brought several grafters (including the chairman of the Police Committee) to justice and the housebreakers and hoodlums who plagued the city with their civil wars were checked by the "reasonable force" which had brought their kind to book in Sheffield.

IMPROVING STATUS

These activities made news and brought Sillitoe's name before the public, but it would be a mistake to see him at this time as nothing more than a gang-buster. He was a "whole" policeman; an innovator, pleading the cause of police science, one of the pioneers in the police force in the use of radio and a supporter of the system of police boxes. Moreover, in his support of his men and his concern for their welfare he did much to improve the status of the police.

In 1943 he was chosen to be, first, Chief Constable of Kent, and shortly afterwards Chief Constable of the Kent joint force, brought into being as a wartime measure by the amalgamation of all the individual forces. This might be termed his last orthodox police appointment, for in 1946 he was selected by Mr. Attlee, the Prime Minister, to be Director General of the Security Service.

He said later that when he took over as head of M.I.5 he knew very little of what his duties would be, although he knew that the Security Service operated on the same basic principles of those of any British force. In his own mind there was no doubt that long and varied experience of police work in Africa and Britain was relevant to the new field. His seven years with M.I.5—from 1946 to 1953—took him to the United States and Canada, to Egypt, Palestine, Kenya, and Malaya in a series of journeys which had never before been undertaken by a chief of the service. Certainly his term of office was a difficult one; public anxiety about security matters was greater than ever before and the difficult problem of detecting the ideological spy became the main task for internal security.

Whether the appointment of one of the most skilled police chiefs in Britain to the post of Director-General of Security Services was an ideal one is open to debate; the qualities that make an outstanding policeman do not necessarily fit him to direct counter-espionage and military security, and there were not wanting those who thought M.I.5 at fault in the cases of Fuchs, Pontecorvo, and Burgess and Maclean.

After his retirement he became a company director, and at the request of the late Sir Harry Oppenheimer undertook an investigation into illicit diamond buying. He was made C.B.E. in 1936, created a knight in 1942, and in 1950 was advanced to K.B.E.

April 6, 1962.

Sydney Silverman, Labour member of Parliament for Nelson and Colne since 1935, and peristent campaigner for the abolition of capital punishment, died in hospital at Hampstead on February 9, 1968. He was 72.

When, a few days before Christmas, 1964, the Commons gave a second reading by a majority of 185 votes to Silverman's Bill to free all types of murder from the death penalty, they conceded to him the most satisfying triumph of his political career. It was the reward of nearly 30 years of dogged endeavour. Although the Commons decision was not the end of the story, it was an impressive indication of how opinion in the Commons had moved in Silverman's direction since his earlier attempts to get the death penalty suspended or abolished. He could justly claim much of the credit for the compromise reform effected in 1957 by which hanging was retained for only five categories of murder, but it fell far short of his ideal. His conviction that the death penalty was a revolting and barbaric outrage on civilized standards gave him no rest from his fight to remove it completely. He brought to this cause all the resources of an uncommonly agile intellect, much tactical skill and a high degree of parliamentary expertise, perfected by incessant practice.

As a politician, Silverman defied facile classification. He was well to the left on many issues and at one time or another he appeared to have been associated with most movements of rebellion or intransigence, from "Keep Left" to C.N.D. But he was too much of an individualist and a freelance—above all, a perfectionist—to find any organization wholly congenial for long. He was all for liberty, particularly his own.

Although he was short of stature there was a dynamic and oddly impressive quality about him with his snowy mop of hair and aggressively bearded chin.

Samuel Sydney Silverman was born in Liverpool on October 8, 1895, the son of the late Mr. M. Silverman of that city. He made his way without any financial backing from the Liverpool Institute to the University of Liverpool, where he was prominent in the Labour Club as a debater with a tongue as sharp as his brain. He was accepted for the honours school of English literature; then came the Military Service Act of 1916. Silverman conscientiously objected and after he had resumed his studies he only took an ordinary degree. He successfully applied for a lectureship in English at the National University of Finland. He remained there until the mid-1920s, returned to Liverpool and entered the University School of Law. He graduated LL.B. with honours and was admitted a solicitor in 1927. He was elected for Nelson and Colne in 1935 and retained the seat at subsequent elections.

He had come out as an opponent of capital punishment before the war, but it was not until April, 1948, that he got the approval of the Commons for a new clause in the Criminal Justice Bill to provide for a five-year experimental suspension of the death penalty. When the Lords reversed this decision, Silverman reluctantly accepted the Labour Government's compromise defining categories of murder, but he voted against them when they yielded to the Lords' resistance to it. A fortnight later he got into the bad books of the party leaders by signing a telegram of good wishes sent by 37 Labour M.P.s to the Nenni Socialists in Italy who were cooperating with Communists in the Popular Front.

As a Jew, Silverman was an ardent supporter of the establishment of a Jewish National Home in Palestine. In matters affecting the treatment of members of his race he often came into conflict with the late Ernest Bevin; they seemed to irritate each other. After one sharp difference of opinion, when the Foreign Secretary had left the House in a rage, Silverman acidly said of him: "He blows in, blows up and blows out." As chairman of the World Jewish Congress and as one of the Parliamentary delegates to the Nazi prison camps after the war, he was passionately concerned that the Jewish survivors should not be denied the chance of making their homes in Palestine.

In 1953 Silverman failed to get leave to bring in a Bill to suspend the death penalty, but in 1956 came his big chance. The way was prepared in February of that year when an abolitionist amendment to a Government motion to retain capital punishment was carried by 31 votes. The Government agreed to find time for a private member's Bill. Quite by chance Silverman got the opportunity to introduce one—the Death Penalty (Abolition) Bill. On March 12, 1956, the Commons on a free vote gave it a second reading, by 286 votes to 262, against the advice of the Government. Silverman's tactical skill in piloting it through the House added greatly to his parliamentary reputation. The Lords rejected the Bill but it was impossible for the Government to let matters rest there. Although they could not concede total abolition, they could not ignore Silverman's moral victory. They compromised by retaining the death penalty for five categories of capital murder in the Homicide Bill which the Home Secretary, Mr. R.A. Butler, conducted through the Commons. The Act received the Royal Assent on March 21, 1957.

He became vice-chairman and then chairman of the "ginger" group who fought under the banner of "Victory for Socialism". In June, 1960, they issued a statement calling for Hugh Gaitskell's resignation and Silverman, in face of angry interruptions, defended their action at the meeting of the Parliamentary Labour Party. Later in the year came the Scarborough conference and Gaitskell's pledge to "fight, fight and fight again" against the unilateralist vote. Silverman, as chairman of V.F.S., issued a long argumentative letter urging Gaitskell to "think, think and think again". He adopted Harold Wilson's line on this issue and supported his candidature for the party leadership.

UNLIKELY SUPPORTERS

With the return of a Labour Government in 1964 Silverman had not to wait long for the chance to test opinion in the new Parliament on the issue of hanging. A free vote on both sides of the House was assured for the second reading, on December 21 that year, of his Murder (Abolition of Death Penalty) Bill, which sought to extend the principle of abolition to those classes of murder which the 1957 Homicide Act had excluded. What he could hardly have expected was the measure of support from unlikely and influential quarters which his own ideas had gathered over the years. The night of the second reading debate was a great occasion for him and he made the most of it. He spoke for nearly an hour and a quarter without a note, pursuing familiar arguments into exhaustive detail. The emotion which nearly overwhelmed him at the end was as sincere as it was moving.

In 1967, Silverman made a venomous attack on the Prime Minister after he had made his "dog's licence" speech to the Parliamentary Labour Party. Silverman called it "the most dangerous attack on social democracy made in this country in my time".

Silverman married in 1933 Nancy, daughter of the late Mr. L. Rubinstein, of Liverpool.

February 10, 1968.

Sir John Hope Simpson, K.B.E., C.I.E., who after a career in the Indian Civil Service carried out a succession of international and Dominion tasks with skill and judgment, died on April 10, 1961, at the age of 92.

He will be remembered for his contribution to the refugee problems following on two world wars, more particularly in the Middle East, and for his contribution to the welfare of China after the disastrous Yangtze floods of the early thirties.

He was born on July 23, 1868, the son of John Hope Simpson, of Sefton Park, Liverpool, who was general manager of the Bank of Liverpool, later merged into Martins Bank. He was educated at Liverpool College (like his six brothers) and at Balliol College, Oxford, and joined the I.C.S. in 1889. In 1904 he became Registrar of Rural Co-operative Credit Societies, which were designed by the Government to save the peasantry from the burdensome exactions of the village *bania* (moneylender). This was a duty welcome to a man of his sympathetic nature. In 1908 he was selected to be president of the Municipal Taxation Committee of the United Provinces. He was acting as Chief Commissioner of the Nicobar and Andaman islands when war broke out in 1914 and his responsibilities in charge of the penal settlement in the mid-Indian Ocean were made the heavier by the exploits of the German cruiser Emden; he spent some anxious days in his official yacht visiting the various islands and communicating such information as he could obtain to the British naval authorities.

Hope Simpson retired from the I.C.S. in 1916, and in 1922 was elected to Parliament in the Liberal interests for the Taunton division of Somerset, but lost the seat in the 1924 general election. In that year he was made chairman of the Indian Colonies Committee which inquired into the grievances of Indian settlers in various parts of the world. In 1926 he was made vice-president of the Refugee Settlement Commission in Athens set up by the League of Nations, and filled the post for four years.

SETTLING REFUGEES

The task of the commission was to resettle the Greek refugees who had been driven out of Anatolia by the victorious nationalist armies of the Turks. This experience was followed in 1930 by his selection by the British Government to take stock of the administration of the mandated territory of Palestine. Sharp conflict had broken out between Jews and Arabs over such matters of detail as the periodical assembly of Jews at the Wall of Weeping, Jerusalem. Hope Simpson's political insight and clear understanding were shown in the successful working out of the measures he recommended in an admirable report.

Still more onerous responsibilities were placed upon him when in 1931 he was chosen to be Director-General of the National Flood Relief Commission, China, under the League of Nations. The appointment was made at the urgent request of the Chinese Government for the loan of an acknowledged expert. The disaster had left behind in the Yangtze valley a scene of indescribable desolation.

There was rapid spread of malaria, dysentery, cholera, and typhus fever. Moreover, the southern bank of the Yangtze was in the possession of the southern communists, who recognized no authority but their own. For three years Hope Simpson was the chief planner of appropriate measures for relief and prevention of such calamities in the future.

From 1934 to 1936 he was in Newfoundland as one of the three British members working with the same number of natives of the country as administrators of the territory. Newfoundland had been for some time a self-governing Dominion, but had encountered serious financial and industrial difficulties, notably in the fields of agriculture and fishing. The work of the commission over a period of two years prepared the way for temporary expedients leading in 1949 to Newfoundland and its dependency in Labrador becoming the tenth Province of the Dominion of Canada.

Hope Simpson was made C.I.E. in 1913, knighted in 1925, and created K.B.E. in 1937.

He married in 1900 Quita, youngest daughter of the late Robert Barclay, of Sedgley New Hall, Prestwich, Manchester, by whom he had two sons and three daughters. She died in 1939 and he married secondly in 1941 Evelyn, widow of W. H. Brookes, and younger twin daughter of J. Forster Hamilton.

April 12, 1961.

Sir Joseph Simpson, K.B.E., the Metropolitan Police Commissioner, died suddenly at his home at Roehampton, Surrey, on March 20, 1968, at the age of 58. He was appointed commissioner in 1958.

Before going to Scotland Yard, Simpson was Assistant Chief Constable of Lincolnshire from 1937 to 1943, Chief Constable of Northumberland from 1943 to 1946, and Chief Constable of Surrey from 1946 to 1956. He was appointed Assistant Commissioner at Scotland Yard in 1956.

He was the first policeman to start his career as a constable and rise through the ranks to Commissioner of Metropolitan Police.

He took over at a time of mounting crime figures, a return to gang warfare, and a deterioration in relations between police and public. In July, 1967, in his annual report, Simpson was hopeful that the crime tide was turning. He reported that relations between police and public had improved. The "have a go" policy was initiated during his time, and he thought it had had a good effect. But in January he warned the public to stay away from armed bandits.

On his appointment as Commissioner of Police in 1958 Simpson set as one of his main tasks the development of a more personal leadership in the Metropolitan Police, one in which the top and the bottom were brought more closely together. His earlier service on the beat in the Bow Street Division, and at various levels of the force, gave him an appreciation of the problems and views of the lower ranks, an attribute which assisted him greatly in his efforts to overcome the somewhat impersonal character of so large an organization. He had the confidence of the ordinary member of the force who knew that in any difficulty he would have a fair and unbiased hearing.

He was much concerned, as Commissioner, with the organization of the Cadet Corps in the Metropolitan Police. Under his guidance the Corps was greatly expanded, and he introduced entirely new methods of training to enable the cadet to continue his education while at the same time developing a sense of discipline and responsibility. Among other aspects of the administration of the Metropolitan Police to which Sir Joseph made valuable contributions were those of crime prevention, the use of police dogs, and the development of good relations between the police and the public, and between the ranks of the force.

As Commissioner he had a series of exceptionally difficult problems to deal with, arising from the handling of certain individual cases by police officers (e.g. Garratt v. Eastmond), appointment of the Royal Commission on the Police, and the cases in which ex-Detective Sergeant Challenor was concerned; and from the demonstrations of the Committee of 100, including the disorders in Trafalgar Square in September, 1961. His personal integrity and determination to see the right thing done had a profound effect on all who came in contact with him, including the members of the Royal Commissions.

Born in 1909, he was educated at Oundle School and Manchester University College of Technology. At Oundle he was captain of football and athletics. He was the Public Schools Champion in the long jump in 1927 and 1928 (a record) and the 440 yards in 1928. He represented Manchester University in Rugby and athletics and was the world's university champion in the 400 metre hurdles in 1930.

After a short period in the cotton trade he joined the Metropolitan police in 1931, and after three years on the beat he attended the new Hendon Police College from 1934 to 1935, where he was the outstanding student.

CALLED TO BAR

He returned to the college on the instructional staff in 1936, and was called to the Bar by Gray's Inn in 1937.

He was a keen rifle shot and cricketer, and latterly devoted a great deal of his time to encouraging athletics and other sports.

Throughout the whole of his police career Simpson set himself the highest of personal standards, and although tolerant of human failings in others he expected those around him to conform to those standards. Perhaps his greatest qualification for high position was the ability to mix with people at all levels. He was as much at home with the youngest member of the police rugby fifteen as he was in the company of the most distinguished in the land, with whom his appointment brought him into daily contact.

He married in 1936 Elizabeth May, daughter of Percy Bowler. They had two sons.

March 21, 1968.

Dr Percy Simpson, editor of Ben Jonson, died on November 14, 1962, at the age of 97.

Percy Simpson was born on November 1, 1865, the son of John Simpson, of Lichfield. Educated at Denstone College and at Selwyn College, of which he was classical scholar, he taught classics and English at his old school and (from 1899 to 1913) at St. Olave's Grammar School. The bent of his nature and the discipline of school and college made him a good classical scholar, but like all men of his and earlier generations he had to make himself a good scholar in his mother tongue without academic assistance. This he did, not without dust and heat, in such time as the life of a busy schoolmaster spared him.

In 1913, at the invitation of Sir Walter Raleigh and the instigation of Charles Cannan, Secretary to the Delegates of the Clarendon Press, he went to Oxford as a Lecturer in English. It had become apparent that some of the works published by the Clarendon Press had failed to profit from the advance in textual and bibliographical method chiefly associated with the names of Greg and McKerrow; and the improvement in these respects in the Elizabethan texts which have come from the Press since 1913 is in part attributable to Simpson and to his teaching in the Oxford School of English.

SHAKESPEARE'S PUNCTUATION

In 1921 he became a Fellow of Oriel, and of all the academic honours which he received, this, together with his election to an honorary fellowship in 1943, gave him greatest pleasure. For 20 years (1914-34) he was librarian of the English School, and from its modest beginnings in 1914 he watched over the interests of his fine library with zealous care and skill. He was Goldsmiths' Reader in English from 1930 till his retirement in 1935. In 1946 at the age of 80 he took pupils once more in a crowded Oriel, and at the age of 79 he established the authenticity of the reading "pertauntlike" in *Love's Labour's Lost* and so disposed of a dozen emendations.

When Simpson went to Oxford in 1913 he was chiefly known for his *Shakespearian Punctuation* (1911) a book which proved that the punctuation of the First Folio of Shakespeare was not so lax and unprincipled as most editors had supposed. But while he published much else of interest and importance, notably his chapters on "Actors and Acting", and "The Masque" in *Shakespeare's England* (1916), the descriptive catalogue (with C. F. Bell) of Inigo Jones's designs for masques and plays at Court (1924), and a pioneer work on *Proof-Reading in the Sixteenth, Seventeenth, and Eighteenth Centuries* (1935), the main task of his life was to edit Jonson.

He began work about the year 1890, and in 1903 joined C. H. Herford, of Manchester—for whom he had the highest regard—as co-editor of the Oxford Jonson; but it was not until 1925 that the two volumes of prolegomena on Jonson, "the Man and his Work", were published. Herford's share was limited in the main to the biographical and critical chapters. The six volumes of the text appeared at intervals from 1927 to 1947.

The textual introductions and the critical apparatus have been thought over-elaborate and like all works of human endeavour they contain mistakes: but when the three volumes of commentary, &c., were published (1950-52), it became yet more clear that this is one of the great editions in our time of an English classic. The annotator of Jonson must possess a wide range of classical and Renaissance learning, and must also be as intimately acquainted with the daily life and speech of Elizabethan England as an annotator of Shakespeare. This range of learning Simpson had as few have ever had it.

At a ceremony at Oriel on his eighty-fifth birthday, the day the first volume of the commentary was published, he was presented by the Delegates of the Press with a specially bound copy and by his friends with a pamphlet containing a "character" and a list of his writings. Other distinctions were honorary doctorates at Cambridge and Glasgow and an honorary fellowship at Selwyn. At the age of 87 he announced that he was turning to Shakespeare, and a new essay on the poet's use of Latin authors is to be found, with older papers, in his last book, *Studies in Elizabethan Drama* (1955).

HELPFUL TO YOUNG SCHOLARS

In 1921 he married Miss Evelyn Spearing, a scholar in her own right; she survives him together with a daughter. In 1953 an only son, who promised to become one of the great authorities on international monetary problems, was accidentally killed while on a skiing holiday at Chamonix.

Simpson was as generous and helpful to all young scholars whom he thought to be in earnest as he was contemptuous of those who fell below the standards he set for himself. Some memory of his tutor's erudition may have given the original impulse to Aldous Huxley's short story with the Jonsonian title "Eupompus gave splendour to art by numbers". He was a tireless walker, and there were few roads and footpaths within 20 miles of Oxford which were not known to him in his Sunday excursions. His irate letters to the *Oxford Times* preserved paths that might have been lost. He continued to walk at an age when most men have taken to the chimney-corner.

November 16, 1962.

Tom Simpson, the outstanding British racing cyclist, died on July 13, 1967, at the age of 29. He was born in co. Durham, on November 30, 1937, but lived most of his formative years in Haworth, Nottinghamshire, and was one of Britain's outstanding professional sportsmen.

A cyclist, he won a national championship in 1956 before going to the Melbourne Olympic Games where as part of 4,000 metres pursuit team he won a bronze medal. Representing England in the 1958 British Commonwealth and Empire Games at Cardiff, he won a silver medal in the individual pursuit in one of the closest finishes ever seen, before leaving for the Continent to try to take the world unpaced hour record at Zurich. Though he did not achieve this he put up the best performance ever ridden by an Englishman, and decided to stay on the Continent, at St. Brieuc, Brittany, to prepare himself for the following year's World Amateur Championships.

After an outstanding season as an amateur he felt himself strong enough to compete in the world professional road championship in Holland, where he gained fourth place behind the French rider, A. Darrigarde, at Zandvoort. In 1960 as a professional he won the Tour of South East France; in 1961 he became the first Englishman to win the Continental classic, the Tour of Flanders. The following year he became the first Englishman to hold the yellow jersey of leadership in the Tour de France and followed this success by setting a new record for the longest single-day race on the Continent from Bordeaux to Paris in 1963.

This was probably his most successful year for he was also second in two other classic races and in the Continent's professional best all-rounder competition, the Super Prestige Pernod.

Early in 1964 he won his first Italian race from Milan to San Remo and then went on to another fourth place in the world road championship at Sallanches as well as taking sixth place in the last Tour de France he was to finish. Although in 1965 he failed to finish in this race, when he was hurt so badly in a crash that doctors feared they might need to amputate his arm, two months afterwards he finally won the world road championship. Within another month he had won his second Italian classic, the Tour of Lombardy, a feat which resulted in his being voted sportsman of the year in Britain. Though he broke his leg in a skiing accident that winter and failed once more through a further crash after a collision with a motor bike in the Tour de France, throughout 1966 his standing among his peers was little diminished. In the spring of 1967 he won the first major race of the season from Paris to Nice and had then settled down to prepare meticulously for the Tour de France.

A man of moderate education, trained as a draughtsman, his quick intelligence and gift for conversation made him an ever-entertaining host or guest in the several languages he had acquired during his nine years living in Brittany, Paris and Ghent, Belgium.

Though he never claimed to be physically the best endowed, he was always convinced that no feat, no honour, was beyond his achieving. Indeed many times he pushed himself beyond all reasonable endurance in an effort to prove still more.

As a sportsman he was outstanding; as a friend he was endearing, as a man he was courageous in a way that only one who has been regarded by his neighbours as eccentric could be.

He leaves a wife, Helen, and two daughters, Jane and Joanne.

July 14, 1967.

Upton Sinclair, left-wing novelist and Pulitzer prize winner, whose writing career spanned more than 60 years, died in New Jersey on November 26, 1968, at the age of 90.

Sinclair, who was married three times, published more than 80 works. He won the Pulitzer Prize in 1943 for his book *Dragon's Teeth,* an account of the rise of fascism in Germany, published in 1942. An earlier book, *The Jungle,* an exposé of the meat packing industry in the Chicago stockyards, shocked the American nation and prompted President Theodore Roosevelt to invite the novelist to the White House. In 1967 he went to the White House again when President Johnson signed the Wholesome Meat Bill which crowned the crusade Sinclair had begun with *The Jungle.*

There were good reasons, no doubt, why Upton Sinclair, for all the stir and excitement he evoked, did not quite attain the literary recognition in the United States which was his due. First, he was a "radical," a socialist of a thoroughgoing kind, in a society still blown by the winds of rugged individualism.

POLITICS FIRST

He himself frequently declared that he was a socialist first and a novelist afterwards. Hence the propagandist and—almost of necessity in the high noon of American industrial capitalism—the "muckraking" emphasis of his whole career of authorship, an emphasis every whit as pronounced in his fiction as in his polemical studies and pamphlets. Thus besides defying popular sentiment in the first place, the creative writer in Upton Sinclair was always subdued to the publicist and journalist. His interest in public affairs was all-embracing; he had something of the critical universality of mind of Bernard Shaw, though he lacked Shaw's aesthetic sensibilities.

Born in Baltimore, Maryland, on September 20, 1878, the child of parents who belonged to the ruined aristocracy of the South, Upton Sinclair went with them to New York when he was 10. His father he described afterwards as a liquor salesman with a taste for his own wares.

At the age of 15, already a student at the City College of New York (where he took his degree four years later), he was making money by composing humorous trifles and light verse, and a year or two later he was earning as much as the equivalent of £14 a week from adventure serials commissioned by boys' magazines and published under various high-sounding naval and military pseudonyms.

LARGE OUTPUT

Before he was 21 he had put into print (he once calculated) more words than are contained in the *Waverley* novels.

He broke away at last from these horrific labours and sat down to write his first really serious novel, *Springtime and Harvest,* which was published in 1901, like most of the books he wrote in middle years, at his own expense. (He had written a first novel at 17 and soon after finished another, *Prince Hagen,* which was offered in 37 markets and always rejected.)

Springtime and Harvest met with little response, as also did *King Midas,* which came out in the same year. Sinclair refused to be discouraged. Published anonymously in 1903, in which year *Prince Hagen* also appeared at last, *The Journal of Arthur Stirling* made more stir, since its air of an authentic diary raised the temperature of the story Sinclair told in it of his own material and intellectual struggles. Then came his novel of the Civil War, *Manassas* (1904) (which he described eventually as "my one book which not the severest critic can say has any propaganda motive.")

The Jungle appeared in 1906, after the publishers, who at first were fearful of handling it, had been satisfied by their own inquiries of its essential truth. It is no exaggeration to say that the novel set the whole English-speaking world agog. Sinclair, it seems, had deliberately taken *Uncle Tom's Cabin* as a model for what he intended to achieve, and his achievement was indeed in some respects comparable. The book marked the climax of a period of profound social disquietude in the United States, where amidst an immediate response of startled horror Sinclair found himself stigmatized as a "professional muckraker" and worse. His writings were loudly assailed, his social experiments—such as his Helicon Home Colony at Englewood, New Jersey—mercilessly mocked.

He did not slacken in his exposure of the evils and injustices of American society. The neglect of some at least of the novels, plays, and essays which he poured out in the years after the publication of *The Jungle* might be excused in part on critical grounds, since the sheer pace at which Sinclair wrote, motives of propaganda apart, was often his artistic undoing. But the neglect, in fact, was seldom a matter of considered judgment. There was no excuse, for instance, for ignoring *Love's Pilgrimage* (1911), which was based upon his early marriage and which is one of his more imaginatively satisfying exercises in fiction.

DIVORCE

After a divorce from his first wife, by whom he had one son, he married in 1913 Mary Craig Kimbrough, and in new and happier domestic circumstances he worked with even more tireless energy. In 1915 he settled in southern California, at Pasadena, where he remained for close on 40 years. Two years later he broke temporarily with the American Socialist movement to support America's entry into the war, but almost at once bore witness to his disillusion in *Jimmie Higgins and The Spy*.

His principal output between 1917 and 1927 was a remarkable series of "economic interpretations" of American social influences—religious, journalistic, educational, literary. In this semi-Marxist analysis of the superstructure of capitalist culture, these volumes—*The Profits of Religion*, *The Brass Check*, *The Goose-Step*, *The Goslings*, *Mammon-art*, and *Money Writes*—demonstrated at once his strength in garnering, selecting and presenting fact, and the weakness of his popular materialist standpoint in interpreting fact. It was with *Oil!* in 1927 that he stepped once more into the leading place among American documentary novelists. Probably this is his most impressive work of fiction, for the power of its nearest rival, *Boston* (1928), which dealt with the Sacco-Vanzetti trial, lay wholly in the accuracy with which he presented the historic facts of the case.

Among the novels of the next few years were *Mountain City* (1930), *Roman Holiday* (1931), *The Wet Parade*—(1931), the last a telling study of Prohibition. Then came an intensive phase of political and public activity, after which the novelist resumed work with more essays in documentary fiction. His biggest undertaking consisted of a chronicle, or series of chronicles, alert and humane in sympathy but frankly journalistic in style, of world politics since 1914. The first volume, *World's End*, appeared in 1940 and was followed by *Between Two Worlds*, *Dragon's Teeth* (which was awarded the Pulitzer Prize), *Wide is the Gate*, *Presidential Agent* and other volumes.

In 1918 Sinclair had become his own publisher in Pasadena in order to issue his books at the cheapest possible price, and it was only with the Lanny Budd volumes that he relinquished that extra burden. He stood as Socialist candidate for Congress for the second time in 1920 (the first was in 1906), for the senate in 1922, for the Governorship of California in 1926 and again in 1930, and surprisingly won the Democratic nomination for the Governorship in 1934 with a programme to end poverty—but the nomination only. He took part in numerous radical movements. Towards the end of his life, while he was still pursuing the odyssey Lanny Budd, his mind turned increasingly towards questions of personal faith and philosophy and rested in the last resort at something like a secular Christianity. In 1953, after half a lifetime in California, he moved to the small town of Buckeye in Arizona. His second wife died in 1961 and his third, Mary Willis, in 1967.

November 27, 1968.

For the death of **Dame Edith Sitwell,** contemporary English poetry is the poorer. Dame Edith died on December 9, 1964, at St. Thomas's Hospital, London at the age of 77.

At any time before the publication of *Gold Coast Customs* in 1929 a common judgment on Dame Edith's poems might have been that they combined great technical virtuosity with a vision of life which seemed oddly precious and private. Even today Dame Edith's work has not been accepted by academic critics as centrally important in the way that Yeats's or Eliot's has. Throughout her career the most discriminating praise of her work came from fellow poets, though some fellow poets, like Geoffrey Grigson, were also among her sharper assailants. Her poetry was not in the Arnoldian sense, a "criticism of life", but was a poetry essentially of praise and transformation. She combined a taste for elaborate and latterly for sweeping technical effects with a basic simplicity of vision: a vision deeply affected in her early poems by childhood memories, and in her later poems by a mixture of deep horror at the violence and cruelty of the world with profound faith in the ultimate goodness of God and holiness of nature.

Her verses always danced rather than walked, her voice was incantatory rather than conversational. The texture of her poems was both enriched and sometimes made a little monotonous by a fondness for certain recurrent symbols; lions, deserts, skeletons, the sun, and for certain favourite colours, green and gold; she was deeply affected by the French symbolists, of whom she had made a profound study, in her attempts at synaesthesia, her association, for instance, of shrillness with greenness. Gardens, the Russian ballet, folk-tales, and the actual physical possession of a voice of far longer breath and richer tonal range than that of any other woman poet of her time, helped to give her work its peculiarly individual quality. With all this, there is also, particularly in her earlier poems, a frequent gaiety and harsh, surprising humour. The total effect of her poetry, like that of her personality, was strange and formidable, and somehow slightly over life-size. Both the verses and the personality lent themselves to criticism, and sometimes even to ridicule, but about both there was a fine aristocratic indifference to common standards that tended to make the criticism and ridicule seem boorish.

There were two Dame Ediths, the formidable bejewelled and turbaned figure who captivated many who had never read a word of her work when she appeared on television with John Freeman; and the dignified and pleasant country gentle woman whom young poets had the privilege sometimes of meeting at literary parties or at her favourite Sesame Club. Underneath all her airs and graces and fantasies there was, in life as in literature, a core of simple and natural good breeding.

A DIFFICULT FATHER

Born at Scarborough on September 7, 1887, Edith Sitwell was the eldest child of Sir George Sitwell, fourth baronet, a man of deep and learned artistic tastes, particularly in gardening, a notable English eccentric, and a difficult father. She spent much of her youth at the family seat, Renishaw Hall, in Derbyshire, which, imaginatively transformed, forms the background to one of her most successful early long poems, *The Sleeping Beauty*. There were occasional visits to Italy and Spain. Unlike her brother, Sir Osbert, Dame Edith never wrote any detailed account of her childhood, but she made it clear that it was unhappy. A lonely girl, not beautiful by the conventional standards of Edwardian times, she relied on the friendship of governesses and servants and the moral support of brothers younger than herself. She began to read poetry when she was 14, but her poetic ambitions were first aroused by encountering Swinburne's *Poems and Ballads* at the age of 17. In temperament and in her technical gifts she was not unlike Swinburne, though her imagination, unlike his, remained all her life one of virginal purity: but, like him, she excelled in creating a mounting rhythmical excitement, and it could be said of her images, as Eliot said of Swinburne's, that they sometimes become mere "points of diffusion."

Edith Sitwell's first verses appeared in the *Daily Mirror*. It was only in 1916, when she was nearly 30, that she threw out a serious challenge with the anthology *Wheels*, which published the work of a number of young poets who had been omitted from Sir Edward Marsh's *Georgian Poetry*. Like some of the poets in Ezra Pound's *Catholic Anthology*, which appeared about the same time, many of the poets who appeared in *Wheels* had been much influenced by the French symbolists; but the emphasis was on verbal music and surprising associations of images rather than on the techniques of ironic and indirect social commentary and criticism which Eliot, for instance, had learnt from Laforgue. Miss Sitwell's own early poetry was especially notable for its preoccupation with what she called "texture". She developed, for this, a critical vocabulary of her own, of light and heavy, or light and dark, of plunging and soaring, of narrow or broad, vowels and diphthongs, which, highly personal though it was, she could use to illuminate vividly the technical qualities she admired in other people's poems.

CONTRAST OF BREVITY

Her remarks on the content and argument of poems were always, in comparison, perfunctory, and prevented her narrow but highly developed special critical gift from being taken at its true value.

The other notable quality of her early poems was the frequent use of transposed imagery, as in:

the unripe snow falls
Like little tunes on the virginals
Whose sound is bright, unripe and sour
As small fruits fall'n before their hour.

There is a rich, almost physical, almost tactual pleasurableness in the detail of these early poems, but it might be said that they explore sensation rather than life, or even that their structural existence is largely that of trellises over which these individual blooms of detail are trained to hang. Certain general preoccupations, with death, with fashion, with ghosts, with gardens, a tone of voice that mingles mockery and exultation, give a common flavour to the early poems, but do not distinguish one sharply from another. But the voice sometimes has a major and ominous richness as in the wonderful opening of *The Sleeping Beauty*:

When we come to that dark house,
Never sound of wave shall rouse
The bird that sings within the blood
Of those who sleep in that dark wood...

or in this couplet from the first version of *Metamorphosis* (1929):

The polar night's huge boulder hath rolled this,
My heart, my Sisyphus, in the abyss.

There is something permanently attractive also in the elegant clownishness of *Bucolic Comedies* and *Facade*. But *Gold Coast Customs* (1929)—in a sense Miss Sitwell's version of *The Waste Land*—expresses a much deeper vision of the horror and hollowness of much contemporary life. Even this, perhaps, has a touch still of the deliberate and provocative "mannerism" of the earlier work. The wish to startle or shock the middle-classes only, perhaps, left Dame Edith in the poems she wrote during the Second World War, collected in 1964 as *The Song of the Cold*. In poems like *Lullaby* and *Song of the Rain*, both of which first appeared in *The Times Literary Supplement*, she seems for the first time completely lost in her subject. There is a new directness of thought and feeling, combined with a new mastery of the long sweeping line and the sustained verse paragraph. She resists the temptation of colourful digression and irrelevant ornament. The repetition of favourite words and phrases, though it was much criticized by, for instance, Geoffrey Grigson, heightens the intimacy of her appeal. The manner of these war-time poems remained, broadly, her manner to the end, and is sustained in volumes like *Gardeners and Astronomers* (1953) and *The Outcasts* (1962).

The Song of the Cold probably marked the moment of Dame Edith's widest general appeal. In later volumes the repetition of favourite effects and allusions, and a certain diffuseness, becomes more noticeable. Dame Edith's thought did not develop, and indeed she was not, as a poet, a "thinker"; but she retained to the end a sustained elevation and intensity of manner, and a purity of religious vision. She is a poet who perhaps wrote too much and who yet, because, as in Swinburne's case, a certain expansiveness is part of her quality, would be difficult to represent justly either in anthologies or in a brief selected volume. A final judgment on her may perhaps rate the earlier poems rather higher and be more selective in its attitude to the later poems than critical fashion now. But the attempt to dismiss her as belonging to the history of publicity rather than poetry is not likely to succeed. Poets as good and as different as W. B. Yeats, Robert Graves, and Roy Campbell all at different times found something to praise in her.

FREQUENT ANTHOLOGIST

She was also a copious writer of prose and a frequent anthologist. Her most recent anthology, *The Atlantic Book of British and American Poetry* (1959), is notable both for its range and for the technical acuteness of some of the notes on individual poets. A critical book, *Aspects of Modern poetry*, published in 1934, had a somewhat stormy passage; she had unconsciously incorporated in it fairly close paraphrases of other contemporary critics she was attacking and had been careless in checking the accuracy of her quotations. She wrote a book on Pope which, while lacking the scholarly equipment of a later critic like Tillotson, and written often in rather too flowery a style, showed a vivid appreciation of Pope's "texture" and did much to revive general interest in him. She wrote also an agreeable book on Bath, and a rather over-loadedly romantic book about Swift. She was fascinated by queens, and wrote two books about Queen Elizabeth (the second, published in 1962, also bringing in Mary Queen of Scots) and one about Queen Victoria. She was not a trained historical scholar in any sense but, relying on secondary sources for her narrative and background, used history or historical biography as an excuse for bringing in bravura set-pieces of picturesque description, or romantic meditation, at which she excelled. The extracts and jottings of *A Poet's Notebook* (1943) gave evidence of the richly wandering range of her reading and of her preoccupation with technique. There was a certain magpie-like quality in her prose, as in some of her poems; phrases, images, episodes attracted her by their glitter. As a polemical correspondent in the newspapers, she had a fine gift for the crushing irrelevance, which was sometimes not so irrelevant as it seemed.

Miss Sitwell was created a Dame of the British Empire in 1954, and had received honorary degrees from the Universities of Leeds, Durham, Oxford, and Sheffield. It is rumoured that, before it was gently hinted to her that this was not done, she used to sign her more formal letters with a triple "D.Litt." As a person, she was tall, handsome, and striking, with a resemblance both to Queen Elizabeth I and to Henry VII of which she was proud. She was often accused of being fond of publicity, but she used her public reputation very largely to help poets, musicians, and artists whom she admired, among them Sir William Walton, Dylan Thomas, and Pavel Tchelitchew. To those who knew her well her combatant spirit and fondness for the crushing snub were less notable than her dignified kindness. She had an aristocratic disdain for compromise and for muffled responses. She was as fond of exotic costume as she was of esoteric imagery. Sargent painted her as a little girl with her brothers, and there are paintings of her in the Tate Gallery by Tchelitchew and Wyndham Lewis (whose work she continued to admire in spite of his virulent attacks on her in criticism and fiction).

December 10, 1964.

Sir Osbert Sitwell, BT., C.H., C.B.E., an author of many and brilliant parts, died on May 4, 1969, at his home in Italy. He was 76.

Poet, novelist, short-story writer, essayist, art critic, and author of a sustained and richly ornate feat of autobiography, Sir Osbert Sitwell belonged in spirit and sympathy to the age of baroque or even to the age of rococo. No writer of his day carried with greater ease and elegance the burden of a passion for superabundant ornamentation. Always the man of taste rather than the man of feeling, he had his own mode of sensibility—the Sitwell mode—with which, together with his sister, Edith, and his brother, Sacheverell, he waged unremitting and uninhibited war upon the philistine. And not upon the philistine only. The Sitwell style of provocation became celebrated in its earliest manifestation, and Sir Osbert, whose aesthetic dislikes and disfavours were of some diversity, brought a majestic assurance to the exhibition of his foibles. Yet the integrity of his pursuit of art was as little in question as the charm of mind and manner which delighted his friends. In his eighteenth-century grandee fashion he was an imposing figure, and an individual and considerable writer.

As poet he explored that part of the Sitwell country where satire flourished most vigorously and at the same time pursued the essentially Sitwellian experience of childhood in deftly invented portraits of types and characters. As essayist and travel writer he was almost unfailingly luxurious and piquant in observation as well as constantly entertaining. As writer on art and architecture he seldom faltered in idiosyncratic conviction and an instinct for iconoclasm or in his delight in rococo. The novelist, notably the author of *Before The Bombardment* and *The Man Who Lost Himself,* was a satirist of commanding powers, with a telling gift both for high comedy and for extravagant farce (both, incidentally, mingling something of Dickens with their contemporary flavour), but was not, perhaps, of a deeply imaginative cast. The short-story writer, again, though bold and diverting, ran all too easily to anecdote. All Sitwell's virtues, however, and with them the defects of his virtues, were summed up in the author of the five astonishing volumes of his celebrated experiment in autobiography. Here the discursive traveller and the unsentimental writer of fiction achieved a faultless elegance of deportment, a Regency dandyism in literary values, a Corinthian richness and brilliance of style. On the recollections of his formative years, and more especially on the elaborate portrait, or gallery of portraits, of his father, the author of *Left Hand, Right Hand*! and the succeeding volumes imposed a Proustian texture of sense and sensibility, a De Quincey-ish reverie and sonority of phrase, a glittering Sitwellian pattern of the significant and the trivial. A rich and rare performance, indeed.

Sir Francis Osbert Sacheverell Sitwell, the fifth baronet, of Renishaw Hall, Derbyshire, who succeeded to the title in 1943, was born on December 6, 1892, the eldest son of Sir George Sitwell, Bt. and Lady Ida Denison, daughter of the first Earl of Londesborough.

PICTURE OF CHILDHOOD

The autobiography fills in with exhaustive detail a childhood picture, which in substance had long been familiar in English literary society, of the offensive and defensive alliance against the world of the Sitwell trio. He was educated at St. David's, Reigate and afterwards at Eton—or, as he himself preferred to say, giving renewed emphasis to his angry and contemptuous dismissal of the English public school, "during the holidays from Eton." In 1911 he joined the Sherwood Rangers and was attached to the 11th Hussars, but next year exchanged into the Grenadier Guards, with which he went to France in 1914. He saw severe fighting, was stung into a sharp sense of the follies and futilities of war and of the usual wartime contrasts of circumstances, and published some of his most bitterly satirical war poems over the signature of "Miles". He left the Army in 1919.

Twentieth-Century Harlequinade and other Poems, by Osbert and Edith Sitwell, had appeared in 1916. *Argonaut and Juggernaut* and *The Winstonburg Line* both came out in 1919, *Who killed Cock Robin* two years later, and *Out of the Flame* two years later still. Here was a satirical poet who encompassed flippancy, indignation, and bitterness in varying proportions, but in whom a natural strength of temperament and resilience of humour were always apparent; here also was a poet with a zest for the revelation of the senses. The prose writer appeared in the six short stories of *Triple Fugue* (1924), in which mere contempt and ridicule too often overcame the spirit of high comedy and the principal source of pleasure lay in the brilliantly evocative descriptions of places and periods; in *Discussions on Travel, Art and Life* (1925), a first instalment, amidst Italian, Sicilian, and south German rococo, of the author's provocative impressions, opinions, and dislikes; and in the novel—a novel that might have gained enormously from a few more touches of ordinary humanity—*Before the Bombardment* (1926), in which he turned a peculiarly masculine and often malicious eye and a gift of witty and mordant phrase upon the commonplaces of existence in the microcosm of Scarborough society before 1914.

It is not possible here to catalogue the complete list of Osbert Sitwell's literary and other ventures; nor is it necessary to do so in order to indicate the place he continued to fill in English letters and lettered society.

"TO BE A SITWELL"

To be a Sitwell, as he would have said, was indication enough. There were two volumes of poetry out of a contemplated trilogy designed to present a personal vision of childhood, both less relaxed in form and style than they appeared to be and both inescapably Sitwellian—*England Reclaimed* (1927) and *Wrack at Tidesend* (1952)—which were to have been completed by a volume of Italian imaginary portraits. There were more discursive travel books—Italian *Winters of Content* (1932) and *Escape with Me* (1939), an Eastern sketch-book with the ruins of Angkor and Peking as the *pièces d'occasion*, more collections of fugitive pieces and more notable works of fiction. The latter included *The Man Who Lost Himself* (1939), a rich and illuminated fantasy, over which hovered the example of Proust, of the life literary; *Miracle on Sinai* (1933), a satire with an echo of *Tancred*—but in a rather more cruel vein; *Those Were the Days* (1938) in its diversity of style a considerable *tour de force*; and among other volumes of short stories, *Dumb Animal* (1930), perhaps the best collection of all, and *Open the Door* (1941). A large volume of *Collected Stories* was published in 1953.

So to the volumes of autobiography: *Left Hand, Right Hand, The Scarlet Tree, Great Morning, Laughter in the next Room,* and *Noble Essences*, the last "a book of characters" published in 1950. They provide lavish entertainment, a social document of singular interest and value, examples of portraiture done with the nicest mingling of affection and witty ruthlessness, a studied record of the growth of artistic sensibility, and an altogether remarkable essay in deliberate, fine writing. In some sort a pendant to them was *The Four Continents* (1954), which reconstructed, in similarly resplendent fashion, scenes of travel in all parts of the world.

He had suffered from Parkinson's disease for some years and announced in 1965 that he would live permanently in Italy. He released his interest in the family settled estates in England to his nephew, Mr. Reresby Sitwell. He was an Hon. LL.D. of St. Andrews and an Hon. D. Litt. of Sheffield University, a Fellow of the Royal Society of Literature, and formerly a trustee of the Tate Gallery.

He was unmarried, and the title passes to his brother, Sacheverell, who was born in 1897.

May 6, 1969.

Dr. R. A. Skelton, Superintendent of the Map Room at the British Museum from 1950 to 1967, died on December 7, 1970. He had established through his promotion of the history of cartography and his own distinguished scholarship an unchallenged international reputation.

Raleigh Ashlin Skelton (Peter Skelton as he was known to his friends and colleagues) was born in 1906 and educated at Aldenham and Pembroke College, Cambridge, where he took an honours degree in modern languages. In 1931, as an assistant keeper, he joined the staff of the Department of Printed Books in the British Museum. In 1936 he married Mary Katherine MacLeod. In the Second World War he served with the Royal Artillery in the Middle East, Italy, and Austria, attaining the rank of major. On his return to the museum after the war his interest in the history of exploration and discovery singled him out for succession to Dr. Edward Lynam as Superintendent of the Map Room. Under his guidance, the Map Room rapidly established itself as a leading centre for cartographic and geographical research.

With tireless energy and enthusiasm Skelton ranged his activities widely in the learned and academic world. He did much to advance the role of the map curator in the profession of of librarianship. As hon. secretary of the Hakluyt Society for 20 years (1946-1966) he supervised the publication of many important texts of travel and exploration, including the Journals of Captain Cook, for which he edited the portfolio of charts. He was elected F.S.A., and served on the councils of the Royal Geographical Society and of the Society for Nautical Research. When the twentieth International Geographical Congress was held in London in 1964, Skelton organized the very successful exhibition "The Growth of London" at the Victoria and Albert Museum, as well as a symposium on the history of cartography. He was for many years on the editorial committee of the learned periodical for the history of cartography, *Imago Mundi,* and at the time of his death was its general editor. As chairman of the Commission for Ancient Maps set up by the International Geographical Union (now a "Working Party") he collaborated in the publication and preparation of a world inventory of early maps. Distinctions awarded to him included the Gold Medal of the Royal Scottish Geographical Society (1965), the Victoria Medal of the Royal Geographical Society (1970), and an Honorary Doctorate of the Memorial University of St. John's, Newfoundland, in 1968.

As a leading authority in his field, Skelton was frequently consulted by American colleagues. In 1962-63 he visited the United States for seven months to act as consultant in maps to Harvard University Library. He gave the Nebenzahl Lectures in Cartography at the Newberry Library, Chicago, in 1966. Not least, he was a major contributor to the Yale University Press volume *The Vinland Map* (1965). His brilliant exposition of the evidence for identifying the map as authentic and c.1440 in date, gave it authority as the only pre-Columbian map to depict the discovery of America by the Norsemen. The publication of the book—which coincided with Columbus Day—aroused widespread controversy and interest. *The Vinland Map* was the most publicized of many publications ranging over the whole field of cartographic history. *Decorative Printed Maps* (1952), *Explorers' Maps* (1958), and his revised edition of Bagrow's *History of Cartography* (1964), are now standard works which have been joined in recent weeks by *County Atlases of the British Isles: A Bibliography*.

Skelton's numerous "Bibliographical Notes" to the facsimile atlases published at Amsterdam by Theatrum Orbis Terrarum have made available to a wide public his expert knowledge of the great European atlases of the fifteenth to seventeenth centuries. Publications in the history of exploration include various essays on Captain Cook and *Magellan's Voyage*, published, like *The Vinland Map*, by Yale University Press.

December 11, 1970.

Mr. Justice Slade, who died on February 10, 1962, at the age of 70, was well known to the public before his appointment to the High Court Bench. In his strenuous career at the Bar he was briefed in many libel actions and criminal cases which attracted public attention and which were given nation-wide publicity. He prepared his cases with the greatest care and thoroughness, and his conduct of them in Court was based on good advocacy and deep experience of the law.

He had an extensive knowledge of both common law and statute law, and a profound grip and understanding of the rules relating to practice and procedure contained in the *Annual Practice*, more familiarly known as the *White Book*. So versed was he in the numerous provisions of this indispensable work that he could cite many of the rules from memory and was equally familiar with the explanatory notes, based on the interpretation and application of the rules and appended to them. Slade had a tendency in some cases which raised a number of issues to treat too many of them as if of equal value. Close and constant study of the *White Book*, necessary though it was to his practice, was not likely to help in resolving this tendency.

A CAUTIOUS MIND

These matters, coupled with his careful, fair, and cautious mind, and not forgetting the keen enthusiasm which he always had for the cases of his clients, sometimes resulted in missing the accurate values of the lights and shades of a case, and when a truer sense of proportion would have been of greater help. This innate tendency, which he himself recognized as a handicap, was not easy to overcome, and would occasionally show itself when, as a Judge, he sat in Chambers to hear appeals on practice and procedure, or in open Court to try cases, with the result that some hearings would be unduly prolonged and the power of decision more difficult to exercise. But of his ability and of his wide knowledge both of substantive and adjectival law there was no question. And all would willingly pay tribute to the fact that he was a patient, conscientious, courteous, and efficient Judge, and one who was personally much liked and greatly respected.

Gerald Osborne Slade, born on October 14, 1891, the younger son of Sir James Benjamin Slade, senior partner in the well-known firm of auctioneers, was educated at Lindisfarne College, Westcliff, Bedford School, and Trinity College, Cambridge, where he took his degree in 1912. In the First World War he served with the Essex Regiment. He was called to the Bar by the Middle Temple in 1921 and joined the South-Eastern Circuit. While a junior he acquired a large practice in the civil courts, and a more limited amount in the criminal courts. He was much in demand in libel actions, a branch of the law in which he had early specialized, and in which he was recognized as one of the leading experts. He edited the late Mr. Justice Frazer's classical work on the subject.

In 1942 he was appointed Recorder of Tenterden. He took silk in the following year, and as a leader he was a conspicuous success; his already large and remunerative practice increased, and in the criminal courts he was called on to plead more often than when he was a junior. The number of cases in which he appeared, even those which caught the public interest, is too long to recite.

COMMISSIONER OF ASSIZE

But it may be recalled that he appeared for Professor Harold Laski in a libel action which he brought against a newspaper. In the criminal law the most important case in which he appeared, from the public point of view, was his defence of William Joyce ("Lord Haw-Haw"), who, after an unsuccessful appeal to the House of Lords, was hanged for treason. Slade, with no merits on the facts in his client's favour, put up a case on the law which won general admiration (and on which there are still divided opinions).

In March, 1948, Slade was appointed a Commissioner of Assize, and in June of the same year was made a Judge of the High Court in succession to Mr. Justice Henn Collins, who had resigned on the grounds of ill-health. He was also then made a Bencher of his Inn. It was also in 1948 that he was knighted.

Among his other activities Slade was Chairman of the Bar Council from 1946 to 1948, and Chancellor of the Diocese of Chelmsford from 1934 to 1948, and of Southwark from 1944 to 1948. As was to be expected he was a member of the Lord Chancellor's Committee on the Law of Defamation, which was set up in 1939. When the committee finally reported some years after the end of the 1939-45 War the conclusions were not as far-reaching as some people had expected. Slade was appointed chairman of the Legal Committee on Medical Partnerships which the Minister of Health set up in 1948 to advise whether the National Health Service Act ought to be amended to secure an equitable result between partners in medical practice.

It was characteristic of Slade—a practice more general these days—never, though bald, to wear a hat during his time at the Bar. And after his appointment to the Bench it was not uncommon to see his upright and athletic figure walking through the streets with his head uncovered. He was a keen and above average lawn tennis player, and the first chairman of the Bar Lawn Tennis Society. Up to 1960 he was playing in matches for the society and, in spite of advancing years, his technical skill enabled him to challenge his opponents with a fine and distinguished game.

In 1917 he married Phyllis Mary, younger daughter of Dr. John Wesley-Smith, of Harrogate. They had four daughters.

February 12, 1962.

Sir William Slater, K.B.E., F.R.S., died at Midhurst on April 19, 1970, after a lifetime of service to agriculture and food production.

He was born on October 19, 1893, and educated at Hulme grammar school, Oldham, and at Manchester University where he graduated with first class honours in chemistry and carried off the Leblane Medal. Rejected for military service because of defective sight, he continued at the university for an M.Sc. and then joined the staff of the chief inspector of explosives. In 1918 he returned to Manchester as an assistant lecturer in chemistry and after a short spell in industry he moved to the physiology department to work with A. V. Hill, whom he later followed to University College London. There he held Beit fellowships for six years, working on biochemical aspects of anaerobiosis in animals and on the metabolism of intestinal parasites.

In 1929, on Hill's recommendation, the trustees of Dartington Hall invited Slater to set up a soil research laboratory and to supervise the scientific aspects of Leonard Elmhirst's exciting experiments in rural economy. It was evident that he had inherited his father's business ability and he was soon given the general management of the trust's commercial enterprises, so gaining valuable experience of mixed farming, fruit growing, pig and poultry farming and cider making. He continued the general oversight of the laboratory which worked on problems ranging from control of potato blight to cobalt deficiency in sheep.

In 1942 Slater went to the Ministry of Agriculture and Fisheries to assist Sir John Fryer in his work for the Agricultural Improvement Council, and when Fryer became Secretary of the Agricultural Research Council, Slater followed him as secretary of the A.I.C., acting also as senior education and advisory officer to the M.A.F. During this period he was associated with Sir James Scott Watson in the creation of the National Agricultural Advisory Service, being especially responsible for its specialist scientific staff, and to him must go much of the credit for the sound foundations on which the N.A.A.S. was built.

In 1949 Slater succeeded Fryer as Secretary of the Agricultural Research Council and during the next 11 years presided over a remarkable expansion of the council's activities, reflected by a rise in its budget from about £1m. to over £6m. In this period five new research institutes were brought into being and links with universities were strengthened by creation of 12 new units; the grant-aiding functions formerly exercised by the Ministry of Agriculture and Fisheries were transferred to the council, which also assumed various other new responsibilities, such as monitoring of radio-active fall-out in the food chain and oversight of food research institutes transferred from the B.S.I.R.

Retirement brought Slater no respite. His experience and personal qualities made him much sought after as an adviser and he was always particularly ready to do anything, as consultant, writer or lecturer, that would contribute to the improvement of living standards in underdeveloped countries. Since 1961, he had been the United Kingdom representative on the Cento scientific council; he led the British delegation to the science committee of Unesco general conferences on several occasions; he served on the Royal Society Unesco Committee and he represented Britain in F.A.O./Unesco discussions on agricultural education. These activities took him to many countries in all of which he made a considerable personal impression. When the Freedom from Hunger campaign was set up in 1961 Slater joined the United Kingdom national committee, to which he brought great experience and breadth of concern and humanity that was an inspiration to all his colleagues. As chairman of the specialist group which considered requests for help from all over the world his judgment was invaluable. It was his concern for the peasant farmer throughout the world which resulted in the Indicative World Plan for agricultural development which is the framework for planning in the seventies.

Slater was appointed K.B.E. in 1951 and elected F.R.S. in 1957. In 1925 he married Hilda Whittenbury who died in 1966 and by whom he had two sons and a daughter.

April 21, 1970.

Air Marshal Sir Leonard Slatter, K.B.E., C.B., D.S.C., D.F.C., died in hospital at Uxbridge on April 14, 1961. He was 66.

Born at Durban, South Africa, on December 8, 1894, and educated there, Leonard Horatio Slatter travelled to Britain when he was about 16 and was a student at Battersea Polytechnic and London University for several years until he left in 1914 to join the Royal Naval Air Service a month after the outbreak of the First World War.

Later in the same year he was posted to the Naval Armoured Car Division, with which he went to France in 1915; he took part in the Second Battle of Ypres and was in action when the Germans launched their first gas attack. He then returned to the R.N.A.S. as an observer and was in the first quota of officers trained at Portsmouth for these duties.

He went back to France in February, 1916, and was attached to the seaplane base at Dunkirk and was later trained as a pilot and passed through Cranwell. He was awarded the Distinguished Service Cross in 1917 "for conspicuous gallantry and skill on many occasions" and he won a bar to this decoration in 1918 for bombing Ostend seaplane station from a height of only 400 feet despite intense anti-aircraft fire. In 1919, after having transferred to the Royal Air Force, he went to south Russia and took part in the operations in support of the White Russians under General Denikin. For these services he was made an O.B.E. In January, 1924, he was promoted to squadron leader and given command of the R.A.F. base at Calafrana, Malta.

LED IN SCHNEIDER CONTEST

His reputation as a pilot was such that in 1926 he was selected by the Air Ministry to form and command the High Speed Flight from which the team was chosen to represent the R.A.F. in the competition for the Schneider Trophy at Venice in the following year. Another highlight in his career between the two wars was a solo flight which he made to South Africa in 1929 in a Blackburn Bluebird.

In 1932, after having commanded three fighter squadrons in turn, he was promoted to wing commander and posted to H.M.S. Courageous as Senior Air Force Officer. This association with the Fleet Air Arm lasted until 1935, when he was given command of the R.A.F. station at Tangmere. In 1937 he went to R.A.F. station Feltwell, in command, and was promoted group captain, and at the outbreak of war he was posted to No. 1 Bomber Group as Senior Air Staff Officer, where he remained until his promotion to air commodore in January, 1940, on appointment as Air Officer in charge of administration at R.A.F Headquarters, Iraq. Soon afterwards he was appointed A.O.C. for the Eritrea and Abyssinia campaign and when this was over he was appointed in October, 1941, to the command of No. 201 Naval Co-operation Group at Alexandria, which operated with the Royal Navy in the Mediterranean. It was in recognition of these services that he received his knighthood in 1942. He remained at Alexandria until his appointment as A.O.C. of No. 15 Group, Coastal Command, in 1943.

As A.O.C. No. 15 Group he was responsible for the conduct of the air side of the Battle of the Atlantic, and it was due to the combined activities of the squadrons under his command and surface vessels of the Royal Navy that enormous convoys of food and war materials were able to reach this country. Not only were the convoys assured safety of passage but, at one period of the battle, U-boats were being sunk at the rate of one a day.

In 1945 Slatter succeeded Sir Sholto Douglas as A.O.C.-in-C. Coastal Command and held the appointment until 1948. He was appointed a Deputy Lieutenant for Bedfordshire in 1951.

He took a keen interest in service sport. He played cricket for the R.A.F. against the Army in eight successive years (1921-28) and against the Royal Navy in 1931; he had also played football and golf for the R.A.F.

He married Cecil Nancy Ashwin, eldest daughter of Colonel C. M. Davies, D.S.O., by whom he had two sons and a daughter.

April 17, 1961.

General Felicjan Slawoj-Skladkowski, Polish Premier at the outbreak of the Second World War, died in London on August 31, 1962. He was 77.

Felicjan Skladkowski was born in Gabin, Poland, on June 9, 1885. He completed medical studies and took up practice before the First World War. He joined the Polish Socialist Party, P.P.S., in 1905. There he came under the influence of Jozef Pilsudski. He joined Pilsudski's Legion in 1914 and took part in the legion's campaign against the Russians from 1914 to 1916. His legionary pseudonym "Slawoj" became part of his name. In connexion with refusal of the oath of allegiance by the legion's officers he was interned by the Germans in 1917, but rejoined active service on Pilsudski's assumption of power in independent Poland in November, 1918, rising eventually to the rank of lieutenant-general. He gradually abandoned both medicine and military service in favour of politics.

After Marshal Pilsudski's *coup d'état* in 1926 Skladkowski became Minister of the Interior. He occupied that post until 1929, and again in the years 1930-31 and 1936-39. In 1936 he was also appointed Prime Minister.

In September, 1939, Skladkowski left Poland with members of his Government when German and Soviet armies were closing in, and was interned in Rumania, where in October he relinquished his Government posts in favour of General Sikorski's new Government in exile. Skladkowski spent the war years mainly in the Middle East, removed from political life, and after the war made his home in England, where he lived in retirement, devoting himself to writing.

Throughout his political career Skladkowski was associated closely with Marshal Pilsudski, as his faithful adherent, and after the latter's death in 1935, with the regime of his successors. Having little political individuality of his own, he is said to have followed blindly the instructions from above. He was, perhaps, little suited to head a Government that had to withstand intense internal opposion from left and right, as well as external pressures by Hitler's Germany and Stalin's Russia, at a most difficult period in Poland's history.

The strain of those pressures was responsible for the growing authoritarianism in the political life of the country during Skladkowski's premiership from 1936 to 1939. As Minister of the Interior in the same period he was connected with some repression of national minorities in the eastern provinces, and had a personal passion for somewhat misguided attempts at raising the sanitary standards in the provinces.

His redeeming qualities were a sense of humour, and undoubted, though limited in range, literary talent for narration, revealed in his books of memoirs: *My Service in the Brigade*, *Benjaminow*, *Administrative Flowers*, and *Shreds of Reports*. The last book, in which his devotion for Pilsudski manifests itself in a moving, if naive, manner is perhaps the best known.

September 10, 1962.

Field Marshal Lord Slim, K.G., G.C.B., G.C.M.G., G.C.V.O., G.B.E., D.S.O., M.C., died on December 14, 1970. He was 79.

His name will be for ever associated with the victorious campaign of the Fourteenth Army in Burma during the Second World War. He was a soldier of the highest ability, with a keen eye for strategy, but his most remarkable quality was his influence over his troops. The campaign in Burma was of a kind that made particularly high calls upon the spirit of the troops, and especially of the European troops, to whom the country was in the popular phrase "a green hell". It is no secret that to build up, and still more to maintain, the spirit of Europeans in these surroundings, with entire absence of any comfort, relaxation, society, or intercourse with civilians of their own race, was a most difficult task. Nor, indeed, can it be denied that in some cases the British units fell below their highest standards before the end of the campaign.

Even Slim could not achieve the impossible in the moral sphere. What can be said is that he worked wonders. The contact between an army commander and his troops is necessarily remote in modern warfare, and therein lies a serious moral danger. Like Montgomery in the Eighth Army, though by rather different methods, Slim contrived to impress his personality on the men he led, Indian as well as British, in one of the most trying and difficult campaigns of modern times. They felt complete confidence in him and indeed gave him their affection, which is something rarer. Yet it hardly needs to be said that personality alone, without generalship, would not have sufficed. The British soldier demands first and foremost of his commanders that he should be "put in with a chance". He always felt that he would be when commanded by Slim.

William Joseph Slim was born on August 6, 1891. There was nothing in his environment or upbringing to indicate that he would adopt the profession of arms and rise to great heights in it. He was educated at King Edward's School, Birmingham, and after leaving followed several avocations; he was a junior clerk, a school teacher, and an engineer. The outbreak of war in 1914 found him a Territorial non-commissioned officer, and on August 22 he was commissioned in The Royal Warwickshire Regiment. He first saw active service on the Gallipoli peninsula. In August 1915, he was seriously wounded in the Battle of Sari Bair, and on discharge from hospital graded as permanently unfit for first-line service.

However, he reappeared in the firing line, this time in France. Next he served in Mesopotamia, where he was wounded again and awarded the Military Cross. On this occasion he was evacuated to India, where on recovery he served as G.S.O. 3 in 1917 and G.S.O. 2 in 1918. In 1919 he transferred to the Indian Army. He joined the 6th Gurkha Rifles, a regiment alongside which he had fought and the bearing of which had deeply impressed him. All his life he was to be an enthusiast about the military qualities of the Gurkha. He was promoted captain in the same year, received a brevet-majority in 1930, and became a substantive major in 1933. From 1934 to 1937 he was an instructor at the Staff College, Camberley, with the local rank of lieutenant-colonel. Between then and the outbreak of war in 1939 he attended the Imperial Defence College.

At an early stage of the war Slim found himself in Sudan, on the Eritrean frontier, in command of the 10th Indian Brigade. He took part in the first offensive against the Italians on that front at Gallabat, but was wounded in early 1941 before the decisive struggle at Keren. On recovery from this third wound of his career he was posted as brigadier-general staff to Lieutenant-General Quinan, but shortly afterwards obtained command of the 10th Indian Division, with which he served in Syria, Persia, and Iraq.

BURMA TASK

He was awarded the D.S.O. for his service during this year.

His next appointment in March, 1942 was far from a promising one. It was to the command of the First Burma Corps, which in fact represented practically the whole of the forces at General Alexander's disposal. At the end of the terrible fighting retreat through jungle and mountains, he was appointed to command the XV Corps in India. For his work in Burma he received the C.B.E. and for that in command of the XV Corps the C.B. Late in 1943 a new army designated the Fourteenth was formed for operations in Burma, and Slim was appointed to command it. He had a great opportunity before him, but also a heavy responsibility. Never so far had British or Indian troops succeeded in defeating the Japanese. The morale of the latter was consequently very high and they went into battle supremely confident of success. Backed by General Giffard, who commanded the army group and was largely responsible for the training, Slim exerted his utmost efforts and ingenuity to implant in his formations the belief that they contained better and more intelligent soldiers than the Japanese and were capable of beating them.

It was only when he had succeeded in this task that he could contemplate a major offensive for the reconquest of Burma. Even then the difficulties were great, since Burma had perforce to be placed low on the list of British priorities as a theatre or war. A country with the slenderest possible military link in communications with India and itself possessing hardly any resources for modern war, so that it depended more than ordinarily upon importations from Britain and the United States, was thus starved by comparison with other theatres.

By cooperation with the Americans, who were interested less in Slim's campaign than in preventing free China from falling under the domination of the Japanese and were prepared to bring in material and supply administrative troops for that purpose, Slim partially overcame one side of this difficulty.

COMMAND OF THE AIR

The other was overcome by the use of air transport, which in this theatre was used with a skill and effectiveness not found in any other. In Burma all depended on the air, not only for the transport of supplies but for transferring whole divisions from one region to another. In February, 1944, when the British offensive was under way but was still being conducted on a relatively small scale, the Japanese struck back, first in the Arakan, the strip of territory on the west coast. Using their favourite simple methods of envelopment, the Japanese gained a temporary tactical success, but they were finally fought down and utterly defeated. This to some extent prejudiced the start of their second and main offensive in Manipur and Assam, directed against India itself, where they hoped to provoke a rising. The battles round Imphal and Kohima none the less developed into a struggle to be measured by months and with fluctuating fortunes. In the end the Japanese were worn out by the stress. Their army, having suffered heavy losses and already showing signs of disintegration, fell back across the Chindwin in the midst of the monsoon of 1944.

FALL OF RANGOON

The Japanese Army did not disintegrate after all, though it was never again to be the same fighting instrument. Using the air for supply with the same effect as in the defensive battles, Slim launched a powerful offensive across the Irrawaddy. Mandalay fell at the end of the third week of March, 1945, and Rangoon not long afterwards. All was not yet finished, and there was in fact some sharp fighting with large bodies of Japanese trapped west of the Sittang and with other forces east of the river which endeavoured to make diversions with the purpose of rescuing these troops.

Slim himself, however, passed on to another task. He had been appointed commander-in-chief of the army group known as "Allied Land Forces South-east Asia", which was to carry out the reconquest of Malaya. For that there was, as it proved, no need. September 9 was the date fixed for the landing, but by that time the unconditional surrender of the Japanese had taken place.

For his services with the Fourteenth Army Slim was promoted K.C.B. in September, 1944. He was also promoted to the rank of general in August, 1945. After his return to England in December, 1945, he was the recipient of further honours, being promoted G.B.E. in 1946.

In 1946 he was allotted the task of reopening, as commandant, the Imperial Defence College at which he had attended as a student. The college was not only restarted but also established on a scale considerably greater than that of before the war. In this period Slim made himself known to the general public as a really admirable speaker and particularly as a broadcaster. In July, 1947, he was offered but refused the post of Commander-in-Chief of the Army of the Dominion of India. In the following September he was appointed a member of the Railway Executive and London Transport Executive set up under the Transport Act earlier in the year.

He became deputy chairman of the Executive, with special responsibility for stores, estates, police and public relations. In view of the war this was an important appointment, but it did not last long. In the following year Slim became Chief of the Imperial General Staff, the appointment taking effect on November 1.

HIGHEST OFFICE

Two months later, on January 4, 1949, he received the baton of a Field Marshal.

On September 3, 1952, his appointment to be Governor-General of Australia was announced. The Prime Minister, Mr. Menzies, had departed from the Labour policy of recommending an Australian for this high office. He naturally came under criticism, which in its turn involved for Slim something less than an ideal start. Again his personality and good humour served him well. Some ruffling of the water did occur; indeed, his very able Prime Minister must have known in advance that it would have been useless to put forward his name if the new Governor-General had to be extremely cautious, and still less if he were expected to utter platitudes. He was sworn in on May 8, 1953.

The publication of his admirable book of war memoirs, *Defeat into Victory*, in 1956 reinforced his position. His appointment was prolonged for two years, and before he left the country in January, 1960, he published another successful book of a very different sort, the lively, amusing and sometimes touching *Unofficial History*. Without exaggeration it may be said that he left in Australia an indelible impression of character, honesty and friendliness, as well as of a powerful mind. In January, 1950, he was promoted to G.C.B. Late in 1952, after his appointment as Governor-General had been announced, he was created G.C.M.G. In 1954, in connexion with the Queen's tour, he was created G.C.V.O. In his last year in Australia he received the Garter and in 1960 he was created a Viscount. He was Governor and Constable of Windsor Castle from 1964 until June this year. In his later years he held a number of directorships.

In person Slim was a big, bluff man with a jutting chin, which gave an air of determination to his countenance. Socially he was an attractive figure and good company at a dinner-table, though not normally talkative. He married in 1926 Aileen, daughter of the Reverend J. A. Robertson, and had one son and one daughter. The former followed his father's footsteps in becoming an officer in the Gurkha Rifles.

December 15, 1970.

Tom Sloan, O.B.E., head of B.B.C. television light entertainment, died on May 13, 1970, in London, at the age of 50.

In December, 1969, in a lecture Sloan said: "If I drop dead tomorrow, I would not mind being remembered for having some responsibility at least for the Black and White Ministrel Show, Hancock, Steptoe and Son, Till Death Us Do Part, Harry Worth, Not in Front of the Children, Dad's Army, Val Doonican and Rolf Harris Shows, and Dixon of Dock Green."

During his nine years as Head of Light Entertainment his production group carried off every major professional award in show business including seven awards at the Montreux International Festival.

Since his appointment as Head of Light Entertainment for B.B.C. Television in 1961, the B.B.C. and its viewers learned from him to accept a wider, tougher and socially more critical view of comedy than was available before. The polite middle-class humour which had previously limited the B.B.C.'s vision of what television amusement should offer, did not die with his accession, but it learned to coexist with the odd ambivalences of "Steptoe and Son", the raucous vigour of "Till Death Us Do Part" and the wild fantasies of "Marty".

PERSONAL VETTING

Tom Sloan's view of his field of activity was extensive: it included not only these deliberately disturbing or provocative reflections of our society but also the recent series of extracts from forgotten films, "The Golden Silents".

Sloan once said: "Comedy ought to reflect life. It is at its best when it does this. I've no intention of giving viewers a marzipan view of life".

"Till Death Us Do Part" was the only show to get Sloan's personal vetting, he said, in 1968. He read every script before rehearsals and saw each finished programme before it was screened. He saw Alf as a kind of television Andy Capp. "Through him", he said, "we expose prejudice, ignorance and bigotry. Of course, Alf is bigoted and stupid, a monster of a man. His wife is a cabbage. His son-in-law a layabout. And his daughter a giggler."

When Sloan joined the light entertainment group in 1955, under Ronnie Waldman, they had six producers who turned out five programmes a week. Some 14 years later he had 34 producers under him, responsible for 16 programmes a week on two channels.

Sloan, the son of a Scottish Free Church Minister, was born in Hertfordshire and educated at Dulwich College. He entered the B.B.C. Sound Effects Department in 1939 and served in the Royal Artillery throughout the war. In 1946 he returned to radio as a talks producer and spent some years as the B.B.C.'s representative in Canada.

His work was governed by the belief that in the new situation of a wealthier and more leisured society the B.B.C.'s survival depended on its power to invert the principles Lord Reith had laid down for it and to offer, instead of "education, information and entertainment" entertainment as a first priority followed by information and education. His view was acceptable and valid because entertainment, to him, meant not only what was cheerfully relaxing but also what was vigorous, thoughtful, stimulating and downright disturbing. He found the writers and the stars to provide and embody what he wanted, and created a space and audience for them.

His last project was the Royal Television Gala due to be recorded on the night he died.

He leaves a widow and four children.

May 14, 1970.

Billy Smart, the celebrated circus proprietor, died on September 25, 1966, at the age of 73. He collapsed while conducting the band as members of the public were visiting his circus zoo at Ipswich.

Smart's career began in the humblest way imaginable. At the age of 15 he was put in charge of a hand roundabout at a fairground in Slough. He determined, however, to be his own employer and, after his marriage in 1914, he set himself up as a fairground proprietor.

LUCK'S CHANGE

At first he met with little success and was obliged to dig gardens and hire out a pony and cart in order to make ends meet. Gradually his luck turned and by 1939 he had built up one of the largest fairs in the country.

It is with the circus, however, that his name is most readily associated. In 1946 he established his own circus and thus achieved what had been the ambition of a lifetime. He toured every part of the British Isles with it and the Billy Smart Circus was also a regular feature of B.B.C. television holiday entertainment programmes.

Apart from being the proprietor of a famous circus Smart was also a showman on the grand scale. On one occasion he rode a circus elephant through the streets of Mayfair and parked it at a meter before inserting a shilling: this was his way of advertising a show for charity. His 20-stone figure and his constant cigar added to his reputation as a public figure.

Smart leaves a widow, six daughters and four sons.

September 26, 1966.

Jan Smeterlin, who died on January 18, 1967, shortly before his seventy-fifth birthday, was one of the last survivors of the romantic, nineteenth-century school of pianists. A compatriot of Chopin, he was one of the Polish master's finest interpreters.

Jan Smeterlin was born in Bielsko, on February 7, 1892. In 1913 he won the state first prize at the Klaviermeisterschule in Vienna. After the First World War he rapidly won a European reputation, and by the early 1930s he had become one of the most widely travelled and sought-after of *virtuosi*. He carried with him an extensive repertoire from the classics to Szymanowski, and while he could provide a fiery, impetuously romantic but firmly controlled account of the big, middle-period Beethoven sonatas, he did more than any other pianist of comparable stature to win acceptance for Szymanowski's work.

By the outbreak of war in 1939 he had settled in England, and though he continually played in public, he began to devote himself to recital work rather than to concerto performances. At the same time, his repertoire tended to narrow until, in recent years, he played little but the works of Chopin. This was not, however, a loss to audiences, for he presented a Chopin who was aristocratic but strong and impulsive, a composer of both power and elegance as well as great nervous energy. Though his playing seemed always ready to submit to the inspiration of the moment, the outlines of the works he played remained firm and their intellectual strength was unimpaired. Perhaps his qualities of energy, grace and control were shown most brilliantly in his playing of the mazurkas, in which subtleties and refinements of rhythm and phrasing intensified the works' combination of dancing vitality and poignant lyricism.

To his friends, Smeterlin was known as one of the most gracious of hosts. Somehow, it seemed, his art extended from the keyboard to the kitchen, for they would speak of his exploits in the preparation of a dinner party with an enthusiasm hardly less vigorous than that with which they applauded his performances in the concert hall.

January 20, 1967.

Sir Ben Smith, P.C., K.B.E., the first Labour Minister of Food, died on May 5, 1964, at his home at Bovey Tracey, Devon.

Everyone knew him as Ben Smith, never as Benjamin; and after his knighthood he was Sir Ben. That he preferred the less formal style of address was an indication of the easy, familiar terms on which he wished to live with people. Straightforward and vigorous in speech, robust in physique, ready to return blow for blow, he retained a geniality of disposition which neither the exacting duties of a trade union leader nor the final disappointment of a political career could lastingly disturb. He had a varied experience before he found a satisfying career in trade union organization and from trade unionism he was borne into politics.

Born in the East End of London in 1879, his boyhood purpose was to go to sea. Trained in the old Warspite he joined the Merchant Service. Then he took a shore job, but the sea called again and he served in the Royal Navy for seven years before being invalided out. But while in the service he won a boxing championship at catch weights. Again returning to civilian life, he first found work in a laundry and later chose a freer and more independent livelihood as the driver of a hansom cab and then of a taxi.

He was now active in trade unionism as a member of the London Cab Drivers' Union, which amalgamated later with the London and Provincial Union of Licensed Vehicle Workers. He recognized, too, that busmen needed organization as well as cabmen and took a notable share in bringing them into the union. One amalgamation followed another till the organization grew into the Transport and General Workers' Union. Ben Smith held the post of a national group organizer. He was becoming widely known in the trade union movement through regular attendance at the Trades Union Congress and, in 1922, he was one of the fraternal delegates to the convention of the American Confederation of Labour.

He entered Parliament in 1923 as the member for the Rotherhithe division of Bermondsey and became a Junior Labour Whip in 1925.

TAXIMAN'S M. P.

But his trade union work was the better known and because of his interest in the welfare of taximen and of the part he took in winning for hackney vehicles the right to drive through Hyde Park he was popularly known as "the taximan's M.P.". In the second Labour Government he was Treasurer of the Household, but his part in parliamentary affairs was not conspicuous. He lost his seat in the overwhelming defeat of the Labour Party in 1931, but was returned again four years later, and when in the third year of the war Churchill partly reshaped his administration Ben Smith became Parliamentary Secretary to the Ministry of Aircraft Production. He went to the United States and Canada to inspect aircraft factories there and was later to go on a longer mission to the United States as Minister Resident in Washington for Supply. He was the first Labour member to hold one of the important Ministerial posts overseas. He had the rank of a Cabinet Minister and was made a Privy Councillor. The contrasting personalities of Lord Halifax, the Ambassador, and Ben Smith, the Minister of Supply, both won the confidence of the American people and Ben Smith did much to encourage understanding of Britain's aims and economic needs after years of exhausting and relentless struggle.

In the Dissolution Honours of 1945 he was made a K.B.E., and in the new Labour Government was given the onerous post of Minister of Food. The times were difficult and in particular the short supplies of wheat and fats and of purchasing power abroad confronted the new Minister with problems he found intractable. He made two visits to Washington in endeavours to obtain help and there was, at the time of the second visit, an apparent lack of direction in his Department which led to confusing and conflicting statements. Already tired of the office—he was perhaps a tired man before he accepted it—Ben Smith resigned. He left silently and without explanation to the House of Commons. Three months later, when the National Coal Board was taking over the administration of the recently nationalized mines, he retired from Parliament and from public life to become chairman of the Board's West Midland Division, an appointment he continued to hold until his illness in June, 1950.

In 1899 he married Mildred Ellen, daughter of Charles Edison, of Peckham, and they had two sons. His wife died in 1959 and in 1961 he married secondly Gertrude Elizabeth, daughter of E. A. Lacey.

May 6, 1964.

Professor David Nichol Smith, who died in Oxford on January 18, 1962, was Merton Professor of English Literature in the University of Oxford from 1929 to 1946. He was 86.

He was born at Edinburgh on September 16, 1875. Educated at George Watson's School and Edinburgh University, he was the first to graduate from Edinburgh (First Class, 1895) in the new Honours Course in English. His elder brother Gregory, a fine scholar whose work is still valued by those who know it, was then Lecturer in English under David Masson, and it was Gregory Smith rather than Masson who planned the course and instructed in it.

WORK ON INDEX

In 1895 George Saintsbury succeeded Masson, and Nichol Smith's first employment was to compile the index to the Professor's *History of Nineteenth-Century Literature*. A scholarship supported him at the Sorbonne for a year, a year in which he laid the foundation of his deep knowledge of English and French criticism in the late seventeenth and in the eighteenth centuries.

In our days when lectureships in English are as plentiful as blackberries we may be surprised that such a man had to wait some six years before obtaining an academic post. The editions of English classics which he published in these lean years were designed for use in schools, yet the sound scholarship and judgment of his later works may be discerned on every page. In 1902 he met Walter Raleigh, then looking for an assistant at Glasgow: a fortunate meeting for both men, for the Oxford English School, and for English scholarship. Each man valued in the other the qualities which he did not himself possess. Except for the years of Nichol Smith's professorship at Armstrong (later King's) College, Newcastle (1904–08), the partnership remained unbroken until Raleigh's death in 1922. Raleigh introduced him to Oxford in 1908 as Goldsmiths' Reader, and in 1921 he was elected to a Fellowship at Merton College, and in 1929 to the Merton Professorship of English Literature, a post which he held till his retirement in 1946.

It cannot be said that he kept abreast of modern developments in poetry or criticism. When a Harvard undergraduate asked him what he thought of W. H. Auden, he answered: "I do not think of him at all." Although he wrote on French and English literature before

Dryden and after Johnson, he was above all an authority on English literature in the late seventeenth and the eighteenth centuries.

He was made free of the best of it by his own preference for clarity and for good sense not necessarily unmixed with sentiment, and he admired the eighteenth century long before that century became the vogue; held that Pope was a poet long before Pope became fashionable. Those who heard him read Pope's verse or Johnson's could not be in doubt of his sincerity. He showed his judgment and learning in several collections of informal lectures, of which the best are in his *Shakespeare and the Eighteenth Century* and the latest was his Clark lectures on Dryden; in such editions as that of Swift's letters to Charles Ford or Johnson's Poems; and in such anthologies as his *Characters and Memoirs of the Seventeenth Century* and his *Oxford Book of Eighteenth Century Verse*.

PUPILS' TRIBUTE

In his later years at Oxford his chief interest was in graduate studies. Pupils came (and still come) to Oxford from many parts of the world to join those who have read the Oxford English School: he took a personal interest in them all, and often helped them to a career. In this and other ways his influence on English studies was wide and deep. Some of his pupils contributed to the volume of essays on the eighteenth century presented to him on his seventieth birthday. It is there stated that the books which mention his name, many as they are, are but a few of those which have been "clarified by his candid scrutiny"; and it is no secret that his judgment and knowledge were greatly valued by the Delegates of the Clarendon Press and their secretary.

He was elected to the British Academy in 1932, and to an Honorary Fellowship at Merton College in 1947, and he received many honorary degrees from Australian, English, French, Scottish, and United States universities. Two visits to America, the first to the Huntington Library in 1936 and the second to Smith College, gave him a taste for travel which he later indulged by visits to Cairo and to Adelaide. Wherever he went he could be sure of meeting old pupils and making new friends.

He married in 1915 Mary, daughter of the Rev. Canon Harford, by whom he had a son and three daughters. His son, an officer in the Royal Air Force, much loved by all who knew him, was killed at Tobruk in 1942.

January 19, 1962.

Former **Detective-Superintendent George "Moonraker" Smith,** who died suddenly in hospital at Bath on October 24, 1970, was a spy-catcher without equal.

Most of the celebrated and treacherous spies ever to operate in Britain for the Russians during the last war and since were tracked down and captured by him.

His talent for undercover work and relentless patience was first spotted as early as 1939 when he was instrumental in arresting a number of I.R.A. terrorists who had been responsible for a series of bomb attacks in Britain. From then on he was attached to the Special Branch and during the war worked closely with M.I.5.

In 1946 he assisted in the inquiries which eventually led to the arrest of Dr. Nunn May, the physicist who passed on information about nuclear power to foreign agents.

Also among his successes was the smashing of the Portland spy ring and the arrest of Gordon Lonsdale, the Krogers, Harry Houghton and Ethel Gee.

There was little of the cloak and dagger image about "Moonraker" Smith, a quiet spoken dapper man who dressed like a city businessman. He shunned publicity and avoided theatricals. After working for months day and night on the Portland case he could have been excused for a dramatic arrest of Lonsdale, probably the most dangerous and intelligent Russian agent ever to work in Britain. But true to form he simply strolled up to Lonsdale, tapped him on the shoulder and said calmly: "It's Scotland Yard for you, my lad."

Two others who can thank Mr. Smith for long prison sentences were atom scientist Klaus Fuchs and Admiralty clerk John Vassall.

Just prior to his retirement in 1963 he was awarded the Queen's Police Medal. At about that time J. Edgar Hoover, head of the F.B.I., wrote to him thanking him for his "international service", a compliment few policemen in the world could claim.

Smith was nicknamed "Moonraker" but none of his senior contemporaries at Scotland Yard is able to remember how he got the name.

Before leaving the police force he had to sign the Official Secrets Act, which, alas, barred him from writing about his fascinating career.

Smith, who was 65 when he died, lived at Edington, Wiltshire. He leaves a widow and a married daughter.

October 27, 1970.

Professor J. L. B. Smith, the man who first traced and identified the coelacanth, a fish believed extinct for some 40 million years, died in Grahamstown on January 7, 1968, at the age of 70.

It was early in 1939 that Smith, then teaching chemistry at Grahamstown University but a passionate spare-time ichthyologist, identified a large heavily-scaled blue fish brought ashore by a trawler at East London a few weeks earlier. The coelacanth, described as the "fish with arms" because of the extraordinary mobility of its pectoral fins, was considered to be a link between fish and amphibians and for long was known only from its fossil remains.

The coelacanth had initially been recognized by Miss Latimer, the enthusiastic curator of the East London museum, who had written to Smith suggesting its early inspection. Christmas postal delays forced Miss Latimer in the absence of instructions to have the fish mounted by a taxidermist, and the putrefying soft parts had to be thrown away.

After the Second World War the quest for a complete coelacanth was renewed; in South Africa leaflets were issued in English, French, and Portuguese offering a reward of £100 for one. No coelacanths were reported until a trader named Eric Hunt took some leaflets to the Comoro group of islands and secured one caught by a native fisherman.

Like the first coelacanth, the second was caught just before Christmas and required expert preservation. Smith persuaded Dr. Malan, then South African Prime Minister, to lend him an aircraft to fetch the new specimen from the island of Anjouan. Most of the brain and other soft parts of the head of this second specimen had gone: the fisherman who had caught the second one in 1952 had beaten it on the head, and the sailors who salted the fish to preserve it had cut the coelacanth open from snout to tail

Several coelacanths, four to five feet long, have since been caught in the Cape of Good Hope and Madagascar regions. They are believed to breed in the Comoro group of islands. But it has been difficult to keep them alive in captivity because the coelacanth rarely comes nearer the sea's surface then 160 fathoms. It is bothered by sunlight, preferring the cold water and heavy pressure of the ocean depths.

In 1958 Smith described his discovery of the coelacanth in a book, *Old Fourlegs*, in which he said he had always been convinced that he was destined to discover "some quite outrageous creature". Smith studied at Stellenbosch University and gained a doctorate of philosophy at Cambridge in 1921. In 1949 he became Professor of Ichthyology at Rhodes University.

January 9, 1968.

Dr. Marian W. Smith (Mrs. H. F. Akehurst), honorary secretary of the Royal Anthropological Institute of Great Britain and Ireland, and a most distinguished anthropologist in her own right, died in New York on May 2, 1961.

Marian Wesley Smith was born in New York on May 10, 1907. When only three years old she was severely afflicted with poliomyelitis, which left one leg partially paralysed for the rest of her life, so that every step which she took required a great effort; yet she scorned mechanical aids, or even the use of a stick.

She learnt and practised anthropology in North America and few American anthropologists can have had a career so distinguished. She was particularly proud to have been the last student of the great Franz Boas at Columbia University, certainly one of the two or three most important thinkers and teachers in the history of anthropological science. She took her M.A. (in philosophy) in 1934 and her Ph.D. in 1938. Among the American institutions where she taught anthropology were Barnard College, Vassar College, and the New York University Graduate School, as well as on the west coast of the United States. Before she reached the age of 40 she had been successively secretary-treasurer, vice-president, president, and editor of the American Ethnological Society (founded in 1842, the year before the Ethnological Society of London, which is now the Royal Anthropological Institute), a remarkable record among the learned societies of the English-speaking world. She also reached high office in the American Association for the Advancement of Science and the American Folklore Society.

She carried out fieldwork of a particularly valuable and illuminating kind not only in her main area of specialization among the Indians of the North-West Coast of America but also in north-western India. Unfortunately a great part of her fieldwork remained to be written up and published at the time of her death, and her colleagues will be anxious to see that everything possible is done to make her papers available to science.

Her publications include monographs on the North-West Coast *The Puyallup-Nisqually*, (1940) and *Archaeology of the Columbia-Fraser Region* (1950), and a large number of articles, many of them outstanding contributions to the theory and philosophy of anthropological science; she also edited *Indians of the Urban Northwest* (1949) and *Asia and North America: Transpacific Contacts* (1953), as well as the forthcoming symposium report *The Artist in Tribal Society*.

In 1952 she married an English industrialist, Mr. H. F. Akehurst, and spent the greater part of her last 10 years living in London in an extremely happy partnership which gave her many opportunities to visit America, as well as Australia and other parts of the world. She quickly made many friends here, and soon took a part-time teaching post in the University of London, where her deep knowledge of the American field and the American tradition in anthropology was of great value. In the spring of 1956 she followed Mr. William Fagg who had spent 17 years in the fairly onerous post of honorary secretary of the Royal Anthropological Institute.

ENDOWMENT FUND

Her charm, generosity and humanity quickly won her the admiration and affection of every one in the institute or who had any dealings with it. Her great vitality, always coupled with a fine sense of humour, enabled her to carry on the honorary secretaryship for nearly four years almost as a full-time job. She handled institute business by herself in all its aspects, even keeping some of the accounts and, in collaboration with the honorary treasurer, Sir George Beresford-Stooke, taking a close interest in its investment policy. Perhaps the most important single event of her secretaryship was the establishment in 1958 of the institute's endowment fund, with a target of £50,000, largely through the great generosity of Mrs. Brenda Z. Seligman (who set aside the £20,000 proceeds of the sale of her famous ivory mask from Benin to form a matching fund) and Mr. Israel Sieff. Marian Smith devoted herself with great energy and resource to raising contributions for the fund, and was deeply disappointed when illness curtailed and finally terminated her efforts before it had reached £20,000.

Constantly, as she worked, she introduced practical innovations which are of permanent value, while at the same time preserving and strengthening traditional procedures which have stood the test of time. Special mention should be made of the highly successful series of symposia—on cross-disciplinary subjects such as race and race relations, tribal art and society, and the domestication of cattle—which she organized and which are now an important part of the institute's activity. But her reforming and conciliating influence pervaded all its work, and the transformation which she effected in it, without ever doing violence to its well established objects, will profoundly affect its future and that of British anthropology itself.

May 9, 1961.

General W. Bedell Smith, who died on August 9, 1961, at the age of 65 in a Washington hospital, was one of a small group of distinguished American soldiers who rendered outstanding service to the Allied cause in the Second World War and went on to carry heavy responsibilities in the political field.

As General Eisenhower's wartime Chief of Staff—a post to which he had risen after steady promotion in spite of lacking the initial advantage of a West Point training—he demonstrated time and again the essential qualities of steadfast loyalty, a thorough mastery of detail, and a supple intellect. Although in a position which did not naturally attract the limelight, his contribution to victory was immense. Inevitably, he was associated with all General Eisenhower's policies, including the more contentious, but he was prepared on occasion to argue against his superior's strategic thinking.

He was once described by General Eisenhower as "a godsend; a master of detail with clear comprehension of main issues". He had, of course, many wartime dealings with Sir Winston Churchill, who admired his tenacity and intellectual ability and superadded to his American sobriquet of "Beetle" the nickname of "the American Bulldog".

In the postwar years he served both Democratic and Republican Administrations impartially. As Truman's Ambassador in Moscow from 1946 to 1949 it fell to him to bear much of the brunt of the early worsening of relations with the Soviet Union. His experience of the Russian character and of Soviet political tactics, as well as his military training, were invaluable to him when he became director of the Central Intelligence Agency.

EISENHOWER'S CHOICE

It was on Eisenhower's personal initiative that his former Chief of Staff went to the State Department as Under-Secretary to Foster Dulles after the Republican victory in 1952. Here, too, Bedell Smith showed his old qualities of loyalty combined with the ability to think for himself.

Walter Bedell Smith was born on October 5, 1895, at Indianapolis, Indiana, the son of a merchant, William Long Smith. He went to the local Roman Catholic school and while still a schoolboy became a private in the Indiana National Guard. He became an undergraduate at the Butler College, Indianapolis, but owing to the illness of his father had to cut short his studies almost immediately in order to contribute to the family income.

At the age of 18 he was an infantry first sergeant, became an officer in 1917, and was sent to France in time to take part in the fighting on the Marne and the Aisne, there sustaining a wound which led to his transfer to Intelligence work in Washington. He now elected to make his career in the Army and read intensively to acquire the knowledge which would have come his way if he had had the normal training at West Point. Stationed at various home camps, and for two years in the Philippines, he rose to the rank of captain in 1929 and 10 years later achieved his majority.

STAFF WORK

A significant milestone was passed in 1937 when, having previously studied for two years at the Command and General Staff School, he graduated from the Army War College, Washington, the United States Army's senior training school. He was now prepared for the staff work which was to be his *métier*.

From the outbreak of war in 1939, United States Army expansion proceeded apace, and with this expansion came recognition of his quality as an officer. In October, 1939, he was called for duty to Washington, first as assistant secretary and then as secretary to the War Department General Staff. The year 1942 marked his emergence as a major military figure in the life of the United States. In February of that year he became the first United States Secretary to the Combined Chiefs of Staff, the function of which was to coordinate the military efforts of Britain and America.

For some time he had attracted the attention of General George C. Marshall, and it was Marshall who now recommended him to General Eisenhower. In September, 1942, holding the temporary rank of brigadier-general, he went to England as Eisenhower's Chief of Staff in the European theatre of operations.

ITALIAN ARMISTICE

The two men worked together in closest collaboration on the North Africa campaign and the invasion of Normandy. It was Bedell Smith who conducted conversations with Italian emissaries in Lisbon and with General Castellano in Sicily, and in September, 1943, signed the Italian armistice terms. It was he, too, who with General Jodl signed the instrument of Germany's unconditional surrender at Theims in May, 1945. He became a major-general in August of the same year.

Early in 1946, at the behest of President Truman, he succeeded Averell Harriman as United States Ambassador to the U.S.S.R. His close observation of conditions in that country was supplemented by considerable knowledge of Russian history.

On his return to America he was offered the post of Under-Secretary of State for European Affairs but refused it, taking instead the much sought-after appointment of commanding general of the First Army, based on Governor's Island, in New York Harbour. His return to military duties was, however, of short duration for in August, 1950, he was appointed director of the Central Intelligence Agency, with its task of gathering and assessing information about the plans and policies of potential enemies of the United States.

TRUSTED COLLEAGUE

The old association between Eisenhower and Bedell Smith was revived in February, 1953, when the President appointed his well trusted colleague to the position of Under-Secretary of State and deputy to the Secretary, John Foster Dulles.

From 1954 until his death Bedell Smith was vice-chairman of the American Machine and Foundry Corporation. In 1956 he was made a member of the National Security Training Command and in 1958 he became one of the special advisers to the Secretary of State on disarmament. He nearly made a dramatic return to political life in the autumn of 1957 when there was a move to appoint him special advisor to the President on foreign affairs. John Foster Dulles was ill at the time and the post might have carried great influence. However, there was strong opposition from Dulles and from Herbert Hoover, junior, who was then acting Secretary of State and the idea was eventually dropped.

He became a full general in July, 1951. He was appointed an honorary K.C.B. in 1944, an honorary G.B.E. in 1945 and was awarded many other honours and decorations, military and civil, including the Distinguished Service Medal (with Oak Leaves), the Legion of Merit, and the Bronze Star Medal.

He married in 1917 Mary Eleanor Cline.

August 11, 1961.

Professor Wilson Smith, F.R.S., the bacteriologist who helped to lay the foundations of influenza virus research, died on July 10, 1965, at Woolton Hill, near Newbury. He was 68.

Wilson Smith was born on June 21, 1897. He was educated at Accrington Grammar School in Lancashire, and left school to pass through the First World War, serving with the 107th Field Ambulance from 1915 to 1919. On demobilization, he entered as a medical student at Manchester University, and qualified as a Bachelor of Medicine and Surgery in 1923.

After qualification, he practised clinical medicine for a time, including a turn of duty as a ship's doctor, and then entered the Diploma in Bacteriology course in Manchester under Professor Topley during 1926. He gained the diploma in 1927, and having married one of Topley's young demonstrators, became Research Assistant at the National Institute for Medical Research, then under the inspiring leadership of Sir Henry Dale. It was at this stage that, possibly influenced by his first chief at the institute, S. R. Douglas, he became interested in viruses, and took the first steps towards joining the small band of pathologists and bacteriologists who were pioneering virological research in Britain.

At this time, severe outbreaks of epidemic influenza were recurring almost yearly as a slowly declining aftermath of the terrible pandemic of 1918-19, and Wilson Smith, together with his colleague, C. H. Andrewes (late Sir Christopher), initiated a line of investigation to test the theory that influenza was caused by a virus. He isolated the first strain of virus by inoculating throat washings from his colleague, who had become a victim of influenza, into ferrets. It is a fitting irony that this first strain was lost by a holocaust of canine distemper which decimated the ferret colony, and that the first influenza virus strain to be successfully established in ferrets, in 1933, was one isolated from Wilson Smith himself. The W.S. strain was the first human strain of influenza virus to be made available for laboratory study, and remains one of the classic strains.

Wilson Smith, together with his colleague, laid the foundations of influenza virus research in his succeeding years at the institute. In 1939 he became Professor of Bacteriology at Sheffield University, which post he held during the Second World War, and subsequently was appointed Professor of Bacteriology at University College Hospital Medical School in 1946. Here he established ultimately one of the first university departments to be devoted wholly to fundamental virus research. In 1949 he was elected Fellow of the Royal Society, and a Fellow of the Royal College of Physicians in 1959.

He resigned his chair in 1960 to become consultant adviser to the Microbiological Research Establishment at Porton, and was awarded the University Graham Gold Medal in the same year.

Virus research is today a complex, rapidly expanding field of scientific endeavour, and in such circumstances it is all too easy to lose sight of the early pioneer contributions from which the field has grown. Although Wilson Smith was a virological pioneer of wide interests, and contributed actively throughout his life many significant experimental observations to diverse aspects of virology, it is his contributions to the foundations of influenza virus research which should perhaps be his most enduring monument.

He leaves a widow, and two married daughters.

July 14, 1965.

Sir Richard Snedden, C.V.O., C.B.E., who spent virtually the whole of his life in work on industrial relations, principally in shipping, died on March 9, 1970. As assistant secretary, secretary and chief executive of the Shipping Federation, he was one of the team of men who kept shipping free of industrial disturbance over a long term of years. He became the first life member of the Federation's executive council in 1962.

He had the confidence and respect of both shipowners and the leaders of the seafarers' societies because of his sincere, almost passionate, devotion to the industry he served. He was ruthless in opposition to anything he believed to be against the interests of that industry, but there was no rancour in him and he had the courage to make short-term concessions for long-term advantages. He was once described as the consummate producer of the unexpected compromise.

Richard Snedden was born in 1900, the eldest son of George Snedden, of Edinburgh. He went to George Watson's College and afterwards to Edinburgh University. He was later to have conferred on him by the university the honorary degree of Doctor of Laws. He studied law and was called to the bar by the Middle Temple in 1925.

He joined the National Confederation of Employers' Organizations (which later became the British Employers' Confederation), serving for six years as assistant secretary and then as joint secretary until 1929 when he was appointed assistant secretary of the Shipping Federation.

To be chief executive officer of an employers' organization demands special qualities, among them the ability to sink individuality and to carry out faithfully a policy not necessarily of his own making. Snedden's complete loyalty and integrity explain the confidence union officials had in him and the great influence he exerted in the shipping industry.

As general manager of the International Shipping Federation and a member of the Governing Body of the International Labour Organization, Snedden was a prominent figure at Geneva or Seattle, Genoa or Colombo—wherever an international conference concerned with labour might be held. Not that he was enamoured of international organizations. At a European regional conference of the I.L.O. at Geneva in 1955 he bluntly criticized the proliferation of international bodies, some of which, he declared, continued in existence even when they had no real work to do. Far too often cooperation was only a label or a slogan and not a policy. He also vigorously opposed the admission of employer-delegates of the Communist *bloc* to membership of the technical committees of the I.L.O.

RARELY AROUSED

Normally he was a quiet speaker, but on occasion both material and delivery could be devastating. He won from the American press the nickname "blockbuster" and it was not an inapt description of his more explosive moments; but he favoured the quiet, persuasive method of negotiation and it was rarely that he was aroused.

Snedden led the British shipowners' delegates at all maritime meetings of the I.L.O. and he had the outstanding compliment paid to him of being elected the chairman and spokesman of the whole international group of shipowners. His appointment in 1952 as the member for the British Employers' Confederation (of whose industrial relations committee he was chairman) on the Governing Body of the I.L.O., made him the representative of the whole of British industry as comprised in the membership of the employers' federations.

Snedden's association with bodies connected with the British Merchant Navy was naturally extensive. He was a representative of the shipowners on the National Maritime Board, which is more than a joint industrial council for the industry for it deals with every aspect of the seafarer's life and employment; vice-chairman of the Merchant Navy Training Board; chairman of the National Sea Training Schools, and chairman of the Merchant Navy Committee of King George's Fund for Sailors.

In 1954 he was given an honorary commission in the Royal Naval Reserve in recognition of the outstanding support he had given to the Reserve. He was made a C.B.E. in 1942 and was knighted in 1951. Norway, Denmark, Sweden and Finland all bestowed decorations on him for his services during the war.

He married in 1926 Janet Catherine, only daughter of Duncan MacDougall and they had one son.

March 10, 1970.

Marshal of the Soviet Union Vassily Danilovich Sokolovsky died on May 10, 1968, at the age of 70. Although he occupied important command positions during the Soviet-German War, Sokolovsky's eminence and authority derived mainly from his services as a military planner. In the first, critical phase of the war, which culminated in the German defeat before Moscow, he served as Zhukov's chief of staff; after an interval as a front commander he returned in the closing stages of the war to his old position as chief of staff to the massive fronts wielded by Koniev and Zhukov.

Important though these services were, it may be that his postwar activity, which included his role as Soviet commander in Berlin during the blockade, and above all his seven years (1953-60) as Chief of the General Staff, will be seen as his prime contribution to Soviet military development. During the vital phase of the modernization of the Soviet forces after Stalin's death, and the later phase of the organization of the Strategic Rocket Forces, Sokolovsky occupied his key position at the General Staff.

Having survived the great military purge of 1937-38, in the autumn of 1939 he was serving as Chief of Staff to the Moscow Military District, a post of distinction and importance. It was in this position that he played a significant part in organizing the motorized supply columns routed through Moscow during the Soviet-Finnish War (1939-40). When formal ranks for senior officers were instituted in 1940, Sokolovsky was appointed a lieutenant-general. When in January, 1941, after the dismissal of General Meretskov, General Zhukov became Chief of the General Staff, Sokolovsky acted as Deputy Chief of the General Staff (replacing General Smorodinov, who went to the Soviet Far East).

During the first stage of the Soviet-German War (the Great Patriotic War), when Zhukov was appointed commander of the Western Front, Sokolovsky again acted as his chief of staff and also as deputy commander. The Military Soviet of the Western Front for the defence of Moscow consisted of General Zhukov (commander), Lieutenant-General Sokolovsky (Chief of Staff) and Lieutenant-General Bulganin (political member). This partnership in command between Zhukov and Sokolovsky continued to be, with certain interruptions, one of the features of higher Soviet military leadership, not least during the war.

On June 14, 1942, while serving with the Bryansk Front, Sokolovsky was promoted to colonel-general, and in August, 1943, became a full General of the Red Army. At that time he commanded the Western Front, taking part in the Soviet exploitation of their success at Kursk and beginning, in association with other fronts, the liberation of Belorussia. In March, 1944, after the winter advance on the Orsha line, Sokolovsky relinquished his front command to become, in May, Chief of Staff to Marshal Koniev, commander of the First Ukranian Front. Almost on the eve of the final Soviet offensive against Berlin on April 13, 1945, in an apparently last-minute switch, Sokolovsky left the First Ukranian Front to become Chief of Staff and Deputy Front commander of Marshal Zhukov's First Belorussian Front. Deputy to Zhukov in occupied Berlin (where Field Marshal Montgomery conferred on him the O.B.E.), he became the Soviet representative on the four-power Control Commission when Zhukov was withdrawn.

In 1946 he was elected a deputy to the Supreme Soviet; in the following year he was made a Marshal of the Soviet Union, and it was thus that he took part in the "Berlin blockade". which ended in Soviet discomfiture. In 1949 he was recalled from his Berlin post and returned to Moscow where he was appointed First Deputy Minister of Defence. He was reelected to the Supreme Soviet in 1950 and in 1952 elected to the Central Committee of the Communist Party. In February, 1953 he replaced Shtemenko as Chief of the General Staff (it is possible that this appointment had become *effective* before the official, open change, late in 1952). This post Sokolovsky held until November, 1960. As Chief of the General Staff, he occupied a key position during the first post-Stalin transformations of the Soviet armed forces, and during the period of intensive reequipping and retraining carried out when Zhukov was Defence Minister (1955-57). In 1956 Sokolovsky was reelected to the Central Commiittee. After the dismissal of Zhukov he retained his post under Marshal Malinovsky, although it was apparent that he was far from satisfied with the reductions in Soviet military strength (conventional forces) proposed and carried out by Mr. Khrushchev. For this opposition, and in the company of Marshal Koniev, he was removed from his post.

OPEN WORK ON STRATEGY

Sokolovsky continued to exercise a powerful influence on the terms and the course of the Soviet "military debate". In 1962 there appeared *Military Strategy* (*Voennaya Strategiya*), edited by Sokolovsky, the first main Soviet work on strategy since 1926 (in open print). The book received the widest attention both inside and outside the Soviet Union.

May 11, 1968.

David Churchill Somervell, who died on January 17, 1965, in his eightieth year, was one of the great teachers of our time.

His father, Robert Somervell, was a revered history master and Bursar of Harrow School. It was Robert Somervell who, according to his pupil, G. M. Trevelyan, first showed him the interest to be found in English history: it was to his teaching, Sir Winston Churchill claimed, that he owed his mastery of the English language. The son went to Harrow and then to Magdalen College, Oxford, and almost instinctively became a schoolmaster in his term. He inherited some of his father's talents and tastes, as well as his gentle modesty. After teaching at Repton for nine years he became in 1919 history master at Tonbridge School, a congenial career to which he devoted the next 31 years of his life. In 1947 he published *A History of Tombridge School* which revealed how deeply his affections were engaged in the life of the school.

Being an energetic and industrious man, he established in these years a national reputation as the author of several useful and reliable historical works. Such books as *English Thought in the Nineteenth Century* (1928), *The British Empire* (1930), and *British Politics Since 1900* (1950) showed the genius of the good schoolmaster for well-ordered, clear and balanced exposition. They came to be widely used and valued among students in sixth forms and at universities, as well as among the general public. They rested not on original research or profound learning, but on wide reading and careful reflection. Their merits were to present knowledge in an attractive form rather than to add to it.

INSPIRED ABRIDGING

Somervell was not only tireless as a teacher; he was also unusually skilled in the craft of literary abridgement. In 1925 he accomplished the task of reducing the two massive Victorian biographies of Disraeli and Gladstone into one short volume which did not deter the reader. The achievement which made him best known was his successful condensation of the 10 large volumes of Arnold Toynbee's *Survey of History* into one volume. Because of what he called his labour of love, thousands of people after the war became familiar with the main ideas of the *Survey*. Somervell had qualities of patience, modesty, energy, and dedication which, combined in the measure in which he united them, produced teaching powers of unusually high excellence. His many grateful pupils, colleagues, and readers will remember him with affection as one who could whet their appetites for further study.

In 1918 he married Dorothea, daughter of the Rev. D. Harford. They had one son and one daughter.

January 20, 1965.

Mary Somerville, O.B.E., died on September 1, 1963, at her home in Bath. She was 65. Although she made history as the first woman to reach the Controller rank in the B.B.C.—

she was Assistant Controller of the Talks Division from 1947 to 1950, and Controller for the ensuing five years—it is for her work in school broadcasting that she will be remembered. A superb producer herself, she taught countless others. Indeed her influence over the whole range of radio production was great and went on through the regular appraisals of programmes the B.B.C. asked her to make after her retirement.

Mary Somerville was born in New Zealand in 1897, the daughter of the Rev. J.A. Somerville. She was educated at the Abbey School, Melrose, Selkirk High School, and Somerville College, Oxford, where she took a degree in English in 1925. Her professional life was bound up with the B.B.C., which she joined in 1925 and to which she devoted herself for 30 years, becoming successively Educational Assistant, Director of School Broadcasting, and Secretary of the Central Council on School Broadcasting, Assistant Controller Talks, and finally Controller Talks.

STARTING THE FERMENT

Mary Somerville did not initiate school broadcasting—the first broadcasts to schools went out in 1924 under the direction of the late T.C. Stobart—but it is rightly associated with her name, because it was she who built up School Broadcasting Department and worked out the close relationship between producer and consumer in which it was firmly grounded—now as then. She subscribed wholeheartedly to Professor Whitehead's view that "education must essentially be a setting in order of a ferment already stirring in the mind". Broadcasting, she thought, could help to start the ferment: the task of setting in order belonged to the teacher. She never forgot that education is a two-way process, and that it was vital for the B.B.C. to know what was happening to the children in the listening schools. The essential data was provided in 1926 by an investigation financed by the Carnegie Trustees in the county of Kent, which set the future pattern for school broadcasting and established a working partnership between the B.B.C. on the one hand, the Board of Education, the local education authorities, and the whole body of teachers on the other.

School broadcasting in sound and TV now employs a staff of over 60; its programmes go out to nearly thirty thousand schools: it is a source of training and advice for visitors from all parts of the world. In so far as such an achievement can ever be credited to one person, that person was Mary Somerville.

TRIUMPHS

She gave 18 years of life to school broadcasting (there were no half-measures in her zeal); she pondered, she pioneered, she fought authority and convinced sceptics; she triumphed.

Mary Somerville was happiest in a position where the hard work was still to be done: she had the courage of her convictions, and because she had both courage and convictions in good measure, her B.B.C. career was not without its stormy passages.

On issues of principle she was never afraid to say "That is *wrong*"; and she won the affection as well as the respect of her colleagues for her ability to stand firmly behind her decisions. When troubles arose, no staff were ever better defended in public, though in private they were often told pretty frankly where their work had fallen short.

Whatever her designation, she was always an educationist in the widest sense of the word. This did not mean that she believed in didactic broadcasting. On the contrary, she disliked it because it was bad radio, and because nothing that was bad radio could be good education. But she judged a broadcast, in whatever context, by the tests she had used in building up school broadcasting: the right relationship between speaker and hearer, and the right use of radio techniques, so that the end product—"what comes out of the box" she called it—was an experience and an extension for its hearers, and not simply an easy alternative to reading.

To the end of her life she had an exceptional capacity for learning new things, and she never lost the ability to revere and admire. Her colleagues were often surprised by the catholicity of her respect for the views of the very varied people she talked to in her private and professional life, until it occurred to them that their own opinions were being treated in the same way.

NEW EXPERIENCE

Perhaps this receptivity to the impact of new experience was the real basis of her contribution to broadcasting. She did not want, in her own words, "to force what was thought good for the public down its throat", but she did believe in providing what was good. She herself had found in broadcasting a source of enrichment: she hoped to make it so for others.

She was appointed O.B.E. in 1935 and in 1943 Manchester University made her an honorary M.A.

She married in 1928 Ralph Penton Brown by whom she had a son. The marriage was dissolved by divorce in 1945. She married secondly in 1962 E. Rowan Davies.

September 2, 1963.

Field Marshal Pibul Songgram, former Prime Minister of Thailand, died in Tokyo on June 11, 1964, at the age of 66. His death closed the career of the most prominent Thai statesman of the present century who was known to his supporters as the founder of the Thai nation.

Songgram was born on July 14, 1897, of a farming family in Nakorn Nayok province. He entered the Royal Military Academy in Bangkok in 1909 and was commissioned in the 7th Artillery in 1914. He attended the artillery training colleges at Poitiers and Fontainebleau between 1924 and 1927. In France he was one of a group of brilliant Thai students which also included Pridi Phanomyong and Khuang Aphaiwong who became first associates and later rivals in his long political career which began in 1932 when a *coup d'état* engineered by military and civilian officials replaced the absolute monarchy with a constitutional regime.

Artillery officers, Pibul Songgram among them, were prominent in the *coup* of June 24, 1932. He was a Minister from 1932 to 1934 in the first four constitutional Cabinets and rose to fame as a result of his dramatically successful suppression of a royalist rebellion in 1933. He joined with Phahon Phonphayuhasena in the overthrow of the civilian-dominated government in 1933 and was Minister of Defence in the Phahon Administration from 1934 to 1938.

TERRITORY RETAKEN

Pibul early came to realize the significance of the rise of Japan in the 1930s and sought to build up the defence strength of Thailand and to create a new sense of nationhood and patriotism. He soon encountered personal and political rivalry and there were three unsuccessful attempts on his life at this period.

Pibul Songgram admired the dynamic policies of the Axis powers and adopted the "leadership principle" in his own methods of government when he became Prime Minister in December, 1938. He opposed radical social policies, fearing that they would split the country in the threatening situation which was developing on the eve of the Second World War. He adopted a positive, flexible policy towards Japan and took advantage of French weakness in 1940 to regain title to territory in Laos and Cambodia which had been under Thai control before the colonial period. Japanese troops landed in Thailand on December 8, 1941, but Pibul entered into an agreement with the invaders and later declared war on the allies.

Pibul Songgram fell from power on July 17, 1944, as the fortunes of war turned against Japan. He remained in political obscurity during the period of ascendancy of Pridi Phanomyong. Pridi was accused of complicity in the death of King Ananda Mahidol in June, 1946, and Pibul was the prime mover in the *coup* which drove him into exile on November 8, 1947.

Pibul regained the premiership in April, 1948 as a champion of anti-communism and led his country into close association with the United States. Thailand became a member of SEATO in 1954 and benefited from the substantial aid programmes that derived from a policy of commitment to the west. Pibul's regime survived attempts to overthrow it by force on four occasions between 1948 and 1952. The attempts of February, 1949 and June, 1951, resulting in street fighting in Bangkok, involved the followers of Pridi Phanomyong who were supported by the Navy.

Towards the end of his last premiership, Pibul came to favour a return to more democratic procedures, influenced perhaps by his world tour undertaken in 1955. He permitted party-political organisation and instituted open air political debates. These were known as the Hyde Park Corner experiment but were soon proscribed since the vast crowds they attracted proved to be antagonistic to the government. A general election held in February, 1957, confirmed Pibul in power but he was involved in charges of electoral malpractice brought against his police chief, Phao Siyanon. His regime survived only until September 16, 1957, when the late Field Marshal Sarit Thanarat, a younger rival, staged a *coup* against it. From that time Pibul lived in exile in the United States and Japan, and became a Buddhist monk during 1960 at Bodh Gaya in India.

Pibul Songgram was an extremely handsome man, of great personal charm. He easily inspired loyalty, especially within the Army, but he was, nevertheless, a controversial figure. His opponents saw him as the chief obstacle to the establishment of a genuine Parliamentary democracy once royal absolutism had been brought to an end. They resented his highly centralized personal rule and categorized his social policies as a mere sham. He was, indeed, a conservative, in the Thai tradition which is by no means obscurantist. He saw the maintenance of a strong independent state in the face of external pressures as the main function of a leader. Foreign policy considerations were paramount in his mind and he certainly succeeded in charting a generally advantageous course for Thailand during a difficult period.

June 13, 1964.

Cécile Sorel, the French actress and music-hall star, whose sheer verve and exuberance had made her into a legendary figure, died in her country house outside Deauville on September 3, 1966, at the age of 92.

Born in September, 1873, she made her first stage appearance in 1889, and in the years that followed became known round the world for her charm and panache. She played before many monarchs, among them Tsar Nicholas II of Russia, leaving a stream of anecdotes in her train. King Fuad of Egypt invited her to his palace in Cairo, and is reported to have said afterwards: "She received me very well."

Cécile Sorel—her real name was Céline Seurre—was never regarded as a great actress, but created her impression by force of personality. Tall and assured, with large eyes and a strong nose, she dominated the scene, first on the stage of the Comédie Française, with whom she acted for 32 years, playing in Molière, Dumas, Victor Hugo and Beaumarchais, and, later, appeared at the Casino de Paris. She joined the Comédie Française in 1901, and among her many triumphs the greatest was her playing of Sapho in the play by Alphonse Daudet. Even there she succeeded in causing a scandal, interrupting the play, at one moment, when the audience were beginning to mock, in order to denounce them all as idiots.

In 1933 Cécile Sorel left the Comédie Française and its classical repertory in order to plunge herself into music-hall. She was then turning 60, but she told a journalist that she wanted to convey "la folie moderne". She appeared at the Casino de Paris, and there achieved new triumphs. Colette wrote that the Casino had formed Cécile Sorel not so much by the physical effort that it demanded as by giving her an atmosphere in which she could give free rein to her feelings. Her majestic manner had become more human. Her smile was no longer directed at an empty sky, but reached the human beings in the audience.

As her autobiography (published in Britain in 1953) showed she was ever a spectacular social figure. Her bed of solid gold and ivory was said at different times to have supported Marie Antoinette and Madame Dubarry; her dining room table was of white marble and she owned a good deal of rather heavy jewelry. She got to know a large number of kings. She was admired by d'Annunzio, who tore up flowers and threw them at her, and by Mussolini who observed to her: "My dear emissary of Heaven, your visit will mark the highest point of my life." She was embraced by Foch, whose medals made an unforgettable imprint on her bare shoulder, and discussed life with Clemenceau at three in the morning on a rough Atlantic crossing.

A woman of great spirit, she understood the large gesture well enough; she knew how to get the very most from a scene. In 1921 a caricature of her in the role of Célimene was exhibited in Paris and she sued the artist for defamation of her beauty, "Je suis belle, je le sais, et je quitterai la scène quand je ne le serais plus".

The gallery immediately moved the offending caricature to a commanding position and posted a copy of her legal process beneath it. Undefeated, she later forced her way through a crowd and broke "with three sharp blows of her fist" the glass covering the picture. She also dislodged the stone of a large ruby ring she happened to be wearing. All looked, but the stone could not be found so she publicly offered a reward of 10,000 francs for its recovery and withdrew to her car after a thoroughly satisfactory afternoon. Later her chauffeur retrieved the missing jewel from the car floor. Thus, as *The Times* Correspondent remarked: "No harm was done to the ring, no harm to the caricature but the actress and the artist have "la plus parisienne des réclames."

Cécile Sorel set off new controversies in August, 1950, when she decided to enter a religious order, the Tiers Ordre de St. François. Giving way once again to her sense of the spectacular, she broke the rules of the order by appearing in public in her habit, and demands were made that she should be expelled. The storm passed, however, and she remained in the order for the rest of her life. Her last public appearance was in March 1966, when she made a point of attending one of the first performances of an Ionesco play—*La Soif et la Faim*—at the Comédie Française.

September 5, 1966.

Queen Victoria Eugénie of Spain, one of the last surviving grandchildren of Queen Victoria, died on April 15, 1969.

She was a strong and gifted personality whose capacity obscured by misfortunes was never fairly tested. Married at 18 she brought to the Spanish royal family the then incurable malaise of some of Queen Victoria's descendants—one of her sons died in early manhood and another as a boy. These matters were not without their influence on her position in Spain which was never an easy one in that she was following an outstanding personality—her mother-in-law, Queen Maria Christina, who had been regent and survived until a few months before the revolution broke out. From 1931 the Queen lived in exile. In the long years away from Spain she is understood to have been a forceful influence in the counsels of her son and grandson—the latter now recognized as the likely Spanish King.

CHRISTENING ERROR

Victoria Eugénie Julia Ena was born at Balmoral—a Golden Jubilee baby—on October 24, 1887. The last name, by which she was always known in the family, was a misreading of her mother's handwriting; it had been intended to mark her Scottish birth with the Gaelic name of Eua. She was the only daughter and second child of Princess Beatrice and Prince Henry of Battenberg—the third of four remarkable brothers. Since the Queen found Princess Beatrice invaluable as a reader and confidential secretary, she and her husband made her home with the Queen. Consequently, Queen Ena and her three brothers brought to life again the nurseries of Osborne, Windsor, and Balmoral after an interval of 30 years.

Her godmother, the Empress Eugénie, who was herself a Spaniard, was almost certainly responsible for encouraging a marriage between Queen Ena and King Alfonso XIII of Spain. Some mutterings were heard at the marriage on account of the supposed lack of ancestry of the bride's father. Queen Mary's excessively royal aunt wrote to her "So Ena is to become Queen of Spain. A Battenberg! Good gracious!" The more immediate difficulty was that she had to change her religion and with anti-Catholic feeling still strong in England the matter needed careful handling. With wisdom, King Edward insisted that no foreign prelate should instruct the Princess, and for this task he chose the then Bishop of Nottingham, who was blessed with the reassuringly English name of Brindle. Bishop Brindle received her into the Roman Catholic Church at San Sebastian. In 1906 she was married to the King in St. Geronimo at Madrid. The occasion has passed into history because of a disgraceful attempt on the lives of the bride and bridegroom, in which several onlookers were killed. King George V. who represented his father, remarked on the Queen's courage and presence of mind in a ghastly ordeal.

ENGLISH WAYS

For the next few years the Queen's time was largely taken up with family cares—she had four sons and two daughters born between 1907 and 1914. Inevitably she was placed in a position of some embarrassment in the first war. Spain was neutral but the Queen was totally English: her appearance and her turn of mind revealed her sympathies, for as an American once bluntly said: "she was as English as a cup of tea". Her youngest brother was killed in 1914—he was in the K.R.R.C.—and his picture stood in the place of honour in her private sitting-room in the palace at Madrid. In the immediate circle of the Spanish royal family things were also difficult because the Queen Dowager was an Austrian archduchess.

The Queen's principal achievement in Spain lay in modernizing and reorganizing the hospital nursing system. Her Red Cross hospital in Madrid was a model, and each year she used to send a detachment of Spanish nurses to study English nursing methods. For this and other reasons her popularity in Spain steadily increased: she returned from a visit to her mother in England a few weeks before the revolution started, and she was given an immense ovation from the people of Madrid—the crowd crying "Down with the Republic". When she was compelled to leave, her departure was not surreptitious: she travelled by the royal train which was driven, according to unvarying tradition by the Duke of Zaragossa, hereditary engine-driver to the royal family.

The last half of her life was lived in exile, adjusting herself from the ancient formalities of Spanish life to the less picturesque realities of modern Europe. She made home at Lausanne in a small but charming chateau, Vielle Fontaine: she separated from King Alfonso but without animosity, and she was with him when he died.

April 16, 1969.

The Infanta Beatrice of Spain died on July 13, 1966, at her home in Spain, at the age of 82.

Although she was largely unfamiliar to the the present generation in Britain, the Infanta Beatrice was one of the most striking members of the English royal family. All through her chequered life in Spain she remained unswerving in her devotion to England. She was always glad to see English people, and they felt immediately at home when they drove through the gates of her beautiful home at the mouth of the Guadalquivir and saw the warning notice, "Look out for cats and dogs".

Her Royal Highness Princess Beatrice Leopoldine Victoria was born on Easter Day, 1884—the youngest of the four dangerously beautiful daughters of the Duke of Edinburgh, Queen Victoria's second son. He had married the only daughter of the Emperor Alexander II 10 years earlier. The Princess, known in the family as "Baby Bee", was born at Eastwell Park, a large country house towards the Kentish coast with views across the North Sea and the Channel. Much of her childhood was spent in Malta when her father had the Mediterranean Command. After 1893 when he became the reigning Duke of Saxe-Coburg-Gotha her home was principally in Germany. She was one of Queen Mary's bridesmaids, and was staying at Osborne during Queen Victoria's last illness and death.

When Beatrice was 25 she married the Infante Alfonso, head of the Orleans branch of the Spanish royal family. He was grandson of the Duke of Montpensier who was the central personality in the international crisis of the Spanish Marriages. But there were great difficulties over the princess's marriage largely on account of religion. She was reluctant to give up her Protestant faith, and for this and other reasons it was thought wiser for them to live away from Spain. (Later the Princess joined the Roman Catholic Church.) They lived largely in Switzerland and it was during this period that the Princess undertook a course at Lucerne University. Later when they returned to Spain they formed part of the immediate family circle of King Alfonso and Queen Ena. When the Revolution broke out in 1931 the Infante accompanied the King on his dramatic drive into exile. The Infanta decided to remain behind in Madrid to look after an aged aunt of her husband's, and she liked to recall that General Franco's brother, Ramon, threatened to burn the house over the heads of the royal ladies unless they left. They remained.

The revolution financially ruined the Infante, and he took work in England in Ford's motor factory. The Infanta made a home for him in a small house at Esher, the charms of which made a great impression on her sister, Queen Marie of Roumania. At the end of the 1930s they returned to Spain, and after the end of the Second World War they went back to the Duke of Montpensier's vast Victorian palace at San Lucar, but when they found that 104 people were living in the house at their expense they decided to move to something more modest. With the excellent artistic taste of the Infanta this made a delightful home where English and American visitors were ever accorded the warmest welcome. The Infanta was very musical—a devoted Wagnerian—and in earlier days she and the Infante were constant visitors to Bayreuth. Her conversation, as Lord Templewood recalled in *Ambassador on Special Mission*, was extraordinarily pithy and brilliant. She enjoyed retailing her memories of England, which were not blurred by discretion. Her scornful comments on the rather colourless personality of General Franco were given without restraint. At one time she and her husband experienced the discomforts of house arrest.

The Infanta had three sons, who were educated at Winchester. The second was killed in action in the civil war, fighting against the Republican Government.

July 14, 1966.

Muggsy Spanier, one of the best of the early jazz cornetists, died on February 12, 1967, at Sausalito, California, at the age of 60.

Of Irish-American parentage, he was born Francis Joseph Spanier on November 9, 1906, in Chicago, Illinois, where he grew up and became a professional musician at the age of 15. During the early and mid-1920s Chicago was the centre of jazz in America and Spanier soon came to model his style on the New Orleans trumpeters who were working there, especially King Oliver.

Although he mostly earned his living during the 1920s playing in large dance bands, he made many recordings with small jazz groups and earned a reputation among his fellow jazz musicians.

When New Orleans jazz fell out of favour in the 1930s, he continued to play with large dance bands, chiefly those of Ted Lewis and Ben Pollack. In 1938 he collapsed and for a while his life was despaired of, but in 1939 he recovered fully to start his own jazz group, which he called his Ragtime Band. Unfortunately he had anticipated the revival of interest in New Orleans jazz by a few years and the band lasted only a year, but after a further retreat into the ranks of the large bands he re-formed a small group and in the postwar years seldom went along without leading his own band.

Although Spanier's music occasionally came close to the pastiche of New Orleans jazz known as Dixieland, his playing at its best was more exciting than that of any of his white contemporaries. As he had neither great inventive powers nor an extensive technique, his style depended largely on a driving open tone sometimes fiery, sometimes smouldering, a superb use of the plunger mute and an instinctive feeling for jazz. He was in fact a marvellous lead player rather than a great soloist, and the best evidence for this is still to be found on the 16 classic records he made with his Ragtime Band in 1939 and the quartet recordings he made with Sidney Bechet in the early 1940s.

February 14, 1967.

Francis Cardinal Spellman, Roman Catholic Archbishop of New York, dean of American Cardinals and best known churchman in the United States, died on December 2, 1967, in St. Vincent's Hospital, New York. He was 78, and had been Archbishop for 28 years and Cardinal for 21.

A Boston Irish grocer's son, Spellman retained throughout his life the easy manner, sentimental touch (his favourite song was "Danny Boy") and paradoxical loyalties of his boyhood. His origins served to explain his social and political conservatism allied with a gregariousness that made him at ease with eminent men at home and abroad as various—one need only name them as examples—as every president from Truman to Johnson.

They explained his passionate American loyalties which took him all over the world, even in his last frail years, as military vicar to the armed forces. In this context his influential activities in the China lobby, his endorsement of the late Joseph McCarthy's anti-communism and his recent consistent call for "victory" in Vietnam were all of a piece.

At the same time, his basic impulses were Eirenic and his public and private statements against anti-Semitism and racial discrimination were well in advance of those of many churchmen of his generation. Indeed, some of his apparent inconsistencies were those of a man who believed deeply in the traditions in which he had been brought up, but was open to persuasion.

Nothing perhaps typified this better than his attitude to the Vatican Council. He had developed a profound and lasting friendship with Pope Pius XII, whom he first met in 1929 when the future Pope was Nuncio in Berlin.

RICHEST DIOCESE

It was Pius XII who had consecrated him archbishop of the richest diocese in the world, and they worked closely to protect what they saw as the real interests of the church in a world in flux.

When the next Pope proposed Vatican II, Spellman helped to finance and plan the council, but in public at least his contribution was lukewarm and cautious. He did not care for collegiality, or the prospect of married deacons, a softer line on mixed marriages or approving references to conscientious objectors.

But in 1965 he played a major part in blocking the conservative attempt to keep the statement on religious liberty from a vote. He worked for a strong declaration exculpating the Jews from sinful responsibility for the crucifixion. And by the end of the council he was taking advice from young American theologians he had previously avoided.

There has probably never been a priest in the American hierarchy with Spellman's capacity for diplomacy behind the scenes, and probably no one person could take the measure of his influence. In public, even those offended by his severity could be won over by his gentle smile and Irish humour—on the other hand, those who felt him too much of the tycoon and administrator were impressed by his impressive and traditional conduct of the celebrant matters of his pastorate. Yet among his clergy he was universally known as "the boss".

His personal generosity was a by-word, and his diocese, although he left most of the public business of raising money to others, was an underpinning of Roman Catholic policy and good works all over the world.

Francis Joseph Spellman was born on May 4, 1889, at Whitman, Massachusetts, one of five children of a small shopkeeper and his wife.

IRISH FORBEARS

Both his parents were of Irish descent. He attended local schools and worked out of school hours, but found time, nevertheless, for baseball and boxing, and during one summer he was the conductor of a tram. In 1907 he entered Fordham College in New York. When, after his graduation, he showed a desire to enter the priesthood he was sent by Cardinal O'Connell, of Boston, to the North American College in Rome where, in 1916, he was given the degree of Doctor of Sacred Theology and ordained in the Church of St. Apollinaris. During the next two years he served as pastor of a church in a Boston suburb. Then he was called to the staff of the archdiocese of Boston, acting, first, as editor of its weekly newspaper and afterwards, for three years, as assistant chancellor of the archdiocese.

In 1925 he returned to Rome with a group making a Holy Year pilgrimage. He had become proficient in Italian and Latin, and at an audience for the pilgrims given by Pope Pius XI he won praise from the Pope by swiftly translating the latter's address into idiomatic English, Largely because of this performance he was shortly afterwards appointed attache to the Office of Secretary of State of the Vatican and translator of Papal broadcasts and encyclicals. He was the first American to receive that appointment. In his new capacity he made much use of American publicity techniques, including mimeographed press "releases", background press conferences and wireless broadcasts, impressing his fellow churchmen with his ability and zeal.

More importantly, his work brought him into contact with a person of great influence in Vatican affairs, Archbishop Eugenio Pacelli, then Papal Nuncio in Germany, later Cardinal Secretary of State and finally Pope Pius XII.

BOTH MOUNTAINEERS

Their acquaintance quickly ripened into friendship with the discovery that they had in common an enthusiasm for mountain climbing. In 1932, when Spellman was appointed titular bishop of Sila, his consecration, by Cardinal Pacelli, was given special significance by the fact that he was wearing the same vestments that Pacelli had worn at his own consecration. In the same year Spellman was sent back to Boston as auxiliary bishop to Cardinal O'Connell and as, in the belief of many, eventually O'Connell's successor. But, contrary to the general expectation, O'Connell lingered on, and for seven years more Spellman continued as auxiliary bishop, serving also as pastor of a church at Newton Center, Massachusetts. Then there came a sudden change in his fortunes. In 1939 Cardinal Pacelli was elevated to the Papacy and one of his first acts was to appoint Spellman Archbishop of New York, the largest and richest of all the Church's sees. Seven years later, in February, 1946, he was made a cardinal.

At the time of his appointment as archbishop he was made Military Vicar of the Armed Forces of the United States throughout the world. He eagerly embraced the opportunities this gave him for wider service and experience, and within a few months after the Japanese attack on Pearl Harbour he started on an 18,000-mile visit to United States Army camps. In the following year he made a second tour, this time travelling more than 46,000 miles visiting American troops in 34 countries. These were the first of an unbroken succession of annual tours made, careless of hardship, during the Second World War, the Korean War, and since.

DELICATE MISSIONS

As it happened, they did more than help to support the morale of the troops. By bringing Spellman into useful contact with Presidents and Prime Ministers throughout the world they made it possible for him, an intensely patriotic citizen, to perform in time many delicate diplomatic missions for Presidents Roosevelt, Truman and Eisenhower.

Spellman's rule in the archdiocese was characterized by efficiency and discipline—some would say ruthlessness. For a long time he did not show publicly the interest in social questions which had occupied his predecessor, Cardinal Hayes, though he had a strong interest in education and in charities. He firmly advocated giving some state aid to parochial schools and this involved him in difficulties with distinguished opponents, particularly Eleanor Roosevelt. He was not, however, an eager controversialist but he could be moved to public expressions of indignation and scorn, as he showed in denouncing the pretensions of communism and in condemning from the pulpit of St. Patrick's Cathedral in 1949 the arrest of Cardinal Mindszenty, of Hungary, and, in later years, "sinful" motion pictures.

He wrote several books, sentimental and devotional, one of them a novel. They were widely popular with Catholics and non-Catholics alike. All the royalties from them, amounting to more than $300,000, he gave to charities.

December 4, 1967.

Alfred Spence, joint assistant managing director of the House of Fraser, and managing director of Harrods, and of the Harrods Group Stores, died on March 15, 1970, at the age of 54. He was also on the boards of the many subsidiary companies of the House of Fraser.

He had been chairman of the Retail Consortium since its formation in 1967, and only recently had had the satisfaction of achieving his objective that it should represent the totality of the retail trade. He was also past chairman of the Retail Distributors Association.

For many years he had taken an active interest in the many charities of the drapery trade, not least in the Linen and Woollen Drapers Cottage Homes, of which he served on the board of management. He was a member of the national executive committee of the Forces Help Societies and the Lord Roberts Workshops.

PRIDE IN TRADE

Alfred Spence, who was born in Perth in 1915, was a draper, and proud of it. On leaving school at the age of 14, he was employed by Caird's of Perth, and subsequently by Robert Simpson's of Glasgow. In 1935 he joined the firm of Fraser Sons, where he rapidly came to the notice of Hugh Fraser (later Lord Fraser of Allander). So much so that at the remarkably early age of 23 he was appointed general manager of Arnott Simpson's, which was Fraser's first major acquisition.

Following World War II, in which he did valuable service in various tank supply depots of the R.A.O.C., he returned to the House of Fraser, and, in appointments of increasing responsibility, grew steadily in Fraser's confidence and affection.

It was in the post-war years that the House of Fraser made giant strides, and Alfred Spence's value to the company grew steadily in step with them. On the formation of the public company in 1948 he was an original director, and the rebuilding of the Middlesbrough store of the Binns Group (acquired in 1953) was the first of six major store developments for which he was responsible. In 1957, when the House of Fraser purchased the Barker Group of stores in Kensington, Spence became a director and first general manager of that group, and completed the rebuilding of John Barker's.

His greatest opportunity came in 1959 when the House of Fraser, after a hard fought battle, won control of Harrods, and Alfred Spence embarked on the difficult task of achieving effective managerial control of that mammoth organization. In no circumstances could it have been easy, and it was due to his tactful, if forceful, perseverance that it was accomplished with remarkable good will. Subsequently his wise direction ensured the steady progress of the group, and in addition he personally supervised the rebuilding of major stores in Glasgow, Liverpool, Birmingham, Sheffield, and, lastly in 1969 in Richmond, Surrey.

In addition to these achievements, he played a considerable part in the building of the Aviemore Centre, which was one of the major preoccupations of the last years of Fraser's life, and was completed after his death.

On the death of Lord Fraser of Allander in 1966, there fell to Spence a large share of the responsibility for advising the present Sir Hugh Fraser in assuming control of a retail empire which even then was achieving a turnover approaching £100m. And in this too he did not fail.

His untimely death is a great sorrow to all who have worked with him at any time in his distinguished career. That career had by no means reached its peak, and the distributive trades will acknowledge sadly that they have lost a leading figure of outstanding drive and ability—and of great personal charm. So too will his many friends in the store trade throughout the world.

During the war he had married Sarah (Sallie) Macdonald, who survives him together with a son and two daughters of that happy marriage. His friends know that however immersed he became in his trade, his family life was an abiding joy to him.

March 16, 1970.

Sir Henry Spencer, managing director of Richard Thomas & Baldwins died on May 31, 1964, at the age of 72. He had been managing director of the company since 1952 and a member of the board since 1949.

Henry Francis Spencer was born in Staffordshire on April 8, 1892. He left school at 13 and went to work in a foundry. By the age of 22 he had his own business as an iron and steel merchant, making sure he had a market for it before persuading a firm to let him have his first load—and the credit to go with it. Later he specialized in steel sheets and after 20 years was said to be the largest distributor of this material in Europe. He played a leading part with the old Ebbw Vale Steel, Iron and Coal Company in promoting the manufacture of high grade sheets, particularly for the motor industry.

In 1935 H. F. Spencer & Co. Ltd, became associated with the Richard Thomas organization when the latter took over the assets of the Ebbw Vale Company, and Spencer joined Richard Thomas as sheet sales controller. He became successively commercial manager, commercial general manager, assistant managing director and finally managing director of Richard Thomas & Baldwins.

He was also a member of the council and executive committee of the British Iron and Steel Federation, and was a member of a number of policy-making committees within the larger orbit of the steel industry.

Spencer was a worried man in 1961 and 1962. Under his direction but paid for with public money a giant steelworks was growing upon green fields and marshlands outside Newport, Monmouthshire. Local critics complained that it was draining labour from all South Wales. Of more consequence to Spencer were the twin ogres of rising costs and falling demand for steel. Cynics forecast that the Government-owned Richard Thomas and Baldwins would have the finest works in the world—but no customers.

"SUPERFLUOUS" PLANT

The situation was not of Spencer's own choosing. In the mid-fifties the Iron and Steel Board had decided that the three British strip steel mills were not adequate to meet future requirements. They recommended another mill should be built with Government help. Mr. Macmillan ultimately made a judgment of Solomon and gave a mill to Scotland and the Llanwern mill to South Wales. He was creating by this decision almost four times more steel-making capacity than the board had recommended.

Spencer recognized from the start that the market was unlikely to grow in time to occupy the Llanwern plant from the day it opened. The position was aggravated when a world surplus in steel shattered international markets in the early sixties. Yet Spencer was determined to see the project through with the maximum efficiency: his determination did not waver. He planned from the start to build the Llanwern works in two-thirds of the time thought reasonable for such a project. He succeeded brilliantly. Main plant orders were placed in late 1959 and early 1960 yet commissioning of the works began early in 1962. Already, at that point, Spencer was thinking ahead to selling the steel and was scouring Europe and farther afield for orders. This foresight was to keep the new works rolling until the boom now being enjoyed by British steel began to be felt in 1963. It was fitting that this works, the great tribulation and the great success of his life, should ultimately have been named the Spencer Works.

FAITH AND SENSE

He had a great capacity for work, and his keen mind had the power to reduce what appeared to be a complicated mass of detail to a simple level. Common sense, faith and a gift for spotting the practical made Spencer the man he was. He rarely looked back but he never forgot his past.

He remained a vigorous, unglossy figure, doing a couple of hours' work before he arrived at his office about 8.30 a.m. and taking papers home at night and at the weekends. He had a dictating machine in his car and sometimes a train compartment reserved for himself, his personal assistant and secretary. He was knighted in 1963.

He married in 1916 Ethel May, only daughter of William Southall, by whom he had a daughter.

June 2, 1964.

Sir Will Spens, who died on November 1, 1962, at Ely at the age of 80, achieved equal distinction in academic life and public administration. As Tutor and Master of Corpus Christi, Cambridge, he was largely responsible for the high reputation which that college achieved between the wars, and for the distinctive character which it has since retained. As regional commissioner for East Anglia during the 1939-45 war he discharged duties of exceptional difficulty and importance with a success which won general admiration. He was Vice-Chancellor of Cambridge from 1931 to 1933.

Born in May, 1882, the son of John Alexander Spens, he was educated at Rugby, at which he became head of the School House. In 1901 he entered King's College, Cambridge, as an Exhibitioner, and in 1903 took a First in Part I of the Natural Science Tripos. Serious illness prevented him from completing the course, but, determined to stay in Cambridge, he accepted a junior post in the Cavendish Laboratory.

In spite of his brilliant academic success he was never whole-heartedly devoted to natural science, and soon turned to theology, a study for which his subtle mind and energetic intelligence no less than his deep Christian convictions admirably fitted him. He became a Fellow of Corpus Christ College in 1907 and for a time contemplated taking Holy Orders.

In 1912 he was appointed Tutor of Corpus and in 1915 published *Belief and Practice,* his only book, which aroused considerable interest in theological circles.

When Spens joined Corpus the college was at a low ebb. He was largely instrumental in securing the election as Fellows of Sir Geoffrey Butler, later Burgess for Cambridge University, Sir Edwin Hoskyns, one of the most eminent theologians of the twentieth century, and A. L. Goodhart, later a most distinguished international lawyer and Master of University College, Oxford. His work was interrupted by the outbreak of war in 1914. Spens, being medically unfit, entered the Foreign Office and in 1917 became Secretary of the Foreign Trade Department, which performed similar functions to those exercised by the Ministry of Economic Warfare in the late war. He proved an admirable administrator and in 1918 was rewarded by being made C.B.E.

PUBLIC ADMINISTRATION

Returning to Cambridge he applied himself again to the task of putting his adopted college in the front rank. With the consent of the governing body he took the decisive step of admitting only Honours men to the college. More generous scholarships, made possible by the judicious administration of finance, enabled the college to develop into a veritable *corps d'élite* and the new policy was justified by the high proportion of firsts and of university prizes gained by its members. He was appointed Master of Corpus in 1927 and held that office for 25 years.

Meantime his interest in public administration did not diminish and he served on a number of committees, including the departmental committee of the War Office on the recruitment of officers. In 1933 he was appointed chairman of the consultative committee of the Board of Education, in which capacity he gave his name to the Spens Report which was regarded by all parties as one of the most remarkable state papers of the inter-war period. He was knighted in 1939. On the outbreak of the last war the Government divided the country for defence purposes into a number of areas over each of which a regional commissioner, to be ultimately responsible for civil defence, was appointed. In the event of one of these areas being cut off by an invasion the regional commissioner would have had immense powers. As it was, the commissioners had the delicate task of supervising relations between the civil and military authorities. Spens was appointed regional commissioner for East Anglia, an area of obvious strategic importance. He discharged his duties with a competence and devotion which won the confidence of all around him. As a mark of their gratitude, the borough of Great Yarmouth elected him its High Steward, an honour which touched Spens very deeply.

CHAIRMAN OF COMMITTEES

In spite of his other preoccupations he did his best to maintain contact with undergraduates. After the war the country's demands on him were not yet exhausted. He was appointed successively chairman of three committees to fix the remuneration of doctors, dentists, and specialists under the National Health Insurance scheme. In 1952, on his retirement from the Mastership he settled in Ely where he became Steward of the cathedral chapter.

Throughout his life Spens had remained devoted to his public school. As chairman of the board of governors from 1944 to 1958 he was mainly responsible for the controversial appointment of Sir Arthur fforde as headmaster in January, 1948. This reflected Spens's conviction that education should be brought into the closest possible contact with contemporary life, and that in the delicate situation of the public schools *vis à vis* the Government the services of a man of the world might prove useful.

Few careers have been more varied or more uniformly successful. As Spens himself used to say, his natural *milieu* was the borderland between theory and practice. In university and public administration he found practical scope for that clear and disinterested judgment which was reflected in his theological writings. Few Masters have had so many outside interests and few have preserved a closer and more sympathetic touch with undergraduates. He had none of the ponderousness of the professional civil servant or the pedantry of the don, and one of his most amiable characteristics was a quiet but pungent wit. His hold on the affections of his friends was deep and strong. It was paradoxically enough, his simplicity, his Christian humility, which made him the beloved spiritual and mental director of generations of undergraduates for close on half a century. As an influence on the lives and outlook of Cambridge men of his day, he was undoubtedly unique. Though a High Tory in politics he had no taste for polemics and was ready to serve the state, whoever might for the moment control it. He held the honorary degree of LL.D. at St. Andrews and Columbia, United States.

In 1912 he married Dorothy Theresa, the elder daughter of Bishop Selwyn of Melanesia, Master of Selwyn College, Cambridge. No tribute to Spens would be complete without mentioning the degree of help to his daily life which he enjoyed from that marriage. He leaves two sons and a daughter.

November 2, 1962.

R.H. Spooner, who died on October 2, 1961, at the age of 80, was one of the most elegant batsmen ever to play cricket for England. His name conjures up memories of what is widely regarded as the "golden age" of English batsmanship in the years before the First World War. For Lancashire and for England he brought a panache and style to the opening of an innings.

It was for this, rather than for the number of runs that he made, that his name became a legend for successive generations of enthusiasts. Even those who never saw him associated his name with graceful and attacking stroke play in an era when batsmen were ready to play their shots without such a numbing awareness of the importance of the result. He personified all that was best in the spirit of amateur batsmanship. Yet so accomplished was his technique that he had also been described as a "right-handed Frank Woolley".

With his brilliance as a batsman went the prowess of an all-round athlete. He was worthy of comparison with the half-dozen best cover-points in the history of the game, and he was also capped for England at Rugby football.

Reginald Herbert Spooner, the second son of the Venerable George Spooner, Archdeacon of Liverpool, was born near Liverpool on October 21, 1880. His skill was soon apparent and by the time of his last year at Marlborough, in 1899, he was an outstanding public schoolboy batsman. On the strength of his reputation there—he played a superb innings of 198 against Rugby at Lord's—he was selected that season for Lancashire and showed himself already a mature player in testing circumstances against Middlesex.

NO AUSTRALIAN TOUR

Largely because of his service in the Boer War, Spooner played no more first-class cricket until 1903. So little did the interruption affect his form that he was invited to tour Australia that winter with the first official M.C.C. side. Unfortunately he was unable to accept, for business reasons, and it was one of the great disappointments of his career that he was never able to play in Australia. He was invited to do so on subsequent occasions, and indeed was to have captained the team of 1920-21 when he was forced to withdraw because of a knee injury. Had he played in Australia at the height of his powers it is quite probable that his success would have been greater than in England, for conditions there have nearly always favoured his style of play—that of the adventurous, wristy batsman who suffers frequent moments of uncertainty at the start of an innings.

As it was, he played in 10 Test matches—seven of them against Australia, beginning in 1905. He made only one Test century, in his first match against South Africa in 1912, and it must be admitted that judged purely on figures his record in the highest class was comparatively disappointing. Yet that century against South Africa, in which he took part in a stand of 124 in 100 minutes with Wilfred Rhodes, showed why his appearance at the crease was always awaited with expectancy.

Moreover, he achieved very many fine performances for Lancashire. With A. C. Maclaren, his partner on so many occasions he took part in what is still the highest opening stand for the county—368 against Gloucestershire at Liverpool in 1903. He played for the county the last time in 1923. He was president of Lancashire County Cricket Club in 1945 and 1946, and was a regular visitor to Old Trafford for Test matches up to 1959.

He played for Liverpool at Rugby football and was awarded his one cap against Wales in the season of 1902-3.

Spooner, who had been wounded in the Boer War, was again wounded when he served in France during the First World War. After his cricketing career was over, he became land agent to Lord Londesborough.

He was twice married. In 1920 he married Margery Lowthorpe-Lutwidge, by whom he had two sons—one of whom, who had been awarded the D.S.O., was killed on active service in 1943. Spooner married secondly in 1940 Lilian Ellerbeck.

October 3, 1961.

Sir William Spooner, K.C.M.G., P.C., M.M., Australian Minister of National Development from 1951 to 1964, died in the Royal Hobart Hospital, Hobart, on July 15, 1966. He was 68. He was Government Leader in the Senate from 1958 to 1964. In January 1966, he was sworn of the Privy Council.

Spooner was born in Sydney on December 23, 1897, and educated at Christ Church School, Sydney. He enlisted in the Australian Imperial Force in 1915, served with the 5th Australian Field Ambulance, was awarded the Military Medal, and was wounded at Ypres. Later he transferred to the Australian Flying Corps and was discharged in 1919 with the rank of Second Lieutenant.

On his return from the war he gained the diploma of Economics and Commerce as an evening student at the University of Sydney. He was a chartered accountant and a member of the firm of Hungerford, Spooner and Co.

PARTY FOUNDER

He helped form the Liberal Party, was chairman of its provisional executive in 1945 and was later elected first New South Wales president of the party. He was its first federal treasurer.

He was elected to the Senate for New South Wales in 1949, 1951, 1955 and 1961, became Minister for Social Services in 1949, Minister in charge of War Service Homes in January, 1951, and Minister for National Development in May, 1951. He had the unusual distinction of going directly into the 1949 Menzies Ministry without previous parliamentary experience. In 1958 he became Vice-President of the Executive Council and in 1958 Leader of the Government in the Senate after the retirement of Senator O'Sullivan.

He was Acting Prime Minister during September, 1962, in the absence overseas of the Prime Minister. In 1963 he was created K.C.M.G. He resigned from the Ministry of National Development in June, 1964, in order to pay more attention to his professional and business interests.

He married in 1924 Catherine Vera Bogle, by whom he had one son and one daughter.

July 16, 1966.

Sir Frank Spriggs, K.B.E., who died on June 11, 1969, at the age of 74, was formerly managing director of the Hawker Siddeley Group of companies. He was a former chairman of Sir W. G. Armstrong Whitworth Aircraft, A. V. Roe & Co., Ltd., Hawker Aircraft Ltd., and Gloster Aircraft Co. Ltd.

He entered the aircraft industry in 1913, joining T. O. M. (now Sir Thomas) Sopwith, at the age of 18 first in the capacity of office boy. He had, however, a mechanical bent and began to apply himself to the workshops.

BACKED THE HURRICANE

Before long he was as skilled as any mechanic and eventually developed the highest technical knowledge of manufacturing, both bodies and engines. Later he left to join the undertakings which were being developed by the Armstrong Siddeley and the Hawker Aircraft Groups.

One of the founders of the Hawker Siddeley Aircraft Company, it was he, as much as any other, who laid the foundation for a sufficient supply of Hawker Hurricanes in time for the Battle of Britain.

Earlier, in 1936, he made a bold decision when he backed the construction of the Hurricane as a private venture.

In 1958 he was succeeded as managing director of Hawker Siddeley by Sir Roy Dobson. He received £75,000 compensation.

June 12, 1969.

Howard Spring, the novelist, author of the best-seller *O Absalom*! and *Fame is the Spur,* died at his home at Falmouth, Cornwall, on May 3, 1965. He was 76 and had been in ill-health for some time. His most recent book *Winds of the Day* was published in 1965.

Spring took to novel writing when he was over 40, and within a few years achieved a secure position in that field. He had spent all his previous working life in journalism working his way up from the humblest beginnings as a messenger.

Robert Howard Spring was born at Cardiff in 1889, the son of a jobbing gardener, and was brought up near the Cardiff docks in conditions of severe poverty. There were nine in the family, of whom seven survived. There were a few good books in the house, and family reading helped to instil the first principles of taste; but the father died when Howard was still at school, and for many years he had a hard struggle for existence.

URGE TO WRITE

He left his elementary school at 12, and after some months as an errand boy, and a further period as office boy to an accountant, he went, at 13, to the *South Wales Daily News* as a general "devil", or messenger. He learnt shorthand, and at evening classes worked at Latin, French, English and mathematics for about five years; and at last he was promoted to the reporting staff. The writing urge took hold of him: he completed a novel, but it was never published; and his first guinea-and-a-half for original work came for a story sent to a new weekly for boys.

In 1911 Spring joined the staff of the *Yorkshire Observer;* in 1913 he transferred to the *Manchester Guardian,* and there he remained as a reporter until 1931. He served in France during the war and was for a time at G.H.Q. Having caught the eye of Lord Beaverbrook by an article in which he referred to Beaverbrook as a "Pedlar of Dreams", he went to London and in 1931 took over the *Evening Standard* book review page in succession to Arnold Bennett. Though his opportunities were necessarily restricted by the conditions obtaining on a popular evening newspaper (which included the reviewing of a large number of books in small space), he became known for his sound taste and prescience.

FIRST BOOK

Spring now turned his mind seriously to original composition, and in 1932 published his first book, *Darkie & Co.,* a pleasant tale for children. His first novel proper appeared in 1934 under the title of *Shabby Tiger*. It drew with insight and humour various aspects of lower middle-class life in Manchester; and in the artist, Faunt, his mistress, the Irish Anna Fitzgerald, the Jewess, Rachel Rosing, and others, it presented a gallery of characters that were well-seen and well-rounded. The career of *Rachel Rosing* was followed further in 1935, and another book for children, *Sampson's Circus* came out in 1936.

With *O Absalom*! (1938) and *Fame is the Spur* (1940) Spring came into the ranks of the "best-sellers" and found himself able to give up journalism for literature. He was now giving evidence of added depth; and *Fame is the Spur* (the story of a Labour leader's rise to power) presented a more powerful character than any he had previously created as well as a comprehensive picture of modern life and times. In 1939 had appeared a third children's book, *Tumbledown Dick*, and a very charming fragment of autobiography called *Heaven Lies About Us,* which gave a plain history of his youthful days of poverty in Cardiff.

He was to write two more essays in autobiography, *In the Meantime* (1942) and *And Another Thing* (1946), this last having as its theme his spiritual development and beliefs.

NO NEED FOR SENSATIONS

The later novels—*There is no Armour*; *The Houses in Between*; *These Lovers Fled Away*; *Time and the Hour* and *I Met a Lady* which appeared at regular intervals until his death, never perhaps equalled the power of his earlier ones but his technique was so sure that it enabled him to write at length without slackening the pace of the story or needing to strengthen it with sensational incidents.

Howard Spring contributed nothing new to the form and shape of the novel as a medium; but inside the limits of the kind he was an able craftsman. His dialogue was easy and natural; his types were recognizable from life; he had a sense both of humour and of pathos, and a wide comprehension of human motive and character. In some of his books perhaps coincidence played too great a part though its incidence in real life is heavy enough. There was no overt political philosophy in Spring's novels, which existed on their own merits as works of art. His work for children was marked by a sure commonsense, and he was never sickly or sentimental.

CHEAP PENS

He did all his writing with a penny penholder (which he had bought as a young man) and ordinary nibs. He worked five mornings each week when engaged on a novel, writing about 1,000 words at each session, to build up a novel of about 150,000 words.

In 1941 when he was living at Mylor, near Falmouth, he received a telephone call from Brendan Bracken, then Minister of Information asking him to come to London. Spring, just back from the dentist's, packed a small suitcase and set off. On arrival in London he was sent to the Admiralty Press Department where he met H. V. Morton. They had been selected by Winston Churchill, then Prime Minister, to accompany him and leading Army, Navy and Air Force advisers on the historic trip across the Atlantic in the battleship Prince of Wales to meet America's President Roosevelt —the meeting which led to the Atlantic Charter.

Spring married Marion Ursula, daughter of G. W. Pye. She was secretary to James Bone, London Editor of the *Manchester Guardian,* and her *Memories and Gardens* was published in 1964. They had two sons.

May 4, 1965.

Admiral Raymond A. Spruance, who died at the age of 83 on December 13, 1969, was one of the most brilliant of the galaxy of talented U.S. naval officers thrown up by the Second World War.

At the time of the Japanese attack in 1941 he was in command of a cruiser division of the Pacific Fleet, and narrowly missed the holocaust in Pearl Harbour. In May 1942, when the Japanese threat to invade the Hawaiian Islands was becoming plain, Admiral Chester Nimitz, the C-in-C., Pacific, selected Spruance to replace Admiral W. F. Halsey, who was ill, in command of the newly created Task Force 16 which included the carriers Enterprise and Hornet. This was a bold decision, as Spruance was not an aviator; but Nimitz's choice was abundantly justified by the outcome of the battle of Midway on June 4. Though Spruance was technically subordinate to Admiral F. J. Fletcher in the Yorktown he showed outstanding tactical skill and initiative, and it was dive bombers from his two ships which accounted for 3 of the 4 Japanese carriers sunk in that decisive encounter.

After a short spell ashore as Chief of Staff to Nimitz, during which plans were made to implement the "island hopping" offensive across the Pacific, in August, 1943, Spruance took command of the Central Pacific Force which had been formed to carry out the first major amphibious operation against the Gilbert Islands. The assault took place on November 20, and although costly in casualties was completely successful. The experience then gained proved invaluable in planning the next leap—to the Marshall Islands; and Spruance then showed his complete mastery of the complex organization and execution of such undertakings across the vast distances of the Pacific Ocean.

The attack on the Marshalls took place at the end of January, 1943, and by the conquest of the group the United States Navy gained vital new advanced bases. The Central Pacific Force, which had by this time increased to an immense size, was now renamed the Fifth Fleet when Spruance was in command, and the Third Fleet when under Admiral Halsey.

TEMPO SPEEDED

While one of them was carrying out an operation the other would be ashore planning the next undertaking. This enabled the tempo of the offensive to be greatly stepped-up.

The next step towards the Philippine Islands was to be the seizure of the Mariana Group, by-passing the isolated Japanese garrisons in the Marshalls. The assault on Saipan in mid-June 1944 led directly to the first major fleet action since Midway the battle of the Philippine Sea. The Japanese then lost three more carriers.

After the conquest of the Marianas Halsey took over the fleet, and it was he who conducted the invasion of the Philippines and fought the battle of LeyteGulf on October 24-25, in which the Japanese suffered a crushing defeat—though not until after some anxious hours had passed. Meanwhile Spruance was planning the assault on Iwo Jima in the Bonin Islands, only some 650 miles from Tokyo. At the end of January 1945 Spruance took over again from Halsey, and on February 19 the assault on Iwo Jima was launched against desperate resistance. Spruance next switched his carrier air power to attacking the Japanese mainland and Okinawa Island in the Nansei Shoto off south-west Japan, which was his next objective. In this undertaking he had the four carriers of the newly arrived British Pacific Fleet under his general command.

Plans were meanwhile being made for the final assault on the Japanese mainland, for which the Third and Fifth fleets, with both their commanders, were to be employed. However, the dropping of the atomic bombs in August rendered this costly and difficult enterprise unnecessary—as indeed Spruance, like Nimitz, had always insisted to be the case.

In the same month Spruance took command of all naval forces in Japanese waters, but in November he succeeded Nimitz, who had become Chief of Naval Operations, as C-in-C., Pacific. In March, 1946, he became President of the Naval War College at Newport, Rhode Island—an appointment on which he had long set his eyes. He retired in 1948. In 1952 President Truman nominated him ambassador to the Philippine Republic, an appointment which President Eisenhower renewed in the following year. He held the post until 1955.

Spruance was a man of quiet and modest personality, but possessed of great powers of organization and outstanding resolution in moments of crisis. He not only won Nimitz's complete confidence, but also that of the thousands of officers and men of the immense fleet which he first trained and then wielded in action with consummate skill. In particular he will be remembered as a master of the complexities and uncertainties of large-scale amphibious warfare. If it was Nimitz who created the supremely successful Pacific strategy, it was Spruance and Halsey who translated the strategy into action.

December 16, 1969.

Sir Henry Spurrier, once chairman and, since ill health forced him to move to quieter waters, president of Leyland Motor Corporation, died at his home near Preston on June 17, 1964, the day after his sixty-sixth birthday. With his death British industry loses one of its most forceful and down to earth personalities.

He was a man to be judged by his actions not his words. The building up of Leylands to be the largest exporter of heavy-duty vehicles in the world; the recent absorption of several smaller vehicles firms; the quiet, deliberate, almost ruthless way in which Standard-Triumph was taken over and knocked into shape—all revealed the steely hand wielded by Henry III (as he was always known in Leylands) in all his business dealings. The attitude of Leylands to the Cuban buses dispute (business before politics) was a typical reflection of where Henry Spurrier stood in the business world; no nonsense, but lots of friendly humour.

Henry Spurrier was born on June 16, 1898, the son of Henry Spurrier, of The Hall, Marston-on-Dove, Derby, and the grandson of yet another Henry, who was in his time a brilliant engineer and constructor. By the time the third Henry went to Repton his father had founded the Leyland Company and had in turn brought in his own father to be its first chairman. The third Henry used to say that his own interest and connection with the firm dated from 1906 when he was only eight years old, because even then he used to potter about the workshops, and he certainly spent most of his holidays from school there. When he left Repton he became apprenticed with the company, and went right through the engineering workshops until he was old enough to join the Royal Flying Corps as a pilot. With it he took part in the Mesopotamia campaign, and was still in it when it became the Royal Air Force.

NOTABLE "EIGHT"

In 1919 he was demobilized, and went back to the Leyland works. He continued his practical and technical training and for some time devoted himself, with his colleagues Parry Thomas and Reld Railton, to developing and perfecting racing cars, particularly the notable "Leyland Eight" in which Parry Thomas gained many world records before his death on Pendine Sands, in South Wales. After the Leyland Eight, however, the company concentrated on the production of heavy vehicles.

Spurrier made rapid progress in the organization and at the outbreak of the Second World War was holding the position of assistant general manager. Leyland became designers and producers of the Centaur, Cromwell, and Comet Cruiser tanks and Sir Henry was made general manager of that particular section. This was an extremely large operation and at one time there were as many as 14 large engineering firms building for the group. In 1942, shortly after his father's death, he was appointed Leyland's general manager, and early in 1949 was made managing director. In 1951 the Leyland-Albion merger was announced, and it was in the same year that he acted as Leyland's chief representative in negotiations with the Ministry of Supply for the building of what was to be the largest tank factory in Europe. He was the controller of this factory, which was completed in 1953, until 1956 when the plant was acquired by the company to further its exports.

In 1957 he became chairman of Leyland, an office he held until June, 1963.

In June, 1955, Leyland Motors Limited absorbed Scammell Lorries Limited, thus widening considerably the range of products manufactured by the group. This range was further extended when, in April, 1961, Leyland took over Standard-Triumph International, a move which Sir Henry himself welcomed among other reasons because it involved him once again in the manufacture of cars—as he had not been since the days of the Leyland Eight. The group was expanded still further when Associated Commercial Vehicles Limited (including A.E.C. and Thornycroft) was taken over in 1962.

In the course of his career Sir Henry was

also a director of the District Bank, part-time member of the Iron and Steel Board, president of the Society of Motor Manufactures and Traders from 1952 to 1953, and a member of the national advisory council of the motor industry. He was knighted in 1955.

Spurrier inherited his father's love of the sea and sailing, and he was keenly interested in ocean racing. He was a prominent member of the Royal Thames Yacht Club.

In 1920 he married Winifred Mary, daughter of Alfred Cope, of Ewell, Surrey, and they had two daughters.

June 19, 1964.

Gideon Stahlberg, international grand master of chess, died on May 26, 1967, in Leningrad, where he had gone to take part in the current international chess tournament.

Gideon Stahlberg, who together with Stoltz and Lundin formed the bulwark of the Swedish international chess team for the past 40 years, was a player who especially impressed by the elegance of his style, His best period in international chess was contained in the years between 1937 and 1954, and his most outstanding tournament performance was probably his first prize at Trenčianske Teplice in 1949.

He played on first board for Sweden in a great number of Olympiads and almost always with success. A prolific writer on the game, he was also a fine linguist with a quite extraordinary memory. By his death Sweden and the world of chess has suffered a severe loss.

May 27, 1967.

Professor Sir Dudley Stamp, C.B.E., F.R.G.S., the British geographer, died on August 8, 1966, while attending the regional Latin American conference of the International Geographic Union in Mexico City. He was 68.

Stamp was one of the most outstanding British geographers of his day. Not a profound master of theory, he made his chief contributions, and great contributions they were, in two main fields: first, in the later 1920s and early 1930s by writing a succession of admirable textbooks at a time when good texts were urgently necessary to support the great development of the subject at home and overseas; secondly, by developing land use studies at home and abroad and applying them to the practical affairs of the workaday world, especially perhaps in regional planning.

Laurence Dudley Stamp was born on March 9, 1898, at Catford, the youngest of a family of seven, of whom the eldest, Josiah, became the first Lord Stamp. Because of almost continuous bad health he had hardly any regular schooling. He nevertheless achieved such brilliant results in the Cambridge Senior Local examinations in 1913 that he was accepted as a student at King's College London, despite his tender age of fifteen years. In the following four years he passed the Intermediate examinations of the University of London in Arts, in Science and in Engineering, and completed Honours courses in both geology and botany. In 1917 he enlisted in the Artists' Rifles, utilising his first leave to sit the Honours examination in Geology. Characteristically he achieved first class honours. Commissioned in the Royal Engineers he served in France, but, being Stamp, he contrived to combine geological investigation in north east France with his military duties, and was able to publish his first research paper and take his M.Sc. degree soon after demobilization in 1919. There followed two years on the geology staff at King's College, by which time he had not merely taken his D.Sc. in geology but as an external student had added the degree of B.A. with first class honours in geography.

A short period as an oil geologist in Burma preceded his appointment in 1923, at the age of 25, as professor of geology and geography in the University of Rangoon. His three years there were marked by an extraordinary amount of geological, botanical and geographical work in Burma, Malaya, China and Indonesia, and earned him the bronze and the gold medals of the Mining and Geological Institute of India.

In 1926 he returned to London to the Cassel Readership in Economic Geography at the London School of Economics. He held that readership till 1945, when, on the retirement of Professor Ll. Rodwell Jones, he was appointed to the Chair of Geography. In 1949 he was translated to the new Chair of Social Geography at the School, and in 1958, at the early age of 60, he retired, and became Professor Emeritus and Honorary Lecturer.

Seen in perspective, 1930 was the critical year for Stamp's great contributions to public service. In that year he began his organization of the Land Utilisation Survey of Great Britain, a project which involved the large-scale field mapping of every acre in Britain and the publication of a complete series of maps, fully coloured, on the one-inch scale. The maps were supplemented by county volumes of text in which the use of land was analysed. Stamp's own *The Land of Britain: Its Use and Misuse* in its masterly handling of the immense detail of the Land Use Maps and the county reports was a landmark in British geography. He also wrote (with S. G. Gilmour) *A Handbook of Commercial Geography*, a school textbook, which ran into the eighteenth edition in 1966. He was editor of the Unesco *History of Land Use in Arid Lands*, which appeared in 1961.

NEW MINISTRY

By the beginning of the Second World War, Stamp's authority in land use had become recognized even in official circles and he was drawn into progressively heavier commitments of government work. In 1941 he was appointed a member of the Uthwatt Committee by Lord Reith, and later in the same year he became vice-chairman of Lord Justice Scott's Committee on Land Utilization in Rural Areas. In the reports of these two committees, especially of the Scott Committee, there was the genesis of the Town and Country Planning Act of 1947, which created the Ministry of Town and Country Planning, and in that report the experience and the influence of Stamp are clearly evident. Another appointment, peculiarly appropriate to his taste and abilities, was to the Royal Commission on Common Land, 1955-58. In addition to his contribution to the investigation and recommendations he was himself responsible for Appendix IV, a very substantial treatment of the geographical distribution of common land.

Meanwhile, in 1942, he had become Chief Adviser on Rural Land Use to the Ministry of Agriculture, a service recognized in 1946 by the award of the C.B.E., and on the formation of the Ministry of Town and Country Planning accepted a similar appointment in that Ministry. His value to the Ministry of Agriculture was further emphasized by his appointment as an official United Kingdom delegate to F.A.O.

In academic circles and pursuits he remained a leader despite the heavy calls of public duties. He qualified by examination for both the D.Sc. and the D.Lit. degrees of the University of London. From 1949, under the auspices of the International Geographical Union, he extended his land use work to a world survey, a daunting task for even his drive and organizing ability. From 1952 to 1956 he was president of the International Geographical Union, and in 1961 undertook the chairmanship of the organizing committee for the 1964 International Geographical Congress in London. He became president of the Royal Geographical Society in 1963. Honorary doctorates from American, Swedish and Polish universities witnessed the international character of his reputation. He was knighted in 1965 for services to land use. In 1965, Stamp was appointed chairman of the Natural Resources Advisory Committee.

More important, however, than what he did was what he was. His zest for life, his friendliness, his generosity of spirit, his love of helping lame dogs over stiles made a host of deeply attached friends over almost the whole world. He married in 1923 Elsa Clara (who died in 1962) daughter of A. U. Rea, and they had one son.

August 10, 1966.

Lord Stanhope, Senior Knight of the Garter P.C., D.S.O., M.C., seventh Earl Stanhope and thirteenth Earl of Chesterfield, died at his home at Chevening, near Sevenoaks, Kent, on August 15, 1967. He was 86.

Lord Stanhope gave his seventeenth-century home, Chevening Manor, with its 3,500-acre-estate and an endowment of £250,000, to the nation in 1959, to be the home of the Prime Minister of the day or a member of the Royal Family. In a memorandum to his will he asked that it should be available for Prince Charles. It will require a legislation.

The seventh Earl Stanhope left no family. Lady Stanhope died in 1940. There are no heirs to the earldoms. The heir to his junior titles, the Stanhope viscounty and barony, is the Earl of Harrington.

Stanhope was First Lord of the Admiralty from 1938 to 1939, in which capacity he once caused no little comment and Parliamentary protest with a speech drawing attention to naval preparedness in a way which the Government—six months after Munich—found a trifle embarrassing. Their action in issuing a "D" notice asking the press not to publish it added to Opposition disquiet, and there were demands for Stanhope's resignation. He held office in the Conservative and National Governments during most of the period between the wars. He entered the Cabinet in 1936, and remained a member of it until 1940. Long experienced in political and official life, Stanhope was a conscientious and hard-working servant of the state. He had, moreover, great personal charm and was a popular and much respected man.

ANCESTRY

James Richard Stanhope, seventh Earl Stanhope, Viscount Stanhope, of Mahon, in the Island of Minorca, and Baron Stanhope, of Elvaston, County Derby, all in the peerage of Great Britain, was born on November 11, 1880, the elder son of the sixth Earl by his marriage with Evelyn Henrietta, only daughter of Richard and Lady Emily Pennefather. The family descended from the first Earl of Chesterfield through James Stanhope who was Commander-in-Chief of the British forces in Spain in 1708 and attained renown by his reduction of Port Mahon in Minorca. When the twelfth Earl of Chesterfield died without issue in 1952, the earldom devolved upon Stanhope but was not claimed. The Stanhope family was also descended by marriage from William, first Earl of Chatham.

Viscount Mahon, as he was called, was educated at Eton (the Rev. Stuart Alexander Donaldson's House) where he was in the Shooting VIII of 1899, and at Magdalen College, Oxford. In 1901 he joined the Grenadier Guards, and served in the South African War. In 1905 he succeeded his father. From 1906 to 1908 he was A.D.C. to the G.O.C., London District. In 1908 he retired as a captain and became a lieutenant-colonel on the Reserve of Officers (Grenadier Guards) and a major in the 4th Battalion, Royal West Kents. From 1910 to 1913 he represented Lewisham on the L.C.C. In 1910 and 1911 he sold his North Devon estate of some 4,450 acres and, the next year, his Derbyshire estate of 2,547 acres.

DEFENSIVE FLEET

On the outbreak of the First World War Stanhope rejoined the Army and serving in France on the general staff became eventually a G.S.O. 1. He was twice mentioned in dispatches, awarded the D.S.O. and M.C. and made a Chevalier of the Légion d'Honneur. In 1918 when Lord Milner was Secretary of State for War, he was appointed to represent the War Office in the House of Lords and to be Parliamentary Secretary to the War Office. In 1923 he became chairman of the Joint Substitution Board and, from 1924 to 1929, was Civil Lord of the Admiralty. It was a time when as the result of the conference on disarmament the Government were concerned with maintaining a fleet for defence only. In 1929 he was sworn of the Privy Council and in 1930 was appointed a trustee of the National Portrait Gallery.

In the first National Government, Stanhope became Parliamentary and Financial Secretary to the Admiralty and in November, 1931, Under-Secretary of State for War. In 1934 he was created a K.G. and, in response to a demand for a Minister to represent the Foreign Office in the House of Lords, was appointed Parliamentary Under-Secretary of State for Foreign Affairs. He held this office during two critical and anxious years. Then in 1936 he became First Commissioner of Works and entered the Cabinet.

EDUCATION POST

In 1937 he succeeded Oliver Stanley as President of the Board of Education. The appointment created some surprise, for though he had attained distinction in the military world and had judgment and experience, he possessed no special knowledge of education. There was, however, a recent Education Act upon the statute book and wise supervision in the Board on the advice of its competent officials was the chief requirement of the time. He remained President until October 1938, when having become Leader of the House of Lords, he succeeded Duff Cooper as First Lord of the Admiralty. It was a position for which he had had several years of training. In March, 1939, he was able to tell the country that the Fleet was both efficient and sufficient for the work it might be called upon to do, and to speak of large additions to it and of great activity in the dockyards.

The speech which was to cause such a commotion was made in April, 1939, at the initiation, on board the Ark Royal, of a new scheme for showing films of the Royal Navy. Having drawn attention to the fact that there was not a full attendance he said that shortly before he left the Admiralty it became necessary to give orders to man the anti-aircraft guns of the Fleet. He added that long before the guests came on board the Ark Royal 16 anti-aircraft guns could have given a warm welcome to "anyone who happened to come this way."

His remarks were reported in the Empire broadcast programme and provoked much comment and excitement. Thereupon the Government in a "D" notice asked the press not to publish the speech, or, if they did, not to ascribe particular importance to it. The matter was raised in the House of Commons and the Opposition demanded Stanhope's resignation. Neville Chamberlain excused him as best he could and Stanhope himself expressed in a personal statement to the House of Lords his regret that his speech should have caused concern.

He said he had been explaining that the reason why there was not a full attendance was because some of the crews were retained on board their own ships in readiness to man their guns, as had been the normal practice in time of tension. He added that no other orders had been given by the Admiralty than that this practice should not be relaxed even on so special an occasion.

An interesting light was thrown on the matter when some of the documents on British Foreign Policy were published in 1951. Volume IV of the third series reproduced a telegram which was sent to the Foreign Secretary on the night before Stanhope's speech by Sir George Ogilvie-Forbes, who was Counsellor at the British Embassy in Berlin. It quoted a statement received from an informant in contact with the German War Ministry to the effect that the first sign of German intentions, which would be kept secret until the last moment, would be a lightning attack on the British Fleet, without either ultimatum or declaration of war. Hitler alone would decide. This message may have been in Stanhope's mind when he said what he did. Indeed he told a newspaper interviewer when the document was published that it had always been his great fear that the Germans would catch the Fleet in port, that he firmly believed that Hitler would make the attempt, and that he did not want him to think it might be a walk-over.

On the outbreak of war he left the Admiralty to become Lord President of the Council, a position which he held until 1940, and in that year he also ceased to be Leader of the House of Lords. From 1941 to 1948 he was chairman of the Standing Committee on Museums and Galleries. He had been a trustee of the National Portrait Gallery since 1930. He helped to carry the Canopy at the coronation of King George VI.

Among Stanhope's chief interests was the National Maritime Museum at Greenwich. He was, from 1927, chairman of the body of trustees which held the Caird and other collections before the museum was established in 1934 by an Act of Parliament of which he himself had charge during its passage through the House of Lords. From 1934 he was chairman of the trustees of the museum as established, and was most assiduous and constant in his performance of his duties, missing only some half-a-dozen meetings during the whole period.

TWO ENTHUSIASTS

He was very largely responsible for directing Sir James Caird's benevolence towards the project, and it is probably true that, without either of these two great enthusiasts, there would be no National Martime Museum today. Stanhope was always readily accessible to the director, and indeed there was hardly a day in which he was not in touch with him. He became president of the Navy Record Society in 1948.

In 1957 it became necessary for him to have his right leg amputated below the knee and to be fitted with an artificial limb. He bore with cheerfulness this limitation on his activities, spending most of his time at his country home, Chevening, near Sevenoaks, where he occupied his later years in writing his memoirs.

In 1921 he married Lady Eileen Agatha Browne, eldest daughter of the sixth Marquess of Sligo. It was a perfect companionship, but to his deep sorrow she died in 1940. There were no children of the marriage.

August 16, 1967.

Sir William Stanier, F.R.S., formerly Chief Mechanical Engineer of the L. M. S. Railway, died on September 27, 1965, at the age of 89.

Brought up amid the great engineering traditions of the Great Western Railway at Swindon—he served under that formidable designer of locomotives George Jackson Churchward—his talent flowered abundantly during his years with the L. M. S.; years in which with Sir Nigel Gresley of the L. N. E. R. breaking records with his improved "Pacifics", the steam locomotive had its high peak in Britain.

Born on May 27, 1876, the son of W. H. Stanier, stores superintendent at Swindon, and educated at Wycliffe College, Stonehouse, he spent the earlier part of his working life in the service of the Great Western Railway, with whom he rose quickly from an engineering apprenticeship in 1892 to the post of Principal Assistant to the Chief Mechanical Engineer in 1923. His thoroughness and originality, anchored to the solid earth by his conviction of the correctness of Swindon engineering practice, made him known in railway circles, and was responsible for his appointment as Chief Mechanical Engineer to the L. M. S. in 1932.

The locomotive stock of the L. M. S. could have been better, when Stanier removed from Swindon to Crewe, and his instructions were to provide the line with a fleet of new types of engine. He boldly transferred Swindon engineering principles to Crewe Works and though the L. M. S. was thus "Great Westernized", his personal charm and integrity, together with the fact that his engines very seldom failed and could be relied on, carried through without strain of difficulty what was nothing less than a major locomotive revolution.

FIRST "PACIFIC"

In 1933 he introduced the first of his Pacifics, the Princess Royal; more followed and the L. M. S. came at last into the fore-front of British railway speed-making. But it was several years before he produced his masterpieces, the Coronation Pacifics—some of which were streamlined—handsome, fast, strong, free-steaming and able to give whatever the enginemen asked of them. As Mr. Hamilton Ellis said in his *British Railway History 1877–1947*, the Coronation Scot was in fact more of a "native" L. M. S. engine than her predecessors. A prolific designer, Stanier produced a notable 2-8-0 freight engine, a fine 4-6-0 series, the "Jubilees", and a memorable mixed traffic engine, the black Class Fives, known familiarly as "Black Staniers" or "Black Fives". They could pull anything, go anywhere and never broke down; many hundreds were built and after nationalization they were to be found all over the British system, even on the Great Western, where they won grudging praise from crews who traditionally look askance at any engine not out of Swindon. Stanier built one interesting experimental Pacific, with non-condensing turbines as its form of propulsion. Though it ran, chiefly between Liverpool and Euston, for some years, its design was never repeated and eventually it was rebuilt as an orthodox Pacific. It came to a sad end, for it was involved in the Harrow disaster of 1952.

When the war came Stanier's work for the L. M. S. was already done, and in 1941 its merit was recognized by electing him president of the Institution of Mechanical Engineers. In 1942 he was seconded as Scientific Adviser to the Ministry of Production, and in 1944 he gave up his position with the L. M. S., though he served still, as required, as a technical consultant. In 1943 he was knighted, and in the next year he was elected a Fellow of the Royal Society. He was also a member of the Aeronautical Research Council and a director of Power Jets Ltd., the company formed to carry on the development of internal combustion turbine and jet propulsion. He was awarded the Gold Medal of the Institution of Locomotive Engineers in 1957 and the James Watt international medal of the Institution of Mechanical Engineers in 1963.

He married in 1906 Ella Elizabeth, daughter of L. L. Morse. They had a son and a daughter. His wife died in 1952.

September 28, 1965.

Sydney Stanley, the man at the centre of a scandal that led to the resignation of a junior member of the Labour Government in 1949, died in Tel Aviv on May 24, 1969. He was in his sixties.

John Belcher resigned as Parliamentary Secretary, Board of Trade, in February, 1949, after giving evidence to a tribunal, headed by Mr. Justice Lynskey, which investigated allegations of irregularities against Ministers and government officials. In its report, the tribunal found adversely against Belcher, who later resigned his seat, and George Gibson, then chairman of the North-western Electricity Board who had recently given up his position as a director of the Bank of England.

In a summary of its findings the tribunal said the allegations which led to its appointment had been that large sums of money had been paid to Ministers and public servants. The report declared: "These allegations, in our view, were largely the result of the statements and activities of Sydney Stanley." It said of Stanley: "He will make any statement, whether true or untrue, if he thinks that it is to his own advantage so to do." During the inquiry Stanley gave evidence for a total of 15½ hours. Allegations concerning football pools were among those investigated. After the tribunal, Clement Attlee, then Prime Minister, told the House of Commons that Stanley was to be deported to Poland as a national of that country. But the Poles would not agree to this step. Stanley disappeared from Britain early in April, 1949, after failing to report to a London police station under a Home Office instruction. He also failed to appear for a bankruptcy examination, and was later reported to be living in Israel, under the name of Sholmo Wulkan. In 1950, he was named in a report set up to look into "contact men" after the Lynskey tribunal.

Stanley was born in Poland, but went to Britain at the age of 12, and was educated there. In 1933 a deportation order was issued against him, but police lost track of him until the outbreak of war.

Although he lived quietly for the most part in Israel, he was unable to resist completely the limelight and the glamour of press attention. Once he told a Paris reporter: "They cannot sell London newspapers unless Stanley's name is in them," On another occasion he called up a British reporter in Paris to give him "the story the whole world has been waiting for". The Russians he said, did not have the atom bomb, and they had called him in to help them get it.

Belcher died in 1964; Gibson in 1953.

May 26, 1969.

Dr. Enid Starkie, C.B.E., F.R.S.L., Reader Emeritus in French Literature at the University of Oxford, and Honorary Fellow of Somerville College, Oxford, died on April 21, 1970. With her death lovers of French literature lost one of the most versatile, energetic and generously gifted women of her generation.

Born in Dublin, Enid Starkie was the eldest daughter of the Right Honourable W. J. M. Starkie, last Minister of Education under the British rule in Ireland and a famous classical scholar. She was the sister of Dr. Walter Starkie and, like him, a person of original and many-sided talent. She was educated at Alexandra College, Dublin, and at the Royal Irish Academy of Music. From Dublin she went to Somerville College, Oxford, with a scholarship in Modern Languages. Leaving Oxford in 1921 with a First, she went to Paris where she lived in great poverty, supporting herself by the meagre but sometimes picturesque jobs available to an indigent foreigner, while she studied for her doctorate. These studies and her stay in Paris were interrupted by her appointment to an assistant lecturership in the University of Exeter. But she was able there to complete the work on Verhaeren which gained her a Sorbonne doctorate and a prize from the French Academy.

After four years in Exeter she returned to Oxford and Somerville in 1929 as lecturer in Modern Languages and, in 1935, she was elected fellow and tutor by Somerville. In 1946 the university, which had already honoured her work on Rimbaud in Abyssinia with the first doctorate to be awarded in the Faculty of Modern Languages, appointed her Reader in French Literature.

These appointments and distinctions came as a tribute to an unusual combination of tutorial gifts, literary perception, and intellectual power, and to the energies which animated the combination and brought it to fruition. From the beginning she had been especially interested in the *mauvais garçons* of nineteenth-century. French literature and two of them, Baudelaire and Rimbaud, were to be her particular study. Baudelaire's life was the subject of her first book, published in 1933, and her next three books all dealt with the life and interpretation of Rimbaud. These were largely pioneer works and were outstanding examples of the scholarly work being done in England in French nineteenth-century literature. Her interest in both poets continued during and after the war: she published her *Arthur Rimbaud* in a revised form (a third edition appeared in 1961) and, after an interlude which resulted in the publication of *Petrus Borel* in 1954, she returned to *Baudelaire* and published the final version of that book in 1957.

There are three other books which not even a brief account of her work can neglect: *André Gide* (1954), a brilliant and concise study of a writer whose friend she was and whose honorary degree from Oxford she had done much to promote; *A Lady's Child* (1941), which recalled her Irish Edwardian childhood and her adolescence in Dublin and Oxford with a candour that was both gentle and bold; and *From Gautier to Eliot* (1960), a study of the influence of French literature on English literature.

To write and to teach—and much of Enid Starkie's time and energy went into teaching, to the enjoyment and profit of both teacher and pupil—these are enough, sometimes more than enough, to exhaust most college tutors.

LIFE ABUNDANT

But she had an abundance of life that clamoured for other expression. She was a force in the politics of Senior Common Room, Faculty Board, and University. Lost causes, when she took them up, tended to be found again. Her life was a rapid alternation of the solitary and the social; a light sleeper, she stole time after midnight to read and to write but at hours when others were awake and forgathering she was seldom absent. Her host might watch his carpet anxiously when her sherry glass gestured the swift movement of her wit but her presence enlivened any party, graduate or undergraduate, and brought not only to the drawing room but also the bars where she occasionally presided something of the atmosphere of a salon.

She abounded in friends; for she liked people if they had life in them. She could identify herself with their interest, and she gave them not merely the pleasure of her conversation and company but her time, her sympathy and her trouble. She never forgot her pupils, as generations of them passed from Oxford but remained her friends. The end of every year found her sending out Christmas cards by the half-thousand to every quarter of the world.

CARE FOR RITUAL

Her memory for birthdays was proverbial and her correspondence must have worn out many a scarlet typewriter. Indeed, in all matters of ritual she was punctilious, from the wearing of her Legion of Honour badge (she was made Officer in 1958) on the lapel of a raincoat to her insistence that married women, however much younger, should precede her through a doorway.

Scarlet and blue were her colours, alternating between the unconventional jacket and trousers which she made her daytime uniform, a uniform with which she startled many an American campus but which in Oxford over the years she established as familiar. In Oxford indeed she exemplified that local rule by which the eccentric if persisted in becomes licensed, and indeed accepted. Unlike most eccentrics, however, Enid Starkie could transcend the tolerance that attempts by assimilation to anaesthetise; she could be effective in the university world of action, whether as a shrewd chairman of her faculty or as an energetic eminence, red rather than grey, confounding the fence-sitters whom she called "hedgers and ditchers" and beating up the votes to have her candidates awarded the Professorship of Poetry.

In 1968 Enid Starkie herself was nominated for election as Professor of Poetry at Oxford although she confessed she had not written any poetry. She was bottom of the poll in the 1961 election, which was won by Robert Graves. She was one of the fieriest supporters of Edmund Blunden when he ran and beat Robert Lowell in the election for the professorship.

Her flat in St. Giles—later its expanded simulacrum, her house in Walton Street—was a refuge to the solitary scholar in her, the tireless nocturnal worker. It was also, in its decor of scarlet and gold, a showpiece of collector's taste, an expression of her at once pugnacious and fastidious personality, and an open house to friends.

In 1965 an unpromising, indeed sinister, medical prognosis induced her to resign her university appointments so that she could give what she had reason to fear would be the small residue of her life to her book on Flaubert, which she published in 1967. She determined to bear her illness with as little embarrassment as possible to her friends and to them she continued to give up much of her time and show a spirit ardent and gay and undiminished. In the words of Ronsard she was: "Belle, courtoise, honeste et de doux entretien."

April 23, 1970.

Dr. Vilhjalmur Stefansson, the Canadian-born Arctic explorer, died in hospital in New Hampshire, United States, on August 26, 1962.

As a young man Stefansson spent nearly a dozen years in the Arctic regions, where he engaged in a succession of expeditions for the purpose of geographical discovery and ethnological research. He was a man of remarkable character, and as an explorer he had distinguishing qualities which ensured a large measure of public attention for his enterprises. He had the ability to live "off the country" in regions where well-provisioned expeditions are generally deemed essential. To emphasise the inherent resources of the Far North in this connexion Stefansson dubbed it with a characteristic touch of exaggeration the "Friendly Arctic."

He was a foremost exponent and protagonist of Eskimo methods of travel and survival and to prepare himself for his Arctic expeditions he had spent several years living with Eskimo tribes.

His parents were Icelanders who emigrated to Canada and were among the pioneer settlers in Northern Manitoba. It was there that Vilhjalmur Stefansson was born in 1879, but he was less than two years of age when the family, after a stern struggle with flood and famine and smallpox, moved southwards across the border into the United States.

Young Vilhjalmur grew up on a North Dakota farm, and when that was sold after his father's death he became a cowboy. Four years later, when still only 18 years of age, he started on a ranch in partnership with some other young fellows, but it was not a financial success, and having developed an ambition to become a poet he decided to work his way through college. He travelled in a train for the first time in his life when he went to the State University of North Dakota, with 53 dollars in his pocket, but by dint of hard work he achieved his object, graduating at the State University of Iowa and from there passing on to Harvard for post-graduate studies. By this time he had given up the idea of being a poet and turned his attention to science, specializing in anthropology.

STUDYING ESKIMO LIFE

Early in 1906, E. de K. Leffingwell, who, with Captain Einar Mikkelsen, was organizing an expedition for the exploration of the Beaufort Sea, invited him to join them as ethonologist for the study of Eskimo life in the Arctic Archipelago.

Stefansson had previously, in 1904 and 1905, paid two visits to Iceland (the second time for archaeological work under the auspices of Harvard), and had written an essay on the early Norse discovery of Greenland. He accepted the invitation to join the Leffingwell-Mikkelsen expedition, but travelled separately and did not work in very close association with the expedition, and returned home in the middle of it in the summer of 1907.

But the spirit of the North had laid hold of him, and in the following year he went back, this time as leader of an expedition, under the auspices of the American Museum of Natural History and the Canadian Geological Survey, which explored in the course of the next four years the little-known region extending from the Mackenzie delta eastward to the Coppermine River, and from Great Bear Lake northwards to the Arctic Archipelago. In Victoria Land, north of the mainland, Stefansson found Eskimo tribes with physical characteristics which led him to suggest that they might be the descendants either of some of the lost members of Franklin's expedition or of the Iceland Scandinavians who disappeared from Greenland in the fifteenth century.

LOST IN GALE

These suggestions attracted widespread attention to his discoveries, and he easily obtained support for another more extended expedition.

The Canadian Government assumed full responsibility and in June 1913, Stefansson again set off. Off the north coast of Alaska, while Stefansson was ashore on a hunting trip, one of his ships was lost through a gale. Most of the ship's company succeeded in making their way over the ice to Wrangel Island and the Siberian Coast, but one party failed to reach Wrangel Island and there were several deaths from sickness. Meanwhile, Stefansson made new plans to pursue his exploration, particularly to ascertain whether, as some supposed, the Beaufort Sea sheltered an unknown "continent". In the spring of 1914 he and two companions started on a journey across the ice of the Beaufort Sea to Banks Land. For a considerable time grave fears were entertained for their safety, but in 1915 word was received that the crossing had been safely accomplished. On this expedition he had two companions, one sledge, and six dogs. They journeyed for three months over drifting pack-ice and then worked from floe to floe as the ice broke up in the warmer weather.

In the spring of 1915, on a journey of some 250 miles from Banks Island north-westward into the unknown Beaufort Sea, nothing was seen of the hypothetical "continent", but to the north-east of Prince Patrick Island, in the region of the discoveries made by Captain Otto Sverdrup on the second Farm expedition, further discoveries were made by Stefansson in 1915, 1916 and 1917, extending the known limits of that part of the Arctic Archipelago and giving greater precision to the maps of the region.

Stefansson's explorations in the Beaufort Sea area, in boldness of concept, in endurance, and in the range of the journeys undertaken, resemble the great expeditions of Nansen and Peary.

In 1918—the expedition's last year—Stefansson himself was incapacitated by a severe attack of typhoid fever. He did not stop work but continued with his idea of setting up a camp on an ice floe which drifted 400 miles to the north, while still making observations. This was the method used by the Russian Papanin in 1937-38. It is the prototype of the scientific stations set up by both Russians and Americans since the Second World War.

The sum total of the expedition's labours in all its sections formed a valuable addition to scientific knowledge of Arctic Canada, both on the mainland and in the vast archipelago to the north.

Stefansson had given fresh evidence of his enterprise, resourcefulness and aptitude for Arctic travel, and on his return the highest honours in the geographical world were bestowed on him, including the Founder's Medal of the Royal Geographical Society. Subsequently there was much controversy in Canada about his conduct of the expedition and his views concerning the "Friendly Arctic". A somewhat irritating suggestion of superiority in his disdain of conventional ideas of Arctic travel, and the tendency of his views to assume the appearance of eccentric "stunts" even while he was most scornful of anything of the kind, did not make for universal popularity. His first book *My Life With the Eskimo* was published in 1913, and he continued to produce new works frequently until very recent years.

Since 1947, he had been curator of the unique Stefansson collection of polar literature at Dartmouth College, New Hampshire. He also was arctic consultant at the college.

In 1941 he married Evelyn Baird, his secretary, who was later to become secretary of the Darmouth Library. She survives him.

August 27, 1962.

John Steinbeck, the American novelist, who died at his home in New York on December 20, 1968, was one of the names most frequently mentioned in the 1940s and 1950s to illustrate the vitality of American letters and demonstrate that American themes, if treated with Steinbeck's breadth and charity, could hold the attention of readers everywhere.

He appeared for a time to express touchingly and courageously ordinary people's rèsistance to the social injustice and oppression that were the consequences of the Depression. He was radical and greathearted without being doctrinaire and revolutionary.

His better stories and novels were translated into many languages, and so clear were the narratives and so basic the characters that the moral issues could be immediately grasped and sympathized with, even by readers used to very different manners and conditions. The international scope of his achievement was recognized in 1962, when he became the seventh American author to win a Nobel Prize for literature—in this award once more pulling level with his great contemporary, Ernest Hemingway, whom he had long seemed to challenge in achievement as well as in popularity.

John Ernst Steinbeck was born at Salinas, California, in 1902. He was educated at the local high school and Stanford University, which he left in 1925 without taking a degree.

NOVELS OF FARMING

After working at a number of jobs, including journalism, he published his first novel, *Cup of Gold,* in 1929. *Cup of Gold* is a romance based on the life of Sir Henry Morgan, the buccaneer, but Steinbeck's second work of fiction, *The Pastures of Heaven* (1932), a series of connected short stories, was set among a farming community in a Californian valley; a theme and setting far more sympathetic to the nature of his inspiration. His second novel, *To a God Unknown* (1933), was an elaborate and largely unsuccessful allegory also set among the farmers in California.

None of these works was very successful, but the fourth, *Tortilla Flat* (1935), a gay, picaresque account of the life of a group of Californian *paisanos* was immediately and deservedly popular. The narrative is skilful, the characterization shrewd, and the tone a pleasant compound of humour and sympathy. *In Dubious Battle* (1936), his next novel, was written in a very different mood. It describes a strike among the fruit pickers in a Californian valley, and shows a keen interest in social conditions. Steinbeck's sympathies were entirely with the strikers and with the men who tried to organize them effectively, at a disastrous personal cost.

The heroes in *Of Mice and Men* (1937) were drawn from the same class. This novelette of two Californian farmhands—Lennie, immensely strong but feeble-minded, and George, his protector—and the tragic issue of their dream of setting up on a farm of their own, made an immediate appeal to both the sophisticated and the general public. Steinbeck adapted the tale for the stage in the following year, and it was equally successful in its new form. It was later filmed with Burgess Meredith, Betty Field and Lon Chaney jr. playing the leading parts. Lewis Milestone was the director.

Steinbeck had by now aroused expectations that he would write something remarkable, and seemed more than to fulfil them in 1939 with the publication of *The Grapes of Wrath.* The hero of the novel is the Joad family itself, rather than any one of the many individual characters, and the theme is its survival in spite of all the obstacles put in its way by nature, poverty, bigotry, and bureaucracy. The action describes how the Joads are driven out of the Dust Bowl of Oklahoma and make the arduous trek to California, the "promised land". The toll is heavy but somehow the family gets through, triumphing in spirit. There are serious charges that can be brought against the novel. The symbolism is obvious, the social thought naive, the characterization sentimental, and the optimism overpowering, but in spite of all that can be urged to its discredit, the novel is one of the most arresting of its time. It was hailed as an "epic", awarded a Pulitzer Prize, and excellently filmed. The book is required reading in every American university where the study of contemporary literature is taken seriously and even if it does not maintain this exceptional position, it will always be valued for its own sake and as a social document of great interest. John Ford was the director and Henry Fonda the star.

Steinbeck was never able to repeat this success, nor, indeed, even to match it. *The Moon is Down* (1942), an account of Norway under the Germans, has merit, but *Cannery Row* (1944) is no more than a slight and whimsical story. *East of Eden* (1952), an attempt at another major novel, which describes the fortunes of a Californian family from the Civil War to the First World War, has occasional power, but dissipates its strength in a complete uncertainty of aim. Steinbeck was unable in any of his later work to master the problems he seems to have set himself, and though several of his books were widely popular, they appeared too small an achievement to be worthy of the author of *The Grapes of Wrath.* His novel, *The Winter of Our Discontent* (1961), a study of corruption in an American small town, is spoilt by sentimentality and the consequent evasion of the moral issues raised. He published an account of his travels through the United States in the company of his pet poodle, *Travels with Charley in Search of America,* in 1962, the year he was awarded the Nobel Prize; proof sufficient that the prize had been earned by his early work.

He was married three times. There were two sons by his second marriage to Gwyn Conger.

December 21, 1968.

Sir Frank Stenton, one of the outstanding English medievalists of his generation, died on September 15, 1967, at the age of 87.

Frank Merry Stenton was born on May 17, 1880, at Southwell and was educated at the Grammar School at that place. Later he proceeded as Scholar to Keble College, Oxford. After taking his degree he engaged for a time in school teaching before joining the staff of University College, Reading, where he became Professor of Modern History in 1912.

He speedily built up a flourishing department, and he was one of those who, under William Childs, were responsible for transforming what had been a small college into an independent university, Stenton, indeed, was never to accept employment elsewhere, and his long services to the university of his choice were recognized by his appointment in 1946 as its Vice-Chancellor. During the five years in which he held that office, many changes in the housing and organization of the University took place, and it was through his leadership, and under his control, that these were successfully effected. The University of Reading owed very much to his loyalty, and to the prestige he gave it, during the early stages of its growth.

It was not however towards university administration that Stenton's interests were mainly directed but towards medieval research, and his best memorial is to be found in his publications. These were, in fact, so numerous that only some of them can here be noted. But in their totality they offer the surest indication of a career which was throughout inspired by a single-minded devotion to scholarship.

SCANDINAVIAN INTEREST

Already between 1905 and 1908 he was contributing editions in translation of Domesday Book to the *Victoria County History* and in the latter year he supplied for the *Heroes of the Nations* series a notable biography of William the Conqueror. His interests in this period were also beginning to turn towards the Scandinavian factor in English development.

In 1910 he produced his *Types of Manorial Structure in the Northern Danelaw*, and 10 years later he compiled a corpus of twelfth-century charters illustrating the social and economic history of that region. These studies were to be summed up in 1927 in his well-known lecture to the British Academy, *The Danes in England*, which has ever since remained the indispensable introduction to the subject.

From the start Stenton had been impressed with the importance of place-name study for the investigation of early English history, and he was one of those most concerned with the foundation of the English Place-Name Society of whose publications he was joint-general-editor from 1924 to 1943. His own contributions to place-name study were themselves numerous, and many of the results of his researches in this field were notably expressed in four remarkable addresses to the Royal Historical Society when he was president of that body from 1939 to 1945.

As the years passed, however, Stenton's interests turned more and more exclusively towards the England of the Anglo-Saxons. So deeply did his personal sympathies become involved in this study that there was even perhaps some danger of a certain insularity in his approach—a tendency to neglect, or to minimize, the importance to English growth of political and ecclesiastical influences imported to England from the continent of Europe. Yet if this tendency existed, it was at most the foible of a great scholar, and the value of his method was demonstrated when there appeared in 1943 what will probably be adjudged to be the greatest of his books. This was the volume on *Anglo-Saxon England* which he contributed to the *Oxford History of England.*

It was immediately acclaimed as a masterpiece of its kind, and it performed much the same service to Anglo-Saxon historical studies as that which J. M. Kemble had rendered a century earlier, summing up the results of a long period of investigation, and indicating the lines upon which future research might most profitably proceed. As an erudite and well-balanced survey of a vast theme it will be long before it is superseded. A critic justly described it as "at once an outstanding contribution to scholarship and a notable addition to literature."

Stenton's publications did not cease with his retirement. He produced in 1955, for instance, an admirable essay on the Latin charters of the Anglo-Saxon period, and in 1957 he contributed to a cooperative work on the Bayeux Tapestry. But during the last years of his life, it was more especially with numismatics as a source of Old English history that he was concerned. He was the driving force in launching the *Sylloge of the Coins of the British Isles* which is now in course of publication, and it was fitting that a volume of studies on Anglo-Saxon coins should have been presented to him on his eightieth birthday.

Stenton's influence on English medieval scholars was profound, and it was not solely through his books that it was exercised. He and Lady Stenton, herself a distinguished medievalist, made their home at Whitley Park Farm, near Reading, and this became a hospitable centre to many who shared their interests. Those who had the privilege of visiting Stenton in his own library carried away an unforgettable impression of his authority, and of the force of his personality.

His energy, which seemed more astonishing in view of his small stature, provided authentic inspiration, and not less remarkable was the generosity with which he was always ready to place his accumulated erudition at the service of others, and particularly of younger men.

His widow survives him, and there are no children.

September 18, 1967.

Cecil Stephenson, who died on November 13 1965, at the age of 76 in the Hampstead studio he had occupied for 45 years, was one of the first abstract painters in England.

Since the thirties he had worked in complete obscurity, except for a single exhibition, his first individual one, in 1960 for which Sir Herbert Read wrote a catalogue introduction. Probably his most important work was done in the middle and late thirties, particularly exciting years for English art, when he worked in close sympathy, and proximity, with Henry Moore, Ben Nicholson, Barbara Hepworth, and the pioneers Naum Gabo and Piet Mondrian, who joined the informal colony of artists in Hampstead when Europe approached war.

Cecil Stephenson was born in 1889 in Bishop Auckland. While attending Darlington Technical College he decided to become an artist, and from 1908-14 he studied at Leeds School of Art, the Royal College of Art, and the Slade which then contained many students who were later to become famous. In 1919 he moved into Sickert's old studio off Parkhill Road, Hampstead, where he lived until his death. At this time he painted in a naturalistic style, but knew little success even at this period of his life, and in 1922 he took up the teaching post at the Northern Polytechnic which he held until 1955.

In 1932 he produced his first abstract paintings and during the thirties he exhibited in many of the collective exhibitions of abstract art, both in Europe and America. For him this yielded little result, but his later paintings of the blitz were bought by the Imperial War Museum, and in 1951 he designed a mural for the Festival of Britain. In 1955 he executed a large window in "Ply Glass" for the British Pavilion at the Brussels Expo., which won him second prize and a silver medal. In 1963 the Tate bought a work of his for the first time—a composition of 1937.

His paintings of the thirties are certainly among the purest produced in England at that time. He was not in the strict sense an innovator; his language of forms and his ideas of space followed the work of European abstract painters such as Maholy-Nagy and Malevich of the decade before. But his use of a consistent scale of colours, and his lucid control of simple forms have kept his work open and fresh, while the more complicated productions of some of his contemporaries have begun to look dated.

A form he made much use of in his paintings of the thirties was a flat upright wedge-shape, producing a rhythm by repeating it at different levels over the canvas, by lightening or darkening it, or by reducing it to a mere outline superimposed on the rest of the group. This is the only period of his work that is at all well known; a fuller evaluation will have to wait until his painting is given the representation it deserves.

November 24, 1965.

Irma Stern, who died in hospital at Cape Town on August 23, 1966, after a long illness, was one of the leading painters in South Africa, where she had a pioneer role in bringing a modern outlook to bear on African life and landscape. She was 71.

She excelled in depicting the vigour and dignity of the tribal Bantu and was the first South African artist to draw upon this wealth of painting material. Rich in colour and strong in design, her work was "modern" in having some relation to that of the German Expressionists, Max Pechstein being a German painter who had a particular influence on her style.

Born in Transvaal, on October 2, 1894, she

received her schooling in Germany and studied art at the Weimar Bauhaus and in Berlin, where she had her first one-man show at the Gallerie Gurlitt in 1919. Until 1929 she regularly exhibited in Berlin and other German cities. From 1929 her disapproval of Nazi policy towards the Jews and her own Jewish origin made her refuse to exhibit any more in Germany.

In South Africa she had a hard struggle for recognition, her first exhibition in Cape Town being visited by the police on the assumption that anything described as "modern" was *ipso facto* immoral. Her quality as an artist, however, was eventually recognized not only in South Africa but internationally. She travelled extensively in Africa and Europe, and exhibited in Paris, Bordeaux, Brussels, Vienna, Amsterdam, Rome, London, and also in the U.S.

She was represented at the Venice Biennale, 1952-58, and at São Paulo, 1957, and won the Oppenheimer Award for the best painting at the "Art, South Africa Today" exhibition at the Durban Art Gallery in 1963. Her work figures in many well known galleries and in Government buildings in Paris, Genoa, Berlin, and Washington. She wrote and illustrated books on the Congo and on Zanzibar.

August 24, 1966.

Josef von Sternberg, one of the most original and controversial film directors in Hollywood during the 1930s, and the discoverer of Marlene Dietrich, died on December 22, 1969. He was 75.

He was a highly intelligent man, something of a *poseur,* quarrelsome, temperamental and frequently at loggerheads with the studios which employed him. He despised the commercialism and banality which he encountered in the American film industry and made many enemies for himself amongst the producers, writers and the stars. Marlene Dietrich said that she owed everything to him, but he churlishly dismissed this acknowledgment as absurd. He could be both ungenerous and autocratic.

His character and outlook were clearly revealed in his autobiography, *Fun in a Chinese Laundry* (a stereotyped title would have been quite out of keeping with the man), a book which often suggested that everyone in the film industry was out of step except the author. But as a text-book for aspiring film directors it proved invaluable. He was a man who thoroughly understood his trade, and his originality of thought is everywhere apparent in it.

His real name was Joe Stern and he was born in Vienna some time in the nineties. His father emigrated to the United States when Joe was three, and sent for the family to join him there when the boy was seven, but poverty soon forced them to return to Austria. At 14 he crossed the Atlantic again and became a messenger boy in a millinery shop. He had already seen a great deal of the world, and what he had seen had provided food for thought in his sharp, analytical and cynical mind. Later he became an assistant to an eccentric who cleaned and repaired old cinema films, and by this channel he entered the rapidly developing film industry. He arrived in Hollywood, moody and resentful, in the early twenties and there directed his first film, *The Salvation Hunters,* in 1924. It aroused considerable controversy, but clearly its maker could not be ignored, and the rebel was received with caution rather than with open arms. Thereafter he directed *Underworld,* in which he claimed later to have inaugurated the gangster cycle, *The Last Command , Dragnet, The Docks of New York* and *The Case of Lena Smith.* The coming of sound was a welcome innovation to anyone as experimentally-minded as he, and in 1929 he made his first sound film, *Thunderbolt,* and soon afterwards he received an urgent request from Emil Jannings, asking that Sternberg should hasten to Berlin and there direct Jannings in his first talking picture, *The Blue Angel.*

Jannings was one of the most temperamental actors in film history, and the clash of these two personalities was both violent and emotional. Faced also with the choice of a leading lady for the film, Sternberg selected a small-time and apparently second-rate young actress named Marlene Dietrich.

The result is legendary. *The Blue Angel* carried both its leading lady and her director to the dizziest heights of universal acclamation. Hollywood humbly begged the truant to return, and Sternberg then made *Morocco, Dishonoured, Shanghai Express, Blonde Venus, The Scarlet Empress* and *The Devil is a Woman,* all for Paramount and each with Marlene Dietrich as his leading lady. They were exotic, artificial and highly flamboyant productions, but the originality and skill of the direction was undeniable. Sternberg continued to direct long after this colourful era of the thirties had ended, and long after Dietrich had—reluctantly—been passed into other directional hands, but the magic of his name diminished, and his acidity towards his fellows increased. At the invitation of Alexander Korda, a producer whom he greatly admired, he went to England in 1937 to direct Charles Laughton in the ill-fated *I, Claudius.*

His later films included *The Shanghai Gesture* (1941), *Macao* (1950) and *Jet Pilot.* In 1953, he made in Japan a fascinating independent film, *The Saga of Anatahan,* about a group of Japanese soldiers and one woman cut off from civilisation.

Von Sternberg was one of the very few film-directors whose style was unmistakable; and as with extreme individualists in any art, opinion was always strongly divided on his merits. What remains undeniable is the extraordinary visual sense which informs his films, the skill with which he manipulated his characteristic properties, weaving intricate effects from glittering nets and painted wooden slats. As an adorner of feminine beauty and a creator of sensuous atmosphere, he was unequalled, and Hollywood was the poorer for allowing his unique talents so often to go to waste.

December 23, 1969.

Mrs. Alfred Sterry (Miss Charlotte Reinagle Cooper), Wimbledon lawn tennis champion five times, died on October 10, 1966, at the age of 96.

She was not only a great lawn tennis player but a great character and always the life and soul of any party—even when she was over 90. She was only three months short of her 91st birthday when she flew unaccompanied down from Scotland during the 1961 Wimbledon to attend the Champions' luncheon, presided over by the president of the All-England Club, H. R. H. the Princess Marina, Duchess of Kent, to mark the 75th year of the championships.

For many years it was her ambition to be the oldest living Wimbledon champion—both in actual age and in the date of her first championship; and when Miss Lottie Dod, who had won the first of her five championships in 1887, died at the age of 88 in Bournemouth during the Wimbledon championships of 1960, Mrs. Sterry was away out on her own.

She was born at Ealing and learnt her tennis at the Ealing Lawn Tennis Club and her first open singles title was won at Ilkley in 1893. Mrs. Sterry won the Wimbledon singles as Miss Cooper in 1895, 1896 and 1898 and then as Mrs. Sterry in 1901 and 1908. During the eight years 1894-1901 following the retirement of the fabulous Miss Lottie Dod, Mrs. G. W. Hillyard and Miss Cooper (Mrs. Sterry) led the field of women's tennis, each of them winning the Wimbledon singles title four times. Mrs. Hillyard died in 1946 at the age of 83.

In 1901, when Mrs. Sterry won the ladies' singles for the fourth time, the men's singles was won by A. W. Gore, and it was curious that the twentieth century should have started with the success at Wimbledon of a man baseliner and a woman volleyer.

In 1907 Mrs. Sterry defeated both Miss M. Sutton (Wimbledon Champion 1905 and 1907) and Mrs. Lambert Chambers in local British tournaments and in 1908, with Miss Sutton not defending, she regained the ladies' singles title at Wimbledon after an interval of seven years—a very remarkable performance—and in doing so she defeated that great champion Mrs. Lambert Chambers. This was the only defeat Mrs. Lambert Chambers sustained from a British player at Wimbledon between 1903 and 1919 (the war years of course intervening). Mrs. Sterry also had many notable singles successes in other championships, being Irish champion in 1895 and 1898, British Covered Court champion in 1895 and Scottish champion in 1899.

SUCCESS AT DOUBLES

She was also an extremely good doubles player, winning the All-England mixed doubles with H. S. Mahony for five successive years from 1894 to 1898, and then with H. L. Doherty in 1900 and with S. E. Casdagli in 1908. As in this latter year she won the All-England ladies' doubles with Miss Garfit, besides being singles champion, she became a treble Wimbledon champion in one year—a very rare achievement. And she also won the triple crown in the Irish championships of 1895 when in addition to the singles she won the ladies' doubles with Miss E. Cooper and the mixed with H. S. Mahony. She won the Irish mixed twice more with H. S. Mahony in 1896 and R. F. Doherty in 1900; also the Irish ladies' championship twice more with Mrs. Hillyard in 1897 and Miss E. Cooper in 1900. She won the British Covered Court mixed doubles in 1898, 1899 and 1900—in each case with R. F. Doherty.

Mrs. Sterry did not defend her singles championship at Wimbledon in 1909 but was runner-up to Mrs. Larcombe in 1912 and reached the final of the ladies' doubles in 1913, 18 years after gaining her first Wimbledon title.

Mrs. Sterry's game was all attack and she came into the net at every opportunity, but it was her supreme steadiness, her equable temperament, and her great tactical ability which was the main reason for her success rather than any brilliancy of stroke. She "had a go" at everyone and everything and her smiling good temper and great sportsmanship made her as popular in her heyday just as did her invincible spirit and irrepressible *joie de vivre* when in her old age she came back to Wimbledon to cheer on the younger generation.

Certainly few champions have enjoyed the game of lawn tennis more than Mrs. Charlotte Sterry. She will be very much missed at Wimbledon.

October 11, 1966.

Adlai Stevenson, the United States Ambassador to the United Nations, who died at the age of 65 on July 14, 1965, had a place in American politics out of all proportion to the offices he held. The ambassadorship to the United Nations and the governorship of Illinois are not regarded as posts of great national power and influence. Nor are defeated presidential candidates normally remembered in history by more than a brief and somewhat mournful mention. Yet while his political career, judged by conventional standards, was not a success, few American politicians of recent times have created such an aura about their name, commanded such unforced affection or such a spontaneous devoted following, or had a greater impact upon American political attitudes.

In a very real sense President Kennedy was Stevenson's political heir, although the two men were never close personally. He possessed the driving ambition, the sheer zest for politics and the capacity for electoral organization that Stevenson lacked. But the projection of the New Frontier owed much to the foundation that Stevenson had built—the concern for serious issues and reasoned debate, the application of liberal and humane reasoning to the whole range of government, the determination not to deal in half truths on a superficial level.

For a number of reasons Stevenson failed to reap the full rewards of what he had sown. To a large extent it was because he was unlucky in his time. Anyone condemned to run twice for the presidency against Eisenhower in the atmosphere of 1952 and 1956 was almost bound to suffer the crippling disadvantage of being "the man who lost twice." He was not as imposing in appearance as he was eloquent in speech; he did not look a President. He lacked that supreme confidence in his own judgment that is necessary for the leadership of a nation the size of the United States. Perhaps even the lively wit of his speeches was a liability to an electorate which expects its politicians to parade their dedication. But he deserves to be honoured for the faith in American idealism that he preserved in the outside world at a difficult time; for the intellectual calibre of that magnificently unsuccessful campaign in 1952; and for the depth of thought and honesty that he always brought to public affairs. Too much may have been made of his indecisiveness. He showed no lack of executive ability in the years when he was Governor of Illinois. He was prepared to outline policy as specifically as it is reasonable to ask of any opposition leader. He took a courageous stand on McCarthyism at a time when other men of eminence were maintaining a prudent silence. Through all his vicissitudes, even in the later years when the fires were rather lower, he showed a mastery of language rarely equalled in the history of American politics.

MIDDLE WEST FAMILY

Adlai Ewing Stevenson, who was born in 1900 in Los Angeles where his father was working for a short time, came of a family rooted firmly in the rich black loam of Illinois. His father's family had been settled in Illinois for 50 years, his mother's family for even longer, and he himself had lived there almost all his life. Both families had reached the Middle West—as so many others have done—after immigration from the British Isles and settlement in the old colonies. The Stevenson family went from Northern Ireland to Pennsylvania in 1748 and sojourned in North Carolina and Kentucky, before settling for good in Bloomington in the agricultural area about 100 miles south-west of Chicago.

The Stevensons—like the Roosevelts, the Tafts and the Adamses—have seldom been far from the centre of the stage. Stevenson's grandfather, another Adlai Stevenson, was Vice-President to Grover Cleveland, and was later a candidate again for the same post with William Jennings Bryan. His father was among those considered when a vice-presidential candidate was being chosen to run in 1928 with Governor Al Smith of New York.

Through his mother, Stevenson was descended from a Northumbrian family which has always been prominent in Republican politics. His maternal great-grandfather, Jesse Fell, was one of Abraham Lincoln's early sponsors. He arranged the famous Lincoln-Douglas debates which, more than anything else, made Lincoln known outside his own state and enabled him to be nominated for the Presidency two years later. So from both sides Stevenson had politics in his blood, and it came from men to whom politics meant the opportunity for public service rather than the chance of personal aggrandisement.

A graduate of Princeton, Stevenson's story was for some years like that of many Americans with a sense of duty. He went to Washington soon after Roosevelt took office and became one of the lawyers in the new Agricultural Adjustment Administration, moving on after a few months to the Federal Alcohol Control Administration, which had been set up in a hurry to cope with the problems resulting from the repeal of prohibition. When the new Administration had settled down, he went back to the law firm in Chicago to which he had previously belonged and to which he returned more than once in the interludes of his public life, most notably, of course, after his defeat in 1952.

YEARS IN NAVY DEPARTMENT

It was not until 1941 that Stevenson had his next job in Washington, but for a year before that he had been practising what was at the time one of the most dangerous trades in the country, chairman for Chicago of William Allen White's Committee to Defend America by Aiding the Allies. Colonel Knox, who had become Secretary of the Navy when Roosevelt decided to bring some Republicans into the Cabinet, appointed him to an undefined position which included doing all Colonel Knox's odd jobs. He stayed in this post until after Colonel Knox's death in the spring of 1944, when he returned to Chicago for another short spell.

While he was in the Navy Department, however, he made a trip to Italy to examine the economic conditions in the liberated part of that country. In his report he gave one of the first warnings in an official doument of the dangers of communism, unless immediate help was given to restore the central industries. Senator McCarthy, who was subsequently to accuse him of being "soft on communism", was many years later in discovering the danger.

Stevenson was soon called back, this time to the State Department, to the task of educating the public about the United Nations before the San Francisco Conference in 1945 and he was sent hastily to the conference itself to ensure that the press were given adequate information on what was happening and on the views of the American delegation.

REPUBLICAN TRIBUTE

After his success in San Francisco, Stevenson was made deputy to Stettinius on the United States delegation to the Preparatory Commission which met in August in London. As Stettinius soon went home because of illness Stevenson was, for most of the time, its effective head and he stayed in London as senior adviser to the American delegation to the first General Assembly. President Truman appointed him an alternate delegate to the General Assemblies in New York in both 1946 and 1947 on the advice of Senator Vandenburg, according to the Senator himself, who wrote to Stevenson that "when I was asked for recommendations... I put your name down as a 'must'. I wish you were devoting all of your time to our foreign affairs at a high level in the State Department"—a remarkable tribute from a great Republican to a future Democratic candidate for the Presidency.

Up to that time the story of Stevenson was that of a man doing a succession of jobs with something more than ordinary efficiency and retiring gracefully to private life again whenever the opportunity offered. He showed no sign of political ability, still less of political ambition. But while he was in Italy during the war he had seen in the Army newspaper the result of a poll in which seven out of 10 parents said they did not want their children to go into public life. He was shocked at this attitude and the memory of his shock probably made him accept when the Democrats in Illinois asked him to run for the Governorship in 1948. The State was a Republican stronghold, and the Democrats had but faint hopes. When Stevenson ran up a majority of more than 570,000 votes, a record in the history of the State, those who knew him best immediately began to wonder whether he was not the perfect candidate for the Presidency in 1952.

His fine record, both as a political manipulator and as an administrator, confirmed this impression, as did his successful campaign against Illinois corruption, and when Truman had made clear he would not stand for reelection, Stevenson's name came increasingly to the fore until he eventually received the nomination in Chicago. It is now clear that after 20 years of power the Democratic sands were temporarily running out and that Stevenson really had no chance of winning the election. The additional weight of General Eisenhower's laurels had pushed the political pendulum too far in favour of the Republicans for mere words—however fine—to pull it back. But though he failed electorally, he did succeed by the calibre of his campaign in raising the whole tone of American political debate. Rarely has any electorate been addressed with such frankness, with such refusal to distort or to descend to the subterfuges of politics.

WORLD TOUR

After his defeat Stevenson made a world tour and on his return he continued to speak frequently, both to keep up interest in the causes near to his heart and to help the Democratic Party pay off its campaign debts. He worked particularly hard in the congressional campaign of 1954, a year which saw the Democrats returned to power in Congress.

By the end of 1955 Stevenson, who had been so reluctant to declare himself in 1952, had made it plain that he was a candidate for the Democratic nomination for the second time. But it was not his for the asking. Senator Kefauver also had presidential ambitions and Stevenson had no choice but to accept the challenge in a number of gruelling primary elections. In the end California gave the palm to Stevenson, but the ordeal was exhausting and somewhat bruising; his opponent accused him, for example, of undue softness toward the South on the race question. This very moderation on a divisive issue was, however, a recommendation to the Democratic convention and, although Truman supported Governor Harriman, Stevenson carried off the nomination. The convention was then allowed to choose its own vice-presidential candidate—a highly imaginative stroke by Stevenson, who sought to draw a comparison between the Democrats and the cut and dried proceedings at the Republican convention. Senator Kefauver won in what later came to be seen as an historic contest against the future President Kennedy.

DISHEARTENING CAMPAIGN

The campaign which followed was a disheartening affair. Drawing the wrong lessons from his previous campaign Stevenson paid too much attention to advice from professional politicians and seemed to be not quite true to himself. The campaign was ineptly managed and an aura of defeat hung about it. Yet it contained some remarkable things. Republicans expressed horror and scorn when Stevenson suggested that atomic texts should be suspended and accused him of gambling with the country's safety. But not long after the election they adopted the idea. The papers on the "New America" which Stevenson produced—dealing with social security, schools, education, and so on—never caught the imagination of voters still beguiled by the combination of peace and prosperity; Stevenson's attacks on their complacency did not get under the skin of many people. Yet this approach foreshadowed the "New Frontier" of President Kennedy. In the end the Democrats' destruction was completed by the Suez crisis although to the logical it seemed to bear out much of what Stevenson had been saying. He suffered a worse defeat than he had in 1952 and held only six southern states.

Probably no candidate could have conquered Eisenhower, then at the height of his popularity. With this consolation Stevenson turned back again to his law practice and to occasional speeches in support of more economic and less military aid; economic growth; and a more flexible use of world financial reserves. Critics might complain that Stevenson was no innovator and no fount of new ideas but he was sensitive to their appearance and graceful and articulate in giving them wider currency.

As time went on the Eisenhower Administration, no longer on the pinnacle of success, would have been glad to use Stevenson's talents and recruit his prestige. At one point he did in fact accept a post as temporary consultant to the State Department but there was a dispute over the terms on which he had agreed to serve and it came to little.

AMBIGUOUS ROLE

As 1960 approached Stevenson continued to protest that he was not a candidate for the Democratic nomination. But to the exasperation of the other candidates, and of his own eager supporters, he also refused to say categorically whether he would reject the nomination if it were offered to him; he also refused to support anyone else. Mrs. Roosevelt, one of his most enthusiastic admirers, was not very successful in obtaining a definite answer although she concluded publicly that Stevenson was in the running. Indeed it was hard to believe that he did not cherish hopes of a deadlock at the convention between Kennedy and Johnson which would give him the nomination for the third time. His behaviour at the convention, which was packed with his own followers, gave further confirmation that he had not abandoned ambition.

The ambiguous part which Stevenson played failed to secure him the nomination; and it may possibly have cost him the post of Secretary of State in the Kennedy Administration. To bind up the wounds of the party Kennedy let it be understood that he might well choose Stevenson but he never made any binding public commitment to this effect. Instead the President offered Stevenson the post of Ambassador to the United Nations with Cabinet status and a voice in foreign policy. No doubt to Stevenson it seemed like a consolation prize and he thought it over—rather ostentatiously—but in the end accepted it.

In the United Nations Stevenson was regarded as one of the founding fathers. He played a large part officially and otherwise in educating American opinion on the need to strengthen and sustain the organization as a force for world peace. He never wavered in his idealistic support, even though on occasion he may have doubted the wisdom of American policies in the organization as expressed, for instance, by his immediate predecessor, Henry Cabot Lodge.

He was greeted by other delegates as an "elder statesman" who had found his spiritual home at last. His eloquent advocacy of liberal causes, however, suffered some diminution when he found himself obliged to espouse American actions in such episodes as the Bay of Pigs in Cuba, and there were times when he seemed to be not as close to the making of decisions in the White House as he might have been.

LOYALTY TO PRESIDENTS

Nevertheless, Stevenson never faltered in his loyalty first to President Kennedy and then to President Johnson and continued to defend the American approach to such controversial questions as the Congo, Vietnam and the Dominican Republic. He found himself embroiled repeatedly in polemics with the Soviet representative on the Security Council. On one occasion, when Cuba was being debated, he told Zorin that he was waiting for an answer to his question and would continue "sitting here until hell freezes over."

With the British delegation, whether headed by Sir Patrick Dean or by Lord Caradon, Stevenson always maintained close and confidential relations. He did much to heal the wounds left by the Anglo-American disagreement over the Suez affair of 1956. He did his best, too, to cultivate delegates from the new countries of Africa, even though at times he was disappointed by their gratuitously critical attitude to his country.

Less than a month before he died, on June 17, Stevenson was given the Honorary Degree of Doctor of Laws by Harvard University, and his citation on that occasion is worth quoting in full. It ran: "Generous spirit, instant spokesman for freedom in the councils of the world; his intelligence and ready wit have informed and enlightened the political experience of a generation."

In private he was a modest, charming, witty companion, always ready with an apposite story or reminiscence, and always ready to listen to his partner. Anyone would brighten when seeing that Stevenson was to be his neighbour at table, for it was a guarantee that the talk would roam over foreign affairs, American internal affairs, and literature with the easiest of step. To add to the pleasure, Stevenson always made it seem that he himself was enjoying himself quite exceptionally well. He had intellect, grace, and unfailing manners.

Stevenson married Ellen Borden in 1928, and they had three sons. The marriage was dissolved in 1949.

July 15, 1965.

Andrew Graham Stewart, who died in a London nursing home on May 7, 1964, at the age of 62, was one of the leading figures in the steel industry, a staunch champion of free enterprise and an outspoken opponent of nationalization. He belonged to that dwindling type of industrialist whose family ties with a great enterprise had not been severed by the advent of the managerial revolution. Quite the reverse in fact. His life was steel and in particular Stewarts and Lloyds, the largest steel tube group in Britain, where he began his career 40 years ago and closed it as chairman and general managing director.

A man with a great capacity for work, he gave himself unstintingly to his industry and his country in general. Quiet but forthright by disposition, with a quiet and keen sense of humour, he inspired a great amount of affection among his many friends in all walks of life.

ON THE SHOP FLOOR

In argument and discussion his views, expressed always at the right moment, carried great conviction. This characterized his uncanny capacity for getting to the heart of the matter. A deep thinker and a wise counsellor, his advice was sought and valued by many. Graham Stewart was a straightforward but unassuming man, ever true to his principles and staunch to his friends.

Stewart, born on August 22, 1901, was a grandson of Andrew Stewart, who founded the Scottish side of the tube manufacturing business of Stewarts and Lloyds in 1860. Educated at Winchester and Cambridge, where he took an engineering degree, Graham Stewart, as he was known to his friends, joined the company in 1924 and spent the next seven years learning in a practical way the business of steel, and particularly of tube-making. He knew hundreds of men personally, for he worked with many of them on the shop floor.

He was appointed a director of the company in 1931 and a managing director later the same year. As assistant general managing director in charge of tube and shell production from 1941 he had much to do with the war record of the company which produced close on 100 million shell cases and projectiles.

He became deputy chairman in 1943, and chairman and general managing director in 1945 on the death of Sir Allan Macdiarmid.

He had travelled about the world on the company's business, but more recently had remained in this country; he spent half of each working week in his London office and the other half at the head office in Glasgow, often making the journey by air to save time.

Stewart, who was president of the British Iron and Steel Federation in 1955, was appointed president-elect in March, 1962. He did not serve a second time as president, however, and at the time of his death had the title of past president. He was a member of the federation's council and executive committee from 1945 until his death and also served on a number of other federation committees. In October, 1956, he was appointed a part-time member of the Iron and Steel Board, an appointment which he relinquished at the end of 1961. He was president of the British Employers' Confederation, 1952-54.

In 1929 he married Barabel Greig, who survives him with their three sons and two daughters. All three sons have entered the company.

May 9, 1964.

Christopher Stone, D.S.O., M.C., died on May 22, 1965, at the age of 82. As an amateur of the gramophone he set a fashion in broadcasting and pioneered the curious and exclusive profession based on the simple act of spinning a disc on a turntable, and talking amiably and informatively about it.

He will be remembered for his disarmingly natural approach to broadcasting at a time when speakers, however eminent or original they may have been, were still subject to the tyranny of the script. For he shared with Sir Walford Davies, C. H. Middleton, and John Hilton a spontaneity and a deceptively effortless delivery which placed him at once on friendly terms with his listeners. His success had a lasting effect on the pattern of radio entertainment. He faced the once unfamiliar microphone with a happy blend of casualness, tolerance and good humour, which British audiences by nature found most engaging. At the same time, in his critical reviews as well as in his spoken comment, Stone could be astringent and penetrating, with the cultured man's contempt for the second-rate.

WROTE EIGHT NOVELS

Christopher Reynolds Stone, the younger son of the late Rev. E. D. Stone, sometime assistant master at Eton, was born on September 19, 1882, and educated at Eton and Christ Church, Oxford, where he was a scholar. In 1914 he enlisted in The Middlesex Regiment, and in the following year was commissioned in The Royal Fusiliers. He served with gallantry from 1914 to 1918, was awarded the Distinguished Service Order and the Military Cross, and was three times mentioned in dispatches.

Stone was the author of eight novels, including *Scars, Valley of Indecision* and *Rigour of the Game.*

His sister Faith (who died in 1960) had married Compton Mackenzie, and it was in 1927 while acting as joint-editor with his brother-in-law of a magazine, *The Gramophone,* that his name became known in a completely new form of entertainment—one of baffling simplicity—which involved playing the latest gramophone records and linking them together with some random remarks. In his own words: "I never had any words written down. I insisted on being free to meander along in my own fashion and tell a few personal stories prompted by the records I played."

Although the B.B.C. dropped him as a paid performer in 1935 because of his association with Radio Luxembourg, they allowed him to take part in B.B.C. charity appeals, which raised £100,000 in four years.

In 1908 he married Alice, daughter of James Wilson and widow of W. M. Chinnery. She died in 1945.

May 24, 1965.

Lord Stopford of Fallowfield, the distinguished anatomist, and Vice-Chancellor of Manchester University from 1934 to 1956, died at his home at Arnside, Westmorland, on March 6, 1961, at the age of 72. He was in the first list of life peers who were created in 1958.

The Rt. Hon. Sir John Sebastian Bach Stopford, K.B.E., F.R.S., Baron Stopford of Fallowfield, of Hindley Green in the county Palatine of Lancaster, was born at Hindley Green, near Wigan, on June 25, 1888, and received his early education at the Manchester Grammar School. He entered the University of Manchester in 1906 and graduated with honours in medicine in 1911. During his undergraduate course he won several prizes and distinctions and in 1915 he received the degree of M.D. with a Gold Medal. His first appointment as a teacher in the University of Manchester was that of Junior Demonstrator in Anatomy in 1912. Thereafter, becoming in turn Senior Demonstrator and Lecturer, he succeeded to the chair of Anatomy on the resignation of Professor (later Sir) Grafton Elliot Smith in 1919.

SERVICE IN WARTIME

It is not surprising that under the inspiration of Elliot Smith Stopford turned his steps to the study of neurological anatomy. His earliest research work was on the distribution of certain blood vessels in the brain and its clinical significance. Later, during the First World War, he was neurologist in turn to the Second Western General Hospital and the Grangethorpe Hospital, and started his investigations on the anatomical basis of sensation, the scientific work for which he is perhaps best known. His views which were set out in a book *Sensation and the Sensory Pathway* were based largely on the clinical studies he had made on the large number of cases of injury to nerves and their consequent changes of sensory function which had come under his observation. In 1927 he was elected a Fellow of the Royal Society. He held the chair of Anatomy until 1937 and was then appointed to the chair of Neurology which he occupied until 1956 when he was made Emeritus Professor.

During his tenure of the chair of Anatomy, Stopford acted as Pro-Vice-Chancellor of the University from 1928 to 1930. He was also Dean of the Medical School for two periods of four and two years respectively. He acted as temporary Vice-Chancellor for six months when Sir Walter Moberly left Manchester to become chairman of the University Grants Committee and in May, 1935, when he was 46 years of age, he was appointed to the Vice-Chancellorship. He had to guide the university through the troubled years of the war and the period of rapid expansion which followed it, for in three years after the cessation of hostilities the number of students doubled. This he did with great success. The Senate of a university is not one of the easiest of bodies to lead; it certainly cannot be driven. His experience of university affairs, his wisdom and thoughtfulness, his firmness and forthrightness when the occasion demanded it, and especially his tact, gained him the affection and admiration of his colleagues. Those who shared with him any of these years of great activity will always be grateful to him for the distinguished services he rendered to the University of Manchester.

MEDICAL EDUCATION

In addition to his work for the university, however, he made valuable contributions nationally to medical education and research. This was done through his membership of the Interdepartmental Committee on Medical Schools of which he was vice-chairman; his many years' membership of the General Medical Council, of which he became Chairman of Business; and his vice-chairmanship of the Managing Trustees of the Nuffield Foundation. To these offices, in which he was able to help the advancement of medical education, must also be added that of membership of the University Grants Committee, where a similar purpose was served. Many years before the National Health Service came into being, the hospital services of the Manchester region were coordinated by the establishment of the Manchester, Salford and Stretford Joint Hospitals Board. He acted as chairman of this board and guided its activities throughout its existence. There is little doubt that its success was an indication, to those who founded the Act, of the type of organization which ought to form a part of a national health service, and this was due in no small way to Stopford's wisdom as its chairman.

When the National Health Service came into operation it was natural that Stopford should be made chairman of the Manchester Regional Hospital Board which had to provide for hospital and specialist services for a considerable part of the North Western area. As might be expected, this appointment was a great success, and the development of this side of the Health Service in the Manchester region worked from the first smoothly and well. In many other ways he gave the benefit of his experience to aid cultural activities both national and local. Examples of these were his chairmanship of the John Rylands Library, the Manchester Royal College of Music, and the Universities Bureau of the British Empire. He was knighted in 1941 and in 1955 was created K.B.E. In 1956 he was made a Freeman of Manchester and a year later the university made him an honorary M.A.

Stopford was born and bred in Lancashire. He was always loyal to it. He did not disdain the outdoor relaxations of the common man and two of them—football and gardening—gave him great pleasure. What was also important, they supplied a complete change of mental activity.

He was a really good half back and played for M. G. S. and Manchester University in that position. As Vice-Chancellor he was a familiar figure on the touchline at all the university's soccer matches. When the university was playing away, and during vacations, he would go to watch Manchester United or Manchester City, in company with—a pleasing expression of the true democracy of the North—the head porter of the university.

His outstanding characteristics were his honesty in expressing his opinions and his wisdom in affairs both great and small. He was a great Vice-Chancellor as well as a distinguished anatomist.

He married, in 1916, Lily, daughter of John Allan, of Blackburn, who was also trained for the medical profession, and they had one son.

March 7, 1961.

The death of **Dr. Milan Stoyadinovich,** the pre-war Prime Minister of Yugoslavia, at the age of 73, was reported in October, 1961, from Buenos Aires.

During his years of power, from 1935 to 1939, Stoyadinovich was notorious for his pro-Fascist policies. He was a close supporter of Hitler and Mussolini and personal friend of Count Ciano. But, although he liked to picture himself as the leader of his people, much of the real authority at this time was exerted by the First Regent, Prince Paul.

Born at Chachak on July 23, 1888, he attended the secondary school and the university in Belgrade and later studied in England, France, and Germany. In 1914 he entered the accountancy section of the Ministry of Finance, where he won swift promotion to become head of the department before resigning in 1919 to start a new career in banking. From 1920 to 1922 he lectured in economics at Belgrade University and became active in the affairs of the Radical Party.

HOPES OF LIBERALISM

Stoyadinovich first came to the fore in national politics when he was appointed Minister of Finance in December, 1922. He remained in this post until April, 1926, with the exception of a few months in 1924. He was elected to the National Assembly in 1923, 1925, and 1927, becoming President of the Assembly's Finance Committee during his third term. While out of office he devoted his time to journalism and broadcasting in addition to his business activities. His newspaper, the *Samouprava,* held strongly pro-Serbian views, yet when Prince Paul called him to the premiership in 1935 there were hopes that he would pursue a liberal policy that would satisfy Croatian aspirations.

These and other expectations proved to be ill-founded. He did little to bring about a more democratic regime, merely easing a little the pressures of the police state. Although he had published a pamphlet in favour of resuming diplomatic relations with the Soviet Union, when he came to conduct foreign policy—he combined the office of Minister of Foreign Affairs with that of Prime Minister—he moved in the opposite direction, forging closer ties with the Fascist states, not the communists. It is true that he was not so much his own master as he would have liked to convey, but there is no reason to suppose that he was forced to adopt such a policy against his will. In 1937 a treaty was signed with Italy. The following February he welcomed the German seizure of Austria. He raised no objection to the dismemberment of Czechoslovakia.

As early as March, 1936, Stoyadinovich only narrowly escaped assassination by another deputy in the Skupshtina. Three shots were fired at the Prime Minister while he was speaking. Yet he remained in office until February, 1939. In April the following year he was interned after a police search of his home, and in 1941 the Yugoslav Government handed him over to the British authorities, who held him in Mauritius until 1948, when he moved to South America. He settled in Argentina and in 1950 became editor of the economic weekly *La Economista.*

October 27, 1961.

John Strachey, M.P., Minister of Food from 1946 to 1950, and Secretary of State for War from 1950 to 1951, died suddenly in a London hospital on July 15, 1963 at the age of 61. He was Labour M. P. for Aston from 1929 to 1931, for Dundee from 1945 to 1950, and since 1950 for West Dundee.

Strachey's outstanding achievement in his later years was to become the most mature ideological thinker of the Labour movement in the fifties and sixties, thus repeating with a difference his eminence as an ideologist of the Left before the war.

Though *The Coming Struggle for Power* (1932) or *The Nature of the Capitalist Crisis* (1935) may remain the best-known of all his books, there was certainly no loss of distinction in his last three major works, *Contemporary Capitalism* (1956), *The End of Empire* (1959) and *On the Prevention of War* (1962). His brilliant essay *The Strangled Cry,* originally published in 1960, showed an insight into the human agony caused by the rise and decadence of communism, which would have been far beyond the powers of an ordinary political writer.

Despite the widely differing titles of his recent books, Strachey saw them as separate parts of a single whole, an attempt to rethink, in the light of his wide political experiences over a quarter of a century, the socialist doctrines of which he had been so radical an exponent. He did this with an intellectual honesty which would have been creditable in any writer but demanded especial courage in one who was also continuously active in national-party politics, where opponents are always ready to point an accusing finger at any one who admits to having changed his views.

During the long years of Labour's opposition since 1951 Strachey continued to be prominent as a front bench spokesman of his party, largely on questions of defence. Characteristically he took the opportunity offered by this post to become one of the very few English politicians or intellectuals to master the complexities of nuclear strategy and to be capable of talking with the American brains trusters on equal terms.

Among the more orthodox worthies of the Labour Party, the stormy character of Strachey's earlier political career may have somewhat diminished the influence to which his writings entitled him and may have caused him to be less close than one might have expected to successive party leaders. But there is no doubt that the current strategic thinking of the Labour Party owes much to his forceful and realistic mind.

In a smaller circle of colleagues in this country, operating in the borderland of politics and academic study, such as Chatham House and the Institute of Strategic Studies, Strachey's contribution to current problems will be sadly missed, and scarcely less in similar circles in India, the United States, and Europe.

For his many close friends his untimely death will leave a gap which they will find it impossible to fill.

MARXIST INFLUENCE

Evelyn John St. Loe Strachey, P.C., M.P., was born on October 21, 1901, and was the only surviving son of John St. Loe Strachey, editor of the *Spectator*. He was educated at Eton and Magdalen College and could have then easily followed in his father's Conservative traditions and been assured of a prosperous position on the paper, but at the university he became interested in socialism and in 1924 joined the I. L. P. The same year he stood as the Labour candidate in the Aston division of Birmingham, and on being defeated, threw himself into the day-to-day activity of the Labour movement, editing the *Socialist Review* and the *Miner*. During the winter of 1927-28 he visited Russia to study conditions in the Soviet mining industry.

In 1929 he stood again for the Aston Division and this time was elected. In the House he was soon seen to be a strong critic of the reformist outlook of most of his Labour colleagues and when in 1931 Sir Oswald Mosley left the Labour Party, he followed and helped him to form his "New Party". But he very soon came to realize the new body's Fascist tendencies and, making a complete break with Mosley, he devoted the greater part of his energies to campaigning against Fascism, both at home and abroad.

All Strachey's writing, from the comparative juvenilia of *Revolution by Reason* (1925), accommodating the influence of Mosley and Wells, Keynes and Marx, was remarkable for its clarity and the free admission of its assumptions. The assumptions changed. Marxism carried him through the thirties, with *The Coming Struggle for Power* (1933), a revolutionary tract, *The Nature of the Capaitalist Crisis* (1935), one of the best Marxist contributions to economic analysis of the depression, and *What Are We to Do?* (1938), which virtually commended the Soviet party model in English dress. The next three years brought a decisive change. *A Programme for Progress* (1940), although it advocated Keynesian ideas only as a transitory step to socialism, has had a great deal to do with modern economic thinking in the Labour Party, and *A Faith to Fight For* (1941), although its praise for British qualities which resisted Nazism may have been unfair to less favoured allies who succumbed, was significant of his emancipation from a Marxist adolescence where truth was revealed: an emancipation he celebrated in the famous essay, *The Strangled Cry*. His great virtue as a political writer was exposition and reconciling of authorities rather than new thinking on his own account. He was not ashamed to confess in later years that much of what he expounded he later had to abandon in the light of common sense and clarity.

IN THE R.A.F.

In 1941 he joined the R.A.F. and after a period as adjutant to a squadron, he was appointed a Public Relations Officer and in a series of effective broadcasts explained the life and background of the men who flew the bombers over Germany. He rose to the rank of wing commander.

In 1943 he had been adopted Labour candidate for Dundee and on being elected at the general election two years later was appointed Under-Secretary for Air. As the Secretary of State for Air, Lord Stansgate, was in the Lords, Strachey was the spokesman for the Air Ministry in the Commons.

In May, 1946, there was a heated controversy about food supplies, and Sir Ben Smith, then Minister of Food, resigned and was succeeded by Strachey. One of his first actions was to fly to Ottawa to negotiate a new long term wheat agreement with Canada, and to Washington to attend the inaugural meeting of the International Emergency Food Council, but before he left he warned that bread rationing might have to be introduced. On his return when he told the House that if bread supplies were not to break down, bread rationing was inescapable, there followed a public uproar with threats of non-cooperation from groups of master bakers, demonstrations by the Housewives League and hosts of petitions.

JUST RATIONS SCHEME

It was hard to devise a workable scheme for such a perishable commodity, but the situation showed little sign of improvement and the Government stood by their decision. When the scheme was eventually put into operation in July, 1946, the controversy soon died down and though there were spasmodic outbreaks of non-cooperation among the bakers, Strachey had the satisfaction of seeing his scheme proved reasonably just and workable and that considerable quantities of flour were saved.

Towards the end of 1946 the Labour Government embarked on the disastrous ground-nuts scheme in East Africa. As a result of investigations of a mission sent out by the Colonial Secretary it was decided to start the large-scale production of groundnuts in selected areas of Tanganyika, Northern Rhodesia, and Kenya. It was hoped to produce substantial supplies of oil and fats. In this scheme Strachey was fully involved, and he brought all his energies to bear on it. It was an ambitious scheme, by which it was hoped to clear by 1953 no fewer than 3,210,000 acres of bush and to produce annually after that about 600,000 tons of ground-nuts at a total cost of £23m. The Overseas Food Corporation, with Sir Leslie Plummer as chairman, was formed and the work began.

But from the very beginning nothing proceeded according to plan, and because of the difficulties encountered in clearing the bush, and the mechanized cultivation of the cleared land, the Overseas Food Corporation submitted, and the Government accepted, in November, 1949 a revised plan which contemplated the clearance of 600,000 acres of bush by 1954. In the succeeding months it became clear that even the revised plans could not be achieved.

To Strachey fell the task of defending the scheme in the House, and it was not easy. He was supported by the Colonial Secretary, of course, but, as Strachey had been largely responsible for its initiation, he had to bear the brunt of Opposition attack.

He is still remembered by many as the man who introduced bread rationing in peace time and for his association with the ill-fated ground nuts scheme yet, in fairness to Strachey, the Ministry of Food would have been a hot potato in any hands and the ground nuts scheme was by no means altogether an ill-conceived one. Strachey was thought by more than one senior civil servant who worked with him to be one of the ablest Labour administrators of the period.

FREED FROM NUTS

It must, however, have been a relief to him when, after a hard-fought battle at Dundee at the general election of 1950, he became Secretary of State for War in the fourth Labour Administration. Freed from the burden of ground-nuts, he took his duties at the War Office very seriously, but he was hardly there long enough to create any lasting impression.

Though the Labour Government were defeated at the general election of October, 1951, Strachey retained his seat at Dundee with a majority of 3,306 in a three-cornered fight, and he held it again in 1955 and 1959.

At the end of his life Strachey made a notable contribution to the discussions of war and peace with his book *On the Prevention of War*, which was published in 1962. He was the only major public figure in England who had taken the trouble, over recent years, to immerse himself in the expert literature and complex researches of the American strategic analysts; and, after long and heated discussions with the thinkers of Harvard and the Rand Corporation, he had come substantially to accept their views about the exacting requirements of a credible strategy of nuclear deterrence based on invulnerable second strike weapons.

These arguments he presented to the lay public with an admirable clarity which no expert had hitherto achieved, together with a deeply perceptive analysis of the effects of the nuclear stalemate upon international relations and of its real as opposed to its chimerical danger. But his synoptic mind led him to a more adventurous conclusion than any other student of the interrelation between strategy and politics has recently attempted. He believed that in effect a world order must now be constructed around an informal condominium of the United States and the Soviet Union whose national interests were beginning rapidly to converge. It is a sad irony that he died on the eve of the important test ban negotiations in Moscow, for he maintained that the fate of the test ban would begin to verify or else falsify his view. He was a member of the council of the Institute for Strategic Studies and played an active part in its work.

He first married, in 1929, Esther, the daughter of P. F. Murphy of New York; this marriage was dissolved by divorce in 1933, and he married secondly in 1933, Celia, daughter of the Rev. A. H. Simpson, by whom he had a son and a daughter.

July 16, 1963.

Philippa Strachey, C.B.E., a pioneer in the struggle for equal rights for women, died on August 23, 1968, at the age of 96.

One of 10 brothers (Lytton Strachey was one) and sisters, she was the third daughter of Lieutenant-General Sir Richard Strachey, R.E., G.C.S.I., F.R.S., by his second marriage to Jane Maria, daughter of John Peter Grant, of Rothiemurchus. Her youth as a member of the famous family whose house in Gordon Square figured so largely in the golden legend of the Bloomsbury set, made it inevitable that she should grow up well aware of the social and philosophic conflict of her day.

In 1907, at the beginning of the great years of the fight for women's suffrage, she became secretary of the London Society for Women's Suffrage, historic progenitor of the Fawcett Society, of which she had been honorary secretary since her retirement from formal office in 1951. Moving in those early days straight into the centre of the constitutional suffrage movement led by Mrs. Henry Fawcett. later Dame Millicent Fawcett, she identified herself completely with the society.

A born administrator who preferred the anonymity of the backroom to the centre of the platform, she had need of all her qualities of judgment, leadership, imaginative thrust and cool-headed tenacity.

One of her first tasks was the organization of the "Mud March" of 1907, the society's first open air rally, when on a bleak February day 3,000 women who had met in Hyde Park marched to the Strand in a gesture of feminine solidarity which astonished London, and set the pattern of future demonstrations there and throughout the country.

Loyal to her colleagues, she inspired loyalty in them. Her memory was phenomenal, and she was a brilliant raconteuse. It is remembered how one day after the Second World War, when documents were being cleared from her society's bombed premises, she seized upon some fragmentary records, filling in from personal recollection every detail of the story of the people and events concerned. In her long life she was able not only to see but to assess the positive results of the movement she served with such devotion. Two great milestones were for her the passing of the Sex Disqualification (Removal) Act in 1919, and as recently as 1955 the acceptance by the Civil Service of the principle of equal pay.

August 26, 1968.

Billy Strayhorn, died in a New York hospital on May 30, 1967, at the age of 51.

No one will ever be able to work out exactly how much the music played by Duke Ellington's orchestra owes to Billy Strayhorn. But certainly his death must affect Ellington deeply. Ever since 1938, when they first met, they had been the closest of musical collaborators.

One debt is obvious: the vast assembly of Strayhorn compositions which the orchestra has featured and still features. He wrote "Take the 'A' train", Ellington's well-known theme-tune. "Lush life", "Some thing to live for", "Passion flower", "Johnny come lately" and many other songs played during the rich Ellington years of the early 1940s were his. So was the fragile and Ravel-influenced "Chelsea bridge". Ellington and Strayhorn never tired of telling the anecdote behind this last tune. It was inspired by a Whistler painting of a bridge across the Thames. It was not, they discovered later, Chelsea bridge at all.

But there was much more to Strayhorn than one-off tunes written for a jazz orchestra. He collaborated with Ellington on many major concert works. "The perfume suite" in the 1940s was the first; in the 1950s came their collaboration on "Such sweet thunder", specially written for the Stratford, Ontario, Shakespeare Festival, and "A drum is a woman".

TWO IN HARMONY

The musical sympathy between the two men was so powerful that members of the orchestra frequently could not recollect precisely where the work of one left off and the other began. Neither could the composers themselves. "Although we feel very differently about life, we really understand what each one of us wants in a composition," Strayhorn said of the musical relationship in 1964. "As a consequence Duke can call me and say 'I've got these notes here and I haven't got the time'. I write it out from there."

Until Strayhorn fell ill in 1966, he and Ellington were almost inseparable on the band's world-wide tours. Yet it is one of the minor mysteries of musical history that Strayhorn virtually never appeared on stage with the orchestra. He often stood in for Duke as pianist on records, playing a light, airy, swinging style which owed something to the French classical Impressionists. "When I play with the band", he said, "I play like its leader. I know what Duke would do in any particular section of a composition."

June 1, 1967.

A. G. Street, who died on July 21, 1966, at the age of 74 was a Wiltshire farmer whose first book, *Farmer's Glory,* written when he was just under 40, won him instant recognition.

The story of Street's early life farming in Wiltshire and Canada had vigour and freshness and showed at once that Street had a real gift for expression. It also showed that he shared with Cobbett and all who feel and write passionately about the land that he was the proud possessor of some good well-nourished prejudices. He wrote in all some 30 books, essays, novels, country calendars and farming commentaries, all readable down-right, and stamped with Street's strong personality, but it is doubtful if he ever equalled *Farmer's Glory*. For years he was a popular broadcaster; he was the original compere for Francis Dillon's programme *Country Magazine* and took part many times in *Any Questions*, where his warmth, shrewdness and fine displays of country argument delivered with his best corn-hall style were heard to advantage.

GOOD TIMES

Arthur George Street was born on April 7, 1892, the son of Henry Street of Ditchampton Farm at Wilton in Wiltshire. He was educated at Dauntsey's School, at West Lavington, near Devizes, but much of his boyhood was spent on his father's farm, on which he worked until he was eighteen. Then in 1911 he emigrated to North West Manitoba where, employed as a farm labourer, he learnt and never forgot the essential differences between the agricultural conditions of Canada and England. In 1914 he returned to his own land, and, having been rejected for the army, again took up work with his father and after the latter's death in 1917 continued to run the family farm.

When agriculture began to enjoy the prosperity that came to it during and for some time after the War, some farmers thought the good times would last for ever. "God help us", wrote Street later, "we actually had late dinner!"

He was not one to bemoan losses when he saw a chance of turning them to profits. He came to the conclusion that corn-growing in England was hopeless, and turned his farm down to grass, and ran it as a dairy farm only. He started a milk round, at first delivering the milk himself, rising every morning at 4.30, including Sundays, canvassing for new customers in the district, and building up a sound business. It was then that Edith Olivier, the novelist, suggested to Street that he should write a book on his experiences, and the changes in farming in Wiltshire, described from the personal point of view.

Much of what became *Farmer's Glory* was written late at night in bed, after hay-making in the wet summer of 1931. Each successive chapter was planned as Street went on his milk round in the early morning, and on wet days he would type out what he had written and correct it. He was greatly encouraged by Richard de la Mare of Faber and Faber who published the book in 1932.

In the same year appeared *Strawberry Roan*, not exactly a novel, but the story of a famous heifer round which were woven the fortunes of a crowd of Wiltshire folk. The book abounded in vivid sketches and confirmed the author's reputation.

There followed *Hedge Trimmings; Land Everlasting; The Endless Furrow; To be a Farmer's Boy; Already Walks Tomorrow;* and many others, indeed for a long period Street published a book a year. His last two which were called *Johnny Cowslip* and *Fish and Chips* came out in 1964.

He left Ditchampton Farm in 1951 to take over Mill Farm at South Newton, Salisbury, because a housing estate was being developed in his old parish and the houses were gradually encroaching on the farming land.

He married in 1918 Vera Florence Foyle by whom he had one daughter.

July 22, 1966.

Anna Louise Strong, the American Communist writer, who lived in Soviet Russia and China for many years died in March, 1970.

She was deported from Russia in 1949, having been accused of spying. In 1955 Tass reported the accusations against her had proved false and she had been fully restored "in her rights". She went to live in Peking where she was friendly with the Communist leaders and for many years issued a newsletter.

Miss Strong settled in China in 1958. She was an honorary member of the Revolutionary Youth Movement, the Red Guards, whose aim was to implement the "cultural revolution" started by Mao Tse-tung in 1965.

Miss Strong was an active campaigner for Mao's China and was a familiar figure at mass rallies, state banquets, and literary meetings in Peking. She had frequent meetings with Mao, Chou En-lai, and other Chinese communist leaders whom she got to know during her five visits to China between 1925 and 1947 when they were fighting for power.

Of enthusiastic temperament, a rebel and a fluent writer from early years, Anna Louise Strong was the daughter of Sydney Strong, a clergyman who was able to graft Darwinist views upon a fundamentalist outlook. She was born at Friend, Nebraska, on November 24, 1885. She studied in Germany for a year before taking her degree at Bryn Mawr in 1903 and later took a Ph.D. degree at Chicago University. She became involved, as a sympathizer of militantly radical views, in labour troubles, and from 1917 onwards longed for Russia. She became a journalist and in 1921 went to Russia as a correspondent with the American Friends' Relief Mission.

That marked the real beginning of her unbounded Communist devotions. On the first stage of her progress towards absolute faith in the inevitability of Communism as a world order she did not know the difference, as she afterwards confessed, between a Bolshevik and a Menshevik. But any lack of knowledge in this respect she made up for by the wholeheartedness of her emotional response as a spectator of the famine on the Volga.

A noted figure among the colony of foreign Communists in Moscow, she took charge of the editorial arrangements for bringing out the *Moscow Daily News* (originally, in 1930, the *Moscow News*, a weekly), designed in the first place for the benefit of American workers in Russia. In 1932 she married Joel Shubin, a Russian.

She had published her first book in 1906, but it was only with the earliest of her numerous books on Russia, *The First Time in History*, which appeared in 1924, that she attracted notice. At once lively and uncritical, naive and independent, her views and observations on Russia were seldom without value and were often genuinely informative. A book of hers of considerable historical value, though it presents a flagrantly one-sided narrative, is *China's Millions* (1928), in which she gave an eye-witness account of the events which culminated in the explusions of Borodin and his advisers by Chiang Kai-shek.

March 30, 1970.

Sir Barnett Stross, Parliamentary Secretary to the Ministry of Health in the 1964 Labour Government, died on May 13, 1967, in University College Hospital London. He was 67. In July, 1965, he announced he would not be contesting the next general election on health grounds.

He was often described as the "unpaid medical practitioner" for the House of Commons because for almost 20 years he had been called on there to attend emergency cases—fellow M. P.s, policemen, and members of the public. Labour M. P. for the Hanley Division from 1945 to 1950, and for Stoke-on-Trent Central from 1950, Stross, who was knighted in the New Year Honours of 1964, was an authority on industrial diseases.

Born in 1899, Barnett Stross was brought to Britain by his Polish parents, political refugees, at the end of the First World War. After taking his medical degrees at Leeds, he started practice in the Potteries in 1926. In 1928 Dr. Stross touched the fringe of medico-politics when he appeared for the Pottery workers before a committee of inquiry into silicosis. Soon afterwards a Bill was passed giving compensation to sufferers from the disease. The pneumoconiosis benefit scheme (1952) and later remedial measures owed much to the persistent campaigning he carried out.

Stross became honorary medical adviser to the Pottery Workers' Society and the North Staffs Miners' Federation. He joined the Labour Party in 1930 and from 1937 gave many years, service to local government as a member, later an Alderman, of Stoke-on-Trent City Council. In the Commons his special interests included industrial health, arts and amenities. He was particularly concerned with problems of nutrition and warned against the danger of lung cancer through smoking.

During the Second World War a lecture by Stross for the Ministry of Food was interrupted by a direct hit and he was extracted from the rubble seriously injured. He was chairman of the Labour Party's art and amenity group, and was the founder of the movement which rebuilt Lidice, the Czech mining village destroyed by the Germans in a mass-murder in 1942. He was honoured by the Czechoslovakian Government.

Stross was made a member of the Historic Buildings Council in 1963. Married in 1922, his wife died in 1961 and, in 1963, he married Miss Gwendolen Chesters, a psychologist and a Children's Home Inspector.

May 15, 1967.

Herbert Strudwick, who died on February 13, 1970, at the age of 90, was one of the greatest and assuredly one of the most popular wicket-keepers of the twentieth century. In a first class professional career dating from 1902 to 1927, he established two world's wicket-keeping records which still stand—his total of 1,493 dismissals (71 in Test matches) and his 1,235 catches. In 1903 he set up another record of 91 victims (71 caught, 20 stumped) in a season, which held good till 1911.

For 25 years Strudwick figured regularly behind the stumps for Surrey, which he served as player and then scorer for 60 years: he appeared in 28 Tests for England between 1911 and 1926 at a time when Australia and South Africa were the sole opponents and would have gained more "caps" had he not been contemporary for a number of his early years with A. A. ("Dick") Lilley, of Warwickshire, the "man in possession" and a better batsman. He toured Australia in 1911-12, 1920-21 and 1924-25 and South Africa in 1909-10 and 1913-14. Additionally he often appeared for Players v. Gentlemen.

EXPOSED TO INJURY

One of the idols of the Surrey crowd, he was always ready to proffer helpful and kindly advice to young players. He never appealed unless certain in his own mind that a batsman was out and his keenness was such that he was often known to chase a ball to the boundary.

In an article, "From Dr. Grace to Peter May", in the 1959 *Wisden*, which was hailed by the critics as one of the best published by "The Cricketers' Bible" for many years, "Struddy" described how hard life was as a professional in his young days, when one dared not stand down through injury for fear of losing a place in the side. Wicket-keepers took a lot of punishment, for their equipment was flimsy compared with that of today and pitches less perfect so that it was difficult to gauge how the ball would come to them. Fred Stedman, Strudwick's predecessor in the Surrey team, used to protect his chest with a copy of the South Western Railway time-table stuffed into his shirt, and once, after receiving a specially heavy blow, he remarked to a team-mate: "I shall have to catch a later train to-night. That one knocked off the 7.30."

Though not regarded as much of a batsman, he hit 93—easily his highest innings—from the Essex bowling at the Oval in 1913, he and H.S. Harrison putting on 134 for the eighth wicket. He also distinguished himself during the tour of the J. W. H. T. Douglas's team in 1920-21 by playing innings of 21 not out and 24 in the second Test match.

February 16, 1970.

Hussein Shaheed Suhrawardy, a former Prime Minister of Pakistan and last chief minister of Bengal before partition in August, 1947, died in Beirut on December 5, 1963, at the age of 70. He was a man of outstanding personality and intelligence who played an always colourful and often highly dextrous role in the politics of Pakistan and pre-independence India.

A son of the late Sir Zahid Suhrawardy, judge of the Calcutta High Court, he was born at Madnapur in 1893, and educated at Calcutta, at the *Madrassah* (a Muslim institution) and St. Xavier's school and college. At Oxford he took honours in jurisprudence, won political economy and political science diplomas, gained the degrees of M.A. and B.C.L., and was then called to the Bar by Gray's Inn. On his return to India he practised in the Calcutta High Court.

When the Calcutta Corporation was given greatly enhanced power by an Act passed in 1923, the city's first mayor was the late C. R. Das, whose preoccupation with wider politics led him to leave municipal matters very much in the hands of Suhrawardy, his deputy, and the late Subhas Chandra Bose, who was the chief executive officer. Suhrawardy remained active in nationalist politics and, in 1937, when provincial autonomy came into force, he was elected to the new Bengal Assembly and given four ministerial portfolios—Finance, Public Health, Local Self-Government, and Labour. In 1943 Suhrawardy, as the minister responsible, was called upon to tackle an acute food shortage. There were formidable obstacles, but his actions and those of the Bengal government itself were later severely criticized by the Bengal Famine Commission.

COMMUNAL RIOTS

In the spring of 1946 he became the chief minister of a Muslim League administration after failing to form a coalition ministry. It was a period of considerable communal disorder which finally led to the "great Calcutta killing", as it was afterwards known, of August 1946. During the troubled time of partition in 1947 he gave courageous support to Mahatma Gandhi. Then he lived with Gandhi in a Calcutta slum in order to emphasize the need for Hindu-Muslim forgiveness and friendship.

Suhrawardy, though a member of the All-India Muslim League Working Committee—the executive of the movement—gave the impression as India moved towards independence that he hoped to make Bengal an independent state after the departure of the British. It is not probable that he seriously considered such a thing could come about, and it is more likely that he was trying to reinforce his bargaining position with the Muslim League leader, Jinnah, with whom he was on bad terms. Nevertheless, when partition came, Jinnah chose Kwaja Nazimuddin, not Suhrawardy, to be the first premier of the newly created state of East Bengal.

For a time after independence Suhrawardy stayed in West Bengal, apparently undecided whether to remain in India or to go to Pakistan. His decision, however, was for Pakistan and in 1949 he formed the Jinnah Awami League, the main support for which he found in East Bengal, although he was in close touch with politicians in west Pakistan and with tribal and religious leaders in the north-west frontier districts. He promised many reforms. In 1954 he was asked to join the central cabinet and accepted the office of Law Minister. But his ambition was to be prime minister. In August, 1955, it seemed likely that he would be asked to form an administration, but it was not until September of the following year that the call finally came. With the slogan "good will to all and malice towards none", Suhrawardy promised a new and dynamic policy. Though, out of office, he had advocated a sort of Nehru-style neutralism, he now became a strong partisan of Seato. He was, however, independent enough to be the first prime minister of a Seato country to visit Peking, where he went a month after taking office.

In October, 1957, the coalition which he led collapsed, mainly because of the activities of the National Awami Party, a splinter group of his own organization. Suhrawardy offered his resignation and it was accepted, though he was convinced that he could have formed a new administration.

OUT OF PUBLIC LIFE

When the Pakistan army took over the government in 1958 all political parties were banned and the new government sought to bring political leaders to trial. In February, 1960, Suhrawardy was warned that he must either retire from political life for six years or face charges of misconduct. Characteristically, he chose to fight, but in July he was found guilty and debarred from public life. He was still, however, a most popular public figure and did everything he could to embarrass the administration of President Ayub Khan until, in January, 1962, he was arrested and sentenced to 12 months' imprisonment for activities which were allegedly endangering the security of the country. When news of his arrest became public there were outbreaks of rioting, especially in East Bengal. Suhrawardy's internment, made not too uncomfortable by an air-conditioned cell, ended in August, 1962, when the government permitted the resumption of political activity. He became one of the leaders of the new National Democratic Front, whose principal demand was for the restoration of the parliamentary system. He stumped the country, drawing large crowds wherever he appeared. His activities upset the government so much that he was even made the subject of a bitter personal attack by the President. Undaunted, Suhrawardy continued his campaign, but in January, 1963, he was taken seriously ill with a heart complaint and was later compelled to go to Europe for medical treatment. He was convalescing in Lebanon at the time of his death.

He was an immensely hard worker with a strong flair for personal publicity. His office was his bedroom, and visitors sat upon a spare bed loaded with files and papers. He loved Western dancing, at which he was expert, and was often to be seen at night clubs. Against the rather grey background of his fellow politicians, Suhrawardy stood out as a flamboyant and rather lonely figure. Pakistani political life will certainly be the drabber for the passing of this colourful personality.

December 6, 1963.

Achmad Sukarno, the first president of the Indonesian Republic, who died on June 21, 1970, was one of those Asian leaders commonly labelled "charismatic" by western writers. He might better be described in terms of the people who adored him as an exponent of Javanese magic.

Undoubtedly his gifts were of the kind needed to hold together a developing nation after the colonial era had ended. He was the father of his people and by many of them was unquestionably accepted as such. He saw himself as the epitome of Asian nationalism and stepped forth whenever this part was called for. In going too far as a potential leader of what he dubbed the "new emerging forces of the post-imperial era" he ran into difficulties. He was much taken up by the Chinese and was drawn more and more into the reading of the world's future prescribed by Mao Tse-tung, a leader with much more substance and foresight. Besides this dubious and in the event fatal attachment Sukarno's most bombastic claims for the new emerging forces began to be made just at the time when scepticism about these countries was beginning to spread in the world at large.

The result was the speedy deflation of Sukarno's image once the first prick had begun to let the air out. The incident which did this was the abortive *coup* in Indonesia on October 1, 1965. It was not a *coup* of Sukarno's doing. It was not even a *coup* of the Indonesian Communist Party's (P.K.I) doing. It was a rising by a few colonels and brigadiers who thought they were ensuring the alliance between the P.K.I. and the President to which Sukarno seemed to be tending. In the event both Sukarno and Aidit (the P.K.I. leader) were seized by the leaders of the *coup* with the aim of aligning them with its purposes. The failure of the *coup* destroyed Sukarno's career as it destroyed, in the most appalling massacre of the postwar period, the P.K.I. and Aidit himself among many other communist leaders.

For some time after the *coup* Sukarno remained in office in a vain attempt to fudge over his damaged reputation. Only at one moment early in 1966 did it seem he might recover his power by skilfully dividing his opponents and using the mass following which was only slowly ebbing away from him. But in March, 1966, the new ruling group under General Suharto exacted the surrender of his powers.

Even then Sukarno denied that anything final had happened, hoping to retain his office and his prestige. At length, after clashes in some Javanese towns between supporters and opponents of the President, Sukarno once again, but this time with indisputable finality, surrendered all his powers to General Suharto at the end of February, 1967.

INDONESIA'S MAKING

For most of his years in office Sukarno's magic worked; his popularity was not spurious or managed. Certainly Indonesia owed much to Sukarno in that 100 million people, scattered over disparate islands, should have found as much in common as they did, or have been swayed as they were by his endless speechmaking. Undoubtedly he held Indonesia together; most strongly after the success with which the Army suppressed the rebellion of 1958, centred in Sumatra but taking its character from a more pro-western and anti-communist attitude than Sukarno would accept. Like others who had served long in the nationalist ranks, what mattered most was the nationalist mystique of the kind that attached to Nehru or to Nasser. Much more than these or any other nationalists Sukarno had to have enemies. For the early years of the republic it was the unwillingly departing colonialists, the Dutch, an enmity specially prolonged by the struggle over West Irian. When this was finally handed over with the aid of American mediation and the sanction of the United Nations Sukarno settled on another issue—the "confrontation" of Malaysia—an issue which brought him into direct conflict with Britain and turned him even more into an inveterate anti-colonialist.

It was during the 1960s that Sukarno began to play more of a world role. The Chinese found Indonesia useful as a base of anti-western propaganda and organization. Sukarno himself veered steadily more and more towards a Chinese view of political change.

He was not an administrator. Financial and economic matters bored him. As in many other newly emergent countries a period of parliamentary rule led to a succession of weak governments with which Sukarno tried to interfere. Gradual estrangement between right and left—represented by the Muslim Masjumi Party and the Socialists on the one hand and the powerful Communist Party on the other—led to a crisis in 1958. Sukarno had at this time proposed to introduce what he called "guided democracy", and this he proceeded to do after the remarkable speed and success with which the rebellion collapsed.

In 1959, the 1945 Constitution was brought back, a consititution giving greater powers to the President. Although the Constituent Assembly which had been sitting for some years refused its approval for this move, Sukarno had no difficulty in dissolving it and proceeding with his plans. Only those parties which supported the old constitution were permitted to continue and the elected Parliament was replaced by a nominated body representing different social groups. Aided by a picked Advisory Council Sukarno restored his own authority at the apex of a triangle of which the other two carefully balanced forces were the Communists and the Army.

Born in 1901, Sukarno soon showed great aptitude for engineering, and before he had graduated from the university he seemed destined for a promising career in the Dutch service. But in the course of his career through the university his enthusiasm for politics led him to make a serious study of the nationalist movement in India, and he formed a high opinion of the value of the techniques of non-cooperation, at that time being practised by Mahatma Gandhi, as a weapon for securing the freedom of Indonesia from Dutch rule. In 1927 he founded the National Party, and at the end of 1929 he experienced his first taste of imprisonment. Again in 1937 he was interned in the island of Flores, and, later, in South Sumatra. He was still exiled from Java when the Japanese overran the Netherlands Indies.

The Japanese released him in 1942, and he agreed to work along with them. His conduct at this time was severely criticized by some of his countrymen; but there can be little doubt that he looked upon the Japanese expulsion of Dutch authority as an important step towards Indonesian freedom, and it was with Japanese assent that on August 17, 1945, he proclaimed jointly with Dr. Hatta, the independence of Indonesia.

June 22, 1970.

Shaikh Sulman bin Hamed Alkhalifah, K.C.M.G., K.C.I.E., the tenth of the Khalifan dynasty to rule Bahrain, died on November 2, 1961 at the age of 67.

Shaikh Sulman succeeded in February, 1942. His father had appointed him as his successor two years before, though the appointment was not made public until the time of his succession. During the 20 years of his reign Bahrain developed under Shaikh Sulman's wise rule from an obscure and comparatively poor Arab State into a place of considerable importance and wealth, although the oil field which supplied most of the revenue is the smallest and least productive in the Persian Gulf.

The Shaikh spent most of the State's revenue on social services and public works, on hospitals and the eradication of malaria, houses for workers, roads, harbours and schools. Bahrain was the first State in the Gulf to provide education for girls. But although Shaikh Sulman modernized the structure of the administration—introducing such features as public councils, a labour law and village development schemes—the growth of education and foreign travel brought with it a certain amount of political unrest which culminated in disorders in 1956, but since then Bahrain has progressed quietly.

Shaikh Sulman possessed the fine qualities of an Arab gentleman. He was generous, courteous and a strict Muslim, but at the same time broad minded towards other religions. He gave valuable land in Manama, the capital, to the Anglican and Catholic communities on which churches were built. He had a shrewd knowledge of men and an aptitude for diplomacy. He was interested in politics and conversant with the happenings in all parts of the Arab world. He was actively concerned in all the developments which were carried out by his Government and would visit sites of new public works and examine with care the maps and plans. The Shaikh was at all times accessible to any of his subjects who wished to petition him; strangers were often surprised when some Arab of no particular importance walked into the Shaikh's audience chamber and engaged him in conversation.

Shaikh Sulman lived plainly in an unostentatious Arab style and did not adopt European dress or habits, although he approved of the modernization of his State and the introduction of Western methods in the schools.

His eldest son, Shaikh Isa bin Sulman, at the age of 28, succeeds to the Shaikhdom, having been publicly appointed Heir Apparent in 1958.

November 3, 1961.

Arthur Hays Sulzberger, chairman of the Board of the *New York Times* since 1957, and publisher of the newspaper for 26 years until 1961 (when his son-in-law Orvil E. Dryfoos succeeded him) died on December 11, 1968, at the age of 77. Sulzberger himself succeeded his father-in-law, Adolph Ochs, in 1935.

During his period as publisher the sale and influence of the *New York Times* expanded remarkably. During the Second World War, Sulzberger was a staunch friend of Britain and saw the growing evils of Nazism before many other newspapermen. The *New York Times* was to become the most stalwart appraiser in American journalism of the British effort.

Sulzberger's deep interest in peace and foreign policy were often dominating influences in the choice of political candidates. Although he felt closer to the liberal internationalist Republicans than to other political groups, party loyalty did not prevent him from backing the candidates he believed best-fitted to promote international understanding. He was to back the late President Kennedy in 1960. The paper was criticized for its comments on the way President Johnson conducted the Vietnam war. In 1963, his son Arthur Ochs Sulzberger became president and publisher of the newspaper.

Arthur Hays Sulzberger, a man of the most deceptive quiet, and mild in manner, was a leading figure among newspaper proprietors in the United States. He did not want the *New York Times* to get too livened up either in Paris or New York. "The good grey Times" he was once reported as saying. "It's done well by that reputation. It's still the best there is." He was determined that the newspaper should continue in the traditions of Adolph Ochs, his father-in-law, who bought the paper as a dying duck and dramatically revived its fortunes with his famous policy of "All the news that's fit to print." Sulzberger spread the circulation of the *New York Times* first throughout the United States and then throughout the world. In his farewell speech when he resigned as publisher he charged the paper to carry on "as an independent newspaper, entirely fearless, free of ulterior influence, and unselfishly devoted to the public welfare without regard to individual advantage or ambition, the claims of party politics, or the voice of religious or personal prejudice or predilection" in the words of his father-in-law's will.

Sulzberger pressed constantly for clearer, more concise, sharper writing, better classification and display of news, and more pictorial reporting. He greatly expanded the *New York Times'* staff, adding foreign and national correspondents, experts in labour, education and science news and other specialists.

Sulzberger once defined his role as publisher as primarily "picking associates and working with them in harmony—talking things out and, on many occasions, being willing to give way rather than to give orders".

Sulzberger never imposed his opinions on the *New York Times* editorial board and never asked that a man write an editorial with which he disagreed. Sometimes he wrote editorials himself, and sometimes wrote letters to the editor and verse that was published under the pen name A. Aitchess (A. H. S.).

CHECK ON PAGES

Sulzberger delegated authority freely, but maintained close touch with details. He kept a small black, gold-cornered pad on which he jotted down innumerable notes about good or bad points in headlines, stories and the like. Often he would eat breakfast in bed, checking and rechecking every page in the *New York Times* and listening to news and music on its radio station, WQXR.

Sulzberger did as much as any man of his day to enhance the good name of journalism in the United States. He had in his own country the reputation of a safe man, who, avoiding extremes in any direction, believed in the wisdom of moderation; but he was none the less firm in principle; and his opinions were invariably based on the deepest and most careful deliberation.

Serious, cool-headed and above all else conscientious, he had a profound sense of the responsibilities of his position, and at all times did his utmost to fulfil them worthily.

Arthur Hays Sulzberger was born in New York City on September 12, 1891, the son of Cyrus L. Sulzberger by his marriage with Rachal Peixotto Hays. He came of an old and respected Jewish family. He was educated at the De Witt Clinton and Horace Mann high schools in the city of his birth and went on to Columbia University, where in 1913 he obtained the degree of Bachelor of Science. He then started work in the cotton goods business with the New York firm of N. Erlanger Blumgart and Company.

In August, 1917, Sulzberger was commissioned as a second lieutenant in the Field Artillery, first Plattsburg Camp, and in the same year married Miss Iphigene B. Ochs, only and beloved child of the late Adolph Ochs, the owner of the *New York Times*.

MARRIED OWNER'S DAUGHTER

Adolph Ochs was in his day one of the most remarkable and successful newspaper proprietors in the United States. He had acquired control of his great daily at a period when its fortunes were at a low ebb and by business ability and journalistic flair had raised it to the position of one of the greatest journals of the world. After his marriage Sulzberger formed a relationship with his father-in-law which was virtually that of a son and heir. In 1919 he joined the staff of the *New York Times* and passing through all its departments, gained an intimate knowledge of the newspaper business. Ochs, who was an extremely active proprietor, kept a firm hand on his paper, and used to travel widely in order to supervise its correspondents and to keep himself in direct touch with developments abroad. He was therefore an ideal mentor for his son-in-law and, profiting by his precepts and examples, Sulzberger was in due course to fit himself for the great position which was in store for him.

On the death of Ochs in 1935 Sulzberger, who was already a director of the *New York Times,* succeeded to its presidency and proprietorship. It was a position which he was admirably qualified both by his disposition and his training to fill. So completely had he shared the views and outlook of his father-in-law that there were no breaks with its established traditions of independence, exactitude and trustworthiness. Any change, indeed, that there was seemed to be in the direction of a greater freedom in judgment and, in 1940, this went so far that the *New York Times* ranged itself in opposition to Roosevelt on the question of the third term.

BREAK WITH TRADITION

In February, 1952, the *New York Times* came out for General Eisenhower, thereby breaking a tradition of never supporting a candidate until after the nominating conventions. Sulzberger had formed a high regard for the General in wartime and had been influential in his appointment to the presidency of Columbia University of which the publisher was a trustee.

Sulzberger's support of President Eisenhower, however, was not without qualification and his most serious disappointment with the candidate arose over the late Senator Joseph R. McCarthy, Wisconsin Republican. Sulzberger urged General Eisenhower to go on record against "McCarthyism" and especially against the Senator's attack on General George C. Marshall whom both Sulzberger and General Eisenhower held in the highest esteem.

At General Eisenhower's invitation, Sulzberger drafted a pro-Marshall statement the President proposed to deliver as part of a speech in the Senator's home state. The statement, however, was deleted from the address because it displeased Wisconsin Republican leaders. Later, in another campaign, President Eisenhower voiced the pro-Marshall remarks but Sulzberger remained deeply disappointed because the candidate had surrendered to political pressures.

The continued threats to civil liberties and the post-war menace of Soviet imperialism and communism led Sulzberger to establish a firm policy for the *New York Times*. At that time he said: "I would not knowingly employ a communist on the news or editorial staff of the *New York Times*. On the other hand. I would not institute a witch hunt to determine if one such existed."

The *New York Times* considered itself the special victim of such a "witch hunt" through an investigation in 1955-56 conducted by Senator James O. Eastland, Mississippi Democrat. He called it a study of communist infiltration of the press, but a large majority of those he summoned were employees or former employees of the *New York Times*.

STAND TAKEN

Concerned by the turn the investigation had taken, Sulzberger cooperated with the Senator and discharged several men, but early in 1956 the *New York Times* took a stand. It charged that it had been singled out for attack because it opposed Senator Eastland's views. On the question of former communists on its staff, the *New York Times* said it would judge each case on its merits.

Sulzberger possessed charm both of appearance and manner. He could be a most intelligent and engaging conversationalist. Although greatly engrossed in the affairs of the *New York Times* he had many other important interests. He was a trustee of the Rockefeller Foundation, of the Baron de Hirsch Fund, the Congregation of Emanu-El, and the Carnegie Institute of Technology, and trustee emeritus of the New York Foundation. He was also a member of the executive committee of the Union of American Hebrew Congregations and the Welfare Council of New York. His sincere interest in Great Britain led him, moreover, to become a Director of the British War Relief Society.

December 12, 1968.

Bernard Sunley, who died of a heart attack on November 21, 1964, at the age of 54, belonged to that dynamic breed of postwar entrepreneurs who from small beginnings managed to amass a fortune early in life and latterly gave freely to a number of charities. Best known in his later years as a property developer both in Britain and overseas, Sunley made his start in life by what he used to call himself "muck-shifting"—the simple non-technical way with a pony and cart. Eventually, after a short interlude in the landscape gardening business, it was earth-moving which brought him the fortune he later employed and multiplied in the property world.

His earth-moving interests were through Blackwood Hodge, a public company of which Sunley was chairman until his death. This acted as agents for, among other products, the Euclid division of General Motors, Cummins Diesel, and other United States groups and the oil engine division of Rolls-Royce. Sunley's property holdings were vested in the Bernard Sunley Investiment Trust, now a group with total assets of £33m. The company was publicly floated in 1959. In January, 1961, Eagle Star Insurance acquired a one-third stake in the trust whose development projects range from office blocks in the City and West End to flats, hotels and shops in the Bahamas.

Sunley was well known for his many gifts to charity and had given about £500,000 in the past year. In February he gave £100,000 to Gordonstoun for a new house which would allow the school to open its sixth form to boys from grammar and technical schools. This followed other £100,000 gifts to the Hertford British Hospital in Paris and to St. Catherine's College, Oxford, and £50,000 to Balliol College, Oxford. Boys' clubs, churches, and an organization for treating alcoholics were among other recipients of gifts of many thousands of pounds at the beginning of 1964.

Among his other interests Sunley was a racehorse owner. One of his horses, Slippery Serpent, started as third favourite in the 1959 Grand National but fell at the thirteenth fence and had to be destroyed.

In his thirties he thought of giving up business for politics. He stood as Conservative candidate for Ealing West in 1945 but was defeated.

November 23, 1964.

The Duke of Sutherland, K.T., P.C., died on February 1, 1963, at the age of 74.

George Granville Sutherland-Leveson-Gower, 5th Duke of Sutherland in the peerage of the United Kingdom, Marquess of Stafford, Earl Gower, Viscount Trentham in that of Great Britain, 23rd Earl of Sutherland and Baron Strathnaver in the peerage of Scotland, Baron Gower in that of England, and a Baronet, was born on August 29, 1888. He was the eldest of the three children of the 4th Duke and Millicent, daughter of the 4th Earl of Rosslyn, who was renowned for her beauty, wit and gifts as a hostess. The happiest of Sutherland's early days were those spent at his Scottish home, Dunrobin. He was educated at Summerfields and Eton and then "crammed for the Army". After some service in the Lovat Scouts, he was commissioned to the Scots Greys in 1909.

Sutherland did not stay in the Army for long, because his keen interest in politics was influenced by the defeat of Lochiel in Sutherland by some 1,600 votes in the first general election of 1910. This made Sutherland determined to try his own fortune at the second election. He put everything into the fight and reduced the adverse majority to 187. Owing to his father's death he never, to his deep regret, sat in the Commons, for he succeeded to the Dukedom in 1913. Before that in 1912 he married Lord Lanesborough's daughter, Lady Eileen Butler, who became a most popular figure in Sutherland. It was typical of Sutherland's delight in big-game hunting, which he had already tried in Canada, Africa, and India, and which became an equal pleasure of his wife, that in the same year, 1912, they went on the first of 30 such journeys, on this occasion to East Africa. On his succession he became Lord Lieutenant of Sutherland.

LLOYD GEORGE CONTROVERSY

It was also in 1913 that the 25-year-old duke became a national figure by engaging in controversy with Lloyd George. The latter had said in a vitriolic speech at Swindon: "Tens of thousands of people are turned out of their homes in order to get sport", adding that it was his own objective to repopulate the glens, reafforest the hillsides, and bring the wasted acres under cultivation. Sutherland endeavoured to expose the baselessness of Lloyd George's allegations by writing to the press offering to sell the Government 200,000 acres at £2 an acre. Lloyd George, after holding an inquiry, rejected the proposal on the ground that the land was not worth the price. Therefore Sutherland offered him double the acreage at about half the price, but again he declined. There was an acrimonious correspondence which produced cartoons which caused a great deal of discussion and amusement at the time and after which little more was heard about the misdeeds of plutocratic landlords. It is an interesting commentary that within a few years Lloyd George and his one-time opponent had become friends, Sutherland serving as a junior Minister in the coalition Government, and through Lloyd George receiving the appointment of Lord High Commissioner to the Church of Scotland.

When the 1914-18 War came, Sutherland offered to lend to the Admiralty for the duration of the war his yacht Catania, and he in turn was offered her command with a commission as Commander, R.N.R. He served first in the Moray Firth and then, after a spell in the British Military Commission to the King of the Belgians, in the Mediterranean and Adriatic mainly on anti-submarine work. At the end of the war he was duty captain at the Admiralty.

In the postwar period he returned to politics by the classic approach of a young peer in a favourable financial position and without the calls on his time and the two-way urging of local problems that a constituency brings. He raised Highland problems in the House of Lords. He became Chancellor of the Primrose League. In addition, however, he became President of the Navy League and also of the Air League, the work of which fed and maintained his abiding interest in flying. He was also actively associated with many voluntary associations for social work. He enjoyed immensely being Lord High Commissioner to the General Assembly of the Church of Scotland, and also being appointed spokesman for the Colonial Office in the House of Lords in June of 1921.

ENTHUSIASM FOR THE AIR

Bonar Law offered him, to his delight, the post of Under-Secretary for Air under Sir Samuel Hoare. Sutherland's enthusiasm was immediately demonstrated by a speech in which he prophesied in glowing words the further progress of flight, and also by his giving a personal prize of £500 for a competition for light aircraft.

After the general election of 1923 Sutherland did not return to office until 1925 and he filled the intervening time by making another unavailing effort for the reform of the House of Lords by the introduction of life peers—a reform which did not come about for another 33 years. Another more successful object of his strong support at this time was the National Playing Fields Association.

In 1925 Baldwin offered him the office of Paymaster General, which he held for three years. He was glad, however, to be moved in 1928 to the post of Under-Secretary for War, where other members of the team were Worthington Evans and Duff-Cooper.

Sutherland, who had been given the Thistle in 1929, was made a Privy Councillor in 1936. In the same year he was offered by King Edward VIII and accepted the Court appointment of Lord Steward of His Majesty's Household. He bore the Orb at the Coronation of King George VI.

His first wife died in 1943, and in 1944 he married Mrs. Claire Dunkerley, daughter of Herbert O'Brien, who survives him. In 1945 he was elected a county councillor for Sutherland, and showed a great interest in arresting the decline of the population of the county which had by that time become reduced to 13,000. In his autobiography, *Looking Back,* he wrote movingly of the wearisome and unrewarding business of trying ever since 1913 to get successive governments to take a more practical and realistic interest in the Highlands.

It is true that Sutherland to the end enjoyed a life of, in the now criticized sense, gracious living. To leave it there would be, however, to ignore two features of his character which were very apparent to his friends, a genuine and wide-ranging desire to serve, and an enthusiasm for his causes which retained its boyish quality well into his seventies.

The Scottish earldom of Sutherland and barony of Strathnaver are inherited by his niece, Elizabeth, who married in 1946 Captain Charles Noel Janson, Welsh Guards. The dukedom and other titles pass to his kinsman, Lord Ellesmere.

February 2, 1963.

Set Svanholm, leading Wagnerian tenor of the postwar decade and formerly director of the Swedish Royal Opera, died on October 4, 1964, at the age of 60.

Set Karl Viktor Svanholm was born in Västerås in 1904; until he entered the Stockholm Conservatory in 1927 he had been an organist, choir trainer, and schoolmaster. He made his operatic debut as a baritone in 1930 at the Swedish Royal Opera, and from 1932 appeared there regularly. From 1936, however, he sang as a tenor and soon established himself as a leading interpreter of the Wagnerian roles. He appeared only twice at Bayreuth but was internationally in great demand, especially as Tristan and Siegfried. He made his Covent Garden debut in the latter role (in *Siegfried*) in November, 1948; subsequently in one *Ring* cycle there he appeared as Loge, Siegmund, and both Siegfrieds, and he had also sung Lohengrin, Walther (in *Meistersinger*) and Tristan at the Royal Opera House. His repertory was by no means confined to Wagner, and indeed was very large: in his home country, at the New York Metropolitan Opera, and in many European opera houses he had appeared in such roles as Florestan, Otello and Radames (and Eisenstein, in English, at a Metropolitan *Die Fledermaus*), while he sang the title role in the Swedish premiere of *Peter Grimes*.

It was for his unusual sensitivity, his keen musical intelligence, and his dramatic insight rather than sheer beauty of voice or heroic stature that Svanholm was so highly esteemed. His reading of Siegfried's Narration in *Götterdämmerung* (which is to be heard on the recording with Kirsten Flagstad, taken from a radio performance) was of particularly high repute. His most recent recordings were of Loge's and Siegmund's parts in the Decca *Das Rheingold* and *Die Walküre* under Georg Solti and Hans Knappertsbusch. As a lieder singer, particularly of the Schubert cycles, he was also noted. From 1956 until 1963 Svanholm was director of the Swedish Royal Opera: in this capacity he visited Edinburgh and London with the company in 1960, singing the role of Erik in *The Flying Dutchman*. He pursued a notably artistic policy, intorducing to Stockholm many contemporary operas (including *The Rape of Lucrctia*, *The Turn of the Screw*, *Mathis der Maler*, *The Rake's Progress* and works by Orff and others) as well as encouraging native talent and reviving such neglected operas as Berlioz's *The Trojans* and Handel's *Alcina*.

October 6, 1964.

The death in a London hospital on January 16, 1962, of **Hannen Swaffer** at the age of 82 removed from the world of journalism one of its best known characters and one of the few survivors of the period in the early days of the century when Lord Northcliffe was moulding the popular newspapers as one knows them today.

"Swaff" was a man of great personality who had friends in all walks of life. He was the champion of many causes from socialism to spiritualism; he was, perhaps, the founder of the modern gossip column; and he was a dramatic critic whose forthright opinions brought him both friends and enemies. His striking appearance with his black hat, sombre clothes, high collar and cravat, and flowing locks made him an outstanding figure in any company.

A POSEUR

But at the same time he was something of a *poseur* who liked to be recognized by the public, and it is possible that few things gave him greater pleasure than to greet and be greeted by his friends at the entrance to the Savoy Grill. Towards the end of his long life he delighted in recalling his adventures in Fleet Street and in telling anecdotes of Lord Northcliffe, Lord Beaverbrook and other newspaper proprietors under whom he had worked. The affection in which he was held was shown by three remarkable gatherings—a luncheon given to him by the Variety Club in 1953 to mark his 50 years in Fleet Street; the celebration of his seventy-fifth birthday a year later when he spoke for just over an hour and rambled over his journalistic life; and a similar function for his eightieth birthday in 1959.

Hannen Swaffer was born at Lindfield, Sussex, on November 1, 1879, and came from a long line of Kentish yeomen farmers. He began his education at Stroud Green and, as he said, continued it in Fleet Street. He started his journalistic career as an apprentice reporter at Folkestone at a weekly wage of five shillings.

BANNED

His first assignment was to criticize a performance by George Grossmith at the local town hall. He expressed his views in the dramatic criticisms so frankly that at the age of 18 he was banned from the Folkestone theatre and in later life he boasted that he had been banned from 12 of the 41 theatres which then stood in London's West End. It was during his Folkestone days that he read Blatchford's *Merrie England* and thereafter he remained an unchanging Socialist. He had further experience in provincial journalism before joining the staff of the *Daily Mail* in 1902. For the next 17 years he worked on papers controlled by Northcliffe, who always referred to him as "The Poet". For a period he was editor of the *Weekly Dispatch* but his most successful achievement was his work for the *Daily Mirror*, which had been founded as a paper for women by Northcliffe. Helped by Swaffer's flair for knowing what the public wanted he transformed it into a brilliantly successful picture paper. In 1913 Swaffer began to write an attractive gossip column in the *Daily Sketch* and next joined the *Daily Graphic*, where his "Mr. London" page became a leading feature. In 1924 he was appointed editor of *The People* but he was not born to occupy the editorial chair.

In 1926 "Swaff" was appointed dramatic critic of the *Daily Express* and the *Sunday Express* and his forthright views quickly brought him into the limelight. Some theatrical managers felt that he did not do their productions justice and barred him from their playhouses. But reconciliation generally followed.

FRONT SEAT

For many years "Swaff" lived in a flat overlooking Trafalgar Square in order, he used to say, to have a front seat when the revolution came. It was a sad blow to him when a new building development forced him to find a new home in the suburbs, which did not suit the temperament of a man who had spent so much of his long life in central London.

The death of his wife in 1956 was a grievous blow, and, although his energy continued unabated, he seemed to his friends to lose some of his old fire and enthusiasm.

January 17, 1962.

Gladys Swarthout, the American mezzo-soprano, died at her villa in Florence in July, 1969, at the age of 64. She had a long career as one of America's leading operatic singers, starred in several films, and played the title role in the televised opera *Carmen*.

Born at Deepwater, Missouri, on Christmas Day, 1904, she had a large and mature voice at an early age. At 13, giving her age as 19, she won an audition for an alto solo post in a Kansas City church. During her first song recital she attracted the attention of a rich Kansas City family and they paid for her further musical training. Her operatic debut took place during the 1924–25 season of the Chicago Civic Opera as the off-stage shepherd in *Tosca*. She sang with this company and the Ravinia Opera Company until 1929 when she was engaged by the New York Metropolitan. Among her principal parts with the Metropolitan were Carmen, Mignon and Adalgisa in *Norma*. She also created leading parts in the first productions of Deems Taylor's *Peter Ibbetson* and of *Merry Mount* by Howard Hanson. She made her first radio broadcast in 1930 in the General Motors Hour. In the mid-1930s she was taken up by Hollywood. This was the period of the "operatic invasion": Grace Moore was starred in *One Night of Love*; Lily Pons in *I Dream Too Much*; Nino Martini in *Here's to Romance*; and Nelson Eddy began his famous partnership with Jeanette MacDonald. Gladys Swarthout starred with John Boles in *Rose of the Rancho* and also appeared in *Give Us this Night*, *Champagne Waltz* with Fred MacMurray, and *Ambush*.

She published an autobiography, *Come Soon, Tomorrow*, in 1945. Dark and handsome, she had a most attractive stage presence. Her first husband, Harry Richmond Kern, died in 1931. Her second husband, Frank M. Chapman jr., died in 1966. He was a singer and her manager.

July 10, 1969.

Queen Louise Alexandra Marie Irene of Sweden, a great granddaughter of Queen Victoria, died on March 7, 1965 at the age of 75.

During her 27 years as Crown Princess under the reign of King Gustaf V and since 1950 as consort to King Gustaf Adolf, she was very much concerned with the care of sick children and the disabled in Sweden. In the First World War she worked as an Auxiliary Nurse in the British Red Cross, and in the Second World War she played an important part in the exchange of disabled prisoners through neutral Swedish ports.

Born in Heiligenberg on July 15, 1889, she was the daughter of Prince Louis Alexander of Battenberg and Princess Victoria of Hessen and Rhein. Her father took the name Mountbatten in 1917, when the titles of Earl of Medina and Marquis of Milford Haven were bestowed on him. His daughter was then known as Lady Louise Mountbatten. She was the sister of Earl Mountbatten of Burma and of Princess Andrew of Greece, mother of the Duke of Edinburgh. Much of her childhood was spent in London and Malta. With her mother she visited the Russian court, and in 1914 she visited Sweden for the first time.

During the first World War, Queen Louise nursed in hospitals in France for the British Red Cross. On November 3, 1923, she was married to Crown Prince Gustaf Adolf of Sweden at St. James's Palace, London.

He had five children from his earlier marriage to Princess Margaret of Connaught, who died in 1920. In the family the Queen was never called anything but "Aunt Louise". Her natural modesty led her to shun publicity at first, but after her husband's accession to the throne in 1950 she became well known to the Swedish people through many visits to all parts of the country.

She was well read in English as well as Swedish and supported her husband's promotion of art and archaeological research. Both of them were fond of gardening at their summer residence, Sofiero in Scania.

Her interest in the care of the sick led her to become patron of several large hospitals, and she played a leading part in the organization of the Swedish Red Cross and Sweden's Women's Army Auxiliary Corps. During the Winter War in Finland, when Swedish families took Finnish children into their homes, Queen Louise personally arranged and visited every day a home for 18 children near Ulriksdal Castle, where she and the then Crown Prince were living.

Tall and slim, at official functions the Queen had the reputation of being a most elegant hostess. She personally supervised all entertaining at the Royal Palace in Stockholm. Since their marriage, the King and Queen made many journeys abroad, including a world tour in 1927. They visited England almost every year, often staying with the Queen's brother, Earl Mountbatten.

March 8, 1965.

Raymond Swing, formerly known as Raymond Gram Swing, who died on December 22, 1968, at the age of 81, had a brilliant career in daily journalism before he became a radio commentator. But it was in this latter capacity that he achieved an international reputation, when for 10 years, beginning in 1935, he interpreted American affairs for the British Broadcasting Corporation.

During part of that time he was acting as New York correspondent for the London *News Chronicle*, was a member of the editorial board of the American publication *The Nation*, and a commentator on foreign affairs for the Columbia, Mutual and American broadcasting systems. Later he became political commentator for the Voice of America, but before then he turned for a time to lecturing. He was frequently called upon by the B.B.C. for discussions of events in the United States; in 1958, he reported from Washington on Alaskan statehood.

He was born at Cortland, New York, in 1887 and was educated at Oberlin College which in later years awarded him the degree of Doctor of Letters and elected him a trustee. This was only one of several honorary degrees given him by American colleges and universities. He began newspaper work in Cleveland, Ohio, in 1906, and afterwards was employed by newspapers in Ohio and Indiana. From 1913 to 1917 he was the Berlin correspondent of the *Chicago Daily News*. Then successively, he was the Berlin correspondent of the *New York Herald* director foreign service of the *Wall Street Journal* and director of the London bureau of the *Philadelphia Public Ledger* and *New York Evening Post*.

RADIO "UNCLE SAM"

In the Second World War, when he made four weekly broadcasts from America, his listeners were numbered in millions and he came to be called the "radio Uncle Sam of the United States Government policy". He was described as taking daily news personally, and being strongly affected by any calamity. He had a deep distrust of big business and advertising. He selected for himself what he should discuss in his broadcasts and what he should include in his reports to newspapers. At no time in his 21 years of foreign correspondence, for example, was there any mention in his dispatches of divorce or murder.

His autobiography *Good Evening*! was published in 1965. Swing married four times and had five children.

December 24, 1968.

Randall Swingler, M.M., who died suddenly in London on June 19, 1967, at the age of 58, was poet, librettist, literary editor of the *Daily Worker*, a distinguished athlete, and a flautist of professional standard. He was godson to Archbishop Randall Davidson.

In the Second World War, when his political views made him ineligible for a commission, he twice won the Military Medal, subsequently concealing this fact which he feared might be open to exploitation. He quietly ceased to be a communist shortly before the Hungarian rising of 1956, and for the last 10 years had been a freelance writer and reviewer. His last sequence of poems was recorded for the B.B.C. soon before his death. He was a brother of Stephen Swingler, Parliamentary Secretary, Ministry of Transport.

SUPPRESSION OF "WORKER"

Randall Carline Swingler was born on May 27, 1909. His father was rector of Cranbrook, Kent, and his mother, Randall Davidson's niece. At Winchester, where he was an exhibitioner, he won a Senior Steeplechase. Much against his housemaster's advice, he abolished beating, subsequently leading his house to win a gratifying number of cups, including that for O.T.C. drill. He went on to New College, where he read Greats and got a running blue as a miler; he also represented the university at cross-country.

After leaving Oxford, he became a schoolmaster for some years. By 1936 he had joined the staff of the *Daily Worker*, whose literary editor he became; from 1937 till that monthly came to an end in May, 1938, he was also editor of the *Left Review*. He was present in the offices on the night of the *Daily Worker's* suppression in 1941, and finished the evening at his friend Claud Cockburn's club. In February, 1941, he founded a new monthly magazine, *Our Time*, of which he was an editor and director until he was called up in the winter of 1941–42.

He became a signaller, then a corporal in the 56th Divisional Signals, with whom he served in the Middle East in the closing stages of the Tunisian battles and throughout the Italian campaign from Salerno to Gorizia. It was in North Italy that he was recommended for his awards, and on the southern shores of Lake Comacchio he had his most gruelling experiences.

After the end of the fighting he came into contact with Tito's partisans, and was thus able himself not only to perform his guard duties in partisan uniform but to run up the Red Flag for his unit's victory parade: a feat which would have got him into real trouble but for good covering up by his colleagues.

After demobilization, he joined Edgell Rickword as co-editor of the greatly expanded *Our Time*, which he eventually led out of the Communist Party's orbit; for its last few numbers he was sole editor, writing more freely under the pseudonym "John Arkright". *Our Time* was followed by the pocket magazine *Circus*, which he edited jointly with John Davenport and Paul Hogarth: in its brief life it published Dylan Thomas's "Advice to a Young Poet" and the first English drawings of André François.

He then withdrew to his Essex home, seldom going to London except in connexion with articles or radio scripts.

For a time he worked on a book on the Czech resistance movement, visiting Prague and Lidice for material. He did a certain amount of part-time teaching and examining, and was a valued reviewer for the *Times Literary Supplement*.

WROTE OPERA

He did not publish very much: two novels, *No Escape* (1937) and *To Town* (1939) and four collections of poems, *Reconstruction and Difficult Morning* (both 1933), *The Years of Anger* (1946) and *The God in the Cave* (1950). Nor did his somewhat romantic, Blakean left-wing writing which made his reputation in the 1930s always fully reflect the strength, courage, and originality of his character. He wrote an opera with Christian Darnton for the 1951 Arts Council competition, and co-operated with such other composers as Alan Bush (notably the words to his piano concerto), Benjamin Britten, Alan Rawsthorne, and Bernard Stevens, with most of whom, as also with Constant Lambert, he was close friends. He married a distinguished pianist, Geraldine Peppin, by whom he had a daughter and a son. He had himself played the flute as a deputy with the London Symphony Orchestra and had a much profounder knowledge of music than most writers. He was also a gifted actor on occasion, though it is difficult to disentangle the recollection from memories of Jean Gabin, whom he much resembled.

June 20, 1967.

Arpad Szakasits, who was President of the Hungarian Republic from 1948–50, and former leader of the Social Democrat Party, died in Budapest on May 3, 1965. He was 77.

In his role as secretary of the Social Democrat party, he made consistent efforts to combat the rise of Fascism in Hungary and to oppose the pro-Nazi policy of successive Hungarian governments, proposing instead an alliance with the Soviet Union. Since 1948 when his party merged with the communists Szakasits had been a willing instrument of the Soviet Union in her bid for power in Central and Eastern Europe after the defeat of Nazi Germany and her satellites.

Arpad Szakasits was born in Budapest in 1888 of a poor family. Material hardships resulting from his father's early death caused his primary education to be neglected and at 13 he augmented the family income by wood-carving. He later became a stonemason, finishing his apprenticeship in 1907. During this time he was active in the labour movement and joined the Construction Workers Union (Memosz), of which he became secretary at an early age. Having been editor of the *Construction Worker*, he was made a member of the editorial board of the Social Democratic paper *Nepszava* in 1918. For his part in the seizure of power by the left extremists under Bela Kun in 1919, he was arrested and imprisoned and after his release he continued his work on *Nepszava*. In the middle twenties he became a member of the central committee of the Social Democrat Party and in 1939 he was elected chief editor of *Nepszava* and secretary of the party.

In 1941, Szakasits was one of the few, mostly Liberals and Social Democrats, who openly criticized the Government for its Fascist tendencies, and at a time when left wing sympathies were illegal in Hungary he printed in his paper the political programme of the Hungarian Independence Front (the name of the illegal Communist organization). In 1942 his connexion with the communist party caused him to be removed from the leadership of the Social Democrat party, but nevertheless he retained a certain influence in the party and tried to form an anti-Fascist popular front.

PRIME MINISTER

After the collapse of Hungary in 1945, Szakasits again became secretary general of the Social Democrats and in the coalition Government formed after the elections in the same year he held the post of Prime Minister. In June 1948, he was instrumental in uniting two of the largest political groups—the Hungarian Communist Party and the Social Democrat Party—into the new communist dominated "Hungarian Working People's Party", of which he made himself chairman. On August 3, 1948, Szakasits became President of the Hungarian Republic.

He remained President until 1950, when together with other leading Social Democrats he was secretly imprisoned. He was known to have been released during 1954, although nothing further was heard of him until 1956, when after a secret retrial he was rehabilitated.

May 4, 1965.

George Szell, for 26 years conductor of the Cleveland Symphony Orchestra, died on July 29, 1970, at the age of 73. He was, like Sir John Barbirolli, one of the dwindling band of conductors who, in spite of the demands of a great international reputation, was prepared to identify himself with a single orchestra and to find his deepest satisfactions in a permanent conductorship.

He had settled in the United States in 1939 and, in subsequent years, had become so completely identified with American musical life and American orchestral style that it was possible for European listeners, noting the qualities of the Cleveland Symphony Orchestra when he conducted, to feel that they were in contact with the quintessentially American orchestra. Szell imbued his players with a tense, apparently unyielding discipline, a lightning alertness of response and the shining, rather metallic tone which often seems to be the special quality of transatlantic players.

George Szell was born in Budapest on June 7, 1897. He appeared as a child pianist and composer by the time he was 11, and studied in Vienna and Leipzig under Mandyczewski, J. B. Forster and Reger. His first appearance in London came in 1908, at a concert with the London Symphony Orchestra in the Albert Hall: as an 11-year-old pianist he played work by Mendelssohn and the programme included an overture which he had composed.

ADVICE TAKEN

It was the advice of Richard Strauss that turned him to conducting, and by the time that he was 20 he was chief conductor of the Strasbourg Opera. He had held important posts in Prague, Darmstadt and Düsseldorf before he was appointed first conductor of the Berlin State Opera in 1924, and in 1927 he became Professor at the Hochschule für Musik. From 1929 to 1937 he was musical director of the German Theatre in Prague and Professor at the German Musical Academy there.

From 1933 until the outbreak of war he appeared frequently in Britain with the London Symphony and Philharmonic Orchestras, the B.B.C. Symphony Orchestra and the Hallé Orchestra, which for a time hoped that he would accept its permanent conductorship in succession to Sir Hamilton Harty. He was for a time conductor of the Scottish Orchestra and of the Residentie Orchestra at The Hague. George Szell was awarded an honorary O.B.E. for services to British music, and was given similar honours in Germany, Austria and Holland.

The United States recognized his quality immediately, and from 1942 for four years he was principal conductor at the Metropolitan Opera, New York. He became principal conductor of the Cleveland Symphony Orchestra in 1946, dividing his time, from 1958 to 1961, between Cleveland and Amsterdam, where he was joint conductor of the Concertgebouw Orchestra. A Chevalier of the Legion of Honour, Szell's services to American music—for he was an eager producer of new music—brought him a sheaf of honorary doctorates and other awards, amongst them the Laurel Leaf Award of the American Composers' Alliance.

His surviving compositions, most notable among which are a piano quintet, a lyric overture and a set of orchestral variations on an original theme, come from early in his career, and it is as a conductor that he must be judged and will be remembered. The idea that he had become imbued with the hard, unrelenting view of music which some Europeans regard as specially American seemed to cause him some sardonic amusement, for he claimed that his speciality was the avoidance of specialization, that he strove to adapt himself to the special demands of every composer whose music he played and to produce the quality of tone which they required; and that these had always been his aims. English musicians who found much to admire in his work when they first became aware of it can, perhaps, bear out his claim, for they found that, at a time when a good deal of English orchestral playing was sloppy, Szell brought to music an unhesitating firmness of line and a sense of unremitting forward movement. No English orchestra, however, knew him for long enough to acquire the sense of almost mechanical discipline—responding, as it were, to the lightest touch on a button—which he gave to the Cleveland Orchestra.

Szell was a first-rate technician. Every gesture had great clarity and definition, and a good deal of the apparent sternness of his interpretations came from his refusal to do anything not immediately justified by the composer's text. Some of the firm severity of his music making, however, came from his own temperament. He had wit, but it was always sardonic. It was obvious that he had no wish to win the love and reverence of his players, nor even to consult them over questions of special instrumental effects. No work, however new, entered his programmes until he was so completely and decisively its master that consultation was unnecessary. He ruled the musicians he conducted, but not with the Latin flamboyances of rage they had endured from Toscanini; his severities were freezing.

August 1, 1970.

Dr. Leo Szilard, a leading American physicist who played an important part in the wartime development of nuclear energy, died on May 30, 1964, at his home at La Jolla, California. He was 66.

Szilard, who was born in Budapest in February, 1898, studied engineering there and received a degree of doctor of philosophy from the University of Berlin in 1922. He taught there from 1925 to 1932. From 1935 to 1937 he lived in England and did research work in nuclear physics at St. Bartholomew's Hospital and at the Clarendon Laboratory at Oxford.

Szilard went to the United States in 1937 and became an American citizen in 1943. He worked on atomic energy at Columbia University before going to the University of Chicago, where he was a professor for many years and a member of the staff of the Enrico Fermi Institute. He left the University of Chicago in 1964 and in April went to La Jolla to accept a position at the Salk Institute for Biological Studies.

While in England he discovered, with Dr.

T. A. Chalmers, an effect which makes it possible in some cases to separate radioactive from stable isotopes of the same chemical element—not completely but simply enough to be still useful in preparing certain radio isotopes for use in research. This is known as the Szilard-Chalmers effect.

Dr. Szilard's main impact was, however, during the period of excited and alarmed interest which followed the discovery by Dr. O. Hahn and Dr. F. Strassmann of the fission of uranium atoms and the guess of Dr. O. R. Frisch and Dr. L. Meitner that fission might not only be caused by the entry of a neutron into a uranium nucleus but also would be accompanied by the release of very large quantities of energy and the emission of further neutrons when the uranium nucleus broke into fragments. Dr. Szilard, working with Dr. W. H. Zinn, was responsible for one of four experiments, all done at more or less the same time, which quickly confirmed that neutrons were indeed emitted in fission—so that in principle a chain reaction was possible.

He was again active, this time in conjunction with Dr. E. Wigner, in moves to bring the possibilities of the fission process to the attention of the American Government. The result of their activity was the setting up of a body that became known as the advisory committee on uranium. It first met on October 1, 1939, and the basis of its discussions, it has been said, was largely provided by a memorandum which Szilard had prepared. The report that the committee agreed only 10 days later, for transmission to President Roosevelt and others, specifically mentioned nuclear power as well as a nuclear bomb as possibilities that could be envisaged. Soon after it was discovered that fission took place only in nuclei of one isotope of uranium—and that the less common one—and it became apparent that if a chain reaction was to develop in natural uranium it would be necessary to provide a material which would slow up the neutrons emitted in fission so as to give them the best chance of bringing about the fission of further atoms. Together with Professor Enrico Fermi, Szilard suggested the use of graphite as a moderator and also the type of lattice structure adopted in the first atomic pile at Chicago and subsequently used with little modification in essentials in all but a very few of the reactors that have since been built.

In 1947 Szilard, who had hoped the bomb would never be used, was refused permission from the State Department to write a letter to Stalin, urging the settlement of international problems. But the letter was later published in a bulletin for atomic scientists.

Szilard shared the 1959 Atoms for Peace award with Dr. Eugene Wigner.

He was not of Fermi's stature as a physicist—few are—but he had qualities of quick imagination combined with persistence which gave him a position of importance during the whole of the early formative period of American work on nuclear energy. He has left his mark on history as well as physics. He is survived by his widow, Dr. Gertrud Weiss Szilard.

June 1, 1964.

T

Jack Tanner, for 15 years president of the Amalgamated Engineering Union, the wealthiest and the second largest trade union in Britain, died on March 3, 1965. He was 75.

"Handsome Jack", as he was nicknamed when he was one of the most popular and best looking men in the Labour movement, had a restless and adventurous youth. As a young man he was stirred by the fire and eloquence of the syndicalists and excited by the Russian revolution, but after a period in the Communist Party he devoted himself to constructive trade union work. The most impressive period of his leadership of the A.E.U. was during the Second World War, when he strove hard to remove muddle in the war industries and to increase production, and was one of the moving spirits in the establishment of the joint production committees. During the postwar period he became very "responsible" and "statesmanlike", but seemed to have lost the fire of his earlier years, and was sometimes accused of weakness in his attitude to communist trouble-makers in his union.

After his retirement in 1954 he became director of Iris (Industrial Research and Information Services, Ltd.), an organization devoted to the exposure of communists in the trade unions.

Tanner was born in 1889, a native of Whitstable. His father was the sports manager at the Alexandra Palace, so that after a while the family lived in London. At 14 he was apprenticed to a small firm of engineers in Southwark, but life in the workshop irked him and he joined the Merchant Navy. After seeing many parts of the world, including the Far East, he returned to London and worked as a turner and fitter. During the First World War he was employed at the Royal Aircraft Factory at Farnborough, but departed after a fight with a non-unionist and spent the latter part of the war with an engineering firm in France.

VISIT TO RUSSIA

From the beginning he had been an active trade unionist and was a keen member of the Shop Stewards Movement and later editor of their journal, *Solidarity*. He helped Tom Mann campaign for "workers' control" and was much influenced by the ideas of Kropotkin. The Russian Revolution in 1917 made a great impression on him and in 1920 he decided to go and see things for himself. He attended the Third International's Second Congress in Leningrad and met Lenin, who described him as "this typical young member of the English proletariat". On his return he became a member of the newly formed British Communist Party, but left after a short while to give all his time to trade union work.

In the postwar depression he found it difficult for 18 months to find a job, but in the end was taken on by the *Evening Standard*. This gave him the opportunity to organize his fellow workers engaged in maintaining newspaper plant and he became well known among the London members of the Amalgamated Engineering Union. In 1926 they elected him a member of the union's London District Committee and three years later the committee's chairman.

In 1930 he gave up his job on the *Evening Standard* to become the A.E.U.'s London organizer. This position brought him into contact with every branch of engineering, and he soon won a reputation for his understanding of the industry's problems. He was well to the left of most of his trade union colleagues and once he had made certain of his facts was merciless in criticism.

DILUTION PROBLEMS

In 1939 he succeeded J. C. Little as the A.E.U.'s president, and shortly after his election, with the outbreak of war, he was involved in the difficult problems of dilution. From the beginning he—more than anyone—realized that it was an "engineers' war" and was prepared to see many of the old safeguards and craft customs disappear provided that his members' standards would not suffer. He carried on continual war against what he called the "plutocratic control" which was responsible for many of the bottlenecks in the armament industry, and in 1940 he was largely responsible for the appointment of the committee on "Skilled Men in the Services" which led to the formation of R.E.M.E., which the A.E.U. looks on almost as a brother.

In 1941 under his auspices the A.E.U. initiated an inquiry into causes of mismanagement and inefficiency in industry. While he did not deny that there were cases of avoidable absenteeism among the men, he defended them against the many charges of slackness and overpayment that were circulating at the time and continued to lay the main blame at the door of the employers. On many occasions he denounced unofficial strikes as being harmful to the war effort and also to the strength of the organized workers, and he always tried to simplify negotiating procedure and machinery and to consolidate the numerous unions which catered for the engineers.

In 1942 he made a tour of the United States' war plants and attended as a fraternal delegate the conference of the American Federation of Labour. He made an outspoken appeal for international labour unity, including an alliance with the Soviet trade unions, and caused a minor sensation by declaring that some of the American factories were less efficient than their British counterparts. At home he was no less outspoken at the Edinburgh T.U.C. in 1941, accusing the then Minister of Aircraft Production of hoping that the Russian and German armies would exterminate each other.

During the latter stage of the war Tanner criticized the Government for not making sufficient preparations for the transition to a peacetime economy. He used his influence to ensure that the nationalization proposals were carried out in full and in particular that they were applied to the steel industry. He was a member of the Engineering Advisory Council and proposed a detailed plan for the whole industry based on the practical needs of the moment and on the continued use of the joint production committees. When the country's economic difficulties became more pronounced in 1947 he was appointed to the Government's Economic Planning Board.

He was chairman of the T.U.C. from 1953–54. He retired from his union office in 1954, on reaching the age limit of 65. In his retirement he served on several public bodies and became a director of the National Fuel Efficiency Service.

March 4, 1965.

Cardinal Domenico Tardini, Cardinal Secretary of State to Pope John XXIII from 1958, died at the Vatican on July 30, 1961. He was 73.

The diplomatic servant and intimate friend of three Popes, Cardinal Tardini was a Pro-Secretary of State for six years in the reign of Pope Pius XII, who announced publicly at a consistory that but for the earnest request of Mgr. Tardini and his fellow Pro-Secretary, Mgr. Montini, he would have elevated both to the Sacred College. When the Pope died in 1958 Tardini was named as Regent of the Secretariat while the seat was vacant, and in one of the first acts of the new Pontificate he was made a Cardinal and appointed Secretary of State and Archpriest of the Vatican Basilica.

A noted theologian in Rome and author of a standard work on sacramental theology, he had served except for nine years exclusively in the Roman Curia. In 1960 after an illness he sought permission to retire, but bowed to the Pope's wish that he should remain, though with the delegation of some of his duties to assistants.

Among his activities outside the scope of his official work was the foundation of the Villa Nazareth in Rome, a home for orphan boys, whom he hoped to train for public life and forms of Catholic Action, and whom he visited daily until he became Secretary of State.

Domenico Tardini was born in Rome on February 29, 1888, and studied for the priesthood at the Roman Seminary, where he took his doctorates of philosophy and theology. He was ordained in 1912.

UNFILLED OFFICE

After nine years as professor of Sacred Theology and Liturgy at the Roman Seminary, Tardini entered the Sacred Congregation of the Sacraments in 1920 and later was appointed as a minutante in the Congregation for Extraordinary Affairs. Domestic Prelate to Pope Pius XI in 1929, he became a member of the Pontifical Academy of St. Thomas Aquinas in 1932 and in the same year visited Dublin in the suite of the Papal Legate to the International Eucharistic Congress there. The following years he was appointed successively a member of the Pontifical Commission for Russia and secretary of the Pontifical Commission for the Interpretation of the Code of Canon Law.

Pope Pius XI had named him as under-secretary of the Congregation of Extraordinary Ecclesiastical Affairs, a post in which he continued under Pope Pius XII, who had been Cardinal Secretary of State to his predecessor, and who reserved to himself many of the decisions normally made by the secretary. When Cardinal Maglione, who had succeeded him, died in 1944 the post was left vacant for the remaining years of the reign; but in 1952 the Pope announced the appointment of two pro-secretaries, Mgr. Tardini for Extraordinary Affairs and Mgr. (now Cardinal) Montini for Ordinary Affairs. At the consistory shortly afterwards when the Pope spoke of his wish to make them both cardinals, he granted them precedence over all other ecclesiastics who were not cardinals and gave them the cardinalatial privileges of preaching or hearing confessions anywhere in the world.

The appointments were without precedent in modern times and continued until the election of Pope John XXIII, who stated immediately afterwards that he regarded the appointment of a secretary of state as a matter of urgency. Accordingly in December of 1958 he elevated Mgr. Tardini as cardinal priest and personally consecrated him as titular Archbishop of Laodicea, in Syria.

In addition to the heavy burden of his work in the secretariat Cardinal Tardini was much engaged during his last three years with preparatory work for the Second Vatican Oecumenical council and with plans for the rebuilding of the Vatican Basilica and with arrangements for the publication of the Pope's pastoral "Mater et Magistra".

July 31, 1961.

Professor R. H. Tawney, F.B.A., a scholar of rare and luminous quality and the most distinguished English economic historian of his generation, who gave new significance and new direction to the study of the 16th and 17th centuries, died on January 16, 1962, in a London nursing home. He was 81.

It is not only as an economic historian of profound scholarship and inspiring temper that R. H. Tawney will be remembered. Few economic historians of his time, it is true, brought to their work so deep a love of learning or so eloquent a passion of moral argument. None, indeed, has combined economic study with moral purpose and the analysis of ideas to quite the same illuminating effect as Tawney in his classic volume, *Religion and the Rise of Capitalism.* But few historians of any kind among his contemporaries have brought history into more fruitful contact with literature or have worked so strongly upon the political ideals of a large body of the unscholarly. One of the pioneer Fabian thinkers, Tawney clearly drew upon Christian doctrine of a not very theological kind for his devoutly egalitarian philosophy. Apart from his work as historian, his was a deeply pervasive influence on Socialist ideals in Britain, not least in the matter of educational opportunity, and in some sort as guide and companion of large sections of organized labour. He will be missed not only by scholars and students but by many among the miners, cotton operatives, and workers in other industries whose cause he made his own.

Richard Henry Tawney, Professor of Economic History in the University of London from 1931 to 1949, and afterwards Emeritus Professor, was born in Calcutta on November 30, 1880, the son of C. H. Tawney, a distinguished Indian civil servant and Sanskrit scholar, and Constance Catherine Fox. He went to school at Rugby, proceeded to Oxford as scholar of Balliol, was a good classic, and took his degree in 1903, though he missed a first. Almost immediately, in the unaffected earnestness of those years, he went to live at the Toynbee Hall University settlement in the East End of London, and until 1906 was secretary of the Children's Country Holiday Fund. Simultaneously, however, his interest in adult education had been deeply aroused, and the founding of the Workers' Educational Association in 1903 gave him an opportunity which he seized with both hands. The W.E.A. was to remain one of the most ardent practical devotions of his life. He became a member of the executive in 1905, retained his membership until 1947, and was president from 1928 until 1944. Possibly the most famous of his classes was that at Rochdale, where a truly remarkable team of students included the late A. P. Wadsworth, afterwards editor of the *Manchester Guardian.* After two years as an assistant lecturer at Glasgow University Tawney was, from 1908 until 1914, a teacher for the Tutorial Classes Committee of Oxford University. It was during this period that he produced his first major work, *The Agrarian Problem in the Sixteenth Century,* a study of striking and in many ways original scholarship of the whole background of the first enclosure movement. Here he defined in as yet somewhat tentative fashion the impact of the rise of capitalism on agriculture and the internal conflicts in English society.

WOUNDED IN BATTLE

When war broke out in 1914 Tawney enlisted as a private in the 22nd Service Battalion, The Manchester Regiment, and was promoted to sergeant. He was severely wounded in the Battle of the Somme in July, 1916, and the effects stayed with him for the rest of his life. However, he was enabled to return to his historical studies, and in 1918 he was elected an honorary Fellow of Balliol. Now followed his most diverse phase of activity. In 1919 he issued the volume, prepared in collaboration with A. E. Bland and P. A. Brown, of *English Economic History: Select Documents.* In the same year he was appointed a member of the Coal Commission over which Lord (then Mr. Justice) Sankey presided, and demonstrated his practical grasp of the economic complexity of the industry and the warmth of his sympathy with the miners' case. A year later came the publication of a pamphlet for the Fabian Society which, subsequently issued in an amplified form under the title of *The Acquisitive Society,* gave reasoned and eloquent force to his condemnation of the moral springs of the capitalist order of society.

The economist and scholar in Tawney was never overcome, or perhaps never more than fugitively overcome, by the idealist and preacher. In 1925 there appeared the three volumes of *Tudor Economic Documents* which he edited jointly with Eileen Power. And in the next year, heralded by essays he had already published on the economic aspect of various contributory causes of the English Civil War and by his introduction to Wilson's *Discourse upon Usury,* appeared what is beyond question his greatest work and not less certainly is one of the noblest pieces of English historical scholarship in modern times, *Religion and the Rise of Capitalism.* Based upon his lectures at the London School of Economics and Political Science, this study of the economic aspect of the Reformation and the growing supremacy of economics in the Puritan tradition owed something, no doubt, to other English and German scholars, Max Weber among them. In the light of later research, not all of its conclusions can be endorsed without reservation. Yet whatever modifications may be necessary, this is a work of profound historical value and of disciplined and often magnificent expression.

MEDIATION IN INDUSTRY

Notable among Tawney's later works is *Equality,* published in 1931, in which he argued the case, now and then in impassioned terms, against what seemed to him to be "the religion of inequality" which had been raised in England and elsewhere upon a basis of class privilege. The book became, in some sort, a text-book for many W.E.A. students. Three months spent in China during that year as one of a mission of four educational experts deputed by the League of Nations to study and advise on the reorganization of education in that country produced a sober and illuminating study, among the earliest on the subject to appear in English, of *Land and Labour in China.* Besides serving as adviser on educational matters to the Labour Party, he had been for many years a member of the Consultative Committee of what was then the Board of Education, and was always available—as in 1936, for instance, when he became a member of the Cotton Trade Conciliation Board—for work of a mediatory character in the conduct of industry and labour.

ADVICE IN WASHINGTON

In the Second World War he acted for a time as adviser on labour conditions and problems to the Embassy at Washington.

Tawney's ancestors had fought as freeholders for Cromwell and Parliament, and the seventeenth century, it might be said, was in his bones. He had always intended, his friends understood, to write a book on the great age of Puritanism and the Levellers in particular, and it is probable that the intractable bulk of material he had accumulated as well as poor health explains in part why he did not. He wrote, he frequently said, slowly and with difficulty. For many years his friends and admirers waited in vain, and then it became known that the book that might one day be looked for from Tawney was not about the Puritan sects but about Lionel Cranfield, the cloth exporter and land speculator who for a brief space was Lord Treasurer under James I. Before that book came out in 1958 Tawney published *The Attack* (1953), a collection of a dozen papers written over a period of more than 30 years, all characteristic in style and sentiment but none strictly concerned with history. The title-piece was an account of the Somme battle in 1916 in which he was wounded, a vividly restrained and telling piece of writing; among the other pieces, some of them Fabian lectures, were two essays on the Webbs. The Cranfield volume—*Business and Politics under James I: Lionel Cranfield as Merchant and Minister*—proved to have been tremendously well worth waiting for. Here, once more, was the economic historian who with splendid scholarship took in his stride the multiform seventeenth-century world of politics and religion, science and ideas. Already, in Tawney's handling of Cranfield's career, the complex of business and politics foreshadows the revolutionary crisis of the century.

Tawney had stood unsuccessfully as a Labour candidate several times, but was perhaps not really fitted for the work of the House of Commons. (Nor, indeed can he have erred in refusing the peerage offered him by Ramsay MacDonald in 1933). The loosely built, untidy figure with a heavy brown moustache and a remote and habitually concentrated look was unmistakably that of a scholar rather than a common-room man. He had a warm, vivid smile, was exceedingly fond of at least one Persian cat, and was somewhat of an ascetic except in friendship.

Bishop Gore, Archbishop Temple, men like Herbert Smith, the miners' leader, and not a few others, knew how great was Tawney's capacity for friendship. He married, in 1909 Annette Jeannie Beveridge (a sister of Lord Beveridge), who died early in 1958. For many years they had lived in Mecklenburgh Square, where in a study lined with books to the ceiling he seemed to be most completely himself, a lover of learning and the humanities, a dreamer of social justice and equality, of generous mind, whose reserve only friendship could penetrate. An honorary Fellow at Peterhouse, Cambridge, as well as of his own college, he had received honorary degrees from the universities of Oxford, Manchester, Birmingham, Sheffield, London, Chicago, Melbourne, and Paris. On the occasion of his eightieth birthday in 1960 a dinner was held in his honour in the House of Commons.

January 17, 1962.

Professor Eva Taylor, Professor of Geography and Head of the Department of Geography, Birkbeck College, London, from 1930 to 1944, died on July 5, 1966, at Wokingham. She was 87. After her retirement she was made Professor Emeritus.

Eva Germaine Rimington Taylor celebrated her 80th birthday in 1959 when she had become almost the only direct remaining link with that small band of pioneers—H. J. Mackinder, H. R. Mill, G. G. Chisholm, and A. J. Herbertson—who formulated and introduced the "new geography" as a university discipline.

The daughter of C. R. Taylor, M.A., LL.D., she was educated at the North London Collegiate School for Girls. She took a degree in chemistry in the University of London, and for two or three years was a Science Mistress at Burton-on-Trent. To improve her qualifications she went up to Oxford to take the Diploma in Education, and it was on the suggestion of the women's tutor, Miss Cooper, that she got interested in the new geography, combining a post at the Convent in Woodstock Road with study at the School of Geography, obtaining the Diploma after two years.

She stayed on to help Professor Herbertson in the preparation of the well-known series of Oxford Wall Maps, and on a vacation course met J. F. Unstead. They collaborated in a series of school texts, and for many years "Unstead and Taylor" swept the new geography teaching in a wide range of schools.

NAVIGATION EXPERT

Some years of part-time lecturing, much writing and the business of bringing up a family followed, and it was not until the end of the First World War that she started lecturing (in 1920) at what is now Queen Mary College—initiating geographical work in the Department of Geology—and in 1921 to evening classes at Birkbeck College, then at its old premises off Fetter Lane, with Unstead in charge of geography. There she developed research interests into what was to prove her major contribution—the geographical work of Tudor and Stuart times. Her books *Tudor Geography, Late Tudor and Early Stuart Geography, Barlow's Brief Summe of Geographie* broke new ground. She became an acknowledged expert not only on the maps and literature of the period, but in navigation and instruments and the work of explorers.

In 1956 she published *The Haven-finding Art* of which Arthur Ransome wrote; "For years I have been badgering publishers to produce such a book as this, telling in language that even I can understand how from earliest times men have found their way about the world".

With M.W.Richey, secretary of the Institute of Navigation, she wrote *The Geometrical Seaman.* Earlier in 1966, in an issue of the institute's journal, Mr. Richey set out her views—she had grave doubts of its authenticity—on the Vinland map.

In 1930 for reasons of health Professor Unstead decided to retire from the Chair of Geography, and Eva Taylor was chosen to succeed him. It was a jump from Demonstrator to Professor, but one fully justified. In the plan-making days of the Second World War she threw herself with enthusiasm into the geographical problems of Town and Country Planning and was appointed by Lord Reith, first Minister of Town and Country Planning, to his Consultative Panel in 1941. She will long be remembered for her advocacy of the "sieve method"—essentially eliminating the areas unsuitable for one reason or another to arrive at a residue of land to be considered for positive planning, and her concept of an industrial area shaped like a coffin, stretching from Lancashire to London, into which industry was tending to concentrate, and some might say to bury itself, to the detriment of peripheral areas. Retiring as Professor Emeritus in 1944 her work was recognized by the Victoria Medal of the Royal Geographical Society in 1947, and an Honorary LL.D. from Aberdeen.

A woman of strong personality and decided views, she expressed herself in debate with great forthrightness but her opinions were always based upon wide knowledge, and commanded respect. She was a stalwart champion of young university workers whom she both bullied and inspired.

July 7, 1966.

By the death of **J. H. Taylor,** at Northam, Devon, on February 10, 1963, at the age of 91, golf lost a venerated and romantic figure, a very great player and the man who more than any other raised the status of professional golf.

In his young days the professional golfer was, save for a few notable exceptions, a cheerful, feckless fellow who lived more or less from hand to mouth and often ended as the caddie from which he had temporarily emerged. It was largely due to Taylor, with his illustrious contemporaries Vardon, Braid and Herd, that the professional became a prosperous, respected and self-respecting member of society. "J.H." was the natural leader of his companions and played the chief part in forming the Professional Golfers' Association, which, without entering into the vexed question of the "closed shop", has unquestionably done a great deal for professional golf. To this cause as to that of artisan golf he devoted much time and a fine, pugnacious enthusiasm.

YOUNG GREENKEEPER

John Henry Taylor was born at Northam on March 10, 1871, the son of a Devon working man. Like other Northam boys he naturally became a caddie at Westward Ho! He had left school at 11 and been in turn a boot boy in the home of Horace Hutchinson's father, a garden boy and a mason's labourer. When he was 17, there was a vacancy on the greenkeeping staff which he joyfully embraced, for he was already a very good player. He tried to enter both the Army and the Navy but ironically enough was rejected for his eyesight, while he was not tall enough for the Metropolitan Police.

At last, when he was 19, his luck turned and with a borrowed sovereign in his pocket he went to Burnham in Somerset as a full blown professional and greenkeeper. The famous Andrew Kirkaldy was then at Winchester and a home and away match was made between them which Taylor won by 4 and 3. Andrew spread the fame of his conqueror who soon afterwards succeeded him at Winchester and there he remained four years, before moving to Wimbledon and utlimately to Mid Surrey.

It was from Winchester that he won his first championship. In 1893 he went to Prestwick, where the astonishing accuracy of his long shots up to the pin, hit firm footed and with a short, sharp punch unlike the orthodox swing of the day, spread consternation among the Scottish professionals. He took them out one by one and knocked them down like ninepins but he had overplayed himself and after one brilliant round collapsed in the championship itself. Next year at Sandwich, however, found him steady as a rock and he won comfortably from the now legendary Douglas Rolland.

He won again at St. Andrews in 1895, coming with a great rush through the rain to catch Herd and in 1896 at Muirfield he tied for first place with Harry Vardon, then just springing into fame. Vardon won the tie and soon afterwards entered upon his invincible period.

Yet Taylor soon bobbed up again, winning once more at St. Andrews in 1900, by magnificent golf, then, after a longer interval in which he was always there or thereabouts, he won at Deal in 1909 and at Hoylake in 1913. This last was his greatest victory and those who saw it will always think that his golf in appalling conditions of rain and wind has never been equalled.

DOMINANT TRIO

It is impossible to enumerate half his other successes; he won the French championship and the *News of the World,* twice each—and he, Vardon and Braid, familiarly known as the Triumvirate, dominated golf for years. The war years told their tale; yet even when he was 53 at Hoylake in 1924, his scores for six rounds (including the two qualifying rounds) were the lowest in all the championship field.

It was characteristic of him that once he realized he could not win, he ceased to compete. Not for him the "cold gradations of decay" though he loved golf as much as ever.

He was a highly strung and emotional man and though he had great control over his emotions, golf "took it out of him" prodigally. He had the compensating quality of this defect, if it was a defect, that once he was over his bad time he was perhaps the most clearly inspired player that ever lived, whom it was vain to pursue. He was a great fighter and most resolute to the point of obstinacy on any point of principle.

SELF-EDUCATED

At the same time he was a most warmhearted and affectionate man and delightful company. Though he had left school so young he had educated himself; he was a devoted reader of Dickens and Boswell, an excellent and on occasions most moving speaker and a fluent writer.

Together with James Braid and Willie Auchterlonie he was made an honorary member of the Royal and Ancient Golf Club, an honour which gave him immense pleasure, and to celebrate his ninetieth birthday the captain and past captains of the club presented him with a silver salver bearing their signatures. In 1957 he was president of the Royal North Devon Club where so many years ago he had started his career.

There have been among professional players of games many men of character but none perhaps more remarkable than he.

Taylor lost his wife shortly after celebrating their diamond wedding in 1956 and six of his family of nine survive him—Mr. J. H. Taylor, schoolmaster and former Oxford golfing blue; Mr. Leslie Taylor, who was his father's assistant professional at the Royal Mid-Surrey, and four daughters.

February 11, 1963.

Captain Sir Patrick Gordon Taylor, G.C., M.C., O.B.E., pioneer aviator, died in Honolulu on December 14, 1966. He was 70.

One of his most famous feats was on a celebration flight across the Tasman Sea with his close friend, Sir Charles Kingsford-Smith, in 1935, when their ancient Southern Cross aircraft ran into trouble. The plane had to turn back to Australia with only two of its three engines working. Taylor, acting as navigator, noticed a stream of smoke issuing from the overloaded port engine. This denoted excessive oil consumption—and the seemingly inevitable loss of another engine. Taylor climbed out along the strut to the useless starboard engine. From it he took oil and transferred it to the smoking port engine. Repeating this every half hour, he enabled the plane to limp back to Australia. He was awarded the O.B.E. in 1937 for averting disaster on the attempted Australia-New Zealand air mail flight in 1935.

From 1942 to 1944 he delivered aircraft across the Atlantic. In 1944 he flew a Catalina from the west coast of Mexico to the little atoll of Clipperton Island and on to Tahiti—surviving a hurricane at the atoll. As recently as 1951 he pioneered another air route—this time across the Southern Pacific by way of the remote, harbourless Easter Island to South America, making the return flight to prove the route thoroughly.

Taylor served in the First World War in the Royal Flying Corps. He made an air crossing of the Indian Ocean, and survey of the air route for the British and Australian Governments in 1939. Later, in 1944, he made a crossing of the Central Pacific and a survey of the air route for the Royal Air Force. He wrote several books—among them *Call to the Winds, Frigate Bird,* and *The Sky Beyond.*

He was awarded the G.C. in 1942, and knighted in 1954.

December 17, 1966.

Robert Taylor, the film star, died on June 8, 1969, in Santa Monica. He was 57.

Robert Taylor, whose real name was S. Arlington Brugh, was born at Filley, Nebraska. He began his career studying medicine, with dramatics as a spare-time interest, but his performance in a college production of *Journey's End* brought him to the notice of a talent-scout and he was immediately put under contract to M.G.M. (he stayed with the same company for 24 years). His first film appearance was in *Andy Hardy* (1934), and his striking good looks soon made him one of Hollywood's principal romantic leads: he appeared in rapid succession in musicals (*Broadway Melody* of 1936), drama (the original *Magnificent Obsession*), and comedy (*The Gorgeous Hussy*, opposite Joan Crawford), before playing Armand Duval to Garbo's *Camille* (1936).

During the rest of the 1930s, his career continued on much the same lines, with *Broadway Melody* of 1938, *A Yank at Oxford*, and the boxing drama *The Crowd Roars* among others. During the forties he turned mainly to dramas and war films, among them *Waterloo Bridge*, with Vivien Leigh, *Bataan*, *Song of Russia* and *Undercurrent*, with Katharine Hepburn, before serving in the U.S. Navy as a lieutenant. His career took on a new lease of life with the arrival of the vogue for expensive costume films: his classical profile and imposing stature made him ideal for such roles as few stars looked better in armour or a toga. Among the films in this cycle were *Ivanhoe*, *Quo Vadis*, *The Knights of the Round Table* and *Quentin Durward*. After this he was seen mainly in Westerns and comedies.

Robert Taylor was never, nor did he lay claim to be, one of Hollywood's greatest acting talents; he had an unobtrusive all-round competence which enabled him to play a wide variety of roles, but basically he was a personality star, the last of filmdom's great matinee idols. When he finally terminated his contract with M.G.M. in 1958, after nearly a quarter of a century, it seemed that there were no more fixed stars in the Hollywood firmament: Robert Taylor and his generation represented glamour to several generations of film-goers, and films will never seem the same without him.

June 9, 1969.

Sir Thomas Taylor, C.B.E., Q.C., Principal and Vice-Chancellor of the University of Aberdeen, died in hospital at Aberdeen on July 19, 1962. He was 65.

Thomas Murray Taylor, the only son of John Taylor, was born in Keith, Banffshire, on May 27, 1897. From the grammar school there, which he left as dux, he proceeded to Aberdeen University, where he graduated in 1919 with first class honours in classics, carrying off at the same time the Fullerton and Ferguson scholarships in that subject. But his ambition was to become a lawyer, and in 1922 he obtained a degree of LL.B. from his Alma Mater. Two years later he was called to the Scottish Bar.

Thereafter his progress was sustained and rapid. Appointed Advocate Depute in 1925 and Senior Advocte Depute in 1934, he was concerned in some of the notable trials of that period; and as a member of various departmental committees, notably that on the salary of Scottish nurses, he played a prominent part in shaping the Scottish scene during troubled and difficult years. His services in this wider field were crowned by his appointment in 1945 as Sheriff of Argyll and interim Sheriff of Renfrew and Bute. At the same time he became a K.C.

But his home country always lay forward in his thoughts, and in 1935 he had returned to Aberdeen as Professor of Law. In this capacity he acquired much fame through the exceptional quality of the orations which he pronounced in promoting graduands to the honorary degree in that faculty. His crowning achievement in this field was his laudation of Sir Winston Churchill in 1946—a speech which so impressed Sir Winston that he specially asked for a copy to be sent to him.

DISTINGUISHED PRINCIPAL

In 1948 he was appointed Principal and Vice-Chancellor of his own university, being the first lawyer to hold that office in the four and a half centuries of her history. His principalship, so unhappily cut short, will mark him out as one of the most distinguished of his line. His intimate knowledge of the university herself, of the social and economic institutions and problems of her hinterland, and of the background, aims and qualities of her students, proved assets of exceptional value in maintaining the distinctive ethos of his Alma Mater; while his wide experience and sagacity qualified him to guide her with a sure and steady hand through the difficulties of the postwar period, and the more recent programme of hectic expansion. Amid many shoals he steered the university forward on an even keel, and the harmony which has prevailed, not only within the university but also in her relations with the town, is in no small measure due to his strong yet conciliatory personality.

In spite of a heavy academic burden that rested on his shoulders Sir Thomas found time to play an important part in Scottish affairs. He was indeed one of the most notable Scotsmen of his time. At different periods he served on the Aberdeen education committee, the North of Scotland College of Agriculture, and the Rowett Institute.

Perhaps his most notable service in this wider field was his chairmanship of the governmental committee which inquired into the crofting system. An earnest Christian and an enthusiastic member of the Church of Scotland, he was a frequent commissioner of the General Assembly, and played a memorable part in the quatercentenary celebrations of the Reformation. In his parish church, the ancient cathedral of St. Machar, he served as an elder, and was a frequent and forceful preacher in King's College chapel. He was also a former president of the Scottish National Council of the Y.M.C.A. He represented his Church abroad on the executive committee of the World Council of Churches, and was chairman of its commission on Christians and the Prevention of War in an Atomic Age.

LAYMAN'S D.D.

In 1944 he was made C.B.E. and 10 years later he was knighted. He received the honorary degrees of LL.D. from St. Andrews and Glasgow and that of D.D.—an unusual distinction for a layman—from Edinburgh.

Personally Taylor was a man of striking presence, tall and handsome, with a native dignity of bearing that was specially marked on academic and public occasions. A Scot to the core, his determined championship of Scottish interests had in it nothing of the petty or bigoted.

He married in 1929 Helen Jardine, a graduate in medicine of Aberdeen, and is survived by his widow and a son and daughter.

July 20, 1962.

Marshal of the Royal Air Force Lord Tedder, G.C.B., who died on June 3, 1967, at the age of 76 was one of the outstanding figures of the Second World War and Chief of the Air Staff from 1946 to 1950. In the campaigns in North Africa he made a great name for himself in his partnerships with Field-Marshals Auchinleck and Lord Alexander and later with General Eisenhower. His cooperation with the latter was continued in North-West Europe and extended to the termination of hostilities with Germany. He had been ill for some time.

COMMAND OF THE AIR

Tedder's experience since first joining the R.F.C. in 1915 had been very wide and varied, and as an administrator at the Air Ministry both on the training and development sides he had done much to build up the powerful weapon which he was called upon to wield. As the Public Orator at Oxford declared when he was made an honorary D.C.L., he was versed in all the arts of war, and thus equipped he evolved new tactical methods, the first principle of which was to gain command of the air. Using these tactics in Africa and Sicily he had exposed the interior of Germany to air attack from its Alpine flank, and in the liberation of France in 1944 he was given a part second only to that of the Supreme Commander.

It was no secret that he did not always see eye to eye with General Montgomery over the conduct of the war in Europe and his side of the matter he described with typical Tedder directness in his memoirs which were published in 1966. Long and detailed, they were fairly entitled *With Prejudice*. They were also well worth reading. Tedder, of course, had been an historian before ever he was a pilot and it is amusing to remember that while at Cambridge he won a prize for an essay on the British Navy of the Restoration. Later in life he was at considerable pains to keep the air forces from falling into the embraces of admirals—and generals.

UNSTUFFY COMMANDER

Tedder's clarity of mind was accompanied by an equal facility of expression which left no room for doubt as to his meaning. His was a complex personality eluding easy analysis. The quizzical humour—like his pipe—was typical Tedder and, as Sir Arthur Harris said, it tended to upset some people, but it played on great and small alike as did his twinkling eye. He was the most unstuffy of great commanders, who could be found sitting cross-legged, jacketless, pipe smouldering, answering questions on a desert air strip. Yet to see him as a squadron "hearty" would be to misread his character entirely.

Tedder was a thoroughly competent, though not a brilliant pilot. Even later in his career, when command and staff duties claimed him, he remained closely in touch with the practical side of flying.

Arthur William Tedder was born on July 11, 1890, the only son of Sir Arthur John Tedder, C.B., Commissioner of Customs and Excise. He was educated at Whitgift Grammar School, Croydon, and at Magdalene College, Cambridge, where he graduated B.A., historical tripos, in 1912, and was awarded the Prince Consort Prize in 1913. He afterwards became an honorary fellow of his college. Soon after he had begun his career in the Colonial Service in Fiji the First World War broke out in 1914 and he went home to serve in The Dorsetshire Regiment, in which he had been commissioned in 1913. From 1915 to 1917 he was with the R.F.C. in France, being seconded in 1916 and from 1918 to 1919 in Egypt.

He was thrice mentioned in dispatches, and in 1919 was awarded a permanent R.A.F. commission as squadron leader. For the three years 1929-31 he was an instructor and assistant commandant at the R.A.F. Staff College, and was promoted to group captain in 1931. From 1932 to 1934 he commanded the Air Armament School at Eastchurch, and then returned to the Air Ministry as Director of Training, with the rank of air commodore from July, 1934. He was nominated as Air Officer Commanding, Far Fast, with headquarters at Singapore from October, 1936, and in the following July was promoted to air vice-marshal. He was appointed C.B. in February, 1937.

TEDDER'S "CARPET"

When the expansion programme of the R.A.F. was well under way in June, 1938, some important changes in the production side of the Air Ministry were announced in the House of Commons by Sir Kingsley Wood, and among them was the nomination of Tedder to the new post of Director-General of Research and Development. This office he held when the Second World War broke out. On the creation of the Ministry of Aircraft Production in 1940 he became Deputy Air Member for Development and Production in August of that year. Three months later, however, he received the first of the operational appointments in which he became famous. He was made Deputy Air Officer Commanding-in-Chief, Middle East, and after six months in this post he succeeded Sir Arthur Longmore as A.O.C.-in-C. During the campaigns in the Western Desert he did much to perfect the cooperation between air and land forces and when the Army under Montgomery began its long advance from El Alamein to Tunisia the technique of the "Tedder carpet", as it was called—the clearance of a pathway through the enemy defences by means of pattern bombing—did much towards the brilliant success achieved.

He was determined to keep his planes and men entire, which was not easy for other commanders of other arms cast covetous eyes on them. But fortunately he won and the fruit of his victory was the brilliant Tactical Air Force.

In January, 1942, he was created a K.C.B., and in the following November received early promotion to G.C.B. At this point, the Air Ministry again claimed Tedder. He was made Vice-Chief of the Air Staff in November, 1942, but was destined to remain only three months.

On February 11, 1943, after his return from the conference at Casablanca with President Roosevelt, Churchill announced in the House of Commons a number of changes in the North African High Command. When the Desert Army passed into the American sphere, it came naturally under the orders of General Eisenhower, who had conducted the landings in North Africa, and under him General Alexander, from the Middle East Command, became Deputy Commander-in-Chief. At the same time, Tedder was appointed Air Commander-in-Chief, Mediterranean, responsible to General Eisenhower for all the air operations in his theatre, and in control also of all the air forces throughout the whole of the Middle East. So began the famous partnership between Eisenhower and Tedder which continued until after Germany was defeated.

PATTERN AGREED

To Tedder must be given the main credit for the consistency of the application of air power both for the campaign in the Mediterranean and for the reentry into Europe. Unlike those who controlled the Luftwaffe, this incisive, penetrating air marshal firmly set the pattern for the allied air offensive in these theatres and welded their air forces into a common instrument of agreed policy. The entry into Sicily and Southern Italy had been greatly facilitated by the attacks on the railway system. This strangling of the enemy's means of communication was extended along the peninsula as the Italian campaign developed. In a far more concentrated form this preparatory bombing of communications preceded the landings in Normandy; it was these paralysing blows, as the Wehrmacht generals conceded, that made the German reactions to the invasion largely nugatory. He became Deputy Supreme Commander to General Eisenhower in December, 1943, and together, in a remarkable spirit of understanding and mutual respect, they advanced to the evening of May 8, 1945, when the instrument of the German surrender was ratified.

Honours justly fell to him with the conclusion of hostilities; he was promoted to the rank of Marshal of the Royal Air Force in September, 1945, and when created a baron in the New Year's honours of 1946, took the title of Baron Tedder, of Glenguin, in the county of Stirling, his birthplace. He was the obvious successor to Lord Portal of Hungerford as Chief of the Air Staff which he became in January, 1946.

UNBALANCED REMNANTS

It was now a very different set of problems he had to contend with in the uneasy postwar years. As he put it himself his service had to undergo a strenuous purgatory. The release scheme—fair in its principles, yet the creator of chronic unbalance in the diminishing force—the advent of the National Service man, the strain of the cold war, the difficulties of adequate recruitment were some of the factors that made his tenure as head of his service a challenging and anxious time.

When he left the Air Ministry at the end of 1949 Tedder had every reason to look forward to a comfortable life in which rewards for his undoubted attainments would not be lacking. He had been made a governor of the B.B.C. and a lucrative directorship was accorded him almost at once. But he forgot his personal inclination and interest to accept the Government's invitation for him to go out to Washington in March, 1950, as Chairman of the British Joint Services Mission and United Kingdom representative on the standing group of the military committee of Nato.

Before he returned to England in May, 1951, he had been made Chancellor of Cambridge University. He was also made vice-chairman of the B.B.C. Board of Governors in 1950. The following year he was appointed chairman of the Royal Commission to investigate Dundee's claims for a university.

From 1954 to 1960 he was chairman of the Standard Motor Co. This was no sinecure; Tedder brought to the task the same quiet sagacity he had shown in military matters.

Lord Tedder was married in 1915 to Rosalinde, daughter of Mr. W. M. Maclardy, of Sydney, New South Wales. She was killed in an air accident in January, 1943, while returning from a visit to the R.A.F. hospital at Benghazi. They had two sons (one was killed on active service) and a daughter. In the following October, he was married at a British Consulate in North Africa to Mrs. Marie de Seton Black, younger daughter of Sir Bruce Seton, Bt., C.B., of Abercorn, and they had one son. Lady Tedder died in 1965. He is succeeded by his son Professor the Hon. Michael Tedder, Roscoe Professor of Chemistry, Queen's College, Dundee.

June 5, 1967.

Dr. William Gladstone Templeman, O.B.E., who played an important part in the discovery of weedkillers, died on November 24, 1970.

After reading botany at King's College London and the Imperial College of Science and Technology, he worked for a short period at Rothamsted Experimental Station before joining the Jealott's Hill Research Station of I.C.I. in 1933. He remained there until his retirement in 1969. For the last 15 years of this period he was deputy director of the station.

Templeman will always have an honoured place in agricultural research for his part in the discovery of the hormone selective weedkillers. This began with an observation in 1940 of the differential effects produced when the artificial plant hormone alpha-naphthyl acetic acid was sprayed on to a mixed population of cereals and broad leaved weeds. Following this observation, collaboration with Dr. W. A. Sexton and Dr. R. E. Slade led to the discovery of the selective weedkillers M.C.P.A. and 2.4-D which were introduced into agriculture in 1946. These weedkillers can justifiably be regarded as initiating a revolution in the growing of cereals in practically every country in the world. The importance of this work was recognized by the Royal Agricultural Society of England in 1958 by the award jointly to Templeman and Dr. Sexton of its Research Medal.

In addition to his service with I.C.I., Templeman had many outside interests. He was on the Council of the Linnean Society from 1958 to 1961 and in the year 1960-61 he served as vice-president. After several years on the Council he was elected president of the Fertilizer Society in 1969. He also gave generously of his time to the Methodist Church and had a lively interest in the welfare of young people. He is survived by an only son.

November 27, 1970.

Lord Tenby, P.C., younger son of the first Earl Lloyd George of Dwyfor, died on February 14, 1967, in St. Thomas's Hospital, London, at the age of 72. He had held office as Minister of Fuel and Power, Minister of Food, and as Home Secretary.

Lord Tenby, for long well known as Major Gwilym Lloyd-George, had qualities very different from those of his famous father. But they were qualities that made him one of the best-liked men in the House of Commons during his 27 years as a member and Minister there. He was never much moved by political ambition and never sought to capitalize the name he bore.

Lloyd-George was a placid and even-tempered man, full of bonhomie and a good companion in any company. He had a lively sense of humour and was renowned in the smoke-room and lobbies for his stock of funny stories. So much liked was he by members of all parties that on two occasions when a vacancy arose there was a strong backing for his nomination as Speaker.

MOVING RIGHT

As a young man he was a good athlete, he played cricket for his college and regiment and was a dependable bat in the Commons cricket team. He was also a sturdy and long-hitting golfer.

After he achieved maturity Lloyd-George was never an enthusiastic political partisan. He was reared as a Liberal and proclaimed his Liberalism throughout his life, even after he had been returned to the House as a Liberal and Conservative M.P. But he found himself increasingly out of sympathy with the Liberal Party and after the Second World War he moved steadily to the right in politics. He said in a public speech in 1948 that "there was no great issue of principle dividing Liberals and Conservatives today" and that he was "prepared to cooperate with anyone in the fight against the Socialist challenge to our liberties".

Gwilym Lloyd-George (he adopted the hyphenated use of the name) was born on December 5, 1894, the former Prime Minister's second son by his marriage to Margaret Owen, afterwards Dame Margaret Lloyd George. Many of his distinctive qualities he inherited from his mother. He was educated at Eastbourne College and Jesus College, Cambridge, of which he became an honorary Fellow in 1953. Throughout the 1914-18 War he was soldiering in France. He rose to the rank of major, commanded a battery of artillery on the Somme and at Passchendaele and was mentioned in dispatches.

In 1922 Lloyd-George was elected Liberal member for Pembroke. He lost the seat in 1924 but regained it in 1929 and then represented the constituency continuously till 1950. In the general election of that year, when he stood as a Liberal and Conservative, he was narrowly beaten by Desmond Donnelly, the present Labour member. After having represented Pembrokeshire for nearly 24 years this defeat was a keen disappointment, but in 1951 Lloyd-George was elected to the House again as Liberal and Conservative member for Newcastle upon Tyne (North).

UNDER LORD WOOLTON

His first Ministerial appointment came in 1931, when he was Parliamentary Secretary to the Board of Trade in Ramsay MacDonald's first National Government. He resigned after three months because he disagreed with the decision to hold an early general election, which he described as "a discreditable manoeuvre by the Tory Party to secure a majority for themselves and their tariff programme". In those early days he shared his family's fierce radicalism and believed ardently in free trade. When the Second World War began Lloyd-George accepted an invitation from Neville Chamberlain to join the Government in his former office as junior Minister at the Board of Trade, although his Liberal colleagues refused to serve in that Government. He continued in office when Churchill formed his Coalition Government and in 1941 was transferred to serve under Lord Woolton as Parliamentary Secretary to the Ministry of Food.

After he had been less than 18 months in this post Churchill gave Lloyd-George his first big task by appointing him to be the first Minister of Fuel and Power. For more than three years, from 1942 until the Coalition was dissolved, Lloyd-George held this exacting post and achieved results which made an outstanding contribution to the nation's war effort.

GAP OVERCOME

The consumption of coal at that time by the war industries was prodigious and coal also had to be found for domestic heating. By stimulating the miners to produce more coal and by persuading consumers of all kinds to exercise rigid economy in its use Lloyd-George won his "battle of the gap" in the sphere of fuel supplies at a time when the prospect was daunting. At the same time the Minister began an extensive reorganization of the coal industry, including the appointment of a National Coal Board to advise him on its wartime control.

When the Conservatives returned to power in 1951 Churchill at once appointed Lloyd-George to be Minister of Food. This office he held for three years and he had the satisfaction of bringing food rationing to an end in the summer of 1954.

Lloyd-George was next appointed Home Secretary, and Minister for Welsh Affairs. As such he was the first Welshman to speak for Wales in the Cabinet. In his three years at the Home Office he developed a harmonious working relationship with his officials. His liberal, but essentially right-wing, views perhaps made it difficult for him to be sympathetic to the parliamentary agitation that was then growing for the abolition of capital punishment. In this, it should be said, he reflected the general views of his colleagues in the Cabinet; but his conduct in debates on these questions lacked parliamentary skill. He was responsible for much of the preparatory work on the Homicide Act of 1957, which modified the law on murder. Lloyd-George, though an abolitionist in 1948, found himself (not unusually for Home Secretaries after the war) a retentionist in office.

He resigned his post in 1957 and accepted a peerage, as Viscount Tenby, of Bulford, in the county of Pembroke. In 1961 he was appointed chairman of the Council on Tribunals, an important organ designed to safeguard the rights of the individual from departmental errors and omissions. Here his qualities of good-heartedness, kindness and concern for liberty found an appropriate mode of expression.

Tenby was also chairman of the governing body of his old school, Eastbourne College. He was for many years president of the University College of Swansea. He had also been president of the London Welsh Rugby Football Club.

He joined the board of directors of Decca in 1962, and the same year succeeded Lord Birkett as president of the Fleming Memorial Fund for Medical Research. He became president of the Football Association of Wales in 1963.

He married in 1921 Edna Gwenfron, daughter of David Jones, of Gwynfa, Denbigh, by whom he had two sons. The heir to the title is the Hon. David Lloyd-George, who was born on November 4, 1922.

February 15, 1967.

Admiral Sir William G. Tennant, K.C.B., C.B.E., M.V.O., who died in Worcester Royal Infirmary on July 26, 1963, at the age of 73, was one of the senior officers who organized the Dunkirk evacuation in 1940, and after service in the Far East, where he survived the loss of his ship, the Repulse, off Malaya, it was fitting that he should be in charge of the operation of preparing, towing, and placing in position of the "Mulberry" harbours and blockships used in the return of the Allied Armies to Normandy.

William George Tennant was born on January 2, 1890, and was the oldest surviving son of the late Lieutenant-Colonel E. W. Tennant, of The Eades, Upton-on-Severn. He was one of the last term of cadets to join the training ship Britannia in May, 1905, and after the cruise in the Highflyer on the North American Station was appointed as midshipman in September, 1906, to the battleship Prince of Wales in the Mediterranean. After specializing in navigation in 1913, he served during the First World War in the destroyers Lizard and Ferret in home waters, the cruiser Chatham at the Dardanelles, and the cruiser Nottingham in the Grand Fleet. After the Nottingham was sunk by submarine in August, 1916, he was appointed to the new cruiser Concord in the Harwich Force, of which he was navigator until April, 1919. A month later he became navigator of the Royal yacht Alexandra, until 1921.

After a year in the battle-cruiser Renown, he was on the staff of the Navigation School from 1922 to 1924. His next ship was the battle-cruiser Repulse, of which he was navigator during her tours to South Africa and South America in 1925 with the Prince of Wales (the Duke of Windsor). He was awarded the M.V.O. on its conclusion, and promoted to commander in December, 1925. After 18 months in the Operations Division at the Admiralty he was appointed in October, 1927 for the course at the R.N. Staff College. During 1934 he attended the course at the Imperial Defence College, and from 1935 to 1937 was flag-captain and chief staff officer in the Arethusa in the 3rd Cruiser Squadron in the Mediterranean. In July, 1937, he became naval instructor on the directing staff of the Imperial Defence College for two years.

When the Second World War broke out he became chief staff officer to the First Sea Lord, Admiral of the Fleet Sir Dudley Pound. In the last week of May, 1940, he went across to Dunkirk as senior naval officer on shore there, and for his good services in organizing the embarkation of the allied armies he was awarded the C.B.

After the last troops had gone on June 3 Tennant and General Alexander (as he then was) inspected the beaches and water-front and left for England together.

THE NORMANDY INVASION

Next he commanded the battle-cruiser Repulse, and in the autumn of 1941 accompanied Admiral Sir Tom Phillips to the Far East, when the Prince of Wales and Repulse were sent there as an advanced wing of the Eastern Fleet. He survived the loss of the Repulse by Japanese air attack on December 10, 1941, and shortly after his return home was promoted to rear-admiral on February 6, 1942. During the next two years he commanded a cruiser squadron of the Eastern Fleet in various operations in the Indian Ocean and Madagascar. Towards the end of 1943 his services were utilized in the planning of the Normandy invasion and in particular with the provision of the prefabricated "Mulberry" harbour.

In a lecture at the Royal United Service Institution in 1945 Rear-Admiral Harold Hickling recalled how in December,1943, when he and Admiral Tennant went to the Admiralty to ask for 60 old ships to sink off Normandy to make the "Gooseberry" breakwaters, "we were very nearly thrown out. As we came away somewhat chastened I said to Tennant: Bill, we came here to get a Gooseberry and all we seem to have got is a raspberry!"

For his services in and connected with the invasion Tennant was made C.B.E. In November, 1944, he was appointed Flag Officer, Levant and Eastern Mediterranean, with acting rank as vice-admiral, and was reappointed on his substantive promotion to that rank in July, 1945. Five months later he was advanced to K.C.B. for distinguished services throughout the war in Europe. He was Commander-in-Chief on the America and West Indies Station from October, 1946, to April, 1949, and was promoted to admiral in October, 1948. He was placed on the retired list in August, 1949. He was chairman of the general council of King George's Fund for Sailors. In 1958 he was made an honorary freeman of Worcester. He had been Lord Lieutenant of the county since 1950.

He married in 1919 Catherine, daughter of the late Major C. H. Blount, R.H.A.

July 27, 1963.

Field Marshal Sarit Thanarat, Prime Minister of Siam, died at an army hospital in Bangkok on December 8, 1963. He was 55.

With his death Siam lost an admired leader who symbolized, for his compatriots, strong rule in a period of national danger. His dramatic rise to supreme power, which began in September, 1957, was welcomed by many both at home and abroad. He was a man with a stern sense of duty, who despite ill-health worked tirelessly in the interests of his nation in the political, economic and social fields within the framework of firm personal control of government.

SUPPORTED COUP

Field-Marshal Sarit Thanarat was born in Bangkok in 1903, son of an officer. He was educated at the Phra Chula Chom Klao Military Academy. On graduation, in 1929, he entered upon the career of a professional soldier. His early appointments were to the training division of the army and he became Commandant of the Infantry Non-Commissioned Officers School in 1939. During the Second World War he undertook regimental duties and as Commander of the 13th Infantry Regiment, he received the Japanese surrender in north Siam in August, 1945.

Sarit Thanarat commanded the King's 1st Guards Infantry Regiment from 1946 to 1949 and it was during this period that his career, which until then had developed on orthodox military lines, began to take on its political aspects. He supported Field-Marshal Pibul Songgram in the *coup d'état* by which the latter regained power on November 8, 1947. After taking a prominent part in the suppression of an attempted revolt in support of Nai Pridi Phanomyong in February, 1949, he was promoted to the rank of general and took command of the 1st Army. He thus gained control of the military forces stationed in the capital. He became Commander-in-Chief of the Army on June 23, 1954, and was Deputy Minister of Defence from 1951–57.

The political career of Sarit Thanarat, who received the baton on January 1, 1956, developed when opposition was growing to Field-Marshal Pibul, who had dominated the political scene for a great part of the time since the establishment of constitutional government in 1932. He was one of a younger group of leaders in the armed services who had not participated in the overthrow of the absolute monarchy. He and Police-General Phao Siyanon emerged as rivals during the last years of Pibul's premiership. From 1955 a liberalization of political method was attempted. The formation of legal political parties was allowed. Sarit Thanarat became Vice-Chairman of the Government party, the Seri Manangkhasila, of which General Phao was Secretary.

In the key elections of February, 1957, considerable opposition to the Government was revealed by the large total of votes polled by other parties. Sarit Thanarat was not involved in the charges made against the Government that it had ensured a majority by illegal electoral practices, and he became something of a national hero as a result of his firm yet tactful handling of the student riots which broke out following the election. He became Minister of Defence in the last Pibul Government but resigned in August, 1957. On September 17 he led the *coup d'état* which resulted in the exile of Field-Marshal Pibul and General Phao. He became Supreme Commander of the Armed Forces but was abroad seeking medical treatment in the United States and the United Kingdom for much of 1958. On October 19 he flew into Bangkok from London and assumed immediate personal control of the Government.

DIRECT RULE

The Constitution was suspended, the National Assembly dissolved and a Constituent Assembly created with the double function of approving legislation and preparing a new Constitution.

Sarit Thanarat was an avowed admirer of the methods of direct rule of such leaders as President de Gaulle. His home policy was firmly directed against Communist subversion. His regime was important for the attempts that were made to improve economic conditions especially in the less well endowed north-eastern provinces. In foreign affairs he fostered his country's special relationship with the United States. He supported the South East Asia Treaty Organization though he believed in a bolder policy towards Laos than was favoured by some of its members.

He enjoyed better relations with the royal family than his predecessors and was invested with the Royal Order of Merit in 1958.

He is survived by his second wife, Than Phu Ying Vichit, whom he married in 1948, and by children.

December 9, 1963.

Ernest Thesiger, C.B.E., the actor, died on January 14, 1961, at his home in London at the age of 81, only a few weeks after he had played his last part in the West End.

A gifted and highly articulate man with varied interests, he had as it were settled for acting as a profession probably because he found his most formidable challenge in it but also his best hope of doing original and first-rate work.

He was born in London on January 15, 1879, the grandson of a Lord Chancellor, the first Lord Chelmsford, and one of the three sons of Sir Edward Pierson Thesiger, K.C.B., Clerk-Assistant in the House of Lords. He went to school at Marlborough, and though it was intended that he should enter the Civil Service, he persuaded his father to send him at the age of 17 to the Slade School, where he was a contemporary of Augustus John and Wyndham Lewis.

At the same time he attended classes at the Guildhall School of Music, dined out, went to parties, and appeared as an amateur actor at charity matinees. Gradually, and surprisingly, one of his own family suggested that he take up the stage professionally, and both Lilian Braithwaite and Robbie Ross having put in a word for him with George Alexander, he was given a job as understudy in a play at the St. James's in 1909.

Charles Hawtrey engaged him for *The Little Damozel*—a play in which the company was commanded to appear at Sandringham on Queen Alexandra's birthday ("even the sky is royal blue," remarked Thesiger)—and Tree put him into a revival of *Othello* in 1912; but soon after the outbreak of the First World War Thesiger was wounded in France while serving with the Queen Victoria Rifles.

THREE YEARS IN FARCE

He returned to the stage in 1915, and having appeared for nearly three years in a farce *A Little Bit of Fluff* and then surprised everyone by making a success in the fey part of the gillie in *Mary Rose,* he went on to establish himself as a very good actor of high comedy.

Shaw, having thought him "magnificent" in a part that was off his beat, Mephistopheles in Marlowe's tragedy, came to adopt Thesiger as one of his favourite and most highly treasured players, telling him at the first rehearsal of *Saint Joan* in 1924, that he already knew far more about the part than the author. He "created" three other Shavian characters: the Microbe in *Too True to be Good*, the British Foreign Secretary complete with monocle and knee breeches in *Geneva*, and Charles II—according to G.B.S. the best of husbands who rules by his wits—in *Good King Charles's Golden Days*.

The pedantic husband in *The Circle*, with his love of beauty and contempt for man; the impoverished nobleman teaching good manners for a living in *Excelsior* (*L'Ecole des Cocottes*); Lord Foppington in *A Trip to Scarborough*; Thesiger accurately took the measure of all such dignified champions of the absurd, not forgetting when it came to Shakespeare, the First Witch in Sir John Gielgud's wartime *Macbeth*, the melancholy Jacques in New York in 1950, and at the Moscow Art Theatre and in London, Polonius to Paul Scofield's Hamlet.

"MY BÊTE NOIRE"

Passion was contrary to his taste and outside his sympathies: "Beethoven is my *bête noire*" was a characteristic declaration of his, and his mere presence on the stage—a twisted pillar of reason—was incongruous in Schiller's *Mary Stuart* at the Old Vic—the last play, but for Enid Bagnold's recent comedy, in which he appeared.

Apart from painting—he had a show in Bond Street during the 1930s—he kept his hands and mind quick to serve things of beauty by embroidery, needlework, the collecting of Victorian mercury glassware, not least perhaps by his punctilious code of good manners. In that he remained faithful to the theatre where he started, Alexander's St. James's.

He married Miss Janette Mary Fernie Ranken in 1917. He was as he put it "engaged in a film studio" for the first time in 1932. He was appointed C.B.E. in 1960, the year following that of his stage jubilee.

January 16, 1961.

Angela Thirkell, a fluent and graceful writer of novels of the English social scene, who enjoyed an even greater success in the United States than in Britain, died on January 29, 1961, at her home in Bramley, Surrey, within a day of her seventy-first birthday.

Her novels, more particularly the earlier ones, had the virtues of gaiety, a fetching inconsequence, and a pretty and at times delicately malicious wit. Comedies of polite manners, illustrating a somewhat narrow world and restricted range of experience, they evoked the graces of living in the country houses of Barsetshire, in which nothing very much happened except that "the County" pursued its leisurely and well-bred occasions, retainers were comic or faithful, and young couples dutifully paired off in the last chapter.

The wit shone rather less brightly in the later novels, the inventive high spirits drooped a little, the admixture of high Tory views grew more pronounced—increasingly the novels tended to become a satirical running commentary or lament on the times, particularly those of an England pinched after the Second World War—but Mrs. Thirkell retained the affections of her English and American public.

Angela Margaret Mackail was born in Kensington on January 30, 1890, the daughter of J. W. Mackail, the classical scholar and Professor of Poetry at Oxford, by his wife, Margaret, only daughter of Sir Edward Burne-Jones. Although in youth she wrote romantic verse—of which Kipling, a frequent visitor in the family circle, was a severe critic—she did not publish anything of note until she was 40. Married in 1911 to Mr. J. Campbell McInnes, she continued to live in London until the marriage was dissolved in 1917; her second marriage, to Mr. G. L. Thirkell, took her to Australia, where she spent some years and where she engaged in journalism and broadcasting.

She went back to England in 1930 and celebrated her return in the following year by publishing an attractive volume of childhood memories, *Three Houses*. A year later came *Ankle Deep*, her first novel, in which her gay humour and verbal felicity made the happiest impression. Then came *High Rising*, *Wild Strawberries*, *O, These Men, These Men*! and the county families of Barsetshire, who appeared and reappeared in them, soon became familiar to a faithful and growing body of readers. *Pomfret Towers* (1938) was, perhaps, one of the best sustained in humorous quality. The outbreak of war did not halt her, neither did the return to the austerities of peace. She wrote in all more than 30 novels, including *Love At All Ages* published two years before she died.

Mrs. Thirkell had two sons by her first marriage—one of whom is Colin McInnes, the novelist—and one son by her second. She was a sister of Denis Mackail, the writer.

January 30, 1961.

Alan Thomas, D.S.O., M.C., who died on November 23, 1969, at the age of 73, left the mark of a strong and modest personality on a variety of activities. Editor of *The Listener* in the palmy years of B.B.C. talks, he carried it on as a weekly journal that was widely read for its intellectual and literary distinction. As a novelist, allowing no concessions to fashion, he earned critical respect and considerable circulation. Serving under Lord Robert Cecil (later Viscount Cecil of Chelwood) on the League of Nations Union, he had made himself respected and won many friends in Geneva as well as in London. As a voluntary worker for St. George's Hospital, and in other medical causes, he showed a devotion and a tact that won him many friends among the doctors.

Alan Thomas was born on August 21, 1896. A classical scholar at Malvern, he won classical and choral scholarships to Clare College, Cambridge, just before the First World War. During it, he served on the western front with the Royal West Kent Regiment, winning the D.S.O. and M.C., and being mentioned in dispatches and four times wounded. After taking his degree in the Law Tripos at Cambridge, he became Barrister-at-Law, Gray's Inn in 1920, and, in the next year, joined the staff of the League of Nations Union.

His experience in the trenches made the work of the League a labour of love; he was passionately convinced of the evils that would be brought about by a second world war. But the gathering gloom of world affairs did not disillusion him or in any way lower his high spirits and subtle sense of comedy. At the most depressing times in the thirties and later he could, in congenial company, cheer a small dinner table or a few friends gathered in a club smoking room, by life-like impersonations of some of the famous figures including Briand and other European statesmen, who had come under his unobtrusive scrutiny; no inflection of voice or peculiarity of idiom escaped him.

EDITED "THE LISTENER"

He stayed with the League of Nations until 1936, and was appointed editor of *The Listener* in 1939. That post he held under the stresses of war-time editing combined with Home Guard duties, and continued in it up to 1958, when he retired. This gave him leisure to return to novel writing which he had intermittently practised in younger days. His early books, among them *The Death of Laurence Vining*, *The Tremayne Case*, *Daggers Drawn*, *The Lonely Years*, *The Stolen Cellini* and *Death of the Home Secretary*, had been well received.

During his later period, he became more and more committed to the study of how a man's professional duties and ambitions may conflict, in the circumstances of modern life, with their domestic affairs. This preoccupation entered into *The Director*, *The Governor*, *The Surgeon*, *The Judge* and *The Professor*. Inflexible loyalty to the standards of conduct he had learnt in youth made him a stern critic of an increasingly permissive society. This was to the taste of many readers who shared his point of view and were held by his skill at telling a story and dealing sympathetically with characters. The sincere individualism of his approach brought him favourable reviews.

In *A Life Apart* (1968), describing his experiences as an infantry officer in the trenches, he made an authentic addition to the literature of the First World War.

He made several excursions into daily journalism, including an assignment in Egypt for the *Manchester Guardian*. A crossword enthusiast, he wrote the "Turnover" article, in May, 1962, celebrating the appearance of the 10,000th puzzle in *The Times*; he began it characteristically with "A decachiliad is not to be sneezed at".

His last years were clouded by a painful illness, involving a serious throat operation, which he faced with his accustomed cool gallantry.

November 25, 1969.

Helen Thomas, who died on April 12, 1967, at her home in Berkshire, was the widow of the poet Edward Thomas, who was killed in Flanders on Easter Monday, April 9, 1917; thus she died three days after the 50th anniversary of his death. She was 89.

At his death they had been married for 18 years and had a son and two daughters. Thomas had written over 20 critical and nature books and only in the last years of his life did he turn to poetry largely under the influence of Robert Frost. Recognition was slow and posthumous. For Helen Thomas, once the icy realization of the finality of Arras began to thaw, her relation with Edward Thomas continued in an extraordinary and inspiring way. She said that more than 20 years after Thomas's death she shortsightedly rushed off a London bus because she was convinced that she had seen him in the street. She always spoke of him with such ringing joy and youth in her voice (even in old age) that this love, with all its hardships, its vicissitudes, came alive and immediate to her listener.

Helen Berenice Noble was the second of the three daughters of James Ashcroft Noble, a literary critic who contributed to the *Spectator*, *The Academy*, *The World*, *The Westminster Gazette* and other papers, and author of several autobiographical and critical books including *The Sonnet in England*. When Helen Noble was 16 her parents, their daughters and son moved to Wandsworth where they led what she was later to describe as a mildly unconventional life which would have been "called Bohemian by the well-to-do of our type". It was a hospitable, Unitarian family and it was on Edward Thomas's first visit to James Ashcroft Noble at the age of 16 in the summer of 1894 that Helen met him. They became close friends, walked in the countryside where he taught her to recognize flowers and birds, fell in love and were married in 1899 while Thomas was still at Oxford.

He came down in 1900 and began earning his living as a free-lance writer—the beginning of a battle against poverty, first in London lodgings, then in rented houses in the southern counties, which continued until he joined the army in 1915 and had, ironically, the freedom to turn to poetry. During those years Helen's optimism and unquestioning love for her husband and their three children alleviated the melancholy to which he was prey throughout his life. There is an excellent portrait of her as wife and mother and of their circle of friends, which included Lascelles Abercrombie, Gordon Bottomley, Wilfrid Gibson and W. H. Davies, in Eleanor Farjeon's *Edward Thomas: the last four years*.

In 1926 Heinemann published *As It Was* by H. T., parts of which had already appeared in the *Adelphi*. It came out in 1927 in the United States, and the Harper edition has an introduction by J. Middleton Murry. This was Helen Thomas's story of their life from first meeting to the birth of their son Mervyn on January 15, 1900. Typical of the acclaim it won was the *Saturday Review's* description as "a *tour de force* of unselfconsciousness". The sequel, *World Without End*, appeared in 1931, continued to their final parting after his last leave at Christmas, 1916, and his return to France. In these books Edward Thomas appears as "David"; both were dedicated "To E.T.".

Harold Nicolson commented: "It is strange that this simple little book will at last bring fame to the poet whose story it tells. For I have no doubt at all that *World Without End* will have an instant, widespread, and a durable success." In the thirty-six years that have elapsed Edward Thomas and his work have received wide attention.

Materially life was difficult for her from 1917; spiritually and intellectually it was bright in her eagerness to help others, to discuss, to learn, to wrest every glow of warmth from life. Whether living in Hampstead or, at the end of her life, in cottages in Wiltshire and Berkshire, friends, gardens, grandchildren and great-grandchildren were tended with undimmed enthusiasm and energy. Above all it was her radiant love for her husband through the half century she lived without him, which showed her greatness of heart and mind and the strength of her gentleness. It was to this aspect of her that Edward Thomas referred when he spoke of himself as:—

"A pine in solitude
Cradling a dove."

April 14, 1967.

Sir Percy Thomas, O.B.E., F.R.I.B.A., who died on August 17, 1969, at his home in Cardiff, was not only a distinguished and successful architect but also a notable public figure in South Wales. He was 85.

He was awarded the Royal Gold Medal for Architecture in 1939. Architects all too seldom seem to find time for other than professional work but Thomas was an exception crowding a mass of activities into his life while remaining, in outward appearance at least, calm and benign with sparkling white hair and pink unwrinkled cheeks. He was twice president of the Royal Institute of British Architects; the only other man to be so elected was Sir William Tite. He was the youngest man ever to be elected to the presidency in the hundred years history of the R.I.B.A. and he proved to be one of the ablest. It was therefore not unnatural that he should be asked to serve again during the difficult later war years and at a time when the Royal Institute found itself faced with big reorganizational problems upon the retirement of Sir Ian McAlister. The R.I.B.A. owes a great deal to Sir Percy Thomas for his work at this time. The fact that he was well known in government circles was of tremendous help.

He was a firm believer in the value of the competition system in architecture. He certainly owed his start in life, and much of his later success to winning such competitions, and this enabled him to build up the largest practice in Wales and one of the largest in the British Isles. His most monumental work was the Swansea Civic Centre, an able piece of planning detailed traditionally but with considerable restraint. His practice included all types of buildings, among them the architectural contribution to the great steel works at Margam.

In Cardiff he had also been responsible for the Technical College and Temple of Peace, the new Welsh College of Advanced Technology and the new buildings of the University College of South Wales and Monmouthshire in addition to the new offices for Glamorgan County Council.

Percy Edward Thomas was born on September 13, 1883, the son of Christmas Thomas, a sea captain. He went to private schools and was articled to E. H. Bruton F.R.I.B.A. of Cardiff. He worked as an assistant in various offices in Lancashire until, in 1911, he won an open competition for the design of Technical College. He became a vice-president of the R.I.B.A. in 1927 and was president in 1935–37 and again 1943–46. He was three times president of the South Wales Institute of Architects.

During the war of 1914–18 Thomas served successively in the Artists Rifles, the Royal Engineers and on the staff of the C. E. XIII Army Corps. He was created O.B.E. (military division) and twice mentioned in dispatches. In the Second World War, his administrative abilities were quickly recognized and he was appointed chairman of the Welsh Board for Industry, an appointment which he held from 1942–55 and at the same time Regional Controller for Wales, Ministry of Production. He also held the rank of Lieut.-Col. in the Home Guard and later became Hon. Col. of 109 Regt. R.E. (T.A.). He was made a J.P. in 1943, a Deputy Lieutenant in 1946, and became High Sheriff of Glamorganshire in 1949.

In 1906 he married Margaret Ethel Turner who died in 1953, they had a son, who later joined his father in practice, and three daughters.

August 18, 1969.

Commander Charles Ralfe Thompson, C.M.G., O.B.E., R.N., who was Personal Assistant to the Prime Minister from 1940 until Churchill left office in 1945, died on August 11, 1966, at his home in London. He was 71.

Second son of R. C. Thompson, member of a Durham shipbuilding family, he was born at Shiney Row, co. Durham, in 1894 and went through Osborne and Dartmouth, first going to sea as a midshipman in the battleship Monarch in 1911. A fantastically keen pioneer airman, he was anxious to make flying his career in the Navy. But ironically enough his application to specialize in this new branch was turned down by Churchill, then First Lord of the Admiralty, soon after the outbreak of the First World War on the grounds that Thompson had not put in enough sea time to entitle him to volunteer. So Thompson became a submarine specialist and he was in command of submarines almost continuously until 1931.

SOUGHT BY CHURCHILL

At a time of retrenchment in the service he was passed over for promotion and became flag lieutenant commander, first to the Commander in Chief Portsmouth, Admiral Sir Arthur Waistell, and then to his successor, Admiral Sir John Kelly. In 1936, when it was decided to create a new post of flag lieutenant to the Board of Admiralty the choice fell on Thompson and he was still carrying out these duties when war was declared and Churchill arrived at the Admiralty. Thompson, by now on the verge of retirement from the Active List, was one of the Duty Officers at the Admiralty. Impressed by his unobtrusive efficiency, his tact and obvious discretion, Churchill asked, when he moved to Downing Street, for Thompson to be permanently attached to his personal staff.

Thompson remained at the Prime Minister's side for the rest of the war, organizing all his journeys by land, sea and air and accompanying him everywhere. When Churchill had to fly home from Bermuda in 1942 after the Washington conference and the passenger list in the flying boat had to be cut to minimum to make room for extra fuel Thompson had to be left behind, "lamenting as bitterly as Lord Ullin in the poem...never before and never afterwards were we separated in these excursions" Churchill afterwards.

INDISPENSABLE "TOMMY"

"Tommy," as he was always known to the Churchill family, became an indispensable member of the Prime Minister's entourage. By nature a modest and extremely self-effacing man, he was content to remain always in the background. But his personal charm and ability to get things done with a minimum of fuss combined with complete unflappability under pressure considerably lightened the burden of the Prime Minister's daily life during those years of stress.

In his younger days an accomplished amateur rider and polo player, he was keenly interested in racing and when he left the Prime Minister's staff he acted for some years as a steward's secretary of the Jockey Club. In 1964 an account of his wartime experiences was given in *The War and Colonel Warden*, a book by Gerald Pawle, based on Thompson's recollections.

Thompson, who was made an O.B.E. in 1939 and C.M.G. in the Prime Minister's list in 1945, was also made a Chevalier of the Legion of Honour for his war services. He was unmarried.

August 12, 1966.

Dorothy Thompson, who died in Lisbon on January 31, 1961, at the age of 66, was held in high esteem in many parts of the world for her work as American feminist leader, newspaper foreign correspondent, broadcaster and columnist, writing in a chain of American journals with a reading public of many millions each week. She was at one time wife of Sinclair Lewis, the American novelist.

Vitality was the outstanding quality of her writing; she could always be trusted to catch her reader's eye; he might disagree with her but he could not ignore her point of view nor the cogency and impressiveness with which she stated it. That same vitality informed her broadcasts; none who heard her memorable talks, instinct with humanity and courage, over the B.B.C. during the war will forget them.

She was born at Lancaster, in the northern part of the state of New York, on July 9, 1894, and went to school in Chicago where she remained until she was 17. Returning to her home she attended the University of Syracuse, not far away, and graduated in 1914. She had found a capacity for learning and speaking foreign languages and continued her studies after graduation at the University of Vienna.

In 1915 she went back to her home, having learnt much of the inside of Europe during the first year of the war. She found the struggle for women's suffrage at its height in the United States and at once threw herself into the battle with energy, taking on the work of director of publicity in the northern part of the state of New York. She then got her first insight into the workings of a newspaper office. The struggle for equal suffrage was soon over and the battle won and she then devoted herself to social work. After three years she found herself well equipped for work on a newspaper with a knowledge of languages and foreign affairs and of social conditions.

In 1920 she was appointed foreign correspondent for the *Philadelphia Public Ledger* which was then attracting attention as a national rather than a local newspaper, and of the *New York Evening Post*, a journal which had at that time a high reputation. She worked for these papers for eight years and during the last four from 1924 till 1928 she was stationed in Berlin as chief of the central European service. She travelled extensively in European countries particularly in Russia where she made long tours investigating so far as she could with thoroughness.

In 1928 she left the staff of the *Ledger* and *Evening Post* and gradually worked up a connexion with a large number of papers in all parts of the United States as a free lance journalist writing chiefly on foreign affairs and matters of interest to women. She travelled extensively in Europe and was well known in most countries. She wrote much of Germany after the Nazi Party came into power in 1933 and was outspoken in her comments on affairs there so that she was more than once at loggerheads with officials and was at last obliged to leave the country. After that she carried on her work mostly in her own country but her long stay in Europe and her knowledge of conditions there enabled her to write and speak with authority. Her broadcasts on European affairs were listened to by many people in all parts of the country and had much to do with formulating American public opinion for she was a clear and attractive speaker.

In the autumn of 1938 she fiercely denounced the German persecution of the Jews and a word dropped by her brought in a large sum of money for the defence of a young Jew who had shot a German official in Paris.

BITING ATTACK

She continued as political columnist for the *New York Herald Tribune* until 1941, at which time she left that paper and thereafter distributed her column throughout the country through a syndicating agency.

In the later years of her life she was less active than she had formerly been but remained a keen follower of causes near her heart and continued to express herself vigorously in print and speech when political events and developments touched near a "cause" that interested her. In 1947 she visited Europe again and spent some time in Poland covering the crucial elections of that year, elections that aroused keen interest throughout the free world. She damned them by saying simply that the voting was "just as free as in Mr. Hitler's elections."

The year 1951 saw her vocally active about the fate of Arabs in Palestine. As a speaker at the Chicago meeting of the anti-Zionist American Council for Judaism, she delivered a biting attack on the new State for allegedly discriminating against its Arabs, saying they were "forced to live as second-rate citizens with serious restrictions on their rights." In 1957 she published a book entitled *The Courage to be Happy*.

Her marriages to Josef Bard and Sinclair Lewis were dissolved, and in 1943 she married, thirdly, Maxim Kopf, the well-known artist and sculptor, and thereafter spent a good deal of time in New Hampshire where Kopf had a studio. He died in Hanover, New Hampshire, in 1958, at the age of 65.

February 1, 1961.

Sylvia Thompson (Mrs. Peter Luling), who died on April 27, 1968, after a sudden illness at the age of 65, was the author of a number of polished and closely observed novels, of which perhaps the best known was her second, *The Hounds of Spring*, which was first published in the mid-1920s and became a best seller.

Her characters, particularly in her earlier books, tended to be people whose private and personal problems were of more concern to them than were problems of the world outside, but she had rich descriptive powers and an undoubted skill in analysing the emotions of a group of people so that even if one did not always find her characters either attractive or sympathetic one generally found them stimulating.

The daughter of Norman Thompson, she was born on September 4, 1902 and educated at "assorted schools", and Somerville College, Oxford. Her first novel was *The Rough Crossing*, then came *The Hounds of Spring*. Her later books included *Winter Comedy; Helena; Breakfast in Bed; Third Act in Venice; Recapture the Moon; The Gulls fly Inland; The People Opposite* and *The Candle's Glory*. With Victor Cunard she wrote a play, *Golden Arrow*, which was put on at the New Theatre, Oxford, in May, 1935, and was later transferred to the Whitehall Theatre, London. The cast included Sir Laurence Olivier, Greer Garson, Cecil Parker and Peter Copley.

She married in 1926 Theodore Dunham (Peter) Luling. They had three daughters.

April 29, 1968.

Arthur Alexander Thomson, M.B.E., novelist, humorist, cricket writer, and for many years a sporting correspondent for *The Times,* died on June 2, 1968, at the age of 74. Few men made their mark with such distinction both in the realm of authorship and day-to-day journalism, and if he was perhaps known to his widest public through his cricket books and writings, his all-round knowledge and professional writing skill had made him an eagerly-read writer on a diversity of topics for more than 40 years.

"A.A." or "Tommy"—he was hardly ever addressed or referred to by one of his Christian names—was born at Harrogate, Yorkshire, on April 7, 1894, and educated at Harrogate Grammar School and King's College London. His early thoughts of entering the scholastic profession were interrupted by the First World War, when he joined the West Yorkshire Regiment and served in France and Mesopotamia. His early boyhood in Yorkshire had formed the subject of his brilliant autobiographical novel, *The Exquisite Burden* (1935), which was re-issued in 1963 and is still in steady demand.

He wrote nearly 60 books in all, including plays, novels, verse, humour and travel books, and in 1953, with *Cricket My Pleasure,* there began his long series of cricket books in which his buoyant philosophy of the game, with all its comedy and character, shone through in rich prose and mellow phrases. There followed, among others, his biography of W. G. Grace, *The Great Cricketer* (1957), *Hirst and Rhodes* (1959) and *Hutton and Washbrook* (1963), and probably no cricket author since Sir Neville Cardus was in his prime had a closer following. Cricket, he only recently declared, gave him more unalloyed pleasure over a longer period than any other single thing.

He had an enormous sense of fun and a perpetual twinkle in his eye, and when, some 10 years ago, he started witing cricket for *The Times,* and then rugger in the winter, his presence in press-boxes throughout the country could guarantee a warm fund of stories, all told with an expressive fervour, that made up for any deficiencies on the field. As an after-dinner speaker at cricket gatherings he was one of the most original and popular of the last decade, and since 1963 he had been president of the Cricket Society.

During the Second World War he worked first at the Air Ministry and then as a lecturer with the Ministry of Information. In the 1966 Birthday Honours List, he was awarded the M.B.E. for services to sports writing.

June 3, 1968.

Dr. David Thomson, Master of Sidney Sussex College, Cambridge, died on February 24, 1970, at the age of 58.

Born in January, 1912, he was a pupil at Sir George Monoux Grammar School, and in 1931 entered Sidney Sussex College with an Open Scholarship in History. During the nineteen thirties his successes were those of an outstanding student: First Class honours in both Parts of the Historical Tripos, the Gladstone Memorial Prize in 1937. He was awarded a Research Fellowship at his College in the following year. In the post-war years he was intensively active in College, Faculty and University affairs, in the development of his own writing and research, and in public debate on international and educational issues. Throughout his working life he showed a rare ability to pursue many interests simultaneously and at a high level.

He was Senior Tutor of his College from 1946-53, which were years of many tutorial problems arising from the return of men from active service, changing periods of national service in peace, changing admissions procedures, growing undergraduate numbers. His tenure of the Mastership, which began in 1957, was notable for a major addition to the college buildings, a reorganization of the college endowments which more than checked the inroads previously made by inflation on its external income, a rapid increase in the number of Fellows, especially in 1962 and the years immediately following, and changing relationships between senior and junior members.

ARCHAIC CUSTOM

He was an excellent administrator, quick, comprehensive and exact in dealing with any business which came his way. No one could ever have answered letters more promptly and fully. This was so even in his early days as Tutor, still in the college's pre-secretarial age, when he himself typed most of his heavy correspondence. The archaic college custom that the Master should be not only chairman but also secretary of the Governing Body and College Council survived into his time, and he filled both roles with distinction. He was a particularly able chairman, well served by his firmness, unfailing good humour, complete knowledge of the business, and the high personal regard in which he was always held by the Fellows over whom he presided. To all college problems, whether they arose from its present working or future development, he brought never less than unshakable good sense, and more often deep wisdom.

Although the college was always his first care, he was generous in his service to the university. From 1950-58 he sat on the Council of the Senate. He had already gained some experience of the working of a university body by his membership of the Board of Extra-Mural studies. This interest in adult education had also led him, while still a young graduate, to teach as a part-time tutor for the Workers' Educational Association, and he was for many years treasurer of the association's Eastern District. Later he was to become chairman of the Governors of the Perse School, at a time when the present school buildings were planned, erected and occupied; and, within the university, he became chairman both of the education syndicate and of the board of governors of the Cambridge Institute of Education. In the decade of the Crowther and Robbins Reports, he was an opponent of the indiscriminate expansion of universities, as he was of that view of them as something other than communities of scholars, pursuing proper academic ends.

He was particularly critical of those who saw universities in terms of industrial plant, to be assessed only in terms of throughput and output and he readily made his views known through broadcasts, articles and public correspondence. In Cambridge he was prominent in the discussion which followed the publication of the Bridges Report in 1962. One of the results of that Report was the setting up of the Colleges' Committee, on which most colleges were represented by their Heads. Thomson was a popular choice as its first chairman.

MANY BOOKS

He was a tower of strength in the History Faculty, not only as chairman of its board from 1958–60 but as a teacher of both graduate and undergraduate students. His range was unusually wide. He lectured and supervized in the fields of politics, political theory, modern British and European history. His deepest and most specialized interest was in the history of modern France, and the importance of his work on this subject was recognized by the creation of a personal Readership in 1969. At various times he was Visiting Professor at Columbia University and a Member of the Institute for Advanced Studies at Princeton.

In whatever field he taught he also published. Most of his many books were those of a teacher, analytical in character interpreting their subjects particularly for undergraduates, sixth-formers, members of adult classes and the intelligent reading public. With original research in the strictest sense he was less concerned, although his Ph.D. thesis on the conception of political party mid-eighteenth century England, and his Zaharoff Lecture on *The Proposal for Anglo-French Union in* 1940, are impressive evidence of what he could achieve in this respect. Certainly his work and influence played their part in promoting the study of contemporary history.

The best of his books stayed long in print and went through a number of editions. *Democracy in France since* 1870, first published in 1946, reached its fourth edition in 1964. *The Babeuf Plot* (1947), *Two Frenchmen: Pierre Laval and Charles de Gaulle* (1951), *France: Empire and Republic, 1850–1940* (1968) were other contributions in the same field. He often broadcast, and contributed regularly to *The Times* on modern French politics.

England in the Nineteenth Century first appeared in 1950 as part of the Pelican History of England; in 1964 he added a companion volume on the twentieth century. He was the first editor of that volume of the new *Cambridge Modern History* devoted to the twentieth century and made a small but much read contribution to the Home University Library on *World History from 1914 to 1961*.

After *Democracy in France* his most outstanding work was *Europe since Napoleon*. Soon after its appearance in 1957 it became part of the reading recommended by University History departments throughout the English-speaking world. His work fully deserved its great success, especially among students. Not only is it extremely well written; it is based on unusually wide reading, on the truest standards of scholarship, on saneness and humanity of outlook.

His help and advice were always worth having, and there were always many who sought them. His breadth of knowledge and experience, his shrewdness and good sense, his complete lack of personal vanity and, not least, his genial and equable temperament, all inspired confidence and affection. Despite the demand made on him by his many responsibilities, those who called never failed to receive a cheerful welcome, or to be given all the time they needed.

His wife, Margaret, helped him to make the Master's Lodge a place of warm friendliness and hospitality, as their many guests, and especially junior and senior members of the College, remember with gratitude.

February 25, 1970.

Rear Admiral Sir George Pirie Thomson, C.B., C.B.E., died on January 24, 1965, at Queen Mary's Hospital, Roehampton, at the age of 77. He will be best remembered for the masterly job he did as Chief Press Censor virtually throughout the war.

Thomson had an eventful and interesting career. Born in Jubbulpore, India, in 1887, he was the son of a civil servant working as a civil engineer in the Public Works Department. His grandfather, William Pirie, was Moderator of the General Assembly of the Church of Scotland and Principal of Aberdeen University, and had the honour of preaching before Queen Victoria. His uncle was Professor of Mathematics at the University of Aberdeen, and one time Senior Wrangler at Cambridge.

He was taken by his parents to Switzerland, where he remained until he reached the age of six, and on his father returning to Edinburgh he himself was unable to speak any language but French. He attended George Watson's College until he was 15, and then joined the Navy, the main reason for his choice being—so he used to say—that his girth troubled him and he felt he might look slimmer in naval uniform. After serving as a cadet he made rapid headway, gaining five "firsts" in passing for lieutenant, and specialized in submarines. During the first year of the 1914–18 War he served as a watch-keeper and German interpreter in the battleship St. Vincent, but in 1915 resumed submarine commands, being awarded the O.B.E. in recognition of his work.

25 YEARS IN SUBMARINES

After the war he continued in this branch of the Navy. Later he became Chief of Staff in China, subsequently commanded the cruiser Devonshire, and from 1937 to 1939 he was second member of the Naval Board of Australia. His service in submarines, at a time when such craft were largely in the experimental stage, totalled 25 years.

Thomson was placed on the retired list, after 35 years' service, in 1939 and he was on holiday in the South of France when Hitler's invasion of Poland sent him back to London immediately. He reported to Churchill, then first Lord of the Admiralty, and was told to report at once at the Ministry of Information to Vice-Admiral Usborne, director of the Censorship Division. At the moment the situation was somewhat chaotic. Steps had been taken in 1938 to allocate personnel as censors in the event of war on the basis that the entire censorship staff would consist of retired officers of the three fighting services. The scheme looked good on paper but it broke down at its first severe test—the sinking of the passenger liner Athenia on September 3, 1939. Usborne insisted that he must have a deputy and Churchill's decision to send Thomson to fill the position paid handsome dividends.

In his entertaining book *Blue Pencil,* Thomson confessed that at that time his experience of the press was limited to reading his newspaper at the breakfast table but he had many assets which made him the ideal man for the job. He had a remarkable facility for making friends; he took prompt decisions which he was prepared to fight for tooth and nail if they were challenged by a higher authority; he trusted the journalists with whom he was working, and as a result they soon came to trust him. It was not surprising, therefore, that he remained at the Ministry for the rest of the war, first as deputy and later for nearly five years as chief press censor.

He had no sympathy with the censor who was not prepared to use commonsense and who preferred to stick to the letter of the Defence Notices under which the censorship operated—however ridiculous the results might be. One of the first persons he met on arriving at the Ministry was a distracted reporter who sought his help over the caption of a picture. It showed girls being issued with gasmasks at a school in Holborn but the censor refused to pass the word *Holborn* in the picture caption. Thomson agreed that the lives of the citizens of London were not likely to be endangered if the enemy knew that there was a girls' school in Holborn. He restored the caption and made a lifelong friend of the journalist.

He was always ready to explain why a story had been stopped and there grew up a system of personal and friendly consultation which helped to make the system of voluntary censorship workable. There was one moment during the war when the voluntary system was threatened from Whitehall and Thomson was one of the men who fought hard and successfully to prevent a compulsory system.

Physically he was not overstrong and the war period at the Ministry of Information must have been a severe strain. He seemed to be always on duty, but never showed annoyance at being awakened during the night if the inquiry was a worthwhile one.

Thomson was one of those who felt that the close liaison which had been established between the fighting services and the press through the committee which controlled the working of the Defence Notice system ought to be continued, and when it was decided to create an organization with the title the Services, Press, and Broadcasting Committee it was unanimously agreed that Thomson should be its secretary. In this post he continued to command the general respect and good will of the press. As he had also been appointed Public Relations Officer of the Latin American Centre, he was able to do his work in the delightful surroundings of Canning House, in Berkeley Square.

On his retirement from the Navy in 1939, with the rank of Rear-Admiral, he was created C.B.E., and in 1946 C.B. He was knighted in the New Year Honours of 1963.

January 26, 1965.

Maurice Thorez, for over 30 years Secretary-General and impregnable head of the French Communist Party and its President since May, 1964, died on July 11, 1964, off the Bulgarian coast while on his way to a holiday in the Soviet Union. He was 64.

He had been a semi-invalid since November, 1950, when he was stricken by a severe cerebral haemorrhage. A Soviet airliner was at once sent to fly him to Moscow for treatment by leading Russian doctors, but when he returned to Paris two and a half years later he was still partially paralysed, and indeed never fully recovered his health. For a long time his public appearances were restricted to a few moments at the opening of important communist gatherings and he who was formerly the party's best and most attractive speaker never again addressed the National Assembly—although he retained his seat until his death. Thorez remained virtually to the end the undisputed master of French communists, putting down intrigue and dissension within the party with firmness and skill, and the unfailing aid of some of the old party stalwarts such as his wife, Jeanette Vermeersch, and his deputy for many years

Jacques Duclos. Although in some ways, such as his slavish adherence to the Moscow line, he did harm to the party and made impossible the Popular Front for which he worked so hard, it is fairly certain that without his leadership the various crises through which the French communist movement passed between 1950 and 1960 would have resulted not, as they did, merely in a decline in membership, but in serious divisions within the party.

Thorez was born in April, 1900, in a mining village in the Pas de Calais, the grandson and probably the son of miners, although there is some doubt about his actual parentage. He was a remarkable child, "first in class and first in catechism, the favourite of the schoolmaster and of the *curé*" and he passed his school-leaving examination at the age of 12.

BEGAN DOWN MINE

Despite his brilliance, there was in those days nothing better for him to do than go down the mine at that tender age. Two years later he became a refugee with his grandfather when the Germans invaded the north of France and he worked as a farm labourer.

He served his regular military service directly after the war, but on his release his former employers refused to take him back on the grounds of his political extremism, so he became a bricklayer and in March 1919 joined the Socialist Party, where he attached himself to a group, headed by Barbusse, that was working for affiliation with the Third (Communist) International. In 1920 the party split over this issue and Thorez became a militant communist, and as such, in the manner of the time, received his first prison sentence, for subversive propaganda among soldiers, in 1927. This he afterwards held to be an advantage since it gave him time to "complete his education". In 1924 he had been appointed party secretary in the Pas de Calais region; a year later he was secretary of the Politbureau; in May, 1932, he was elected to the Chamber of Deputies for the Ivry (Seine) constituency; and in 1933 he became secretary-general of the Communist Party and all-powerful leader of the French communists, not at that time a very extensive group. It was however to his energy and intelligence and, indeed, to some extent to his attractive personality—he was a handsome, jovial man who loved good living—that the gradual growth of the party in the prewar years was mainly due.

ANTI-NAZI CAMPAIGN

He led a bitter campaign against Nazi Germany in the late thirties and supported the Government's rearmament programme—until the Germano-Soviet Pact of August, 1939. This took the French communists entirely by surprise because then, and frequently in later years, Moscow did not trouble to inform the subservient French party of impending changes in policy. Twenty-one of the 72 Communist Deputies resigned from the party but Thorez himself valiantly changed course in mid-stream. In October, when Daladier began a wholesale arrest of French communists, Thorez, who had been called up, deserted from the French Army, escaped to Belgium and some months later found his way to Russia. For this he was sentenced *in absentia* in November, 1939, to six years' imprisonment for desertion *à l'intérieur en temps de guerre*.

During General de Gaulle's visit to Moscow, in October, 1944, Stalin interceded with him for Thorez, who was granted an amnesty and allowed to return to France, where, so strong and so contemptuous of facts is communist propaganda, he was given a hero's welcome. This was the period when, profiting by the Soviet alliance and their own record in the Resistance, the communists were, with the Socialists and the M.R.P., at the head of affairs and in fact Thorez was a great help to de Gaulle; he persuaded his followers to work with a will towards the rebuilding of France, to accept the unavoidable privations and refrain from strikes and unreasonable wage claims, and to agree to the dissolution of their armed force, the *milices patriotiques*. In two elections the communists, with over five million votes, emerged as the strongest single party and Thorez was not only Minister of State and then Vice-Premier in three governments, but a serious candidate for the Premiership.

At the same time there is no doubt that he was anxious to remain in the Government and to make the communists "a progressive but national party". When, however, in April, 1947, Thorez and the other Communist Ministers openly opposed the Government's wages and prices policy Ramadier obtained their resignation—much to Thorez's fury—and the honeymoon with the other tripartite parties was at an end. There was a period of high industrial unrest led by the communists, and during the active phase of the cold war Thorez, in and outside Parliament, was vehement in his attacks upon French policy and strong in his support of the Soviet attitude. Then came his stroke and his departure for Moscow. By the time he returned, in 1953, economic conditions had improved and the cold war lessened in intensity, and although they still polled around five million votes in any general election, and were still the largest and most disruptive party in Parliament the communists ceased to weigh so heavily on national affairs. Thorez constantly opposed General de Gaulle after his return to power and also, for ideological reasons which were never either clear or convincing, the negotiations leading to the Algerian settlement.

July 13, 1964.

James Thurber died in a New York hospital on November 2, 1961. He was 66.

As illustrator and writer he commanded the affectionate devotion of readers on both sides of the Atlantic to a degree perhaps not surpassed by any American author since Mark Twain. His stories, illustrated fables, humorous drawings, fairy-tales for grown-ups and apparently casual comments on the society of his day combine the fantasy of Carroll with the throwaway, salty wisdom of Will Rogers.

Conventional as only a state capital can be, Columbus, Ohio, is nevertheless a town in which, according to James Grover Thurber, who was born there on December 8, 1894, almost anything is likely to happen and in which almost everything does. Its greatest modern eccentric, Mary Thurber, who died in 1956, aged 89, was renowned for practical jokes of formidable proportions and was well equipped to mother one of America's finest comic talents.

Of his father little has been recorded except that on "The Night the Bed Fell" (the title of one of the most immediately popular among the short autobiographical pieces in *My Life and Hard Times*, 1933), it fell not on Charles L. Thurber, asleep in the attic, but on his son. Thurber was educated at Ohio State University, where two years of military drill were compulsory; thus, as the First World War concluded, he found himself studying the tactics of the Civil War.

In 1918 he joined the State Department and was posted to the American Embassy in Paris as a code clerk. Colonel House, it was said, had cabled for more code books, but as his message was wrongly deciphered, got clerks instead. Two years later Thurber returned home and working successively on the Columbus *Evening Dispatch*, the Paris edition of the *Chicago Tribune*, and, briefly, the New York *Evening Post*, earned the title by which he preferred to describe himself—newspaperman. How in fact anyone whom he was supposedly interviewing ever got in a word puzzled his more orthodox colleagues, for the flow of Thurber's talk was already compulsive.

A FLAWLESS MAGAZINE

It was not a newspaper, however, but a new magazine which, in 1927 and for the rest of his life, provided Thurber with the perfect outlet for his many-sided brilliance. The *New Yorker* was two years old; Harold Ross, its prickly, unpredictable founder, determined that Thurber, of all people, should become its ideal managing editor, coordinating staff, contributors and contents and bringing forth each Thursday an entirely flawless magazine. In his *The Years with Ross* (1959) Thurber has chronicled how, whenever he said he wanted to write, not to edit, Ross would snarl, "Writers are a dime a dozen. What I want is an editor." Fortunately Thurber's administrative powers proved as scanty as his contributions were fluent and versatile. His unsigned "Talk of the Town" paragraphs, his stories, often deriving from his own family's rich store of characters, and later his drawings became an integral part of the *New Yorker*. Many of his best pieces first appeared there: "The Secret Life of Walter Mitty", "The Day the Dam Broke", "If Grant Had Been Drinking at Appomattox", to name but a few. Since then they have reappeared in his own collections, such as *The Thurber Carnival* (1945), *The Beast in Me* (1949) and *Alarms and Diversions* (1957), and have been anthologized and translated all over the world.

His drawings found their first champion in his *New Yorker* colleague E. B. White. When they collaborated on *Is Sex Necessary*? their American publisher stared in discomfiture at the illustrations and said, "I gather this is a rough idea of the kind of drawing you want in the book". "These *are* the drawings that go in the book", answered White. They had all been shown to Ross and rejected. For some reason, perhaps because Paul Nash was one of the first to recognize Thurber's genius as a draughtsman, Ross regarded the drawings as an odd fad of the English. He soon realized his mistake and printed as many as he could get. Dogs, seals, warring men and women, pretentious ladies who "come from haunts of coot and hern"—have not all these in 30 years grown even closer to their Thurber prototypes? Certainly there can be few comic artists whose pictures leap so instantaneously to mind on re-reading merely the captions: "All right, have it your own way—you heard a seal bark"; "Touché!", and "That's my first wife up there, and this is the *present* Mrs. Harris". This last, as "The Lady on the Bookcase", provided the title for a characteristic essay on his drawings by Thurber himself.

When Thurber's sight began to fail, Ross was quick to come to the rescue by cutting up old drawings, fitting them together as new compositions and recaptioning them. Thurber lost his left eye in an accident when he was only six. Until he was 45 he could see well enough with glasses, but then complications set in; he underwent a series of operations but within a few years was totally blind. Helped by the devoted care of his wife (who herself at one stage suffered from a detached retina) and by his own phenomenally retentive memory, he let blindness interfere very little either with his writing or with his conviviality.

Tall, thin, and with a mop of startlingly white hair, he was gay and attractive to meet. His talk, increasingly monological with the years, was uproarious and the social disadvantages of blindness seemed to bother him not at all. He had a warm regard for Britain, which he visited regularly and often said that the British had been quicker than his fellow-countrymen to recognize his quality as a writer. For this reason the suggestion, voiced by one or two reviewers in England (but by none in America), that in *The Years with Ross* he had been less than just to his former editor wounded him deeply.

James Thurber's other books include *The Middle-Aged Man on the Flying Trapeze*, *Fables for Our Time*, *Thurber's Dogs*, *The Thirteen Clocks*, *The Wonderful O*, *Lanterns and Lances*, and a play, *The Male Animal*, written in collaboration with Elliott Nugent and successfully produced in New York and London.

He was twice married, first, in 1921, to Althea Adams and secondly, in 1935, to Helen Wismer, and leaves a daughter by his first wife.

November 3, 1961.

Lord Thurso, K.T., P.C., C.M.G., died at his Twickenham home on June 15, 1970, after a long illness. As Sir Archibald Sinclair he led the Liberal Party during the critical decade 1935–45; he brought to public life fine gifts of character, liveliness and endurance.

Endowed with striking good looks and charm of manner, he won a distinctive position for himself both with supporters and opponents—a position which was strengthened by his integrity and his power of driving through to the heart of any problem. The position which was achieved by his small following in the House of Commons in the 1930s—the Liberals then numbered 17—was out of all proportion to their strength and was in a measure due to the personal authority of his leadership. Some indication of this is suggested by the pressure brought to bear on him to fortify and rejuvenate Neville Chamberlain's Government at the outbreak of war in 1939; when Churchill joined that Government as First Lord he strongly urged this course both on Sinclair and on Chamberlain.

When Churchill became Prime Minister Sinclair was made Secretary of State for Air, remaining in that office for the duration of the war and until the break up of the wartime coalition.

PARENTS DIED

Archibald Henry Macdonald Sinclair, the first Viscount Thurso in the peerage of the United Kingdom and the fourth baronet, was born on October 22, 1890. His mother, Mabel Sands, an American lady of great beauty, died a few days after he was born, and his father, Clarence Granville Sinclair, died when he was five. Consequently Archibald Sinclair was brought up by his grandfather, Sir Tollemache Sinclair, third baronet, to whom he was heir, and by his uncle and aunt, General and Mrs. Owen Williams. Owing to the remoteness of Caithness, where the family property lay, much of Sinclair's boyhood was spent at Temple House, Berkshire, with General and Mrs. Williams. The former was a friend of King Edward and provided a background for the conventional pastimes of fashionable life which were at no time naturally congenial to Sinclair. He was somewhat reserved, underneath an expansive manner, and the ordinary pleasantries of social life did not come easily to him. He had a small impediment in speech and he often lamented that he was a poor hand at the companionship of the smoking-room in the House of Commons. Yet among friends he was delightful company, ever lively and courteous. He went to Eton, where he did not specially distinguish himself but is remembered for his pertinacity in argument, and then to Sandhurst. On passing out he joined the Life Guards (1st and 2nd).

He succeeded his grandfather when he was 22. His imagination was from the first captured by the possibilities of flight and he spent some time shortly before the First World War in experimenting with a primitive aircraft of his own, with some rather novel features, which he kept at Shoreham airfield.

During the war he served in France and he was, for some time, adjutant of the battalion of the Royal Scots Fusiliers which was commanded by Churchill. Although he knew Churchill before, this comradeship in the field helps to explain a friendship which coloured the whole of his political life. In the closing months of the war he married Marigold, daughter of Colonel and Lady Angela Forbes, by whom he had a family of two sons and two daughters.

After the war he became personal military secretary to Churchill at the War Office, following him to the Colonial Office as private secretary in 1922. In the autumn of that year he was returned to Parliament for his own constituency of Caithness and Sutherland. He was at this time a Churchillian Liberal and rather naturally gravitated towards the Lloyd George section of the party. His maiden speech in the House of Commons was, appropriately enough, devoted to air matters and in particular to the importance of an independent Air Force and to the vulnerability of Great Britain in air attack. He held his seat throughout the spate of elections between 1922 and 1924 and his reputation in the House steadily grew.

In 1930 he became Chief Liberal Whip: this was a position which greatly taxed both his diplomacy and forbearance because the party was falling apart under the vagaries of Lloyd George's leadership and the difficulties created by Sir John Simon and his following. Simon roundly told Sinclair in the summer of 1931 that the party had reached the depths of humiliation. In the autumn of that year Sinclair, with the other Liberal leaders, joined the National Government and became Secretary of State for Scotland. Like many other progressive leaders—Lord Grey at Howick, Rosebery at Dalmeny, or Gladstone at Hawarden—he was inclined to disappear and become inaccessible in his native land, but Liberal policy was often fashioned in private gatherings of his Liberal colleagues in the summer at Thurso or on the Caithness moors, where Sinclair, in the kilt and surrounded by his attractive family, was seen at his splendid best.

Some discussions leading to the departure of the Free Trade Ministers from the National Government took place at Thurso in the summer of 1932. Sinclair, in company with his Liberal and Labour colleagues, made a defiant departure from the Government in September, 1932.

PARTY LEADER

When Sir Herbert Samuel lost his seat at the 1935 election, Sinclair was chosen to succeed him as leader of the Parliamentary party. In the four years which intervened between his election as leader and the outbreak of war, Sinclair enormously enhanced his reputation. Admittedly the situation favoured him. With a body of followers —small but compact and loyal—he was in close alliance with his old chief, Churchill, as the indignant critics of the foreign policy of the Baldwin and Chamberlain eras. Many observers felt that the Liberal criticism of the Government was more resoundingly effective than that of the official opposition. Lord Cecil was only voicing an opinion which was general when he said at that period that "Sir Archibald Sinclair was the only Liberal leader of recent times who has infused vigour and reality into his party."

When war began Sinclair rejected all overtures from Neville Chamberlain, and some of his strictures on that Prime Minister were resented. When Churchill succeeded Chamberlain he immediately offered Sinclair the Air Ministry. In this post he was not automatically a member of the War Cabinet and his followers felt with some justice that as the leader of a party in a coalition he ought to have a seat in the War Cabinet. On the other side there was feeling that so far as office was concerned the Liberals, in the words of Churchill, had plenty of sail for their small hull. He remained as Secretary of State for five years and history will probably echo an observation of Lord Beaverbrook that he was the best Air Minister "in our experience." Of the extent of his work the public knew little. Though he never failed in many rounded phrases to pay tribute to the service of which he was the parliamentary head he scarcely did himself justice either in public speeches or in the House of Commons. His best work was done in Cabinet and few Ministers can have fought with more tenacious loyalty for their department than he did. Certainly with a less determined Secretary of State the manpower needed to sustain the bomber offensive could never have been kept. While the exact value of the bomber offensive is likely to be long debated, Sinclair's conviction that, in the circumstances of the time, it was our only effective means of grappling with the Germans was widely understood even by critics at the time. He set a high standard of courage, cheerfulness, attention to detail and hard work which were an encouragement throughout the department.

During the war he rather slipped from the memory of the public because he made few speeches and took no part in politics. He scarcely visited his home in Caithness during the war and this helps to explain his totally unexpected defeat at the General Election of 1945 by 60 votes. He failed by 269 votes to regain his old seat at the 1950 general election, and did not stand again the following year.

In the New Year Honours of 1952 he was created a Viscount, but because of the ill-health which dogged him in later years he did not take his seat in the House of Lords until the summer of 1954—and it was not until 1956 that he made his maiden speech in the Upper Chamber. In 1954 he was appointed to the Political Honours Scrutiny Committee, remaining a member until 1961.

The viscounty now passes to his son, the Hon. Robin Sinclair.

June 17, 1970.

Dr. Paul Tillich, whose lectures, essays and books led him to be regarded by many in Britain as the most significant contemporary theologian, died in Chicago on October 22, 1965, at the age of 79.

The third and last volume of his *magnum opus—Systematic Theology*—was published in Britain in 1964,

Tillich's great achievement in theology was the construction of a system of apologetics that was essentially modern and yet in so many ways seemed a revival of Liberalism. Perhaps he was unique among theologians because of his ability to relate theology to such different interests as depth-psychology and politics. Certainly the uniqueness of his own theology was that it was a serious attempt to construct a system which answered the fundamental questions raised by philosophers, psychologists, artists and politicians. The volumes of sermons which he published give some idea of the power of his preaching. To many he seemed to be both prophet and philosopher and hundreds of American students hailed him as the Master.

Paul Johannes Tillich was born on August 20, 1886, near Guben. The son of a Lutheran pastor of conservative outlook, he grew up to revere the Protestant tradition to which he belonged. His early years were spent in eastern Germany, but in 1900 the family moved to Berlin where Tillich became a pupil at a humanistic *Gymnasium,* matriculating in the theological faculties of Berlin, Tübingen, and Halle. In 1911 he obtained the degree of Doctor of Philosophy of Breslau, and in 1921 the degree of Licentiat of Theology of Halle. He served in the First World War as an Army chaplain, and after the end of the war became a *Privatdozent* of Theology at the University of Berlin.

Thus he began his academic life as a theologian, and though he taught in the philosophy faculties of Dresden, Leipzig, Frankfurt, Columbia, and Yale he always insisted that he was primarily a theologian. The reason for this was that he regarded the Christian message as the answer to what he called "the existential question of our ultimate concern." As a theologian, however, he regarded nothing human as alien to him, and he was one of the strongest supporters of the religious socialist movement in Germany.

PROLIFIC WRITING

Throughout his life he maintained this interest in politics; and though he was not active in American politics he taught his students to look upon religious socialism, if and wherever it could be found, as the embodiment of the biblical prophetic message. After five years in Berlin Tillich moved to Marburg in 1924 to occupy a Chair of Theology, and while he was in Marburg he began work on his *Systematic Theology,* which was not to appear until 25 years later.

He was not long in Marburg, nor again in Dresden and Leipzig, and in 1929 he accepted the Chair of Philosophy at Frankfurt University. His activities there brought him into conflict with the growing Nazi movement, and as soon as Hitler gained power Tillich was dismissed. Fortunately the distinguished American theologian Reinhold Niebuhr happened to be in Germany at the time and he invited Tillich to join him in Union Theological Seminary. So at the age of 47 Tillich emigrated to the United States of America.

The bulk of his prolific writing had been in essay form, and the three most important books of those published originally in Germany have appeared under the English titles: *The Religious Situation*, *The Interpretation of History* and *The Protestant Era.*

Tillich's American career was singularly sucsessful and he was hailed as the most important of America's theologians. A judgment which was widely quoted was that "what Whitehead was to American philosophy Tillich has been to American theology". Most of his time was spent in Union Theological Seminary in New York City, where for almost 20 years he was Professor of Philosophical Theology. If he added lustre to the glorious Union Seminary it gave him a prominent platform in the American theological forum. People came from all over the continent of America to study under him, and scores of young theologians came annually to sit at his feet. Indeed he was already a legend in Union Seminary long before he left in 1955 on reaching retirement age. He had been Gifford Lecturer in 1953-54, and when he returned to the United States in 1955 he was invited by Harvard University to become University Professor. Judged by American standards he was indeed *mirabile doctus,* but the more cautious judgment of British scholars was not as immediately commendatory.

HONEST TO GOD

In the 1960s Tillich, who had already delivered the Firth Lectures at Nottingham, subsequently published as *Love, Power and Justice,* became well known in Britain through the enthusiastic exposition of his thought in the Bishop of Woolwich's *Honest to God.* His *Shaking of the Foundations* has run into several editions as a Pelican paperback, a new volume of sermons followed under the title *The Eternal Now,* and a book based on the dialogues which he so enjoyed with American students, *Ultimate Concern,* is about to be published in London.

Inevitably Tillich's grand style, originating in the idealism of nineteenth-century Germany, has seemed out of keeping both with the empiricist secularism of British philosophy and with the Catholic or Evangelical orthodoxy which dominates official British religion. Four recent books have been devoted to a scholarly critique of Tillich's theological system from various points of view, and a symposium has been published to reflect the cautious but definite interest of Roman Catholics. This criticism became sharp and popular after the Bishop of Woolwich's controversial best seller.

But it is only fair to add that no British Christian has recently arisen to match Tillich. In the book of essays in his honour, *Religion and Culture,* other leading theologians—Barth, Brunner and Boultmann among them—gave of their best to demonstrate the breadth and depth of his concern. This was a company of giants, emerging against an apocalyptic background of war and revolution and responding with their varied restatements of what Tillich called the "new being" disclosed in Jesus. In such company many British criticisms would seem, however justified in detail, somewhat impertinent in tone.

October 25, 1965.

Dr. E. M. W. Tillyard, O.B.E., who retired from the Mastership of Jesus College, Cambridge, in 1959, died at Cambridge on May 24, 1962. His death deprives his college, the University of Cambridge, and the world of English scholarship and criticism of one of their best known and most highly-respected figures. He was 73.

Eustace Mandeville Wetenhall Tillyard was

in every sense a Cambridge man. Born in Cambridge in 1889, the son of a former Mayor of the Borough (as it then was), and educated at the Perse School and Jesus College, he lived in Cambridge all his life, apart from his years of service in the First World War and his many academic tours in later life. And to Cambridge—the town itself and the surrounding countryside, his College, the University, and above all the Faculty of English—his heart was fully dedicated.

LIAISON WITH GREEKS

Tillyard began as a classical scholar and an archaeologist. After gaining first in both parts of the Classical Tripos and being awarded the Craven Studentship, he went to Athens in 1911 to study at the British School of Archaeology there. This bore fruit after the war in his first book, *The Hope Vases* (1923). It also led to a knowledge of Modern Greek which caused him, after seeing active service as an infantry officer with the B.E.F. (1915–16), to be seconded to the Salonica Force (1916-19) and later to be chosen to act as Liaison Officer with the Greek G.H.Q. (1918-19). His distinguished work in this field was recognized by an O.B.E., a Greek M.C., and three mentions in dispatches.

Returning to Cambridge after the war, Tillyard threw all his energies into the task of building up the newly-established English School in the University. Of the small group of dons who were trying to achieve academic respectability for what was then still a Cinderella subject, Tillyard was one of the most energetic and successful. Many of the best students from numerous Colleges became his pupils, and all were inspired by his faith in English as an academic discipline, and helped by the enthusiasm and sanity of his teaching, as well as by his personal kindness and good-humour. "You should go to Tillyard", was the wise advice given by H.M. Chadwick to some who had been disheartened by certain ancestral voices prophesying disaster for Cambridge English. Although not one of the Founding Fathers of the School, he rapidly became one of its central figures and its leading statesman—a position which, in spite of many changes in organization and personnel, he never really lost until his retirement from his University Lectureship in 1954. His influence was not mainly due to his very considerable gifts as a University politician; it was essentially the result of his whole-hearted devotion to the cause of English. Others may have won more widespread celebrity as scholars or as critics, but everyone in Cambridge knew that Tillyard, because of his selfless and unremitting thought and care for the good of the School, was its chief mainstay.

MILTON RE-LIVED

All the while, and especially after 1930 (by which time the new English Tripos was fairly launched), he found time to produce an impressive series of books. Recognition (and the Litt.D. degree) came with his *Milton* (1930), perhaps his best and most deservedly admired work. Aided by his own Puritan and classical upbringing he was able to relive Milton's life and illuminate his poetry by constant reference to his inmost meaning and purpose. Tillyard followed up this success by several other books on Milton: *Milton's Correspondence and Academic Exercises* (1932), *The Miltonic Setting* (1938), *Studies in Milton* (1951), and *The Metaphysicals and Milton* (1956); these led to his being acknowledged, both here and in America, as our foremost Miltonist.

But Tillyard, always simmering with ideas, ventured also into many other fields, not always with equal success, but never without distinction. His three books on Shakespeare—*Shakespeare's Last Plays* (1938), *Shakespeare's History Plays* (1944), and *Shakespeare's Problem Plays* (1950)—though enterprising and suggestive, were relatively lightweight performances, lacking the authority of his Miltonic work. In preparing for them, however, he was impelled to write what has become his most widely read book, *The Elizabethan World Picture* (1943), in which he lucidly and concisely summarized the conclusions of scholars about the continuity of medieval and Elizabethan ideas and symbols. His lifelong preoccupation with the Epic, in its classical and Miltonic forms, and in its various other manifestations in fiction and history, found expression in the most massive of all his productions, *The English Epic and its Background* (1954), and in its sequel, *The Epic Strain in the English Novel* (1958), both of which afforded impressive proof of the depth and width of his scholarship and understanding.

Also in 1958 appeared *The Muse Unchained*, described in its sub-title as "An Intimate Account of the Revolution in English Studies at Cambridge". This enthralling little book was criticized by some who had been led by by the titlepage to expect an account of the more recent developments. But the book admirably fulfilled its avowed intention, which was to describe the emergence of English from the chrysalis stage, its growth towards independence and freedom after 1919, and its palmy days up to about 1930. In what he called "the tricky business of blending fact with gossip and personalities" Tillyard was notably successful, and the book will be relished if only for its graphic portaits of the "Patriarchs" (Furnivall, Skeat. Verrall, &c.), and above all of the "Founders" (H. M. Chadwick, Mansfield Forbes, Q. H. F. Stewart) and their allies and successors.

IN NO COTERIE

Tillyard's central position in the world of English studies was acknowledged in many ways: by his election to a Fellowship of the British Academy, by his presidency of the International Association of University Professors of English (1953-56), by his presidency of the English Association (1957-58), and by the many invitations he received (and often accepted) to lecture in the United States, Canada, Germany and other places. In all his writing and teaching Tillyard preserved his integrity and independence; he never joined any coterie, never adopted any extreme or sectarian position, nor turned aside for long into the tempting but dangerous fields of psychology, sociology, or the "history of ideas".

Not only in Cambridge, but far beyond it, his passing will be mourned by his many friends and former pupils. In all public matters—as Master, as lecturer, or on Faculty and other Boards—he combined dignity and sanity with an unassuming and ingratiating manner, and his judgments were always well considered and weighty. As a man he was at once frank and reserved, simple and subtle. He loved open-air exercise, and it was when out walking that he gave himself most freely. Perhaps only those who shared his walks with him, round the Cambridge footpaths, in Italy, or in the Alps, discovered to the full his capacity for good companionship and true friendship, his sanguine temper, his flow of rich talk and his occasional flights of drollery, and knew that they all arose from the essential goodness and innocence of his heart.

In 1919 he married Phyllis, daughter of Henry M. Cooke by whom he had one son and two daughters.

May 25, 1962.

Marshal Semyon Timoshenko, who died at the age of 75 on March 31, 1970, was a dashing cavalry officer who helped stem the Nazi invasion of Russia as Defence Commissar in the early 1940s.

One of the original Red Army commanders, the square-jawed grim-faced soldier spanned the Soviet period of history. He remained in favour with Stalin while the dictator carried out his pre-war purge which decimated the Army leadership.

Timoshenko, a former peasant from Bessarabia who was over six feet tall, was generally credited with having halted the German drive on Moscow.

Russia's veteran soldier went on to collect further Orders of Lenin. (He received his fifth and last on his seventy-fifth birthday in February, 1970). He was also twice made a Hero of the Soviet Union—the highest Soviet military honour.

Semyon Konstantinovich Timoshenko was born in 1875 in the village of Furmanka in Bessarabia. His family were poor peasants and the young Timoshenko, after attending the village school, worked as a barrel maker. In 1915 Timoshenko was called up to the Imperial Russian Army; after six months with a training regiment he was dispatched to the Oranienbaum Regiment as a machine gunner, from which he was subsequently posted to a cavalry division. With the outbreak of the Russian Revolution, Timoshenko took some part in the revolutionary agitation among the disaffected soldiery, but after the Bolshevik seizure of power in November, 1917 he moved to southern Russia where he joined a partisan detachment early in 1918 and was elected a platoon commander. Once in the Kuban this partisan force formed itself into the "first Revolutionary Cavalry Guards Regiment" under Timoshenko's command.

Timoshenko and his men now entered the Red Army and in the autumn of 1918 fought at Tsaritsyn, where Timoshenko was attached to the 10th Red Army commanded by Voroshilov. Throughout the siege of Tsaritsyn, where Stalin and Voroshilov opposed both the White troops and Trotsky's authority, Timoshenko commanded a cavalry brigade and it was as a brigade commander that he joined Budënny and Voroshilov in the first Cavalry Army, an elite Red Army formation. Timoshenko's success in the fighting against Denikin in 1919 led to his promotion to divisional commander (6th Cavalry Division); his exploits in Denikin's rear earned him recognition as one of the foremost commanders in the first Cavalry Army, whose troopers included Zhukov. During the Soviet-Polish war in 1920 Timoshenko operated at the Zhitomir break through in June and in August he took command of the 4th Cavalry Division; at the close of 1920 he also took part in the final campaign against Wrangel in the Crimea, where he was severely wounded and forced to convalesce.

MET LENIN

In 1920 Timoshenko was dispatched as a delegate of the first Cavalry Army to the eighth Congress of Soviets where he met Lenin for the first time. With the end of the civil war, Timoshenko remained in the Red Army and in 1922 completed the higher command course at the Military Academy. In 1927 he continued his military education by completing further command courses for senior officers. In 1930 he attended the course for commander-commissars at the Military-Political Academy. In 1933 Timoshenko took up the post of deputy commander of the Byelo Russian military district, a key appointment in a key command where the first Soviet experiments with large-scale armoured units were taking place; in 1935, after a period studying the organization and tactics of foreign armies, Timoshenko took up a senior appointment in the Kiev Military District, another major post in the Soviet military system.

Since 1918 Timoshenko had been associated with Voroshilov, Stalin and Budënny, the core of the first Cavalry Army. When Stalin launched the military purge in June, 1937, he spared these old associates and Timoshenko was despatched as commander of the North Caucasus Military District in June, transferred to the Caucasus in September and then switched to the Kiev command in February, 1938.

ESCAPED PURGE

Having survived the military purge Timoshenko took a prominent part in the Soviet occupation of Poland in 1939. But his rise to wider fame came with the Soviet-Finnish war, when he supervised the storming of the Mannerheim Line and commanded the final phase of the operations which ultimately battered down Finnish resistance. For these exploits he was made a Hero of the Soviet Union. After the Red Army's dismal showing in the "winter war" Stalin decided to reorganize the Soviet forces and entrusted this task to Timoshenko; Voroshilov was removed as Defence Commissar. Timoshenko took his place and was appointed Marshal of the Soviet Union on May 7, 1940. Timoshenko put into operation extensive modernization schemes, a more realistic training programme and was associated with the strict and formal discipline, including the obligatory salute, introduced into the Red Army.

When Hitler attacked the Soviet Union on June 22, 1941, Timoshenko was Defence Commissar and Zhukov Chief of the General Staff; both have been blamed in some measure for Soviet unpreparedness. In the first confused days of the war Timoshenko acted as a temporary commander in chief, but then Stalin took over the post of Defence Commissar and early in July Timoshenko was sent to take command of the Western Military District.

BLITZKRIEG HALTED

During the early autumn Timoshenko organized the Soviet defence against the German advance at the centre, earning the reputation of having halted the German blitzkrieg at Smolensk. In the late autumn he was moved to the south-western front where at the end of November his forces launched a successful counterattack, recapturing Rostov-on-Don, forcing back German troops and precipitating a major crisis in the German High Command.

In the spring of 1942 Timoshenko advocated a major Soviet attack on Kharkov for which Stalin gave special permission and appreciable reinforcements. But this offensive failed and the Soviet south-western front was then ripped apart in May, a rout which Timoshenko could not prevent and which led to the uncovering of the approaches to Stalingrad and the Caucasus. This marked the end of Timoshenko's wartime career as a front commander. In February, 1943 he appeared as Stavka "Coordinator" in the Leningrad area and in the summer of 1944 he played the same role in "coordinating" the operations of the several Ukrainian fronts striking into Rumania and Bulgaria.

Unlike the majority of his fellow marshals, Timoshenko refused to commit himself at length in memoirs about his military career and wartime commands; he contributed a small piece on the Rostov-on-Don operations in a volume published in Moscow in 1968. Otherwise he elected to remain both silent and aloof.

April 2, 1970.

Madge Titheradge died on November 14, 1961, at the age of 74.

It is many years since illness brought her career to a close but older playgoers will still remember with pleasure a long series of polished performances by her in most kinds of straight play and in pantomime. They will recall the husky voice, sprightly air and graceful figure of the actress who was born in Australia in July, 1887, and first appeared on the London stage as one of Kingsley's "Water Babies" before her sixteenth birthday. Three years later she was with Tree and in another three could boast that she had played in London with Coquelin *aîné*. After the Coquelin season she joined Lewis Waller, being seen in *Henry the Fifth* and *A Butterfly on the Wheel*—the play in which she made her first appearance in America. A tour of Australia followed and she was Peter Pan in London in 1914. Thereafter came a number of variegated parts at Drury Lane, where she showed that she could enact a highly strung heroine of melodrama and the principal boy in pantomime with equal facility. Thus in 1916 she was in the "autumn drama" *The Best of Luck*; in successive pantomimes she was "principal boy" and after a season of film work in California she returned to Drury Lane in 1920 for what proved to be a spectacular success for the theatre, herself and the leading man, Godfrey Tearle, the stage version of Robert Hichens's novel *The Garden of Allah*.

As Desdemona, in a fair wig, she played opposite Godfrey Tearle in 1921, and as Beatrice—a happier piece of casting—she had Henry Ainley for her Benedick in 1926. She continued to partner Ainley in Pierre Frondaie's drama *Prince Fazil* but in later years she was allowed to return to comedy and rang the changes on some effects already made by her in such light plays of the earlier 1920s as Maugham's *The Camel's Back*, Milne's *To Have the Honour* (with Gerald du Maurier), Vajda's *Grounds for Divorce* (with Owen Nares), Molnar's *The Guardsman* (with Seymour Hicks), and Savoir's *Bluebeard's Eighth Wife*. In the English version of this piece Madge Titheradge was able to indulge in her favourite stage pastime of graciously baiting the opposite sex during a run of 14 months.

Two of her appearances in the later 1920s were in plays by Noel Coward: *The Queen was in the Parlour* and *Home Chat*. She and the author had first met back-stage in 1914, when Coward, aged 15, was playing Slightly to Madge Titheradge's Peter Pan at the Duke of York's. The star came face to face with the young actor on the stairs, shook his hand and said: "My name's Madge; what's yours?"

"A never-to-be-forgotten, most characteristic gesture", Coward recorded.

Madge Titheradge left the stage for five years, but made her return in 1932 to be directed by Coward in *Theatre Royal* and Jacques Deval's *Mademoiselle*. She was in poor health and suffering pain during *Mademoiselle*, and after one more play—in 1938—she retired.

Her father was a well known actor, George S. Titheradge, and Dion Titheradge, actor and playwright, was her brother. Her marriage to Charles Quartermaine, the actor, was dissolved, and in 1928 she married an American business man, Edgar Park, who died 10 years later.

November 15, 1916.

Palmiro Togliatti, the Italian communist leader, who died in Yalta on August 21, 1964, at the age of 71, was the most eminent communist outside of the Russian or Chinese leadership, possessing profound experience of the movement from its beginning. He was also the most able politician in Italy, though for some time he had been a sick and tired man.

In his neat double-breasted suits Togliatti

looked typically middle-class. With this went an academic manner and a precise, sharp sort of mental liveliness. The caustic edge to his tongue heightened the impression which some people had of talking to a schoolmaster or university professor; the benign, harmless-looking smile might set one wondering how appropriate he would have looked in the clothes of a priest—those of a bishop probably, for the superficial judgment that he might have looked well as a cardinal of the church was rather belied by his general manner. The greatest prelates are inclined to come from simple homes or princely ones; they seldom look so bourgeois as Togliatti. The mistake would have been, of course, to take this appearance as implying any degree of mediocrity. By temperament he preferred moderation to violence but had no inclination towards half measures. He placed much value on intellectual argument, at which he was a master, but when other methods were ordered or seemed to him necessary there could be no doubt of his decisiveness or of his callousness, even if some of the most cold-blooded actions attributed to him have never been proved.

DISLIKE OF VIOLENCE

His moderation and dislike of violence have lately been shown most clearly in his work in international communist affairs where flexibility was his watchword. His last journey to Russia was almost certainly a final effort at persuading the Russians to show more subtlety in dealing with the Chinese problem. In Italy the clearest picture which will remain of him with many devoted communists is the rather harsh and autocratic side of his nature displayed at the national organizational conference of his party held at Naples in March when his illness and fatigue enhanced his lack of patience for the views of others. Their respect for him was naturally immense but they could not have liked their demands for change being argued so brusquely—however clearly—aside, while they themselves were peremptorily told by their leader to go home and get on with their work.

Palmiro Togliatti was born at Genoa on March 26, 1893, into a lower middle class family. As a boy he showed the love of close study and of reading which marked his character throughout his life. His schooling was no charge on his parents and it was because of his intention of continuing to find backing for his higher education that he stood one November day in 1911 in the courtyard of Turin University waiting to take a scholarship examination. It was an occasion which was to influence his whole future life. Among the other candidates was a young dark-eyed Sardinian whose intense face was later to be seen in almost any room where two or three Italian communists were gathered together; Antonio Gramsci did not do as well as Togliatti in that examination but was to precede him as leader of the party which they were both to have a hand—though not an immediate one in Togliatti's case—in founding.

While he studied law and philology at the university, Togliatti also studied socialism, both from books and from personal contacts. He and his group of left-wing friends built up close ties with men working in the factories at Turin, which was Italy's great industrial centre. This must have helped him. Togliatti was not the man to be loved as a matter of course by the masses in spite of the description of him which used to be part of the routine of public introductions as "our beloved leader"; he nevertheless had a gift for commanding popular loyalty. This was combined of course with an unequalled grasp on the structure of the party, in itself an asset demanding the respect and obedience of his followers.

In the First World War he served for two years in the Medical Corps before being released for reasons of health. He then rejoined Gramsci in Turin where the two socialists faced the significance of the Russian Revolution.

REVIEW FOR REVOLUTION

On May 1, 1919, they and other friends, including the present Senator Terracini, founded a review called *L'Ordine Nuovo* to publicize their theories which were based on the assertion that the Russian Revolution was not an experience to be limited to Russia alone.

The Italian communist party itself came into being at Leghorn on January 21, 1921, when the pro-communist wing at the socialist national congress broke away and formed its own party. Togliatti himself played little part in the dramatic events leading to the split. He was not elected to the first central committee, though others with less experience were given seats. He concerned himself at the time with the business of taking over the Turin edition of the socialist newspaper *Avanti* for the benefit of the new party. He took his seat the following year after he had moved to Rome to found and edit another daily newspaper *Il Comunista*. His chance to prove himself came in 1923. Gramsci was in Russia; Bordiga, the Neapolitan who had played the leading part in founding the party, was under arrest; Terracini was in hiding. Gramsci proposed to the Russians that Togliatti should for the time being be placed in charge of the party's affairs. With the rise of Fascism the communists were increasingly persecuted and the acting secretary's work was now to organize a semi-clandestine body, a task made more difficult by the deterioration in relations with the socialists.

FATAL SENTENCE

When Gramsci himself was arrested in 1926 and sentenced by the Fascists to a long—and fatal—term of imprisonment the way was clear for Togliatti to take over formally, on the Comintern's nomination, the secretaryship of the Italian party and he held this post until his death.

He had by this time already made his start in Moscow as one of the Italian representatives to the Comintern. He was there in fact when Gramsci was arrested. He was already apparently intent on pleasing the Russians. In the great feuds which marked the rise of Stalin he moved with agility from attachment to one or other of the emerging dictator's rivals and ended safely. In 1935 he was made secretary of the Comintern. From the following year until 1939 he was responsible for the political morale of the communist units in Spain, dividing his time between Madrid, Moscow and France where he maintained contact with the remains of the Italian party.

He returned to Italy in March, 1944, after an absence of 18 years, landing by boat at Naples. Showing none of the disadvantages usually felt by returning exiles, he had in a matter of days joined Badoglio's Government, taking his oath to the King like any monarchist. This was the first of many surprises with which he was to tax, and sometimes confuse, his less mentally agile colleagues. The prompt entry into government was the beginning of his policy of achieving power by constitutional means which was the essence of his action since the war. He maintained it with extraordinary dexterity, surviving at the same time the upheavals in the communist movement of which the process of destalinization harmed him most. The idea of a mass communist party was his own invention, designed to suit Italian conditions.

INSISTENCE ON LEGALITY

He made of it the largest communist party in the west and the second largest political party in Italy. Perhaps the best example of his insistence on legality was his intervention in the riots which took place in a number of Italian cities in the summer of 1960 as a largely left wing protest against the late Signor Tambroni's acceptance of neo-fascist support for his Christian Democratic government. Togliatti hurried back from Moscow. The agitation ended and there can be little doubt that prompt insistence from him brought about the restoration of calm.

His methods brought periodic restiveness among his colleagues. Up to the last, none of them, however, had any clear idea of how to put pressure for change upon him. His constitutional approach placed a strain as well on some of the rank and file and at his death the party was having to face problems of failing enthusiasm because of the apparent lack of real revolutionary outlook. Electorally, nevertheless, his cause increasingly prospered.

He spent much of his last energies attempting to moderate the course of the Russian quarrel with China. The quarrel was incidentally first shown in its full intensity to the western world from the platform of the Italian Communist Party's national congress held in Rome in December, 1962, in the bitter exchanges with the Chinese fraternal delegates. Togliatti's position was quite clear. He was loyal to Moscow in spite of the annoyance which he several times suffered as a result of Khrushchev's unpredictability. He felt that the Chinese were wrong; at the same time he disagreed with the Russian handling of the dispute. The Russian insistence on an international communist conference to discuss the differences with China seemed to him to be particularly wrongheaded and an invitation to make final the split; he constantly, though unsuccessfully, advised against it.

Another of his main contributions to the theoretical side of the relations with the Russian party was his invention of polycentrism. He put forward the word, newly coined, in a newspaper interview in June 1956. It was fairly widely misunderstood and the expressions of western contentment with the thought that he was proposing a breaking down of the structure of international communism was enough to make the Russians express their disapproval. What he was apparently meaning to express, however, was the need for national parties to be free to adapt their methods to suit prevailing conditions in their own countries without impinging on the ideological unity of the movement. In fact it was an attempt at defining in words the policy which he applied as far as he could in Italy from the day of his return from exile.

In the final phase of his thinking he refused to allow the party to use its full weight in opposing the series of centre-left governments, in which his former allies, the Socialists, had moved into alliance with the Christian Democrats.

August 22, 1964.

Queen Salote of Tonga, who had reigned over the Pacific island group which Captain Cook called "the Friendly Islands" since 1918, died in hospital in Auckland, New Zealand, on December 15, 1965, She was 65.

Queen Salote was born at Nukualofa, the capital of the Kingdom of Tonga, last independent monarchy of the South Seas, on March 13, 1900. She was the elder daughter of King George II, who left no sons, and succeeded her father in April, 1918, being crowned in October of the same year.

She was the third sovereign of the dynasty of Tupou, for her father and predecessor had succeeded his great-grandfather King George I, who laid the foundations of Tonga as a modern Christian state in 1845 and died in 1893 at the patriarchal age of 96 after firmly establishing his reputation as the "Grand Old Man of the Pacific". King George I and his wife embraced Christianity in 1831, when they took at their baptisms the names of George and Salote (the Polynesian form of Charlotte) in honour of our King George III and his Consort, Queen Charlotte. The names George and Salote have persisted in the Tupou dynasty ever since.

Queen Salote, who was educated in New Zealand, was an ardent Methodist and spoke English so perfectly that anyone hearing her talk without seeing her would have taken her for a member of an English-speaking race.

INDEPENDENT KINGDOM

She personally drafted the more important of her state documents and dispatches, and her English prose had in its limpidity and dignity something of the qualities of the best seventeenth-century English writing. A woman of majestic height (over 6ft. 3in.) and deportment, and yet of great simplicity of manner, she was an ideal constitutional sovereign, deeply loved and revered by her people no less for her sagacity and wise leadership as for her descent, which the Tongas, genealogically minded as are all the Polynesian peoples, trace back to the tenth century.

Tonga is not a British Protectorate but an independent kingdom under British protection, the Treaty of Friendship and Protection having been concluded between the British Government and King George II of Tonga in 1900. It has been the aim and result of British protection to reinforce and uphold Tongan independence; and the Tongan rulers, Government, and people responded enthusiastically in the two Great Wars.

When the Queen celebrated the twentieth anniversary of her coronation in 1938, King George VI said in his telegram of congratulation: "The period of your reign has been one of steady and peaceful progress in the development of your kingdom. Medical and health services have been extended, roads have been built, educational facilities have increased, and communications between the islands have been improved by the provision of wireless services." At her Silver Jubilee in 1943 both King George VI and Churchill paid tribute in warm terms to the manner in which the Queen and her people had placed all the resources of the kingdom at the disposal of the Empire's war effort.

In 1951 the Queen's heir and Prime Minister, Prince Tungi, paid his first visit to England as the guest of the British Government in connexion with the Festival of Britain and, after a stay in London, toured the provinces to inspect agricultural institutions. Queen Salote herself paid her first visit two years later for the Coronation of Queen Elizabeth II. Her braving of the rain during the Coronation procession in her carriage, which she insisted on keeping open, endeared her to the London crowds; and this episode, together with a majestic personality radiating friendliness, made her the outstanding overseas figure at the celebrations. Such was the popularity she won in Britain that June babies were christened Charlotte in her honour, a racehorse was named after her, and she was the subject of topical songs.

ROYAL VISITORS

Before returning to her own country Queen Salote visited Scotland, Northern Ireland and the Continent, reaching Tonga in time to prepare for the visit of Queen Elizabeth II and the Duke of Edinburgh to her island kingdom. The two days which Queen Elizabeth and her consort spent in Tonga were among the most picturesque events of the Royal Tour of 1953-54.

In 1962 the Royal Mint produced for the Kingdom of Tonga a remarkable series of three gold coins whose face value equals respectively £16, £8 and £4, bearing Queen Salote's effigy on the obverse and the Tongan arms on the reverse. They are the first gold coins to be produced at the Royal Mint for 150 years to consist of gold alloyed only with silver.

In the year before her accession Queen Salote married her cousin Prince Uiliami (William) Tungi, C.B.E., who for several years preceding his death in 1941 was also her Prime Minister. By him her Majesty had three sons, the eldest of whom, Prince Tupouto'a, who after his father's death assumed his title of Tungi, now succeeds to the throne as King after having been his mother's Prime Minister since 1949.

Queen Salote was created a D.B.E., in 1932, and a G.B.E. in 1945 on the occasion of the centenary of the unification of the Kingdom of Tonga by the Queen's great-great-grandfather, George I. She was personally invested with the G.C.V.O. by Queen Elizabeth during the latter's visit to Tonga, and she was also an Associate Dame of the Order of St. John of Jerusalem. In November 1965 she received the further and highly appropriate distinction of becoming the first Dame Grand Cross of the Order of St. Michael and St. George.

In July 1965, celebrations were held in Tonga to mark the length of the Queen's reign, which on June 20 surpassed that of King George Tupou I, who reigned in Tonga for 47 years.

December 16, 1965.

Athol Gordon Townley, the former Australian Defence Minister and Ambassador-designate to Washington, died in Mercy Hospital, Melbourne, on December 24, 1963, at the age of 56. He had been a Cabinet Minister since 1951, and at various times administered the portfolios of Social Services, Air and Civil Aviation, Immigration, Defence Production and Supply.

Townley's qualities were quickly recognized after he was first elected to the House of Representatives in 1949 for the Tasmanian seat of Denison and within 18 months he was promoted to the Government, becoming Minister for Social Services. A Hobart pharmaceutical chemist in private life, he was regarded as the Cabinet expert on the Government's pharmaceutical benefits scheme, although he never held the Health portfolio under which the scheme is administered. He also spoke with special knowledge in Cabinet on aviation matters, as he held both private and commercial flying licences. His World War II service with the Royal Australian Navy, in which he reached the rank of lieutenant-commander, gave him a more than lay knowledge for his frequent meetings with the Service Chiefs of Staff as Defence Minister, the office to which he was appointed in 1958.

To a higher than average administrative ability, Townley added an easy familiarity of manner and a well-developed capacity to mix with people which made him as at home among Asians on visits to Singapore and Malaya as he was at the smoke socials of the suburban football and cricket clubs of his electorate. His willingness to fit snugly into the society he was with led him into occasional political indiscretions such as the donning of an Indonesian Army uniform when inspecting troops during a visit to that country at the height of the Indonesian campaign to gain West New Guinea. This brought wide criticism in Australia, not only from his political opponents, but it was typical of the man that he faced such criticism direct. Immediately on his return to Australia he allowed himself to be questioned by a television panel and largely disarmed his critics.

His reputation as a successful negotiator was enhanced when, just before the November, 1963, elections, he flew to the United States and arranged for the purchase by Australia of the TFX bomber as a replacement for the Royal Australian Air Force's Canberras—although the decision was one which aroused controversy at home and abroad.

Two statements provide the key to Townley's defence policies: "The defence programme", he told the House, "has been framed against the strategic background that any outbreak of war is likely to be of the bushfire type. Our strategy is to prevent it spreading". And again: "Friendship with Indonesia is the most important thing for Australia's future."

Townley had been described as a typical Australian who could not be anything else. After the general election of November, 1963, which gave the Government an increased majority, Townley was nominated to succeed Sir Howard Beale as Australian Ambassador in Washington, and would have taken up the appointment in March, 1964.

Townley was born in Hobart, Tasmania, on October 3, 1907, but looked younger than his 56 years, although a series of illnesses over his last 18 months had left their mark. He was educated at Hobart high and technical schools and the University of Tasmania.

He is survived by his widow, whom he married in 1934, and their only son. An older brother was for some years a member of the Tasmania House of Assembly.

December 27, 1963.

Spencer Tracy, the film actor, died on June 10, 1967, at the age of 67.

"When I go", said Tracy once, "a whole epoch will have ended." The comment was made dispassionately, without conceit, for his attitude to life was far too philosophical and objective for any indulgence in the self-adulation which characterized so many of his contemporaries. A difficult man in the studios in many ways, he was temperamental through perversity rather than self-esteem. He disliked on principle anyone who tried to push him about.

When he spoke of an epoch, he was thinking of the film star era that dominated Hollywood in the thirties and which was itself dominated by the M.G.M. studios, who carried the star system to its ultimate peak. Garbo, Gable, Robert Taylor. Norma Shearer, Myrna Loy, William Powell, Jean Harlow, Jeanette MacDonald, Mickey Rooney and Judy Garland were but a few of the names which Louis B. Mayer created. And when Mayer died in 1957, it was Spencer Tracy who read the funeral oration. That, too, marked the end of an epoch.

When Tracy spoke of an epoch, he was also thinking of the qualities which made a star in those days. Personality allied to an expert technique was the answer. The star system called for no outstanding histrionic ability, and Spencer Tracy never thought of himself as a great actor. He looked upon himself as a professional who thoroughly understood his trade.

Tough, honest and indomitable, a man of sober authority and rugged good sense, he became a symbol on the screen of all those qualities which represented the pioneering spirit of America. There was nothing fancy about Tracy. He was never seen as the great lover or the debonair seducer. Throughout his career he was at his best when he represented the plain and solid citizen who spoke up for what he believed to be right. A man of the people.

He was born in Milwaukee, Wisconsin, on April 5, 1900, and was educated at the Wisconsin University. He then studied for the stage at the American Academy of Dramatic Art.

NEW YORK DEBUT

His New York debut was made at the Garrick Theatre in October, 1922, and for the next eight years he appeared in the theatre with reasonable frequency and success.

In 1930 he played a ruthless gangster in the Broadway production *The Last Mile*. Hollywood, at that time, was just beginning to interest itself in the melodramatic possibilities of the gangster film, and so Tracy was summoned to the Coast by the Fox Film Company to play in tough parts. He did not like these parts, and became troublesome to his new employers, who were happy enough to let him go to M.G.M. But here again he was required at first to play only tough-guy parts—in *Riffraff* opposite Jean Harlow, and *Whipsaw* with Myrna Loy.

His first real opportunity came with the production of one of Mayer's most ambitious pictures—*San Francisco* with Jeanette MacDonald and Clark Gable. Tracy to the surprise of everyone, including himself, was cast as a priest. This was in 1936, and the same year saw the release of another unusual picture in which he played the leading part. In *Fury*, directed by Fritz Lang, Tracy was seen as an innocent man who is almost lynched by a mob who suspect him of kidnapping. It was one of the best pictures ever to come out of the M.G.M. studios and it firmly established Tracy as a star. The following year saw him appear as the Portuguese fisherman in the Kipling story *Captains Courageous*, and although he was apprehensive about taking the part, which was very different from anything he had done previously, he achieved another success and won his first Academy Award. His second came within a year, for his performance as Father Flanagan in *Boys' Town*.

EPOCH ENDED

Tracy worked for 21 years for M.G.M., but his contract was cancelled by mutual agreement in 1955—a year after the cancellation of that between M.G.M. and Clark Gable. The star epoch was already dying, and the old brigade at M.G.M. were drifting away. Tracy, like Gable, was unmoved. He knew that there were still many good years of action in him and he was not sorry to be parted from Mayer. In spite of the oration at Mayer's funeral, he had never had much regard for the man; for Tracy was far less gullible than some.

"As Tracy gets older, he acts less and less", wrote a critic of him in his later days. He might have added that his technique became ever more skilful and mature. To this later period belong such notable films as *Bad Day at Black Rock, The Mountain, The Old Man and the Sea, Devil at Four O'clock, Inherit the Wind,* in which another old-timer, Fredric March, put up a tremendous performance against him, and *Judgment at Nuremberg*, in which he played a judge at the Nuremberg trial.

By now he was something of a grand old man of the cinema—a little tetchy, a bit cynical, and as stubborn as of old, but still philosophical, and with a sense of humour. "I hear that you're quite impossible now on the set", a friend once said to him in these later days. "That", said Tracy indignantly, "is only about 98 per cent true."

He missed his old associates greatly—Gable, Cooper, Bogart, and all the others of the golden epoch of stardom. But he never went to see his old films. The epoch was dying, and he had no wish to be reminded of its past glories. He will be remembered as one of the best examples of it.

Tracy had been a sick man for several years, and he knew that his days were numbered, but he continued to appear in films because idleness was an anathema to him. Wherever possible he sought out another of the old brigade to play opposite him. Katharine Hepburn was his favourite, a sparring partner of many epics, and another experienced veteran of the M.G.M. team. A resolute and independent thinker like himself, who had never submitted weakly to the Mayer regime. A professional, too, to the fingertips, as he was himself. His death came shortly after they had completed *Guess who's coming to Dinner*, in which they were directed by Stanley Kramer.

During his life he never sought publicity and never wished for his private life to be described. He was married in 1923 to Louise Treadwell and had one son born in 1932. By the end of his apprenticeship with M.G.M. he and Gary Cooper were together the most skilled and highly professional film actors in the business—players who had ceased to act consciously in the studio because they did the right thing by instinct. They understood the camera and the camera understood them. An epoch has ended with his death as he forecast. And the opening words of his speech at Mayer's funeral return to the memory: "It is the Book of Genesis which says: there were giants in those days. . . ."

June 12, 1967.

Jack Train, who died on December 19, 1966, at the age of 64 in London, was one of the stalwart and accomplished band of comedians who wrung a new type of radio comedy from the strains and misfortunes of the Second World War. As a member of the team which created *Itma,* he brought to life a series of strangely eccentric personalities who ranked second only to that of Tommy Handley, the prime mover of the programme, in their fantastic reality. Train made the phrase "I don't mind if I do" famous. As himself, a quick-witted, slow-speaking fantastic, he was an indispensable member of the *Twenty Questions* "panel".

Train was born in Plymouth on November 28, 1902. It was during his service in the Navy in the First World War that he began to exploit his comic talent as a semi-professional entertainer. Leslie Hore-Belisha, who later became Minister for War in the National Government, heard his act when he was entertaining sailors at Devonport, advised him to turn professional, and arranged an audition for him, with the result that in 1928 he reached the West End in a revue, *Many Happy Returns,* at the Duke of York's Theatre. After a spell in R. C. Sherriff's play *Journey's End*—his one invasion of the "straight theatre"—Train spent five years as a "straight man" to Nervo and Knox.

It was, however, radio that developed his unusual gifts and became his essential medium.

FUN IN "FUNF"

He first broadcast in 1928 and was heard on the air intermittently before 1939, when he became one of the original members of the *Itma* company, with which he remained until the death of Tommy Handley in 1949 put an end to the programme. The multi-voiced Train was a variety of unforgettable personalities—the German Funf, who was both fundamentally menacing and naturally funny, always worsted because a streak of toiling, teutonic literalness in his mental composition made it almost impossible for him to understand what was said to him; Claude, the removal man and general dogsbody whose extreme courtesy was equalled only by that of his partner, Cecil; and finally, Colonel Chinstrap, the sound of whose voice carried the unmistakable aroma of vintage port and brandy, and whose speciality was less a drinker's expertise than a drinker's insatiable appetite and extreme cunning in satisfying it. Colonel Chinstrap remains a part of the national mythology,

Itma and *Twenty Questions,* in which Train showed himself to be capable of wild flights of fantasy without a script writer to prompt him, occupied most of his time after 1939, but he was still seen occasionally on the stage in variety and in pantomime.

Train was also a member of the *Guess My Story* panel on radio, and acted in many films, including *Tom Tom Topla, Colonel Bogey* and *The Twenty Questions Murder Mystery.* He was twice married and leaves a widow.

December 20, 1966.

Professor M. W. Travers, the distinguished chemist, and oldest member by election of the Royal Society, whose ranks he joined in 1904, died on August 25, 1961, at the age of 89.

He was the biographer of Sir William Ramsay (1852-1916), with whom he collaborated in the discovery of the inert elementary gases, neon, krypton, and xenon.

Morris William Travers was born on January 24, 1872, the son of William Travers, M.D., F.R.C.S., of London, and was educated at Blundell's School, Tiverton, University College London, taking his D.Sc. in 1898, and the University of Nancy. He was appointed assistant Professor of Chemistry at his old college (which later made him a Fellow) in 1898 and six years later he was given the chair of physics at University College, Bristol. He was to have a close association with Bristol, for he was honorary Professor, Fellow, and Nash Lecturer in the university from 1927 to 1937 and was later made Professor Emeritus.

From 1906 to 1914 Travers was Director of the Indian Institute of Science, and from 1914 to 1919 scientific director of Duroglass, Ltd. He became president of the Society of Glass Technology in 1922 and later an honorary Fellow. He was vice-president and Melchett medallist, Institute of Fuel, in 1930 and was made an honorary member three years later. In 1936 he was president of the Faraday Society and from 1929 to 1932 a member of the Fuel Research Board. In the Second World War he served as a technical consultant at the Ministry of Supply. He published *The Experimental Study of Gases; The Discovery of the Rare Gases;* and the admirable life of Sir William Ramsay (1957). In preparing the biography Travers had access to Ramsay's laboratory notebooks and to the papers left after Lady Ramsay's death in 1937. The business of examining and arranging this mass of material was interrupted by the outbreak of war in 1939 and was not resumed until 1948. The book was finally written between the author's eighty-first and eighty-third birthdays.

Travers married in 1909 Dorothy, daughter of Robert J. Gray, by whom he had a son and a daughter.

August 29, 1961.

Dr. Sidney Joseph Mazzini Trenaman died on December 28, 1961, at his home in Leeds, at the age of 51. He married Margaret Shaw in 1936, and she survives him with two daughters.

Dr. Trenaman was educated at Greenwich Central School, the Lycée Montaigne, Paris, and King's College London, where he took his intermediate B.A. He wanted all the education he could get, and in order to pay for it he spent some years in a variety of jobs, including working for a grocer and travelling with Cooks tours. In 1929 he joined the B.B.C. as a shorthand-typist in the Advertisement Department, and, apart from two intervals—one for war service and one for a secondment to Oxford to read for a B.Litt.—remained with the corporation for the main part of his working life, leaving it only in 1959 to build up a Television Research Unit at Leeds University as the first holder of the Granada Fellowship.

During the war he was in charge of a group of delinquent soldiers and responsible for their reeducation in special training units—an imaginative and successful experiment which was later described in his book, *Out of Step,* published by Methuen in 1952. In 1945 he went to East Africa to inaugurate an army education scheme, returning to the B.B.C. at the end of that year as an assistant in the analysis section of the then Listener Research Department. In 1949 he was appointed assistant to the B.B.C.'s Further Education Officer to work on an experimental analysis of the new possibilities for broadcasting in the field of further education. He provided the statistical background to a report which formed the basis of the B.B.C.'s future policy for further education, and in 1952 he became Further Education Liaison Officer—a new post which involved making a detailed study of the world of adult and further education, and maintaining a close liaison with organizations and individuals so that their needs and interests could be reflected in broadcasting. He threw himself heart and soul into this work, measuring the changing attitudes of different sections of the public to educational broadcasting, yet never forgetting that the figures on his graphs were made up of people. He also spent a long time in building up a wide circle of valuable consultants.

ADULT EDUCATION

By 1955 he came to the conclusion that he needed to spend more time on pure research, and with the good will of the B.B.C. he was seconded to Oxford, where he chose as the subject of his thesis "The Attitudes to Opportunities for Further Education in relation to Education and Environment in Samples of the Adult Population". The first part of the project, for which he was awarded a B.Litt., was completed in 1957, and his D.Phil. thesis, which was an extension of it, only a few months before his death. His Leeds studies on television as a means of communication are in this sense only an extension of work he had begun elsewhere.

Much of his research has confirmed the view that there is a fund of common sense in the general public which cannot be affected by the more extreme forms of persuasion. This, among other things, emerged from his Leeds study, *Television and the Political Image,* written in collaboration with Denis McQuail and published by Methuen in 1961.

On other occasions his conclusions were more disturbing. After completing his first thesis his findings were widely publicized—in *Adult Education,* in a talk in 1958 to the annual conference of the Library Association, and, following this, in the national press, where they were the subject of more than one special article. He made clear what many adult educationists had already begun to suspect, but he also made it memorable, summing up what he found in the phrase *an educationally stratified society.* "Educationally speaking", he wrote, "the population appears to be an hierarchy, pyramidal in distribution of attitudes and participation, rich and complex at the top, impoverished at the bottom. The trend is for further education opportunities of all kinds to reinforce and extend the top, not to change the main structure."

REJECTION OF CULTURE

Could this structure be changed? He was worried by the effect of the process of selection for secondary education on those who are not chosen for grammar schools, and summed it up on one occasion by saying that "culture has rejected them, and they in turn reject culture". At the same time he believed that it would be possible to prevent the development of two separate cultural "nations" by catering for the conscious and unconscious educational interests of a large intermediate group, consisting mainly of skilled craftsmen, and representing some 55 per cent of the population. He had great faith in the power of the informal educational medium—television in particular—to bridge this gap in an acceptable way.

Dr. Trenaman's views, while based on sound scholarship, were also founded in his personal beliefs. He was the best sort of humanitarian, prepared to underwrite his beliefs in the individual by working for the handicapped and the under-privileged: in what free time he had he served on the Howard League, and visited discharged prisoners, many of whom became personal friends and kept in touch with him for the rest of his life.

Those who had the privilege of working with Dr. Trenaman will not forget his patience and integrity; his charm and kindness; and his occasional persuasiveness. He was a person of rich interests, a good pianist and a skilled Morris dancer; and for good measure, he had his outbursts of Celtic temper (with obstructions, never with people).

His work has given a new impetus to educational research and new insight into the responsibilities of the mass media. But perhaps his most important legacy for those concerned with education is his optimism. Dr. Trenaman got his education, and built his career, in spite of a succession of setbacks. He discovered something positive in each of his army delinquents. He made his plans on the basis of what was right, and not of what was possible; and in the end, more often than not, he achieved the impossible.

January 9, 1962.

Professor G. M. Trevelyan, O.M., C.B.E., F.R.S., the historian, died at his home at Cambridge on July 20, 1962, at the age of 86.

George Macaulay Trevelyan was the third son of Sir George Otto Trevelyan Bt., O.M., biographer, politician, and historian; the grandson of Sir Charles Trevelyan, first baronet, who reformed and established the high tradition of our modern Civil Service; and the great-nephew of Lord Macaulay. He was born on February 16, 1876. His mother was Caroline, daughter of Robert Philips, the Manchester merchant and Liberal politician, and herself an artist and musician.

Of the Trevelyans it has been written, "they stand together, handing on their torch of austere intellectual light, a group peculiarly English, though their minds are often concerned with international affairs." And it was in the great house of Welcombe, at Shakespeare's Stratford, and still more at Hallington, the beautiful family home among the moorlands and traditions of the Northumbrian border, that he grew up, in an atmosphere of intellectual Liberalism, cultivated and exclusive, but in contact with many of the best writers and statesmen of both England and America.

At Harrow he came under the influence of the great educator Edward Bowen and of the historian Townshend Warner. Already as a boy his intellectual integrity and forceful character, intolerant of insincerity, impetuous for ordered freedom, had determined the lines of his life's work—to write history, and to complete the story which Macaulay had left unfinished and from which his father had been diverted by politics and literature. Great poetry was through all his life his favourite reading, and it was the poetic aspect of history, the human tragedy and comedy in progress, which fascinated him. A scholarship to Trinity College brought him into the History School founded by F. W. Maitland and Lord Acton. To Maitland, and to a critical familiarity with the writings of Carlyle and Macaulay, he felt that his own work owed most. At Cambridge, his surplus energy plunged him for a time into contemporary movements for social reform. He taught at the Working Men's College and was one of a prominent group of young reformers which produced *The Heart of Empire*, a constructive programme after the example of *Essays in Reform* of an earlier generation. He spoke also once, and then memorably, at the Union, in defence of Dreyfus. But he never varied in his judgment that his gifts did not lie in the sphere of politics or of public life, and position for its own sake had never any attraction for him. Heredity and fortune, he felt, had set him free to write history, and not for a living, and he must justify the indulgence by the devotion of his life to this work.

LOVE OF THE ENGLISH SCENE

During this period George Meredith as a friend, and Wordsworth's and Milton's poetry as lifelong companions, inspired his second enthusiasm—which became to him as a religion—the preservation of the beauty and character of the historic English scene. He wrote an admirable study of the *Poetry and Philosophy of George Meredith* and since the "book-mindedness" of his family was complemented in his case by a strenuous love of the open air and wilder natural scenery, he disciplined himself into becoming a rapid and tireless walker and hill-climber, and, incidentally, a fine game-shot.

Upon moving to London he revived the Sunday Tramps, first founded by Leslie Stephen, and he wrote later of his two legs as his "two doctors, during the troubled years of a young man's realization that the world is not created to make him happy". Dark, vehement, eagle-like, at once ardent and austere; with sombre moods responding sensitively to public error or private sympathy, and alternating with an emphatic humour and the tremendous Trevelyan laugh, he stood out a notable figure among his distinguished contemporaries. He was elected Fellow of Trinity College in 1898 and in early years proved a brilliant lecturer; but he left Cambridge to be the more free to write.

His first published history was *England in the Age of Wycliffe*; but probably he first became known to a wider public as the author of a remarkable essay, *If Napoleon had won Waterloo,* contributed to a competition in the great days of the *Westminster Gazette*. A *History of England under the Stuarts* followed, and demonstrated his unusual gifts as a lucid writer of military campaigns no less than of social development. To train himself in political research, he undertook the authorized *Life of John Bright*, whom his father in politics had particularly admired. But during the 10 years of his prime, his passion for human freedom and for its story and protagonists found its right outlet in the great Garibaldi trilogy, *Garibaldi and the Defence of the Roman Republic, Garibaldi and the Thousand, Garibaldi and the Making of Italy*. This work of genius, its combination of the new scientific with the great literary tradition, the European range of its scholarship, its human understanding, and the poetry of its style placed him at once in the front rank of historians.

FRIEND OF ITALY

It also brought him the friendship of Italy; and during the years of the First World War, when his sight precluded him from combatant service, this friendship marked him out to become the commandant of a volunteer Red Cross Field Ambulance and Hospital which rendered conspicuously gallant service on the Isonzo and Piave fronts, and proved an invaluable ambassador to the Italian armies during the crucial years. He insisted on sharing with his drivers many of their most dangerous tasks under fire, and was awarded the Italian Silver Medal for Valour and, later, appointed C.B.E. To increase our knowledge of the Italian effort, he returned home to issue *Scenes from Italy's War*, dramatic accounts of the alpine warfare; but he had rejoined in time to meet the Caporetto retreat and to help to re-form his scattered unit.

He next published a *Life of Lord Grey of the Reform Bill*, for he was happiest writing in the Whig tradition. A *History of England in the 19th Century* was followed by a complete *History of England;* each of them in one volume, and each a masterpiece of selection, arrangement and vivid delineation of character and scene.

Content in his own sphere of work, it was with difficulty that he was induced in 1928 to accept the Cambridge Regius professorship in Modern History. The appointment was more than justified by the personal distinction which his spiritual force and learning lent to his university. During his professorship he achieved his early purpose of completing Macaulay's history, although upon the briefer scale dictated by modern taste. The three volumes, *Blenheim, Ramillies,* and *The Peace and the Protestant Succession* are the artistic product of matured powers; although it may seem that their concentration has deprived them of something of the fire and lively humanity of the great Garibaldi epic. A shorter study, *The English Revolution*, and *Clio*, a collection of essays of great literary merit and charm, also appeared. He was by now recognized as our leading historian and the influence of his thought and style may be traced in such historic utterances as the stately periods of King George the Fifth's address to the two Houses of Parliament in Westminster Hall.

In the Life of his father, Sir George Otto Trevelyan, he set a model of proportionate biography, perfect in its reticence, justice, and grave affection. The *Life of Lord Grey of Fallodon* was for him a new departure, in its treatment of a career devoted as much to nature and to books as to public affairs. His friendship with Edward Grey, the tastes and sentiments they shared as neighbouring squires and sportsmen qualified him, he hoped, to make the attempt. His success was perhaps as much due to his own deepening understanding of the emotional springs of human action.

Self-discipline, magnanimity, and what had been termed his ethical passion had brought the stormy intellectualism of his youth, an essential aristocracy of mind and some social diffidence, into a serene relationship with ordinary living. To this, two great sorrows in an otherwise fortunate life may have contributed; the death of his elder son, a child of extraordinary promise, and the defection of Italy, for which country he had laboured and written so devotedly, first to Fascism and then to the enemies of freedom and of England. His *English Social History: A Survey of Six Centuries,* which he wrote during the Second World War and which, published in 1944, attained immediate and significant popularity, marks a phase of distaste for all politics and a parallel intensification of his interest in the continuous beauty and development of the English scene.

MASTER OF TRINITY

He had looked forward to retiring to Hallington, the Northumbrian home he had inherited from a branch of his family, to his library and country pursuits. But the Mastership of Trinity College falling vacant early in the war, the unanimous wishes of those both within and without the university were allowed again to prevail. Possibly a further inducement was the German raiding of the historic buildings then in progress. It was a call that appealed to his temperament, to hold what might prove to be a post of danger, in the spirit of Sir Walter Scott's "Abbot". "My appointment would probably have pleased Macaulay and my father as much as the destruction of Holland House would have pained them", was his own estimate at the time. The nobility and historical romance of the college buildings was a setting after his heart. He wrote the history of the college, a masterly epitome of the history of our country as seen through one of its institutions; and his Mastership was made memorable by his dignified fulfilment of all its obligations even under war difficulties, by the weighty eloquence of his occasional Addresses, by the affectionate respect with which he was sought out by the learned men of two continents, and by his own sympathetic attitude to younger men and towards the changing order; for if his personality had something of the impressiveness of an earlier tradition, he could and did dispense with its trappings as with its prejudices.

Earlier he had accepted the chairmanship of the executive committee of the National Trust, when it was still in its beginnings, and for many years he devoted his inspiring energy and no inconsiderable fortune to extending its scope and winning for it the national and central position it now holds. He was as zealous in protecting the amenities of Cambridge. Trusteeships of the British Museum and of the National Portrait Gallery he accepted as responsibilities also proper to the historical sphere within which he was resolved to remain. The presidency of the Youth Hostels Association he undertook in the same interest, of the guardianship and right enjoyment of our English scenic inheritance. Among many honorary distinctions from many countries he once spoke of the bestowal of the Order of Merit and of an Honorary Fellowship of Oriel College as having satisfied early in life any personal ambition—for the reason that in both honours he succeeded his father.

LAST WRITINGS

His last writings, a collection of historical essays both brilliant and weighty, contained a terse autobiographical account of his development as a historian—"all that matters of me", he wrote, "and, with that, I have packed wheel barrow and wheeled myself off the stage."

After his retirement in 1951 from the Mastership of Trinity he lived quietly either in his house in West Road or in Northumberland, where his small estate of Hallington, which had fallen to him through so strange a providence, brought him ever deeper and surer happiness. Happiness came to him, too, in his period of retirement through various public marks of affection and esteem. In 1953 he was asked to deliver the Clark Lectures, an honour usually accorded to someone whose *métier* is literature. In these lectures, reprinted as *A Layman's Love of Letters,* he was able to give expression to his lifelong passion for great poetry; and few who heard them will forget the force with which they were delivered or the excitement with which they were received. A few years later the Trevelyan Lecturers were founded, to be delivered yearly in his honour on an historical subject; and at about the same time the Trevelyan Scholarships, a more unusual but no less successful way of honouring him, and commemorating his name. In his last years failing eyesight robbed him of the pleasure of reading and writing and he found consolation by reciting to himself the long tracts of poetry that he knew by heart. One of the last things he wrote was a centenary article on Macaulay for *The Times* in 1959.

He was most happily and equally married with Janet, daughter of Humphry and Mary Ward, the novelist, herself an historian of Italy and a public-spirited organizer who took her mother's foundation, the Play Centres of London, through many years of difficult increase to a triumphant conclusion in their adoption by the London County Council; upon which occasion she was made a Companion of Honour. His daughter Mary (wife of the Bishop of Ripon) is the author of a *History of William of Orange* and of a large work on Wordsworth; and his son Humphrey (a Fellow of King's) of philosophical studies in Goethe.

A great critic said of him "A great historian, he is equally a poet; history is to him always the Muse: each of his books, in its close-woven pattern and rhythm, is a poem, and a poem built upon truth." He will be remembered no less as a great Englishman, one who consecrated an individual genius to preserving the best of our English heritage, to continuing and developing a high national tradition of literary history, and to making it acceptable to a new age.

July 23, 1962.

General Rafael Leonidas Trujillo, who was assassinated on May 30, 1961, at the age of 69, had been the undisputed ruler of the Dominican Republic for over 30 years and was one of the last of the old-fashioned military dictators of South America. His regime was noted for the cruelty with which all opposition was repressed and most of the normal human freedoms eliminated, but also for the material benefits which it brought for his people. It was above all things an efficient dictatorship—efficient in its organization of widespread social services and efficient in maintaining itself in power for a long period.

Born in San Cristobal on October 24, 1891, he was the third of 11 children of a poor family. His first job was as a telegraph operator, but in 1918 he joined the National Constabulary organized by the United States Marines during their occupation of the Republic. In 1921 he graduated from the Haina Military Academy, and his subsequent rise was rapid. A major when the United States Marines left the country in 1924, he was chief of staff by 1928, and the nation's ruler two years later when the previous president was gaoled.

After much bloodshed his control became absolute. His posts varied. For some of the time he was president. For many years he was Commander-in-Chief of the Armed Forces. Sometimes he held a variety of Ministerial posts. But his precise title did not matter. Restorer of Financial Independence, First Journalist, Maximum Leader—it made no difference. Wherever it came from, the voice of command was the same.

The sweets of office were denied neither to himself nor to his family. Businesses were divided among his relatives while he personally dominated the salt, tobacco and beer industries. It was calculated that he and his relatives owned between them one-third of the cultivated land. Many of his family were appointed to posts of distinction. His brother, General Hector Trujillo, was nominally president for eight years.

He came to power with the old capital, Santo Domingo, in ruins after a hurricane. Now a new modern city, Ciudad Trujillo, stands in its place. But he was not only concerned with the shop window. The hospitals, schools and roads built under the Trujillo regime spread throughout the whole state. The contrast between the Dominican Republic under Trujillo and Haiti under its various rulers or Cuba under Batista was most striking.

In these respects his rule was enlightened but he never trusted to the unfettered judgment of his subjects to appreciate it. There was only one political party—although he had announced his intention of holding free elections, with an opposition, in 1962. There were no freedom of the press, no right of assembly, and no independent trade unions. The Republic has proportionately a larger army than any other Latin American state. There were the secret police, arbitrary arrests, torture and summary executions.

These methods may have kept the regime in power but they did not remove discontent. Opposition came principally from the middle classes, even, at times, the officers of the armed forces. There was very little evidence of it among the masses. But in recent years he faced increasing opposition from the Roman Catholic Church. In January, 1960, the six bishops of the republic issued a pastoral letter calling for civil liberties and an amnesty for political prisoners. Soon afterwards the secret police arrested hundreds of people who were said to be in a conspiracy against the regime. Most of them were sentenced to 30 years' hard labour as "agents of international communism".

Perhaps the most serious blow to his position came in August, 1960 when the Organization of American States indicted him for his involvement in a plot to assassinate President Romulo Betancourt of Venezuela. Diplomatic relations were severed. A ban was imposed on the sale of arms and ammunition to the Republic and in January, 1961, further economic sanctions were approved. Tourism declined and the economy, always based on a slender foundation, was seriously threatened.

With growing opposition within, with increasing hostility from his neighbours, particularly Castro's Cuba, and with so many Dominican exiles waiting for the chance to pounce, Trujillo's fall had been predicted in many quarters.

He had been married three times and had four children.

June 2, 1961.

Constantin Tsaldaris, who was Prime Minister and Foreign Minister of Greece at a time when, after the Second World War, his country was engaged in a life or death struggle against militant communism, died on November 15, 1970, in Athens. He was 86.

He was largely responsible for the fact that Greece survived her vicissitudes and remained a faithful ally of the West. Born at Alexandria in 1884, the son of one of the many prosperous Greeks of Egypt, "Dino", as he was known to his friends, was sent to Athens for his education. He obtained a law degree at Athens University and continued his studies in London, Berlin and Florence. When he returned from his travels he joined the Greek civil service and was appointed in 1916 to the important post of Prefect of Patras and, later, of Corfu. After a period of inactivity during King Constantine's exile, he assumed the Governorship of Crete upon the King's return in 1920, and held that office until 1922.

He was first elected member of Parliament under the banner of the Liberal Party which then opposed the Populists led by his uncle Panayis Tsaldaris. In 1928 he joined the Populists and between 1933 and 1935 he was under-secretary of Posts, Telephones and Telegraphs in his uncle's Cabinet, and was later head of the Prime Minister's political bureau. After the death of Panayis Tsaldaris in 1936, he was elected to be member of the governing body of the Populist Party which soon afterwards, however, was forced to suspend all activity with the advent of the Metaxas dictatorship in 1936.

MONARCHY ISSUE

Constantine Tsaldaris reappeared on the Greek political scene after the end of the Second World War when the main issue was whether Greece would remain a monarchy or not. A staunch royalist himself, he was chosen by the Populist Party soon after its sweeping electoral victory in 1946, to be leader of the party and head of the Populist Government which carried out the referendum and ultimately brought about the return of King George to Greece. He held power for 10 months, but as the danger of communist domination imposed a more representative government, he relinquished the premiership and became Minister of Foreign Affairs under Maximos, Sophoulis and Diomidis. He held that post until 1950. It was during this period that Constantine Tsaldaris displayed considerable diplomatic acumen by securing for his country both the moral and material support of the Western powers. He represented Greece at the Peace Conference, induced the United Nations to dispatch a team to investigate the real causes of communist sedition in Greece, and was instrumental in bringing about the so-called Truman Doctrine in 1947 which helped Greece defeat the armed Communist bid for power and launched the country on its postwar economic recovery.

Constantine Tsaldaris's career as a political leader ended in 1950 when his party lost the elections and gradually began to disintegrate under the blows of economic scandals which were attributed to his entourage. His own integrity and honesty were never put to doubt. The entry into politics of Field Marshal Papagos precipitated Tsaldaris's complete loss of control over the Greek Right wing. His deputies gradually sided with the Field Marshal and, after the latter's death, with Constantine Karamanlis, once one of his followers.

He failed in the 1952 elections, but was reelected in Parliament with two followers in 1956 when he joined the Opposition's Popular Front with the pro-communists. He failed again in 1958 and had since retired from active politics. He is survived by his wife, Nadine.

November 16, 1970.

Moise Tshombe, the former Congolese Prime Minister and one time self-styled president of the breakaway Katanga province, died in Algeria on June 29, 1969. He was 49. He had been detained near Algiers since he was kidnapped at gunpoint two years earlier from exile in Spain.

The Congo-Kinshasa Government had pressed for Tshombe's extradition to face charges of high treason. Although the Algerian supreme court recommended that he be handed over President Boumedienne never sanctioned this.

In the early days of independence of the Congo, Tshombe, as provincial president of his home province of Katanga, declared the Congo's richest province independent of the rest of the country. For nearly three years secession was maintained in defiance of the United Nations and of virtually all African nationalist opinion and was ended only after a war fought on behalf of the central Congolese Government by the United Nations.

The secession ended early in 1963 and Tshombe went into exile in Europe. Yet eighteen months later he was back, not to Katanga but Leopoldville (now Kinshasa), as Prime Minister of the very central Government which had struggled for so long to bring about his downfall.

KIDNAPPED IN SPAIN

He was Prime Minister of the Congo from July, 1964 until his dismissal by President Kasavubu in October, 1965. Again he went into exile in Europe, living in Madrid. It was from Spanish territory that he was kidnapped when his aircraft was hijacked in July, 1967.

For the great majority of Africans, certainly the majority of African politicians, Tshombe was more than an odd man out. He was an object of execration, whose name became synonymous with treason. There were several reasons for this. One was his vision to lead Katanga to secession—and his success in defying the central Government and the U.N.—in a continent where secessionist sentiments are unacceptable. Another was his readiness to use Europeans not only for economic support but in military action against fellow Africans. This he did as president of Katanga, where he relied heavily on an army of white mercenaries.

He recruited more mercenaries, many of them as before from South Africa and Rhodesia, as Prime Minister of the Congo for his campaign against the rebels who held large parts of the country. He also earned much abuse by committing the Americans and Belgians to rescue white prisoners of rebels by an air-lift from Stanleyville in 1964.

A third reason for Tshombe's unpopularity among Africans, and in some ways the most important, was his alleged complicity in the murder of Patrice Lumumba, the deposed Congolese Prime Minister, who had been sent under guard by the then central Congolese Government into the care of Tshombe, his arch opponent.

It was mainly this accusation against Tshombe which led some African and Arab leaders to refuse to sit down at the same table with him when he arrived in Cairo in October, 1964, to attend a non-aligned conference. Tshombe was under guard with his staff for some days in a former palace on the outskirts of Cairo until he left for Paris.

One of the charges frequently levelled against Tshombe was that he was a stooge of the Europeans. In evidence was called the fact that he maintained close and friendly relations with the Belgians, and particularly the directors of the Union Minière after his declaration of secession. For many Africans, Tshombe was simply a puppet, manipulated by European interests. For many Europeans, on the other hand, he was a genuine African nationalist, sensible enough, unlike many African leaders, to see on which side his bread was buttered.

NO STOOGE

On an objective view, Tshombe must be acquitted of the accusation of being a stooge. He was very much a personality in his own right, cheerfully and skilfully using Europeans by playing on the desires of business interests for stability above all, at a time when the Congo was in chaos. There is no doubt that he could not have maintained secession for so long without the active support of European interests. This is by no means the same thing as saying that he was the puppet of these interests.

Moise Tshombe was a shrewd and clever negotiator, whose considerable charm was admitted even by many who disliked everything he stood for. He had a gift for flexibility—or, as some might prefer to call it, deliberate ambiguity—that made him a difficult man to deal with but which at the same time enabled him to hold together the disparate elements in Katanga and later, in a remarkable way, similarly opposing factions in the Congo as a whole. As a popular leader he had an undoubted flair, and the capacity, for generating genuine popular enthusiasm.

Sir Roy Welensky, in his book *Welensky's 4000 Days,* summed Tshombe up as "a remarkable man, honest, brave and highly intelligent". Dr. Conor Cruise O'Brien, who as U.N. representative in Katanga had many a brush with Tshombe, paints a different picture in his book *To Katanga and Back*. One of the habits which particularly turned Africans against Tshombe was his friendship with Sir Roy Welensky, from whom he obtained much moral, and some practical, support.

COURAGE

Yet of Tshombe's courage there is plenty of evidence. Perhaps the most telling is the fact that he returned to the Congo in 1964, not knowing whether he was going to power or to execution. After his removal from the premiership he was in fact tried in absence by a military court which sentenced him to death in March, 1967. A month or so earlier there had been rumours that Tshombe was raising more mercenaries in preparation for a return to power.

His great failing as an African leader was that he was completely out of sympathy with the trends of nationalist thought and indeed manifestly despised them. He was a manipulator, who seemed seriously lacking in sensitivity, blatantly living a European life in Europe except when actually in power. This set people against him far more than his readiness to use European assistance, which, after all, many African leaders have done.

Tshombe was born in November, 1919, at Musumba, in Katanga and was educated in American Methodist mission schools. The son of a wealthy businessman, he went into his father's business (a chain of stores and an hotel), but proved to be a failure, and was three times declared bankrupt. Under Belgian rule the Tshombes were bourgeois and Tshombe himself was an *involue*—a citizen.

In the early 1950s he entered local politics, sitting as a member of the Katanga provincial council, and in 1959 was one of the founders of the Katangese party Conakat, of which he became president.

Until the round table conference of 1960, which arranged the Congo's independence, however, Tshombe, like other Congolese politicians, was scarcely known. At this conference he was a strong advocate of a loose confederal rather than a federal arrangement, with large powers left in provincial hands. He was also a firm believer in continuing economic links with the Belgians.

After independence and his secession declaration, he attended in 1961 a conference in Coquilhatville with other Congolese leaders. At one stage, in disagreement, he walked out and was promptly arrested and held prisoner. It was announced that he would be tried for treason, but by the intervention of General Mobutu he was released, and he returned to Katanga in time for the first anniversary of secession, and to a royal welcome.

Tshombe married a daughter of the paramount chief of the Balunda, his own tribe, and they had 10 children.

After his dismissal as Prime Minister he wrote a book, *Quinze mois de gouvernement au Congo*, published in 1966.

July 1, 1969.

Elias Tsirimokos, who became Prime Minister of Greece for 30 days during the eventful summer of 1965, died on July 13. 1968 aged 61.

He was a frustrated socialist in a country which spurns ideology in favour of personalities. Realization of this axiom came late in his 30-year-long political career, and shortly before his untimely death he had reconciled himself to realities to a degree that could have ensured his political survival but for the rapid and dramatic deterioration of his health which coincided with the suspension of constitutional rule by the military in April, 1967.

He was born in Lamia, central Greece, in a family which had a long political tradition. His father and grandfather had been Cabinet Ministers and Speakers of Parliament. In 1926, he graduated in law at Athens University. He pursued post-graduate studies in Paris before returning to Athens in 1931 to establish a law practice specializing in criminal law.

His baptism of fire in Greek politics came in the short-lived Parliament of 1936 in which he was elected as a Liberal deputy. During the Greek-Italian war, he served as a volunteer truck-driver and took part in the Albanian campaign. He became better known during the enemy occupation of Greece, 1941-44, when he was active in the resistance movement, having founded his first political group, "The Union of Popular Democracy", in 1941. In March, 1944, a few months before the liberation of Greece by the allies, he was appointed Secretary for Justice in the communist-dominated Political Committee of National Liberation (P.E.E.A.), which became known as the Government of the Mountains.

He had his first proper ministerial post in the Liberation Government of Papandreou, as Minister of National Economy. His resignation, together with those of three Communist Ministers, signalled the December 1944 communist uprising which plunged Greece into her first post-war bloodbath. He was one of the negotiators for the Communist Front in the 1945 Varkiza agreement which ended the hostilities.

COMMUNIST BRAND

His association with the Greek communists branded his political career at a time when passions ran high and political extremism was *de rigueur*. He was elected in the 1950 elections at the head of his party, but failed in 1951, 1952, and again in 1956, although he had rejoined the Liberals. In 1958 he was elected as an independent on the pro-communist ticket for Athens. After the elections, he dissociated himself from the extreme left-wing and founded the "Democratic Union" Party and in 1961 he was one of the eight splinter-party leaders who joined forces to form the Centre Union under George Papandreou.

When the Centre Union came to power in 1963, he was elected president of Parliament, but when he sought the same post after the 1964 election which consolidated the Centre Union victory, he was turned down by Papandreou. He led a revolt within the party, which first revealed the lack of cohesion in the Centre Union that later led to its downfall.

By January, 1965, he had patched his dispute with the Prime Minister, and became Minister of Interior, an appointment which soon had the right-wing opposition clamouring that Papandreou was turning left. It was ironic that when, after his dispute with Papandreou in July, 1965, King Constantine failed in the first attempt to set up a government, he should have been chosen on August 18, 1965, to be the new Prime Minister with the promise of support from the same right-wing critics. He deserted the Centre Union and held power at a critical time for the regime. He displayed a determination and forcefulness in quelling the communist-led pro-Papandreou riots in Athens, and restored order for the first time since the outbreak of the July crisis.

His leftist background, however, was the main cause of his failure to remain in office. This deterred Markezinis, influential leader of of the small Progressive Party, and the Tsirimokos Cabinet was defeated in a confidence vote in Parliament.

He served as deputy Prime Minister and

Foreign Minister in the Government of Stefanopoulos, who succeeded him, but by April, 1966, his unstinted support to Archbishop Makarios, President of Cyprus, versus General Grivas, the Athens-appointed commander-in-chief in Cyprus, brought him at loggerheads with the rest of the Cabinet. He resigned and attempted to bring down the Stefanopoulos government, without success. He remained, together with a nephew who is also a deputy, an independent member of Parliament.

His wife and one daughter survive him.

July 15, 1968.

Sophie Tucker, who died in New York on February 9, 1966, was, like the Roxy Music-Hall, one of the apparently immovable fixtures of American show-business; except that when the Roxy Music Hall, being merely brick and stone, went the way of all brick and stone, Miss Tucker went right on singing.

She was that rare thing in show business, the complete original; not only the last of the red-hot mommas. but the model, and the greatest of the breed.

There is some confusion about precisely where and when she was born. She was certainly in Boston at an early age. Some books say she was born there on January 13, 1884; according to another account she was born in Russia, child of Jewish parents, and taken to America at the age of three months. At any rate, she spent most of her youth in New England, her parents keeping a small hotel and restaurant at Hartford, Connecticut.

She began by singing popular songs to the patrons of her parent's restaurant, then started to perform professionally in the area, and in 1906 went to New York, where she took Tucker as her stage name and got a job singing in a music-hall on 16th Street. Improbably, it was with a black-face act that she first made some sort of name; but so the story goes, she one night lost her costumes and make-up box while on tour with a burlesque show and, discovering that she needed no special costume and make-up to hold her audiences, decided from that moment to perform just as a straight singer.

"SOME OF THESE DAYS"

It was at this phase of her career that she acquired the label of "red hot momma"—a singer of sentimental and on occasion suggestive songs laced with torch songs and blues. This was how she appeared in her first major New York show, the *Ziegfeld Follies* of 1909, at the New York Jardin de Paris, and two years later the image received its permanent confirmation when the Negro composer Shelton Brooks gave her the song that she made famous, and that in a measure made her famous, "Some of These Days". She continued a string of successful appearances in the United States, and in 1922 made her first London appearance, in cabaret to begin with and then at the Palladium and other variety theatres around the country. So busy and popular was she that (so it was stated in a court case in 1926) at the time she was playing cabaret at the Kit Kat Club (1925) she was also doing so much outside work in cabaret and private entertaining that she was giving at least seven performances a day.

In 1929, always ready to try something new, Sophie Tucker appeared in one of the early talkies, *Honky Tonk*, in a role carefully tailored for her so that she could sing a number of her most famous songs. In 1934 she played in a Command Performance before King George V and Queen Mary.

During the war she worked tirelessly entertaining the troops as "the last of the red-hot mommas", and though in her later career she gracefully allowed the red heat to pale to a rosy nostalgic glow, concentrating more on the sentimental and even slightly sententious songs like "Life Begins at Forty" and "My Yiddisher Momma", she could still raise a laugh with a risque double entendre or put over a comic song like "Nobody Loves a Fat Girl" with all her old aplomb.

February 11, 1966.

Professor William Ernest Stephen Turner, O.B.E., F.R.S., Emeritus Professor of Glass Technology in the University of Sheffield, died on October 27, 1963. He was 82.

Turner was educated at King Edward VI Grammar School, Birmingham. He graduated as B.Sc. of the University of London and was a post-graduate student of the University of Birmingham, where in 1904 he received the Master's Degree. In 1911 he was awarded the D.Sc. of the University of London.

He was appointed as assistant lecturer in the University of Sheffield in 1904 to teach physical chemistry and in 1907 took charge of the Honours School in this subject. In 1914 he had already established a reputation in the field of molecular association, having published some 25 papers and a monograph, but his main life work began shortly after the outbreak of the First World War when he proposed that a University Scientific Advisory Committee be set up to deal with the technical problems arising in local industry from the cutting off of supplies of previously imported raw materials and manufactured products This committee was formed and he became secretary. Many inquiries came from the local glass industry and Dr. Turner suggested that as there was nobody on the university staff having any knowledge of glass and glass-making he should do what he could to help. In a short time he visited some 40 glass works in south Yorkshire and came to the conclusion that the time was ripe to apply science systematically to the problems of the glass industry. He presented this conclusion in a report to the University Council in the spring of 1915 and advocated the creation of a university department to provide teaching and research in glass manufacture. The department was created in June 1915, and at first classes were held in local centres of industry but within two years courses at graduate level were set up at the university.

From then on Turner devoted himself with a tremendous concentration to the field of study which he himself named "Glass Technology". The department was the first of its kind in the world and rapidly became noteworthy not only for its subject but for the manner of its organization. An advisory committee was soon formed which in a few years became the Glass Delegacy and the governing body of the department; on this body academic representation was about equal with representation of industry. The department not only taught but also undertook research, much of the kind one would expect to be undertaken now by a research association, and perhaps on some waves it was even closer to industry than such bodies are able to get in that members of the staff were frequently dispatched to glass works in order to help with solving problems which had arisen on the factory floor.

BREAKING DOWN SECRECY

Turner also soon realized that communication of ideas was a necessity if science was going to make any progress in helping the glass industry and in 1917 he formed the Society of Glass Technology. This society arranged meetings and published a journal in which appeared the papers read to those meetings. Visits were also arranged to works not only in Britain but abroad and these activities did a great deal to break down the secrecy which until that time had obtained among the various parts of the industry. With the help of a small staff Turner carried on all these activities, producing annually a volume of some 500 pages, but at the same time he was active in building up his department. After a few years in an attic in the chemistry department the work moved to a laboratory in the applied science department and to small, newly built premises in Badger Lane, Sheffield, and then again to a bigger place, an old glass works in Darnall. However, in 1937 to Turner's great pride and tremendous credit the department moved to its present buildings known as Elmfield, Northumberland Road, Sheffield, on a site contiguous with other university buildings. Turner lavished great care on the preparation of plans and the raising of money for these buildings and exerted a great influence on their appearance not only externally but in providing such things as a mosaic showing the history of glass on the wall of the museum. The museum itself contains many beautiful pieces of glass presented by him.

INTERNATIONAL BODY

Inspired by the success of the journeys abroad which he arranged for the Society of Glass Technology, Turner in 1933 was the prime mover in organizing the first International Congress on Glass. Shortly afterwards the International Commission on Glass was formed and he became the first president. On his retirement from that office 20 years later he was made honorary president. An internationalist at heart, he was active in reviving the work of the commission in 1948 and the congress in 1953 after the cessation of activities during the war. He retired from active work in the Department of Glass Technology at the end of 1945. He continued for another eight years or so as editor of the journal. In 1955 to Turner's dismay it was decided that the existing organization of the department was no longer in accord with the demands of the time and two new bodies were formed, the British Glass Industry Research Association to undertake the industrial work, and the Department of Glass Technology to continue the university work. As the Society of Glass Technology, which had used rooms in the department for its offices for many years, had left in 1953 to occupy a small office building near by, Turner's creation was split into three a situation to which Turner never really became reconciled. Nevertheless he was not opposed to change and when, in 1959, it was suggested that the journal of which he had been editor for some 35 years should cease to publish in its present form and should be replaced by two other journals, one dealing with glass technology and one dealing with the physics and chemistry of glasses, he was an enthusastic supporter of the idea.

All this work still left time for other pursuits. Whenever opportunity permitted he would climb in the mountains of Switzerland and he was a great walker on the moors near Sheffield; for a short time he was president of the University Mountaineering Club. For many years too he was an active worker in organizations concerned with social welfare; for example, he and his first wife were active class leaders at the Helen Wilson Settlement in Neepsend, Sheffield. Turner was twice married; his first wife died in 1939. There were two sons and two daughters of this marriage; the younger son, Professor Eric Turner, is Director of the Institute of Classical Studies in the University of London. In 1943 Turner married, secondly, Helen Munro the artist, well known for her work in glass-decoration.

He was the easiest man to entertain, he loved music and always had interesting stories to tell of his travels.

Among the many honours bestowed on Turner, he was made O.B.E. in 1918 and elected a Fellow of the Royal Society in 1938.

October 31, 1963.

Randolph Turpin, the former middleweight boxing champion of the world, was found dead at his home in Leamington, Warwickshire, on May 17, 1966. He was 37.

Turpin, who won the world middleweight title in 1951, was called "the most exciting fighter raised in Britain for a generation". But the years of his greatness in the ring were overshadowed first by his struggles to reach the top and later by financial difficulties in spite of the £150,000 he was believed to have earned from boxing.

Turpin was born at Leamington on June 7, 1928. He was the son of a white woman and a merchant seaman from British Guiana, who died from the long term effects of German gassing in the First World War in 1929. Mrs. Turpin had to bring up five children on a tiny pension and her sons, Dick, Jackie, and later Randolph, took up self-defence for fear they might have to face colour prejudice.

Dick eventually became the first coloured boxer to hold a British professional boxing title and Jackie did well as a featherweight. But it was Randolph, with victories in the A.B.A. championships of 1945 and 1946, who eventually proved to have the most talent.

EUROPEAN TITLE

Turpin turned professional in 1946 and five years later he won the British middleweight championship by beating Albert Finch in five rounds. The next year he took only 48 seconds to gain the vacant European title and four more victories inside the distance brought him to challenge the renowned American, Sugar Ray Robinson, for the world championship at Earls Court on July 10, 1951.

The boxing reporters nearly all favoured Robinson, who had lost only once in 133 fights. But Turpin was quietly confident in his remarkably strong body and his unusually long reach for a middleweight. And Robinson, possibly regarding the match a little too lightheartedly after a hectic tour of Europe, had to take so many left jabs and left hooks to the head that he was beaten on points over 15 rounds. The rapturous crowd sang "For he's a jolly good fellow".

Yet Turpin reigned as world champion for only 64 days. In September, 1951, he went to New York for the return bout with Robinson and the American again seemed close to defeat when he was cut by his left eyebrow in the tenth round. But Robinson fought back tigerishly, put Turpin down for nine seconds and was hammering his opponent with blows to the head when the referee stopped the fight.

SLOWER REFLEXES

After that defeat Turpin continued to box at the top level, winning the British and Empire light-heavyweight titles from Don Cockell and challenging unsuccessfully for the world middleweight championship at a time when it was vacant. But his reflexes became slower and he was much easier to hit. After one defeat he said: "I could see the punches coming but I couldn't get out of the way."

The end came on September 9, 1958, in his seventy third professional fight when Yolande Pompey knocked him out in four and a half minutes boxing. After that it was a battle, not against the other man's fists, but against rapidly diminishing money. The world champion who once said "I was fleeced right, left and centre by those around me" was declared bankrupt in 1962.

Work in a Midlands scrapyard and as a professional wrestler brought in only small sums and Turpin was left with only the memories of the nights of greatness when "I just hit the other boys and they fell over."

May 18, 1966.

Lord Twining, G.C.M.G., M.B.E., Governor of Tanganyika from 1949 to 1958, died on July 21, 1967, at the age of 68. Lord Twining was one of the most remarkable of the post-war colonial Governors. A regular soldier in the early years of his life, he carried with him into his career as a colonial servant much of the soldier's forthrightness and preference for personal contacts over office administration. During his governorship, he guided Tanganyika through the crucial period which saw the first awakening of political consciousness. In manner he was bluff, boisterous and possessed of a schoolboyish sense of humour. A strong personality, of untiring energy, he gave a sense of purpose and direction to his subordinates and to ordinary people of all races in Tanganyika. As a hobby, he made himself a leading expert on the Crown Jewels of Europe on which he wrote a book.

MARRIED THE DOCTOR

Edward Francis Twining was born in 1899, the son of the Rev. W.H.G. Twining. He was educated at Lancing and Sandhurst, whence he was commissioned to The Worcestershire Regiment in 1918. From there he was seconded to the 4th (Uganda) Battalion of the King's African Rifles. After 12 years as a regular officer, he sent in his papers and joined the Colonial administrative service. Sir Philip Mitchell once related how, when Governor of Uganda, he first had his attention drawn to Twining. While perusing the annual reports from the districts, his eye was caught by a paragraph in that from Twining, in which it was stated that, during the year, the relations betwen the administrative and medical services had much improved. On inquiry he found that Twining had married the medical officer. At the outbreak of war, Twining was appointed Director of Labour in Mauritius, a post which he held until he was transferred to the West Indies as Administrator of St. Lucia, in the Windward Islands. Two years later he became Governor of North Borneo.

It was in 1949 that he was called to the task which became in a sense his life work, the Governorship of the United Nations Trust Territory of Tanganyika. This vast and backward country had had a chequered history. First opened up in a rough and ready way by the Germans, who had built the railways and introduced the sisal industry, it had served as a battle ground during the First World War and lain somewhat fallow as a League of Nations mandatory territory under British administration between the wars. It had enjoyed the rule of one great colonial administrator, Donald Cameron, during this period, but by the time Twining took it over the after-effects of another world war and the repercussions of the disastrous groundnuts scheme had left much confusion that called for specially energetic action. This, in a governorship lasting nearly 10 years, Twining provided.

In the economic field, he did much to encourage established industries, such as sisal growing and diamond mining, which were owned and managed by the immigrant races, British, Asian, and European. He also worked hard to increase the African's stake in the cash economy of the country at every point. Dar-es-Salaam is a tribute to the success he achieved in encouraging secondary industries to settle.

Twining's most notable achievements were in the field of race relations. By example rather than precept he succeeded in a remarkable degree in breaking down the social barriers between the three communities; and a happy and constructive period of Tanganyikan history unrolled itself beneath his aegis. The Twinings were everywhere about the countryside and Vernon Bartlett has related how he once saw Lady Twining pose at a garden party as a female William Tell while Indian girls shot at an apple on her head with bows and arrows. Twining spent much of his time on safari, travelling in a private train which hauled two flat-trucks carrying cars up and down the central line. His method was to halt for several days in sidings, where people from far and wide could come to confer with him: and then to range in the cars more deeply into the bush. In this way he was able to impress the whole countryside with the boisterous vigour of his personality and also to keep a keen eye on the functioning of the administrative services. It was all very much personal rule.

As the years passed, Twining addressed himself more and more to the political problems of the country. As a Trust Territory, Tanganyika underwent a biennial inspection by a United Nations visiting mission and he attended the Trusteeship Council of the United Nations to give a personal account of his stewardship. Their reports, which varied very much in quality, all had this in common, that they urged the acceleration of political advancement on democratic lines. Twining's first constitution, instituted in 1952, contented itself with establishing parity between the three races. It left ultimate control of the country firmly in official hands. There were no elected seats. But Twining foresaw the necessity of anticipating demand and before he retired had introduced measures providing for a franchise on a qualitative basis and for the appointment of unofficials of all races.

July 24, 1967.

Giuseppe Ungaretti, the Italian poet, died in Milan on June 3, 1970, at the age of 82.

His death removes one of the most youthful spirits as well as one of the two or three finest poets to have written in Italy during his own long lifetime.

The trinity of Ungaretti, Quasimodo and Montale, all brilliantly personal poets, one—Quasimodo—a winner of the Nobel prize, is a credit to any country. Their appeal is direct and unextravagant, free of gestures and rhetoric but none the less Italian for that. Only Montale survives.

Of the three Ungaretti was the oldest and the best known to the general public. Quasimodo was rather morose and Montale is by nature retiring. But Ungaretti liked to appear on the television screen, happily gave interviews to the weekly magazines and maintained his boyish dress and vitality into his eighties.

Ungaretti was born by chance in Alexandria. His parents came from Lucca and his father was employed in the cutting of the Suez Canal. His father died young and Ungaretti was brought up by his mother who had a shop in an Alexandria suburb.

At the age of 26 he went to Paris passing, as he went, through Florence, Rome and Milan. The experience of these cities of his native origins deeply moved him. In Paris he studied at the Sorbonne and lived the life of a bohemian with such friends as Pea the anarchist and Kavaks the Greek poet, both of whom he had met in Egypt. In 1914 he enrolled in the Italian army, fighting on the Carso and in 1917 was with the Italian Army corps in France. He married in Paris and in 1920 settled in Rome. His first published work was *Il Porto Sepolto,* a book of verses produced at Udine in 1916 of which 80 copies were printed. Three years later he published his *L'Allegria,* which was one of the genuinely innovating works in modern Italian literature.

Ungaretti had an Italian clarity of mind. He also had a freedom of imagination seen by some of his admirers to have had an oriental element; and, of course, there was the attraction towards France and contemporary French poets. This equipment, added to his natural sensitivity, enabled him to react to the grandiloquent style associated with D'Annunzio and the near prose forms of some of the *crepuscolari.*

With another two volumes of poetry behind him, Ungaretti left Italy in 1936 for Brazil, taking the chair of Italian Literature at Sao Paulo largely because of lack of funds. While in Brazil he suffered the loss of his only son. In 1942 he asked to be allowed to return to Italy. The effect of the war following his own private catastrophe inspired the *Il Dolore,* published in 1947.

Ungaretti loved travel and wrote vividly about his journeys while continuing his poetic output. He translated Shakespeare and Racine. After his return to Italy from Brazil he held the chair of modern and contemporary literature at Rome university until he reached the retiring age of 70. He took over the presidency of the European Community of Writers at the age of 74.

June 4, 1970.

Sir Stanley Unwin, the distinguished publisher, chairman of George Allen and Unwin, and director of several other publishing firms, died in London on October 13, 1968. He was 83.

Energetic and businesslike, possessed of a shrewd grasp of affairs that matched the bent of his intellectual interests, Unwin left his imprint not only upon the publishing concerns with which he was closely connected but upon English publishing generally. Nobody knew more about the economics of publishing, and few were more active in all public affairs that bore on the printing, publishing and distribution of English books at home and abroad. He was president during 1933-35 of the Publishers' Association of Great Britain, whose influence and prestige owed not a little to him personally, and was president of the International Publishers' Congress during 1936-38. From its inception in 1934 Unwin was an enthusiast for the work of the British Council, on whose Executive Committee he served, and whose interests he helped to safeguard from whatever quarter they were threatened.

Born on December 19, 1884, the son of Edwin Unwin and Elizabeth Spicer, Stanley Unwin came to publishing almost by the light of nature. After his schooling at Abbotsholme he entered the publishing business of his uncle, T. Fisher Unwin, set himself industriously to study every aspect of the profession, made a special study of the book trade at Leipzig, and soon found himself well equipped to direct his own publishing business. His was the assured hand that built up the wide-ranging interests, notably in international affairs, the social sciences, philosophy and psychology, of the firm of Allen and Unwin, whose progress was marked by the incorporation of several other firms. At one time or another Unwin was associated with the guidance of the affairs of John Lane, the Bodley Head; Methuen; Chapman and Hall; Simpkin Marshall; the Book Centre; and the old established printing house of Unwin Brothers Ltd., Woking.

His book, *The Truth About Publishing,* first published in 1926 and often revised, is in its own kind a classic, an invaluable work of exposition, dealing with costs and commerce, rights and royalties, printing and publicity and a great deal more, from which everybody concerned with the writing, manufacture or sale of books will derive benefit. Now and then, perhaps, its point of view is peculiar to Unwin himself, but that does not impair the usefulness of the book, which has been translated into many foreign languages.

In 1934 he published, in *Two Young Men See the World,* an account based on their letters home at the time of a journey of 20 years before which he and Seven Storr had made to South Africa, Australia, New Zealand, Japan and some of the South Sea islands for the purpose of studying bookselling conditions in those regions. Nobody worked harder to promote the sale of British books abroad, and following the logic of his own saying: "Trade follows the Book", Unwin was a great traveller all his life. Until a very late age he played a remarkably skilful game of lawn tennis. Quite recently not even the heat of Washington in early summer could subdue his enthusiasm for the game; and he could be heard offering to players not unknown to American or European championships advice about the exact place on the court where best to receive certain deliveries. In 1960 he published, in *The Truth About a Publisher,* a full and frank account of his activities, his interests, and his business success.

Unwin, who was knighted in 1946 and made K.C.M.G. in 1966, received Belgian, French and Czechoslovak decorations and was an Hon. LL.D. of Aberdeen University. Exceptionally happy in his home life, he married, in 1914, Mary, daughter of Rayner Storr; they had two sons and a daughter.

October 15, 1968.

Sir Boris Uvarov, K.C.M.G., F.R.S., a worldwide authority on locust migration and on the classification of orthopterous insects, died on March 18, 1970, at the age of 81.

Boris Petrovitch Uvarov was born on November 5, 1888, at Uralsk in south-eastern Russia, and was the third son of a bank cashier who was also a lover of open-air life. After leaving school he entered first the Mining Academy at Ekaterinoslav (now Dniepropetrovsk) and second the Faculty of Natural Sciences at St. Petersburg University, taking his degree in 1910. He had studied insects since his schooldays, and was at once appointed entomologist to the crown cotton estates at Merv in Transcaspia. He resigned after a year, because the management wanted immediate practical result without the necessary scientific investigation, and in 1911 he joined the Department of Agriculture at St. Petersburg and was sent to study locusts in the Northern Caucasus. At 23 he became the first director of the Entomological Bureau at Stavropol and in three years had established its reputation and had developed scientific locust control in the region. His observations led him to the conclusion—so startling that he withheld publication of it for some years—that swarming and non-swarming locusts, which appeared so different as then to be thought specifically distinct, were in fact phases of the same insect.

WORLD REPUTATION

In 1915 Uvarov was chosen to organize plant-protection stations in Transcaucasia, and was appointed director of the Tiflis Bureau which served the central provinces there. In the next five years he contributed greatly to the entomological exploration of the region and in 1919 became Professor of Zoology in the State University of Tiflis, which after the revolution became the capital of the new Georgian republic. Conditions, and especially rampant Georgian nationalism, made things difficult for Uvarov at Tiflis, but the presence of British troops in Georgia enabled him to resume contact with European science, and in 1920 he was given an appointment in London at the Imperial Bureau (later Institute) of Entomology. This he held for 25 years.

In this post Uvarov built up a world-wide reputation as a general entomologist, an expert on the Orthoptera, and a leading authority on the locust problem, to the understanding of which his theory of phase transformation of locusts provided a clue. His work *Locusts and Grasshoppers,* published in 1928, was an able summary of our knowledge at that time and has been an essential work of reference.

In 1929 the British Government put him in charge of the investigations of Locust Committees of the Economic Advisory Council in Africa, and he at once realized the need to organize the work internationally. In 1930 the first international locust conference held at Rome recognized London as the centre for information. Investigations in which many Governments cooperated were carried out in most of Africa, Arabia and India, in order to discover the original sources of locust invasions.

The results, analysed in London, gave a coherent picture which strikingly supported Uvarov's phase theory. Plagues of the three distinct species of locust in Africa were found to originate in certain restricted areas, where they survived between whiles as locusts of the solitary phase. Uvarov's work during the period was the inspiration and guidance of the field workers of various nations. By 1938 results were clear enough to form a basis for an international plan, for the study and control of locusts, especially in their "outbreak areas" where successful control might lead to a radical solution of the problem. The outbreak of the war prevented operation of the scheme except in the case of the Red Locust. During the Second World War he made many flights to various parts of East Africa and the Middle East where locust plagues threatened to create famine behind the Allied armies. After the war the plan was completed and international services were set up to deal also with the Migratory and Desert locusts. Uvaroy's services were in wide demand as a consultant.

In 1945 the London centre was formally taken over by the Colonial Office (now the Department of Technical Cooperation), as the Anti-Locust Research Centre, with Sir Boris as the first director. The work of the centre was gradually expanded particularly in the fields of research and training. He retired in 1959 but continued to work at the centre, especially on a new edition of his book on locusts and grasshoppers.

Uvarov was elected a Fellow of the Royal Society in 1950 and received recognition from a number of foreign learned bodies.

March 19, 1970.

Roger Vailland, the French writer, author of *La Loi* and other novels, died on May 11, 1965, at his home near Bourg-en-Bresse.

He was born on October 16, 1907. He first appeared before the public in 1945, with a left-wing existentialist novel entitled *Drôle de jeu.* This is a seemingly autobiographical novel about a nihilistic intellectual who overcomes the temptation to suicide by throwing himself into a life of violent political action. Its hero is drawn to communism at the age of 21 not because he has any vision of a better socialist future but because he likes the idea of rebellion for its own sake. But although Vailland was thus critical of the motives which led men like himself to communism he nevertheless maintained, for some years at least, that communism represented a valid *ethos.* In one of his critical essays, *Le Surréalisme contre la révolution* (1948) he argued that surrealists were cured of their moral weakness by the discipline that had been entailed by their collaboration with the French Communist Party. It was some time, even so, before Vailland himself actually joined the party.

That his opinions were even more communist than many party members' was evident in 1952, when he wrote a play, *Le Colonel Foster plaidera coupable,* which depicted the Americans as the instigators and villains of the Korean war. The play was banned in France by Pinay, but Vailland had the satisfaction of seeing it performed in Russia and in all the satellite capitals. He took out a party card at the time of the "Go-home-Ridgway" demonstrations in Paris. Then the Hungarian revolution, and its ruthless suppression by the Russians in 1956, led Vailland to break quickly and finally with the Communist Party.

PICTURE OF ITALIAN LIFE

His new-found independence of view had a bracing effect on his work. His novel *La Loi,* which won the Prix Goncourt in 1957, was a masterly picture of life in a meridional Italian village. Although its perspective was unmistakably French, Vailland revealed a sympathy for residual Italian feudalism unexpected in a former Marxist. His next novel, *La Fête,* published in English as *The Sovereigns,* was less popular, but showed an even more confident command of technique, and established Vailland as a leading exponent of the more realistic kind of French fiction, albeit at a time when the *nouveau roman* was putting that kind of fiction somewhat out of fashion.

Vailland's last book to be published in Paris was *La Truite,* which recently appeared in English translation as *A Young Trout.* This novel was a marked success with the critics and the reading public and seemed to indicate a return to the author's best after he had dispersed his talent for some years in miscellaneous script-writing for the cinema. where, perhaps, his best-known work was the script of *Les Liaisons Dangereuses.*

He left at least one uncompleted book at his death.

May 13, 1965.

Professor Charles Valentine, who died on May 26, 1964, at his home at Wythall, Worcestershire, was Professor of Education at Birmingham University from 1919 to 1946 and subsequently Professor Emeritus. He was 84.

Among educationists and psychologists the name of C. W. Valentine is always associated with the *British Journal of Educational Psychology* which he founded in 1931 and edited so brilliantly for 25 years. Replacing the *Forum of Education* which he had also founded and edited for nearly a decade, the new journal was an immediate success, achieving an international reputation and contributing greatly to the creation of the influential position which psychology now holds in the field of education. Even so the journal would never have survived the financial stringencies of the depression or the frustrations and shortages of the war years had Professor Valentine not only edited it but also acted as its publisher and managed its finances with very little help outside the gratuitious labour of his own family. When he resigned his editorship in 1955 the status of the journal was assured, its finances were sound and its future certain.

Valentine's work may be seen as of two

kinds. First, there were his attacks upon contemporary educational problems, and second, were his lifelong interests which only became manifest to the outside world when he wrote his major books in his mature years. In the first category his work ranged so widely that there are few fundamental educational problems in which he was not a pioneer worker. His early work before the First World War was a painstaking investigation into the well-known horizontal-vertical illusion, but he was never greatly interested in laboratory experiments and soon became involved in trying to assess the relative merits of two methods of teaching reading to children. He thus initiated a line of research very much alive today.

He was among the first to doubt the efficiency of the methods of selection used in educational selections. He showed, for example, that in many cases there was little relationship between the placement of children in secondary schools and their subsequent academic progress. This work attracted a great deal of attention and led to the volume of work on the "eleven plus" which has made it, with all its faults, probably the most reliable and valid large-scale instrument of selection anywhere. Equally important findings on the unreliability of university awards have never been followed up to any extent though the need is clearly apparent.

Rejecting the influence of the discredited view that the mind consists of a number of discrete faculties which can be strengthened and improved by appropriate training, Valentine saw that much in the curriculum was inappropriate for the children in the schools.

REFORM OVER LATIN

He studied the problem with special reference to the teaching of Latin and, by casting severe doubts upon its value for the majority of children, he speeded a general reform which culminated in the relaxing of university requirements in that subject.

In 1939, Valentine was too old for active service but at once placed himself at the disposal of the government and agreed to produce an elementary text book for n.c.o.s and officers on the applications of psychology to training, selection, morale and discipline. With characteristic thoroughness he undertook a course of elementary infantry training to see at first hand, from the ranks, the problems he had to deal with.

These are only examples of the way Valentine turned his energy to contemporary problems, others included his critical appraisal of Freud's work and his great contribution to the mental testing movement. But these held up his most important work, which in 1942 gave his *magnum opus, The Psychology of Early Childhood,* which is based upon the day-to-day observation of his own five children over nearly 20 years, but is also a synoptic survey of many other studies of children and deals with the fundamental theoretical bases of child psychology. An equally long enduring interest was Valentine's concern for aesthetics. His first book on the topic was published in 1913; his last under the same title, *The Experimental Psychology of Beauty*, appeared in 1962.

Charles Wilfrid Valentine, son of the Rev. Harry Valentine, was born in 1879 and educated at Nottingham High School, Preston Grammar School, University College Aberystwyth (where he was an Exhibitioner) graduating B.A. at London University, while at Downing College, Cambridge, where he was Foundation Scholar in Moral Sciences, he took a double First in Philosophy and Psychology.

He taught in secondary schools for seven years and then spent a period as lecturer in psychology to St. Andrews Provincial Committee and as assistant in education in the University of St. Andrews before being appointed to the chair of Education in Queen's University of Belfast. From 1919 to 1925 Valentine was chairman of the Birmingham Higher Education Sub-Committee. He was president of the Psychology Section of the British Association in 1930 and president of the British Psychological Society in 1947 and 1948.

May 29, 1964.

Vittorio Valletta, the honorary president of Fiat, the last of Italy's great captains of industry, and the man who, more than any other single industrialist, shaped and inspired Italy's post-war "economic miracle", died on August 10, 1967. He was 84.

A brilliant and intense man, he also had the incisive foresight to make two recent decisions of signal importance for Italy. One was his early support for the current "Centre-left" formula of Socialist participation in the Coalition Government. The second was his perception of and stunningly successful invasion of the virgin East European automotive market.

Born on July 28, 1883, at Sampierdarena, near Genoa, Valletta moved to Turin, where he took a degree in economic and social sciences. He soon demonstrated a formidable capacity for work when he earned his way through university by teaching at night school because his father, an Army official, could not give him enough money. He also worked as an art and music critic for a Turin newspaper. After school he did such an outstanding job of re-organizing the labour and administrative structure at a paper plant that his services came to the attention of other Turin industrialists.

Among these was the young Giovanni Agnelli, who founded Fiat ("Fiat" stands for Fabbrica Italiana Automobili Tirinese) in 1899. Valletta's canny management insight was soon recognized by Agnelli who befriended the young scholar who had become a professor at a Turin institute of economics. Prior to and during the First World War, Valletta and Agnelli worked on a consultative basis to develop Fiat's efficiency at producing wartime material. During the war Valletta served as a pilot, training which later resulted in the development of Fiat's aviation division which is among Europe's most advanced industries.

On April 1, 1921, "the professor", as people already called the precocious young man, was called by Giovanni Agnelli to join Fiat. Although he continued his scholastic career on a part-time basis, the growing automative industry claimed almost all his time. His hard-headed brilliance and ability to work 20 hours a day took him on a meteoric rise through the Fiat hierarchy. Joining Fiat as central administrative director, he became director general and in 1928 the managing director and general director until the outbreak of the Second World War.

During the war, he and a handful of Fiat executives remained at Turin during massive bombardment of Fiat's huge Mirafiori plant.

GERMANS RESTRAINED

During the Nazi occupation, Valletta was instrumental in helping prevent the Germans from completely stripping the plant's equipment. At the war end, Senator Agnelli died and Valletta was named his successor. After a brief period in England in 1945, he returned to become a member of a management committee named by the allies to run Fiat. In 1946, he was made president, a position he held until 1966, when he was named honorary president for life and Signor Gianni Agnelli was made president.

Before the Second World War, it was Valletta who conceived of mass-producing tiny cheap cars. The legendary "Topolino" (little mouse) was the precursor of today's best-selling air-cooled Fiat 500D, which many experts have called the best city car built today. The ubiquitous 500 has done more to motorize Italy than any other car.

Under his direction Fiat grew into a physically enormous industry—the Mirafiori plant is one of the largest plants in the world—with sales that skyrocketed from £13m. in 1946 to £85m. in 1950 and £570m. in 1966. Only a few days ago Valletta read what must have been satisfying news, that Fiat will probably displace Volkswagen as Europe's largest single carmaker in 1967.

"The professor's" influence was principally felt in the organization and management of Fiat. Emphasizing highly centralized management decisions, the Turin headquarters could make rapid changes far faster than many competitors. In 1964 a fully developed 1,000 c.c. saloon was scrapped in favour of the 850 model, developed in a matter of months, which market trends indicated would be more popular.

BIG INVESTMENT

Investing more than £287m. in plant between 1946 and 1960, Fiat created a massively diversified industrial group that emphasized vertical integration. Today Fiat, or one of its numerous subsidiaries, produces almost 100,000 separate components from raw materials. Although this once gave Fiat great flexibility it is now one of the characteristics that Signor Gianni Abnelli is said to be changing.

Early on, Valletta saw the changing patterns in the world car industry and the threat of American domination. In 1964 he initiated talks with Volkswagen's Dr. Heinz Nordhoff to discuss cooperation in production and marketing. But Nordhoff rejected the approach as did France's Renault. Even earlier, however, in 1962 Valletta had made a highly significant visit to Moscow where he initiated discussions that four years later were to result in the signing of the largest single automotive contract signed in history.

Fiat's £115 million contract to build a car assembly plant in Russia, that would quadruple Russia's current annual production of 200,000 cars, was a landmark. It opened the hitherto virgin car markets in East Europe to Western companies. Fiat's cue was speedily followed by Renault, B.M.C. and others but it was Fiat that got the plums. Today, Fiat assembly plants are being built in Russia, Poland and Bulgaria and the principal automobile plant in Yugoslavia was built by Fiat in 1954.

Although he will be credited for Fiat's extraordinary post-war growth and the penetration of Eastern Europe, Valletta leaves a heritage for his successor that is not entirely problem free. A family-dominated and aged management, self-financing, that is increasingly strained to meet the needs of a growing industry, and the artificially awkward structure created by the once useful vertical integration are all problems that Signor Agnelli is, however, admirably well equipped to deal with.

A member of many economic organizations, Valletta was named one of Italy's five senators for life by President Saragat in November, 1966. It was a fitting honour of which he was said to have been singularly proud.

August 11, 1967.

Tony Vandervell, millionaire industrialist and former racing driver, died on March 10, 1967, at the age of 68.

For many years chief of the Vanwall car racing team, Guy Anthony Vandervell was reputed to have spent £250,000 on putting British Grand Prix cars on the map with the Vanwall racing car. His fortune came largely from the international motor-bearings business he built up. In 1964 he turned his company into a public one and its shares were quoted on the Stock Exchange for the first time to a value of £10m.

Since his firm went public Vandervell had waived his right to dividends and bonus worth over £1,000,000. Up to mid-1966 he had forgone £763,000 and in January he again gave up his right to dividends worth almost £300,000. In November, 1965, the House of Lords, by a majority decision, finally rejected his appeal against an order to pay surtax relating to dividends on shares which he had transferred to the Royal College of Surgeons to provide £150,000 to found a Chair of Pharmacology. The tax on his gift came to almost £250,000—surtax of £162,000 for 1958-59 and £87,500 for 1959-60. He recently estimated his personal fortune at more than £10m.

His father, the late Mr. Charles Anthony Vandervell, whose C.A.V. company was a pioneer of car electrical equipment, left £262,000 but none of it went to his son because, as the will put it, he was "so exceptionally successful in business".

Tony Vandervell was born in 1898 and had known all about petrol engines since he was a child. He raced his first motor cycle when he was 15.

He joined the Army in the First World War and became a dispatch rider, later getting a commission as a workshop officer in the R.A.S.C. On demobilization, he joined his father's company to learn the business but in 1926, after C.A.V. amalgamated with Lucas and Rotax, he became unhappy about the clash of personalities between the three firms, and a year later he resigned.

Some years later he became interested in a new "Thinwall" bearing being produced in America and in 1932 he formed a company, Vandervell Products, for the manufacture under licence of Thinwall bearings in England. It exported bearings to motor and machinery manufacturers all over the world. Vandervell became convinced it would be possible to build an effective racing car in Britain. Thus, in 1947, when Raymond Mays announced his plan of organizing a team of British Grand Prix cars if the motor industry would assist with finance and components, Vandervell was one of the first to pledge support as a member of the British Motor Racing Committee.

He and his mechanics, however, ultimately produced a racing car of their own. Named the Vanwall, it made its first competition appearance at Silverstone in May, 1954. Though it had teething troubles, its first big success came when, driven by Stirling Moss, it won the International Trophy at Silverstone in 1955.

In July, 1957, the Vanwall won a world championship event at the European and British Grand Prix at Aintree and went on from there to win seven out of 12 world championship races. Vandervell found that his whole life was taken up with work and motor racing.

Vandervell succeeded in a field which had been monopolized by the Germans and the Italians. He did it because he was a firstclass engineer who worked hard and expected others to do the same. In 1959, mainly for health reasons, he decided to give up motor racing. This was the year in which he was awarded the Ferodo Gold Trophy for the most outstanding British contribution to motor racing in 1958.

It was the third time he had taken the trophy—the others were in 1954 and 1957—so he became the outright winner. In 1958 Vanwall cars had also won the Manufacturers' World Championship. In 1960, however, Vandervell returned to motor racing with a new Vanwall car.

Vandervell lived at Stoke Poges, Buckinghamshire. In 1962 his son Colin claimed that he had been kidnapped from Stowe School. A court action by Vandervell, against the school for an interim injunction to allow his son to return, was later withdrawn.

REASON FOR SUCCESS

Vandervell's death comes just a month after his third marriage. His bride was Miss Marian Moore, 45, who had been his private secretary for 20 years. The marriage took place quietly at Chelsea Register Office. His two previous marriages were dissolved.

March 11, 1967.

Georges van Houten, who died in Rome on June 23, 1964, was one of the rare survivors of that wonderfully gifted group of artists who worked in Paris before the 1914-18 War. Through his patron, Duret, a man of unique integrity and judgment, he came into contact not only with artists, but with many of the leading men of action in France at that time. He painted their portraits, and in doing so gained a remarkable insight into the political life of France, at its best and its worst; and came to know also the émigrés from Imperial Russia in whose houses the *ancien régime* was preserved like a fantastic fossil from a previous age.

CHOSE TO PAINT

Van Houten was born in Amsterdam, the son of a well-known industrialist. As a boy he made the choice, in face of bitter parental opposition, of painting rather than business, and as a result was turned out of his home at 16 to make his own life. He found his way to Paris, and by 1914 his work was already attracting attention. When he was in his early twenties Duret noticed a picture by him in Blot's gallery, invited him to his house and commissioned immediately a full-length portrait of himself, later shown in the salon—a successor to portraits of Duret by Whistler and Vuillard. Van Houten had been one of the early admirers of van Gogh, from whose teacher, Jacob Schmidt, he also had learnt in Antwerp; and some of the early work shows that influence strongly. Another powerful influence was that of Toulouse-Lautrec, whose vitality and merciless characterization had a great appeal for him. He enlisted in the Belgian Army in 1914, and after the war resumed his painting in Paris. At a famous retrospective exhibition of the past 40 years of painting in Paris in 1924 van Houten showed half a dozen pictures, one of which, the Bridge at St. Rafael, is now in Oxford. By this date his work was becoming known in Amsterdam and in Copenhagen also. In both cities he had brilliantly successful exhibitions. But by temperament he was suspicious of success and disliked the advertisement which it brought.

RECOGNITION DELAYED

At this critical moment of his career two things happened that transformed his existence. An uncle left him money, a modest fortune which under his shrewd management gave him an income large enough not to need to worry about selling a picture again; while a group of his rivals, including Matisse and Braque, the latter of whom incidentally was an artist whose work he much admired, jealous (so he thought) of the ascendancv of a foreigner with Duret, conspired (as he believed) to prevent his election to the Salon. He had recently married. When Duret first met his wife, he said. "Mrs. van Houten, your husband is a great artist. But he must die." Recognition did not come to the living. Certainly Paris was not the place for him. On Duret's advice he went to work in Denmark, then in Berlin. But he painted less and less, and as he grew older more time was spent in travel and study of the work he specially admired: Michelangelo, Titian, Velasquez, Rubens, Rembrandt. During the Second World

War he and his wife lived in America. But, influenced again by his memories of Duret, who had spent 10 years in exile in England after 1870 and had come to admire it enormously, van Houten found that the place where he was happiest was London. Yet London did not suit his health, and eventually he built a house in Tangier, where he furiously resumed painting.

GEORGE MOORE SKETCH

Many of his own works given late to Oxford University belong to this time, and there are good pictures among them. But the promise of his early work with its vivid characterization and power was perhaps never fully realized. Fortunately in the Oxford benefaction there are some pictures of the earlier period also. After the death of his wife in 1959 he became a wanderer, and for the last three years lived in Rome. He gave to Oxford University (with which his only connexion was his admiration for England) a small group of works of art that he had at various times acquired: among them the important Degas portrait sketch of George Moore—a sketch of which he thought little (it had indeed been given him in part payment for one of his own portraits); a magnificent Tang Dynasty horse; and the remarkable little sketch book of a Japanese artist, possibly Hokusai, given him by Duret who brought it back in 1874 from a journey which was one of the first signs of a European interest in Japanese art.

Van Houten was short and slight, walked to the end of his life bolt upright, and spoke lively, if unorthodox, English, with a charming French accent. "Pay attention" he would say, as one steered him hazardously across the Via Veneto, listening to his vigorous protests about the Doria Velasquez ("of course zey ave ruined ze skirt wiz ze cleaning but fortunately zey 'ave left ze 'ead")—"pay attention". His caustic comments on Americans, on Italians, on de Gaulle, were not to be taken too seriously, and he had an unusual sympathy which won him, unasked, the casual friendship of the young. But he was uncompromising and direct, still trouncing doctors and surgeons ruthlessly during his last illness. He died a lonely and a proud figure, making no concessions, and expecting none.

June 25, 1964.

General Georges Philias Vanier, P.C., D.S.O., M.C., who died on March 5, 1967, in Ottawa at the age of 78, filled a greater variety of posts, civilian and military, culminating in the Governor-Generalship of his native land, than any Canadian of his time.

Vanier was born on St. George's Day, April 23, 1888, in Montreal. The family had settled in Canada in the days of the "new France" of Cartier and de Champlain; and he was educated at the Loyola College in Montreal and Laval University, Quebec. He was called to the Quebec Bar in 1911 but on the outbreak of war in 1914 immediately helped to recruit and organize the famous Canadian unit known as the Van Doos, with which he went to France, where he rapidly rose to the rank of Colonel, was awarded the D.S.O., M.C. and bar, and the Legion of Honour. He was wounded in both legs, one of which had to be amputated. Returning to Canada he was chosen as A.D.C. first by Lord Byng and then by Lord Willingdon when they were Governors-General of Canada in the 1920s.

In 1928, still a soldier, he was sent to Geneva, where he was to spend several of the inter-war years. He served first as representative of his country on the Advisory Commission of the League of Nations for military, naval and air questions; and was seconded from the Army in 1928 to be technical adviser in the Canadian Advisory Office on all matters concerned with disarmament. Four years later he was transferred to London with the rank of Secretary and Counsellor in the Canadian High Commissioner's Office, serving there from 1935 under Vincent Massey, whom he was later to succeed as Governor-General of Canada. In all these posts he was valued for his sound and unprejudiced advice; it was not his nature to be an improviser or to insist unduly upon his own point of view.

Then in 1938 he became a diplomatist—he was appointed Canadian Minister to France. Two years later, when the country was overrun by the Germans, he escaped, in company with the British Ambassador, Sir Ronald Campbell, and the South African Minister to France, in a fishing boat. They had been told that a British cruiser was searching for them, which, however, they failed to contact. After many hours of being tossed about they picked up a message that another ship was being sent, which duly found them and which, much to the delight of Vanier, turned out to be a Canadian destroyer.

FRIEND OF DE GAULLE

Back in Canada he was appointed a member of the joint Canadian-U.S.A. Board of Defence and joint chairman of the Civilian Recruiting Committee and at the same time he was O.C. the Quebec military district. In 1943 he was, typically, both given the rank of general and sent on his first purely diplomatic mission, that of Minister to the Allied Governments which had taken refuge in London, and to de Gaulle's "Committee of National Liberation". He became a personal friend of the French leader, and when de Gaulle moved his headquarters to Algiers Vanier was sent there as representative of Canada; and in the same year, 1944, when de Gaulle reached Paris, he was formally appointed Canadian Ambassador to France. No post could have been more congenial to Vanier, and he and Madame Vanier, as soon as circumstances permitted, made the Canadian Embassy in the Avenue Foch a centre of Parisian society life. How deeply he won the appreciation and affection of the French was shown by the title of *Citoyen d'Honneur* conferred upon him by three separate towns, Lille, Dijon, and Dieppe.

He always considered himself first and foremost a soldier; and it was in his military uniform that he was sworn in as Governor-General (September 15, 1959). It was also typical of him that he began his short speech on that occasion by saying "My first words are a prayer"—that God might bless his work in Canada. He became very much in demand as a speaker, and this ardent Roman Catholic showed a remarkable capacity for uttering serious truths in unassuming language. He spoke with equal facility in English and French, often using both languages in the same speech.

As Queen's representative in Canada for his last seven years Vanier, despite his physical infirmities, travelled extensively in Canada from the shores of Newfoundland to the Pacific coast and in the remote regions of the Arctic. This he did because he was deeply conscious of the need for unity in Canada. Indeed, in his centenary message early in 1967 he made a plea for unity. In nearly all his speeches there were references to this theme coupled with the need for understanding between the English and the French Canadians, the two founding races of the nation.

Few incumbents of Rideau Hall have looked the part as much as Vanier with his tall, erect, military figure, his white moustache, the limp and his array of medals on ceremonial occasions.

MODERN OUTLOOK

But he was not a figure from a Gilbert and Sullivan opera, even if in these days some in Canada speak of the office of the Queen's representative as a kind of anachronism. He was modern in outlook, particularly in his views on the youth of the country and about such questions as where Canada was going and what she wanted to do. He always emphasized the necessity for strengthening the family life and was instrumental in sponsoring a conference on this subject. He believed strongly in the Christian disciplines which he thought were in some cases best brought out in the comradeship of service life. He was a great favourite with children and his annual Christmas gatherings at Rideau Hall for the under-privileged youth of the capital were a delight to all who attended them.

Despite his frail appearance, towards the end of his life, he could exercise his right to advise the Prime Minister of the day and, on occasions, did so. Indeed he was very sensitive to all that was going on in Canada in the difficult sixties and did much to try to keep the nation together. It is probably true to say that there was never a more respected governor-general than Vanier, who, free fom any political partisanship, was in the eyes of his people a great Canadian. He wrote two short books, *Un Canadien parle aux Français* and *Paroles de Guerre*.

The Vaniers had four sons and a daughter. Their eldest son is a Trappist monk and their daughter became paediatrician in London's leading hospital for children.

March 6, 1967.

Georges Vantongerloo, the Belgian artist, who died in Paris on October 8, 1965, at the age of 78, was not so much a painter or sculptor in the traditional and professional sense as one who gave visual form to philosophic and scientific ideas.

He could accurately be termed a philosopher, for he dealt, through the medium of paint and plastic constructions, with general causes and principles, with him an urge to "understand space" gradually extended to a study of the universe and a conception of infinity. A believer in progress, in art as in science, he held that art in the age of the atom must necessarily be different from that of the "era of the paraffin lamp" (as he described the time when he was born). His own work was certainly a new and remarkable departure though not only in comparison with nineteenth century work but even when compared with that of such contemporaries as Klee, Kandinsky or Mondrian.

Georges Vantongerloo was born in Antwerp on November 24, 1886. He studied art in Antwerp and Brussels and for some years contributed to the triennial Salons of Brussels paintings on fairly conventional impressionist lines. He arrived at a turning-point of development about the year 1914 when, painting the "Head of a Child", he has recorded he suddenly became aware that the subject was quite irrelevant to his wish to "express space".

At The Hague in the following two years, the figures he painted became secondary in importance to the system of brush strokes which indicated their presence; and the trend towards abstraction was completed in the course of his relation with the promoters of the "de Stijl" movement in Holland in 1917. The general aim of that movement, it may be recalled, was to find a common denominator for all the arts of design which would reunite them and allow of their consistent application to utilitarian as well as to purely aesthetic ends. Both were reflected for a number of years in his productions. He used the basic rectangular formula which Piet Mondrian had adapted from Cubism, an example of the infectiousness of style rather than of personal cooperation, for it seems to have been a long time before they actually met; yet paintings of Vantongerloo's "de Stijl" period are not dissimilar in their geometric "stained-glass" effect from those produced by Mondrian and Theo van Doesburg.

SPECULATIVE DESIGNS

Settling in France in 1927, he produced between 1928 and 1931 designs for practical undertakings, including airports which have a look prophetic of the present day, but seemed to have abandoned them as a hindrance to purely speculative thought and likewise to have rebelled against the confines of geometry as a systematic means of producing works of art. Even as early as 1917 a series of "Reflections", in the aphoristic manner of early twentieth-century artists, published in the "de Stijl" magazine looked far beyond the combination of horizontals and verticals in quasi-architectural form, into questions of volume and void and the vibrations "from which spring life and perpetual motion". The "Construction in a Sphere" produced in 1917 during his stay at The Hague strikingly demonstrated his conception of the infinities of void and volume contained within a simple form.

One gets the impression that in his later phase Vantongerloo came to canvas and paint with reluctance as if to a medium which might lead a puritanical philosopher from his strait path into pitfalls and temptations. He retired, during the war which began in 1939 and after it, into an eremitic seclusion, in which his most characteristic expression was attained. The "Radiation" of 1954, ascetic in suggestion, shows how different his course had been from that of Mondrian and makes a pronounced contrast with so gay and graphic a piece of painting as the latter's "Broadway Boogie-Woogie".

His studio was a kind of laboratory for the production of objects in plexiglass and wire which resulted from his contemplation of "light, radiation and outer space", and it is characteristic of his thought that he considered the aurora borealis—"the result of the action of electrons in a magnetic field"—the essence of natural beauty. The scientifically titled plastic conceptions of his later years are his best works, strange gems of design evolving from solitary cogitation in which he declared himself to have nothing in common with any school or "ism" of modern art.

Though from 1922 onwards his paintings and constructions figured in numerous exhibitions in Europe and the United States he was isolated enough in his later years to be referred to on the occasion of the retrospective exhibition, held in London at the New London Gallery in 1962, as a "great unknown". It would scarcely be appropriate to describe him as a great painter or sculptor, so much did he dissociate himself from the making of works of art, but in the visible expression of experimental thought he was unique.

October 14, 1965.

Edgar Varèse died in a New York hospital on November 6, 1965, at the age of 79.

So an important chapter in the history of twentieth-century music, perhaps even more momentous than can yet be appreciated, has ended. In his youth he was a pupil of Vincent D'Ingy and a protégé of Richard Strauss; but his own musical world was not one that they, or even his contemporaries, could recognize. Varèse explored it dauntlessly and scientifically, undismayed by hostility or incomprehension. He remained a leader of the musical vanguard all his life, and only towards the end of it received some of the honour (instead of notoriety) that his energies merited.

Edgar Varèse was born in Paris on December 22, 1885, of a French father and Italian mother. He composed an opera when he was 12, but his parents did not wish him to be a musician and, after studying mathematics and science, it was in defiance that he entered the Schola Cantorum where his teachers were D'Ingy and Roussel; he also studied with Widor. He destroyed his early compositions, so that his name was initially made as choir-trainer, conductor and concert promoter. He spent some time in Berlin, where he met Strauss, Busoni and Hofmannsthal, who wrote the libretto for Varese's *Oedipus und die Sphinx*. Varèse's war service was terminated by ill-health, and in 1915 he emigrated to the United States of which he subsequently became a citizen.

As a composer Varèse, at any rate from this period onwards, pursued a pugnacious and unpopular path of abandoning the most familiar elements of musical composition, consonant harmony, thematic development, lyrical melody. In his *Oftrandes* (1922) the soprano voice and stringed instruments provide a recognizable link with traditional music, but *Hyperprism* (1923) for wind and percussion perplexed early audiences by its ruthless dynamism and rebarbative textures.

MUSIC FOR SIRENS

Leopold Stokowski was one of Varèse's persistent champions in America, from the premiere of *Ameriques* (1926) onwards. *Ionization* (1931) further pursued virgin territory with an instrumentation for 41 percussion instruments and two sirens. Sometimes Varèse seemed to be no more than reviving the rhythmic primitivism of Stravinsky's *Rite of Spring*, though *Octandre* (1924) and *Density 21.5* for solo flute (1935) showed individually along more easily intelligible lines.

In his later years Varese composed much for electronic instruments. His *Deserts* (1954) for wind, percussion and tape is a particularly impressive example of his challenging work in this field, and his *Poème Electronique*, relayed over 400 loudspeakers at the Brussels Exhibition in 1958, and subsequently recorded on disc, has vivid imaginative impact. Varèse's ear for sonority and richly original mind can be recognized even if, as yet, his place in musical history cannot confidently be determined.

November 8, 1965.

Sophocles Venizelos, the Greek Liberal leader and former Prime Minister, who died suddenly on February 6, 1964, at the age of 70, was a leading member of the Centre Union Party, and until recently served as deputy Prime Minister and Foreign Minister in the Papandreou Government. His handling of the initial phases of the Cyprus crisis was masterful and constructive. It was he who, in an attempt to avert clashes between the Greek and Turkish army contingents in Cyprus, proposed that both forces should be placed under the orders of a British military commander. His proposal did much to save the situation which could escalate into a full-fledged conflict between Greece and Turkey.

LIBERAL HERITAGE

The son of the late Eleftherios Venizelos, he inherited the Liberal Party, founded by his father in 1949 when the then leader, Themistocles Sophoulis, died. But his approach to domestic politics had at times been desultory. In 1946 he quit the Liberal Party, of which he was deputy leader, and founded the party of Venizelosist Liberals, only to return to the Liberal Party as deputy leader in 1947 and then as leader in 1949. In 1953 he announced his decision to retire from politics and handed over his party to Papandreou. He changed his mind two years later and as Papandreou refused to return this political loan he split the Liberals and formed the Liberal Democratic Union by withdrawing 25 loyal deputies from Papandreou's share of the party.

In 1957 he agreed to a re-merger of this group and Papandreou's, the two of them acting as co-leaders. In 1959 he encouraged General Grivas's political ambitions by integrating the Liberals in the General's National Regeneration Movement, but when Grivas decided that the people did not really want him, Venizelos promptly negotiated a coalition with Markezinis, the Progressive leader, only to arrange with Papandreou shortly afterwards (1961) the creation of the Centre Union.

He was born in Crete in 1894 and joined the Greek officer cadet school in 1911. Until 1920 he took part in the Balkan wars, and was later in the First World War, and in the abortive Asia Minor campaign. He resigned his commission as an artillery major to enter politics and was elected in 1920 deputy for Chanea, his birthplace. After his father's electoral defeat he joined him in his voluntary exile and did not take up his seat in the Assembly. The 1922 Revolutionary Committee recalled him to active service and posted him as military attaché in Paris, a post he held until 1930, when he retired with the rank of colonel.

He re-entered politics in 1936 after his father's death, becoming one of a triumvirate which regulated party affairs in the absence of a leader. The Metaxas dictatorship followed and as all political activities were suspended he left for Paris and later lived in New York. As Navy Minister in the Tsouderos Cabinet in exile in May, 1943, he saw the outbreak of the communist revolt in the Greek warships in Alexandria and became Prime Minister in order to suppress it.

He was again Prime Minister twice in 1950 and conducted the elections in 1951. He held a number of ministerial posts between 1944 and 1952. As Minister of Foreign Affairs he aided the restoration of Greek-Yugoslav and Greek-Italian relations and it was he who negotiated Greece's membership of Nato. He was a gifted statesman although his attitude towards domestic politics suggested adherence to the principle of "no holds barred".

He is survived by his widow and one married daughter.

February 8, 1964.

General Sir Walter Venning, G.C.B., C.M.G., C.B.E., M.C., who died on June 19, 1964, at the age of 82, was Quartermaster General to the Forces from 1939 to 1942 and Director General of the British Supply Mission in Washington from 1942 to 1945.

He was an Army administrator on the grand scale. It was due to the superb organization which he created and directed that the mobilization of the Regular Army in 1939, the embodiment of the Territorial Army and the embarkation of the expeditionary force were carried out with such astonishing smoothness. During the first three years of the war while he was still the Quartermaster General he was responsible for the tremendous expansion of the Q side of the Army in meeting the requirements of the forces across the world. A month after his retirement in 1942 on reaching the age limit of 60 he was recalled and appointed to Washington where he rendered invaluable service as head of the British Supply Mission.

Venning was given his first appointment on the administrative side of the staff on the Western Front in 1915, and he displayed such remarkable ability that for the rest of his service he was given an almost unbroken succession of staff appointments. He acquired a unique knowledge of Army administration in all its aspects. His calm, efficiency and resource in emergency were remarkable and he endeared himself to his subordinates and to all with whom he worked by his modesty and sympathetic understanding. Their confidence in him was complete for they recognized him as being in the front rank of administrators.

AT YPRES

Walter King Venning was born on January 17, 1882, the son of Edward Venning, Ceylon Civil Service. He went to Clifton College and from Sandhurst was gazetted to a commission in the Duke of Cornwall's Light Infantry in May, 1901. He served with the West African Field Force for three years from 1907. In 1912 he became adjutant of a Territorial battalion, the 12th County of London (Rangers). Here he did excellent work as was proved when the Rangers took the field in the war. He accompanied the battalion to France at the end of 1914 but after some months in and out of the line at Ypres he was selected for an appointment at G.H.Q.

From May, 1915, until March, 1916, he worked at G.H.Q. in France as Deputy Assistant Adjutant General. He then followed home his old chief, Sir Nevil Macready, who had become Adjutant General at the War Office, and was appointed A.A.G. in the Directorate of Personal Services, a post which he held until 1919. He was created C.M.G. in 1918 and was mentioned three times in dispatches. While serving with the Rangers he had won the Military Cross.

During his last few weeks at the War Office he acted as Deputy Director of Personal Services and then, at the beginning of March when preparations were being made for reopening the staff college, he was selected to instruct in administrative staff duties. He left Camberley in 1922 to resume his former work at the War Office where he stayed for the next five years.

In 1927 he went to Aldershot as A.A. and Q.M.G. of the First Division, and was appointed D.A. and Q.M.G. at the headquarters of the Eastern Command in India in July, 1929. From 1931 to 1934 he commanded the 2nd (Rawalpindi) Infantry Brigade, and then returned to the War Office as Director of Movement and Quartering.

In 1939 he was appointed Quartermaster General to the Forces. The wartime story of his department was one of rapid development and constant planning ahead. He began planning for the equipment of the Second Front as soon as the battered Army returned from Dunkirk.

It was his policy to get businessmen into his staff and he constantly paid tribute to the way in which they aided him. He established the happiest relations with the commercial firms engaged in the provision of equipment and of staff for wartime depots and workshops at home and overseas. One of his greatest problems was the provision of accommodation not only for the rapidly expanding forces but for stores and ammunition. By 1942 hundreds of square miles of covered and outside storage accommodation had been created. In the provision of equipment perhaps the most picturesque example was the baling, packing and dispatch to Russia of enough greatcoat cloth to stretch from the White Sea to the Black Sea. He introduced a catering system under which over 100,000 soldiers and women of the A.T.S. were employed and which reduced wastage of food to an infinitesimal quantity.

Venning went to Washington as a civilian and there he succeeded Edward P. Taylor. In his new post his profound knowledge of Army stores and requirements was invaluable, and his work with his American colleagues was a considerable factor in the successful organization of the flow of supplies required for the campaign in western Europe.

He was Colonel of the D.C.L.I. from 1935 to 1947 and Colonel Commandant R.E.M.E. from 1942 to 1950. He was A.D.C. General to the King from 1941 to 1942. He was created G.C.B. in 1942.

He married Marcia, daughter of Surgeon General J. C. Dorman, of Kinsale, co. Cork, in 1912 and they had two sons. She died in 1946 and he married secondly in 1954 Vera, daughter of A. E. Thomas-Haime and widow of Roland Weightman.

June 22, 1964.

Dr. Hendrik Verwoerd, the South African Prime Minister, who was assassinated on September 6, 1966, at the age of 64, was a quiet, almost gentle purveyor of extreme policies. Not all South Africans would classify him as an extremist. In his electoral triumph in the March before his death he had to rebuff assaults from the right as well as the left. But in his eight years as Prime Minister he led South Africa farther down the path of a police state, he intensified the policies of apartheid, he allowed his country to become even more diplomatically isolated in the world.

Verwoerd stood for policies with which most people in the outside world found themselves in total disagreement. But he advocated them with sincerity and with the quiet avuncular air of a family lawyer.

His handling of the Rhodesian crisis was a particular case in point. There is no reason to doubt that he shared the sympathy of most white South Africans for the Smith regime. But he also recognized that too open support could endanger relations with Britain and draw the fire of the rest of the world on to South Africa.

This was not the first assassination attempt on his life. In April, 1960, shortly after the Sharpeville shootings, he was shot in the face at close range after opening an international trade fair. In spite of serious injury he made a swift recovery, and by the time of his death he was in full political control of white South African opinion.

BORN IN HOLLAND

He was the first of the six Prime Ministers (including himself) since the Union not to have been born in the country and not to have any links with the emotional past such as made his predecessors the men they were. He had no memories, as Botha and Smuts had, of a resistance against imperialism that had mellowed into working on terms of friendly equality with the British; nor was there anything in his family background to make him react in the opposite way to Botha and Smuts, as Hertzog had done. He had no reason to expect that Afrikaans-speaking South Africans would accept him as their leader as they had Malan and Strydom. Yet he lived to rule over them with dictatorial disregard for anyone's opinion except his own.

He was born in Holland on September 8, 1901, and, although the founding fathers of White South Africa came from the Low Countries and thereabouts, a Dutchman was unusual in 1903. That was the year in which his parents took him to the Cape. His early years marked him as a scholarly, and, indeed, as a pedantic type of lad. He did well at his books and is remembered by his contemporaries as having shown a detached indifference to games. His father was a missionary of the Dutch Reformed Church who moved on into Southern Rhodesia. The story has often been told of Verwoerd, as a schoolboy in Bulawayo, being offered a scholarship and saying that he wanted to return to the Union.

His headmaster asked him why he wanted to have anything to do with that "nest of rebels." This may have helped him to decide against going to Oxford and in favour of a round of European universities—Hamburg, Leipzig, and Berlin—in the tradition of Afrikaner intellectuals. After taking several degrees he went back to his adopted home and was made Professor of Applied Psychology (a novel chair) at his old university, Stellenbosch. It was at this point of his career that he first became a public figure. He protested, with some of his fellow professors who went on deputation to the Government, when it was being proposed to allow Jews from Hitler's Germany to find asylum in South Africa. From this it was a natural transition to enter politics on the narrow Nationalist side and to become a member of the Broederbond, the society which is, to any Nationalist Cabinet in South Africa, what the submerged bulk of an iceberg is to the visible tip.

SYMPATHY FOR HITLER

Again following the tradition of Afrikaner intellectuals, in 1937 he turned political journalist, becoming editor in chief of *Die Transvaaler*. There he made himself a famous, and indeed a notorious, figure. Like Dr. Malan and so many other Nationalists, he hoped that Hitler would win the war and (in spite of having seen something of Europe) was convinced that Britain would collapse. His paper was blatantly anti-British and he did not scruple to falsify the news.

The Johannesburg *Star* pointed this out in print and Verwoerd sued his rival for libel. He lost, being told by Mr. Justice Millin (the husband of Sarah Gertrude Millin) that he had no grounds for objecting because "he had allowed his paper to be made a tool of the Nazis in South Africa and he knew it." Resilient as ever, Verwoerd again came into the public eye during the royal visit of 1947, when his paper studiously limited itself to reporting that some traffic congestion had been caused by the presence of some visitors from oversea.

Such proofs of his loyalty to extreme Afrikanerdom did not help him at the general election of 1948, even though Smuts went down and the still-continuing reign of the Nationalists began. His defeat at the poll was compensated for by a seat in the Senate. That was the foundation of his political fortunes. Upon that he built up the position which ended in dictatorship. Dr. Malan had won the 1948 election on the slogan of *apartheid*. But neither he, nor anyone else in the party, had thought it out, or regarded it as anything more than a promising way of putting the "Ou Baas," Smuts, on his back. Verwoerd proceeded to do the thinking.

THEORY OF APARTHEID

He worked out the theory of *apartheid* so thoroughly that he astonished and delighted the *plaateland* upon which votes in the South African Parliament depend. He told the voters that the Bantu could be denied a say in politics, or a right to hold property outside the reserves, and that this could be done without in any way suggesting that the black man was inferior to the white. God, for all man knew, had made men of different colours equal in their potentialities of development. But they must develop separately. Hence the doctrine of Bantustan, which Verwoerd—and this was his strength—sincerely believed in.

It was an obvious and enormous improvement on the traditional Boer theory that the Old Testament provides divine justification for keeping the sons of Ham in their place. Verwoerd went politically from strength to strength. By the time that Malan gave way to Strydom he was the most powerful man in the most key position in the party. Had Havenga beaten Strydom, Verwoerd might have suffered a reverse. But, as things turned out, he was so strong after Strydom had died in 1958 that he jumped over Mr. Swart (now State President) and Dr. Dönges—doing so because the party caucus had fallen under his spell and in spite of the frightened apprehension of a majority in the Cabinet.

Having taken office, he proceeded to clear the way for a republic outside the Commonwealth, making no real pretence of regarding a republic within the Commonwealth as more than a halfway house. That was easy enough for all South Africans to understand because it represents the point of view of the average Afrikaner.

What was harder to disentangle was the opportunist from the ideological side of Verwoerd's native policy. He had performed the remarkable feat of persuading voters in his own camp that, sooner or later, they would have to spend more money on making a reality of Bantustan. Until he brought off this quite genuinely believed-in piece of advocacy, the voters had thought that money spent on the "kaffirs" was money wasted.

He had spent very large sums of public money but nothing remotely on the scale that was needed to carry out his theories. That these theories were advanced because he believed in them as a matter of principle is generally accepted in South Africa.

REASSURING FIGURE

It would be untrue to say that his adopted countrymen, even in his own party, liked him. He was not one of them, to be quarrelled with at times, but to be understood and held in affection, as were Strydom and Malan, and, above all, as Hertzog was and (even though with reservations on the backveld) as Smuts and Botha were.

Verwoerd was aloof,' and yet somehow his appearance made people feel that he was more warm than that: the unassuming, amiable look on that healthy face, the high complexion and the white hair seemed at first sight reassuring. The tall figure—he was well over six feet—and the blue eyes (even if they were rather small and rather strained, if you looked into them hard) did not suggest a fanatic.

Or did they? It is remarkable that men of fiercely different opinions in South African politics all agreed that they were consumed with curiosity by that question mark. If there is a Boswell or, perhaps, an Afrikaner Clarendon (as there may be) history will learn more than is now publicly known of Verwoerd.

In private life he was a domestic family man. He married in 1927 Elizabeth, daughter of W. J. Schoombee, and they had seven children.

September 7, 1966.

Admiral of the Fleet Sir Philip Vian, G.C.B., K.B.E., D.S.O., who died on May 27, 1968, at the age of 73, had perhaps the most distinguished record of service at sea of any British naval officer during the Second World War.

His name was virtually unknown outside the Navy until, on February 17, 1940, the destroyer Cossack, which he commanded, ran alongside and boarded the German raider supply ship Altmark in a Norwegian fjord and rescued the 299 British Merchant Navy men who had been captured by the pocket battleship Graf Spee and were being taken back to Germany through Norwegian territorial waters.

The cry of the Cossack's boarding party to the prisoners confined in the Altmark's holds, "The Navy is here", rang throughout the free world at a depressing period. This feat gained for Vian the first of his three D.S.O.s. He continued in command of the 4th Destroyer Flotilla, composed of the famous Tribal Class ships, during the very arduous Norwegian campaign of April-May, 1940, and took part in the landings in southern Norway and in the subsequent evacuation of the troops sent on what Churchill called that "ramshackle operation". Then in May, 1941 Vian, still in the same command, figured in the final phase of the pursuit of the Bismarck. His flotilla shadowed the giant battleship, and attacked her with torpedoes during the night before she was sunk, thereby helping to deliver her into the hands of Admiral Tovey's battleships.

Having been specially promoted Rear-Admiral in July, 1941, Vian hoisted his flag in the cruiser Nigeria, and was ordered to take a squadron to the Arctic to evacuate the Norwegian settlement on Spitsbergen and investigate German activity on Jan Mayen Island.

RAMMED AND SUNK

On his return journey he became involved in a mêlee in a Norwegian fjord, and rammed and sank the German warship Bremse. In October of the same year he hoisted his flag in the new light cruiser Naiad, and took command of the 15th Cruiser Squadron to the Mediterranean Fleet under Sir Andrew Cunningham. In this appointment Vian added greatly to his growing fame. The Mediterranean Fleet was at the time faced with grave difficulties in supporting the Army in the western desert and supplying Malta, in face of the much superior Italian navy and the powerful Axis air forces stationed in Crete and Sicily.

Vian was repeatedly placed in charge of the hazardous convoy operations undertaken to relieve Malta from the east. It was, however, while he was searching for an enemy convoy bound for north Africa that in March, 1942, his flagship was sunk by a U-boat. Vian was picked up, and nine days later left Alexandria with his flag in the Cleopatra to escort another convoy to Malta.

This led to the Second Battle of Sirte, when by very skilful tactics Vian held off a far stronger Italian force which endeavoured to bar the convoy's progress. For this action Vian was made K.B.E. In the following June he led another, but unsuccessful, attempt to relieve Malta, shortly after which he returned to England.

Vian's next appointment was to command the assault force which was assembling in England to take part in the invasion of Sicily in July, 1943. His success in the new field of amphibious warfare led naturally to participation in the landings on the Italian mainland at Salerno in the following September. For that undertaking he commanded a number of escort carriers, whose function it was to supply fighter cover until the Allied Air Forces were established on shore. Vian was next selected to command the Eastern (British) Task Force in the Normandy invasion, and returned home to take part in the planning of that great undertaking. For his services on that occasion he was made K.C.B.

After the successful return of the Allied armies to Europe the Admiralty turned their attention to building up the Eastern Fleet to join the Americans in the final phase of the Pacific War. In November, 1944, Vian took command of the carrier task force which was to be the carrier task force which was to be the spearhead of the British Pacific Fleet, with his flag in the Indomitable. On the way to Australia early in 1945 he carried out the successful air attacks on the oil refineries at Palembang in Sumatra, and in April of that year his squadron of four fleet carriers took part in the assault on Okinawa.

After joining in final air attacks on the Japanese mainland Vian's force was dispersed, and he himself, now a Vice-Admiral, returned home in the Implacable. In September 1946, after no less than 14 years of continuous service in command at sea, he joined the Board of Admiralty as Fifth Sea Lord. His final service, from 1950 to 1952, was as Commander in-Chief, Home Fleet.

Philip Louis Vian was born on June 15, 1894, the son of Alsager Vian, and joined the Royal Navy as a cadet in May, 1907.

Vian was without doubt an exacting officer to serve. He never spared himself, and he expected his subordinates never to fall below his own very high standard. Towards failure, especially in time of war, he could act harshly, and that occasionally led him to be somewhat less than fair to subordinates. But of his leadership in times of stress and danger, and especially in battle, there can be no two opinions. To him is due a large share of the credit for bringing the Mediterranean Fleet through its great ordeal of 1941-42.

Vian published in 1960 a volume of memoirs entitled *Action This Day,* but his natural modesty evidently prevented him giving an uninhibited account of his war service. After retirement he became a director of the Midland Bank and of the North British and Mercantile Insurance Company.

He married in 1929 Marjorie, daughter of Colonel D. P. Haig, O.B.E., of Highfields Park, Withyham, Sussex. They had two daughters.

May 29, 1968.

Queen Victoria Eugenie of Spain—See under **Spain.**

Lieutenant-Colonel Valentine Vivian, C.M.G., C.B.E., former member of the Indian Police force who became Vice-Chief of the Secret Intelligence Service, died on April 15, 1969. He was responsible for counter-espionage during the Second World War and he was Director of Security for the S.I.S.

It was Vivian who, while honourably attempting to introduce new blood into the service, selected Kim Philby—whose father St. John had been one of Vivian's friends in India. Ironcially, Vivian's star "intellectual" in the Intelligence Service was later to become notorious as "The Third Man" who defected to the Russians and did considerable harm to the system he had infiltrated.

Vivian, lean and elegant, with crinkled hair and a monocle, who had been largely responsible for the influx of dons, journalists and writers at the beginning of the war, was later to come under criticism for not having brought to light Philby's past Communist associations.

Vivian, known as "Vee-Vee" to the staff, was an amiable man. He embodied one of the most solidly-established traditions of British intelligence-work at the time, in that he came from the Indian police. Son of Comley Vivian, the portrait painter, Valentine Patrick Terrel, Vivian was born on March 17, 1886, and joined the Indian Police in 1906—retiring in 1925. He was attached to the Foreign Office from 1923 to 1951. In the First World War he served in Palestine and Turkey and was mentioned in dispatches. He received the O.B.E. in 1918; the C.B.E. in 1923; and the C.M.G. in 1947.

Vivian became head of Section V—the counter-espionage section of S.I.S.—before the war; Philby was later to take over command of the Iberian sub-section—but by that time Vivian was Vice-Chief of the Secret Service. Vivian's faith was that Philby could rescue Section V by bridging the gap between the "Indians" and the intellectuals. It was a faith which was brilliantly justified and no doubt accounted for Vivian's subsequent powerful patronage of Philby within the Service.

April 16, 1969.

---

von . . .—See under various substantive surnames.

Marshal Klimenti Yefrimovitch Voroshilov, a former President of the Soviet Union, who died on December 3, 1969, at the age of 88, was at one time credited with the creation of the Red Army between the two world wars.

Later research into Russian documents and revelations by those close to events have suggested that, successful as he may have been in the revolutionary wars, he was no longsighted military thinker, no friend to innovation, and that when in power he actually opposed the mechanization of Soviet forces. Nonetheless, Voroshilov—the first Marshal of the Soviet Union—seems to have retained for a long time what may be called popular appeal; he was seen as the patriot soldier of humble birth whose knapsack had indeed contained a baton.

"Klim" Voroshilov was one of the oldest Bolsheviks—a worker turned soldier. Most of his early years were spent in South Russia engaged in underground political activity in preparation for the Russian Revolution, in which, as a revolutionary soldier and guerrilla leader, he played a conspicuous part. His name was especially associated with the defence of Tsaritsyn (later Stalingrad, now Volgograd). It was at this time that he rose to fame as a military leader.

In 1961 he was accused at a party congress of complicity in some of Stalin's purges and confessed his sins but a year later he was reelected to the Praesidium of the Supreme Soviet. Vital and hearty, he was a first class horseman to whom William Bullitt when United States Ambassador in the 1930s had introduced the pleasures of polo.

Klimenti Yefrimovitch Voroshilov was born on February 4, 1881, in the village of Verkhne,

Dnepropetrovsk. At the age of seven he worked underground in the mines of the Don basin and later took to tending the flocks of a local landowner. He entered a school for the first time at the age of 13 and two years later, having learnt to read and write, he went to work in an English-owned locomotive factory in Lugansk, where he became a crane operator in the iron foundry. At the age of 18 he organized and led the first strike ever known in the district, after which he was dismissed, his passport labelled "Unreliable".

REVOLT AND PRISON

Between 1900 and 1903 he wandered round the Ukraine engaged in underground political activity under the assumed name of Plakhov; but unlike Lenin and Stalin, this alias never remained with him. He was able to return in 1903 to Lugansk, where he worked as an electrical fitter, becoming chairman of the Lugansk group of the Social Democratic Party. As chairman of the Lugansk workers' committee, he led them in revolt in 1905, for which he was imprisoned for several months. In the following year he was sent by the Lugansk workers as a delegate to the fourth congress of the Social Democratic Party in Stockholm, where he met Lenin and Stalin for the first time and became their staunch supporter against the Mensheviks. In the following year he was sent to London as a delegate of the fifth congress and, on his return, was arrested and sentenced to three years' exile in Archangel.

He managed to escape from the north and proceeded to Baku to work under the direction of Stalin, and from then on until war broke out in 1914 his story is one of continual arrests and exiles. During the 1914 War he avoided military service and worked instead in munition factories in Tsaritsyn and Petrograd in order to disseminate Bolshevik propaganda among the workers. In 1917 he turned up again in Lugansk as editor of the newspaper Donets Proletariat, busy organizing the industrial workers for the coming revolution. He began his military career in Petrograd after the October Revolution as chairman of the committee for the defence of the city, and early in the following year he returned to Lugansk to organize guerrilla warfare. After failures with his guerrillas against the Germans at Kharkov, he fell back on Lugansk and began his long retreat with 15,000 soldiers and 30,000 refugees across the Donets, Don, and Volga to Tsaritsyn—a distance of some 650 miles. On his arrival at besieged Tsaritsyn he was appointed Commander-in-Chief of the defences and Commander of the Tenth Army. As the pressure of the counter revolutionaries increased, Stalin arrived from Moscow to take over the work of Political Commissar, leaving Voroshilov to concentrate on the military defence.

In 1918 a violent antagonism flared up between Minister of War Trotsky, on the one hand, and Stalin and Voroshilov on the other. Stalin was eventually recalled and Trotsky arrived in Tsaritsyn to inform Voroshilov that unless he obeyed his orders he would have him shot, whereupon Voroshilov gave up the command and was transferred to the Ukraine. In 1919, as People's Commissar for the Military Region of Kharkov and Commander of the Fourteenth Army, he was sent together with Stalin and Budënny to stem the advance of Denikin, who had reached a point some 200 miles south of Moscow. After the capture of Orel and Kursk by Voroshilov the Germans retreated, and shortly after he was appointed Commissar for Home Affairs of the Ukraine Soviet Republic.

He saw service in the Polish-Russian war in 1920 under his military rival, General Tukhachevsky, and soon afterwards he was sent against Wrangel, whom he defeated in the Crimea. In March, 1921, he quelled the Kronstadt rising and in the same year, at the tenth congress of the Communist Party, he was elected for the first time to the executive committee of that body. He also fought in 1921 in the Far East against Manchurian war lords over the question of the Chinese Eastern Railway. In 1922 he held the military command of the North Caucasus and on the death of Lenin in 1924 he was hastily appointed to the vital command of the Moscow area, to replace General Tukhachevsky, a partisan of Trotsky who was moved out of harm's way to Central Asia. On the death of Michael Frunze in 1925 Voroshilov was appointed People's Commissar for Naval and Military Affairs and chairman of the revolutionary committee and shortly afterwards was made a member of the Politburo. His position was now secure; Trotsky, his former superior, was discredited and his old rival Tukhachevsky was relegated to a subordinate position. In 1934 he became People's Commissar for Defence, which post he held until 1940.

After the murder of Kirov, Stalin's close friend, 16 Trotskyites including Kamenev, Zinoviev, and Smirnov were tried and executed in 1936 for conspiring against the lives of Stalin, Voroshilov, and others. Voroshilov's main task between the wars was supposed to be the building up of the Soviet armed forces.

On the eve of the Second World War he headed the Russian delegation that discussed a military pact with the French and British General Staffs.

FORCES UNREADY

In May, 1940, Voroshilov was released from the War Ministry, made a Deputy Premier and appointed chairman of the Committee on Defence. But when the attack came Russia proved poorly prepared.

Stalin took over the chairmanship of the defence committee and sent Voroshilov to the Leningrad front. It was all but overwhelmed. Voroshilov, in eclipse, was sent to organize reserves in the Urals; then to head the Asiatic armies that figured in the brief final clash with Japan in Manchuria.

After the war he was head of the Control Commission in Hungary until 1947. From 1946 onwards he was a member of the Politburo and a Deputy Chairman of the Council of Ministers, and in 1953, on Stalin's death, he became Chairman of the Praesidium of the Supreme Soviet—in effect, President of the U.S.S.R. He paid an official visit to China in 1957 and to India in 1960, the year in which he stepped down as president of the Soviet Union to be replaced by Brezhnev who a year later conferred on him the Order of Lenin.

That was in March. In October at the twenty-second party congress he was named by Khrushchev as a member of the anti-party group which had tried to unseat him in 1957 and it was said that Voroshilov had admitted his errors at the party's central executive meeting which had expelled the group. Some days later—with Voroshilov listening—the chairman of the session read the old Marshal's confession of anti-party sins in which he insisted that he was "deeply dedicated to the Soviet Communist Party and people".

His reelection in the spring of 1962 to the Praesidium came as a surprise and was seen as a sign of opposition to the de-Stalinization campaign. Later that year he published a long article in *Pravda* defending Khrushchev's foreign policy.

In 1968 the old marshal published a volume of his memoirs, entitled *Life Stories*: it described his early life as a worker in the Ukrainian city of Lugansk.

December 4, 1969.

W

Helen Waddell, the author of *The Wandering Scholars*, one of the most delightful works of medieval scholarship written in our time, died on March 5, 1965, at the age of 75.

Among those who have opened our eyes to the dawning romanticism and the humanism of the early Middle Ages Helen Waddell stood out for the grace of her learning, her love of fine literature and her poet's gift of translation. Others have conveyed, in sympathetic commentary and in accomplished English versions, the felicity of the secular Latin lyric of the ninth to the twelfth centuries, but few have interpreted so well its poetic impulse or captured with so haunting an effect the tenderness and passion to which it rises in, for instance, the poets of the *Carmina Burana*.

The daughter of the Rev. Hugh Waddell, of co. Down, a distinguished Orientalist and scholar, who went to the Far East and accepted a chair at the Imperial University of Japan. Helen Waddell was born in Tokyo on May 31, 1889. She received her education at Victoria College and Queen's University, Belfast, was a member of Somerville College, Oxford, from 1920 to 1922, and Cassell Lecturer for St. Hilda's in 1921; held a lectureship at Bedford College, London, during 1922 and 1923; and in the latter year was given her opportunity by the award of a Susette Taylor Fellowship from Lady Margaret Hall, which permitted her to spend the next two years in research in Paris. Out of that research came, in 1927, *The Wandering Scholars*.

It was a pioneering work in many ways. Beginning with the poems of the *Anthologia Latina* and the poets of Charlemagne's Court (though these, it might be said, were scarcely wandering scholars), Miss Waddell disclosed with ardent historical feeling and literary sensibility, with at times a wonderful freshness of romantic perception also, the tradition that came to flower at St. Gall.

Two years later came her anthology of *Medieval Latin Lyrics*. The selection, as an anthologist's should, gave clear evidence of her personal taste and, whatever might be said of the omission of the noblest sacred verse of three centuries or more, might well be thought justified by the sensuous intensity of the happiest of her translations, more particularly of the nature poems, the love lyrics and the drinking songs. One third of the poems in the volume were extracts from the *Carmina Burana*, and among the more familiar names those of Alcuin and Abelard stood out at either extremity of the period. It was to the latter that Helen Waddell returned in a novel, *Peter Abelard*, published in 1933, which evoked with a scholar's love and fidelity the poetry and philosophy of the schools of Paris and the appearances and modes of living of the medieval world.

HERMITS' SAYINGS

Miss Waddell's other work was varied but not extensive. She had produced a small volume of translations from the Chinese in 1913, had written an essay on John of Salisbury, a book of medieval Latin for schools, and an introduction to the Paris and Blecheley Diaries of the Rev. William Cole, and in 1931 had published a wholly charming translation of *Manon Lescaut*. This in turn led to a play, *The Abbé Prévost*, written in 1933 and produced two years later, which now and then followed a course almost parallel to the novel's and had some engaging moments, but which lacked a sufficiently strong sense of drama and the theatre. In 1934 she published a small volume, *Beasts and Saints*, which gracefully recounted from Latin sources a number of pious fairy stories of the mutual charities between flies, mice, frogs, crocodiles, geese on the one hand and various pre-Franciscan saints on the other. The lives and sayings of the eremites of the Egyptian and Syrian deserts in the early centuries of the Church's history provide the theme of *The Desert Fathers* (1936), a volume of translated excerpts from the *Vitae Patrum*, in which she sought to reveal the kernel of ascetic tradition in the west. In 1949 she published *Stories from Holy Writ*, a retelling of Bible stories.

March 6, 1965.

Professor L. R. Wager, F.R.S., Professor of Geology in the University of Oxford since 1950, died suddenly on November 20, 1965, at the age of 61.

Lawrence Rickard Wager was born on February 5, 1904, the son of a schoolmaster in the Yorkshire dales, and was educated at Leeds Grammar School and Pembroke College, Cambridge, where he read for the Natural Sciences Tripos, taking a First Class in Geology in 1926. At Cambridge Wager numbered among his teachers Hutchinson, Marr, and Harker, and it was to Harker that he always felt he owed his real awakening to the science of petrology. Wager became president of the Cambridge Mountaineering Club and, with the reputation of being one of the best young mountaineers and rockclimbers in Britain, was invited to join Gino Watkins's British Arctic air route expedition to eastern Greenland in 1930-31. This experience largely determined the course of much of Wager's subsequent scientific work, and it is for his exhaustive and far-reaching researches in East Greenland, and especially into the now geologically classic Skaergaard layered basic intrusion, first visited during Watkins's expedition, that his name will be chiefly remembered by future generations of petrologists.

In 1929 Wager was appointed as the second member of the staff of the vigorous young geology department at Reading University, under H. L. Hawkins, a post he held until 1943. In 1932 he again visited East Greenland as a member of Ejnar Mikkelsen's expedition, while 1933 saw him away in the Himalayas as a member of Hugh Ruttledge's Everest team, when, with Wyn Harris, Wager reached 28,000ft, in a final attempt to gain the summit. He also managed to carry out a good deal of incidental geological work, including a fine geomorphological study of the evolution of the drainage pattern of that corner of the Himalayan range and foothills.

In 1935-36 he organized his own British East Greenland Expedition to continue work on the Skaergaard and Kangerdlugssuak intrusions. The expedition wintered in Greenland and included his wife, his brother H. G. Wager, and W. A. Deer, the latter of whom was to be his collaborator in the classic Skaergaard researches and in future Greenland ventures.

LEADER IN THE FIELD

Their joint account of the Skaergaard intrusion, judged by many to be the most significant single contribution yet made to the science of igneous petrology, was published in 1939. Those who were his companions on expeditions all remember with gratitude Wager's remarkable powers of leadership in the field under trying conditions. He had the gift, shared by certain rare leaders, of inspiring a kind of blind faith in his ability, due to his deep understanding of the factors controlling the spirit and stamina of his party, to the cautious commonsense which governed all his decisions, and to his insistence upon the detailed organization of any venture in which he was concerned.

As a result of the experience of the interpretation of aerial photographs which he had gained on his Greenland expeditions, Wager entered the photographic reconnaissance section of the Royal Air Force shortly after the outbreak of war, serving spells in the Middle East and in Arctic Russia, and being mentioned in dispatches.

DEVELOPMENTS IN DURHAM

Wager was released from the Air Force in 1944 in order to take the chair of geology at Durham. Starting with three rooms and a three-man staff, he steadly built up his department during the postwar years and was able to continue and enhance its already high reputation. He resumed his research work, consolidating his deep and lasting interest in geochemistry with a detailed study of the behaviour of trace elements in the rocks and minerals of the Skaergaard intrusion. He also began field and laboratory work on the intrusive rocks of central Skye. In 1946 he was elected a Fellow of the Royal Society.

In 1950 Durham lost him to the chair of geology at Oxford and a professorial fellowship at University College. Here he took over a larger department, but ill-equipped for modern research. With characteristic vigour, Wager set about rectifying this. He quickly attracted an enthusiastic research school and in a few years made Oxford one of the leading centres in Britain for the study of petrology and geochemistry. He was quick to see the significance for geology of the postwar development of newer and more refined methods for the radiometric dating of rocks, and set up in Oxford the first laboratory in Britain for this kind of work. Though much involved in administration Wager still found time for his own petrological research, and an important new phase in his detailed work on the Skaergaard intrusion was initiated by a further expedition to east Greenland with W. A. Deer and others in 1953. He also turned more and more towards the bigger and more generalized problems of vulcanicity and of the nature and genesis of the earth's mantle and crust. Wager took a great interest in the publication of geological results, and was largely responsible for initiating *Geochimica et Cosmochimica Acta* in 1950 and the *Journal of Petrology* in 1960.

STIMULATOR OF IDEAS

As a geologist and explorer, Wager's merits were recognized by numerous distinctions. He was full of ideas, though he sometimes found difficulty in expressing them clearly to others. He had an immense range of geological interests. He loved in vacations to spend some time at his farm at Litton in Yorkshire, where he did much of his scientific writing, and would often go out with map, rucksack and hammer to map the local Yoredale rocks. He was deeply interested in the history of science and amassed an enviable library of early works in geology and related sciences.

As a colleague and head of department Wager was wonderful. Completely loyal towards his staff and students, he devoted endless time to helping them with even their smallest personal, academic, and scientific problems. He never took a decision hurriedly but viewed every problem from all angles so as to get the best possible answer. Terribly self-critical and an absolute perfectionist, he was not overlavish with praise, but if one shared his high standards and capacity for sustained work all went well. He was invariably stimulating: 10 minutes' discussion with him could provide enough ideas for several months of work; and he was adept at encouraging ventures into new fields of interest, even if his colleagues sometimes felt that he had a somewhat Churchillian tendency to bite off more than they could easily chew. Between him and his closest friends there developed the strongest ties of affection, and they knew him as the true, generous, and open hearted man he was.

His wife, Phyllis Margaret Worthington, whom he married in 1934, was his constant and unfailing support in all he did, and organized his home in such a manner that the Wagers' hospitality was an experience to be remembered. He had two sons and three daughters.

November 22, 1965.

Wieland Wagner, who died in a Munich hospital on October 16, 1966, was probably the most controversial figure to arise in the world of opera since the Second World War. As director and designer, engaged in the production of familiar and time-hallowed works and passionately involved in an aesthetic which dismissed as irrelevancies the stage practices of the past, his work at first stimulated quite as much acrimony as delight. To those sympathetic to his aims he seemed to achieve triumphs of architectural simplicity; his opponents saw him as an iconoclast at whose touch romantic beauties withered and classic nobilities crumbled in ruin. He was 49.

Wieland Adolf Gottfried Wagner, the son of Siegfried Wagner and grandson of the composer, was born in Bayreuth on January 5, 1917. He was educated at the Bayreuth Gymnasium and the Kunsthochschule in Munich, and began his career as stage designer and director with the Opera at Altenburg. In 1951, with his younger brother Wolfgang, he revived the Bayreuth Festival, reopening his grandfather's Festival Theatre for the first time since the end of the war in 1945.

In the years since then the revolutionary impact of his ideas has continually startled audiences, for, to his mind, any production as much as five years old was necessarily stale and ripe for rethinking, so that year after year devout audiences flocking to Bayreuth were asked to readjust attitudes they had adjusted perhaps only a year before. The violent shock of his staging of *Der Ring des Nibelungen* in the early 1950s had not yet passed into numbed acceptance before his production in 1963, noticeably different in stage pictures and details if not in effect and principles, renewed its effect.

The revolutionary force of Wieland Wagner's production is best seen in his treatment of his grandfather's work. Richard Wagner's scores are carefully marked with stage directions demanding visual effects which are, almost invariably, illustrated in the music; the Gods enter Valhalla over a rainbow bridge; the door of Hunding's hut flies open to flood the enraptured Sieglinde and Siegmund with light after Siegmund has drawn from the roof tree the miraculous sword revealed by a sudden flame from the fire; in Siegmund's hands the sword shatters on Wotan's spear: in Siegfried's it shatters Wotan's spear. The visual effects, magnificently stageworthy in their nineteenth-century romantic way, elucidate the music, but to Wieland Wagner they seemed either dated or irrelevant; if they are actions made explicit in the orchestra, they need not be seen, and if the orchestra does not allude to them, they are pointless.

Therefore his productions worked for and achieved a puritanical, almost naked simplicity in place of the crowded naturalism that Wagner had instituted and that his widow Cosima had held sacrosanct throughout her long reign over the Bayreuth Festival. A tilted ellipse created a stage within the stage; decors often impressively beautiful were, nevertheless, as simple as possible, and lighting, brilliantly handled and powerfully suggestive, supplied all the rest that he wished the audience to be given, for, to Wieland Wagner, the man at the lighting controls was not less important than the conductor in the orchestra pit. Unncessary movement on the stage was avoided and, though a cut in the 1963 production of *Götterdämmerung* disturbed many of his well-wishers, the music was left to work in freedom even though not only *Parsifal* but Wagner's other works and even Beethoven's *Fidelio* took on the look of stage oratorio in which lighting, decor, and grouping created often magnificent pictures.

The principles which governed his work were clear and explicitly stated. "My generation has been, and still is, concerned not to luxuriate in aesthetic conceptions as if these were defined immutably for all time but to seek out the inner laws inherent in a work of genius", he wrote in his "Afterword" to Sir Victor Gollancz's very critical *The "Ring" at Bayreuth:* "what Richard Wagner as a practical man of the theatre laid down as a guide to the production of his operas interests us only in a historical sense". In 1957, in an interview given to *The Times*, he explained that in his view "a style of production applicable to 1957 was not suitable to 1937 and will not do for 1967. All that the producer can do is to make that work of art significant for his audiences at that very moment."

These doctrines he practised not only in Bayreuth but, as the influence of the "Bayreuth revolution" spread, in many of the great German opera houses. A production of *Fidelio* for the Stuttgart Opera was taken in 1955 to Paris, and eventually provided London audiences with their first view of Wieland Wagner's work.

RARE THEATRICAL GENIUS

He worked as guest-director in the Operas of Naples, Munich, Hamburg, Berlin—where he was responsible for an excitingly primitive *Aida* in 1961, and Paris, where, in 1964, his treatment of Strauss's *Salome*, a development of his production in Berlin in 1962, seemed almost to reverse the traditional style of production, finding stillness in the great dance and movement where other directors attempt motionlessness. His death comes (Georg Solti, who regards him as "one of the few theatrical geniuses of our age", expläins) after plans had been made for him to come to Covent Garden for a new production of *Tannhäuser*.

Wieland Wagner's influence, however, travelled to theatres which he himself did not visit. The present Covent Garden production of *The Ring* has designs by Leslie Hurry which accept his simplifications, and Hans Hotter, its director, "has been in constant artistic association with him", Hotter says, "since I sang almost all the leading Wagner roles in my repertory at Bayreuth". Hotter is the world's veteran Wotan, but, he says: "Among the few people who have had any profound influence on the formation and development of my artistic instincts, Wieland Wagner held a prominent place." That influence will, it now seems, work powerfully in the world of opera for many years to come.

In 1941 Wieland Wagner married the choreographer Miss Gertrud Ressinger. He leaves a widow and four children.

October 18, 1966.

Sir Edward Wakefield, BT., C.I.E., who died on January 14, 1969, at the age of 65, was the first British High Commissioner for Malta after the island became independent in 1964. From 1950 to 1962 he was Conservative M.P. for West Derbyshire. Earlier he had a distinguished and varied career in the Indian Civil Service, which he described in *Past Imperative*, published in 1966.

A brother of Lord Wakefield of Kendal he was born on July 24, 1903, the third son of Dr. R.W. Wakefield and educated at Haileybury and Trinity College, Cambridge, where he took a first in the classical Tripos Parts I and II. He entered the Indian Civil Service in 1927, and in 1930 was appointed to the Political Department. He had the experience of being at various times Chief Minister of a Mohammedan State, of a Sikh State and of a Hindu State. He served in the Punjab, Rajputana, Kathiawar, Baluchistan, Central India, Tibet and the Persian Gulf. He was Chief Minister of Kalat State from 1933 to 1936, of Nabha State from 1939 to 1941, and of Rewa State from 1943 to 1945. From 1946 until India achieved political independence in August 1947, he was Joint Secretary to the Political Department in Delhi, where he served under Lord Wavell and Lord Mountbatten.

He refused gratifying and well-deserved offers from the two successive governments to remain with them, but after spending much of his life in the service of the Crown, he did not feel disposed to serve a different master.

He was awarded the bronze medal of the Royal Humane Society for saving life from drowning in 1936. He was made C.I.E. in 1945 and received a baronetcy in 1962.

GOVERNMENT OFFICES

In 1954, Wakefield was appointed an Assistant Whip, and he became a Lord Commissioner of the Treasury in 1956. He was promoted to be Comptroller of H.M. Household in October, 1958, and was Vice-Chamberlain from 1959 to 1960. From 1960 to 1962 he was Treasurer of the Household.

In March, 1962, he was chosen to be the first Commissioner for Malta under the new Constitution and early in September, 1964, became first High Commissioner after the island attained independence.

He married in 1929 Constance Lalage, daughter of Sir John Thompson, K.C.S.I., K.C.I.E. They had two sons and two daughters. Their elder daughter died in the Quetta earthquake of 1935 and the younger daughter in 1962. Their heir is the elder son Edward Humphry Tyrrel Wakefield.

January 16, 1969.

Lieutenant-Colonel H.B.T. Wakelam, who was well known as sporting journalist, author and B.B.C. commentator, died on July 10, 1963, in the Essex County Hospital at Colchester at the age of 70. He gave the first running commentary ever broadcast in Britain—the Rugby international between England and Wales at Twickenham in 1927.

Teddy Wakelam qualified for the job of a running commentator on the wireless on the strength of an exceptionally quick mind already shown in public as a Harlequin forward. Almost needless to add, he belonged to the rugby type known as a "backrow specialist" which was also emerging about the same time. He was in fact splendidly equipped for the experiment of describing a game of Rugby as it went along—something no one had ever visualized before as a serious proposition. Later he was called upon to use his practical knowledge of sport to describe other great games, including lawn tennis and cricket. In 1938 he gave the first television commentary of a Test match when England played Australia at Lord's.

The B.B.C., for their part, had practically nothing to go on when the idea of the running commentary was more or less forced on them, or rather on the attention of members of their staff who knew very little about the games they were asked to present over the wireless. Some of the very first commentators, discovered in the oddest places, had to be almost dragged by the scruff of the neck to various London Rugby grounds and there invited to describe—into a microphone—what was going on, whether they knew the players or not. One of the experimenters, himself being experimented upon, was told that he could give the players numbers if he could not think of their names. The oddest situations thereupon arose and fortunately they never reached the public ear.

NEVER LOST FOR WORDS

It said much for Wakelam's courage, enterprise, and quickness of mind, not to mention his choice of words when going full tilt, not always having the clearest view of what was going on some distance away on the playing field below, sometimes in horrible weather, that he emerged as such a resounding success. For that undoubtedly he was—no matter what a few unbelieving critics occasionally said about "making it up as he went along". Certainly Wakelam fairly earned his place in the history of wireless.

Henry Blythe Thornhill Wakelam was born on May 8, 1893, the son of Henry Titus Wakelam and Mary Whitfield. He was educated at Marlborough and Pembroke College, Cambridge, going up to the university in 1911, when there was a galaxy of talent in Cambridge sport. Wakelam played Rugby football for the university—though without obtaining a blue—and, coming to the notice of Adrian Stoop, began his long connexion with the Harlequins. After the war he captained them in 1921-22 and also became a vice-president.

Wakelam joined the Army at the outbreak of the war, and obtained a commission in the 2nd City of London Regiment, Royal Fusiliers. His war experience was varied, as he served in Malta, France, Gallipoli, Egypt, Palestine, and Poland; before going to Gallipoli he had been transferred to the Regualr Army, R.H. and R.F.A. He was twice mentioned in dispatches and wounded. When hostilities ceased he was on special service in France, assisting General Haller's Polish Army to return to Poland across Germany.

RUGBY CORRESPONDENT

Wakelam resigned his commission in 1921 and went into business. In 1928, the year after his first commentary, he became Rugby correspondent of *The Morning Post*. He was also the author of a number of books on sport.

From 1936 to 1939 he was a War Office lecturer (A.A.G., T.A.). In 1940 he was appointed to G.H.Q. Middle East and two years later became a propaganda officer in north Syria.

In 1922 he married Vera Harriet Greenhill, who survives him with a daughter.

July 12, 1963.

Anton Walbrook, the actor, who died on August 9, 1967, had laid the foundations of his career in his native Austria and in Germany in the days before the Nazi regime. Like a number of his "non-Aryan" colleagues, he was faced during the 1930s with the problem of reestablishing himself outside Central Europe in English-speaking films and in the English theatre, and he had been notably successful in solving it.

Adolph Anton Wilhelm Wohlbrück, the descendant of a long line of professional performers, and the son of a clown also named Adolph Wohlbrück, was born in Vienna on November 19, 1900, and went on the stage in 1920. Among directors Max Reinhardt, and among leading players Paul Wegener and Hermine Korner, not to mention the public, soon recognized him as a very capable "juvenile"; and in 1934, three years after his debut on the screen, he participated in the international success of the Austrian film *Maskerade* and was engaged by R.K.O. for all three versions, English-speaking, German-speaking and French-speaking of *Michael Strogoff*. While in Hollywood he dropped the unpopular first name of Adolph. As Anton Walbrook he went to work in England in 1937, appearing on the screen as the Prince Consort to Anna Neagle's Queen in *Victoria the Great*, and on the stage in Noel Coward's *Design for Living*, in the part created by Alfred Lunt in the New York production some years earlier.

During the Second World War he followed up his success in Britain as a film actor by his performances in *Dangerous Moonlight* (with Sally Gray and featuring the enormously popular Warsaw Concerto), *Gaslight, 49th Parallel*, and *The Life and Death of Colonel Blimp*, and was in one of the big successes of the London Theatre, Lillian Hellman's *Watch on the Rhine*, in the role of a German political refugee in the United States.

The only classic parts he played in English were Herman in a film of Pushkin's *The Queen of Spades* and Hjalmar Ekdal to Mai Zetterling's Hedwige in a revival of *The Wild Duck*. He found opportunities, however, of showing his competence and hereditary adaptability in long-running stage musicals such as *Call Me Madam*, at the Coliseum, and *Wedding in Paris*, at the Hippodrome; for, as a critic put it, playing a singing part he did not sing, but was effective through the force of good listening and good timing and, it might be added, of improvisation in the matter of comic dance steps. He had not attempted on beginning to work in England to change his style radically, but he judiciously toned it down while slyly drawing attention to his individuality at moments.

In 1948 he was seen as the director of a ballet company, to Moira Shearer's young ballet dancer, in the colour film *The Red Shoes*. During the 1950s he made two films in France, the well known *La Ronde* and *Lola Montez*, both for Max Ophüls, and in England Otto Preminger's film version of *Saint Joan*, in which he was cast as Bishop Cauchon to the Joan of Jean Seberg.

Later he returned to work in his mother tongue in Central Europe, and it was while on stage at the Kleine Komödie in Munich that he suffered a heart attack in April, 1967. He had become a naturalized British subject in 1947. He was unmarried.

August 10, 1967.

Dr. Arthur Waley, C.H., who died on June 27, 1966, did more by the elegance, vitality and lucidity of his translations from the Chinese and Japanese to introduce the English-speaking world to the literature and civilization of the Far East than anyone of his generation. He freed oriental studies from the charge of pedantry and the distortion of patronage which had affected them in the later nineteenth century, and brought them into the main stream of intelligent reading.

An orientalist who never set foot in Asia, a profound scholar who never filled a university post, a poet who was content to be the interpreter of the work of others, a linguist who penetrated the meaning of the most difficult of Chinese and Japanese classical texts, without having received formal instruction in those languages, a master of English prose and verse forms—Arthur Waley was a survivor from that most brilliant Cambridge generation of the years before the outbreak of the 1914-18 War. A precocious classical scholar from Rugby, he found at King's, where he proceeded in 1907, the refinement of sensibility and the play of wit which quickly developed his aesthetic sense and a philosophy of life, scorn of pretentiousness and horror of the dull or the flippant. The circle round Lowes Dickinson, G. E. Moore, and J. M. E. McTaggart withdrew from the "clatter of thought". Waley may have formed half-consciously a penchant for eastern studies at this time, especially from Lowes Dickinson who travelled to China and Japan in 1912 as first Albert Kahn Travelling Fellow.

ASSISTANT TO BINYON

But Waley has himself told how casual and apparently accidental his introduction to oriental studies appeared to him to be. In the Cambridge of 1910 his chance of getting a Fellowship was very remote; and his family provided an opening in an export business with South America. He never got farther than Spain, however, for from this lot he sought refuge in the British Museum Print Room, to which he was appointed in the summer of 1913. But, finding the routine of cataloguing prints tedious, he exchanged into the new oriental side as assistant to the first chief, Laurence Binyon the poet, who proved an ideal friend during the 18 years that Waley stayed in the service of the museum. He began studying both Chinese and Japanese, and was soon wishing to share the pleasure he was getting from reading Chinese poetry with his friends. From this wish came the publication in 1918 of his translation of *One Hundred and Seventy Chinese Poems*, many of them already published in the first volume of the Bulletin of the newly founded school of Oriental Studies. That he had by then, in four years, read several thousand Chinese poems is less remarkable than that these translations should have stood the test of time, both for their rendering and as poetry. In them appeared at once his mastery of English, direct, informal and apparently effortless, but rhythmical and evocative. It was appropriate that he should have received in 1953 the Queen's Medal for Poetry; for his influence on poets was considerable, especially in his flexible use of stress in lines of unequal length, in which he experimented before the publication of Hopkins's poetry by Robert Bridges.

Otherwise the museum years bore fruit mainly in translations from the Japanese; first selections of classical poems and Nô plays (1921), and then of the great classic *Tale of Genji*, which appeared in six volumes between 1925 and 1933, and was hailed in far wider circles as a masterpiece of prose, and indeed as adding a classic to the world's roll. The mixtures of fastidiousness and informality of the language exactly suited his temperament; and he again showed his sympathy with the Heian period in Japan—which was in its culture a continuation of the preceding Tang peiod in China, but with an even greater aesthetic emphasis on the art of calligraphy—by his rendering in 1928 of the best part of the *Pillow-book of Sei Shônagon*.

SYMPATHY FOR NEW CHINA

Freed from official duties in 1930, Waley deepened his studies. In 1934 he published a study of the Tao Te-ching under the title of *The Way and its Power*, in which he sought to expose the ancient religious beliefs of China, which had been overlaid by Confucian interpretation. In 1937-38 there followed annotated translations of the *Book of Songs* and the *Analects*, and in 1939 *Three Ways of Thought in Ancient China*, in which he displayed and studied the unparalleled fecundity of ideas in the time of the "Hundred Schools", which he judged to be of immediate interest at that junction in world history. For although Waley never chose to visit the Far East, finding himself all the sight-seeing which he needed, he was far from being distinterested in current affairs, and was conspicuously sympathetic towards the new China. Indeed by preserving a detachment he was able the more effectively to reveal permanent values.

This astringent view of the confrontation of east and west in the nineteenth century was notably shown in his presentation of the *Opium War through Chinese Eyes*, published in 1958, all the more effective for the understatement in which it relates this shameful episode. But Waley remained a student of thought and literature rather than of institutions or history, and was at his happiest in rendering the allegorical fairy story *Monkey* (1942), which was translated into five European languages and more widely appreciated than any of his books since the *Tale of Genji*. In 1952 appeared its sequel, *The Real Tripitaka*, in which he told the true story of the life and travels of Hsuan Tsang, the T'ang dynasty pilgrim to India and translator of Buddhist canonical texts into Chinese.

T'ANG POETS

Meanwhile he had returned to his early interest in the T'ang poets Li Po and Po Chü-i, devoting to each a volume in which their lives and times were illuminated by translations, linked by brilliant sketches of the social and political background in eighth and ninth century China. Even in the more purely Sinological studies like the rendering with commentary of the *Nine Songs* of pre-Han shamans; or the anthology of *Ballads and Stories from Tun-huang*, Waley's text conveys the freshness of popular songs and folk-stories. This was something which greatly interested him, and he was at his best tracing the Cinderella story back to the Chinese southern borderlands in the eighth century.

Paradoxically, while enjoying lifelong friendship with painters like Clive and Vanessa Bell and Duncan Grant, Waley took a remote interest in Chinese and Japanese painting. His *Introduction to the Study of Chinese Painting* is mainly about the literary tradition of Chinese criticism, while his official *Catalogue of the Paintings recovered from Tun-huang by Sir Aurel Stein* is concerned with Buddhist iconography and not art-history.

Waley's last published work, a miscellany, *The Secret History of the Mongols and Other Pieces* (1964), besides its translation of the history of Mongol growth until after the death of Chinggis Khan, collected other translations from the Ainu and Syriac, as well as Waley's normal excursions in Japanese and Chinese. The volume also included original short stories and poems by Waley himself.

A lifelong inhabitant of Bloomsbury, Waley was a familiar figure on his bicycle riding between Gordon Square and the Museum, in early days wearing a broad-brimmed black hat which he would raise punctiliously to ladies whom he recognized en route. His fine profile, ascetic look, and slightly abstracted air intimidated those who had not experienced his kindness, especially to the young and the foreigner. He was in fact extremely sociable, enjoying conversation, music and ballet, and had a great gift for friendship. Skiing was an annual pleasure, first in Austria and later in Norway; and he loved mountains.

Arthur David Waley was born in 1889, the son of David Frederick Schloss and Rachel Sophia Waley, and assumed the name of Waley by deed-poll in 1914. He was a Fellow of the British Academy and of the School of Oriental and African Studies; an honorary Fellow of King's since 1946, and received the honorary Lit.D. from Oxford. He was created C.B.E. in 1952 and Companion of Honour in 1956.

He married, in the month before his death, Alison Grant Robinson.

June 28, 1966.

Charles Clement Walker, C.B.E., who died on September 30, 1968, at the age of 91, headed the technical side of the de Havilland organization for 40 years, and was respected internationally as one of the great men of aviation's formative decades.

Born on August 25, 1877, educated at Highgate School and University College, apprenticed with John Abbot and Co., Gateshead-on-Tyne, and articled to a Westminster civil engineer, J. J. Taylor, he joined Captain Geoffrey de Havilland (later Sir Geoffrey) at Hendon in February, 1915, to lead the structural and aerodynamics departments of the Aircraft Manufacturing Co., Ltd. Nearly a third of the British and American aircraft in the 1914-18 war and almost all the combat aeroplanes of the United States forces, were of de Havilland design.

When The de Havilland Aircraft Co., Ltd., was formed on September 25, 1920, Walker was a founder director and Chief Engineer. In a continuity of team leadership that was one of the secrets of de Havilland success he held this position up to his retirement 25 years later.

BASIC RESPONSIBILITY

Walker was, throughout, D.H.'s right-hand man on the technical side, largely responsible for the basic formulae of aircraft, guiding technical policy, and strongly influencing the character of what became the de Havilland world enterprise, with a war-time payroll of 38,000 people.

With keen foresight he advocated variable propeller pitch back in the early 1920s; its adoption in the famous Comet racer of 1934 led to de Havilland being ready to build the main share of the R.A.F.'s propellers in the 1939-1945 war.

He persistently urged the economy of speed obtained through clean form, when people held that speed had to be paid for. The Mosquito, advantageously sacrificing defensive guns for speed, was the world's fastest aircraft for 2½ years of the war. The first jet airliner, also named the Comet, historically proved the point afresh in 1949; a developed version is to be the R.A.F.'s ocean reconnaissance aircraft of the 1970s.

Walker did valuable advisory work for various bodies, was on the Advisory Committee to the war-time Minister of Aircraft Production, served many years on the council of the Society of British Aircraft Constructors.

Charles Walker's rich influence on the policy and people of de Havilland Aircraft came from his remarkable integrity and character, Kind, guileless, self-effacing, forthright, calm, wise, full of faith and twinkling with humour, he was a tower of strength when times were bad, and always an inspiration to rising engineers around him. He saw the best in everyone. Clear and penetrating in technical matters, he insisted upon reducing complexities to plain language in a refreshing, often amusing way. The theory that apes at typewriters must eventually produce a Shakespearian sonnet led him to argue against over-theorizing: "Well, the sands of the seashore are re-arranged a good deal, but how often do you see them form a portrait of the Kaiser?" He was elected honorary F.R.Ae.S., and F.I.Ae.S.

Crippled by poliomyelitis from boyhood he was nevertheless a powerful swimmer and a short-handicap golfer. As a young man he had a fine bass voice, approaching professional quality. While a lover of the arts his inquiring mind was ever seeking to understand natural phenomena in such fields as geography, meteorology, astronomy, space and relativity, migrations and evolution, and he was a fascinating conversationalist and companion.

He married in 1916 Eileen Hood. Their only child, David, was killed in the war, when night flying with the R.A.F.

October 1, 1968.

Henry Agard Wallace, the best known member of Roosevelt's New Deal Cabinets, and Vice-President of the United States from 1941 to 1945, died on November 18, 1965, at the age of 77 in hospital in Danbury, Connecticut.

A visionary and humanitarian, he symbolized better than any other American of his time the instinctive generosity, the single-minded idealism and the troubled consciences of American liberals. But he was irresponsible and politically inept; and his vanity, and a tendency toward wishful thinking, led him astray.

Wallace was born in Iowa in 1888 into a dynasty of agricultural leaders; his father was Secretary of Agriculture in the 1920s. Wallace took his degree in agriculture and for 23 years he acted as associate editor and editor of the paper *Wallace's Farmer*. He was a brilliant breeder of new strains of plants and animals and laid the foundation of a flourishing business. The family was Republican, but Wallace left the party in 1928 in disgust at its disastrous farm policies.

Wallace did not become a Democrat officially until 1936; but in 1933 Roosevelt made him his first Secretary of Agriculture. Farmers were then in the pit of the depression and to save them Wallace initiated a programme of supporting farm prices in return for restriction of production. It is strange to reflect that the same price-supporting policies helped, by assuring bumper crops, to save the world from starvation during and after the war and that they are still in effect to the financial embarrassment of the Government.

At the time it simply seemed strange that the man demanding curbs on production should be the Henry Wallace whose hybrid maize had been responsible for such miraculous increase in productivity. Restriction of planting was not enough and Wallace invited farmers to plough under their growing cotton and to sell the Government their young pigs and sows to be turned into fertilizer. This destruction seemed shocking when so many Americans were short of food and clothing, but it was based on the belief that foreign markets—lost because of America's high tariffs—were not likely to be won back and that farm income could regain its former parity with industrial income only by fitting production to the domestic market.

Temporarily, restriction had the desired effect and when the Supreme Court declared the Act unconstitutional in 1936 a substitute, lightly disguised as soil conservation, was hurried through Congress. In 1938 a new long-term Act was adopted. Based on the idea of the "ever-normal granary", it bore the mark of Wallace's close study of the Bible and of the fearful droughts of 1935-36. It put great emphasis on conservation of the land; Wallace had a mystical and not misplaced faith in what he was to call "quietness and strength of grass".

In 1940, when Roosevelt decided to stand for an unprecedented third term, he decided that his running-mate must be Wallace, whose progressive ideas appealed strongly to farmers, small businessmen, the trade unions, and racial minorities. Wallace was looked upon with suspicion by both the professional politicians and the party's conservatives, and only the President's insistence won the nomination for him.

During the War Wallace headed the Board of Economic Warfare (until he lost a savage quarrel with Jesse Jones) and other boards dealing with economic priorities. But the titles of his books show that he was looking ahead to the problems of the postwar period: *Democracy Reborn*, *The Century of the Common Man* and *Sixty Million Jobs*. At that time his ideas excited much derision. Who, in 1945, could foresee an economy providing 60 million jobs? Yet today employment is far higher.

SECRETARY OF COMMERCE

In 1944, when the President decided to stand for a fourth term, the party managers realized that he might not be able to complete it, and demanded a new Vice President. Wallace had made many enemies among the conservatives, but even some of his friends, particularly among the trade unions, had come to doubt whether he had the stability and judgment needed in the White House. The choice fell on Truman. Roosevelt made Wallace Secretary of Commerce, a post in which, if Roosevelt had lived, Wallace might have put into practice his ideas about a planned, expanding economy and full employment. Fearing as much, Congress took away from the Secretary of Commerce his powers over the Reconstruction Finance Corporation before confirming Wallace.

Relations with Russia were, however, to prove Wallace's downfall—like that of other liberals of his time. Hopeful, naive, he became convinced that the tough policy of the State Department was responsible for Russian intransigence—instead of the other way about. He attacked the Baruch plan for controlling atomic energy as unfair to Russia; misrepresented it, and, after his mistakes were pointed out, continued to do so. He attacked American policy as war-like. The crisis came over a speech at Madison Square Garden in 1946 which the President, in an absent-minded moment, had passed. The Secretary of State threatened to resign and Wallace had to go.

TRUMAN'S VICTORY

Wallace had long felt that he, not Truman, was Roosevelt's spiritual heir and he began to attack the President for betraying the New Deal. In return, Truman accused Wallace, with more accuracy, of having become the prisoner of the Communists. Wallace, in calmer days, had recognized that the creation of a third party to the left of the Democrats could lead only to a Republican victory, but he was bitten by the presidential bug and accepted the nomination of the Progressive Party, a liberal group with Communists in the driver's seat.

It was expected that Wallace would win about three million votes and cost the Democrats the White House in 1948. In fact he won only a trifle over one million and did not prevent the re-election of Truman, although in New York he gave the state to the Republicans. One reason for the fiasco was prosperity; another was Wallace's unpopular pro-Russian policy; a third the wildness of his campaign. In the south he talked inflammatory nonsense about non-existent lynchings in New York; he justified the Russian coup in Czechoslovakia as a move to forestall seizure of power by the American Ambassador. He was even grudging about the Marshall Plan. Not until 1952 did Wallace admit publicly that he had been deceived by the Russians, but in 1951 he said that he would never again stand for public office. He retired to his 130-acre farm about 50 miles from New York, and devoted most of his time to his first love—plant genetics.

In 1914 he married Miss Ilo Browne. They had three children.

November 19, 1965.

Lurleen Wallace, Governor of Alabama, died on May 7, 1968, at the age of 41.

Although she came into office riding on the coat-tails of her husband, Mrs. Wallace, Alabama's first woman governor and the third in the United States history, always strove to overcome the circumstances surrounding her election and to make her mark in history as a "good governor". Like the famous Mirian "Ma" Ferguson of Texas in 1924, Mrs. Wallace followed her husband in office as a means of perpetuating his political power. George Wallace had been blocked in his bid to succeed himself in the 1966 elections when the state Senate refused to approve his succession bill. Her position also gave him the time to launch his independent campaign for the presidency in 1968.

At her inauguration Mrs. Wallace promised that she would continue her husband's policies and would continue his fight against integration and federal bureaucracy.

Many observers noted that between her and her husband, who was maintained on a dollar a year retainer as "assistant to the Governor", there was a political relationship similar to that between a Queen and a Prime Minister. Mrs. Wallace would perform state ceremonies, greet visitors to the capitol and make official visits, while Wallace would draw up the outlines of state policy, with which his wife was unfamiliar, and see that this was carried out.

When in April, 1967, Mrs. Wallace threatened to seize control of the public schools to prevent integration and at the same time requested an increase in the state police force her words were obviously those of her husband and she seemed visibly uncomfortable mouthing them.

DEFIED DECREE

At the time, government officials feared a repetition of Mr. Wallace's renowned "stand in the school-house door" in 1963; a vain attempt to block the integration of the University of Alabama.

She defied the decree of a federal district court in March, 1967, ordering a racial balance to be achieved in schools by the autumn. Demanding that the State legislature serve a "cease and desist" order on the judges, she said: "They have made their decree—now let them enforce it."

In June, 1967, 400 Negro demonstrators marched to the state capital demanding that she should hear their grievances or relinquish office. But they were halted at barricades—while Mrs. Wallace watched them through binoculars.

In office she overcame the shyness that she had shown as a retiring housewife and appeared as a woman with ideas of her own, and a strong state presence, especially in non-political speeches. One of her first acts as governor was to tour the state's infamously deprived mental hospitals, after which she sent the legislature a priority programme to secure more money to improve conditions.

Born on September 19, 1926, the daughter of Henry Burns of Tuscaloosa, Mrs. Wallace was brought up in the same fundamentalist and tee-total atmosphere as her husband. Her early ambition was to be a nurse and she attended Tuscaloosa Business College. She later took a job in a small store, where she met her future husband while he was working nearby as a lorry driver for the State Highway Department. They were married in May 1943, shortly before Mr. Wallace entered the Army. Mrs. Wallace is survived by two sons and two daughters.

May 8, 1968.

Dr. Bruno Walter, who died on February 17, 1962, at the age of 85 after a heart attack at his home in Beverly Hills, California, was a conductor of international fame whose art was universally admired but whose career was more chequered by anti-Semitic persecution than any other musician of the same status, for neither Busch nor Furtwängler, who were his contemporaries, was a Jew. Born in Berlin and educated there in essentially German surroundings he encountered race-hostility at Munich long before Nazidom made it the official policy of the German nation. It did not end when the German occupation of Austria in 1938 turned him out of Vienna, for though he and his wife were speedily granted French nationality war and the German occupation drove him from Europe to settle for the rest of his life in the United States.

Walter, which he adopted as his surname, was the second prenomen of Schlesinger. He was born on September 15, 1876. He describes in his autobiography, which he wrote at the age of 68 and called *Theme and Variations,* how he got his education at the Stern Conservatoire, and how he abandoned the careers of pianist and composer for which he was being trained, being fired to become a conductor after hearing and seeing Hans von Bülow, whom Walter names as the first of the great conductors.

Walter's conducting career began at Cologne Opera on March 13, 1894, when he conducted Lortzing's *Der Waffenschmied*. Work in other opera houses followed, including the Berlin Royal Opera and the Hamburg Opera, where he first met and worked with Gustav Mahler. Walter's most formative experience began in 1901 when Mahler called him to the Vienna Royal Opera: formative not only because he was working with Mahler the setter of new operatic standards, and with Mahler the composer whose works Walter championed all his life, but because Walter's interpretative style was to become identifiably Viennese; he bore four nationalities in the course of his life, but his musical passport was permanently stamped Vienna.

MUNICH FESTIVALS

Walter remained at the Vienna Opera after his mentor left in 1907; he added the Singakademie to his duties, and after Mahler's death conducted the first performance of the ninth symphony and *Das Lied von der Erde.* Foreign engagements began to come his way, led by the Royal Philharmonic Society in London for whom he conducted a concert in 1909; a year later Beecham invited him to direct *Tristan und Isolde* and the premiere of Ethel Smyth's *The Wreckers* at Covent Garden. In 1913 he was invited to follow Mottl as General Music Director at Munich. For the next nine years he worked unremittingly at Munich, organizing its festivals and more than maintaining the already high reputation of its opera. But there was opposition, and in 1922 he was superseded on some trivial excuse. The time had not come when racial prejudice could be openly quoted as the reason. Still all Germany was open to him; in 1925 he accepted an appointment as conductor at the Charlottenburg Opera in Berlin, and he also became conductor of the famous Gewandhaus concerts at Leipzig. Outside Germany he took a leading part in building up the reputation of the summer festival at Salzburg, and when Covent Garden once more reverted to internationalism he directed the German seasons of the London Opera Syndicate from 1924 onwards.

TROUBLE IN BERLIN

The performances which Walter conducted at Covent Garden during these years, particularly those of *Der Rosenkavalier* and *Die Fledermaus*, belong to the most glorious pages of the Opera House's history. There is a famous story of how Walter, at a Covent Garden rehearsal, once addressed his colleagues for four hours in four languages without once falling into the wrong language.

Trouble, however, followed him to Berlin in 1929 over a scheme for reorganization which he and Herr Tietjen, the General Intendant, proposed together. Walter offered his resignation, which was not immediately accepted. He held on to his German activities until 1933, when the Nazi Ministry for Propaganda prohibited him from appearing in either Leipzig or Berlin. By this time Sir Thomas Beecham had taken control of Covent Garden, so there was no longer room for Walter there. His interests became the more concentrated in Austria, and he had received an appointment, which virtually amounted to the direction of the Vienna State Opera, only two years before the Schuschnigg government capitulated to the invader. No more Salzburg; no more Vienna. A domicile in France and occasional festivals in Switzerland and concerts in England became his lot for the time being, until war uprooted him once more and he became a resident in the United States. In 1946 he revisited England to conduct the L.P.O. and was received as before with warm appreciation of his distinctive qualities.

Subsequently he went to several Edinburgh Festivals at the first of which in 1947 he discovered Kathleen Ferrier as an ideal exponent of Mahler's *Lied von der Erde.* This was the beginning of a musical association that lasted till the singer's death in 1953. Walter went to London from New York specially to conduct at a concert in her memory at the Festival Hall. Walter also went to Edinburgh with the Paris Conservatoire Orchestra, the New York Philharmonic-Symphony Orchestra (of which he was musical director from 1947 until 1957) and twice with the Vienna Philharmonic.

LAST TIME IN LONDON

He last appeared in London in 1955 when he conducted the B.B.C. Symphony Orchestra, and should have returned in 1957, but for a heart attack, to conduct the concert at which he was awarded the gold medal of the Royal Philharmonic Society. But since the war he had not conducted opera in Britain (though he was in charge of the Metropolitan Opera's bicentenary production of *The Magic Flute* in New York), and Londoners particularly missed his Wagner, which was memorable for the great span of its rhythm that never collapsed under the full sensuousness which he found and realized in the music.

He continued to conduct concerts and to make gramophone records until quite recently. A volume of essays, *Of Music and Musicians,* was published in English only in 1961. Walter was married and had two daughters, one of whom was killed in tragic circumstances in 1939; his wife died in 1945. Among honours conferred upon him was a doctorate of music of Edinburgh University; he was a Commander of the French Legion of Honour, and a Grand Officer of the Dutch Order of Orange Nassau.

Walter's method has been contrasted with Toscanini's. It was said that Toscanini incited and spurred on his players, but Walter drew them out. He had an enormous sense of beauty of tone and phrase: he luxuriated in it. His musical sympathies were wide but his special field was the German opera from Gluck to Strauss. That sense of beauty found satisfaction in Bruckner and Mahler, whose symphonies he delighted to champion. His performance of Bizet's *Carmen* in Vienna shortly before his banishment was considered almost a miracle of production and musical presentation. But his heart was given primarily to German music, which made his tragedy the deeper, though he himself said, "I am never homesick because my home is in music".

February 19, 1962.

John Walter, for many years a chief proprietor and a director of *The Times* died at his home in Hove on August 11, 1968, at the age of 95.

A great-great-grandson of the John Walter who, in 1785, founded the newspaper which became *The Times*, he was born in London on August 8, 1873, in the lifetime of his grandfather John Walter III, then principal proprietor; his father being Arthur Fraser Walter, who afterwards succeeded to his own father's position. His mother was the eldest daughter of the Rev. T. A. Anson, of Longford Rectory, Derbyshire, and grand-daughter of General Sir George Anson. She died in 1935 at the age of 88.

John Walter was educated at Eton, where he was in Mr H. G. Wintle's house and had the Rev. S. R. James as his tutor; in 1892 he was in the shooting VIII. He went on to Christ Church, Oxford, where he graduated with honours (Lit. Hum.) in 1897. Both by family tradition and by practical training in Printing House Square, which he entered as soon as he left Oxford, he became well fitted as a young man to regard *The Times* as the permanent seat of his duties in life; and during his long and intimate connexion with the paper his first interest was *The Times* and everything that concerned it. One of the first things he learnt to do was to operate the Kastenbein composing machine. In his early days he acted as assistant to Blowitz, the Paris Correspondent. John Walter was master of a plain, terse English and a good linguist, commanding French, German and Spanish. He was of particular service to *The Times* in Spain for two extensive periods; he also served at The Hague and in Lisbon, and travelled in many parts of Europe and in America on special missions for *The Times*. His presence and manner made him persona grata wherever he went, whether as guest or as a host. Inside Printing House Square itself he was a friendly mentor to succeeding generations of staff.

John Walter became chairman of The Times Publishing Company Limited on the death of his father, Arthur Fraser Walter, on February 22, 1910. John Walter had borne a full share in all the internal crises that convulsed Printing House Square during the long period of adversity that followed the verdict of the Parnell Commission. *The Times* was then a partnership of numerous proprietors of minute fractions of the 16 original shares into which they had become divided in the course of a century. In the decade 1898-1908, *The Times* became associated with the enterprise of selling the Encyclopaedia Britannica by payment in instalments, a device unfamiliar to that generation and scandalous to many of the small proprietors.

SALE ORDERED

They reproached, admonished, and forced the family to agree to modernize its capital structure by turning the eighteenth-century partnership-at-will into a limited liability company. After opposing the Encyclopaedia scheme, they placed their grievances before the Court of Chancery, which ordered *The Times* to be sold at the best price.

In 1906 plans were made for the formation of The Times Limited and a constitution was drafted to which approval was secured by November, 1907. Sir Alexander Henderson was called in to advise and he suggested that Cyril Arthur Pearson be approached. By December 12 the heads of an agreement between Arthur Fraser Walter and Pearson had been approved. Meanwhile, in conditions of the greatest secrecy, Moberly Bell, Manager of *The Times*, had been in touch with Lord Northcliffe (then Alfred Harmsworth). In court on March 16, 1908, Moberly Bell represented an unnamed competitor, who was prepared to pay what proved to be the best price. Thus Harmsworth secured control of *The Times,* and became, in all essentials, its owner for life.

It was in these conditions that John Walter succeeded his father as chairman. The position was never tranquil and became less so when Northcliffe's health worsened.

RESPECT FOR NORTHCLIFFE

None the less, Walter had a profound and enduring respect for Northcliffe. Many years after, he described their first meeting in the Ritz Hotel in Paris, Northcliffe in a blue serge suit, a large lock of brown hair falling over his forehead. "Here was a man who knew neither doubt nor hesitation", wrote Walter. Of their later relationship Walter remarked: "We got on better apart", adding: "There was a quality of greatness in him which distinguished him at once from the common run of men. He treated me as a busy father treats his son, indulgently as a rule, but with bursts of wrathful impatience if I opposed him." He impressed on John Walter that he had set his heart on restoring the fortunes of the paper and how important it was that Walter should second his efforts, saying: "After all, it is your business. Your people made it and you have a son to inherit it. I am only here to put it on its legs again."

During the 12 years of their partnership, the agreement stood that John Walter should have the right, at Northcliffe's death, to exercise an option to purchase *The Times* at the best price. In 1922 it was announced that Northcliffe's shares had been acquired by John Walter in association with Major the Hon. John J. Astor (later Lord Astor of Hever). John Walter became co-chief proprietor of *The Times* with Lord Astor of Hever, served as vice-chairman of The Times Publishing Company Limited and as chairman of The Times Book Company Limited. He was for many years a director of the Guardian Assurance Company.

In February, 1960, Walter was hurt in a motor accident, but in spite of the fact that pneumonia followed his injuries he made a remarkable recovery. He rarely went to London after his accident and in the summer of 1960 he retired from the boards of The Times Publishing Company and The Times Book Company. He remained, however, with Lord Astor of Hever, and Mr. Gavin Astor, a chief proprietor until the merger with *The Sunday Times*. In 1961 he was received into the Roman Catholic Church.

John Walter was not a businessman by inclination and only a strong sense of family duty enabled him to accept without demur his destined role in Printing House Square. He did not inherit the dynastic absorption in mechanical contrivance that in his grandfather, John Walter III, had resulted in the revolutionary inventions of stereotyping and the rotary press upon which the printing trade, at home and abroad, still depends. Persons were of greater concern to him than machines.

FAITH IN P.H.S.

The inflexibility in matters of principle that distinguished him was accompanied by an unshakable faith in men, and particularly in his colleagues at Printing House Square. He was a shrewd and lively observer of affairs, with a fine sense of humour. To *The Times* he had an unremitting devotion. A scrupulous conscientiousness was manifest in all his dealings however trivial. John Walter's manner was mild, his courtesy mellow. He was ready to welcome all, of whatever rank. A certain diffidence obstructed his passage to the centre of society, and he was apt to stay on the fringe of a gathering. Though slow to offer conversation without encouragement, he was generous in friendship. His colleagues in Printing House Square held him in great affection.

John Walter was an accomplished watercolourist and at one time amused himself by painting political satires and social caricatures. He was interested in many country pursuits. As a young man he was a cricketer, and a patron of newspaper cricket. He was also, in his earlier years, a patron of agriculture in Berkshire. For some years he served in the 4th Battalion, The Royal Berkshire Regiment (T.A.) and became captain and honorary major.

John Walter married, first, in 1903, Phyllis,

daughter of Colonel C. E. Foster, of The Northamptonshire Regiment; she died in 1937, leaving two sons and two daughters surviving. In 1939 he married secondly Rosemary, only daughter of the late Mr. J. A. Crawford. I.C.S. Mr. Walter's elder son is John, born in 1908.

August 12, 1968.

Dr. Edmund Frederic Warburg, who died on June 9, 1966, at the age of 58, was a botanist with an international reputation as a plant taxonomist.

He was Warburg of Clapham, Tutin and Warburg, a trio revered by all botanists.

He was born on March 22, 1908 and owed his early interest in botany to his father, Sir Otto Warburg, a former chairman of the London County Council and a keen amateur botanist and horticulturist. Father and son together developed this interest to the point at which they became leading experts in the scientific study of the native and the garden flora of Britain and also of the flora of the French Riviera. Already as an undergraduate at Cambridge Edmund was publishing joint papers with his father in the *Journal* of the Horticultural Society.

After leaving Marlborough in 1927 Warburg ("Heff" to his friends) went up to Trinity College, Cambridge, as an entrance scholar in mathematics. He was subsequently elected to a Senior Scholarship and was placed in the first class in both parts of the Natural Sciences Tripos, reading botany for Part II. His first researches, in the new field of cytotaxonomy, were carried out under the supervision of Miss Edith Saunders and earned him his Ph.D. degree and a Research Fellowship of Trinity in 1933. After some years in Cambridge he joined the staff of Bedford College, London, but soon after the outbreak of war he joined the R.A.F. and was engaged in the interpretation of aerial photographs. After the war he was invited to the staff of the Oxford Department of Botany as Curator of the Druce Herbarium, where he had remained ever since. In 1964 he was elected Reader in Plant taxonomy and became a Fellow of New College.

Warburg is perhaps best known for his part in the production of the *Flora of the British Isles* by Clapham, Tutin and Warburg. This was the first comprehensive scientific flora of this country to be produced for over 70 years and was quite outstanding for its scientific quality. His considerable contribution to the research for this great work included among others the section on Rosaceae, which had been one of his long-standing interests

OUTSTANDING BRYOLOGIST

Warburg's scientific reputation is not only based upon his work with flowering plants. He was also one of the outstanding bryologists of his generation. He prepared, besides many short papers in bryophytes, the third edition of the Census Catalogue of British Mosses for the Bryological Society, of which he was president in 1962 and 1963.

Heff was the most reticent and modest of men. As a scientist he was content to publish only a few works of real weight. His great influence arose from his enthusiasm for his subject, his common sense and moderation in discussion and his immense patience with pupils, colleagues and amateur botanists of all kinds. He was a devoted and highly valued member of the Ashmolean Natural History Society as well as of the Botanical and Bryological Societies of the British Isles. His influence in biological matters in the Oxford Department of Botany and in the university generally was, in spite of his modesty and self-effacement, very great, and a steady stream of young men worked under his supervision even in days when research in taxonomic botany had become unfashionable.

In 1948 he married Primrose Churchman, of Melton, Suffolk. They had two sons and one daughter.

June 11, 1966.

Professor Otto Warburg, a Jewish Nobel prize-winning biochemist who was so famous that the Nazis dared not imprison him, died on August 1, 1970, in west Berlin at the age of 86. He was also a leading cancer resarcher.

In 1931, Warburg won the Nobel Prize in Physiology and Medicine for his work on the nature and functioning of respiratory enzymes and ferments, the catalysators of the chemical process in a living cell. Thirteen years later he was offered a second Nobel Prize, but was not allowed to receive the award under Hitler's ban.

In 1966, Warburg told a conference of Nobel prize-winners that cancer in most of its forms could be avoided if people would take the necessary preventive measures. "There is no illness whose cause is better known and which has been traced back farther into physics and chemistry," he said. Warburg, then head of the Max Planck Institute for cell physiology in west Berlin, said cancer occurred when oxygen in body cells was replaced by zymosis (fermentation). Zymosis was caused when free oxygen did not reach the cells in sufficient quantity, or when the enzymes carrying oxygen to the cells were damaged, he said.

Warburg also won many other international awards. In 1934 he became a foreign member of the Royal Society, London, and in 1952 of the "Pour Le Mérite" order. He never accepted professorship and concentrated solely on research.

He devoted much time to helping younger scientists such as Adolf Butenandt, the German biochemist who determined the structure of male and female sex hormones, and Richard Kuhn, the Austrian chemist. Kuhn and Butenandt were also prevented by the Nazi decree from accepting Nobel Prize awards in 1938 and 1939 respectively.

Born in Freiburg-im-Breisgau on October 8, 1883, he obtained his doctorate in chemistry at Berlin in 1906 and in medicine at Heidelberg in 1911. He was a prominent figure in the colony of institutes at Berlin-Dahlem for a number of years. In 1931 an entirely new institute was built for him, named the Kaiser Wilhelm Institut für Zellphysiologie. He first became known through his researches at the marine biological station at Naples on the metabolism of various types of ova.

In 1963 Warburg was awarded a doctor's degree "honoris causa" by Oxford University.

August 4, 1970.

Dr. Harry Ward, national chairman of the American Civil Liberties Union for its first 20 years and sometime professor of Christian Ethics at Union Theological Seminary, died at his home in New Jersey, in December, 1962.

A famous exponent of moral indignation, he was in the forefront of pacific and social causes for 60 years. His last public activity was signing an open letter appealing to President Kennedy to end the Vietnam War in 1963, when he was 90. Not long before, at a birthday celebration when he was guest of honour of 100 religious leaders and scholars, he spoke for nearly an hour on the lessons of his career.

A slender, delicate figure—"luminous", as one supporter described his physical appearance—he was a well-ordered and effective speaker, an English Methodist immigrant who never became wholly reconciled to what he found in America and laboured unceasingly for change.

Born in London, he went to the United States in 1891 and plunged into social welfare and the Methodist Ministry. He studied at Northwestern University, Chicago, and at Harvard; began his ministry as Head Resident of a Methodist Settlement in Chicago in 1898; and served in many pastorates before his appointment to the seminary in 1916. He retired in 1941.

As a teacher he was quiet, coaxing, a propounder of questions rather than a dogmatist.

UNPOPULAR STANDS

As a public figure he was a stubborn advocate of unpopular positions. He helped to found the Methodist Federation of Social Service in 1907 and was general secretary from 1911 to 1944. He was national chairman of the Civil Liberties Union from 1920 to 1940. In 1927 at a symposium he called capitalism a state of mind and a religion of which all the world but the United States was sceptical. In 1933 he called for an overhaul of the immigration laws to let in refugees. For the next eight years, in face of prevailing isolationism, he denounced the atrocities of Germans and Japanese, culminating in a call for United States involvement in Europe in 1939.

In the same year he admitted that the Communist Party subscribed to the American League for Peace and Democracy, which he had founded in 1934, but denied that the party determined the league's foreign policy. In 1953 the Unamerican Activities Committee of Congress released secret testimony that he was one of three Methodist Ministers who were communist conspirators. Like the others, he denied it. He said that he had never been a member of any political party and based his judgments on Christian teaching.

He did indeed give Russia the benefit of the doubt, spoke frequently for American-Soviet friendship, and published a favourable essay called *The Soviet Spirit* in 1945. He wrote many other books on religion, social ethics and economic theory.

He is survived by two sons, Professor Gordon Ward, of the American University, Beirut, and Mr. Lynn Ward, a well-known graphic artist.

December 12, 1966.

Beatrice Warde collapsed and died suddenly on September 14, 1969, at her home in Epsom. She was 68. She was widely known as an authority on typography not because the subject interested her for its own sake but because, in her view, "it helps other people to communicate with the clarity which their ideas deserve."

Born in New York on September 20, 1900, the daughter of a remarkable literary figure, May Lamberton Becker, and of Gustav L. Becker, a composer and musical pedagogue, her first post after graduation from Barnard College at Columbia University was as assistant librarian from 1921-25 at the Typographic Library of the American Type Founders Company in Jersey City.

In 1925 she went to Europe with her husband, Frederic Warde, a gifted typographic designer with a difficult temperament. They separated after she had settled in England as editor of the *Monotype Recorder* with the Monotype Corporation. This post was secured largely on the strength of her remarkable investigations into the origins of the so-called Garamond types. Her account of this investigation was published in *The Fleuron*, at that time edited by Stanley Morison, who was also typographical adviser to the Monotype Corporation. The joint efforts of Morison and Mrs. Warde for that organization did much to establish its leading position in the manufacture and sale of type designs.

In the final volume of *The Fleuron* Mrs. Warde contributed an essay on the work of Eric Gill, whose Monotype Perpetua type she later used with magnificent effect in what is perhaps her best known piece of writing and design: a poster "This is a Printing Office.." which has been frequently reprinted, translated, and parodied. Sixteen of her essays on typography were published in book form under the title *The Crystal Goblet* in 1955.

As a research scholar she also produced a valuable monograph on the French eighteenth century type designer and type founder P.S. Fournier, but it was her gift for the spoken rather than the written word which made her such a popular and influential figure on four continents. Less than three years ago, she boasted that what she was really good at was "standing up on front of an audience with no preparation at all and for fifty minutes refusing to let them wriggle an ankle."

Her resonant voice, deep-pitched with an American burr, conveyed a riveting blend of conviction and enthusiasm; it kept up an urgent momentum in discussions by means of a crescendo, or a tremolo, whenever she agreed or disagreed with an interjection. Both in speech and in prose, she was fastidious in her choice of words, and she took great pains to explain precisely what a word was meant to convey in her own context.

The generosity of her nature dictated much of her important work. The English language was so rich an instrument of communication that it had to be shared with others; so she took a most active part in the affairs of the English-speaking Union and became one of its governors. A similar post with the St. Bride Printing Library resulted from her need to share her excitement in the literature of printing, but still more important was her indefatigable work for printing schools, where she was much in demand as a speaker. A specially drawn map of the British Isles, elegantly lettered with the names of all the schools where she had lectured, was presented to her in 1961 by a group of printing school teachers; no other gift gave her greater satisfaction.

She had been brought up in the Dutch Reformed Church, but after periods as a Unitarian and later as a freethinker, she entered the Catholic Church in 1941.

Her work as a writer, lecturer and typographical designer will remain on record. What will be be mourned is the loss of a personality that combined intelligence, energy and generosity in rare degree.

Frederic Warde died in 1939.

September 16, 1969.

Dr. Eric John Warlow-Davies, managing director of Bristol Siddeley Engines, Limited, who died on June 28, 1964, had among his responsibilities leadership of the Anglo-French team working on the development of the engine for the Concord supersonic air liner. He was 54.

He was chairman of the Committee of Directors (Engines) formed by Bristol Siddeley and the company's French collaborators on the Concord project, S.N.E.C.M.A., to manage joint work on the Bristol Siddeley Olympus 593 engine. Selection of the 593 was partly the result of Warlow-Davies's earlier energetic interest in establishing the "family" of Olympus engines.

A third generation Australian, Warlow-Davies was born at Broken Hill, New South Wales. He was educated at Hutchins School, Hobart, Tasmania, at the University of Tasmania where he completed his B.Sc. degree, obtaining the 1931 Rhodes Scholarship for Tasmania, and at Oxford where he took his B.A. with first class Honours followed by a D.Phil. In 1937 from Oxford he joined the Royal Aircraft Establishment as a junior scientific officer in the mechanical test department. The following year he became a technical assistant in the research department of the former London Midland Scottish Railway Company where he worked on problems of fatigue failure.

In 1941 he returned to his early association with aviation by joining Rolls-Royce, serving with this company in Britain and Canada, finally as general manager and chief engineer of Rolls-Royce of Canada. In 1953 he joined the former engine division of the Bristol Aeroplane Company, the following year being appointed Assistant Chief Engineer and subsequently Deputy Chief Engineer with a seat on the board of the engine division. When the Bristol Aero Engines Company was formed in 1956 he was appointed a director. On the formation of the present Bristol Siddeley Engines in 1959 he was appointed a special director and chief engineer, and in 1961 a full director.

A bachelor, he was a keen member of the Veteran Car Club and owned a 1904 Humberette car which he entered at many meetings.

June 30, 1964.

Albert Warner, one of the four Warner brothers who started with a 100-seat movie house and built a multi-million dollar film dynasty, died on November 26, 1967, at his apartment at Miami Beach, Florida. He was 84.

His death means that Jack L. Warner is the only survivor of the film-making brothers. Albert Warner had been a winter resident in Miami Beach since 1936.

The Warners pioneered talkies with Al Jolson's *Jazz Singer* that set off a revolution in the film industry and rocketed the value of Warner Brothers \$230m. dollars in 1930. Until Warner Brothers combined with another film company earlier this year, Jack Warner had served as president while Albert remained on the board of directors.

The brothers began motion picture production starting with Warner Brothers features made at a studio in St. Louis in 1912, moving west with the rest of the industry later. They suspended their venture at Santa Paula, California, in 1914, because of heavy competition and returned to exhibition and distribution. They were back three years later when they filmed *My Four Years in Germany* (based on the book of that name by James W. Gerard, United States Ambassador in Berlin from 1913 to 1917) and grossed nearly \$2m. They built a studio on Sunset Boulevard in Hollywood, formed Vitaphone to experiment with sound films and exploded into modern talkies with Al Jolson and *The Jazz Singer*. Through the years that followed, Warner Brothers grew to be one of the biggest studios.

Vice-president and treasurer, Albert Warner, in New York, held a seat on the board of directors, handled distribution and ran financial matters. He ceased to be active in Warner Brothers about 10 years ago. He was married twice. A year ago he and his wife gave \$1,500,000 to create the Albert and Bessie Warner pavilion at Mount Sinai hospital in Miami Beach, where he had been a patient in 1964. Two of his brothers died before him—Sam on the day before the 1927 opening of *The Jazz Singer*, and Harry in 1958.

November 28, 1967.

Sir Pelham Warner, M.B.E., died on January 30, 1963, at the age of 89. With his death cricket loses one of its greatest advocates and most trusted friends.

In his playing days scarcely an honour eluded him, and the same was so when he retired. As a prolific writer about the game he had a distinctive and pleasant style, which was allied to a very long memory, and in committee his authority and soundness of judgment were much in demand. He became a legendary figure at Lord's neatly dressed, gently spoken, always optimistic, and with the experience of a lifetime spent close to cricket. In 1950 he was president of M.C.C., 47 years after captaining their first touring team in Australia, and the members' stand, built in 1958 between the pavilion and the grandstand, was named after him.

Nobody ever lived who took the game more seriously. He did not care for festive country house or indeed any cricket except the three-day first class match. Anything else was a trifling with the great game, and very seldom did he take any part in such matches.

Pelham Francis Warner was born at Port of Spain, Trinidad, on October 2, 1873, the son of Charles William Warner, C.B. His father was for many years Attorney General of Trinidad, and it was in the West Indies that he spent his early boyhood, acquiring an affection for those islands which he never lost. At the age of 13 he was sent to England, where he soon found the way to Lord's, and in 1887 he went to Rugby School. There he was coached by Tom Emmett, a renowned Yorkshire cricketer. He had four years in the eleven, the last two as captain, and while still at school he met, either on or off the field, many famous players. Warner was at that time a good, but not a great, batsman, and at Oriel College, Oxford, he did not get a Blue until his third year. He used to relate how G. J. Mordaunt, the Oxford captain of 1895, came up to him in the field when the University were playing M.C.C. and said, "Plum, I think you would look very nice in a dark blue cap!"

CONSISTENT BATSMAN

His advance into the top flight of cricketers was due as much to his complete devotion to the game and infinite capacity for taking pains as to any great natural ability. With his studies behind him cricket became his life. He took his Bar final examination in 1896, soon after going down from Oxford, and a month later he embarked on the first of his many cricket tours, to the West Indies under Lord Hawke. On his return he made his first century at Lord's, for M.C.C. against Yorkshire, and that winter he led a side to the United States. In 1898 he went to South Africa for the first time, again under Lord Hawke, who had a considerable influence on his career. At Johannesburg he scored 132 not out in his first Test match, and he began the following summer by making 150 for Middlesex against Yorkshire at Lord's, the Yorkshire attack having Rhodes, Hirst, Haigh, Jackson, and Wainwright. Wisden called this "emphatically the innings of his life" and he was by now among the best and most consistent batsmen in England, having in spite of his slight physique, a remarkable facility for playing fast bowling. In 1901 he represented the Gentlemen against the Players at Lord's for the first time, putting on 105 in an opening partnership with C. B. Fry in the first innings, and his sixth tour abroad was with an unofficial side to New Zealand and Australia in 1902-03.

A year later Warner was appointed captain of the first M.C.C. touring team without, up to this time, having played in a home Test match. Many expected the honour to go to A. C. Maclaren, and yet no one could have excelled Warner in the performance of his duties. When the side left for Australia, England's reputation was waning, and victory in the rubber by 3 matches to 2 was largely the result of the brilliance of R.E. Foster, Hayward, Tyldesley, and B.J.T. Bosanquet—who in this series introduced the googly to Test cricket—and the thorough captaincy and steady batting of Warner. The latter gave close attention to every phase of a match. Hardly a point escaped him, which was important on the perfect Australian wickets against such batsmen as Trumper, Hill, Duff and Noble.

A CELEBRATED SIDE

Warner's next visit to Australia was with his celebrated side of 1911-12. In the meantime he had lost heavily in South Africa, and Australia had regained the Ashes. England, in fact, were no longer champions. But Warner's team—F. R. Foster, Hobbs and Rhodes to the fore—beat Australia by four matches to one. Lord Harris believed them to be just about the best side he had ever seen, and it was sad that the tour should have been marred when the captain himself was struck down by a serious illness after making 151 against South Australia at Adelaide in his first and only innings of the tour. Although he began the season of 1912 by scoring three centuries within 10 days of each other at Lord's the effort took a lot out of him and in his own opinion he was never the same batsman again. With the 1914-18 War intervening, the last playing triumph that was left to him was to lead Middlesex to a glorious and thrilling victory in the County Championship in 1920. "It was not his batting but his skill as a captain that made his final season memorable", said Wisden for 1921. The decisive match with Surrey which gave Middlesex their ninth successsive victory was his last at Lord's and provided a moving finale. He had scored almost 30,000 runs in first-class cricket including 60 centuries. After his retirement his unfailing optimism and infectious enthusiasm were devoted to writing about the game or to its administration.

AS AN ADMINISTRATOR

From 1921 to 1934 he was Cricket Correspondent to the *Morning Post*; he became editor of the *Cricketer*, a paper in which he retained a close interest until his death; and he wrote more than a dozen books about the game he loved so well. At various periods, too, he was on the M.C.C. committee, and he was chairman of the Test Match Selection Committee in 1926, in 1931-32, and again from 1935-38. He returned to Australia as joint manager with R. C. N. Palairet of the M.C.C. team during the controversial tour of 1932-33 when body-line howling raised its ugly head. His tact, charm, and modesty were valuable assets then in dealing with an unpleasant situation, and his many services to cricket were recognized when he was knighted in 1937. Although in his middle sixties there was yet much energy and zeal left in him, and when war came again in 1939 he worked ceaselessly at Lord's to keep cricket alive, acting as assistant secretary of M.C.C. and providing splendid entertainment for a harassed public.

Perhaps his crowning moment came when, in May, 1950 he was nominated president of M.C.C. by the Duke of Edinburgh. It was a fitting tribute to a dedicated life. Yet there was still a final honour for the M.C.C. to bestow upon him when in May, 1961, he was made the first life vice-president in the history of the club.

Wherever cricket is played he was well known and greatly respected. The game ran always in his veins, and the thought of it kept him young in spirit. Indeed, the name of "Plum" Warner will always be affectionately imprinted upon the history of cricket.

He married in 1904 Agnes, daughter of the late Henry Blyth, of Portland Place, London. She died in 1955 and he is survived by two sons and a daughter of the marriage.

January 31, 1963.

Sir George Waters, for 20 years editor of *The Scotsman* and a member of the first Royal Commission on the Press, died at his home in Edinburgh on December 15, 1967. He was 87.

George Alexander Waters was born at Thurso on July 28, 1880, and was educated at Thurso Academy, George Watson's College, Edinburgh and Edinburgh University, where he obtained his M.A. with first class honours in English in 1902 and in the following year was a Vans Dunlop scholar in English poetry. From 1903 to 1904 he studied at Berlin University and at the Sorbonne in Paris. For a short period he served as a teacher but then became a sub-editor on the *Weekly Scotsman*. He was soon transferred to the editorial staff of *The Scotsman* and he spent the rest of his journalistic life on that newspaper. In 1908 he became a leader writer and reviewer. He was promoted to be chief assistant and deputy editor in 1919 and editor in 1924, holding that office for 20 years.

Waters was a man of broadminded sympathies. While he was primarily interested in Scottish affairs he also had a keen insight into foreign affairs with the result that *The Scotsman* was accepted as the outstanding spokesman for Scotland. His views on his own country were always listened to with respect by members of the Cabinet, from whichever political party it happened to come.

BETTER LOOKING PAGES

In his efforts to improve the technical side of newspaper production he had largely transformed the appearance of *The Scotsman* in the years before 1939. Its financial services were expanded; he vastly improved the appearance of the book page, and special articles on the arts were introduced. The reproduction of the pictures was developed enormously and his letters to the editor feature was a notable one. The shortage of newsprint made it essential that many of those features should be suspended in wartime but he lived long enough to see the contents of the paper restored to the high standard which he had himself established.

His appointment to be a member of the first Royal Commission on the Press in 1947 was received with general approval both in Scotland and in Fleet Street. Although by that time he was 66 he threw himself into his new task with great energy and enthusiasm. When the report was signed in June, 1949, he made one important reservation to it. While he accepted whole-heartedly the recommendation in favour of setting up a General Council of the Press on a voluntary basis, he was unable to agree that it would be strengthened by the inclusion of lay members, apart from an independent chairman. He believed that it would be given a better start and would realize more fully what was expected of it if the responsibility for order, decency and progress within the press was left to the sense of honour and duty of those who owned and conducted it.

Waters received the honorary degree of LL.D. from St. Andrews University in 1938 and the knighthood conferred on him in 1944 was hailed as a well-deserved tribute not only to the editor of *The Scotsman* but to the "quality" press as a whole. Two years later he was created a Chevalier of the Legion of Honour. He married in 1919 Mina, daughter of John Waters, a Thurso bank manager, and there was one daughter of the marriage.

December 18, 1967.

Norman E. Wates, chairman of Wates Limited, building and civil engineering contractors, died on July 21, 1969, in London at the age of 64.

In addition to being chairman of one of the largest family businesses in the construction industry, he played an active part in many organizations concerned with improving housing standards, and the technological advance of the industry. He was a founder member of the formative committee of the National Housebuilders' Registration Council as far back as 1935. In 1957 he became a member of the Central Housing Advisory Committee set up by the Ministry of Housing and Local Government. He was a member of the Parker Morris committee whose report in 1961 so strongly influenced housing standards. He was a member of the National Economic Development Committee for the building industry and was also on the urban renewal sub-committee.

Wates was born in 1905 when the housebuilding firm started by his father—Edward Wates—four years earlier was still relatively modest. He joined the family business in 1925. Wates very early showed his belief that building, the "Cinderella" of the big industries, could profit from modern methods of accountancy, management and quality control. In the 1930s he made the first of his many tours across the United States, studying their business and management techniques as well as building design and methods.

During the war the company's activities were directed towards the war effort and among other appointments he was an adviser to the Admiralty on specialist concrete structures. In the immediate postwar years while helping to develop the contracting side of the company he was able to implement his long-felt ideas on education. He anticipated the technological advances construction would take in the years to come. In 1947 he inaugurated the first indentured student scheme in the company.

Wates's recognition of the educational needs of the industry brought him in contact with the inaugural body which formed the London Business School. He was a foundation governor of the United Westminster Schools foundation, was a member of the council of the King's College Hospital medical school, and was elected to the court of governors of the London School of Economics in 1968.

In his private life he was an equally active man well-known for his skill and enthusiasm in ocean racing (he was Rear Commodore of the Royal Thames Yacht Club and a committee member of the Royal National Lifeboat Institution). He was co-founder, with his brothers, of the Wates Foundation, whose charitable aims embraced the arts and sciences.

In 1929 he married Miss Margaret Sidwell.

July 22, 1969.

A.T.L.Watkins, who was killed in a motor accident on July 31, 1965, was—under the name of Arthur Watkyn—one of those playwrights who devote their talents to the provision of acceptable, fundamentally good-natured drama. Invariably unpretentious but invariably skilful and fluent, his plays engaged the interest and affections of the West End theatre-goer, sometimes for considerable periods.

Arthur Thomas Levi Watkins was born in Aberystwyth on July 27, 1907, and educated at Tonbridge School. A classics scholarship took him to Christ Church, Oxford, where his first play, *Cavalier*, was produced by the Oxford Repertory Company in 1932. This was followed three years later by *Backward Boy* and in 1936 by *Muted Strings*, a wholeheartedly romantic study of Beethoven.

During the Second World War Watkins held an administrative post in the Home Office, relinquishing it in 1947 and becoming secretary to the British Board of Film Censors, a position he occupied for nine years, in 1948; he was instrumental in abolishing the "H Certificate" category for films and replacing it with the more inclusive "X Certificate". In 1957 he became vice-president, and in 1958 president, of the British Film Producers' Association.

Watkins's greatest successes in the theatre began with *For better, for worse ....* which reached the West End in 1952 and offered satisfying parts to several younger actors who have since attained some eminence. *Not in the Book*, which ran for 600 performances after its opening at the Criterion Theatre in April, 1958, proved to be his highwater mark. *The Geese are Getting Fat*, two years later, was agreeably diverting, and in 1962 *Out of Bounds* allowed Sir Michael Redgrave to please large audiences with an amusing romp.

If the dramatic revolution after 1956 left him unmoved—*Amber for Anna*, his last play, did not achieve a lengthy run—he was one of the type of technically expert, engagingly entertaining playwrights whom the theatre always needs, if only to provide the jam which adds sweetness to its bread and butter.

August 3, 1965.

Sir Alfred Watson, who died on March 1, 1967, in Beckenham, Kent, at the age of 92, was for many years the chief associate of J. A. Spender in the guidance of the *Westminster Gazette*, and in 1925 accepted the editorship of the *Statesman*, Calcutta, where his independence of judgment led to two attempts on his life, both falling just short of success, at the hands of Bengali terrorists.

Alfred Henry Watson was born in 1874 at Newcastle upon Tyne, the son of Aaron Watson (1850-1926) who was at different times editor of the *Newcastle Leader*, the *Shields Gazette* and the London *Echo*. After education at Rutherford College, Newcastle, Alfred entered on his journalistic career at the age of 16. He began a brief experience in the Press Gallery of the House of Commons when only 19. He became leader writer and special correspondent of his father's paper, the *Newcastle Leader*, in 1894, and in the following year was made its London correspondent. He joined the staff of the *Westminster Gazette* in 1902, and in the next 21 years filled successively the posts of news editor, general manager, managing editor, and chief leader writer. The "seagreen incorruptible" had in J.A. Spender, F.C. Gould, incomparable cartoonist, and Alfred Watson an outstanding combination of value to the then powerful Liberal Party. For two years Watson edited the *Weekly Westminster*.

TERRORISTS' THREAT

In 1925, soon after the *Westminster Gazette* entered upon its short term of life as a morning paper, Watson accepted the editorship of the Calcutta *Statesman*, and a little later became the Bengal Correspondent of *The Times*. A younger brother of his took up the managership, and the *Statesman* advanced in influence and prestige. Notwithstanding the economic slump of the period they were able to carry into effect a long-talked of project of simultaneous publication at Delhi. This brought about a greatly increased circulation in Northern India, and also early delivery of the journal to officialdom at Delhi and Simla, the two seats of the Central Government.

It was common knowledge that Watson's name was high on the black lists of the Bengali terrorists. He made light of the danger, and expressed to personal friends his pained regret that the police authorities urged him to carry a revolver for his own protection. The menace was never allowed to interfere either with unflinching expressions of editorial opinion or his cheerful good humour when once the office was left behind. In the first attempt on his life on August 5, 1932, a revolver was thrust through the window of his car and fired point blank at his face, but missed. His attacker, an engineering student, immediately committed suicide. The relief of his fellow countrymen at his escape found humorous expression in the legend that the unfound bullet was believed to be still lodged in the jungle of Watson's bushy upstanding head of hair.

A second attempt on Watson's life was made by a gang of youths on September 28, 1932. He was again in his car with his English secretary when at a traffic regulation point another car ran up alongside and crashed into the side of his saloon. There was a rapid burst of fire, shattering the glass windows round his head. He was wounded in both arms. Two of the assailants poisoned themselves, while the others escaped in a taxicab, and subsequently six men were brought to trial. Watson spent the next three weeks in hospital and was then peremptorily ordered by his doctors to "quit India". Early in the summer of that year he had been knighted, and thereupon entertained to dinner by leading citizens of Calcutta, both Indian and British. He had been chairman in India of the Empire Press Union and leader of the Rotary movement in that country.

REFORM MOVEMENT

Watson returned home to take an active part in the advocacy of the constitutional reforms embodied in the Government of India Act, 1935, by serving as vice-chairman of the Union of Britain and India, which was created to counter the opposition to the reforms organized by the India Defence League.

He had a long record of service to the National Liberal Club and in 1954 his eightieth birthday was celebrated by a dinner at the club under the chairmanship of Lord Samuel.

He married in 1903 Isa Morland, daughter of John Beck. She died in 1927 and he married secondly in 1940 Rose Ada Gros. She was his secretary who was with him when he was attacked in India and made vigorous attempts to protect him.

His younger brother Arthur was a former managing editor of the *Daily Telegraph.*

March 2, 1967.

Professor Sir James Anderson Scott Watson, C.B.E., M.C., former professor of Rural Economy at Oxford and Edinburgh, chief scientific and agricultural adviser to the Ministry of Agriculture, and Director-General of the National Agriculture Advisory Service 1948-54, died on August 5, 1966 at his home in London. He was 76.

James Anderson Scott Watson was born on November 16, 1889, the second of the six sons of William Watson of Downieken, Dundee. He left school at the age of 14 and went to work on his father's farm, but after a year of this went up to Edinburgh University to study agriculture. He graduated in 1908, having won nearly all the class medals at Edinburgh and a two-year post-graduate scholarship, which later enabled him to pursue his studies at the University of Berlin and at Iowa State College of Agriculture.

In 1910, Scott Watson was appointed an Assistant in the University Department of Agriculture at Edinburgh and the following year was made a lecturer. He served in France during the First World War until invalided home in 1918 after being awarded the M.C. He returned to Edinburgh University as lecturer and in 1922 was appointed professor of Agriculture and Rural Economy. During this period he wrote (with J. A. More) his *Agriculture—The Science and Practice of British Farming,* which remains an important text-book on the subject.

PROGRESSIVE FARMERS

In 1925, Scott Watson was appointed to succeed Sir William Somerville in the Sibthorpian Chair of Rural Economy at Oxford, which he held until 1944. From 1931-45 he combined with his other duties the editorship of the Journal of the Royal Agricultural Society, and in addition wrote a *History of the Royal Agricultural Society.* An easy fluent style and catholic interests, humane, technical and scientific, were shown in a number of books. During his Oxford period he was much engaged in lectures and conferences where the most intelligent and progressive farmers gathered together and no such educational and advisory services could have been more highly appreciated. Even in his more popular writings and addresses, Scott Watson preserved his intellectual integrity and his balanced views. The range and firmness of technical and scientific knowledge shown in his more academic and in his advisory work was very remarkable. But he was an omnivorous reader, and a prodigious worker, and his personal relations with agricultural scientists in all branches were such as opened to him the stores of their knowledge. His real genius was shown in his power of interpreting knowledge in the simplest terms which were appropriate, and in his powers of exposition and persuasion.

IN NORTH AMERICA

The Government decided in 1942 to create two new posts, namely, those of Agricultural Attaché to the Embassy in Washington and Agricultural Adviser to the British High Commissioner in Canada. Scott Watson was appointed to fill both positions. His practical knowledge and his understanding of rural problems enabled him to win the respect and affection of both farmers and their leaders in America. On his return in 1944, he was appointed Chief Education and Advisory Officer at the Ministry of Agriculture and had the task of inaugurating the National Agricultural Advisory Service. In 1948 he was appointed Chief Scientific and Agricultural Adviser to the Ministry of Agriculture and was also appointed to the new post of Director-General of the N.A.A.S. He retired in 1954. He was created a Knight Bachelor in the Birthday Honours in 1949, having previously been made a C.B.E. in 1946. He was president of the British Agricultural History Society, 1953, and a development commissioner in 1955-56.

Scott Watson was not highly successful as an administrator. He was too considerate of other views, too tender towards susceptibilities in his immediate environment, inclined to discount the more distant or indirect interest. The interests of British agriculture might have been better served, had he retained academic freedom and given fully, without administrative taint, of his knowledge and inspiration to the younger generation of technologists. But no man of his period gave better or more highly valuable services to British agriculture.

Scott Watson married, in 1914, Jeanie (who died in 1962), elder daughter of Provost Carmichael of Coldstream. They had one son (killed on active service) and three daughters.

August 8, 1966.

Sam Watson, veteran miners' leader and a former chairman of the Labour Party, died on May 7, 1967, at his home, Bede Rest, Durham, aged 69.

From humble beginnings in a cottage in Donkin's Row in the Durham village of Boldon Colliery, Watson rose to become an international figure but resisted all temptation to enter Parliament or move to London. He declared that his life's work was to serve the Durham minner.

He started work at the age of 14 at Boldon Colliery for 1s. 4d. a shift. To improve his education he joined the vicar's literary class and he also learnt at the bedside of his father, crippled by a pit accident.

At 20 he became secretary of Boldon miners' lodge and at 38 Durham miners elected him as an agent. Watson often described this as one of his greatest successes. It was to prove a stepping stone that led to opportunities of great influence and of service to his fellow men. For it was followed by his appointment as secretary of Durham area of the National Union of Mineworkers and it was in that role that he became nationally and internationally known.

Parliament was open to him with the prospect of a ministerial post in a Labour government. His reply was always a courteous refusal.

He never forgot that education had been one of the mainstays of progress of the Labour and trade union movement. After his retirement from the N.U.M. in 1963 he continued to give up his Sunday afternoons to carry on a tutorial class attended by a band of both young and mature men. Among those who have acknowledged the help which that class gave them in their earlier years is Norman Pentland, M.P. for Chester-le-Street.

For 22 years Watson was a member of the national executive of the Labour Party and in 1949 party chairman. He travelled widely, his favourite destination being Israel. He made many Israeli friends and in return Israel named a room in its new senate house "The Sam Watson Room".

Watson became a J.P., a director of North East Trading Estates, chairman of the Durham executive council of the National Health Service, and a member of the court of the University of Durham which conferred on him the honorary degree of Doctor of Civil Law.

Traveller, writer, and orator, he took part in many great occasions but there is no doubt which was the greatest event to him. It was the Big Meeting—the Durham miners' gala which he considered the greatest unorganized democratic demonstration in the world.

No one argued with him about that, nor questioned his own contribution to the change in character of the Big Meeting from being in its early days an indignant claim for the miners' rights to a joyous celebration of achievement. To take that further, one of Watson's most treasured documents was a statement of 27 improvements in the conditions of miners and their families—one for each of his years of service at Durham area union headquarters. Among them were the highest-ever wages, five-day week, pension schemes, modernization of colliery houses, and free pit-head baths.

After his retirement from the N.U.M., the coal board and the Electricity Council benefited from his part-time membership.

He is survived by his wife, son, and daughter.

May 8, 1967.

Dame Katherine C. Watt, the first Chief Nursing Officer at the Ministry of Health, died on November 1, 1963, in St. George's Hospital, where she had been a member of the Board of Governors for some years.

Dame Katherine Watt's quiet manner and soft voice hid a somewhat dynamic personality which with typical Scottish persistence she brought to bear in all she did. In guiding the build-up of the Civil Nursing Reserve, including the organization of the ambulance trains, her tact and judgment and service experience enabled her to carry the voluntary organizations with her—St. John's Ambulance Brigade, British Red Cross Society and W.V.S.—upon whom so much depended at that time.

As the first Chief Nursing Officer at the Ministry of Health her work was of a pioneering nature and she could be seen in and out of the senior officials' offices constantly putting over the nursing point of view. She was known and recognized by all the matrons in the country and her personal intervention on their behalf was paramount. She had a strong human side and will always be remembered for her kindly attitude and personal concern for nurses everywhere. Her work for other countries may be less well known but she was a great traveller and her influence abroad was immense. She sought out experienced nurses and persuaded them to go far afield to show what British nursing meant and to help to build up those countries' nursing services.

Katherine Christie Watt, second daughter of James Christie Watt of Glasgow, took her nursing training at the Western Infirmary, Glasgow, and served in the First World War, 1916-19, at home and abroad. She joined Princess Mary's Royal Air Force Nursing Service in 1919 and was Matron-in-Chief from 1930 to 1938.

She travelled abroad visiting hospitals from early 1938 until appointed Principal Matron for Emergency Bed Service, Ministry of Health, in June, 1939, when she helped to create the Civil Nursing Reserve. Her appointment as Chief Nursing Officer to the new Division of Nursing, Ministry of Health, in April, 1941, was the first of its kind and Dame Katherine left behind her a legacy of wise and balanced advice.

TRAVEL ABROAD

She retired from this post in 1948 and from then until 1950, as Chief Nursing Adviser to the Ministry, she travelled extensively and gave many countries abroad, not only throughout the Commonwealth, the benefit of her wide administrative experience. Her kindness and her quiet unfailing wit endeared her to people in many corners of the world.

Since her retirement from the Ministry of Health she had continuously given of her time and experience to the Royal Air Force Benevolent Fund, the Nation's Fund for Nurses, the Committee of the Princess Ts-Hai Memorial Hospital, Addis Ababa, the Lebanon Hospital for Mental Diseases, and many other causes.

She was made C.B.E. in 1935 and raised to D.B.E. 10 years later.

November 4, 1963.

Evelyn Waugh, the novelist, died at his home at Combe Florey on April 10, 1966. He was 62.

Waugh was essentially an artist in prose. In an age where care for the exact word, for the form of a sentence and for good grammar are all too rare, Waugh set himself from the first a high standard of writing. Whether he was engaged on his earlier works of unreal and high spirited satire, on one of his more serious books of later life, of a defence of religion or even some casual *pièce d'occasion* of a sharp letter to the press, one could always be certain that his conscience would require him to find for it the exact phrase. Though not himself a deep classical scholar he had a great reverence for the disciplinary virtues of the Latin language—of that which "had fought and conquered the centuries"—and felt that those who had "little Latin and less Greek" were likely to fail in piety towards the English language. He thought such disrespect for language almost the supreme sign of a failing culture.

DISTASTE

It was this disrespect which he found in the younger writers and which was the main cause of his distaste for them. He did not conceal his dislike of the movement within the Catholic Church for the substitution of a vernacular for the Latin liturgy, thinking that with the loss of Latin the Mass would be robbed of much of the sense of awe which it had held throughout the ages.

He himself professed to find this carefulness for the exact phrase, more clearly than in any other modern writer, in Monsignor Knox, whose biography he wrote and for whom his admiration was high, but Monsignor Knox expressed himself most naturally in parody or in translation. Waugh expressed himself most naturally in satire. He imposed upon himself a most strict economy of language. None of his books is long. He believed in saying what he had to say and then closing down. The same is true of his sentences. No long speeches are put into the mouths of his characters. They say what they have to say in a sentence or two. He had no ear for music and he imposed on himself the same discipline which he imposed on his charcters in his own descriptive passages. He had no belief in irrelevant padding to create an atmosphere. He never told the reader anything that was not strictly necessary for the understanding of his story. There were no literary allusions or cultural references. His own opinions were only discoverable through his mockery of the follies of his characters.

IN HIS BLOOD

The second son of Arthur Waugh, sometime chairman of the publishing firm of Chapman and Hall, and younger brother of Alec Waugh, the novelist, Evelyn Arthur St. John Waugh was born on October 28, 1903 and educated at Lancing and Hertford College, Oxford. Literature was in his blood and from the time of his coming down from Oxford he gave himself to writing. His first book, a study of Rossetti, appeared in 1928, and this was followed shortly after in the same year by his first novel, *Decline and Fall.* It is as a novelist that he is mainly remembered.

In his earliest books—*Decline and Fall* and *Vile Bodies*—he appeared before the public as the chronicler and satirist of the Bright Young People of society's life, holding up to scorn with exquisite wit the futility of their lives. His second period—the period of *Black Mischief, A Handful of Dust* and *Scoop*—was a period of transition. Of the characters in those books some were what might be called two-dimensional characters, figures of farce, too unreal to arouse condemnation or sympathy, but there were also in those books characters, like Tony Last in *A Handful of Dust,* who were more nearly real people, demanding real moral judgments. With *Brideshead Revisited,* published in 1945, we enter on Waugh's third period. He came of a strongly clerical family, and even in his earlier works, where he appeared superficially to be a mere chronicler of futility, it was possible to trace an interest in, and a respect for, religion—in, for instance, the character of Father Rothschild in *Vile Bodies.*

ROMAN CATHOLIC

In 1930 Waugh was received into the Roman Catholic Church by Father Martin D'Arcy. His reception did not immediately make any dramatic difference to his writing, but in 1935 as an act of friendship to Father D'Arcy, who was then the Master of Campion Hall at Oxford, he wrote the life of Edmund Campion. It won him the Hawthornden Prize in 1936. The intimate study of the Elizabethan martyr marked a turning point in his life. It deepened his religious faith and henceforward religion was unquestioningly his outstanding interest, and the form which his religious faith took gave him an ever increasing antipathy to the social, political and artistic fashions and furniture of the modern world, which were, he thought, leading it to inevitable catastrophe. After having served in the Second World War first in the Royal Marines and afterwards in the Royal Horse Guards and having taken part in the Battle of Crete, he published immediately after the war *Brideshead Revisited.* This is a study of an old aristocratic Catholic family and the reaction of the members of that family to their religion. It is the first of what may be called Waugh's three-dimensional novels—novels in which we are presented with characters in all of whom we are asked to believe as real people. The same demand was made in his next two full-length books, *Helena,* a study of the Finding of the True Cross, by the Emperor Constantine's mother, Helena, and his three-volume war-time novel, *Men at Arms* (which won the James Tait Black Prize) and *Officers and Gentlemen.* Meanwhile he had by no means lost his gift for extravagance and satire, as was shown in *The Loved One* and in *Scott-King's Modern Europe* and in *The Ordeal of Gilbert Pinfold* he showed a devastating capacity for self-portraiture, offering a picture of himself which betrayed a full awareness of those faults of temper and snobbery of which his critics often accused him.

For many years he had enjoyed an intimate friendship with Monsignor Ronald Knox, for whom both as a man and as a writer he had a deep reverence, considering him the first prose-writer of our time. Monsignor Knox made Waugh his literary executor, and on his death in 1957 Waugh wrote his biography. It was of all his works that by which he set the highest store, and it was undoubtedly a deep disappointment to him when some readers, freely admitting the book's literary greatness, nevertheless complained that the portrait of Ronald Knox was not wholly attractive and that Waugh had transferred unjustly to Ronald Knox something of his own sourness towards life.

In 1964 appeared the first volume of his autobiography, written with great distinction and entitled *A Little Learning.* It carried his life up to the end of his Oxford career. His book *The Loved One* was recently filmed.

LIKED PRIVACY

As a young man Waugh enjoyed the attractions of London society, in which he was a prominent figure, but with middle age and after the war he came increasingly to dislike the noise and bustle of town life. He developed eccentric habits to guard his privacy, such as a refusal to speak on the telephone or a notice on his garden gates "No Admission On Business", and it was increasingly difficult to get him to move from his houses in the West Country—first at Stinchcombe, in Gloucestershire, and afterwards at Combe Florey, near Taunton, in Somerset—except to travel on a ship to some place outside Europe, which he did regularly in the early months of every year to avoid the rigours of the English winter. He did not care for country pursuits nor mix much with his neighbours. Yet the picture of him as a recluse or a misanthropist would be unjust. Though continually complaining of boredom and disliking any crush of acquaintances he remained deeply devoted to a select circle of friends, to whom he was always the most generous and amusing of hosts.

His first marriage in 1928 to the Hon. Evelyn Gardner, fourth daughter of the first and last Baron Burghclere, was dissolved by divorce in 1930 and he married secondly in 1937 Laura, the daughter of the Hon. Aubrey Herbert, by whom he had three sons and three daughters.

April 11, 1966.

Naunton Wayne, the actor and entertainer who died in hospital at Tolworth, Surrey, on November 17, 1970, was an artist who knew exactly both the limitations of his talents and the areas of strength within them. He was 69.

From revue—he was a skilled and ingratiating compere—to innumerable films and West End plays all he did was effective, precisely calculated and usually good-humouredly funny. At the same time all his work had a distinct personality of its own: he presented an intricate series of variations on the theme of the comic Englishman in whom the English are always eager to recognize themselves. Naunton Wayne was not simply the vacuous, golden-hearted aristocrat who, like Bertie Wooster, succeeds in extricating himself from perilous situations.

AGAINST THE WORLD

He was, each of his successes assured us, a man battling, with intense mental activity, against a world of almost insoluble problems; that most of them were trivial, and that conversational irrelevancies attracted him more than conversational points, was an indication not of the silliness but of the complexity of his world. The high-breeding could become petulant when another world collided with his own.

Henry Wayne Davies (he changed his name by deed poll in 1933) was the son of a solicitor, born in Llanwonno, Glamorganshire, on June 22, 1901. He was educated at Clifton College and began his career in 1920 as a member of a concert party on Barry Island. Ten years as an entertainer in similar companies enabled him to develop an easy, nonchalant way of winning an audience's sympathy and took him, as a revue compere, to London. He made his first appearance at the Victoria Palace in 1928 as an entertainer and he also appeared at the Palladium, the Coliseum, and the Holborn Empire. For nearly a year he compered the non-stop variety at the London Pavilion.

His first big success came in *1066 and All That,* the musical adaptation of Sellers and Yeatman's perversion of schoolbook English history in which it was Naunton Wayne's function, performed with entire ease and an apparent delight in punning, to give a semblance of continuity to a series of detached sketches.

Never without a role, and always capable of playing it effectively, Wayne found himself drawn more and more into the straight theatre and into a memorable film partnership with the late Basil Radford, usually opposing a quick-witted oneupmanship to his partner's slower, deliberately elephantine obstinacy. In *The Lady Vanishes* they were unforgettably involved in the murderous skullduggeries of Central European politics while hastening across the continent to reach Manchester in time for a test match. In *Dead of Night* they provided a light-hearted interlude in an anthology of ghost stories, sinking to the moral abyss in which, for the sake of love, they cheated each other at golf.

In *Arsenic and Old Lace,* at the Strand in 1942, Wayne occupied the role of the journalist nephew who discovers his old-world aunts to be well-intentioned mass murderers, achieving a performance in which horror and bewilderment were expressed within a natural sang-froid. At the end of a run of nearly 1,300 performances, he scored another success in Benn Levy's *Clutterbuck,* playing for the only time against instead of with Basil Radford as the intellectual novelist baffled and defeated by Radford's invincible obtuseness.

The range of his abilities and the validity of the national type in which he specialized was demonstrated by his appearance as Mr. Sedley, in the musical version of *Vanity Fair* seen in 1962. In 1964, in William Douglas Home's *The Reluctant Peer,* he played the Earl of Lister during the play's first year and then took over the role of Beecham, the butler. He was in *Justice is a Woman* at the Vaudeville in 1966 and *Oh Clarence*! at the Lyric in 1968.

He continued from time to time to appear in cabaret, and performed frequently on television and radio. The passage of time did nothing to slow his quick-wittedness or to remove the mischievous quality by which the observant could sense that his playing was often a joke at the expense of what we like to regard as national characteristics.

November 18, 1970.

Helene Weber, one of the German pioneer women politicians, died on July 25, 1962, in a Bonn hospital, at the age of 81.

Devoting her life to Roman Catholic social work and the political and social emancipation of women, Frau Weber was able, after the setting up of the Federal Republic, to play an influential role within the Christian Democrat Party, whom she represented in the Bundestag continuously up to the time of her death, in getting legislation passed for the equal status of women in west Germany.

Frau Weber, who was born in Wuppertal-Elberfeld, North Rhine-Westphalia, spent five years teaching in a state primary school before studying history at Bonn and Grenoble Universities. She was already busy in social work, however, and in 1916 was given charge of the newly founded school of social welfare of the German Catholic Women's Federation in Cologne. In 1919 she joined the Prussian Ministry of Social Welfare, specializing in youth questions and social education. From 1924 until 1933 she also represented the Zentrum Party in the Reichstag. When the Nazis came to power she was immediately dismissed from the Ministry, but carried on with social work in a private sphere.

After the Second World War Frau Weber

joined in efforts to build up a Catholic women's organization again and became a member of the newly founded Christian Democrat Party. In 1946 she was elected to the North Rhine-Westphalian Landtag, then in the British occupation zone. In the Bundestag she became chairman of the women's committee and, because of her age and experience, quickly became an influential figure within Christian Democrat circles. Often in the Bundestag she was to be seen at the beginning of the morning session greeting and talking animatedly to Dr. Adenauer.

On her seventy-fifth birthday Frau Weber received the Grosse Bundesverdienstkreuz, the highest civil award in west Germany, and a citation from Pope Pius XII praising her life-long social work. She was also a former president of the German Catholic Women's Federation and of the German Catholic Social Workers Association.

July 27, 1962.

Professor Sir Charles Webster, K.C.M.G., Stevenson Professor of International History, London School of Economics, from 1932 to 1953 and since the latter year Professor Emeritus, died on August 21, 1961, in a London hospital. He was 75.

Charles Kingsley Webster was born on April 25, 1886, the son of Daniel Webster, of Freshfield, Liverpool. He was educated at Merchant Taylors' School, Crosby, before going to King's College, Cambridge, as a scholar in 1904. At the time of his election to a Fellowship in 1909 he had already decided to make the study of nineteenth-century British foreign policy his life work, and to produce a definitive history of it for the period from 1815 to 1878. This great project was never completed, for the wars and politics of the twentieth century were soon to provide distractions, but his masterly volumes on the foreign policy of Castlereagh and Palmerston were a substantial contribution. He returned to his home town as Professor of Modern History at Liverpool University in 1914 and the year following married Nora Violet, daughter of R. P. Harvey, of Florence.

He served as a subaltern in the R.A.S.C. in England and France from 1915 to 1917, and as a member of the General Staff at the War Office in 1917-18. He then joined the team of historians which was preparing material for the use of the peace negotiators, and was secretary of the Military Section of the British delegation to the Paris peace conference in 1918-19. A brochure which he wrote on the Congress of Vienna was circulated in the hope that it would assist the delegates; and although President Wilson impatiently rejected such historical aids Webster did not lose his belief in the contribution that the historian can make to contemporary history.

A man of great vitality and enthusiasm, he found himself after the war one of the few established academic specialists in international affairs, a field of study which was only just coming into its own in the British universities. One side of his activity during the next two decades was to popularize these studies in the universities and the country at large by his robust and effective speaking, and he was an active supporter of the Royal Institute of International Affairs from its foundation. As a writer, however, he never sought to be a popularizer of history; his volumes on nineteenth-century diplomacy are models of austere professional competence which have a somewhat limited appeal outside academic circles but have done a great deal to establish high standards within them.

He was Wilson Professor of International Politics at Aberystwyth from 1922 to 1932, and the unusually generous terms of appointment of this chair gave full scope to his interests, for the Professor was allowed and indeed encouraged to travel widely. In 1926 he visited the University of Vienna as Ausserordentlich Professor and lectured at the Nobel Institute in Oslo; in 1927 he lectured on the Concert of Europe at the University of Calcutta. From 1928 to 1932 he held a part-time appointment as Professor of History at Harvard University. His reputation was established by his first important book, *The Foreign Policy of Castlereagh, 1815–1822* (1925), which was followed by *The Foreign Policy of Castlereagh, 1812-1815* in 1931. Another product of his Aberystwyth-Harvard period was a study of League of Nations machinery, written in conjunction with Mr. Sidney Herbert, *The League of Nations in Theory and Practice* (1933).

THE U.N. CHARTER

Then in 1932 he joined the staff of the London School of Economics in the newly created Stevenson Chair of International History, an appointment which he held until his retirement. This was a "teaching" chair parallel to the "research" chair held by Dr. A. J. Toynbee. He made a great impact on the university as a lecturer and director of research in modern diplomatic history, and his study of Palmerston's foreign policy was well advanced when it was interrupted by the Second World War.

It was, however, with the taking over of the Chatham House Foreign Research Service (to which he had returned) by the Foreign Office as its research department that his most characteristic contribution to British foreign policy began. He became the deputy director of the new organization and then was transferred later in 1943 to the Reconstruction Department, where he worked very closely with Gladwyn Jebb; he and Jebb were jointly responsible for the greater part of the British contribution to the drafting of the United Nations Charter. In July, 1944, he was a delegate to the Dumbarton Oaks Conference, and from April to June, 1945, one of the senior advisers to the United Kingdom Delegation to the United Nations Conference at San Francisco. He was frequently the British spokesman in the committee which devised the security chapters of the Charter. His previous acquaintance with the work of the League of Nations was of the greatest value to the British Government in avoiding the pitfalls into which the drafters of the Covenant had fallen; to him as much as to anyone can go the credit for producing a Charter which, whatever its defects, had marked advantages over its predecessor. He wrote the *Commentary on the United Nations Charter*, which was published by the Foreign Office as a White Paper.

Later, from September, 1945, to April, 1946, he was Special Adviser to the Minister of State on United Nations Affairs, with the particular duty of advising on the work of the Preparatory Commission and the Executive Committee of the new United Nations Organization. In 1946 he was created a K.C.M.G.

ACADEMIC DON

Webster was by this stage a very eminent figure in academic life. A fellow of the British Academy since 1930, he was its president from 1950 to 1954, and Foreign Secretary of the Academy from 1955 to 1958. He returned to his chair and to historical study after the war, and published *The Foreign Policy of Palmerston, 1830-41*, in two volumes in 1951. The work was perhaps too long to suit some modern tastes in historical writing, but it showed all his earlier mastery of the source material and the diplomatic complexities of the Metternich era. Then after his retirement in 1953 he was able to give his full time for the next six years to the writing, in conjunction with Dr. Noble Frankland, of the official history of the British bomber offensive in World War II.

He was above all a great academic don. His exceptionally long professorial life, his fund of self-confident reminiscence, his fine presence and combative temperament, were familiar to students and colleagues for nearly 50 years. Many thought him to be too much of an optimist about the future of the world. He had on the professional side a keen interest in the technique of historical research, and was fond of expounding scholarly ingenuities in his own field, which he had himself done much to devise. Always forceful and ready to engage in argument, he had no hard feelings for those who stood up to him. Above all, perhaps, his career is notable for the consistency with which he followed an academic path largely of his own choice and invention in one of the Cinderella subjects of pre-1914 Cambridge.

August 23, 1961.

Tom Webster, a sporting cartoonist of great vitality, fertility and resource, died on June 20, 1962, at his London home. He was 71.

It was characteristic of Webster's art that it aroused the interest of people not greatly interested in sport at all or highly skilled in judging its finer points; for he had a far-seeing sense of character which enabled him to seize on droll aspects of personality or demeanour and bring out their inherent fun.

Gilbert Tom Webster was born at Bilston, Staffordshire, on July 17, 1890, and was educated at Wolverhampton. He began to draw at an early age, and when only 13 or 14 had already an uncommon facility with the pencil. But never at any time did he have any formal art training. Before he was 20 he won a prize offered by the *Birmingham Weekly Post* for a humorous drawing; and this helped him to secure a post as cartoonist to the *Brmingham Sports Argus*, with which paper he remained for some four years. Just before the First World War he spent a short time as political cartoonist on the *Daily Citizen*. In the war itself he served from start to finish with the Royal Fusiliers.

In 1919 Webster began to build his wide national reputation when he was appointed sports cartoonist to the *Daily Mail*. His "spiky" line, his extreme facility in catching and registering personal idiosyncrasies, the unexpected turns he gave to sporting situations, his apt and acid verbal commentaries, all combined to give him, within a very short space of time, an almost unexampled popularity. He soon acquired an intimate knowledge of the sporting world of London and its environs, and dealt with football, cricket, racing, golf, boxing, tennis, athletics, and billiards.

Webster visited America in August, 1920. In 1924 he played a considerable part in arranging the revue *Cartoons* at the Criterion Theatre. During the announcement of the general election results in 1929 a great screen was erected in Trafalgar Square, and on it Webster cartoons were built up and projected. In 1936 he was one of the artists commissioned to decorate the Queen Mary, and for the gymnasium of that ship he evolved an extraordinary sporting panorama in oils thinly laid on—this being his first experiment in colour. It comprised 14 panels showing some of the most prominent personages in the sporting world.

He issued year after year *Tom Webster's Annual*, which contained some of his best production of the 12 months. He liked to meet and draw robust characters; and he would rapidly seize on any peculiarity (such as a bowler's delivery) or any point relating to training, draw out the inwardness of it, and extract from it the utmost fun. It was he who made a national joke of the famous racehorse Tishy, which was reputed to cross its forelegs when running.

He retired from the *Daily Mail* in 1940. Four years later he came out of retirement to join Kemsley Newspapers, moving to the *News Chronicle* in 1953, and retiring finally in 1956.

Webster was a wit not only in his work but in his private life. He quickly saw through pretentiousness and sham; his sense of comedy was lively and alert.

In September, 1929, in New York, Webster married Mae Flynn. The marriage was dissolved in 1933. In 1935 he married Ida Michael, by whom he had one son and two daughters.

June 22, 1962.

Josiah Wedgwood, one of the outstanding master potters of the twentieth century, died on May 5, 1968, at the age of 68, less than five months after retiring as chairman of the Stoke-on-Trent pottery firm of Josiah Wedgwood Ltd. After his retirement as chairman, he accepted the specially created post of honorary Life President of Wedgwoods.

Wedgwood, the second son of the first Lord Wedgwood, was born on October 20, 1899, and educated at Bedales School and London University. From 1922 to 1926 he was first Secretary, then Director of the Rural Industries Bureau.

He first joined the family firm in 1928 as company secretary at the original works in Etruria and was later to plan and direct the move to the present works in Barlaston which are now one of the largest pottery factories in the world. From 1930 to 1961 he was managing director and he held the post as chairman from 1947 until the end of 1967.

Wedgwood was vice-chairman of the British Pottery Manufacturers' Federation from 1942 to 1945, and a director of the Bank of England from 1942 to 1946. In 1949 he was elected a member of the Monopolies and Restrictive Practices Commission on which he served until 1953.

Always keenly interested in art and design, he commissioned many outside artists to work for Wedgwood, among them Arnold Machin and Richard Guyatt. From 1948 to 1949 he was chairman of the Advisory Council of the Royal College of Art and he was one of the original members of the Council of Industrial Design. In 1929 he published *The Economics of Inheritance*.

May 6, 1968.

Dr. Kurt Weigelt, who organized the revival of the German Lufthansa after the Second World War, died on August 4, 1968. He was 84. Weigelt helped as a financial expert to set up the original Lufthansa and was a board member from 1925 until the end of the war in 1945, when it temporarily ceased to exist. He retired in 1960.

Weigelt, who came from an old Berlin family, passed the "Abitur" (higher school-leaving examination) in 1904 at the Graue Kloster Gymnasium in Berlin. In 1912, after a preparatory juridical voluntary period, he passed the Assessors' Examination. He studied law and political economy; his Doctors' Examination (Jena, 1909) dealt, in both subjects, with the system of tariff agreements which was new at that time.

During his time as a junior barrister, Weigelt was appointed by Colonial Minister Dernburg to a board made up of five members, whose task was to make the preparations for the systemization of the rights of natives, for the Imperial Colonial Office.

Following study trips to Egypt (proposals for the establishment of a cooperative society), Tripolitania, Cyrenaika, Syria, Palestine and Asia Minor (partly working for German newspapers), Weigelt was employed by the Deutsche Bank in 1913, which sent him to America. After negotiations lasting several months, he succeeded in restoring the Lehigh Coke Co. in South Bethlehem. Upon his return, he became assistant to Carl Helfferich—later the Imperial Minister of Finance—in his well-known negotiations concerning Central Africa.

After a short expedition to Turkey on behalf of the Admiralty, he took over the organization of the supplying of rubber, oils and fats, under Walter Rathenau (Military Raw Materials Department). He was head of this department until his appointment to the Executive Board of the Deutsche Petroleum AG in 1918. In this position, and, at the same time, as deputy director of the Deutsche Bank, he took an authoritative part in the negotiations for the sale of all German petroleum concerns abroad and also the sale of the German railways in the Near East, which he successfully concluded in 1927.

During the years directly after the First World War, Weigelt commenced his important activities for German civil aviation. As member of the executive board of the Deutsche Petroleum AG, and later, upon being appointed to the executive board of the Deutsche Bank, he was concerned in establishing the Deruluft airline of the Deutsche Aerolloyd, in the increasing of the capital of the SCADTA (Columbia) and, in particular, in the establishment of the old Lufthansa, German Airlines.

In the aviation committee of the International Chamber of Commerce in Paris, of which he was chairman for 10 years, he was able to represent German interests. As a direct continuation of this capacity immediately after the Second World War, he took care of the preservation of the remains of the old Lufthansa.

August 6, 1968.

Victor Weisz—"Vicky"—one of the foremost newspaper cartoonists, died on February 23, 1966, at his home in London at the age of 52.

Vicky was a "foreigner" with an English sense of fun. He knew the worlds of Lewis Carroll and A.A.Milne as well as he knew the policies of the Left Wing Socialists with whom he was so much in sympathy.

In spite of the many protests received from outraged readers—"acidic" was a familiar epithet—he was not unkind. Unlike Sir David Low, Vicky was not a great draughtsman, but his qualities were perfectly suited to his ideas—in which he was enviably fecund. It was not uncommon for him to produce two major drawings in one day.

Though perhaps not a very profound thinker, Vicky knew his mind and was unshaken in his beliefs; so much so that he was able to react and comment upon the changing political scene with remarkable speed and, given his point of view, sharp precision.

In spite of the fervent propagation of his beliefs, and the controversial "straight" cartoons of Topolski-like refugees and starving children, he will probably be best remembered for his transformation of Harold Macmillan into the hyperactive "Supermac"—a character based with heavy irony on the American cartoon strip character "Superman".

LEFT GERMANY

Vicky was born in Berlin of Hungarian parents on April 25, 1913. He worked for the Berliner's *12 Uhr Blatt* and published his first anti-Hitler cartoon in 1928. When the Nazis came to power, Vicky left Germany and went to England. When he arrived in 1935, he knew of only three British politicians—Chamberlain, Churchill and

Baldwin—but with intensive research he became well-equipped to join the *News Chronicle* in 1941. After 14 years he left, when that newspaper refused to print a biting cartoon on Kenya. He later joined the *Daily Mirror* and in 1958 Lord Beaverbrook persuaded him to become the *Evening Standard* cartoonist; he kept the complete political freedom of expression he had demanded all his life, and soon created "Supermac" with sprouting wings.

Since 1954 he had also worked regularly for the *New Statesman*. He exhibited paintings at the Lefevre Galleries and the Modern Art Gallery.

A lifelong socialist, Vicky never took out a Labour Party card. It would have impeded his freedom of criticism, he once said. His work, as he himself admitted, was probably best when in opposition to the government. But even after the Labour Party came to power in 1964, Vicky's unabating curiosity about politicians ensured a continuing sharp edge to his drawings.

February 24, 1966.

Harry Welchman, perhaps the most popular musical comedy hero on the London stage in the years between the wars, died at Penzance on January 3, 1966, at the age of 79.

The Desert Song, The Student Prince, The New Moon, The Maid of the Mountains, The Vagabond King, and the other tuneful high romantic shows of his time—he had played and sung in them all. Tall and handsome with a charming speaking and singing voice, Welchman was also a vigorous athlete; he played, as he said himself, "all games" and as a schoolboy had a place in the Somerset County hockey team.

Born at Barnstaple on February 24, 1886, the son of Colonel Welchman, Bengal Cavalry, he was educated at Weston-super-Mare and went straight from school to make his first appearance on the stage in a musical comedy in which Ada Reeve was touring. His great chance came at Christmas, 1906, while playing in pantomine. He was noticed by Robert Courtneidge, father of Cicely Courtneidge, to whom so many young players of that generation owed so much. Under his management Welchman played in many notable successes, including *Tom Jones, The Arcadians, The Mousmé. The Pearl Girl,* and *The Cinema Star*. The 1914-18 War interrupted his stage career but after demobilization from the Royal Artillery he appeared under Sir Charles Cochran's management with Alice Delysia in the production of *Afgar* at the London Pavilion. In 1921 he went to Daly's Theatre, where he registered two notable successes as the Grand Duke in *Sybil* and as Colonel Belovar in *The Lady of the Rose*, which contained a famous duet in which Welchman tried without success to storm the affections of the heroine, played by Phyllis Dare.

A season of management at the Adelphi was followed by perhaps the greatest of all Welchman's successes, his apperance as the Red Shadow in *The Desert Song*, which ran for more than 400 performances at Drury Lane. The part was a double one, for Welchman alternated between the quixotic leader of the Riff Irregulars and the apparently weak-willed son of the Army colonel who is trying to capture the Red Shadow. He was back at Drury Lane in 1929 to sing in *The New Moon*. Other successes like *Silver Wings* and *Viktoria and her Hussar* were followed by a provincial tour as Captain Hook in *Peter Pan*, a revival of *The Desert Song* at the Coliseum and a picturesque performance as Francois Villon in *The Vagabond King*.

At Christmas, 1946, and again a year later, Welchman gave a vigorous performance of Long John Silver in *Treasure Island*. He appeared in the film of *The Maid of the Mountains,* but although his work was always polished and professional he made no special reputation on the screen.

In 1947 he bought four cottages in Cornwall and, equipped with a seven pound hammer and a chisel, set about making himself a comfortable home. He insisted he was not thinking of retiring, and as late as 1959, at the age of 73, he was back on the boards in the role of Lord Mortlake in John Osborne's play *The World of Paul Slickey*. In 1960 the B.B.C. chose him as the subject for one of its *This is Your Life* television programmes.

He was twice married, first to Jean Challenor and, after their marriage was dissolved, to Sylvia Forde.

January 4, 1966.

Sumner Welles, United States Under-Secretary of State from 1937 to 1943, died on September 24, 1961, at the age of 68.

As a professional diplomatist, as a supporter and colleague of the late President Roosevelt, and as an exponent first of American foreign policy and later of the aims of the Allied Powers during the first four years of the Second World War Welles made a reputation which neither his lack of a political following nor his enforced resignation from the State Department in 1943 was able to affect. Deprived of office he used his freedom for positive ends. He continued to plead with the United States and with the rest of the world for the application of those qualities of reason, cooperation, and conciliation in dealings between Governments which had been his guide in his official life.

Welles, who was born in New York on October 14, 1892, came from the same social group that produced Franklin Roosevelt, and the two men had an early connexion when Welles, as a boy of 13, was a page at Roosevelt's wedding. After Groton and Harvard, Welles entered the service of the State Department in 1915 as secretary to the Embassy in Tokyo. Two years later he went to Buenos Aires, and in 1920 he returned to Washington as assistant chief of the Latin American affairs division of the State Department. A year later, when he was 28, he became head of the division, the youngest man to hold the post in the history of the department.

In 1922 he left this position, but with his interests now fixed on Latin American affairs—even before he went to Japan he had expressed a preference for work in South America—he continued to serve the State Department in various ways. He was commissioner to the Dominican Republic in 1922 and he acted as the personal representative of President Coolidge when he offered mediation in the Honduras revolution of 1925. In 1929 he made another official visit to the Dominican Republic. By now, however, he had become a critic of the official American attitude to its neigbours in the south, and he published *Naboth's Vineyard—Eighty Years of Dominican History*. It was not only a history but a call for a more liberal approach to the other Americas. Here he was presenting in outline the conception of relations in the Western Hemisphere which, backed by President Roosevelt, became known after 1933 as the Good Neighbour policy.

Welles did much to secure the nomination of Roosevelt as Democratic candidate for the Presidency at the party convention in Chicago in 1932. He was a party man of a quieter kind, and his appearances at conventions were correct but slightly self-conscious. But he was a Democrat of the most effective quality in his support of Roosevelt, and he was responsible in the main for shaping the plank on foreign policy which the Democrats offered in their platform of 1932.

Early in the first term of Roosevelt's presidency Welles was made an Assistant Secretary of State. Cordell Hull had already been appointed Secretary of State, and for the next 10 years the names of Cordell Hull and Sumner Welles were linked—though not always in agreement—whenever United States foreign policy was discussed.

CLOSE TO PRESIDENT

In 1937 Welles was promoted from Assistant to Under-Secretary of State, and henceforth, during Cordell Hull's periods of illness, he acted as Secretary of State. It was a duty that he readily undertook. He was close to the President; he was an organizer; and he had his own ideas of the part that the United States should take in world affairs. With the encroachments of Hitler in Europe as a sombre inspiration Welles broadened his diplomatic view, not only for the preservation of his Latin American policy but, as he saw so clearly, for the ultimate security of the United States. In December, 1938, as Acting Secretary of State, he spoke out against the Nazis' treatment of the Jews; and in April, 1939, at the Founder's Day celebrations at the University of Virginia, of which Thomas Jefferson was the "father", he asked, with an eye on events in Europe: "Would Jefferson maintain, as do some undoubtedly sincere persons in our own country, that the ever more rapid spread by conquest and by violence of such doctrines of persecution and of tyranny over the face of the earth can leave unendangered our own liberties which he proclaimed?"

In this, as in other speeches, Welles could be taken to be speaking as much for Roosevelt as for himself; and when the President decided, soon after the outbreak of war in 1939, to send a representative to Europe on a fact-finding mission it was no surprise that he chose Welles for the task. "This forlorn hope", as Welles later described it, was an attempt to discover on behalf of the President whether there remained any possibility of establishing a just and permanent peace. It was bound to cause speculation and some false hopes, and it needed a diplomatist of Welles's balance to save it from doing harm. But from his meetings with Chamberlain, Daladier, Hitler, and Mussolini in February and March, 1940, he took back the information that the President then needed.

THE ATLANTIC CHARTER

Eighteen months later Welles accompanied Roosevelt in his meetings with Mr. Churchill which produced the Atlantic Charter and from this time until his resignation in 1943 he was concerned with the essence of American policy. There had been recurring rumours that Cordell Hull differed from Welles on policy, though from the public expressions of the two men it was difficult to see where these differences could lie. Other reports—and they were probably nearer the truth—had it that there was a clash of personality between them. Supporters of Hull said that Welles was a difficult subordinate; critics of Hull said that while the Secretary of State had the power, it was the Under-Secretary who had the ideas.

Hull's version of events was published in 1948 in his memoirs. He recorded there that before going to the Quebec conference in 1943 the President called in Welles and requested his resignation. He said he and the President had discussed "the Welles problem" and were in agreement that he must resign. The then Secretary complained that his deputy had a readiness to make major decisions from time to time without consulting his chief. He also wrote with some bitterness that Welles visited the President without the Secretary's knowledge.

In the end, on September 25, 1943, after nearly a month of speculation and doubt, Roosevelt announced that he had regretfully accepted Welles's resignation and that Mr. Edward Stettinius, the former Lend-Lease administrator, would succeed him. It was announced on behalf of Welles that he had wished to resign on account of his wife's health. Though Welles himself needed no face-saver, this was one, and it convinced nobody. Roosevelt, it was believed, could not ignore Cordell Hull's political following in the South when it came to a choice between the two men. Thus he had to part with a loyal colleague and a public servant of the highest ability.

This was the end of Welles's official career. In his retirement he contributed regularly for a number of years to the American press through a syndicate and wrote several books.

Welles was three times married.

September 25, 1961.

Bombardier Billy Wells, who was the British heavyweight boxing champion from 1911 to 1919, died at his home in Ealing on June 11, 1967, at the age of 79.

The measure of the impact which Wells had upon professional boxing can be gauged from the fact that his reputation survived the passing of the years. "Beautiful Billy" was an idol of the British sporting public during his active career, which ended in 1925, but as long after as 1966 he was the guest of honour of the National Sporting Club.

Wells started boxing when serving with the Army and he beat his first five professional opponents inside the distance. In 1911 he won the British title by knocking out Iron Hague and he did not lose the championship until Joe Beckett beat him in five rounds in 1919.

He had the longest reign as British heavyweight champion until his record was beaten by the present holder, Henry Cooper, who defends the title at Wolverhampton this evening. Internationally Wells often failed to live up to expectation and twice he was knocked out by Georges Carpentier, of France.

On paper the record of Wells is none too impressive. But the public, though knowing in their hearts that he could not take a really hard punch, persisted in their belief in a man who lacked the temperament for the big occasion. He remained "the ring's Henry Irving who rarely made us laugh but frequently made us sob", as a contemporary wrote.

Technically he fulfilled all the ideas then held of a classic stylist of the ring. His straight left was like a rapier, his right could land with shattering force and his upright stance and marvellous physique brought women in evening gowns to a boxing match for the first time. They came again and again because Wells was always a dramatic figure whether in victory or defeat.

If Wells had fought in the days of television interviews he would have been an even greater national hero. For the looks of a matinée idol were backed by a personality full of charm and entirely without malice. By his sportsmanship and appearance he transformed boxing from the brutish pastime of prize-fighting into an acceptable part of society's pleasure.

Every schoolboy could look up to him as an example, for he summed up William Hazlitt's remark about the prize-fighters, "The best men were the best behaved." Henry Cooper acted almost as if he was in the presence of royalty whenever he was with Wells, and the sons of those who had supported him through thick and thin held him equally high in their esteem. Bombardier Billy Wells had no feet of clay.

June 13, 1967.

George Western, the piano-playing member of the Western Brothers variety partnership, died at Weybridge, Surrey, on August 16, 1969. He was 74, and had been ill for some weeks.

His partner Kenneth, who was really his cousin, created the lyrics for their act, while George composed the music. Their partnership, started in 1925, lasted until Kenneth's death in 1963.

Their stock-in-trade comprised immaculate evening dress, the old school tie, monocles and the catch phrase "Play the game, you cads", uttered in a drawling voice.

The humour of the Western Brothers depended on a social situation which no longer exists. They were, they pretended, the bad boys who had succeded in passing through a public school unaffected by its character-training, its ethos and its moral code.

They had not themselves been educated at public schools, but their mockery of public school standards was admiringly affectionate. Their elegance, their monocled arrogance and their classy, deliberately rather phoney, accents lost their amusing relevance at some point in the late 1940s.

George Western, shorter and less bulky than his stage "brother", matched his partner's lyrics with catchy if not very memorable tunes which owed a great deal to the tradition of the music hall. He sat at the piano against which his partner negligently leaned. George shared with Kenneth the ability to convince audiences in the days before television "satire" but their entirely good-humoured, cleverly-timed act, innocent of any possible effect, was somehow an impudent mockery of the establishment. At the same time they showed that even the raffish ne'er-do-well found its standards inescapable.

The real criticism, though it was neither profound nor violent, was aimed at those who did not accept the loyalties and the codes which social tradition had sanctified. To them, their act was all a joke, but it was a joke growing out of social realities which they shared with audiences of all classes. George's music meant much to it, for it was entirely static and as effective by radio as it was in the theatre.

Six years ago, with the death of his stage brother, George started a new career, a far cry from the glamorous microphone or stage years—he took over a sweet and tobacco kiosk at Weybridge station. He was still running the kiosk until his last illness.

August 19, 1969.

The fourth Duke of Westminster, P.C., D.S.O., died on February 25, 1967, at his home, Saighton Grange, near Chester. He was 60.

The Duke—Gerald Hugh Grosvenor—succeeded to the title in 1963. He married Sally, daughter of George Perry, in 1945, but had no children, and his heir is his brother, Lieutenant-Colonel Lord Robert Grosvenor. The Duke was a big landowner with acres in Mayfair and Belgravia, London. Educated at Eton and the Royal Military College Sandhurst, he joined the 9th Lancers in 1926. He became a Lieutenant-Colonel in 1942 and served in the North African campaign, winning the D.S.O.

In 1964 he was made Lord Steward of the Royal Household and a Privy Councillor. From 1952 to 1964 he was a member of the Queen's Bodyguard, Yeomen of the Guard. The Duke was a former High Sheriff of Cheshire, a Deputy-lieutenant of the county, Honorary Colonel of the Cheshire Yeomanry, a Freeman of Chester, and a director of Chester Race Company.

The Grosvenors are an old Norman family who became enormously wealthy, with big estates in Canada, Australia and South Africa, as well as in London. After the death of the second duke in 1953, the family had to pay more than £11m. in duty on estates said to be worth between £40m. and £60m. The third duke, a bachelor, who died in 1963 at the age of 68, was said to be head of what was still the greatest estate-owning family in the country. Some of the family's millions have been settled on 15-year-old Gerald Cavendish Grosvenor, son and heir of the new duke.

February 27, 1967.

General Weygand, who died on January 28, 1965, in Paris at the age of 98, was a remarkable instance of a soldier who gained the highest distinction as a staff officer but failed as a commander when separated from the great chief whose right hand he had been. When he took over the supreme command in 1940 he was past the age at which a soldier may be expected to be at his best, and the military situation was virtually irretrievable. This does not alter the fact that as Chief of the General Staff and Vice-President of the Supreme War Council he had misinterpreted the developments of modern war.

Maxime Weygand was not of French birth, but was born in Brussels on January 21, 1867. There were various rumours as to his parentage which he neither confirmed nor denied, saying only that he was "sans origines." He entered Saint-Cyr in 1886, and in 1888 passed out into the 4th Dragoons. An excellent horseman, and not without means, he found military life agreeable. He rode in military steeplechases, and sought higher things only in his own arm of the service. There, however, he was eager for advancement. He went to the cavalry school of Saumur for an instructor's course, from which he passed out first. The high reputation which he gained at Saumur brought him relatively rapid promotion to lieutenant-colonel, and in 1913 to the Centre of Higher Military Studies, without having passed through the Ecole de Guerre.

PARTNERSHIP WITH FOCH

On the outbreak of war in 1914 he had returned to regimental duty with the 5th Hussars, which formed part of the XX Corps under Foch, in the Morhange offensive in Lorraine. When Foch assumed command of an army to fill a gap in the centre of the French line he was told to take with him Weygand and another officer as chief and sub-chief of the staff. Actually the other was to have been chief, but Foch, finding that Weygand was the senior, appointed him, though he was not a staff college graduate, and Foch himself was the very embodiment of the staff college.

All through the war, as Foch mounted the ladder, the two worked together in perfect harmony. Weygand possessed a prodigious memory and an infinite capacity for detail. He served Foch faithfully, completely effacing his own personality, and giving up all his hopes of exercising an independent command. Foch and Weygand became one of the most illustrious combinations in military annals. Only once were they even partially separated. That was when, in December, 1917, Weygand was appointed French military representative on the Supreme War Council of the Allies at Versailles. Yet as Foch was at the same time Chief of the General Staff in Paris they were not far apart and in constant communication. When Foch was appointed allied commander-in-chief he again took Weygand with him.

After the war Weygand served, still with Foch, as Secretary-General to the Inter-Allied Military Commission. In 1920 he was sent to Poland at the time of the Russian invasion. His moral influence at Warsaw was considerable, but it is clear that he had no part in the plan conceived and executed by Pilsudski, which resulted in the complete defeat of the Russians.

In 1923 Weygand was appointed High Commissioner for Syria and Commander-in-Chief of the French Army in the Levant. He did much to restore order in Syria, but, suspected of right-wing tendencies by the Radical Party, which had triumphed in the elections of 1924, he was recalled. His next post was that of Director of the Centre of Higher Military Studies. In January, 1930, he became Chief of the General Staff, and in the following year succeeded Pétain as Vice-President of the Supreme War Council, the highest military post, since the Minister of War was *ex officio* President. In 1931 he was elected to the French Academy, an honour sometimes bestowed on great soldiers without "literary baggage" but appropriate in his case since he was an admirable writer.

SUMMONED TO PARIS

On reaching the age limit in 1935 Weygand went into retirement, but was listed for further employment if the occasion arose. He had bought the beautiful château of Coatamour, near Morlaix, so becoming a close neighbour of Foch, at Trofonteuniou. He also had a house in Paris and engaged in various business enterprises, becoming a director of the Suez Canal Company. On the outbreak of war in 1939 he was sent out to Syria as Commander-in-Chief in the Levant. His service in the Near East was comparatively uneventful, but in January, 1940, he paid an official visit to Turkey, where he was received by President Inönü. He was, of course, in constant touch with General (later Field-Marshal Lord Wavell) Sir Archibald Wavell at Cairo.

The first disasters in France brought him home post-haste on the summons of the President of the Council, Reynaud, and on May 19 1940, he was appointed Chief of the General Staff of the National Defence and Commander-in-Chief in all theatres. But the hopes which were entertained that he would restore the situation so gravely compromised under the leadership of General Gamelin were not to be realized. The French Army dissolved into disconnected remnants, and it was on his advice that Marshal Pétain demanded an armistice from the Germans.

Little was heard of Weygand in the gloomy months which followed, but in October he was dispatched to North Africa as Delegate-General of the French Government. He made constant tours, which extended to the French West African colonies. With the natives his prestige was undiminished; in France he was the only man beside Pétain who could be said to retain any. It is known that he took a strong stand against French military cooperation with Germany. At all events, while he remained in North Africa German penetrations were to some extent limited, and the most reasonable view is that he played for time with much skill.

It is perhaps surprising that he should have been allowed to stay at his post for over a year. In November, 1941, "at the express demand of Hitler," he was removed from it and the office itself, which had been virtually that of a "viceroy", was suppressed. At the same time Weygand returned to France and passed once more into complete obscurity. In September, 1942, however, there came an astonshing report that General Giraud, who had escaped from Germany, was staying with Weygand at the latter's villa at Cannes. That the Germans themselves considered he had taken a hand in planning General Giraud's moves was proved by the promptitude with which they arrested him after crossing the demarcation line of what had hitherto been unoccupied France in the following November. Later he was imprisoned at Schloss Ober Asperg, where he was treated with some consideration and lived in the villa of the camp commandant.

Weygand was released from captivity in 1945 and returned to France. He was then 78, embittered, suspect to the new leaders of France, and anyway, past the age for active service. He took no further part in public life and devoted himself to his admirable writings which included some memoirs of absorbing interest, and a few directorships. As was to be expected, however, he was strongly opposed to President de Gaulle's Algerian policy and although far less vocal than some other senior French soldiers, occasionally took an opportunity of stating his views. One occurred when he was called as a witness during the trial of the men accused of organizing the abortive counter-revolution in Algiers in January, 1960.

OPPOSITION TOTAL

He was then, as he said, "94 in three weeks time", and as a former representative of France in Algeria, Tunisia and Morocco, he roundly condemned self-determination for Algeria. No one, he declared, had the right "to deprive France of a part of her patrimony" and he gave it as his opinion that "France and her Army should keep Algeria". In his day the "fraternal union between Muslims and Europeans had been absolutely total."

Weygand married in 1900 Renée de Forsanz, who came of an old Breton family, and they had two sons. He had many British friends, despite the fact that, on the evidence of many senior British officers who were serving in France in May and June 1940, he was then savagely anti-British and laid the blame for the defeat of the Allied army upon the British forces, particularly the R.A.F. Like so many other French generals he considered that the French was "the finest army in the world" and could not be defeated by any fault of its own.

It was remarkable to what trouble he would put himself if his aid were solicited on any historical matter relating to his old master,

Marshal Foch, of whom he used to say that he lived only to guard his memory. It is perhaps not a fanciful psychological interpretation of his later career to say that he never recovered fully from the effects of his self-effacement in the service of Foch and that the development of his own personality suffered thereby.

January 29, 1965.

Albert Whelan, a polished entertainer of the variety stage, died in London on February 19, 1961, at the age of 85.

To hear his mellifluous whistling of the first few bars of his signature tune "Lustige Brüder," instantly identified him to thousands of B.B.C. listeners, and those thousands more who knew him on the music hall stage could see in imagination as the tune continued the leisurely removal of the immaculate gloves, muffler, overcoat, and top hat in which he always made his entrance.

He was, perhaps, the first entertainer to use a signature tune and he kept his throughout the more than half a century in which he was a leading variety artist. He was extremely versatile and could sing a comic song, a serious ballad, play the piano and the violin, dance, and give a wide range of impersonations. For a time he joined the late Billy Bennett in the black-faced act of Alexander and Mose.

His timing was perfect and his performance was always smooth, polished, and satisfying. Moreover, he was an eloquent speaker, and his broadcast tribute on the death of Vesta Tilley (Lady de Frece), his contemporary on the music hall stage during much of his long career, was a memorable achievement.

COME BACK AT 80

At the age of 80 he returned to the West End stage at the Windmill Theatre, appearing for six shows a day. His performance clearly demonstrated his ability to hold his own against any of the new-comers to variety. He lost a leg when he was 82, but even this did not defeat him and only in September, 1960, he appeared in a television broadcast.

Born in Melbourne, Australia, on May 5, 1875, the son of Aaron Waxman he was educated at Carlton College, Melbourne.

He first tried accountancy as a profession but forsook it for engineering. Caught up in the gold rush that was at its height in Western Australia in 1894, he was prospecting for gold at Coolgardie when he discovered that he had a natural gift for entertaining. In order to make some money, he took part in camp shows for the miners and became very popular. Leaving the goldfields, he gained further experience, and then went to England.

His first appearance in London was in October, 1901, at the old Empire Theatre, Leicester Square, as a scarecrow dancer. He then played in a Liverpool pantomime and later was given the part of Ichabod Bronson in *The Belle of New York* which was put on at the Adelphi; he was himself responsible for producing the first act. In spite of its immediate and continued success he decided that there was a more alluring future for him as an individual artist.

In subsequent years he became one of the leading favourites of music hall patrons in in all parts of the country. His material was of a high quality, his humour wholesome, and his act invariably clever. Numbers which he popularized included "The Preacher and the Bear," "I am a Business Man," "Three Trees," and "Won't You Tell Me the Lady's Name?"

February 20, 1961.

John Rex Whinfield, C.B.E., who, with his colleague, Dr. James Dickson, invented Terylene, died on July 6, 1966, at his home in Dorking. He was 65.

Whinfield dipped a glass needle into a thick liquid in a test-tube, and drew off a thin fibre a few inches long. "Ah, I thought so", he said. The fibre was Terylene, a new synthetic fibre, made out of anti-freeze liquid. It happened in 1941 while he was working with Dickson in the laboratories of the Calico Printers' Association at Accrington, Lancashire.

Whinfield was born on February 16, 1901, at Sutton, Surrey, and educated at Merchant Taylors' School, and Caius College, Cambridge. In 1923, when he was starting his career, he went to see C. F. Cross, who, with his colleague, Bevan, had discovered rayon in 1892. Whinfield worked—without payment—for Cross in his small laboratory at Lincolns' Inn for a year. Then he wanted to get married: so he got a paid job with the Calico Printers' Association as a research chemist. By 1933 he had his own laboratory, and two years later became obsessed with the idea of synthetic fibre; he refused to believe that nylon was the end of discovery in synthetic fabrics.

During the war, Whinfield was an assistant director of chemical research and development for the Ministry of Supply, and worked on men's clothing. He joined I.C.I. at Welwyn Garden City in 1947, became a member of the I.C.I. Terylene Council in 1952, and a director of the I.C.I. Fibres Division. He was awarded the C.B.E. in 1954. He retired in 1963.

July 7, 1966.

General Sir Lashmer Whistler, G.C.B., K.B.E., D.S.O., who died on July 4, 1963, in the Cambridge Military Hospital, Aldershot, at the age of 64, made his name in the Second World War as a leader of troops in battle.

Lord Montgomery, under whom he served both in North Africa and in North-West Europe, described him as "probably the finest fighting brigadier in the British Army". The division he commanded in the last year of the war was involved in some of the hardest fighting; between the landing in Normandy and the German surrender it had 16,000 casualties. His units often suffered from extreme exhaustion and were weakened by the influx of raw recruits. Whistler understood well the psychological problem of keeping up their morale and the maintenance of high efficiency in face of such difficulties. He was respected for his courage in action, and he inspired confidence and affection in his men by his interest in their welfare.

Every unit under his command realized that he followed their smallest actions with the closest attention. After a tough fight at the Mühlen Fleuth Bridge in the winter battle before the crossing of the Rhine, he wrote to the Commanding Officer of the East Yorkshires, the regiment chiefly involved, "Will you let all ranks know that I shall come and tell them, as soon as I possibly can, how moved I have been by their very gallant action", and he ordered the Sappers to place a board on the bridge with the East Yorkshire crest and name, an imaginative gesture which gave enormous satisfaction to the battalion.

Lashmer Gordon Whistler was born on September 3, 1898, the son of Colonel A. E. Whistler, Indian Army. He was educated at Harrow and at the Royal Military College, Sandhurst, from which he was commissioned in the Royal Sussex Regiment in 1917. In the First World War he saw six months' service on the Western Front, where he was wounded, and in 1919 he was again on active service for a few months in Russia during the anti-Bolshevik operations. He was one of the comparatively few officers who rose to high rank without graduating at the Staff College.

Between the wars he served in Germany, India, Egypt, the Sudan, and Palestine, as well as in England, and he was an adjutant for the exceptionally long period of seven years, four of them with the Territorial Army. He did not reach the rank of major till 21 years after being commissioned, but when the Second World War broke out, a year after his promotion to field rank, he very soon made his mark as a first-class leader.

THE WESTERN DESERT

In 1940 he took the 4th Battalion of his regiment to France, where he won the first of his three D.S.O.s. Two years later he was given command of a lorry-borne infantry brigade, the 131st, in the Western Desert. This brigade was composed of three battalions of the Queen's Royal Regiment, and was attached to the 7 Armoured Division, the famous "Desert Rats". Its role was to carry out tasks which could not be undertaken by tanks, such as mopping up the battlefield, night patrolling and night attacks, and outflanking movements over ground where tanks could not operate. Whistler commanded the Queen's Brigade all through the advance from Alamein to Tunisia, and was awarded a bar to his D.S.O. for his fine leadership.

His brigade was next in action in the landing at Salerno, for which it was put under the orders of General Mark Clark, and it took part in the crossing of the Volturno River in October 1943. Whistler was promoted to Major-General in 1944 and was transferred to the 3 Infantry Division, which he took over on the eve of the assault on Caen. He led this division throughout the campaign in North-West Europe. His services were marked by the award of a third bar to his D.S.O.

Soon after the German surrender, he took his

division to Palestine, where it was employed against the Jewish extremists who carried on a campaign of rioting and sabotage during the early part of Sir Alan Cunningham's regime as High Commissioner. A year later he was appointed G.O.C. Egypt, but he had not been long there before he was transferred to India as G.O.C.-in-C., British Troops. This was a post created by Field Marshal Montgomery, then C.I.G.S.-designate, with the object of safeguarding the interests of the British forces under the new Indian Government, and, in Montgomery's words, "he proved to be the right man for the job".

After this appointment had come to an end, he held a succession of peace-time commands. In 1948 he was appointed G.O.C. Troops in the Sudan and Kaid of the Sudan Defence Force; in 1950 G.O.C. Northumbrian District and 50 Territorial Division; in 1951 G.O.C.-in-C. West Africa; and in 1953 G.O.C.-in-C. Western Command. He retired from the Army in 1957, but he served for a further year as chairman of the Committee on the New Army which was set up to examine subjects of reorganization, recruiting and the welfare of the troops.

He married in 1926 Esmé Keighly, who, with two daughters, survives him.

July 6, 1963.

Sir Arthur Whitaker, K.C.B., past-president of the Institution of Civil Engineers and Civil Engineer-in-Chief of the Admiralty from 1940 to 1954, died on June 13, 1968, at the age of 74. He was one of the great maritime civil engineers of his generation.

It was as Civil Engineer-in-Chief, Admiralty, and later as president of the Institution of Civil Engineers that he became known to and greatly respected by the whole of his profession throughout the Commonwealth.

During the last war the extent and variety of the work done under his direction was enormous, covering the whole of the civil engineering works for the Navy throughout the world. The reputation of the C.E.-in-C. Department, established under his leadership, has survived the demise of the department in 1963.

Many of his wartime staff came from outside the department and today are leaders of the profession in various fields. By his drive and sense of purpose and service, he welded them and his permanent staff into such an efficient and loyal team that the bonds then forged have never been loosened. "The Chief", although essentially a shy man, was a hard task-master who drove them to their limits. He seemed to know what people were capable of and they responded to his challenge.

Apart from his Admiralty department, he had one abiding interest to which he gave devoted service—the Institution of Civil Engineers. He believed that its role was fundamental to the development of the science and practice of civil engineering and to the standing of the profession: he regarded it as a great honour when he was elected president in 1957.

Fredrick Arthur Whitaker was born in Ladysmith, South Africa. He was educated in Liverpool and attended Liverpool University, where he took a first. Created C.B. in 1941 and K.C.B. in 1945, he was made a Commander of the Legion of Honour in 1947 and Honorary D.Eng. (Liverpool) in 1960. He was a member of the Dover Harbour Board for 14 years and of the Commission Consultative Internationale des Traveaux of the Suez Canal Company from 1952. From 1954 to 1962 he was a partner in the firm of Livesey & Henderson, consulting engineers.

He is survived by his widow, Florence, the daughter of John Overend, and by a son and two daughters.

June 14, 1968.

Dorothy Hale White, widow of "Mark Rutherford," the Victorian novelist, died on July 27, 1967, at the age of 90.

Dorothy Vernon Horace Smith was born in Bromley, Kent, on January 31, 1877, daughter of Horace Smith, metropolitan magistrate and minor poet. Physically a healthy girl, famed in her county as a demon over-arm bowler in an era of lobs and long skirts, she suffered in youth from a searing sense of sin. She had always, she once wrote, been religiously inclined, "though not always wholesomely so", and at 22 she "passed through a dark cloud; but God had been with me in the cloud, and I came out of it with the desire for service". Service for the next 40 years, except for the brief interlude of her marriage, meant running classes and clubs for working-class children on Church of England principles. Her understanding of young people and her complete freedom from cant or priggishness come out clearly in her two books about her work, *Twelve Years with My Boys* (anonymous, 1912), and *The Children's Parish* (1934). The qualities which especially endeared her to her pupils were an indestructible innocence and faith in human nature, and a bubbling sense of fun. A favourite word of the heroines of her Edwardian novels remained a favourite with her to the end of her life: she liked everything to be "jolly".

In 1907 Dorothy Smith's first novel, *Miss Mona*, fell into the hands of William Hale White, who thought it full of faults but determined to meet its author. The outcome of the meeting is well known to readers of biographies of Mark Rutherford. She was thirty, he was seventy-five: they fell in love at sight; three and a half years later he rose from his invalid couch to marry her; two years later he died. The joys and stresses of these few years of intimacy are described, almost day by day, in her book *The Groombridge Diary* (1924), a book which explicitly contains only diary extracts pertinent to their mutual relationship; the omissions, many readers must have felt, and her other diaries, ought one day to be published, if only to prove, what is already implicit between the lines, that Dorothy was a fascinating personality in her own right.

Meanwhile she had herself published two other novels, *Frank Burnet* in 1909 and *Isabel* in 1911. The former, which an American critic described not long ago as "possibly a masterpiece", is a moral fable about weakness and strength of character, written with great intelligence and gusto. *Isabel* is a somewhat disquieting book about a husband-hunting miss, curiously cynical from so generous minded a writer, but a singularly observed picture of middle-class suburban life in the early years of the century: the author seems to have been working off the discontents of her young spinsterhood before entering, in maturity and confidence, upon a marriage which could have had no charms for her flighty heroine.

After her husband's death Mrs. White returned to live with her parents, first in Beckenham and later in Sherborne, Dorset. Apart from the books already mentioned she did no more writing. She was not, as Hale White early remarked, a particularly "literary" person; her energies went into her "children's parish". A few years ago a friend asked a local contractor whether he would do some small necessary job in her house, and do it quietly, quickly, and cheaply. "Mrs. White?", replied this former parishioner, now a prosperous forty; "why, I'd do anything for Mrs. White; she taught me to play cricket". It was more of a tribute than the mere words imply.

July 28, 1967.

General Sir John Whiteley, G.B.E., K.C.B., M.C., who died on May 20, 1970, at the age of 73, was Deputy Chief of the Imperial General Staff from 1949 to 1953.

It was on the staff that he made his name, and he served with conspicuous success in a series of high staff appointments during the Second World War and after it. He made a valuable contribution by his happy cooperation with the Americans by whom he was held in great respect as well as affection. He was a man of splendid character and his modesty and sense of humour made him a delightful colleague to work with.

John Francis Martin Whiteley was born on June 7, 1896, the son of J. J. Whiteley, and educated at Blundell's School and the Royal Military Academy, from which he was commissioned in 1915 in the Royal Engineers. In the First World War he served in the Balkans and the Middle East, winning the Military Cross and a mention in dispatches.

Early in 1940 he was posted to G.H.Q. Cairo, where he was Brigadier, General Staff, and Deputy Director of Military Operations, first under Wavell and then under Auchinleck. In 1941 he was Auchinleck's envoy to London to explain the situation in the Western Desert to the Prime Minister and the reasons why Auchinleck was resisting Churchill's pressure to advance the date of the projected autumn offensive against Rommel. In 1942 he was Chief of Staff to Ritchie in the operations which culminated in the disastrous Battle of Gazala and the loss of Tobruk. Later he was transferred to Eisenhower's headquarters as British Deputy Chief of Staff, and there played a notable part in the planning and direction of the final phases of the operations in Tunisia and in the invasion of Sicily and Italy.

When Eisenhower was appointed Supreme Commander for Overlord, Whiteley was one of the staff officers he took with him to England. He was promoted Major General and was appointed first to the Intelligence and then to the Planning and Operations Section of Supreme Allied Headquarters, where he remained until the end of the war. Eisenhower has placed on record how greatly he valued his services as "a constant adviser in whom he reposed the greatest confidence".

After a few months in Germany as Assistant Chief of Staff in the Control Commission, Whiteley was appointed Army Instructor at the Imperial Defence College to initiate the postwar courses under Sir William Slim as Commandant. In 1947 he was selected for an exchange of appointments with Canada, and became Commandant of the Canadian National Defence College, being replaced at the Imperial Defence College by General Simon, of the Canadian Army.

His next appointment was as Deputy C.I.G.S. at the War Office and he served in this post from 1949 till 1953. In 1953 he was promoted General and took up his last appointment as chairman of the British Joint Services Mission, Washington, and United Kingdom representative on the Standing Group of the Military Committee of the North Atlantic Treaty Organization. It fell to him, as the representative of the British Chiefs of Staff, to conduct the discussions on the introduction of tactical atomic weapons and the consequent adjustments to defence plans.

He married in 1929 Margaret, daughter of F. Anderson, and had a son and a daughter.

May 22, 1970.

Paul Whiteman, the American band leader, died on December 29, 1967, in Doylestown, Pennsylvania. He was 77. Perhaps the biggest figure in the pop bandleading world of the 1920s his band gave the first performance of George Gershwin's *Rhapsody in Blue* at the Aeolian Hall, New York, in 1924. In 1930 he starred in a lavishly made picture called *The King of Jazz*, one of the first film musicals; it was memorable for another reason; for Bing Crosby, who had earlier attracted Whiteman's attention when singing in a trio called The Rhythm Boys, also had a part in it. Crosby left the band after making the film to launch himself on his career as a singer.

Though many famous jazzmen passed through Whiteman's band, among them Bix Beiderbecke, Frankie Trumbauer, Eddie Lang, Joe Venuti, Red Norvo and the Dorsey brothers, Tommy and Jimmy, jazz critics challenged Whiteman's right to the title King of Jazz. One of them, Wilder Hobson, wrote in *American Jazz Music*: Whiteman drew very little from the jazz language except some of its simpler rhythmic patterns.

He was born in Denver, Colorado, in 1890, and started his musical career as a violinist before soaring to fame with his big band. In 1926 he toured England and principal European cities. In recent years he had worked as musical director with the American Broadcasting Company in New York.

December 30, 1967.

John Whiting, who died at the Royal Marsden Hospital, London, on June 16, 1963, at the age of 45, was one of the most inventive and strikingly individual dramatists of his generation, and will retain a distinctive niche in British theatrical history not only on account of the inherent qualities of his works (which are considerable) but as the main precursor in the early 1950s of that "new British drama" which arrived on the scene with explosive suddenness in 1956.

John Whiting was born in Salisbury on November 15, 1917, and was early drawn to the stage. After leaving school he trained as an actor at R.A.D.A. and appeared briefly on the stage before joining the Army in 1939. Demobbed in 1945, he went back to acting, and soon began to write in his spare time, first narrative prose and then, at the suggestion of a friend, drama. His first play, *Conditions of Agreement*, was put away unproduced and rewritten for television in 1960 as *A Walk in the Desert* (unsuccessfully, in its author's opinion). In 1947 he wrote *Saint's Day*, a violent and highly wrought symbolic drama, but that also failed to find a producer and so instead he turned to the light fantastic in a mode popular at the time (it was the heyday of Christopher Fry's verse drama) with *A Penny for a Song*, which was his first work to be produced, at the Haymarket in 1951.

BADLY RECEIVED

If the effect of this was uncontroversial—everyone found it charming, at least in parts—the impact of *Saint's Day*, produced later the same year at the Arts and awarded first prize in the Arts Council's Festival of Britain play competition, was very different. Most critics did not like or understand the play, which was certainly by the standards of his later work uncontrolled and immature, but it also received eloquent support; in letters to *The Times*, for instance, Sir Tyrone Guthrie and Peter Brook described it as "the product of a new and extraordinary theatrical mind", and Dame Peggy Ashcroft and Sir John Gielgud called it "moving, beautiful, and fascinating". Evidently, even to those who most disliked the play (and it was a work which could leave no one merely indifferent), Whiting was a dramatist to be reckoned with.

His next play, *Marching Song* (1954), though it was no more lucky commercially than its predecessors, showed a new power and maturity; indeed arguably it remains Whiting's most completely successful work. A formidably intelligent psychological drama about a crucial decision in the life of a disgraced general, it is written with restrained intensity and a perfect command of the English language at its most lucid, and has long seemed to demand reassessment in a theatre which now, nearly 10 years later, should prove far more receptive to what the author has to say and his uncompromising way of saying it. Unfortunately *Marching Song's* commercial failure appears to have disillusioned Whiting with the theatre, or perhaps theatrical managers with him, and for the next seven years no new play by him was seen in London, though he made some excellent translations from Anouilh and a "bitter comedy" called *The Gates of Summer* closed on tour in 1956.

Just when it seemed that Whiting might be permanently lost to the theatre, though, he was commissioned by the Royal Shakespeare Company to write the first new play to be staged by their London branch at the Aldwych, and the result was *The Devils*, suggested by Mr. Aldous Huxley's book *The Devils of Loudon*. With this at least he achieved a decisive popular success, and his command of dark theatrical eloquence summoned up comparison with Webster and the greater Jacobeans. He was immediately commissioned to write another play for the company, as well as revising *Penny for a Song* for revival at the Aldwych in 1962, and completed also a one-act play called *No Why*, as yet unproduced, and two film scripts.

As a dramatist John Whiting was in reach of the first rank, even if in his completed works he never quite achieved it. He was an incisive critic (for some time he wrote as drama critic of *The London Magazine*) and his fine critical intelligence prevented him from ever, after *Saint's Day*, going too far, but in artistic creations those who never go too far perhaps never go quite far enough. Nevertheless in *Marching Song* in particular he wrote a play which seems likely to last, and at the time of his death he appeared to be at the beginning of a fruitful new phase in his career. The British theatre, even in its present flowering, can ill afford to lose the plays he might have written had he lived long enough to achieve his full potential stature.

June 17, 1963.

Jimmy Wilde, world flyweight boxing champion from 1916 to 1923, died on March 10, 1969, at Whitchurch Hospital, Cardiff. He was 76.

Wilde was regarded by many venerable critics of pugilism as pound for pound the greatest boxer the world has ever seen.

"Pound for pound" is the important phrase for Wilde. He rarely weighed more than 7st. 5lb. in his prime—the flyweight limit is 8st. Yet in his long and illustrious career he beat many featherweights of around 9st. and was reportedly capable of holding his own with much heavier men.

Born in Pontypridd on May 12, 1892, Wilde earned the ring name of "The Ghost with a Hammer in his Hand" because of his extraordinarily powerful punch which belied his frail appearance. The story is told that in his first professional bout in London the promoter did not want Wilde to enter the ring because he feared for the safety of the bird-like little Welshman. Wilde, in tears, finally was allowed to box and won on a first round knockout.

Wilde learnt his trade fighting in the boxing booths and in unofficial contests in back alleys. He must have had several hundred of these valuable encounters before he began his career proper. The record books list him as having scored 125 victories, 76 of them inside the distance, but ignore all the countless knockouts of his formative years.

What is more certain is that Wilde suffered defeat only on four occasions and each time had the odds stacked against him. When unwell he was beaten by the Scot, Tancy Lee, in the seventeenth round. He was narrowly outpointed by the American bantamweight, Pal Moore over three rounds (the decision produced a riot), and he was also defeated inside the distance by the American bantamweight, Pete Herman, when outweighed by many pounds. In the last bout of his career Wilde lost his world title to Pancho Villa in New York through a seventh round knockout, but that was in 1923 and he was past his best.

Those who saw him in action claim that Wilde was not a particularly stylish boxer to watch, but he could sway out of reach almost by instinct.

Younger enthusiasts of boxing have only seen a spidery figure flicking across the screen in the few films made of Wilde's contests, but the dazzling talent is there to be spotted.

Wilde had so much legend weaved round his little frame even in his life-time that few could appreciate the identity or the worth of the quiet man who came to the ringside as a journalist in the 1950s. His unobtrusive manner sometimes caused him to be pushed aside and it is recalled that he watched a title bout perched on a press photographer's box.

Those who saw him at his best are now few. The story of his greatness may become so distorted that the young may believe it an exaggeration by those in love with the past. But he was perhaps the most talented man ever to slip on the gloves.

March 11, 1969.

Georges Wildenstein, whose death occurred on June 11, 1963, was at one time called "the Duveen of France", though such a term could convey only in part the nature of his activities and his international reputation in the realm of art.

He was, it is true, one of the most famous art dealers of this century, conducting with great success and discernment a business with world-wide ramifications and building shrewdly on the foundations left by his father, Nathan Wildenstein. From his father, who went to Paris from Alsace-Lorraine after the Franco-Prussian war and made a fortune as a picture-dealer, he inherited both wealth and a flair for art. The Wildenstein Galleries of Paris, New York, Buenos Aires and London (the latter member of this group of Houses opened in 1937) are testimony to the family spirit of enterprise. Yet Georges Wildenstein, in addition to being a dealer, was eminent as a scholar and art historian and his reputation was soundly based on the scrupulous and exact research and the wide and in some respects unrivalled knowledge he applied to the study of French painting. He was one of the greatest authorities in Europe on eighteenth-century art and his numerous books included important works on Lancret, Chardin, Maurice Quentin Latour, and Fragonard. His book on Fragonard, with its catalogue and "chronological résumé of documents", the result of the labours of nearly half a century, first published in English in 1960, was hailed in *The Times Literary Supplement* as a foundation of Fragonard studies "never likely to be replaced". He applied himself with no less zeal to the study of such modern masters as Renoir, Sisley, Seurat and Gauguin.

EDITOR AND WRITER

As a writer he deprecated "effusion" and his own manner was stately and marked by a sober regard for fact, though his literary activity was not only considerable in amount, including hundreds of articles as well as books, but extended to the direction of periodicals, the *Gazette des Beaux Arts*, an old established magazine of learned studies to which he gave fresh life and, from 1946, the weekly art-newspaper *Arts*, which with broader appeal was planned to chronicle events and trends in literature, music, stage and film as well as the visual "fine arts".

During the last war, from 1941 to 1946, he edited the monthly journal *La République Française* at New York as a contribution to the French cause. His truly prodigious activity as editor included the long series of monographs on French masters in the *Collection d'Art Française* of the *Editions Les Beaux Arts*. His knowledge and abilities were freely placed at the national service. Of the great number of exhibitions for which he was responsible, many were organized on behalf of the French Government. He was entrusted with the important task of drawing up the inventory of treasures of art in France which was designed as far as possible to avoid, and to minimize, destruction by the allied armies in the process of liberation.

The quality of the exhibitions for which his gallery was responsible was exemplified earlier in 1963 by the exhibition of paintings by the Impressionists and some of their contemporaries, held at the Bond Street Gallery. From many splendid exhibitions of the past one might pick out the "Five Centuries of French Art" shown in the French Pavilion of the International Exhibition of New York, 1939, as representative.

GIFTS TO THE LOUVRE

Georges Wildenstein was born on March 16, 1892, at Paris and was educated at the Lycée Carnot. He collaborated with his father during the latter's lifetime in the family business. His enterprise was later shown by such a *coup* as the acquisition in 1936 of the famous Schmitz collection of nineteenth-century French art for £150,000, and it may be recalled that only this year (1963), by agreement with the heirs of Pierre Bonnard, his gallery shared in the partition of the great collection of 700-800 oils and 5,000 drawings which Bonnard left.

In addition to his work as art historian Wildenstein was noted for many disinterested uses of his fortune. He made numerous gifts of works of art to the Louvre and other French museums and founded and endowed the American Institute of France with the aim of promoting the exchange of research students between the two countries. In 1941 he placed £2,000 at the service of General de Gaulle and the *Armée du Salut*. He was made Commander of the Legion of Honour in 1938 and in April, 1963, was gratified by his appointment as Member of the Institut de France. A typical Frenchman in many ways he had, among other traits, a rooted suspicion of the English climate, so that in London even in summer, he was never without an overcoat.

He married in 1913, Mlle. Jane Lévi, by whom he had a son and a daughter.

June 13, 1963.

L. Dana Wilgress, the Canadian diplomat, who died in Ottawa on July 22, 1969, at the age of 76, was High Commissioner in Britain from 1949 to 1952, and Canadian Permanent Representative to the North Atlantic Treaty Organization (Nato) Council in Paris from 1953 to 1958.

He was chairman of the General Agreement on Tariffs and Trade (G.A.T.T.) from 1948 to 1951. From 1959 to 1966 he was Canadian chairman of the Canada-United States Joint Defence Board.

He was born on October 20, 1892, in Vancouver, B.C., and graduated in 1914 from McGill University with a B.A. degree and first-class honours in economics and political science.

He joined the Commercial Intelligence Service of the Department of Trade and Commerce in 1914, and later served as Trade Commissioner in Omsk, Vladivostok, and Hamburg. In 1918 he investigated trade opportunities in south China and carried out similar investigations in south eastern Europe and other European countries in 1920 and 1921. He visited Russia in the period from 1921 to 1923 and again in 1936.

In 1942 he was appointed Canadian Minister to the USSR, and in 1944 became Ambassador when the Canadian Mission in that country was elevated to an Embassy.

Wilgress was adviser to the Canadian delegation to the Imperial Economic Conference held in Ottawa in 1932. He was chairman of the Canadian delegation to the preparatory commission of the United Nations Assembly in London in 1945.

He was appointed Minister to Switzerland in 1947, when a Canadian Legation was established in Berne. This posting allowed him to represent Canada at almost all of the significant international conferences of the time. During his stay in London as High Commissioner from 1949 to 1952 he became an outstandingly popular figure in the public and social life of the capital. Having originally entered diplomacy on its economic and commercial side he was well-qualified to be chairman of the contracting parties to Gatt as well as leading his national delegation at the two Torquay conferences. He returned home in 1952 to become Under-Secretary of State for External Affairs.

July 24, 1969.

Princess Wilhelmina of the Netherlands—See under **Netherlands.**

Louis Wilkinson, who died on September 12, 1966, at Westcot Barton, near Oxford, may be most widely known as Louis Marlow, under which pseudonym he wrote many novels. Under his own name he will be remembered as the friend, biographer, and editor of the Powys brothers, as a gifted lecturer on English literature, and as a ripe and rewarding personality with a genius for friendship. He was 84.

Louis Umfreville Wilkinson was born at Aldeburgh on December 17, 1881, the only son of a clergyman who owned a preparatory school. From his father's school he went to Radley, where he showed his independent character and judgment by opening a correspondence with Oscar Wilde, then in Reading Gaol. "I cannot but think of your cruel and unjust fate whenever I pass through Reading on my way to Radley", he wrote in the first letter of a correspondence that continued till Wilde's death four years later. Wilde told Robert Ross that this schoolboy of 16 was the first stranger who had written to him sympathetically after his imprisonment.

His career at Oxford lasted only four terms. Finding themselves unable to accept the Christian faith, Wilkinson and three other members of his college indulged in "mock Masses and Confession", which the humourless authorities condemned as organized "blasphemies". When the four were sent down in December, 1901, their case was taken up by Henry Labouchere's *Truth* in an indictment of "a varsity Star Chamber".

Wilkinson was always grateful for the wiser tolerance of St. John's College, Cambridge, where he spent three years before taking his degree and publishing his first novel, *The Puppets' Dallying*, in 1905. Among Cambridge contemporaries he made friendships lasting all their lives with Llewelyn Powys, J.C. Squire, Ronald Storrs, and Ralph Straus. Even in such distinguished company he was so outstanding that he was nicknamed "the Archangel"; for his intellectual powers, epigrammatic wit, and sense of fun were allied to a handsome presence—tall and elegant in build, he had finely boned features, auburn hair, and piercing hazel eyes.

By the time he left Cambridge, he had fallen under the influence of John Cowper Powys, the elder brother of his Cambridge friend.

CONTRASTS

Apparently fitted to be himself a leader, he inevitably felt resentment at finding himself a disciple, yet he never escaped from the Powys spell. As he related in the autobiographical novel, *Swan's Milk* (1934), he was fascinated by Powys's genius yet repelled by his eccentricities, which he satirized in the character of Jack Welsh in his second novel, *The Buffoon* (1916).

His own fastidious taste and economy of style were alike offended by the undisciplined prodigality of Powys's genius; he declared himself unable to read Powys's long novels, and always preferred to praise the work of the younger brothers, T. F. and Llewelyn Powys. Yet when he wrote his study of the three brothers, *Welsh Ambassadors* (1936), it was John Cowper Powys who dominated the book. Their friendship survived all such criticism as well as the lives of nearly all their mutual friends; one of Wilkinson's last undertakings was the editing of *The Letters of John Cowper Powys to Louis Wilkinson* (1958), a selection of letters received during 21 years of their long intimacy.

When Wilkinson left Cambridge, Powys was earning his living in America as a lecturer on English literature; persuaded similarly to capitalize his fine presence and deep, rich voice, Wilkinson modelled his style of dramatic delivery on Powys's. For some 15 years—till his first marriage with Frances Gregg ended in divorce—he travelled the United States as an itinerant lecturer. After a brief unhappy experience in the advertising business, he married the gifted young novelist, Ann Reid, and resumed his writing of novels.

During the war years he took up again work as a university extension lecturer and served on the committee of the Royal Society of Literature. His last novels were a satirical fantasy, *The Devil in Crystal* (1944), and a sequel to *Swan's Milk, Forth Beast!* (1946); he often talked of writing another novel, but like his friend, Somerset Maugham, found himself out of sympathy with the modern idiom.

With his wide reading and judicious taste, he might have ranked high among contemporary critics, but he recoiled from reviewing as a chore likely to interfere with his enjoyment of life.

Four times married, he is survived by a son of his first marriage, Mr. Oliver Wilkinson, the dramatist, and by a daughter of his second marriage with Ann Reid. After living for many years in or near London, he settled at the Dorset village of Hazelbury Bryan after his fourth marriage to Joan Lamburn, a writer of charming verse and children's books, who died in 1956.

September 13, 1966.

Jess Willard, the former world heavyweight boxing champion, who won the title from Jack Johnson and lost it to Jack Dempsey, died on December 15, 1968. He was 86.

Originally a Kansas cowboy, Willard stood 6ft. 6in. and weighed 17 stone. He had beaten few boxers of standing when he met the great Negro boxer Johnson at Havana in April, 1915. He was large and slow and he had great courage but he lacked Johnson's natural gifts. The fight was set for 45 rounds. As a contemporary account makes very plain popular sympathy was with Willard; Johnson as usual was laughing and the crowd jeered at him. For many rounds Johnson had it all his own way but by the early twenties the fight had degenerated and Willard was now on top. In the twenty-sixth round he caught Johnson on the jaw with one of his swings and the fight was over.

Willard's reign as heavyweight champion was not a distinguished one. It was not until July, 1919, that he met Jack Dempsey at Toledo, Ohio. Dempsey was five inches shorter and 58lb. lighter—but 13 years younger. He attacked from the first bell, and in the next few rounds he had Willard down many times. Willard, always brave, stuck it out until the fourth round, and they then carried him out with a fractured jaw, his nose crushed, and his left cheek open to the bone.

Willard's career in boxing did not start until he was 28 years old in 1911, and he was 43 when he fought his last match in 1923.

He and his wife had lived quietly for many years in a modest cottage in La Crescenta, Los Angeles. In April, 1966, a freeway project forced the Willards to sell the home and move to nearby Sunland.

Jack Johnson, who had a chequered career, was born in 1878 and died in 1946.

December 16, 1968.

Lord Williams of Barnburgh, who died on March 29, 1967, at the age of 79, was Minister of Agriculture from 1945 until 1951.

He had an unusually long connexion as a political head in that department with which he was also associated during the 1939-45 War as Joint Parliamentary Secretary from May, 1940, until May, 1945. Both in the war years and afterwards when Labour came to power he was concerned with many agricultural reforms and a policy aimed (solely) at obtaining more food from our own land and livestock. He was a modest and painstaking man who established himself as an authority on agriculture in the Parliamentary Labour Party by hard work and close study. His knowledge of the subject and his love of it earned him the respect and regard of the farming community, and he was able to maintain always the most cordial relations with the various organizations representing the farming community.

Thomas Williams was born on March 18, 1888, the seventh of 14 children raised by a Derbyshire miner. He attended an elementary school and at the age of 11 followed his father to the pit. For some years he was a checkweighman at a colliery in South Yorkshire and he gained some administrative experience as an official of the Yorkshire Miners' Association. Then in 1922 he entered Parliament as the Labour member for Don Valley, a seat which he held until 1959. In the first Labour Government of 1924 he was Parliamentary Private Secretary to the Minister of Agriculture and thereafter he steadily accumulated the knowledge of farming which soon established him as one of Labour's foremost spokesmen on the subject in the House of Commons and outside.

When Churchill formed his Coalition in May 1940, and appointed R. S. Hudson as Minister of Agriculture, Tom Williams was the obvious choice as his aide in the Commons and the two men, though differing widely in temperament, worked well together in the rapid, and successful development of agricultural production. In their five years together they saw British agriculture transformed from the sluggish state of prewar days to an unprecedented peak of efficiency. The War Agricultural Executive Committees were developed as administrative and supervising agents in all counties with some 4,000 farmers working on a voluntary basis as district and parish representatives. Mechanization was introduced to an extent never known before, the Women's Land Army and thousands of civilian volunteers were added to the labour force, and the most detailed survey since the Domesday Book was carried out over land in use for food production.

For the few weeks between the end of the Coalition and the Labour victory in July, 1945, Williams was out of office, but with Labour's return he was back at the Ministry of Agriculture, and this time as its political head. He soon made it clear that there were to be no drastic changes of policy; the aim was to be stability for the industry and a fair reward for those engaged in it. Inevitably, there was some reaction from the strenuous endeavour of the war years but Williams continued to warn farmers that there was no cause for relaxation and the scarcity of bread grains in Europe told its own grim story. In November of that year he again announced the system of guaranteed prices and assured markets for the main farm products, a policy which was a legacy from the Coalition.

These and other measures were embodied in the Agriculture Act which he put through the Commons in 1947. It was largely agreed policy and welcomed by all parties. It enshrined the guaranteed prices and assured markets, provided for annual and special reviews of the condition of the agricultural industry, established the Land Commission, gave increased security of tenure, revised the county executive committees and laid down standards of food husbandry.

In spite of some friction engendered by the compulsory powers which the Ministry continued to possess in the immediate postwar period relations between its head and the main farming organization were probably more cordial than they have been since. It was a common saying of the time that if farmers could have Tom Willams as Minister in a Tory Administration they would for once be really happy.

MINISTRY'S HIGHER STATUS

He was certainly the only Minister of Agriculture of whom it could be reputed that he had gone over the head of the Chancellor of the Exchequer to the Cabinet for more money at a price review and got away with it. He clearly regarded his office as an end in itself and not as merely a politician's stepping-stone—an attitude which did much to raise its status.

He was perhaps fortunate in that the problems of surplus, which bedevilled the agricultural politics of the 1950s, had hardly come to a head while he was still in office. Nor had the Ministries of Agriculture and Food yet been merged, leading to a dual responsibility on the part of their joint head.

During his last years in office he sometimes showed signs that the arthritis which plagued him was trial to the temper. But for the most part he bore it with a philosophic fortitude.

Out of office he retained to the end the affection and confidence of many who differed with him politically, and was a familiar figure on all major agricultural occasions. He shared with his fellow Parliamentary Secretary in the wartime Ministry, the Duke of Norfolk, a proper Yorkshire interest in the Turf.

He was created a life peer in 1961. He was a member of the Political Honours Scrutiny Committee. In 1965 he published his autobiography, *Digging for Britain*.

He married in 1910 Elizabeth Ann, daughter of Thomas Andrews. They had a son and a daughter.

March 31, 1967.

The Right Reverend A. T. P. Williams, D.D., Bishop of Winchester from 1952 to 1961, and chairman of the committee which prepared the *New English Bible*, died at Bridport, Dorset, on February 18, 1968. He was 79.

His was not one of those "names which make news". He wrote little, and his deep humility, the wise and cautious reserve of his utterances, and his scorn for anything which might even seem meretricious prevented him from attracting the wide-spread attention of the general public; but by his colleagues, and by all those who came under his personal care, in the great charges in education and the Church to which he was successively called, he was held in deep respect and great affection.

Alwyn Terrell Petre Williams, Prelate to the Most Noble Order of the Garter from 1952 to 1961, was born on July 20, 1888, son of John Terrell Williams. Educated at Rossall and at Jesus College, Oxford, where he was a Scholar, he took a First Class in Mods, followed by Firsts in *Lit Hum*, and History. He also, in 1909, won the Gladstone History Essay Prize. Elected a fellow of All Souls College in 1911, he was ordained in 1913. In 1915 the headmaster of Winchester College, Dr. M. J. Rendall, invited him to help with the teaching of history. Rendall was quick to perceive his quality, and said to him: "Williams carries more guns, and is less conscious of them, than any young man whom I have ever known." He had no hesitation, when the Second Mastership—the Mastership in College, with the care of the Seventy Scholars—fell vacant at the end of the year, in offering it to Williams; nor did it come as any surprise that he was elected to succeed Rendall as headmaster in 1924.

In this capacity he served for 10 years, a "decennium", as one of his colleagues wrote in the name of them all on his retirement, "*omnium consensu nimium breve*". In the headmaster was prefigured the bishop to be. During this period, one of the happiest in his life, his personal qualities came to their full maturity.

A fully articulated science "side" had already been implanted into a school with traditions almost exclusively classical; now it remained to do the same for the modern linguists and modern historians. A "modern side", in this sense, was created by Williams upon deep and lasting foundations. But in the main Winchester was called, during his headmastership, to quiet consolidation, and to an equally quiet progress in details, upon its inherited foundations. This precisely suited his cast of mind, with its distrust of "enthusiasm" in the large and its willingness to spend itself without stint upon improvement in particulars. Church history was his special subject; his *Anglican Tradition in the Life of England*, a short survey, is a distillation of his ripe knowledge in this field.

In 1934 he was appointed Dean of Christ Church. There, in the wider setting of College, Cathedral, and University, he showed the same qualities of administrative grasp and personal self-giving as he had manifested at Winchester. In 1939 he was appointed Bishop of Durham. He quickly won, and retained, the confidence of his clergy and laity. A Northerner himself by birth and upbringing, he found work in the North congenial, its historical associations absorbing, and its countryside a source of refreshment. In 1952 he was translated to Winchester. This was another homecoming. It was at Winchester, at the outset of his career, that he had first shown himself to be a true pastor; and it was there, at its culmination, that he was honoured and loved as an equally true pastor pastorum.

Williams was not one of the most widely known among the Bishops. He had no love for the public platform or for popular "causes": even in Convocation he did not speak very frequently, though his interventions carried much weight. He was chairman of the Archbishops' Commission on Training for the Ministry, the report of which was published in 1944. Made a Doctor of Divinity at Oxford by decree as early as 1925 he received honorary doctorates of Divinity from the Universities of Durham, St. Andrews, and Glasgow, and an honorary D.Litt., from Southampton.

He married, in 1914, Margaret Grace, daughter of Colonel Charles Stewart. There were no children of the marriage. His wife died in 1958.

February 20, 1968.

Bransby Williams, actor and music-hall performer, who was especially well known for his impersonations of characters from the novels of Dickens, died on December 3, 1961, in a nursing home at Streatham, S.W. He was 91.

Bransby Williams was born at Hackney on August 14, 1870. Though he was originally intended for the Church, his early employment was with a firm of tea merchants and in a paper works. He began as a youth to perform in amateur theatricals, and then took small professional engagements performing at Saturday variety shows and working men's clubs at two shillings or five shillings a night. He then spent some years in stock companies, and on August 26, 1896, made his first regular music-hall appearance, at the London, Shoreditch, where he gave imitations of Irving, Tree, Wyndham, and other actors. He immediately got a West End engagement at the Tivoli, and in 1897 began his renderings of Dickens characters. These remained for many years his chief stock in trade, and included Micawber, Uriah Heep, Little Nell's grandfather, and many more, all acted with a certain richness and broad sense of character, though without much subtlety. He also had a long repertoire of imitations of performers whom he had known and watched on both the music-hall and legitimate stages. These he sometimes gave in a little sketch of an old stagedoor keeper remembering the stars of the past. Occasionally he would vary his turn by reciting Shakespearian speeches, and as a reciter, too, he was the first to render Milton Hayes's famous pieces, "The Green Eye of the Little Yellow God", and "The Whitest Man I Know".

A well-built, handsome man, with black hair and a square jaw, Williams generally appeared wearing a tail-coat with brass buttons and black knee-breeches and stockings. He did not, however, confine himself to the variety stage and in the twenties acted in a number of plays, sometimes in London but mostly in the provinces. He tackled such theatrically famous things as Irving's old double part of Lesurques and Dubose in *The Lyons Mail*, and was not afraid even to tackle *Hamlet* at Birmingham in March, 1923. He was a very competent actor, in an extremely old-fashioned way, speaking resonantly and clearly, and making great play of stage business. When in 1922 he doubled the parts of Micawber and Peggotty in *David Copperfield* at Brixton, it was greeted as a remarkable *tour de force*, though complaint was made that Williams, for the sake of contrast, took an unjustifiable liberty in rendering Micawber as a drunken buffoon. In recent years he often appeared in television, tackling the new medium with modesty and professional competence. When he was 88 he was the subject of a B.B.C. television programme in the "This is Your Life" series. In 1959 a committee, of which Lord Birkett was chairman, launched an appeal on his behalf.

His eldest son, a captain in the Royal Flying Corps, was killed in 1918.

December 4, 1961.

The Right Reverend Henry Herbert Williams, C.H., D.D., Bishop of Carlisle from 1920 to 1946 and previously Principal of St. Edmund Hall, Oxford, died on September 29, 1961, at Chester. He was 88.

One of the very ablest members of the Bench of Bishops, he was at the same time one of the most retiring. Outside the dioceses of Oxford and Carlisle he was perhaps best known to the general public for his chairmanship of the Archbishops' Commission on the Ministry of Women, which was set up as a consequence of the report of the Committee on the Ministry of the Church to the 1930 Lambeth Conference.

Dr. Williams's unstinting devotion to the care of his diocese was another cause which contributed to preventing him—to the regret of many—from playing the part in the affairs of the Church as a whole which his intellectual abilities warranted. He had contributed brilliant articles on ethical subjects to the *Encyclopaedia Britannica*. His article on "will" in particular was considered one of the ablest statements ever penned of the issues in the controversy between libertarianism and determinism. The case against the latter, based on the facts of moral consciousness, can rarely have been stated more cogently or more fairly. He repeated the substance of the arguments in one of the best official sermons ever preached before the British Association for the Advancement of Science. He was a useful member of the Church and State Commission and other bodies, an efficient and beloved diocesan, and both at Oxford and later in the diocese of Carlisle a spiritual inspiration to innumerable thoughtful men and women.

Short in stature, he looked out on the world from under bushy eyebrows that were a little reminiscent of Archbishop Lord Davidson. He combined a shrewd but kindly understanding of men and affairs with the learning—always worn lightly—of a scholar. He was distrustful of new organizations, maintaining that "the Church of England already possesses all the machinery necessary for its life and needs if it had the will to use it", and he himself never spared pains to make existing organizations work. Any memoir would be incomplete if it did not make some mention of his leadership in offering help from the diocese of Carlisle to a southern diocese which had suffered heavily from air raids; or of the scene in the Diocesan Conference, of September, 1941, when the Bishop of Penrith referred to the fact that Dr. Williams had completed 21 years as Bishop of the Diocese and the whole Conference stood up to express a tribute of good wishes. He was made C.H. in 1945 and retired in 1946.

Born at Poppleton, York, on December 19, 1872, Williams was the eldest son of the Rev. J. Williams, Vicar of Poppleton. He was educated at St. Peter's School, York, and at Queen's College, Oxford, where he was Hastings Exhibitioner, took a second in Classical Moderations and a first in Literae Humaniores and won the Aubrey Moore studentship. He was ordained in 1900, from 1899 to 1914 he was a Fellow of Hertford College, Oxford, and from 1913 to 1920 Principal of St. Edmund Hall. He was a Tutor of Hertford College from 1909 to 1914 and rector of Gatcombe from 1914 to 1917. He was a Select Preacher at Oxford in 1909-10, 1918-19 and in 1938, and at Cambridge in 1921 and 1926. He was consecrated Bishop of Carlisle in August, 1920. He was made an Honorary Fellow of Queen's College, Hertford College, and of St. Edmund Hall.

He married in 1902 Maud Elizabeth, third daughter of the late J. Y. Sargent, Fellow of Hertford College. There were no children.

September 30, 1961.

Hugh Williams, the actor and playwright, died on December 7, 1969, in a London hospital. He was 65.

Born on March 6, 1904, Hugh Anthony Glanmor Williams went to school at Haileybury and studied at R.A.D.A. Having gained an experience of $2\frac{1}{2}$ years at the Liverpool Playhouse, he found it, as he admitted, "astonishingly easy", thanks to engagements in comedy in the West End, on an Australian tour with Irene Vanbrugh and on the road in the United States, to become a successful actor.

He was seen regularly on the London stage, in the 1930s, some of the roles he played having more of the stuff of serious drama in them: roles such as that of the aristocratic burglar in *Grand Hotel*, the spoilt boy in *The Green Bay Tree*, Darcy in *Pride and Prejudice*, and the eldest son in *Dear Octopus*, which he took over from John Gielgud.

After his war service he was seen in such "testing" roles as the barrister husband in the New York production of *The Cocktail Party* and Trigorin in *The Seagull*, but his appearances in Verneuil's *Affairs of State* and in *Book of the Month* were in comedy of a much more conventional type, mildly satirical, mildly sentimental. This was the pattern he followed when, during a period of unemployment, he wrote with his wife, the actress Margaret Vyner, *Plaintiff in a Pretty Hat*. Successfully produced in 1956, with himself in the part of an urbane Welsh peer, it was followed by *The Happy Man* and by *The Grass is Greener* which, with Williams again playing a peer, trim in figure, lethargic in movement, quick in wind—Cary Grant's role in the film version—broke box office records at the St. Martin's.

The author-actor had for his stage partner Joan Greenwood in *The Irregular Verb to Love* and Susan Hampshire in *Past Imperfect*. He did not appear in *The Flip Side*, but that play was still running and *Charlie Girl* was already in its third year, when the Williams's *Let's All Go Down the Strand*, made its appearance in 1967. In *His, Hers and Theirs*, produced last week, Williams had the cooperation of Dame Gladys Cooper for the second time, and that of his actor-son Simon Williams. As Margaret Williams herself put it, she and her husband liked to see people on the stage looking clean and well dressed and the plays they wrote were to be considered not statements, just remarks. They believed, however, and wished to affirm their belief, that married couples should stay married.

Most of Williams's film work was done in British films, *Rome Express*, Korda's *An Ideal Husband* and *The Gift Horse* being among them.

His marriage to Miss Gwynne Whitby, the actress, was dissolved in 1940. There were two daughters of the marriage. By his second marriage to Margaret Vyner, he had two sons and a daughter.

December 8, 1969.

Sir Ifor Williams, the eminent Welsh scholar and author, and Emeritus Professor of Welsh Language and Literature at the University College of North Wales, Bangor, died at his home in North Wales on November 4, 1965. He was 84.

Ifor Williams, one of the foremost Celtic scholars of his time, was born at Tregarth, a quarry village near Bangor, in 1881. His father was a quarryman; his maternal grandfather, Hugh Derfel Hughes, was a poet and hymn writer of some note.

As a boy Ifor Williams's health was bad: he used to say that his literary and linguistic taste was formed during the periods when he was ill and unable to get about and had no resources other than books. At first he intended to become a minister in the Presbeterian Church of Wales, but although he continued to preach as a layman during the greater part of his life he did not seek ordination.

He took his degree in the University of Wales in 1905 and in the following year was appointed scholar assistant in Welsh at Bangor. In 1907 he was appointed assistant lecturer in the department. In 1919 he became independent lecturer in Welsh literature, the lectureship becoming a chair a year later. In 1929, on the death of Sir John Morris-Jones, the two chairs were merged and he became Professor of Welsh Language and Literature. He retired in 1947 and was knighted in the same year.

In 1938 he was elected a Fellow of the British Academy and in 1939 a Fellow of the Society of Antiquaries. He had been chairman of the Board of Celtic Studies of the University of Wales and of the Ancient Monuments Board for Wales and a member of the Royal Commission on Ancient Monuments in Wales and Monmouthshire. He held the D. Litt. degree of his University. He married in 1913, Myfanwy, daughter of the late Henry Jones, of Pont Lyfni, Caernarvonshire. They had a son and a daughter who survive him. His wife died last year.

LITERARY DETECTIVE

Williams was a personality as well as a scholar. He had a gift that might almost be called genius for interpreting words and sentences that had puzzled generations of scholars, and he could make the process of interpretation interesting and even fascinating for people who were not scholars at all in the strict sense. Thus, in the introduction to what is probably his greatest work, his edition of the sixth-century poem *Y Gododdin*, and in his edition of the poems commonly attributed to Llywarch Hen (*Canu Aneirin*, 1938 and *Canu Llywarch Hen*, 1935) he makes the unfolding of what may be called the case really enthralling without deviating from the canons of careful scholarship.

The same thing may be said of his editing of some other Welsh poets, including the work of Dafydd ap Gwilym and his contemporaries, and his book on Welsh placenames. As a writer, lecturer, broadcaster, and in general conversation he could not be other than entertaining. He had a keen sense of humour and he was not afraid of telling a story against himself.

His main interests were linguistic and grammatical rather than literary, and when Sir John Morris-Jones was professor of Welsh and Ifor Williams lecturer in Welsh literature it used to be said that the roles might have been reversed, for Sir John was a poet and a literary critic of note as well as a Celtic scholar. But Williams's prose was good and although he confined himself, with the exception of a few essays, to his own subject his introductions rank as contributions to the Welsh literature of his time. In addition to the editing of Welsh texts he was editor of the Bulletin of the Board of Celtic Studies, and joint editor of *Y Traethodydd*, the oldest Welsh quarterly.

With Mr. Robert Richards, M.P., he had also been editor of the monthly *Tyddynnwr*. He translated Ibsen's *A Doll's House* for the Bangor College Players, a version in which he sought to discover a flexible stage language that would combine the dignity of literary Welsh with the ease of the spoken language.

After his retirement, he continued to write, and to take the liveliest interest in all aspects of Celtic studies.

November 5, 1965.

Iolo Williams, who died on January 18, 1962, at the age of 71, will be missed by many friends in remarkably diverse circles of London and Welsh life. His tall, stooping, scholarly figure—he was careless of appearances and distinguished without conscious effort like a don of the best academic vintage—could be seen daily both entering Printing House Square and the Athenaeum and strolling through museums, picture galleries, and the Zoo.

He looked a veteran surviving from an age of greater style than the present and this appearance was confirmed by chronology. Williams would speak as naturally of his years at Rugby and King's with Rupert Brooke and other vanished and almost legendary contemporaries as he did of the latest acquisition by the Tate or a rare bird just seen in Norfolk or (theme always dear to his heart) some advance in the cultural field in Wales. He moved as easily in conversation (and he was a gifted talker and listener) from Edwardian to up-to-date topics and he never gave the slightest impression of having aged in spirit.

The warm, kindly flame that burnt inside that large body, kept its brightness undimmed through illness and in the face of setbacks to some of the causes he cared for most. A Liberal of the old school, with no nonsense about a small "l", he had a Gladstonian rectitude and a stern radicalism in his bones which made him, for instance, an almost fanatical apostle of temperance. Gravity in the classic sense was his and piety. He stood four square on principle.

TRUE HUMANIST

But he was unbending without being dour. A delicious relish for the lighter side of things would often cause a quick smile and a chuckle to enliven his companions. His memory for old music hall songs was remarkable and he would sing his favourites with humour and gusto.

The range of his interests and his deep knowledge of so many subjects marked him as a true humanist.

He will be especially remembered for the *Early English Water-Colours* and for his studies in eighteenth-century bibliography and verse. But as botanist, ornithologist and literary critic he made his mark.

Iolo Aneurin Williams was born at Middlesbrough on June 18, 1890, the son of the late Aneurin Williams, who sat as Liberal M.P. for Plymouth and later for the North-West and the Consett divisions of Durham, and grandson of Edward Williams, a notable Middlesbrough ironmaster who became president of the Iron and Steel Institute. A more distant ancestor was that other Edward Williams who was better known as Iolo Morganwg, the Welsh bard and antiquary.

Williams was educated at Rugby School and at King's College, Cambridge. In his youth his health gave some anxiety, but he thrived in the bracing air of Hindhead, where his father made his home, and there developed a life-long interest in natural history. His early interest in folk-song was shown by his contribution to E. W. Swanton's *Byegone Haslemere* of a paper on the folk-songs of the neighbourhood. With Clive Carey he undertook some active field-work in collecting old songs from those who still sang them. He became for a time the honorary secretary of the Folk Song Society and later wrote the book on *English Folk Song and Dance* in the English Heritage Series.

WAR SERVICE

At the beginning of the 1914–18 War Williams served in the London Intelligence Department. In October, 1914, he crossed to the Continent with the Red Cross, and in 1915 joined the Army as a second lieutenant, serving with various units in England until July, 1916. From then until 1920 he was attached to the Claims Commission and Directorate of Hirings and Requisitions, B.E.F., being graded as staff captain.

In 1915 and 1919 Williams published two small books of poetry; much of his verse has charm—sometimes a grave charm—and an almost eighteenth-century sensibility, conveyed with economy of means. On returning to civilian life he settled down to steady work as an author and freelance journalist. In 1920 he became bibliographical correspondent of the *London Mercury*, and he continued in that capacity until the *Mercury* ceased independent publication in 1939. He also wrote bibliographical articles for the *Publisher and Bookseller* and for the *Bookman*, and was an active contributor to *The Observer* for many years.

Williams's growing interest in the minor poets of the eighteenth century was shown in his pleasant anthology *Byways round Helicon* (1922) and in his *Shorter Poems of the Eighteenth Century* (1923); these were books that played their part in the revival of interest in eighteenth-century literature between the wars. He also prepared an edition of Sheridan's plays, while his *Elements of Book-Collecting* (1927) was a useful and unusual handbook.

So far as the *minutiae* of eighteenth-century bibliography was concerned, Williams was undoubtedly a pioneer. Stimulated perhaps by the appearance of Wise's Ashley Library Catalogue, he compiled *Seven Eighteenth Century Bibliographies* (1924) which was the first work to investigate problems of eighteenth-century bibliography, apart from the works of a few major writers.

He was responsible for the popularity of what are called Poetical Miscellanies, a feature of eighteenth-century verse publishing which had previously been virtually ignored.

Williams was a first-class field botanist. Although he did not publish much himself, the writings of many other botanists were enriched with his notes and observations. He described a species of brome-grass new to Britain, and in 1947 he contributed a volume on *Flowers of Marsh and Stream* to the King Penguin series. His amazingly quick eye for spotting inconspicuous rarities and his rich store of out-of-the-way knowledge on British plants made him an ideal companion on a botanical expedition.

ENGLISH WATER COLOURS

Studies in bibliography and book illustration led Williams to the drawings and water colours of the earlier English School, and the interest that he showed in collecting and writing about these was of much the same type as his study of birds and flowers. The pleasures of the chase and discovery were transferred from field and hedgerow to shops and portfolios. He delighted in finding examples that bore new names, and he brought together a large and very interesting collection showing as many varieties of any artist's work as came within his reach. In this the impulse was not merely the stamp-collector's search for rare specimens; he had a simple and direct interest in the more human aspects of the drawings, especially that of representation, and this unsophisticated humanity of his outlook gave a special value to his words when he came to deal with contemporary work, because it was perfectly adapted to indicate to those in need of guidance precisely those works on the walls of galleries which would give them the pleasure that he had received himself.

Williams inherited his father's politics and twice unsuccessfully contested Chelsea as a Liberal. He also derived from his father a keen interest in proportional representation, and was for a time honorary treasurer of the Proportional Representation Society. He was a vice-president of the Bibliographical Society, a trustee of the Watts Gallery, Compton, a member of the council of the National Museum of Wales, and had been a member of the council and a vice-president of the Zoological Society of London. It gave him great pleasure to be made in 1960 an honorary member of the Gorsedd of Bards. An unflagging student of Welsh, he took every chance to speak, read and write the language.

Williams had contributed on occasion to *The Times* and its *Literary Supplement* before he joined the staff of the paper as its Museums Correspondent in 1936. It was a task for which a collector's enthusiasm and a multiplicity of interests fully qualified him. But he was much more than a specialist and for the past 25 years he added distinction and scholarship to many sides of the paper including its leading articles. His modesty and constant friendliness, added to an encyclopaedic knowledge which was always conscientiously placed at the service of *The Times*, made him an invaluable, and indeed an irreplaceable colleague.

In 1920 he was married to Francion Elinor, daughter of the late A. R. Dixon, of Cedaredge, Colorado, United States, and there were a son and two daughters of the marriage.

January 19, 1962.

Dr. Ivy Williams, the first woman to be called to the English Bar, died at her home in Oxford on February 18, 1966. She was 88.

Dr. Williams, an hon. fellow and former tutor at St. Anne's College, Oxford, was called to the English Bar in May, 1922, six months after Ulster-born Miss Frances Kyle was called to the Irish Bar. Dr. Williams earned her priority by gaining a Certificate of Honour at the Final Bar Examination.

Born in September, 1877, she lived in Oxford for almost the whole of her long life. The only daughter of George St. Swithin Williams, an Oxford solicitor, she was educated privately, and at 19 became a member of the Society of Oxford Home Students, now St. Anne's College. To this body, originally drawn from girls living in their own homes, she remained loyally devoted throughout her life, watching and sharing in its development.

She took a second class in Jurisprudence in 1900, and in the B.C.I. examination in 1902. At the same time she was taking the London University examinations, and received the LL.D. in 1903. Oxford, though allowing women to take their examinations, as yet refused them full membership of the University.

DEGREES FOR WOMEN

But as soon as degrees were opened to women, Ivy Williams received her B.C.L. in October, 1920.

In January, 1920, when women were first admitted to the Inns of Court, she had joined the Inner Temple, under the sponsorship of Sir John Simon; and in May, 1922, was called to the Bar by Sir Henry Dickens on a Final Bar Examination Certificate of Honour (1st Class), which excused her two terms' dinners. In 1923, on publication of *The Sources of Law in the Swiss Civil Code*, she was awarded the degree of D.C.L. at Oxford In 1925 she published *The Swiss Civil Code: English Version, with Notes and Vocabulary*. Studious and reserved, Ivy Williams never practised, but preferred an academic career. From 1920 to 1945 she was Tutor and Lecturer in Law to the Society of Oxford Home Students. During these years most women who studied law at Oxford were under her wise and scholarly direction. Her own distinction enabled her to enlist some of the chief members of the Law Faculty to help in the teaching of her pupils, to whom she herself was an inspiration by her dedicated study of law. When no longer pupils, they could count on her advice and encouragement in their careers, so that by both precept and example she continued to play her part in the slow and difficult advance of women to their present position in the legal profession and in the universities.

ENDOWED SCHOLARSHIPS

She was elected Honorary Fellow of St. Anne's College in 1956. She endowed two law scholarships at Oxford—one of them open to women only—in memory of her brother, Captain Winter Williams, Barrister-at-Law.

Dr. Williams was twice appointed to positions outside her University, serving in 1930 as Delegate to the Hague Conference for the Codification of International Law under Sir Maurice Gwyer, and in 1932 as a member of the Aliens Deportation Advisory Committee under Roland Vaughan Williams.

In many ways also she gave of her best to her generation, both by her wisdom and strong good sense and by many unobtrusive acts of kindness. To her friends she leaves a memory, not only of steadfast friendship and of high aims and achievement, but of shining integrity of intellect and character. In her later years she faced severe physical disabilities with courage and serenity. Realizing that her eyesight was failing, she took up the study of Braille and became an authority on work for the blind. Her Braille Primer, published for the N.I.B. in 1948, passed into more than one edition, while she herself had correspondence pupils in many parts of Britain, whom she taught to read and write Braille, almost to the end of her long life. Of no one could it more truly be said that she "turned her necessity to glorious gain", using in old age for the service of others the powers and enthusiasm which had won her distinction in her youth.

February 19, 1966.

Dr. J. A. Williamson, the historian of the great age of maritime enterprise and of British colonial expansion, died on December 31, 1964, at his home at Chichester. He was 78.

As a historian, the author of a standard work like *A Short History of British Expansion* or of a brillant sketch like *Great Britain and the Empire*, Williamson was no doubt in the line of Seeley and his successors, though his vision and intellectual purpose were both his own. As a historical writer, blessed with imagination and a flexible style, he drew upon the resources of a rich acquaintance with the literature of exploration and discovery and especially upon the fruits of his love for the Elizabethan voyagers and geographers. He had a guiding sense of the unbroken continuity of the processes of English history.

The acquisition of the Empire and Commonwealth did not, in his view, disturb this continuity, but rather exhibited the constancy with which the same geographical factors made themselves felt. In a series of impressively vivid volumes Williamson ranged over the centuries of the influence of sea power and of the growth of the idea of liberty as these shaped the evolution of island and Empire. His contributions of new material were often considerable. Few, indeed, had a greater respect for evidence in writing history. To his gifts of clear narrative and sober and sane judgment were added a passion for accuracy that entailed endlessly patient research at the Public Record Office and at the British Museum and Bodleian Libraries.

SCHOOLMASTERING

James Alexander Williamson was born in 1886, the son of James Ireland Williamson, and was educated at Watford Grammar School and London University, where he took his degree in 1906. Much of his most important work was done while he was engaged in schoolmastering. From 1910 until 1937, with only an interruption for service in the Army during 1914–19, he was an assistant master at Westminster City School. His first book, *Maritime Enterprise, 1485–1558*, appeared in 1913 and already exhibited the qualities of patient research and the graces of literary style which were to mark his work as a whole. It was from this as yet somewhat circumscribed study that Williamson developed his *Short History of British Expansion* (1923), his earliest work after his release from the Army and a shining example of accurate, vivid, and measured historical writing. Here he demonstrated with quiet cogency that the British Empire was based upon sea power. This central thesis was given fresh illustration in most of the studies that followed during the next seven or eight years—among them *English Colonies in Guiana and The Amazon, 1604–1658*, which filled a hitherto blank space in our Colonial history; *The Caribee Islands under the Proprietary Patents*, which resumed the early history of the West Indies; *Sir John Hawkins, the Time and the Man;* and *The Voyages of the Cabots and the English Discovery of North America under Henry VII and Henry VIII*.

BREADTH OF VIEW

In 1931 Williamson produced *The Evolution of England*, which he himself described as "a commentary on the facts". It is a first-rate piece of work in its way, perhaps just a shade overwritten here and there, but graphic, pithy, of fine proportion and distinguished in its emphasis on geography by a remarkable breadth of view. The last book he wrote before abandoning schoolmastering was *The British Empire and Commonwealth* (1935), and then, in another phase of sustained energy, came *The Age of Drake* (1938), in which he collected together new material contributed by several hands and produced a volume at once sober and stirring; an edition of Dampier's *Voyage to New Holland* (1939); *The Ocean in English History* (*1941*), consisting of his Ford lectures at Cambridge for 1939–40—a survey of sea power through the centuries; *A Notebook of Empire History*, designed for students and teachers; *Great Britain and the Empire* (1944), which he styled "a discursive history", and in which all the elements of his theme were organized into a balanced and stimulating unity; and a short book on *Cook and the Opening of the Pacific* (1946).

HAWKINS AND DRAKE

Finally there came *Hawkins of Plymouth* (1949); *Sir Francis Drake*, in Collins's Brief Lives series (1951); *The Tudor Age* (1953); *George and Robert Stephenson* (1958); *The English Channel: a History* (1959); and *The Cabot Voyages and British Discovery under Henry VII* (1962).

Williamson made notable contributions to the Cambridge History of the British Empire and was a contributor also to various magazines and historical journals. He was a vice-president of the Historical Association and of the Hakluyt Society.

January 2, 1965.

Lord Wilmot of Selmeston, P.C., died on July 22, 1964, at the age of 69. For some years before his elevation to the peerage in 1950 he had been a prominent member of the Labour Party in the House of Commons, and was Minister of Supply from 1945 to 1947. In this office he occupied a key position in the changeover from war to peacetime production.

He first came into the public eye in the autumn of 1933 when, as John Wilmot, he was chosen to be Labour candidate at an historic by-election at East Fulham. This contest, though confused by many local issues, was fought largely on the question of rearmament. Wilmot won a sensational victory which was a major factor in persuading Stanley Baldwin, who subsequently succeeded Ramsay MacDonald as Prime Minister in the National Government, to modify his rearmament plans and change his policy for the general election of 1935.

Wilmot's early training as a banker made him recognized as one of his party's experts on finance and taxation. He had a genial manner, allied to a concise, persuasive way of speaking. These two assets made him a valuable member of all kinds of committees.

John Wilmot was born on April 2, 1895. His father, Charles Wilmot, was an engraver. Educated at Hither Green Central School John was only 15 when his father died. He was compelled to leave school and to take on the job of office-boy with a firm of marine insurance brokers. He continued his studies at King's College and the Chelsea Polytechnic. At the former he won the Gilbart Prize in Banking, and subsequently joined the staff of the Westminster Bank.

PROGRESS AT THE BANK

He had already become interested in politics and joined the Labour Party in 1911. After serving during the First World War as an aircraftman in the Royal Naval Air Service, in 1919 he helped to form the Labour Party's Lewisham branch, being elected treasurer. Although East Lewisham was a strong Conservative seat, Wilmot was three times Labour candidate at Parliamentary elections there, and in 1929 brought the Conservative majority down to less than 400. These activities did not prevent his making progress at the bank, where he was promoted to the general manager's staff and to the secretaryship of the Anglo-Russian Bank.

After his by-election victory at East Fulham in 1933 (he converted the Conservative majority of 14,000 into a Labour majority of 4,800) Wilmot became active in the House of Commons on many subjects, in particular on foreign policy and armaments and his own special subject, finance. His success, however, was shortlived as he lost the seat in 1935 and did not return to Westminster until after winning another by-election at Kennington in 1939.

In 1937 Wilmot had been elected an Alderman of the London County Council and when war broke out was Chairman of the London Fire Brigade. He held this post during some of the worst air raids. In 1940 he became Parliamentary Private Secretary to the Minister of Economic Warfare and in 1942 to the President of the Board of Trade. In 1944 his special talents were given real scope when he was appointed Joint Parliamentary Secretary to the Ministry of Supply. By this time the supply of war materials was relatively well organized, but each day there was still a full quota of old problems to be straightened out, and the mass of new problems which would come with the end of the war increasingly made their presence felt. Wilmot soon appeared as a believer in the maintenance of economic controls if the dangers of postwar inflation were to be avoided, and after the Labour victory in 1945, when he was returned as M.P. for Deptford and was himself raised to the Minister's chair, this became the essence of his policy. He was also given the powers formerly vested in the Minister of Aircraft Production and had the difficult task of welding the two ministries into one, and supervising the switch-over to peacetime production.

STEEL NATIONALIZATION

One of the major controversies during his first year of office was over the future of the iron and steel industry. He was chairman of the committee which considered the proposals of the Iron and Steel Federation for the industry's future and he led the debate in the House in which it became clear that the Government were in favour of eventually nationalizing appropriate sections of the industry. After this he had to face vehement attacks from some of the back-benchers of his own party in discussions on the personnel of the board to control the industry during the transitional period, and on the form nationalization should take. During this year the Government also had to face up to the implications of atomic energy, and as Minister of Supply he was vested with exceptionally wide powers to control its development. In addition to being concerned with the modernization of industry as a whole, Wilmot was particularly charged with the production of civilian aircraft and the exploitation of new developments such as jet propulsion.

In October, 1947, Wilmot resigned his office as Minister of Supply. Though he denied that there had been any differences with his colleagues about the policy to be adopted for the iron and steel industry, there was no doubt that his plans had been subjected to severe criticism. He was offered a peerage, which he declined, stating that he preferred to remain a member of the House of Commons. In January, 1950, however, his name appeared in the New Year Honours list, and he was gazetted Baron Wilmot of Selmeston, in the county of Sussex.

The innumerable committees of which Wilmot had been a member included the Cohen Committee on Company Law Reform, the Select Committee on Rebuilding the Houses of Parliament, and the L.C.C.'s Town Planning, Housing and Public Health and Parliamentary committees. He was chairman of the latter committee. He was twice elected to the Labour Party's National Executive and served on the Executive Committee of the Workers' Travel Association.

In 1944 he served on a Parliamentary mission to study conditions in the West Indies. He had been chairman of the Governors of the Old Vic and of the Glyndebourne Festival Society.

and was a member of the National Theatre Board. Together with Lord Latham he formed the Shareholders' Protection Association, and as a business man became well known in the City.

July 24, 1964.

Sir Edward Wilshaw, K.C.M.G., president of Cable and Wireless (Holding) Ltd. and chairman or director of many other companies, who spent more than 60 years in the cable and wireless service, died on March 3, 1968, at the age of 88 in London.

Wilshaw played a large part in hastening better telegraphic communications between countries. He was the author of the Imperial Communications scheme, launched shortly before the Second World War. For nearly half a century he helped to guide the company from the days of hand-tapped Morse code practically into the satellite age.

The company was nationalized in 1947. Wilshaw had stonewalled his way through two years and nearly 100 meetings with the Treasury, and came out with good compensation terms. He was then approaching 70. He fought a battle with a cash-and-carry minority among the shareholders, and started Cable and Wireless on its very successful career as an investment company. In 1964, he relinquished the governorship of the company, and became its president.

Wilshaw possessed the technical knowledge and scientific experience, business acumen, and a capacity for getting along with men, necessary to develop and control the worldwide expansion of telegraphic communications.

Edward Wilshaw, the son of a shipyard chairman, was born on June 3, 1879. He joined the Eastern Telegraph Co. as a junior clerk in 1894. From the moment that he got his foot on the bottom rung of the ladder, he set himself the task of mastering the cable network. His progress was modest but persistent, until, in 1928, he was appointed general manager and secretary of Imperial & International Communications on the amalgamation of the Empire cable and wireless services.

Within a decade he was directing companies in the realm of communications controlling capital totalling more than £100m.; he had produced the Imperial Communications scheme; he had an eye and a hand on a network of more than 300,000 miles. From 1936 to 1946 he was, in addition to the Government-approved managing director and chairman of Cable & Wireless, managing director of all its subsidiary companies. In 1947, when the company was nationalized, Wilshaw retired as chairman and managing director, but remained as governor. During his period of control the flat rate for all Empire telegrams had been instituted and he had started a profit-sharing scheme for the staff.

In December, 1939, soon after Wilshaw had been created K.C.M.G., he was presented with a replica of the star of the Order in diamonds and rubies set in platinum, at a staff gathering. The fund for the presentation had been collected in 39 different currencies.

In addition to his directorates in the many cable and wireless concerns, Wilshaw was on the boards of several other companies. He had been for many years General Commissioner of Income Tax and of Land Tax for the Havering Division of the county of Essex, president of the Chartered Institute of Secretaries, and vice-president of the Royal Society of St. George.

Wilshaw was a great and enthusiastic Londoner, and for many years a member of the Court of the Guild of Freemen. As befitted a descendant of Thomas Wilshaw, an Elder Brother of Trinity House, who succeeded Pepys as Comptroller of the Navy, he was a past Prime Warden of the Company of Shipwrights, as well as a Liveryman of the Company of Coopers.

Wilshaw was an honorary LL.D. of London, a magistrate and a Deputy Lieutenant for Essex, and one of Her Majesty's Lieutenants of the City of London. In 1912 he married Myn, daughter of William Moar, of Orkney. They had two daughters.

March 4, 1968.

Field Marshal Lord Wilson, who died on December 31, 1964, at the age of 83, rose to the highest rank and honours in the 1939-45 War and carried out his work in a number of senior appointments with calm efficiency. He was completely dependable rather than brilliant and in particular enjoyed the confidence of the then Prime Minister and Minister of Defence, Mr. Churchill.

Henry Maitland Wilson was born on September 5, 1881, the son of Arthur Maitland Wilson of Stowlangtoft Hall, Suffolk. His uncle, Lieutenant-General Sir H. F. M. Wilson, served with distinction in the 1914-18 War. On his mother's side he was descended from Admiral Lord Howe and Lord Raglan, British Commander-in-Chief in the Crimea. He followed his uncle to Eton, Sandhurst, and the Rifle Brigade, in which he was commissioned in 1900. He took part in the South African War, receiving the Queen's and King's Medals, each with two clasps. Having been promoted captain in 1908 and appointed adjutant of the Oxford University O.T.C. in 1911, Wilson went out to France in 1914. In the course of the war he acted as brigade major, G.S.O.2, and G.S.O.1, was awarded the D.S.O., and was twice mentioned in dispatches. He was promoted major in 1915 and after the war, in 1919, received a brevet lieutenant-colonelcy. In the same year he passed through the Staff College.

Between the two great wars Wilson saw no active service and his promotion was relatively slow, so that he fell behind several of his contemporaries. He was, however, always considered an outstanding instructor and trainer of troops. For a brief period in 1920 he acted as instructor at the Royal Military College Sandhurst, moving on in the same capacity to the Staff College, where he remained until 1924. From 1927 to 1930 he commanded the 1st Battalion The Rifle Brigade and in the latter year returned to the Staff College as G.S.O.1 with the now extinct rank of colonel on the staff. Next, after a period on half-pay, he took over command of the 6th Brigade. He was promoted major-general in 1935, being then some nine years older—almost a generation in military life—than men who just afterwards received particularly rapid promotion to the same rank, such as Generals Alexander, Freyberg, and Holmes. In 1937 he succeeded General Wavell in command of the 2nd Division at Aldershot. There his full worth was seen, and his superior, General Dill, considered him the best peacetime divisional commander with whom he had come in contact. He received the C.B. in that year.

CAMPAIGN IN SYRIA

Wilson reached the rank of lieutenant-general in 1938 and on the eve of the 1939-45 War was Commander-in-Chief, British Troops, Egypt. In the first British offensive against the Italians he commanded the striking force, known then as the Army of the Nile, but directed the victorious operations only as far as the frontier, their conduct then passing into the hands of the corps commander, General O'Connor. For his part in this campaign Wilson was advanced to K.C.B. In 1941 he commanded the ill-fated expedition to Greece, a task in which no man could have succeeded, though he did all that was humanly possible. His next campaign, in the same year, was in Syria. This was, as he himself afterwards confessed in a broadcast speech, a painful though very necessary undertaking: painful because it involved hostilities against our former French allies, necessary because Syria and Lebanon could not be allowed to fall under Axis contol. The French fought stoutly and delivered a daring counter-offensive, but Wilson, completely unmoved by an unexpected set-back, stuck to his plan and carried the operations to a successful conclusion. In the course of that year he was promoted general and made G.B.E.

In December, 1941, he took over command of the Ninth Army in Syria and Palestine, in the Middle East Command. In the following summer, however, when the German success in Southern Russia seemed likely to lead to an invasion of Persia, the command was split up and a new independent command, Persia-Iraq, to which Wilson was appointed, was created.

LEVANT FAILURE

This appointment came to an end in February, 1943, when General Alexander was transferred to French North Africa and Wilson succeeded him as Commander-in-Chief, Middle East. Egypt was by now further removed than formerly from the fighting, but Wilson became involved in an unsuccessful venture in the Levant which was very strongly criticized in this country. This was the occupation of the islands of Cos, Leros, and Samos, in September, 1943.

It had been hoped that the Italians would have secured Rhodes after the armistice, but they had allowed themselves to be disarmed by the German section of the garrison, though it was much smaller than their own, and without the benefit of the Rhodes airfields it was impossible to provide air cover for either the land or naval forces fighting in the smaller islands or endeavouring to keep them supplied. Nor could German landings be prevented and after very hard fighting the greater proportion of the survivors of the garrisons were captured by the enemy. Writing of this improvised expedition in his postwar dispatch, Wilson described it pointedly as carried out "on orders from London".

In January, 1944, on the return to England of General Eisenhower to prepare for the invasion of north-west Europe, Wilson was appointed Supreme Allied Commander, Mediterranean. He exercised strategic control over the chief campaign, that in Italy, though the operations were directly conducted by Alexander. He was always optimistic about the possibilities of the Italian theatre. His remarkable reports to the Combined Chiefs of Staff—which take the place of the conventional British dispatches because he was an international commander—show that he believed, and urged, that if the armies and air forces in Italy were kept up to strength and the landing in the south of France was abandoned it would be possible to penetrate to the plain of the Danube. In this he was supported by Alexander, who wrote of his armies, as they were in early June, 1944: "Neither the Apennines nor even the Alps should prove a serious obstacle to their enthusiasm and skill." However, other considerations prevailed and the armies in Italy were progressively weakened. For his work in the Mediterranean Wilson was advanced to G.C.B.

SUCCEEDED DILL

In November, 1944, Sir John Dill, Senior British Military Representative on the Combined Chiefs of Staffs Committee in the United States, died in Washington. Wilson was appointed to succeed him. Before he reached Washington (in January, 1945), he was promoted to the rank of field marshal. He remained in the United States until the spring of 1947—sufficient proof that he gave satisfaction to both sides. He was awarded the Distinguished Service Medal by President Truman in November, 1945, was appointed A.D.C. General to the King in January, 1946, and on March 12 of that year had conferred upon him the dignity of a barony of the United Kingdom. He took the style and title of Baron Wilson of Libya and of Stowlangtoft in the county of Suffolk. From 1955 to 1960 he was Constable of the Tower of London.

Wilson has been described as "large, genial, quiet, and imperturbable". His bulk, which had earned him the sobriquet of "Jumbo" as a comparatively junior officer, did not connote a lethargic mind, and he possessed an excellent tactical eye. In spite of his weight, he was an enthusiastic follower of hounds up to the time of the war, and this big man, on a horse built on a somewhat similar scale, kept as close up as many who had the advantage over him of 20 years and three or four stones but yet considered themselves fairly hard riders.

He married in 1914 Hester Mary, daughter of Philip James Digby Wykeham, of Tythrop House, Oxfordshire, and had one son and one daughter.

January 1, 1965.

Charles Edwin Wilson, the former president of the General Motors Corporation, who was Secretary of Defence under President Eisenhower for four years from 1953 to 1957, died in his sleep on September 26, 1961, at his plantation in Louisiana. He had been living in semi-retirement since leaving the Pentagon and suffered a heart attack several years ago.

It is Wilson's misfortune that the difficult and sometimes stormy years he spent at the head of the Defence Department are likely to obscure in the public memory the much more successful period of his life in Detroit. To him belongs much of the credit for the remarkable arms production effort sustained in the United States during the Second World War and he was later responsible for the revolutionary General Motors cost-of-living wage formula after the war.

In public life he was a controversial figure and his relations with Congress were strained from the beginning, partly because he insisted on referring to the legislators as "you men" and partly because he appeared reluctant to dispose of his General Motors shares. Wilson subsequently modified the appellation to "gentlemen" and his stock rose slightly on Capitol Hill but he always refused to add "sir".

However, Wilson was Secretary of Defence for longer than any other man has been and he gave his President loyal and tireless service. He won affection from the general public as a man prepared to laugh at his own mistakes and respect from others for his knowledge of technical matters. It was his fate to be in charge of the armed forces at a time when the transition from the military concepts of the Second World War to those of the missile age were exacerbating service rivalries, and he was criticized on occasion for showing insufficient firmness or control. President Eisenhower once told him in this connexion: "You have got to be prepared to be the most unpopular man in the Government".

But it was his tendency to allow an unfortunate phrase to pass his lips that was the principal cause of Wilson's becoming such a controversial figure. He was never allowed to forget "What is good for General Motors is good for the country" (although what he really said was: "I thought what was good for our country was good for General Motors and vice versa") and he is said to have remarked about outer space "What is up there anyway?"

HUNTERS PREFERRED

Once when trying to explain why he did not favour areas of unemployment with defence contracts, he said: "I have always liked bird dogs better than kennel dogs myself. You know, one who will get out and hunt for food rather than sit and yell".

Charles Erwin Wilson, the son of Thomas Erwin Wilson, was born in Minerva, Ohio, on July 18, 1890, and was educated at public schools there and in Pennsylvania. After four years at the Carnegie Institute of Technology in Pittsburgh he became a student apprentice in the Westinghouse Electric and Manufacturing Company at a salary of 18 cents an hour. In 1912 when he was 21 he designed the first motor car starter to be made by Westinghouse and later that year he married Jessie Ann Curtis, by whom he had three sons and three daughters.

He won steady promotion and in 1919 joined General Motors as an engineer and sales manager. He became a vice-president in 1929, a director in 1934, and six years later became acting president.

He later succeeded as president in his own right and while he ran General Motors he was responsible for the production of about a fourth of the tanks, armoured cars and aircraft engines built in the United States, almost half the machine guns and carbines, two-thirds of the heavier lorries, and thousands of transport aircraft. He took a particular interest in labour relations and was an inveterate opponent of the "closed shop", which he once compared with compulsory membership of the Nazi Party.

September 27, 1961.

Edith Bolling Wilson, second wife of President Woodrow Wilson, died on December 28, 1961, at her home in Washington. She was 89.

In recent years Mrs. Wilson lived in some seclusion, to emerge only occasionally in connexion with the Woodrow Wilson Memorial Commission and the Freedom from Hunger Programme, but she was remembered as a steadfast companion and ardent champion of President Wilson in the First World War and during and after the Versailles conferences. She alone knew the secret code used by the President to communicate with Colonel House, and she sat in on many of the private conferences in the White House.

The late President sought her advice constantly, and depended heavily upon their affectionate relationship especially after his crippling stroke in 1919. She was not free from criticism. Members of the cabinet complained during this period that they were not allowed to see the President: and indeed all government business passed through her hands, as did executive orders and messages to Congress.

The last months in the White House were known as Mrs. Wilson's regency, although stewardship would have been a better word, and newspapers referred to her as the acting President. Nevertheless, many Americans remember her as the first First Lady to play a considerable role in the history of the republic and certainly according to her own lights she rose magnificently to the occasion.

Edith Bolling was born on October 15, 1872, the seventh child of a Virginian gentleman who claimed descent from Pocahontas, the daughter of King Powhaten, and John Rolfe. The Bollings were proud of their Indian blood and their standing in the aristocratic society of Virginia, but the family lost almost everything except its gentility in the civil war. Edith Bolling's first marriage was to Norman Galt, a Washington jeweller, who died in 1908. She met President Wilson in the White House early in 1915 and they were married the same year.

At the time the United States was almost in a state of war with Mexico. An unsuccessful expedition was mounted against Pancho Villa, but this proved to be only a romantic overture; the election campaign, which was narrowly won, quickly followed, and two months afterwards Germany launched its unrestricted submarine attack against all shipping.

Until Wilson left the White House the marriage was intimately involved in affairs of state. Personal difficultics, especially with the daughters of the President's first marriage, were gracefully avoided, and what little happiness Wilson enjoyed in his last years was provided by his wife. Edith Wilson's regency —*Liberty* magazine claimed that for six and one half months she was acting President, secretary of the President, and the Secretary of State—could not have been regarded by either of them as an unusual arrangement.

In fact, the stewardship lasted only a few weeks, and it is doubtful that Mrs. Wilson realized the power that she wielded. She faced a constitutional crisis alone. Her husband, the President of the United States, was seriously ill, and he had duties that could not be delegated, and could only be temporarily postponed.

Mrs. Wilson insisted afterwards that she never interfered in affairs of state except when directed by the President's physician, Dr. Dercum, who however advised her at the beginning that it was necessary for Wilson to remain in office and that her assistance was vital. The recommendation of the Secretary of State that the vice-President assume the powers of the Presidency was rejected, and Mrs. Wilson's stewardship was established.

She received every official paper, letter, and document addressed to the President. If possible the department concerned was asked to deal with important matters, but if the President's attention was considered necessary Mrs. Wilson made a brief digest of the situation and read to her husband. She also claimed that she never made a single decision regarding the disposition of public affairs, but only decided what was important and when it should be given to the President. This however required a statesmanship of high order, and it was maintained until Wilson's health improved.

Mrs. Wilson published her memoirs in 1939.

December 30, 1961.

The Right Reverend Henry Albert Wilson, C. B. E., D. D., Bishop of Chelmsford from 1929 to 1950, died on July 16, 1961, at the age of 84.

Wilson was a tremendous driving force in diocesan administration, a trenchant writer and a fearless speaker. A broadminded Liberal Evangelical, he laid continual emphasis on the comprehensiveness of the Church of England and on the supreme need of Church unity in face of the perils without, and of the opportunities of the mission fields.

Born at Port Bannatyne, Bute, on September 6, 1876, Henry Albert Wilson was the son of Thomas Alexander Wilson, of Glasgow, and Mary Proctor, of Newtown Butler, co. Fermanagh. He was educated at Corpus Christi College, Cambridge, where he took an honours degree in 1898, and was ordained in 1899 to the curacy of Christ Church, Hampstead. After five years there he was appointed vicar of Norbiton, Kingston-upon-Thames, and during his tenure of that benefice the various parochial activities were greatly strengthened and a mission church was built.

In 1915, on the resignation of Canon L'Estrange Fawcett, he was appointed by the Simeon Trustees to the benefice of Cheltenham, and in 1917 was appointed Rural Dean of Cheltenham. Here the qualities which were later to mark his episcopate found considerable scope both in parochial organization and in the chairmanship of the Cheltenham Conference. Indeed, his outspoken leadership was an important factor in making this conference one of the most important Evangelical gatherings in the country. On his elevation to the episcopate it was transferred to Oxford, where the tradition was carried on by the first Master of St. Peter's Hall, Bishop Chavasse.

RISKED FRIENDSHIPS

Wilson was equally active in diocesan affairs. From 1921 to 1928 he was an honorary canon of Gloucester; from 1923 to 1928 an honorary chaplain to the Bishop of Gloucester; and from 1922 to 1929 a Proctor in Convocation for the diocese. His independence of mind and his sense of the importance of Church unity were very evident in the Prayer Book controversy when, although there were parts of the projected new Prayer Book which he strongly disliked, he supported it—thereby risking many a longstanding friendship among Evangelicals. His decision once taken, he did not waver or hesitate, but urged with characteristic vigour both in Convocation and in the correspondence columns of *The Times* that discipline and unity demanded acceptance of the Measure.

Special mention should be made of the new public school for girls, St. Monica's, Clacton-on-Sea, which owes so much to the Bishop's efforts, private as well as public. The Bishop's "London-over-the-Border" Fund and other funds were instrumental in providing churches, schools and religious ministrations for hundreds of thousands of people who came to live in the new areas, and permanently enlarged the work and responsibilities of the diocese.

The Bishop was an outspoken commentator on world affairs, especially such matters as Japanese aggression in China, the Italian use of mustard gas against Abyssinian villages, and the bombing of Barcelona. He did not hesitate to describe Nazi theories and actions as Satanic or to upbraid the Vatican for failure to denounce various actions and policies of the dictators. He was at one time president of the British Soviet Society.

Wilson had a quite exceptional flair for popular writing and it might have been said of him that when he was ordained the world of letters lost a first class journalist. Many of his episcopal pronouncements attracted notice and were widely quoted in the press simply because they stated in a really arresting way well known facts and common sense views about religion. On one occasion he suggested that nine famous hymns should be banned in the diocese for 12 months, in order to give people an opportunity of hearing and appreciating other hymns, writing that he was "astonished at the very narrow choice of hymns to which we now seem to have restricted ourselves". He went on to criticize some hymns as "deplorable in their teaching". He observed:—

"One of these hymns tells us that after death we shall be 'lying each within our narrow bed', and another tells us that we shall be 'asleep within the tomb'. This conception of churchyards and cemeteries as places where dead people are sleeping may be widely held by ignorant people, but it is not the teaching of the Christian religion, and it is a lamentable thing that we should be making this prevailing ignorance darker still by singing hymns that teach that false view."

The Bishop had little patience with those who complain that the Church "does not give a lead" in national and international affairs. Not only did he himself express many opinions on a wide range of public affairs. He defended explicitly his right to do so. "There appears to be a superstition," he would observe, "cherished in political circles, that an intelligent opinion on Spain, Abyssinia, Naziism, &c., can only be forthcoming from a member of Parliament!" He would emphasize that Christianity was not simply "a consolation or a set of opinions", but a whole "way of living", "The systematic teaching of the Christian religion in our churches *is* the lead"

Bishop Wilson's ready pen made his monthly letter to his diocese one of the most widely read and quoted of such letters, but he found time to write books. *Episcopacy and Unity* published in 1912 expressed very clearly some of his most fundamental convictions. Other books of his were *The Faith of a Little Child* (1913), *The Creed of a Young Churchman* (1915), *The Master and his Friends* (1925), *At the Lord's Table* (1927), and *Reflections of a Back-Bench Bishop* (1948). He was a Select Bishop Preacher at Cambridge in 1930, 1939 and 1959, and at Oxford in 1932. In 1953 he was made C.B.E.

He married Dorothy Mary Marston, daughter of G. W. Daniels, Hampstead, and had two sons and two daughters.

July 17, 1961.

Dr. J. Dover Wilson, C. H., the distinguished Shakespearian scholar and a noted educationist, died on January 15, 1969, at his home at Balerno, Midlothian. He was 87.

He brought to his Shakespeare studies over a period of more than thirty years unusual powers of concentration, lively judgment, and unfailing enthusiasm. His distinctive contribution lay in the field of textual criticism. He called in history, psychology, and other aids to the study and interpretation of Shakespeare's plays, but only after he had first addressed himself to the task of establishing the text. In this primary aim, which he pursued all through the volumes of *The New Shakespeare* issued by the Cambridge University Press, in the editorship of which he was alone after the death of Sir Arthur Quiller-Couch, Dover Wilson exhibited an acuteness, and at times a boldness, of imagination that set him apart from the run of textual critics of Shakespeare. His own work certainly gives striking support to the view he maintained that it was only after the problems of the text had been persuasively solved, or at any rate fairly met, that the critic would proceed with advantage to the interpretation of the dialogue and the elucidation of the plot by way of arriving at an estimate of character and of the play itself. This doctrine he established most effectively, perhaps, in his study of Hamlet, where his textual analysis yielded a number of novel and illuminating conclusions.

John Doyer Wilson was born in London on July 13, 1881, the son of Edwin Wilson, of Cambridge, whose distinguished work as a lithographer was well known to an earlier generation of scientists. From Lancing he went up to Gonville and Caius College, Cambridge. He was Members' Prizeman in 1902 and Harness Prizeman in 1904, having in between gained a second class in the history tripos. His teaching career began with a year as assistant master at Whitgift Grammar School. In 1906 he married Dorothy, daughter of the late Canon Baldwin, and went to the University of Helsingfors as English Lecturer, returning three years later to a lectureship at Goldsmiths' College, University of London.

TEACHING OF ENGLISH

In 1912 he was appointed a special inspector in the technological branch of the Board of Education (as it then was), and continued in that capacity from 1912 until 1924. As an educationist Dover Wilson's special interest was in the speaking and writing of English, and fuller opportunity to develop his ideas came when he was appointed to the chair of Education in the University of London at King's College. This post he held from 1924 until 1935. A year later he succeeded Professor H. J. C. Grierson in the Regius professorship of Rhetoric and English Literature at Edinburgh, and continued in that appointment until 1945.

Even before he had left Cambridge Dover Wilson had chosen to devote his critical abilities to Shakespearian study. His original bent towards history and his professional interest in education were both pressed into the service of his first book, *Life in Shakespeare's England* (1911), an anthology designed to illustrate the social atmosphere of the Elizabethan age. But textual problems engaged him increasingly, and in the leisure that his work for the Board of Education allowed him he produced, in collaboration with Professor A. W. Pollard, the *Stolne and Surreptitious Shakespearian Texts* (1919), and, in collaboration with Professor Pollard and others, *Shakespeare's Hand in the Play of Sir Thomas More* (1923). The first mature fruit of his studies, however, appeared in the stimulating small volume he published in 1932 under the title of *The Essential Shakespeare.* Dover Wilson himself described the book, which was a summing-up of his personal views and discoveries about Shakespeare, as "a biographical adventure". At once soberly thoughtful and entertaining, it made a telling figure of Shakespeare as dramatic poet, though it also speculated a little freely on the man. Dover Wilson saw in the fall of Essex the great tragedy of Shakespeare's life and in Hamlet Shakespeare's attempt to understand Essex.

In 1934 and the following year appeared the full results of his 20 years' study of Hamlet.

KEY TO "HAMLET"

First, there were the two volumes of *The Manuscript of Shakespeare's Hamlet and the Problems of the Transmission*. Then, in *What Happens in Hamlet*, he reviewed the whole intricate question of the plot of the play, arriving in the end at the ingenious and by no means unplausible theory that a missing stage direction lay beneath the mountain of critical doubt and confusion on the subject. If only, Dover Wilson maintained, it can be assumed, as it should be assumed, that Hamlet overheard the plot hatched between Polonius and Claudius—why, then, a great deal which is now obscure or contradictory becomes intelligible and illuminated, and with that transformation the plot of Hamlet can be shown to be completely watertight. This was the author's most formidable undertaking. Eight years later, in 1943, he brought a not dissimilar apparatus of curiosity and reasoning to the view of Shakespeare's Histories which he expounded in *The Fortunes of Falstaff*.

In 1963, Dover Wilson published *Shakespeare's Sonnets: An Introduction for the Use of Historians and Others* in which he argued that the dark lady of the sonnets was unknown. He did not agree with Dr. Rowse that Sir William Harvey was Mr. W. H.: for him William Herbert was behind the initials W. H. The previous year Dover Wilson had published *Shakespeare's Happy Comedies*—which were his views on Shakespeare's first 10 comedies, *Errors* to *Merry Wives*; he stressed his enjoyment of them in this work.

Dover Wilson was no cloistered scholar. He was a Life Trustee of Shakespeare's Birthplace and a trustee of the National Library of Scotland. He was a popular lecturer in the best sense, whether to a learned, or an unlearned, audience. He had the manner of one who had just discovered the secret of Shakespeare for the first time and was anxious to share it with his listeners; and his listeners, whether in Cambridge or in Cairo or in Lille, quickly responded to the appeal. Nor were his interests confined to the Elizabethan age. When, to his surprise, he became Professor of Education, he soon developed an enthusiasm for the classics of the subject. He promoted a series (*Landmarks in the History of Education*) with his faithful Cambridge publishers and himself edited *Culture and Anarchy* for the series.

To the end he preserved a boyish zest for scholarship and for life. An enthusiastic, though not very skilful, golfer, he was always happy in the belief that he was improving. Many honours came to him: he was a Companion of Honour, a Fellow of the British Academy and an honorary doctor of several universities at home and abroad. What gave him especial pleasure was his honorary Fellowship of Caius, where he was regularly, and affectionately, welcomed on his visits to Cambridge. The deepest sorrow of his life was the death of his only son, Godfrey, on active service in South Africa in 1944; but he was fortified by his Christian faith and by the staunch devotion of his wife who, after 55 years of wedded happiness, died in 1961. Two daughters survive him. He married secondly in 1963 Elizabeth Wintringham, daughter of Sir Joseph Arkwright, F.R.S.

January 17, 1969.

The Right Reverend John Leonard Wilson, K.C.M.G., Bishop of Birmingham from 1953 to 1969, died on August 18, 1970. He was 72.

In the Second World War he was tortured by the Japanese. When the war was over he baptized and confirmed a group of Japanese soldiers, including some of his captors.

Wilson, who regularly led the service which closes the Albert Hall Festival of Remembrance, was one of those who thought that the purpose of Remembrance Day should be reassessed in 1967. That year he tabled a motion at the Church Assembly calling for the day also to be observed "for dedication to the service of mankind in the pursuit of peace and justice" among other things.

He was born on November 23, 1897, the son of a Gateshead clergyman, who was always to be his son's acknowledged exemplar. He was educated at St. John's School, Leatherhead. In the First World War he joined The Durham Light Infantry as a private, saw service in France, and gained his commission. From the Army he went to the disused Knutsford jail where F. R. Barry, later Bishop of Southwell, had been made Principal of a Training College for Service Ordinands. Here Wilson's Christian liberalism, derived from his father, was informed and fortified and he proceeded to the Queen's College, Oxford, to read a shortened course in theology.

At Oxford, the main influence upon him was that of Streeter, then approaching the height of his powers, and Wilson drew from the religious and moral, perhaps more than from the intellectual, depths of that complex nature. From Queen's he went to Wycliffe, not to Ripon Hall. Of the latter he was much later to become a Governor, and in 1957 he also became President of the Modern Churchmen's Union, but his native hue and piety was Evangelical rather than Modernist.

In 1924 he was ordained to his first curacy. Wilson was popular and full of projects, as a curate should be. He inaugurated what was probably the First Children's Church in the Midlands; and climbed the spire of St. Michael's in answer to a steeplejack who had bantered him on the relative difficulties of their jobs.

In 1927 he went out to Cairo to take over the C.M.S. Boys' School and to join the group which Temple Gairdner was forming to make a fresh endeavour in the spirit of Christian liberalism to win the obdurate heart of Islam.

After a year as curate-in-charge of St. John's, Neville Cross, he went to be vicar of Eighton Banks. This mining parish was at the bottom of the abyss of Tyneside's unemployment.

In 1935 he went to Roker, one of the "Priestman Churches" and so came to Sunderland, that breeding ground of Bishops. Again his ministry was popular, but after three years he responded to the call of his old friend, Hall of Hongkong, and went to be Dean and Archdeacon of the colony in 1938. When in 1941 there fell vacant the see of the crucially important Singapore, it need now be no secret that it was on the pressing representations of the colonial authorities that Wilson was appointed to it.

In wartime Singapore, the apathy of perpetual afternoon had given place to the hectic frivolity of a drawn-out last evening. Yet already Wilson, by his ability to mix so freely and through his hospitable home, had persuaded many men and women to listen again to the Gospel, and already had extended the missionary and social work of his church, when, in 1942, the Prince of Wales and the Repulse, having called at the base, were blown up in the South China Sea. In the swift debacle that ensued, Wilson and his clergy played an important steadying part in evacuating the British families. His own wife and children went to Australia, where his fifth child was born. There followed for him some four years in an internment camp, where his gifts of religious and social leadership, his understanding of defeat, his essentially masculine humour and fund of racy stories, were taxed to the utmost. He would conduct the camp physical exercises to the exhortation: Lift up your hearts. Meantime, Christian, Chinese, Malayans and Indians had remained faithful, and impervious to the blandishments of their Japanese liberators. Surreptitious contacts were maintained between them and the camp and these the Japanese sought to crush.

FLUNG INTO CHANGI

For a time, indeed, unaccountably, they permitted the Bishop to officiate occasionally in his Cathedral; then as unaccountably immured him in the notorious Changi Jail, where some 950 persons were to die, 567 of them British.

The conditions of confinement were in themselves lethal; squatting timelessly. Wilson taught a fellow captive poems of Keats drawing from his capacious memory. Wilson was tortured, unavailingly, partly to make him confess the names of his contacts, partly to force him to recant his faith and so to end his influence, partly as a matter of protocol for all prisoners: he bore the marks all his life. Then, unaccountably, he was returned to the camp and his emaciated frame miraculously nursed back to some health. When the war was over he baptized and confirmed a group of Japanese soldiers, including some of his captors, and always treasured a silk panel they presented to him. For his part in these events, which moved all England, he was made a C.M.G. in 1946.

In 1948 he became Dean of Manchester, where William Greer was now Bishop, and in 1949, Assistant Bishop. There was no abatement of his abounding energy. Again he and his wife made a wide circle of friends. He raised £90,000 for the restoration of the bombed Cathedral.

In 1953, Wilson was chosen to be Bishop of Birmingham. There could have been no more difficult assignment of the kind, nor any more imaginative a choice. The administration of the Diocese had run down; many of the vast new housing estates were unchurched and more being built. Barnes had been highly respected, and better loved than gossip had it, but he had left a rebellious group of Anglo-Catholics, and, on the other side, some clergy engaged in experiments and idiosyncratic actions which, if not so blatantly illegal, were mostly inexpedient. The appointment of another avowed Modernist with a strong sense of the Church and a flair for knowing men, proved to be the eirenic answer.

He could be masterful, impetuous, sometimes passionate. He had his share of ambition, but where his love of truth or righteousness was plainly engaged he was forthright, regardless of the consequence to himself. He relished the good things of life and could forgo them, possessing that touch of earth necessary to a leader of men. He was generous. In an age assigned to the common man, by an uncommon one, Wilson was an outstanding bishop.

Wilson married in 1930 Doris Ruby Phillips. They had three sons and one daughter.

August 19, 1970.

Lord Winster, a former Minister of Civil Aviation and Governor of Cyprus from 1946 to 1949, died on June 7, 1961, at his home in Crowborough, Sussex. He was 76.

Before his elevation to the peerage in 1942 he was Lieutenant-Commander Reginald Fletcher, R. N. (retd.), and had sat in the House of Commons for several years, first as a Liberal and then as a Labour member. He was recognized as an authority on naval strategy, about which he had written extensively.

Always a Radical in political outlook, his adherence to the Labour Party in 1929 came as no surprise to his friends, but he never fully succeeded in gaining the ear of the House of Commons.

As Minister of Civil Aviation he strove to build up Britain's air services, but in spite of his undoubted abilities he found himself hampered and frustrated at almost every turn. As Governor and Commander-in-Chief of Cyprus, too, he found his hands were to a large extent tied by vacillation in Whitehall, and he was bitterly disappointed when attempts to inaugurate constitutional reforms failed.

After his resignation, he spoke on occasions in the House of Lords, but his utterances often seemed to be those of a disappointed and frustrated man. He had a ready wit, and while in the Commons he unearthed more than one mare's nest in connexion with naval matters. He could hit hard in debate when necessary, but his verbal darts left no sting behind. Though a loyal member of the Labour Party, he frequently gave the impression of detachment from purely party issues. His concern was invariably for vital national interests, particularly in defence affairs.

The Right Hon. Reginald Thomas Herbert Fletcher, K.C.M.G., first Baron Winster, of Witherslark, co. Westmorland, was born in 1885, the eldest son of Nicholas and Dinah Fletcher, of Rampholme, Windermere. He chose the Royal Navy as his profession, and in the 1914–18 War served in destroyers and with the Grand Fleet as a lieutenant-commander. When he retired he turned his attention to politics. His Westmorland family were traditionally Conservative in outlook, but Fletcher's views were more to the left, and he won Basingstoke for the Liberal Party in 1923. He lost it in 1924, and was unsuccessful at a by-election in the Tavistock division of Devon in October, 1928.

His political ideas, however, were gradually inclining more to the left as he became dissatisfied with the steadily declining Liberal fortunes.

GAINED SEAT FOR LABOUR

In 1929 he joined the Labour Party, and at the general election of 1935 he won the Nuneaton division of Warwickshire, turning a Conservative majority of 2,564 votes into a Labour margin of 5,237.

This was a notable achievement, and Fletcher was looked upon by some colleagues as one of the coming men in the Labour Party. But the outbreak of the Second World War in 1939 saw him recalled to the Royal Navy. He was first posted to the London docks, where he worked long hours supervising the fitting of guns to merchant ships. Next he became chief staff officer at the Grimsby naval base, where he dealt with East Coast convoys.

When A. V. Alexander (afterwards Lord Alexander of Hillsborough) became First Lord of the Admiralty in the wartime Coalition Government, he invited Fletcher to become his parliamentary private secretary. Fletcher held this post until December, 1941, and in the following year he was raised to the peerage.

His peerage and those conferred at the same time on three other members of the Labour Party were not, as was explained in the announcement issued from 10, Downing Street, political honours or rewards. They were "a special measure of state...designed to strengthen the Labour Party in the Upper House where its representation is disproportionate, at a time when a Coalition Government of three parties is charged with the direction of affairs".

The creations certainly added to the debating strength not only of Labour but also of the House of Lords as a whole. Lord Winster spoke there with a still more marked sense of detachment from party than in the Lower House. The war was then in a comparatively early stage, and he was critical of certain phases of its central direction. He was part author of a publication on *The Air Defence of Great Britain,* and he contributed to several publications. He was one of the signatories, along with Lord Chatfield, Field Marshal Lord Milne, Sir John Salmond and Lord Hankey, to the notable statement on the unity of all arms for total war which appeared in *The Times* in October, 1943.

After the overwhelming Labour political victory in the summer of 1945, Attlee chose Winster to be Minister of Civil Aviation. This was a job after Winster's own heart, and he devoted all his energies to the building up of British postwar air services. One of his aims was the cheapening of air travel and he was a great believer in the extension of Commonwealth air services and cooperation on routes in the United States territories, and in Australia, New Zealand, and British territories. To this end he travelled widely abroad, and attended in 1946 the Pacific Civil Aviation Conference at Wellington, New Zealand.

In October, 1946, Winster was appointed Governor and Commander-in-Chief of Cyprus. He arrived in Nicosia by air on his sixty-second birthday but, in accordance with the advice of the Ethnarchy Council, the public in general remained aloof. Winster's term of office could not, unhappily, be described as a success. He was not by temperament suited for his difficult task and for all his efforts he was unable to carry through the constitutional reforms envisaged in 1946. It is no secret that he was often at loggerheads with Whitehall, and he never wavered from the view that the island should be retained within the Empire.

He left Cyprus after two years of a politically troubled governorship. He had been created K.C.M.G. in the birthday honours in June, 1948, and in the following month intimated his intention to resign, though he continued in office until February, 1949. After that he appeared less and less in the public eye.

Lord Winster married in 1909, Elspeth, daughter of the Rev. H. J. Lomax, of Abbotswood, Buxted, Sussex. There were no children of the marriage.

June 9, 1961.

Lord Winterton, who died on August 26, 1962, at the age of 79, was a parliamentary personality of rare and vivid quality. A man of great courage, often explosively outspoken, he won a unique place in the House of Commons, where he sat continuously for 47 years. For eight of them he was "Father of the House", a title which belied the perennial youthfulness of his mind and an unquenchable vitality, enriched by endearing mannerisms which contributed notably to the gaiety of the Lower House.

He held office in four Governments, and his elevation to Cabinet rank in 1938 was regarded by many as an overdue recognition of his talents. But it is as a pugnacious, irrepressible private member that he will best be remembered—a "House of Commons man", *par excellence*, always quick to defend the traditional rights and usages of Parliament, even in the middle of a great war. He was emphatic that Parliament should not be considered a "negligible factor" in wartime, and he made it his business in consort with Mr. Shinwell—an alliance dubbed "arsenic and old lace"—to offer such critical comment on the conduct of the late war as he deemed necessary. His loyalty to and close friendship with Mr. Churchill did not prevent his challenging some of his great leader's judgments, and the House enjoyed more than one brisk encounter between them.

TALL ANGULAR FIGURE

The Commons seemed a duller place when Winterton retired from it. He was translated to the Upper House in 1952 by the conferment on him of a United Kingdom peerage—his Earldom was an Irish title with no seat in the Lords. His tall, angular figure, clothed in high-buttoned jacket and rather short, narrow trousers, had been for so long a much prized ornament of the green benches. Arms tightly folded, long legs entwined, he was always ready to uncoil like a spring to raise points of order or to expatiate on some matter of the "gravest constitutional importance". The House had become familiar with signs which betokened that "Eddie Winterton" was on the boil over some injustice to a fellow citizen or some affront to the dignity of Parliament. The lean torso would sway backwards and forwards on the bench, choler would mantle his face, and he would rub his long hands so violently together that he must have generated no little heat. It is recorded that he thus once dislocated a thumb. If his anger was quickly aroused and vehemently expressed, it was always utterly free from malice. For all his hard-hitting, Winterton never lost the respect, and even won the affection of his opponents.

Probably the greatest joy of his parliamentary career came to him when he was charged with the chairmanship of the select committee on the rebuilding of the House of Commons. He could have desired no worthier monument than the new Chamber which arose from the ashes of the old.

The Right Hon. Edward Turnour, P.C., 6th Earl Winterton (created in 1766 in the peerage of Ireland) first Baron Turnour of Shillinglee, co. Sussex, in the peerage of the United Kingdom, was born in 1883. He was the only child of the fifth Earl and Lady Georgiana Susan Hamilton, daughter of the first Duke of Abercorn. Winterton was educated at Eton and at New College, Oxford. He had scarcely attained his majority when he was elected to Parliament in the Conservative interest by the Horsham Division of Sussex in November, 1904. Subject to boundary changes (Horsham and Worthing from 1918 to 1945 and the Horsham Division of West Sussex thereafter) he remained M.P. for these parts until his retirement in 1951.

NO RESPECTER OF PERSONS

In opposition he began to achieve his early notoriety as an *enfant terrible* of the Tory benches. It was one way of sustaining the spirits of a shattered Party. He cared little for the conventions, and neither individual standing nor dignity was a protection against his attacks. About 1911 he compiled a pocket book intended for the use of militant M.P.s. It contained discreditable facts for the disparagement of Government supporters. Once the author in a hurry turned up the wrong man and hurled the wrong missile. There was an apology.

During the War he went with the Sussex Yeomanry to Gallipoli. Later he joined the Imperial Camel Corps in the Egyptian Expeditionary force of 1916, and saw service in Palestine and Arabia. In March, 1922, he was appointed Under-Secretary for India. His views on Indian affairs were more progressive than those he held on Ireland. He was Chancellor of the Duchy of Lancaster from 1937 to 1939.

In March, 1938, he entered the Cabinet to act as Deputy Secretary of State for Air and Vice-President of the Air Council, and to represent the Secretary of State, Lord Swinton, in the Commons. At that time the Ministry was under heavy attack to which reasons of security prevented a complete answer, and it was Winterton's task to fight the critics. He records with characteristic frankness in his book *Orders of the Day* what happened when he rose to speak in a debate early in May, 1938. "I crashed, bringing down the administration of Lord Swinton with me." Believing that any Minister who had thus failed in a big debate should resign, he asked to be relieved of his duties at the Air Ministry. Soon afterwards he was appointed Under-Secretary of State at the Home Office. In 1938 he became chairman of an intergovernmental committee on refugees and remained so until 1945.

On January 30, 1939, he resigned the Duchy of Lancaster and accepted the unpaid office of Paymaster General. In the Churchill Government he had no place. He was asked if he would permit his name to be submitted to the King for an important appointment overseas, but preferred to remain an M.P. and to be Father of the House.

During the period of Labour rule after the War, Winterton was a member of Churchill's shadow Cabinet, exercising with relish those gifts of plain speaking in debate and pungency in interjection which rejoiced his friends and infuriated his opponents.

In 1932 Lord Winterton published *Pre-War*, an unpretentious book of memoirs which covered the decade 1904-1914. After his retirement from the Commons he brought out in 1953 *Orders of the Day*, and two years later *Fifty Tumultuous Years.*

His widow, the Hon. Cecilia Monica Wilson, only daughter of the second Baron Nunburnholme, outlives him but there were no children of the marriage and no heir to the United Kingdom barony. The Winterton earldom and the other Irish titles pass to a distant kinsman, Flight Sergeant Robert Chad Turnour, of the Royal Canadian Air Force.

August 28, 1962.

Sir William Wiseman, tenth baronet, C.B., C.M.G., chairman of the committee in the United States of the Dollar Exports Council, died in a New York hospital on June 17, 1962, at the age of 77. He was for many years one of the most prominent British residents in the United States.

In the First World War, as chief of the intelligence service attached to the British Embassy at Washington, he played as a natural diplomatist a role of great importance. Colonel House discovered in him a kindred spirit, and there sprang up between the two men a friendship which had significant effects. The close cooperation which existed between the United States and Great Britain at the middle period of the war and after it was, indeed, largely due to their mutual comprehension. Thus it was that he came into immediate association with the leaders of both the British and American Governments, and rendered services of great value to his country. After the war he stayed on in the United States. Few Englishmen over the years have known that country so intimately, or been so well qualified to advise their own Government in regard to American affairs. The first Lord Reading once said of him, "Wiseman is well named".

William George Eden Wiseman was born on February 1, 1885. He was the eldest son of the ninth Baronet by his marriage with Sarah Elizabeth, daughter of Lewis Langworthy. In 1893 he succeeded to the family title. He was educated at Winchester and at Jesus College, Cambridge. In 1905 he successfully represented Cambridge against Oxford in the inter-University boxing. As a young man he had business interests in Canada and travelled widely in North and Central America. Having been a lieutenant in the Cardigan Artillery R.G.A., he became in the First World War a captain in the 6th (Service) Battalion.

CONFIDENTIAL MESSAGE

Gassed at the front, Wiseman was sent to the United States as Intelligence Officer attached to the British Embassy. On one occasion in 1916 Sir Cecil Spring Rice, the British Ambassador, sent him to make a confidential communication to Colonel House. House was much impressed by him and from that time until the United States entered the war, Wiseman was confidential intermediary between Colonel House and the British Government. The numerous allusions to him in *The Intimate Papers of Colonel House* indicate the measure of his influence. During the Peace Conference he was a Lieutenant-Colonel on the Staff of Military Intelligence and was chief adviser on American Affairs to the British Delegation in Paris. In recognition of his services he was created a C.M.G. in 1917 and a C.B. in 1918.

After the Armistice Wiseman made his home in the United States, and became a partner in the New York Banking house of Kuhn, Loeb and Company. In 1929 during an investigation by a United States Senate Sub-Committee of the activities of William B. Shearer a so-called "British Secret Document" extracts of which had been published over Shearer's signature in the *Gaelic American* came under consideration.

EXPLANATION

It was alleged to be a copy of a report sent years before by Wiseman to Lloyd George which detailed the ways and means of making the United States a British Colony. Wiseman, who on the purported date of the document had been at the Peace Conference, telegraphed to the chairman of the sub-committee recalling that on first seeing it he had passed it on *pour rire* to Colonel House, President Wilson, and the State Department who had concurred that it was a clumsy forgery.

During and after the Second World War Wiseman continued to reside in the United States where, as a prominent citizen of New York, his advice and help was always at the disposal of British officials.

In 1908 he married Florence Marjorie Hulton, daughter of the Rev. G. F. Sams, Rector of Emberton, Buckinghamshire, by whom he had three daughters. That marriage was dissolved in 1933 and in 1944 he married Mrs. Joan Mary Leseur, daughter of Arthur Phelps, of Harrow. There was one son of this marriage, John William Wiseman, to whom the baronetcy now passes.

June 18, 1962.

Dr. Helen Marion Wodehouse, Mistress of Girton College, Cambridge, from 1931 to 1942, died on October 20, 1964, at the age of 84.

Born on October 12, 1880, at the Rectory, Bratton Fleming, north Devon, she was the eldest daughter of Philip John Wodehouse, Rector of Bratton Fleming, formerly Fellow of Gonville and Caius College, Cambridge, and of Marion Bryan Wallas, sister of Graham Wallas. From Notting Hill High School, where her aunt, Miss K. T. Wallas, was Mathematical Mistress, she gained the Clothworkers' Exhibition in Mathematics at Girton College in 1898, and read first for the Mathematical Tripos, and, in her fourth year, for the Tripos in Mental and Moral Sciences. In 1902 she was awarded the Gilchrist Fellowship for professional training, and a year later attained the Diploma in Education at Birmingham University.

AT BRISTOL UNIVERSITY

From 1903 to 1911 Miss Wodehouse held the position of assistant lecturer in Philosophy at the University and became a Doctor of Philosophy in 1907. These years at Birmingham, where for the greater part of the time she lived with her uncle and aunt, Professor and Mrs. J. H. Muirhead, were always remembered by her with particular happiness. When Bingley Training College was opened by the West Riding County Councll in 1911 Dr. Wodehouse was appointed the first principal, and her work at Bingley, from 1911 to 1919, was in no small degree responsible for the high reputation which the college attained in the educational world. After the war she was appointed to the new chair of Education created to coordinate the training work of the men and women students at Bristol University, and in 1931, when Miss Major retired from the Mistress-ship of Girton College, Dr. Wodehouse was invited by the Council to succeed her. She retired from the Mistress-ship in 1942.

At Girton, perhaps even more than at Bingley and Bristol, her intellectual powers and her administrative ability were conspicuous. The early years of her Mistress-ship was a period of consolidation after the rapid development of the college during the postwar years. Her guidance then and from 1939-42 was of rare value. Throughout, her personal relations with senior and junior members of college were especially happy. She had the "gift of accessibility". It allowed her to give time and interest to problems demanding judgment and practical sympathy and to understand and appreciate changing conditions and ideas.

Dr. Wodehouse's published work included *The Logic of Will; The Presentation of Reality; Nights and Days and other Lay Sermons; God the Prisoner; A Survey of the History of Education* (1924)*; The Scripture Lesson in the Elementary School* (1926)*; Temples and Treasuries* (1935)*; Selves and their Good* (1936)*;* and *One Kind of Religion.*

October 22, 1964.

Sir Donald Wolfit, C.B.E., actor, for some 20 years actor-manager, and to the end of his days a proud servant of the theatre, died in hospital in London on February 17, 1968, at the age of 65.

Once he had found his feet at the age of 35, he put into practice a scheme for raising and leading a touring company of his own with a Shakespearian repertoire. With the outbreak of the Second World War two years later, his plans developed: his theatrical pioneering became in the London of the Blitz, in the blacked-out provincial towns, later in many Service camps, a form of National Service for himself and his company, an unsubsidized contribution to the war effort. It is for this missionary aspect of his work, which distinguished it for some years after the war ended, that he will probably be remembered, but it does not exhaust the whole of Wolfit. When he had given up management and had no more thoughts of playing Shakespearian leads, save possibly on radio, he continued to talk theatre, to believe in theatre and to act in theatre, to say nothing of films.

One of the five children of W. P. Wolfit, who worked for a firm of brewers, Donald Wolfit was born on April 20, 1902, at Newark-on-Trent and grew up in a home which he described as poor but never impoverished, but in which the theatre was ignored. As a boy he recited and sang at concerts during the First World War, and in 1920, with a paternal loan of £30 in his pocket, he exchanged a teaching job at a school in Eastbourne for a studentship, at first unpaid, in Charles Doran's Shakespeare Company.

FIRST CHANCE

In those days there were 150 companies touring during the spring and autumn seasons and after two years with Doran, Wolfit was two more years on the road before joining Matheson Lang at the New Theatre, London, in 1924. Lang gave him his first real chance in 1928, and a year later he was engaged by Harcourt Williams for the latter's first season at the Old Vic. Barry Jackson used him for a Canadian tour and in Shaw's *Too True to Be Good*, and in 1933 the success of his Hamlet in the First Quarto version at the Arts Theatre Club kindled his ambition to do Shakespeare under his own management. After two seasons at Stratford on Avon under Ben Iden Payne, he was ready to make his bid, setting out on a nine-week tour with five plays in the repertoire and with Phyllis Neilson-Terry, daughter of his old chief Fred Terry, as leading lady. When all expenses had been paid, he had lost just under £80.

He brought a company to the West End for the first time during the "phoney war", and he held out at the Strand during the Blitz when almost all other theatres were closed, giving lunchtime programmes of scenes from Shakespeare or "potted" plays before going on Home Guard duty in Surrey at night.

Violet and Irene Vanbrugh toured with him in 1941, but he was back in London that Christmas and again in each of the four remaining years of the war, once with Molière and Ibsen in the bill, more often with a Shakespearian repertoire. Otherwise he was on the road, and for E.N.S.A. he carried out special tours of garrison theatres, of R.A.F. stations, of liberated western Europe and of Egypt. During the immediate postwar period he twice crossed the Atlantic. His own repertoire had grown, the outstanding characters in it being probably Shylock (his most frequent role), Volpone, Richard III, Lear (probably his masterpiece) and Ibsen's Solness.

To these he added, before a disagreement on policy caused him to leave, Tamburlaine and Lord Ogleby in *The Clandestine Marriage* at the Old Vic in 1951. At the King's, Hammersmith, during 1953 his repertoire was largely classical; in 1958 he toured in a double bill of Kleist and Wedekind; and in the meantime he did London seasons of plays by contemporary authors such as Fritz Hochwalder and Henry de Montherlant.

RETURN TO FILMS

Wolfit had first appeared in films in 1934, and in 1952 he returned to film-making, replacing Robert Newton in the role of Svengali in a new version of Du Maurier's novel. He also helped out other theatrical managements in the West End by taking over the ex-docker colonial governor in *His Excellency* from Eric Portman, a Highland laird in *Keep in a Cool Place* from Roger Livesey, and Pastor Manders in *Ghosts* (to Flora Robson's Mrs. Alving) from Michael Hordern. At one Christmas he was seen as Captain Hook, at another as Long John Silver. In New York early in 1963 he played the working class father, a part created by Bernard Miles, in the Lancashire comedy *All In Good Time*, and in the London of the 1960s he played an unscrupulous Fleet Street editor, progressing in the words of *The Times* critic from the eupeptic to the apoplectic, and—in his last West End run—succeeding John Clements as Elizabeth Barrett's father in the musical, *Robert and Elizabeth*. After the days of his Shakespearian management, he gave many recitals alone or in company with his wife, Rosalind Iden the actress, in Nairobi, in Ethiopia, in Rome and Milan, and in South Africa. His last important television play *Ghosts* (with himself as Manders to Celia Johnson's Mrs. Alving) and his last film, *Decline and Fall* (with himself playing Evelyn Waugh's headmaster of a private school) have yet to be shown.

Wolfit's policy of maintaining a company led by himself was practicable only because he worked on a low budget. He valued his financial independence and he believed in the system of individual control which he had inherited from Terry and Lang, but he paid a price for gearing a whole production to his own performance by becoming willy nilly more isolated from his professional peers than was good for his work. He would protest, however, that the atmosphere of his companies can't have been all that uninspiring to the young, since the payroll of his actors had included such future writers as Harold Pinter and Ronald Harwood.

Wolfit was appointed C.B.E. in 1950 and knighted in 1957. His first two marriages, to Miss Chris Castor the actress and to Miss Susan Anthony, were dissolved. His third wife, Miss Rosalind Iden, daughter of Ben Iden Payne, was associated with him in his actor-management from the beginning. Wolfit had two daughters, one being Miss Margaret Wolfit the actress, and a son. He published his autobiography *First Interval* in 1955, succeeded Leslie Henson as President of the Royal General Theatrical Fund, and was for a time Honorary Chairman of the Carl Rosa Trust.

February 19, 1968.

Sir Walter Womersley, first baronet, Minister of Pensions in the war-time Coalition Government, died in London on March 15, 1961. He was 83.

He was for 21 years Conservative member of Parliament for Grimsby, and became Minister of Pensions in 1939 when the war clouds were gathering once again over Europe. His department soon began to have new calls upon it, in addition to those remaining from the First World War. Womersley brought to his office a combination of shrewd judgment and broad sympathy. He knew what it was to be brought up the hard way, and no deserving case ever failed to receive favourable consideration from him.

His business training proved of considerable help in his planning for rehabilitation after the war. He would take pride in describing himself as "the only retail trader in the Government", and he took the view that the first priority after the war should be given to servicemen and others on war work who had left their businesses and wished to return to them. But he was never able to carry through his plans, for, like many of his colleagues, he lost his seat at the general election in the summer of 1945, and did not reenter Parliament.

TO WORK AT TEN

Walter James Womersley was born at Bradford on February 5, 1878. He was the son of William Womersley, of that city, and educated at Usher Street board school. When only 10 years old he was compelled to go to work as a half-timer in a Bradford factory; two years later he was employed as a shop boy in a ready-made tailor's.

"But we made bespoke clothes too", he once told the House of Commons. "I could measure you for a suit any time."

At 18 he became the manager of a retail shop, and at 21 started in business on his own account.

Later he became senior partner in Womersley and Stamp, a firm of furnishers and general merchants in Grimsby, a town which he was to serve for many years of public life. In local government he received a training which stood him in good stead later. In 1911 he became a member of Grimsby Town Council and he was mayor in 1922–23. By that time a wider sphere of public service was opening to him. In 1924 he was elected Conservative member of Parliament for Grimsby and he held the seat until 1945. He also became president of the National Chamber of Trade.

In spite of the hardships of his early life, Womersley had no use for socialism. He was a Conservative to the backbone, and he was never happier than when engaged in political warfare with his Labour opponents, no matter whether in Parliament or outside. He first came into the House of Commons when his party was in office with a substantial majority. Like other backbench supporters of the Government he did not have the opportunities of gaining distinction granted to members of the Opposition, but he began, nevertheless, to make an impression by his forceful qualities and by the forthright common sense which marked his contributions to debate. He had no pretensions to oratory and his speeches, coloured by native dialect, were direct and even blunt. Having made one point in the fewest words he would pass on to the next without any effort to elaborate.

Having served for a few months in 1931 as Parliamentary Private Secretary to Sir Kingsley Wood, who was then Parliamentary Secretary to the Board of Education, Womersley became in the same year a Junior Lord of the Treasury and acted as an Assistant Whip till 1935. In that year he was appointed Assistant Postmaster General and obtained wide and useful ministerial experience.

Four years later he became Minister of Pensions in the National Government led by Neville Chamberlain. Soon the Second World War broke out, and brought the searchlight of criticism to bear on Womersley and his department. By common consent the Minister emerged well from the test. As always, he gave wholehearted service. He was sympathetic and helpful in cases of distress, and he mastered all phases of the work of his Ministry.

He had been knighted in 1934, and in 1941 was sworn of the Privy Council. The result of the general election of 1945 was a bitter blow, for Grimsby chose the Labour candidate, Mr. Kenneth Younger, by a majority of 9,643. In the resignation honours Womersley received a baronetcy.

He married in 1905 Annie, daughter of Alderman John Stamp, of Bradford, by whom he had two sons and one daughter. His elder son died when a boy and the baronetcy now passes to Peter John Walter Womersley, the only child of Womersley's second son, who was killed in action in Italy in 1944.

March 17, 1961.

The Very Reverend Dr. Christopher Woodforde, Dean of Wells, died on August 12, 1962, at the age of 54.

He was born in 1907, the son of R. E. H. Woodforde. Brought up in Somerset he was educated at King's School, Bruton, and at Peterhouse, Cambridge, and these two regions, Somerset and East Anglia, were the poles round which his life turned. His theology was studied at Wells and he became deacon in 1930 and priest in 1932.

The short stories he was later to write for boys—or was it for adults: there was a curious matter of fact maturity about them?—suggest a sensitive introvert childhood deeply appreciative of the country, with a remarkable insight into its past history and intense curiosity about its works of craftsmanship and of imagination. His first curacy was in King's Lynn and he went back to Somerset to a country rectory in 1936.

It was at this time that his antiquarian interests began to find their focus in the study of stained glass, his work on which was to become that of a leading authority. His first book, *Stained Glass in Somerset, 1250–1830*, was rapidly recognized as being in its way a classic. It was followed by his survey of the Norwich School, a book in which accounts of the windows of four of the most important East Anglian churches were introduced by a characteristically laconic catalogue of the known Norwich glaziers of the medieval period, and followed by an examination of a later history of the medieval glass and the disasters it suffered in the sixteenth and seventeenth centuries.

The Stained Glass of New College, Oxford appeared in 1951. Here he had, in plenty, the documentary evidence he loved, and he printed *in extenso* the three-cornered correspondence between the Warden, the Dean of Exeter and the glazier Peckitt. It was typical of him that he let the correspondence speak for itself and chose not to emphasize the vivid picture it gives, of a governing body grumbling at Peckitt's high prices and unsuitable productions, and finally commissioning through the back door (in this instance the headmaster of Winchester) the Reynolds window, "a landmark if also a low water mark in the history of English glass painting", as he was later to describe it.

A USEFUL SURVEY

English Stained and Painted Glass, 1954, is a useful but in some ways disappointing book: useful because it is a survey of the whole field and refers the reader with excellent judgment to the best work done through the centuries; disappointing because on the technical side it is perfunctory and because in general his style had now become so terse as to be almost unreadable. Perhaps it was the highly critical atmosphere of an Oxford common room that made him avoid saying anything which might lay his work open to attack.

It may have been something of the kind also which made him reject after long consideration the task of editing the English section of the international corpus of stained glass, a task for which he was eminently well qualified. But while he was distinguished as a scholar, what he enjoyed most was the days spent in the company of those expert craftsmen who looked to him for advice; and the delicate problem of restoring the William of Wykeham glass in Winchester College Chapel, a job in which he collaborated with the distinguished antiquary John Harvey and that notable craftsman, Dennis King, was brilliantly solved, thanks to their cooperation.

Woodforde was invited to New College as chaplain by Warden Smith, who thought well of his book on the Somerset glass, in 1948, and he went with the highest hopes. In many ways an Oxford common room should have suited him admirably; but if anyone expected him to settle down to a life of research, maintaining the chapel services because that was the chaplain's obligation, they were mistaken. He looked on himself as a pastor as well as a priest and those undergraduates who penetrated his somewhat formidable reserve came to set great store by the warmth of his friendship and shrewdness of his judgment. Yet he found as time went on that what seemed primarily to be expected of an Oxford chaplain was that he should not interfere. He was out of sympathy with many of the attitudes of postwar Oxford and not being a man who could compromise he did not conceal his disapproval.

In 1935 he married Muriel Forster, who died in 1951 after an illness for him almost as painful as for the sufferer herself. This blow drove him further into isolation. His last few years at Oxford were unhappy.

INITIAL STORMS

The offer of the deanery at Wells in 1959 seemed as if it might be the perfect answer. So perhaps it would have been if he had survived the storms of the initial phase. He was determined that the cathedral for which he had an almost proprietary feeling should be maintained in a way worthy of its superb fabric and came to think that this could only be done if radical changes were made in the teeth of opposition. He was frustrated by lack of funds, a lack which became something of an obsession. Playing his hand as it seemed to him in isolation, he would speak (by all accounts) to his diocesan or in chapter with a candour that his more conventional associates, unaware of the man behind the mask, no doubt found lacking in charity. Nevertheless, for an outsider to visit the cathedral in the last months of Woodforde's life was to appreciate immediately the excellence of his stewardship.

The Church of England is made richer from time to time by the emergence of individuals whose strength lies in their fearlessness, their great ability, their unwillingness to accept any man as master. But when such a man has the temperamental shyness and the profound reserve of Woodforde the part is not an easy one and his few intimate friends knew how the battles in which he found himself engaged lacerated him. There was a mellowness of which they were conscious which might if there had been time have made his tenure of the deanery one of the great periods in its history.

His book of short stories, already mentioned, was followed by a sensitive study of a boy growing up, *The Testimony of John*, a copy of which reached him a few days before his death; and he had just finished a more ambitious novel. These books were the expression of a sympathetic humanity which at Wells found its other main outlet in his contacts with the cathedral school. He was always at his best with young people. With them he knew real happiness.

He was Litt. D. of Cambridge and D. Litt. of Oxford and from 1950 to 1953 Prebendary of Chichester. He leaves one son.

August 13, 1962.

W. M. Woodfull, O.B.E., who died on August 11, 1965, near Brisbane, at the age of 67, was one of the most popular and successful cricket captains that Australia has ever had. He was the first Australian since Joe Darling, at the turn of the century, to lead two winning teams in England. But his greatest service to cricket was probably his wise and balanced leadership of his country throughout the distasteful "bodyline" controversy.

Both as batsman and captain Woodfull was a man for the connoisseur of the game. With his short backlift and intense concentration, the most notable feature of his batting was his sturdy defence. It was not for nothing that he was named "the unbowlable". He and Ponsford were the opening pair who time and again wore down the bowling before the appearance of the more scintillating Bradman. Woodfull's batting was consequently more valuable to the team than exciting to the spectators. Similarly, his captaincy was of the quietly effective kind. Shrewd in tactical judgment, popular with his players, though a firm disciplinarian, he was not a man for the flamboyant gesture.

William Maldon Woodfull was born at Maldon in Victoria on August 22, 1897, and played his first cricket up-country with little coaching. In 1922 he first played for his State, and his first appearance against the M.C.C. was against A.E.R. Gilligan's team in the winter of 1924–25.

Woodfull's first tour of England was in 1926, when he scored centuries in the Tests at Leeds and Old Trafford, and headed the team's averages for all matches on the tour with an aggregate of 1,912 runs at an average of 57.93. On his return to Australia he had another successful season, sharing in a partnership of 375 with Ponsford for Victoria against New South Wales—still the second highest Australian opening stand in first-class cricket. In 1928–29 against Percy Chapman's triumphant team Woodfull was again in excellent form, scoring three centuries in the Tests.

RECOVERY OF ASHES

He first captained Australia in 1930, the season when Bradman first made his presence really felt in Test cricket. That was undoubtedly the main factor in the recovery of the Ashes, but Woodfull himself scored 155 in the Lord's Test and won a fine reputation with his leadership. This stood him in good stead during the unhappy "bodyline" series of 1932–33. He was one of the direct sufferers, receiving a severe blow over the heart from a ball by Larwood in the third Test. Amidst all the strain it was not surprising that his batting fell off a little and he could not prevent an English victory, but although feelings ran so high the situation could have been much worse if a more intemperate personality had been leading Australia.

Woodfull returned to Britain in 1934 and concluded his career on an appropriately successful note. Although his own batting was not as formidable as on previous tours, the Ashes were regained and, even more important, happy relations on and off the field were restored.

Throughout his career Woodfull scored 2,300 runs in Test cricket, 49 centuries, seven of them in Test cricket and all but one of those against England.

A schoolmaster by profession, he was appointed Principal of Melbourne High School in 1956 retiring in 1962. In the New Year's Honours List of 1963 he received the O.B.E. for services to education.

August 12, 1965.

Dorothy Woodman, companion and co-worker for close upon 40 years of Kingsley Martin, died in September, 1970.

In the early twenties, while still a student at University College, Exeter, she developed from the evangelical Liberalism of her family to a Labour and Socialist outlook; her outstanding qualities of heart and brain and her great organizing ability were from that time placed untiringly at the service of so many groups and societies which were endeavouring to put a little decency into the world.

Dorothy Woodman was a farmer's daughter, born in 1902 of Wiltshire country stock, who attained higher education and an honours degree through her own exertions. Before ever she had left school she had taken to music, learned the organ and (more unusual in a village girl) had been taught Sanskrit by a young Wiltshire poet, so foreshadowing her lifelong interest in India. After leaving university she took at once to work for "just causes" in the political world. For a time she was secretary to the Women's International League, but as Kingsley Martin says in his autobiography, she was rather much of a firebrand for them, and fairly soon moved on to a similar post in the Union of Democratic Control, founded by E. D. Morel. It was in that capacity that she first met Kingsley Martin, then the newly-appointed editor of the *New Statesman,* and began the association which meant so much to him and steadied him so profoundly for the rest of his life—in the cottage at Dunmow in Essex, where they foregathered with so many of the friends of H. G. Wells and the Red Countess of Warwick, in London flats, and later on the Downs above Lewes, close to where the University of Sussex was soon to arise.

Kingsley edited and wrote for his paper; Dorothy in the thirties fought steadily against fascism and imperialism; she visited the mother and sister of Dimitrov during the Reichstag trial; she attended and reported the famous meeting of the British fascists at Olympia; she organized the China Campaign Committee; worked with Krishna Menon and the India League, and with Jomo Kenyatta when he was a student in London, and of course for the Republicans in Spain.

During the war she made it her business to find out and publish in the *New Statesman* all she could about the movements of resistance in the occupied countries and to help the refugees. She organized support for Tito in Yugoslavia, and by the time the war ended had become increasingly involved in the struggle for independence, not only in India, but in Burma, Indonesia and Vietnam. Besides being great friends of Nehru and other leading Indians, she and Kingsley were the only unofficial British guests at the 1948 ceremony of hoisting the new Burmese flag at Rangoon. After the war, particularly after Kingsley had retired from the *New Statesman,* their interest and reputation in India and Burma increased enormously. Dorothy became a recognized authority on Far Eastern questions; she wrote several books, some on the Far East.

She was with Kingsley when he died unexpectedly in Cairo, and after his death continued to work for the causes they had in common. In 1969, at Mrs. Gandhi's invitation, she went to India to make personal presentation of his Indian library to the Nehru University. But the shock of his death had been very great, and the work she did afterwards put a strain on her which eventually became too much for her. Her spirit, her liveliness and her determination will long survive in the memories of those who knew her personally and the many more who are profoundly greateful for all that she did.

October 2, 1970.

Sir John Woods, G.C.B., M.V.O., formerly Permanent Secretary at the Board of Trade and the Ministry of Production, and a director of the English Electric Company Ltd., died at his home at Haywards Heath on December 1, 1962. He was 68.

Sir John Harold Edmund Woods—but his true Christian names were known to few, for he was universally and affectionately known as "John Henry"—had the distinction of outstanding success in two separate careers: in the public service at the Treasury and Board of Trade, and in industry after his retirement from the Civil Service at the age of 56.

His achievements were the more remarkable in that he carried through life the severe wounds he received when serving with the Royal Fusiliers in France in the 1914–18 War. His war wounds were an essential part of his personality. The visible sign of his disability was the effort he had to make to move his thick-set frame, leaning heavily on a stick. So the first impression was of awkwardness. But that was immediately followed by other and stronger impressions, chiefly of his energy, gaiety and acute perception; and these remained the dominant features of his character through all his time as a civil servant and industrialist.

Born on April 20, 1895, the eldest son of the Rev. J. H. Woods, he was educated at Christ's Hospital and Balliol College, Oxford, and entered the Treasury in 1920. There may have been a time in his earlier days in the Treasury when his capacity for enjoying life concealed his strength of character. A "clubbable" man and excellent company, the young Woods was in some danger of earning a reputation for getting things done by telling the right story rather than by arguing the merits of the case. But Woods had outgrown any such judgments by the 1930s. His powers had then matured and the Treasury recognized them by giving him a special assignment, the provision of Government credit for employment-giving work such as the new Cunarders of that era.

This was activity that exactly suited him. It gave him the opportunity to test his intelligence and strength of character in negotiations with men of high calibre in industry and the world of finance. Above all it was personal work and productive of positive results. For he never had great aptitude or liking for the intricacies of management, nor were the critical functions of the Treasury congenial to him.

"ACCOUNTANT DOCTORS"

This was an era when the Treasury had much to do with a series of "accountant-doctors"—outstanding members of the accountancy profession who gave their guidance to the Treasury in the use of public funds to rescue or stimulate industry, like Sir William McClintock, Sir John Morison and Sir Andrew Macharg. The respect of such men was not lightly given. Woods secured their respect and their admiration. With Woods it was spontaneous to keep his friendships in good repair, and these and other friendships in the world of industrial finance continued and were strengthened in the war years and after.

In 1937 he was appointed Principal Private Secretary to the Chancellor of the Exchequer, first to Neville Chamberlain and then to Sir John Simon. Woods had already served with distinction six years before as Private Secretary to Philip Snowden as Chancellor, then as Lord Privy Seal. Snowden was one of his heroes, and Woods always had much to say of his courage and integrity.

The 1930s were an heroic period for Chancellors' private secretaries. Woods's two predecessors had gone straight from their posts to be permanent heads of major departments of state. Woods's performance was at least as impressive as that of his predecessors. But he ended his spell in the Chancellor's office in a bleaker climate. By now the country was at war, the Treasury under a cloud. Woods stayed in the Treasury in charge of the division responsible for controlling expenditure on defence material. For the time he was a dispirited man and seemed to have lost heart. He had suffered much physically and otherwise from the First World War and like other colleagues who had been through the experience the prospect of a Second World War gave him, to use his own words, "the horrors".

In time however, Woods found he had two significant contributions to make to war finance. The first was in the price fixing of munitions contracts. He was not, of course, operating single handed in this matter, but on him fell the main responsibility for formulating Treasury policy. On several occasions he gave evidence on contract procedure to the Public Accounts Committee and by his clear and cogent evidence made himself a reputation which he was to confirm when later he came before the Committee as an accounting officer.

EQUIPMENT OF THE ARMY

The other issue of munitions finance on which Woods had a decisive influence centred on the equipment of the Army. In this field he found himself in alliance with the then Director General of Army Requirements who later became Lord Sinclair. In 1943 Sinclair was appointed chief executive of the Ministry of Production and Woods left the Treasury to become Permanent Secretary of that department. This alliance continued after the war, for in 1945 when the Labour Government fused the Ministry of Production and the Board of Trade, Woods (now Sir John Woods, K.C.B.) moved to the Board of Trade as Permanent Secretary and Sinclair with him.

Woods was now, at the age of 50, the permanent head of a great department with a large organization to control and varied and rapidly shifting functions to perform. In addition his Minister was a key member of the new government, for the President of the Board of Trade was Sir Stafford Cripps. The tasks were large and diverse enough—the conversion of war to civilian production, export promotion, the administration of controls carried over from war into peace, and supervising the efficiency of private industry under threat of nationalization. In all these matters Woods had full scope for his talents as policy adviser—at least while Sir Stafford Cripps was President and there was no doubt of the Board of Trade's primacy.

When Cripps became Chancellor and the centre of gravity shifted to the Treasury, Woods was made a member of the Economic Planning Board, and at the Board of Trade was still responsible for the administrative machine. He was not, however, at his best in dealing with the problems of administering a larger scale organization. Indeed a born organizer might well have been daunted by the problem of making an efficient machine out of such a heterogeneous empire. Woods could be tough and even brutal when advising on policy. He found it hard to be tough and could never be brutal when faced by staff problems.

INTO INDUSTRY

Woods left the public service in 1951. He was now 56 years old and glad to be released from the strain of holding perhaps the most arduous post in the Civil Service at the time. He was also glad of the opportunities for positive and creative activity which he felt he could find in private industry. There he soon made for himself a special position both as a shrewd judge of men and of issues in the board room, and as a link between industry and government with a special gift for mediating between the two. He was much sought after as a representative of business. He was a member and former president of the National Institute of Economic and Social Research, a Visiting Fellow of Nuffield College, and a Governor of the Administrative Staff College.

It was perhaps inevitable that in this industrial period he showed less of the vitality for which he had been famous in the Civil Service. He was older, he had his health to consider, he knew he must husband his energy and he had much to live for. He became more detached and calm, but there was no falling off in the shrewdness and penetration of his judgment, backed as it was by the combination of great experience in government and in industry.

This combination proved to be of special value in the contribution that he made as a member of the Radcliffe Committee on the Working of the Monetary System.

Woods was also a prominent layman of the Church of England, being a member of the Church Assembly and serving on a number of the Church's central committees, particularly those concerned with finance. He was also chairman of the National Hospital for Nervous Diseases.

In 1930 he married Molly, daughter of N. H. Baker. They had one son and one daughter.

December 3, 1962.

Professor S. W. Wooldridge C.B.E., F.R.S., Professor of Geography at King's College, London, died on April 25, 1963, at the age of 62.

Sydney William Wooldridge was born on November 16, 1900, the son of Lewis William Wooldridge. He received his early education at Glendale County School, Wood Green, and while still a schoolboy showed a characteristic industriousness by attending classes at Birkbeck College, which had not yet become a college of the university. As a fulltime student he entered King's College, London, taking a first-class degree in geology in 1921, an M.Sc. in 1923, and a D.Sc. in 1927.

By this time he had joined the staff at King's in the Geology and Geography Department, becoming Lecturer in 1927 and Reader in 1942. In 1928 the Council of the Geological Society awarded him a grant from the Daniel Pigeon Fund to further his work on the glaciation of the London Basin, and in 1936 a similar award was made him from the Lyell Geological Fund. In 1942 he shared with David Linton the Murchison grant of the Royal Geographical Society. On the retirement of Professor Eva Taylor, in 1944, he migrated to Birkbeck as Professor, but when the Chair of Geography at King's fell vacant in 1947, returned to fill it. This move was something of a wrench—his years at Birkbeck had been happy ones, spent among students of maturer years, and he returned there as visitor and visiting lecturer as often as possible, and was, at the time of his death, on the staff of Birkbeck College as Honorary Lecturer in Geography.

His geographical interests always centred in Britain, and he used to say that "the eyes of the fool are on the ends of the earth". When, in the 1930s and later, he played golf, he would say that his eye for the lie of the land improved his game, and vice versa. Many are the young men who were encouraged by him to explore the rocks of south-east England in their leisure time.

Some of his work lay outside colleges. He served with the Observer Corps during the Second World War, first at Bristol, where King's had evacuated, then in the London area: and he was awarded the C.B.E. in recognition of his services on the Advisory Committee on Sand and Gravel appointed by the Minister of Town and Country Planning in June, 1946, which reported in 1948. In 1949 and 1950 he was president of the Institute of British Geographers, in 1950 of Section E of the British Association, and in 1954 of the Geographical Association. In 1957 he received the Victoria Medal of the Royal Geographical Society and he became F.R.S. in 1959.

His published work was mainly about the geology and geomorphology of the London Basin and the Weald, and in 1956 he collected 16 of his papers into a volume he called *The Geographer as Scientist, Essays on the Scope and Nature of Geography*. His other written work was done mainly in collaboration—with David Linton (*The Structure Surface and Drainage of South East England*), with R.S. Morgan (*Geomorphology*), with Frederick Goldring (*The Weald*), with G. F. Hutchings (*London's Countryside*), and with W. G. East (*The Spirit and Purpose of Geography*).

He was always interested in theology, and did some lay-preaching as a Congregationalist. It was amusing that he should find himself at a college so Anglican as King's, who disputed his right as a Congregationalist to partake in Communion in the college. When in 1960 he went to Cheshunt College and the Department of Geography at Cambridge to write a geography of south-east England, it was feared that his time would be mainly spent on theological discussion.

As a person he was extremely likeable, and students must have felt able to approach him without feeling intimidated. He spoke to a first-year student in the blunt good-natured way that he spoke to everybody. With his colleagues he was noted for frankness, both in praise and blame. He was inclined to bluster but never bore resentment. His tone of voice suggested that all was vanity, and also, in his later years, that all was vexation of spirit, too. Usually he spoke as he tugged at his pipe.

He married Edith Mary Stephens in 1934. There were no children of the marriage. His widow survives him.

April 27, 1963.

James Woolf, who died in Hollywood on May 30, 1966, at the age of 46, had been for nearly 20 years one of the most consistently successful, commercially and sometimes artistically, of British film producers.

He came of a family early involved in the cinema: his father, Cecil Woolf, was the founder of General Film Distributors and something of a legend in the British film industry in the 1920s. James Woolf began to learn about making films, as have a number of film producers, by first learning to sell them, in the publicity department of a major Hollywood studio. On the death of his father, he and his brother John took over the family interests and soon branched out on their own as directors of Independent Film Distributors, and of a producing company, Romulus Films. In this John Woolf was the main financial brain, and James primarily in charge of artistic policy. "Artistic" would be an optimistic word for most of their earlier efforts, though films like James Woolf's first personal production, *I'll Get You For This*, starring George Raft in 1948, or *Cosh Boy*, or *Women of Twilight*, served their turn, entertained many and made enough money to permit Romulus Films to gamble on a few more ambitious productions. Oddly enough, it was one of the latter, *The African Queen*, directed by John Huston, which first fulfilled the promise of *Pandora and the Flying Dutchman* that one day James Woolf would produce films with artistic pretensions which were also highly effective popular entertainment; and with the world success of *The African Queen* Romulus Films found themselves on the international film map.

Later Woolf productions varied in quality, but among them were two more John Huston films of some interest, *Moulin Rouge* and *Beat the Devil*. At about the same time the Woolf brothers figured in the unlikely role of financial backers for Korda after the collapse of British Lion; and thus they were responsible for underwriting such notable Korda productions as Olivier's *Richard III*, David Lean's *Summertime*, and Carol Reed's *A Kid for Two Farthings*. Among James Woolf's own productions in the mid-1950s were *I Am a Camera* and *The Story of Esther Costello*, neither more than a partial success; but in 1959 he retrieved his position with *Room at the Top*, Jack Clayton's version of John Braine's best-selling novel. This, however much its producer might subsequently fulminate against the shoddiness and superficiality, and, above all, the amateurishness—as he saw it—of much of the British cinema's New Wave, played perhaps a more important part than any other film in setting the wave in motion.

In 1963 the Woolf brothers ran into some trouble from the Film Distributors' Defence Organization as a result of their refusal to withhold their old cinema films from television, and there was talk of a complete boycott on their films in British cinemas. Relatively undeterred, James Woolf went to Hollywood, and there produced *King Rat*, with a British writer-director, Bryan Forbes (with whom he had previously made *The L-Shaped Room*), and a nearly all-British cast.

If few of his films made cinema history, one at least, *Room at the Top*, came near to it, and several of the others were among the most accomplished pieces of entertainment to emerge from the postwar British cinema.

June 1, 1966.

Leonard Woolf died on August 14, 1969, at the age of 88.

His death removes from the scene a distinguished man of a type more common in earlier generations perhaps than it is today. Though never a commanding public figure in literature, he had a delightful style of his own—markedly in the four volumes of autobiography (*Sowing*, 1880-1904; *Growing*, 1904–11; *Beginning Again*, 1911-18, and *Downhill All the Way*, 1919-39) which he produced late in life—and as author, critic, and publisher he exerted for many years a significant influence on educated literary opinion. Similarly in politics, though he neither held nor sought any position of importance, his books, his work as editor, especially of the *Political Quarterly*, and his untiring service on bodies such as the Labour Party's Advisory Committee and the International Bureau of the Fabian Society, ensured that his advice carried a great deal of weight in the counsels of the political left.

In middle life his name was strongly linked with that of the long-extinct "Bloomsbury Group", which derived from the local habitation of a number of the most brilliant and cultivated minds of the day who set up house in and about what is today the precinct of the University of London. Here Leonard and his wife Virginia established the Hogarth Pess, long known for the outstanding appearance as well as the literary quality of its products; here lived Lytton Strachey, for a time the Group's best known author, his brother James, Clive and Vanessa Bell (Virginia Woolf's sister), Maynard Keynes and Lydia Lopokova, and a host of others, whose lofty cultivation of the pleasures of mind and taste combined with a perceptible contempt for those of lesser attainments made the word "Bloomsbury" something of an irritant to the outsider. Woolf himself, however, partly because of his strong political affiliations to the cause of Labour, shared to only a minor extent in the assumptions of superiority.

Leonard Sidney Woolf was born on November 25, 1880, one of the fairly large family of Sidney Woolf, Q.C., and was educated at St. Paul's School and Trinity College, Cambridge.

POVERTY'S EXTREMES

His youthful experience—including a vivid impression of the extremes of poverty then visible even in the Royal Borough of Kensington—were fascinatingly described in the first volume of his autobiography, *Sowing* (1960). The St. Paul's which he attended was the school of Sir Compton Mackenzie and *Sinister Street*; but unlike his distinguished contemporary, he had nothing good to say of it, of the classical discipline through which he was put, or of Walker, its famous High Master. It was as one released from prison that he reached Cambridge, where he came rapidly under the influence of the philosopher G. E. Moore, and has left us a charming account of eager Cambridge youth in early Edwardian days; it was then that he came into contact with the family of Sir Leslie Stephen, whose daughter, Virginia, he married in 1912.

From 1904 to 1911 Woolf served in the Ceylon Civil Service, arriving there, as he recounted in his book *Growing* (1961), an unreflecting agent of the British Empire, and returning, after a variety of formative experiences, all poised to become a spearhead of anti-imperialism. His first published work, however, *The Village in the Jungle*, which appeared the year after his marriage is a delicate study of the values of the primitive mind and little more, and shortly afterwards politics—wartime politics—claimed his attention.

Through the Cambridge Fabians, of whom Rupert Brooke and Hugh Dalton are the best remembered lights, he had come into contact with Beatrice and Sidney Webb. In 1912 and 1913, after their campaign for reform of the Poor Law had ended, the Webbs were engaged in founding a Research Department for the study of social problems from a Socialist angle, and in 1915 Woolf was engaged by the Fabian Society to write a study of the possibilities of an international governing authority after the war. This work, published first as a supplement to the young *New Statesman* and subsequently as a book under the title *International Government* was Woolf's first outstanding production: its claim to be at least one of the earliest blue-prints for the League of Nations has never been disputed.

He followed it up, in 1920 by a devastating indictment, called *Empire and Commerce in Africa*, of the story of the European capitalist scramble for that continent. From then on his position as an authority in left-wing political thought was assured. Arthur Henderson, then secretary of the reorganized Labour Party, invited him to serve as honorary secretary of the party's advisory committees on international and imperial affairs—not always the easiest of assignments: he became editor of the *International Review* in 1919, and of the international section of the *Contemporary Review* in 1920 and 1921.

Politically, he was a committed man from the First World War onwards. Though he was literary editor of the Liberal *Nation* from 1923–30, it was a literary connexion only; because he was a Guild Socialist while Guild Socialism endured, working chairman of the International section of the New Fabian Research Bureau and the Fabian Society from 1931 to 1953, co-editor of the left-wing Political *Quarterly* from its foundation until 1959, and a member of the Board of the *New Statesman and Nation* to which he was a frequent contributor until he grew old. He was never, however, a blind supporter of any cause or person; while deeply appreciative of the Webbs, he was critical of their methods and attitudes, and impatient of Labour Party leaders when they seemed to him stupid or illiberal. His own philosophic outlook was never very clearly formulated. In the first volume of *After the Deluge* (1931) he appeared to be beginning a very interesting study of the psychology of mankind in the mass and its effects on the course of history, recalling Graham Wallas's seminal *Human Nature in Politics* of more than 20 years back: but as in Wallas's case also the follow-up was disappointing. Neither in the second volume (1939), nor in *Principia Politica* (1953), did he seem to have quite made up his mind where he stood or whether he was an optimist or a pessimist about the future of mankind.

August 15, 1969.

H. Bruce Woolfe, C.B.E., one of the pioneers of the British film industry during the difficult years which followed the end of the First World War, died on December 6, 1965.

The names of other pioneers of this era, such as Herbert Wilcox and Michael Balcon, may perhaps come more readily to mind for their achievements were largely in the sphere of popular entertainment, and it was left to Bruce Woolfe to concentrate on the education and documentary side of British film production, especially in so far as it concerned children. He was a quiet and self-effacing man who did not step readily into the limelight. But to those who remember these early, struggling years of the twenties when the British film industry did not generally amount to very much in the eyes of the world, the work of Bruce Woolfe will be recalled with gratitude.

Woolfe entered the film industry as a salesman during its virile infancy before the first war. Unfortunately much of this early impetus was lost during the war years, and Hollywood quickly monopolized the cinemas of the world during the silent twenties which followed. In 1919, after his demobilization from the Army, Woolfe made a modest start in the film world by initiating a documentary series on wild life called *Secrets of Nature*, with a studio which was a converted Army hut in Elstree. Later he launched out into a far more ambitious field of production by filming outstanding events of the war, including Zeebrugge, Ypres, Mons and the Battle of Coronel and the Falkland Islands.

SECRETS OF NATURE

By 1926 he was head of British Instructional Films, with well-appointed studios at Welwyn Garden City, and it was in this year that he showed his inspiration by taking on his staff as a script writer an inexperienced university teacher named Mary Field, and put to work on the floor of the studio as an assistant director an equally inexperienced young graduate from Oxford named Anthony Asquith.

Each handsomely repaid his confidence in them. Mary Field soon became the inspiration behind the *Secrets of Nature* series, which she made with a rare understanding, not only of the medium of the cinema, but also of the mind of children, to whom documentary films had previously been something of a bore, while Anthony Asquith went on to become one of the most brilliant of the younger school of British film directors.

Bruce Woolfe himself remained largely in the background, but he became the first Film Producers' Representative on the Board of Trade Advisory Committee, and in 1935 he was awarded three gold medals and four diplomas for short films shown at the Brussels Film Exhibition. During his film career he served on many committees of inquiry, and joined Children's Entertainment Films as member of the Film Production Committee on its formation in 1944. He was later trade member on the Ministry of Education Committee for the Preparation and Production of Visual Aids, and he was also a member of the British Film Academy and the honorary president of the Association of Specialized Film Producers. The British Film Industry has good reason to remember the name of Bruce Woolfe with pride and affection.

December 8, 1965.

Lord Woolton, who died on December 14, 1964, at the age of 81, had a career remarkable not only for success but for variety. As a young social worker in the back streets of Liverpool, as a captain of commerce in Lewis's Ltd., as the non-party Minister of Food during the Second World War, and as the brilliantly partisan chairman of the Conservative Party in the postwar years—in all these widely differing roles he triumphed. Yet so different were they from each other that each new departure provoked surprise and doubt. After all, the qualities of the social reformer are not normally those of the business tycoon; commercial success does not necessarily augur well for the tasks of national administration amid the pitfalls of Parliament; nor does a coalition Minister above party seem an obvious choice as a party political boss.

Yet each time Woolton confounded his critics. His work at the Ministry of Food must always be judged an integral part of the nation's war effort. It would also be hard to exaggerate his contribution to the postwar transformation of the Conservative Party. While others were refurbishing the doctrine, he was improving the efficiency of the machine and the attractiveness of the image. He added something of his own to the technique of party political warfare in Britain.

Avuncular in manner, perceptive in judgment, and thorough in action, he was repeatedly underestimated by his critics at large. He had a broader mind and a stronger will than might have been recognized from that bland smile and hearty chuckle. Above all, he had those immense assets, the ability to profit from his mistakes and to work within his limits.

The Rt. Hon. Sir Frederick James Marquis, P.C., C.H., first Earl of Woolton, Viscount Walberton, of Walberton in the County of Sussex, Viscount Woolton and Baron Woolton, of Liverpool, in the County of Lancaster in the Peerage of the United Kingdom, was born at Manchester on August 24, 1883, only son of Thomas Robert Marquis.

INTEREST IN SOCIAL WORK

He was educated at Manchester Grammar School—he was later to become a Governor—and at the University of Manchester, where he was awarded a research fellowship in economics. As a result of his work he was made a Fellow of the Royal Statistical Society. In 1908 he went to Liverpool to become warden of the David Lewis Men's Clubs and the University Settlement. As student of economic and social questions he gathered round him a group of eager social workers, and social work continued to be one of his chief interests.

In the war of 1914–18 he was rejected for military service on medical grounds, but he held various posts at the War Office in connexion with the Allied Commission and Raw Materials sections and then became secretary to the Leather Control Board and Controller of Civilian Boots. He was quick to grasp the details of the boot trade, and showed such ability in regard to it that he was required during the two years after the war to reorganize the Boot Manufacturers' Federation. Then he was asked by the late Alderman Cohen to join the directorate of Lewis's Limited, the large general stores, whose headquarters were at Liverpool. "It is", Cohen wrote, "the first time I have asked anybody who is not of my faith and my family to join my band." At first he was on the staff side of the business, a valuable experience; later on he became director of merchandising, and in 1928 was appointed joint managing director of the company. Under his control it prospered and extended its operations, and Marquis as time went on joined the boards of other well-known businesses. In 1936 he succeeded the late H. L. Cohen as chairman of Lewis's and its associated companies.

Meanwhile his well-organized gift for administration led to his appointment to various Government committees and to organizations connected with distribution and with education. From 1930 to 1933 he was a member of the Overseas Trade Development Council, from 1930 to 1934 a member of the Advisory Council of the Board of Trade, in 1933 was appointed to the Advisory Council of the Post Office, and in 1937 to the Cadman Committee on Civil Aviation. He was knighted in 1935. During the period of his business activities in Liverpool he played a prominent part in the social and intellectual life of the city, was chairman of the Liverpool Medical Research Council and a member of the University Council of Liverpool as well as of the Manchester University, of which he later became Chancellor.

CLOTHING THE ARMY

He had, therefore, achieved both a local and general reputation when in 1939 the decision of the Government to double the Territorial Army led to his appointment as Honorary Adviser to the Secretary of State for War for the purpose of clothing the Army. In four months he had completed his task. Meanwhile he had been created a baron, and in September, 1939, was appointed Director-General of Equipment and Stores, Ministry of Supply.

When, in April, 1940, Neville Chamberlain asked him to join the Government as Minister of Food, Woolton made clear his reluctance to get involved in politics, for which he said he said he had neither liking nor capacity. He resigned his directorships and started upon his new duties with much trepidation. After giving his first parliamentary answer from an inadequate brief, he heard a peer say to a Minister: "You must never let this feller speak in the House again." But he had the immense advantage of knowing the outlook of ordinary people. Churchill told him later that they thought of him as a philanthropist, not as a businessman. Almost immediately he launched a campaign to give guidance on the best use of comestibles and he put new heart into the staff of his department—with the timely and imaginative help of King George VI. Woolton put over the door the slogan: "We not only cope. We care."

In spite of his problems and the huge scale of his responsibilities for the provisioning and rationing of the country, he was able to evolve a national policy of wide scope. In the autumn of 1942 he explained that in order to free ships for the North African campaign he had recourse to the great reserve stocks which had been accumulated, and that in consequence the public had not noticed any change. He never seemed to be at a loss. In all modesty he claimed that his successes were not due to any capacity he had except that for choosing men. In 1942 he was created a C.H.

In November, 1943, it was announced that Lord Woolton had relinquished the office he had held with such marked distinction to become Minister of Reconstruction. It was an open recognition of the resource he had shown and the confidence he had won. For the first time a Minister of Churchill's Government was given full authority to deal with all aspects of postwar reconstruction policy. He was given, moreover, a seat in the War Cabinet in order to confer on him the necessary status. He had been loath to accept a post which would bring him into the arena of political argument. But it was largely on account of his independence of party affiliations that Churchill chose him.

In his appreciation of his new task Lord Woolton gave a leading place to the provision of decent homes for those who were serving in the forces, and was swift to urge local authorities to get on with their plans. From the outset he made it clear that he would make no promises until he knew that they could be fulfilled. It was yet another indication of his understanding of a public which, although he never courted it unduly, he never forgot. He had no department, and there was some anxiety whether his powers were wide enough for the scope of his undertaking, for it was felt that a fresh and massive impetus was required; but the man himself seemed to supply the answer.

In 1944 he announced the Government's proposals for the creation of a Ministry of Social Insurance, the provision of family allowances, and a comprehensive Social Insurance Bill, thus foreshadowing the policy followed by the Labour Party when it gained power in 1945. Until then he had described himself as a "political neuter," but in the hour of its defeat he joined the Conservative Party because, as he said at the time, he believed that, "however well-intentioned the other people now in office may be, if they pursue their policy to the end it will be disastrous for the economic life of this country and for personal freedom".

Lord Woolton's beaming geniality—the "Uncle Fred" side of his character, at which his critics were wont to mock—masked a steely resolve which had a startling impact on the party to which he gave his unstinted loyalty.

FORMIDABLE

He brought to its affairs the same efficiency and energy which had made him such a formidable—some would say ruthless—figure in the business world. It has been said that he took the party machinery to bits and rebuilt it from top to bottom. But he was not content merely to create a smooth-running mechanism. He harnessed it to the wills, energies, and emotions of those whose cause it was to serve. He has been described as perhaps the most successful party boss the country has ever known.

His presence at party conferences was always the focus of affectionate acclaim, never so movingly demonstrated as when illness suddenly struck him down at the conference of 1952. For a time his recovery was despaired of and this critical phase created a widely shared sense of personal anxiety. His spectacular recruiting drives had done much to broaden the social composition of the party, which he firmly refused to regard as merely a party of the well-to-do.

SHREWD PUBLICITY

His business training had given him a shrewd and expert facility in the arts of publicity and he neglected no modern method of propagating his political beliefs. His great poster compaigns will always be a lively memory of the electoral battles he launched. In public speech, not least in election broadcasts, he kindled the hopes and imagination of his supporters with vivid phrases which often laid him open to the bitter attacks of his opponents. There was, for instance, the celebrated "red meat" broadcast of the 1951 campaign. He seemed indifferent to the furore it created until his chance came two years later. Then in a speech at a local fete he observed mildly: "I ventured to remark in a broadcast that I thought a little more red meat would help us. We have got it now."

Another of his broadcast utterances brought him under fierce controversial heat. He had denied in October, 1951, what he called an election story that the Conservatives would cut the food subsidies, though he was careful to add: "What we want to do is to get rid of the need for subsidies." When on Budget day, 1952, a decision to reduce the food subsidies was announced this was seized on by the Opposition as a repudiation of Lord Woolton, who had been appointed Lord President of the Council (the post he held in the "caretaker" Government of 1945) with the task of supervising and coordinating the policies of the Ministries of Food and Agriculture.

In any case there had been much opposition at this time to the appointment of coordinating ministers or "overlords," and the circumstances gave fresh fuel to Labour Party criticism of Lord Woolton. They demanded that he should resign, but his offer to do so was firmly scouted by Winston Churchill, who reaffirmed in glowing terms his confidence in his colleague.

HUE AND CRY

A month or two later he was under attack again for having said in a Lords debate that the work of the coordinating ministers was not a responsibility to Parliament. Churchill stoutly defended Woolton. "Certainly", he said, "I am not likely to throw him over because of a hue and cry started on the benches opposite."

After his illness Lord Woolton did not resume his coordinating duties in connexion with food and agriculture, and in November, 1952, he was appointed Chancellor of the Duchy of Lancaster with a seat in the Cabinet. A viscounty was conferred on him in the Coronation Honours List of the succeeding June. He had made a good recovery from his illness and in September he was given the additional post of Minister of Materials—remaining a member of the Cabinet—to complete the work of winding up the Ministry. After the election victory of 1955, which owed so much to his endeavours, there was much speculation about his future. In the June of that year he resigned the chairmanship of the Conservative Party. In December he resigned from ministerial office also and accepted an earldom. Two years later he was elected president of the National Union of Conservative and Unionist Associations.

He married in 1912 Maud, the youngest daughter of Thomas Smith, who died in September, 1961. In 1962 he married secondly Dr. Margaret Elured Thomas. There were a son and a daughter of his first marriage. His son, Viscount Walberton, now succeeds to the earldom.

December 15, 1964.

Max Woosnam who died on July 14, 1965, at the age of 72, was an Olympic gold medallist for lawn tennis and had played Association football for Corinthians, Chelsea, Manchester City, and England. The son of Canon Woosnam. Maxwell Woosnam was born on September 6, 1892, and educated at Winchester and Trinity College, Cambridge. He joined the Montgomery Yeomanry in 1914 and later served with the Royal Welch Fusiliers. For over 30 years he was on the staff of I.C.I., retiring in 1954.

ALL-ROUNDER

Max Woosnam was one of the great all-round ball games players of his time—and indeed of any other time. At any game which demanded the quick coordination of eye, foot, hand, and body he was quite outstanding, and these qualities, combined with a powerful physique, brought him many successes in the world of sport. It was only because he played so many games and was essentially an amateur who could only play games in his spare time that he was not more famous. Also, of course, the First World War provided a great barrier to his athletic career, as it did to so many other athletes.

He was a brilliant boy cricketer at Winchester and in 1911 made a century at Lord's for the Public Schools XI against M.C.C. At Cambridge he won blues for cricket, athletics, golf, soccer, lawn tennis and real tennis. Perhaps his greatest athletic achievement was at soccer, where, in the 1920s, he played first for Chelsea and then for Manchester City (whom he captained), and also for England. He was probably the best amateur centre half of his day and there were very few better in the ranks of the professionals.

He did a great deal for professional football in England, and he had a fantastic following in Manchester. When he was carried off the field with a broken leg there were amazing expressions of sympathy from his many admirers in the Manchester crowd.

LAWN TENNIS SUCCESSES

At lawn tennis he won the singles championship of Lancashire in 1920, and in that year represented England at the Olympic tournament in Antwerp, where he won a Gold Medal in the men's doubles with O. G. N. Turnbull, and a Silver Medal in the mixed with Miss K. McKane (now Mrs. Leslie Godfree). In 1921 Max Woosnam won the men's doubles at Wimbledon with Randolph Lycett, and reached the final of the mixed doubles; he represented England in the Davis Cup doubles match against Spain, where, partnered by Lycett, he defeated the strong Spanish pair of Manuel Alonso and Count de Gomar. In that year he also captained the British side against Australasia at Pittsburgh, U.S.A., where he played in both singles and doubles. Perhaps his favourite doubles partner was the British International and Wimbledon doubles champion, Leslie Godfree, with whom he had many successes.

In later years Max Woosnam had played a leading part on the administrative side of the game in the International Lawn Tennis Club of Great Britain, of which he was a vice-president.

GAY SPIRIT

He brought a spirit of gaiety and adventure to all the games he played, and into his everyday life. Whatever game he played, or whatever else he did, he did with all his might—and he took his defeats with the same good temper and serenity as he took his victories.

He bore a severe chest complaint, from which he had suffered to an increasing degree for many years, with unbelievable courage.

To say that Max Woosnam will be missed in the world of sport is an understatement. His death leaves a gap which can never be filled, and he leaves behind him a host of friends and admirers.

July 16, 1965.

Sir Frank Worrell, the great West Indian cricketer, died on March 13, 1967, in Kingston, Jamaica, at the age of 42. His death was a profound shock to cricket lovers around the world for it was little more than three years since he ended his first class career as captain of the triumphant West Indian touring team in England. He was one of the finest all-rounders in the history of the game, remembered as much for his leadership as his play. It was he who moulded the West Indian Test team from a group of talented, entertaining but erratic individuals into probably the finest side in the world. In doing this he not only won personal fame but raised the status and dignity of the West Indian coloured cricketer.

Frank Mortimer Maglinne Worrell was born at Bridgetown on August 1, 1924. As nearly a natural cricketer as may be—for he was never coached and rarely practised—he was a leading figure in the remarkable upsurge of Barbadian cricket in the 1940s. He was an outstanding player from boyhood; at Combermere School he was primarily an orthodox slow left-arm bowler and as such—and a number eleven batsman—was first chosen for Barbados—when he was 17. A year later while still at school, sent in as "night watchman" he went on next morning to make 64 and to establish himself as a batsman. In the same West Indian season he scored 188, the first of his 40 centuries, against Trinidad. In 1943–44 at 19, he made 308 not out in an unfinished partnership of 502 with John Goddard, a record for the fourth wicket which he and Walcott broke two years later with an unbroken 574, also against Trinidad. When world cricket recommenced after the Second World War, he and his fellow Barbadian batsmen, Walcott and Weekes, were the legendary "three Ws".

Worrell was the most orthodox of the three; his self-taught technique was so correct that he seemed incapable of a crooked stroke. Lithely built and superbly balanced, he was a stylist with an elegantly unhurried air, although his wide range of strokes, off front or back foot, was based on rapid movement into correct position. His cutting was delicate, his driving, for all its easy execution, powerful; he was strong on both sides of the wicket; and he combined ability to relax when not actually playing with the unremitting concentration of those who build long innings.

CHANGE OF BOWLING

The demands of League cricket changed his bowling method from slow to fast-medium left arm; he exploited English conditions in sharp movement off the seam and his pace from the pitch was so hostile as at times to be little short of genuinely fast. Latterly his speed declined but to the end of his Test career his experience and control enabled him to seal up an end. He was a safe fieldsman and a clean catcher anywhere and latterly his fielding at silly mid-on was a considerable tactical asset for his bowlers.

As a young man he was markedly sensitive to criticism and some schoolday bitternesses rankled so deeply that, in 1947, he made his home in Jamaica. So it was as a Jamaican player that he established his Test place in the series of 1947–48 against England.

His performances brought him the offer which few West Indian cricketers have found it financially possible to resist and in 1948 he joined the Central Lancashire League club, Radcliffe.

YEARS IN LEAGUE

There, and subsequently with Norton and Church, he spent some dozen happy and successful years as a league professional. Meanwhile, he read first optics and then economics at Manchester University. He contrived, however, to take part in all the West Indies' Tests of that period except those of 1958–59 in India which coincided with the final terms before he took a B.A. (Admin.) degree. He made three tours of India with Commonwealth sides.

For the team of 1950, which was the first from the West Indies to win a Test, and a rubber, in England, he was top of the batting averages with 539 runs at 89.83 and made an important contribution to team-balance by his fast-medium bowling. At Trent Bridge after taking three important English wickets he scored 261, then the highest innings by a West Indian in a Test in England.

In the West Indian side which was beaten in Australia in 1951–52 he emerged as a genuine all rounder of Test standard. Apart from his technical ability, the quality of his temperament was strikingly apparent in Goddard's defeated and dispirited team of 1957 in England, when he made good the lack of an opening batsman and opened the bowling. He took seven English wickets in the innings at Headingley and finished second in the batting and first in the bowling averages for Tests.

It was now apparent that only internal politics could prevent him from captaining the West Indies. He himself wisely took little part in the occasionally acrimonious controversy which ended when he was asked to take the 1960–61 team to Australia; the first time a coloured West Indian had been appointed to the captaincy of a touring side.

On that tour, which included the famous tied Test at Brisbane, cricket in Australia was raised to such heights of public esteem as it had not reached since the days of Bradman. Australian opinion was reflected in the institution of the "Worrell Trophy" for all future series between the two countries.

TWO AIMS

When he captained the touring side of 1963 to England, he was almost 39, a veteran by West Indian standards; indeed, all his famous contemporaries of the 1940s had retired from Test cricket. He himself was no longer the player he had been but, as batsman, bowler and fielder, he was still useful and he was one of the few men whose captaincy was so oustanding as to make a major contribution to a side's strength. He declared his purpose as not merely to win the Test series, but also to make such an impression as to bring West Indies to England again appreciably before the 1971 season of the Conference schedule. He achieved both his aims. The West Indies won the rubber 3–1.

Worrell's captaincy was outstanding. Sharp in tactical perception, astute in attack and defence, quietly spoken, yet firm to the brink of ruthlessness, he outwitted his opponents and sustained his colleagues. As lately as 1957 a West Indian team had crumpled psychologically in face of defeat. Now, at one crisis after another, Worrell, with what sometimes seemed exaggerated calm, held them steady. His achievement may best be described as instilling in his players a professional attitude and stability which has endured. As in Australia, his side's cricket roused such immense public interest as achieved his second design. In the following winter the tour programme was revised, bringing another West Indian team to England in 1966.

By the time that decision was taken, Worrell had returned home to a magnificent public reception, the post of Warden in the University of the West Indies at Kingston and a seat in the Jamaican Senate; a knighthood followed in the New Year Honours of 1964. In 1966 he was appointed Dean of Students for the branch of the University of the West Indies in Trinidad.

EASILY FIT

He was a non-smoker who kept enviably fit with a minimum of training. Convivial and conversational, he would talk gaily far into the night in his pleasant, slightly husky voice; he was quick and flexible in debate, fond of England and his many English friends, courteous in manner and he only rarely revealed the depth of his feeling on racial matters.

In 51 Test Matches he scored 3,860 runs at an average of 49.48 and took 69 wickets at 38.37.

He married Velda Brewster of Barbados in 1948; they had one daughter.

March 14, 1967.

Sir Evelyn Wrench, K.C.M.G., founder of the Overseas League (since 1959 the Royal Overseas League) and the English-Speaking Union, and chairman and former editor of the *Spectator*, died on November 11, 1966, at the age of 84.

The only surviving son of the Right Hon. Frederick Wrench, of Killacoona, co. Dublin, an Irish Land Commissioner, John Evelyn Leslie Wrench was born at Brookeborough, co.Fermanagh, on October 29, 1882, and educated at Summer Fields, near Oxford, and at Eton. When travelling on the Continent, to learn languages necessary to the diplomatic career at which he then aimed, Evelyn Wrench became depressed with the lead which the Continent then had over England in the picture postcard business, and when only 18 founded a firm in England which rapidly became the biggest there, and with the affairs of which he was preoccupied from 1900 to 1904. Over-rapid expansion, having regard to the capital available, ultimately caused the venture to fall, but in circumstances which did nothing to diminish the reputation for enterprise, character and ability which his first successes in the field had won for him.

Among those who had been attracted by his qualities was Lord Northcliffe, whose staff Evelyn Wrench joined in 1904, and with whom he remained for eight years, serving his chief on many special tasks and missions, and also holding at different times the posts of editor of the *Overseas Daily Mail,* of the Continental edition of the *Daily Mail,* and of the *Weekly Despatch,* and of sales manager for the Amalgamated Press.

VISION OF EMPIRE

The further successes which undoubtedly awaited Evelyn Wrench in the newspaper field were, however, of less interest to him than the vision he had acquired, on a visit in 1906 to Canada and the United States, of the mission of the peoples of the Empire, to which he increasingly longed to make a more direct personal contribution. He therefore resigned his newspaper posts and embarked on a round-the-world Empire tour, from which he returned to found what was at first called the Overseas Club, later renamed the Overseas League.

While continuing to serve with this organization, which made rapid progress, and undertook much war work (a notable aspect of which was an Empire Fund to provide tobacco for the troops), Wrench also served a brief second term as editor of the Paris Edition of the *Daily Mail,* joined the Royal Air Force, in which he reached the rank of Major, served as principal private secretary to Lord Rothermere when the latter was Air Minister, and finally was deputy to Lord Beaverbrook in the latter's capacity as Controller for the Dominions and the United States of the Ministry of Information. For his war services he was made C.M.G.

In 1918 with the encouragement and help of the then Canadian High Commissioner, Sir George Perley, and American Ambassador, Walter Hines Page, and others from Great Britain, the Dominions and the United States, Wrench was inspired by the wartime partnership of the English-speaking peoples to found a second organization, the English-Speaking Union. This shortly after the war absorbed the oldest of Anglo-American voluntary societies, the Atlantic Union, founded in 1897 by Sir Walter Besant, which in 1920 was duplicated by a sister society, with the same name, in the United States.

To the Overseas League, where he was secretary as well as founder, and the English-Speaking Union, where he served two terms as chairman, and a long period as honorary secretary, Wrench devoted much of his time between the wars. Wrench's appetite for work was keen, and he added to his work for the two organizations which he had founded service on the *Spectator*. He became a contributor in 1922, later joined the board, bought control from St. Loe Strachey in 1925, and was editor from 1925 to 1932. He remained chairman for the rest of his life, although he sold out his controlling shareholding to the present proprietor, Ian Gilmour, M.P.

During the inter-war years Wrench suffered his second failure, although, like his first with the picture postcard business which he started as a schoolboy, one which reflected credit on him. This was with the All Peoples Association, which he founded in 1930, to do in the wider field what the Overseas League was doing in the inter-Empire field, and the English-Speaking Union in the Commonwealth-American field. The period 1930 to 1939 was one in which forces too powerful for any voluntary organization to make way against were threatening any vision of universal, international amity, and the specific field of Anglo-German understanding, in which the All Peoples Association tried to be helpful, became, as Munich and the war approached, an increasingly difficult one to cultivate successfully.

In 1937 he married his first cousin, Hylda Lady de Voeux, daughter of Sir Victor Brooke, sister of Sir Alan Brooke (later Viscount Alanbrooke), and aunt of Viscount Brookeborough.

WORLD TOUR

Late in 1940 they embarked on a world tour, and found themselves when in India on its homeward leg unable to proceed farther. They sought ways of being helpful, and quickly found them in efforts to help the American officers and men reaching India for the war, and to promote contacts between these, the British in India, and the Indians themselves. So valuable was their work that Wrench was appointed by the Viceroy to the specially created post of American Relations Officer to the Government of India, in which he served from 1942 to 1944.

After the war he devoted himself increasingly to writing. To earlier books, *Uphill* and *Struggle,* which were personal memoirs, and his two wartime books, *I Loved Germany* and *Immortal Years,* he added after the war *Francis Yeats Brown: A Portrait, Transatlantic London, Geoffrey Dawson and our Times,* and *Alfred Lord Milner: The Man of No Illusions.* The two latter books were based on extensive research into the private papers of Dawson and Milner, to which Wrench was given special access by their families, and also drew much on his personal acquintance with both men, and personal recollections of the events with which they had been concerned.

On his eightieth birthday, the English-Speaking Union launched a trust fund to be named after Wrench for travel grants to be awarded to categories of his choice. He was advanced to K.C.M.G. in 1960.

A man of deep religious convictions, profoundly devoted to the service of his fellow men, Wrench had great grace, sensitivity and charm, and an infectious enthusiasm which was as marked late in his life as it had been when he was a young man.

November 12, 1966.

Lord Wright, P.C., G.C.M.G., a former Master of the Rolls and Lord of Appeal, died on June 27, 1964, at his home near Marlborough. He was 94.

Robert Alderson Wright's career owed nothing either to birth or to fortune. He was the son of John Wright, Marine Superintendent of South Shields. Born on October 15, 1869, he was educated privately and at Trinity College, Cambridge, and graduated in 1896 with a first class in the Classical Tripos. He was a Fellow of Trinity from 1899 to 1905, and was called to the Bar by the Inner Temple in 1900, in his thirty-second year.

Wright was a pupil of Mr. (afterwards Lord Justice) Scrutton, then at the height of his very large commercial practice. From the close of the last century the Commercial Court had begun to be the stepping-stone to many promotions to the Bench, and, as the leaders passed upwards, firstrate juniors in that branch had great opportunities for advancement. By 1917, the year in which he took silk, Wright had achieved a high position in the confidence of the City firms of commercial solicitors. While the 1914–18 War brought a decline in the ordinary mercantile business of the Courts, the Prize Court was a valuable source of additional profit, and the end of the war brought an aftermath of litigation. From that time onward Wright was in nearly every important commercial case before the Courts, and was frequently briefed before the House of Lords and the Judicial Committee of the Privy Council. Though he had an attractive vein of dry humour, his advocacy, like that of several of his contemporaries in commercial practice, was lugubrious rather than brisk.

When in May, 1925, Mr. Justice Lush resigned, Wright's nomination by Lord Cave, then Lord Chancellor, to fill the vacancy was received by the profession with great satisfaction. He made an excellent Judge, and showed more patience on the Bench than was expected from a somewhat irritable manner, for which perhaps overwork was responsible, occasionally displayed at the Bar. In his earlier days on the Bench he was a Judge of the silent type, but it was noticed that latterly in the House of Lords and Privy Council he developed the habit of maintaining a running commentary on the arguments of counsel.

TWO NOTABLE TRIALS

As the commercial cases which he usually tried were not widely reported in the press, his name was little known to the public. Towards the close of his career as a Judge of the King's Bench Division, however, it fell to him to preside over two of the most remarkable cases of their day—Banco de Portugal v. Waterlow and Sons, Ltd., and the trial of Lord Kylsant. The first of these arose out of a criminal conspiracy of which Waterlows, the well-known printers, were the innocent victims. They were induced to print a large number of notes in the belief that the Bank of Portugal had given authority, and the notes were put into circulation in Portugal. The hearing of the action before Wright occupied 21 days, at the end of 1930, and he gave judgment for the bank for £569,421. In July, 1931, he presided at the trial of Lord Kylsant at the Central Criminal Court on charges of publishing, as chairman of the Royal Mail Steam Packet Company, false balance-sheets and a false prospectus. On the first charge he was acquitted, but he was convicted on the second and sentenced to 12 months' imprisonment. Wright's handling of this intricate case greatly enhanced his already high reputation as a Judge, and on the resignation of Lord Dunedin as a Lord of Appeal, in April, 1932, he was singled out at once among about three Judges as likely to be promoted. His appointment was entirely justified, and at a time when the House of Lords and Privy Council had never been stronger in legal talent his presence added even greater strength to those Courts. His legal path had lain among the type of litigation which comes before the final tribunals, and at the Privy Council his fine mind soon made itself master of the intricacies of Indian litigation.

In 1935 an unusual break occurred in Wright's judicial career. Lord Hanworth, shortly before his death, had resigned the Mastership of the Rolls in October, and at the time the Government was in some difficulty in filling the post satisfactorily. Wright was invited to take it on the understanding that, on the first vacancy arising among the Lords of Appeal, he would be at liberty to resume his former office. The Mastership of the Rolls, with its appanages, at that time the Record Office, as well as the control of solicitors, is recognized as the most onerous of judicial posts, and Wright, who was neither young nor very robust when he assumed it, was understood to feel the strain and was somewhat annoyed that the resignation of one of the Lords of Appeal was delayed beyond its expected time. However, in April 1937, a vacancy occurred, and Wright, to his great satisfaction, resumed his former duties as a Lord of Appeal which he carried out until his resignation in 1947.

WAR CRIMES COMMISSION

In February, 1945, he was elected chairman of the United Nations War Crimes Commission. The object of this commission was the collection of material on which the charges subsequently investigated at the trials at Nuremberg were based. During their inquiries the members of the commission visited Germany and inspected the camps where the worst crimes had been perpetrated. Later, at the invitation of the Australian Government, Lord Wright went by air to Japan to attend the trials of the war criminals there. He also visited Washington for consultation with the American authorities. It was generally agreed that the work of the Nuremberg Tribunal was greatly facilitated by the care and speed with which the commission had performed their duties. For these services he was made a G.C.M.G. in 1948.

He was made a Bencher of his Inn in 1923, and elected Treasurer in 1946. For a time Wright was chairman of the committee concerned with law revision, a topic much under discussion at the present time. He had been Deputy High Steward of Cambridge University which conferred on him the degree of Hon. LL.D., as also did the Universities of Birmingham, London, and Toronto.

In his younger days Wright had been a mountaineer and was a member of the Alpine Club. He was also a keen horseman, a taste shared by the lady whom he married in 1928, Margery Avis, daughter of F. J. Bullows, of Sutton Coldfield.

June 29, 1964.

Lawrence Wright, the music publisher and songwriter, died on May 16, 1964, in a Blackpool hospital at the age of 76.

Wright, who opened an office in Denmark Street over 50 years ago, was known as "The father of Tin Pan Alley". Of his songs, many of them written under the pseudonym of Horatio Nicholls, perhaps the best known was "Among my Souvenirs". His output over the years was prodigious, and he also wrote "That Old-Fashioned Mother of Mine", "Shepherd of the Hills". "Mistakes", "Wyoming Lullaby", "Old Father Thames", and "Babette", among many others.

Born in Leicester on February 15, 1888, he began his career by opening a music shop there at the age of 18. He wrote songs about every important national or local event and soon won a measure of success. For the coronation of King George V he composed the march "Long May He Reign".

Feeling the need to expand, he went to London and set up as a publisher in Denmark Street. As a songwriter his first big success was "Blue Eyes", written just before the 1914–18 War. During the war he enlisted and was in the air service. It was while in a barrack room one night that he had the idea for "Are We Downhearted—No", one of the famous trench songs of that war.

"Among my Souvenirs" was widely popular when it was written in 1927, and suddenly, in 1959, it had a remarkable comeback, winning a place in the top 10 after the American singer Connie Francis recorded it.

May 18, 1964.

Fritz Wunderlich, who died in Heidelberg in September, 1966, from injuries received in a fall, was the leading German lyric tenor of the present day. He was 36.

Born in 1930 at Kusel, he studied at Freiburg and became a student singer at the Freiburg Opera in 1953. Two years later he joined the Stuttgart Opera, making his debut as a Master in *Die Meistersinger* and soon afterwards singing Tamino in *Die Zauberflöte*—a role of which he has come to be regarded as the leading interpreter. He sang with the Frankfurt Opera from 1958 to 1960; since then he has been jointly with the Vienna, Munich and Frankfurt companies, and has appeared frequently as a guest elsewhere, for example at Stuttgart and Hamburg, and at the Salzburg Festival.

Wunderlich appeared in Britain several times: as Don Ottavio in the last Covent Garden revival of *Don Giovanni,* as Ferrando in the Hamburg State Opera production of *Cosi fan tutte* at the 1965 Edinburgh Festival, in *Das Lied von der Erde* at the Festival Hall, and at the Edinburgh Festival which finished just before his death. He there sang Tamino and gave a recital of lieder, a field in which he had only lately begun to appear substantially. While he was best known internationally for the sweet tone, smooth delivery, and beautiful line of his Mozart singing (Belmonte in *Die Entführung aus dem Serail* was another of his outstanding roles), his repertory was wide: from Monteverdi and Bach (he took part in recordings of the B Minor Mass and the St. Matthew Passion) to Strauss, Orff and a range of operetta roles. Among the roles he created was Tiresias in *Oedipus*. Recently his voice had gained in substance and it seemed that he was reaching the peak of a distinguished career.

September 19, 1966.

Sir Myles Wyatt, C.B.E., chairman of British United Airways, died at his home, Alresford Hall, Colchester, on April 14, 1968. He was 64.

Wyatt was educated at Radley and New College, Oxford, which he left in 1926 to join the Commissioners for the Port of Calcutta. He retired in 1934 and joined Airwork Ltd. as general manager. It was then a small pioneering business, which built, among other things, Heston airport, from which Chamberlain departed for Munich.

In 1960 Wyatt announced the formation of British United Airways, now Britain's largest independent operating company whose network of scheduled services from Gatwick includes East, West and Central Africa, the Canary Islands, western Europe and South America.

Wyatt was chairman of Air Holdings, the parent concern of a large number of air transport, aero engineering and aviation servicing companies, principally British United Airways, the largest independent airline in Europe. The forerunner of this large private enterprise complex with assets of £34m. was Airwork, founded in 1928, of which Wyatt was ultimately managing director.

Before the war Airwork concentrated on technical support services for civil and Government aviation activities, in Britain and overseas, but after 1945, led by Wyatt, the company expanded into the civil airline, engineering and helicopter operating sectors of the industry. Many of the smaller independent airlines which came into being in the late 1940s were acquired by Airwork and formed into a major independent air transport group operating trooping and charter flights and pioneering inclusive tour air holiday travel.

In 1960 Airwork was merged with Hunting-Clan to form British United Airways which under Wyatt's chairmanship has bought nearly £30m. worth of British jet airliners during seven years and developed worldwide scheduled air services. Air Holdings was formed in 1961 as a financial umbrella for the group.

Recently Wyatt was concerned with setting up an executive sales team to sell the 50 Rolls-Royce powered Lockheed L. 1011 air buses ordered by Air Holdings. Wyatt visited the United States to finalize this deal which clinched a multi-million pound order for Rolls-Royce engines for the giant American air bus.

Wyatt was outspoken in his demands for a "fair crack of the whip" for the independent airline operators who, he said, should have a powerful organization.

Wyatt was a keen yachtsman, Admiral of the Royal Ocean Racing Club and a former owner of Bloodhound, which was sold to the Queen and the Duke of Edinburgh in 1962. He afterwards commissioned the magnificent Tyger, one of the largest ocean-going yachts in Britain with an overall length of more than 88 feet.

Tyger seldom, if ever, appeared on the racing scene but made several notable cruises. Wyatt won the Royal Cruising Club challenge cup for a voyage Iceland to Spitsbergen and home by way of Norway and the Faroës.

Wyatt was created C.B.E. in 1954 and knighted in the 1963 Birthday Honours. Married in 1929, he leaves a widow and two children.

April 16, 1968.

Sir Bruce Wycherley, M.C., president and formerly managing director of the Abbey National Building Society, died on March 17, 1965, at the age of 70.

He was a well-known and much-liked figure in many aspects of life in the City of London, and his interest in and affection for it were not a whit diminished when he forsook Moorgate for Baker Street in January, 1944.

Robert Bruce Wycherley (invariably called by his second name) was born on April 5, 1894, at Hadnall in Shropshire, where his father was a Methodist minister. As a result of that calling, the family moved to Settle in Yorkshire, where the son was educated and also acquired that love of the organ which remained with him throughout his life. Here, too, were developed the character and the ability which justify the addition of his name to the long list of sons of the manse (his ancestry was of course partly Scottish) who have achieved distinction in after life.

At 17 Wycherley entered the West Riding Education Department at Wakefield but, like so many of his generation, war both unsettled his career and widened his horizons. His war record was distinguished. He served for four years (mainly in France), won the Military Cross and a bar, both in 1918, and returned as a captain, aged 24.

He was restless and ambitious and after two years as secretary of the West Riding War Pensions Division obtained the appointment of secretary of the Halifax District Engineering Employers Association. Here he gained much experience of men and affairs, the value of which he subsequently freely acknowledged.

It was not until he was 35 that he found his true métier when he became assistant secretary of the then National Building Society. It was typical of him that he stepped down from first to second place, and it proved a true case of *reculer pour mieux sauter* for he soon rose to be general manager and then managing director. This position he retained until the amalgamation of the Abbey Road and the National on January 1, 1944, when he became joint managing director until the retirement of the late Sir Harold Bellman from managerial office four years later.

SHREWD JUDGMENT

Wycherley rapidly made his mark among his colleagues. Tall, broad-shouldered, and genial, his was an easily remembered figure at any gathering, but behind the geniality lay a keen brain and shrewd judgment which soon came to be recognized and appreciated. He served on the council of the Building Societies Association for over 30 years and was chairman during the exceptionally difficult years of 1943 to 1946. On retiring from the council he was elected a vice-president. He was a past-chairman of the Metropolitan Association of Building Societies and a vice-president of the International Union of Building Societies and of the Building Societies Institute.

Outside his office his main interests, which he served devotedly, were in free-masonry (in which he held past grand rank) and in the City of London, of which he was a freeman. He was a past-president of the Chartered Institute of Secretaries and of the City Livery Club and a member of the Court of the Innholders Company. He greatly enjoyed good food, good wine and good company and one likes to think that he derived this pleasant trait from the Restoration dramatist from whom he was descended.

WITTY FLASHES

For many years he was a frequent, congenial and welcome diner-out in the City and the West End. He wrote easily and well and his speeches were always carefully prepared by himself. He was not, however, a ready speaker but when he spoke without notes (which he rarely did) he delighted his hearers with unexpected flashes of wit which he normally reserved for private conversation.

Wycherley married first Lena Winifred, daughter of Edward Land Harrison, of Wakefield, by whom he had a daughter. After her death in 1942 he married Margaret Brown, daughter of William Leitch Morton of Forfar, by whom also he had a daughter. He was happy in his home life and a generous and devoted husband, father, and grandfather.

Wycherley was a big man in every way, big in frame, big in heart, and big in outlook. He had a gift of leadership and carried great influence in building society circles, where his counsels, almost invariably of moderation, were widely respected. His knighthood, conferred in 1953, brought great pleasure to his wide circle of friends. Like most big men, he was not easily roused but he could be vehement when he thought it necessary.

In 1962 he was stricken with severe illness and underwent three major operations in 12 days. That he survived them at all is a tribute to his vitality and determination but, to the great regret of his friends, they forced a severe curtailment of his activities, though he made a valiant but only partial recovery which earned him unstinted admiration. He was, however, obliged to withdraw from active management of the Abbey National Building Society though remaining a director and he was greatly pleased by being elected president of the society—the first person to be so honoured.

March 18, 1965.

Patrick Wymark, the actor, was found dead in his hotel in Melbourne, Australia, on October 20, 1970, three days before he was due to appear in the leading role in *Sleuth* at the Playbox Theatre there. He was 44.

Wymark's name became a household word in Britain with the creation of the Independent Television series *The Planemakers.* As Sir John Wilder, he added dimensions—not, perhaps, entirely comprehended in an efficient but possibly too dramatic script—to a character seen one-dimensionally as a power-hungry, ruthlessly ambitious tycoon whose deepest conviction seemed to be that the aircraft industry, like marriage, existed for his personal advancement. Wymark allowed this stereotype to develop odd corners of sardonic humour and humanity as well as a suggestion that his centre, though unreachable, was quite soft. It was natural that so forceful a TV characterization should live again in a second series, *The Power Game,* to expand his industrial interests, flirt with politics and find an enemy as ruthless and ambitious as himself. Wymark's work in *The Power Game* brought him an "Actor of the Year" award.

Patrick Wymark was born A. K. A. Cheeseman at Cleethorpes, Lincolnshire, on July 11, 1926. He was educated at Wintringham Grammar School, Grimsby, and University College London, before he went to the Old Vic School for theatrical training. He first appeared on the stage in 1951 with the Old Vic Company, with which he toured South Africa in the following year. In 1953 and 1954 he was Artist in Residence at Stanford University, California, where he produced several plays.

From 1955 to 1958, with the Royal Shakespeare Company, Wymark showed himself to be a Shakespearian actor of considerable range, from comic "heavy" roles like Sir Toby Belch, Pompey in *Measure for Measure,* Dogberry in *Much Ado about Nothing,* and Stephano in *The Tempest* to odder characterizations like Macbeth's Porter and Marullus in *Julius Caesar.* Lance in *Two Gentlemen of Verona* found him capable of an earthy innocence and Bottom in *A Midsummer's Night's Dream*, of finding the role's fantastic poetry. Outside the Shakespearean repertory he was impressive as Büchner's Danton in *Danton's Death*, and with the Royal Shakespeare Company after 1960 he was Bosola in *The Duchess of Malfi* and Epihodov in *The Cherry Orchard*, and was seen in John Whiting's *The Devils*. At the Mermaid, in 1965, he was King John in John Arden's *Left-Handed Liberty*. His films included *The Criminal, Dr. Syn, Operation Crossbow*, and the new film *Cromwell* in which he was Strafford, and he was frequently seen on television in roles outside the series which made him famous among those who rarely visit the theatre.

An actor of considerable genial humanity and imagination as well as of the driving force that won him his reputation on television, Wymark did not allow himself to be trapped by his success in front of the cameras. His return to the stage was a thing he took always for granted. He leaves a widow and four children.

October 21, 1970.

Diana Wynyard, C.B.E., the actress, who died on May 13, 1964, had shown herself over a a long period of varied work to be not less remarkable for all-round competence than she was conspicuous by her beauty and the graciousness of her stage personality. While her beauty made her stand out and drew the attention of an audience, something demure and cool in temperament counteracted this, causing her performance to drop back into place and blend with the ensemble.

The daughter of Edward and Margaret Cox, she was born in London on January 16, 1906, received the names Dorothy Isobel, and attended Woodford School, Croydon. There, together with a pupil two years junior to herself, the future Dame Peggy Ashcroft, she produced Shakespeare plays and studied elocution in Gwen Lally's class. Under the name of Diana Wynyard she made her debut in London in 1925, but the foundations of her career were laid at the Playhouse, Liverpool, during two seasons' work as a member of William Armstrong's company. On getting her chance in London at the end of that time in a comedy of Walter Hackett's at the St. Martin's in 1929, she was equipped to take it. The beauty of this unknown girl caused quite a stir on the opening night, and was remarked upon by Charles Morgan in his notice in *The Times* the next day.

PART IN "CAVALCADE"

Nine months later at the same theatre Nigel Playfair and Diana Wynyard were co-stars. She essayed Belinda in his revival of Congreve's *The Old Bachelor* at the Lyric, Hammersmith, unsuccessfully as it happened; but this was followed at once by an engagement on the stage in the United States and in turn by the opportunity of making several big films in Hollywood including that of Noel Coward's *Cavalcade*. After an appearance in London as Charlotte Brontë in a drama by Clemence Dane, she was back in Hollywood, and on returning there for the second time in 1934, she was, in the words of Sir Tyrone Guthrie, all set to be a big star.

No new part of suitable weight presented itself till the heroine of Coward's comedy *Design for Living*, first played by Lynn Fontanne in New York, devolved upon her at the Haymarket in 1939. She proved during the war years and the postwar period that she was now also capable of handling dramatic parts in plays by Lillian Hellman and Emlyn Williams and in films such as *The Prime Minister* and Alexander Korda's *An Ideal Husband*. This development was carried farther during two seasons of Shakespeare at Stratford upon Avon, the first under Sir Barry Jackson, the second under Anthony Quayle, followed by a tour of Australia with the Memorial Theatre Company in 1949–50.

ADVENTUROUS CHOICE

Denis Cannan, John Whiting, André Roussin, Maxwell Anderson, Tennessee Williams, Lillian Hellman and Peter Ustinov were among the contemporary dramatists in whose plays she took leading parts during the 1950s and early 1960s. The first two authors, regarded in those days as being "difficult", were helped to obtain a hearing by her performances in, respectively, *Captain Carvallo* and *Marching Song*.

Audiences, once having discovered Diana Wynyard, expected much of her, and it was as though she resolved to keep faith with them, if in no other way, at least by being adventurous in her choice of plays. Certainly she was adventurous. If she scarcely received due credit for this, it was probably because something in her bearing and her attitude towards any role deprecated fervour and excitement on the parts of an audience. She was a restraining influence in the theatre, an enemy of emotional self-indulgence whether on the stage or in the auditorium. The values of her performance often seemed to be a criticism of the values of the play and of the theatre generally.

Diana Wynyard was made a C.B.E., in 1953. Her first marriage to Sir Carol Reed, the film director, and her second marriage to Mr. Tibor Csato were both dissolved.

May 14, 1964.

X

Dr. Alfred Bitini Xuma, whose death in South Africa was reported on January 28, 1962, was one of the architects of the African National Congress, of which he was president-general throughout the 1940s. He was also one of the considerable number of Africans of his generation (he was in his late 60s) who achieved eminence in his profession and who had travelled widely overseas.

At the age of 19 he went to study at Tuskegee Institute in Alabama, choosing scientific agriculture as his subject. Soon after he transferred to a medical course at the University of Minnesota. He received his M.D. at Northwestern University. Subsequently he studied gynaecology in Austria and took further degrees at Glasgow and Edinburgh.

He lived and practised in Sophiatown until compelled, by the Western Area's Resettlement Scheme, to sell his house to a white man and move to an area where Africans were permitted to live under the Group Areas Act. Thus, in 1958, he once again started a medical practice in Dube Township.

YOUNG MEN TO THE FORE

Under Xuma's leadership the organization of the African National Congress was greatly improved, and a country-wide system of provincial committees linked with the national executive was established. Young men were brought in and encouraged to voice their opinions, and of him Albert Luthuli has written: "Until Dr. Xuma's time older men did not encourage younger men to join Congress, let alone participate in leading it. The organization therefore stood in dire need of the ideas and energies of young men. Xuma brought the young men in, and the impact which the vigorous Youth League made on Congress as a whole was considerable and beneficial."

It was these young men who eventually, in 1949, voted Xuma from power. The reason for their dissatisfaction was his refusal to support the Youth League's Programme of Action which advocated an end to representations and deputations, and called for country-wide demonstrations, strikes and civil disobedience.

Before his replacement Xuma had brought another important innovation to Congress, that of collaboration with non-African organization opposing the Government's racial policy. In particular he worked with the Indian National Congress, led by Dr. Yusef Dadoo, when it mounted its campaign against the Asiatic Land Tenure Act—known as the "Ghetto Act"—in 1946. In this way he showed himself to be a man moved to action by human suffering rather than by any racialist feeling of his own.

AT THE UNITED NATIONS

In the same year Xuma gave his support to the Hereros in South West Africa by supporting a petition to the United Nations from the Chiefs of Bechuanaland which urged that South Africa should not incorporate the mandated territory of South West Africa. He went to the United Nations to seek the support of member states for this petition.

Xuma met his wife during a visit to the United States in 1938. Mrs. Xuma was then studying at Columbia University. On marriage she returned with her husband to South Africa, where, although retaining her American citizenship, she identified herself closely with her husband's work among the rapidly growing African population of Johannesburg.

Xuma's son has studied medicine in Britain and his daughter is one of the few remaining African students of Social Science at the University of Witwatersrand.

January 30, 1962.

Sir Harold E. Yarrow, G.B.E., second baronet, who died on April 19, 1962, at his home in Renfrewshire at the age of 77, was chairman of Yarrow and Co., Ltd., Glasgow shipbuilders and engineers. He was also chairman of the Clydesdale and North of Scotland Bank.

Harold Edgar Yarrow was the eldest of the three sons of Sir Alfred Fernandez Yarrow, the first Baronet and the founder of Yarrow and Co., whom he succeeded in 1932. He was born on August 11, 1884, and was educated at Bedford Grammar School, where also he received some basic instruction in engineering. His father being determined that his son should learn the family business on equal terms with those whom he was later to supervise, Harold had to pass the entrance examination required of would-be Yarrow apprentices before entering on his own apprenticeship, though he did not serve it in the Yarrow yard.

Having obtained experience in the pattern shop, foundry, machine, and erecting shops, and in the drawing office, at the age of 18 Yarrow entered his father's drawing office. Water-tube boiler design was then very much in the empirical stage and one of his first assignments was to take part in some boiler trials which, in 1903, formed the subject of the first of his numerous papers read to professional bodies.

YOUTHFUL TRIUMPH

It was entitled "A Description of some Evaporative Trials of one of the Water-tube Boilers for the Chilian Ironclad 'Constitution' " (later taken into the Royal Navy as H.M.S. Swiftsure) and was delivered "with fear and trembling", as he recalled half a century later, before the Junior Institution of Engineers. As a technical report it was a highly creditable performance for a youth who was not yet 19.

At that time the Yarrow shipyard was still in Poplar, but in 1906–07 the entire establishment was transferred to Scotstoun, on the Clyde. Yarrow was sent there at an early stage, while the new buildings were still under construction, and was closely concerned with the laying out and equipment of the shops and building berths, from which the first launch took place in July, 1908. Five years later his father went south to live in Hampshire, leaving Harold Yarrow as managing director at Scotstoun. It was a position of great responsibility, and he was still only 29, but he was to prove himself fully equal to the demands that it entailed.

BURDENS SHARED

At the outbreak of war in 1914 Alfred Yarrow returned to Scotstoun and, without disturbing Harold in his position, undoubtedly helped him greatly to bear the burdens of the war years; but there were heavy burdens still to come after the war, when the depression of the thirties almost brought shipbuilding to a standstill. Harold Yarrow met them by launching out into a new field, that of supplying boilers for power stations and other industrial plants on land; even to the extent, in conjunction with the late Sir Nigel Gresley, of constructing a water-tube boiler for a locomotive, No. 10,000, for the London and North Eastern Railway. No. 10,000 was not a success, but the land boiler side of the business grew to encouraging dimensions and provided experience which was useful when shipbuilding began to recover and the Admiralty came into the market again, wanting destroyers of higher performance, and with boilers of greater individual output, then they had ever had before.

BELIEF IN RESEARCH

Similar trends in merchant ships soon became evident and Yarrow's work, backed by much quiet research at Scotstoun, greatly influenced them; it is significant that whereas the Cunarder Queen Mary has 24 boilers, the later Queen Elizabeth has only 12. Like father, he was a strong believer in research, especially of the ad hoc variety arising out of observed needs and inspired by men of practical experience: a policy which bore fruit when the shipbuilding history of the Second World War and the years that followed more or less repeated that of the first. During the Second World War he became chairman of the Ministry of Supply's Scotland Area Board.

He was a member of a number of professional institutions, but his principal activities in this field were naturally in connexion with the institutions directly concerned with shipbuilding and marine engineering. He was an honorary vice-president of the Royal Institution of Naval Architects, which he had entered as one of its original students on the establishment of that grade in 1904 and in which he was the first student to present a paper—an excellent factual report describing the effect of depth of water on the speed of destroyers, for which he was awarded an Institution Premium. He was elected an Associate Member in 1910 and transferred to Member in 1915. Three years later he was elected to the Council, on which he served continuously thereafter. He was twice president of the Institution of Engineers and Shipbuilders in Scotland; on the first occasion in 1921 and again in 1957, the Institution's centenary year.

He was twice married: first in 1906 to Eleanor Etheldreda (who died in 1934), daughter of the Rev. Canon W. H. M. H. Aitken, by whom he had a son, Eric Grant Yarrow, who now succeeds to the title, and three daughters; and, secondly, in 1935, to Rosalynde, daughter of the late Sir Oliver Lodge, F.R.S., by whom he had a daughter.

INSPIRED TEAM

Like his father, he had the gift of inspiring teamwork. When decisions, technical or other, had to be made, he could make them as firmly as any industrialist, yet always leaving the impression that the ruling was not a fiat from on high, but the result of conference between man and man. To some he probably seemed reserved, but the reserve was more apparent than real; he was by nature thoughtful, but he was also a conversationalist of memorable charm and much shrewd observation.

April 21, 1962.

His Majesty the Imam al-Nasr Ahmad ibn Yahya, Hamid al-Din, Imam of the Zeidis and second **King of Yemen,** reported officially as having died on September 18, 1962, will be remembered for his success in preserving his kingdom virtually intact against all the political and social ideas of the twentieth century, and for the uncompromising manner in which he prosecuted the claims of his dynasty over Aden.

Ahmad, eldest of the 14 sons of the Iman Yahya, grew up in troubled times. He seems to have decided early that an Imam had not only to be orthodox and quite ruthless but to inspire fear. It is generally believed that as a boy he slept at night with a cord tied tightly round his neck to make his eyes protrude. Short and stocky, and immensely powerful, he grew at one time a forked beard with one prong shorter than the other, but his huge bulging eyes were certainly his most alarming feature.

Ahmad was not his father's favourite, and it was only in 1927 he proclaimed him as Crown Prince. He also appointed him Governor-General of Southern Yemen, where his harsh rule made him generally disliked. He had the rivalries of his own brothers, notably Hussein and his father's favourite, Abdullah, as well as other candidates to contend with. There was a vast net of intrigue concerned with the succession, and his most formidable rival was the head of the powerful Al-Wazir family, Sayyid Abdullah, a much more commanding personality then even Ahmad and extremely intelligent.

FIGHT FOR RECOGNITION

In 1937 Yahya had to engage in a more elaborate campaign to secure recognition of Ahmad by his rivals. He often remonstrated with his son, sometimes by telegraph, on account of his cruelties which alienated support. During the war the whole royal family from the Imam downwards incurred much dislike through the trading monopoly they built up, but Ahmad and his brother Abdullah were regarded as the worst offenders.

This monopoly greatly stimulated the Free Yemeni movement in Aden and pressure for reforms increased. In 1946 Ahmad himself visited Aden for discussions with the malcontents, but Imamic policy was not sensibly modified. The Imam's ninth son, Ibrahim, later left for Aden and joined the Free Yemenis. In September, 1947, a Press campaign in favour of revolution began, and in January, 1948, an attempt was made on the Imam's life. A month later he was machine-gunned to death outside Sana. Abdullah al-Wazir was proclaimed and set up a reformist government. Ahmad promised his brother Hassan that he should succeed him, and with another brother, Abbas, the three went north, where Ahmad was acknowledged as Imam and the brothers marched on Sana with a force of tribesmen. Resistance quickly collapsed and Abdullah al-Wazir was executed. Ibrahim, who had come from Aden, was imprisoned and very shortly died of "heart-failure"

Ahmad took the title of al-Nasr. He avoided Sana, residing at Ta'iz. In his domestic policy he proceeded cautiously, and in 1951 granted an amnesty to a number of the conspirators against his father. Reforms were sought and some approved but his policy remained based on preservation of the regime. The Free Yemenis therefore continued aloof and hostile. In his relations with the British Ahmad continued to insist that the Aden Protectorate was legally a part of southern Yemen.

TURNING THE TABLES

In April, 1955, his brother Abdullah led a *coup* against him, with another brother, Abbas, supporting the revolution in Sana. Imam Ahmad was imprisoned in Ta'iz and signed an instrument of abdication. His son Badr hurried to Hajjah, collected a large force of Hashid and Bakil tribesmen, and marched on Ta'iz. There, allegiances were uncertain and the revolutionaries wavering. The Imam in his prison seized a Bren gun from a slack guard and overcame his captors.

The tables were quickly turned. Abdullah and Abbas were imprisoned and soon after excuted at Hajjah. There was a spate of other executions. Hassan was in Cairo when the revolution took place and the Imam now appointed his son Badr as Prime Minister and Crown Prince. This rankled with Hassan in view of his brother's promises to him and he stayed out of the country.

Badr was regarded as a moderate. His father, forced to recognize the pressure of events, used him as his travelling envoy abroad. Towards the end of 1957 he went to London for a conference on frontier demarcation which proved fruitless. He went on to Moscow, Warsaw, Prague, and Peking, where promises of military, technical and other help soon resulted in the arrival of armaments and a considerable number of Russians, Chinese, and other Communist technicians in Yemen. In March, 1958, Yemen joined the United Arab Republic in a strange manifestation of Arab unity called the United Arab states. This association fell to pieces in 1961, when the Imam, together with the kings of Jordan and Saudi Arabia became the main targets of Cairo propaganda. President Nasser described conditions in Yemen as "against the law of justice and the law of God". The Imam replied in kind, and wrote a poem attacking socialism.

OVERDOSE OF MORPHINE

In April, 1959, the Imam Ahmad flew to Rome with a large retinue and was shortly followed by his brother Hassan. In spite of his powerful constitution he had long suffered from indisposition, principally arthritis, which caused him considerable pain. An unfortunate concubine administered to him an overdose of morphine and serious drug-poisoning ensued.

His departure was a break with all precedent for it has been held that even Zeidi prayers would be invalid in an Imam's absence. He returned to Yemen in August and at the end of the following March a further unsuccessful attempt against his life was made. He was, however, wounded.

The Imam Ahmad and his father were absolute monarchs. There was hardly a detail of administration with which they did not personally deal. While Imam Yahya's rule was tyrannical and oppressive, that of his son exceeded it in harshness. But Ahmad's personal courage was never in doubt and he never forfeited the support of the powerful and fanatical tribes in the north, whom a Turkish Governor-General described in 1911 as of a quality which could "subdue all Europe".

September 20, 1962.

Wing Commander Forest Frederick Edward Yeo-Thomas, G.C., M.C., who died on February 26, 1964, in Paris at the age of 61, three times parachuted into France during the war of 1939–45 to organize and work with the French resistance movement. Betrayed eventually to the Gestapo, who shamefully used him, he spent some time in Buchenwald and in a Jewish extermination camp. Finally, after some further heartbreaking adventures, he reached the American lines.

The citation which accompanied the award of his George Cross in 1946 stated "... he endured brutal treatment and torture without flinching and showed the most amazing fortitude and devotion to duty throughout his service abroad during which he was under the constant threat of death". In addition to the G.C. he was awarded the M.C. and Bar and the Croix de Guerre. In July, 1963, he was promoted Commander of the Legion of Honour.

Yeo-Thomas was born on June 17, 1902, of an English family which had lived in France since 1855. He was educated in France and in England. Although under age, he served with the Allied armies in the latter part of the 1914–18 War and subsequently fought with the Poles against the Russians during 1919 and 1920. He was captured by the Bolsheviks and sentenced to death but escaped the night before he was due to be shot—an experience that was to be repeated two decades later. Between the wars he worked in Paris, from 1932 as a director of the fashion house of Molyneux.

SEIZED BY GESTAPO

He enlisted in the R.A.F. in 1939, became a sergeant-interpreter with the Advanced Air Striking Force, and was later commissioned. Early in 1943 he dropped by parachute into France to get in touch with the underground movement, and on his return in April he brought with him a United States Army Air Corps officer who, having no French, was in danger of capture. Later the same year he went back to France to find out what the Maquis needed in the way of weapons and supplies. Six times he was all but captured, but he contrived to keep his liberty and returned to England. In February, 1944, he made his last visit to France, and a month later was betrayed and seized by the Gestapo. He was interrogated for four days, was beaten and tortured, the Germans attempting to break his spirit by immersing him head downwards in ice-cold water while his legs and arms were chained. They were unsuccessful. The questioning went on for two months, and he was offered his freedom on the condition that he gave the Gestapo the information they wanted. He all but lost an arm through blood poisoning caused by the chains cutting one of his wrists. After twice attempting to escape Yeo-Thomas was confined in solitude in Fresnes prison for four months; for some weeks he was in a darkened cell and was given little food. Through all he remained steadfast, inspiring his fellow prisoners by his infectious spirits.

After further bold attempts to escape from Compiègne, where he had been transferred with a party of other prisoners, he was sent to Buchenwald, where, in his own words, "I conveniently died of typhus on October 13, 1944, after getting into the 'guinea pig' block and changed my identity to that of a Frenchman named Choquet". The day after an order for his execution arrived.

He was now moved to work commandos at Gleina and Rehmsdorf, where as a hospital orderly he almost miraculously survived. With 20 others, whom he led, he escaped in April, 1945, from the train in which they were being moved once more. On his recapture he impersonated a dead French officer and succeeded for the last time in escaping and thus regained the allied lines. This period of his life is recorded in Bruce Marshall's book *The White Rabbit,* one of his many soubriquets, "Shelley" being the one by which he was most often known.

After the war he at first returned to Molyneux and in 1950 he joined the Federation of British Industries as their representative in France, which he remained until his death. To his new task he brought his characteristic qualities of loyalty and service and his understanding of the French scene, and the special regard in which he was held enabled him to render great assistance to the F.B.I. and many of its members.

February 27, 1964.

Marshal Andrei Yeremenko, who commanded the Soviet forces at the Battle of Stalingrad in 1942, died in Moscow in November, 1970.

Yeremenko was born in 1892 in the Ukrainian village of Markoyka. He joined the imperial Russian Army in 1913 and served as a cavalryman in the First World War, becoming a Communist Party member in 1918 and entering the Red Army in 1919, where he served with Second Cavalry Army. After the civil war, Yeremenko remained in the Red Army, became a regimental commander in 1923 and after graduating from the Frunze Academy in 1935 took command of 14th Cavalry Division, followed by 6th Cossack Corps in 1938; in 1940 he switched to armour and took over 3rd Mechanised Corps.

He was recalled at the beginning of the Soviet-German war to the European theatre after a brief spell as an Army commander in the Soviet Far East, and became, in turn, Deputy-Commander and Commander of the Western Front, assuming command of the Bryansk front in August, 1941, but here he failed to check Guderian's armoured drive into the Ukraine. After recovering from a severe wound he took over 4th Shock Army on the North-Western front in the winter of 1941–42 and in August, 1942, was sent to the South-Eastern front in the initial stages of the battle for

Stalingrad, where he played an important part in the defensive battle and in the subsequent Soviet counter-offensive. In the summer of 1943 he moved to the Kalinin front, and in 1944 commanded the Coastal (Black Sea) Army and latterly Second Baltic Front, taking part in the capture of Riga.

After the war he commanded several military districts and was appointed a Marshal in 1955, taking up a post as General Inspector in the Ministry of Defence in 1958. He produced a series of memoirs which lauded Khrushchev's military talents and also inflated his own wartime role.

November 20, 1970.

F. R. S. Yorke, F.R.I.B.A. who died on June 10, 1962, at the age of 55, was senior partner in the well-known firm of architects Yorke, Rosenberg and Mardall. He was created C.B.E. in the Birthday Honours earlier in that month.

He was, as architect, journalist, and writer, one of the pioneers of the modern movement in this country. With Wells Coates, Morton Shand, and a handful of others he founded in 1932 the Modern Architectural Research Group (M.A.R.S.) as the British component of Les Congrès Internationals d'Architecture Moderne (C.I.A.M.) and, although both these organization have now been wound up, they played, in their time, a leading role in the introduction and development of good architecture as we know it today. Yorke was the first honorary secretary of the M.A.R.S. group. At this time he was assistant editor of the *Architects Journal* and compiler and editor of *Specification.* The latter appointment he held until his death. He also wrote several books on houses while carrying on a small and selective private practice. For this combination of work he was much revered by the young architects and students of the day. In 1944 he went into partnership with Eugene Rosenberg and Cyril Mardall and his own architectural personality in this very successful combination tended to become submerged. He was a great character, a countryman at heart with all the naughtiness of the typical British small boy apparent for all to see on his perpetually cheerful face.

GATWICK AIRPORT

Throughout his life he was a great traveller in search of architectural information and on these occasions he combined pleasure with business on a large scale. He is reported several times to have defeated his Russian hosts at their own game and yet to have been on parade fresh as a daisy ready for more exhausting talking and visiting on the following day. He was not easily tired. This remarkable sense of well-being remained with him throughout his long and distressing illness, and in spite of physical handicaps which would have crushed many men Yorke remained boisterous and quite unaltered in spirit until his death.

His firm, which in 1961 moved into a fine building of its own design in the City of London, carried out buildings of all kinds. Leaders in school design, they have also been responsible for a number of technical colleges, hospitals and housing schemes. Yorke took particular interest in the design and construction of the new and extended Gatwick airport which was opened in 1958. At that time revolutionary in conception, it differed radically in planning and in the technique of passenger handling from Frederick Gibberd's great scheme at Heathrow.

Francis Reginald Stevens Yorke was born on December 3, 1906. He was the son of an architect, F. W. B. Yorke, F.R.I.B.A., and was educated at Chipping Campden School and the University of Birmingham School of Architecture.

BREEDER OF CATTLE

During the Second World War he was a member of the team of architects working under Sir William Holford on the design of camps, factories, and ordnance depots for the Government.

Yorke had many recreations; he collected modern paintings, drawings, and sculpture, he had a fine library and a collection of curious objects of all kinds. All these were housed in a delightful roof-top flat over the firm's offices. His love of these indoor pursuits was, however, secondary to his love of the countryside, where he was a notable breeder of cattle and a keen fly fisherman. Best of all he probably liked standing about with a crowd of his vast number of friends, preferably at a party, or in a pub, just talking.

In 1930 he married Thelma Austin Jones, who survives him with twin daughters of the marriage.

June 11, 1962.

Shigeru Yoshida, the former Japanese Prime Minister, died on October 20, 1967, at his home at Oiso. He was 89.

Japan was fortunate, in the spiritual and material collapse which followed defeat and surrender, to have at the helm during the crucial years of the Occupation and of her newly recovered sovereignty a man of the stamp and calibre of Yoshida. For seven years and two months, the longest tenure of office of any Japanese Prime Minister, he steered his country with sureness and skill—and sublime indifference to opposition—between the combined shoals of revolution from the Left and reaction from the Right, giving it that basis of free institutions and parliamentary Government, and of unequivocal alignment with the free world, upon which it could begin the task of economic and social reconstruction it has since achieved.

It was inevitable, in the circumstances, when traditional behaviour and beliefs were violently challenged from every side, and no less by the Occupation authorities themselves, that Yoshida should have been a highly controversial figure almost to the end of his life. His very character was a challenge: he never suffered fools gladly, and never concealed the fact. His political enemies felt the lash of his contemptuous wit; his fellow Ministers and his subordinates the impact of a sharp mind and relentless energy that brooked no obstacle, tergiversation or delay.

Yoshida's undying claim to the gratitude of his countrymen is that, by example and leadership, he enabled them to come to terms with the inexorable catastrophe of a defeat they had experienced for the first time in their history, and the unpalatable but purifying necessity of a foreign occupation; and gradually to rediscover their faith in themselves and in the nation.

He was born in Tokyo on September 22, 1878, the fifth son of Tsuna Takeuchi, a samurai and liberal patriot from Kochi, in Shikoku Island, and a member of the Tosa clan designed with Satsuma and Choshu to play a leading role in the Meiji Restoration of 1868. Yoshida once said jokingly that he owed his life to the Meiji Restoration—a reference to the practice of smothering unwanted infants at birth. In 1880 he was adopted by Kenzo Yoshida, a wealthy merchant of Fukui, near Kyoto, a practice common with younger sons of good family, and inherited a substantial fortune from him when he died in 1887.

After graduation from Tokyo Imperial University in 1906 he entered the Foreign Ministry. Three years later he married Tsuruko, eldest daughter of Count Makino, the Lord Privy Seal, and one of the confidants of the Emperor Meiji, a step destined to give his career a very substantial impulse by associating him with the powerful aristocracy in close contact with the Court. His first appointment abroad was as Consul-General in Mukden in 1925, and his first taste of politics came with the Vice-Ministership of Foreign Affairs in 1928, in the Tanaka Cabinet. Two years later he was Ambassador to Rome, and in 1936, Hirota wished to appoint him Foreign Minister in his new cabinet, but had to surrender before strong protests of the Army, to whom Yoshida was already highly suspect as a staunch liberal, and an outspoken opponent of the growing power of the military in politics. It enabled him, however, to go to England as Ambassador, an experience which confirmed him in his predilection for all things English.

EXILE AND PRISON

He was retired in 1939, as a result of his disapproval of the policies of the militarists, rapidly leading Japan to war; and after the conflict broke out two years later, he remained more or less in exile till the end, suffering a few months' imprisonment for opposing the continuation of hostilities. At the end of the war, he was 67, a retired diplomatist and a country gentleman, who had never been in politics. But his reputation as a consistent, and courageous critic of the men who had led Japan to catastrophe, marked him for office once the country had utterly broken with her past. He succeeded Shigemitsu at the Foreign Ministry in the first cabinet after the surrender, and retained the portfolio in the Shidehara cabinet that followed it. But his real emergence to the forefront of Japanese politics occurred almost by default. Jehiro Hatoyama, the president of the Liberal Party, about to become Prime Minister in May, 1946, was suddenly "purged" by the Occupation authorities; and Yoshida was appointed in his stead, on the understanding, it was believed, that once "depurged", Hatoyama would resume leadership of the party and the Government. But this was not to happen until 1954.

Yoshida had, with the greatest reluctance, assumed the burden of power at a time when the country was in a state of moral and material collapse, with thousands of destitute repatriates pouring in from Japan's former overseas possessions; a population on the brink of famine staved off only by American aid, the machinery of Government disorientated and disorganized by the "purge" of all officials who had held any post of authority under the former regime; industry at a standstill, and unemployment soaring; and the Communists and fellow-travellers revelling in their new-found freedom, with at that time the blessing of the Occupation, and fishing to their hearts' content in troubled waters. On top of it all, there was the problem of SCAP, always well-meaning, but frequently clumsy and ill-advised in its desire to remake Japan in the democratic image, as a peaceful, largely pastoral state.

Except for a period of 16 months between 1947 and 1948, he was Prime Minister without interruption, displaying a resilience unequalled in Japanese politics, and formed five cabinets. His reward came in 1951, when he went to San Francisco to sign the Peace Treaty with the United States, and the Security Treaty which he regarded as the corner-stone of Japanese defence in her then utterly disarmed state.

IMPACT OF KOREAN WAR

He had, however, with the pragmatism and common sense which always characterized him, supported the Occupation's efforts to give Japan an embryonic armed force when, under the impact of the Korean conflict, the impracticability of the 1948 "peace" Constitution was blatantly disclosed. An ingenious interpretation of the war-renouncing clause made possible the creation of the National Police Reserve, which, after the Peace Treaty, became the National Safety Force, in the teeth of violent opposition from the Socialist Party and the combined Leftwing forces in the country. It was the so-called "reverse course", which also led to the adoption of strict measures to stamp out Communist activities and to the prosecution of Communist leaders.

As time went on, both his own party and the country grew restive under Yoshida's rule. His electoral margins dwindled, and after 1952 the Liberals had less than a majority though still the largest party in the Diet. Hatoyama, who had returned to politics after the country regained its sovereignty, led a group of followers out of the ruling party in 1953, and returned to the fold a few months later. But the factional struggles within conservative ranks to unseat Yoshida increased in intensity the following year, especially during his extended world tour which took him to London, where he was received by the Queen. The year 1954 was a bad year for Japan. The Liberal Party was severely shaken by the uncovering of a scandal involving shipbuilding contracts. The adverse balance of payments the preceding year forced the adoption of a rigid deflationary policy which caused bankruptcies among small businesses and much hardship. The move to bring about a merger between the Liberals and the Progressives (equally conservative) without Yoshida gathered much momentum during his absence. When he returned his rivals presented him with a virtual *fait accompli*, and he surrendered the Premiership to Hatoyama in December.

From that time on he led a life of purposeful leisure at his villa of Oiso, after the example of one of his illustrious predecessors, Saionji, who for two decades exercised a decisive influence on affairs from his retreat at Okitsu. For Yoshida, it was a retirement from active politics, but not from political life. He continued to make his presence strongly felt behind the scenes, and while his counsel was less unchallenged than the prewar *genros*', it carried great weight in conservative ranks.

October 21, 1967.

Salah Ben Youssef, the Tunisian lawyer and politician, who was shot dead on August 12, 1961, was born in the island of Jerba in 1908, being five years younger than President Bourguiba. Like the latter he was a leading figure in the neo-Destour party from its foundation in 1934, and shared with its other leaders the vicissitudes of prison and exile.

When Bourguiba, having failed to reach an agreement with the Free French in 1946, fled in disguise to Egypt, Salah Ben Youssef, as secretary-general of the party, became responsible for its reorganization. About this time he was described by a British visitor as an "energetic, buoyant, and boisterous person, very obviously a leader, impulsive and outspoken". In 1950 when the Chenik government of negotiation was formed Ben Youssef became Minister of Justice, the first neo-Destour member to hold governmental office. At this period he supported the policy of achieving the party's aims by collaboration with the French Government. In 1951 he accompanied the Premier to Paris to present the Tunisian proposals. When these were rejected in December it was Salah Ben Youssef who presented the appeal from the Tunisian Government to the security council. Two months later on March 25, 1952, the French Resident General arrested those Tunisian ministers who were in the country.

ESCAPE THROUGH BELGIUM

Ben Youssef, however, who was in Paris, managed to escape over the Belgian frontier and from there to Cairo. Here he proved more susceptible to Arab League influences than Bourguiba had been and when, four years later, the latter approved the conventions for internal autonomy which had been negotiated as the result of the Mendes-France undertaking, Ben Youssef opposed the agreement. He never had the reputation of Bourguiba for personal integrity and it was widely believed that he was influenced by personal ambition and the hope of supplanting Bourguiba by assuming an ultra-patriotic attitude.

After unsuccessful attempts had been made at a reconciliation, Ben Youssef was deposed from the office of secretary-general but invited to justify his conduct before the party congress at Sfax in February, 1956. Instead of doing so he organized violence which had to be suppressed by police and military action. On January 28 his house was raided, though he himself escaped to Cairo, and treasonable documents were seized together with a number of weapons and explosives and a large sum of money.

In March, 1956, the achievement of complete independence removed any justification for his conduct and he became completely discredited outside his home district. He nevertheless continued to agitate from Egypt and in March, 1958, an emissary of his was detected on the Tunisian frontier with letters seeking to organize the assassination of Bourguiba. Recent reports suggested that if the Bizerta affair should be long drawn out it might result in a certain revival of Ben Youssef's influence.

August 15, 1961.

Queen Marie of Yugoslavia, who died at her London home on June 22, 1961, was the widow of King Alexander, whose assassination at Marseilles in October, 1934, brought her son, King Peter, to the throne.

She was born at Gotha on January 9, 1899, the second daughter of King Ferdinand of Rumania by his marriage with Princess Marie of Saxe-Coburg-Gotha and the sister of ex-King Carol of Rumania. She was, therefore, a granddaughter of H.R.H. Alfred Duke of Edinburgh, who succeeded to the Duchy of Saxe-Coburg-Gotha, and a great-grand-daughter of Queen Victoria. She was also closely allied to the Royal House of Russia, for the Duchess of Edinburgh had been before her marriage the Grand Duchess Marie Alexandrovna, the only daughter of Tsar Alexander II.

Known from her birth as "Princess Mignon" the future Queen Marie of Yugoslavia, who had had an English nurse, received a careful education, and its character, under the guidance of her mother, continued to be English in all essentials. She was her father's favourite child and became his companion in his morning rides, his unofficial amanuensis and reader and his partner in quiet indoor games. When Rumania entered the war she did Red Cross work with her mother and sister and, as a hospital nurse at Dobruga, first came into contact with her future subjects, the wounded of a volunteer regiment fighting under the Russian Imperial Standard.

After the Armistice Queen Marie of Rumania sent her to Heathfield School. A good musician, she already spoke English perfectly, for her mother never lost touch with Britain and the Rumanian Royal Family were frequently at Eastbourne for holidays, spending on each occasion some time at Windsor or Balmoral.

In January, 1922, the engagement was announced of Princess Marie to King Alexander of the Serbs, Croats and Slovenes—the name of the kingdom was changed to Yugoslavia in 1929.

The Royal Wedding, at which King George VI, then Duke of York, was *Koom*, or chief witness, was solemnized according to rites of the Orthodox Church at Belgrade on June 8, 1922. The honeymoon was spent in the charmingly situated Castle of Windisgratz. On September 6, 1923, she gave birth to a son, the future King Peter.

The early years of the Queen's marriage were clouded by the political difficulties which afflicted the land of her adoption. It was torn by a constitutional struggle between the Serbs and Croats. In December 1928 the King, who did his utmost to hold a just balance, faced the twenty-fifth Cabinet crisis in 10 years. Then, weary of the bickerings of the politicians, he abolished the constitution and appointed an administration of picked men as instruments of a Royal dictatorship. Meanwhile two other royal children had been born, Prince Tomislav in 1928 and Prince Andrew in 1929.

It was probably only a change of plans that saved the Queen from sharing her husband's fate. Owing to rough seas and the state of her health she was travelling by rail. After her husband's death she returned to England frequently and made her home there from 1938 onwards.

June 23, 1961.

King Peter II, of Yugoslavia, third and last monarch of a united Yugoslavia, who died on November 5, 1970, in hospital at Los Angeles at the age of 47, was born in Belgrade in 1923, the eldest son of King Alexander and of Queen Marie, daughter of King Ferdinand of Rumania. He was the great great grandson, in direct male descent, of Karageorge, who, in 1804, led the Serbian peasants of the province of Belgrade in the revolt which started the emancipation of the Balkans from Ottoman rule. On his mother's side, he was in the same degree of descent from Queen Victoria through Alfred, Duke of Edinburgh, Queen Marie's maternal grandfather.

In October, 1934, after the assassination in Marseilles of his father, he was brought back from school in England to succeed to the throne at the age of 11, under a regency headed by his uncle, Prince Paul. His minority coincided with a difficult period of increasing pressure by the Axis Powers linked to a constitutional crisis and the Croatian problem. It was the Prince-Regent's giving way to that pressure that anticipated King Peter's assumption of the royal prerogative by six months in 1941, for no sooner had the instruments of adherence to the Anti-Comintern Pact been signed, than a military conspiracy took over control in Belgrade on March 27, and, amid popular enthusiasm, brought together all the party leaders to form a broadly based government to face the situation of crisis. The coup had been carried out in King Peter's name and the Regents resigned, but on April 6 that year the Germans and their allies attacked Yugoslavia. Peter was immediately sent away from the air-bombed capital, and in mid-April he was flown to Greece, where the Government was soon to join him.

In June, 1941, the King arrived in England where he was welcomed. To those who hoped for a restoration of a united Yugoslavia, after an Allied victory, in the non-communist camp, and more especially among the fighters and sympathizers of General Mihailovich's "Yugoslav Home Army", he was the symbol of Yugoslavia's survival as a nominal legal entity and as an idea. But to many Serbs, especially those persecuted under the rule of the Axis-protected Croatian ustashas, and who struggled, not for the Yugoslav ideal, or legal continuity, or the Western alliance, but for survival, he became more simply the symbol of their dismembered Serbian nation to which emotionally they reverted after the destruction of the Yugoslav state.

In 1943 a crisis arose over the King's wish to marry deemed by some of his advisers to be inopportune. It marked the end of the all-party government and its replacement by a new cabinet whose existence depended on the confidence of the monarch and on the toleration of Churchill who was looking more and more to Tito's Communist-led People's Liberation Army and less and less to Mihailovich and the Yugoslav Home Army.

In November, 1943, at a congress of Tito's partisans, a virtual counter-government was set up under their leader, while the London government was denied any right, and King Peter forbidden to return from exile. Soon after, the Allies dropped General Mihailovich, and hailed Marshal Tito as the acknowledged leader of the Yugoslav resistance. Churchill, however, felt a moral obligation to Peter and tried to reach a compromise with Tito which would protect the monarchy.

THREE MONTHS' PRESSURE

This entailed, after the King's marriage to Princess Alexandra of Greece in London in March, 1944, pressing him to change his government and give up General Mihailovich. After three months of such pressure, the King gave in, but it was not until June (almost a week after Churchill's anticipated announcement in the Commons that King Peter had accepted the resignation of his Cabinet, and without the previous resignation of this administration) that he entrusted Dr. Subasich with the task of forming a new government.

Having tried to play a personal political role over and above the heads of his country's traditional parties, King Peter thereafter became a simple instrument. The new government had been called into being by the British for the express purpose of coming to an agreement with Tito, and Subasich went off for a meeting with Tito on the Adriatic island of Vis. He recognized the administration set up by Tito's movement over the regions under its control as the only authority on Yugoslav territory, and his partisans as the only legitimate fighting force. The communist leader's only real concession was that the issue of the monarchy would not be raised while the war lasted. In view of Yugoslavia's impending liberation, further steps were taken to appease Tito and obtain a single united provisional government. A royal decree abolished the position of Chief of Staff of the High Command, held by General Mihailovich, and King Peter personally broadcast an appeal to his subjects to rally round Marshal Tito.

In November, 1944 Subasich once again met Marshal Tito, this time in liberated Belgrade. They agreed that, pending complete liberation, the King would remain abroad and delegate the exercise of the royal prerogative to a regency appointed in consultation with Tito. A provisional government would be set up from Subasich's Cabinet and Tito's committee until a constituent assembly had been elected, and had decided on the organization of the postwar regime. King Peter refused to sanction this new agreement.

The British Government pressed the King to accept the realities of the situation. Churchill having told the Commons on January 18, 1945, that "if we were so unfortunate as not to be able to obtain the consent of King Peter, the matter would have, in fact, to go ahead, his assent being presumed", the King reluctantly gave way. By the end of February, final agreement was reached on the composition, according to Marshal Tito's wishes, of the Regency and government. More pressure got the regents appointed by royal decree and Tito's new provisional government (with Subasich as Foreign Minister) was granted formal recognition by the Allies.

MONARCHY ENDED

In August, King Peter, alleging that the Tito-Subasich agreements had, in many instances, been disregarded and that the Regents had not been allowed to carry out the constitutional duties for which they had been appointed, withdrew the authority he had delegated to them. It was held in Yugoslavia by the new government that he did not have the power to do so, and his objections were disregarded. The communists were well in control of the machinery of the state by November, when the elections were held. Marshal Tito's list received over 90 per cent of ballots cast, and the first act of the Constituent Assembly, which met on November 29, 1945, was to abolish the monarchy.

Succeeding his murdered father at 11, proclaimed of age by a military coup before he was 18, deposed at 24 by the communists, driven away by the Germans and prevented from returning by Tito's partisans, Peter II reigned effectively in his country for 10 days in 1941 and thereafter lived in exile. He was placed in the limelight at an early age, with neither maturity nor preparation. Unwittingly he became a symbol first of resistance to Nazism in 1941, then of resistance to communism in 1944, and for a while tried to act a personal political part far above his abilities, in most difficult circumstances. The role which he was made to play was too large for the youth he was. Since the end of the war, he lived mostly in France, in dwindling financial circumstances and dwindling health.

From his marriage to Princess Alexandra, daughter of King Alexander of Greece, he had a son, Prince Alexander, born in London in 1945.

November 6, 1970.

Prince Felix Yusupov, who died in Auteuil, Paris, on September 27, 1967, at the age of 81, was the leader of the group who assassinated Rasputin in 1916.

He was born in St. Petersburg on April 17, 1887, and belonged, on his mother's side, to one of the oldest and richest families in Russia. The Prince's father was Governor-General of Moscow for a brief spell. Educated at Oxford, he married the Princess Irina, niece of the Tsar, in 1914.

The 1914-1918 War was to give him a place in history. Towards the end of 1916 the Russian armies were in the throes of defeat. There were murmurs against the deafness of the Tsar, but the most subversive threats were against Rasputin and his influence over the Empress.

Prince Felix made up his mind that the only way to revive the Russian armies and also the Russian people was to get rid of Rasputin.

By December, 1916, all was ready. Drinks and cakes filled with cyanide of potassium were prepared downstairs for Rasputin by Prince Felix. The Prince's collaborators were to remain upstairs till all was over and then help in the hiding of the body. The plan went wrong, for Rasputin swallowed enough supposedly poisoned cakes to kill a man in 30 seconds. Doubtless the Prince remembered the stories about the superhuman qualities of Rasputin. He became nervous. Eventually he took his revolver and shot Rasputin near the heart. The Prince was about to run upstairs to summon his friends, when he saw Rasputin moving and making his way to a side door leading to a back courtyard. Purishkevitch, a member of the Duma, came to the rescue and ended Rasputin's life with two shots.

The grisly deed was committed on the night and morning of December 29 and 30, 1916. The news gave satisfaction to numerous people, but when the body of Rasputin was discovered, the Tsar and the Empress were indignant. The Grand Duke Dmitri was exiled to Persia, and Prince Felix was escorted to Rakitnoe in the province of Kursk and ordered to remain there.

The Yusupov family, including father, son and their wives, survived the revolution and were brought away from Yalta.

September 28, 1967.

Z

Ossip Zadkine, who died on November 25, 1967, at his home in Paris, may fairly be called a great sculptor if only on the strength of one remarkable work which has touched the imagination of the world and has a significance for everyone, whether versed or not in the language of modern art, "The Destroyed City" monument commemorating the destruction of Rotterdam by bombing in 1940. It is a work well described by Lewis Mumford as "an image as terrible in its immediacy as Picasso's 'Guernica', yet conceived with a power that promises the resurrection Rotterdam has experienced." It could not, as this critic remarked, be received as just another titillating horror. It contained a great weight of emotion and meaning. But Zadkine was also a very prolific artist. He produced in all more than four hundred sculptures and thousands of drawings, watercolours, engravings, and tapestry designs. He was in the forefront of the School of Paris as an inventor and manipulator of forms, of volumes and hollows treated with a flexible variation of skill.

With invention of this kind which relates him to the Cubist movement he had a poetic imagination which preserved him from being merely the exponent of a technique and enabled him to express a wide range of emotion, not only that arising from the tragedy of war. He had his own mythology. "Orpheus", he said, "has always haunted me" and the figure of Orpheus, so identified with his lyre that instrument and player seem one, is another of his remarkable conceptions. He had an admiration for genius in art which is movingly conveyed in his monument to Van Gogh at Auvers-sur-Oise, a statue which rejects all superficial cleverness of treatment in the effort to come close to the impassioned sincerity of his subject. He found inspiration in the Bible, in music, poetry and the venerable aspects of natural form. During a stay on a Sussex farm where he was commissioned to make a wood-carving for his friend, the painter Edward Wadsworth, the trunk of an elm tree brought down in a storm aroused all his love for transforming old trees into sculpture and kept him, he said, "working like a demon".

Zadkine was born on July 14, 1890, in Smolensk, where his father was a teacher of Latin and Greek and one of the local intelligentsia. His mother, Sophie Lester, was descended from a Scottish family that had settled in Russia as shipbuilders in the time of Peter the Great. He went to England as a boy and was befriended in London by David Bomberg, but soon returned home and his beginnings as an artist can be dated from student days in Paris and his meeting in 1912 with the poets, painters and sculptors of the avant-garde: Apollinaire, Max Jacob, Picasso, Archipenko and others. After service in the French Army, for which he volunteered in 1915, he began to gain critical notice early in the 1920s and from then onwards his work was widely exhibited and admired. He married a young painter, Valentine Prax, who shared his enthusiasms and ideas. He had several exhibitions in England, at Tooth's Gallery in 1928, at the Whitworth Art Gallery, Manchester, in 1935, at the Leicester Gallery in 1952 and at the Tate Gallery (Arts Council) in 1961. Major exhibitions in Paris were those at the Musée d'Art Moderne in 1949 and the Maison de la Pensée Française in 1958. He worked at his sculpture, taught and lectured in the United States for a period.

The many books on Zadkine and his sculpture include the study (1962) by Jean Cassou, who was one of the first to recognize his ability. His own writings include an account of how he became a sculptor, a record of impressions in Greece and a book of his poems with his own drawings published in London in 1964.

November 27, 1967.

General Fazlullah Zahedi, Iranian Ambassador to the United Nations at Geneva, who died there on September 3, 1963, will be chiefly remembered as the Prime Minister who restored order in his country after the dangerous chaos into which it had been plunged by Moussadek.

Born about 1890 in Hamadan, he came to the notice of the late Reza Shah Pahlevi while serving under him and from 1922 onwards held a number of military posts. In 1942, after the Allied occupation of Iran, he came to the unfavourable notice of the British military authorities while commanding the Iranian forces in the south, and Sir Fitzroy Maclean in his book *Eastern Approaches* vividly describes his arrest of General Zahedi, who remained under detention until after the war. From 1949 his rise was rapid, for he was appointed in succession Chief of Police, a Senator, and Minister of the Interior; but from the time when Moussadek came to power in 1951 he found himself in strong opposition to the latter's policy and twice, in August, 1952, and again in July, 1953, was constrained to take "sanctuary" in the Parliament building after violently criticizing him in the Senate.

CRITICAL PHASE

By August, 1953, the situation in Iran had become critical. Moussadek's nationalization of the oil industry, while it had made him a hero in the eyes of the masses, had had the effect, in the face of firm western opposition, of undermining the Iranian economy and had thus alienated many powerful elements among the property-owning classes, including the religious leader Kashani; and to maintain his own position Moussadek had been compelled to call in any elements prepared to support him, not excluding the Tudeh (communist) Party, and to arrogate to himself ever more far-reaching powers. Finally, however, he overreached himself by coming into direct conflict with the Shah, the only remaining centre of resistance to his pretensions; and on August 13 the Shah signed a decree dismissing Moussadek and appointing Zahedi in his place. Moussadek rejected the decree and arrested the officer who brought it, and a state of anarchy supervened, with Tudeh-inspired mobs calling for the deposition of the Shah and establishment of the republic, the Prime Minister in hiding, and the Shah in flight abroad. But suddenly the situation was reversed; now the mobs were reviling Moussadek and calling for the Shah, and were joined by the troops and police; Zahedi emerged from hiding and took control; and on August 22 he was able to announce the arrest of Moussadek and the assumption of full powers by the legal Government.

The Shah returned in triumph, and a new regime was instituted with a loyal army as its guarantor. The Tudeh Party was forced underground, diplomatic relations with Great Britain (broken by Moussadek) restored and after complex negotiations with the western powers an oil agreement was signed under which Iranian oil again flowed in world markets and its revenues into Iran's economy.

In 1955 Zahedi, his main task accomplished, handed over the Premiership and retired to

Switzerland, where in 1958 he was appointed to represent his country at the United Nations organs in Geneva.

His son is the present Iranian Ambassador at the Court of St. James's.

September 4, 1963.

Alexander Zawadski, chairman of the Council of State in Poland and a member of the Polish Politburo, died in Warsaw on August 7, 1964, at the age of 65.

He had held this post, the counterpart to the presidency in Poland, since 1952 and his period in office therefore spanned the old diehard regime, the crisis of 1956 and the return to power of Mr. Gomulka. A Bolshevik of the old guard, the only one of the present government to have been in the Soviet Union at the time of the October Revolution of 1917, he had earned a reputation for ruthlessness and subservience to Moscow and it is thought that in 1956 he originally supported the orthodox ruling communists, but at the last moment switched to Gomulka. His retention in office provided at least an appearance of continuity between one regime and the next.

Born in Silesia in 1899, he worked first as a miner and then served in the Russian Army during the First World War. He joined the Red Guards and fought in the Revolution. On his return to Poland in 1925 he was sent to prison for subversion, but a few years later was exchanged with a political prisoner in the U.S.S.R., and by 1935 had risen to the rank of colonel in the N.K.V.D., the secret police. In 1936, at the beginning of the great Soviet purge, he was arrested on a charge of espionage and was sent to a forced labour camp, but two years later was allowed to go back to Poland where he was once more arrested—by the anti-Communist Polish authorities—and was serving a long sentence there at the outbreak of the Second World War. He returned subsequently to Russia, served with the Soviet forces and was at Stalingrad and in the advance westwards into Poland. By 1945 he was general of brigade.

POLITICS IN ARMY

In August of that year, after a period as chief of the political department of the Polish Army—a post where he was responsible for political indoctrination in the Army—he became the first communist Governor of Silesia and, a Silesian by birth himself, was successful to a considerable degree in winning the confidence of the population. He was recalled from Silesia in October, 1948, on his appointment to the Politburo and the Party Secretariat, and the following January became Vice-Premier. In 1950 he was coopted to the Council of State and was given the post of chairman of the Central Council of the Trade Unions, where he undertook a purge of the non-communists. He relinquished this office in 1952 when he became chairman of the Council of State. Zawadski was married and had two children.

August 8, 1964.

Hans Zehrer, chief editor of the well-known Hamburg daily newspaper *Die Welt*, who died on August 23, 1966, in Berlin at the age of 67, was a powerful influence in the German press over a period of 40 years. Throughout his life he held strong views of a kind usually associated with the right in politics, and in his youth was one of the leading members of a group of intellectuals who were strong critics of the weaknesses of the Weimar Republic.

Although it was later said of him that his writings during the late twenties and early thirties did much to prepare the ground for the advent of National Socialism, it must be added that when Hitler actually came to power in 1933 his differences with the Nazis quickly became sufficiently acute for him to be suspended by Goebbels and forbidden to exercise his profession.

Born in 1899 in Berlin, Zehrer studied medicine, psychology, history and theology, then plunged early into journalism. In 1923 he became editor of the *Vossische Zeitung*, and after 1929, editor of the monthly journal *Die Tat*. These were probably his most influential years, when he and a group of young intellectuals around him, who claimed to be "neither left nor right" in their ideas, came out in favour of a strong central government in opposition to the feeble later stages of the Weimar Republic.

In later years Zehrer was director of the German publishing firm of Gerhard Stalling in Oldenburg and fought as a soldier in the Second World War. He wrote a number of novels under a pseudonym, and also film manuscripts.

When *Die Welt* (which was founded by the British after the war) was handed over to German management in 1953, the owner, Axel Springer, made Zehrer chief editor. Zehrer's editorials were strongly anti-communist during the period after Stalin's death. He had no use for Khrushchev. In 1958 he and Springer visited Moscow, and Zehrer, on his return to Germany, expressed his bitter feelings at the Soviet refusal to do anything for the reunification of Germany. In November, 1963, he moved to Berlin but continued to be editor of the paper until his death.

August 25, 1966.

Professor Fritz Zernike, who won the Nobel Prize for Physics in 1953, died on March 10 1966, in Groningen, Holland. He was awarded the Nobel Prize for the invention of the phase-contact microscope, allowing the study of fine structures of living organisms. He was 77.

He was born in Amsterdam on July 16, 1888. He was educated in the University of Amsterdam, and obtained his doctorate there in 1915. He then worked in the department of astronomy in the University of Groningen as professor extraordinarius of mathematical physics and theoretical mechanics, becoming full professor in 1920. His researches contributed to optics and other branches of physics. His earliest work in optics was concerned with problems relating to astronomical telescopes, and in 1934 he published a defraction theory of the Foucalt knife-edge test for the figure of telescopic mirrors, and discovered the so-called polynomials of the phase-contrast method. He realized that this method could be applied to the microscope and its use in microscopy proved most valuable in medical and biological research. He was awarded the Rumford medal of the Royal Society in 1952.

He retired as Professor of Theoretical and Technical Physics and Theoretical Mechanics at the University of Groningen in 1958, after 48 years of work there. He was visiting professor at the Johns Hopkins University, Baltimore, in 1948. Two years previously he had been made a member of the Netherlands Academy of Science. In 1956 he became a Foreign Member of the Royal Society. He was twice married.

Zernike was a versatile physicist who made it possible to examine normal and healthy living cells under the microscope—that is, without need to use chemical stains to make the structure of the cells visible. His phase contrast microscope enables structure to be seen in colourless and transparent objects provided only that they differ locally in the extent to which they refract or bend light waves. It is thus a routine instrument in biological and medical research. As well as being used to show structure and to see what happens, for example, when cells divide, it can also be applied to some extent as a means of analysis.

Zernike was at the same time an able theorist and a good practical physicist. Without the first type of ability he would hever have been led to phase contrast microscopy—for his first serious work in optics was on a theory of a commonly-used test for the accuracy of telescope mirrors. This was in 1934. Neither would he have seen, as he did almost at once, that an approach which he had adopted in his telescope mirror research could be applied to the opposite extreme of microscopy. Without practical skill he could not have arrived at a neat and simple method of giving effect to his idea.

Important as his invention was, his real achievement was to take a new look at a subject which to almost everyone else at the time seemed to be already finished and complete, apart from quite minor improvements in detailed design. His researches paved the way for a whole new family of optical microscopes, not just one single device. His earlier work included research both in statistics and on electrical instruments.

March 16, 1966.

Lord Zetland, Secretary of State for India from June, 1935, to May, 1940, and sometime Governor of Bengal, died at Aske, Yorkshire, on February 6, 1961, at the age of 84.

He had a knowledge and appreciation of the philosophy and culture of India possessed by no previous holders of those great offices. He was a traveller, author, parliamentarian, administrator, and sportsman, and he filled many honorary offices of importance; but India held the first place in his affections.

The Rt. Hon. Sir Lawrence John Lumley

Dundas, K.G., P.C., G.C.S.I., G.C.I.E., second Marquess of Zetland and Earl of Zetland, Earl of Ronaldshay in the county of Orkney, and Baron Dundas, of Aske, in the county of York, and a baronet, was born on June 11, 1876, eldest son of the first Marquess and Lady Lilian Lumley, third daughter of the ninth Earl of Scarbrough. He followed his father to Harrow and Trinity College, Cambridge. He took a commission in the 1st North Riding of Yorkshire (Western Division) Royal Artillery, and later as a Yorkshire landowner was active in promoting the Territorial movement.

Modelling himself on Lord Curzon, on whose Viceregal staff he served in 1900 as A.D.C., he devoted much of his early manhood to travel and exploration. He visited Persia, India, Ceylon, and Burma and made two long journeys across Asia between the Caspian Sea and Japan.

FACILE WRITER

He did some shooting in the Himalayas, but politics always attracted him, and he employed a facile pen to write travel books with a strong political flavour. His *Sport and Politics Under an Eastern Sky* in 1902 was followed two years later by *On the Outskirts of Empire in Asia*. He published in 1908 *A Wandering Student in the Far East* and in 1911 *An Eastern Miscellany*.

Meanwhile at a by-election in 1907 he entered the strongly Liberal Parliament of the day as Unionist Member for Hornsey which he was to represent for nine years. His selection at the close of 1916 to succeed Lord Carmichael as Governor of Bengal evoked strong Nationalist criticism on the alleged ground that his books showed him to have a Curzonian outlook and to be out of sympathy with Indian aspirations. He could not have taken office at a time of greater difficulty. When he went out the War had still 18 months to run, the revolutionary movement in Bengal was at its height, and later came the rise of non-cooperation and the final culminating disorders in Calcutta during the cold weather of 1921-22. The horizon was obscured by financial difficulties, and there soon came anxious consideration of the best means to give effect to the famous declaration of British policy of progressive stages towards Indian independence made by Sir Edwin Montagu, then Secretary of State for India, on August 20, 1917.

It was soon found that the youthful enthusiasm for British achievement in the East expressed by Ronaldshay (as he then was) in his books was compatible with a liberal outlook. The close study which he gave to the thought and philosophy of India and his unaffected admiration for the intellectual ability, the courtesy and warm-hearted generosity of the people of Bengal, made a deep impression. Readily accessible, frank in the expression of his views, and possessing the precise mind and cool judgment which enabled him to grasp problems quickly and take rapid decisions, he soon won general confidence. During his tour in India to confer with the Viceroy, Lord Chelmsford, Edwin Montagu wrote in his diary "Ronaldshay is alive and has some driving force."

The Governor had a gift of selecting good colleagues, whom he never let down. When the reforms took effect he had two British and five Indian colleagues in the bifurcated Cabinet. The measures necessary to maintain order and to assert the authority of the law, drastic though they had to be, were taken with the full assent of Ronaldshay's Ministers. In spite of straitened resources he extended irrigation, improved agriculture, strengthened the rural cooperative movement, and inaugurated a great anti-malarial campaign. Though the revolutionary movement had become endemic, he saw it decaying and the non-cooperation troubles subsiding.

On vacating office in the spring of 1922 Ronaldshay, already appointed G.C.I.E., was made G.C.S.I., and sworn of the Privy Council. The Knighthood of the Garter was conferred in 1942. He did not attempt to reenter the House of Commons but settled down to his books and papers, to the management of his Yorkshire property, and to the many calls of an unofficial kind which he accepted. Zetland had inherited his father's love of racing, and was a Steward of the Jockey Club from 1928 to 1931.

RACING INTERESTS

From his stud he turned out a number of winners, though in his own words they fell just short of the highest class. His racing colours —the famous white jacket with red spots first registered in 1774—were especially familiar at Yorkshire race meetings. Zetland served the usual term as a most knowledgeable president of the Royal Geographical Society, and was a trustee from 1925 to 1947. As a lover of Indian art he was an active President of the India Society, now the Royal India, Pakistan and Ceylon Society, and for a time he similarly served the Royal Asiatic Society. Especially notable was his chairmanship of the National Trust.

After returning from Bengal he wrote a trilogy of books on India and her borders. The first was *Lands of the Thunderbolt. Sikhim, Chumbi and Bhutan*—the result of close study of Buddhism and brief mountaineering holidays. Then came *India: a Bird's Eye View* and *The Heart of Aryavarta*. These works showed his penetration of the inner mind of India, and his close understanding of political unrest and the other multiform reactions against the supremacy which western thought had claimed for itself.

LIFE OF CURZON

A literary effort with a more general appeal awaited him, for he was invited by Lord Curzon's literary executors to write his biography. By the express instructions of the subject, a separate volume was devoted to the Viceregal years, and therefore the life extended over three volumes, published at quarterly intervals in 1928. Ronaldshay made judicious use of the vast material placed at his disposal, and he wrote with commendable frankness, showing a capacity to view Curzon alike with the eyes of an intimate friend and with those of a critical publicist. In 1929 Zetland (as he had then become in that year) edited *The Letters of Disraeli to Lady Bradford and Lady Chesterfield*. In 1932 he made a further valuable contribution to Victorian history by writing the authorized biography of the first Lord Cromer. In this instance a single volume sufficed since Evelyn Baring had recorded his main achievements in *Modern Egypt*.

The frequent predictions that Zetland would ascend to Viceregal *gadi* were so persistent and widespread at the close of 1925 when Lord Reading's time was nearing completion, that he himself expected nomination. It was, as he privately admitted, a bitter disappointment not to be chosen after nearly 30 years of almost uninterrupted study of Eastern problems.

Similar prophecies were made when the Statutory Commission on Indian Reforms was to be set up towards the close of 1927. By a kind of universal nomination, voiced in *The Times*, Zetland was one of the British delegates to the successive sessions of the Indian Round Table Conference in London.

On the reconstruction of the Baldwin Cabinet in the middle of 1935 he succeeded Sir Samuel Hoare (later Lord Templewood) as Secretary of State for India. No previous holder of the office had gone to it so well equipped with knowledge of India and her storied past. The selection was welcomed by all sections, including the Services, and with especial warmth in Bengal.

THE INDIA BILL

The India Bill had had a stormy passage through the Commons, and it fell to Zetland to be its pilot in the Upper House, where right wing opponents had entertained some hope of defeating the measure by the help of the "backwoodsmen". The fact that, though many unwonted faces were seen in the Chamber, the second reading was carried by a substantial majority was due in no small degree to the persuasive reasonableness of the Minister, and to his readiness to yield on some minor matters while firm on points of broad principle.

When in the spring of 1940 Neville Chamberlain resigned the Premiership and Mr. Winston Churchill succeeded him, Zetland was replaced at the India Office by L. S. Amery.

That same spring he had a remarkable escape from death. He was on the platform with Sir Michael O'Dwyer at the meeting at Caxton Hall when O'Dwyer was shot dead by Udam Singh. Zetland, like Sir Louis Dane and Lord Lamington, was struck by a bullet from the assassin's pistol and hit in the ribs.

During his five years of strenuous labour in Whitehall Zetland had managed to maintain many of his outside activities, for he had a lifelong habit of systematic economy of time and effort. He had the high honour of bearing the Sword of State at the Coronation of King George VI in 1937. His last years were spent almost entirely at his Yorkshire home at Aske, and from 1945 to 1951 he was Lord Lieutenant of the North Riding. He was from 1923 to 1956 Provincial Grand Master of the Freemasons of the North and East Ridings of Yorkshire. The office had been held continuously by members of his family since the formation of the Province in 1821. On reaching octogenarian rank, Zetland yielded to the frequent solicitations of old friends to write his memoirs. Under the title of "*Essayez*", *the Memoirs of Lawrence Second Marquess of Zetland* (1957) he wrote of his experiences in touching life at so many different angles.

Zetland married in 1907 Cicely, daughter of Colonel Mervyn Archdale. He made repeated allusions in the autobiography to her most helpful companionship. Two sons and three daughters were born to them. The younger son, Bruce Thomas Dundas, was killed in the last war when serving in the R.A.F. Lord Zetland is succeeded by the elder son, the Earl of Ronaldshay, who was born on November 1, 1908, married in 1936 Penelope, daughter of Colonel Ebenezer Pike, of Ditcham Park, Petersfield and has three sons and a daughter.

February 7, 1961.

Konni Zilliacus, Labour member of Parliament for the Gorton division of Manchester since 1955, died in St. Bartholomew's Hospital, London, on July 6, 1967, at the age of 72. He had sat as member for Gateshead from 1945 to 1950.

It was impossible to fit Zilliacus easily into any known political category, whether as extreme left-winger, fellow-traveller, or crypto-communist. In the eyes of some he appeared at times to be one or all of these things, but somehow he managed to elude precise definition as any of them. His immense fecundity of ideas overflowed all over the place, carrying him into excesses of unorthodoxy which he could defend with elaborate logic as being in strictest accord with the true Socialist canon. He was always convinced that it was the others who were out of step. But this did not save him from being expelled from the party from May, 1949, to February, 1952, for persistent opposition to his Government's foreign policy, or from being suspended in March, 1961.

He was a constant thorn in the flesh of his party leaders who did not accept his claim to be the keeper of their political consciences, but he was generally liked in the party and in the House even by those who detested his views as highly dangerous. As a speaker he was fluent to the point of prolixity. He had an easy command of many languages, and his passion for foreign affairs carried him far and wide and sometimes into awkward situations. His memory teemed with facts and precedents which he would quote with telling effect, and few could rival his skill and knowledgeability as a controversialist.

COURAGE AND ABILITY

None could doubt his great ability or question his courage. If he carried his independence of mind sometimes near the extreme of eccentricity it was an amiable quality which mellowed with the years and earned him a unique place in political life and increasingly affectionate tolerance of a rich and colourful personality.

Konni Zilliacus was born in Kobe, Japan, on September, 13, 1894. He owed much to his mixed parentage. He was the son of Konni Zilliacus, a distinguished Finnish-Swedish author and journalist, and his wife Lilian Maclaurin Grafe, who was of Scottish-American extraction. After primary education in Brooklyn, Finland and Sweden, he went to Bedales and then to Yale, where he graduated first of his year with a Ph. B. In the 1914–18 War he served in the Royal Flying Corps and as an intelligence officer with the British military mission in Siberia. Between the wars he was a member of the information section of the League of Nations Secretariat and was highly regarded for his drive and energy. He spent the Second World War at the Ministry of Information.

Gateshead sent him to Parliament in 1945 with a thumping majority over the sitting Liberal National member. His ardour for close collaboration with Russia seemed unexceptionable enough, but by 1947 he was attacking his Government's conduct of foreign policy, and his persistent criticism of Ernest Bevin did not go down well with the Labour hierarchy. In the same year he interviewed Stalin and joined with 12 other Labour M.P.s in a message of good will to the German Peoples' Congress in the Soviet sector of Berlin, which was tartly disowned by the Parliamentary Labour Party.

Zilliacus came in for sterner admonishment in April, 1948, as one of 21 Labour M.P.s who had signed what was known as the "Nenni telegram". They claimed that their message of greeting had been addressed to the Italian Socialist Party and not to the Nenni-Communist combination, but they were warned that they would be expelled from the British Labour Party unless they undertook to desist from organized opposition to party policy. Characteristically, Zilliacus gave a carefully guarded undertaking, refusing to pledge himself always to agree with whatever the N.E.C. might do.

In December of that year he was adopted as prospective Labour candidate for East Gateshead, but the N.E.C. refused to endorse his candidature in spite of the pleadings of the local party. The Labour leadership had become increasingly incensed at what they regarded as his consistent opposition to the Government's policy. A speech he made at the communist-sponsored world congress of the "Partisans of Peace" helped to harden the N.E.C. in their decision in May, 1949, to expel him. He was not the only left-winger on whom official displeasure fell at that time and he was certainly not the least vociferous in his defence. He lashed the party leaders as "ersatz Tories" and with four colleagues decided to form a "Labour Independence Group" in the Commons.

YEARS OF WAITING

He fought the 1950 election as a Labour Independent candidate for East Gateshead, but came at the bottom of the poll. He made more than one attempt to get back to the Commons. In February, 1952, the National Executive with much hesitation allowed him to rejoin the Labour Party and in 1955 he was returned for Gorton with a majority of 269. Thereafter for a time he managed to avoid conflict with the party leadership.

Then towards the end of 1960 he was in trouble again over a speech attacking Gaitskell's leadership of the party and a pamphlet in the same vein. The trade union group of M.P.s conveyed a protest to the Shadow Cabinet. Zilliacus refused to appear before the Deputy Leader and the Chief Whip, and when the National Executive in February, 1961, officially deplored his conduct in writing, for a communist journal, an article highly critical of the British Labour Party, he replied at great length that he would continue to write articles to give effect to decisions of the Labour Party conferences. That put the fat in the fire and a month later the N.E.C. decided on his suspension from the Parliamentary Party. He reiterated that in writing for the Soviet and east European press he was acting in the spirit of a previous conference resolution, but the party conference in 1961 endorsed his suspension, against a minority show of hands.

It was ironical that Zilliacus, who had always made a great point about the constitutional sanctity of conference resolutions, should himself be the victim of one. However, Gorton remained loyal to him, giving him a majority of more than 4,000 in 1964 and nearly doubling it in 1966, and he continued to contribute to the Commons his own highly individual version of what Labour policy should be and exactly how its custodians had failed to carry out their charge. He produced about 17 books on political topics and many pamphlets and articles.

He married first, in 1918, Eugenia Nowicka, and they had one son and one daughter; his second wife was Janet Harris, whom he married in 1942, and they had one daughter.

July 7, 1967.

King Zog of Albania—See under **Albania.**

Arnold Zweig, the Jewish novelist, playwright and poet, died in east Berlin on November 26, 1968, at the age of 81.

His international fame rested on, and will continue to rest on, one book, *Der Streit um den Sergeanten Grischa* (1928) or The Case of Sergeant Grischa, the best of the many German war novels that appeared during the Weimar Republic.

Arnold Zweig, the son of a saddle-maker, was born in Glogau, Silesia, on November 10, 1887. He wrote his first story in 1909, but held it back from publication until 1938. It is based on his experiences in the university of Munich and in the city's art circles.

In 1920 Zweig had his first conflict with National Socialism, and two years later this antagonism caused him to leave Bavaria. While serving as a volunteer in the German Army he had planned a play based on his experiences; he had come to think of literature as the vehicle for a social and political message, and the result was another play, published in 1921. It had no success, and Zweig turned it into the novel about Sergeant Grischa. Its success in this form was immediate and world-wide. It was translated into English and some 16 other languages. Its anti-militarism was fashionable at the time, but it differed from such realistic war novels as Remarque's *All Quiet on the Western Front*.

Later Zweig made this book the central part

of a great trilogy; he called it "a trilogy of transition", meaning the passing into a new age. The two other novels were called *Education before Verdun* and *The Crowning of a King*. The latter was designed to show up the political abdication of the German ruling class and the surrender to the middle and lower classes. In 1933 he was barely able to make his escape to Palestine. His works were publicly burnt by the Nazis, with those of other well known Jewish or "anti-national" writers.

Meanwhile Zweig had become almost blind as the result of an ailment he had contracted at the front. But his inventiveness and imaginative vigour were undiminished, and he went on to dictate work after work. At first in exile, for example, his novel, *De Vriendt Goes Home*, of which an English translation was published in 1934, describing dispassionately conditions in Palestine. Then he was invited by a Soviet official to return to the more congenial atmosphere of Germany, and there he went on with his writing.

In 1950, on the death of Heinrich Mann, he was elected president of the east German Academy of Arts. In 1960 he paid a visit to London, and there was some talk about his settling in England. But he returned to east Germany, under communist domination, and the president of the "German Democratic Republic" conferred on him the national prize for literature. In 1958 Zweig had been to Moscow to receive the Lenin prize.

November 27, 1968.

INDEX OF OBITUARIES AND TRIBUTES 1961–1970

EXPLANATION OF INDEX

This index has been compiled from the last edition of *The Times* each day, for the years 1961 to 1970. It contains references to all obituaries—including the 'after rules' the short death notices at the foot of the Obituary Section of the paper—and tributes, published during the period.

Where a name is printed in black type, it signifies that the full text of the Obituary is reprinted in the main section of this book, which is arranged in alphabetical order.

In each entry the first numeral(s) indicate the day of the month, the second the page, and the letter the column: for reference purposes the columns of each page are supposed to be lettered from left to right—a,b, c,d,e,f,g,h. The final numerals appearing in parenthesis indicate the year. Thus July 15, 9c (62) denotes the issue of July 15, Page 9, column 3, of the year 1962.

The first date after each name refers to the date the obituary appeared in *The Times,* and each subsequent date refers to a tribute; the only exception being where the letter (t) appears, thus indicating that there was no obituary and that all references are to tributes.

A

B

C

Cove, Capt. George E.—Mar. 30, 14f (67)
Cove, William G.—Mar. 19, 15b (63); 28, 17b (63)
Coventry, Rt. Rev. Harry B.—(t.) June 20, 17a (63)
Coventry, Maj. John—July 7, 10f (69)
Coverdale, Harry—Nov. 8, 12d (65)
Covernton, Alfred L.—Jan. 6, 14b (61)
Cowan, Andrew W.—Nov. 30, 14b (64)
Cowan, Colin J.—Nov. 22, 18c (62)
Cowan, Jimmy—June 22, 10h (68)
Cowell, Henry—Dec. 17, 17c (65)
Cowland, Rear-Adm. William G.—Apr. 22, 15b (66)
Cowley, Lord—Aug. 30, 12e (62)
Cowley, Lord—Mar. 25, 10h (68)
Cowley, Charles—Apr. 11, 10h (68)
Cowley, Wilfred—(t.) Oct. 5,12d (65)
Cowper, Col. Lionel I.—Jan. 20, 10h (68)
Cox, Prof. A. H.—Feb. 20, 16e (61)
Cox, Charles L.—June 1, 12a (63)
Cox, Air Comdre. Claude R.—Aug. 21, 10g (61)
Cox, Cuthbert M.—Mar. 15, 17a (62)
Cox, Edwin H.—Aug. 1, 12f (61)
Cox, Ida—Nov. 13, 10g (67)
Cox, Sir Ivor—June 12, 15a (64)
Cox, Katherine—(t.) Sep. 12, 10h (67)
Cox, Kenelon—(t.) Nov. 20, 12h (68)
Cox, Dr. Leslie R.—Aug. 12, 10e (65)
Cox, Brig. Sir Matthew—Sep. 12,12g (66)
Cox-Ife, William—Mar. 28, 12h (68)
Coxon, Charles L.—May 30, 14e (62)
Coxwell, Charles B.—Nov. 10, 10g (67)
Crabbe, Lady—Jan. 14, 12h (70)
Crabbe, Col. Sir John—Nov. 2, 19a (61)
Crabbe, Rt. Rev. R. P.—Oct. 24, 10e (64)
Crabos, Rene—June 18, 19a (64)
Crabtree, Charles H.—Sep. 13, 10g (66)
Crabtree, Norman V.—Apr. 19, 10g (67)
Crace, Adm. Sir John G.—May 13, 12h (68)
Craig, Lady—Jan. 13, 6g (68)
Craig, Lady Juliet—Apr. 29, 10h (68)
Craig, J. M.—Feb. 21, 8g (70)
Craig, Edward Gordon—July 30, 10f (66); Aug. 1, 12g (66); 4, 12e (66)
Craig, Sir Ernest G.—Apr. 30, 10g (66)
Craig, James T.—(t.) May 14, 10g (69)
Craig, Prof. John—(t.) Oct. 10, 16f (70)
Craig, Prof. John D.—May 16, 14f (68); 18, 12h (68)
Craig, Col. Noel N. L.—Nov. 5, 12h (68)
Craig, Thomas—Mar. 9, 10h
Cranbrook, Dowager Lady—Mar. 25, 10g (68)
Crandall, Charles F.—Nov. 9, 12b (63)
Crane, Lady—Aug. 25, 10e (65)
Crane, Edward M.—Apr. 16, 18c (64)
Crane, Prof. Ronald S.—Sep. 2, 12g (67)
Cranfund, Sir James G.—Apr. 13, 10g (70)
Crankshaw, Lt.-Col. Sir Eric N. S.—June 27, 12g (66)
Cranston, William P.—Nov. 15, 12h (67)
Cranworth, Lord—Jan. 6, 12e (64); 7, 12b (64); 10, 14a (64); 14, 11a (64)
Cranworth, Lady—Nov. 17, 14e (66)
Craske, Arthur H. G.—May 10, 12g (67); 18, 12h (67)
Crathorne, Lady—May 20, 12f (69)
Craufurd, Vice Adm. A. G.—May 1, 12e (65)
Craufurd, Sir Alexander J.—July 16, 12g (66)
Craven, Lord—Jan. 29, 15g (65)
Craven, Lady Anna—Sept. 26, 13b (61)
Craven, Lady Cothelia—May 20, 10e (61)
Craven, Cicely—(t.) Feb. 15, 18d (62)
Craven, Rt. Rev. George L.—Mar. 16, 16g (67)
Craw, Sir Henry—Jan. 29, 15a (64)
Crawford, Lady Augusta—Dec. 21, 12e (61)
Crawford, Lady Marion—Nov. 22, 14e (63)
Crawford, Dr. Arthur M.—July 16, 12e (62)
Crawford, Bobby—Oct. 26, 15e (65)
Crawford, Eileen M. E.—Aug. 22, 10g (66)
Crawford, Rev. Ernest A.—Oct. 30, 10f (65)
Crawford, John N.—May 4, 12e (63); 8, 14f (63)
Crawford, John V.—Feb. 28, 12h (68)
Crawford, Gen. Sir Kenneth N.—Mar. 7, 15d (61); 10, 22d (61)
Crawford, Robert M.—Mar. 14, 17b (61)
Crawford, Robert McK.—Aug. 17, 10g (67)
Crawfurd-Price, Walter H.—Oct. 24, 12f (67)
Crawley, Alice—June 3, 10c (63)
Crawley-Boevey, Barbara Lady—Oct. 10, 17c (62)
Crawley-Boevey, Sir Launcelot V. H.—July 6, 10g (68)
Crawshaw, Lady—Sep. 7, 15c (64)
Crawshay-Williams, Lt.-Col. Eliot—May 12, 10d (62)
Cray, Canon Frank M.—(t.) Sep. 4, 10h (67)
Craze, Olive—Aug. 4, 12f (61)
Creagh, Maj.-Gen. Sir Michael—Dec. 16, 10g (70); 21, 12g (70); 29, 10h (70)
Creed, Charles—July 19, 12g (66)
Creed, Dr. Richard S.—July 9, 23b (64)
Creed, Dr. S.—Jan. 31, 8h (70)
Creed, Sir Thomas—May 13, 10e (69)
Creggan, Dr. George T.—Dec. 28, 8h (67)
Creighton, Lady—Feb. 15, 12f (66)
Creighton, Rev. Cuthbert—Apr. 23, 15d (63); 26, 17e (63)
Creighton, Rear-Adm. Sir Kenelm—Feb. 28, 12 (63)
Cremona, Paul—Oct. 28, 15a (63)
Crerar, Air Comdre. Finlay—Aug. 13, 10e (65)
Crerar, Gen. H. D. G.—Apr. 2, 18a (65); 6, 14e (65)
Crespi, Vittorio—July 20, 12a (63)
Crespigny, A. V. M. Hogh V. C. de—June 28, 10g (69)
Cressall, Maud—May 30, 14e (62)
Cresswell, Fenwick—Jan. 11, 10f (66)
Creswell, Rear-Adm. George H.—Apr. 24, 10g (67)
Cressy-Marcks, Violet—Sep. 16, 12g (70)
Crew, J. C.—June 1, 14e (65)
Crewdson, Eric—Feb. 8, 12g (67)
Crewdson, Brig. Wilson T. O.—Dec. 9, 10f (61)
Crewe, Lady—Mar. 14, 14g (67); 15, 14e (67); 17, 16f (67)
Crews, Dr. Cynthia M.—(t.) Sep. 11, 10h (69)
Cribbett, Lady—Nov. 18, 20b (63)
Cribbett, Sir W. C. George—May 25, 12e (64); June 3, 15c (64); 8, 12e (64)
Crichton, Lady—July 25, 14g (61)
Crichton, Arthur O.—July 14, 10h (70)
Crichton, Lilian M.—Mar. 7, 14d (66)
Crichton, Lt.-Col. Michael H.—Apr. 21, 10g (70); 25, 10h (70)
Crichton, Robert—Mar. 18, 14e (66)
Crichton-Stuart, Capt. Lord—June 27, 12g (69)
Crichton-Stuart, Lady—Mar. 28, 10d (64)
Crick, Monte—Apr. 8, 10g (69)
Crick, Rev. Thomas—Nov. 16, 10g (70)
Crickmore, K.—Apr. 15, 14e (65)
Cridlan, Evelyn M.—(t.) Apr. 7, 17a (61)
Cringle, Lt. William—(t.) Jan. 4, 10e (62)
Cripps-Day, Francis H.—July 15, 12b (61)
Crisp, Raymond J. S.—Nov. 29, 12f (66)
Cristie-Miller, Lt.-Col. Sir Geoffry—Apr. 5, 10h (69)
Critchett, Lady—May 8, 16c (62)
Critchley, Brig.-Gen. Alfred C.—Feb. 11, 14 (63); 14, 14e (63); 15, 12g (63)
Crivon, Robert—(t.) Sep. 16, 10g (68)
Croce, Adele—Feb. 28, 15b (64)
Crocker, Edward S.—Apr. 8, 10h (68)
Crocker, Gen. Sir John—Mar. 11, 12d (63); 30, 10e (63)
Crockett, H. L.—Jan. 24, 14d (64)
Crockford, Walter—May 23, 10h (67)
Crocombe, Leonard—Nov. 21, 12g (68)
Croft, Dowager Lady—Dec. 2, 16e (66)
Croft, Sir Arthur—Feb. 14, 15c (61)
Croft, Lt.-Col. Richard P.—Feb. 28, 16b (61); Mar. 2, 18g (61)
Croft, Sir William—Aug. 20, 10e (64); 21, 10d (64)
Croft-Murray, Amy—(t.) May 17, 19a (61)
Crofton, Lady—Mar. 2, 18g (61)
Crofton, Maj. Arthur M. L.—June 16, 10e (62)
Crofton, Maj. Sir Malby R. H.—Jan. 23, 14c (62)
Crole, G. B.—(t.) Apr. 9, 17a (65)
Cromartie, Lady—May 21, 12e (62)
Crombe, Henri-Philippe—Feb. 7, 12g (69)
Crombie, Charles—Apr. 22, 12h (67)
Crombie, Sir James—May 24, 10g (69); 29, 12g (69)
Cromer, Lady—Nov. 7, 16d (61)
Crommelynck, Fernand—Mar. 19, 12h (70)
Crompton, Richmal—Jan. 13, 8f (69)
Cromwell, Lord—Oct. 22, 10f (66)
Cronshaw, Cecil J. T.—Jan. 7, 10c (61); 11, 17a (61)
Crook, A. H.—(t.) Nov. 10, 17c (61)
Crookenden, Col. Arthur—Dec. 24, 10g (62); 29, 8d (62); Jan. 10, 12e (63)
Crookshank, Lord—Oct. 18, 17a (61); 20, 15b (61); 25, 15a (61)
Croome, William I.—May 2, 12f (67)
Cropper, Arthur C.—May 2, 12g (67)
Crosby, Caresse—Jan. 27, 10g (70); 28, 12g (70)
Crosby, Everett—July 16, 12g (66)
Crosfield, Lady—Jan. 18, 13a (63); 21, 13b (63)
Crosfield, Lt.-Col. George R.—Aug. 23, 10e (62); 24, 10e (62)
Cross, Sir Alexander—May 14, 17c (63); 20, 16b (63)
Cross, Dorothy M.—Sep. 1, 8g (62)
Cross, Dr. Frank L.—Dec. 31, 10g (68); Jan. 1, 10f (69); 4, 8g (69)
Cross, Maj. Frank N.—Nov. 1, 12g (67)
Cross, Henry A.—Nov. 26, 14d (65)
Cross, John K.—Feb. 1, 14g (67)
Cross, Kenneth—Jan. 18, 10f (68)
Cross, Prof. Kenneth G. W.—June 19, 10g (67)
Cross, Robert—June 17, 15b (64)
Cross, Sir Ronald—June 4, 10g (68); 12, 12g (68)
Cross, Weimar—Oct. 28, 12a (61)
Cross, Maj. William—May 4, 12h (67)
Cross, Zora—Jan. 24, 14d (64)
Crosse, Edinund M.—(t.) July 9, 12e (63)
Crosse, F. G.—(t.) June 5, 12b (65)
Crossley, Edward—May 8, 10f (69)
Crosswell, Noel A.—Nov. 30, 14b (64)
Crosthwaite, Lady—Oct. 15, 23d (65)
Crosthwaite, Maj. John S.—Sep. 18, 15b (63)
Crosthwaite, Sir William—May 14, 12f (68)
Crouch, Dr. Henry C.—(t.) Jan. 7, 10f (63)
Crouse, Russell—Apr. 5, 12e (66)
Crow, Sir Alwyn—Feb. 6, 10e (65)
Crow, John W.—Nov. 4, 12g (69); 6, 12f (69); 11, 12g (69)
Crowden, Prof. Guy P.—Nov. 23, 14e (66)
Crowder, Sir John E.—July 11, 12e (61)
Crowdy, Mary—(t.) Nov. 10, 17c (61)
Crowdy, Dame Rachel—Oct. 12, 12c (64)
Crowe, Capt. J.—Mar. 3, 14e (65)
Crowther, Alexander C.—June 3, 14f (66)
Crowther, Dr. Charles—Dec. 9, 15a (64)
Croy, Princess de—June 22, 10g (68); 24, 10h (68)
Croy-Solre, Prince de—Dec. 28, 8e (65)
Crozier, Rt.Rev. Dr. John W.—Feb. 16, 14d (66)
Cruickshank, Prof. E. W. H.—Jan. 2, 13b (65)
Cruikshank, Prof. John—Oct. 11, 12g (66)
Cruikshank, Col. Martin M.—Oct. 13, 14e (64)
Cruikshank, Stewart—June 29, 14g (66)
Crump, Jack—Apr. 16, 10e (66)
Crump, Norman—Jan. 24, 14d (64)
Crutchley, G. E. V.—Aug. 18, 10h (69)
Cruttendon, William—Apr. 16, 12f (70)
Cruz, Pabon—Dec. 2, 12h (69)
Cryer, Leonard H.—June 28, 15b (61)
Csokor, Prof. F. T.—Jan. 10, 10h (69)
Cubitt, George E. S.—Sep. 19, 14f (66)
Cuckney, A. V. M. Ernest J.—Nov. 9, 14d (65)
Cudlipp, Percy—Nov. 6, 16a (62); 15, 15a (62)
Cuffe, Sir George E.—May 7, 18a (62); 11, 19d (62)
Cuke, Sir Archibald—Sep. 26, 12f (68)
Cull, Anders E. K.—(t.) May 7, 12f

D

E

F

G

H

I

J

K

L

M

N

O

Q

R

S

T

U

V

W

(61)
Western, George—Aug. 19, 10h (69)
Western, Kenneth—Jan. 25, 13e (63)
Westman, Prof. Knut—Nov. 1, 12h (67)
Westmeath, Lady—Apr. 10, 12h (68)
Westminster, Duke of—Feb. 23, 10d (63); Mar. 1, 14e (67)
Westminster, Fourth Duke of—Feb. 27, 14g (67)
Westminister, Duchess of—Jan. 22, 12g (70)
Westoll, Capt. James—July 29, 8h (69)
Weston, Lady—June 16, 14g (66)
Weston, Sir Arthur A.—Oct. 28, 12g (69)
Weston, Brig. John L.—June 22, 10d (63)
Weston, Reta L.—Mar. 18, 12g (67)
Westrop, Capt. A. R.—Sep. 1, 10g (65)
Westropp, Edward—Jan. 23, 14b (62)
Westwater, Robert H.—Nov. 17, 10f (62)
Westwood, John D.—Aug. 31, 10g (64)
Wetenhall, Percy—(t.) June 28, 17a (62)
Wethey, Capt. Edwin H.—Dec. 24, 10b (63)
Wetter, Ernest—Aug. 14, 10g (63)
Weve, Prof. Henricus J. M.—Jan. 5, 13c (62)
Wexler, Dr. Harry—Aug. 13, 10e (62)
Weyers, Susanna J.—Aug. 13, 10g (66)
Weygand, Gen. M.—Jan. 29, 14d (65)
Weyman, Lt.-Col. Arthur—Sep. 27, 8g (69)
Whalen, Grover A.—Apr. 21, 10d (62)
Whaley, Maj. Herbert E.—Feb. 12, 15e (62)
Whalley, Ursula—(t.) Sep. 12, 17c (62)
Whanslow, H. W.—Apr. 1, 14e (65)
Wharton, Lord—July 15, 10g (69)
Whately, Comdr. Richard F. A.—Mar. 4, 10h (68)
Whates, Harold R. G.—Dec. 4, 15c (61)
Whatley, N.—Apr. 3, 10f (o5)
Whatmough, Prof. Joshua—Apr. 30, 18b (64)
Wheatcroft, A.—Jan. 25, 14e (65)
Wheatcroft, Kenneth D.—Jan. 4, 10d (64)
Wheatley, Grace—Dec. 2, 12h (70)
Wheatley-Crowe, Capt. Henry S.—Sep. 21, 12h (67)
Wheeler, Lady—May 18, 22a (61)
Wheeler, Lady Dorothea—Sep. 10, 12d (63)
Wheeler, Lady Mavis—Oct. 24, 14h (70)
Wheeler, Bert—Jan. 20, 10h (68)
Wheeler, Lt.-Cdr. D. R.—Mar. 15, 16a (65)
Wheeler, Brig. Sir Edward O.—Mar. 21, 15a (62)
Wheeler, H. E. O.—(t.) Mar. 13, 16c (63)
Wheeler, Capt. Sidney G.—(t.) Jan. 16, 13a (62)
Wheeler, Sybil G.—Feb. 12, 15e (62)
Wheeler, Prof. Thomas S.—Dec. 14, 16e (62)
Wheeler-Cuffe, Lady—Mar. 10, 14f (67)
Whelan, Albert—Feb. 20, 16f (61)
Whelan, William P.—Feb. 12, 10e (66)
Wheldon, Sir Wynn P.—Nov. 13, 15a (61); 15, 17b (61)
Wheler, Charles W. G.—Jan. 3, 12c (62)
Wherry, Albert E. K.—June 4, 19f (62)
Whiddington, Prof. Richard—June 15, 10c (70)
Whineray, Bruce—(t.) Nov. 17, 12h (70)
Whinfield, John R.—July 7, 15d (66)
Whipple, Dorothy—Sep. 15, 14g (66); 21, 12g (66)
Whistler, Gen. Sir Lashmer—July 6, 10f (63); 12, 13f (63); 17, 15b (63); 30, 12e (63)
Whitaker, Sir Arthur—June 14, 10e (68)
Whitaker, Frank—Feb. 19, 15e (62)
Whitaker, Maj. William H. B.—Mar. 25, 12f (63)
Whitbread, Madeline—(t.) Sep. 6, 16a (61)
Whitburgh, Lord—Oct. 2, 12h (67)
Whitcher, Alec E.—Apr. 21, 10d (62)
White, Lady—Mar. 7, 14f (62)
White, Lady—Jan. 6, 14d (66)
White, Lady—May 17, 10g (67)
White, Lady Margery—Aug. 7, 8f (65)
White, Sir Bernard—July 13, 14b (64)
White, Dr. Charles F.—June 30, 14g (66); July 6, 14f (66)
White, Dorothy Hale—July 28, 10g (67)
White, Sir Dymoke—May 27, 10h (68)
White, Dr. F. Norman—June 6, 14c (64); 9, 15a (64)
White, Florence—Apr. 14, 22c (61)
White, Francis—July 15, 10g (69); 21, 10h (69)
White, A.V.M. G. Halford—Jan. 19, 12f (65)
White, Geoffrey—Mar. 8, 10h (69)
White, Lt.-Col. Geoffrey C.—Oct. 17, 15d (61); 19, 17b (61); 25, 15b (61)
White, George—Oct. 12, 12h (68)
White, George R. B.—Mar. 29, 12f (66); Apr. 1, 14f (66)
White, Sir George S.—Jan. 20, 14a (64)
White, Gilbert—Feb. 14, 17d (62)
White, H. G.—Feb. 20, 14a (65)
White, H. Lee—Sep. 30, 12h (69)
White, Henry—Feb. 7, 17b (64)
White, Herbert M. O.—Nov. 25, 14a (63)
White, John—July 22, 12g (64)
White, John C.—Dec. 5, 13g (68)
White, John C.—May 3, 15a (61); 5, 20d (61)
White, John W. B.—Jan. 18, 14b (62)
White, Josh—Sep. 8, 10h (69)
White, Prof. Leonard W. T.—Oct. 26, 15e (65); 29, 19b (65)
White, Oswald—Dec. 31, 12g (70)
White, Terence H.—Jan. 18, 15f (64)
White, Gen. Thomas D.—Dec. 24, 10a (65)
White, Tommy—Aug. 15, 10h (67)
White, Walter—July 2, 12f (66); Apr. 18, 10g (67)
Whitehead, Alan O.—Mar. 4, 16a (64)
Whitehead, Ernest C.—July 6, 25b (61)
Whitehead, Ven. Louis G.—(t.) June 2, 23c (61)
Whitehouse, Sheldon—(t.) Aug. 25, 10e (65)
Whitehouse, Dr. William H.—July 10, 13a (63)
Whitelaw, Anne W.—Aug. 20, 10g (66)
Whitelaw, Nan—Aug. 26, 8h (69)
Whitelegg, Harold G.—(t.) May 31, 16a (63)
Whiteley, Lady—Dec. 16, 12a (61)
Whiteley, Alfred H.—May 26, 12h (67)
Whiteley, Clifford—July 24, 10h (69)
Whiteley, Gen. Sir John—May 22, 10g (70); 26, 10g (70)
Whiteley, William—Sep. 12, 10h (67)
Whiteman, Paul—Dec. 30, 8g (67)
Whitfield, B. G.—(t.) Sep. 17, 10f (69)
Whitefield, Edwin—(t.) Mar. 12, 17d (64)
Whitford, A. V. M. Sir John—Aug. 13, 10g (66)
Whitham, Maj.-Gen. G. S.—Sep. 2, 10h (70)
Whithouse, Frederick P.—Oct. 10, 14e (61)
Whiting, Frederic—Aug. 4, 8e (62)
Whiting, John—June 17, 16d (63); July 2, 12f (63)
Whitlard, Prof. Walter F.—Mar. 8, 14e (66)
Whitley, Lady—Mar. 8, 15c (65)
Whitley, Lady—May 18, 14g (66)
Whitley, Brig.-Gen. Sir Edward—Dec. 1, 14f (66)
Whitley, Rev. George—Nov. 12, 17a (64)
Whitley, Mary—Sep. 11, 12h (70)
Whitley-Jones, Ernest—July 13, 14f (65)
Whitley-Lavarack Maj. A.—(t.) Mar. 21, 15d (62); 22, 17a (62)
Whitlock, Alan C.—Jan. 8, 10e (66)
Whitmore, Col. Sir Francis H. D. C.—June 13, 12f (62)
Whitney, George—July 23, 13b (63)
Whitney, Jack—May 18, 14g (66)
Whitney, Capt. Robert G. E.—July 12, 12f (66)
Whittaker, Francis C.—Oct. 1, 14d (63)
Whittaker, Bishop Frank—Dec. 12, 14b (61)
Whittaker, Prof. K.—Sep. 2, 10g (70)
Whittaker, Maj.-Gen. R. F. E.—Feb. 20, 14f (67); 21, 12g (67)
Whittingham, Lady—Mar. 15, 12f (66)
Whittington, Charles H.—Nov. 22, 17b (61)
Whittle, Frank—June 19, 14b (62)
Whittle, Ven. John T.—Jan. 28, 10f (69)
Whitton, Ivor—July 4, 12g (67)
Whittuck, Brig. Gerald E. M.—May 10, 12h (68)
Whitty, Maj.-Gen. Henry M.—Sep. 19, 13d (61); 22, 18c (61)
Whitwill, Col. Mark—Apr. 21, 10f (67)
Whitworth, Lady—Sep. 17, 12h (70)
Whitworth, Charles S.—Sep. 17, 15a (63)
Whitworth, Mrs. Geoffrey—(t.) Dec. 11, 17c (64)
Whorf, Richard—Dec. 16, 14f (66)
Whyte, Dr. A. F.—(t.) Mar. 4, 15f (65)
Whyte, Dorothy—(t.) May 8, 10g (67)
Whyte, Sir Frederick—July 31, 10h (70)
Whyte, Marjorie—(t.) Aug. 9, 10f (63)
Wibault, Michel—Jan. 24, 15b (63)
Wickard, Claude—May 1, 10f (67); 8, 10h (67)
Wickham, Lady—May 11, 19c (61)
Wickham, Florence—Oct. 22, 12e (62)
Wickham, Brig. John C.—May 21, 10g (70)
Wickham, Maj. John L.—Aug. 1, 14a (62); 4, 8e (62)
Wickham, Gp.-Capt. Peter R. W.—May 2, 10g (70)
Wickham, Comdr. Tom—June 8, 12g (67)
Wieler, Brig. L. F. E.—Feb. 2, 14e (65)
Wiener, Dr. Alfred—Feb. 6, 14e (64)
Wiener, Prof. Norbert—Mar. 20, 20c (64)
Wienken, Rt. Rev. Heinrich—Jan. 23, 21b (61)
Wierzynski, Kazimierz—Feb. 19, 10f (69)
Wieschoff, Heinrich A.—Sep. 20, 17b (61)
Wieth, Mogens—Sep. 11, 17g (62); 14, 13c (62)
Wifstrand, Naina—Oct. 26, 12h (68)
Wiggin, Lady—Jan. 21, 13b (63); Feb. 7, 14e (63)
Wiggins, Rev. Clare A.—July 9, 14f (65); 17, 8e (65)
Wigglesworth, Air Comdr. C. George—Aug. 10, 10e (61)
Wight, Sir Gerald R.—May 22, 17a (62)
Wight, John S.—Jan. 23, 15c (63); 24, 15b (63)
Wightwick, Humphrey W.—May 10, 18c (62)
Wigley, Lady—July 15, 10g (69)
Wigley, H. de Winton—June 18, 14e (62); 22, 15b (62)
Wigley, Rev. Henry T.—May 29, 12h (70)
Wigley, Thomas—(t.) Mar. 30, 17d (61)
Wigley, W. C. S.—Oct. 5, 10h (70)
Wigman, George—Jan. 2, 12b (62)
Wigram, Dr. Loftus E.—July 5, 21c (63)
Wihuri, Antti—Dec. 29, 8d (62)
Wilberforce-Bell, Lady—July 22, 12f (65)
Wilock, Gp.-Capt. Clifford A. B.—Jan. 15, 12e (62)
Wilcox, Fred M.—Sep. 26, 10e (64)
Wilcox, Grafton—Feb. 18, 12e (64)
Wilde, Agnes M.—(t.) Apr. 2, 18b (62)
Wilde, Jimmy—Mar. 11, 12g (69); 12, 12h (69)
Wilde, Prof. Johannes—Sep. 15, 12h (70); 21, 10h (70)
Wildenstein, Georges—June 13, 17c (63)
Wilder, Richard J.—May 10, 18c (62)
Wildgans, Fredrich—Nov. 12, 14f (65)
Wilding, Longworth A.—Aug. 28, 10d (63)
Wildman-Lushington, Maj.-Gen. G. L.—Feb. 4, 12g (70)
Wiles, Sir Gilbert—Sep. 12, 15d (61); 14, 17b (61); 20, 17a (61)
Wiles, Sir H.—May 22, 10d (65)
Wiles, Philip—May 19, 12h (67)
Wiles, Walter G.—May 25, 16e (66)
Wiley, Alexander—Oct. 28, 10g (67)
Wiley, Arthur E.—Aug. 14, 10e (64)
Wiley, John C.—Feb. 4, 10f (67)
Wilgress, Dana—July 24, 10g (69)
Wilhelmina, Princess of the Netherlands—see under Netherlands
Wilkie, A.—Jan. 8, 10g (70)
Wilkie, Alexander M.—Aug. 15, 10g (66)
Wilkie, Doris M.—Apr. 22, 22b (63)
Wilkie, Hugh G.—Mar. 15, 12h (69)
Wilkie, Reginald J.—Aug. 14, 10e (62)
Wilkins, Miss E.—Feb. 26, 15a (65)
Wilkins, Dr. Frederick J.—Oct. 28, 15a (65); 30, 10f (65)
Wilkins, H. E. B.—Feb. 18, 14e (65); 19, 15a (65)
Wilkins, Brig. Robert J.—Aug. 27, 10f (69)
Wilkins, Dr. W. H.—Apr. 27, 14f (66)
Wilkinson, Lady—Jan. 7, 12c (64)
Wilkinson, C. T. A.—Dec. 21, 12g (70)
Wilkinson, Denys C.—(t.) Apr. 11, 13b

X

Y

Z